GO TO Page

35?*

Rand McNally
Cosmopolitan
World Atlas

Rand McNally
Cosmopolitan
World Atlas

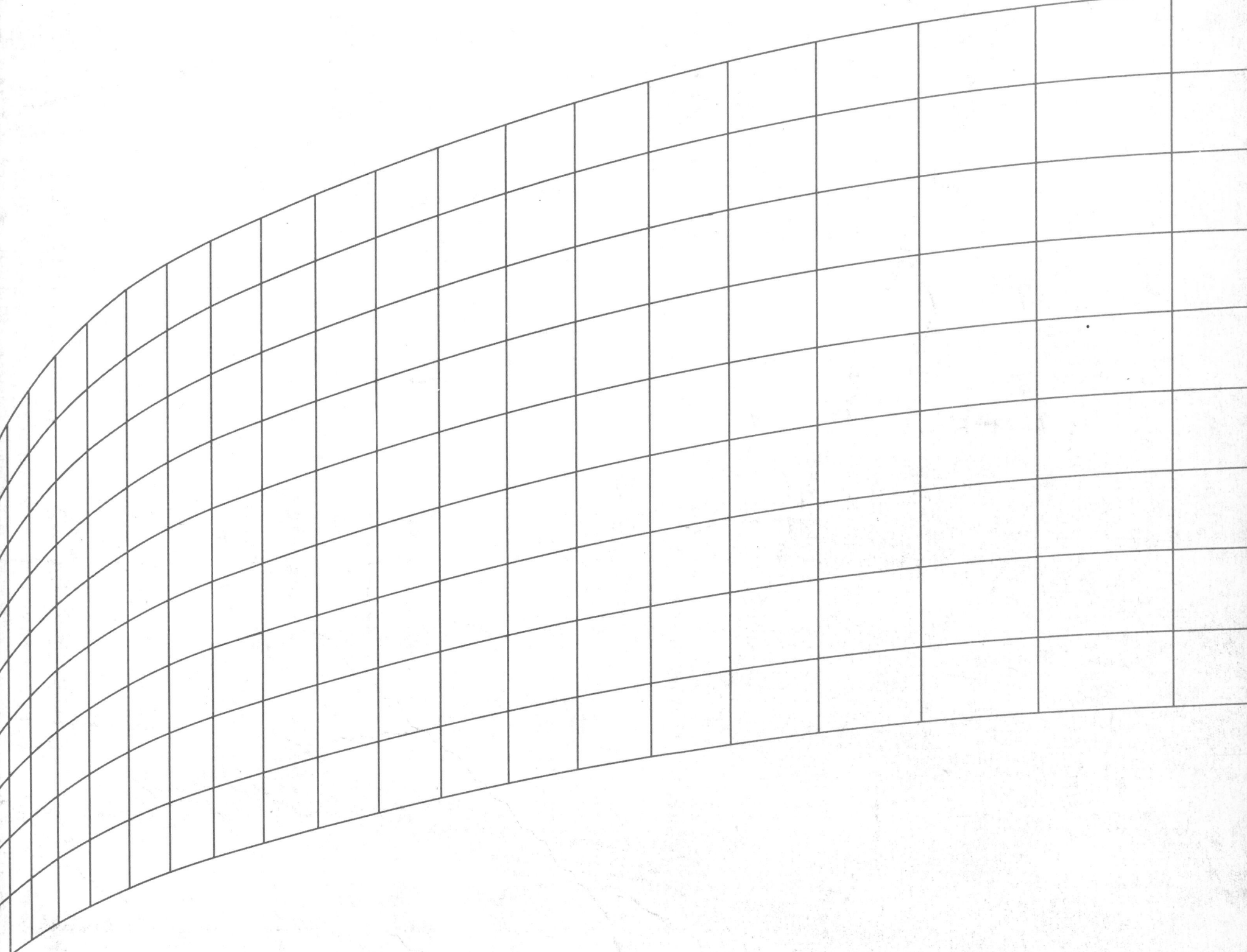

Rand McNally & Company Chicago / New York / San Francisco

Photo Credits: viii, United States Geological Survey; xiii, Bob and
Ira Spring; xiv, xv, National Aeronautics and Space Administration;
xv, FPG/Wendler; xvii, Alpha Photo/Lanks; xix, upper, xxxiii,
Brazilian Embassy; xix, lower, xxviii, right, George Hunter; xxii,
Apollo Photo Group/Perceval; xxiii, Photo Researchers, Inc./
G.R. Roberts; xxiv, xxxvi, left, Marvin W. Mikesell; xxv, left, PFI/
Charles E. Rotkin; xxv, right, Howard S. Sochurek; xxvii, Grant
Heilman; xxviii, Consulate General of Japan; xxxi, left, Woodfin
Camp/Marc and Evelyne Bernheim; xxxi, right, John LaDue; xxxii,
Illinois Department of Transportation; xxxiv, Weyerhaeuser
Company; xxxvi, right, Time, Inc./Carl Iwasaki; xxxvii, Harold M.
Mayer; xxxviii, Embassy of Japan.
Map Credits: xv, After Lester E. Klimm; xxx, After Brian J.L. Berry.

Contents

Introduction to the Atlas

The new edition of the **Cosmopolitan World Atlas** integrates reference, environment, travel, and metropolitan maps; latest population figures; and geographical facts to furnish basic, comprehensive information about the world in which we live.

The opening graphic essay, "Human Patterns and Imprints," focuses upon the interaction of people and the land and the impact this has upon our environment.

Through the use of maps, photographs, captions, and text, the differences in the distribution of population are explained along with factors that influence settlement patterns and the utilization of natural resources. The article closes by relating people's inventiveness and available resources to the opportunities and challenges confronting us today.

In total, the essay gives meaning to the patterns and features we come in contact with every day as well as building a foundation for better interpreting the maps and tables in the atlas.

Following the introductory section, and related to it, is the environment-map series. These maps show the ten ways in which people have fashioned the land. The colors and patterns are chosen to create a visual impression of the earth's surface environment.

Included in the atlas and following the environment series is a twelve-page section of United States travel maps, showing major roads, major cities and towns, the topography of the land, and historic and natural places of national interest.

The Cosmo Series Maps — the reference maps and the heart of the atlas — are grouped on a broad regional basis. Each region is introduced with a full-color global view, showing the area as it might appear from high above the earth. With each global view a short description of the region is provided, along with a locator map indicating the political divisions of that region.

Within the regions the basic organization of the Cosmo Series Maps is retained. Each of the great landmasses of the earth is shown as a whole and then divided into major continental regions. All the regional maps for a given continent are drawn on the same scale. Thus it is possible to make direct visual comparisons of the sizes of countries and the distances between places by turning from one map to another. Smaller areas are shown in greater detail on larger-scale maps that use even multiples of these regional scales. The United States and Canada sections contain individual state and province maps, which supply the necessary detail for this area of the world. Small marginal maps show the location of areas covered by the maps. This coverage was designed to enable the user to compare areas and see the relationships among them.

The index at the back of the book includes in one alphabetical listing the names that appear on the Cosmo Series Maps. Often the form of a name commonly used in English-speaking countries differs from the local, official name. On the maps, the English name of major cities and physical features is used, and the local, official name is often included in parentheses after the English form. Both forms appear in the index. For other features, the official form is given first on the map, with the customary English form in parentheses. This policy has been followed as an aid to English-speaking readers.

In general, place-name spellings follow the recommendations of the United States Board on Geographic Names, which determines the official government spelling of foreign geographical names. For some areas and languages, however, more anglicized names are used than the board recommends for official maps. For the spelling of place-names in the United States, the United States Postal Guide is the authority followed.

Included in the atlas is a section of U.S. metropolitan area maps. These maps (all drawn at the same scale to facilitate comparison) depict in detail twelve major U.S. urban areas. A special index listing all communities shown follows the maps.

This edition of the **Cosmopolitan World Atlas** is highlighted by a table showing the 1980 census populations of U.S. cities, towns, counties, and states. The latest 1980 census material has been used to develop the table, which is arranged alphabetically by state.

Updated general information and geographical facts about the United States, U.S. populations traced from 1650 to 1980, and largest metropolitan areas of the United States are other features of the atlas.

Supplementary information about the world is included in a world political information table that lists pertinent facts about each country and major political subdivision of the world. Other tables document facts about world mountains, oceans, lakes, rivers, islands, and metropolitan areas. Another extensive table gives world cities, towns, political divisions, and their populations.

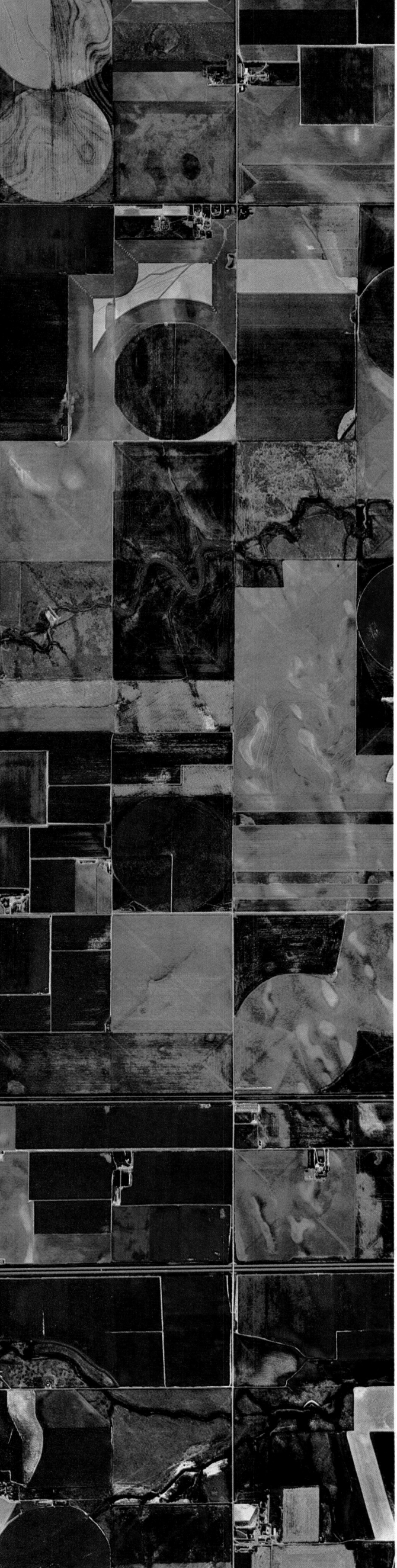

Human Patterns and Imprints

Marvin W. Mikesell
Professor of Geography, University of Chicago

No part of the earth is beyond the reach of human activity. We have climbed Mount Everest, penetrated the densest jungle, camped at the North and South poles, and explored the depths of the oceans. Now, when we are reaching out to the most distant planets of the solar system, we may believe that the earth has been effectively tamed and settled.

People have been almost everywhere, but human settlements are not distributed evenly or randomly over the earth, nor are the patterns and imprints of our occupancy the same from place to place. In fact, our cities and farms, villages and industries occupy only limited areas of the world, and even these regions are unevenly settled. For example, the great sprawling cities along the eastern seaboard of the United States lie near miles of uninhabited land, some of it virtual wilderness. The dense rural population of Egypt is concentrated in a narrow valley surrounded by the vast desert of northwestern Africa. For every "boom town," with its vigorous and rapid growth, there is a "ghost town," abandoned when resources ran out. And our impressive ability to improve and alter the environment is countered by air and water pollution, soil erosion, and other processes that destroy some areas or make them unfit for human habitation. Our environment, part natural and part artificial, still presents a major challenge to human understanding.

The Human Mosaic. The high altitude infra-red image of the Goodland, Kansas, area illustrates a variety of humanity's patterns and imprints. Vegetation shows red, lack of vegetation blue and green.

The World and Human Geography

We will attempt to build a foundation for understanding our world by looking at the historical distribution of human population, the patterns of settlement and land use, and the ways we have modified nature to suit our needs. The detailed maps in this atlas illustrate many of the varied patterns of human activity. While the maps give us a broad perspective of our world, they show us only part of the story. Much of what follows is an attempt to deal more fully with the features that appear as lines or colored areas on the maps and illustrations. Perhaps the starting point for an understanding of our world is the general belief among many scholars that there is a fundamental

. . . Our environment, part natural and part artificial, still presents a major challenge to human understanding. . .

order and logic in the distribution of people and their activities and creations, a "human geography" controlled by nature and culture. If we can increase our understanding of this order and logic, perhaps we can deal more intelligently with some of the problems facing us now.

Photographs taken from satellites and other spacecraft reveal the varied patterns and imprints of the human race, how we have marked and changed the earth's surface. Our first task is to try to understand why human population is so unevenly distributed. Although different growing seasons and levels of rainfall help explain the worldwide contrast between crowded and empty areas, various cultural factors also must be considered.

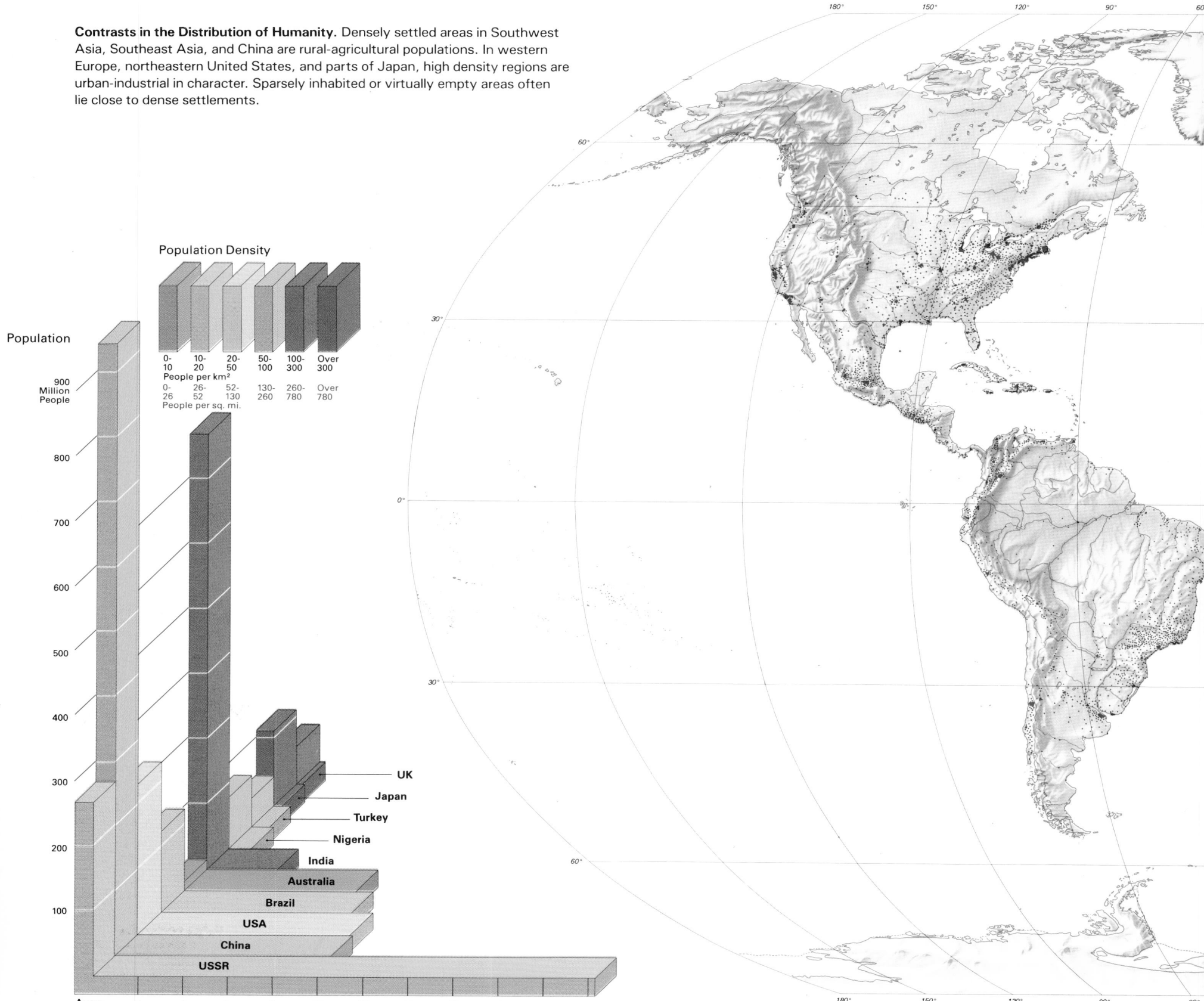

Contrasts in the Distribution of Humanity. Densely settled areas in Southwest Asia, Southeast Asia, and China are rural-agricultural populations. In western Europe, northeastern United States, and parts of Japan, high density regions are urban-industrial in character. Sparsely inhabited or virtually empty areas often lie close to dense settlements.

Population Density

| 0-10 | 10-20 | 20-50 | 50-100 | 100-300 | Over 300 |
People per km²
| 0-26 | 26-52 | 52-130 | 130-260 | 260-780 | Over 780 |
People per sq. mi.

Population

900 Million People

800

700

600

500

400

300

UK
Japan
Turkey
Nigeria

200

India
Australia
Brazil

100

USA
China
USSR

Area   2   4   6   8   10   12   14   16   18   20   22 Million km²

People, Land, and Density. The graph shows the differences in the number of people, the land area, and the population density for 10 nations of the world. The world's population of over 4 billion averages about 75 people per square mile (30 per square kilometer). Density variations can be explained by a combination of natural and cultural factors.

In our exploration of how humanity has used the earth, the year A.D. 1500, just before European expansion overseas, serves as a particularly important landmark. The progressive settlement of the Americas was a continuation of the process started by early European explorers, as are the recent pioneer settlements in Brazil, Siberia, and Australia. Modern patterns of land use, contrasting forms of rural and urban settlements, the location of industries, and the availability of energy sources all influence where people will settle. The last of our human patterns, vast transportation and communication networks, is another important indicator of economic development and land use.

Satellite photographs have also made us more aware that our environment, the earth and its atmosphere, is a closed system, intricately balanced and often highly vulnerable to human activity. That we have destroyed as well as built is evident in the many scarred areas people have left behind them. The decline of air and water quality

has been a consequence of the Industrial Revolution that began in the 18th and 19th centuries. But deforestation and erosion are equally serious and are much older problems, dating back some 10,000 years to the beginning of farming in the Near East. In the 20th century, we tend to think of artificial environments—heated and air conditioned—as the answer to our search for more comfortable habitats. While opportunities in this area may seem limitless, management of the real world outside our structures remains a serious challenge to human ingenuity. Realizing that the world is a closed system may help us find solutions to our energy and population problems that will work with the environment.

. . . Our environment is a closed system, intricately balanced and often highly vulnerable to human activity . . .

x

The task of describing and interpreting our world is a continuous one, for the patterns and imprints we try to explain are always changing. Our study of the past can help us understand the present and perhaps allow us to see a few years into the future. But beyond that point, we cannot tell where our human ingenuity will take us.

Crowded and Empty Areas of the Earth

Everyone knows that the world is experiencing a human "population explosion." Faced with this challenge, we may forget that substantial regions of the earth are *under*populated or virtually empty.

The most densely settled parts of the earth appear in two dissimilar regions: the industrial areas of Europe, the United States, and Japan; and the predominantly rural areas of India, China, and Southeast Asia. The industrial regions date from the mid-18th and 19th centuries, when emerging technology increased people's productive capacity

and encouraged the development of large urban districts. The heavily populated rural areas of India, China, and other Asian countries reflect nearly 4,000 years of an agricultural civilization.

Other regions of the world offer striking contrasts between crowded and open places. In the Soviet Union, a narrow band of population stretches along the Trans-Siberian railway. The crowded area of Canada's southern Ontario is a dramatic counterpart to the open stretches farther north. In Japan, the well-populated island of Honshū lies just south of the more sparsely settled island of Hokkaidō. The eastern shores of the Mediterranean Sea, with the crowded coastal fringe of Israel, Lebanon, and Syria, stand out

---

. . . Regions of the world offer striking contrasts between crowded and open places . . .

---

sharply against the barren land beyond. But perhaps the clearest illustration is the dramatic difference between Java and Iceland, two countries approximately equal in size but vastly different in population.

The United States, with slightly over 226,000,000 inhabitants and an area of about 3,600,000 square miles (9,500,000 square kilometers), is only moderately crowded. Settlement is fairly dense from the major urban areas along the Atlantic seaboard and the Great Lakes to as far west as Texas, Oklahoma, Kansas, Nebraska, and the Dakotas. Beyond that point, until reaching the urban areas of the Pacific Coast, lack of adequate rainfall restricts settlements to river valleys, along transportation lines, and near sites of valuable resources.

Natural Limits on Growth. To explain the uneven distribution of humanity, we must look at several natural and cultural factors. Perhaps the most

xi

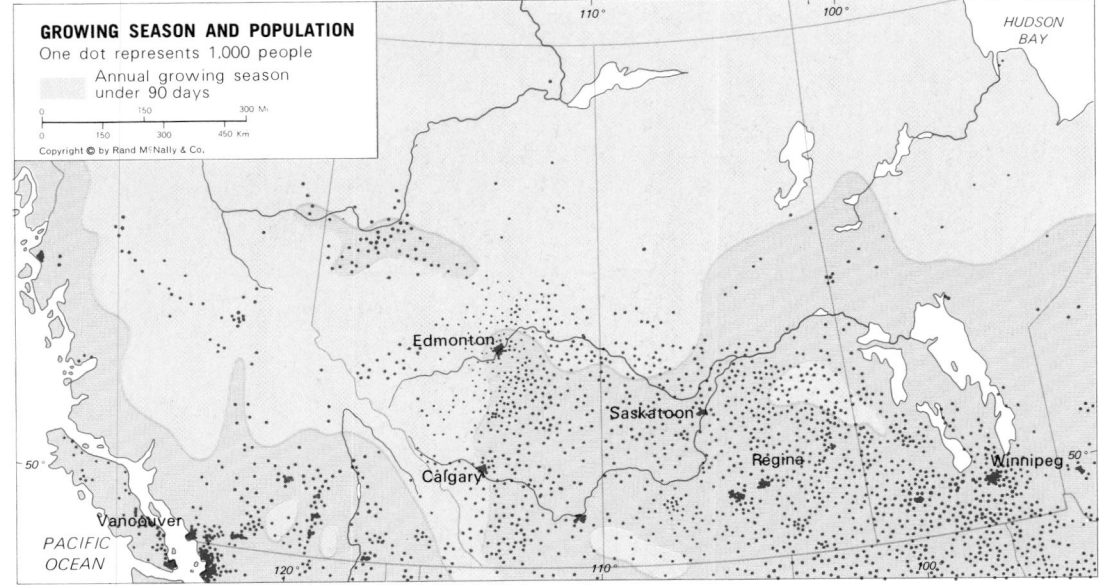

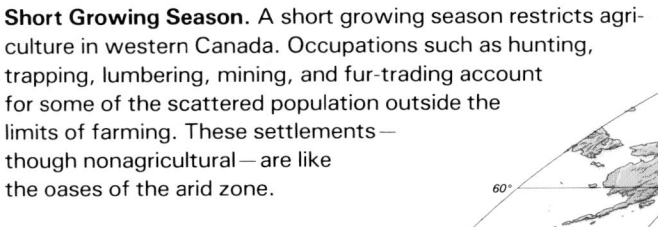

Short Growing Season. A short growing season restricts agriculture in western Canada. Occupations such as hunting, trapping, lumbering, mining, and fur-trading account for some of the scattered population outside the limits of farming. These settlements— though nonagricultural—are like the oases of the arid zone.

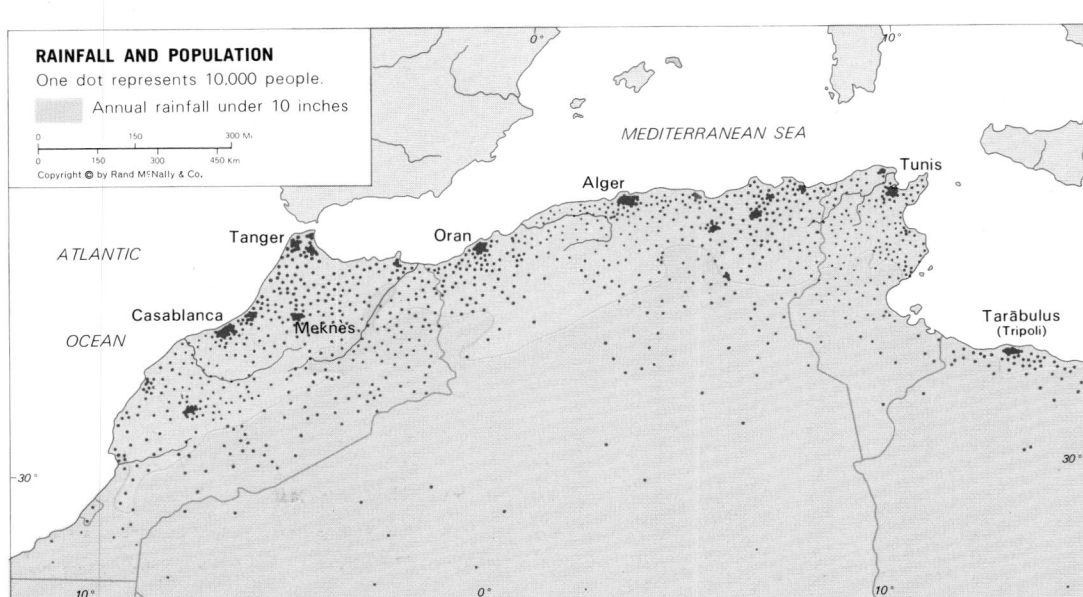

Too Dry. Cereal farming in northwestern Africa requires at least 10 inches (25.4 centimeters) of rainfall each year. As a result, the dense rural population has settled mainly in the coastal hills. But rural settlement does not terminate abruptly, for wells and dams supply water for irrigation. Nevertheless, population is sparse where average rainfall drops below 10 inches a year.

important are the limits that nature imposes on agricultural development. Many areas are too dry or too mountainous or have growing seasons too short to support a large, stable population. While people have settled in harsh climates such as the

---

. . . To explain the uneven distribution of humanity, we must look at several natural and cultural factors. . .

Sahara, northern Siberia, and Antarctica, such settlements are small and likely to remain so. Thus, for the most part, we can mark off the earth's rich and fertile regions as the effective limits of the habitable world.

Growing Season. The most severe limitation on human settlement is the length of the growing season. Areas with less than 90 days free of frost are not suitable for most forms of agriculture. Without an adequate local supply of food, settlements cannot grow beyond a certain population size. Inadequate growing seasons partly explain why large areas of Canada and Siberia remain empty, but other factors also limit settlement in the world's northlands. Portions of these regions are extremely dry, which limits plant growth. The vegetation of the Arctic zone consists of mosses, sedges, lichens, and other species which are referred to as tundra. The lack of trees is explained by the short growing season and the permanently frozen subsoil. Move southward and you will find tundra replaced by taiga, a forest of fir, spruce,

larch, and other conifers. These vast forested regions constitute an important resource in Canada, Scandinavia, and the Soviet Union. Unfortunately, the thin, acidic soil that develops under such forests is too infertile to sustain permanent agricultural settlements.

Aridity. Human settlement is also seriously limited by the lack of adequate precipitation. In general, farming is not practical where annual rainfall averages less than 10 inches (25.4 centimeters). In areas where rainfall occurs mainly in the hottest part of the year and averages less than 20 inches (51 centimeters) annually, farming may be marginal.

The great arid and semiarid regions of the world were once populated by bands of nomadic farmers and herders and by oasis dwellers. Today, nomadism is declining as a way of life and in some areas has disappeared altogether, making the great desert regions of North Africa and Southwest Asia more desolate than ever before. In contrast, population in the desert areas of the United States has increased sharply. Air conditioning and water piped in from underground reservoirs have made cities such as Tucson, Phoenix, and Las Vegas more attractive. Converting salt water to fresh, a practical but still expensive process, will eventually enable more acres of arid and semiarid land to be cultivated.

Mountainous Regions. A substantial part of the world is too mountainous or simply too high for people to settle. The "timberline" on mountains is similar to the forest-tundra boundary of the Arctic region. This line varies with latitude, from about

8,000 feet (2,438 meters) in the European Alps to about 14,000 feet (4,267 meters) in the tropics. Above the line, growing seasons are too short for cultivation, although alpine pastures may be grassy enough to raise domestic herds. Also, many areas of the earth are too rough or rocky to support farming. Settlements in these regions are too scattered to appear on the map. Although Tibet has about 1,300,000 inhabitants, it is sparsely populated for its size. The upper slopes of the Alps and many other mountain ranges are also virtually without human habitation. Only when mountains are exposed to rain-bearing winds, as in Southwest Asia, can they support large, populous settlements.

Living on the Edge. The smaller maps emphasize the importance of natural limits on population distribution. Length of growing season in Canada and precipitation in northwestern Africa restrict the

---

. . . There is a fundamental order and logic in the distribution of people and their activities and creations. . .

---

number and range of settlements in both areas. Since non-agricultural opportunities are limited in these regions, population centers reflect where farmers have successfully cultivated the lands.

In western Canada a short growing season has restricted settlement. There can be little agriculture except that based on grazing where the growing seasing is less than three months long. But settlement does not end abruptly, for some appears

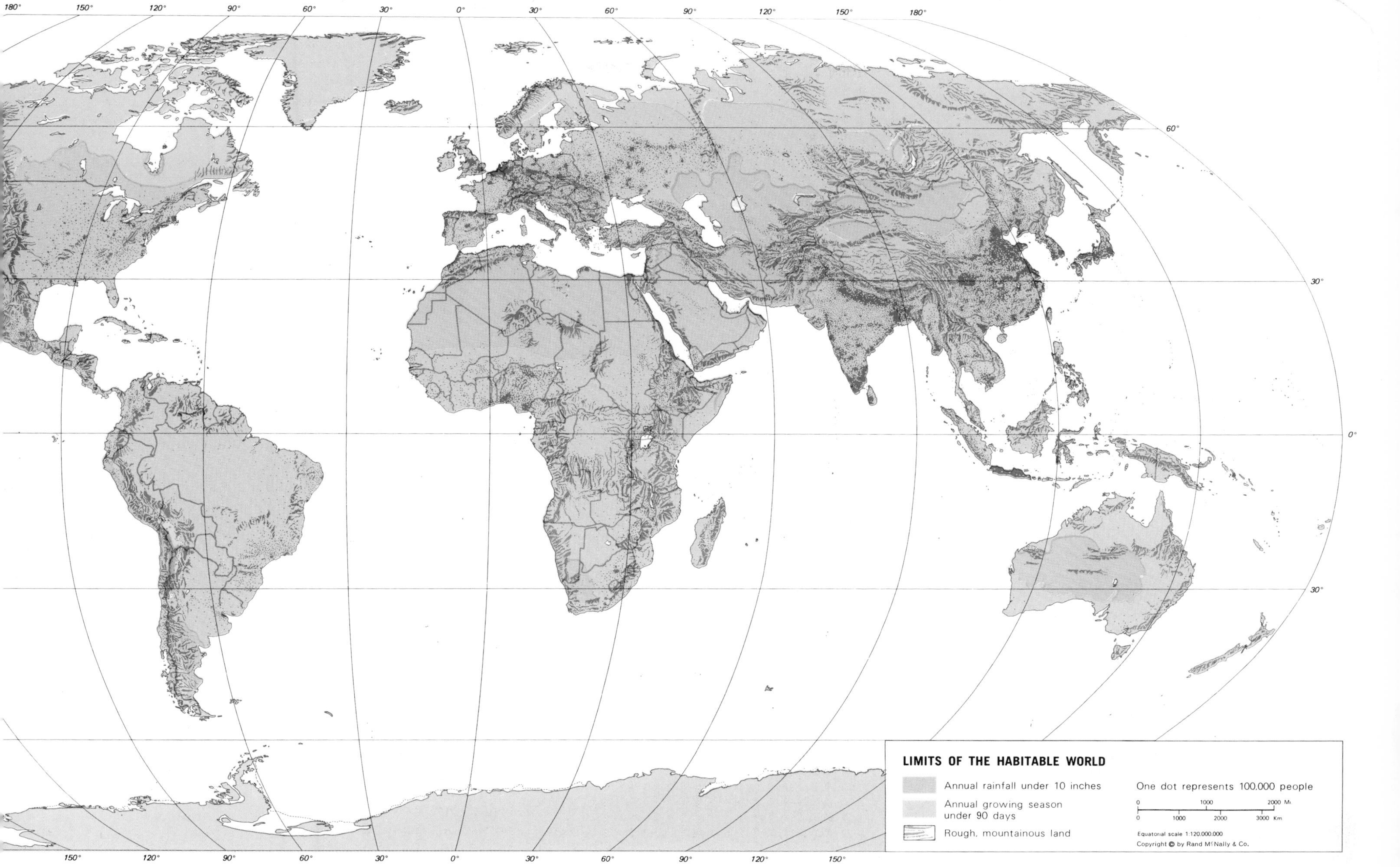

LIMITS OF THE HABITABLE WORLD

Annual rainfall under 10 inches

Annual growing season
under 90 days

Rough, mountainous land

One dot represents 100,000 people

Equatorial scale 1:120,000,000
Copyright © by Rand M⁹Nally & Co.

in the colder zone. Hunting, trapping, fishing, fur-trading, lumbering, mining, and transportation and government jobs account for the scattered population outside the limits of farming.

In northwestern Africa, cereal farming requires abundant rainfall. As a result, the dense rural population has settled mainly in the coastal hills. However, as in western Canada, settlement does not end abruptly, for wells tap underground water and dams divert streams flowing from the Atlas Mountains. Nevertheless, irrigation farming is more restricted than rain agriculture. The pattern of population distribution shows a break where average precipitation drops below 10 inches (25.4 centimeters) a year.

Perhaps nowhere else in the world is the contrast between inhabited and uninhabited land so dramatic as in the Nile Delta and surrounding desert lands. The photograph taken from an orbiting spacecraft highlights the stark contrast between the fertile valley and the bleak, arid land to the west and south. Average annual rainfall at Cairo, at the southern edge of the delta, is only slightly over 1 inch (2.54 centimeters). At Alexandria, on the northern edge, moist winds from the Mediterranean Sea raise the total to 7 inches (17.78 centimeters), still insufficient for farming without irrigation. As a result, the population of Egypt is confined to the floodplain and delta of the Nile River—the crowded homeland of 40,000,000 Egyptians.

Culture and Human Settlement. Cultural factors also influence where people are likely to settle. The contrast between major urban areas and uninhab-

Most Desirable Regions. As the map illustrates, humanity has chosen to settle in the richest and most fertile regions of the earth. These areas combine adequate rainfall and growing season with terrain that is neither too rough or mountainous. Abundant mineral deposits as well as people's ability to develop natural resources also explain settlement preferences. In contrast, regions with less hospitable climates, such as deserts, equatorial zones, and the poles, have discouraged dense settlement.

Humanity's Boldness. In sight of the Myrdals Glacier, a farmer in Iceland has succeeded in extending the limits of the habitable world. Cultural developments, such as hybrid crops that mature faster, make farming—and permanent settlement—possible in these harsh northern latitudes.

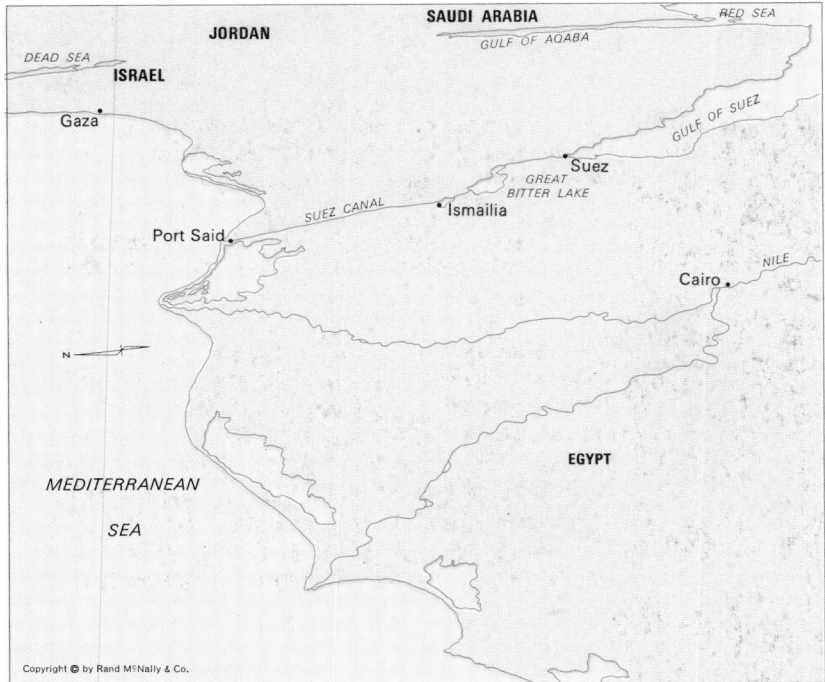

Map of the Nile Delta shown in the photograph below.

An Astronaut's View. The photograph of the Nile Delta, taken from the spacecraft Gemini IV, points out the sharp contrast between crowded, fertile land in the foreground and the desert beyond. An average annual rainfall of only 1 to 7 inches (2.54 to 17.78 centimeters) in this region cannot support agriculture without irrigation. As a result, the population of Egypt lives on the floodplain and delta of the Nile River.

Urban Crowding. New York City (far left) is an example of the densely settled human urban landscape that develops when multiple factors are present to offer employment opportunity. It is a typical setting for the life and work of many Americans and others in the world living in industrial-commercial societies.

Humanized Rural. This part of Vermont typifies the ''empty'' regions adjacent to the heavily populated northeastern metropolitan areas of the United States. The soil, terrain, and climate limit economic opportunity and thus permanent settlement, even though scenery and recreational potential make it an attractive place in which to live. It is sobering to realize that despite our great urban centers, sparsely inhabited land accounts for the major portion of the earth's surface.

ited land in the northeastern United States is a good example. A vast and almost continuous zone of urban development, a megalopolis, stretches from Washington, D. C., to Boston. This region offers innumerable employment opportunities, has an intricate network of communication, and can boast of all the facilities and resources associated with one of the world's greatest concentrations of population. This complex of homes, schools, indus-

---

...A vast and almost continuous zone of urban development stretches from Washington, D. C. to Boston...

---

try, stores and supermarkets, highways, parking lots, train and air terminals, and hospitals is a zone best described as a cultural landscape.

This urbanized area, as so many other built-up areas, has its counterpart in uninhabited or sparsely settled lands close by. Urban zones are limited mainly by their network of communication and transportation. People will commute an hour, even two, to their jobs, but not three or four hours. Outlying regions, beyond the range of commuting, especially in hilly or poorly drained areas, serve as sites for resorts, retirement communities, and small market towns. In general, the persistence of these communities runs counter to the trend for people to move from rural to urban areas. And, in the past decade, cities in the North and Northeast have been losing their populations to the less urbanized South and Southwest. For some, milder climate has become more attractive than commercial opportunities. Also, rising labor and energy costs have forced many businesses to relocate in the so-called Sun Belt—in some instances, taking their workers with them.

The association of crowded and empty land is also evident in Europe. As in the United States, the first areas to be abandoned were those where agriculture was poor. The pattern included shifts from mountain land to lowland, dry land to irrigated land, and poorer land to richer land. Many people gave up rural livelihoods for the greater promise of commerce and industry. For example, the trend to settle the alpine slopes was reversed when industries keyed to water power sprang up in the valleys. Since the industrial process that encourages this shift in population is not yet evident in many areas of the world, we cannot speak of a global trend toward rural depopulation.

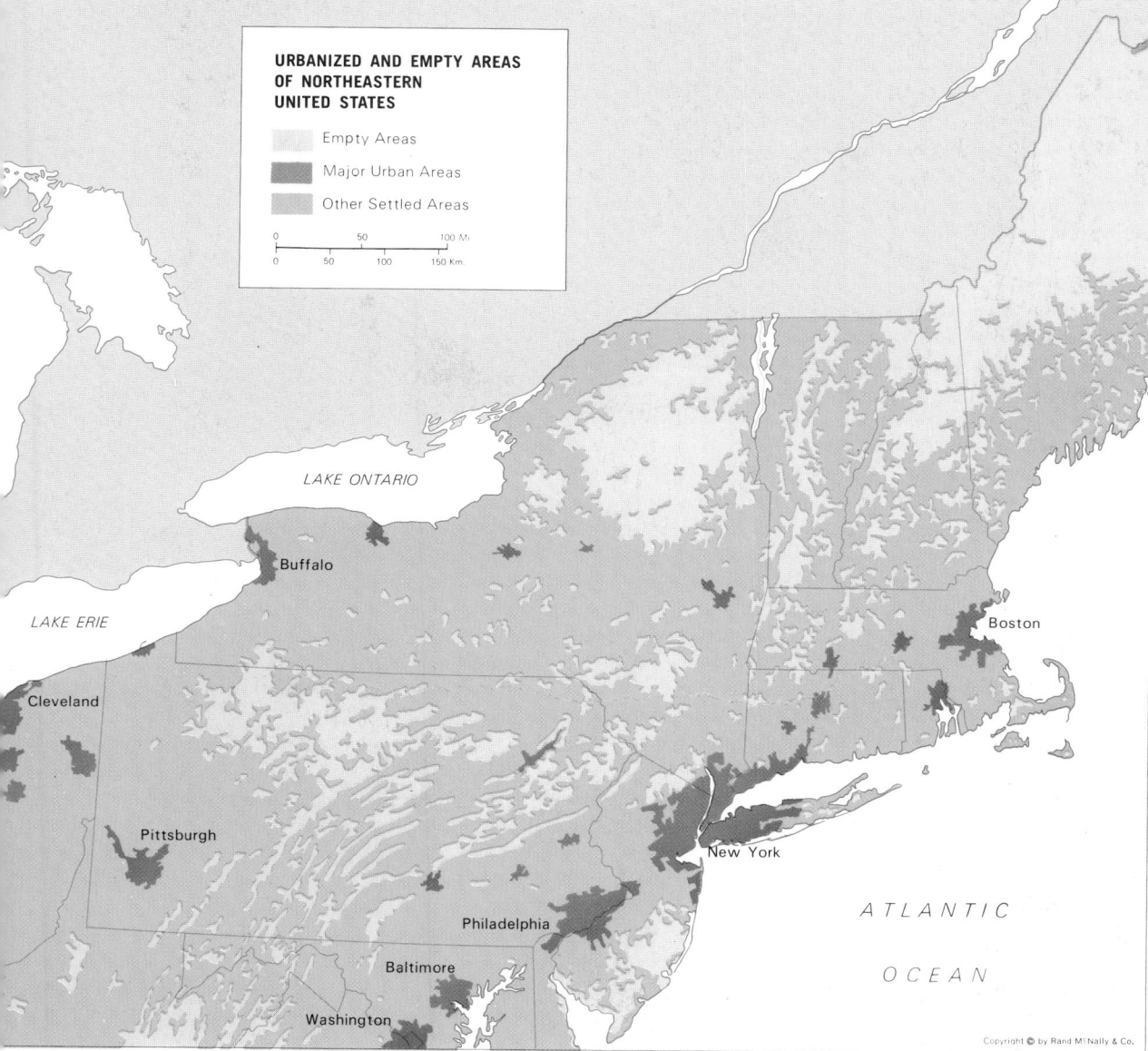

URBANIZED AND EMPTY AREAS OF NORTHEASTERN UNITED STATES

Empty Areas
Major Urban Areas
Other Settled Areas

0   50   100 Mi.
0   50   100   150 Km.

LAKE ONTARIO

Buffalo

LAKE ERIE

Cleveland

Boston

Pittsburgh

New York

Philadelphia

Baltimore

ATLANTIC OCEAN

Washington

Copyright © by Rand McNally & Co.

Cultural and Natural Factors Combine. Cultural incentives such as employment opportunities found in the cities of the northeastern United States help explain the dense urban settlement along the seaboard. Gray areas near these urban sprawls outside the commuting range depict hilly or poorly drained land with little economic potential. This natural restriction, together with the cultural factor of better employment opportunities in cities, has accelerated the movement of people from rural to urban areas.

Our "Permanent" Patterns. We are so used to thinking of ourselves as "conquerors of the world," it is well to remember that many of our imprints and settlements have not lasted. Each generation has left a new pattern of ghost towns and abandoned land. To understand the complex forces behind our patterns of settlement and abandonment, advance and retreat, we must bear in mind that the earth's resources are exhaustible and that each generation is governed by its own goals and values. The current energy crisis has made us keenly aware of how dependent our great urban and industrial centers are on adequate energy supplies. Should those supplies be disrupted or destroyed, the megalopolis could rapidly become a "ghost town."

Historical Forces

Before giving further consideration to the factors that influence the distribution of human settlement and economic activities, we must go back several centuries. The human geography of our world cannot be adequately explained without taking into account the forces that have shaped it over many hundreds of years.

Patterns of Land Use—A.D. 1500. Perhaps the most significant event in the evolution of the world's cultural landscapes is the extraordinary expansion of European culture. We can best show the impact of this expansion by looking at the pattern of land use at about A.D. 1500, on the eve of the European movement into Africa, Asia, and the Americas. The nearby world map depicts only the

---

. . . It is well to remember that many of our imprints and settlements have not lasted . . .

---

most significant features of that pattern: the distribution of agricultural and nonagricultural livelihoods, including the ranges of important natural resources.

Eight Major Centers. By 1500, agriculture had spread over most of the Old World and a substantial part of the New World. The diffusion of crops and domesticated animals came primarily from eight major regions or centers in the world. Scholars have not yet been able to determine the exact ages of these centers and their possible connections with one another. Yet archaeological evidence suggests that cereal farming, especially wheat, barley, and maize, may have been practiced before other types of cultivation. In any case, each of the centers contributed several plant foods and various domesticated animals, to world agriculture.

From the standpoint of Western culture, the most important center was located in Southwest Asia and the Mediterranean region. Here the cultivation of cereals, vegetables, and tree crops, and the herding of sheep and goats, provided the foundation for what may have been the world's oldest system of agriculture. In contrast, Europe was not an important center of innovation. Only one significant crop, oats, is thought to have been domesticated north of the Alps. Most of Europe's crops were introduced from Southwest Asia. The crop complexes of East, South, and Southeast Asia spread throughout these regions and into Africa.

Livelihood Patterns in the Old World. Agricultural civilizations took several forms. In Europe, Northwest Africa, Southwest Asia, and Central Asia, cereal farming, horticulture, and livestock used for plowing were common features. In the tropical regions of Africa and Asia, root crops were combined with cereal farming and, in some cases, replaced it. Plows were supplanted by hoes and other hand tools. Population density was heaviest in East and South Asia and in Europe. Although somewhat less populated, the area of North Africa and Southwest Asia included densely settled river valleys where cultivation depended on irrigation.

. . . The diffusion of crops and domesticated animals came primarily from eight major centers in the world . . .

By 1500, most of these regions had developed cities or urban districts. The agricultural areas of the Old World had also witnessed the development of several major religions, different systems of writing, and the rise and fall of kingdoms and vast empires. On the eve of its expansion overseas, Europe was evolving from a rather backward peninsula of Asia into a formidable military, political, and economic power.

The nonagricultural areas of the Old World were restricted to the northern part of Europe and Asia, where growing seasons are too short for farming. Certain isolated patches of nonagricultural areas were also found in the tropical forests of Central Africa and Southeast Asia. Pygmy and Negrito

---

The Birth of Agriculture. The wide-ranging agricultural landscapes of the earth in A.D. 1500 originated in eight major centers from which domesticated crops and animals had been disseminated for many hundreds of years. The chart below lists crops and animals associated with each major center.

Northeast Africa	millets sorghums	lentils peas	cucumbers sesame	melons	coffee cotton	cats dogs	donkey
Southwest Asia and Mediterranean	barley rye wheat	peas	onions	almonds date palm fig grapevine olive		cattle? dogs dromedary camel goat pig?	pigeon sheep
Central Asia		lentils peas	onions turnips	apple cherries melons pears walnut	hemp	bactrian camel dogs horse reindeer yak	
South and Southeast Asia			eggplant taro yam	banana citrus fruits mango	black pepper sugar cane	cats cattle? chicken dogs	ducks goose pig water buffalo
East Asia	millets rice sorghums	soy beans	cabbages radishes	apricot peaches persimmon plums	mulberry silkworm tea	dogs chicken? pig?	
Eastern South America		beans peanut	manioc squashes sweet potato	cashew pineapple	cacao tobacco	dogs ducks	
Andean Highlands			oca potato squashes ulluco	strawberry		alpaca guinea pig llama	
Mexico and Central America	maize	beans	red pepper squashes tomatoes	avocado		dogs turkey	

Plural endings, e.g., onions, indicate that several varieties are involved. Question marks indicate uncertainty as to area or areas of origin.

Mexico and Central America

180°
60°
30°
0°
30°
60°
180°

tribes in these latter areas lived by hunting and by gathering wild plants. A more specialized livelihood based on herding reindeer was practiced by some of the people in Scandinavia and the Arctic fringe of Siberia. Nonagricultural livelihoods were also found in the arid and semiarid regions of Southwest Africa. While the cereal-farming, pastoral, and oasis economy of North Africa would have suited the southwest area as well, the economy could not spread through the humid tropical environment of Central Africa. Agriculture also failed to move beyond the East Indian islands into Australia.

Diffusion of Crops in the New World. At the time of the first voyages across the Atlantic, agriculture had already spread over substantial areas of the New World. For the most part, it involved the diffusion of two crop complexes. One from Central America included maize, beans, and squashes, and the other from South America consisted of manioc and sweet potatoes. The crop complex of the Andean highlands—potatoes and potatolike plants (oca, ulluco)—provided the food base for the vast Inca empire.

To the north, agriculture was restricted to Central America and Mexico (the Mayan and Aztec civilizations), the forest lands of the eastern half of the United States and along the rivers in the southwestern United States. The crop complex of Mexico and Central America could not survive in the short growing season north of the Great Lakes, nor did it spread into the semiarid lands of the Great Plains. The most impressive example of the diffusion of agriculture was the extraordinary distribution of maize, from southern Chile to the St. Lawrence

Flourishing Civilizations. The ruined terraces and buildings of this 15th-century Inca city at Machu Picchu, Peru, offer dramatic evidence of the material accomplishments of one of the New World's most highly developed civilizations.

The World Stage Set for Development. Just prior to the expansion of European culture into almost every area of the world, people's livelihoods were related to various forms of farming, hunting, fishing, and plant gathering. The map shows the likely distribution of these activities and the eight major centers of innovation. Most of these areas had also developed sophisticated urban centers.

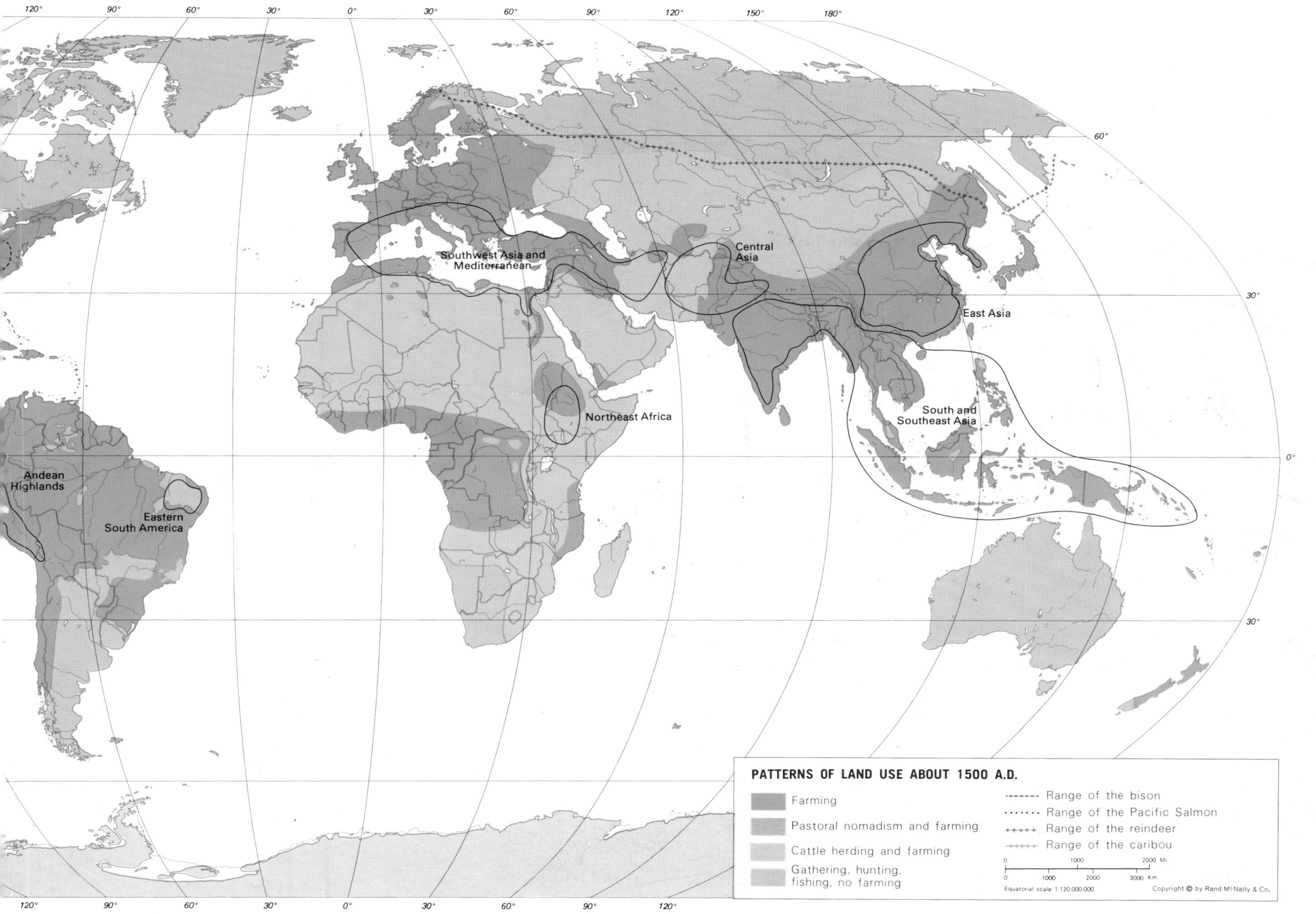

PATTERNS OF LAND USE ABOUT 1500 A.D.

Farming

Pastoral nomadism and farming

Cattle herding and farming

Gathering, hunting, fishing, no farming

------- Range of the bison
.... Range of the Pacific Salmon
+++++ Range of the reindeer
++++++ Range of the caribou

0   1000   2000 Mi.
0   1000   2000   3000 Km
Equatorial scale 1:120,000,000   Copyright © by Rand McNally & Co.

Southwest Asia and Mediterranean

Central Asia

East Asia

Northeast Africa

South and Southeast Asia

Andean Highlands

Eastern South America

Valley and the Great Lakes region of North America, a chain spanning two continents.

The nonagricultural areas of the New World included the semiarid environment of central Argentina, which could not support tropical crops, as well as the colder regions of southern Argentina and Chile. In restricted areas of the tropical forests, throughout South America, scattered groups practiced hunting, fishing, and plant gathering to support themselves. In North America, salmon and bison provided the basis for some groups' livelihoods, but for the most part people obtained their sustenance from plants as well as from fish or game. The richest source of plant food was from acorns of the oak forests of California.

Livelihood patterns of people in the New World can help us distinguish between civilized and primitive areas. Mexico, Central America, the northern fringe of South America, and the Andean highlands—areas where agriculture was well established—all had advanced civilizations, with urban areas, elaborate political organizations, distinct social levels, and sophisticated art and architecture. In many ways, these areas compared favorably to civilized regions of the Old World. Except for weaknesses in military technology—

absence of riding animals, iron, and gunpowder—these New World civilizations might have been able to resist the Europeans.

European Expansion and Colonization. From the time of Columbus until the middle of the 17th century, Europeans did not try to establish many settlements overseas. They were more interested in acquiring the spices, silks, tea, and other goods of the Orient, and the gold and silver of Central and South America. As in the Spanish conquest of the Aztec and Inca empires, the motto "God, gold, and glory" seemed to inspire most early European ventures abroad.

In time, European occupation of new lands assumed two forms: "farm colonization" in the temperate regions of North America, Australia, New Zealand, and South Africa, and "plantation colonization" in the tropical regions of Central and South America, Central Africa, and Asia.

Farm Colonization. Farm colonization began when fur trading, fishing, and other commercial enterprises gave way to subsistence farming. As more and more settlers immigrated to the New World, they reproduced the European settlement patterns of hamlets, villages, and towns. This population pushed steadily westward and even-

tually occupied territories larger and richer than the European homeland.

Plantations. Plantation colonization developed in areas that possessed valuable natural resources for European markets but were less attractive as permanent settlements. The plantation economy was generally based on certain crops or raw materials, such as sugar cane and rubber, which were grown or collected for export. Europeans acted as overseers of native laborers, usually local people but later slaves from West Africa. Plantations worked best in the tropics, where cheap labor, year-long growing seasons, and a host of valuable crops or raw materials insured a handsome return for colonists involved in the enterprise. The European plantation economy persisted into the 19th century in the Americas and even later in Africa and Asia. Eventually, the abolition of slavery; competition from beet sugar, artificial dyes, new fibers, and textiles; and the rise of nationalism brought the age of European colonization to a close.

New "Frontiers". The vast lands opened to pioneer settlement in the 19th century have all been occupied. Frontiers today are marginal or remote areas that earlier settlers passed by: the interior of Brazil, the eastern flanks of the Andes, the drier edges of the cultivated areas of the Soviet Union, the tropical environment of northern Australia, and the mining frontiers of Canada and Siberia. Although these frontiers are not likely to attract many people, some government attempts to settle people in the tropical areas of Brazil are in

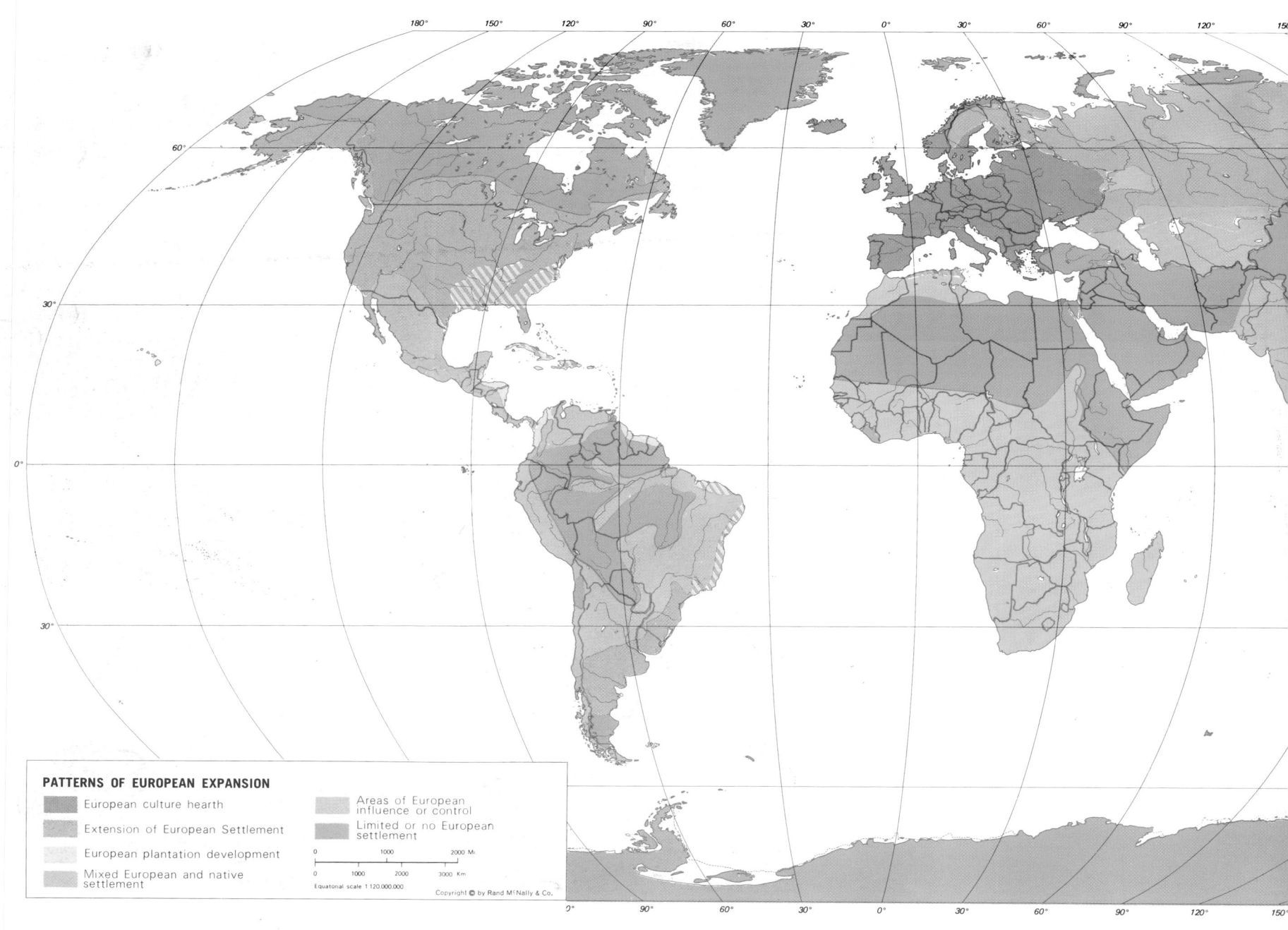

PATTERNS OF EUROPEAN EXPANSION

- European culture hearth
- Extension of European Settlement
- European plantation development
- Mixed European and native settlement
- Areas of European influence or control
- Limited or no European settlement

0   1000   2000 Mi.
0   1000   2000   3000 Km.
Equatorial scale 1:120,000,000

Copyright © by Rand McNally & Co.

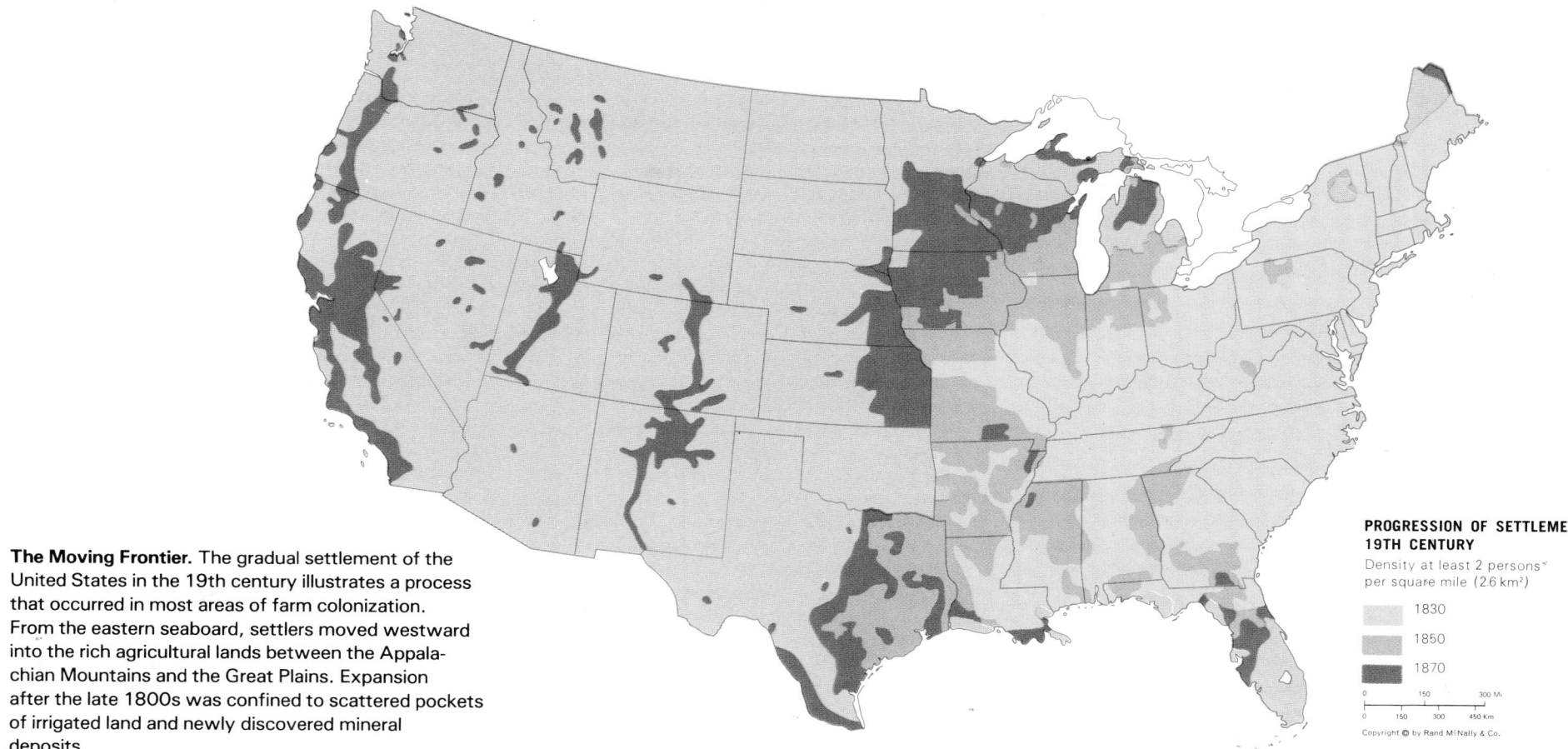

PROGRESSION OF SETTLEMENT 19TH CENTURY

Density at least 2 persons* per square mile (2.6 km²)

- 1830
- 1850
- 1870

0 150 300 Mi.
0 150 300 450 Km.

The Moving Frontier. The gradual settlement of the United States in the 19th century illustrates a process that occurred in most areas of farm colonization. From the eastern seaboard, settlers moved westward into the rich agricultural lands between the Appalachian Mountains and the Great Plains. Expansion after the late 1800s was confined to scattered pockets of irrigated land and newly discovered mineral deposits.

European Influence Causes Change. After A.D. 1500, European settlement and the associated culture had its most dramatic extension in North America and South America. Europe's influence and control, however, touched most areas of the world, including many regions that have achieved independent statehood in recent decades. Only China and Japan remained outside the main sphere of European influence until the late 19th and early 20th centuries.

Edge of a Tropical Frontier. This agricultural village in the state of Pará, Brazil, is one of many government-sponsored attempts to permanently settle people in one of the last land frontiers on earth.

Pioneering the Arctic Fringe. Houses and service connections of Inuvik, Northwest Territories, Canada, are lifted above the permanently frozen land. Strong goverment support is needed to establish settlements on the world's arctic lands in Alaska and the Soviet Union as well as this area of Canada.

the experimental stage. For the most part, however, it is not an exaggeration to suggest that the age of European exploration and settlement in the 19th century marks the last chapter in the history of our occupation of the earth. Since then, population movement has meant concentration rather than expansion, as nations experience the effects of industrialization and urban development.

Modern Patterns of Land Use

European expansion encouraged patterns of land use substantially different from those in existence before Columbus's time. Vast areas are still relatively empty, but within most of the habitable world, rural landscapes have been significantly modified.

Land Use. Today small portions of the earth, corresponding to dense urban populations, are devoted to manufacturing and commerce. Yet these areas control much of the world's wealth and political power. Agricultural surplus is possible where mechanization and relatively low population allow high productivity yields per person. In some fertile

Vanishing Ways of Life. Livelihoods based on hunting and gathering, once practiced over large parts of the New World in A.D. 1500, are now limited to the northern fringe of Canada and a few isolated areas in the tropical forests of South America. Elsewhere in the world, this most primitive form of livelihood is practiced by only a few thousand people in Europe and Asia, many living on reservations. By the end of this century, hunting and gathering as a way of life may disappear.

Nomadic life, which once prevailed over the deserts and steppes of the Old World, has also declined. In the Soviet Union, it has all but disappeared. It is discouraged, officially or unofficially, in most of the countries in North Africa and Southwest Asia. Nomads are no longer able to serve as sovereigns of oases or guardians of trade

Asian lands, overpopulation means that many people exist at starvation levels, even though crop yields are high. Vast arid, equatorial, polar, and mountainous regions still sustain human settlement but only at subsistence level. Development of these zones offers one of the greatest challenges to our ingenuity for extending the area of human settlement.

routes; these responsibilities have been assumed by governments. In many parts of the world, old trade routes have been abandoned and transportation mechanized. Impoverished by the loss of their privileged social and economic positions, nomadic peoples have become more willing to seek employment in towns and cities. At present, nomads are predominant in only two countries: Mauritania and Somalia. Elsewhere, even in Saudi Arabia, suppression combined with increased opportunities for settled life is discouraging this ancient livelihood.

Commercial Farming. The decline of pastoral nomadism has not affected the world's production of meat, milk, hides, and other animal products. Commercial stock raising is an important feature

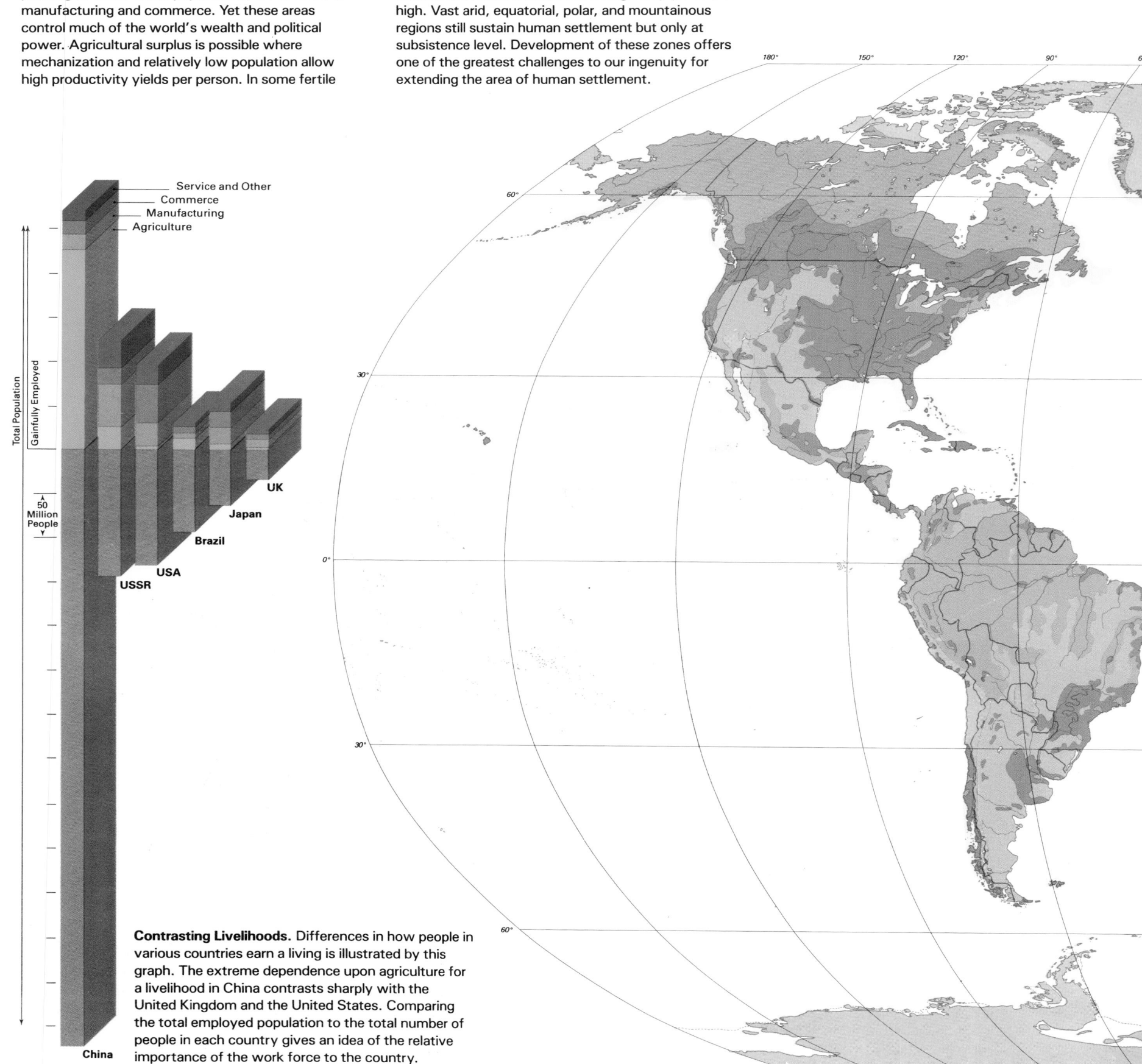

Contrasting Livelihoods. Differences in how people in various countries earn a living is illustrated by this graph. The extreme dependence upon agriculture for a livelihood in China contrasts sharply with the United Kingdom and the United States. Comparing the total employed population to the total number of people in each country gives an idea of the relative importance of the work force to the country.

of the economy in the semiarid regions of Argentina, Australia, Mexico, and the United States. Beef or pork production is an essential part of agriculture in the American Midwest and most of Europe. And dairy farming is not only a major economic factor in such countries as Denmark, Switzerland, the Netherlands, Ireland, and New Zealand, it is often a conspicuous feature of land use near most cities in the Western world.

In some regions, particularly the United States, industrialization has transformed crop raising. Many small, family-owned farms have given way to huge commercial agri-business firms. Using advanced methods of fertilization and mechanized harvesting, these agricultural businesses can raise enough food to feed the population of the United States and still export surplus to other countries.

Subsistence Farming. It would be a mistake, however, to believe that rural life has undergone profound changes everywhere in the world. The semiindustrial agriculture of Europe and the United States is not characteristic of much of Africa, Latin America, or Asia. In these regions, subsistence farming is still the main way of life. It may shift from one area to another, as in the tropical forest of Africa and Southeast Asia, or serve as the basis for peasant village economies found in many areas of the non-Western world. Subsistence farming usually means that food is produced for local consumption only. But farmers may also practice a certain amount of specialization in raising livestock or crops and trade their surplus for a variety of other products—including imports from the outside world. For example, at

tribal markets in remote areas of North Africa you will find tea, kerosene, ballpoint pens, sunglasses, and a host of other items from around the globe.

Nevertheless, the large areas devoted to subsistence farming represent small, essentially closed economic systems. It is in these areas that the challenge of economic development is greatest, for this type of farming is often the struggle of an impoverished people to wrest a living from tiny plots of land. Even rich land does not necessarily mean rich people, for such regions are often

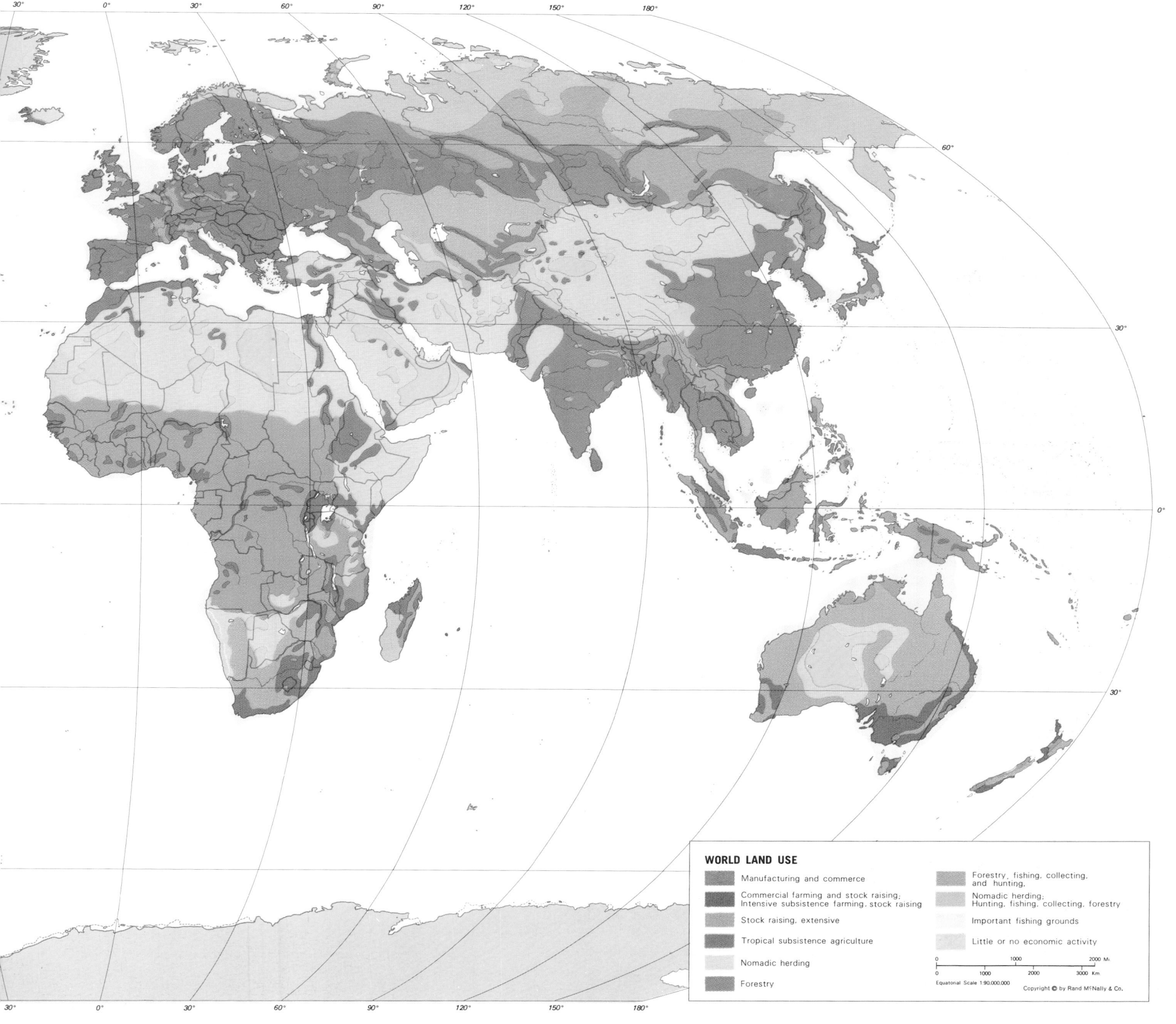

WORLD LAND USE

- Manufacturing and commerce
- Commercial farming and stock raising; Intensive subsistence farming, stock raising
- Stock raising, extensive
- Tropical subsistence agriculture
- Nomadic herding
- Forestry
- Forestry, fishing, collecting, and hunting.
- Nomadic herding; Hunting, fishing, collecting, forestry
- Important fishing grounds
- Little or no economic activity

0   1000   2000 Mi.
0   1000   2000   3000 Km.
Equatorial Scale 1:90,000,000

Copyright © by Rand M°Nally & Co.

seriously overcrowded. Few areas in the world are more fertile than the Nile and Ganges valleys, and few areas have experienced more poverty and suffering.

Release from such grinding poverty and toil is possible only where industries can provide an alternative to rural life and where systems of transportation and storage permit farming on a

---

. . . Release from grinding poverty and toil is possible only where industries can provide an alternative to rural life. . .

---

large scale. For example, the source of food for cities in the United States is incredibly complex—potatoes from Maine, citrus fruits from Florida or California, coffee from Brazil, bananas from Central America, and so on. However, underlying and supporting this pattern of consumption is the

mechanized agriculture of the United States, a system that yields maximum results from a relatively small investment of labor. While not as mechanized, farming in much of Western Europe follows the same pattern.

Hunger versus Plenty—a Worldwide Problem.

The map depicting world land use patterns carries additional meanings. Its various categories provide a basis for distinguishing between regions of hunger and plenty, tradition and innovation, and above all between areas of declining rural livelihood and places where no other way of life is possible. Such contrasts may seem remote to people in the United Kingdom or the United States, where only 5 to 10 percent of the population is employed in food production. But the social and political implications of hunger and poverty constitute a grave threat to the stability of the world, a threat that wealthier nations cannot afford to ignore.

Manufacturing and Commerce.
Only a small portion of the earth's surface is devoted to manufacturing and commerce—the foundation of wealth and national power. These areas coincide with major urban districts. In the United States, cities account for slightly over 1 percent of the territory, yet provide employment and residence for nearly 70 percent of the population. Australia, a large and sparsely populated country, is even more highly urbanized. Only in the United Kingdom, the Netherlands, and West Germany do urban areas cover a substantial part of the land. This situation, perhaps more than any other, demonstrates the truth of our earlier generalization about the uneven distribution of humanity.

. . . The social and political implications of hunger and poverty constitute a grave threat to the stability of the world. . .

The lighter, wedge-shaped area on each map represents the region pictured in the accompanying photograph.

Clustered Settlement. In many areas of Europe, rural settlement consists of a tight cluster of houses and other buildings located in the midst of surrounding fields. Varennes, France, shown in this photograph and map, is such a settlement. Numerous factors have contributed to the development of these rural clusters: local water supplies, the convergence of communication lines, the mutual need for protection, and social or economic circumstances that encourage close residential communities.

Settlements

Human settlement is either concentrated into hamlets, villages and cities or dispersed into scattered farmsteads.

Patterns of Rural Settlement. Every culture has created its own distinctive pattern. Throughout history, wherever rural people live together and travel to their fields, the settlements are in tight clusters, usually near lines of communication and reliable sources of water. Dispersed settlements may be strung out along roads, on dikes in poorly drained areas, or along rivers. Scattered settlements are found in many parts of the world: Australia and New Zealand, the British Isles, Argentina, and most of Canada and the United States. Often such settlements reflect widely dispersed sources of water or hilly terrain. They may also be the result of a particular system of land subdivision, an explanation that accounts for the way farm communities are scattered in the United States.

However, environment or methods of land subdivision alone do not explain patterns of rural settlement. When all factors are considered, the most basic issue is culture, the particular style

---

. . . Settlement patterns reflect cultural tradition for people tend to live in the manner of their ancestors. . .

---

and preferences of a people. Some prefer to live in compact villages and commute to their fields; others prefer to settle on the banks of rivers; and still others are content to live in widely scattered houses in the midst of their fields. Also, settlement patterns tend to reflect cultural tradition more than personal choice. In most parts of the world, and especially in rural areas, people tend to live in the manner of their ancestors, repeating patterns established over long periods of time.

Urban Development Patterns. The pattern of urban development also varies from culture to culture. In most of North America, most cities are laid out in a grid pattern, with streets intersecting one another at right angles. Other features include a distinctive profile, with tall buildings in the heart of the city giving way to lower structures and then to single-family and apartment dwellings. American cities usually have well-defined zones: residential, industrial, commercial, and so on. The quality of residences tends to improve as you travel to the outskirts of the city. In these outlying regions, urban and rural areas may blend into an "urban sprawl." In a culture strongly influenced by the automobile, it is not surprising that newer shopping districts are usually built in suburban areas or as narrow strips along highways.

In Europe, the pattern of city development

Linear Settlement. A special linear settlement pattern near Beauharnois, Canada, developed under the seignorial, or landlord, system in the French-speaking areas of Canada during the latter half of the 17th century. Narrow strips of land, some only 100 yards (60 meters) wide, fronted the St. Lawrence River and extended back from the banks for a half mile or so. This type of rural settlement contrasts with those in northern France, the homeland of most pioneer settlers of the St. Lawrence Valley.

Scattered Settlement. When farm buildings and houses are situated on the individual farmstead they serve, as shown by the map and photo near Taunton, England, a dispersed pattern of settlement develops. A common feature of the agricultural landscape of the United States and Canada, this scattered form of settlement can also be seen in Europe and many other parts of the world.

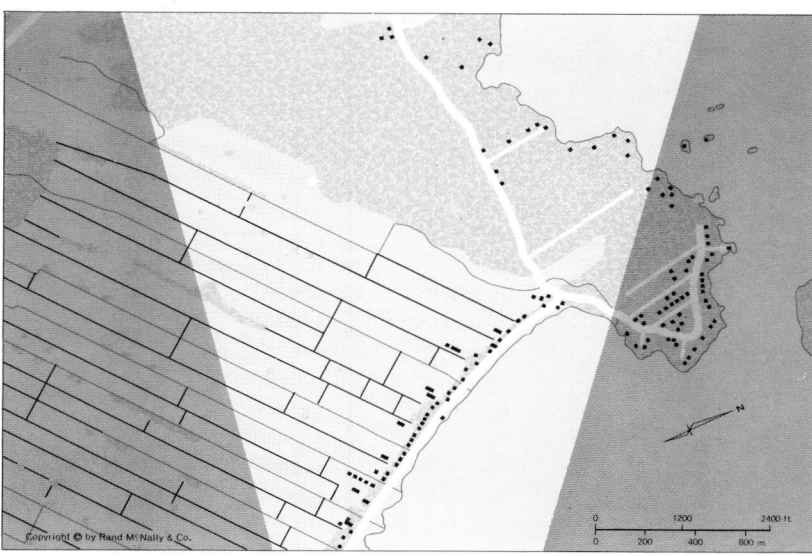

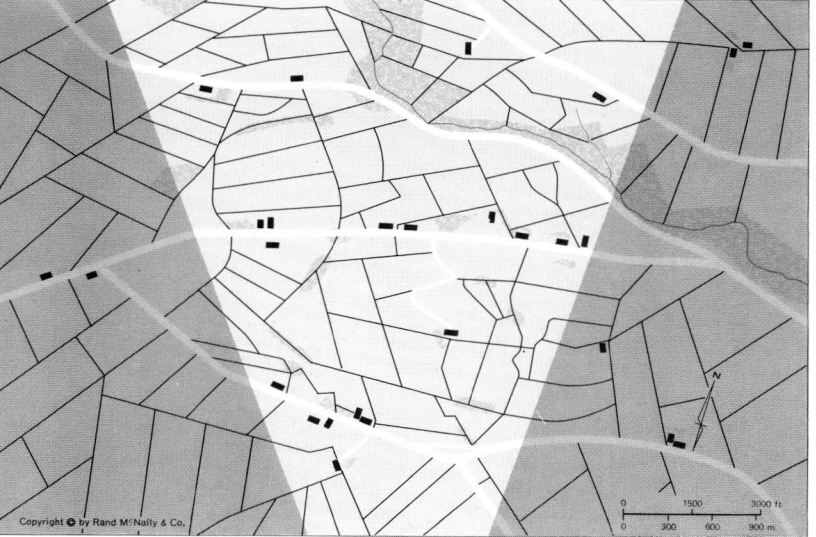

is more complex. The basic structure of most European cities was established long before the automobile arrived on the scene, and streets tend to be more irregular and narrow. Zoning is usually less distinct, with more specialty shops and fewer well-defined central business districts or "downtown" areas. The focal point of such cities tends to be religious or political rather than commercial. As a result, urban sprawl is less evident, and there is usually a sharper distinction between urban and rural landscapes. Since the skyscraper does not yet dominate European cities, the urban profile is less clearly outlined than in the United States. If a geometric pattern is evident, more often than not it

has been imposed on an older, more haphazard design.

Once we move beyond the realm of Western civilization, we encounter widely different city patterns, as the photograph of Fès, in Morocco, clearly illustrates. Since Fès is walled, it begins and ends abruptly. Its profile is low, for most buildings have only two or three stories. Streets are narrow alleys, often with dead ends, since they were built without regard for motor vehicles. Fès has several quarters, but these are culturally rather than economically defined. The Andalusian quarter was founded by refugees from the Christian reconquest of Spain, while the Kairouani quarter takes its name from the original inhabitants, who came from the Tunisian city of el-Kairouan. Unlike American or European cities, Fès has no clear distinction between residential and commercial or industrial districts. Crafts and trade activi-

ties are spread along particular lanes; craft workers and merchants usually live above or behind their shops. The focal point of the entire city, as with many cities of the Middle East, is a large mosque containing the tomb of the patron saint of the city. Smaller mosques serve as focal points for particular quarters. But as a visitor to Fès, you would have a hard time determining where the "downtown" of the city is located.

Similar urban patterns can be found in the traditional cities of the Middle East and elsewhere in Asia. Modern quarters, of course, have a different character. The new quarter of the ancient city of Damascus is laid out in wide, regular streets not

Irregular City Pattern. Many traditional urban developments in North Africa and Southwest Asia resemble this medieval walled city of Fès, Morocco. Compact and seemingly haphazard arrangements of narrow streets, twisted alleys, low houses, and tiny courtyards characterize these cities. The lack of more substantial thoroughfares indicates that such towns were designed long before motor traffic came on the scene.

Copyright © by Rand McNally & Co.

unlike those found in an American city. Where European influence has been strong, especially in former colonial areas, two distinctly different cities often exist side by side. Old and New Delhi and the ancient and modern quarters of Jerusalem are particularly striking examples of this dual pattern. In time, contrasting styles may eventually blend. Nevertheless, it is still possible to speak of "Western" and "Eastern" patterns of urban development. This fact illustrates one of the most important principles of human geography—that each culture has a distinctive urban style.

Distribution of World Industry

The process of industrialization, which began in Europe in the 18th century, so thoroughly transformed society that it has often been described as a revolution. Perhaps "evolution" would be an equally appropriate term, for the inventions, economic changes, and social transformations of this process have helped shape human history during the past three centuries.

Key Inventions of the Industrial Revolution. The Industrial Revolution was founded on a series of key inventions. Perhaps the most influential were improved spinning and weaving machines, the steam engine, the railway locomotive, and the factory system of production characterized by specialized tasks.

The significance of these technological advances cannot be overestimated. They constitute the foundation of the modern economy in Europe, the United States, Japan, and the Soviet Union. It is striking to note that a large number of major inventions occurred over a fairly brief time, and most of them can be credited to Europeans and Americans.

Radial Pattern. The photograph and map of Paris, France (left), illustrates the world's most notable example of a radial plan. It was used in the 19th-century redevelopment of the French capital with the Arc de Triomphe at its center. Based on the principle of a wheel hub and spokes, the plan was conceived in the 18th century by the architect L'Enfant for the capital of the United States.

Rectangular Grid Pattern. Although widespread in the world, the rectangular, or grid, street pattern is most characteristic of cities in the United States and Canada. San Francisco, even though built on hilly terrain, is an example of the north-south and east-west orientation of streets intersecting at right angles; this layout was chosen in response to a uniform national survey system.

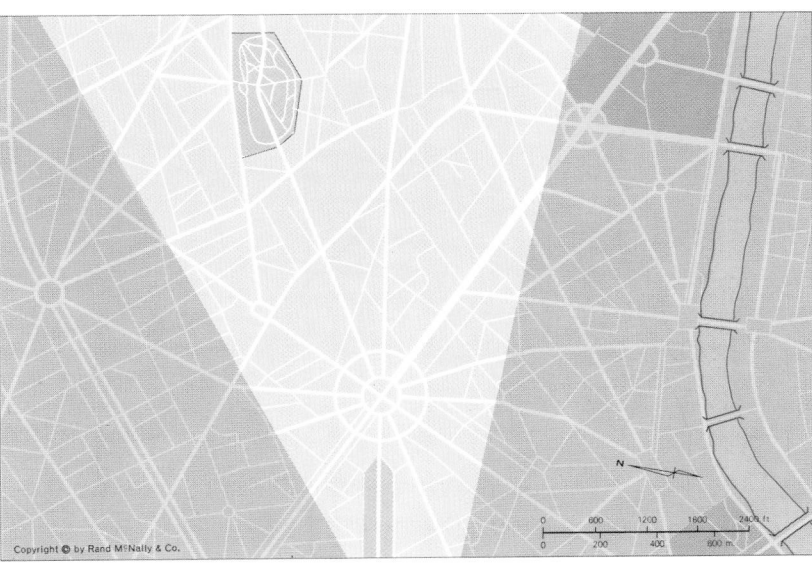

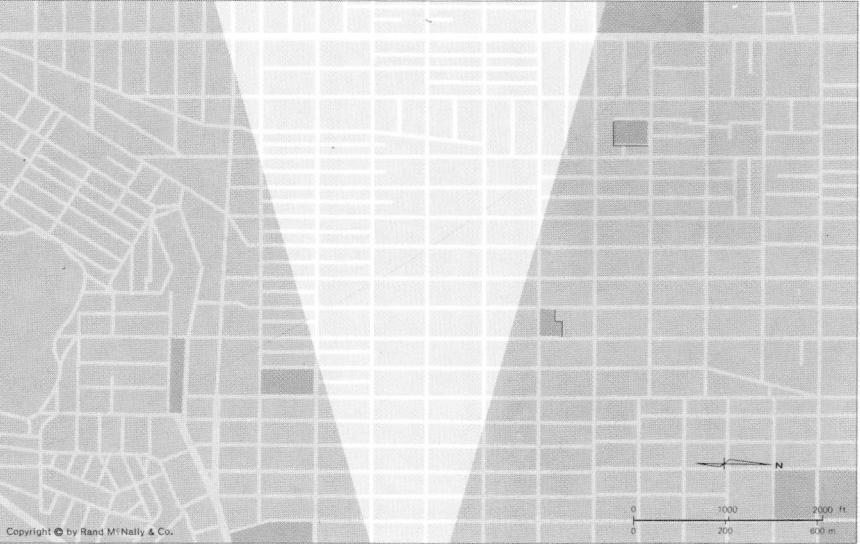

The Industrial Revolution is indeed an achievement of Western civilization, and it may be the only one destined to spread over the entire world.

Taken together, several technological changes had far-reaching effects on the nature of produc-

---

. . . Control of or access to resources required for heavy industry is necessary for any country that hopes to be a major world power . . .

---

tion and employment in the Western world. These include (1) the use of new basic materials, especially steel; (2) the use of new sources of energy (steam engines, petroleum, electricity, and internal combustion engines); (3) a great increase in production with a smaller investment of labor; (4) a radical reorganization of work, from small, family enterprises to large factories with elaborate subdivisions of labor; (5) important developments in transportation partly needed to carry raw materials to factories and ship finished products to markets; and (6) an increased application of science to industry.

These innovations not only permitted the mass production of goods but meant an increased use of certain natural resources such as oil, natural gas, coal, aluminum, and other minerals. Population tended to concentrate in those areas where abundant raw materials were discovered.

Resources and Manufacturing. Europe and the United States, with their large deposits of coal and iron ore, have the raw materials necessary for steel production. The United States is also well endowed with petroleum and natural gas. The extraordinary abundance of resources in the United States was underscored in World War II. The interruption of international commerce resulted in only minor shortages of critical raw materials such as rubber and tin. In contrast, Germany's economy was seriously hampered when the country could no longer get adequate petroleum supplies. The Japanese Empire, whose industry depended on imports of raw materials, lost the war when it lost command of the sea. Control of or access to the resources required for heavy industry, and especially steel production, is necessary for any country that hopes to be a major world power. The United States and the Soviet Union—great rivals since World War II—are particularly rich in this regard.

But natural resources alone do not account for the distribution of manufacturing in the world. For example, tiny Switzerland is a major producer of watches and other precision instruments, whereas the Middle East, with its huge reserves of petroleum, has few other important industries. Besides raw materials, power, and fuel, industrial development requires a skilled labor force; sufficient capital for construction, maintenance, and research; transportation facilities; and access to

---

. . . The Industrial Revolution may be the only one destined to spread over the entire world . . .

---

effective markets. Also, government planning, tariffs, monetary incentives, and economic or political alliances influence industrial development. Thus, the existence of one of the world's major deposits of natural gas in the Sahara does not mean that Algeria will automatically develop a vast petrochemical industry. Nor is the impressive water-power potential in central Africa likely to promote large-scale industries in the near future. On the other hand, government policies may encourage industrial developments that other countries would not consider efficient. For

example, the steel mill at Karabük in Turkey is not economical by European or American standards. Yet the foundry is regarded as a national asset by the Turkish government.

Location of Industrial Areas. Thus, an entire range of factors influences the location of industries and industrial development. Neither the general pattern nor specific cases of industrialization can be adequately explained without keeping these factors in mind. Yet we can make some general observations about the location of industrial regions.

The Americas. In North America, industrial sites coincide with concentrations of resources or with urban districts large enough to provide adequate markets for finished goods. This is especially true of the diversified industrial districts of the Pacific Coast. The main centers of steel production—the Lower Great Lakes region, southeastern Canada, and the northeastern United States—profit from large deposits of iron ore and the transportation network of the Great Lakes. This region, heavily populated, is also blessed with abundant labor and a large market. On the Atlantic Coast, the Piedmont has replaced New England as America's leading textile center and is now a diversified district similar to those on the West Coast. The Gulf region benefits from its port facilities and rich deposits of petroleum and natural gas.

In South America, industrial districts are confined primarily to the main urban centers of the continent: Rio de Janeiro–São Paulo, Buenos Aires, and Santiago. Only Rio de Janeiro and São Paulo have profited from readily accessible deposits of iron ore and coal. Venezuela has important reserves of petroleum and iron ore but

---

. . . Government policies may encourage industrial development that other countries would not consider efficient . . .

---

lacks an adequate labor force or national market to sustain major industrial development. The same can be said for Chile's abundant copper deposits.

Europe, the Soviet Union, and Japan. Four major industrial districts of Europe—Midlands-Lancashire, Belgium and northern France, the Ruhr basin, and Silesia (Śląsk)—coincide with significant deposits of iron ore or coal. The Po Valley in Italy profits from abundant and accessible hydroelectric power. Yet the presence in this area of such important industries as the Fiat automobile works is not a reflection of natural resources but of individual initiative and collective skills. Also, the southern industrial district of Sweden, which has profited from the rich deposits of iron ore in the northern part of the country, is not tied primarily to this one resource.

On the other hand, the pattern of industrial development in the Soviet Union is directly tied to resources. One exception is the Moscow-Gorki district, which—like Buenos Aires or the Po Valley —is more a reflection of local labor supplies and large urban markets than of abundant raw materials. Both the Donbas and the Kuzbas basins have large reserves of coal, with the Donbas also rich in iron ore and hydroelectric power. The Urals region is blessed with a variety of industrial resources, including iron ore, coal, and petroleum. In southern Manchuria, local supplies of coal and iron ore—originally developed by the Japanese— now serve as the base for China's major manufacturing region.

Japan itself is nearly equal to the United States and the Soviet Union in overall industrial production, followed closely by West Germany. Indeed, the impressive growth in Japan in shipbuilding, electrical and optical industries, textiles, automobiles, and many other enterprises is the result of human rather than natural resources.

Key Inventions (1764-1964) These and many other technological innovations revolutionized the nature of production and employment and greatly increased the use of natural resources. Since 1964 people have been aided in their use of the world's resources by widespread use of computer technology, earth-monitoring satellites, and breakthroughs in genetic research.

Key Inventions (1764-1964)		
1764	Spinning Jenny	ENGLAND
1765	Steam Engine	ENGLAND
1769	Self-propelled Steam Vehicle	FRANCE
1783	Puddling Iron Furnace	ENGLAND
1785	Power Loom	ENGLAND
1786	Threshing Machine	SCOTLAND
1793	Cotton Gin	UNITED STATES
1802	Steamboat	UNITED STATES
1811	Cylinder Printing Press	GERMANY
1824	Portland Cement	ENGLAND
1825	Steam Locomotive	ENGLAND
1831	Electric Generator	ENGLAND
1834	Reaper	UNITED STATES
1839	Vulcanization of Rubber	UNITED STATES
1839	Photography *(Daguerreotype)*	FRANCE
1844	Telegraphy	UNITED STATES
1846	Rotary Printing Press	UNITED STATES
1850	Corn Picker	UNITED STATES
1851	Refrigerating Machine	UNITED STATES
1855	Bessemer Process Steel	ENGLAND
1859	Gas Engine	FRANCE
1859	Oil Well Drilling	UNITED STATES
1861	Passenger Elevator	UNITED STATES
1866	Open-hearth Steel Furnace	UNITED STATES
1867	Reinforced Concrete	FRANCE
1869	Railway Air Brake	UNITED STATES
1876	Telephone	UNITED STATES
1876	Four-cycle Gas Engine	GERMANY
1879	Incandescent Light	UNITED STATES
1882	Steam Turbine	FRANCE
1884	Photographic Roll Film	UNITED STATES
1884	Linotype	UNITED STATES
1884	Artificial Silk *(rayon)*	FRANCE
1888	Pneumatic Tire	IRELAND
1892	Diesel Engine	GERMANY
1892	Electric Motor *(A.C.)*	UNITED STATES
1892	Gasoline Automobile	UNITED STATES
1893	Motion Pictures	UNITED STATES
1895	Wireless Telegraphy	ITALY
1900	Caterpillar Tractor	UNITED STATES
1903	Airplane	UNITED STATES
1906	Radio Vacuum Tube	UNITED STATES
1907	Plastic *(Bakelite)*	UNITED STATES
1911	Air Conditioning	UNITED STATES
1913	Radio Receiver	UNITED STATES
1913	Talking Motion Pictures	UNITED STATES
1925	Television	SCOTLAND - UNITED STATES
1926	Liquid-propelled Rocket	UNITED STATES
1928	Autogiro	UNITED STATES
1931	Cyclotron	UNITED STATES
1935	Radiolocator *(radar)*	SCOTLAND
1937	Nylon	UNITED STATES
1937	Jet Aircraft Engine	ENGLAND
1937	Xerography	UNITED STATES
1939	Helicopter	GERMANY - UNITED STATES
1942	Nuclear Reactor	UNITED STATES
1946	Computer	UNITED STATES
1947	Transistor	UNITED STATES
1956	Nuclear Power Station	ENGLAND
1957	Earth-Orbiting Satellite	SOVIET UNION
1959	Fuel Cell	UNITED STATES
1960	Laser	UNITED STATES
1962	Communications Satellite	UNITED STATES
1964	Microcircuitry	UNITED STATES

Indelible Imprint. Near Hibbing, Minnesota, the mining of iron ore—the most useful of the world's metals and a foundation of the industrial strength of the United States—has been carried on for over 100 years. Open-pit mining of iron ore and strip mining of coal have radically altered the earth's surface in many areas—vivid evidence of human modification of the environment.

Keys to Industrial Development. Of all the world's natural resources, fossil fuels have been the most essential for industrial development. (The map shows their distribution favors countries in the northern hemisphere.) Even with rising costs, fossil fuels continue to serve as major energy sources because of abundant reserves and the recent discovery of vast new deposits. Though scattered and less accessible than previously uncovered reserves, these deposits are still cheaper to develop and transport than newer sources of energy, including electricity.

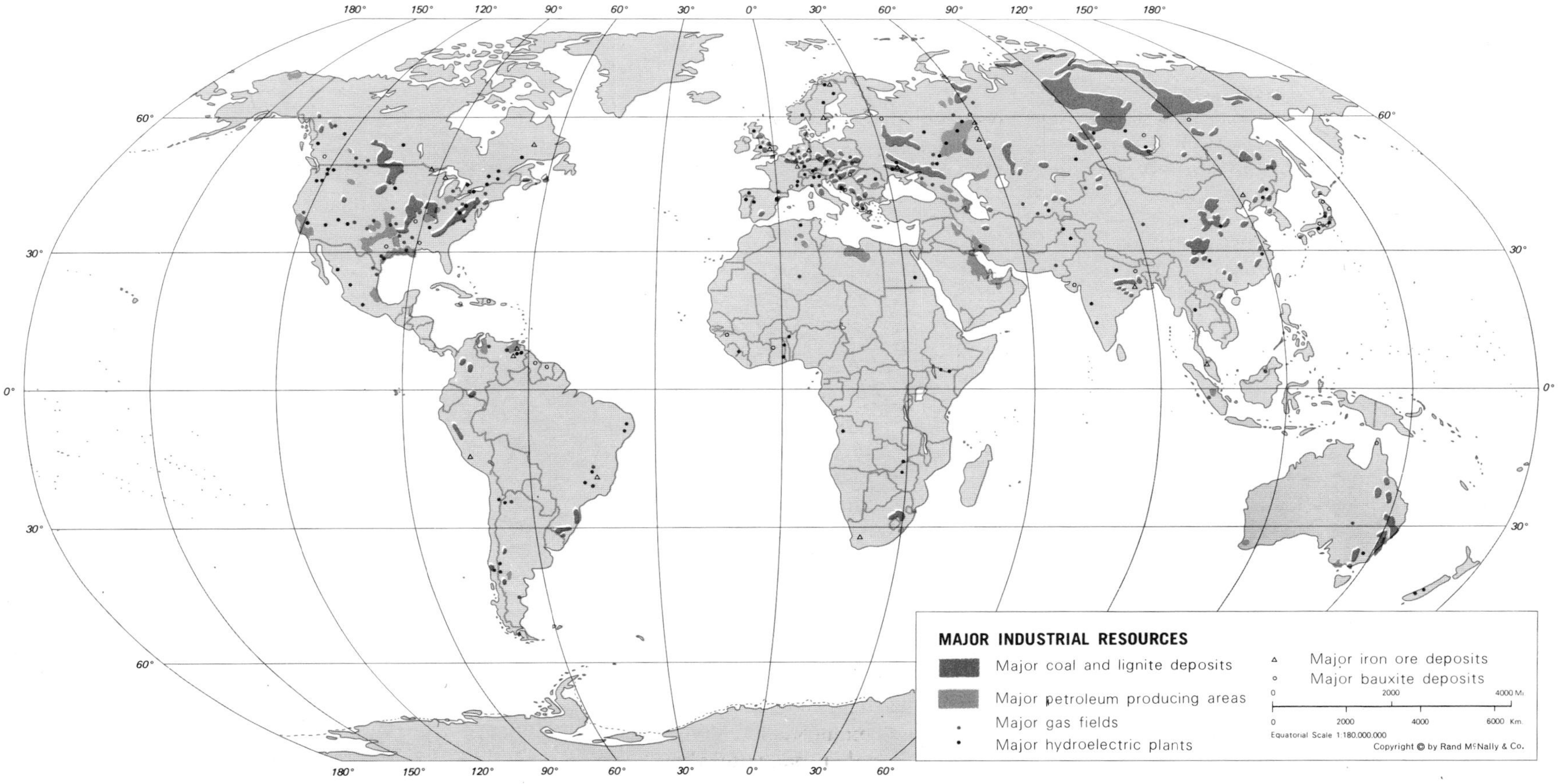

MAJOR INDUSTRIAL RESOURCES
Major coal and lignite deposits
Major petroleum producing areas
Major gas fields
Major hydroelectric plants
Major iron ore deposits
Major bauxite deposits
Equatorial Scale 1:180,000,000
Copyright © by Rand McNally & Co.

Japan lacks important sources of coking coal, iron and other metallic ores, petroleum, and many other resources essential to modern industry. Yet skillful management and abundant, relatively cheap labor have enabled the Japanese to meet the high costs of importing raw materials and still compete successfully with such resource-rich nations as West Germany, the United Kingdom, and the United States.

Other Regions. Industrial development in other areas of the world reflects a mixture of natural resources and cultural influences. India has only one major industrial district, the product of

---

. . . The very life of the world as we know it is highly dependent on adequate, cost-effective sources of energy . . .

---

government encouragement and local supplies of iron ore and coal. Australia's development is virtually coincident with its major population centers. Southwest Asia has no major manufacturing, while China is struggling to modernize its industries. But from an industrial point of view,

Africa remains the least developed continent. The only exceptions are the mining industries in the Johannesburg region keyed to some of the world's richest deposits of gold, uranium, and diamonds.

The map of the United States manufacturing region shows the concentration of employment in that area. Many natural, economic, and political factors have encouraged development in this region. The original basis of the heavy industries was the iron ore of Michigan and Minnesota and coking coal of the Appalachian Mountains. Other industries were drawn by ample water power, transportation by way of the Great Lakes, the rich agriculture of the region, an elaborate system of roads and railways, and the presence of millions of workers and consumers. Similar factors account for the great industrial complex of northern France, Belgium, and West Germany.

Current Trends. In the past two decades, other patterns in industrial development have emerged. Light industries, such as electronics, food processing, even automotive assembly, have been moving to suburban areas outside major cities in the United States and parts of Western Europe. Suburbs offer low-cost labor and lower tax rates.

However, this trend is highly dependent on the private automobile, since most workers cannot get to their jobs any other way. As a result, this type of population and industry shift is not feasible in many parts of the world.

Light industries are also moving their assembly and labor-intensive processes overseas to plants in Taiwan, the Philipines, Mexico, and Korea. In time, other industries may also transfer their operations to these countries to take advantage of lower tax rates and reduced labor costs. According to business observers, we are already entering the age of the "international product," whose various components are manufactured and assembled in factories all over the world.

Energy—Crisis and Opportunity

Energy resources are essential to industrial development in both advanced and less developed nations. The availability and cost of energy set limits on economic growth as much as the length of the growing season and available moisture restrict agriculture. Without fuel for transportation, most of the world would be paralyzed. Factories would close and cities eventually die. The very life of the

Heavy and Light Industry. The needs of different types of industry lead them to locate in different environments. Heavier industrial plants, such as those of the Kawasaki District of Japan, still tend to cluster together near harbors and railroad yards. Location here points out the importance of efficient transportation to an industry that uses large quantities of bulk raw materials to manufacture finished goods for a world market. Lighter industrial establishments have tended to migrate from crowded inner-city areas to the less crowded and less expensive sites of suburbia, as in the area shown at far right, near Toronto, Canada.

Complex Distribution of Industry. Many of the major industrial regions of the world are located close to major resource areas. However, it is a mistake to assume, based on this one fact, that natural resources always attract industry. A full range of factors must be considered—technology, politics, market, labor force, as well as resources—to understand why industry locates where it does.

MAJOR INDUSTRIAL REGIONS

Major industrial concentrations

Equatorial Scale 1:180,000,000

Copyright © by Rand McNally & Co.

world as we know it is highly dependent on adequate, cost-effective sources of energy.

Effects of the Crisis. Ironically, most of the world's major industrial countries, such as West Germany and Japan, are deficient in petroleum, while countries that export abundant quantities of oil, such as Libya and Nigeria, have little industrial development. Escalating energy costs have put pressure on many nations, creating problems of inflation and rising national debts. But industrialized countries can still afford to pay for imported fuel with goods that petroleum-exporting states want—automobiles, electrical goods, technical expertise, and so on.

Nations that suffer the most are both oil deficient and economically poor. They cannot pay the higher prices exacted by such oil cartels as OPEC (Organization of Petroleum Exporting Countries). While the industrialized nations must worry about reducing their use of automobiles,

poorer nations must worry about growing enough food to feed their people.

In the past few decades, energy has expanded from the industrial arena—how to find, develop, and transport reserves—into the political arena as well. Third-world countries are forming alliances to offset the industrial power of the more developed nations. For example, OPEC has been able to gain recognition as an international business and political force. Founded in 1960, the 18-member organization includes not only Arab states but Venezuela, Nigeria, Indonesia, and Ecuador. But the industrialized nations have a potentially powerful cartel of their own. These countries, particularly the United States, produce the major share of food in the world. Grain embargoes can be as effective in some cases as oil embargoes. As a result, a tug of war involving food and energy may develop in the next decade or two, with poorer nations caught between these international cartels.

The Search for New Sources. The energy crisis represents an opportunity as well. Most industrial nations are pursuing alternative means of generating the energy they need. It is important to remember that petroleum dependency is relatively

recent in human history, a product of 20th-century settlement and industrial technology. Since for many years petroleum and coal were relatively inexpensive, alternative forms of energy production were not explored. Now, with rising oil and gas prices, solar power, nuclear energy, shale oil, and wind and water power are being seriously examined. Nations have invested heavily in nuclear energy, but recent accidents have dramatized some of the risks involved in using this form of energy;

and no one has yet found a foolproof method for disposing of nuclear by-products. Solar, wind, water, and geothermal power represent clean, renewable sources of energy that can be used effectively in many parts of the world. Also, simply altering the way homes and commercial buildings are constructed can save energy and make use of solar collectors or prevailing winds.

Currently, even more sophisticated methods are being tried. In Hawaii, a state that must import petroleum for 92 percent of its electricity needs, 14,000 solar panels are used in heating water. A giant windmill on the north coast of Oahu is part of a complex that will feed power to the Hawaiian Electric Company. Off the island of Hawaii, a floating rig draws its own power from the interaction of warm and cold sea water, a process known as ocean thermal energy conversion.

Weighing Our Choices. Our search for alternative energy sources means we are confronted with difficult choices regarding the environment. In many parts of the world, oil dependency can be lessened by using more coal; often this means accepting higher levels of air pollution. We can develop the vast reserves of oil shale found in the Rocky Mountains of the United States, but huge quantities of earth must be mined to extract the oil. As a result, we may destroy the natural environment in the process. How we choose to acquire additional energy will have considerable impact on the political, economic, and natural environment of the world. Energy solutions must benefit not only industrial and resource-rich nations but poorer countries as well if we are to create a stable and balanced world economy.

Concentration and Dispersion. The major industrial zone in the United States is also the most heavily populated area. The original basis of the heavy industries was the iron ore of Michigan and Minnesota and the coking coal of the Appalachian range. However, many industries are moving to the margins which offer fresh, low cost labor and tax benefits. The same attractions are inducing companies to move their labor intensive operations overseas.

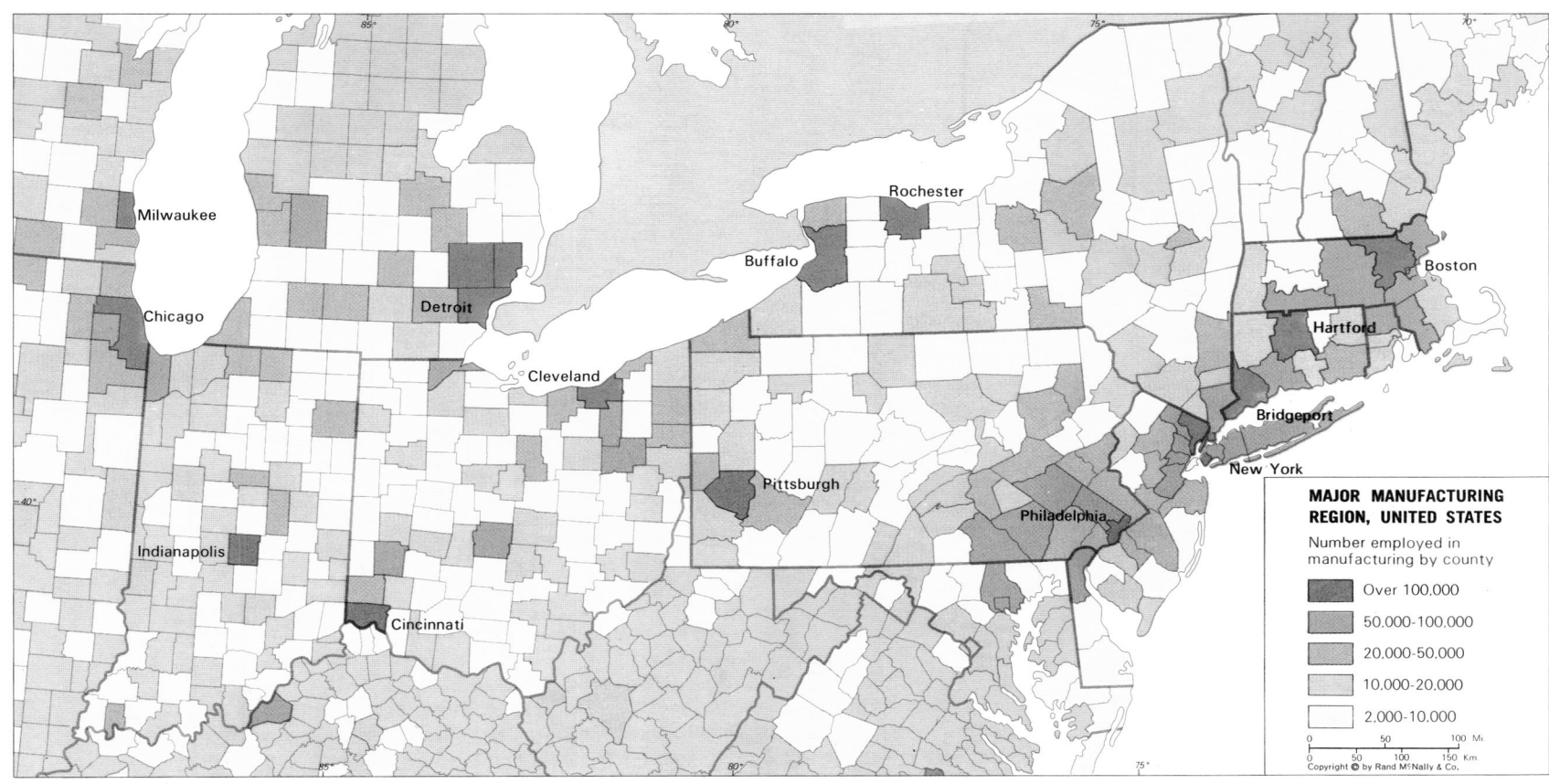

MAJOR MANUFACTURING REGION, UNITED STATES

Number employed in manufacturing by county

- Over 100,000
- 50,000-100,000
- 20,000-50,000
- 10,000-20,000
- 2,000-10,000

0   50   100 Mi
0   50   100   150 Km
Copyright © by Rand McNally & Co.

Trade Centers. The maps graphically portray the importance of trade centers in establishing a pattern of settlement within an area. Red lines show the travel of people to central places to buy goods and services. In Spain (map at lower right), as in Iowa, large centers grow to provide a greater range of goods and services than smaller centers and to attract customers from the widest area. The size and spacing of these interdependent places show an ordered pattern as it progresses from the smallest village to the largest city. Development of transportation and methods of food production and storage are among the factors that help create the settlement pattern.

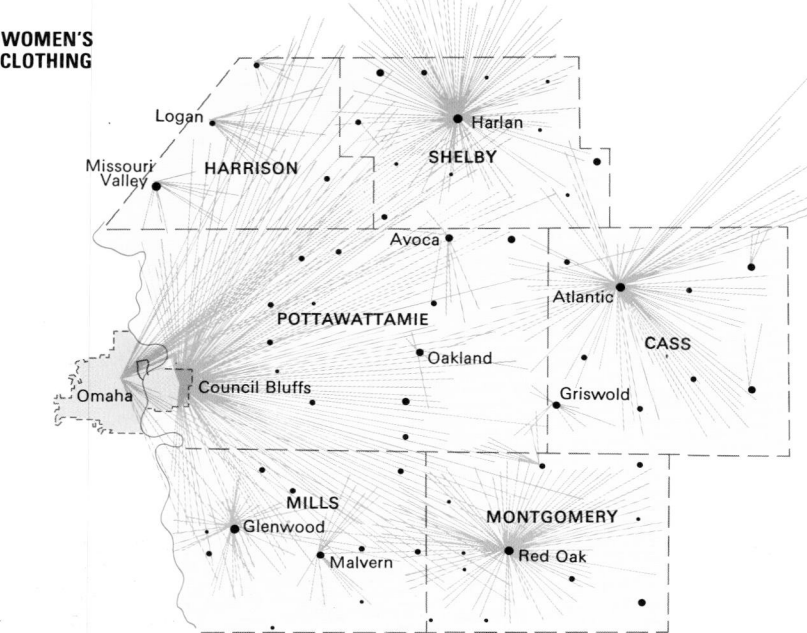

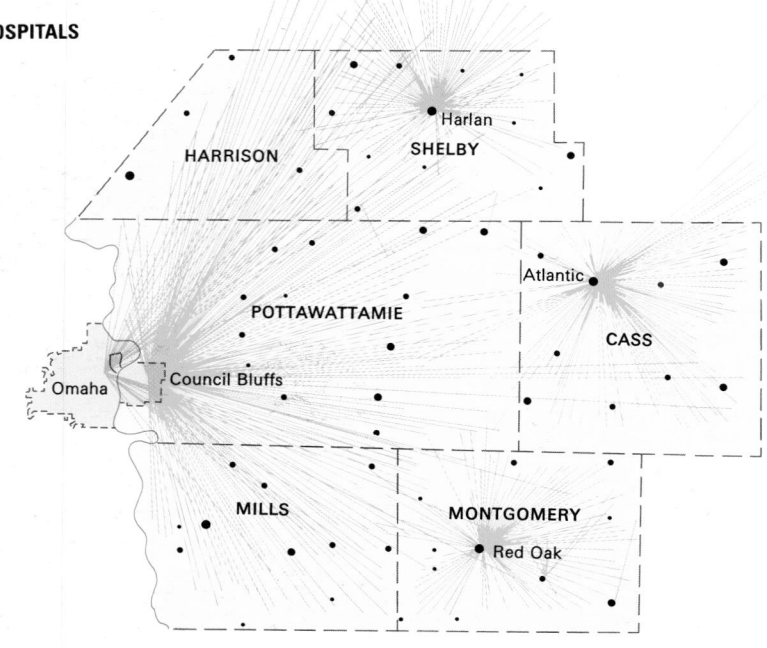

Settlements as Trade Centers

So far in our attempt to understand human patterns and imprints, we have looked at some of the factors that influence the location and design of rural communities and cities. Now we need to consider another element: the role of towns as trade centers.

Each urban settlement acts as a central place offering goods and services to the people within its trade area. The number and type of goods or services available depends largely on the size of the town or urban settlement. Even the smallest towns will have a post office, grocery store, and perhaps a clothing shop, a doctor, a dentist, and church and school. However, the chances are remote that a large department store or hospital would be attracted to these small towns. There would not be enough business to make such facilities economical or profitable. Each of the goods or services offered by a town will attract people from a certain area or zone. When added together, these zones constitute the trade area, or "hinterland," of a center.

The Settlement Hierarchy. When you examine the trade patterns of villages, towns, and cities in a particular area, a type of "settlement hierarchy" emerges. This concept can be used to explain the size and spacing of these trade centers. In general, the principle of a "hierarchy" can be applied to most settled regions of the world. In well-populated areas, settlements tend to fall into distinctive categories. At the base of the system are rural villages of about 500 inhabitants; next come towns with 1,000 to 2,000 people, small cities with populations of 5,000 to 10,000, and finally larger cities with perhaps 50,000. Each of these settlements is subordinate, both economically and culturally, to one or more metropolitan areas of 200,000 or more people. In turn, these areas are subordinate to national urban districts with up to several million inhabitants. That the larger centers with their wide range of goods and services have

Settlement Hierarchy — Northeastern Spain. The map of this region indicates which trade areas are the first choice of consumers. There is a rather even distribution of main cities and towns, each with differently shaped trade areas. Each hinterland begins from one focal point and gradually extends outward. Dominant towns in this region are subordinate to Barcelona or Madrid.

larger trade centers is not surprising. That they incorporate the functions of small centers is less obvious but true in most parts of the world. As a result, we can say that within a settlement hierarchy, cities, towns, and villages are both dependent on and independent of one another, since their functions and clientele tend to overlap somewhat. Naturally, the largest urban centers will draw customers from the widest area. These principles are illustrated in the accompanying maps of southwestern Iowa and northeastern Spain.

Southwestern Iowa. Since most of the settlements in this area have grocery stores, the first map merely hints at the attraction of the larger cities. Most consumers will travel only short distances to buy their food. But the pattern for women's clothing is quite different. Many of the smaller towns lack such goods or are less attractive to consumers; people will drive to larger cities such as Atlantic, Red Oak, Harlan, and Omaha/ Council Bluffs to find what they want. The pattern for visits to hospitals is even more pronounced. Only the larger urban centers provide this service. As a result, people bypass smaller towns and cities, and travel to the center offering the health care they need.

Looking at the maps, we can make some generalizations about the settlement hierarchy of southwestern Iowa. Obviously, Omaha is the dominant urban center since it draws from the entire six-county area. Council Bluffs, on the other hand, has a more restricted trade area since shoppers tend to bypass it in favor of Omaha. Atlantic, Red Oak, and Harlan are far enough from Omaha to have their own substantial hinterlands. Of course, the predominance of Omaha is not absolute. Residents of southwestern Iowa may have to rely on Chicago or

even New York for some goods and services. The principles underlying these trade patterns can be applied in other areas of the world as well.

Northeastern Spain. A similar hierarchical picture is evident in the trade areas of northeastern Spain. The map of this region makes no distinction among different goods or services. Instead, it merely indicates which trade areas are the first choice of consumers. Several important features can be seen at a glance. Notice the rather even distribution of main cities and towns, and the different shapes of their hinterlands or trade areas. Each trade area begins from one focal point and gradually extends outward until it overlaps and competes with other areas. Also, notice the gap between the hinterlands of Sangüesa Jaca, Huesca, and Babastro, and those of Tudela, Zaragoza, and Alcañiz. This gap coincides with the forbidding Ebro steppe, a sparsely settled region between the irrigated valley of the Ebro River and the dry-farmed piedmont of the Pyrenees. The primary center of the Ebro Valley is Zaragoza, which lies in the midst of a large plain of irrigated grain fields and orchards. Not only do trade routes within the valley converge on Zaragoza; the city also serves as a stopping-off point for those traveling on to France, Catalonia (Cataluña), the Basque Provinces (Vascongadas), and the plateau of central Spain. However, like Omaha, Zaragoza is not the predominant city, for residents of northeastern Spain may have to travel to Barcelona or Madrid for some goods and services. The same can be said for Lyon in regard to Paris, of Kiev in relation to Moscow, and even of Kandahar in regard to Kabul.

The study of trade areas and consumer patterns helps us understand how the settlement hierarchy evolves. Very often, improvements in transportation result in the concentration of goods and services within a few larger centers. A rural district with poor roads or few motor vehicles will have a number of small trading centers that serve a regular clientele. When the roads are improved and more people acquire trucks and automobiles, customers will bypass these smaller centers for the

attractions of larger cities. Perhaps these cities offer a rich assortment of goods, more services, or lower prices. Also, the longer trip to a large center may be a matter of convenience; people can buy several goods or services in one place. These possibilities explain why smaller towns tend to decline as communications and transportation improve and why people within a city may pass up neighborhood shops in favor of a trip "downtown."

Market Centers. Not all cities in the world have central business districts like those in the United States. But most urban centers have at least one district that can be called commercial. Moreover, in regions where storage facilities are poor, cities provide markets where rural people can sell their produce to urban customers. Such markets are still found in some cities of Europe and are common in African, Asian, and Latin American towns.

Finally, it should be remembered that commerce in a particular trade area depends to some extent on the characteristics of production. In the mountains of southwestern Asia, the largest markets are found in regions where people raise or produce complementary goods. For example, one group may cultivate cereal crops, another fruits and

vegetables, and still another may make pottery or special tools. The existence of such markets enables families engaged in subsistence farming to specialize in certain crops or products and trade their surplus. The situation in which families are totally self-sufficient, producing everything they need, is more mythical than real. Even in the most primitive areas, where the economy is small-scale and exchange based on barter, markets are a vital feature of people's livelihoods.

Open-Air Market. Abidjan's market in Ivory Coast, Africa, provides an effective means for rural peoples to offer their products to urban consumers. Local markets of this nature are often the only method for exchanging goods in Africa, Asia, and Latin America, or wherever storage and transportation facilities are inadequate. Such markets are also found in some European cities.

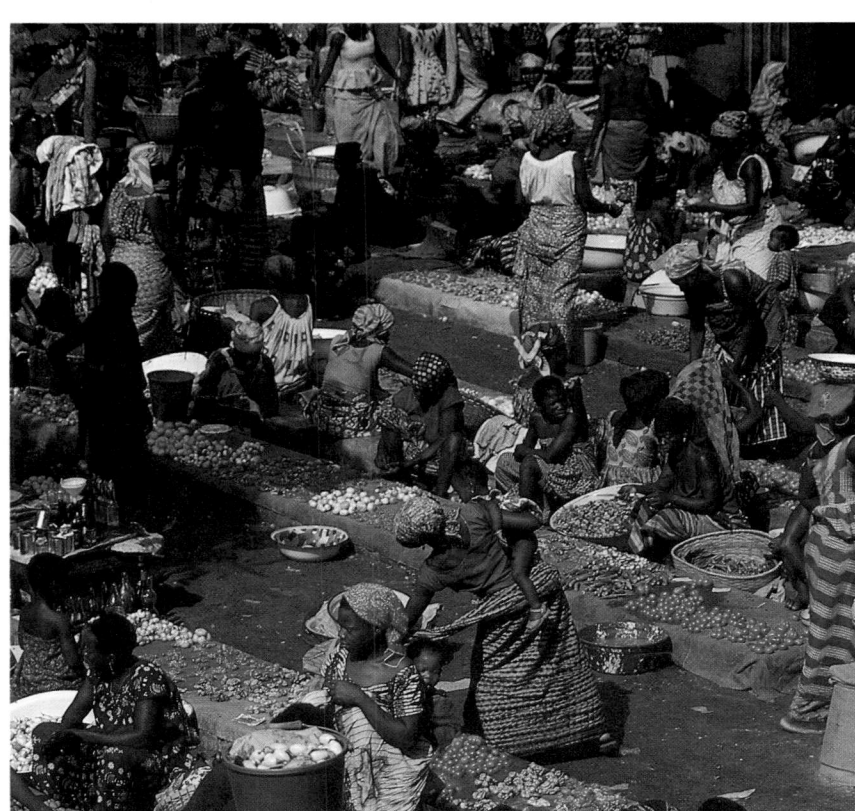

The Modern Market. The modern shopping center of Europe and North America serves much the same purpose as an open-air market—the sale of goods and services to customers. But there the resemblance ends. A complex transportation network supplies the center with a wide variety of goods. Many centers, like the district in Stockholm, Sweden, pictured here, draw customers from a wide area and often replace neighborhood shopping districts or downtown centers.

Development of Transportation

The development of transportation is closely related to the growth of urban and industrial areas. Cities depend on the supply lines and routes that converge on them. Likewise, no industry can survive without adequate facilities to import raw materials and export finished products. A look at the surface transportation networks of the world clearly reveals the uneven distribution of our human patterns and imprints.

Networks Around the World. The greatest system of surface transportation appears in Europe and the United States, where virtually every inhabited district is accessible by car, bus, or train. This elaborate pattern carries over into the populated areas of Canada, thinning only at the edge of settled territory. The more open network of the Soviet Union follows the well-populated area west of the Ural Mountains and a narrower zone of cultivated land wedged between the dry regions of central Asia and the vast Siberian forests.

South America presents some of the world's most striking contrasts. Between the well-developed and generally accessible plains of Argentina and the underdeveloped interior of Brazil is an enormous difference in population density and level of economic organization. Development of the Amazon basin and huge rain forest area has spurred construction of roads and highways. Previously, communication depended entirely on inland water routes. The Pan American Highway, stretching from Mexico through Central America and down the Pacific Coast to Chile, is a major link among Latin American nations. Feeder roads off this highway connect smaller cities and farm communities to ports and market centers.

The transportation pattern of Africa is more complicated. The continent is largely underdeveloped, though the Union of South Africa and the northern parts of Morocco, Algeria, and Tunisia are exceptions. The greatest contrast in transportation patterns appears between the arid regions of the Sahara and the cultivated zone extending from Senegal across the continent to Ethiopia. Egypt is a special case. For countless centuries, the Nile

---

. . . The distribution of transportation facilities reflects patterns of social and cultural development . . .

River has served as a great natural highway, delaying the country's road and rail development. However, the government is beginning to construct settlements in outlying desert areas, and roadways will be vital in maintaining lines of communication with the Nile Delta.

Vast regions of the Asian continent are sparsely settled. In the mountainous and dry sections, transportation facilities are poor or nonexistent. The relatively well-developed network of roads and railways in India and Pakistan reflects British initiative in reproducing an essentially European pattern. The network in Australia clearly defines inhabited and uninhabited parts of the country and underscores the importance of the few roads and single railway cutting across the interior desert. However, if mining industries in the "outback" regions expand, there will be a corresponding increase in the number of highways and rail lines. In East Asia, Japan alone possesses a transportation system comparable to that of Europe or the United States.

Transportation, Economics, and Culture. There are many ways to measure economic development: average income, energy consumption, and so on. Transportation facilities are perhaps not a refined indicator of economic development, but their

Sophisticated Surface Transportation. Trails of blurred light from moving automobiles on an expressway near Peoria, Illinois, close to the heart of the North American continent, serve to dramatize the advanced development of the surface transportation of the United States.

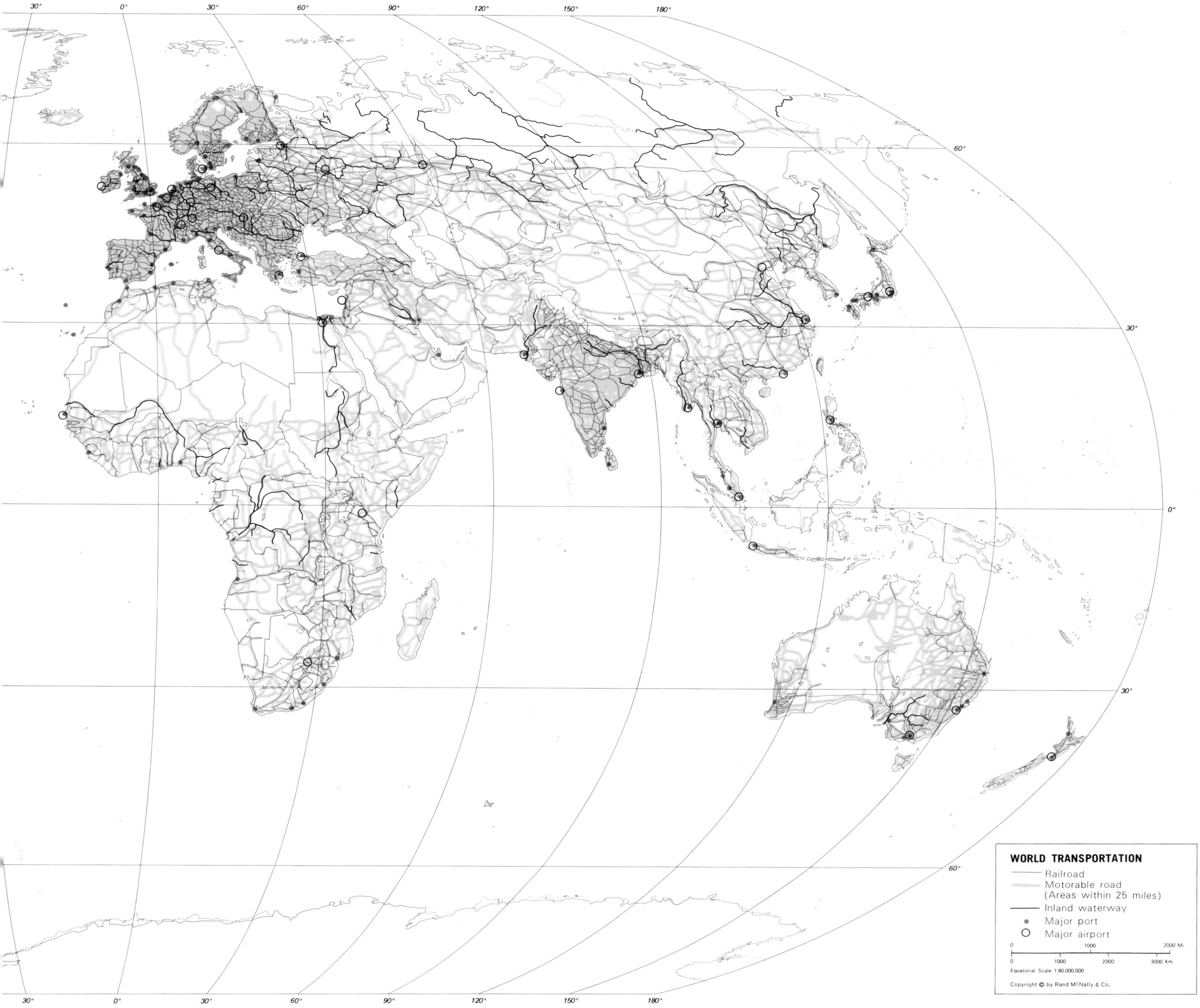

Map gridlines and degree labels (top): 30° 0° 30° 60° 90° 120° 150° 180°

60°

30°

0°

30°

60°

Map gridlines and degree labels (bottom): 30° 0° 30° 60° 90° 120° 150° 180°

WORLD TRANSPORTATION
- Railroad
- Motorable road (Areas within 25 miles)
- Inland waterway
- ● Major port
- ○ Major airport

0   1000   2000 Mi.
0   1000   2000   3000 Km.

Equatorial Scale 1:90,000,000
Copyright © by Rand McNally & Co.

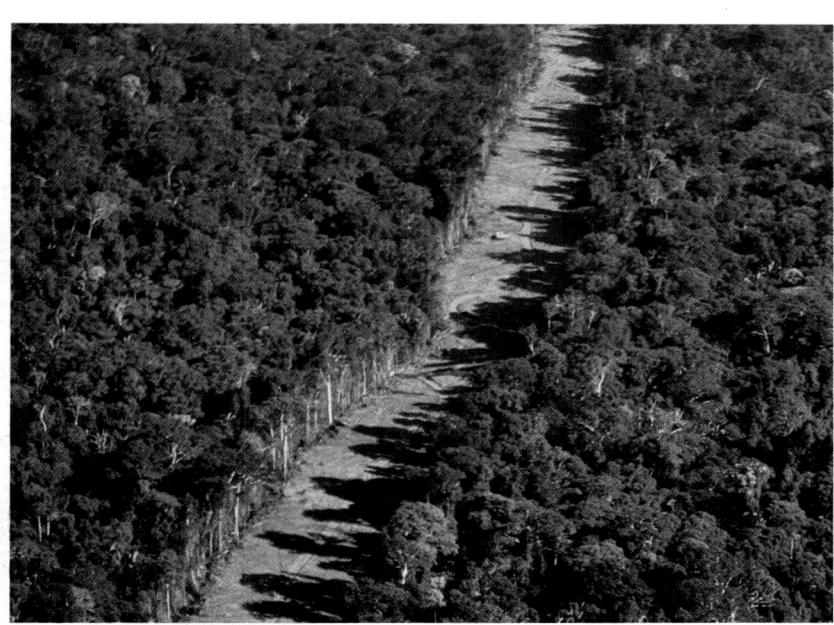

Transportation Systems Related to Progress. World transportation networks are most heavily concentrated in the urban and industrial areas of Europe and North America. The communication system provided by such a network contributes to the rapid dissemination of ideas, methods, and tools, and thus to the cultural evolution of these areas. In sharp contrast, the lack of transportation and communication systems in less developed countries is as much a barrier to progress as overpopulation or lack of resources.

Building a Transportation System. The Trans-Amazon Highway stretches from Recifé, Brazil, to Pucallapa, Peru. A portion of the "highway" in Amazonas, a state in northwestern Brazil, near the center of South America, pictured here, represents a country's transportation system in the early stages of development.

xxxiii

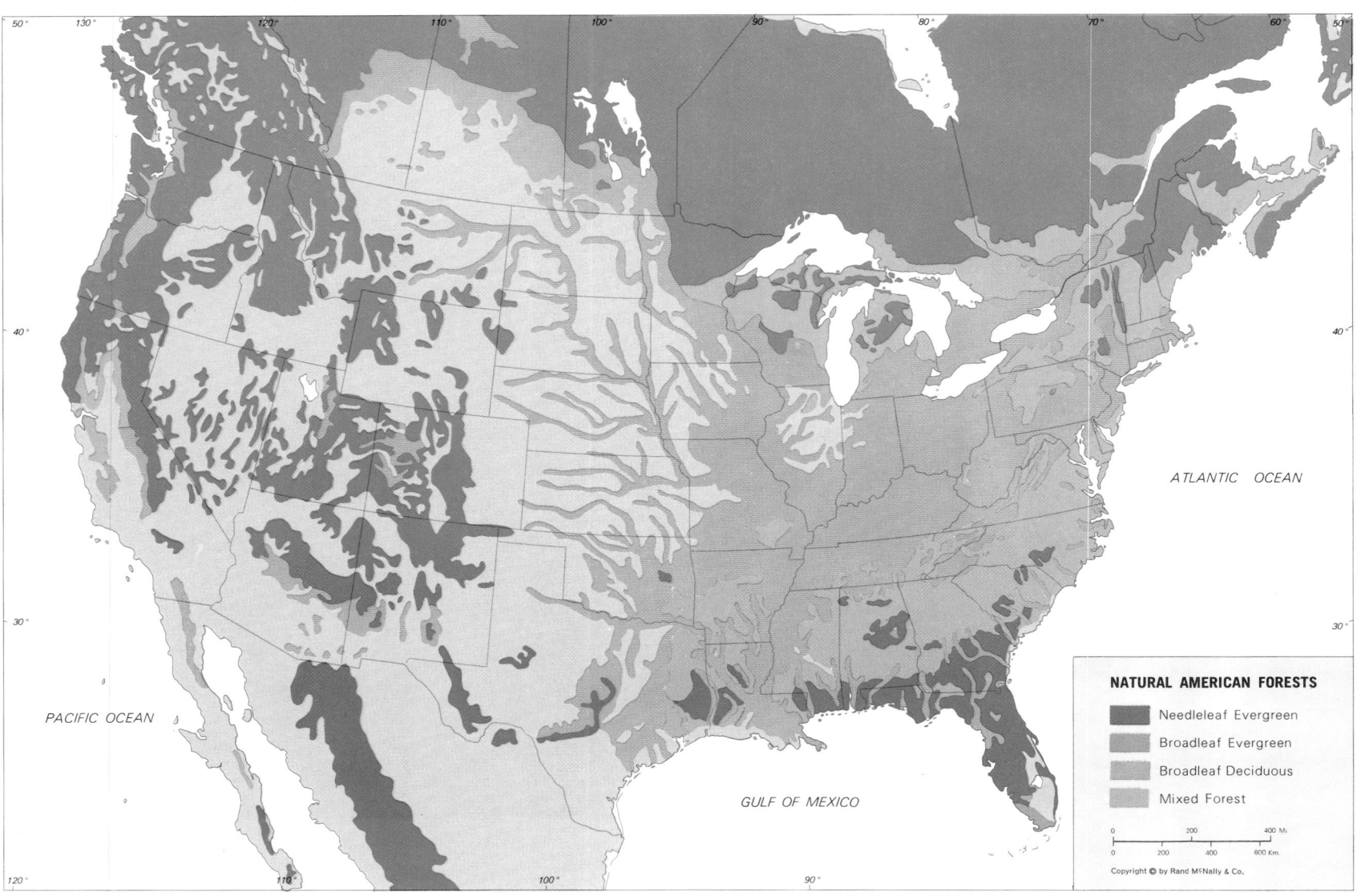

NATURAL AMERICAN FORESTS

Needleleaf Evergreen
Broadleaf Evergreen
Broadleaf Deciduous
Mixed Forest

PACIFIC OCEAN

ATLANTIC OCEAN

GULF OF MEXICO

Copyright © by Rand McNally & Co.

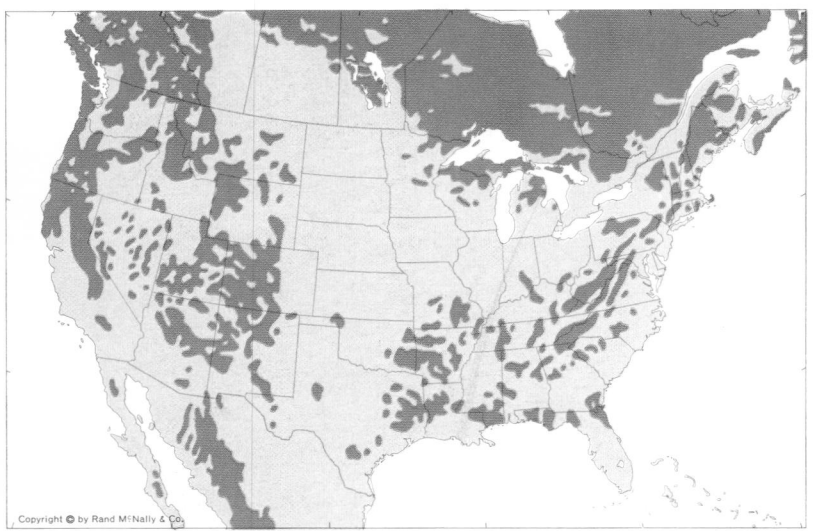

AMERICAN FORESTS—PRESENT STANDS

Copyright © by Rand McNally & Co.

patterns present a striking picture of the different concentrations of human activity around the globe. The fact that people find it easy to move from Hamburg to Rome or from New York to San Francisco but find it much harder to travel from Rio de Janeiro to the interior of Brazil or from Algiers to the Congo tells us a great deal about the state of economic development in these areas. Moreover, the distribution of transportation facilities reflects patterns of social and cultural development as well. The complex transportation network in France means that virtually every field, factory, and home in this country is connected into a nationwide system of communications. In contrast, people in areas not well served by roads and railways may not be exposed to new ideas and methods. In short, whether a nation is connected into a vital network of communication or relatively isolated has a significant impact on its rate of cultural evolution.

Modifying the Environment

As people have spread over the earth, they have not only settled and improved the land, they have destroyed it as well. Substantial regions of the planet have been stripped of their native vegetation and become desert and semidesert areas. Animals once numbering in the thousands or millions have become extinct or are now found mainly in zoos. As the Brazilian forests are cleared, ecologists fear that many species of plants and animals are being exterminated. While we have made headway in preserving many endangered species, many others remain on the edge of extinction.

Clearing the Land. Perhaps the most conspicuous result of our efforts to modify the environment has been the removal or alteration of plant life. Except for the great forests of northern Canada and Siberia, all of the world's major vegetation zones

show signs of clearing or burning, and the grazing of domestic animals. In the tropical rain forests, scattered groups may farm an area for a short time and then move on; to clear away forest, they burn off trees or kill them by stripping a complete circle of their bark. At the edge of these tropical rain forests is a zone of tall grass and scattered trees, usually referred to as "savanna." For the most part, savannas are created and maintained by fires set each year to clear the land for farming or pasture. In the drier parts of this zone, savanna gives way to grass and low shrubs (steppe). Beyond such vegetation lie desert zones consisting of plants that germinate quickly after infrequent rains, perennials with deep or widespreading roots, and succulent species like the cactus that can store moisture.

One of the best known examples of how human activity has modified native vegetation can be found in the Mediterranean area of the Old World.

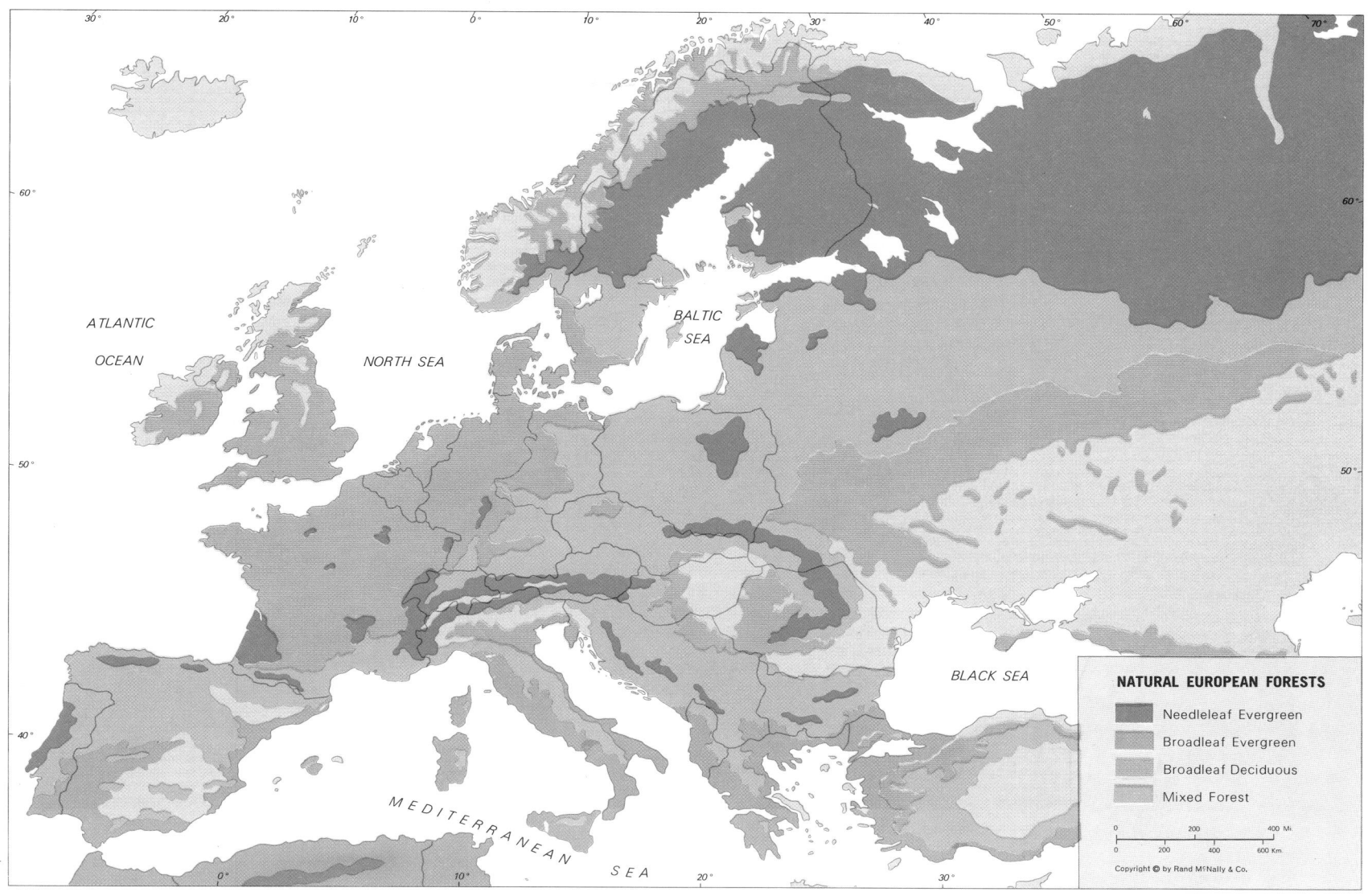

NATURAL EUROPEAN FORESTS

- Needleleaf Evergreen
- Broadleaf Evergreen
- Broadleaf Deciduous
- Mixed Forest

0   200   400 Mi
0   200   400   600 Km

Copyright © by Rand M⁹Nally & Co.

Deforestation. The larger maps on these pages show the probable extent of forest before humanity began clearing large areas for farming. Agriculture and industrial development have reduced the forest cover to the limited regions shown on the smaller maps. Deforestation of an equal magnitude has taken place in Asia, Africa, and other regions of the world where people have sacrificed forests for fuel as well as for farming and industry.

Reforestation. In this photograph, taken in western Washington, acres of new trees (foreground) are planted as mature trees are harvested. Reforestation of this type is now a standard procedure by which government and industry attempt to perpetuate renewable forest resources and stabilize the forest environment.

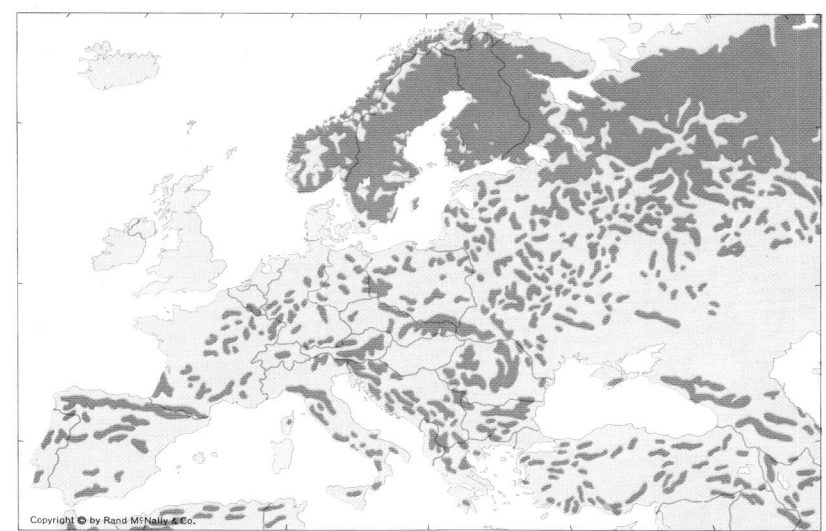

Copyright © by Rand M⁹Nally & Co.

EUROPEAN FORESTS—PRESENT STANDS

... The most conspicuous result of our efforts to modify the environment has been the removal or alteration of plant life...

In this region of ancient agricultural and pastoral livelihood, most of the original forest has been destroyed or reduced to scrub. That this is not the natural character of the land is suggested by vegetation growing on protected sites. Cemeteries in northwestern Africa are sacred ground, and trees found there are seldom disturbed. As a result, many cemeteries resemble small forests with their tall trees and deep, spreading shade. The removal of this shade from the surrounding land exposes the earth to the sun's heat and changes the climate at ground level. This change creates a favorable environment for the invasion of plants from nearby steppes or desert lands. Thus, the widely held belief that the Sahara is expanding is true. However, the cause is not a change in the atmosphere but centuries of clearing away forests to make room for human settlement.

The great, mid-latitude zones of both the Old World and New World were once covered with a mixed forest of evergreen and deciduous, broadleaf, and coniferous trees. Now this region is the most heavily populated in the world. Indeed, the process of clearing forests is so advanced in China that it is almost impossible to reconstruct that country's native vegetation patterns. Europe and the United States still have substantial forested regions, but most of these forests represent second or third growth and may be of a different species than the original stands. This is especially true of parts of Western Europe and the "cut-over" districts around the Great Lakes in the United States. Many of the surviving forests in the south-eastern United States are actually commercial plantations.

In Europe, human settlements have replaced much of the continent's forests. In contrast, from the beginning of the Christian era until the 10th century, most of the area north of the Alps was so heavily forested that it presented a living barrier to agricultural settlement. The clearing of this vast forest represents one of the most impressive and difficult accomplishments of medieval society. In England, the process was carried out so vigorously that by the 17th century it was difficult to find enough timber for shipbuilding. The same problem had frustrated other maritime powers: Spain, Portugal, the city-states of northern Italy, Rome, Greece, and Phoenicia (Lebanon).

Soil Erosion. The clearing and destruction of the world's forests has had serious consequences for the soil. In some cases, it has meant a change in the

xxxv

structure of the chemical composition of the earth; in others, the loss of part or all of the soil through erosion. Some erosion is inevitable in any area where soil is exposed to running water or wind; nor is all erosion destructive. Earth washed from hilly or mountainous regions may enrich flood-plains that sustain thousands, even millions, of people. Nevertheless, in many areas, accelerated soil erosion caused by human activity is one of the more obvious results of our modification of the earth and one of our most serious problems.

. . .Nature often requires centuries to repair what human cultivation may have destroyed in a single decade. . .

Erosion may take several forms. The most spectacular is gully erosion, whereby the earth is washed away to form deep channels that may evolve into intricate networks. This hazard is greatest where slopes are steep, protective vegetation has been cleared away, and poor cultivation methods have been used or the area has been overgrazed. The land eventually becomes unfit for agriculture. If abandoned by farmers and herders, the slopes may be recolonized by native vegetation. But nature, however forgiving, often requires centuries to repair what human cultivation may have destroyed in a single decade. Other forms of erosion include "sheet wash," when topsoil is removed without forming gullies. Landslides and mudslides carry away hundreds of square acres of productive land. Also, large amounts of topsoil can be removed by wind, a process that in the 1930's created the famous Dust Bowl of the American Great Plains.

Each of these destructive processes has taken a heavy toll of productive land. The humid tropics have probably suffered the most, for rainfall in this zone is often torrential. Central America, South America, and Southwest Asia show dramatic evidence of erosion. However, to cope with the problem, farmers have built elaborate terraces, improved the soil with mud from river valleys, and used various types of fertilizer. As a result, areas of relatively low productivity have supported some of the largest populations in the world. Most areas of the earth, however, have suffered serious depletion of the soil. It is not an exaggeration to say that this vital resource has been continuously damaged since humanity first began practicing agriculture some 10,000 years ago. The implications of this fact are especially serious today, when we are faced with a population explosion and the prospect of widespread famine.

Pollution: The High Cost of Progress

Our modifications of the environment are not restricted to vegetation, animal life, and the soil. We are now aware that the earth's air and water have also undergone radical changes at our hands. The term "pollution" covers a wide range of processes, from oil spills and automobile exhausts to nuclear and chemical wastes. The earth's atmosphere and hydrosphere are closed circulating systems, much like the circulatory system in a human being. At one time, the waste products of our civilization were probably insignificant enough to be dispersed by these systems without harming the air or water. But this is certainly not the case today. One of the consequences of urbanization and industrialization has been a rapid increase in air and water contamination. In the city of Chicago alone, over 15 million tons of coal are burned to heat homes and businesses and to generate electricity. As if this were not enough, more than 2 million automobiles in the city discharge vast quantities of carbon monoxide, sulphur dioxide, and hydrocarbons into the atmosphere. Waste, detergents, and water contaminated by pesticides and other chemicals are discharged into the Chicago River and Lake Michigan. The same process takes place in major industrial cities around the world.

Air Quality. Air pollution is especially serious in areas where temperature inversions occur. Occasionally, a layer of cooler air may form near the ground. Since this air is heavier and more stable than warm air, it forms a "lid," or temperature inversion, over an area. Pollutants cannot rise and disperse; they remain trapped in the colder air. Inversions like this are common in the Los Angeles area, which is also flanked on three sides by mountains that prevent the air from moving horizontally. When you consider that the city also has the world's greatest concentration of automobiles, numerous refineries and industries, and huge amounts of garbage and trash, it is not surprising that Los Angeles suffers from a severe smog problem.

Similar problems plague other industrialized urban areas. In the port city of Yokkaichi, Japan, near Nagoya, schoolchildren wear masks to protect themselves from air polluted by nearby petrochemical plants. In December of 1952, a combination of unusually heavy fog and smog in London filled the hospitals with patients suffering from acute respiratory diseases. It is estimated that during this period, 4,000 more people died than would have under normal circumstances.

. . . The earth's air and water have undergone radical changes at our hands. . .

Although the most ominous feature of air pollution is its hazard to human health, it also damages buildings and crops. Air pollutants corrode, tarnish, and crack a wide variety of materials. The stone and statuary on the great medieval cathedrals of Europe have probably suffered more damage during the past century than in all of their previous history. Native vegetation and crops also suffer from the effects of pollution. Evergreen trees cannot grow in cities located within the industrial zone of the northeastern United States. Moreover, Los Angeles smog has damaged the vegetable and citrus crops of southern California. In many cities, wilted leaves on trees and shrubs and the corroded metal of buildings are mute testimony to the same process.

Scientists concerned with air quality have also taken a harder look at the effects of clearing away extensive tracts of vegetation. Plants provide much of the free oxygen in our atmosphere. As more forest areas are cut back or burned off, scientists

Soil Depletion. The severely eroded slope near Bab-Taza, Morocco (left), is the result of overgrazing and improper methods of cultivation. With protective vegetation gone, heavy rains carve a maze of gullies into the slope, making future cultivation increasingly difficult. Water erosion of this sort is one of several ways in which fertile soil has been depleted since the beginning of agriculture, approximately 10,000 years ago.

Air Pollution. Smoke from the Heyden, Arizona, copper smelter shows that air pollution is not restricted to large urban districts; it occurs wherever industrial wastes are discharged into the atmosphere. Though some areas are seemingly free from air pollution, it is important to realize that our earth's atmosphere is shared by all. Because the atmosphere is a closed system, it has a limited capacity to absorb pollutants and still support abundant life.

Water Pollution. The Cuyahoga River, pictured here as it enters Lake Erie, at Cleveland, Ohio, is an example of a river in a heavily populated area that carries industrial wastes, sewage, and detergents into the inland lakes and, finally, to the world's oceans. Recent legislation by federal, state, and local governments bordering the Great Lakes has curbed the discharge of such pollutants. This type of cooperative effort is essential if rivers, lakes, and their related marine environments are to be saved from extinction.

worry that the loss of so much vegetation may lessen air quality. They are watching the commercial development of Brazilian rain forests with particular concern. This region is thought to provide a significant part of the oxygen for the Western hemisphere.

Water Pollution. The problem of water pollution is also most serious near cities and industrial establishments, though oceanographers have found contaminants in all the world's seas as well. Discharges of phosphates, pesticides, industrial wastes, and sewage into lakes and rivers damage fish and plant life and contaminate drinking water in most cities. Coastal areas are threatened by massive oil spills from offshore drilling or shipwrecks of supertankers carrying millions of gallons of petroleum. Most recently, chemical "dumping grounds" have been discovered where chemical wastes have been illegally or improperly buried near populated areas. These chemicals often seep into the earth and contaminate ground water or hidden springs and well water used for cooking and drinking. Also, containers of nuclear waste material disposed of in the sea are not always adequately sealed. Material leaking into the environment will remain radioactive for thousands of years before decaying into stable elements.

Restoring the Environment. Over the past two decades, environmentalists, consumer groups, and government agencies have focused their attention on the problem of pollution. Action by these groups has resulted in various environmental protection regulations, in some cases on both a national and international level. The results have been mixed, but promising. In Chicago, air quality has been

dramatically improved over a 15-year period. Lake Erie, once considered devoid of life, has also made a striking comeback. Fish and plant life now flourish where once only sediment and decaying algae could be found.

Even more promising in the long run are experiments in the design of electrically powered vehicles, attempts to recycle liquid wastes, and the use of solid waste for building materials and landfill. Optimists point to technological breakthroughs in solar, wind, and geothermal power for private homes and small- to medium-sized businesses.

...Environmentalists, consumer groups, and government agencies have focused their attention on the problem of pollution ... The results have been mixed, but promising...

Conservation and more efficient use of energy resources also reduces waste materials and helps cut down on pollution. Thanks to international agreements, the threat posed by fallout from thermonuclear explosions is less serious than it was previously. Many nations recognize the need for such agreements regarding the construction of nuclear power plants and the disposal of plutonium by-products.

Nevertheless, much remains to be done. If economic growth and development are carried on without adequate safeguards, the deterioration of our air, soil, and water is likely to continue. The future quality of our environment rests on the priorities we choose and our ability to cooperate as a world community.

Artificial Environments

A clear distinction between a natural and an artificial environment is difficult to make, because the influence of humanity is evident almost everywhere. Nevertheless, we can start by pointing to the historic and even prehistoric efforts of people to create a more comfortable settlement.

Keeping Warm. Caves were probably the first artificial environments. They offered shelter and, with the discovery of fire, warmth to prehistoric peoples. Since the earliest times, people have lived in such forbidding regions as Alaska and southern Chile. The ice and snow huts built by Eskimos were well-insulated dwellings. While the Indians of southern Chile were less skilled in constructing shelters, they had the imagination and boldness to carry fires in their canoes. By the time of the Roman Empire, people had devised methods of heating large buildings and water used for public baths. The stone castles of medieval Europe may have been chilly and drafty, but there is reason to believe that the peasant huts clustered nearby were warm and relatively comfortable. Although people have often had to work and travel in harsh climates, they have long been able to create warm shelters.

Cooling Off. Defense against excessive heat is a more complicated affair. But even here it is easy to point out how human beings have dealt with the problem. In the Middle East, covered streets helped block the sun's rays. Wetted grass mats were placed over the doorways of houses in India. In the American Southwest, Indians used thick

---

. . . A clear distinction between a natural and an artificial environment is difficult to make, because the influence of humanity is evident almost everywhere. . .

---

adobe walls to keep out the oppressive summer heat. The use of fans and other devices to circulate the air or reduce humidity are refinements of an ancient quest.

Early methods of modern air conditioning began in the textile industry. Steam pots were used to increase humidity and help reduce breakage and static electricity. In the 1920s, new techniques of refrigeration began to appear. The first use of air conditioning for human comfort occurred in an American motion-picture theater in 1922. After World War II, central air conditioning was installed in office buildings, factories, restaurants, and other businesses, whereas smaller units began to appear in houses.

Air conditioning is now a requirement of life in the hotter regions of the United States, especially the Southeast and the Southwest. Life during the torrid summer months may be a series of short trips from one air-conditioned place to another. Exposure to the "real world" may be as limited as in Alaska or Siberia during the bitterly cold winter months. Within the last few decades, air conditioning has been used in large shopping centers and sports arenas; often these facilities are enclosed under one roof or dome. New office buildings in all but the most temperate regions have air conditioning features built into their basic design.

Cities "Under Glass." If we have been able to air-condition entire shopping centers and sports complexes, why not larger areas? This prospect is made more intriguing by the development of structural domes, which are relatively inexpensive and can be built virtually to any scale. Thus, a dome comparable to the one housing the Civic Arena in

---

. . . Not even an artificial environment with total and infallible control of temperature and humidity would be without its problems and hazards. . .

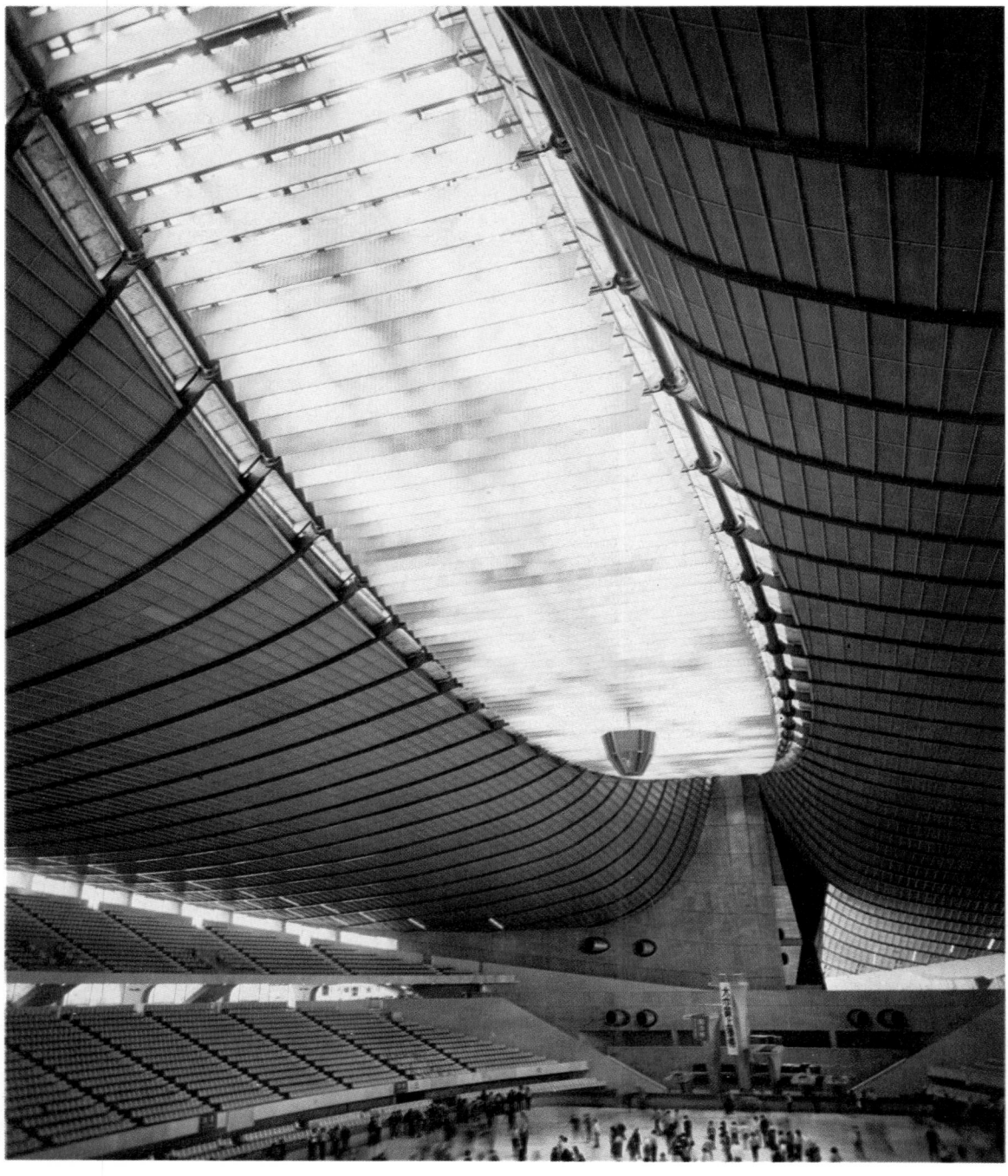

Artificial Environments. The Yoyogi Sports Center in Tōkyō, Japan, was built for the 1964 Olympics. It is now used as a recreation center and stands as one of the first in an increasing number and variety of large, self-contained artificial environments.

Pittsburgh could be as high as the tallest skyscraper. In this case, it would be possible to air-condition an entire city.

This awesome prospect should not overshadow the obstacles still facing us in our efforts to build comfortable, healthy environments. Although air conditioning can filter out pollutant particles, gaseous contaminants pass through unimpeded. Nor are we likely to discover an effective substitute for the beneficial qualities of sunlight. Not even an artificial environment with total and infallible control of temperature and humidity would be without its problems and hazards. A world of artificial environments may help us solve part of our problems in constructing comfortable habitats. But whether this is a desirable or even humane solution remains to be seen.

Evolution of Our Patterns and Imprints

The story of our gradual settlement of the planet can be divided into at least three distinctive phases, with a fourth phase slowly emerging.

Expansion Without Agriculture. The first phase began about 100,000 years ago, probably in Africa. Moving in small bands and supporting themselves by hunting and by gathering wild plants, various groups spread from tropical environments to all the earth's major climatic zones. Population remained low during this long migration, and vast areas were left unoccupied. Yet the remarkable adaptability of the human species enabled people to survive in dense rain forests, deserts, even on the edge of the Arctic Circle. Many experts feel that the isolation of these groups from one another, plus the high rate of infant deaths and the inbred genetic makeup of each people, helped create the physical characteristics still evident in our races. The precarious nature of hunting and gathering as a way of life did not permit any elaborate subdivision of labor or the development of more than subsistence skills. The family or clan remained the essential economic and social unit. If astronauts could have orbited the earth in 50,000 B.C., or even 15,000 B.C., they would not have seen any indications of modification of the environment.

Expansion and Concentration with Agriculture. The situation changed dramatically about 10,000 years ago, when humanity entered into the second phase—agricultural development. Plants and animals were domesticated, and people began to enjoy a relatively steady, abundant food supply. It is not known exactly where this crucial innovation took place. Most authorities favor the foothill region of the Near East, where they believe wheat and barley were the first cultivated crops and sheep and goats the first animals domesticated. Cultivation may also have begun several thousand years ago in the warm, humid environments of South and Southwest Asia. And in the New World, evidence suggests that maize agriculture in Mexico is ancient as Near East wheat cultivation.

. . . The story of our gradual settlement of the planet can be divided into at least three distinctive phases, with a fourth phase slowly emerging. . .

The development of agriculture enabled human settlements to increase significantly. In some areas, population jumped a hundred-fold as people learned to plant, irrigate, and harvest crops. Abundant food production freed some people to develop skills such as pottery, crafts, tool manufacturing, and weaving. Societies began to separate into special castes of warriors, priests, and merchants. From the eight major centers of innovation, agriculture expanded to all areas of the earth where cultivation and raising livestock were possible. A major exchange of crops and animals occurred after the European conquest of the New World. European settlers and pioneers cultivated the last great agricultural frontiers in the 19th century. Similar pioneer settlements, though on a much smaller scale, are found in South America and regions of Canada and the Soviet Union.

This 10,000-year period of rapid progress also saw humanity alter and modify vast areas of the environment. Clearing forests for agriculture and overgrazing lands encouraged soil erosion and turned some regions into virtual desert. In our hypothetical orbiting of the earth, an astronaut in 5,000 B.C. would have spotted cultivated fields, clearings in forests, eroded slopes, and countless other signs of the beneficial and destructive aspects of human activity.

Concentration—Urbanization and the Industrial Age. The middle of the 19th century signaled the third phase in the great adventure of the human expansion and settlement over the earth. An era of rapid scientific innovation ushered in the industrial age. As industry and commerce developed, people moved from rural areas into crowded urban centers, abandoning agriculture for the more varied economic opportunities found in cities. The trend toward concentration marked a reversal of previous population movements, a fact often overlooked in accounts of humanity's use of the earth. As a result, many areas of the world are now less occupied than prior to the Industrial Revolution. Although the distinction between crowded and empty lands was always evident during the period of agricultural expansion, the difference became more pronounced after people could leave rural areas. Convergence on urban and industrial sites meant a concentrated and magnified impact on the environment—often with damaging results. Air and water pollution, thought to be a 20th century dilemma, plagued industrial areas of Europe and the United States in the latter half of the 19th century.

Suburbanization. The fourth stage, suburbanization, is not yet a global trend. However, it is such a striking feature in North America and many European cities that it may well foreshadow a worldwide pattern. City growth initially fostered a concentration of population and industry. But subsequent development led to a new phase of expansion. The process began with the first streetcar lines extending out from the heart of the city. Houses could be built along these lines, allowing people to live beyond walking distance from their places of work. Today, expressways and rail transport enable millions of American and European suburbanites to live miles from where they work, shop, or find recreation and entertainment. In most of these cities, commuting from the suburbs to the downtown area takes about one hour, round trip. Where before people thought little of walking 2 or 3 miles to work, commuters today regard traveling 20 or 30 miles as equally routine.

Suburban growth, unfortunately, has often meant inner city decay, a problem facing most major American and European cities. Also, the process has encouraged the development of shopping centers and industrial districts in widely scattered suburban areas. The congestion associated with "rush hour" is complicated by traffic moving from suburb to suburb.

It is too early to predict whether suburbanization will occur in other nations as well. Most people in African and Asian countries still live close to where they work or combine their shops and homes into one. Moreover, even between Europe and the United States, the trend toward suburban growth differs significantly, since in Europe more people must rely on public transportation. Regardless of the transportation network that supports it, suburban sprawl often encroaches on agricultural land. Strasbourg, France, is expanding into the vineyards of the Rhine Valley, and Tel Aviv, Israel, is slowly reducing the citrus orchards of the Mediterranean coast. The growth of the huge Los Angeles metropolitan area has been at the expense of one of the nation's richest agricultural counties. Also, escalating fuel costs may encourage a new era of population concentration as commuting becomes more and more expensive. On the other hand, if more inexpensive sources of energy are developed and transportation facilities expanded, the current trend of suburban sprawl may actually accelerate. In any case, the movement of people from urban districts to outlying areas is likely to be an important chapter in the story of human settlement on our planet.

Epilogue

We began our look at the patterns and imprints of humanity with the observation that people have been virtually everywhere on the planet Earth. At

---

. . . We can hope that we will act more wisely in the future to live within the limits of our earth . . .

---

times our presence has been beneficial, at times destructive. But it has always changed the appearance of the earth's surface. In the course of 100,000 years, humanity has developed from small hunting and gathering societies into nation states. Advanced methods of agriculture and industrialization have given us some measure of control over natural forces and have enabled us to increase our population dramatically. We have constructed elaborate artificial environments and intricate cultural landscapes. The imprint of our species is deep and widespread.

Our transformed human geography shows signs of failure as well. Environmental pollution and our consumption of nonrenewable resources are straining the earth's ability to support our expanding industrial economies. War and famine threaten the future of many nations, and the gap between rich and poor countries continues to widen at an alarming rate. Always, the specter of nuclear warfare hangs over each succeeding generation.

As we strive to create new patterns and imprints on the earth, we cannot tell if our evolving creation will result in a more attractive and productive world. We do know it will be different. We can hope that as we become more aware of our effect upon the environment, we will act more wisely in the future in order to live within the limits of our earth for the well-being of all humanity.

Four Phases of Human Settlement

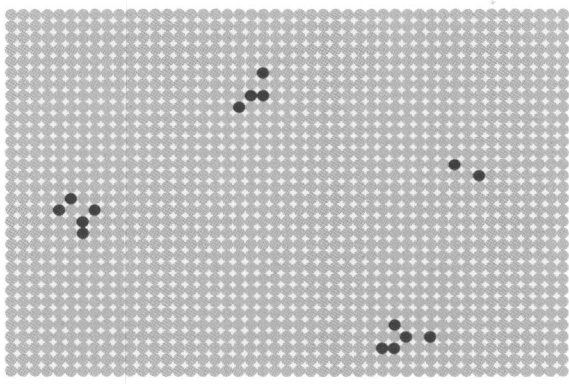

First Phase: Expansion without Agriculture. About 100,000 years ago, hunters and food gatherers spread from tropical environments to all the earth's major climatic regions, with insignificant modification of the environment.

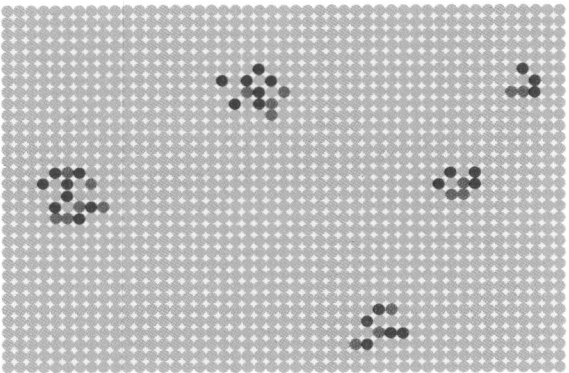

Second Phase: Expansion with Agriculture. Agricultural development evolved about 10,000 years ago and proceeded to expand to all areas where crop cultivation and livestock raising were possible, accompanied by deforestation and soil erosion.

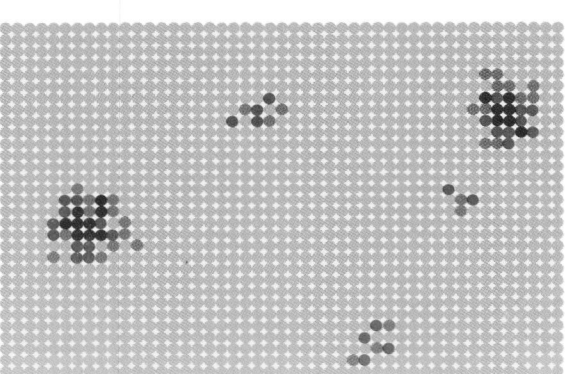

Third Phase: Concentration with Industrialization and Urbanization. Movement of the rural population to the urban centers began about 150 years ago and reversed the previous population movements. Convergence on urban and industrial sites accelerated pollution of air and water and the exhaustion of nonrenewable resources.

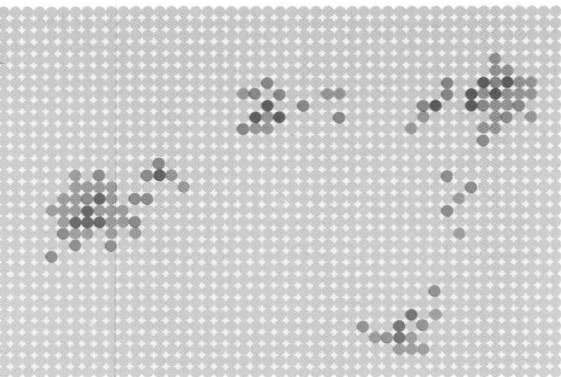

Fourth Phase: Suburbanization. A feature of urban industrial societies is the recent phase of expansion away from the cities, which has been facilitated by efficient transportation systems. Often, suburbs spring up at the expense of agricultural land.

Environment Maps

The environment-map series shows the general nature of the environment, whether natural or modified by man. The appearance and/or general activity which characterize an area were the conditions for its being classified in one of the map categories. Inclusion in a category was determined largely by the percent of the area covered by urban development, crops (including pasture), trees, or grass. On these small-scale maps, no attempt was made to depict specific crops or the productivity of the area.

Ten major environments were depicted and the categories identified and described in the legend below. The colors and patterns for each category were chosen to illustrate the results of man's activity. Hill shading was used to show land configuration. Together, these design elements create a visual impression of the surface environment.

Naturally, when mapping any distribution it is necessary to limit the number of categories. Therefore, some gradations of meaning exist within the limits of the chosen categories. For example, the grassland, grazing-land category identifies the lush pampas of Argentina and the savanna of Africa as well as the steppes of the Soviet Union. Furthermore, in areas of cropland certain enclaves which might not be defined as cropland are included within the boundary. Tracts such as these, through the process of generalization were included within the boundary of the dominant environment surrounding them. Finally, it should be pointed out that boundaries on these maps, as on all maps, are never absolute but mark the center of transitional zones between categories.

Actual urban shapes were shown where metropolitan areas are of a large areal extent. A red dot indicates concentrated urbanized development where actual shapes would be indistinguishable at the map scale. Black dots were used to locate selected places important as locational reference points.

From these maps one may make comprehensive observations about the extent and distribution of the major world environments. For example, the urban areas of the world are limited in extent, although over 40 percent of the world's population lives in these areas. Together, the categories of cropland and cropland associated with woodland or grazing land apply to relatively small portions of the earth's surface. Conversely, vast areas of each continent show man's limited influence on the natural environment. The barren lands, wasteland, and tundra, the sparse grass and steppe land, and the tropical rain forests are notable in this respect.

Environment Map Legend

URBAN
Major areas of contiguous residential, commercial, and industrial development.

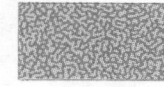
FOREST, WOODLAND
Extensive wooded areas with little or no cropland.

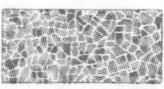
CROPLAND
Cultivated land predominates (includes pasture, irrigated land, and land in crop rotation).

SWAMP, MARSHLAND
Extensive wetland areas (includes mangroves).

CROPLAND AND WOODLAND
Cultivated land interrupted by small wooded areas.

TUNDRA
Areas of lichen, shrubs, small trees, and wetland.

CROPLAND AND GRAZING LAND
Cultivated land with grassland and rangeland.

SHRUB, SPARSE GRASS; WASTELAND
Desert shrub and short grass, growing singly or in patches. Wasteland includes sand, salt flats, etc. (Extensive wastelands shown by pattern).

GRASSLAND, GRAZING LAND
Extensive grassland and rangeland with little or no cropland.

BARREN LAND
Icefields, glaciers, permanent snow, with exposed rock.

. OASIS
Important small areas of cultivation within grassland or wasteland.

• Selected cities as points of reference.

Urban
Cropland
Cropland & Woodland
Cropland & Grazing Land
Grassland, Grazing Land
Forest, Woodland
Swamp, Marshland
Tundra
Shrub, Sparse Grass, Wasteland (pattern)
Barren Land
Oasis

Reykjavik

ATLANTIC

OCEAN

North
Sea

Glasgow
Belfast
MANCHESTER
Dublin

LONDON
Amsterdam
Antwerp

Brest

PARIS   Seine
Loire   Strasbourg

Bay of Biscay

La Coruña
Bordeaux   Garonne
Lyon
Bilbao   Zürich
Douro   Milan
PYRENEES   Genoa
MADRID   Ebro   Marseille
Lisbon
Sevilla   BARCELONA   CORSICA
ROME
ISLAS BALEARES   SARDINIA   Naples
Tanger
Oran   Algiers   Palermo
Casablanca   Tunis   SICILY
ATLAS   MOUNTAINS   MALTA
Mediterranean   Sea

Trondheim

Bergen
Oslo
Göteborg
Copenhagen

Narvik   Murmansk

Gulf of Bothnia
Ume

Helsinki   LENINGRAD
Tallinn
Stockholm

Baltic   Sea
Riga
Kaliningrad
Minsk
Hamburg   Elbe   BERLIN
Essen   Leipzig   Oder   Warsaw   Pripyat
Frankfurt
Prague   Kraków   L'vov
Munich   Danube   CARPA
VIENNA
Zagreb   Tisza   BUDAPEST
Venice
Sava   Belgrade   Bucharest
Adriatic   Danube
Sea   Sofia
Tirane
Aegean
Sea
Tyrrhenian Sea
Athens
CRETE

Longitude West of Greenwich   0°   Longitude East of Greenwich   10°   20°

Conic Projection

0   50   100   200   300   400   500 Miles
0   100   200   400   600   800 Kilometers

xlii

White Sea

q:

Nar'yan-Mar

Pechora

Archangelsk

Ob'

Irtysh

Novosibirsk

Ob'

Omsk

U R A L S

Perm'

SVERDLOVSK

Karaganda

Kirov

Vologda

Kazan'

Kama

Ufa

Magnitogorsk

Balkhash

Volga

Gorki

Kuybyshev

Orsk

MOSCOW

Tula

Volga

Saratov

Ural

Kzyl-Orda

Syr-Dar'ya

Aral'skoye
More
(Aral Sea)

PESKI
KYZYLKUM

DEPRESSION

VOLGOGRAD

CASPIAN

Kiev

Khar'kov

Don

Volga

Amu Dar'ya

Dnepropetrovsk

Donetsk

Astrakhan

PESKI KARAKUMY

Dnepr

MANYCH

DEPRESSION

Odessa

Krasnodar

Caspian

Ashkhabad

C A U C A S U S   M T S.

TBILISI

BAKU

Sea

İSTANBUL

Black   Sea

Yerevan

ELBURZ   MTS.

TEHRAN

DASHT-E-KAVIR

Ankara

Kerman

BOROS

AS LARI

Tigris

Euphrates

ZAGROS

MOUNTAINS

Nicosia

CYPRUS

Baghdad

Beirut

Abādān

B-550000-95   -2°

COPYRIGHT BY

RAND McNALLY & COMPANY

MADE IN U.S.A.

xliii

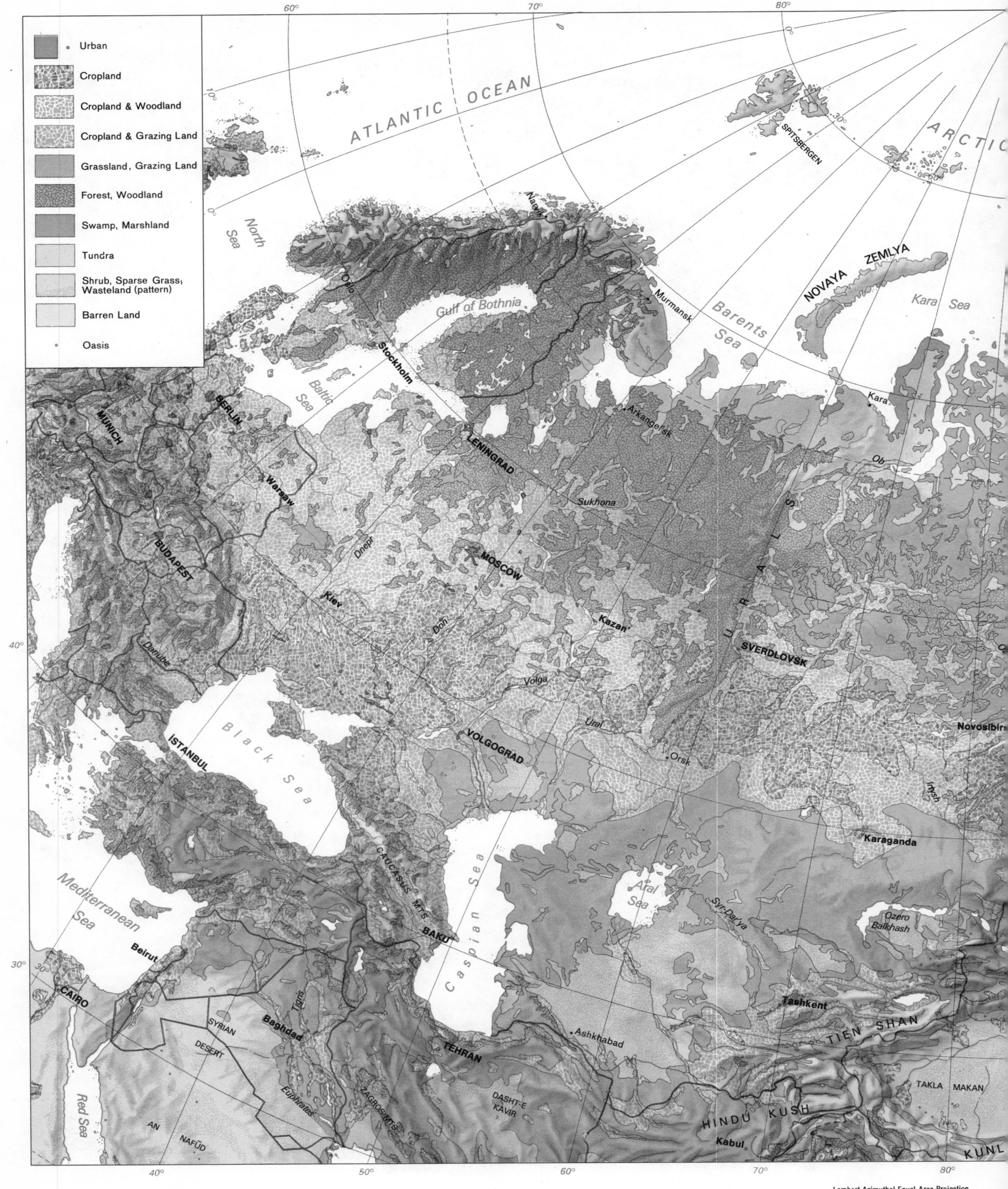

Urban

Cropland

Cropland & Woodland

Cropland & Grazing Land

Grassland, Grazing Land

Forest, Woodland

Swamp, Marshland

Tundra

Shrub, Sparse Grass,
Wasteland (pattern)

Barren Land

Oasis

ATLANTIC OCEAN

ARCTIC

SPITSBERGEN

NOVAYA ZEMLYA

Kara Sea

Barents Sea

Murmansk

North Sea

Gulf of Bothnia

Narva

Arkange'sk

Oslo

Stockholm

Baltic Sea

BERLIN

LENINGRAD

Kara

MUNICH

Warsaw

Sukhona

Ob

BUDAPEST

Dnepr

MOSCOW

Kazan

SVERDLOVSK

Kiev

Don

Ural

Novosibirs

40°

Danube

Volga

ISTANBUL

Black Sea

VOLGOGRAD

Orsk

Irtysh

Karaganda

Mediterranean Sea

CAUCASUS Mts

BAKU

Caspian Sea

Aral Sea

Syr-Dar'ya

Ozero Balkhash

Beirut

30°   30°

Tashkent

CAIRO

SYRIAN

Baghdad

Ashkhabad

TIEN SHAN

Tigris

DESERT

TEHRAN

Red Sea

Euphrates

ZAGROS Mts

DASHT-E KAVIR

TAKLA MAKAN

AN

NAFŪD

HINDU KUSH

Kabul

KUNL

Lambert Azimuthal Equal-Area Projection

OCEAN

70°

Anadyrskiy
Zaliv

80°

East
Siberian
Sea

60°

50°

150°

Ambarchik

Bering

Sea

120°

Laptev
Sea

180°

90°

Ilirney

170°

Nordvik

POLUOSTROV
KAMCHATKA

Magadan

Petropavlovsk-
Kamchatskiy

KHREBET GYDAN

Olenëk

GORY
PUTORANA

Lena

Yakutsk

160°

Sea
of
Okhotsk

Tura

SAKHALIN

Lena

Komsomolsk-
na-Amure

150°

Amur

Krasnoyarsk

MTS.

HOKKAIDŌ

40°

Lake
Baikal

Argun

KHINGAN

Haerhpin

Sapporo

Irkutsk

GREATER

Vladivostok

HONSHŪ

Ulaan Baatar

MUKDEN

Sea
of
Japan

TOKYO

ALTAI

MTS.

GOBI (DESERT)

SEOUL

140°

Tihua

PEKING

30°

Yellow
Sea

KYŪSHŪ

Hwang Ho

Chengchou

PACIFIC

East
China
Sea

OCEAN

SHANGHAI

Yangtze

B-568500-96 -1-1-1°
COPYRIGHT BY
RAND MCNALLY & COMPANY
MADE IN U.S.A.

MOUNTAINS

90°

100°

110°

120°

130°

0   100   200   400   600   800 Miles

0   150   300   600   900   1200 Kilometers

xlv

Mediterranean Sea
Red Sea
CAUCASUS MTS
Caspian Sea
BAKU
Beirut
CAIRO
SYRIAN
Baghdad
Tigris
TEHRAN
Ashkhabad
Tashkent
Syr-Dar'ya
Karaganda
Ozero Balkhash
Aral Sea
DESERT
Euphrates
ZAGROS MTS
DASHT-E KAVIR
TIEN SHAN
AN NAFUD
Persian Gulf
Kermān
HINDU KUSH
KUNLU
TAKLA MAKAN
Kabul
Mecca
Riyadh
Rawalpindi
PLATE
Muscat
KARACHI
DELHI
AR RUB' AL KHĀLĪ
Indus
DANAKIL
Aden
Gulf of Aden
Berbera
Arabian Sea
Nāgpur
BOMBAY
WESTERN GHATS
EASTERN GHATS
MADRAS
Calicut
SRI LANKA
Colombo
INDIAN OCEAN

Legend:
- Urban
- Cropland
- Cropland & Woodland
- Cropland & Grazing Land
- Grassland, Grazing Land
- Forest, Woodland
- Swamp, Marshland
- Tundra
- Shrub, Sparse Grass; Wasteland (pattern)
- Barren Land
- Oasis

Lambert Azimuthal Equal-Area Projection

ALTAI MTS.

Tihua

GOBI (DESERT)

Ulaan Baatar

GREATER KHINGAN MTS.

Harbin

Vladivostok

Sea of Japan

HONSHŪ

TOKYO

MUKDEN

SEOUL

Yellow Sea

KYŪSHŪ

PEKING

East China Sea

PACIFIC OCEAN

Hwang Ho

Chengchou

SHANGHAI

MOUNTAINS

WUHAN

CHUNGKING

T'aipei

Tropic of Cancer

TAIWAN

TIBET

Mekong

K'unming

CANTON

HIMALAYAS

Brahmaputra

Ganges

Philippine Sea

CALCUTTA

Hanoi

HAINAN TAO

Mandalay

Salween

Mekong

MANILA

Cebu

South

China

Sea

MINDANAO

Bay of

Bengal

Rangoon

BANGKOK

HO CHI MINH CITY

Gulf of Thailand

Andaman Sea

Celebes Sea

Manado

Kota Kinabalu

Kuching

Medan

SINGAPORE

BORNEO

CELEBES

SUMATRA

Ujung Pandang

Equator

Java Sea

JAKARTA

JAVA

0   100   200   400   600   800 Miles
0   150   300   600   900   1200 Kilometers

90°   100°   110°   120°

40°

30°

20°

130°

10°

0°

10°

xlvii

Lambert Azimuthal Equal-Area Projection

Urban
Cropland
Cropland & Woodland
Cropland & Grazing Land
Grassland, Grazing Land
Forest, Woodland
Swamp, Marshland
Shrub, Sparse Grass;
Wasteland (pattern)
Barren Land

Oasis

INDIAN OCEAN

Gulf of Aden
Aden
Berbera
DANAKIL
Asmera
Khartoum
Blue Nile
Addis Ababa
White Nile
Mogadishu
Mountain Nile
Nairobi
Dar-es-Salaam
Lake Victoria
Uele
Kisangani
Lake Tangayika
Lake Nyasa
Bangui
Congo (Zaire)
Ubangi
Blantyre
Lubumbashi
Harare
Kasai
Lusaka
Congo (Zaire)
Kinshasa
Zambezi
Luanda
Limpopo
Johannesburg
Durban
Orange
KALAHARI DESERT
Windhoek
NAMIB DESERT
Orange
Cape Town

SEYCHELLES
COMORO ISLANDS
Mozambique Channel
MADAGASCAR
Antananarivo
Tropic of Capricorn

INDIAN OCEAN

| 0 | 100 | 200 | 400 | 600 | 800 Miles |
| 0 | 150 | 300 | 600 | 900 | 1200 Kilometers |

Legend

- Urban
- Cropland
- Cropland & Woodland
- Cropland & Grazing Land
- Grassland, Grazing Land
- Forest, Woodland
- Swamp, Marshland
- Shrub, Sparse Grass, Wasteland (pattern)
- Barren Land

Lambert Azimuthal Equal-Area Projection

I

NEW GUINEA

NEW BRITAIN

rt Moresby

SOLOMON ISLANDS

Coral Sea

Cairns

Townsville

VANUATU

NEW CALEDONIA

ÎLES LOYAUTÉ

Nouméa

Rockhampton

GREAT DIVIDING RANGE

Brisbane

SYDNEY

Canberra

GREAT DIVIDING RANGE

MELBOURNE

Tasman Sea

TASMANIA

Hobart

Equator

KIRIBATI

P A C I F I C   *O C E A N*

SAMOA ISLANDS

Pago Pago

FIJI ISLANDS

Suva

TONGA ISLANDS

Auckland

NORTH ISLAND

SOUTHERN ALPS

Wellington

Christchurch

SOUTH ISLAND

Dunedin

STEWART ISLAND

P A C I F I C   *O C E A N*

150° 160° 170° 180° 170° 160°

0° 10° 20° 30° 40°

B-590200-96 -1-1-3

0 100 200 400 600 800 Miles
0 150 300 600 900 1200 Kilometers

li

ATLANTIC

OCEAN

Tropic of Cancer

Equator

Fortaleza

Recife

Salvador

São Francisco

Belém

Brasília

Cuiabá

MATO GROSSO

Georgetown

Manaus

Amazon

Port of Spain
TRINIDAD

Orinoco

CARACAS

Negro

SELVAS

Caribbean Sea

Maracaibo

San Juan

PUERTO
RICO

La Paz

HISPANIOLA

BAHAMAS

LLANOS

Rio Branco

Kingston

JAMAICA

Barranquilla

BOGOTÁ

Iquitos

CUBA

Havana

Quito

Panamá

LIMA

ANDES

Lambert Azimuthal Equal-Area Projection

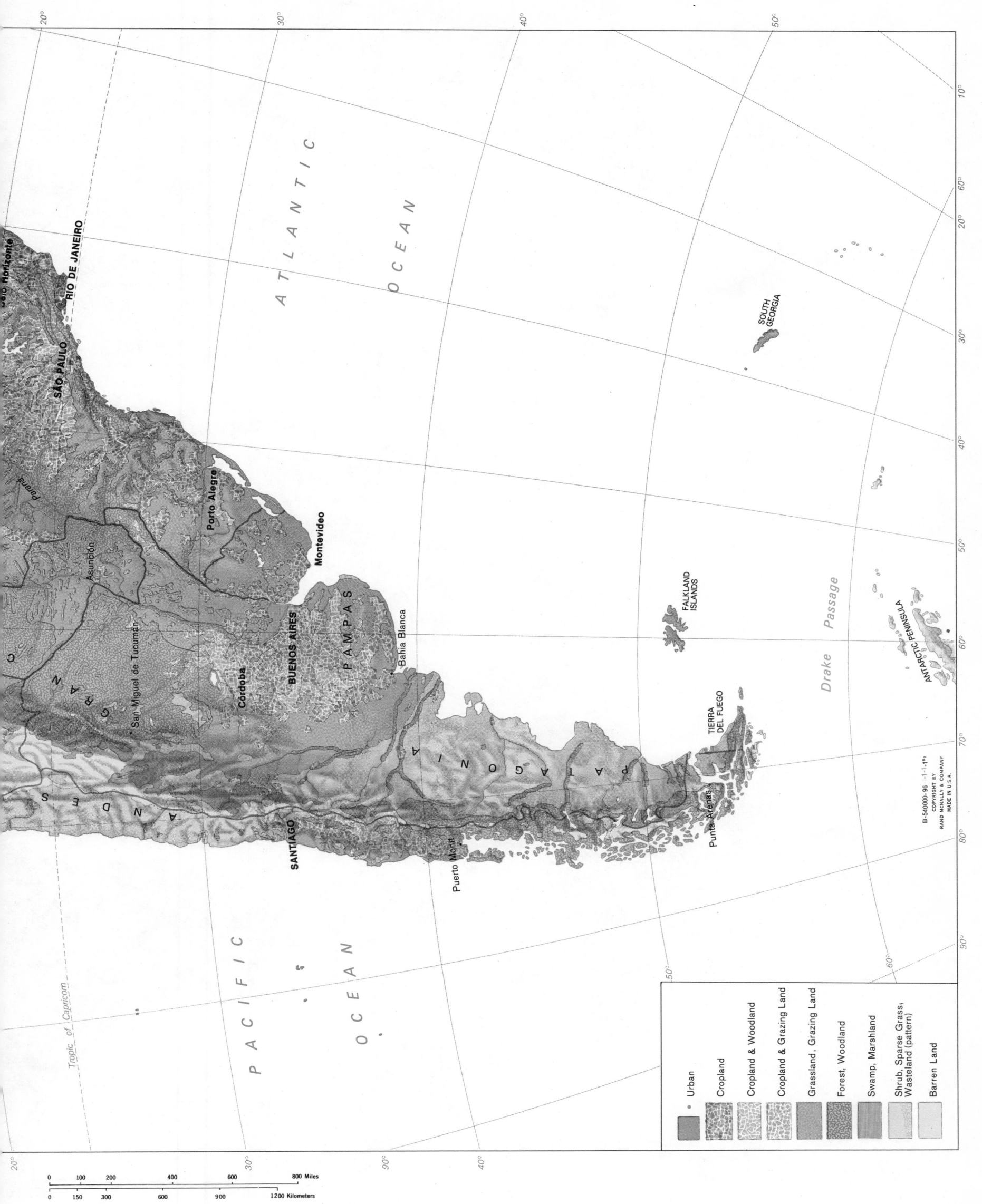

ATLANTIC

OCEAN

Belo Horizonte

RIO DE JANEIRO

SÃO PAULO

SOUTH
GEORGIA

Porto Alegre

Paraná

Asunción

Montevideo

PAMPAS

Buenos Aires

San Miguel de Tucumán

Córdoba

BUENOS AIRES

Bahía Blanca

FALKLAND
ISLANDS

GRAN

ANDES

SANTIAGO

Puerto Montt

PATAGONIA

Punta Arenas

TIERRA
DEL FUEGO

Drake   Passage

ANTARCTIC PENINSULA

PACIFIC

OCEAN

Tropic of Capricorn

Urban
Cropland
Cropland & Woodland
Cropland & Grazing Land
Grassland, Grazing Land
Forest, Woodland
Swamp, Marshland
Shrub, Sparse Grass,
Wasteland (pattern)
Barren Land

0   100   200   400   600   800 Miles

0   150   300   600   900   1200 Kilometers

GREENLAND

Arctic Circle

Godthab

Labrador Sea

Baffin Bay

ELLESMERE ISLAND

BAFFIN ISLAND

UNGAVA PENINSULA

DEVON ISLAND

Hudson Bay

MELVILLE ISLAND

BANKS ISLAND

VICTORIA ISLAND

Cambridge Bay

Churchill

ARCTIC OCEAN

North Pole

Beaufort Sea

Great Slave Lake

Peace

Edmonton

Red Riv.

BROOKS RANGE

Yukon

Fairbanks

Calgary

ROCKY MOUNTAINS

Bering Strait

Nome

ALASKA RANGE

Anchorage

Juneau

Gulf of Alaska

Prince Rupert

Vancouver

Seattle

Bering

Sea

Columbia

Portland

PACIFIC OCEAN

ALEUTIAN ISLANDS

Lambert Azimuthal Equal-Area Projection

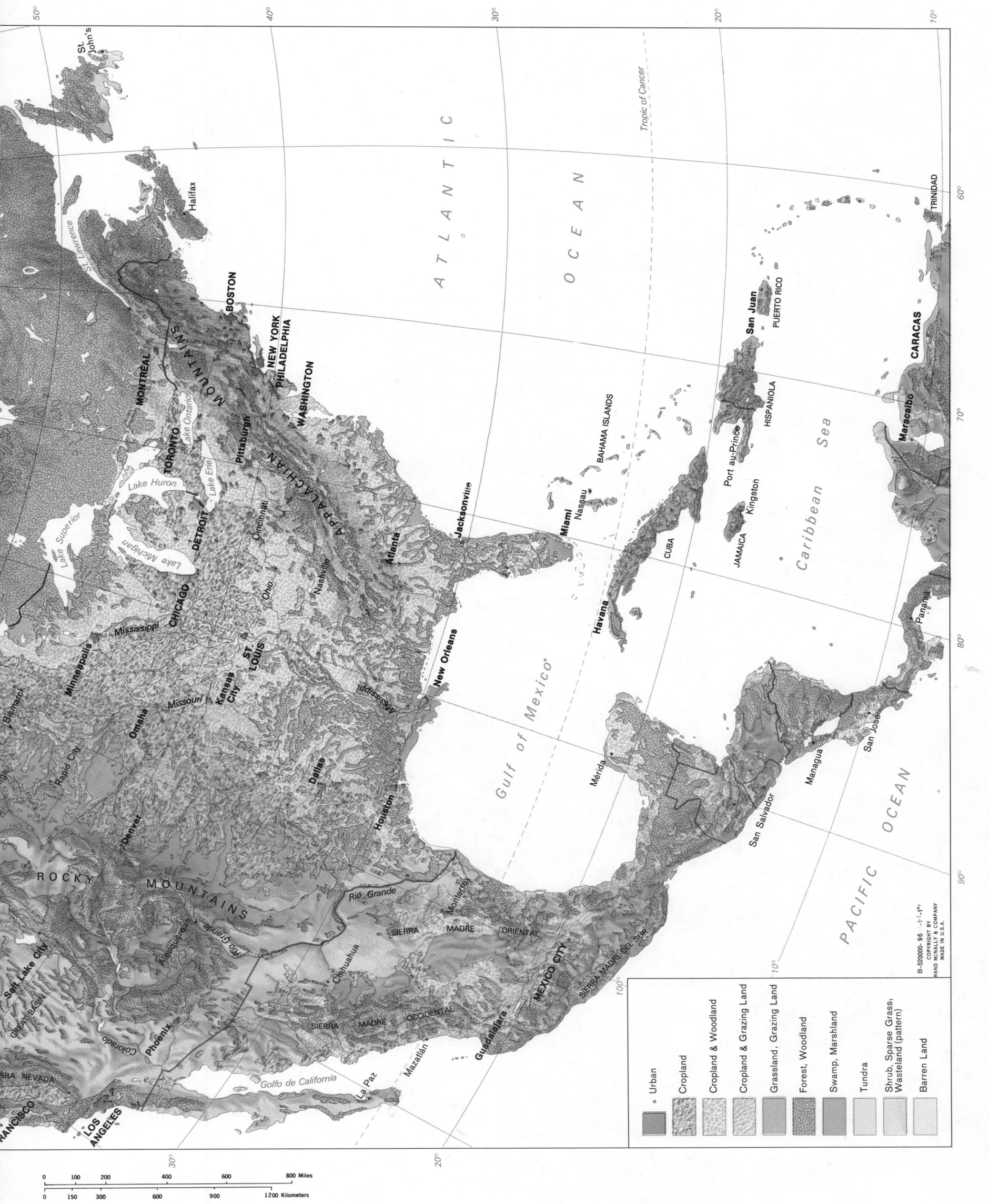

ATLANTIC

OCEAN

Tropic of Cancer

St. John's

Halifax

St. Lawrence

BOSTON

NEW YORK

PHILADELPHIA

WASHINGTON

MONTREAL

TORONTO

Lake Ontario

Lake Erie

Lake Huron

Lake Superior

Lake Michigan

DETROIT

Pittsburgh

Cincinnati

APPALACHIAN MOUNTAINS

CHICAGO

Nashville

Ohio

Atlanta

Jacksonville

Miami

Nassau

BAHAMA ISLANDS

San Juan

PUERTO RICO

Port au-Prince

HISPANIOLA

Kingston

JAMAICA

CUBA

Havana

Caribbean Sea

Maracaibo

CARACAS

TRINIDAD

Mississippi

ST. LOUIS

Kansas City

Missouri

Minneapolis

Bismarck

Omaha

Rapid City

Dallas

Mississippi

New Orleans

Houston

Gulf of Mexico

Mérida

Managua

San José

San Salvador

Panamá

Denver

ROCKY MOUNTAINS

Río Grande

Monterrey

SIERRA MADRE ORIENTAL

Chihuahua

SIERRA MADRE OCCIDENTAL

Río Grande

Albuquerque

Salt Lake City

GREAT BASIN

Colorado

Phoenix

SIERRA NEVADA

Golfo de California

La Paz

Mazatlán

Guadalajara

MEXICO CITY

SIERRA MADRE DEL SUR

SAN FRANCISCO

LOS ANGELES

PACIFIC OCEAN

B-520000- 96 -1-1-1*1
COPYRIGHT BY
RAND McNALLY & COMPANY
MADE IN U.S.A.

Urban
Cropland
Cropland & Woodland
Cropland & Grazing Land
Grassland, Grazing Land
Forest, Woodland
Swamp, Marshland
Tundra
Shrub, Sparse Grass,
Wasteland (pattern)
Barren Land

| 0 | 100 | 200 | 400 | 600 | 800 Miles |
| 0 | 150 | 300 | 600 | 900 | 1200 Kilometers |

Urban
Cropland
Cropland & Woodland
Cropland & Grazing Land
Grassland, Grazing Land
Forest, Woodland
Swamp, Marshland
Shrub, Sparse Grass, Wasteland (pattern)
Barren Land
Polyconic Projection
0 50 100 200 300 400 Miles
0 75 150 300 450 600 Kilometers
ATLANTIC OCEAN
PACIFIC OCEAN
Gulf of Mexico
Gulf of California
Gulf of St. Lawrence
ROCKY MOUNTAINS
APPALACHIAN MOUNTAINS
SIERRA MADRE ORIENTAL
SIERRA MADRE OCCIDENTAL
GREAT BASIN
CASCADE RANGE
OZARK PLATEAU
Lake Superior
Lake Michigan
Lake Huron
Lake Erie
Lake Ontario
Lake Winnipeg
Great Salt Lake
NEW YORK
BOSTON
PHILADELPHIA
WASHINGTON
DETROIT
CHICAGO
ST. LOUIS
TORONTO
MONTREAL
LOS ANGELES
SAN FRANCISCO
New Orleans
Houston
Dallas
Miami
Jacksonville
Atlanta
Memphis
Denver
El Paso
Phoenix
San Diego
Seattle
Vancouver
Minneapolis
Kansas City
Winnipeg
Oklahoma City
Omaha
Indianapolis
Cincinnati
Pittsburgh
Cleveland
Buffalo
Milwaukee
Norfolk
Salt Lake City
D-520500-96-1-1-1
COPYRIGHT BY RAND McNALLY & COMPANY
MADE IN U.S.A.

United States Travel Maps

A United States travel map has been divided into six regions—Alaska and Hawaii, the Pacific States, North Central States, South Central States, Northeast States, and Southeast States, as a convenience to the traveler in planning a route between adjoining states.

The map shows all major highways and all major cities and towns. It shows the topography of the land, including mountains, lakes, and reservoirs. For the vacationer, the map also locates major National Park Service areas—national parks, monuments, seashores, and recreation areas.

Elevations are indicated in meters, Interstate highway distances in miles and kilometers, and other road distances in miles.

Map Legend

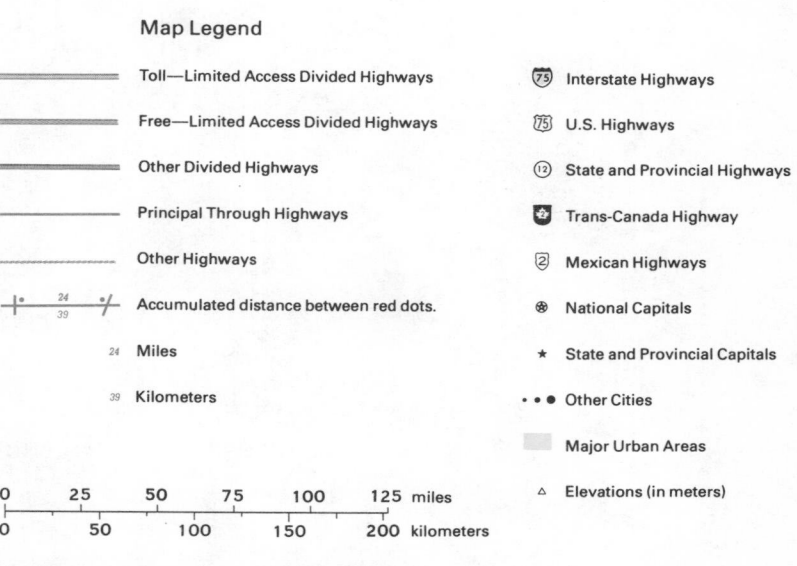

Toll—Limited Access Divided Highways	🛡 Interstate Highways
Free—Limited Access Divided Highways	🛡 U.S. Highways
Other Divided Highways	🛡 State and Provincial Highways
Principal Through Highways	🛡 Trans-Canada Highway
Other Highways	🛡 Mexican Highways
Accumulated distance between red dots.	✦ National Capitals
24 Miles	★ State and Provincial Capitals
39 Kilometers	• • ● Other Cities
	Major Urban Areas
	△ Elevations (in meters)

```
0      25     50     75     100    125  miles
0         50       100      150     200  kilometers
```

Scale 1: 3,900,000 One inch equals approximately 62 miles.
One centimeter equals approximately 39 kilometers.

ALBERS CONICAL EQUAL AREA PROJECTION

CANADA
UNITED STATES
ALBERTA
SASKATCHEWAN
BRITISH COLUMBIA
MONTANA
IDAHO
WASHINGTON
OREGON
WYOMING
UTAH
NEVADA
CALIFORNIA
VANCOUVER
Victoria
SEATTLE
Tacoma
Olympia
PORTLAND
Salem
Eugene
Spokane
Boise
Billings
Great Falls
Helena
Butte
Missoula
Bozeman
Pocatello
Idaho Falls
Twin Falls
Ogden
Lethbridge
Medicine Hat
Yakima
Walla Walla
Lewiston
CLEARWATER MOUNTAINS
SALMON RIVER MOUNTAINS
BLUE MOUNTAINS
BEAVERHEAD MOUNTAINS
LEWIS RANGE
MADISON RANGE
CABINET MOUNTAINS
PURCELL MTS
OCHOCO MTS.
KLAMATH MOUNTAINS
SNAKE RIVER PLAIN
GREAT SANDY DESERT
HARNEY BASIN
YELLOWSTONE NATIONAL PARK
GRAND TETON NAT'L PARK
OLYMPIC NATIONAL PARK
CRATER LAKE NAT'L PARK

PACIFIC OCEAN
SAN FRANCISCO
LOS ANGELES
SAN DIEGO
Sacramento
Oakland
San Jose
Stockton
Fresno
Bakersfield
Reno
Las Vegas
Phoenix
Tucson
Yuma
Flagstaff
Prescott
Tijuana
Mexicali
Ensenada
Santa Barbara
San Bernardino
Riverside
Barstow
Needles
Kingman
SIERRA NEVADA
COAST RANGES
SACRAMENTO VALLEY
MOJAVE DESERT
GREAT BASIN
DEATH VALLEY
GRAND CANYON
PAINTED DESERT
COLORADO PLATEAU
COCONINO PLATEAU
MOGOLLON RIM
IMPERIAL VALLEY
DESIERTO DE ALTAR
UNITED STATES
MEXICO
NEVADA
CALIFORNIA
ARIZONA
UTAH
COLORADO
NEW MEXICO
SONORA
BAJA CALIFORNIA NORTE
© RAND McNALLY & CO.

CANADA
UNITED STATES
ALBERTA
SASKATCHEWAN
MANITOBA
MONTANA
NORTH DAKOTA
SOUTH DAKOTA
WYOMING
NEBRASKA
COLORADO
KANSAS
UTAH
IDAHO
NEW MEXICO
ROCKY MOUNTAINS
LITTLE BELT MOUNTAINS
BIG BELT MOUNTAINS
MADISON RANGE
ABSAROKA RANGE
BIGHORN MOUNTAINS
BIG HORN BASIN
WYOMING BASIN
WYOMING RANGES
WASATCH RANGE
UINTA MOUNTAINS
LARAMIE MOUNTAINS
FRONT RANGE
SANGRE DE CRISTO MTS
SAN JUAN MOUNTAINS
ROAN PLATEAU
BOOK CLIFFS
YAMPA PLATEAU
WILLISTON BASIN
COTEAU DU MISSOURI
BAD LANDS
BLACK HILLS
SAND HILLS
BLUE HILLS UPLAND
SOURIS PLAIN
FORT PECK INDIAN RESERVATION
FORT BELKNAP INDIAN RESERVATION
ROCKY BOYS INDIAN RESERVATION
CROW INDIAN RESERVATION
NORTHERN CHEYENNE INDIAN RESERVATION
FORT BERTHOLD INDIAN RESERVATION
TURTLE MOUNTAIN INDIAN RESERVATION
STANDING ROCK INDIAN RESERVATION
CHEYENNE RIVER INDIAN RESERVATION
CROW CREEK INDIAN RESERVATION
PINE RIDGE INDIAN RESERVATION
ROSEBUD INDIAN RESERVATION
WIND RIVER INDIAN RESERVATION
UINTAH AND OURAY INDIAN RESERVATION
UTE MOUNTAIN INDIAN RESERVATION
SOUTHERN UTE INDIAN RESERVATION
CUSTER BATTLEFIELD NAT'L MON.
BIGHORN CANYON NAT'L RECR. AREA
YELLOWSTONE NATIONAL PARK
GRAND TETON NAT'L PARK
THEODORE ROOSEVELT NAT'L PARK
DEVILS TOWER NAT'L MON.
MOUNT RUSHMORE NAT'L MEM.
WIND CAVE NAT'L PARK
BADLANDS NAT'L PARK
AGATE FOSSIL BEDS NATIONAL MONUMENT
SCOTTS BLUFF NAT'L MON.
FOSSIL BUTTE NATIONAL MONUMENT
FLAMING GORGE NATIONAL RECREATION AREA
DINOSAUR NAT'L MON.
ROCKY MOUNTAIN NAT'L PARK
SHADOW MOUNTAIN NAT'L RECR. AREA
COLORADO NAT'L MON.
ARCHES NAT'L PARK
CANYONLANDS NATIONAL PARK
BLACK CANYON OF THE GUNNISON NAT'L MON.
CURECANTI NAT'L RECR. AREA
GREAT SAND DUNES NAT'L MON.
MESA VERDE NAT'L PARK
GLEN CANYON NATIONAL RECREATION AREA
NATURAL BRIDGES NAT'L MON.
RAINBOW BRIDGE NAT'L MON.
MONUMENT VALLEY
AZTEC RUINS NAT'L MON.
CAPULIN MOUNTAIN NAT'L MON.
Great Falls
Havre
Shelby
Lewistown
Helena
Bozeman
Livingston
Billings
Miles City
Glendive
Sidney
Glasgow
Wolf Point
Williston
Minot
Bismarck
Mandan
Dickinson
Jamestown
Devils Lake
Rapid City
Pierre
Sheridan
Buffalo
Gillette
Casper
Rawlins
Rock Springs
Green River
Laramie
Cheyenne
Scottsbluff
North Platte
McCook
Sterling
Fort Collins
Greeley
Longmont
Boulder
DENVER
Aurora
Colorado Springs
Pueblo
Grand Junction
Durango
Trinidad
Garden City
Dodge City
Liberal
Hays
© RAND McNALLY & CO.

CANADA
UNITED STATES
MANITOBA
MINNESOTA
ONTARIO
MICHIGAN
NORTH DAKOTA
SOUTH DAKOTA
WISCONSIN
IOWA
ILLINOIS
MISSOURI
KANSAS
NEBRASKA
OKLAHOMA
INDIANA
TENNESSEE
LAKE SUPERIOR
LAKE MICHIGAN
ISLE ROYALE
ISLE ROYALE NATIONAL PARK
KEWEENAW PENINSULA
MESABI RANGE
SUPERIOR UPLAND
OZARK PLATEAU
SALEM UPLAND
VOYAGEURS NAT'L PARK
GRAND PORTAGE NAT'L MON.
APOSTLE ISLANDS NATIONAL LAKESHORE
PICTURED ROCKS NATIONAL LAKESHORE
SLEEPING BEAR DUNES NATIONAL LAKESHORE
EFFIGY MOUNDS NAT'L MON.
PIPESTONE NAT'L MON.
GEORGE WASHINGTON CARVER NAT'L MON.
RED LAKE INDIAN RESERVATION
LEECH LAKE INDIAN RESERVATION
WHITE EARTH INDIAN RESERVATION
NETT LAKE INDIAN RESERVATION
SISSETON INDIAN RES.
MENOMINEE INDIAN RES.
POTAWATOMIE INDIAN RESERVATION
WINNEBAGO INDIAN RESERVATION
SANTEE INDIAN RESERVATION
DOOR PENINSULA
Fargo
Moorhead
Grand Forks
Duluth
Superior
MINNEAPOLIS
St. Paul
Rochester
St. Cloud
Bemidji
International Falls
Thunder Bay
Marquette
Green Bay
Madison
MILWAUKEE
CHICAGO
Rockford
Peoria
Springfield
Des Moines
Cedar Rapids
Davenport
Dubuque
Waterloo
Sioux City
Sioux Falls
Omaha
Lincoln
Topeka
KANSAS CITY
Wichita
ST. LOUIS
Columbia
Jefferson City
Springfield
Grand Rapids
Kalamazoo
South Bend
Gary
INDIANAPOLIS
Terre Haute
Evansville
Nashville
Paducah
Cape Girardeau

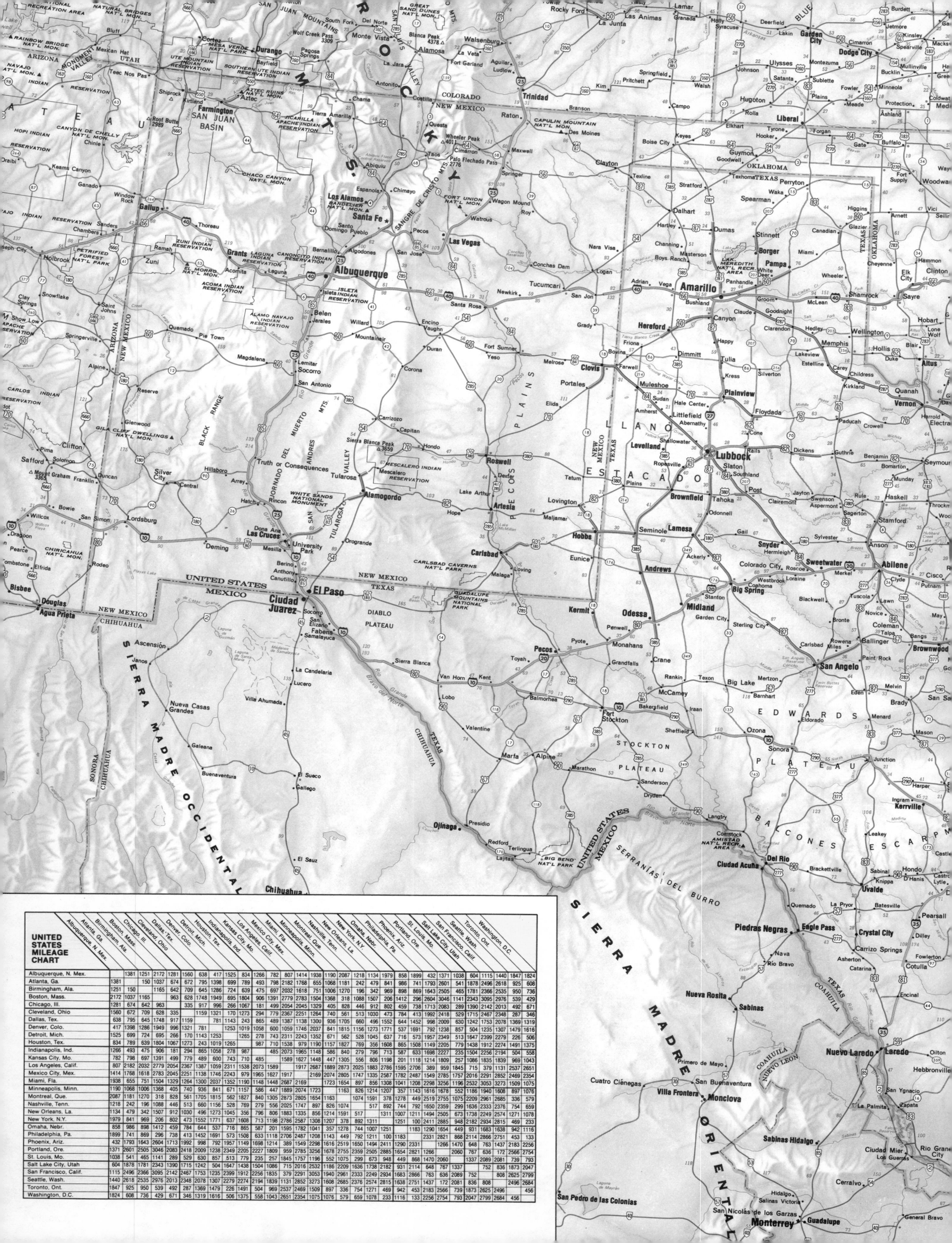

UNITED STATES MILEAGE CHART	Albuquerque, N. Mex.	Atlanta, Ga.	Birmingham, Ala.	Boston, Mass.	Chicago, Ill.	Cleveland, Ohio	Dallas, Tex.	Denver, Colo.	Detroit, Mich.	Houston, Tex.	Indianapolis, Ind.	Kansas City, Mo.	Los Angeles, Calif.	Mexico City, Mex.	Miami, Fla.	Minneapolis, Minn.	Montreal, Que.	Nashville, Tenn.	New Orleans, La.	New York, N.Y.	Omaha, Nebr.	Philadelphia, Pa.	Phoenix, Ariz.	Portland, Ore.	St. Louis, Mo.	Salt Lake City, Utah	San Francisco, Calif.	Seattle, Wash.	Toronto, Ont.	Washington, D.C.
Albuquerque, N. Mex.		1381	1251	2172	1281	1560	638	417	1525	834	1266	782	807	1414	1938	1190	2087	1218	1134	1979	858	1899	432	1371	1038	604	1115	1440	1847	1824
Atlanta, Ga.	1381		150	1037	674	672	795	1398	699	789	493	798	2182	1768	655	1068	1181	242	479	841	986	741	1793	2601	541	1878	2496	2618	925	608
Birmingham, Ala.	1251	150		1165	642	709	645	1286	724	639	475	697	2032	1618	751	1006	1270	196	342	969	898	869	1643	2505	465	1781	2366	2535	950	736
Boston, Mass.	2172	1037	1165		963	628	1748	1949	695	1804	906	1391	2779	2783	1504	1368	318	1088	1507	206	1412	296	2604	3046	1141	2343	3095	2976	539	429
Chicago, Ill.	1281	674	642	963		335	917	996	266	1067	181	499	2054	2045	1329	405	828	446	912	802	459	738	1713	2083	289	1390	2142	2013	492	671
Cleveland, Ohio	1560	672	709	628	335		1159	1321	170	1273	294	779	2367	2251	1264	740	561	513	1030	473	784	413	1992	2418	529	1715	2467	2348	287	346
Dallas, Tex.	638	795	645	1748	917	1159		781	1143	243	865	489	1387	1138	1300	936	1705	660	496	1552	644	1452	998	2009	630	1242	1753	2078	1369	1319
Denver, Colo.	417	1398	1286	1949	996	1321	781		1253	1019	1058	600	1059	1746	2037	841	1815	1156	1273	1771	537	1691	792	1238	857	504	1235	1307	1479	1616
Detroit, Mich.	1525	699	724	695	266	170	1143	1253		1265	278	743	2311	2243	1352	671	562	528	1045	637	716	573	1957	2349	513	1647	2399	2279	226	506
Houston, Tex.	834	789	639	1804	1067	1273	243	1019	1265		987	710	1538	979	1190	1157	1827	769	356	1608	865	1508	1149	2205	779	1438	1912	2274	1491	1375
Indianapolis, Ind.	1266	493	475	906	181	294	865	1058	278	987		485	2073	1965	1148	586	840	279	796	713	587	633	1698	2227	235	1504	2256	2194	504	558
Kansas City, Mo.	782	798	697	1391	499	779	489	600	743	710	485		1589	1627	1448	447	1305	556	806	1198	201	1118	1214	1809	257	1086	1835	1839	969	1043
Los Angeles, Calif.	807	2182	2032	2779	2054	2367	1387	1059	2311	1538	2073	1589		1917	2687	1889	2873	2025	1883	2786	1595	2706	389	959	1845	715	379	1131	2537	2651
Mexico City, Mex.	1414	1768	1618	2783	2045	2251	1138	1746	2243	979	1965	1627	1917		2169	2074	2805	1747	1335	2587	1782	2487	1549	2785	1757	2016	2291	2852	2469	2354
Miami, Fla.	1938	655	751	1504	1329	1264	1300	2037	1352	1190	1148	1448	2687	2169		1723	1654	897	856	1308	1041	1208	2298	3256	1196	2532	3053	3273	1509	1075
Minneapolis, Minn.	1190	1068	1006	1368	405	740	936	841	671	1157	586	447	1889	2074	1723		1163	826	1214	1207	357	1143	1616	1678	552	1186	1940	1608	897	1076
Montreal, Que.	2087	1181	1270	318	828	561	1705	1815	562	1827	840	1305	2873	2805	1654	1163		1074	1591	378	1278	449	2519	2755	1075	2209	2961	2685	336	579
Nashville, Tenn.	1218	242	196	1088	446	513	660	1156	528	769	279	556	2025	1747	897	826	1074		517	892	744	792	1650	2359	299	1636	2333	2376	754	659
New Orleans, La.	1134	479	342	1507	912	1030	496	1273	1045	356	796	806	1883	1335	856	1214	1591	517		1311	1007	1211	1494	2505	673	1738	2249	2574	1271	1078
New York, N.Y.	1979	841	969	206	802	473	1552	1771	637	1608	713	1198	2786	2587	1308	1207	378	892	1311		1251	100	2411	2885	948	2182	2934	2815	469	233
Omaha, Nebr.	858	986	898	1412	459	784	644	537	716	865	587	201	1595	1782	1041	357	1278	744	1007	1251		1183	1290	1654	449	931	1683	1638	942	1116
Philadelphia, Pa.	1899	741	869	296	738	413	1452	1691	573	1508	633	1118	2706	2487	1208	1143	449	792	1211	100	1183		2331	2821	868	2114	2866	2751	453	133
Phoenix, Ariz.	432	1793	1643	2604	1713	1992	998	792	1957	1149	1698	1214	389	1549	2298	1616	2519	1650	1494	2411	1290	2331		1266	1470	648	763	1437	2183	2256
Portland, Ore.	1371	2601	2505	3046	2083	2418	2009	1238	2349	2205	2227	1809	959	2785	3256	1678	2755	2359	2505	2885	1654	2821	1266		2060	767	636	172	2566	2754
St. Louis, Mo.	1038	541	465	1141	289	529	630	857	513	779	235	257	1845	1757	1196	552	1075	299	673	948	449	868	1470	2060		1337	2089	2081	739	793
Salt Lake City, Utah	604	1878	1781	2343	1390	1715	1242	504	1647	1438	1504	1086	715	2016	2532	1186	2209	1636	1738	2182	931	2114	648	767	1337		752	836	1873	2047
San Francisco, Calif.	1115	2496	2366	3095	2142	2467	1753	1235	2399	1912	2256	1835	379	2291	3053	1940	2961	2333	2249	2934	1683	2866	763	636	2089	752		808	2625	2799
Seattle, Wash.	1440	2618	2535	2976	2013	2348	2078	1307	2279	2274	2194	1839	1131	2852	3273	1608	2685	2376	2574	2815	1638	2751	1437	172	2081	836	808		2496	2684
Toronto, Ont.	1847	925	950	539	492	287	1369	1479	226	1491	504	969	2537	2469	1509	897	336	754	1271	469	942	453	2183	2566	739	1873	2625	2496		456
Washington, D.C.	1824	608	736	429	671	346	1319	1616	506	1375	558	1043	2651	2354	1075	1076	579	659	1078	233	1116	133	2256	2754	793	2047	2799	2684	456	

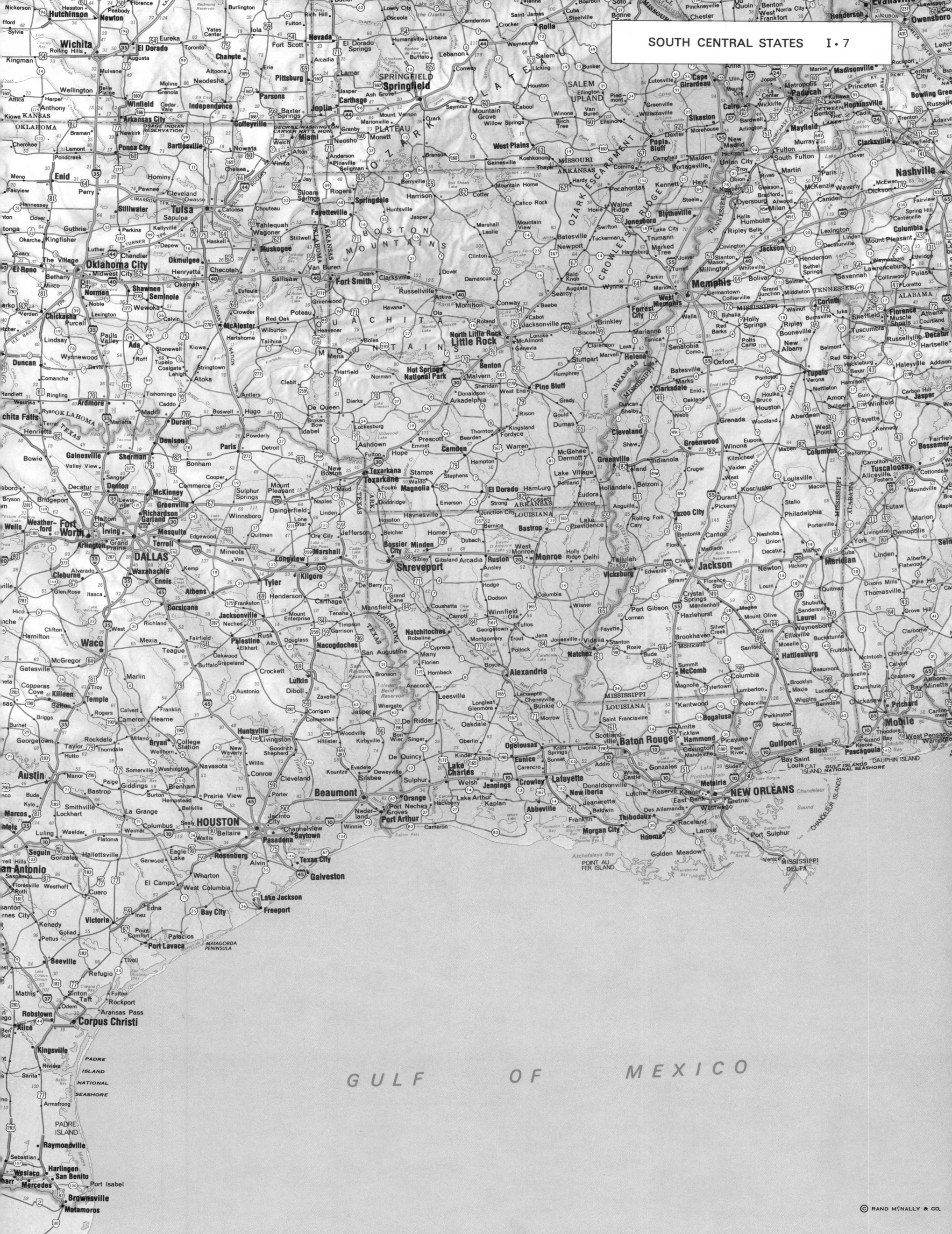
GULF OF MEXICO
OKLAHOMA
KANSAS
MISSOURI
ARKANSAS
TENNESSEE
MISSISSIPPI
ALABAMA
LOUISIANA
TEXAS
OZARK PLATEAU
BOSTON MOUNTAINS
OUACHITA MOUNTAINS
CROWLEY'S RIDGE
OZARK ESCARPMENT
SALEM UPLAND
SPRINGFIELD PLATEAU
PADRE ISLAND NATIONAL SEASHORE
MATAGORDA PENINSULA
MISSISSIPPI DELTA
CHANDELEUR ISLANDS
GULF ISLANDS NATIONAL SEASHORE
Wichita
Hutchinson
Tulsa
Oklahoma City
Springfield
Fort Smith
Little Rock
Memphis
Nashville
Jackson
Shreveport
Dallas
Fort Worth
Waco
Austin
San Antonio
HOUSTON
Galveston
Beaumont
Port Arthur
Lake Charles
Baton Rouge
NEW ORLEANS
Mobile
Gulfport
Biloxi
Corpus Christi
Brownsville
Matamoros
Texarkana
Monroe
Vicksburg
Alexandria
Lafayette
Tuscaloosa
Meridian
Hattiesburg
Paducah
Evansville
Owensboro
© RAND McNALLY & CO.

CANADA
UNITED STATES
ONTARIO
MICHIGAN
MINNESOTA
WISCONSIN
IOWA
ILLINOIS
INDIANA
OHIO
KENTUCKY
MISSOURI
ARKANSAS
TENNESSEE
LAKE SUPERIOR
LAKE MICHIGAN
LAKE HURON
ISLE ROYALE
ISLE ROYALE NATIONAL PARK
PUKASKWA NATIONAL PARK
VOYAGEURS NAT'L PARK
GRAND PORTAGE NAT'L MON.
APOSTLE ISLANDS NATIONAL LAKESHORE
PICTURED ROCKS NATIONAL LAKESHORE
SLEEPING BEAR DUNES NATIONAL LAKESHORE
KEWEENAW PENINSULA
HURON MOUNTAINS
MESABI RANGE
SUPERIOR UPLAND
MANITOULIN ISLAND
GEORGIAN BAY ISLANDS NAT. PARK
POINT PELEE NAT. PARK
MAMMOTH CAVE NATIONAL PARK
MOUND CITY GROUP NAT'L MON.
SALEM UPLAND
Thunder Bay
Duluth
Superior
International Falls
Sault Ste. Marie
Sudbury
Marquette
MINNEAPOLIS
St. Paul
MILWAUKEE
Madison
Green Bay
CHICAGO
Rockford
Peoria
Springfield
ST. LOUIS
Davenport
Cedar Rapids
Grand Rapids
Lansing
Flint
DETROIT
Windsor
London
Toledo
CLEVELAND
Akron
Youngstown
Columbus
Dayton
CINCINNATI
INDIANAPOLIS
Fort Wayne
South Bend
Louisville
Lexington
Evansville
Paducah
Charleston
Huntington
Kalamazoo
Saginaw
Bay City
Port Huron
Sarnia
Erie

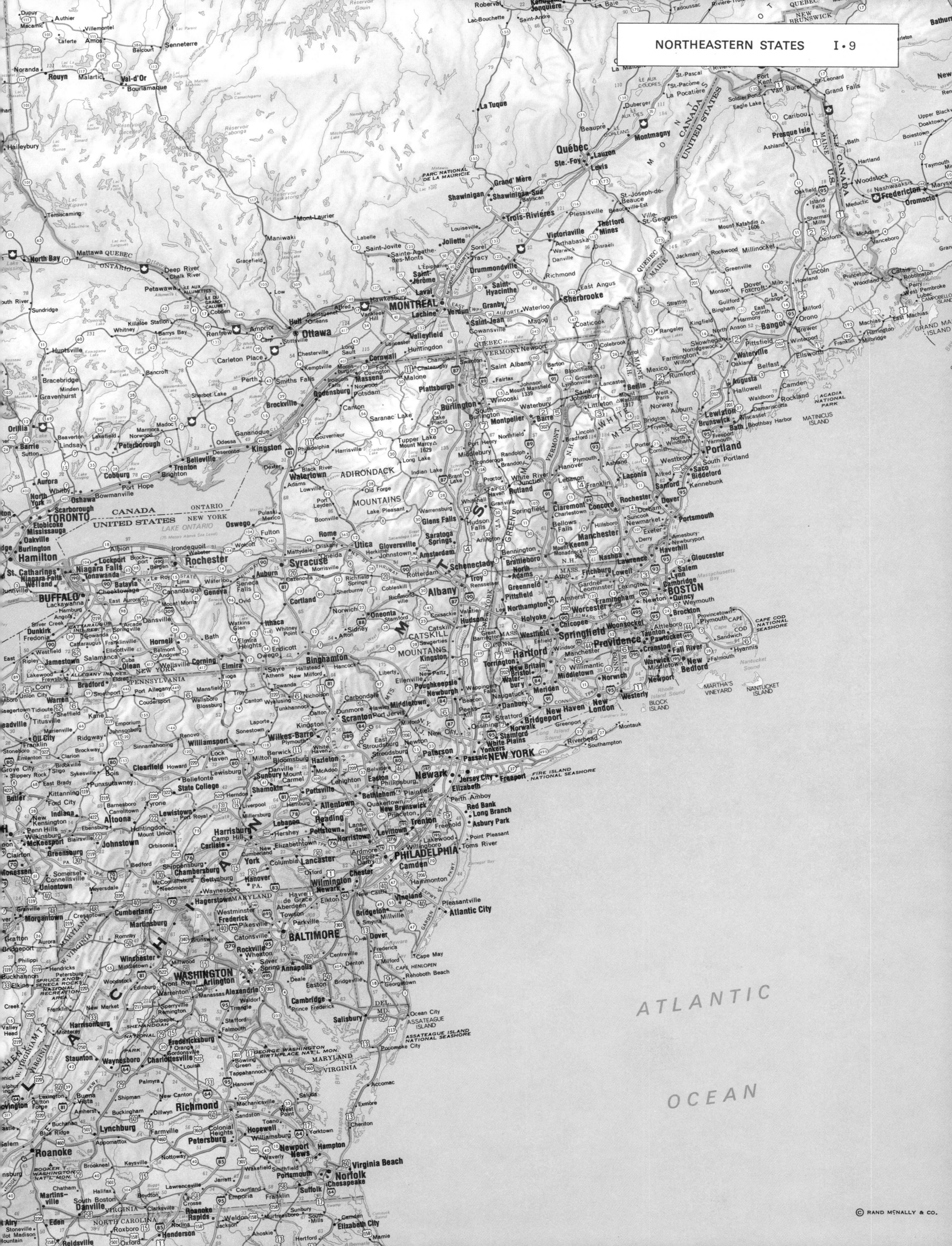
ATLANTIC
OCEAN
CANADA
UNITED STATES
ONTARIO
QUEBEC
NEW YORK
PENNSYLVANIA
MARYLAND
VIRGINIA
NORTH CAROLINA
W. VIRGINIA
MAINE
VERMONT
N.H.
MASS.
CONN.
NEW BRUNSWICK
LAKE ONTARIO
ADIRONDACK
MOUNTAINS
CATSKILL
MOUNTAINS
WHITE MTS.
GREEN MTS.
MONTREAL
Ottawa
Québec
TORONTO
Hamilton
BUFFALO
Rochester
Syracuse
Albany
BOSTON
Providence
Hartford
New Haven
NEW YORK
Newark
PHILADELPHIA
BALTIMORE
WASHINGTON
Richmond
Norfolk
Portland
Bangor
Atlantic City
Virginia Beach
Harrisburg
Scranton
Wilkes-Barre
Allentown
Springfield
Worcester
CAPE COD NATIONAL SEASHORE
FIRE ISLAND NATIONAL SEASHORE
ASSATEAGUE ISLAND NATIONAL SEASHORE
ACADIA NATIONAL PARK
MARTHA'S VINEYARD
NANTUCKET ISLAND
BLOCK ISLAND
© RAND McNALLY & CO.

GULF OF MEXICO
OZARK PLATEAU
BOSTON MOUNTAINS
OUACHITA MOUNTAINS
OZARK ESCARPMENT
CROWLEY'S RIDGE
SALEM UPLAND
OKLAHOMA
ARKANSAS
MISSOURI
TEXAS
LOUISIANA
MISSISSIPPI
TENNESSEE
ALABAMA
KENTUCKY
FLORIDA
Oklahoma City
Tulsa
Muskogee
Okmulgee
McAlester
Ardmore
Durant
Enid
Stillwater
Ponca City
Bartlesville
Norman
Shawnee
Chickasha
Sherman
Denison
Gainesville
Denton
McKinney
Paris
Fort Worth
Arlington
DALLAS
Irving
Mesquite
Garland
Richardson
Tyler
Longview
Marshall
Kilgore
Waco
Temple
Bryan
College Station
Huntsville
Lufkin
Nacogdoches
Palestine
Corsicana
Athens
HOUSTON
Pasadena
Baytown
Beaumont
Port Arthur
Orange
Texas City
Galveston
Freeport
Lake Jackson
Bay City
Victoria
Port Lavaca
Corpus Christi
Aransas Pass
Rockport
MATAGORDA PENINSULA
Texarkana
Fort Smith
Fayetteville
Springdale
Rogers
Joplin
Carthage
Springfield
West Plains
Poplar Bluff
Cape Girardeau
Sikeston
Paducah
Cairo
Hopkinsville
Bowling Green
Nashville
Clarksville
Jackson
Memphis
West Memphis
Jonesboro
Blytheville
Batesville
Conway
North Little Rock
Little Rock
Pine Bluff
Hot Springs National Park
Arkadelphia
Camden
El Dorado
Magnolia
Hope
Helena
Stuttgart
Greenville
Greenwood
Clarksdale
Cleveland
Tupelo
Columbus
Oxford
Corinth
Florence
Muscle Shoals
Sheffield
Decatur
Huntsville
Birmingham
Bessemer
Tuscaloosa
Meridian
Selma
Jackson
Vicksburg
Yazoo City
Natchez
Hattiesburg
Laurel
McComb
Biloxi
Gulfport
Pascagoula
Mobile
Prichard
Pensacola
Fort Walton Beach
Shreveport
Bossier City
Monroe
Ruston
Minden
Natchitoches
Alexandria
Lake Charles
Lafayette
New Iberia
Opelousas
Crowley
Jennings
Abbeville
Baton Rouge
Hammond
Houma
Thibodaux
Morgan City
Metairie
Kenner
NEW ORLEANS
Gretna
Slidell
Bogalusa
Port Sulphur
Venice
MISSISSIPPI DELTA
CHANDELEUR ISLANDS
Chandeleur Sound
Breton Sound
Atchafalaya Bay
POINT AU FER ISLAND
CAT ISLAND
GULF ISLANDS NATIONAL SEASHORE
DAUPHIN ISLAND
Mississippi Sound
Lake Pontchartrain
Sabine Pass

ATLANTIC
OCEAN
BAHAMAS
APPALACHIAN
ATLANTA
Charlotte
Columbia
Augusta
Savannah
Charleston
Macon
Columbus
Jacksonville
Tallahassee
Gainesville
Orlando
Tampa
St. Petersburg
West Palm Beach
Fort Lauderdale
MIAMI
Key West
FLORIDA KEYS
Nassau
NEW PROVIDENCE
GRAND BAHAMA
ANDROS ISLAND
Raleigh
Wilmington
Knoxville
Chattanooga
Greenville
Asheville
Daytona Beach
Myrtle Beach
Fort Myers
Sarasota
© RAND McNALLY & CO.

ALASKA

ARCTIC OCEAN
Beaufort Sea
Chukchi Sea
BERING SEA
Gulf of Alaska
PACIFIC OCEAN
Norton Sound
Bristol Bay
Anadyrskij Zaliv
Bering Strait
UNION OF SOVIET SOCIALIST REPUBLICS
ČUKOTSKIJ POLUOSTROV
Anadyr
Providenija
Dal'stroja
Naukan
POINT BARROW
Barrow
Wainwright
CAPE HALKETT
Deadhorse
MARTIN POINT
CAPE LISBURNE
Point Hope
BROOKS RANGE
GATES OF THE ARCTIC NATIONAL PARK
ENDICOTT MOUNTAINS
KOBUK VALLEY NATIONAL PARK
Noatak
Kotzebue
Kiana
Noorvik
Selawik
Shishmaref
SEWARD PENINSULA
Teller
Nome
Venetie
Fort Yukon
Circle
Nulato
Galena
Ruby
Kaltag
Manley Hot Springs
College
Fairbanks
Nenana
Delta Junction
McKinley Park
DENALI NATIONAL PARK
Mount McKinley 6194
Mount Brooks 3639
ALASKA RANGE
McGrath
KUSKOKWIM MOUNTAINS
Talkeetna
Glennallen
Nabesna
WRANGELL MOUNTAINS
Chitina
Valdez
Cordova
Willow
Palmer
Wasilla
Chugiak
Mount Torbert 3479
Anchorage
Whittier
Kenai
Soldotna
Seward
Homer
Seldovia
KENAI PENINSULA
KENAI FJORDS NATIONAL PARK
CHUGACH MOUNTAINS
WRANGELL-ST. ELIAS NATIONAL PARK
Mount Saint Elias 5489
Mount Logan 5950
SAINT ELIAS MOUNTAINS
LAKE CLARK NATIONAL PARK
TAYLOR MOUNTAINS
Newhalen
Dillingham
Togiak
Naknek
KATMAI NATIONAL PARK
CAPE DOUGLAS
AFOGNAK ISLAND
Kodiak
KODIAK ISLAND
SITKALIDAK ISLAND
TUGIDAK ISLAND
SITKINAK ISLAND
CHIRIKOF ISLAND
ALASKA PENINSULA
Sand Point
SHUMAGIN ISLANDS
UNIMAK ISLAND
KRENITZIN ISLANDS
FOX ISLANDS
UNALASKA ISLAND
UMNAK ISLAND
ISLANDS OF THE FOUR MOUNTAINS
ATKA ISLAND
ALEUTIAN ISLANDS
PRIBILOF ISLANDS
SAINT LAWRENCE ISLAND
SAINT MATTHEW ISLAND
NUNIVAK ISLAND
Emmonak
Alakanuk
Kotlik
Mountain Village
Saint Marys
Pilot Station
Chevak
Hooper Bay
Tununak
Toksook Bay
Kipnuk
Bethel
Akiachak
Akiak
Napakiak
Napaskiak
Aniak
Eagle
Dawson
OGILVIE MOUNTAINS
Elsa
Mayo
DAWSON RANGE
Carmacks
Haines Junction
Whitehorse
Teslin
Watson Lake
Ross River
PELLY MOUNTAINS
SELWYN MOUNTAINS
MACKENZIE MOUNTAINS
RICHARDSON MOUNTAINS
YUKON
NORTHWEST TERRITORIES
BRITISH COLUMBIA
UNITED STATES
CANADA
ALASKA
RICHARDS ISLAND
Tuktoyaktuk
Inuvik
Aklavik
Fort Good Hope
COAST MOUNTAINS
Atlin
Cassiar
Skagway
Haines
GLACIER BAY NATIONAL PARK
Juneau
Douglas
Hoonah
Angoon
CHICHAGOF ISLAND
Sitka
BARANOF ISLAND
Mount Edgecumbe
Kake
KUPREANOF ISLAND
Petersburg
Wrangell
ZAREMBO ISLAND
WRANGELL ISLAND
Stewart
PRINCE OF WALES ISLAND
Ketchikan
Metlakatla
Prince Rupert
ALEXANDER ARCHIPELAGO
QUEEN CHARLOTTE ISLANDS
GRAHAM ISLAND
LATOUCHE ISLAND
0 100 200 300 miles
0 100 200 300 400 kilometers

BERING SEA
ALEUTIAN ISLANDS
ATTU ISLAND
NEAR ISLANDS
BULDIR ISLAND
KISKA ISLAND
SEMISOPOCHNOI ISLAND
RAT ISLANDS
AMCHITKA ISLAND
TANAGA ISLAND
KANAGA ISLAND
GREAT SITKIN ISLAND
KAGALASKA ISLAND
PACIFIC OCEAN

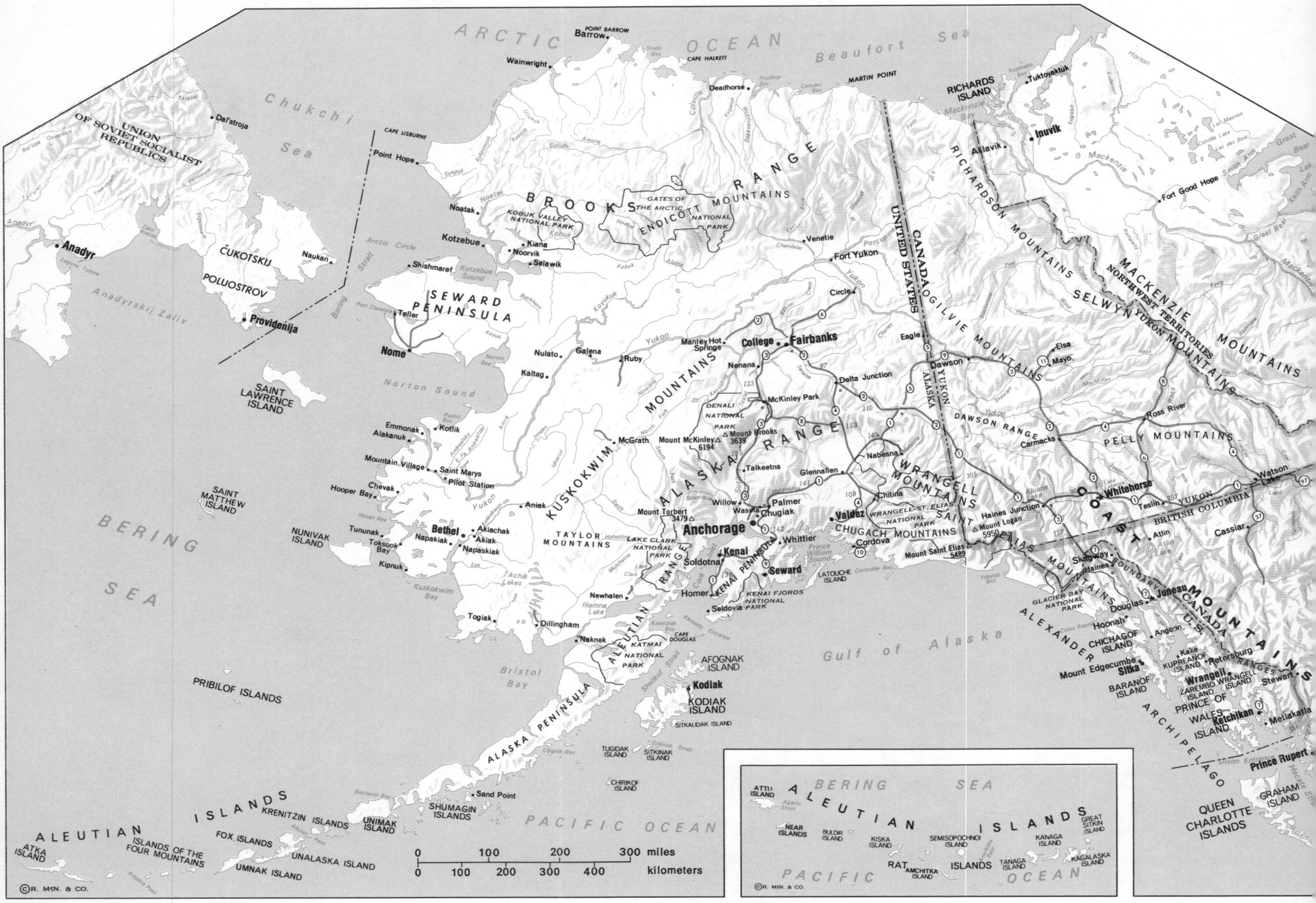

HAWAII

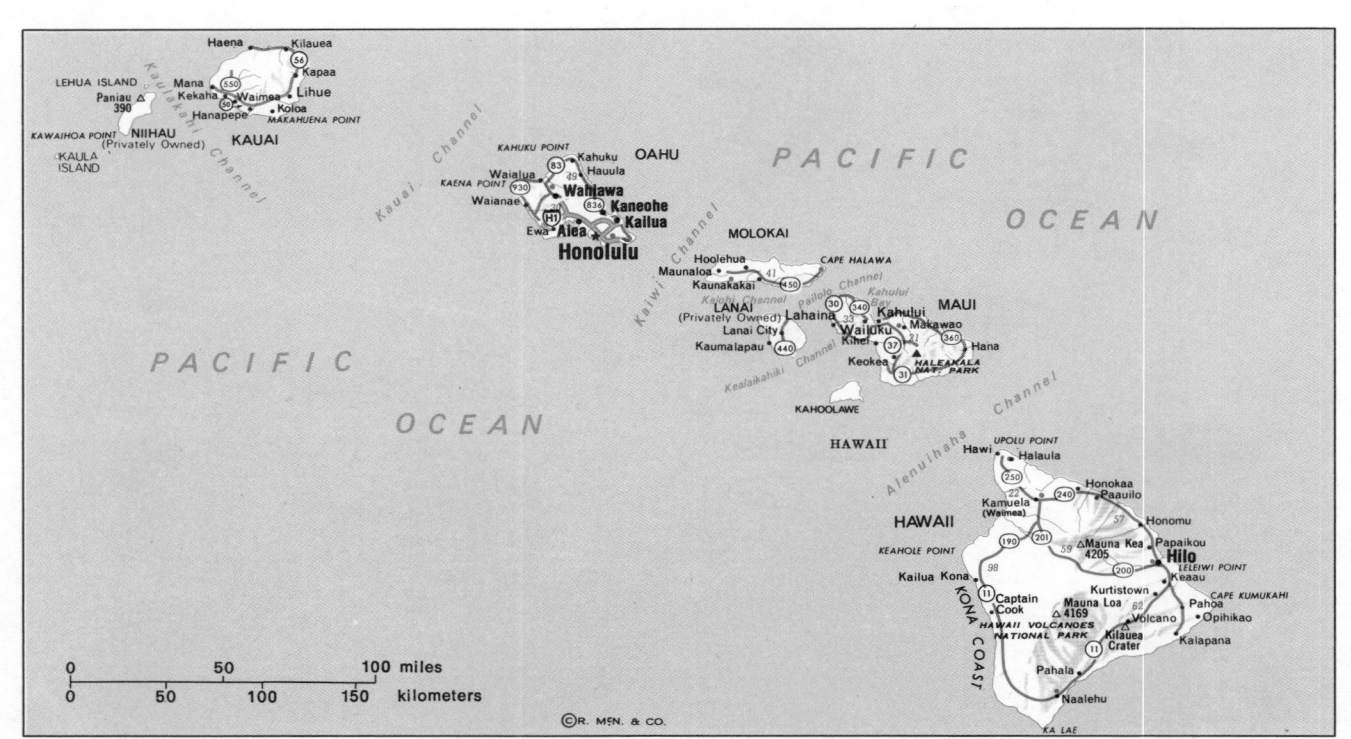

World Reference Maps

In the atlas the world has been mapped on a broad regional basis, not country by country. Introducing each of the regions is a global view of that region, showing how the land might appear in its summer mantle of vegetation if viewed from far out in space. Accompanying text characterizes the region's physical geography, and a simple multicolored outline map identifies the countries of this world region.

Following each of these global views are the Cosmo Series Maps of the region, with each great landmass shown as a whole and subsequently broken down into major continental regions.

As an example, on pages 7A-7B there is a global view of Europe, and this introduces the Cosmo Series Maps that follow on pages 8-32.

All the regional maps for each continent are drawn on the same scale. Thus it is possible to make direct visual comparisons of the sizes of countries and the distances between places by turning from one map to another. For instance, North America is mapped in three regions— Mexico, United States, Canada—all at the scale of 1:12,000,000. South America's regions are shown at the scale of 1:8,000,000, Europe's, Asia's, and Australia's regions at the scale of 1:16,000,000, and Africa's at the scale of 1:11,400,000.Smaller areas are shown in detail on larger scale sectional maps, which use even multiples of the regional scales. The United States and Canada have individual maps of each state and province.

The maps carry as many political subdivisions as space will permit. Counties are shown on all U.S. state maps and on the maps of appropriate Canadian provinces. Other countries may not be mapped on a large enough scale to show administrative subdivisions. For some of these countries, the names of larger administrative subdivisions appear without the boundaries. In others, regions with historical significance are shown.

I·13

Maps and Map Projections

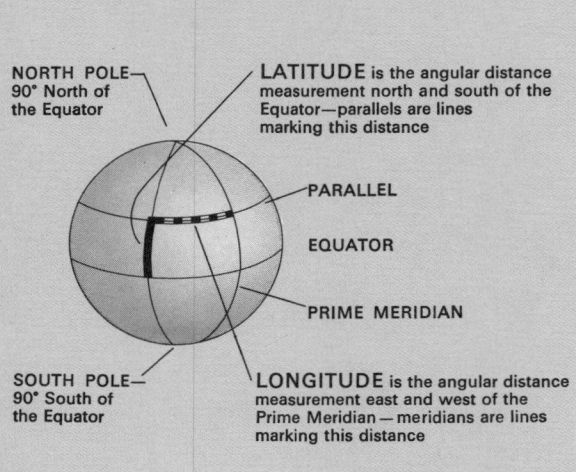

NORTH POLE—
90° North of
the Equator

LATITUDE is the angular distance
measurement north and south of the
Equator—parallels are lines
marking this distance

PARALLEL

EQUATOR

PRIME MERIDIAN

SOUTH POLE—
90° South of
the Equator

LONGITUDE is the angular distance
measurement east and west of the
Prime Meridian—meridians are lines
marking this distance

CONIC PROJECTIONS

Simple Conic

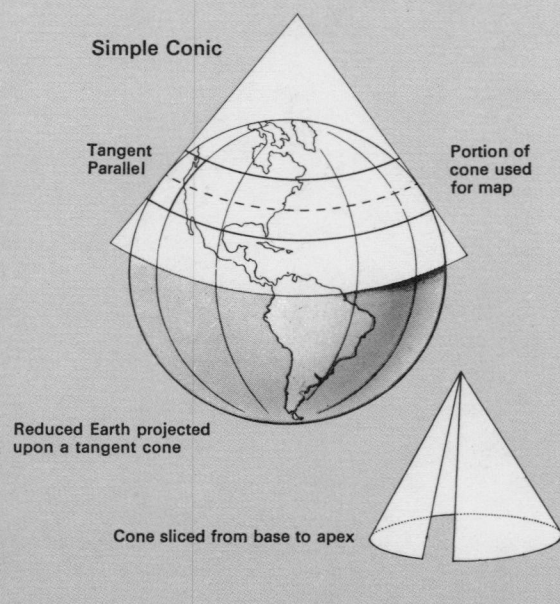

Tangent
Parallel

Portion of
cone used
for map

Reduced Earth projected
upon a tangent cone

Cone sliced from base to apex

Cone developed
onto a flat surface

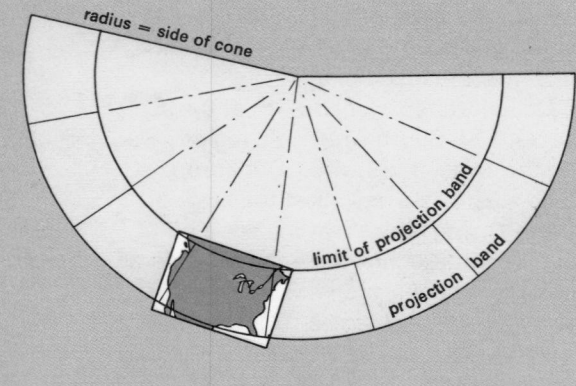

radius = side of cone

limit of projection band

projection band

From the earliest crude drawing to the latest highly accurate, skillful execution, maps have played a very important part in man's understanding of the planet upon which he lives. Maps expand our conceptions about areas. The following pages are designed to point up some significant elements of maps which are useful in intelligently interpreting them and the variety of information they contain. These sections are *Map Projections*, *Map Scale*, *Map Symbols*, and the *Index Reference System*.

MAP PROJECTIONS

The systematic arrangement of parallels and meridians on a plane or flat surface is the framework upon which a map is constructed, and this orderly network is called a map projection. Projections are actually developed through the use of mathematical formulae. The process can best be comprehended by visualizing the following four steps.

1. The earth reduced to a small sphere.
2. Geometric forms—cone, cylinder, plane surface—placed upon or around this sphere.
3. Transferral of the Earth's imaginary grid of parallels and meridians to one of these forms.
4. The form flattened, producing the projection.

Conic Projections

The Simple Conic or Conic as it is often called, the Lambert Conformal Conic, and the Polyconic, as their names imply, are all conically derived. Most of the maps in the atlas utilize these three conic projections. Parallels and meridians are projected onto a cone that is tangent to the reduced earth. Slicing the cone from its base to apex and flattening it onto a flat surface results in the *Simple Conic Projection*. Along the line that is tangent to the surface, the scale of the map is true. This line, usually a parallel, is called a *standard parallel*. As regions away from this line are mapped, the alterations of scale, shape, areal size, and direction increase.

Cylindrical Projections

By projecting the Earth's grid onto a tangent cylinder, we can achieve a series of parallels and meridians at right angles to one another, as they are on the Earth.

The three cylindrical projections illustrated here show how the same outlined regions look on all three. Notice that on all the maps there is a difference between the regions' areal extent; however, the difference is minimized by the Miller Projection. Comparison of the shapes of the regions with those on a globe shows the Mercator indicating this property most accurately. Other cylindrical projections enable the areas to be correctly shown while distorting the shapes of the landmasses.

Plane Projections

Here transformation of the sphere directly to a tangent flat surface is the method of projection. The *Lambert Azimuthal Equal Area Projection* is one upon which the correct relationships between areas have been maintained. For instance, Greenland and the lower portion of the Arabian Peninsula, which are approximately the same in areal extent, appear to be so on the Lambert Azimuthal Equal Area Projection. Notice, however, that although Africa's area is shown correctly, it has been stretched in one direction and compressed in another, thus altering its shape and the scale of the projection.

Equal Area Projections of the World

To show the world in its entirety on a flat surface so that areas may be compared intelligently, is extremely difficult without altering the shapes of areas beyond recognition. Cylindrical projections do not accomplish this, and plane and conic projections also do not represent the whole world this way. Two projections are frequently used today to accomplish this—the *Homolographic* and the *Sinusoidal*. Each retains the equal area property of the sphere, although each sacrifices uniform scale and invites some extreme shape compression and shearing in the polar areas of the projections.

In summary, where maps cover approximately a hemisphere of the Earth's surface, extreme distortion of some type is evidenced. On most of the maps in the atlas, however, individual choices of projections have been made to present a realistic picture of the Earth. With these maps the user may compare sizes of areas, shapes of landmasses, and measure distances and directions as accurately as necessary.

CYLINDRICAL PROJECTIONS

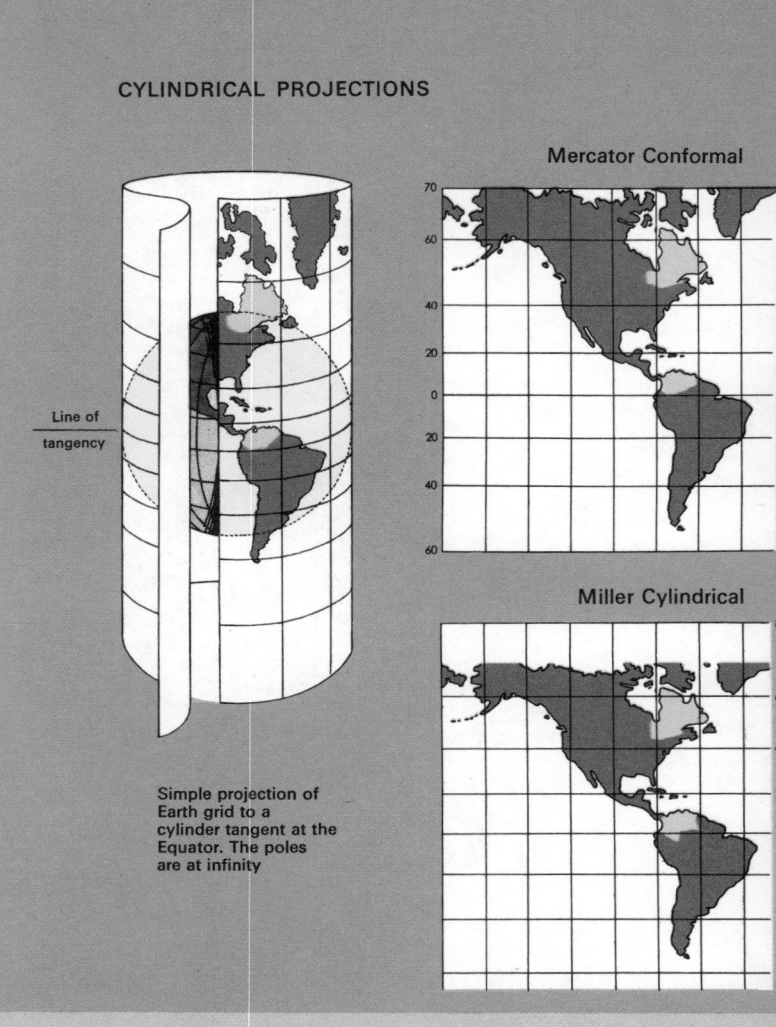

Line of
tangency

Mercator Conformal

Miller Cylindrical

Simple projection of
Earth grid to a
cylinder tangent at the
Equator. The poles
are at infinity

PLANE PROJECTIONS

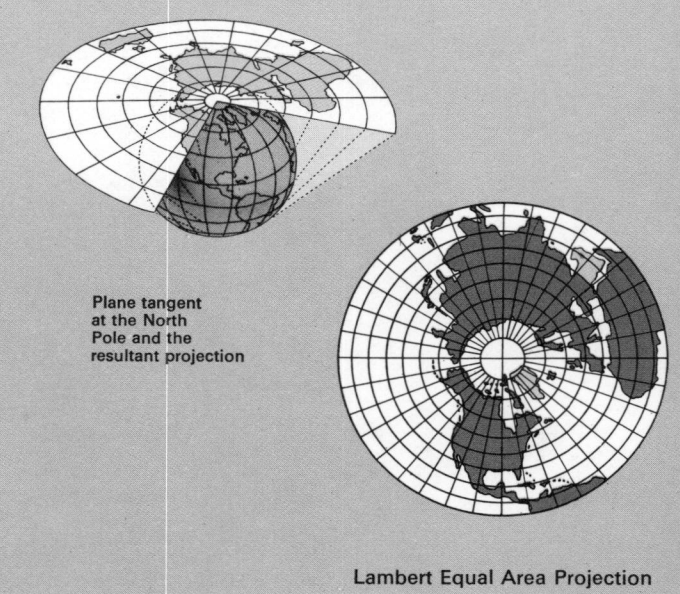

Plane tangent
at the North
Pole and the
resultant projection

Lambert Equal Area Projection

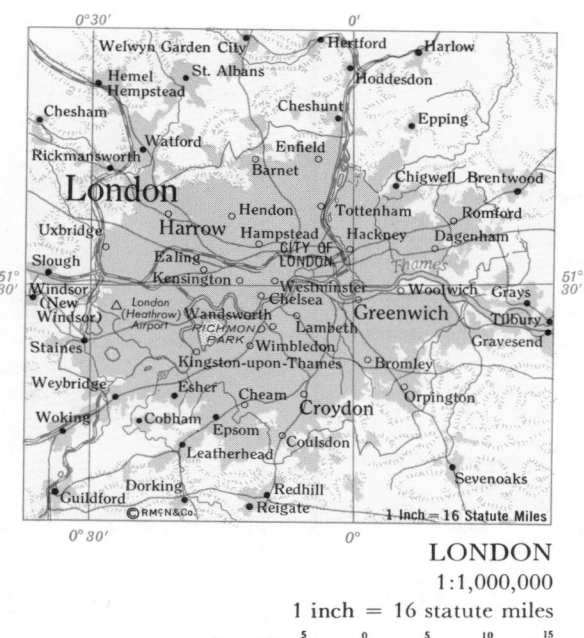

LONDON
1:1,000,000

1 inch = 16 statute miles

Statute Miles 5 0 5 10 15

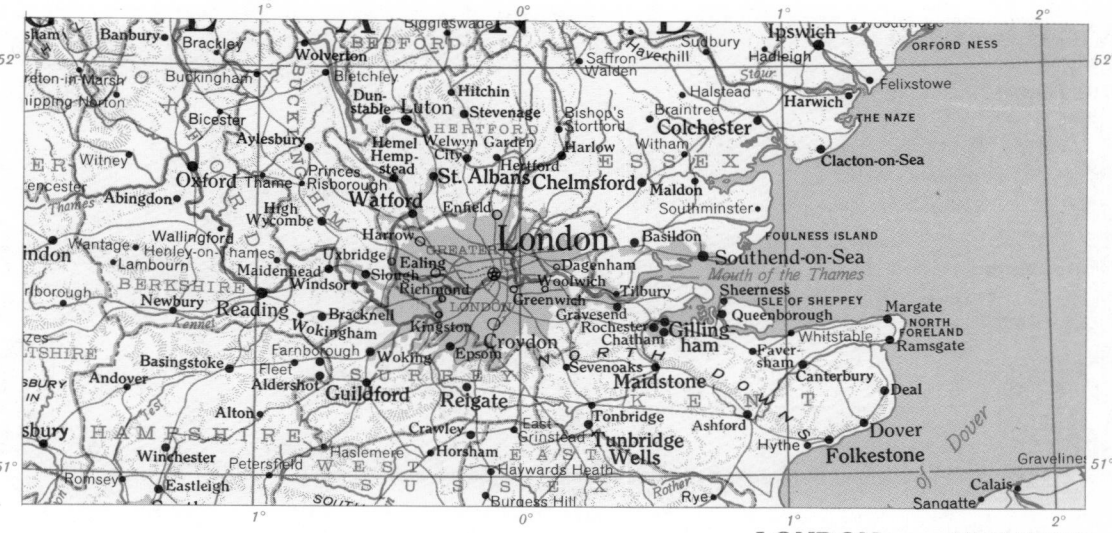

LONDON AND VICINITY
1:2,000,000

1 inch = 32 statute miles

Statute Miles 5 0 5 10 20 30

MAP SCALE

The scale of a map is the relationship it has with the area it represents. It usually is determined by measuring the distance between two places on the map and relating this to the distance between the same two places on the Earth's surface. This relationship may be stated in a number of different ways. Three commonly used methods are the representative fraction, a written statement, and a graphic portrayal. Each of the four maps on this page has its scale stated by these three methods.

The *representative fraction* is written either $\frac{1}{1,000,000}$ or 1:1,000,000. The map unit is always given as one, and the number of similar units this map unit represents on the Earth's surface is written as the denominator of the fraction, or after the colon. Thus, 1 inch or 1 centimeter on the London map in the upper left of the page represents 1,000,000 inches or 1,000,000 centimeters on the Earth's surface. In order to determine how many miles on the Earth 1 inch on the map represents, divide 63,360 (the number of inches in one mile) into 1,000,000. This results in the *written scale* being stated 1 inch represents approximately 16 miles. To further simplify the written scale by a *graphic portrayal*, a distance measured on the map may be converted to the Earth miles it represents by reading directly off the scale. The measured distance from London to Glasgow on the 1:16,000,000 scale map is 1.35 inches, which represents approximately 340 miles, the actual distance on the Earth's surface.

Because the Earth is spherical in shape and the map representing this sphere is flat, a degree of stretching and compressing has taken place in the projection of the sphere to the flat surface. (See the preceding section on projections). Inconsistency of scale from place to place on all maps is one of the results of this flattening process. The size relationship of map measurement to Earth measurement (scale) may not be exactly as stated on all parts of the map. Generally, as one moves away from the standard parallels, or the midsection of the map, toward the periphery, the stated scale changes. Because most of the Cosmo Series Maps encompass relatively small portions of the Earth's surface, the change in scale is of little consequence for general map use.

On world maps, however, where the scale varies greatly from one latitude to another, a varying graphic scale is employed. See the Graphic Linear Scale employed on the world map on pages 2 and 3. This permits accurate measurements at various parallels of latitude. At parallel 45°, 1 inch represents approximately 1,000 miles; at parallel 60° 1 inch represents approximately 700 miles.

As the scale of a map increases, the amount of information and detail shown increases, that is, the representative fraction and scale become larger. Notice in the four examples on this page how the increase in scale makes possible an increase in the number of cities shown, in the detail of the coastline, and in the intricacy and number of rivers.

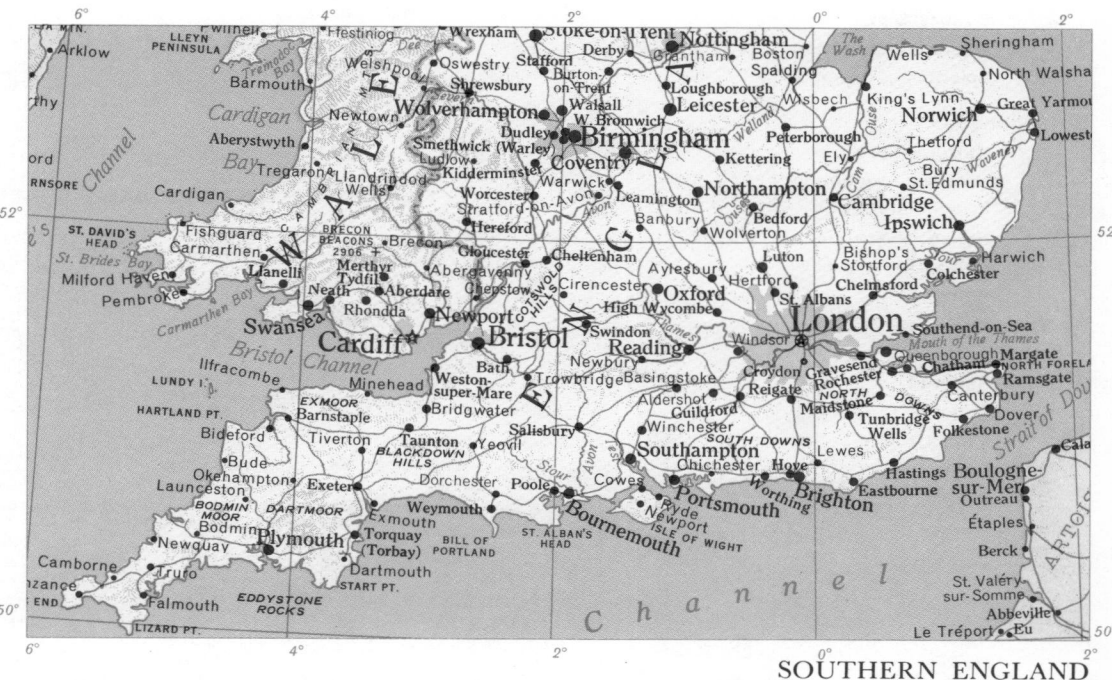

SOUTHERN ENGLAND
1:4,000,000

1 inch = 64 statute miles

Statute Miles 25 0 25 50 75

NORTHWEST EUROPE
1:16,000,000

1 inch = 252 statute miles

Statute Miles 100 0 100 200 300

MAP SYMBOLS

CULTURAL FEATURES

Political Boundaries

═══ International
――― Secondary (State, province, etc.)
――― County

Populated Places

Cities, towns, and villages

· · • • ● ● Symbol size represents population of the place

Chicago
Gary
Racine
Glenview
Edgewood

Type size represents relative importance of the place.

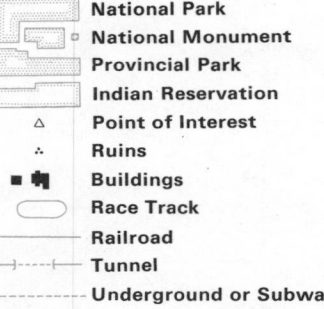 Corporate area of large U.S. and Canadian cities and urban area of other foreign cities

Major Urban Area
Area of continuous commercial, industrial, and residential development in and around a major city

○ Community within a city
⊕ Capital of major political unit
☆ Capital of secondary political unit
◉ Capital of U.S. state or Canadian province
○ County Seat
▲ Military Installation
⊙ Scientific Station

Miscellaneous

National Park
National Monument
Provincial Park
Indian Reservation
△ Point of Interest
∴ Ruins
■ ▬ Buildings
▭ Race Track
― Railroad
―‖― Tunnel
――― Underground or Subway
Dam
Bridge
Dike

LAND FEATURES

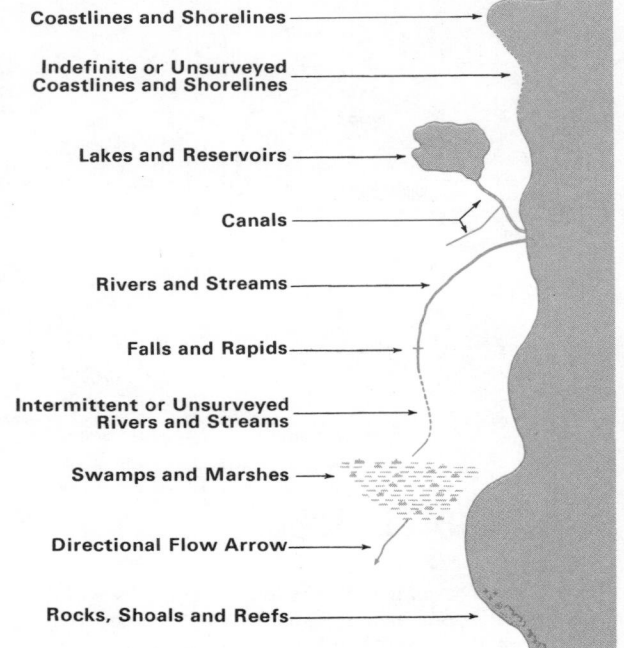

Ranges
Peaks
Passes — LITTLE PASS
Point of Elevation above sea level — 8,520 FT.
Escarpments, Bluffs, Cliffs, and Plateaus — PLATEAU
Glaciers
Volcanoes
Lava Flows
Sand Dunes
Deserts

WATER FEATURES

Coastlines and Shorelines
Indefinite or Unsurveyed Coastlines and Shorelines
Lakes and Reservoirs
Canals
Rivers and Streams
Falls and Rapids
Intermittent or Unsurveyed Rivers and Streams
Swamps and Marshes
Directional Flow Arrow
Rocks, Shoals and Reefs

TYPE STYLES USED TO NAME FEATURES

A S I A	Continent	PANTELLERIA (ITALY)	Country of which unit is a dependency in parentheses
DENMARK CANADA	Country, State, or Province	SRI LANKA (CEYLON)	Former or alternate name
BÉARN	Region, Province, or Historical Region	Rome (Roma)	Local or alternate city name
CROCKETT	County	Naval Air Station	Military Installation
		MESA VERDE SAN XAVIER	National Park or Monument, Provincial Park, Indian Res.,

UINTA DESERT — Major Terrain Features
MT. MORIAH — Individual Mountain
STROMBOLI NUNIVAK — Island or Coastal Feature
Ocean Lake River Canal — Hydrographic Features

Note: Size of type varies according to importance and available space. Letters for names of major features are spread across the extent of the feature.

THE INDEX REFERENCE SYSTEM

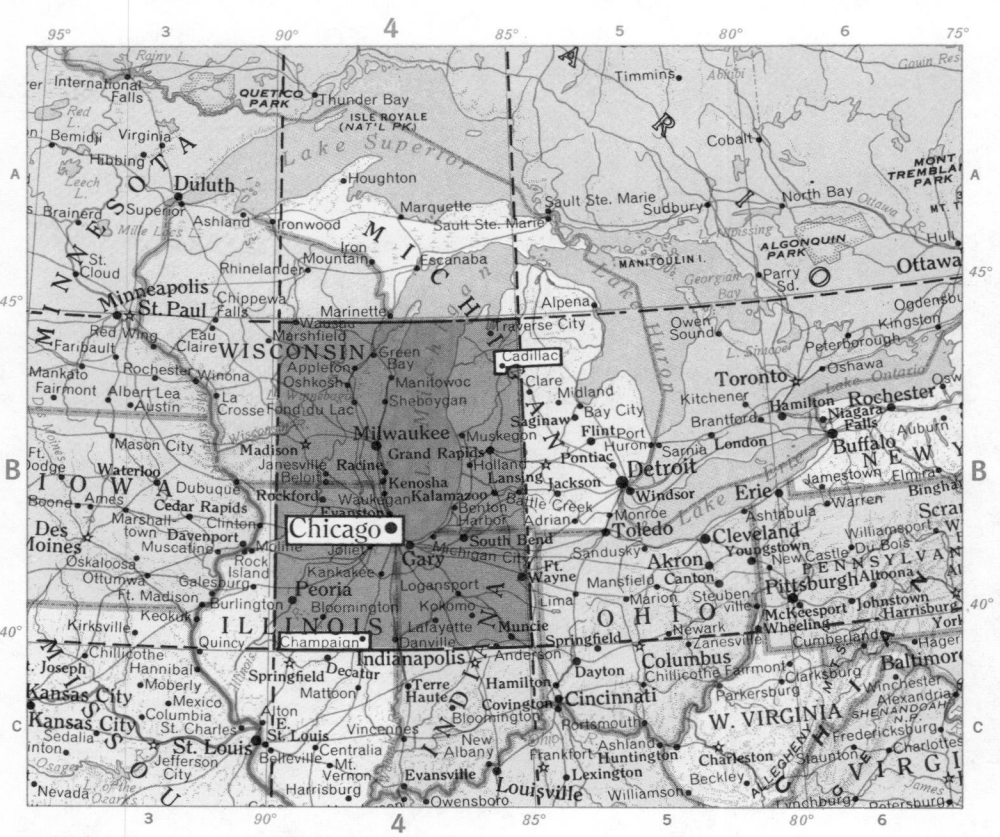

Place	Location	Index Key	Page
Cadillac, Que., Can		*h11	73
Cadillac, Sask., Can		H2	70
Cadillac, Fr		E3	14
Cadillac, Wexford, Mich		B4	90
Cadiz, San Bernardino, Calif		E6	82
Cadiz, Trigg, Ky		D2	94
Cadron, creek, Ark		B3	81
Caen, Fr		C3	14
Caetité, Braz		D2	57
Calcutta, India		D8	39
Cambridge, Eng		B8	12
Catania, It		F5	21
Ceará, state, Braz		C3	57
Chamblee, DeKalb, Ga		h8	87
Chambly, Que., Can		D4	73
Chambord, Que., Can		A5	73
Champagne, former prov., Fr		C5	14
Champaign, Champaign, Ill		B4	90
Champdore, lake, Que., Can		g8	75
Champerico, Guat		C2	62
Champéry, Switz		D2	19
Champex, Switz		D3	19
Champigneulles, Fr		F6	15
Champion, Chase, Nebr		D4	103
Champlain, co., Que., Can		B4	73
Champlain, lake, N.Y., Vt		B2	120
Champotón, Mex		D6	63
Changchou, China		E8	34
Chanthaburi, Thai		F5	38
Chaparral, Col		C2	60
Charleville-Mézières, Fr		C6	14
Chatham, Eng		B2	12
Chiapa de Corzo, Mex		D6	63
Chiapas, state, Mex		D6	63
Chiba, Jap		I10, n19	37
Chiba, pref., Jap		*I10	37
Chibemba, Ang		E1	48
Chibougamau, Que., Can		k12	73
Chicago, Cook, Ill		B4	90
Chichaoua, Mor		C3	44
Chichen Itzá, ruins, Mex		C7	63
Chichester, Eng		D7	12
Chickasaw, co., Iowa		A5	92
Chiclana, Sp		D2	20
Chiclayo, Peru		C2	58
Columbus, Franklin, Ohio		C3	111

The indexing system used in this atlas is based upon the conventional pattern of parallels and meridians used to indicate latitude and longitude. The index samples beside the map indicate that the cities of *Chicago, Cadillac*, and *Champaign* are all located in *B4*. Each index key letter, *in this case "B,"* is placed between corresponding degree numbers of latitude in the vertical borders of the map. Each index key number, *in this case "4,"* is placed between corresponding degree numbers of longitude in the horizontal borders of the map. Crossing of the parallels above and below the index letter with the meridians on each side of the index number forms a confining "box" in which the given place is certain to be located. It is important to note that location of the place may be anywhere in this confining "box."

Insets on many foreign maps are indexed independently of the main maps by separate index key letters and figures. All places indexed to these insets are identified by the lower case reference letter in the index key. A diamond-shaped symbol in the margin of the map is used to separate the insets from the main map and also to separate key letters and numbers where the spacing of the parallels and meridians is great.

Place-names are indexed to the location of the city symbol. Political divisions and physical features are indexed to the location of their names on the map.

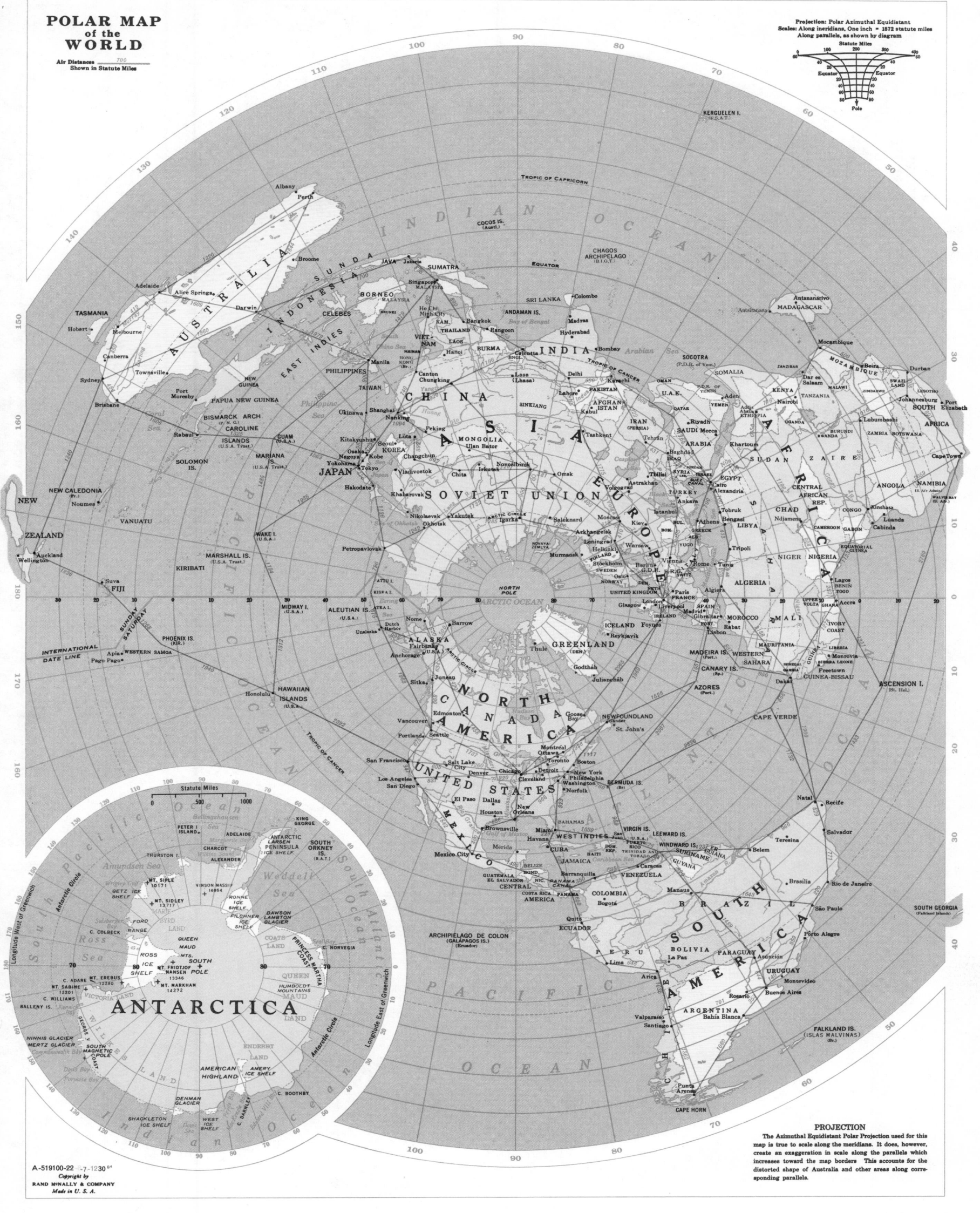

Polar Map
of the
WORLD

Air Distances
Shown in Statute Miles

Projection: Polar Azimuthal Equidistant
Scales: Along meridians, One inch = 1872 statute miles
Along parallels, as shown by diagram

Statute Miles

ANTARCTICA

Statute Miles
0   500   1000

PROJECTION

The Azimuthal Equidistant Polar Projection used for this map is true to scale along the meridians. It does, however, create an exaggeration in scale along the parallels which increases toward the map borders. This accounts for the distorted shape of Australia and other areas along corresponding parallels.

A-519100-22   7-1230
Copyright by
RAND McNALLY & COMPANY
Made in U.S.A.

1

COMPARATIVE WORLD TIME
(Legal Clock Time)

In comparing the time of one zone with another, consider the zone numbers as hours, then by subtracting find the difference in time. The lower zone number represents the earlier hour and the higher zone number the later hour. (If the difference is greater than 12 hours, subtract this difference from 24 hours to find the nearest time difference.)

Antarctica has no legal time.

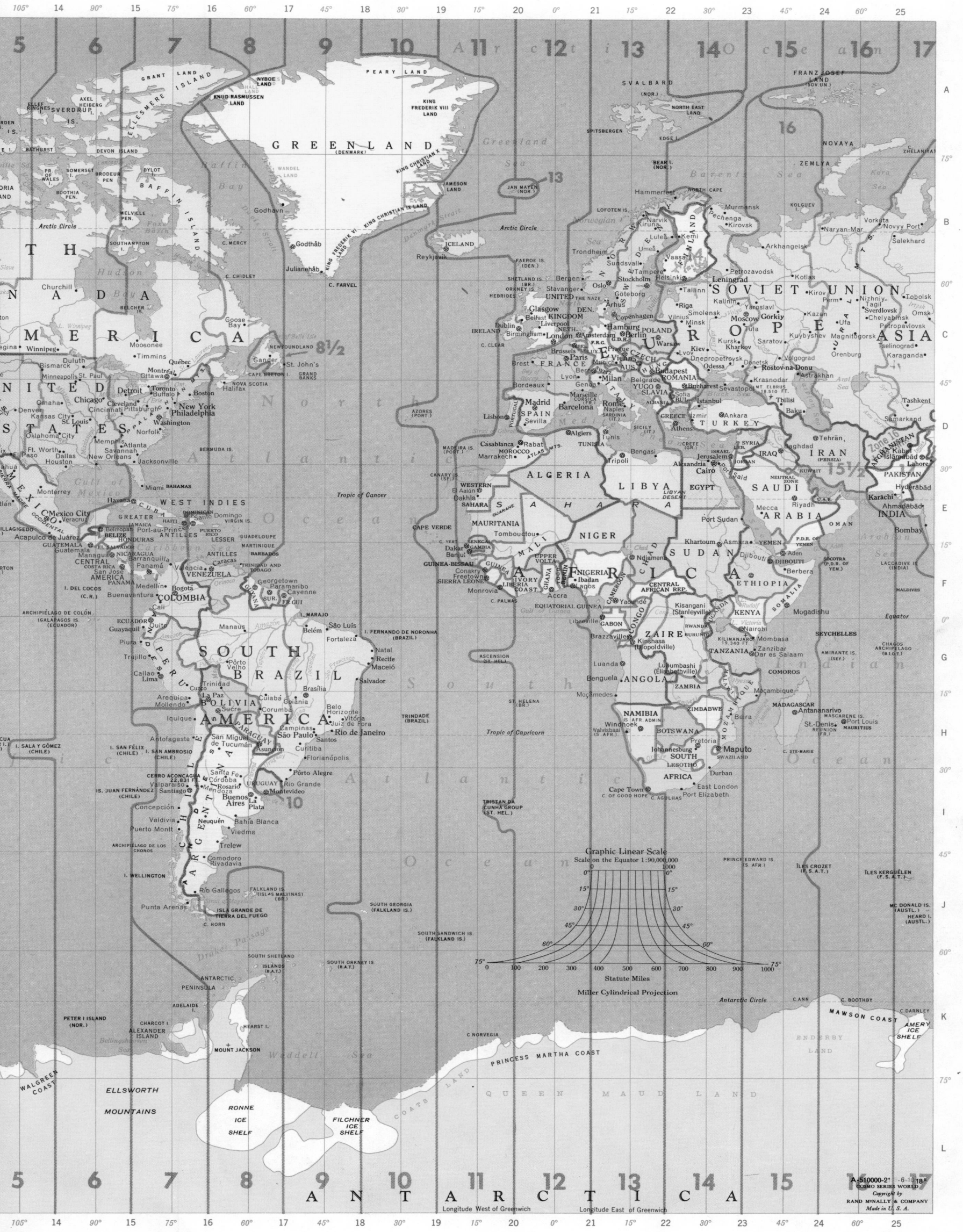

Graphic Linear Scale
Scale on the Equator 1:90,000,000
Statute Miles
Miller Cylindrical Projection
Longitude West of Greenwich
Longitude East of Greenwich
GREENLAND
SOUTH AMERICA
AFRICA
EUROPE
ASIA
SOVIET UNION
ANTARCTICA
North Atlantic Ocean
South Atlantic Ocean
Indian Ocean
Tropic of Cancer
Tropic of Capricorn
Arctic Circle
Antarctic Circle
Equator
Copyright by RAND McNALLY & COMPANY
Made in U. S. A.

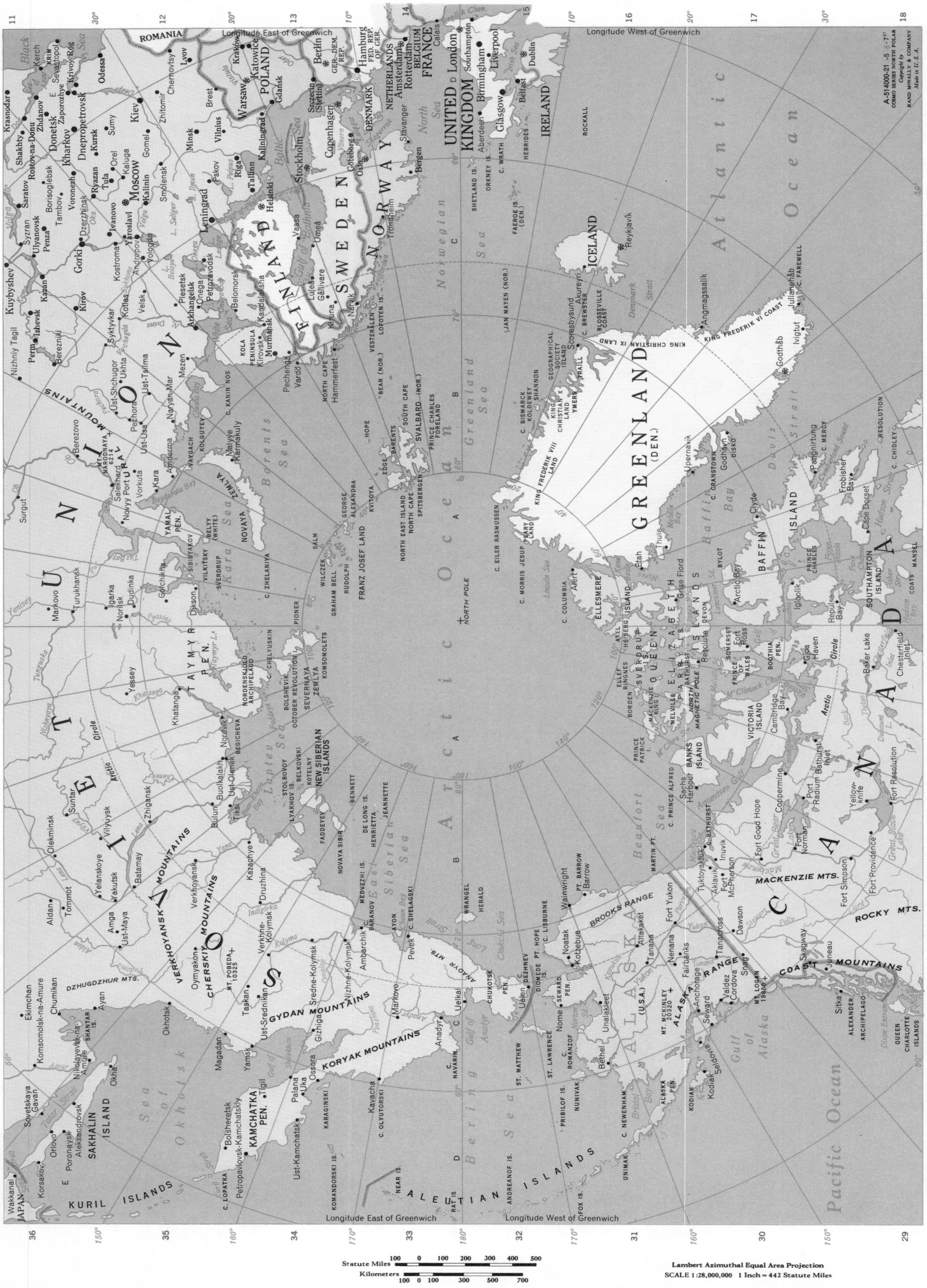

ROMANIA, POLAND, Berlin, Hamburg, GER.-DEM. REP., FED. REP. OF GER., NETHERLANDS, Amsterdam, Rotterdam, BELGIUM, FRANCE, Calais, London, UNITED KINGDOM, Birmingham, Glasgow, Belfast, IRELAND, Dublin, Liverpool, Southampton, Aberdeen, Bergen, Stavanger, Trondheim, NORWAY, SWEDEN, FINLAND, Stockholm, Göteborg, Oslo, Copenhagen, DENMARK, Helsinki, Leningrad, Tallinn, Riga, Vilnius, Minsk, MOSCOW, Kiev, Warsaw, Gdansk, Katowice, Krakow, Szczecin, Kaliningrad, ICELAND, Reykjavik, ROCKALL, SHETLAND IS., ORKNEY IS., HEBRIDES, FAEROE IS. (DEN.), JAN MAYEN (NOR.), GREENLAND (DEN.), King Frederik VIII Land, King Christian IX Land, King Frederik VI Coast, Scoresbysund, Angmagssalik, Julianehåb, Godthåb, Ivigtut, Upernavik, Godhavn, DISKO, C. FAREWELL, ELLESMERE ISLAND, BAFFIN ISLAND, Baffin Bay, Davis Strait, Frobisher Bay, SOUTHAMPTON ISLAND, PRINCE CHARLES, COATS ISLAND, MANSEL, Hudson Strait, VICTORIA ISLAND, BANKS ISLAND, Cambridge Bay, PRINCE PATRICK, MELVILLE IS., CANADA, Yellowknife, Fort Providence, Baker Lake, Chesterfield Inlet, Great Bear Lake, Great Slave Lake, Coppermine, MACKENZIE MTS., ROCKY MTS., Fort Good Hope, Fort Norman, Inuvik, Dawson, Fort Yukon, ALASKA (U.S.A.), Fairbanks, Anchorage, Juneau, MT. MCKINLEY 20320, MT. LOGAN 19850, BROOKS RANGE, ALASKA RANGE, COAST MOUNTAINS, Sitka, Kodiak, ALEUTIAN ISLANDS, PT. BARROW, Nome, Bethel, Bering Sea, KAMCHATKA PEN., SAKHALIN ISLAND, KURIL ISLANDS, JAPAN, Sea of Okhotsk, Magadan, Petropavlovsk-Kamchatskiy, U.S.S.R., Verkhoyansk, CHERSKIY MOUNTAINS, KORYAK MOUNTAINS, GYDAN MOUNTAINS, VERKHOYANSK MOUNTAINS, URAL MOUNTAINS, NEW SIBERIAN ISLANDS, SEVERNAYA ZEMLYA, FRANZ JOSEF LAND, NOVAYA ZEMLYA, SPITSBERGEN, SVALBARD (NOR.), NORTH CAPE, Murmansk, Arkhangelsk, Gorki, Kazan, Perm, Sverdlovsk, Omsk, Novosibirsk, NORTH POLE, Arctic Ocean, Barents Sea, Kara Sea, Laptev Sea, East Siberian Sea, Chukchi Sea, Beaufort Sea, Greenland Sea, Norwegian Sea, Atlantic Ocean, Pacific Ocean

Longitude East of Greenwich
Longitude West of Greenwich

A-514000-21 -5 -7⁸¹
COSMO SERIES NORTH POLAR
Copyright by
RAND MCNALLY & COMPANY
Made in U.S.A.

Statute Miles 100 0 100 200 300 400 500
Kilometers 100 0 100 300 500 700

Lambert Azimuthal Equal Area Projection
SCALE 1:28,000,000 1 Inch = 442 Statute Miles

4

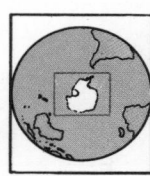

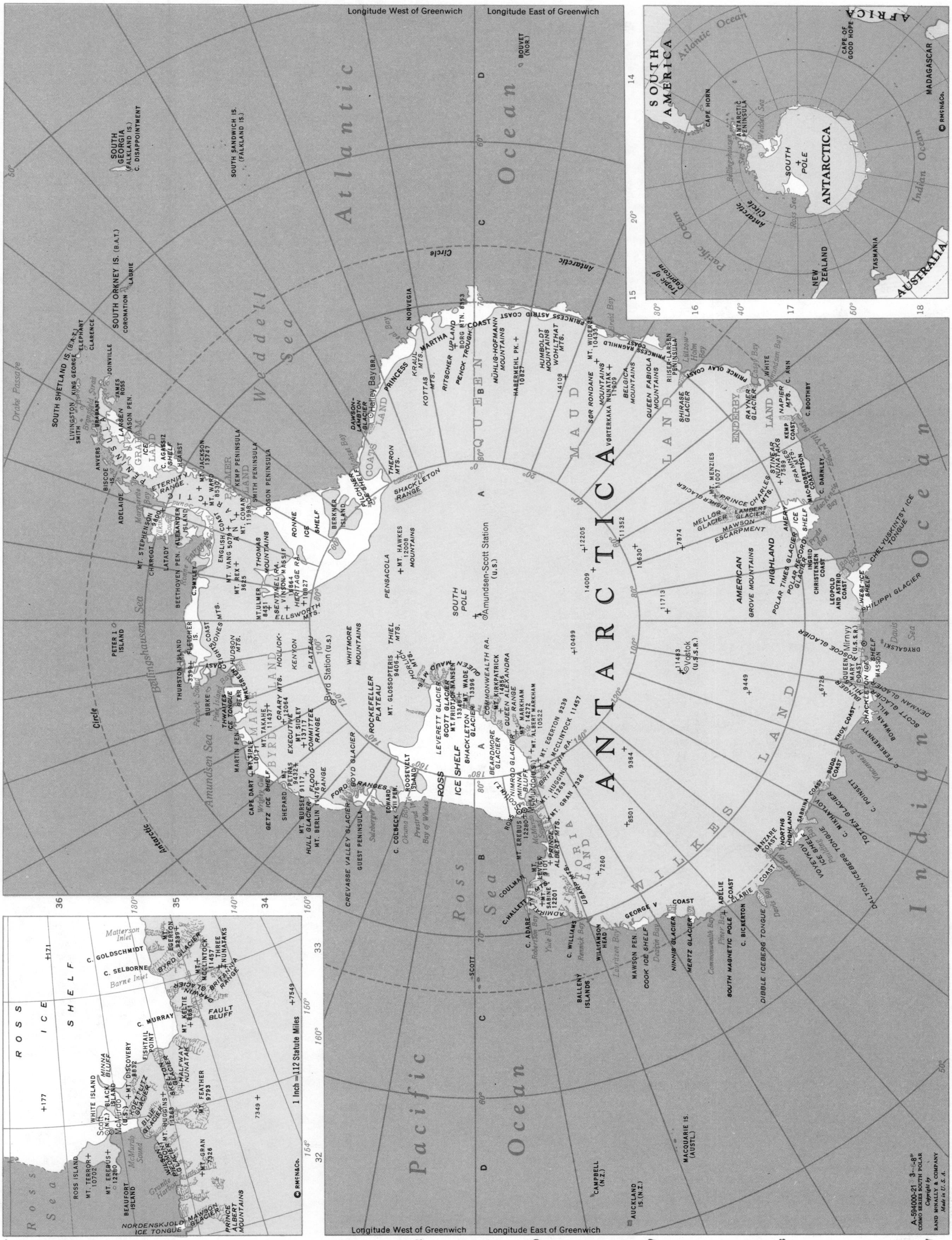

Main map labels:

Longitude West of Greenwich · Longitude East of Greenwich

ANTARCTICA

SOUTH POLE

Amundsen-Scott Station (U.S.)

Byrd Station (U.S.)

Vostok (U.S.S.R.)

QUEEN MAUD LAND

MARIE BYRD LAND

WILKES LAND

VICTORIA LAND

ENDERBY LAND

ELLSWORTH LAND

PALMER LAND

GRAHAM LAND

AMERICAN HIGHLAND

Atlantic Ocean

Indian Ocean

Pacific Ocean

Weddell Sea

Ross Sea

Amundsen Sea

Bellingshausen Sea

Drake Passage

Antarctic Circle

RONNE ICE SHELF

ROSS ICE SHELF

FILCHNER ICE SHELF

SHACKLETON RANGE

PENSACOLA MTS.

THIEL MTS.

WHITMORE MOUNTAINS

ROCKEFELLER PLATEAU

KENYON PLATEAU

ELLSWORTH MTS.

BERKNER ISLAND

ROOSEVELT ISLAND

COMMONWEALTH RA.

QUEEN ALEXANDRA RANGE

QUEEN MAUD MTS.

BEARDMORE GLACIER

SCOTT GLACIER

LEVERETT GLACIER

MT. HAWKES 12009

MT. MARKHAM 14856

MT. KIRKPATRICK 14856

MT. SIDLEY 13717

VINSON MASSIF 16860

HUMBOLDT MOUNTAINS

MÜHLIG-HOFMANN MOUNTAINS

BELGICA MOUNTAINS

SØR RONDANE MOUNTAINS

PRINCE CHARLES MTS.

LAMBERT GLACIER

MAWSON ESCARPMENT

GROVE MOUNTAINS

RAYNER GLACIER

NAPIER MTS.

PRINCE OLAV COAST

PRINCESS ASTRID COAST

PRINCESS RAGNHILD COAST

LEOPOLD AND ASTRID COAST

KNOX COAST

SABRINA COAST

CLARIE COAST

ADÉLIE COAST

GEORGE V COAST

OATES COAST

SHIRASE GLACIER

DENMAN GLACIER

SCOTT GLACIER

TOTTEN GLACIER

NINNIS GLACIER

MERTZ GLACIER

SOUTH MAGNETIC POLE

DIBBLE ICEBERG TONGUE

SHACKLETON ICE SHELF

WEST ICE SHELF

AMERY ICE SHELF

MACROBERTSON LAND

PRINCESS ELIZABETH LAND

WILHELM II LAND

QUEEN MARY COAST

KAISER WILHELM II LAND

BOUVET IS. (NOR.)

PETER I ISLAND

THURSTON ISLAND

ALEXANDER ISLAND

ANTARCTIC PENINSULA

ADELAIDE ISLAND

CHARCOT ISLAND

LARSEN ICE SHELF

COATS LAND

THERON MTS.

MAWSON

MIRNY (U.S.S.R.)

MACQUARIE IS. (AUSTL.)

CAMPBELL IS. (N.Z.)

AUCKLAND IS. (N.Z.)

BALLENY ISLANDS

SOUTH GEORGIA (FALKLAND IS.)

C. DISAPPOINTMENT

SOUTH SANDWICH IS. (FALKLAND IS.)

SOUTH ORKNEY IS. (B.A.T.)

CORONATION · LAURIE

SOUTH SHETLAND IS. (B.A.T.)

KING GEORGE · ELEPHANT · CLARENCE

LIVINGSTON · SMITH · JOINVILLE · JAMES ROSS

ANVERS · BRABANT

Scale / projection:

Lambert Azimuthal Equal Area Projection
SCALE 1:28,000,000   1 Inch = 442 Statute Miles

Statute Miles 100 0 100 200 300 400 500

Kilometers 100 0 100 300 500 700

A-594000-21 3-54*
COMO SELLER SOUTH POLAR
Copyright by
RAND M?NALLY & COMPANY
Made in U.S.A.

Inset map (top right):

SOUTH AMERICA · AFRICA · AUSTRALIA · MADAGASCAR · NEW ZEALAND · TASMANIA

CAPE HORN · CAPE OF GOOD HOPE

ANTARCTICA · SOUTH POLE

Antarctic Circle · Tropic of Capricorn

Atlantic Ocean · Pacific Ocean · Indian Ocean

ANTARCTIC PENINSULA

Ross Sea · Weddell Sea

© R M?N & CO.

Inset map (bottom left):

ROSS ICE SHELF

ROSS ISLAND

MT. EREBUS 12280

MT. TERROR 10702

ROSS SEA

McMurdo Sound

McMURDO (U.S.)

SCOTT BASE (N.Z.)

WHITE ISLAND

BLACK ISLAND

MINNA BLUFF

BEAUFORT ISLAND

FAULT BLUFF

PRINCE ALBERT MOUNTAINS

BRITANNIA RANGE

BYRD GLACIER

NORDENSKJOLD ICE TONGUE

MAWSON GLACIER

MATTERSON INLET

1 Inch = 112 Statute Miles

© R M?N & CO.

ATLANTIC OCEAN

Longitude West of Greenwich

Longitude East of Greenwich

Statute Miles 200 0 200 600 1000 1400

Kilometers 200 0 200 600 1000 1400 1800 2200

Modified Polyconic Projection

SCALE 1:60,728,000 1 Inch = 960 Statute Miles

A-598100-21 -3-3-22-
COSMO SERIES ATLANTIC

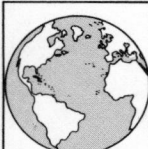

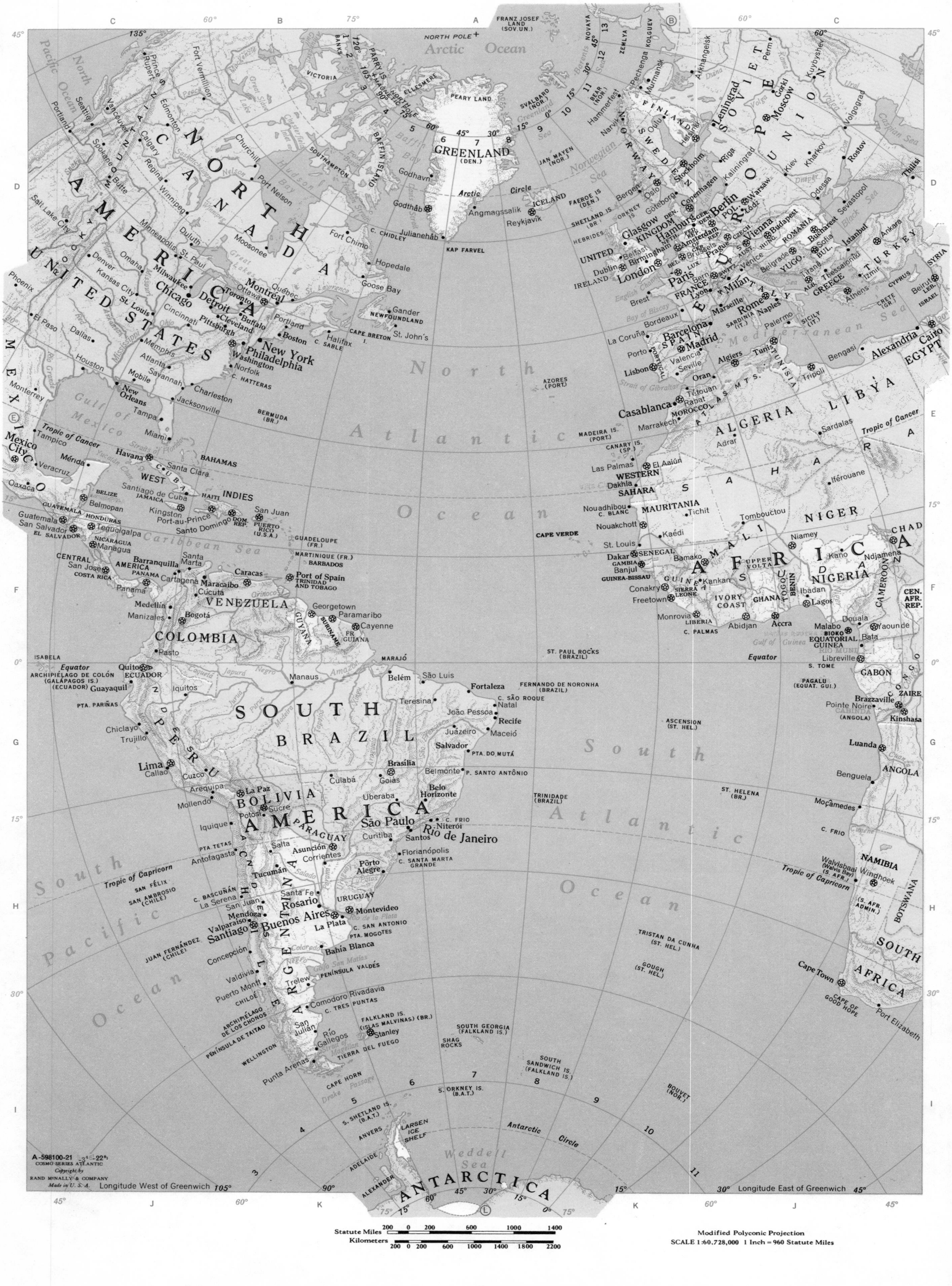

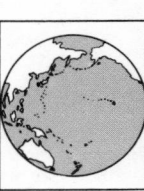

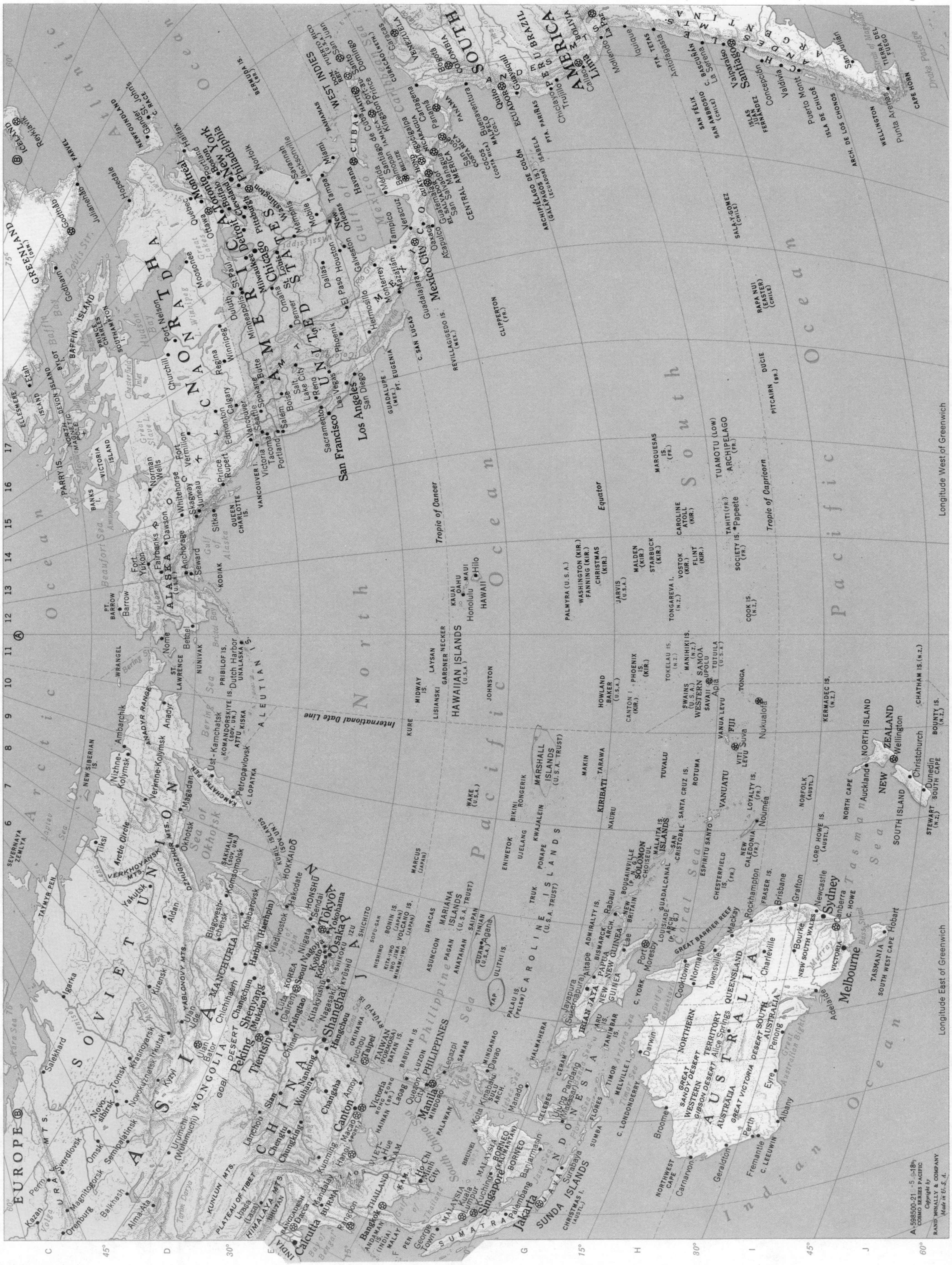

Modified Secant Conic Projection
SCALE 1:66,800,000 1 Inch = 1,040 Statute Miles

Statute Miles 200 0 200 600 1000 1400
Kilometers 200 0 200 600 1000 1400 1800 2200

EUROPE

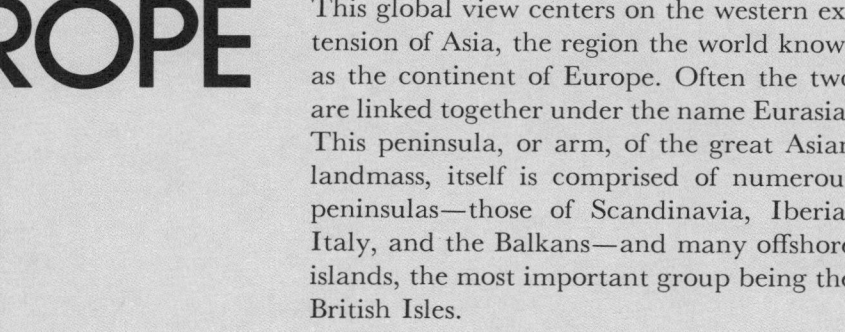

This global view centers on the western extension of Asia, the region the world knows as the continent of Europe. Often the two are linked together under the name Eurasia. This peninsula, or arm, of the great Asian landmass, itself is comprised of numerous peninsulas—those of Scandinavia, Iberia, Italy, and the Balkans—and many offshore islands, the most important group being the British Isles.

The thrust of this arm of Asia into the Atlantic Ocean, the North and Mediterranean seas provides a clear-cut western terminus. But the limits of Europe are not so clearly defined on its eastern flank where no natural barriers exist. For the sake of a "boundary" geographers have come to recognize the low Ural Mountains and the Ural River, the Caspian Sea, the Caucasus Mountains, and the Black Sea as the eastern and southeastern border.

From Europe's eastern limits, where the north to south dimension is approximately 2,500 miles, the irregularly shaped continent tapers toward the southwest and the surrounding bodies of water. Through Europe's history its miles of coastline encouraged contact with the other continents, and the seas became avenues of exchange for culture, politics, and technology with other regions of the world.

Internally Europe embraces a varied landscape comparable to no other region of its size in the world: In a total area of only 3,825,000 square miles are found extremes from zero winters and dry steppes in the east to year-round humid, mild climates in the west; extremes in elevation from the heights of the Alps to the below-sea-level Belgian and Netherlands coasts; and a variation in the distribution of inhabitants from the densely populated, industrialized northwest to the sparsely peopled areas in the agricultural south and east. Thirty-three independent nations, each with its own national, religious, cultural, and political heritage, adds to this variegated landscape.

Because much of Europe is neither too hot or cold, or too high or low, a great extent of its land has been developed, aided by an impressive river-canal system, dominated by the Rhine and Danube. Its natural and cultural wealth has made possible an economic-social-political system which has long influenced the economic, political, and social structure of the rest of the world.

Today, because of its density of population, strategic location, politics, history, economic strength, and cultural tradition, Europe still may rightfully and strongly claim to be one of the hubs of the world.

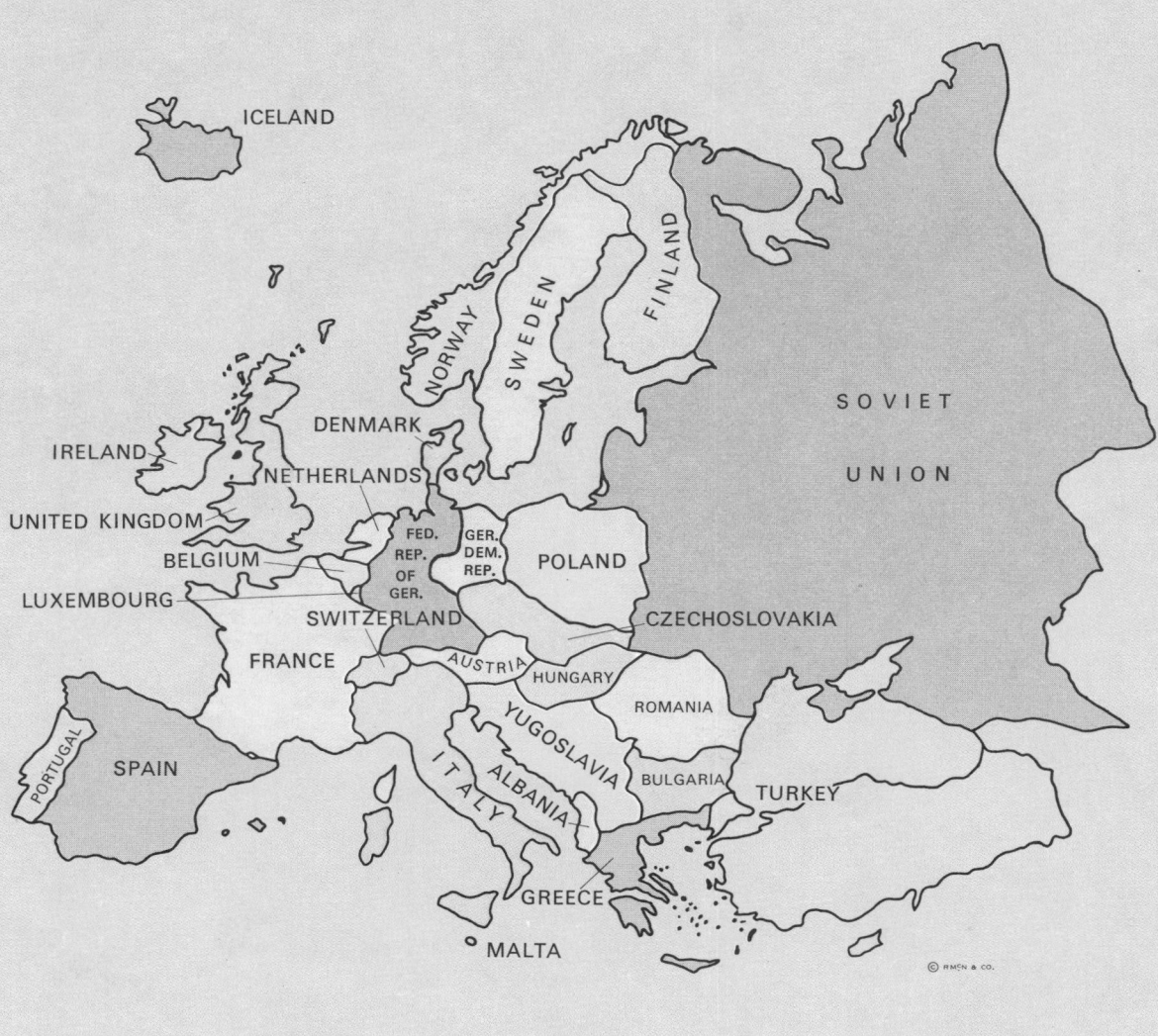

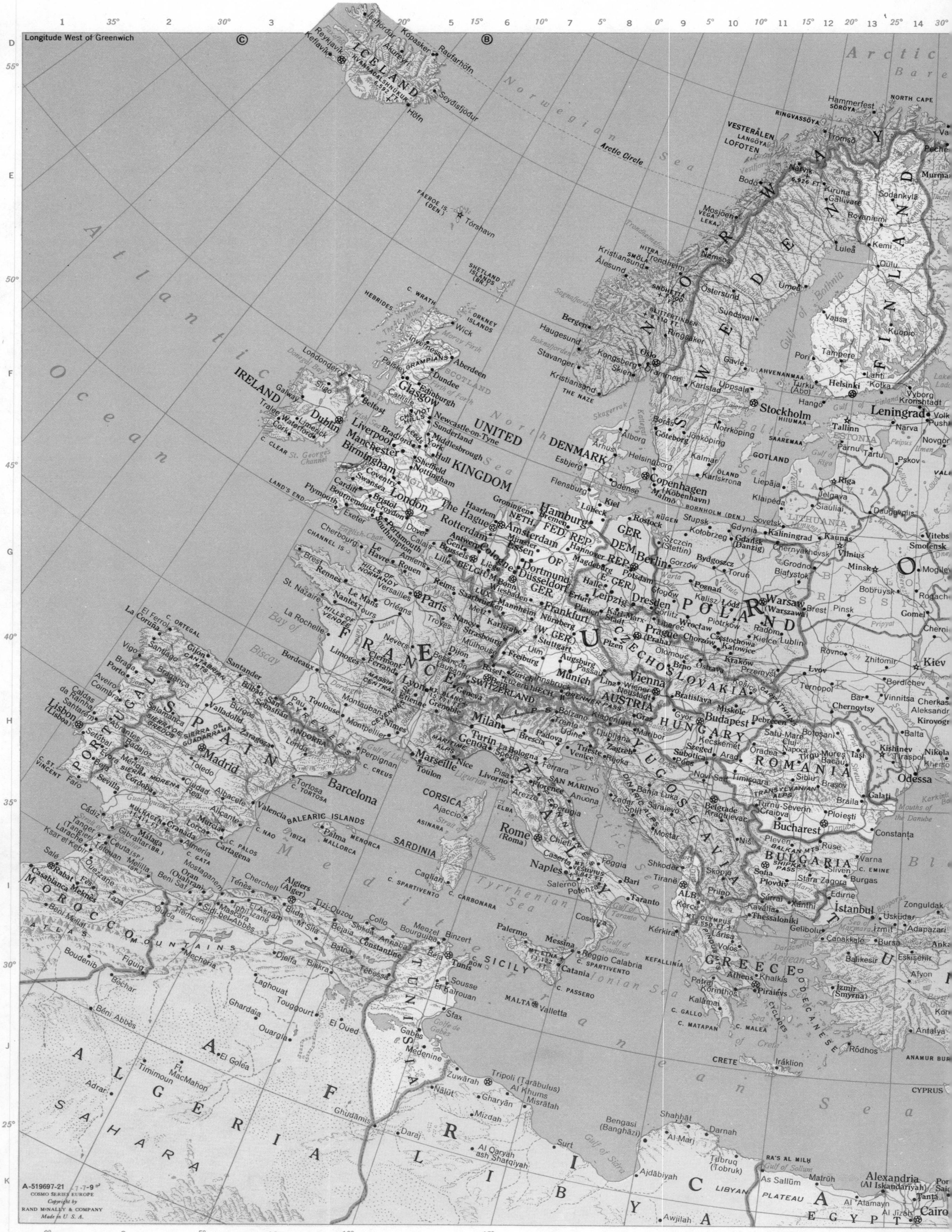

Longitude West of Greenwich

A-519697-21 7-7-9
COSMO SERIES EUROPE
Copyright by
RAND McNALLY & COMPANY
Made in U.S.A.

Statute Miles 100 0 100 200 300
Kilometers 100 0 100 200 300 400

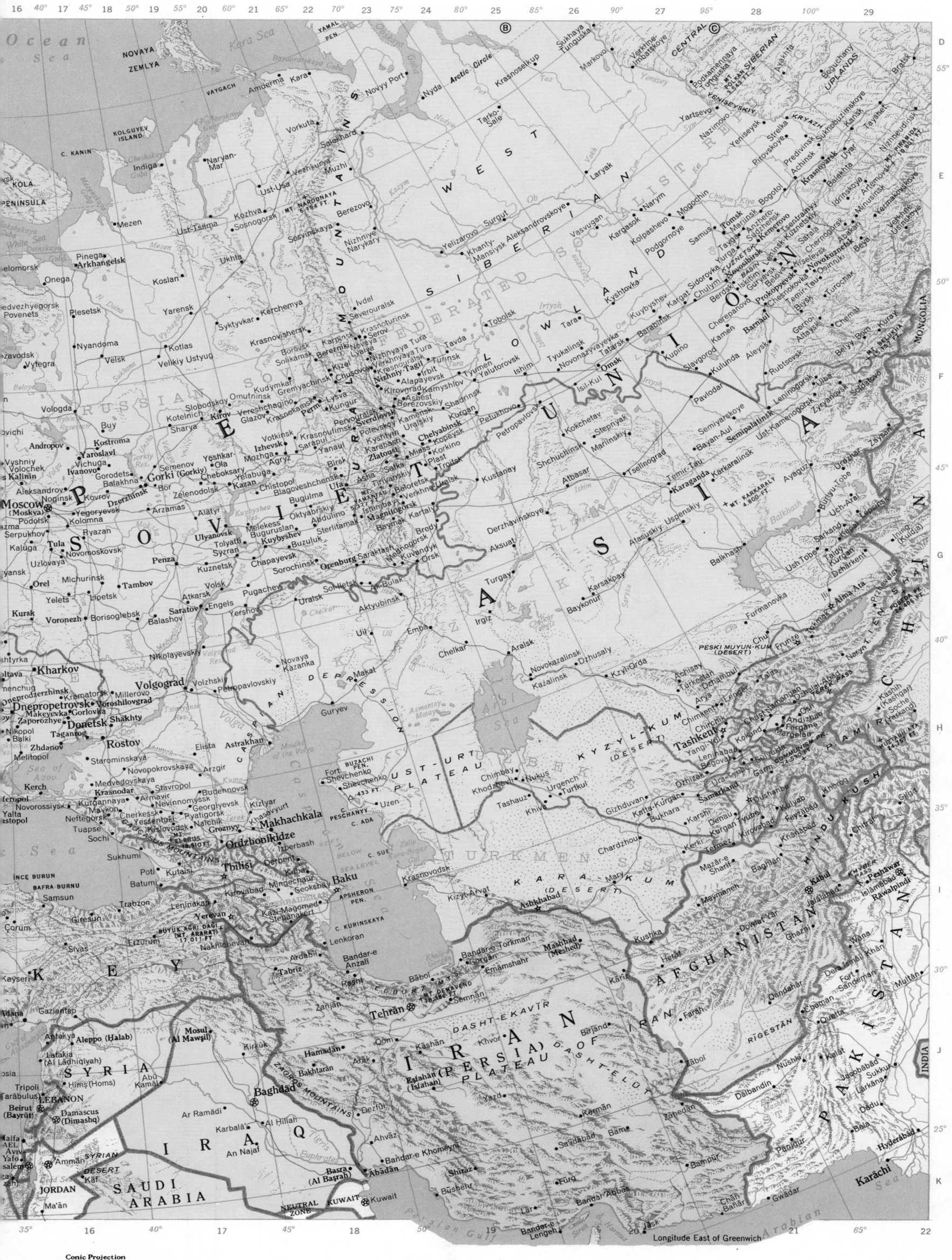

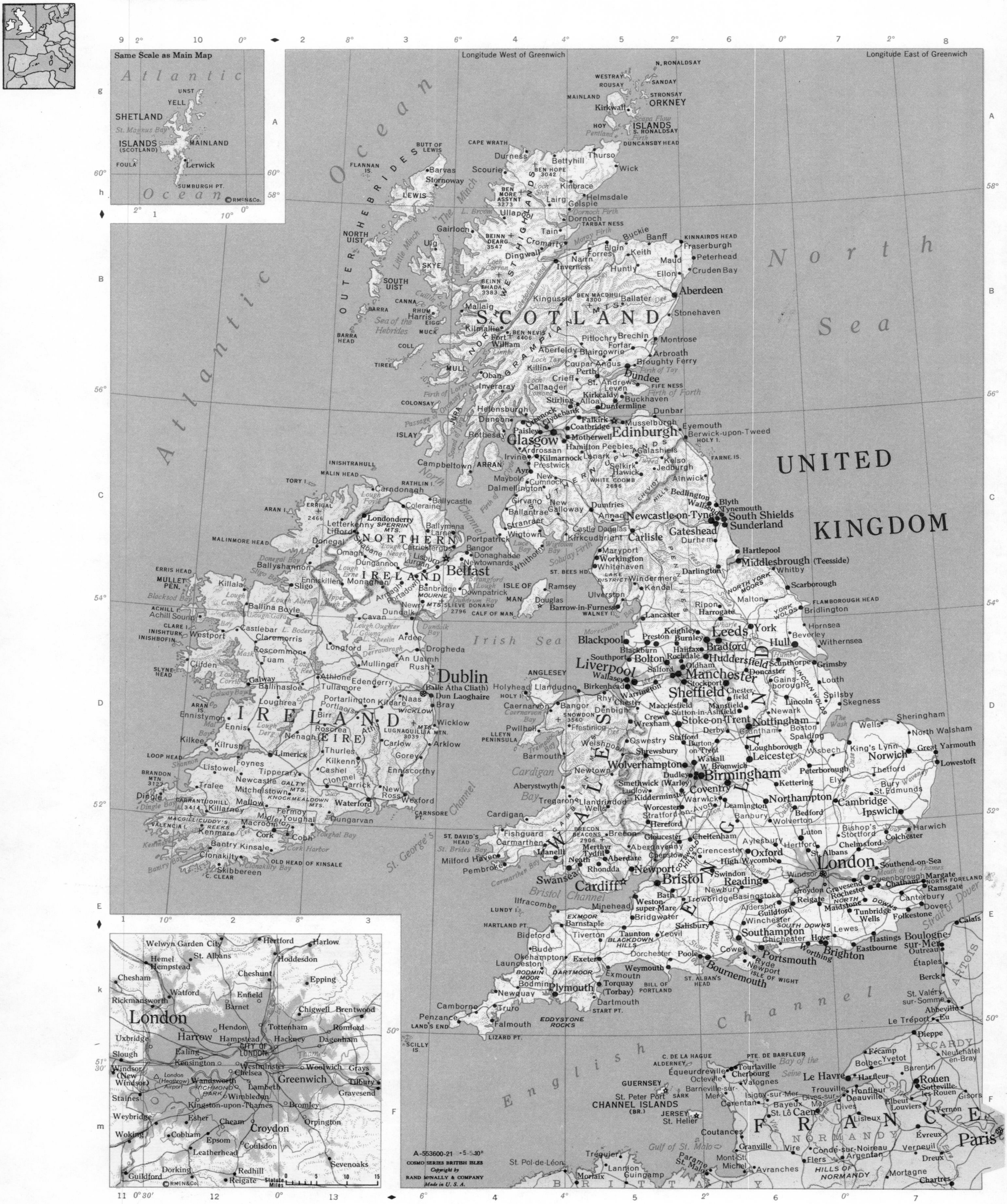

Same Scale as Main Map

Longitude West of Greenwich · Longitude East of Greenwich

A-553600-21 • 5-5-30*
COSMO SERIES BRITISH ISLES
Copyright by
RAND McNALLY & COMPANY
Made in U.S.A.

Statute Miles 25 0 25 50 75
Kilometers 25 0 50 100

Conic Projection
SCALE 1:4,000,000 1 Inch = 63 Statute Miles

Lambert Conformal Conic Projection
SCALE 1 : 2,000,000 1 Inch = 32 Statute Miles

Statute Miles

Kilometers

Longitude West of Greenwich

A-551700-21 -4 -8°
COSMO SERIES IRELAND
Copyright by
RAND McNALLY & COMPANY
Made in U.S.A.

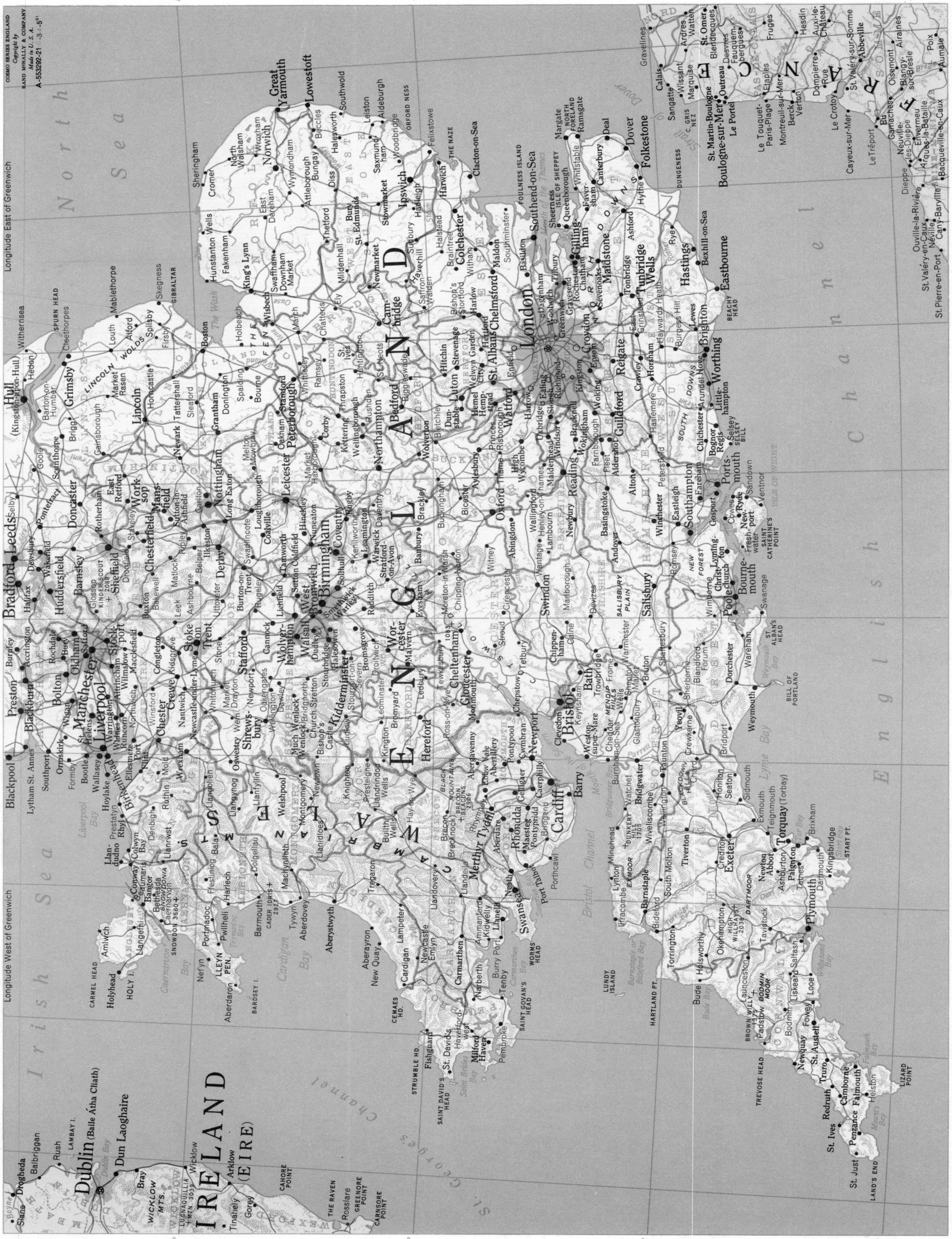

Statute Miles 5 0 5 10 20 30 40 50

Kilometers 5 0 5 10 20 30 40 50 60

Lambert Conformal Conic Projection

SCALE 1:2,000,000 1 Inch = 32 Statute Miles

Lambert Conformal Conic Projection
SCALE 1 : 2,000,000 1 Inch = 32 Statute Miles

Statute Miles 5 0 5 10 20 30 40 50
Kilometers 5 0 5 10 20 30 40 50 60

Longitude West of Greenwich

Statute Miles 25 0 25 50 75

Kilometers 25 0 25 50 100

Conic Projection
SCALE 1:4,000,000 1 Inch = 63 Statute Miles

A-550900-21 -5-6-11°
COSMO SERIES FRANCE

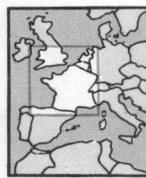

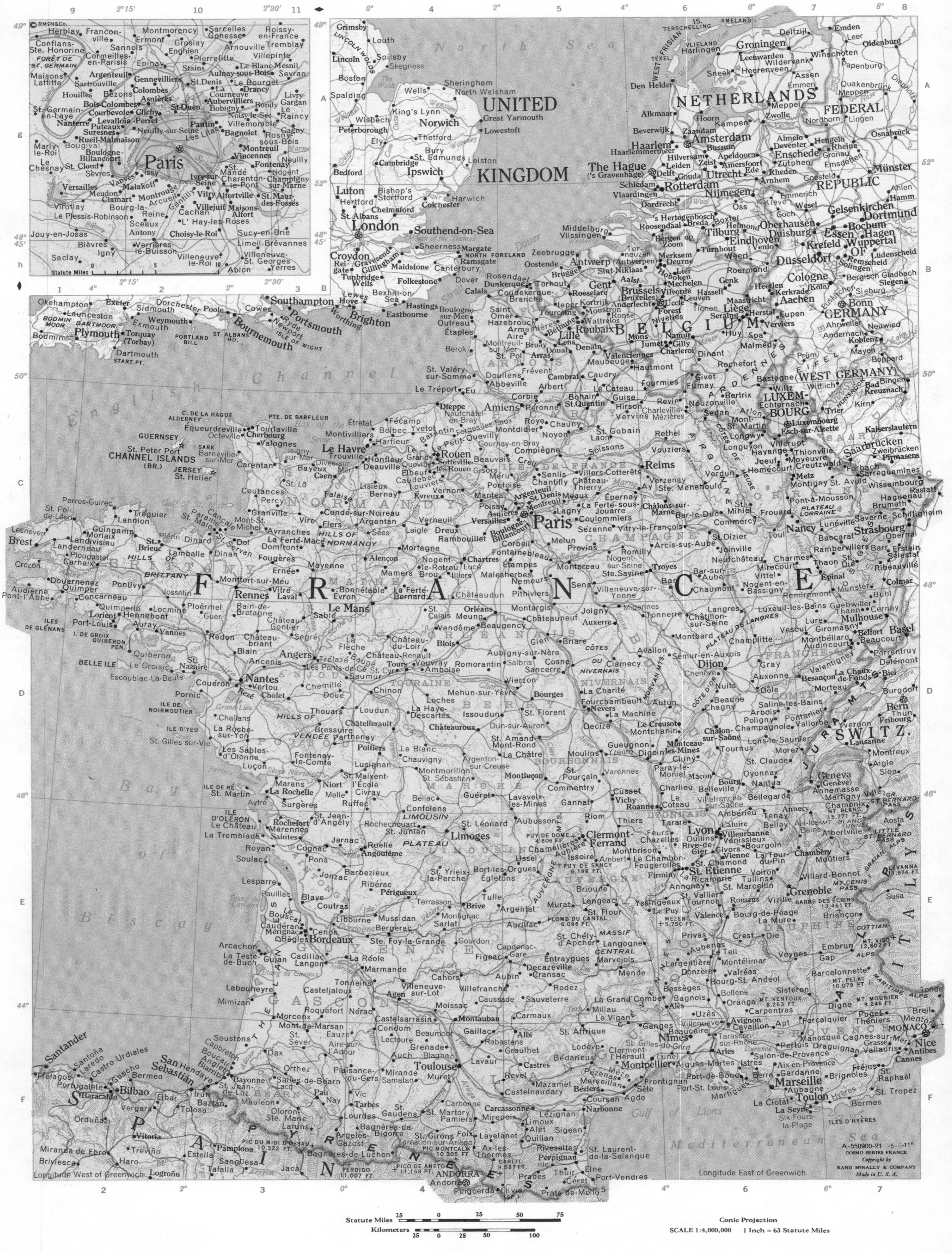

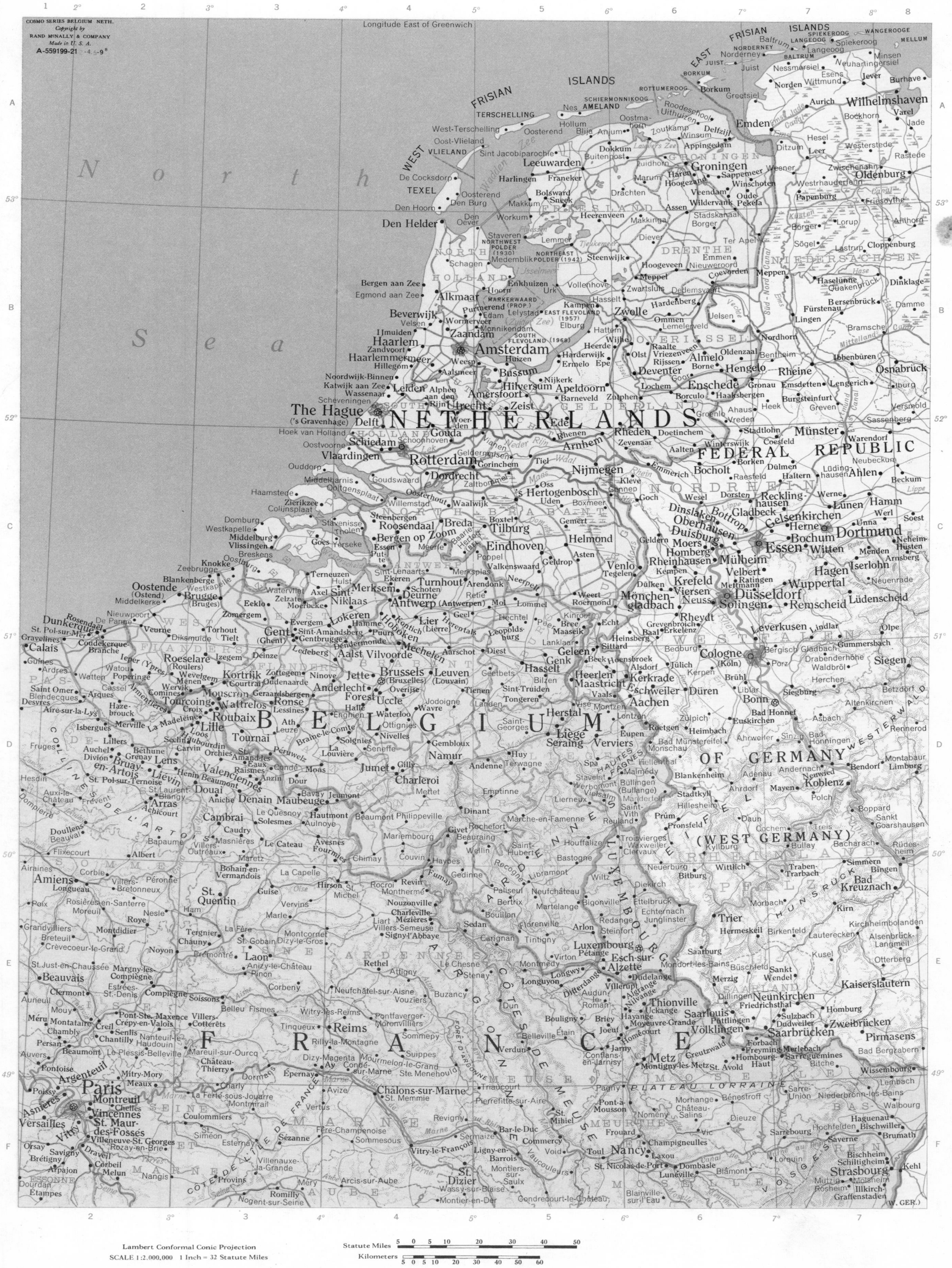

Lambert Conformal Conic Projection
SCALE 1:2,000,000   1 Inch = 32 Statute Miles

Statute Miles 5 0 5 10 20 30 40 50
Kilometers 5 0 5 10 20 30 40 50 60

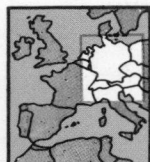

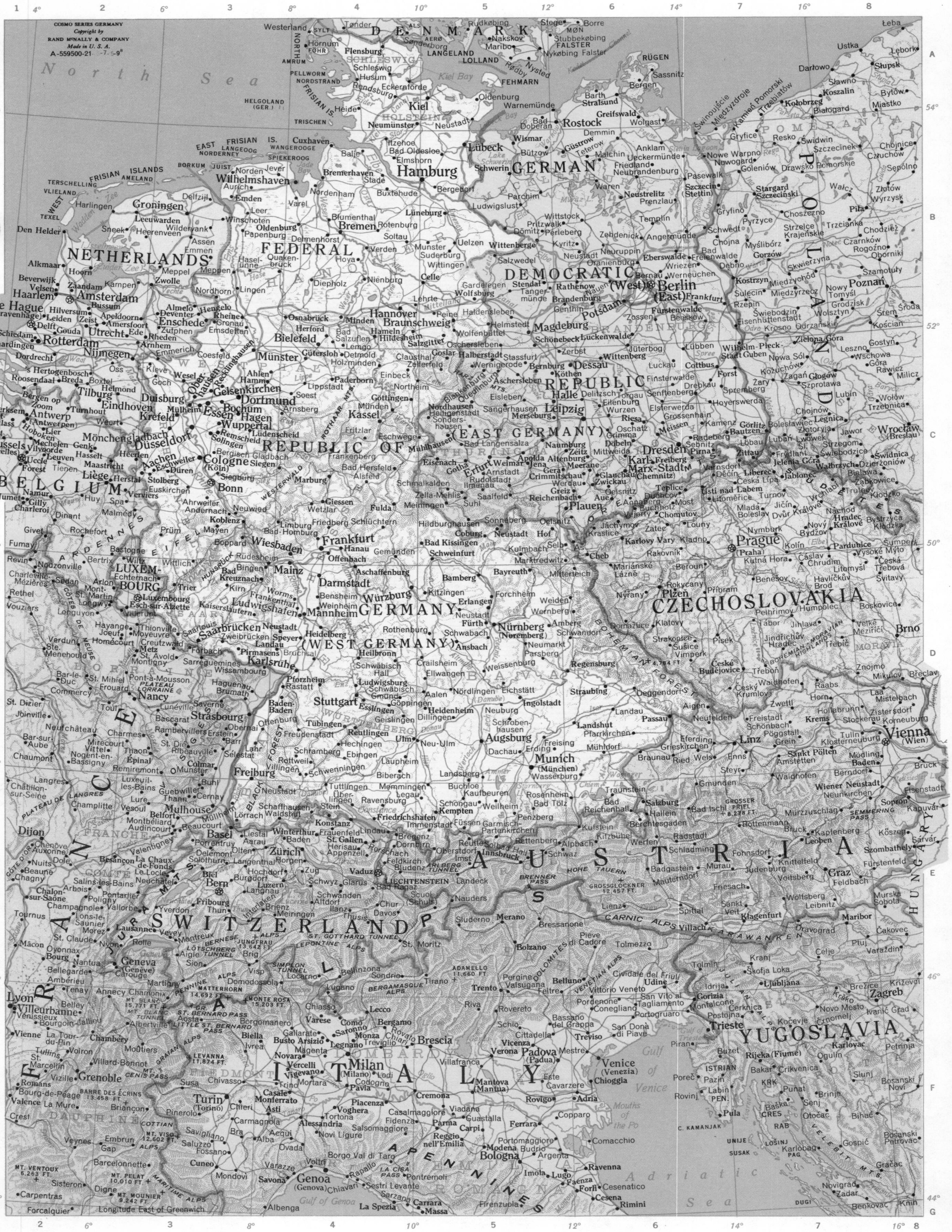

Statute Miles 25 0 25 50 75
Kilometers 25 0 25 50 100

Conic Projection
SCALE 1:4,000,000   1 Inch = 63 Statute Miles

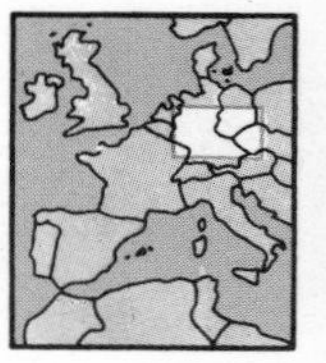

POLAND

GERMAN DEMOCRATIC REPUBLIC (EAST GERMANY)

FEDERAL REPUBLIC OF GERMANY (WEST GERMANY)

CZECHOSLOVAKIA

AUSTRIA

FRANCE

NETHERLANDS

Berlin (West) · Berlin (East)

Prague (Praha)

Lambert Conformal Conic Projection
SCALE 1:2,000,000   1 Inch = 32 Statute Miles

Statute Miles 5 0 5 10 20 30 40 50
Kilometers 5 0 5 10 20 30 40 50 60

Statute Miles 5 0 5 10 20 30 40 50
Kilometers 5 0 5 10 20 30 40 50 60

Lambert Conformal Conic Projection
SCALE 1:2,000,000   1 Inch = 32 Statute Miles

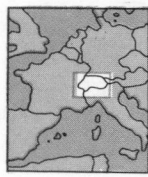

Lambert Conformal Conic Projection
SCALE 1 : 1,100,000   1 Inch = 17 Statute Miles

Statute Miles 5 0 5 10 20 30
Kilometers 5 0 5 10 20 30 40

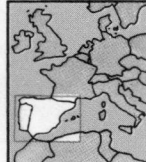

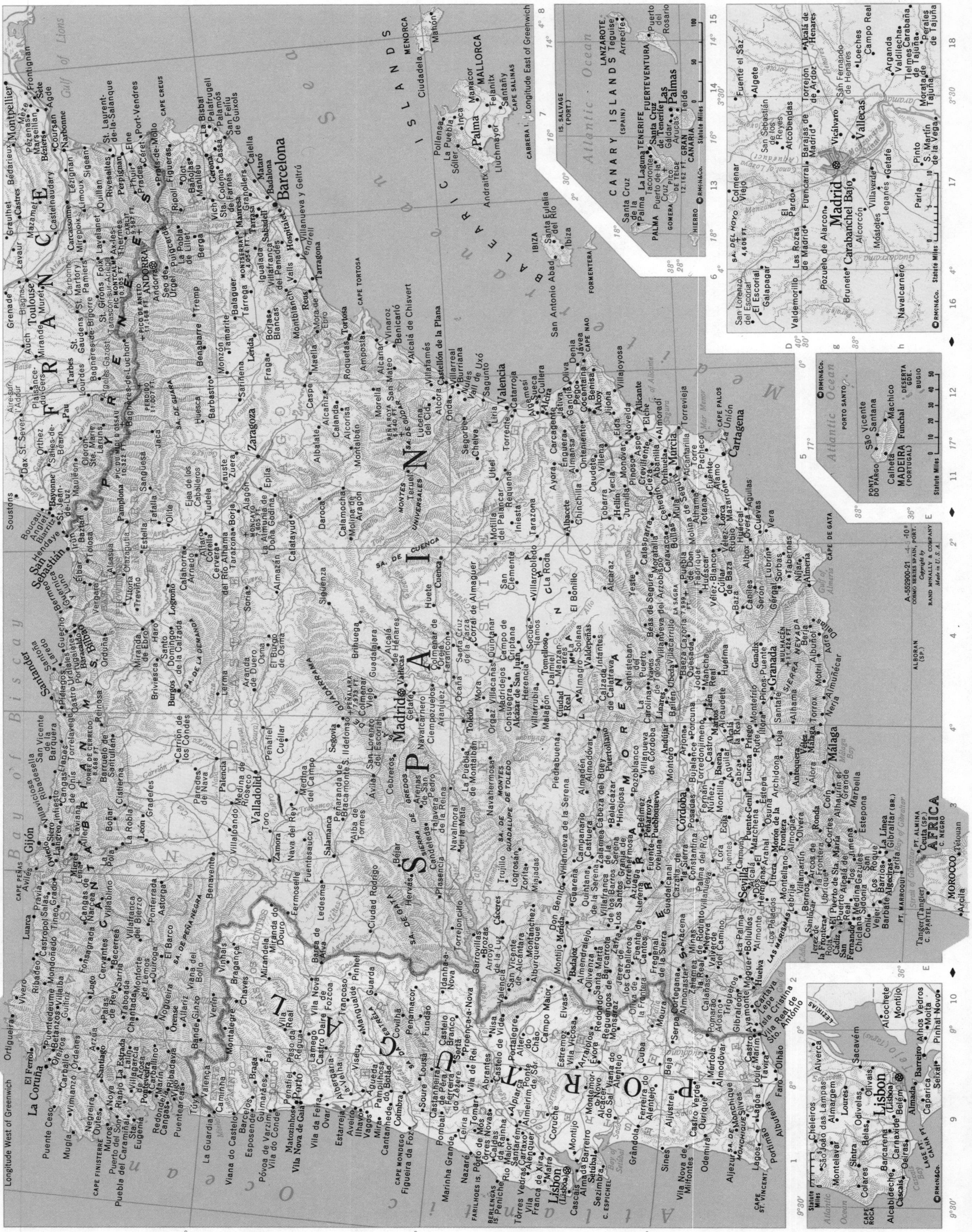

Statute Miles 25 0 25 50 75

Kilometers 25 0 25 50 100

Conic Projection

SCALE 1:4,000,000   1 Inch = 63 Statute Miles

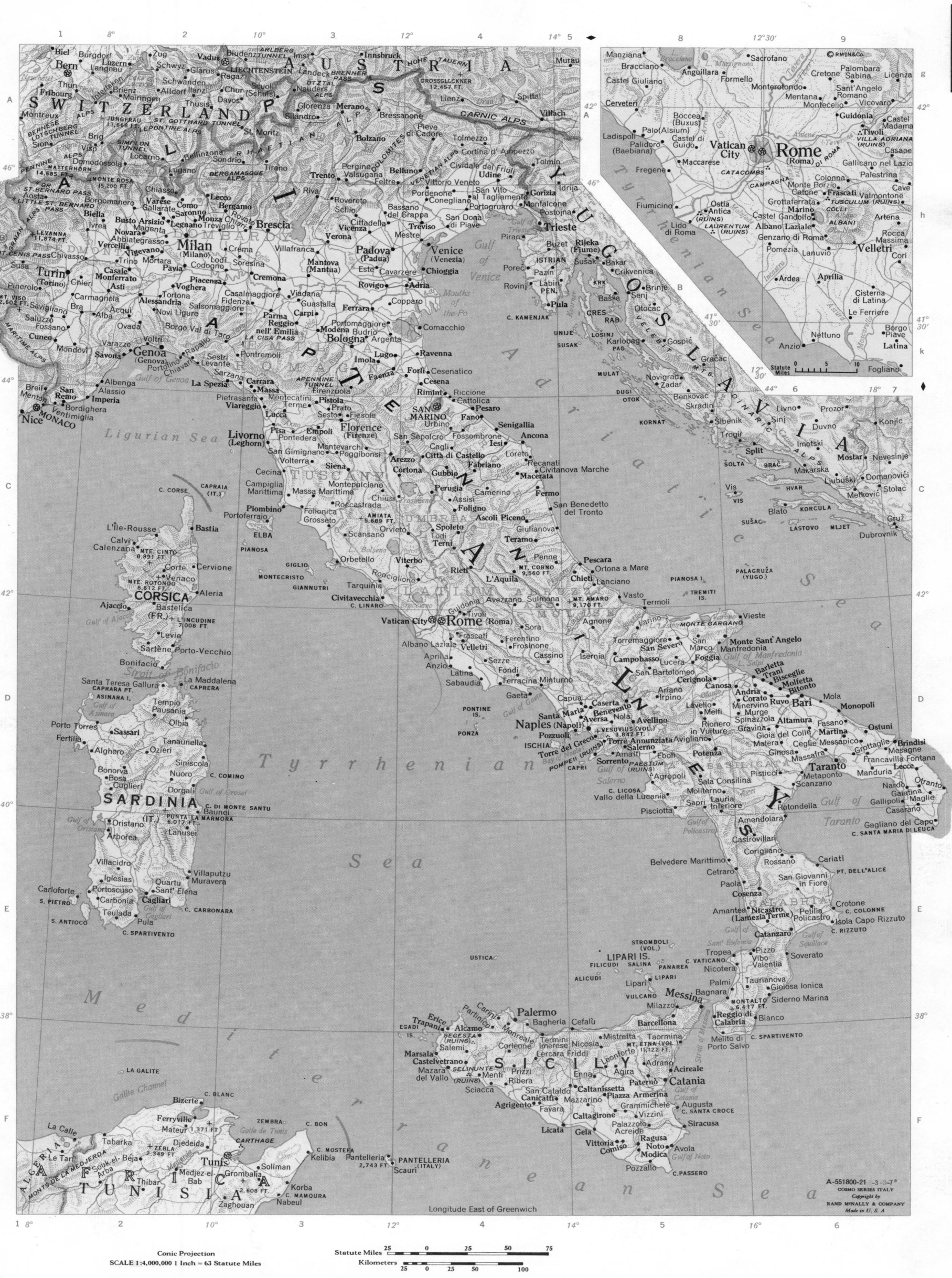
SWITZERLAND
AUSTRIA
YUGOSLAVIA
ALPS
APENNINES
CORSICA (FR.)
SARDINIA (IT.)
SICILY
TUSCANY
UMBRIA
LATIUM
ABRUZZI
MOLISE
BASILICATA
CALABRIA
LOMBARDY
PIEDMONT
AFRICA
TUNISIA
ALGERIA
Ligurian Sea
Tyrrhenian Sea
Adriatic Sea
Mediterranean Sea
Gulf of Venice
Gulf of Genoa
Gulf of Taranto
Strait of Bonifacio
Strait of Messina
Galite Channel
Rome (Roma)
Vatican City
Milan (Milano)
Turin (Torino)
Genoa (Genova)
Venice (Venezia)
Florence (Firenze)
Bologna
Naples (Napoli)
Palermo
Messina
Catania
Bari
Taranto
Trieste
Livorno (Leghorn)
Padova (Padua)
Mantova (Mantua)
Cagliari
Bastia
Ajaccio
Pescara
Ancona
Perugia
Nice
MONACO
SAN MARINO
Bern
Tunis
Bizerte
LIPARI IS.
MT. ETNA (VOL.) 11,122 FT.
VESUVIUS (VOL.) 3,842 FT.
MONTE ROSA 15,200 FT.
MATTERHORN 14,685 FT.
MT. CORNO 9,560 FT.
PANTELLERIA (ITALY)
ELBA
CAPRI
ISCHIA
Statute Miles
Conic Projection
SCALE 1:4,000,000 1 Inch = 63 Statute Miles
Statute Miles 25 0 25 50 75
Kilometers 25 0 25 50 100
Longitude East of Greenwich
A-551800-21
COSMO SERIES ITALY
Copyright by RAND McNALLY & COMPANY
Made in U. S. A.

Statute Miles 25 0 25 50 75

Kilometers 25 0 25 50 100

Conic Projection
SCALE 1:4,000,000   1 Inch = 63 Statute Miles

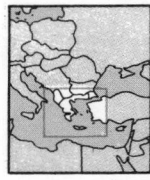

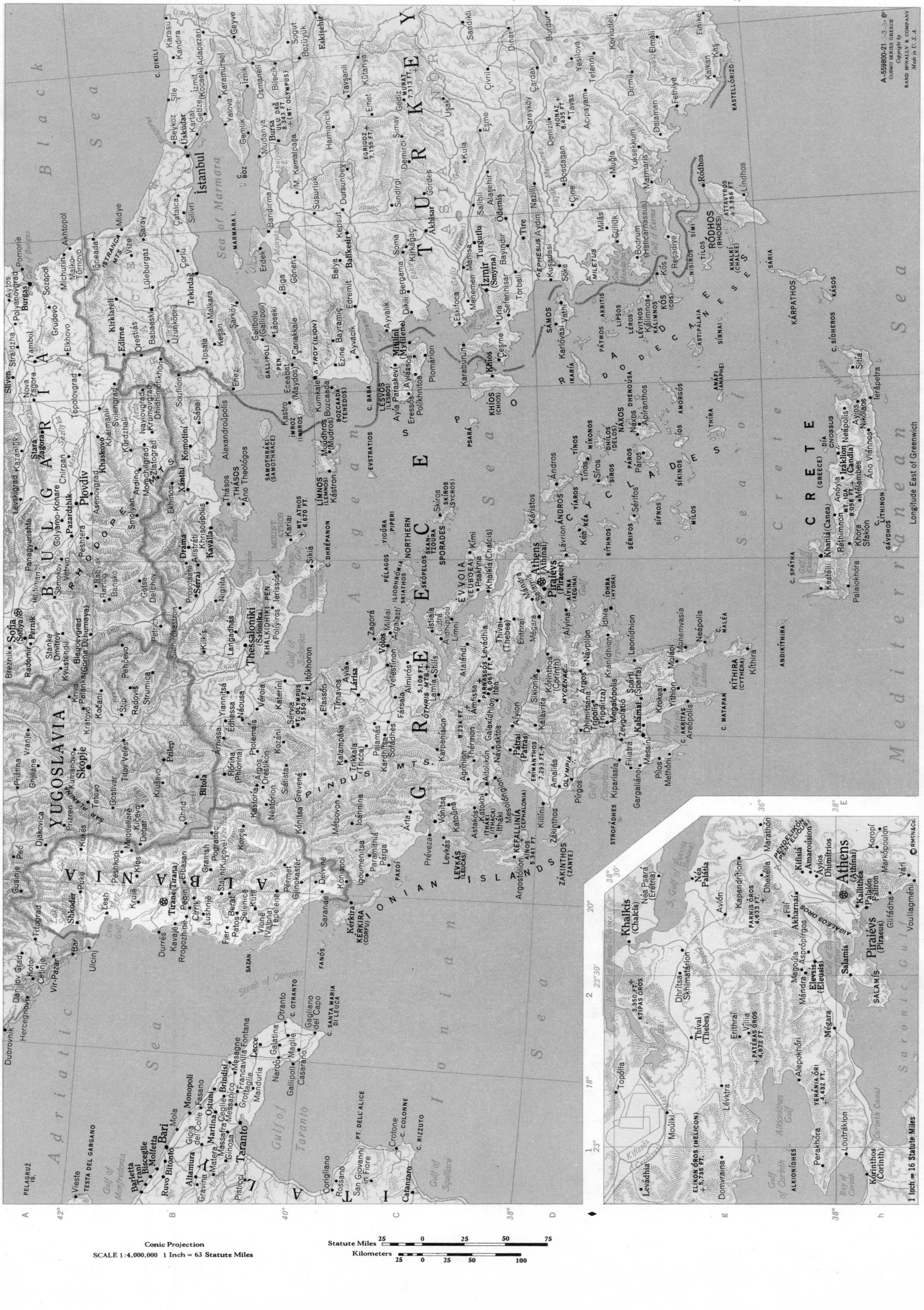

Conic Projection

SCALE 1:4,000,000   1 Inch = 63 Statute Miles

Statute Miles
25   0   25   50   75

Kilometers
25   0   25   50   100

1 Inch = 16 Statute Miles

A-559800-21
COSMO SERIES GREECE
Copyright by
RAND M?NALLY & COMPANY
Made in U.S.A.

DENMARK AND NORTHERN GERMANY

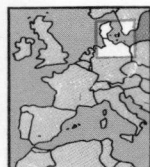

COSMO SERIES DENMARK
Copyright by
RAND McNALLY & COMPANY
Made in U. S. A.
A-550600-21- -4-4-6[B]
Longitude East of Greenwich
SWEDEN
FEDERAL REPUBLIC OF GERMANY
NIEDERSACHSEN (WEST GERMANY)
GERMAN DEMOCRATIC REPUBLIC (EAST GERMANY)
POLAND
JUTLAND
SJAELLAND
FYN
LOLLAND
FALSTER
BORNHOLM
RÜGEN
FEHMARN
NORTH FRISIAN ISLANDS
SCHLESWIG-HOLSTEIN
MECKLENBURG
BRANDENBURG
SACHSEN-ANHALT
Skagerrak
Kattegat
Baltic Sea
North Sea
Helgoland Bay
Kiel Bay
Mecklenburg Bay
Pomeranian Bay
Kadet Channel
Fehmarn Strait
Store Baelt
Lille Baelt
Øresund (The Sound)
Copenhagen (København)
Århus
Ålborg
Odense
Esbjerg
Randers
Kolding
Vejle
Horsens
Helsingør
Helsingborg
Malmö
Lund
Göteborg
Halmstad
Hamburg
Kiel
Lübeck
Flensburg
Bremen
Bremerhaven
Wilhelmshaven
Cuxhaven
Hannover
Rostock
Stralsund
Wismar
Schwerin
Greifswald
Szczecin (Stettin)
Berlin (West)
Berlin (East)
Potsdam
Brandenburg
Statute Miles 5 0 5 10 20 30 40 50
Kilometers 5 0 5 10 20 30 40 50 60
Lambert Conformal Conic Projection
SCALE 1:2,000,000 1 Inch = 32 Statute Miles

Longitude West of Greenwich

Longitude East of Greenwich

Same Scale as Main Map

Conic Projection
SCALE 1:8,000,000 1 Inch = 126 Statute Miles

Statute Miles 50 0 50 100 150

Kilometers 50 0 50 100 200

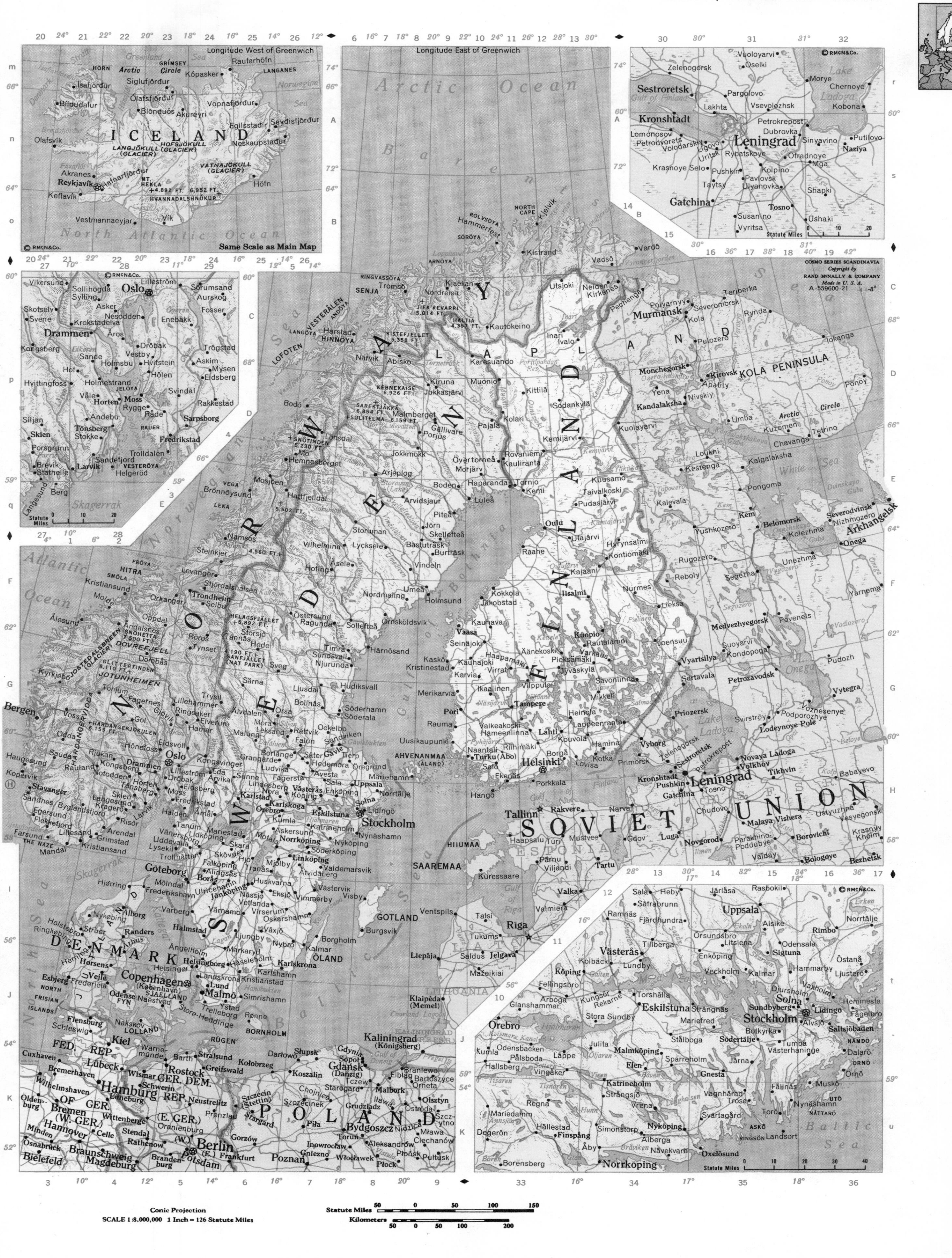

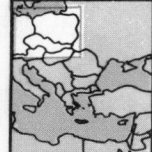

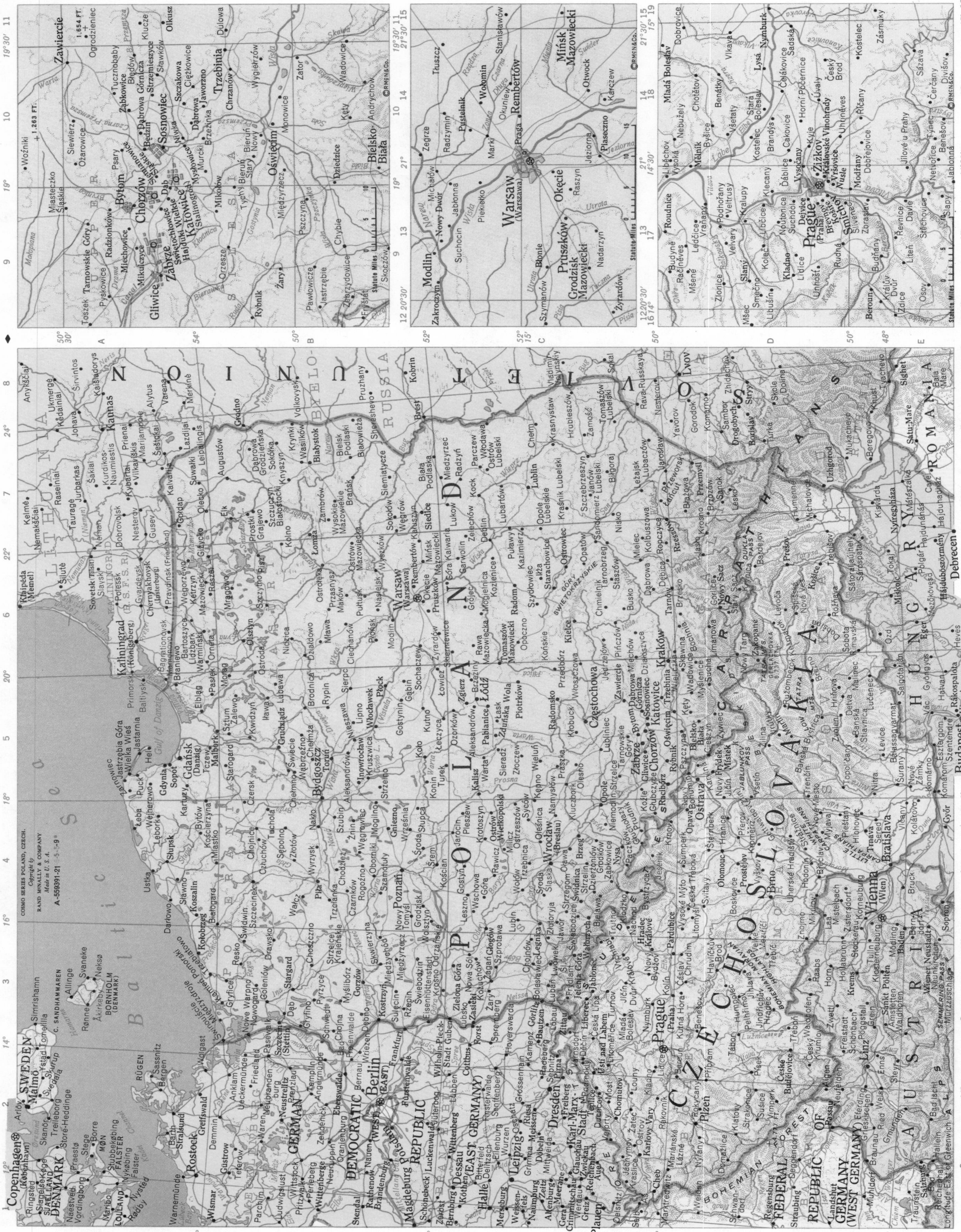

The annexation of Lithuania, Latvia and Estonia in 1940 by the Soviet Union has never been officially recognized by the United States Government.

SOVIET UNION

Longitude East of Greenwich

Conic Projection
SCALE 1:8,000,000 1 Inch = 126 Statute Miles

Statute Miles 50 0 50 100 150
Kilometers 50 0 50 100 200

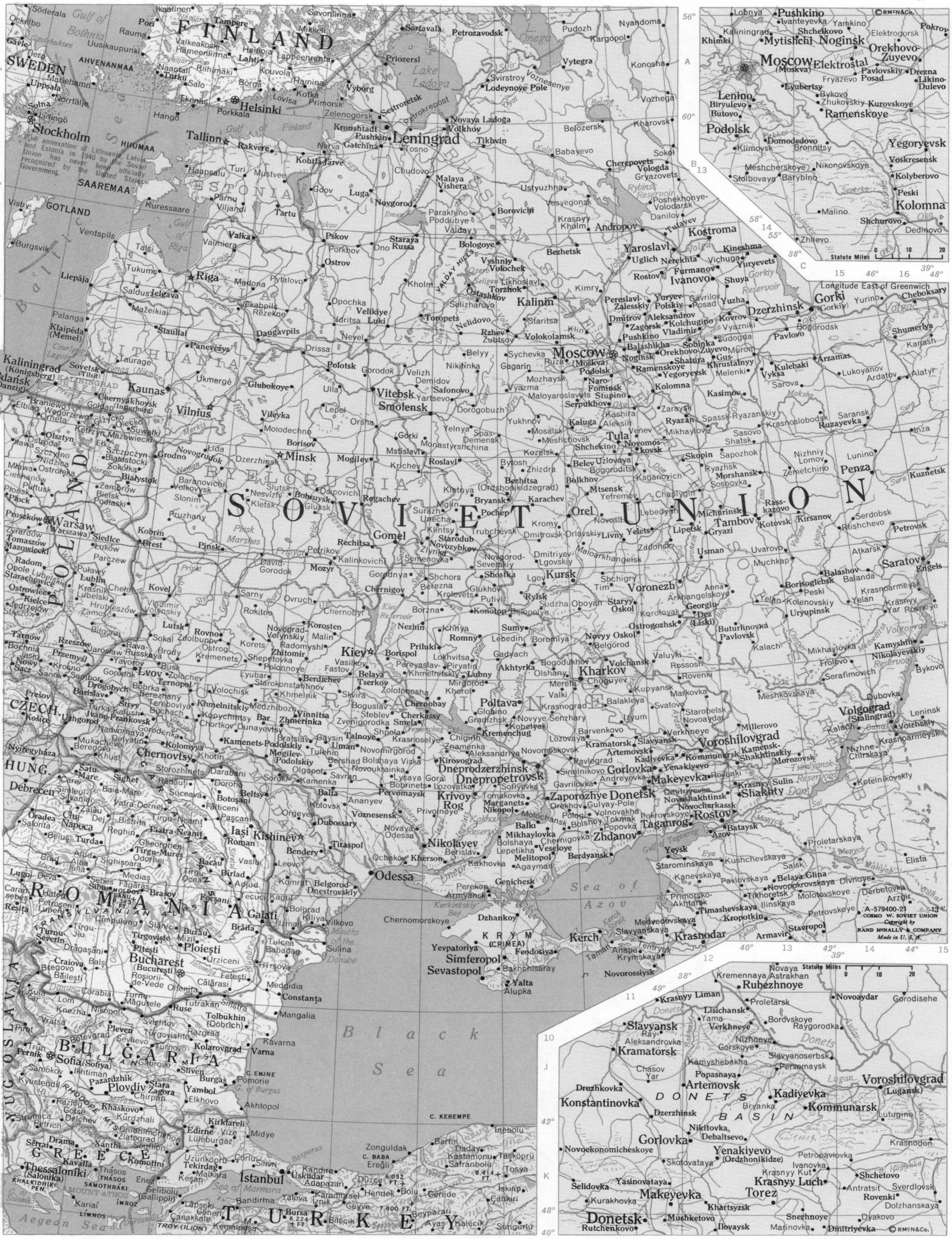

Statute Miles 100 0 100 200 300 400 500
Kilometers 100 0 100 300 500 700

Lambert Azimuthal Equal Area Projection
SCALE 1:28,000,000   1 Inch = 442 Statute Miles

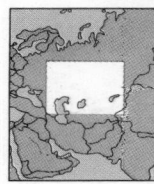

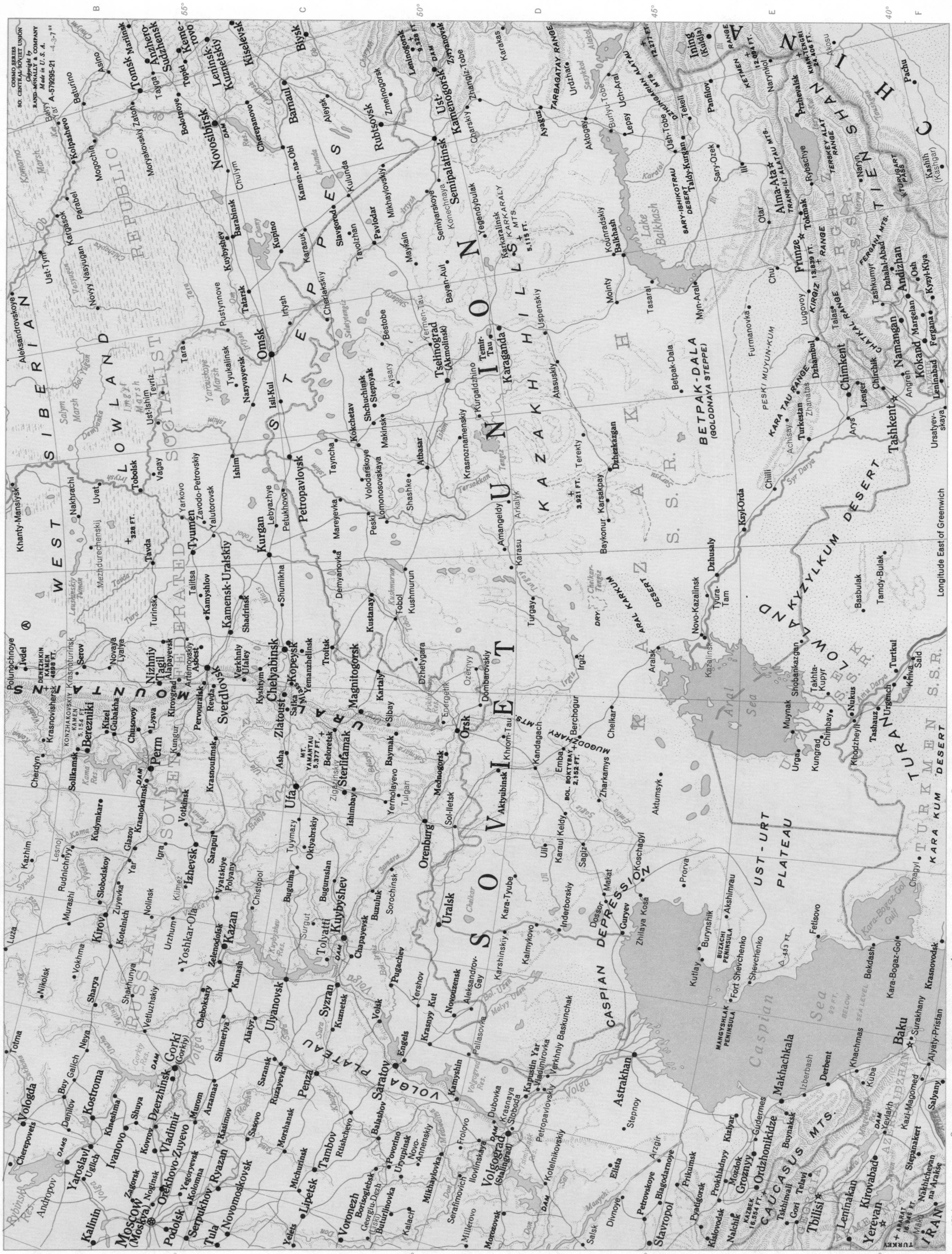

Sinusoidal Projection

SCALE 1: 11,400,000 1 Inch = 180 Statute Miles

Statute Miles 50 0 50 100 150 200 250

Kilometers 50 0 50 100 150 200 250 300

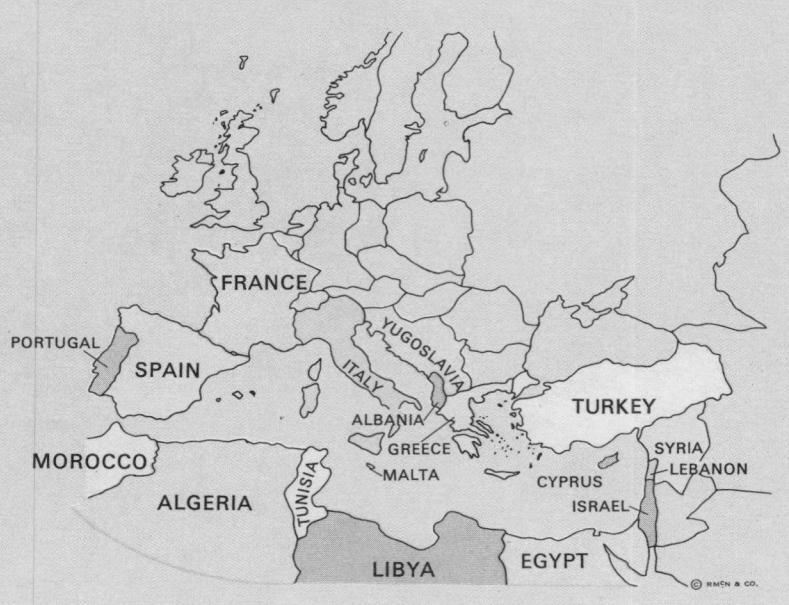

Southern Europe, extreme Southwest Asia, and the rim of North Africa, all integral parts of their respective continents, also belong to another significant world region. As lands that hem in the Mediterranean Sea, the waterway of the ancients, their history began early, and the climate provided by this body of water led to distinctive crops and cultures.

The Mediterranean region curves from the Biblical lands of the Middle East westward 2,500 miles to the Portuguese coast, and back again across the top of Africa to the Sinai Peninsula. Besides the Mediterranean itself, the region includes peninsulas, islands, and a thin, scalloped, often mountainous coastal strip. Both the sea and the general characteristics associated with the region are confined on the west and east by the constrictions at Gibraltar and the Suez. The Pyrenees, Alps, Balkan Mountains, and Black Sea on the north, and the Atlas Mountains and the North African desert on the south form the region's limits.

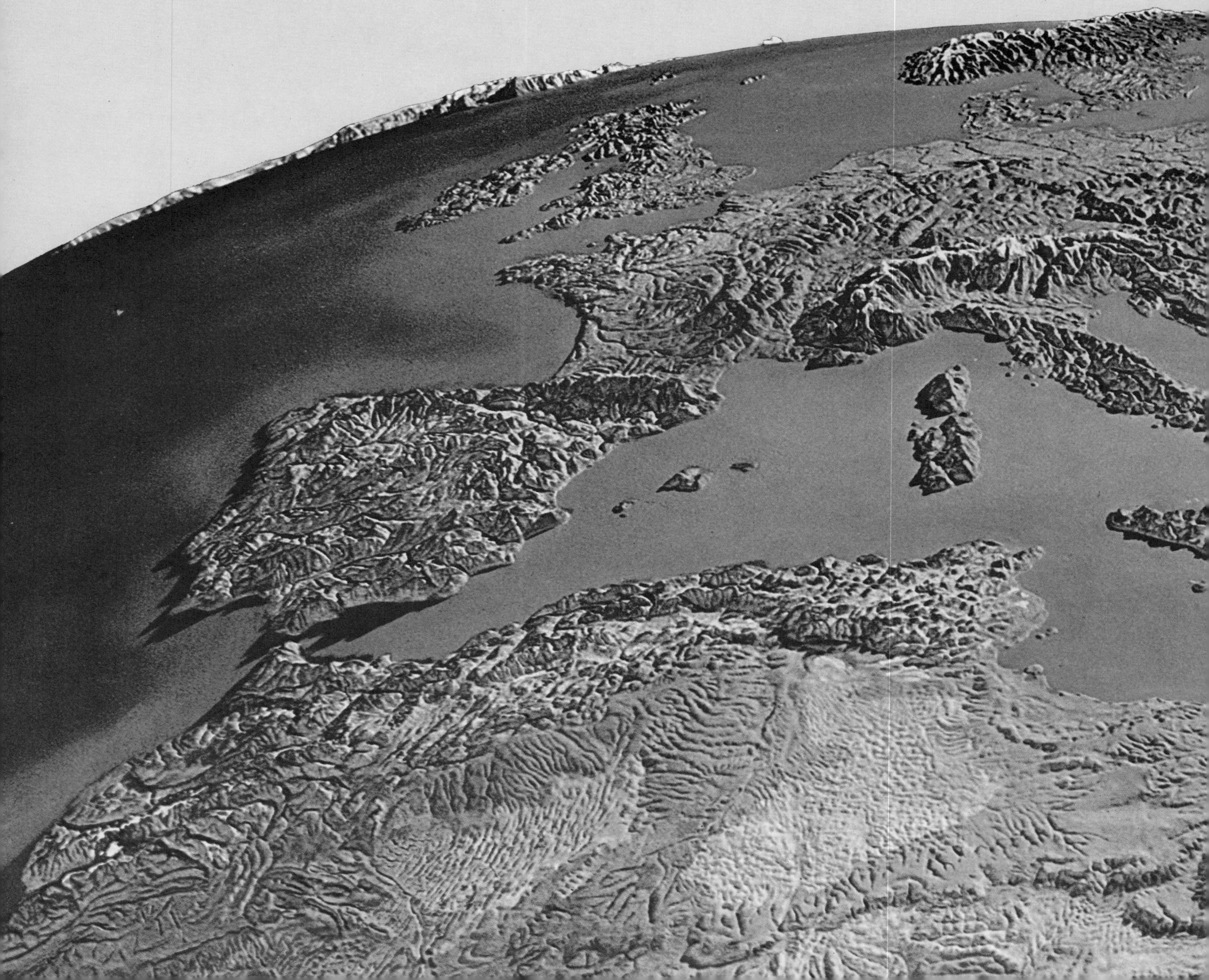

Although the Iberian, Italian, Balkan, and Anatolian peninsulas are imposing physical features, the Mediterranean Sea itself is the dominant element of the region's landscape. Upon this sea, which nature has segmented into two basins by the boot of Italy

and the island of Sicily, were developed the navigation techniques of the Western World. Over this body of water a commerce of goods and ideas flowed and still flows between Asia, Africa, and Europe. And from it many of the Italian, Spanish, and Portuguese explorers of the 1400's and 1500's sailed to discover and conquer new lands.

The rugged shores of the Mediterranean, insular and peninsular, with hot, dry summers and mild, moist winters have long presented man a challenging landscape from which to extract a living. By growing olive trees and grapevines, whose long roots sustain them through the dry summer, by cultivating barley and wheat, and by grazing sheep where little else can subsist on the rugged terrain, man has met this challenge. The scenic beauty of the azure sky and sea and the mountainous terrain—the Rivieras of France, Spain, and Italy, the Balkan coast and islands—contribute to a long famous and steadily expanding tourist economy.

Though the efforts to conquer the rugged natural elements have been heroic, most of the significant economic development has taken place on the few lowland plains and valleys of the region. The Nile Valley of Egypt, the Languedoc region of France,

the Guadalquivir Valley of Spain, and the Po Plain of Italy are representative. Here milder natural conditions have aided agricultural success. Coupled with what little industrial expansion has taken place, these areas have bolstered the total economy. Still the economy of these few widely separated, thriving pockets is not dynamic enough to absorb immigrants from the fairly dense rural population. In recent years thousands of workers have left for the industries of Northern Europe.

It is difficult to realize that in the rough land of the Mediterranean are buried many of the roots of Western civilization. Here Greek, Roman, and Byzantine cultures flourished and passed on their heritage to the far reaches of the earth. Around the shores of the Mediterranean, too, Christianity and Islam have their roots. Although today the major power centers are removed from the region, strong national feelings still prevail, based in good measure on the fact that each nation has played a role in world history. So, although the Mediterranean lands display similarities in climate, economy, and physical make-up, the variety of individual cultures and strong traditions that exist continue to defy political unification.

THE MEDITERRANEAN

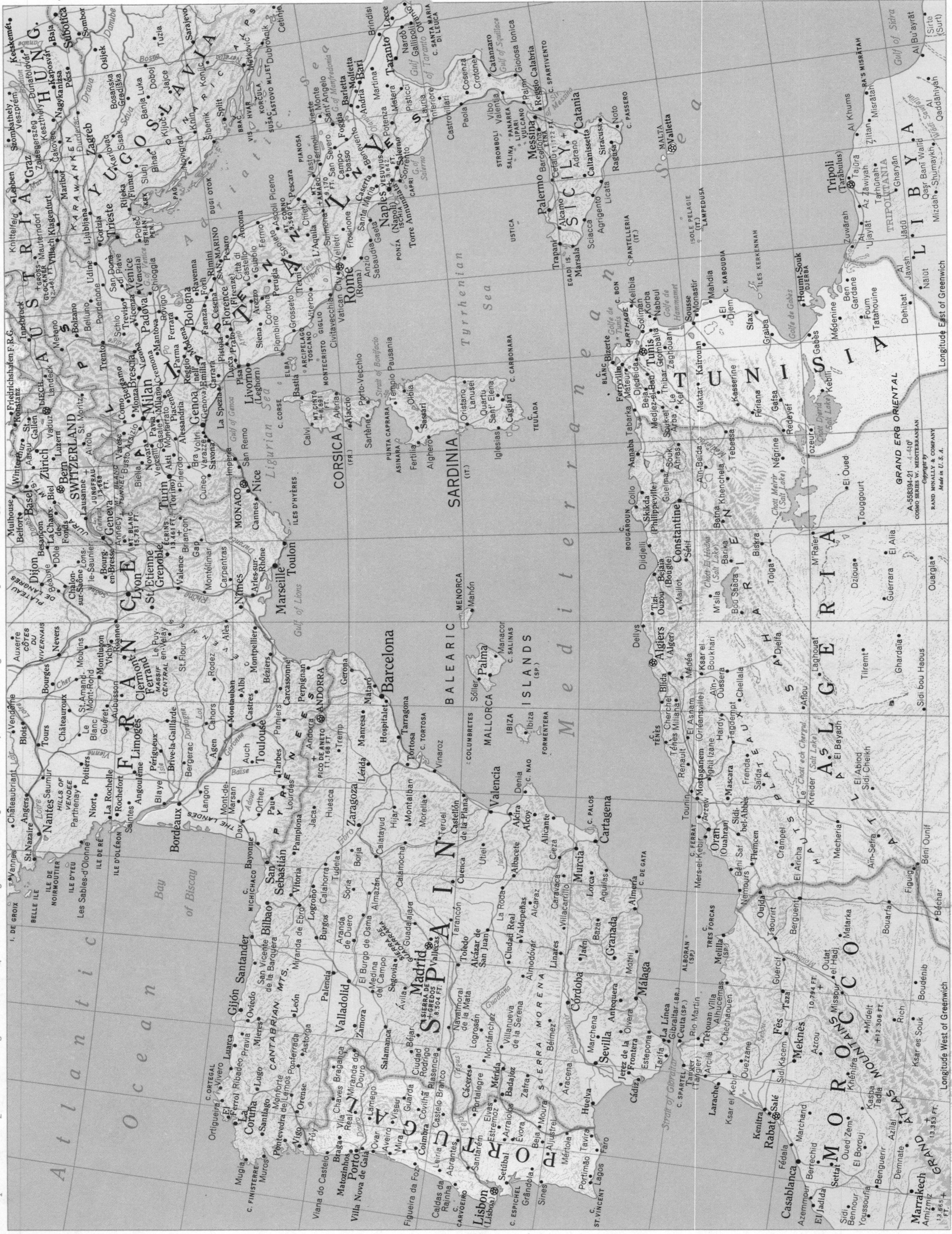

Statute Miles 50 0 50 100 150

Kilometers 50 0 50 100 200

Lambert Conformal Conic Projection
SCALE 1 : 8,000,000 1 Inch = 126 Statute Miles

For Eastern Iraq, see map of Iran and Afghanistan.

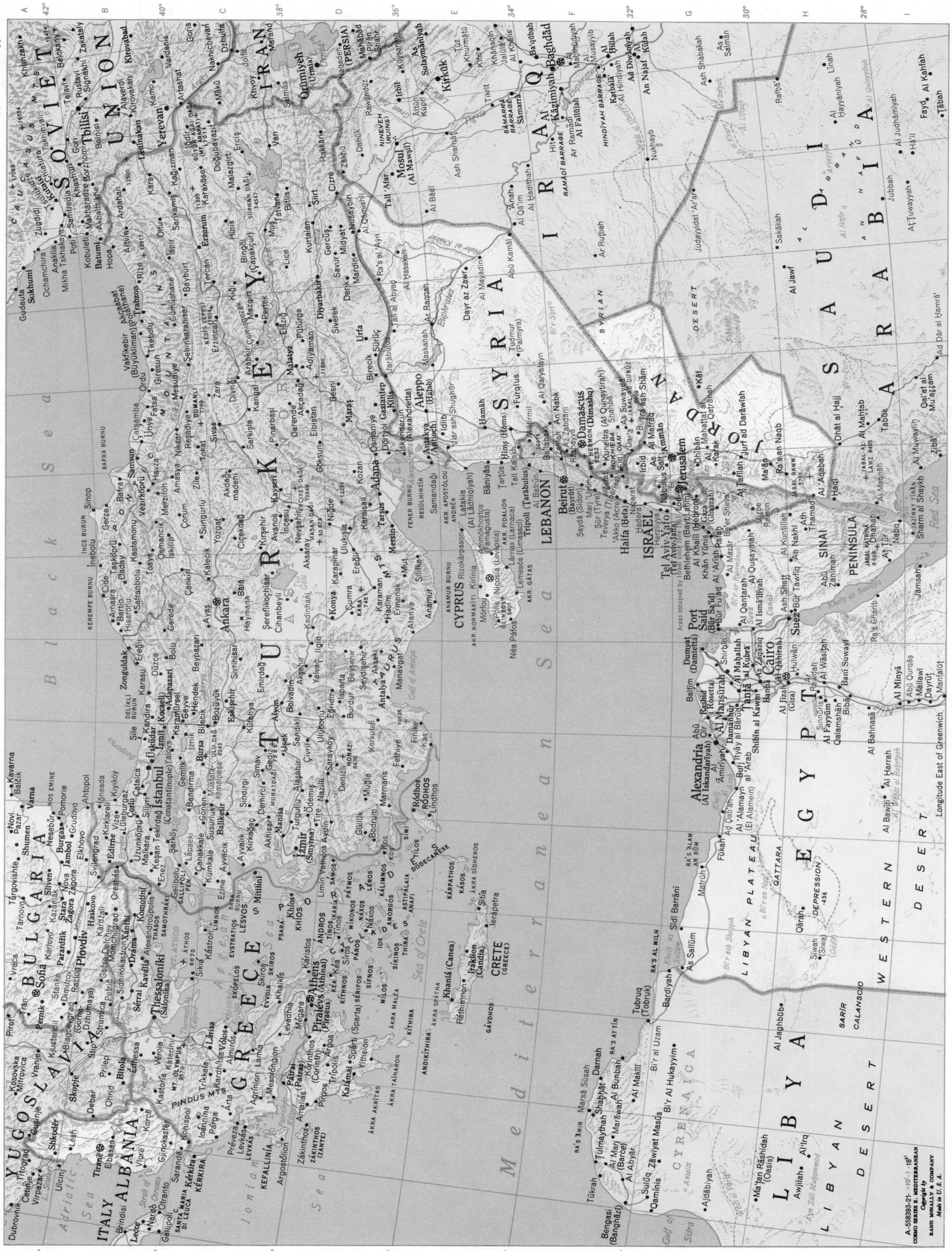

Lambert Conformal Conic Projection
SCALE 1 : 8,000,000   1 Inch = 126 Statute Miles

Statute Miles

Kilometers

A-558393-21-10/71-18
COSMO SERIES E. MEDITERRANEAN
Copyrighted by
RAND M9NALLY & COMPANY
Made in U.S.A.

JERUSALEM
1 Inch = 1 Statute Mile

1" = 16 Statute Miles

Longitude East of Greenwich

Areas occupied by Israel since June 1967

Statute Miles 5 0 5 10 20 30 40 50
Kilometers 5 0 5 10 20 30 40 50 60

Lambert Conformal Conic Projection
SCALE 1:2,000,000 1 Inch = 32 Statute Miles

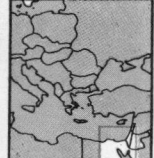

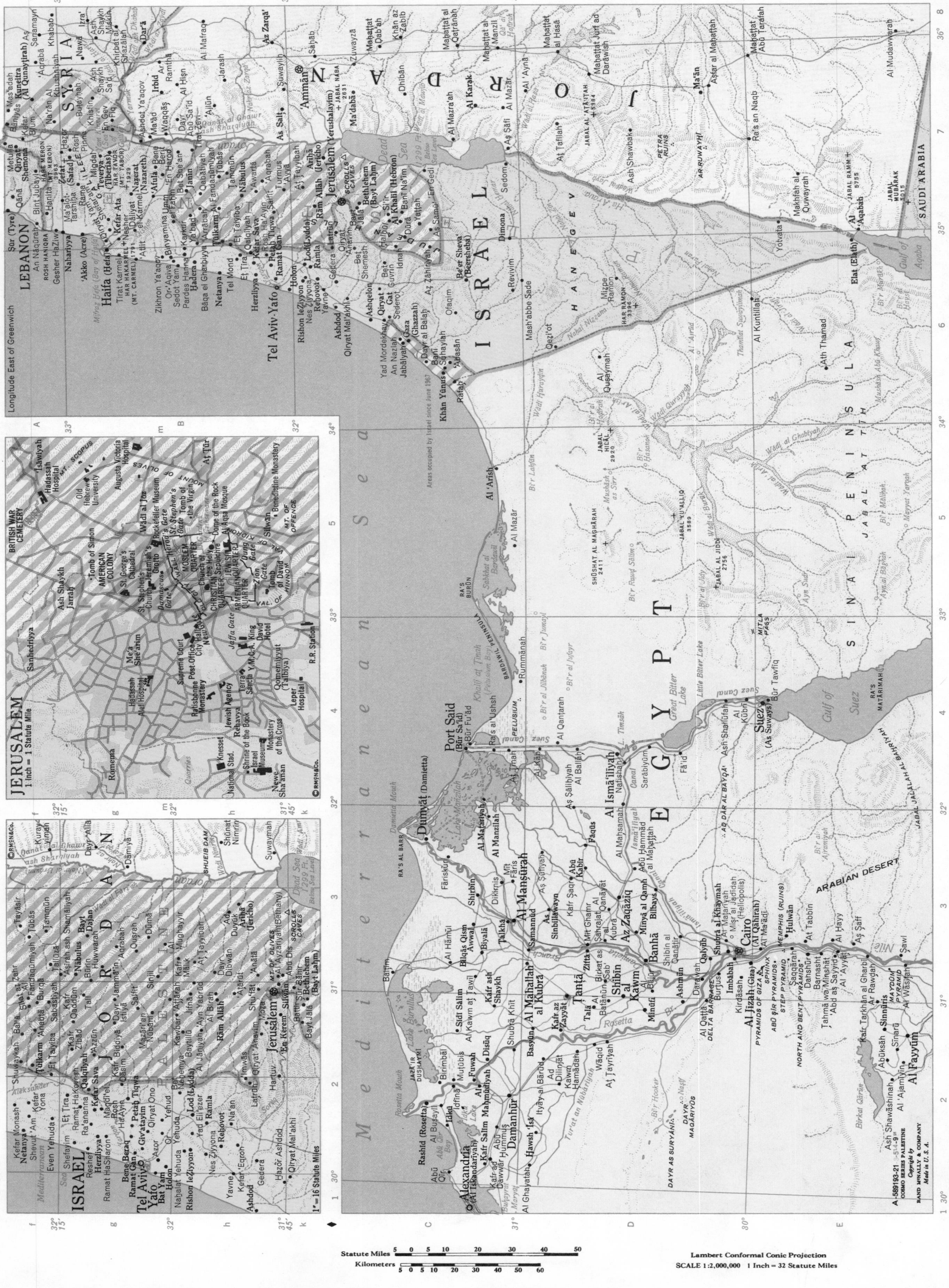

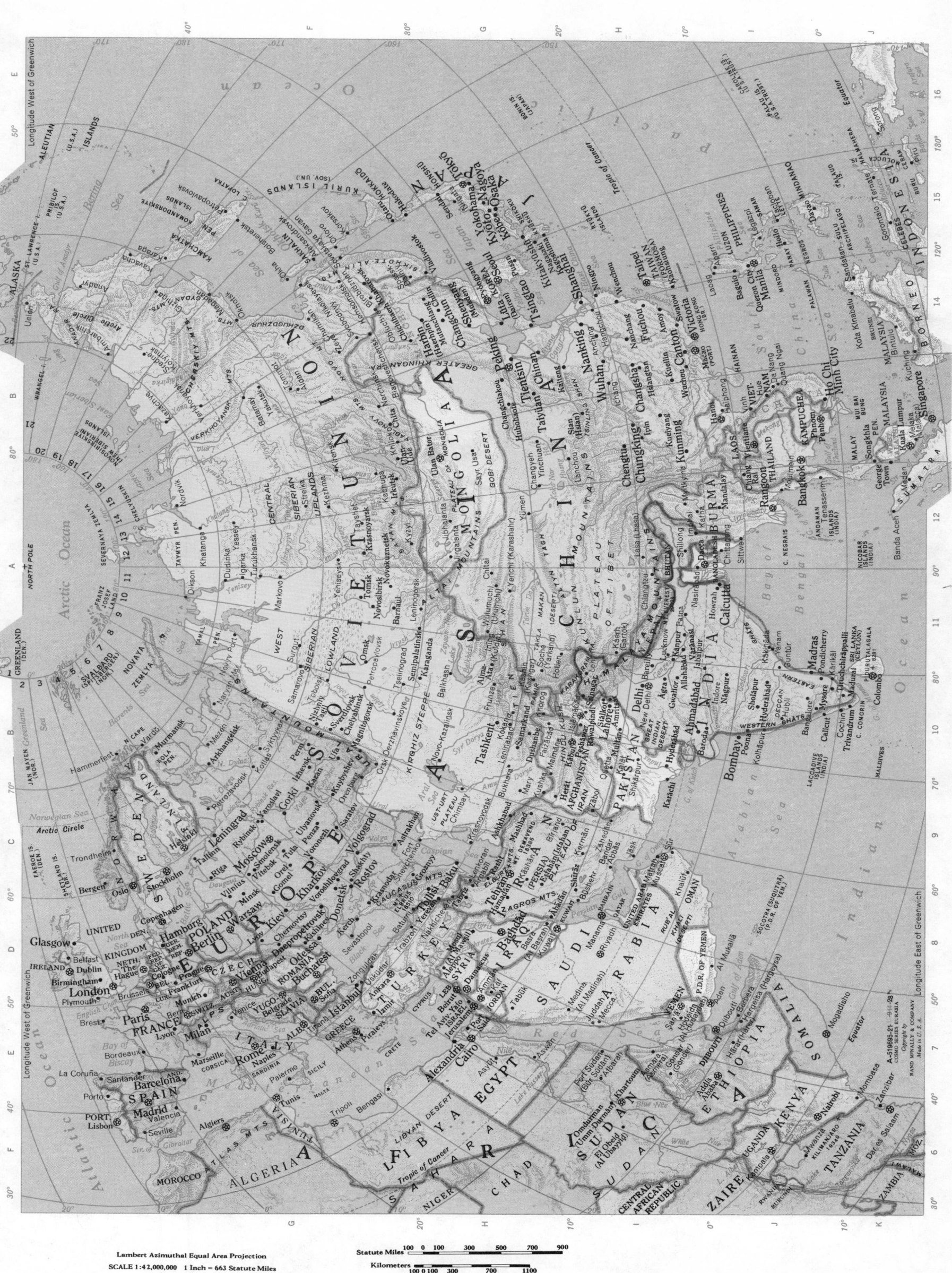

Lambert Azimuthal Equal Area Projection

SCALE 1:42,000,000 1 Inch = 663 Statute Miles

Statute Miles

Kilometers

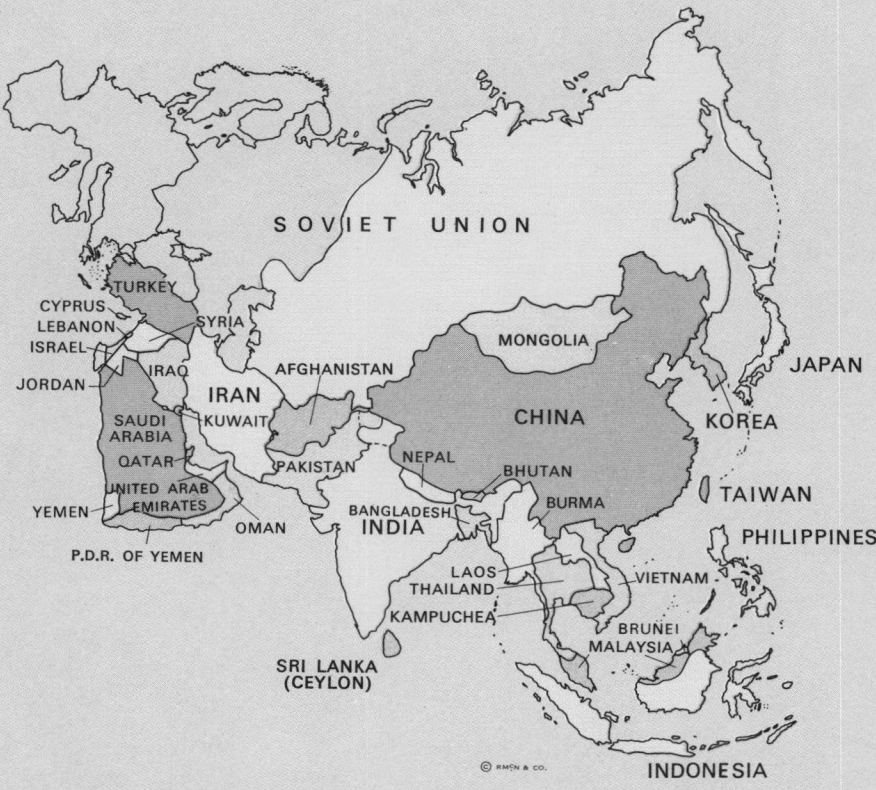

ASIA

Asia, the massive giant of continents, spreads its 17,085,000 square miles from polar wastes to regions of tropical abundance, and from Oriental to Occidental hearthlands. Much of Asia's vastness, however, is occupied by deserts, steppes, and by frozen and near-frozen wastes. Rugged upland areas stretch from Turkey and Iran, through the two-mile-high Tibetan Plateau, to the Bering Strait, leaving only one-third of Asia suitable for human habitation. These barriers also separate the two dominant, sharply contrasting parts of Asia—the realm made up of Southwest, South, and Southeast Asia from that of "European" Asia.

Rimming the south and east coasts of the continent are the most densely populated regions of the world, each dominated by a life-giving river system—the Tigris-Euphrates, the Indus and Ganges, the Brahmaputra, the Irrawaddy and Salween, the Menam and Mekong, the Yangtze and Hwang Ho, as well as innumerable small river valleys, plains, and islands. Separated from one another by deserts, massifs, and seas these regions account for over one-half of the world's population.

The civilizations associated with this population (where rural densities frequently may exceed 1,000 people per square mile) were developed largely upon the strength of intensive agricultural systems. Today these systems occupy more than 60 per cent of the populace, who manage only to win a bare subsistence. Changeover from subsistence agricultural economic systems to industrialized economies has been successful only in Japan and parts of the U.S.S.R.

North of the great Gobi Desert and the mountain barriers of the interior is the second Asia which, on almost every hand, differs from the southern portion of the continent. In the far north severe climatic elements send temperatures to −90°F., and permanently frozen ground impedes growth of vegetation. Only the scattered settlements next to the Trans-Siberian Railway give the area an indication of development. The activities of most of the populace are clearly directed toward Europe rather than Asia.

These two realms of the Asian continent do share two common characteristics. One is vast, yet generally inaccessible, natural resources—extensive forests, minerals, and hydroelectric potential—and the second is the drive to industrialize in order to "catch up" to the general material well-being of the Western World.

In the future, as the common characteristics, resources and drive, are developed, Asia's two realms may witness a change. A material way of life may result consistent with their heritage and historic contributions to the world.

CHINA, MONGOLIA, KOREA, JAPAN AND TAIWAN

Statute Miles 100 0 100 200 300

Kilometers 100 0 100 200 300 400

Polyconic Projection

SCALE 1:16,000,000 1 Inch = 252 Statute Miles

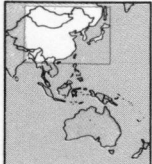

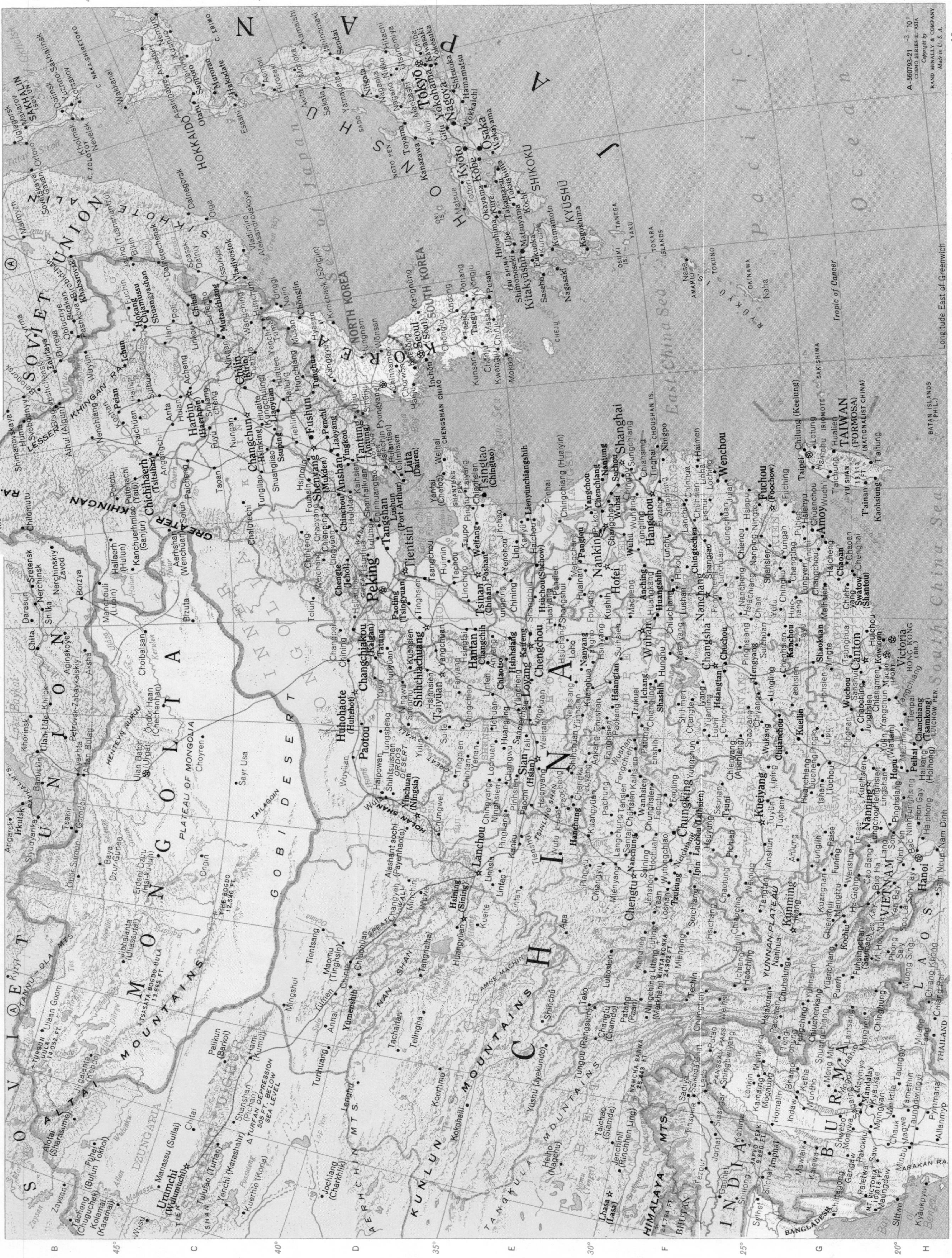

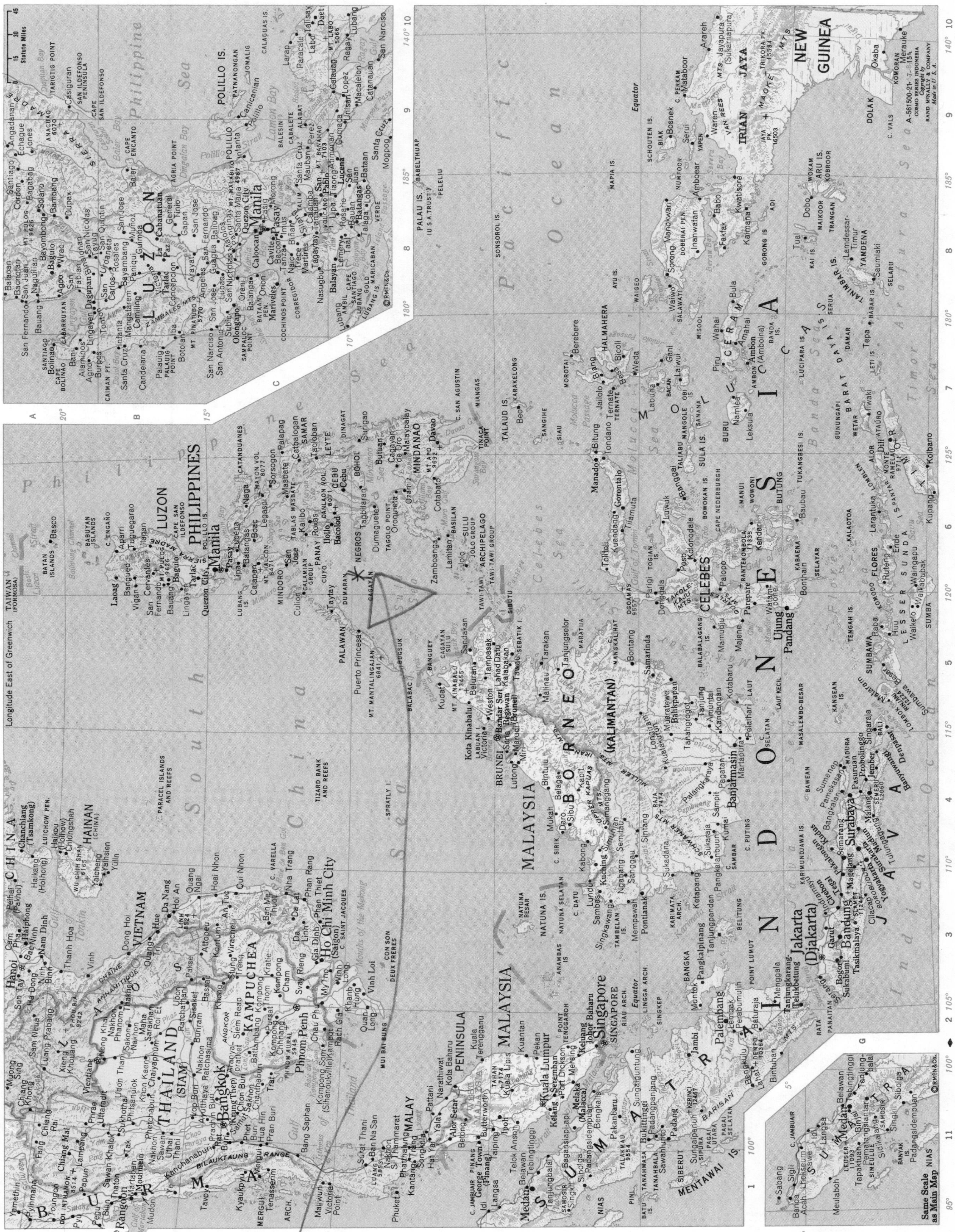

Polyconic Projection
SCALE 1:16,000,000 1 Inch = 252 Statute Miles

Statute Miles
100   0   100   200   300

Kilometers
100   0   100   200   300   400

Same Scale as Main Map

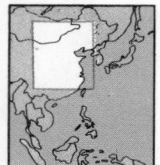

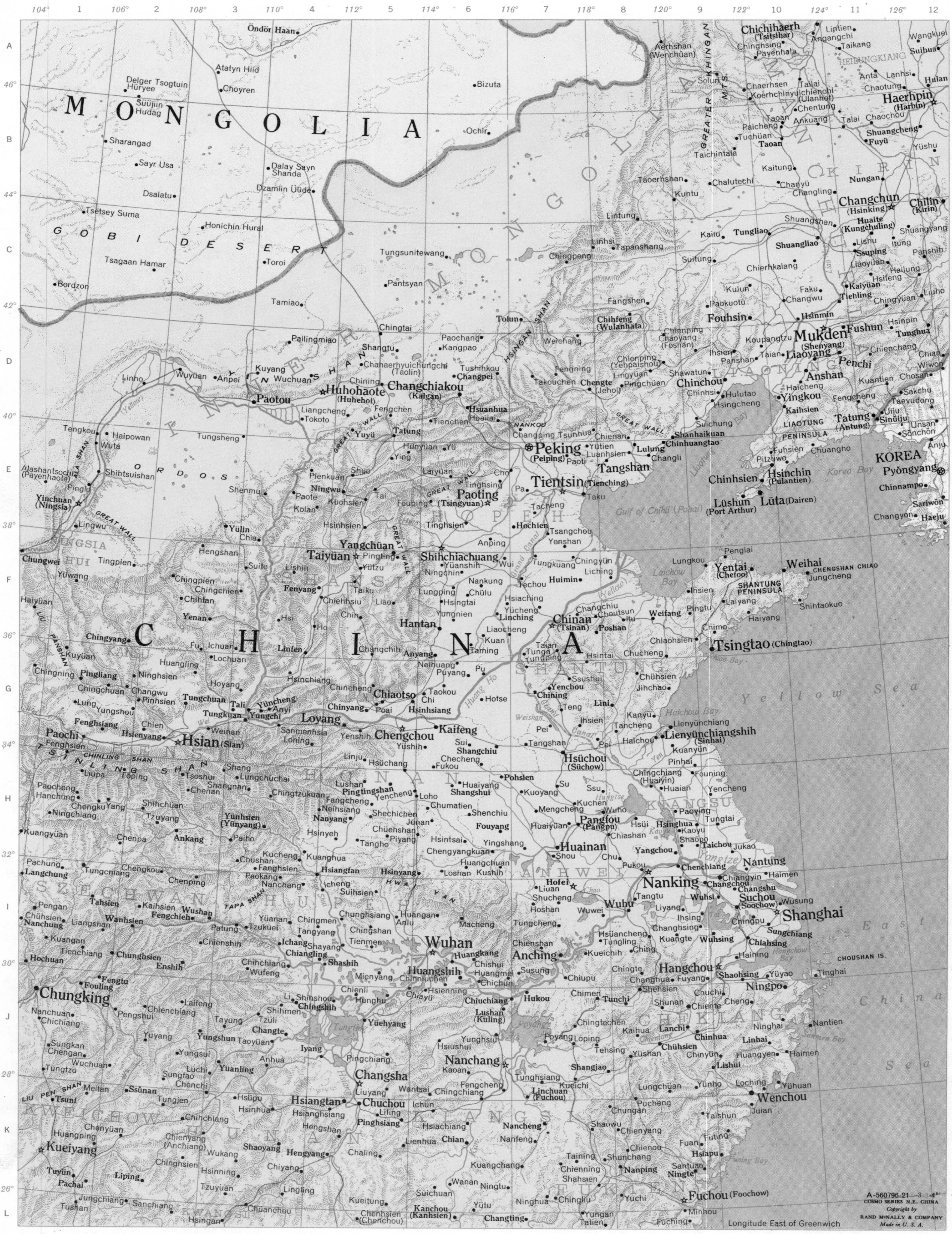

MONGOLIA

GOBI DESERT

C H I N A

KOREA

Peking (Peiping)
Tientsin (Tienching)
Paoting (Tsingyuan)
Taiyüan
Hsian (Sian)
Loyang
Chengchou
Kaifeng
Mukden (Shenyang)
Changchun (Hsinking)
Haerhpin (Harbin)
Chilin (Kirin)
Chichihaerh (Tsitsihar)
Tsingtao (Chingtao)
Chinan (Tsinan)
Nanking
Shanghai
Hangchou
Wuhan
Chungking
Changsha
Nanchang
Wenchou
Fuchou (Foochow)
Pyongyang

Huhohaote (Huhehot)
Paotou
Yinchuan (Ningsia)
Changchiakou (Kalgan)
Shihchiachuang
Hantan
Tangshan
Chinchou
Anshan
Fushun
Lüshun (Port Arthur)
Lüta (Dairen)
Weihai
Yentai (Chefoo)
Hsüchou (Süchow)
Pangfou (Pengpu)
Huainan
Hofei
Anching
Huangshih
Ningpo

Gulf of Chihli (Pohai)
Korea Bay
Yellow Sea
East China Sea
Laichow Bay
Haichow Bay

SHANTUNG PENINSULA
LIAOTUNG PENINSULA
GREATER KHINGAN MTS.
GREAT WALL
TSINLING SHAN
TAPA SHAN

Longitude East of Greenwich

A-560796-21 -3 -4
COSMO SERIES N.E. CHINA
Copyright by
RAND McNALLY & COMPANY
Made in U.S.A.

Statute Miles   50   0   50   100   150
Kilometers   50   0   50   100   200

Lambert Conformal Conic Projection
SCALE 1 : 8,000,000   1 Inch = 126 Statute Miles

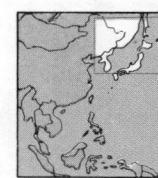

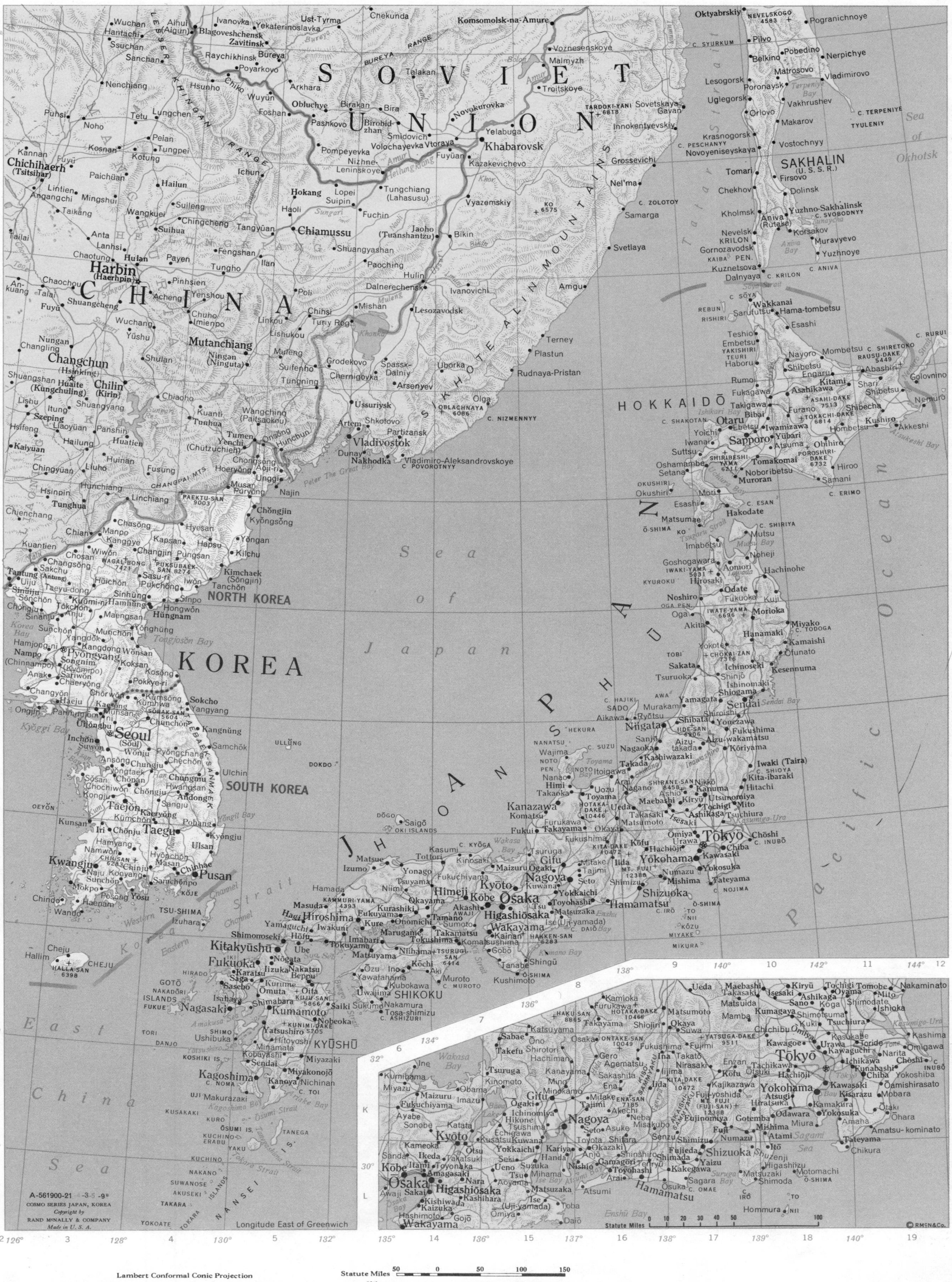

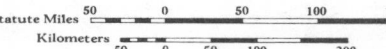

Lambert Conformal Conic Projection
SCALE 1 : 8,000,000   1 Inch = 126 Statute Miles

Statute Miles

Kilometers

BURMA

CHINA

LAOS

THAILAND (SIAM)

KAMPUCHEA (CAMBODIA)

VIET-NAM

HAINAN (CHINA)

MALAYSIA

SUMATRA

INDONESIA

BORNEO

Mandalay · Maymyo · Mogok · Lashio · Hsipaw · Mong Nai · Lantsang · Fuhsingchen (Ssumao) · Hokou · Ha Giang · Cao Bang · Nanning · Yulin (Waitlam) · Loting

Rangoon · Pegu · Henzada · Bassein · Moulmein · Thaton

Chiang Mai · Chiang Rai · Lampang · Nan · Vientiane · Nong Khai · Udon Thani · Sakon Nakhon · Thakhek · Hue · Da Nang

Bangkok · Krung Thep · Nakhon Ratchasima · Ubon Ratchathani · Nakhon Sawan · Phitsanulok · Khon Kaen

Phnom Penh · Battambang · Siem Reap · Kompong Cham · Kratie

Ho Chi Minh City (Saigon) · Gia Dinh · Bien Hoa · Phan Thiet · Da Lat · Nha Trang · Qui Nhon

Hanoi · Haiphong · Nam Dinh · Thanh Hoa · Vinh · Dong Hoi · Quang Tri

Haikou (Hoihow) · Chengmai · Chanchiang

George Town (Pinang) · Ipoh · Kuala Lumpur · Kelang · Melaka (Malacca) · Johor Baharu · Singapore

Medan · Pematangsiantar · Tebingtinggi · Banda Aceh

Kuching

Andaman Sea · Gulf of Thailand · South China Sea · Gulf of Tonkin · Gulf of Martaban · Mergui Archipelago

Statute Miles
Kilometers

Lambert Conformal Conic Projection
SCALE 1:8,000,000 1 Inch = 126 Statute Miles

A-561100-21
COSMO SERIES INDOCHINA, THAILAND
Copyright by
RAND M⸱NALLY & COMPANY
Made in U.S.A.

Longitude East of Greenwich

38

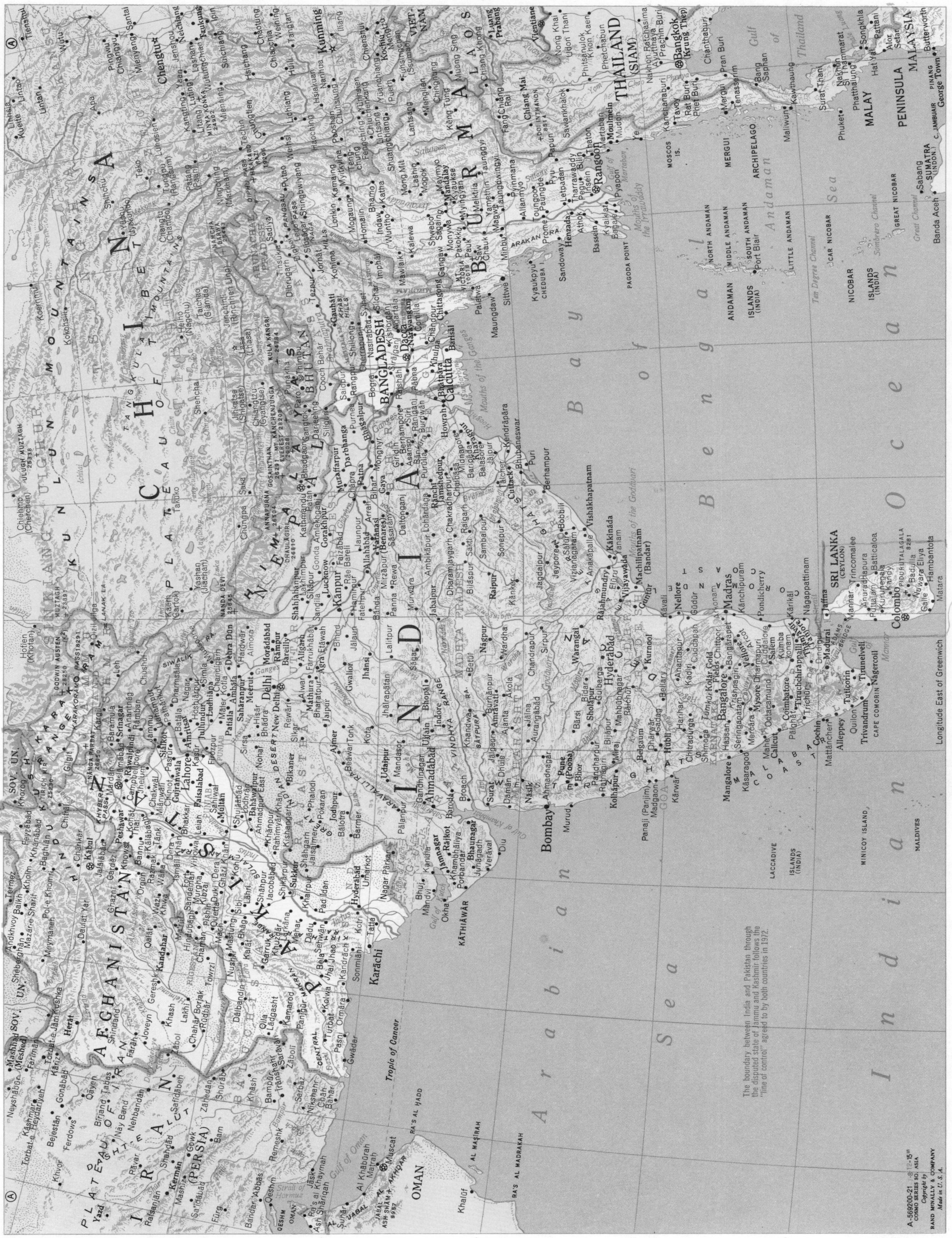

The boundary between India and Pakistan through the disputed state of Jammu and Kashmir follows the "line of control" agreed to by both countries in 1972.

Polyconic Projection
SCALE 1:16,000,000   1 inch = 252 Statute Miles

Statute Miles   100   0   100   200   300
Kilometers   100   0   100   200   300   400

A-569200-21 -8′ 12″-15′ H
COSMO SERIES NO. ASIA
Copyright by
RAND McNALLY & COMPANY
Made in U.S.A.

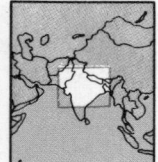

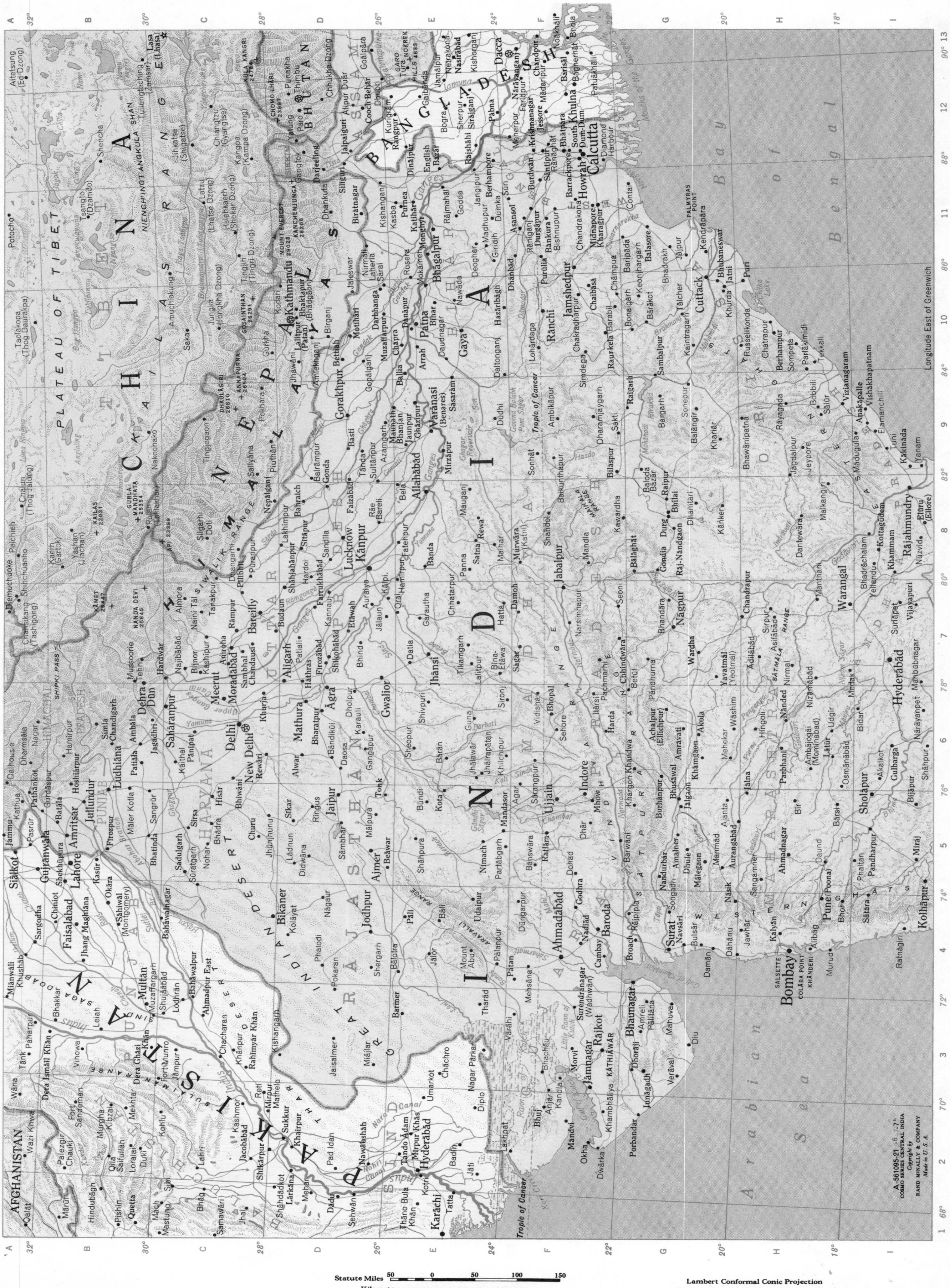

Statute Miles 50 0 50 100 150
Kilometers 50 0 50 100 200

Lambert Conformal Conic Projection
SCALE 1 : 8,000,000   1 Inch = 126 Statute Miles

A-561095-21
COSMO SERIES CENTRAL INDIA
Copyright by
RAND McNALLY & COMPANY
Made in U.S.A.

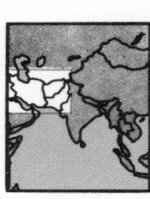

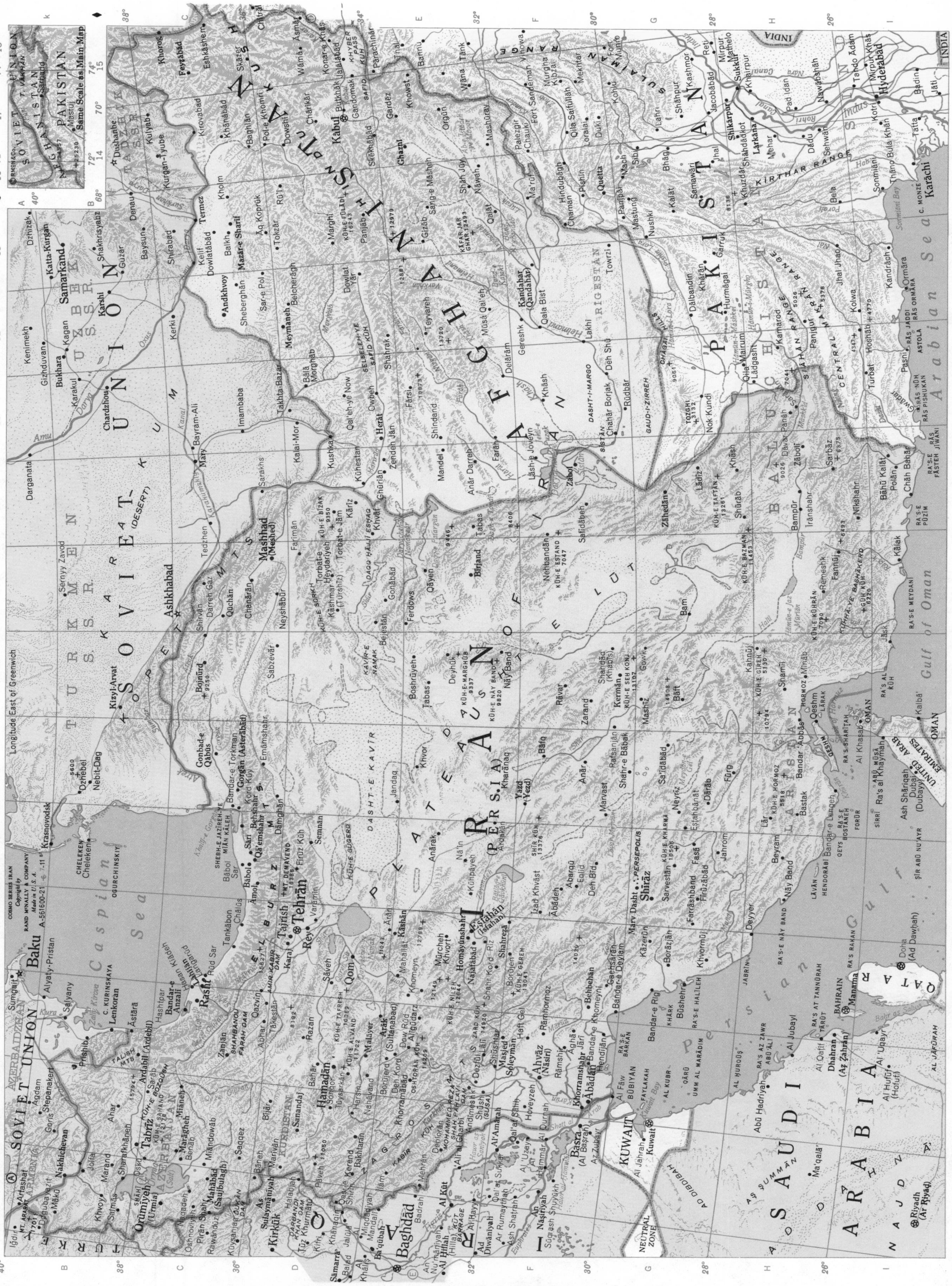

Lambert Conformal Conic Projection
SCALE 1 : 8,000,000 1 Inch = 126 Statute Miles

Statute Miles 50 0 50 100 150
Kilometers 50 0 50 100 200

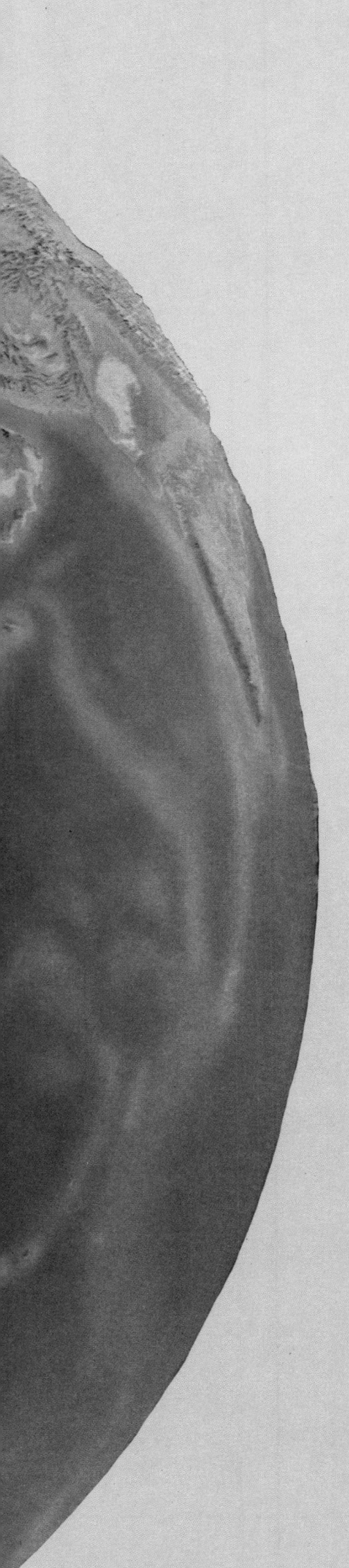

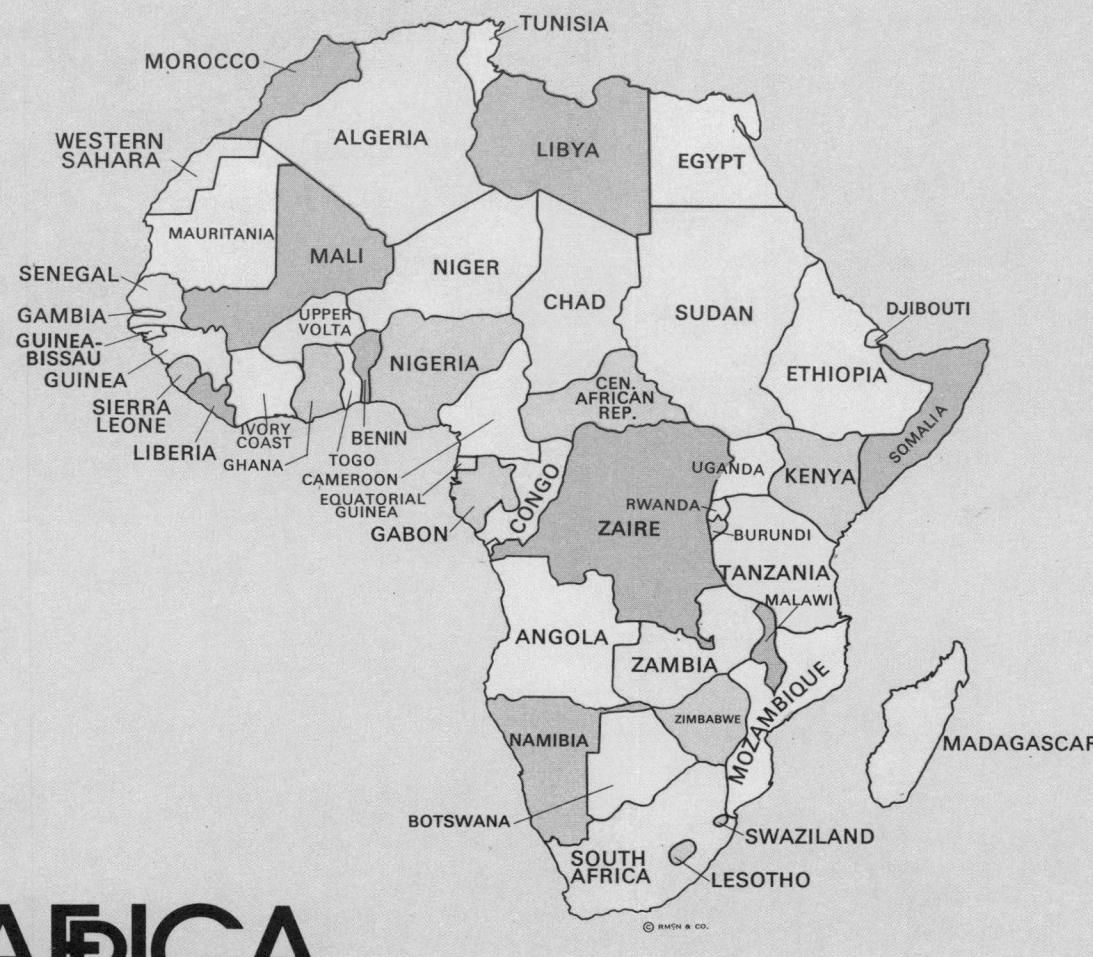

AFRICA

For centuries most of Africa's 11,685,000 square miles was unknown to outsiders. Access by one available avenue, the Nile, was impeded by the cataracts above Aswan. Since much of the interior is upland or plateau, usually dropping off rather sharply near the coasts, most of Africa's great rivers have rapids or falls close to the seaboard and so have not provided convenient routes to the interior. Moreover, the coastline is very regular, with few of the natural harbors of the other continents.

Once penetrated, much of the interior proved inhospitable to man. In the north, the world's largest desert, the immense expanse of the Sahara, blocks Africa's north rim from the central and southern portions. Near the other end of Africa, the Kalahari Desert helps separate the pleasant southernmost portion from the rest of the continent. In the center, the vast Congo Basin, humid, thinly settled, and unattractive, runs from the Atlantic seaboard east to the foot of the rugged highlands of East Africa, marked by the Rift Valley, which can be identified by the string of elongated lakes.

Africa's most important internal boundary is the Sahara. North of it the Mediterranean coastal countries are Moslem in tradition and have had close connections with Europe and the Near East. South of the Sahara are the many rich and varied cultures of Negroid tribal Africa. Unlike in many ways though they are, Mediterranean and Black Africa have until recently shared a common history of domination by non-African colonial powers. As late as 1945 there were only four independent nations in the entire continent. Now, spurred by the forces of nationalism, one new nation after another has emerged.

Past developments in communications, transport, education, and agricultural and industrial techniques, though limited, have formed a legacy from the old colonial powers on which the new African nations can build. Resources of iron ore, gold, oil, copper, timber, and a host of other vital raw materials are available. And there are many areas where climate and soil conditions are conducive to commercial agriculture, particularly for peanuts and cacao.

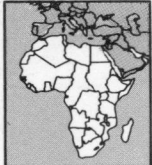

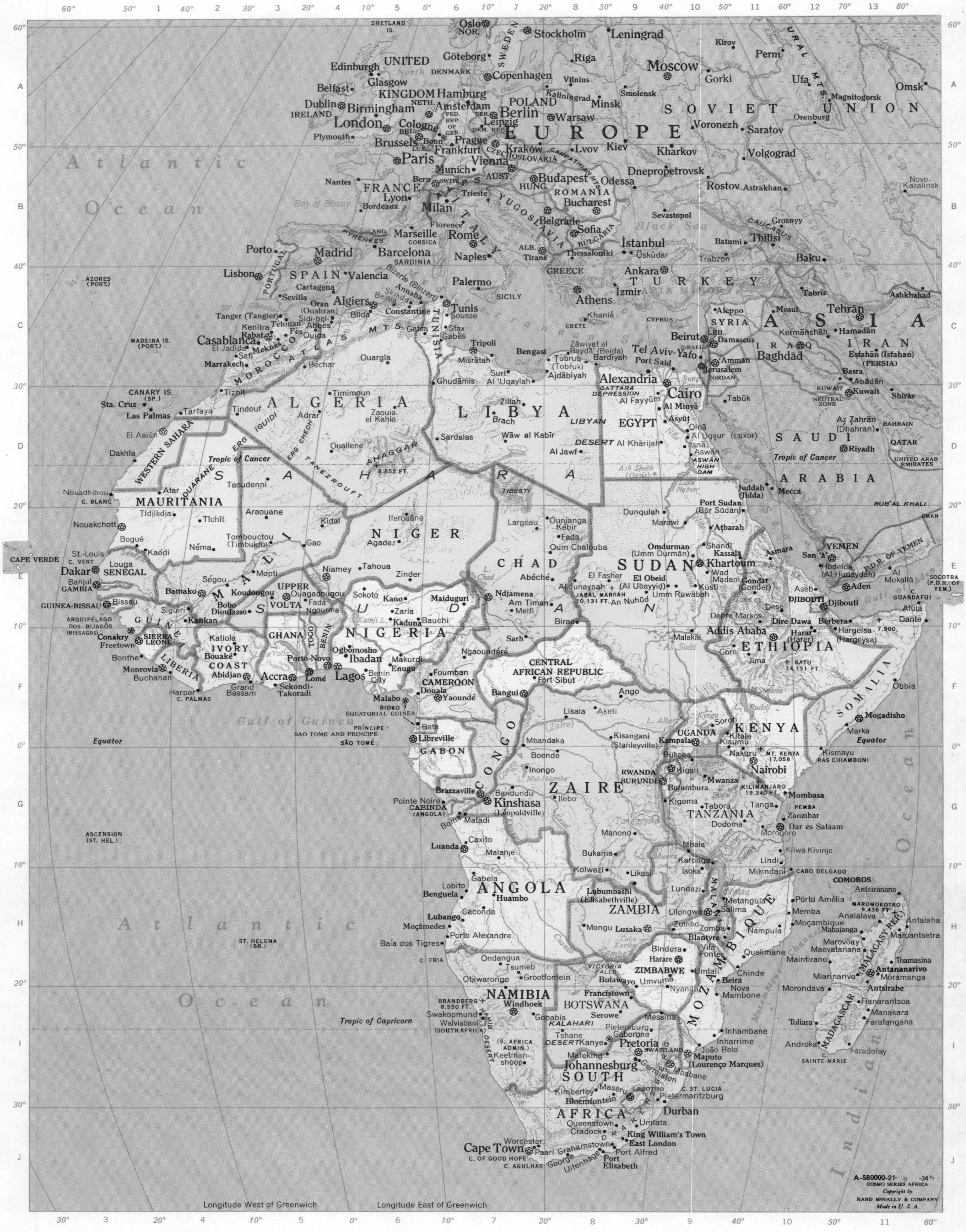

AFRICA

60° 50° 1 40° 30° 2 20° 10° 3 0° 4 10° 5 20° 6 30° 7 40° 50° 10 11 60° 70° 12 13 80°

Atlantic Ocean

SHETLAND IS.

Oslo NOR. Stockholm Leningrad Kirov Perm Omsk

Edinburgh UNITED Göteborg Copenhagen Riga Moscow Gorki Ufa Magnitogorsk

Glasgow KINGDOM Hamburg Amsterdam Berlin Minsk Voronezh Saratov Orenburg S O V I E T   U N I O N

Belfast Birmingham NETH. Leipzig Warsaw Smolensk Novo-Kazalinsk

IRELAND Dublin London Cologne FED. REP. OF GER. DEM. REP. POLAND Kiev Kharkov Volgograd

Plymouth Brussels Bonn Prague CZECHOSLOVAKIA Lvov Dnepropetrovsk Rostov Astrakhan

Paris Frankfurt Munich Vienna AUST. Budapest ROMANIA Odessa Sevastopol CAUCASUS Groznyy

Nantes FRANCE Bern SWITZ. HUNG. Bucharest Belgrade Sofia BULGARIA İstanbul Batumi Tbilisi Baku

Bordeaux Lyon Milan Trieste YUGOSLAVIA Thessaloníki Üsküdar Trabzon Caspian Sea

Marseille CORSICA Florence Rome ALB. Tiranë GREECE Ankara TURKEY İzmir ASIA MINOR Tabrīz Ashkhabad

Porto Madrid Barcelona Naples SARDINIA Athens CRETE CYPRUS Aleppo Mosul Tehrān IRAN (PERSIA)

Lisbon SPAIN Valencia Palermo SICILY Khaniá Beirut LEB. Damascus SYRIA Kermānshāh Hamadān Eşfahān (Isfahan)

Cartagena Sevilla Algiers Tunis Sousse Tel Aviv-Yafo ISRAEL Amman IRAQ Baghdād Basra Ābādān Shīrāz

Tanger (Tangier) Oran (Ouahran) Blida Constantine Sfax Gabès Port Said Jerusalem JORDAN KUWAIT Kuwait NEUTRAL ZONE BAHRAIN QATAR

Casablanca Rabat Fes Oujda Tripoli Misrātah Surt Al 'Uqaylah Ajdābiyā Alexandria Cairo Tabūk Az Zahrān (Dhahran) Riyadh UNITED ARAB EMIRATES

Marrakech Béchar Ghudāmis Bengasi (Beida) Tubruq (Tobruk) Bardiyah Al Fayyūm Al Minyā SAUDI RUB' AL KHALI OMAN

CANARY IS. (SP.) Tiznit Timimoun Adrar Zillah Brach Asyūt Al Khārijah Tropic of Cancer Juddah (Jidda) Mecca ARABIA

Sta. Cruz Las Palmas Tarfaya Tindouf AHAGGAR 9,852 FT. Zaouia el Kahla Wāw al Kabīr TIBESTI Aswān ASWÂN HIGH DAM Port Sudan (Būr Sūdān)

El Aaiún WESTERN SAHARA Atar Taoudenni Araouane Largeau Ounianga Kébir Dunqulah Marawi 'Atbarah San 'ā' YEMEN Hodeida (Al Hudaydah)

Nouadhibou C. BLANC MAURITANIA Tidjikdja Tîchît Kidal Agadez NIGER CHAD El Fasher Omdurman (Umm Durmān) SUDAN Khartoum Asmara P.D.R. OF YEMEN

Nouakchott Bogué Kaédi Néma Tombouctou (Timbuktou) Gao Tahoua Zinder Abéché Am Timan Al Junaynah JABAL MARRAH 10,131 FT. El Obeid (Al Ubayyid) Wad Madani (Gonder) Gondar Aden Al Mukallā

CAPE VERDE St-Louis Louga DAKAR SENEGAL Bamako Ségou Mopti MALI Niamey Sokoto Kano Maiduguri Melfi Birao CENTRAL AFRICAN REPUBLIC Umm Ruwābah Kūstī Débré Markos Dire Dawa Berbera Hargeisa 7,900 Atula Dante

Banjul GAMBIA Bissau GUINEA-BISSAU Siguiri Kankan UPPER VOLTA Ouagadougou Fada Ngourma Zaria Kaduna Bauchi Ndjamena Sarh Ngaoundéré Fort-Sibut Malakal Addis Ababa Harar (Harer) SOCOTRA (P.D.R. OF YEM.)

ARQUIPÉLAGO DOS BIJAGÓS (BISSAGOS) Conakry Freetown SIERRA LEONE Katiola Bouaké GHANA BENIN NIGERIA Ogbomosho Makurdi Enugu Foumban CAMEROON Bangui Ango ETHIOPIA BATU 14,131 FT. Jima Gore DJIBOUTI Djibouti

Bonthe Monrovia LIBERIA IVORY COAST Abidjan Accra Lomé Ibadan Lagos Benin City Douala Yaoundé SOMALIA Obbia

Buchanan Harper C. PALMAS Grand Bassam Sekondi-Takoradi Malabo BIOKO EQUATORIAL GUINEA Bata Lisala Aketi Kisangani (Stanleyville) UGANDA Sorot Kitale KENYA Marka Mogadishu RAS CHIAMBONI

Gulf of Guinea SAO TOME AND PRINCIPE PRÍNCIPE SÃO TOMÉ Libreville GABON Mbandaka Boende Bukoba Kampala Kisumu MT. KENYA 17,058 Nairobi Equator Kismayu

Equator ASCENSION (ST. HEL.) Brazzaville CONGO Kinshasa (Léopoldville) Inongo Lac Mai-Ndombe ZAIRE RWANDA Bujumbura BURUNDI Kigali Mwanza KILIMANJARO 19,340 FT. Mombasa

Pointe Noire CABINDA (ANGOLA) Boma Matadi Ilebo Bandundu Kigoma Tabora TANZANIA Tanga PEMBA Zanzibar

Luanda Caxito Manono Bukama Dodoma Dar es Salaam Morogoro

Malanje Kolwezi Likasi Mbala Karonga Lindi Mikindani CABO DELGADO COMOROS Antsiranana

Lobito Benguela ANGOLA Gabela Huambo Lubumbashi (Elisabethville) Isoka Mbeya Porto Amélia Memba Antalaha

Lubango Caconda ZAMBIA Lundazi Metangula Salima Moçambique Mahajanga Analalava Maroantsetra

Moçâmedes Porto Alexandre Mongu Lusaka Lilongwe Zumbo Zomba Nampula Marovoay Maevatanana Antananarivo

Baía dos Tigres Blantyre Vila Fontes Quelimane Maintirano Miarinarivo Moramanga MADAGASCAR Toamasina

C. FRIA Ondangua Tsumeb VICTORIA FALLS Bindura Harare Chinde Nova Mambone Morondava Antsirabe

Otjiwarongo Grootfontein ZIMBABWE Umtali Beira Nyanda Fianarantsoa Manakara

BRANDBERG 6,550 FT. Francistown Bulawayo Umvuma Inhambane Morondava Toliara Farafangana

NAMIBIA Windhoek BOTSWANA Messina João Belo Androka Faradofay SAINTE-MARIE

Swakopmund Tsumeb Gobabis Pietersburg Inharrime Tropic of Capricorn

Walvisbaai (SOUTH AFRICA) KALAHARI Gaborone Maputo (Lourenço Marques) SWAZILAND

Tropic of Capricorn Tshane DESERT Kanye Pretoria Mafeking Johannesburg SOUTH

Keetmanshoop (S. AFRICA ADMIN.) Kimberley Maseru LESOTHO Pietermaritzburg Durban

Atlantic Ocean Bloemfontein AFRICA Queenstown Umtata C. ST. LUCIA Indian Ocean

Cape Town Worcester Paarl Cradock Grahamstown King William's Town East London

C. OF GOOD HOPE George Uitenhage Port Alfred Port Elizabeth C. AGULHAS

Longitude West of Greenwich Longitude East of Greenwich

A-580000-21 -34½ COSMO SERIES AFRICA Copyright by RAND McNALLY & COMPANY Made in U.S.A.

30° 3 20° 4 10° 5 0° 6 10° 7 20° 8 30° 9 40° 10 50° 11 60°

Statute Miles 100 0 100 300 500 700 900

Kilometers 100 0 100 300 500 700 900 1100 1300

Sinusoidal Projection SCALE 1:36,313,000 1 Inch = 565 Statute Miles

42

Sinusoidal Projection
SCALE 1:11,400,000   1 Inch = 180 Statute Miles

Statute Miles
50 0 50 100 150 200 250
50 0 50 100 150 200 250 300

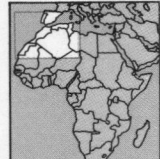

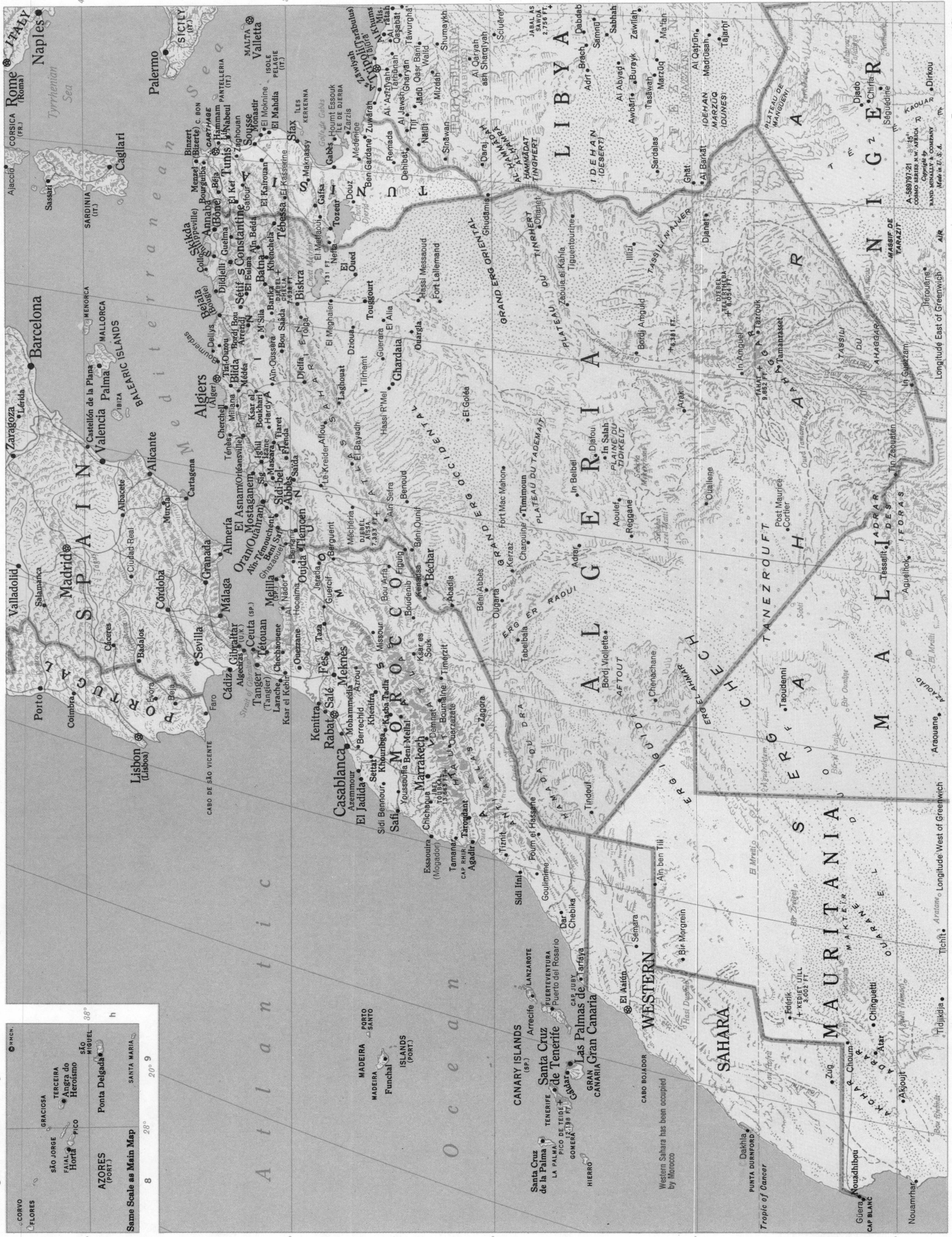

Statute Miles 50 25 0 50 100 150 200 250

50 0 50 100 150 200 250 300

Sinusoidal Projection
SCALE 1: 11,400,000   1 Inch = 180 Statute Miles

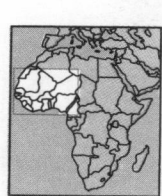

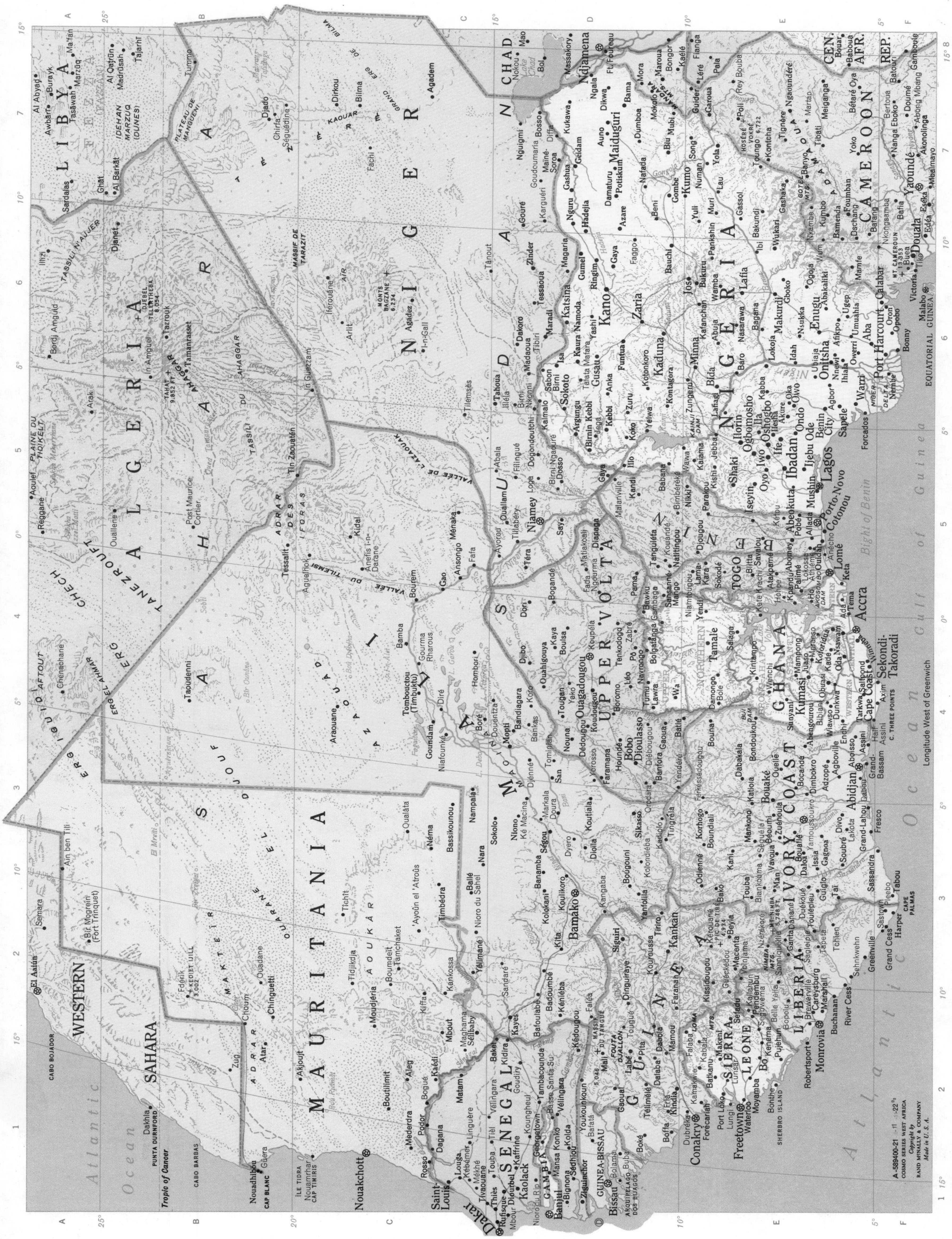

LIBYA

ALGERIA

NIGER

CHAD

NIGERIA

CAMEROON

CEN. AFR. REP.

MALI

MAURITANIA

WESTERN SAHARA

SENEGAL

GUINEA

UPPER VOLTA

GHANA

TOGO

BENIN

IVORY COAST

LIBERIA

SIERRA LEONE

GAMBIA

GUINEA-BISSAU

NORTHERN

EQUATORIAL GUINEA

Atlantic Ocean

Gulf of Guinea

Bight of Benin

Tropic of Cancer

Lake Chad

Ndjamena

Kano

Kaduna

Zaria

Maiduguri

Lagos

Ibadan

Accra

Abidjan

Bamako

Dakar

Nouakchott

Conakry

Freetown

Monrovia

Niamey

Ouagadougou

Tombouctou (Timbuktu)

Gao

Tamanrasset

El Aaiún

MT. CAMEROON 13,353

TAHAT 9,853 FT.

Sinusoidal Projection
SCALE 1 : 11,400,000   1 Inch = 180 Statute Miles

Statute Miles
50 25 0   50   100   150   200   250

Kilometers
50 0   50   100   150   200   250 300

A-58600-21 — 11 -'22¾
COSMO SERIES: WEST AFRICA
Copyright by
RAND McNALLY & COMPANY
Made in U.S.A.

45

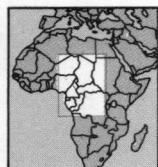

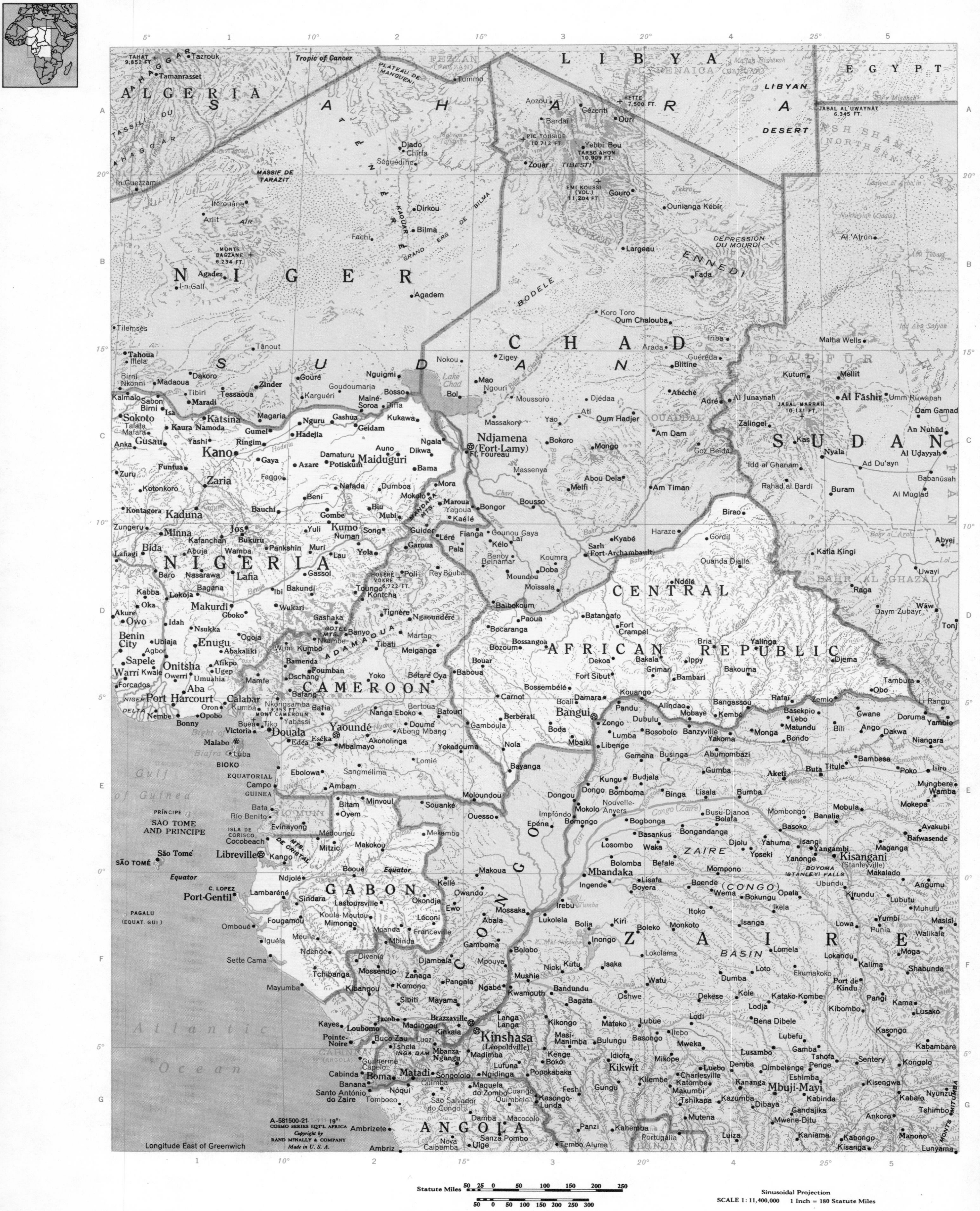

ALGERIA   LIBYA   EGYPT

SAHARA   DESERT

Tropic of Cancer

NIGER   CHAD   SUDAN

NIGERIA

CAMEROON

CENTRAL AFRICAN REPUBLIC

EQUATORIAL GUINEA

SAO TOME AND PRINCIPE

GABON   CONGO   ZAIRE

Gulf of Guinea

Atlantic Ocean

Equator

ZAIRE BASIN

ANGOLA

Statute Miles 50 25 0 50 100 150 200 250

50 0 50 100 150 200 250 300

Sinusoidal Projection
SCALE 1 : 11,400,000   1 Inch = 180 Statute Miles

Longitude East of Greenwich

A-581500-21
COSMO SERIES EQ'T'L AFRICA
Copyright by
RAND McNALLY & COMPANY
Made in U.S.A.

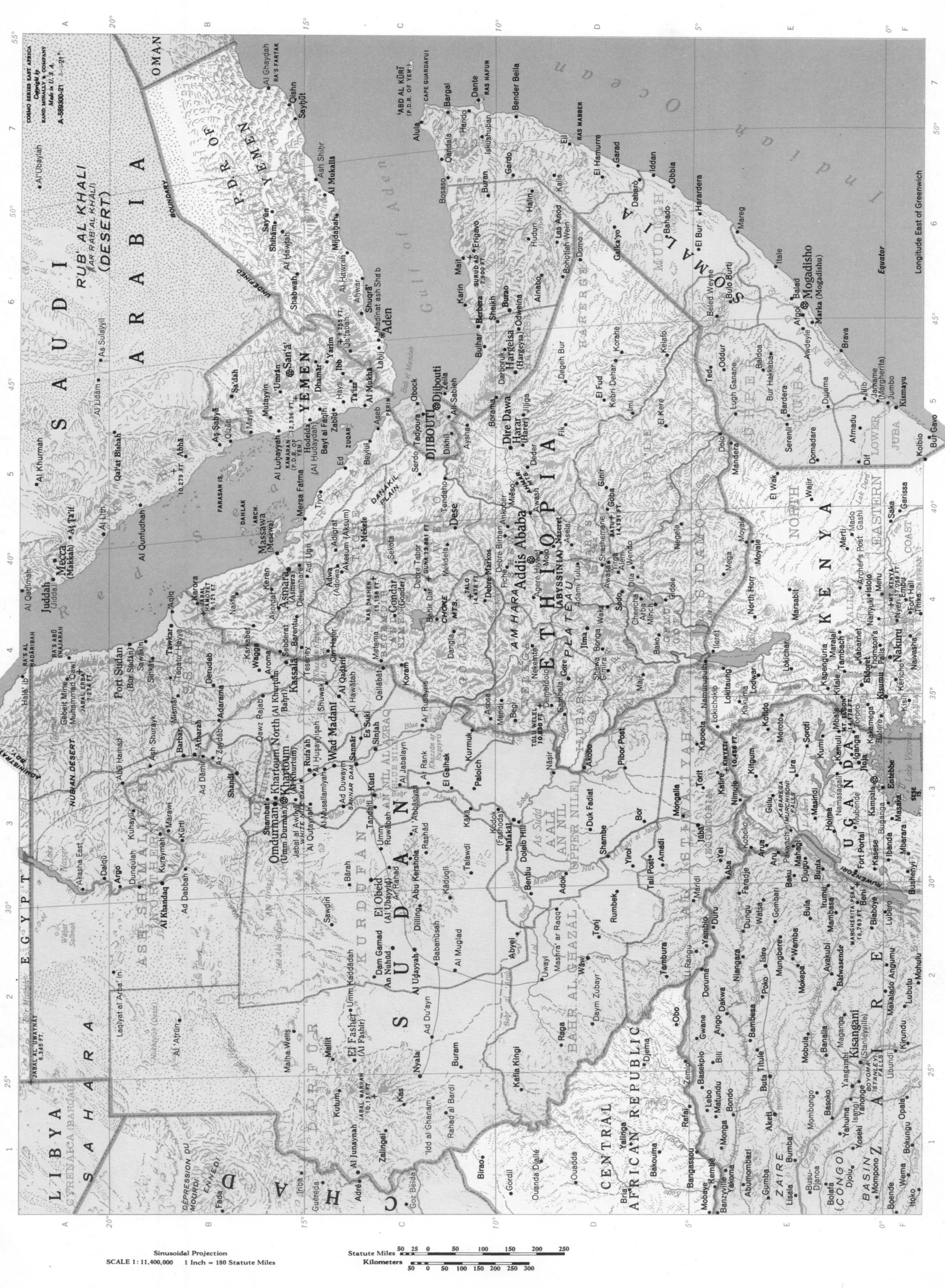

Sinusoidal Projection
SCALE 1: 11,400,000   1 Inch = 180 Statute Miles

Statute Miles   50 25 0   50   100   150   200   250
Kilometers   50 0   50   100   150   200   250   300

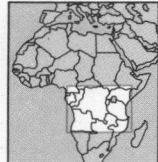

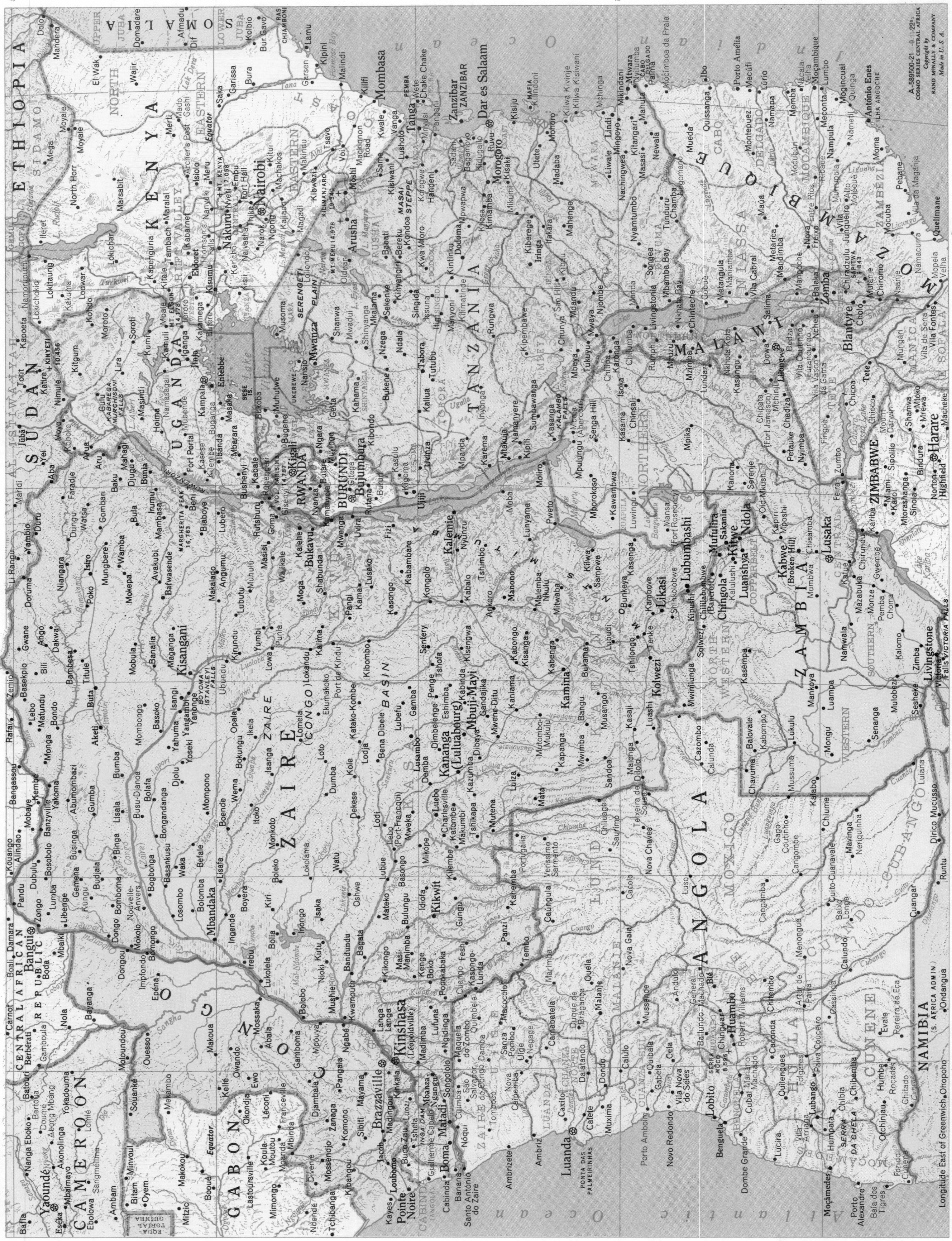

Statute Miles 50 0 50 100 150 200 250

50 0 50 100 150 200 250 300

Sinusoidal Projection

SCALE 1: 11,400,000   1 Inch = 180 Statute Miles

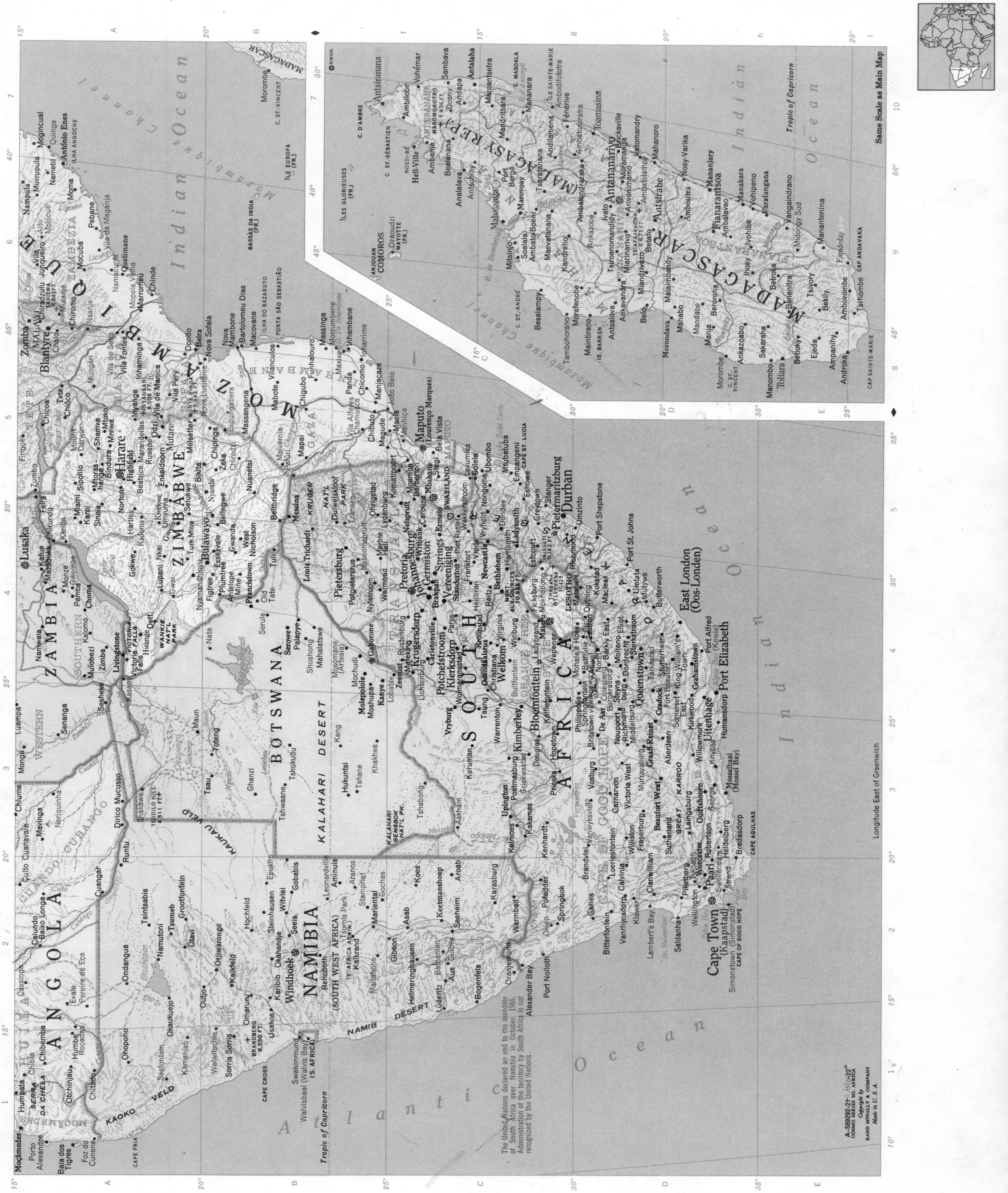

The United Nations declared an end to the mandate of South Africa over Namibia in October 1966. Administration of the territory by South Africa is not recognized by the United Nations.

Same Scale as Main Map

Sinusoidal Projection
SCALE 1:11,400,000   1 Inch = 180 Statute Miles

Statute Miles 50 25 0   50   100   150   200   250
Kilometers 50 0 50 100 150 200 250 300

A-589292-21- 111⅛22⁸
COSMO SERIES SO. AFRICA
Copyright by
RAND McNALLY & COMPANY
Made in U.S.A.

AUSTRALIA & OCEANIA

This region of the world is composed of the island continent of Australia, the substantial islands of New Zealand and New Guinea, clusters of smaller islands, and the many pinpoint atolls scattered throughout the expanse of the central and southern Pacific. Extreme isolation and their island nature are common characteristics held by these realms, but other similarities are few.

Australia's size compares with that of the forty-eight conterminous United States. Dry air masses sweep across the western interior from the west, creating the largest desert outside of the Sahara. Along the eastern coast higher temperatures and humidity have combined to produce climates conducive to a varied agricultural system, and therefore, the population is concentrated along this favorable coastal strip. The mountains of the east tend to isolate the population in a number of distinct clusters. Sydney, Melbourne, Brisbane, and Adelaide are the four principal centers, acting as chief exporters of the wool and wheat, and the importers, manufacturers, and distributors for the continent.

New Zealand, like Australia, is an enclave of a European settlement in the Pacific. Upon the vegetation of this climatically mild area the descendants of European settlers have established a thriving economy based upon the exportation of butter, beef, and mutton. The mountainous spine running the length of New Zealand provides some magnificent scenery and the gamut of climatic types.

New Guinea is closely related to both Indonesia and Melanesia, and so links Southeast Asia with Oceania. Although much larger, it typifies the larger islands of the Southwestern Pacific. Like New Guinea, these islands have a mountainous core and narrow, alluvial coastal plains. Upon the plains, under tropical heat and humidity, a variety of tropical agricultural products are raised and some of the islands, such as Fiji, have well developed commercial economies.

Unlike New Guinea and the larger islands are the speck-like atolls scattered throughout the central and southern Pacific. These South Sea Islands are famed for isolation, mild climate, and scenic beauty. But their size, limited resources, and small population, keep their economies at a subsistence level.

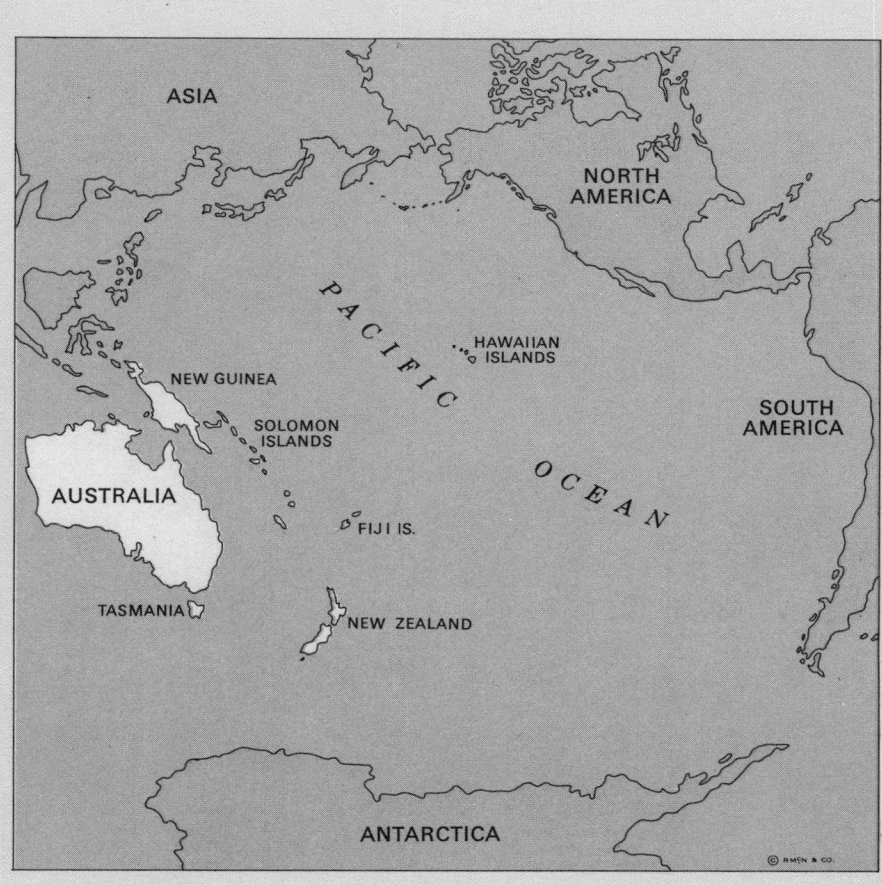

Statute Miles 100 0 100 200 300

Kilometers 100 0 100 200 300 400

Lambert Azimuthal Equal Area Projection
SCALE 1:16,000,000 1 Inch = 252 Statute Miles

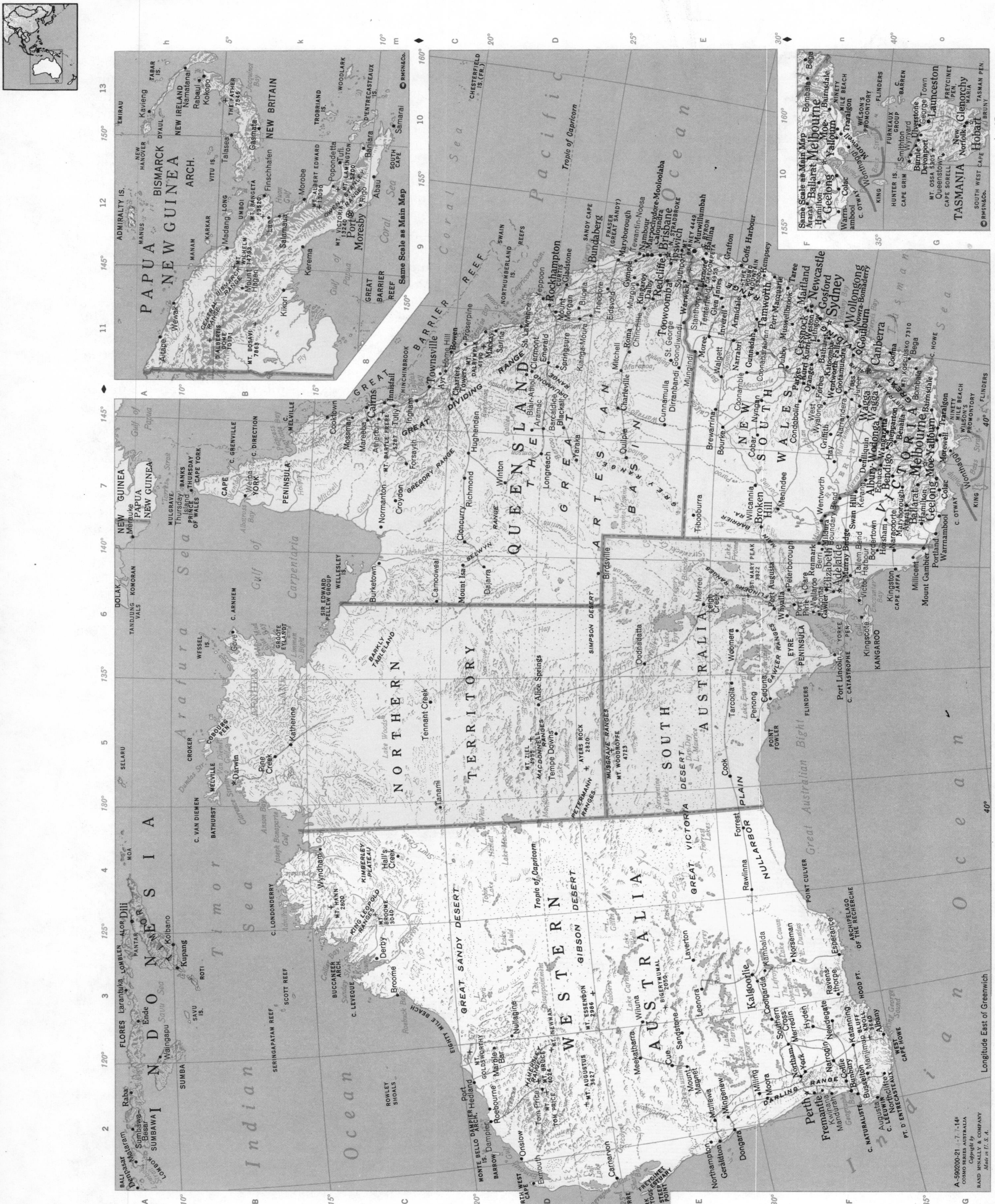

Lambert Conformal Conic Projection
SCALE 1 : 8,000,000 1 Inch = 126 Statute Miles

Statute Miles 50 0 50 100 150
Kilometers 50 0 50 100 200

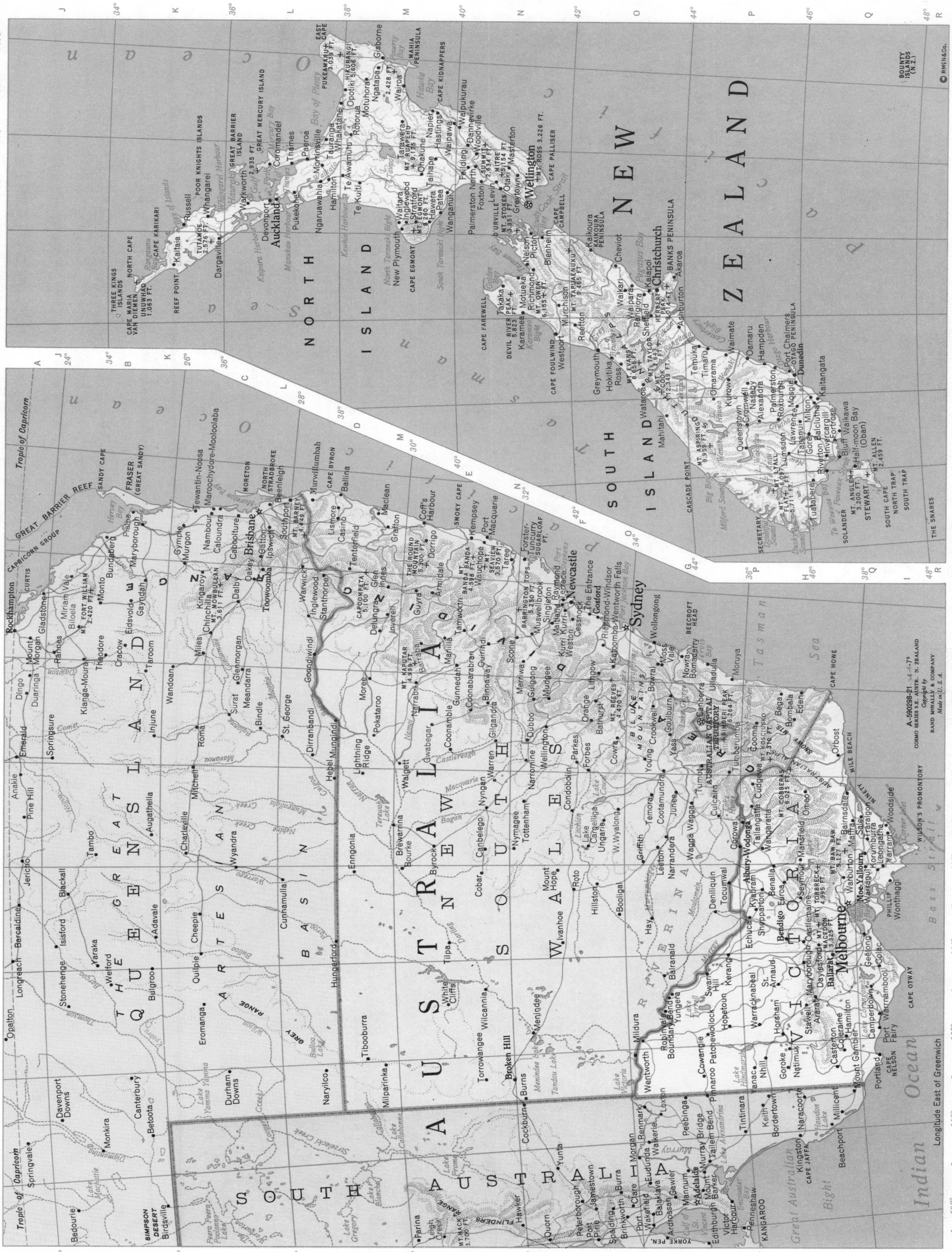

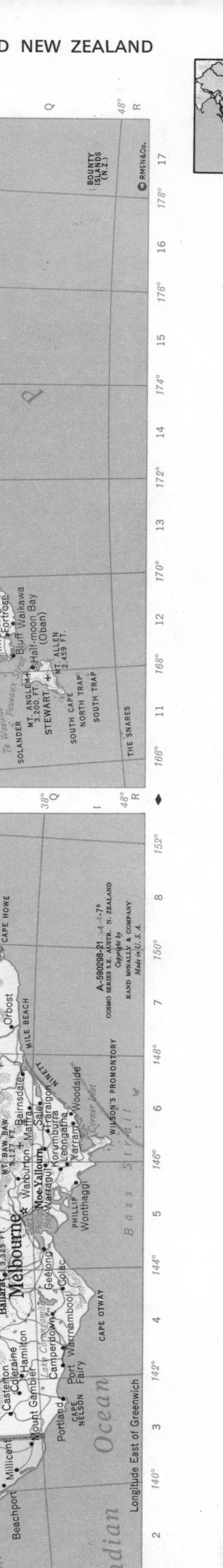

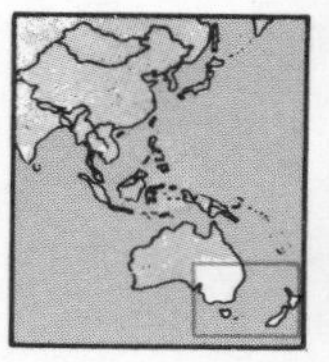

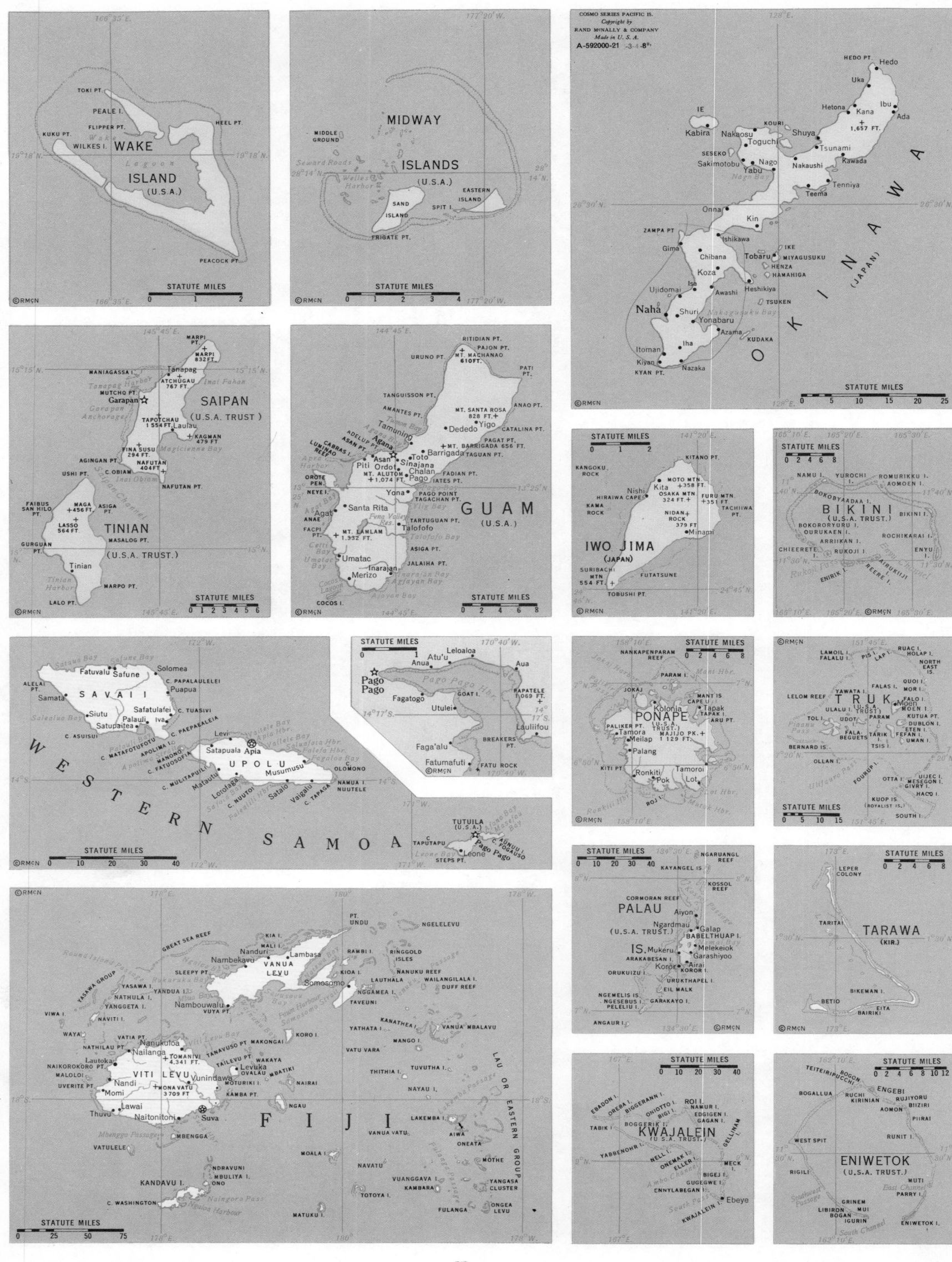
WAKE ISLAND (U.S.A.)
TOKI PT.
PEALE I.
FLIPPER PT.
KUKU PT.
WILKES I.
HEEL PT.
PEACOCK PT.
STATUTE MILES
MIDWAY ISLANDS (U.S.A.)
MIDDLE GROUND
SAND ISLAND
EASTERN ISLAND
SPIT I.
FRIGATE PT.
COSMO SERIES PACIFIC IS.
Copyright by RAND McNALLY & COMPANY
Made in U. S. A.
A-592000-21
OKINAWA (JAPAN)
HEDO PT.
Hedo
Uka
IE
Kabira
Nakaosu
Toguchi
Shuya
Hetona
Kana
Ibu
Ada
1,657 FT.
Tsunami
Kawada
Nakaushi
Sakimotobu
Nago
Yabu
Teema
Tenniya
Onna
Kin
ZAMPA PT.
Gima
Ishikawa
Chibana
Tobaru
Koza
Awashi
Heshikiya
Uji-domai
Naha
Shuri
Yonabaru
Azama
Iha
Itoman
Kiyan
KYAN PT.
Nazaka
KUDAKA
TSUKEN
MIYAGUSUKU
HENZA
HAMAHIGA
SAIPAN (U.S.A. TRUST)
MARPI PT.
MARPI 832 FT.
MANIAGASSA I.
Tanapag
ATCHUGAU 767 FT.
MUTCHO PT.
Garapan
TAPOTCHAU 1 554 FT.
Laulau
KAGMAN 479 FT.
FINA SUSU 294 FT.
AGINGAN PT.
NAFUTAN 404 FT.
USHI PT.
C. OBIAM
NAFUTAN PT.
TINIAN (U.S.A. TRUST.)
FAIBUS SAN HILO PT.
MAGA 456 FT.
ASIGA PT.
LASSO 564 FT.
MASALOG PT.
GURGUAN PT.
Tinian
MARPO PT.
LALO PT.
GUAM (U.S.A.)
RITIDIAN PT.
PAJON PT.
URUNO PT.
MT. MACHANAO 610 FT.
PATI PT.
TANGUISSON PT.
AMANTES PT.
MT. SANTA ROSA 828 FT.
ANAO PT.
Yigo
Dededo
Tamuning
CATALINA PT.
Agana
PAGAT PT.
MT. BARRIGADA 656 FT.
Barrigada
TAGUAN PT.
Asan
Piti
Ordot
Toto
Sinajana
Chalan Pago
MT. ALUTOM 1,074 FT.
FADIAN PT.
OROTE PEN.
NEYE I.
Yona
PAGO POINT
TAGACHAN PT.
Santa Rita
Agat
ANAE
TARTUGUAN PT.
FACPI PT.
MT. LAMLAM 1,332 FT.
Talofofo
ASIGA PT.
Umatac
JALAIHA PT.
Inarajan
Merizo
COCOS I.
IWO JIMA (JAPAN)
KITANO PT.
KANGOKU ROCK
Nishi
Kita
MOTO MTN +358 FT.
OSAKA MTN 324 FT.
FURU MTN. +351 FT.
HIRAIWA CAPE
KAMA ROCK
NIDAN ROCK 379 FT.
TACHIIWA PT.
Minami
SURIBACHI MTN 554 FT.
FUTATSUNE
TOBUSHI PT.
BIKINI (U.S.A. TRUST.)
NAMU I.
YUROCHI
ROMURIKKU I.
AOMOEN I.
BOKOBYAADAA I.
BOKORORYURU I.
OURUKAEN I.
ARRIIKAN I.
ROCHIKARAI I.
CHIEERETE I.
RUKOJI I.
ENYU I.
ENIRIK I.
REERE I.
AIRUKIIJI
WESTERN SAMOA
SAVAII
Fatuvalu
Safune
Solomea
ALELAI PT.
Samata
C. PAPALAULELEI
Puapua
Safatulafei
C. TUASIVI
Siutu
Palauli
Iva
Satupaitea
C. ASUISUI
C. MATAFOTUFOTU
APOLIMA I.
MANONO I.
C. FATUOSOFIA
UPOLU
Levi
Apia
Satapuala
Musumusu
OLOMONO
C. MULITAPUILI
Mataut
Lorofaga
C. NUUTOI
Satalo
Vaigalu
C. TAPAGA
NAMUA I.
NUUTELE
Pago Pago
Leloaloa
Atu'u
Anua
Aua
Fagatogo
GOAT I.
PAPATELE 1,069 FT.
Utulei
Lauliifou
BREAKERS PT.
Faga'alu
Fatumafuti
FATU ROCK
TUTUILA (U.S.A.)
C. TAPUTAPU
Leone
STEPS PT.
C. FOGAUSO
AUNUU I.
PONAPE (U.S.A. TRUST.)
NANKAPENPARAM REEF
PARAM I.
JOKAJ
MANT IS
CAPE
Kolonia
Tapak
TAPAK I.
ARU PT.
PALIKER PT.
Tamora
Meilap
MAJIJO PK. 1 129 FT.
Palang
KITI PT.
Ronkiti
Pok
Tamoroi
Lot
ROJ I.
TRUK (U.S.A. TRUST)
LAMOIL I.
FALALU I.
PIS I.
LAP I.
RUAC I.
HOLAP I.
NORTH EAST IS.
QUOI I.
MOR I.
FALAS I.
YAWATA I.
LELOM REEF
ULALU I.
FALO I.
Moen
MOEN I.
TOL I.
UDOT
PARAM
KUTUA PT.
DUBLON I.
ETEN I.
FEFAN I.
UMAN I.
FALA-BEGUETS
TARIK
TSIS I.
BERNARD IS.
OLLAN I.
FOURUP I.
OTTA I.
UIJEC I.
MESEGON I.
GIVRY I.
HACO I.
KUOP IS.
SOUTH I.
PALAU IS. (U.S.A. TRUST.)
NGARUANGL REEF
KAYANGEL IS.
KOSSOL REEF
CORMORAN REEF
Aiyon
Ngardmau
Galap
BABELTHUAP I.
Melekeiok
Garashiyoo
Mukeru
ARAKABESAN I.
Airai
Koror
KOROR I.
ORUKUIZU I.
URUKTHAPEL I.
EIL MALK
NGEMELIS IS.
NGESEBUS I.
PELELIU I.
GARAKAYO I.
ANGAUR I.
TARAWA (KIR.)
LEPER COLONY
TARITAI
BIKEMAN I.
BETIO
EITA
BAIRIKI
FIJI
PT. UNDU
NGELELEVU
KIA I.
MALI I.
GREAT SEA REEF
Nanduri
Lambasa
Nambekavu
VANUA LEVU
RAMBI I.
RINGGOLD ISLES
SLEEPY PT.
NANUKU REEF
YASAWA GROUP
YASAWA I.
YANDUA I.
Somosomo
KIOA I.
LAUTHALA
WAILANGILALA I.
DUFF REEF
NATHULA I.
YANGGETA I.
Nambouwalu
NGGAMEA I.
TAVEUNI
VIWA I.
NAVITI I.
VUYA PT.
KANATHEA I.
VANUA MBALAVU
YATHATA I.
WAYA
VATIA PT.
KORO I.
MANGO I.
NATHILAU PT.
Nanukuloa
TANAVUSO PT.
MAKONGAI
Nailanga
Lautoka
TOMANIVI 4,341 FT.
TAILEVU PT.
WAKAYA
VATU VARA
LAU OR EASTERN GROUP
NAIKOROKORO PT.
Levuka
OVALAU
MBATIKI
MALOLO I.
VITI LEVU
Vunindawa
THITHIA I.
TUVUTHA I.
UVERITE PT.
Nandi
MOTURIKI I.
NAIRAI
Momi
MONAVATU 3 709 FT.
NAYAU I.
KAMBA PT.
Lawai
Thuvu
Naitonitoni
Suva
NGAU
LAKEMBA I.
VANUA VATU
AIWA
MBENGGA
ONEATA
VATULELE I.
MOALA I.
MOTHE
NDRAVUNI
MBULIYA I.
ONO
NAVATU
VUANGGAVA I.
KAMBARA
YANGASA CLUSTER
KANDAVU I.
TOTOYA I.
C. WASHINGTON
MATUKU I.
FULANGA
ONGEA LEVU
KWAJALEIN (U.S.A. TRUST.)
EBADON I.
OMEBA I.
BIGGERANN I.
ROI I.
NAMUR I.
ENNUBIRR I.
GAGAN I.
TABIK I.
YABBENOHR I.
GELLINAM
NELL I.
MECK I.
BIGEJ I.
GUGEGWE I.
ENNYLABEGAN I.
Ebeye
KWAJALEIN I.
ENIWETOK (U.S.A. TRUST.)
TEITEIRIPUCCHI
BOGON
ENGEBI
BOGALLUA
RUCHI
KIRINIAN
RUJIYORU
BIIZIRI
AOMON
PIIRAI
WEST SPIT
RUNIT I.
RIGILI
MUTI
PARRY I.
GRINEM
LIBIRON
BOGAN
MUI
IGURIN
ENIWETOK I.
©RMcN

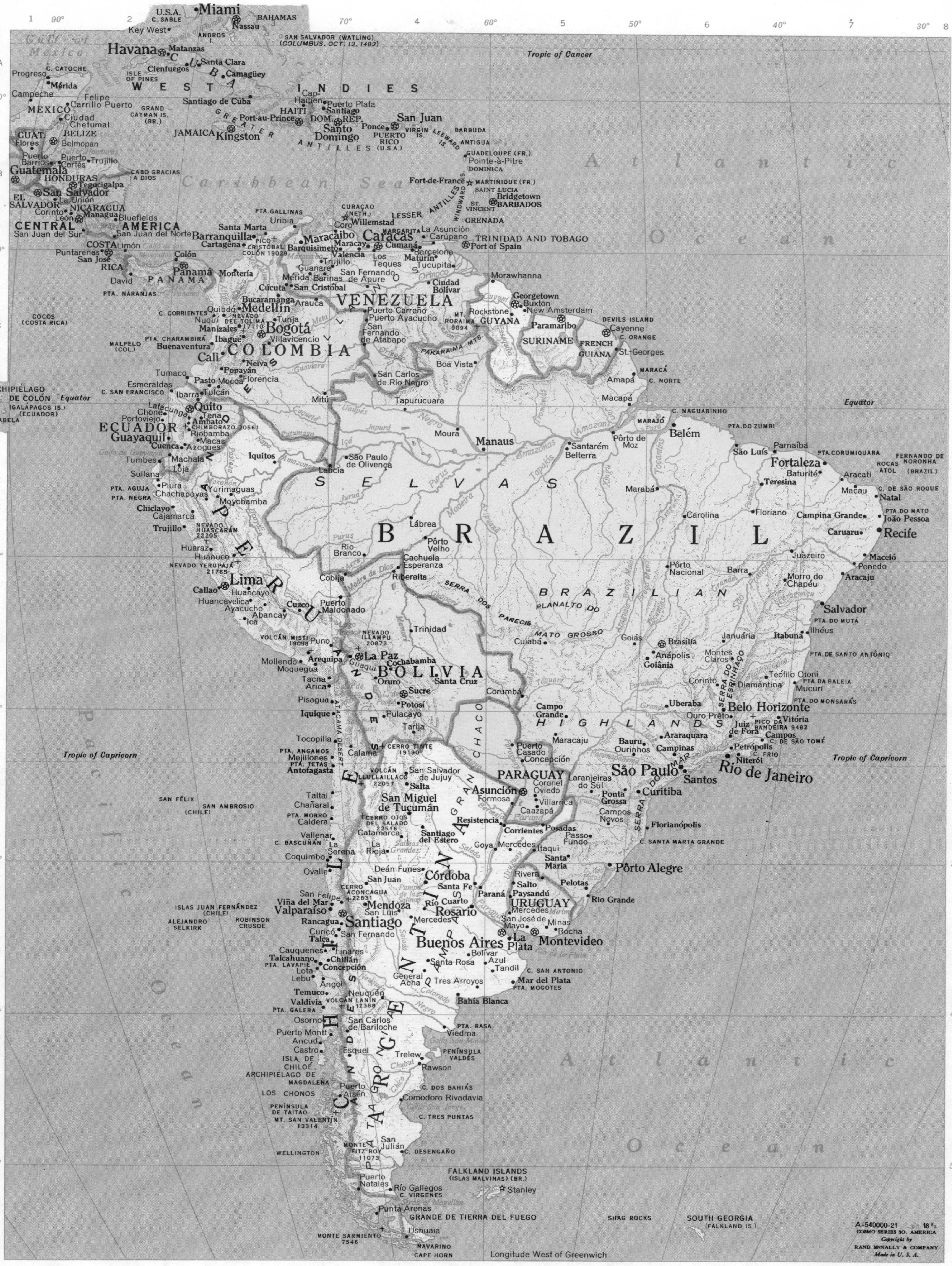

BRAZIL

Sinusoidal Projection
SCALE 1 : 29,465,000   1 Inch = 465 Statute Miles

Statute Miles 100 0 100   300   500   700
Kilometers 100 0 100 300 500 700 900 1100

A-540000-21
COSMO SERIES SO. AMERICA
Copyright by
RAND M⊂NALLY & COMPANY
Made in U.S.A.

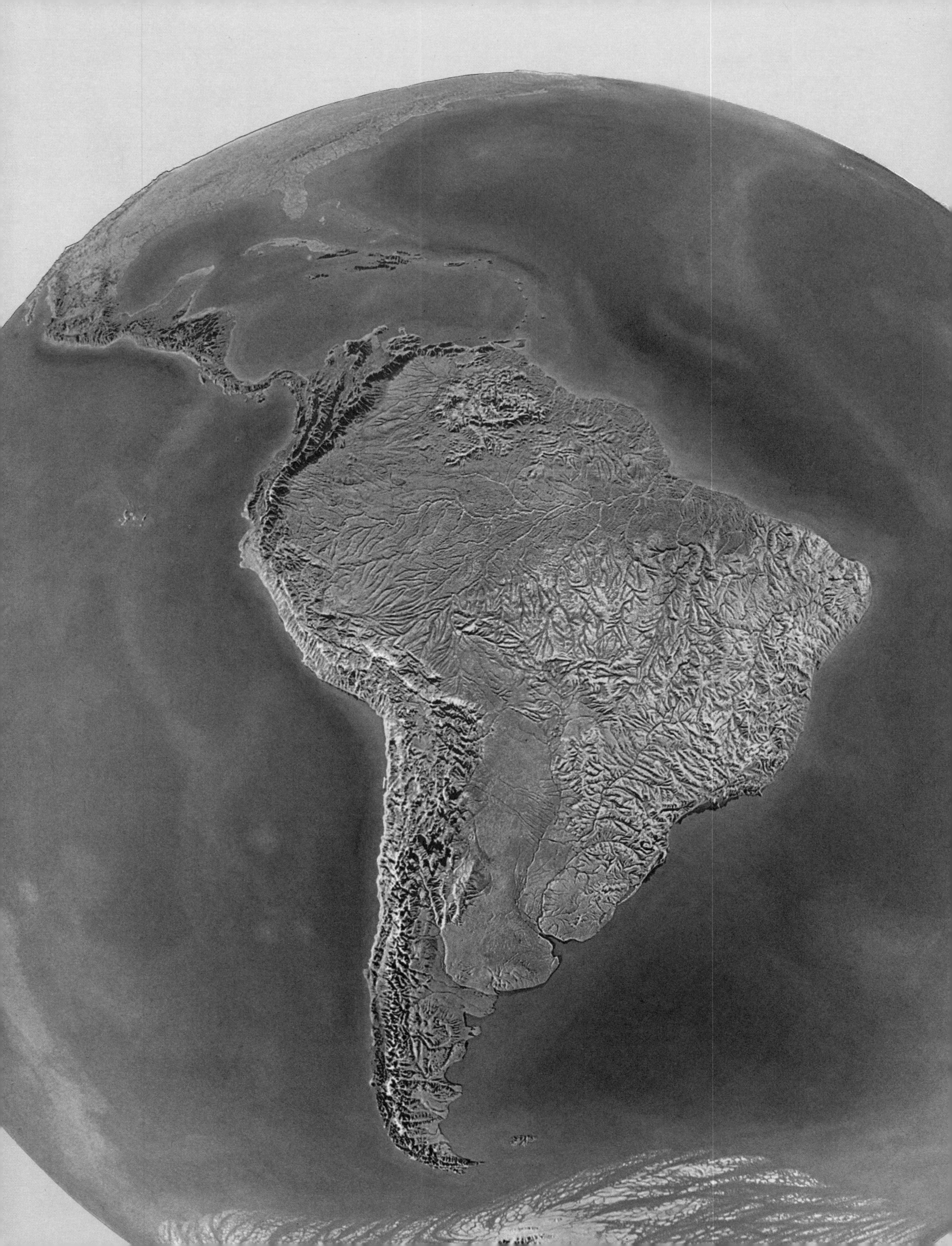

SOUTH AMERICA

Triangularly shaped South America is surrounded by water except at the narrow Isthmus of Panama. No great peninsulas extend into its seas or oceans, and its outlines are more regular than those of most other continents.

The Andes Mountains rise like a wall along the western shores, and this formidable chain runs the entire length of the continent, rising to altitudes of over 20,000 feet. It is the longest continuous mountain chain in the world.

The bulk of the continent slopes eastward from the eastern face of the Andes. From north to south, landforms include plains drained by the Orinoco and the eroded plateau areas of the Guiana and Brazilian highlands, the tropical lowlands of the Amazon Basin, savanna called the Gran Chaco, which is drained by the Paraná-Paraguay-Plata river systems, the pampas, and the plains of Patagonia.

The shape of the continent, its position astride the Equator, the water surrounding it, and the mountainous terrain have resulted in a variety of climates. The area east of the Andes from Venezuela to Northern Argentina, is dominated by moisture-laden air masses of the Atlantic. This two-thirds of the continent has a tropical or subtropical environment. Most of the remaining portion is under the influence of the relatively dry, cool Pacific air masses, which create the driest region in the world —the Atacama Desert of Chile. These cool Pacific air masses, too, on crossing the Andes in the narrow southern portion of the continent, create the Patagonian Desert of Argentina. In the higher altitudes of the mountain chain climates familiar to mid and upper latitudes are found.

Much of the interior of South America is still inaccessible, owing to extensive regions of mountains or jungle. Most of the settlement has been around the periphery of the continent. Spanish and Portuguese settlers, and later Germans and Italians, have developed highly specialized commercial economies in certain of the peripheral areas. Around Buenos Aires, São Paulo, Santiago, Bogotá economies based on agricultural products have been developed— wheat, beef, coffee, citrus fruit to name a few. Exported minerals—oil from Venezuela, tin from Bolivia, and copper from Chile— are economic mainstays of other countries.

Longitude West of Greenwich

Statute Miles 50 0 50 100 150

Kilometers 50 0 50 100 150 200

Oblique Conic Conformal Projection
SCALE 1:8,000,000 1 Inch = 126 Statute Miles

Same Scale as Main Map

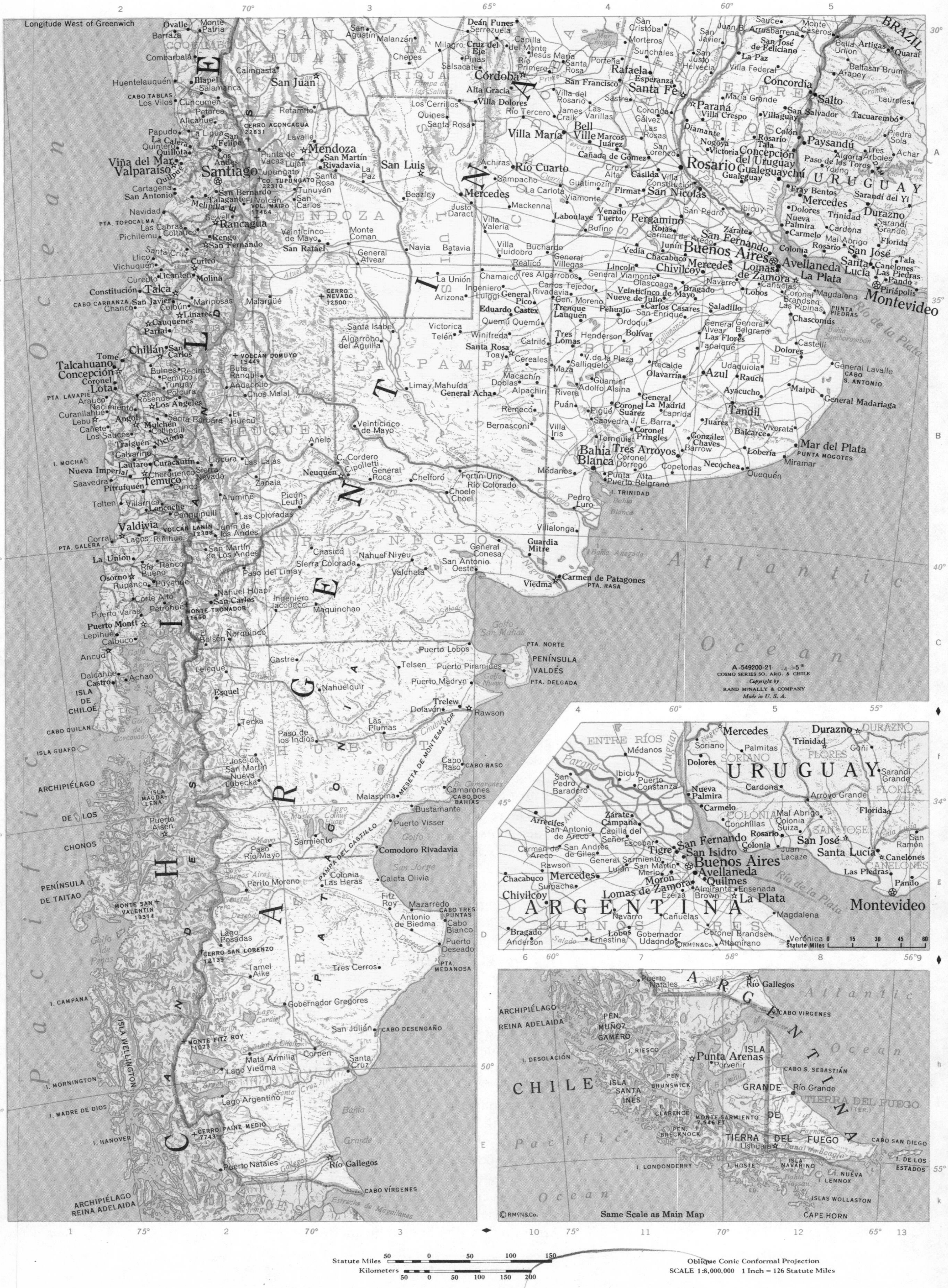

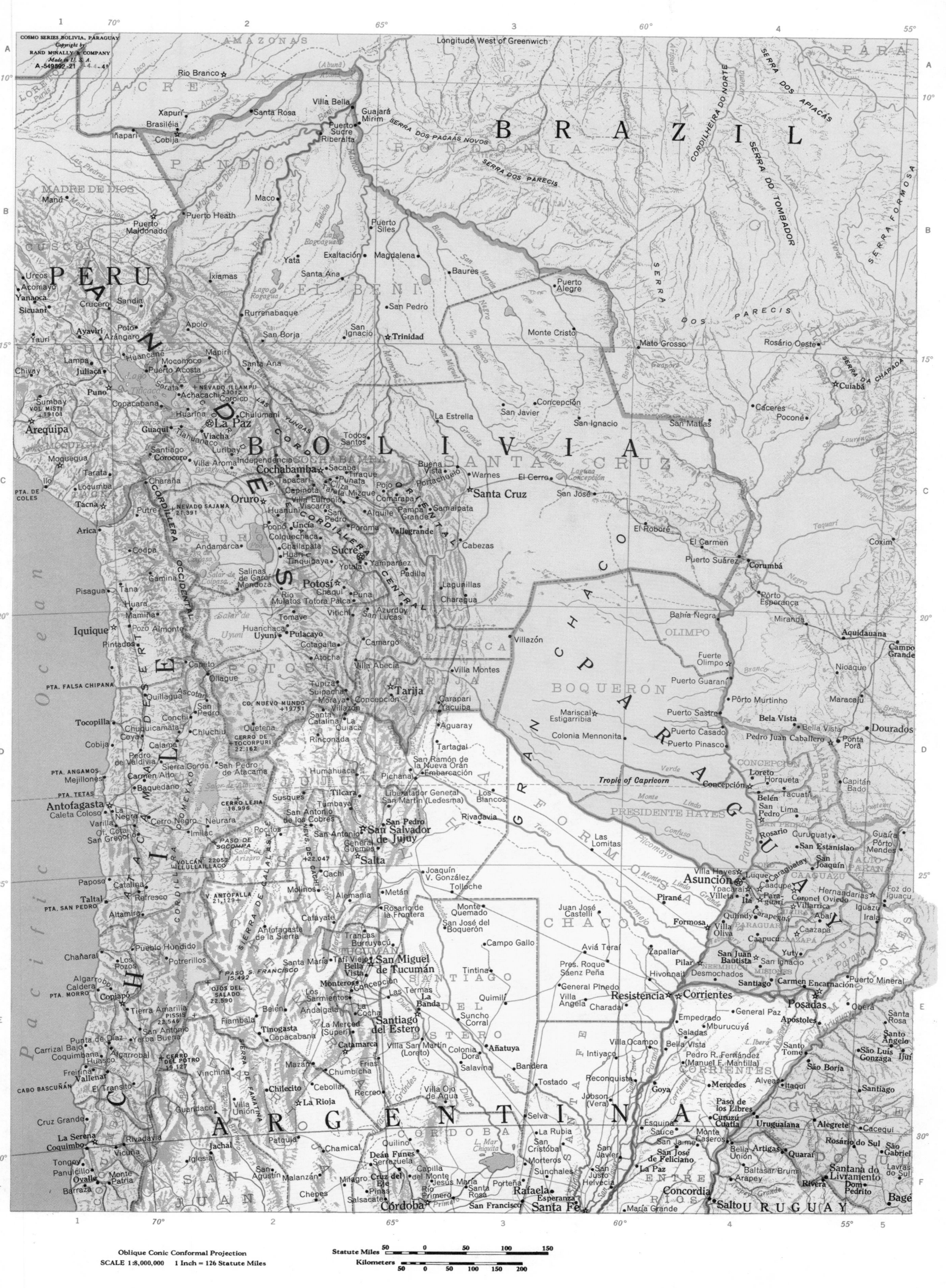
COSMO SERIES BOLIVIA, PARAGUAY
Copyright by RAND McNALLY & COMPANY
Made in U. S. A.
A-549592-21
Longitude West of Greenwich
BRAZIL
PERU
BOLIVIA
PARAGUAY
ARGENTINA
CHILE
URUGUAY
ANDES
Pacific Ocean
Tropic of Capricorn
GRAN CHACO
Rio Branco
Cobija
Riberalta
Puerto Heath
Trinidad
La Paz
Cochabamba
Santa Cruz
Oruro
Sucre
Potosí
Tarija
Corumbá
Cuiabá
Arequipa
Puno
Iquique
Antofagasta
Copiapó
La Serena
Coquimbo
Asunción
Concepción
Villa Hayes
Encarnación
Posadas
Corrientes
Resistencia
Formosa
Salta
San Salvador de Jujuy
San Miguel de Tucumán
Santiago del Estero
Catamarca
La Rioja
Córdoba
Santa Fe
Rafaela
Paraná
Concordia
Salto
Uruguaiana
Oblique Conic Conformal Projection
SCALE 1:8,000,000 1 Inch = 126 Statute Miles
Statute Miles 50 0 50 100 150
Kilometers 50 0 50 100 150 200

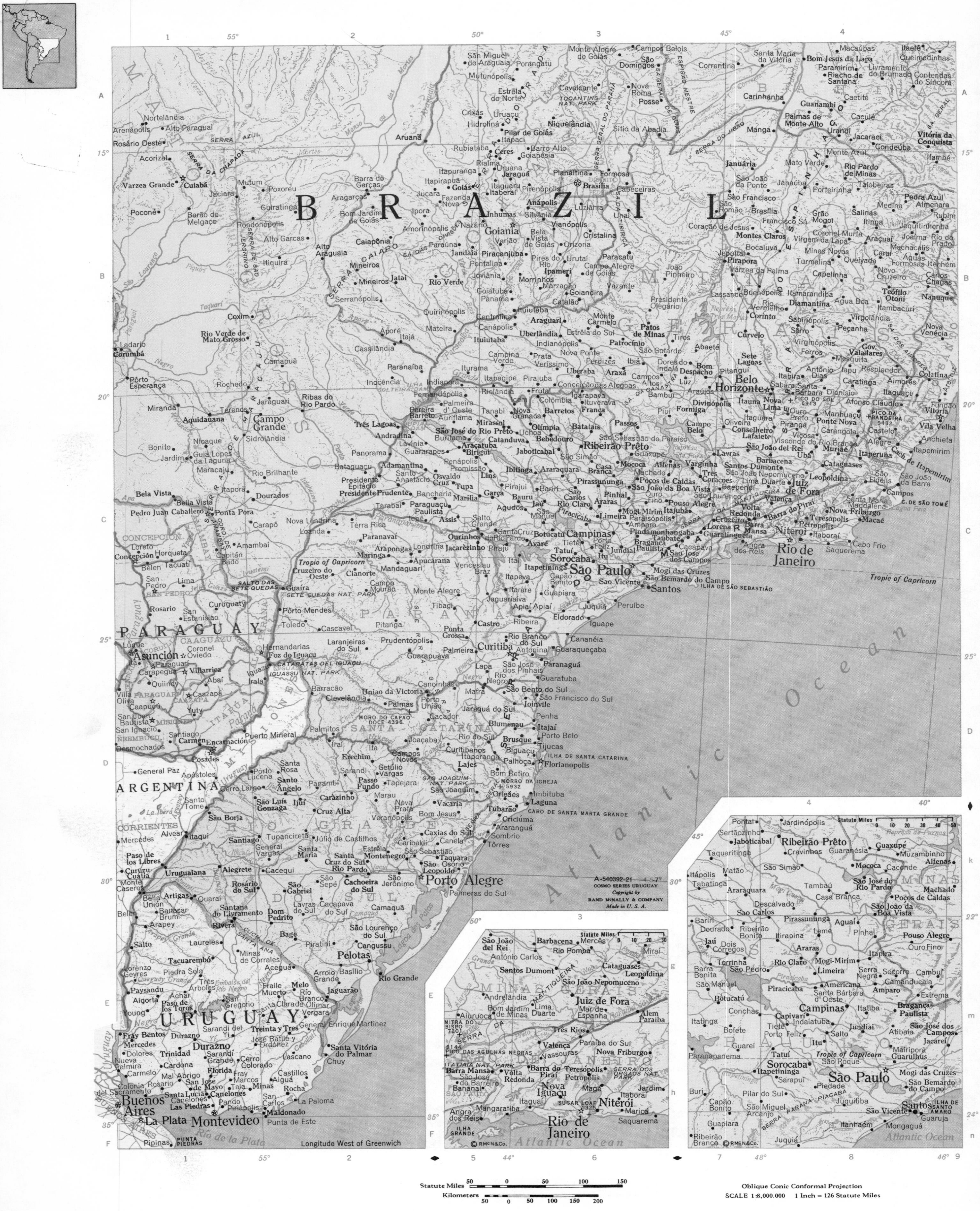

Oblique Conic Conformal Projection
SCALE 1:8,000,000   1 Inch = 126 Statute Miles

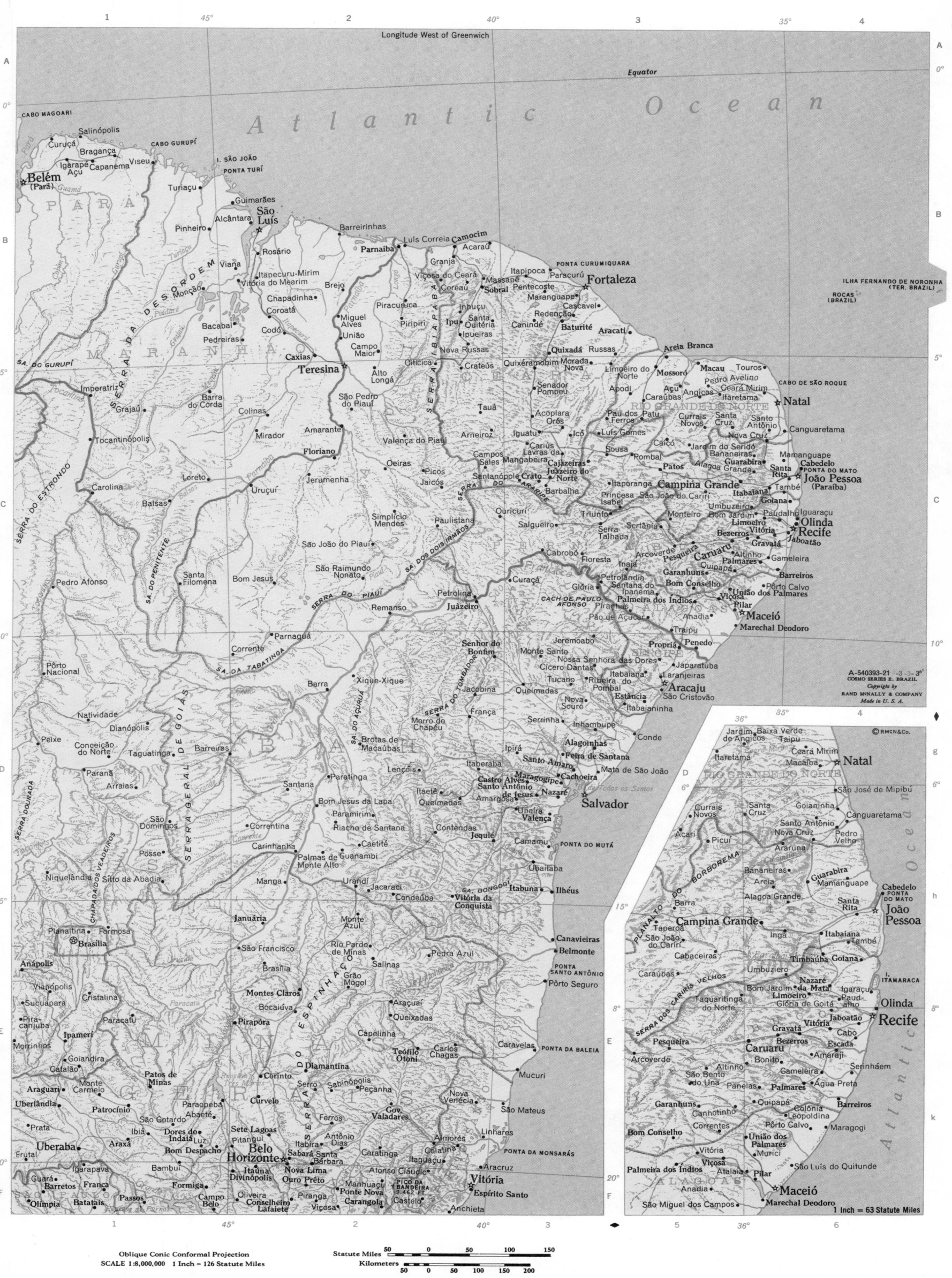

EASTERN BRAZIL

Longitude West of Greenwich

Equator

Atlantic Ocean

A-540393-21 -3-3-3ᴿ¹
COSMO SERIES E. BRAZIL
Copyright by
RAND MᶜNALLY & COMPANY
Made in U. S. A.

© RMᶜN&Co.

Oblique Conic Conformal Projection
SCALE 1:8,000,000   1 Inch = 126 Statute Miles

Statute Miles   50 0 50 100 150
Kilometers   50 0 50 100 150 200

1 Inch = 63 Statute Miles

COLOMBIA

ECUADOR

PERU

BRAZIL

BOLIVIA

CHILE

VENEZUELA

Pacific Ocean

Equator

ARCHIPIÉLAGO DE COLÓN
(GALÁPAGOS IS.)
(ECUADOR)

Same Scale as Main Map

A-549400-21
COSMO SERIES PERU, ECUADOR
Copyright by
RAND McNALLY & COMPANY
Made in U. S. A.

Longitude West of Greenwich

Statute Miles 50 0 50 100 150

Kilometers 50 0 50 100 150 200

Oblique Conic Conformal Projection
SCALE 1:8,000,000 1 Inch = 126 Statute Miles

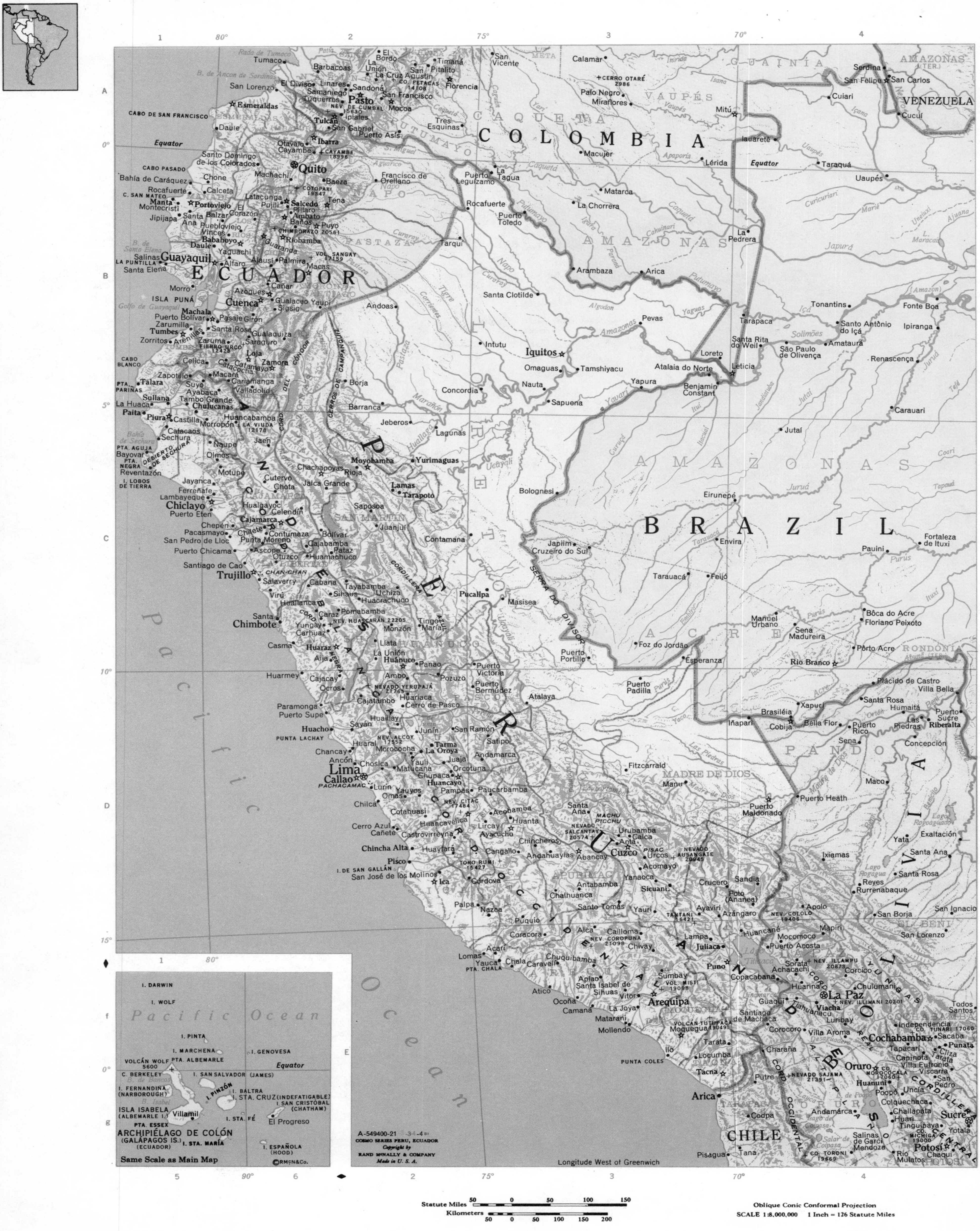

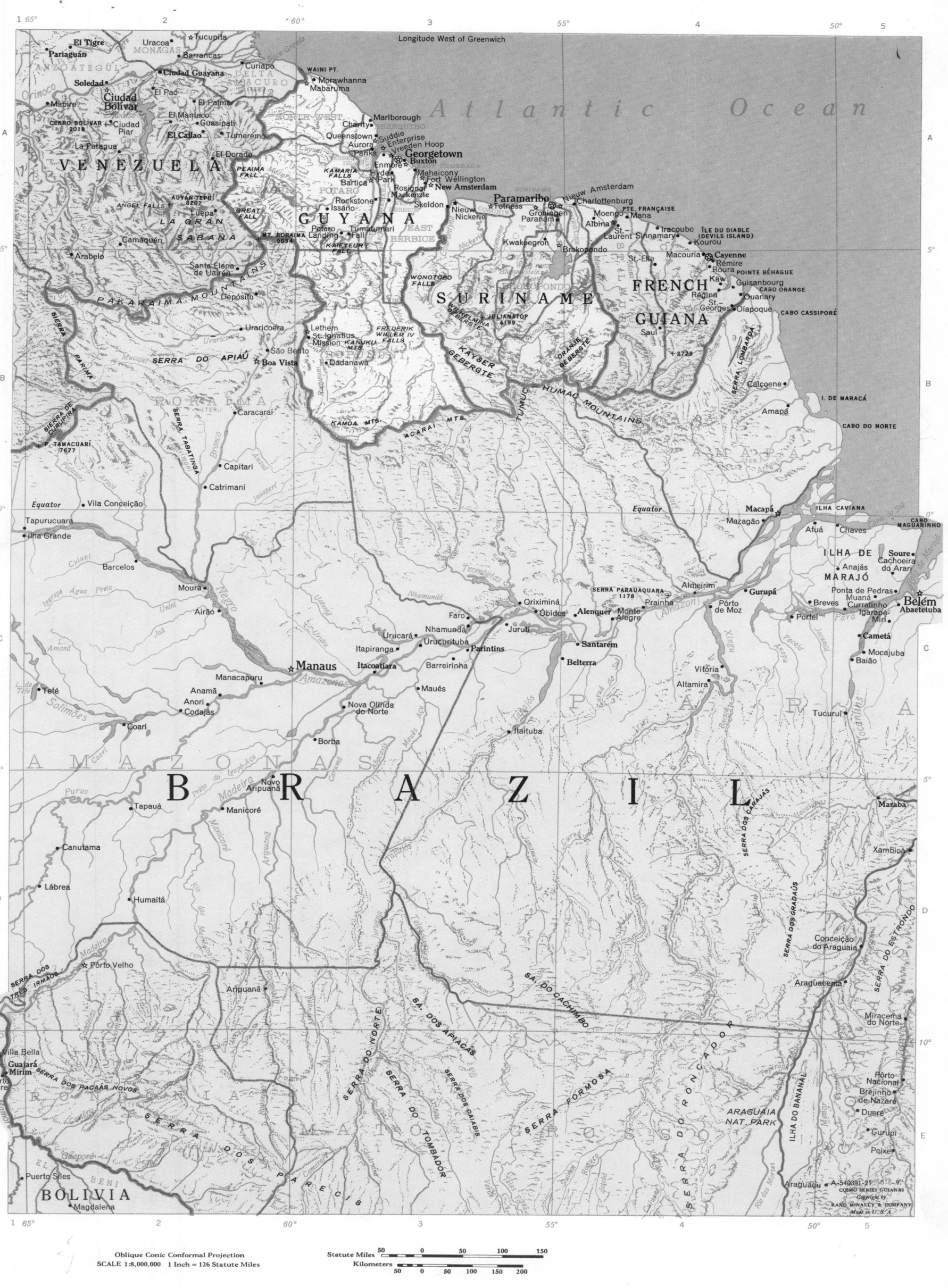
Longitude West of Greenwich
Atlantic Ocean
VENEZUELA
GUYANA
SURINAME
FRENCH GUIANA
BRAZIL
BOLIVIA
AMAZONAS
PARÁ
AMAPÁ
RORAIMA (TER.)
RONDÔNIA
MATO GROSSO
Equator
El Tigre
Pariaguán
Uracoa
Tucupita
Barrancas
Curiapo
Ciudad Guayana
Soledad
Ciudad Bolívar
Mapire
El Pao
El Palmar
El Manteco
Guasipati
CERRO BOLÍVAR 2018
Ciudad Piar
El Callao
Tumeremo
La Paragua
El Dorado
ANGEL FALLS
AUYAN-TEPUÍ 2602
Luepa
LA GRAN SABANA
Camaquén
Arabelo
Santa Elena de Uairén
PAKARAIMA MOUNTAINS
Depósito
SIERRA PARIMA
Uraricoera
SERRA DO APIAÚ
São Bento
Boa Vista
Caracaraí
SERRA TABATINGA
SIERRA DE CURUPIRA
P. TAMACUARÍ 7677
Capitari
Catrimani
Vila Conceição
WAINI PT.
Morawhanna
Mabaruma
NORTH WEST
Marlborough
Charity
Queenstown
Suddie
Aurora
Enterprise
Parika
Vreeden Hoop
Georgetown
Buxton
Enmore
Hyde Park
Mahaicony
Fort Wellington
Bartica
KAMARIA FALLS
PEAIMA FALL
Rosignol
New Amsterdam
Mackenzie
Rockstone
Skeldon
Issano
MT. RORAIMA 9094
GREAT FALL
Potaro Landing
Tumatumari Fall
KAIETEUR FALL
EAST BERBICE
Lethem
St. Ignatius Mission
KANUKU MTS.
Dadanawa
FREDERIK WILLEM IV FALLS
KAMOA MTS.
ACARAI MTS.
Nieuw Nickerie
Totness
Paramaribo
Groningen
Paranam
Nieuw Amsterdam
Charlottenburg
Moengo
Albina
PTE. FRANÇAISE
Mana
St.-Laurent
Iracoubo
Sinnamary
ÎLE DU DIABLE (DEVILS ISLAND)
Kourou
WONOTOBO FALLS
Kwakoegron
Brokopondo
JULIANATOP 4199
WILHELMINA GEBERGTE
KAYSER GEBERGTE
ORANJE GEBERGTE
TUMUC HUMAC MOUNTAINS
St.-Elie
Macouria
Cayenne
Rémire
Roura
Kaw
POINTE BÉHAGUE
Guisanbourg
CABO ORANGE
Régina
St.-Georges
Ouanary
Oiapoque
CABO CASSIPORÉ
Saül
2723
SERRA LOMBARDA
Calçoene
I. DE MARACÁ
Amapá
CABO DO NORTE
Macapá
Mazagão
ILHA CAVIANA
CABO MAGUARINHO
Afuá
Chaves
ILHA DE MARAJÓ
Soure
Cachoeira do Arari
Anajás
Ponta de Pedras
Muaná
Breves
Curralinho
Belém
Abaetetuba
Igarapé-Miri
Gurupá
Portel
Cametá
Mocajuba
Baião
Tucuruí
Almeirim
Prainha
Pôrto de Moz
SERRA PARAUAQUARA 1178
Monte Alegre
Alenquer
Óbidos
Oriximiná
Santarém
Belterra
Faro
Juruti
Nhamundá
Urucará
Itapiranga
Urucurituba
Parintins
Itacoatiara
Barreirinha
Maués
Manaus
Manacapuru
Anamã
Anori
Codajás
Tefé
Coari
Nova Olinda do Norte
Borba
Novo Aripuanã
Manicoré
Tapauá
Canutama
Lábrea
Humaitá
Tapurucuara
Ilha Grande
Barcelos
Moura
Airão
Vitória
Altamira
Itaituba
Marabá
Xambioá
Conceição do Araguaia
Araguacema
Miracema do Norte
Pôrto Nacional
Brejinho de Nazaré
Dueré
Gurupi
Peixe
Araguaçu
SERRA DOS CARAJÁS
SERRA DOS GRADAÚS
SERRA DO ESTRONDO
SA. DO CACHIMBO
SA. DOS APIACÁS
SERRA DOS CAIABIS
SERRA DO NORTE
SERRA DO TOMBADOR
SERRA FORMOSA
SERRA DO RONCADOR
ARAGUAIA NAT. PARK
ILHA DO BANANAL
SERRA DOS PARECIS
SERRA DOS PACAÁS NOVOS
SERRA DOS TRÊS IRMÃOS
Pôrto Velho
Aripuanã
Vila Bella
Guajará-Mirim
Puerto Sucre
Puerto Siles
Magdalena
PANDO
BENI
Amazonas
Solimões
Negro
Madeira
Purus
Tapajós
Xingu
Tocantins
Araguaia
Trombetas
Branco
A-540391-21
RAND McNALLY & COMPANY
Made in U. S. A.
Oblique Conic Conformal Projection
SCALE 1:8,000,000 1 Inch = 126 Statute Miles
Statute Miles 50 0 50 100 150
Kilometers 50 0 50 100 150 200

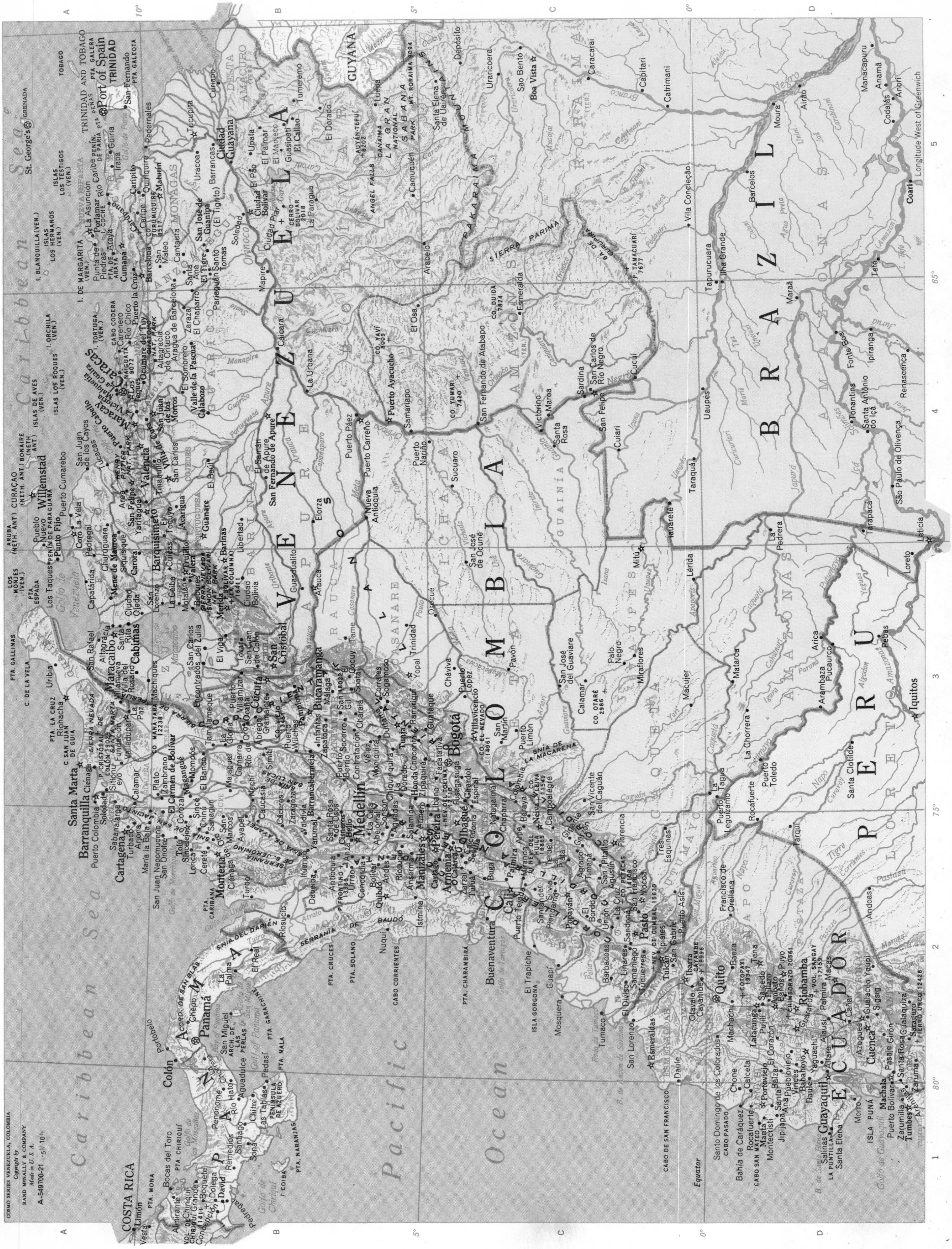

Statute Miles 50 0 50 100 150
Kilometers 50 0 50 100 150 200

Oblique Conic Conformal Projection
SCALE 1:8,000,000 1 Inch = 126 Statute Miles

COSMO SERIES VENEZUELA, COLOMBIA
Copyright
RAND MCNALLY & COMPANY
Made in U. S. A.
A-549700-21

A-520000-21 -3-7-9
COSMO SERIES NO. AMERICA
Copyright by
RAND McNALLY & COMPANY
Made in U. S. A.

Same Scale as Main Map

© RM&Co.

Longitude West of Greenwich

Lambert Azimuthal Equal Area Projection
SCALE 1:31,977,000 1 Inch = 490 Statute Miles

Statute Miles 100 0 100 200 300 400 500 600 700 800

Kilometers 100 0 100 200 400 600 800 1000

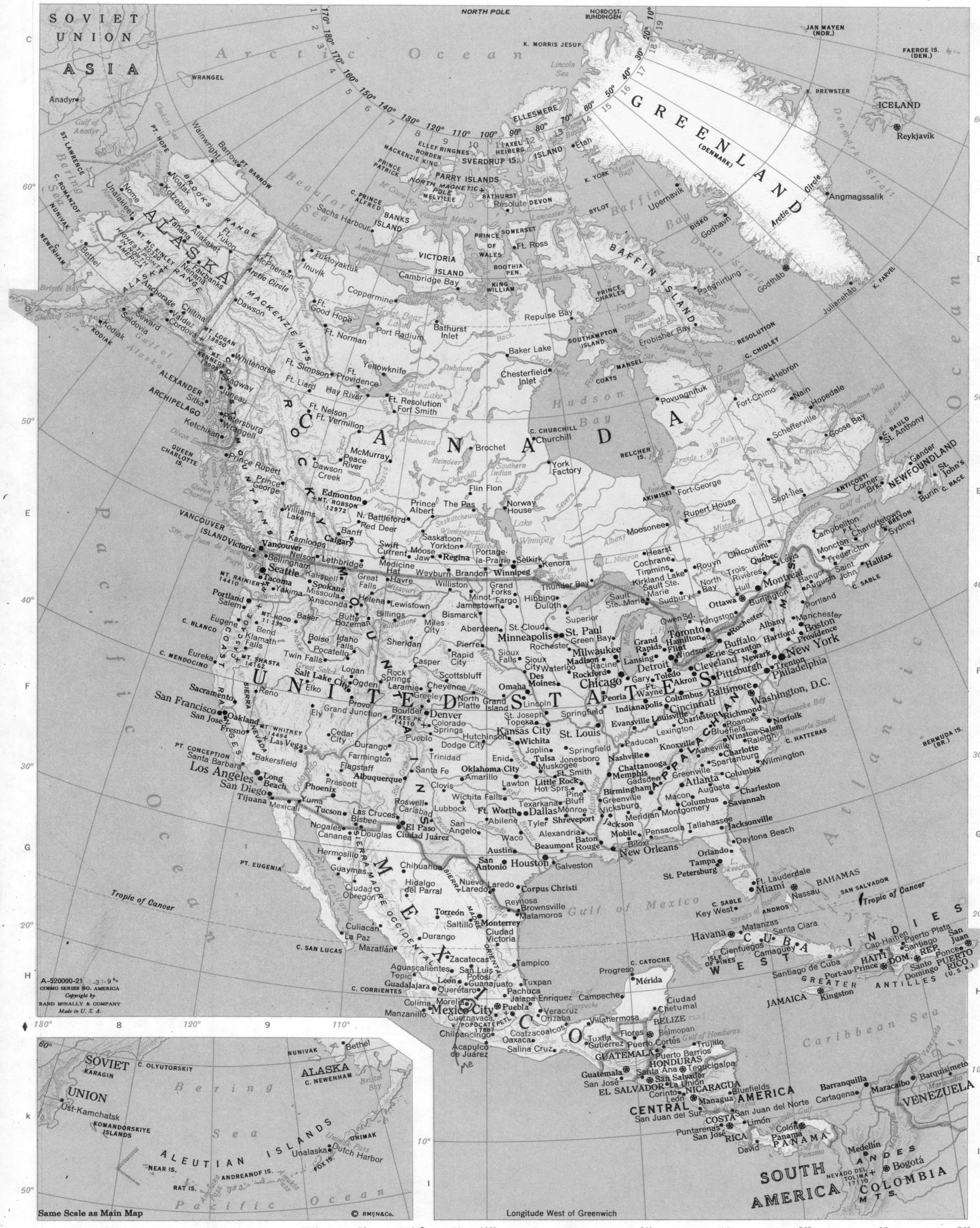

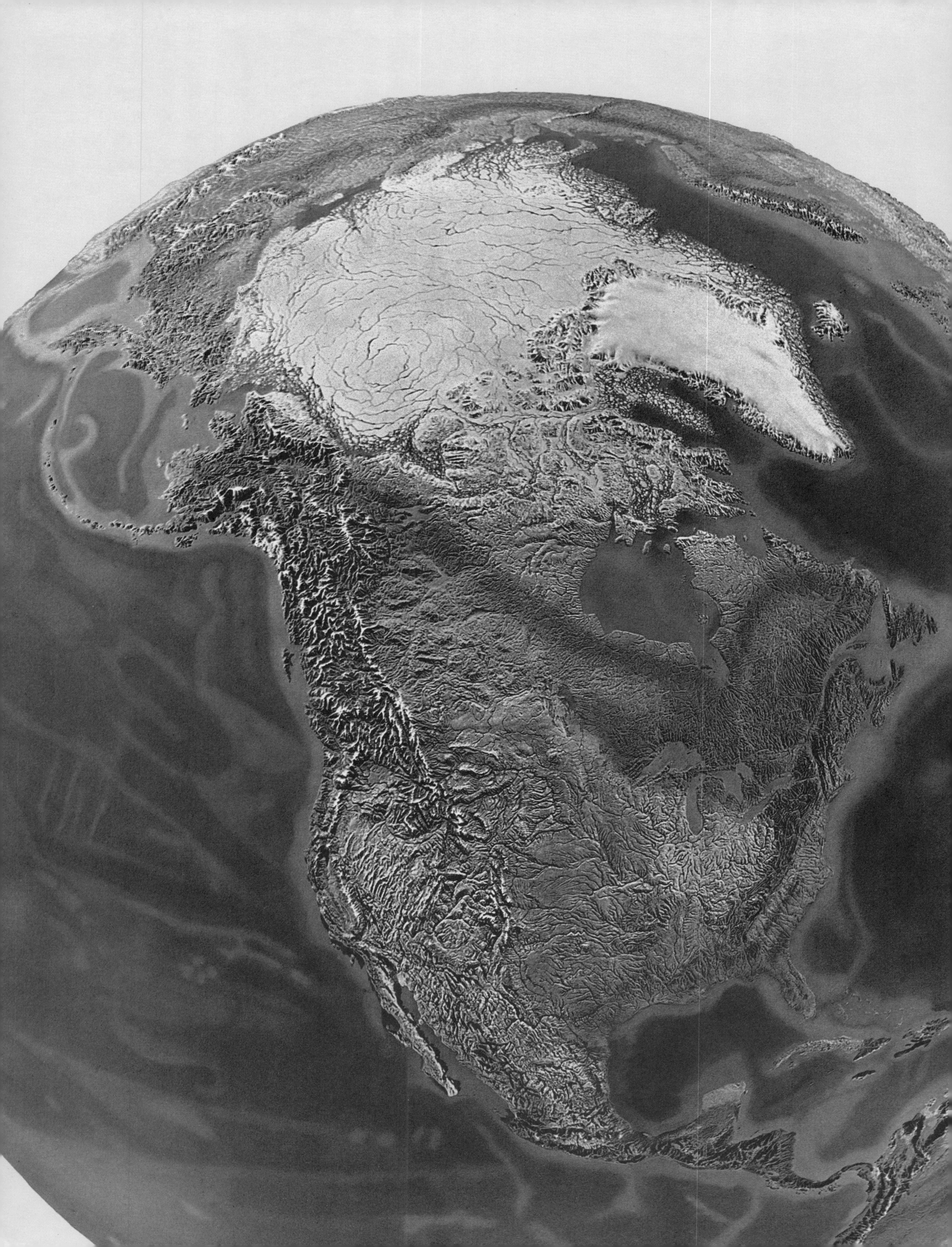

Physically the North American continent extends from the ice-covered Arctic Ocean in the north to the tropical Isthmus of Panama in the south. North America, like Africa and South America, tapers from north to south. Canada, the United States, and Mexico occupy over 85 per cent of its total area of nearly 9,500,000 square miles. Central America, the West Indies, and Greenland make up the remainder.

Within this vast area, differences, rather than similarities, abound. All major types of climate can be found in North America ranging from the cold, perpetual ice cap of Greenland to the hot, moist tropical rain forests of Central America. Landforms vary from the towering chain of the Rocky Mountains, through the high plateau of Mexico, the relatively low Appalachian Highland, the featureless expanses of the Arctic tundra, the regularity of the Great Plains, and the fertile fields of the interior lowlands and coastal plains. Soils, vegetation, temperature, precipitation—all reflect the differences that can be expected over such an area.

Similarly, the development of agriculture and industry has varied considerably over the North American continent. Modern methods and the extensive use of machinery characterize agriculture in the flat to gently rolling areas of Midwestern United States and the Prairie Provinces of Canada. Stock-grazing is prevalent in the more arid areas of the continent. Agriculture in Middle America is characterized by the extensive use of hand labor. Here subtropical crops are important, for instance, bananas in Central America and sugar cane in the West Indies.

Early settlement, access to raw materials, a well developed transportation network, and a density of population providing both labor and markets have led to a heavy concentration of industrial development in the northeast quarter of the United States and the southeastern rim of Canada. Other industrial development has taken place in scattered locations in southern and western United States and in the largest cities of Middle America.

NORTH AMERICA

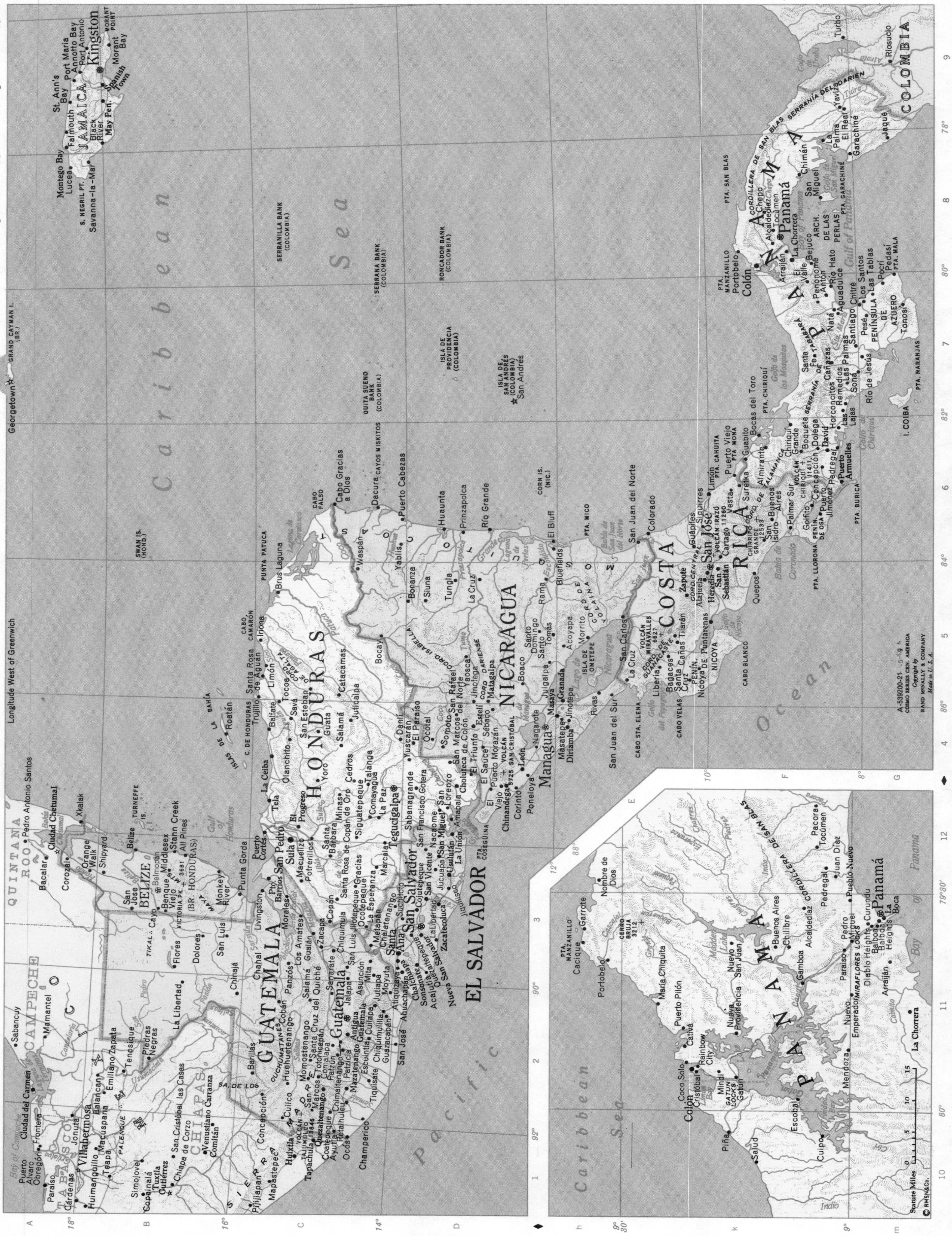

Oblique Conic Conformal Projection
SCALE 1:6,000,000 1 Inch = 95 Statute Miles

Statute Miles 25 0 25 75 125
Kilometers 25 0 25 75 125 175

Oblique Conic Conformal Projection
SCALE 1:12,000 000 1 Inch = 189 Statute Miles

Statute Miles 50 25 0 50 100 150 200 250

Kilometers 50 0 100 200 300

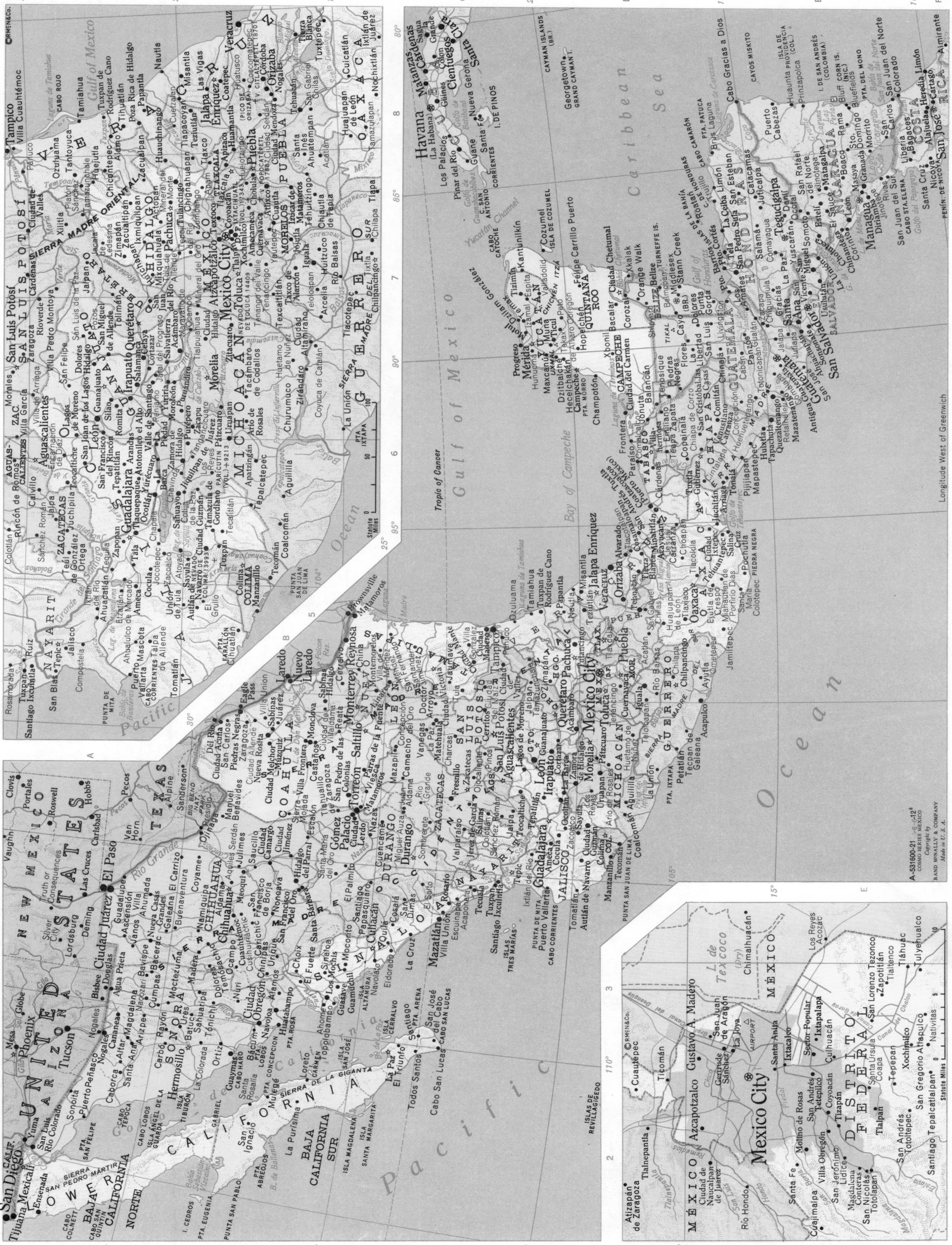

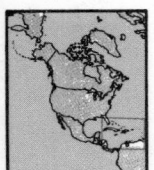

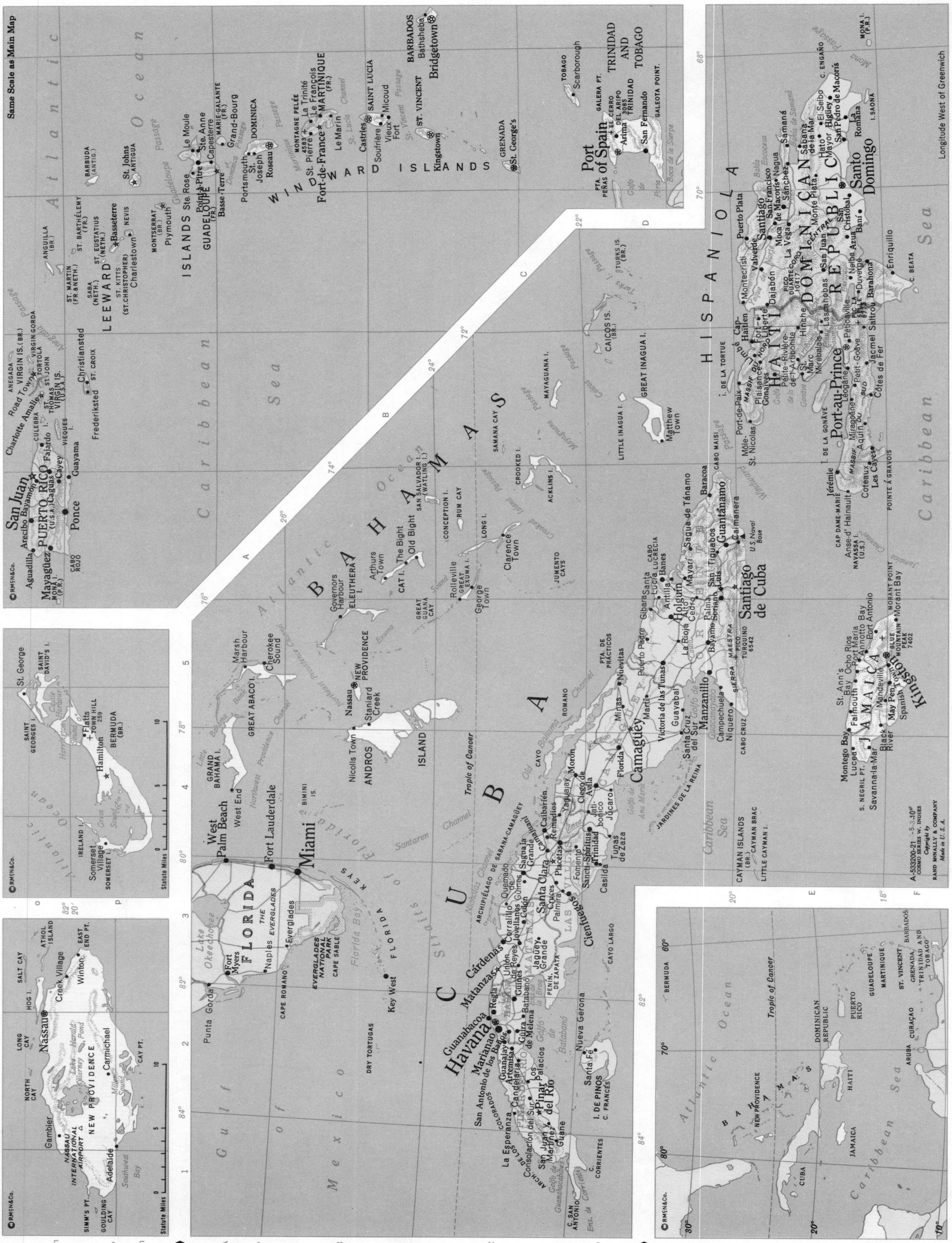

Same Scale as Main Map

Atlantic Ocean

BARBUDA (ANTIG.)
ANGUILLA (BR.)
ST. MARTIN (FR.&NETH.)
ST. BARTHÉLEMY (FR.)
SABA (NETH.)
ST. EUSTATIUS (NETH.)
ST. KITTS (ST. CHRISTOPHER)
NEVIS
MONTSERRAT (BR.)
Plymouth
Charlestown
Basseterre
St. Johns ★ ANTIGUA

LEEWARD ISLANDS

GUADELOUPE (FR.)
Ste. Rose
Le Moule
Ste. Anne
Capesterre
Pointe-à-Pitre
Basse-Terre
MARIE-GALANTE (FR.)
Grand-Bourg
DOMINICA
Portsmouth
St. Joseph
Roseau ⊛
MONTAGNE PELÉE
La Trinité
St. Pierre
MARTINIQUE (FR.)
Le François
Fort-de-France ⊛
Le Marin
SAINT LUCIA
Castries ★
Soufrière
Vieux Fort
Micoud
ST. VINCENT
Kingstown ⊛
GRENADA
St. George's

WINDWARD ISLANDS

BARBADOS
Bathsheba ⊛
Bridgetown ⊛

TOBAGO
Scarborough
GALERA PT.
TRINIDAD AND TOBAGO
Port of Spain ⊛
PTA. DE PEÑAS
EL CERRO DEL ARIPO
TRINIDAD
Arima
San Fernando
GALEOTA POINT
Boca de la Sierpe

MONA (P.R.)

HISPANIOLA

DOMINICAN REPUBLIC
Puerto Plata
Montecristi
Dajabón
Santiago
Moca
La Vega
San Francisco de Macorís
Nagua
Samaná
Sabana de la Mar
Monte Plata
El Seibo
Higüey
Hato Mayor
San Pedro de Macorís
Santo Domingo ★
C. ENGAÑO
I. SAONA
C. RAFAEL
Baní
Azua
Bani
Barahona
Neiba
San Juan
Comendador
Enriquillo
C. BEATA

HAITI
Cap-Haïtien
Port-de-Paix
Môle St. Nicolas
I. DE LA TORTUE
Fort-Liberté
Plaisance
Gonaïves
Petite-Rivière-de-l'Artibonite
Hinche
St. Marc
Mirebalais
Port-au-Prince ★
Léogâne
Petit-Goâve
Miragoâne
Jacmel
Côtes de Fer
Jérémie
Corail
Pestel
Anse-d'Hainault
Cap Dame-Marie
Aquin
Coteaux
Les Cayes
Pointe à Gravois
I. DE LA GONÂVE
NAVASSA (U.S.)

Caribbean Sea

VIRGIN IS. (BR.)
ANEGADA
Road Town
TORTOLA
VIRGIN GORDA
ST. JOHN
ST. THOMAS
Charlotte Amalie
VIRGIN IS. (U.S.)
ST. CROIX
Christiansted
Frederiksted

PUERTO RICO (U.S.)
San Juan ★
Aguadilla
Arecibo
Bayamón
Mayagüez
MONA I. (P.R.)
Caguas
Cayey
Guayama
Ponce
CABO ROJO

BAHAMAS
MAYAGUANA I.
GREAT INAGUA I.
Matthew Town
LITTLE INAGUA I.
TURKS IS. (BR.)
CAICOS IS. (BR.)
SAMANA CAY
CROOKED I.
ACKLINS I.
LONG I.
Clarence Town
RUM CAY
SAN SALVADOR I. (WATLING I.)
CONCEPTION I.
CAT I.
The Bight
Old Bight
ELEUTHERA I.
GREAT EXUMA I.
George Town
GREAT GUANA CAY
EXUMA CAYS
JUMENTO CAYS
Rolleville
Arthurs Town
Governors Harbour
NEW PROVIDENCE
Nassau ⊛
Staniard Creek
ANDROS ISLAND
Nicolls Town
Marsh Harbour
Cherokee Sound
GREAT ABACO I.
GRAND BAHAMA I.
West End
BIMINI IS.

CUBA
Havana ⊛ ★
Guanabacoa
Marianao
Regla
Matanzas
Cárdenas
Colón
Jovellanos
Unión de Reyes
Jagüey Grande
PEN. DE ZAPATA
Cienfuegos
Santa Clara
Sagua la Grande
Caibarién
Remedios
Placetas
Sancti Spíritus
Trinidad
Casilda
Sancti Spíritus
Ciego de Ávila
Morón
Júcaro
Camagüey
Nuevitas
Santa Cruz del Sur
Victoria de las Tunas
Manzanillo
Bayamo
Niquero
CABO CRUZ
Holguín
Gibara
Banes
Antilla
Mayarí
San Germán
Palma Soriano
SIERRA MAESTRA
TURQUINO 6542
Santiago de Cuba
Guantánamo
Baracoa
Sagua de Tánamo
CABO MAISÍ
U.S. Naval Base
PTA. DE PRÁCTICOS
Nueva Gerona
I. DE PINOS
C. FRANCÉS
Los Palacios
Consolación del Sur
Candelaria
San Cristóbal
Artemisa
Guanajay
Pinar del Río
La Esperanza
San Juan y Martínez
Guane
C. CORRIENTES
C. SAN ANTONIO

FLORIDA
West Palm Beach
Fort Lauderdale
Miami
Key West
Fort Myers
Everglades
Naples
CAPE SABLE
CAPE ROMANO
EVERGLADES NATIONAL PARK
Lake Okeechobee
FLORIDA KEYS
DRY TORTUGAS
Gulf of Mexico

Atlantic Ocean

Caribbean Sea

CAYMAN ISLANDS
GRAND CAYMAN I.
CAYMAN BRAC
LITTLE CAYMAN I.

JAMAICA
Montego Bay
Falmouth
St. Ann's Bay
Ocho Rios
Port Maria
Port Antonio
MORANT POINT
Kingston ★
Spanish Town
Mandeville
May Pen
Black River
Savanna-la-Mar
Lucea
S. NEGRIL PT.
BLUE MOUNTAIN PEAK 7402
Annotto Bay
Morant Bay

BERMUDA (BR.)
St. George
SAINT DAVID'S I.
SAINT GEORGE'S I.
Hamilton ★
Somerset Village
IRELAND ISLAND
SOMERSET I.
TOWN HILL 259

NEW PROVIDENCE
NORTH CAY
HOG I.
Nassau ★
INTERNATIONAL AIRPORT
Adelaide
Carmichael
Gambier
Creek Village
Winton
SALT CAY
ATHOL ISLAND
EAST END PT.
LONG CAY
CAY PT.
Southwest Bay
SIMM'S PT.
GOULDING CAY

Statute Miles 25 0 25 75 125
Kilometers 25 0 25 75 125 175

Oblique Conic Conformal Projection
SCALE 1:6,000,000 1 Inch = 95 Statute Miles

A-533200-21 -5-:-30°
COMBO SERIES W. INDIES
Copyright by
RAND McNALLY & COMPANY
Made in U.S.A.

Longitude West of Greenwich

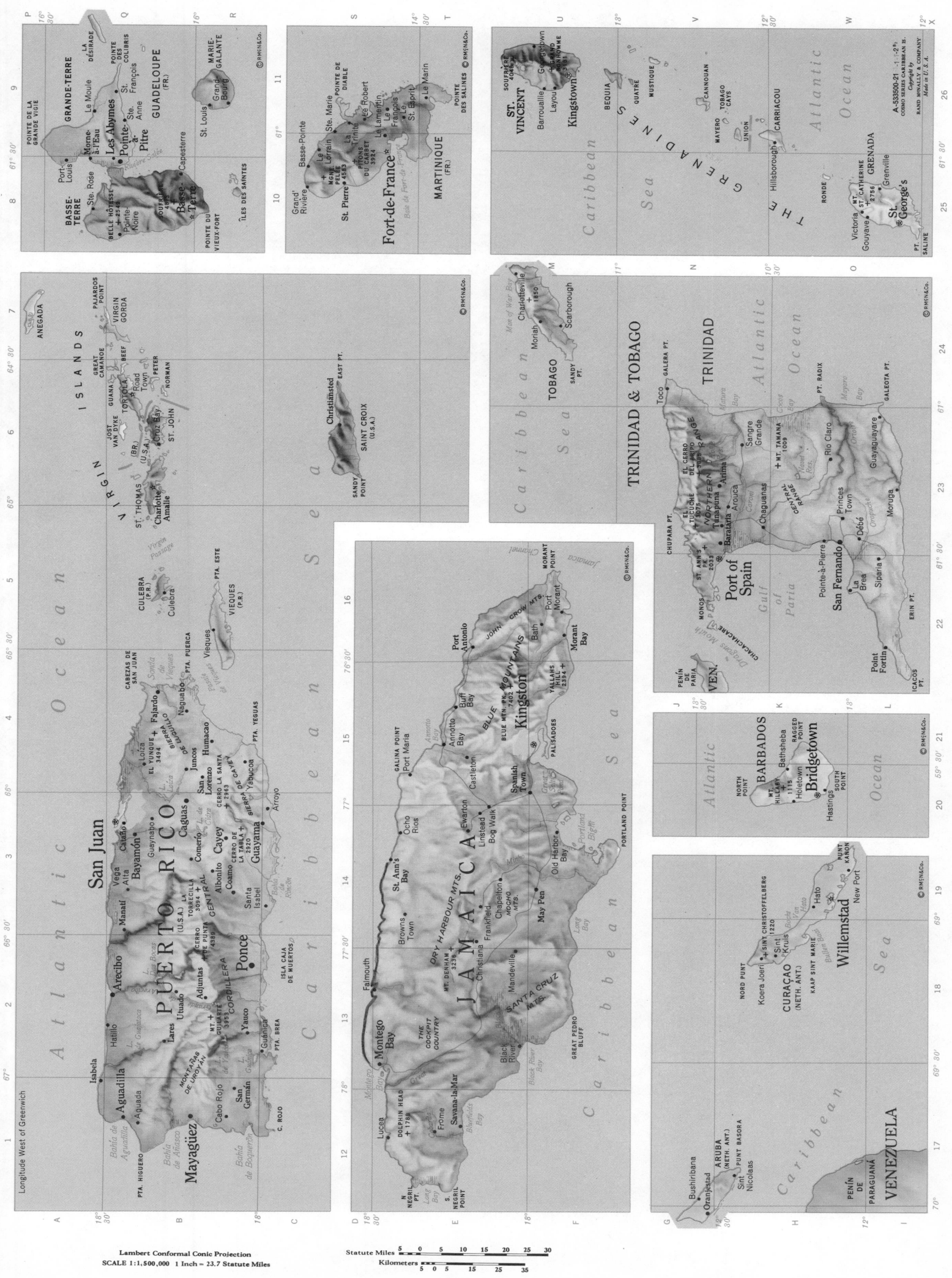

Lambert Conformal Conic Projection
SCALE 1:1,500,000 1 Inch = 23.7 Statute Miles

Statute Miles 5 0 5 10 15 20 25 30
Kilometers 5 0 5 15 25 35

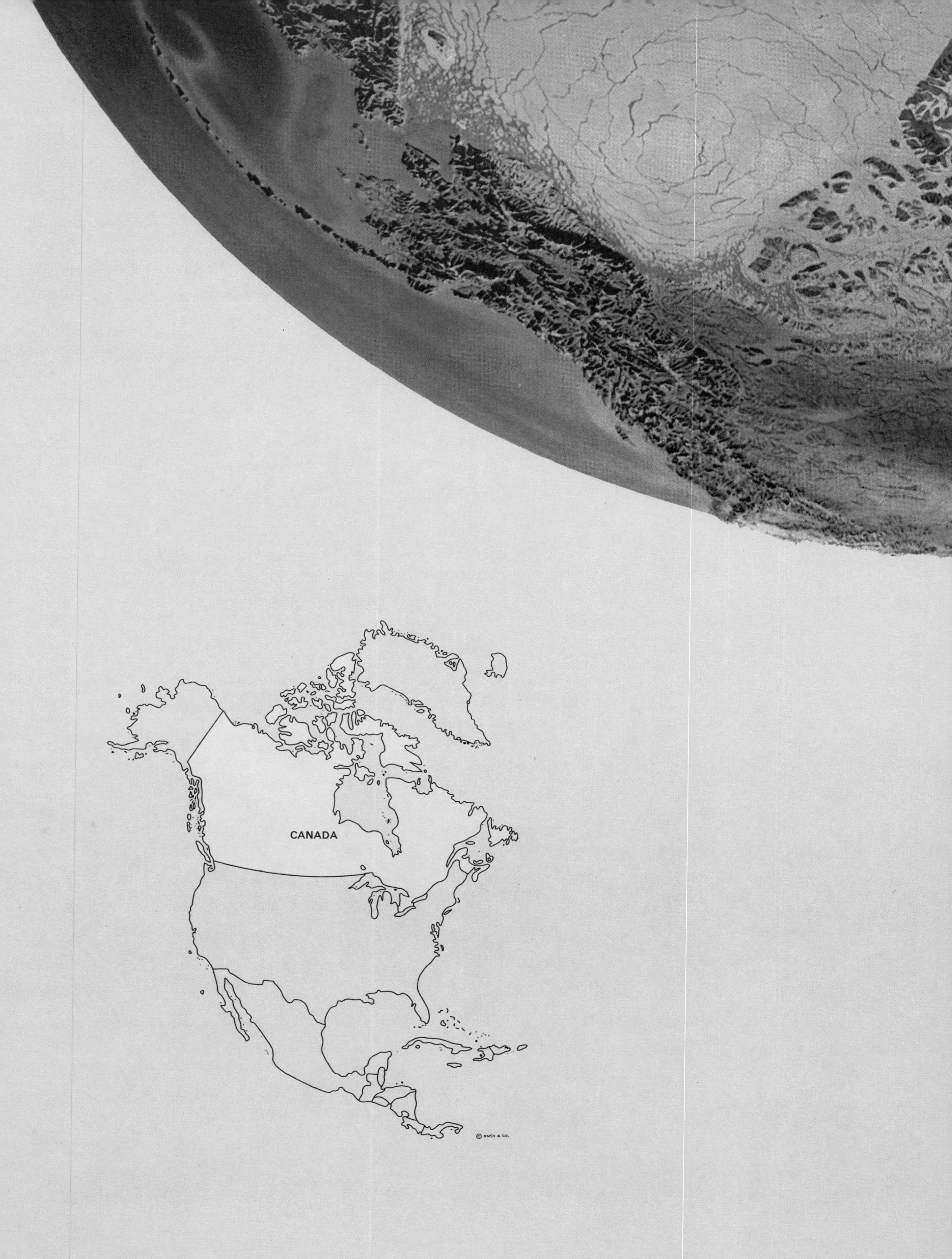

CANADA

© RAND & CO.

CANADA

Canada, the largest single political entity in the Western Hemisphere, occupies the great territorial expanse of northern North America. It crosses the breadth of the continent from ocean to ocean and extends from the frozen wastes of the Arctic to the northern bounds of the United States. Although Canada is second only to the Soviet Union in total land area, it does not share the population density of other territorial giants. Only a narrow strip of land adjacent to the boundary of the United States possesses the agricultural and industrial activities to support any substantial concentration of population. Here, within a hundred miles of the United States' northern boundary, 90 per cent of Canada's population is concentrated.

The geographic location of Canada has profoundly influenced the economic development of the country. Proximity to the Polar region has provided the hostile, barren tundra and has placed Canada within the path of the frigid air masses moving southward over North America. The great glacial movements from the north during the Ice Age scoured much of Canada, leaving a shield-shaped region whose broad base lies along the northern lands from Great Bear Lake to the Maritimes and whose apex dips into the State of Minnesota. The Laurentian, or Canadian, Shield occupies more than half of the country's total area. Such was the thoroughness of the glaciers that only in a few places did they leave even a veneer of soil suitable for concentrated agriculture. Today the Interior Plains and the St. Lawrence Valley have adequate soils and climate to be intensively cultivated. The rugged western portion of the North American continent reaches its greatest heights in British Columbia and the Yukon, also limiting the amount of agricultural activity.

Although the scoured rock of the Canadian Shield, the rugged terrain, and the climate limit Canada's agriculture, these same factors contribute to the vast natural resources of the country. Contained in the ancient glaciated rocks of the Shield and the western mountain chains is much of the mineral wealth of Canada —gold, uranium, iron ore. Under the dry plains lying to the east of the Rocky Mountains are the recently tapped oil reserves of Alberta. And on both the rocks of the Shield and the terrain of the west tracts of coniferous forests flourish, providing the raw material for lumber and wood-pulp industries. In these same areas great hydroelectric potential abounds.

Transportation has proved an impetus to the exploitation of the wilderness frontiers and provided a link between the southeastern urban centers and the outlying trading centers. The completion of the Canadian Pacific Railroad in 1886 bound the Prairie Provinces and British Columbia to the financial, commercial, and industrial centers of Ontario, Quebec, and the Maritime Provinces. The Trans-Canada Highway augmented the ties. Joint development of the St. Lawrence Seaway with the United States has further enhanced the movement of grain and other agricultural products from the interior through the Great Lakes.

British and French influences shaped the early development of the country, but most of modern Canada owes its cultural heritage to Great Britain. Only the Province of Quebec still bears the imprint of its French settlers.

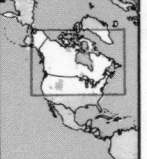

Lambert Conformal Conic Projection
SCALE 1:12,000.000   1 Inch = 189 Statute Miles

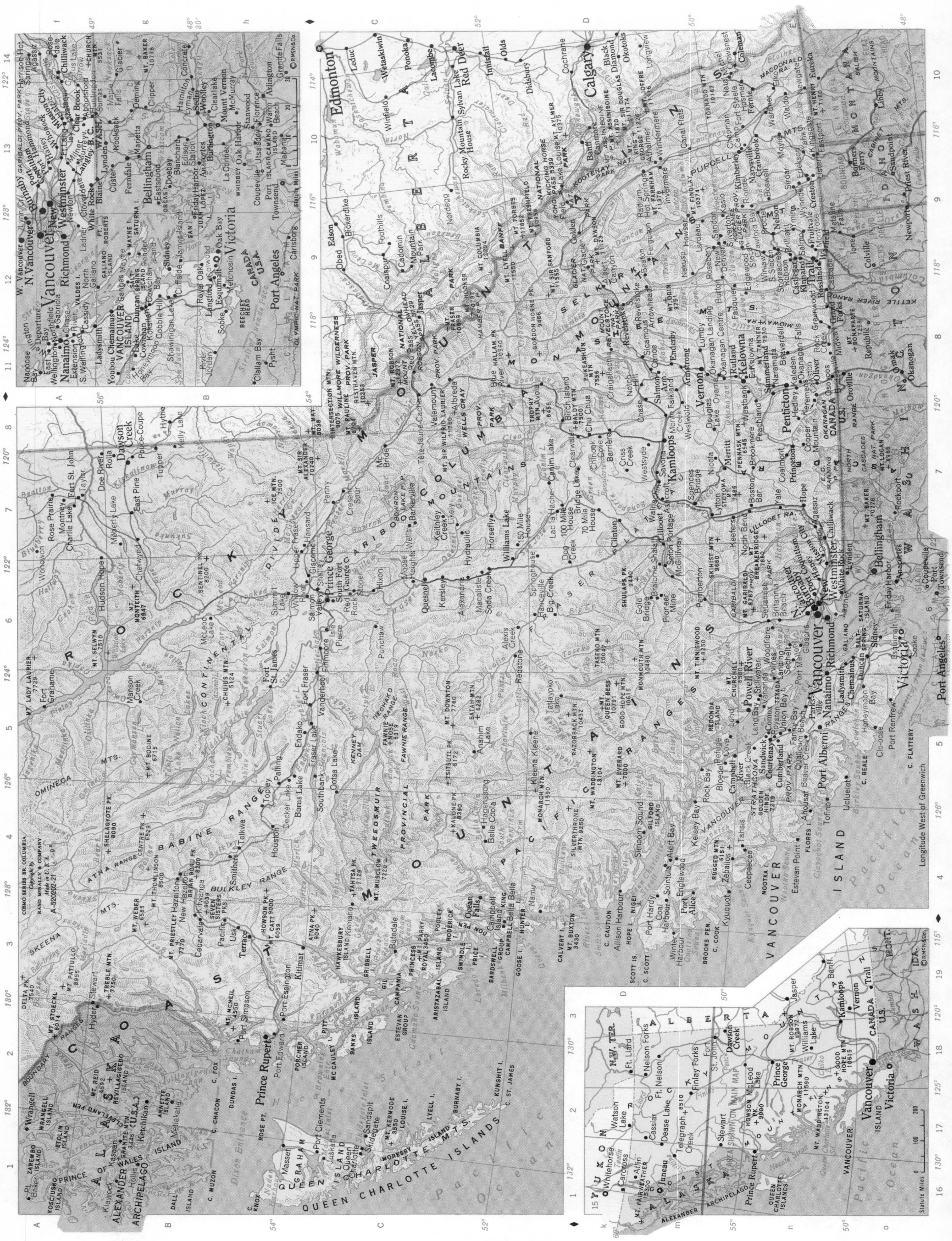

Statute Miles 10 0 10 20 30 40 50 60 70 80 90 100

Kilometers 10 0 10 20 30 40 50 60 70 80 90 100 120 140

Oblique Cylindrical Projection
SCALE 1:4,255,000 1 Inch = 67 Statute Miles

Oblique Cylindrical Projection
SCALE 1:3,110,000 1 Inch = 49 Statute Miles

Statute Miles 10 0 10 20 30 40 50 60 70

Kilometers 10 0 10 20 40 60 80 100

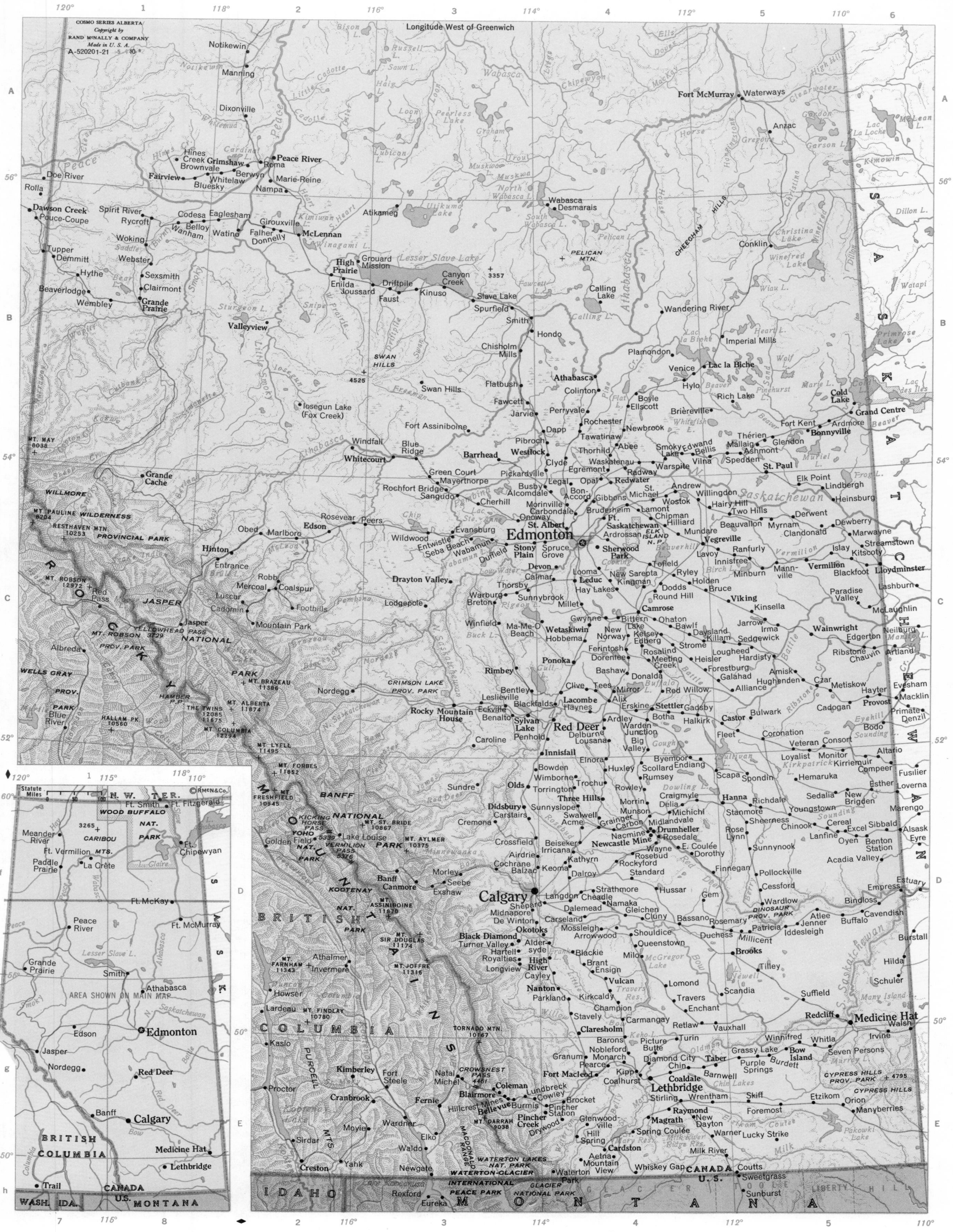

Longitude West of Greenwich

Statute Miles 10 0 10 20 30 40 50 60

Kilometers 10 0 10 20 40 60 80

Oblique Cylindrical Projection

SCALE 1:2,827,000 1 Inch = 44 Statute Miles

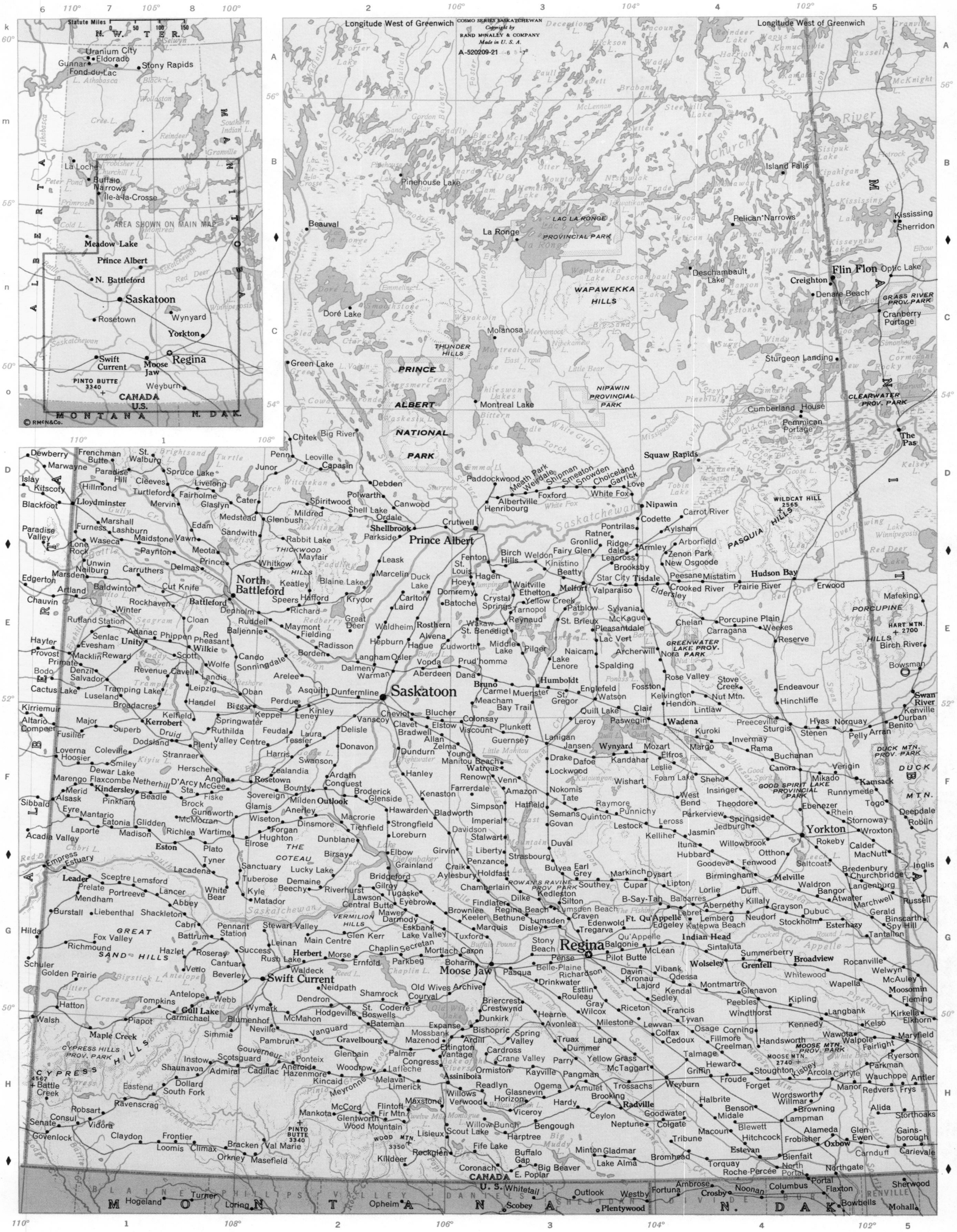

Longitude West of Greenwich

Oblique Cylindrical Projection
SCALE 1:3,167,000 1 Inch = 50 Statute Miles

Statute Miles 10 0 10 20 30 40 50 60 70

Kilometers 10 0 10 20 40 60 80 100

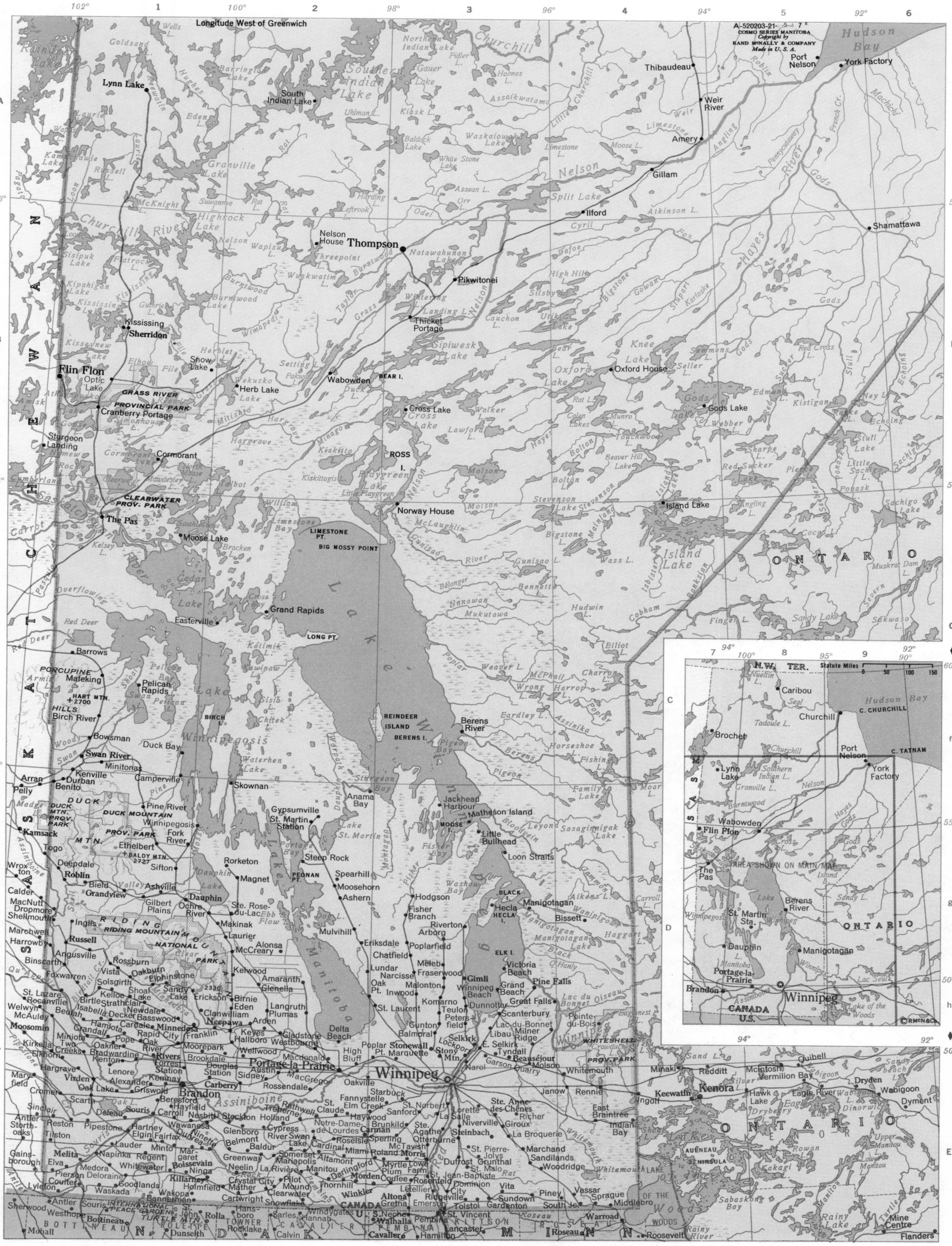

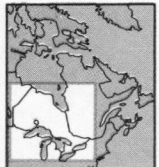

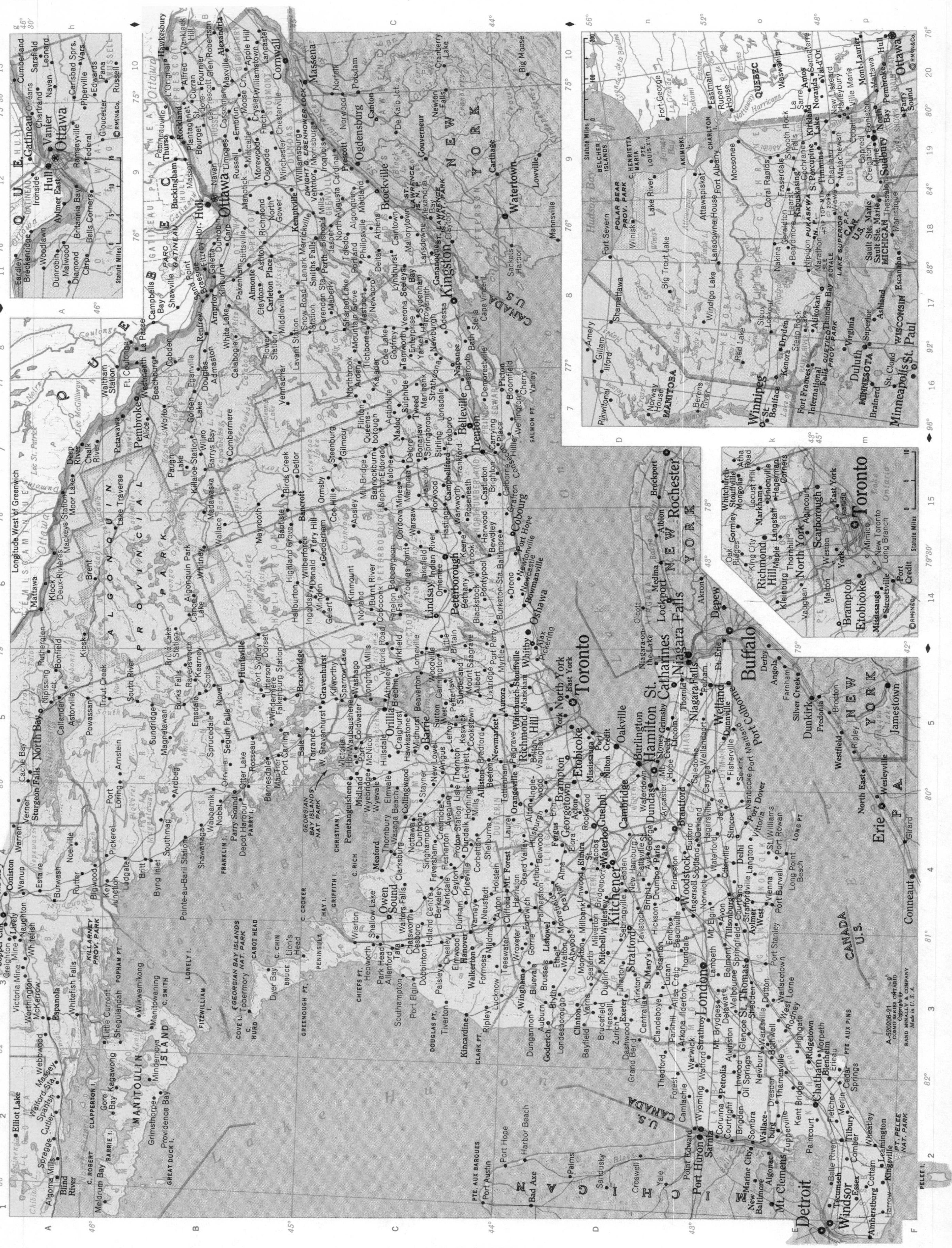

Statute Miles 5 0 5 10 20 30 40 50
Kilometers 5 0 5 15 25 35 45 55 65 75

Oblique Cylindrical Projection
SCALE 1:2,226,000 1 Inch = 35 Statute Miles

A-500206-21 RAND MCNALLY & COMPANY
Made in U.S.A.

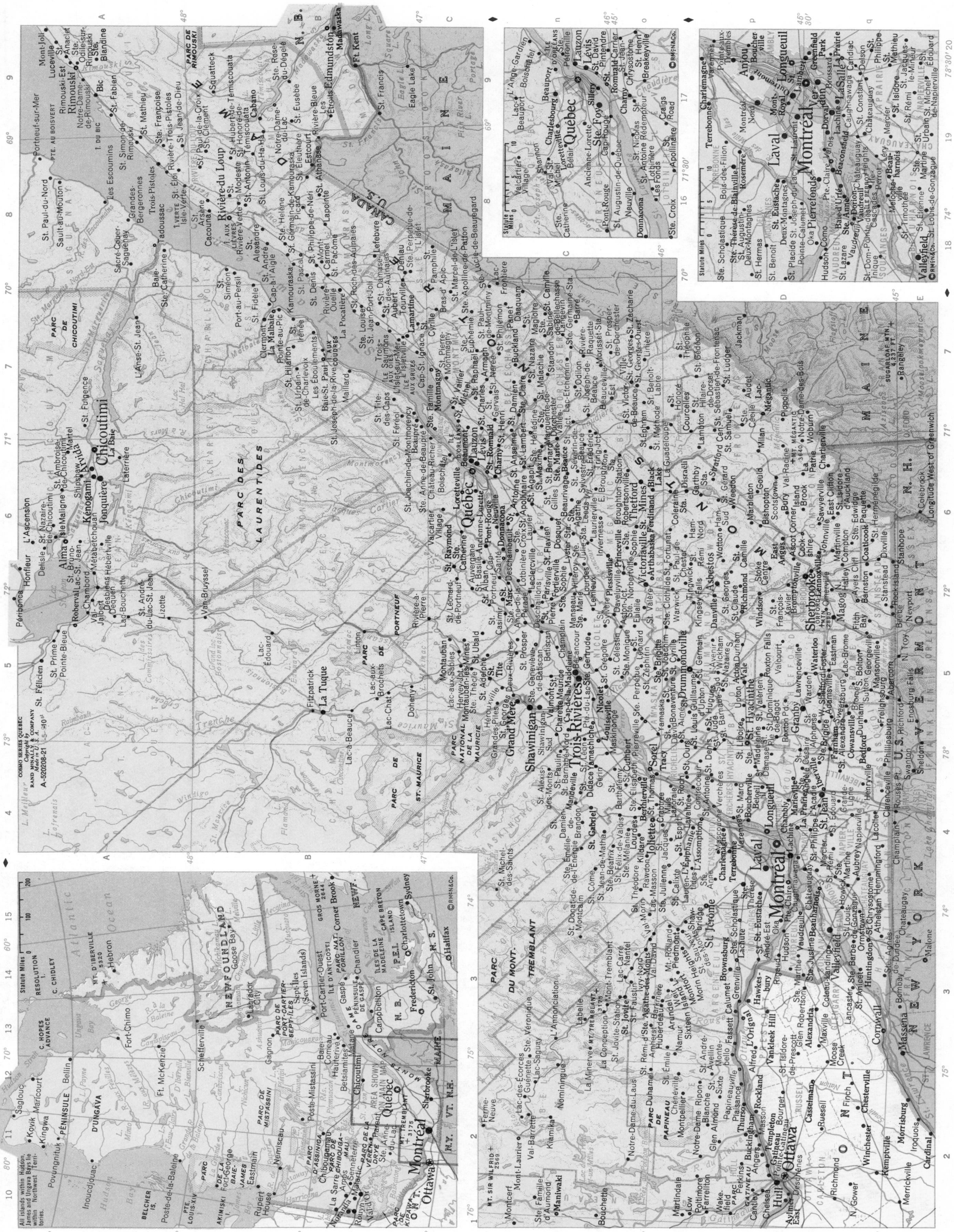

Oblique Cylindrical Projection
SCALE 1:1,929,000 1 Inch = 30.5 Statute Miles

Statute Miles 5 0 5 10 20 30 40
Kilometers 5 0 5 15 25 35 45 55

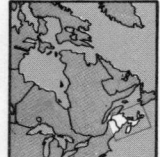

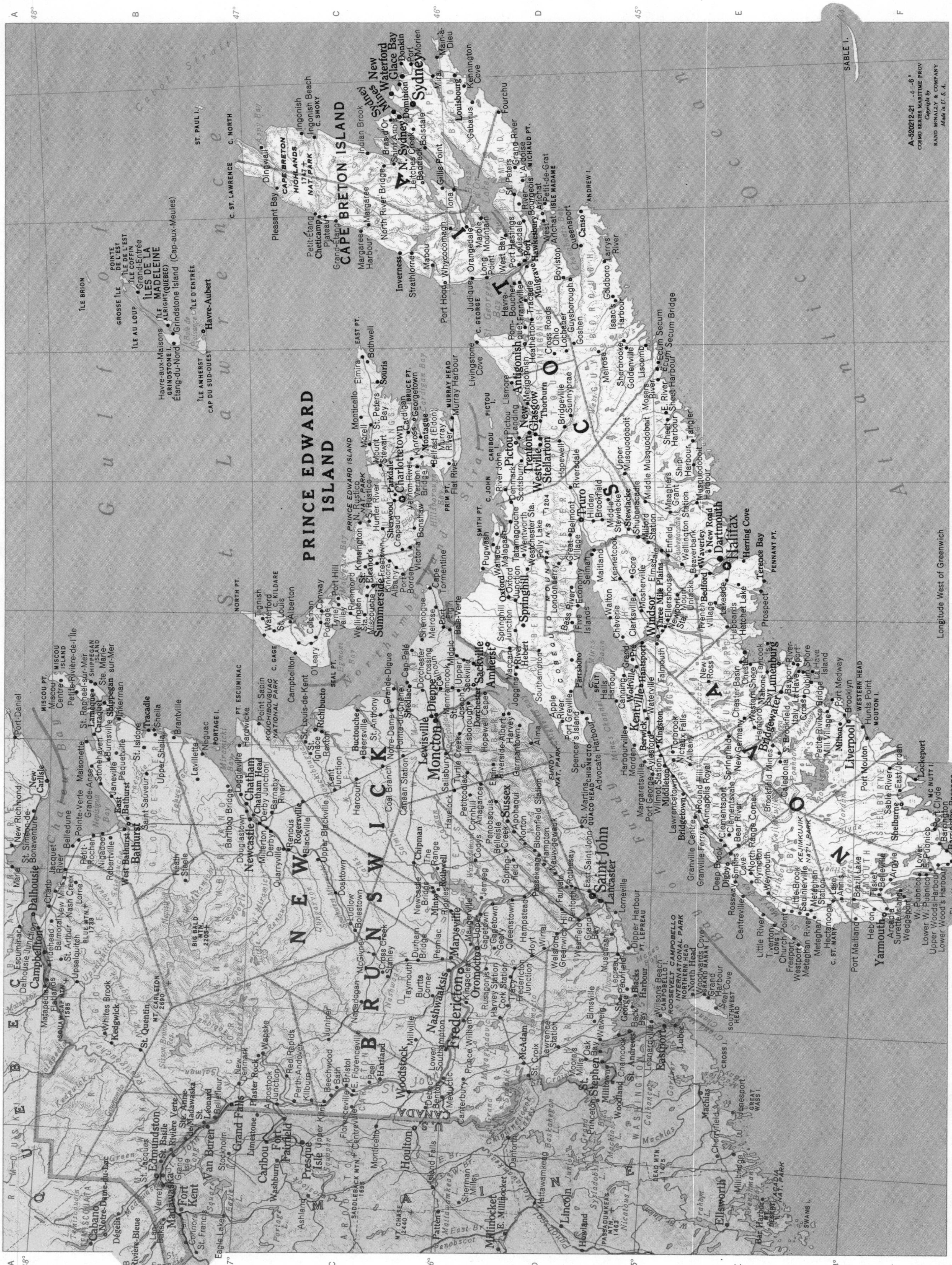

PRINCE EDWARD ISLAND

NEW BRUNSWICK

NOVA SCOTIA

CAPE BRETON ISLAND

CAPE BRETON HIGHLANDS NAT'L PARK

Statute Miles 5 0 5 10 20 30 40 50
Kilometers 5 0 5 15 25 35 45 55 65 75

Oblique Cylindrical Projection
SCALE 1:2,312,000 1 Inch = 36.5 Statute Miles

A-500212-21 -4-6°

COSMO SERIES MARITIME PROV.
Copyright
RAND McNALLY & COMPANY
Made in U.S.A.

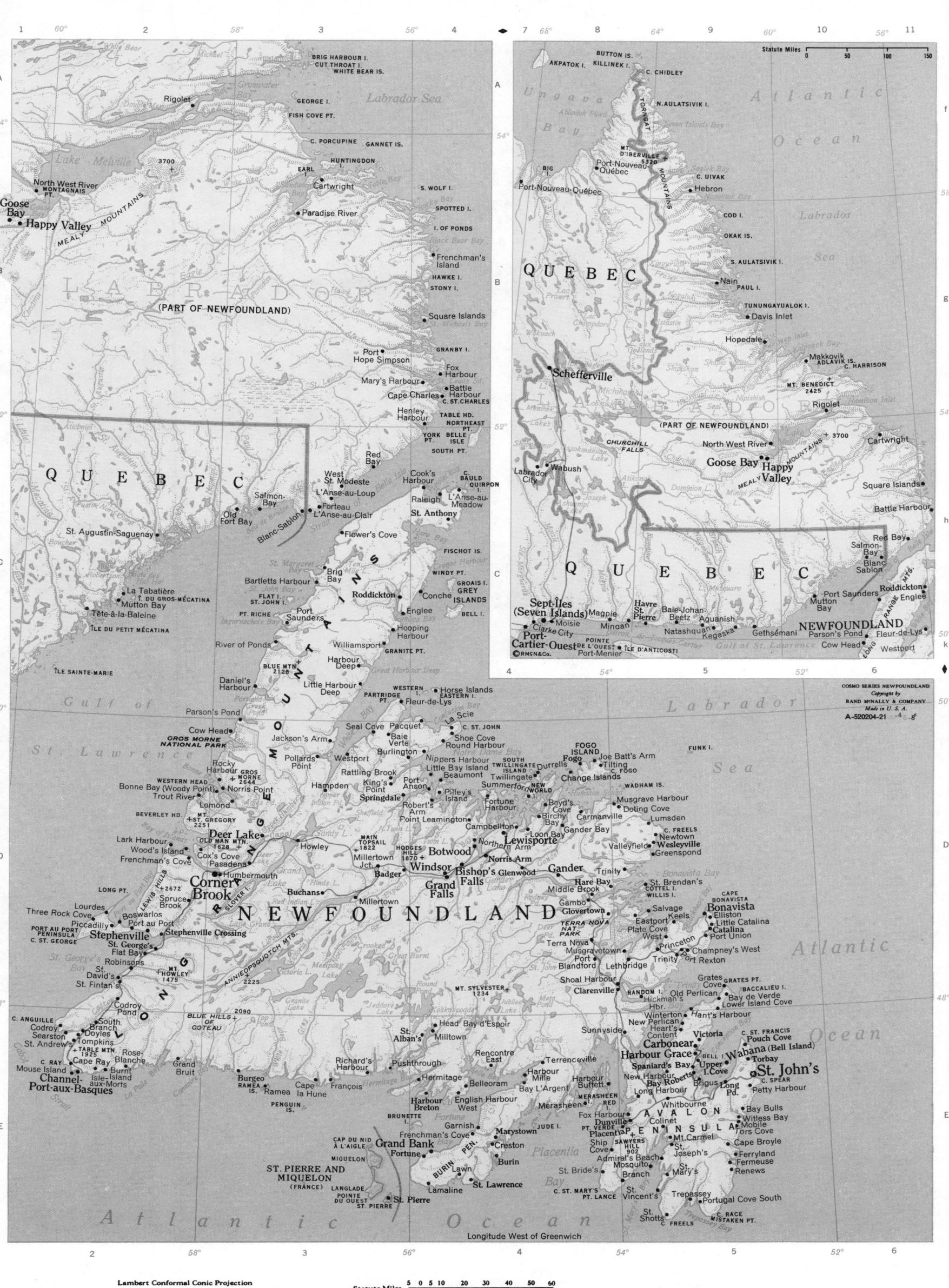

Lambert Conformal Conic Projection
SCALE 1 : 3,000,000 1 Inch = 47 Statute Miles

Statute Miles 0 5 10 20 30 40 50 60
Kilometers 0 5 10 20 30 40 50 60 70 80

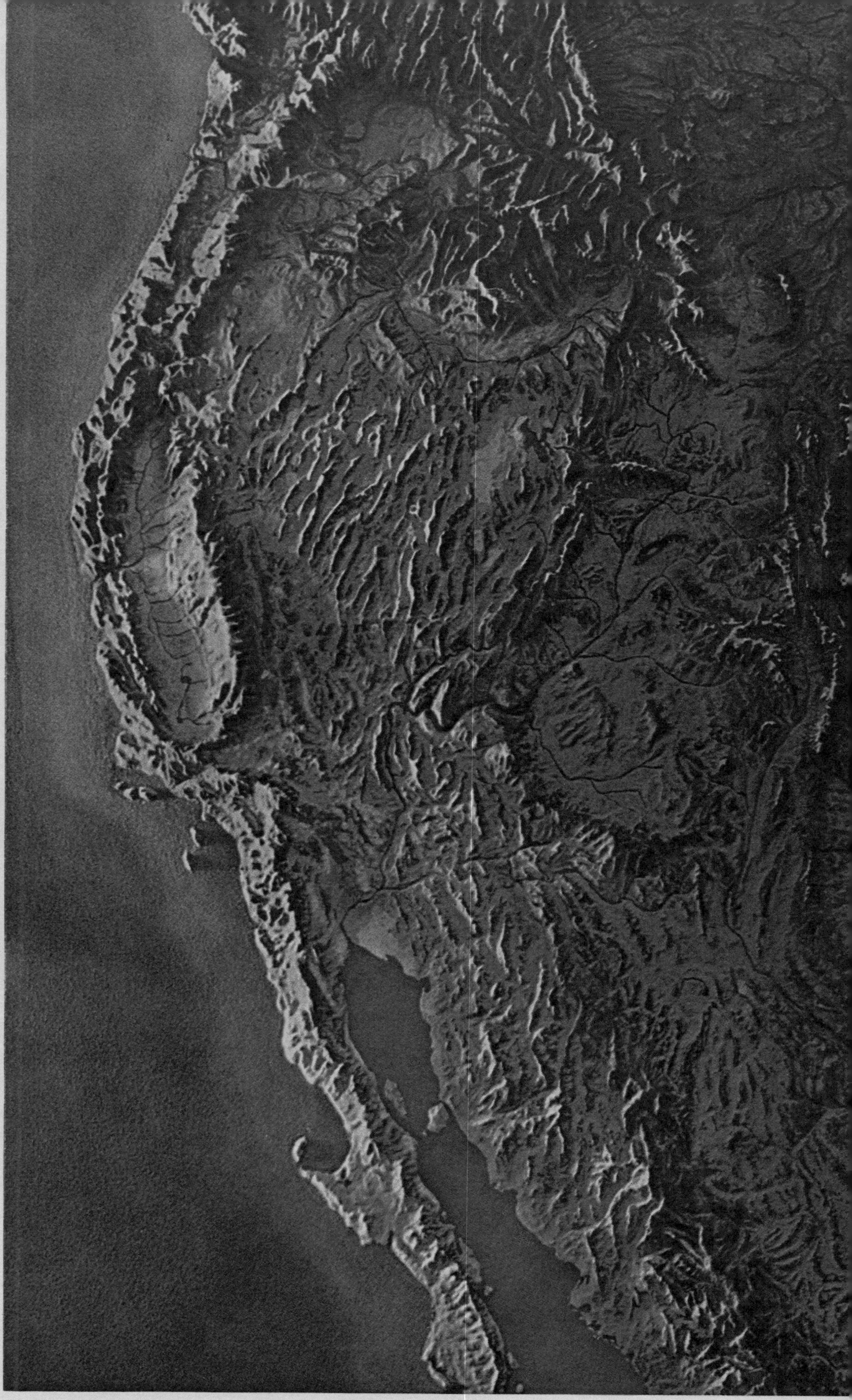

Today the world's strongest and most prosperous major power, the United States, has developed in less than two centuries from a modest group of British colonies huddled along the Atlantic coastline of a new and undeveloped continent. This tremendous expansion in population, area, wealth, and power has had its roots partly in the richness of the natural resources America has had to offer to a new and growing nation. But perhaps equally important have been the human resources of initiative, political stability, and religious faith brought by America's first settlers and augmented by later arrivals from the Old World.

The landscape of the United States today reflects many patterns. First, there is the fundamental pattern of the terrain from east to west—the Atlantic Coastal Plain, the low but rugged Appalachian Highlands, the great interior lowland, drained by the Mississippi and its tributaries and merging on the south into the Gulf Coastal Plain, the long chain of the Rockies, the high and arid Great Basin with its many ranges and plateaus, and finally the Cascades, Sierras, and the other mountains and valleys of the Pacific coast. On this variety of terrain, the forces of climate and natural vegetation

THE UNITED STATES

have combined to produce different soils. Man, in turn, has developed different kinds of farming in response to the particular conditions of each section—dairying along the northern frontier in the East; corn and livestock on the rich soils of the Midwest; cotton, orchards, or cattle in the South; wheat on the drier lands of the Great Plains;

cattle and sheep raising in the more rugged, drier areas of the West; and special fruit and vegetable crops in scattered local areas, but especially in the Far West and the South.

Just as the pattern of American agriculture reflects that of climate and soils, so does that of American manufacturing reflect the distribution of natural resources. Here the

pattern becomes more complex, since industries use many raw materials, and nearness to markets today is more important for many factories than nearness to supplies.

Roughly two-thirds of U.S. manufacturing is concentrated in the northeast quarter of the nation. This degree of localization reflects the interplay of many factors, including the early start of many industries in or near Boston, New York, Philadelphia; resources of water power, coal, and iron ore in the Appalachians-Great Lakes region; accessibility to the major harbors of the Atlantic seaboard and through them contact with Europe; and convenient inland water and rail routes across the Appalachians and Midwest, focusing in New York on the east and Chicago on the west.

Recent times have seen the South and Far West making giant strides in the development of manufacturing, and the gap between these areas and the manufacturing belt has narrowed, especially as their number of consumers has increased.

A-520500-21 -5-1-

COSMO SERIES UNITED STATES

Same Scale as Main Map

HAWAIIAN ISLANDS

ALASKA

ALEUTIAN ISLANDS

Statute Miles 0 150 300

Statute Miles 50 25 0 50 100 150 200 250

Kilometers 50 0 100 200 300

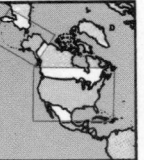

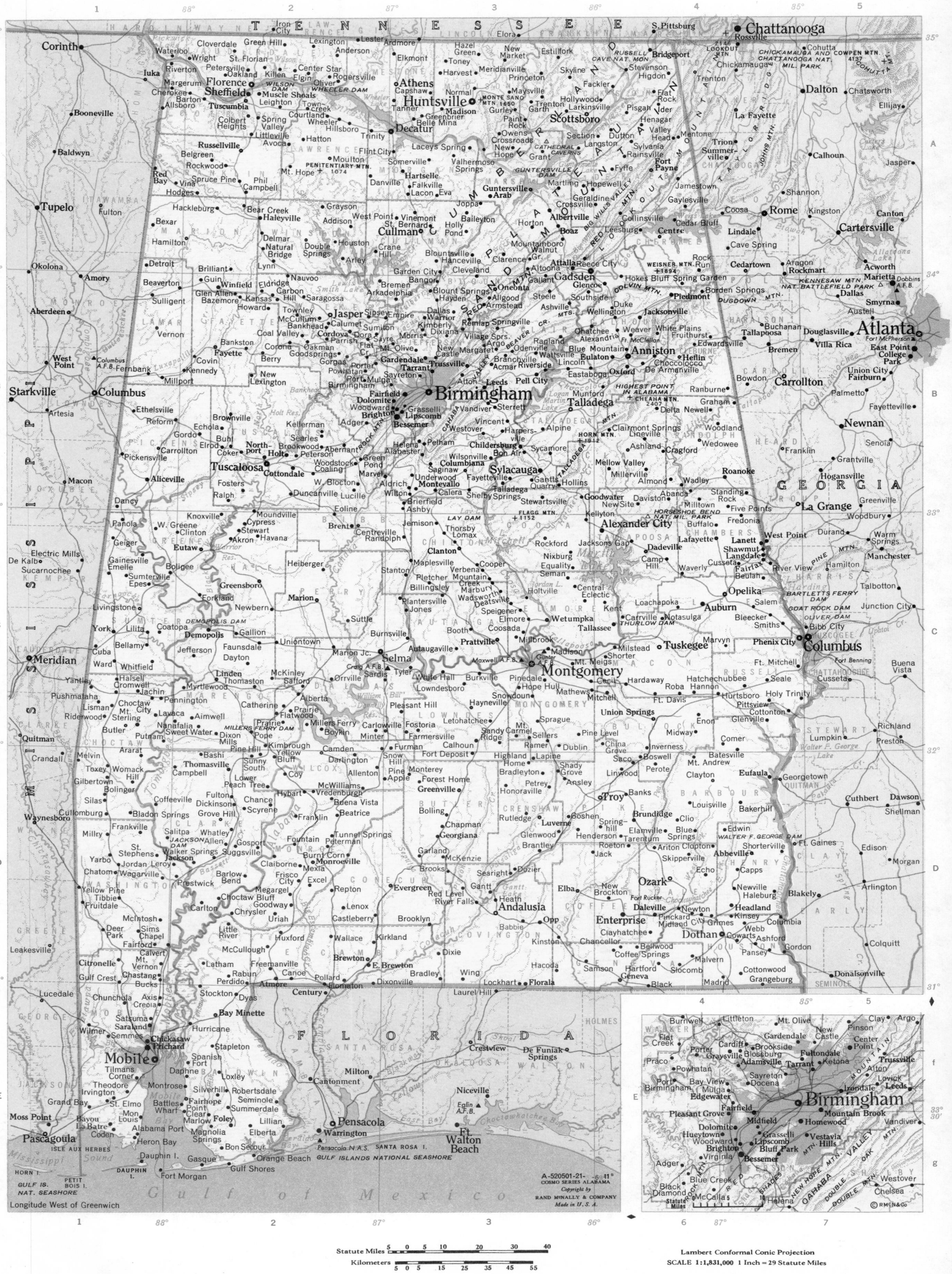

ALABAMA

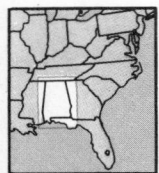

Statute Miles 5 0 5 10 20 30 40
Kilometers 5 0 5 15 25 35 45 55

A-520501-21   -6-41
COSMO SERIES ALABAMA
Copyright by
RAND McNALLY & COMPANY
Made in U.S.A.

Longitude West of Greenwich

Lambert Conformal Conic Projection
SCALE 1:1,831,000 1 Inch = 29 Statute Miles

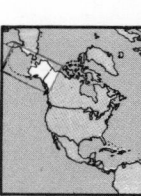

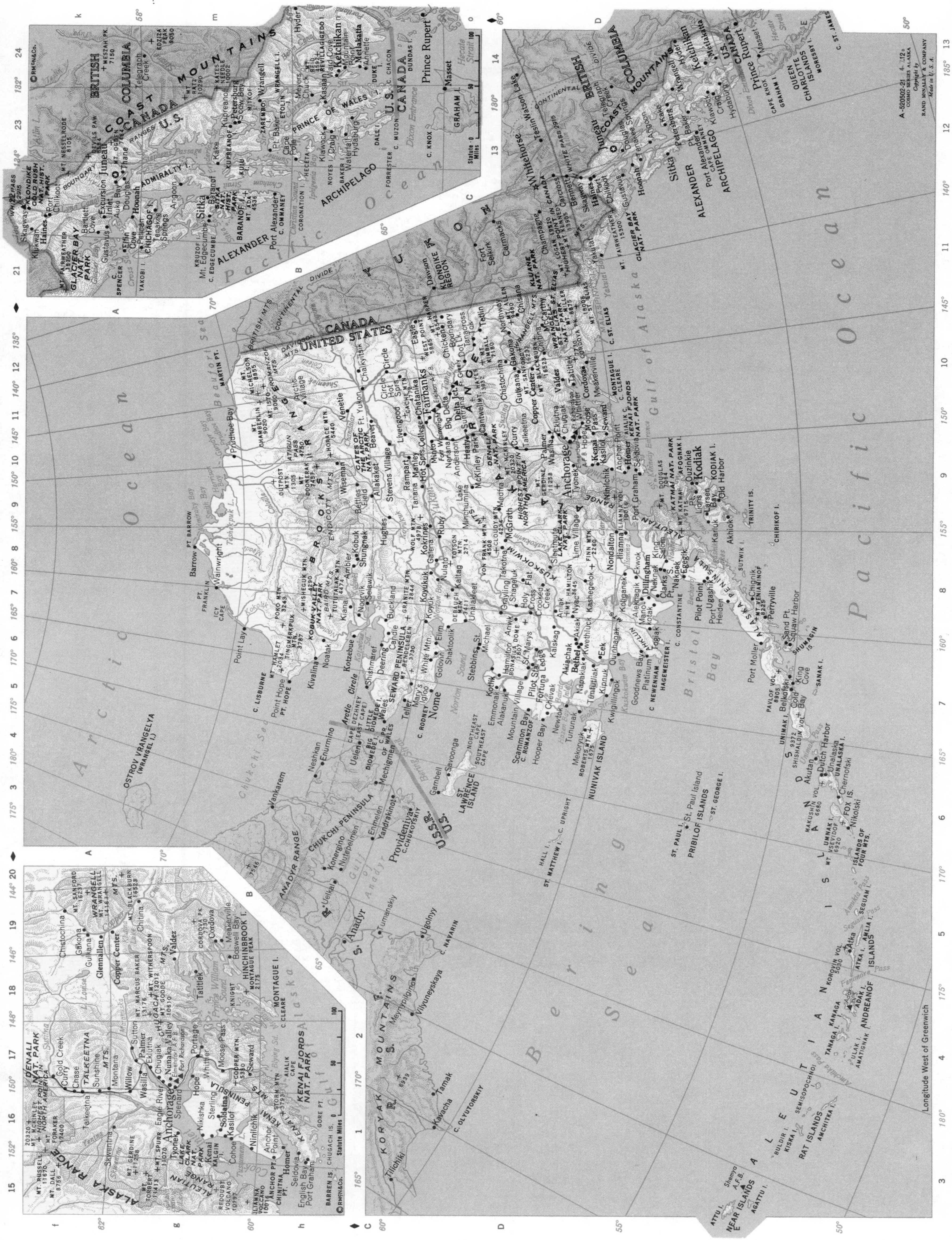

Polyconic Projection
SCALE 1:12,000,000 1 Inch = 189 Statute Miles

Statute Miles 50 25 0 50 100 150 200 250
Kilometers 50 0 100 200 300

Statute Miles 10 0 10 20 30 40 50 60 70 80 90

Kilometers 10 0 10 20 40 60 80 100 120

Lambert Conformal Conic Projection
SCALE 1:2,725,000 1 Inch = 43 Statute Miles

Longitude West of Greenwich

A-520503-21- COSMO SERIES ARIZONA
Copyright by RAND McNALLY & COMPANY Made in U. S. A.

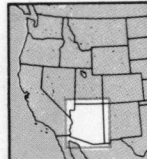

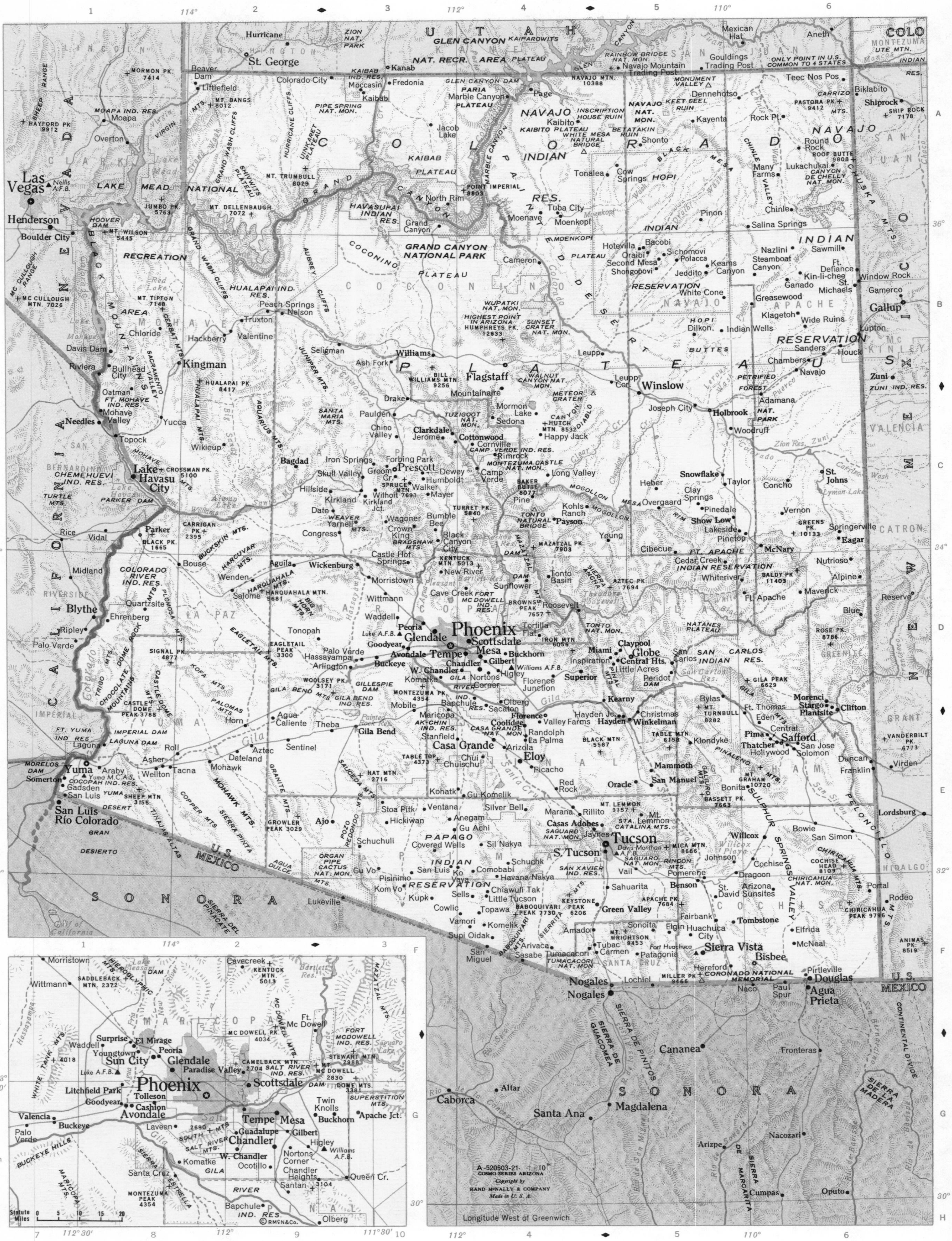

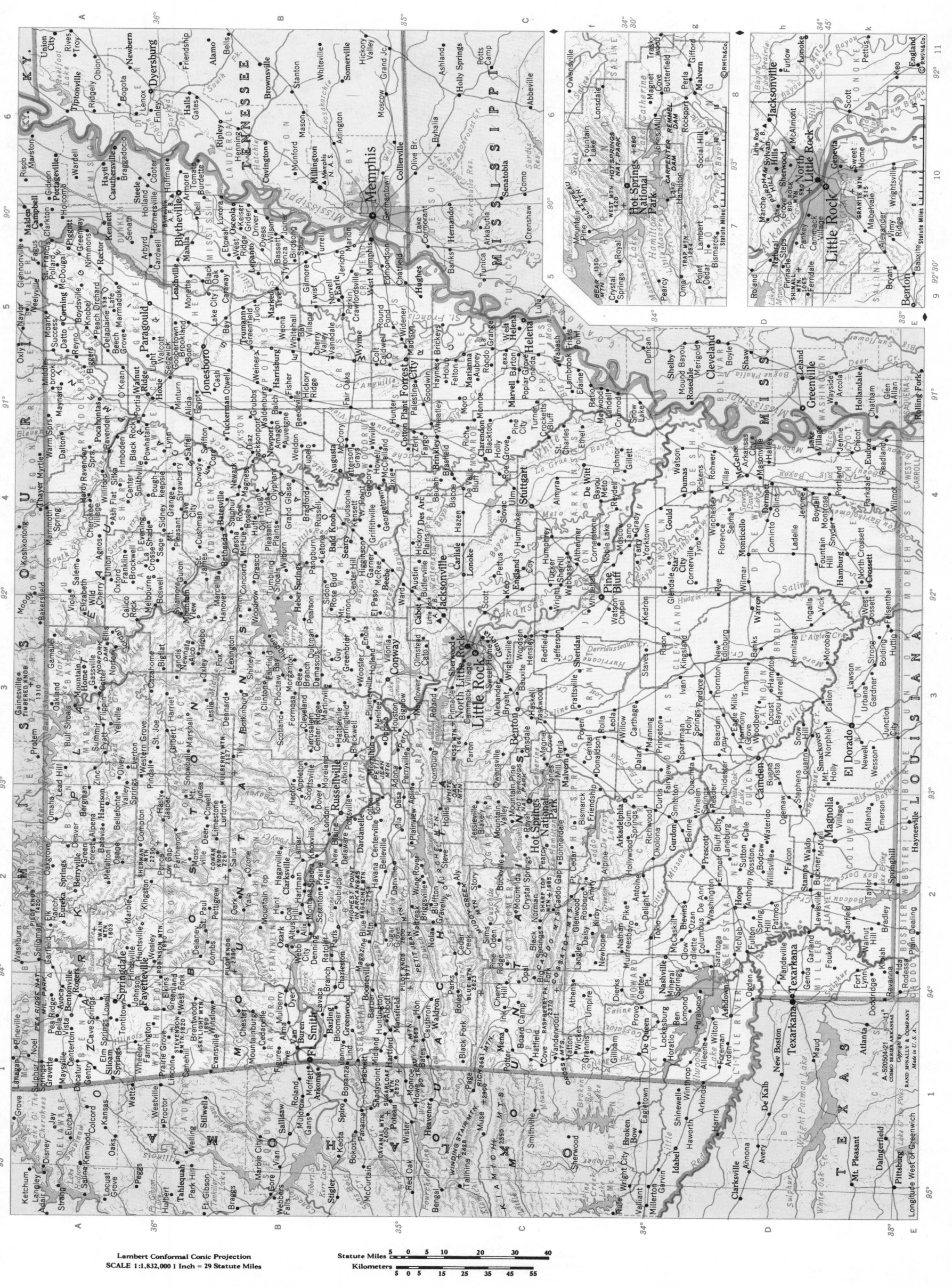

Lambert Conformal Conic Projection
SCALE 1:1,832,000 1 Inch = 29 Statute Miles

Statute Miles 5 0   5   10   20   30   40

Kilometers 5 0   15   25   35   45   55

A-520504-21
Copyright by
RAND M~NALLY & COMPANY
Made in U.S.A.

CALIFORNIA

A-520505-21-7-10-14
COSMO SERIES CALIFORNIA
Copyright by
RAND McNALLY & COMPANY
Made in U. S. A.

Longitude West of Greenwich

Statute Miles 10 0 10 20 30 40 50 60 70 80 90

Kilometers 10 0 10 20 40 60 80 100 120

Lambert Conformal Conic Projection
SCALE 1:3,733,000 1 Inch = 59 Statute Miles

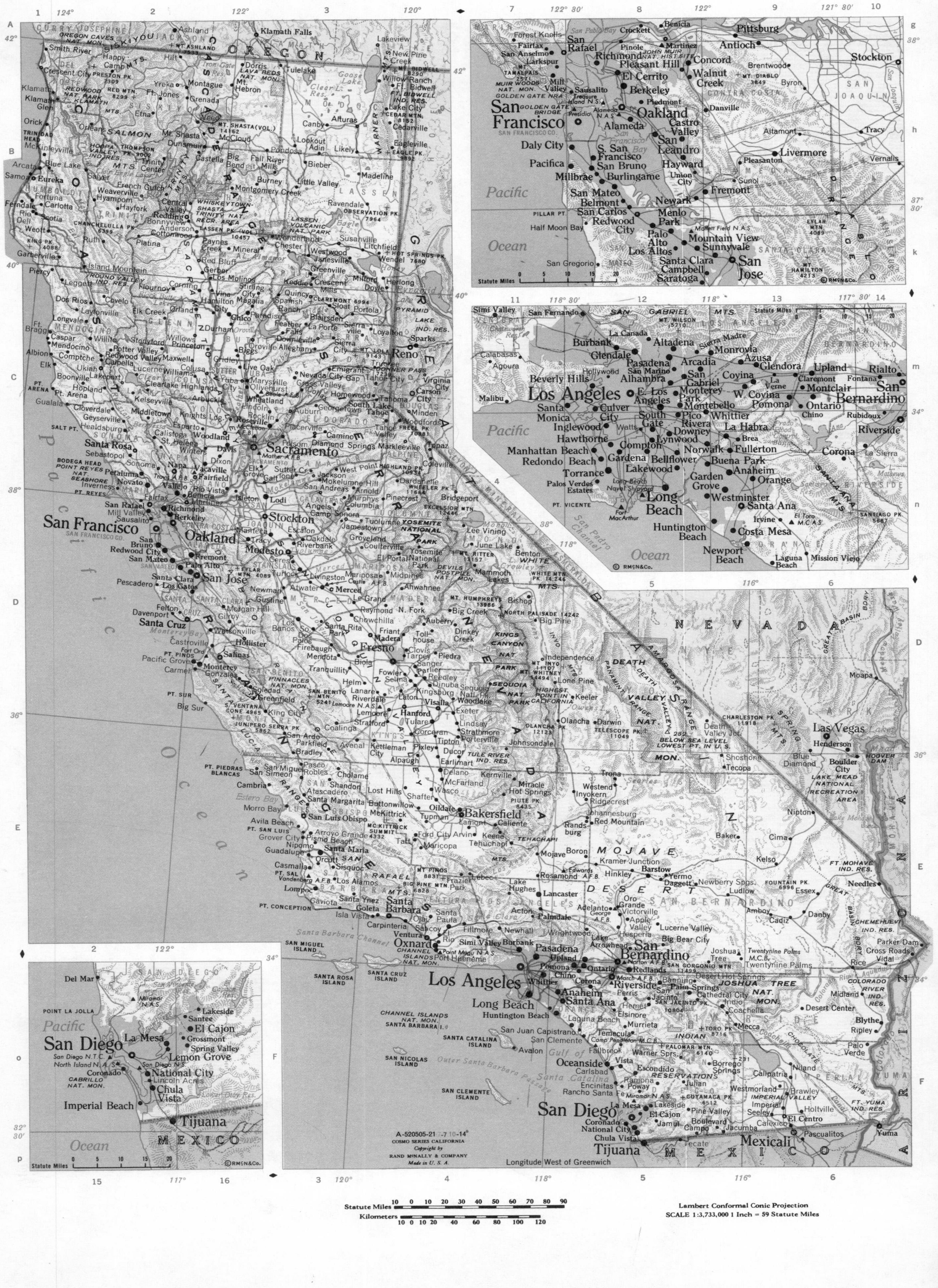

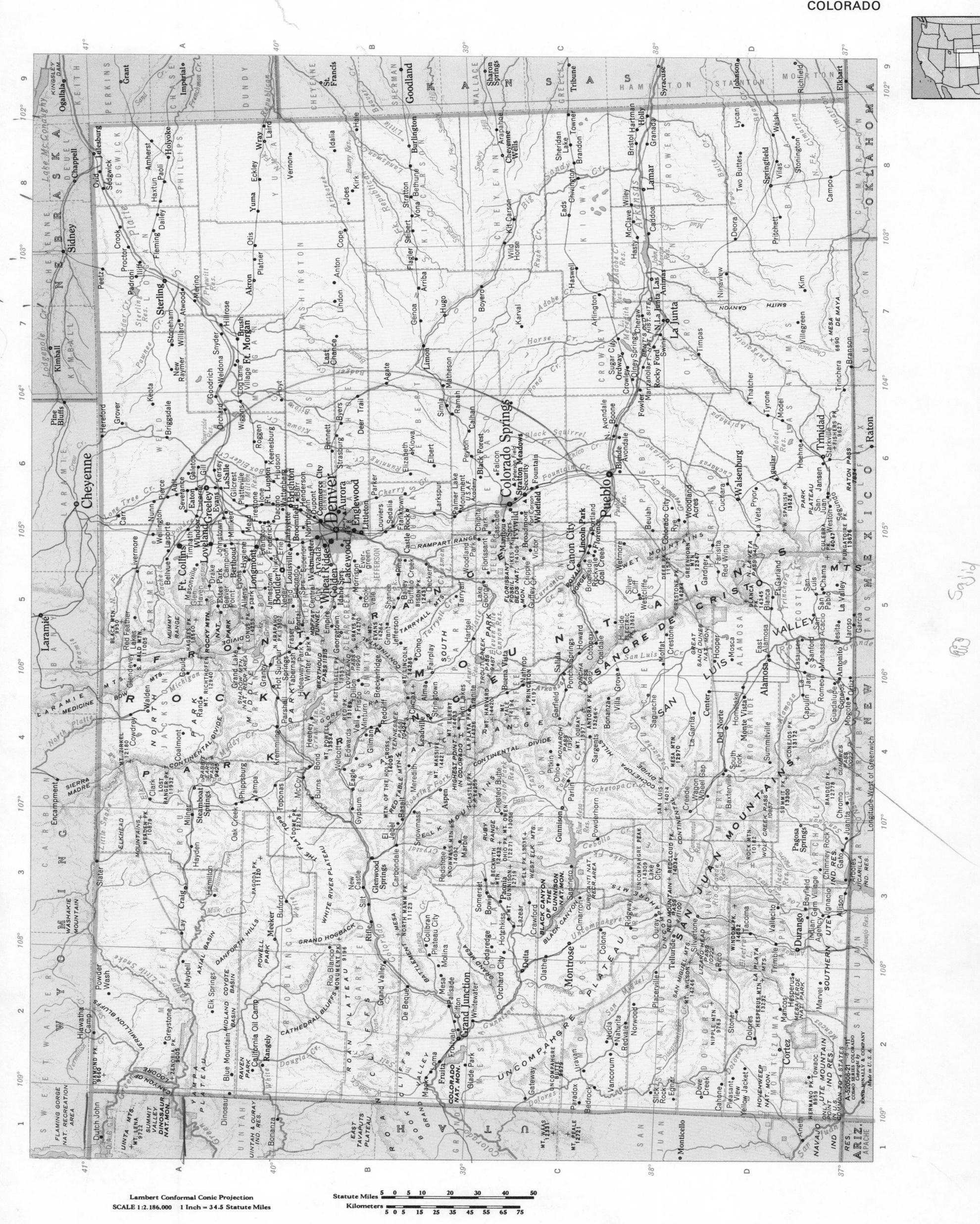

Lambert Conformal Conic Projection
SCALE 1:2,186,000   1 Inch = 34.5 Statute Miles

Statute Miles 5 0 5 10   20   30   40   50
Kilometers 5 0 5 15 25 35 45 55 65 75

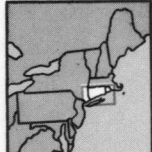

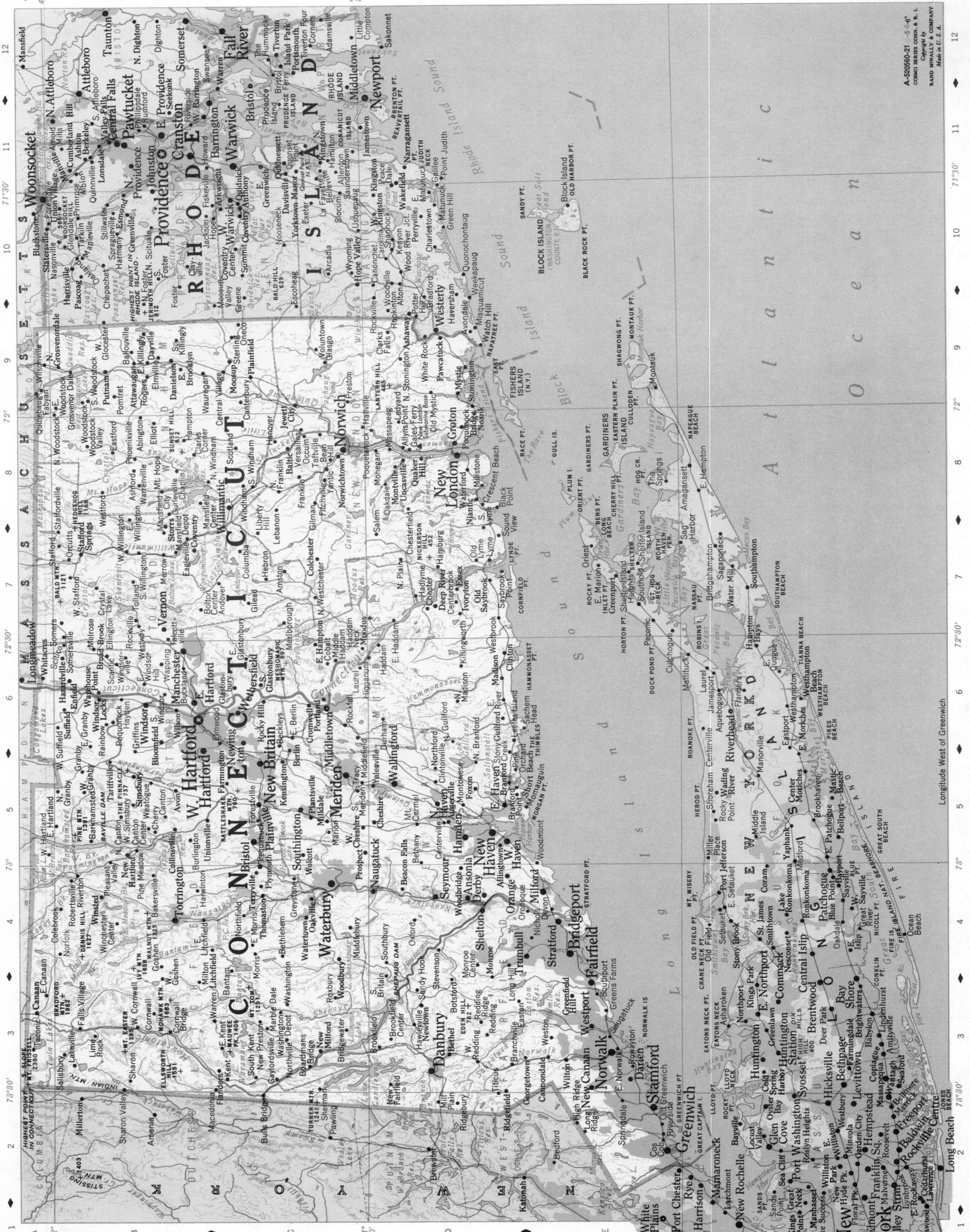

A-520560-21 -5-6-6"
COSMO SERIES CONN. & R. I.
Copyright by
RAND M?NALLY & COMPANY
Made in U.S.A.

Statute Miles
Kilometers

Lambert Conformal Conic Projection
SCALE 1:731,000 1 Inch = 11.5 Statute Miles

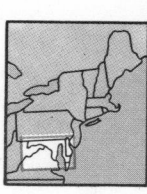

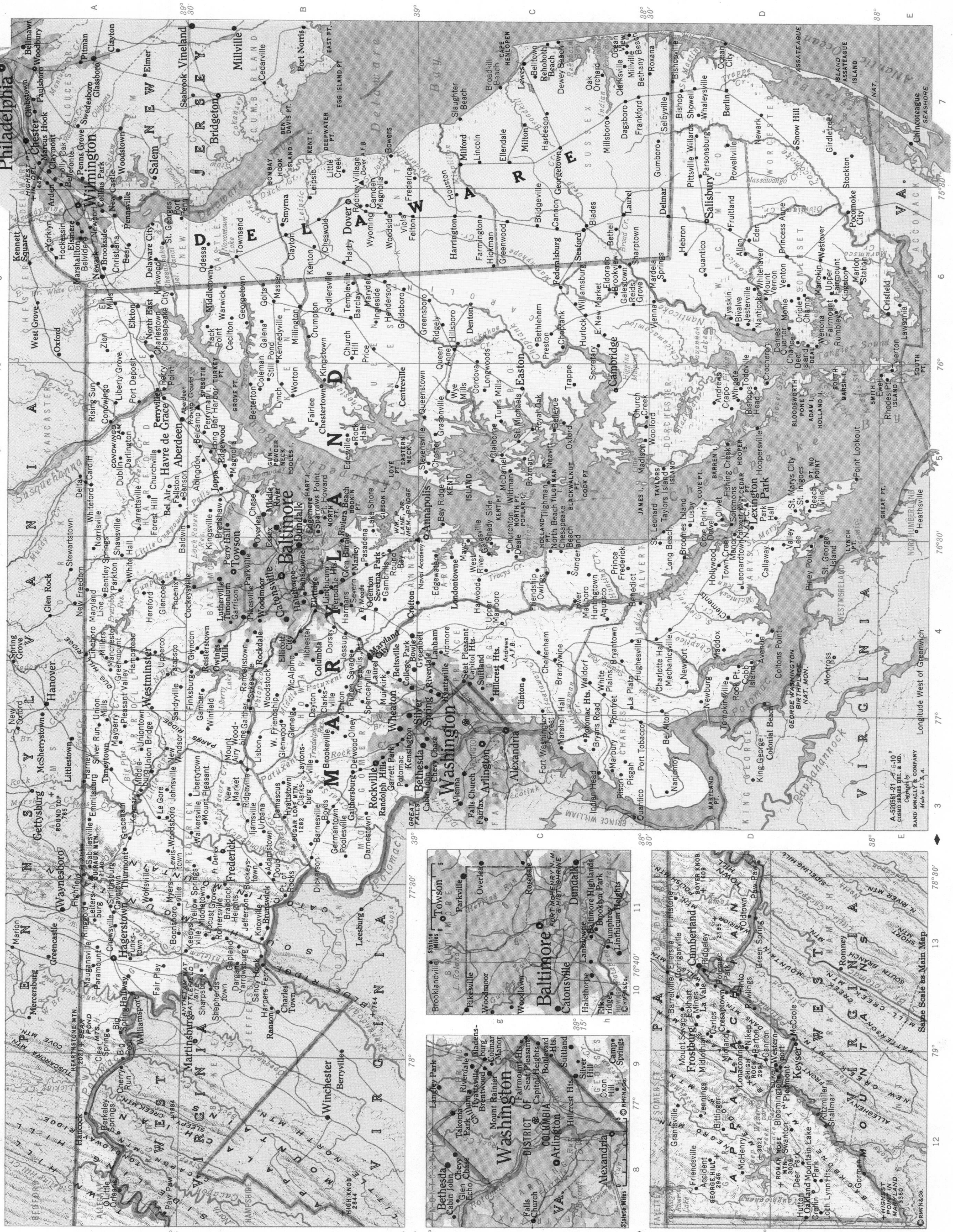

Lambert Conformal Conic Projection
SCALE 1:985,000 1 Inch = 15.5 Statute Miles

Statute Miles 5 0 5 10 15 20
Kilometers 5 0 5 10 15 20 25 30

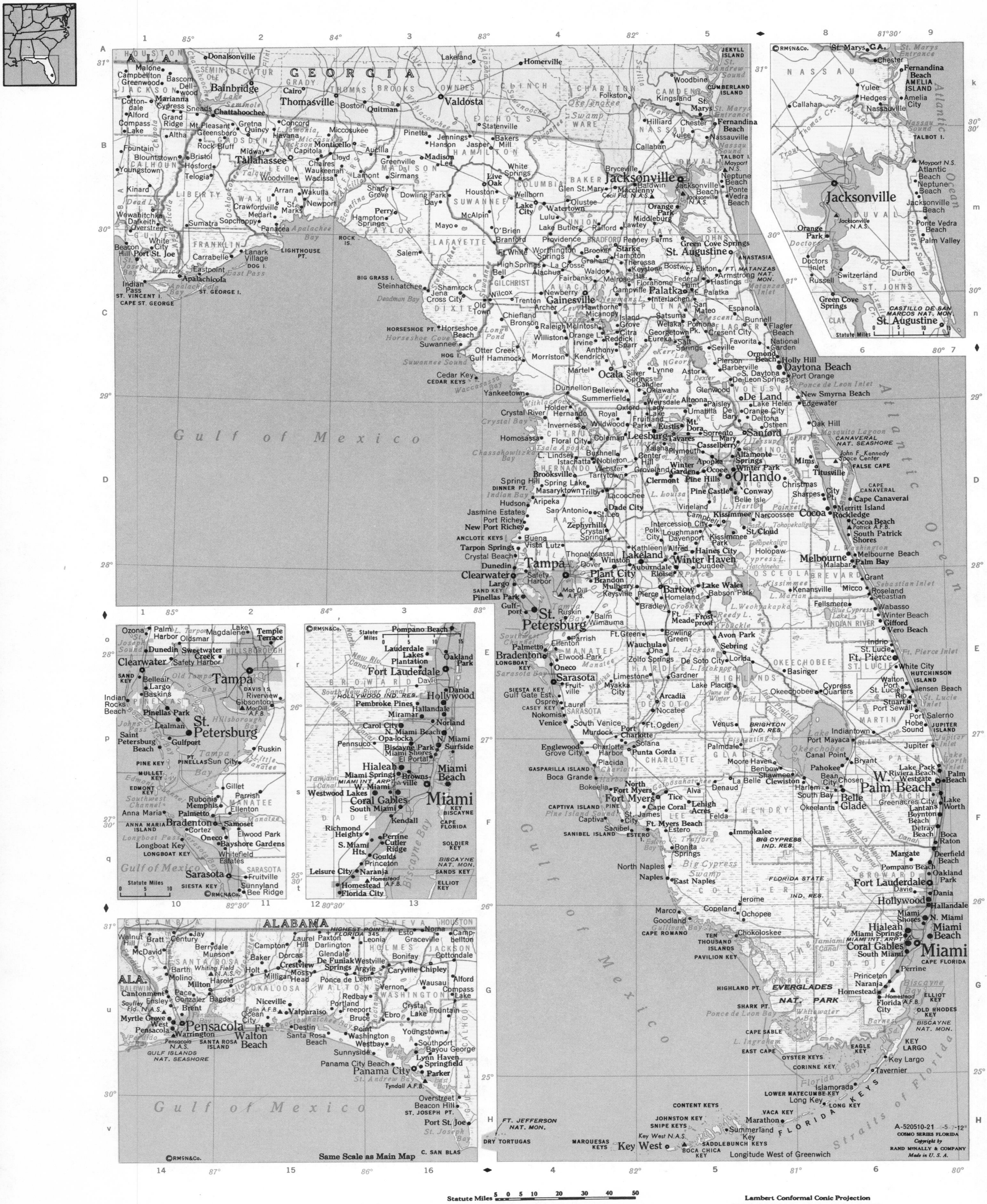

FLORIDA

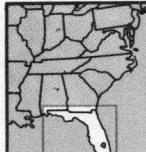

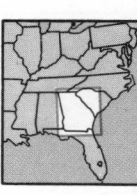

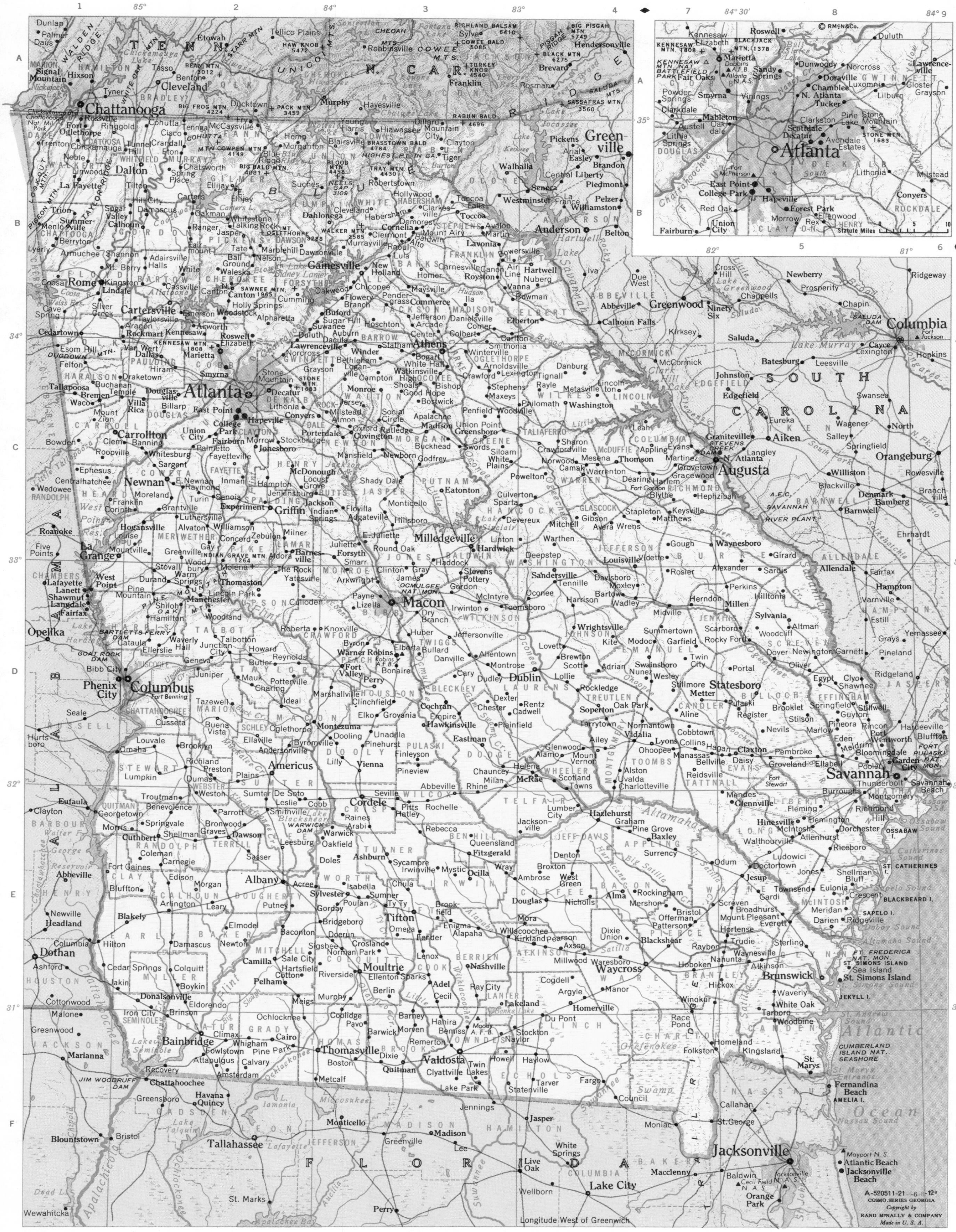

Lambert Conformal Conic Projection
SCALE 1:1,962,000   1 Inch = 31 Statute Miles

Statute Miles
5 0 5 10   20   30   40

Kilometers
5 0 5 15 25 35 45 55

A-520511-21 -6- 12*
COSMO SERIES GEORGIA
Copyright by
RAND MCNALLY & COMPANY
Made in U.S.A.

Statute Miles 5 0 5 10 20 30 40 50

Kilometers 5 0 5 10 20 30 40 50 60

Lambert Conformal Conic Projection

SCALE 1:2,000,000 1 Inch = 32 Statute Miles

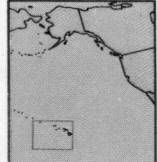

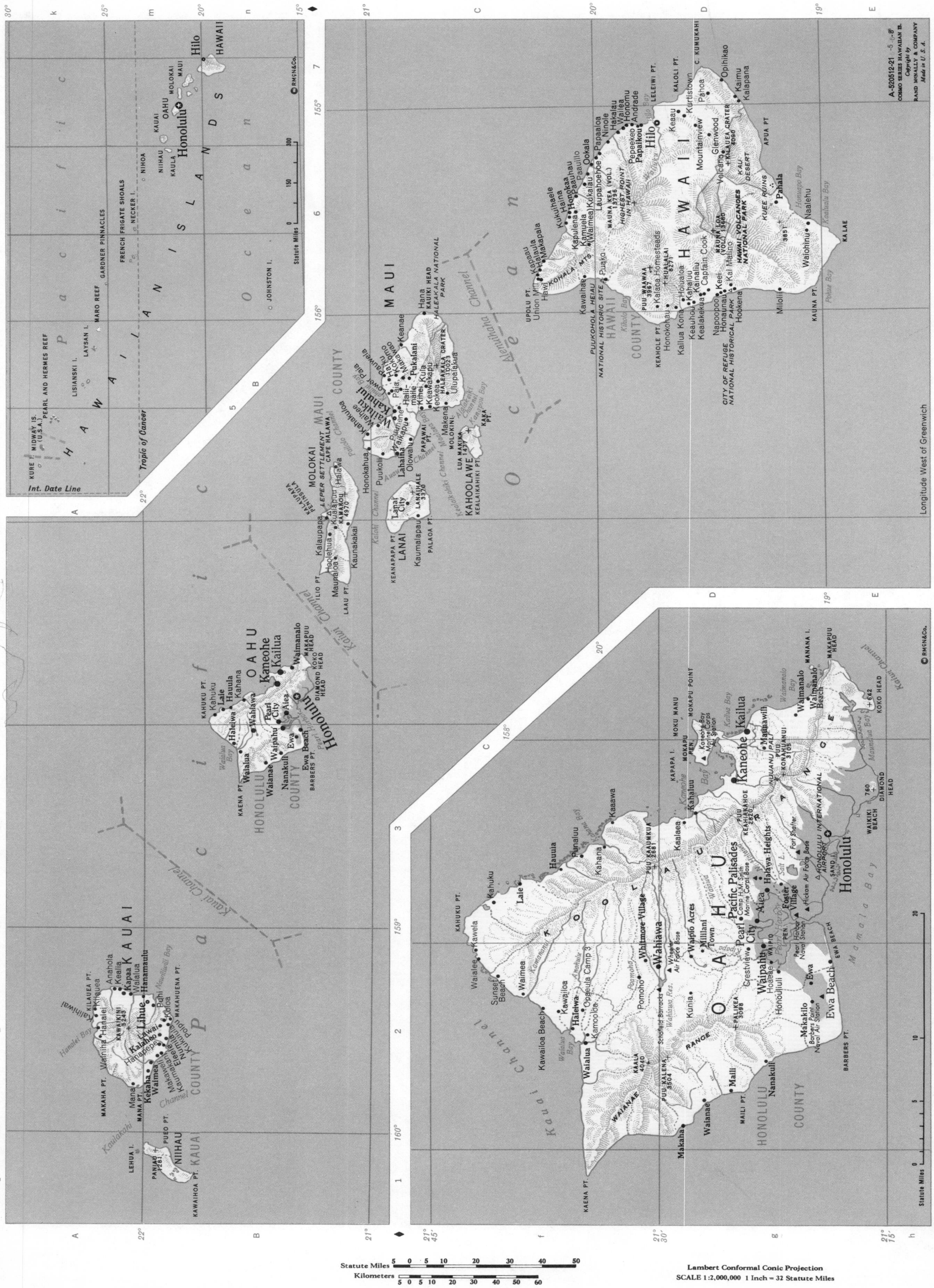

COSMO SERIES IDAHO
Copyright by RAND McNALLY & COMPANY
Made in U. S. A.
A-520513-21 -4-6-75

Longitude West of Greenwich

BRITISH COLUMBIA
ALBERTA
CANADA
UNITED STATES
MONTANA
OREGON
WASHINGTON
WYOMING
NEVADA
UTAH
HUMBOLDT
ELKO
BOX ELDER
CACHE
RICH

WATERTON
GLACIER NATIONAL PARK
INTERNATIONAL PEACE PARK
BLACKFEET INDIAN RESERVATION
FLATHEAD INDIAN RES.
COEUR D'ALENE IND. RES.
NEZ PERCE IND. RES.
HELLS CANYON NAT. RECR. AREA
SAWTOOTH NAT. RECR. AREA
CRATERS OF THE MOON NAT. MON.
YELLOWSTONE NATIONAL PARK
GRAND TETON NAT. PARK
FORT HALL IND. RES.
DUCK VALLEY IND. RES.
FT. MCDERMITT IND. RES.
Mountain Home A.F.B.
Malmstrom A.F.B.

ROCKY MOUNTAINS
BITTERROOT RANGE
CLEARWATER MOUNTAINS
SALMON RIVER MOUNTAINS
SAWTOOTH RANGE
LEMHI RANGE
LOST RIVER RANGE
BEAVERHEAD MTS.
CENTENNIAL MTS.
SNAKE RIVER RANGE
BIG BELT MOUNTAINS
LITTLE BELT MOUNTAINS
CABINET MOUNTAINS
PURCELL MOUNTAINS
COEUR D'ALENE MOUNTAINS
SWAN RANGE
MISSION RANGE
LEWIS RANGE
GARNET RANGE
FLINT CREEK RANGE
ANACONDA RANGE
PIONEER MTS.
TOBACCO ROOT MTS.
BLUE MOUNTAINS
WALLOWA MOUNTAINS
SEVEN DEVILS MTS.
OWYHEE MTS.
SNAKE RIVER PLAIN
LAVA BEDS
CONTINENTAL DIVIDE

Spokane
Coeur d'Alene
Lewiston
Moscow
Pullman
Sandpoint
Bonners Ferry
Wallace
Kellogg
St. Maries
Grangeville
Orofino
Kamiah
McCall
Weiser
Payette
Ontario
Emmett
Caldwell
Nampa
Boise
Mountain Home
Gooding
Jerome
Twin Falls
Burley
Rupert
Hailey
Sun Valley
Ketchum
Challis
Salmon
Arco
Idaho Falls
Blackfoot
Pocatello
American Falls
Rexburg
St. Anthony
Ashton
Driggs
Soda Springs
Montpelier
Preston
Malad City
Missoula
Kalispell
Whitefish
Hamilton
Anaconda
Butte
Helena
Great Falls
Bozeman
Livingston
Dillon
Choteau
Conrad
Shelby
Cut Bank
Browning
Fort Benton
Jackson
Afton

Lambert Conformal Conic Projection
SCALE 1:2,633,000 1 Inch = 41.5 Statute Miles

Statute Miles 5 0 5 10 20 30 40 50 60
Kilometers 5 0 5 15 25 35 45 55 65 75

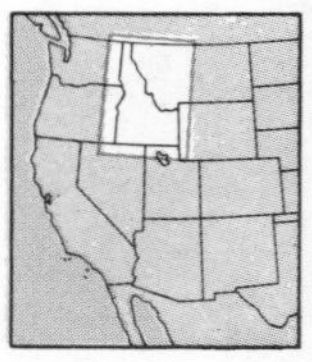

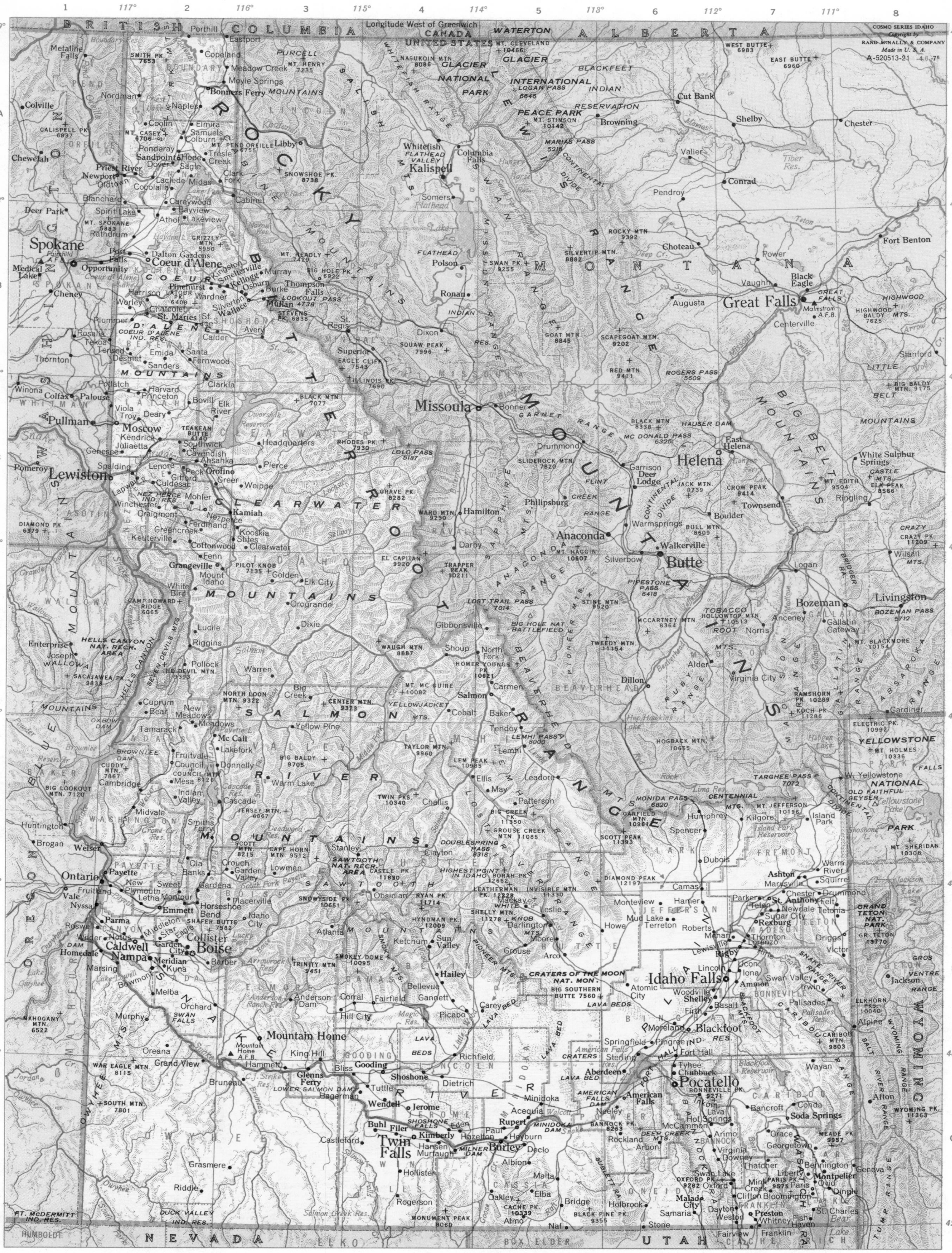

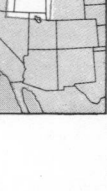

CHARLES MOUND 1235 HIGHEST PT. IN ILL.

Longitude West of Greenwich

Statute Miles 5 0 5 10 20 30 40

Kilometers 5 0 5 15 25 35 45 55

Lambert Conformal Conic Projection

SCALE 1:1,997,000 1 Inch = 31.5 Statute Miles

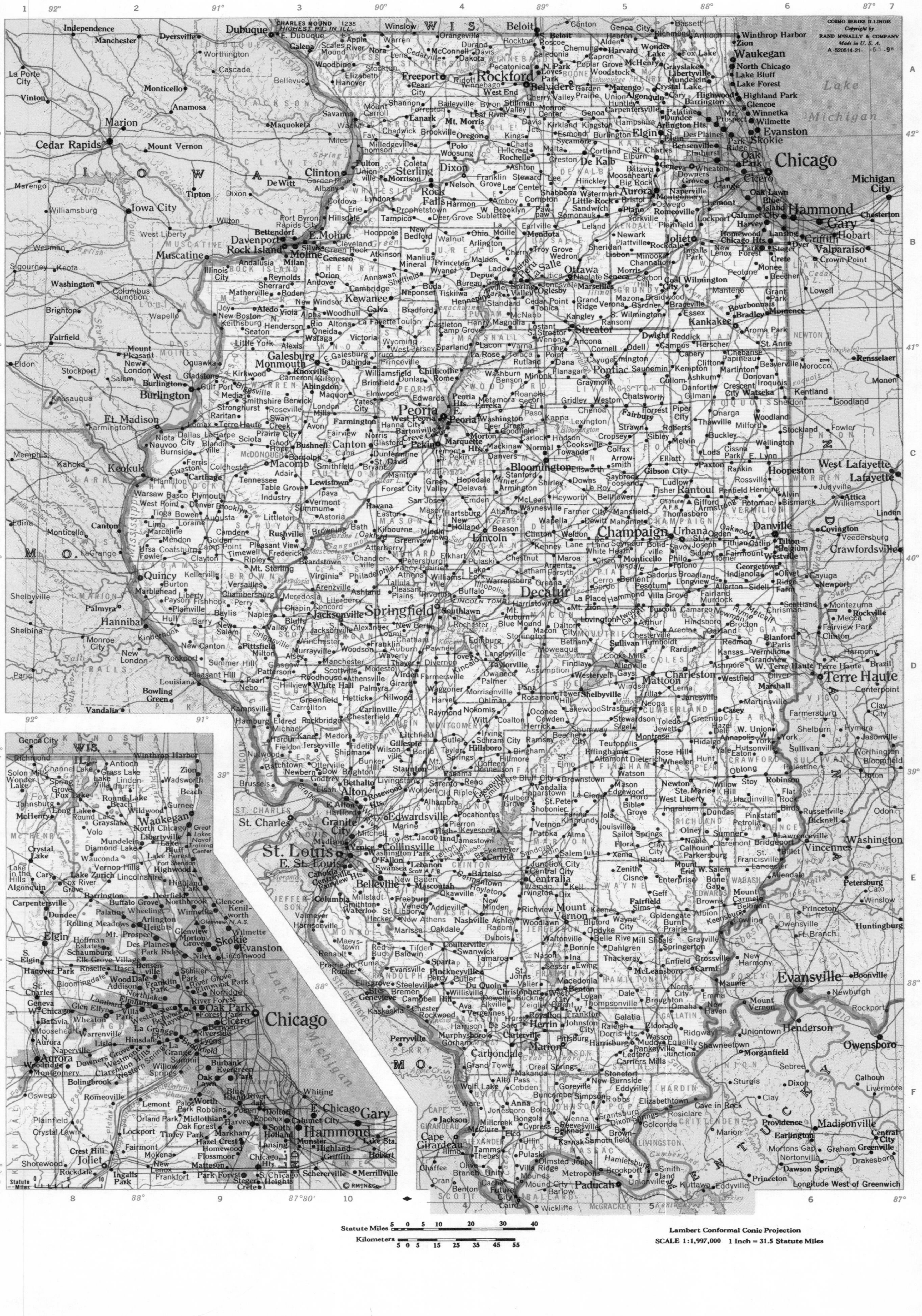

Lambert Conformal Conic Projection
SCALE 1:1,465,000 1 Inch=23 Statute Miles

Statute Miles 5 0 5 10 15 20 25 30

Kilometers 5 0 5 15 25 35

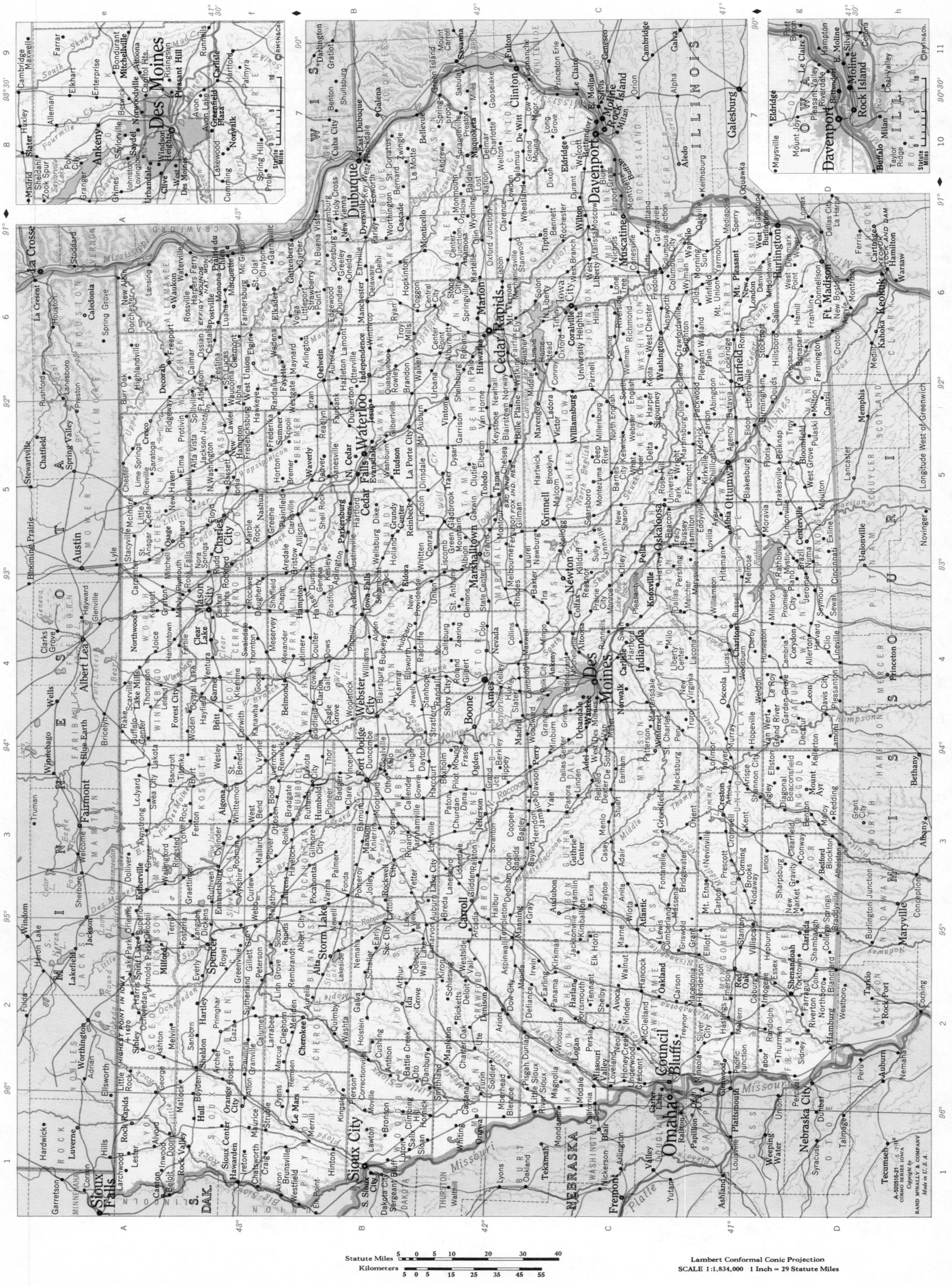

Statute Miles 5 0 5 10 20 30 40
Kilometers 5 0 5 15 25 35 45 55

Lambert Conformal Conic Projection
SCALE 1:1,834,000   1 Inch = 29 Statute Miles

A-800916-21   COSMO SERIES, IOWA
Copyright by
RAND McNALLY & COMPANY
Made in U.S.A.

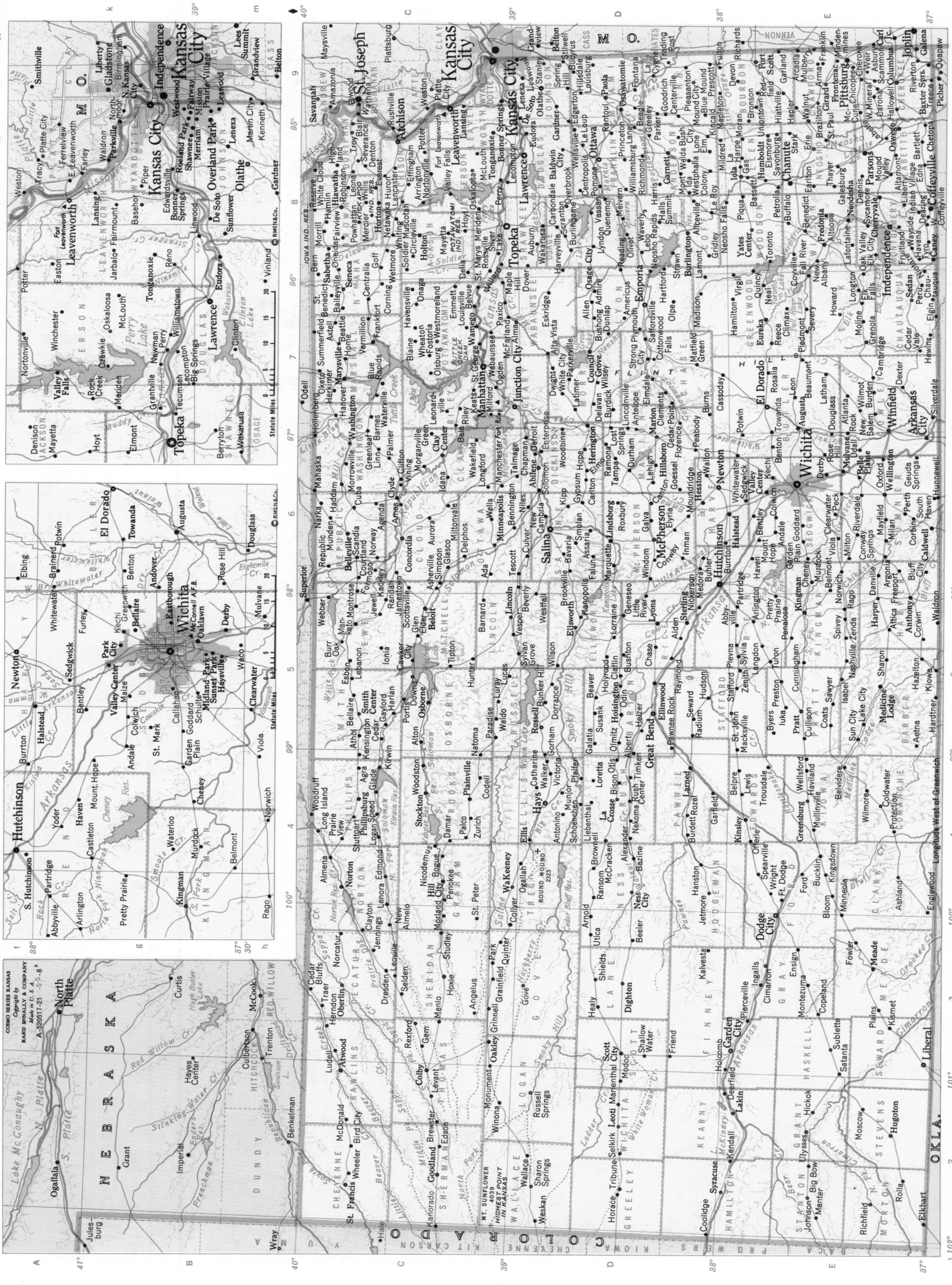

Lambert Conformal Conic Projection
SCALE 1:2,208,000 1 Inch = 35 Statute Miles

Statute Miles
Kilometers

COSMO SERIES KANSAS
Copyright by
RAND M^cNALLY & COMPANY
Made in U.S.A.
A-520517-21

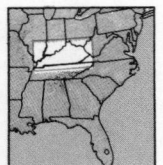

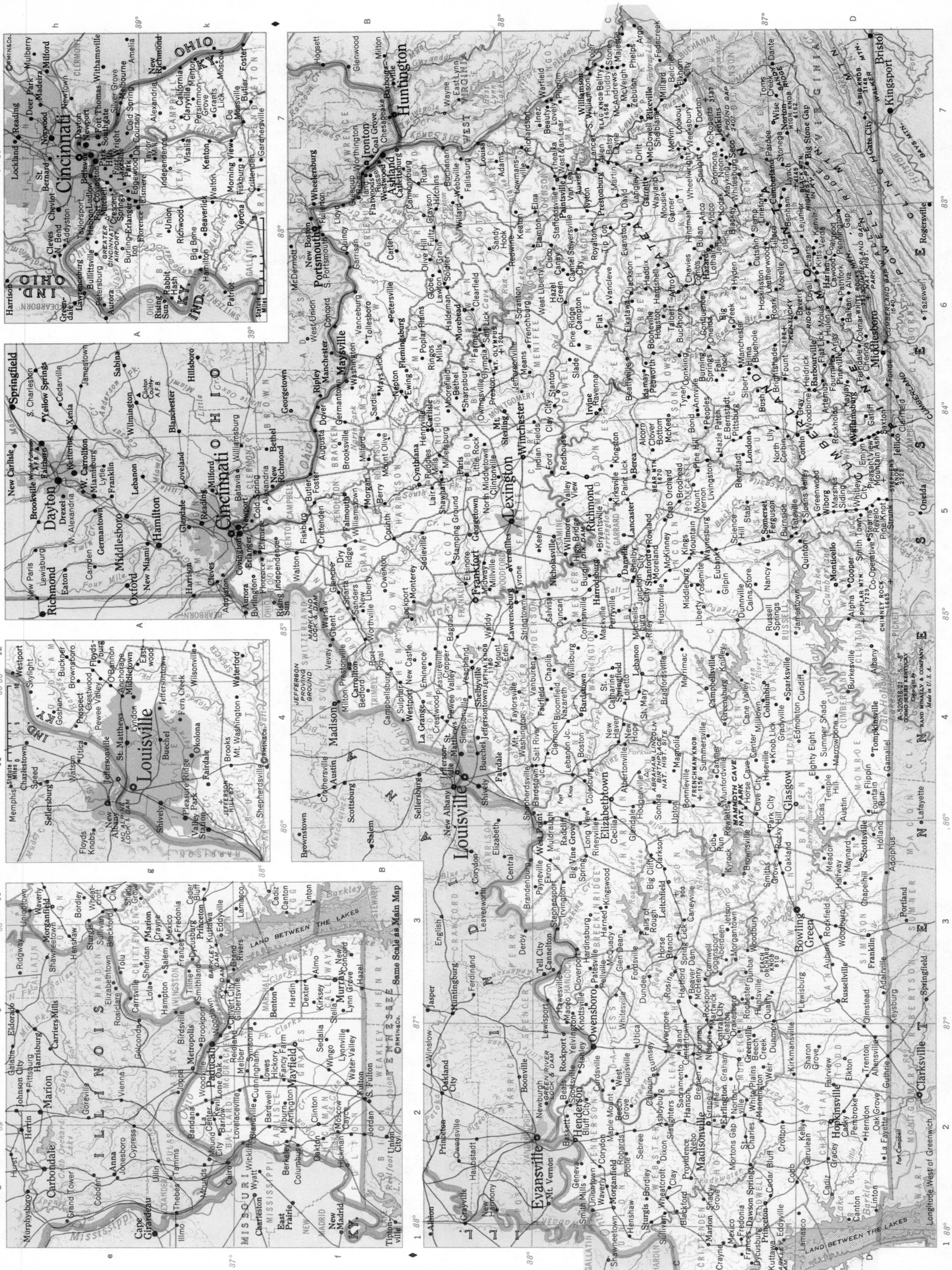

Statute Miles 5 0 5 10 20 30 40

Kilometers 5 0 5 10 20 30 40 50 60

Lambert Conformal Conic Projection
SCALE 1:1,738,000 1 Inch = 27 Statute Miles

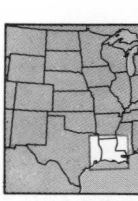

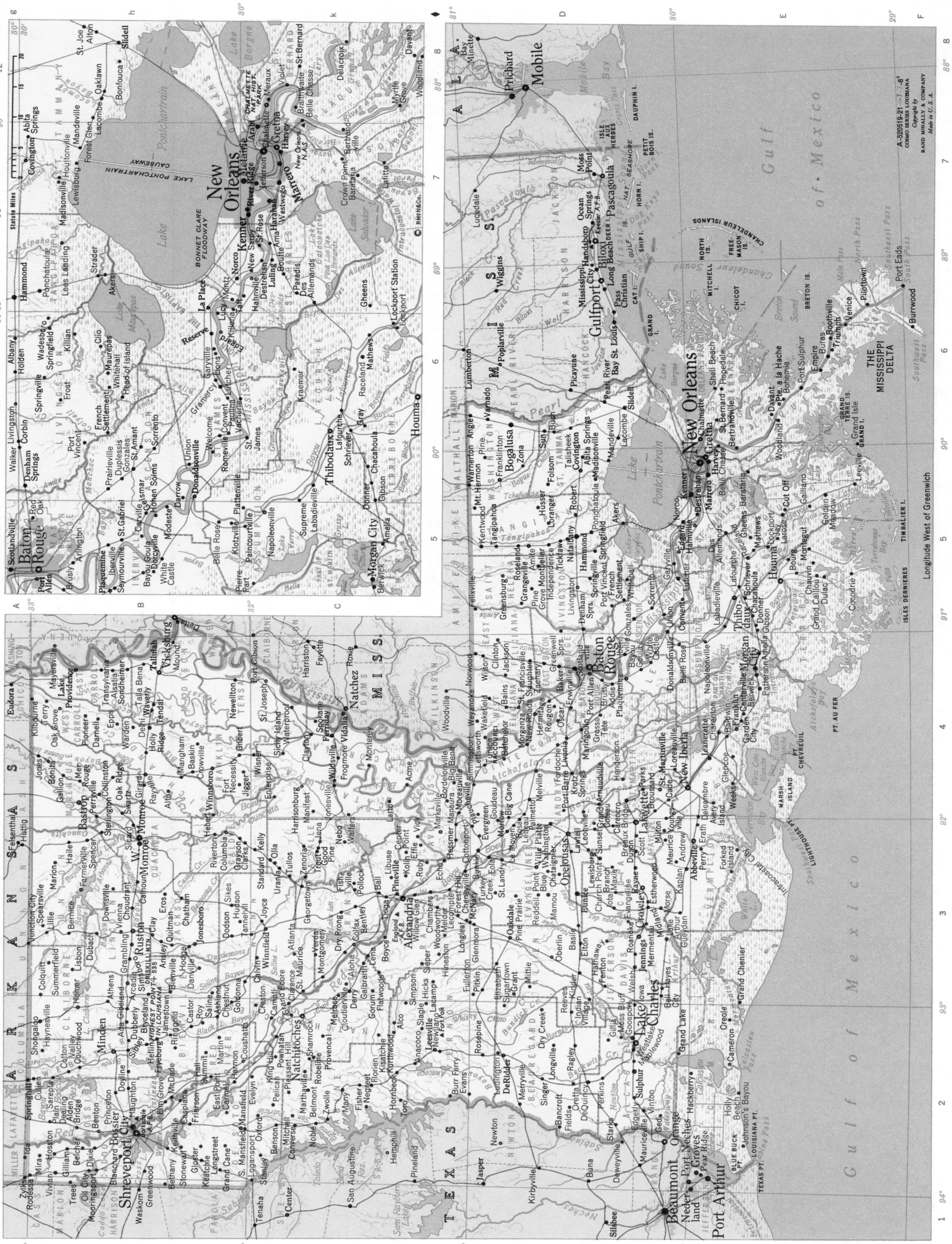

Lambert Conformal Conic Projection
SCALE 1:2,083,000 1 Inch = 33 Statute Miles

Statute Miles 5 0 5 10 20 30 40
Kilometers 5 0 5 15 25 35 45 55

Atlantic Ocean

Longitude West of Greenwich

A-520520-21 -5-6-8
COSMO SERIES MAINE
Copyright by
RAND McNALLY & COMPANY
Made in U. S. A.

Statute Miles 5 0 5 10 20 30

Kilometers 5 0 5 10 20 30 40

Lambert Conformal Conic Projection
SCALE 1:1,581,000 1 Inch = 25 Statute Miles

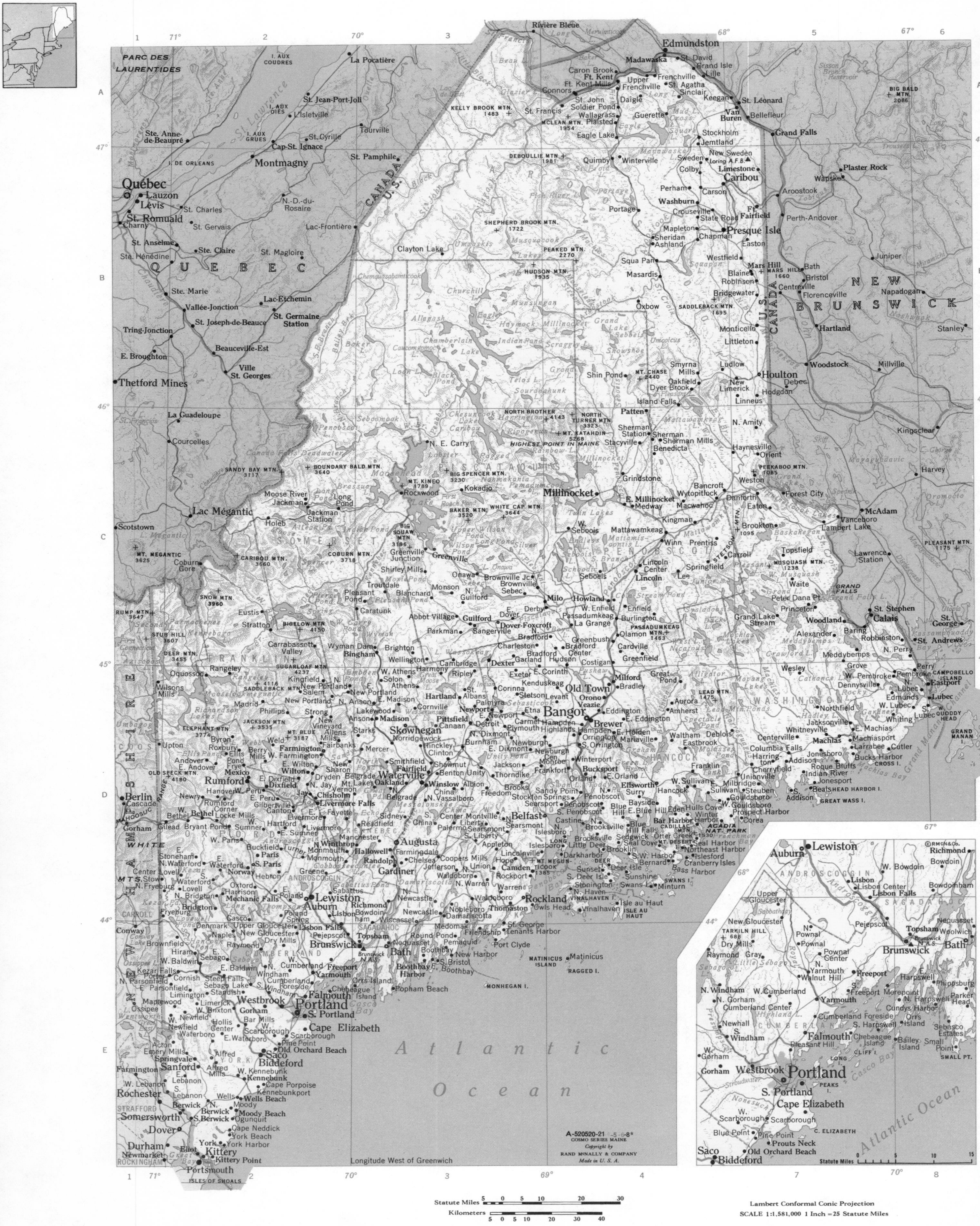

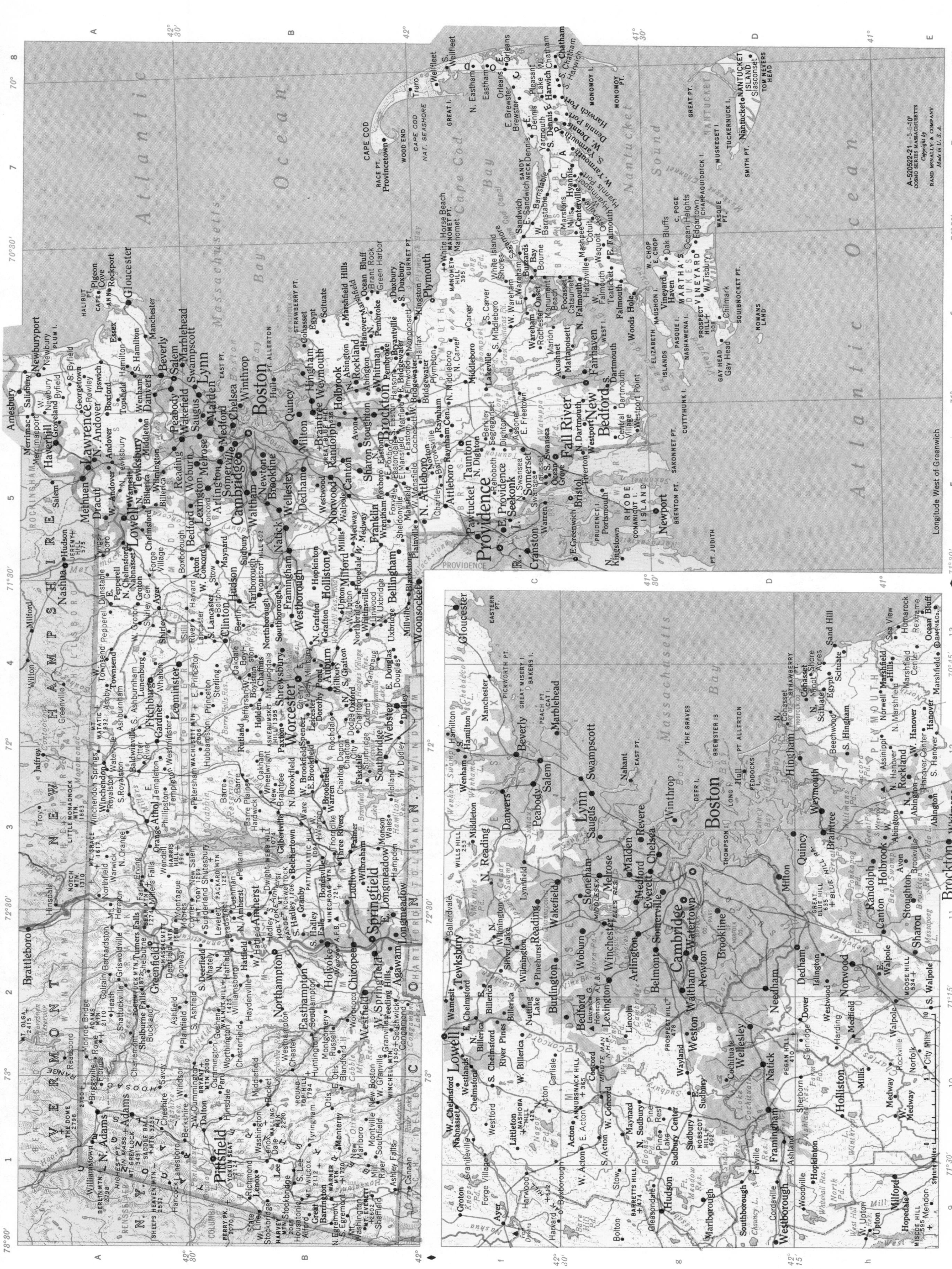

Lambert Conformal Conic Projection
SCALE 1:978,000   1 Inch = 15.5 Statute Miles

Statute Miles
Kilometers

A-50522-21
COSMO SERIES MASSACHUSETTS
Copyright by
RAND M�NALLY & COMPANY
Made in U.S.A.

MICHIGAN

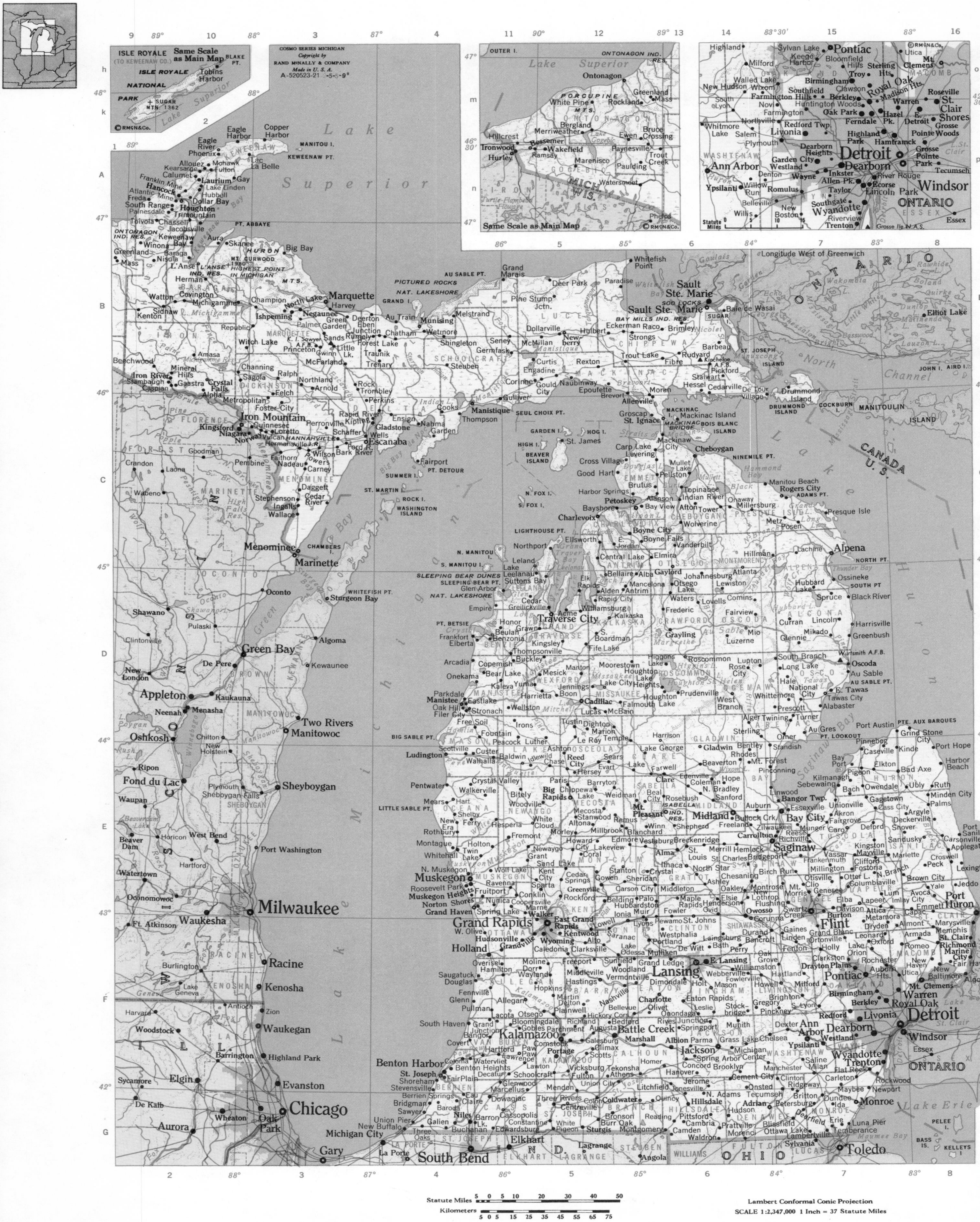

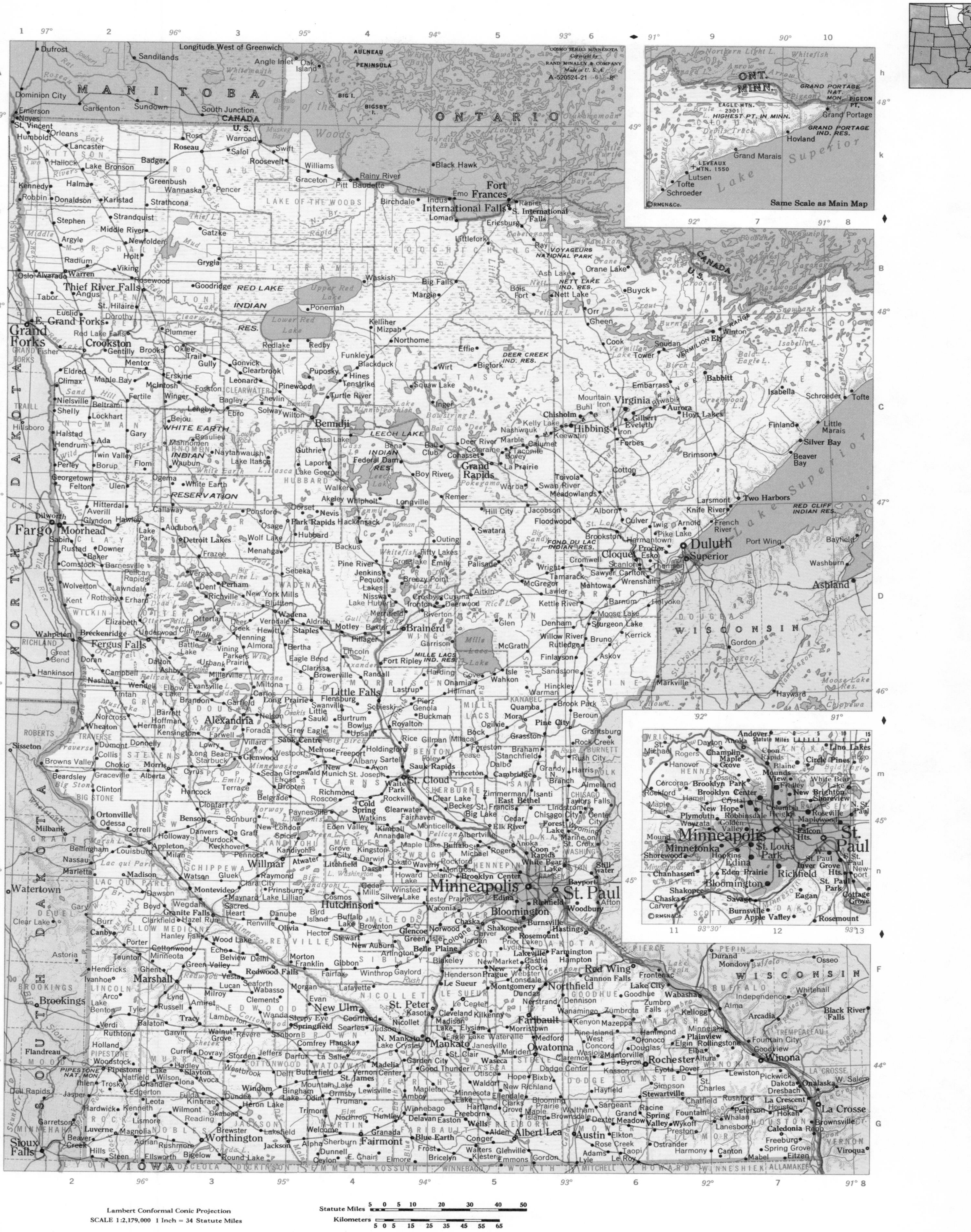

Longitude West of Greenwich

COSMO SERIES MINNESOTA
Copyright by
RAND M?NALLY & COMPANY
Made in U. S. A.
A-520524-21

Same Scale as Main Map

Lambert Conformal Conic Projection
SCALE 1:2,179,000   1 Inch = 34 Statute Miles

Statute Miles
Kilometers

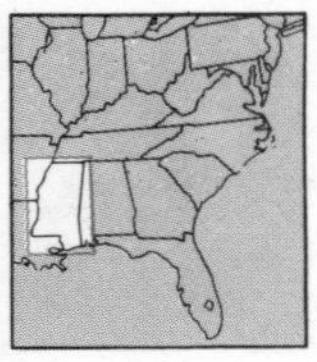

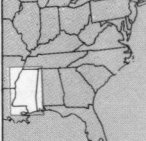

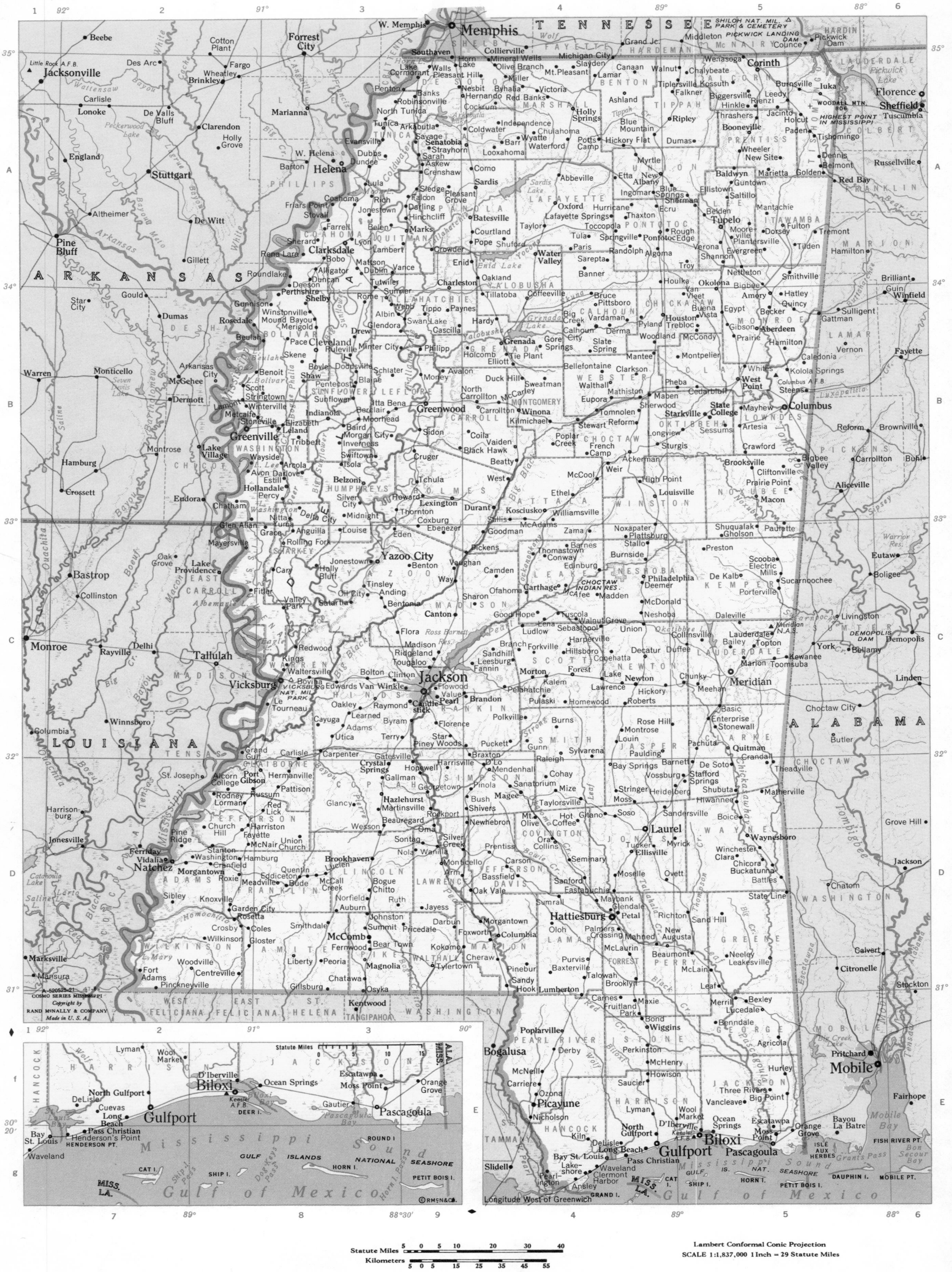
TENNESSEE
ARKANSAS
LOUISIANA
ALABAMA
Memphis
Jackson
Vicksburg
Greenville
Greenwood
Columbus
Tupelo
Meridian
Hattiesburg
Laurel
Natchez
Gulfport
Biloxi
Pascagoula
Mobile
Monroe
Jacksonville
Pine Bluff
Helena
Clarksdale
Yazoo City
Corinth
Florence
Sheffield
Bogalusa
Picayune
McComb
Brookhaven
Starkville
Oxford
Grenada
Cleveland
Canton
Gulf of Mexico
Mississippi Sound
GULF ISLANDS NATIONAL SEASHORE
CHOCTAW INDIAN RES.
HIGHEST POINT IN MISSISSIPPI
WOODALL MTN. 806
Longitude West of Greenwich
Statute Miles 5 0 5 10 20 30 40
Kilometers 5 0 5 15 25 35 45 55
Lambert Conformal Conic Projection
SCALE 1:1,837,000 1 Inch = 29 Statute Miles
COSMO SERIES MISSISSIPPI
Copyright by RAND McNALLY & COMPANY
Made in U. S. A.

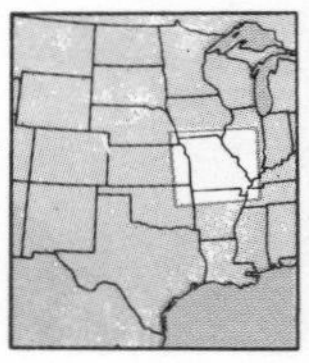

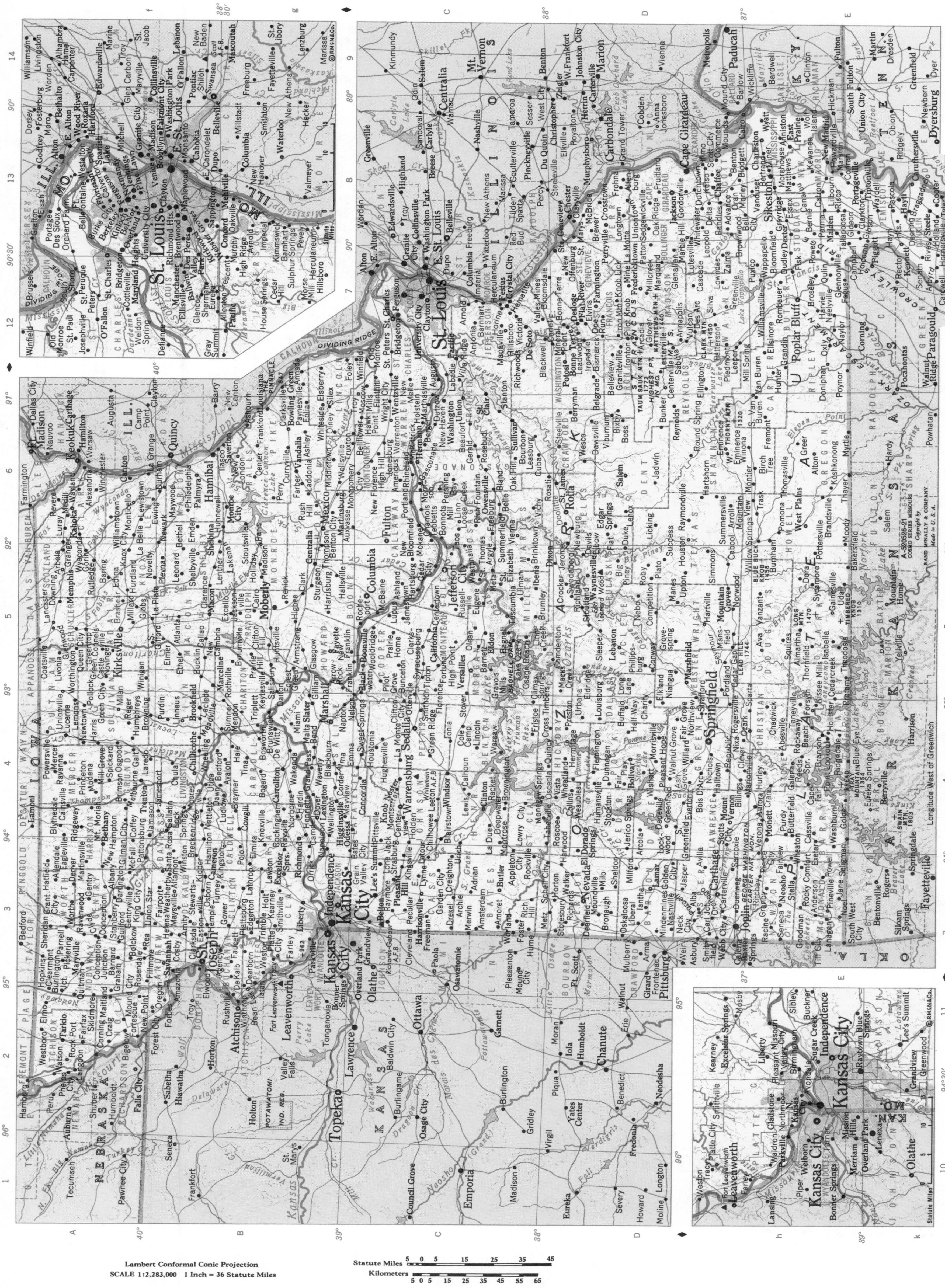
St. Louis
Kansas City
Springfield
Independence
St. Joseph
Columbia
Jefferson City
Joplin
Cape Girardeau
Topeka
Lawrence
Leavenworth
Hannibal
Quincy
Paducah
Olathe
I O W A
N E B R A S K A
K A N S A S
I L L I N O I S
A R K A N S A S
O Z A R K S
Lambert Conformal Conic Projection
SCALE 1:2,283,000 1 Inch = 36 Statute Miles
Statute Miles 5 0 5 15 25 35 45
Kilometers 5 0 5 15 25 35 45 55 65

Statute Miles 10 0 10 20 30 40 50 60 70

Kilometers 10 0 10 30 50 70 90

Lambert Conformal Conic Projection

SCALE 1:3,000,000 1 Inch = 47.5 Statute Miles

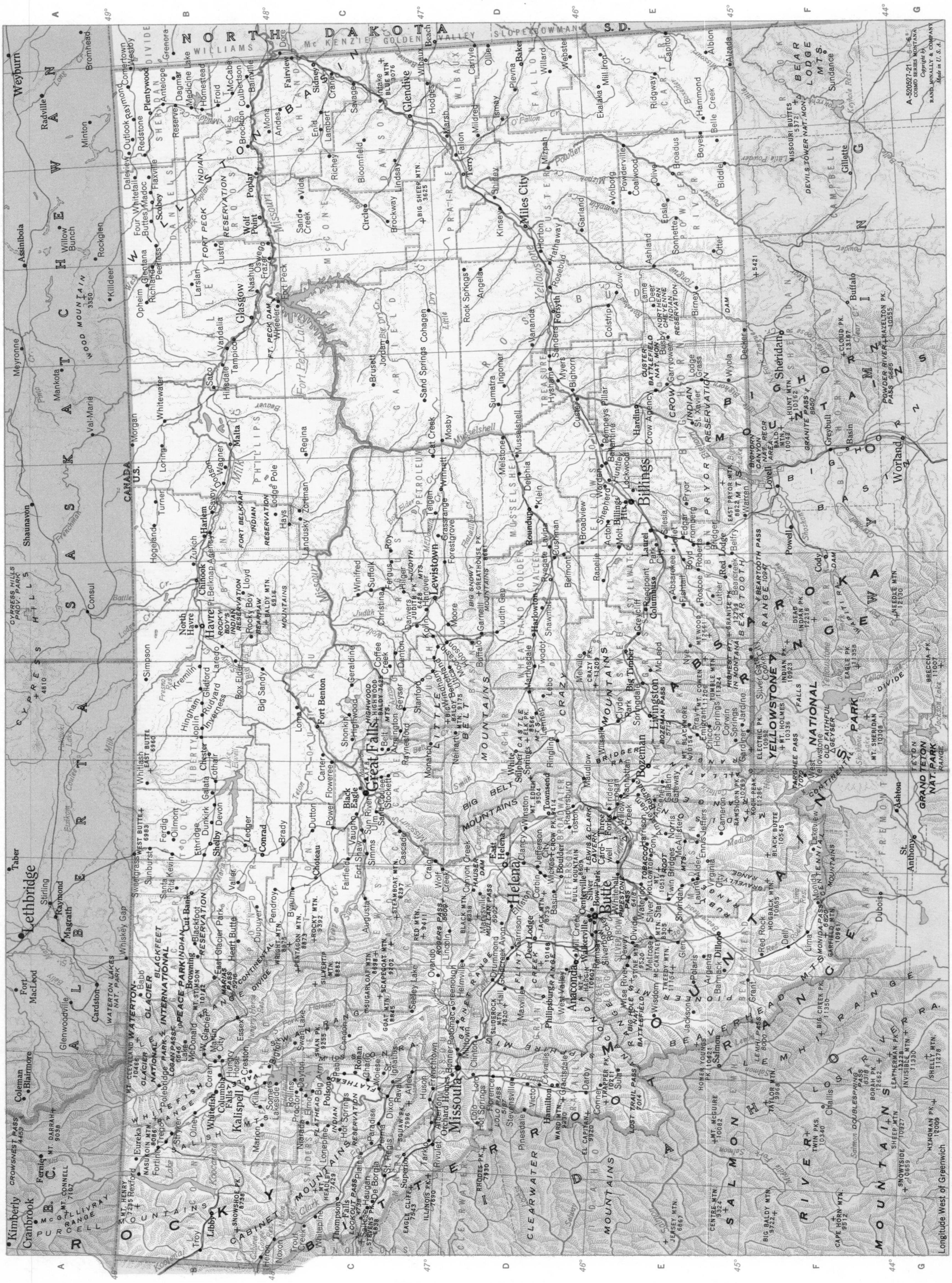

Lambert Conformal Conic Projection
SCALE 1:2,460,000 1 Inch = 39 Statute Miles

Statute Miles 5 0 5 10 20 30 40 50 60
Kilometers 5 0 5 15 35 55 75 95

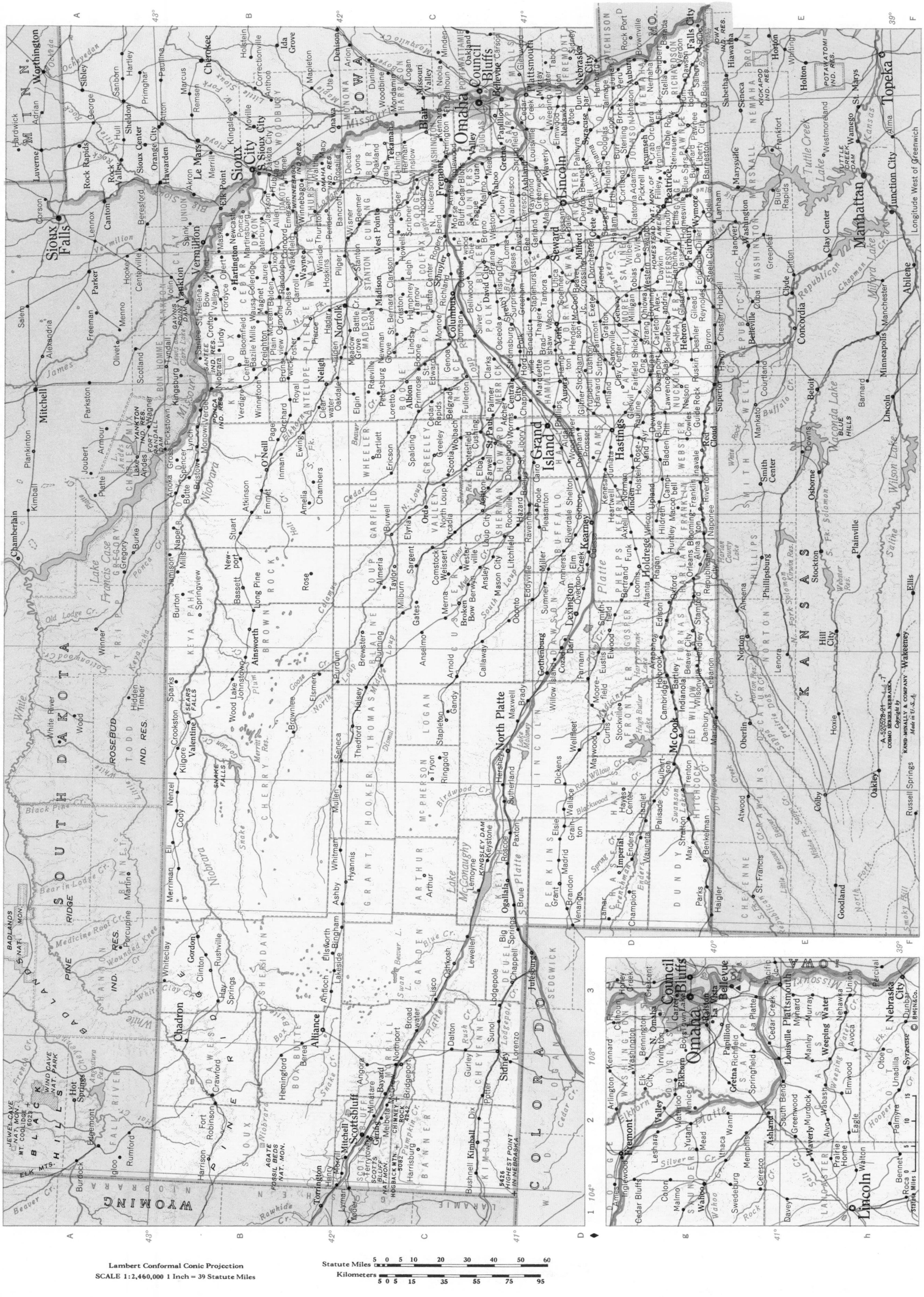

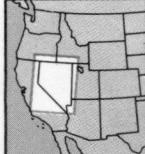

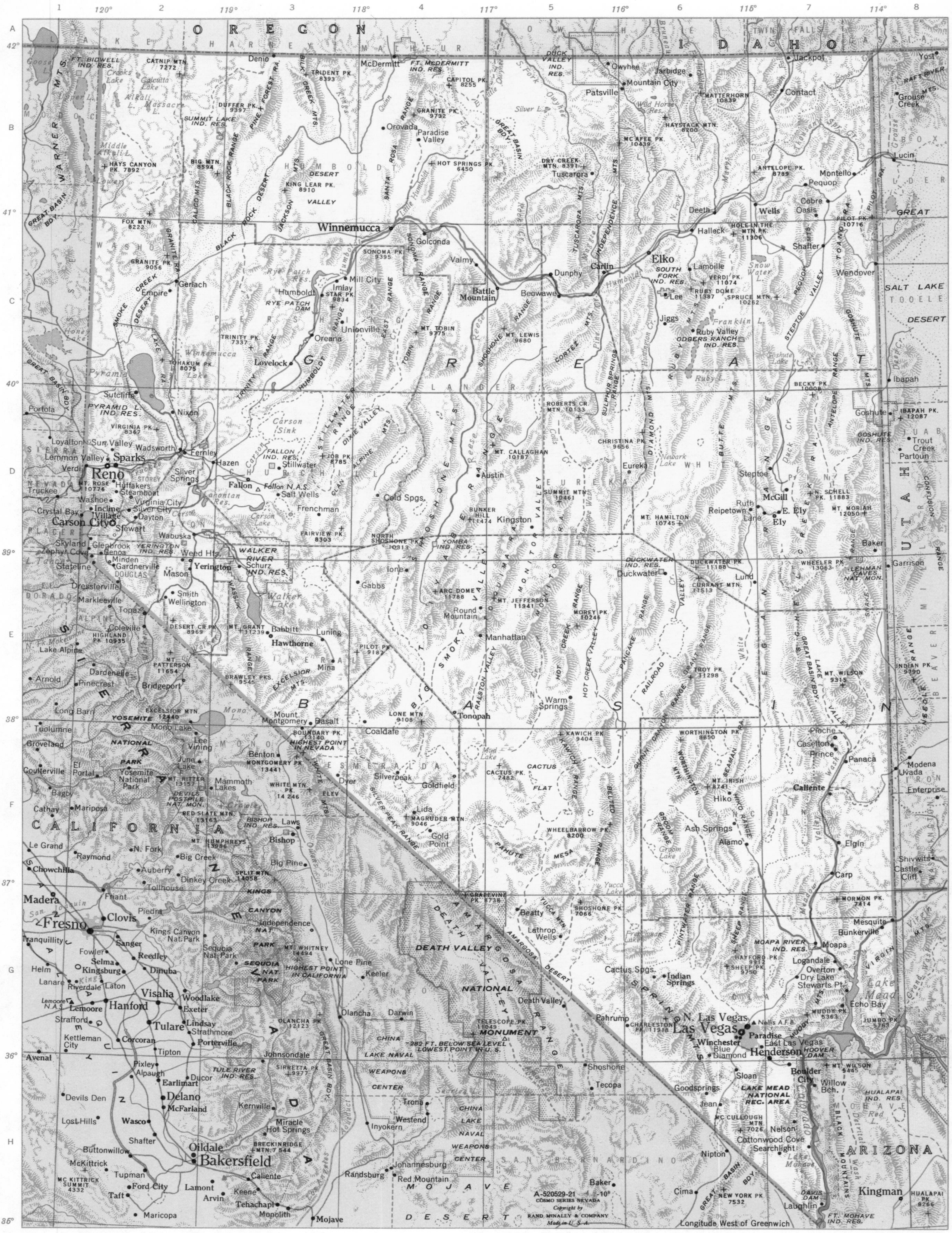

OREGON
IDAHO
CALIFORNIA
UTAH
ARIZONA

GREAT BASIN

HUMBOLDT DESERT

Denio · McDermitt · Ft. McDermitt Ind. Res. · Owyhee · Jarbidge · Jackpot · Yost
Catnip Mtn. 7272 · Trident Pk. 8393 · Capitol Pk. 8255 · Duck Valley Ind. Res. · Mountain City · Contact
Duffer Pk. 9397 · Orovada · Paradise Valley · Matterhorn 10839 · Pequop
Summit Lake Ind. Res. · Hot Springs Pk. 6450 · Dry Creek Mtn. 8391 · Tuscarora · Antelope Pk. 8789 · Montello
Big Mtn. 8594 · King Lear Pk. 8910 · Deeth · Wells · Cobre
Winnemucca · Golconda · Valmy · Elko · Lamoille · Wendover
Sonoma Pk. 9395 · Dunphy · Carlin · South Fork Ind. Res. · Verdi Pk. 11074
Battle Mountain · Beowawe · Ruby Dome 11387
Gerlach · Empire · Mill City · Imlay · Lee · Jiggs
Humboldt · Star Pk. 9834 · Mt. Lewis 9680 · Ruby Valley · Odgers Ranch Ind. Res.
Rye Patch Dam · Unionville · Mt. Tobin 9775 · Franklin L.
Lovelock · Oreana · Austin · Eureka · Ibapah
Tohakum Pk. 8075 · Roberts Cr. Mtn. 10133 · Goshute

Sutcliffe · Nixon · Carson Sink · Mt. Callaghan 10187 · Christina Pk. 9656 · Steptoe
Pyramid L. Ind. Res. · Fernley · Stillwater · Mt. Hamilton 10745 · Reipetown · McGill
Reno · Sparks · Fallon · Fallon N.A.S. · Eureka · Ely · E. Ely
Carson City · Virginia City · Cold Spgs. · Bunker Hill 11474 · Kingston · Mt. Moriah 12050
Minden · Gardnerville · Yerington · Schurz Ind. Res. · Ione · Gabbs · Duckwater · Baker
Walker Lake · Arc Dome 11788 · Mt. Jefferson 11941 · Morey Pk. 10246 · Wheeler Pk. 13063 · Lehman Caves Nat. Mon.
Hawthorne · Babbitt · Luning · Round Mountain · Current Mtn. 11513 · Lund · Garrison
Bridgeport · Mina · Manhattan · Troy Pk. 11298 · Mt. Wilson 9315
Mono Lake · Basalt · Lone Mtn. 9108 · Tonopah · Worthington Pk. 8850 · Pioche
Boundary Pk. 13140 Highest Point in Nevada · Coaldale · Warm Springs · Kawich Pk. 9404 · Caselton · Prince
Benton · Montgomery Pk. 13441 · Dyer · Silverpeak · Cactus Flat · Mt. Irish 8741 · Panaca · Modena
White Mtn. 14246 · Goldfield · Hiko · Caliente
Bishop · Laws · Lida · Magruder Mtn. 9046 · Ash Springs · Alamo · Elgin
Big Pine · Gold Point · Wheelbarrow Pk. 8200 · Carp
Split Mtn. 14058 · Grapevine Pk. 8738 · Beatty · Shoshone Pk. 7066 · Mormon Pk. 7414 · Mesquite · Bunkerville
Independence · Lathrop Wells · Moapa River Ind. Res. · Moapa
Mt. Whitney 14494 · Death Valley · Pahrump · Indian Springs · Overton · Echo Bay
Lone Pine · Charleston Pk. 11918 · N. Las Vegas · Nellis A.F.B. · Jumbo Pk. 5760
Keeler · Telescope Pk. · Las Vegas · Winchester · Paradise · Henderson · Hoover Dam
Olancha · Darwin · Death Valley National Monument · 282 Ft. Below Sea Level Lowest Point in U.S. · Blue Diamond · Boulder City · Mt. Wilson
Johnsondale · China Lake Naval Weapons Center · Shoshone · Sloan · Nelson · Searchlight · Kingman
Randsburg · Red Mountain · Tecopa · Goodsprings · Jean · Cottonwood Cove · Laughlin · Ft. Mohave Ind. Res.
Mojave · Baker · Cima · New York Pk. 7532 · Davis Dam

Statute Miles 5 0 5 10 20 30 40 50 60 70 80
Kilometers 5 0 10 20 40 60 80 100 120

Lambert Conformal Conic Projection
SCALE 1:2,630,000 1 Inch = 41.5 Statute Miles

A-520529-21 Cosmo Series Nevada
Copyright by RAND McNALLY & COMPANY
Made in U.S.A.
Longitude West of Greenwich

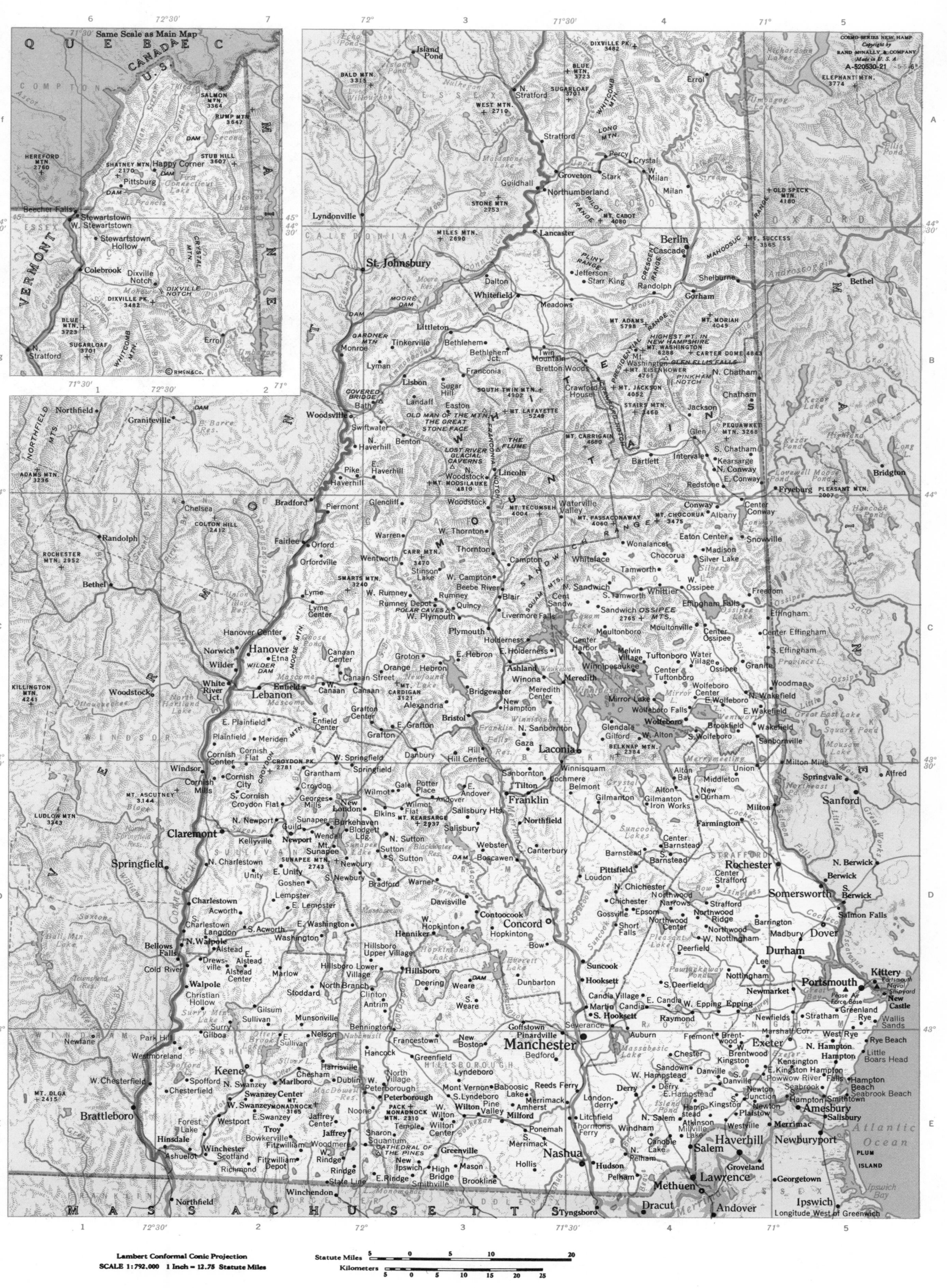

Same Scale as Main Map

Lambert Conformal Conic Projection
SCALE 1:792,000   1 Inch = 12.75 Statute Miles

Statute Miles

Kilometers

NEW JERSEY

A-520531-21 -6-8-13'
COSMO SERIES NEW JERSEY
Copyright by
RAND McNALLY & COMPANY
Made in U. S. A.

Longitude West of Greenwich

Statute Miles 5 0 5 10 15
Kilometers 5 0 5 10 15 20

Lambert Conformal Conic Projection
SCALE 1:849,000 1 Inch = 13 Statute Miles

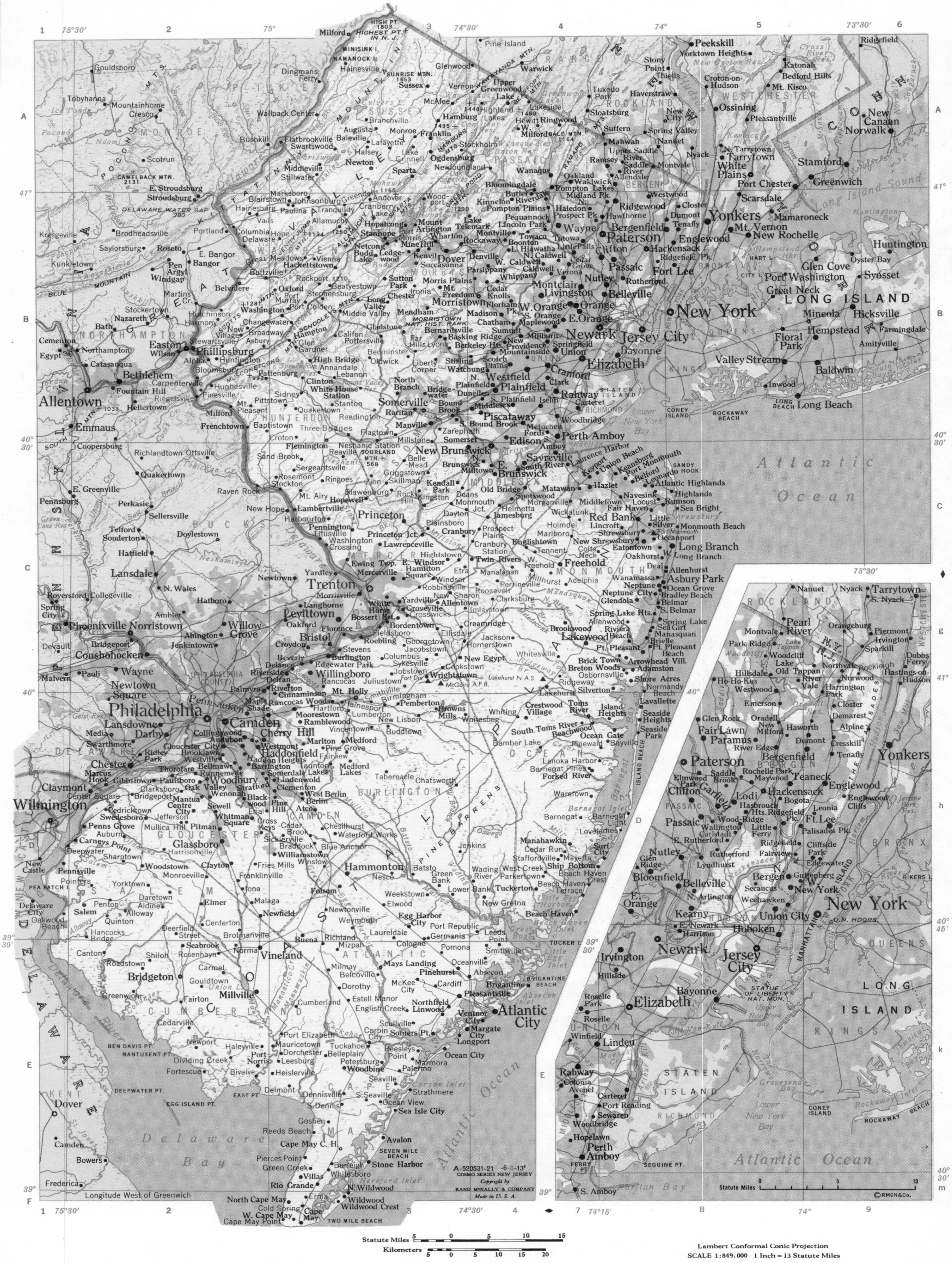

A-520532-21 -5-8-10th
COSMO SERIES NEW MEXICO

Longitude West of Greenwich

1 Inch = 22.5 Statute Miles

Lambert Conformal Conic Projection
SCALE 1:2,600,000 1 Inch = 41 Statute Miles

Statute Miles 10 0 10 20 30 40 50 60 70 80 90

Kilometers 10 0 10 20 40 60 80 100 120

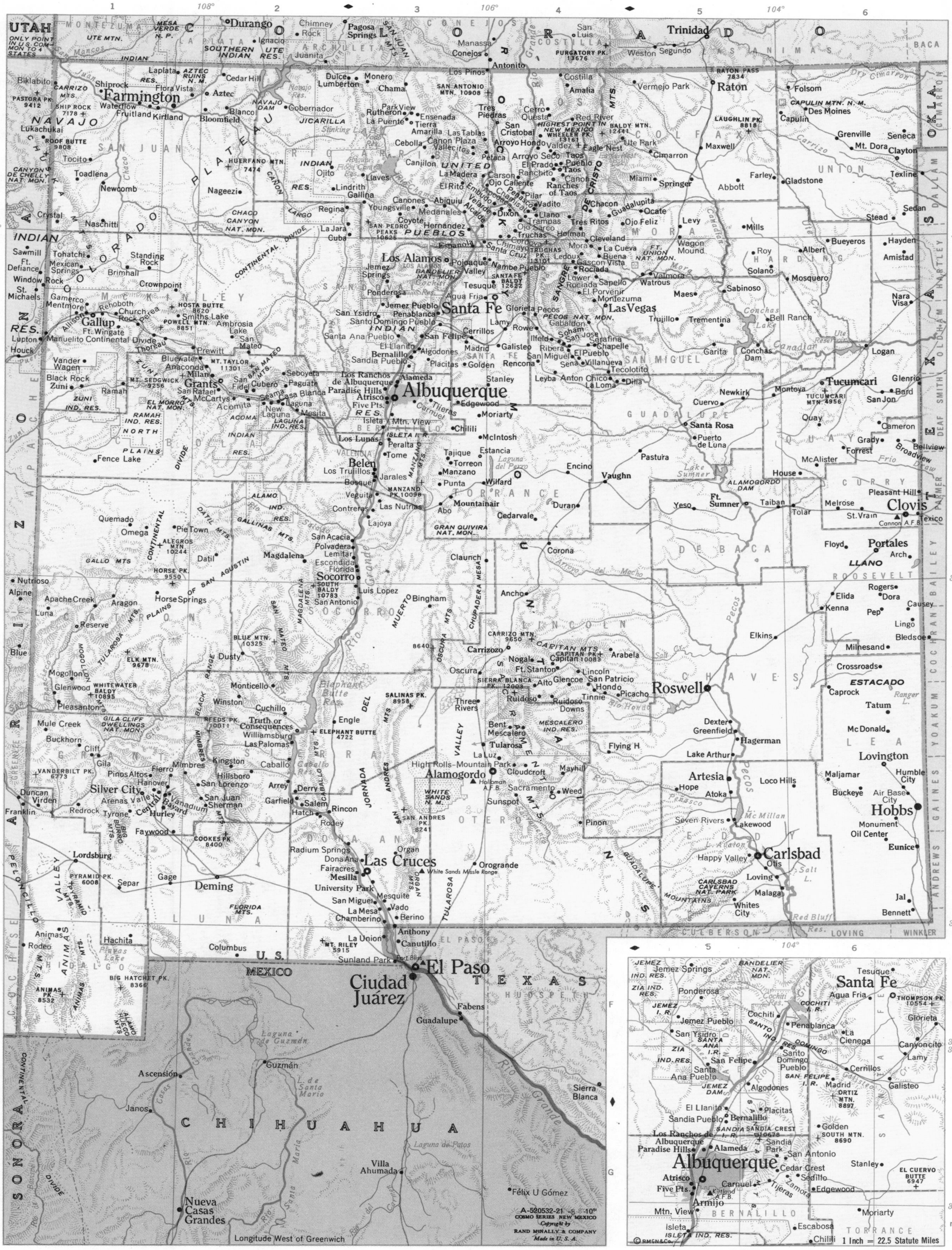

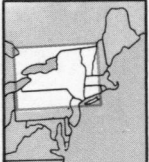

Statute Miles 5 0 5 10 20 30 40

Kilometers 5 0 5 15 25 35 45 55

Lambert Conformal Conic Projection
SCALE 1:1,862,000   1 Inch = 29 Statute Miles

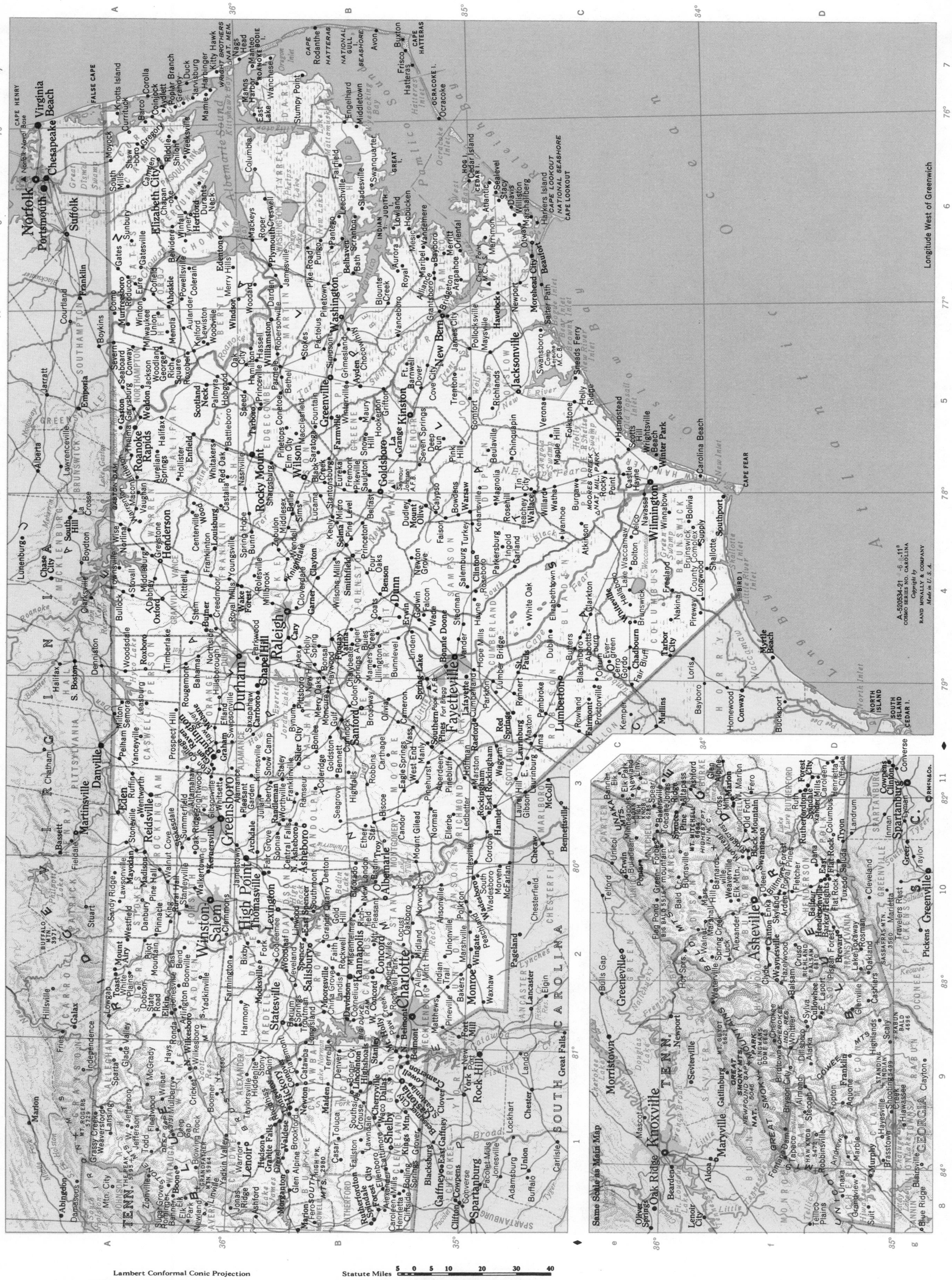

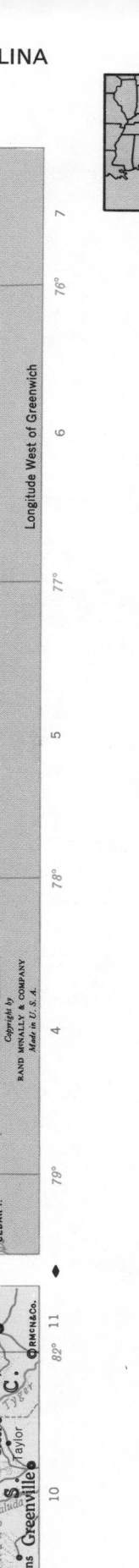

Lambert Conformal Conic Projection
SCALE 1:1,950,000   1 Inch = 31 Statute Miles

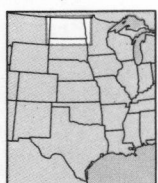

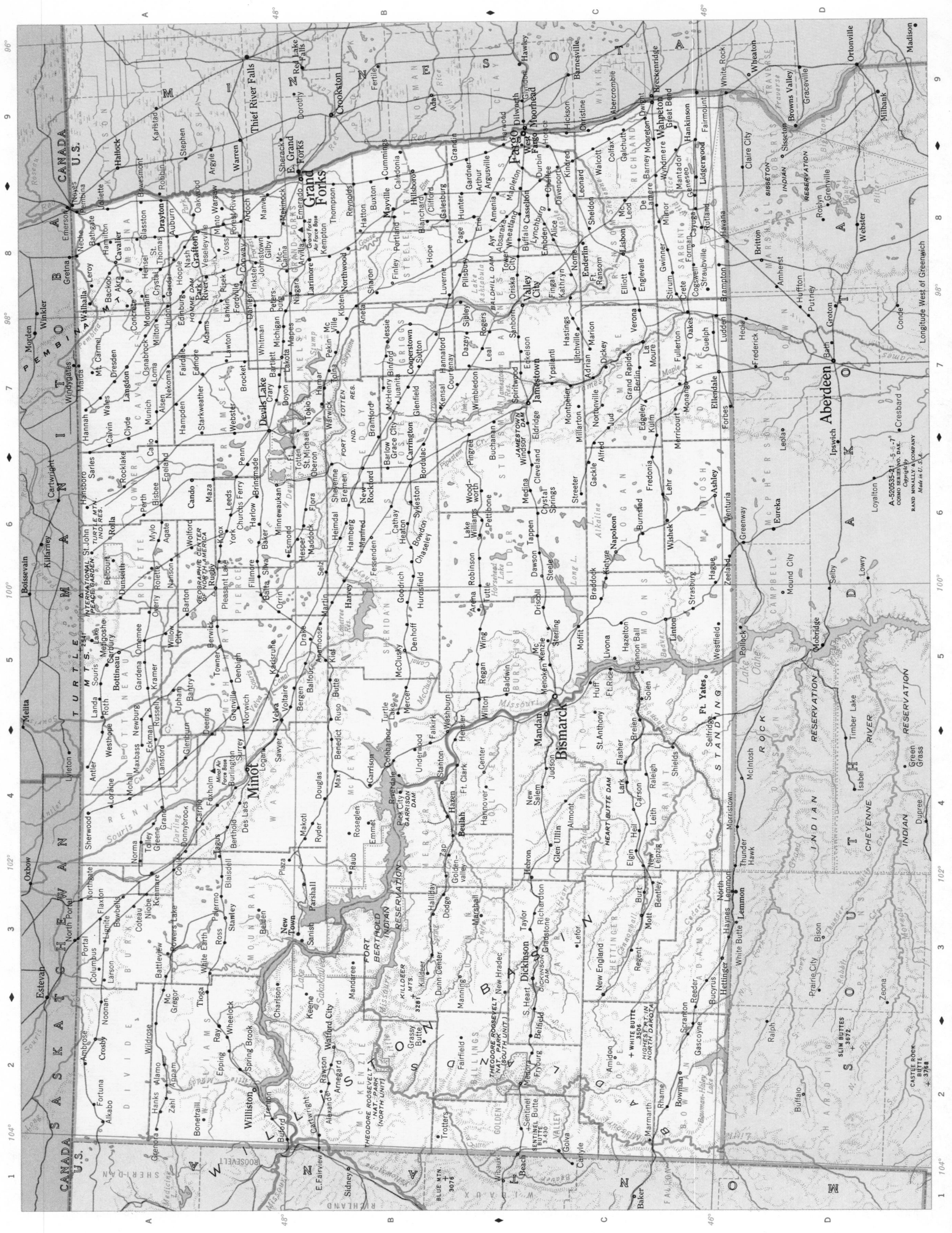

Statute Miles 5 0 5 10 20 30 40 50 60
Kilometers 5 0 5 15 25 35 45 55 65 75

Lambert Conformal Conic Projection
SCALE 1:2,091,000 1 Inch = 33 Statute Miles

Lambert Conformal Conic Projection
SCALE 1:1,714,000 1 Inch = 27 Statute Miles

Statute Miles 5 0 5 10 20 30 40
Kilometers 5 0 5 15 25 35 45 55

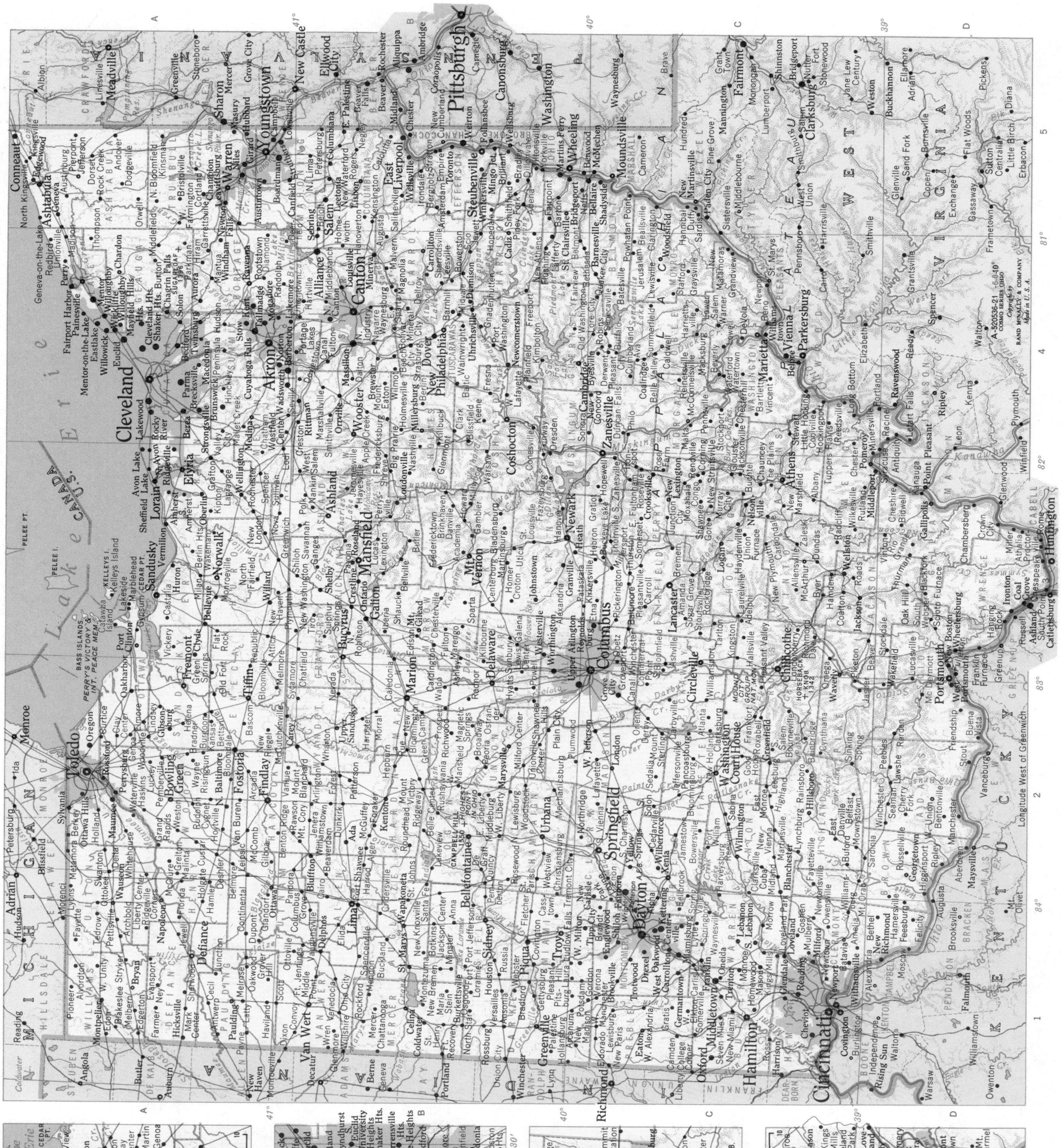

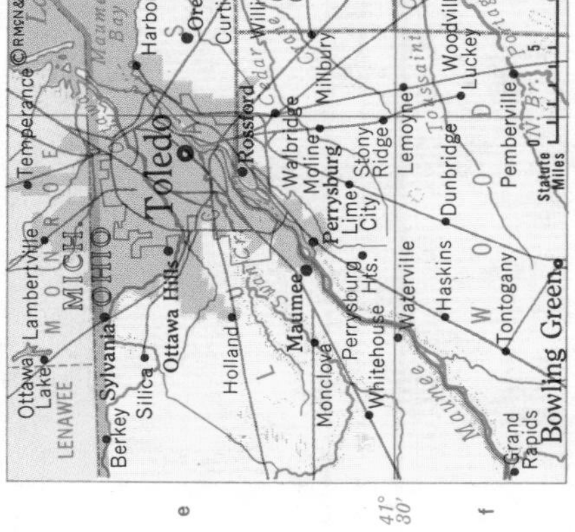

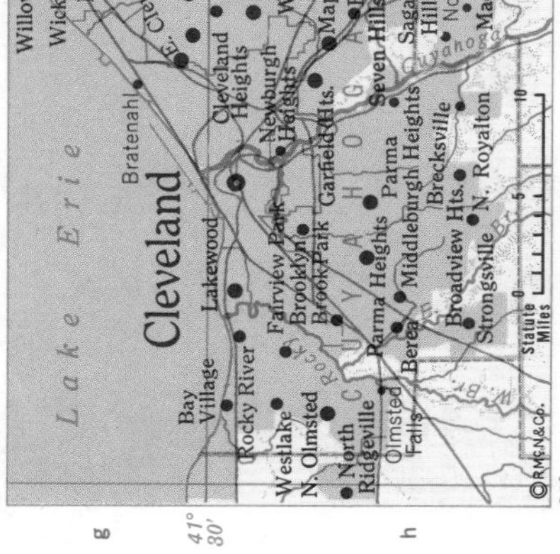

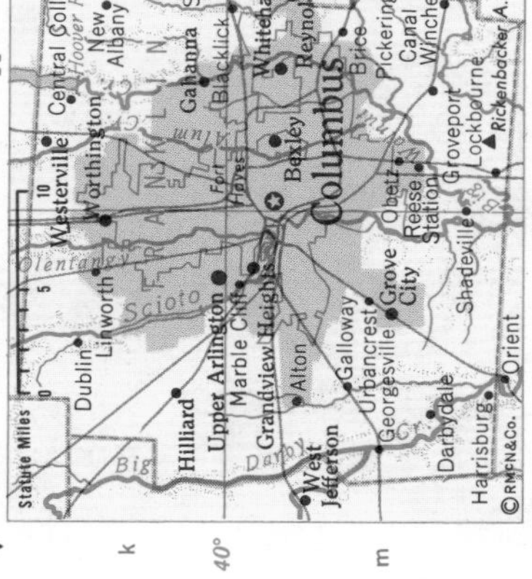

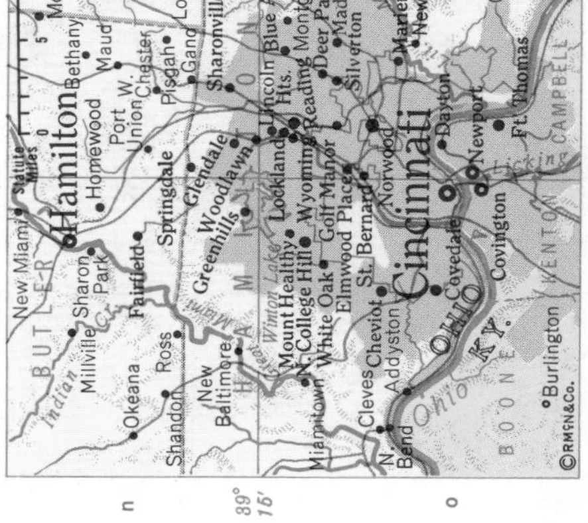

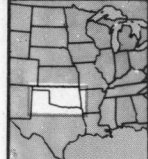

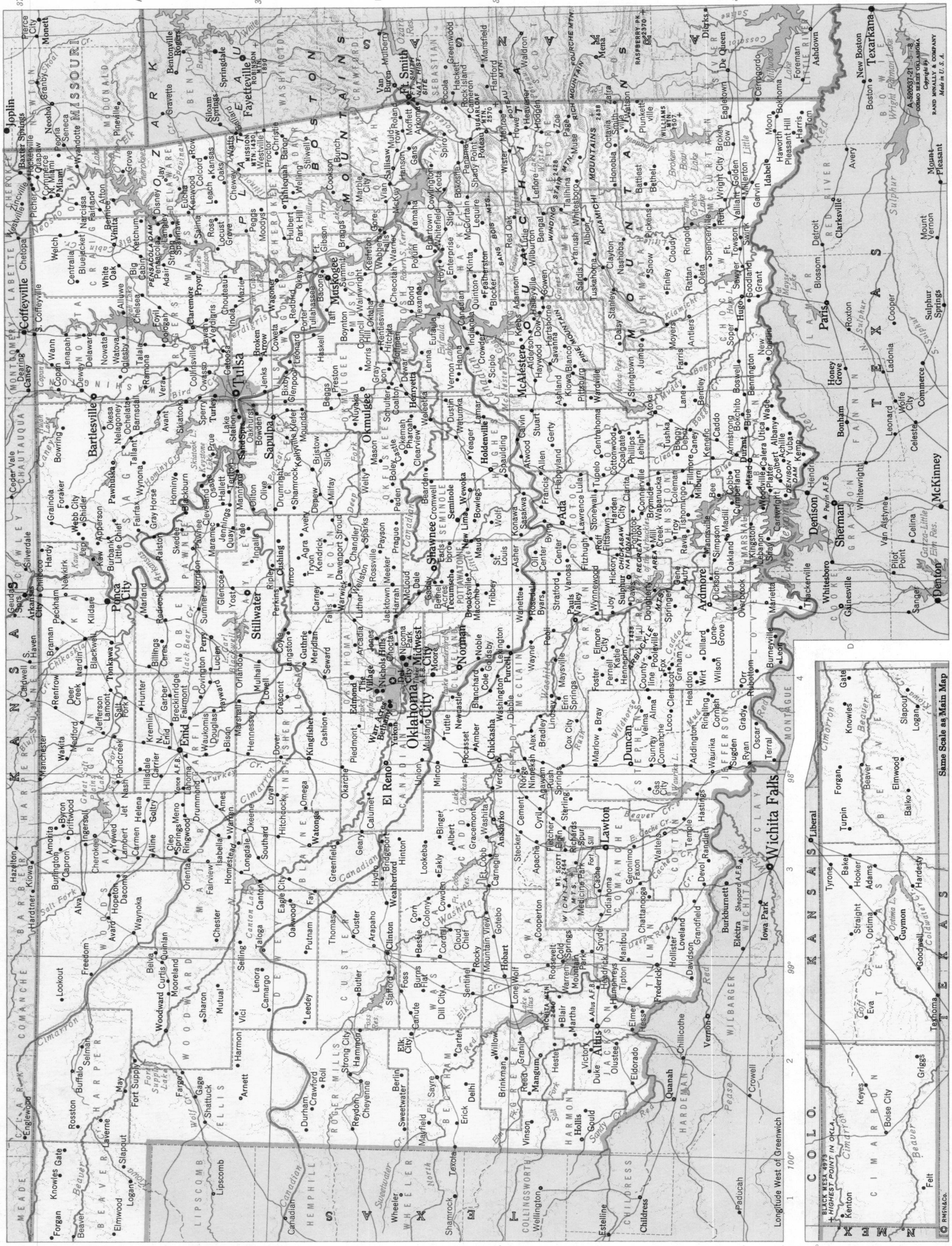

Statute Miles 5 0 5 10 20 30 40
Kilometers 5 0 5 15 25 35 45 55

Lambert Conformal Conic Projection
SCALE 1:1,957,000 1 Inch = 31 Statute Miles

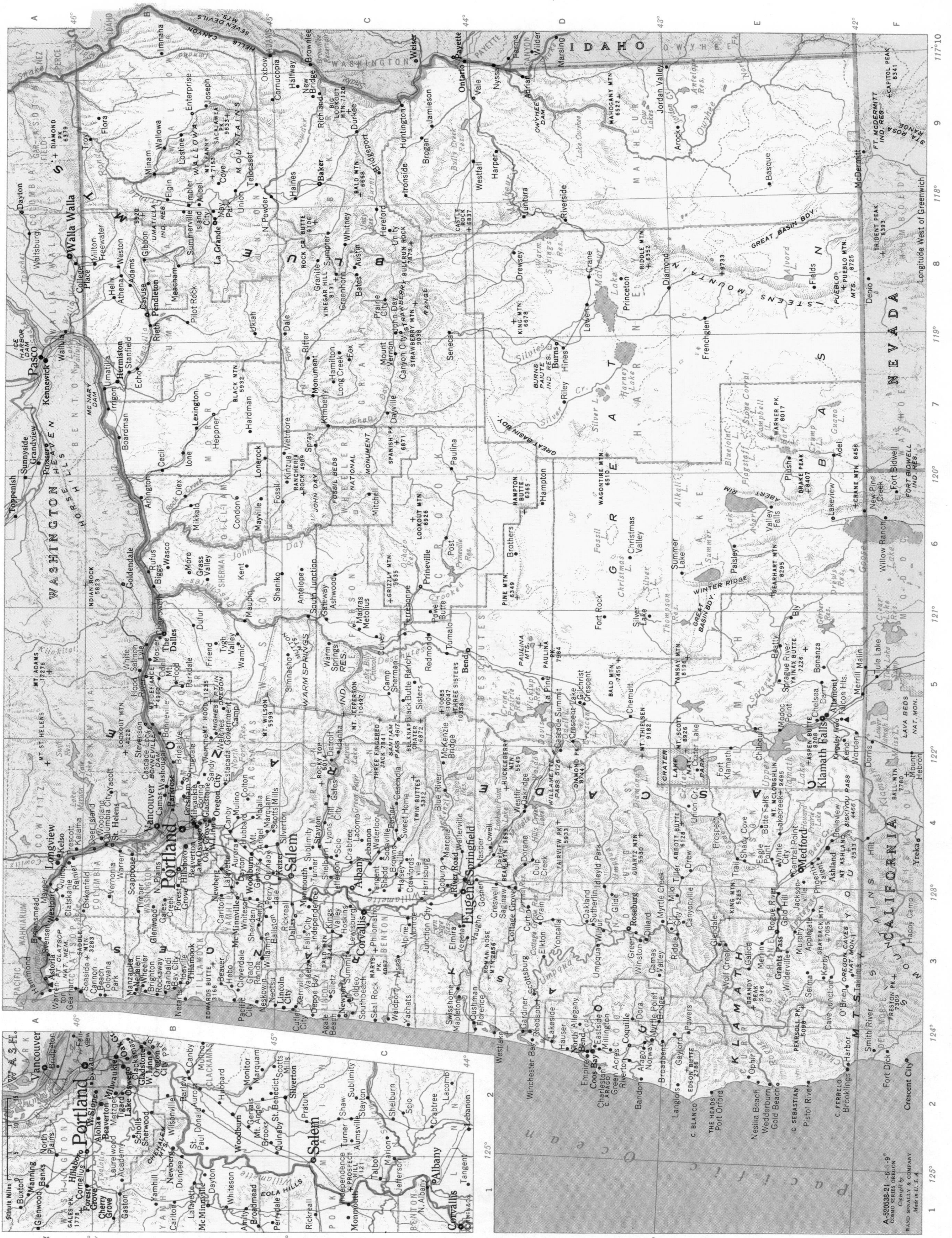

Lambert Conformal Conic Projection
SCALE 1:2,329,000   1 Inch = 37 Statute Miles

Statute Miles
Kilometers

A-520538-21 -6 -9°
Compiled and Printed by
RAND M°NALLY COMPANY
Made in U.S.A.

Statute Miles 5 0 5 10 20 30
Kilometers 5 0 5 15 25 35 45

Lambert Conformal Conic Projection
SCALE 1:1,593,000 1 Inch = 25 Statute Miles

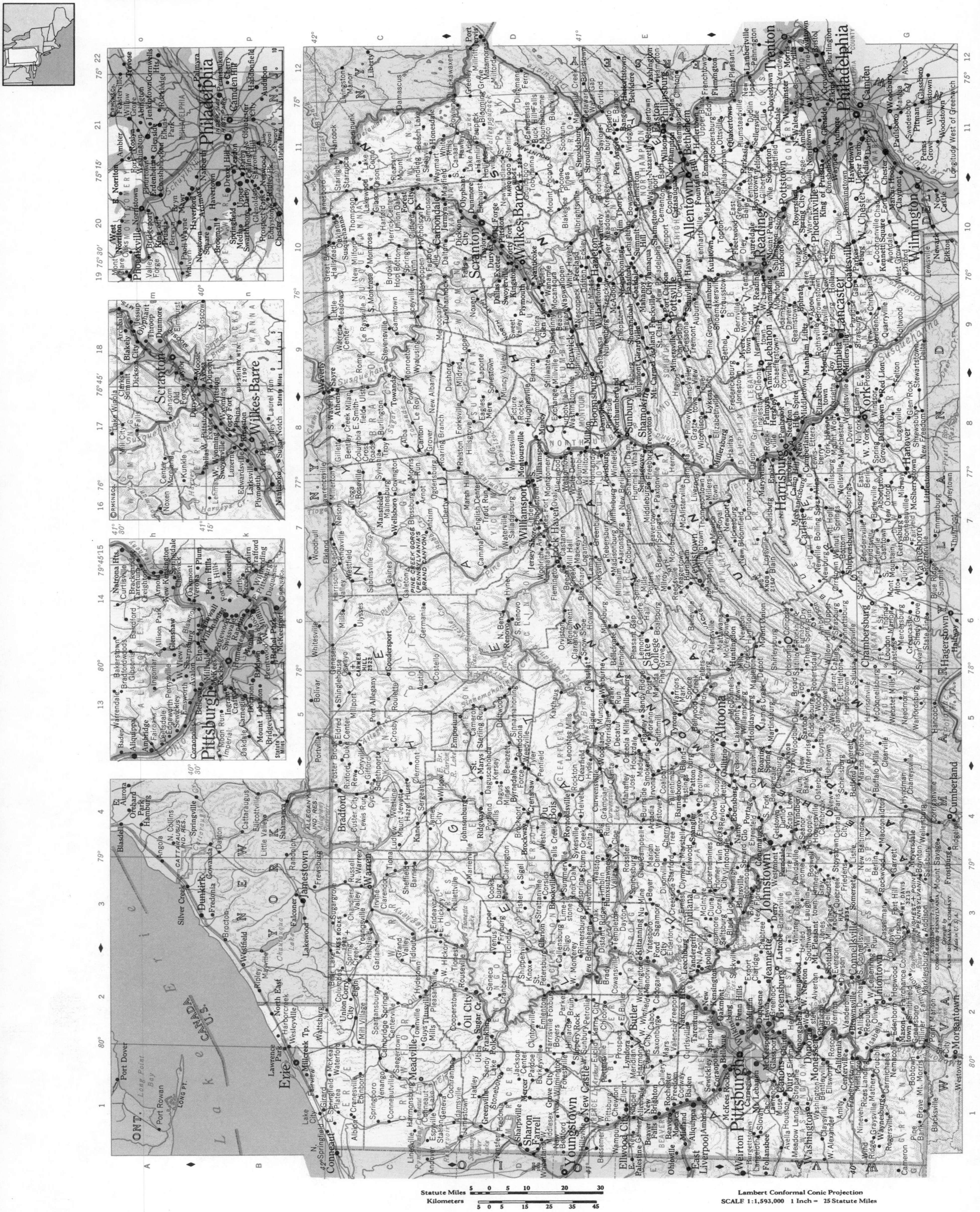

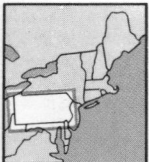

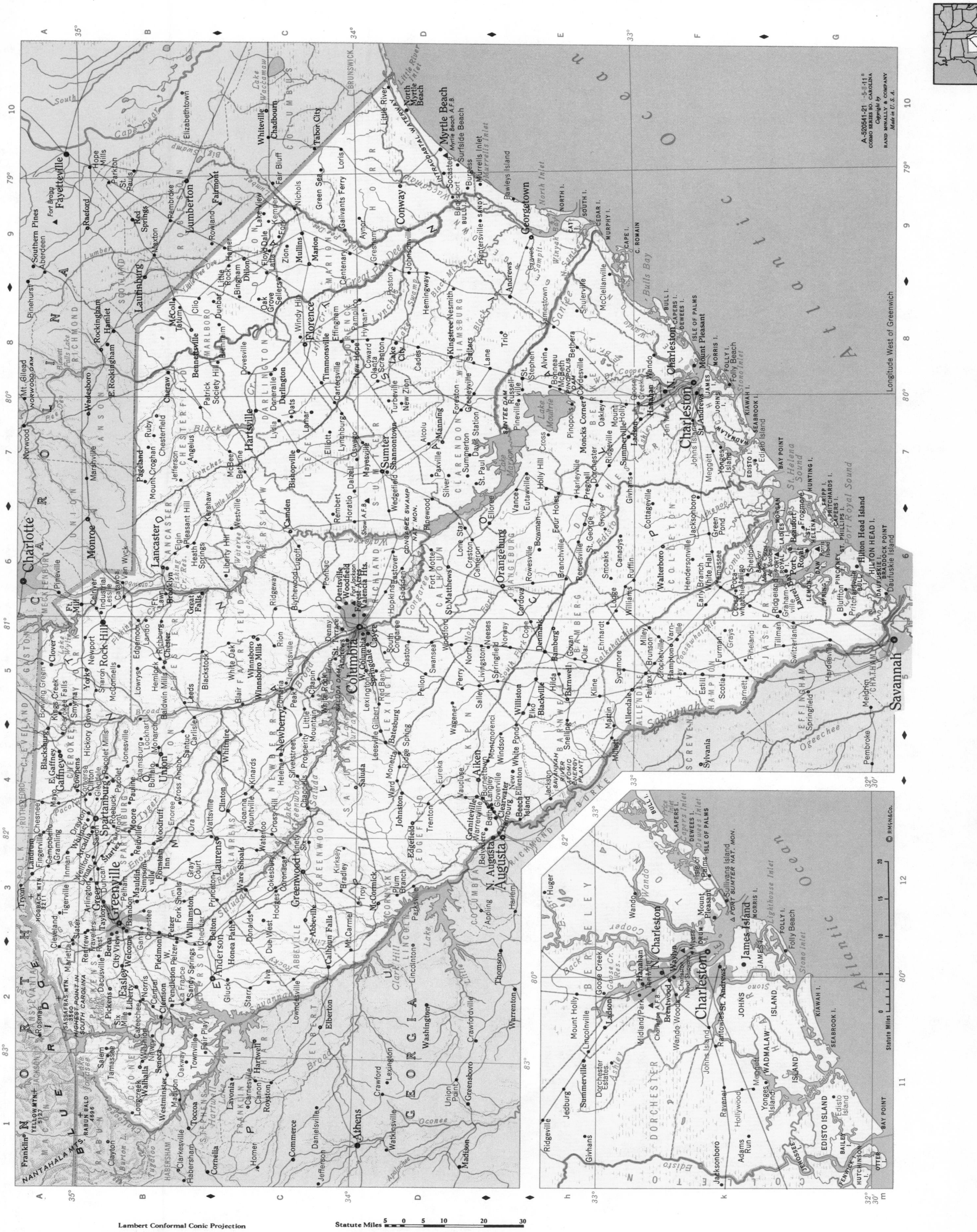

A-520541-21 -5-8-61 B
CG60 SERIES SO CAROLINA
Copyright by
RAND McNALLY & COMPANY
Made in U.S.A.

Lambert Conformal Conic Projection
SCALE 1:1,566,000   1 Inch = 25 Statute Miles

Statute Miles 5 0 5 10 20 30
Kilometers 5 0 5 15 25 35 45

Longitude West of Greenwich

Statute Miles 5 0 5 10 20 30 40 50 60

Kilometers 5 0 5 15 25 35 45 55 65 75

Lambert Conformal Conic Projection

SCALE 1:2,091,000 1 Inch = 33 Statute Miles

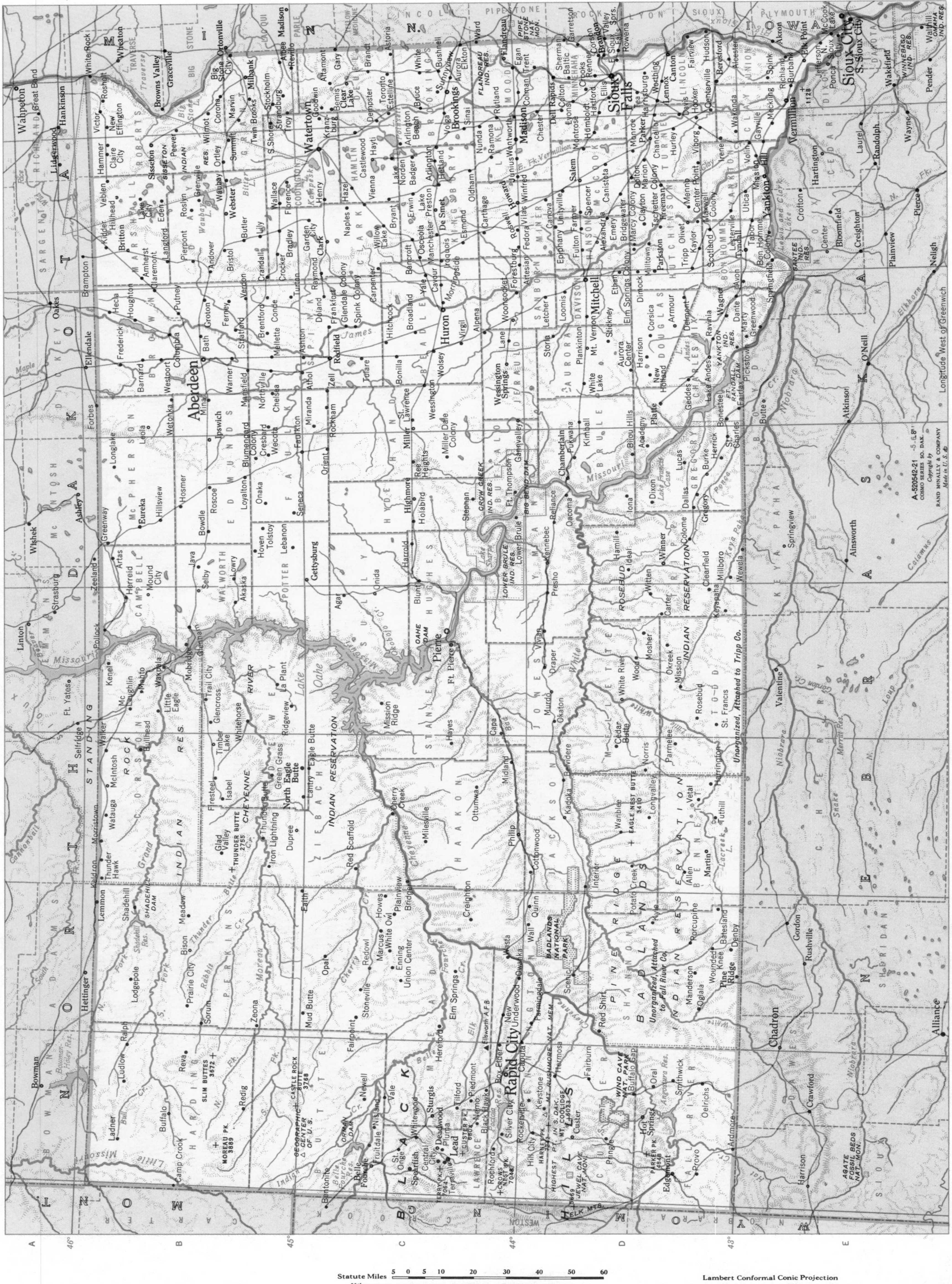

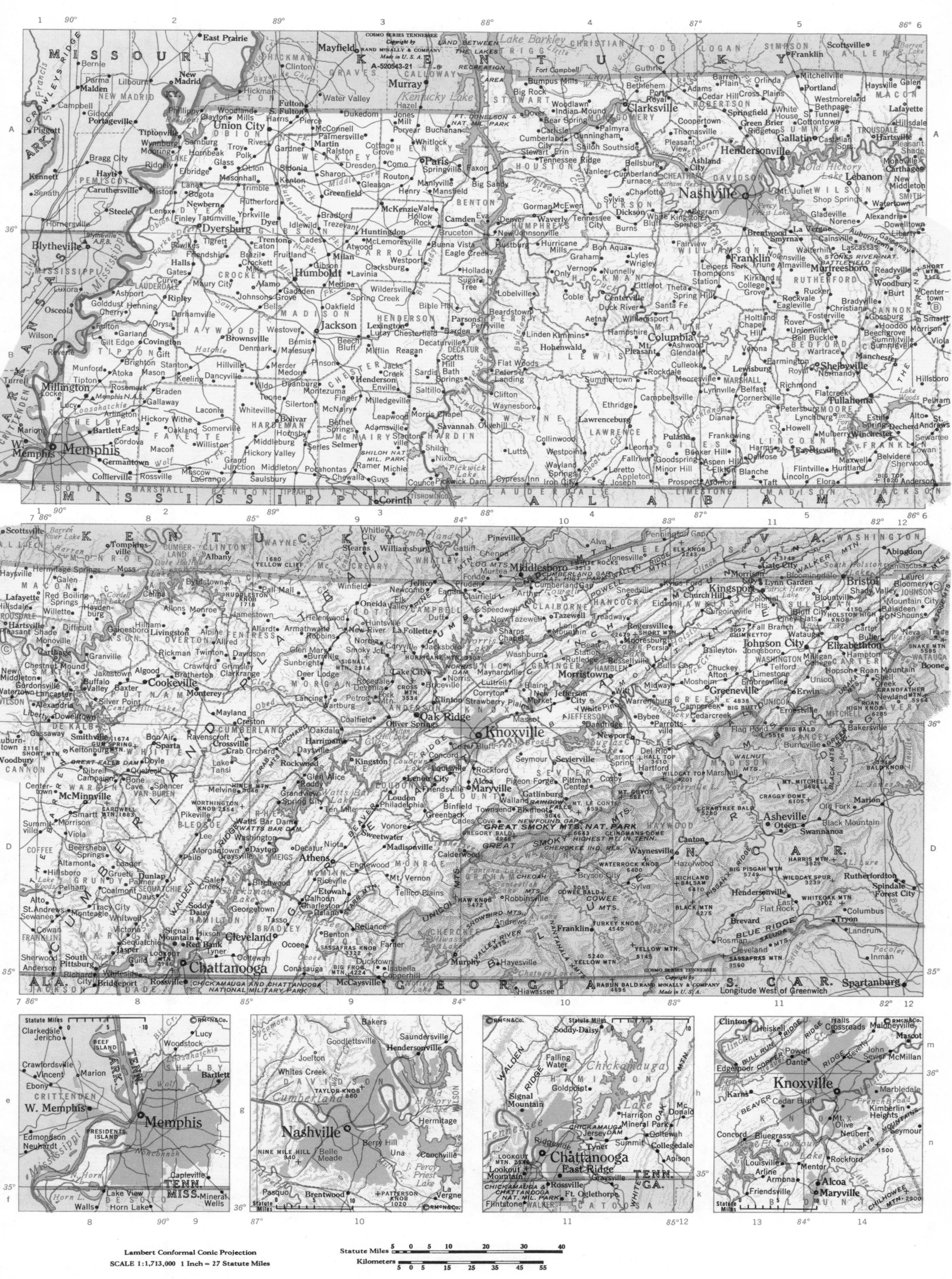

Lambert Conformal Conic Projection
SCALE 1:1,713,000 1 Inch = 27 Statute Miles

Statute Miles

Kilometers

Same Scale as Main Map

Statute Miles 10 0 10 20 30 40 50 60 70 80 90 100

Kilometers 10 0 10 20 40 60 80 100 120 140

Lambert Conformal Conic Projection

SCALE 1:4,118,000 1 Inch = 65 Statute Miles

Longitude West of Greenwich

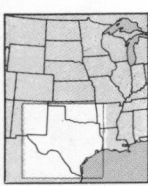

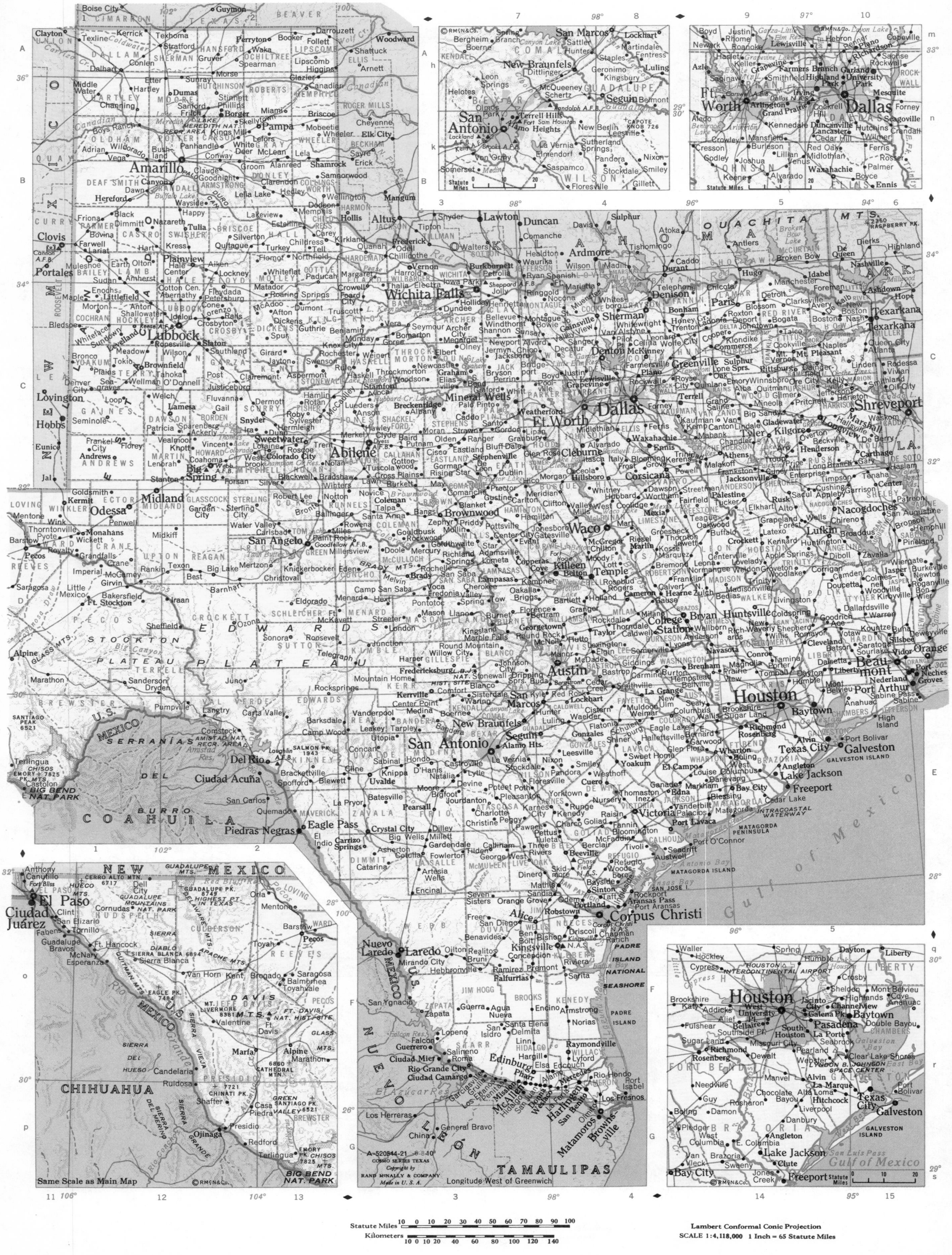

Longitude West of Greenwich

A-520545-21 -6-8-9
COSMO SERIES UTAH
Copyright by
RAND McNALLY & COMPANY
Made in U. S. A.

Lambert Conformal Conic Projection
SCALE 1:2,100,000 1 Inch = 33 Statute Miles

Statute Miles 5 0 5 10 20 30 40 50 60

Kilometers 5 0 5 20 30 40 50 60 70 80

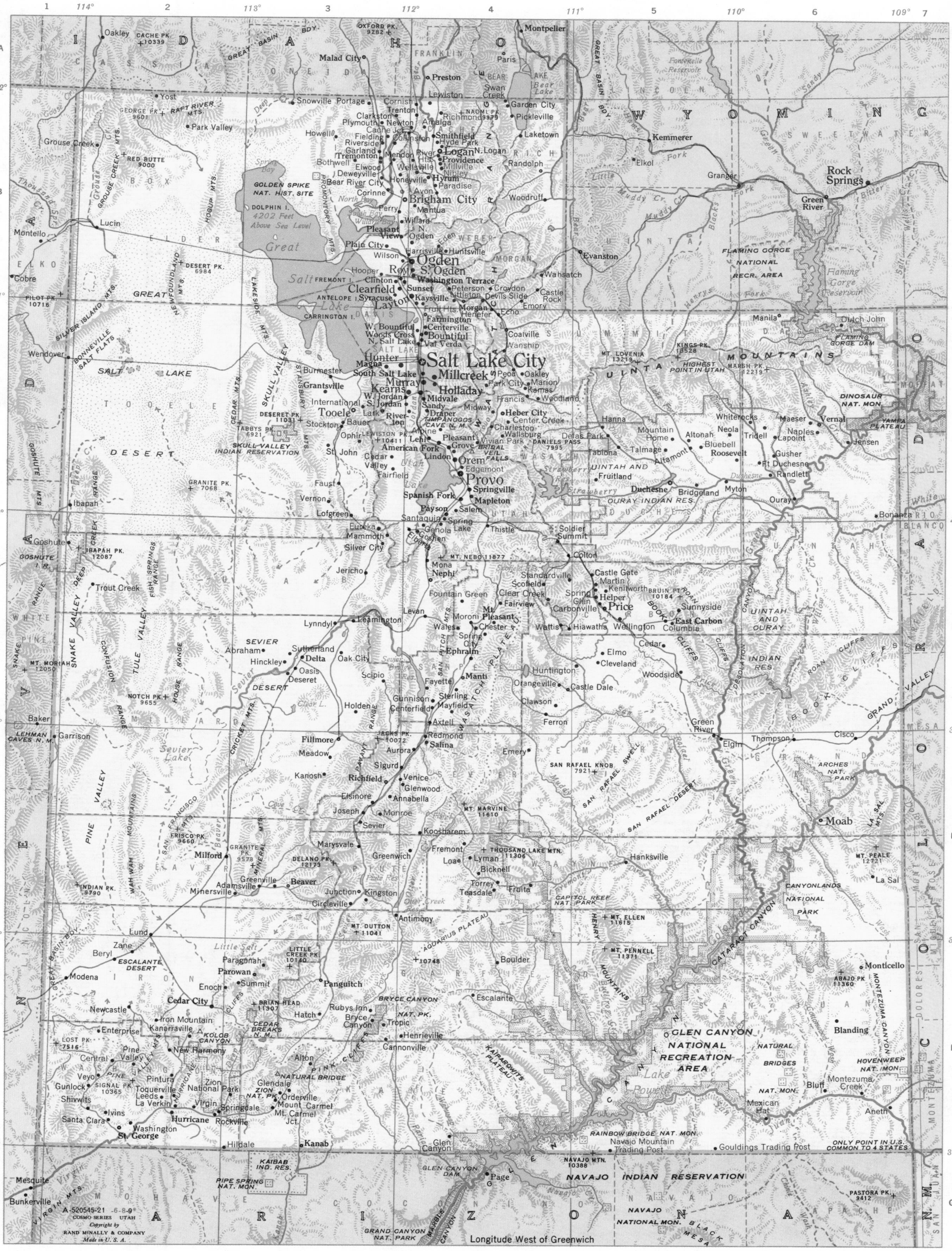

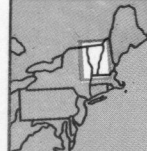

SCALE 1:903,000 1 Inch = 14.25 Statute Miles

Statute Miles

Kilometers

Lambert Conformal Conic Projection

Longitude West of Greenwich

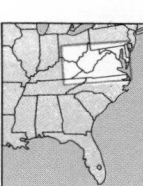

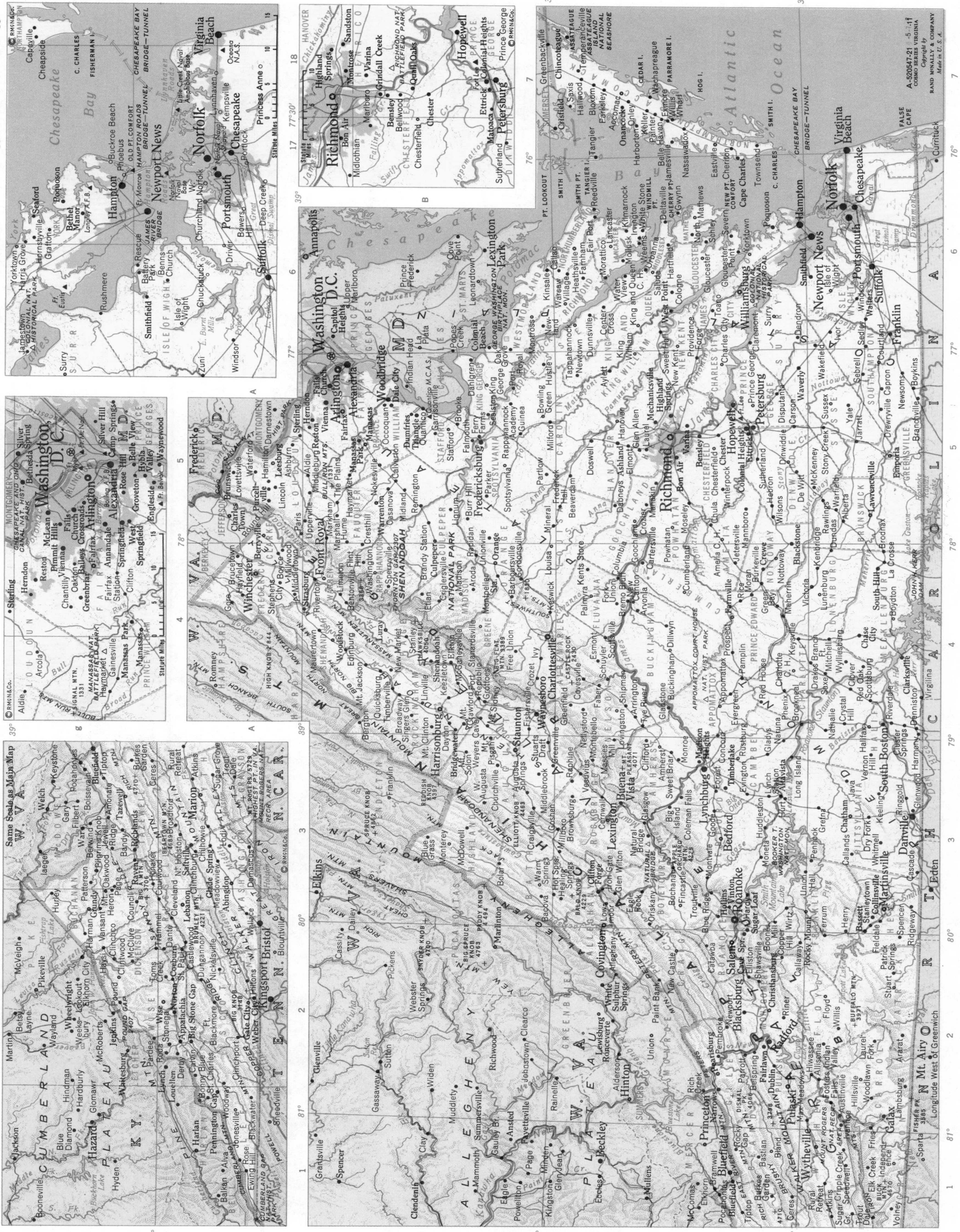

Lambert Conformal Conic Projection
SCALE 1:1,822,000 1 Inch = 29 Statute Miles

Statute Miles 5 0 5 10 20 30 40
Kilometers 5 0 5 15 25 35 45 55

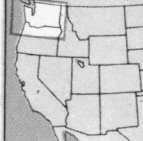

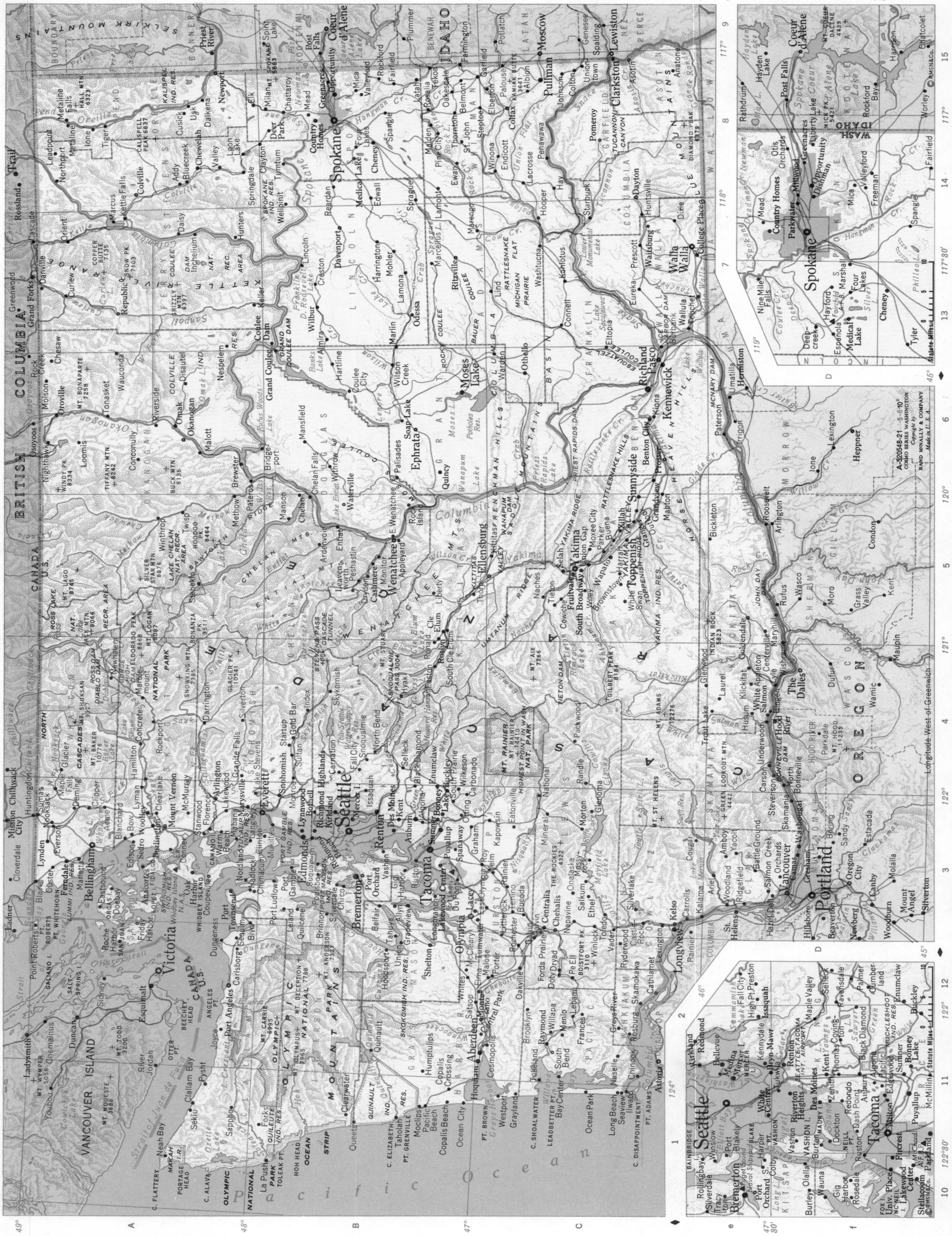

Lambert Conformal Conic Projection
SCALE 1:2,091,000 1 Inch = 33 Statute Miles

Statute Miles 5 0 5 10 20 30 40 50
Kilometers 5 0 5 15 25 35 45 55 65

Lambert Conformal Conic Projection
SCALE 1:2,091,000 1 Inch = 33 Statute Miles

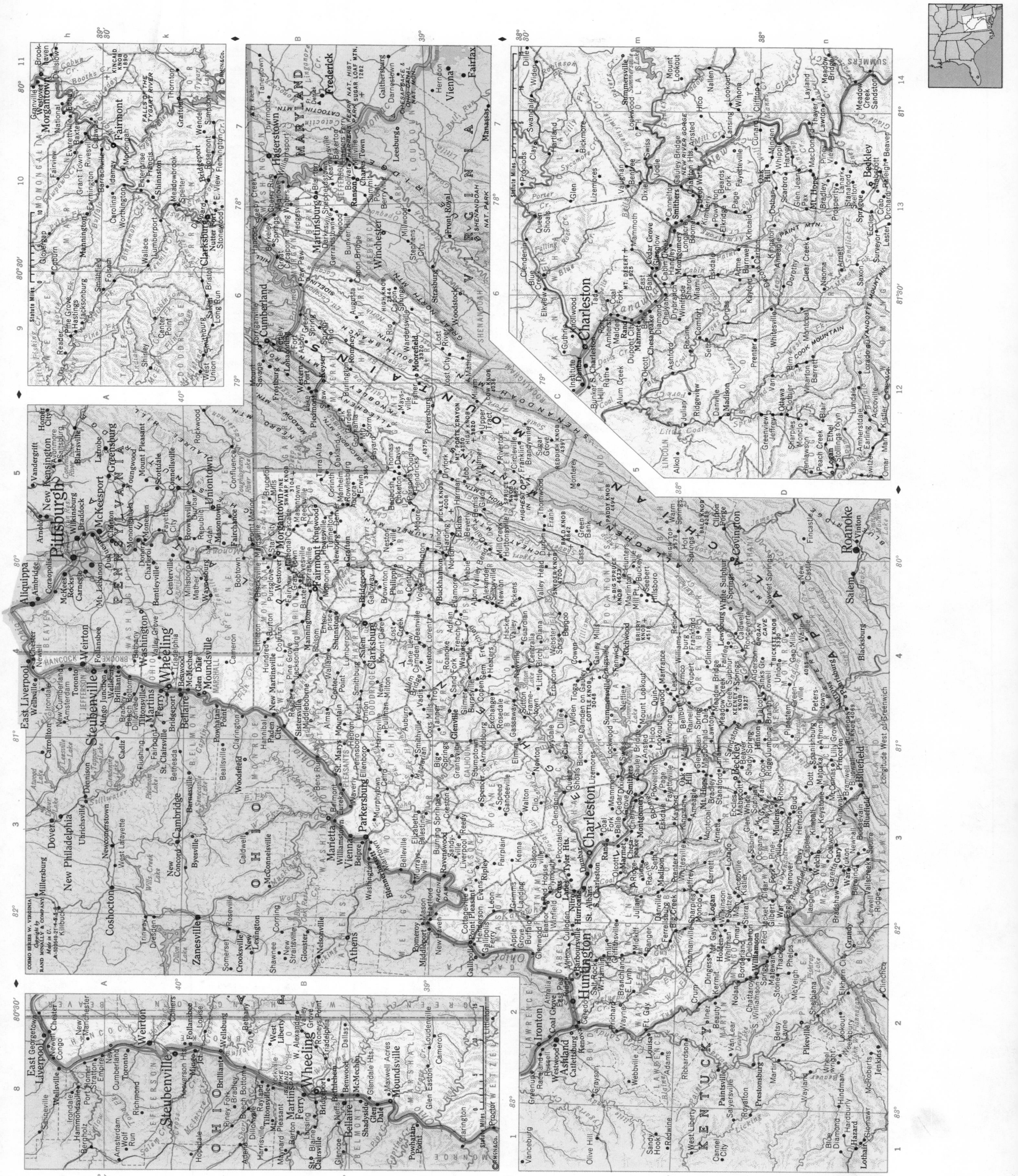

Lambert Conformal Conic Projection
SCALE 1:1,704,000   1 Inch = 27 Statute Miles

Statute Miles
Kilometers

COSMO SERIES W. VIRGINIA
Copyright by
RAND MCNALLY & COMPANY
A-328604-21-1-5-5

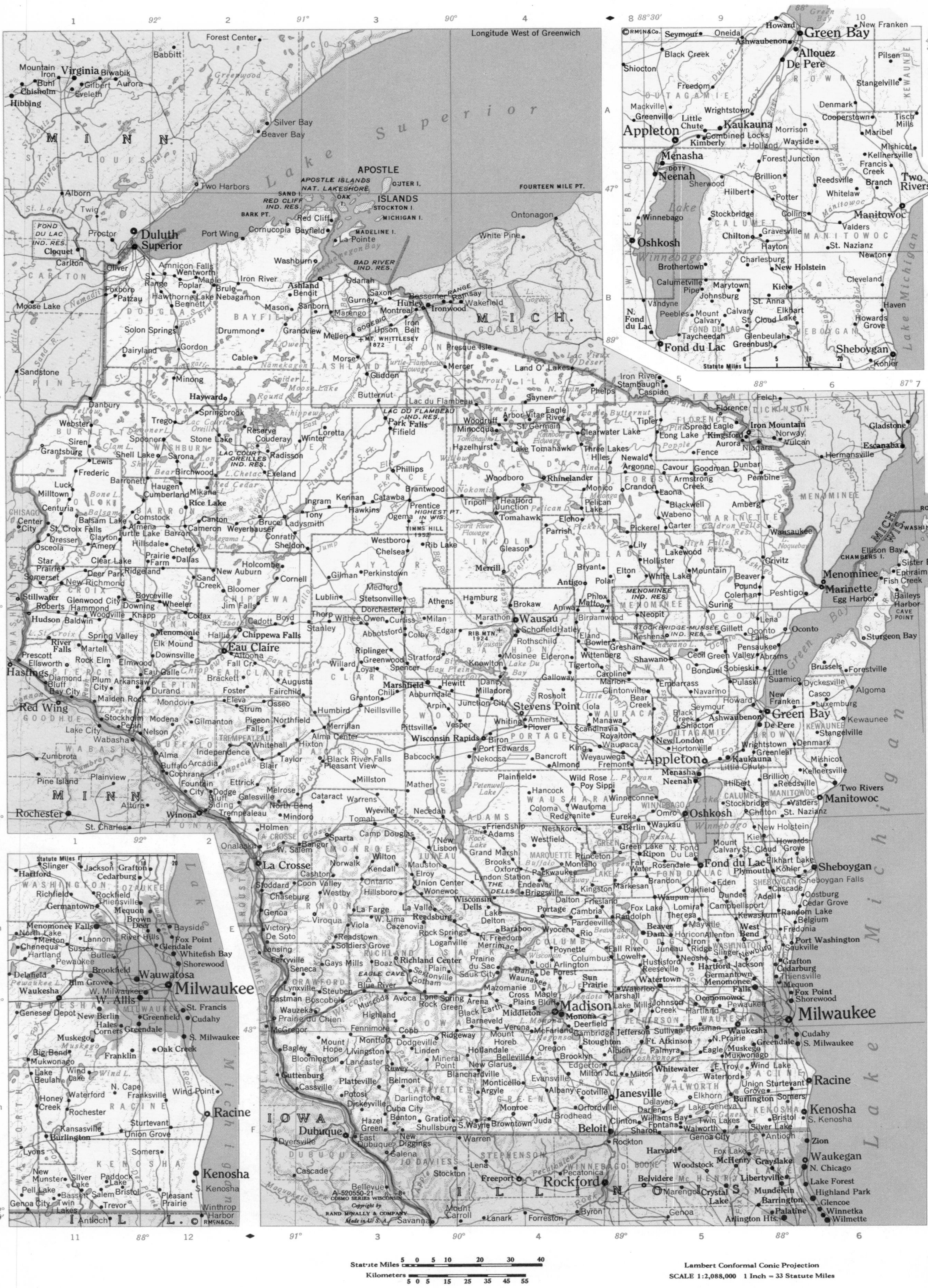

Longitude West of Greenwich

Lake Superior

APOSTLE ISLANDS

MICH.

Lake Michigan

Green Bay

Milwaukee

Madison

Lambert Conformal Conic Projection
SCALE 1:2,088,000   1 Inch = 33 Statute Miles

Statute Miles
Kilometers

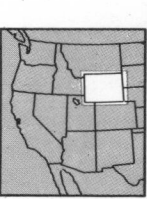

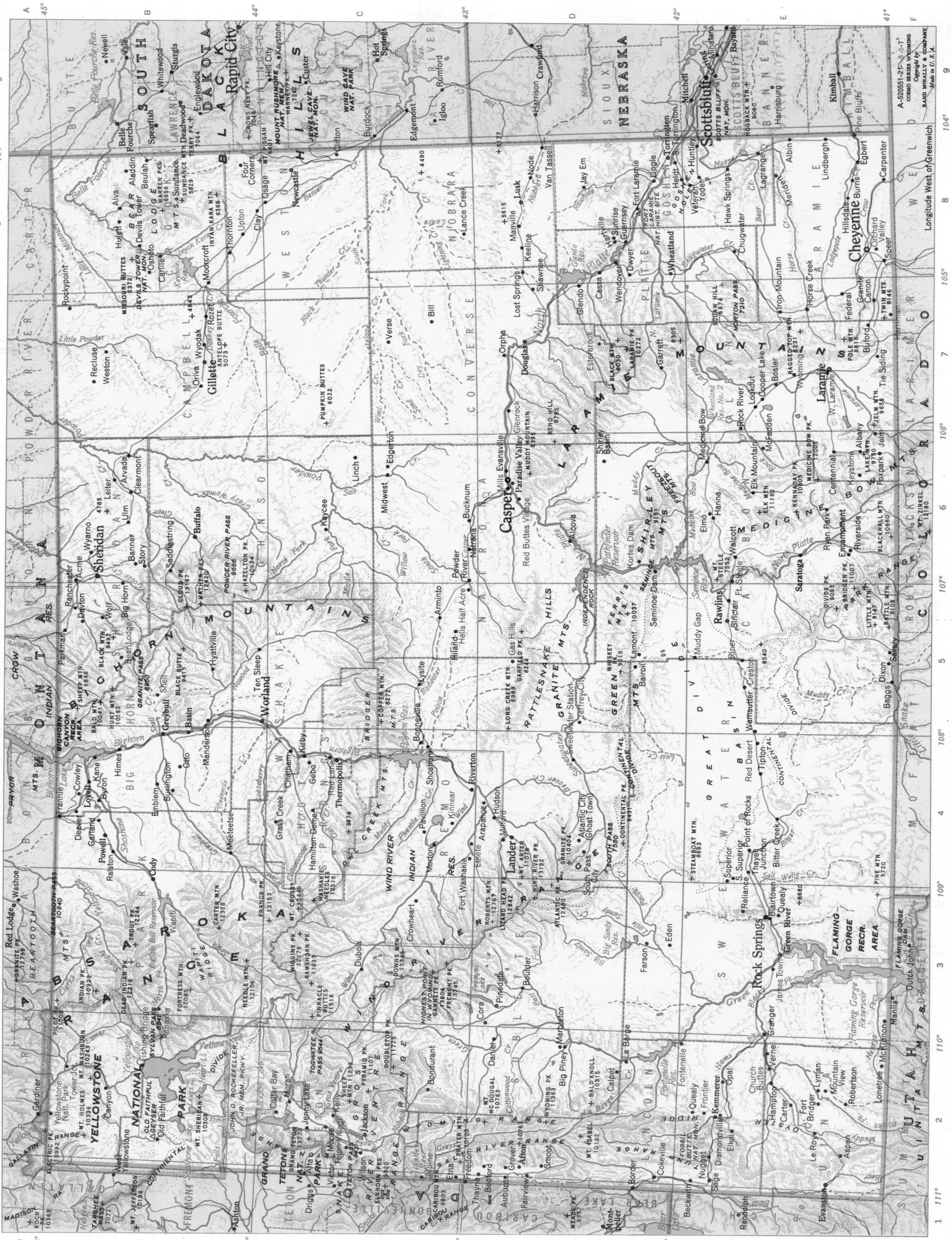

Lambert Conformal Conic Projection
SCALE 1:2,186,000   1 Inch = 34.5 Statute Miles

Statute Miles 5 0 5 10   20   30   40   50
Kilometers 5 0 5 15   25   35   45   55   65   75

Longitude West of Greenwich

A-520551-21°-√5-7'
COMPILED BY RAND M°NALLY & COMPANY
Copyright by
RAND M°NALLY & COMPANY
Made in U.S.A.

Introduction to Special United States and World Geographical Information Sections

In the pages that follow, the editors of the atlas have provided factual information of geographic interest on the fifty U.S. states, the world, the continents and individual foreign countries. These pages are designed to supplement the reference maps (Cosmo Series) with data not readily available from the maps themselves. Here will be found answers to many of the questions raised by those who use the atlas, particularly questions that ask "how large?" "how many?" and "when?"

United States Geographical Information

A series of tables summarizing general geographical and historical facts about the United States, including extremes of elevation, distance, dimensions, temperature, and rainfall follows the map section. The historical growth of the country's territory is charted, as is the course of settlement. Land and water areas and the 1980, 1970, and 1960 populations of all of the states are conveniently listed, and each state's rank in area and in population is also included.

Next, the largest metropolitan areas of the United States are ranked according to their 1980 population. This table also gives the populations for the central cities of these metropolitan areas.

1980 Census Populations of U.S. Cities, Towns, Counties, and States. Concluding the tabular section on the United States is an extensive table, totaling thirty-two pages, which is arranged alphabetically by state and lists the populations of U.S. cities, towns, counties, and states. Populations are also listed for all U.S. counties or political units equivalent to counties.

World Geographical Information

The World Political Information Table is the first of the tables containing world information. For each political unit listed the table specifies the latest estimated population, area in square miles, population density, capital, largest city, and principal languages. In addition, the table states the precise political or administrative status of the units listed and classifies them into major types. Under the heading of World Facts and Comparisons appear the answers to many frequently asked questions. Here are the basic facts about the earth's movements and measurements, as well as information on the physiographic and temperature extremes found in each of the continents. The population growth of the continents is summarized for the period since the year 1650, and the twenty-five countries with the largest populations and areas are listed.

Following World Facts and Comparisons are listings of the major physical features of the world, including mountains, oceans and seas, lakes, rivers, and islands. Each list includes the outstanding features in each category and provides ready answers to questions about which of two mountains is higher, which of two rivers is longer, and many similar queries.

Next is a table ranking the largest metropolitan areas of the world. Concluding the section on world information is a seventeen-page table of world cities and their populations (excluding those populations in the United States). This population table is arranged alphabetically by country and includes every important foreign urban center. Major political subdivisions (states, provinces, etc.) are also listed for the leading countries.

Index

The final pages of the atlas are devoted to an explanation of the index and a 100-page index of alphabetized places found on the reference maps of the atlas.

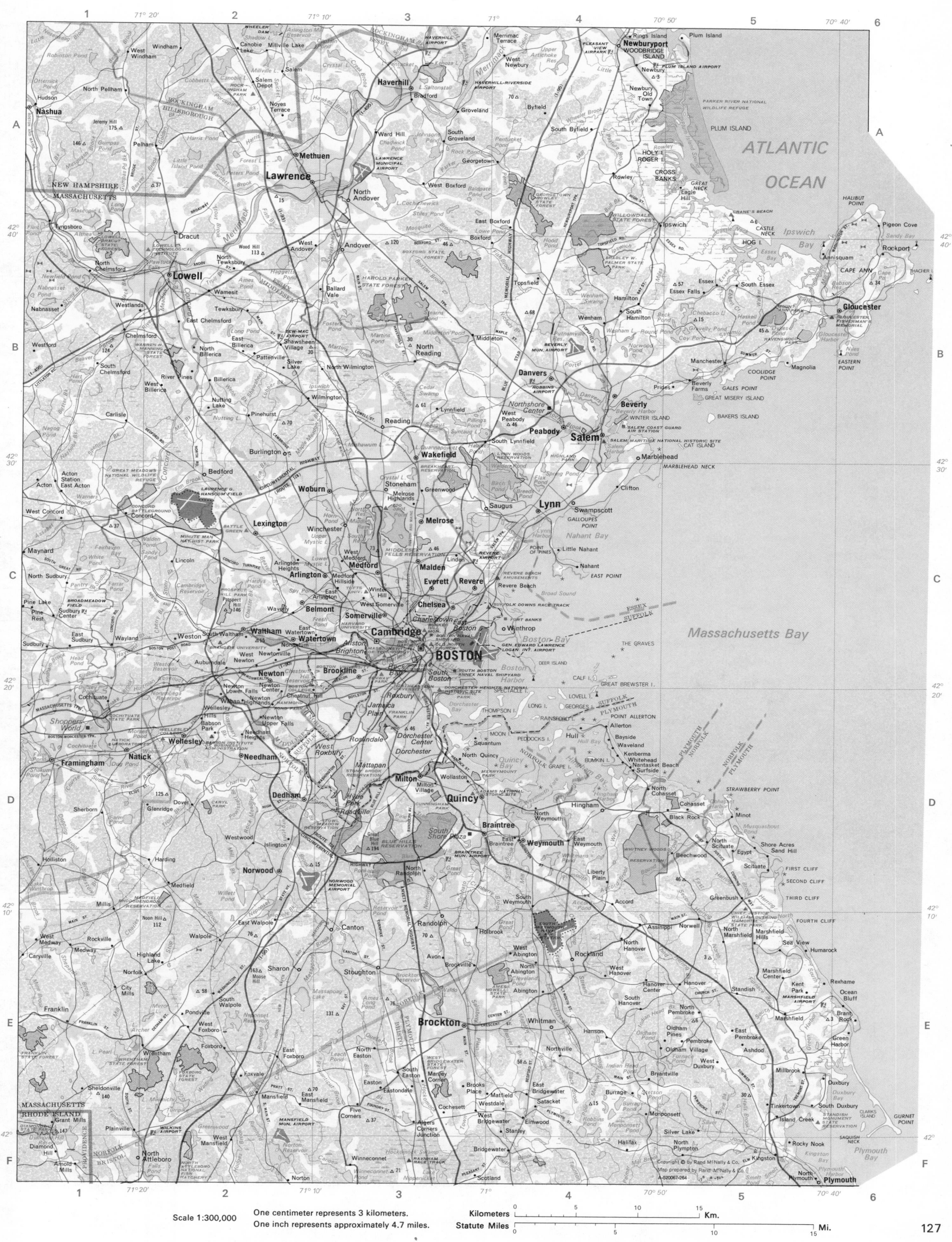

Scale 1:300,000
One centimeter represents 3 kilometers.
One inch represents approximately 4.7 miles.

Kilometers
Statute Miles

127

1 2 3 4 5 6
74° 40′
74° 30′
74° 20′
74° 10′
74°
A B C D E F G
41° 10′
41°
40° 50′
40° 40′
40° 30′
40° 20′
NEW YORK
NEW JERSEY
Newark
Paterson
Passaic
Hackensack
Jersey City
Elizabeth
Plainfield
Morristown
Perth Amboy
New Brunswick
Princeton
Somerville
Bayonne
Hoboken
Union City
Clifton
Montclair
Bloomfield
Livingston
Summit
Westfield
Rahway
Linden
Piscataway
Red Bank
STATEN ISLAND
Manhattan
Brooklyn
Raritan Bay
Sandy Hook Bay
Lower New York Bay
RAMAPO MTS
FIRST WATCHUNG MOUNTAIN
SECOND WATCHUNG MOUNTAIN
GERMANY FLATS

Scale 1:300,000

One centimeter represents 3 kilometers.
One inch represents approximately 4.7 miles.

Kilometers

Statute Miles

Copyright © by Rand McNally & Co.
Map prepared by Rand McNally & Co.
A-520060-264

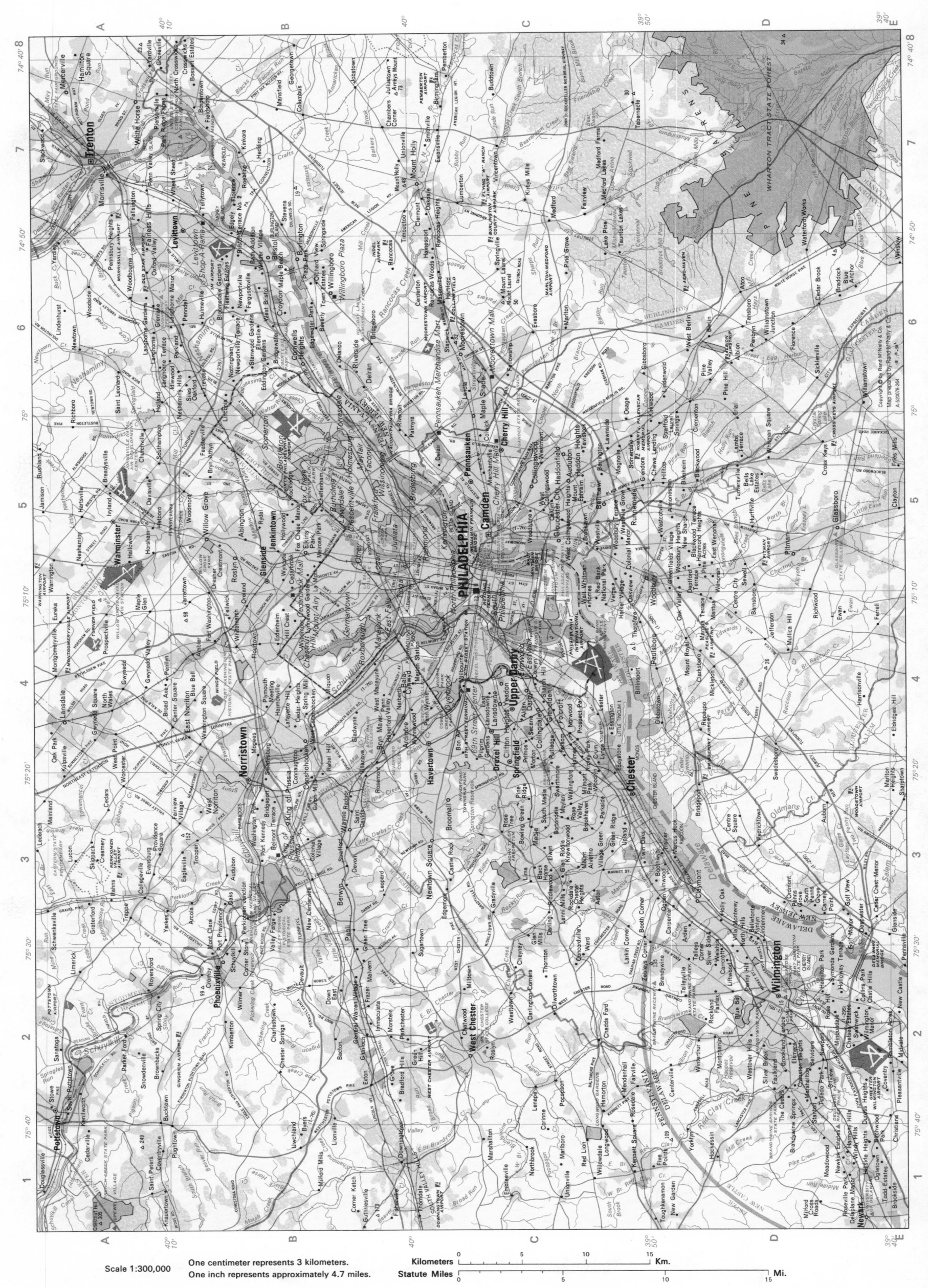

Scale 1:300,000
One centimeter represents 3 kilometers.
One inch represents approximately 4.7 miles.

Kilometers
Km.
Statute Miles
Mi.

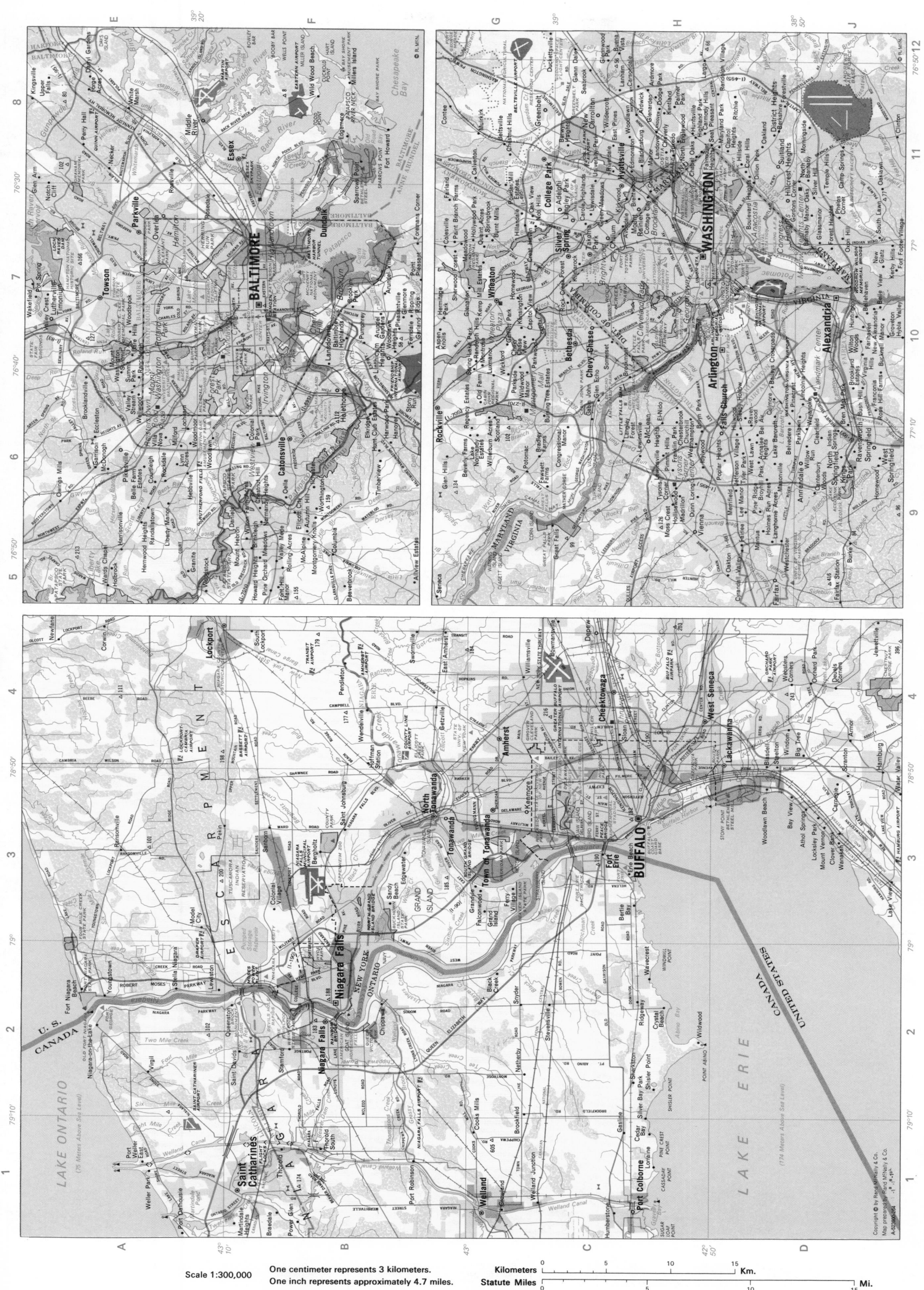

Scale 1:300,000
One centimeter represents 3 kilometers.
One inch represents approximately 4.7 miles.

Kilometers
Statute Miles

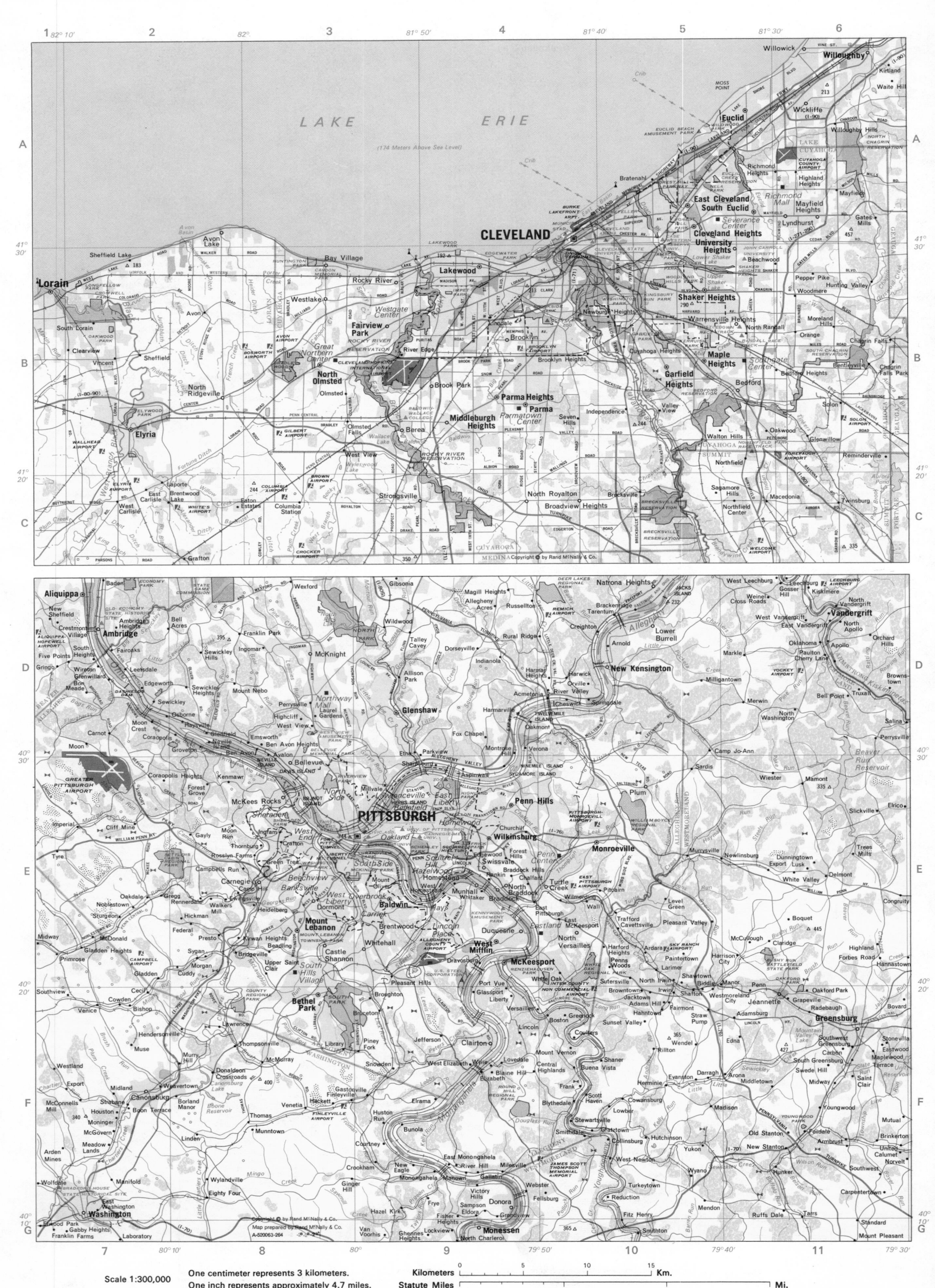

Scale 1:300,000

One centimeter represents 3 kilometers.
One inch represents approximately 4.7 miles.

Kilometers

Statute Miles

Scale 1:300,000   One centimeter represents 3 kilometers.
One inch represents approximately 4.7 miles.

Kilometers |0   5   10   15| Km.
Statute Miles |0   5   10   15| Mi.

Copyright © by Rand McNally & Co.
Map Prepared by Rand McNally & Co.
A-500061-294

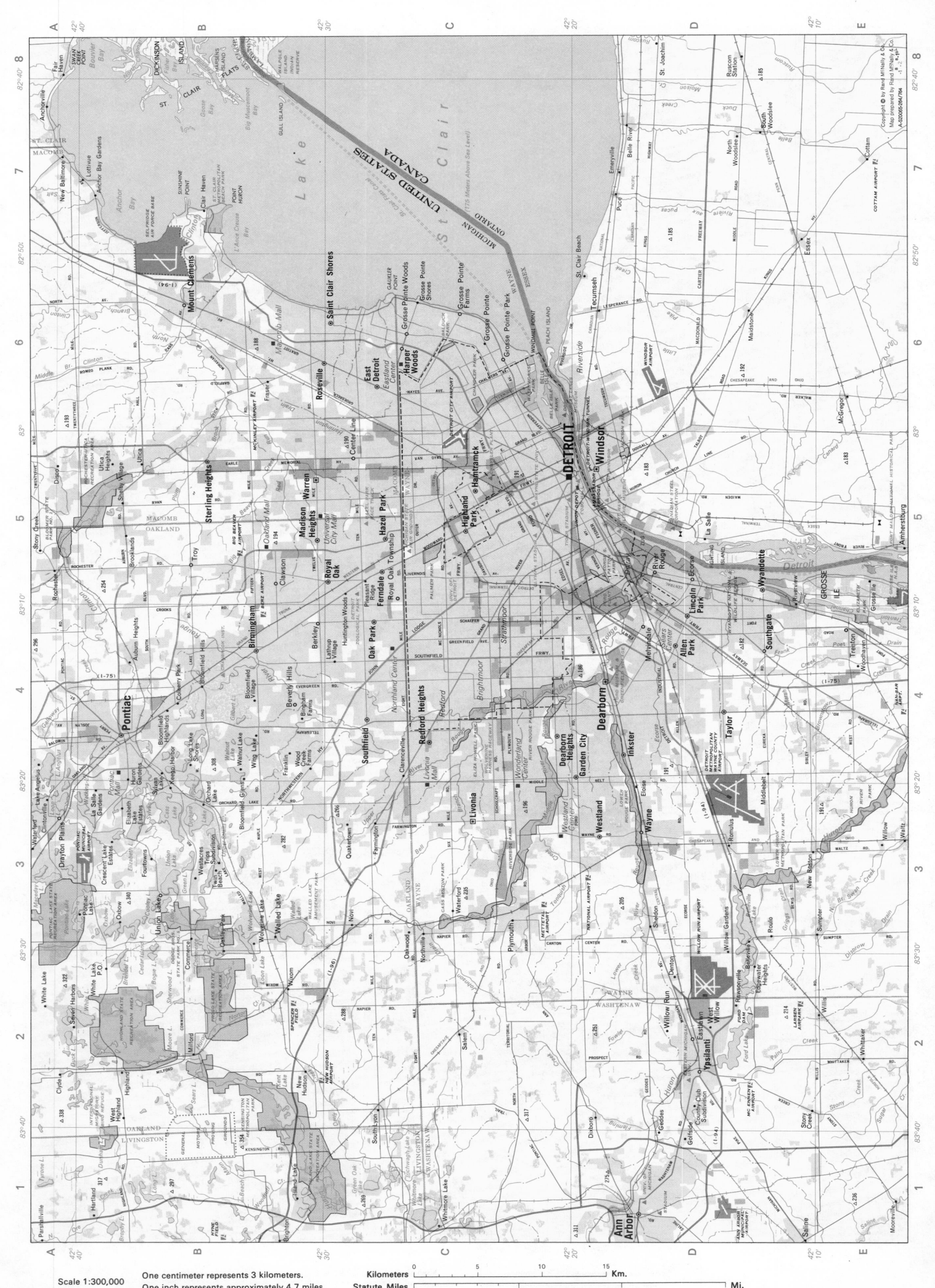

Scale 1:300,000

One centimeter represents 3 kilometers.
One inch represents approximately 4.7 miles.

Kilometers 0   5   10   15   Km.

Statute Miles 0   5   10   15   Mi.

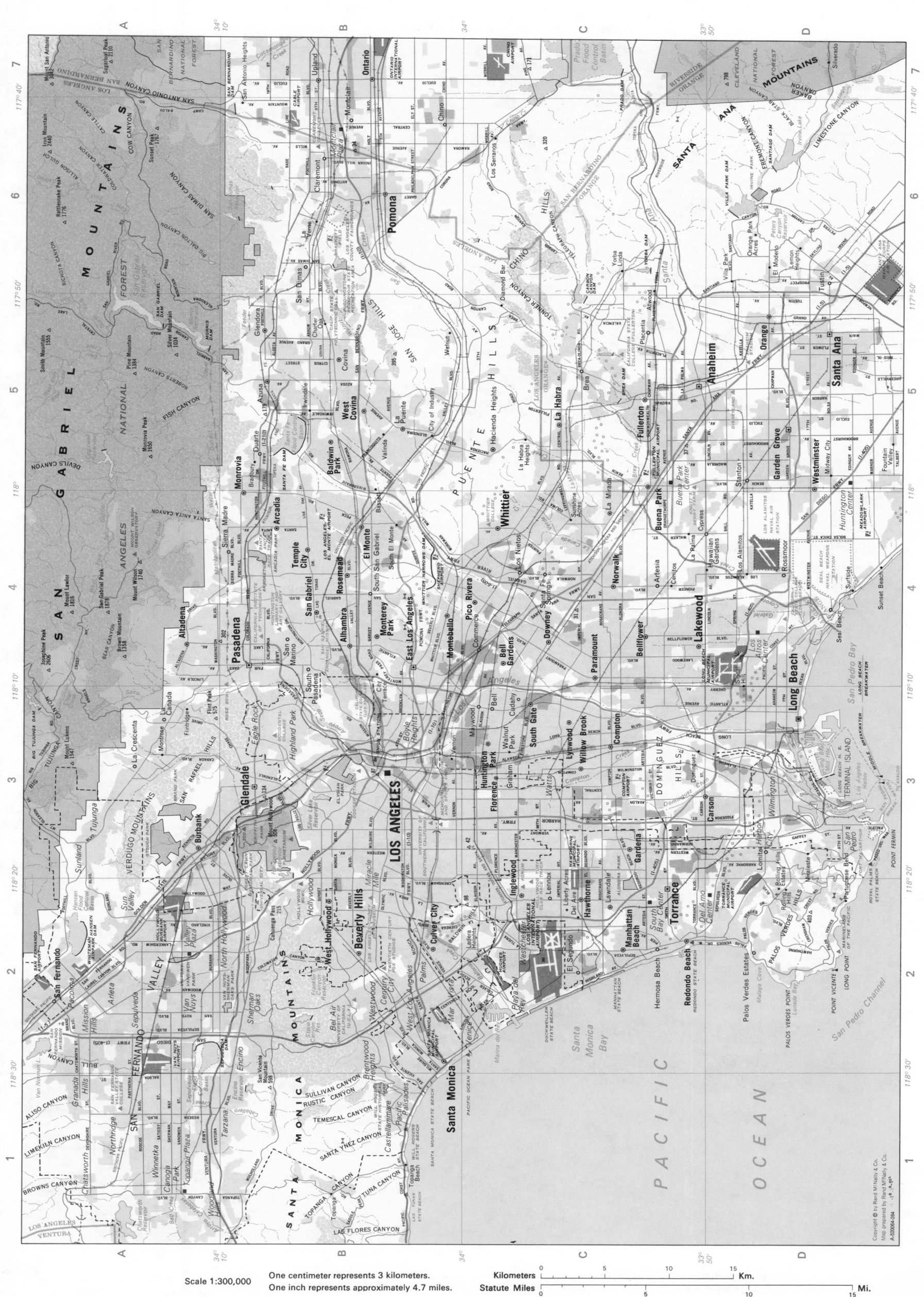

Scale 1:300,000
One centimeter represents 3 kilometers.
One inch represents approximately 4.7 miles.

Kilometers
Statute Miles

0   5   10   15
Km.

0   5   10   15
Mi.

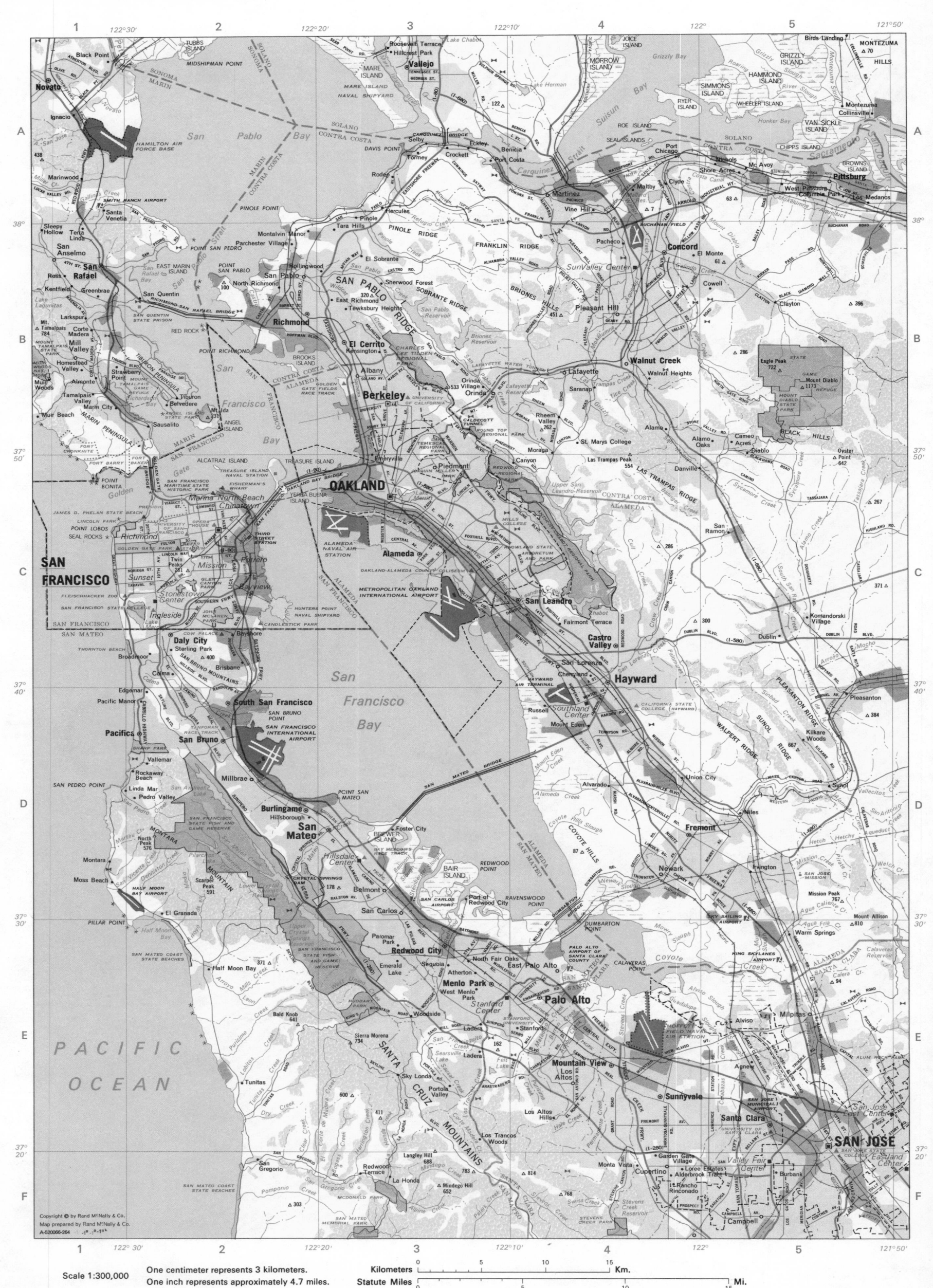

Scale 1:300,000

One centimeter represents 3 kilometers.
One inch represents approximately 4.7 miles.

Kilometers

Statute Miles

Index for U.S. Metropolitan Area Maps

NOTE: This index lists in alphabetical order all cities, towns, and other localities shown on the maps on pages 127–136. Neighborhoods and local area names that occur within cities are shown in *italic* type.

137

131 F7 Dundalk, Md.
129 E3 Dunellen, N.J.
129 E10 Dunewood, N.Y.
132 E11 Dunningtown, Pa.
131 G9 Dunn Loring, Va.
132 E9 Duquesne, Pa.
129 E3 Durham Park, N.J.
130 D2 Duross Heights, Del.
127 E5 Duxbury, Mass.
133 F5 Dyer, Ind.

E

127 A5 Eagle Hill, Mass.
135 B3 *Eagle Rock, Calif.*
130 B3 Eagleville, Pa.
127 C1 East Acton, Mass.
131 B4 East Amherst, N.Y.
127 C3 East Arlington, Mass.
129 E7 East Atlantic Beach, N.Y.
127 B2 East Billerica, Mass.
127 C3 *East Boston, Mass.*
127 A4 East Boxford, Mass.
127 D4 East Braintree, Mass.
127 E4 East Bridgewater, Mass.
129 F3 East Brunswick, N.J.
132 C2 East Carlisle, Ohio
127 B2 East Chelmsford, Mass.
129 C7 Eastchester, N.Y.
133 F5 East Chicago, Ind.
133 F4 East Chicago Heights, Ill.
132 A5 East Cleveland, Ohio
134 C6 East Detroit, Mich.
130 B4 *East Falls, Pa.*
129 D9 East Farmingdale, N.Y.
127 E2 East Foxboro, Mass.
133 F4 East Hazel Crest, Ill.
129 D8 East Hills, N.Y.
129 B6 East Irvington, N.Y.
129 D10 East Islip, N.Y.
129 F5 East Keansburg, N.J.
130 C4 East Lansdowne, Pa.
134 D2 Eastlawn, Mich.
132 E9 *East Liberty, Pa.*
135 B4 East Los Angeles, Calif.
127 E2 East Mansfield, Mass.
132 E10 East McKeesport, Pa.
129 D8 East Meadow, N.Y.
129 E2 East Millstone, N.J.
132 F9 East Monongahela, Pa.
129 D5 East Newark, N.J.
129 D6 *East New York, N.Y.*
130 B4 East Norriton, Pa.
129 C10 East Northport, N.Y.
129 C8 East Norwich, N.Y.
127 E3 Easton, Mass.
127 E3 Eastondale, Mass.
129 D4 East Orange, N.J.
136 E4 East Palo Alto, Calif.
129 C5 East Paterson, N.J.
127 E5 East Pembroke, Mass.
131 H11 East Pines, Md.
132 E10 East Pittsburgh, Pa.
136 B3 East Richmond, Calif.
129 E8 East Rockaway, N.Y.
129 D5 East Rutherford, N.J.
129 C11 East Setauket, N.Y.
127 C1 East Sudbury, Mass.
132 D11 East Vandergrift, Pa.
129 B7 East View, N.Y.
127 E2 East Walpole, Mass.
132 D7 East Washington, Pa.
127 C2 East Watertown, Mass.
130 D5 East Wenonah, N.J.
127 D4 East Weymouth, Mass.
129 B7 East White Plains, N.Y.
130 C4 *Eastwick, Pa.*
132 F11 Eastwood, Pa.
132 C2 Eaton Estates, Ohio
131 E6 Eccleston, Md.
136 A3 Eckley, Calif.
134 D5 Ecorse, Mich.
130 B6 Eddington Gardens, Pa.
130 C3 Eddystone, Pa.
130 B7 Edgely, Pa.
136 D2 Edgemar, Calif.
131 F8 Edgemere, Md.
130 C3 Edgemont, Pa.
129 D6 Edgewater, N.J.
131 B3 Edgewater, N.Y.
134 D2 Edgewater Heights, Mich.
130 B6 Edgewater Park, N.J.
132 E9 Edgewood, Pa.
132 D7 Edgeworth, Pa.
129 E3 Edison, N.J.
133 C3 *Edison Park, Ill.*
131 H11 Edmonston, Md.
132 F11 Edna, Pa.
127 D5 Egypt, Mass.
132 F8 Eightyfour, Pa.
136 B3 El Cerrito, Calif.
132 F9 Eldora, Pa.
130 E4 Eldridges Hill, N.J.
136 D2 El Granada, Calif.
129 E4 Elizabeth, N.J.
132 F9 Elizabeth, Pa.
134 B3 Elizabeth Lake Estates, Mich.
133 C2 Elk Grove Village, Ill.
130 B5 Elkins Park, Pa.
131 F6 Elkridge, Md.
130 B6 Ellerslie, Pa.
131 F6 Ellicott City, Md.
133 D2 Elmhurst, Ill.
129 D6 *Elmhurst, N.Y.*
135 D6 El Modeno, Calif.
129 D7 Elmont, N.Y.
135 B4 El Monte, Calif.
129 B7 Elmsford, N.Y.
130 C4 *Elmwood, Pa.*
127 E4 Elmwood, Mass.
133 D3 Elmwood Park, Ill.
131 H10 El Nido, Va.
134 C3 Eloise, Mich.
132 F9 Elrama, Pa.
132 E11 Elrico, Pa.
135 C2 El Segundo, Calif.
130 D2 Elsmere, Del.
136 B3 El Sobrante, Calif.
129 C9 Elwood, N.Y.
132 G7 Elwood Park, Pa.
130 C3 Elwyn, Pa.
132 B2 Elyria, Ohio
130 C1 Embreeville, Pa.
136 E3 Emerald Lake, Calif.
129 C5 Emerson, N.J.
136 C3 Emeryville, Calif.
132 D8 Emsworth, Pa.
135 B2 *Encino, Calif.*
129 C6 Englewood, N.J.
133 E4 *Englewood, Ill.*
129 C6 Englewood Cliffs, N.J.
130 B4 Erdenheim, Pa.
130 D5 Erial, N.J.
131 F8 Essex, Md.
127 B5 Essex, Mass.
127 B5 Essex Falls, Mass.
129 D4 Essex Fells, N.J.
130 C4 Essington, Pa.
132 D9 Etna, Pa.
132 A5 Euclid, Ohio
130 A4 Eureka, Pa.
130 A3 Evansburg, Pa.
133 C3 Evanston, Ill.
132 F10 Evanston, Pa.
127 C3 Everett, Mass.
129 F5 Everett, N.J.
133 E3 Evergreen Park, Ill.
130 C6 Evesboro, N.J.
130 D4 Ewan, N.J.
130 C7 Ewansville, N.J.
132 E8 Ewingsville, Pa.
132 E11 Export, Pa.
132 F7 Export, Pa.
130 B2 Exton, Pa.

F

130 D2 Fairfax, Del.
131 H9 Fairfax, Va.
131 J9 Fairfax Station, Va.
129 C4 Fairfield, N.J.
129 E10 Fair Harbor, N.Y.
134 A8 Fair Haven, Mich.
129 F5 Fair Haven, N.J.
131 J10 Fairhaven, Va.
131 G11 Fairland, Md.
129 C5 Fair Lawn, N.J.
131 H9 Fairlee, Va.
130 A6 Fairless Hills, Pa.
133 F1 Fairmont, Ill.
132 F10 Fairmont, Pa.
136 C4 Fairmont Terrace, Calif.
131 H11 Fairmount Heights, Md.
132 D7 Fairoaks, Pa.
129 B7 Fairview, N.J.
130 C7 Fairview, N.J.
129 F5 Fairview, N.J.
129 D6 Fairview, N.Y.
132 B3 Fairview Park, Ohio
130 B3 Fairview Village, Pa.
130 C2 Fairville, Pa.
131 C3 Falconwood, N.Y.
131 H9 Falls Church, Va.
130 A7 Fallsington, Pa.
129 E3 Fanwood, N.J.
129 D2 Far Hills, N.J.
134 C3 Farmington, Mich.
129 D9 Farmingville, N.Y.
129 F3 Farrington Lake Heights, N.J.
129 E7 *Far Rockaway, N.Y.*
130 D2 Faulkland, Del.
131 G9 Fawsett Farms, Md.
130 B5 Feasterville, Pa.
132 E8 Federal, Pa.
133 C2 Feehanville, Ill.
130 C6 Fellowship, N.J.
132 F10 Fellsburg, Pa.
130 B4 Fellwick, Pa.
130 B6 Fergusonville, Pa.
131 F7 Ferndale, Md.
134 C5 Ferndale, Mich.
133 F3 Fernway, Ill.
130 D4 Ferrell, N.J.
131 C3 Ferry Village, N.Y.
130 B7 Fieldsboro, N.J.
129 D2 Fieldstone, N.J.
129 E2 Finderne, N.J.
132 F8 Finleyville, Pa.
129 D11 Fire Island Pines, N.Y.
132 F9 Fisher Heights, Pa.
130 B1 Fisherville, Pa.
132 G10 Fitz Henry, Pa.
127 E3 Five Corners, Mass.
132 D7 Five Points, Pa.
130 D1 Five Points, Pa.
129 E1 Flagtown, N.J.
129 C1 Flanders, N.J.
129 E6 *Flatbush, N.Y.*
130 B6 Fleetwing Estates, Pa.
135 A3 Flintridge, Calif.
129 D7 Floral Park, N.Y.
135 C3 Florence, Calif.
130 D6 Florence, N.J.
129 D3 Florham Park, N.J.
133 F3 Flossmoor, Ill.
130 B4 Flourtown, Pa.
133 D1 Flowerfield, Ill.
129 D7 *Flushing, N.Y.*
130 C4 Folcroft, Pa.
130 C4 Folsom, Pa.
131 F5 Font Hill Manor, Md.
132 E11 Forbes Road, Pa.
129 E4 Fords, N.J.
131 F7 Foremans Corner, Md.
132 E8 Forest Grove, Pa.
131 J10 Forest Heights, Md.
132 E9 Forest Hills, Pa.
129 D6 *Forest Hills, N.Y.*
133 B1 Forest Lake, Ill.
133 D3 Forest Park, Ill.
131 F6 *Forest Park, Md.*
133 C2 Forest River, Ill.
133 E3 Forest View, Ill.
131 H11 Forestville, Md.
131 E8 Forge Acres, Md.
131 J10 Fort Foote Village, Md.
131 F8 Fort Howard, Md.
129 C6 Fort Lee, N.J.
131 A2 Fort Niagara Beach, N.Y.
130 B4 Fort Washington, Pa.
136 D3 Foster City, Calif
135 D5 Fountain Valley, Calif.
134 B3 Fourtowns, Mich.
127 E2 Foxboro, Mass.
132 D9 Fox Chapel, Pa.
130 B5 *Fox Chase, Pa.*
130 B5 Fox Chase Manor, Pa.
132 F11 Foxdale, Pa.
127 E2 Foxvale, Mass.
127 D1 Framingham, Mass.
132 F10 Frank, Pa.
130 B5 *Frankford, Pa.*
133 F2 Frankfort, Ill.
127 E1 Franklin, Mass.
134 B4 Franklin, Mich.
129 B2 Franklin, N.J.
132 G7 Franklin Farms, Pa.
129 C4 Franklin Lakes, N.J.
133 D2 Franklin Park, Ill.
129 F2 Franklin Park, N.J.
132 D8 Franklin Park, Pa.
131 H10 Franklin Park, Va.
134 B6 Fraser, Mich.
130 B2 Frazer, Pa.
129 E8 Freeport, N.Y.
136 D4 Fremont, Calif.
129 D7 *Fresh Meadows, N.Y.*
130 E5 Fries Mills, N.J.
132 F9 Frye, Pa.
135 C5 Fullerton, Calif.

G

132 G7 Gabby Heights, Pa.
133 A2 Gages Lake, Ill.
132 F3 Gallatin, Pa.
129 D2 Galloping Hill, N.J.
135 C3 Gardena, Calif.
129 D6 *Garden Bay Manor, N.Y.*
134 D4 Garden City, Mich.
129 D8 Garden City, N.Y.
129 D7 Garden City Park, N.Y.
136 F4 Garden Gate Village, Calif.
135 D5 Garden Grove, Calif.
129 C5 Garfield, N.J.
132 B5 Garfield Heights, Ohio
131 F7 Garland, Md.
131 G10 Garrett Park, Md.
131 E6 Garrison, Md.
129 E4 Garwood, N.J.
133 F5 Gary, Ind.
132 F9 Gastonville, Pa.
132 A6 Gates Mills, Ohio
132 E8 Gayly, Pa.
134 D1 Geddes, Mich.
130 B2 General Warren Village, Pa.
131 H10 *Georgetown, D.C.*
127 A4 Georgetown, Mass.
130 B8 Georgetown, N.J.
133 F6 Georgia Heights, Ind.
130 B4 *Germantown, Pa.*
131 B4 Getzville, N.Y.
132 G9 Ghennes Heights, Pa.
130 C6 Gibbsboro, N.J.
130 D4 Gibbstown, N.J.
132 D9 Gibsonia, Pa.
129 D3 Gillette, N.J.
133 B1 Gilmer, Ill.
132 F8 Ginger Hill, Pa.
129 C3 Glacier Hills, N.J.
132 E7 Gladden, Pa.
132 E7 Gladden Heights, Pa.
129 D2 Gladstone, N.J.
130 B4 Gladwyne, Pa.
130 D5 Glassboro, N.J.
131 J11 Glassmanor, Md.
132 F9 Glassport, Pa.
131 G10 Glenallen, Md.
131 H11 Glenarden, Md.
131 E8 Glen Arm, Md.
133 C3 Glencoe, Ill.
129 C8 Glen Cove, N.Y.
135 B3 Glendale, Calif.
133 D1 Glendale Heights, Ill.
135 B5 Glendora, Calif.
130 C5 Glendora, N.J.
131 H10 Glen Echo, Md.
133 D1 Glen Ellyn, Ill.
133 D1 Glen Ellyn Countryside, Ill.
132 D8 Glenfield, Pa.
131 G9 Glen Hills, Md.
130 A6 Glenlake, Pa.
130 B2 Glenloch, Pa.
130 C3 Glen Mills, Pa.
131 F7 Glenmore, Md.
131 H12 Glenn Dale, Md.
131 H12 Glennwood Park, Md.
133 D1 Glen Oak, Ill.
130 C4 Glenolden, Pa.
130 C3 Glen Riddle, Pa.
129 D4 Glen Ridge, N.J.
127 D2 Glenridge, Mass.
129 C5 Glen Rock, N.J.
132 D9 Glenshaw, Pa.
130 B5 Glenside, N.J.
130 E3 Glenside, Pa.
133 C3 Glenview, Ill.
133 C2 Glenview Countryside, Ill.
129 B6 Glenville, N.Y.
132 D7 Glenwillard, Pa.
132 B6 Glenwillow, Ohio
133 F4 Glenwood, Ill.
129 D8 Glenwood Landing, N.Y.
127 B6 Gloucester, Mass.
130 C5 Gloucester City, N.J.
133 C3 Golf, Ill.
129 C2 Golf Hill, N.J.
130 D3 Golf Manor, N.J.
133 C2 Golf Park Terrace, Ill.
134 D1 Golfside, Mich.
130 D3 Golf View, N.J.
133 E2 Golfview Hills, Ill.
129 B3 Gordon Lakes, N.J.
131 H11 Gordons Corner, Md.
132 D11 Gosser Hill, Pa.
130 C3 Gradyville, Pa.
132 C2 Grafton, Ohio
135 C3 Graham, Calif.
135 A1 *Granada Hills, Calif.*
131 C3 Grand Island, N.Y.
132 F9 Grandview, Pa.
129 B6 Grand View-on-Hudson, N.Y.
131 C3 Grandyle, N.Y.
131 E5 Granite, Md.
127 E1 Grant Mills, R. I.
132 F11 Grapeville, Pa.
130 A3 Graterford, Pa.
132 F10 Gratztown, Pa.
133 A1 Grayslake, Ill.
131 G9 Great Falls, Va.
129 E5 *Great Kills, N.Y.*
129 D7 Great Neck, N.Y.
129 D7 Great Neck Estates, N.Y.
129 D11 Great River, N.Y.
129 D10 Great River, N.Y.
131 G11 Greenbelt, Md.
136 B1 Greenbrae, Calif.
129 E3 Green Brook, N.J.
127 D5 Greenbush, Mass.
129 B10 Green Farms, N. Y.
130 D5 Greenfields Village, N.J.
127 E6 Green Harbor, Mass.
130 C2 Green Hill, Pa.
129 C2 Green Hut Park, N.J.
129 E2 Green Knoll, N.J.
131 H11 Green Meadows, Md.
133 B2 Green Oaks, Ill.
132 F10 Greenock, Pa.
129 B3 Green Pond, N.J.
130 C3 Green Ridge, Pa.
132 F11 Greensburg, Pa.
132 E8 Green Tree, Pa.
130 B2 Green Tree, Pa.
129 D3 Green Village, N.J.
129 B7 Greenville, N.Y.
129 D6 *Greenwich Village, N.Y.*
127 C3 Greenwood, Mass.
132 E7 Gregg, Pa.
133 F5 Griffith, Ind.
129 F2 Griggstown, N.J.
132 D7 Gringo, Pa.
134 E5 Grosse Ile, Mich.
134 C6 Grosse Pointe, Mich.
134 C6 Grosse Pointe Farms, Mich.
134 C6 Grosse Pointe Park, Mich.
134 C6 Grosse Pointe Shores, Mich.
134 C6 Grosse Pointe Woods, Mich.
130 B2 Grove, Pa.
127 A3 Groveland, Mass.
129 G2 Grovers Mills, N.J.
132 D8 Groveton, Pa.
131 J10 Groveton, Va.
130 A7 Groveville, N.J.
130 B3 Gulph Mills, Pa.
130 B1 Guthriesville, Pa.
129 D5 Guttenberg, N.J.
130 A4 Gwynedd, Pa.
130 A4 Gwynedd Square, Pa.
130 A4 Gwynedd Valley, Pa.

H

135 C5 Hacienda Heights, Calif.
129 C5 Hackensack, N.J.
132 F8 Hackett, Pa.
130 C5 Haddonfield, N.J.
130 C5 Haddon Heights, N.J.
132 F10 Hahntown, Pa.
130 C7 Hainesport, N.J.
133 A1 Hainesville, Ill.
129 C4 Haledon, N.J.
129 C9 Halesite, N.Y.
131 F6 Halethorpe, Md.
133 B2 Half Day, Ill.
136 E2 Half Moon Bay, Calif.
127 F4 Halifax, Mass.
130 A5 Hallowell, Pa.
129 B2 Hamburg, N.J.
131 D4 Hamburg, N.Y.
131 E7 *Hamilton, Md.*
127 B4 Hamilton, Mass.
130 D2 Hamilton Park, Del.
130 A8 Hamilton Square, N.J.
133 F4 Hammond, Ind.
130 D5 Hammond Heights, N.J.
130 C2 Hamorton, Pa.
134 C5 Hamtramck, Mich.
132 E11 Hannastown Pa.
131 F6 Hanover, Md.
127 E5 Hanover, Mass.
129 D3 Hanover, N.J.
127 E4 Hanover Center, Mass.
127 E4 Hanson, Mass.
135 D3 *Harbor City, Calif.*
129 E7 Harbor Isle, N.Y.
127 D2 Harding, Mass.
132 E10 Harford Heights, Pa.
130 C5 Harker Village, N.J.
129 D6 *Harlem, N.Y.*
132 D10 Harmar Heights, Pa.
132 D9 Harmarville, Pa.
130 B4 Harmonville, Pa.
129 F5 Harmony, N.J.
130 D1 Harmony Hills, Del.
134 C6 Harper Woods, Mich.
129 C6 Harrington Park, N.J.
129 C7 Harrison, N.J.
129 D5 Harrison, N.Y.
132 E11 Harrison City, Pa.
131 E6 Harrisonville, Md.
130 D4 Harrisonville, N.J.
130 C6 Hartford, N.J.
134 B1 Hartland, Mich.
129 B7 Hartsdale, N.Y.
130 A5 Hartsville, Pa.
133 F4 Harvey, Ill.
132 D10 Harwick, Pa.
133 D3 Harwood Heights, Ill.
131 F6 Harwood Park, Md.
129 C5 Hasbrouck Heights, N.J.
133 E2 Hastings, Ill.
129 C6 Hastings-on-Hudson, N.Y.
130 A5 Hatboro, Pa.
129 D10 Hauppauge, N.Y.
129 E3 Haven Homes, N.J.
130 B4 Haverford, Pa.
127 A3 Haverhill, Mass.
130 C4 Havertown, Pa.
135 D4 Hawaiian Gardens, Calif.
129 C6 Haworth, N.J.
135 C2 Hawthorne, Calif.
129 B7 Hawthorne, N.J.
129 C5 Hawthorne, N.Y.
133 B1 Hawthorn Woods, Ill.
132 E9 *Hays, Pa.*
132 D8 Haysville, Pa.
136 C4 Hayward, Calif.
133 F4 Hazel Crest, Ill.
133 E3 Hazel Green, Ill.
132 F9 Hazel Kirk, Pa.
134 C5 Hazel Park, Mich.
132 G9 *Hazelwood, Pa.*
129 F4 Hazlet, N.J.
129 C11 Head of the Harbor, N.Y.
131 E6 Hebbville, Md.
130 B7 Hedding, N.J.
133 F4 *Hegewisch, Ill.*
132 E8 Heidelberg, Pa.
129 F3 Helmetta, N.J.
129 D8 Hempstead, N.Y.
132 F8 Hendersonville, Pa.
136 A3 Hercules, Calif.
132 F10 Herminie, Pa.
131 G10 Hermitage Park, Md.
135 C2 Hermosa Beach, Calif.
131 E6 Hernwood Heights, Md.
129 E7 Hewitt, N.J.
129 C3 Hibernia, N.J.
132 E8 Hickman, Pa.
133 E3 Hickory Hills, Ill.
129 D8 Hicksville, N.Y.
132 D8 Highcliff, Pa.
133 F5 Highland, Ind.
134 B2 Highland, Mich.
132 E11 Highland, Pa.
132 A6 Highland Heights, Ohio
133 D1 Highland Hills, Ill.
133 A1 Highland Lake, Ill.
127 E2 Highland Lake, Mass.
129 A3 Highland Lakes, N.J.
135 B3 *Highland Park, Calif.*
133 B3 Highland Park, Ill.
131 H11 Highland Park, Md.
134 C5 Highland Park, Mich.
129 F3 Highland Park, N.J.
129 F6 Highlands, N.J.
131 F7 *Highlandtown, Md.*
129 F3 High Point Manor, N.J.
133 B3 Highwood, Ill.
131 G11 Hillandale, Md.
129 B4 Hillburn, N.Y.
129 B5 Hillcrest, N.Y.
130 B4 Hill Crest, Pa.
131 H11 Hillcrest Heights, Md.
136 A3 Hillcrest Park, Calif.
136 D2 Hillsborough, Calif.
129 B5 Hillsdale, N.J.
133 D2 Hillside, Ill.
131 H11 Hillside, Md.
129 D4 Hillside, N.J.
129 D7 *Hillside, N.Y.*
130 D1 Hillside Heights, Del.
129 D7 Hillside Manor, N.Y.
130 D5 Hilltop, N.J.
131 H9 Hillwood, Va.
127 D4 Hingham, Mass.
133 E2 Hinsdale, Ill.
129 D5 Hoboken, N.J.
130 D1 Hockessin, Del.
133 E2 Hodgkins, Ill.
133 C1 Hoffman Estates, Ill.
131 B4 Hoffman Station, N.Y.
129 C5 Ho-Ho-Kus, N.J.
133 F4 Holbrook, Ill.
131 E5 Holbrook, Md.
127 E3 Holbrook, Mass.
129 D11 Holbrook, N.Y.
130 A6 Holland, Pa.
131 H9 Hollinswood, Va.
129 D7 *Hollis, N.Y.*
127 D1 Holliston, Mass.
130 D2 Holloway Terrace, Del.
130 D3 Holly Oak, Del.
135 B2 *Hollywood, Calif.*
130 B5 Hollywood, Pa.
131 G11 Hollywood Park, Md.
129 F4 Holmdel, N.J.
130 C4 Holmes, Pa.
130 C5 *Holmesburg, Pa.*
131 H9 Holmes Run Acres, Va.
129 D11 Holtsville, N.Y.
132 E9 Homestead, Pa.
129 D3 Homestead Park, N.J.
136 B1 Homestead Valley, Calif.
133 E3 Hometown, Ill.
133 F3 Homewood, Ill.
131 J9 Homewood, Md.
132 E9 *Homewood, Pa.*
131 G10 Homewood, Va.
133 F3 Homewood Acres, Ill.
129 C2 Hopatcong, N.J.
129 E4 Hopelawn, N.J.
133 C2 Horatio Gardens, Ill.
130 C5 Horsham, Pa.
132 E7 Houston, Pa.
129 E6 *Howard Beach, N.Y.*
131 F5 Howard Heights, Md.
133 C3 Hubbard Woods, Ill.
127 A1 Hudson, N.H.
127 D4 Hull, Mass.
130 B6 Hulmeville, Pa.
127 E5 Humarock, Mass.
132 F11 Hunker, Pa.
131 F6 Hunt Club Estates, Md.
129 C9 Huntington, N.Y.
131 J10 Huntington, Va.
129 C9 Huntington Bay, N.Y.
135 C3 Huntington Park, Calif.
129 C9 Huntington Station, N.Y.
134 C5 Huntington Woods, Mich.
132 B6 Hunting Valley, Ohio
131 H11 Huntsville, Md.
129 C2 Hurdtown, N.J.
130 D5 Hurffville, N.J.
134 B3 Huron Gardens, Mich.
132 F9 Huston Run, Pa.
132 F10 Hutchinson, Pa.
131 H11 Hyattsville, Md.
131 J10 Hybla Valley, Va.
133 E4 *Hyde Park, Ill.*
127 D3 *Hyde Park, Mass.*

I

130 B6 Idlewood, Pa.
131 H9 Idylwood, Va.
136 A1 Ignacio, Calif.
131 F6 Ilchester, Md.
130 B2 Immaculata, Pa.
132 D7 Imperial, Pa.
132 B5 Independence, Ohio
133 B2 Indian Creek, Ill.
133 E2 Indian Head Park, Ill.
132 D9 Indianola, Pa.
131 J9 Indian Springs, Va.
133 F1 Ingalls Park, Ill.
136 C2 *Ingleside, Calif.*
135 C2 Inglewood, Calif.
132 D8 Ingomar, Pa.
132 E8 Ingram, Pa.
134 D4 Inkster, Mich.
133 C1 Inverness, Ill.
129 E7 Inwood, N.Y.
127 A4 Ipswich, Mass.
129 D2 Ironia, N.J.
133 D3 *Irving Park, Ill.*
136 D5 Irvington, Calif.
131 F6 *Irvington, Md.*
129 B6 Irvington, N.J.
129 D4 Irvington, N.Y.
132 F10 Irwin, Pa.
135 B5 Irwindale, Calif.
129 E4 Iselin, N.J.
127 E5 Island Creek, Mass.
134 B1 Island Lake, Mich.
129 E8 Island Park, N.Y.
127 D2 Islington, Mass.
129 D10 Islip, N.Y.
129 D10 Islip Terrace, N.Y.
133 D1 Itasca, Ill.
133 B1 Ivanhoe, Ill.
130 A5 Ivyland, Pa.

J

129 D6 *Jackson Heights, N.Y.*
132 F10 Jacktown, Pa.
129 D7 *Jamaica, N.Y.*
127 D3 *Jamaica Plain, Mass.*
129 F3 Jamesburg, N.J.
130 A5 Jamison, Pa.
130 B4 Jarrettown, Pa.
132 F11 Jeannette, Pa.
130 D4 Jefferson, N.J.
132 F9 Jefferson, Pa.
133 D3 *Jefferson Park, Ill.*
131 H9 Jefferson Village, Va.
130 B5 Jenkintown, Pa.
129 D8 Jericho, N.Y.
129 D5 Jersey City, N.J.
131 D4 Jewettville, N.Y.
130 B7 Jobstown, N.J.
133 F1 Joliet, Ill.
130 B7 Juliustown, N.J.
130 B5 *Juniata, Pa.*
133 E2 Justice, Ill.

K

129 F5 Keansburg, N.J.
129 D5 Kearny, N.J.
129 E4 Keasbey, N.J.
129 E4 Keasby Heights, N.J.
134 B3 Keego Harbor, Mich.
133 D1 Keeneyville, Ill.
131 G10 Kemp Mill Estates, Md.
127 D4 Kenberma, Mass.
129 F2 Kendall Park, N.J.
133 C3 Kenilworth, Ill.
129 D4 Kenilworth, N.J.
130 A2 Kenilworth, Pa.
132 E8 Kenmawr, Pa.
131 C3 Kenmore, N.Y.
130 C1 Kennett Square, Pa.
136 B3 Kensington, Calif.
131 G10 Kensington, Md.
129 E6 *Kensington, N.Y.*
130 C5 *Kensington, Pa.*
136 B1 Kentfield, Calif.
131 H11 Kentland, Md.
127 E5 Kent Park, Mass.
129 C2 Kenvil, N.J.
133 E4 *Kenwood, Ill.*
131 J11 Kerby Hills, Md.
129 F4 Keyport, N.J.
133 B1 Kildeer, Ill.
136 D5 Kilkare Woods, Calif.
131 H10 Kilmarock, Md.
130 B2 Kimberton, Pa.
130 B3 King of Prussia, Pa.
129 C10 Kings Park, N.Y.
131 J9 Kings Park, Va.
129 D7 Kings Point, N.Y.
127 F5 Kingston, Mass.
129 F2 Kingston, N.J.
131 E8 Kingsville, Md.
130 B7 Kinkora, N.J.
129 C3 Kinnelon, N.J.
130 C7 Kirbys Mills, N.J.
131 H11 Kirkwood, Md.
130 D5 Kirkwood, N.J.
132 A6 Kirtland, Ohio
132 E8 Kirwan Heights, Pa.
132 D11 Kiskimere, Pa.
129 E10 Kismet, N.Y.
130 B3 Knauertown, Pa.
133 B2 Knollwood, Ill.
130 C3 Knowltonwood, Pa.
136 C5 Komandorski Village, Calif.
130 A3 Kulpsville, Pa.
130 D3 Kynlyn, Del.

L

132 D7 Laboratory, Pa.
135 A3 La Canada, Calif.
131 D4 Lackawanna, N.Y.
135 A3 La Crescenta, Calif.
136 E3 Ladera, Calif.
135 C2 Ladera Heights, Calif.
136 B4 Lafayette, Calif.
129 B1 Lafayette, N.J.
130 B4 Lafayette Hill, Pa.
133 E2 La Grange, Ill.
133 E2 La Grange Highlands, Ill.
133 E2 La Grange Park, Ill.
135 C5 La Habra, Calif.
135 C5 La Habra Heights, Calif.
136 F3 La Honda, Calif.
134 A4 Lake Angelus, Mich.
131 H10 Lake Barcroft, Va.
133 B2 Lake Bluff, Ill.
133 B2 Lake Forest, Ill.
129 C2 Lake Forest, N.J.
129 B2 Lake Grinnell, N.J.
129 C3 Lake Hiawatha, N.J.
129 C2 Lake Hopatcong, N.J.
129 C3 Lake Intervale, N.J.
129 C1 Lake Lackawanna, N.J.
129 B3 Lake Lookover, N.J.
129 B2 Lake Mohawk, N.J.
129 E3 Lake Nelson, N.J
131 G9 Lake Normandy Estates, Md.
130 C6 Lake Pine, N.J.
129 D11 Lake Ronkonkoma, N.Y.
129 B2 Lake Stockholm, N.J.
129 D7 Lake Success, N.Y.
129 B2 Lake Tamarack, N.J.
129 C3 Lake Telemark, N.J.
131 D3 Lake View, N.Y.
133 D4 *Lakeview, Ill.*
135 C4 Lakewood, Calif.
132 B4 Lakewood, Ohio
133 B1 Lake Zurich, Ill.
130 D5 Lambs Terrace, N.J.
135 C4 La Mirada, Calif.
130 B5 La Mott, Pa.
129 C2 Landing, N.J.
131 H11 Landover, Md.
130 A6 Langhorne, Pa.
131 H9 Langhorne Acres, Va.
130 A6 Langhorne Gardens, Pa.
130 B6 Langhorne Manor, Pa.
130 A6 Langhorne Terrace, Pa.
131 H11 Langley Park, Md.
131 H11 Lanham, Md.
130 A4 Lansdale, Pa.
131 F7 Lansdowne, Md.
130 C4 Lansdowne, Pa.
133 F4 Lansing, Ill.
135 C4 La Palma, Calif.
132 C2 Laporte, Ohio
135 B5 La Puente, Calif.
129 C7 Larchmont, N.Y.
131 H12 Largo, Md.
132 E10 Larimer, Pa.
130 C3 Larkin Corner, Pa.
136 B1 Larkspur, Calif.
134 B3 La Salle Gardens, Mich.
134 C4 Lathrup Village, Mich.
129 C8 Lattingtown, N.Y.
132 D8 Laurel Gardens, Pa.
129 C9 Laurel Hollow, N.Y.
129 E4 Laurel Homes, N.J.
130 D5 Laurel Springs, N.J.
129 F4 Laurence Harbor, N.J.
135 B6 La Verne, Calif.
135 C2 Lawndale, Calif.
130 B5 *Lawndale, Pa.*
133 D3 *Lawndale, Ill.*
130 C5 Lawnside, N.J.
127 A2 Lawrence, Mass.
129 E7 Lawrence, N.Y.
132 F8 Lawrence, Pa.
132 E9 *Lawrenceville, Pa.*
130 A3 Lederach, Pa.
129 C2 Ledgewood, N.J.
132 D11 Leechburg, Pa.
131 H9 Lee Manor, Va.
132 D7 Leetsdale, Pa.
135 D6 Lemon Heights, Calif.
133 E2 Lemont, Ill.
130 C2 Lenape, Pa.
130 C3 Lenni Mills, Pa.
135 C2 Lennox, Calif.
130 C6 Lenola, N.J.
129 F5 Leonardo, N.J.
129 C6 Leonia, N.J.
130 B3 Leopard, Pa.
130 C4 Lester, Pa.
132 E10 Level Green, Pa.
129 D8 Levittown, N.Y.
130 B7 Levittown, Pa.
131 H9 Lewinsville, Va.
131 H9 Lewinsville Heights, Va.
131 H11 Lewisdale, Md.
131 A2 Lewiston, N.Y.
127 C2 Lexington, Mass.
132 F9 Liberty, Pa.
135 C2 Liberty Acres, Calif.
129 E2 Liberty Corner, N.J.
131 E6 Liberty Manor, Md.
127 D4 Liberty Plain, Mass.
133 B2 Libertyville, Ill.
132 F8 Library, Pa.
130 D2 Liftwood, Del.
130 C3 Lima, Pa.
130 A2 Limerick, Pa.
127 C2 Lincoln, Mass.
132 F9 Lincoln, Pa.
133 F3 Lincoln Estates, Ill.
131 J10 Lincolnia Heights, Va.
134 D4 Lincoln Park, Mich.
129 C4 Lincoln Park, N.J.
132 E9 *Lincoln Place, Pa.*
133 B2 Lincolnshire, Ill.
133 C3 Lincolnwood, Ill.
133 F2 Lincolnwood Hills, Ill.
130 B6 Linconia, Pa.
129 G5 Lincroft, N.J.
136 D2 Linda Mar, Calif.
127 C3 Linden, Mass.
129 E4 Linden, N.J.
132 F8 Linden, Pa.
129 D9 Lindenhurst, N.Y.
130 A6 Lindenhurst, Pa.
130 D3 Lindenmere, Del.
130 D6 Lindenwold, N.J.
129 B3 Lindy Lake, N.J.
132 B4 Linndale, Ohio
131 F7 Linthicum Heights, Md.
130 D3 Linwood, Pa.
130 B2 Lionville, Pa.
133 E1 Lisle, Ill.
129 C4 Little Falls, N.J.
129 C5 Little Ferry, N.J.
127 C4 Little Nahant, Mass.

129 D7 *Little Neck, N.Y.*
129 F5 Little Silver, N.J.
129 D4 Livingston, N.J.
134 C3 Livonia, Mich.
129 C9 Lloyd Harbor, N.Y.
131 E6 Lochearn, Md.
133 F1 Lockport, Ill.
131 A4 Lockport, N.Y.
131 D3 Locksley Park, N.Y.
132 G9 Lockview, Pa.
129 F5 Locust, N.J.
129 C8 Locust Valley, N.Y.
129 C5 Lodi, N.J.
130 B5 *Logan, Pa.*
133 D3 *Logan Square, Ill.*
133 D1 Lombard, Ill.
135 D3 Lomita, Calif.
129 E10 Lonelyville, N.Y.
135 D3 Long Beach, Calif.
129 E8 Long Beach, N.Y.
133 B2 Long Grove, Ill.
129 D6 *Long Island City, N.Y.*
134 B4 Long Lake Shores, Mich.
130 C1 Longwood, Pa.
129 B2 Longwood Lake, N.J.
133 D4 *Loop, Ill.*
132 B1 Lorain, Ohio
136 F4 Loree Estates, Calif.
135 D4 Los Alamitos, Calif.
136 E4 Los Altos, Calif.
136 E4 Los Altos Hills, Calif.
135 B3 Los Angeles, Calif.
136 A5 Los Medanos, Calif.
135 C4 Los Nietos, Calif.
136 C6 Los Serranos, Calif.
136 E3 Lost Trancos Woods, Calif.
133 F5 Lottaville, Ind.
134 A7 Lottivue, Mich.
132 F9 Lovedale, Pa.
132 F10 Lowber, Pa.
127 B2 Lowell, Mass.
129 C2 Lower Bershire Valley, N.J.
132 D10 Lower Burrell, Pa.
130 A3 Lucon, Pa.
130 C7 Lumberton, N.J.
132 E11 Lusk, Pa.
131 E7 Lutherville-Timonium, Md.
131 G10 Luxmanor, Md.
129 E7 Lynbrook, N.Y.
129 D5 Lyndhurst, N.J.
132 A6 Lyndhurst, Ohio
127 C4 Lynn, Mass.
131 E6 Lynn Acres, Md.
130 B5 Lynnewood Gardens, Pa.
127 B3 Lynnfield, Mass.
135 C3 Lynwood, Calif.
133 F4 Lynwood, Ill.
133 E3 Lyons, Ill.
129 D2 Lyons Sta., N.J.
129 C3 Lyonsville, N.J.

M

131 F6 McAlpine, Md.
133 F3 MacArthur, Ill.
136 A5 McAvoy, Calif.
132 F7 McConnells Mill, Pa.
133 E2 McCook, Ill.
132 E11 McCullough, Pa.
132 E7 McDonald, Pa.
131 E6 McDonogh, Md.
132 C5 Macedonia, Ohio
132 F7 McGovern, Pa.
132 E9 McKeesport, Pa.
132 E8 McKees Rocks, Pa.
132 D8 McKnight, Pa.
131 G9 McLean, Va.
132 F8 McMurray, Pa.
129 D3 Madison, N.J.
132 F10 Madison, Pa.
134 B5 Madison Heights, Mich.
129 F4 Madison Park, N.J.
129 D2 Madisonville, N.J.
131 H9 Madrillon, Va.
132 D9 Magill Heights, Pa.
130 C5 Magnolia, N.J.
127 B5 Magnolia, Mass.
129 B5 Mahwah, N.J.
130 A3 Mainland, Pa.
127 C3 Malden, Mass.
136 A4 Maltby, Calif.
130 B2 Malvern, Pa.
129 D7 Malverne, N.Y.
129 C7 Mamaroneck, N.Y.
132 E11 Mamont, Pa.
130 B4 *Manayunk, Pa.*
127 B5 Manchester, Mass.
129 C7 Manhasset, N.Y.
135 C2 Manhattan Beach, Calif.
132 F7 Manifold, Pa.
127 E3 Manley Corner, Mass.
132 E11 Manor, Pa.
129 C7 Manorhaven, N.Y.
132 F9 Manown, Pa.
127 E2 Mansfield, Mass.
132 B7 Mansfield, N.J.
130 D4 Mantua, N.J.
131 H9 Mantua, Va.
130 D4 Mantua Terrace, N.J.
129 E2 Manville, N.J.
132 B6 Maple Beach, Pa.
130 A4 Maple Glen, Pa.
132 B5 Maple Heights, Ohio
130 C6 Maple Shade, N.J.
129 D4 Maplewood, N.J.
132 F11 Maplewood Terrace, Pa.
127 B4 Marblehead, Mass.
129 C3 Marcella, N.J.
130 D3 Marcus Hook, Pa.
135 C2 *Marina, Calif.*
136 B1 Marin City, Calif.
136 A1 Marinwood, Calif.
133 E2 Marion Hills, Ill.
133 F3 Markham, Ill.
132 D11 Markle, Pa.
130 C1 Marlboro, Pa.
133 F2 Marley, Ill.
130 C6 Marlton, N.J.
130 E3 Marlton Heights, N.J.
130 D2 Marshallton, Del.
130 C1 Marshallton, Pa.
127 E5 Marshfield, Mass.
127 E5 Marshfield Center, Mass.
127 E5 Marshfield Hills, Mass.
136 A4 Martinez, Calif.
129 E2 Martinsville, N.J.
135 B2 *Mar Vista, Calif.*
131 H11 Maryland Park, Md.
130 C6 Masonville, N.J.
131 H9 Masonville, Va.
129 D6 *Maspeth, N.Y.*
129 D9 Massapequa, N.Y.
129 D9 Massapequa Park, N.Y.
129 F4 Matawan, N.J.
127 E4 Matfield, Mass.
129 C8 Matinecock, N.Y.
127 D3 *Mattapan, Mass.*
130 B5 *Mayfair, Pa.*
132 A6 Mayfield, Ohio
132 A6 Mayfield Heights, Ohio
127 C1 Maynard, Mass.
135 C3 Maywood, Calif.
133 D2 Maywood, Ill.
129 C5 Maywood, N.J.
133 F5 Meadowdale, Ind.
132 D7 Meadow Lands, Pa.
130 D1 Meadowood, Del.
131 G10 Meadowood, Md.
127 D2 Medfield, Mass.
127 C3 Medford, Mass.
130 C7 Medford, N.J.
130 C7 Medford Farms, N.J.
127 C3 Medford Hillside, Mass.
130 C7 Medford Lakes, N.J.
130 C3 Media, Pa.
133 D1 Medinah, Ill.
127 E1 Medway, Mass.
127 C3 Melrose, Mass.
129 D6 *Melrose, N.Y.*
127 C3 Melrose Highlands, Mass.
133 D2 Melrose Park, Ill.
130 B5 Melrose Park, Pa.
129 D9 Melville, N.Y.
134 D4 Melvindale, Mich.
130 C2 Mendenhall, Pa.
129 D2 Mendham, N.J.
132 F10 Mendon, Pa.
136 E3 Menlo Park, Calif.
129 E3 Menlo Park, N.J.
129 E4 Menlo Park Terrace, N.J.
130 A7 Mercerville, N.J.
130 C5 Merchantville, N.J.
129 C3 Meriden, N.J.
130 C4 Merion Station, Pa.
129 E8 Merrick, N.Y.
131 H9 Merrifield, Va.
127 A3 Merrimac Terrace, Mass.
133 E3 Merrionette Park, Ill.
132 D11 Merwin, Pa.
127 A2 Methuen, Mass.
133 B2 Mettawa, Ill.
129 E3 Metuchen, N.J.
129 D3 Meyersville, N.J.
130 D4 Mickleton, N.J.
134 D4 Middlebelt, Mich.
132 B4 Middleburgh Heights, Ohio
129 F2 Middlebush, N.J.
131 F8 Middle River, Md.
129 E3 Middlesex, N.J.
127 B3 Middleton, Mass.
129 F5 Middletown, N.J.
132 F11 Middletown, Pa.
129 C10 Middleville, N.Y.
132 F7 Midland, Pa.
129 E5 *Midland Beach, N.Y.*
129 C5 Midland Park, N.J.
133 F3 Midlothian, Ill.
130 E2 Midvale, Del.
132 F11 Midway, Pa.
132 E7 Midway, Pa.
135 D5 Midway City, Calif.
132 F9 Milesville, Pa.
131 E6 Milford, Md.
134 B2 Milford, Mich.
130 D1 Milford Cross Roads, Del.
130 B1 Milford Mills, Pa.
130 C4 Millbourne, Pa.
136 E2 Millbrae, Calif.
127 E5 Millbrook, Mass.
129 C2 Millbrook, N.J.
131 F8 Millers Island, Md.
132 D10 Milligantown, Pa.
129 D2 Millington, N.J.
127 D1 Millis, Mass.
129 C8 Mill Neck, N.Y.
129 F2 Millstone, N.J.
129 F3 Milltown, N.J.
130 C2 Milltown, Pa.
132 E9 Millvale, Pa.
136 B1 Mill Valley, Calif.
127 A2 Millville Lake, N.H.
130 C3 Milmont Park, Pa.
136 E5 Milpitas, Calif.
127 D3 Milton, Mass.
127 D3 Milton Village, Mass.
129 C2 Mine Hill, N.J.
129 D8 Mineola, N.Y.
127 D5 Minot, Mass.
130 D2 Minquadale, Del.
130 B4 Miquon, Pa.
135 B2 *Miracle Mile, Calif.*
135 D3 Miraleste, Calif.
136 C2 *Mission, Calif.*
135 A2 *Mission Hills, Calif.*
131 A3 Model City, N.Y.
130 B4 Mogees, Pa.
133 F2 Mokena, Ill.
132 F9 Monessen, Pa.
132 F7 Moninger, Pa.
129 G6 Monmouth Beach, N.J.
129 F6 Monmouth Hills, N.J.
129 F2 Monmouth Junction, N.J.
132 F9 Monongahela, Pa.
127 E4 Monponsett, Mass.
129 B2 Monroe, N.J.
132 E10 Monroeville, Pa.
135 B4 Monrovia, Calif.
129 B5 Monsey, N.Y.
135 B2 Montalvin Manor, Calif.
136 D1 Montara, Calif.
136 F4 Monta Vista, Calif.
130 D2 Montchanin, Del.
135 B6 Montclair, Calif.
129 D4 Montclair, N.J.
130 B2 Mont Clare, Pa.
135 B4 Montebello, Calif.
135 B4 Monterey Park, Calif.
136 A5 Montezuma, Calif.
131 F6 Montgomery Knolls, Md.
130 A4 Montgomeryville, Pa.
135 A3 Montrose, Calif.
131 G10 Montrose, Md.
132 D9 Montrose Hill, Pa.
129 B5 Montvale, N.J.
129 C3 Montville, N.J.
132 D7 Moon, Pa.
129 D5 Moonachie, N.J.
132 D7 Moon Crest, Pa.
132 E8 Moon Run, Pa.
130 C6 Moorestown, N.J.
134 E1 Mooreville, Mich.
136 B4 Moraga, Calif.
132 B6 Moreland Hills, Ohio
132 E8 Morgan, Pa.
133 E3 *Morgan Park, Ill.*
129 F4 Morganville, N.J.
131 J11 Morningside, Md.
129 D3 Morris Plains, N.J.
129 D3 Morristown, N.J.
130 A7 Morrisville, Pa.
132 B2 Morstein, Pa.
130 C4 Morton, Pa.
133 C3 Morton Grove, Ill.
136 D1 Moss Beach, Calif.
131 H9 Moss Crest, Va.
129 C3 Mountain Lakes, N.J.
129 D3 Mountainside, N.J.
129 B3 Mountain Spring Lakes, N.J.
135 E4 Mountain View, Calif.
130 B4 *Mount Airy, Pa.*
130 C3 Mount Alverno, Pa.
129 C2 Mount Arlington, N.J.
129 E2 Mount Bethel, N.J.
134 B6 Mount Clemens, Mich.
136 D4 Mount Eden, Calif.
130 C5 Mount Ephraim, N.J.
129 C2 Mount Fern, N.J.
129 D2 Mount Freedom, N.J.
133 E3 *Mount Greenwood, Ill.*
131 F6 Mount Hebron, Md.
130 C7 Mount Holly, N.J.
129 C2 Mount Hope, N.J.
130 C6 Mount Laurel, N.J.
132 E8 Mount Lebanon, Pa.
132 D8 Mount Nebo, Pa.
132 E9 Mount Oliver, Pa.
132 G11 Mount Pleasant, Pa.
133 C2 Mount Prospect, Ill.
131 H11 Mount Rainier, Md.
130 D4 Mount Royal, N.J.
131 D3 Mount Vernon, N.Y.
129 C6 Mount Vernon, N.Y.
132 F10 Mount Vernon, Pa.
131 E6 *Mount Washington, Md.*
131 E6 Mount Washington Summit, Md.
130 C3 Moylan, Pa.
136 B1 Muir Beach, Calif.
131 G11 Muirkirk, Md.
136 B1 Muir Woods, Calif.
130 D4 Mullica Hill, N.J.
133 B2 Mundelein, Ill.
132 E9 Munhall, Pa.
132 F8 Munntown, Pa.
129 D7 Munsey Park, N.Y.
133 F5 Munster, Ind.
132 F8 Murry Hill, Pa.
132 E10 Murrysville, Pa.
132 F7 Muse, Pa.
129 D8 Muttontown, N.Y.
132 F11 Mutual, Pa.

N

127 B1 Nabnasset, Mass.
127 C4 Nahant, Mass.
127 D4 Nantasket Beach, Mass.
129 B5 Nanuet, N.Y.
130 B4 Narberth, Pa.
127 A1 Nashua, N.H.
129 E9 Nassau Shores, N.Y.
127 D1 Natick, Mass.
130 C4 National Park, N.J.
132 D10 Natrona Heights, Pa.
129 F5 Navesink, N.J.
133 D4 *Near North Side, Ill.*
131 E8 Necker, Md.
127 D2 Needham, Mass.
127 D2 Needham Heights, Mass.
130 A5 Neshaminy, Pa.
130 B6 Neshaminy Hills, Pa.
129 C1 Netcong, N.J.
132 D8 Neville Island, Pa.
131 J10 New Alexandria, Va.
136 D4 Newark, Calif.
130 D1 Newark, Del.
129 D4 Newark, N.J.
134 B7 New Baltimore, Mich.
134 D3 New Boston, Mich.
129 E5 *New Brighton, N.Y.*
129 F3 New Brunswick, N.J.
129 E3 New Brunswick Heights, N.J.
132 B5 Newburgh Heights, Ohio
127 A4 Newbury, Mass.
127 A4 Newbury Old Town, Mass.
127 A4 Newburyport, Mass.
131 H11 New Carrollton, Md.
129 D8 New Cassel, N.Y.
130 E2 New Castle, Del.
130 B3 New Centerville, Pa.
129 B6 New City, N.Y.
132 F9 New Eagle, Pa.
131 A4 Newfane, N.Y.
129 B3 Newfoundland, N.J.
130 D1 New Garden, Pa.
131 J10 New Glatz, Md.
129 B5 New Hempstead, N.Y.
134 B2 New Hudson, Mich.
129 D7 New Hyde Park, N.Y.
132 D10 New Kensington, Pa.
130 D1 Newkirk Estates, Del.
133 F2 New Lenox, Ill.
132 E11 Newlinsburg, Pa.
129 C5 New Milford, N.J.
129 F5 New Monmouth, N.J.
130 D2 Newport, Del.
130 B6 Newportville, Pa.
130 B6 Newportville Terrace, Pa.
130 B3 New Providence, N.J.
129 C7 New Rochelle, N.Y.
130 D5 New Sharon, N.J.
132 D7 New Sheffield, Pa.
129 G5 New Shrewsbury, N.J.
129 B5 New Square, N.Y.
132 F11 New Stanton, Pa.
127 C2 Newton, Mass.
127 D2 Newton Center, Mass.
127 D2 Newton Highlands, Mass.
127 D2 Newton Lower Falls, Mass.
127 D2 Newton Upper Falls, Mass.
127 C2 Newtonville, Mass.
130 A6 Newtown, Pa.
130 C3 Newtown Square, Pa.
129 E6 *New Utrecht, N.Y.*
129 D5 New Vernon, N.J.
129 C6 New York, N.Y.
131 B2 Niagara Falls, N.Y.
136 A5 Nichols, Calif.
136 D5 Niles, Calif.
133 C3 Niles, Ill.
129 C10 Nissequogue, N.Y.
129 E3 Nixon, N.J.
131 G11 Nob Hills, Md.
132 E7 Noblestown, Pa.
127 C2 Nonantum, Mass.
133 D1 Nordic Park, Ill.
127 E2 Norfolk, Mass.
131 F6 Normandy Heights, Md.
133 D3 Norridge, Ill.
130 B3 Norristown, Pa.
127 E4 North Abington, Mass.
129 D9 North Amityville, N.Y.
127 A3 North Andover, Mass.
132 D11 North Apollo, Pa.
130 D5 North Arlington, N.J.
127 F2 North Attleboro, Mass.
129 D10 North Babylon, N.Y.
131 J11 North Barnaby, Md.
136 C2 *North Beach, Calif.*
129 D8 North Bellmore, N.Y.
129 D5 North Bergen, N.J.
127 B2 North Billerica, Mass.
132 E9 North Braddock, Pa.
129 E1 North Branch, N.J.
133 C3 Northbrook, Ill.
130 C1 Northbrook, Pa.
129 F3 North Brunswick, N.J.
129 C4 North Caldwell, N.J.
132 G9 North Charleroi, Pa.
127 B1 North Chelmsford, Mass.
133 B2 North Chicago, Ill.
127 D4 North Cohasset, Mass.
130 B8 North Crosswicks, N.J.
127 E3 North Easton, Mass.
129 E3 North Edison, N.J.
131 H11 North Englewood, Md.
133 C1 Northern Aire Estates, Ill.
136 E3 North Fair Oaks, Calif.
133 C3 Northfield, Ill.
132 B5 Northfield, Ohio
132 C5 Northfield Center, Ohio
132 B5 Northfield Village, Ohio
133 C4 Northfield Woods, Ill.
133 D1 North Glen Ellyn, Ill.
129 D10 North Great River, N.Y.
129 C4 North Haledon, N.J.
127 E4 North Hanover, Mass.
130 D2 North Hills, Del.
133 B1 North Hills, Ill.
129 D7 North Hills, N.Y.
135 B2 *North Hollywood, Calif.*
132 E10 North Irwin, Pa.
133 D2 Northlake, Ill.
129 D9 North Lindenhurst, N.Y.
129 E8 North Long Beach, N.Y.
127 E5 North Marshfield, Mass.
129 D9 North Massapequa, N.Y.
129 D8 North Merrick, N.Y.
129 D7 North New Hyde Park, N.Y.
132 B3 North Olmsted, Ohio
133 D3 *North Park, Ill.*
129 D11 North Patchogue, N.Y.
129 C7 North Pelham, N.Y.
127 A1 North Pelham, N.H.
127 E5 North Pembroke, Mass.
130 C4 *North Philadelphia, Pa.*
129 E3 North Plainfield, N.J.
127 F5 North Plympton, Mass.
129 C9 Northport, N.Y.
127 D3 North Quincy, Mass.
132 B6 North Randall, Ohio
127 D3 North Randolph, Mass.
127 B3 North Reading, Mass.
136 B2 North Richmond, Calif.
135 A1 *Northridge, Calif.*
132 B2 North Ridgeville, Ohio
133 D3 North Riverside, Ill.
129 D8 North Rockville Centre, N.Y.
132 C4 North Royalton, Ohio
127 D5 North Scituate, Mass.
132 E8 *North Side, Pa.*
131 J9 North Springfield, Va.
129 E3 North Stelton, N.J.
127 C1 North Sudbury, Mass.
129 B6 North Tarrytown, N.Y.
127 B2 North Tewksbury, Mass.
131 B3 North Tonawanda, N.Y.
129 B6 Northvale, N.J.
129 D7 North Valley Stream, N.Y.
132 D11 North Vandergrift, Pa.
132 E10 North Versailles, Pa.
127 E4 Northville, Mass.
134 C3 Northville, Mich.
130 A4 North Wales, Pa.
132 D11 North Washington, Pa.
127 D4 North Weymouth, Mass.
129 B7 North White Plains, N.Y.
127 B3 North Wilmington, Mass.
127 F2 Norton, Mass.
132 F11 Norvelt, Pa.
135 C4 Norwalk, Calif.
127 E5 Norwell, Mass.
127 D2 Norwood, Mass.
129 C6 Norwood, N.J.
130 C4 Norwood, Pa.
133 D3 *Norwood Park, Ill.*
131 E8 Notch Cliff, Md.
130 B6 Nottingham, Pa.
133 E3 Nottingham Park, Ill.
136 A1 Novato, Calif.
134 C3 Novi, Mich.
127 A2 Noyes Terrace, N.H.
129 D5 Nutley, N.J.
127 B2 Nutting Lake, Mass.
129 B6 Nyack, N.Y.

O

129 E10 Oak Beach, N.Y.
133 D2 Oak Brook, Ill.
133 D2 Oakbrook Terrace, Ill.
129 C7 Oakdale, N.J.
129 D11 Oakdale, N.Y.
132 E7 Oakdale, Pa.
133 D2 Oakdale Woods, Ill.
130 B6 Oakford, Pa.
132 F11 Oakford Park, Pa.
133 F3 Oak Forest, Ill.
136 C3 Oakland, Calif.
131 H11 Oakland, Md.
129 B4 Oakland, N.J.
132 D11 *Oakland, Pa.*
129 D7 *Oakland Gardens, N.Y.*
131 J11 Oaklawn, Md.
133 E3 Oak Lawn, Ill.
134 B3 Oakley Park, Mich.
130 C5 Oaklyn, N.J.
132 E9 Oakmont, Pa.
130 A2 Oak Park, Pa.
134 C4 Oak Park, Mich.
133 D3 Oak Park, Ill.
129 B3 Oak Ridge, N.J.
129 C2 Oak Ridge Lake, N.J.
130 B3 Oaks, Pa.
131 H9 Oakton, Va.
129 E3 Oak Tree, N.J.
130 D5 Oak Valley, N.J.
131 G11 Oak View, Md.
130 C5 Oakview, N.J.
132 B5 Oakwood, Ohio
129 E11 Ocean Bay Park, N.Y.
129 E11 Ocean Beach, N.Y.
127 E6 Ocean Bluff, Mass.
129 E8 Oceanside, N.Y.
131 F6 Oella, Md.
130 D3 Ogden, Pa.
129 B2 Ogdensburg, N.J.
130 D1 Ogletown, Del.
132 D9 Oklahoma, Pa.
129 D9 Old Bethpage, N.Y.
129 D8 Old Brookville, N.Y.
131 G10 Old Farm, Md.
129 C11 Old Field, N.Y.
129 B8 Old Greenwich, Conn.
127 E5 Oldham Pines, Mass.
127 E5 Oldham Village, Mass.
132 F11 Old Stanton, Pa.
129 B6 Old Tappan, N.J.
129 D8 Old Westbury, N.Y.
132 B3 Olmsted, Ohio
132 B3 Olmsted Falls, Ohio
130 B5 *Olney, Pa.*
133 F3 Olympia Fields, Ill.
135 B7 Ontario, Calif.
129 C5 Oradell, N.J.
135 D5 Orange, Calif.
129 D4 Orange, N.J.
132 B6 Orange, Ohio
129 B6 Orangeburg, N.Y.
135 D6 Orange Park Acres, Calif.
132 D11 Orchard Hills, Pa.
134 B3 Orchard Lake, Mich.
131 D4 Orchard Park, N.Y.
130 B6 Orchard View, N.J.
130 D3 Ordmont, N.J.
130 B4 Oreland, Pa.
136 B3 Orinda, Calif.
136 B3 Orinda Village, Calif.
133 F2 Orland Park, Ill.
132 D10 Orville, Pa.
130 C5 Osage, N.J.
132 D8 Osborne, Pa.
129 B6 Ossining, N.Y.
129 F3 Outcalt, N.J.
132 E9 *Overbrook, Pa.*
130 C4 *Overbrook, Pa.*
131 E7 Overlea, Md.
131 E6 Owings Mills, Md.
134 B3 Oxbow, Mich.
130 A6 Oxford Valley, Pa.
131 J11 Oxon Hill, Md.
129 C8 Oyster Bay, N.Y.
129 C8 Oyster Bay Cove, N.Y.
129 D6 *Ozone Park, N.Y.*

P

136 B4 Pacheco, Calif.
136 D2 Pacifica, Calif.
136 D2 Pacific Manor, Calif.
135 B1 *Pacific Palisades, Calif.*
135 A2 *Pacoima, Calif.*
131 G11 Paint Branch Farms, Md.
132 E10 Paintertown, Pa.
133 C1 Palatine, Ill.
129 B6 Palisades, N.Y.
129 C6 Palisades Park, N.J.
131 H11 Palmer Park, Md.
135 B2 *Palms, Calif.*
130 B5 Palmyra, N.J.
136 E4 Palo Alto, Calif.
136 E3 Palomar Park, Calif.
133 F3 Palos Gardens, Ill.
133 E3 Palos Heights, Ill.
133 E3 Palos Hills, Ill.
133 E2 Palos Park, Ill.
135 D2 Palos Verdes Estates, Calif.
130 B3 Paoli, Pa.
135 C4 Paramount, Calif.
129 C5 Paramus, N.J.
136 B2 Parchester Village, Calif.
130 B2 Parkchester, Pa.
133 A2 Park City, Ill.
130 A2 Parker Ford, Pa.
130 B6 Parkland, Pa.
133 C3 Park Ridge, Ill.
129 B5 Park Ridge, N.J.
130 A7 Park Ridge Farms, N.J.
133 C3 Park Ridge Manor, Ill.
131 A2 Parkside, Md.
130 C3 Parkside, Pa.
132 D9 Parkview, Pa.
131 E7 Parkville, Md.
131 A2 Parkwood, Md.
132 B4 Parma, Ohio
132 B4 Parma Heights, Ohio
134 A1 Parshallville, Mich.
129 C3 Parsippany, N.J.
135 B4 Pasadena, Calif.
129 C5 Passaic, N.J.
129 D11 Patchogue, N.Y.
129 C4 Paterson, N.J.
127 B2 Pattenville, Mass.
130 D4 Paulsboro, N.J.
132 D11 Paulton, Pa.
127 B4 Peabody, Mass.
129 B5 Pearl River, N.Y.
130 D3 Pedricktown, N.J.
136 D2 Pedro Valley, Calif.
131 A3 Pekin, N.Y.
127 A2 Pelham, N.H.
129 C7 Pelham, N.Y.
129 C7 Pelham Manor, N.Y.
130 C7 Pemberton, N.J.
127 E5 Pembroke, Mass.
130 D6 Penbryn, N.J.
131 B4 Pendleton, N.Y.
132 B2 Penfield Junction, Ohio
130 A4 Penllyn, Pa.
132 F11 Penn, Pa.
130 B6 Penndel, Pa.
132 E9 Penn Hills, Pa.
130 C5 Pennsauken, N.J.
130 A7 Pennsbury Heights, Pa.
130 D3 Penns Grove, N.J.
129 G2 Penns Neck, N.J.
130 E2 Pennsville, N.J.
130 B4 Penn Valley, Pa.
130 A7 Penn Valley, Pa.
132 F10 Penn Woods, Pa.
130 C4 Penn Wynne, Pa.
130 D2 Penny Hill, Del.
132 B6 Pepper Pike, Ohio
129 C4 Pequannock, N.J.
130 B3 Perkiomen Junction, Pa.
131 E8 Perry Hall, Md.
132 D8 Perrysville, Pa.
132 D11 Perrysville, Pa.
129 E4 Perth Amboy, N.J.
131 J11 Phelps Corner, Md.
130 C5 Philadelphia, Pa.
133 F4 Phoenix, Ill.
130 B2 Phoenixville, Pa.
135 C4 Pico Rivera, Calif.
136 C3 Piedmont, Calif.
129 B6 Piermont, N.Y.
130 A7 Piersonville, N.J.
127 A6 Pigeon Cove, Mass.
131 E6 Pikesville, Md.
130 C4 Pilgrim Gardens, Pa.
131 H9 Pimmit Hills, Va.
130 D5 Pine Acres, N.J.
129 D10 Pine Aire, N.Y.
129 C4 Pine Brook, N.J.
131 H10 Pinecrest, Va.
130 C6 Pine Grove, N.J.
130 D6 Pine Hill, N.J.
127 B2 Pinehurst, Mass.
127 C1 Pine Lake, Mass.
129 D9 Pinelawn, N.Y.
131 F5 Pine Orchard Meadows, Md.
127 C1 Pine Rest, Mass.
130 C3 Pine Ridge, Pa.
131 H9 Pine Ridge, Va.
130 D6 Pine Valley, N.J.
132 F9 Piney Fork, Pa.
136 A3 Pinole, Calif.
129 E3 Piscataway, N.J.
132 E10 Pitcairn, Pa.
130 D5 Pitman, N.J.
136 A5 Pittsburg, Calif.
132 E8 Pittsburgh, Pa.
135 C5 Placentia, Calif.
129 E3 Plainfield, N.J.
129 F2 Plainsboro, N.J.
129 D9 Plainview, N.Y.
127 E1 Plainville, Mass.
129 D7 Plandome, N.Y.
129 D7 Plandome Heights, N.Y.
129 D7 Plandome Manor, N.Y.
135 C2 *Playa del Rey, Calif.*
130 B6 Plaza Park, N.J.
136 B4 Pleasant Hill, Calif.
132 E9 Pleasant Hills, Pa.
136 D5 Pleasanton, Calif.
134 C5 Pleasant Ridge, Mich.
132 E10 Pleasant Valley, Pa.
130 E2 Pleasantville, Del.
131 F7 Pleasantville, Md.
129 B7 Pleasantville, N.Y.
129 E2 Pluckemin, N.J.
132 E10 Plum, Pa.
133 C1 Plum Grove Estates, Ill.
127 A5 Plum Island, Mass.
127 F5 Plymouth, Mass.
134 C3 Plymouth, Mich.
130 B4 Plymouth Meeting, Pa.
129 B7 Pocantico Hills, N.Y.
130 C2 Pocopson, Pa.
129 E8 Point Lookout, N.Y.
129 E11 Point O' Woods, N.Y.
131 F7 Point Pleasant, Md.
135 B6 Pomona, Calif.
129 B5 Pomona, N.Y.
129 B5 Pomona Heights, N.Y.
129 B4 Pompton Lakes, N.J.
129 C4 Pompton Plains, N.J.
127 E2 Pondville, Mass.
134 B4 Pontiac, Mich.
134 B3 Pontiac Lake, Mich.
131 H9 Poplar Heights, Va.
129 C11 Poquott, N.Y.
133 D3 *Portage Park, Ill.*
129 B8 Port Chester, N.Y.
136 A4 Port Chicago, Calif.
136 A3 Port Costa, Calif.
129 C11 Port Jefferson, N.Y.
129 C11 Port Jefferson Station, N.Y.
130 B3 Port Kennedy, Pa.
129 F5 Port Monmouth, N.J.
129 C1 Port Morris, N.J.
136 D3 Port of Redwood City, Calif.
136 E3 Portola Valley, Calif.
130 B3 Port Providence, Pa.
129 E4 Port Reading, N.J.
135 D2 Portuguese Bend, Calif.
132 F9 Port Vue, Pa.
129 D7 Port Washington, N.Y.
133 F3 Posen, Ill.
129 E3 Possumtown, N.J.
131 G9 Potomac, Md.
136 C2 *Potrero, Calif.*
131 E7 Pot Spring, Md.
129 D4 Pottersville, N.J.
130 A2 Pottstown, Pa.
131 G11 Powder Mill Estates, Md.
133 B2 Prairie View, Ill.
132 E8 Presto, Pa.
127 B5 Prides, Mass.
130 C4 Primos, Pa.
132 E7 Primrose, Pa.
129 F2 Princeton, N.J.
129 G2 Princeton Junction, N.J.
133 C2 Prospect Heights, Ill.
133 C2 Prospect Meadows, Ill.
129 C4 Prospect Park, N.J.
130 C4 Prospect Park, Pa.
129 G3 Prospect Plains, N.J.
129 C2 Prospect Point, N.J.
130 A4 Prospectville, Pa.
130 A3 Providence Square, Pa.
130 B1 Pughtown, Pa.
133 E4 *Pullman, Ill.*
131 F7 Pumphrey, Md.

Q

131 G10 Quaint Acres, Md.
134 C3 Quakertown, Mich.
129 B7 Quarry Heights, N.Y.
127 D3 Quincy, Mass.

R

132 F11 Radebaugh, Pa.
130 B3 Radnor, Pa.
130 A3 Rahns, Pa.
129 E4 Rahway, N.J.
129 C3 Rainbow Lakes, N.J.
129 B4 Ramapo, N.Y.
130 E2 Rambleton Acres, Del.
129 B5 Ramsey, N.J.
133 F5 Ranburn Woods, Ind.
131 E6 Ranchleigh, Md.
136 F4 Rancho Rinconado, Calif.
130 B6 Rancocas, N.J.
130 C6 Rancocas Heights, N.J.
130 C6 Rancocas Woods, N.J.
131 E6 Randallstown, Md.
127 E3 Randolph, Mass.
131 G10 Randolph Hills, Md.
131 H11 Randolph Village, Md.
132 E9 Rankin, Pa.
131 A3 Ransomville, N.Y.
129 E2 Raritan, N.J.
131 H10 Ravensworth, Va.
131 H10 Ravenwood, Va.
134 D2 Rawsonville, Mich.
127 B3 Reading, Mass.
127 D3 *Readville, Mass.*
129 D2 Rebel Hill, N.J.
130 B3 Rebel Hill, Pa.
130 C4 Red Bank, N.J.
129 F5 Red Bank, N.J.
134 C4 *Redford, Mich.*
134 C4 Redford Heights, Mich.
130 C1 Red Lion, Pa.
135 C2 Redondo Beach, Calif.
132 F10 Reduction, Pa.
136 E3 Redwood City, Calif.
136 F3 Redwood Terrace, Calif.
131 G9 Regency Estates, Md.
129 D6 *Rego Park, N.Y.*
132 B6 Reminderville, Ohio
132 E8 Rennerdale, Pa.
130 D4 Repaupo, N.J.
127 C3 Revere, Mass.
127 C4 Revere Beach, Mass.
127 E5 Rexhame, Mass.
133 F5 Rexville, Ind.
136 B4 Rheem Valley, Calif.
130 A5 Richboro, Pa.
130 C5 *Richmond, Pa.*
136 B2 Richmond, Calif.
136 C2 *Richmond, Calif.*
129 E5 *Richmond, N.Y.*
132 A6 Richmond Heights, Ohio
129 D6 *Richmond Hill, N.Y.*
129 E4 *Richmond Valley, N.Y.*
130 D4 Richwood, N.J.
130 C3 Riddlewood, Pa.
129 D2 Ridge Acres, N.J.
129 C5 Ridgefield, N.J.
129 C5 Ridgefield Park, N.J.
133 F1 Ridgewood, Ill.
133 E2 Ridgewood, Ill.
129 C5 Ridgewood, N.J.
129 D6 *Ridgewood, N.Y.*
130 C4 Ridley Park, Pa.
132 F10 Rillton, Pa.
127 A4 Rings Island, Mass.
129 B4 Ringwood, N.J.
131 F7 Rippling Ridge, Md.
131 H11 Ritchie, Md.
133 F4 Riverdale, Ill.
131 H11 Riverdale, Md.
129 C4 Riverdale, N.J.
129 C6 *Riverdale, N.Y.*
132 B3 Riveredge, Ohio
129 C5 River Edge, N.J.
133 D3 River Forest, Ill.
133 D3 River Grove, Ill.
132 F9 River Hill, Pa.
127 B2 River Pines, Mass.
129 F5 River Plaza, N.J.
134 D5 River Rouge, Mich.
133 E3 Riverside, Ill.
130 B6 Riverside, N.J.

129 B8 Riverside, Conn.
130 B5 Riverton, N.J.
129 C5 River Vale, N.J.
132 D10 River Valley, Pa.
134 D5 Riverview, Mich.
129 E3 Riverview Manor, N.J.
133 C2 Riverwoods, Ill.
133 F3 Robbins, Ill.
129 E11 Robbins Rest, N.Y.
133 E3 Roberts Park, Ill.
129 F4 Robertsville, N.J.
129 C5 Rochelle Park, N.J.
134 A5 Rochester, Mich.
129 C2 Rockaway, N.J.
136 D2 Rockaway Beach, Calif.
129 C3 Rockaway Neck, N.J.
129 E7 *Rockaway Park, N.Y.*
129 E6 *Rockaway Point, N.Y.*
129 C3 Rockaway Valley, N.J.
131 H10 Rock Creek Forest, Md.
131 E6 Rockdale, Md.
130 C3 Rockdale, Pa.
130 D2 Rockland, Del.
127 E4 Rockland, Mass.
129 B6 Rockland Lake, N.Y.
130 B5 Rockledge, Pa.
129 B6 Rockleigh, N.J.
127 B6 Rockport, Mass.
127 E1 Rockville, Mass.
131 G10 Rockville, Md.
129 E8 Rockville Centre, N.Y.
129 F2 Rocky Hill, N.J.
127 F5 Rocky Nook, Mass.
132 B3 Rocky River, Ohio
136 A3 Rodeo, Calif.
130 B7 Roebling, N.J.
133 C3 *Rogers Park, Ill.*
131 E7 *Roland Park, Md.*
131 F5 Rolling Acres, Md.
135 D2 Rolling Hills, Calif.
135 D2 Rolling Hills Estates, Calif.
133 C1 Rolling Meadows, Ill.
136 B3 Rollingwood, Calif.
133 F1 Romeoville, Ill.
134 D1 Romulus, Mich.
133 B2 Rondout, Ill.
129 D11 Ronkonkoma, N.Y.
136 A3 Roosevelt Terrace, Calif.
131 F7 Rosedale, Md.
129 E7 *Rosedale, N.Y.*
130 C2 Rosedale, Pa.
130 D2 Rose Hill, Del.
131 J10 Rose Hill Farms, Va.
133 E4 *Roseland, Ill.*
129 D4 Roseland, N.J.
133 D1 Roselle, Ill.
129 E4 Roselle, N.J.
129 E4 Roselle Park, N.J.
135 B4 Rosemead, Calif.
133 D2 Rosemont, Ill.
130 B4 Rosemont, Pa.
130 C3 Rose Tree, Pa.
130 C3 Rose Valley, Pa.
134 B6 Roseville, Mich.
130 D1 Roseville Park, Del.
127 D3 *Roslindale, Mass.*
130 C2 Roslyn, Pa.
130 B5 Roslyn, Pa.
129 D7 Roslyn Estates, N.Y.
129 D8 Roslyn Harbor, N.Y.
129 D8 Roslyn Heights, N.Y.
136 B1 Ross, Calif.
133 F5 Ross, Ind.
132 E8 Rosslyn Farms, Pa.
135 D4 Rossmoor, Calif.
131 E8 Rossville, Md.
134 D3 Roulo, Mich.
133 A1 Round Lake, Ill.
133 A1 Round Lake Park, Ill.
127 A4 Rowley, Mass.
130 B4 *Roxborough, Pa.*
127 D3 *Roxbury, Mass.*
129 E6 *Roxbury, N.Y.*
134 C5 Royal Oak, Mich.
134 C4 Royal Oak Township, Mich.
130 A2 Royersford, Pa.
129 B2 Rudeville, N.J.
132 F11 Ruffs Dale, Pa.
129 F5 Rumson, N.J.
130 C5 Runnemede, N.J.
132 D10 Rural Ridge, Pa.
130 A5 Rushland, Pa.
136 D4 Russell, Calif.
129 D7 Russell Gardens, N.Y.
132 D9 Russellton, Pa.
129 D5 Rutherford, N.J.
130 C4 Rutledge, Pa.
130 B5 Rydal, Pa.
129 C7 Rye, N.Y.

S

129 C5 Saddle Brook, N.J.
129 B5 Saddle River, N.J.
129 D7 Saddle Rock, N.Y.
132 C5 Sagamore Hills, Ohio
129 D7 *Saint Albans, N.Y.*
132 F11 Saint Clair, Pa.
134 C6 Saint Clair Shores, Mich.
130 B3 Saint Davids, Pa.
129 E5 *Saint George, N.Y.*
129 C11 Saint James, N.Y.
131 B3 Saint Johnsburg, N.Y.
130 A6 Saint Leonard, Pa.
136 B4 St. Marys College, Calif.
130 A1 Saint Peters, Pa.
127 B4 Salem, Mass.
134 C2 Salem, Mich.
127 A2 Salem, N.H.
127 A2 Salem Depot, N.H.
132 D11 Salina, Pa.
134 D1 Saline, Mich.
132 F9 Sampson, Pa.
136 B1 San Anselmo, Calif.
135 B6 San Antonio Heights, Calif.
130 A2 Sanatoga, Pa.
131 B3 Sanborn, N.Y.
136 D2 San Bruno, Calif.
136 C2 San Carlos, Calif.
127 D5 Sand Hill, Mass.
135 B6 San Dimas, Calif.
129 C7 Sands Point, N.Y.
131 B3 Sandy Beach, N.Y.
135 A2 San Fernando, Calif.
136 C2 San Francisco, Calif.
135 B4 San Gabriel, Calif.
136 F2 San Gregorio, Calif.
136 E5 San Jose, Calif.
136 C3 San Leandro, Calif.
136 C3 San Lorenzo, Calif.
135 B4 San Marino, Calif.
136 D3 San Mateo, Calif.
136 B3 San Pablo, Calif.
135 D3 *San Pedro, Calif.*
136 B2 San Quentin, Calif.
136 B1 San Rafael, Calif.
136 C5 San Ramon, Calif.
129 C10 San Remo, N.Y.
135 D5 Santa Ana, Calif.
136 E5 Santa Clara, Calif.
135 C4 Santa Fe Springs, Calif.
135 B2 Santa Monica, Calif.
136 A1 Santa Venetia, Calif.
136 B4 Saranap, Calif.
136 F4 Saratoga, Calif.
132 E10 Sardis, Pa.
127 E4 Satacket, Mass.
129 B9 Saugatuck, Conn.
127 C3 Saugus, Mass.
136 B2 Sausalito, Calif.
129 F3 Sayreville, N.J.
129 D11 Sayville, N.Y.
129 C7 Scarsdale, N.Y.
133 C1 Schaumburg, Ill.
133 D2 Schiller Park, Ill.
130 B2 Schuylkill, Pa.
130 A3 Schwenksville, Pa.
127 D5 Scituate, Mass.
129 E3 Scotch Plains, N.J.
131 G10 Scotland, Md.
127 F3 Scotland, Mass.
132 F10 Scott Haven, Pa.
131 D3 Scranton, N.Y.
129 F6 Sea Bright, N.Y.
131 H11 Seabrook, Md.
129 C8 Sea Cliff, N.Y.
135 D4 Seal Beach, Calif.
131 H11 Seat Pleasant, Md.
127 E5 Sea View, Mass.
129 E11 Seaview, N.Y.
130 C4 Secane, Pa.
129 D5 Secaucus, N.J.
129 C3 Sedgefield, N.J.
136 A3 Selby, Calif.
129 C11 Selden, N.Y.
131 G9 Seneca, Md.
135 A2 *Sepulveda, Calif.*
136 E3 Sequoia, Calif.
129 C11 Setauket, N.Y.
134 A2 Seven Harbors, Mich.
132 B4 Seven Hills, Ohio
129 E4 Sewaren, N.J.
130 D5 Sewell, N.J.
132 D7 Sewickley, Pa.
132 D8 Sewickley Heights, Pa.
132 D8 Sewickley Hills, Pa.
132 F10 Shafton, Pa.
132 B5 Shaker Heights, Ohio
132 F10 Shaner, Pa.
127 E2 Sharon, Mass.
130 C4 Sharon Hill, Pa.
132 E9 Sharpsburg, Pa.
130 E3 Sharptown, N.J.
127 B2 Shawsheen Village, Mass.
132 E10 Shawtown, Pa.
129 E6 *Sheepshead Bay, N.Y.*
132 B2 Sheffield, Ohio
132 B2 Sheffield Lake, Ohio
134 B5 Shelby Village, Mich.
134 D3 Sheldon, Mich.
127 E1 Sheldonville, Mass.
132 E8 *Sheraden, Pa.*
127 D1 Sherborn, Mass.
135 B2 *Sherman Oaks, Calif.*
133 C2 Sherri Park, Ill.
136 B3 Sherwood Forest, Calif.
131 G10 Sherwood Forest, Md.
127 D5 Shore Acres, Mass.
136 A5 Shore Acres, Calif.
129 G5 Shrewsbury, N.J.
130 D6 Sicklerville, N.J.
135 B4 Sierra Madre, Calif.
135 D3 Signal Hill, Calif.
130 B6 Siles, Pa.
135 D7 Silverado, Calif.
130 D2 Silver Brook, Del.
131 J11 Silver Hill, Md.
132 B2 Silver Lake, Mass.
127 E5 Silver Lake, Mass.
130 D3 Silver Side, Del.
131 H10 Silver Spring, Md.
130 D2 Silview, Del.
129 F1 Skillman, N.J.
130 A3 Skippack, Pa.
133 C3 Skokie, Ill.
136 E3 Sky Londa, Calif.
130 A7 Slackwood, N.J.
136 B1 Sleepy Hollow, Calif.
131 H10 Sleepy Hollow, Va.
132 E11 Slickville, Pa.
131 C4 Sloan, N.Y.
129 B4 Sloatsburg, N.Y.
129 D2 Sloping Hills, N.J.
129 E3 Smalleytown, N.J.
132 F10 Smithdale, Pa.
129 B3 Smiths Mills, N.J.
132 G10 Smithton, Pa.
129 C10 Smithtown, N.Y.
129 C10 Smithtown Pines, N.Y.
130 C7 Smithville, N.J.
132 F9 Snowden, Pa.
130 A2 Snowdenville, Pa.
132 B6 Solon, Ohio
130 C5 Somerdale, N.J.
131 H10 Somerset, Md.
129 F3 Somerset, N.J.
130 B5 *Somerton, Pa.*
127 C3 Somerville, Mass.
129 E2 Somerville, N.J.
129 F4 South Amboy, N.J.
130 A5 Southampton, Pa.
133 C1 South Barrington, Ill.
127 C3 *South Boston, Mass.*
129 E2 South Bound Brook, N.J.
129 E1 South Branch, N.J.
129 D6 *South Brooklyn, N.Y.*
127 A4 South Byfield, Mass.
127 B1 South Chelmsford, Mass.
133 E4 *South Chicago, Ill.*
127 E5 South Duxbury, Mass.
127 E2 South Easton, Mass.
135 B4 South El Monte, Calif.
127 B5 South Essex, Mass.
132 A5 South Euclid, Ohio
129 D9 South Farmingdale, N.Y.
134 C4 Southfield, Mich.
129 D7 South Floral Park, N.Y.
134 D4 Southgate, Mich.
135 C3 South Gate, Calif.
132 F11 South Greensburg, Pa.
127 A3 South Groveland, Mass.
129 C5 South Hackensack, N.J.
127 D5 South Hamilton, Mass.
127 E4 South Hanover, Mass.
132 D7 South Heights, Pa.
129 D8 South Hempstead, N.Y.
133 F4 South Holland, Ill.
129 D9 South Huntington, N.Y.
131 J11 South Lawn, Md.
131 B4 South Lockport, N.Y.
132 B3 South Lorain, Ohio
127 B3 South Lynnfield, Mass.
134 C3 South Lyon, Mich.
130 C3 South Media, Pa.
129 B6 South Nyack, N.Y.
129 D4 South Orange, N.J.
135 B4 South Pasadena, Calif.
130 D3 South Penns Grove, N.J.
130 C4 *South Philadelphia, Pa.*
129 E3 South Plainfield, N.J.
130 A2 South Pottstown, Pa.
129 F3 South River, N.J.
136 D2 South San Francisco, Calif.
135 B4 South San Gabriel, Calif.
129 C11 South Setauket, N.Y.
133 E4 *South Shore, Ill.*
132 E9 *South Side, Pa.*
133 E3 South Stickney, Ill.
129 E7 South Valley Stream, N.Y.
132 F7 Southview, Pa.
127 E2 South Walpole, Mass.
127 C2 South Waltham, Mass.
132 F11 Southwest, Pa.
129 D8 South Westbury, N.Y.
132 F11 Southwest Greensburg, Pa.
127 D4 South Weymouth, Mass.
129 B6 Sparkill, N.Y.
131 F8 Sparrows Point, Md.
129 B2 Sparta, N.J.
129 B2 Sparta Lake, N.J.
129 F3 Spotswood, N.J.
131 G11 Springbrook, Md.
130 A2 Spring City, Pa.
129 E2 Springdale, N.J.
132 D10 Springdale, Pa
129 D4 Springfield, N.J.
130 C4 Springfield, Pa.
131 J9 Springfield, Va.
131 G10 Spring Lake Park, Md.
130 B4 Spring Mill, Pa.
130 B6 Springside, N.J.
129 B5 Spring Valley, N.Y.
130 C6 Springville, N.J.
132 E9 *Squirrel Hill, Pa.*
131 G11 Standard, Pa.
127 E5 Standish, Mass.
136 E4 Stanford, Calif.
129 D11 Stanhope, N.J.
127 E4 Stanley, Mass.
135 D5 Stanton, Calif.
130 D2 Stanton, Del.
130 C6 Stanwick, N.J.
130 B6 Stanwood Gardens, Pa.
130 D4 Steelton, N.Y.
131 A2 Stella Niagara, N.Y.
129 E3 Stephenville, N.J.
134 B5 Sterling Heights, Mich
136 C2 Sterling Park, Calif.
130 B7 Stevens, N.J.
129 D7 Stewart Manor, N.Y.
132 F10 Stewartsville, Pa.
133 E3 Stickney, Ill.
129 D3 Stirling, N.J.
129 B2 Stockholm, N.J.
127 C3 Stoneham, Mass.
133 D2 Stone Park, Ill.
132 F11 Stonevilla, Pa.
129 C11 Stony Brook, N.Y.
134 A5 Stony Creek, Mich.
134 D2 Stony Creek, Mich.
131 F6 Stony Run, Md.
127 E3 Stoughton, Mass.
130 A2 Stowe, Pa.
132 F7 Strabane, Pa.
130 B3 Strafford, Pa.
130 D5 Stratford, N.J.
134 C5 *Strathmoor, Mich.*
136 B1 Strawberry Point, Calif.
132 F10 Straw Pump, Pa.
132 C3 Strongsville, Ohio
132 E7 Sturgeon, Pa.
129 C2 Succasunna, N.J.
127 C1 Sudbury, Mass.
127 C1 Sudbury Center, Mass.
129 B5 Suffern, N.Y.
129 B5 Suffern Park, N.Y.
130 C2 Sugartown, Pa.
131 H11 Suitland, Md.
133 E3 Summit, Ill.
129 D3 Summit, N.J.
131 E6 Summit Park, Md.
134 E3 Sumpter, Mich.
135 A3 *Sunland, Calif.*
133 F3 Sunny Crest, Ill.
136 E4 Sunnyvale, Calif.
136 D5 Sunol, Calif.
129 D3 Sunrise Park, N.J.
136 C2 *Sunset, Calif.*
135 D4 Sunset Beach, Calif.
129 F2 Sunset Hill Garden, N.J.
133 C3 Sunset Trailer Park, Ill.
132 F10 Sunset Valley, Pa.
135 C4 Sunshine Acres, Calif.
135 A2 *Sun Valley, Calif.*
135 D4 Surfside, Calif.
127 D4 Surfside, Mass.
132 E10 Sutersville, Pa.
127 C4 Swampscott, Mass.
129 B2 Swannanoa, N.J.
130 D2 Swanwyck, Del.
130 C3 Swarthmore, Pa.
132 F11 Swede Hill, Pa.
130 D4 Swedesboro, N.J.
130 B3 Swedesburg, Pa.
132 E9 Swissvale, Pa.
131 B4 Swormville, N.Y.
132 E8 Sygan, Pa.
133 B1 Sylvan Lake, Ill.
134 B2 Sylvan Lake, Mich.
130 D2 Symonds Gardens, Del.
129 D8 Syosset, N.Y.

T

130 C7 Tabernacle, N.J.
127 C3 Tabor, N.J.
130 B5 *Tacony, Pa.*
131 H10 Takoma Park, Md.
132 D9 Talley Cavey, Pa.
130 D2 Talleys Corner, Del.
130 D2 Talleyville, Del.
129 B5 Tallman, N.Y.
136 B1 Tamalpais Valley, Calif.
130 D6 Tansboro, N.J.
129 D6 Tappan, N.Y.
136 B3 Tara Hills, Calif.
132 D10 Tarentum, Pa.
132 F11 Tarrs, Pa.
129 B6 Tarrytown, N.Y.
135 B1 *Tarzana, Calif.*
130 C6 Taunton Lakes, N.J.
130 C5 Tavistock, N.J.
134 D4 Taylor, Mich.
129 D3 Taylortown, N.J.
129 C5 Teaneck, N.J.
133 C3 Techny, Ill.
135 B4 Temple City, Calif.
131 J11 Temple Hills, Md.
129 C6 Tenafly, N.J.
136 B1 Terra Linda, Calif.
129 C11 Terryville, N.Y.
129 C5 Teterboro, N.J.
127 B2 Tewksbury, Mass.
132 B3 Tewksbury Heights, Calif.
130 D2 The Cedars, Del.
132 F8 Thomas, Pa.
129 D7 Thomaston, N.Y.
132 F8 Thompsonville, Pa.
132 E8 Thornburg, Pa.
132 C1 Thorndale, Pa.
133 F4 Thornton, Ill.
132 C2 Thornton, Pa.
129 B7 Thornwood, N.Y.
130 C4 Thorofare, N.J.
129 D7 *Throgs Neck, N.Y.*
136 B2 Tiburon, Calif.
133 B1 Timber Lake, Ill.
133 D2 Timber Trails, Ill.
131 F6 Timberview, Md.
130 B7 Timbuctoo, N.J.
127 E5 Tinkertown, Mass.
133 F3 Tinley Park, Ill.
130 B5 *Tioga, Pa.*
130 D1 Todd Estates, Del.
131 B3 Tonawanda, N.Y.
135 B1 Topanga, Calif.
135 B1 Topanga Beach, Calif.
127 B4 Topsfield, Mass.
136 A3 Tormey, Calif.
135 C2 Torrance, Calif.
130 B5 *Torresdale, Pa.*
129 C4 Totowa, N.J.
130 D1 Toughkenamon, Pa.
129 C3 Towaco, N.J.
130 B6 Town Estates, N.J.
131 C3 Town of Tonawanda, N.Y.
131 E7 Towson, Md.
132 E10 Trafford, Pa.
130 D3 Trainer, Pa.
130 A3 Trappe, Pa.
132 E11 Trees Mills, Pa.
129 C6 *Tremont, N.Y.*
134 E4 Trenton, Mich.
130 A7 Trenton, N.J.
130 B6 Trevose, Pa.
134 B3 Trips Subdivision, Mich.
133 E2 Tristate Village, Ill.
130 B3 Trooper, Pa.
134 B5 Troy, Mich.
129 C3 Troy Hills, N.J.
132 D11 Truxall, Pa.
129 C7 Tuckahoe, N.Y.
135 A3 *Tujunga, Calif.*
130 B7 Tullytown, Pa.
136 E2 Tunitas, Calif.
132 F10 Turkeytown, Pa.
130 D5 Turnersville, N.J.
132 E10 Turtle Creek, Pa.
135 D6 Tustin, Calif.
131 H11 Tuxedo, Md.
130 D2 Tuxedo Park, Del.
134 B3 Twin Beach, Mich.
133 C2 Twin Oaks, Ill.
130 C3 Twin Oaks, Pa.
132 C6 Twinsburg, Ohio
131 H9 Tyler Park, Va.
127 A1 Tyngsboro, Mass.
132 E7 Tyre, Pa.
131 H9 Tysons Corner, Va.

U

129 D4 Union, N.J.
129 F4 Union Beach, N.J.
136 D4 Union City, Calif.
129 D5 Union City, N.J.
129 D8 Uniondale, N.Y.
134 B3 Union Lake, Mich.
130 B7 Unionville, N.J.
130 C1 Unionville, Pa.
132 F11 United, Pa.
132 B5 University Heights, Ohio
131 H11 University Park, Md.
135 B7 Upland, Calif.
130 C3 Upland, Pa.
129 C2 Upper Berkshire Valley, N.J.
129 C8 Upper Brookville, N.Y.
130 C4 Upper Darby, Pa.
131 E8 Upper Falls, Md.
129 B6 Upper Nyack, N.Y.
129 B5 Upper Saddle River, N.J.
132 E8 Upper Saint Clair, Pa.
133 D3 *Uptown, Ill.*
134 B5 Utica, Mich.
134 B5 Utica Heights, Mich.
130 B1 Uwchland, Pa.

V

129 B7 Valhalla, N.Y.
135 B5 Valinda, Calif.
136 A3 Vallejo, Calif.
136 D2 Vallemar, Calif.
129 B6 Valley Cottage, N.Y.
131 E7 Valley Crest, Md.
130 B3 Valley Forge, Pa.
131 F5 Valley Mede, Md.
131 E6 Valley Stream, Md.
129 E7 Valley Stream, N.Y.
133 D1 Valley View, Ill.
132 B5 Valley View, Ohio
132 D11 Vandergrift, Pa.
135 A2 *Van Nuys, Calif.*
132 G9 Van Voorhis, Pa.
132 F8 Venetia, Pa.
132 F7 Venice, Pa.
135 C2 *Venice, Calif.*
129 C5 Verga, N.J.
135 B3 Vernon, Calif.
133 B2 Vernon Hills, Ill.
129 D4 Verona, N.J.
132 D9 Verona, Pa.
132 F9 Versailles, Pa.
129 C2 Victory Gardens, N.J.
132 F9 Victory Hills, Pa.
131 H9 Vienna, Va.
130 C3 Village Green, Pa.
129 C10 Village of the Branch, N.Y.
130 D3 Villa Monterey, Del.
130 B3 Villanova, Pa.
131 E6 Villa Nova, Md.
135 D6 Villa Park, Calif.
133 D2 Villa Park, Ill.
132 B2 Vincent, Ohio
130 C7 Vincentown, N.J.
136 A4 Vine Hill, Calif.
129 E3 Vineyard Homes, N.J.
129 B5 Viola, N.Y.
131 J10 Virginia Hills, Va.

W

127 D2 Waban, Mass.
132 A6 Waite Hill, Ohio
131 E7 Wakefield, Md.
127 B3 Wakefield, Mass.
129 B5 Waldwick, N.J.
132 E8 Walkers Mill, Pa.
132 E10 Wall, Pa.
134 B3 Walled Lake, Mich.
130 C3 Wallingford, Pa.
129 C5 Wallington, N.J.
135 B5 *Walnut, Calif.*
136 B4 Walnut Creek, Calif.
136 B4 Walnut Heights, Calif.
134 B4 Walnut Lake, Mich.
135 C3 Walnut Park, Calif.
127 E2 Walpole, Mass.
127 C2 Waltham, Mass.
132 B5 Walton Hills, Ohio
130 C4 Walt Whitman Homes, N.J.
134 E3 Waltz, Mich.
127 B3 Wamesit, Mass.
131 D3 Wanakah, N.Y.
129 B4 Wanaque, N.J.
129 D8 Wantagh, N.Y.
130 C2 Ward, Pa.
127 A3 Ward Hill, Mass.
131 E5 Wards Chapel, Md.
130 A5 Warminster, Pa.
136 E5 Warm Springs, Calif.
134 B5 Warren, Mich.
129 E3 Warren, N.J.
132 B5 Warrensville Heights, Ohio
130 A5 Warrington, Pa.
132 F7 Washington, Pa.
131 H10 Washington, D.C.
130 B3 Washington Park, Pa.
130 B4 Washington Square, Pa.
129 D2 Washington Valley, N.J.
129 E3 Watchung, N.J.
134 A3 Waterford, Mich.
134 C3 Waterford, Mich.
130 D6 Waterford Works, N.J.
129 D11 Water Island, N.Y.
127 C2 Watertown, Mass.
131 D3 Water Valley, N.Y.
135 C3 *Watts, Calif.*
133 B1 Wauconda, Ill.
133 A3 Waukegan, Ill.
127 D4 Waveland, Mass.
127 C2 Waverly, Mass.
127 C1 Wayland, Mass.
134 D3 Wayne, Mich.
129 C4 Wayne, N.J.
130 B3 Wayne, Pa.
132 F7 Weavertown, Pa.
132 F9 Webster, Pa.
131 D4 Webster Corners, N.Y.
129 D5 Weehawken, N.J.
132 D11 Weinel Cross Roads, Pa.
127 D2 Wellesley, Mass.
127 D2 Wellesley Hills, Mass.
131 E6 Wellwood, Md.
130 D2 Welshire, Del.
132 F10 Wendel, Pa.
131 B4 Wendelville, N.Y.
127 B4 Wenham, Mass.
130 D5 Wenonah, N.J.
127 E4 West Abington, Mass.
134 B3 Westacres, Mich.
129 D9 West Amityville, N.Y.
127 B2 West Andover, Mass.
129 D9 West Babylon, N.Y.
130 D6 West Berlin, N.J.
127 B2 West Billerica, Mass.
127 A3 West Boxford, Mass.
127 E3 West Bridgewater, Mass.
130 B6 West Bristol, Pa.
133 E1 Westbury, Ill.
129 D8 Westbury, N.Y.
129 C4 West Caldwell, N.J.
132 C2 West Carlisle, Ohio
135 C2 *Westchester, Calif.*
133 D2 Westchester, Ill.
129 C7 *Westchester, N.Y.*
130 C2 West Chester, Pa.
131 H9 Westchester, Va.
130 C5 West Collingswood, N.J.
130 C5 West Collingswood Heights, N.J.
127 C1 West Concord, Mass.
130 B4 West Conshohocken, Pa.
130 D5 Westcotville, N.J.
135 B5 West Covina, Calif.
133 D2 Westdale, Ill.
127 E4 Westdale, Mass.
127 E5 West Duxbury, Mass.
132 F9 West Elizabeth, Pa.
132 E8 *West End, Pa.*
133 E2 Western Springs, Ill.
129 E3 Westfield, N.J.
127 B1 Westford, Mass.
127 E2 West Foxboro, Mass.
131 H9 Westhampton, Va.
127 E4 West Hanover, Mass.
133 F2 Westhaven, Ill.
129 D8 West Hempstead, N.Y.
134 B2 West Highland, Mich.
135 B2 West Hollywood, Calif.
132 E9 West Homestead, Pa.
129 C9 West Huntington, N.Y.
129 D10 West Islip, N.Y.
129 F5 West Keansburg, N.J.
132 B3 Westlake, Ohio
134 D3 Westland, Mich.
132 F7 Westland, Pa.
127 B1 Westlands, Mass.
131 H9 West Lawn, Va.
132 D11 West Leechburg, Pa.
132 E8 *West Liberty, Pa.*
135 B2 *West Los Angeles, Calif.*
132 E8 West Manayunk, Pa.
127 F2 West Mansfield, Mass.
127 C3 West Medford, Mass.
127 E1 West Medway, Mass.
136 E3 West Menlo Park, Calif.
132 E9 West Mifflin, Pa.
129 B3 West Milford, N.J.
129 E2 West Millington, N.J.
135 D5 Westminster, Calif.
133 E2 Westmont, Ill.
130 C5 Westmont, N.J.
132 F10 Westmoreland City, Pa.
127 A4 West Newbury, Mass.
127 C2 West Newton, Mass.
132 F10 West Newton, Pa.
129 D5 West New York, N.J.
130 B5 West Norriton, Pa.
129 B6 West Nyack, N.Y.
127 C2 Weston, Mass.
129 D4 West Orange, N.J.
129 C4 West Paterson, N.J.
127 B4 West Peabody, Mass.
136 A5 West Pittsburg, Calif.
130 A4 West Point, Pa.
133 E4 *West Pullman, Ill.*
127 D3 *West Roxbury, Mass.*
129 D11 West Sayville, N.Y.
131 C4 West Seneca, N.Y.
127 C3 West Somerville, Mass.
131 J10 West Springfield, Va.
130 C2 Westtown, Pa.
132 D11 West Vandergrift, Pa.
132 B3 Westview, Ohio
132 D8 West View, Pa.
130 C5 Westville, N.J.
130 C5 Westville Grove, N.J.
134 D2 West Willow, Mich.
127 A1 West Windham, N.H.
135 B2 *Westwood, Calif.*
127 D2 Westwood, Mass.
129 C5 Westwood, N.J.
132 D8 Wexford, Pa.
131 J9 Weyanoke, Va.
127 D4 Weymouth, Mass.
129 C2 Wharton, N.J.
133 D1 Wheaton, Ill.
131 G10 Wheaton, Md.
130 B7 Wheat Sheaf, Pa.
133 C2 Wheeling, Ill.
129 D3 Whippany, N.J.
132 E9 Whitaker, Pa.
132 E9 Whitehall, Pa.
127 D4 Whitehead, Mass.
130 A7 White Horse, N.J.
134 A2 White Lake, Mich.
134 B2 White Lake P. O., Mich.
131 E8 White Marsh, Md.
130 B4 Whitemarsh, Pa.
129 C2 White Meadow Lake, N.J.
132 E10 White Oak, Pa.
133 D2 White Pines, Ill.
129 B7 White Plains, N.Y.
129 D7 *Whitestone, N.Y.*
132 E11 White Valley, Pa.
133 E5 Whiting, Ind.
127 E4 Whitman, Mass.
130 D5 Whitman Square, N.J.
134 C1 Whitmore Lake, Mich.
134 E2 Whittaker, Mich.
135 C4 Whittier, Calif.
129 F4 Wickatunk, N.J.
131 G10 Wickford, Md.
132 A6 Wickliffe, Ohio
132 E11 Wiester, Pa.
131 H11 Wildercroft, Md.
133 A2 Wildwood, Ill.
132 D9 Wildwood, Pa.
131 F8 Wild Wood Beach, Md.
131 G10 Wildwood Manor, Md.
132 E9 Wilkinsburg, Pa.
131 G10 Willerburn Acres, Md.
129 E2 William Bradley Estates, N.J.
129 C7 *Williams Bridge, N.Y.*
129 D6 *Williamsburg, N.Y.*
130 D6 Williamstown, N.J.
130 D6 Williamstown Junction, N.J.
131 C4 Williamsville, N.Y.
130 B6 Willingboro, N.J.
134 E2 Willis, Mich.
129 D8 Williston Park, N.Y.
132 A6 Willoughby, Ohio
132 A6 Willoughby Hills, Ohio
134 E3 Willow, Mich.
136 C3 Willow Brook, Calif.
133 E2 Willowbrook, Ill.
130 C1 Willowdale, Pa.
134 D3 Willow Gardens, Mich.
130 B5 Willow Grove, Pa.
132 A6 Willowick, Ohio
134 D2 Willow Run, Mich.
131 G9 Willow Run, Va.
133 E2 Willow Springs, Ill.
130 B2 Wilmer, Pa.
132 E10 Wilmerding, Pa.
133 C3 Wilmette, Ill.
135 D3 *Wilmington, Calif.*
130 D2 Wilmington, Del.
127 B2 Wilmington, Mass.
130 D2 Wilmington Manor, Del.
133 A2 Wilson, Ill.
131 F6 Wilton Farm Acres, Md.
131 J10 Wilton Woods, Va.
127 C3 Winchester, Mass.
130 B6 Winder Village, Pa.
127 A2 Windham, N.H.
131 D4 Windom, N.Y.
130 D1 Windy Hills, Del.
129 E4 Winfield, N.J.
134 B4 Wing Lake, Mich.
127 F5 Winneconnet, Mass.
135 A1 *Winnetka, Calif.*
133 C3 Winnetka, Ill.
130 E6 Winslow, N.J.
127 C3 Winter Hill, Mass.
130 D2 Winterthur, Del.
127 C4 Winthrop, Mass.
133 E3 Wireton, Ill.
132 D7 Wireton, Pa.
130 B5 *Wissinoming, Pa.*
134 B2 Wixom, Mich.
127 C3 Woburn, Mass.
132 F7 Wolfdale, Pa.
127 D3 Wollaston, Mass.
134 B3 Wolverine Lake, Mich.
129 E4 Wood Acres, N.J.
130 A6 Woodbourne, Pa.
129 E4 Woodbridge, N.J.
131 E7 Woodbrook, Md.
130 D5 Woodbury, N.J.
129 D9 Woodbury, N.Y.
130 D5 Woodbury Heights, N.J.
130 C5 Woodbury Terrace, N.J.
129 B5 Woodcliff Lake, N.J.
134 B4 Wood Creek Farms, Mich.
133 D2 Wood Dale, Ill.
134 E4 Woodhaven, Mich.
129 D6 *Woodhaven, N.Y.*
135 A1 *Woodland Hills, Calif.*
133 E4 *Woodlawn, Ill.*
129 C6 *Woodlawn, N.Y.*
131 F6 Woodlawn, Md.
131 H11 Woodlawn, Md.
131 D3 Woodlawn Beach, N.Y.
131 F7 Woodlawn Heights, Md.
130 C3 Woodlyn, Pa.
130 C5 Woodlynne, N.J.
129 E7 Woodmere, N.Y.
132 B6 Woodmere, Ohio
130 B5 Woodmont, Pa.
131 E2 Woodmoor, Md.
129 C2 Woodport, N.J.
129 C5 Wood-Ridge, N.J.
133 E1 Woodridge, Ill.
129 E7 Woodsburgh, N.Y.
129 D6 *Woodside, N.Y.*
136 E3 Woodside, Calif.
130 A6 Woodside, Pa.
129 E2 Woods Tavern, N.J.
131 F5 Woodstock, Md.
133 C2 Woodview Manor, Ill.
130 A3 Worcester, Pa.
133 E3 Worth, Ill.
131 F6 Worthington, Md.
127 E2 Wrentham, Mass.
133 F5 Wright, Ind.
129 D9 Wyandanch, N.Y.
134 D5 Wyandotte, Mich.
132 F10 Wyano, Pa.
129 B4 Wyckoff, N.J.
132 F8 Wyllie Hills, Pa.
132 F9 Wylie, Pa.
130 B5 Wyncote, Pa.
130 B4 Wyndmoor, Pa.
130 C4 Wynnewood, Pa.

Y

130 A6 Yardley, Pa.
130 A7 Yardville, N.J.
130 C4 Yeadon, Pa.
130 A3 Yerkes, Pa.
129 C6 Yonkers, N.Y.
135 C6 Yorba Linda, Calif.
133 D2 York Center, Ill.
133 D2 Yorkfield, Ill.
130 D1 Yorklyn, Del.
131 A2 Youngstown, N.Y.
132 F11 Youngwood, Pa.
134 D2 Ypsilanti, Mich.
132 F10 Yukon, Pa.

Z

129 E2 Zarephath, N.J.
130 C3 Zebleys Corner, Pa.

U.S. State General Information

STATE	CAPITAL	LARGEST CITY	ENTERED UNION AS STATE Date of Entry	Rank of Entry	Greatest N-S Measurement (miles)	Greatest E-W Measurement (miles)	HIGHEST POINT Location	Altitude (feet)	STATE FLOWER	STATE BIRD	STATE NICKNAME
Alabama	Montgomery	Birmingham	Dec. 14, 1819	22	330	200	Cheaha Mountain	2,407	Camellia	Yellowhammer	Yellowhammer
Alaska	Juneau	Anchorage	Jan. 3, 1959	49	1,332	2,250	Mt. McKinley	20,320	Forget-me-not	Willow Ptarmigan	Last Frontier
Arizona	Phoenix	Phoenix	Feb. 14, 1912	48	390	335	Humphreys Peak	12,633	Saguaro Cactus	Cactus Wren	Grand Canyon
Arkansas	Little Rock	Little Rock	June 15, 1836	25	240	275	Magazine Mtn.	2,753	Apple Blossom	Mockingbird	Land of Opportunity
California	Sacramento	Los Angeles	Sept. 9, 1850	31	800	375	Mt. Whitney	14,494	Golden Poppy	California Valley Quail	Golden
Colorado	Denver	Denver	Aug. 1, 1876	38	270	380	Mt. Elbert	14,433	Rocky Mountain Columbine	Lark Bunting	Centennial
Connecticut*	Hartford	Hartford	Jan. 9, 1788	5	75	90	S. slope of Mt. Frissell	2,380	Mountain Laurel	Robin	Constitution
Delaware*	Dover	Wilmington	Dec. 7, 1787	1	95	35	Ebright Road, New Castle Co.	442	Peach Blossom	Blue Hen Chicken	First
District of Columbia	Washington	Washington	March 3, 1791	..	15	15	Tenleytown	410	American Beauty Rose	Wood Thrush	.....
Florida	Tallahassee	Jacksonville	March 3, 1845	27	460	400	N. boundary, Walton Co.	345	Orange Blossom	Mockingbird	Sunshine
Georgia*	Atlanta	Atlanta	Jan. 2, 1788	4	315	250	Brasstown Bald (mtn.)	4,784	Cherokee Rose	Brown Thrasher	Peach
Hawaii	Honolulu	Honolulu	Aug. 21, 1959	50	.....	1,600	Mauna Kea	13,796	Red Hibiscus	Nene (Hawaiian Goose)	Aloha
Idaho	Boise	Boise	July 3, 1890	43	480	305	Borah Peak	12,662	Syringa	Mountain Bluebird	Gem
Illinois	Springfield	Chicago	Dec. 3, 1818	21	380	205	Charles Mound	1,235	Violet	Cardinal	Prairie
Indiana	Indianapolis	Indianapolis	Dec. 11, 1816	19	265	160	Near Spartanburg	1,257	Peony	Cardinal	Hoosier
Iowa	Des Moines	Des Moines	Dec. 28, 1846	29	205	310	N. W. corner Osceola Co.	1,670	Wild Rose	Eastern Goldfinch	Hawkeye
Kansas	Topeka	Wichita	Jan. 29, 1861	34	205	410	Mt. Sunflower	4,039	Sunflower	Western Meadowlark	Sunflower
Kentucky	Frankfort	Louisville	June 1, 1792	15	175	350	Black Mountain	4,145	Goldenrod	Kentucky Cardinal	Bluegrass
Louisiana	Baton Rouge	New Orleans	April 30, 1812	18	275	300	Driskill Mountain	535	Magnolia	Pelican	Pelican
Maine	Augusta	Portland	March 15, 1820	23	310	210	Mt. Katahdin	5,268	White Pine	Chickadee	Pine Tree
Maryland*	Annapolis	Baltimore	April 28, 1788	7	120	200	Backbone Mountain	3,360	Black-eyed Susan	Baltimore Oriole	Old Free
Massachusetts*	Boston	Boston	Feb. 6, 1788	6	110	190	Mt. Greylock	3,491	Mayflower	Chickadee	Old Bay
Michigan	Lansing	Detroit	Jan. 26, 1837	26	400	310	Mt. Curwood	1,980	Apple Blossom	Robin	Wolverine
Minnesota	St. Paul	Minneapolis	May 11, 1858	32	400	350	Eagle Mtn.	2,301	Showy Lady's-slipper	Loon	Gopher
Mississippi	Jackson	Jackson	Dec. 10, 1817	20	340	180	Woodall Mountain	806	Magnolia	Mockingbird	Magnolia
Missouri	Jefferson City	St. Louis	Aug. 10, 1821	24	280	300	Taum Sauk Mountain	1,772	Hawthorne	Bluebird	Show Me
Montana	Helena	Billings	Nov. 8, 1889	41	315	570	Granite Peak	12,799	Bitterroot	Western Meadowlark	Big Sky
Nebraska	Lincoln	Omaha	March 1, 1867	37	210	415	S.W. corner Kimball Co.	5,426	Goldenrod	Western Meadowlark	Cornhusker
Nevada	Carson City	Las Vegas	Oct. 31, 1864	36	485	315	Boundary Peak	13,143	Shrub Sagebrush	Mountain Bluebird	Silver
New Hampshire*	Concord	Manchester	June 21, 1788	9	185	90	Mt. Washington	6,288	Purple Lilac	Purple Finch	Granite
New Jersey*	Trenton	Newark	Dec. 18, 1787	3	166	70	High Point	1,803	Purple Violet	Eastern Goldfinch	Garden
New Mexico	Santa Fe	Albuquerque	Jan. 6, 1912	47	390	350	Wheeler Peak	13,161	Yucca	Roadrunner	Land of Enchantment
New York*	Albany	New York	July 26, 1788	11	310	330	Mt. Marcy	5,344	Rose	Bluebird	Empire
North Carolina*	Raleigh	Charlotte	Nov. 21, 1789	12	200	520	Mt. Mitchell	6,684	Dogwood	Cardinal	Tar Heel
North Dakota	Bismarck	Fargo	Nov. 2, 1889	39	210	360	White Butte	3,506	Wild Prairie Rose	Western Meadowlark	Flickertail
Ohio	Columbus	Cleveland	March 1, 1803	17	230	205	Campbell Hill	1,550	Scarlet Carnation	Cardinal	Buckeye
Oklahoma	Oklahoma City	Oklahoma City	Nov. 16, 1907	46	210	460	Black Mesa	4,973	Mistletoe	Scissor-tailed Flycatcher	Sooner
Oregon	Salem	Portland	Feb. 14, 1859	33	290	375	Mt. Hood	11,239	Oregon Grape	Western Meadowlark	Beaver
Pennsylvania*	Harrisburg	Philadelphia	Dec. 12, 1787	2	180	310	Mt. Davis	3,213	Mountain Laurel	Ruffed Grouse	Keystone
Rhode Island*	Providence	Providence	May 29, 1790	13	50	35	Jerimoth Hill	812	Violet	Rhode Island Red	Little Rhody
South Carolina*	Columbia	Columbia	May 23, 1788	8	215	285	Sassafras Mountain	3,560	Carolina Jessamine	Carolina Wren	Palmetto
South Dakota	Pierre	Sioux Falls	Nov. 2, 1889	40	240	360	Harney Peak	7,242	Pasque	Ringnecked Pheasant	Coyote
Tennessee	Nashville	Memphis	June 1, 1796	16	120	430	Clingmans Dome	6,643	Iris	Mockingbird	Volunteer
Texas	Austin	Houston	Dec. 29, 1845	28	710	760	Guadalupe Peak	8,751	Bluebonnet	Mockingbird	Lone Star
Utah	Salt Lake City	Salt Lake City	Jan. 4, 1896	45	345	275	Kings Peak	13,528	Sego Lily	Seagull	Beehive
Vermont*	Montpelier	Burlington	March 4, 1791	14	155	90	Mt. Mansfield	4,393	Red Clover	Hermit Thrush	Green Mountain
Virginia*	Richmond	Norfolk	June 25, 1788	10	205	425	Mt. Rogers	5,729	Flowering Dogwood	Cardinal	Old Dominion
Washington	Olympia	Seattle	Nov. 11, 1889	42	230	340	Mt. Rainier	14,410	Rhododendron	Willow Goldfinch	Evergreen
West Virginia	Charleston	Huntington	June 20, 1863	35	200	225	Spruce Knob	4,862	Rhododendron	Cardinal	Mountain
Wisconsin	Madison	Milwaukee	May 29, 1848	30	300	290	Timms Hill	1,952	Violet	Robin	Badger
Wyoming	Cheyenne	Cheyenne	July 10, 1890	44	275	365	Gannett Peak	13,804	Indian Paint Brush	Meadowlark	Equality
United States	Washington, D.C.	New York	...	..	275	365	Mt. McKinley, Alaska	20,320	.....	Bald Eagle	.....

*One of the Thirteen Original States.

U.S. Population by State or Colony 1650-1980

STATES	1980	1970	1960	1950	1940	1920	1900	1880	1860	1840	1820	1800	1790	1770	1750	1700	1650
Alabama	3,893,978	3,444,165	3,266,740	3,061,743	2,832,961	2,348,174	1,828,697	1,262,505	964,201	590,756	127,901						
Alaska	401,851	302,173	226,167	128,643	72,524	55,036	63,592	33,426									
Arizona	2,718,425	1,772,482	1,302,161	749,587	499,261	334,162	122,931	40,440									
Arkansas	2,286,419	1,923,295	1,786,272	1,909,511	1,949,387	1,752,204	1,311,564	802,525	435,450	97,574	14,273						
California	23,667,837	19,953,134	15,717,204	10,586,223	6,907,387	3,426,861	1,485,053	864,694	379,994								
Colorado	2,889,735	2,207,259	1,753,947	1,325,089	1,123,296	939,629	539,700	194,327	34,277								
Connecticut	3,107,576	3,032,217	2,535,234	2,007,280	1,709,242	1,380,631	908,420	622,700	460,147	309,978	275,248	251,002	237,946	183,881	111,280	25,970	4,139
Delaware	594,317	548,104	446,292	318,085	266,505	223,003	184,735	146,608	112,216	78,085	72,749	64,273	59,096	35,496	28,704	2,470	185
District of Columbia	638,432	756,510	763,956	802,178	663,091	437,571	278,718	177,624	75,080	33,745	23,336	8,144					
Florida	9,746,421	6,789,443	4,951,560	2,771,305	1,897,414	968,470	528,542	269,493	140,424	54,477							
Georgia	5,463,087	4,589,575	3,943,116	3,444,578	3,123,723	2,895,832	2,216,331	1,542,180	1,057,286	691,392	340,989	162,686	82,548	23,375	5,200		
Hawaii	964,691	769,913	632,772	499,794	422,770	255,881	154,001	32,610									
Idaho	944,038	713,008	667,191	588,637	524,873	431,866	161,772										
Illinois	11,427,414	11,113,976	10,081,158	8,712,176	7,897,241	6,485,280	4,821,550	3,077,871	1,711,951	476,183	55,211						
Indiana	5,490,260	5,193,669	4,662,498	3,934,224	3,427,796	2,930,390	2,516,462	1,978,301	1,350,428	685,866	147,178	5,641					
Iowa	2,913,808	2,825,041	2,757,537	2,621,073	2,538,268	2,404,021	2,231,853	1,624,615	674,913	43,112							
Kansas	2,364,236	2,249,071	2,178,611	1,905,299	1,801,028	1,769,257	1,470,495	996,096	107,206								
Kentucky	3,660,257	3,219,311	3,038,156	2,944,806	2,845,627	2,416,630	2,147,174	1,648,690	1,155,684	779,828	564,317	220,955	73,677	15,700			
Louisiana	4,206,098	3,643,180	3,257,022	2,683,516	2,363,880	1,798,509	1,381,625	939,946	708,002	352,411	153,407						
Maine⁴	1,125,030	993,663	969,265	913,774	847,226	768,014	694,466	648,936	628,279	501,793	298,335	151,719	96,540	31,257	27,505	4,958	1,305
Maryland	4,216,941	3,922,399	3,100,689	2,343,001	1,821,244	1,449,661	1,188,044	934,943	687,049	470,019	407,350	341,548	319,728	202,599	141,073	29,604	4,504
Massachusetts⁴	5,737,081	5,689,170	5,148,578	4,690,514	4,316,721	3,852,356	2,805,346	1,783,085	1,231,066	737,699	523,287	422,845	378,787	235,308	188,000	55,941	16,603
Michigan	9,262,070	8,875,083	7,823,194	6,371,766	5,256,106	3,668,412	2,420,982	1,636,937	749,113	212,267	8,896						
Minnesota	4,075,970	3,805,069	3,413,864	2,982,483	2,792,300	2,387,125	1,751,394	780,773	172,023								
Mississippi	2,520,631	2,216,912	2,178,141	2,178,914	2,183,796	1,790,618	1,551,270	1,131,597	791,305	375,651	75,448	8,850					
Missouri	4,916,759	4,677,399	4,319,813	3,954,653	3,784,664	3,404,055	3,106,665	2,168,380	1,182,012	383,702	66,586						
Montana	786,690	694,409	674,767	591,024	559,456	548,889	243,329	39,159									
Nebraska	1,569,825	1,483,791	1,411,330	1,325,510	1,315,834	1,296,372	1,066,300	452,402	28,841								
Nevada	800,493	488,738	285,278	160,083	110,247	77,407	42,335	62,266	6,857								
New Hampshire	920,610	737,681	606,921	533,242	491,524	443,083	411,588	346,991	326,073	284,574	244,161	183,858	141,885	62,396			
New Jersey	7,365,011	7,168,164	6,066,782	4,835,329	4,160,165	3,155,900	1,883,669	1,131,116	672,035	373,306	277,575	211,149	184,139	117,431	71,393	14,010	
New Mexico	1,303,445	1,016,000	951,023	681,187	531,818	360,350	195,310	119,565	93,516								
New York	17,558,072	18,241,266	16,782,304	14,830,192	13,479,142	10,385,227	7,268,894	5,082,871	3,880,735	2,428,921	1,372,812	589,051	340,120	162,920	76,696	19,107	4,116
North Carolina	5,881,385	5,082,059	4,556,155	4,061,929	3,571,623	2,559,123	1,893,810	1,399,750	992,622	753,419	638,829	478,103	393,751	197,200	72,984	10,720	
North Dakota³	652,717	617,761	632,446	619,636	641,935	646,872	319,146	36,909									
Ohio	10,797,624	10,652,017	9,706,397	7,946,627	6,907,612	5,759,394	4,157,545	3,198,062	2,339,511	1,519,467	581,434	45,365					
Oklahoma⁵	3,025,495	2,559,253	2,328,284	2,233,351	2,336,434	2,028,283	790,391										
Oregon	2,633,149	2,091,385	1,768,687	1,521,341	1,089,684	783,389	413,536	174,768	52,465								
Pennsylvania	11,864,751	11,793,909	11,319,366	10,498,012	9,900,180	8,720,017	6,302,115	4,282,891	2,906,215	1,724,033	1,049,458	602,365	434,373	240,057	119,666	17,950	
Rhode Island	947,154	949,723	859,488	791,896	713,346	604,397	428,556	276,531	174,620	108,830	83,059	69,122	68,825	58,196	33,226	5,894	785
South Carolina	3,122,814	2,590,516	2,382,594	2,117,027	1,899,804	1,683,724	1,340,316	995,577	703,708	594,398	502,741	345,591	249,073	124,244	64,000	5,704	
South Dakota³	690,768	666,257	680,514	652,740	642,961	636,547	401,570	98,268	4,837								
Tennessee	4,591,120	3,924,164	3,567,089	3,291,718	2,915,841	2,337,885	2,020,616	1,542,359	1,109,801	829,210	422,823	105,602	35,691	1,000			
Texas	14,227,574	11,196,730	9,579,677	7,711,194	6,414,824	4,663,228	3,048,710	1,591,749	604,215								
Utah	1,461,037	1,059,273	890,627	688,862	550,310	449,396	276,749	143,963	40,273								
Vermont	511,456	444,732	389,881	377,747	359,231	352,428	343,641	332,286	315,098	291,948	235,981	154,465	85,425	10,000			
Virginia⁶	5,346,797	4,648,494	3,966,949	3,318,680	2,677,773	2,309,187	1,854,184	1,512,565	1,219,630	1,025,227	938,261	807,557	691,737	447,016	231,033	58,560	18,731
Washington	4,132,204	3,409,169	2,853,214	2,378,963	1,736,191	1,356,621	518,103	75,116	11,594								
West Virginia⁶	1,950,258	1,744,237	1,860,421	2,005,552	1,901,974	1,463,701	958,800	618,457	376,688	224,537	136,808	78,592	55,873				
Wisconsin	4,705,642	4,417,933	3,951,777	3,434,575	3,137,587	2,632,067	2,069,042	1,315,497	775,881	30,945							
Wyoming	469,557	332,416	330,066	290,529	250,742	194,402	92,531	20,789									
Total	226,549,010	203,235,298	179,323,175	151,325,798	132,164,569	106,021,537	76,212,168	50,189,209	31,443,321	17,069,453[2]	9,638,453	5,308,483	3,929,214	2,148,076	1,170,760	250,888	50,368

1 All figures prior to 1890 exclude uncivilized Indians. Figures for 1650 through 1770 include only the British colonies that later became the United States. No areas are included prior to their annexation to the United States. However, many of the figures refer to territories prior to their admission as States. U.S. total includes Alaska from 1880 through 1970 and Hawaii from 1900 through 1970.

2 U.S. total for 1840 includes 6,100 persons on public ships in service of the United States, not credited to any State.

3 South Dakota figure for 1860 represents entire Dakota Territory. North and South Dakota figures for 1880 are for the parts of Dakota Territory which later constituted the respective States.

4 Maine figures for 1770 through 1800 are for that area of Massachusetts which became the State of Maine in 1820. Massachusetts figures exclude Maine from 1770 through 1800, but include it from 1650 through 1750. Massachusetts figure for 1650 also includes population of Plymouth (1,566), a separate colony until 1691.

5 Oklahoma figure for 1900 includes population of Indian Territory (392,060).

6 West Virginia figures for 1790 through 1860 are for that area of Virginia which became West Virginia in 1863. These figures are excluded from the figures for Virginia from 1790 through 1860.

Geographical Facts about the United States

ELEVATION

The highest elevation in the United States is Mount McKinley, Alaska, 20,320 feet.

The lowest elevation in the United States is in Death Valley, California, 282 feet below sea level.

The average elevation of the United States is 2,500 feet.

EXTREMITIES

Direction	Location	Latitude	Longitude
North	Point Barrow, Alaska	71°23′N.	156°29′W.
South	Ka Lae (point) Hawaii	18°56′N.	155°41′W.
East	West Quoddy Head, Maine	44°49′N.	66°57′W.
West	Cape Wrangell, Alaska	52°55′N.	172°27′E.

The two places in the United States separated by the greatest distance are Kure Island, Hawaii, and Mangrove Point, Florida. These points are 5,848 miles apart.

LENGTH OF BOUNDARIES

The total length of the Canadian boundary of the United States is 5,525 miles.

The total length of the Mexican boundary of the United States is 1,933 miles.

The total length of the Atlantic coastline of the United States is 2,069 miles.

The total length of the Pacific and Arctic coastline of the United States is 8,683 miles.

The total length of the Gulf of Mexico coastline of the United States is 1,631 miles.

The total length of all coastlines and land boundaries of the United States is 19,841 miles.

The total length of the tidal shoreline and land boundaries of the United States is 96,091 miles.

GEOGRAPHIC CENTERS

The geographic center of the United States (including Alaska and Hawaii) is in Butte County, South Dakota at 44°58′N., 103°46′W.

The geographic center of North America is in North Dakota, a few miles west of Devils Lake, at 48°10′N., 100°10′W.

EXTREMES OF TEMPERATURE

The highest temperature ever recorded in the United States was 134°F., at Greenland Ranch, Death Valley, California, on July 10, 1913.

The lowest temperature ever recorded in the United States was —76°F., at Tanana, Alaska, in January, 1886.

PRECIPITATION

The average annual precipitation for the United States is approximately 29 inches.

Hawaii is the wettest state, with an average annual rainfall of 82.48 inches. Nevada, with an average annual rainfall of 8.81 inches, is the driest state.

The greatest local average annual rainfall in the United States is at Mt. Waialeale, Kauai, Hawaii, 460 inches.

Greatest 24-hour rainfall in the United States, 23.22 inches at New Smyrna, Florida, October 10–11, 1924.

Extreme minimum rainfall records in the United States include a total fall of only 3.93 inches at Bagdad, California, for a period of 5 years, 1909–13, and an annual average of 1.78 inches at Death Valley, California.

Heavy snowfall records include 76 inches at Silver Lake, Colorado, in 1 day; 42 inches at Angola, New York, in 2 days; 87 inches at Giant Forest, California, in 3 days; and 108 inches at Tahoe, California, in 4 days.

Greatest seasonal snowfall, 1,000.3 inches, more than 83 feet, at Paradise Ranger Station, Washington, during the winter of 1955–56.

Historical Facts about the United States

TERRITORIAL ACQUISITIONS

Accession	Date	Area (sq. mi.)	Cost in Dollars
Original territory of the Thirteen States	1790	888,685	
Purchase of Louisiana Territory, from France	1803	827,192	$11,250,000.00
By treaty with Spain: Florida	1819	58,560 }	$ 5,000,000.00
Other areas	1819	13,443 }	
Annexation of Texas	1845	390,144	
Oregon Territory, by treaty with Great Britain	1846	285,580	
Mexican Cession	1848	529,017	$15,000,000.00
Gadsden Purchase, from Mexico	1853	29,640	$10,000,000.00
Purchase of Alaska, from Russia	1867	586,412	7,200,000.00
Annexation of Hawaiian Islands	1898	6,450	
Puerto Rico, by treaty with Spain	1899	3,435	
Guam, by treaty with Spain	1899	212	
American Samoa, by treaty with Great Britain and Germany	1900	76	
Virgin Islands, by purchase from Denmark	1917	133	$25,000,000.00
Total		3,618,979	$73,450,000.00

Note: The Philippines, ceded by Spain in 1898 for $20,000,000.00, were a territorial possession of the United States from 1898 to 1946. On July 4, 1946 they became the independent republic of the Philippines.

Note. The Canal Zone, ceded by Panama in 1903 for $10,000,000.00, was a territory of the United States from 1903 to 1979. As a result of treaties signed in 1977, sovereignty over the Canal Zone reverted to Panama in 1979.

WESTWARD MOVEMENT OF CENTER OF POPULATION

Year	U.S. Population Total at Census	Approximate Location
1790	3,929,214	23 miles east of Baltimore, Md.
1800	5,308,483	18 miles west of Baltimore, Md.
1810	7,239,881	40 miles northwest of Washington, D.C.
1820	9,638,453	16 miles east of Moorefield, W. Va.
1830	12,866,020	19 miles southwest of Moorefield, W. Va.
1840	17,069,453	16 miles south of Clarksburg, W. Va.
1850	23,191,876	23 miles southeast of Parkersburg, W. Va.
1860	31,443,321	20 miles southeast of Chillicothe, Ohio
1870	39,818,449	48 miles northeast of Cincinnati, Ohio
1880	50,155,783	8 miles southwest of Cincinnati, Ohio
1890	62,947,714	20 miles east of Columbus, Ind.
1900	75,994,575	6 miles southeast of Columbus, Ind.
1910	91,972,266	Bloomington, Ind.
1920	105,710,620	8 miles southeast of Spencer, Ind.
1930	122,775,046	3 miles northeast of Linton, Ind.
1940	131,669,275	2 miles southeast of Carlisle, Ind.
1950	150,697,361	8 miles northwest of Olney, Ill.
1960	179,323,175	6 miles northwest of Centralia, Ill.
1970	204,816,296	5 miles southeast of Mascoutah, Ill.
1980	226,504,825	Near DeSoto, Mo.

State Areas and Populations

STATE	Land Area square miles	Water Area* square miles	Total Area* square miles	Area Rank land area	1980 Resident Population	1980 Population per square mile	1970 Population	1960 Population	1950 Population	Population Rank 1980	Population Rank 1970	Population Rank 1960
Alabama	50,766	938	51,704	28	3,893,978	77	3,444,165	3,266,740	3,061,743	22	21	19
Alaska	570,833	20,171	591,004	1	401,851	0.7	302,173	226,167	128,643	50	50	50
Arizona	113,510	492	114,002	6	2,718,425	24	1,772,482	1,302,161	749,587	29	33	35
Arkansas	52,082	1,109	53,191	27	2,286,419	44	1,923,295	1,786,272	1,909,511	33	32	31
California	156,297	2,407	158,704	3	23,667,837	151	19,953,134	15,717,204	10,586,223	1	1	2
Colorado	103,598	496	104,094	8	2,889,735	28	2,207,259	1,753,947	1,325,089	28	30	33
Connecticut	4,872	147	5,019	48	3,107,576	638	3,032,217	2,535,234	2,007,280	25	24	25
Delaware	1,933	112	2,045	49	594,317	307	548,104	446,292	318,085	47	46	46
District of Columbia	63	6	69	. .	638,432	10,134	756,510	763,956	802,178	. .	. .	. .
Florida	54,157	4,511	58,668	26	9,746,421	180	6,789,441	4,951,560	2,771,305	7	9	10
Georgia	58,060	854	58,914	21	5,463,087	94	4,589,575	3,943,116	3,444,578	13	15	16
Hawaii	6,427	46	6,473	47	964,691	150	769,913	632,772	499,794	39	40	43
Idaho	82,413	1,153	83,566	11	944,038	11	713,008	667,191	588,637	41	42	42
Illinois	55,646	2,226	57,872	24	11,427,414	205	11,113,976	10,081,158	8,712,176	5	5	4
Indiana	35,936	481	36,417	38	5,490,260	153	5,193,669	4,662,498	3,934,224	12	11	11
Iowa	55,965	310	56,275	23	2,913,808	52	2,825,041	2,757,537	2,621,073	27	25	24
Kansas	81,783	499	82,282	13	2,364,236	29	2,249,071	2,178,611	1,905,299	32	28	28
Kentucky	39,674	740	40,414	37	3,660,257	92	3,219,311	3,038,156	2,944,806	23	23	22
Louisiana	44,520	3,230	47,750	33	4,206,098	94	3,643,180	3,257,022	2,683,516	19	20	20
Maine	30,995	2,270	33,265	39	1,125,030	36	993,663	969,265	913,774	38	38	36
Maryland	9,838	623	10,461	42	4,216,941	429	3,922,399	3,100,689	2,343,001	18	18	21
Massachusetts	7,826	460	8,286	45	5,737,081	733	5,689,170	5,148,578	4,690,514	11	10	9
Michigan	56,959	40,148	97,107	22	9,262,070	163	8,875,083	7,823,194	6,371,766	8	7	7
Minnesota	79,548	7,066	86,614	14	4,075,970	51	3,805,069	3,413,864	2,982,483	21	19	18
Mississippi	47,234	457	47,691	31	2,520,631	53	2,216,912	2,178,141	2,178,914	31	29	29
Missouri	68,945	752	69,697	18	4,916,759	71	4,677,399	4,319,813	3,954,653	15	13	13
Montana	145,388	1,657	147,045	4	786,690	5.4	694,409	674,767	591,024	44	43	41
Nebraska	76,639	711	77,350	15	1,569,825	20	1,483,791	1,411,330	1,325,510	35	35	34
Nevada	109,895	667	110,562	7	800,493	7.3	488,738	285,278	160,083	43	47	49
New Hampshire	8,992	286	9,278	44	920,610	102	737,681	606,921	533,242	42	41	45
New Jersey	7,468	319	7,787	46	7,365,011	986	7,168,164	6,066,782	4,835,329	9	8	8
New Mexico	121,336	258	121,594	5	1,303,445	11	1,016,000	951,023	681,187	37	37	37
New York	47,379	5,358	52,737	30	17,558,072	371	18,241,266	16,782,304	14,830,192	2	2	1
North Carolina	48,843	3,826	52,669	29	5,881,385	120	5,082,059	4,556,155	4,061,929	10	12	12
North Dakota	69,299	1,403	70,702	17	652,717	9.4	617,761	632,446	619,636	46	45	44
Ohio	41,004	3,782	44,786	35	10,797,624	263	10,652,017	9,706,397	7,946,627	6	6	5
Oklahoma	68,656	1,301	69,957	19	3,025,495	44	2,559,253	2,328,284	2,233,351	26	27	27
Oregon	96,187	889	97,076	10	2,633,149	27	2,091,385	1,768,687	1,521,341	30	31	32
Pennsylvania	44,892	1,155	46,047	32	11,864,751	264	11,793,909	11,319,366	10,498,012	4	3	3
Rhode Island	1,054	158	1,212	50	947,154	899	949,723	859,488	791,896	40	39	39
South Carolina	30,207	909	31,116	40	3,122,814	103	2,590,516	2,382,594	2,117,027	24	26	26
South Dakota	75,956	1,164	77,120	16	690,768	9.1	666,257	680,514	652,740	45	44	40
Tennessee	41,154	989	42,143	34	4,591,120	112	3,924,164	3,567,089	3,291,718	17	17	17
Texas	262,015	4,790	266,805	2	14,227,574	54	11,196,730	9,579,677	7,711,194	3	4	6
Utah	82,076	2,826	84,902	12	1,461,037	18	1,059,273	890,627	688,862	36	36	38
Vermont	9,273	341	9,614	43	511,456	55	444,732	389,881	377,747	48	48	47
Virginia	39,700	1,063	40,763	36	5,346,797	135	4,648,494	3,966,949	3,318,680	14	14	14
Washington	66,512	1,627	68,139	20	4,132,204	62	3,409,169	2,853,214	2,378,963	20	22	23
West Virginia	24,124	112	24,236	41	1,950,258	81	1,744,237	1,860,421	2,005,552	34	34	30
Wisconsin	54,424	11,789	66,213	25	4,705,642	86	4,417,933	3,951,777	3,434,575	16	16	15
Wyoming	96,988	820	97,808	9	469,557	4.8	332,416	330,066	290,529	49	49	48
United States	3,539,341	139,904	3,679,245	. .	226,549,010	64	203,235,298	179,323,175	151,325,798	. .	. .	. .

*Includes the United States area of the Great Lakes.

Largest Metropolitan Areas of the United States, 1980

This table ranks the largest cities of the United States according to metropolitan area population. The Ranally Metropolitan Area (RMA) populations reflect Rand McNally's exclusive definition of metropolitan areas. Each RMA includes one or more central cities, as well as socially and economically integrated surrounding areas. The table also indicates central city populations and compares the latest available data to the previous census. Populations are rounded totals. 1980 populations reflect final census data.

Rank 1980	Metropolitan Area	RMA Abbrev.	Metro Area Population Census 4/1/80	Census 4/1/70	%Change 1970-80	City Population Census 4/1/80	%Change 1970-80
1	New York, NY-NJ-CT	N.Y.	16,573,600	17,326,300	-4.3	7,538,800	-10.5
	New York, NY					7,071,600	-10.4
	Newark, NJ					329,200	-13.8
	Paterson, NJ					138,000	-4.7
2	Los Angeles, CA	L.A.	9,840,200	8,716,600	12.9	2,968,600	5.6
3	Chicago, IL-IN-WI	CHI	7,803,800	7,676,200	1.7	3,005,100	-10.8
4	Philadelphia-, PA-NJ-DE-MD	PHIL-	5,153,900	5,285,400	-2.5	1,850,500	-13.3
	Philadelphia, PA					1,688,200	-13.4
	Trenton, NJ					92,100	-12.1
	Wilmington, DE					70,200	-12.7
5	San Francisco-Oakland-San Jose, CA	SF-O-	4,665,500	4,274,900	9.1	1,647,700	7.2
	San Francisco, CA					679,000	-5.1
	Oakland, CA					339,300	-6.2
	San Jose, CA					629,400	36.9
6	Detroit, MI-CAN.	DET	4,399,000	4,492,900	-2.1	1,310,500	-18.8
	Detroit, MI					1,202,500	-20.6
	Ann Arbor, MI					108,000	7.3
7	Boston, MA-NH	BOS	3,738,800	3,763,700	-.7	899,000	-8.1
	Boston, MA					563,000	-12.2
	Lowell, MA					92,400	-1.9
	Lawrence, MA					63,200	-5.5
	Haverhill, MA					46,900	1.7
	Brockton, MA					95,200	7.0
	Salem, MA					38,300	-5.7
8	Washington, DC-MD-VA	WASH	3,220,700	2,992,600	7.6	638,400	-15.6
9	Dallas-Fort Worth, TX	D-FW	2,811,800	2,263,200	24.2	1,289,300	4.1
	Dallas, TX					904,100	7.1
	Fort Worth, TX					385,200	-2.1
10	Houston, TX	HOU	2,689,200	1,871,100	43.7	1,595,100	29.3
11	Miami-Fort Lauderdale, FL	MIA-	2,689,100	1,914,400	40.5	500,200	5.4
	Miami, FL					346,900	3.6
	Fort Lauderdale, FL					153,300	9.8
12	Cleveland, OH	CLEV	2,218,300	2,360,600	-6.0	573,800	-23.6
13	St. Louis, MO-IL	ST. L	2,216,100	2,295,700	-3.5	452,800	-27.2
14	Pittsburgh, PA	PGH	2,165,100	2,302,600	-6.0	424,000	-18.5
15	Seattle-Tacoma, WA	SEAT-	2,077,100	1,823,500	13.9	706,700	-4.3
	Seattle, WA					493,800	-7.0
	Tacoma, WA					158,500	2.7
	Everett, WA					54,400	1.5
16	Minneapolis-St. Paul, MN-WI	MPLS-	1,978,000	1,869,100	5.8	641,200	-13.9
	Minneapolis, MN					371,000	-14.6
	St. Paul, MN					270,200	-12.8
17	Atlanta, GA	ATL	1,950,600	1,541,300	26.6	425,000	-14.1
18	Baltimore, MD	BAL	1,883,100	1,865,100	1.0	786,700	-13.1
19	San Diego, CA-MEX.	SDGO	1,597,000	1,206,800	32.3	875,500	25.5
20	Phoenix, AZ	PHOE	1,483,500	950,500	56.1	790,000	35.2
21	Cincinnati-, OH-KY-IN	CIN-	1,476,600	1,445,300	2.2	448,700	-13.9
	Cincinnati, OH					385,500	-15.0
	Hamilton, OH					63,200	-6.9
22	Denver, CO	DEN	1,414,200	1,103,100	28.2	492,400	-4.3
23	Milwaukee, WI	MILW	1,358,600	1,375,400	-1.2	636,300	-11.3
24	Kansas City, MO-KS	K.C.	1,254,600	1,222,700	2.6	448,000	-11.7
25	Portland, OR-WA	POR	1,220,100	997,800	22.3	368,100	-3.1
26	New Orleans, LA	N.O.	1,175,800	1,042,000	12.8	557,900	-6.0
27	Buffalo-Niagara Falls, NY-CAN.	BUF-	1,154,600	1,265,200	-8.7	429,300	-21.7
	Buffalo, NY					357,900	-22.7
	Niagara Falls, NY					71,400	-16.6
28	Indianapolis, IN	IND	1,104,200	1,053,100	4.9	700,800	-6.2
29	Hartford-New Britain, CT	H-NB	1,055,700	1,039,100	1.6	210,200	-12.9
	Hartford, CT					136,400	-13.7
	New Britain, CT					73,800	-11.5
30	San Antonio, TX	SANT	1,012,300	846,600	19.6	786,000	20.1
31	Columbus, OH	COL	943,300	886,700	6.4	565,000	4.6
32	Dayton-Springfield, OH	DAY-	898,000	934,000	-3.9	266,100	-18.1
	Dayton, OH					193,500	-20.4
	Springfield, OH					72,600	-11.4
33	Providence-, RI-MA	PROV-	897,900	891,200	.8	273,900	-9.6
	Providence, RI					156,800	-12.5
	Pawtucket, RI					71,200	-7.5
	Woonsocket, RI					45,900	-1.9
34	Louisville, KY-IN	LOU	881,100	848,500	3.8	298,700	-17.4
35	Sacramento, CA	SAC	848,800	684,000	24.1	275,700	7.2
36	Memphis, TN-AR-MS	MEM	843,200	772,400	9.2	646,200	3.6
37	Rochester, NY	ROCH	809,500	805,400	.5	241,700	-18.1
38	Norfolk-Portsmouth, VA	NORF-	795,600	725,800	9.6	371,600	-11.3
	Norfolk, VA					267,000	-13.3
	Portsmouth, VA					104,600	-5.8
39	Honolulu, HI	HON	762,900	630,500	21.0	365,000	12.3
40	Oklahoma City, OK	O.C.	742,000	627,300	18.3	403,500	9.6
41	Albany-Schenectady-Troy, NY	A-S-T	740,300	727,000	1.8	226,300	-11.8
	Albany, NY					101,700	-12.2
	Schenectady, NY					68,000	-12.8
	Troy, NY					56,600	-10.0
42	San Bernardino-Riverside, CA	SBDO-	715,300	577,000	24.0	289,400	17.2
	San Bernardino, CA					118,800	11.1
	Riverside, CA					170,600	21.8
43	St. Petersburg-, FL	ST. PET-	699,800	509,300	37.4	324,100	20.8
	St. Petersburg, FL					238,600	10.4
	Clearwater, FL					85,500	64.1
44	Birmingham, AL	BIR	697,900	666,200	4.8	286,800	-4.7
45	Salt Lake City, UT	S.L.C.	686,200	503,700	36.2	163,000	-7.3
46	Jacksonville, FL	JAX	615,300	548,500	12.2	540,900	7.3
47	Akron, OH	AKR	614,100	635,300	-3.3	237,200	-13.9
48	Nashville, TN	NASH	608,400	520,100	17.0	455,700	7.0
49	Tampa, FL	TAM	573,100	442,700	29.5	271,600	-2.2
50	Toledo, OH-MI	TOL	571,200	566,600	.8	354,600	-7.4
51	Tulsa, OK	TUL	569,100	460,300	23.6	360,900	-9.2
52	Orlando, FL	ORL	568,300	367,400	54.7	128,300	29.6
53	Flint, MI	FLN	550,200	523,300	5.1	159,600	-17.4
54	Omaha-Council Bluffs, NE-IA	OMA-	548,400	525,500	4.4	378,500	-7.0
	Omaha, NE					322,100	-7.1
	Council Bluffs, IA					56,400	-6.5
55	Richmond, VA	RICH	548,100	494,500	10.8	219,200	-12.1
56	Syracuse, NY	SYR	546,200	546,900	-.1	170,100	-13.8
57	Allentown-Bethlehem-Easton, PA-NJ	AL-B-E	534,200	504,300	5.9	200,200	-5.6
	Allentown, PA					103,800	-5.6
	Bethlehem, PA					70,400	-3.2
	Easton, PA					26,000	-11.9
58	New Haven-Meriden, CT	N. HAV-	500,500	488,700	2.4	183,200	-5.4
	New Haven, CT					126,100	-8.4
	Meriden, CT					57,100	2.0
59	Youngstown-Warren, OH-PA	YNGS-	497,000	505,400	-1.7	172,000	-15.9
	Youngstown, OH					115,400	-18.1
	Warren, OH					56,600	-10.9
60	Tuscon, AZ	TUC	495,200	324,800	52.5	336,500	28.0
61	Knoxville-, TN	KNOX-	490,000	419,400	16.8	220,200	1.6
	Knoxville, TN					175,000	.2
	Maryville, TN					17,500	26.8
	Oak Ridge, TN					27,700	-2.1
62	Grand Rapids, MI	GDR	488,200	444,300	9.9	181,800	-8.0
63	Springfield-Holyoke, MA	SPRG-	485,800	498,300	-2.5	197,000	-7.9
	Springfield, MA					152,300	-7.1
	Holyoke, MA					44,700	-10.8
64	El Paso, TX-NM-MEX.	ELP	484,300	358,600	35.1	425,300	32.0
65	Charlotte, NC	CHRLT	479,200	416,800	15.0	315,500	30.7
66	Scranton Wilkes-Barre, PA	SCR-	467,400	478,300	-2.3	139,700	-13.6
	Scranton, PA					88,100	-14.2
	Wilkes-Barre, PA					51,600	-12.4
67	Albuquerque, NM	ALBU	445,400	327,400	36.0	332,300	35.9
68	Bridgeport, CT	BRDG	444,600	445,500	-.2	142,500	-8.9
69	Baton Rouge, LA	B.R.	441,800	337,400	30.9	238,900	44.0
70	Las Vegas, NV	LASV	441,600	261,900	68.6	164,700	30.9
71	South Bend-Elkhart, IN-MI	S.B.-	437,500	422,800	3.5	151,000	-10.5
	South Bend, IN					109,700	-12.7
	Elkhart, IN					41,300	-4.4
72	Austin, TX	AUS	422,700	292,800	44.4	345,900	36.4
73	Harrisburg, PA	HRBG	404,600	371,700	8.9	53,300	-21.7
74	West Palm Beach, FL	WPB	394,600	236,600	66.8	63,300	10.3
75	Little Rock, AR	L.R.	380,800	310,500	22.6	167,700	26.6
76	Fresno, CA	FRES	377,900	306,100	23.5	235,800	42.3
77	Greensboro-High Point, NC	GRNS-	371,100	334,100	11.1	219,400	5.8
	Greensboro, NC					155,600	8.0
	High Point, NC					63,800	.9
78	Wichita, KS	WICH	367,400	350,400	4.9	279,800	1.2
79	Worcester, MA	WORC	361,200	358,100	.9	161,800	-8.4
80	Chattanooga, TN-GA	CHTN	360,000	317,300	13.5	169,700	41.5
81	Mobile, AL	MOB	353,500	305,900	15.6	200,500	5.5
82	Charleston, SC	CHAS	349,100	280,500	24.5	69,900	4.5
83	Columbia, SC	COL	345,000	286,000	20.6	101,200	-10.8
84	Beaumont-Port Arthur-Orange, TX	B-PA-O	339,400	315,600	7.5	204,800	2.7
	Beaumont, TX					118,100	.5
	Port Arthur, TX					63,100	9.9
	Orange, TX					23,600	-3.7
85	Greenville, SC	GRNV	329,400	266,900	23.4	58,200	-5.2
86	Lansing, MI	LANS	329,200	303,200	8.6	130,400	-.8
87	Davenport-Rock I.-Moline, IA-IL	D-RI-M	328,200	310,900	5.6	196,500	.8
	Davenport, IA					103,300	4.9
	Rock Island, IL					46,800	-6.8
	Moline, IL					46,400	-1.1
88	Des Moines, IA	DES	323,200	300,700	7.5	191,000	-5.2
89	Ventura-Oxnard, CA	V-OX	321,400	242,000	32.8	186,200	44.1
	Ventura, CA					78,000	34.5
	Oxnard, CA					108,200	52.0
90	Peoria, IL	PEOR	317,000	299,500	5.8	124,200	-2.2
91	Spokane, WA-ID	SPOK	316,200	263,800	19.9	171,300	.5
92	Newport News-Hampton, VA	NN-H	314,600	299,100	5.2	267,500	3.3
	Newport News, VA					144,900	4.8
	Hampton, VA					122,600	1.5
93	Canton-Massillon, OH	CAN-	311,200	311,100	.0	123,700	-13.3
	Canton, OH					93,100	-15.4
	Massillon, OH					30,600	-5.8
94	Fort Wayne, IN	FTWA	307,700	292,500	5.2	172,300	-3.4
95	Colorado Springs, CO	CSPG	303,500	230,600	31.6	214,800	58.5
96	Shreveport, LA-TX	SHRE	299,000	266,500	12.2	205,800	13.0
97	Jackson, MS	JAC	295,000	238,800	23.5	202,900	31.8
98	Stockton, CA	STOC	291,500	241,800	20.6	149,800	36.2
99	Madison, WI	MAD	287,300	259,600	10.7	170,600	-.7
100	Sarasota-Bradenton, FL	SAR-B	284,200	187,800	51.3	79,100	29.2
	Sarasota, FL					48,900	21.6
	Bradenton, FL					30,200	43.8
101	Raleigh, NC	RAL	282,800	216,900	30.4	150,300	22.4
102	Winston-Salem, NC	WNS	278,400	236,700	17.6	138,600	3.7
103	Corpus Christi, TX	CRPX	277,100	243,800	13.7	231,000	13.0
104	Lexington, KY	LEX	262,900	217,900	20.7	204,200	88.9
105	Huntington-Ashland, WV-KY-OH	HNTG-	261,900	248,200	5.5	90,800	-12.3
	Huntington, WV					63,700	-14.3
	Ashland, KY					27,100	-7.2
106	Utica-Rome, NY	UT-R	259,900	281,800	-7.8	119,400	-15.6
	Utica, NY					75,600	-17.3
	Rome, NY					43,800	-12.6
107	Charleston, WV	CHAS	249,300	238,800	4.4	64,000	-10.5
108	Rockford, IL	RKFD	247,500	244,900	1.1	139,700	-5.2
109	New London-Norwich, CT-RI	N. LON-	244,600	237,600	2.9	66,900	-8.7
	New London, CT					28,800	-8.9
	Norwich, CT					38,100	-8.6
110	Binghamton, NY-PA	BING	240,500	248,600	-3.3	55,900	-12.8
111	Augusta, GA-SC	AUG	238,200	209,500	13.7	47,500	-20.7
112	Erie, PA	ERIE	237,300	228,100	4.0	119,100	-7.9
113	Fayetteville, NC	FAY	236,200	202,700	16.5	59,500	11.2
114	Macon-, GA	MAC-	235,900	209,700	12.5	156,800	.6
	Macon, GA					116,900	-4.5
	Warner Robins, GA					39,900	19.1
115	Columbus, GA-AL	COL	235,100	231,600	1.5	169,400	1.7
116	Bakersfield, CA	BAK	231,700	187,600	23.5	105,700	52.1
117	Poughkeepsie, NY	POK	231,200	205,300	12.6	29,800	-6.9
118	Evansville, IN-KY	EV	230,400	214,100	7.6	130,500	-6.0
119	Pensacola, FL	PENS	229,200	199,000	15.2	57,600	-3.2
120	Portland, ME	POR	225,200	203,500	10.7	61,600	-5.4
121	Kalamazoo, MI	KZOO	223,600	208,800	7.1	79,700	-6.9
122	Montgomery, AL	MTGY	223,600	183,400	21.9	177,900	33.4
123	Ogden, UT	OGD	221,700	175,500	26.3	64,400	-7.3
124	York, PA	YORK	220,000	199,100	10.5	44,600	-11.3
125	Eugene, OR	EUG	216,900	171,400	26.5	105,700	33.8
126	Provo, UT	PRVO	214,400	133,500	60.6	74,100	39.5
127	Oceanside-Vista, CA	OC-V	214,100	130,900	63.6	112,500	72.5
	Oceanside, CA					76,700	89.4
	Vista, CA					35,800	44.9
128	Waterbury, CT	WATB	213,900	204,100	4.8	103,300	-4.4
129	Reading, PA	READ	213,500	212,400	.5	78,700	-10.2
130	Roanoke, VA	ROAN	213,300	190,500	12.0	100,200	8.8
131	Savannah, GA	SAV	210,400	192,900	9.1	141,700	19.8
132	Lancaster, PA	LANC	209,700	189,200	10.8	54,700	-5.2
133	Huntsville, AL	HNTS	203,800	193,000	5.6	142,500	2.3
134	Durham-Chapel Hill, NC	DUR-	203,100	170,000	19.5	132,900	9.3
	Durham, NC					100,500	5.3
	Chapel Hill, NC					32,400	23.7

Populations of United States Cities, Towns, Counties, and States

This table lists alphabetically by state populations for approximately 20,000 places in the United States. Most populations are from the 1980 census. The populations given for unincorporated places, not available from the 1980 census, are Rand McNally estimates or 1970 census figures. These population figures are identified by a circle (○).

Populations followed by a triangle (▲) represent township or New England "town" populations. These "town" populations usually include a central village of the same name, as well as other nearby communities and surrounding rural areas.

If a place is within a metropolitan area, the name of the Ranally Metropolitan Area (RMA) is designated in an abbreviated form after the place-name. Each RMA includes one or more central cities, as well as socially and economically integrated surrounding areas. The central city for each RMA is identified by the use of CAPITAL LETTERS.

ALABAMA

1980 Census 3,893,978

CITIES

Abbeville . . . 3,155
Adamsville BIR . . . 2,498
Addison . . . 746
Akron . . . 604
Alabaster BIR . . . 9,885
Albertville . . . 12,039
Aldrich . . . 600 ○
Alexander City . . . 13,807
Aliceville . . . 3,207
Altoona . . . 928
Andalusia . . . 10,415
ANNISTON ANNI . . . 29,523
Arab . . . 5,967
Ardmore . . . 1,096
Ariton . . . 844
Ashford DOTH . . . 2,165
Ashland . . . 2,052
Ashville . . . 1,489
Athens HNTS . . . 14,558
Atmore . . . 8,789
Attalla GAD . . . 7,737
Auburn OP-AU . . . 28,471
Autaugaville . . . 843
Axis . . . 600 ○
Babbie . . . 553
Bay Minette . . . 7,455
Bayou La Batre . . . 2,005
Bayview BIR . . . 830 ○
Beatrice . . . 558
Bellamy . . . 750 ○
Berry . . . 916
Bessemer BIR . . . 31,729
BIRMINGHAM BIR . . . 286,799
Blountsville . . . 1,509
Bluff Park BIR . . . 12,000 ○
Boaz . . . 7,151
Bon Secour . . . 600 ○
Brantley . . . 1,151
Brent . . . 2,862
Brewton . . . 6,680
Bridgeport . . . 2,974
Brighton BIR . . . 5,308
Brilliant . . . 871
Brookside BIR . . . 1,409
Brookwood . . . 492
Brundidge . . . 3,213
Butler . . . 1,882
Cahaba Heights BIR . . . 3,800 ○
Calera . . . 2,035
Calvert . . . 500 ○
Camden . . . 2,406
Camp Hill . . . 1,628
Carbon Hill . . . 2,452
Carrollton . . . 1,104
Castleberry . . . 847
Cedar Bluff . . . 1,129
Center Point BIR . . . 23,317
Centre . . . 2,351
Centreville . . . 2,504
Chatom . . . 1,122
Chelsea . . . 600 ○
Cherokee . . . 1,589
Chickasaw MOB . . . 7,402
Childersburg . . . 5,084
Citronelle . . . 2,841
Clanton . . . 5,832
Clayhatchee . . . 560
Clayton . . . 1,589
Cleveland . . . 487
Clio . . . 1,224
Coaling . . . 500 ○
Coden . . . 500 ○
Coffeeville . . . 448
Colbert Heights FLO- . . . 500 ○
Collinsville . . . 1,383
Columbia . . . 881
Columbiana . . . 2,655
Coosada MTGY . . . 980
Cordova . . . 3,123
Cottondale TUSC . . . 2,300 ○
Cottonwood . . . 1,352
Courtland . . . 456
Creola . . . 1,652
Crossville . . . 1,222
Cuba . . . 486
Cullman . . . 13,084
Dadeville . . . 3,263
Daleville . . . 4,250
Daphne MOB . . . 3,406
De Armanville ANNI . . . 450 ○
DECATUR DEC . . . 42,002
Demopolis . . . 7,678
Dixiana BIR . . . 600 ○
Docena BIR . . . 1,140 ○
Dolomite BIR . . . 2,400 ○
Dora BIR . . . 2,327
DOTHAN DOTH . . . 48,750
Double Springs . . . 1,057
Dozier . . . 494
East Brewton . . . 3,012
Eclectic . . . 1,124
Edgewater BIR . . . 1,400 ○
Elba . . . 4,355
Elberta . . . 491
Enterprise . . . 18,033
Eufaula . . . 12,097
Eulaton ANNI . . . 1,869
Eutaw . . . 2,444
Evergreen . . . 4,171
Fairfield BIR . . . 13,242
Fairhope MOB . . . 7,286
Falkville . . . 1,310
Fayette . . . 5,287
Flint City DEC . . . 673
Flomaton . . . 1,882
Florala . . . 2,165
FLORENCE FLO- . . . 37,029
Foley . . . 4,003
Fort Deposit . . . 1,519
Fort Payne . . . 11,485
Frisco City . . . 1,424
Fulton . . . 606
Fultondale BIR . . . 6,217
Fyffe . . . 1,305
GADSDEN GAD . . . 47,565
Gallant . . . 550 ○
Garden City . . . 655
Gardendale BIR . . . 8,495
Geneva . . . 4,866
Georgiana . . . 1,993
Geraldine . . . 911
Glencoe GAD . . . 4,648
Goodwater . . . 1,895
Gordo . . . 2,112
Grand Bay PSCG . . . 3,185
Grant . . . 632
Graysville BIR . . . 2,642
Greenhill . . . 550 ○
Green Pond . . . 500 ○
Greensboro . . . 3,248
Greenville . . . 7,807
Grove Hill . . . 1,912
Guin . . . 2,418
Gulf Shores . . . 1,349
Guntersville . . . 7,041
Gurley . . . 735
Hackleburg . . . 883
Haleyville . . . 5,306
Hamilton . . . 5,093
Hanceville . . . 2,220
Harpersville . . . 934
Hartford . . . 2,647
Hartselle . . . 8,858
Hayneville . . . 864
Hazel Green . . . 1,503
Headland . . . 3,327
Heflin ANNI . . . 3,014
Helena BIR . . . 2,130
Hokes Bluff GAD . . . 3,216
Holly Pond . . . 493
Hollywood . . . 1,110
Holt TUSC . . . 4,300 ○
Homewood BIR . . . 21,412
Hoover BIR . . . 19,792
Hueytown BIR . . . 14,585
Huguley . . . 2,947
HUNTSVILLE HNTS . . . 142,513
Hurtsboro . . . 752
Irondale BIR . . . 6,510
Irvington MOB . . . 450 ○
Jackson . . . 6,073
Jacksonville ANNI . . . 9,735
Jasper . . . 11,894
Jemison . . . 1,828
Kennedy . . . 604
Kent . . . 500 ○
Ketona BIR . . . 600 ○
Killen FLO- . . . 747
Kimberly BIR . . . 1,043
Kinsey DOTH . . . 1,239
Kinston . . . 604
Lafayette . . . 3,647
Lanett . . . 6,897
Leeds BIR . . . 8,638
Leighton FLO- . . . 1,218
Lexington . . . 884
Lillian . . . 600 ○
Lincoln . . . 2,081
Linden . . . 2,773
Lineville . . . 2,257
Lipscomb BIR . . . 3,741
Lisman . . . 638
Littleville FLO- . . . 1,262
Livingston . . . 3,187
Lockhart . . . 547
Louisville . . . 791
Loxley . . . 804
Luverne . . . 2,639
Lynn . . . 554
McCalla BIR . . . 500 ○
McKenzie . . . 605
Madison HNTS . . . 4,057
Madison MTGY . . . 500 ○
Malvern . . . 558
Maplesville . . . 754
Margaret . . . 757
Marion . . . 4,467
Mentone . . . 476
Meridianville HNTS . . . 1,403
Midfield BIR . . . 6,203
Midland City DOTH . . . 1,903
Midway . . . 593
Millbrook MTGY . . . 3,101
Millport . . . 1,287
Millry . . . 956
MOBILE MOB . . . 200,452
Monroeville . . . 5,674
Montevallo . . . 3,965
MONTGOMERY MTGY . . . 177,857
Montrose MOB . . . 1,200 ○
Morris BIR . . . 623
Moulton . . . 3,197
Moundville . . . 1,310
Mountain Brook BIR . . . 19,718
Mount Olive BIR . . . 1,900 ○
Mount Vernon . . . 1,038
Munford ANNI . . . 600 ○
Muscle Shoals FLO- . . . 8,911
New Brockton . . . 1,392
New Castle BIR . . . 1,000 ○
New Hope HNTS . . . 1,546
New Market . . . 550 ○
Newton . . . 1,540
Newville . . . 814
Normal HNTS . . . 5,000 ○
Northport TUSC . . . 14,291
Notasulga . . . 876
Oakman . . . 770
Odenville . . . 724
Ohatchee . . . 860
Oneonta . . . 4,824
OPELIKA OP-AU . . . 21,896
Opp . . . 7,204
Owens Cross Roads HNTS . . . 804
Oxford ANNI . . . 8,939
Ozark . . . 13,188
Parrish . . . 1,583
Pelham BIR . . . 6,759
Pell City . . . 6,616
Perdido . . . 1,100 ○
Peterman . . . 500 ○
Peterson TUSC . . . 550 ○
Petersville FLO- . . . 2,000 ○
Phenix City COL . . . 26,928
Phil Campbell . . . 1,549
Piedmont . . . 5,544
Pinckard . . . 771
Pine Hill . . . 510
Pinson BIR . . . 1,600 ○
Pisgah . . . 699
Plantersville . . . 650 ○
Pleasant Grove BIR . . . 7,102
Point Clear MOB . . . 1,812
Prattville MTGY . . . 18,647
Prichard MOB . . . 39,541
Ragland . . . 1,860
Rainbow City GAD . . . 6,299
Rainsville . . . 3,907
Red Bay . . . 3,232
Red Level . . . 504
Reece City GAD . . . 718
Reform . . . 2,245
River Falls . . . 669
Riverside . . . 849
Roanoke . . . 5,896
Robertsdale . . . 2,306
Rockford . . . 494
Rogersville . . . 1,224
Russellville . . . 8,195
Rutledge . . . 496
St. Bernard . . . 600 ○
St. Elmo MOB . . . 450 ○
Samson . . . 2,402
Saraland MOB . . . 10,308
Satsuma MOB . . . 3,822
Sayreton BIR . . . 550 ○
Scottsboro . . . 14,758
Section . . . 821
Selma . . . 26,684
Semmes MOB . . . 1,200 ○
Sheffield FLO- . . . 11,903
Shelby . . . 600 ○
Silverhill . . . 624
Sipsey BIR . . . 678
Slocomb . . . 2,153
Smiths COL . . . 900 ○
Southside GAD . . . 5,141
Spanish Fort MOB . . . 3,415
Springville . . . 1,476
Spruce Pine . . . 600 ○
Stapleton . . . 900 ○
Steele . . . 795
Stevenson . . . 2,568
Sulligent . . . 2,130
Sumiton BIR . . . 2,815
Summerdale . . . 546
Sycamore . . . 900 ○
Sylacauga . . . 12,708
Sylvania . . . 1,156
Talladega . . . 19,128
Tallassee . . . 5,583
Tanner HNTS . . . 550 ○
Tarrant City BIR . . . 8,148
Theodore MOB . . . 6,392
Thomaston . . . 679
Thomasville . . . 4,387
Thorsby . . . 1,422
Tillmans Corner MOB . . . 5,000 ○
Town Creek . . . 1,201
Townley . . . 500 ○
Trinity DEC . . . 1,328
Troy . . . 12,945
Trussville BIR . . . 3,507
TUSCALOOSA TUSC . . . 75,211
Tuscumbia FLO- . . . 9,137
Tuskegee . . . 13,327
Underwood . . . 750 ○
Union Springs . . . 4,431
Uniontown . . . 2,112
Valhermoso Springs . . . 550 ○
Valley Head . . . 609
Vernon . . . 2,609
Vestavia Hills BIR . . . 15,722
Vincent . . . 1,652
Vinemont . . . 615
Wadley . . . 532
Walnut Grove . . . 510
Warrior BIR . . . 3,260
Weaver ANNI . . . 2,765
Webb DOTH . . . 448
Wedowee . . . 908
West Blocton . . . 1,147
Wetumpka MTGY . . . 4,341
Whatley . . . 450 ○
Wilmer MOB . . . 581
Wilsonville . . . 914
Wilton . . . 642
Winfield . . . 3,781
York . . . 3,392

COUNTIES

Autauga . . . 32,259
Baldwin . . . 78,556
Barbour . . . 24,756
Bibb . . . 15,723
Blount . . . 36,459
Bullock . . . 10,596
Butler . . . 21,680
Calhoun . . . 119,761
Chambers . . . 39,191
Cherokee . . . 18,760
Chilton . . . 30,612
Choctaw . . . 16,839
Clarke . . . 27,702
Clay . . . 13,703
Cleburne . . . 12,595
Coffee . . . 38,533
Colbert . . . 54,519
Conecuh . . . 15,884
Coosa . . . 11,377
Covington . . . 36,850
Crenshaw . . . 14,110
Cullman . . . 61,642
Dale . . . 47,821
Dallas . . . 53,981
De Kalb . . . 53,658
Elmore . . . 43,390
Escambia . . . 38,440
Etowah . . . 103,057
Fayette . . . 18,809
Franklin . . . 28,350
Geneva . . . 24,253
Greene . . . 11,021
Hale . . . 15,604
Henry . . . 15,302
Houston . . . 74,632
Jackson . . . 51,407
Jefferson . . . 671,324
Lamar . . . 16,453
Lauderdale . . . 80,546
Lawrence . . . 30,170
Lee . . . 76,283
Limestone . . . 46,005
Lowndes . . . 13,253
Macon . . . 26,829
Madison . . . 196,966
Marengo . . . 25,047
Marion . . . 30,041
Marshall . . . 65,622
Mobile . . . 364,980
Monroe . . . 22,651
Montgomery . . . 197,038
Morgan . . . 90,231
Perry . . . 15,012
Pickens . . . 21,481
Pike . . . 28,050
Randolph . . . 20,075
Russell . . . 47,356
St. Clair . . . 41,205
Shelby . . . 66,298
Sumter . . . 16,908
Talladega . . . 73,826
Tallapoosa . . . 38,766
Tuscaloosa . . . 137,541
Walker . . . 68,660
Washington . . . 16,821
Wilcox . . . 14,755
Winston . . . 21,953

ALASKA

1980 Census 401,851

CITIES

Alakanuk . . . 522
ANCHORAGE ANCH . . . 174,431
Anderson . . . 517
Angoon . . . 465
Barrow . . . 2,267
Bethel . . . 3,576
Chevak . . . 466
College FRBK . . . 800 ○
Cordova . . . 1,879
Craig . . . 527
Delta Junction . . . 945
Dillingham . . . 1,563
Emmonak . . . 567
FAIRBANKS FRBK . . . 22,645
Fort Yukon . . . 619
Galena . . . 765
Gambell . . . 445
Glennallen . . . 511
Haines . . . 993
Homer . . . 2,209
Hoonah . . . 680
Hooper Bay . . . 627
Juneau . . . 19,528
Kake . . . 555
Kenai . . . 4,324
Ketchikan . . . 7,198
King Cove . . . 460
King Salmon . . . 545
Kodiak . . . 4,756
Kotzebue . . . 2,054
Kwethluk . . . 454
Metlakatla . . . 1,056
Mountain Village . . . 583
Nenana . . . 470
Nikishka . . . 1,109
Nome . . . 2,301
Noorvik . . . 492
Palmer ANCH . . . 2,141
Petersburg . . . 2,821
Point Hope . . . 464
St. Paul . . . 551
Sand Point . . . 625
Savoonga . . . 491
Seldovia . . . 479
Seward . . . 1,843
Sitka . . . 7,803
Skagway . . . 768
Soldotna . . . 2,320
Sterling . . . 919
Togiak . . . 470
Tok . . . 589
Unalakleet . . . 623
Unalaska . . . 1,322
Valdez . . . 3,079
Wasilla . . . 1,559
Wrangell . . . 2,184
Yakutat . . . 449

ARIZONA

1980 Census 2,718,425

CITIES

Aguila . . . 600 ○
Ajo . . . 5,189
Alpine . . . 500 ○
Apache Junction PHOE . . . 10,013
Arizona Sunsites . . . 900 ○
Ash Fork . . . 600 ○
Avondale PHOE . . . 8,168
Bagdad . . . 2,331
Benson . . . 4,253
Bisbee . . . 7,154
Black Canyon City . . . 600 ○
Bouse . . . 450 ○
Bowie . . . 600 ○
Buckeye . . . 3,434
Bullhead City . . . 5,000 ○
Bylas . . . 1,175
Cameron . . . 500 ○
Camp Verde . . . 1,125
Casa Grande . . . 14,971
Casas Adobes TUC . . . 5,300 ○
Cashion PHOE . . . 3,014
Catalina Foothills TUC . . . 1,500 ○
Cave Creek . . . 1,589
Central Heights . . . 1,500 ○
Chandler PHOE . . . 29,673
Chandler Heights PHOE . . . 750 ○
Chinle . . . 2,815
Chino Valley . . . 2,858
Cibecue . . . 950 ○
Clarkdale . . . 1,512
Claypool . . . 2,362
Clifton . . . 4,245
Colorado City . . . 450 ○
Congress . . . 450 ○
Coolidge . . . 6,851
Cornville . . . 800 ○
Cottonwood . . . 4,550
Crane YUMA . . . 2,400 ○
Dennehotso . . . 500 ○
Douglas . . . 13,058
Dreamland Villa PHOE . . . 3,200 ○
Duncan . . . 603
Eagar . . . 2,791
Ehrenberg . . . 900 ○
El Mirage PHOE . . . 4,307
Eloy . . . 6,240
Flagstaff . . . 34,743
Florence . . . 5,375
Fort Defiance . . . 3,431
Fredonia . . . 1,040
Gadsden . . . 500 ○
Ganado . . . 1,200 ○
Gila Bend . . . 1,585
Gilbert PHOE . . . 5,717
Glendale PHOE . . . 97,172
Globe . . . 6,886
Goodyear PHOE . . . 2,923
Grand Canyon . . . 1,348
Greasewood . . . 450 ○
Green Valley TUC . . . 7,999
Guadalupe PHOE . . . 4,506
Hayden . . . 1,205
Heber . . . 600 ○
Holbrook . . . 5,785
Hotevilla . . . 700 ○
Houck . . . 600 ○
Huachuca City . . . 1,661
Indian Ridge Estates TUC . . . 2,300 ○
Joseph City . . . 900 ○
Kayenta . . . 3,343
Keams Canyon . . . 600 ○
Kearny . . . 2,646
Kingman . . . 9,257
Kykotsmovi Village . . . 600 ○
Lake Havasu City . . . 15,909
Lakeside . . . 1,333
Laveen PHOE . . . 600 ○
Litchfield Park PHOE . . . 3,657
Little Acres . . . 600 ○
Lukachukai . . . 1,049
McNary . . . 1,320
Mammoth . . . 1,906
Many Farms . . . 1,364

○ Rand McNally estimate (not reported in census).
▲ Population of entire township or "town", including rural areas.
● Independent city. Population not included in county total.

ARIZONA continued

Marana 1,674
Maricopa 900 ○
Mayer 950 ○
Mesa PHOE 152,453
Miami 2,716
Moenkopi 900 ○
Mohave Valley 750 ○
Morenci 1,200 ○
Mountainaire 700 ○
Naco 800 ○
NOGALES NOGLS 15,683
Oracle 2,484
Page 4,907
Paradise Valley PHOE 11,711
Parker 2,542
Patagonia 980
Payson 5,068
Peach Springs 600 ○
Peoria PHOE 12,307
PHOENIX PHOE 790,044
Picacho 550 ○
Pima 1,599
Pine 500 ○
Pinetop 1,527
Plantsite 1,500 ○
Polacca 600 ○
Prescott 20,055
Quartzsite 600 ○
Riviera 4,500 ○
Sacaton 1,951
Safford 7,010
Sahuarita 600 ○
St. David 950 ○
St. Johns 3,368
Salome 600 ○
San Carlos 2,668
San Luis 1,946
San Manuel 5,443
Scottsdale PHOE 88,622
Sedona 5,368
Seligman 950 ○
Sells 1,864
Shonto 600 ○
Show Low 4,298
Sierra Vista 24,937
Silver Bell 600 ○
Snowflake 3,510
Somerton 5,761
South Tucson TUC 6,554
Springerville 1,452
Stanfield 900 ○
Stargo 1,038
Sun City PHOE 40,505
Superior 4,600
Surprise PHOE 3,723
Tacna 500 ○
Taylor 1,915
Tempe PHOE 106,920
Thatcher 3,374
Tolleson PHOE 4,433
Tombstone 1,632
Tuba City 5,045
TUCSON TUC 336,503
Twin Knolls PHOE 4,700 ○
Valencia 1,300 ○
Velda Rose Estates PHOE 2,250 ○
Wellton 911
Whiteriver 1,400 ○
Wickenburg 3,535
Willcox 3,243
Williams 2,266
Window Rock 2,230
Winkelman 1,060
Winslow 7,921
Wittmann 700 ○
Yarnell 950 ○
Youngtown PHOE 2,254
YUMA YUMA 43,950

COUNTIES

Apache 52,108
Cochise 85,686
Coconino 75,008
Gila 37,080
Graham 22,862
Greenlee 11,406
La Paz 12,557
Maricopa 1,509,262
Mohave 55,865
Navajo 67,629
Pima 531,443
Pinal 90,918
Santa Cruz 20,459
Yavapai 68,145
Yuma 77,997

ARKANSAS

1980 Census 2,286,419

CITIES

Alma FTSM 2,755
Altheimer 1,231
Altus 441
Amity 859
Arkadelphia 10,168
Arkansas City 668
Ashdown 5,282
Ash Flat 524
Atkins 3,002
Augusta 3,496
Bald Knob 2,756
Barling FTSM 3,761
Batesville 8,263
Bay 1,605
Bearden 1,191
Beebe 3,599
Bella Vista 2,589
Belleville 571
Benton L.R. 17,717
Bentonville 8,756
Berryville 2,966
Biscoe 486
Black Rock 848
Blytheville 23,844
Bonanza 553
Bono 967
Booneville 3,718
Bradford 950
Bradley 790
Brinkley 4,909
Brookland 840
Bryant L.R. 2,682
Bull Shoals 1,312
Cabot L.R. 4,806
Calico Rock 1,046
Calion 638
Camden 15,356
Cammack Village L.R. 920
Caraway 1,165
Carlisle 2,567
Carthage 568
Cave City 1,634
Charleston 1,748
Cherokee Village 3,200 ○
Cherry Valley 729
Clarendon 2,361
Clarksville 5,237
Clinton 1,284
Coal Hill 859
Conway 20,375
Corning 3,650
Cotter 920
Cotton Plant 1,323
Crawfordsville 685
Crossett 6,706
Cushman 556
Danville 1,698
Dardanelle 3,621
Decatur 1,013
De Queen 4,594
Dermott 4,731
Des Arc 2,001
Desha 750 ○
De Valls Bluff 738
De Witt 3,928
Diaz 1,192
Dierks 1,249
Dover 948
Dumas 6,091
Dyer 608
Dyess 446
Earle 3,517
Elaine 991
El Dorado 25,270
Elkins 579
Elm Springs FAY- 781
Emerson 444
Emmet 475
England 3,186
Eudora 3,840
Eureka Springs 1,989
Farmington FAY- 1,283
FAYETTEVILLE FAY- 36,608
Flippin 1,072
Fordyce 5,175
Foreman 1,377
Forrest City 13,803
FORT SMITH FTSM 71,626
Garland City 660
Gassville 859
Gentry 1,468
Gillett 927
Gilmore 503
Glenwood 1,402
Gosnell 3,215
Gould 1,671
Grady 597
Gravette 1,218
Greenbrier 1,423
Green Forest 1,609
Greenland FAY- 622
Greenwood 3,317
Grubbs 546
Gurdon 2,707
Hackett 505
Hamburg 3,394
Hampton 1,627
Hardy 643
Harrisburg 1,921
Harrison 9,567
Hartford 613
Hartman 517
Haskell 1,074
Hazen 1,636
Heber Springs 4,944
Hector 449
Helena 9,598
Hensley 450 ○
Hickory Ridge 478
Holly Grove 754
Hope 10,290
Horatio 989
HOT SPRINGS NATIONAL PARK HTSPR 36,228
Hoxie 2,961
Hughes 1,919
Humnoke 442
Humphrey 872
Huntington 662
Huntsville 1,394
Huttig 976
Imboden 661
Jacksonville L.R. 27,589
Jasper 519
Johnson FAY- 519
Joiner 725
Jonesboro 31,530
Jones Mill 850 ○
Judsonia 2,025
Junction City 813
Keiser 962
Kensett 1,751
Knobel 503
Lake City 1,842
Lake Hamilton HTSPR 1,054
Lakeview 512
Lake Village 3,088
Lamar 708
Lavaca FTSM 1,092
Leachville 1,882
Leola 481
Lepanto 1,964
Leslie 501
Lewisville 1,476
Lexa 500 ○
Lincoln 1,422
LITTLE ROCK L.R. 167,744
Lockesburg 616
London 859
Lonoke 4,128
Lowell FAY- 1,078
Luxora 1,739
Mabelvale L.R. 550 ○
McAlmont L.R. 1,600 ○
McCrory 1,942
McGehee 5,671
McNeil 725
McRae 641
Madison 1,238
Magazine 799
Magnet Cove 500 ○
Magnolia 11,909
Malvern 10,163
Mammoth Spring 1,158
Mandeville 700 ○
Manila 2,553
Mansfield 1,000
Marianna 6,220
Marion MEM 2,996
Marked Tree 3,201
Marmaduke 1,168
Marshall 1,595
Marvell 1,724
Mayflower L.R. 1,381
Melbourne 1,619
Mena 5,154
Mineral Springs 936
Monette 1,186
Monticello 8,958
Montrose 641
Morrilton 7,355
Mountainburg 595
Mountain Home 8,066
Mountain Pine 1,068
Mountain View 2,147
Mount Ida 1,023
Mulberry 1,444
Murfreesboro 1,883
Nashville 4,554
Newark 1,128
Newport 8,339
Norman 539
Norphlet 756
North Crossett 3,513
North Little Rock L.R. 64,388
Ola 1,121
Oppelo 486
Osceola 8,881
Oxford 520
Ozark 3,597
Palestine 976
Pangburn 673
Pankey 450 ○
Paragould 15,248
Paris 3,991
Parkdale 471
Parkin 2,035
Patterson 567
Pea Ridge 1,488
Perryville 1,058
Piggott 3,762
PINE BLUFF PNBLF 56,636
Plainview 752
Plumerville 785
Pocahontas 5,995
Portia 480
Portland 701
Pottsville 564
Prairie Grove 1,708
Prescott 4,103
Quitman 556
Rector 2,336
Redfield 745
Reyno 521
Rison 1,325
Rockport 528
Rogers 18,086
Russellville 15,591
Salem 1,424
Searcy 13,612
Sheridan 3,042
Sherwood L.R. 11,383
Siloam Springs 7,940
Smackover 2,453
Sparkman 622
Springdale FAY- 23,458
Stamps 2,859
Star City 2,066
Stephens 1,366
Strong 785
Stuttgart 10,941
Subiaco 744
Sulphur Springs 496
Summit 506
Sweet Home L.R. 1,100 ○
Swifton 859
Sylvan Hills L.R. 2,900 ○
Taylor 657
TEXARKANA TEXR- 21,459
Thornton 711
Tontitown FAY- 615
Traskwood 459
Trumann 6,395
Tuckerman 2,078
Turrell 1,041
Tyronza 777
Van Buren FTSM 12,020
Vilonia 736
Waldo 1,685
Waldron 2,642
Walnut Ridge 4,152
Ward 981
Warren 7,646
Watson Chapel PNBLF 900 ○
Weiner 750
West Crossett 1,466
West Fork 1,526
West Helena 11,367
West Memphis MEM 28,138
Wheatley 523
White Hall PNBLF 2,680
Wickes 464
Wilmar 747
Wilmot 1,227
Wilson 1,115
Wilton 495
Woodson 600 ○
Wrightsville L.R. 1,400
Wynne 7,805
Yellville 1,044

COUNTIES

Arkansas 24,175
Ashley 26,538
Baxter 27,409
Benton 78,115
Boone 26,067
Bradley 13,803
Calhoun 6,079
Carroll 16,203
Chicot 17,793
Clark 23,326
Clay 20,616
Cleburne 16,909
Cleveland 7,868
Columbia 26,644
Conway 19,505
Craighead 63,239
Crawford 36,892
Crittenden 49,499
Cross 20,434
Dallas 10,515
Desha 19,760
Drew 17,910
Faulkner 46,192
Franklin 14,705
Fulton 9,975
Garland 70,531
Grant 13,008
Greene 30,744
Hempstead 23,635
Hot Spring 26,819
Howard 13,459
Independence 30,147
Izard 10,768
Jackson 21,646
Jefferson 90,718
Johnson 17,423
Lafayette 10,213
Lawrence 18,447
Lee 15,539
Lincoln 13,369
Little River 13,952
Logan 20,144
Lonoke 34,518
Madison 11,373
Marion 11,334
Miller 37,766
Mississippi 59,517
Monroe 14,052
Montgomery 7,771
Nevada 11,097
Newton 7,756
Ouachita 30,541
Perry 7,266
Phillips 34,772
Pike 10,373
Poinsett 27,032
Polk 17,007
Pope 39,021
Prairie 10,140
Pulaski 340,597
Randolph 16,834
St. Francis 30,858
Saline 53,161
Scott 9,685
Searcy 8,847
Sebastian 95,172
Sevier 14,060
Sharp 14,607
Stone 9,022
Union 48,573
Van Buren 13,357
Washington 100,494
White 50,835
Woodruff 11,222
Yell 17,026

CALIFORNIA

1980 Census 23,667,837

CITIES

Acton 900 ○
Adelanto 2,164
Adin 575 ○
Agoura Hills L.A. 600 ○
Ahwahnee 900 ○
Alameda SF-O- 63,852
Albany SF-O- 15,130
Alhambra L.A. 64,767
Alondra L.A. 12,096
Alpaugh 900 ○
Altadena L.A. 40,983
Alturas 3,025
Alum Rock SF-O- 16,890
Anaheim L.A. 219,494
Anderson REDD 7,381
Angels Camp 2,302
ANTIOCH ANT-P 42,683
Apple Valley 14,305
Aptos S.CRZ 7,039
Arbuckle 1,306
Arcade SAC 37,600 ○
Arcadia L.A. 45,993
Arcata EUR 13,838
Arden SAC 52,000 ○
Arnold 2,385
Arroyo Grande 11,290
Artesia L.A. 14,301
Arvin 6,863
Ashland SF-O- 13,893
Atascadero 16,232
Atherton SF-O- 7,797
Atwater MRCD- 17,530
Auberry 1,100 ○
Auburn 7,540
Avalon L.A. 2,022
Avenal 4,137
Avila Beach 600 ○
Avocado Heights L.A. 11,721
Azusa L.A. 29,380
Baker 650 ○
BAKERSFIELD BAK 105,735
Baldwin Park L.A. 50,554
Banning 14,020
Barstow 17,690
Beaumont 6,818
Bell L.A. 25,450
Bellflower L.A. 53,441
Bell Gardens L.A. 34,117
Belmont SF-O- 24,505
Benicia SF-O- 15,376
Berkeley SF-O- 103,328
Beverly Hills L.A. 32,367
Bieber 600 ○
Big Bear City 3,500 ○
Big Creek 700 ○
Biggs 1,413
Big Pine 1,510
Big Sur 520 ○
Biola 800 ○
Bishop 3,333
Bloomington SBDO- 18,888
Blue Lake 1,201
Blythe 6,805
Boonville 1,000 ○
Boron 2,040
Borrego Springs 1,405
Brawley 16,337
Brea L.A. 27,913
Brentwood ANT-P 4,434
Broderick SAC 9,900 ○
Buena Park L.A. 64,165
Burbank L.A. 84,625
Burlingame SF-O- 26,173
Burney 3,187
Buttonwillow 1,350
Byron 900 ○
Calabasas L.A. 900 ○
Calavo Gardens SDGO 6,100 ○
CALEXICO CLEX 14,412
Calipatria 2,636
Calistoga 3,879
Calwa FRES 6,640
Camarillo V-OX 37,797
Cambria 3,061
Cambrian Park SF-O- 4,000 ○
Camino 900 ○
Campbell SF-O- 31,039
Canby 450 ○
Capitola S.CRZ 9,095
Cardiff By The Sea SDGO 10,054
Carlotta 500 ○
Carlsbad OC-V 35,490
Carmel MTRY 4,707
Carmichael SAC 43,108
Carpinteria S.BAR 10,835
Carson L.A. 81,221
Caspar 550 ○
Castella 525 ○
Castle Park SDGO 6,300 ○
Castro Valley SF-O- 44,011
Castroville SLNS 4,396
Cathedral City 11,096
Cedarville 950 ○
Central Valley REDD 3,424
Ceres MOD 13,281
Cerritos L.A. 53,020
Cherryland SF-O- 9,425
Chester 1,756
CHICO CHICO 26,716
Chino L.A. 40,165
Chowchilla 5,122
Chula Vista SDGO 83,927
Citrus Heights SAC 85,911
Claremont L.A. 31,028
Cloverdale 3,989
Clovis FRES 33,021
Coachella 9,129
Coalinga 6,593
Colfax 981
Colton SBDO- 15,201
Columbia 950 ○
Colusa 4,075
Commerce L.A. 10,509
Comptche 555 ○
Compton L.A. 81,230
Concord SF-O- 103,763
Corcoran 6,454
Corning 4,745
Corona L.A. 37,791
Coronado SDGO 18,790
Corte Madera SF-O- 8,074
Costa Mesa L.A. 82,562
Cottonwood REDD 1,553
Coulterville 500 ○
Covelo 1,448
Covina L.A. 38,743
Crescent City 3,075
Crockett SF-O- 2,900 ○
Cucamonga L.A. 55,250
Cudahy L.A. 18,275
Culver City L.A. 38,139
Cupertino SF-O- 37,037
Cypress L.A. 40,391
Daggett 650 ○
Daly City SF-O- 78,427
Danville SF-O- 26,143
Davis 36,640
Del Aire L.A. 3,900 ○
Delano 16,491
Del Mar SDGO 5,017
Desert Hot Springs 5,941
Diamond Bar L.A. 28,045
Diamond Springs 2,287
Dinuba 9,907
Dixon 7,541
Dorris 836
Downey L.A. 82,602
Downieville 950 ○
Doyle 900 ○
Duarte L.A. 16,766
Dublin SF-O- 13,496
Dunsmuir 2,253
Durham CHICO 950 ○

○ Rand McNally estimate (not reported in census).
▲ Population of entire township or "town", including rural areas.
● Independent city. Population not included in county total.

○ Rand McNally estimate (not reported in census).
▲ Population of entire township or "town", including rural areas.
● Independent city. Population not included in county total.

COLORADO continued

El Jebel 900 ○
Englewood DEN 30,021
Erie 1,254
Estes Park 2,703
Evans GRLY 5,063
Evergreen DEN 6,376
Federal Heights DEN 7,846
Firestone 1,204
Flagler 550
Florence 2,987
FORT COLLINS FTCL 65,092
Fort Lupton DEN 4,251
Fort Morgan 8,768
Fountain CSPG 8,324
Fowler 1,227
Fraser 470
Frederick 855
Frisco 1,221
Fruita 2,810
Georgetown 830
Gilcrest 1,025
Glendale DEN 2,496
Glenwood Springs 4,637
Golden DEN 12,237
Granada 557
Granby 963
GRAND JUNCTION GDJC 27,956
GREELEY GRLY 53,006
Green Mountain Falls CSPG 607
Greenwood Village DEN 5,729
Gunnison 5,785
Gypsum 743
Haxtun 1,014
Hayden 1,720
Holly 969
Holyoke 2,092
Hotchkiss 849
Hudson 698
Hugo 776
Idaho Springs 2,077
Ignacio 667
Indian Hills DEN 900 ○
Ivywild CSPG 4,000 ○
Johnstown 1,535
Julesburg 1,528
Keenesburg 541
Kersey 913
Kremmling 1,296
Lafayette DEN 8,985
La Jara 858
La Junta 8,338
Lakewood DEN 113,808
Lamar 7,713
Laporte FTCL 900 ○
La Salle GRLY 1,929
Las Animas 2,818
La Veta 611
Leadville 3,879
Limon 1,805
Lincoln Park 3,426
Littleton DEN 28,631
Log Lane Village 709
Longmont 42,942
Louisville BOUL 5,593
Loveland 30,215
Lyons 1,137
Manassa 945
Mancos 870
Manitou Springs CSPG 4,475
Manzanola 459
Meeker 2,356
Milliken 1,506
Minturn 1,060
Monte Vista 3,902
Montrose 8,722
Monument CSPG 690
Morrison DEN 478
Mountain View DEN 584
Mountain View FTCL 1,693 ○
Naturita 819
Nederland 1,212
New Castle 563
Niwot BOUL 500 ○
Northglenn DEN 29,847
North La Junta 1,076
Norwood 478
Nucla 1,027
Oak Creek 929
Olathe 1,262
Orchard City 1,914
Orchard Mesa GDJC 4,876
Ordway 1,135
Otis 534
Ouray 684
Pagosa Springs 1,331
Palisade 1,551
Palmer Lake CSPG 1,130
Paonia 1,425
Perl-Mack DEN 6,002
Pierce 878
Platteville 1,662
Pleasant View DEN 4,500 ○
PUEBLO PUEB 101,686
Rangely 2,113
Rifle 3,215
Rocky Ford 4,804
Saguache 656
Salida 4,870
Sanford 687
San Luis 842
Security CSPG 11,000 ○
Sheridan DEN 5,377
Sherrelwood DEN 11,450 ○
Silt 923
Silverton 794
Simla 494
Skyway CSPG 3,600 ○
Southglenn DEN 3,800 ○
Southwood DEN 2,600 ○
Springfield 1,657
Steamboat Springs 5,098
Sterling 11,385
Stratton 705
Stratton Meadows CSPG 6,223 ○
Swink 668
Telluride 1,047
Thornton DEN 40,343
Trinidad 9,663
Uravan 800 ○
USAF Academy CSPG 8,655
Vail 3,553
Walden 947
Walsenburg 3,945
Walsh 884
Wellington 1,215
Western Hills DEN 6,000 ○
Westminster DEN 50,211
Wheat Ridge DEN 30,293
Widefield CSPG 7,500 ○
Wiggins 531
Windsor 4,277
Winter Park 480
Woodland Acres 800 ○
Woodland Park 2,634
Wray 2,131
Yampa 472
Yuma 2,824

COUNTIES

Adams 245,944
Alamosa 11,799
Arapahoe 293,621
Archuleta 3,664
Baca 5,419
Bent 5,945
Boulder 189,625
Chaffee 13,227
Cheyenne 2,153
Clear Creek 7,308
Conejos 7,794
Costilla 3,071
Crowley 2,988
Custer 1,528
Delta 21,225
Denver 492,365
Dolores 1,658
Douglas 25,153
Eagle 13,320
Elbert 6,850
El Paso 309,424
Fremont 28,676
Garfield 22,514
Gilpin 2,441
Grand 7,475
Gunnison 10,689
Hinsdale 408
Huerfano 6,440
Jackson 1,863
Jefferson 371,753
Kiowa 1,936
Kit Carson 7,599
Lake 8,830
La Plata 27,195
Larimer 149,184
Las Animas 14,897
Lincoln 4,663
Logan 19,800
Mesa 81,530
Mineral 804
Moffat 13,133
Montezuma 16,510
Montrose 24,352
Morgan 22,513
Otero 22,567
Ouray 1,925
Park 5,333
Phillips 4,542
Pitkin 10,338
Prowers 13,070
Pueblo 125,972
Rio Blanco 6,255
Rio Grande 10,511
Routt 13,404
Saguache 3,935
San Juan 833
San Miguel 3,192
Sedgwick 3,266
Summit 8,848
Teller 8,034
Washington 5,304
Weld 123,438
Yuma 9,682

CONNECTICUT

1980 Census 3,107,576

CITIES

Abington 500 ○
Addison H-NB 1,100 ○
Ansonia BRDG 19,039
Attawaugan 450 ○
Avon H-NB 11,201 ▲ 1,434
Bakersville H-NB 450 ○
Ballouville 500 ○
Baltic N.LON- 1,500 ○
Bantam TORR 860
Beacon Falls WATB 3,995 ▲ 1,500 ○
Bel Aire Estates N.LON- 900 ○
Berlin H-NB 15,121 ▲ 2,000 ○
Bethany N.HAV- 4,330 ▲ 890 ○
Bethel DANB 8,755
Bethlehem WATB 2,573 ▲ 1,762
Black Point Beach Club N.LON- 500 ○
Bloomfield H-NB 18,608 ▲ 7,400 ○
Blue Hills H-NB 6,600 ○
Branford N.HAV- 23,363 ▲ 5,438
Branford Hills N.HAV- 2,200 ○
Branford Point N.HAV- 700 ○
BRIDGEPORT BRDG 142,546
Bristol H-NB 57,370
Broad Brook H-NB 1,548 ○
Brookfield DANB 12,872 ▲ 1,000 ○
Brookfield Center DANB 900 ○
Brooklyn 5,691 ▲ 900 ○
Canaan 1,160
Candlewood Isle DANB 750 ○
Candlewood Shores DANB 1,950 ○
Cannondale N.Y. 1,300 ○
Canton H-NB 7,635 ▲ 1,680
Centerbrook 900 ○
Central Village 1,200 ○
Cheshire N.HAV- 21,788 ▲ 5,722
Chester 3,068 ▲ 1,388
Clinton N.HAV- 11,195
Colchester H-NB 7,761 ▲ 3,190
Collinsville H-NB 2,555
Coventry H-NB 8,895 ▲ 3,769
Cromwell H-NB 10,100 ○
Crystal Lake H-NB 500 ○
DANBURY DANB 60,470
Danielson 4,553
Darien N.Y. 18,892
Dayville 1,100 ○
Deep River 3,994 ▲ 2,495
Derby BRDG 12,346
Durham H-NB 5,143 ▲ 2,641
Eagleville H-NB 450 ○
East Berlin H-NB 900 ○
East Brooklyn 1,251
East Canaan 800 ○
Eastford 1,028 ▲ 500 ○
East Granby H-NB 4,102 ▲ 500 ○
East Haddam 5,621 ▲ 600 ○
East Hampton H-NB 8,572 ▲ 2,152
East Hartford H-NB 52,563
East Hartland 700 ○
East Haven N.HAV- 25,036
East Lyme N.LON- 13,870 ▲ 700 ○
East River N.HAV- 1,800 ○
East Windsor H-NB 1,850 ○
Ellington H-NB 9,711 ▲ 1,000 ○
Enfield H-NB 42,695 ▲ 8,151
Essex 5,078 ▲ 2,501
Fairfield BRDG 54,849
Fall Mountain Lake H-NB 730 ○
Falls Village 500 ○
Farmington H-NB 16,407 ▲ 2,000 ○
Field Crest Estates N.LON- 1,200 ○
Fitchville N.LON- 600 ○
Gales Ferry N.LON- 1,191
Georgetown N.Y. 1,834
Giants Neck N.LON- 1,150 ○
Glastonbury H-NB 24,327 ▲ 7,049
Goshen 1,706 ▲ 450 ○
Granby H-NB 7,956 ▲ 1,192
Green Manorville H-NB 3,250 ○
Greenwich N.Y. 59,565
Grosvenor Dale 700 ○
Groton N.LON- 41,062 ▲ 10,086
Groton Long Point N.LON- 800 ○
Guilford N.HAV- 17,375 ▲ 2,555
Haddam H-NB 6,383 ▲ 600 ○
Hadlyme 450 ○
Hamden N.HAV- 51,071
HARTFORD H-NB 136,392
Harwinton TORR 4,889 ▲ 3,293
Hazardville H-NB 5,436
Hebron H-NB 5,453 ▲ 500 ○
Heritage Village WATB 5,200 ○
Higganum H-NB 1,660
Hitchcock Lake WATB 1,600 ○
Honeypot Glen N.HAV- 900 ○
Huckleberry Hill H-NB 700 ○
Indian Neck N.HAV- 2,200 ○
Ivoryton 950 ○
Jewett City N.LON- 3,294
Kensington H-NB 7,502
Kent 2,505 ▲ 500 ○
Lake Beseck H-NB 500 ○
Lakeside WATB 900 ○
Lakeville 1,200 ○
Leffingwell N.LON- 450 ○
Litchfield TORR 7,605 ▲ 1,489
Lords Point N.LON- 460 ○
Lyme N.LON- 500 ○
Madison N.HAV- 14,031 ▲ 2,069
Manchester H-NB 49,761
Mansfield Center H-NB 1,043
Marion H-NB 800 ○
Marlborough H-NB 4,746 ▲ 1,039
Meriden N.HAV- 57,118
Middlebury WATB 5,995 ▲ 3,900 ○
Middlefield H-NB 3,796 ▲ 600 ○
Middle Haddam H-NB 500 ○
Middletown H-NB 39,040
Milford BRDG 49,101
Milldale H-NB 1,100 ○
Monroe BRDG 14,010 ▲ 760 ○
Monroe Center BRDG 6,950 ○
Montville N.LON- 16,455 ▲ 1,711
Moodus H-NB 1,179
Moosup 3,308
Mystic N.LON- 2,333
Naugatuck WATB 26,456
Nautilus Park N.LON- 6,500 ○
New Britain H-NB 73,840
New Canaan N.Y. 17,931
New Fairfield
DANB 11,260 ▲ 2,150 ○
New Hartford H-NB 4,884 ▲ 1,310
NEW HAVEN N.HAV- 126,101
Newington H-NB 28,841
NEW LONDON N.LON- 28,842
New Milford DANB 19,420 ▲ 5,186
New Preston 1,209
Newtown DANB 19,107 ▲ 2,022
Niantic N.LON- 3,151
Noank N.LON- 1,406
Norfolk 2,156 ▲ 1,500 ○
North Branford
N.HAV- 11,554 ▲ 5,200 ○
Northfield TORR 600 ○
Northford N.HAV- 2,800 ○
North Grosvenor Dale 1,856
North Haven N.HAV- 22,080
North Windham H-NB 750 ○
Norwalk N.Y. 77,767
Norwich N.LON- 38,074
Oakville WATB 8,737
Old Mystic N.LON- 500 ○
Old Saybrook 9,287 ▲ 1,857
Oneco 500 ○
Orange N.HAV- 13,237
Oxford BRDG 6,634 ▲ 900 ○
Pawcatuck N.LON- 5,216
Pequabuck H-NB 1,400 ○
Pine Bridge WATB 870 ○
Pine Orchard N.HAV- 1,500 ○
Plainfield 12,774 ▲ 2,799
Plainville H-NB 16,401
Plantsville H-NB 5,700 ○
Pleasure Beach N.LON- 1,356
Plymouth WATB 10,732 ▲ 1,000 ○
Pomfret 2,775 ▲ 500 ○
Poquonock H-NB 900 ○
Poquonock Bridge N.LON- 2,549
Portland H-NB 8,383
Prospect WATB 6,807
Putnam 8,580 ▲ 6,855
Quaker Hill N.LON- 2,052
Quinebaug 1,088
Redding N.Y. 7,272 ▲ 800 ○
Ridgefield N.Y. 20,120 ▲ 6,066
Rockfall H-NB 500 ○
Rocky Hill H-NB 14,559
Rogers 500 ○
Salisbury 3,896 ▲ 900 ○
Sandy Hook DANB 950 ○
Saybrook Manor 1,140
Seymour BRDG 13,434
Sharon 2,623 ▲ 900 ○
Shelton BRDG 31,314
Sherwood Manor H-NB 6,303
Short Beach N.HAV- 1,200 ○
Simsbury H-NB 21,161 ▲ 5,488
Somers H-NB 8,473 ▲ 1,643
Somersville H-NB 750 ○
Southbury WATB 14,156 ▲ 900 ○
South Glastonbury H-NB 1,600 ○
Southington H-NB 36,879 ▲ 17,400 ○
South Windham H-NB 1,399
South Windsor
H-NB 17,198 ▲ 10,200 ○
Southwood Acres H-NB 9,779
South Woodstock 1,319
Stafford H-NB 9,268 ▲ 500 ○
Stafford Springs H-NB 3,392
Staffordville H-NB 600 ○
Stamford N.Y. 102,466
Stevenson BRDG 450 ○
Stonington N.LON- 16,220 ▲ 1,228
Stony Creek N.HAV- 700 ○
Storrs H-NB 11,394
Stratford BRDG 50,541
Suffield H-NB 9,294 ▲ 1,122
Tariffville H-NB 1,324
Terryville H-NB 5,234
Thomaston WATB 6,276 ▲ 3,500 ○
Thompson 8,141 ▲ 500 ○
Tolland H-NB 9,694 ▲ 500 ○
TORRINGTON TORR 30,987
Trumbull BRDG 32,989
Uncasville N.LON- 1,597
Unionville H-NB 4,900 ○
Vernon H-NB 27,974
Wallingford N.HAV- 37,274
Washington 3,657 ▲ 600 ○
Washington Depot 600 ○
WATERBURY WATB 103,266
Waterford N.LON- 17,843 ▲ 2,736
Watertown WATB 19,489 ▲ 6,000 ○
Wauregan 900 ○
Weatogue H-NB 2,249
Wequetequock N.LON- 800 ○
Westbrook 5,216 ▲ 2,035
West Goshen 600 ○
West Granby H-NB 600 ○
West Hartford H-NB 61,301
West Haven N.HAV- 53,184
West Mystic N.LON- 3,364
Weston N.Y. 8,284 ▲ 1,200 ○
Westport N.Y. 25,290
West Simsbury H-NB 2,140
West Stafford H-NB 450 ○
West Suffield H-NB 500 ○
Wethersfield H-NB 26,013
Whitacres H-NB 2,500 ○
Willimantic H-NB 14,650 ○
Wilton N.Y. 15,351 ▲ 6,500 ○
Windham H-NB 21,062 ▲ 700 ○
Windsor H-NB 25,204 ▲ 17,517
Windsor Locks H-NB 12,190
Winsted 8,092
Wolcott WATB 13,008 ▲ 5,500 ○
Woodbridge N.HAV- 7,600 ○
Woodbury WATB 6,942 ▲ 1,290
Woodmont BRDG 1,797

COUNTIES

Fairfield 807,143
Hartford 807,766
Litchfield 156,769
Middlesex 129,017
New Haven 761,337
New London 238,409
Tolland 114,823
Windham 92,312

DELAWARE

1980 Census 594,317

CITIES

Arden PHIL- 516
Bear PHIL- 950 ○
Bellefonte PHIL- 1,279
Belvidere PHIL- 1,100 ○
Birchwood Park PHIL- 1,500 ○
Blades 664
Briar Park DOVR 600 ○
Bridgeville 1,238
Brookside PHIL- 15,255
Camden DOVR 1,757
Canterbury DOVR 500 ○
Capitol Park DOVR 900 ○
Carrcroft PHIL- 800 ○
Castle Hills PHIL- 1,950 ○
Chalfonte PHIL- 2,200 ○
Chelsea Estates PHIL- 1,500 ○
Chestnut Hill Estates PHIL- 2,000 ○
Christiana PHIL- 500 ○
Clarksville 450 ○
Claymont PHIL- 10,022
Clayton DOVR 1,216
Cleland Heights PHIL- 1,500 ○
Collins Park PHIL- 2,850 ○
Delaware City PHIL- 1,858
Delmar SLSB 948
DOVER DOVR 23,507
Dunleith PHIL- 2,700 ○
Du Ross Heights PHIL- 600 ○
Edgemoor PHIL- 7,397
Elsmere PHIL- 6,493
Fairfax PHIL- 2,850 ○
Felton DOVR 547
Frankford 828
Frederica DOVR 864
Garfield Park PHIL- 1,000 ○
Georgetown 1,710
Graylyn Crest PHIL- 5,000 ○
Greenwood 578
Gwinhurst PHIL- 1,400 ○
Harmony Hills PHIL- 1,350 ○
Harrington 2,405
Hockessin PHIL- 950 ○
Holloway Terrace PHIL- 1,000 ○
Jefferson Farms PHIL- 2,400 ○
Kent Acres DOVR 900 ○
Laurel 3,052
Leedom Estates PHIL- 1,300 ○
Lewes 2,197
Lincoln 500 ○
Manor Park Apartments PHIL- 800 ○
Marshallton PHIL- 3,950 ○
Meadowood PHIL- 2,260 ○
Middletown 2,946
Midway 500 ○
Milford 5,366
Millsboro 1,233
Milton 1,359
Minquadale PHIL- 1,700 ○
Newark PHIL- 25,247
New Castle PHIL- 4,907
Newkirk Estates PHIL- 600 ○
Newport PHIL- 1,167
Ocean View 495
Penn Acres PHIL- 1,950 ○
Penny Hill PHIL- 700 ○
Rambleton Acres PHIL- 1,500 ○
Rehoboth Beach 1,730
Rodney Village DOVR 1,100 ○
St. Georges PHIL- 500 ○
Seaford 5,256
Selbyville 1,251
Silview PHIL- 1,650 ○
Smyrna DOVR 4,750
Stanton PHIL- 5,495
Stratford PHIL- 2,100 ○
Swanwyck Estates PHIL- 1,700 ○
Talleyville PHIL- 6,880
Todd Estates PHIL- 2,050 ○
Willow Run PHIL- 1,950 ○
Wilmington PHIL- 70,195
Wilmington Manor PHIL- 2,000 ○
Wilmington Manor Gardens
PHIL- 1,600 ○
Windy Hills PHIL- 1,300 ○
Wyoming DOVR 960
Yorklyn PHIL- 600 ○

COUNTIES

Kent 98,219
New Castle 398,115
Sussex 97,983

DISTRICT OF COLUMBIA

1980 Census 638,432

CITIES

WASHINGTON WASH 638,432

FLORIDA

1980 Census 9,746,421

CITIES

Alachua 3,561
Alford 548
Altamonte Springs ORL 22,028
Altha 478
Altoona 1,300 ○
Alva 1,200 ○
Anna Maria SAR-B 1,537
Anthony 1,200 ○
Apalachicola 2,565
Apopka ORL 6,019
Arcadia 6,002
Archer 1,230
Astor 950 ○
Atlantic Beach JAX 7,847
Atlantis WPB 1,325
Auburndale WNHV 6,501
Avon Park 8,026
Azalea Park ORL 8,301
Babson Park 950 ○
Bagdad 1,479
Baker 600 ○
Baldwin JAX 1,526
Balm 600 ○
Bartow 14,780
Baskin ST.PET- 800 ○
Bayou George PNCY 1,500 ○
Bayshore Gardens SAR-B 14,945
Bee Ridge SAR-B 3,313
Bellair JAX 5,200 ○
Belle Glade 16,535
Belle Isle ORL 2,848
Belleview 1,913
Biscayne Gardens MIA- 13,000 ○
Biscayne Park MIA- 3,088
Blountstown 2,632
Boca Grande 1,200 ○
Boca Raton MIA- 49,447
Bokeelia 900 ○
Bonifay 2,534
Bonita Springs 3,400 ○
Bostwick 500 ○
Bowling Green 2,310

○ Rand McNally estimate (not reported in census).
▲ Population of entire township or "town", including rural areas.
● Independent city. Population not included in county total.

Boynton Beach 35,624
Bradenton SAR-B 30,228
Bradley 1,108
Brandon TAM 29,100 ○
Branford 622
Bratt 550 ○
Brent PENS 4,500 ○
Bristol 1,044
Broadview Park MIA- 6,022
Bronson 853
Brooksville 5,582
Browardale MIA- 7,409
Brownsville MIA- 18,058
Bryant 500 ○
Buena Vista 3,000 ○
Bunche Park MIA- 4,000 ○
Bunnell 1,816
Bushnell 983
Callahan 869
Callaway PNCY 7,154
Campbell 2,941
Canal Point 950 ○
Candler 500 ○
Cantonment PENS 3,200 ○
Cape Canaveral COCO 5,733
Cape Coral 32,103
Captiva 1,200 ○
Carol City MIA- 47,349
Carrabelle 1,304
Carver Ranch Estates MIA- 5,600 ○
Caryville 633
Casselberry ORL 15,247
Cedar Key 700
Center Hill 751
Century 1,805
Charlotte Harbor 2,084
Chattahoochee 5,332
Chiefland 1,986
Chipley 3,330
Christmas 1,200 ○
Citra 1,500 ○
City Of Sunrise MIA- 39,681
Clair-Mel City TAM 7,000 ○
Clearwater ST.PET- 85,528
Clermont 5,461
Clewiston 5,219
COCOA COCO 16,096
Cocoa Beach COCO 10,926
Cocoa West COCO 6,432
Coconut Creek MIA- 6,288
Coleman 1,022
Conway ORL 16,000 ○
Cooper City MIA- 10,140
Copeland 700 ○
Coral Gables MIA- 43,241
Cortez SAR-B 1,450 ○
Cottondale 1,056
Crawfordville 1,110
Crescent City SAR-B 1,722
Cresthaven MIA- 2,400 ○
Crestview 7,617
Cross City 2,154
Crystal Beach ST.PET- 1,450 ○
Crystal Lake LKLD 6,827
Crystal River 2,778
Crystal Springs 800 ○
Cutler Ridge MIA- 20,886
Cypress Quarters 1,479
Dade City 4,923
Dania MIA- 11,796
Davenport 1,509
Davie MIA- 28,963
DAYTONA BEACH D.BCH 54,176
De Bary 4,980
Deerfield Beach MIA- 39,193
De Funiak Springs 5,563
De Land 15,354
De Leon Springs 1,669
Delray Beach 34,468
Deltona 14,000 ○
Destin FTWL 3,672
Doctors Inlet JAX 600 ○
Dover TAM 2,354
Dundee 2,227
Dunedin ST.PET- 30,203
Dunnellon 1,427
East Naples 9,000 ○
East Palatka 1,613
Eastpoint 1,246
Edgewater 6,726
Ellenton SAR-B 1,561
Eloise WNHV 1,408
El Portal MIA- 2,055
Elwood Park 500 ○
Englewood 9,633
Ensley PENS 3,850 ○
Estero 950 ○
Eustis 9,453
Fairbanks 500 ○
Fairview Shores ORL 6,100 ○
Fellsmere 1,161
Fernandina Beach 7,224
Flagler Beach 2,208
Florahome 600 ○
Floral City 1,181
Florida City MIA- 6,174
Fort Lauderdale MIA- 153,279
Fort Meade 5,546
FORT MYERS FTMY 36,638
Fort Myers Beach 5,753
Fort Ogden 900 ○
FORT PIERCE FTPI 33,802
FORT WALTON BEACH FTWL 20,829
Fountain 600 ○
Freeport 669
Frostproof 2,995
Fruitland Park 2,259
Fruitville SAR-B 3,070
GAINESVILLE GAIN 81,371
Gibsonton TAM 3,700 ○
Gifford 6,240
Glen Saint Mary 462
Glenwood 950 ○
Golden Beach MIA- 612
Gonzalez PENS 6,084
Goodland 1,000 ○
Goulds MIA- 7,078
Graceville 2,918
Grand Ridge 591
Grant 900 ○
Greenacres City WPB 8,780
Green Cove Springs 4,154
Greensboro 562
Greenville 1,096
Greenwood 577
Gretna 1,557
Grove City 1,932
Groveland 1,992
Gulf Breeze PENS 5,478
Gulf Gate Estates SAR-B 9,248
Gulfport ST.PET- 11,180
Haines City 10,799
Hallandale MIA- 36,517
Hampton 466
Harlem 2,669
Hastings 636
Havana 2,782
Hawthorne 1,303
Hedges 900 ○
Hernando 1,653
Hialeah MIA- 145,254
High Springs 2,491
Hilliard 1,869
Hobe Sound 6,822
Holden Heights ORL 8,000 ○
Holiday 15,400 ○
Holly Hill D.BCH 9,953
Hollywood MIA- 121,323
Holt 780 ○
Homeland 500 ○
Homestead MIA- 20,668
Homosassa 1,426
Hosford 700 ○
Hudson 5,799
Immokalee 11,038
Indian Harbour Beach MELB 5,967
Indian Rocks Beach ST.PET- 3,717
Indiantown 3,383
Intercession City 950 ○
Interlachen 848
Inverness 4,095
Inwood WNHV 6,668
Islamorada 1,441
JACKSONVILLE JAX 540,920
Jacksonville Beach JAX 15,462
Jasmine Estates 3,500 ○
Jasper 2,093
Jay 633
Jennings 749
Jensen Beach 6,639
Jerome 675 ○
Jupiter WPB 9,868
Kathleen LKLD 1,866
Kenansville 700 ○
Kendall MIA- 51,000 ○
Key Largo 7,447
Keystone Heights 1,056
Key West 24,382
Kissimmee 15,487
La Belle 2,287
Lacoochee 1,720
Lady Lake 1,193
Lagrange TITUS 460 ○
Lake Alfred WNHV 3,134
Lake Butler 1,830
Lake City 9,257
Lake Forest MIA- 5,400 ○
Lake Helen 2,047
LAKELAND LKLD 50,158
Lake Magdalene TAM 13,331
Lake Mary 2,853
Lake Park WPB 6,909
Lake Placid 963
Lake Wales 8,466
Lake Worth WPB 27,048
Lanark Village 650 ○
Lantana WPB 8,048
Largo ST.PET- 58,977
Lauderdale Lakes MIA- 25,426
Lauderhill MIA- 37,271
Laurel 1,500 ○
Laurel Hill 610
Lawtey 692
Lealman ST.PET- 19,873
Leesburg 13,191
Lehigh Acres 9,604
Leisure City MIA- 17,905
Leto TAM 9,003
Lighthouse Point MIA- 11,488
Live Oak 6,732
Lockhart ORL 10,571
Longboat Key SAR-B 4,843
Longwood ORL 10,029
Lorida 620 ○
Loughman 800 ○
Lutz TAM 5,555
Lynne 500 ○
Lynn Haven PNCY 6,239
Macclenny 3,851
Madison 3,487
Maitland ORL 8,763
Malabar MELB 1,118
Malone 897
Marathon 7,568
Marco 4,679
Margate MIA- 35,900
Marianna 7,006
Masaryktown 800 ○
Mayo 891
MELBOURNE MELB 46,536
Melbourne Beach MELB 2,713
Melrose 1,700 ○
Melrose Park MIA- 5,672
Memphis SAR-B 5,501
Merritt Island COCO 30,708
MIAMI MIA- 346,865
Miami Beach MIA- 96,298
Miami Shores MIA- 9,244
Miami Springs MIA- 12,350
Micanopy 737
Micco 3,585
Middleburg 2,500 ○
Midway 450 ○
Milligan 500 ○
Milton 7,206
Mims TITUS 7,583
Miramar MIA- 32,813
Molino 1,456
Monticello 2,994
Moore Haven 1,250
Mount Dora 5,883
Mulberry 2,932
Myrtle Grove PENS 14,238
Naples 17,581
Naranja MIA- 5,000 ○
Neptune Beach JAX 5,248
Newberry 1,826
New Port Richey 11,196
New Smyrna Beach 13,557
Niceville FTWL 8,543
Nocatee 1,300 ○
Nokomis 3,108
Norland MIA- 19,471
North Andrews Gardens MIA- 8,967
North Fort Myers FTMY 17,200 ○
North Lauderdale MIA- 18,653
North Miami MIA- 42,566
North Miami Beach MIA- 36,553
North Naples 7,950
North Palm Beach WPB 11,344
North Port 6,205
Oak Hill 938
Oakland 658
Oakland Park MIA- 22,944
Ocala 37,170
Ocean City FTWL 5,582
Ocoee ORL 7,803
Odessa 950 ○
Okeechobee 4,225
Oklawaha 1,200 ○
Oldsmar TAM 2,608
Old Town 550 ○
Olustee 450 ○
Olympia Heights MIA- 33,112
Oneco SAR-B 6,417
Opa-Locka MIA- 14,460
Orange City 2,795
Orange Lake 1,000 ○
Orange Park JAX 8,766
ORLANDO ORL 128,291
Ormond Beach D.BCH 21,378
Osprey SAR-B 1,660
Osteen 900 ○
Ozona ST.PET- 1,500 ○
Pace 5,006
Pahokee 6,346
Paisley 600 ○
Palatka 10,175
Palm Bay MELB 18,560
Palm Beach WPB 9,729
Palm Beach Gardens WPB 14,407
Palmetto SAR-B 8,637
Palm Harbor ST.PET- 5,215
Palm Springs WPB 8,166
Panacea 950 ○
PANAMA CITY PNCY 33,346
Panama City Beach PNCY 2,148
Parker PNCY 4,298
Parrish 950 ○
Paxton 659
Pembroke Pines MIA- 35,862
Penney Farms 630
PENSACOLA PENS 57,619
Perrine MIA- 16,129
Perry 8,254
Pierson 1,085
Pine Castle ORL 9,992
Pine Hills ORL 26,000 ○
Pinellas Park ST.PET- 32,811
Pinewood MIA- 7,900 ○
Placida 700 ○
Plantation MIA- 48,653
Plant City 17,064
Plymouth 2,700 ○
Polk City 576
Pomona Park 791
Pompano Beach MIA- 58,021
Pompano Beach Highlands MIA- 9,000 ○
Ponce de Leon 454
Ponte Vedra Beach JAX 1,700 ○
Port Charlotte 25,770
Port Orange D.BCH 18,756
Port Richey 2,165
Port Salerno 4,511
Port St. Joe 4,027
Port St. Lucie FTPI 14,690
Princeton MIA- 5,300 ○
Punta Gorda 6,797
Quincy 8,591
Reddick 657
Richmond Heights MIA- 8,577
Rio 1,205
Riverview TAM 3,200 ○
Riviera Beach WPB 26,489
Rockledge COCO 11,877
Rocky Creek TAM 7,800 ○
Roseland 1,607
Rubonia SAR-B 550 ○
Ruskin 5,117
Safety Harbor ST.PET- 6,461
St. Augustine 11,985
St. Cloud 7,840
St. James City 1,298
St. Leo 917
St. Lucie FTPI 593
ST. PETERSBURG ST.PET- 238,647
St. Petersburg Beach ST.PET- 9,354
Salt Springs 1,500 ○
Samoset SAR-B 5,747
San Antonio 529
Sanford 23,176
Sanibel 3,363
San Mateo 950 ○
Santa Rosa Beach 950 ○
SARASOTA SAR-B 48,868
Satellite Beach MELB 9,163
Satsuma 950 ○
Sebastian 2,831
Sebring 8,736
Seminole Park ST.PET- 8,000 ○
Seville 800 ○
Sharpes COCO 1,250 ○
Silver Springs 1,082
Sneads 1,690
Solana 1,408
Sopchoppy 444
Sorrento 950 ○
South Bay 3,886
South Daytona D.BCH 11,252
South Miami MIA- 10,895
South Miami Heights MIA- 18,000 ○
South Patrick Shores MELB 9,816
Southport PNCY 1,992
South Venice 8,075
Sparr 1,100 ○
Springfield PNCY 7,220
Spring Hill 6,468
Starke 5,306
Steinhatchee 800 ○
Stuart 9,467
Summerfield 550 ○
Sun City 700 ○
Sunnyland SAR-B 650 ○
Sunnyside 600 ○
Surfside MIA- 3,763
Sweetwater Creek TAM 18,000 ○
Switzerland 2,400 ○
TALLAHASSEE TALL 101,547
Tamarac MIA- 29,376
TAMPA TAM 271,598
Tarpon Springs 13,251
Tavares 4,398
Tavernier 1,834
Temple Terrace TAM 11,097
Thonotosassa TAM 1,500 ○
Tice FTMY 6,645
TITUSVILLE TITUS 31,910
Treasure Island ST.PET- 6,316
Trenton 1,131
Trilby 950 ○
Uleta MIA- 10,000 ○
Umatilla 1,872
Valparaiso FTWL 6,142
Venice 12,153
Vernon 885
Vero Beach 16,176
Wabasso 2,157
Waldo 993
Warrington PENS 15,792
Watertown 600 ○
Wauchula 2,986
Webster 856
Weirsdale 1,500 ○
Welaka 492
Westchester MIA- 20,000 ○
Westgate WPB 2,100 ○
West Melbourne MELB 5,078
West Miami MIA- 6,076
WEST PALM BEACH WPB 63,305
West Pensacola PENS 24,371
Westwood Lakes MIA- 11,478
Wewahitchka 1,742
White City 725 ○
White City FTPI 4,110
White Springs 781
Whitfield Estates SAR-B 3,000 ○
Wildwood 2,665
Williston 2,240
Wilton Manors MIA- 12,742
Wimauma 1,477
Winston LKLD 5,500 ○
Winter Beach 700 ○
Winter Garden 6,789
WINTER HAVEN WNHV 21,119
Winter Park ORL 22,339
Winter Springs ORL 10,475
Woodville 1,768
Yalaha 950 ○
Yankeetown 600
Zephyrhills 5,742
Zolfo Springs 1,495

COUNTIES

Alachua 151,369
Baker 15,289
Bay 97,740
Bradford 20,023
Brevard 272,959
Broward 1,018,257
Calhoun 9,294
Charlotte 58,460
Citrus 54,703
Clay 67,052
Collier 85,971
Columbia 35,399
Dade 1,625,724
De Soto 19,039
Dixie 7,751
Duval 571,003
Escambia 233,794
Flagler 10,913
Franklin 7,661
Gadsden 41,674
Gilchrist 5,767
Glades 5,992
Gulf 10,658
Hamilton 8,761
Hardee 19,379
Hendry 18,599
Hernando 44,469
Highlands 47,526
Hillsborough 646,960
Holmes 14,723
Indian River 59,896
Jackson 39,154
Jefferson 10,703
Lafayette 4,035
Lake 104,870
Lee 205,266
Leon 148,655
Levy 19,870
Liberty 4,260
Madison 14,894
Manatee 148,442
Marion 122,488
Martin 64,014
Monroe 63,188
Nassau 32,894
Okaloosa 109,920
Okeechobee 20,264
Orange 471,016
Osceola 49,287
Palm Beach 576,758
Pasco 193,661
Pinellas 728,531
Polk 321,652
Putnam 50,549
St. Johns 51,303
St. Lucie 87,182
Santa Rosa 55,988
Sarasota 202,251
Seminole 179,752
Sumter 24,272
Suwannee 22,287
Taylor 16,532
Union 10,166
Volusia 258,762
Wakulla 10,887
Walton 21,300
Washington 14,509

GEORGIA

1980 Census 5,463,087

CITIES

Abbeville 985
Acworth ATL 3,648
Adairsville 1,739
Adel 5,592
Adrian 756
Ailey 579
Alamo 993
Alapaha 771
ALBANY ALB 83,245
Allenhurst 606
Alma 3,819
Alpharetta ATL 3,128
Alto 618
Americus 16,120
Aragon 855
Arlington 1,572
Ashburn 4,766
ATHENS ATH 42,549
ATLANTA ATL 425,022
Attapulgus 623
Auburn ATL 692
AUGUSTA AUG 47,532
Austell ATL 3,939
Avondale Estates ATL 1,313
Baconton 763
Bainbridge 10,553
Baldwin 1,080
Ball Ground 640
Barnesville 4,887
Baxley 3,586
Belvedere Park ATL 17,766
Berlin 538
Bibb City COL 667
Blackshear 3,222
Blairsville 530
Blakely 5,880
Bloomingdale SAV 1,855
Blue Ridge 1,376
Bogart ATH 819
Boston 1,424
Bowdon 1,743
Bowman 890
Bremen 3,966
Bronwood 524
Brooklet 1,035
Broxton 1,117
BRUNSWICK BRUNS 17,605
Buchanan 1,019
Buena Vista 1,544
Buford ATL 6,578
Butler 1,959
Byromville 567
Byron MAC- 1,661
Cairo 8,777
Calhoun 5,855
Camilla 5,414
Canon 704
Canton 3,601
Carnesville 465
Carrollton 14,078
Cartersville 9,247
Cataula 500 ○
Cave Spring 883
Cedartown 8,619
Chamblee ATL 7,137
Chatsworth 2,493
Chickamauga CHTN 2,232
Chicopee 900 ○
Clarkdale ATL 550 ○
Clarkesville 1,348
Clarkston ATL 4,539
Claxton 2,694
Clayton 1,838
Cleveland 1,578
Cobbtown 494
Cochran 5,121
Colbert ATH 498
College Park ATL 24,632
Collins 639
Colquitt 2,065
COLUMBUS COL 169,441
Comer 930
Commerce 4,092
Conyers ATL 6,567
Coolidge 736
Cordele 11,184
Cornelia 3,203
Covington ATL 10,586
Crawfordville 594
Cumming ATL 2,094
Cusseta COL 1,218
Cuthbert 4,340
Dacula ATL 1,577
Dahlonega 2,844
Dallas ATL 2,508
Dalton 20,548
Danville 529
Darien 1,731
Dawson 5,699
Dearing 539
Decatur ATL 18,404
Demorest 1,130

○ Rand McNally estimate (not reported in census).
▲ Population of entire township or "town", including rural areas.
● Independent city. Population not included in county total.

Dexter 527
Dock Junction BRUNS 6,189
Doerun 1,062
Donalsonville 3,320
Doraville ATL 7,414
Douglas 10,980
Douglasville ATL 7,641
Dublin 16,083
Duluth ATL 2,956
Dunaire ATL 5,400 ○
Dunwoody ATL 5,100 ○
East Ellijay 469
Eastman 5,330
East Newnan 1,495
East Point ATL 37,486
Eatonton 4,833
Eden SAV 450 ○
Edison 1,128
Elberta MAC- 500 ○
Elberton 5,686
Eldorado 1,000 ○
Elizabeth ATL 1,500 ○
Ellaville 1,684
Ellenwood ATL 500 ○
Ellijay 1,507
Emerson ATL 1,110
Enigma 574
Evans AUG 800 ○
Experiment 3,000 ○
Fairburn ATL 3,466
Fairmount 842
Fair Oaks ATL 8,486
Fargo 600 ○
Fayetteville ATL 2,715
Fitzgerald 10,187
Flovilla 458
Flowery Branch ATL 755
Folkston 2,243
Forest Park ATL 18,782
Forsyth 4,624
Fort Gaines 1,260
Fort Oglethorpe CHTN 5,443
Fort Valley 9,000
Franklin 711
Gainesville 15,280
Garden City SAV 6,895
Georgetown 935
Gibson 730
Glennville 4,144
Glenwood 824
Gordon 2,768
Gracewood AUG 500 ○
Grantville 1,110
Gray MAC- 2,145
Grayson ATL 464
Greensboro 2,985
Greenville 1,213
Gresham Park ATL 6,232
Griffin 20,728
Grovetown AUG 3,384
Guyton 749
Haddock 700 ○
Hagan 880
Hahira 1,534
Hamilton 495
Hampton ATL 2,059
Hapeville ATL 6,166
Hardwick 6,000 ○
Harlem AUG 1,485
Harrison 456
Hartwell 4,855
Hawkinsville 4,372
Hazlehurst 4,298
Helena 1,390
Hephzibah 1,452
Hiawassee 491
Hilltonia 515
Hinesville 11,309
Hiram ATL 1,030
Hoboken 514
Hogansville 3,362
Holly Springs ATL 687
Homeland 683
Homer 734
Homerville 3,112
Hoschton 490
Ideal 619
Irwinton 841
Jackson 4,133
Jasper 1,556
Jefferson 1,820
Jeffersonville 1,473
Jesup 9,418
Jonesboro ATL 4,132
Kennesaw ATL 5,095
Kingsland 2,008
Kingston 733
La Fayette 6,517
La Grange 24,204
Lakeland 2,647
Lake Park VALD 448
La Vista ATL 5,200 ○
Lavonia 2,024
Lawrenceville ATL 8,928
Leary 783
Leesburg 1,301
Lenox 965
Leslie 470
Lilburn ATL 3,765
Lincoln Park 1,755
Lincolnton 1,406
Lindale ROME 2,958
Lithia Springs ATL 9,145
Lithonia ATL 2,637
Lizella MAC- 600 ○
Locust Grove ATL 1,479
Loganville ATL 1,841
Louisville 2,823
Ludowici 1,286
Lula 857
Lumber City 1,426
Lumpkin 1,335
Luthersville 597
Lyerly 482
Lyons 4,203
Mableton ATL 20,200 ○
McCaysville 1,219
McDonough ATL 2,778
MACON MAC- 116,896
McRae 3,409
Madison 2,954
Manchester 4,796
Marietta ATL 30,829
Marshallville 1,540
Maysville 619
Meigs 1,231
Menlo 611
Metter 3,531
Midville 670
Milan 1,115
Milledgeville 12,176
Millen 3,988
Milstead ATL 1,157 ○
Monroe 8,854
Montezuma 4,830
Monticello 2,382
Morrow ATL 3,791
Morven 471
Moultrie 15,105
Mountain City 701
Mount Airy 670
Mount Berry ROME 500 ○
Mount Vernon 1,737
Mount Zion 445
Nahunta 951
Nashville 4,831
Nelson 562
New Holland 800 ○
Newnan 11,449
Newton 711
Nicholls 1,114
Norcross ATL 3,367
Norman Park 757
North Atlanta ATL 22,800 ○
North Druid Hills ATL 8,700 ○
Oakdale ATL 800 ○
Oakwood 723
Ochlocknee 627
Ocilla 3,436
Oglethorpe 1,305
Omega 996
Oxford ATL 1,750
Palmetto ATL 2,086
Panthersville ATL 11,366
Patterson 763
Pavo 830
Peach Orchard AUG 14,000 ○
Peachtree City 6,429
Pearson 1,827
Pelham 4,306
Pembroke 1,400
Pendley Hills ATL 5,800 ○
Perry MAC- 9,453
Pine Lake ATL 901
Pine Mountain 984
Pineview 564
Plains 651
Pooler SAV 2,543
Portal 694
Porterdale ATL 1,451
Port Wentworth SAV 3,947
Poulan 818
Powder Springs ATL 3,381
Quitman 5,188
Raoul 1,400 ○
Ray City 658
Red Oak ATL 1,200 ○
Reidsville 2,296
Remerton VALD 443
Reynolds 1,298
Rhine 590
Richland 1,802
Richmond Hill 1,177
Rincon SAV 1,988
Ringgold CHTN 1,882
Riverdale ATL 7,121
Roberta 859
Rochelle 1,626
Rockmart 3,623
ROME ROME 29,928
Rossville CHTN 3,851
Roswell ATL 23,337
Royston 2,404
Rutledge 694
St. Marys 3,596
St. Simons Island BRUNS 6,566
Sandersville 6,137
Sandy Springs ATL 20,300 ○
Sardis 1,180
Sargent 700 ○
SAVANNAH SAV 141,651
Scottdale ATL 8,770
Screven 872
Senoia 900
Shannon ROME 2,040
Shellman 1,254
Siloam 446
Smithville 867
Smyrna ATL 20,312
Snellville ATL 8,514
Social Circle 2,591
Soperton 2,981
South Decatur ATL 24,000 ○
Sparks 1,353
Sparta 1,745
Springfield 1,075
Statenville 650 ○
Statesboro 14,866
Statham 1,101
Stillmore 527
Stockbridge ATL 2,103
Stone Mountain ATL 4,867
Sugar Hill ATL 2,473
Summerville 4,878
Suwanee ATL 1,026
Swainsboro 7,602
Sycamore 474
Sylvania 3,352
Sylvester 5,860
Talbotton 1,140
Tallapoosa 2,647
Tate 900 ○
Temple 1,520
Tennille 1,709
Thomaston 9,682
Thomasville 18,463
Thomson 7,001
Thunderbolt SAV 2,165
Tifton 13,749
Tignall 733
Toccoa 9,104
Toomsboro 673
Trenton CHTN 1,636
Trion 1,732
Tucker ATL 18,200 ○
Tunnel Hill 936
Twin City 1,402
Tybee Island SAV 2,240
Ty Ty 618
Unadilla 1,566
Union City ATL 4,780
Union Point 1,750
Uvalda 646
VALDOSTA VALD 37,596
Vidalia 10,393
Vienna 2,886
Villa Rica ATL 3,420
Waco 471
Wadley 2,438
Waleska 450
Walthourville 905
Warner Robins MAC- 39,893
Warrenton 2,172
Warwick 488
Washington 4,662
Watkinsville ATH 1,240
Waverly Hall 913
Waycross 19,371
Waynesboro 5,760
West Point 4,305
Whigham 507
White 501
Whitesburg 775
Willacoochee 1,166
Winder 6,705
Windsor Forest SAV 7,288 ○
Winterville ATH 621
Woodbine 910
Woodbury 1,738
Woodland 664
Woodstock ATL 2,699
Woodville 455
Wrens 2,415
Wrightsville 2,526
Young Harris 687
Zebulon 995

COUNTIES

Appling 15,565
Atkinson 6,141
Bacon 9,379
Baker 3,808
Baldwin 34,686
Banks 8,702
Barrow 21,354
Bartow 40,760
Ben Hill 16,000
Berrien 13,525
Bibb 150,256
Bleckley 10,767
Brantley 8,701
Brooks 15,255
Bryan 10,175
Bulloch 35,785
Burke 19,349
Butts 13,665
Calhoun 5,717
Camden 13,371
Candler 7,518
Carroll 56,346
Catoosa 36,991
Charlton 7,343
Chatham 202,226
Chattahoochee 21,732
Chattooga 21,856
Cherokee 51,699
Clarke 74,498
Clay 3,553
Clayton 150,357
Clinch 6,660
Cobb 297,718
Coffee 26,894
Colquitt 35,376
Columbia 40,118
Cook 13,490
Coweta 39,268
Crawford 7,684
Crisp 19,489
Dade 12,318
Dawson 4,774
Decatur 25,495
De Kalb 483,024
Dodge 16,955
Dooly 10,826
Dougherty 100,718
Douglas 54,573
Early 13,158
Echols 2,297
Effingham 18,327
Elbert 18,758
Emanuel 20,795
Evans 8,428
Fannin 14,748
Fayette 29,043
Floyd 79,800
Forsyth 27,958
Franklin 15,185
Fulton 589,904
Gilmer 11,110
Glascock 2,382
Glynn 54,981
Gordon 30,070
Grady 19,845
Greene 11,391
Gwinnett 166,903
Habersham 25,020
Hall 75,649
Hancock 9,466
Haralson 18,422
Harris 15,464
Hart 18,585
Heard 6,520
Henry 36,309
Houston 77,605
Irwin 8,988
Jackson 25,343
Jasper 7,553
Jeff Davis 11,473
Jefferson 18,403
Jenkins 8,841
Johnson 8,660
Jones 16,579
Lamar 12,215
Lanier 5,654
Laurens 36,990
Lee 11,684
Liberty 37,583
Lincoln 6,716
Long 4,524
Lowndes 67,972
Lumpkin 10,762
McDuffie 18,546
McIntosh 8,046
Macon 14,003
Madison 17,747
Marion 5,297
Meriwether 21,229
Miller 7,038
Mitchell 21,114
Monroe 14,610
Montgomery 7,011
Morgan 11,572
Murray 19,685
Muscogee 170,108
Newton 34,489
Oconee 12,427
Oglethorpe 8,929
Paulding 26,110
Peach 19,151
Pickens 11,652
Pierce 11,897
Pike 8,937
Polk 32,382
Pulaski 8,950
Putnam 10,295
Quitman 2,357
Rabun 10,466
Randolph 9,599
Richmond 181,629
Rockdale 36,747
Schley 3,433
Screven 14,043
Seminole 9,057
Spalding 47,899
Stephens 21,763
Stewart 5,896
Sumter 29,360
Talbot 6,536
Taliaferro 2,032
Tattnall 18,134
Taylor 7,902
Telfair 11,445
Terrell 12,017
Thomas 38,098
Tift 32,862
Toombs 22,592
Towns 5,638
Treutlen 6,087
Troup 50,003
Turner 9,510
Twiggs 9,354
Union 9,390
Upson 25,998
Walker 56,470
Walton 31,211
Ware 37,180
Warren 6,583
Washington 18,842
Wayne 20,750
Webster 2,341
Wheeler 5,155
White 10,120
Whitfield 65,775
Wilcox 7,682
Wilkes 10,951
Wilkinson 10,368
Worth 18,064

HAWAII

1980 Census 964,691

CITIES

Aiea HON 15,200 ○
Anahola 915
Captain Cook 2,008
Crestview HON 1,000 ○
Eleele 580
Ewa HON 2,637
Ewa Beach HON 14,369
Foster Village HON 3,700 ○
Haiku 619
Halawa Heights HON 7,000 ○
Haleiwa HON 2,412
Haliimaile 741
Hana 643
Hanalei 483
Hanamaulu 3,227
Hanapepe 1,417
Hauula HON 2,997
Hawi 795
HILO HILO 35,269
Holualoa 1,243
Honaunau 600 ○
Honokaa 1,936
HONOLULU HON 365,048
Honomu HILO 559
Honouliuli HON 600 ○
Kaaawa HON 959
Kahaluu HON 2,925
Kahuku HON 935
Kahului 12,978
Kailua HON 35,812
Kailua Kona 4,751
Kainaliu 512
Kalaheo 2,500
Kaneohe HON 29,919
Kapaa 4,467
Kapaau 612
Kaumakani 888
Kaunakakai 2,231
Keaau 775
Kealakekua 1,033
Kealia 700 ○
Kekaha 3,260
Keokea 900 ○
Kihei 5,644
Kilauea 895
Koloa 1,457
Kualapuu 502
Kula 1,300 ○
Kunia HON 550 ○
Kurtistown 1,200 ○
Lahaina 6,095
Laie HON 4,643
Lanai City 2,092
Laupahoehoe 500
Lawai 950 ○
Lihue 4,000
Lower Paia 1,500
Maili HON 5,026
Makaha HON 6,582
Makakilo City HON 7,691
Makaweli 700 ○
Maunaloa 633
Maunawili HON 2,200 ○
Mililani Town HON 21,365
Mountain View 540
Naalehu 1,168
Nanakuli HON 8,185
Pauilo 755
Pacific Palisades HON 9,500 ○
Pahala 1,619
Pahoa 923
Paia 1,000 ○
Papaikou HILO 1,567
Pauwela 468
Pearl City HON 33,000 ○
Pepeekeo HILO 1,800 ○
Poipu 685
Puhi 991
Pukalani 3,950
Puunene 572
Sunset Beach HON 800 ○
Volcano 900 ○
Wahiawa HON 16,911
Waialua HON 4,051
Waianae HON 5,000 ○
Waikapu 698
Wailua 1,587
Wailuku 10,260
Waimalu HON 3,600 ○
Waimanalo HON 3,562
Waimanalo Beach HON 4,161
Waimea HON 600 ○
Waimea 1,569
Waipahu HON 29,139
Waipio Acres HON 4,091
Whitmore Village HON 2,318

COUNTIES

Hawaii 92,053
Honolulu 762,565
Kalawao 144
Kauai 39,082
Maui 70,847

IDAHO

1980 Census 944,038

CITIES

Aberdeen 1,528
American Falls 3,626
Ammon IDFL 4,669
Arco 1,241
Ashton 1,219
Bancroft 505
Bellevue 1,016
Blackfoot 10,065
BOISE BOIS 102,160
Bonners Ferry 1,906
Buhl 3,629
Burley 8,761
Caldwell 17,699
Carey 600 ○
Cascade 945
Challis 758
Chubbuck POC 7,052
Clark Fork 449
Coeur d'Alene 21,177
Cottonwood 941
Council 917
Craigmont 617
Dalton Gardens 1,795
Deary 539
Downey 645
Driggs 727
Eagle BOIS 2,620
Elk City 670 ○
Emmett 4,605
Fernwood 680 ○
Filer 1,645
Firth 460
Fort Hall 900 ○
Fruitland 2,559
Garden City BOIS 4,571
Genesee 791
Georgetown 544
Glenns Ferry 1,374
Gooding 2,949
Grace 1,216
Grangeville 3,666
Hagerman 602
Hailey 2,109
Hansen 1,078
Hayden 2,586
Hazelton 496
Heyburn 2,889
Homedale 2,078
Horseshoe Bend 700
IDAHO FALLS IDFL 39,734
Inkom 830
Iona IDFL 1,072
Jerome 6,891
Juliaetta 522

○ Rand McNally estimate (not reported in census).
▲ Population of entire township or "town", including rural areas.
● Independent city. Population not included in county total.

Kamiah 1,478
Kellogg 3,417
Ketchum 2,200
Kimberly 2,307
Kingston 1,000 ○
Kooskia 784
Kuna 1,767
Lapwai 1,043
Lava Hot Springs 467
LEWISTON LEW 27,986
Lewisville 502
Lincoln IDFL 700 ○
McCall 2,188
McCammon 770
Mackay 541
Malad City 1,915
Marsing 786
Menan 605
Meridian BOIS 6,658
Middleton 1,901
Montpelier 3,107
Moscow 16,513
Mountain Home 7,540
Mullan 1,269
Nampa 25,112
New Meadows 576
New Plymouth 1,186
Nezperce 517
Oakley 663
Orofino 3,711
Osburn 2,220
Paris 707
Parma 1,820
Paul 940
Payette 5,448
Pierce 1,060
Plummer 634
POCATELLO POC 46,340
Post Falls SPOK 5,736
Potlatch 819
Preston 3,759
Priest River 1,639
Rathdrum 1,369
Rexburg 11,559
Rigby 2,624
Riggins 527
Ririe 555
Roberts 466
Rupert 5,476
St. Anthony 3,212
St. Maries 2,794
Salmon 3,308
Samuels 650 ○
Sandpoint 4,460
Shelley IDFL 3,300
Shoshone 1,242
Silverton 750 ○
Smelterville 776
Soda Springs 4,051
Spirit Lake 834
Star 600 ○
Sugar City 1,022
Sun Valley 545
Teton 559
Troy 820
Twin Falls 26,209
Ucon IDFL 833
Wallace 1,736
Weippe 828
Weiser 4,771
Wendell 1,974
Wilder 1,260

COUNTIES

Ada 173,036
Adams 3,347
Bannock 65,421
Bear Lake 6,931
Benewah 8,292
Bingham 36,489
Blaine 9,841
Boise 2,999
Bonner 24,163
Bonneville 65,980
Boundary 7,289
Butte 3,342
Camas 818
Canyon 83,756
Caribou 8,695
Cassia 19,427
Clark 798
Clearwater 10,390
Custer 3,385
Elmore 21,565
Franklin 8,895
Fremont 10,813
Gem 11,972
Gooding 11,874
Idaho 14,769
Jefferson 15,304
Jerome 14,840
Kootenai 59,770
Latah 28,749
Lemhi 7,460
Lewis 4,118
Lincoln 3,436
Madison 19,480
Minidoka 19,718
Nez Perce 33,220
Oneida 3,258
Owyhee 8,272
Payette 15,825
Power 6,844
Shoshone 19,226
Teton 2,897
Twin Falls 52,927
Valley 5,604
Washington 8,803

ILLINOIS

1980 Census 11,427,414

CITIES

Abingdon 4,210
Addison CHI 29,826
Albion 2,285
Aledo 3,881
Alexis 1,076
Algonquin CHI 5,834
Alsip CHI 17,134
Altamont 2,389
Alton ST.L. 34,171
Amboy 2,377
Anna 5,408
Annawan 908
Antioch CHI 4,419
Arcola 2,714
Argenta DEC 994
Arlington Heights CHI 66,116
Aroma Park KANK 673
Arthur 2,122
Ashland 1,351
Ashton 1,140
Assumption 1,283
Astoria 1,370
Athens 1,371
Atkinson 1,138
Atlanta 1,807
Atwood 1,464
Auburn 3,616
Augusta 764
Aurora CHI 81,293
Ava 811
Avon 1,019
Barrington CHI 9,029
Barry 1,487
Bartlett CHI 13,254
Bartonville PEOR 6,137
Batavia CHI 12,574
Beardstown 6,338
Beckemeyer 1,119
Beecher 2,024
Belleville ST.L 41,580
Bellwood CHI 19,811
Belvidere RKFD 15,176
Bement 1,770
Benld 1,638
Bensenville CHI 16,106
Benton 7,778
Berkeley CHI 5,467
Berwyn CHI 46,849
Bethalto ST.L 8,630
Bethany 1,550
Blandinsville 886
Bloomingdale CHI 12,659
BLOOMINGTON BLMNG 44,189
Blue Island CHI 21,855
Blue Mound 1,338
Bolingbrook CHI 37,261
Boulder Hill CHI 9,333
Bourbonnais KANK 13,280
Bradford 924
Bradley KANK 11,519
Braidwood 3,429
Breese 3,516
Bridgeport 2,330
Bridgeview CHI 14,155
Brighton ST.L 2,364
Brimfield 890
Broadview CHI 8,618
Brookfield CHI 19,395
Brookport PAD 1,128
Brownstown 708
Buda 668
Buffalo Grove CHI 22,230
Bunker Hill 1,700
Burbank CHI 28,462
Bushnell 3,811
Byron 2,035
Cahokia ST.L. 18,904
Cairo 5,931
Calumet City CHI 39,697
Calumet Park CHI 8,788
Cambridge 2,217
Camp Point 1,285
Canton 14,626
Carbondale 26,414
Carlinville 5,439
Carlyle 3,388
Carmi 6,452
Carol Stream CHI 15,472
Carpentersville CHI 23,272
Carrier Mills 2,268
Carrollton 2,816
Carterville 3,445
Carthage 2,978
Cary CHI 6,640
Casey 3,026
Catlin DANV 2,226
Central City 1,505
Centralia 15,126
Centreville ST.L 9,747
Cerro Gordo 1,553
CHAMPAIGN CH-U 58,267
Chandlerville 842
Charleston 19,355
Chatham SPRG 5,597
Chatsworth 1,187
Chebanse KANK 1,191
Chenoa 1,847
Cherry 541
Cherry Valley RKFD 946
Chester 8,401
CHICAGO CHI 3,005,072
Chicago Heights CHI 37,026
Chicago Ridge CHI 13,473
Chillicothe PEOR 6,176
Chrisman 1,413
Christopher 3,086
Cicero CHI 61,232
Cissna Park 825
Clarendon Hills CHI 6,870
Clay City 1,038
Clayton 889
Clifton 1,390
Clinton 8,014
Coal City 3,028
Cobden 1,210
Colchester 1,729
Colfax 920
Collinsville ST.L 19,613
Columbia ST.L 4,269
Coulterville 1,118
Country Club Hills CHI 14,676
Countryside CHI 6,290
Creal Springs 845
Crest Hill CHI 9,252
Crestwood CHI 10,852
Crete CHI 5,417
Creve Coeur PEOR 6,851
Crossville 944
Crystal Lake CHI 18,590
Crystal Lawns CHI 2,800 ○
Cuba 1,648
Dallas City 1,408
Danvers 921
DANVILLE DANV 38,985
Darien CHI 14,536
DECATUR DEC 93,896
Deerfield CHI 17,430
DE KALB DKLB 33,157
Delavan 1,973
Depue 1,873
De Soto 1,589
Des Plaines CHI 55,374
Divernon 1,081
Dixon 15,710
Dolton CHI 24,766
Dongola 886
Downers Grove CHI 42,691
Dundee CHI 3,551
Du Quoin 6,594
Durand 1,073
Dwight 4,146
Earlville 1,382
East Alton ST.L 7,096
East Chicago Heights CHI 5,347
East Dubuque DUB 2,194
East Galesburg GLSB 928
East Moline D-RI-M 20,907
East Peoria PEOR 22,385
East St. Louis ST.L 55,200
Edinburg 1,231
Edwardsville ST.L 12,480
Effingham 11,270
Elburn CHI 1,224
Eldorado 5,198
Elgin CHI 63,668
Elizabeth 772
Elizabethtown 478
Elk Grove Village CHI 28,679
Elkville 973
Elmhurst CHI 44,276
Elmwood 2,117
Elmwood Park CHI 24,016
El Paso 2,676
Enfield 890
Equality 831
Erie 1,725
Eureka PEOR 4,306
Evanston CHI 73,706
Evansville 863
Evergreen Park CHI 22,260
Fairbury 3,544
Fairfield 5,954
Fairmont CHI 2,600 ○
Fairview Heights ST.L 12,414
Farina 594
Farmer City 2,252
Farmington 3,118
Findlay 868
Fisher 1,572
Flanagan 978
Flat Rock 493
Flora 5,379
Flossmoor CHI 8,423
Forest Park CHI 15,177
Forrest 1,246
Forreston 1,384
Fox Lake CHI 6,831
Fox River Grove CHI 2,515
Frankfort CHI 4,357
Franklin Grove 965
Franklin Park CHI 17,507
Freeburg ST.L 2,989
Freeport 26,266
Fulton CLNT 3,936
Galatia 1,042
Galena 3,878
GALESBURG GLSB 35,305
Galva 3,185
Gardner 1,322
Geneseo D-RI-M 6,373
Geneva CHI 9,881
Genoa 3,276
Georgetown DANV 4,220
Gibson City 3,498
Gillespie 3,740
Gilman 1,913
Girard 2,246
Glasford PEOR 1,201
Glen Carbon ST.L 5,197
Glencoe CHI 9,200
Glendale Heights CHI 23,163
Glen Ellyn CHI 23,743
Glenview CHI 33,131
Glenwood CHI 10,538
Godfrey ST.L 2,600 ○
Golconda 960
Grafton 1,024
Grand Tower 748
Granite City ST.L 36,815
Grant Park 1,038
Granville 1,537
Grayslake CHI 5,260
Grayville 2,313
Greenfield 1,090
Greenup 1,655
Greenview 830
Greenville 5,271
Gridley 1,246
Griggsville 1,301
Gurnee CHI 7,693
Hamilton 3,509
Hampshire 1,735
Hanna City PEOR 1,361
Hanover 1,069
Hanover Park CHI 28,848
Hardin 1,107
Harrisburg 10,410
Harristown DEC 1,456
Hartford ST.L 1,887
Harvard 5,126
Harvey CHI 35,810
Harwood Heights CHI 8,228
Havana 4,277
Hazel Crest CHI 13,973
Hebron 786
Henry 2,740
Herrin 10,708
Heyworth 1,598
Hickory Hills CHI 13,778
Highland 7,122
Highland Park CHI 30,599
Highwood CHI 5,455
Hillsboro 4,408
Hillside CHI 8,279
Hinckley 1,447
Hinsdale CHI 16,726
Hoffman Estates CHI 37,272
Homer 1,279
Hometown CHI 5,324
Homewood CHI 19,724
Hoopeston 6,411
Hopedale 913
Huntley CHI 1,646
Hurst 938
Hutsonville 705
Illiopolis 1,118
Ipava 661
Itasca CHI 7,129
Jacksonville 20,284
Jerseyville 7,506
Johnston City 3,873
Joliet CHI 77,956
Jonesboro 1,842
Joppa 535
Justice CHI 10,552
KANKAKEE KANK 29,635
Kansas 791
Karnak 646
Keithsburg 936
Kenilworth CHI 2,708
Ken Rock RKFD 5,945 ○
Kewanee 14,508
Kincaid 1,591
Kinmundy 945
Kirkland 1,155
Kirkwood 1,008
Knoxville GLSB 3,432
Lacon 2,135
Ladd 1,337
La Grange CHI 15,636
La Grange Highlands CHI 7,100 ○
La Grange Park CHI 13,359
La Harpe 1,471
Lake Bluff CHI 4,434
Lake Forest CHI 15,245
Lake In The Hills CHI 5,651
Lake Zurich CHI 8,225
La Moille 734
Lanark 1,483
Lansing CHI 29,039
La Salle 10,347
Lawrenceville 5,652
Lebanon ST.L 3,245
Lemont CHI 5,640
Lena 2,295
Le Roy 2,870
Lewistown 2,758
Lexington 1,806
Libertyville CHI 16,520
Lincoln 16,327
Lincolnwood CHI 11,921
Lindenhurst CHI 6,220
Lisle CHI 13,638
Litchfield 7,204
Livingston 949
Lockport CHI 9,192
Lombard CHI 36,879
London Mills 587
Louisville 1,166
Loves Park RKFD 13,873
Lovington 1,313
Lyons CHI 9,925
McHenry CHI 11,949
Mackinaw 1,354
McLean 836
McLeansboro 2,960
Macomb 19,863
Macon DEC 1,300
Madison ST.L 5,301
Mahomet CH-U 1,986
Manito 1,869
Mansfield 921
Manteno 3,155
Marengo 4,361
Marine 957
Marion 14,031
Marissa 2,568
Markham CHI 15,172
Maroa 1,760
Marseilles 5,114
Marshall 3,655
Martinsville 1,298
Mascoutah ST.L 4,962
Mason City 2,719
Matteson CHI 10,223
Mattoon 19,293
Maywood CHI 27,998
Mazon 828
Melrose Park CHI 20,735
Mendon 979
Mendota 7,134
Meredosia 1,272
Metamora PEOR 2,482
Metropolis 7,171
Midlothian CHI 14,274
Milan D-RI-M 6,371
Milford 1,716
Milledgeville 1,209
Millstadt ST.L 2,736
Minier 1,261
Minonk 2,039
Mokena CHI 4,578
Moline D-RI-M 46,407
Momence 3,297
Monmouth 10,706
Montgomery CHI 3,630
Monticello 4,753
Mooseheart CHI 600 ○
Morris 8,833
Morrison 4,605
Morrisonville 1,208
Morton PEOR 14,178
Morton Grove CHI 23,747
Mound City 1,102
Mounds 1,669
Mount Carmel 8,908
Mount Carroll 1,936
Mount Morris 2,989
Mount Olive 2,357
Mount Prospect CHI 52,634
Mount Pulaski 1,783
Mount Sterling 2,186
Mount Vernon 17,193
Moweaqua 1,922
Mulberry Grove 707
Mundelein CHI 17,053
Murphysboro 9,866
Naperville CHI 42,601
Nashville 3,186
Nauvoo 1,133
Neoga 1,736
New Athens 1,937
New Baden ST.L 2,476
New Berlin 834
New Boston 731
New Haven 559
New Lenox CHI 5,792
Newman 1,079
Newton 3,186
New Windsor 863
Niles CHI 30,363
Noble 832
Nokomis 2,656
Normal BLMNG 35,672
Norridge CHI 16,483
Norris City 1,515
North Aurora CHI 5,205
Northbrook CHI 30,778
North Chicago CHI 38,774
Northfield CHI 4,889
Northlake CHI 12,166
North Park RKFD 15,806
North Riverside CHI 6,764
Oak Brook CHI 6,676
Oak Forest CHI 26,096
Oakland 1,035
Oak Lawn CHI 60,590
Oak Park CHI 54,887
Oakwood DANV 1,627
Oblong 1,840
Odell 1,083
Odin 1,285
O'Fallon ST.L 12,173
Oglesby 3,979
Okawville 1,337
Olive Branch 550 ○
Olney 9,026
Onarga 1,269
Oneida 765
Oquawka 1,533
Oreana DEC 999
Oregon 3,559
Orient 480
Orion D-RI-M 2,013
Orland Park CHI 23,045
Oswego CHI 3,021
Ottawa 18,166
Palatine CHI 32,166
Palestine 1,718
Palmyra 864
Palos Heights CHI 11,096
Palos Hills CHI 16,654
Palos Park CHI 3,150
Pana 6,040
Paris 9,885
Park Forest CHI 26,222
Park Forest South CHI 6,245
Park Ridge CHI 38,704
Patoka 662
Pawnee 2,577
Paw Paw 839
Paxton 4,258
Pecatonica 1,732
Pekin PEOR 33,967
PEORIA PEOR 124,160
Peoria Heights PEOR 7,453
Peotone 2,832
Percy 1,053
Peru 10,886
Petersburg 2,419
Phoenix CHI 2,850
Pinckneyville 3,319
Piper City 905
Pittsfield 4,170
Plainfield CHI 3,777
Plano CHI 4,875
Pleasant Hill 1,112
Pleasant Plains 688
Plymouth 649
Pocahontas 866
Polo 2,643
Pontiac 11,227
Port Byron D-RI-M 1,289
Posen CHI 4,642
Prairie Du Rocher 701
Princeton 7,342
Princeville 1,712
Prophetstown 2,141
Prospect Heights CHI 11,823
QUINCY QUIN 42,554
Ramsey 1,058
Rankin 727
RANTOUL RNTL 20,161
Raymond 957
Red Bud 2,850
Richmond CHI 1,068
Richton Park CHI 9,403
Ridge Farm DANV 1,096
Ridgway 1,245

○ Rand McNally estimate (not reported in census).
▲ Population of entire township or "town", including rural areas.
● Independent city. Population not included in county total.

Riverdale CHI 13,233
River Forest CHI 12,392
River Grove CHI 10,368
Riverside CHI 9,236
Roanoke 2,001
Robbins CHI 8,853
Robinson 7,285
Rochelle 8,982
Rockdale CHI 1,913
Rock Falls 10,633
ROCKFORD RKFD 139,712
Rock Island D-RI-M 46,821
Rockton BLOIT 2,313
Rolling Meadows CHI 20,167
Romeoville CHI 15,519
Roodhouse 2,364
Roselle CHI 17,683
Roseville 1,254
Rosewood Heights ST.L 5,085
Rosiclare 1,441
Rossville 1,363
Round Lake Beach CHI 12,921
Royalton 1,320
Rushville 3,348
St. Anne KANK 1,421
St. Charles CHI 17,492
St. David 786
St. Elmo 1,611
St. Francisville 1,040
St. Joseph CH-U 1,900
Salem 7,813
Sandoval 1,734
Sandwich CHI 5,361
San Jose 784
Sauk Village CHI 10,906
Savanna 4,529
Saybrook 882
Schaumburg CHI 53,355
Schiller Park CHI 11,458
Schram City 708
Seneca 2,098
Sesser 2,238
Shabbona 851
Shannon 938
Shawneetown 1,841
Sheffield 1,130
Shelbyville 5,259
Sheldon 1,215
Silvis D-RI-M 7,130
Skokie CHI 60,278
Somonauk 1,344
South Beloit BLOIT 4,088
South Chicago Heights CHI 3,757
South Elgin CHI 5,970
South Holland CHI 24,977
South Jacksonville 3,382
South Pekin PEOR 1,243
South Streator 2,334
South Wilmington 747
Sparta 4,976
SPRINGFIELD SPRG 100,054
Spring Valley 5,822
Staunton 4,744
Steeleville 2,240
Steger CHI 9,269
Sterling 16,281
Stewardson 745
Stickney CHI 5,893
Stockton 1,872
Stonington 1,184
Streamwood CHI 23,456
Streator 14,795
Stronghurst 865
Sullivan 4,526
Summit CHI 10,110
Sumner 1,238
Swansea ST.L 5,347
Sycamore DKLB 9,219
Tampico 966
Taylorville 11,386
Teutopolis 1,414
Tilden 1,025
Tilton DANV 2,405
Tinley Park CHI 26,178
Tiskilwa 990
Toledo 1,284
Tolono CH-U 2,434
Toluca 1,471
Tonica 695
Toulon 1,390
Tower Hill 715
Tremont PEOR 2,096
Trenton ST.L 2,504
Troy ST.L 3,772
Tuscola 4,327
Urbana CH-U 35,978
Utica 1,067
Valmeyer 898
Vandalia 6,104
Venice ST.L 3,480
Vermont 885
Vernon Hills CHI 9,827
Vienna 1,420
Villa Grove 2,707
Villa Park CHI 23,155
Viola 1,144
Virden 3,899
Virginia 1,825
Walnut 1,513
Wamac 1,665
Warren 1,595
Warrenville CHI 7,519
Warsaw 1,842
Washburn 1,206
Washington PEOR 10,364
Washington Park ST.L 8,223
Waterloo ST.L 4,646
Waterman 943
Watseka 5,543
Wauconda CHI 5,688
Waukegan CHI 67,653
Waverly 1,537
Wayne City 1,132
Westchester CHI 17,730
West Chicago CHI 12,550
West City 886
Western Springs CHI 12,876
West Frankfort 9,543
Westmont CHI 17,353
West Peoria PEOR 5,219
West Salem 1,145
Westville DANV 3,573
Wheaton CHI 43,043
Wheeling CHI 23,266
White Hall 2,935
Williamsville 996
Willow Springs CHI 4,147
Wilmette CHI 28,221
Wilmington 4,424
Winchester 1,716
Windsor 1,228
Winnebago RKFD 1,644
Winnetka CHI 12,772
Winthrop Harbor CHI 5,427
Witt 1,205
Wood Dale CHI 11,251
Woodhull 901
Woodridge CHI 21,763
Wood River ST.L 12,446
Woodstock 11,730
Worden 953
Worth CHI 11,592
Wyanet 1,069
Wyoming 1,614
Yates City 860
Yorkville CHI 3,422
Zeigler 1,858
Zion CHI 17,865

COUNTIES

Adams 71,622
Alexander 12,264
Bond 16,224
Boone 28,630
Brown 5,411
Bureau 39,114
Calhoun 5,867
Carroll 18,779
Cass 15,084
Champaign 168,392
Christian 36,446
Clark 16,913
Clay 15,283
Clinton 32,617
Coles 52,260
Cook 5,253,628
Crawford 20,818
Cumberland 11,062
De Kalb 74,628
De Witt 18,108
Douglas 19,774
Du Page 658,858
Edgar 21,725
Edwards 7,961
Effingham 30,944
Fayette 22,167
Ford 15,265
Franklin 43,201
Fulton 43,687
Gallatin 7,590
Greene 16,661
Grundy 30,582
Hamilton 9,172
Hancock 23,877
Hardin 5,383
Henderson 9,114
Henry 57,968
Iroquois 32,976
Jackson 61,649
Jasper 11,318
Jefferson 36,558
Jersey 20,538
Jo Daviess 23,520
Johnson 9,624
Kane 278,405
Kankakee 102,926
Kendall 37,202
Knox 61,607
Lake 440,388
La Salle 112,033
Lawrence 17,807
Lee 36,328
Livingston 41,381
Logan 31,802
McDonough 37,467
McHenry 147,897
McLean 119,149
Macon 131,375
Macoupin 49,384
Madison 247,661
Marion 43,523
Marshall 14,479
Mason 19,492
Massac 14,990
Menard 11,700
Mercer 19,286
Monroe 20,117
Montgomery 31,686
Morgan 37,502
Moultrie 14,546
Ogle 46,338
Peoria 200,466
Perry 21,714
Piatt 16,581
Pike 18,896
Pope 4,404
Pulaski 8,840
Putnam 6,085
Randolph 35,652
Richland 17,587
Rock Island 166,759
St. Clair 267,531
Saline 28,448
Sangamon 176,070
Schuyler 8,365
Scott 6,142
Shelby 23,923
Stark 7,389
Stephenson 49,536
Tazewell 132,078
Union 17,765
Vermilion 95,222
Wabash 13,713
Warren 21,943
Washington 15,472
Wayne 18,059
White 17,864
Whiteside 65,970
Will 324,460
Williamson 56,538
Winnebago 250,884
Woodford 33,320

INDIANA
1980 Census 5,490,260

CITIES

Advance 559
Akron 1,045
Albany MUN 2,625
Albion 1,637
Alexandria AND 6,028
Amboy 450
Amo 444
ANDERSON AND 64,695
Andrews 1,243
Angola 5,486
Arcadia IND 1,801
Ardmore S.B.- 3,400 ○
Argos 1,547
Arlington 500 ○
Ashley 841
Atlanta IND 657
Attica 3,841
Auburn FTWA 8,122
Aurora CIN- 3,816
Austin 4,857
Avilla 1,272
Bainbridge 644
Bargersville IND 1,647
Bass Lake 1,500 ○
Batesville 4,152
Battle Ground LAF 812
Bedford 14,410
Beech Grove IND 13,196
Berne 3,300
Beverly Shores CHI 864
Bicknell 4,713
Birdseye 533
Black Oak CHI 10,000 ○
Blanford T.H. 700 ○
Bloomfield 2,705
BLOOMINGTON BLMNG 52,044
Bluffton 8,705
Boonville EV 6,300
Boswell 810
Bourbon 1,522
Brazil T.H. 7,852
Bremen 3,565
Bristol S.B.- 1,203
Brook 926
Brooklyn IND 889
Brookston 1,701
Brookville 2,874
Brownsburg IND 6,242
Brownstown 2,704
Butler 2,509
Cambridge City 2,407
Camden 618
Campbellsburg 695
Cannelton 2,373
Carlisle 717
Carmel IND 18,272
Carthage 886
Cayuga 1,258
Cedar Lake CHI 8,754
Centerville RICH 2,284
Chalmers 554
Chandler EV 3,043
Charlestown LOU 5,596
Chesterfield AND 2,701
Chesterton IND 900 ○
Chesterton CHI 8,531
Chrisney 537
Churubusco 1,638
Cicero IND 2,557
Clarks Hill 653
Clarksville LOU 15,164
Clay City 883
Claypool 464
Clayton IND 703
Clermont 1,671
Clinton T.H. 5,267
Cloverdale 1,357
Coalmont 450 ○
Coatesville 474
Colfax 823
Collegeville 1,059
Columbia City 5,091
COLUMBUS COL 30,614
Connersville 17,023
Converse 1,279
Corydon 2,724
Covington 2,883
Crawfordsville 13,325
Cromwell 458
Crothersville 1,747
Crown Point CHI 16,455
Culver 1,601
Cumberland IND 3,375
Cynthiana 874
Dale 1,693
Daleville AND 1,749
Dana 803
Danville IND 4,220
Darlington 811
Dayton LAF 781
Decatur 8,649
Delphi 3,042
Demotte 2,559
Denver 589
Dillsboro CIN- 1,038
Dublin 979
Dubois 550 ○
Dugger 1,118
Dunkirk 3,180
Dunlap S.B.- 2,500 ○
Dyer CHI 9,555
Earl Park 469
East Chicago CHI 39,786
Eaton MUN 1,804
Edgewood AND 2,215
Edinburgh COL 4,856
Edwardsport 459
Elberfeld 640
Elizabethtown COL 603
Elkhart S.B.- 41,305
Ellettsville BLMNG 3,328
Elnora 756
Elwood AND 10,867
English 633
Etna Green 522
EVANSVILLE EV 130,496
Fairland IND 900 ○
Fairmount MRN 3,286
Fairview Park T.H. 1,545
Farmersburg 1,240
Farmland MUN 1,560
Ferdinand 2,192
Fillmore 550 ○
Fishers IND 2,008
Flora 2,303
Floyds Knobs LOU 500 ○
Fontanet T.H. 450 ○
Fort Branch 2,504
Fortville IND 2,787
FORT WAYNE FTWA 172,349
Fountain City RICH 839
Fowler 2,319
Francesville 944
Francisco 612
Frankfort 15,168
Franklin IND 11,563
Frankton AND 2,080
Freelandville 680 ○
Freetown 600 ○
Fremont 1,180
French Lick 2,265
Galveston KOK 1,822
Garrett FTWA 4,751
Gary CHI 151,953
Gas City MRN 6,370
Gaston MUN 1,150
Geneva 1,430
Georgetown LOU 1,494
Goodland 1,200
Goshen S.B.- 19,665
Gosport 729
Grabill FTWA 658
Grandview 670
Greencastle 8,403
Greendale CIN- 3,795
Greenfield IND 11,299
Greensburg 9,254
Greentown KOK 2,265
Greenville LOU 537
Greenwood IND 19,327
Griffith CHI 17,026
Hagerstown 1,950
Hamilton 587
Hamlet 738
Hammond CHI 93,714
Hanna 500 ○
Hanover 4,054
Harlan FTWA 1,000 ○
Harmony T.H. 613
Hartford City 7,622
Hatfield 600 ○
Haubstadt 1,389
Hebron CHI 2,696
Heltonville 500 ○
Henryville LOU 1,132
Highland CHI 25,935
Hillsboro 561
Hoagland FTWA 650 ○
Hobart CHI 22,987
Holland 683
Holton 487
Home Corner MRN 500 ○
Homecroft IND 831
Home Place IND 2,000 ○
Hope COL 2,185
Howe 500 ○
Hudson 447
Hudson Lake 1,347
Huntertown FTWA 1,265
Huntingburg 5,376
Huntington 16,202
Hymera 1,054
Idaville 625 ○
INDIANAPOLIS IND 700,807
Indian Heights KOK 4,277
Ingalls AND 909
Ireland 450 ○
Jamestown 924
Jasonville 2,497
Jasper 9,097
Jeffersonville LOU 21,220
Jonesboro MRN 2,279
Kendallville 7,299
Kennard 441
Kentland 1,936
Kewanna 711
Kingman 566
Kirklin 662
Knightstown 2,325
Knightsville T.H. 763
Knox 3,674
KOKOMO KOK 47,808
Koontz Lake 1,436
Kouts 1,619
La Crosse 713
Ladoga 1,151
LAFAYETTE LAF 43,011
La Fontaine 946
Lagrange 2,164
Lagro 549
Lake Station CHI 14,294
Laketon 500 ○
Lake Village 650 ○
Lakeville S.B.- 629
Lanesville LOU 570
Lapaz 651
Lapel AND 1,881
La Porte 21,796
Laurel 819
Lawrence IND 25,591
Lawrenceburg CIN- 4,403
Lebanon IND 11,456
Leesburg 629
Leo FTWA 800 ○
Lewisville 577
Liberty 1,844
Ligonier 3,134
Linden 700
Linton 6,315
Lizton 456
Logansport 17,731
Long Beach MICH 2,262
Loogootee 3,100
Lowell CHI 5,827
Lynn 1,250
Lynnville 566
Lyons 782
Madison 12,472
Marengo 892
MARION MRN 35,874
Markle 975
Martinsville IND 11,311
Matthews MRN 745
Mecca 482
Medaryville 731
Medora 853
Memphis LOU 500 ○
Mentone 973
Merrillville CHI 27,677
Mexico 850 ○
MICHIGAN CITY MICH 36,850
Michigantown 453
Middlebury S.B.- 1,665
Middletown AND 2,978
Milan 1,566
Milford 1,153
Millersburg S.B.- 809
Milltown 1,006
Milroy 900 ○
Mishawaka S.B.- 40,201
Mitchell 4,641
Monon 1,540
Monroe 739
Monroe City 569
Monroeville 1,372
Monrovia IND 450 ○
Montezuma 1,352
Monticello 5,162
Montpelier 1,995
Mooreland 479
Moores Hill 566
Mooresville IND 5,349
Morgantown 897
Morocco 1,348
Morristown 989
Mount Vernon 7,656
Mulberry 1,225
MUNCIE MUN 77,216
Munster CHI 20,671
Nappanee 4,694
Nashville 705
New Albany LOU 37,103
Newburgh EV 2,906
New Carlisle 1,439
New Castle 20,056
New Goshen T.H. 500 ○
New Harmony 945
New Haven FTWA 7,101
New Market 608
New Palestine IND 749
New Paris S.B.- 1,062
Newport 704
New Washington 600 ○
New Whiteland IND 4,502
Noblesville IND 12,056
North Judson 1,653
North Liberty 1,211
North Manchester 5,998
North Salem 581
North Terre Haute T.H. 1,500 ○
North Vernon 5,768
North Webster 709
Oakland City 3,301
Oaktown 776
Odon 1,463
Oldenburg 770
Oolitic 1,495
Orestes AND 539
Orleans 2,161
Osceola S.B.- 1,990
Osgood 1,554
Ossian FTWA 1,945
Otterbein 1,118
Otwell 500 ○
Owensville 1,261
Oxford 1,327
Palmyra LOU 692
Paoli 3,637
Paragon 538
Parker City MUN 1,414
Patoka 832
Pekin 1,125
Pendleton AND 2,130
Pennville 805
Perrysville 532
Peru 13,764
Petersburg 2,987
Pierceton 1,086
Pittsboro IND 891
Plainfield IND 9,191
Plainville 556
Pleasant Lake 500 ○
Plymouth 7,693
Portage CHI 27,409
Porter CHI 3,441
Portland 7,074
Poseyville 1,247
Princes Lakes 937
Princeton 8,976
Redkey 1,537
Remington 1,268
Rensselaer 4,944
Reynolds 632
Richland 550 ○
RICHMOND RICH 41,349
Ridgeville 933
Rising Sun 2,478
Riverhaven FTWA 700 ○
Roachdale 958
Roann 548
Roanoke 1,174
Rochester 5,050

○ Rand McNally estimate (not reported in census).
▲ Population of entire township or "town", including rural areas.
● Independent city. Population not included in county total.

Rockport	2,590
Rockville	2,785
Rocky Ripple IND	778
Rome City	1,319
Rosedale T.H.	744
Roseland S.B.-	832
Rossville	1,148
Royal Center	908
Royerton MUN	650 ○
Rushville	6,113
Russiaville KOK	973
St. Bernice	900 ○
St. Joe FTWA	546
St. John CHI	3,974
St. Mary-of-the-Woods T.H.	650 ○
St. Marys S.B.-	1,700 ○
St. Meinrad	500 ○
St. Paul	976
Salem	5,290
Sandborn	576
Santa Claus	514
Schererville CHI	13,209
Scottsburg	5,068
Seelyville T.H.	1,374
Sellersburg LOU	3,211
Selma MUN	1,056
Seymour	15,050
Sharpsville KOK	617
Shelburn	1,259
Shelby CHI	700 ○
Shelbyville IND	14,989
Sheridan IND	2,200
Shipshewana	466
Shirley AND	919
Shoals	967
Silver Lake	576
SOUTH BEND S.B.-	109,727
South Haven CHI	6,679
South Milford	500 ○
Southport IND	2,266
South Whitley	1,575
Speed LOU	650 ○
Speedway IND	12,641
Spencer BLMNG	2,732
Spiceland	940
Spring Grove RICH	469
Star City	500 ○
Staunton T.H.	607
Stockwell	500 ○
Stroh	450 ○
Sullivan	4,774
Summitville AND	1,085
Sunman	924
Swayzee	1,127
Sweetser MRN	944
Syracuse	2,579
Taylorsville COL	1,247
Tell City	8,704
TERRE HAUTE T.H.	61,125
Thorntown	1,468
Tipton	5,004
Topeka	876
Trafalgar	466
Trail Creek MICH	2,581
Tri-Lakes	1,356
Troy	550
Underwood LOU	500 ○
Union City	3,908
Union Mills	550 ○
Upland MRN	3,335
Utica LOU	501
Vallonia	500 ○
Valparaiso CHI	22,247
Van Buren	935
Veedersburg	2,261
Versailles	1,560
Vevay	1,343
Vincennes	20,857
Wabash	12,985
Wakarusa S.B.-	1,281
Waldron IND	800 ○
Walkerton	2,051
Wallen FTWA	1,200 ○
Walton KOK	1,202
Wanatah	879
Warren	1,254
Warren Park IND	1,803
Warsaw	10,647
Washington	11,325
Waterloo	1,951
Waveland	559
Waynetown	915
West Baden Springs	796
West College Corner	614
Westfield IND	2,783
West Lafayette LAF	21,247
West Lebanon	946
Westpoint	500 ○
Westport	1,450
West Terre Haute T.H.	2,806
Westville	2,887
Wheatfield	755
Wheatland	532
Wheeler CHI	600 ○
Whitestown IND	497
Whiting CHI	5,630
Wilkinson AND	493
Williamsport	1,747
Winamac	2,370
Winchester	5,659
Windfall	911
Winona Lake	2,827
Winslow	1,017
Wolcott	923
Wolcottville	890
Wolflake	450 ○
Woodburn FTWA	1,002
Worthington	1,574
Yorktown MUN	3,945
Zanesville	550 ○
Zionsville IND	3,948

COUNTIES

Adams	29,619
Allen	294,335
Bartholomew	65,088
Benton	10,218
Blackford	15,570
Boone	36,446
Brown	12,377
Carroll	19,722
Cass	40,936
Clark	88,838
Clay	24,862
Clinton	31,545
Crawford	9,820
Daviess	27,836
Dearborn	34,291
Decatur	23,841
De Kalb	33,606
Delaware	128,587
Dubois	34,238
Elkhart	137,330
Fayette	28,272
Floyd	61,205
Fountain	19,033
Franklin	19,612
Fulton	19,335
Gibson	33,156
Grant	80,934
Greene	30,416
Hamilton	82,027
Hancock	43,939
Harrison	27,276
Hendricks	69,804
Henry	53,336
Howard	86,896
Huntington	35,596
Jackson	36,523
Jasper	26,138
Jay	23,239
Jefferson	30,419
Jennings	22,854
Johnson	77,240
Knox	41,838
Kosciusko	59,555
Lagrange	25,550
Lake	522,965
La Porte	108,632
Lawrence	42,472
Madison	139,336
Marion	765,233
Marshall	39,155
Martin	11,001
Miami	39,820
Monroe	98,785
Montgomery	35,501
Morgan	51,999
Newton	14,844
Noble	35,443
Ohio	5,114
Orange	18,677
Owen	15,841
Parke	16,372
Perry	19,346
Pike	13,465
Porter	119,816
Posey	26,414
Pulaski	13,258
Putnam	29,163
Randolph	29,997
Ripley	24,398
Rush	19,604
St. Joseph	241,617
Scott	20,422
Shelby	39,887
Spencer	19,361
Starke	21,997
Steuben	24,694
Sullivan	21,107
Switzerland	7,153
Tippecanoe	121,702
Tipton	16,819
Union	6,860
Vanderburgh	167,515
Vermillion	18,229
Vigo	112,385
Wabash	36,640
Warren	8,976
Warrick	41,474
Washington	21,932
Wayne	76,058
Wells	25,401
White	23,867
Whitley	26,215

IOWA

1980 Census 2,913,808

CITIES

Ackley	1,900
Adair	883
Adel	2,846
Afton	985
Agency OTUM	657
Ainsworth	547
Akron	1,517
Albert City	818
Albia	4,184
Albion	739
Alden	953
Algona	6,289
Allerton	670
Allison	1,132
Alta	1,720
Alton	986
Altoona DES	5,764
Amana	600 ○
AMES AMES	45,775
Anamosa	4,958
Anita	1,153
Ankeny DES	15,429
Anthon	687
Aplington	1,027
Arcadia	454
Arlington	498
Armstrong	1,153
Arnolds Park	1,051
Ashton	441
Atlantic	7,789
Audubon	2,841
Aurelia	1,143
Avoca	1,650
Avon Lake DES	600 ○
Badger	653
Bancroft	1,082
Batavia	525
Battle Creek	919
Baxter	951
Bayard	637
Beacon	530
Bedford	1,692
Belle Plaine	2,903
Bellevue	2,450
Belmond	2,505
Bennett	458
Bettendorf D-RI-M	27,381
Blairstown	695
Bloomfield	2,849
Blue Grass D-RI-M	1,377
Bonaparte	489
Bondurant DES	1,283
Boone	12,602
Boyden	708
Breda	502
Brighton	804
Britt	2,185
Brooklyn	1,509
Buffalo D-RI-M	1,569
Buffalo Center	1,233
BURLINGTON BUR	29,529
Burt	689
Bussey	579
Calamus	452
Callender	446
Calmar	1,053
Camanche CLNT	4,725
Cambridge	732
Capitol Heights DES	815 ○
Carlisle DES	3,073
Carroll	9,705
Carson	716
Carter Lake OMA-	3,438
Cascade	1,912
Casey	473
Cedar Falls WATL	36,322
CEDAR RAPIDS CEDR	110,243
Center Point	1,591
Centerville	6,558
Central City	1,067
Chariton	5,116
Charles City	8,778
Charlotte	442
Charter Oak	615
Cherokee	7,004
Churdan	540
Cincinnati	598
Clarence	1,001
Clarinda	5,458
Clarion	3,060
Clarksville	1,424
Clear Lake MSCY	7,458
Clermont	602
CLINTON CLNT	32,828
Clive DES	6,064
Coggon	639
Colesburg	463
Colfax	2,234
Collins	451
Colo	808
Columbus Junction	1,429
Conrad	1,133
Coon Rapids	1,448
Coralville IACY	7,687
Corning	1,939
Correctionville	935
Corwith	480
Corydon	1,818
Council Bluffs OMA-	56,449
Crescent	547
Cresco	3,860
Creston	8,429
Dakota City	1,072
Dallas	451
Dallas Center	1,360
Danbury	492
Danville BUR	994
DAVENPORT D-RI-M	103,264
Dayton	941
Decorah	8,068
Delhi	511
Delmar	633
Delta	482
Denison	6,675
Denver WATL	1,647
DES MOINES DES	191,003
De Soto	1,035
De Witt	4,512
Dexter	678
Dike	987
Donnellson	972
Doon	537
Dow City	616
Dows	771
DUBUQUE DUB	62,321
Dumont	815
Duncombe	504
Dunkerton	718
Dunlap	1,374
Durant	1,583
Dyersville	3,825
Dysart	1,355
Eagle Grove	4,324
Earlham	1,140
Earling	520
Earlville	844
Early	670
Eddyville	1,116
Edgewood	900
Eldon	1,255
Eldora	3,063
Eldridge D-RI-M	3,279
Elgin	702
Elkader	1,688
Elk Horn	746
Elliott	493
Ellsworth	480
Elma	714
Emerson	502
Emmetsburg	4,621
Epworth	1,380
Essex	1,001
Estherville	7,518
Evansdale WATL	4,798
Everly	796
Exira	978
Fairbank	980
Fairfax CEDR	683
Fairfield	9,428
Farley	1,287
Farmington	869
Farnhamville	461
Farragut	603
Fayette	1,515
Fonda	863
Fontanelle	805
Forest City	4,270
FORT DODGE FTDO	29,423
Fort Madison	13,520
Fredericksburg	1,075
Fremont	730
Fruitland	461
Garnavillo	723
Garner	2,908
Garwin	626
George	1,241
Gilbert AMES	805
Gilbertville WATL	740
Gilman	642
Gilmore City	626
Gladbrook	970
Glenwood	5,280
Glidden	1,076
Goldfield	789
Gowrie	1,089
Graettinger	923
Grand Junction	970
Grand Mound	674
Grandview	473
Granger	619
Greene	1,332
Greenfield	2,243
Greenfield Plaza DES	2,100 ○
Grimes DES	1,973
Grinnell	8,868
Griswold	1,176
Grundy Center	2,880
Guthrie Center	1,713
Guttenberg	2,428
Hamburg	1,597
Hampton	4,630
Harlan	5,357
Hartford	761
Hartley	1,700
Hawarden	2,722
Hawkeye	512
Hazleton	877
Hedrick	847
Hiawatha CEDR	4,825
Hills	547
Hinton	659
Holstein	1,477
Hopkinton	774
Hospers	655
Hubbard	852
Hudson WATL	2,267
Hull	1,714
Humboldt	4,794
Humeston	671
Huxley AMES	1,884
Ida Grove	2,285
Independence	6,392
Indianola DES	10,843
Inwood	755
IOWA CITY IACY	50,508
Iowa Falls	6,174
Ireton	588
Janesville WATL	840
Jefferson	4,854
Jesup	2,343
Jewell	1,145
Johnston DES	2,617
Kalona	1,862
Kanawha	756
Kellogg	654
Keokuk	13,536
Keosauqua	1,003
Keota	1,034
Keystone	618
Kingsley	1,209
Klemme	620
Knoxville	8,143
Lake City	2,006
Lake Mills	2,281
Lake Park	1,123
Lakeside	589
Lake View	1,291
Lakewood DES	900 ○
Lamoni	2,705
Lamont	554
Lansing	1,181
La Porte City WATL	2,324
Larchwood	701
Latimer	441
Laurens	1,606
Lawler	534
Lawton	447
Le Claire D-RI-M	2,899
Le Grand	921
Lehigh	654
Le Mars	8,276
Lenox	1,338
Leon	2,094
Letts	473
Lewis	497
Lime Springs	476
Lisbon CEDR	1,458
Little Rock	490
Livermore	490
Logan	1,540
Lohrville	521
Lone Tree	1,014
Long Grove	596
Lost Nation	524
Lovilia	637
Lovington DES	850 ○
Lowden	717
McGregor	945
Madrid	2,281
Malvern	1,244
Manchester	4,942
Manilla	1,020
Manly	1,496
Manning	1,609
Manson	1,924
Mapleton	1,495
Maquoketa	6,313
Marathon	442
Marcus	1,206
Marengo	2,308
Marion CEDR	19,474
Marquette	528
Marshalltown	26,938
MASON CITY MSCY	30,144
Massena	518
Maxwell	783
Maynard	561
Mechanicsville	1,166
Mediapolis	1,685
Melbourne	732
Melcher	953
Merrill	737
Middletown BUR	487
Milford	2,076
Milo	778
Milton	567
Minden	483
Missouri Valley	3,107
Mitchellville DES	1,530
Monona	1,530
Monroe	1,875
Montezuma	1,485
Monticello	3,641
Montrose	1,038
Moravia	706
Morning Sun	959
Moulton	762
Mount Ayr	1,938
Mount Pleasant	7,322
Mount Vernon CEDR	3,325
Moville	1,273
Murray	703
Muscatine	23,467
Mystic	665
Nashua	1,846
Neola	839
Nevada AMES	5,912
New Albin	609
Newell	913
Newhall	899
New Hampton	3,940
New Hartford	764
New London	2,043
New Market	554
New Sharon	1,225
Newton	15,292
New Virginia	512
Nora Springs	1,572
North Cedar WATL	1,950 ○
North English	990
North Liberty IACY	2,046
Northwood	2,193
Norwalk DES	2,676
Norway	633
Norwoodville DES	1,400 ○
Oakland	1,552
Oakville	470
Ocheyedan	599
Odebolt	1,299
Oelwein	7,564
Ogden	1,953
Okoboji	559
Olin	735
Onawa	3,283
Orange City	4,588
Orleans	546
Osage	3,718
Osceola	3,750
Oskaloosa	10,989
Ossian	829
Otho FTDO	692
OTTUMWA OTUM	27,381
Oxford	676
Oxford Junction	600
Pacific Junction	511
Palo CEDR	529
Panora	1,211
Parkersburg	1,968
Paullina	1,224
Pella	8,349
Perry	7,053
Peterson	470
Plainfield	469
Pleasant Hill DES	3,493
Pleasant Valley D-RI-M	750 ○
Pleasantville	1,531
Plymouth	463
Pocahontas	2,352
Polk City DES	1,658
Pomeroy	895
Postville	1,475
Prairie City	1,278
Preston	1,120
Primghar	1,050
Princeton	965
Quasqueton	599
Radcliffe	593
Readlyn	858
Redfield	959
Red Oak	6,810
Reinbeck	1,808
Remsen	1,592
Riceville	919
Richland	600
Ringsted	557
Riverdale D-RI-M	462
Riverside	826
Robins CEDR	726
Rockford	1,012
Rock Rapids	2,693
Rock Valley	2,706
Rockwell	1,039
Rockwell City	2,276
Roland	1,005
Rolfe	796
Royal	522
Rudd	460
Russell	593
Ruthven	769

○ Rand McNally estimate (not reported in census).
▲ Population of entire township or "town", including rural areas.
● Independent city. Population not included in county total.

Sabula 824
Sac City 3,000
St. Ansgar 1,100
St. Charles 507
Salem 463
Sanborn 1,398
Saydel DES 4,200 ○
Saylorville DES 780 ○
Schleswig 868
Scranton 748
Sergeant Bluff SXCY 2,416
Seymour 1,036
Sheffield 1,224
Shelby 665
Sheldon 5,003
Shell Rock 1,478
Shellsburg 771
Shenandoah 6,274
Sibley 3,051
Sidney 1,308
Sigourney 2,330
Sioux Center 4,588
SIOUX CITY SXCY 82,003
Sioux Rapids 897
Slater AMES 1,312
Sloan 978
Solon CEDR 969
Spencer 11,726
Spirit Lake 3,976
Springville 1,165
Stacyville 538
Stanhope 492
Stanton 747
Stanwood 705
State Center 1,292
Storm Lake 8,814
Story City 2,762
Stratford 806
Strawberry Point 1,463
Stuart 1,650
Sully 828
Sumner 2,335
Sutherland 897
Swea City 813
Swisher CEDR 654
Tabor 1,088
Tama 2,968
Thompson 668
Thornton 442
Tipton 3,055
Titonka 607
Toledo 2,445
Traer 1,703
Treynor 981
Tripoli 1,280
Underwood 448
Union 515
University Heights IACY 1,069
University Park 645
Urbana 574
Urbandale DES 17,869
Ute 479
Vail 490
Van Horne 682
Van Meter 747
Ventura MSCY 614
Victor 1,046
Villisca 1,434
Vinton 5,040
Walcott D-RI-M 1,425
Walker 733
Wall Lake 892
Walnut 897
Wapello 2,011
Washburn WATL 1,400 ○
Washington 6,584
WATERLOO WATL 75,985
Waukee DES 2,227
Waukon 3,983
Waverly 8,444
Wayland 720
Webster City 8,572
Wellman 1,125
Wellsburg 761
Wesley 598
West Bend 941
West Branch IACY 1,867
West Burlington BUR 3,371
West Des Moines DES 21,894
West Liberty 2,723
West Point 1,133
West Union 2,783
What Cheer 803
Wheatland 840
Whiting 734
Whittemore 647
Williamsburg 2,033
Wilton 2,502
Windsor Heights DES 5,474
Winfield 1,042
Winterset 4,021
Winthrop 767
Woodbine 1,463
Woodward 1,212
Wyoming 702
Zearing 630

COUNTIES

Adair 9,509
Adams 5,731
Allamakee 15,108
Appanoose 15,511
Audubon 8,559
Benton 23,649
Black Hawk 137,961
Boone 26,184
Bremer 24,820
Buchanan 22,900
Buena Vista 20,774
Butler 17,668
Calhoun 13,542
Carroll 22,951
Cass 16,932
Cedar 18,635
Cerro Gordo 48,458
Cherokee 16,238
Chickasaw 15,437
Clarke 8,612
Clay 19,576
Clayton 21,098
Clinton 57,122
Crawford 18,935
Dallas 29,513
Davis 9,104
Decatur 9,794
Delaware 18,933
Des Moines 46,203
Dickinson 15,629
Dubuque 93,745
Emmet 13,336
Fayette 25,488
Floyd 19,597
Franklin 13,036
Fremont 9,401
Greene 12,119
Grundy 14,366
Guthrie 11,983
Hamilton 17,862
Hancock 13,833
Hardin 21,776
Harrison 16,348
Henry 18,890
Howard 11,114
Humboldt 12,246
Ida 8,908
Iowa 15,429
Jackson 22,503
Jasper 36,425
Jefferson 16,316
Johnson 81,717
Jones 20,401
Keokuk 12,921
Kossuth 21,891
Lee 43,106
Linn 169,775
Louisa 12,055
Lucas 10,313
Lyon 12,896
Madison 12,597
Mahaska 22,867
Marion 29,669
Marshall 41,652
Mills 13,406
Mitchell 12,329
Monona 11,692
Monroe 9,209
Montgomery 13,413
Muscatine 40,436
O'Brien 16,972
Osceola 8,371
Page 19,063
Palo Alto 12,721
Plymouth 24,743
Pocahontas 11,369
Polk 303,170
Pottawattamie 86,561
Poweshiek 19,306
Ringgold 6,112
Sac 14,118
Scott 160,022
Shelby 15,043
Sioux 30,813
Story 72,326
Tama 19,533
Taylor 8,353
Union 13,858
Van Buren 8,626
Wapello 40,241
Warren 34,878
Washington 20,141
Wayne 8,199
Webster 45,953
Winnebago 13,010
Winneshiek 21,876
Woodbury 100,884
Worth 9,075
Wright 16,319

KANSAS

1980 Census 2,364,236

CITIES

Abilene 6,572
Alma 925
Almena 517
Altamont 1,054
Altoona 564
Americus 915
Andale 538
Andover WICH 2,801
Anthony 2,661
Arcadia 460
Argonia 587
Arkansas City 13,201
Arlington 631
Arma 1,676
Ashland 1,096
Atchison 11,899
Attica 730
Atwood 1,665
Auburn 890
Augusta WICH 6,968
Axtell 470
Baldwin City 2,829
Basehor K.C. 1,483
Baxter Springs 4,730
Bel Aire WICH 2,395
Belle Plaine WICH 1,706
Belleville 2,805
Beloit 4,367
Bennington 579
Benton 609
Bird City 546
Blue Rapids 1,280
Bonner Springs K.C. 6,266
Bucklin 786
Buhler 1,188
Burden 518
Burlingame 1,239
Burlington 2,901
Burrton 976
Caldwell 1,401
Callahan WICH 900 ○
Caney 2,284
Canton 926
Carbondale TOP 1,518
Cawker City 640
Cedar Vale 848
Centralia 486
Chanute 10,506
Chapman 1,255
Chase 753
Cheney 1,404
Cherokee 775
Cherryvale 2,769
Chetopa 1,751
Cimarron 1,491
Claflin 764
Clay Center 4,948
Clearwater 1,684
Clifton 695
Clyde 909
Coffeyville 15,185
Colby 5,544
Coldwater 989
Colony 474
Columbus 3,426
Colwich WICH 935
Concordia 6,847
Conway Springs 1,313
Cottonwood Falls 954
Council Grove 2,381
Cunningham 540
Dearing 475
Deerfield 538
Delphos 570
Derby WICH 9,786
De Soto 2,061
Dighton 1,390
Dodge City 18,001
Douglass 1,450
Downs 1,324
Eastborough WICH 854
Easton 460
Edgerton 1,214
Edna 537
Edwardsville K.C. 3,364
Effingham 634
El Dorado 11,551
Elkhart 2,243
Ellinwood 2,508
Ellis 2,062
Ellsworth 2,465
Elwood ST.JO 1,275
Emporia 25,287
Enterprise 839
Erie 1,415
Eskridge 603
Eudora 2,934
Eureka 3,425
Fairway K.C. 4,619
Florence 729
Fort Scott 8,893
Fowler 592
Frankfort 1,038
Fredonia 3,047
Frontenac 2,586
Galena JOP 3,587
Galva 651
Garden City 18,256
Garden Plain 775
Gardner K.C. 2,392
Garnett 3,310
Gas 543
Geneseo 496
Girard 2,888
Glasco 710
Glen Elder 491
Goddard WICH 1,427
Goodland 5,708
Great Bend 16,608
Greenleaf 462
Greensburg 1,885
Halstead 1,994
Hanover 802
Harper 1,823
Hartford 551
Haven 1,125
Haviland 770
Hays 16,301
Haysville WICH 8,006
Herington 2,930
Hesston 3,013
Hiawatha 3,702
Highland 954
Hill City 2,028
Hillsboro 2,717
Hoisington 3,678
Holcomb 816
Holton 3,132
Holyrood 567
Hope 468
Horton 2,130
Howard 965
Hoxie 1,462
Hoyt 536
Hugoton 3,165
Humboldt 2,230
HUTCHINSON HUCH 40,284
Independence 10,598
Inman 947
Iola 6,938
Jamestown 440
Jetmore 862
Jewell 589
Johnson 1,244
Junction City 19,305
Kanopolis 729
KANSAS CITY K.C. 161,148
Kensington 681
Kingman 3,563
Kinsley 2,074
Kiowa 1,409
La Crosse 1,618
La Cygne 1,025
La Harpe 687
Lakin 1,823
Lansing LEAV 5,307
Larned 4,811
LAWRENCE LAWR 52,738
LEAVENWORTH LEAV 33,656
Leawood K.C. 13,360
Lebanon 440
Lebo 966
Lecompton 576
Lenexa K.C. 18,639
Lenora 444
Leon 667
Leoti 1,869
Le Roy 701
Lewis 551
Liberal 14,911
Lincoln 1,599
Lindsborg 3,155
Linn 483
Little River 529
Logan 720
Louisburg 1,744
Lucas 524
Lyndon 1,132
Lyons 4,134
McCune 528
Macksville 546
McLouth 700
McPherson 11,753
Madison 1,099
Maize WICH 1,294
Manhattan 32,644
Mankato 1,205
Marion 1,951
Marquette 639
Marysville 3,670
Meade 1,777
Medicine Lodge 2,384
Melvern 481
Meriden TOP 707
Merriam K.C. 10,794
Midland Park WICH 1,350 ○
Milford 465
Miltonvale 588
Minneapolis 2,075
Minneola 712
Mission K.C. 8,643
Mission Hills K.C. 3,904
Moline 553
Montezuma 730
Moran 643
Mound City 755
Moundridge 1,453
Mount Hope 791
Mulberry 647
Mulvane WICH 4,254
Natoma 515
Neodesha 3,414
Ness City 1,769
Newton 16,332
Nickerson 1,292
Norton 3,400
Nortonville 692
Norwich 476
Oaklawn WICH 4,200 ○
Oakley 2,343
Oberlin 2,387
Ogden 1,804
Olathe K.C. 37,258
Olpe 477
Onaga 752
Osage City 2,667
Osawatomie 4,459
Osborne 2,120
Oskaloosa 1,092
Oswego 2,218
Ottawa 11,016
Overbrook 930
Overland Park K.C. 81,784
Oxford 1,125
Ozawkie 472
Paola 4,557
Park City WICH 4,056
Parsons 12,898
Peabody 1,474
Perry 907
Phillipsburg 3,229
Piper K.C. 730 ○
Pittsburg 18,770
Plains 1,044
Plainville 2,458
Pleasanton 1,303
Pomona 868
Potwin 563
Prairie Village K.C. 24,657
Pratt 6,885
Pretty Prairie 655
Protection 684
Quinter 951
Ransom 448
Richmond 510
Riley 779
Riverton JOP 550 ○
Roeland Park K.C. 7,962
Rose Hill WICH 1,557
Rossville 1,045
Russell 5,427
Sabetha 2,297
St. Francis 1,610
St. John 1,501
St. Marys 1,598
St. Paul 746
SALINA SLN 41,843
Satanta 1,117
Scammon 501
Scandia 480
Scott City 4,154
Scranton 664
Sedan 1,579
Sedgwick 1,471
Seneca 2,389
Severy 447
Sharon Springs 982
Shawnee K.C. 29,653
Silver Lake TOP 1,350
Smith Center 2,240
Solomon 1,018
South Hutchinson HUCH 2,226
Spearville 693
Spring Hill 2,005
Stafford 1,425
Sterling 2,312
Stockton 1,825
Strong City 675
Sublette 1,293
Sunset Park WICH 1,050 ○
Syracuse 1,654
Thayer 517
Tonganoxie 1,864
TOPEKA TOP 118,690
Toronto 466
Towanda 1,332
Tribune 955
Troy 1,240
Turon 481
Udall 891
Ulysses 4,653
Valley Center WICH 3,300
Valley Falls 1,189
Victoria 1,328
WaKeeney 2,388
Wakefield 803
Wamego 3,159
Washington 1,488
Waterville 694
Wathena ST.JO 1,418
Waverly 671
Weir 705
Wellington 8,212
Wellsville 1,612
Westmoreland 598
Westwood K.C. 1,783
White City 534
Whitewater 751
WICHITA WICH 279,835
Wilson 978
Winchester 570
Winfield 11,866
Yates Center 1,998

COUNTIES

Allen 15,654
Anderson 8,749
Atchison 18,397
Barber 6,548
Barton 31,343
Bourbon 15,969
Brown 11,955
Butler 44,782
Chase 3,309
Chautauqua 5,016
Cherokee 22,304
Cheyenne 3,678
Clark 2,599
Clay 9,802
Cloud 12,494
Coffey 9,370
Comanche 2,554
Cowley 36,824
Crawford 37,916
Decatur 4,509
Dickinson 20,175
Doniphan 9,268
Douglas 67,640
Edwards 4,271
Elk 3,918
Ellis 26,098
Ellsworth 6,640
Finney 23,825
Ford 24,315
Franklin 22,062
Geary 29,852
Gove 3,726
Graham 3,995
Grant 6,977
Gray 5,138
Greeley 1,845
Greenwood 8,764
Hamilton 2,514
Harper 7,778
Harvey 30,531
Haskell 3,814
Hodgeman 2,269
Jackson 11,644
Jefferson 15,207
Jewell 5,241
Johnson 270,269
Kearny 3,435
Kingman 8,960
Kiowa 4,046
Labette 25,682
Lane 2,472
Leavenworth 54,809
Lincoln 4,145
Linn 8,234
Logan 3,478
Lyon 35,108
McPherson 26,855
Marion 13,522
Marshall 12,787
Meade 4,788
Miami 21,618
Mitchell 8,117
Montgomery 42,281
Morris 6,419
Morton 3,454
Nemaha 11,211
Neosho 18,967
Ness 4,498
Norton 6,689
Osage 15,319
Osborne 5,959
Ottawa 5,971
Pawnee 8,065
Phillips 7,406
Pottawatomie 14,782
Pratt 10,275
Rawlins 4,105
Reno 64,983
Republic 7,569
Rice 11,900
Riley 63,505
Rooks 7,006
Rush 4,516
Russell 8,868
Saline 48,905
Scott 5,782
Sedgwick 367,088
Seward 17,071
Shawnee 154,916
Sheridan 3,544
Sherman 7,759

○ Rand McNally estimate (not reported in census).
▲ Population of entire township or "town", including rural areas.
● Independent city. Population not included in county total.

Smith	5,947
Stafford	5,694
Stanton	2,339
Stevens	4,736
Sumner	24,928
Thomas	8,451
Trego	4,165
Wabaunsee	6,867
Wallace	2,045
Washington	8,543
Wichita	3,041
Wilson	12,128
Woodson	4,600
Wyandotte	172,335

KENTUCKY

1980 Census 3,660,257

CITIES

Adairville	1,105
Albany	2,083
Alexandria CIN-	4,735
Anchorage LOU	1,726
Arjay	650 ○
Arlington	511
Artemus	500 ○
Ashland HNTG-	27,064
Auburn	1,467
Augusta	1,455
Auxier	900 ○
Barbourville	3,333
Bardstown	6,155
Bardwell	988
Barlow	746
Beattyville	1,068
Beauty	450 ○
Beaver Dam	3,185
Bedford	835
Belfry	900 ○
Bellevue CIN-	7,678
Benham	936
Benton	3,700
Berea	8,226
Betsy Layne	900 ○
Bloomfield	954
BOWLING GREEN BOWLG	40,450
Brandenburg	1,831
Brodhead	686
Brooks LOU	1,344
Brooksville	680
Brownsville	674
Buechel LOU	6,855
Bulan	440 ○
Burgin	1,008
Burkesville	2,051
Burlington CIN-	550 ○
Burnside	775
Butler	663
Cadiz	1,661
Calhoun	1,080
Calvert City PAD	2,388
Campbellsburg	714
Campbellsville	9,245
Campton	486
Caneyville	642
Cannonsburg	600 ○
Carlisle	1,757
Carrollton	3,967
Catlettsburg HNTG-	3,005
Cave City	2,098
Cawood	800 ○
Cecilia	500 ○
Centertown	462
Central City	5,214
Clarkson	666
Clay	1,356
Clay City	1,276
Clearfield	1,250
Clinton	1,720
Cloverport	1,585
Cold Spring CIN-	2,117
Columbia	3,710
Combs	700 ○
Corbin	8,075
Corydon	874
Covington CIN-	49,567
Crab Orchard	843
Crescent Springs CIN-	1,944
Crestwood LOU	531
Crittenden	597
Crofton	823
Cromona	700 ○
Cumberland	3,712
Cynthiana	5,881
Danville	12,942
Dayton CIN-	6,979
Dixon	533
Dorton	600 ○
Drakesboro	798
Drift	600 ○
Dry Ridge	1,250
Earlington	2,011
East Bernstadt	700 ○
Eddyville	1,949
Edgewood CIN-	7,239
Edmonton	1,448
Elizabethtown	15,380
Elkhorn City	1,446
Elkton	1,815
Elsmere CIN-	7,203
Eminence	2,260
Erlanger CIN-	14,466
Evarts	1,234
Fairdale LOU	7,315
Falmouth	2,482
Ferguson	1,009
Fern Creek LOU	16,866
Flat Lick	700 ○
Flatwoods HNTG-	8,354
Flemingsburg	2,835
Florence CIN-	15,586
Fordsville	561
Fort Mitchell CIN-	7,310
Fort Thomas CIN-	16,012
Fort Wright CIN-	4,481
Fourmile	500 ○
Frankfort	25,973
Franklin	7,738
Fredonia	535
Frenchburg	550
Fullerton PTSM	500 ○
Fulton	3,137
Gamaliel	456
Garrison	650 ○
Georgetown LEX	10,972
Glasgow	12,958
Grahn	500 ○
Grapevine	900 ○
Gray	750 ○
Grayson HNTG-	3,423
Greensburg	2,377
Greenup HNTG-	1,386
Greenville	4,631
Guthrie	1,361
Hanson	485
Hardin	545
Hardinsburg	2,211
Harlan	3,024
Harrodsburg	7,265
Hartford	2,512
Hawesville	1,036
Hazard	5,371
Hazel	465
Hebron CIN-	500 ○
Heidrick	600 ○
Henderson EV	24,834
Hickman	2,894
Highview LOU	13,286
Hillview LOU	5,196
Hima	700 ○
Hindman	876
Hitchins	700 ○
Hodgenville	2,531
HOPKINSVILLE HPKNV	27,318
Horse Cave	2,045
Hyden	488
Independence CIN-	8,581
Irvine	2,889
Irvington	1,409
Island	532
Jackson	2,651
Jamestown	1,441
Jeffersontown LOU	15,795
Jeffersonville	1,528
Jenkins	3,271
Junction City	2,045
Kenvir	950 ○
Kitts	500 ○
Kuttawa	560
La Center	1,044
La Grange	2,971
Lakeside Park CIN-	3,062
Lancaster	3,365
Langley	600 ○
Lawrenceburg	5,167
Lebanon	6,590
Lebanon Junction	1,581
Leitchfield	4,533
Lejunior	600 ○
Lewisburg	972
Lewisport	1,832
LEXINGTON LEX	204,165
Liberty	2,206
Livermore	1,672
London	4,002
Lone Oak PAD	443
Long View	650 ○
Lookout	550 ○
Loretto	954
Lothair	600 ○
Louisa	1,832
LOUISVILLE LOU	298,694
Lovely	700 ○
Loyall	1,210
Ludlow CIN-	4,959
Lynch	1,614
Lyndon LOU	2,283
McHenry	582
McKee	759
McRoberts	1,106
McVeigh	800 ○
Madisonville	16,979
Magnolia	450 ○
Manchester	1,838
Maple Mount	500 ○
Marion	3,392
Marshes Siding	500 ○
Martin	827
Maryville LOU	6,000 ○
Mayfield	10,705
Maysville	7,983
Melbourne CIN-	628
Melvin	700 ○
Middlesboro	12,251
Midway LEX	1,445
Millersburg	987
Milton	718
Monticello	5,677
Morehead	7,789
Morganfield	3,781
Morgantown	2,000
Mortons Gap	1,201
Mount Sterling	5,820
Mount Vernon	2,334
Mount Washington LOU	3,997
Muldraugh	1,752
Munfordville	1,783
Murray	14,248
Nazareth	700 ○
New Castle	832
New Haven	926
Newport CIN-	21,587
Nicholasville LEX	10,319
North Corbin	1,000 ○
North Middletown	637
Nortonville	1,336
Oak Grove	2,088
Okolona LOU	20,039
Olive Hill	2,539
Oneida	600 ○
OWENSBORO OWNS	54,450
Owenton	1,341
Owingsville	1,419
PADUCAH PAD	29,315
Paintsville	3,815
Paris	7,935
Park City	614
Park Hills CIN-	3,500
Pembroke	636
Perryville	841
Pewee Valley LOU	982
Phelps	1,120 ○
Pikeville	4,756
Pine Knot	1,389
Pineville	2,599
Pittsburg	620 ○
Pleasure Ridge Park LOU	27,332
Pleasureville	837
Prestonsburg	4,011
Princeton	7,073
Prospect LOU	1,981
Providence	4,434
Raceland HNTG-	1,970
Radcliff	14,519
Ravenna	793
Revelo	550 ○
Richmond	21,705
Rineyville	450 ○
Robards	500 ○
Rockport	511
Russell HNTG-	3,824
Russell Springs	1,831
Russellville	7,520
Sacramento	538
St. Matthews LOU	14,409
Salem	833
Salyersville	1,352
Sandy Hook	627
Science Hill	655
Scottsville	4,278
Sebree	1,516
Shelbiana	500 ○
Shelby City	700 ○
Shelbyville	5,329
Shepherdsville LOU	4,454
Shively LOU	16,645
Silver Grove CIN-	1,260
Simpsonville	642
Smithland	512
Smiths Grove	767
Somerset	10,649
Southgate CIN-	2,833
South Portsmouth PTSM	550 ○
South Williamson	1,016
Spottsville	500 ○
Springfield	3,179
Staffordsville	700 ○
Stamping Ground	562
Stanford	2,764
Stanton	2,691
Stearns	1,557
Sturgis	2,293
Summersville	450 ○
Symsonia	550 ○
Tateville	725 ○
Taylor Mill CIN-	4,509
Taylorsville	801
Thealka	500 ○
Toler	500 ○
Tollesboro	808
Tompkinsville	3,077
Trenton	465
Union CIN-	601
Uniontown	1,169
Upton	731
Valley Station LOU	20,000 ○
Vanceburg	1,939
Van Lear	2,035
Veachland	700 ○
Verda	1,133
Versailles LEX	6,427
Vicco	456
Vine Grove	3,583
Walton CIN-	1,651
Warfield	450
Warsaw	1,328
Washington	624
Wayland	601
Weeksbury	700 ○
West Liberty	1,381
West Point	1,339
West Van Lear	900 ○
Wheelwright	865
White Plains	859
Whitesburg	1,525
Whitesville	788
Whitley City	1,683
Wickliffe	1,034
Williamsburg	5,560
Williamstown	2,502
Wilmore LEX	3,787
Winchester	15,216
Wingo	606
Woodbine	500 ○
Woodlawn PAD	1,200 ○
Worthington HNTG-	1,948

COUNTIES

Adair	15,233
Allen	14,128
Anderson	12,567
Ballard	8,798
Barren	34,009
Bath	10,025
Bell	34,330
Boone	45,842
Bourbon	19,405
Boyd	55,513
Boyle	25,066
Bracken	7,738
Breathitt	17,004
Breckinridge	16,861
Bullitt	43,346
Butler	11,064
Caldwell	13,473
Calloway	30,031
Campbell	83,317
Carlisle	5,487
Carroll	9,270
Carter	25,060
Casey	14,818
Christian	66,878
Clark	28,322
Clay	22,752
Clinton	9,321
Crittenden	9,207
Cumberland	7,289
Daviess	85,949
Edmonson	9,962
Elliott	6,908
Estill	14,495
Fayette	204,165
Fleming	12,323
Floyd	48,764
Franklin	41,830
Fulton	8,971
Gallatin	4,842
Garrard	10,853
Grant	13,308
Graves	34,049
Grayson	20,854
Green	11,043
Greenup	39,132
Hancock	7,742
Hardin	88,917
Harlan	41,889
Harrison	15,166
Hart	15,402
Henderson	40,849
Henry	12,740
Hickman	6,065
Hopkins	46,174
Jackson	11,996
Jefferson	684,565
Jessamine	26,065
Johnson	24,432
Kenton	137,058
Knott	17,940
Knox	30,239
Larue	11,922
Laurel	38,982
Lawrence	14,121
Lee	7,754
Leslie	14,882
Letcher	30,687
Lewis	14,545
Lincoln	19,053
Livingston	9,219
Logan	24,138
Lyon	6,490
McCracken	61,310
McCreary	15,634
McLean	10,090
Madison	53,352
Magoffin	13,515
Marion	17,910
Marshall	25,637
Martin	13,925
Mason	17,760
Meade	22,854
Menifee	5,117
Mercer	19,011
Metcalfe	9,484
Monroe	12,353
Montgomery	20,046
Morgan	12,103
Muhlenberg	32,238
Nelson	27,584
Nicholas	7,157
Ohio	21,765
Oldham	27,795
Owen	8,924
Owsley	5,709
Pendleton	10,989
Perry	33,763
Pike	81,123
Powell	11,101
Pulaski	45,803
Robertson	2,270
Rockcastle	13,973
Rowan	19,049
Russell	13,708
Scott	21,813
Shelby	23,328
Simpson	14,673
Spencer	5,929
Taylor	21,178
Todd	11,874
Trigg	9,384
Trimble	6,253
Union	17,821
Warren	71,828
Washington	10,764
Wayne	17,022
Webster	14,832
Whitley	33,396
Wolfe	6,698
Woodford	17,778

LOUISIANA

1980 Census 4,206,098

CITIES

Abbeville	12,391
Abita Springs N.O.	1,072
Addis B.R.	1,320
Albany	857
ALEXANDRIA ALEX	51,565
Ama N.O.	875 ○
Amelia MRGCY	3,617
Amite	4,301
Anacoco	820
Anandale ALEX	2,000 ○
Arabi N.O.	10,248
Arcadia	3,403
Arlington B.R.	850 ○
Arnaudville	1,679
Avery Island	575 ○
Avondale N.O.	6,699
Baker B.R.	12,865
Baldwin	2,644
Ball ALEX	3,405
Barataria	1,123
Basile	2,635
Bastrop	15,527
BATON ROUGE B.R.	238,876
Bawcomville MONR	2,500 ○
Bayou Cane HOMA	15,723
Bayou Goula	800 ○
Belle Chasse N.O.	5,412
Belle Rose	700 ○
Benton	1,864
Bernice	1,956
Berwick	4,466
Blanchard SHRE	1,128
Bogalusa	16,976
Bonfouca N.O.	480 ○
Bonita	503
Boothville	600 ○
Bossier City SHRE	50,817
Bourg HOMA	2,073
Boutte	1,200 ○
Boyce	1,198
Breaux Bridge LAF	5,922
Bridge City N.O.	2,500 ○
Broussard LAF	2,923
Brownfields B.R.	1,800 ○
Brownsville MONR	3,000 ○
Brusly B.R.	1,762
Bunkie	5,364
Buras	2,600 ○
Cameron	1,736
Campti	1,069
Carencro LAF	3,712
Carville	1,037
Centerville	500 ○
Chalmette N.O.	33,847
Charenton	950 ○
Chatham	714
Chauvin	3,338
Cheneyville	865
Choudrant	809
Church Point	4,599
Claiborne MONR	2,000 ○
Clarence	612
Clarks	931
Clayton	1,204
Clinton	1,919
Colfax	1,680
Columbia	687
Converse	449
Cooper Road SHRE	10,000 ○
Cottonport	1,911
Cotton Valley	1,445
Coushatta	2,084
Covington	7,892
Crowley	16,036
Crown Point	950 ○
Cullen	1,869
Cut Off	5,049
Delcambre	2,216
Delhi	3,290
Denham Springs B.R.	8,563
De Quincy	3,966
De Ridder	11,057
Des Allemands	2,920
Destrehan N.O.	2,382
Dodson	469
Donaldsonville	7,901
Doyline	801
Dry Prong	526
Dubach	1,161
Duson LAF	1,253
Elizabeth	454
Elton	1,450
Empire	630 ○
Epps	672
Erath	2,259
Erwinville	475 ○
Estherwood	691
Eunice	12,479
Farmerville	3,768
Fenton	491
Ferriday	4,472
Florien	964
Fordoche	676
Forest Glen	600 ○
Forest Hill	494
Forest Park MONR	1,500 ○
Fountain Place B.R.	9,200 ○
Franklin	9,584
Franklinton	4,119
French Settlement	761
Galliano	5,159
Garyville	2,856
Gibsland	1,354
Gilbert	800
Glenmora	1,479
Golden Meadow	2,282
Goldonna	526
Gonzales B.R.	7,287
Good Pine	900 ○
Grambling	4,226
Gramercy	3,211
Grand Caillou	1,400 ○
Grand Coteau LAF	1,165
Grand Ecore	450 ○
Grand Isle	1,982
Gray	4,000 ○
Grayson	564
Greensburg	662
Greenwood SHRE	1,043
Gretna N.O.	20,615
Grosse Tete	749
Gueydan	1,695
Hackberry	800 ○
Hahnville N.O.	2,947
Hammond	15,960
Harahan N.O.	11,384
Harrisonburg	610
Harvey N.O.	15,000 ○
Haughton SHRE	1,510
Hayes	830 ○
Haynesville	3,454
Henderson	1,560
Hessmer	743
Hineston	500 ○
Hodge	708
Homer	4,307
Hornbeck	470
Hosston	480
HOUMA HOMA	32,602
Independence	1,684
Inniswold B.R.	1,800 ○

○ Rand McNally estimate (not reported in census).
▲ Population of entire township or "town", including rural areas.
● Independent city. Population not included in county total.

LOUISIANA continued

Iota 1,326
Iowa 2,437
Jackson 3,878
Jeanerette 6,511
Jefferson N.O. 15,550
Jena 4,375
Jennings 12,401
Jonesboro 5,061
Jonesville 2,828
Joyce 900 ○
Junction City 727
Kaplan 5,016
Kennedy Heights N.O. 2,000 ○
Kenner N.O. 66,382
Kentwood 2,667
Killian 611
Killona 600 ○
Kinder 2,603
Kraemer 500 ○
Krotz Springs 1,374
Lacombe N.O. 5,146
LAFAYETTE LAF 80,584
Lafayette Southwest LAF 5,500 ○
Lafitte 1,312
Lafourche 600 ○
Lagonda MRGCY 5,805
Lake Arthur 3,615
LAKE CHARLES LKCH 75,226
Lake Providence 6,361
La Place 16,112
Larose 5,234
Lawtell 1,014
Lecompte 1,661
Leesville 9,054
Leonville 1,143
Libuse ALEX 700 ○
Live Oak Manor N.O. 1,500 ○
Livingston 1,260
Livonia 980
Lockport 2,424
Logansport 1,565
Loreauville 860
Lucy 450 ○
Luling N.O. 4,006
Lutcher 4,730
Madisonville N.O. 799
Mamou 3,194
Mandeville N.O. 6,076
Mangham 867
Mansfield 6,485
Mansura 2,074
Many 3,988
Maringouin 1,291
Marion 989
Marksville 5,113
Marrero N.O. 36,548
Martin 584
Mathews 900 ○
Maurice LAF 478
Melville 1,764
Meraux N.O. 4,100 ○
Mermentau 771
Mer Rouge 802
Merryville 1,286
Metairie N.O. 164,160
Mimosa Park N.O. 3,737
Minden 15,084
MONROE MONR 57,597
Montegut 800 ○
Montgomery 843
Montz 500 ○
Mooringsport SHRE 911
Moreauville 853
MORGAN CITY MRGCY 16,114
Morganza 846
Morrow 460 ○
Morse 835
Moss Bluff LKCH 7,004
Napoleonville 829
Natalbany 700 ○
Natchitoches 16,664
Newellton 1,726
NEW IBERIA NWIB 32,766
Newllano 2,213
NEW ORLEANS N.O. 557,927
New Roads 3,924
New Sarpy N.O. 2,249
Norco N.O. 4,416
North Merrydale B.R. 3,500 ○
Oakdale 7,155
Oak Grove 2,214
Oberlin 1,764
Oil City 1,323
Olla 1,603
Opelousas 18,903
Paincourtville 2,004
Paradis 800 ○
Parks 545
Patterson MRGCY 4,693
Paulina 980 ○
Pearl River N.O. 1,693
Pierre Part 3,153
Pine Prairie 734
Pineville ALEX 12,034
Pitkin 750 ○
Plain Dealing 1,213
Plaquemine 7,521
Pointe a la Hache 600 ○
Ponchatoula 5,469
Port Allen B.R. 6,114
Port Barre 2,625
Port Sulphur 3,318
Port Vincent B.R. 450
Provencal 695
Raceland 6,302
Rayne 9,066
Rayville 4,610
Reddell 550 ○
Red Oaks B.R. 2,000 ○
Reserve 7,288
Ringgold 1,655
River Ridge N.O. 17,146
Roanoke 600 ○
Roseland 1,346
Rosepine 953
Ruston 20,585
St. Bernard 720 ○
St. Francisville 1,471
St. Joseph 1,687
St. Martinville 7,965
St. Rose N.O. 2,800 ○
Samtown ALEX 4,125 ○
Sarepta 831
Schriever 500 ○
Scotlandville B.R. 15,113
Scott LAF 2,239
Seymourville 2,891
SHREVEPORT SHRE 205,820
Sicily Island 691
Siegle MONR 1,400 ○
Simmesport 2,293
Simpson 534
Simsboro 553
Slaughter B.R. 729
Slidell N.O. 26,718
Sorrento 1,197
South Mansfield 1,463
Springhill 6,516
Starks 780 ○
Sterlington MONR 1,400
Stonewall 1,175
Sulphur LKCH 19,709
Sunset LAF 2,300
Swartz MONR 450 ○
Tallulah 11,341
Tangipahoa 493
Thibodaux 15,810
Tickfaw 571
Tioga ALEX 1,200 ○
Triumph 1,600 ○
Trout 500 ○
Tullos 776
Union 600 ○
Urania 849
Vacherie 2,169
Vidalia NCHZ 5,936
Vienna 519
Ville Platte 9,201
Vinton 3,631
Violet N.O. 6,000 ○
Vivian 4,225
Walker B.R. 2,957
Washington 1,266
Waterproof 1,339
Welcome 450 ○
Welsh 3,515
Westlake LKCH 5,246
West Monroe MONR 14,993
Westwego N.O. 12,663
White Castle 2,160
Willow Glen 500 ○
Wilson 656
Winnfield 7,311
Winnsboro 5,921
Wisner 1,424
Youngsville LAF 1,053
Zachary B.R. 7,297
Zwolle 2,602

COUNTIES

Acadia 56,427
Allen 21,408
Ascension 50,068
Assumption 22,084
Avoyelles 41,393
Beauregard 29,692
Bienville 16,387
Bossier 80,721
Caddo 252,437
Calcasieu 167,223
Caldwell 10,761
Cameron 9,336
Catahoula 12,287
Claiborne 17,095
Concordia 22,981
De Soto 25,727
East Baton Rouge 366,191
East Carroll 11,772
East Feliciana 19,015
Evangeline 33,343
Franklin 24,141
Grant 16,703
Iberia 63,752
Iberville 32,159
Jackson 17,321
Jefferson 454,592
Jefferson Davis 32,168
Lafayette 150,017
Lafourche 82,483
La Salle 17,004
Lincoln 39,763
Livingston 58,806
Madison 15,682
Morehouse 34,803
Natchitoches 39,863
Orleans 557,927
Ouachita 139,241
Plaquemines 26,049
Pointe Coupee 24,045
Rapides 135,282
Red River 10,433
Richland 22,187
Sabine 25,280
St. Bernard 64,097
St. Charles 37,259
St. Helena 9,827
St. James 21,495
St. John the Baptist 31,924
St. Landry 84,128
St. Martin 40,214
St. Mary 64,253
St. Tammany 110,869
Tangipahoa 80,698
Tensas 8,525
Terrebonne 94,393
Union 21,167
Vermilion 48,458
Vernon 53,475
Washington 44,207
Webster 43,631
West Baton Rouge 19,086
West Carroll 12,922
West Feliciana 12,186
Winn 17,253

MAINE

1980 Census 1,125,030

CITIES

Alfred 1,890▲ 500 ○
Andover 470 ○
Anson 2,226▲ 900 ○
Ashland 1,865▲ 800 ○
Auburn LEW- 23,128
AUGUSTA AUG 21,819
Bailey Island BR-BA 650 ○
BANGOR BANG 31,643
Bar Harbor 4,124▲ 2,685
Bar Mills POR 825 ○
Bath BR-BA 10,246
Belfast 6,243
Berwick DOV- 4,149▲ 2,378
Bethel 2,340▲ 1,225 ○
Biddeford POR 19,638
Bingham 1,184▲ 1,074
Blaine 922▲ 620 ○
Blue Hill 1,644▲ 700 ○
Boothbay 2,308▲ 450 ○
Boothbay Harbor 2,207
Bradley BANG 1,149▲ 625 ○
Brewer BANG 9,017
Bridgton 3,528▲ 1,639
Brownville Junction 775 ○
BRUNSWICK BR-BA 10,990
Bucksport 4,345▲ 2,853
Calais 4,262
Camden 4,584▲ 3,743
Canton 500 ○
Cape Elizabeth POR 7,838
Cape Porpoise 500 ○
Caribou 9,916
Castine 1,304▲ 550 ○
Chisholm 1,796
Clinton 2,696▲ 1,305
Corinna 1,887▲ 950 ○
Cornish 600 ○
Cumberland Center POR 2,015
Cumberland Foreside POR 1,000 ○
Damariscotta 1,493▲ 950 ○
Danforth 500 ○
Dexter 4,286▲ 3,118
Dixfield 2,389▲ 1,725
Dover-Foxcroft 4,323▲ 2,974
Dryden 500 ○
Eagle Lake 600 ○
East Hampden BANG 950 ○
East Holden 570 ○
East Millinocket 2,361
Eastport 1,982
East Wilton 500 ○
Eliot PTSM 4,948▲ 2,450 ○
Ellsworth 5,179
Fairfield WATRVL 6,113▲ 3,169
Falmouth POR 6,853
Farmingdale AUG 2,535▲ 2,014
Farmington 6,730▲ 3,583
Fort Fairfield 4,376▲ 2,282
Fort Kent 4,826▲ 2,375
Freeport POR 5,863▲ 1,906
Frenchville 1,450▲ 615 ○
Friendship 585 ○
Fryeburg 2,715▲ 1,644
Gardiner AUG 6,485
Gorham POR 10,101▲ 4,052
Grand Isle 460 ○
Gray POR 4,344▲ 900 ○
Greenville 1,839▲ 1,640
Greenville Junction 600 ○
Guilford 1,793▲ 1,235
Hallowell AUG 2,502
Hampden BANG 5,250▲ 2,300 ○
Hampden Highlands BANG 1,540 ○
Harrison 1,667▲ 465 ○
Hartland 1,669▲ 1,041
Houlton 6,766▲ 5,730
Howland 1,602
Island Falls 981▲ 650 ○
Jackman 1,003▲ 800 ○
Jay 5,080▲ 500 ○
Jonesport 1,512▲ 1,050
Kennebunk 6,621▲ 3,294
Kennebunkport 2,952▲ 1,685
Kezar Falls 900 ○
Kingfield 1,083▲ 700 ○
Kittery PTSM 9,314▲ 5,465
Kittery Point PTSM 1,260
LEWISTON LEW- 40,481
Limestone 8,719▲ 1,334
Lincoln 5,066▲ 3,524
Lisbon LEW- 8,769▲ 1,200 ○
Lisbon Center LEW- 625 ○
Lisbon Falls LEW- 4,370
Littleton 1,009▲ 600 ○
Livermore Falls 3,572▲ 2,441
Lubec 2,045▲ 990 ○
Machias 2,458▲ 1,277
Madawaska 5,282▲ 4,165
Madison 4,367▲ 2,788
Manchester AUG 1,949▲ 600 ○
Mapleton 1,895▲ 500 ○
Mars Hill 1,892▲ 1,500 ○
Mattawamkeag 1,000▲ 750 ○
Mechanic Falls LEW- 2,616
Medway 1,871▲ 525 ○
Mexico 3,698▲ 3,207
Milbridge 1,306▲ 465 ○
Milford BANG 2,160▲ 1,688
Millinocket 7,567
Milo 2,624▲ 2,255
Monmouth LEW- 2,888▲ 500 ○
Monson 500 ○
Moody 515 ○
Newcastle 1,227▲ 490 ○
New Harbor 450 ○
Newport 2,755▲ 1,748
Norridgewock 2,552▲ 1,318
North Anson 600 ○
North Berwick 2,878▲ 1,436
North Bridgton 500 ○
Northeast Harbor 550 ○
North Vassalboro WATRVL 850 ○
North Windham POR 5,492
Norway 4,042▲ 2,653
Oakfield 847▲ 500 ○
Oakland WATRVL 5,162▲ 3,387
Ogunquit 1,492
Old Orchard Beach POR 6,291
Old Town BANG 8,422
Orono BANG 10,578
Orrs Island BR-BA 500 ○
Oxford 3,143▲ 625 ○
Patten 1,368▲ 1,057
Phillips 1,092▲ 700 ○
Pine Point POR 700 ○
Pittsfield 4,125▲ 3,117
Portage 450 ○
Port Clyde 500 ○
PORTLAND POR 61,572
Presque Isle 11,172
Princeton 994▲ 800 ○
Randolph AUG 1,834
Rangeley 1,023▲ 700 ○
Raymond POR 2,251▲ 500 ○
Richmond 2,627▲ 1,578
Rockland 7,919
Rockport 2,749▲ 1,000 ○
Rumford 8,240▲ 6,256
Sabattus LEW- 3,081▲ 1,234
Saco POR 12,921
Sanford 18,020▲ 10,268
Sangerville 1,219▲ 550 ○
Scarborough POR 11,347▲ 2,280
Searsport 2,309▲ 1,348
Sebago Lake POR 600 ○
Sherman Mills 450 ○
Skowhegan 8,098▲ 6,517
South Berwick DOV- 4,046▲ 2,120
South Bristol 600 ○
South Paris 2,128
South Portland POR 22,712
Southwest Harbor 1,855▲ 1,052
South Windham POR 1,350 ○
Springvale 2,940
Stonington 1,273▲ 700 ○
Strong 1,506▲ 700 ○
Thomaston 2,900▲ 2,348
Topsham BR-BA 6,431▲ 4,657
Union 1,569▲ 500 ○
Unity 1,431▲ 445 ○
Van Buren 3,557▲ 3,282
Veazie BANG 1,610
Vinalhaven 1,211▲ 900 ○
Waldoboro 3,985▲ 1,195
Washburn 2,028▲ 1,221
Waterboro 2,943▲ 500 ○
WATERVILLE WATRVL 17,779
Wells 8,211▲ 850 ○
Westbrook POR 14,976
West Cumberland POR 800 ○
West Enfield 440 ○
West Paris 1,390▲ 500 ○
West Scarborough POR 700 ○
Wilton 4,382▲ 2,262
Windham Center POR 500 ○
Winslow WATRVL 8,057▲ 5,903
Winter Harbor 1,120▲ 900 ○
Winterport BANG 2,675▲ 1,126
Winthrop AUG 5,889▲ 3,264
Wiscasset 2,832▲ 1,350 ○
Woodland 1,363
Woolwich BR-BA 2,156▲ 500 ○
Yarmouth POR 6,585▲ 2,981
York PTSM 8,465▲ 3,130 ○
York Beach PTSM 860 ○
York Harbor PTSM 1,400 ○

COUNTIES

Androscoggin 99,657
Aroostook 91,331
Cumberland 215,789
Franklin 27,447
Hancock 41,781
Kennebec 109,889
Knox 32,941
Lincoln 25,691
Oxford 48,968
Penobscot 137,015
Piscataquis 17,634
Sagadahoc 28,795
Somerset 45,049
Waldo 28,414
Washington 34,963
York 139,666

MARYLAND

1980 Census 4,216,941

CITIES

Aberdeen 11,533
Abingdon BAL 450 ○
ANNAPOLIS ANPLS 31,740
Annapolis Junction BAL 600 ○
Ardmore WASH 900 ○
Arundel Village BAL 5,300 ○
Ashton WASH 1,010 ○
Aspen Hill WASH 9,800 ○
Avenel WASH 5,600 ○
BALTIMORE ● BAL 786,741
Baltimore Highlands BAL 6,750 ○
Barton CUMB 617
Bay Ridge ANPLS 1,989
Bel Air BAL 7,814
Belcamp BAL 650 ○
Beltsville WASH 12,760
Benedict 700 ○
Berlin 2,162
Bethesda WASH 63,022
Birchwood City WASH 8,000 ○
Bladensburg WASH 7,691
Boonsboro HAG- 1,908
Boulevard Heights WASH 1,700 ○
Bowie WASH 33,695
Braddock Heights 4,223
Bradshaw BAL 800 ○
Brandywine WASH 1,319
Brentwood WASH 3,000
Brooklandville BAL 500 ○
Brooklyn Park BAL 2,800 ○
Broomes Island 450 ○
Brunswick 4,572
Bryans Road WASH 3,739
Cabin John WASH 1,500 ○
Calverton WASH 7,649
Cambridge 11,703
Camp Springs WASH 2,500 ○
Capitol Heights WASH 3,271
Cardiff BAL 450 ○
Cavetown HAG- 1,533
Cecilton 508
Centreville 2,018
Charlestown PHIL- 720
Charlotte Hall 1,000 ○
Chase BAL 700 ○
Cheltenham WASH 500 ○
Chesapeake Beach WASH 1,408
Chesapeake City PHIL- 899
Chester ANPLS 600 ○
Chestertown 3,300
Cheverly WASH 5,751
Chillum WASH 14,900 ○
Churchton WASH 800 ○
Clarksburg WASH 600 ○
Clear Spring HAG- 477
Clinton WASH 16,438
Cockeysville BAL 17,013
College Park WASH 23,614
Colmar Manor WASH 1,286
Coltons Point 500 ○
Columbia WASH 52,518
Corriganville CUMB 1,020
Cresaptown CUMB 4,645
Crisfield 2,924
Crofton WASH 12,009
CUMBERLAND CUMB 25,933
Damascus WASH 4,129
Darlington BAL 500 ○
Dayton BAL 700 ○
Deale WASH 3,008
Deal Island 500 ○
Deer Park 486
Delmar SLSB 1,232
Denton 1,927
Derwood WASH 550 ○
District Heights-Forestville WASH 6,799
Dorsey BAL 1,186
Dublin BAL 500 ○
Dundalk BAL 71,293
Easton 7,536
Eckhart Mines CUMB 1,333
Edgemere BAL 7,800 ○
Edgewater ANPLS 800 ○
Edgewood BAL 19,455
Edmondson Heights BAL 5,000 ○
Elk Ridge BAL 2,100 ○
Elkton PHIL- 6,468
Ellerslie CUMB 1,150 ○
Ellicott City BAL 4,000 ○
Emmitsburg 1,552
Essex BAL 39,614
Fairmount Heights WASH 1,616
Federalsburg 1,952
Ferndale BAL 2,600 ○
Fishing Creek 650 ○
Forest Hill BAL 550 ○
Forestville WASH 16,401
Fort Howard BAL 1,050 ○
Fort Washington Forest WASH 1,800 ○
Frederick 28,086
Friendsville 511
Frostburg CUMB 7,715
Fruitland SLSB 2,694
Fulton WASH 600 ○
Funkstown HAG- 1,103
Gaithersburg WASH 26,424
Galesville WASH 600 ○
Gambrills WASH 650 ○
Garrett Park WASH 1,178
Garrison BAL 750 ○
Germantown WASH 9,721
Glen Burnie BAL 30,000 ○
Glyndon BAL 1,100 ○
Grantsville 498
Grasonville ANPLS 1,910
Greenbelt WASH 17,332
Greensboro 1,253
HAGERSTOWN HAG- 34,132
Halethorpe BAL 20,163
Halfway HAG- 8,659
Hampstead BAL 1,293
Hancock 1,887
Harmans BAL 600 ○
Havre de Grace 8,763
Hebron SLSB 714
Hereford BAL 600 ○
Hillcrest Heights 24,900 ○
Hillcrest Heights WASH 17,021
Hughesville WASH 1,208
Hurlock 1,690
Hyattsville WASH 12,709
Indian Head WASH 1,381
Jarrettsville BAL 1,485
Jessup BAL 4,288
Joppa BAL 11,348
Keedysville HAG- 476
Kensington WASH 1,822
Kettering WASH 6,972
Kingstown 1,192
Kingsville BAL 2,824
Lake Shore BAL 2,100 ○
Langley Park WASH 11,100 ○
Lanham WASH 7,300 ○
Lansdowne BAL 10,000 ○
La Plata WASH 2,484
Laurel WASH 12,103
La Vale CUMB 5,500 ○
Lawsonia 1,687
Leonardtown 1,448
Lexington Park 10,361
Libertytown 500 ○
Linthicum Heights BAL 7,457
Loch Lynn Heights 503

○ Rand McNally estimate (not reported in census).
▲ Population of entire township or "town", including rural areas.
● Independent city. Population not included in county total.

Lonaconing CUMB 1,420
Londontowne WASH 3,500 ○
Long Bar Harbor 700 ○
Long Beach 900 ○
Lutherville-Timonium BAL 16,871
Lynne Acres BAL 7,700 ○
McAlpine BAL 2,500 ○
Manchester BAL 1,830
Marbury WASH 1,189
Margate BAL 4,800 ○
Marion Station 500 ○
Marley BAL 4,800 ○
Maryland City WASH 6,250 ○
Maugansville HAG- 1,707
Mayo WASH 1,500 ○
Middle River BAL 26,756
Middletown 1,748
Midland CUMB 601
Millington 546
Montgomery Village WASH 16,600 ○
Mountain Lake Park 1,597
Mount Airy WASH 2,450
Mount Rainier WASH 7,361
Mount Savage CUMB 1,640
New Carrollton WASH 12,632
New Windsor 799
North Beach WASH 1,504
North East PHIL- 1,469
Oakland 1,994
Ocean City 4,946
Odenton BAL 7,500 ○
Olney WASH 10,000 ○
Owings Mills BAL 9,526
Oxford 754
Oxon Hill WASH 8,100 ○
Palmer Park WASH 7,986
Paramount HAG- 1,878
Parkville BAL 35,159
Parsonsburg SLSB 500 ○
Pasadena BAL 3,900 ○
Perry Hall BAL 13,455
Perryman BAL 1,819
Perry Point 500 ○
Pikesville BAL 20,000 ○
Piney Point 900 ○
Pittsville 519
Pocomoke City 3,558
Poolesville 3,428
Port Deposit 664
Potomac WASH 22,800 ○
Potomac Heights WASH 2,456
Preston 498
Prince Frederick 1,805
Princess Anne 1,499
Pumphrey BAL 3,300 ○
Queenstown 491
Randallstown BAL 20,500 ○
Randolph Hills WASH 500 ○
Reisterstown BAL 19,385
Ridgely 933
Rising Sun 1,160
Riverdale WASH 4,761
Riviera Beach BAL 5,600 ○
Rockdale BAL 4,200 ○
Rock Hall 1,511
Rockville WASH 43,811
Rosedale BAL 19,956
St. Marys City 900 ○
St. Michaels 1,301
SALISBURY SLSB 16,429
Savage BAL 2,000 ○
Seabrook WASH 7,100 ○
Seat Pleasant WASH 5,217
Secretary 487
Severn BAL 20,147
Severna Park BAL 21,253
Shady Side WASH 2,877
Sharpsburg HAG- 721
Sharptown 654
Silver Hill WASH 2,400 ○
Silver Spring WASH 64,100 ○
Smithsburg HAG- 833
Snow Hill 2,192
Solomons 500 ○
South Laurel WASH 8,500 ○
Spencerville WASH 1,100 ○
Stevensville ANPLS 450 ○
Sudlersville 443
Suitland WASH 24,800 ○
Sykesville BAL 1,712
Takoma Park WASH 16,231
Taneytown 2,618
Thurmont 2,934
Tilghman 900 ○
Town Creek Manor 900 ○
Towson BAL 51,083
Trappe 739
Union Bridge 927
Upper Marlboro WASH 828
Waldorf WASH 9,782
Walkersville 2,212
Westernport 2,706
West Friendship BAL 500 ○
Westminster BAL 8,808
Westover 525 ○
Wheaton WASH 48,600 ○
White Plains WASH 5,167
Willards 540
Williamsport HAG- 2,153
Woodlawn BAL 8,000 ○
Woodmoor BAL 7,600 ○
Woodsboro 506
Woodstock BAL 700 ○

COUNTIES

Allegany 80,548
Anne Arundel 370,775
Baltimore 655,615
Calvert 34,638
Caroline 23,143
Carroll 96,356
Cecil 60,430
Charles 72,751
Dorchester 30,623
Frederick 114,792
Garrett 26,498
Harford 145,930
Howard 118,572
Kent 16,695
Montgomery 579,053
Prince George's 665,071
Queen Anne's 25,508
St. Mary's 59,895
Somerset 19,188
Talbot 25,604
Washington 113,086
Wicomico 64,540
Worcester 30,889

MASSACHUSETTS

1980 Census 5,737,081

CITIES

Abington BOS 13,517
Acton BOS 17,544▲ 2,500 ○
Acushnet N.BED 8,704▲ 6,400 ○
Adams PTSF 10,381
Agawam SPRG- 26,271▲ 10,300 ○
Amesbury BOS 13,971
AMHERST AMH 17,773
Andover BOS 26,370▲ 8,445
Arlington BOS 48,219
Ashburnham FTCH- 4,075▲ 1,150 ○
Ashby FTCH- 2,311▲ 600 ○
Ashfield 1,458▲ 600 ○
Ashland BOS 9,165
Assinippi BOS 1,400 ○
Assonet F.R. 900 ○
Athol 10,634
Attleboro PROV- 34,196
Auburn WORC 14,845
Avon BOS 5,026
Ayer 6,993
Baldwinville 1,709
Ballardvale BOS 1,300 ○
Barnstable 30,898▲ 2,033
Barre 4,102▲ 1,136
Barre Plains 550 ○
Becket 1,339▲ 500 ○
Bedford BOS 13,067
Belchertown SPRG- 8,339▲ 2,531
Bellingham BOS 14,300
Belmont BOS 26,100
Berkshire PTSF 500 ○
Berlin BOS 2,215▲ 550 ○
Bernardston 1,750▲ 700 ○
Beverly BOS 37,655
Billerica BOS 36,727▲ 6,400 ○
Blackstone PROV- 6,570▲ 5,100 ○
Blandford 1,038▲ 800 ○
Bolton BOS 2,530▲ 500 ○
Bondsville SPRG- 1,906
BOSTON BOS 562,994
Bourne 13,874▲ 800 ○
Boxborough BOS 3,126▲ 500 ○
Boxford BOS 5,374▲ 1,841
Boylston WORC 3,470▲ 950 ○
Braintree BOS 36,337
Brant Rock BOS 1,500 ○
Brewster 5,226▲ 1,744
Bridgewater BOS 17,202▲ 6,781
Brimfield SPRG- 500 ○
Brockton BOS 95,172
Brookfield WORC 2,397▲ 1,037
Brookline BOS 55,062
Brooks Place BOS 500 ○
Brookville BOS 950 ○
Bryantville BOS 1,500 ○
Burlington BOS 23,486
Buzzards Bay 3,375
Byfield BOS 950 ○
Cambridge BOS 95,322
Canton BOS 18,182
Carlisle BOS 3,306▲ 600 ○
Carver BOS 6,988▲ 650 ○
Cataumet 800 ○
Centerville 3,640
Chaffin WORC 3,700 ○
Charlemont 1,149▲ 500 ○
Charlton City WORC 1,100 ○
Chartley PROV- 600 ○
Chatham 6,071▲ 1,922
Chelmsford BOS 31,174
Chelsea BOS 25,431
Cherry Valley WORC 1,400 ○
Cheshire PTSF 3,124▲ 1,100 ○
Chester 1,123▲ 750 ○
Chesterfield 1,000▲ 550 ○
Chicopee SPRG- 55,112
Clinton 12,771
Cochituate BOS 6,126
Cohasset BOS 7,174▲ 5,300 ○
Concord BOS 16,293▲ 6,400 ○
Conway 1,213▲ 600 ○
Cordaville BOS 1,384
Cotuit 1,300 ○
Dalton PTSF 6,797
Danvers BOS 24,100
Dedham BOS 25,298
Deerfield 4,517▲ 550 ○
Dennis 12,360▲ 900 ○
Dennis Port 2,570
Dighton TAUN 5,352▲ 900 ○
Dorothy Pond WORC 1,900 ○
Dover BOS 4,703▲ 2,051
Dracut BOS 21,249
Dudley WORC 8,717▲ 3,700 ○
Dunstable BOS 1,671▲ 900 ○
Duxbury BOS 11,807▲ 1,685
East Acton BOS 1,200 ○
East Billerica BOS 2,900 ○
East Brewster 700 ○
East Bridgewater
BOS 9,945▲ 3,300 ○
East Brookfield
WORC 1,955▲ 1,443
East Dennis 800 ○
East Douglas WORC 1,683
East Falmouth 5,181
East Foxboro BOS 500 ○
East Freetown N.BED 500 ○
Eastham 3,472▲ 1,100 ○
Easthampton SPRG- 15,580
East Longmeadow SPRG- 12,905
East Mansfield BOS 500 ○
East Millbury WORC 1,000 ○
Eastondale BOS 900 ○
East Orleans 1,200 ○
East Pepperell 2,212
East Sudbury BOS 1,500 ○
East Templeton 980 ○
East Walpole BOS 4,900 ○
East Wareham 1,000 ○
Edgartown 2,204▲ 1,138
Egypt BOS 1,100 ○
Elmwood BOS 750 ○
Essex BOS 2,998▲ 1,490
Everett BOS 37,195
Fairhaven N.BED 15,759
FALL RIVER F.R. 92,574
Falmouth 23,640▲ 4,200 ○
Fayville BOS 1,000 ○
Feeding Hills SPRG- 8,500 ○
Fiskdale 1,859
FITCHBURG FTCH- 39,580
Forge Village BOS 1,400 ○
Foxboro BOS 5,697
Foxvale BOS 500 ○
Framingham BOS 65,113
Franklin BOS 18,217
Gardner 17,900
Georgetown BOS 5,687▲ 2,600 ○
Gilbertville 1,029
Gloucester BOS 27,768
Grafton WORC 11,238▲ 2,000 ○
Granby SPRG- 5,380▲ 1,302
Graniteville BOS 1,000 ○
Gray Gables 500 ○
Great Barrington 7,405▲ 3,150
Greenfield 14,198
Green Harbor BOS 2,000 ○
Groton 6,154▲ 1,264
Groveland BOS 4,300 ○
Hadley AMH 4,125▲ 890 ○
Halifax BOS 5,513▲ 900 ○
Hamilton BOS 6,960▲ 1,000 ○
Hampden SPRG- 4,745▲ 700 ○
Hanover BOS 11,358▲ 2,500 ○
Hanover Center BOS 1,000 ○
Hanson BOS 8,617▲ 2,120
Hardwick 2,272▲ 500 ○
Harvard 12,170▲ 900 ○
Harwich 8,971▲ 1,000 ○
Harwich Port 1,900 ○
Harwood BOS 900 ○
Hatfield NHAMP 3,045▲ 1,251
Haverhill BOS 46,865
Haydenville NHAMP 900 ○
Hingham BOS 20,339▲ 12,800 ○
Hinsdale PTSF 1,707▲ 950 ○
Holbrook BOS 11,140
Holden WORC 13,336▲ 3,900 ○
Holliston BOS 12,622
Holyoke SPRG- 44,678
Hopedale BOS 3,905
Hopkinton BOS 7,114▲ 2,542
Housatonic 1,314
Hubbardston 1,797▲ 500 ○
Hudson BOS 14,156
Hull BOS 9,714
Huntington 1,804▲ 950 ○
Hyannis 8,000 ○
Hyannis Port 1,150 ○
Indian Mound Beach 800 ○
Ipswich BOS 11,158▲ 4,548
Island Creek BOS 450 ○
Islington BOS 5,100 ○
Jefferson WORC 800 ○
Kingston BOS 7,362▲ 4,405
Lakeville BOS 5,931▲ 1,948
Lancaster 6,334▲ 900 ○
Lanesboro PTSF 950 ○
Lawrence BOS 63,175
Lee PTSF 6,247▲ 2,140
Leicester WORC 9,446▲ 3,400 ○
Lenox PTSF 6,523▲ 2,668
Lenox Dale PTSF 600 ○
Leominster FTCH- 34,508
Lexington BOS 29,479
Lincoln BOS 7,098▲ 3,300 ○
Linwood WORC 1,100 ○
Littleton BOS 6,970▲ 3,109
Longmeadow SPRG- 16,301
Lowell BOS 92,418
Ludlow SPRG- 18,150
Lunenburg FTCH- 8,405▲ 1,789
Lynn BOS 78,471
Lynnfield BOS 11,267
Malden BOS 53,386
Manchaug WORC 1,000 ○
Manchester BOS 5,424
Manomet BOS 950 ○
Mansfield BOS 13,453▲ 6,786
Marblehead BOS 20,126
Marion N.BED 3,932▲ 1,438
Marlborough BOS 30,617
Marshfield BOS 20,916▲ 4,421
Marshfield Hills BOS 2,308
Marstons Mills 600 ○
Mashpee 3,700▲ 500 ○
Matfield BOS 700 ○
Mattapoisett N.BED 5,597▲ 3,159
Maynard BOS 9,590
Medfield BOS 10,220▲ 6,108
Medford BOS 58,076
Medway BOS 8,447▲ 4,300 ○
Melrose BOS 30,055
Mendon BOS 3,108▲ 900 ○
Merrimac BOS 4,451▲ 2,300 ○
Merrimacport BOS 450 ○
Methuen BOS 36,701
Middleboro BOS 7,012
Middleton BOS 4,135
Milford BOS 23,390
Millbury WORC 11,808▲ 5,700 ○
Millers Falls 1,101
Millis BOS 6,908▲ 3,777 ○
Millville PROV- 1,693
Milton BOS 25,860
Minot BOS 800 ○
Monponsett BOS 600 ○
Monson SPRG- 7,315▲ 2,167
Montague 8,011▲ 900 ○
Monterey 818▲ 500 ○
Monument Beach 1,500 ○
Morningdale WORC 1,150 ○
Mount Hermon 600 ○
Nabnasset BOS 4,800 ○
Nahant BOS 3,947
Nantucket 5,087▲ 3,229
Natick BOS 29,461
Needham BOS 27,901
NEW BEDFORD N.BED 98,478
New Braintree 671▲ 600 ○
Newbury BOS 4,529▲ 900 ○
Newburyport BOS 15,900
Newton BOS 83,622
Norfolk BOS 6,363▲ 450 ○
North Abington BOS 4,700 ○
North Acton BOS 900 ○
North Adams 18,063
North Amherst AMH 5,616
NORTHAMPTON NHAMP 29,286
North Andover BOS 20,129
North Attleboro PROV- 21,095
North Billerica BOS 6,700 ○
Northborough
WORC 10,568▲ 5,670
Northbridge
WORC 12,246▲ 3,321 ○
North Brookfield
WORC 4,150▲ 2,543
North Carver BOS 700 ○
North Cohasset BOS 900 ○
North Dartmouth N.BED 6,000 ○
North Dighton TAUN 1,174
North Eastham 1,318
North Easton BOS 6,100 ○
North Falmouth 1,800 ○
Northfield 2,386▲ 1,182
North Grafton WORC 3,400 ○
North Hanover BOS 900 ○
North Hatfield NHAMP 450 ○
North Marshfield BOS 450 ○
North Oxford WORC 1,550 ○
North Pembroke BOS 2,215
North Reading BOS 11,455
North Scituate BOS 4,100 ○
North Sudbury BOS 1,700 ○
North Swansea F.R. 950 ○
North Tewksbury BOS 1,400 ○
North Truro 700 ○
North Uxbridge WORC 1,400 ○
North Wilmington BOS 4,200 ○
Norton PROV- 12,690▲ 2,035
Norwell BOS 9,182▲ 800 ○
Norwood BOS 29,711
Nutting Lake BOS 2,400 ○
Oak Bluffs 1,984
Oakdale WORC 600 ○
Ocean Bluff BOS 2,500 ○
Ocean Grove F.R. 4,000 ○
Ocean Heights 500 ○
Oldham Village BOS 900 ○
Onset BOS 1,493
Orange 6,844▲ 3,942
Orleans 5,306▲ 1,811
Osterville 1,799
Otis 963▲ 500 ○
Otter River 600 ○
Oxford WORC 11,680▲ 6,369
Palmer SPRG- 11,389▲ 3,854
Paxton WORC 3,762▲ 1,800 ○
Peabody BOS 45,976
Pelham AMH 1,112▲ 500 ○
Pembroke BOS 13,487▲ 1,800 ○
Pepperell 8,061▲ 2,076
Petersham 1,024▲ 550 ○
Pigeon Cove BOS 1,700 ○
Pinehurst BOS 6,588
Pine Lake BOS 800 ○
Pine Rest BOS 900 ○
PITTSFIELD PTSF 51,974
Plainville PROV- 5,857
Plymouth BOS 35,913▲ 7,232
Pocasset 2,000 ○
Point Independence BOS 700 ○
Princeton WORC 2,425▲ 600 ○
Provincetown 3,536
Quincy BOS 84,743
Randolph BOS 28,218
Raynham TAUN 9,085▲ 2,124
Raynham Center TAUN 3,776
Reading BOS 22,678
Revere BOS 42,423
Rexhame BOS 550 ○
River Pines BOS 3,700 ○
Rochdale WORC 1,105
Rochester N.BED 3,205▲ 450 ○
Rock BOS 500 ○
Rockland BOS 15,695
Rockport BOS 6,345▲ 4,600 ○
Rowley BOS 3,867▲ 1,321
Russell SPRG- 1,570▲ 650 ○
Rutland WORC 4,334▲ 2,312
Sagamore 1,152
Sagamore Beach 800 ○
Salem BOS 38,264
Salisbury BOS 5,973▲ 3,265
Sand Hill BOS 1,750 ○
Sandwich 8,727▲ 1,784
Saugus BOS 24,746
Scituate BOS 17,317▲ 5,351
Seekonk PROV- 12,269
Sharon BOS 13,601
Sheffield 2,743▲ 1,100 ○
Shelburne Falls 2,046
Sherborn BOS 4,049▲ 950 ○
Shirley 5,124▲ 1,630
Shore Acres BOS 1,200 ○
Shrewsbury WORC 22,674
Silver Lake BOS 3,400 ○
Somerset F.R. 18,813
Somerville BOS 77,372
South Acton BOS 4,600 ○
South Amherst AMH 4,861
Southampton SPRG- 4,137▲ 500 ○
South Ashburnham FTCH- 1,123
South Barre 600 ○
Southborough BOS 6,193▲ 1,600 ○
Southbridge 16,665
South Carver BOS 600 ○
South Chatham 950 ○
South Dartmouth N.BED 7,000 ○
South Deerfield 1,926
South Dennis 1,500 ○
South Duxbury BOS 2,985
South Easton BOS 1,400 ○
South Egremont 600 ○
South Grafton WORC 3,000 ○
South Hadley
SPRG- 16,399▲ 8,900 ○
South Hadley Falls SPRG- 5,600 ○
South Hamilton BOS 2,900 ○
South Hanover BOS 950 ○
South Harwich 900 ○
South Hingham BOS 5,200 ○
South Lancaster 2,329
South Lee PTSF 500 ○
South Swansea F.R. 1,700 ○
South Walpole BOS 1,600 ○
South Wellfleet 600 ○
Southwick SPRG- 7,382▲ 1,400 ○
South Yarmouth 7,525
Spencer WORC 10,774▲ 6,350
SPRINGFIELD SPRG- 152,319
Sterling WORC 5,440▲ 1,200 ○
Stockbridge PTSF 2,328▲ 1,109
Stoneham BOS 21,424
Stoughton BOS 26,710
Stow BOS 5,144▲ 1,100 ○
Sturbridge 5,976▲ 1,891
Sudbury BOS 14,027▲ 2,200 ○
Sudbury Center BOS 2,900 ○
Sunderland AMH 2,929▲ 600 ○
Sutton WORC 5,855▲ 500 ○
Swampscott BOS 13,837
Swansea F.R. 15,461▲ 750 ○
TAUNTON TAUN 45,001
Teaticket 2,000 ○
Templeton 6,070▲ 900 ○
Tewksbury BOS 24,635▲ 11,500 ○
Thorndike SPRG- 1,000 ○
Three Rivers SPRG- 3,322
Topsfield BOS 5,709▲ 2,647
Touisset F.R. 1,300 ○
Townsend FTCH- 7,201▲ 1,266
Truro 1,486▲ 500 ○
Turners Falls 4,711
Upton BOS 3,886▲ 1,500 ○
Uxbridge WORC 8,374▲ 3,500 ○
Vineyard Haven 1,704
Wakefield BOS 24,895
Wales 1,177▲ 500 ○
Walpole BOS 18,859▲ 5,274
Waltham BOS 58,200
Wamesit BOS 2,700 ○
Ware 8,953▲ 6,806
Wareham 18,457▲ 2,493
Warren 3,777▲ 1,548
Watertown BOS 34,384
Wayland BOS 12,170▲ 5,500 ○
Webster WORC 14,480
Wellesley BOS 27,209
Wellfleet 2,209▲ 950 ○
Wenham BOS 3,897
West Abington BOS 2,000 ○
West Acton BOS 5,800 ○
West Andover BOS 3,700 ○
West Barnstable 500 ○
West Billerica BOS 2,000 ○
Westborough WORC 13,619
West Boylston
WORC 6,204▲ 3,500 ○
West Bridgewater
BOS 6,359▲ 2,100 ○
West Brookfield 3,026▲ 1,423
West Chatham 1,398
West Concord BOS 5,331
West Dennis 2,030
West Falmouth 1,200 ○
Westfield SPRG- 36,465
Westford BOS 13,434▲ 1,000 ○
West Groton 950 ○
West Hanover BOS 1,600 ○
West Hyannisport 1,200 ○
West Mansfield BOS 500 ○
West Medway BOS 2,269 ○
Westminster FTCH- 5,139▲ 950 ○
West Newbury BOS 2,861▲ 950 ○
Weston BOS 11,169
West Pelham AMH 450 ○
Westport F.R. 1,850 ○
Westport Point F.R. 450 ○
West Springfield SPRG- 27,042
West Stockbridge
PTSF 1,280▲ 800 ○
West Townsend FTCH- 700 ○
West Upton BOS 1,000 ○
West Wareham 1,837
West Warren SPRG- 1,200 ○
Westwood BOS 13,212▲ 6,500 ○
West Yarmouth BOS 3,882
Weymouth BOS 55,601
Whalom FTCH- 1,400 ○
Whately 1,341▲ 450 ○
White Horse Beach BOS 800 ○
White Island Shores 950 ○
Whitinsville WORC 5,379
Whitman BOS 13,534
Wilbraham SPRG- 12,053▲ 3,379
Williamsburg NHAMP 2,237▲ 950 ○
Williamstown 8,741▲ 4,798
Wilmington BOS 17,471
Winchendon 7,019▲ 4,030
Winchester BOS 20,701
Winthrop BOS 19,294
Woburn BOS 36,626
Woods Hole 1,080
WORCESTER WORC 161,799
Wrentham BOS 7,580▲ 1,400 ○
Yarmouth 18,449▲ 900 ○
Yarmouth Port 2,490

COUNTIES

Barnstable 147,925
Berkshire 145,110
Bristol 474,641

○ Rand McNally estimate (not reported in census).
▲ Population of entire township or "town", including rural areas.
● Independent city. Population not included in county total.

- Dukes 8,942
- Essex 633,676
- Franklin 64,317
- Hampden 443,018
- Hampshire 138,813
- Middlesex 1,367,034
- Nantucket 5,087
- Norfolk 606,587
- Plymouth 405,437
- Suffolk 650,142
- Worcester 646,352

MICHIGAN

1980 Census 9,262,070

CITIES

- Adrian 21,276
- Akron 538
- Alanson 508
- Albion 11,059
- Algonac DET 4,412
- Allegan 4,576
- Allen Park DET 34,196
- Alma 9,652
- Almont DET 1,857
- Alpena 12,214
- Amasa 600 ○
- Ann Arbor DET 107,969
- Armada DET 1,392
- Ashley 570
- Athens 960
- Atlanta 650 ○
- Auburn BC-M 1,921
- Auburn Heights DET 4,000 ○
- Au Gres 768
- Augusta BTLCK 913
- Bad Axe 3,184
- Baldwin 674
- Bancroft FLN 618
- Bangor 2,001
- Bangor Township BC-M 17,494 ○
- Baraga 1,055
- Baroda BNTH- 627
- Barron Lake S.B.- 1,600 ○
- Bath LANS 600 ○
- BATTLE CREEK BTLCK 56,339
- BAY CITY BC-M 41,593
- Bay Port 800 ○
- Beaverton 1,025
- Beecher FLN 17,178
- Belding 5,634
- Bellaire 1,063
- Belleville DET 3,366
- Bellevue 1,289
- BENTON HARBOR BNTH- 14,707
- Benton Heights BNTH- 6,787
- Benzonia 466
- Bergland 700 ○
- Berkley DET 18,637
- Berrien Springs S.B.- 2,042
- Bertrand S.B.- 5,000 ○
- Bessemer 2,553
- Beulah 454
- Beverly Hills DET 11,598
- Big Rapids 14,361
- Birch Run FLN 1,196
- Birmingham DET 21,689
- Blissfield 3,107
- Bloomfield Hills DET 3,985
- Bloomingdale 537
- Boyne City 3,348
- Breckenridge 1,495
- Bridgeport SAG 3,500 ○
- Bridgman BNTH- 2,235
- Brighton DET 4,268
- Brimley 500 ○
- Britton 693
- Bronson 2,271
- Brooklyn JAC 1,110
- Brown City 1,163
- Buchanan S.B.- 5,142
- Burr Oak 853
- Burton FLN 29,976
- Cadillac 10,199
- Caledonia GDR 722
- Calumet 1,013
- Canton DET 5,000 ○
- Capac 1,377
- Carleton DET 2,786
- Caro 4,317
- Carrollton SAG 7,482
- Carson City 1,229
- Carsonville 622
- Caseville 851
- Caspian 1,038
- Cass City 2,258
- Cassopolis S.B.- 1,933
- Cedar Springs GDR 2,615
- Cedarville 900 ○
- Cement City JAC 539
- Center Line DET 9,293
- Central Lake 895
- Centreville 1,202
- Champion 500 ○
- Charlevoix 3,296
- Charlotte 8,251
- Chassell 700 ○
- Cheboygan 5,106
- Chelsea DET 3,816
- Chesaning FLN 2,656
- Clare 3,300
- Clarkston DET 968
- Clawson DET 15,103
- Climax BTLCK 619
- Clinton 2,342
- Clio FLN 2,669
- Coldwater 9,461
- Coleman 1,429
- Coloma BNTH- 1,833
- Colon 1,190
- Columbiaville FLN 953
- Comstock KZOO 5,310 ○
- Concord 900
- Constantine 1,680
- Coopersville 2,889
- Corunna 3,206
- Covert 600 ○
- Crystal 600 ○
- Crystal Falls 1,965
- Cutlerville GDR 8,256
- Davison FLN 6,087
- Dearborn DET 90,660
- Dearborn Heights DET 67,706
- Decatur 1,915
- Deckerville 887
- Deerfield 957
- De Tour Village 466
- DETROIT DET 1,202,463
- De Witt LANS 3,165
- Dexter DET 1,524
- Dimondale LANS 1,008
- Dollar Bay 900 ○
- Dorr GDR 500 ○
- Douglas 948
- Dowagiac 6,307
- Drayton Plains DET 18,000 ○
- Drummond Island 500 ○
- Dryden 650
- Dundee 2,575
- Durand FLN 4,206
- East Detroit DET 38,280
- East Grand Rapids GDR 10,914
- East Jordan 2,185
- Eastlake 514
- East Lansing LANS 51,392
- East Tawas 2,584
- Eastwood KZOO 7,186
- Eaton Rapids 4,510
- Eau Claire S.B.- 573
- Eben Junction 450 ○
- Ecorse DET 14,447
- Edmore 1,176
- Edwardsburg S.B.- 1,135
- Elberta 556
- Elk Rapids 1,504
- Elkton 953
- Elsie 1,022
- Engadine 500 ○
- Erie TOL 700 ○
- Escanaba 14,355
- Essexville BC-M 4,378
- Evart 1,945
- Ewen 500 ○
- Fairgrove 691
- Fair Haven DET 900 ○
- Fair Plain BNTH- 8,289
- Fairview 500 ○
- Farmington DET 11,022
- Farmington Hills DET 58,056
- Farwell 804
- Fennville 934
- Fenton FLN 8,098
- Ferndale DET 26,227
- Flat Rock DET 6,853
- FLINT FLN 159,611
- Flushing FLN 8,624
- Fowler 1,021
- Fowlerville 2,289
- Frankenmuth SAG 3,753
- Frankfort 1,603
- Fraser DET 14,560
- Frederic 500 ○
- Freeland BC-M 1,364
- Freeport 479
- Fremont 3,672
- Fruitport MUS 1,143
- Fulton 750 ○
- Gaines FLN 440
- Galesburg KZOO 1,822
- Galien 692
- Garden City DET 35,640
- Gaylord 3,011
- Genesee FLN 950 ○
- Gladstone 4,533
- Gladwin 2,479
- Gobles 816
- Grand Blanc FLN 6,848
- Grand Haven MUS 11,763
- Grand Ledge LANS 6,920
- GRAND RAPIDS GDR 181,843
- Grandville GDR 12,412
- Grant 683
- Grass Lake 900 ○
- Grayling 1,792
- Greenville 8,019
- Greilickville 1,000 ○
- Grosse Ile DET 9,320
- Grosse Pointe DET 5,901
- Grosse Pointe Park DET 14,515
- Grosse Pointe Woods DET 18,886
- Gwinn 1,408
- Hamilton 800 ○
- Hamtramck DET 21,300
- Hancock 5,122
- Hanover JAC 490
- Harbor Beach 2,000
- Harbor Springs 1,567
- Harper Woods DET 16,361
- Harrison 1,700
- Harrisville 559
- Hart 1,888
- Hartford BNTH- 2,493
- Hartland DET 450 ○
- Harvey 1,341
- Haslett LANS 7,025
- Hastings 6,418
- Hazel Park DET 20,914
- Hemlock BC-M 1,362
- Hermansville 700 ○
- Hesperia 876
- Higgins Lake 500 ○
- Highland DET 1,000 ○
- Highland Park DET 27,909
- Hillsdale 7,432
- HOLLAND HLND 26,281
- Holly FLN 4,874
- Holt LANS 10,097
- Homer 1,791
- Hopkins 536
- Houghton 7,512
- Houghton Lake 1,500 ○
- Houghton Lake Heights 2,449
- Howard City 1,118
- Howell DET 6,976
- Hubbell 1,278
- Hudson 2,545
- Hudsonville GDR 4,844
- Huntington Woods DET 6,937
- Ida TOL 1,000 ○
- Imlay City 2,495
- Inkster DET 35,190
- Ionia 5,920
- Iron Mountain 8,341
- Iron River 2,426
- Ironwood 7,741
- Ishpeming 7,538
- Ithaca 2,950
- JACKSON JAC 39,739
- Jenison GDR 16,330
- Jonesville 2,172
- KALAMAZOO KZOO 79,722
- Kaleva 445
- Kalkaska 1,654
- Keego Harbor DET 3,083
- Kent City 860
- Kentwood GDR 30,438
- Kinde 600
- Kingsford 5,290
- Kingsley 664
- Laingsburg 1,145
- Lake City 843
- Lake Linden 1,181
- Lake Odessa 2,171
- Lake Orion DET 2,907
- Lakeview 1,139
- Lambertville TOL 6,341
- L'Anse 2,500
- LANSING LANS 130,414
- Lapeer FLN 6,198
- Laurium 2,678
- Lawrence 903
- Lawton 1,558
- Leland 600 ○
- Leslie 2,110
- Lewiston 600 ○
- Lexington 765
- Lincoln Park DET 45,105
- Linden FLN 2,174
- Litchfield 1,353
- Livonia DET 104,814
- Lowell GDR 3,707
- Ludington 8,937
- Luna Pier TOL 1,443
- Luzerne 500 ○
- Lyons 708
- McBain 519
- Mackinac Island 479
- Mackinaw City 820
- Madison Heights DET 35,375
- Mancelona 1,432
- Manchester 1,686
- Manistee 7,665
- Manistique 3,962
- Manton 1,212
- Maple Rapids 683
- Marcellus 1,134
- Marenisco 600 ○
- Marine City 4,414
- Marion 816
- Marlette 1,761
- Marne 500 ○
- Marquette 23,288
- Marshall 7,201
- Martin 447
- Marysville PTHU 7,345
- Mason LANS 6,019
- Maybee 490
- Mayville 958
- Melvindale DET 12,322
- Memphis 1,171
- Mendon 951
- Menominee 10,099
- Merrill BC-M 851
- Metamora 552
- Michigan Center JAC 5,244
- Middleton 500 ○
- Middleville GDR 1,797
- Midland BC-M 37,269
- Milan DET 4,182
- Milford DET 5,041
- Millington FLN 1,237
- Mio 1,500 ○
- Mohawk 950 ○
- Moline GDR 800 ○
- MONROE MONR 23,531
- Montague MUS 2,332
- Montrose FLN 1,706
- Morenci 2,110
- Morley 507
- Mount Clemens DET 18,806
- Mount Morris FLN 3,246
- Mount Pleasant 23,746
- Muir 698
- Mulliken 550
- Munising 3,083
- MUSKEGON MUS 40,823
- Muskegon Heights MUS 14,611
- Nashville 1,628
- Negaunee 5,189
- Newaygo 1,271
- New Baltimore DET 5,439
- Newberry 2,120
- New Boston DET 1,200
- New Buffalo MICH 2,821
- New Era 534
- New Haven DET 1,871
- New Hudson DET 800 ○
- New Lothrop 646
- Newport DET 900 ○
- Niles S.B.- 13,115
- North Adams 565
- North Branch 896
- North Lake 500 ○
- North Muskegon MUS 4,024
- Northport 611
- Northville DET 5,698
- Norton Shores MUS 22,025
- Norway 2,919
- Novi DET 22,525
- Oak Hill 1,000 ○
- Oak Park DET 31,537
- Okemos LANS 8,882
- Olivet 1,604
- Onaway 1,084
- Onekama 582
- Onsted 670
- Ontonagon 2,182
- Ortonville DET 1,190
- Oscoda 2,431
- Otisville FLN 682
- Otsego KZOO 3,802
- Otter Lake FLN 456
- Ovid 1,712
- Owosso 16,455
- Oxford DET 2,746
- Painesdale 650 ○
- Palmer 900 ○
- Parchment KZOO 1,817
- Parma JAC 873
- Paw Paw 3,211
- Peck 606
- Pellston 565
- Pentwater 1,165
- Perry LANS 2,051
- Petersburg 1,222
- Petoskey 6,097
- Pewamo 488
- Pickford 500 ○
- Pigeon 1,247
- Pinckney DET 1,390
- Pinconning BC-M 1,430
- Plainfield Heights GDR 5,000 ○
- Plainwell KZOO 3,751
- Plymouth DET 9,986
- Pontiac DET 76,715
- Portage KZOO 38,157
- Port Austin 839
- PORT HURON PTHU 33,981
- Portland 3,963
- Port Sanilac 598
- Powers 490
- Pullman 500 ○
- Quincy 1,569
- Quinnesec 900 ○
- Ramsay 1,068 ○
- Rapid River 700 ○
- Ravenna 951
- Reading 1,203
- Redford Township DET 58,441
- Reed City 2,221
- Reese 1,645
- Remus 450 ○
- Republic 1,000 ○
- Richland KZOO 486
- Richmond DET 3,536
- River Rouge DET 12,912
- Riverview DET 14,569
- Rives Junction JAC 450 ○
- Rochester DET 7,203
- Rock 475 ○
- Rockford GDR 3,324
- Rockwood DET 3,346
- Rogers City 3,923
- Romeo DET 3,509
- Romulus DET 24,857
- Roosevelt Park MUS 4,015
- Roscommon 834
- Rose City 661
- Roseville DET 54,311
- Rothbury 522
- Royal Oak DET 70,893
- Rudyard 900 ○
- SAGINAW SAG 77,508
- St. Charles SAG 2,276
- St. Clair 4,780
- St. Clair Shores DET 76,210
- St. Ignace 2,632
- St. Johns 7,376
- St. Joseph BNTH- 9,622
- St. Louis 4,107
- Saline DET 6,483
- Sandusky 2,216
- Sanford BC-M 864
- Saranac 1,421
- Saugatuck 1,079
- SAULT STE. MARIE SOO 14,448
- Sawyer 550 ○
- Schoolcraft KZOO 1,359
- Scottville 1,241
- Sebewaing 2,046
- Shelby 1,624
- Shepherd 1,534
- Shoreham BNTH- 742
- Southfield DET 75,568
- Southgate DET 32,058
- South Haven 5,943
- South Lyon DET 5,214
- South Range 861
- Sparta GDR 3,373
- Spring Arbor JAC 2,101
- Springfield BTLCK 5,917
- Spring Lake MUS 2,731
- Springport 675
- Stambaugh 1,442
- Standish 1,264
- Stanton 1,315
- Stephenson 967
- Sterling 457
- Sterling Heights DET 108,999
- Stevensville BNTH- 1,268
- Stockbridge 1,213
- Sturgis 9,468
- Sunfield 591
- Suttons Bay 504
- Swartz Creek FLN 5,013
- Tawas City 1,967
- Taylor DET 77,568
- Tecumseh 7,320
- Tekonsha 755
- Temperance TOL 3,500 ○
- Three Oaks 1,774
- Three Rivers 7,015
- Tower 500 ○
- Traverse City 15,516
- Trenton DET 22,762
- Troy DET 67,102
- Ubly 862
- Union City 1,667
- Union Lake DET 12,000 ○
- Union Pier 1,039
- Unionville 578
- Utica DET 5,282
- Vanderbilt 525
- Vandercook Lake JAC 4,975
- Vassar 2,727
- Vermontville 832
- Vicksburg KZOO 2,224
- Vulcan 600 ○
- Wakefield 2,591
- Waldron 570
- Walker GDR 15,088
- Walled Lake DET 4,748
- Warren DET 161,134
- Waterford DET 64,250
- Watersmeet 700 ○
- Watervliet BNTH- 1,867
- Waverly LANS 6,700 ○
- Wayland 2,023
- Wayne DET 21,159
- Webberville 1,535
- Weidman 450 ○
- West Branch 1,785
- Westland DET 84,603
- Westphalia 896
- West Willow DET 5,400 ○
- Westwood KZOO 8,519
- White Cloud 1,101
- Whitehall MUS 2,856
- White Pigeon 1,478
- White Pine 1,142
- Whitmore Lake DET 2,920
- Williamston LANS 2,981
- Willow Run DET 6,400 ○
- Winn 450 ○
- Wixom DET 6,705
- Wolf Lake MUS 3,876
- Woodhaven DET 10,902
- Wyandotte DET 34,006
- Wyoming GDR 59,616
- Yale 1,814
- Ypsilanti DET 24,031
- Zeeland HLND 4,764
- Zilwaukee SAG 2,201

COUNTIES

- Alcona 9,740
- Alger 9,225
- Allegan 81,555
- Alpena 32,315
- Antrim 16,194
- Arenac 14,706
- Baraga 8,484
- Barry 45,781
- Bay 119,881
- Benzie 11,205
- Berrien 171,276
- Branch 40,188
- Calhoun 141,557
- Cass 49,499
- Charlevoix 19,907
- Cheboygan 20,649
- Chippewa 29,029
- Clare 23,822
- Clinton 55,893
- Crawford 9,465
- Delta 38,947
- Dickinson 25,341
- Eaton 88,337
- Emmet 22,992
- Genesee 450,449
- Gladwin 19,957
- Gogebic 19,686
- Grand Traverse 54,899
- Gratiot 40,448
- Hillsdale 42,071
- Houghton 37,872
- Huron 36,459
- Ingham 275,520
- Ionia 51,815
- Iosco 28,349
- Iron 13,635
- Isabella 54,110
- Jackson 151,495
- Kalamazoo 212,378
- Kalkaska 10,952
- Kent 444,506
- Keweenaw 1,963
- Lake 7,711
- Lapeer 70,038
- Leelanau 14,007
- Lenawee 89,948
- Livingston 100,289
- Luce 6,659
- Mackinac 10,178
- Macomb 694,600
- Manistee 23,019
- Marquette 74,101
- Mason 26,365
- Mecosta 36,961
- Menominee 26,201
- Midland 73,578
- Missaukee 10,009
- Monroe 134,659
- Montcalm 47,555
- Montmorency 7,492
- Muskegon 157,589
- Newaygo 34,917
- Oakland 1,011,793
- Oceana 22,002
- Ogemaw 16,436
- Ontonagon 9,861
- Osceola 18,928
- Oscoda 6,858
- Otsego 14,993
- Ottawa 157,174
- Presque Isle 14,267
- Roscommon 16,374
- Saginaw 228,059
- St. Clair 138,802
- St. Joseph 56,083
- Sanilac 40,789
- Schoolcraft 8,575
- Shiawassee 71,140
- Tuscola 56,961
- Van Buren 66,814
- Washtenaw 264,740
- Wayne 2,337,891
- Wexford 25,102

○ Rand McNally estimate (not reported in census).
▲ Population of entire township or "town", including rural areas.
● Independent city. Population not included in county total.

MINNESOTA

1980 Census 4,075,970

CITIES

Ada 1,971
Adams 797
Adrian 1,336
Aitkin 1,770
Akeley 486
Albany 1,569
Albert Lea 19,200
Albertville MPLS- 564
Alden 687
Alexandria 7,608
Amboy 606
Andover MPLS- 9,387
Annandale 1,568
Anoka MPLS- 15,634
Appleton 1,842
Apple Valley MPLS- 21,818
Arden Hills MPLS- 8,012
Argyle 741
Arlington 1,779
Arnold DUL- 1,350 ○
Ashby 486
Atwater 1,128
Aurora 2,670
Austin 23,020
Avon 804
Bagley 1,321
Balaton 752
Barnesville 2,207
Barnum 464
Battle Lake 708
Baudette 1,170
Baxter 2,625
Bayport MPLS- 2,932
Becker 601
Belgrade 805
Belle Plaine 2,754
Bemidji 10,949
Benson 3,656
Bertha 510
Big Falls 490
Bigfork 457
Big Lake 2,210
Bird Island 1,372
Biwabik 1,428
Blackduck 653
Blaine MPLS- 28,558
Blooming Prairie 1,969
Bloomington MPLS- 81,831
Blue Earth 4,132
Bovey 813
Braham 1,015
Brainerd 11,489
Brandon 473
Breckenridge 3,909
Brewster 559
Bricelyn 487
Brooklyn Center MPLS- 31,230
Brooklyn Park MPLS- 43,332
Brooten 647
Browerville 693
Brownsdale 691
Browns Valley 887
Brownton 697
Buffalo 4,560
Buffalo Lake 782
Buhl 1,284
Burnsville MPLS- 35,674
Butterfield 634
Byron ROCH 1,715
Caledonia 2,691
Calumet 469
Cambridge 3,287
Canby 2,143
Cannon Falls 2,653
Carlton 862
Carver MPLS- 642
Cass Lake 1,001
Center City MPLS- 458
Ceylon 543
Champlin MPLS- 9,006
Chanhassen MPLS- 6,359
Chaska MPLS- 8,346
Chatfield 2,055
Chisago City MPLS- 1,634
Chisholm 5,930
Chokio 559
Circle Pines MPLS- 3,321
Clara City 1,574
Claremont 591
Clarissa 663
Clarkfield 1,171
Clarks Grove 620
Clearbrook 579
Cleveland 699
Clinton 622
Cloquet 11,142
Cohasset 600 ○
Cokato 2,056
Cold Spring 2,294
Coleraine 1,116
Cologne 545
Columbia Heights MPLS- 20,029
Comfrey 548
Cook 800
Coon Rapids MPLS- 35,826
Corcoran MPLS- 4,252
Cosmos 571
Cottage Grove MPLS- 18,994
Cottonwood 924
Crookston 8,628
Crosby 2,218
Crosslake 1,064
Crystal MPLS- 25,543
Danube 590
Dassel 1,066
Dawson 1,901
Dayton MPLS- 4,070
Deer River 907
Deerwood 580
Delano MPLS- 2,480
Detroit Lakes 7,106
Dilworth FAR- 2,585
Dodge Center 1,816
DULUTH DUL- 92,811
Eagan MPLS- 20,700
Eagle Bend 593
Eagle Lake MNKT 1,470
East Bethel MPLS- 6,626
East Grand Forks GDFK 8,537
Eden Prairie MPLS- 16,263
Eden Valley 763
Edgerton 1,123
Edina MPLS- 46,073
Elbow Lake 1,358
Elgin 667
Elk River MPLS- 6,785
Ellendale 555
Ellsworth 629
Elmore 882
Ely 4,820
Elysian 454
Emmons 465
Erskine 585
Esko 500 ○
Evansville 571
Eveleth 5,042
Eyota 1,244
Fairfax 1,405
Fairmont 11,506
Falcon Heights MPLS- 5,291
Faribault 16,241
Farmington MPLS- 4,370
Fergus Falls 12,519
Fertile 869
Fisher 453
Floodwood 648
Foley 1,606
Forest Lake MPLS- 4,596
Fosston 1,599
Franklin 512
Frazee 1,284
Freeport 563
Fridley MPLS- 30,228
Fulda 1,308
Gaylord 1,933
Gibbon 787
Gilbert 2,721
Glencoe 4,396
Glenville 851
Glenwood 2,523
Glyndon 882
Golden Valley MPLS- 22,775
Goodhue 657
Good Thunder 560
Goodview 2,567
Graceville 780
Grand Marais 1,289
Grand Meadow 965
Grand Rapids 7,934
Granite Falls 3,451
Greenbush 817
Grove City 596
Hallock 1,405
Halstad 690
Ham Lake MPLS- 7,832
Hancock 877
Harmony 1,133
Harris 678
Hastings MPLS- 12,827
Hawley 1,634
Hayfield 1,243
Hector 1,252
Henderson 739
Hendricks 737
Henning 832
Herman 600
Hermantown DUL- 6,759
Heron Lake 783
Hibbing 21,193
Hill City 533
Hills 598
Hinckley 963
Hoffman 631
Hokah 686
Holdingford 635
Hopkins MPLS- 15,336
Houston 1,057
Howard Lake 1,240
Hoyt Lakes 3,186
Hugo MPLS- 3,771
Hutchinson 9,244
International Falls 5,611
Inver Grove Heights MPLS- 17,171
Ironton 537
Isanti 858
Isle 573
Ivanhoe 761
Jackson 3,797
Janesville 1,897
Jasper 731
Jordan MPLS- 2,663
Kandiyohi 447
Karlstad 934
Kasota 739
Kasson 2,827
Keewatin 1,443
Kellogg 440
Kelly Lake 900 ○
Kenyon 1,529
Kerkhoven 761
Kiester 670
Kimball 651
La Crescent LACRO 3,674
Lafayette 507
Lake Benton 869
Lake City 4,505
Lake Crystal MNKT 2,078
Lake Elmo MPLS- 5,296
Lakefield 1,845
Lake Park 716
Lakeville MPLS- 14,790
Lamberton 1,032
Lanesboro 923
La Prairie 536
Le Center 1,967
Le Roy 930
Lester Prairie 1,229
Le Sueur 3,763
Lewiston 1,226
Lindstrom MPLS- 1,972
Lino Lakes MPLS- 4,966
Litchfield 5,904
Little Canada MPLS- 7,102
Little Falls 7,250
Littlefork 918
Long Prairie 2,859
Lonsdale 1,160
Luverne 4,568
Lyle 576
Mabel 861
McGregor 447
McIntosh 681
Madelia 2,130
Madison 2,212
Madison Lake 592
Mahnomen 1,283
MANKATO MNKT 28,646
Mantorville 705
Maple Grove MPLS- 20,525
Maple Lake 1,132
Mapleton 1,516
Maplewood MPLS- 26,990
Marble 757
Marine On St. Croix MPLS- 543
Marshall 11,161
Mazeppa 680
Medford 775
Melrose 2,409
Menahga 980
Mendota Heights MPLS- 7,288
Milaca 2,104
MINNEAPOLIS MPLS- 370,951
Minneota 1,470
Minnesota Lake 744
Minnetonka MPLS- 38,683
Montevideo 5,845
Montgomery 2,349
Monticello 2,830
Moorhead FAR- 29,998
Moose Lake 1,408
Mora 2,890
Morgan 975
Morris 5,367
Morristown 639
Morton 549
Motley 444
Mound MPLS- 9,280
Mounds View MPLS- 12,593
Mountain Iron 4,134
Mountain Lake 2,277
Nashwauk 1,419
New Brighton MPLS- 23,269
New Hope MPLS- 23,087
New London 812
Newport MPLS- 3,323
New Prague 2,952
New Richland 1,263
New Ulm 13,755
New York Mills 972
Nicollet 709
North Branch 1,597
Northfield 12,562
North Mankato MNKT 9,145
North St. Paul MPLS- 11,921
Norwood 1,219
Oakdale MPLS- 12,123
Oklee 536
Olivia 2,802
Onamia 691
Orono MPLS- 6,845
Oronoco ROCH 574
Ortonville 2,550
Osakis 1,355
Osseo MPLS- 2,974
Owatonna 18,632
Parkers Prairie 917
Park Rapids 2,976
Paynesville 2,140
Pelican Rapids 1,867
Pequot Lakes 681
Perham 2,086
Pierz 1,018
Pike Lake DUL- 1,004
Pine City 2,489
Pine Island 1,977
Pine River 881
Pipestone 4,887
Plainview 2,416
Plymouth MPLS- 31,615
Preston 1,478
Princeton 3,146
Prinsburg 557
Prior Lake MPLS- 7,284
Proctor DUL- 3,180
Ramsey MPLS- 10,093
Randall 527
Raymond 723
Redlake 600 ○
Red Lake Falls 1,732
Red Wing 13,736
Redwood Falls 5,210
Renville 1,493
Rice 499
Richfield MPLS- 37,851
Richmond 867
Robbinsdale MPLS- 14,422
ROCHESTER ROCH 57,890
Rockford MPLS- 2,408
Rockville 597
Rogers MPLS- 652
Rollingstone 528
Roseau 2,272
Rosemount MPLS- 5,083
Roseville MPLS- 35,820
Rothsay 476
Round Lake 480
Royalton 660
Rush City 1,198
Rushford 1,478
Sabin 446
Sacred Heart 666
St. Charles 2,184
St. Clair 655
ST. CLOUD ST.CLD 42,566
St. Francis 1,184
St. James 4,346
St. Joseph ST.CLD 2,994
St. Louis Park MPLS- 42,931
St. Michael MPLS- 1,519
St. Paul MPLS- 270,230
St. Peter 9,056
Sanborn 518
Sandstone 1,594
Sartell ST.CLD 3,427
Sauk Centre 3,709
Sauk Rapids ST.CLD 5,793
Scanlon 1,050
Sebeka 774
Shakopee MPLS- 9,941
Sherburn 1,275
Shoreview MPLS- 17,300
Shorewood MPLS- 4,646
Silver Bay 2,917
Silver Lake 698
Slayton 2,420
Sleepy Eye 3,581
Soudan 950 ○
South International Falls 2,806
South St. Paul MPLS- 21,235
Spicer 909
Springfield 2,303
Spring Grove 1,275
Spring Valley 2,616
Staples 2,887
Starbuck 1,224
Stephen 898
Stewart 616
Stewartville ROCH 3,925
Stillwater MPLS- 12,290
Taylors Falls 623
Thief River Falls 9,105
Tower 640
Tracy 2,478
Trimont 805
Truman 1,392
Twin Valley 907
Two Harbors 4,039
Tyler 1,353
Ulen 514
Vadnais Heights MPLS- 5,111
Verndale 504
Virginia 11,056
Wabasha 2,372
Wabasso 745
Waconia MPLS- 2,638
Wadena 4,699
Waite Park ST.CLD 3,496
Walker 970
Walnut Grove 753
Wanamingo 717
Warren 2,105
Warroad 1,216
Waseca 8,219
Waterville 1,717
Watkins 757
Waverly 470
Welcome 855
Wells 2,777
Westbrook 978
West Concord 762
West St. Paul MPLS- 18,527
Wheaton 1,969
White Bear Lake MPLS- 22,538
Willmar 15,895
Windom 4,666
Winnebago 1,869
Winona 25,075
Winsted 1,522
Winthrop 1,376
Woodbury MPLS- 10,297
Worthington 10,243
Wykoff 482
Wyoming MPLS- 1,559
Zimmerman 1,074
Zumbrota 2,129

COUNTIES

Aitkin 13,404
Anoka 195,998
Becker 29,336
Beltrami 30,982
Benton 25,187
Big Stone 7,716
Blue Earth 52,314
Brown 28,645
Carlton 29,936
Carver 37,046
Cass 21,050
Chippewa 14,941
Chisago 25,717
Clay 49,327
Clearwater 8,761
Cook 4,092
Cottonwood 14,854
Crow Wing 41,722
Dakota 194,279
Dodge 14,773
Douglas 27,839
Faribault 19,714
Fillmore 21,930
Freeborn 36,329
Goodhue 38,749
Grant 7,171
Hennepin 941,411
Houston 18,382
Hubbard 14,098
Isanti 23,600
Itasca 43,069
Jackson 13,690
Kanabec 12,161
Kandiyohi 36,763
Kittson 6,672
Koochiching 17,571
Lac qui Parle 10,592
Lake 13,043
Lake of the Woods 3,764
Le Sueur 23,434
Lincoln 8,207
Lyon 25,207
McLeod 29,657
Mahnomen 5,535
Marshall 13,027
Martin 24,687
Meeker 20,594
Mille Lacs 18,430
Morrison 29,311
Mower 40,390
Murray 11,507
Nicollet 26,929
Nobles 21,840
Norman 9,379
Olmsted 92,006
Otter Tail 51,937
Pennington 15,258
Pine 19,871
Pipestone 11,690
Polk 34,844
Pope 11,657
Ramsey 459,784
Red Lake 5,471
Redwood 19,341
Renville 20,401
Rice 46,087
Rock 10,703
Roseau 12,574
St. Louis 222,229
Scott 43,784
Sherburne 29,908
Sibley 15,448
Stearns 108,161
Steele 30,328
Stevens 11,322
Swift 12,920
Todd 24,991
Traverse 5,542
Wabasha 19,335
Wadena 14,192
Waseca 18,448
Washington 113,571
Watonwan 12,361
Wilkin 8,454
Winona 46,256
Wright 58,681
Yellow Medicine 13,653

MISSISSIPPI

1980 Census 2,520,631

CITIES

Abbeville 448
Aberdeen 7,184
Ackerman 1,598
Amory 7,307
Anguilla 950
Arcola 588
Artesia 520
Ashland 532
Baldwyn 3,427
Batesville 4,692
Bay Saint Louis 7,850
Bay Springs 1,884
Bear Town 1,277
Beaumont 1,112
Belmont 1,420
Belzoni 2,982
Benoit 499
Bentonia 518
Bigpoint 900 ○
Biloxi GUL-B 49,311
Blue Mountain 867
Bogue Chitto 600 ○
Bolton 664
Booneville 6,199
Brandon JAC 9,626
Brookhaven 10,800
Brooklyn 800 ○
Brooksville 1,038
Bruce 2,208
Buckatunna 700 ○
Bude 1,092
Burnsville 889
Byhalia 757
Caledonia 497
Calhoun City 2,033
Canton 11,116
Carriere 500 ○
Carthage 3,453
Cary 470
Charleston 2,878
Clarksdale 22,384
Cleveland 14,524
Clinton JAC 14,660
Coffeeville 1,129
Coldwater 1,505
Collins 2,131
Columbia 7,733
COLUMBUS COL 27,503
Como 1,378
Corinth 13,839
Crawford 495
Crenshaw 1,019
Crowder 789
Cruger 540
Crystal Springs 4,902
Decatur 1,148
De Kalb 1,159
De Lisle GUL-B 600 ○
Derma 793
D'Iberville GUL-B 9,000 ○
D'Lo 463
Drew 2,528
Duck Hill 706
Duncan 501
Durant 2,889
Ecru 687
Edwards 1,515
Elliott 1,200 ○
Ellisville LAUR 4,652
Enterprise 607
Escatawpa PSCG 5,367
Ethel 486
Eupora 2,048
Fayette 2,033
Fernwood 600 ○
Flora 1,507
Florence JAC 1,111
Flowood JAC 943
Forest 5,229
Foxworth 1,000 ○
Friars Point 1,400
Fulton 3,238
Gautier PSCG 8,917

○ Rand McNally estimate (not reported in census).
▲ Population of entire township or "town", including rural areas.
● Independent city. Population not included in county total.

MISSISSIPPI continued

Glen Allan 600 ○
Glendale HATT 1,329
Gloster 1,726
Goodman 1,285
GREENVILLE GRNV 40,613
Greenwood 20,115
Grenada 12,641
GULFPORT GUL-B 39,676
Gunnison 708
Hamilton 500 ○
Harriston 450 ○
Hatley 497
HATTIESBURG HATT 40,829
Hazlehurst 4,437
Heidelberg 1,098
Henderson's Point GUL-B 1,114
Hernando MEM 2,969
Hickory 670
Hickory Flat 458
Hollandale 4,336
Holly Springs 7,285
Horn Lake MEM 4,326
Houlka 710
Houston 3,745
Hurley 600 ○
Indianola 8,221
Inverness 1,034
Isola 834
Itta Bena 2,904
Iuka 2,846
JACKSON JAC 202,895
Jonestown 1,231
Kilmichael 906
Kiln 650 ○
Kings VICK 1,165
Kosciusko 7,415
Lake 524
Lakeshore 800 ○
Lambert 1,624
Lauderdale 750 ○
LAUREL LAUR 21,897
Leakesville 1,120
Leland 6,667
Lexington 2,628
Liberty 669
Long Beach GUL-B 7,967
Lorman 650 ○
Louisville 7,323
Lucedale 2,429
Lumberton 2,217
Maben 855
McComb 12,331
McLain 688
McNeill 500 ○
Macon 2,396
Madison JAC 2,241
Magee 3,497
Magnolia 2,461
Mantachie 732
Marion MRID 771
Marks 2,260
Mathiston 632
Meadville 575
Mendenhall 2,533
MERIDIAN MRID 46,577
Merigold 574
Metcalfe GRNV 952
Mississippi State 4,600 ○
Monticello 1,834
Moorhead 2,358
Morgantown NCHZ 3,288
Morton 3,303
Moselle 500 ○
Moss Point PSCG 18,998
Mound Bayou 2,917
Mount Olive 993
NATCHEZ NCHZ 22,209
Nettleton 1,911
New Albany 7,072
New Augusta 589
Newhebron 470
Newton 3,708
North Carrollton 859
North Gulfport GUL-B 6,660
North Tunica 1,026
Noxapater 516
Oakland 540
Ocean Springs GUL-B 14,504
Okolona 3,409
Olive Branch MEM 2,067
Orange Grove GUL-B 2,700 ○
Osyka 581
Oxford 9,882
Pace 519
PASCAGOULA PSCG 29,318
Pass Christian GUL-B 5,014
Pearl JAC 18,602
Pearlington 600 ○
Pelahatchie 1,445
Perkinston 650 ○
Petal HATT 8,476
Philadelphia 6,434
Picayune 10,361
Pickens 1,386
Plantersville 920
Pontotoc 4,723
Poplarville 2,562
Port Gibson 2,371
Potts Camp 525
Prentiss 1,465
Purvis 2,256
Quitman 2,632
Raleigh 998
Raymond JAC 1,967
Richton 1,205
Ridgeland JAC 5,461
Ripley 4,271
Rolling Fork 2,590
Rosedale 2,793
Roxie 591
Ruleville 3,332
Saltillo 1,271
Sanatorium 700 ○
Sandersville LAUR 800
Scooba 511
Senatobia 5,013
Shannon 680
Shaw 2,461
Shelby 2,540
Sherman 499
Shubuta 626
Shuqualak 554
Sidon 450
Sledge 699
Smithville 866
Southaven MEM 16,441
Star 500 ○
Starkville 15,169
State Line 484
Stonewall 1,345
Summit 1,753
Sumner 452
Sumrall 1,197
Sunflower 1,027
Taylorsville 1,387
Tchula 1,931
Terry JAC 655
Thomastown 500 ○
Tie Plant 450 ○
Tunica 1,361
Tupelo 23,905
Tutwiler 1,174
Tylertown 1,976
Union 1,931
Utica 865
Vaiden 924
Vancleave 1,330
Vardaman 1,009
Verona 2,497
VICKSBURG VICK 25,434
Victoria 950 ○
Walnut 513
Washington 900 ○
Water Valley 4,147
Waveland 4,186
Waynesboro 5,349
Webb 782
Weir 553
Wesson 1,313
West Point 9,123
Wheeler 600 ○
Wiggins 3,205
Winona 6,177
Winstonville 486
Woodville 1,512
Woolmarket GUL-B 670 ○
Yazoo City 12,092

COUNTIES

Adams 38,071
Alcorn 33,036
Amite 13,369
Attala 19,865
Benton 8,153
Bolivar 45,965
Calhoun 15,664
Carroll 9,776
Chickasaw 17,851
Choctaw 8,996
Claiborne 12,279
Clarke 16,945
Clay 21,082
Coahoma 36,918
Copiah 26,503
Covington 15,927
DeSoto 53,930
Forrest 66,018
Franklin 8,208
George 15,297
Greene 9,827
Grenada 21,043
Hancock 24,496
Harrison 157,665
Hinds 250,998
Holmes 22,970
Humphreys 13,931
Issaquena 2,513
Itawamba 20,518
Jackson 118,015
Jasper 17,265
Jefferson 9,181
Jefferson Davis 13,846
Jones 61,912
Kemper 10,148
Lafayette 31,030
Lamar 23,821
Lauderdale 77,285
Lawrence 12,518
Leake 18,790
Lee 57,061
Leflore 41,525
Lincoln 30,174
Lowndes 57,304
Madison 41,613
Marion 25,708
Marshall 29,296
Monroe 36,404
Montgomery 13,366
Neshoba 23,789
Newton 19,944
Noxubee 13,212
Oktibbeha 36,018
Panola 28,164
Pearl River 33,795
Perry 9,864
Pike 36,173
Pontotoc 20,918
Prentiss 24,025
Quitman 12,636
Rankin 69,427
Scott 24,556
Sharkey 7,964
Simpson 23,441
Smith 15,077
Stone 9,716
Sunflower 34,844
Tallahatchie 17,157
Tate 20,119
Tippah 18,739
Tishomingo 18,434
Tunica 9,652
Union 21,741
Walthall 13,761
Warren 51,627
Washington 72,344
Wayne 19,135
Webster 10,300
Wilkinson 10,021
Winston 19,474
Yalobusha 13,139
Yazoo 27,349

MISSOURI

1980 Census 4,916,759

CITIES

Adrian 1,484
Advance 1,054
Affton ST.L 23,181
Alba 474
Albany 2,152
Allenton ST.L 500 ○
Alma 445
Alton 721
Anderson 1,237
Antonia ST.L 500 ○
Appleton City 1,257
Arcadia 683
Archie 753
Arnold ST.L 19,141
Ash Grove 1,157
Ashland 1,021
Atlanta 441
Aurora 6,437
Auxvasse 858
Ava 2,761
Avondale K.C. 612
Ballwin ST.L 12,656
Barnhart ST.L 800 ○
Bell City 539
Belle 1,233
Bellefontaine Neighbors ST.L 12,082
Bel-Nor ST.L 2,047
Belton K.C. 12,708
Benton 674
Berkeley ST.L 15,922
Bernie 1,975
Bertrand 688
Bethany 3,095
Billings 911
Birch Tree 622
Bismarck 1,625
Black Jack ST.L 5,293
Bland 662
Bloomfield 1,795
Blue Springs K.C. 25,936
Bolivar 5,919
Bonne Terre 3,797
Booneville 6,959
Bourbon 1,259
Bowling Green 3,022
Braggadocio 450 ○
Branson 2,550
Braymer 986
Breckenridge 523
Breckenridge Hills ST.L 5,666
Brentwood ST.L 8,209
Bridgeton ST.L 18,445
Brookfield 5,555
Brunswick 1,272
Bucklin 713
Buckner K.C. 2,848
Buffalo 2,217
Bunker 673
Burke City ST.L 2,600 ○
Burlington Junction 657
Butler 4,107
Cabool 2,090
Cainsville 496
California 3,381
Calverton Park ST.L 1,717
Camdenton 2,303
Cameron 4,519
Campbell 2,134
Canton 2,435
CAPE GIRARDEAU CPGIR 34,361
Cardwell 831
Carl Junction JOP 3,937
Carrollton 4,700
Carterville JOP 1,973
Carthage 11,104
Caruthersville 7,958
Cassville 2,091
Castle Point ST.L 6,500 ○
Cedar Hill ST.L 1,512
Center 669
Centralia 3,537
Chaffee 3,241
Chamois 546
Charleston 5,230
Chillicothe 9,089
Clarence 1,147
Clarksville 585
Clarkton 1,228
Clayton ST.L 14,273
Cleveland 485
Clever 551
Clinton 8,366
Cole Camp 1,022
COLUMBIA COL 62,061
Concord ST.L 20,896
Concordia 2,129
Conway 601
Cooter 479
Corder 483
Crane 1,185
Crestwood ST.L 12,815
Creve Coeur ST.L 11,743
Crocker 979
Crystal City ST.L 3,618
Cuba 2,120
Dearborn 547
Deepwater 475
Dellwood ST.L 6,200
Delta 524
Desloge 3,581
De Soto ST.L 5,993
Des Peres ST.L 7,953
Dexter 7,043
Dixon 1,402
Doe Run 900 ○
Doniphan 1,921
Doolittle 701
Downing 462
Drexel 908
Duenweg JOP 703
East Prairie 3,713
Edgerton 584
Edina 1,520
Eldon 4,342
El Dorado Springs 3,868
Ellington 1,215
Ellisville ST.L 6,233
Elsberry 1,272
Elvins 1,548
Eminence 614
Essex 545
Eureka ST.L 3,862
Excelsior Springs K.C. 10,424
Exeter 588
Fairfax 835
Fair Grove 863
Farber 503
Farmington 8,270
Fayette 2,983
Ferguson ST.L 24,549
Festus ST.L 7,574
Fisk 450
Flat River 4,443
Florissant ST.L 55,372
Fordland 569
Forsyth 1,010
Frankford 443
Fredericktown 4,036
Freeburg 554
Freeman 485
Fulton 11,046
Gainesville 707
Gallatin 2,063
Garden City 1,021
Gerald 921
Gideon 1,240
Gladstone K.C. 24,990
Glasgow 1,336
Glasgow Village ST.L 7,200 ○
Glencoe ST.L 500 ○
Glendale ST.L 6,035
Golden City 900
Goodman 1,030
Gower 1,276
Grain Valley K.C. 1,327
Granby 1,908
Grandview K.C. 24,561
Grant City 1,068
Gray Summit ST.L 500 ○
Green City 719
Greenfield 1,394
Green Ridge 488
Greenwood K.C. 1,315
Hale 529
Hallsville 624
Hamilton 1,582
Hannibal 18,941
Hardin 688
Harrisonville K.C. 6,372
Hartville 576
Hayti 3,964
Hayti Heights 1,023
Hazelwood ST.L 15,992
Herculaneum ST.L 2,293
Hermann 2,695
Higbee 817
Higginsville 4,595
High Ridge ST.L 900 ○
Hillsboro ST.L 1,508
Holcomb 632
Holden 2,195
Hollister 1,439
Hopkins 634
Horine ST.L 850 ○
Hornersville 704
Houston 2,157
Howardville 536
Humansville 907
Iberia 852
Illmo CPGIR 1,368
Imperial ST.L 950 ○
Independence K.C. 111,797
Ironton 1,743
Jackson CPGIR 7,827
Jamesport 651
Jasper 1,012
JEFFERSON CITY JFCY 33,619
Jennings ST.L 17,217
Jonesburg 614
JOPLIN JOP 39,023
Kahoka 2,101
KANSAS CITY K.C. 448,033
Kearney 1,433
Kelso CPGIR 455
Kennett 10,145
Keytesville 689
King City 1,063
Kinloch ST.L 4,455
Kirksville 17,167
Kirkwood ST.L 27,987
Knob Noster 2,040
La Belle 845
Laclede 445
Laddonia 726
Ladue ST.L 9,369
La Grange 1,217
Lake Ozark 534
Lamar 4,053
La Monte 1,054
Lanagan 440
Lancaster 855
La Plata 1,423
Lathrop 1,732
Lawson 1,743
Leadwood 1,371
Lebanon 9,507
Lees Summit K.C. 28,741
Leeton 604
Lemay ST.L 35,424
Lewistown 502
Lexington 5,063
Liberal 701
Liberty K.C. 16,251
Licking 1,272
Lilbourn 1,463
Lincoln 819
Linn 1,211
Lockwood 971
Louisiana 4,261
Lowry City 676
Lutesville 865
Macon 5,680
Madison 656
Malden 6,096
Manchester ST.L 6,351
Mansfield 1,423
Maplewood ST.L 10,960
Marble Hill 601
Marceline 2,938
Marionville 1,920
Marshall 12,781
Marshfield 3,871
Marston 742
Marthasville 543
Maryland Heights ST.L 5,676
Maryville 9,558
Matthews 547
Maysville 1,187
Mehlville ST.L 22,900 ○
Memphis 2,105
Mercer 442
Mexico 12,276
Milan 1,947
Miner 1,182
Moberly 13,418
Monett 6,148
Monroe City 2,557
Montgomery City 2,101
Montrose 498
Morehouse 1,220
Morley 745
Moscow Mills 484
Mound City 1,447
Mountain Grove 3,976
Mountain View 1,664
Mount Vernon 3,341
Murphy ST.L 8,121
Naylor 602
Neelyville 474
Neosho 9,493
Nevada 9,044
New Bloomfield 519
Newburg 743
New Florence 731
New Franklin 1,228
New Haven 1,581
New London 1,161
New Madrid 3,204
Nixa SPRG 2,662
Noel 1,228
Norborne 931
Normandy ST.L 5,174
North Kansas City K.C. 4,507
Northmoor K.C. 506
Northwoods ST.L 5,831
Novinger 626
Oakville ST.L 1,100 ○
Odessa 3,088
O'Fallon ST.L 8,677
Olivette ST.L 7,952
Oran 1,266
Oregon 901
Oronogo JOP 525
Orrick 922
Osage Beach 1,992
Osceola 841
Otterville 472
Overland ST.L 19,620
Owensville 2,241
Ozark SPRG 2,980
Pacific ST.L 4,410
Palmyra 3,469
Paris 1,598
Parkville K.C. 2,091
Parma 1,081
Pattonsburg 502
Peculiar K.C. 1,571
Perry 836
Perryville 7,343
Pevely ST.L 2,732
Piedmont 2,359
Pierce City 1,391
Pilot Grove 745
Pilot Knob 722
Pine Lawn ST.L 6,600
Pineville 504
Platte City K.C. 2,114
Plattsburg 2,095
Pleasant Hill K.C. 3,301
Pleasant Valley K.C. 1,545
Point Lookout 900 ○
Polo 583
Poplar Bluff 17,139
Portage Des Sioux 488
Portageville 3,470
Potosi 2,528
Princeton 1,264
Purdy 928
Puxico 833
Queen City 783
Qulin 545
Raymore K.C. 3,154
Raytown K.C. 31,831
Reeds Spring 461
Republic SPRG 4,485
Rich Hill 1,471
Richland 1,922
Richmond 5,499
Richmond Heights ST.L 11,516
Ridgeway 516
Risco 446
Rock Hill ST.L 5,702
Rock Port 1,511
Rogersville SPRG 741
Rolla 13,303
Russellville 667
St. Ann ST.L 15,921
St. Charles ST.L 43,557
St. Clair 3,485
Ste. Genevieve 4,481
St. James 3,328
St. Johns ST.L 7,854

○ Rand McNally estimate (not reported in census).
▲ Population of entire township or "town", including rural areas.
● Independent city. Population not included in county total.

- ST. JOSEPH ST.JO. . . . 76,691
- ST. LOUIS ● ST.L. . . . 452,801
- St. Mary . . . 565
- St. Paul ST.L. . . . 607
- St. Peters ST.L . . . 15,700
- Salem . . . 4,454
- Salisbury . . . 1,975
- Sappington ST.L . . . 11,388
- Sarcoxie . . . 1,381
- Savannah ST.JO . . . 4,184
- Scott City CPGIR . . . 4,630
- Sedalia . . . 20,927
- Seligman . . . 508
- Senath . . . 1,728
- Seneca . . . 1,853
- Seymour . . . 1,535
- Shelbina . . . 2,169
- Shelbyville . . . 645
- Sheldon . . . 491
- Shrewsbury ST.L . . . 5,077
- Sikeston . . . 17,431
- Slater . . . 2,492
- Smithton . . . 559
- Smithville K.C. . . . 1,873
- South Shore . . . 450 ○
- South West City . . . 516
- Spanish Lake ST.L . . . 20,632
- Sparta . . . 743
- SPRINGFIELD SPRG . . . 133,116
- Stanberry . . . 1,387
- Steele . . . 2,419
- Steelville . . . 1,470
- Stewartsville . . . 832
- Stockton . . . 1,432
- Stover . . . 1,041
- Strafford SPRG . . . 1,121
- Sturgeon . . . 901
- Sugar Creek K.C. . . . 4,305
- Sullivan . . . 5,461
- Summersville . . . 551
- Sweet Springs . . . 1,694
- Taos . . . 759
- Tarkio . . . 2,375
- Thayer . . . 2,211
- Tipton . . . 2,155
- Trenton . . . 6,811
- Troy . . . 2,624
- Union ST.L . . . 5,506
- Unionville . . . 2,178
- University City ST.L . . . 42,690
- Urich . . . 509
- Valley Park ST.L . . . 3,232
- Van Buren . . . 850
- Vandalia . . . 3,170
- Verona . . . 592
- Versailles . . . 2,406
- Viburnum . . . 836
- Vienna . . . 514
- Walnut Grove . . . 504
- Warrensburg . . . 13,807
- Warrenton . . . 3,219
- Warsaw . . . 1,494
- Washington . . . 9,251
- Waverly . . . 941
- Wayland . . . 498
- Waynesville . . . 2,879
- Weaubleau . . . 464
- Webb City JOP . . . 7,309
- Webster Groves ST.L . . . 23,097
- Wedgewood ST.L . . . 5,700 ○
- Wellington . . . 780
- Wellsville . . . 1,546
- Wentzville ST.L . . . 3,193
- West Alton ST.L . . . 500 ○
- Weston . . . 1,440
- West Plains . . . 7,741
- Wheaton . . . 548
- Willard SPRG . . . 1,799
- Willow Springs . . . 2,215
- Windsor . . . 3,058
- Winfield . . . 592
- Winona . . . 1,050
- Wright City . . . 1,179
- Wyatt . . . 441

COUNTIES

- Adair . . . 24,870
- Andrew . . . 13,980
- Atchison . . . 8,605
- Audrain . . . 26,458
- Barry . . . 24,408
- Barton . . . 11,292
- Bates . . . 15,873
- Benton . . . 12,183
- Bollinger . . . 10,301
- Boone . . . 100,376
- Buchanan . . . 87,888
- Butler . . . 37,693
- Caldwell . . . 8,660
- Callaway . . . 32,252
- Camden . . . 20,017
- Cape Girardeau . . . 58,837
- Carroll . . . 12,131
- Carter . . . 5,428
- Cass . . . 51,029
- Cedar . . . 11,894
- Chariton . . . 10,489
- Christian . . . 22,402
- Clark . . . 8,493
- Clay . . . 136,488
- Clinton . . . 15,916
- Cole . . . 56,663
- Cooper . . . 14,643
- Crawford . . . 18,300
- Dade . . . 7,383
- Dallas . . . 12,096
- Daviess . . . 8,905
- De Kalb . . . 8,222
- Dent . . . 14,517
- Douglas . . . 11,594
- Dunklin . . . 36,324
- Franklin . . . 71,233
- Gasconade . . . 13,181
- Gentry . . . 7,887
- Greene . . . 185,302
- Grundy . . . 11,959
- Harrison . . . 9,890
- Henry . . . 19,672
- Hickory . . . 6,367
- Holt . . . 6,882
- Howard . . . 10,008
- Howell . . . 28,807
- Iron . . . 11,084
- Jackson . . . 629,266
- Jasper . . . 86,958
- Jefferson . . . 146,183
- Johnson . . . 39,059
- Knox . . . 5,508
- Laclede . . . 24,323
- Lafayette . . . 29,925
- Lawrence . . . 28,973
- Lewis . . . 10,901
- Lincoln . . . 22,193
- Linn . . . 15,495
- Livingston . . . 15,739
- McDonald . . . 14,917
- Macon . . . 16,313
- Madison . . . 10,725
- Maries . . . 7,551
- Marion . . . 28,638
- Mercer . . . 4,685
- Miller . . . 18,539
- Mississippi . . . 15,726
- Moniteau . . . 12,068
- Monroe . . . 9,716
- Montgomery . . . 11,537
- Morgan . . . 13,807
- New Madrid . . . 22,945
- Newton . . . 40,555
- Nodaway . . . 21,996
- Oregon . . . 10,238
- Osage . . . 12,014
- Ozark . . . 7,961
- Pemiscot . . . 24,987
- Perry . . . 16,784
- Pettis . . . 36,378
- Phelps . . . 33,633
- Pike . . . 17,568
- Platte . . . 46,341
- Polk . . . 18,822
- Pulaski . . . 42,011
- Putnam . . . 6,092
- Ralls . . . 8,984
- Randolph . . . 25,460
- Ray . . . 21,378
- Reynolds . . . 7,230
- Ripley . . . 12,458
- St. Charles . . . 144,107
- St. Clair . . . 8,622
- St. Francois . . . 42,600
- Ste. Genevieve . . . 15,180
- St. Louis . . . 974,180
- Saline . . . 24,919
- Schuyler . . . 4,979
- Scotland . . . 5,415
- Scott . . . 39,647
- Shannon . . . 7,885
- Shelby . . . 7,826
- Stoddard . . . 29,009
- Stone . . . 15,587
- Sullivan . . . 7,434
- Taney . . . 20,467
- Texas . . . 21,070
- Vernon . . . 19,806
- Warren . . . 14,900
- Washington . . . 17,983
- Wayne . . . 11,277
- Webster . . . 20,414
- Worth . . . 3,008
- Wright . . . 16,188

MONTANA

1980 Census . . . 786,690

CITIES

- Absarokee . . . 750 ○
- Anaconda . . . 12,518
- Augusta . . . 450 ○
- Baker . . . 2,354
- Belgrade . . . 2,336
- Belt . . . 825
- Bigfork . . . 1,080
- Big Sandy . . . 835
- Big Timber . . . 1,690
- BILLINGS BIL . . . 66,824
- Billings Heights BIL . . . 8,480
- Black Eagle GTFA . . . 1,100 ○
- Boulder . . . 1,441
- Bozeman . . . 21,645
- Bridger . . . 724
- Broadus . . . 712
- Browning . . . 1,226
- BUTTE BUT . . . 37,205
- Cascade . . . 773
- Chester . . . 963
- Chinook . . . 1,660
- Choteau . . . 1,798
- Circle . . . 931
- Colstrip . . . 1,476
- Columbia Falls . . . 3,112
- Columbus . . . 1,439
- Conrad . . . 3,074
- Crow Agency . . . 750 ○
- Culbertson . . . 887
- Cut Bank . . . 3,688
- Darby . . . 581
- Deer Lodge . . . 4,023
- Dillon . . . 3,976
- East Glacier Park . . . 500 ○
- East Helena . . . 1,647
- Ekalaka . . . 620
- Ennis . . . 660
- Eureka . . . 1,119
- Fairfield . . . 650
- Fairview . . . 1,366
- Forsyth . . . 2,553
- Fort Belknap Agency . . . 500 ○
- Fort Benton . . . 1,693
- Fort Peck . . . 600 ○
- Fromberg . . . 469
- Gardiner . . . 600 ○
- Glasgow . . . 4,455
- Glendive . . . 5,978
- GREAT FALLS GTFA . . . 56,725
- Hamilton . . . 2,661
- Hardin . . . 3,300
- Harlem . . . 1,023
- Harlowton . . . 1,181
- Havre . . . 10,891
- Havre North . . . 1,230
- Helena . . . 23,938
- Hot Springs . . . 601
- Hungry Horse . . . 900 ○
- Hysham . . . 449
- Joliet . . . 580
- Jordan . . . 485
- Kalispell . . . 10,648
- Lakeside . . . 500 ○
- Lame Deer . . . 600 ○
- Laurel BIL . . . 5,498
- Lewistown . . . 7,104
- Libby . . . 2,748
- Lincoln . . . 500 ○
- Livingston . . . 6,994
- Lockwood BIL . . . 1,600 ○
- Lodge Grass . . . 486
- Lolo . . . 2,418
- Malta . . . 2,367
- Manhattan . . . 988
- Martin City . . . 500 ○
- Miles City . . . 9,602
- MISSOULA MSLA . . . 33,388
- Nashua . . . 495
- Orchard Homes MSLA . . . 4,000 ○
- Philipsburg . . . 1,138
- Pinesdale . . . 458
- Plains . . . 1,116
- Plentywood . . . 2,476
- Polson . . . 2,798
- Poplar . . . 995
- Red Lodge . . . 1,896
- Ronan . . . 1,530
- Roundup . . . 2,119
- Rudyard . . . 600 ○
- St. Ignatius . . . 877
- St. Regis . . . 600 ○
- Scobey . . . 1,382
- Seeley Lake . . . 800 ○
- Shelby . . . 3,142
- Sheridan . . . 646
- Sidney . . . 5,726
- Somers . . . 800 ○
- Stanford . . . 595
- Stevensville . . . 1,207
- Sunburst . . . 476
- Superior . . . 1,054
- Terry . . . 929
- Thompson Falls . . . 1,478
- Three Forks . . . 1,247
- Townsend . . . 1,587
- Troy . . . 1,088
- Valier . . . 640
- Vaughn . . . 2,270
- Victor . . . 450 ○
- Walkerville BUT . . . 887
- West Yellowstone . . . 735
- Whitefish . . . 3,703
- Whitehall . . . 1,030
- White Sulphur Springs . . . 1,302
- Wibaux . . . 782
- Wolf Point . . . 3,074

COUNTIES

- Beaverhead . . . 8,186
- Big Horn . . . 11,096
- Blaine . . . 6,999
- Broadwater . . . 3,267
- Carbon . . . 8,099
- Carter . . . 1,799
- Cascade . . . 80,696
- Chouteau . . . 6,092
- Custer . . . 13,109
- Daniels . . . 2,835
- Dawson . . . 11,805
- Deer Lodge . . . 12,518
- Fallon . . . 3,763
- Fergus . . . 13,076
- Flathead . . . 51,966
- Gallatin . . . 42,865
- Garfield . . . 1,656
- Glacier . . . 10,628
- Golden Valley . . . 1,026
- Granite . . . 2,700
- Hill . . . 17,985
- Jefferson . . . 7,029
- Judith Basin . . . 2,646
- Lake . . . 19,056
- Lewis and Clark . . . 43,039
- Liberty . . . 2,329
- Lincoln . . . 17,752
- McCone . . . 2,702
- Madison . . . 5,448
- Meagher . . . 2,154
- Mineral . . . 3,675
- Missoula . . . 76,016
- Musselshell . . . 4,428
- Park . . . 12,869
- Petroleum . . . 655
- Phillips . . . 5,367
- Pondera . . . 6,731
- Powder River . . . 2,520
- Powell . . . 6,958
- Prairie . . . 1,836
- Ravalli . . . 22,493
- Richland . . . 12,243
- Roosevelt . . . 10,467
- Rosebud . . . 9,899
- Sanders . . . 8,675
- Sheridan . . . 5,414
- Silver Bow . . . 38,092
- Stillwater . . . 5,598
- Sweet Grass . . . 3,216
- Teton . . . 6,491
- Toole . . . 5,559
- Treasure . . . 981
- Valley . . . 10,250
- Wheatland . . . 2,359
- Wibaux . . . 1,476
- Yellowstone . . . 108,035
- Yellowstone National Park . . . 66

NEBRASKA

1980 Census . . . 1,569,825

CITIES

- Ainsworth . . . 2,256
- Air Park West LINC . . . 3,100 ○
- Albion . . . 1,997
- Alda GDIS . . . 601
- Alliance . . . 9,920
- Alma . . . 1,369
- Ansley . . . 644
- Arapahoe . . . 1,107
- Arlington . . . 1,117
- Arnold . . . 813
- Ashland . . . 2,274
- Atkinson . . . 1,521
- Auburn . . . 3,482
- Aurora . . . 3,717
- Axtell . . . 602
- Bancroft . . . 552
- Bassett . . . 1,009
- Battle Creek . . . 948
- Bayard . . . 1,435
- Beatrice . . . 12,891
- Beaver City . . . 775
- Beaver Crossing . . . 458
- Beemer . . . 853
- Bellevue OMA- . . . 32,145
- Benkelman . . . 1,235
- Bennet . . . 523
- Bennington OMA- . . . 631
- Bertrand . . . 775
- Big Springs . . . 505
- Blair . . . 6,418
- Bloomfield . . . 1,393
- Blue Hill . . . 883
- Blue Springs . . . 521
- Boys Town OMA- . . . 622
- Bridgeport . . . 1,668
- Broken Bow . . . 3,979
- Burwell . . . 1,383
- Butte . . . 529
- Cairo . . . 737
- Callaway . . . 579
- Cambridge . . . 1,206
- Campbell . . . 441
- Cedar Bluffs . . . 632
- Cedar Rapids . . . 447
- Central City . . . 3,083
- Ceresco . . . 836
- Chadron . . . 5,933
- Chappell . . . 1,095
- Clarks . . . 445
- Clarkson . . . 817
- Clay Center . . . 962
- Coleridge . . . 673
- Columbus . . . 18,057
- Cozad . . . 4,453
- Crawford . . . 1,315
- Creighton . . . 1,341
- Crete . . . 4,872
- Crofton . . . 948
- Crown Point OMA- . . . 700 ○
- Culbertson . . . 767
- Curtis . . . 1,014
- Dakota City SXCY . . . 1,440
- Davenport . . . 445
- David City . . . 2,514
- Debolt OMA- . . . 800 ○
- Decatur . . . 723
- Deshler . . . 997
- De Witt . . . 642
- Dodge . . . 815
- Doniphan . . . 696
- Dorchester . . . 611
- Eagle . . . 832
- Edgar . . . 705
- Elgin . . . 807
- Elkhorn OMA- . . . 1,344
- Elm Creek . . . 862
- Elmwood . . . 598
- Elwood . . . 716
- Emerson . . . 874
- Eustis . . . 460
- Ewing . . . 520
- Exeter . . . 807
- Fairbury . . . 4,885
- Fairfield . . . 543
- Fairmont . . . 767
- Falls City . . . 5,374
- Fort Calhoun . . . 641
- Franklin . . . 1,167
- Fremont . . . 23,979
- Friend . . . 1,079
- Fullerton . . . 1,506
- Geneva . . . 2,400
- Genoa . . . 1,115
- Gering . . . 7,760
- Gibbon . . . 1,531
- Gordon . . . 2,245
- Gothenburg . . . 3,479
- GRAND ISLAND GDIS . . . 33,180
- Grant . . . 1,270
- Greeley . . . 597
- Greenwood . . . 587
- Gretna OMA- . . . 1,609
- Hartington . . . 1,730
- Harvard . . . 1,217
- Hastings . . . 23,045
- Hay Springs . . . 794
- Hebron . . . 1,906
- Hemingford . . . 1,023
- Henderson . . . 1,072
- Hershey . . . 633
- Hickman . . . 687
- Holdrege . . . 5,624
- Homer . . . 564
- Hooper . . . 932
- Howells . . . 677
- Humboldt . . . 1,176
- Humphrey . . . 799
- Imperial . . . 1,941
- Indianola . . . 856
- Irvington OMA- . . . 500 ○
- Juniata . . . 703
- Kearney . . . 21,751
- Kenesaw . . . 854
- Kimball . . . 3,120
- Laurel . . . 1,031
- La Vista OMA- . . . 9,588
- Leigh . . . 509
- Lexington . . . 7,040
- LINCOLN LINC . . . 171,932
- Long Pine . . . 521
- Loomis . . . 447
- Louisville . . . 1,022
- Loup City . . . 1,368
- Lyman . . . 551
- Lyons . . . 1,214
- McCook . . . 8,404
- Macy . . . 500 ○
- Madison . . . 1,950
- Mead . . . 506
- Milford . . . 2,108
- Minatare . . . 969
- Minden . . . 2,939
- Mitchell . . . 1,956
- Morrill . . . 1,097
- Mullen . . . 720
- Murray . . . 465
- Nebraska City . . . 7,127
- Neligh . . . 1,893
- Nelson . . . 733
- Newman Grove . . . 930
- Norfolk . . . 19,449
- North Bend . . . 1,368
- North Oaks OMA- . . . 600 ○
- North Omaha OMA- . . . 1,100 ○
- North Platte . . . 24,509
- Oakland . . . 1,393
- Ogallala . . . 5,638
- OMAHA OMA- . . . 322,133
- O'Neill . . . 4,049
- Orchard . . . 482
- Ord . . . 2,658
- Orleans . . . 527
- Osceola . . . 975
- Oshkosh . . . 1,057
- Osmond . . . 871
- Overton . . . 633
- Oxford . . . 1,109
- Palmer . . . 487
- Palmyra . . . 512
- Papillion OMA- . . . 7,725
- Pawnee City . . . 1,156
- Paxton . . . 568
- Pender . . . 1,318
- Peru . . . 998
- Pierce . . . 1,535
- Plainview . . . 1,483
- Plattsmouth OMA- . . . 6,295
- Plymouth . . . 506
- Polk . . . 440
- Ponca . . . 1,057
- Ralston OMA- . . . 5,952
- Randolph . . . 1,106
- Ravenna . . . 1,296
- Red Cloud . . . 1,300
- Roanoke OMA- . . . 900 ○
- Rushville . . . 1,217
- St. Edward . . . 891
- St. Paul . . . 2,094
- Sargent . . . 828
- Schuyler . . . 4,151
- Scottsbluff . . . 14,156
- Scribner . . . 1,011
- Seward . . . 5,713
- Shelby . . . 724
- Shelton . . . 1,046
- Sidney . . . 6,010
- Silver Creek . . . 496
- South Sioux City SXCY . . . 9,339
- Spalding . . . 645
- Spencer . . . 596
- Springfield . . . 782
- Stanton . . . 1,603
- Sterling . . . 526
- Still Meadow OMA- . . . 950 ○
- Stratton . . . 499
- Stromsburg . . . 1,290
- Stuart . . . 641
- Sunnyslope OMA- . . . 770 ○
- Superior . . . 2,502
- Sutherland . . . 1,238
- Sutton . . . 1,416
- Syracuse . . . 1,638
- Tecumseh . . . 1,926
- Tekamah . . . 1,886
- Terrytown . . . 727
- Tilden . . . 1,012
- Trenton . . . 796
- Utica . . . 689
- Valentine . . . 2,829
- Valley . . . 1,716
- Valparaiso . . . 484
- Verdigre . . . 617
- Wahoo . . . 3,555
- Wakefield . . . 1,125
- Walthill . . . 847
- Waterloo OMA- . . . 450
- Wauneta . . . 746
- Wausa . . . 647
- Waverly LINC . . . 1,726
- Wayne . . . 5,240
- Weeping Water . . . 1,109
- West Point . . . 3,609
- Wilber . . . 1,624
- Winnebago . . . 902
- Wisner . . . 1,335
- Wood River . . . 1,334
- Wymore . . . 1,841
- York . . . 7,723
- Yutan . . . 631

COUNTIES

- Adams . . . 30,656
- Antelope . . . 8,675
- Arthur . . . 513
- Banner . . . 918
- Blaine . . . 867
- Boone . . . 7,391
- Box Butte . . . 13,696
- Boyd . . . 3,331
- Brown . . . 4,377

○ Rand McNally estimate (not reported in census).
▲ Population of entire township or "town", including rural areas.
● Independent city. Population not included in county total.

Buffalo	34,797
Burt	8,813
Butler	9,330
Cass	20,297
Cedar	11,375
Chase	4,758
Cherry	6,758
Cheyenne	10,057
Clay	8,106
Colfax	9,890
Cuming	11,664
Custer	13,877
Dakota	16,573
Dawes	9,609
Dawson	22,304
Deuel	2,462
Dixon	7,137
Dodge	35,847
Douglas	397,038
Dundy	2,861
Fillmore	7,920
Franklin	4,377
Frontier	3,647
Furnas	6,486
Gage	24,456
Garden	2,802
Garfield	2,363
Gosper	2,140
Grant	877
Greeley	3,462
Hall	47,690
Hamilton	9,301
Harlan	4,292
Hayes	1,356
Hitchcock	4,079
Holt	13,552
Hooker	990
Howard	6,773
Jefferson	9,817
Johnson	5,285
Kearney	7,053
Keith	9,364
Keya Paha	1,301
Kimball	4,882
Knox	11,457
Lancaster	192,884
Lincoln	36,455
Logan	983
Loup	859
McPherson	593
Madison	31,382
Merrick	8,945
Morrill	6,085
Nance	4,740
Nemaha	8,367
Nuckolls	6,726
Otoe	15,183
Pawnee	3,937
Perkins	3,637
Phelps	9,769
Pierce	8,481
Platte	28,852
Polk	6,320
Red Willow	12,615
Richardson	11,315
Rock	2,383
Saline	13,131
Sarpy	86,015
Saunders	18,716
Scotts Bluff	38,344
Seward	15,789
Sheridan	7,544
Sherman	4,226
Sioux	1,845
Stanton	6,549
Thayer	7,582
Thomas	973
Thurston	7,186
Valley	5,633
Washington	15,508
Wayne	9,858
Webster	4,858
Wheeler	1,060
York	14,798

NEVADA
1980 Census 800,493

CITIES

Babbitt	1,800 ○
Battle Mountain	2,749
Beatty	900 ○
Boulder City	9,590
Caliente	982
Carlin	1,232
Carson City ●	32,022
Crystal Bay	1,200 ○
East Las Vegas LASV	6,449
Elko	8,758
Ely	4,882
Eureka	500 ○
Fallon	4,262
Fernley	1,200 ○
Gabbs	811
Gardnerville	2,800 ○
Hawthorne	3,741
Henderson LASV	24,363
Indian Springs	900 ○
Jackpot	500 ○
LAS VEGAS LASV	164,674
Lemmon Valley RENO	2,000 ○
Lovelock	1,680
McGill	1,419
Mesquite	700 ○
Minden	1,300 ○
New Washoe City	2,543
North Las Vegas LASV	42,739
Overton	1,111
Owyhee	700 ○
Pahrump	1,000 ○
Panaca	550 ○
Paradise LASV	45,000 ○
Pioche	700 ○
RENO RENO	100,756
Ruth	735 ○
Skyland	500 ○
Sparks RENO	40,780
Stateline	1,500 ○
Sunrise Manor LASV	44,155
Sun Valley RENO	8,822
Tonopah	1,952
Topaz Ranch Estates	500 ○
Verdi RENO	800 ○
Virginia City	600 ○
Weed Heights	650 ○
Wells	1,218
Winchester LASV	19,728
Winnemucca	4,140
Yerington	2,021
Zephyr Cove	1,300 ○

COUNTIES

Churchill	13,917
Clark	463,087
Douglas	19,421
Elko	17,269
Esmeralda	777
Eureka	1,198
Humboldt	9,449
Lander	4,076
Lincoln	3,732
Lyon	13,594
Mineral	6,217
Nye	9,048
Pershing	3,408
Storey	1,503
Washoe	193,623
White Pine	8,167

NEW HAMPSHIRE
1980 Census 920,610

CITIES

Alstead 1,461 ▲	500 ○
Alton 2,440 ▲	900 ○
Alton Bay	900 ○
Amherst NSHUA 8,243 ▲	750 ○
Antrim 2,208 ▲	1,142
Ashland 1,807 ▲	1,479
Atkinson BOS 4,397 ▲	900 ○
Bartlett 1,566 ▲	700 ○
Bedford MNCH 9,481 ▲	1,300 ○
Belmont 4,026 ▲	900 ○
Bennington 890 ▲	500 ○
Berlin	13,084
Bethlehem 1,784 ▲	700 ○
Bow CONC 4,015 ▲	500 ○
Bradford 1,115 ▲	450 ○
Bristol 2,198 ▲	1,258
Campton 1,694 ▲	600 ○
Canaan 2,456 ▲	600 ○
Canobie Lake BOS	800 ○
Center Harbor 808 ▲	500 ○
Center Ossipee	500 ○
Charlestown 4,417 ▲	1,294
Chester BOS 2,006 ▲	500 ○
Claremont	14,557
Colebrook 2,459 ▲	1,131
CONCORD CONC	30,400
Contoocook CONC	1,499
Conway 7,158 ▲	1,781
Danville BOS 1,318 ▲	500 ○
Derry BOS 18,875 ▲	12,248
DOVER DOV-	22,377
Dublin 1,303 ▲	600 ○
Durham 10,652 ▲	8,448
East Derry BOS	600 ○
East Hampstead BOS	900 ○
Enfield 3,175 ▲	1,581
Epping 3,460 ▲	1,384
Exeter 11,024 ▲	8,947
Farmington DOV- 4,630 ▲	3,284
Fitzwilliam 1,795 ▲	600 ○
Franconia 743 ▲	600 ○
Franklin	7,901
Fremont 1,333 ▲	450 ○
Gilmanton 1,941 ▲	600 ○
Gilsum 652 ▲	500 ○
Goffstown MNCH 11,315 ▲	2,500 ○
Gorham 3,322 ▲	2,180
Greenfield 972 ▲	500 ○
Greenland PTSM 2,129 ▲	600 ○
Greenville 1,988 ▲	1,447
Groveton	1,389
Hampstead BOS 3,785 ▲	500 ○
Hampton 10,493 ▲	6,779
Hampton Beach	900 ○
Hampton Falls 1,372 ▲	500 ○
Hanover 9,119 ▲	6,861
Henniker 3,246 ▲	1,538
Hillsboro	1,797
Hinsdale 3,631 ▲	1,546
Hooksett MNCH 7,303 ▲	1,868
Hudson NSHUA 14,022 ▲	6,248
Jaffrey 4,349 ▲	2,684
Keene	21,449
Kingston BOS 4,111 ▲	900 ○
Laconia	15,575
Lancaster 3,401 ▲	2,134
Lebanon	11,134
Lincoln 1,313 ▲	950 ○
Lisbon 1,517 ▲	1,151
Little Boars Head PTSM	500 ○
Littleton 5,558 ▲	4,480
Londonderry MNCH 13,598 ▲	950 ○
MANCHESTER MNCH	90,936
Marlborough 1,846 ▲	1,184
Meredith 4,646 ▲	1,202
Merrimack NSHUA 15,406 ▲	1,200 ○
Milford NSHUA 8,685 ▲	6,269
Millville Lake BOS	600 ○
Milton DOV- 2,438 ▲	1,000 ○
NASHUA NSHUA	67,865
New Castle PTSM	975
Newfields 817 ▲	700 ○
New Ipswich FTCH- 2,433 ▲	500 ○
New London 2,935 ▲	1,335
Newmarket 4,290 ▲	3,749
Newport 6,229 ▲	4,388
Newton BOS 3,068 ▲	450 ○
Newton Junction BOS	450 ○
North Branch	800 ○
North Conway	2,104
Northfield 3,051 ▲	1,340 ○
North Hampton PTSM 3,425 ▲	1,000 ○
North Salem BOS	600 ○
North Stratford	650 ○
North Swanzey	950 ○
North Walpole	950 ○
North Woodstock	600 ○
Pelham BOS 8,090 ▲	500 ○
Peterborough 4,895 ▲	2,100 ○
Pinardville MNCH	4,500 ○
Pittsfield CONC 2,889 ▲	1,584
Plaistow BOS 5,609 ▲	1,800 ○
Plymouth 5,094 ▲	3,628
PORTSMOUTH PTSM	26,254
Raymond MNCH 5,453 ▲	1,192
Rochester DOV-	21,560
Rollinsford DOV- 2,319 ▲	1,173
Rye PTSM 4,508 ▲	800 ○
Rye Beach PTSM	600 ○
Salem BOS 24,124 ▲	11,500 ○
Sanbornville	800 ○
Seabrook BOS 5,917 ▲	700 ○
Somersworth DOV-	10,350
South Hooksett MNCH	1,200 ○
Stratham 2,507 ▲	500 ○
Sunapee 2,312 ▲	900 ○
Suncook CONC	4,698
Swanzey Center	700 ○
Tilton 3,387 ▲	1,230 ○
Troy 2,131 ▲	1,318
Walpole 3,188 ▲	700 ○
Warner 1,963 ▲	700 ○
Warren 650 ▲	450 ○
West Chesterfield	450 ○
West Peterborough	500 ○
Westport	450 ○
West Swanzey	1,022
Westville BOS	700 ○
Whitefield 1,681 ▲	1,005
Wilton NSHUA	1,310
Winchester 3,465 ▲	1,732
Winnisquam	600 ○
Wolfeboro 3,968 ▲	1,800 ○
Wolfeboro Falls	500 ○
Woodsville	1,195

COUNTIES

Belknap	42,884
Carroll	27,931
Cheshire	62,116
Coos	35,147
Grafton	65,806
Hillsborough	276,608
Merrimack	98,302
Rockingham	190,345
Strafford	85,408
Sullivan	36,063

NEW JERSEY
1980 Census 7,365,011

CITIES

Absecon ATCY	6,859
Adamston N.Y.	1,300 ○
Allendale N.Y.	5,901
Allenhurst N.Y.	912
Allentown PHIL-	1,962
Allenwood N.Y.	500 ○
Alloway	1,370
Alpha AL-B-E	2,644
Alpine N.Y.	1,549
Andover N.Y.	892
Annandale N.Y.	1,040
Arrowhead Village N.Y.	3,100 ○
Asbury Park N.Y.	17,015
Atco PHIL-	2,100 ○
ATLANTIC CITY ATCY	40,199
Atlantic Highlands N.Y.	4,950
Audubon PHIL-	9,533
Avalon	2,162
Avon by the Sea N.Y.	2,337
Barnegat	1,012
Barnegat Light	619
Barrington PHIL-	7,418
Basking Ridge N.Y.	4,800 ○
Bay Head N.Y.	1,340
Bayonne N.Y.	65,047
Bayville N.Y.	900 ○
Beach Haven	1,714
Beachwood N.Y.	7,687
Bedminster N.Y.	500 ○
Belford N.Y.	6,000 ○
Belle Mead	600 ○
Belleville N.Y.	35,367
Bellmawr PHIL-	13,721
Belmar N.Y.	6,771
Belvidere	2,475
Bergenfield N.Y.	25,568
Berkeley Heights N.Y.	12,549
Berlin PHIL-	5,786
Bernardsville N.Y.	6,715
Beverly PHIL-	2,919
Blackwood PHIL-	5,219
Blairstown	700 ○
Bloomfield N.Y.	47,792
Bloomingdale N.Y.	7,867
Bloomsbury	864
Blue Anchor PHIL-	500 ○
Bogota N.Y.	8,344
Boonton N.Y.	8,620
Bordentown PHIL-	4,441
Bossert Estates PHIL-	2,800 ○
Bound Brook N.Y.	9,710
Bradley Beach N.Y.	4,772
Branchville	870
Breton Woods N.Y.	1,300 ○
Bridgeport PHIL-	900 ○
BRIDGETON BRDGT	18,795
Bridgewater N.Y.	5,800 ○
Brielle N.Y.	4,068
Brigantine ATCY	8,318
Broadway	450 ○
Brooklawn PHIL-	2,133
Brookwood N.Y.	4,000 ○
Browns Mills	10,568
Budd Lake N.Y.	6,523
Buena VINL-	3,642
Burleigh	600 ○
Burlington PHIL-	10,246
Butler N.Y.	7,616
Caldwell N.Y.	7,624
Califon N.Y.	1,023
Camden PHIL-	84,910
Cape May	4,853
Cape May Court House	3,597
Carlstadt N.Y.	6,166
Carmel VINL-	500 ○
Carneys Point PHIL-	7,574
Carteret N.Y.	20,598
Cedar Brook PHIL-	500 ○
Cedar Grove N.Y.	12,600
Cedar Knolls N.Y.	3,000 ○
Cedar Run	450 ○
Cedarville	990 ○
Centre City PHIL-	2,500 ○
Chatham N.Y.	8,537
Cherry Hill PHIL-	68,785
Chesilhurst PHIL-	1,590
Chester N.Y.	1,433
Cinnaminson PHIL-	16,072
Clark N.Y.	16,699
Clarksboro PHIL-	800 ○
Clayton PHIL-	6,013
Clementon PHIL-	5,764
Cliffside Park N.Y.	21,464
Cliffwood Beach N.Y.	6,300 ○
Clifton N.Y.	74,388
Clinton N.Y.	1,910
Closter N.Y.	8,164
Cold Spring	850 ○
Collingswood PHIL-	15,838
Cologne ATCY	500 ○
Colts Neck N.Y.	500 ○
Columbus PHIL-	700 ○
Cranberry Lake N.Y.	600 ○
Cranbury N.Y.	1,255
Cranford N.Y.	24,573
Cresskill N.Y.	7,609
Crestwood Village N.Y.	7,965
Crosswicks PHIL-	550 ○
Dayton N.Y.	900 ○
Deal N.Y.	1,952
Deans N.Y.	600 ○
Deepwater PHIL-	650 ○
Delanco PHIL-	3,730
Delran PHIL-	14,811
Demarest N.Y.	4,963
Denville N.Y.	14,380
Dividing Creek	500 ○
Dorchester	500 ○
Dorothy	600 ○
Dover N.Y.	14,681
Dumont N.Y.	18,334
Dunellen N.Y.	6,593
East Brunswick N.Y.	37,711
East Hanover N.Y.	9,319
East Newark N.Y.	1,923
East Orange N.Y.	77,878
East Rutherford N.Y.	7,849
East Windsor N.Y.	15,000 ○
Eatontown N.Y.	12,703
Edgewater N.Y.	4,628
Edgewater Park PHIL-	9,273
Edison N.Y.	70,193
Egg Harbor City ATCY	4,618
Elizabeth N.Y.	106,201
Elmer PHIL-	1,569
Elmwood Park N.Y.	18,377
Elwood	900 ○
Emerson N.Y.	7,793
Englewood N.Y.	23,701
Englewood Cliffs N.Y.	5,698
Englishtown N.Y.	976
Erial PHIL-	900 ○
Erma	1,200 ○
Essex Fells N.Y.	2,363
Estell Manor	848
Ewing Township PHIL-	34,842
Fairfield N.Y.	7,987
Fair Haven N.Y.	5,679
Fair Lawn N.Y.	32,229
Fairton BRDGT	1,107
Fairview N.Y.	10,519
Fanwood N.Y.	7,767
Far Hills N.Y.	677
Farmingdale N.Y.	1,348
Fellowship PHIL-	1,900 ○
Fieldsboro PHIL-	597
Flagtown N.Y.	800 ○
Flanders N.Y.	6,000 ○
Flemington N.Y.	4,132
Florence PHIL-	5,000 ○
Florham Park N.Y.	9,359
Folsom	1,892
Forked River	1,600 ○
Fort Lee N.Y.	32,449
Franklin N.Y.	4,486
Franklin Lakes N.Y.	8,769
Franklinville PHIL-	900 ○
Freehold N.Y.	10,020
Frenchtown	1,573
Garfield N.Y.	26,803
Garwood N.Y.	4,752
Gibbstown PHIL-	5,404
Gladstone N.Y.	2,038
Glassboro PHIL-	14,574
Glendola N.Y.	2,300 ○
Glendora PHIL-	5,632
Glen Gardner N.Y.	834
Glen Ridge N.Y.	7,855
Glen Rock N.Y.	11,497
Gloucester City PHIL-	13,121
Green Brook N.Y.	4,500 ○
Green Creek	500 ○
Groveville PHIL-	1,200 ○
Guttenberg N.Y.	7,340
Hackensack N.Y.	36,039
Hackettstown N.Y.	8,850
Haddonfield PHIL-	12,337
Haddon Heights PHIL-	8,361
Hainesport PHIL-	900 ○
Haledon N.Y.	6,607
Hamburg N.Y.	1,832
Hamilton Square PHIL-	10,000 ○
Hammonton	12,298
Hampton N.Y.	1,614
Hancocks Bridge	600 ○
Harrington Park N.Y.	4,532
Harrison N.Y.	12,242
Hasbrouck Heights N.Y.	12,166
Haworth N.Y.	3,509
Hawthorne N.Y.	18,200
Hazlet N.Y.	23,013
Heislerville	600 ○
Helmetta N.Y.	955
High Bridge N.Y.	3,435
Highland Lakes N.Y.	2,888
Highland Park N.Y.	13,396
Highlands N.Y.	5,187
Hightstown N.Y.	4,581
Hillsdale N.Y.	10,495
Hillside N.Y.	21,440
Hoboken N.Y.	42,460
Ho Ho Kus N.Y.	4,129
Holmdel N.Y.	800 ○
Hopatcong N.Y.	15,531
Hope N.Y.	450 ○
Hopewell PHIL-	2,001
Huntington AL-B-E	700 ○
Ironia N.Y.	900 ○
Irvington N.Y.	61,493
Island Heights N.Y.	1,575
Jackson N.Y.	600 ○
Jamesburg N.Y.	4,114
Jersey City N.Y.	223,532
Keansburg N.Y.	10,613
Kearny N.Y.	35,735
Kendall Park N.Y.	7,419
Kenilworth N.Y.	8,221
Kenvil N.Y.	3,000 ○
Keyport N.Y.	7,413
Kingston	900 ○
Kinnelon N.Y.	7,770
Lake Hiawatha N.Y.	14,000 ○
Lakehurst N.Y.	2,908
Lake Telemark N.Y.	1,216
Lakewood N.Y.	22,863
Lambertville PHIL-	4,044
Lanoka Harbor	700 ○
Laurence Harbor N.Y.	5,000 ○
Lavallette N.Y.	2,072
Lawnside PHIL-	3,042
Lawrenceville PHIL-	1,800 ○
Lebanon N.Y.	820
Ledgewood N.Y.	1,100 ○
Leesburg	700 ○
Leonardo N.Y.	3,600 ○
Leonia N.Y.	8,027
Liberty Corner N.Y.	800 ○
Lincoln Park N.Y.	8,806
Lincroft N.Y.	4,100 ○
Linden N.Y.	37,836
Lindenwold PHIL-	18,196
Linwood ATCY	6,144
Little Falls N.Y.	11,496
Little Ferry N.Y.	9,399
Little Silver N.Y.	5,548
Livingston N.Y.	28,040
Locust N.Y.	700 ○
Lodi N.Y.	23,956
Long Branch N.Y.	29,819
Longport ATCY	1,249
Long Valley N.Y.	1,682
Lumberton PHIL-	700 ○
Lyndhurst N.Y.	20,326
McAfee N.Y.	500 ○
McKee City	600 ○
Madison N.Y.	15,357
Magnolia PHIL-	4,881
Mahwah N.Y.	7,500 ○
Malaga VINL-	950 ○
Manahawkin	1,469
Manasquan N.Y.	5,354
Mantua PHIL-	1,900 ○
Manville N.Y.	11,278
Maple Shade PHIL-	20,525
Maplewood N.Y.	22,950
Margate City ATCY	9,179
Marlboro N.Y.	5,700 ○
Marlton PHIL-	9,411
Marmora	500 ○
Matawan N.Y.	8,837
Mauricetown	500 ○
Mays Landing	2,054
Maywood N.Y.	9,895
Medford PHIL-	1,800 ○
Medford Lakes PHIL-	4,958
Mendham N.Y.	4,899
Mercerville PHIL-	15,500 ○
Merchantville PHIL-	3,972
Metuchen N.Y.	13,762
Middlesex N.Y.	13,480
Middletown N.Y.	62,298
Midland Park N.Y.	7,381
Milford	1,368
Millburn N.Y.	19,543
Millstone N.Y.	530
Milltown N.Y.	7,136
Millville VINL-	24,815
Mine Hill N.Y.	3,250 ○
Mizpah	600 ○
Monmouth Beach N.Y.	3,318
Monmouth Junction N.Y.	2,579
Montclair N.Y.	38,321
Montvale N.Y.	7,318
Montville N.Y.	2,700 ○
Moonachie N.Y.	2,706
Moorestown PHIL-	15,596
Morganville N.Y.	900 ○
Morris Plains N.Y.	5,305
Morristown N.Y.	16,614
Mountain Lakes N.Y.	4,153
Mountainside N.Y.	7,118
Mount Arlington N.Y.	4,251
Mount Ephraim PHIL-	4,863
Mount Freedom N.Y.	1,700 ○

○ Rand McNally estimate (not reported in census).
▲ Population of entire township or "town", including rural areas.
● Independent city. Population not included in county total.

Mount Holly PHIL- 10,818
Mullica Hill PHIL- 1,050
National Park PHIL- 3,552
Navesink N.Y. 1,500 ○
Neptune N.Y. 28,366
Neptune City N.Y. 5,276
Netcong N.Y. 3,557
Newark N.Y. 329,248
New Brunswick N.Y. 41,442
New Egypt 2,111
Newfield VINL- 1,563
Newfoundland N.Y. 900 ○
New Gretna 550 ○
New Milford N.Y. 16,876
New Providence N.Y. 12,426
Newton N.Y. 7,748
Newtonville VINL- 500 ○
Norma VINL- 800 ○
North Arlington N.Y. 16,587
North Bergen N.Y. 47,019
North Brunswick N.Y. 22,220
North Caldwell N.Y. 5,832
North Cape May 4,029
Northfield ATCY 7,795
North Haledon N.Y. 8,177
North Plainfield N.Y. 19,108
Northvale N.Y. 5,046
North Wildwood 4,714
Norwood N.Y. 4,413
Nutley N.Y. 28,998
Oakhurst N.Y. 4,600 ○
Oakland N.Y. 13,443
Oaklyn PHIL- 4,223
Oak Valley PHIL- 7,000 ○
Ocean City ATCY 13,949
Ocean Gate N.Y. 1,385
Ocean Grove N.Y. 4,200 ○
Oceanport N.Y. 5,888
Oceanville ATCY 600 ○
Ogdensburg N.Y. 2,737
Old Bridge N.Y. 12,500 ○
Old Tappan N.Y. 4,168
Oldwick N.Y. 450 ○
Oradell N.Y. 8,658
Orange N.Y. 31,100
Oxford 1,587
Palisades Park N.Y. 13,732
Palmyra PHIL- 7,085
Paramus N.Y. 26,474
Parkertown 500 ○
Park Ridge N.Y. 8,515
Parsippany N.Y. 8,000 ○
Passaic N.Y. 52,463
Paterson N.Y. 137,970
Paulsboro PHIL- 6,944
Pedricktown PHIL- 900 ○
Pemberton 1,198
Pennington PHIL- 2,109
Pennsauken PHIL- 33,775
Penns Grove PHIL- 5,760
Pennsville PHIL- 12,467
Pequannock N.Y. 13,776
Perth Amboy N.Y. 38,951
Phillipsburg AL-B-E 16,647
Pine Hill PHIL- 8,684
Pinehurst ATCY 1,500 ○
Pinewald N.Y. 900 ○
Piscataway N.Y. 42,223
Pitman PHIL- 9,744
Plainfield N.Y. 45,555
Plainsboro N.Y. 800 ○
Pleasantville ATCY 13,435
Point Pleasant N.Y. 17,747
Point Pleasant Beach N.Y. 5,415
Pomona ATCY 2,358
Pompton Lakes N.Y. 10,660
Port Elizabeth 500 ○
Port Monmouth N.Y. 3,600 ○
Port Morris N.Y. 600 ○
Port Norris 1,730
Port Republic ATCY 837
Princeton 12,035
Princeton 13,683 ○
Princeton Junction N.Y. 2,419
Prospect Park N.Y. 5,142
Quinton PHIL- 500 ○
Rahway N.Y. 26,723
Ramblewood PHIL- 6,475
Ramsey N.Y. 12,899
Rancocas PHIL- 600 ○
Rancocas Woods PHIL- 1,400 ○
Raritan N.Y. 6,128
Red Bank N.Y. 12,031
Richland VINL- 800 ○
Ridgefield N.Y. 10,294
Ridgefield Park N.Y. 12,738
Ridgewood N.Y. 25,208
Ringoes PHIL- 650 ○
Ringwood N.Y. 12,625
Rio Grande 2,016
Riverdale N.Y. 2,530
River Edge N.Y. 11,111
Riverside PHIL- 7,941
Riverton PHIL- 3,068
River Vale N.Y. 9,489
Riviera Beach N.Y. 2,000 ○
Robbinsville PHIL- 550 ○
Rochelle Park N.Y. 5,603
Rockaway N.Y. 6,852
Rocky Hill 717
Roebling PHIL- 3,600 ○
Roosevelt 835
Roseland N.Y. 5,330
Roselle N.Y. 20,641
Roselle Park N.Y. 13,377
Rosenhayn VINL- 750 ○
Rumson N.Y. 7,623
Runnemede PHIL- 9,461
Rutherford N.Y. 19,068
Saddle Brook N.Y. 14,084
Saddle River N.Y. 2,763
Salem PHIL- 6,959
Sayreville N.Y. 29,969
Scotch Plains N.Y. 20,774
Sea Bright N.Y. 1,812
Seabrook BRDGT 1,411
Sea Girt N.Y. 2,650
Sea Isle City 2,644
Seaside Heights N.Y. 1,802

Seaside Park N.Y. 1,795
Secaucus N.Y. 13,719
Sewell PHIL- 1,900 ○
Shiloh BRDGT 604
Ship Bottom 1,427
Shore Acres N.Y. 1,300 ○
Shrewsbury N.Y. 2,962
Sicklerville PHIL- 850 ○
Silverton N.Y. 7,236
Slackwood PHIL- 8,100 ○
Somerdale PHIL- 5,900
Somerset N.Y. 21,731
Somers Point ATCY 10,330
Somerville N.Y. 11,973
South Amboy N.Y. 8,322
South Belmar N.Y. 1,566
South Bound Brook N.Y. 4,331
South Hackensack N.Y. 2,229
South Orange N.Y. 15,864
South Plainfield N.Y. 20,521
South River N.Y. 14,361
South Toms River N.Y. 3,954
Sparta N.Y. 8,498
Spotswood N.Y. 7,840
Springfield N.Y. 13,955
Spring Lake N.Y. 4,215
Spring Lake Heights N.Y. 5,424
Stanhope N.Y. 3,638
Stewartsville AL-B-E 900 ○
Stirling N.Y. 2,000 ○
Stockholm N.Y. 600 ○
Stockton PHIL- 643
Stone Harbor 1,187
Stratford PHIL- 8,005
Succasunna N.Y. 9,000 ○
Summit N.Y. 21,071
Surf City 1,571
Sussex 2,418
Sutton Park N.Y. 2,500 ○
Swedesboro PHIL- 2,031
Teaneck N.Y. 39,007
Tenafly N.Y. 13,552
Thorofare PHIL- 1,400 ○
Three Bridges N.Y. 650 ○
Tinton Falls N.Y. 7,740
Titusville PHIL- 900 ○
Toms River N.Y. 7,465
Totowa N.Y. 11,448
Towaco N.Y. 1,400 ○
Trenton PHIL- 92,124
Tuckahoe 650 ○
Tuckerton 2,472
Twin Rivers N.Y. 7,742
Union N.Y. 50,184
Union Beach N.Y. 6,354
Union City N.Y. 55,593
Upper Greenwood Lake N.Y. 2,734
Upper Saddle River N.Y. 7,958
Vail Homes N.Y. 995
Ventnor City ATCY 11,704
Vernon N.Y. 900 ○
Verona N.Y. 14,166 ○
Villas 5,909
Vincentown PHIL- 800 ○
VINELAND VINL- 53,753
Waldwick N.Y. 10,802
Wallington N.Y. 10,741
Wanaque N.Y. 10,025
Waretown 1,175
Washington 6,429
Washington Crossing PHIL- 500 ○
Washington Township N.Y. 9,550
Watchung N.Y. 5,290
Waterford Works PHIL- 600 ○
Wayne N.Y. 46,474
Weehawken N.Y. 13,168
Wenonah PHIL- 2,303
West Berlin PHIL- 3,300 ○
West Caldwell N.Y. 11,407
West Cape May 1,091
West Creek 500 ○
Westfield N.Y. 30,447
West Long Branch N.Y. 7,380
West Milford N.Y. 1,600 ○
Westmont PHIL- 5,700 ○
West New York N.Y. 39,194
West Orange N.Y. 39,400 ○
West Paterson N.Y. 11,293
Westville PHIL- 4,786
Westwood N.Y. 10,714
Wharton N.Y. 5,485
White Horse PHIL- 10,098
White House Station N.Y. 1,300 ○
White Meadow Lake N.Y. 8,429
Whitesboro 900 ○
Whiting 700 ○
Whitman Square PHIL- 2,600 ○
Wildwood 4,913
Wildwood Crest 4,149
Williamstown PHIL- 5,768
Willingboro PHIL- 39,912
Winfield N.Y. 1,785
Winslow PHIL- 500 ○
Woodbine 2,809
Woodbury PHIL- 10,353
Woodcliff Lake N.Y. 5,644
Woodlynne PHIL- 2,578
Woodport N.Y. 500 ○
Wood-Ridge N.Y. 7,929
Woodstown PHIL- 3,250
Wrightstown 3,031
Wyckoff N.Y. 15,500
Yardville PHIL- 8,400 ○

COUNTIES

Atlantic 194,119
Bergen 845,385
Burlington 362,542
Camden 471,650
Cape May 82,266
Cumberland 132,866
Essex 851,304
Gloucester 199,917
Hudson 556,972
Hunterdon 87,361
Mercer 307,863
Middlesex 595,893
Monmouth 503,173
Morris 407,630
Ocean 346,038
Passaic 447,585
Salem 64,676
Somerset 203,129
Sussex 116,119
Union 504,094
Warren 84,429

NEW MEXICO

1980 Census 1,303,445

CITIES

Adobe Acres ALBU 3,400 ○
Agua Fria S.FE 850 ○
Alameda ALBU 7,800 ○
Alamogordo 24,024
ALBUQUERQUE ALBU 332,336
Alcalde 800 ○
Anthony ELP 3,285
Arenas Valley 500 ○
Armijo ALBU 18,900 ○
Arroyo Seco 500 ○
Artesia 10,385
Aztec 5,512
Bayard 3,036
Belen ALBU 5,617
Bernalillo ALBU 3,012
Black Rock 500 ○
Bloomfield 4,881
Capitan 762
Carlsbad 25,496
Carrizozo 1,222
Cedar Crest 900 ○
Central 1,968
Chama 1,090
Chamisal 600 ○
Chimayo 1,993
Church Rock 500 ○
Cimarron 888
Clayton 2,968
Cloudcroft 521
CLOVIS CLOV 31,194
Cordova 600 ○
Crownpoint 1,134
Cuba 609
Deming 9,964
Dexter 882
Dulce 1,648
Edgewood 600 ○
El Prado 700 ○
Espanola 6,803
Estancia 830
Eunice 2,970
Fairacres LSCR 600 ○
Farmington 31,222
Five Points ALBU 5,500 ○
Flora Vista 500 ○
Fort Sumner 1,421
Fort Wingate 900 ○
Fruitland 700 ○
Gallup 18,167
Grants 11,439
Hagerman 936
Hanover 500 ○
Happy Valley 630 ○
Hatch 1,028
High Rolls Mountain Park 650 ○
Hobbs 29,153
Hurley 1,616
Isleta ALBU 1,246
Jal 2,675
Jemez Pueblo 1,503
Kirtland 2,358
Laguna 800 ○
La Luz 1,194
La Mesa 900 ○
LAS CRUCES LSCR 45,086
Las Vegas 14,322
Logan 735
Lordsburg 3,195
Los Alamos 11,039
Los Lunas ALBU 3,525
Los Padillas ALBU 2,500 ○
Los Ranchos de Albuquerque ALBU 2,857
Los Trujillos 500 ○
Loving 1,355
Lovington 9,727
Magdalena 1,022
Melrose 649
Mescalero 1,259
Mesilla LSCR 2,029
Mexican Springs 500 ○
Milan 3,747
Mora 900 ○
Moriarty 1,276
Mountainair 1,170
Mountain View ALBU 1,900 ○
New Laguna 600 ○
Ojo Caliente 500 ○
Organ 500 ○
Pajarito ALBU 2,000 ○
Paradise Hills ALBU 5,096
Pecos 885
Penasco 900 ○
Placitas 450 ○
Pojoaque Valley 900 ○
Portales 9,940
Pueblo of Acoma 500 ○
Questa 1,202
Ramah 600 ○
Ranchos de Taos 1,411
Raton 8,225
Rio Rancho ALBU 9,985
ROSWELL RSWL 39,676
Ruidoso 4,260
Ruidoso Downs 949
San Antonio 500 ○
San Juan Pueblo 600 ○
San Rafael 560 ○
Santa Clara Pueblo 450 ○
Santa Cruz 600 ○
SANTA FE S.FE 49,299
Santa Rosa 2,469
Santo Domingo Pueblo 2,082
Shiprock 7,237
Silver City 9,887
Socorro 7,173
Springer 1,657
Sunland Park ELP 3,377
Taos 3,369
Taos Pueblo 1,030 ○
Tatum 896
Tesuque S.FE 1,014
Texico 958
Thoreau 1,099
Tierra Amarilla 800 ○
Tohatchi 1,011
Truth or Consequences 5,219
Tucumcari 6,765
Tularosa 2,536
Tyrone 950 ○
University Park LSCR 4,353
Vaughn 737
Waterflow 500 ○
Zuni 5,551

COUNTIES

Bernalillo 420,261
Catron 2,720
Chaves 51,103
Cibola 30,347
Colfax 13,667
Curry 42,019
De Baca 2,454
Dona Ana 96,340
Eddy 47,855
Grant 26,204
Guadalupe 4,496
Harding 1,090
Hidalgo 6,049
Lea 55,993
Lincoln 10,997
Los Alamos 17,599
Luna 15,585
McKinley 56,536
Mora 4,205
Otero 44,665
Quay 10,577
Rio Arriba 29,282
Roosevelt 15,695
Sandoval 34,799
San Juan 81,433
San Miguel 22,751
Santa Fe 75,360
Sierra 8,454
Socorro 12,566
Taos 19,456
Torrance 7,491
Union 4,725
Valencia 30,768

NEW YORK

1980 Census 17,558,072

CITIES

Accord 500 ○
Adams 1,701
Adams Center 1,519
Addison 2,028
Afton 982
Akron 2,971
ALBANY A-S-T 101,727
Albertson N.Y. 5,561
Albion ROCH 4,897
Alden BUF- 2,488
Alexandria Bay 1,265
Alfred 4,967
Allegany 2,078
Almond 568
Altamont A-S-T 1,292
Amagansett 2,188
Amenia 1,183
Amherst BUF- 66,100 ○
Amityville N.Y. 9,076
Amsterdam A-S-T 21,872
Andover 1,120
Angelica 982
Angola BUF- 2,292
Antwerp 749
Apalachin BING 1,227
Aquebogue 1,800 ○
Arcade 2,052
Ardsley N.Y. 4,183
Arkport 811
Arkville 600 ○
Arlington POK 11,305
Armonk N.Y. 2,238
Athens 1,738
Atlanta 750 ○
Attica 2,659
AUBURN AUB 32,548
Aurora 926
Au Sable Forks 2,100 ○
Averill Park A-S-T 1,337
Avoca 1,144
Avon ROCH 3,006
Babylon N.Y. 12,388
Bainbridge 1,603
Baldwin N.Y. 31,630
Baldwinsville SYR 6,446
Ballston Spa A-S-T 4,711
Balmville NWBG 2,919
Barker 535
Barryville 600 ○
Batavia 16,703
Bath 6,042
Bayberry SYR 6,500 ○
Bayport N.Y. 9,282
Bay Shore N.Y. 33,200 ○
Bayville N.Y. 7,034
Beacon POK 12,937
Bedford Hills N.Y. 3,200 ○
Belfast 900 ○
Bellmore N.Y. 18,106
Bellport N.Y. 2,809
Belmont 1,024
Bemus Point JMST 444
Bergen ROCH 976
Bethpage N.Y. 16,840
Big Flats ELM- 2,892
BINGHAMTON BING 55,860
Black River WATN 1,384
Blasdell BUF- 3,288
Blauvelt N.Y. 4,900 ○
Bloomingdale 608
Bohemia N.Y. 9,308
Bolivar 1,345
Bolton Landing 1,500 ○
Boonville 2,344
Brant Lake 700 ○
Brentwood N.Y. 48,800 ○
Brewster N.Y. 1,650
Briarcliff Manor N.Y. 7,115
Bridgehampton 1,941
Brighton ROCH 35,776
Broadalbin A-S-T 1,415
Brockport ROCH 9,776
Brocton 1,416
Bronxville N.Y. 6,267
Brookfield 600 ○
Brookville N.Y. 3,290
Brownville WATN 1,099
BUFFALO BUF- 357,870
Burnt Hills A-S-T 2,000 ○
Cairo 1,281
Caledonia ROCH 2,188
Callicoon 500 ○
Cambridge 1,820
Camden 2,667
Canajoharie 2,412
Canandaigua 10,419
Canaseraga 700
Canastota 4,773
Candor 917
Canisteo 2,679
Canton 7,055
Cape Vincent 785
Carle Place N.Y. 5,470
Carthage 3,643
Cassadaga 821
Castile 1,135
Castleton on Hudson A-S-T 1,627
Cato SYR 475
Catskill 4,718
Cattaraugus 1,200
Cayuga Heights ITH 3,170
Cazenovia SYR 2,599
Cedarhurst N.Y. 6,162
Celoron JMST 1,405
Centereach N.Y. 30,136
Center Moriches N.Y. 5,703
Central Bridge 500 ○
Central Islip N.Y. 26,000 ○
Central Square SYR 1,418
Central Valley N.Y. 1,705
Chadwicks UT-R 1,500 ○
Champlain 1,410
Chappaqua N.Y. 5,100 ○
Chateaugay 869
Chatham A-S-T 2,001
Chaumont 620
Chazy 800 ○
Cheektowaga BUF- 92,145
Chenango Bridge BING 2,600 ○
Chenango Forks BING 500 ○
Cherry Creek 677
Cherry Valley 684
Chester N.Y. 1,910
Chestertown 750 ○
Chili Center ROCH 5,300 ○
Chittenango SYR 4,290
Churchville ROCH 1,399
Cincinnatus 500 ○
Clayton 1,816
Cleveland SYR 855
Clifton Knolls A-S-T 4,200 ○
Clifton Springs 2,039
Clinton UT-R 2,107
Clyde 2,491
Clymer 500 ○
Cobleskill 5,272
Cohocton 902
Cohoes A-S-T 18,144
Cold Spring Harbor N.Y. 5,336
Colonie A-S-T 8,869
Colton 450 ○
Commack N.Y. 34,719
Congers N.Y. 7,123
Conklin BING 1,900 ○
Constantia SYR 1,254
Cooperstown 2,342
Copake 700 ○
Copenhagen 656
Copiague N.Y. 20,132
Coram N.Y. 24,752
Corfu 689
Corinth 2,702
Corning ELM- 12,953
Cornwall On Hudson NWBG 3,164
Cortland 20,138
Coxsackie 2,786
Croghan 703
Croton-on-Hudson N.Y. 6,889
Crown Point 900 ○
Cuba 1,739
Cutchogue 1,400 ○
Dalton 500 ○
Dannemora 3,770
Dansville 4,979
Deer Park N.Y. 30,394
Delanson 448
Delevan 1,113
Delhi 3,374
Delmar A-S-T 8,423
Depew BUF- 19,819
Deposit 1,897
Derby BUF- 1,200 ○
DeRuyter 542
De Witt SYR 9,024
Dexter WATN 1,053
Dix Hills N.Y. 10,500 ○
Dobbs Ferry N.Y. 10,053
Downsville 950 ○
Dryden ITH 1,761
Dundee 1,556

○ Rand McNally estimate (not reported in census).
▲ Population of entire township or "town", including rural areas.
● Independent city. Population not included in county total.

NEW YORK continued

Dunkirk 15,310
Earlville 985
East Aurora BUF- 6,803
Eastchester N.Y. 20,305
East Glenville A-S-T 6,537
East Half Hollow Hills N.Y. 9,000 ○
East Hampton 1,886
East Hills N.Y. 7,160
East Islip N.Y. 13,852
East Marion 1,500 ○
East Meadow N.Y. 39,317
East Northport N.Y. 20,187
East Patchogue N.Y. 18,139
Eastport N.Y. 2,000 ○
East Randolph 655
East Rochester ROCH 7,596
East Rockaway N.Y. 10,917
East Vestal BING 5,300 ○
Eden BUF- 3,000
Edmeston 600 ○
Edwards 561
Elba 750
Elizabethtown 650 ○
Ellenville 4,405
Ellicottville 713
ELMIRA ELM- 35,327
Elmira Heights ELM- 4,279
Elmont N.Y. 27,592
Elmsere A-S-T 5,500 ○
Elwood N.Y. 11,847
Endicott BING 14,457
Endwell BING 13,745
Etna ITH 500 ○
Evans Mills 651
Fair Haven 976
Fairmount SYR 8,400 ○
Fairport ROCH 5,970
Fairview POK 5,852
Falconer JMST 2,778
Farmingdale N.Y. 7,946
Farmingville N.Y. 13,398
Fillmore 563
Fishkill POK 1,555
Floral Park N.Y. 16,805
Florida MIDD 1,947
Flower Hill N.Y. 4,558
Fonda A-S-T 1,006
Forestville 804
Fort Ann GLFLS 509
Fort Covington 1,200 ○
Fort Edward GLFLS 3,561
Fort Plain 2,555
Frankfort UT-R 2,995
Franklin 440
Franklin Square N.Y. 29,051
Franklinville 1,887
Fredonia 11,126
Freeport N.Y. 38,272
Freeville ITH 449
Frewsburg JMST 1,908
Friendship 1,461
Fulton SYR 13,312
Galeville SYR 5,600 ○
Gang Mills ELM- 2,300
Garden City N.Y. 22,927
Garden City Park N.Y. 7,712
Garrison N.Y. 650 ○
Gasport LOCK 1,339
Gates ROCH 29,756
Geneseo 6,746
Geneva 15,133
Ghent 600 ○
Gilbertsville 455
Glasco KNGST 1,179
Glen Cove N.Y. 24,618
Glenham POK 2,832
Glen Head N.Y. 6,800 ○
GLENS FALLS GLFLS 15,897
Gloversville 17,836
Gorham 800 ○
Goshen MIDD 4,874
Gouverneur 4,285
Gowanda 2,713
Grand Gorge 800 ○
Granville 2,696
Great Neck N.Y. 5,604
Great Neck Estates N.Y. 2,936
Greece ROCH 63,700 ○
Greene 1,747
Green Island A-S-T 2,696
Greenlawn N.Y. 13,869
Greenport 2,273
Greenville N.Y. 8,706
Greenwich 1,955
Greenwood 450 ○
Greenwood Lake N.Y. 2,809
Groton 2,313
Hadley 850 ○
Haines Falls 700 ○
Half Hollow Hills N.Y. 7,800 ○
Hamburg BUF- 10,582
Hamilton 3,725
Hammondsport 1,065
Hampton Bays 6,000 ○
Hannibal SYR 680
Harrison N.Y. 23,046
Harrisville 937
Hartsdale N.Y. 10,216
Hartwick 600 ○
Hastings-on-Hudson N.Y. 8,573
Hauppauge N.Y. 20,960
Haverstraw N.Y. 8,800
Hawthorne N.Y. 5,010
Hemlock ROCH 500 ○
Hempstead N.Y. 40,404
Henrietta ROCH 1,200 ○
Herkimer UT-R 8,383
Hermon 490
Heuvelton 777
Hewlett N.Y. 6,986
Hicksville N.Y. 43,245
Highland POK 3,967
Highland Falls 4,187
Hillcrest N.Y. 5,733
Hilton ROCH 4,151
Hobart 473
Holbrook N.Y. 24,342
Holland BUF- 1,347
Holland Patent UT-R 534
Holley ROCH 1,882
Homer 3,635
Honeoye Falls ROCH 2,410
Hoosick Falls 3,609
Hopewell Junction POK 1,754
Hornell 10,234
Horseheads ELM- 7,348
Houghton 1,604
Hudson 7,986
Hudson Falls GLFLS 7,419
Huntington N.Y. 19,569
Huntington Bay N.Y. 1,783
Huntington Station N.Y. 28,769
Hurley KNGST 4,905
Hurleyville 500 ○
Hyde Park POK 2,550
Ilion UT-R 9,450
Indian Lake 450 ○
Interlaken 685
Inwood N.Y. 8,228
Irondequoit ROCH 57,648
Irvington N.Y. 5,774
Island Park N.Y. 4,847
Islip N.Y. 13,438
Islip Terrace N.Y. 5,588
ITHACA ITH 28,732
JAMESTOWN JMST 35,775
Jasper 450 ○
Jay 500 ○
Jeffersonville 554
Jericho N.Y. 12,739
Johnson City BING 17,126
Johnstown 9,360
Jordan SYR 1,371
Keene 450 ○
Keeseville 2,025
Kenmore BUF- 18,474
Kennedy JMST 500 ○
Kerhonkson 1,646
Kinderhook A-S-T 1,377
Kings Point N.Y. 5,234
KINGSTON KNGST 24,481
Lackawanna BUF- 22,701
Lacona 582
LaFargeville 500 ○
Lake Delta UT-R 2,400 ○
Lake Erie Beach BUF- 4,625
Lake George 1,047
Lake Grove N.Y. 9,692
Lake Katrine KNGST 2,011
Lake Luzerne 1,150 ○
Lake Placid 2,490
Lake Ronkonkoma N.Y. 9,600 ○
Lake View BUF- 4,600 ○
Lakeville ROCH 950 ○
Lakewood JMST 3,941
Lancaster BUF- 13,056
Larchmont N.Y. 6,308
Larchmont North N.Y. 11,500 ○
Latham A-S-T 11,182
Lawrence N.Y. 6,175
Leicester 462
Leonardsville 500 ○
Le Roy 4,900
Levittown N.Y. 57,045
Lewiston BUF- 3,326
Liberty 4,293
Lima ROCH 2,025
Limestone 466
Lindenhurst N.Y. 26,919
Little Falls 6,156
Little Valley 1,203
Livingston Manor 1,436
Livonia ROCH 1,238
Lloyd Harbor N.Y. 3,405
Locke 500 ○
LOCKPORT LOCK 24,844
Locust Grove N.Y. 9,670
Long Beach N.Y. 34,073
Long Lake 500 ○
Loudonville A-S-T 11,480
Lowville 3,364
Lyndonville 916
Lyon Mountain 950 ○
Lyons 4,160
Lyons Falls 755
Macedon ROCH 1,400
McGraw 1,188
Machias 850 ○
Madrid 800 ○
Mahopac N.Y. 7,681
Maine BING 700 ○
Malone 7,668
Malverne N.Y. 9,262
Mamaroneck N.Y. 17,616
Manchester ROCH 1,698
Manhasset N.Y. 8,485
Manlius SYR 5,241
Manorhaven N.Y. 5,384
Marathon 1,046
Margaretville 755
Marion ROCH 1,080
Marlboro NWBG 2,275
Massapequa N.Y. 24,454
Massapequa Park N.Y. 19,779
Massena 12,851
Mastic N.Y. 10,413
Mastic Beach N.Y. 8,318
Mattituck N.Y. 3,923
Mattydale SYR 7,511
Mayfield 944
Mayville 1,626
Mechanicville A-S-T 5,500
Medford N.Y. 20,418
Medina 6,392
Melville N.Y. 8,139
Menands A-S-T 4,012
Merrick N.Y. 24,478
Mexico SYR 1,621
Middleburgh 1,358
Middle Granville 600 ○
Middleport LOCK 1,995
MIDDLETOWN MIDD 21,454
Middleville 647
Milford 514
Millbrook POK 1,343
Millerton 1,013
Mineola N.Y. 20,757
Minetto 1,629
Mineville 1,000 ○
Mohawk UT-R 2,956
Monroe N.Y. 5,996
Monsey N.Y. 12,380
Montauk 2,828
Montgomery NWBG 2,316
Monticello 6,306
Montour Falls ELM- 1,791
Mooers 549
Moravia 1,582
Moriah 500 ○
Morris 681
Morrisonville 1,721
Morristown 461
Morrisville 2,707
Mountain Dale 1,200 ○
Mount Kisco N.Y. 8,025
Mount Morris 3,039
Mount Upton 500 ○
Mount Vernon N.Y. 66,713
Munnsville 499
Nanuet N.Y. 12,578
Napanoch 1,260
Naples 1,225
Narrowsburg 700 ○
Nassau A-S-T 1,285
Nassau Shores N.Y. 5,600 ○
Natural Bridge 650 ○
Nedrow SYR 3,000 ○
Nesconset N.Y. 10,706
Newark 10,017
Newark Valley BING 1,190
New Baltimore 700 ○
New Berlin 1,392
NEWBURGH NWBG 23,438
New Cassel N.Y. 9,635
New City N.Y. 35,869
Newcomb 800 ○
Newfane LOCK 3,120
New Hyde Park N.Y. 9,801
New Lebanon 800 ○
New Paltz 4,938
Newport UT-R 746
New Rochelle N.Y. 70,794
Newton Falls 560 ○
New Windsor NWBG 7,812
New Woodstock SYR 450 ○
NEW YORK N.Y. 7,071,639
Niagara Falls BUF- 71,384
Nichols BING 613
Niskayuna A-S-T 17,471
Norfolk 1,599
North Amityville N.Y. 13,140
North Babylon N.Y. 19,019
North Bellmore N.Y. 20,360
North Collins BUF- 1,496
North Creek 850 ○
Northeast Henrietta ROCH 12,000 ○
North Great River N.Y. 11,416
North Lindenhurst N.Y. 11,511
North Massapequa N.Y. 21,385
North Merrick N.Y. 12,848
North New Hyde Park N.Y. 15,114
North Norwich 500 ○
North Patchogue N.Y. 7,126
Northport N.Y. 7,651
North Rose 700 ○
North Syracuse SYR 7,970
North Tarrytown N.Y. 7,994
North Tonawanda BUF- 35,760
North Valley Stream N.Y. 14,530
Northville 1,304
North Wantagh N.Y. 12,677
Norwich 8,082
Norwood 1,902
Nunda 1,169
Nyack N.Y. 6,428
Oakdale N.Y. 8,090
Oakfield 1,791
Oceanside N.Y. 33,639
Odessa ELM- 613
Ogdensburg 12,375
Olcott LOCK 1,571
Old Bethpage N.Y. 6,215
Old Forge 1,061
Old Village N.Y. 9,168
Olean 18,207
Oneida 10,810
Oneonta 14,933
Ontario ROCH 750 ○
Orchard Park BUF- 3,671
Orient 1,500 ○
Oriskany UT-R 1,680
Oriskany Falls UT-R 802
Ossining N.Y. 20,196
Oswego 19,793
Otego 1,089
Ovid 666
Owego BING 4,364
Oxford 1,765
Oyster Bay N.Y. 6,497
Painted Post ELM- 2,196
Palmyra ROCH 3,729
Panama 511
Parish SYR 535
Parksville 500 ○
Patchogue N.Y. 11,291
Patterson N.Y. 950 ○
Pavilion 550 ○
Pawling POK 1,996
Pearl River N.Y. 15,893
Peconic 1,056
Peekskill N.Y. 18,236
Pelham N.Y. 6,848
Pelham Manor N.Y. 6,130
Penfield ROCH 9,600 ○
Penn Yan 5,242
Perry 4,198
Peru 1,716
Petersburg 500 ○
Phelps 2,004
Philadelphia 855
Philmont 1,539
Phoenicia 700 ○
Phoenix SYR 2,357
Pine Bush NWBG 1,255
Pine Island MIDD 950 ○
Plainview N.Y. 28,037
Plattsburgh 21,057
Pleasant Valley POK 1,255
Pleasantville N.Y. 6,749
Poland UT-R 553
Port Byron AUB 1,400
Port Chester N.Y. 23,565
Port Dickinson BING 1,974
Port Ewen KNGST 2,813
Port Henry 1,450
Port Jefferson N.Y. 6,731
Port Jefferson Station N.Y. 8,500 ○
Port Jervis 8,699
Portland 600 ○
Port Leyden 740
Portville 1,136
Port Washington N.Y. 14,521
Potsdam 10,635
Pottersville 600 ○
POUGHKEEPSIE POK 29,757
Prattsburg 750 ○
Prattsville 500 ○
Pulaski 2,415
Randolph 1,398
Ransomville BUF- 1,401
Ravena A-S-T 3,091
Raymondville 600 ○
Red Creek 645
Red Hook 1,692
Redwood 600 ○
Remsen UT-R 621
Rensselaer A-S-T 9,047
Rhinebeck POK 2,542
Richburg 494
Richfield Springs 1,561
Richmondville 792
Ridgemont ROCH 16,177
Ripley 1,205
Riverhead 6,339
ROCHESTER ROCH 241,741
Rockville Centre N.Y. 25,412
Roessleville A-S-T 11,685
Rome UT-R 43,826
Ronkonkoma N.Y. 20,200 ○
Roosevelt N.Y. 14,109
Roslyn Heights N.Y. 6,546
Rotterdam A-S-T 22,933
Round Lake A-S-T 791
Rouses Point 2,266
Roxbury 700 ○
Rushford 500 ○
Rushville 548
Rye N.Y. 15,083
Sackets Harbor 1,017
Sag Harbor 2,581
St. James N.Y. 12,122
St. Johnsville 1,974
St. Regis Falls 950 ○
Salamanca 6,890
Salem 959
Sandy Creek 765
San Remo N.Y. 9,000 ○
Saranac Lake 5,578
Saratoga Springs A-S-T 23,906
Saugerties KNGST 3,882
Savannah 640 ○
Savona ELM- 932
Sayville N.Y. 12,013
Scarsdale N.Y. 17,650
Schaghticoke A-S-T 677
Schenectady A-S-T 67,972
Schenevus 625
Schoharie 1,016
Schroon Lake 1,000 ○
Schuylerville 1,256
Scotia A-S-T 7,280
Scottsville ROCH 1,789
Sea Cliff N.Y. 5,364
Seaford N.Y. 16,117
Selden N.Y. 17,259
Seneca Falls 7,466
Shandaken 500 ○
Shelter Island 1,115
Sherburne 1,561
Sherman 775
Sherrill 2,830
Shirley N.Y. 18,082
Shortsville ROCH 1,669
Sidney 4,861
Sidney Center 600 ○
Silver Creek BUF- 3,088
Silver Springs 801
Sinclairville 772
Skaneateles SYR 2,789
Sloan BUF- 4,529
Sloatsburg N.Y. 3,154
Smithtown N.Y. 23,700 ○
Sodus ROCH 1,790
Sodus Point ROCH 1,334
Solvay SYR 7,140
Sound Beach N.Y. 8,071
Southampton 4,000
South Bethlehem A-S-T 500 ○
South Corning ELM- 1,195
South Dayton 661
South Fallsburg 2,196
South Farmingdale N.Y. 16,439
South Glens Falls GLFLS 3,714
South Huntington N.Y. 18,854
South New Berlin 450 ○
South Nyack N.Y. 3,602
Southold 4,770
South Otselic 450 ○
Southport ELM- 8,329
South Stony Brook N.Y. 9,100 ○
South Valley Stream N.Y. 5,462
South Westbury N.Y. 9,732
Spencer 863
Spencerport ROCH 3,424
Springs 3,197
Spring Valley N.Y. 20,537
Springville 4,285
Springwater 500 ○
Staatsburg POK 950 ○
Stamford 1,240
Stillwater A-S-T 1,572
Stony Brook N.Y. 7,100 ○
Stony Creek 450 ○
Stony Point N.Y. 8,686
Stottville 1,387
Suffern N.Y. 10,794
Sylvan Beach UT-R 1,243
Syosset N.Y. 9,818
SYRACUSE SYR 170,105
Tappan N.Y. 8,267
Tarrytown N.Y. 10,648
Terryville N.Y. 7,200 ○
Theresa 827
Thornwood N.Y. 1,300 ○
Three Mile Bay 600 ○
Ticonderoga 2,938
Tillson KNGST 1,529
Tivoli 711
Tomkins Cove N.Y. 700 ○
Tonawanda BUF- 18,693
Tonawanda BUF- 72,795
Troy A-S-T 56,638
Trumansburg ITH 1,722
Tuckahoe N.Y. 6,076
Tully SYR 1,049
Tupper Lake 4,478
Unadilla 1,367
Uniondale N.Y. 20,016
Union Springs AUB 1,201
University Gardens N.Y. 5,400 ○
UTICA UT-R 75,632
Valatie A-S-T 1,620
Valhalla N.Y. 8,000 ○
Valley Cottage N.Y. 8,214
Valley Stream N.Y. 35,769
Van Etten 559
Vestal BING 6,000 ○
Vestal Center BING 900 ○
Victor ROCH 2,370
Waddington 980
Wading River 2,500 ○
Walden NWBG 5,659
Wallkill NWBG 2,064
Walton 3,329
Wampsville 569
Wantagh N.Y. 19,817
Wappingers Falls POK 5,110
Warrensburg 2,834
Warsaw 3,619
Warwick N.Y. 4,320
Waterford A-S-T 2,405
Waterloo 5,303
WATERTOWN WATN 27,861
Waterville UT-R 1,672
Watervliet A-S-T 11,354
Watkins Glen ELM- 2,440
Waverly 4,738
Wayland 1,846
Webster ROCH 5,499
Weedsport SYR 1,952
Wellsburg ELM- 647
Wellsville 5,769
West Amityville N.Y. 6,623
West Babylon N.Y. 41,699
West Bay Shore N.Y. 5,118
Westbury N.Y. 13,871
West Carthage 1,824
West Chazy 700 ○
West Elmira ELM- 5,485
Westfield 3,446
West Haverstraw N.Y. 9,181
West Hempstead N.Y. 18,536
West Huntington N.Y. 3,500 ○
West Islip N.Y. 23,000 ○
Westmere A-S-T 6,881
West Point 8,105
Westport 613
West Sayville N.Y. 8,185
West Seneca BUF- 51,210
Westvale SYR 6,169
West Webster ROCH 10,600 ○
West Winfield 979
Whitehall 3,241
White Plains N.Y. 46,999
Whitesboro UT-R 4,460
Whitesville 600 ○
Whitney Point BING 1,093
Willard 1,339
Williamson ROCH 1,768
Williamsville BUF- 6,017
Williston Park N.Y. 8,216
Willsboro 950 ○
Wilmington 500 ○
Wilson LOCK 1,259
Winthrop 550 ○
Witherbee 920 ○
Wolcott 1,496
Woodbourne 1,155 ○
Woodmere N.Y. 17,205
Woodstock KNGST 2,280
Worcester 950 ○
Wyandanch N.Y. 13,215
Wyoming 507
Yonkers N.Y. 195,351
Yorkshire 1,236
Yorktown N.Y. 7,100 ○
Yorktown Heights N.Y. 6,000 ○
Yorkville UT-R 3,115
Youngstown BUF- 2,191

COUNTIES

Albany 285,909
Allegany 51,742
Bronx 1,168,972
Broome 213,648
Cattaraugus 85,697
Cayuga 79,894
Chautauqua 146,925
Chemung 97,656
Chenango 49,344
Clinton 80,750
Columbia 59,487
Cortland 48,820
Delaware 46,824
Dutchess 245,055
Erie 1,015,472
Essex 36,176
Franklin 44,929
Fulton 55,153
Genesee 59,400
Greene 40,861
Hamilton 5,034
Herkimer 66,714
Jefferson 88,151

○ Rand McNally estimate (not reported in census).
▲ Population of entire township or "town", including rural areas.
● Independent city. Population not included in county total.

Kings 2,231,028
Lewis 25,035
Livingston 57,006
Madison 65,150
Monroe 702,238
Montgomery 53,439
Nassau 1,321,582
New York 1,428,285
Niagara 227,354
Oneida 253,466
Onondaga 463,920
Ontario 88,909
Orange 259,603
Orleans 38,496
Oswego 113,901
Otsego 59,075
Putnam 77,193
Queens 1,891,325
Rensselaer 151,966
Richmond 352,029
Rockland 259,530
St. Lawrence 114,347
Saratoga 153,759
Schenectady 149,946
Schoharie 29,710
Schuyler 17,686
Seneca 33,733
Steuben 99,217
Suffolk 1,284,231
Sullivan 65,155
Tioga 49,812
Tompkins 87,085
Ulster 158,158
Warren 54,854
Washington 54,795
Wayne 84,581
Westchester 866,599
Wyoming 39,895
Yates 21,459

NORTH CAROLINA

1980 Census 5,881,385

CITIES

Aberdeen 1,945
Ahoskie 4,887
Albemarle 15,110
Alexander Mills 643
Alliance 616
Andrews 1,621
Angier RAL 1,709
Ansonville 794
Apex RAL 2,847
Arapahoe 467
Archdale GRNS- 5,326
Arden ASHE 500 ○
Arlington 872
Asheboro 15,252
ASHEVILLE ASHE 53,583
Atlantic 900 ○
Aulander 1,214
Aurora 698
Ayden 4,361
Badin 1,514
Bailey 685
Balfour 1,772
Banner Elk 1,087
Barker Heights 1,267
Barnardsville 500 ○
Battleboro RKYMT 632
Bayboro 759
Beaufort 3,826
Belfast GLDS 950 ○
Belhaven 2,430
Belmont CHRLT 4,607
Benson 2,792
Bessemer City GAST 4,787
Bethel 1,825
Beulaville 1,060
Biltmore Forest ASHE 1,499
Biscoe 1,334
Black Creek 523
Black Mountain 4,083
Bladenboro 1,428
Blowing Rock 1,337
Boger City 2,252
Boiling Springs 2,381
Bolton 563
Bonnie Doone FAY 5,950
Boone 10,191
Boonville 1,028
Brevard 5,323
Bridgeton 461
Broadway 908
Brookford HICK 467
Bryson City 1,556
Buies Creek 1,939
Bunn 505
Bunnlevel 500 ○
Burgaw 1,738
BURLINGTON BUR 37,266
Burnsville 1,452
Butner 4,240
Buxton 700 ○
Calypso 689
Candor 868
Canton 4,631
Caroleen 1,000 ○
Carolina Beach WILM 2,000
Carrboro DUR- 8,030
Carthage 925
Cary RAL 21,763
Cashiers 533
Castle Hayne WILM 1,087
Catawba 509
Chadbourn 1,975
Chapel Hill DUR- 32,421
CHARLOTTE CHRLT 315,473
Cherokee 600 ○
Cherryville 4,844
China Grove KANN- 2,081
Chocowinity 644
Claremont 880
Clarkton 664
Clayton RAL 4,091
Clemmons WNS 7,401
Cleveland 595
Cliffside 600 ○
Clinton 7,552
Clyde 1,008
Coats 1,385
Cofield 465
Columbia 758
Columbus 727
Concord KANN- 16,942
Conover 4,245
Conway 678
Cooleemee 1,448
Cordova 1,200 ○
Cornelius CHRLT 1,921
Cove City 500
Cramerton GAST 1,869
Creedmoor 1,641
Cricket 2,307
Cross Mill 1,200 ○
Crouse 900 ○
Cullowhee 2,000 ○
Cumberland FAY 900 ○
Dallas GAST 3,340
Dana 500 ○
Davidson CHRLT 3,241
Davis 500 ○
Delco 550 ○
Denton 949
Dobson 1,222
Dover 600
Drexel 1,392
Dublin 477
Dunn 8,962
DURHAM DUR- 100,538
East Bend 602
East Flat Rock 3,365
East Laurinburg 536
East Spencer SLSB 2,150
Eden 15,672
Edenton 5,357
Efland 600 ○
Elizabeth City 14,004
Elizabethtown 3,551
Elkin 2,858
Elk Park 535
Ellenboro 560
Ellerbe 1,415
Elm City 1,561
Elon College BUR 2,873
Enfield 2,995
Engelhard 600 ○
Enka ASHE 5,567
Erwin 2,828
Fair Bluff 1,095
Fair Grove GRNS- 1,500 ○
Fairmont 2,658
Faison 636
Faith SLSB 552
Fallston 614
Farmville 4,707
FAYETTEVILLE FAY 59,507
Flat Rock 1,200 ○
Fletcher 700 ○
Forest City 7,688
Four Oaks 1,049
Franklin 2,640
Franklinton 1,394
Franklinville 607
Fremont GLDS 1,736
Fuquay-Varina RAL 3,110
Garland 885
Garner RAL 10,073
Garysburg 1,434
Gaston 883
GASTONIA GAST 47,333
Gibson 533
Gibsonville BUR 2,865
Glen Alpine 645
Glen Raven BUR 2,755
Glenville 500 ○
GOLDSBORO GLDS 34,705
Graham BUR 8,674
Grandy 600 ○
Granite Falls HICK 2,580
Granite Quarry SLSB 1,294
Grantsboro 550 ○
GREENSBORO GRNS- 155,642
Greenville 35,740
Grifton 2,179
Grimesland 453
Grover 597
Hallsboro 500 ○
Hamilton 638
Hamlet 4,720
Hampstead 700 ○
Harkers Island 1,901
Harmony 470
Hatteras 700 ○
Havelock 17,718
Haw River BUR 1,858
Hays 900 ○
Hazelwood 1,811
Henderson 16,095
Hendersonville 6,862
Henrietta 1,412
Hertford 1,941
HICKORY HICK 23,426
Hiddenite 800 ○
Highlands 653
High Point GRNS- 63,808
High Shoals GAST 586
Hillsborough 3,019
Hobgood 483
Hobucken 450 ○
Holly Ridge 465
Holly Springs RAL 688
Hookerton 460
Hope Mills FAY 5,600
Hot Springs 678
Hudson 2,888
Indian Trail CHRLT 811
Jackson 720
JACKSONVILLE JAX 22,586
James City 700 ○
Jamestown GRNS- 2,148
Jamesville 604
Jefferson 1,086
Jonesville 1,752
KANNAPOLIS KANN- 34,564
Kenansville 931
Kenly 1,433
Kernersville WNS 6,849
King WNS 5,000 ○
Kings Mountain GAST 9,080
Kinston 25,234
Kitty Hawk 849
Knightdale RAL 985
Lafayette FAY 4,100 ○
La Grange 3,147
Lake Waccamaw 1,133
Landis KANN- 2,092
Laurel Hill 2,314
Laurinburg 11,480
Lawndale 469
Lenoir 13,748
Lewiston Woodville 671
Lexington 15,711
Liberty 1,997
Lilesville 588
Lillington 1,948
Lincolnton 4,879
Littleton 820
LOCUST 1,590
Longview HICK 3,587
Louisburg 3,238
Lowell GAST 2,917
Lowland 600 ○
Lucama 1,070
Lumberton 18,241
Macclesfield 504
McGrady 500 ○
Madison 2,806
Magnolia 592
Maiden 2,574
Manteo 902
Maple Hill 550 ○
Marble 700 ○
Marion 3,684
Marshall 809
Marshallberg 600 ○
Mars Hill 2,126
Marshville 2,011
Matthews CHRLT 1,648
Maury 450 ○
Maxton 2,711
Mayodan 2,627
Maysville 877
Mebane BUR 2,782
Middlesex 837
Midland 600 ○
Mint Hill CHRLT 9,695
Misenheimer 1,250 ○
Mocksville 2,637
Moncure 600 ○
Monroe CHRLT 14,587
Montreat 741
Mooresville 8,575
Morehead City 4,359
Morganton 15,060
Morven 765
Mount Airy 6,862
Mount Gilead 1,423
Mount Holly CHRLT 4,530
Mount Olive HICK 4,876
Mount Pleasant KANN- 1,210
Moyock 700 ○
Mulberry 1,210
Murfreesboro 3,007
Murphy 2,070
Nags Head 1,020
Nashville RKYMT 3,033
New Bern 14,557
Newland 722
New London 454
Newport 1,883
Newton 8,128
Newton Grove 564
Norlina 901
North Belmont CHRLT 5,000 ○
North Wilkesboro 3,260
Norwood 1,818
Oakboro 587
Oak City 475
Oak Ridge GRNS- 950 ○
Ocracoke 600 ○
Old Fort 752
Olivia 500 ○
Oriental 536
Oteen ASHE 2,200 ○
Oxford 7,603
Parkton 564
Parkwood DUR- 3,420
Parmele 484
Paw Creek CHRLT 1,700 ○
Peachland 506
Pembroke 2,698
Pikeville 662
Pilot Mountain 1,090
Pinebluff 935
Pine Hall 500 ○
Pinehurst 1,746
Pine Level 953
Pinetops 1,465
Pineville CHRLT 1,525
Pink Hill 644
Pinnacle 600 ○
Pisgah Forest 1,899
Pittsboro 1,332
Pleasant Garden GRNS- 1,991
Plymouth 4,571
Polkton 762
Princeton 1,034
Princeville 1,508
Raeford 3,630
RALEIGH RAL 150,255
Ramseur 1,162
Randleman 2,156
Red Springs 3,607
Reidsville 12,492
Rhodhiss HICK 727
Richlands 825
Rich Square 1,057
Ridgecrest 500 ○
Roanoke Rapids 14,702
Robbins 1,256
Robbinsville 814
Robersonville 1,981
Rockingham 8,300
Rockwell SLSB 1,339
Rockwell Park CHRLT 2,600 ○
ROCKY MOUNT RKYMT 41,283
Rocky Point 600 ○
Ronda 457
Roper 795
Roseboro 1,227
Rose Hill 1,508
Rosman 512
Rougemont 500 ○
Rowland 1,841
Roxboro 7,532
Royal Pines ASHE 2,000 ○
Ruffin 600 ○
Rural Hall WNS 1,336
Rutherfordton 3,434
St. Pauls 1,639
Salemburg 742
Salisbury SLSB 22,677
Salter Path 600 ○
Saluda 607
Sanford 14,773
Saxapahaw 500 ○
Scotland Neck 2,834
Seaboard 687
Selma 4,762
Shallotte 680
Sharpsburg RKYMT 997
Shelby 15,310
Siler City 4,446
Skyland ASHE 2,200 ○
Smithfield 7,288
Sneads Ferry 600 ○
Snow Hill 1,374
Southern Pines 8,620
South Gastonia GAST 2,000 ○
South Mills 300 ○
Southmont 700 ○
Southport 2,824
Sparta 1,687
Spencer SLSB 2,938
Spindale 4,246
Spring Hope 1,254
Spring Lake FAY 6,273
Spruce Pine 2,282
Stanley CHRLT 2,341
Stanleyville WNS 5,039
Stantonsburg 920
Star 816
State Road 800 ○
Statesville 18,622
Stedman 723
Stokesdale GRNS- 1,070
Stoneville 1,054
Stony Point 1,150
Summerfield GRNS- 1,680
Sunbury 500 ○
Swannanoa ASHE 5,586
Swanquarter 450 ○
Swansboro 976
Swepsonville 900 ○
Sylva 1,699
Tabor City 2,710
Tarboro 8,634
Taylorsville 1,103
Thomasville GRNS- 14,144
Toast 2,339
Troutman 1,360
Troy 2,702
Tryon 1,796
Tuxedo 950 ○
Valdese 3,364
Vanceboro 833
Vander FAY 1,671
Vass 828
Verona JAX 600 ○
Wade FAY 474
Wadesboro 4,206
Wagram 617
Wake Forest RAL 3,780
Walkertown WNS 2,100 ○
Wallace 2,903
Walnut 550 ○
Walnut Cove 1,147
Wanchese 1,105
Warrenton 908
Warsaw 2,910
Washington 8,418
Waxhaw 1,208
Waynesville 6,765
Weaverville ASHE 1,495
Weeksville 450 ○
Weldon 1,844
Wendell 2,222
West Concord KANN- 3,200 ○
West End 900 ○
Westfield 600 ○
West Jefferson 822
West Marion 1,596
Whitakers 924
Whiteville 5,565
Whitsett BUR 500 ○
Whittier 500 ○
Wilkesboro 2,335
Williamston 6,159
WILMINGTON WILM 44,000
Wilson 34,424
Wilsons Mills 580 ○
Windsor 2,126
Winfall 634
Wingate CHRLT 2,615
WINSTON-SALEM WNS 138,583
Winterville 2,052
Winton 825
Wise 500 ○
Woodland 861
Wrightsville Beach WILM 2,910
Yadkinville 2,216
Yanceyville 1,511
Youngsville 486
Zebulon 2,055

COUNTIES

Alamance 99,319
Alexander 24,999
Alleghany 9,587
Anson 25,649
Ashe 22,325
Avery 14,409
Beaufort 40,355
Bertie 21,024
Bladen 30,491
Brunswick 35,777
Buncombe 160,934
Burke 72,504
Cabarrus 85,895
Caldwell 67,746
Camden 5,829
Carteret 41,092
Caswell 20,705
Catawba 105,208
Chatham 33,415
Cherokee 18,933
Chowan 12,558
Clay 6,619
Cleveland 83,435
Columbus 51,037
Craven 71,043
Cumberland 247,160
Currituck 11,089
Dare 13,377
Davidson 113,162
Davie 24,599
Duplin 40,952
Durham 152,785
Edgecombe 55,988
Forsyth 243,683
Franklin 30,055
Gaston 162,568
Gates 8,875
Graham 7,217
Granville 34,043
Greene 16,117
Guilford 317,154
Halifax 55,286
Harnett 59,570
Haywood 46,495
Henderson 58,580
Hertford 23,368
Hoke 20,383
Hyde 5,873
Iredell 82,538
Jackson 25,811
Johnston 70,599
Jones 9,705
Lee 36,718
Lenoir 59,819
Lincoln 42,372
McDowell 35,135
Macon 20,178
Madison 16,827
Martin 25,948
Mecklenburg 404,270
Mitchell 14,428
Montgomery 22,469
Moore 50,505
Nash 67,153
New Hanover 103,471
Northampton 22,584
Onslow 112,784
Orange 77,055
Pamlico 10,398
Pasquotank 28,462
Pender 22,262
Perquimans 9,486
Person 29,164
Pitt 90,146
Polk 12,984
Randolph 91,300
Richmond 45,481
Robeson 101,610
Rockingham 83,426
Rowan 99,186
Rutherford 53,787
Sampson 49,687
Scotland 32,273
Stanly 48,517
Stokes 33,086
Surry 59,449
Swain 10,283
Transylvania 23,417
Tyrrell 3,975
Union 70,380
Vance 36,748
Wake 301,327
Warren 16,232
Washington 14,801
Watauga 31,666
Wayne 97,054
Wilkes 58,657
Wilson 63,132
Yadkin 28,439
Yancey 14,934

NORTH DAKOTA

1980 Census 652,717

CITIES

Arthur 445
Ashley 1,192
Beach 1,381
Belcourt 1,803
Belfield 1,274
Berthold 485
Beulah 2,908
BISMARCK BIS- 44,485
Bottineau 2,829
Bowbells 587
Bowman 2,071
Burlington MNOT 762
Cando 1,496
Carrington 2,641
Carson 469
Casselton 1,661
Cavalier 1,505
Center 900
Cooperstown 1,308
Crosby 1,469
Devils Lake 7,442
Dickinson 15,924

○ Rand McNally estimate (not reported in census).
▲ Population of entire township or "town", including rural areas.
● Independent city. Population not included in county total.

NORTH DAKOTA continued

Drake ... 479
Drayton ... 1,082
Dunseith ... 625
Edgeley ... 843
Elgin ... 930
Ellendale ... 1,967
Emerado ... 596
Enderlin ... 1,151
Fairmount ... 480
FARGO FAR- ... 61,383
Fessenden ... 761
Finley ... 718
Forman ... 629
Fort Totten ... 750 ○
Fort Yates ... 771
Gackle ... 456
Garrison ... 1,830
Glenburn ... 454
Glen Ullin ... 1,125
Grafton ... 5,293
GRAND FORKS GDFK ... 43,765
Gwinner ... 725
Hankinson ... 1,158
Harvey ... 2,527
Hatton ... 787
Hazen ... 2,365
Hebron ... 1,078
Hettinger ... 1,739
Hillsboro ... 1,600
Horace ... 494
Jamestown ... 16,280
Kenmare ... 1,456
Killdeer ... 790
Kindred ... 568
Kulm ... 570
Lakota ... 963
La Moure ... 1,077
Langdon ... 2,335
Larimore ... 1,524
Leeds ... 678
Lidgerwood ... 971
Linton ... 1,561
Lisbon ... 2,283
McClusky ... 658
McVille ... 626
Maddock ... 677
Mandan BIS- ... 15,513
Mayville ... 2,255
Medina ... 521
Michigan ... 502
Milnor ... 716
Minnewaukan ... 461
MINOT MNOT ... 32,843
Minto ... 592
Mohall ... 1,049
Mott ... 1,315
Napoleon ... 1,103
Neche ... 471
New England ... 825
New Rockford ... 1,791
New Salem ... 1,081
New Town ... 1,335
Northwood ... 1,240
Oakes ... 2,112
Park River ... 1,844
Parshall ... 1,059
Pembina ... 673
Portland ... 627
Powers Lake ... 466
Ray ... 766
Richardton ... 699
Riverdale ... 500 ○
Rolette ... 667
Rolla ... 1,538
Rugby ... 3,335
St. Thomas ... 528
Stanley ... 1,631
Stanton ... 623
Steele ... 796
Strasburg ... 623
Surrey MNOT ... 999
Thompson ... 785
Tioga ... 1,597
Towner ... 867
Turtle Lake ... 802
Underwood ... 1,329
Valley City ... 7,774
Velva ... 1,101
Wahpeton ... 9,064
Walhalla ... 1,429
Washburn ... 1,767
Watford City ... 2,119
West Fargo FAR- ... 10,099
Westhope ... 741
Williston ... 13,336
Wilton ... 950
Wishek ... 1,345
Wyndmere ... 550
Zap ... 511

COUNTIES

Adams ... 3,584
Barnes ... 13,960
Benson ... 7,944
Billings ... 1,138
Bottineau ... 9,239
Bowman ... 4,229
Burke ... 3,822
Burleigh ... 54,811
Cass ... 88,247
Cavalier ... 7,636
Dickey ... 7,207
Divide ... 3,494
Dunn ... 4,627
Eddy ... 3,554
Emmons ... 5,877
Foster ... 4,611
Golden Valley ... 2,391
Grand Forks ... 66,100
Grant ... 4,274
Griggs ... 3,714
Hettinger ... 4,275
Kidder ... 3,833
La Moure ... 6,473
Logan ... 3,493
McHenry ... 7,858
McIntosh ... 4,800
McKenzie ... 7,132
McLean ... 12,383
Mercer ... 9,404
Morton ... 25,177
Mountrail ... 7,679
Nelson ... 5,233
Oliver ... 2,495
Pembina ... 10,399
Pierce ... 6,166
Ramsey ... 13,048
Ransom ... 6,698
Renville ... 3,608
Richland ... 19,207
Rolette ... 12,177
Sargent ... 5,512
Sheridan ... 2,819
Sioux ... 3,620
Slope ... 1,157
Stark ... 23,697
Steele ... 3,106
Stutsman ... 24,154
Towner ... 4,052
Traill ... 9,624
Walsh ... 15,371
Ward ... 58,392
Wells ... 6,979
Williams ... 22,237

OHIO

1980 Census ... 10,797,624

CITIES

Aberdeen ... 1,566
Ada ... 5,669
Addyston CIN- ... 1,195
Adelphi ... 472
Adena ... 1,062
AKRON AKR ... 237,177
Albany ... 905
Alexandria ... 489
Alger ... 992
ALLIANCE ALLI ... 24,315
Amanda ... 720
Amelia CIN- ... 1,108
Amherst CLEV ... 10,638
Amsterdam ... 783
Andover ... 1,205
Anna ... 1,038
Ansonia ... 1,267
Antwerp ... 1,765
Apple Creek ... 741
Arcadia ... 580
Arcanum ... 2,002
Archbold ... 3,318
Arlington ... 1,187
Ashland ... 20,326
Ashley ... 1,057
ASHTABULA ASHT ... 23,449
Ashville COL ... 2,046
Athens ... 19,743
Attica ... 865
Aurora CLEV ... 8,177
Austinburg ... 600 ○
Avon CLEV ... 7,241
Avondale DAY- ... 5,000 ○
Avon Lake CLEV ... 13,222
Bainbridge ... 1,042
Baltic ... 563
Baltimore ... 2,689
Barberton AKR ... 29,751
Barnesville ... 4,633
Barton WHL ... 1,039
Bascom ... 550 ○
Batavia CIN- ... 1,896
Bay Village CLEV ... 17,846
Beach City ... 1,083
Beachwood CLEV ... 9,983
Beallsville ... 601
Beavercreek DAY- ... 31,589
Beaverdam ... 492
Bedford CLEV ... 15,056
Bedford Heights CLEV ... 13,214
Bellaire WHL ... 8,241
Bellbrook DAY- ... 5,174
Belle Center ... 930
Bellefontaine ... 11,888
Bellevue ... 8,187
Bellville MANS ... 1,714
Belmont ... 714
Beloit ALLI ... 1,093
Belpre PRKB ... 7,193
Berea CLEV ... 19,567
Bergholz ... 914
Berlin Heights CLEV ... 756
Bethel CIN- ... 2,231
Bethesda ... 1,429
Bettsville ... 752
Beverly ... 1,471
Bexley COL ... 13,405
Blacklick Estates COL ... 11,223
Blanchester ... 3,202
Bloomdale ... 744
Bloomingburg ... 869
Bloomville ... 1,019
Blue Ash CIN- ... 9,506
Bluffton ... 3,310
Boardman YNGS- ... 39,161
Bolivar CAN- ... 989
Boston Heights CLEV ... 781
Botkins ... 1,372
Bowerston ... 487
Bowling Green ... 25,728
Bradford ... 2,166
Bradner ... 1,175
Bratenahl CLEV ... 1,485
Brecksville CLEV ... 10,132
Bremen ... 1,432
Brentwood CIN- ... 5,508
Brewster ... 2,321
Bridgeport WHL ... 2,642
Bridgetown CIN- ... 11,460
Brilliant STU- ... 1,751
Bristolville YNGS- ... 500 ○
Broadview Heights CLEV ... 10,920
Brooklyn CLEV ... 12,342
Brook Park CLEV ... 26,195
Brookville DAY- ... 4,322
Brunswick CLEV ... 28,104
Bryan ... 7,879
Buchtel ... 585
Buckeye Lake NWRK ... 2,521
Bucyrus ... 13,433
Buffalo ... 800 ○
Burton CLEV ... 1,401
Butler MANS ... 991
Byesville ... 2,572
Cadiz ... 4,058
Cairo ... 596
Calcutta E.LIV- ... 1,121
Caldwell ... 1,935
Caledonia MRN ... 759
Cambridge ... 13,573
Camden ... 1,971
Campbell YNGS- ... 11,619
Canal Fulton AKR ... 3,481
Canal Winchester COL ... 2,749
Canfield YNGS- ... 5,535
CANTON CAN- ... 93,077
Cardington ... 1,665
Carey ... 3,674
Carroll COL ... 641
Carrollton ... 3,065
Castalia SNDSK ... 973
Cedarville ... 2,799
Celina ... 9,137
Centerburg ... 1,275
Centerville DAY- ... 18,886
Chagrin Falls CLEV ... 4,335
Champion YNGS- ... 5,270 ○
Chardon CLEV ... 4,434
Chauncey ... 1,050
Chesapeake HNTG- ... 1,370
Cheviot CIN- ... 9,888
Chillicothe ... 23,420
Christiansburg ... 593
Churchill YNGS- ... 7,700 ○
CINCINNATI CIN- ... 385,457
Circleville ... 11,700
Clarington ... 558
Clarksburg ... 483
Clarksville ... 525
CLEVELAND CLEV ... 573,822
Cleveland Heights CLEV ... 56,438
Clyde ... 5,489
Coal Grove HNTG- ... 2,602
Coalton ... 639
Coldwater ... 4,220
Columbiana ... 4,987
COLUMBUS COL ... 565,032
Columbus Grove ... 2,313
Conesville ... 451
Conneaut ... 13,835
Continental ... 1,179
Convoy ... 1,140
Coolville ... 649
Corning ... 789
Cortland YNGS- ... 5,011
Coshocton ... 13,405
Covedale CIN- ... 5,830
Covington ... 2,610
Crestline ... 5,406
Creston ... 1,828
Cridersville LIMA ... 1,843
Crooksville ... 2,766
Croton ... 444
Crown City ... 513
Cumberland ... 461
Curtice TOL ... 800 ○
Cuyahoga Falls AKR ... 43,890
Cygnet ... 646
Dalton CAN- ... 1,357
Danville ... 1,127
DAYTON DAY- ... 193,536
Deerfield ... 450 ○
Deer Park CIN- ... 6,745
Defiance ... 16,810
De Graff ... 1,358
Delaware ... 18,780
Delhi Hills CIN- ... 7,650 ○
Delphos ... 7,314
Delta TOL ... 2,831
Dennison ... 3,398
Deshler ... 1,870
Dillonvale WHL ... 912
Dover ... 11,782
Doylestown AKR ... 2,493
Dresden ... 1,646
Drexel DAY- ... 2,250 ○
Duncan Falls ZAN ... 1,200 ○
Dunkirk ... 954
East Cleveland CLEV ... 36,957
East Fultonham ... 650 ○
Eastlake CLEV ... 22,104
East Liberty ... 480 ○
EAST LIVERPOOL E.LIV- ... 16,687
East Palestine ... 5,306
East Sparta CAN- ... 868
Eaton DAY- ... 6,839
Edgerton ... 1,813
Edgewood ASHT ... 3,099
Edison ... 504
Edon ... 947
Eldorado ... 509
Elida LIMA ... 1,349
Elmore ... 1,271
Elmwood Place CIN- ... 2,840
Elyria CLEV ... 57,538
Empire STU- ... 484
Englewood DAY- ... 11,329
Euclid CLEV ... 59,999
Fairborn DAY- ... 29,702
Fairfield CIN- ... 30,787
Fairlawn AKR ... 6,100
Fairpoint ... 600 ○
Fairport Harbor CLEV ... 3,357
Fairview Park CLEV ... 19,311
Fayette ... 1,222
Fayetteville ... 478
Felicity ... 929
FINDLAY FIND ... 35,594
Fletcher ... 498
Flushing ... 1,266
Forest ... 1,633
Forest Park CIN- ... 18,675
Fort Jennings ... 538
Fort Loramie ... 977
Fort Recovery ... 1,370
Fort Shawnee LIMA ... 4,541
Fostoria ... 15,743
Frankfort ... 1,008
Franklin MIDD ... 10,711
Frazeysburg ... 1,025
Fredericksburg ... 511
Fredericktown ... 2,299
Freeport ... 525
Fremont ... 17,834
Friendship ... 600 ○
Gahanna COL ... 18,001
Galion ... 12,391
Gallipolis ... 5,576
Gambier ... 2,056
Garfield Heights CLEV ... 34,938
Garrettsville ... 1,769
Geneva ... 6,655
Genoa TOL ... 2,213
Georgetown ... 3,467
Germantown DAY- ... 5,015
Gettysburg ... 545
Gibsonburg ... 2,479
Girard YNGS- ... 12,517
Glandorf ... 746
Glendale CIN- ... 2,368
Glouster ... 2,211
Gnadenhutten ... 1,320
Golf Manor CIN- ... 4,317
Grafton CLEV ... 2,231
Grand Rapids ... 962
Grandview Heights COL ... 7,420
Granville NWRK ... 3,851
Gratis ... 809
Green Camp ... 475
Greenfield ... 5,150
Greenhills CIN- ... 4,927
Green Springs ... 1,568
Greenville ... 12,999
Greenwich ... 1,458
Groesbeck CIN- ... 9,594
Grove City COL ... 16,816
Groveport COL ... 3,286
Grover Hill ... 486
Hamden ... 1,010
Hamersville CIN- ... 688
Hamilton CIN- ... 63,189
Hamler ... 625
Hannibal ... 650 ○
Hanover NWRK ... 926
Hanoverton ... 490
Harrison CIN- ... 5,855
Harrod LIMA ... 506
Hartville CAN- ... 1,772
Haskins ... 568
Haydenville ... 500 ○
Hayesville ... 518
Heath NWRK ... 6,969
Hebron NWRK ... 2,035
Hicksville ... 3,929
Highland Heights CLEV ... 5,739
Hilliard COL ... 8,008
Hillsboro ... 6,356
Hiram ... 1,360
Holgate ... 1,315
Holland TOL ... 1,048
Homewood CIN- ... 2,550 ○
Hopedale ... 857
Howard ... 450 ○
Hubbard YNGS- ... 9,245
Huber Heights DAY- ... 35,480
Huber South DAY- ... 4,800 ○
Hudson CLEV ... 4,615
Huron SNDSK ... 7,123
Independence CLEV ... 6,607
Irondale E.LIV- ... 535
Ironton HNTG- ... 14,290
Jackson ... 6,675
Jackson Center ... 1,310
Jacksonville ... 651
Jamestown ... 1,702
Jefferson ... 2,952
Jeffersonville ... 1,252
Jeromesville ... 582
Jewett ... 972
Johnstown ... 3,158
Junction City ... 754
Kent AKR ... 26,164
Kenton ... 8,605
Kenwood CIN- ... 9,928
Kettering DAY- ... 61,186
Killbuck ... 937
Kings Mills CIN- ... 500 ○
Kingston ... 1,208
Kingsville ASHT ... 1,243
Kinsman ... 800 ○
Kirtland CLEV ... 5,969
Lafferty ... 600 ○
Lagrange CLEV ... 1,258
Lakemore AKR ... 2,744
Lakeside ... 950 ○
Lakeview ... 1,089
Lakewood CLEV ... 61,963
LANCASTER LANC ... 34,953
La Rue ... 861
Laura DAY- ... 501
Laurelville ... 591
Leavittsburg YNGS- ... 2,220 ○
Lebanon DAY- ... 9,636
Leesburg ... 1,019
Leetonia ... 2,121
Leipsic ... 2,171
Lewisburg ... 1,450
Lexington MANS ... 3,823
Liberty Center ... 1,111
LIMA LIMA ... 47,827
Lincoln Heights CIN- ... 5,259
Lincoln Village COL ... 10,548
Lindsey ... 571
Linworth COL ... 650 ○
Lisbon ... 3,159
Lockland CIN- ... 4,292
Lodi CLEV ... 2,942
Logan ... 6,557
London ... 6,958
Lorain CLEV ... 75,416
Lore City ... 443
Loudonville ... 2,945
Louisville CAN- ... 7,996
Loveland CIN- ... 9,106
Loveland Park CIN- ... 1,653
Lowell ... 729
Lowellville YNGS- ... 1,558
Lucas MANS ... 753
Lucasville PTSM ... 3,349
Luckey TOL ... 895
Lynchburg ... 1,205
Lyndhurst CLEV ... 18,092
Lyons ... 596
McArthur ... 1,912
McClure ... 694
McComb ... 1,608
McConnelsville ... 2,018
McDermott PTSM ... 550 ○
Macedonia CLEV ... 6,571
McGuffey ... 646
Madeira CIN- ... 9,341
Madison CLEV ... 2,291
Magnolia ... 986
Malta ... 956
Malvern ... 1,032
Manchester ... 2,313
MANSFIELD MANS ... 53,927
Mantua CLEV ... 1,041
Maple Heights CLEV ... 29,735
Marble Cliff COL ... 630
Marblehead ... 679
Mariemont CIN- ... 3,295
MARIETTA MRIET ... 16,467
MARION MRN ... 37,040
Marshallville AKR ... 788
Martins Ferry WHL ... 9,331
Martinsville ... 539
Marysville ... 7,414
Mason CIN- ... 8,692
Massillon CAN- ... 30,557
Masury SHAR ... 1,836
Mauds CIN- ... 600 ○
Maumee TOL ... 15,747
Mayfield Heights CLEV ... 21,550
Mechanicsburg ... 1,792
Medina CLEV ... 15,268
Mendon ... 749
Mentor CLEV ... 42,065
Mentor-on-the-Lake CLEV ... 7,919
Metamora ... 556
Miamisburg DAY- ... 15,304
Miamitown CIN- ... 650 ○
Middleburg Heights CLEV ... 16,218
Middlefield CLEV ... 1,997
Middle Point ... 709
Middleport ... 2,971
MIDDLETOWN MIDD ... 43,719
Midvale ... 654
Milan SNDSK ... 1,569
Milford CIN- ... 5,232
Milford Center ... 764
Millbury TOL ... 955
Millersburg ... 3,247
Millersport ... 844
Mineral City ... 884
Minerva ... 4,549
Mingo Junction STU- ... 4,834
Mogadore AKR ... 4,190
Monfort Heights CIN- ... 9,745
Monroe MIDD ... 4,256
Monroeville ... 1,329
Montgomery CIN- ... 10,088
Montpelier ... 4,431
Moraine DAY- ... 5,325
Morral ... 454
Morrow CIN- ... 1,254
Mount Blanchard ... 492
Mount Carmel CIN- ... 900 ○
Mount Gilead ... 2,911
Mount Healthy CIN- ... 7,562
Mount Orab CIN- ... 1,573
Mount Sterling COL ... 1,623
Mount Vernon ... 14,323
Mount Victory ... 667
Mowrystown ... 475
Mulberry CIN- ... 800 ○
Murray City ... 579
Napoleon ... 8,614
Navarre CAN- ... 1,343
Neffs WHL ... 1,106
Negley ... 900 ○
Nevada ... 945
NEWARK NWRK ... 41,200
New Athens ... 440
New Boston PTSM ... 3,188
New Bremen ... 2,393
Newburgh Heights CLEV ... 2,678
New Carlisle DAY- ... 6,498
Newcomerstown ... 3,986
New Concord ... 1,860
New Holland ... 783
New Knoxville ... 760
New Lexington ... 5,179
New London ... 2,449
New Madison ... 1,008
New Matamoras ... 1,172
New Miami CIN- ... 2,980
New Paris RICH ... 1,709
New Philadelphia ... 16,883
Newport ... 950 ○
New Richmond CIN- ... 2,769
New Straitsville ... 937
Newton Falls YNGS- ... 4,960
Newtown CIN- ... 1,817
New Vienna ... 1,133
New Washington ... 1,213
New Waterford ... 1,314
Niles YNGS- ... 23,088
North Baltimore ... 3,127
North Bend CIN- ... 546
North Bloomfield ... 500 ○
Northbrook CIN- ... 8,357
North Canton CAN- ... 14,228
North College Hill CIN- ... 11,114
North Fairfield ... 525
Northfield CLEV ... 3,913
North Industry CAN- ... 3,250 ○
North Kingsville ASHT ... 2,939
North Lewisburg ... 1,072
North Lima YNGS- ... 900 ○

○ Rand McNally estimate (not reported in census).
▲ Population of entire township or "town", including rural areas.
● Independent city. Population not included in county total.

Place	Population
North Olmsted CLEV	36,486
Northridge DAY-	5,559
Northridge DAY-	9,720
North Ridgeville CLEV	21,522
North Royalton CLEV	17,671
Northwood TOL	5,495
Norton AKR	12,242
Norwalk	14,358
Norwood CIN-	26,342
Oak Harbor	2,678
Oak Hill	1,713
Oakwood CLEV	3,786
Oakwood DAY-	9,372
Oakwood	886
Oberlin CLEV	8,660
Obetz COL	3,095
Ohio City	881
Olmsted Falls CLEV	5,868
Oneida MIDD.	1,650 ○
Ontario MANS	4,123
Oregon TOL	18,675
Orrville	7,511
Orwell	1,067
Ottawa	3,874
Ottawa Hills TOL	4,065
Ottoville	833
Owensville CIN-	858
Oxford	17,655
Page Manor DAY-	9,300 ○
Painesville CLEV	16,391
Pandora	977
Park Layne DAY-	5,372
Parkman CLEV	600 ○
Parma CLEV	92,548
Parma Heights CLEV	23,112
Pataskala COL	2,284
Paulding	2,754
Payne	1,399
Peebles	1,790
Pemberville	1,321
Peninsula CLEV	604
Pepper Pike CLEV	6,177
Perry CLEV	961
Perry Heights CAN-	9,206
Perrysburg TOL	10,215
Perrysville MANS	836
Petersburg YNGS-	950 ○
Pettisville	500 ○
Philo ZAN	799
Pickerington COL	3,917
Piketon	1,726
Piney Fork	500 ○
Pioneer	1,133
Piqua	20,480
Pitsburg	460
Plain City	2,102
Pleasant City	481
Pleasant Hill	1,051
Pleasantville LANC	780
Plymouth	1,939
Pomeroy	2,728
Portage Lakes AKR	11,310
Port Clinton	7,223
Port Jefferson	482
PORTSMOUTH PTSM	25,943
Port Washington	622
Powhatan Point	2,181
Proctorville HNTG-	975
Prospect	1,159
Quaker City	698
Quincy	633
Racine	908
Randolph AKR	800 ○
Ravenna AKR	11,987
Rawson	477
Reading CIN-	12,843
Redbird CLEV	1,600 ○
Reedurban CAN-	6,650 ○
Republic	656
Reynoldsburg COL	20,661
Richmond Dale	650 ○
Richmond Heights CLEV	10,095
Richwood	2,181
Ridgeville Corners	600 ○
Ripley	2,174
Risingsun	698
Rittman	6,063
Rockbridge	450 ○
Rock Creek	652
Rockford	1,245
Rocky River CLEV	21,084
Rootstown AKR	650 ○
Roseland MANS	3,000 ○
Roseville	1,915
Rossford TOL	5,978
Rudolph	600 ○
Rushsylvania	610
Russellville	445
Rutland	635
Sabina	2,799
Sagamore Hills CLEV	4,700 ○
St. Bernard CIN-	5,396
St. Clairsville WHL	5,452
St. Henry	1,596
St. Marys	8,414
St. Paris	1,742
Salem	12,869
Salineville	1,629
SANDUSKY SNDSK	31,360
Sardinia	826
Sardis	500 ○
Scio	1,003
Seaman	1,039
Sebring ALLI	5,078
Senecaville	458
Seven Hills CLEV	13,650
Seven Mile CIN-	841
Seville	1,568
Shadyside WHL	4,315
Shaker Heights CLEV	32,487
Sharonville CIN-	10,108
Shawnee	924
Sheffield Lake CLEV	10,484
Shelby	9,646
Sherwood	915
Shiloh DAY-	4,600 ○
Shiloh	857
Shreve	1,608
Sidney	17,657
Silverton CIN-	6,172
Smithfield STU-	1,308
Smithville	1,467
Solon CLEV	14,341
Somerset	1,432
South Charleston	1,682
South Euclid CLEV	25,713
South Lebanon CIN-	2,700
South Vienna	464
South Webster	886
South Zanesville ZAN	1,739
Spencer	764
Spencerville	2,184
Springboro DAY-	4,962
Springdale CIN-	10,111
Springfield DAY-	72,563
Spring Valley	541
STEUBENVILLE STU-	26,400
Stockport	558
Stony Ridge TOL	450 ○
Stoutsville	537
Stow AKR	25,303
Strasburg	2,091
Streetsboro CLEV	9,055
Strongsville CLEV	28,577
Struthers YNGS-	13,624
Stryker	1,423
Summit Station COL	700 ○
Sunbury COL	2,101
Swanton TOL	3,424
Sycamore	1,059
Sylvania TOL	15,527
Syracuse	946
Tallmadge AKR	15,269
The Plains	2,044
The Village of Indian Hill CIN-	5,521
Thornville	838
Thurston	527
Tiffin	19,549
Tiltonsville WHL	1,750
Tipp City DAY-	5,595
TOLEDO TOL	354,635
Toronto STU-	6,934
Trenton MIDD	6,401
Trinway	500 ○
Trotwood DAY-	7,802
Troy	19,086
Twinsburg CLEV	7,632
Uhrichsville	6,130
Union DAY-	5,219
Union City	1,716
Uniontown AKR	1,500 ○
Unionville	500 ○
University Heights CLEV	15,401
Upper Arlington COL	35,648
Upper Sandusky	5,967
Urbana	10,762
Urbancrest COL	880
Utica	2,238
Vandalia DAY-	13,161
Van Wert	11,035
Vermilion CLEV	11,012
Verona DAY-	571
Versailles	2,384
Wadsworth AKR	15,166
Wakeman CLEV	906
Walbridge TOL	2,900
Wapakoneta LIMA	8,402
Warren YNGS-	56,629
Warrensville Heights CLEV	16,565
Warsaw	765
Washington Court House	12,682
Waterford	600 ○
Waterville TOL	3,884
Wauseon	6,173
Waverly	4,603
Wayne	894
Waynesburg	1,160
Waynesville DAY-	1,796
Wellington	4,146
Wellston	6,016
Wellsville E.LIV-	5,095
West Alexandria DAY-	1,313
West Carrollton DAY-	13,148
West Chester CIN-	700 ○
Westerville COL	23,414
West Farmington	563
Westfield Center CLEV	791
West Jefferson COL	4,448
West Lafayette	2,225
Westlake CLEV	19,483
West Liberty	1,653
West Manchester	448
West Mansfield	716
West Milton DAY-	4,119
Weston	1,708
West Portsmouth PTSM	4,095
West Salem	1,357
West Union	2,791
West Unity	1,639
Wheelersburg PTSM	4,796
Whitehall COL	21,299
Whitehouse TOL	2,137
White Oak CIN-	9,563
Wickliffe CLEV	16,790
Wickliffe YNGS-	7,700 ○
Wilberforce DAY-	2,512
Willard	5,720
Williamsburg CIN-	1,952
Williamsport	792
Willoughby CLEV	19,329
Willoughby Hills CLEV	8,612
Willowick CLEV	17,834
Wilmington	10,431
Winchester	1,080
Windham YNGS-	3,721
Wintersville STU-	4,724
Woodbourne DAY-	6,000 ○
Woodlawn CIN-	2,715
Woodsfield	3,145
Woodville	2,050
Wooster	19,289
Worthington COL	15,016
Wyoming CIN-	8,282
Xenia DAY-	24,653
Yellow Springs DAY-	4,077
Yorkville WHL	1,447
YOUNGSTOWN YNGS-	115,436
ZANESVILLE ZAN	28,655

COUNTIES

County	Population
Adams	24,328
Allen	112,241
Ashland	46,178
Ashtabula	104,215
Athens	56,399
Auglaize	42,554
Belmont	82,569
Brown	31,920
Butler	258,787
Carroll	25,598
Champaign	33,649
Clark	150,236
Clermont	128,483
Clinton	34,603
Columbiana	113,572
Coshocton	36,024
Crawford	50,075
Cuyahoga	1,498,400
Darke	55,096
Defiance	39,987
Delaware	53,840
Erie	79,655
Fairfield	93,678
Fayette	27,467
Franklin	869,126
Fulton	37,751
Gallia	30,098
Geauga	74,474
Greene	129,769
Guernsey	42,024
Hamilton	873,224
Hancock	64,581
Hardin	32,719
Harrison	18,152
Henry	28,383
Highland	33,477
Hocking	24,304
Holmes	29,416
Huron	54,608
Jackson	30,592
Jefferson	91,564
Knox	46,304
Lake	212,801
Lawrence	63,849
Licking	120,981
Logan	39,155
Lorain	274,909
Lucas	471,741
Madison	33,004
Mahoning	289,487
Marion	67,974
Medina	113,150
Meigs	23,641
Mercer	38,334
Miami	90,381
Monroe	17,382
Montgomery	571,697
Morgan	14,241
Morrow	26,480
Muskingum	83,340
Noble	11,310
Ottawa	40,076
Paulding	21,302
Perry	31,032
Pickaway	43,662
Pike	22,802
Portage	135,856
Preble	38,223
Putnam	32,991
Richland	131,205
Ross	65,004
Sandusky	63,267
Scioto	84,545
Seneca	61,901
Shelby	43,089
Stark	378,823
Summit	524,472
Trumbull	241,863
Tuscarawas	84,614
Union	29,536
Van Wert	30,458
Vinton	11,584
Warren	99,276
Washington	64,266
Wayne	97,408
Williams	36,369
Wood	107,372
Wyandot	22,651

OKLAHOMA

1980 Census 3,025,495

CITIES

City	Population
Achille	480
Ada	15,902
Adair	508
Afton	1,174
Alex	769
Allen	998
Altus	23,101
Alva	6,416
Anadarko	6,378
Antlers	2,989
Apache	1,560
Arapaho	851
Ardmore	23,689
Arkoma FTSM	2,175
Arnett	714
Asher	659
Atoka	3,409
Avant	461
Barnsdall	1,501
Bartlesville	34,568
Beaver	1,939
Beggs	1,428
Bethany O.C.	22,038
Bethel Acres	2,314
Billings	632
Binger	791
Bixby TUL	6,969
Blackwell	8,400
Blair	1,092
Blanchard O.C.	1,688
Boise City	1,761
Bokchito	628
Bokoshe	556
Boswell	702
Bowlegs	522
Boynton	518
Bray	591
Bristow	4,702
Broken Arrow TUL	35,761
Broken Bow	3,965
Buffalo	1,381
Burns Flat	2,431
Byng	833
Cache	1,661
Caddo	923
Calera	1,390
Calumet	469
Canton	854
Canute	676
Carmen	516
Carnegie	2,016
Carney	622
Cashion	547
Catoosa TUL	1,561
Cement	884
Chandler	2,926
Checotah	3,454
Chelsea	1,754
Cherokee	2,105
Cheyenne	1,207
Chickasha	15,828
Chilocco	500 ○
Choctaw O.C.	7,520
Chouteau	1,559
Claremore TUL	12,085
Clayton	833
Cleo Springs	514
Cleveland	2,972
Clinton	8,796
Coalgate	2,001
Colbert	1,122
Colcord	530
Collinsville TUL	3,556
Comanche	1,937
Commerce	2,556
Cookson	500 ○
Copan	960
Cordell	3,301
Corn	542
Countyline	500 ○
Covington	715
Coweta TUL	4,554
Cowlington	546
Crescent	1,651
Cushing	7,720
Custer City	530
Cyril	1,220
Davenport	974
Davidson	501
Davis	2,782
Delaware	544
Del City O.C.	28,523
Depew	682
Dewar	1,048
Dewey	3,545
Dickson	996
Dill City	649
Disney	464
Dover	570
Drummond	482
Drumright	3,162
Duke	484
Duncan	22,517
Durant	11,972
Dustin	498
Eagletown	500 ○
Eakly	452
Edmond O.C.	34,637
Eldorado	688
Elgin	1,003
Elk City	9,579
Elmore City	582
El Reno	15,486
ENID ENID	50,363
Erick	1,375
Eufaula	3,159
Fairfax	1,949
Fairland	1,073
Fairview	3,370
Fittstown	500 ○
Fletcher	1,074
Forgan	611
Fort Cobb	760
Fort Gibson MSKOG	2,477
Fort Supply	559
Fort Towson	789
Frederick	6,153
Gage	667
Garber	1,215
Geary	1,700
Geronimo	726
Glencoe	490
Glenpool TUL	2,706
Goldsby O.C.	603
Goodwell	1,186
Gore	445
Gotebo	457
Gracemont	503
Grandfield	1,445
Granite	1,617
Grove	3,378
Guthrie	10,312
Guymon	8,492
Haileyville	832
Hammon	866
Harrah O.C.	2,897
Hartshorne	2,380
Haskell	1,953
Healdton	3,769
Heavener	2,776
Helena	710
Hennessey	2,287
Henryetta	6,432
Hinton	1,432
Hobart	4,735
Holdenville	5,469
Hollis	2,958
Hominy	3,130
Hooker	1,788
Howe	562
Hugo	7,172
Hulbert	633
Hydro	938
Idabel	7,622
Inola	1,550
Jay	2,100
Jenks TUL	5,876
Jones O.C.	2,270
Kansas	491
Kellyville	960
Keota	661
Keyes	557
Kiefer TUL	912
Kingfisher	4,245
Kingston	1,171
Kiowa	866
Konawa	1,711
Krebs	1,754
Lahoma	537
Lake Station TUL	800 ○
Lamont	571
Langley	582
Langston	443
Laverne	1,563
LAWTON LAWT	80,054
Leedey	499
Lexington	1,731
Lindsay	3,454
Locust Grove	1,179
Lone Grove	3,369
Lone Wolf	613
Luther O.C.	1,159
McAlester	17,255
McCurtain	549
McLoud O.C.	4,061
Madill	3,173
Mangum	3,833
Mannford	1,610
Mannsville	568
Marietta	2,494
Marlow	5,017
Maud	1,444
Maysville	1,396
Medford	1,419
Meeker	1,032
Miami	14,237
Midwest City O.C.	49,559
Minco	1,489
Moore O.C.	35,063
Mooreland	1,383
Morris	1,288
Morrison	671
Mounds TUL	1,086
Mountain Park	557
Mountain View	1,189
Muldrow	2,538
MUSKOGEE MSKOG	40,011
Mustang O.C.	7,496
Newcastle O.C.	3,076
Newkirk	2,413
Nichols Hills O.C.	4,153
Nicoma Park O.C.	2,588
Noble O.C.	3,497
Norman O.C.	68,020
North Enid ENID	992
North Miami	544
Nowata	4,270
Oakhurst TUL	2,000 ○
Oakland	485
Oaks	591
Ochelata	480
Oilton	1,244
Okarche	1,064
Okay MSKOG	554
Okeene	1,601
Okemah	3,381
OKLAHOMA CITY O.C.	403,484
Okmulgee	16,263
Olustee	721
Oologah	798
Owasso TUL	6,486
Paden	448
Panama	1,425
Paoli	573
Pauls Valley	5,664
Pawhuska	4,771
Pawnee	1,688
Perkins	1,762
Perry	5,796
Picher	2,180
Piedmont O.C.	2,016
Pocola	3,268
Ponca City	26,238
Pond Creek	949
Porter	642
Porum	668
Poteau	7,089
Prague	2,208
Prue	554
Pryor	8,483
Purcell	4,638
Quapaw	1,097
Quinton	1,228
Ralston	495
Ramona	567
Randlett	461
Ravia	487
Red Oak	676
Ringling	1,561
Ripley	451
Roff	729
Roland	1,472
Rush Springs	1,451
Ryan	1,083
Salina	1,115
Sallisaw	6,403
Sand Springs TUL	13,121
Sapulpa TUL	15,853
Savanna	828
Sayre	3,177
Seiling	1,103
Seminole	8,590
Sentinel	1,016
Shattuck	1,759
Shawnee	26,506
Shidler	708
Skiatook TUL	3,596

○ Rand McNally estimate (not reported in census).
▲ Population of entire township or "town", including rural areas.
● Independent city. Population not included in county total.

Snyder 1,848
Soper 465
South Coffeyville 873
Sparks 772
Spavinaw 623
Sperry TUL 1,276
Spiro 2,221
Springer 679
Sterling 702
Stigler 2,630
Stillwater 38,268
Stilwell 2,369
Stonewall 672
Stratford 1,459
Stringtown 1,047
Stroud 3,148
Sulphur 5,516
Taft MSKOG 489
Tahlequah 9,708
Talihina 1,387
Taloga 446
Tecumseh 5,123
Temple 1,339
Terral 604
Texhoma 785
Thomas 1,515
Tipton 1,475
Tishomingo 3,212
Tonkawa 3,524
TULSA TUL 360,919
Tupelo 542
Turley TUL 6,336
Tuttle 3,051
Tyrone 928
Union City 558
Valliant 927
Velma 831
Verden 625
Vian 1,521
Vici 845
Village O.C. 11,114
Vinita 6,740
Wagoner 6,191
Wakita 526
Walters 2,778
Wanette 473
Wapanucka 472
Warner 1,310
Warr Acres O.C. 9,940
Washington 477
Watonga 4,139
Waukomis 1,551
Waurika 2,369
Wayne 621
Waynoka 1,377
Weatherford 9,640
Webbers Falls 461
Welch 697
Weleetka 1,195
Wellston 802
Westville 1,049
Wetumka 1,725
Wewoka 6,280
Wilburton 2,996
Wilson 1,585
Wister 982
Woodward 13,610
Wright City 1,168
Wynnewood 2,615
Wynona 780
Yale 1,652
Yukon O.C. 17,112

COUNTIES

Adair 18,575
Alfalfa 7,077
Atoka 12,748
Beaver 6,806
Beckham 19,243
Blaine 13,443
Bryan 30,535
Caddo 30,905
Canadian 56,452
Carter 43,610
Cherokee 30,684
Choctaw 17,203
Cimarron 3,648
Cleveland 133,173
Coal 6,041
Comanche 112,456
Cotton 7,338
Craig 15,014
Creek 59,016
Custer 25,995
Delaware 23,946
Dewey 5,922
Ellis 5,596
Garfield 62,820
Garvin 27,856
Grady 39,490
Grant 6,518
Greer 7,028
Harmon 4,519
Harper 4,715
Haskell 11,010
Hughes 14,338
Jackson 30,356
Jefferson 8,294
Johnston 10,356
Kay 49,852
Kingfisher 14,187
Kiowa 12,711
Latimer 9,840
Le Flore 40,698
Lincoln 26,601
Logan 26,881
Love 7,469
McClain 20,291
McCurtain 36,151
McIntosh 15,562
Major 8,772
Marshall 10,550
Mayes 32,261
Murray 12,147
Muskogee 67,033
Noble 11,573
Nowata 11,486
Okfuskee 11,125
Oklahoma 568,933
Okmulgee 39,169
Osage 39,327
Ottawa 32,870
Pawnee 15,310
Payne 62,435
Pittsburg 40,524
Pontotoc 32,598
Pottawatomie 55,239
Pushmataha 11,773
Roger Mills 4,799
Rogers 46,436
Seminole 27,465
Sequoyah 30,749
Stephens 43,419
Texas 17,727
Tillman 12,398
Tulsa 470,593
Wagoner 41,801
Washington 48,113
Washita 13,798
Woods 10,923
Woodward 21,172

OREGON

1980 Census 2,663,149

CITIES

Albany 28,067
Aloha POR 10,000 ○
Altamont 19,805
Amity 1,092
Applegate 800 ○
Arlington 521
Ashland 14,943
Astoria 9,998
Athena 965
Aumsville SAL 1,432
Aurora POR 523
Baker 9,471
Bandon 2,311
Banks POR 489
Barview 1,462
Bay City 986
Beaverton POR 31,926
Bend 17,263
Bly 750 ○
Boardman 1,261
Boring POR 500 ○
Brookings 3,384
Brownsville 1,261
Bunker Hill 1,555
Burns 3,579
Canby POR 7,659
Cannon Beach 1,187
Canyon City 639
Canyonville 1,288
Carlton 1,302
Cascade Locks 838
Cave Junction 1,023
Cedar Hills POR 8,000 ○
Central Point MEDF 6,357
Charleston 700 ○
Chenoweth 2,820
Chiloquin 778
Clackamas POR 3,250 ○
Clatskanie 1,648
Coburg EUG 699
Columbia City POR 678
Condon 783
Coos Bay 14,424
Coquille 4,481
Cornelius POR 4,462
CORVALLIS CORV 40,960
Cottage Grove 7,148
Cove 451
Crescent 700 ○
Creswell 1,770
Culver 514
Dallas 8,530
Dayton 1,409
Depoe Bay 723
Dillard 1,000 ○
Drain 1,148
Dufur 560
Dundee POR 1,223
Eagle Point MEDF 2,764
Eastside 1,601
Echo 624
Elgin 1,701
Elmira EUG 500 ○
Enterprise 2,003
Errol Heights POR 7,800 ○
Estacada 1,419
EUGENE EUG 105,664
Fairview POR 1,749
Falcon Heights 800 ○
Falls City 804
Florence 4,411
Forest Grove POR 11,499
Fossil 535
Foster 600 ○
Four Corners SAL 11,331
Garden Home POR 5,500 ○
Gardiner 600 ○
Garibaldi 999
Gaston 471
Gates 455
Gearhart 967
Gervais SAL 799
Gilbert POR 4,000 ○
Gilchrist 600 ○
Gladstone POR 9,500
Glendale 712
Glenwood EUG 1,600 ○
Glide 900 ○
Gold Beach 1,515
Gold Hill 904
Grand Ronde 550 ○
Grants Pass 15,032
Green 3,897
Gresham POR 33,005
Halsey 693
Hammond 516
Happy Valley POR 1,499
Harbor 2,856
Harrisburg EUG 1,881
Hauser 630 ○
Hayesville SAL 9,213
Heppner 1,498
Hermiston 9,408
Hillsboro POR 27,664
Hines 1,632
Hood River 4,329
Hubbard POR 1,640
Huntington 539
Independence SAL 4,024
Irrigon 700
Island City 477
Jacksonville MEDF 2,030
Jefferson 1,702
Jennings Lodge POR 3,000 ○
John Day 2,012
Jordan Valley 473
Joseph 999
Junction City EUG 3,320
Keizer SAL 18,592
Keno 900 ○
Kerby 550 ○
Klamath Falls 17,590
Lafayette 1,215
La Grande 11,743
Lake Oswego POR 22,527
Lakeside 1,453
Lakeview 2,770
La Pine 900 ○
Lebanon 10,413
Lincoln City 5,469
Lowell EUG 661
Lyons 877
McMinnville 14,080
McNulty POR 1,805
Madras 2,235
Malin 539
Manzanita 443
Mapleton 900 ○
Marcola 500 ○
Marlene Village POR 1,500 ○
Maupin 495
May Park 800 ○
Maywood Park POR 845
MEDFORD MEDF 39,603
Merlin 500 ○
Merrill 809
Metolius 451
Metzger POR 5,544
Midway POR 19,000 ○
Mill City 1,565
Milton-Freewater 5,086
Milwaukie POR 17,931
Molalla 2,992
Monmouth SAL 5,594
Mount Angel 2,876
Mount Vernon 569
Myrtle Creek 3,365
Myrtle Point 2,859
Newberg POR 10,394
Newport 7,519
North Albany 4,499
North Bend 9,779
North Plains POR 715
Nyssa 2,862
Oak Grove POR 11,640
Oakland 886
Oakridge 3,729
Odell 600 ○
Ontario 8,814
Oregon City POR 14,673
Pacific City 1,500 ○
Parkrose POR 21,108
Pendleton 14,521
Philomath CORV 2,673
Phoenix MEDF 2,309
Pilot Rock 1,630
PORTLAND POR 368,139
Port Orford 1,061
Powell Butte 600 ○
Powellhurst POR 9,000 ○
Powers 819
Prairie City 1,106
Prineville 5,276
Prospect 1,200 ○
Rainier LNGV 1,655
Raleigh Hills POR 6,517
Redmond 6,452
Reedsport 4,984
Riddle 1,265
River Road EUG 10,370
Rockaway 906
Rockwood POR 11,000 ○
Rogue River 1,308
Roseburg 16,644
Russellville POR 6,500 ○
St. Helens POR 7,064
SALEM SAL 89,233
Sandy POR 2,905
Santa Clara EUG 14,288
Scappoose POR 3,213
Scio 579
Seal Rock 800 ○
Seaside 5,193
Shady Cove 1,097
Sheridan 2,249
Sherwood POR 2,386
Siletz 1,001
Silverton 5,168
Sisters 696
South Medford MEDF 2,898
Springfield EUG 41,621
Stanfield 1,568
Stayton 4,396
Sublimity 1,077
Sutherlin 4,560
Svensen 650 ○
Sweet Home 6,921
Talent MEDF 2,577
Tangent 478
Terrebonne 900 ○
The Dalles 10,820
Tigard POR 17,543
Tillamook 3,981
Toledo 3,151
Tri-City 3,439
Troutdale POR 5,908
Tualatin POR 7,483
Tumalo 500 ○
Turner SAL 1,116
Tygh Valley 500 ○
Umatilla 3,199
Union 2,062
Vale 1,558
Veneta EUG 2,449
Vernonia 1,785
Waldport 1,274
Wallowa 847
Warm Springs 500 ○
Warren POR 800 ○
Warrenton 2,493
Welches 500 ○
Wemme 500 ○
West Haven POR 3,400 ○
West Linn POR 11,358
Weston 719
Westport 500 ○
West Slope POR 5,364
White City MEDF 5,445
Willamina 1,749
Wilsonville POR 2,920
Winchester Bay 900 ○
Winston 3,359
Wolf Creek 600 ○
Woodburn SAL 11,196
Yachats 482
Yamhill 690
Yoncalla 805

COUNTIES

Baker 16,134
Benton 68,211
Clackamas 241,911
Clatsop 32,489
Columbia 35,646
Coos 64,047
Crook 13,091
Curry 16,992
Deschutes 62,142
Douglas 93,748
Gilliam 2,057
Grant 8,210
Harney 8,314
Hood River 15,835
Jackson 132,456
Jefferson 11,599
Josephine 58,855
Klamath 59,117
Lake 7,532
Lane 275,226
Lincoln 35,264
Linn 89,495
Malheur 26,896
Marion 204,692
Morrow 7,519
Multnomah 562,647
Polk 45,203
Sherman 2,172
Tillamook 21,164
Umatilla 58,861
Union 23,921
Wallowa 7,273
Wasco 21,732
Washington 245,860
Wheeler 1,513
Yamhill 55,332

PENNSYLVANIA

1980 Census 11,864,751

CITIES

Abington Township PHIL- 59,084
Adamstown 1,119
Akron 3,471
Albion 1,818
Alburtis AL-B-E 1,428
Alden SCR- 800 ○
Aliquippa PGH 17,094
ALLENTOWN AL-B-E 103,758
Allison 1,040 ○
Allison Park PGH 5,600 ○
ALTOONA ALT 57,078
Ambler PHIL- 6,628
Ambridge PGH 9,575
Annville LEB 4,493
Apollo PGH 2,212
Archbald SCR- 6,295
Arnold PGH 6,853
Ashland 4,235
Ashley SCR- 3,512
Aspinwall PGH 3,284
Aston PHIL- 14,530
Athens 3,622
Auburn 999
Austin 740
Avalon PGH 6,240
Avella STU- 950 ○
Avis WMSPT 1,718
Avoca SCR- 3,536
Avondale PHIL- 891
Avonmore 1,234
Baden PGH 5,318
Bairdford PGH 950 ○
Baldwin PGH 24,714
Bally 1,051
Bangor 5,006
Barnesboro 2,741
Bath AL-B-E 1,953
Beaver PGH 5,441
Beaverdale JNST 1,000 ○
Beaver Falls PGH 12,525
Beaver Meadows HAZ 1,078
Bedford 3,326
Bellefonte STCOL 6,300
Belle Vernon PGH 1,489
Belleville 1,689
Bellevue PGH 10,128
Bellwood ALT 2,114
Bensalem PHIL- 52,368
Bentleyville WASH 2,525
Benton 981
Berlin 1,999
Bernville READ 798
Berwick 11,850
Berwyn PHIL- 9,300 ○
Bessemer 1,293
Bethel Park PGH 34,755
Bethlehem AL-B-E 70,419
Biglerville 991
Big Run 822
Birdsboro 3,481
Black Lick 1,313
Blairsville 4,166
Blakely SCR- 7,438
Blandburg 775 ○
Blawnox PGH 1,653
Bloomsburg 11,717
Blossburg 1,757
Blue Ridge Summit 800 ○
Bobtown 1,008
Boiling Springs HRBG 2,323
Bolivar 706
Boswell JNST 1,480
Boyertown PTSTN 3,979
Brackenridge PGH 4,297
Braddock PGH 5,634
Bradenville PGH 1,100 ○
Bradford 11,211
Brentwood PGH 11,859
Bridgeville PGH 6,154
Bristol PHIL- 10,867
Brookhaven PHIL- 7,912
Brookville 4,568
Broomall PHIL- 23,642
Brownsville 4,043
Burgettstown PGH 1,867
Burnham 2,457
BUTLER BUTL 17,026
Cadogan 459 ○
Cairnbrook 1,081
California 5,703
Cambridge Springs 2,102
Camp Hill HRBG 8,422
Canadensis 800 ○
Canonsburg PGH 10,459
Canton 1,959
Carbondale 11,255
Carlisle 18,314
Carmichaels 630
Carnegie PGH 10,099
Carnot PGH 6,000 ○
Castle Shannon PGH 10,164
Catasauqua AL-B-E 6,711
Catawissa 1,568
Cecil 900 ○
Cementon AL-B-E 1,200 ○
Centerville 4,207
Central City JNST 1,496
Centre Hall STCOL 1,233
Chambersburg 16,174
Charleroi PGH 5,717
Cheltenham Township PHIL- 35,509
Chester PHIL- 45,794
Chester Township PHIL- 5,687
Cheswick PGH 2,336
Chicora BUTL 1,192
Christiana COAT 1,183
Clairton PGH 12,188
Clarendon 776
Claridge PGH 900 ○
Clarion 6,198
Clarks Summit SCR- 5,272
Claysburg ALT 1,346
Claysville WASH 1,029
Clearfield 7,580
Cleona LEB 2,003
Clifton Heights PHIL- 7,320
Clymer 1,761
Coaldale 2,762
Coalport 739
COATESVILLE COAT 10,698
Cochranton 1,240
Collegeville PHIL- 3,406
Collingdale PHIL- 9,539
Colonial Park HRBG 10,000 ○
Columbia 10,466
Colver 1,165
Conemaugh JNST 2,128
Confluence 968
Conneautville 971
Connellsville 10,319
Conshohocken PHIL- 8,591
Conway PGH 2,747
Coopersburg AL-B-E 2,595
Coplay AL-B-E 3,130
Coral 700 ○
Coraopolis PGH 7,308
Cornwall LEB 2,653
Corry 7,149
Coudersport 2,791
Crabtree PGH 950 ○
Crafton PGH 7,623
Creighton PGH 1,658
Cresson 2,184
Cressona PTSVL 1,810
Crucible 800 ○
Curtisville PGH 1,404
Curwensville 3,116
Dallas SCR- 2,679
Dallastown YORK 3,949
Dalton SCR- 1,383
Danville 5,239
Darby PHIL- 11,513
Dauphin HRBG 901
Dawson 661
Dayton 648
Delta 692
Denver 2,018
Derry LTROB 3,072
Devon PHIL- 6,700 ○
Dickson City SCR- 6,699
Dillsburg HRBG 1,733
Distant 575 ○
Dixonville 900 ○
Donald Son 465 ○
Donora PGH 7,524
Dormont PGH 11,275
Dover YORK 1,910
Downingtown COAT 7,650

○ Rand McNally estimate (not reported in census).
▲ Population of entire township or "town", including rural areas.
● Independent city. Population not included in county total.

Doylestown PHIL- 8,717
Drifton HAZ 900 ○
Du Bois 9,290
Duboistown WMSPT 1,218
Duke Center 900 ○
Dunbar 1,369
Duncannon HRBG 1,645
Duncansville ALT 1,355
Dunlo JNST 950 ○
Dunmore SCR- 16,781
Dupont SCR- 3,460
Duquesne PGH 10,094
Duryea SCR- 5,415
Dushore 692
East Bangor 955
East Berlin YORK 1,054
East Brady 1,153
East Greenville 2,456
East Norriton PHIL- 12,711
Easton AL-B-E 26,027
East Petersburg LANC 3,600
East Pittsburgh PGH 2,493
East Stroudsburg 8,039
East Washington WASH 2,241
Ebensburg 4,096
Economy PGH 9,538
Eddystone PGH 2,555
Edenborn 500 ○
Edgewood PGH 4,382
Edgeworth PGH 1,738
Edinboro 6,324
Edwardsville SCR- 5,729
Eldred 965
Elizabethtown HRBG 8,233
Elizabethville 1,531
Elkland 1,974
Ellport PGH 1,290
Ellsworth PGH 1,228
Ellwood City PGH 9,998
Elmhurst SCR- 953 ○
Elmora 950 ○
Elrama 800 ○
Elysburg 1,477
Emmaus AL-B-E 11,001
Emporium 2,837
Emsworth PGH 3,074
Enola HRBG 3,600 ○
Ephrata 11,095
ERIE ERIE 119,123
Ernest 584
Espy 1,571
Etna PGH 4,534
Evans City BUTL 2,299
Everett 1,828
Everson 1,032
Exeter SCR- 5,493
Export PGH 1,143
Factoryville SCR- 924
Fairchance UNTN 2,106
Fairoaks PGH 1,854
Fairview ERIE 1,855
Falls Creek 1,208
Farrell SHAR 8,645
Fayetteville 3,202
Ferndale JNST 2,204
Fleetwood 3,422
Flemington 1,416
Folcroft PHIL- 8,231
Ford City 3,923
Forest City 1,924
Forest Hills PGH 8,198
Forty Fort SCR- 5,590
Fountain Hill AL-B-E 4,805
Fox Chapel PGH 5,049
Frackville 5,308
Franklin OILC-F 8,146
Franklin Park PGH 6,135
Fredericktown 1,052
Freedom PGH 2,272
Freeland HAZ 4,285
Freemansburg AL-B-E 1,879
Freeport PGH 2,381
Galeton 1,462
Gallitzin ALT 2,315
Gap 1,000 ○
Garrett 563
Geistown JNST 3,304
Gettysburg 7,194
Girard ERIE 2,615
Girardville 2,268
Glassport PGH 6,242
Glen Lyon SCR- 2,352
Glenolden PHIL- 7,633
Glen Rock YORK 1,662
Grampian 464
Grassflat 750 ○
Great Bend BING 740
Greencastle HAG- 3,679
Greensburg PGH 17,558
Green Tree PGH 5,722
Greenville 7,730
Grove City 8,162
Halifax HRBG 909
Hallstead BING 1,280
Hamburg 4,011
HANOVER HANV 14,890
Harmony PGH 1,334
HARRISBURG HRBG 53,264
Harrisville 1,033
Hastings 1,574
Hatboro PHIL- 7,579
Hatfield PHIL- 2,533
Hawk Run 750 ○
Hawley 1,181
Hawthorn 547
HAZLETON HAZ 27,318
Hegins 900 ○
Heilwood 700 ○
Hellam YORK 1,428
Hellertown AL-B-E 6,025
Herminie PGH 2,000 ○
Hermitage SHAR 16,365 ○
Herndon 483
Hershey HRBG 13,249
Highspire HRBG 2,959
Hillsville 915 ○
Hollidaysburg ALT 5,892
Homer City 2,248
Homestead PGH 5,092
Honesdale 5,128
Honey Brook COAT 1,164
Hooversville JNST 863
Hopwood UNTN 2,420
Horsham PHIL- 9,900
Houston PGH 1,568
Houtzdale 1,222
Howard 838
Hughesville 2,174
Hummels Wharf 1,474
Huntingdon 7,042
Hyndman 1,106
Imperial PGH 3,200 ○
Indiana 16,051
Ingram PGH 4,346
Irvona 644
Irwin PGH 4,995
Isabella 700 ○
James City 450 ○
Jamestown 854
Jeannette PGH 13,106
Jefferson PGH 8,643
Jenkintown PHIL- 4,942
Jenners 800 ○
Jermyn SCR- 2,411
Jerome JNST 1,196
Jersey Shore WMSPT 4,631
Jessup SCR- 4,974
Jim Thorpe AL-B-E 5,263
Johnsonburg 3,938
JOHNSTOWN JNST 35,496
Jonestown LEB 814
Juniata Terrace 631
Kane 4,916
Kennett Square PHIL- 4,715
Kersey 600 ○
Kingston SCR- 15,681
Kittanning 5,432
Knox 1,364
Knoxville 650
Koppel PGH 1,146
Kulpmont 3,675
Kutztown 4,040
Lake City ERIE 2,384
Lakemont ALT 1,500 ○
LANCASTER LANC 54,725
Lanesboro BING 465
Langeloth 1,112
Langhorne PHIL- 1,697
Lansdale PHIL- 16,526
Lansdowne PHIL- 11,891
Lansford 4,466
Larksville SCR- 4,410
Latrobe LTROB 10,799
Lattimer Mines 650 ○
Laureldale READ 4,047
Laurel Run SCR- 725
Lawrence PGH 970 ○
LEBANON LEB 25,711
Leechburg PGH 2,682
Leetsdale PGH 1,604
Lehighton AL-B-E 5,826
Lewisburg 5,407
Lewis Run 677
Lewistown 9,830
Ligonier 1,917
Lilly 1,462
Linesville 1,198
Lititz LANC 7,590
Littlestown HANV 2,870
Liverpool 809
Lock Haven 9,617
Loretto 1,395
Lower Burrell PGH 13,200
Lucernemines 1,195
Ludlow 800 ○
Luzerne SCR- 3,703
Lykens 2,181
Lyndora BUTL 3,000 ○
McAdoo HAZ 2,940
McCandless PGH 26,250
McClure 1,024
McConnellsburg 1,178
McKeesport PGH 31,012
McKees Rocks PGH 8,742
McSherrystown HANV 2,764
Macungie AL-B-E 1,899
Madera 900 ○
Mahaffey 513
Mahanoy City 6,167
Manchester YORK 2,027
Manheim 5,015
Mansfield 3,322
Mapleton Depot 591
Marcus Hook PHIL- 2,638
Marienville 900 ○
Marietta 2,740
Mars PGH 1,803
Martinsburg ALT 2,231
Marysville HRBG 2,452
Masontown 4,909
Matamoras 2,111
Mather 860 ○
Mayfield SCR- 1,812
Meadow Lands PGH 1,200 ○
Meadville 15,544
Mechanicsburg HRBG 9,487
Media PHIL- 6,119
Mercer SHAR 2,532
Mercersburg 1,617
Meyersdale 2,581
Middleburg 1,357
Middletown HRBG 10,122
Midland E.LIV- 4,310
Midway PGH 1,187
Mifflin 648
Mifflinburg 3,151
Mifflintown 783
Mifflinville 1,341
Mildred 800 ○
Milesburg STCOL 1,309
Milford 1,143
Millcreek ERIE 44,303 ○
Millersburg 2,770
Millerstown 550
Millersville LANC 7,668
Mill Hall 1,744
Millheim 800
Millsboro 900 ○
Millvale PGH 4,772
Millville 975
Milroy 1,594
Milton 6,730
Minersville PTSVL 5,635
Mocanaqua 990 ○
Mohnton READ 2,156
Monaca PGH 7,661
Monessen PGH 11,928
Monongahela PGH 5,950
Monroeville PGH 30,977
Mont Alto HAG- 1,592
Mont Clare PHIL- 950 ○
Montgomery 1,653
Montoursville WMSPT 5,403
Montrose 1,980
Moon Run PGH 700 ○
Moosic SCR- 6,068
Morrisdale 600 ○
Morrisville PHIL- 9,845
Moscow SCR- 1,536
Mount Carmel 8,190
Mount Holly Springs 2,068
Mount Jewett 1,053
Mount Joy 5,680
Mount Lebanon PGH 34,414
Mount Pleasant 5,354
Mount Pocono 1,237
Mount Union 3,101
Mount Wolf YORK 1,517
Muncy 2,700
Munhall PGH 14,535
Murrysville PGH 16,036
Muse PGH 1,000 ○
Myerstown LEB 3,131
Nanticoke SCR- 13,044
Nanty Glo JNST 3,936
Narberth PHIL- 4,496
Natrona Heights PGH 13,252 ○
Nazareth AL-B-E 5,443
Neffsville LANC 1,300 ○
Nemacolin 1,235
Nescopeck 1,768
Nesquehoning 3,346
New Bethlehem 1,441
New Bloomfield HRBG 1,109
New Brighton PGH 7,364
NEW CASTLE NWCS 33,621
New Cumberland HRBG 8,051
New Florence JNST 855
New Freedom 2,205
New Holland 4,147
New Hope 1,473
New Kensington PGH 17,660
Newmanstown 1,417
New Milford 1,040
New Oxford HANV 1,921
New Philadelphia PTSVL 1,341
Newport HRBG 1,600
Newtown Square PHIL- 11,775 ○
Newville 1,370
New Wilmington 2,774
Nicholson 945
Norristown PHIL- 34,684
Northampton AL-B-E 8,240
North Apollo PGH 1,487
North Bend 700 ○
North Braddock PGH 8,711
North East ERIE 4,568
Northumberland 3,636
North Versailles PGH 13,294
North Wales PHIL- 3,391
North Warren 1,232
North York YORK 1,755
Norwood PHIL- 6,647
Noxen 800 ○
Nuremberg 800 ○
Oakdale PGH 1,955
Oakland BING 734
Oakmont PGH 7,039
Ohioville E.LIV- 4,217
OIL CITY OILC-F 13,881
Old Forge SCR- 9,304
Oliver UNTN 3,777
Olyphant SCR- 5,204
Orwigsburg PTSVL 2,700
Osceola Mills 1,466
Oxford 3,633
Palmerton AL-B-E 5,455
Palmyra HRBG 7,228
Paoli PHIL- 5,277
Parker 808
Parkesburg COAT 2,578
Patton 2,441
Pen Argyl 3,388
Penbrook HRBG 3,006
Penn Hills PGH 57,632
Pennsburg 2,339
Perkasie PHIL- 5,241
PHILADELPHIA PHIL- 1,688,210
Philipsburg 3,533
Phoenixville PHIL- 14,165
Pine Grove 2,244
Pitcairn PGH 4,175
PITTSBURGH PGH 423,959
Pittston SCR- 9,930
Plains SCR- 5,455
Pleasant Gap STCOL 1,859
Pleasant Hills PGH 9,604
Pleasantville 1,099
Plum PGH 25,390
Plymouth SCR- 7,605
Point Marion MORG 1,642
Polk OILC-F 1,884
Portage JNST 3,510
Port Allegany 2,593
Port Royal 835
Port Vue PGH 5,316
POTTSTOWN PTSTN 22,729
POTTSVILLE PTSVL 18,195
Prospect Park PHIL- 6,593
Punxsutawney 7,479
Quakertown 8,867
Quarryville 1,558
Rankin PGH 2,892
READING READ 78,686
Reamstown 1,308
Red Lion YORK 5,824
Reedsville 1,023
Renovo 1,812
Republic UNTN 1,400 ○
Revloc 800 ○
Reynoldsville 3,016
Ridgway 5,604
Ridley Park PHIL- 7,889
Rimersburg 1,096
Roaring Spring ALT 2,962
Robertsdale 550 ○
Robinson 660 ○
Rochester PGH 4,759
Rockledge PHIL- 2,538
Rockwood 1,058
Roscoe PGH 1,123
Roseto 1,484
Rossiter 750 ○
Rothsville LANC 1,263
Roulette 1,500 ○
Rouseville OILC-F 734
Royersford PHIL- 4,243
Russell 800 ○
Saegertown 942
Sagamore 850 ○
St. Clair PTSVL 4,037
St. Marys 6,417
Salisbury 817
Saltsburg 964
Sandy Lake 779
Saxton 814
Sayre 6,951
Scalp Level JNST 1,186
Schaefferstown 800 ○
Schuylkill Haven PTSVL 5,977
Scottdale 5,833
Scott Township PGH 20,413
SCRANTON SCR- 88,117
Selinsgrove 5,227
Sellersville PHIL- 3,143
Sewickley PGH 4,778
Shamokin 10,357
Shamokin Dam 1,622
SHARON SHAR 19,057
Sharon Hill PHIL- 6,221
Sharpsburg PGH 4,351
Sharpsville SHAR 5,375
Sheffield 1,471
Shenandoah 7,589
Sheppton 650 ○
Shickshinny 1,192
Shillington READ 5,601
Shinglehouse 1,310
Shippensburg 5,261
Shoemakersville READ 1,391
Shrewsbury 2,688
Simpson 2,200 ○
Slatington AL-B-E 4,277
Slickville PGH 1,178
Sligo 798
Slippery Rock 3,047
Slovan 900 ○
Smethport 1,797
Smithfield 1,084
Somerset 6,474
Souderton PHIL- 6,657
South Connellsville 2,296
South Fork JNST 1,401
South Renovo 663
South Waverly 1,176
South Williamsport WMSPT 6,581
Spangler 2,399
Spring City PHIL- 3,389
Springdale PGH 4,418
Springfield PHIL- 25,326
Spring Garden YORK 11,127 ○
Spring Grove YORK 1,832
STATE COLLEGE STCOL 36,130
Steelton HRBG 6,484
Stewartstown 1,072
Stockertown AL-B-E 661
Stoneboro 1,177
Stowe PTSTN 3,860
Stowe Township PGH 9,202
Strabane PGH 1,900 ○
Strasburg LANC 1,999
Strattanville 555
Stroudsburg 5,148
Sugarcreek OILC-F 5,954
Sugar Notch SCR- 1,191
Summerville 830
Summit Hill 3,418
Sunbury 12,292
Susquehanna BING 1,994
Swarthmore PHIL- 5,950
Swissvale PGH 11,345
Swoyerville SCR- 5,795
Sykesville 1,537
Tamaqua 8,843
Tarentum PGH 6,419
Taylor SCR- 7,246
Telford PHIL- 3,507
Temple READ 1,486
Templeton 700 ○
Terre Hill 1,217
Throop SCR- 4,166
Tidioute 844
Titusville 6,884
Tobyhanna 700 ○
Topton 1,818
Towanda 3,526
Tower City 1,667
Trafford PGH 3,662
Tremont 1,796
Tresckow HAZ 1,128
Trevorton 2,192
Troy 1,381
Tunkhannock 2,144
Turtle Creek PGH 6,959
Twin Rocks 700 ○
Tyrone 6,346
Union City 3,623
UNIONTOWN UNTN 14,510
United PGH 950 ○
Upper Darby PHIL- 84,054
Upper St. Clair PGH 19,023
Valley Forge 950 ○
Valley View 1,722
Vanderbilt 689
Vandergrift PGH 6,823
Verona PGH 3,179
Vintondale JNST 697
Walnutport AL-B-E 2,007
Wampum PGH 851
Wanamie SCR- 600 ○
Warminster PHIL- 35,463
Warren 12,146
Warrendale PGH 800 ○
WASHINGTON WASH 18,363
Waterford ERIE 1,568
Watsontown 2,366
Waymart 1,248
Waynesboro HAG- 9,726
Waynesburg 4,482
Weatherly HAZ 2,891
Webster PGH 900 ○
Wellsboro 3,805
Wesleyville ERIE 3,998
West Chester PHIL- 17,435
West Decatur 600 ○
West Fairview HRBG 1,426
Westfield 1,268
West Grove PHIL- 1,820
West Hazleton HAZ 4,871
West Lawn READ 1,686
West Leisenring 700 ○
West Middlesex SHAR 1,064
West Mifflin PGH 26,322
West Milton 775 ○
Westmont JNST 6,113
West Newton PGH 3,387
West Norriton PHIL- 14,034
West Pittsburg 1,133
West Pittston SCR- 5,980
West Reading READ 4,507
West View PGH 7,648
West Wyoming SCR- 3,288
West York YORK 4,526
Whitehall PGH 15,143
Whitehall AL-B-E 8,055
White Haven 1,218
White Oak PGH 9,480
Whitney LTROB 500 ○
Wiconisco 1,321
Wilcox 900 ○
Wilkes-Barre SCR- 51,551
Wilkinsburg PGH 23,669
Williamsburg 1,400
WILLIAMSPORT WMSPT 33,401
Williamstown 1,664
Wilmerding PGH 2,421
Wilson AL-B-E 7,564
Winburne 650 ○
Windber JNST 5,585
Windgap 2,651
Windsor YORK 1,205
Womelsdorf 1,827
Wood 500 ○
Woodland 600 ○
Worthington 760
Wrightsville LANC 2,365
Wyalusing 716
Wyoming SCR- 3,655
Wyomissing READ 6,551
Yardley PHIL- 2,533
Yatesboro 700 ○
Yeadon PHIL- 11,727
Yeagertown 1,305
YORK YORK 44,619
York Haven YORK 746
Youngsville 2,006
Youngwood PGH 3,749
Zelienople PGH 3,502

COUNTIES

Adams 68,292
Allegheny 1,450,195
Armstrong 77,768
Beaver 204,441
Bedford 46,784
Berks 312,509
Blair 136,621
Bradford 62,919
Bucks 479,180
Butler 147,912
Cambria 183,263
Cameron 6,674
Carbon 53,285
Centre 112,760
Chester 316,660
Clarion 43,362
Clearfield 83,578
Clinton 38,971
Columbia 61,967
Crawford 88,869
Cumberland 179,625
Dauphin 232,317
Delaware 555,029
Elk 38,338
Erie 279,780
Fayette 159,417
Forest 5,072
Franklin 113,629
Fulton 12,842
Greene 40,476
Huntingdon 42,253
Indiana 92,281
Jefferson 48,303
Juniata 19,188
Lackawanna 227,908
Lancaster 362,346
Lawrence 107,150
Lebanon 108,582
Lehigh 272,349
Luzerne 343,079
Lycoming 118,416
McKean 50,635
Mercer 128,299
Mifflin 46,908
Monroe 69,409
Montgomery 643,371
Montour 16,675
Northampton 225,418
Northumberland 100,381
Perry 35,718
Philadelphia 1,688,210
Pike 18,271
Potter 17,726
Schuylkill 160,630

○ Rand McNally estimate (not reported in census).
▲ Population of entire township or "town", including rural areas.
● Independent city. Population not included in county total.

PENNSYLVANIA continued

Snyder 33,584
Somerset 81,243
Sullivan 6,349
Susquehanna 37,876
Tioga 40,973
Union 32,870
Venango 64,444
Warren 47,449
Washington 217,074
Wayne 35,237
Westmoreland 392,184
Wyoming 26,433
York 312,963

RHODE ISLAND
1980 Census 947,154

CITIES

Albion PROV- 1,200 ○
Allenton PROV- 600 ○
Anthony PROV- 4,500 ○
Arnold Mills PROV- 600 ○
Ashaway N.LON- 1,747
Ashton PROV- 875 ○
Barrington PROV- 16,174
Berkeley PROV- 930 ○
Block Island 620 ○
Bradford N.LON- 1,354
Bristol PROV- 20,128
Carolina 500 ○
Central Falls PROV- 16,995
Charlestown 4,800 ▲ 1,200 ○
Chepachet PROV- 900 ○
Coventry PROV- 27,065 ▲ 8,000 ○
Cranston PROV- 71,992
Cumberland Hill PROV- 5,421
Davisville PROV- 550 ○
Diamond Hill PROV- 1,150 ○
East Greenwich PROV- 10,211
East Providence PROV- 50,980
Esmond PROV- 3,500 ○
Forestdale PROV- 450 ○
Glendale PROV- 600 ○
Greenville PROV- 7,576
Harmony PROV- 800 ○
Harris PROV- 1,000 ○
Harrisville PROV- 1,224
Hope PROV- 490 ○
Hope Valley 1,414
Island Park NWPT 1,000 ○
Jamestown NWPT 4,040
Johnston PROV- 24,907
Kingston 5,479
La Fayette PROV- 680 ○
Lonsdale PROV- 4,100 ○
Manville PROV- 3,100 ○
Mapleville PROV- 900 ○
Middletown NWPT 3,350 ○
Mount View PROV- 560 ○
Narragansett 12,088 ▲ 3,342
NEWPORT NWPT 29,259
North Kingstown PROV- 21,938 ▲ 3,100 ○
North Providence PROV- 29,188
Oakland PROV- 500 ○
Pascoag PROV- 3,807
Pawtucket PROV- 71,204
Peace Dale 3,100 ○
Portsmouth NWPT 14,257 ▲ 4,300 ○
PROVIDENCE PROV- 156,804
Quidnessett PROV- 3,300 ○
Quidnick PROV- 2,300 ○
Saylesville PROV- 3,200 ○
Shannock 600 ○
Slatersville PROV- 2,000 ○
South Hopkinton N.LON- 500 ○
Tiverton F.R. 13,526 ▲ 7,653
Union Village PROV- 2,400 ○
Valley Falls PROV- 10,892
Wakefield 3,400 ○
Warren PROV- 10,640
Warwick PROV- 87,123
Watch Hill N.LON- 500 ○
West Barrington PROV- 3,700 ○
Westerly N.LON- 18,580 ▲ 14,093
West Kingston 700 ○
West Warwick PROV- 27,026
Woonsocket PROV- 45,914
Wyoming 600 ○
Yorktown Manor PROV- 2,500 ○

COUNTIES

Bristol 46,942
Kent 154,163
Newport 81,383
Providence 571,349
Washington 93,317

SOUTH CAROLINA
1980 Census 3,122,814

CITIES

Abbeville 5,833
Adams Run 600 ○
Aiken 14,978
Alcolu 600 ○
Allendale 4,400
ANDERSON AND 27,546
Andrews 3,129
Arcadia SPRT 2,088
Arlington SPRT 600 ○
Aynor 643
Baldwin 700 ○
Bamberg 3,672
Barnwell 5,572
Batesburg 4,023
Bath AUG 2,242
Beaufort 8,634
Beech Island AUG 1,300 ○
Belton 5,312
Belvedere AUG 6,859
Bennettsville 8,774
Berea GRNV 7,500 ○
Bethune 481
Bishopville 3,429
Blacksburg 1,873
Blackville 2,840
Bluffton 541
Bowling Green 850 ○
Bowman 1,137
Branchville 1,769
Brandon GRNV 2,170 ○
Brentwood CHAS 2,000 ○
Brooklyn 1,800 ○
Brunson 590
Bucksport 1,125
Buffalo 1,641
Calhoun Falls 2,491
Camden 7,462
Cameron 536
Campobello SPRT 472
Carlisle 503
Cateechee 500 ○
Cayce COL 11,701
Central 1,914
CHARLESTON CHAS 69,855
Cheraw 5,654
Chesnee 1,069
Chester 6,820
Chesterfield 1,432
City View GRNV 1,662
Clearwater AUG 3,967
Clemson 8,118
Clifton SPRT 800 ○
Clinton 8,596
Clio 1,031
Clover 3,451
COLUMBIA COL 101,229
Conestee GRNV 540 ○
Converse SPRT 1,173
Conway 10,240
Cowpens SPRT 2,023
Cross Hill 604
Darlington 7,989
Denmark 4,434
Denny Terrace COL 1,885 ○
Dentsville COL 5,000 ○
Dillon 7,065
Doneraile 1,276
Drayton SPRT 1,443
Due West 1,366
Duncan SPRT 1,259
Easley GRNV 14,264
East Gaffney 4,092
Eastover 899
Edgefield 2,713
Elgin 900 ○
Elliott 500 ○
Elloree 909
Enoree 1,107
Estill 2,308
Eureka 1,627
Eutawville 615
Fairfax 2,154
FLORENCE FLO 29,842
Folly Beach CHAS 1,478
Forest Acres COL 6,062
Fort Lawn 471
Fort Mill 4,162
Fountain Inn GRNV 4,226
Gaffney 13,453
Gantt GRNV 1,600 ○
Gaston COL 960
Georgetown 10,144
Glendale SPRT 1,049
Gloverville 2,619
Gluck AND 650 ○
Goose Creek CHAS 17,811
Graniteville 1,158
Gray Court 988
Great Falls 2,601
Greeleyville 593
GREENVILLE GRNV 58,242
Greenwood 21,613
Greer GRNV 10,525
Hampton 3,143
Hanahan CHAS 13,224
Hardeeville 1,250
Harleyville 606
Hartsville 8,939
Heath Springs 979
Hemingway 853
Hilton Head Island 11,239
Holly Hill 1,785
Hollywood CHAS 729
Honea Path 4,114
Hopkins COL 1,600 ○
Inman SPRT 1,554
Irmo COL 3,957
Isle of Palms CHAS 3,421
Iva 1,369
Jackson 1,771
Jacksonboro 450 ○
James Island CHAS 24,124
Jefferson 651
Jenkinsville 500 ○
Joanna 1,839
Johnsonville 1,421
Johnston 2,624
Jonesville 1,201
Kershaw 1,993
Kingstree 4,147
Ladson CHAS 13,246
La France AND 800 ○
Lake City 6,731
Lake View 939
Lamar 1,333
Lancaster 9,703
Lando 850 ○
Landrum 2,141
Lane 554
Langley AUG 1,714
Latta 1,804
Laurel Bay 5,238
Laurens 10,587
Leesville 2,296
Leslie RKHL 1,102
Lexington COL 2,131
Liberty 3,167
Lincolnville CHAS 808
Little River 500 ○
Little Rock 450 ○
Loris 2,193
Lugoff 2,939
Lyman SPRT 2,194
Lynchburg 534
McBee 774
McColl 2,677
McCormick 1,725
Manning 4,746
Marietta GRNV 900 ○
Marion 7,700
Mauldin GRNV 8,143
Mayesville SUMT 663
Mayo SPRT 900 ○
Midland Park CHAS 1,300 ○
Monarch Mills 2,353
Moncks Corner 4,179
Montmorenci 900 ○
Mount Pleasant CHAS 15,660
Mullins 6,068
Murrells Inlet 2,410
Myrtle Beach 18,446
Neeses 557
Newberry 9,866
New Ellenton 2,628
Nichols 606
Ninety Six 2,249
Norris 903
North 1,304
North Augusta AUG 13,593
North Charleston CHAS 62,504
North Myrtle Beach 3,960
Norway 518
Olanta 699
Orangeburg 14,933
Pacolet 1,556
Pacolet Mills 1,051
Pageland 2,720
Pamplico 1,213
Pawleys Island 2,200 ○
Pelham 450 ○
Pendleton AND 3,154
Pickens 3,199
Piedmont GRNV 2,992
Pinewood 689
Pinopolis 500 ○
Port Royal 2,977
Prosperity 803
Ravenel CHAS 1,655
Reidville GRNV 460 ○
Ridgeland 1,143
Ridge Spring 969
Ridgeville 603
ROCK HILL RKHL 35,327
Roebuck SPRT 1,083
St. Andrews CHAS 9,908
St. Andrews COL 20,245
St. George 2,134
St. Matthews 2,496
St. Stephen 1,850
Salley 584
Saluda 2,752
Sandy Springs AND 1,100 ○
Saxon SPRT 1,200 ○
Scranton 861
Seneca 7,436
Shannontown SUMT 7,900 ○
Simpsonville GRNV 9,037
Six Mile 470
Slater GRNV 1,000 ○
Socastee 1,082
Society Hill 848
South Congaree COL 2,113
SPARTANBURG SPRT 43,826
Springdale COL 2,985
Springfield 604
Startex SPRT 1,006
Sullivans Island CHAS 1,867
Summerton 1,173
Summerville CHAS 9,473
SUMTER SUMT 24,921
Surfside Beach 2,522
Swansea 888
Taylors GRNV 12,100 ○
Timmonsville 2,112
Travelers Rest GRNV 3,017
Turbeville 549
Union 10,523
Valencia Heights COL 4,786
Varnville 1,948
Vaucluse 450 ○
Wagener 903
Walhalla 3,977
Walterboro 6,209
Wando Woods CHAS 5,253
Ware Shoals 2,370
Warrenville 1,029
Watts Mills 1,324
Waylyn CHAS 2,400 ○
Welcome GRNV 6,922
Wellford SPRT 2,143
West Columbia COL 11,044
Westminster 3,114
West Pelzer 944
Whitmire 2,038
Whitney SPRT 1,800 ○
Williamston 4,310
Williston 3,173
Windy Hill FLO 1,622
Winnsboro 2,919
Winnsboro Mills 1,890
Woodfield COL 5,560 ○
Woodruff 5,171
Yemassee 789
York RKHL 6,412

COUNTIES

Abbeville 22,627
Aiken 105,630
Allendale 10,700
Anderson 133,235
Bamberg 18,118
Barnwell 19,868
Beaufort 65,364
Berkeley 94,745
Calhoun 12,206
Charleston 276,573
Cherokee 40,983
Chester 30,148
Chesterfield 38,161
Clarendon 27,464
Colleton 31,776
Darlington 62,717
Dillon 31,083
Dorchester 59,028
Edgefield 17,528
Fairfield 20,700
Florence 110,163
Georgetown 42,461
Greenville 287,895
Greenwood 57,847
Hampton 18,159
Horry 101,419
Jasper 14,504
Kershaw 39,015
Lancaster 53,361
Laurens 52,214
Lee 18,929
Lexington 140,353
McCormick 7,797
Marion 34,179
Marlboro 31,634
Newberry 31,242
Oconee 48,611
Orangeburg 82,276
Pickens 79,292
Richland 269,572
Saluda 16,136
Spartanburg 203,023
Sumter 88,243
Union 30,764
Williamsburg 38,226
York 106,720

SOUTH DAKOTA
1980 Census 690,768

CITIES

Aberdeen 25,851
Alcester 885
Alexandria 588
Arlington 991
Armour 819
Aurora 507
Avon 576
Baltic 679
Belle Fourche 4,692
Beresford 1,865
Big Stone City 672
Bison 457
Black Hawk RAP 1,608
Bowdle 644
Box Elder RAP 3,186
Brandon SXFL 2,589
Bridgewater 653
Bristol 445
Britton 1,590
Brookings 14,951
Buffalo 453
Burke 859
Canistota 626
Canton 2,886
Castlewood 557
Centerville 892
Chamberlain 2,258
Clark 1,351
Clear Lake 1,310
Colman 501
Colton 757
Corsica 644
Crooks 594
Custer 1,830
Deadwood 2,035
De Smet 1,237
Dupree 562
Edgemont 1,468
Elk Point 1,661
Elkton 632
Estelline 719
Eureka 1,360
Faith 576
Faulkton 981
Flandreau 2,114
Fort Pierre 1,789
Freeman 1,462
Froehlich Addition SXFL 750 ○
Garretson 963
Gettysburg 1,623
Gregory 1,503
Groton 1,230
Harrisburg 558
Hartford 1,207
Hayward Addition SXFL 725 ○
Herreid 570
Highmore 1,055
Hill City 535
Hot Springs 4,742
Hoven 615
Howard 1,169
Humboldt 487
Huron 13,000
Ipswich 1,153
Irene 523
Jefferson 592
Kadoka 832
Kimball 752
Lake Andes 1,029
Lake Preston 789
Lead 4,330
Lemmon 1,871
Lennox 1,827
Leola 645
McCook Lake SXCY 600 ○
McLaughlin 754
Madison 6,210
Marion 830
Martin 1,018
Menno 793
Milbank 4,120
Miller 1,931
Mission 748
Mitchell 13,916
Mobridge 4,174
Murdo 723
Newell 638
New Underwood 517
North Eagle Butte 1,354
North Sioux City SXCY 1,992
Norton Acres SXFL 800 ○
Onida 851
Parker 999
Parkston 1,545
Philip 1,088
Pierre 11,973
Pine Ridge 3,059
Plankinton 644
Platte 1,334
Presho 760
RAPID CITY RAP 46,492
Redfield 3,027
Rosebud 600 ○
Rosholt 446
St. Francis 766
Salem 1,486
Scotland 1,022
Selby 884
SIOUX FALLS SXFL 81,343
Sisseton 2,789
Spearfish 5,251
Springfield 1,377
Sturgis 5,184
Tabor 460
Tea 729
Timber Lake 660
Tripp 804
Tyndall 1,253
Valley Springs 801
Vermillion 10,136
Viborg 812
Volga 1,221
Wagner 1,453
Wall 770
Watertown 15,649
Waubay 675
Webster 2,417
Webster Grove SXFL 540 ○
Wessington Springs 1,203
White 474
White River 561
Whitewood 821
Wilmot 507
Winner 3,472
Woonsocket 799
Yankton 12,011

COUNTIES

Aurora 3,628
Beadle 19,195
Bennett 3,044
Bon Homme 8,059
Brookings 24,332
Brown 36,962
Brule 5,245
Buffalo 1,795
Butte 8,372
Campbell 2,243
Charles Mix 9,680
Clark 4,894
Clay 13,689
Codington 20,885
Corson 5,196
Custer 6,000
Davison 17,820
Day 8,133
Deuel 5,289
Dewey 5,366
Douglas 4,181
Edmunds 5,159
Fall River 8,439
Faulk 3,327
Grant 9,013
Gregory 6,015
Haakon 2,794
Hamlin 5,261
Hand 4,948
Hanson 3,415
Harding 1,700
Hughes 14,220
Hutchinson 9,350
Hyde 2,069
Jackson 3,437
Jerauld 2,929
Jones 1,463
Kingsbury 6,679
Lake 10,724
Lawrence 18,339
Lincoln 13,942
Lyman 3,864
McCook 6,444
McPherson 4,027
Marshall 5,404
Meade 20,717
Mellette 2,249
Miner 3,739
Minnehaha 109,435
Moody 6,692
Pennington 70,361
Perkins 4,700
Potter 3,674
Roberts 10,911
Sanborn 3,213
Shannon 11,323
Spink 9,201
Stanley 2,533
Sully 1,990
Todd 7,328
Tripp 7,268
Turner 9,255
Union 10,938
Walworth 7,011
Yankton 18,952
Ziebach 2,308

○ Rand McNally estimate (not reported in census).
▲ Population of entire township or "town", including rural areas.
● Independent city. Population not included in county total.

TENNESSEE

1980 Census 4,591,120

CITIES

City	Population
Adams	600
Adamsville	1,453
Alamo	2,615
Alcoa KNOX-	6,870
Alexandria	689
Algood	2,406
Allardt	654
Altamont	679
Ardmore	835
Ashland City NASH	2,329
Athens	12,080
Atoka MEM	691
Atwood	1,143
Bartlett MEM	18,599
Baxter	1,411
Beersheba Springs	643
Bell Buckle	450
Bells	1,571
Benton	1,115
Bethel Springs	873
Big Sandy	650
Blaine	1,147
Bloomingdale KNGSP	9,000 ○
Blountville KNGSP	2,554
Bluff City BRIS-	1,121
Bolivar	6,597
Bradford	1,146
Brentwood NASH	9,431
Briceville KNOX-	800 ○
Brighton	976
BRISTOL BRIS-	23,986
Brownsville	9,307
Bruceton	1,579
Bulls Gap	821
Burns	777
Byrdstown	884
Calhoun	590
Camden	3,279
Campaign	500 ○
Carson Spring	600 ○
Carthage	2,672
Caryville	2,039
Cedar Bluff Two KNOX-	2,000 ○
Celina	1,580
Centerville	2,824
Chapel Hill	861
Charleston	756
Charlotte	788
CHATTANOOGA CHTN	169,728
Church Hill KNGSP	4,110
CLARKSVILLE CLRKV	54,777
Cleveland	26,415
Clifton	773
Clinton KNOX-	5,785
Coalmont	625
Collierville MEM	7,839
Collinwood	1,064
Colonial Heights KNGSP	6,744
Columbia	26,571
Cookeville	20,535
Cornersville	722
Counce	600 ○
Covington	6,065
Cowan	1,790
Crab Orchard	1,065
Cross Plains	655
Crossville	6,394
Dandridge	1,383
Dayton	5,913
Decatur	1,069
Decaturville	1,004
Decherd	2,233
Dickson	7,040
Dover	1,197
Dresden	2,256
Ducktown	583
Dunlap	3,681
Dyer	2,442
Dyersburg	15,856
Eagleville	444
East Ridge CHTN	21,236
Elizabethton JNSC-	12,431
Elkton	540
Englewood	1,840
Erin	1,614
Erwin	4,739
Estill Springs	1,324
Ethridge	548
Etowah	3,758
Fairview NASH	3,648
Fall Branch KNGSP	1,340
Fayetteville	7,559
Finley	1,014
Franklin NASH	13,227
Friendship	763
Friendsville KNOX-	694
Gadsden	683
Gainesboro	1,119
Gallatin	17,191
Gallaway	804
Gates	729
Gatlinburg	3,210
Germantown MEM	22,431
Gibson	458
Gleason	1,335
Goodlettsville NASH	8,327
Gordonsville	893
Graysville	1,380
Greenback	546
Greenbrier NASH	3,180
Greeneville	14,097
Greenfield	2,109
Grimsley	600 ○
Halls	2,444
Hampton JNSC-	2,236
Harriman	8,303
Hartsville	2,674
Henderson	4,449
Hendersonville NASH	26,561
Henning	638
Hohenwald	3,922
Hollow Rock	955
Hornbeak	452
Humboldt	10,209
Huntingdon	3,962
Huntland	983
Huntsville	519
Iron City	482
Jacksboro	1,722
JACKSON JAC	49,258
Jamestown	2,364
Jasper	2,633
Jefferson City	5,612
Jellico	2,798
JOHNSON CITY JNSC-	43,617
Jonesboro JNSC-	2,829
Kenton	1,551
KINGSPORT KNGSP	32,027
Kingston KNOX-	4,441
Kingston Springs	1,017
KNOXVILLE KNOX-	175,045
Lafayette	3,808
La Follette	8,198
Lake City KNOX-	2,335
Lake Tansi	500 ○
La Vergne NASH	5,495
Lawrenceburg	10,184
Lebanon	11,872
Lenoir City KNOX-	5,777
Lewisburg	8,760
Lexington	5,934
Linden	1,087
Livingston	3,372
Lobelville	993
Loretto	1,612
Loudon	3,943
Luttrell	962
Lynchburg	668
Lynn Garden KNGSP	7,213
McEwen	1,352
McKenzie	5,405
McMinnville	10,683
Madisonville	2,884
Manchester	7,250
Martin	8,898
Maryville KNOX-	17,480
Mascot KNOX-	2,203
Mason	471
Maury City	989
Maynardville	924
Medina	687
MEMPHIS MEM	646,174
Michie	530
Middleton	596
Milan	8,083
Millington MEM	20,236
Minor Hill	564
Monteagle	1,126
Monterey	2,610
Morgantown	600 ○
Morrison	587
Morrison City KNGSP	2,032
Morristown	20,530
Moscow	499
Mosheim	1,539
Mountain City	2,125
Mount Juliet NASH	2,879
Mount Pleasant	3,375
Munford MEM	2,336
Murfreesboro	32,845
NASHVILLE NASH	455,651
Newbern	2,794
New Johnsonville	1,824
New Market	1,216
Newport	7,580
New Tazwell	1,677
Niota	765
Nolensville	500 ○
Norris KNOX-	1,374
Oakland	472
Oak Ridge KNOX-	27,662
Obion	1,282
Oliver Springs KNOX-	3,659
Oneida	3,494
Ooltewah CHTN	900 ○
Palmer	1,027
Paris	10,728
Parsons	2,422
Pegram NASH	1,081
Petersburg	681
Petros	1,286
Philadelphia	507
Pigeon Forge	1,822
Pikeville	2,085
Pittman Center	488
Portland	4,030
Pulaski	7,184
Puryear	624
Red Bank CHTN	13,129
Red Boiling Springs	1,173
Riceville	500 ○
Ridgely	1,932
Ripley	6,366
Roan Mountain	1,108
Robbins	450 ○
Rockford KNOX-	567
Rockwood	5,767
Rogersville	4,368
Russellville	1,069
Rutherford	1,378
Rutledge	1,058
St. Joseph	897
Sale Creek	900 ○
Samburg	465
Savannah	6,992
Scotts Hill	668
Selmer	3,979
Sevierville	4,556
Sewanee	2,298
Sharon	1,134
Shelbyville	13,530
Sherwood	450 ○
Signal Mountain CHTN	5,818
Smithville	3,839
Smyrna NASH	9,200
Sneedville	1,110
Soddy-Daisy CHTN	8,388
Somerville	2,264
South Fulton	2,735
South Pittsburg	3,636
Sparta	4,864
Spencer	1,126
Spring City	1,951
Springfield	10,814
Spring Hill	989
Stanton	540
Summitville	600 ○
Sunbright	500 ○
Surgoinsville	1,536
Sweetwater	4,725
Tazewell	2,090
Tellico Plains	698
Tennessee Ridge	1,325
Tiptonville	2,438
Tracy City	1,444
Trenton	4,601
Trezevant	921
Trimble	722
Troy	1,093
Tullahoma	15,800
Unicoi	600 ○
Union City	10,436
Vonore	528
Wartburg	761
Wartrace	540
Watertown	1,300
Waverly	4,405
Waynesboro	2,109
Westmoreland	1,754
Westover JAC	500 ○
White Bluff	2,055
White House	2,225
White Pine	1,900
Whiteville	1,270
Whitwell	1,783
Winchester	6,103
Woodbury	2,160

COUNTIES

County	Population
Anderson	67,346
Bedford	27,916
Benton	14,901
Bledsoe	9,478
Blount	77,770
Bradley	67,547
Campbell	34,923
Cannon	10,234
Carroll	28,285
Carter	50,205
Cheatham	21,616
Chester	12,727
Claiborne	24,595
Clay	7,676
Cocke	28,792
Coffee	38,311
Crockett	14,941
Cumberland	28,676
Davidson	477,811
Decatur	10,857
De Kalb	13,589
Dickson	30,037
Dyer	34,663
Fayette	25,305
Fentress	14,826
Franklin	31,983
Gibson	49,467
Giles	24,625
Grainger	16,751
Greene	54,422
Grundy	13,787
Hamblen	49,300
Hamilton	287,740
Hancock	6,887
Hardeman	23,873
Hardin	22,280
Hawkins	43,751
Haywood	20,318
Henderson	21,390
Henry	28,656
Hickman	15,151
Houston	6,871
Humphreys	15,957
Jackson	9,398
Jefferson	31,284
Johnson	13,745
Knox	319,694
Lake	7,455
Lauderdale	24,555
Lawrence	34,110
Lewis	9,700
Lincoln	26,483
Loudon	28,553
McMinn	41,878
McNairy	22,525
Macon	15,700
Madison	74,546
Marion	24,416
Marshall	19,698
Maury	51,095
Meigs	7,431
Monroe	28,700
Montgomery	83,342
Moore	4,510
Morgan	16,604
Obion	32,781
Overton	17,575
Perry	6,111
Pickett	4,358
Polk	13,602
Putnam	47,690
Rhea	24,235
Roane	48,425
Robertson	37,021
Rutherford	84,058
Scott	19,259
Sequatchie	8,605
Sevier	41,418
Shelby	777,113
Smith	14,935
Stewart	8,665
Sullivan	143,968
Sumner	85,790
Tipton	32,930
Trousdale	6,137
Unicoi	16,362
Union	11,707
Van Buren	4,728
Warren	32,653
Washington	88,755
Wayne	13,946
Weakley	32,896
White	19,567
Williamson	58,108
Wilson	56,064

TEXAS

1980 Census 14,227,574

CITIES

City	Population
Abernathy	2,904
ABILENE ABIL	98,315
Addison D-FW	5,553
Alamo MCAL	6,289
Alamo Heights SANT	6,252
Albany	2,450
Alice	20,961
Allen D-FW	8,314
Alpine	5,465
Alto	1,203
Alvarado	2,701
Alvin HOU	16,515
AMARILLO AMA	149,230
Anahuac	1,840
Andrews	11,061
Angleton FREP-	13,929
Anson	2,831
Anthony ELP	2,640
Aransas Pass CRPX	7,173
Archer City	1,862
Arlington D-FW	160,113
Arp	939
Asherton	1,574
Aspermont	1,357
Athens	10,197
Atlanta	6,272
AUSTIN AUS	345,890
Azle D-FW	6,097
Baird	1,696
Balch Springs D-FW	13,746
Ballinger	4,207
Bartlett	1,567
Bastrop	3,789
Bay City	17,837
Baytown HOU	56,923
BEAUMONT B-PA-O	118,102
Bedford D-FW	20,821
Beeville	14,574
Bellaire HOU	14,950
Bellmead WACO	7,569
Bellville	2,860
Belton TMPL	10,660
Benavides	1,978
Benbrook D-FW	13,579
Big Lake	3,404
Big Spring	24,804
Big Wells	939
Bishop	3,706
Bloomington	1,884
Blossom	1,487
Boerne SANT	3,229
Boling	850 ○
Bonham	7,338
Borger	15,837
Bowie	5,610
Brackettville	1,676
Brady	5,969
Brazoria FREP-	3,025
Breckenridge	6,921
Bremond	1,025
Brenham	10,966
Bridge City B-PA-O	7,667
Bridgeport	3,737
Brookshire	2,175
Brownfield	10,387
BROWNSVILLE BRNS	84,997
Brownwood	19,396
BRYAN BRY	45,917
Burkburnett WIFL	10,668
Burleson D-FW	11,734
Burnet	3,410
Caldwell	2,953
Calvert	1,732
Cameron	5,721
Canadian	3,491
Canton	2,845
Canutillo ELP	4,000 ○
Canyon	10,724
Canyon Lake	6,000 ○
Carrizo Springs	7,112
Carrollton D-FW	40,595
Carthage	6,447
Castroville SANT	1,821
Cedar Hill D-FW	6,849
Celina	1,520
Center	5,827
Centerville	799
Channelview HOU	17,471
Charlotte	1,443
Chico	890
Childress	5,817
Chillicothe	1,052
Chilton	650 ○
Cisco	4,517
Clarendon	2,220
Clarksville	4,917
Cleburne D-FW	19,218
Cleveland HOU	5,977
Clifton	3,063
Cloverleaf HOU	17,317
Clute FREP-	9,577
Cockrell Hill D-FW	3,262
Coleman	5,960
College Station BRY	37,272
Colleyville D-FW	6,700
Colorado City	5,405
Columbus	3,923
Comanche	4,075
Comfort	1,226
Commerce	8,136
Conroe HOU	18,034
Coolidge	810
Cooper	2,338
Copperas Cove KILL	19,469
CORPUS CHRISTI CRPX	231,134
Corrigan	1,770
Corsicana	21,712
Cotulla	3,912
Crandall	831
Crane	3,622
Crockett	7,405
Crosbyton	2,289
Cross Plains	1,240
Crowell	1,509
Crowley D-FW	5,852
Crystal City	8,334
Cuero	7,124
Daingerfield	3,030
Daisetta	1,177
Dalhart	6,854
DALLAS D-FW	904,078
Dawson	747
Dayton	4,908
Decatur	4,104
Deer Park HOU	22,648
De Kalb	2,217
De Leon	2,478
Del Rio	30,034
Denison SHRM-	23,884
Denton D-FW	48,063
Denver City	4,704
De Soto D-FW	15,538
Devine SANT	3,756
Diboll LUFK	5,227
Dickinson GLV-	7,505
Dilley	2,579
Dimmitt	5,019
Donna	9,952
Dublin	2,723
Dumas	12,194
Duncanville D-FW	27,781
Eagle Lake	3,921
Eagle Pass	21,407
Eastland	3,747
Edcouch	3,092
Eden	1,294
EDINBURG EDIN	26,013
Edna	5,650
El Campo	10,462
Eldorado	2,061
Electra	3,755
Elgin	4,535
EL PASO ELP	425,259
Elsa	5,061
Encinal	704
Ennis	12,110
Euless D-FW	24,002
Everman D-FW	5,387
Fabens	4,285
Fairfield	3,505
Falfurrias	6,103
Farmers Branch D-FW	24,863
Farmersville	2,360
Farwell	1,354
Ferris D-FW	2,228
Flatonia	1,070
Floresville	4,381
Floydada	4,193
Forest Hill D-FW	11,684
Forney D-FW	2,483
Fort Davis	950 ○
Fort Stockton	8,688
Fort Worth D-FW	385,164
Franklin	1,349
Frankston	1,255
Fredericksburg	6,412
FREEPORT FREP-	13,444
Freer	3,213
Friendswood HOU	10,719
Friona	3,809
Fritch	2,299
Gainesville	14,081
Galena Park HOU	9,879
GALVESTON GLV-	61,902
Garland D-FW	138,857
Gatesville	6,260
Georgetown	9,468
George West	2,627
Giddings	3,950
Gilmer	5,167
Gladewater LNGV	6,548
Glen Rose	2,075
Goldthwaite	1,783
Goliad	1,990
Gonzales	7,152
Gorman	1,258
Graham	9,170
Granbury	3,332
Grand Prairie D-FW	71,462
Grand Saline	2,709
Granger	1,236
Grapeland	1,634
Grapevine D-FW	11,801
Greater Richland Area D-FW	7,977
Greenville	22,161
Groesbeck	3,373
Groves B-PA-O	17,090
Groveton	1,262
Grulla	1,442
Hale Center	2,297
Hallettsville	2,865
Hallsville LNGV	1,556
Haltom City D-FW	29,014
Hamilton	3,189
Hamlin	3,248
Harker Heights KILL	7,345
HARLINGEN HRL	43,543
Haskell	3,782
Hearne	5,418
Hebbronville	4,684
Hemphill	1,353
Hempstead	3,456
Henderson	11,473
Henrietta	3,149
Hereford	15,853
Hewitt WACO	5,247
Hico	1,375
Highland Park D-FW	8,909
Highlands HOU	6,467
Hillsboro	7,397
Hitchcock GLV-	6,103
Hondo	6,057
Honey Grove	1,973

○ Rand McNally estimate (not reported in census).
▲ Population of entire township or "town", including rural areas.
● Independent city. Population not included in county total.

TEXAS continued

HOUSTON HOU 1,595,138
Hubbard 1,676
Humble HOU 7,588
Huntington LUFK 1,672
Huntsville 23,936
Hurst D-FW 31,420
Idalou LUB 2,348
Ingleside CRPX 5,436
Iowa Park WIFL 6,184
Iraan 1,358
Irving D-FW 109,943
Italy 1,306
Itasca 1,600
Jacinto City HOU 8,953
Jacksboro 4,000
Jacksonville 12,264
Jasper 6,959
Jefferson 2,643
Johnson City 872
Jones Creek FREP- 2,634
Jourdanton 2,743
Junction 2,593
Karnes City 3,296
Katy 5,660
Kaufman 4,658
Keene D-FW 3,013
Keller D-FW 4,156
Kemp 1,035
Kenedy 4,356
Kennedale D-FW 2,594
Kerens 1,582
Kermit 8,015
Kerrville 15,276
Kilgore 11,331
KILLEEN KILL 46,296
Kingsville 28,808
Kirby SANT 6,435
Kirbyville 1,972
Klein HOU 9,000 ○
Knox City 1,546
Kountze 2,716
Kyle 2,093
Ladonia 761
La Feria HRL 3,495
La Grange 3,768
Lake Jackson FREP- 19,102
La Marque GLV- 15,372
Lamesa 11,790
Lampasas 6,165
Lancaster D-FW 14,807
La Porte HOU 17,053
LAREDO LAR 91,449
League City HOU 16,578
Leakey 468
Lefors 829
Leonard 1,421
Leon Valley SANT 9,088
Levelland 13,809
Lewisville D-FW 24,273
Liberty 7,945
Lindale 2,180
Linden 2,443
Littlefield 7,409
Little Mexico 600 ○
Live Oak SANT 8,183
Livingston 4,928
Llano 3,071
Lockhart 7,953
Lockney 2,334
Lometa 666
LONGVIEW LNGV 62,762
Loraine 929
Lott 865
LUBBOCK LUB 173,979
LUFKIN LUFK 28,562
Luling 5,039
Lyford 1,618
Lytle SANT 1,920
Mabank 1,443
MCALLEN MCAL 66,281
McCamey 2,436
McGregor 4,513
McKinney D-FW 16,256
McLean 1,160
Madisonville 3,660
Malakoff 2,082
Mansfield D-FW 8,102
Marble Falls 3,252
Marfa 2,466
Marlin 7,099
Marshall 24,921
Mart 2,324
Mason 2,153
Matador 1,052
Mathis 5,667
Memphis 3,352
Menard 1,697
Mercedes 11,851
Meridian 1,330
Merkel 2,493
Mesquite D-FW 67,053
Mexia 7,094
MIDLAND MIDL 70,525
Midlothian D-FW 3,219
Miles 720
Mineola 4,346
Mineral Wells 14,468
Mission MCAL 22,653
Missouri City HOU 24,423
Monahans 8,397
Mont Belvieu HOU 1,730
Moody 1,385
Morton 2,674
Mount Pleasant 11,003
Mount Vernon 2,025
Muleshoe 4,842
Munday 1,738
Nacogdoches 27,149
Naples 1,908
Natalia SANT 1,264
Navasota 5,971
Nederland B-PA-O 16,855
Needville 1,417
New Boston 4,628
New Braunfels 22,402
Newcastle 688
Newton 1,620
Nixon 2,008
Nocona 2,992

North Richland Hills D-FW 30,592
Oakwood 606
Odem 2,363
ODESSA ODES 90,027
O'Donnell 1,200
Olmos Park SANT 2,069
Olney 4,060
Olton 2,235
Orange B-PA-O 23,628
Orange Grove 1,212
Overton 2,430
Ozona 3,766
Paducah 2,216
Palacios 4,667
Palestine 15,948
Pampa 21,396
Panhandle 2,226
Paris 25,498
Pasadena HOU 112,560
Pearland HOU 13,248
Pearsall 7,383
Pecos 12,855
Perryton 7,991
Pharr MCAL 21,381
Phillips 1,729
Pilot Point 2,211
Pineland 1,111
Pittsburg 4,245
Plainview 22,187
Plano D-FW 72,331
Pleasanton 6,346
Port Arthur B-PA-O 63,053
Port Isabel 3,769
Portland CRPX 12,023
Port Lavaca 10,911
Port Neches B-PA-O 13,944
Post 3,961
Poteet 3,086
Prairie View 3,993
Premont 2,984
Presidio 1,603
Quanah 3,890
Queen City 1,748
Quitman 1,893
Ralls 2,422
Ranger 3,142
Raymondville 9,493
Refugio 3,898
Richardson D-FW 72,496
Richmond HOU 10,526
Rio Grande City 8,930
Rio Hondo 1,673
Rising Star 1,204
River Oaks D-FW 6,890
Robinson WACO 6,074
Robstown CRPX 12,100
Roby 814
Rockdale 5,611
Rockport 3,686
Rocksprings 1,317
Rockwall D-FW 5,939
Rogers 1,242
Roma 3,384
Roscoe 1,628
Rosebud 2,076
Rosenberg HOU 17,840
Rotan 2,284
Round Rock AUS 12,740
Rowlett D-FW 7,522
Royse City D-FW 1,566
Rule 1,015
Runge 1,244
Rusk 4,681
Sabinal 1,827
St. Jo 1,071
SAN ANGELO SANG 73,240
SAN ANTONIO SANT 786,023
San Augustine 2,930
San Benito HRL 17,988
Sanderson 1,241
San Diego 5,225
Sanger 2,574
San Isidro 700 ○
San Juan MCAL 7,608
San Marcos 23,422
San Saba 2,847
Santa Anna 1,535
Schertz SANT 7,262
Schulenburg 2,469
Seabrook HOU 4,670
Seagoville D-FW 7,304
Seagraves 2,596
Sealy 3,875
Seguin 17,854
Seminole 6,080
Seymour 3,657
Shallowater LUB 1,932
Shamrock 2,834
SHERMAN SHRM- 30,413
Shiner 2,213
Silsbee 7,684
Sinton 6,044
Slaton LUB 6,804
Smithville 3,470
Snyder 12,705
Somerville 1,814
Sonora 3,856
Sour Lake 1,807
South Houston HOU 13,293
Southside Place HOU 1,366
Spearman 3,413
Spring HOU 3,000 ○
Spur 1,690
Stamford 4,542
Stanton 2,314
Stephenville 11,881
Sterling City 915
Stinnett 2,222
Stockdale 1,265
Stratford 1,917
Strawn 694
Sudan 1,091
Sugar Land HOU 8,826
Sulphur Springs 12,804
Sundown 1,511
Sunray 1,952
Sweeny 3,538
Sweetwater 12,242
Taft 3,686

Tahoka 3,262
Talco 751
Taylor 10,619
Teague 3,390
TEMPLE TMPL 42,354
Terrell D-FW 13,269
Terrell Hills SANT 4,644
TEXARKANA TEXR- 31,271
Texas City GLV- 41,201
The Colony D-FW 11,586
Thorndale 1,300
Thorntonville 717
Three Rivers 2,133
Throckmorton 1,174
Timpson 1,164
Trinidad 1,130
Trinity 2,620
Troup 1,911
Tulia 5,033
Turkey 644
TYLER TYL 70,508
Universal City SANT 10,720
University Park D-FW 22,254
Uvalde 14,178
Valley Mills 1,236
Van 1,881
Van Alstyne 1,860
Van Horn 2,772
Vernon 12,695
VICTORIA VICT 50,695
Vidor B-PA-O 12,464
WACO WACO 101,261
Waelder 942
Wallis 1,138
Watauga D-FW 10,284
Waxahachie D-FW 14,624
Weatherford D-FW 12,049
Weimar 2,128
Wellington 3,043
Weslaco 19,331
West 2,485
West Columbia FREP- 4,109
West University Place HOU 12,010
Wharton 9,033
Wheeler 1,584
Whitesboro 3,197
White Settlement D-FW 13,508
Whitewright 1,760
Whitney 1,631
WICHITA FALLS WIFL 94,201
Willis 1,674
Windcrest SANT 5,332
Wink 1,182
Winnsboro 3,458
Winters 3,061
Wolfe City 1,594
Woodsboro 1,974
Woodville 2,821
Woodway WACO 7,091
Wortham 1,187
Yoakum 6,148
Yorktown 2,498
Zapata 3,831

COUNTIES

Anderson 38,381
Andrews 13,323
Angelina 64,172
Aransas 14,260
Archer 7,266
Armstrong 1,994
Atascosa 25,055
Austin 17,726
Bailey 8,168
Bandera 7,084
Bastrop 24,726
Baylor 4,919
Bee 26,030
Bell 157,820
Bexar 988,971
Blanco 4,681
Borden 859
Bosque 13,401
Bowie 75,301
Brazoria 169,587
Brazos 93,588
Brewster 7,573
Briscoe 2,579
Brooks 8,428
Brown 33,057
Burleson 12,313
Burnet 17,803
Caldwell 23,637
Calhoun 19,574
Callahan 10,992
Cameron 209,727
Camp 9,275
Carson 6,672
Cass 29,430
Castro 10,556
Chambers 18,538
Cherokee 38,127
Childress 6,950
Clay 9,582
Cochran 4,825
Coke 3,196
Coleman 10,439
Collin 144,576
Collingsworth 4,648
Colorado 18,823
Comal 36,446
Comanche 12,617
Concho 2,915
Cooke 27,656
Coryell 56,767
Cottle 2,947
Crane 4,600
Crockett 4,608
Crosby 8,859
Culberson 3,315
Dallam 6,531
Dallas 1,556,390
Dawson 16,184
Deaf Smith 21,165
Delta 4,839
Denton 143,126
De Witt 18,903
Dickens 3,539

Dimmit 11,367
Donley 4,075
Duval 12,517
Eastland 19,480
Ector 115,374
Edwards 2,033
Ellis 59,743
El Paso 479,899
Erath 22,560
Falls 17,946
Fannin 24,285
Fayette 18,832
Fisher 5,891
Floyd 9,834
Foard 2,158
Fort Bend 130,962
Franklin 6,893
Freestone 14,830
Frio 13,785
Gaines 13,150
Galveston 195,738
Garza 5,336
Gillespie 13,532
Glasscock 1,304
Goliad 5,193
Gonzales 16,949
Gray 26,386
Grayson 89,796
Gregg 99,495
Grimes 13,580
Guadalupe 46,708
Hale 37,592
Hall 5,594
Hamilton 8,297
Hansford 6,209
Hardeman 6,368
Hardin 40,721
Harris 2,409,547
Harrison 52,265
Hartley 3,987
Haskell 7,725
Hays 40,594
Hemphill 5,304
Henderson 42,606
Hidalgo 283,323
Hill 25,024
Hockley 23,230
Hood 17,714
Hopkins 25,247
Houston 22,299
Howard 33,142
Hudspeth 2,728
Hunt 55,248
Hutchinson 26,304
Irion 1,386
Jack 7,408
Jackson 13,352
Jasper 30,781
Jeff Davis 1,647
Jefferson 250,938
Jim Hogg 5,168
Jim Wells 36,498
Johnson 67,649
Jones 17,268
Karnes 13,593
Kaufman 39,038
Kendall 10,635
Kenedy 543
Kent 1,145
Kerr 28,780
Kimble 4,063
King 425
Kinney 2,279
Kleberg 33,358
Knox 5,329
Lamar 42,156
Lamb 18,669
Lampasas 12,005
La Salle 5,514
Lavaca 19,004
Lee 10,952
Leon 9,594
Liberty 47,088
Limestone 20,224
Lipscomb 3,766
Live Oak 9,606
Llano 10,144
Loving 91
Lubbock 211,651
Lynn 8,605
McCulloch 8,735
McLennan 170,755
McMullen 789
Madison 10,649
Marion 10,360
Martin 4,684
Mason 3,683
Matagorda 37,828
Maverick 31,398
Medina 23,164
Menard 2,346
Midland 82,636
Milam 22,732
Mills 4,477
Mitchell 9,088
Montague 17,410
Montgomery 127,222
Moore 16,575
Morris 14,629
Motley 1,950
Nacogdoches 46,786
Navarro 35,323
Newton 13,254
Nolan 17,359
Nueces 268,215
Ochiltree 9,588
Oldham 2,283
Orange 83,838
Palo Pinto 24,062
Panola 20,724
Parker 44,609
Parmer 11,038
Pecos 14,618
Polk 24,407
Potter 98,637
Presidio 5,188
Rains 4,839
Randall 75,062
Reagan 4,135

Real 2,469
Red River 16,101
Reeves 15,801
Refugio 9,289
Roberts 1,187
Robertson 14,653
Rockwall 14,528
Runnels 11,872
Rusk 41,382
Sabine 8,702
San Augustine 8,785
San Jacinto 11,434
San Patricio 58,013
San Saba 5,841
Schleicher 2,820
Scurry 18,192
Shackelford 3,915
Shelby 23,084
Sherman 3,174
Smith 128,366
Somervell 4,154
Starr 27,266
Stephens 9,926
Sterling 1,206
Stonewall 2,406
Sutton 5,130
Swisher 9,723
Tarrant 860,880
Taylor 110,932
Terrell 1,595
Terry 14,581
Throckmorton 2,053
Titus 21,442
Tom Green 84,784
Travis 419,573
Trinity 9,450
Tyler 16,223
Upshur 28,595
Upton 4,619
Uvalde 22,441
Val Verde 35,910
Van Zandt 31,426
Victoria 68,807
Walker 41,789
Waller 19,798
Ward 13,976
Washington 21,998
Webb 99,258
Wharton 40,242
Wheeler 7,137
Wichita 121,082
Wilbarger 15,931
Willacy 17,495
Williamson 76,521
Wilson 16,756
Winkler 9,944
Wise 26,575
Wood 24,697
Yoakum 8,299
Young 19,083
Zapata 6,628
Zavala 11,666

UTAH

1980 Census 1,461,037

CITIES

Alpine 2,649
American Fork PRVO 13,524
Annabella 463
Aurora 874
Ballard 558
Bear River City 540
Beaver 1,792
Belmont Heights 600 ○
Bennion S.L.C. 950 ○
Blanding 3,118
Bluffdale S.L.C. 1,300
Bountiful S.L.C. 32,877
Brigham City 15,596
Carbonville 500 ○
Castle Dale 1,910
Cedar City 10,972
Centerfield 653
Centerville S.L.C. 8,069
Circleville 445
Clarkston 562
Clearfield OGD 17,982
Cleveland 522
Clinton OGD 5,777
Coalville 1,031
Copperton 850 ○
Corinne 512
Cottonwood S.L.C. 11,554
Cottonwood Heights S.L.C. 18,000 ○
Delta 1,930
Draper S.L.C. 5,521
Duchesne 1,677
East Carbon 1,942
Eastwood Hills S.L.C. 1,200 ○
Elsinore 612
Elwood 481
Enoch 678
Enterprise 905
Ephraim 2,810
Escalante 652
Eureka 670
Fairview 916
Farmington S.L.C. 4,691
Ferron 1,718
Fillmore 2,083
Fountain Green 578
Fruit Heights OGD 2,728
Garland 1,405
Genola 630
Glenwood 447
Goshen 582
Granite 650 ○
Granite Park S.L.C. 5,554
Grantsville 4,419
Green River 1,048
Gunnison 1,255
Harrisville OGD 1,371
Heber City 4,362

○ Rand McNally estimate (not reported in census).
▲ Population of entire township or "town", including rural areas.
● Independent city. Population not included in county total.

Helper 2,724
Henefer 547
Herriman 600 ○
Highland PRVO 2,435
Highlands 500 ○
Hildale 1,009
Hinckley 464
Holladay S.L.C. 22,189
Honeyville 915
Huntington 2,316
Huntsville 577
Hurricane 2,361
Hyde Park LOGN 1,495
Hyrum LOGN 3,952
Ivins 600
Kamas 1,064
Kanab 2,148
Kaysville OGD 10,250
Kearns S.L.C. 21,353
Lark 500 ○
La Verkin 1,174
Layton OGD 26,393
Lehi PRVO 6,848
Levan 453
Lewiston 1,438
Lindon PRVO 2,796
LOGAN LOGN 26,844
Maeser 2,216
Magna S.L.C. 13,138
Manti 2,080
Mantua 484
Mapleton PRVO 2,726
Mendon 663
Midvale S.L.C. 10,146
Midway 1,194
Milford 1,293
Millcreek S.L.C. 24,150
Millville LOGN 848
Minersville 552
Moab 5,333
Mona 536
Monroe 1,476
Monticello 1,929
Morgan 1,896
Moroni 1,086
Mount Olympus S.L.C. 6,068
Mount Pleasant 2,049
Murray S.L.C. 25,750
Myton 500
Naples 1,502
Neola 550 ○
Nephi 3,285
Newton 623
Nibley LOGN 1,036
North Logan LOGN 2,258
North Ogden OGD 9,309
North Salt Lake S.L.C. 5,548
Oakley 470
OGDEN OGD 64,407
Orangeville 1,309
Orem PRVO 52,399
Panguitch 1,343
Paradise 542
Park City 2,823
Park Terrace S.L.C. 850 ○
Parowan 1,836
Payson PRVO 8,246
Perry 1,084
Peruvian Park S.L.C. 600 ○
Plain City OGD 2,379
Pleasant Grove PRVO 10,833
Price 9,086
Providence LOGN 2,675
PROVO PRVO 74,108
Randolph 659
Redmond 619
Redwood S.L.C. 2,000 ○
Richfield 5,482
Richmond 1,705
Riverdale OGD 6,031
River Heights LOGN 1,211
Riverton S.L.C. 7,293
Roosevelt 3,842
Roy OGD 19,694
St. George 13,146
Salem PRVO 2,233
Salina 1,992
SALT LAKE CITY S.L.C. 163,034
Sandy S.L.C. 52,210
Santa Clara 1,091
Santaquin 2,175
Smithfield LOGN 4,993
South Jordan S.L.C. 7,492
South Ogden OGD 11,366
South Salt Lake S.L.C. 10,413
Spanish Fork PRVO 9,825
Spring City 671
Spring Glen 800 ○
Springville PRVO 12,101
Sunnyside 611
Sunset OGD 5,733
Syracuse OGD 3,702
Taylorsville S.L.C. 17,448
Tooele 14,335
Tremonton 3,464
Trenton 447
Union S.L.C. 3,100 ○
Val Verda S.L.C. 6,422
Vernal 6,600
Washington 3,092
Washington Terrace OGD 8,212
Wellington 1,406
Wellsville 1,952
Wendover 1,099
West Bountiful S.L.C. 3,556
West Jordan S.L.C. 27,315
West Point OGD 2,170
West Valley City S.L.C. 72,509
White City S.L.C. 7,267
Willard 1,241
Woods Cross S.L.C. 4,263

COUNTIES

Beaver 4,378
Box Elder 33,222
Cache 57,176
Carbon 22,179
Daggett 769
Davis 146,540
Duchesne 12,565
Emery 11,451
Garfield 3,673
Grand 8,241
Iron 17,349
Juab 5,530
Kane 4,024
Millard 8,970
Morgan 4,917
Piute 1,329
Rich 2,100
Salt Lake 619,066
San Juan 12,253
Sanpete 14,620
Sevier 14,727
Summit 10,198
Tooele 26,033
Uintah 20,506
Utah 218,106
Wasatch 8,523
Washington 26,065
Wayne 1,911
Weber 144,616

VERMONT

1980 Census 511,456

CITIES

Alburg 1,352▲ 496
Arlington 2,184▲ 800 ○
Barre MTPLR- 9,824
Barton 2,990▲ 1,062
Bellows Falls 3,456
Bennington 15,815▲ 9,349
Bethel 1,715▲ 1,016
Bomoseen RUTL 500 ○
Bradford 2,191▲ 831
Brandon 4,194▲ 1,925
Brattleboro 8,596
Bristol 3,293▲ 1,793
BURLINGTON BUR 37,712
Castleton RUTL 3,637▲ 600 ○
Center Rutland RUTL 475 ○
Chelsea 1,091▲ 500 ○
Chester 2,791▲ 500 ○
Chester Depot 500 ○
Danville 1,705▲ 450 ○
Derby 4,222▲ 598
Derby Line 874
Dorset 1,648▲ 550 ○
East Arlington 600 ○
East Barre MTPLR- 900 ○
East Middlebury 550 ○
East Montpelier 2,205▲ 600 ○
East Poultney 450 ○
Enosburg Falls 1,207
Essex BUR 14,392▲ 800 ○
Essex Junction BUR 7,033
Fair Haven 2,819
Forest Dale 500 ○
Gilman 550 ○
Graniteville MTPLR- 1,800 ○
Groton 667▲ 440 ○
Hardwick 2,613▲ 1,476
Hartford 7,963▲ 600 ○
Hartland 2,396▲ 500 ○
Hyde Park 2,021▲ 475
Hydeville RUTL 500 ○
Island Pond 1,216
Jeffersonville 491
Jericho BUR 3,575▲ 1,340
Johnson 2,581▲ 1,393
Ludlow 2,414▲ 1,352
Lyndonville 1,401
Manchester 3,261▲ 563
Manchester Center 1,719
Middlebury 7,574▲ 5,591
Milton BUR 6,829▲ 1,411
MONTPELIER MTPLR- 8,241
Morrisville 2,074
Newport 4,756
North Bennington 1,685
North Clarendon RUTL 500 ○
Northfield MTPLR- 5,435▲ 2,033
Northfield Falls MTPLR- 600 ○
North Springfield 750 ○
North Troy 717
Norwich 2,398▲ 1,000 ○
Orleans 983
Pittsford 2,590▲ 666
Plainfield MTPLR- 1,249▲ 599
Poultney 3,196▲ 1,554
Proctor RUTL 1,998
Putney 1,850▲ 1,100 ○
Quechee 500 ○
Randolph 4,689▲ 2,217
Richford 2,206▲ 1,471
Richmond BUR 3,159▲ 865
Riverton MTPLR- 500 ○
Rochester 1,054▲ 500 ○
RUTLAND RUTL 18,436
St. Albans 7,308
St. Johnsbury 7,938▲ 7,150
St. Johnsbury Center 450 ○
Saxtons River 593
Shaftsbury 3,001▲ 700 ○
South Barre MTPLR- 1,301
South Burlington BUR 10,679
South Royalton 700 ○
South Ryegate 450 ○
Springfield 10,190▲ 5,603
Stamford 773▲ 500 ○
Stowe 2,991▲ 531
Swanton 5,141▲ 2,520
Vergennes 2,273
Wallingford 1,893▲ 1,141
Warren 956▲ 500 ○
Waterbury 4,465▲ 1,892
Waterbury Center 500 ○
Websterville MTPLR- 600 ○
West Pawlet 500 ○
West Rutland RUTL 2,351
White River Junction 2,582
Wilder 1,461
Williamstown MTPLR- 2,284▲ 650 ○
Wilmington 1,808▲ 545 ○
Winooski BUR 6,318
Woodstock 3,214▲ 1,178

COUNTIES

Addison 29,406
Bennington 33,345
Caledonia 25,808
Chittenden 115,534
Essex 6,313
Franklin 34,788
Grand Isle 4,613
Lamoille 16,767
Orange 22,739
Orleans 23,440
Rutland 58,347
Washington 52,393
Windham 36,933
Windsor 51,030

VIRGINIA

1980 Census 5,346,797

CITIES

Abingdon 4,318
Accomac 522
Alexandria● WASH 103,217
Altavista 3,849
Amelia Court House 600 ○
Amherst LYNCH 1,135
Annalee Heights WASH 1,750 ○
Annandale 31,000 ○
Appalachia 2,418
Appomattox 1,345
Arlington WASH 152,599
Arvonia 700 ○
Ashland RICH 4,640
Atkins 1,352
Austinville 800 ○
Baileys Crossroads WASH 4,600 ○
Bassett MRTNV 2,034
Bedford● 5,991
Belle Haven 589
Belle View WASH 3,500 ○
Bellwood RICH 950 ○
Bensley RICH 3,400 ○
Berryville 1,752
Big Stone Gap 4,748
Blacksburg 30,638
Blackstone 3,624
Bland 450 ○
Bluefield 5,946
Blue Ridge ROAN 2,347
Boissevain 980 ○
Bon Air RICH 16,224
Bowling Green 665
Boydton 486
Boykins 791
Bridgewater 3,289
BRISTOL● BRIS- 19,042
Broadway 1,234
Brodnax 492
Brookfield WASH 2,600 ○
Brookneal 1,454
Broyhill Park WASH 3,600 ○
Buchanan 1,205
Bucknell Manor WASH 2,300 ○
Buena Vista● 6,717
Burke WASH 21,000 ○
Burkeville 606
Callao 450 ○
Cape Charles 1,512
Castlewood 2,420
Cave Spring ROAN 15,200 ○
Centreville WASH 4,000 ○
Chantilly WASH 3,600 ○
Chapel Square WASH 2,000 ○
Charlotte Court House 568
CHARLOTTESVILLE● CHRLTV 39,916
Chase City 2,749
Chatham 1,390
Cheriton 695
Chesapeake● NORF- 114,486
Chester RICH 11,728
Chilhowie 1,265
Chincoteague 1,607
Christiansburg 10,345
Clarksville 1,468
Clifton Forge● 5,046
Clinchco 1,500 ○
Clintwood 1,369
Cloverdale ROAN 850 ○
Coeburn 2,625
Collinsville MRTNV 7,517
Colonial Beach 2,474
Colonial Heights● PET- 16,509
Courtland 976
Covington● 9,063
Craigsville 845
Crewe 2,325
Crozet 2,553
Culpeper 6,621
Dahlgren 575 ○
Dale City WASH 33,127
Damascus 1,330
Dante 1,083
DANVILLE● DANV 45,642
Dayton 1,017
Deltaville 1,082
Dillwyn 596
Drakes Branch 617
Dublin 2,368
Dumfries WASH 3,214
Dunn Loring Woods WASH 2,800 ○
Edinburg 752
Elkton 1,520
Elliston 800 ○
Emporia● 4,840
Engleside WASH 24,058
Ewing 500 ○
Exmore 1,300
Fairfax● WASH 20,537
Fairlawn 1,405
Falls Church● WASH 9,515
Falmouth 1,500 ○
Farmville 6,067
Ferrum 500 ○
Ferry Farms 1,600 ○
Fieldale MRTNV 1,190
Fishersville 700 ○
Franklin● 7,308
Fredericksburg● 15,322
Fries 758
Front Royal 11,126
Gainesville WASH 600 ○
Galax● 6,524
Gate City KNGSP 2,494
Glade Spring 1,722
Glasgow 1,259
Glen Allen RICH 2,300 ○
Glenwood DANV 2,276
Glenwood Farms RICH 3,300 ○
Gloucester 900 ○
Gloucester Point NN-H 2,500 ○
Goochland 450 ○
Gordonsville 1,421
Grafton NN-H 900 ○
Greenbriar WASH 6,200 ○
Gretna 1,255
Grindall Creek RICH 1,900 ○
Grottoes 1,369
Groveton WASH 6,300 ○
Groveton Gardens WASH 2,600 ○
Grundy 1,699
Halifax 772
Hamilton 598
Hampton● NN-H 122,617
Harrisonburg● 24,655
Hayfield WASH 2,300 ○
Herndon WASH 11,449
Highland Springs RICH 7,900 ○
Hillsville 2,123
Hollins ROAN 12,295
Honaker 1,475
Hopewell● PET- 23,397
Hurt 1,481
Hybla Valley WASH 4,000 ○
Independence 1,112
Iron Gate 620
Irvington 567
Ivanhoe 600 ○
Jarratt 614
Jefferson Manor WASH 2,300 ○
Jefferson Village WASH 2,500 ○
Jewell Ridge 600 ○
Jonesville 874
Kenbridge 1,539
Keysville 704
Kilmarnock 945
Kings Park WASH 6,000 ○
Kings Park West WASH 6,000 ○
La Crosse 734
Lake Barcroft WASH 1,800 ○
Lake Ridge WASH 11,072
Lakeside RICH 11,400 ○
Laurel RICH 3,000 ○
Lawrenceville 1,484
Lebanon 3,206
Leesburg WASH 8,357
Lexington● 7,292
Loch Lomond WASH 3,608
Louisa 932
Lovettsville 613
Lovingston 550 ○
Lowmoor 800 ○
Luray 3,584
LYNCHBURG● LYNCH 66,743
McKenney 473
McLean WASH 24,000 ○
Madison Heights LYNCH 14,146
Manassas● WASH 15,438
Manassas Park● WASH 6,524
Mantua Hills WASH 1,600 ○
Marion 7,287
Marlboro RICH 950 ○
Marshall 600 ○
MARTINSVILLE● MRTNV 18,149
Mathews 650 ○
Matoaca PET- 1,967
Max Meadows 550 ○
Meadowview 950 ○
Mechanicsville RICH 2,969
Merrifield WASH 7,525
Middleburg 619
Middletown 841
Midlothian RICH 1,000 ○
Milford 500 ○
Montrose RICH 3,400 ○
Montross 456
Montvale 450 ○
Monument Heights RICH 3,100 ○
Mount Jackson 1,419
Mount Sidney 550 ○
Narrows 2,516
Nassawadox 630
Newington WASH 2,500 ○
New Market 1,118
NEWPORT NEWS● NN-H 144,903
Nickelsville 464
NORFOLK● NORF- 266,979
North Springfield WASH 7,000 ○
Norton● 4,757
Oakton WASH 12,500 ○
Onancock 1,461
Onley 526
Orange 2,631
Parksley 979
Parrott 525 ○
Pearisburg 2,128
Pembroke 1,302
Pennington Gap 1,716
PETERSBURG● PET- 41,055
Pimmit Hills WASH 6,658
Pocahontas 708
Poquoson● NN-H 8,726
Portsmouth● NORF- 104,577
Pound 1,086
Pulaski 10,106
Purcellville 1,567
Quail Oaks RICH 2,000 ○
Quantico WASH 621
Radford● 13,456
Raven 4,000
Reedville 500 ○
Reston WASH 36,407
Rich Creek 746
Richlands 5,796
RICHMOND● RICH 219,214
Ridgeway MRTNV 858
Riverdale 500 ○
ROANOKE● ROAN 100,220
Rocky Mount 4,198
Rose Hill WASH 5,600 ○
Rose Hill 800 ○
Rural Retreat 1,083
Rushmere 1,070
Rustburg LYNCH 600 ○
St. Paul 973
Salem● ROAN 23,958
Saltville 2,376
Sandston RICH 4,500 ○
Seaford NN-H 2,500 ○
Sedley 500 ○
Shenandoah 1,861
Smithfield NORF- 3,718
South Boston● 7,093
South Hill 4,347
Springfield WASH 12,500 ○
Stafford WASH 650 ○
Stanley 1,204
Stanleytown MRTNV 1,761
Staunton● 21,857
Stephens City 1,179
Sterling WASH 16,080
Stonega 450 ○
Strasburg 2,311
Stratford Landing WASH 2,800 ○
Stuart 1,131
Stuarts Draft 1,776
Suffolk● NORF- 47,621
Sugar Grove 1,027
Sugarland Run WASH 6,258
Sugar Loaf ROAN 6,500 ○
Tangier 771
Tappahannock 1,821
Tazewell 4,468
Timberlake LYNCH 8,700 ○
Timberville 1,510
Toano 750 ○
Trammel 500 ○
Triangle WASH 4,770
Troutville ROAN 496
Urbanna 518
Vansant 2,708
Varina RICH 2,000 ○
Victoria 2,004
Vienna WASH 15,469
Vinton ROAN 8,027
Virginia Beach● NORF- 262,199
Wakefield 1,355
Warrenton WASH 3,907
Warsaw 771
Waverly 2,284
Waynesboro● 15,329
Waynewood WASH 5,000 ○
Weber City KNGSP 1,543
Westham RICH 3,600 ○
West Point 2,726
West Springfield WASH 18,000 ○
Williamsburg● 9,870
Willston WASH 2,800 ○
Winchester● 20,217
Windsor 985
Wise 3,894
Woodbridge WASH 24,004
Woodlawn 1,689
Woodstock 2,627
Wytheville 7,135

COUNTIES

Accomack 31,268
Albemarle 55,783
Alleghany 14,333
Amelia 8,405
Amherst 29,122
Appomattox 11,971
Arlington 152,599
Augusta 53,732
Bath 5,860
Bedford 34,927
Bland 6,349
Botetourt 23,270
Brunswick 15,632
Buchanan 37,989
Buckingham 11,751
Campbell 45,424
Caroline 17,904
Carroll 27,270
Charles City 6,692
Charlotte 12,266
Chesterfield 141,372
Clarke 9,965
Craig 3,948
Culpeper 22,620
Cumberland 7,881
Dickenson 19,806
Dinwiddie 22,602
Essex 8,864
Fairfax 595,754
Fauquier 35,889
Floyd 11,563
Fluvanna 10,244
Franklin 35,740
Frederick 34,150
Giles 17,810
Gloucester 20,107
Goochland 11,761
Grayson 16,579
Greene 7,625
Greensville 10,903
Halifax 30,599
Hanover 50,398
Henrico 180,735
Henry 57,654
Highland 2,937
Isle of Wight 21,603
James City 22,763
King and Queen 5,968
King George 10,543

○ Rand McNally estimate (not reported in census).
▲ Population of entire township or "town", including rural areas.
● Independent city. Population not included in county total.

King William 9,334
Lancaster 10,129
Lee 25,956
Loudoun 57,427
Louisa 17,825
Lunenburg 12,124
Madison 10,232
Mathews 7,995
Mecklenburg 29,444
Middlesex 7,719
Montgomery 63,285
Nelson 12,204
New Kent 8,781
Northampton 14,625
Northumberland 9,828
Nottoway 14,666
Orange 18,063
Page 19,401
Patrick 17,647
Pittsylvania 66,147
Powhatan 13,062
Prince Edward 16,456
Prince George 25,733
Prince William 144,703
Pulaski 35,229
Rappahannock 6,093
Richmond 6,952
Roanoke 72,945
Rockbridge 17,911
Rockingham 52,054
Russell 31,761
Scott 25,068
Shenandoah 27,559
Smyth 33,345
Southampton 18,731
Spotsylvania 34,435
Stafford 40,470
Surry 6,046
Sussex 10,874
Tazewell 50,511
Warren 21,200
Washington 46,487
Westmoreland 14,041
Wise 43,863
Wythe 25,522
York 35,463

WASHINGTON

1980 Census 4,132,204

CITIES

Aberdeen 18,739
Albion 631
Algona SEAT- 1,467
Allyn 900 ○
Anacortes 9,013
Arlington SEAT- 3,282
Asotin LEW 943
Auburn SEAT- 26,417
Bainbridge Island Winslow SEAT- 2,196
Battle Ground POR 2,774
Belfair 450 ○
Bellevue SEAT- 73,903
BELLINGHAM BELNG 45,794
Benton City 1,980
Bingen 644
Black Diamond SEAT- 1,170
Blaine 2,363
Bonney Lake SEAT- 5,328
Bothell SEAT- 5,345
BREMERTON BREM 36,208
Brewster 1,337
Bridgeport 1,174
Brinnon 600 ○
Bryn Mawr SEAT- 1,500 ○
Buckley SEAT- 3,143
Bucoda 519
Buena 800 ○
Burbank 700 ○
Burien SEAT- 18,000 ○
Burlington 3,894
Camas 5,681
Carbonado SEAT- 456
Carnation 913
Carson 950 ○
Cashmere 2,240
Castle Rock 2,162
Cathlamet 635
Centralia 11,555
Central Park 2,709
Chehalis 6,100
Chelan 2,802
Cheney 7,630
Chewelah 1,888
Chico BREM 750 ○
Chimacum 600 ○
Chinook 650 ○
Clallam Bay 600 ○
Clarkston LEW 6,903
Clearlake 900 ○
Cle Elum 1,773
Clinton SEAT- 2,000 ○
Colfax 2,780
College Place 5,771
Colville 4,510
Concrete 592
Connell 1,981
Copalis Beach 900 ○
Cosmopolis 1,575
Coulee City 510
Coulee Dam 1,412
Country Homes SPOK 4,000 ○
Coupeville 1,006
Custer 500 ○
Darrington 1,064
Davenport 1,559
Dayton 2,565
Deer Park 2,140
Deming 450 ○
Des Moines SEAT- 9,456
Dishman SPOK 10,169
Du Pont SEAT- 559
Eastgate SEAT- 8,341
East Olympia OLYM 700 ○
Eastsound 900 ○
East Wenatchee 1,640
Eatonville 998
Edgewood SEAT- 1,800 ○
Edmonds SEAT- 27,679
Ellensburg 11,752
Elma 2,720
Entiat 445
Enumclaw SEAT- 5,427
Ephrata 5,359
Everett SEAT- 54,413
Everson 898
Fairfield 582
Fall City 1,528
Federal Way SEAT- 16,872
Ferndale BELNG 3,855
Fircrest SEAT- 5,477
Fords Prairie 2,582
Forks 3,060
Friday Harbor 1,200
Fruitvale YAK 3,967
Garfield 599
Gig Harbor SEAT- 2,429
Gold Bar 794
Goldendale 3,575
Grand Coulee 1,180
Grandview 5,615
Granger 1,812
Granite Falls SEAT- 911
Grapeview 500 ○
Grayland 600 ○
Greenacres SPOK 3,900 ○
Hadlock 1,752
Harrington 507
Hazel Dell POR 5,500 ○
Hoodsport 900 ○
Hoquiam 9,719
Ilwaco 604
Ione 594
Issaquah SEAT- 5,536
Kalama 1,216
Kelso LNGV 11,129
Kenmore SEAT- 7,281
Kennewick P-K-R 36,756
Kennydale SEAT- 2,000 ○
Kent SEAT- 22,961
Kettle Falls 1,087
Kirkland SEAT- 18,779
Kittitas 782
Klickitat 700 ○
Lacey OLYM 13,940
La Conner 633
Lakes District SEAT- 54,533
Lake Stevens SEAT- 1,660
Lakewood SEAT- 500 ○
Langley SEAT- 650
La Push 600 ○
Leavenworth 1,522
Lexington LNGV 1,907
Liberty Lake SPOK 1,599
Lind 567
Long Beach 1,199
Longbranch SEAT- 900 ○
LONGVIEW LNGV 31,052
Loon Lake 650 ○
Lyle 700 ○
Lynden 4,022
Lynnwood SEAT- 22,641
Mabton 1,248
McCleary 1,419
Manson 500 ○
Maple Valley 900 ○
Marysville SEAT- 6,257
Mead SPOK 1,650 ○
Medical Lake 3,600
Medina SEAT- 3,220
Mercer Island SEAT- 21,522
Millwood SPOK 1,717
Milton SEAT- 3,162
Mineral 500 ○
Moclips 700 ○
Monroe SEAT- 2,869
Montesano 3,247
Morton 1,264
Moses Lake 10,629
Mossyrock 463
Mountlake Terrace SEAT- 16,534
Mount Vernon 13,009
Moxee City 687
Mukilteo SEAT- 1,426
Naches 644
Napavine 611
Naselle 900 ○
Neah Bay 1,200 ○
Newport 1,665
Newport Hills SEAT- 6,000 ○
Nordland 500 ○
North Bend 1,701
North City SEAT- 6,250 ○
Oakesdale 444
Oak Harbor 12,271
Oakville 537
Ocean City 500 ○
Ocean Park 1,500 ○
Odessa 1,009
Okanogan 2,326
Olalla BREM 450 ○
OLYMPIA OLYM 27,447
Omak 4,007
Onalaska 560 ○
Opportunity SPOK 21,241
Orchards POR 4,300 ○
Oroville 1,483
Orting SEAT- 1,787
Othello 4,454
Otis Orchards SPOK 4,100 ○
Pacific SEAT- 2,261
Pacific Beach 1,200 ○
Packwood 950 ○
Palouse 1,005
Parker 550 ○
Parkland SEAT- 23,355
Parkwater SPOK 4,850 ○
PASCO P-K-R 18,425
Pateros 555
Pe Ell 617
Peshastin 900 ○
Point Roberts 750 ○
Pomeroy 1,716
Port Angeles 17,311
Port Ludlow 500 ○
Port Orchard BREM 4,787
Port Townsend 6,067
Poulsbo BREM 3,453
Preston SEAT- 500 ○
Prosser 3,896
Pullman 23,579
Puyallup SEAT- 18,251
Quilcene 1,200 ○
Quincy 3,525
Rainier 891
Randle 600 ○
Ravensdale SEAT- 500 ○
Raymond 2,991
Reardan 498
Redmond SEAT- 23,318
Redondo 900 ○
Renton SEAT- 30,612
Republic 1,018
Richland P-K-R 33,578
Richmond Beach SEAT- 6,700 ○
Richmond Highlands SEAT- 24,463
Ridgecrest SEAT- 7,300 ○
Ridgefield POR 1,062
Ritzville 1,800
Riverton Heights SEAT- 14,182
Rochester 900 ○
Rockford 442
Rock Island 491
Rollingbay SEAT- 700 ○
Rosalia 572
Roslyn 938
Ruston SEAT- 612
St. John 529
Salmon Creek POR 1,900 ○
SEATTLE SEAT- 493,846
Seaview 500 ○
Sedro Woolley 6,110
Sekiu 600 ○
Selah YAK 4,500
Sequim 3,013
Shelton 7,629
Silverdale BREM 1,500 ○
Skyway SEAT- 8,500 ○
Snohomish SEAT- 5,294
Snoqualmie SEAT- 1,370
Soap Lake 1,196
South Bend 1,686
South Broadway YAK 3,500
South Cle Elum 449
South Colby BREM 500 ○
South Wenatchee 1,376
Spanaway SEAT- 8,868
SPOKANE SPOK 171,300
Sprague 473
Stanwood SEAT- 1,646
Startup 450 ○
Steilacoom SEAT- 4,886
Stevenson 1,172
Sultan SEAT- 1,578
Sumas 712
Sumner SEAT- 4,936
Sunnyside 9,225
Suquamish BREM 1,498
Tacoma SEAT- 158,501
Taholah 800 ○
Tekoa 854
Tenino 1,280
Tieton 528
Toledo 637
Tonasket 985
Toppenish 6,517
Town and Country SPOK 5,578
Tracyton BREM 2,304
Trout Lake 550 ○
Tukwila SEAT- 3,578
Tumwater OLYM 6,705
Twisp 911
Union Gap YAK 3,184
University Place SEAT- 20,381
Vancouver POR 42,834
Waitsburg 1,035
Walla Walla 25,618
Wapato 3,307
Warden 1,479
Washougal 3,834
Waterville 908
Wenatchee 17,257
Westport 1,954
White Center SEAT- 18,000 ○
White Salmon 1,853
White Swan 600 ○
Wilbur 1,122
Winlock 1,052
Wishram 675 ○
Woodland 2,341
Yacolt 544
YAKIMA YAK 49,826
Yelm 1,294
Zenith SEAT- 900 ○
Zillah 1,599

COUNTIES

Adams 13,267
Asotin 16,823
Benton 109,444
Chelan 45,061
Clallam 51,648
Clark 192,227
Columbia 4,057
Cowlitz 79,548
Douglas 22,144
Ferry 5,811
Franklin 35,025
Garfield 2,468
Grant 48,522
Grays Harbor 66,314
Island 44,048
Jefferson 15,965
King 1,269,749
Kitsap 147,152
Kittitas 24,877
Klickitat 15,822
Lewis 56,025
Lincoln 9,604
Mason 31,184
Okanogan 30,663
Pacific 17,237
Pend Oreille 8,580
Pierce 485,667
San Juan 7,838
Skagit 64,138
Skamania 7,919
Snohomish 337,720
Spokane 341,835
Stevens 28,979
Thurston 124,264
Wahkiakum 3,832
Walla Walla 47,435
Whatcom 106,701
Whitman 40,103
Yakima 172,508

WEST VIRGINIA

1980 Census 1,950,258

CITIES

Accoville 900 ○
Alderson 1,375
Alum Creek 500 ○
Amherstdale 800 ○
Anawalt 652
Ansted 1,952
Athens 1,147
Barboursville HNTG- 2,871
Barrackville FAIRM 1,815
Barrett 700 ○
Baxter FAIRM 500 ○
Bayard 540
Beaver BECK 1,122
BECKLEY BECK 20,492
Beech Bottom STU- 507
Belington 2,038
Belle CHAS 1,621
Belmont 887
Benwood WHL 1,994
Berkeley Springs 789
Berwind 500 ○
Bethany STU- 1,336
Beverly 475
Blennerhassett PRKB 3,537
Blue Creek 500 ○
Bluefield 16,060
Bluewell 2,752
Bolivar 672
Boomer 1,051
Bradley BECK 1,704
Bradshaw 750
Bramwell 989
Brenton 1,041
Bridgeport CLRKB 6,604
Brookhaven MORG 1,661
Brownton 600 ○
Buckhannon 6,820
Buffalo 1,034
Bunker Hill 500 ○
Bunker Hill CHAS 800 ○
Burnsville 531
Cabin Creek 900 ○
Cameron 1,474
Cannelton 500 ○
Caretta 850 ○
Carolina 650 ○
Cedar Grove CHAS 1,479
Ceredo HNTG- 2,255
Chapmanville 1,164
CHARLESTON CHAS 63,968
Charles Town 2,857
Charlton Heights 600 ○
Charmco 800 ○
Chattaroy 1,383
Chelyan CHAS 950 ○
Chesapeake CHAS 2,364
Chester E.LIV- 3,297
CLARKSBURG CLRKB 22,371
Clay 940
Clendenin CHAS 1,373
Clothier 600 ○
Coalwood 900 ○
Colliers STU- 600 ○
Cowen 723
Crab Orchard BECK 3,337
Craigsville 1,562
Cross Lanes CHAS 3,500 ○
Culloden CHAS 2,931
Cunard 450 ○
Danville 727
Davis 979
Davy 882
Deep Water 500 ○
Delbarton 981
Dellslow 700 ○
Despard CLRKB 1,434
Diamond 500 ○
Dixie 450 ○
Drybranch CHAS 500 ○
Dunbar CHAS 9,285
Dupont City CHAS 900 ○
East Bank CHAS 1,155
East Pea Ridge HNTG- 1,900 ○
East View CLRKB 1,222
Eccles BECK 1,162
Eckman 600 ○
Eleanor CHAS 1,282
Elizabeth 856
Elkins 8,536
Elkview CHAS 1,161
Enterprise 1,110
Ethel 900 ○
Fairlea 1,888
FAIRMONT FAIRM 23,863
Fairview 759
Farmington FAIRM 583
Fayetteville 2,366
Flemington CLRKB 452
Follansbee STU- 3,994
Fort Ashby CUMB 1,205
Fort Gay 886
Gary 2,233
Gassaway 1,225
Gauley Bridge 1,177
Gilbert 757
Glasgow CHAS 1,031
Glen Dale WHL 1,875
Glendale Heights WHL 700 ○
Glen Jean 900 ○
Glenville 2,155
Glen White 500 ○
Grafton 6,845
Grantsville 788
Grant Town FAIRM 987
Granville MORG 992
Great Cacapon 500 ○
Guthrie CHAS 600 ○
Hamlin 1,219
Handley CHAS 633
Harrisville 1,673
Hartford 556
Harvey 500 ○
Henderson 604
Henlawson 900 ○
Hico 700 ○
Hinton 4,622
Holden 1,500 ○
Hooverson Heights STU- 3,111
Hundred 485
HUNTINGTON HNTG- 63,684
Hurricane CHAS 3,751
Iaeger 833
Idamay 800 ○
Institute CHAS 1,500 ○
Jeffrey 900 ○
Jodie 450 ○
Julian 700 ○
Junior 591
Kearneysville 500 ○
Kenova HNTG- 4,454
Kermit 705
Keyser 6,569
Keystone 902
Kimball 871
Kimberly 700 ○
Kincaid 725 ○
Kingwood 2,877
Kistler 800 ○
Knollwood CHAS 700 ○
Lanark BECK 600 ○
Lansing 500 ○
Lester BECK 626
Lewisburg 3,065
Lilly Grove 600 ○
Logan 3,029
Longacre 450 ○
Lost Creek 604
Lumberport 939
Mabscott BECK 1,668
Mc Comas 800 ○
Mc Mechen WHL 2,402
Madison 3,228
Malden CHAS 950 ○
Mammoth CHAS 600 ○
Man 1,333
Mannington 3,036
Marlinton 1,352
Marlowe HAG- 700 ○
Marmet CHAS 2,196
Martinsburg 13,063
Mason 1,432
Masontown 1,052
Matewan 822
Matoaka 613
Maxwell Acres WHL 1,000 ○
Maybeury 800 ○
Meadow Bridge 530
Meadowbrook CLRKB 500 ○
Miami 500 ○
Middlebourne 941
Mill Creek 801
Milton HNTG- 2,178
Minden 950 ○
Monongah FAIRM 1,132
Montgomery 3,104
Moorefield 2,257
MORGANTOWN MORG 27,605
Moundsville WHL 12,419
Mount Clare 800 ○
Mount Gay 2,000 ○
Mount Hope 1,849
Mullens 2,919
Naoma 600 ○
Nettie 600 ○
New Cumberland STU- 1,752
Newell E.LIV- 2,032
New Haven 1,723
New Manchester STU- 600 ○
New Martinsville 7,109
Nitro CHAS 8,074
Nutter Fort CLRKB 2,078
Oak Hill 7,120
Oceana 2,143
Odd 550 ○
Omar 800 ○
Paden City 3,671
Page 600 ○
PARKERSBURG PRKB 39,946
Parsons 1,937
Paw Paw 644
Pennsboro 1,652
Petersburg 2,084
Peterstown 648
Philippi 3,194
Piedmont 1,491
Pineville 1,140
Piney View BECK 1,193
Poca CHAS 1,142
Pocatalico CHAS 2,450
Point Pleasant 5,682
Powellton 1,339
Pratt CHAS 821
Princeton 7,922
Prosperity BECK 1,298
Pursglove MORG 600 ○
Quinwood 460
Racine 650 ○
Rainelle 1,983
Raleigh BECK 800 ○
Rand CHAS 2,500 ○
Ranson 2,471
Ravenswood 4,126

○ Rand McNally estimate (not reported in census).
▲ Population of entire township or "town", including rural areas.
● Independent city. Population not included in county total.

Reader 700 ○
Red Jacket 850 ○
Reedsville 564
Rhodell 472
Richwood 3,568
Ridgeley CUMB 994
Ridgeview 500 ○
Ripley 3,464
Rivesville FAIRM 1,327
Roderfield 950 ○
Romney 2,094
Ronceverte 2,312
Rowlesburg 966
Rupert 1,276
St. Albans CHAS 12,402
St. Marys 2,219
Salem 2,706
Scarbro 500 ○
Seth 800 ○
Shady Spring BECK 1,786
Sharples 500 ○
Shepherdstown 1,791
Shinnston 3,059
Sissonville CHAS 900 ○
Sistersville 2,367
Smithers 1,482
Sophia BECK 1,216
South Charleston CHAS 15,968
Spelter 450 ○
Spencer 2,799
Sprague BECK 700 ○
Squire 800 ○
Stanaford BECK 2,016
Star City MORG 1,464
Stollings 950 ○
Stonewood CLRKB 2,058
Summersville 2,972
Sutton 1,192
Switzer 1,034
Tad CHAS 500 ○
Talcott 450 ○
Terra Alta 1,946
Thomas 747
Triadelphia WHL 1,461
Tunnelton 510
Tyler Heights CHAS 3,200 ○
Union 743
Valley Grove WHL 597
Vallscreek 900 ○
Van 500 ○
Verdunville 900 ○
Vienna PRKB 11,618
Wallace 900 ○
War 2,158
Wayne 1,495
Webster Springs 939
Weirton STU- 25,371
Welch 3,885
Wellsburg STU- 3,963
West Hamlin HNTG- 643
West Liberty WHL 744
Weston 6,250
Westover MORG 4,884
West Union 1,090
WHEELING WHL 43,070
White Sulphur Springs 3,371
Whitesville 689
Whitman 1,651
Wilkinson 700 ○
Williamson 5,219
Williamstown MRIET 3,095
Winfield CHAS 885
Winifrede CHAS 900 ○
Yukon 750 ○

COUNTIES

Barbour 16,639
Berkeley 46,775
Boone 30,447
Braxton 13,894
Brooke 31,117
Cabell 106,835
Calhoun 8,250
Clay 11,265
Doddridge 7,433
Fayette 57,863
Gilmer 8,334
Grant 10,210
Greenbrier 37,665
Hampshire 14,867
Hancock 41,053
Hardy 10,030
Harrison 77,710
Jackson 25,794
Jefferson 30,302
Kanawha 231,414
Lewis 18,813
Lincoln 23,675
Logan 50,679
McDowell 49,899
Marion 65,789
Marshall 41,608
Mason 27,045
Mercer 73,942
Mineral 27,234
Mingo 37,336
Monongalia 75,024
Monroe 12,873
Morgan 10,711
Nicholas 28,126
Ohio 61,389
Pendleton 7,910
Pleasants 8,236
Pocahontas 9,919
Preston 30,460
Putnam 38,181
Raleigh 86,821
Randolph 28,734
Ritchie 11,442
Roane 15,952
Summers 15,875
Taylor 16,584
Tucker 8,675
Tyler 11,320
Upshur 23,427
Wayne 46,021
Webster 12,245
Wetzel 21,874
Wirt 4,922
Wood 93,627
Wyoming 35,993

WISCONSIN

1980 Census 4,705,642

CITIES

Abbotsford 1,901
Adams 1,744
Adell 545
Albany 1,051
Algoma 3,656
Allenton 700 ○
Allouez GRBY 14,882
Alma 848
Alma Center 454
Almena 526
Almond 477
Altoona EAUC 4,393
Amery 2,404
Amherst 701
Antigo 8,653
APPLETON APP 58,913
Arcadia 2,109
Arena 451
Argyle 720
Arlington 440
Ashland 9,115
Ashwaubenon GRBY 14,486
Athens 988
Auburndale 641
Augusta 1,560
Avoca 505
Baldwin 1,620
Balsam Lake 749
Bangor 1,012
Baraboo 8,081
Barneveld 579
Barron 2,595
Bay City 543
Bayfield 778
Bayside MILW 4,724
Bear Creek 454
Beaver Dam 14,149
Belgium 892
Belleville 1,302
Belmont 826
BELOIT BLOIT 35,207
Beloit North BLOIT 5,457
Benton 983
Berlin 5,478
Big Bend MILW 1,345
Birnamwood 688
Biron 698
Black Creek 1,097
Black Earth 1,145
Black River Falls 3,434
Blair 1,142
Blanchardville 803
Bloomer 3,342
Bloomington 743
Bonduel 1,160
Boscobel 2,662
Boyceville 862
Boyd 660
Brandon 862
Brillion 2,907
Bristol CHI 500 ○
Brodhead 3,153
Brookfield MILW 34,035
Brooklyn 627
Brown Deer MILW 12,921
Bruce 905
Buffalo 894
Burlington 8,385
Butler MILW 2,059
Cadott 1,247
Cambria 680
Cambridge 844
Cameron 1,115
Campbellsport 1,740
Camp Douglas 589
Cascade 615
Casco 484
Cashton 827
Cassville 1,270
Cecil 445
Cedarburg MILW 9,005
Cedar Grove 1,420
Centuria 711
Chenequa MILW 532
Chetek 1,931
Chilton 2,965
Chippewa Falls EAUC 12,270
Clear Lake 899
Cleveland 1,270
Clinton BLOIT 1,751
Clintonville 4,567
Cochrane 512
Colby 1,496
Coleman 852
Colfax 1,149
Columbus 4,049
Combined Locks APP 2,573
Coon Valley 758
Cornell 1,583
Crandon 1,969
Crivitz 1,041
Cross Plains MAD 2,156
Cuba City 2,129
Cudahy MILW 19,547
Cumberland 1,983
Dallas 477
Dane 518
Darien 1,152
Darlington 2,300
Deerfield 1,466
De Forest MAD 3,367
Delafield MILW 4,083
Delavan 5,684
Delavan Lake 2,082
Denmark 1,475
De Pere GRBY 14,892
Dickeyville DUB 1,156
Dodgeville 3,458
Dorchester 613
Dousman MILW 1,153
Dresser 670
Durand 2,047
Eagle MILW 1,008
Eagle Lake 1,000 ○
Eagle River 1,326
East Troy MILW 2,385
EAU CLAIRE EAUC 51,509
Eden 534
Edgar 1,194
Edgerton JNSV 4,335
Elcho 450 ○
Eleva 593
Elkhart Lake 1,054
Elkhorn 4,605
Elk Mound 737
Ellsworth 2,143
Elm Grove MILW 6,735
Elmwood 885
Elroy 1,504
Embarrass 496
Ettrick 462
Evansville 2,835
Fairchild 577
Fall Creek 1,148
Fall River 850
Fennimore 2,212
Florence 575 ○
FOND DU LAC FDLC 35,863
Fontana 1,764
Footville 794
Forestville 455
Fort Atkinson 9,785
Fountain City 963
Fox Lake 1,373
Fox Point MILW 7,649
Francis Creek MNTW- 589
Franklin MILW 16,871
Frederic 1,039
Fredonia MILW 1,437
Fremont 510
French Island LACRO 4,118
Friendship 744
Galesville 1,239
Gays Mills 627
Genoa City CHI 1,202
Germantown MILW 10,729
Gillett 1,356
Glendale MILW 13,882
Glenwood City 950
Glidden 550 ○
Goodman 450 ○
Grafton MILW 8,381
Grantsburg 1,153
GREEN BAY GRBY 87,899
Greendale MILW 16,928
Greenfield MILW 31,353
Green Lake 1,208
Greenwood 1,124
Gresham 534
Hales Corners MILW 7,110
Hallie EAUC 950 ○
Hammond 991
Hartford 7,159
Hartland MILW 5,559
Hayward 1,698
Hazel Green 1,282
Hewitt 470
Highland 860
Hilbert 1,176
Hillsboro 1,263
Holmen LACRO 2,411
Horicon 3,584
Hortonville APP 2,016
Howard GRBY 8,240
Howards Grove-Millersville SHEB 1,838
Hudson MPLS- 5,434
Hurley 2,015
Hustisford 874
Independence 1,180
Iola 957
Iron Belt 520 ○
Iron Ridge 766
Iron River 650 ○
Jackson MILW 1,817
JANESVILLE JNSV 51,071
Jefferson 5,647
Johnson Creek 1,136
Juda 450 ○
Junction City 523
Juneau 2,045
Kaukauna APP 11,310
Kendall 486
KENOSHA CHI 77,685
Keshena 750 ○
Kewaskum 2,381
Kewaunee 2,801
Kiel 3,083
Kimberly APP 5,881
King 750 ○
Kohler SHEB 1,651
Lac du Flambeau 900 ○
LA CROSSE LACRO 48,347
Ladysmith 3,826
La Farge 746
Lake Delton 1,158
Lake Geneva 5,612
Lake Mills 3,670
Lake Nebagamon 780
Lake Tomahawk 600 ○
Lake Wazeecha 2,176
Lake Wissota EAUC 1,788
Lancaster 4,076
Land O'Lakes 500 ○
Lannon MILW 987
Laona 700 ○
Lena 585
Little Chute APP 7,907
Livingston 642
Lodi 1,959
Lomira 1,446
Lone Rock 577
Loyal 1,252
Luck 997
Luxemburg 1,040
Lyons 540 ○
McFarland MAD 3,783
MADISON MAD 170,616
Manawa 1,205
MANITOWOC MNTW- 32,547
Maple Bluff MAD 1,351
Marathon WAUS 1,552
Marinette 11,965
Marion 1,348
Markesan 1,446
Marshall 2,363
Marshfield 18,290
Mauston 3,284
Mayville 4,333
Mazomanie 1,248
Medford 4,035
Mellen 1,046
Melrose 507
Menasha APP 14,728
Menomonee Falls MILW 27,845
Menomonie 12,769
Mequon MILW 16,193
Mercer 950 ○
Merrill 9,578
Merrillan 587
Merton MILW 1,045
Middleton MAD 11,848
Milltown 732
Milton JNSV 4,092
MILWAUKEE MILW 636,297
Mineral Point 2,259
Minocqua 900 ○
Minong 557
Mishicot MNTW- 1,503
Mondovi 2,545
Monona MAD 8,809
Monroe 10,027
Montello 1,273
Montfort 616
Monticello 1,021
Montreal 887
Mosinee WAUS 3,015
Mount Calvary 585
Mount Horeb 3,251
Mukwonago MILW 4,014
Muscoda 1,331
Muskego MILW 15,277
Necedah 773
Neenah APP 22,432
Neillsville 2,780
Nekoosa 2,519
Neopit 1,065
Neosho 575
New Auburn 466
New Berlin MILW 30,529
Newburg 783
New Glarus 1,763
New Holstein 3,412
New Lisbon 1,390
New London 6,210
New Richmond 4,306
Niagara 2,079
North Fond du Lac FDLC 3,844
North Freedom 616
North Hudson MPLS- 2,218
North Lake MILW 600 ○
North Prairie MILW 938
Norwalk 517
Oak Creek MILW 16,932
Oakfield 990
Oconomowoc MILW 9,909
Oconto 4,505
Oconto Falls 2,500
Okauchee MILW 1,950 ○
Okauchee Lake MILW 2,000 ○
Omro OSH 2,763
Onalaska LACRO 9,249
Oostburg SHEB 1,647
Oregon MAD 3,876
Orfordville 1,143
Osceola 1,581
OSHKOSH OSH 50,016
Osseo 1,474
Owen 998
Paddock Lake CHI 2,207
Palmyra 1,515
Pardeeville 1,594
Park Falls 3,192
Pell Lake CHI 1,826
Pembine 475 ○
Pepin 890
Peshtigo 2,807
Pewaukee MILW 4,637
Phelps 700 ○
Phillips 1,522
Pittsville 810
Plain 676
Plainfield 813
Platteville 9,580
Pleasant Prairie CHI 500 ○
Pleasant View 700 ○
Plover 5,310
Plum City 505
Plymouth 6,027
Poplar 569
Portage 7,896
Port Edwards 2,077
Port Washington MILW 8,612
Potosi 736
Poynette 1,447
Poy Sippi 500 ○
Prairie du Chien 5,859
Prairie du Sac 2,145
Prentice 605
Prescott MPLS- 2,654
Princeton 1,479
Pulaski 1,875
RACINE RAC 85,725
Randolph 1,691
Random Lake 1,287
Redgranite 976
Reedsburg 5,038
Reedsville 1,134
Reeseville 649
Rhinelander 7,873
Rib Lake 945
Rice Lake 7,691
Richland Center 4,997
Ridgeway 503
Rio 785
Ripon 7,111
River Falls 9,019
River Hills MILW 1,642
Roberts 833
Rochester RAC 746
Rosendale 725
Rosholt 520
Rothschild WAUS 3,338
St. Cloud 560
St. Croix Falls 1,497
St. Francis MILW 10,095
St. Nazianz 738
Salem CHI 900 ○
Sauk City 2,703
Saukville MILW 3,494
Schofield WAUS 2,226
Seymour 2,530
Sharon 1,280
Shawano 7,013
SHEBOYGAN SHEB 48,085
Sheboygan Falls SHEB 5,253
Shell Lake 1,135
Shiocton 805
Shorewood MILW 14,327
Shorewood Hills MAD 1,837
Shullsburg 1,484
Silver Lake CHI 1,598
Siren 896
Sister Bay 564
Slinger MILW 1,612
Soldiers Grove 622
Solon Springs 590
Somerset 860
South Kenosha CHI 875 ○
South Milwaukee MILW 21,069
South Wayne 495
Sparta 6,934
Spencer 1,754
Spooner 2,365
Spring Green 1,265
Spring Valley 982
Stanley 2,095
Stetsonville 487
Stevens Point 22,970
Stockbridge 567
Stoddard 762
Stoughton MAD 7,589
Stratford 1,385
Strum 944
Sturgeon Bay 8,847
Sturtevant RAC 4,130
Sun Prairie MAD 12,931
Superior DUL- 29,571
Suring 581
Sussex MILW 3,482
Theresa 766
Thiensville MILW 3,341
Thorp 1,635
Three Lakes 600 ○
Tigerton 865
Tomah 7,204
Tomahawk 3,527
Trempealeau 956
Trevor CHI 700 ○
Turtle Lake 762
Twin Lakes CHI 3,474
Two Rivers MNTW- 13,354
Union Grove CHI 3,517
Valders MNTW- 984
Verona MAD 3,336
Vesper 554
Viola 696
Viroqua 3,716
Wabeno 900 ○
Walworth 1,607
Washburn 2,080
Waterford RAC 2,051
Waterloo 2,393
Watertown 18,113
Waukesha MILW 50,365
Waunakee MAD 3,866
Waupaca 4,472
Waupun 8,132
WAUSAU WAUS 32,426
Wausaukee 648
Wautoma 1,629
Wauwatosa MILW 51,308
Wauzeka 580
Webster 610
West Allis MILW 63,982
West Bend 21,484
Westby 1,797
Westfield 1,033
West Milwaukee MILW 3,535
Weston WAUS 8,775
West Salem LACRO 3,276
Weyauwega 1,549
Whitefish Bay MILW 14,930
Whitehall 1,530
Whitelaw MNTW- 649
Whitewater 11,520
Whiting 2,050
Wild Rose 741
Williams Bay 1,763
Wilton 465
Wind Lake MILW 2,400 ○
Wind Point RAC 1,695
Winnebago OSH 1,433
Winneconne OSH 1,935
Wisconsin Dells 2,521
Wisconsin Rapids 17,995
Withee 509
Wittenberg 997
Wonewoc 842
Woodruff 1,200 ○
Woodville 725
Wrightstown APP 1,169
Wyocena 548

COUNTIES

Adams 13,457
Ashland 16,783
Barron 38,730
Bayfield 13,822
Brown 175,280
Buffalo 14,309
Burnett 12,340

○ Rand McNally estimate (not reported in census).
▲ Population of entire township or "town", including rural areas.
● Independent city. Population not included in county total.

Calumet	30,867
Chippewa	52,127
Clark	32,910
Columbia	43,222
Crawford	16,556
Dane	323,545
Dodge	75,064
Door	25,029
Douglas	44,421
Dunn	34,314
Eau Claire	78,805
Florence	4,172
Fond du Lac	88,964
Forest	9,044
Grant	51,736
Green	30,012
Green Lake	18,370
Iowa	19,802
Iron	6,730
Jackson	16,831
Jefferson	66,152
Juneau	21,037
Kenosha	123,137
Kewaunee	19,539
La Crosse	91,056
Lafayette	17,412
Langlade	19,978
Lincoln	26,555
Manitowoc	82,918
Marathon	111,270
Marinette	39,314
Marquette	11,672
Menominee	3,373
Milwaukee	964,988

Monroe	35,074
Oconto	28,947
Oneida	31,216
Outagamie	128,730
Ozaukee	66,981
Pepin	7,477
Pierce	31,149
Polk	32,351
Portage	57,420
Price	15,788
Racine	173,132
Richland	17,476
Rock	139,420
Rusk	15,589
St. Croix	43,262
Sauk	43,469
Sawyer	12,843
Shawano	35,928
Sheboygan	100,935
Taylor	18,817
Trempealeau	26,158
Vernon	25,642
Vilas	16,535
Walworth	71,507
Washburn	13,174
Washington	84,848
Waukesha	280,203
Waupaca	42,831
Waushara	18,526
Winnebago	131,772
Wood	72,799

WYOMING
1980 Census 469,557

CITIES

Afton	1,481
Basin	1,349
Big Piney	530
Buffalo	3,799
Byron	633
CASPER CASP	51,016
CHEYENNE CHEY	47,716
Cody	7,512
Cokeville	515
Cowley	455
Dayton	701
Diamondville	1,000
Douglas	6,030
Dubois	1,067
Edgerton	510
Encampment	611
Evanston	6,621
Evansville CASP	2,335
Fox Farm CHEY	2,850
Freedom	450 ○
Gillette	13,652
Glenrock	2,736
Green River	12,807
Greybull	2,277
Guernsey	1,512
Hanna	2,288
Hudson	514
Jackson	4,511

Jeffrey City	1,882
Kemmerer	3,273
Lander	7,867
Laramie	24,410
Lingle	475
Lovell	2,447
Lusk	1,650
Lyman	2,284
Marbleton	537
Medicine Bow	953
Meeteetse	512
Midwest	638
Mills CASP	2,139
Moorcroft	1,014
Mountain View CASP	1,500 ○
Mountain View	628
Newcastle	3,596
Orchard Valley CHEY	3,321
Pine Bluffs	1,077
Pinedale	1,066
Powell	5,310
Ranchester	655
Rawlins	11,547
Reliance	500 ○
Riverton	9,247
Rock Springs	19,458
Saratoga	2,410
Sheridan	15,146
Shirley Basin	450 ○
Shoshoni	879
Sinclair	586
South Laramie	1,500 ○
South Superior	586
Story	700 ○

Sundance	1,087
Thermopolis	3,852
Torrington	5,441
Upton	1,193
Wamsutter	681
West Laramie	2,000 ○
Wheatland	5,816
Worland	6,391
Wright	1,117

COUNTIES

Albany	29,062
Big Horn	11,896
Campbell	24,367
Carbon	21,896
Converse	14,069
Crook	5,308
Fremont	38,992
Goshen	12,040
Hot Springs	5,710
Johnson	6,700
Laramie	68,649
Lincoln	12,177
Natrona	71,856
Niobrara	2,924
Park	21,639
Platte	11,975
Sheridan	25,048
Sublette	4,548
Sweetwater	41,723
Teton	9,355
Uinta	13,021
Washakie	9,496
Weston	7,106

○ Rand McNally estimate (not reported in census).
▲ Population of entire township or "town", including rural areas.
● Independent city. Population not included in county total.

World Political Information Table

This table lists all countries and dependencies in the world, U.S. States, Canadian provinces, and other important regions and political subdivisions. Besides specifying the form of government for all political areas, the table classifies them into five groups according to their political status. Units labeled **A** are independent sovereign nations. Units labeled **B** are independent as regards internal affairs, but for purposes of foreign affairs they are under the protection of another country.

Areas under military government are also labeled **B**. Units labeled **C** are colonies, overseas territories, dependencies, etc., of other countries. Together the **A**, **B**, and **C** areas comprise practically the entire inhabited area of the world. Units labeled **D** are States, provinces, Soviet Republics, or similar major administrative subdivisions of important countries. Units in the table with no letter designation are regions or other areas that do not constitute separate political units by themselves.

Country, Division, or Region English (Conventional)	Area* in sq. mi.	Estimated Population 1/1/84	Pop. per sq. mi.	Form of Government and Political Status	Capital: Largest City (unless same)	Predominant Language
Afars and Issas, *see* Djibouti	...	...	...			
†Afghanistan	250,000	14,165,000	57	Socialist Republic ... A	Kābul	Dari, Pushtu
Africa	11,700,000	519,800,000	44		......; Cairo	
Alabama	51,704	4,010,000	78	State (U.S.) ... D	Montgomery; Birmingham	English
Alaska	591,004	465,000	0.8	State (U.S.) ... D	Juneau; Anchorage	English, Indian, Eskimo
†Albania	11,100	2,600,000	234	Socialist Republic ... A	Tiranë	Albanian
Alberta	255,285	2,365,000	9.3	Province (Canada) ... D	Edmonton	English
†Algeria	919,595	21,290,000	23	Socialist Republic ... A	Algiers	Arabic, French, Berber
American Samoa	77	35,000	455	Unincorporated Territory (U.S.) ... C	Pago Pago	Samoan, English
Andaman and Nicobar Islands	3,202	205,000	64	Territory (India) ... D	Port Blair	Andaman, Nicobar Malay
Andorra	175	39,000	223	Co-Principality (Spanish and French protection) ... B	Andorra	Spanish, French
†Angola	481,353	7,735,000	16	Socialist Republic ... A	Luanda	Portuguese, native languages
Anguilla	35	7,000	200	Associated State (U.K.) ... B	The Valley; South Hill	English
Anhwei	50,193	51,700,000	1,030	Province (China) ... D	Hofei, Huainan	Chinese
Antarctica	5,405,000	...(1)				
†Antigua and Barbuda	170	80,000	471	Parliamentary State (Comm. of Nations) ... A	Saint John's	English
Arabian Peninsula	1,160,000	23,505,000	20		......; Riyadh	Arabic
†Argentina	1,068,301	28,955,000	27	Republic ... A	Buenos Aires	Spanish
Arizona	114,002	2,965,000	26	State (U.S.) ... D	Phoenix	English
Arkansas	53,191	2,315,000	44	State (U.S.) ... D	Little Rock	English
Armenian S.S.R.	11,506	3,200,000	278	Soviet Socialist Republic (U.S.S.R.) ... D	Yerevan	Armenian, Russian
Aruba	75	69,000	920	Division of Netherlands Antilles (Neth.) ... D	Oranjestad	Dutch, Spanish, English, Papiamento
Ascension	34	1,100	32	Dependency of St. Helena (U.K.) ... C	Georgetown	English
Asia	17,240,000	2,863,400,000	166		......; Tōkyō	
†Australia	2,967,909	15,535,000	5.2	Parliamentary State (Federal) (Comm. of Nations) ... A	Canberra; Sydney	English
Australian Capital Territory	939	235,000	250	Territory (Australia) ... D	Canberra	English
†Austria	32,377	7,575,000	234	Federal Republic ... A	Vienna (Wien)	German
Azerbaidzhan S.S.R.	33,436	6,370,000	190	Soviet Socialist Republic (U.S.S.R.) ... D	Baku	Turkish, Russian, Armenian
Azores	868	240,000	276	Autonomous Region (Portugal) ... D	Ponta Delgada	Portuguese
Baden-Württemberg	13,804	9,255,000	670	State (Federal Republic of Germany) ... D	Stuttgart	German
†Bahamas	5,382	225,000	42	Parliamentary State (Comm. of Nations) ... A	Nassau	English
Bahrain	256	400,000	1,563	Constitutional Monarchy ... A	Manama	Arabic, English
Balearic Islands	1,936	695,000	359	Province of Spain (Baleares) ... D	Palma	Spanish
Baltic Republics	67,182	7,655,000	114	Part of U.S.S.R. (3 republics) ... D	......; Rīga	Lithuanian, Latvian, Estonian, Russian
†Bangladesh	55,598	95,600,000	1,719	Republic (Comm. of Nations) ... A	Dacca	Bangla, English
†Barbados	166	250,000	1,506	Parliamentary State (Comm. of Nations) ... A	Bridgetown	English
Bavaria (Bayern)	27,238	10,920,000	401	State (Federal Republic of Germany) ... D	Munich (München)	German
†Belgium	11,781	9,870,000	838	Constitutional Monarchy ... A	Brussels (Bruxelles)	French, Dutch (Flemish)
†Belize	8,866	155,000	17	Parliamentary State (Comm. of Nations) ... A	Belmopan; Belize City	English, Spanish, Indian languages
Benelux	28,672	24,655,000	860	Economic Union	......; Brussels (Bruxelles)	Dutch, French, Luxumbourgish
†Benin	43,484	3,655,000	84	Socialist Republic ... A	Porto-Novo; Cotonou	French, native languages
Berlin (West)	185	1,880,000	10,162	State (Federal Republic of Germany) ... D	Berlin (West)	German
Bermuda	21	68,000	3,238	Colony (U.K.) ... C	Hamilton	English
†Bhutan	18,147	1,400,000	77	Monarchy (Indian protection) ... B	Thimbu	Dzongkha, English, Nepalese dialects
Bioko	785	77,000	98	Province of Equatorial Guinea ... D	Malabo	Spanish, English
†Bolivia	424,164	6,160,000	15	Republic ... A	Sucre and La Paz; La Paz	Spanish, Quechua, Aymara
Bophuthatswana(6)	15,610	1,400,000	89	Bantu Homeland (South African protection) ... D	Mmabatho	Sesotho, Afrikaans
Borneo, Indonesian (Kalimantan)	208,287	7,185,000	34	Part of Indonesia (4 provinces) ...	......; Banjarmasin	Bahasa Indonesia
†Botswana	231,805	1,020,000	4.4	Republic (Comm. of Nations) ... A	Gaborone	Setswana, English
†Brazil	3,265,075	133,100,000	41	Federal Republic ... A	Brasília; São Paulo	Portuguese
Bremen	156	690,000	4,423	State (Federal Republic of Germany) ... D	Bremen	German
British Columbia	366,255	2,840,000	7.8	Province (Canada) ... D	Victoria; Vancouver	English
British Honduras, *see* Belize	...	...	...			
British Indian Ocean Territory	23	......(1)	...	Colony (U.K.) ... C		
British Solomon Islands, *see* Solomon Islands	...	...	...			
Brunei	2,226	215,000	92	Constitutional Monarchy (Comm. of Nations) ... A	Bandar Seri Begawan	Malay, Chinese, English
†Bulgaria	42,823	9,370,000	219	Socialist Republic ... A	Sofia (Sofiya)	Bulgarian
†Burma	261,228	37,505,000	144	Socialist Republic ... A	Rangoon	Burmese, ethnic languages
†Burundi	10,747	4,625,000	430	Republic ... A	Bujumbura	Kirundi, French, Swahili
†Byelorussian S.S.R.	80,155	9,925,000	124	Soviet Socialist Republic (U.S.S.R.) ... D	Minsk	Byelorussian, Polish, Russian
California	158,704	25,300,000	159	State (U.S.) ... D	Sacramento; Los Angeles	English
Cambodia, *see* Kampuchea	...	...	...			
†Cameroon	183,569	9,125,000	50	Republic ... A	Yaoundé; Douala	English, French, native languages
†Canada	3,831,033	25,100,000	6.6	Parliamentary State (Federal) (Comm. of Nations) ... A	Ottawa; Toronto	English, French
Canary Islands (Islas Canarias)	2,808	1,470,000	524	......; Part of Spain (2 provinces) ...	......; Las Palmas de Gran Canaria	Spanish
†Cape Verde	1,557	310,000	199	Republic ... A	Praia	Portuguese, Crioulo
Cayman Islands	100	19,000	190	Colony (U.K.) ... C	Georgetown	English
Celebes	73,057	11,125,000	152	Part of Indonesia (4 provinces)	......; Ujung Pandang	Bahasa Indonesia, Malay-Polynesian languages
Ceylon, *see* Sri Lanka	...	...	...			
†Chad	495,755	4,785,000	9.7	Provisional Military Government ... A	Ndjamena	French, Arabic, native languages
Channel Islands	75	133,000	1,773		......; St. Helier	English, French
Chekiang	38,996	40,500,000	1,039	Province (China) ... D	Hangchou	Chinese
†Chile	292,135	11,740,000	40	Republic ... A	Santiago	Spanish
China (excl. Taiwan)	3,630,747	1,046,530,000	288	Socialist Republic ... A	Peking (Beijing); Shanghai	Chinese dialects
China (Nationalist), *see* Taiwan	...	...	...			
Christmas Island	52	3,200	62	External Territory (Australia) ... C	......; Flying Fish Cove	Chinese, Malay, English
†Ciskei(6)	3,205	690,000	215	Bantu Homeland (South African protection) ... B	Bisho; Mdantsane	Xhosa, Afrikaans
Cocos (Keeling) Islands	5.4	500	92	External Territory (Australia) ... C		Malay, English
†Colombia	439,737	30,285,000	69	Republic ... A	Bogotá	Spanish
Colorado	104,094	3,130,000	30	State (U.S.) ... D	Denver	English
Commonwealth of Nations	10,670,000	1,667,050,000	156	Political Union	......; London	
†Comoros	838	395,000	471	Federal Republic ... A	Moroni	Swahili, French, Arabic
†Congo	132,047	1,720,000	13	Republic ... A	Brazzaville	French, native languages
Connecticut	5,019	3,165,000	631	State (U.S.) ... D	Hartford	English

* Areas include inland water.
† Member of the United Nations (1983).
... None, or not applicable.
(1) No permanent population.
(6) Bophuthatswana, Ciskei, Transkei, and Venda are not recognized by the United Nations.

World Political Information Table (continued)

Country, Division, or Region English (Conventional)	Area* in sq. mi.	Estimated Population 1/1/84	Pop. per sq. mi.	Form of Government and Political Status	Capital: Largest City (unless same)	Predominant Language
Cook Islands	91	18,000	198	Self-governing Territory (New Zealand protection) ... B	Avarua	Malay-Polynesian languages, English
Corsica	3,352	235,000	70	Part of France (2 departments)	......; Ajaccio	French, Italian
†Costa Rica	19,730	2,395,000	121	Republic. ... A	San José	Spanish
†Cuba	44,218	9,850,000	223	Socialist Republic ... A	Havana (La Habana)	Spanish
Curaçao	171	180,000	1,053	Division of Netherlands Antilles (Neth.) ... D	Willemstad	Dutch, Spanish, English, Papiamento
†Cyprus	3,572	665,000	186	Republic (Comm. of Nations) ... A	Nicosia	Greek, Turkish
†Czechoslovakia	49,378	15,415,000	312	Federal Socialist Republic ... A	Prague (Praha)	Czech, Slovak, Hungarian
Dahomey, see Benin.						
Delaware	2,045	615,000	301	State (U.S.) ... D	Dover; Wilmington	English
†Denmark	16,633	5,110,000	307	Constitutional Monarchy ... A	Copenhagen (København)	Danish
Denmark and Possessions	857,177	5,210,000	6.1		Copenhagen (København)	Danish, Faroese, Eskimo
District of Columbia	69	625,000	9,058	District (U.S.) ... D	Washington	English
†Djibouti	8,880	350,000	39	Republic. ... A	Djibouti	Somali, French, Afar, Arabic
†Dominica	290	74,000	255	Republic (Comm. of Nations). ... A	Roseau	English, French
†Dominican Republic	18,704	5,975,000	319	Republic. ... A	Santo Domingo	Spanish
†Ecuador	109,483	9,410,000	86	Republic. ... A	Quito; Guayaquil	Spanish, Quechua
†Egypt	386,643	46,465,000	120	Socialist Republic ... A	Cairo (Al Qāhirah)	Arabic, English, French
Ellice Islands, see Tuvalu						
†El Salvador	8,124	5,140,000	633	Republic. ... A	San Salvador	Spanish
England	50,362	46,465,000	923	Administrative division of U.K. ... D	London	English
†Equatorial Guinea	10,831	310,000	29	Republic. ... A	Malabo	Spanish, English, native languages
Estonian S.S.R.	17,413	1,530,000	88	Soviet Socialist Republic (U.S.S.R.) ... D	Tallinn	Estonian, Russian
†Ethiopia	472,434	31,790,000	67	Provisional Military Government ... A	Addis Ababa	Amharic, Arabic, native languages
Eurasia	21,080,000	3,535,800,000	168		......; Tōkyō	
Europe	3,840,000	672,400,000	175		......; London	
Faeroe Islands	540	45,000	83	Part of Danish Realm. ... B	Tórshavn	Danish, Faroese
Falkland Islands (Islas Malvinas) (excl. Dependencies).	4,700	2,000	0.4	Colony (U.K.)(3). ... C	Stanley	English
†Fiji	7,055	675,000	96	Parliamentary State (Comm. of Nations) ... A	Suva	English, Fijian, Hindustani
†Finland	130,558	4,860,000	37	Republic. ... A	Helsinki	Finnish, Swedish
Florida	58,668	10,825,000	185	State (U.S.) ... D	Tallahassee; Miami	English
†France (excl. Overseas Depts.	211,208	54,730,000	259	Republic. ... A	Paris	French
France and Possessions	260,661	56,345,000	216		Paris	French
French Guiana	35,135	78,000	2.2	Overseas Department (France) ... D	Cayenne	French
French Polynesia	1,544	160,000	104	Overseas Territory (France) ... C	Papeete	Malay-Polynesian languages, French
French West Indies	1,112	615,000	553		......; Fort-de-France	French
Fukien	47,877	27,000,000	564	Province (China) ... D	Fuchou	Chinese
†Gabon	103,347	940,000	9.1	Republic. ... A	Libreville	French, native languages
Galapagos Islands (Archipiélago de Colón)	3,075	6,000	2.0	Province of Ecuador (Galápagos) ... D	Puerto Baquerizo Moreno	Spanish
†Gambia	4,361	660,000	151	Republic (Comm. of Nations) ... A	Banjul	English, native languages
Georgia	58,914	5,790,000	98	State (U.S.) ... D	Atlanta	English
Georgian S.S.R.	26,911	5,195,000	193	Soviet Socialist Republic (U.S.S.R.) ... D	Tbilisi	Georgic, Armenian, Russian
†German Democratic Republic	41,768	16,725,000	400	Socialist Republic ... A	Berlin (East)	German
†Germany, Federal Republic of (incl. West Berlin)	96,016	61,480,000	640	Federal Republic ... A	Bonn; Essen	German
Germany (Entire)	137,784	78,205,000	568		......; Essen	German
†Ghana	92,100	14,670,000	160	Provisional Military Government (Comm. of Nations) ... A	Accra	English, native languages
Gibraltar	2.3	31,000	13,478	Colony (U.K.) ... C	Gibraltar	Spanish, English
Gilbert Islands, see Kiribati						
Great Britain, see United Kingdom						
†Greece	50,944	9,905,000	194	Republic. ... A	Athens (Athínai)	Greek
Greenland	840,004	54,000	0.06	Part of Danish Realm ... B	Godthåb	Danish, Eskimo
†Grenada	133	105,000	789	Parliamentary State (Comm. of Nations) ... A	Saint George's	English
Guadeloupe (incl. Dependencies)	687	310,000	451	Overseas Department (France) ... D	Basse-Terre; Pointe-à-Pitre	French, Creole
Guam	209	117,000	560	Unincorporated Territory (U.S.) ... C	Agana	English, Chamorro
†Guatemala	42,042	7,815,000	186	Republic. ... A	Guatemala	Spanish, Indian languages
Guernsey (incl. Dependencies)	30	58,000	1,933	Bailiwick (U.K.). ... C	St. Peter Port	English, French
†Guinea	94,926	5,500,000	58	Republic. ... A	Conakry	Native languages, French
†Guinea-Bissau	13,948	835,000	60	Republic. ... A	Bissau	Native languages, Portuguese
†Guyana	83,000	835,000	10	Republic (Comm. of Nations) ... A	Georgetown	English
†Haiti	10,714	5,185,000	484	Republic. ... A	Port-au-Prince	Creole, French
†Hamburg	292	1,630,000	5,582	State (Federal Republic of Germany) ... D	Hamburg	German
Hawaii	6,473	1,020,000	158	State (U.S.) ... D	Honolulu	English, Japanese, Hawaiian
Heilungkiang	177,607	34,000,000	191	Province (China) ... D	Harbin	Chinese, Mongolian
Hesse (Hessen)	8,152	5,590,000	686	State (Federal Republic of Germany) ... D	Wiesbaden; Frankfurt am Main	German
Hispaniola	29,418	11,160,000	379		......; Santo Domingo	French, Spanish, Creole
Holland, see Netherlands						
Honan	64,093	77,440,000	1,208	Province (China) ... D	Chengchou	Chinese
†Honduras	43,277	4,155,000	96	Republic. ... A	Tegucigalpa	Spanish
Hong Kong	410	5,360,000	13,073	Colony (U.K.) ... C	Victoria; New Kowloon	Chinese, English
Hopeh	73,359	55,150,000	752	Province (China) ... D	Shihchiachuang; Tangshan	Chinese
Hunan	81,081	56,200,000	693	Province (China) ... D	Changsha	Chinese
†Hungary	35,921	10,685,000	297	Socialist Republic ... A	Budapest	Hungarian (Magyar)
Hupeh	69,498	49,815,000	717	Province (China) ... D	Wuhan	Chinese
†Iceland	39,769	235,000	5.9	Republic. ... A	Reykjavík	Icelandic
Idaho	83,566	1,000,000	12	State (U.S.) ... D	Boise	English
Illinois	57,872	11,530,000	199	State (U.S.) ... D	Springfield; Chicago	English
†India (incl. part of Jammu and Kashmir)	1,237,061	738,240,000	597	Federal Republic (Comm. of Nations) ... A	New Delhi; Calcutta	Hindi, English, Bengali, Tegulu, Marathi, and other languages
Indiana	36,417	5,505,000	151	State (U.S.) ... D	Indianapolis	English
†Indonesia	741,101	157,560,000	213	Republic. ... A	Jakarta	Bahasa Indonesia, Malay-Polynesian languages
Inner Mongolia	424,772	20,200,000	48	Autonomous Region (China) ... D	Huhohaote; Paotou	Mongolian
Iowa	56,275	2,920,000	52	State (U.S.) ... D	Des Moines	English
Iran	636,296	43,335,000	68	Republic. ... A	Tehrān	Farsi, Turkish, Kurdish, Arabic
†Iraq	167,925	14,530,000	87	Republic. ... A	Baghdād	Arabic, Kurdish
†Ireland	27,136	3,555,000	131	Republic. ... A	Dublin	English, Irish Gaelic
Isle Of Man	227	67,000	295	Self-governing Territory (U.K. protection) ... B	Douglas	English
†Israel	7,848	4,055,000	517	Republic. ... A	Jerusalem (Yerushalayim); Tel Aviv-Yafo	Hebrew, Arabic, English
Israeli Occupied Areas.	2,703	1,285,000	475		......; Gaza (Ghazzah)	Hebrew, Arabic, English
†Italy	116,319	56,685,000	487	Republic. ... A	Rome; Milano	Italian
†Ivory Coast	123,847	8,980,000	73	Republic. ... A	Abidjan and Yamoussoukro; Abidjan	French, native languages
†Jamaica	4,244	2,310,000	544	Parliamentary State (Comm. of Nations) ... A	Kingston	English
†Japan	145,834	119,680,000	821	Constitutional Monarchy ... A	Tōkyō	Japanese
Java (incl. Madura)	51,038	97,500,000	1,910	Part of Indonesia (5 provinces) ... D	......; Jakarta	Bahasa Indonesia, Chinese, English
Jersey	45	75,000	1,667	Bailiwick (U.K.). ... C	St. Helier	English, French
†Jordan	35,135	2,420,000	69	Constitutional Monarchy ... A	'Ammān	Arabic, English
†Kampuchea	69,898	7,180,000	103	Socialist Republic ... A	Phnom Penh	Khmer (Cambodian)
Kansas	82,282	2,415,000	29	State (U.S.) ... D	Topeka; Wichita	English
Kansu	150,580	20,405,000	136	Province (China) ... D	Lanchow	Chinese, Mongolian, Tibetan dialects
Kashmir, Jammu and	86,024	9,335,000	109	In dispute (India and Pakistan)	......; Srīnagar and Jammu; Srīnagar	Urdu, Kashmiri, Dogri, Balti, Ladakhi, Punjabi

* Areas include inland water.
† Member of the United Nations (1983).
... None, or not applicable.
(3) Claimed by Argentina.

World Political Information Table (continued)

Country, Division, or Region English (Conventional)	Area* in sq. mi.	Estimated Population 1/1/84	Pop. per sq. mi.	Form of Government and Political Status	Capital: Largest City (unless same)	Predominant Language
Kazakh S.S.R.	1,049,155	15,445,000	15	Soviet Socialist Republic (U.S.S.R.) D	Alma-Ata	Turkish, Russian
Kentucky	40,414	3,740,000	93	State (U.S.) D	Frankfort; Louisville	English
†Kenya	224,961	18,915,000	84	Republic (Comm. of Nations) A	Nairobi	English, Swahili, native languages
Kerguelen Islands (Iles Kerguèlen)	2,700	92	0.03	Part of French Southern and Antarctic Territory (France) C	...	French
Kiangsi	62,162	34,640,000	557	Province (China) D	Nanchang	Chinese
Kiangsu	38,996	63,000,000	1,616	Province (China) D	Nanking	Chinese
Kirghiz S.S.R.	76,641	3,745,000	19	Soviet Socialist Republic (U.S.S.R.) D	Frunze	Turkish, Farsi, Russian
Kiribati	291	62,000	213	Republic (Comm. of Nations) A	Bairiki	Gilbertese, English
Kirin	69,498	23,545,000	339	Province (China) D	Changchun	Chinese, Mongolian, Korean
Korea, North	46,540[4]	19,400,000	417	Socialist Republic A	Pyŏngyang	Korean
Korea, South	38,025[4]	40,945,000	1,077	Republic A	Seoul (Sŏul)	Korean
Korea (Entire)	85,052	60,345,000	710	...	......; Seoul (Sŏul)	Korean
†Kuwait	6,880	1,705,000	248	Constitutional Monarchy A	Kuwait	Arabic, English
Kwangsi	89,190	37,990,000	426	Autonomous Region (China) D	Nanning	Chinese, Thai
Kwangtung	84,942	61,750,000	727	Province (China) D	Canton	Chinese
Kweichow	67,182	29,825,000	444	Province (China) D	Guiyang	Chinese, Thai
Labrador	112,826	30,000	0.3	Part of Newfoundland Province (Canada) ...	......; Labrador City	English, Eskimo
†Laos	91,429	4,035,000	44	Socialist Republic A	Viangchan	Lao, French
Latin America	7,916,000	392,965,000	50	...	......; Mexico City (Ciudad de México)	Spanish, Portuguese
Latvian S.S.R.	24,595	2,600,000	106	Soviet Socialist Republic (U.S.S.R.) D	Riga	Latvian, Russian
†Lebanon	4,015	2,960,000	737	Republic A	Beirut (Bayrūt)	Arabic, French, English
†Lesotho	11,720	1,460,000	125	Monarchy (Comm. of Nations) A	Maseru	Sesotho, English
Liaoning	57,915	37,260,000	643	Province (China) D	Shenyang (Mukden)	Chinese, Mongolian
†Liberia	43,000	2,260,000	53	Provisional Military Government A	Monrovia	Native languages, English
†Libya	679,362	3,415,000	5.0	Socialist Republic A	Tripoli	Arabic
Liechtenstein	62	27,000	435	Constitutional Monarchy A	Vaduz	German
Lithuanian S.S.R.	25,174	3,525,000	140	Soviet Socialist Republic (U.S.S.R.) D	Vilnius	Lithuanian, Polish, Russian
Louisiana	47,750	4,505,000	94	State (U.S.) D	Baton Rouge; New Orleans	English
Lower Saxony (Niedersachsen)	18,311	7,250,000	396	State (Federal Republic of Germany) D	Hannover	German
†Luxembourg	999	365,000	365	Constitutional Monarchy A	Luxembourg	Luxembourgish, French, German, English
Macao	6.0	370,000	61,667	Overseas Province (Portugal) D	Macao	Chinese dialects
†Madagascar	226,658	9,620,000	42	Socialist Republic A	Antananarivo	French, Malagasy
Madeira Islands (Arquipélago da Madeira)	307	240,000	782	Autonomous Region (Portugal) D	Funchal	Portuguese
Maine	33,265	1,160,000	35	State (U.S.) D	Augusta; Portland	English
Malagasy Republic, *see* Madagascar	...	...	...	...	...	...
†Malawi	45,747	6,510,000	142	Republic (Comm. of Nations) A	Lilongwe; Blantyre	Chichewa, English
Malaya	50,700	12,575,000	248	Part of Malaysia (11 States) ...	......; Kuala Lumpur	Bahasa Malaysia, English, Chinese, Tamil
†Malaysia	128,430	15,165,000	118	Federal Constitutional Monarchy (Comm. of Nations) A	Kuala Lumpur	Bahasa Malaysia, English, Chinese, Tamil
†Maldives	115	160,000	1,391	Republic A	Male	Divehi
†Mali	478,766	7,600,000	16	Republic A	Bamako	French, Bambara
†Malta	122	365,000	2,992	Republic (Comm. of Nations) A	Valletta	English, Maltese
Manitoba	251,000	1,055,000	4.2	Province (Canada) D	Winnipeg	English
Maritime Provinces (excl. Newfoundland)	51,963	1,711,000	33	Part of Canada (3 provinces) ...	......; Halifax	English
Marshall Islands	70	33,000	471	Part of Trust Territory of the Pacific Islands (U.S. administration) B	Majuro (island); Jarej-Uliga-Delap	Malay-Polynesian languages, English
Martinique	425	305,000	718	Overseas Department (France) D	Fort-de-France	French, Creole
Maryland	10,461	4,325,000	413	State (U.S.) D	Annapolis; Baltimore	English
Massachusetts	8,286	5,785,000	698	State (U.S.) D	Boston	English
†Mauritania	397,955	1,805,000	4.5	Provisional Military Government A	Nouakchott	Arabic, French
†Mauritius (incl. Dependencies)	790	1,000,000	1,266	Parliamentary State (Comm. of Nations) A	Port Louis	French, Creole, English
Mayotte	144	57,000	396	Overseas Department (France) D	Dzaoudzi	Swahili, French
†Mexico	761,604	75,750,000	99	Federal Republic A	Mexico City (Ciudad de México)	Spanish
Michigan	97,107	9,195,000	95	State (U.S.) D	Lansing; Detroit	English
Micronesia, Federated States of	271	78,000	288	Part of Trust Territory of the Pacific Islands (U.S. administration) B	Kolonia	Malay-Polynesian languages, English
Middle America	1,056,000	130,665,000	124	...	......; Mexico City (Ciudad de México)	Spanish, English
Midway Islands	2.0	2,300	1,150	Unincorporated Territory (U.S.) C	...	English
Minnesota	86,614	4,230,000	49	State (U.S.) D	St. Paul; Minneapolis	English
Mississippi	47,691	2,630,000	55	State (U.S.) D	Jackson	English
Missouri	69,697	5,035,000	72	State (U.S.) D	Jefferson City; St. Louis	English
Moldavian S.S.R.	13,012	4,075,000	313	Soviet Socialist Republic (U.S.S.R.) D	Kishinev	Moldavian, Russian, Ukrainian
Monaco	0.6	28,000	46,667	Constitutional Monarchy A	Monaco	French, Italian, English, Monegasque
†Mongolia	604,250	1,845,000	3.1	Socialist Republic A	Ulan Bator	Khalka Mongol
Montana	147,045	815,000	5.5	State (U.S.) D	Helena; Billings	English
Montserrat	40	12,000	300	Colony (U.K.) C	Plymouth	English
†Morocco (excl. Western Sahara)	172,414	23,045,000	134	Constitutional Monarchy A	Rabat; Casablanca	Arabic, Berber, French
†Mozambique	302,329	13,360,000	44	Socialist Republic A	Maputo	Portuguese, native languages
Muscat and Oman, *see* Oman	...	...	...	...	...	...
Namibia (excl. Walvis Bay)	318,261	1,095,000	3.4	Under South African Administration[5] C	Windhoek	Afrikkans, German, native languages
Nauru	8.2	8,200	1,000	Republic (Comm. of Nations) A	Uaboe District;	Nauruan, English
Nebraska	77,350	1,610,000	21	State (U.S.) D	Lincoln; Omaha	English
†Nepal	56,135	15,960,000	284	Constitutional Monarchy A	Kathmandu	Nepali, Tibeto-Burman languages
†Netherlands	15,892	14,420,000	907	Constitutional Monarchy A	Amsterdam and The Hague; Amsterdam	Dutch
Netherlands Guiana, *see* Suriname	...	...	...	...	...	...
Netherlands Antilles	383	275,000	718	Self-governing Territory (Netherlands protection) B	Willemstad	Dutch, Spanish, English, Papiamento
Nevada	110,562	955,000	8.6	State (U.S.) D	Carson City; Las Vegas	English
New Brunswick	28,354	715,000	25	Province (Canada) D	Fredericton; Saint John	English, French
New Caledonia (incl. Dependencies)	7,358	148,000	20	Overseas Territory (France) C	Nouméa	Malay-Polynesian languages, French
New England	66,674	12,580,000	189	Part of U.S. (6 states) ...	......; Boston	English
Newfoundland	156,185	580,000	3.7	Province (Canada) D	St. John's	English
Newfoundland (excl. Labrador)	43,359	550,000	13	Part of Newfoundland Province, Canada ...	......; St. John's	English
New Hampshire	9,278	980,000	106	State (U.S.) D	Concord; Manchester	English
New Hebrides, *see* Vanuatu	...	...	...	...	...	...
New Jersey	7,787	7,555,000	970	State (U.S.) D	Trenton; Newark	English
New Mexico	121,594	1,415,000	12	State (U.S.) D	Santa Fe; Albuquerque	English, Spanish
New South Wales	309,433	5,435,000	18	State (Australia) D	Sydney	English
New York	52,737	17,555,000	333	State (U.S.) D	Albany; New York	English
†New Zealand	103,883	3,300,000	32	Parliamentary State (Comm. of Nations) A	Wellington; Auckland	English, Maori
†Nicaragua	50,193	3,060,000	61	Republic A	Managua	Spanish
†Niger	489,191	5,905,000	12	Provisional Military Government A	Niamey	French, Hausa, native languages
†Nigeria	356,669	84,945,000	238	Federal Republic (Comm. of Nations) A	Lagos	Hausa, Ibo, Yoruba, English

* Areas include inland water.
† Member of the United Nations (1983).
. . .None, or not applicable.
(4) The 1,262 km² or 487 sq mi of the demilitarized zone are not included in either North or South Korea.
(5) In October 1966 the United Nations terminated the South African mandate over Namibia, a decision which South Africa did not accept.

Country, Division, or Region English (Conventional)	Area* in sq. mi.	Estimated Population 1/1/84	Pop. per sq. mi.	Form of Government and Political Status		Capital: Largest City (unless same)	Predominant Language
†Ningsia Hui................	25,483	4,185,000	164	Autonomous Region (China)	D	Yinchuan	Chinese
Niue.....................	102	3,000	29	Self-governing Territory (New Zealand).....	B	Alofi	Malay-Polynesian languages, English
Norfolk Island............	14	2,300	164	External Territory (Australia)	C	Kingston	English
North America............	9,410,000	391,100,000	42			......; New York	
North Borneo, see Sabah.....	......	......					
North Carolina...........	52,669	6,170,000	117	State (U.S.)...................	D	Raleigh; Charlotte	English
North Dakota............	70,702	675,000	9.5	State (U.S.)...................	D	Bismarck; Fargo	English
Northern Ireland..........	5,452	1,560,000	286	Administrative division of United Kingdom...............	D	Belfast	English
Northern Mariana Islands......	184	19,000	103	Part of Trust Territory of the Pacific Islands (U.S. administration)	B	Saipan (island); Chalan Kanoa	Malay-Polynesian languages, English
Northern Territory, Austl.......	520,280	130,000	0.2	Territory (Australia)	D	Darwin	English, Aboriginal languages
North Rhine-Westphalia (Nordrhein-Westfalen)......	13,153	16,980,000	1,291	State (Federal Republic of Germany)	D	Düsseldorf; Essen	German
Northwest Territories........	1,304,903	49,000	0.04	Territory (Canada)	D	Yellowknife	English, Eskimo, Indian
†Norway (incl. Svalbard and Jan Mayen)........	149,158	4,140,000	28	Constitutional Monarchy	A	Oslo	Norwegian (Riksmål and Landsmål)
Nova Scotia..............	21,425	870,000	41	Province (Canada)...............	D	Halifax	English
Oceania (incl. Australia)........	3,290,000	24,000,000	7.3			......; Sydney	
Ohio....................	44,786	10,825,000	242	State (U.S.)...................	D	Columbus; Cleveland	English
Oklahoma................	69,957	3,250,000	46	State (U.S.)...................	D	Oklahoma City	English
†Oman..................	82,030	990,000	12	Monarchy	A	Muscat; Matrah	Arabic
Ontario..................	412,582	8,875,000	22	Province (Canada)...............	D	Toronto	English
Oregon..................	97,076	2,715,000	28	State (U.S.)...................	D	Salem; Portland	English
Orkney Islands	376	19,000	51	Part of Scotland, U.K. Orkney Island Area)		Kirkwall	English
Pacific Islands, Trust Territory of the	717	143,000	199	U.N. Trusteeship (Administered by U.S.)....	B	Saipan (island); Jarej-Uliga-Delap	Malay-Polynesian languages, English
†Pakistan (incl. part of Jammu and Kashmir)......	319,867	100,580,000	314	Federal Republic	A	Islāmābād; Karāchi	Urdu, English, Punjabi, Sindhi
Palau	192	13,000	68	Part of Trust Territory of the Pacific Islands (U.S. administration)	B	Koror	Malay-Polynesian languages, English
†Panama................	29,762	2,200,000	74	Republic.....................	A	Panamá	Spanish, English
†Papua New Guinea...........	178,703	3,155,000	18	Parliamentary State (Comm. of Nations)....	A	Port Moresby	Papuan and Negrito languages, English
†Paraguay...............	157,048	3,575,000	23	Republic.....................	A	Asunción	Spanish, Guraní
Peking	6,487	9,735,000	1,501	Autonomous City (China)	D	Peking (Beijing)	Chinese
Pennsylvania..............	46,047	11,885,000	258	State (U.S.)...................	D	Harrisburg; Philadelphia	English
Persia, see Iran...........	......	......					
†Peru..................	496,224	19,555,000	39	Republic.....................	A	Lima	Spanish, Quechua, Aymara
†Philippines	115,831	52,720,000	455	Republic.....................	A	Manila	Pilipino, English, Spanish
Pitcairn (excl. Dependencies) ...	1.8	54	30	Colony (U.K.)	C	Adamstown	English
†Poland.................	120,728	36,725,000	304	Socialist Republic	A	Warsaw (Warszawa); Katowice	Polish
†Portugal................	35,516	10,230,000	288	Republic.....................	A	Lisbon (Lisboa)	Portuguese
Portuguese Guinea, see Guinea-Bissau.........	......	......					
Prairie Provinces...........	757,985	4,420,000	5.8	Part of Canada (3 provinces)		......; Winnipeg	English
Prince Edward Island	2,184	126,000	58	Province (Canada)...............	D	Charlottetown	English
Puerto Rico...............	3,515	3,365,000	957	Commonwealth (U.S. protection).......	B	San Juan	Spanish, English
†Qatar.................	4,247	270,000	64	Monarchy	A	Doha	Arabic, English
Quebec..................	594,860	6,600,000	11	Province (Canada)...............	D	Québec; Montréal	French, English
Queensland...............	667,000	2,470,000	5.2	State (Australia)................	D	Brisbane	English
Reunion	969	540,000	557	Overseas Department (France)	D	Saint-Denis	French
Rhineland-Palatinate (Rheinland-Pfalz)...............	7,663	3,625,000	473	State (Federal Republic of Germany)	D	Mainz	German
Rhode Island.............	1,212	960,00	792	State (U.S.)...................	D	Providence	English
Rhodesia, see Zimbabwe......	......	......					
Rodrigues	42	34,000	810	Part of Mauritius		......; Port Mathurin	English, French
†Romania...............	91,699	23,025,000	251	Socialist Republic	A	Bucharest (Bucureşti)	Romanian, Hungarian, German
Russian Soviet Federated Socialist Republic	6,592,846	142,705,000	22	Soviet Federated Socialist Republic (U.S.S.R.)..................	D	Moscow (Moskva)	Russian, Finno-Ugric languages, Farsi, Turkish, Mongolian
†Rwanda...............	10,169	5,380,000	529	Republic.....................	A	Kigali	French, Kinyarwanda
†Saar (Saarland)..........	992	1,055,000	1,064	State (Federal Republic of Germany)	D	Saarbrücken	German
Sabah.................	29,388	1,130,000	38	State (Malaysia)................	D	Kota Kinabalu	Bahasa Malaysia, Chinese, English, native languages
St. Christopher-Nevis.........	104	45,000	433	Parliamentary State (Comm. of Nations)....	A	Basseterre	English
St. Helena (incl. Dependencies)...........	162	6,000	37	Colony (U.K.)	C	Jamestown	English
†St. Lucia..............	238	120,000	504	Parliamentary State (Comm. of Nations)....	A	Castries	English, French
St. Pierre and Miquelon	93	6,100	66	Overseas Department (France)	D	Saint-Pierre	French
†St. Vincent and the Grenadines	150	136,000	350	Parliamentary State (Comm. of Nations)....	A	Kingstown	English
San Marino...............	24	22,000	917	Republic.....................	A	San Marino	Italian
†Sao Tome and Principe........	372	89,000	239	Republic.....................	A	São Tomé	Portuguese, native languages
Sarawak................	48,342	1,460,000	30	State (Malaysia)................	D	Kuching	Bahasa Malaysia, Chinese, English, native languages
Sardinia	9,301	1,590,000	171	Part of Italy (Sardegna Autonomous Region)...................	D	Cagliari	Italian
Saskatchewan	251,700	1,000,000	4.0	Province (Canada)...............	D	Regina	English
†Saudi Arabia............	830,000	10,220,000	12	Monarchy	A	Riyadh	Arabic
Scandinavia (incl. Finland and Iceland).............	510,000	22,740,000	45			......; Copenhagen (København)	Swedish, Danish, Norwegian, Finnish, Icelandic
Schleswig-Holstein..........	6,070	2,605,000	429	State (Federal Republic of Germany)	D	Kiel	German
Scotland................	30,416	5,175,000	170	Administrative division of U.K.	D	Edinburgh	English, Scots Gaelic
†Senegal...............	75,955	6,190,000	81	Republic.....................	A	Dakar	Wolof, French, native languages
†Seychelles	171	65,000	380	Republic (Comm. of Nations)........	A	Victoria	French, Creole, English
Shanghai................	2,239	12,455,000	5,563	Autonomous City (China)	D	Shanghai	Chinese
Shansi..................	61,004	26,380,000	432	Province (China)................	D	Taiyüan	Chinese
Shantung................	59,074	77,440,000	1,311	Province (China)................	D	Tsinan (Chinan); Tsingtao (Chingtao)	Chinese
Shensi..................	76,062	30,140,000	396	Province (China)................	D	Sian	Chinese
Shetland Islands............	551	27,000	19	Part of Scotland, U.K. (Shetland Island Area)		Lerwick	English
Siam, see Thailand...........	......	......					
Sicily...................	9,926	4,880,000	492	Part of Italy (Sicilia Autonomous Region)................	D	Palermo	Italian
†Sierra Leone............	27,925	3,825,000	137	Republic (Comm. of Nations)........	A	Freetown	English, Krio, native languages
†Singapore..............	224	2,540,000	11,339	Republic (Comm. of Nations)........	A	Singapore	Chinese, Malay, English, Tamil
Sinkiang................	635,910	13,710,000	22	Autonomous Region (China)	D	Urumchi	Turkish, Mongolian, Tungus
†Solomon Islands..........	11,506	260,000	23	Parliamentary State (Comm. of Nations)....	A	Honiara	Malay-Polynesian languages, English
†Somalia...............	246,200	7,160,000	29	Socialist Republic	A	Mogadishu (Muqdisho)	Somali, Arabic, English, Italian
†South Africa (incl. Walvis Bay)..................	434,674	24,465,000	56	Republic.....................	A	Pretoria and Cape Town; Johannesburg	English, Afrikaans, native languages
South America............	6,860,000	262,300,000	38			......; São Paulo	
South Australia	380,070	1,370,000	3.6	State (Australia)................	D	Adelaide	English
South Carolina............	31,116	3,280,000	105	State (U.S.)...................	D	Columbia; Charleston	English
South Dakota.............	77,120	705,000	9.1	State (U.S.)...................	D	Pierre; Sioux Falls	English

* Areas include inland water.
† Member of the United Nations (1983).
... None, or not applicable.

Country, Division, or Region English (Conventional)	Area* in sq. mi.	Estimated Population 1/1/84	Pop. per sq. mi.	Form of Government and Political Status	Capital: Largest City (unless same)	Predominant Language
Southern Yemen, see Yemen, People's Democratic Republic of	....	....	...			....
South Georgia (incl. Dependencies)	1,580	22	0.01	Dependency of Falkland Islands (U.K.)(3) C		English, Norwegian
South West Africa, see Namibia Soviet Union, see Union of Soviet Socialist Republics	....	....	...			....
†Spain	194,882	38,350,000	197	Constitutional Monarchy .... A	Madrid	Spanish
Spanish North Africa (Sp.)(2)	12	136,000	11,333	Five Possessions (No Central Government) C	......; Cueta	Spanish, Arabic, Berber
Spanish Sahara, see Western Sahara	....	....	...			....
†Sri Lanka	24,962	15,510,000	621	Socialist Republic (Comm. of Nations)...... A	Colombo	Sinhala, Tamil, English
†Sudan	967,500	20,500,000	21	Republic. .... A	Khartoum	Arabic, native languages, English
Sumatra	182,860	29,935,000	164	Part of Indonesia (7 provinces) .... A	......; Medan	Bahasa Indonesia, English, Chinese
†Suriname	63,037	375,000	5.9	Republic. .... A	Paramaribo	Dutch, English, Sranang Tongo
Svalbard	23,958	4,200	0.2	Part of Norway .... A	......; Longyearbyen	Norwegian, Russian
†Swaziland	6,704	615,000	92	Monarchy (Comm. of Nations) ...... A	Mbabane; Manzini	English, siSwati
†Sweden	173,780	8,350,000	48	Constitutional Monarchy .... A	Stockholm	Swedish
Switzerland	15,943	6,470,000	406	Federal Republic .... A	Bern; Zürich	German, French, Italian
†Syria	71,498	10,635,000	149	Socialist Republic .... A	Damascus (Dimashq)	Arabic
Szechwan	216,217	103,710,000	480	Province (China) .... D	Chengtu; Chunking	Chinese, Tibetan dialects
Tadzhik S.S.R.	55,251	4,100,000	74	Soviet Socialist Republic (U.S.S.R.) ..... D	Dushanbe	Tadzhik, Turkish, Russian
Taiwan	13,900	18,870,000	1,358	Republic. .... A	Taipei	Chinese dialects
†Tanzania	364,900	20,005,000	55	Republic (Comm. of Nations). .... A	Dar es Salaam	Swahili, English, native languages
Tasmania	26,383	435,000	16	State (Australia)................. D	Hobart	English
Tennessee	42,143	4,765,000	113	State (U.S.) .... D	Nashville; Memphis	English
Texas	266,805	15,565,000	58	State (U.S.) .... D	Austin; Dallas	English, Spanish
†Thailand	198,115	51,230,000	259	Constitutional Monarchy .... A	Bangkok (Krung Thep)	Thai
Tibet	471,044	2,095,000	4.4	Autonomous Region (China) .... D	Lasa (Lhasa)	Tibetan dialects
Tientsin	4,247	8,165,000	1,923	Autonomous City (China) .... D	Tientsin	Chinese
†Togo	21,925	2,825,000	129	Republic. .... A	Lomé	Native languages, French
Tokelau	3.9	1,500	385	Island Territory (New Zealand). C	......; Fakaofo	Malay-Polynesian languages, English
Tonga	270	104,000	385	Constitutional Monarchy (Comm. of Nations) .... A	Nuku'alofa	Tongan, English
Transcaucasia	71,853	14,765,000	205	Part of U.S.S.R. (3 republics) .... D	......; Baku	Russian, Armenian, Georgic, Turkish
Transkei(6)	15,831	2,495,000	158	Bantu Homeland (South African protection) .... B	Umtata	Xhosa, Afrikaans
†Trinidad and Tobago	1,980	1,220,000	616	Republic (Comm. of Nations). .... A	Port of Spain	English
Tristan da Cunha	40	300	7.5	Dependency of St. Helena (U.K.) C	Edinburgh	English
Trucial States, see United Arab Emirates	....	....	...			....
Tsinghai	277,993	4,185,000	15	Province (China) .... D	Hsining	Tibetan dialects, Mongolian; Turkish, Chinese
†Tunisia	63,170	6,905,000	109	Republic. .... A	Tunis	Arabic, French
†Turkey	300,948	47,715,000	159	Republic. .... A	Ankara; İstanbul	Turkish, Kurdish, Arabic
Turkey in Europe	9,175	4,495,000	490	Part of Turkey.	......; İstanbul	Turkish
Turkmen S.S.R.	188,456	2,980,000	16	Soviet Socialist Republic (U.S.S.R.) .... D	Ashkhabad	Turkish, Russian
Turks and Caicos Islands.	166	8,000	48	Colony (U.K.) C	Grand Turk	English
Tuvalu	10	7,800	780	Parliamentary State (Comm. of Nations) .... A	Funafuti	English, Tuvaluan
†Uganda	91,134	14,140,000	155	Republic (Comm. of Nations). .... A	Kampala	English, Swahili, Luganda, native languages
†Ukrainian S.S.R.	233,090	51,420,000	221	Soviet Socialist Republic (U.S.S.R) .... D	Kiev	Ukrainian, Russian
†Union of Soviet Socialist Republics	8,600,383	273,380,000	32	Federal Socialist Republic .... A	Moskow (Moskva)	Russian and other Slavic languages various and other Altaic and Indo-European languages
U.S.S.R. in Europe	1,920,789	177,360,000	92	Part of U.S.S.R.	......; Moskow (Moskva)	Russian and other Slavic languages
†United Arab Emirates	32,278	1,450,000	45	Federation of Monarchs. .... A	Abu Dhabi	Arabic, English, Farsi
United Arab Republic, see Egypt.	....	....	...			....
†United Kingdom	94,249	56,010,000	594	Constitutional Monarchy (Comm. of Nations) .... A	London	English, Gaelic
United Kingdom and Possessions	102,311	61,715,000	603	....	London	English
†United States	3,679,245	235,310,000	64	Federal Republic .... A	Washington; New York	English
United States and Possessions	3,683,901	239,075,000	65	....	Washington; New York	English, Spanish
†Upper Volta	105,869	6,525,000	62	Provisional Military Government .... A	Ouagadougou	French, native languages
†Uruguay	68,037	2,980,000	44	Republic. .... A	Montevideo	Spanish
Utah	84,902	1,640,000	19	State (U.S.) .... D	Salt Lake City	English
Uzbek S.S.R.	172,742	16,565,000	96	Soviet Socialist Republic (U.S.S.R.) .... D	Tashkent	Turkish, Sart, Russian
†Vanuatu	5,714	129,000	23	Republic (Comm. of Nations). .... A	Port-Vila	Bislama, French, English
Vatican City	0.2	700	3,500	Ecclesiastical State. .... A	Vatican City	Italian, Latin
Venda(6)	2,774	390,000	141	Bantu Homeland (South African protection) .... B	Thohoyandou; Makearela	Venda, Afrikaans
†Venezuela	352,144	15,325,000	44	Federal Republic .... A	Caracas	Spanish
Vermont	9,614	530,000	55	State (U.S.) .... D	Montpelier; Burlington	English
Victoria	87,884	4,100,000	47	State (Australia) .... D	Melbourne	English
Vietnam	127,242	58,070,000	456	Socialist Republic .... A	Hanoi; Ho Chi Minh City	Vietnamese
Virginia	40,763	5,615,000	138	State (U.S.) .... D	Richmond; Norfolk	English
Virgin Islands (U.S.)	133	104,000	782	Unincorporated Territory (U.S.) C	Charlotte Amalie	English, Spanish
Virgin Islands, British	59	13,000	220	Colony (U.K.) C	Road Town	English
Wake Island	3.0	400	133	Unincorporated Territory (U.S.) C		English
Wales	8,019	2,810,000	350	Administrative division of U.K. .... D	Cardiff	English, Welsh
Wallis and Futuna	98	12,000	122	Overseas Territory (France) C	Mata-Utu; Ono	French, Uvean, Futunan
Washington	68,139	4,290,000	63	State (U.S.) .... D	Olympia; Seattle	English
Western Australia	975,920	1,360,000	1.4	State (Australia) .... D	Perth	English
Western Sahara	102,703	150,000	1.5	Occupied by Morocco C	El Aaiún	Arabic
†Western Samoa	1,097	160,000	146	Constitutional Monarchy (Comm. of Nations) .... A	Apia	Samoan, English
West Indies	92,000	29,995,000	326	....	......; Havana	Spanish, English, French, Creole
West Virginia	24,236	1,985,000	82	State (U.S.) .... D	Charleston; Huntington	English
White Russia, see Byelorussian S.S.R.	....	....	...			....
Wisconsin	66,213	4,835,000	73	State (U.S.) .... D	Madison; Milwaukee	English
Wyoming	97,808	535,000	5.5	State (U.S.) .... D	Cheyenne	English
†Yemen	75,290	6,285,000	83	Republic. .... A	San'a'	Arabic
†Yemen, People's Democratic Republic of	128,560	2,185,000	17	Socialist Republic .... A	Aden	Arabic
†Yugoslavia	98,766	22,915,000	232	Federal Socialist Republic .... A	Belgrade (Beograd)	Serbo-Croatian, Slovene, Macedonian
Yukon Territory	186,300	25,000	0.1	Territory (Canada) .... D	Whitehorse	English, Eskimo, Indian
Yunnan	147,105	33,910,000	231	Province (China) .... D	Kunming	Chinese, Tibetan dialects, Khmer
†Zaire	905,567	31,705,000	35	Republic. .... A	Kinshasa (Léopoldville)	French, English, Lingala, Swahili, Kikongo, Tshiluba
†Zambia	290,586	6,435,000	22	Republic (Comm. of Nations). .... A	Lusaka	English, native languages
Zanzibar	950	540,000	568	Part of Tanzania .... D	Zanzibar	Swahili, English, native languages
Zimbabwe	150,804	8,510,000	56	Republic (Comm. of Nations). .... A	Harare (Salisbury)	English, native languages
World	57,740,000	4,733,000,000	82	....	......; Tōkyō	....

* Areas include inland water.
† Member of the United Nations (1983).
. . . None, or not applicable.
(2) Comprises Ceuta, Melilla, and several small islands.
(6) Bophuthatswana, Ciskei, Transkei, and Venda are not recognized by the United Nations.

World Facts and Comparisons

MOVEMENTS OF THE EARTH

The earth makes one complete revolution around the sun every 365 days, 5 hours, 48 minutes, and 46 seconds.

The earth makes one complete rotation on its axis in 23 hours and 56 minutes.

The earth revolves in its orbit around the sun at a speed of 66,700 miles per hour.

The earth rotates on its axis at an equatorial speed of more than 1,000 miles per hour.

MEASUREMENTS OF THE EARTH

Estimated age of the earth, at least 3 billion years.
Equatorial diameter of the earth, 7,926.68 miles.
Polar diameter of the earth, 7,899.99 miles.
Mean diameter of the earth, 7,918.78 miles.
Equatorial circumference of the earth, 24,902.45 miles.
Polar circumference of the earth, 24,818.60 miles.

Difference between equatorial and polar circumference of the earth, 83.85 miles.

Weight of the earth, 6,600,000,000,000,000,000,000 tons, or 6,600 billion billion tons.

Total area of the earth, 196,940,400 square miles.

Total land area of the earth (including inland water and Antarctica), 57,740,000 square miles.

THE EARTH'S INHABITANTS

Total population of the earth is estimated to be 4,733,000,000 (January 1, 1984).

Estimated population density of the earth, 82 per square mile.

THE EARTH'S SURFACE

Highest point on the earth's surface, Mount Everest, China (Tibet)–Nepal, 29,028 feet.

Lowest point on the earth's land surface, shores of the Dead Sea, Israel-Jordan, 1,299 feet below sea level.

Greatest ocean depth, the Marianas Trench, south of Guam, Pacific Ocean, 36,198 feet.

EXTREMES OF TEMPERATURE AND RAINFALL OF THE EARTH

Highest temperature ever recorded, 136.4°F. at Al 'Azīzīyah, Libya, Africa, on September 13, 1922.

Lowest temperature ever recorded, −126.9°F. at Vostok, Antarctica, on August 24, 1960.

Highest mean annual temperature, 88°F. at Lugh Ferrandi, Somalia.

Lowest mean annual temperature, −67°F. at Vostok, Antarctica.

At Cilaos, Réunion Island, in the Indian Ocean, 74 inches of rainfall was reported in a 24-hour period, March 15-16, 1952. This is believed to be the world's record for a 24-hour rainfall.

An authenticated rainfall of 366 inches in 1 month—July, 1861— was reported at Cherrapunji, India. More than 131 inches fell in a period of 7 consecutive days in June, 1931. Average annual rainfall at Cherrapunji is 450 inches.

The Continents

CONTINENT	Area (sq. mi.)	Population Estimated Jan. 1, 1984	Population per sq. mi.	Mean Elevation (feet)	Highest Elevation (Feet)	Lowest Elevation (Feet)	Highest Recorded Temperature	Lowest Recorded Temperature
North America	9,410,000	391,100,000	42	2,000	Mt. McKinley, United States (Alaska), 20,320	Death Valley, California, 282 below sea level	Death Valley, California 134°F.	Snag, Yukon, Canada, −81°F.
South America	6,860,000	262,300,000	38	1,800	Mt. Aconcagua, Argentina, 22,831	Salinas Chicas, Argentina, 138 below sea level	Rivadavia, Argentina, 120°F.	Sarmiento, Argentina, −27.4°F.
Europe	3,840,000	672,400,000	175	980	Mt. Elbrus, Soviet Union, 18,510	Caspian Sea, Soviet Union—Iran, 92 below sea level	Sevilla (Seville), Spain, 122°F.	Ust-Shchugor, Soviet Union, −67°F.
Asia	17,240,000	2,863,400,000	166	3,000	Mt. Everest, China (Tibet)-Nepal, 29,028	Dead Sea, Israel-Jordan, 1,299 below sea level	Tirat Zvi, Israel, 129.2°F.	Oymyakon, Soviet Union, −89.9°F.
Africa	11,700,000	519,800,000	44	1,900	Mt. Kilimanjaro, Tanzania, 19,340	Lac Assal, Djibouti, 509 below sea level	Al 'Azīzīyah, Libya, 139.4°F.	Ifrane, Morocco, −11.2°F.
Oceania, incl. Australia	3,290,000	24,000,000	7	.....	Mt. Wilhelm, Papua New Guinea, 14,793	Lake Eyre, South Australia, 52 below sea level	Cloncurry, Queensland, Australia, 127.5°F.	Charlotte Pass, New South Wales, Australia, −8°F.
Australia	2,967,909	15,535,000	5	1,000	Mt. Kosciusko, New South Wales, 7,310	Lake Eyre, South Australia, 52 below sea level	Cloncurry, Queensland, 127.5°F.	Charlotte Pass, New South Wales, −8°F.
Antarctica	5,405,000	Uninhabited	...	6,000	Vinson Massif, 16,864	Unknown	Esperanza (Antarctic Peninsula), 58.3°F.	Vostok, −126.9°F.
World	57,740,000	4,733,000,000	82	.....	Mt. Everest, China (Tibet)-Nepal, 29,028	Dead Sea, Israel-Jordan, 1,299 below sea level	Al 'Azīzīyah, Libya, 136.4°F.	Vostok, −126.9°F.

Approximate Population of the World   1650-1984*

AREA	1650	1750	1800	1850	1900	1914	1920	1939	1950	1984
North America	5,000,000	5,000,000	13,000,000	39,000,000	106,000,000	141,000,000	147,000,000	186,000,000	219,000,000	391,100,000
South America	8,000,000	7,000,000	12,000,000	20,000,000	38,000,000	55,000,000	61,000,000	90,000,000	111,000,000	262,300,000
Europe	100,000,000	140,000,000	190,000,000	265,000,000	400,000,000	470,000,000	453,000,000	526,000,000	530,000,000	672,400,000
Asia	335,000,000	476,000,000	593,000,000	754,000,000	932,000,000	1,006,000,000	1,000,000,000	1,247,000,000	1,418,000,000	2,863,400,000
Africa	100,000,000	95,000,000	90,000,000	95,000,000	118,000,000	130,000,000	140,000,000	170,000,000	199,000,000	519,800,000
Oceania, incl. Australia	2,000,000	2,000,000	2,000,000	2,000,000	6,000,000	8,000,000	9,000,000	11,000,000	13,000,000	24,000,000
Australia					4,000,000	5,000,000	6,000,000	7,000,000	8,000,000	15,535,000
World	550,000,000	725,000,000	900,000,000	1,175,000,000	1,600,000,000	1,810,000,000	1,810,000,000	2,230,000,000	2,490,000,000	4,733,000,000

*Figures prior to 1984 are rounded to the nearest million.   Figures in italics represent very rough estimates.

Largest Countries of the World in Population

	Population 1/1/84
1 China (excl. Taiwan)	1,046,530,000
2 India (incl. part of Jammu and Kashmir)	738,240,000
3 Soviet Union	273,380,000
4 United States	235,310,000
5 Indonesia	157,560,000
6 Brazil	133,100,000
7 Japan	119,680,000
8 Pakistan (incl. part of Jammu and Kashmir)	100,580,000
9 Bangladesh	95,600,000
10 Nigeria	84,945,000
11 Mexico	75,750,000
12 Federal Republic of Germany (incl. West Berlin)	61,480,000
13 Vietnam	58,070,000
14 Italy	56,685,000
15 United Kingdom	56,010,000
16 France	54,730,000
17 Philippines	52,720,000
18 Thailand	51,230,000
19 Turkey	47,715,000
20 Egypt	46,465,000
21 Iran	43,335,000
22 South Korea	40,945,000
23 Spain	38,350,000
24 Burma	37,505,000
25 Poland	36,725,000

Largest Countries of the World in Area

	Area (sq. mi.)
1 Soviet Union	8,600,383
2 Canada	3,831,033
3 United States	3,679,245
4 China (excl. Taiwan)	3,630,747
5 Brazil	3,265,075
6 Australia	2,967,909
7 India (incl. part of Jammu and Kashmir)	1,237,061
8 Argentina	1,068,301
9 Sudan	967,500
10 Algeria	919,595
11 Zaire	905,567
12 Greenland	840,004
13 Saudi Arabia	830,000
14 Mexico	761,604
15 Indonesia	741,101
16 Libya	679,362
17 Iran	636,296
18 Mongolia	604,250
19 Peru	496,224
20 Chad	495,755
21 Niger	489,191
22 Angola	481,353
23 Mali	478,766
24 Ethiopia	472,434
25 Colombia	439,737

Principal Mountains of the World

North America

Mountain	Height (Feet)
McKinley, △Alaska (△United States; △North America)	20,320
Logan, △Canada (△St. Elias Mts.)	19,520
Citlaltépetl (Orizaba), △Mexico	18,701
St. Elias, Alaska–Canada	18,008
Popocatépetl, Mexico	17,887
Foraker, Alaska	17,400
Ixtacihuatl, Mexico	17,343
Lucania, Yukon, Canada	17,147
Whitney, △California	14,494
Elbert, △Colorado (△Rocky Mts.)	14,433
Massive, Colorado	14,421
Harvard, Colorado	14,420
Rainier, △Washington (△Cascade Range)	14,410
Williamson, California	14,375
Blanca Pk., Colorado (△Sangre de Cristo Range)	14,345
Uncompahgre Pk., Colorado (△San Juan Mts.)	14,309
Grays Pk., Colorado (△Front Range)	14,270
Evans, Colorado	14,264
Longs Pk., Colorado	14,255
Wrangell, Alaska	14,163
Shasta, California	14,162
Pikes Peak, Colorado	14,110
Colima, Nevado de, Mexico	13,993
Tajumulco, △Guatemala (△Central America)	13,846
Gannett Pk., △Wyoming	13,804
Mauna Kea, △Hawaii (△Hawaii I.)	13,796
Grand Teton, Wyoming	13,766
Mauna Loa, Hawaii	13,680
Kings Pk., △Utah	13,528
Cloud Pk., Wyoming (△Big Horn Mts.)	13,175
Wheeler Pk., △New Mexico	13,161
Boundary Pk., △Nevada	13,143
Gunnbjörn, △Greenland	13,120
Waddington, Canada (△Coast Mts.)	13,104
Robson, Canada (△Canadian Rockies)	12,972
Granite Pk., △Montana	12,799
Borah Pk., △Idaho	12,662
Humphreys Pk., △Arizona	12,633
Chirripó Grande, △Costa Rica	12,533
Adams, Washington	12,307
San Gorgonio, California	11,502
Chiriquí, △Panama	11,411
Hood, △Oregon	11,239
Lassen Pk., California	10,457
Duarte, Pico, △Dominican Rep. (△West Indies)	10,417
Haleakala, Hawaii (△Maui)	10,023
Parícutin, Mexico	9,213
La Selle, Pic, △Haiti	8,773
Guadalupe Pk., △Texas	8,751
Olympus, Washington (△Olympic Mts.)	7,965
Monte Cristo, △El Salvador–Guatemala–Honduras	7,936
Blue Mountain Pk., △Jamaica	7,402
Harney Pk., △South Dakota (△Black Hills)	7,242
Mitchell, △North Carolina (△Appalachian Mts.)	6,684
Clingmans Dome, North Carolina–△Tennessee (△Great Smoky Mts.)	6,643
Turquino, Pico, △Cuba	6,542
Washington, △New Hampshire (△White Mts.)	6,288
Rogers, △Virginia	5,729
Marcy, △New York (△Adirondack Mts.)	5,344
Katahdin, △Maine	5,268
Kawaikini, Hawaii (△Kauai)	5,243
Spruce Knob, △West Virginia	4,862
Pelée, △Martinique	4,583
Mansfield, △Vermont (△Green Mts.)	4,393
Punta, Cerro de, △Puerto Rico	4,389
Black Mtn., △Kentucky	4,145
Kaala Pk., Hawaii (△Oahu)	4,050

South America

Mountain	Height (Feet)
Aconcagua, △Argentina (△Andes Mts.; △South America)	22,831
Ojos del Salado, Argentina–△Chile	22,590
Tupungato, Argentina–Chile	22,310
Pissis, Argentina	22,241
Mercedario, Argentina	22,211
Huascarán, △Peru	22,205
Llullaillaco, Argentina–Chile	22,057
Yerupaja, Peru	21,765
Incahuasi, Argentina–Chile	21,719
Sajama, Nevado, △Bolivia	21,391
Illimani, Bolivia	21,201
Chimborazo, △Ecuador	20,561
Cotopaxi, Ecuador	19,347
Misti, Peru	19,098
Cristóbal Colón, △Colombia	19,029
Huila, Colombia (△Cordillera Central)	18,865
Bolívar (La Columna), △Venezuela	16,411
Fitz Roy, Argentina	11,073
Neblina, Pico da, △Brazil	9,888

△Highest mountain in state, country, range, or region named.

Europe

Mountain	Height (Feet)
Elbrus, Soviet Union (△Caucasus Mts.; △Europe)	18,510
Dykh-Tau, Soviet Union	17,070
Shkhara, Soviet Union	16,594
Kazbek, Soviet Union	16,512
Blanc, Mont, △France–△Italy (△Alps)	15,771
Rosa, Monte (Dufourspitze) △Switzerland	15,200
Weisshorn, Switzerland	14,803
Matterhorn, Italy–Switzerland	14,685
Finsteraarhorn, Switzerland	14,026
Jungfrau, Switzerland	13,668
Grossglockner, △Austria	12,457
Teide, Pico de, △Spain (△Canary Is.)	12,162
Mulhacén, △Spain (continental)	11,424
Aneto, Pico de, Spain (△Pyrenees)	11,168
Etna, Italy (△Sicily)	11,122
Perdido (Perdu), Spain	11,007
Clapier, France-Italy (△Maritime Alps)	9,993
Zugspitze, Austria–△Germany, Fed. Rep. of	9,721
Coma Pedrosa, Andorra	9,665
Musala, △Bulgaria	9,592
Corno, Italy (△Apennines)	9,560
Olympus, △Greece	9,550
Triglav, △Yugoslavia	9,393
Korab, △Albania–Yugoslavia	9,068
Ginto, France (△Corsica)	8,891
Gerlachovka, △Czechoslovakia (△Carpathian Mts.)	8,737
Moldoveanu, △Romania	8,343
Rysy, Czechoslovakia–△Poland	8,199
Glittertinden, △Norway (△Scandinavia)	8,110
Parnassós, Greece	8,061
Idhi (Ida), Greece (△Crete)	8,058
Pico, △Portugal (△Azores Is.)	7,713
Hvannadalshnúkur, △Iceland	6,952
Kebnekaise, △Sweden	6,926
Estrela, △Portugal (continental)	6,539
Narodnaya, Soviet Union (△Ural Mts.)	6,184
Marmora, Punta la, Italy (△Sardinia)	6,017
Hekla, Iceland	4,747
Nevis, Ben, △United Kingdom (△Scotland)	4,406
Haltia, △Finland–Norway	4,357
Vesuvius, Italy	3,842
Snowdon, △Wales	3,560
Carrantuohill, △Ireland	3,414
Kékes, △Hungary	3,330
Scafell Pikes, △England	3,210

Asia

Mountain	Height (Feet)
Everest, △China (△Tibet)–△Nepal (△Himalaya Mts.; △Asia; △World)	29,028
Godwin Austen (K2), China–△Pakistan (△Kashmir) (△Karakoram Range)	28,250
Kanchenjunga, Nepal–△India	28,208
Makalu, China (Tibet)–Nepal	27,824
Dhaulagiri, Nepal	26,810
Nanga Parbat, Pakistan (Kashmir)	26,650
Annapurna, Nepal	26,504
Gasherbrum, Pakistan (Kashmir)	26,470
Gosainthan, China (Tibet)	26,291
Nanda Devi, India	25,645
Rakaposhi, Pakistan (Kashmir)	25,550
Kamet, India	25,447
Namcha Barwa, China (Tibet)	25,443
Gurla Mandhata, China (Tibet)	25,354
Ulugh Muztagh, China (△Kunlun Mts.)	25,338
Tirich Mir, Pakistan (△Hindu Kush)	25,230
Minya Konka, China	24,902
Muztagh Ata, China	24,787
Kula Kangri, △Bhutan	24,784
Communism Pk., △Soviet Union (△Pamir-Alay Mts.)	24,590
Pobeda Pk., China–Soviet Union (△Tien Shan)	24,406
Lenin Pk., Soviet Union	23,406
Api, Nepal	23,399
Khan-Tengri, Soviet Union	22,949
Kailas, China (Tibet)	22,031
Hkakabo Razi, △Burma–China	19,296
Demavend, △Iran	18,386
Ararat, △Turkey	17,011
Jaya Pk., △Indonesia (△New Guinea)	16,503
Klyuchevskaja Sopka, Soviet Union (△Kamchatka)	15,584
Trikora Pk., Indonesia	15,584
Belukha, Soviet Union	14,783
Tabun Bogdo (Khuitun), China–△Mongolia–Soviet Union (△Altai Mts.)	14,291
Turgun Uula, Mongolia	14,052
Kinabalu, △Malaysia (△Borneo)	13,455
Hsinkao, △Taiwan (Formosa)	13,113
Erciyeş, Turkey	12,848
Kerinci, Indonesia (△Sumatra)	12,467
Fuji, △Japan (△Honshu)	12,388
Hadūr Shuʻayb, △Yemen (△Arabian Peninsula)	12,336
Rindjani, Indonesia (△Lombok)	12,224
Semeru, Indonesia (△Java)	12,060
Munku-Sardyk, Mongolia–Soviet Union (△Sayan Mts.)	11,453
Rantekombola, Indonesia (△Celebes)	11,335
Saʻuda, Qurnet es, △Lebanon	10,131
Shām, Jabal ash, △Oman	9,957
Apo, △Philippines (△Mindanao	9,692
Pulog, Philippines (△Luzon)	9,626
Bia, Phou, △Laos	9,242
Hermon, Lebanon–△Syria	9,232
Paektu-san, China–△Korea	9,003
Anai Mudi, △India (peninsular)	8,841
Inthanon, Doi, △Thailand	8,514
Pidurutalagala, △Sri Lanka	8,281
Mayon, Philippines (Luzon)	8,077
Asahi, Japan (△Hokkaido)	7,513
Tahan, Gunong, Malaysia (△Malaya)	7,174
Olimbos, △Cyprus	6,401
Kuju-San, Japan (△Kyushu)	5,866
Meron, △Israel	3,963
Carmel, Israel	1,791

Africa

Mountain	Height (Feet)
Kilimanjaro (Kibo), △Tanzania (△Africa)	19,340
Kirinyaga (Kenya), △Kenya	17,058
Margherita Pk., △Zaire–△Uganda	16,763
Ras Dashen, △Ethiopia	15,158
Meru, Tanzania	14,978
Elgon, Kenya–Uganda	14,178
Toubkal, Jbel, △Morocco (△Atlas Mts.)	13,665
Cameroun, △Cameroon	13,353
Thabana Ntlenyana, △Lesotho	11,425
Koussi, Emi, △Chad (△Tibesti Mts.)	11,204
Injasuti, △South Africa	11,182
Neiges, Piton des, △Reunion	10,069
Santa Isabel, △Equatorial Guinea (△Bioko)	9,868
Tahat, △Algeria (△Ahaggar Mts.)	9,852
Maromokotro, △Madagascar	9,436
Pico, △Cape Verde	9,281
Kātrīnā, Jabal, △Egypt	8,668
São Tomé, Pico de, △Sao Tome	6,640

Oceania

Mountain	Height (Feet)
Wilhelm, △Papua New Guinea	14,793
Giluwe, Papua New Guinea	14,330
Bangeta, Papua New Guinea	13,520
Victoria, Papua New Guinea (△Owen Stanley Range)	13,240
Cook, △New Zealand (△South Island)	12,349
Ruapehu, New Zealand (△North Island)	9,175
Balbi, △Solomon Is. (△Bougainville)	9,000
Egmont, New Zealand	8,260
Sinewit, Papua New Guinea (△Bismarck Archipelago)	8,000
Orohena, △Fr. Polynesia (△Tahiti)	7,352
Kosciusko, △Australia (△New South Wales)	7,310
Silisili, Mauga, △Western Samoa	6,095
Panié, △New Caledonia	5,341
Ossa, Australia (△Tasmania)	5,305
Bartle Frere, Australia (△Queensland)	5,287
Humboldt, New Caledonia	5,282
Woodroffe, Australia (△South Australia)	4,723
Tomaniivi (Victoria), △Fiji (△Viti Levu)	4,341
Bruce, Australia (△Western Australia)	4,024

Antarctica

Mountain	Height (Feet)
Vinson Massif (△Antarctica)	16,864
Kirkpatrick	14,856
Markham	14,272
Jackson	13,747
Sidley	13,717
Wade	13,396

Great Oceans and Seas of the World

OCEANS AND SEAS	Area (sq. mi.)	Average Depth (feet)	Greatest Depth (feet)
Pacific Ocean	63,855,000	14,050	36,201
Atlantic Ocean	31,744,000	12,690	27,651
Indian Ocean	28,371,000	13,000	24,442
Arctic Ocean	5,427,000	5,010	17,880
Mediterranean Sea	967,000	4,780	16,420
South China Sea	895,000	5,420	18,090

OCEANS AND SEAS	Area (sq. mi.)	Average Depth (feet)	Greatest Depth (feet)
Bering Sea	876,000	4,710	16,800
Caribbean Sea	750,000	7,310	24,580
Gulf of Mexico	596,000	4,960	14,360
Okhotsk, Sea of	590,000	2,760	11,400
East China Sea	482,000	620	9,840
Yellow Sea	480,000	150	300

OCEANS AND SEAS	Area (sq. mi.)	Average Depth (feet)	Greatest Depth (feet)
Hudson Bay	476,000	402	850
Japan, Sea of	389,000	4,490	12,280
North Sea	222,000	310	2,170
Black Sea	178,000	3,610	7,360
Red Sea	169,000	1,610	7,370
Baltic Sea	163,000	180	1,440

Principal Lakes of the World

LAKES	Area (sq. mi.)
Caspian, Soviet Union–Iran (salt)	152,084
Superior, United States–Canada	31,820
Victoria, Kenya–Uganda–Tanzania	26,828
Aral, Soviet Union (salt)	26,518
Huron, United States–Canada	23,010
Michigan, United States	22,400
Great Bear, Canada	12,275
Baykal, Soviet Union	12,159
Great Slave, Canada	10,980
Tanganyika, Zaire–Tanzania–Burundi–Zambia	10,965
Nyasa, Malawi–Tanzania–Mozambique	10,900
Erie, United States–Canada	9,940
Winnipeg, Canada	9,465

LAKES	Area (sq. mi.)
Ontario, United States–Canada	7,540
Ladoga, Soviet Union	7,092
Balkhash, Soviet Union	6,678
Chad, Chad–Nigeria–Cameroon	△6,300
Onega, Soviet Union	3,821
Eyre, Australia (salt)	△3,700
Titicaca, Peru–Bolivia	3,500
Athabasca, Canada	3,120
Nicaragua, Nicaragua	2,972
Rudolf, Kenya–Ethiopia (salt)	2,473
Reindeer, Canada	2,467
Issyk-Kul, Soviet Union	2,393
Urmia, Iran (salt)	△2,229

LAKES	Area (sq. mi.)
Torrens, Australia (salt)	△2,200
Albert, Uganda–Zaire	2,162
Vänern, Sweden	2,156
Winnipegosis, Canada	2,103
Bangweulu, Zambia	△1,900
Nipigon, Canada	1,870
Manitoba, Canada	1,817
Great Salt, United States (salt)	1,700
Koko Nor (Ching Hai), China	1,650
Dubawnt, Canada	1,600
Gairdner, Australia (salt)	△1,500
Lake of the Woods, United States–Canada	1,485
Van, Turkey (salt)	1,470

△ Due to seasonal fluctuations in water level, areas of these lakes vary considerably.

Principal Rivers of the World

River	Length (miles)
Nile, Africa	4,132
Amazon (Amazonas), South America	3,900
Mississippi–Missouri–Red Rock, North America	3,860
Ob-Irtysh, Asia	3,461
Yangtze (Chang), Asia	3,430
Huang Ho (Yellow), Asia	2,903
Congo (Zaïre), Africa	2,900
Amur, Asia	2,802
Irtysh, Asia	2,747
Lena, Asia	2,653
Mackenzie, North America	2,635
Mekong, Asia	2,600
Niger, Africa	2,590
Yenisey, Asia	2,566
Missouri, North America	2,466
Paraná, South America	2,450
Mississippi, North America	2,348
Plata-Paraguay, South America	2,300
Volga, Europe	2,293
Madeira, South America	2,060
Indus, Asia	1,980
Purús, South America	1,900
St. Lawrence, North America	1,900
Rio Grande, North America	1,885
Brahmaputra (Yalutsangpu), Asia	1,800
Orinoco, South America	1,800
São Francisco, South America	1,800
Yukon, North America	1,800
Danube, Europe	1,770
Darling, Australia	1,750
Salween, Asia	1,730
Euphrates (Firat), Asia	1,675
Syr Darya, Asia	1,653
Zambezi, Africa	1,650
Tocantins, South America	1,640
Araguaia, South America	1,630

River	Length (miles)
Amu Darya, Asia	1,628
Kolyma, Asia	1,615
Murray, Australia	1,600
Ganges, Asia	1,550
Pilcomayo, South America	1,550
Angara, Asia	1,549
Ural, Asia	1,522
Vilyuy, Asia	1,513
Arkansas, North America	1,450
Colorado, North America (U.S.–Mexico)	1,450
Irrawaddy, Asia	1,425
Dnepr, Europe	1,420
Aldan, Asia	1,392
Negro, South America	1,305
Paraguay, South America	1,290
Kama, Europe	1,261
Juruá, South America	1,250
Xingú, South America	1,230
Don, Europe	1,224
Ucayali, South America	1,220
Columbia, North America	1,214
Saskatchewan, North America	1,205
Peace, North America	1,195
Orange, Africa	1,155
Tigris, Asia	1,150
Sungari, Asia	1,140
Pechora, Europe	1,118
Tobol, Asia	1,093
Snake, North America	1,038
Uruguay, South America	1,025
Red, North America	1,018
Churchill, North America	1,000
Marañón, South America	1,000
Ohio, North America	981
Magdalena, South America	950
Roosevelt (River of Doubt), South America	950
Godavari, Asia	930

River	Length (miles)
Si, Asia	930
Oka, Europe	920
Canadian, North America	906
Dnestr, Europe	876
Brazos, North America	870
Salado, South America	870
Fraser, North America	850
Parnaíba, South America	850
Colorado, North America (Texas)	840
Rhine, Europe	820
Narbada, Asia	800
Athabasca, North America	765
Donets, Europe	735
Pecos, North America	735
Green, North America	730
Elbe, Europe	720
James, North America	710
Ottawa, North America	696
White, North America	690
Cumberland, North America	687
Gambia, Africa	680
Yellowstone, North America	671
Tennessee, North America	652
Gila, North America	630
Vistula (Wisła), Europe	630
Loire, Europe	625
Tagus (Tajo) (Tejo), Europe	625
North Platte, North America	618
Albany, North America	610
Tisza (Tisa), Europe	607
Back, North America	605
Ouachita, North America	605
Cimarron, North America	600
Sava, Europe	585
Nemunas (Niemen), Europe	582
Branco, South America	580
Oder, Europe	565

Principal Islands of the World

Island	Area (sq. mi.)
Greenland, Arctic Region	840,000
New Guinea, Oceania	316,856
Borneo, Indonesia–Malaysia–Brunei	286,967
Madagascar, Indian Ocean	227,800
Baffin, Canadian Arctic	183,810
Sumatra, Indonesia	182,860
Honshū, Japan	88,930
Great Britain, North Atlantic Ocean	88,756
Ellesmere, Canadian Arctic	82,119
Victoria, Canadian Arctic	81,930
Celebes, Indonesia	72,986
South Island, New Zealand	58,093
Java, Indonesia	50,745
North Island, New Zealand	44,281
Cuba, West Indies	44,218
Newfoundland, North Atlantic Ocean	43,359
Luzon, Philippines	40,814
Iceland, North Atlantic Ocean	39,800
Mindanao, Philippines	36,906
Ireland, North Atlantic Ocean	32,596
Novaya Zemlya, Soviet Arctic	31,390
Hokkaidō, Japan	29,950

Island	Area (sq. mi.)
Hispaniola, West Indies	29,530
Sakhalin, Soviet Union	29,344
Tasmania, Australia	26,383
Sri Lanka (Ceylon), Indian Ocean	25,332
Banks, Canadian Arctic	23,230
Devon, Canadian Arctic	20,861
Tierra del Fuego, Argentina-Chile	18,600
Kyūshū, Japan	16,215
Melville, Canadian Arctic	16,141
Southampton, Hudson Bay, Canada	15,700
West Spitsbergen, Arctic Region	15,260
New Britain, Oceania	14,592
Taiwan (Formosa), China Sea	13,885
Hainan, South China Sea	13,127
Timor, Timor Sea	13,094
Prince of Wales, Canadian Arctic	12,830
Vancouver, Canada	12,408
Sicily, Mediterranean Sea	9,926
Somerset, Canadian Arctic	9,370
Sardinia, Mediterranean Sea	9,301
Shikoku, Japan	7,245
North East Land, Svalbard Group	6,350

Island	Area (sq. mi.)
Ceram, Indonesia	6,046
New Caledonia, Oceania	5,671
Flores, Indonesia	5,513
Samar, Philippines	5,124
Negros, Philippines	4,903
Palawan, Philippines	4,500
Panay, Philippines	4,448
Jamaica, West Indies	4,232
Hawaii, Oceania	4,030
Cape Breton, Canada	3,970
Bougainville, Oceania	3,880
Mindoro, Philippines	3,794
Cyprus, Mediterranean Sea	3,572
Kodiak, Gulf of Alaska	3,569
Puerto Rico, West Indies	3,435
Corsica, Mediterranean Sea	3,352
Crete, Mediterranean Sea	3,217
New Ireland, Oceania	3,205
Leyte, Philippines	3,090
Wrangel, Soviet Arctic	2,819
Guadalcanal, Oceania	2,500
Long Island, United States	1,620

Largest Metropolitan Areas of the World, 1981

This table lists the major metropolitan areas of the world according to their estimated population on January 1, 1981. For convenience in reference, the areas are grouped by major region, and the number of areas in each region and size group is given.

There are 27 areas with more than 5,000,000 population each; these are listed in rank order of estimated population, with the world rank given in parentheses following the name. For example, New York's 1981 rank is second. Below the 5,000,000 level, the metropolitan areas are listed alphabetically within region, not in order of size.

For ease of comparison, each metropolitan area has been defined by Rand McNally & Company according to consistent rules. A metropolitan area includes a central city, neighboring communities linked to it by continuous built-up areas, and more distant communities if the bulk of their population is supported by commuters to the central city. Some metropolitan areas have more than one central city, for example Tōkyō–Yokohama or San Francisco–Oakland–San Jose.

POPULATION CLASSIFICATION	UNITED STATES and CANADA	LATIN AMERICA	EUROPE (excl. U.S.S.R.)	U.S.S.R.	ASIA	AFRICA–OCEANIA
Over 15,000,000 (4)	New York, U.S. (2)	Mexico City, Mex. (4)			Tōkyō–Yokohama, Jap. (1) Ōsaka–Kōbe–Kyōto, Jap. (3)	
10,000,000–15,000,000 (6)		São Paulo, Braz. (5) Buenos Aires, Arg. (10)	London, Eng. (8)	Moscow (6)	Seoul, Kor. (7) Calcutta, India (9)	
5,000,000–10,000,000 (17)	Los Angeles, U.S. (11) Chicago, U.S. (17) Philadelphia–Trenton–Wilmington, U.S. (26)	Rio de Janeiro, Braz. (12)	Paris, Fr. (13) Essen–Dortmund–Duisburg (The Ruhr), Ger., Fed. Rep. of (27)	Leningrad (23)	Bombay, India (14) Shanghai, China (16) Manila, Phil. (18) Jakarta, Indon. (19) Delhi–New Delhi, India (20) Peking, China (21) Tehrān, Iran (22) Bangkok, Thai. (24) Karāchi, Pak. (25)	Cairo, Eg. (15)
3,000,000–5,000,000 (31)	Boston, U.S. Detroit, U.S.–Windsor, Can. San Francisco–Oakland–San Jose, U.S. Washington, U.S.	Bogotá, Col. Caracas, Ven. Lima, Peru Santiago, Chile	Athens, Greece Barcelona, Sp. Berlin, Ger. İstanbul, Tur. Madrid, Sp. Milan, It. Rome, It.		Baghdād, Iraq Chungking, China Dacca, Bngl. Lahore, Pak. Madras, India Mukden, China Nagoya, Jap. Pusan, Kor. Rangoon, Bur. Taipei, Taiwan Tientsin, China Victoria, Hong Kong Wuhan, China	Alexandria, Eg. Johannesburg, S. Afr. Sydney, Austl.
2,000,000–3,000,000 (45)	Cleveland, U.S. Dallas–Fort Worth, U.S. Houston, U.S. Miami–Fort Lauderdale, U.S. Montréal, Can. Pittsburgh, U.S. St. Louis, U.S. San Diego, U.S.–Tijuana, Mex. Seattle–Tacoma, U.S. Toronto, Can.	Belo Horizonte, Braz. Guadalajara, Mex. Havana, Cuba Medellín, Col. Monterrey, Mex. Porto Alegre, Braz. Recife, Braz.	Birmingham, Eng. Brussels, Bel. Bucharest, Rom. Budapest, Hung. Hamburg, Ger., Fed. Rep. of Katowice–Bytom–Gliwice, Pol. Lisbon, Port. Manchester, Eng. Naples, It. Warsaw, Pol.	Donetsk–Makeyevka Kiev Tashkent	Ahmādābād, India Ankara, Tur. Bangalore, India Canton, China Chengtu, China Harbin, China Ho Chi Minh City (Saigon), Viet. Hyderābād, India Sian, China Singapore, Singapore	Algiers, Alg. Casablanca, Mor. Kinshasa, Zaire Lagos, Nig. Melbourne, Austl.
1,500,000–2,000,000 (35)	Atlanta, U.S. Baltimore, U.S. Minneapolis–St. Paul, U.S. Phoenix, U.S.	Salvador, Braz. San Juan, P.R.	Amsterdam, Neth. Cologne, Ger., Fed. Rep. of Copenhagen, Den. Frankfurt am Main, Ger., Fed. Rep. of Glasgow, Scot. Leeds–Bradford, Eng. Liverpool, Eng. Munich, Ger., Fed. Rep. of Stuttgart, Ger., Fed. Rep. of Turin, It. Vienna, Aus.	Baku Gorki Kharkov	Bandung, Indon. Chittagong, Bngl. Colombo, Sri Lanka Damascus, Syria Fukuoka, Jap. Hanoi, Viet. Hiroshima–Kure, Jap. Kanpur, India Kaohsiung, Taiwan Kitakyūshū–Shimonoseki, Jap. Nanking, China Pune, India Surabaya, Indon. Taegu, Kor.	Cape Town, S. Afr.
1,000,000–1,500,000 (86)	Buffalo–Niagara Falls, U.S.–St. Catharines–Niagara Falls, Can. Cincinnati, U.S. Denver, U.S. El Paso, U.S.–Ciudad Juárez, Mex. Hartford–New Britain, U.S. Indianapolis, U.S. Kansas City, U.S. Milwaukee, U.S. New Orleans, U.S. Portland, U.S. San Antonio, U.S. Vancouver, Can.	Barranquilla, Col. Brasília, Braz. Cali, Col. Córdoba, Arg. Curitiba, Braz. Fortaleza, Braz. Guatemala, Guat. Guayaquil, Ec. Montevideo, Ur. Rosario, Arg. Santo Domingo, Dom. Rep.	Antwerp, Bel. Belgrade, Yugo. Bilbao, Sp. Dublin, Ire. Düsseldorf, Ger., Fed. Rep. of Hannover, Ger., Fed. Rep. of Lille, Fr. Łódź, Pol. Lyon, Fr. Mannheim, Ger., Fed. Rep. of Marseille, Fr. Newcastle–Sunderland, Eng. Nürnberg, Ger., Fed. Rep. of Porto, Port. Prague, Czech. Rotterdam, Neth. Sofia, Bul. Stockholm, Swe. Valencia, Sp.	Chelyabinsk Dnepropetrovsk Kazan Kuybyshev Minsk Novosibirsk Odessa Omsk Perm Rostov-na-Donu Saratov Sverdlovsk Tbilisi Ufa Volgograd Yerevan	Anshan, China Beirut, Leb. Chengchou, China Dairen, China Faisalabad (Lyallpur), Pak. Fushun, China Hsinking, China Izmir, Tur. Kuala Lumpur, Mala. Kunming, China Kuwait, Kuw. Lanchou, China Lucknow, India Nāgpur, India Pyŏngyang, Kor. Rāwalpindi–Islāmābād, Pak. Sapporo, Jap. Shihchiachuang, China Taiyuan, China Tel Aviv–Yafo, Isr. Tsinan, China Tsingtao, China	Abidjan, I.C. Addis Ababa, Eth. Brisbane, Austl. Durban, S. Afr. Khartoum, Sud. Tunis, Tun.
Total by Region (224)	34	28	50	24	72	16

Population of Foreign Cities and Towns, Countries and Important Political Divisions

This table includes every urban center of 50,000 or more population in the world (excluding the United States), as well as many other important or well-known cities and towns. The table also lists major political subdivisions (states, provinces, etc.) of the leading countries.

The population figures are all from recent censuses (designated C) or official estimates (designated E), except for a few cities for which only unofficial estimates are available (designated UE). The date of the census or estimate is specified for each country. Individual exceptions are dated in parentheses or with a dagger symbol (‡ or †).

For many cities, a second population figure is given accompanied by a star (★). The starred population refers to the city's entire metropolitan area, including suburbs. These metropolitan areas have been defined by Rand McNally & Company, following consistent rules to facilitate comparisons among the urban centers of various countries. Where a place is part of the metropolitan area of another city, that city's name is specified in parentheses preceded by (★). Some important places that are considered to be secondary central cities of their areas are designated by (★★) preceding the name of the metropolitan area's main city. A population marked with a triangle (▲) refers to an entire municipality, commune, or other district, which includes rural areas in addition to the urban center itself. The names of capital cities appear in CAPITALS; the largest city in each country is designated by the symbol (•).

For more recent population totals for countries, see the Rand McNally population estimates in the table on pages 35X-39X. For lists of the largest metropolitan areas, see pages 43X (world) and 2X (United States). For a list of U.S. cities and towns, see pages 3X-34X.

AFGHANISTAN / Afghānestān

1973 E....................18,294,000

Andkhvoy (1975 E)....46,000
Baghlān....29,000
Chārikār....19,000
Ghaznī....24,000
Herāt (1975 E)....157,000
Jalālābād (1975 E)....58,000
•KĀBUL (1975 E)....749,000
Kandahār (Qandahār) (1975 E)....209,000
Khānābād....18,000
Kholm....22,000
Mazār-e-Sharīf (1975 E)....97,000
Meymaneh (1975 E)....29,000
Pol-e-Khomrī....25,000
Qondūz....46,000
Sheberghān....17,000

ALBANIA / Shqipëri

1976 E....................2,482,000

Berat (1975 E)....30,000
Durrës....61,000
Elbasan....50,700
Fier (1975 E)....28,000
Gjirokastër (1975 E)....22,000
Kavajë (1973 E)....19,900
Korçë....50,900
Lushnje (1975 E)....21,000
Shkodër....62,500
Stalin (Kuçovë) (1971 E)....14,300
•TIRANË....192,300
Vlorë (Valona)....58,400

ALGERIA / Algérie

1974 E....................16,275,000

Aïn Beïda....40,011
Aïn Benian (★Algers) (1966 C)....17,653
Aïn M'Lila (1966 C) (44,662▲)....12,632
Aïn Sefra (26,234▲)....13,100
Aïn Taya (★Algiers) (1966 C)....22,542
Aïn Témouchent....47,977
•ALGIERS (ALGER) (★1,800,000)....1,503,720
Annaba (Bône)....313,174
Arzew (1966 C)....13,080
Barika (1966 C) (40,957▲)....13,689
Batna (115,138▲)....91,500
Béchar (Colomb-Béchar)....71,081
Bejaïa (Bougie) (103,996▲)....80,000
Béni Saf (1966 C) (23,368▲)....18,507
Biskra....84,971
Blida....158,947
Bordj Bou Arreridj (85,545▲)....66,400
Bordj Ménaïel (87,736▲)....38,700
Boufarik (109,234▲)....77,700
Bouguerra (1966 C) (21,401▲)....13,373
Bouira (50,007▲)....26,800
Bou Saâda....36,433
Chelghoum el Aïd (1966 C) (27,985▲)....15,031
Cherchell (40,308▲)....17,100
Collo (40,860▲)....14,100
Constantine....350,183
Dellys (31,729▲)....13,700
Djelfa (1966 C) (30,304▲)....25,472
Djidjelli (61,545▲)....43,500
Douéra....55,993
El Affroun (67,566▲)....47,500
El Arba (1966 C) (22,857▲)....14,415
El Asnam (Orléansville) (114,327▲)....80,500
El Bayadh (33,743▲)....21,200
El Eulma (54,406▲)....41,500
El Goléa (1966 C) (16,679▲)....13,708
El Meghaier (1966 C) (23,506▲)....11,324
El Oued (1966 C) (43,547▲)....11,429
Fouka (1966 C)....10,208
Frenda (23,349▲)....16,400
Ghardaïa (85,230▲)....55,200
Ghazaouet (29,592▲)....16,600
Guelma (1966 C)....39,817
Guerrara (1966 C) (14,173▲)....12,546
Hadjout (32,334▲)....27,100
Hamma Bouziane (1966 C) (21,040▲)....11,472
Hammam Bou Hadjar (1966 C) (14,637▲)....11,219
Khemis Miliana (63,370▲)....41,400
Khenchela (49,922▲)....40,900
Koléa (48,133▲)....35,900
Ksar el Boukhari (36,986▲)....18,400
Laghouat (60,249▲)....41,900
Lakhdaria (53,780▲)....30,800
Maghnia (44,777▲)....31,000
Mascara (82,468▲)....70,600
Mecheria....23,681
Médéa (102,336▲)....70,700
Mers el Kébir (1966 C) (20,193▲)....5,624
Mila (1966 C) (33,007▲)....12,733
Miliana (46,217▲)....27,200
Mohammadia (49,730▲)....30,000
Mostaganem....101,780
M'Sila (1966 C) (36,930▲)....19,883
Oran (Ouahran)....485,139
Ouargla (69,509▲)....26,200
Oued Zenati (81,036▲)....31,900
Relizane....65,918
Rouiba (★Algiers) (87,540▲)....20,300
Saïda (59,344▲)....51,800
Sétif....157,065
Sidi bel Abbès....151,148
Sig (41,725▲)....33,900
Skikda (Philippeville)....127,968
Souk Ahras (60,551▲)....48,800
Sour el Ghozlane (67,205▲)....32,100
Tébessa....58,008
Tiaret....63,039
Tighennif (1966 C) (25,839▲)....11,834
Tizi-Ouzou (223,702▲)....108,000
Tlemcen....115,054
Touggourt (65,935▲)....34,800

AMERICAN SAMOA

1970 C....................27,159

•PAGO PAGO....2,451

ANDORRA

1971 C....................20,550

•ANDORRA....2,000

ANGOLA

1970 C....................5,673,046

Benguela....40,996
Cabinda....21,124
Huambo (Nova Lisboa)....61,885
Lobito....59,528
•LUANDA....475,328
Lubango (Sá da Bandeira)....31,674
Malanje....31,599

ANGUILLA

1974 C....................6,519

•South Hill....774
THE VALLEY....760

ANTIGUA

1970 C....................65,525

•ST. JOHNS....21,814

ARGENTINA

1970 C....................23,364,431

Almirante Brown (★Buenos Aires)....245,017
Avellaneda (★Buenos Aires)....337,538
Azul....36,023
Bahía Blanca (1979 E)....253,000
Balcarce....26,461
Berazategui (★Buenos Aires)....127,740
Berisso (★La Plata)....58,833
Bolívar....18,643
Bragado....23,366
•BUENOS AIRES (1979 E) (★10,300,000)....2,978,000
Campana (★Buenos Aires)....33,919
Cañada de Gómez....20,611
Caseros (Tres de Febrero) (★Buenos Aires)....313,460
Catamarca (★64,410)....57,228
Chivilcoy....37,190
Cipolletti....23,768
Comodoro Rivadavia....72,906
Concepción del Uruguay....38,967
Concordia....72,136
Córdoba (1979 E) (★1,026,000)....985,000
Corrientes (1979 E)....186,000
Cruz del Eje....23,401
Curuzú-Cuatiá....20,636
Cutral-Có....19,404
Ensenada (★La Plata)....39,154
Esquel....13,771
Esteban Echeverría (★Buenos Aires)....111,150
Florencio Varela (★Buenos Aires)....98,446
Formosa....61,071
General Pico....21,897
General Roca....29,320
General San Martín (★Buenos Aires)....360,573
General Sarmiento (★Buenos Aires)....315,457
Godoy Cruz (★Mendoza)....112,481
Goya....39,367
Gualeguay....20,401
Gualeguaychú....40,661
Guaymallén (★Mendoza)....112,081
Junín....59,020
La Banda (★Santiago del Estero)....33,032
Lanús (★Buenos Aires)....449,824
La Plata (1979 E) (★557,000)....435,000
La Rioja....46,090
Las Heras (★Mendoza)....67,789
Lomas de Zamora (★Buenos Aires)....410,806
Luján (★Buenos Aires)....38,393
Maipú....34,839
Mar del Plata (1979 E)....417,000
Mendoza (1979 E) (★677,000)....125,000
Mercedes (*San Luis Prov.*)....40,052
Mercedes (*Buenos Aires Prov.*) (★Buenos Aires)....39,760
Merlo (★Buenos Aires)....188,868
Moreno (★Buenos Aires)....114,041
Morón (★Buenos Aires)....485,983
Necochea....39,868
Neuquén....43,070
Olavarría....52,453
Paraná....127,635
Pergamino....56,078
Pilar (★Buenos Aires)....34,372
Posadas....97,514
Presidencia Roque Sáenz Peña....38,620
Punta Alta....36,805
Quilmes (★Buenos Aires)....355,265
Rafaela....43,695
Reconquista....25,333
Resistencia (1979 E)....183,000
Río Cuarto....88,852
Río Gallegos....27,833
Rosario (1979 UE) (★975,000)....810,000
Salta (1979 E)....254,000
San Carlos de Bariloche....26,799
San Fernando (★Buenos Aires)....119,565
San Francisco (★48,896)....45,023
San Isidro (★Buenos Aires)....250,008
San Juan (1979 E) (★310,000)....115,000
San Justo (★Buenos Aires)....659,193
San Lorenzo (★Rosario)....56,487
San Luis....50,771
San Martín....24,300
San Miguel de Tucumán (1979 E) (★442,000)....375,000
San Nicolás de los Arroyos....64,730
San Rafael....58,237
San Salvador de Jujuy....82,637
Santa Fe (1979 E)....282,000
Santa Rosa....33,649
Santiago del Estero (★140,000)....105,127
Tandil....65,876
Tartagal....23,696
Tigre (★Buenos Aires)....152,335
Trelew....24,214
Tres Arroyos....37,991
Ushuaia....5,373
Venado Tuerto....35,677
Vicente López (★Buenos Aires)....285,178
Villa Krause (★San Juan)....47,794
Villa María....56,087
Zárate....54,772

AUSTRALIA

1979 E....................14,423,500

Adelaide (★933,300)....13,400
Albury (★54,900)....36,600
Alice Springs (1976 C)....14,149
Ashfield (★Sydney)....42,850
Auburn (★Sydney)....48,400
Ballarat (★73,200)....38,400
Bankstown (★Sydney)....159,500
Bendigo (★59,600)....33,300
Blacktown (★Sydney)....179,350
Blue Mountains (★Sydney)....51,150
Botany (★Sydney)....36,150
Box Hill (★Melbourne)....49,200
Brighton (★Melbourne)....35,000
Brisbane (★1,014,700)....702,000
Brisbane Water (★Sydney) (1976 C)....54,819
Broadmeadows (★Melbourne)....112,300
Broken Hill....28,600
Brunswick (★Melbourne)....44,800
Bundaberg (★41,900)....32,500
Burnside (★Adelaide)....37,800
Cairns (★53,000)....36,000
Camberwell (★Melbourne)....88,700
Campbelltown (★Adelaide)....42,300
Campbelltown (★Sydney)....78,000
CANBERRA (★241,500)....221,000
Canning (★Perth)....48,350
Canterbury (★Sydney)....131,900
Caulfield (★Melbourne)....74,700
Coburg (★Melbourne)....57,100
Croydon (★Melbourne)....36,400
Dandenong (★Melbourne)....54,700
Darwin (1976 C) (★46,655)....39,193
Doncaster and Templestowe (★Melbourne)....89,100
Drummoyne (★Sydney)....32,700
Dubbo....22,850
Enfield (★Adelaide)....70,200
Essendon (★Melbourne)....50,300
Fairfield (★Sydney)....120,850
Footscray (★Melbourne)....51,700
Frankston (★Melbourne)....80,300
Fremantle (★Perth)....23,500
Geelong (★141,100)....15,200
Glenorchy (★Hobart) (1980 C)....42,400
Gosnells (★Perth)....46,850
Heidelberg (★Melbourne)....67,000
Hobart (1980 E) (★170,200)....49,020
Holroyd (★Sydney)....82,600
Hurstville (★Sydney)....66,950
Ipswich (★Brisbane)....71,200
Kalgoorlie (★19,300)....9,400
Keilor (★Melbourne)....76,800
Knox (★Melbourne)....83,100
Kogarah (★Sydney)....47,850
Ku-ring-gai (★Sydney)....103,100
Lake Macquarie (★Newcastle)....140,450
Launceston (1980 E) (★86,100)....32,300
Leichhardt (★Sydney)....62,550
Lismore....31,900
Liverpool (★Sydney)....95,950
Mackay (★44,800)....21,800
Maitland (★Newcastle)....38,950
Malvern (★Melbourne)....45,900
Manly (★Sydney)....36,350
Marion (★Adelaide)....69,700
Marrickville (★Sydney)....90,150
Melbourne (★2,739,700)....65,800
Melville (★Perth)....56,900
Mitcham (★Adelaide)....59,500
Moe....16,300
Moorabbin (★Melbourne)....102,900
Mount Gambier (★20,750)....18,950
Mount Isa....26,800
Newcastle (★379,800)....139,400
Northcote (★Melbourne)....53,000
North Sydney (★Sydney)....47,900
Nunawading (★Melbourne)....95,900
Oakleigh (★Melbourne)....55,400
Orange....30,650
Parramatta (★Sydney)....134,300
Penrith (★Sydney)....94,000
Perth (★883,600)....88,850
Port Adelaide (★Adelaide)....36,400
Port Augusta (★15,650)....14,400
Port Lincoln (★11,050)....10,250
Port Pirie (★14,900)....12,150
Prahran (★Melbourne)....47,900
Preston (★Melbourne)....87,900
Queanbeyan (★Canberra)....20,100
Randwick (★Sydney)....123,750
Redcliffe (★Brisbane)....41,200
Ringwood (★Melbourne)....37,900
Rockdale (★Sydney)....86,650
Rockhampton (★54,600)....53,900
Ryde (★Sydney)....91,900
St. Kilda (★Melbourne)....52,400
Salisbury (★Adelaide)....83,800
Sandringham (★Melbourne)....32,600
Shellharbour (★Wollongong)....41,650
Shepparton (★34,100)....23,200
South Perth (★Perth)....31,400
Southport (Gold Coast) (★128,000)....102,500
South Sydney (★Sydney)....32,100
Springvale (★Melbourne)....79,000
Stirling (★Perth)....169,350
Sunshine (★Melbourne)....94,600
•Sydney (★3,193,300)....49,750
Tamworth....32,650
Tea Tree Gully (★Adelaide)....63,300
Toowoomba....72,500
Townsville (★96,100)....84,900
Unley (★Adelaide)....35,700
Wagga Wagga....38,150
Waverley (★Melbourne)....121,500
Waverley (★Sydney)....64,050
West Torrens (★Adelaide)....46,100
Whyalla (★31,150)....31,000
Willoughby (★Sydney)....52,250
Wollongong (★223,950)....172,350
Woodville (★Adelaide)....76,600
Woollahra (★Sydney)....54,500

AUSTRIA / Österreich

1971 C....................7,456,745

Bruck an der Mur (★50,000)....16,359
Dornbirn....33,810
Graz (1976 E) (★275,000)....250,900
Innsbruck (1976 E) (★150,000)....120,400
Kapfenberg (★★Bruck)....26,001
Klagenfurt (1973 L)....82,512
Leoben (★48,000)....35,153
Linz (1976 E) (★290,000)....208,000
Salzburg (1976 E) (★165,000)....139,000
Sankt Pölten (1973 L)....50,144
Steyr (★54,000)....40,578
Stockerau (★Vienna) (1976 L)....12,768
Ternitz (1978 L)....16,343
Traun (★Linz)....20,843
•VIENNA (WIEN) (1979 E) (★1,925,000)....1,572,300
Villach (1973 L)....50,993
Wels (★59,000)....47,279
Wiener Neustadt (★41,000)....34,774
Wolfsberg (1974 L)....29,002

BAHAMAS

1970 C....................168,812

Freeport....15,286
•NASSAU (★101,503)....3,233

BAHRAIN / Al-Bahrayn

1971 C....................216,078

Al-Muḥarraq (★Manama)....37,577
•MANAMA (★145,000)....89,112

BANGLADESH

1974 C....................76,398,120

Barisāl....98,127
Bhairab Bazar....43,702
Bogra....47,154
Brāhmanbāria....62,407
Chāndpur....51,668
Chittagong (★1,200,000)....497,026
Chuadanga....36,381
Comilla....86,446
•DACCA (★2,750,000)....1,563,517
Dinājpur....61,866
Doublemooring (★Chittagong)....125,453
Farīdpur....46,232
Ghorāsāl....34,321
Gopālpur....39,066
Jamālpur....60,261
Jessore (★82,817)....76,168
Jhenida....34,020
Khulna....521,543
Kishorganj....35,605
Kurigram....30,129
Kushtia....36,199
Mādārīpur....32,488
Mymensingh (★182,153)....76,036
Naogaon....34,395
Nārāyanganj (★★Dacca)....201,450
Narsingdi....39,140
Nawābganj....46,059
Noākhāli....32,490
Pābna....62,254
Pānchlāish (★Chittagong)....127,839
Pārbatipur....10,604
Rājshāhi (Rampur Boalia) (★132,909)....96,645
Rangpur....72,829
Saidpur....90,132
Sātkhira....40,507
Sherpur....35,578
Sirājganj....74,457
Sitākunda (★Chittagong)....99,929
Sylhet....59,546
Tangail....51,863
Tongi (★Dacca)....67,420

BARBADOS

1970 C....................238,141

•BRIDGETOWN (★115,000)....8,789

BELGIUM / Belgique / België

1980 E....................9,855,110

Provinces

Antwerpen (Anvers)....1,573,647
Brabant....2,220,699
Hainaut (Henegouwen)....1,308,931
Liège (Luik)....1,005,947
Limburg (Limbourg)....710,715
Luxembourg (Luxemburg)....222,317
Namur (Namen)....404,481
Oost-Vlaanderen; Flandre Orientale (East Flanders)....1,330,134
West-Vlaanderen; Flandre Occidentale (West Flanders)....1,078,239

Cities

Aalst (Alost) (★Brussels)....79,340
Anderlecht (★Brussels)....95,969
Antwerp (Antwerpen) (★1,105,000)....194,073
Arlon (23,218▲)....17,400
Ath (Aat) (24,171▲)....14,400
Auderghem (★Brussels)....31,174
Bastogne (11,357▲)....6,700
Berchem (★Antwerp)....46,368
Berchem-Sainte-Agathe (Sint-Agatha-Berchem) (★Brussels)....18,792
Beveren (★Antwerp) (40,510▲)....20,300
Binche....33,743
Borgerhout (★Antwerp)....44,369
Braine-l'Alleud (★Brussels)....29,116
Brasschaat (★Antwerp)....31,663
Brugge (Bruges) (★217,000)....118,243
•BRUSSELS (BRUXELLES) (BRUSSEL) (★2,400,000)....143,957
Charlerol (★495 000)....221,911
Châtelet (★Charleroi)....38,753

C Census. E Official estimate. UE Unofficial estimate.
L Population within municipal limits of year specified. • Largest city in country.

★ Population or designation of metropolitan area, including suburbs (see headnote).
▲ Population of an entire municipality, commune, or district, including rural area.
‡† Year of information specified at start of country.

Dendermonde....................40,856
Deurne (*Antwerp).............78,646
Edegem (*Antwerp).............23,422
Eeklo............................19,541
Ekeren (*Antwerp).............30,347
Etterbeek (*Brussels)...........46,856
Eupen...........................17,072
Evere (*Brussels)...............29,772
Forest (Vorst) (*Brussels).......51,314
Ganshoren (*Brussels)..........21,593
Geel (31,450▲)...................17,300
Genk (**Hasselt)................61,512
Gent (Ghent) (*470,000)........241,695
Geraardsbergen (Grammont)
(30,447▲).......................14,900
Halle (Hal) (*Brussels)..........32,124
Hamme..........................22,938
Harelbeke (*Kortrijk)............25,213
Hasselt (*275,000)...............64,439
Herentals........................23,682
Herstal (*Liège).................39,190
Hoboken (*Antwerp)............34,640
Huy.............................18,038
Ieper (Ypres) (34,446▲)...........21,000
Ixelles (*Brussels)..............76,545
Izegem..........................26,237
Jette (*Brussels)................40,361
Knokke-Heist....................28,757
Kortrijk (Courtrai) (*200,000)....76,424
La Louvière (*148,000)..........76,892
Leuven (Louvain) (*167,000).....85,632
Liège (Luik) (*765,000)..........220,183
Lier (*Antwerp).................31,319
Lokeren.........................33,126
Maasmechelen....................33,262
Mechelen (Malines) (*120,000)...77,667
Menen...........................33,972
Merksem (*Antwerp)...........41,202
Mol (29,474▲)...................16,600
Molenbeek St.-Jean
(Sint-Jans-Molenbeek)
(*Brussels)...................70,958
Mons (Bergen) (*250,000).......96,784
Mortsel (*Antwerp).............26,834
Mouscron (Moeskroen)
(*Lille, France)................54,553
Namur (*143,000)...............100,712
Nivelles (21,318▲)...............16,300
Oostende (Ostende) (*120,000)..70,125
Oudenaarde (Audenarde)
(27,308▲).......................13,600
Roeselare (Roulers).............51,752
Ronse (Renaix)..................24,463
Saint-Gilles (Sint-Gillis)
(*Brussels)...................47,932
Schaerbeek (Schaarbeek)
(*Brussels)..................109,005
Schoten (*Antwerp)............31,180
Seraing (*Liège)................65,371
Sint-Niklaas (St.-Nicolas).......68,080
Sint-Truiden (St.-Trond)
(36,160▲).......................17,000
Soignies (23,344▲)...............11,600
Spa..............................9,766
Tienen (Tirlemont)...............32,842
Tongeren (Tongres) (29,375▲)...18,400
Tournai (Doornik) (69,862▲).....46,700
Turnhout........................37,652
Uccle (Ukkel) (*Brussels).......75,861
Verviers (*103,000).............56,209
Veurne (Furnes) (11,212▲)........7,500
Vilvoorde (*Brussels)...........33,644
Waregem........................32,088
Waterloo (*Brussels)............24,536
Watermael-Boitsfort
(*Brussels)...................24,965
Wilrijk (*Antwerp)..............43,161
Woluwe-St.-Lambert
(*Brussels)...................46,823
Woluwe-St.-Pierre (*Brussels)...39,166
Zottegem (25,152▲)...............13,000

BELIZE

1972 E..........................127,200

•Belize City.......................41,500
BELMOPAN (1971 E)..............5,000
Corozal............................5,000
Orange Walk.......................6,100
Punta Gorda.......................2,200
San Ignacio........................4,600
Stann Creek.......................7,400

BENIN (DAHOMEY)

1975 E........................3,112,000

•Cotonou.........................178,000
PORTO-NOVO....................104,000

BERMUDA

1970 C...........................52,330

•HAMILTON (*13,757)..............2,060
St. George.........................1,604

BHUTAN / Druk-Yul

1977 E........................1,232,000

THIMBU............................8,982

BOLIVIA

1976 C........................4,647,816

Cobija.............................3,636
Cochabamba......................205,002
•LA PAZ..........................654,713
Oruro............................124,121
Potosí............................77,334
Santa Cruz.......................256,946
SUCRE............................62,207
Tarija............................39,087
Trinidad..........................27,583

BOTSWANA

1971 C..........................574,094

Francistown.......................18,613
•GABORONE (GABERONES)....18,799
Kanye............................10,664
Lobatse..........................11,936
Mahalapye.......................12,056
Mochudi..........................6,945
Molepolole........................9,448
Serowe...........................15,723

BRAZIL / Brasil

1975 E......................107,145,200

States

Acre.............................249,100
Alagoas........................1,786,200
Amapá (Ter.)....................142,100
Amazonas.......................1,089,100
Bahia...........................8,438,900
Ceará...........................5,111,600
Distrito Federal (Brasília).......763,000
Espírito Santo..................1,725,100
Fernando de Noronha (Ter.)
(1970 C)..........................1,239
Goiás...........................3,558,100
Maranhão.......................3,330,000
Mato Grosso (1978 L)...........753,700
Mato Grosso do Sul (1978 L)..1,253,200
Minas Gerais...................12,550,600
Pará............................2,544,300
Paraíba.........................2,675,100
Paraná..........................8,449,200
Pernambuco....................‡5,853,400
Piauí...........................1,988,200
Rio de Janeiro.................10,400,200
Rio Grande do Norte...........1,855,700
Rio Grande do Sul..............7,457,600
Rondônia (Ter.).................141,300
Roraima (Ter.)...................48,200
Santa Catarina..................3,351,400
São Paulo......................20,636,900
Sergipe..........................992,400

‡Includes 1975 estimated population for Fernando de Noronha

Cities (1970 C or †1975 E)

Alagoinhas.......................53,891
Alegrete.........................45,522
Alvorada.........................39,485
Americana........................62,387
Anápolis.........................89,405
Andradina........................43,465
Anil..............................37,719
Apucarana........................41,800
Aracaju.........................179,512
Araçatuba........................85,660
Araguari.........................48,702
Arapiraça........................43,875
Arapongas........................36,628
Araraquara.......................82,607
Araras...........................40,945
Araxá............................31,498
Arcoverde........................33,308
Assis............................45,531
Bagé.............................57,036
Barbacena........................57,766
Barra do Piraí...................42,713
Barra Mansa
(**Volta Redonda)..............75,006
Barretos.........................53,050
Bauru...........................120,178
Bayeux (*João Pessoa)..........34,681
Belém (*660,000)................565,097
Belford Roxo (*Rio de Janeiro).173,427
Belo Horizonte (*1,945,000)..†1,557,464
Blumenau.........................85,942
Boa Vista (*Roraima Ter.*)..........16,720
Boa Vista (*Santa Catarina State*).33,503
Botucatu.........................42,252
Bragança Paulista................39,573
BRASÍLIA (1975 UE) (*750,000).350,000
Brusque..........................32,427
Cabedelo (*João Pessoa).........12,811
Cachoeira do Sul.................50,001
Cachoeiro de Itapemirim.........58,968
Camarajibe (*Recife).............41,216
Campina Grande..................163,206
Campinas........................328,629
Campo Grande....................130,792
Campos..........................153,310
Campos Elyseos
(*Rio de Janeiro).............104,636
Canoas (*Porto Alegre).........148,798
Carapicuíba (*São Paulo)........54,907
Caruaru.........................101,006
Cascavel.........................33,809
Cataguases.......................32,515
Catanduva........................48,446
Cavaleiro (*Recife)..............58,811
Caxias...........................31,089
Caxias do Sul...................107,487
Coelho da Rocha
(*Rio de Janeiro)..............100,781
Colatina.........................46,012
Conselheiro Lafaiete.............44,894
Corumbá..........................48,607
Crato............................36,836
Criciúma.........................50,430
Cruz Alta........................43,568
Cruzeiro.........................42,366
Cubatão (*Santos)...............37,255
Cuiabá...........................83,621
Curitiba (*680,000).............483,038
Curvelo..........................30,225
Diadema (*São Paulo)............68,552
Divinópolis......................69,872
Duque de Caxias
(*Rio de Janeiro)..............256,582
Erechim..........................32,426
Feira de Santana................127,105
Florianópolis...................115,665
Fortaleza (*1,175,000).......†1,109,837
Franca...........................86,852
Garanhuns........................49,579
Goiânia.........................362,152
Governador Valadares...........125,174
Guaratinguetá....................55,069
Guarujá (*Santos)...............30,741
Guarulhos (*São Paulo)........221,639
Ijuí..............................31,879
Ilhéus...........................58,529
Imperatriz.......................34,709
Inhomirim (*Rio de Janeiro)....40,322
Ipatinga.........................35,808
Ipiíba (*Rio de Janeiro)........55,486
Itabira..........................40,143
Itabuna..........................89,928
Itajaí............................54,135
Itajubá..........................42,485
Itapetinga.......................30,578
Itapetininga.....................42,331
Itaquari (*Vitória)..............64,559
Itaúna...........................32,731
Itu..............................35,907
Ituiutaba........................46,784
Jaboatão (*Recife)...............52,537
Jacareí..........................48,684
Jaú..............................40,989
Jequié...........................62,341
João Monlevade..................38,689
João Pessoa (*310,000).........197,398
Joinvile.........................77,760
Juàzeiro.........................36,273
Juàzeiro do Norte................79,796
Juiz de Fora....................218,832
Jundiaí.........................145,785
Lajes............................82,325
Lavras...........................35,489
Limeira..........................77,243
Limoeiro.........................30,726
Lins.............................38,080
Londrina........................156,675
Lorena...........................39,653
Macapá...........................51,567
Maceió..........................242,860
Manaus..........................284,118
Marília..........................73,165
Maringá..........................51,620
Mauá (*São Paulo)..............101,569
Mesquita (*Rio de Janeiro).....93,926
Mogi das Cruzes (*São Paulo)..90,330
Monjolo (*Rio de Janeiro)......46,793
Montes Claros....................81,572
Mossoró..........................77,251
Muriaé...........................34,118
Muribeca dos Guararapes
(*Recife).......................74,963
Nanuque..........................34,714
Natal...........................250,787
Neves (*Rio de Janeiro)........112,912
Nilópolis (*Rio de Janeiro).....86,720
Niterói (*Rio de Janeiro).....†376,033
Nova Friburgo....................65,732
Nova Iguaçu
(*Rio de Janeiro)..............331,457
Nôvo Hamburgo
(*Porto Alegre)..................81,248
Olinda (*Recife)................187,553
Olinda (*Rio de Janeiro)........41,378
Osasco (*São Paulo)............283,303
Ourinhos.........................40,733
Paranaguá........................51,510
Parnaíba.........................57,031
Parque Industrial
(*Belo Horizonte)...............80,572
Passo Fundo......................69,135
Passos...........................39,184
Patos............................39,850
Patos de Minas...................42,215
Paulo Afonso.....................38,494
Pelotas.........................150,278
Petrolina........................37,801
Petrópolis (*Rio de Janeiro)...116,080
Pinheirinho (*Curitiba)..........50,302
Piracicaba......................125,490
Poços de Caldas..................51,844
Ponta Grossa.....................92,344
Porto Alegre (*1,760,000)....†1,043,964
Porto Velho......................41,146
Presidente Prudente..............91,188
Queimados (*Rio de Janeiro)....62,560
Recife (*2,100,000)...........†1,249,821
Ribeirão Prêto..................190,897
Rio Branco.......................34,531
Rio Claro........................69,240
Rio de Janeiro (*8,235,000)..†4,857,716
Rio Grande.......................98,863
Salvador (*1,270,000).........†1,237,373
Santa Maria.....................120,667
Santana do Livramento...........48,448
Santarém.........................51,123
Santo André (*São Paulo)......415,025
Santo Ângelo.....................36,020
Santos (*610,000)...............341,317
São Bernardo do Campo
(*São Paulo)..................187,368
São Caetano do Sul
(*São Paulo)..................150,171
São Carlos.......................74,835
São Gonçalo (*Rio de Janeiro).161,392
São João del Rei.................45,019
São João de Meriti
(*Rio de Janeiro)..............163,934
São José do Rio Prêto..........108,319
São José dos Campos...........130,118
São Leopoldo (*Porto Alegre)...62,861
São Luís........................167,529
São Mateus (*Rio de Janeiro)...38,393
•São Paulo (*9,900,000).......†7,198,608
São Vicente (*Santos)..........116,075
Sapucaia do Sul
(*Porto Alegre).................41,154
Sete Lagoas......................61,063
Sete Pontes (*Rio de Janeiro)...53,766
Sobral...........................51,864
Sorocaba........................165,990
Taboão da Serra (*São Paulo)...40,959
Taubaté..........................98,933
Teófilo Otoni....................64,568
Teresina........................181,071
Teresópolis......................53,462
Três Lagoas......................40,157
Tubarão..........................51,121
Uberaba.........................108,576
Uberlândia......................110,463
Uruguaiana.......................60,667
Varginha.........................36,447
Vicente de Carvalho (*Santos)..59,767
Vila Velha (Espírito Santo)
(*Vitória).......................43,177
Vitória (*345,000)..............121,978
Vitória da Conquista.............82,477
Vitória de Santo Antão...........41,130
Volta Redonda (*205,000)......120,645

BRITISH VIRGIN ISLANDS

See Virgin Islands, British

BRUNEI

1971 C..........................136,256

•BANDAR SERI BEGAWAN
(BRUNEI) (*37,000)..........17,410
Seria.............................20,824

BULGARIA / Bălgarija

1979 E........................8,846,417

Asenovgrad (1969 E)............38,500
Blagoevgrad
(Gorna Dzhumaya)............57,457
Burgas..........................165,994
Dimitrovgrad (1969 E)...........44,200
Gabrovo..........................78,092
Gorna Oryakhovitsa (1969 E).....28,300
Karlovo (Levskigrad) (1969 E)...22,900
Karnobat (Polyanovgrad)
(1969 E)........................20,500
Kazanlŭk.........................56,483
Khaskovo.........................82,636
Kŭrdzhali........................52,487
Kyustendil.......................52,118
Lom (1969 E).....................29,100
Lovech (1969 E)..................40,000
Mikhaylovgrad (1969 E)..........34,200
Nova Zagora (1969 E)............21,000
Panagyurishte (1969 E)..........21,800
Pazardzhik.......................71,933
Pernik (Dimitrovo)...............91,428
Petrich (1969 E)..................21,900
Pleven..........................122,916
Plovdiv.........................342,000
Razgrad (1969 E).................35,600
Ruse............................170,594
Samokov (1969 E).................23,800
Sevlievo (1969 E)................21,900
Shumen (Kolarovgrad)............92,157
Silistra..........................53,085
Sliven...........................96,090
Smolyan (1969 E).................20,300
•SOFIA (SOFIYA) (*1,133,733).1,047,920
Stanke Dimitrov (1969 E).........37,800
Stara Zagora....................133,201
Svishtov (1969 E)................22,900
Tolbukhin (Dobrich)..............94,132
Tŭrgovishte (Eski Dzhumaya)
(1969 E)........................31,100
Varna...........................286,382
Veliko Tŭrnovo (Tŭrnovo).......62,565
Vidin............................58,213
Vratsa...........................64,697
Yambol...........................81,477

BURMA / Myanma

1977 E.......................31,512,000

Bassein.........................138,000
Chauk (1953 C)...................24,466
Henzada (1970 E).................85,000
Insein (*Rangoon) (1973 C)....143,625
Kanbe (*Rangoon) (1973 C)....253,600
Mandalay........................458,000
Meiktila (1953 C)................25,180
Mergui (1953 C)..................33,697
Monywa (1953 C)..................26,172
Moulmein........................188,000
Myaungmya (1953 C)..............24,532
Myingyan (1970 E)................65,000
Myitkyina (1953 C)...............12,833
Pakokku (1953 C).................30,943
Pegu............................135,000
Prome (Pyè) (1970 E)............65,000
•RANGOON (*3,000,000).......2,276,000
Sagaing (1953 C).................15,439
Sittwe (Akyab) (1970 E)..........82,000
Tavoy (1970 E)...................53,000
Thaton (1953 C)..................38,047
Thingangyun (*Rangoon)
(1973 C).......................141,210
Toungoo (1953 C).................31,589
Yenangyaung (1953 C)............24,416

BURUNDI

1976 E........................3,864,000

•BUJUMBURA.....................157,000
Gitega (1970 E)..................15,000
Muyinga (1970 E).................19,000

CAMBODIA

See Kampuchea

CAMEROON / Cameroun

1976 C........................7,663,246

Bafoussam........................62,239
Bamenda..........................48,111
•Douala..........................458,246
Foumban..........................33,944
Garoua...........................63,900
Kumba............................44,175
Maroua...........................67,187
Ngaoundere.......................38,992
Nkongsamba.......................71,298
Victoria..........................27,016
YAOUNDÉ.........................313,706

CANADA

1976 C......................22,992,604

CANADA/ALBERTA.......1,838,037

Banff..............................3,410
Blairmore (*7,292)................2,321
Brooks.............................6,339
Calgary..........................469,917
Camrose..........................10,104
Cardston...........................3,043
Claresholm.........................3,276
Coaldale...........................3,654
Drayton Valley.....................4,303
Drumheller.........................6,154
Edmonton (*554,228)..........461,361
Edson..............................4,038
Fort MacLeod.......................3,067
Fort McMurray....................15,424
Fort Saskatchewan
(*Edmonton).....................8,304
Grand Cache........................4,116
Grande Prairie....................17,626
High River.........................3,598
Hinton.............................6,731
Jasper.............................3,404
Lacombe............................3,888
Leduc..............................8,576
Lethbridge.......................46,752
Lloydminster (*Alta. and Sask.*)...10,311
Medicine Hat (*36,326)..........32,811
Olds...............................3,658
Peace River........................4,840
Pincher Creek......................3,448
Ponoka.............................4,636
Redcliff (*Medicine Hat)........3,006
Red Deer.........................32,184
Rocky Mountain House.............3,432
St. Albert (*Edmonton)..........24,129
St. Paul...........................4,337
Sherwood Park (*Edmonton).....26,534
Slave Lake.........................3,561
Spruce Grove.......................6,907
Stettler............................4,182
Taber...............................5,296
Vegreville..........................4,158
Wainwright.........................3,890
Westlock............................3,721
Wetaskiwin.........................6,754
Whitecourt.........................3,878

CANADA/ BRITISH COLUMBIA.....2,466,608

Burnaby (*Vancouver)........131,599
Campbell River...................11,781
Castlegar..........................6,255
Chemainus..........................2,129
Chilliwack (*37,525).............8,634
Clear Brook........................4,849
Comox (*Courtenay)..............5,359
Courtenay (*19,012)..............7,733
Cranbrook........................13,510
Creston............................3,552
Dawson Creek.....................10,528
Duncan (*20,410).................4,106
Esquimalt (*Victoria)...........15,053
Fernie..............................4,608
Fort Nelson.........................2,916
Fort St. John.......................8,947
Kamloops..........................58,311
Kelowna...........................51,955
Kimberley...........................7,111
Kitimat............................11,791
Ladysmith...........................4,004
Langley (*Vancouver)...........10,123
MacKenzie...........................5,266
Merritt..............................5,680
Mission City.......................8,278
Nanaimo...........................40,336
Nelson..............................9,235
New Westminster
(*Vancouver)....................38,393
North Vancouver
(*Vancouver)....................31,934
Oak Bay (*Victoria)..............17,658
Penticton..........................21,344
Port Alberni (*26,254)...........19,585
Port Coquitlam (*Vancouver)....23,926
Port Moody (*Vancouver).......11,649
Powell River.......................13,694
Prince George.....................59,929
Prince Rupert......................14,754
Quesnel.............................7,637
Richmond (*Vancouver)..........80,034
Sidney (*Victoria)................6,732
Smithers............................3,783
Summerland.........................6,724
Terrace (*15,000).................10,251
Trail (*15,649).....................9,976
Vancouver (*1,166,348).......410,188
Vernon (*22,541)..................17,546
Victoria (*218,250)...............62,551
West Vancouver (*Vancouver)..37,144
White Rock (*Vancouver)........12,497
Williams Lake (*15,966)...........6,199

CANADA/MANITOBA.....1,021,506

Brandon...........................34,901
Churchill...........................1,699
Dauphin.............................9,109
Flin Flon (*Man. and Sask.*)
(*10,306)........................8,560
Morden..............................3,886
Neepawa.............................3,508
Portage-la-Prairie.................12,555
Selkirk..............................9,862
Steinbach...........................5,979
Swan River..........................3,742
The Pas.............................6,602
Thompson...........................17,291
Winkler.............................3,749
Winnipeg (*578,217)...........560,874

C Census. E Official estimate. UE Unofficial estimate.
L Population within municipal limits of year specified. • Largest city in country.

* Population or designation of metropolitan area, including suburbs (see headnote).
▲ Population of an entire municipality, commune, or district, including rural area.
‡† Year of information specified at start of country.

CANADA/ NEW BRUNSWICK........677,250

Bathurst (★19,500)........16,301
Beresford (★Bathurst)........3,199
Campbellton (★11,144)........9,282
Caraquet (★5,678)........3,950
Chatham (★★Newcastle)........7,601
Dalhousie........5,640
Dieppe (★Moncton)........7,460
Edmundston (★15,851)........12,710
Fairvale (★Saint John)........3,258
Fredericton........45,248
Grand Falls........6,223
Minto........3,714
Moncton (★77,571)........55,934
Newcastle (★18,419)........6,423
Oromocto........10,276
Quispamsis (★Saint John)........4,968
Riverview (★Moncton)........14,177
Sackville........5,755
St. Basile (★Edmundston)........3,072
Saint John (★112,974)........85,956
St. Stephen........5,264
Shediac........4,216
Sussex........3,938
Woodstock........4,869

CANADA/ NEWFOUNDLAND........557,725

Bay Roberts (★5,640)........4,072
Bishop's Falls........4,504
Bonavista........4,299
Botwood........4,554
Carbonear (★11,326)........5,026
Channel-Port-aux-Basques........6,187
Conception Bay South (St. John's)........9,743
Corner Brook........25,198
Deer Lake........4,546
Gander........9,301
Grand Bank........3,802
Grand Falls (★15,078)........8,729
Happy Valley........8,075
Labrador City (★15,781)........12,012
Lewisporte........3,782
Marystown........5,915
Mount Pearl (★St. John's)........10,193
St. John's (★143,390)........86,576
Springdale........3,513
Stephenville........10,284
Wabana........4,824
Wabush (★Labrador City)........3,769
Windsor (★Grand Falls)........6,349

CANADA/ NORTHWEST TERRITORIES........42,609

Fort Smith........2,288
Frobisher Bay........2,320
Hay River........3,268
Inuvik........3,116
Pine Point........1,915
Yellowknife........8,256

CANADA/NOVA SCOTIA...828,571

Amherst........10,263
Antigonish........5,442
Bible Hill (★Truro)........4,266
Bridgewater........6,010
Dartmouth (★Halifax)........65,341
Glace Bay (★★Sydney)........21,836
Halifax (★267,991)........117,882
Kentville (★12,973)........5,056
Liverpool........3,336
Louisbourg........1,519
New Glasgow (★23,513)........10,672
New Waterford (★Sydney)........9,223
North Sydney (★★Sydney Mines)........8,319
Pictou........4,588
Port Hawkesbury........4,008
Sackville........14,590
Springhill........5,220
Stellarton (★New Glasgow)........5,366
Sydney (★88,614)........30,645
Sydney Mines (★35,455)........8,965
Truro (★27,551)........12,840
Westville (★New Glasgow)........4,251
Windsor........3,702
Yarmouth........7,801

CANADA/ONTARIO........8,264,465

Ajax (★Toronto)........20,774
Amherstburg........5,566
Amherstview........5,295
Ancaster (★Hamilton)........14,255
Arnprior (★10,662)........6,111
Atikokan........5,668
Aurora (★Toronto)........14,249
Aylmer West........5,125
Barrie (★49,228)........34,389
Belleville........35,311
Blackburn Hamlet (★Ottawa)........8,290
Bracebridge........8,428
Bradford........5,080
Brampton (★Toronto)........103,459
Brantford (★82,800)........66,950
Brockville (★26,883)........19,903
Burlington (★Hamilton)........104,314
Caledon (★Toronto)........22,434
Cambridge (Galt) (★★Kitchener)........72,383
Capreol........4,089
Carleton Place........5,256
Chatham........38,685
Cobourg (★20,256)........11,421
Cochrane........4,974
Collingwood........11,114
Collins Bay (★Kingston)........6,897
Cornwall........46,121
Deep River........5,565
Delhi........3,929
Dryden........6,799
Dundas (★Hamilton)........19,179
Dunnville........11,642
East York (★Toronto)........106,950
Elliot Lake........8,849
Elmira........7,034
Espanola........5,926
Essex (★Windsor)........5,577
Etobicoke (★Toronto)........297,109
Exeter........3,494
Fergus (★11,727)........6,001
Fort Erie........24,031
Fort Frances........9,325
Gananoque........5,103
Goderich........7,385
Gravenhurst........7,986
Grimsby (★Hamilton)........15,567
Guelph (★70,388)........67,538
Haileybury (★12,596)........4,939
Haldimand........16,375
Halton Hills........34,477
Hamilton (★529,371)........312,003
Hanover........5,691
Hawkesbury (★11,306)........9,789
Hearst........5,195
Huntsville........11,123
Ingersoll........8,198
Iroquois Falls........6,887
Kanata (★Ottawa)........6,304
Kapuskasing........12,676
Kenora (★12,519)........10,565
Kincardine........4,182
Kingston (★90,741)........56,032
Kingsville (★11,836)........4,692
Kirkland Lake........13,567
Kitchener (★272,158)........131,870
Lambeth (★London)........2,876
Leamington........11,169
Lincoln........14,460
Lindsay........13,062
Listowel........5,126
London (★270,383)........240,392
Manitouwadge Lake........3,507
Marathon........2,258
Markham (★Toronto)........56,206
Meaford........4,319
Midland (★26,239)........11,568
Milton........20,756
Mississauga (★Toronto)........250,017
Mount Forest........3,376
Nanticoke........19,489
Napanee........4,844
Newcastle........31,928
New Hamburg........3,628
New Liskeard (★Haileybury)........5,601
Newmarket (★Toronto)........24,795
Niagara Falls (★★St. Catharines)........69,423
Niagara-on-the-Lake (★St. Catharines)........12,485
Nickel Centre (★Sudbury)........13,157
North Bay (★53,961)........51,639
North York (★Toronto)........558,398
Oakville (★Toronto)........68,950
Onaping Falls........6,776
Orangeville........12,021
Orillia........24,412
Oshawa (★135,196)........107,023
OTTAWA (★693,288)........304,462
Owen Sound........19,525
Paris (★Brantford)........6,713
Parry Sound........5,501
Pelham (★St. Catharines)........10,071
Pembroke (★18,468)........14,927
Penetanguishene (★Midland)........5,460
Perth........5,675
Petawawa (★14,326)........5,815
Peterborough (★65,293)........59,683
Petrolia........4,393
Pickering (★Toronto)........27,879
Picton........4,629
Port Colborne (★St. Catharines)........20,536
Port Elgin (★9,481)........5,069
Port Hope........9,788
Prescott........4,975
Rayside-Balfour (★Sudbury)........16,035
Renfrew........8,617
Richmond Hill (★Toronto)........34,716
St. Catharines (★301,921)........123,351
St. Marys........4,843
St. Thomas........27,206
Sarnia (★81,342)........55,576
Sault Ste. Marie (★81,992)........81,048
Scarborough (★Toronto)........387,149
Simcoe........14,189
Smiths Falls (★13,327)........9,279
Stoney Creek (★Hamilton)........30,294
Stratford........25,657
Strathroy........7,769
Sturgeon Falls........6,400
Sudbury (★157,030)........97,604
Tecumseh (★Windsor)........5,326
Thorold (★St. Catharines)........14,944
Thunder Bay (★119,253)........111,476
Tilbury........4,248
Tillsonburg........9,404
Timmins........44,747
•Toronto (★2,803,101)........633,318
Trenton (★32,634)........15,465
Valley East (★Sudbury)........19,591
Vanier (Eastview) (★Ottawa)........19,812
Vaughan (Woodbridge) (★Toronto)........17,782
Walden (★Sudbury)........10,453
Walkerton........4,626
Wallaceburg........11,132
Waterloo (★Kitchener)........46,623
Wawa (Jamestown)........4,272
Welland (★★St. Catharines)........45,047
Whitchurch Stouffville (★Toronto)........12,884
Whitby (★Oshawa)........28,173
Windsor (★247,582)........196,526
Woodstock........26,779
York (★Toronto)........141,367

CANADA/PRINCE EDWARD ISLAND........118,229

Charlottetown (★24,837)........17,063
Kensington........1,150
Montague........1,827
Parkdale (★Charlottetown)........2,172
St. Eleanors (★Summerside)........2,495
Sherwood (★Charlottetown)........5,602
Souris........1,447
Summerside (★14,145)........8,592

CANADA/QUEBEC........6,234,445

Acton Vale........4,326
Alma........25,638
Amos........9,213
Amqui........3,949
Ancienne-Lorette (Notre-Dame-de-Lorette) (★Québec)........11,694
Anjou (★Montréal)........36,596
Arthabaska (★Victoriaville)........5,907
Asbestos (★14,395)........9,075
Aylmer East (★Ottawa)........25,714
Baie-Comeau (★26,635)........11,911
Baie-d'Urfé (★Montréal)........3,955
Baie-St. Paul........4,062
Beaconsfield (★Montréal)........20,417
Beauceville........4,276
Beauharnois (★Montréal)........7,665
Beauport (★Québec)........55,339
Beaupré (★7,490)........2,821
Bécancour........9,043
Beloeil (★Montréal)........15,913
Berthierville........4,249
Black Lake (★Thetford Mines)........4,051
Blainville (★Montréal)........12,517
Boisbriand (★Montréal)........10,132
Bois-des-Filion (★Montréal)........4,346
Boucherville (★Montréal)........25,530
Bromptonville........2,992
Brossard (★Montréal)........37,641
Brownsburg (★Lachute)........3,114
Buckingham........14,328
Cabano........3,193
Candiac (★Montréal)........7,166
Cap-aux-Meules (★6,847)........1,305
Cap-Chat........3,617
Cap-de-la-Madeleine (★Trois-Rivières)........32,126
Carignan (★Montréal)........3,585
Chambly (★Montréal)........11,815
Chandler........4,011
Chapais........3,147
Charlemagne (★Montréal)........4,025
Charlesbourg (★Québec)........63,147
Charny (★Québec)........6,461
Châteauguay (★Montréal)........36,329
Château-Richer (★Québec)........3,075
Chibougamau........10,536
Chicoutimi (★128,643)........57,737
Clermont........3,518
Coaticook........6,392
Côte-St.-Luc (★Montréal)........25,721
Cowansville........11,902
Deux-Montagnes (★Montréal)........8,957
Dolbeau (★13,924)........8,451
Dollard-des-Ormeaux (★Montréal)........36,837
Donnacona (★7,876)........5,800
Dorion-Vaudreuil (Dorion) (★Montréal)........5,843
Dorval (★Montréal)........19,131
Drummondville (★45,018)........29,286
Drummondville-Sud (★Drummondville)........9,420
East Angus........4,417
East Broughton Station (★2,562)........1,191
Farnham........6,476
Forestville (★4,358)........1,819
Gaspé........16,842
Gatineau (★Ottawa)........73,479
Granby (★41,462)........37,132
Grande-Rivière........4,390
Grand'Mere (★Shawinigan)........15,999
Greenfield Park (★Montréal)........18,430
Hampstead (★Montréal)........7,562
Hauterive (★Baie-Comeau)........14,724
Havre-St.-Pierre........3,208
Hébertville-Station (★3,621)........1,362
Hudson (★Montréal)........4,480
Hull (★Ottawa)........61,039
Iberville (★St.-Jean)........8,897
Île-Perrot (★Montréal)........5,272
Joliette (★30,116)........18,118
Jonquière (★★Chicoutimi)........60,691
Kirkland (★Montréal)........7,476
La Baie........20,116
Lac-Brome........4,117
Lachenaie (★Montréal)........7,118
Lachine (★Montréal)........41,503
Lachute (★15,042)........11,928
Lac-Mégantic........6,457
La Malbaie (★5,135)........4,069
La Pocatière........4,319
Laprairie (★Montréal)........9,173
La Salle (★Montréal)........76,713
La Sarre........4,978
L'Assomption (★Montréal)........4,832
La Tuque........12,067
Lauzon (★Québec)........12,663
Laval (Ville de Laval) (★Montréal)........246,243
LeMoyne (★Montréal)........7,202
Lévis (★Québec)........17,819
Longueuil (★Montréal)........122,429
Loretteville (★Québec)........14,767
Louiseville........3,993
Magog (★14,598)........13,290
Malartic........5,092
Maniwaki........5,969
Marieville (★Montréal)........4,853
Mascouche (★Montréal)........14,266
Matane........12,726
Mercier (Ste.-Philomène) (★Montréal)........4,957
Métabetchouan........3,016
Mirabel........13,486
Mistassini (★Dolbeau)........5,473
Mont-Joli........6,508
Mont-Laurier........8,565
Montmagny........12,326
Montréal (★2,802,485)........1,080,546
Montréal-Est (★Montréal)........4,372
Montréal-Nord (★Montréal)........97,250
Montréal-Ouest (★Montréal)........5,980
Mont-Royal (★Montréal)........20,514
Mont-St.-Hilaire (★Montréal)........7,688
Murdochville........3,704
Napierville........2,166
New Richmond........4,295
Nicolet........4,818
Noranda (★★Rouyn)........9,809
Notre-Dame-des-Prairies........5,714
Otterburn Park (★Montréal)........4,159
Outremont (★Montréal)........27,089
Percé........5,198
Pierrefonds (★Montréal)........35,402
Pierreville (★2,510)........1,311
Pincourt (★Montréal)........7,892
Plessisville........7,238
Pohénégamook........3,627
Pointe-aux-Trembles (★Montréal)........35,618
Pointe-Claire (★Montréal)........25,917
Pontiac........3,365
Pont-Rouge........3,342
Port-Cartier........8,139
Portneuf (★3,225)........1,320
Price........2,461
Princeville........3,852
Québec (★542,158)........177,082
Rawdon........2,808
Repentigny (★Montréal)........26,698
Richmond........4,021
Rimouski (★30,225)........27,897
Rivière-du-Loup........13,103
Roberval........8,543
Rock Island (★3,548)........1,230
Rosemère (★Montréal)........7,112
Rouyn (★27,487)........17,678
Roxboro (★Montréal)........7,106
Ste.-Adèle (★6,273)........4,186
Ste.-Agathe-des-Monts........5,435
St.-Ambroise-de-Chicoutimi........3,169
Ste.-Anne-de-Bellevue (★Montréal)........3,738
Ste.-Anne-des-Monts (★7,606)........5,945
St.-Antoine (★St.-Jérôme)........6,872
St.-Basile-le-Grand (★Montréal)........5,843
St.-Boniface-de-Shawinigan........2,680
St.-Bruno (★Montréal)........21,272
Ste.-Catherine (★Montréal)........5,036
St.-Césaire........2,701
St.-Constant (★Montréal)........7,659
St.-David-de-l'Auberivière (★Québec)........4,386
St.-Eustache (★Montréal)........21,248
St.-Félicien........4,985
St.-Ferdinand (Bernierville)........2,182
Ste.-Foy (★Québec)........71,237
Ste.-Geneviève (★Montréal)........2,869
St.-Georges-Ouest (★Ville-St.-Georges)........6,478
St.-Hubert (★Montréal)........49,706
St.-Hyacinthe (★40,202)........37,500
St.-Jacques........2,095
St.-Jean (★50,363)........34,363
St.-Jérôme (★36,489)........25,175
St.-Joseph-de-Beauce........3,213
St.-Joseph-de-Sorel (★Sorel)........2,811
St.-Jovite........3,595
Ste.-Julie (★Montréal)........8,666
St.-Lambert (★Montréal)........20,318
St.-Laurent (★Montréal)........64,404
St.-Léonard (★Montréal)........78,452
St.-Luc (★St.-Jean)........7,103
St.-Marc-des-Carrières........2,625
Ste.-Marie-de-Beauce........4,462
St.-Pamphile........3,450
St.-Paul-l'Ermite (★Montréal)........6,107
St.-Pierre (★Montréal)........6,039
St.-Raymond........3,742
St. Rémi........4,866
St.-Romuald-d'Etchemin (★Québec)........9,160
Ste.-Thérèse-de Blainville (★Montréal)........17,479
St.-Tite........3,128
Sayabec........1,818
Schefferville........3,429
Senneterre........4,289
Sept-Îles (Seven Islands)........30,617
Shawinigan (★55,414)........24,921
Shawinigan-Sud (★Shawinigan)........11,155
Sherbrooke (★104,505)........76,804
Sillery (★Québec)........13,580
Sorel (★37,029)........19,666
Témiscaming........2,165
Terrebonne (★Montréal)........11,204
Thetford Mines (★28,826)........20,784
Thurso........3,066
Tracy (★Sorel)........12,284
Trois-Pistoles........4,554
Trois-Rivières (★98,583)........52,518
Trois-Rivières-Ouest (★Trois-Rivières)........10,564
Val-Bélair (★Québec)........10,716
Val-d'Or (★21,378)........19,915
Valleyfield (Salaberry-de) (★35,920)........29,716
Vanier (Québec-Ouest) (★Québec)........10,683
Varennes (★Montréal)........6,469
Vaudreuil (★Montréal)........5,630
Verdun (★Montréal)........68,013
Victoriaville (★27,732)........21,825
Ville-St.-Georges (★15,083)........8,605
Warwick........2,865
Waterloo........4,746
Westmount (★Montréal)........22,153
Windsor........5,637

CANADA/ SASKATCHEWAN........921,323

Assiniboia........2,738
Battleford (★North Battleford)........2,569
Biggar........2,491
Canora........2,689
Esterhazy........2,894
Estevan........8,847
Hudson Bay........2,280
Humboldt........4,265
Kamsack........2,726
Kindersley........3,523
Lloydminster (*Sask. and Alta.*)........10,311
Maple Creek........2,330
Meadow Lake........3,662
Melfort........5,141
Melville........5,149
Moose Jaw (★34,829)........32,581
Nipawin........4,317
North Battleford (★16,124)........13,158
Prince Albert........28,631
Regina (★151,191)........149,593
Rosetown........2,551
Saskatoon........133,750
Shaunavon........2,183
Swift Current........14,264
Tisdale........3,026
Unity........2,244
Uranium City........1,765
Weyburn........8,892
Wynyard........2,045
Yorkton........14,119

CANADA/YUKON........21,836

Dawson........838
Elsa........456
Faro........1,544
Watson Lake........808
Whitehorse........13,311

CAPE VERDE / Cabo Verde

1970 C........272,071
•Mindelo........28,797
PRAIA........21,494

CAYMAN IS.

1970 C........10,652
•GEORGETOWN........3,975

CENTRAL AFRICAN REPUBLIC
République centrafricaine

1971 E........1,637,000
Bambari (1968 E)........35,300
•BANGUI........187,000
Bouar (1968 E)........24,600

CHAD / Tchad

1975 E........4,030,000
Abéché........32,000
Kélo........18,500
Koumra........18,800
Moundou........45,000
•NDJAMENA (FORT-LAMY)........224,000
Sarh (Fort-Archambault)........50,000

CHILE

1970 C........8,880,889
Angol........22,123
Antofagasta........138,821
Apoquindo (★Santiago)........90,722
Arica........87,726
Calama........45,863
Chillán........87,555
Concepción (★395,000)........175,853
Conchalí (★Santiago)........246,046
Copiapó........45,194
Coquimbo........50,405
Coronel........37,312
Curicó........41,262
Iquique........65,040
La Cisterna (★Santiago)........246,537
La Granja (★Santiago)........163,882
La Serena........61,897
Las Rejas (★Santiago)........44,681
Linares........37,913
Lo Prado Arriba (★Santiago)........112,548
Los Ángeles........49,175
Lota........48,166
Ñuñoa (★Santiago)........280,733
Osorno........68,815
Ovalle........31,756
Providencia (★Santiago)........85,678
Puente Alto (★Santiago)........61,077
Puerto Montt........62,726
Punta Arenas........61,813
Quillota........35,488
Quilpué (★Valparaíso)........40,163
Quinta Normal (★Santiago)........138,007
Rancagua........86,404
Renca (★Santiago)........68,440
San Antonio........46,744
San Bernardo (★Santiago)........100,225
San Fernando........27,997
San Miguel (★Santiago)........320,883
•SANTIAGO (★2,925,000)........517,473
Talca........94,449
Talcahuano (★★Concepción)........152,755
Temuco........110,335
Tocopilla........22,241
Tomé........29,597
Valdivia........82,362
Vallenar........26,800
Valparaíso (★530,000)........250,358
Victoria........16,509
Villa Alemana........29,605
Viña del Mar (★Valparaíso)........188,811

C Census. E Official estimate. UE Unofficial estimate.
L Population within municipal limits of specified year. • Largest city in country.

★ Population or designation of metropolitan area, including suburbs (see headnote).
▲ Population of an entire municipality, commune, or district, including rural area.
‡† Year of information specified at start of country.

CHINA / Zhongguo

1975 UE.................930,500,000

Provinces

Anhwei..................45,900,000
Chekiang..................35,600,000
Fukien....................21,000,000
Heilungkiang..............29,300,000
Honan....................67,200,000
Hopeh....................55,100,000
Hunan....................49,000,000
Hupeh....................43,600,000
Inner Mongolia
(Auton. Region)..........8,000,000
Kansu....................19,500,000
Kiangsi..................26,400,000
Kiangsu..................62,100,000
Kirin....................20,900,000
Kwangsi Chuang
(Auton. Region)..........30,000,000
Kwangtung................51,200,000
Kweichow.................24,800,000
Liaoning.................43,000,000
Ningsia Hui (Auton. Region).2,800,000
Peking (Auton. City)........8,000,000
Shanghai (Auton. City).....11,300,000
Shansi...................23,000,000
Shantung.................78,100,000
Shensi...................27,700,000
Sinkiang Uighur
(Auton. Region)..........8,900,000
Szechwan.................99,800,000
Tibet (Auton. Region).......1,600,000
Tientsin (Auton. City)........7,000,000
Tsinghai..................3,600,000
Yünnan...................26,100,000

Cities

Ach'eng........................60,000
Amoy (Hsiamen).............300,000
Anching (Huaining)..........135,000
Anshan...................1,050,000
Anshun........................50,000
Anta...........................60,000
Anyang.......................175,000
Canton (Kuangchou).........2,500,000
Chanchiang (Tsamkong).......200,000
Changchiakou (Kalgan).......300,000
Changchih.....................100,000
Changchou (Wuchin)..........300,000
Changchou (Lungchi)..........110,000
Changchun (Hsinking).......1,300,000
Changsha.....................840,000
Changshu......................95,000
Changte......................125,000
Chaoan........................95,000
Chaoching.....................75,000
Chaotung (Tientsaokang)......65,000
Chaoyang (*Kwangtung Prov.*)....60,000
Chaoyang (*Liaoning Prov.*).....120,000
Chenchiang (Chinkiang).......225,000
Chengchou..................1,100,000
Chenghai......................50,000
Chengte (Jehol)..............120,000
Chengtu....................1,800,000
Chenhsien.....................60,000
Chiahsing....................150,000
Chiamussu (Kiamusze)........300,000
Chian.........................110,000
Chiangmen (Sunwui)..........120,000
Chiaohsien....................45,000
Chiaotso......................275,000
Chiawang......................50,000
Chichihaerh (Tsitsihar)........850,000
Chiehyang (Kityang)............65,000
Chihfeng......................75,000
Chihsi........................325,000
Chilin (Kirin)................775,000
Chinan (Tsinan).............1,125,000
Chinchou.....................450,000
Chingchiang (Huaiyin)........100,000
Chingshih......................65,000
Chingtechen (Fouliang).......300,000
Chinhsi........................50,000
Chinhsien......................75,000
Chinhua........................55,000
Chinhuangtao.................275,000
Chining (*Inner Mongolia A.R.*)..100,000
Chining (*Shantung Prov.*)......130,000
Chiuchiang (Kiukiang).........100,000
Choutsun......................50,000
Chüanchou....................130,000
Chuchou.......................250,000
Chühsien......................50,000
Chungking (Chungching)....2,900,000
Chungshan (Shekki)............90,000
Erhlien........................60,000
Foshan (Fatshan).............125,000
Fouhsin (Fusin)..............350,000
Fouyang.......................90,000
Fuchou (Foochow).............725,000
Fuhsien.......................85,000
Fushun.....................1,150,000
Haerhpin (Harbin)...........2,400,000
Haicheng......................90,000
Haikou (Hoihow)..............275,000
Hailaerh (Hulun)...............85,000
Hami (Kumul)..................50,000
Hanchung (Nancheng)...........90,000
Hangchou.....................900,000
Hanku........................100,000
Hantan.......................480,000
Hengyang.....................350,000
Hochuan.......................60,000
Hofei.........................450,000
Hokang (Haoli)................250,000
Hopi..........................100,000
Hopu..........................50,000
Hsian (Sian)................1,900,000
Hsiangfan.....................110,000
Hsiangtan (Siangtan)..........325,000
Hsienyang......................85,000
Hsikueituchi...................50,000
Hsinghua.......................85,000
Hsingtai......................115,000
Hsinhsiang (Sinsiang).........250,000
Hsinhui........................50,000
Hsining (Sining)..............300,000
Hsinwen........................50,000
Hsinyang......................100,000
Hsüanhua......................140,000
Hsüchang......................100,000
Hsüchou (Süchow).............800,000
Huaian.........................50,000
Huainan.......................400,000
Huaipei........................75,000
Huaite (Kungchuling)...........75,000
Huangshih.....................140,000
Huatien........................55,000
Huhohaote (Huhehot)...........450,000
Huichou (Huiyang).............80,000
Hulan..........................75,000
Hunchiang......................50,000
Ichang........................120,000
Ichun..........................90,000
Ining (Kuldja)..................90,000
Ipin (Suifu)...................250,000
Itu............................50,000
Iyang.........................110,000
Kaifeng.......................350,000
Kaiyüan........................50,000
Kanchou (Kanhsien)...........140,000
Kashih (Kashgar)..............100,000
Kochiu........................100,000
Koerhchinyuichienchi
(Ulanhot)......................80,000
Kolamai (Karamai)..............60,000
Kueilin.......................250,000
Kueiyang......................800,000
Kunming (Yunnanfu).........1,225,000
Lanchou.......................950,000
Lasa (Lhasa)...................80,000
Liaoyang......................250,000
Liaoyüan (Shuangliao).........250,000
Lienyünchiangshih (Sinhai)....250,000
Linching.......................65,000
Linchuan.......................55,000
Linfen.........................50,000
Linshi.........................90,000
Linhsia........................65,000
Liuan..........................55,000
Liuchou.......................300,000
Liyüchiang.....................50,000
Loho...........................60,000
Loshan.........................70,000
Loyang........................750,000
Luchou (Luhsien)..............175,000
Lüshun (Port Arthur)...........40,000
Lüta (Dairen) (1,700,000▲).....1,100,000
Maanshan.......................60,000
Manchouli (Lupin)..............65,000
Maoming.......................100,000
Meihsien.......................50,000
Mienyang.......................50,000
Minhang........................60,000
Mukden (Shenyang)..........3,300,000
Mutanchiang...................350,000
Nancha.........................50,000
Nanchang......................700,000
Nanchung......................225,000
Nanking....................1,800,000
Nanning (Yungning)............350,000
Nanping........................50,000
Nantung.......................275,000
Nanyang........................60,000
Neichiang.....................225,000
Nientzushan....................50,000
Ningpo (Ninghsien)............300,000
Paicheng......................125,000
Paiyin.........................50,000
Pangfou (Pangpu)..............400,000
Paochi........................250,000
Paoting (Tsingyuan)...........350,000
Paotou........................650,000
Paoying........................50,000
Peian..........................80,000
Peihai (Pakhoi)................95,000
Peipiao.......................100,000
PEKING (PEIPING)
(8,000,000▲)...............5,400,000
Penchi........................500,000
Pinghsiang....................120,000
Pingliang......................80,000
Pingtingshan...................85,000
Pohsien........................90,000
Poshan........................100,000
Putehachi (Yalu)...............55,000
Sanmenhsia.....................60,000
Sanming........................55,000
Shangchiu.....................100,000
•Shanghai (11,300,000▲).......8,100,000
Shangjao.......................60,000
Shangshui (Chouchiakou)........90,000
Shaohsing.....................150,000
Shaokuan (Kükong).............100,000
Shaoyang......................215,000
Shashih.......................120,000
Shihchiachuang................940,000
Shihkuaikou....................50,000
Shuangyashan..................150,000
Soche (Yarkand)................60,000
Ssuping (Szeping).............165,000
Suchou (Soochow)..............750,000
Suhsien........................50,000
Suihua.........................70,000
Suining........................60,000
Sungchiang.....................60,000
Swatow (Shantou)..............325,000
Tachangchen....................50,000
Taian..........................50,000
Taichou (Tai).................175,000
Taiyüan (Yangkü)...........1,350,000
Tangshan (1980 UE)............650,000
Tantung (Antung)..............300,000
Taoan..........................75,000
Tatung........................350,000
Techou.........................70,000
Teyang.........................50,000
Tiehling.......................75,000
Tienshui.......................85,000
Tientsin (Tienching)
(7,000,000▲)...............4,500,000
Tinghsien (Ting)...............40,000
Titao..........................50,000
Tsangchou (Tsanghsien)........100,000
Tsaochuang.....................75,000
Tsingtao (Chingtao).........1,200,000
Tsuni.........................250,000
Tukou.........................120,000
Tunchi.........................65,000
Tungchuan......................75,000
Tunghsien......................80,000
Tunghua.......................175,000
Tungkuan.......................55,000
Tungliao.......................60,000
Tunglinghsien..................65,000
Tungtai........................50,000
Tunhua.........................60,000
Tuyün..........................75,000
Tzukung.......................325,000
Tzupo (Changtien) (900,000▲)....60,000
Wanhsien......................120,000
Weifang.......................240,000
Wenchou.......................260,000
Wuchou (Tsangwu)..............160,000
Wuhan......................3,000,000
Wuhsi (Wusih).................700,000
Wuhsing........................90,000
Wuhu..........................325,000
Wulumuchi (Urumchi)...........400,000
Wutungchiao....................45,000
Yaan...........................50,000
Yangchiang.....................60,000
Yangchou (Chiangtu)...........175,000
Yangchüan.....................275,000
Yencheng.......................60,000
Yenchi.........................90,000
Yentai (Chefoo)...............150,000
Yingchengtsu...................50,000
Yinchuan (Ningsia)............125,000
Yingkou.......................175,000
Yingkou (Tashihchiao)..........50,000
Yüehyang.......................60,000
Yümenshih......................90,000
Yützu..........................90,000

COLOMBIA

1973 C....................22,551,811

Armenia (1979 E) (★205,000)....164,000
Barrancabermeja (1979 E)......115,000
Barranquilla (1979 E)
(★950,000)....................859,000
Bello (★Medellín)..............121,204
•BOGOTÁ (1979 E)
(★4,150,000)................4,067,000
Bucaramanga (1979 E)
(★470,000)....................402,000
Buenaventura (1979 E)..........144,000
Buga (84,057▲)..................71,016
Caicedonia......................23,567
Calarcá (★Armenia) (49,936▲)....29,349
Caldas..........................27,394
Cali (1979 E) (★1,340,000)......1,293,000
Cartagena (1979 E).............388,000
Cartago (77,890▲)...............69,154
Ciénaga (89,723▲)...............42,546
Cúcuta (1979 UE)...............355,000
Dos Quebradas (★Pereira)........37,837
Duitama (48,459▲)...............36,551
Envigado (★Medellín)............69,921
Espinal.........................32,475
Facatativá......................27,892
Florencia.......................31,817
Floridablanca
(★Bucaramanga)..................38,446
Fusagasugá......................25,456
Girardot (★78,000)..............61,829
Ibagué (1979 E)................257,000
Ipiales.........................30,871
Itagüí (★Medellín)..............96,972
La Dorada.......................30,962
Líbano (42,832▲)................19,132
Lorica (59,757▲)................18,251
Magangué (62,746▲)..............34,396
Manizales (1979 UE)............252,000
Medellín (1979 E)
(★2,025,000)................1,477,000
Montería (1979 E)..............123,000
Neiva (1979 E).................145,000
Ocaña...........................38,352
Palmira (1979 E)...............168,000
Pamplona........................31,817
Pasto (1979 E).................171,000
Pereira (1979 UE)(★325,000)....260,000
Popayán (1977 E)................88,768
Pradera.........................15,732
Puerto Berrío...................19,579
Quibdó (1977 E).................33,588
Ríohacha (1977 E)...............35,000
Santa Marta (1979 UE)..........155,000
Santa Rosa de Cabal
(★Pereira) (42,717▲)............28,368
Sevilla.........................31,143
Sincelejo (1977 E)..............86,569
Sogamoso (67,738▲)..............48,891
Soledad (★Barranquilla).........64,469
Sonsón..........................15,990
Tuluá (1979 E).................113,000
Tumaco (87,448▲)................38,742
Tunja (1977 E)..................64,551
Valledupar (1979 E)............164,000
Villavicencio (1979 E).........133,000

COMOROS / Comores

1974 E.........................292,000

•MORONI.........................12,000
Mutsamudu (1966 C)...............7,652

CONGO (PEOPLE'S REPUBLIC OF THE CONGO)

1970 C.......................1,089,300

•BRAZZAVILLE...................175,000
Jacob (1969 E)...................18,000
Loubomo (1969 E).................15,000
Pointe-Noire....................135,000

COOK IS.

1971 C..........................21,227

•AVARUA (1961 E)..................4,000

COSTA RICA

1976 E.......................1,993,800

Alajuela.........................35,000
Cartago..........................23,100
Desamparados (★San José)........32,700
Guadalupe (★San José)...........29,100
Heredia..........................24,200
Liberia (18,000▲)................11,600
Limón (43,800▲)..................31,900
Puntarenas.......................29,000
•SAN JOSÉ (1978 E) (★519,400)..239,800
San Juan (★San José)............19,600
San Pedro (★San José)...........25,100
San Vicente (★San José).........16,400

CUBA

1970 C.......................8,553,400

Amancio Rodríguez (37,900▲)....12,300
Artemisa.........................31,200
Banes (39,300▲)..................27,100
Baracoa (35,600▲)................20,900
Bauta (★Havana) (25,400▲)........21,100
Bayamo (1976 E) (88,994▲)........68,900
Camagüey (1976 E)...............230,891
Camajuaní (32,300▲)..............15,900
Cárdenas.........................55,700
Chaparra (51,000▲)................8,400
Ciego de Avila (1976 E)
(66,542▲)........................57,700
Cienfuegos (1976 E)
(92,210▲)........................86,600
Colón (40,800▲)..................26,000
Consolación del Sur (42,000▲)...15,100
Contramaestre (43,900▲)..........22,900
Cruces (32,100▲).................19,100
Florida (37,500▲)................32,700
Fomento (33,600▲)................12,900
Guanabacoa (★Havana).............69,700
Guantánamo (1976 E).............155,217
Güines (45,300▲).................41,400
Guisa (44,100▲)...................9,000
•HAVANA (LA HABANA)
(1976 E) (★2,000,000).........1,961,674
Holguín (1976 E) (160,965▲).....129,800
Manzanillo (88,900▲).............77,900
Matanzas (1976 E)................99,003
Mayarí (34,000▲).................17,600
Mayarí Arriba (31,400▲)...........2,300
Morón (31,100▲)..................29,000
Niquero (36,500▲)................11,300
Nueva Gerona (1976 E)
(28,342▲)........................24,300
Nuevitas (21,500▲)...............20,700
Palma Soriano (59,600▲)..........41,200
Pinar del Río (1976 E)...........89,978
Placetas (48,400▲)...............32,300
Sagua la Grande (41,900▲)........35,800
San Antonio de los Baños
(30,000▲)........................25,300
Sancti-Spíritus (1976 E)
(67,569▲)........................58,600
San Germán (30,200▲).............12,400
San José de las Lajas (33,600▲).24,900
San Juan y Martínez (45,700▲)....11,100
San Luis (35,000▲)...............17,400
Santa Clara (1976 E)............152,361
Santiago de Cuba (1976 E).......326,066
Santiago de las Vegas
(★Havana)........................29,300
Trinidad (37,000▲)...............31,500
Vertientes (32,600▲).............14,000
Victoria de las Tunas (1976 E)
(65,767▲)........................54,400

CYPRUS / Kípros /Kıbrıs

1974 E.........................639,000

Ammókhostos (Famagusta).........39,400
Kirínia...........................3,900
Lárnax (Larnaca).................19,800
Lemesós (Limassol) (★80,600)....55,000
•NICOSIA (LEVKOSÍA)
(★117,100).......................51,000
Páfos.............................9,100

CZECHOSLOVAKIA / Československo

1979 E......................15,280,148

Banská Bystrica..................66,279
Beroun (★26,000).................18,149
Bratislava......................374,860
Břeclav..........................24,258
Brno............................372,793
České Budějovice (Budweis)......89,399
Cheb.............................31,030
Chomutov.........................49,960
Děčín............................48,424
Frýdek-Místek (★Ostrava)........54,112
Gottwaldov (Zlín)................82,926
Havířov (★Ostrava)...............93,832
Havlíčkův Brod...................24,859
Hlohovec (★26,000)...............16,815
Hodonín..........................25,504
Hradec Králové...................93,165
Humenné..........................26,885
Jablonec [nad Nisou].............39,692
Jihlava..........................50,995
Karlovy Vary (Karlsbad)..........61,212
Karviná (★★Ostrava)..............80,017
Kladno (★86,000).................66,370
Kolín............................31,169
Komárno..........................30,886
Košice..........................200,943
Krnov............................26,393
Kroměříž.........................26,166
Levice...........................25,610
Liberec (★96,000)................85,119
Liptovský Mikuláš................23,795
Litvínov.........................23,572
Lučenec..........................26,300
Martin...........................56,294
Michalovce.......................28,012
Mladá Boleslav...................43,876
Most.............................61,411
Náchod...........................19,812
Nitra............................72,140
Nové Zámky.......................32,694
Nový Jičín.......................31,101
Olomouc.........................102,501
Opava............................59,481
Orlová (★Ostrava)................30,938
Ostrava (★745,000)..............325,473
Pardubice........................93,042
Piešťany.........................30,070
Písek............................28,067
Plzeň (Pilsen)..................169,466
Poprad...........................36,428
Považská Bystrica................24,747
•PRAGUE (PRAHA)
(★1,275,000)..................1,193,345
Přerov...........................47,933
Prešov...........................69,453
Příbram..........................36,441
Prievidza........................38,948
Prostějov........................48,516
Ružomberok.......................26,803
Sokolov..........................27,338
Spišská Nová Ves.................31,537
Šumperk..........................29,872
Tábor............................31,005
Teplice..........................53,822
Třebíč...........................27,708
Trenčín..........................47,832
Třinec...........................34,226
Trnava...........................61,617
Trutnov..........................27,402
Uherské Hradiště.................35,909
Ústí nad Labem (★103,000)........80,309
Valašské Meziříčí................24,485
Vsetín...........................29,023
Žilina...........................67,204
Znojmo...........................35,711
Zvolen...........................35,754

DENMARK / Danmark

1980 E.......................5,122,065

Åbenrå (21,172▲).................18,200
Albertslund (★Copenhagen)........30,425
Ålborg..........................153,948
Århus...........................244,839
Ballerup-Måløv (★Copenhagen).48,938
Brøndby (★Copenhagen)............38,034
•COPENHAGEN (KØBENHAVN)
(★1,470,000)....................498,850
Esbjerg..........................79,310
Fredericia.......................45,820
Frederiksberg (★Copenhagen)......88,287
Frederikshavn.....................35,038
Gentofte (★Copenhagen)...........67,300
Gladsakse (★Copenhagen)..........64,954
Glostrup (★Copenhagen)...........19,573
Haderslev (29,973▲)..............23,100
Helsingør (Elsinore).............56,566
Herlev (★Copenhagen).............28,530
Herning (56,033▲)................47,900
Hillerød.........................33,686
Hjørring (34,456▲)...............24,900
Høje Tåstrup (★Copenhagen)....43,292
Holbæk (29,578▲).................23,300
Holstebro (36,777▲)..............29,900
Horsens..........................54,533
Hvidovre (★Copenhagen)...........50,608
Køge (34,511▲)...................30,300
Kolding..........................55,769
Lyngby (Kongens Lyngby)-
Tårbæk (★Copenhagen)..........52,013
Middelfart.......................17,996
Næstved (45,237▲)................39,800
Odense..........................168,528
Randers..........................62,486
Rødovre (★Copenhagen)............38,020
Roskilde.........................48,746
Silkeborg (46,774▲)..............40,300
Søllerød (★Copenhagen)...........31,920
Sønderborg.......................27,790
Svendborg (37,996▲)..............33,200
Tårnby (★Copenhagen).............42,075
Vejle............................49,471
Viborg (38,757▲).................32,600

DJIBOUTI

1971 E.........................125,000

•DJIBOUTI........................40,000

DOMINICA

1970 C..........................70,302

•ROSEAU..........................10,157

DOMINICAN REPUBLIC / República Dominicana

1976 E.......................4,835,207

Baní.............................31,763
Barahona.........................53,912
Bonao............................32,132
La Romana........................49,498
La Vega..........................41,658
Mao (Valverde)...................32,723
Moca.............................32,621
Puerto Plata.....................44,113
San Cristóbal....................36,504
San Francisco de Macorís.........60,821
San Juan [de la Maguana].........43,417
San Pedro de Macorís.............66,022
Santiago [de los Caballeros]...219,846
•SANTO DOMINGO..................979,608

C Census. E Official estimate. UE Unofficial estimate.
L Population within municipal limits of year specified. • Largest city in country.

★ Population or designation of metropolitan area, including suburbs (see headnote).
▲ Population of an entire municipality, commune, or district, including rural area.
‡† Year of information specified at start of country.

ECUADOR

1974 C....6,521,710

Ambato (1976 E)....80,000
Azogues....10,939
Babahoyo....28,345
Chone....23,647
Cuenca (1978 E)....128,788
Esmeraldas....60,132
Guaranda....11,387
•Guayaquil (1978 E)....1,022,010
Ibarra....41,057
Jipijapa....19,719
Latacunga....22,106
Loja....47,268
Machala....68,379
Manta....63,514
Milagro....53,058
Pasaje....20,822
Portoviejo....59,404
Quevedo....43,123
QUITO (1978 E)....742,858
Riobamba....58,029
Santo Domingo....30,487
Tulcán....24,443

EGYPT / Miṣr

1966 C....30,083,419

Abnūb....31,195
Abū Kabīr....41,789
Abū Tīj....28,161
Akhmīm....44,829
Al-'Arīsh....††40,338
Al-Badārī....26,531
Alexandria (Al-Iskandarīyah) (1978 E) (★2,850,000)....2,409,000
Al-Fashn....27,746
Al-Fayyūm (1976 C)....167,081
Al-Ḥawāmidīyah (★Cairo)....36,227
Al-Ismā'īlīyah (Ismailia) (1976 C) (★185,000)....145,478
Al-Jīzah (Giza) (★Cairo) (1976 C)....1,246,713
Al Madīnah al Fikrīyah....21,504
Al-Maḥallah al Kubrā (1976 C)....292,853
Al-Manshāh....25,027
Al-Manṣūrah (El Mansura) (1976 C) (★290,000)....257,866
Al-Manzilah....33,298
Al-Maṭarīyah....41,105
Al-Minyā (1976 C)....146,423
Al Qanāṭir al Khayrīyah....22,477
Al-Quṣayr....5,525
Al-Qūṣīyah....25,991
Al-Uqṣur (Luxor)....77,578
Armant....38,308
Ashmūn....32,168
Ash Shuhadā'....21,947
As-Sallūm....2,483
As-Sinbillāwayn....40,686
Aswān (1976 C)....144,377
Asyūṭ (1976 C)....213,983
Aṭ Ṭalibīyah....20,438
Az-Zaqāzīq (1976 C)....202,637
Bahtīm (★Cairo)....32,510
Banhā....63,849
Banī Mazār....34,053
Banī Suwayf (1976 C)....118,148
Bibā....22,871
Bilbays....58,070
Bilqās Qism Awwal....41,067
Biyalā....33,008
Būsh....21,174
•CAIRO (AL QĀHIRAH) (1978 E) (★8,500,000)....5,278,000
Damanhūr (1976 C)....188,927
Dayrūṭ....27,646
Dishnā....21,857
Disūq....45,580
Dumyāṭ (Damietta) (1975 E)....113,200
Fāqūs....40,561
Fuwah....30,654
Giheina al Gharbiya....24,203
Ḥawsh 'Īsá....30,006
Idfū....27,326
Idkū....42,239
Isnā....27,383
Jirjā....44,150
Kafr ad-Dawwār (★Alexandria) (1976 C)....160,554
Kafr ash-Shaykh....51,544
Kafr az-Zayyāt....34,084
Kafr Salīm (★Alexandria)....40,381
Kawm Umbū....27,227
Maghāghah....33,211
Mallawī....59,938
Manfalūṭ....34,132
Minūf....48,256
Minyā al-Qamḥ....31,533
Mīt Ghamr (★82,000)....43,665
Nafīshah (★Al-Ismā'īlīyah)....29,483
Port Said (Bur Sa'īd) (1978 E)....271,000
Qalyūb....49,303
Qinā....68,536
Qūṣ....27,462
Rashīd (Rosetta)....36,711
Samālūṭ....37,861
Samannūd....29,749
Sāqiyat Makkī....22,967
Sawhāj (1976 C)....101,758
Shibīn al-Kawm (1976 C)....102,844
Shirbīn....25,089
Shubrā al-Khaymah (★Cairo) (1976 C)....393,700
Sīdī Sālim....21,096
Sinnūris....34,855
Suez (As Suways) (1978 E)....204,000
Ṭahṭā....38,915
Ṭalā....25,448
Ṭanṭā (1976 C)....284,636
Ṭimā....29,293
Warrāq al-'Arab (★Cairo)....31,263
Ziftá (★★Mīt Ghamr)....37,883

††31,733 per 1967 census taken by Israeli occupation authorities.

EL SALVADOR

1977 E....4,255,000

Ahuachapán (63,600▲)....18,100
Chalchuapa (51,200▲)....22,000
Delgado (★San Salvador) (77,100▲)....53,600
Mejicanos (★San Salvador) (85,000▲)....70,500
Nueva San Salvador (63,500▲)....44,000
San Miguel (144,900▲)....72,900
•SAN SALVADOR (★720,000)....397,100
Santa Ana (189,000▲)....112,800
San Vicente (56,900▲)....21,500
Sonsonate (61,000▲)....40,100
Soyapango (★San Salvador) (56,900▲)....32,700
Usulután (57,600▲)....25,100
Zacatecoluca (71,500▲)....20,200

EQUATORIAL GUINEA / Guinea Ecuatorial

1965 C....254,684

Bata (1960 C) (27,024▲)....4,000
•MALABO (SANTA ISABEL) (37,152▲)....17,500

ETHIOPIA / Yaitopya

1978 E....29,408,200

•ADDIS ABABA....1,125,340
Asmera....373,827
Bahir Dar....45,955
Dabra-Mārk'os....35,818
Debre Zeyt....43,654
Desē....65,571
Dirē Dawa....72,202
Gonder....67,790
Hārer....55,401
Jimā....56,278
Keren....33,368
Mak'alē....41,235
Mitsiwa....29,064
Nazreth (Adāmā)....61,468

FAEROE IS. / Føroyar

1977 E....41,575

•TÓRSHAVN....11,586

FALKLAND ISLANDS

1972 C....1,957

•STANLEY....1,081

FIJI

1976 C....588,068

Lautoka (★28,847)....22,672
•SUVA (★117,827)....63,628

FINLAND / Suomi

1978 E....4,758,088

Espoo (Esbo) (★Helsinki)....129,758
Hämeenlinna....41,303
•HELSINKI (HELSINGFORS) (★885,000)....484,879
Hyvinkää....37,104
Iisalmi....22,131
Imatra....36,593
Joensuu....43,940
Jyväskylä (★86,000)....62,937
Kajaani....33,662
Kotka....61,320
Kouvola (★53,000)....30,524
Kuopio....73,567
Kuusankoski (★★Kouvola)....22,649
Lahti (★109,000)....94,980
Lappeenranta....53,393
Mikkeli....27,919
Nokia (★Tampere)....23,612
Oulu (★112,000)....93,497
Pori....79,815
Rauma....30,429
Tampere (★241,000)....165,519
Turku (Åbo) (★221,000)....164,586
Vaasa (Vasa)....53,774
Vantaa (Vanda) (★Helsinki)....127,403
Varkaus....24,536

FRANCE

1980 E....53,589,000

Regions and Departments

ALSACE....1,560,000
Bas-Rhin....904,300
Haut-Rinh....655,700
AQUITAINE....2,576,700
Dordogne....365,800
Gironde....1,089,000
Landes....292,000
Lot-et-Garonne....287,800
Pyrénées-Atlantiques (Basses-Pyrénées)....542,100
AUVERGNE....1,319,500
Allier....365,400
Cantal....160,500
Haute-Loire....199,300
Puy-de-Dôme....594,300
BASSE-NORMANDIE....1,314,000
Calvados....579,100
Manche....444,600
Orne....290,300
BOURGOGNE....1,589,600
Côte-d'Or....474,100
Nièvre....239,500
Saône-et-Loire....569,000
Yonne....307,000
BRETAGNE....2,652,800
Côtes-du-Nord....531,700
Finistère....817,800
Ille-et-Vilaine....731,600
Morbihan....571,700
CENTRE....2,224,000
Cher....319,100
Eure-et-Loir....352,700
Indre....243,000
Indre-et-Loire....498,700
Loiret....521,900
Loir-et-Cher....288,600
CHAMPAGNE-ARDENNE....1,346,600
Ardennes....300,700
Aube....286,900
Haute-Marne....205,700
Marne....553,300
CORSE (CORSICA)....229,400
Corse-du-Sud....102,400
Haute-Corse....127,000
FRANCHE-COMTÉ....1,085,800
Belfort, Territoire de....132,000
Doubs....492,500
Haute-Saône....223,500
Jura....237,800
HAUTE-NORMANDIE....1,638,500
Eure....443,800
Seine-Maritime....1,194,700
ÎLE-DE-FRANCE....10,064,700
Essonne....1,087,600
Hauts-de-Seine....1,350,000
Paris....2,050,500
Seine-et-Marne....889,400
Seine-Saint-Denis....1,292,400
Val-de-Marne....1,226,000
Val-d'Oise....921,000
Yvelines....1,247,800
LANGUEDOC-ROUSSILLON....1,832,100
Aude....265,200
Gard....500,000
Hérault....685,500
Lozère....72,300
Pyrénées-Orientales....309,100
LIMOUSIN....733,500
Corrèze....238,600
Creuse....138,100
Haute-Vienne....356,800
LORRAINE....2,312,900
Meurthe-et-Moselle....716,500
Meuse....191,400
Moselle....1,007,200
Vosges....397,800
MIDI-PYRÉNÉES....2,272,100
Ariège....135,500
Aveyron....268,300
Gers....167,200
Haute-Garonne....816,600
Hautes-Pyrénées....222,200
Lot....148,300
Tarn....334,900
Tarn-et-Garonne....179,100
NORD-PAS-DE-CALAIS....3,920,300
Nord....2,521,300
Pas-de-Calais....1,399,000
PAYS DE LA LOIRE....2,860,800
Loire-Atlantique....977,700
Maine-et-Loire....652,700
Mayenne....264,700
Sarthe....499,500
Vendée....466,200
PICARDIE....1,714,600
Aisne....527,200
Oise....642,100
Somme....545,300
POITOU-CHARENTES....1,537,200
Charente....334,200
Charente-Maritime....499,800
Deux-Sèvres....338,000
Vienne....365,200
PROVENCE-ALPES-CÔTE D'AZUR....3,873,100
Alpes-de-Haute-Provence (Basses-Alpes)....115,800
Alpes-Maritimes....862,600
Bouches-du-Rhône....1,715,400
Hautes-Alpes....99,800
Var....667,300
Vaucluse....412,200
RHÔNE-ALPES....4,930,800
Ain....398,000
Ardèche....252,000
Drôme....366,700
Haute-Savoie....483,400
Isère....903,900
Loire....735,500
Rhône....1,478,900
Savoie....312,400

Cities (1975 C)

Aix-en-Provence....110,659
Aix-les-Bains....22,210
Ajaccio....50,726
Albi....46,162
Alençon....33,680
Alès (★67,513)....44,245
Alfortville (★Paris)....38,057
Amiens (★152,997)....131,476
Angers (★188,695)....137,587
Angoulême (★100,528)....47,221
Annecy (★103,543)....53,262
Antibes (★★Cannes)....55,960
Antony (★Paris)....57,540
Arcachon (★38,000)....13,892
Argenteuil (★Paris)....102,530
Arles (50,059▲)....37,340
Armentières (★58,000)....26,346
Arras (★79,783)....46,446
Asnières [-sur-Seine] (★Paris)....75,431
Athis-Mons (★Paris)....30,737
Aubervilliers (★Paris)....72,976
Aulnay-sous-Bois (★Paris)....78,137
Aurillac....30,863
Autun....21,556
Auxerre....38,342
Avignon (★162,562)....90,786
Avranches....10,136
Bagneux (★Paris)....40,674
Bagnolet (★Paris)....35,906
Barentin (★12,000)....10,773
Bar-le-Duc....19,288
Bastia (★56,984)....50,718
Bayeux....13,457
Bayonne (★121,474)....42,938
Beauvais....54,089
Belfort (★75,795)....54,615
Besançon (★126,349)....120,315
Béthune (★145,155)....26,982
Béziers (★88,619)....84,029
Biarritz (★★Bayonne)....27,595
Blois....49,778
Bobigny (★Paris)....43,125
Bois-Colombes (★Paris)....26,657
Bondy (★Paris)....48,333
Bordeaux (★612,456)....223,131
Boulogne-Billancourt (★Paris)....103,578
Boulogne-sur-Mer (★100,581)....48,440
Bourg-en-Bresse....42,181
Bourges (★86,041)....77,300
Brest (★190,812)....166,826
Briançon....9,489
Brive-la-Gaillarde....51,864
Bron (★Lyon)....44,563
Bruay-en-Artois (★116,340)....25,714
Caen (★181,390)....119,474
Cagnes [-sur-Mer] (★Nice) (29,538▲)....23,353
Cahors....20,311
Calais (★100,327)....78,820
Caluire-et-Cuire (★Lyon)....43,041
Cambrai (★51,357)....39,049
Cannes (★210,000)....70,527
Carcassonne....42,154
Carmaux (★23,000)....13,208
Castres....45,978
Châlons-sur-Marne (★63,407)....52,275
Chalon-sur-Saône (★72,407)....58,187
Chambéry (★88,081)....54,415
Chamonix-Mont-Blanc....6,285
Champigny-sur-Marne (★Paris)....80,291
Chantilly....10,552
Charleville-Mézières (★69,124)....60,176
Chartres (★72,246)....38,928
Châteauroux (★66,836)....53,429
Châtellerault (★66,836)....37,080
Châtenay-Malabry (★Paris)....30,497
Châtillon (★Paris)....26,574
Chatou (★Paris)....26,550
Chaumont....27,226
Chauny (★21,000)....14,405
Chelles (★Paris)....36,516
Cherbourg (★82,539)....32,536
Chinon....5,391
Choisy-le-Roi (★Paris)....38,705
Cholet....52,976
Clamart (★Paris)....52,952
Clermont-Ferrand (★253,244)....156,900
Clichy (★Paris)....47,764
Cognac....22,237
Colmar (★83,435)....64,771
Colombes (★Paris)....83,390
Compiègne (★57,210)....37,699
Concarneau (18,759▲)....15,096
Corbeil-Essonnes (★Paris)....38,859
Courbevoie (★Paris)....54,488
Coutances....8,349
Creil (★77,225)....32,509
Créteil (★Paris)....59,023
Dax (★27,000)....19,137
Deauville....5,664
Decazeville (★26,000)....10,231
Denain (★★Valenciennes)....26,204
Dieppe (★40,000)....25,822
Dijon (★208,432)....151,705
Dinard....9,234
Dives-sur-Mer (★11,500)....5,872
Dole....29,295
Douai (★210,508)....45,239
Douarnenez....19,096
Drancy (★Paris)....64,430
Dreux....33,101
Dunkerque (★186,314)....83,163
Elbeuf (★48,000)....19,116
Épernay....29,677
Épinal (★53,522)....39,525
Épinay-sur-Seine (★Paris)....46,578
Étaples (★22,000)....10,559
Eu (★21,000)....8,626
Évreux....47,412
Fécamp....21,910
Foix....9,599
Fontaine (★Grenoble)....25,036
Fontainebleau (★36,000)....16,778
Fontenay-sous-Bois (★Paris)....46,475
Forbach (★62,000)....25,244
Fougères....26,610
Fréjus (★50,000)....28,851
Gagny (★Paris)....36,772
Gap (28,233▲)....25,052
Garges-lès-Gonesse (★Paris)....37,927
Gennevilliers (★Paris)....50,290
Givors (★35,000)....21,968
Granville....13,330
Grasse (34,579▲)....24,442
Grenoble (★389,088)....166,037
Guebwiller (★25,566)....11,072
Guéret....14,855
Haguenau....25,147
Hayange (★75,000)....20,426
Hendaye....9,470
Hénin-Beaumont (Hénin-Liétard) (★★Lens)....26,359
Houilles (★Paris)....30,345
Hyères (★★Toulon) (36,123▲)....29,611
Issy-les-Moulineaux (★Paris)....47,561
Ivry-sur-Seine (★Paris)....62,856
Jœuf (★30,000)....10,649
La Baule-Escoublac (★St.-Nazaire)....15,006
La Ciotat (32,721▲)....29,319
La Courneuve (★Paris)....37,958
La Garenne-Colombes (★Paris)....24,038
La Grand' Combe (★17,500)....10,452
Lambersart (★Lille)....29,642
Laon....27,914
La Rochelle (★100,649)....75,367
La Roche-sur-Yon....44,713
La Seyne-sur-Mer (★Toulon)....51,155
Laval....51,544
Le Blanc-Mesnil (★Paris)....49,107
Le Creusot....33,366
Le Grand-Quevilly (★Rouen)....31,963
Le Havre (★264,422)....217,881
Le Mans (★192,057)....152,285
Lens (★328,741)....40,199
Le Perreux-sur-Marne (★Paris)....28,333
Le Puy-en-Velay (★41,000)....26,594
Les Sables-d'Olonne (★29,000)....17,463
Levallois-Perret (★Paris)....52,523
Le Vésinet (★Paris)....17,986
L'Hay-les-Roses (★Paris)....31,412
Libourne....21,651
Liévin (★Lens)....33,070
Lille (★1,015,000)....172,280
Limoges (★167,664)....143,689
Lisieux....25,521
Livry-Gargan (★Paris)....32,917
Loches....6,738
Lomme (★Lille)....29,255
Longwy (★83,000)....20,131
Lons-le-Saunier....20,942
Lorient (★105,797)....69,769
Lourdes....17,870
Lunéville....22,709
Lyon (★1,170,660)....456,716
Mâcon....39,344
Maisons-Alfort (★Paris)....54,146
Maisons-Laffitte (★Paris)....23,504
Malakoff (★Paris)....34,121
Mantes-la-Jolie....42,465
Marcq-en-Baroeul (★Lille)....36,126
Marignane (★Marseille)....26,477
Marseille (★1,070,912)....908,600
Martigues (38,373▲)....26,897
Massy (★Paris)....41,344
Maubeuge (★105,000)....35,399
Mazamet (★28,000)....14,440
Meaux....42,243
Melun (★77,272)....37,705
Mende....10,451
Menton (★34,000)....25,129
Mérignac (★Bordeaux)....50,652
Metz (★181,191)....111,869
Meudon (★Paris)....52,806
Millau....21,907
Montargis (★50,200)....18,380
Montauban (48,053▲)....35,940
Montbéliard (★132,343)....30,425
Montceau-les-Mines (★51,385)....28,177
Mont-de-Marsan....26,166
Montélimar....28,058
Montereau-faut-Yonne....21,568
Montigny-lès-Metz (★Metz)....24,519
Montluçon (★71,988)....56,468
Montmorency (★Paris)....20,860
Montpellier (★211,430)....191,354
Montreuil-sous-Bois (★Paris)....96,587
Montrouge (★Paris)....40,304
Morlaix (19,237▲)....17,256
Moulins (★42,000)....26,067
Moyeuvre-Grande (★77,000)....12,523
Mulhouse (★218,743)....117,013
Nancy (★280,569)....107,902
Nanterre (★Paris)....95,032
Nantes (★453,500)....256,693
Narbonne....39,342
Neuilly-sur-Seine (★Paris)....65,983
Nevers (★59,424)....45,480
Nice (★437,566)....344,481
Nîmes (★131,638)....127,933
Niort (★64,128)....62,267
Nogent-sur-Marne (★Paris)....25,634
Noisy-le-Grande (★Paris)....26,662
Noisy-le-Sec (★Paris)....37,734
Noyon....13,889
Orange (25,371▲)....20,779
Orléans (★209,234)....106,246
Orly (★Paris)....26,109
Oullins (★Lyon)....27,772
Oyonnax....23,007
Palaiseau (★Paris)....28,716
Pantin (★Paris)....42,739
Paray-le-Monial....11,545
•PARIS (1980 E) (★9,450,000)....2,050,500
Pau (★126,859)....83,498
Périgueux (★57,830)....35,120
Perpignan (★117,689)....106,426
Pessac (★Bordeaux)....51,360
Poissy (★Paris)....37,431
Poitiers (★98,554)....81,313
Pont-à-Mousson (★23,000)....14,830
Pontoise (★Paris)....27,240
Port-de-Bouc....21,424
Privas....10,808
Puteaux (★Paris)....35,514
Quimper....55,977
Reims (★197,021)....178,381
Rennes (★229,310)....198,305
Rezé (★Nantes)....35,730
Rive-de-Gier (★38,000)....17,706
Roanne (★83,561)....55,195
Rochefort....28,155
Rodez (★35,000)....25,550
Romainville (★Paris)....26,260
Romans-sur-Isère (★46,000)....33,030
Rosny-sous-Bois (★Paris)....35,784
Roubaix (★★Lille)....109,553
Rouen (★388,711)....114,927
Royan (★29,000)....18,062
Rueil-Malmaison (★Paris)....62,727
St.-Avold (★28,000)....17,955
St. Brieuc (★82,148)....52,559
St.-Chamond....40,250
St.-Cloud (★Paris)....28,560
St. Cyr-l'École (★Paris)....16,537
St.-Denis (★Paris)....96,132
St.-Dié....25,423
St.-Dizier....37,266
Saintes....26,691
St.-Étienne (★334,846)....220,070

C Census. E Official estimate. UE Unofficial estimate.
L Population within municipal limits of year specified. • Largest city in country.
★ Population or designation of metropolitan area, including suburbs (see headnote).
▲ Population of an entire municipality, commune, or district, including rural area.
‡† Year of information specified at start of country.

St.-Étienne-du-Rouvray (★Rouen) 37,242
St.-Germain-en-Laye (★Paris) 37,509
St.-Jean-de-Luz (★23,000) 11,854
St.-Lô 23,221
St.-Malo 45,030
St.-Martin-d'Hères (★Grenoble) .. 38,052
St.-Maur-des-Fossés (★Paris) 80,920
St.-Nazaire (★119,418) 69,251
St.-Omer (★27,000) 16,932
St.-Ouen (★Paris) 43,588
St.-Quentin (★75,056) 67,243
St.-Tropez 4,523
Salon-de-Provence 34,576
Sarcelles (★Paris) 55,007
Sarreguemines 25,729
Sartrouville (★Paris) 42,253
Saumur 32,515
Savigny-sur-Orge (★Paris) 34,607
Schiltigheim (★Strasbourg) 30,144
Sedan 23,995
Senlis 13,639
Sens 26,463
Sète 39,258
Sèvres (★Paris) 21,149
Soissons (★49,000) 30,009
Sotteville (★Rouen) 31,659
Stains (★Paris) 35,545
Strasbourg (★390,000) 253,384
Suresnes (★Paris) 37,537
Talence (★Bordeaux) 34,127
Tarbes (★78,645) 54,897
Thann (★28,187) 8,519
Thionville (★141,881) 43,020
Thonon-les-Bains 26,354
Toul (★23,000) 16,454
Toulon (★378,430) 181,801
Toulouse (★509,939) 373,796
Tourcoing (★★Lille) 102,239
Tours (★245,631) 140,686
Trouville-sur-Mer (★16,000) 6,618
Troyes (★126,611) 72,167
Tulle 20,100
Valence (★104,330) 68,460
Valenciennes (★350,599) 42,473
Vannes 40,359
Vanves (★Paris) 22,528
Vénissieux (★Lyon) 74,347
Verdun 23,621
Versailles (★Paris) 94,145
Vesoul 18,173
Vichy (★59,062) 32,117
Vienne 27,830
Vierzon 35,699
Villefranche (★Nice) 7,200
Villefranche-sur-Saône (★42,000) 30,341
Villejuif (★Paris) 55,606
Villemomble (★Paris) 28,727
Villeneuve-d'Ascq (★Lille) 36,769
Villeneuve-St.-Georges (★Paris) .. 31,664
Villeurbanne (★Lyon) 116,535
Vincennes (★Paris) 44,261
Viry-Châtillon (★Paris) 32,411
Vitry-le-François 19,372
Vitry-sur-Seine (★Paris) 87,316
Voiron (★31,000) 19,420
Wattrelos (★Lille) 45,440

FRENCH GUIANA / Guyane française

1974 C 55,125

•CAYENNE 30,461
St.-Laurent-du-Maroni 3,182

FRENCH POLYNESIA / Polynésie française

1977 C 137,382

•PAPEETE (★42,000) 23,453

GABON

1976 E 530,000

Lambaréné 24,000
•LIBREVILLE 251,000
Port-Gentil 85,000

GAMBIA

1978 E 569,000

•BANJUL (BATHURST) (★88,000) 45,600

GAZA STRIP

1967 C 356,261

•GAZA (GHAZZAH) 118,272
Jabālyah 43,604
Khān Yūnis 52,997
Rafaḩ 49,812

GERMAN DEMOCRATIC REPUBLIC (EAST GERMANY) / Deutsche Demokratische Republik

1978 E 16,751,375

Altenburg 54,281
Annaberg-Buchholz 25,584
Apolda 28,961
Arnstadt 29,820
Aschersleben 35,259
Aue 30,053
Bautzen 47,450
•BERLIN, EAST (OST-BERLIN) (★★Berlin) 1,128,983
Bernburg 43,221
Bitterfeld (★105,000) 24,644
Blankenburg 18,143
Borna 23,326
Brandenburg 94,505
Burg [bei Magdeburg] 28,805
Coswig (★Dresden) 26,250
Cottbus 107,623
Crimmitschau 27,208
Delitzsch 24,124
Dessau (★135,000) 101,322
Döbeln 27,549
Dresden (★640,000) 514,508
Eberswalde 50,994
Eilenburg 21,969
Eisenach 49,850
Eisenhüttenstadt 48,677
Eisleben 27,785
Erfurt 208,800
Falkensee (★Berlin) 24,442
Finsterwalde 23,335
Forst [Lausitz] 27,030
Frankfurt an der Oder 77,175
Freiberg 50,808
Freital (★Dresden) 46,626
Fürstenwalde [Spree] 33,570
Gera 121,251
Glauchau 29,690
Görlitz 81,963
Gotha 58,369
Greifswald 60,636
Greiz 36,606
Güstrow 36,794
Halberstadt 47,919
Halle (★485,000) 232,543
Halle-Neustadt (★Halle) 91,860
Heidenau (★Dresden) 20,644
Hennigsdorf bei Berlin (★Berlin) 26,899
Hettstedt 19,646
Hoyerswerda 70,133
Ilmenau 24,026
Jena 102,025
Karl-Marx-Stadt (Chemnitz) (★460,000) 313,850
Köthen [Anhalt] 34,651
Lauchhammer 25,710
Leipzig (★710,000) 563,980
Leuna (★Halle) (1977 E) 10,132
Limbach-Oberfrohna (★Karl-Marx-Stadt) 24,272
Lübbenau [Spreewald] 22,365
Luckenwalde 27,677
Ludwigsfelde 20,081
Magdeburg (★395,000) 283,109
Meissen 40,858
Merseburg (★★Halle) 51,684
Mühlhausen (Thomas-Müntzer-Stadt) 43,678
Naumburg [an der Saale] 34,675
Neubrandenburg 73,258
Neuruppin 25,258
Neustrelitz 27,342
Nordhausen 46,317
Oranienburg (★Berlin) 24,258
Parchim 22,998
Pirna 48,233
Plauen 79,190
Potsdam (★Berlin) 126,262
Prenzlau 22,283
Quedlinburg 29,179
Radebeul (★Dresden) 35,497
Rathenow 32,341
Reichenbach [Vogtland] 25,909
Riesa 51,411
Rostock 224,834
Rudolstadt 31,435
Saalfeld [Saale] 33,876
Salzwedel 22,732
Sangerhausen 33,454
Schneeberg 21,842
Schönebeck 44,485
Schwedt [Oder] 52,228
Schwerin 115,950
Senftenberg 31,447
Sömmerda 21,933
Sondershausen 23,148
Sonneberg 28,663
Spremberg 22,582
Stassfurt 26,404
Stendal 42,942
Stralsund 73,889
Strausberg (★Berlin) 22,930
Suhl 42,324
Torgau 21,627
Waren 23,322
Weimar 62,803
Weissenfels 40,958
Weisswasser 29,632
Werdau 21,028
Wernigerode 35,435
Wilhelm-Pieck-Stadt Guben 36,826
Wismar 57,055
Wittenberg [Lutherstadt] 53,211
Wittenberge 32,893
Wolfen (★★Bitterfeld) 34,284
Zeitz 44,135
Zittau 41,822
Zwickau (★170,000) 123,446

GERMANY, FEDERAL REPUBLIC OF (WEST GERMANY) / Bundesrepublik Deutschland

1979 E 61,439,342

States

BADEN-WÜRTTEMBERG 9,190,052
BAYERN (BAVARIA) 10,870,968
BERLIN (WEST) 1,902,250
BREMEN 695,115
HAMBURG 1,653,043
HESSEN (HESSE) 5,576,085
NIEDERSACHSEN (LOWER SAXONY) 7,234,000
NORDRHEIN-WESTFALEN (NORTH RHINE-WESTPHALIA) 17,017,075
RHEINLAND-PFALZ (RHINE-LAND-PALATINATE) 3,633,195
SAARLAND 1,068,555
SCHLESWIG-HOLSTEIN 2,599,004

Cities

Aachen (★540,000) 242,971
Aalen (★80,000) 62,854
Achern 20,442
Achim (★Bremen) 27,442
Ahaus 27,824
Ahlen 53,681
Ahrensburg (★Hamburg) 25,416
Albstadt 48,192
Alfeld (Leine) 23,447
Alsdorf (★Aachen) 46,328
Altena 24,729
Amberg 44,541
Andernach (★★Neuwied) 26,897
Ansbach 38,338
Arnsberg 78,282
Aschaffenburg (★145,000) 59,054
Augsburg (★390,000) 245,940
Aurich 34,344
Backnang 29,104
Baden-Baden 49,399
Bad Harzburg (★Goslar) 25,095
Bad Hersfeld 28,240
Bad Homburg (★Frankfurt) 50,909
Bad Honnef am Rhein (★Bonn) .. 20,877
Bad Kissingen 22,331
Bad Kreuznach 41,255
Bad Nauheim (★Frankfurt) 26,852
Bad Neuenahr-Ahrweiler 26,027
Bad Oeynhausen 44,126
Bad Oldesloe 20,009
Bad Reichenhall 17,919
Bad Salzuflen (★★Herford) 51,181
Bad Vilbel (★Frankfurt) 25,875
Baesweiler (★Aachen) 23,471
Balingen 29,638
Bamberg (★120,000) 71,993
Barsinghausen (★Hannover) 32,699
Bayreuth (★89,000) 70,210
Beckum 37,952
Bensheim 32,874
Berchtesgaden 8,276
Bergheim (Erft) (★Cologne) 53,205
Bergisch Gladbach (★Cologne) . 101,007
Bergkamen (★Essen) 47,533
Berlin, West- (★3,775,000) 1,902,250
Biberach 28,122
Bielefeld (★525,000) 312,357
Bietigheim-Bissingen (★Stuttgart) 33,982
Bingen 23,837
Böblingen (★Stuttgart) 41,065
Bocholt 65,346
Bochum (★★Essen) 402,988
BONN (★555,000) 286,184
Borken 31,939
Bornheim (★Bonn) 33,819
Bottrop (★Essen) 114,510
Brake 17,511
Bramsche 23,762
Braunschweig (Brunswick) (★335,000) 261,669
Bremen (★800,000) 556,128
Bremerhaven (★190,000) 138,987
Bretten 22,615
Brilon 24,439
Bruchsal 37,232
Brühl (★Cologne) 43,012
Buchholz in der Nordheide (★Hamburg) 27,999
Bückeburg 20,626
Bünde 39,871
Burgdorf (★Hannover) 27,949
Butzbach 21,096
Buxtehude (★Hamburg) 31,162
Calw 22,881
Castrop-Rauxel (★Essen) 79,264
Celle 72,804
Cloppenburg 20,681
Coburg 45,906
Coesfeld 31,093
Cologne (Köln) (★1,815,000) 976,136
Crailsheim 24,636
Cuxhaven 58,891
Dachau (★Munich) 34,162
Darmstadt (★305,000) 138,661
Datteln (★Essen) 37,004
Deggendorf 30,455
Delmenhorst (★★Bremen) 72,140
Detmold 67,116
Dillingen (★Saarlouis) 20,722
Dinslaken (★Essen) 58,334
Dormagen (★Cologne) 55,826
Dorsten (★Essen) 68,862
Dortmund (★★Essen) 609,954
Duderstadt 22,886
Duisburg (★★Essen) 559,066
Dülmen 38,074
Düren (★110,000) 86,308
Düsseldorf (★1,225,000) 594,770
Einbeck 28,923
Elmshorn 41,628
Emden 51,607
Emmendingen 24,448
Emmerich 29,378
Emsdetten 30,900
Ennepetal (★Essen) 35,965
Erftstadt (★Cologne) 42,905
Erkelenz 35,579
Erkrath (★Düsseldorf) 42,637
Erlangen (★★Nürnberg) 100,760
Eschwege 24,097
Eschweiler (★★Aachen) 53,065
Espelkamp 23,124
•Essen (★5,125,000) 652,501
Esslingen (★Stuttgart) 91,733
Ettlingen (★Karlsruhe) 36,259
Euskirchen 44,593
Fellbach (★Stuttgart) 41,653
Filderstadt (★Stuttgart) 36,757
Flensburg (★103,000) 88,810
Forchheim 28,932
Frankenthal (★Mannheim) 43,511
Frankfurt am Main (★1,880,000) 628,203
Frechen (★Cologne) 43,161
Freiburg (★220,000) 174,121
Freising 34,252
Friedrichshafen 51,541
Fulda (★79,000) 57,114
Fürstenfeldbruck (★Munich) 31,354
Fürth (★★Nürnberg) 98,266
Gaggenau 28,611
Garbsen (★Hannover) 57,406
Garmisch-Partenkirchen 27,765
Geldern 25,730
Gelsenkirchen (★★Essen) 306,323
Georgsmarienhütte (★Osnabrück) 30,857
Gevelsberg (★Essen) 31,138
Giessen (★160,000) 76,485
Gifhorn 33,006
Gladbeck (★Essen) 80,434
Goch 28,634
Göppingen (★155,000) 53,034
Goslar (★84,000) 52,815
Göttingen 128,118
Greven 28,414
Grevenbroich (★Düsseldorf) 58,644
Gronau (★Enschede, Netherlands) 41,042
Gummersbach 48,344
Gütersloh (★★Bielefeld) 77,792
Hagen (★★Essen) 220,676
Haltern (★Essen) 30,783
Hamburg (★2,260,000) 1,653,043
Hameln (★72,000) 59,005
Hamm 171,595
Hanau [am Main] (★★Frankfurt) . 86,144
Hannover (★1,005,000) 535,854
Hattingen (★Essen) 57,255
Heidelberg (★★Mannheim) 128,773
Heidenheim (★89,000) 48,470
Heilbronn (★230,000) 111,426
Heinsberg 36,343
Helmstedt 26,816
Hemer 32,891
Hennef (★Siegburg) 28,835
Heppenheim (★Mannheim) 23,908
Herford (★120,000) 62,977
Herne (★Essen) 183,065
Herten (★Essen) 69,400
Herzogenrath (★Aachen) 42,425
Hilden (★Düsseldorf) 52,708
Hildesheim (★139,000) 102,512
Hof 53,398
Hofheim am Taunus (★Frankfurt) 33,262
Homburg (★★Zweibrücken) 41,581
Höxter 32,457
Hückelhoven 34,919
Hürth (★Cologne) 50,654
Ibbenbüren 42,149
Idar-Oberstein 35,811
Ingolstadt (★135,000) 89,467
Iserlohn 94,478
Itzehoe 33,707
Jülich 30,495
Kaarst (★Düsseldorf) 37,595
Kaiserslautern (★138,000) 99,197
Kamen (★Essen) 43,278
Kamp-Lintfort (★Essen) 37,859
Karlsruhe (★485,000) 271,417
Kassel (★370,000) 196,224
Kaufbeuren 42,204
Kempen (★Essen) 30,101
Kempten 57,390
Kerpen (★Cologne) 53,932
Kiel (★335,000) 250,750
Kirchheim (★Stuttgart) 31,756
Kleve (Cleves) 44,036
Koblenz (★180,000) 113,795
Königswinter (★Bonn) 34,935
Konstanz 67,948
Krefeld (★★Essen) 222,750
Kreuztal (★Siegen) 30,295
Kulmbach 28,324
Laatzen (★Hannover) 33,919
Lage 32,044
Lahr 35,516
Lampertheim (★Mannheim) 31,307
Landau 36,502
Landshut 55,538
Langen (★Frankfurt) 29,198
Langenfeld (★Düsseldorf) 46,590
Langenhagen (★Hannover) 46,825
Leer 31,316
Lehrte (★Hannover) 38,271
Leichlingen (★Cologne) 24,616
Leinfelden-Echterdingen (★Stuttgart) 35,044
Lemgo 39,512
Leonberg (★Stuttgart) 37,848
Leverkusen (★Cologne) 161,453
Lingen 43,864
Lippstadt 61,692
Löhne 37,111
Lörrach (★Basel, Switzerland) 41,522
Lübeck (★265,000) 222,120
Lüdenscheid 74,561
Ludwigsburg (★Stuttgart) 81,049
Ludwigshafen (★★Mannheim) 160,479
Lüneburg 62,198
Lünen (★Essen) 85,685
Mainz (★★Wiesbaden) 186,200
Mannheim (★1,395,000) 303,247
Marburg an der Lahn 74,724
Marl (★Essen) 89,441
Meerbusch (★Düsseldorf) 49,794
Melle 40,757
Memmingen 37,885
Menden [Sauerland] 53,101
Meppen 28,062
Merzig 30,008
Meschede 31,352
Mettmann (★Düsseldorf) 36,724
Minden (★125,000) 77,989
Moers (★Essen) 100,110
Mönchengladbach (★410,000) .. 258,001
Monheim (★Düsseldorf) 39,932
Mülheim an der Ruhr (★Essen) 182,465
Münden 26,047
Munich (München) (★1,940,000) 1,299,693
Münster 267,478
Nettetal 37,366
Neuburg an der Donau 23,945
Neu Isenburg (★Frankfurt) 35,899
Neumarkt in der Oberpfalz 30,226
Neumünster 80,331
Neunkirchen (★135,000) 52,216
Neuss (★Düsseldorf) 149,333
Neustadt am Rübenberge (★Hannover) 37,941
Neustadt an der Weinstrasse .. 50,405
Neu-Ulm (★Ulm) 47,263
Neuwied (★150,000) 60,461
Niederkassel (★Cologne) 25,460
Nienburg 30,207
Nordenham (★★Bremerhaven) .. 30,320
Norderstedt (★Hamburg) 64,302
Nordhorn 48,580
Northeim 32,307
Nürnberg (★1,025,000) 484,184
Nürtingen (★Stuttgart) 35,046
Oberammergau 4,800
Oberhausen (★★Essen) 229,613
Oberursel (★Frankfurt) 39,477
Oelde 27,335
Oer-Erkenschwick (★Essen) 26,702
Offenbach (★Frankfurt) 111,310
Offenburg 50,471
Oldenburg 136,155
Osnabrück (★270,000) 158,150
Paderborn 109,218
Papenburg 27,420
Passau 50,323
Peine 47,559
Pforzheim (★220,000) 106,677
Pinneberg (★Hamburg) 36,823
Pirmasens 50,250
Pulheim (★Cologne) 43,501
Rastatt 36,942
Ratingen (★Düsseldorf) 89,039
Ravensburg (★74,000) 42,081
Recklinghausen (★Essen) 119,472
Regensburg (★200,000) 132,399
Remagen (★Bonn) 14,342
Remscheid (★★Wuppertal) 129,507
Rendsburg 32,860
Reutlingen (★155,000) 94,737
Rheda-Wiedenbrück (★Bielefeld) 37,723
Rheinbach (★Bonn) 21,609
Rheinberg (★Essen) 26,205
Rheine 71,525
Rodgau (★Frankfurt) 34,854
Rosenheim 51,485
Rottenburg am Neckar 31,468
Rottweil 23,732
Rüsselsheim (★★Wiesbaden) 62,606
Saarbrücken (★390,000) 194,452
Saarlouis (★115,000) 39,028
Salzgitter 113,427
Sankt Augustin (★Bonn) 47,288
Sankt Ingbert 41,896
Sankt Wendel 26,880
Schleswig 30,118
Schmallenberg 24,929
Schorndorf (★Stuttgart) 33,527
Schwabach (★Nürnberg) 34,693
Schwäbisch Gmünd 56,621
Schwäbisch Hall 31,548
Schweinfurt (★110,000) 53,035
Schwelm (★Wuppertal) 31,207
Schwerte (★Essen) 47,333
Seelze (★Hannover) 30,293
Seevetal (★Hamburg) 35,409
Selb 21,428
Siegburg (★160,000) 34,475
Siegen (★205,000) 112,740
Sindelfingen (★Stuttgart) 54,163
Singen 43,653
Soest 40,373
Solingen (★★Wuppertal) 166,654
Speyer 43,663
Springe 30,528
Stade 42,519
Steinfurt 32,090
Stolberg (★★Aachen) 57,552
Straubing 42,718
Stuttgart (★1,935,000) 581,989
Sundern (Sauerland) 25,400
Trier (★125,000) 95,736
Troisdorf (★★Siegburg) 57,733
Tübingen 72,167
Tuttlingen 31,555
Uelzen 36,536
Ulm (★210,000) 99,560
Unna (★Essen) 56,903
Velbert (★Essen) 93,302
Verden 24,275
Viernheim (★Mannheim) 29,645
Viersen (★★Mönchengladbach) .. 81,419
Villingen-Schwenningen 78,465
Voerde (★Essen) 31,442
Völklingen (★★Saarbrücken) 44,901
Waiblingen (★Stuttgart) 44,968
Warendorf 32,909
Warstein 28,413
Wedel (★Hamburg) 30,075
Weiden 44,319
Weinheim (★Mannheim) 41,498
Wermelskirchen (★Wuppertal) .. 34,730
Wesel 56,760
Wetzlar (★105,000) 52,138
Wiesbaden (★795,000) 273,267
Wilhelmshaven (★135,000) 99,426
Willich (★Essen) 38,916
Witten (★Essen) 106,185
Wolfenbüttel (★★Braunschweig) 50,218
Wolfsburg 126,942
Worms (★★Mannheim) 73,505
Wunstorf (★Hannover) 37,318
Wuppertal (★870,000) 394,605
Würselen (★Aachen) 34,802
Würzburg (★205,000) 127,370
Zweibrücken (★105,000) 35,074

C Census. E Official estimate. UE Unofficial estimate.
L Population within municipal limits of year specified. • Largest city in country.

★ Population or designation of metropolitan area, including suburbs (see headnote).
▲ Population of an entire municipality, commune, or district, including rural area.
‡† Year of information specified at start of country.

GHANA

1970 C ... 8,559,313

•ACCRA (★738,498) ... 633,880
Bawku ... 20,567
Bolgatanga ... 18,896
Cape Coast ... 71,594
Ho ... 24,199
Keta ... 14,446
Koforidua ... 46,235
Kumasi ... 345,117
Nkawkaw ... 23,219
Nsawam ... 25,518
Obuasi ... 31,005
Oda ... 20,957
Sekondi-Takoradi ... 160,868
Tamale ... 83,653
Tarkwa ... 14,702
Tema ... 60,767
Wa ... 21,374
Winneba ... 30,778
Yendi ... 22,072

GIBRALTAR

1979 E ... 29,760

•GIBRALTAR ... 29,760

GREECE / Ellás

1971 C ... 8,768,641

Agrínion (★41,794) ... 30,973
Aiyáleo (★Athens) ... 79,961
Aíyion (★23,756) ... 18,829
Akharnaí (Acharnae) ... 24,621
Alexandroúpolis ... 22,995
Amaliás ... 14,177
Amaroúsion (★Athens) ... 27,112
Ambelókipoi (★Thessaloníki) ... 24,892
Árgos ... 18,890
Árta ... 19,498
•ATHENS (ATHÍNAI) (★2,540,241) ... 867,023
Ayía Varvára (★Athens) ... 26,409
Áyioi Anáryiroi (★Athens) ... 26,094
Áyios Dhimítrios (★Athens) ... 40,968
Dháfni (★Athens) ... 26,608
Dráma ... 29,692
Édhessa ... 13,967
Elevsís (Eleusis) ... 18,535
Ermoúpolis (Síros) (★16,082) ... 13,502
Flórina (Phlorina) ... 11,164
Galátsion (★Athens) ... 27,240
Glifádha (★Athens) ... 23,449
Grevená ... 8,016
Ilioúpolis (★Athens) ... 49,215
Ioánnina (Yanina) ... 40,130
Iráklion (Candia) (★84,710) ... 77,506
Iráklion (★Athens) ... 24,302
Kaisarianí (★Athens) ... 26,833
Kalámai (★40,402) ... 39,133
Kalamákion (★Athens) ... 26,957
Kalamariá ... 36,978
Kallithéa (★Athens) ... 82,438
Kardhítsa ... 25,685
Kastoría ... 15,407
Kateríni (★30,512) ... 28,808
Kavála ... 46,234
Keratsínion (★Athens) ... 67,672
Kérkira (Corfu) ... 28,630
Khaïdhárion (★Athens) ... 34,673
Khálandrion (★Athens) ... 35,944
Khalkís (Chalcis) ... 36,300
Khaniá (Canea) (★53,026) ... 40,564
Khíos (Chios) (★30,021) ... 24,084
Kifisiá (★Athens) ... 20,082
Komotiní ... 28,896
Koridhallós (★Athens) ... 47,335
Kórinthos (Corinth) ... 20,773
Kozáni ... 23,240
Lamía ... 37,872
Lárisa ... 72,336
Levádhia (Lebadea) ... 15,445
Mégara ... 17,294
Néa Ionía (★Athens) ... 54,906
Néa Liósia (★Athens) ... 56,217
Néa Smírni (★Athens) ... 42,512
Níkaia (★Athens) ... 86,269
Palaión Fáliron (★Athens) ... 35,066
Pátrai (Patras) (★120,847) ... 111,607
Peristérion (★Athens) ... 118,413
Piraiévs (Piraeus) (★★Athens) ... 187,362
Pírgos (Pyrgos) ... 20,599
Ródhos (Rhodes) ... 32,092
Salamís ... 18,256
Sérrai ... 39,897
Spárti (Sparta) (★13,432) ... 10,549
Thessaloníki (Salonika) (★557,360) ... 345,799
Thívai (Thebes) ... 15,971
Tríkkala ... 34,794
Trípolis (Tripolitza) ... 20,209
Véroia ... 29,528
Víron (★Athens) ... 44,021
Vólos (★88,096) ... 51,290
Xánthi ... 24,867
Zákinthos ... 9,339
Zografós (★Athens) ... 56,722

GREENLAND / Grønland

1977 E ... 49,719

Angmagssalik ... 1,023
Egedesminde ... 3,347
•GODTHÅB ... 8,545
Holsteinsborg ... 3,741
Julianehåb ... 2,670
Sukkertoppen ... 2,937
Thule ... 357

GRENADA

1976 E ... 109,609

•ST. GEORGE'S (★26,000) ... 10,000

GUADELOUPE

1974 C ... 324,530

BASSE-TERRE (★25,202) ... 15,457
Capesterre (18,143▲) ... 6,861
Les Abymes (★Pointe-à-Pitre) (53,605▲) ... 10,573
•Pointe-à-Pitre (★59,000) ... 23,889

GUAM

1980 C ... 105,816

•AGANA (★25,000) ... 881
Dededo ... 23,659

GUATEMALA

1973 C ... 5,211,929

Amatitlán ... 15,372
Antigua Guatemala ... 17,692
Chiquimula ... 16,181
Coatepeque ... 15,949
Escuintla ... 37,180
•GUATEMALA (★945,000) ... 717,322
Mazatenango ... 24,156
Puerto Barrios ... 19,696
Quezaltenango ... 45,977
Retalhuleu ... 20,222

GUERNSEY

1971 C ... 53,734

•ST. PETER PORT (★36,000) ... 16,303

GUINEA / Guinée

1967 E ... 3,702,000

•CONAKRY (1967 C) ... 197,267
Kankan ... 50,000
Kindia ... 45,000
Labé ... 26,000
Mamou ... 18,000
Nzérékoré ... 26,000
Siguiri ... 15,000

GUINEA-BISSAU

1970 C ... 487,448

•BISSAU ... 71,169

GUYANA

1976 E ... 783,000

•GEORGETOWN (★187,056) ... 72,049
New Amsterdam (1970 C) ... 17,782

HAITI / Haïti

1975 E ... 4,583,785

Cap-Haïtien ... 52,220
Gonaïves ... 33,837
Jérémie ... 19,227
Les Cayes ... 24,931
Pétionville (★Port-au-Prince) (1971 C) ... 35,257
•PORT-AU-PRINCE (1978 E) (★800,000) ... 745,700
Port-de-Paix ... 16,151
St.-Marc ... 19,354

HONDURAS

1977 E ... 2,998,700

Choluteca ... 29,300
Comayagua (1974 C) ... 15,941
El Progreso ... 32,800
La Ceiba ... 44,900
La Lima (1974 C) ... 14,631
Puerto Cortés ... 30,200
San Pedro Sula ... 172,900
•TEGUCIGALPA ... 316,800
Tela ... 22,700

HONG KONG

1976 C ... 4,402,990

Kowloon (★★Victoria) ... 749,600
New Kowloon (★Victoria) ... 1,628,880
Tai Wan Tsun (Ngau Tau Kok) (★Victoria) (1961 C) ... 53,836
Tsun Wan (★Victoria) ... 455,270
•VICTORIA (HONG KONG) (★3,975,000) ... 1,026,870

HUNGARY / Magyarország

1980 C ... 10,710,000

Ajka ... 30,000
Baja ... 39,000
Békés (22,000▲) ... 17,900
Békéscsaba (66,000▲) ... 57,400
•BUDAPEST (★2,600,000) ... 2,060,000
Cegléd (40,000▲) ... 32,500
Csongrád (22,000▲) ... 19,100
Debrecen ... 195,000
Dunaújváros ... 60,000
Eger ... 60,000
Érd (★Budapest) ... 40,000
Esztergom ... 31,000
Gödöllő (★Budapest) ... 26,000
Gyöngyös ... 38,000
Győr ... 125,000
Gyula (34,000▲) ... 29,300
Hajdúböszörmény (32,000▲) ... 28,600
Hajdúszoboszló ... 24,000
Hatvan ... 24,000
Hódmezővásárhely (54,000▲) ... 45,100
Jászberény (31,000▲) ... 24,900
Kaposvár ... 73,000
Karcag ... 24,000
Kazincbarcika ... 37,000
Kecskemét (93,000▲) ... 74,200
Kiskunfélegyháza (36,000▲) ... 27,300
Kiskunhalas (31,000▲) ... 22,700
Komló ... 30,000
Makó ... 30,000
Miskolc ... 210,000
Mohács (21,000▲) ... 17,700
Mosonmagyaróvár ... 30,000
Nagykanizsa ... 48,000
Nagykőrös (27,000▲) ... 21,600
Nyíregyháza (107,000▲) ... 84,600
Orosháza (36,000▲) ... 31,500
Ózd ... 47,000
Pápa ... 32,000
Pécs ... 170,000
Salgótarján ... 49,000
Sopron ... 56,000
Szeged ... 175,000
Székesfehérvár ... 102,000
Szekszárd ... 34,000
Szentes (35,000▲) ... 30,600
Szolnok ... 77,000
Szombathely ... 82,000
Tata ... 24,000
Tatabánya ... 75,000
Törökszentmiklós (26,000▲) ... 22,500
Vác ... 34,000
Várpalota ... 28,000
Veszprém ... 55,000
Zalaegerszeg ... 55,000

ICELAND / Ísland

1979 E ... 226,724

Akureyri ... 13,137
Hafnarfjördur (★Reykjavík) ... 12,158
Keflavík ... 6,539
Kópavogur (★Reykjavík) ... 13,533
•REYKJAVIK (★120,085) ... 83,536

INDIA / Bhārat

1976 E ... 609,264,000

(total excludes Sikkim, annexed in 1975)

States

Andaman and Nicobar Islands (Ter.) ... 128,000
Andhra Pradesh ... 47,944,000
Arunachal Pradesh (Ter.) ... 520,000
Assam ... 17,354,000
Bihār ... 61,790,000
Chandīgarh (Ter.) ... 285,000
Dādra and Nagar Haveli (Ter.) ... 83,000
Delhi (Ter.) ... 5,116,000
Goa, Damān and Diu (Ter.) ... 954,000
Gujarāt ... 30,269,000
Haryana ... 11,221,000
Himāchal Pradesh ... 3,657,000
Jammu and Kashmīr ... 5,120,000
Karnataka (Mysore) ... 32,448,000
Kerala ... 23,955,000
Lakshadweep (Ter.) ... 36,000
Madhya Pradesh ... 47,167,000
Mahārāshtra ... 56,341,000
Manipur (Ter.) ... 1,195,000
Meghalaya ... 1,125,000
Mizoram (pop. included with Assam)
Nāgāland ... 557,000
Orissa ... 24,391,000
Pondicherry (Ter.) ... 524,000
Punjab ... 14,954,000
Rājasthān ... 29,005,000
Sikkim (1971 E) ... 196,852
Tamil Nadu (Madras) ... 45,434,000
Tripura (Ter.) ... 1,731,000
Uttar Pradesh ... 96,172,000
West Bengal ... 49,788,000

Cities (1971 C)

Abohar ... 58,925
Achalpur (Ellichpur) (★66,451) ... 42,326
Adilābād ... 30,368
Ādoni ... 85,311
Agartala (★100,264) ... 59,625
Āgra (★634,622) ... 591,917
Āgra Cantonment (★Āgra) ... 37,074
Ahmadābād (★1,950,000) ... 1,585,544
Ahmadnagar (★148,405) ... 118,236
Aijal ... 31,740
Ajmer (★264,291) ... 262,851
Akola ... 168,438
Akot ... 41,534
Alandur (★Madras) ... 65,039
Alīgarh ... 252,314
Alīpur Duār (★54,454) ... 36,667
Allahābād (★513,036) ... 490,622
Alleppey ... 160,166
Almora (★20,881) ... 19,671
Alwar ... 100,378
Amalāpuram ... 30,518
Amalner ... 55,544
Ambāla (★186,126) ... 83,633
Ambāla Cantonment (★Ambāla) ... 102,493
Ambarnāth (★Bombay) ... 56,276
Ambāsamudram (★49,255) ... 27,709
Ambattur (★Madras) ... 45,586
Āmbūr ... 54,011
Amrāvati (Amraoti) (★221,277) ... 193,800
Amreli (★43,794) ... 39,520
Amritsar (★458,029) ... 407,628
Amroha ... 82,702
Anakapalle ... 57,273
Ānand ... 59,155
Anantapur ... 80,069
Arcot (★75,911) ... 30,230
Arkonam ... 43,347
Arni ... 38,664
Arrah ... 92,919
Aruppukkottai ... 62,223
Asansol (★925,000) ... 155,968
Ashoknagar-Kalyangarh (★Hābra) ... 41,916
Āttūr ... 41,569
Aurangābād (★165,253) ... 150,483
Avadi (★Madras) ... 77,413
Azamgarh ... 40,963
Badagara ... 53,938
Bāgalkot ... 51,746
Bahraich ... 73,931
Baidyabāti (★Calcutta) ... 54,130
Balasore ... 46,239
Ballarpur ... 34,268
Ballia ... 47,101
Balrāmpur ... 36,191
Bālurghāt ... 67,088
Bānda ... 50,575
Bangalore (★1,750,000) ... 1,540,741
Bangaon ... 50,538
Bānkura ... 79,129
Bansbāria (★Calcutta) ... 61,748
Bāpatla ... 41,947
Baranagar (★Calcutta) ... 136,842
Bārāsat (★Calcutta) ... 42,642
Baraut ... 31,264
Bareilly (★326,106) ... 296,248
Barmer ... 38,630
Barnāla ... 31,388
Baroda (Vadodara) (★467,487) ... 466,696
Barrackpore (★Calcutta) ... 96,889
Bārsi ... 62,374
Basīrhāt ... 63,816
Basti ... 49,635
Batāla (★76,488) ... 58,200
Beāwar ... 66,114
Begusarai (★44,084) ... 35,736
Behāla (South Suburban) (★Calcutta) ... 272,600
Belgaum (★213,872) ... 192,427
Bellampalle ... 30,290
Bellary ... 125,183
Berhampore (*West Bengal state*) (★78,909) ... 72,605
Berhampur (*Orissa state*) ... 117,662
Bettiah ... 51,018
Betūl ... 30,862
Bhadrakh ... 40,487
Bhadrāvati (★101,358) ... 40,203
Bhadreswar (★Calcutta) ... 45,586
Bhāgalpur ... 172,202
Bhandāra ... 39,423
Bharatpur (★69,902) ... 68,036
Bhatinda (★65,318) ... 53,684
Bhātpāra (★Calcutta) ... 204,750
Bhaunagar (★225,974) ... 225,358
Bhavāni (★56,696) ... 23,114
Bhilai (Bhilainagar) (★245,124) ... 157,173
Bhīlwāra ... 82,155
Bhīmavaram ... 63,762
Bhind (★45,794) ... 42,371
Bhiwandi (★Bombay) ... 79,576
Bhiwāni ... 73,086
Bhopāl (★384,859) ... 298,022
Bhubaneswar ... 105,491
Bhuj (★52,861) ... 52,177
Bhusāwal (★104,708) ... 96,800
Bīdar ... 50,670
Bihar ... 100,046
Bijāpur ... 103,931
Bijnor ... 43,290
Bīkaner (★208,894) ... 188,518
Bilāspur (★130,740) ... 98,410
Bīr (Bhir) ... 49,965
Bishnupur ... 38,135
Bodhan ... 37,589
Bodināyakkanūr ... 54,176
Bokāro Steel City (★107,159) ... 94,007
Bolāngir ... 35,748
Bombay (★6,750,000) ... 5,970,575
Botād ... 32,179
Broach (Bharuch) (★92,251) ... 91,589
Budaun ... 72,204
Budge Budge (★Calcutta) ... 51,039
Bulandshahr ... 59,505
Bulsār (Valsad) (★54,966) ... 43,254
Būndi ... 34,279
Burdwān ... 143,318
Burhānpur (★105,335) ... 105,246
Buxar ... 31,691
•Calcutta (★9,100,000) ... 3,148,746
Calicut (Kozhikode) ... 333,979
Cambay ... 62,097
Cannanore (★59,912) ... 55,162
Chaibāsā ... 35,386
Chākdaha ... 46,345
Chakradharpur (★34,967) ... 22,709
Chālakudi ... 37,562
Chālisgaon ... 41,720
Champdāni (★Calcutta) ... 58,596
Chandannagar (Chandernagore) (★Calcutta) ... 75,238
Chandausi ... 53,393
Chandīgarh (★232,940) ... 218,743
Chandrapur ... 75,134
Changanācheri ... 48,545
Chāpra (★98,401) ... 83,101
Chhatarpur ... 32,271
Chhindwāra (★53,508) ... 53,492
Chidambaram (★57,658) ... 48,811
Chikmagalūr ... 41,639
Chilakalūrupet ... 41,543
Chingleput ... 38,419
Chīrāla ... 54,487
Chitradurga ... 50,254
Chittaranjan ... 40,736
Chittoor ... 63,035
Chopda ... 32,656
Churu (★53,185) ... 52,502
Cochin ... 439,066
Coimbatore (★750,000) ... 356,368
Cooch Behār (★62,664) ... 53,684
Coonoor (★70,813) ... 38,007
Cuddalore ... 101,335
Cuddapah ... 66,195
Cumbum ... 40,796
Cuttack (★205,759) ... 194,068
Dabhoi ... 37,892
Dabra (★21,430) ... 18,623
Dalhousie (★5,123) ... 4,296
Daltonganj ... 32,367
Damān ... 17,317
Damoh (★59,983) ... 59,489
Dānāpur (★Patna) ... 42,694
Darbhanga ... 132,059
Darjeeling ... 42,873
Datia ... 36,439
Dāvangere ... 121,110
Dehra Dūn (★203,464) ... 166,073
Dehri ... 46,037
Delhi (★4,500,000) ... 3,706,558
Delhi Cantonment (★Delhi) ... 57,339
Deoband ... 38,194
Deoghar (★45,060) ... 40,356
Deolāli (★★Nāsik) ... 55,436
Deoria ... 38,161
Dewās (★51,866) ... 51,545
Dhānbād (★600,000) ... 79,838
Dhār ... 36,172
Dhārāpuram ... 34,500
Dharmapuri ... 40,086
Dholka ... 35,520
Dholpur ... 31,865
Dhorāji (★60,080) ... 59,773
Dhrāngadhra ... 40,791
Dhubri (★45,589) ... 36,503
Dhule ... 137,129
Dibrugarh ... 80,348
Digboi (★32,388) ... 16,538
Dindigul ... 128,429
Dohad (★51,406) ... 44,506
Dombivli (★Bombay) ... 51,108
Dum-Dum (★Calcutta) ... 31,363
Durg (★★Bhilai) ... 67,892
Durgāpur ... 206,638
Dwarka ... 17,801
Elūru (Ellore) ... 127,023
English Bāzār (★68,026) ... 61,335
Erode (★169,613) ... 105,111
Etah ... 33,514
Etāwah ... 85,894
Faizābād (★109,806) ... 102,835
Farīdābād New Township (★Delhi) ... 85,762
Farrukhābād (★110,835) ... 102,768
Fatehābād ... 22,630
Fatehpur ... 54,665
Fatehpur Sikri ... 13,561
Fāzilka ... 36,281
Fīrozābād ... 133,863
Fīrozpur (Ferozepore) (★97,709) ... 49,545
Gadag ... 95,426
Garden Reach (★Calcutta) ... 154,913
Garulia (★Calcutta) ... 44,271
Gauhāti (★200,377) ... 123,783
Gaya ... 179,884
Ghāziābād (★Delhi) ... 118,836
Ghāzīpur ... 45,635
Giridih ... 40,308
Godhra (★66,853) ... 66,403
Gonda ... 52,662
Gondal (★55,329) ... 54,928
Gondia ... 77,992
Gopichettipālaiyam ... 36,356
Gorakhpur ... 230,911
Govindpura (★Bhopāl) ... 53,922
Gūdalūr ... 32,843
Gudivāda ... 61,068
Gudiyāttam (★67,966) ... 63,007
Gūdūr ... 33,778
Gulbarga ... 145,588
Guna ... 40,006
Guntakal ... 66,320
Guntūr ... 269,991
Gurdāspur ... 32,064
Gurgaon ... 57,151
Gwalior (★406,140) ... 384,772
Hābra (★93,351) ... 51,435
Hājīpur ... 41,890
Haldwāni ... 52,205
Hālisahar (★Calcutta) ... 68,906
Hānsi ... 41,108
Hāpur ... 71,266
Hardoi ... 46,639
Hardwār (★79,277) ... 77,864
Harihar ... 33,888
Haripād ... 31,145
Hassan ... 51,325
Hāthras ... 74,349
Hazāribāgh ... 54,818
Hindupur ... 42,959
Hinganghāt ... 44,349
Hingoli ... 31,948
Hisār ... 89,437
Hooghly-Chinsura (★Calcutta) ... 105,241
Hoshiārpur ... 57,691
Hospet ... 65,196
Howrah (★Calcutta) ... 737,877
Hubli-Dhārwār ... 379,166
Hyderābād (★2,000,000) ... 1,607,396
Ichalkaranji ... 87,731
Imphāl ... 100,366
Indore (★560,936) ... 543,381
Itārsi (★46,866) ... 44,191
Jabalpur (★534,845) ... 426,224
Jabalpur Cantonment (★Jabalpur) ... 50,195
Jagādhri (★115,020) ... 35,094
Jagannāthnagar (★Rānchī) ... 55,663
Jagraon ... 32,999
Jagtiāl ... 30,900
Jaipur (★636,768) ... 615,258
Jālgaon ... 106,711
Jālna ... 91,099
Jalpaiguri ... 55,159
Jamālpur (★★Monghyr) ... 61,731
Jammu (★164,207) ... 155,338
Jāmnagar (★227,640) ... 199,709
Jamshedpur (★456,146) ... 341,576
Jaora ... 37,235
Jaridih Bazar (★69,321) ... 33,084
Jaunpur ... 80,737
Jetpur (★41,943) ... 41,926

C Census. E Official estimate. UE Unofficial estimate.
L Population within municipal limits of year specified. • Largest city in country.

★ Population or designation of metropolitan area, including suburbs (see headnote).
▲ Population of an entire municipality, commune, or district, including rural area.
‡† Year of information specified at start of country.

Jeypore 34,319
Jhānsi (*198,135) 173,292
Jharia (**Dhānbād) 45,236
Jind 38,161
Jodhpur 317,612
Jorhāt (*70,674) 30,247
Jullundur (*329,830) 296,106
Junāgadh (*95,900) 95,485
Kadaiyanallūr 50,295
Kadiri 33,810
Kairāna 32,353
Kaithal 45,199
Kākināda 164,200
Kālol (*Ahmadābād) 50,321
Kalyān (*Bombay) 99,547
Kamarhati (*Calcutta) 169,404
Kāmthi (*Nāgpur) 53,412
Kānchipuram (Conjeeveram) (*119,693) 110,657
Kānchrāpāra (*Calcutta) 78,768
Kānpur (*1,320,000) 1,154,388
Kānpur Cantonment (*Kānpur) 69,452
Kapadvanj 30,748
Kapūrthala 35,482
Karād 42,329
Kāraikkudi (*88,371) 55,449
Kāranja 31,150
Karimganj 31,618
Karīmnagar 48,918
Karnāl 92,784
Karūr 65,706
Kāsaragod 34,984
Kāsganj 46,467
Kāshīpur 33,457
Katihār (*80,121) 67,014
Kayankulam (Kayamkulam) 54,102
Kerkend (*Dhānbād) 51,314
Khadki (Kirkee) (*Pune) 65,497
Khāmgaon 53,692
Khammam 56,919
Khandwa (*85,403) 84,517
Khanna 34,182
Kharagpur (*161,257) 61,783
Khargone 41,316
Khurja 50,245
Kilikollūr 41,871
Kishanganj 36,893
Kishangarh 37,405
Kohima 21,545
Kolār 43,418
Kolār Gold Fields (*118,861) 76,112
Kolhāpur (*267,513) 259,050
Konnagar (*Calcutta) 34,424
Kota 212,991
Kot Kapūra (*34,116) 33,907
Kottagūdem 75,542
Kottayam 59,714
Kovilpatti 48,509
Krishnanagar 85,923
Kulti (**Asansol) 29,665
Kumbakonam (*119,655) 113,130
Kundla 37,957
Kurichi (*Coimbatore) 40,537
Kurnool 136,710
Lakhīmpur 43,752
Lalitpur 34,462
Lātūr 70,156
Leh 5,519
Lucknow (*840,000) 749,239
Lucknow Cantonment (*Lucknow) 39,338
Ludhiāna (*401,176) 397,850
Machilīpatnam (Bandar) 112,612
Madras (*3,200,000) 2,469,449
Madakulam (*Madurai) 46,317
Madanapalle 36,458
Madgaon (Margao) (*48,593) 41,655
Madhubani 32,919
Madurai (*725,000) 549,114
Mahbūbnagar 51,756
Mahuva 39,497
Mainpuri 43,849
Mālegaon 191,847
Māler Kotla (*48,859) 48,536
Malkāpur 35,476
Manappārai 32,092
Mandasor (*56,988) 52,347
Mandya 72,132
Mangalagiri 32,850
Mangalore (*215,122) 165,174
Mannārgudi 42,783
Mānsa 31,351
Mathura (*140,150) 132,028
Maunath Bhanjan 64,058
Māyūram 60,195
Meerut (*367,754) 270,993
Meerut Cantonment (*Meerut) 85,415
Mehsāna (Mahesāna) (*51,713) 51,598
Melappālaiyam (*Tirunelveli) 47,731
Mettupālaiyam 48,365
Mettūr 38,380
Mhow (*63,739) 59,037
Midnapore 71,326
Mira (**Sāngli) 77,606
Mirzāpur 105,939
Modinagar 43,470
Moga (*61,625) 55,270
Mokameh 38,164
Monghyr (*164,205) 102,474
Morādābād (*272,652) 258,590
Morena 44,901
Mormugão 44,065
Morvi 60,976
Motihāri (*40,352) 37,032
Muktsar 36,750
Murtazāpur 23,141
Murwāra (Katni) (*86,535) 54,864
Mussoorie 18,038
Muzaffarnagar 114,783
Muzaffarpur 126,379
Mysore 355,685
Nabadwip 94,204
Nābha 34,761
Nadiād 108,269
Nāgappattinam (*74,019) 68,026
Nāgaur 36,448
Nāgda 32,569

Nāgercoil 141,288
Nagīna 37,066
Nāgpur (*950,000) 866,076
Naihāti (*Calcutta) 82,080
Naini Tāl (*25,167) 23,986
Najībābād 42,586
Nalgonda 33,126
Nānded 126,538
Nandurbār 54,070
Nandyāl 63,193
Nangi (*Calcutta) 47,555
Narasapur 36,147
Narasaraopet 43,467
Nārnaul 31,875
Nāsik (*271,681) 176,091
Navsāri (*80,101) 72,979
Nawābganj 35,395
Neemuch (*49,748) 47,113
Nellikkuppam 37,638
Nellore 133,590
NEW DELHI (**Delhi) 301,801
Neyveli 58,285
Nipāni 35,116
Nizāmābād 115,640
North Barrackpore (*Calcutta) 76,335
North Dum-Dum (*Calcutta) 63,873
Nowgong 56,537
Ongole 53,330
Ootacamund 63,310
Orai 42,513
Outer Burnpur (*Asansol) 56,900
Pālakollu 36,196
Pālanpur 42,114
Pālayankottai (**Tirunelveli) 70,070
Pālghāt 95,788
Pāli 49,834
Pallavaram (*Madras) 51,374
Palni (*51,664) 49,575
Palwal 36,207
Panaji (Panjim) (Nova Goa) (*59,258) 34,953
Pānchur (*Calcutta) 59,021
Pandharpur 53,638
Pandu (*Gauhati) 38,876
Pānihāti (*Calcutta) 148,046
Pānīpat 87,981
Panruti 34,065
Paramagudi 48,880
Parbhani 61,570
Parli 31,078
Pātan 64,519
Pattukkottai 37,682
Pathānkot (*78,192) 76,355
Patiāla (*151,041) 148,686
Patna (*625,000) 473,001
Periyakulam 41,561
Petlād 39,535
Phagwāra (*55,012) 50,863
Pīlibhīt 68,273
Pimpri-Chinchwad (*Pune) 83,542
Pithāpuram 31,391
Pollāchi (*93,838) 68,655
Pondicherry (*153,325) 90,637
Ponnāni 35,723
Porbandar (*106,727) 96,881
Port Blair 26,218
Proddatūr 70,822
Pudukkottai 66,384
Pulgaon 33,382
Puliyangudi 38,742
Pune (Poona) (*1,175,000) 856,105
Pune Cantonment (*Pune) 77,774
Puri 72,674
Purnea (*71,311) 56,484
Purūlia 57,708
Quilon 124,208
Rabkavi Banhatti 37,509
Rāe-Bareli 38,765
Rāichūr 79,831
Raiganj 43,191
Raigarh (*48,049) 46,745
Raipur (*205,986) 174,518
Rājahmundry (*188,805) 165,912
Rājapālaiyam 86,952
Rājkot 300,612
Rāj-Nāndgaon (*55,827) 41,183
Rājpur (*Calcutta) 33,604
Rāmanāthapuram 36,122
Rāmpur 161,417
Rānāghāt 47,815
Rānchī (*255,551) 175,934
Rānībennur 40,749
Rānīganj (**Asansol) 40,104
Ratangarh 31,506
Ratlām (*119,247) 106,666
Ratnāgiri 37,551
Raurkela (*172,502) 125,426
Rewa 69,182
Rewāri 43,885
Rishīkesh 17,646
Rishra (*Calcutta) 63,486
Rohtak 124,755
Roorkee (*62,456) 47,561
Sāgar (*154,785) 118,574
Sahāranpur 225,396
Sāhibganj 35,640
Salem (*416,440) 308,716
Sāmalkot ‡34,607
Sambalpur (*105,085) 64,675
Sambhal 86,323
Sāngli (*201,597) 115,138
Sāntipur 61,166
Sardārshahr 37,703
Sāsarām 48,282
Sātāra 66,433
Satna (*62,162) 57,531
Secunderābād Cantonment (*Hyderābād) 94,416
Sehore 35,657
Seoni 38,396
Serampore (*Calcutta) 102,023
Shāhābād 33,408
Shāhjahānpur (*144,065) 135,604
Shāmli 36,959
Shikohābād 31,442
Shillong (*122,752) 87,659
Shimoga 102,709

Shivpuri (*50,858) 42,120
Sholāpur 398,361
Sidhpur (*41,334) 40,521
Sīkar 70,987
Silchar 52,596
Silīguri (*136,343) 97,484
Simla 55,368
Sindri (**Dhānbād) 46,385
Singānallūr (*Coimbatore) 112,206
Sirsa 48,808
Sītāpur 66,715
Sivakāsi (*60,753) 44,883
Siwān 33,162
Sonīpat 62,393
South Dum-Dum (*Calcutta) 174,342
Sri Gangānagar (Gangānagar) 90,042
Srīkākulam 45,179
Srīnagar (*423,253) 403,413
Srīrangam (*Tiruchchirāppalli) 51,069
Srīvilliputtūr 53,855
Sūjāngarh 39,073
Sultānpur 32,330
Surat (*493,001) 471,656
Surendranagar (*97,251) 66,667
Sūri 30,110
Tādepallegūdem 43,610
Tādpatri 31,618
Tāmbaram (*Madras) 58,805
Tandā 41,611
Tanuku 34,197
Tellicherry 68,759
Tenāli 102,937
Tenkāsi 42,627
Tezpur 39,870
Thāna (*Bombay) 170,675
Thanjāvūr (Tanjore) 140,547
Theni-Allinagaram 34,854
Tindivanam 45,058
Tinsukia 54,911
Tiruchchirāppalli (Trichinopoly) (*475,000) 307,400
Tiruchendūr (*55,636) 18,126
Tiruchengodu 36,990
Tirunelveli (*266,688) 108,498
Tirupati (*71,984) 65,843
Tiruppattūr 40,357
Tiruppur (*151,127) 113,302
Tiruvannāmalai 61,370
Tiruvottiyūr (*Madras) 82,853
Titāgarh (*Calcutta) 88,218
Tonk 55,866
Trichūr 76,241
Trivandrum 409,627
Tumkūr 70,476
Tuticorin (*181,913) 155,310
Udaipur 161,278
Udamalpet 39,311
Udgīr 30,647
Ujjain (*208,561) 203,278
Ulhāsnagar (*Bombay) 168,462
Upleta 35,326
Uttarpara-Kotrung (*Calcutta) 67,568
Valparai 95,175
Vāniyambādi (*57,686) 51,810
Vārānasi (Benares) (*606,271) 583,856
Vellore (*178,554) 139,082
Verāval (*75,520) 58,771
Vidisha 43,212
Vijayawāda (*344,607) 317,258
Vikramasingapuram 40,274
Villupuram 60,242
Viramgām 43,790
Virudunagar 61,902
Vishākhapatnam (*363,467) 352,504
Visnagar 34,863
Vizianagaram 86,608
Warangal 207,520
Wardha 69,037
Yādgīr 32,756
Yamunānagar (**Jagādhri) 72,594
Yavatmāl 64,836

INDONESIA

1979 E 144,911,000

Island Groups

BORNEO, INDONESIAN (KALIMANTAN) 6,406,000
CELEBES 10,605,000
JAVA AND MADURA 90,780,000
LESSER SUNDA ISLANDS ‡8,153,000
MOLUCCAS 2,481,000
SUMATRA 26,486,000

†Total excludes Timor Timur, annexed in 1976

Cities (‡1971 C or 1961 C)

Amahai 18,256
Ambon (Amboina) (1976 E) 91,000
Amuntai 27,383
Balikpapan ‡137,340
Banda Aceh (Kutaradja) ‡53,668
Bandung (*1,250,000) ‡1,201,730
Bangil 28,275
Bangkalan 22,514
Banjarmasin ‡281,673
Bantul 30,572
Banyuwangi ‡89,103
Baubau 21,060
Bekasi ‡45,694
Bengkulu ‡31,866
Binjai ‡59,882
Blitar ‡67,856
Blora ‡53,504
Bogor ‡195,882
Bojonegoro ‡52,597
Bondowoso 35,760
Brebes ‡44,456
Bukittinggi ‡63,132
Ciamis 35,189
Cianjur (Tjiandjur) 62,546
Cilacap (Tjilatjap) ‡82,043
Cimahi (Tjimahi) ‡72,367
Cirebon (Tjirebon) ‡178,529
Denpasar ‡88,142

Dili (1970 C) (65,451▲) 6,730
Ende 26,843
Garut ‡81,234
Gorontalo ‡82,328
Gresik ‡48,561
Indramayu 25,710
•JAKARTA (DJAKARTA) (1979 UE) (*6,500,000) 6,400,000
Jambi (Telanaipura) ‡158,559
Jayapura (Sukarnapura) (1976 E) 61,054
Jember ‡122,712
Jepara 18,921
Jombang ‡45,450
Kediri ‡178,865
Klaten 33,400
Kotabumi 37,496
Krawang ‡61,361
Kualakapuas 18,573
Kudus ‡87,767
Kuningan 21,542
Kupang ‡52,698
Lahat ‡41,030
Langsa ‡55,016
Lawang 35,852
Lhokseumawe 28,386
Lumajang ‡48,995
Madiun ‡136,147
Magelang ‡110,308
Magetan 26,818
Majalengka 14,361
Majene 24,259
Makale 32,578
Malang ‡422,428
Manado ‡169,684
Martapura ‡69,729
Medan ‡635,562
Mojokerto ‡60,013
Nganjuk 23,499
Ngawi 29,220
Padang ‡196,339
Padangpanjang ‡30,711
Padangsidempuan ‡49,090
Pakanbaru ‡145,030
Palangkaraya ‡27,132
Palembang ‡582,961
Palopo 29,724
Palu 16,977
Pamekasan ‡41,416
Pangkalpinang ‡74,733
Parepare ‡72,538
Pasuruan ‡75,266
Pati ‡46,037
Payakumbuh ‡63,388
Pekalongan ‡111,537
Pemalang ‡77,672
Pematangsiantar ‡129,232
Perabumulih 41,951
Pinrang 23,818
Ponorogo ‡67,711
Pontianak ‡217,555
Praya 26,729
Probolinggo ‡82,008
Purbolinggo 22,698
Purwakarta ‡49,703
Purwokerto ‡94,023
Purworejo ‡52,956
Raba 29,881
Rangkasbitung 30,822
Salatiga ‡69,831
Samarinda ‡137,521
Semarang ‡646,590
Serang ‡56,263
Sibolga ‡42,223
Sidoarjo ‡41,254
Singaraja ‡42,289
Singkawang 35,169
Situbondo ‡55,348
Solok ‡24,771
Sragen 25,685
Subang ‡42,437
Sukabumi ‡96,242
Sungaipenuh 36,766
Surabaya (*1,400,000) ‡1,332,249
Surakarta ‡414,285
Tangerang ‡50,893
Tanjungbalai ‡33,604
Tanjungkarang-Telukbetung ‡198,986
Tanjungpandan 29,412
Tanjungpinang 37,638
Tarutung 24,998
Tasikmalaya ‡136,004
Tebingtinggi ‡30,314
Tegal ‡105,752
Ternate 24,287
Tidore 26,160
Tual 38,403
Tuban 38,575
Tulungagung ‡68,899
Ujung Pandang (Makasar) ‡434,766
Watampone ‡54,720
Yogyakarta (Jogjakarta) ‡342,267

IRAN / Īrān

1976 C 33,591,875

Ābādān 296,081
Ahvāz 329,006
Āmol 68,782
Arāk 114,507
Ardabīl 147,404
Bābol 67,790
Bakhtarān 290,861
Bandar 'Abbās 89,103
Bandar-e Anzalī (Bandar-e Pahlavī) 55,978
Behbehān (1966 C) 39,874
Behshahr (1966 C) 26,032
Bīrjand (1966 C) 25,854
Bojnūrd (1966 C) 31,248
Borūjerd 100,103
Dezfūl 110,287
Emāmshahr (Shahrūd) (1966 C) 30,767
Eşfahān (Isfahan) 671,825
Gonbad-e Qābūs 59,868
Gorgān 88,348

Hamadān 155,846
Homāyunshahr (1966 C) 46,836
Jahrom (1966 C) 38,236
Karaj 138,774
Kāshān 84,545
Kāzerūn 51,309
Kermān 140,309
Khorramābād 104,928
Khorramshahr 146,709
Khvoy 70,040
Lāhījān (1966 C) 25,725
Lār (1966 C) 21,576
Mahābād (1966 C) 28,610
Malāyer (1966 C) 28,434
Marāgheh 60,820
Marand (1966 C) 23,818
Marv Dasht (1966 C) 25,498
Mashhad (Meshed) 670,180
Masjed Soleymān 77,161
Mīāneh (1966 C) 28,447
Najafābād 76,236
Neyshābūr 59,101
Orūmīyeh (Rezā'īyeh) 163,991
Qā'emshahr (Shāhī) 63,289
Qazvīn 138,527
Qom 246,831
Qūchān (1966 C) 29,133
Rasht 187,203
Sabzevār 69,174
Sanandaj 95,834
Sārī 70,936
Semnān (1966 C) 31,058
Shīrāz 416,408
Tabrīz 598,576
•TEHRĀN (*4,700,000) 4,496,159
Torbat-e Ḩeydarīyeh (1966 C) 30,106
Yazd 135,978
Zāhedān 92,628
Zanjān 99,967

IRAQ / Al-'Irāq

1970 E 9,465,800

Ad-Dīwānīyah 62,300
Al-'Amārah 80,100
Al-Başrah (Basra) 370,900
Al-Fallūjah (1965 C) 38,072
Al-Ḩillah (Hilla) 128,800
Al-Kūfah (1965 C) 30,862
Al-Mawşil (Mosul) 293,100
An-Najaf 179,200
An-Nāşirīyah 62,400
Ar-Ramādī (1965 C) 28,723
As-Samāwah (1965 C) 33,473
As-Sulaymānīyah 98,100
Az-Zubayr (1965 C) 41,408
•BAGHDĀD (*2,183,800) 1,300,000
Ba'qūbah (1965 C) 34,575
Irbīl 107,400
Karbalā' 107,500
Kirkūk 207,900
Kūt al-Imāra (Al-Kūt) (1965 C) 42,116
Sāmarrā (1965 C) 24,746
Tall 'Afar (1965 C) 36,837

IRELAND / Eire

1979 C 3,368,217

An Uaimh (Navan) (*7,000) 4,277
Arklow (Inbhear Mór) 8,446
Athlone (Áth Luain) (*12,500) 9,760
Ballina (Béal Átha an Fheadha) 6,941
Ballinasloe (Béal Átha na Sluagh) 6,461
Bray (Brí Chualann) (*Dublin) 21,672
Carlow (Ceatharlach) 11,404
Carrick-on-Suir (Carraig na Siúire) 5,510
Castlebar (Caisleán an Bharraigh) 6,482
Clonmel (Cluain Meala) 12,411
Cobh 6,670
Cork (Corcaigh) (*175,000) 138,267
Drogheda (Droichead Átha) 22,555
Droichead Nua (1971 C) 5,053
•DUBLIN (BAILE ÁTHA CLIATH) (*1,110,000) 544,586
Dundalk (Dún Dealgan) 25,281
Dungarvan (Dún Garbháin) 6,578
Dún Laoghaire (*Dublin) 54,244
Ennis (Inis) (*12,000) 6,277
Enniscorthy (Inis Coirthe) 5,253
Galway (Gaillimh) 36,824
Kilkenny (Cill Choinnigh) (*14,800) 10,075
Killarney (Cill Áirne) 7,724
Limerick (Luimneach) (*80,000) 60,665
Mallow (Mala) 6,609
Monaghan (Muineachán) 6,173
Mullingar (Muileann Cearr) (1971 C) (*9,245) 6,790
Naas (Nás na Ríogh) (*Dublin) 7,740
Nenagh (Aonach Urmhumhan) 5,647
New Ross (Ros Mhic Treoin) 5,230
Portlaoise (1971 C) (*6,470) 3,902
Sligo (Sligeach) 16,836
Thurles (Durlas Éile) 7,436
Tipperary (Tiobrad Árann) 4,929
Tralee (Tráighlí) 15,011
Tuam (Tuaim) (1971 C) (*4,952) 3,808
Tullamore (Tulach Mhór) 7,720
Waterford (Port Láirge) (*42,000) 32,617
Wexford (Loch Garman) 11,848
Youghal (Eochaill) 5,739

ISLE OF MAN

1976 C 61,723

•DOUGLAS (*28,500) 20,262
Peel 3,338
Ramsey 5,458

C Census. E Official estimate. UE Unofficial estimate.
L Population within municipal limits of specified year. • Largest city in country.

* Population or designation of metropolitan area, including suburbs (see headnote).
▲ Population of an entire municipality, commune, or district, including rural area.
‡† Year of information specified at start of country.

ISRAEL / Yisra'el

1979 E ... †3,836,200

'Afula ... 19,700
'Akko (Acre) (★Haifa) ... 37,900
Ashdod ... 62,300
Ashqelon ... 52,000
Bat Yam (★Tel Aviv-Yafo) ... 130,100
Be'er Sheva' (Beersheba) ... 107,000
Bene Beraq (★Tel Aviv-Yafo) ... 89,600
Dimona ... 27,800
Elat (Elath) ... 18,900
Giv'atayim (★Tel Aviv-Yafo) ... 49,300
Hadera ... 37,800
Haifa (Hefa) (★415,000) ... 229,300
Herzliyya (★Tel Aviv-Yafo) ... 56,400
Holon (★Tel Aviv-Yafo) ... 128,400
JERUSALEM (YERUSHALAYIM) (AL-QUDS) *(includes Old City area occupied in 1967)* (★420,000) ... 398,200
Kefar Ata (★Haifa) ... 31,400
Kefar Sava (★Tel Aviv-Yafo) ... 38,100
Lod (Lydda) ... 39,400
Nahariyya ... 28,200
Nazerat (Nazareth) (★63,000) ... 40,400
Nazerat 'Illit (★Nazerat) ... 21,400
Nes Ziyyona ... 13,700
Netanya ... 95,900
Or Yehuda (★Tel Aviv-Yafo) ... 19,400
Petah Tiqwa (★Tel Aviv-Yafo) ... 117,000
Qiryat Bialik (★Haifa) ... 27,500
Qiryat Gat ... 24,300
Qiryat Motzkin (★Haifa) ... 23,200
Qiryat Ono (★Tel Aviv-Yafo) ... 22,500
Qiryat Shemona ... 15,800
Qiryat Yam (★Haifa) ... 28,400
Ra'anana (★Tel Aviv-Yafo) ... 29,700
Ramat Gan (★Tel Aviv-Yafo) ... 120,400
Ramat HaSharon (★Tel Aviv-Yafo) ... 30,100
Ramla ... 40,600
Rehovot ... 63,700
Rishon le Ziyyon (★Tel Aviv-Yafo) ... 87,800
•Tel Aviv-Yafo (Tel Aviv-Jaffa) (★1,350,000) ... 336,300
Teverya (Tiberias) ... 28,300
Tirat Karmel (★Haifa) ... 15,500
Umm el Fahm ... 18,600
Zefat ... 15,500

ITALY / Italia

1979 E ... 56,999,047

Regions and Provinces

ABRUZZI ... 1,239,738
Chieti ... 372,791
L'Aquila ... 302,480
Pescara ... 291,592
Teramo ... 272,875
APULIA, see PUGLIA
BASILICATA (LUCANIA) ... 618,703
Matera ... 204,273
Potenza ... 414,430
CALABRIA ... 2,078,264
Catanzaro ... 748,166
Cosenza ... 735,673
Reggio di Calabria ... 594,425
CAMPANIA ... 5,457,838
Avellino ... 440,712
Benevento ... 294,438
Caserta ... 753,207
Napoli (Naples) ... 2,945,181
Salerno ... 1,024,300
EMILIA-ROMAGNA ... 3,964,538
Bologna ... 937,136
Ferrara ... 385,503
Forlì ... 598,672
Modena ... 590,547
Parma ... 399,560
Piacenza ... 280,981
Ravenna ... 361,634
Reggio nell'Emilia ... 410,505
FRIULI-VENEZIA GIULIA ... 1,245,130
Gorizia ... 146,600
Pordenone ... 274,550
Trieste ... 291,581
Udine ... 532,399
LAZIO (LATIUM) ... 5,059,174
Frosinone ... 464,439
Latina ... 434,787
Rieti ... 143,983
Roma (Rome) ... 3,747,003
Viterbo ... 268,962
LIGURIA ... 1,844,779
Genova ... 1,065,846
Imperia ... 229,936
La Spezia ... 244,558
Savona ... 304,439
LOMBARDIA (LOMBARDY) ... 8,941,704
Bergamo ... 890,540
Brescia ... 1,015,350
Como ... 772,532
Cremona ... 333,403
Mantova ... 380,413
Milano ... 4,065,584
Pavia ... 519,369
Sondrio ... 175,188
Varese ... 789,325
MARCHE (MARCHES) ... 1,415,563
Ancona ... 434,091
Ascoli Piceno ... 354,667
Macerata ... 292,728
Pesaro e Urbino ... 334,077
MOLISE ... 334,091
Campobasso ... 238,564
Isernia ... 95,527
PIEMONTE (PIEDMONT) ... 4,531,141
Alessandria ... 472,865
Asti ... 217,982
Cuneo ... 548,236
Novara ... 509,830
Torino (Turin) ... 2,380,674
Vercelli ... 401,554
PUGLIA (APULIA) ... 3,917,029
Bari ... 1,471,563
Brindisi ... 400,092
Foggia ... 692,245
Lecce ... 778,830
Taranto ... 574,299
SARDEGNA (SARDINIA) ... 1,601,586
Cagliari ... 730,333
Nuoro ... 278,267
Oristano ... 157,151
Sassari ... 435,835
SICILIA (SICILY) ... 4,999,032
Agrigento ... 489,020
Caltanissetta ... 295,817
Catania ... 1,014,493
Enna ... 204,114
Messina ... 686,764
Palermo ... 1,206,291
Ragusa ... 276,312
Siracusa ... 397,818
Trapani ... 428,403
TOSCANA (TUSCANY) ... 3,600,233
Arezzo ... 313,801
Firenze ... 1,209,407
Grosseto ... 223,661
Livorno ... 346,395
Lucca ... 388,576
Massa-Carrara ... 205,535
Pisa ... 388,560
Pistoia ... 266,526
Siena ... 257,772
TRENTINO-ALTO ADIGE ... 876,249
Bolzano ... 432,073
Trento ... 444,176
UMBRIA ... 808,351
Perugia ... 579,311
Terni ... 229,040
VALLE D'AOSTA ... 114,591
VENETO (VENETIA) ... 4,351,313
Belluno ... 224,829
Padova ... 813,289
Rovigo ... 254,466
Treviso ... 716,250
Venezia (Venice) ... 844,391
Verona ... 774,347
Vicenza ... 723,741

Cities

Abano Terme ... 16,115
Acerra (★Naples) (37,629▲) ... 33,100
Acireale (49,813▲) ... 30,600
Adrano ... 34,190
Afragola (★Naples) ... 58,927
Agrigento ... 51,725
Alassio ... 13,943
Alba ... 31,309
Albano Laziale (★Rome) (27,889▲) ... 22,000
Alberobello ... 9,983
Alcamo ... 43,593
Alessandria ... 101,684
Alghero (37,892▲) ... 31,700
Altamura ... 49,878
Amalfi ... 6,446
Ancona ... 108,371
Andria ... 83,734
Anzio ... 27,223
Aosta ... 39,072
Arezzo ... 92,245
Ascoli Piceno ... 56,200
Assisi (24,910▲) ... 19,400
Asti ... 79,407
Augusta ... 38,181
Avellino ... 59,324
Aversa (★Naples) ... 51,837
Avezzano (34,353▲) ... 29,800
Avola ... 30,565
Bagheria ... 41,373
Barcellona Pozzo di Gotto (37,737▲) ... 26,000
Bari (★460,000) ... 387,266
Barletta ... 81,414
Bassano del Grappa ... 37,801
Battipaglia (40,604▲) ... 32,200
Belluno ... 37,003
Benevento (62,524▲) ... 52,800
Bergamo (★340,000) ... 125,544
Biella ... 55,857
Bisceglie ... 46,962
Bitonto ... 48,052
Bollate (★Milan) ... 43,115
Bologna (★550,000) ... 471,554
Bolzano (Bozen) ... 106,199
Bordighera (12,014▲) ... 9,600
Brescia ... 212,265
Bresso (★Milan) ... 34,245
Brindisi ... 89,241
Busto Arsizio (★Milan) ... 81,139
Cagliari (★305,000) ... 241,472
Caltagirone ... 38,525
Caltanissetta (61,461▲) ... 54,700
Camaiore (31,110▲) ... 22,700
Camerino (8,085▲) ... 3,400
Campobasso ... 47,316
Canicattì ... 32,603
Canosa di Puglia ... 30,781
Cantù ... 36,664
Capannori (43,972▲) ... 36,900
Capua ... 18,435
Carbonia ... 33,162
Carpi (59,824▲) ... 51,800
Carrara (★★Massa) ... 70,227
Casale Monferrato ... 42,711
Cascina ... 35,073
Caserta ... 67,257
Casoria (★Naples) ... 67,242
Cassino (32,181▲) ... 27,200
Castel Gandolfo (★Rome) (5,953▲) ... 3,400
Castellammare di Stabia (★Naples) ... 74,452
Castelvetrano ... 31,382
Catania (★515,000) ... 398,426
Catanzaro ... 93,845
Cattolica ... 15,811
Cava de' Tirreni (★Salerno) (51,611▲) ... 45,500
Cefalù (13,624▲) ... 11,600
Cerignola (51,349▲) ... 45,300
Cesano Maderno (★Milan) ... 32,637
Cesena (90,269▲) ... 68,100
Cesenatico (20,222▲) ... 15,900
Chiavari ... 30,508
Chieri (31,012▲) ... 26,400
Chieti ... 57,140
Chioggia (53,611▲) ... 38,200
Chivasso ... 27,064
Ciampino (★Rome) ... 30,561
Cinisello Balsamo (★Milan) ... 80,387
Cittadella (17,182▲) ... 7,000
Città di Castello (37,497▲) ... 28,600
Civitanova Marche (36,002▲) ... 31,500
Civitavecchia ... 48,342
Collegno (★Turin) ... 46,326
Cologno Monzese (★Milan) ... 51,855
Como (★160,000) ... 96,665
Conegliano (36,000▲) ... 29,500
Corato ... 41,623
Corsico (★Milan) ... 43,769
Cortina d'Ampezzo ... 8,326
Cosenza (★130,000) ... 102,338
Crema ... 34,742
Cremona ... 82,056
Crotone ... 57,009
Cuneo ... 55,784
Desio (★Milan) ... 33,051
Domodossola ... 20,704
Eboli ... 29,044
Empoli ... 45,725
Enna ... 29,370
Ercolano (Resina) (★Naples) ... 57,114
Erice ... 26,282
Este ... 18,283
Faenza (55,538▲) ... 40,100
Fano (53,273▲) ... 44,000
Fasano (36,420▲) ... 23,300
Favara ... 33,046
Fermo (35,186▲) ... 27,000
Ferrara (152,752▲) ... 125,200
Fiesole (★Florence) ... 14,760
Florence (Firenze) (★660,000) ... 462,690
Foggia ... 157,727
Foligno (52,580▲) ... 46,300
Forlì (110,523▲) ... 92,500
Francavilla Fontana ... 34,565
Frascati (★Rome) ... 19,587
Frattamaggiore (★Naples) ... 38,134
Frosinone ... 45,725
Gaeta ... 24,437
Gallarate (★Milan) ... 47,741
Gela ... 75,201
Genoa (Genova) (★855,000) ... 782,476
Giugliano in Campania (★Naples) ... 42,347
Gorizia ... 42,580
Gravina in Puglia ... 36,628
Grosseto (69,699▲) ... 61,600
Grottaglie ... 28,477
Grugliasco (★Turin) ... 34,202
Gubbio (32,164▲) ... 9,900
Guidonia Montecelio (★Rome) ... 48,821
Iesi (Jesi) (41,974▲) ... 35,600
Iglesias ... 29,561
Imola (60,234▲) ... 48,000
Imperia ... 42,159
Isernia (19,121▲) ... 14,500
Ivrea ... 28,650
L'Aquila ... 66,644
La Spezia (★192,000) ... 117,761
Latina (94,910▲) ... 83,200
Lecce ... 90,121
Lecco ... 52,806
Legnago ... 27,044
Legnano (★Milan) ... 49,600
Lentini ... 34,350
Licata ... 42,250
Limbiate (★Milan) ... 32,815
Lissone (★Milan) ... 30,482
Livorno (Leghorn) ... 176,757
Lodi ... 43,927
Loreto (10,851▲) ... 6,000
Lucca ... 91,256
Lucera (33,307▲) ... 28,500
Lugo (34,518▲) ... 20,300
Macerata (44,492▲) ... 37,700
Maddaloni (33,228▲) ... 26,100
Magenta ... 23,627
Manduria ... 30,488
Manfredonia (53,052▲) ... 45,800
Mantova ... 64,008
Marino (★Rome) ... 30,464
Marsala (86,051▲) ... 50,400
Martina France (44,340▲) ... 32,600
Massa (★145,000) ... 66,060
Matera ... 50,424
Mazara del Vallo ... 43,825
Merano (Meran) ... 34,460
Messina ... 271,660
•Milan (Milano) (★3,800,000) ... 1,677,109
Milazzo (30,710▲) ... 20,500
Modena ... 180,428
Modica (47,742▲) ... 31,400
Molfetta ... 66,699
Moncalieri (★Turin) ... 65,066
Monfalcone ... 31,053
Monopoli (44,017▲) ... 29,800
Monreale ... 25,416
Montecatini Terme ... 21,843
Montepulciano (14,255▲) ... 9,500
Monte Sant'Angelo ... 17,421
Monza (★Milan) ... 123,834
Naples (Napoli) (★2,740,000) ... 1,223,228
Nardò (30,916▲) ... 24,200
Nettuno (29,321▲) ... 25,300
Nicastro (Lamezia Terme) (62,069▲) ... 29,800
Nichelino (★Turin) ... 45,092
Nocera Inferiore (51,533▲) ... 43,300
Nola (29,282▲) ... 22,400
Novara ... 101,947
Novi Ligure ... 31,783
Nuoro ... 36,503
Oristano ... 29,769
Orvieto (23,414▲) ... 17,500
Otranto ... 4,748
Paderno Dugnano (★Milan) ... 38,885
Padova (★280,000) ... 242,216
Pagani ... 32,713
Palermo ... 693,949
Parma ... 176,945
Partinico ... 28,162
Paternò ... 48,992
Pavia ... 87,005
Perugia ... 139,871
Pesaro ... 90,705
Pescara ... 137,059
Piacenza ... 108,888
Pinerolo ... 36,589
Piombino ... 39,659
Pisa ... 103,772
Pistoia (94,344▲) ... 84,300
Poggibonsi ... 26,743
Pompei (★Naples) (22,526▲) ... 13,300
Pontedera ... 28,254
Pordenone ... 52,106
Portici (★Naples) ... 83,372
Portoferraio ... 11,212
Portofino ... 773
Potenza ... 64,513
Pozzuoli (★Naples) (70,429▲) ... 61,400
Prato (★201,000) ... 158,229
Ragusa (66,545▲) ... 55,200
Rapallo ... 29,809
Ravello (2,387▲) ... 1,400
Ravenna (139,392▲) ... 102,300
Reggio di Calabria ... 181,293
Reggio nell'Emilia ... 130,005
Rho (★Milan) ... 49,657
Riccione ... 31,688
Rieti (43,277▲) ... 38,700
Rimini ... 127,714
Riva [del Garda] ... 13,240
Rivoli (★Turin) ... 50,992
ROME (ROMA) (★3,195,000) ... 2,911,671
Rosignano Marittimo ... 29,402
Rovereto ... 33,082
Rovigo ... 52,588
Salerno (★240,000) ... 161,997
Salsomaggiore Terme ... 17,982
San Benedetto del Tronto ... 46,256
San Donà di Piave (32,058▲) ... 22,500
San Gimignano (7,521▲) ... 2,800
San Giorgio a Cremano (★Naples) ... 65,245
San Remo (63,423▲) ... 52,400
San Severo ... 54,914
Santa Maria Capua Vetere ... 32,529
Saronno ... 36,683
Sassari ... 119,597
Sassuolo ... 39,471
Savona (★120,000) ... 78,216
Scandicci (★Florence) ... 54,102
Schio ... 36,388
Sciacca (36,148▲) ... 32,300
Senigallia (40,567▲) ... 34,500
Seregno (★Milan) ... 37,717
Sesto Fiorentino (★Florence) ... 44,862
Sesto San Giovanni (★Milan) ... 98,151
Settimo Torinese (★Turin) ... 44,895
Siena ... 63,961
Siracusa ... 116,755
Sorrento (★42,900) ... 16,868
Spoleto (37,593▲) ... 32,200
Taranto ... 247,681
Teramo (51,768▲) ... 41,000
Termini Imerese ... 26,815
Terni ... 113,241
Tivoli (★Rome) ... 46,201
Todi (17,244▲) ... 3,900
Torre Annunziata (★Naples) ... 57,659
Torre del Greco (★Naples) ... 101,905
Trani ... 43,243
Trapani (72,036▲) ... 62,400
Trento ... 99,052
Treviso ... 89,121
Trieste ... 260,291
Turin (Torino) (★1,670,000) ... 1,160,686
Udine (★128,000) ... 102,973
Urbino (16,211▲) ... 13,000
Varese ... 91,100
Venice (Venezia) (★445,000) ... 355,865
Verbania ... 33,384
Vercelli ... 54,063
Verona ... 269,763
Viareggio ... 59,600
Vicenza ... 117,571
Vigevano ... 67,034
Villa San Giovanni (12,106▲) ... 9,000
Viterbo (58,529▲) ... 50,000
Vittoria ... 50,739
Vittorio Veneto ... 30,897
Voghera ... 42,781

IVORY COAST / Côte d'Ivoire

1978 E ... 7,613,000

Abengourou (1975 C) ... 31,239
•ABIDJAN ... 1,100,000
Agboville (1975 C) ... 27,192
Bouaké ... 230,000
Daloa ... 70,000
Danane (1975 C) ... 19,872
Dimbokro (1975 C) ... 30,986
Divo (1975 C) ... 37,896
Gagnoa (1975 C) ... 42,362
Grand-Bassam (1975 C) ... 25,808
Korhogo (1975 C) ... 47,657
Man ... 55,000
Séguéla (1975 C) ... 12,587

JAMAICA

1978 E ... 2,137,300

•KINGSTON ... 665,050
Mandeville (1970 C) ... 14,421
May Pen (1970 C) ... 26,074
Montego Bay (1970 C) ... 43,754
Ocho Rios (1970 C) ... 6,900
Port Antonio (1970 C) ... 10,538
Savanna-la-Mar (1970 C) ... 11,759
Spanish Town (1970 C) ... 40,731

JAPAN

1979 E ... 116,133,000

Districts and Prefectures

CHUBU ... 19,844,000
Aichi ... 6,176,000
Fukui ... 792,000
Gifu ... 1,945,000
Ishikawa ... 1,110,000
Nagano ... 2,071,000
Niigata ... 2,437,000
Shizuoka ... 3,420,000
Toyama ... 1,098,000
Yamanashi ... 795,000
CHUGOKU ... 7,557,000
Hiroshima ... 2,723,000
Okayama ... 1,865,000
Shimane ... 782,000
Tottori ... 599,000
Yamaguchi ... 1,588,000
HOKKAIDŌ ... 5,532,000
Hokkaidō ... 5,532,000
KANTŌ (KWANTŌ) ... 34,428,000
Chiba ... 4,617,000
Gumma ... 1,826,000
Ibaraki ... 2,503,000
Kanagawa ... 6,809,000
Saitama ... 5,309,000
Tochigi ... 1,768,000
Tōkyō ... 11,596,000
KINKI ... 21,158,000
Hyōgo ... 5,139,000
Kyōto ... 2,515,000
Mie ... 1,674,000
Nara ... 1,190,000
Ōsaka ... 8,487,000
Shiga ... 1,063,000
Wakayama ... 1,090,000
KYŪSHŪ ... 13,985,000
Fukuoka ... 4,527,000
Kagoshima ... 1,770,000
Kumamoto ... 1,776,000
Miyazaki ... 1,141,000
Nagasaki ... 1,592,000
Ōita ... 1,224,000
Okinawa ... 1,096,000
Saga ... 859,000
SHIKOKU ... 4,143,000
Ehime ... 1,499,000
Kagawa ... 995,000
Kōchi ... 828,000
Tokushima ... 821,000
TŌHOKU ... 9,486,000
Akita ... 1,251,000
Aomori ... 1,514,000
Fukushima ... 2,015,000
Iwate ... 1,411,000
Miyagi ... 2,054,000
Yamagata ... 1,241,000

Cities (1975 C or †1979 E)

Abashiri (43,825▲) ... 34,900
Abiko (★Tōkyō) ... 76,218
Ageo (★Tōkyō) ... †163,985
Aioi ... 42,008
Aizu-wakamatsu ... †113,175
Akashi (★Ōsaka) (1980 C) ... 254,873
Akishima (★Tōkyō) ... 83,864
Akita (1980 C) ... 284,830
Akō ... 49,583
Amagasaki (★Ōsaka) (1980 C) ... 523,657
Amagi (42,725▲) ... 25,700
Anan (60,439▲) ... 37,200
Anjō ... †121,178
Aomori (1980 C) ... 287,609
Arao (★Ōmuta) (58,296▲) ... 47,300
Arida ... 34,865
Asahikawa (1980 C) ... 352,620
Asaka (★Tōkyō) ... 81,755
Ashibetsu (36,520▲) ... 29,100
Ashikaga ... †165,024
Ashiya (★Ōsaka) ... 76,211
Atami ... 51,437
Atsugi (★Tōkyō) ... †136,652
Ayabe (43,490▲) ... 29,000
Ayase (★Tōkyō) ... 50,365
Beppu ... †137,477
Bibai (38,416▲) ... 29,200
Bisai ... 54,247
Chiba (★Tōkyō) (1980 C) ... 746,428
Chichibu ... 61,798
Chigasaki (★Tōkyō) ... †168,849
Chikugo ... 39,520
Chikushino (★Fukuoka) ... 47,741
Chiryū (★Nagoya) ... 47,209
Chita (★Nagoya) ... 56,560
Chitose ... 61,031
Chōfu (★Tōkyō) ... †179,631
Chōshi ... 90,374
Daitō (★Ōsaka) ... †115,678
Ebetsu ... 77,624
Ebina (★Tōkyō) ... 59,783
Fuchū *(Hiroshima pref.)* ... 50,217
Fūchū (★Hiroshima) *(Hiroshima pref.)* ... 47,538
Fuchū (★Tōkyō) ... †190,048
Fuji (1980 C) (★325,000) ... 205,752
Fujieda (101,216▲) ... †72,000
Fujiidera (★Ōsaka) ... 59,515
Fujimi (★Tōkyō) ... 70,391
Fujinomiya (★★Fuji) (106,524▲) ... †82,800
Fujioka (49,169▲) ... 30,000
Fujisawa (★Tōkyō) (1980 C) ... 300,181
Fuji-yoshida ... 51,976
Fukaya (75,748▲) ... 53,100
Fukuchiyama (60,003▲) ... 43,000
Fukui (1980 C) ... 240,264
Fukuoka (1980 C) (★1,575,000) ... 1,088,617
Fukuroi (42,581▲) ... 25,700
Fukushima (1980 C) ... 262,847
Fukuyama (1980 C) ... 346,031
Funabashi (★Tōkyō) (1980 C) ... 479,437
Furukawa (54,356▲) ... 31,100
Fussa (★Tōkyō) ... 46,457
Futtsu ... 56,653

C Census. E Official estimate. UE Unofficial estimate.
L Population within municipal limits of year specified. • Largest city in country.

★ Population or designation of metropolitan area, including suburbs (see headnote).
▲ Population of an entire municipality, commune, or district, including rural area.
‡† Year of information specified at start of country.

Gamagōri 85,282
Gifu (1980 C) 410,368
Ginowan 53,835
Gose (★Ōsaka) 37,554
Gotemba (62,722▲) 49,300
Gushikawa 42,133
Gyōda 66,069
Habikino (★Ōsaka) †102,217
Hachinohe (1980 C) 238,208
Hachiōji (★Tōkyō) (1980 C) 387,162
Hadano (★Tōkyō) †118,528
Hagi (52,724▲) 42,100
Hakodate (1980 C) 320,152
Hamada 50,316
Hamakita (67,180▲) 49,600
Hamamatsu (1980 C) 490,827
Hanamaki (65,826▲) 38,200
Handa 85,824
Hannō (★Tōkyō) 55,926
Haranomachi (43,483▲) 26,800
Hashima (52,570▲) 40,500
Hatogaya (★Tōkyō) 56,693
Hekinan 60,680
Higashihiroshima (★Hiroshima) 66,231
Higashikurume (★Tōkyō) †106,566
Higashimatsuyama 57,684
Higashimurayama (★Tōkyō) †119,684
Higashiōsaka (★Ōsaka) (1980 C) 521,635
Higashiyamato (★Tōkyō) 58,464
Hikari (★Tokuyama) 48,794
Hikone 85,066
Himeji (1980 C) 446,255
Himi (61,789▲) 38,600
Hino (★Tōkyō) †142,982
Hirakata (★Ōsaka) (1980 C) 353,360
Hiratsuka (★Tōkyō) (1980 C) 214,299
Hirosaki (173,550▲) †112,300
Hiroshima (1980 C) (★1,525,000) 899,394
Hisai 36,587
Hita (63,969▲) 47,300
Hitachi (1980 C) 204,612
Hōfu (109,762▲) †86,100
Honjō 51,090
Hōya (★Tōkyō) 91,546
Hyūga (53,448▲) 40,600
Ibaraki (★Ōsaka) (1980 C) 234,059
Ichihara (★Tōkyō) (1980 C) 216,395
Ichikawa (★Tōkyō) (1980 C) 364,244
Ichinomiya (1980 C) 253,138
Ichinoseki (59,122▲) 36,000
Iida (77,112▲) 51,900
Iizuka (★103,000) 75,417
Ikeda (★Ōsaka) †101,872
Ikoma (★Ōsaka) 48,848
Imabari †123,928
Imaichi (46,760▲) 29,800
Imari (60,913▲) 36,600
Ina (54,468▲) 32,500
Inagi (★Tōkyō) 43,924
Inazawa (★Nagoya) 88,606
Innoshima 41,683
Inuyama (★Nagoya) 58,731
Iruma (★Tōkyō) 83,997
Isahaya (73,341▲) 49,400
Ise (Uji-yamada) †105,624
Isehara (★Tōkyō) 61,616
Isesaki †104,300
Ishinomaki †119,758
Ishioka (43,679▲) 30,400
Itami (★Ōsaka) †177,745
Itō 68,072
Itsukaichi (★Hiroshima) 64,885
Iwai 38,304
Iwaki (Taira) (1980 C) (342,076▲) 271,800
Iwakuni †112,200
Iwakura (★Nagoya) 41,935
Iwamizawa (72,305▲) 56,800
Iwata 67,665
Iwatsuki (★Tōkyō) (83,825▲) 60,900
Iyo-mishima 38,409
Izumi (★Ōsaka) †122,464
Izumi (*Kagoshima pref.*) 37,483
Izumi (★Sendai) 70,087
Izumi-ōtsu (★Ōsaka) 66,250
Izumi-sano (★Ōsaka) 86,139
Izumo (71,568▲) 47,700
Joetsu †126,474
Jōyō (★Ōsaka) 58,923
Kadoma (★Ōsaka) †142,167
Kaga (61,599▲) 47,400
Kagoshima (1980 C) 505,077
Kainan 53,250
Kaizuka (★Ōsaka) 79,506
Kakamigahara †112,802
Kakegawa (61,731▲) 38,600
Kakogawa (★Ōsaka) (1980 C) 212,232
Kamagaya (★Tōkyō) 63,288
Kamaishi 68,981
Kamakura (★Tōkyō) †173,331
Kameoka (58,184▲) 36,400
Kamifukuoka (★Tōkyō) 58,332
Kanazawa (1980 C) 417,681
Kanonji (44,131▲) 31,700
Kanoya (67,951▲) 38,500
Kanuma (81,799▲) 55,800
Karatsu 75,224
Kariya (★Nagoya) †103,643
Karuizawa 13,951
Kasai (50,161▲) 30,600
Kasaoka (63,413▲) 42,700
Kashihara (★Ōsaka) †105,691
Kashiwa (★Tōkyō) (1980 C) 239,199
Kashiwara (★Ōsaka) 63,586
Kashiwazaki (80,351▲) 53,500
Kasuga (★Fukuoka) 55,160
Kasugai (★Nagoya) (1980 C) 244,114
Kasukabe (★Tōkyō) †151,083
Katano (★Ōsaka) 52,732
Katsuta 79,996
Kawachi-nagano (★Ōsaka) 66,936
Kawagoe (★Tōkyō) 259,317
Kawaguchi (★Tōkyō) (1980 C) 379,357
Kawanishi (★Ōsaka) †128,861

Kawanoe 35,961
Kawasaki (★Tōkyō) (1980 C) 1,040,698
Kazo (45,183▲) 27,900
Kesennuma 66,616
Kimitsu 76,016
Kiryū †132,950
Kisarazu †108,065
Kishiwada (★Ōsaka) †179,038
Kitaibaraki (44,332▲) 33,500
Kitakami (48,759▲) 28,200
Kitakyūshū (1980 C) (★1,515,000) 1,065,084
Kitami (91,519▲) 73,000
Kitamoto (★Tōkyō) 46,632
Kiyose (★Tōkyō) 60,574
Kobayashi 38,325
Kōbe (★★Ōsaka) (1980 C) 1,367,392
Kōchi (1980 C) 300,830
Kodaira (★Tōkyō) †156,758
Kōfu †197,803
Koga (★Tōkyō) 55,973
Koganei (★Tōkyō) †103,487
Kokubunji (★Tōkyō) 88,159
Komae (★Tōkyō) 70,043
Komaki (★Nagoya) †101,299
Komatsu †103,606
Komatsushima (42,203▲) 32,300
Kōnan 90,426
Kōnosu (★Tōkyō) 51,632
Kōriyama (1980 C) (286,497▲) 195,700
Koshigaya (★Tōkyō) (1980 C) 223,243
Kudamatsu (★★Tokuyama) 55,825
Kuki (★Tōkyō) 45,797
Kumagaya †134,347
Kumamoto (1980 C) 525,613
Kunitachi (★Tōkyō) 64,495
Kurashiki (1980 C) 403,785
Kurayoshi (50,785▲) 34,800
Kure (★★Hiroshima) (1980 C) 234,550
Kurume (1980 C) 216,974
Kusatsu (★Ōsaka) 64,873
Kushiro (1980 C) 214,694
Kuwana 83,440
Kyōto (★★Ōsaka) (1980 C) 1,472,993
Machida (★Tōkyō) (1980 C) 295,354
Maebashi (1980 C) 265,171
Maizuru (97,780▲) 82,600
Marugame 65,662
Masuda (50,734▲) 34,400
Matsubara (★Ōsaka) †135,741
Matsudo (★Tōkyō) (1980 C) 400,870
Matsue †134,190
Matsumoto †190,780
Matsuyama (1980 C) 401,682
Matsuzaka (112,870▲) †81,800
Mihara 83,679
Miki (★Ōsaka) (55,731▲) 41,200
Minamiashigara 36,928
Minō (★Ōsaka) 79,621
Mino-kamo 37,524
Misato (★Tōkyō) 79,355
Misawa (37,437▲) 28,600
Mishima (★★Numazu) 89,248
Mitaka (★Tōkyō) †166,514
Mito (1980 C) 215,563
Mitsuke (40,954▲) 30,900
Miura 47,888
Miyako 61,912
Miyakonojō (127,528▲) †82,200
Miyazaki (1980 C) 264,858
Mizusawa (52,266▲) 34,700
Mobara 64,942
Mōka (47,345▲) 20,700
Mombetsu (32,825▲) 28,000
Moriguchi (★Ōsaka) †164,716
Morioka (1980 C) 229,123
Moriyama 41,439
Mukō (★Ōsaka) 45,886
Muroran (★220,000) †162,731
Musashi-murayama (★Tōkyō) 50,842
Musashino (★Tōkyō) †138,874
Mutsu 44,646
Nagahama 54,064
Nagano (1980 C) (324,360▲) 244,300
Nagaoka †178,201
Nagaokakyo (★Ōsaka) 65,557
Nagareyama (★Tōkyō) †103,864
Nagasaki (1980 C) 447,091
Nagoya (1980 C) (★3,700,000) 2,087,884
Naha (1980 C) 295,801
Nakama (★Kitakyūshū) 43,145
Nakatsu (59,111▲) 44,200
Nakatsugawa (51,183▲) 36,800
Nanao (49,493▲) 38,800
Nankoku (42,832▲) 25,500
Nara (★Ōsaka) (1980 C) 297,893
Narashino (★Tōkyō) †120,257
Narita (50,915▲) 30,500
Naruto (61,959▲) 50,600
Natori (46,730▲) 29,700
Naze 46,335
Nemuro 45,817
Neyagawa (★Ōsaka) (1980 C) 255,864
Nichinan (52,171▲) 38,200
Niigata (1980 C) 457,783
Niihama †133,178
Niitsu (58,970▲) 42,900
Niiza (★Tōkyō) †119,991
Nikkō 26,279
Nishinomiya (★Ōsaka) (1980 C) 410,329
Nishio (82,524▲) 62,600
Nishiwaki 38,108
Nobeoka †136,572
Noboribetsu (★Muroran) 50,885
Noda (★Tōkyō) 78,193
Nōgata 58,551
Noshiro (59,215▲) 43,600
Numata (45,255▲) 32,000
Numazu (1980 C) (★435,000) 203,699
Obihiro †150,337
Ōbu (★Nagoya) 56,211
Ōda 37,449
Ōdate (71,828▲) 50,200
Odawara †177,047
Ōfunato (39,632▲) 32,700
Ōgaki †141,877

Ōita (1980 C) 360,484
Ojiya (44,375▲) 26,900
Ōkawa 50,395
Okaya 61,776
Okayama (1980 C) 545,737
Okazaki (1980 C) 262,370
Okegawa (★Tōkyō) 48,034
Okinawa 91,347
Ōme (★Tōkyō) 86,152
Ōmi-hachiman (★Ōsaka) (51,537▲) 34,100
Ōmiya (★Tōkyō) (1980 C) 354,082
Ōmura (60,919▲) 44,200
Ōmuta (★225,000) †163,436
Ōno (*Fukui pref.*) (41,918▲) 25,800
Ōno (*Hyōgo pref.*) 40,576
Onojo (★Fukuoka) 52,169
Onoda (★Ube) 43,804
Onomichi †102,190
Ōsaka (1980 C) (★15,200,000) 2,648,158
Ōta †120,472
Ōtake 38,457
Otaru †185,737
Ōtawara (42,332▲) 22,900
Ōtsu (★Ōsaka) (1980 C) 215,318
Ōtsuki 36,766
Oyama (125,565▲) †81,000
Rumoi 36,882
Ryūgasaki (40,565▲) 25,000
Sabae (57,252▲) 45,700
Saga †162,038
Sagamihara (★Tōkyō) (1980 C) 439,257
Saijō (52,615▲) 39,100
Saiki (52,863▲) 42,200
Sakado (★Tōkyō) 51,230
Sakai (★Ōsaka) (1980 C) 810,120
Sakaide 67,624
Sakaiminato 35,821
Sakata (101,454▲) †73,900
Saku (56,143▲) 32,500
Sakura (★Tōkyō) (80,804▲) 61,500
Sakurai (54,314▲) 42,800
Sanda (★Ōsaka) 35,261
Sanjō 81,806
Sano 75,844
Sapporo (1980 C) (★1,450,000) 1,401,758
Sasebo (1980 C) 251,188
Sawara (48,670▲) 26,000
Sayama (★Tōkyō) †121,433
Seki 53,881
Sendai (*Kagoshima pref.*) (61,788▲) 34,700
Sendai (*Miyagi pref.*) (1980 C) (★925,000) 664,799
Sennan (★Ōsaka) 46,741
Seto †119,473
Settsu (★Ōsaka) 76,704
Shibata (74,025▲) 48,700
Shibukawa 47,071
Shijōnawate (★Ōsaka) 52,368
Shimabara (45,179▲) 34,000
Shimada 68,820
Shimizu (★★Shizuoka) (1980 C) 241,578
Shimminato (★Takaoka) 44,700
Shimodate (57,778▲) 36,500
Shimonoseki (★★Kitakyūshū) (1980 C) 268,964
Shingū 39,023
Shinjō (42,227▲) 28,100
Shiogama (★Sendai) 59,235
Shiojiri (47,421▲) 29,200
Shirakawa (42,685▲) 32,300
Shizuoka (1980 C) (★735,000) 458,342
Sōja 47,027
Sōka (★Tōkyō) †186,759
Suita (★Ōsaka) (1980 C) 332,413
Sukagawa (54,922▲) 33,700
Sumoto (44,137▲) 35,700
Suwa 49,594
Suzaka 49,513
Suzuka (152,431▲) †106,900
Tachikawa (★Tōkyō) †142,793
Tagajō (★Sendai) 44,862
Tajimi 68,901
Takaishi (★Ōsaka) 66,824
Takamatsu (1980 C) 316,662
Takaoka (★220,000) †174,334
Takarazuka (★Ōsaka) †179,394
Takasago (★Ōsaka) 77,080
Takasaki (1980 C) 221,432
Takatsuki (★Ōsaka) (1980 C) 340,722
Takawa 61,464
Takayama 60,504
Takefu (65,012▲) 48,700
Takehara 36,273
Takikawa 50,090
Tama (★Tōkyō) 65,466
Tamana (42,837▲) 28,100
Tamano 78,516
Tanabe (66,999▲) 51,800
Tanashi (★Tōkyō) 67,433
Tatebayashi 66,410
Tateyama (56,139▲) 40,700
Tatsuno 39,646
Tendō (48,082▲) 27,900
Tenri (62,909▲) 45,200
Toba 29,346
Tochigi 83,189
Toda (★Tōkyō) 77,137
Tokai (★Nagoya) 95,457
Tōkamachi (50,211▲) 33,400
Toki 63,324
Tokoname 54,865
Tokorozawa (★Tōkyō) (1980 C) 236,477
Tokushima (1980 C) 249,343
Tokuyama (★255,000) †111,347
•TŌKYŌ (1980 C) (★25,800,000) 8,349,209
Tomakomai †146,088
Tomioka (46,821▲) 29,200
Tondabayashi (★Ōsaka) 91,393
Toride (★Tōkyō) 52,816
Tosu 50,733
Tottori †128,789
Towada (54,365▲) 27,900

Toyama (1980 C) 305,054
Toyoake (★Nagoya) 45,837
Toyohashi (1980 C) 304,274
Toyokawa †102,484
Toyonaka (★Ōsaka) (1980 C) 403,185
Toyooka (46,210▲) 33,000
Toyota (1980 C) 281,609
Tsu †144,587
Tsubame 43,265
Tsuchiura †110,912
Tsuruga 60,205
Tsuruoka (95,932▲) 74,600
Tsushima 58,241
Tsuyama (79,907▲) 56,500
Ube (★222,000) †167,732
Ueda †110,340
Ueno (59,716▲) 42,500
Uji (★Ōsaka) †150,869
Uozu 48,419
Urawa (★Tōkyō) (1980 C) 358,180
Usa (50,677▲) 25,400
Usuki (39,163▲) 28,200
Utsunomiya (1980 C) 377,748
Uwajima 70,428
Wakayama (1980 C) 401,462
Wakkanai 55,464
Warabi (★Tōkyō) 76,311
Yachiyo (★Tōkyō) †132,989
Yaizu †103,544
Yamagata (1980 C) 236,984
Yamaguchi (111,725▲) †80,800
Yamato (★Tōkyō) †165,858
Yamato-kōriyama (★Ōsaka) 71,001
Yamato-takada (★Ōsaka) 58,637
Yame 38,843
Yao (★Ōsaka) (1980 C) 272,706
Yashio (★Tōkyō) 56,127
Yatsushiro (107,200▲) †80,000
Yawata (★Ōsaka) 50,131
Yawatahama (45,259▲) 34,700
Yokkaichi (1980 C) 255,442
Yokohama (★★Tōkyō) (1980 C) 2,773,322
Yokosuka (★Tōkyō) (1980 C) 421,112
Yonago †125,291
Yonezawa (91,974▲) 71,400
Yono (★Tōkyō) 71,044
Yūbari 50,131
Yukuhashi (53,750▲) 39,300
Zama (★Tōkyō) 80,562
Zushi (★Tōkyō) 56,298

JERSEY

1976 C 74,470
•ST. HELIER (★45,000) 26,343

JORDAN / Al-Urdunn

1979 E 2,152,273
Al-'Aqabah ('Aqaba) 26,986
Al-Karak 11,805
Al-Khalīl (Hebron) (††1971 E) 43,000
Al-Mafraq (1973 E) 15,500
•AMMĀN 648,587
Arīḥā (Jericho) (††1967 C) 6,829
Ar-Ramthā (1973 E) 19,000
As-Salt 32,866
Az-Zarqā' 215,687
Bayt Laḥm (Bethlehem) (††1971 E) 25,000
Irbid 112,864
Janīn (††1971 E) 20,000
Jerusalem (★Jerusalem, Israel) (††1976 E) 90,000
Ma'ān 11,308
Nābulus (††1971 E) 64,000

††Located in area occupied by Israel in 1967. See note under Israel.

KAMPUCHEA / Kâmpŭchéa Prâchéathĭpâtéyy

1962 C 5,728,711
Battambang 38,780
Kompong Cham 28,532
•PHNUM PÉNH 393,995

KENYA

1979 C 15,322,000
Eldoret 50,000
Kisumu 150,000
Mombasa 342,000
•NAIROBI 835,000
Nakuru 93,000
Nyeri 36,000
Thika 41,000

KOREA, NORTH / Chosŏn Minjujuŭi In'min Konghwaguk

1967 E 12,700,000
Aoji (1944 C) 39,616
Ch'ŏngjin 265,000
Haeju 115,000
Hamhŭng (1944 C) 112,184
Hŭngnam (1944 C) 143,600
Kaesŏng 140,000
Kilchu (1944 C) 30,026
Kimch'aek (Sŏngjin) 265,000
Najin (1944 C) 34,338
Namp'o (Chinnamp'o) 130,000
Ongjin (1949 C) 32,965
Pukch'ŏng (1944 C) 30,709
•P'YONGYANG 840,000
Sariwŏn (1944 C) 42,957
Sinŭiju 165,000
Songnim (1944 C) 53,035
Tanch'ŏn (1944 C) 32,761
Wŏnsan 215,000

KOREA, SOUTH / Taehan-Min'guk

1978 E 37,019,000
Andong (101,494▲) 85,000
Anyang (★Seoul) 187,887
Bucheon (★Seoul) 163,341
Ch'angwŏn 70,707
Chech'ŏn (80,124▲) 55,400
Cheju (152,486▲) 83,100
Chinhae 108,730
Chinju 174,918
Ch'ŏnan (109,324▲) 76,800
Ch'ŏngju 223,016
Chŏngŭp (1975 C) (54,864▲) 37,600
Chŏnju 348,053
Ch'unch'ŏn 152,606
Ch'ungju (110,091▲) 76,500
Chungmu 71,511
Inch'ŏn (★★Seoul) 936,497
Iri (132,272▲) 109,800
Kangnŭng (102,153▲) 67,100
Kimch'ŏn (70,348▲) 53,200
Kumi 89,612
Kunsan 167,422
Kwangju 694,646
Kyŏngju (113,921▲) 68,100
Masan 391,874
Mokp'o 210,922
Namwŏn (55,043▲) 37,900
P'ohang (1975 C) (134,404▲) 110,000
Pusan 2,879,570
Pyŏngtaek 56,324
Samch'ŏnp'o (61,701▲) 37,100
Sangju (55,242▲) 29,500
Seongnam (★Seoul) 324,064
•SEOUL (SŎUL) (1979 E) (★10,775,000) 8,114,000
Sŏkch'o 71,737
Songjŏng (47,070▲) 29,900
Sunch'ŏn (114,588▲) 76,900
Suwŏn (★Seoul) 266,135
Taegu 1,487,098
Taejŏn 508,574
Ŭijŏngbu (★Seoul) 117,849
Ulsan (364,456▲) 247,000
Wŏnju 131,047
Yŏngju (1975 C) (70,793▲) 50,800
Yŏsu 151,337

KUWAIT / Al-Kuwayt

1975 C 994,837
Abraq Khīṭān (★Kuwait) 59,443
Al-Farwānīyah (★Kuwait) 44,875
Al-Jahrah (★Kuwait) 52,302
As-Sālimīyah (★Kuwait) 113,943
Ḥawallī (★Kuwait) 130,565
•KUWAIT (Al-Kuwayt) (★780,000) 78,116

LAOS / Lao

1973 E 3,181,000
Louangphrabang 43,000
Pakxé 44,860
Savannakhet 50,691
Sayaboury 13,760
•VIANGCHAN (VIENTIANE) 174,229

LEBANON / Al-Lubnān

1970 E 2,126,355
Ba'labakk (Baalbek) 16,000
•BEIRUT (BAYRŪT) (★1,010,000) 474,870
Ṣaydā (Sidon) 34,000
Ṣūr (Tyre) 12,500
Ṭarābulus (Tripoli) 157,320
Zaḥlah 29,500

LESOTHO

1972 E 972,000
•MASERU 17,000

LIBERIA

1974 C 1,503,368
Buchanan 23,994
•MONROVIA 204,210

LIBYA / Lībiyā

1970 E 1,938,000
Ajdābiyah (1964 C) 15,400
Beida (1964 C) 12,800
Benghāzī (Bengasi) 170,000
Darnah (Derna) (1964 C) 21,400
Misrātah 44,000
•TRIPOLI (ṬARĀBULUS) 264,000
Ṭubruq (Tobruk) (1964 C) 15,900

LIECHTENSTEIN

1977 E 24,715
•VADUZ 4,704

LUXEMBOURG

1976 E 358,000
Bettembourg 7,100
Clervaux (1970 C) 1,428
Diekirch 5,500
Differdange (★Esch-sur-Alzette) 18,000
Dudelange 14,600
Echternach (1970 C) 3,792
Esch-sur-Alzette (★98,000) 27,600
Ettelbruck 6,100
•LUXEMBOURG (★110,000) 79,300
Pétange (★★Longwy, France) 12,100
Sanem (★Esch-sur-Alzette) 10,900
Wtilz (1970 C) 3,920

C Census. E Official estimate. UE Unofficial estimate.
L Population within municipal limits of year specified. • Largest city in country.

★ Population or designation of metropolitan area, including suburbs (see headnote).
▲ Population of an entire municipality, commune, or district, including rural area.
‡† Year of information specified at start of country.

MACAO

1970 C 248,636
•MACAO (★248,636) 241,413

MADAGASCAR / Madagasikara

1977 E 8,520,000
•ANTANANARIVO (TANANARIVE) 484,000
Antsirabe (85,000▲) 45,000
Antsiranana 43,000
Fianarantsoa 73,000
Mahajanga 71,000
Manakara (1972 E) (25,070▲) 23,225
Marovoay (1972 E) 20,780
Toamasina 83,000
Toliara 49,000

MALAWI

1977 C 5,561,821
•Blantyre 229,000
LILONGWE 102,924
Mzuzu 16,000
Zomba 16,000

MALAYSIA

1970 C 10,319,324
Alor Setar (★85,748) 66,179
Ayer Itam (★Pinang) 25,640
Batu Pahat 53,291
Bentong 22,683
Bukit Mertajam 26,631
Butterworth (★★Pinang) 61,187
Chukai 12,514
George Town (Pinang) (★450,000) 270,019
Ipoh (★257,309) 247,689
Johor Baharu (★Singapore) 136,229
Kajang 21,950
Kampar 26,591
Kangar 8,758
Kelang 113,607
Keluang 43,272
Kota Baharu (★69,756) 55,052
Kota Kinabalu (Jesselton) 40,939
•KUALA LUMPUR (★750,000) 451,728
Kuala Terengganu (★59,494) 53,353
Kuantan 43,358
Kuching 63,535
Kulim 18,505
Melaka (Malacca) (★99,782) 86,357
Miri 35,702
Muar (Bandar Maharani) 61,218
Petaling Jaya (★Kuala Lumpur) 93,447
Sandakan 42,413
Segamat 17,796
Seremban (★90,062) 79,915
Sibu 50,635
Sungai Petani 35,959
Sungai Siput 21,383
Taiping 54,645
Tawau 24,247
Telok Anson 44,524

MALDIVES

1978 C 143,046
•MALE 29,555

MALI

1972 E 5,257,000
•BAMAKO (1976 C) 404,022
Gao 17,000
Kati (1971 E) 13,800
Kayes 37,000
Kita (1971 E) 11,700
Koulikoro 15,000
Koutiala 16,000
Mopti 43,000
Nioro du Sahel (1971 E) 13,200
San 18,000
Ségou 40,000
Sikasso 29,000
Tombouctou (Timbuktu) (1971 E) 11,900

MALTA

1979 E 346,970
Birkirkara (★Valletta) 16,832
Cospicua (★Valletta) 9,440
Gzira (★Valletta) 10,046
Hamrun (★Valletta) 13,875
Msida (★Valletta) 12,448
Paola (★Valletta) 11,974
Qormi (★Valletta) 15,784
Rabat 11,823
Sliema (★Valletta) 20,095
•VALLETTA (★215,000) 14,042
Victoria *(Gozo I.)* 5,249
Zabbar (★Valletta) 10,366
Zejtun 10,252

MARTINIQUE

1974 C 324,832
•FORT-DE-FRANCE (★113,556) 98,807
Le Lamentin (23,145▲) 7,558
Saint-Pierre 5,358
Schœlcher (★Fort-de-France) (14,749▲) 13,792

MAURITANIA / Mauritanie

1971 E 1,190,000
Atar (1967 E) 8,500
Kaédi (1967 E) 10,000
Nouadhibou (1966 E) 11,000
•NOUAKCHOTT 35,000

MAURITIUS

1978 E 924,663
Beau Bassin (★Port Louis) 83,714
Curepipe (★Port Louis) 54,356
•PORT LOUIS (★405,000) 142,853
Quatre Bornes (★Port Louis) 53,835
Vacoas-Phoenix (★Port Louis) 51,793

MEXICO / México

1976 E 62,329,000

States

Aguascalientes 430,000
Baja California Norte 1,253,000
Baja California Sur 181,000
Campeche 337,000
Chiapas 1,933,000
Chihuahua 2,000,000
Coahuila 1,334,000
Colima 317,000
Distrito Federal (Federal District) 8,906,000
Durango 1,122,000
Guanajuato 2,811,000
Guerrero 2,013,000
Hidalgo 1,409,000
Jalisco 4,157,000
México 6,245,000
Michoacán 2,805,000
Morelos 866,000
Nayarit 699,000
Nuevo León 2,344,000
Oaxaca 2,337,000
Puebla 3,055,000
Querétaro 618,000
Quintana Roo 131,000
San Luis Potosí 1,527,000
Sinaloa 1,714,000
Sonora 1,414,000
Tabasco 1,054,000
Tamaulipas 1,901,000
Tlaxcala 498,000
Veracruz 4,917,000
Yucatán 904,000
Zacatecas 1,097,000

Cities (1970 C)

Acámbaro 32,257
Acaponeta 11,844
Acapulco [de Juárez] (1978 E) 421,100
Acayucan 21,173
Actopan 11,037
Agua Dulce 21,060
Agua Prieta 20,754
Aguascalientes (1978 E) 247,800
Alvarado 15,792
Ameca 21,018
Amecameca [de Juárez] 16,276
Apatzingán 44,849
Apizaco 21,189
Arandas 18 934
Arriaga 13,193
Atlixco 41,967
Atotonilco el Alto 16,271
Autlán de Navarro 20,398
Caborca 20,771
Campeche (1978 E) 103,600
Cananea 17,518
Cárdenas 15,643
Celaya (1978 E) 114,400
Cerro Azul 20,259
Chihuahua (1978 E) 369,500
Chilpancingo [de los Bravos] 36,193
Cholula [de Rivadabia] 15,399
Ciudad Acuña 30,276
Ciudad Camargo 24,030
Ciudad Chetumal 23,685
Ciudad del Carmen 34,656
Ciudad de Valles 47,587
Ciudad Guzmán 48,166
Ciudad Hidalgo 24,692
Ciudad Ixtepec 14,025
Ciudad Jiménez 18,095
Ciudad Juárez (★★El Paso, Tex.) (1978 E) 597,100
Ciudad Lerdo (★Torreón) 19,803
Ciudad Madero (★Tampico) (1978 E) 135,100
Ciudad Mante 51,247
Ciudad Melchor Múzquiz 18,868
Ciudad Mendoza (★Orizaba) 18,696
Ciudad Obregón (1978 E) 173,000
Ciudad Serdán 9,581
Ciudad Victoria (1978 E) 121,400
Coatepec 21,542
Coatzacoalcos (1978 E) 120,100
Colima 58,450
Comalcalco 14,963
Comitán [de Domínguez] 21,249
Córdoba (1978 E) 116,100
Cortazar 25,794
Cosamaloapan 19,766
Cumauhtéoc 26,598
Cuautla 13,946
Cuernavaca (1978 E) 226,600
Culiacán (1978 E) 302,200
Delicias 52,446
Dolores Hidalgo 16,849
Durango (1978 E) 218,600
Ecatepec de Morelos (★Mexico City) 11,899
El Grullo 10,538
Empalme 24,927
Encarnación de Díaz 10,474
Ensenada 77,687
Escuinapa de Hidalgo 16,442
Fresnillo [de González Echeverría] 44,475
Garza García (★Monterrey) 20,934
Gómez Palacio (★★Torreón) (1978 E) 100,200
Guadalajara (1978 E) (★2,350,000) 1,813,100
Guadalupe (★Monterrey) 51,899
Guamúchil 17,151
Guanajuato 36,809
Guasave 26,080
Guaymas 57,492
Hermosillo (1978 E) 299,700
Hidalgo del Parral 57,619
Huajuapan de León 13,822
Huamantla 15,565
Huatabampo 18,506
Huauchinango 16,826
Huixtla 15,737
Iguala 45,355
Irapuato (1978 E) 155,600
Izúcar de Matamoros 21,164
Jacona de Plancarte 22,724
Jalapa Enríquez (1978 E) 191,100
Jalostotitlán 11,719
Jerez de García Salinas 20,325
Juchitán [de Zaragoza] 30,218
La Barca 18,055
Lagos de Moreno 33,782
La Paz 46,011
La Piedad [Cavadas] 34,963
Las Choapas 20,166
Léon [de los Aldamas] (1978 E) 590,000
Linares 24,456
Loma Bonita 15,804
Los Mochis (1978 E) 111,800
Los Reyes 19,452
Magdalena 10,281
Manzanillo 20,777
Martínez de la Torre 17,203
Matamoros (★★Brownsville, Tex.) (1978 E) 186,500
Matamoros de la Laguna 15,125
Matehuala 28,799
Matías Romero 13,200
Mazatlán (1978 E) 177,700
Meoqui 12,308
Mérida (1978 E) 263,200
Mesa de Tijuana (★San Diego, Calif.) 50,094
Mexicali (1978 E)(★355,000) 338,400
•MEXICO CITY (CIUDAD DE MÉXICO) (1978 E) (★14,400,000) 8,988,200
Minatitlán (1978 E) 112,600
Mineral del Monte 8,887
Monclova (1978 E) 130,900
Montemorelos 18,642
Monterrey (1978 E) (★1,925,000) 1,054,000
Morelia (1978 E) 239,400
Moroleón 25,620
Motul de Felipe Carrillo Puerto 12,949
Navojoa 43,817
Netzahualcóyotl (★Mexico City) 580,438
Nogales (*Sonora*) 52,108
Nogales (*Veracruz*) (★Orizaba) 14,254
Nueva Rosita 34,706
Nuevo Casas Grandes 20,023
Nuevo Laredo (★★Laredo, Tex.) (1978 E) 214,200
Oaxaca [de Juárez] (1978 E) 131,200
Ocotlán 35,367
Ojinaga 12,757
Orizaba (1978 E) (★265,000) 118,400
Pachuca [de Soto] (1978 E) 105,200
Pánuco 14,277
Papantla [de Olarte] 26,773
Parras de la Fuente 18,707
Pátzcuaro 17,299
Pénjamo 9,245
Piedras Negras 41,033
Poza Rica de Hidalgo (1978 E) 188,900
Progreso 17,518
Puebla [de Zaragoza] (1978 E) 678,000
Puerto Vallarta 24,155
Puruándiro 9,956
Querétaro (1978 E) 176,200
Reynosa (1978 E) 218,700
Río Bravo 39,018
Ríoverde 16,804
Romita 11,947
Rosario 10,276
Sabinas 20,538
Sabinas Hidalgo 17,439
Sahuayo 28,727
Salamanca 61,039
Salina Cruz 22,004
Saltillo (1978 E) 245,700
Salvatierra 18,975
San Andrés Tuxtla 24,267
San Cristóbal de las Casas 25,700
San Francisco del Oro 12,116
San Francisco del Rincón 27,079
San Juan de los Lagos 19,570
San Juan del Río 15,422
San Juan Teotihuacán (★Mexico City) 2,238
San Luis de la Paz 12,654
San Luis Potosí (1978 E) 315,200
San Luis Río Colorado 49,990
San Martín Texmelucan 23,355
San Miguel de Allende 24,286
San Miguel el Alto 7,909
San Nicolás de los Garzas (★Monterrey) 28,803
San Pedro de las Colonias 26,882
Santa Ana Chiautempan 12,327
Santa Bárbara 16,978
Santa Cruz de Juventino Rosas 15,859
Santa Inés Zacatelco 14,117
Santa Rosalía 7,356
Santiago Ixcuintla 17,321
Sayula 14,339
Silao 31,825
Sombrerete 11,077
Tala 15,744
Tamazula de Gordiano 13,521
Tamazunchale 12,302
Tampico (1978 E) (★420,000) 240,000
Tangancícuaro [de Arista] 12,650
Tapachula 60,620
Taxco de Alarcón 27,089
Tecomán 31,625
Tecuala 12,461
Tehuacán 47,497
Tehuantepec 16,179
Teocaltiche 13,745
Tepatitlán [de Morelos] 29,292
Tepic (1978 E) 133,400
Tequila 11,839
Texcoco [de Mora] (★Mexico City) 18,044
Teziutlán 23,948
Ticul 14,341
Tierra Blanca 22,727
Tijuana (★★San Diego, Calif.) (1978 E) 535,000
Tizimín 18,343
Tlalnepantla (★Mexico City) 45,575
Tlapacoyan 13,172
Tlaquepaque (★Guadalajara) 59,760
Tlaxcala [de Xicohténcatl] 9,972
Toluca [de Lerdo] (1978 E) 222,900
Tonalá 15,611
Torreón (1978 E) (★450,000) 268,700
Tulancingo 35,799
Tuxpan *(Jalisco)* 14,693
Tuxpan *(Nayarit)* 20,322
Tuxpan de Rodríguez Cano *(Veracruz)* 33,901
Tuxtepec 17,700
Tuxtla Gutiérrez (1978 E) 101,700
Umán 8,371
Unión de Tula 6,399
Uriangato 14,626
Uruapan [del Progreso] (1978 E) 138,300
Valladolid 14,663
Valle de Santiago 16,517
Valle Hermoso 19,278
Venustiano Carranza 23,624
Veracruz [Llave] (1978 E) (★365,000) 295,300
Vicente Guerrero *(Tlaxcala)* 18,280
Vicente Guerrero *(Veracruz)* (★Orizaba) 11,688
Villa Frontera 25,761
Villahermosa (1978 E) 165,500
Xicotepec de Juárez 12,656
Yautepec 13,952
Yurécuaro 13,611
Yuriria 10,085
Zaachila 7,270
Zacapu 31,989
Zacatecas 50,251
Zacatepec 16,839
Zacoalco de Torres 11,343
Zamora de Hidalgo 57,775
Zapopan (★Guadalajara) 18,512
Zapotiltic 11,733
Zihuatanejo 4,879
Zitácuaro 36,911
Zumpango 12,923

MONACO

1975 E 25,000
•MONACO (★50,000) 25,000

MONGOLIA / Mongol Ard Uls

1969 C 1,197,600
Cecerleg (Tsetserleg) 12,400
Choibalsan 20,500
Darchan 22,800
Jirgalanta (Chovd) 12,400
Süchbaatar 10,000
•ULAN BATOR (URGA) (1970 E) 287,000

MONTSERRAT

1970 C 11,458
•PLYMOUTH 1,267

MOROCCO / Al-Magreb

1971 C 15,379,259
Agadir 61,192
Beni-Mellal 53,826
Berkane 39,015
Berrechid 20,113
•Casablanca (Dar-el-Beida) (★1,575,000) 1,506,373
El-Jadida (Mazagan) 55,501
Essaouira (Mogador) 30,061
Fès (Fez) 325,327
Fkih Ben Salah 26,918
Jerada 30,633
Kenitra 139,206
Khemisset 21,811
Khenifra 25,526
Khouribga 73,667
Ksar-el-Kebir 48,262
Ksar-es-Souk 16,775
Larache 45,710
Marrakech 332,741
Meknès 248,369
Mohammedia (Fedala) 70,392
Nador 32,490
Ouarzazate 11,142
Oued-Zem 33,323
Ouezzane 33,267
Oujda 175,532
RABAT (★540,000) 367,620
Safi 129,113
Salé (★★Rabat) 155,557
Sefrou 28,607
Settat 42,325
Sidi Ifni 13,650
Sidi Kacem 26,831
Sidi Slimane 20,398
Tanger (Tangier) 187,894
Taroudant 22,272
Taza 55,157
Tétouan 139,105
Villa Alhucemas (Al Hoceima) 18,686
Youssoufia 22,435

MOZAMBIQUE / Moçambique

1970 C 8,168,933
Beira 110,752
Inhambane 24,090
João Belo 63,494
•MAPUTO (LOURENÇO MARQUES) 341,922
Nampula 120,188
Quelimane 71,289
Tete 51,453
Villa Cabral 41,251

NAMIBIA

1970 C 722,867
Gobabis 4,428
Keetmanshoop 10,297
Lüderitz 6,642
Mariental 4,629
Otjiwarongo 8,018
Rehoboth 5,363
Swakopmund 5,681
Tsumeb 12,338
•WINDHOEK 61,260

NEPAL / Nepāl

1971 C 11,555,983
Bhaktapur 40,112
Birātnagar 45,100
•KATHMANDU (★215,000) 150,402
Lalitpur (★Katmandu) 59,049
Nepālganj 23,523

NETHERLANDS / Nederland

1980 E 14,091,014
(includes 1,546 persons with no fixed residence in any province)

Provinces

Drenthe 418,479
Dronten 19,658
Friesland 583,989
Gelderland 1,694,416
Groningen 553,709
Lelystad 38,971
Limburg 1,069,038
North Brabant (Noord-Brabant) 2,051,195
North Holland (Noord-Holland) 2,307,646
Overijssel 1,018,208
Southern IJsselmeer Polders (Zuidelijke IJsselmeerpolders) (not part of any province) 6,872
South Holland (Zuid-Holland) 3,083,555
Utrecht 895,464
Zeeland 348,268

Cities

Aalsmeer 20,486
Alkmaar (★107,000) 71,245
Almelo 63,381
Alphen aan den Rijn 51,780
Amersfoort (★128,678) 88,097
Amstelveen (★Amsterdam) 69,488
•AMSTERDAM (★1,810,000) 716,919
Apeldoorn 138,164
Arnhem (★287,305) 127,846
Assen 45,036
Bergen op Zoom 43,715
Beverwijk (★Amsterdam) 35,980
Breda (★151,236) 117,259
Brunssum (★Heerlen) 26,281
Bussum (★Amsterdam) 35,316
Castricum (★Amsterdam) 22,783
De Bilt (★Utrecht) 32,397
Delft (★The Hague) 83,939
Delfzijl 25,433
Den Helder 61,761
Deventer 64,561
Doetinchem (36,995▲) 27,800
Dordrecht (★195,792) 107,453
Edam-Volendam (★Amsterdam) 23,091
Ede (82,829▲) 43,500
Eindhoven (★369,352) 194,451
Emmen (89,763▲) 35,500
Enschede (★285,000) 143,042
Geldrop (★Eindhoven) 26,474
Geleen (★181,250) 35,371
Goes 30,193
Gorinchem 28,957
Gouda 58,784
Groningen (★200,467) 161,322
Haarlem (★Amsterdam) 158,291
Haarlemmermeer (77,657▲) 10,600
Harderwijk 30,174
Harlingen 15,427
Heemstede (★Amsterdam) 26,729
Heerenveen (36,729▲) 20,400
Heerlen (★267,003) 71,102
Helmond 58,490
Hengelo (★★Enschede) 75,216
Hilversum (★Amsterdam) 92,964
Hoensbroek (★Heerlen) 22,748
Hoogeveen (43,645▲) 33,000
Hoorn 39,300
IJmuiden (Velsen) (★Amsterdam) 61,202
Kampen 30,353
Katwijk aan Zee 38,163
Kerkrade (★Heerlen) 47,001
Leeuwarden 84,518
Leiden (★173,386) 103,046
Lelystad (38,971▲) 9,900
Maassluis (★Rotterdam) 32,937
Maastricht (★145,346) 109,285
Meppel 22,377
Middelburg 38,077
Nijmegen (★217,951) 147,614
Oldenzaal 28,134
Oss 43,462

C Census. E Official estimate. UE Unofficial estimate.
L Population within municipal limits of year specified. • Largest city in country.

★ Population or designation of metropolitan area, including suburbs (see headnote).
▲ Population of an entire municipality, commune, or district, including rural area.
‡† Year of information specified at start of country.

Papendrecht (★Dordrecht)......24,995
Purmerend (★Amsterdam)......32,565
Renkum (★Arnhem) (34,168▲)....12,600
Rheden (★Arnhem) (48,637▲)....10,100
Ridderkerk (★Rotterdam)........45,908
Rijswijk (★The Hague)..........52,605
Roermond........................37,539
Roosendaal.......................54,838
Rotterdam (★1,085,000).........579,194
Schiedam (★Rotterdam)..........74,895
's-Hertogenbosch (★183,583)....87,897
Sittard (★★Geleen)..............33,702
Sliedrecht.......................22,504
Sneek.............................28,457
Soest (★Amersfoort).............40,581
Spijkenisse (★Rotterdam).......36,863
Tegelen (★Venlo)................18,079
Terneuzen (35,393▲).............22,200
THE HAGUE ('s-GRAVENHAGE)
(★775,000).......................456,886
Tiel................................28,919
Tilburg (★216,873)..............151,799
Utrecht (★481,875)..............237,037
Valkenswaard (★Eindhoven)......27,441
Veendam...........................28,169
Veenendaal........................39,210
Veldhoven (★Eindhoven).........33,382
Venlo (★86,000)..................62,595
Vlaardingen (★Rotterdam).......79,531
Vlissingen (Flushing) (45,726▲)..26,200
Voorburg (★The Hague)..........44,227
Vught (★'s-Hertogenbosch)......23,582
Waalwijk...........................28,514
Wageningen........................30,447
Wassenaar (★The Hague).........26,989
Weert (38,311▲)...................27,800
Winschoten........................21,101
Woerden...........................23,715
Zaanstad (Zaandam)
(★Amsterdam)....................128,809
Zeist (★Utrecht).................61,532
Zoetermeer (★The Hague)........63,832
Zutphen............................31,767
Zwijndrecht (★★Dordrecht).......39,641
Zwolle.............................82,190

NETHERLANDS ANTILLES / Nederlandse Antillen

1960 C........................188,914

Kralendijk *(Bonaire)* (1953 E)......600
Oranjestad *(Aruba)* (1965 E).....14,700
•WILLEMSTAD *(Curaçao)*
(★94,133)..........................43,547

NEW CALEDONIA / Nouvelle-Calédonie

1976 C........................133,233

•NOUMEA (★70,600)..............56,100

NEW HEBRIDES
see Vanuatu

NEW ZEALAND

1979 E........................3,144,700

•Auckland (★775,000)............147,600
Birkenhead (★Auckland).........20,600
Blenheim...........................17,450
Christchurch (★309,000).........171,300
Dunedin (★113,000)...............81,600
East Coast Bays (★Auckland)...24,500
Gisborne (★32,000)...............30,000
Hamilton (★97,400)...............90,900
Hastings (★★Napier)..............35,500
Invercargill (★53,800)...........49,900
Lower Hutt (★Wellington).......65,100
Manukau (★Auckland)............143,500
Masterton (★21,200)..............19,650
Mount Albert (★Auckland).......28,300
Mount Eden (★Auckland).........19,500
Mount Roskill (★Auckland)......34,800
Mount Wellington (★Auckland)..20,500
Napier (★110,600).................47,900
Nelson (★42,800)..................33,100
New Plymouth (★44,700).........38,300
Palmerston North (★64,900).....58,800
Papakura (★Auckland)............22,200
Papatoetoe (★Auckland)..........23,100
Porirua (★Wellington).............42,500
Rotorua (★47,400).................37,700
Takapuna (★Auckland)............63,700
Tauranga (★49,000)................34,300
Timaru (★30,100)...................29,500
Tokoroa.............................19,150
Upper Hutt (★Wellington)........31,300
Wainuiomata (★Wellington)
(1978 E)............................19,650
Waitemata (★Auckland)...........81,900
Wanganui (★39,800)...............37,500
WELLINGTON (★349,900).........137,600
Whangarei (★39,600)..............35,900

NICARAGUA

1978 E........................2,451,418

Bluefields..........................18,252
Chinandega.........................44,435
Granada.............................56,232
León................................81,647
•MANAGUA..........................552,900
Masaya..............................47,276
Matagalpa..........................26,986
Rivas................................16,222

NIGER

1977 E........................5,098,000

Maradi...............................45,900
•NIAMEY............................225,300
Tahoua...............................31,300
Zinder...............................58,400

NIGERIA

1963 C........................55,670,052

Aba (1975 E)......................177,000
Abeokuta (1975 E)...............253,000
Ado-Ekiti (1975 E)...............213,000
Afikpo...............................36,096
Agege...............................45,986
Akure...............................71,106
Awka................................48,725
Bauchi...............................37,778
Benin City (1975 E).............136,000
Bida..................................55,007
Calabar (1975 E).................103,000
Deba..................................60,679
Ede (1975 E)......................182,000
Effon-Alaiye.......................67,090
Ejigbo................................46,410
Enugu (1975 E)...................187,000
Epe...................................44,268
Gombe...............................47,265
Gusau................................69,231
Ibadan (1975 E)..................847,000
Ife (1975 E).......................176,000
Igboho...............................46,776
Ihiala.................................40,198
Ijebu-Igbo..........................43,180
Ijebu-Ode...........................68,543
Ijero Ekiti..........................41,935
Ikare.................................61,696
Ikerre (1975 E)...................145,000
Ikire.................................54,022
Ikirun................................79,516
Ikorodu..............................81,024
Ikot Ekpene.........................38,107
Ila (1975 E)........................155,000
Ilawe.................................80,833
Ilegboro.............................44,543
Ilesha (1975 E)...................224,000
Ilobu.................................87,223
Ilorin (1975 E)....................282,000
Inisa..................................52,482
Ise Ekiti..............................45,323
Iseyin (1971 E)....................115,000
Iwo (1975 E).......................214,000
Jos.....................................90,402
Kaduna (1975 E)..................202,000
Kano (1975 E).....................399,000
Katsina (1971 E)..................109,000
Kishi...................................42,374
Kumo..................................64,878
Lafia...................................53,667
•LAGOS (1975 E) (★1,450,000)..1,060,800
Maiduguri (1975 E)..............189,000
Makurdi..............................53,967
Minna.................................59,988
Mushin (★Lagos) (1975 E)......197,000
Nguru.................................43,234
Offa....................................86,425
Ogbomosho (1975 E).............432,000
Oka....................................62,761
Ondo..................................74,343
Onitsha (1975 E).................220,000
Oshogbo (1975 E)................282,000
Owo...................................89,693
Oyo (1975 E)......................152,000
Port Harcourt (1975 E)..........242,000
Sapele................................61,007
Shagamu.............................51,371
Shaki..................................76,290
Shomolu (★Lagos).................64,731
Sokoto................................89,817
Ugep..................................44,945
Warri..................................55,254
Zaria (1975 E).....................224,000

NORWAY / Norge

1979 E........................4,073,000

Ålesund..............................34,744
Arendal (1980 E) (★20,000).......11,400
Bergen (1980 E) (★238,000).....209,000
Bodø..................................32,163
Drammen (1980 E) (★71,000).....49,700
Eigersund............................11,694
Fredrikstad (1980 E) (★48,000)....28,000
Gjøvik................................26,150
Grimstad.............................13,588
Halden................................26,810
Hamar................................16,053
Hammerfest..........................7,457
Harstad...............................21,579
Haugesund...........................27,081
Horten................................13,476
Kongsberg...........................20,385
Kongsvinger.........................17,018
Kristiansand.........................60,722
Kristiansund.........................18,412
Larvik (1980 E) (★16,500)..........8,300
Lillehammer.........................21,762
Mandal...............................11,847
Mo (1970 C).........................21,033
Molde.................................20,886
Moss..................................25,407
Namsos...............................11,640
Narvik................................19,202
Notodden............................12,973
•OSLO (1980 E) (★725,000).....‡454,819
Porsgrunn (★★Skien) (1980 E)...31,365
Ringerike............................26,839
Sandefjord...........................34,405
Sandnes (★Stavanger) (1980 E)..36,200
Sarpsborg (1980 E) (★37,500).....12,100
Skien (1980 E) (★78,815)...........47,450
Stavanger (1980 E) (★128,000)....90,000
Steinkjer.............................20,526
Tønsberg (1980 E) (★35,000)........9,200
Tromsø...............................45,360
Trondheim..........................134,683
Vadsø..................................6,054

OMAN / 'Umān

1962 E........................565,000

•Maṭraḥ..............................14,000
MUSCAT (MASQAṬ)....................6,000

PACIFIC ISLANDS TRUST TERRITORY

1973 C........................114,773

Island Groups

Caroline Islands....................75,394
Mariana Islands (excl. Guam)...14,335
Marshall Islands....................25,044

PAKISTAN / Pākistān

1972 C........................64,979,732

(excl. population in section of Jammu and Kashmir occupied by Pakistan)

Abbottābād (★47,122).............27,963
Ahmadpur East......................43,312
Bahāwalnagar........................50,991
Bahāwalpur (★133,782)..........115,660
Baldia (★Karāchi)..................79,529
Bannu (★43,795)....................33,000
Bhakkar..............................34,638
Burewala.............................57,741
Campbellpore (★29,172)...........21,633
Chakwāl..............................29,143
Chārsadda...........................45,555
Chiniot...............................70,108
Dādu..................................30,184
Dera Ghāzi Khān....................72,343
Dera Ismāīl Khān (★58,778)......57,296
Faisalabad (Lyallpur).............823,343
Gujrānwāla (★360,478)............323,880
Gujrāt...............................100,333
Gwādar...............................15,758
Hāfizābād.............................61,597
Hyderābād (★660,000)............600,796
ISLĀMĀBĀD (★★Rāwalpindi)....77,000
Jacobābād............................57,596
Jhang Maghiāna....................131,843
Jhelum (★70,157)...................63,676
Kamālia...............................50,934
Kāmoke...............................50,257
•Karāchi (1975 E) (★4,500,000)..2,800,000
Karāchi Cantonment
(★Karāchi).........................133,176
Kasūr................................102,531
Khānewāl.............................67,746
Khānpur...............................49,235
Kohāt (★65,202).....................48,096
Lahore (★2,200,000)...............2,022,577
Lahore Cantonment (★Lahore)..147,165
Landhi Korangi (★Karāchi).....551,236
Lārkāna...............................71,893
Leiah..................................33,549
Mardān (★115,194)................105,157
Miānwāli..............................48,304
Mīrpur-Khās.........................81,965
Multān (★538,949)..................504,365
Nawābshāh...........................81,045
New Karāchi No. 1 (★Karāchi)..85,398
New Karāchi No. 2 (★Karāchi)..67,682
Nowshera (★55,916)................31,101
Okāra (★101,052)...................84,334
Orangi (★Karāchi).................109,979
Peshāwar (★284,833)..............219,562
Quetta (★158,026)..................137,659
Rahīmyār Khān (★85,699)..........74,262
Rāwalpindi (★725,000).............372,919
Rāwalpindi Cantonment
(★Rāwalpindi)......................241,890
Sāhiwāl (Montgomery)............106,648
Sargodha (★200,460)...............166,391
Shekhūpura..........................80,560
Shikārpur.............................70,924
Shujāābād.............................24,422
Siālkot (★203,650)..................183,685
Sibi....................................19,989
Sukkur...............................158,781
Turbat.................................27,671
Wah Cantonment...................107,510

PANAMA / Panamá

1970 C........................†1,472,280

†Includes former Canal Zone

Balboa (★Panamá)..................2,569
Balboa Heights (★Panamá)..........232
Colón (1976 E) (★82,000)..........73,600
David..................................35,677
Gamboa................................2,102
La Chorrera..........................25,873
•PANAMÁ (1978 E) (★645,000)...439,800
Puerto Armuelles...................12,015
San Miguelito (★Panamá)
(1977 E).............................135,100
Santiago...............................14,595

PAPUA NEW GUINEA

1977 E........................2,905,000

Lae.....................................45,100
Madang................................20,100
•PORT MORESBY.....................106,600
Rabaul.................................13,400
Wewak..................................18,100

PARAGUAY

1972 C........................2,357,955

•ASUNCIÓN (1978 E) (★655,000).463,700
Caacupé...............................7,278
Concepción...........................19,392
Coronel Oviedo......................13,786
Encarnación..........................23,343
Fernando de la Mora
(★Asunción).........................36,834
Lambaré (★Asunción)...............31,656
Luque (★Asunción)..................13,921
Paraguarí..............................5,036
Pedro Juan Caballero...............21,033
Pilar...................................12,506
Villa Hayes...........................4,749
Villarrica.............................17,687

PERU / Perú

1972 C........................13,572,052

Arequipa (★304,653)...............98,605
Ayacucho (★43,304)...............34,593
Barranco (★Lima)...................46,449
Barrio Obrero Industrial
(★Lima)...............................238,402
Breña (★Lima).......................123,345
Cajamarca............................37,608
Callao (★★Lima)....................196,919
Cerro de Pasco (★47,178).........35,975
Chiclayo (★189,685)...............148,932
Chimbote.............................159,045
Chorrillos (★Lima)..................87,021
Cuzco (★120,881)...................67,658
Huacho................................36,697
Huancayo (★115,693)...............64,777
Huánuco...............................41,123
Ica.....................................73,883
Iquitos................................111,327
Jesús María (★Lima)................82,988
Juliaca................................38,475
La Victoria (★Lima)................265,157
•LIMA (★3,250,000).................340,339
Lince (★Lima).........................82,749
Magdalena del Mar (★Lima).......54,855
Miraflores (★Lima)..................93,926
Pisco..................................41,429
Piura (★126,702)....................81,683
Pucallpa...............................57,525
Pueblo Libre (★Lima)...............76,279
Puno...................................41,166
Rímac (★Lima)......................165,340
San Isidro (★Lima)..................61,682
Sullana................................60,112
Surco (★Lima)........................70,949
Surquillo (★Lima)...................89,201
Tacna..................................55,752
Trujillo (★241,882).................127,535
Tumbes................................32,972
Vitarte (★Lima)......................54,417

PHILIPPINES / Pilipinas

1975 C........................42,070,660

Angeles..............................151,164
Antipolo (40,944▲)..................35,672
Bacolod..............................223,392
Bacoor (★Manila)....................62,225
Baguio................................97,449
Baliuag...............................61,624
Batangas (125,363▲)................18,592
Biñan (★Manila).....................67,444
Bocaue................................40,577
Butuan (132,682▲)...................53,578
Cabanatuan (115,258▲)..............32,003
Cadiz (127,653▲)....................26,581
Cagayan de Oro (165,220▲)........37,272
Calamba (97,432▲)..................33,321
Calapan (55,608▲)...................13,982
Caloocan (★Manila).................397,201
Cavite (★160,000)...................82,456
Cebu (★500,000)....................413,025
Cotabato (67,097▲)..................49,134
Dagupan..............................90,092
Davao (484,678▲)...................214,849
General Santos (Dadiangas)
(91,154▲).............................37,527
Gingoog (66,577▲)...................16,590
Ilagan (70,075▲).....................12,234
Iligan (118,778▲)....................10,367
Iloilo.................................227,027
Iriga (75,885▲)......................13,938
Isabela (Basilan) (27,261▲)........7,204
Jolo...................................37,623
Koronadal (62,764▲)................15,066
La Carlota (40,984▲)...............20,251
Laoag (66,259▲).....................31,336
Lapu-Lapu............................79,484
Las Piñas (★Manila)................81,610
Legazpi (88,378▲)...................37,724
Lingayen (59,034▲).................16,096
Lipa (106,094▲).....................18,330
Lucena................................92,336
Maasin (54,737▲)....................12,348
Makati (★Manila)...................334,448
Malabon (★Manila).................174,878
Malaybalay (65,198▲)...............10,207
Malolos...............................83,491
Mandaluyong (★Manila)...........182,267
Mandaue (★Cebu)...................75,904
•MANILA (★5,500,000)..........1,479,116
Marawi................................63,332
Marikina (★Manila).................168,453
Mati (73,125▲).......................18,188
Mecauayan (★Manila)...............60,225
Muntinglupa (★Manila).............94,563
Naga..................................83,337
Navotas (★Manila)...................97,098
Olongapo............................147,109
Ormoc (89,466▲)....................13,075
Ozamiz (71,559▲)...................17,372
Pagadian (66,062▲).................28,645
Parañaque (★Manila)...............158,974
Pasay (★Manila)....................254,999
Pasig (★Manila).....................209,915
Puerto Princesa (45,709▲).........18,480
Quezon City (★Manila)............956,864
Roxas (Capiz) (71,305▲)...........18,869
Sagay (95,421▲).....................32,417
San Carlos (*Negros Occidental Prov.*) (90,982▲).....................23,950
San Carlos (*Pangasinan Prov.*)
(90,882▲).............................12,003
San Fernando (*La Union Prov.*)
(61,166▲).............................14,133
San Fernando (*Pampanga Prov.*)..98,382
San Juan del Monte (★Manila).122,492
San Pablo (116,607▲)...............42,489
San Pedro............................43,439
Santa Cruz...........................52,672
Santa Rosa (★Manila)...............47,639
Tacloban (80,707▲).................63,693
Tagbilaran............................37,335
Tagig (★Manila).....................73,702
Valenzuela (★Manila)..............150,605
Zamboanga (265,023▲)..............53,678

POLAND / Polska

1979 E........................35,414,000

Będzin (★Katowice)...............75,000
Biała Podlaska.......................38,100
Białystok............................218,700
Bielawa (Langenbielau)
(★★Dzierżoniów)...................32,100
Bielsko-Biała........................160,300
Bolesławiec (Bunzlau)..............39,200
Brzeg (Brieg)........................35,300
Bydgoszcz...........................343,800
Bytom (Beuthen)
(★★Katowice).......................231,600
Chełm.................................51,200
Chojnice..............................31,100
Chorzów (★★Katowice)............149,900
Częstochowa........................232,400
Dąbrowa Górnicza
(★Katowice).........................137,300
Dzierżoniów (Reichenbach)
(★85,000).............................35,800
Elbląg (Elbing).....................108,100
Ełk (Lyck).............................37,300
Gdańsk (Danzig) (★820,000).....449,200
Gdynia (★★Gdańsk)................232,500
Gliwice (Gleiwitz)
(★★Katowice).......................195,300
Głogów (Glogau)....................49,200
Gniezno...............................61,100
Gorzów Wielkopolski
(Landsberg)..........................102,500
Grudziądz.............................88,700
Inowrocław............................65,100
Jarosław...............................34,900
Jastrzębie Zdrój.....................97,800
Jaworzno (★Katowice)..............88,200
Jelenia Góra (Hirschberg).........86,000
Kalisz.................................97,700
•Katowice (★2,590,000)...........351,300
Kędzierzyn-Koźle (Heydebreck).68,700
Kielce................................181,000
Knurów (★Katowice).................40,200
Kołobrzeg (Kolberg).................37,500
Konin..................................65,300
Koszalin (Köslin).....................90,000
Kraków (★780,000).................706,100
Krosno................................38,000
Kutno.................................40,500
Legionowo (★Warsaw)..............37,200
Legnica (Liegnitz)...................88,400
Leszno................................47,500
Łódź (★1,025,000).................830,800
Łomża................................38,100
Lubin (Lüben)........................63,000
Lublin (★345,000)..................297,600
Mielec................................41,300
Mysłowice (★Katowice).............78,100
Nowa Sól (Neusalz)..................38,000
Nowy Sącz............................62,600
Nysa (Neisse)........................40,700
Olsztyn (Allenstein)...............130,400
Opole (Oppeln)......................114,000
Ostrowiec Świętokrzyski............62,300
Ostrów Wielkopolski.................61,400
Oświęcim.............................44,200
Otwock (★Warsaw)...................47,400
Pabianice (★Łódź)...................69,800
Piekary Śląskie (★Katowice).......63,500
Piła (Schneidemühl).................57,200
Piotrków Trybunalski................70,900
Płock..................................99,800
Poznań (★610,000)..................545,600
Pruszków (★Warsaw)................49,000
Przemyśl..............................60,100
Pszczyna..............................34,800
Puławy.................................44,800
Racibórz (Ratibor)...................52,900
Radom................................187,600
Radomsko.............................39,900
Ruda Śląska (★Katowice)..........156,800
Rybnik................................118,200
Rzeszów..............................116,900
Siedlce................................52,500
Siemianowice Śląskie
(★Katowice)..........................77,200
Skarżysko-Kamienna.................49,500
Słupsk (Stolp).......................84,200
Sopot (Zoppot) (★Gdańsk).........51,800
Sosnowiec (★★Katowice)...........241,700
Stalowa Wola.........................52,200
Starachowice.........................48,400
Stargard Szczeciński.................57,200
Starogard Gdański....................43,300
Suwałki................................38,500
Świdnica (Schweidnitz)..............55,700
Świętochłowice (★Katowice).......57,700
Świnoujście (Swinemünde)..........46,000
Szczecin (Stettin) (★425,000)....388,000
Szczecinek (Neustettin).............35,200
Tarnobrzeg............................35,200
Tarnów................................102,800
Tarnowskie Góry (★Katowice).....65,900
Tczew..................................52,300
Tomaszów Mazowiecki...............62,800
Toruń.................................170,100
Tychy (★Katowice)..................160,700
Wałbrzych (Waldenburg)
(★195,000)..........................132,900
Wałcz (Deutsch Krone)...............22,000
WARSAW (WARSZAWA)
(★2,080,000)......................1,576,600
Wejherowo.............................41,600
Włocławek............................104,400
Wodzisław Śląski....................104,500
Wołomin (★Warsaw).................30,600
Wrocław (Breslau)..................609,100
Zabrze (Hindenburg)
(★★Katowice)......................195,000
Zamość................................45,700
Żary (Sorau)...........................34,700
Zawiercie..............................61,600
Zduńska Wola.........................38,200
Zgierz (★Łódź).......................52,100
Zgorzelec..............................32,800
Zielona Góra (Grünberg)............98,000
Żyrardów (★Warsaw)................36,700

C Census. E Official estimate. UE Unofficial estimate.
L Population within municipal limits of specified year. • Largest city in country.

★ Population or designation of metropolitan area, including suburbs (see headnote).
▲ Population of an entire municipality, commune, or district, including rural area.
‡† Year of information specified at start of country.

PORTUGAL

1970 C	**8,568,703**
Almada (★Lisbon)	38,714
Amadora (★Lisbon)	66,189
Angra do Heroísmo (*Azores Is.*)	14,328
Aveiro	20,651
Barreiro (★Lisbon)	53,200
Beja	15,909
Braga	49,693
Bragança	10,001
Coimbra	56,568
Covilhã	27,018
Évora	24,003
Faro	20,687
Funchal (*Madeira Is.*)	40,057
Guimarães	25,113
Horta (*Azores Is.*)	6,025
•LISBON (LISBOA) (1975 E) (★1,950,000)	829,900
Matosinhos (★Porto)	22,475
Montijo (★Lisbon)	25,949
Moscavide (★Lisbon)	21,647
Odivelas (★Lisbon)	25,978
Piedade (★Lisbon)	21,004
Ponta Delgada (*Azores Is.*)	21,262
Portimão	10,389
Porto (Oporto) (1975 E) (★1,150,000)	335,700
Póvoa de Varzim	17,555
Queluz (★Lisbon)	25,913
Santarem	18,069
Setúbal	50,730
Sintra (★Lisbon) (1960 C)	7,705
Vila do Conde	16,390
Vila Nova de Gaia (★Porto)	50,219
Viseu	16,636

PUERTO RICO

1980 C	**3,187,570**
Adjuntas (18,617▲)	5,184
Aguadilla (52,627▲)	20,879
Aibonito (22,230▲)	9,369
Arecibo (86,660▲)	48,586
Bayamón (★San Juan)	184,854
Cabo Rojo (33,909▲)	10,254
Caguas (★San Juan) (118,020▲)	87,218
Carolina (★San Juan)	147,100
Cataño (★San Juan)	26,318
Cayey (40,927▲)	23,315
Cidra (28,135▲)	6,065
Coamo (30,752▲)	12,834
Corozal (28,218▲)	5,891
Fajardo (32,011▲)	26,845
Guánica (18,784▲)	9,627
Guayama (40,137▲)	21,044
Guayanilla (21,012▲)	6,191
Guaynabo (★San Juan)	65,091
Humacao (45,916▲)	19,135
Isabela (37,451▲)	12,097
Juncos (25,433▲)	7,898
Manatí (36,480▲)	17,254
Mayagüez (★132,814)	82,703
Ponce (★252,420)	161,260
San Germán (32,941▲)	13,093
•SAN JUAN (★1,535,000)	422,701
San Lorenzo (32,333▲)	8,886
San Sebastian (35,877▲)	10,792
Trujillo Alto (★San Juan) (51,389▲)	41,097
Utuado (34,384▲)	11,049
Vega Alta (★San Juan) (28,225▲)	10,584
Vega Baja (★San Juan) (46,841▲)	18,020
Yabucoa (30,589▲)	6,782
Yauco (37,682▲)	14,598

QATAR / Qaṭar

1971 E	**160,000**
•DOHA (AD-DAWḤAH)	95,000

REUNION / Réunion

1974 C	**476,675**
Le Port (25,068▲)	21,621
•ST. DENIS (103,512▲)	80,802
St. Pierre (46,060▲)	22,022

RHODESIA see Zimbabwe

ROMANIA / România

1978 E	**21,854,622**
Aiud	25,929
Alba-Iulia	44,870
Alexandria	39,531
Arad	174,411
Bacău	135,841
Baia-Mare	107,945
Bîrlad	57,954
Bistriţa	48,959
Blaj	21,465
Bocşa	21,317
Borşa	25,427
Botoşani	68,325
Brăila	200,435
Braşov	268,226
•BUCHAREST (BUCUREŞTI) (★2,050,000)	1,858,418
Buzău	102,868
Călăraşi	50,601
Caracal	31,433
Caransebeş	28,437
Carei	24,473
Cîmpia Turzii	23,750
Cîmpina	33,554
Cîmpulung	33,329
Cluj Napoca	273,199
Codlea	23,691
Constanţa (★301,758)	267,612
Craiova	230,721
Cugir	27,892
Curtea de Argeş	26,081
Dej	33,350
Deva	65,009
Dorohoi	22,332
Drobeta-Turnu-Severin	80,200
Făgăraş	35,831
Feteşti	28,257
Focşani	60,038
Galaţi	252,592
Gheorghe Gheorghiu-Dej	43,282
Giurgiu	53,072
Hunedoara	81,963
Huşi	23,652
Iaşi	278,545
Lugoj	45,957
Lupeni	27,857
Mangalia	30,404
Medgidia	41,792
Mediaş	66,795
Miercurea Ciuc	33,884
Odorheiu Secuiesc	30,756
Olteniţa	25,185
Oradea	179,780
Petroşani (★74,000)	41,720
Piatra-Neamţ	83,168
Piteşti	133,081
Ploieşti (★270,000)	206,138
Rădăuţi	22,750
Reghin	31,035
Reşiţa	90,664
Rîmnicu-Sărat	29,246
Rîmnicu-Vîlcea	72,915
Roman	53,797
Roşiori de Vede	29,462
Săcele	31,615
Satu-Mare	107,852
Sebeş	26,881
Sfîntu Gheorghe	45,739
Sibiu	157,519
Sighetul Marmaţiei	39,095
Sighişoara	33,359
Slatina	50,683
Slobozia	33,701
Suceava	66,527
Tecuci	37,423
Timişoara	277,779
Tîrgovişte	67,024
Tîrgu-Jiu	67,694
Tîrgu-Mureş	136,679
Tîrnăveni	26,877
Tulcea	66,054
Turda	56,350
Turnu-Măgurele	33,404
Vaslui	42,718
Vulcan	29,216
Zalău	35,734
Zărneşti	24,317

RWANDA

1978 C	**4,819,000**
Butare	21,700
•KIGALI	117,700
Ruhengeri	16,000

ST. HELENA
(excl. Dependencies)

1976 C	**5,147**
•JAMESTOWN	1,516

ST. KITTS-NEVIS

1970 C	**47,457**
•BASSETERRE (*St. Kitts*)	13,055
Charlestown (*Nevis*)	1,880

SAINT LUCIA

1978 E	**117,500**
•CASTRIES	47,600

ST. PIERRE & MIQUELON / Saint-Pierre-et-Miquelon

1974 C	**5,840**
•ST.-PIERRE	5,232

ST. VINCENT

1970 C	**89,129**
•KINGSTOWN (★23,782)	17,258

SAN MARINO

1977 E	**20,000**
•SAN MARINO	4,628

SAO TOME & PRINCIPE / São Tomé e Príncipe

1970 C	**73,631**
•SÃO TOMÉ	17,380

SAUDI ARABIA / Al-'Arabīyah as-Sa'ūdīyah

1974 C	**7,012,642**
Abhā	30,150
Ad-Dammām	127,844
Al-Hufūf (Hofuf)	101,271
Al-Jawf (1961 UE)	20,000
Al-Khubar	48,817
Al-Madīnah (Medina)	198,186
Al-Mubarraz	54,325
Al-Qaṭīf (1961 UE)	30,000
At-Tā'if	204,857
Aẓ-Ẓahrān (Dhahran) (1974 UE)	25,000
Buraydah	69,940
Ḥā'il	40,502
Juddah (Jidda)	561,104
Khamīs Mushayṭ	49,581
Mecca (Makkah)	366,801
Najran	47,501
Qal'at Bīshah (1961 UE)	20,000
Qīzān	32,812
•RIYADH (AR-RIYĀḌ)	666,840
Tabūk	74,825
Yanbu' (1961 UE)	20,000

SENEGAL / Sénégal

1976 C	**5,085,388**
•DAKAR	798,792
Diourbel	51,000
Kaolack	106,899
Rufisque (★Dakar) (1973 E)	54,000
Saint-Louis	88,000
Thiès	117,333
Ziguinchor	73,000

SEYCHELLES

1971 C	**52,437**
•VICTORIA	13,622

SIERRA LEONE

1974 C	**2,730,000**
Bo	30,000
Bonthe (1963 C)	6,230
•FREETOWN (★335,000)	274,000
Kenema	15,000
Kissy (★Freetown) (1963 C)	13,143
Koidu (1963 C)	11,706
Lunsar (1963 C)	12,132
Makeni	12,000
Port Loko (1963 C)	5,809

SINGAPORE

1980 E	**2,390,800**
•SINGAPORE (★2,600,000)	2,390,800

SOLOMON ISLANDS

1976 C	**196,823**
•HONIARA	14,942

SOMALIA / Somaliya

1972 E	**2,941,000**
Afgoi (1964 C)	16,575
Berbera (1966 E)	14,000
Hargeisa (1966 E)	42,000
Kismayu (1968 C)	17,872
Marka (Merca) (1967 E)	17,700
•MOGADISHU (MOGADISCIO)	230,000

SOUTH AFRICA / Suid-Afrika

1970 C	**21,794,328**
Provinces	
Cape (Kaap)	6,827,756
Natal	4,315,847
Orange Free State (Oranje-Vrystaat)	1,749,671
Transvaal	8,901,054
Cities	
Alberton (★Johannesburg)	23,988
Alexandra (★Johannesburg)	57,040
Aliwal North	12,311
Beaufort West	17,862
Bellville (★Cape Town)	49,026
Benoni (★Johannesburg)	151,294
Bethal	17,337
Bethlehem	29,918
Bishop Levis (★Cape Town)	26,386
Bloemfontein (★182,329)	149,836
Boksburg (★Johannesburg)	106,126
Brakpan (★Johannesburg)	73,210
CAPE TOWN (KAAPSTAD) (★1,125,000)	697,514
Carletonville	93,096
Clermont (★Durban)	26,125
Cradock	20,822
De Aar	18,057
Dundee	17,162
Durban (★1,040,000)	736,852
East London (Oos-Londen) (★190,000)	119,727
Edendale (★Pietermaritzburg)	41,194
Edenvale (★Johannesburg)	25,126
Elsies River (★Cape Town)	64,539
Ermelo	19,036
Ga-Rankuwa	45,631
George	24,625
Germiston (★★Johannesburg)	221,972
Goodwood (★Cape Town)	31,592
Graaff-Reinet	22,392
Grahamstown	41,302
Grassy Park (★Cape Town)	32,709
Hammarsdale	21,657
Harrismith	16,082
•Johannesburg (★2,550,000)	654,232
Kempton Park (★Johannesburg)	37,205
Kimberley	105,258
Klerksdorp (★175,000)	63,558
Kroonstad	51,988
Krugersdorp (★Johannesburg)	92,725
Ladysmith	28,920
Mabopane	22,559
Madadeni	32,398
Mafeking	6,515
Mariannhill (★Durban)	22,484
Mdantsane (★East London)	67,501
Middelburg	26,942
Mosselbaai	17,574
Nelspruit	25,092
Newcastle	14,407
Nigel	41,179
Odendaalsrus (★29,026)	15,603
Orkney (★★Klerksdorp)	22,117
Oudtshoorn	26,907
Paarl	49,244
Parow (★Cape Town)	60,768
Parys	17,447
Pietermaritzburg (★160,855)	114,822
Pietersburg	27,174
Port Elizabeth (★475,869)	392,231
Potchefstroom	57,443
Potgietersrus	6,667
PRETORIA (★575,000)	545,450
Queenstown	39,304
Randburg (★Johannesburg)	46,011
Randfontein (★Johannesburg)	50,481
Roodepoort-Maraisburg (★Johannesburg)	115,366
Rustenburg	22,303
Sandton (★Johannesburg)	49,022
Sasolburg (★Vereeniging)	29,056
Soweto (★Johannesburg)	602,043
Springs (★Johannesburg)	142,812
Standerton	21,038
Stellenbosch	29,955
Stilfontein (★Klerksdorp)	70,661
Strand (★Cape Town)	24,503
Tembisa (★Johannesburg)	83,637
Uitenhage (★★Port Elizabeth)	70,517
Umlazi (★Durban)	123,495
Umtata	25,216
Upington	28,632
Vanderbijlpark (★★Vereeniging)	80,375
Vereeniging (★310,188)	172,549
Virginia	46,138
Welkom (★132,880)	67,472
Westonaria (★Johannesburg)	36,253
Witbank	37,456
Worcester	41,198
Zwelitsha	22,131

SOVIET UNION
See Union of Soviet Socialist Republics

SPAIN / España

1978 E	**38,141,157**
Regions and Provinces	
ANDALUSIA (ANDALUCÍA)	6,560,445
Almería	418,471
Cádiz	1,016,340
Córdoba	751,833
Granada	780,848
Huelva	427,991
Jaén	677,756
Málaga	1,013,346
Sevilla	1,473,860
ARAGON (ARAGÓN)	1,204,244
Huesca	218,364
Teruel	157,454
Zaragoza	828,426
ASTURIAS	1,172,301
Oviedo	1,172,301
BALEARIC IS. (BALEARES)	642,702
Baleares	642,702
BASQUE PROVINCES (VASCONGADAS)	2,192,755
Álava	256,883
Guipúzcoa	714,690
Vizcaya	1,221,182
CANARY IS. (CANARIAS)	1,410,665
Las Palmas	704,389
Santa Cruz de Tenerife	706,276
CATALONIA (CATALUÑA)	6,071,953
Barcelona	4,724,063
Gerona	467,749
Lérida	358,430
Tarragona	521,711
ESTREMADURA (EXTREMADURA)	1,110,457
Badajoz	666,389
Cáceres	444,068
GALICIA	2,895,467
La Coruña	1,126,202
Lugo	418,770
Orense	447,980
Pontevedra	902,515
LEON (LEÓN)	1,156,113
León	549,709
Salamanca	368,833
Zamora	237,571
MURCIA	1,300,878
Albacete	343,868
Murcia	957,010
NAVARRE (NAVARRA)	511,699
Navarra	511,699
NEW CASTILE (CASTILLA LA NUEVA)	6,010,575
Ciudad Real	498,205
Cuenca	226,496
Guadalajara	143,520
Madrid	4,659,478
Toledo	482,876
OLD CASTILE (CASTILLA LA VIEJA)	2,261,956
Ávila	194,913
Burgos	368,302
Logroño	252,110
Palencia	192,102
Santander	515,109
Segovia	153,771
Soria	104,595
Valladolid	481,054
VALENCIA	3,638,947
Alicante	1,142,323
Castellón	430,845
Valencia	2,065,779
Cities (1975 C or ‡1978 E)	
Aguilas (18,900▲)	16,900
Albacete	‡107,725
Alcalá [de Guadaira] (39,593▲)	33,500
Alcalá de Henares (★Madrid)	‡114,788
Alcalá la Real (20,184▲)	9,300
Alcantarilla	21,891
Alcázar de San Juan	26,930
Alcira	35,428
Alcobendas (★Madrid)	‡57,951
Alcorcón (★Madrid)	‡124,348
Alcoy	‡65,078
Algeciras	‡92,933
Algemesí	23,623
Algorta (66,306▲)	‡29,500
Alicante	‡235,868
Almadén	10,312
Almendralejo	22,074
Almería	‡136,720
Andújar (34,459▲)	28,400
Antequera (40,113▲)	27,500
Aranjuez	31,275
Arcos de la Frontera (24,867▲)	15,500
Arizgoiti (Basauri) (★Bilbao) (55,303▲)	‡46,800
Arrecife (*Canary Is.*)	25,201
Ávila	‡38,105
Avilés (★129,000)	‡90,458
Badajoz (112,573▲)	‡89,500
Badalona (★Barcelona)	‡216,041
Baracaldo (★Bilbao)	‡123,178
Barcelona (★3,975,000)	‡1,902,713
Baza (20,113▲)	14,400
Bilbao (★995,000)	‡452,921
Burgos	‡148,487
Burjasot (★Valencia)	30,739
Burriana	23,846
Cabra (20,140▲)	15,900
Cáceres	‡64,539
Cádiz (★230,000)	‡156,328
Camas (★Sevilla)	23,840
Carmona	21,548
Cartagena (165,557▲)	‡135,200
Castellón de la Plana	‡118,648
Chiclana [de la Frontera]	31,711
Cieza	28,228
Ciudad Real	‡48,871
Córdoba	‡276,255
Cornellá (★Barcelona)	‡95,933
Cuenca	‡39,064
Daimiel	16,986
Don Benito	26,117
Dos Hermanas	47,800
Écija (33,505▲)	25,400
Éibar	37,838
Elche (165,203▲)	‡136,400
Elda	‡53,558
El Ferrol del Caudillo (★126,000)	‡90,317
El Puerto de Santa María	‡52,350
Esplugas Llobregat (★Barcelona)	38,110
Figueras	28,102
Gandía (41,565▲)	32,600
Gavá (★Barcelona)	30,586
Gerona	‡85,522
Getafe (★Madrid)	‡128,523
Gijón	‡256,904
Granada	‡229,108
Granollers (★Barcelona)	36,366
Guadalajara	‡49,130
Guadix (19,234▲)	14,900
Guernica y Luno (17,271▲)	11,704
Hellín (22,327▲)	16,109
Hospitalet (★Barcelona)	‡294,280
Huelva	‡125,810
Huesca	‡38,986
Ibiza	20,552
Igualada	30,024
Irún	‡54,781
Jaén	‡91,198
Játiva	22,613
Jerez de la Frontera (183,534▲)	‡137,700
La Coruña	‡228,637
La Línea	‡57,940
Langreo (Sama de Langreo) (63,128▲)	‡10,600
La Orotava (*Canary Is.*) (30,190▲)	9,300
Las Palmas de Gran Canaria (*Canary Is.*)	‡357,158
Leganés (★Madrid)	‡151,353
Léon (★144,000)	‡122,827
Lérida (108,212▲)	‡86,100
Linares (56,356▲)	‡50,520
Logroño	‡104,928
Loja (22,001▲)	11,700
Lorca (65,806▲)	27,400
Lucena	29,373
Lugo (72,686▲)	‡60,900
•MADRID (★4,415,000)	‡3,367,438
Mahón	21,619
Málaga	‡467,637
Manacor	24,275
Manresa	‡68,213
Marbella (59,445▲)	‡35,200
Martos (21,375▲)	16,300
Mataró	‡98,589
Mérida	38,319
Mieres (62,826▲)	‡22,200
Miranda de Ebro	35,354
Mislata (★Valencia)	26,100
Morón de la Frontera (26,047▲)	22,700
Móstoles (★Madrid)	‡108,290
Motril (35,471▲)	28,100
Murcia (290,414▲)	‡190,600
Onteniente	26,297
Orense (89,485▲)	‡77,600
Orihuela (51,163▲)	‡20,000
Oviedo	‡181,556
Palencia	‡67,755
Palma [de Mallorca]	‡287,389
Pamplona	‡175,833

C Census. E Official estimate. UE Unofficial estimate.
L Population within municipal limits of year specified. • Largest city in country.

★ Population or designation of metropolitan area, including suburbs (see headnote).
▲ Population of an entire municipality, commune, or district, including rural area.
‡† Year of information specified at start of country.

Peñarroya-Pueblonuevo........13,579
Plasencia........28,574
Ponferrada........‡53,400
Pontevedra (64,722▲)........‡33,500
Portugalete (★Bilbao)........‡57,053
Prat de Llobregat (★Barcelona).‡57,330
Priego [de Córdoba] (20,560▲)...12,300
Puente-Genil (25,277▲)........21,900
Puerto de la Cruz *(Canary Is.)* (50,173▲)........37,100
Puertollano........‡52,722
Rentería (★San Sebastián)......46,329
Reus........‡84,986
Ronda (30,099▲)........22,100
Rota........25,702
Rubí (★Barcelona)........35,855
Sabadell (★Barcelona)........‡188,344
Sagunto........‡57,840
Salamanca........‡144,446
San Adrián de Besós (★Barcelona)........37,286
San Baudilio de Llobregat (★Barcelona)........‡67,321
San Cristóbal de la Laguna (Canary Is.) (114,183▲)........‡24,900
San Fernando (★★Cádiz)........‡69,123
Sanlúcar (43,867▲)........31,500
San Sebastián (★290,000)......‡176,023
Santa Coloma de Gramanet (★Barcelona)........‡143,568
Santa Cruz de Tenerife *(Canary Is.)*........‡186,949
Santander........‡176,363
Santiago de Compostela (83,841▲)........‡61,100
Santurce-Antiguo (★Bilboa)....‡55,159
Segovia........‡49,583
Sestao (★Bilbao)........41,399
Sevilla (Seville) (★740,000).....‡630,329
Soria........‡29,315
Sueca........22,522
Talavera de la Reina........‡60,964
Tarragona........‡109,969
Tarrasa (★Barcelona)........‡160,403
Telde *(Canary Is.)* (58,503▲).....‡17,300
Teruel........‡24,856
Toledo........‡56,414
Tomelloso........26,089
Torrejón de Ardoz (★Madrid)...‡63,500
Torrelavega (55,695▲)........‡25,900
Torrente (★Valencia)........46,686
Tortosa (47,246▲)........20,400
Ubeda........30,223
Valencia (★1,140,000)........‡750,994
Valladolid........‡315,486
Vall de Uxó........25,087
Vélez-Málaga (38,249▲)........18,700
Vich........27,615
Vigo........‡260,059
Villanueva y Geltrú........41,229
Vitoria........‡185,271
Zamora........‡55,822
Zaragoza (Saragossa)........‡563,375

SPANISH NORTH AFRICA / Plazas de Soberanía en el Norte de África

1978 E........120,719
•Ceuta........64,567
Melilla........56,152

SRI LANKA

1977 E........13,940,000
Anuradhapura........38,000
Badulla........38,000
Battaramulla (★Colombo) (1971 C)........43,057
Batticaloa........40,000
•COLOMBO (★1,540,000)........616,000
Dalugama (★Colombo) (1971 C)..41,200
Dehiwala-Mount Lavinia (★Colombo)........169,000
Galle........79,000
Jaffna........118,000
Kalutara........32,000
Kandy........103,000
Kegalla........14,000
Kotikawatta (★Colombo) (1971 C)........43,764
Kotte (★Colombo)........102,000
Kurunegala........28,000
Maharagama (★Colombo) (1971 C)........40,378
Matale........34,000
Matara........40,000
Moratuwa (★Colombo)........104,000
Negombo........63,000
Ratnapura........32,000
Trincomalee........46,000

SUDAN / As-Sūdān

1973 C........12,427,795
Al-Fāshir........51,932
Al-Junaynah........35,424
Al-Khurṭūm Baḥrī (Khartoum North (★Khartoum)........150,991
Al-Qaḍārif........66,465
Al-Ubayyiḍ (El Obeid)........90,060
'Aṭbarah........66,116
Būr-Sūdān (Port Sudan)........132,631
Jūbā........56,737
Kassalā........98,751
•KHARTOUM (AL-KHARṬŪM) (★790,000)........333,921
Kūstī........65,257
Malakāl........34,898
Nyala........59,852
Umm Durmān (Omdurman) (★★Khartoum)........299,401
Wad Madanī........106,776
Wāw........52,752

SURINAME

1971 C........384,900
•PARAMARIBO (★175,000).....102,300

SWAZILAND

1976 C........494,534
•Manzini (★26,000)........10,019
MBABANE........23,109

SWEDEN / Sverige

1979 E........8,303,010

Counties
Älvsborg........424,240
Blekinge........154,135
Gävleborg........293,959
Göteborg och Bohus........713,242
Gotland........55,261
Halland........229,211
Jämtland........134,653
Jönköping........302,475
Kalmar........241,448
Kopparberg........285,545
Kristianstad........278,917
Kronoberg........172,401
Malmöhus........743,133
Norrbotten........266,983
Örebro........274,223
Östergötland........392,390
Skaraborg........268,702
Södermanland........252,026
Stockholm........1,524,266
Uppsala........241,722
Värmland........284,615
Västerbotten........241,898
Västernorrland........267,895
Västmanland........259,670

Cities
Alingsås (29,109▲)........19,800
Angelholm (29,397▲)........16,700
Arvika (26,962▲)........13,600
Avesta (26,471▲)........18,600
Boden (28,770▲)........20,200
Bollnäs (27,683▲)........11,100
Borås........102,914
Borlänge........46,318
Enköping (32,286▲)........18,800
Eskilstuna........90,414
Eslöv (26,939▲)........14,000
Falkenberg (34,610▲)........14,800
Falun (50,079▲)........31,600
Gällivare (24,661▲)........8,500
Gävle........87,364
Göteborg (Gothenburg) (★665,000)........434,699
Halmstad (75,663▲)........50,400
Härnösand (27,616▲)........19,400
Hässleholm (48,751▲)........17,000
Helsingborg........101,370
Huddinge (★Stockholm)........66,038
Hudiksvall (37,336▲)........15,200
Järfälla (★Stockholm)........52,442
Jönköping........107,652
Kalmar (52,657▲)........32,200
Karlshamn (31,907▲)........17,400
Karlskoga........37,070
Karlskrona (60,270▲)........33,400
Karlstad........73,904
Katrineholm (32,308▲)........22,700
Kiruna........30,177
Koping (27,291▲)........19,700
Kristianstad (68,675▲)........31,300
Kristinehamn (27,166▲)........20,700
Kungsbacka (42,905▲)........13,400
Landskrona........37,027
Lidingö (★Stockholm)........37,390
Linköping........111,866
Ljungby (27,097▲)........13,400
Ludvika........31,976
Luleå........67,190
Lund........78,003
Malmö (★305,000)........235,111
Mariestad (24,377▲)........16,200
Mjölby (25,885▲)........12,700
Mölndal (★Göteborg)........47,692
Motala (41,945▲)........25,100
Nacka (★Stockholm)........56,825
Nässjö (31,891▲)........18,200
Norrköping........119,993
Norrtälje (40,400▲)........31,200
Nyköping (63,918▲)........31,000
Örebro........116,877
Örnsköldsvik (60,665▲)........29,600
Oskarshamn (28,021▲)........19,000
Östersund (55,440▲)........41,000
Piteå (38,146▲)........17,400
Ronneby (30,270▲)........12,000
Sandviken........43,139
Skellefteå (73,647▲)........29,800
Skövde (45,847▲)........30,200
Söderhamn (31,264▲)........14,200
Södertälje (★Stockholm)........79,396
Sollefteå (26,133▲)........8,900
Sollentuna (★Stockholm)........45,864
Solna (★Stockholm)........51,324
•STOCKHOLM (★1,384,310)........649,384
Sundyberg (★Stockholm)........25,676
Sundsvall (94,358▲)........52,500
Täby (★Stockholm)........46,142
Trelleborg (34,473▲)........22,300
Trollhättan........49,846
Uddevalla (46,139▲)........32,300
Umeå (79,930▲)........52,800
Uppsala........145,032
Vänersborg (34,613▲)........20,600
Varberg (43,829▲)........19,800
Värnamo (30,156▲)........15,700
Västerås........117,257
Västervik (41,303▲)........21,000
Växjö (63,763▲)........41,500
Vetlanda (28,714▲)........12,400
Visby (Gotland) (55,261▲)........20,200

SWITZERLAND / Schweiz/Suisse/Svizzera

1980 E........6,314,200
Aarau (★51,100)........15,900
Adliswil (★Zürich)........16,100
Allschwil (★Basel)........18,000
Altdorf........8,200
Appenzell........5,300
Arbon (★15,100)........11,500
Arosa (1970 C)........2,717
Baar (★Zug)........15,300
Baden (★67,300)........13,900
Basel (Bâle) (★575,000)........180,900
Bellinzona (★33,700)........17,200
BERN (BERNE) (★282,400).....141,300
Biel (Bienne) (★87,000)........56,800
Bolligen (★Bern)........32,500
Bülach........12,200
Burgdorf (★17,900)........14,900
Château d'Oex (1970 C)........3,203
Chiasso........8,900
Chur (Coire)........32,500
Davos........11,200
Delémont........11,600
Einsiedeln........9,700
Emmen (★Luzern)........22,800
Frauenfeld........18,600
Fribourg (Freiburg) (★51,800)....37,700
Genève (Geneva) (★425,000)...151,100
Glarus........5,800
Grenchen (★25,300)........16,800
Herisau........13,900
Illnau (★Zürich)........14,600
Interlaken (1970 C)........4,735
Köniz (★Bern)........34,400
Kreuzlingen........16,100
Kriens (★Luzern)........21,200
La Chaux-de-Fonds........38,100
Langenthal (★21,900)........13,400
Lausanne (★225,200)........128,800
Lauterbrunnen (1970 C)........3,431
Le Locle........12,600
Liestal (★Basel)........11,700
Locarno (★41,600)........15,100
Lugano (★69,100)........28,000
Luzern (Lucerne) (★156,400).....62,400
Martigny........11,100
Meiringen (1970 C)........3,759
Monthey........11,400
Montreux (★★Vevey)........20,200
Morges (★19,100)........13,300
Neuchâtel (Neuenburg) (★59,000)........34,900
Nyon........12,500
Olten (★47,200)........19,200
Opfikon (★Zürich)........11,200
Riehen (★Basel)........20,600
Rorschach (★23,000)........9,800
Sankt Gallen (St.-Gall) (★112,000)........73,800
Schaffhausen (Schaffhouse) (★51,300)........31,900
Schwyz........12,100
Sierre........14,200
Sion (Sitten)........23,400
Solothurn (Soleure) (★34,500)...15,600
Thun (Thoune) (★65,400)........37,000
Uster........23,000
Vernier (★Genève)........28,000
Vevey (★60,400)........15,700
Wädenswil........18,300
Wettingen (★Baden)........18,200
Wil (★21,500)........15,100
Winterthur (★106,800)........86,100
Wohlen (★15,700)........11,600
Yverdon (Iferten)........20,800
Zug (Zoug) (★52,200)........21,900
•Zürich (★780,000)........374,200

SYRIA / As-Sūrīyah

1978 E........8,401,100
Aleppo (Ḥalab)........878,000
Al-Ḥasakah........29,900
Al-Lādhiqīyah (Latakia)........204,000
Al-Qāmishlī (1970 C)........47,714
Ar-Raqqah........48,500
As-Suwaydā'........30,400
•DAMASCUS (DIMASHQ) (1979 E) (★1,550,000)........1,156,000
Dayr az-Zawr........99,100
Dūmā (★Damascus) (1970 C)....30,980
Ḥamāh........180,000
Ḥimṣ (Homs)........306,000
Idlib........52,600
Mukhayyam al-Yarmūk (★Damascus) (1970 C)........64,273

TAIWAN / T'aiwan

1977 E........16,813,127
Changhua (166,612▲)........129,000
Chiai........252,972
Chilung (Keelung)........345,392
Chungho (★T'aipei)........175,778
Chungli (Chunli) (180,689▲).....151,000
Chutung........52,000
Fengshan (Kaohsiunghsien) (★Kaohsiung)........177,982
Fengyüan (T'aichunghsien) (121,491▲)........94,000
Hsichih........51,000
Hsinchu........233,459
Hsinchuang (★T'aipei)........124,609
Hsintien (★T'aipei)........145,809
Hsinying (T'ainanhsien)........45,000
Hualien........101,010
Ilan (78,983▲)........66,000
Kangshan........58,000
Kaohsiung (★1,480,000)........1,172,977
Lotung........49,000
Lukang (Luchiang)........32,000
Makung (Penghuhsien)........23,000
Miaoli........66,000
Nant'ou........60,000
Panch'iao (T'aipeihsien) (★T'aipei)........314,848
Peikang........31,000
P'ingtung........182,114
Sanch'ung (★T'aipei)........292,909
Shulin (★T'aipei)........54,000
T'aichung........585,205
T'ainan........572,590
•T'AIPEI (★3,825,000)........2,196,237
T'aitung (111,647▲)........78,000
T'aoyüan........163,404
Touliu (Yünlin)........31,000
Yungho (★T'aipei)........162,731

TANZANIA

1978 C........17,557,000
Arusha........48,000
•DAR-ES-SALAAM........870,000
Dodoma (1970 E)........28,000
Iringa (1967 C)........21,746
Morogoro (1970 E)........30,000
Moshi........52,000
Mwanza........171,000
Tabora (1970 E)........23,000
Tanga........144,000
Ujiji (1967 C)........21,369
Zanzibar (1975 E)........80,000

THAILAND / Prathet Thai

1972 E........36,286,000
Ayutthaya........46,664
•BANGKOK (KRUNG THEP) (★3,375,000)........3,133,834
Ban Pong........22,036
Chachoengsao........27,071
Chiang Mai........93,353
Chon Buri........46,368
Hat Yai........57,255
Hua Hin........24,041
Khon Kaen........35,055
Lampang........42,007
Lop Buri........33,302
Nakhon Phanom........21,019
Nakhon Pathom........37,807
Nakhon Ratchasima........77,397
Nakhon Sawan........51,378
Nakhon Si Thammarat........50,761
Narathiwat........24,069
Nong Khai........24,680
Nonthaburi (★Bangkok)........25,654
Pattani........26,243
Phayao........22,217
Phet Buri........32,928
Phitsanulok........70,649
Phuket........38,493
Rat Buri........34,966
Samut Prakan (★Bangkok)........44,916
Samut Sakhon........39,982
Sara Buri........23,300
Songkhla........50,687
Suphan Buri........20,128
Surat Thani (Ban Don)........35,560
Surin........27,995
Trang........35,859
Ubon Ratchathani........52,236
Udon Thani........70,110
Warin Chamrap........25,850
Yala........39,983

TOGO

1977 E........2,348,000
•LOMÉ........229,400
Palimé........25,500
Sokodé........33,500

TONGA

1976 C........90,085
•NUKUALOFA........18,312

TRINIDAD & TOBAGO

1977 E........1,118,500
Arima (1970 C)........11,792
Débé (★Port of Spain) (1970 UE)........13,200
Point Fortin (1970 C)........7,738
•PORT OF SPAIN (★395,000)........42,950
Princess Town (1970 C)........7,784
San Fernando (★73,000)........36,650
San Juan (★Port of Spain) (1970 C)........30,802
Scarborough *(Tobago)* (1970 C)...1,724
Tunapuna (★Port of Spain) (1970 C)........11,984

TUNISIA / Tunisie

1975 C........5,588,209
Ariana (★Tunis)........47,833
Béja........39,226
Bizerte (Binzert)........62,856
Gabès........40,585
Gafsa........42,225
Hammam Lif (★Tunis)........35,634
Kairouan........54,546
Kasserine........22,594
La Goulette (★Tunis)........41,912
Le Bardo (★Tunis)........49,367
Menzel Bourguiba........42,111
Moknine........26,035
Monastir........26,759
Msaken........33,559
Nabeul........30,476
Sfax (★260,000)........171,297
Sousse........69,530
•TUNIS (★915,000)........550,404

TURKEY / Türkiye

1980 C........45,217,556
(Cities designated (E) are in Turkey in Europe)
Adana........568,513
Adapazarı........131,400
Adıyaman........55,030
Afyonkarahisar........73,832
Akhisar........60,061
Aksaray........65,306
Akşehir........40,418
Alaşehir........25,605
Alibeyköy (★İstanbul) (1975 C)...33,387
Amasya........48,010
ANKARA (★2,290,000)........2,203,729
Antakya (Antioch)........91,551
Antalya........176,446
Aydın........71,576
Bafra........50,167
Balıkesir........124,122
Bandırma........53,187
Batman........86,034
Bayburt........22,540
Bayrampaşa (E) (★İstanbul) (1975 C)........157,367
Bergama........34,386
Bolu........38,400
Bolvadin........30,733
Bornova (★İzmir)........54,965
Buca (★İzmir) (1975 C)........70,715
Burdur........44,750
Bursa........466,178
Çamdibi (★İzmir) (1975 C)........42,376
Çanakkale........39,943
Çankiri........35,040
Çarşamba........28,524
Ceyhan........57,097
Çorlu (E)........45,675
Çorum........76,020
Denizli........134,673
Diyarbakır........233,289
Düzce........37,659
Edirne (E)........71,927
Elâzığ........142,787
Ereğli *(Konya prov.)*........61,100
Ereğli *(Zonguldak prov.)*........50,096
Erzincan........73,335
Erzurum........190,121
Esenler (E) (★İstanbul) (1975 C)..49,379
Eskişehir........309,335
Gaziantep........371,000
Gebze (★İzmit)........58,212
Gelibolu (Gallipoli) (E)........14,554
Giresun........46,068
Gölcük........45,006
İnegöl........45,314
İskenderun (Alexandretta)........120,985
Isparta........91,544
•İstanbul (E) (★4,765,000)........2,853,539
İzmir (Smyrna) (★1,190,000)........753,749
İzmit (Kocaeli)........191,340
Kadirli........38,125
Kâğıthane (E) (★İstanbul) (1975 C)........164,448
Karabük........84,975
Karaköse (Ağrı)........41,103
Karaman........51,868
Kars........58,651
Kartal (★İstanbul)........67,627
Kastamonu........35,636
Kayseri........273,362
Keşan (E)........28,428
Kilis........58,686
Kırıkhan........47,688
Kırıkkale........175,235
Kırklareli (E)........36,183
Kırşehir........50,063
Konya........325,850
Kozan........42,410
Küçükçekmece (★İstanbul) (1975 C)........58,709
Kütahya........101,087
Lüleburgaz (E)........35,643
Malatya........184,390
Manisa........93,970
Maraş........177,919
Mardin........37,750
Mersin........215,300
Merzifon........32,031
Muğla........27,162
Muş........40,297
Mustafakemalpaşa........40,099
Nazilli........64,015
Nevşehir........37,106
Niğde........39,972
Nizip........39,267
Ödemiş........40,652
Ordu........52,080
Osmaniye........84,338
Polatlı........43,514
Reyhanli........30,843
Rize........41,740
Salihli........51,638
Samsun........198,266
Siirt........42,692
Silvan........44,412
Sinop........18,381
Sivas........173,831
Siverek........30,000
Söke........37,362
Tarsus........120,270
Tatvan........40,324
Tekirdağ (E)........51,327
Tire........32,242
Tokat........60,369
Trabzon........107,412
Turgutlu........55,575
Turhal........47,364
Urfa........148,434
Uşak........70,822
Uzunköprü (E)........27,706
Van........93,823
Viranşehir........41,934
Yozgat........36,220
Zile........30,066
Zonguldak (★195,000)........108,661

C Census. E Official estimate. UE Unofficial estimate.
L Population within municipal limits of year specified. • Largest city in country.

★ Population or designation of metropolitan area, including suburbs (see headnote).
▲ Population of an entire municipality, commune, or district, including rural area.
‡† Year of information specified at start of country.

TURKS & CAICOS IS.

1970 C 5,607
•GRAND TURK 2,287

UGANDA

1969 C 9,548,847
Arua 10,837
Bugembe 46,884
Entebbe 21,096
Fort Portal 7,949
Gulu 18,170
Jinja 52,509
Kabale 8,234
•KAMPALA 330,700
Lugazi 12,000
Masaka 12,987
Mbale 23,544
Soroti 12,398
Tororo 15,977

UNION OF SOVIET SOCIALIST REPUBLICS / Sojuz Sovetskich Socialističeskich Respublik

1980 E 264,486,000
UNION OF SOVIET SOCIALIST REPUBLICS IN EUROPE 172,022,000

Soviet Socialist Republics

Byelorussia (White Russia) 9,611,000
Estonia 1,474,000
Latvia 2,529,000
Lithuania 3,420,000
Moldavia 3,968,000
Russian Soviet Federated Socialist Republic (part) 101,067,000
Ukraine 49,953,000

Cities (1974 E, ‡1980 E)

Abdulino 25,000
Agryz 19,000
Akhtubinsk 44,000
Akhtyrka 43,000
Alatyr 46,000
Aleksandriya ‡84,000
Aleksandrov ‡61,000
Aleksin ‡68,000
Almetyevsk ‡111,000
Alytus ‡57,000
Andropov ‡241,000
Antratsit (★★Krasnyy Luch) ‡62,000
Apatity ‡64,000
Apsheronsk 33,000
Arkhangelsk ‡387,000
Armavir ‡163,000
Artemovsk ‡88,000
Arzamas ‡95,000
Astrakhan ‡465,000
Atkarsk 30,000
Avdeyevka (★Donetsk) 33,000
Azov ‡76,000
Bakhchisaray 20,000
Balakhna (★Gorkiy) 37,000
Balakleya 31,000
Balakovo ‡156,000
Balashikha (★Moscow) ‡119,000
Balashov ‡94,000
Baranovichi ‡135,000
Bataysk (★Rostov-na-Donu) ‡91,000
Belaya Kalitva 35,000
Belaya Tserkov ‡157,000
Belebey 39,000
Belgorod ‡248,000
Belgorod-Dnestrovskiy 37,000
Belorechensk 38,000
Beloretsk ‡72,000
Beltsy ‡128,000
Bendery ‡104,000
Berdichev ‡81,000
Berdyansk ‡124,000
Berezniki ‡186,000
Bezhetsk 30,000
Bobruysk ‡197,000
Bogoroditsk 32,000
Bogorodsk (★Gorkiy) 37,000
Bologoye 34,000
Bor (★Gorkiy) ‡63,000
Borislav 36,000
Borisoglebsk ‡67,000
Borispol' 36,000
Borisov ‡115,000
Borovichi ‡60,000
Brest ‡186,000
Brezhnev ‡319,000
Brovary (★Kiev) ‡60,000
Bryanka (★Stakhanov) ‡63,000
Bryansk ‡401,000
Bugulma ‡81,000
Buguruslan ‡54,000
Buy 28,000
Buynaksk 42,000
Buzuluk ‡77,000
Chapayevsk ‡85,000
Chaykovskij ‡71,000
Cheboksary ‡323,000
Chekhov ‡53,000
Cherepovets ‡274,000
Cherkassy ‡234,000
Cherkessk ‡92,000
Chernigov ‡245,000
Chernovtsy ‡221,000
Chernyakhovsk (Insterburg) 34,000
Chervonograd ‡56,000
Chistopol ‡65,000
Chusovoy ‡57,000
Daugavpils ‡117,000
Debaltsevo 37,000
Derbent ‡71,000
Dimitrov (★★Krasnoarmeysk) ‡59,000
Dimitrovgrad (Melekess) ‡108,000
Dmitrov ‡59,000
Dneprodzerzhinsk (★★Dnepropetrovsk) ‡253,000
Dnepropetrovsk (★1,460,000) ‡1,083,000
Dobropolye 31,000
Dolgoprudnyy (★Moscow) ‡66,000
Domodedovo (★Moscow) 39,000
Donetsk (*Donetsk obl.*) (★2,075,000) ‡1,032,000
Donetsk (*Rostov obl.*) 42,000
Donskoy (★Novomoskovsk) 34,000
Drogobych ‡68,000
Druzhkovka (★Kramatorsk) ‡66,000
Dubna ‡56,000
Dzerzhinsk (★Gorkiy) ‡260,000
Dzerzhinsk (★Gorlovka) 46,000
Dzhankoy 46,000
Elektrostal ‡141,000
Elista ‡72,000
Engels (★★Saratov) ‡165,000
Fastov ‡52,000
Feodosiya ‡78,000
Frolovo 38,000
Fryazino (★Moscow) 39,000
Furmanov 41,000
Galich 21,000
Gatchina (★Leningrad) ‡76,000
Gelendzhik 31,000
Georgiu-Dezh (Liski) ‡52,000
Georgiyevsk ‡55,000
Glazov ‡83,000
Glukhov 30,000
Gomel ‡393,000
Gorkiy (Gorki) (★1,900,000) ‡1,358,000
Gorlovka (★700,000) ‡337,000
Gorodets 35,000
Gremyachinsk 27,000
Grodno ‡202,000
Groznyy ‡377,000
Gryazi 42,000
Gubakha 32,000
Gubkin ‡65,000
Gudermes 34,000
Gukovo ‡69,000
Gusev 23,000
Gus-Khrustalnyy ‡72,000
Ilichevsk 43,000
Ingulets 35,000
Inta ‡51,000
Ishimbay ‡58,000
Ivano-Frankovsk ‡159,000
Ivanovo ‡466,000
Ivanteyevka (★Moscow) 41,000
Izberbash 20,000
Izhevsk ‡562,000
Izmail ‡84,000
Izyum ‡61,000
Jelgava ‡69,000
Jurmala (★Rīga) ‡62,000
Kagul 31,000
Kakhovka 35,000
Kalinin ‡416,000
Kaliningrad (★Moscow) ‡135,000
Kaliningrad (Königsberg) ‡361,000
Kaluga ‡270,000
Kalush ‡61,000
Kamenets-Podolskiy ‡86,000
Kamenka 32,000
Kamensk-Shakhtinskiy ‡72,000
Kamyshin ‡112,000
Kanash 46,000
Kandalaksha 43,000
Kapsukas 33,000
Kashira 42,000
Kasimov 34,000
Kaspiysk 42,000
Kaunas ‡377,000
Kazan (★1,050,000) ‡1,002,000
Kerch ‡158,000
Kharkov (★1,750,000) ‡1,464,000
Khartsyzsk (★Donetsk) ‡59,000
Khasavyurt ‡67,000
Kherson ‡324,000
Khimki (★Moscow) ‡120,000
Khmelnitskiy ‡179,000
Kiev (Kiyev) (★2,430,000) ‡2,192,000
Kimovsk 44,000
Kimry ‡58,000
Kinel' 40,000
Kineshma ‡102,000
Kirishi 34,000
Kirov (*Kirov obl.*) ‡392,000
Kirov (*Kaluga obl.*) 30,000
Kirovo-Chepetsk ‡74,000
Kirovograd ‡242,000
Kirovsk (*Murmansk obl.*) 40,000
Kirovsk (*Voroshilovgrad obl.*) (★Stakhanov) 40,000
Kishinev ‡519,000
Kislovodsk ‡102,000
Kizel 42,000
Klaipėda (Memel) ‡178,000
Klimovsk (★Moscow) ‡55,000
Klin ‡92,000
Klintsy ‡69,000
Kobrin 28,000
Kohtla-Järve ‡73,000
Kolchugino 43,000
Kolomna ‡149,000
Kolomyya ‡53,000
Kolpino (★Leningrad) ‡118,000
Kommunarsk (★Stakhanov) ‡120,000
Konakovo 33,000
Kondopoga 32,000
Konotop ‡84,000
Konstantinovka ‡113,000
Korosten ‡66,000
Kostroma ‡255,000
Kotel'nich 31,000
Kotlas ‡63,000
Kotovsk (*Odessa obl.*) 39,000
Kotovsk (*Tambov obl.*) 36,000
Kovel 40,000
Kovrov ‡144,000
Kramatorsk (★445,000) ‡180,000
Krasnoarmeysk (★155,000) ‡61,000
Krasnodar ‡572,000
Krasnodon 46,000
Krasnogorsk (★Moscow) ‡80,000
Krasnokamsk ‡56,000
Krasnyy Luch (★230,000) ‡107,000
Krasnyy Sulin 43,000
Kremenchug ‡212,000
Krichev 28,000
Krivoy Rog ‡657,000
Kronshtadt (★Leningrad) (1970 C) 39,477
Kropotkin ‡71,000
Krymsk (Krymskaya) 43,000
Kstovo (★Gorkiy) ‡60,000
Kudymkar (1975 E) 27,000
Kulebaki 46,000
Kumertau ‡54,000
Kungur ‡80,000
Kupyansk 34,000
Kurganinsk 38,000
Kursk ‡383,000
Kuybyshev (★1,440,000) ‡1,226,000
Kuznetsk ‡94,000
Labinsk ‡55,000
Leningrad (★5,360,000) ‡4,119,000
Leninogorsk ‡68,000
Lida ‡67,000
Liepāja ‡108,000
Lipetsk ‡405,000
Lisichansk (★365,000) ‡120,000
Livny 42,000
Lobnya (★Moscow) ‡53,000
Lomonosov (★Leningrad) 43,000
Lozovaya ‡55,000
Lubny ‡55,000
Luga 35,000
Lutsk ‡146,000
Lvov ‡676,000
Lysva ‡75,000
Lytkarino (★Moscow) 42,000
Lyubertsy (★Moscow) ‡162,000
Lyubotin 33,000
Lyudinovo 36,000
Makeyevka (★★Donetsk) ‡439,000
Makhachkala ‡261,000
Marganets ‡51,000
Marks 22,000
Maykop ‡130,000
Mednogorsk 36,000
Melitopol ‡163,000
Michurinsk ‡102,000
Mikhaylovka ‡59,000
Millerovo 37,000
Mineralnyye Vody ‡68,000
Minsk (★1,330,000) ‡1,295,000
Mogilev ‡300,000
Molodechno ‡74,000
Monchegorsk ‡53,000
Morshansk (1977 E) 50,000
•MOSCOW (MOSKVA) (★11,950,000) ‡7,915,000
Mozdok 33,000
Mozhga 41,000
Mozyr ‡75,000
Mtsensk 34,000
Mukachevo ‡74,000
Murmansk ‡388,000
Murom ‡116,000
Mytishchi (★Moscow) ‡143,000
Naberezhnyye Chelny see Brezhnev
Nalchik ‡211,000
Naro-Fominsk ‡57,000
Narva ‡74,000
Neftekamsk ‡72,000
Nevinnomyssk ‡106,000
Nezhin ‡71,000
Nikolayev ‡449,000
Nikopol ‡149,000
Nizhnekamsk ‡139,000
Noginsk ‡120,000
Novaya Kakhovka ‡54,000
Novgorod ‡192,000
Novocheboksarsk ‡89,000
Novocherkassk ‡185,000
Novo-Ekonomicheskoye (★★Krasnoarmeysk) (1970 C) 31,214
Novograd-Volynskiy 44,000
Novokuybyshevsk (★Kuybyshev) ‡110,000
Novomoskovsk (*Dnepropetrovsk obl.*) ‡70,000
Novomoskovsk (*Tula obl.*) (★370,000) ‡147,000
Novopolotsk ‡70,000
Novorossiysk ‡162,000
Novoshakhtinsk ‡105,000
Novo-Troitsk ‡97,000
Novovolynsk 44,000
Novozybkov 39,000
Obninsk ‡76,000
Odessa (★1,120,000) ‡1,057,000
Odintsovo (★Moscow) ‡104,000
Oktyabr'sk 33,000
Oktyabr'skiy ‡91,000
Onega 25,000
Ordzhonikidze (*Severo-Osetinsk obl.*) ‡283,000
Ordzhonikidze (*Dnepropetrovsk obl.*) 39,000
Orekhovo-Zuyevo (★200,000) ‡133,000
Orel ‡309,000
Orenburg ‡471,000
Orsha ‡113,000
Orsk ‡252,000
Otradnyy 46,000
Panevėžys ‡104,000
Pärnu ‡51,000
Pavlograd ‡111,000
Pavlovo ‡69,000
Pavlovskiy Posad ‡71,000
Pechora ‡57,000
Penza ‡490,000
Pereslavl-Zalesskiy 33,000
Pereval'sk (★Stakhanov) 32,000
Perm (★1,075,000) ‡1,008,000
Pervomaysk (★Stakhanov) (*Voroshilovgrad obl.*) 46,000
Pervomaysk (*Nikolayev obl.*) ‡73,000
Petrodvorets (★Leningrad) ‡74,000
Petrovsk 34,000
Petrozavodsk ‡238,000
Pinsk ‡93,000
Podolsk (★Moscow) ‡203,000
Polotsk ‡72,000
Poltava ‡282,000
Priluki ‡66,000
Prokhladnyy 44,000
Pskov ‡177,000
Pugachev 35,000
Pushkin (★Leningrad) ‡89,000
Pushkino ‡71,000
Pyatigorsk ‡112,000
Ramenskoye (★Moscow) ‡79,000
Rasskazovo 40,000
Rechitsa ‡62,000
Reutov (★Moscow) ‡62,000
Rēzekne 34,000
Rīga (★920,000) ‡843,000
Rodniki 30,000
Rogachëv 20,000
Romny ‡53,000
Roslavl ‡56,000
Rossosh' 38,000
Rostov 31,000
Rostov-na-Donu (★1,075,000) ‡946,000
Rovenki ‡62,000
Rovno ‡185,000
Rtishchevo 41,000
Rubezhnoye (★★Lisichansk) ‡66,000
Ruzayevka 44,000
Ryazan ‡462,000
Rybinsk see Andropov
Rybnitsa 39,000
Rzhev ‡69,000
Safonovo ‡53,000
Salavat ‡140,000
Salsk ‡58,000
Saransk ‡271,000
Sarapul ‡107,000
Saratov (★1,090,000) ‡864,000
Serdobsk 37,000
Serpukhov ‡141,000
Sevastopol ‡308,000
Severodonetsk (★★Lisichansk) ‡115,000
Severodvinsk (Molotovsk) ‡203,000
Severomorsk ‡51,000
Shakhtersk (★★Torez) ‡70,000
Shakhty ‡212,000
Shchekino ‡71,000
Shchelkovo (★Moscow) ‡101,000
Shebekino 36,000
Shepetovka 42,000
Shostka ‡82,000
Shumerlya 35,000
Shuya ‡72,000
Šiauliai ‡121,000
Sibay 40,000
Simferopol ‡307,000
Slantsy 42,000
Slavyansk (★★Kramatorsk) ‡141,000
Slavyansk-na-Kubani ‡55,000
Slobodskoy 36,000
Slutsk 39,000
Smela ‡63,000
Smolensk ‡305,000
Snezhnoye (★Torez) ‡67,000
Sochi ‡291,000
Sokol 48,000
Soligorsk ‡68,000
Solikamsk ‡102,000
Solnechnogorsk (★Moscow) 37,000
Solntsevo (★Moscow) ‡62,000
Sovetsk 40,000
Stakhanov (Kadiyevka) (★590,000) ‡108,000
Staraya Russa 37,000
Staryy Oskol ‡123,000
Stavropol ‡265,000
Sterlitamak ‡224,000
Stryy ‡56,000
Stupino ‡71,000
Sumy ‡233,000
Suzdal (1959 C) 9,000
Sverdlovsk ‡75,000
Svetlogorsk ‡56,000
Svetlovodsk (Kremges) 41,000
Syktyvkar ‡175,000
Syzran ‡168,000
Taganrog ‡278,000
Tallinn ‡436,000
Tambov ‡270,000
Tartu ‡106,000
Ternopol ‡149,000
Teykovo 42,000
Tikhoretsk ‡64,000
Tikhvin ‡61,000
Timashevsk 31,000
Tiraspol 142,000
Tokmak 39,000
Tolyatti (Stavropol) ‡517,000
Torez (Chistyakovo) (★295,000) ‡87,000
Torzhok (1977 E) 50,000
Tuapse ‡61,000
Tula (★615,000) ‡518,000
Tuymazy 42,000
Ufa (★1,000,000) ‡986,000
Uglich 37,000
Ukhta ‡89,000
Ulyanovsk ‡473,000
Uman ‡80,000
Uryupinsk 39,000
Ust'-Labinsk 38,000
Uzhgorod ‡93,000
Uzlovaya (★★Novomoskovsk) ‡65,000
Valuyki 30,000
Velikiye Luki ‡103,000
Velikiy Ustyug 38,000
Ventspils 44,000
Vichuga ‡52,000
Vidnoye 40,000
Vilnius ‡492,000
Vinnitsa ‡323,000
Vitebsk ‡303,000
Vladimir ‡301,000
Vogodonsk ‡109,000
Volgograd (Stalingrad) (★1,230,000) ‡939,000
Volkhov 48,000
Vologda ‡241,000
Volsk ‡65,000
Volzhsk ‡53,000
Volzhskiy (★Volgograd) ‡214,000
Vorkuta ‡101,000
Voronezh ‡796,000
Voroshilovgrad (Lugansk) ‡469,000
Voskresensk ‡77,000
Votkinsk ‡92,000
Voznesensk 39,000
Vyatskiye Polyany 35,000
Vyazma ‡52,000
Vyazniki 44,000
Vyborg ‡77,000
Vyksa ‡54,000
Vyshniy Volochek ‡71,000
Yalta ‡81,000
Yaroslavl ‡603,000
Yartsevo 39,000
Yasinovataya 39,000
Yefremov ‡53,000
Yegoryevsk ‡73,000
Yelabuga 35,000
Yelets ‡112,000
Yenakiyevo (★★Gorlovka) ‡115,000
Yessentuki ‡79,000
Yevpatoriya ‡95,000
Yeysk ‡72,000
Yoshkar-Ola ‡207,000
Yuryev-Polskiy 23,000
Zagorsk ‡108,000
Zaporozhye ‡799,000
Zavolzh'ye 38,000
Zelenodolsk ‡85,000
Zelenograd (★Moscow) ‡132,000
Zelenokumsk 30,000
Zhdanov ‡507,000
Zheleznodorozhnyy (★Moscow) ‡78,000
Zheleznogorsk ‡67,000
Zheltyye Vody ‡53,000
Zhigulevsk (1977 E) 50,000
Zhitomir ‡250,000
Zhlobin 29,000
Zhmerinka 38,000
Zhukovskiy ‡92,000

UNION OF SOVIET SOCIALIST REPUBLICS IN ASIA 92,464,000

Soviet Socialist Republics

Armenia 3,074,000
Azerbaidzhan 6,112,000
Georgia 5,041,000
Kazakh S.S.R. 14,858,000
Kirghiz S.S.R. 3,588,000
Russian Soviet Federated Socialist Republic (part) 37,298,000
Tadzhik S.S.R. 3,901,000
Turkmen S.S.R. 2,827,000
Uzbek S.S.R. 15,765,000

Cities (1974 E, ‡1980 E)

Abakan ‡133,000
Abay 41,000
Abovyan (★Yerevan) 32,000
Achinsk ‡117,000
Akhaltsikhe 19,000
Aktyubinsk ‡197,000
Alapayevsk (1977 E) 52,000
Aldan 20,000
Aleysk 37,000
Ali-Bayramly 38,000
Alma-Ata (★970,000) ‡928,000
Almalyk ‡102,000
Andizhan ‡233,000
Angarsk ‡241,000
Angren ‡108,000
Anzhero-Sudzhensk ‡107,000
Aral'sk 39,000
Arkalyk (1975 E) 35,000
Arsenyev ‡61,000
Artem ‡69,000
Artemovskiy 38,000
Arys 28,000
Asbest ‡80,000
Asha 38,000
Ashkhabad ‡318,000
Asino 31,000
Atbasar 39,000
Ayaguz 40,000
Baku (★1,800,000) ‡1,030,000
Balkhash ‡78,000
Barabinsk 37,000
Barnaul (★600,000) ‡542,000
Batumi ‡124,000
Bayram-Ali 36,000
Bekabad (Begovat) ‡69,000
Belogorsk ‡64,000
Belovo ‡112,000
Berdsk (★Novosibirsk) ‡68,000
Berezovskiy (★Sverdlovsk) 39,000
Berezovskiy (*Kemerovo obl.*) 37,000
Birobidzhan ‡70,000
Biysk ‡213,000
Blagoveshchensk ‡175,000
Bratsk ‡219,000
Bukhara ‡188,000
Chardzhou ‡143,000
Chebarkul' 42,000
Chelkar 20,000
Chelyabinsk (★1,215,000) ‡1,042,000
Cheremkhovo ‡75,000
Chernogorsk ‡73,000
Chimkent ‡327,000
Chirchik (★Tashkent) ‡134,000
Chita ‡308,000
Chu 35,000
Chust 31,000
Dudinka (1975 E) 23,000
Dushanbe ‡501,000
Dzhalal-Abad ‡55,000
Dzhambul ‡270,000
Dzhetygara 39,000
Dzhezkazgan ‡92,000
Dzhizak ‡71,000
Echmiadzin (★Yerevan) 37,000
Ekibastuz ‡74,000

C Census. E Official estimate. UE Unofficial estimate.
L Population within municipal limits of year specified. • Largest city in country.

★ Population or designation of metropolitan area, including suburbs (see headnote).
▲ Population of an entire municipality, commune, or district, including rural area.
‡† Year of information specified at start of country.

Fergana ‡177,000
Frunze ‡543,000
Gagra 22,000
Geokchay 30,000
Gori ‡57,000
Gorno-Altaysk (1975 E) 39,000
Gulistan (1975 E) 39,000
Guryev ‡134,000
Igarka 16,000
Irbit ‡52,000
Irkutsk ‡561,000
Ishim ‡62,000
Iskitim ‡60,000
Kachkanar 38,000
Kafan 31,000
Kagan 38,000
Kamen-na-Obi 40,000
Kamensk-Uralskiy ‡189,000
Kamyshlov 31,000
Kansk ‡100,000
Karaganda ‡577,000
Karpinsk 37,000
Karshi ‡113,000
Kartaly 44,000
Katta-Kurgan ‡54,000
Kemerovo ‡478,000
Kentau ‡52,000
Kerki (1967E) 18,000
Khabarovsk ‡538,000
Khanty-Mansiysk (1975 E) 26,000
Khiva 26,000
Khodzheyli 40,000
Kholmsk 43,000
Khorog (1975 E) 15,000
Kirovabad ‡237,000
Kirovakan ‡149,000
Kiselevsk (★★Prokopyevsk) ‡122,000
Kokand ‡154,000
Kokchetav ‡106,000
Komsomolsk-na-Amure ‡269,000
Kopeysk (★Chelyabinsk) ‡146,000
Korkino ‡63,000
Korsakov 40,000
Krasnokamensk 54,000
Krasnotur'insk ‡61,000
Krasnoufimsk 40,000
Krasnouralsk 40,000
Krasnovodsk ‡53,000
Krasnoyarsk ‡807,000
Kuba 19,000
Kulyab ‡57,000
Kurgan ‡316,000
Kurgan-Tyube 39,000
Kushva 43,000
Kustanay ‡169,000
Kutaisi ‡197,000
Kuybyshev 44,000
Kyakhta 16,000
Kyshtym 39,000
Kyzyl ‡67,000
Kyzyl-Kiya 33,000
Kzyl-Orda ‡159,000
Leninabad ‡132,000
Leninakan ‡210,000
Leninogorsk ‡54,000
Leninsk 31,000
Leninsk-Kuznetskiy ‡133,000
Lenkoran 38,000
Lesozavodsk 38,000
Magadan ‡124,000
Magnitogorsk ‡410,000
Margelan ‡112,000
Mariinsk 40,000
Mary ‡76,000
Mezhdurechensk ‡93,000
Miass ‡152,000
Mingechaur ‡61,000
Minusinsk ‡61,000
Myski 38,000
Nakhichevan-na-Arakse (1975 E) 37,000
Nakhodka ‡136,000
Namangan ‡234,000
Naryn (1975 E) 26,000
Navoy ‡86,000
Nazarovo ‡55,000
Nazyvayevsk 15,000
Nebit-Dag ‡73,000
Nefteyugansk 51,000
Nev'yansk 31,000
Nikolayevsk-na-Amure 33,000
Nizhneudinsk 42,000
Nizhnevartovsk ‡122,000
Nizhniy Tagil ‡400,000
Norilsk ‡182,000
Novoaltaysk (★Barnaul) ‡50,000
Novokazalinsk (1970 C) 34,815
Novokuznetsk ‡545,000
Novosibirsk (★1,460,000) ‡1,328,000
Nukus ‡113,000
Omsk (★1,040,000) ‡1,028,000
Osh ‡173,000
Osinniki ‡60,000
Partizansk (Suchan) 49,000
Pavlodar ‡281,000
Pervouralsk ‡130,000
Petropavlovsk ‡209,000
Petropavlovsk-Kamchatskiy ‡219,000
Polevskoy ‡64,000
Poti (1977 E) 54,000
Prokopyevsk (★395,000) ‡266,000
Przhevalsk ‡52,000
Razdan 33,000
Revda ‡63,000
Rezh 34,000
Rubtsovsk ‡158,000
Rudnyy ‡111,000
Rustavi (★Tbilisi) ‡132,000
Rybachye 33,000
Samarkand ‡481,000
Saran ‡56,000
Satka 44,000
Semipalatinsk ‡286,000
Serov ‡101,000
Shadrinsk ‡82,000
Shakhtinsk ‡51,000
Shchuchinsk 46,000
Sheki (Nukha) 44,000
Shevchenko ‡116,000
Spassk-Dalniy ‡53,000
Sukhumi ‡116,000
Sumgait (★Baku) ‡196,000
Surgut ‡121,000
Sverdlovsk (★1,450,000) ‡1,225,000
Svobodnyy ‡75,000
Taldy-Kurgan ‡91,000
Tashauz ‡87,000
Tashkent (★2,015,000) ‡1,816,000
Tavda 47,000
Tayshet 35,000
Tbilisi (★1,240,000) ‡1,080,000
Temirtau ‡215,000
Termez ‡58,000
Tobolsk ‡64,000
Tokmak ‡60,000
Tomsk ‡431,000
Troitsk ‡83,000
Tselinograd (Akmolinsk) ‡237,000
Tskhinvali (1975 E) 34,000
Tulun ‡52,000
Turkestan ‡69,000
Tyumen ‡369,000
Ulan-Ude ‡305,000
Uralsk ‡170,000
Ura-Tyube 36,000
Urgench ‡103,000
Usolye-Sibirskoye ‡104,000
Ussuriysk ‡148,000
Ust-Ilimsk ‡76,000
Ust-Kamenogorsk ‡280,000
Ust-Kut ‡51,000
Verkhniy Ufaley 38,000
Verkhnyaya Pyshma (★Sverdlovsk) 40,000
Verkhnyaya Salda ‡55,000
Vladivostok ‡558,000
Yakutsk ‡155,000
Yangi-Yul ‡64,000
Yerevan (★1,155,000) ‡1,036,000
Yermak 40,000
Yurga ‡80,000
Yuzhno-Sakhalinsk ‡143,000
Zima (1977 E) 51,000
Zlatoust ‡199,000
Zugdidi 41,000
Zyryanovsk ‡52,000

UNITED ARAB EMIRATES / Ittiḥād al-Imārāt al-'Arabīyah

1968 C 180,200

ABU DHABI (ABŪ ẒABY) (1973 E) 50,000
'Ajmān 3,725
Al Fujayrah 760
Ash Shāriqah 19,200
•Dubai (Dubayy) (1970 E) 60,000
Ra's al Khaymah 5,300
Umm al Qaywayn 2,900

UNITED KINGDOM

1979 E 55,880,000

Political Divisions

ENGLAND 46,396,100
WALES 2,774,700
SCOTLAND 5,167,000
NORTHERN IRELAND 1,542,200

ENGLAND

Metropolitan Counties

Greater London 6,877,100
Greater Manchester 2,648,300
South York 1,301,300
Tyne & Wear 1,155,900
West Midlands 2,696,000
West York 2,064,100

Non-metropolitan Counties

Avon 924,200
Bedford 498,800
Berks 682,000
Buckingham 535,800
Cambridge 579,300
Cheshire 926,500
Cleveland 568,600
Cornwall & Isles of Scilly 419,300
Cumbria 469,900
Derby 898,300
Devon 952,100
Dorset 591,100
Durham 603,200
East Sussex 654,600
Essex 1,446,700
Gloucester 497,100
Hampshire 1,459,500
Hereford & Worcester 617,900
Hertford 952,000
Humberside 849,600
Isle of Wight 115,300
Kent 1,456,100
Lancashire 1,369,700
Leicester 836,300
Lincoln 533,800
Merseyside 1,531,600
Norfolk 686,300
Northampton 523,300
Northumberland 289,800
North York 663,200
Nottingham 974,100
Oxford 542,100
Shropshire 369,500
Somerset 415,500
Stafford 999,900
Suffolk 597,600
Surrey 993,700
Warwick 468,900
West Sussex 643,800
Wilts 516,400

Cities *(1979 E or ‡1973 E)

Abingdon (★Oxford) ‡20,130
Accrington (Hyndburn) (★★Blackburn) 79,400
Adur (★Brighton) 57,700
Aldershot (Rushmoor) (★London) 81,000
Aldridge-Brownhills (Walsall) *‡89,370*
Andover ‡27,620
Ashford ‡36,380
Ashton-under-Lyne (Tameside) (★★Manchester) 218,500
Aycliffe (1971 C) 20,190
Aylesbury ‡41,420
Banbury ‡31,060
Barnsley 221,800
Barnstaple ‡17,820
Barrow-in-Furness 71,100
Basildon (★London) 148,200
Basingstoke ‡60,910
Bath 83,900
Batley (★Leeds) ‡41,630
Battle (1971 C) 4,987
Bebington (Wirral) *‡62,500*
Bedford ‡74,390
Bedworth (Nuneaton) *‡41,600*
Beeston & Stapleford (★Nottingham) ‡65,360
Benfleet (Castle Point) (★London) 84,400
Berkhamsted (★London) ‡15,920
Berwick-upon-Tweed ‡11,610
Bexhill-on-Sea ‡34,680
Birkenhead (Wirral) (★Liverpool) 342,300
Birmingham (★2,660,000) 1,033,900
Bishop Auckland ‡32,940
Bishop's Stortford (★London) ‡21,720
Blackburn (★221,900) 142,500
Blackpool (★275,000) 145,400
Bletchley ‡33,450
Blyth (Blyth Valley) 75,700
Blyth Valley see Blyth
Bodmin ‡10,430
Bognor Regis ‡34,620
Bolton (★★Manchester) 260,100
Bootle (★Liverpool) ‡71,160
Boston ‡26,700
Bournemouth (★315,000) 144,200
Bracknell (★London) (1971 C) 33,953
Bradford (★★Leeds) 461,600
Bradford-on-Avon ‡8,310
Braintree ‡26,300
Brentwood (★London) ‡58,690
Bridgwater ‡26,700
Bridlington ‡26,920
Brighouse (★Halifax) ‡35,320
Brighton (★425,000) 152,700
Bristol (★635,000) 408,000
Broadstairs and St. Peters ‡21,670
Bromsgrove (★Birmingham) ‡41,430
Broxbourne see Cheshunt
Burgess Hill (★London) ‡20,030
Burnham-on-Sea ‡12,690
Burnley (★160,000) 92,300
Burton-upon-Trent ‡49,480
Bury (★★Manchester) 178,600
Bury St. Edmunds ‡26,800
Buxton ‡20,050
Camborne-Redruth ‡43,970
Cambridge 101,600
Cannock (Cannock Chase) (★Birmingham) 83,600
Cannock Chase see Cannock
Canterbury ‡34,510
Carlisle ‡70,930
Carlton (Gedling) (★Nottingham) 102,800
Castleford (★Leeds) ‡37,650
Castle Point see Benfleet
Caterham & Warlingham (★London) ‡35,840
Chatham (Medway) (★London) 147,400
Cheadle and Gatley (Stockport) *‡62,460*
Chelmsford (★London) ‡58,320
Cheltenham 85,000
Chertsey (Runnymede) (★London) 72,800
Chesham (★London) ‡20,830
Cheshunt (Broxbourne) (★London) 79,200
Chester ‡61,370
Chesterfield (★127,000) 96,300
Chester-le-Street (★Newcastle) ‡20,720
Chichester ‡20,940
Chigwell (★London) ‡54,220
Chippenham ‡18,550
Chorley (★★Preston) ‡31,800
Christchurch (★Bournemouth) 38,600
Cirencester ‡14,500
Clacton-on-Sea ‡39,380
Cleethorpes (★Grimsby) ‡37,200
Clevedon ‡15,140
Coalville ‡28,740
Colchester ‡79,600
Consett (★Newcastle) ‡35,080
Corby 53,000
Coventry (★655,000) 339,300
Cowes ‡19,190
Crawley (★London) 71,800
Crewe ‡50,450
Crosby (★Liverpool) ‡56,750
Cuckfield (★London) ‡26,500
Darlington ‡85,120
Dartford (★London) ‡44,130
Dartmouth ‡6,720
Dawley ‡30,720
Deal ‡26,840
Derby (★270,000) 215,900
Dewsbury (★★Leeds) ‡50,560
Doncaster (★160,000) ‡81,530
Dorchester ‡13,880
Dorking (★London) ‡22,410
Dover ‡34,160
Dronfield (★Sheffield) ‡20,000
Dudley (★★Birmingham) 296,000
Dunstable (★Luton) ‡32,090
Durham ‡29,490
Eastbourne 73,100
East Grinstead (★London) ‡19,420
Eastleigh (★Southampton) ‡46,340
East Retford ‡18,260
Ellesmere Port (★Liverpool) ‡63,870
Elmbridge see Walton and Weybridge
Ely ‡10,630
Epsom and Ewell (★London) 70,500
Esher (Elmbridge) *‡63,970*
Eton (★London) ‡4,950
Evesham ‡14,090
Exeter 95,600
Exmouth ‡26,840
Falmouth ‡17,530
Fareham (★Portsmouth) 85,000
Farnham (★London) ‡33,140
Faversham ‡15,010
Felixstowe ‡19,460
Fleet (★London) ‡22,930
Fleetwood (★★Blackpool) ‡30,070
Folkestone ‡45,610
Formby (★Liverpool) ‡24,850
Frimley & Camberley (★London) ‡47,390
Frome ‡13,780
Gainsborough ‡17,440
Gateshead (★Newcastle) 212,200
Gedling see Carlton
Gillingham (★London) 92,800
Glastonbury ‡6,580
Glossop (★Manchester) ‡24,820
Gloucester (★115,000) 91,300
Goole ‡17,920
Gosport (★Portsmouth) 79,400
Grantham ‡27,830
Gravesend (Gravesham) (★London) 95,900
Gravesham see Gravesend
Great Yarmouth ‡49,410
Grimsby (★145,000) 91,900
Guildford (★London) ‡58,470
Halesowen (Dudley) *‡54,120*
Halifax (★173,000) ‡88,580
Haltemprice (★Hull) ‡54,850
Halton see Widnes
Harlow (★London) 79,100
Harrogate ‡64,620
Hartlepool (★★Middlesbrough) 95,100
Harwich ‡15,280
Hastings 74,200
Havant (★Portsmouth) 116,100
Haverhill ‡14,550
Heanor ‡24,590
Hemel Hempstead (★London) ‡71,150
Hemsworth ‡14,680
Henley-on-Thames ‡11,860
Hereford 46,800
Herne Bay ‡26,510
Hertford (★London) ‡20,760
Hertsmere (★London) 87,800
Hexham ‡9,820
High Wycombe ‡61,190
Hinckley (★★Coventry) ‡49,310
Hitchin ‡29,190
Horsham (★London) ‡26,770
Hove (★Brighton) 87,800
Hucknall (★Nottingham) ‡27,110
Huddersfield (★209,000) ‡130,060
Huntingdon & Godmanchester ‡17,200
Huyton-with-Roby (Knowsley) (★Liverpool) 179,700
Hyndburn see Accrington
Hythe ‡12,210
Ilkeston (★Nottingham) ‡33,690
Ipswich 118,900
Keighley (Bradford) *‡56,040*
Kendal ‡22,440
Kenilworth (★Coventry) ‡19,730
Keswick ‡4,790
Kettering ‡44,480
Kidderminster ‡49,960
King's Lynn ‡29,990
Kingston-upon-Hull (Hull) (★350,000) 274,500
Kingswood (★Bristol) 82,100
Kirkby (Knowsley) *‡59,100*
Knowsley see Huyton-with-Roby
Lancaster (★100,000) ‡50,570
Leamington Spa (★★Coventry) ‡44,950
Leatherhead (★London) ‡40,830
Leeds (★1,540,000) 724,300
Leek ‡19,460
Leicester (★480,000) 276,600
Leighton-Linslade ‡22,590
Letchworth ‡31,520
Lewes ‡14,170
Leyland (South Ribble) (★Preston) 96,100
Lichfield ‡23,690
Lincoln 71,900
Littlehampton ‡20,320
Liverpool (★1,535,000) 520,200
•LONDON (★11,050,000) 6,877,100
Longbenton (North Tyneside) *‡50,120*
Long Eaton (★Nottingham) ‡33,560
Loughborough ‡49,010
Lowestoft ‡53,260
Ludlow (1971 C) 7,466
Luton (★215,000) 160,300
Lymington ‡36,760
Lytham St. Annes (★Blackpool) ‡42,120
Macclesfield ‡45,420
Maidenhead (★London) ‡48,210
Maidstone ‡72,110
Malvern ‡30,420
Manchester (★2,800,000) 479,100
Mansfield (★198,000) ‡58,450
Margate ‡50,290
Market Harborough ‡15,230
Marlborough ‡6,370
Matlock ‡20,300
Medway see Chatham
Melton Mowbray ‡20,680
Middlesbrough (★580,000) 153,000
Middleton (Rochdale) *‡53,340*
Morecambe [& Heysham] (★★Lancaster) ‡42,010
Morley (Leeds) *‡44,790*
Nelson (★★Burnley) ‡31,220
Newark-upon-Trent ‡24,760
Newbury ‡24,850
Newcastle-under-Lyme (★★Stoke-on-Trent) ‡75,940
Newcastle-upon-Tyne (★1,295,000) 287,300
Newmarket ‡13,370
Newport ‡22,430
Newton Abbot ‡19,940
Northampton 154,900
North Tyneside see Tynemouth
Northwich ‡17,710
Norwich (★220,000) 119,300
Nottingham (★645,000) 278,600
Nuneaton (★★Coventry) 110,300
Oadby and Wigston (★Leicester) 52,300
Oakengates ‡17,340
Oakham ‡7,280
Oldham (★★Manchester) 223,500
Ormskirk (★Liverpool) ‡28,860
Oxford (★240,000) 122,400
Penrith ‡11,400
Penzance ‡19,360
Peterborough ‡72,270
Peterlee (1971 C) 21,836
Plymouth (★295,000) 255,500
Poole (★★Bournemouth) 115,500
Portsmouth (★490,000) 191,000
Preston (★245,000) 126,200
Queenborough-in-Sheppey ‡31,550
Ramsgate ‡40,090
Rawtenstall ‡20,950
Rayleigh (★London) ‡26,740
Reading (★200,000) 138,400
Redditch (★Birmingham) 64,300
Reigate and Banstead (★London) 114,000
Rickmansworth (★London) ‡29,030
Ripon ‡12,580
Rochdale (★★Manchester) 209,000
Rochester (Medway) (★London) ‡56,030
Rotherham (★★Sheffield) 248,800
Rugby ‡60,380
Runnymede see Chertsey
Rushden ‡21,840
Rushmoor see Aldershot
Ryde ‡23,170
Rye ‡4,530
Saint Albans (★London) 124,300
St. Austell [with Fowey] ‡32,710
St. Helens 188,700
Sale (Trafford) *‡59,060*
Salford (★Manchester) 252,600
Salisbury ‡35,460
Sandwell see Smethwick
Sandwich ‡4,420
Scarborough ‡43,300
Scunthorpe 67,200
Seaford ‡18,020
Seaham (★Newcastle) ‡22,470
Selby ‡11,590
Sevenoaks (★London) ‡18,160
Sheffield (★705,000) 544,200
Shrewsbury ‡56,120
Sittingbourne & Milton ‡32,830
Skelmersdale [& Holland] (★Manchester) ‡35,850
Slough (★London) 98,400
Smethwick (Sandwell) (★Birmingham) 306,900
Solihull (★Birmingham) 198,300
Southampton (★410,000) 207,800
Southend-on-Sea (★London) 154,700
Southport (★★Liverpool) ‡86,030
South Ribble see Leyland
South Shields (South Tyneside) (★★Newcastle) 162,600
South Tyneside see South Shields
Spenborough (★Leeds) ‡41,460
Spennymoor ‡19,050
Stafford ‡54,860
Staines (Spelthorne) (★London) 93,500
Stamford ‡14,980
Stanley (★Newcastle) ‡42,280
Stevenage 73,100
Stockport (★Manchester) 291,700
Stockton-on-Tees (★★Middlesbrough) 171,800
Stoke-on-Trent (★445,000) 257,200
Stourbridge (Dudley) *‡56,530*
Stratford-on-Avon ‡20,080
Stretford (Trafford) (★Manchester) 224,000
Stroud ‡19,600
Sudbury ‡8,860
Sunderland (★★Newcastle) 300,800
Sutton Coldfield (Birmingham) *‡83,630*
Sutton-in-Ashfield (★★Mansfield) ‡40,330
Swadlincote ‡21,060
Swindon (Thamesdown) 143,800
Tameside see Ashton-under-Lyne
Tamworth 60,300
Taunton ‡37,570
Tewkesbury ‡9,210
Thamesdown see Swindon
Thetford ‡15,690
Thornton Cleveleys (★Blackpool) ‡27,090
Thurrock (★London) 127,100
Tiverton ‡16,190
Todmorden ‡14,540
Tonbridge (★London) ‡31,410
Torquay (Torbay) 108,700
Trafford see Stretford

(England continued)

C Census. E Official estimate. UE Unofficial estimate.
L Population within municipal limits of year specified. • Largest city in country.
★ Population or designation of metropolitan area, including suburbs (see headnote).
▲ Population of an entire municipality, commune, or district, including rural area.
‡† Year of information specified at start of country.
* Italicized place names are now a part of the city shown in parentheses following the place name. These changes are part of the April 1974 reorganization of local administrative areas.

(England continued)

Trowbridge....‡20,120
Truro....‡15,690
Tunbridge Wells....‡44,800
Tynemouth (North Tyneside) (★Newcastle)....193,000
Ulverston....‡12,370
Wakefield (★★Leeds)....‡58,490
Wallasey (Wirral)....‡94,520
Walsall (★★Birmingham)....263,400
Walton and Weybridge (Elmbridge) (★London)....110,000
Wansbeck....61,000
Warrington....168,200
Warwick (★★Coventry)....‡17,870
Watford (★London)....76,500
Wellingborough....‡39,570
Wells....‡8,960
Welwyn Garden City (★London)....‡39,900
West Bridgford (★Nottingham)....‡28,340
West Bromwich (Sandwell)....‡162,740
Weston-super-Mare....‡51,960
Weymouth and Portland....57,700
Whitby....‡12,710
Whitehaven....‡26,260
Whitstable....‡26,980
Widnes (Halton)....120,700
Wigan (★★Manchester)....311,200
Wilmslow (★Manchester)....‡31,250
Winchester....‡31,070
Windermere....‡7,860
Windsor (New Windsor) (★London)....‡29,660
Winsford....‡26,920
Wirral see Birkenhead
Woking (★London)....80,500
Wokingham....‡22,390
Wolverhampton (★★Birmingham)....258,200
Worcester....75,000
Workington....‡28,260
Worksop....‡36,590
Worthing (★★Brighton)....90,600
Yeovil....‡26,180
York (★140,000)....100,900

WALES

Counties

Clwyd....385,100
Dyfed....325,600
Gwent....435,900
Gwynedd....226,300
Mid Glamorgan....537,500
Powys....107,100
South Glamorgan....390,600
West Glamorgan....366,600

Cities (1973 E)

Aberdare....38,030
Abertillery (★Newport)....20,550
Aberystwyth....10,900
Bangor....16,030
Barry (★Cardiff)....42,780
Brecon....6,460
Bridgend....14,690
Caernarfon....8,840
Caerphilly (★Cardiff)....42,190
•CARDIFF (1979 E) (★625,000)....282,000
Carmarthen....12,860
Colwyn Bay....25,370
Ebbw Vale....25,670
Flint....15,070
Islwyn (★Newport) (1979 E)....63,400
Llandudno....17,700
Llanelli....25,870
Merthyr Tydfil....53,680
Milford Haven....13,960
Monmouth....7,000
Neath (★★Swansea)....27,280
Newport (1979 E) (★310,000)....132,800
Pembroke....14,570
Pontypool (Torfaen) (★★Newport) (1979 E)....90,400
Pontypridd (★Cardiff)....34,180
Port Talbot (★132,000)....50,200
Prestatyn....15,480
Rhondda (★★Cardiff) (1979 E)....81,800
Rhyl....22,150
Swansea (1979 E) (★270,000)....186,900
Torfaen see Pontypool
Wrexham....39,530

SCOTLAND

Regions (1979 E)

Borders....99,938
Central....271,177
Dumfries and Galloway....142,547
Fife....340,170
Grampian....469,168
Highland....190,507
Lothian....750,728
Orkney (Island Area)....18,134
Shetland (Island Area)....22,111
Strathclyde....2,431,101
Tayside....401,661
Western Isles (Island Area)....29,758

Cities (‡1979 E or 1974 E)

Aberdeen....‡209,189
Airdrie (Monklands) (★Glasgow)....38,833
Alloa....13,498
Arbroath....23,207
Ardrossan (★★Irvine)....11,166
Ayr (★97,000)....47,991
Bearsden and Milngavie (★Glasgow)....‡38,812
Clydebank (★Glasgow)....‡52,835
Cumbernauld (★Glasgow)....‡49,300
Dumbarton (★Glasgow)....25,440
Dumfries....29,431
Dundee....‡190,793
Dunfermline (★124,893)....53,418
East Kilbride (★Glasgow)....‡76,000
EDINBURGH (★635,000)....‡455,126
Elgin....17,589
Falkirk (★142,058)....36,589
Forfar....11,395
•Glasgow (★1,830,000)....‡794,316
Glenrothes (★★Kirkcaldy)....‡36,500
Grangemouth (★★Falkirk)....24,347
Hamilton (★Glasgow)....‡107,490
Hawick....16,378
Helensburgh (★Glasgow)....13,956
Inverclyde (Greenock)....‡102,598
Inverness....36,595
Irvine (★97,000)....‡57,900
Johnstone (★Glasgow)....23,603
Kilmarnock (★82,000)....50,318
Kirkcaldy (★148,028)....50,063
Kirkintilloch (★Glasgow)....26,845
Kirkwall....4,814
Lerwick....6,307
Livingston....‡35,900
Monklands (Coatbridge)....‡109,645
Montrose....10,112
Motherwell (★Glasgow)....‡150,857
Oban....6,410
Paisley (Renfrew) (★Glasgow)....94,025
Perth....44,066
Peterhead....14,994
Port Glasgow (Inverclyde)....22,278
Prestwick (★Ayr)....13,138
Renfrew (★★Glasgow)....‡214,534
St. Andrews....13,137
Stirling (★58,000)....29,818
Stranraer....10,170
Thurso....9,107
Wick....7,842

NORTHERN IRELAND

Cities (1971 C)

Armagh....13,606
•BELFAST (1978 E) (★710,000)....354,400
Castlereagh (★Belfast) (1978 E)....63,900
Enniskillen....9,679
Larne....18,482
Lisburn (★Belfast)....31,836
Londonderry (1973 E) (★87,000)....51,200
Lurgan (★59,000)....25,431
Newry....20,279
Newtownabbey (★Belfast) (1978 E)....75,000
North Down (Bangor) (★Belfast) (1978 E)....61,500
Omagh....14,594
Portadown (★★Lurgan)....22,207

UPPER VOLTA / Haute-Volta

1977 E....6,390,000

Bobo Dioulasso....120,000
Koudougou....38,000
•OUAGADOUGOU....180,000
Ouahigouya....27,000

URUGUAY

1975 C....2,763,964

Artigas....29,256
Canelones (1963 C)....14,180
Colonia del Sacramento (1963 C)....12,839
Dolores (1963 C)....12,483
Durazno....25,811
Florida....25,030
Fray Bentos (1963 C)....20,755
La Paz (★Montevideo) (1963 C)....13,204
Las Piedras (★Montevideo)....53,983
Maldonado (1963 C)....15,361
Melo....38,260
Mercedes....34,667
Minas....35,433
•MONTEVIDEO (★1,350,000)....1,229,748
Paysandú....62,412
Rivera....49,013
Rocha (1963 C)....19,063
Salto....71,881
San Carlos (1963 C)....13,663
San José de Mayo....28,427
Santa Lucía (1963 C)....12,630
Tacuarembó....34,157
Treinta y Tres....25,757
Trinidad (1963 C)....15,460

VANUATU

1979 C....112,596

•VILA (★14,801)....10,158

VATICAN CITY / Città del Vaticano

1977 E....723

VENEZUELA

1971 C....10,721,522

Acarigua....56,743
Altagracia de Orituco....18,717
Anaco....29,003
Araure....22,466
Bachaquero....17,896
Barcelona....78,201
Barinas....56,329
Barquisimeto....330,815
Baruta (★Caracas)....121,066
Boconó....15,915
Cabimas....118,037
Cagua....29,601
Calabozo....38,360
Caraballeda (★Caracas)....20,725
•CARACAS (★2,475,000)....1,658,500
Caripito....19,053
Carora....36,115
Carúpano....50,935
Catia La Mar (★Caracas)....62,200
Chacao (★Caracas)....78,528
Chivacoa....19,210
Ciudad Bolívar....103,728
Ciudad Guayana (Santo Tomé de Guayana)....143,540
Ciudad Ojeda (Lagunillas)....83,083
Coro....68,701
Cumaná....119,751
El Tigre....49,801
El Tocuyo....19,351
El Vigía....20,970
Guacara....38,793
Guanare....34,148
Guarenas (★Caracas)....33,374
Guatire (★Caracas)....18,604
Güigüe....18,067
La Guaira (★Caracas)....20,344
La Victoria....40,731
Los Dos Caminos (★Caracas)....59,211
Los Teques (★Caracas)....63,106
Machiques....18,898
Maiquetía (★Caracas)....59,238
Maracaibo....651,574
Maracay....255,134
Mariara....24,284
Maturín....98,188
Mérida....74,214
Morón....19,451
Ocumare del Tuy....24,229
Palo Negro....19,173
Petare (★Caracas)....227,727
Porlamar....31,985
Pozuelos....44,011
Puerto Cabello....72,103
Puerto la Cruz....63,276
Punta Cardón....18,182
Punto Fijo....55,483
San Antonio del Táchira....20,342
San Carlos....21,029
San Carlos del Zulia....26,762
San Cristobal....151,717
San Felipe....42,905
San Fernando de Apure....38,960
San José de Guanipa....22,530
San Juan de Colón....16,615
San Juan de los Morros....38,265
San Mateo....17,389
Táriba....15,683
Trujillo....25,921
Tucupita....21,417
Turmero....43,832
Upata....22,793
Valencia....367,171
Valera....76,740
Valle de la Pascua....36,809
Villa de Cura....27,832
Villa del Rosario....17,491
Yaritagua....21,363
Zaraza....15,480

VIETNAM / Viet-nam Dan-chu Cong-hoa

1967 E....37,073,000

Bac-ninh (1960 C)....22,520
Ban-me-thuot....37,500
Bien-hoa....52,200
Cam-pha (1971 E)....90,000
Cam-ranh....46,600
Can-tho....61,100
Chau-phu (1971 E)....40,400
Da-lat (1971 E)....86,600
Da-nang (1971 E)....437,700
Gia-dinh (★Saigon) (1968 E)....151,100
Ha-dong (1960 C)....25,001
Hai-duong (1960 C)....24,752
Hai-phong (1971 E) (650,000▲)....400,000
HANOI (1971 E)....1,600,000
•Ho Chi Minh City (Than-pho Ho Chi Minh) (Saigon) (1971 E) (★2,750,000)....1,804,900
Hon-gai (1960 C)....35,412
Hue (1971 E)....199,900
Khanh-hung....40,300
Long-xuyen....45,800
My-tho....62,700
Nam-dinh (1960 C)....86,132
Nha-trang....59,600
Phan-rang....21,900
Phan-thiet....58,300
Phu-cuong (1971 E)....34,400
Phu-vinh (1971 E)....51,500
Pleiku....23,700
Quang-tri (1971 E)....16,900
Quan-long....33,500
Qui-nhon....50,000
Rach-gia....56,000
Sa-dec....34,800
Truc-giang....45,200
Vinh (1960 C)....43,954
Vinh-loi....41,700
Vinh-long (1971 E)....35,300
Vung-tau....54,200

VIRGIN ISLANDS, BRITISH

1970 C....10,484

•ROAD TOWN....2,183

VIRGIN ISLANDS OF THE U.S.

1970 C....62,468

•CHARLOTTE AMALIE....12,220
Christiansted....3,020

WALLIS AND FUTUNA
Wallis et Futuna

1976 C....9,192

MATA-UTU....558
•Ono....624

WESTERN SAHARA

1974 E....108,000

•EL AAIÚN (ÁIÚN)....20,000

WESTERN SAMOA

1976 C....151,983

•APIA....32,099

YEMEN / Al-Yaman

1979 E....5,785,000

Hodeida (Al Ḩudaydah) (1978 E)....106,080
Mocha (Al-Mukhā) (1975 C)....1,110
•ŞAN'Ā'....192,045
Ta'izz (1975 C)....81,000

YEMEN, PEOPLE'S DEMOCRATIC REPUBLIC OF / Al-Yaman ash-Sha'bīyah

1973 E....1,555,000

•ADEN (1977 E)....271,600
Al Mukallā (1970 E)....65,000
Madīnat ash Sha'b (Al-Ittiḩad) (1966 UE)....10,000

YUGOSLAVIA / Jugoslavija

1976 E....21,560,000

People's Republics

Bosnia-Hercegovina (Bosna i Hercegovina)....4,029,000
Croatia (Hrvatska)....4,530,000
Macedonia (Makedonija)....1,784,000
Montenegro (Crna Gora)....565,000
Serbia (Srbija)....8,860,000
Slovenia (Slovenija)....1,792,000

Cities (1971 C)

Banja Luka....89 866
Bečej....26,470
•BELGRADE (BEOGRAD) (★1,150,000)....770,140
Bihać....24,026
Bijeljina....24,722
Bitola....65,851
Bor....29,039
Brčko....25,422
Čačak....38,170
Celje....31,788
Cetinje....11,892
Djakovica....29,638
Dubrovnik....31,106
Karlovac....47,532
Kikinda....37,487
Kosovska Mitrovica....42,241
Kragujevac....71,180
Kraljevo....27,817
Kranj....27,209
Kruševac....29,469
Kumanovo....46,406
Leskovac....44,255
Ljubljana....173,662
Maribor....97,167
Mostar....47,606
Nikšić....28,547
Niš....127,178
Novi Pazar....29,072
Novi Sad....141,712
Ohrid....26,370
Osijek....93,912
Pančevo (★Belgrade)....54,269
Peč....42,113
Pirot....29,228
Požarevac....33,121
Prilep....48,242
Priština....69,524
Prizren....41,661
Pula....47,414
Rijeka....132,933
Šabac....42,307
Sarajevo....244,045
Šibenik....30,090
Sisak....38,421
Skopje....312,092
Slavonski Brod....38,762
Smederevo....40,289
Sombor....43,971
Split....151,875
Sremska Mitrovica....31,921
Štip....27,289
Subotica....88,787
Svetozarevo....27,542
Tetovo....35,792
Titograd....54,509
Titovo Užice....34,312
Titov Veles....36,026
Tuzla....53,825
Valjevo....26,367
Varaždin....34,270
Vinkovci....29,072
Vranje....25,685
Vršac....34,231
Vukovar....30,149
Zadar....43,187
Zagreb....566,084
Zaječar....27,677
Zenica....51,279
Zrenjanin....59,580

ZAIRE / Zaïre

1974 E....24,222,000

Bandundu (1970 C)....74,467
Boma (1970 E)....61,100
Bukavu....182,000
Gandajika (1970 E)....60,100
Goma (1970 E)....48,600
Isiro (1970 E)....49,300
Kabinda (1970 E)....60,500
Kalemie (Albertville) (1970 E)....62,300
Kamina (1970 E)....56,300
Kananga (Luluabourg)....601,000
Kikwit....150,000
•KINSHASA (LÉOPOLDVILLE) (1975 E)....2,202,000
Kisangani (Stanleyville)....311,000
Kolwezi (1970 E)....81,600
Likasi (Jadotville) (1970 C)....146,394
Lubumbashi (Élisabethville)....404,000
Matadi....144,000
Mbandaka (Coquilhatville)....134,000
Mbanza Ngungu (1970 E)....55,800
Mbuji-Mayi (Bakwanga)....337,000
Mwene-Ditu (1970 E)....71,100

ZAMBIA

1980 E....5,834,000

Chililabombwe (Bancroft)....77,000
Chingola....192,000
Kabwe (Broken Hill)....147,000
Kalulushi....60,000
Kitwe....341,000
Livingstone....80,000
Luanshya....164,000
•LUSAKA....641,000
Mufulira....187,000
Ndola....323,000

ZIMBABWE

1982 C....7,539,000

Bulawayo (★413,800)....97,700
Chinhoyi (★24,300)....6,500
Gweru (★78,900)....25,400
•HARARE (SALISBURY) (★656,000)....122,800
Hwange (★39,200)....17,500
Kadoma (★44,600)....6,400
Kwekwe (★47,600)....16,500
Nyanda (★30,600)....14,400
Mutare (★69,600)....22,600
Zvishavane (★26,800)....2,500

C Census. E Official estimate. UE Unofficial estimate.
L Population within municipal limits of year specified. • Largest city in country.
★ Population or designation of metropolitan area, including suburbs (see headnote).
▲ Population of an entire municipality, commune, or district, including rural area.
‡† Year of information specified at start of country.
* Italicized place names are now a part of the city shown in parentheses following the place name. These changes are part of the April 1974 reorganization of local administrative areas.

EXPLANATION OF THE INDEX AND ABBREVIATIONS

This universal index includes in a single alphabetical list all important names that appear on the reference maps. For ease in index usage and interpretation, two kinds of type are used to distinguish political names from those of physical features and points of interest. All political names (cities, towns, counties, districts, states, provinces, countries, etc.) are set in roman type. Physical features, and points of interest (rivers, mountains, lakes, bays, hills, straits, islands, national parks, etc.) are set in *italic* type. The supplementary descriptive information with each index entry varies with its political or physical classification.

POLITICAL NAMES

The more important names and political divisions shown on the maps are listed in the index. Each place name is followed by its location; the map index key; and the page number of the map.

County and State locations are given for all places in the United States. Province and country locations are given for all places in Canada. All other place name entries show only country locations.

The index reference key, always a letter and figure combination, and the map page are the last items in each entry. Because some places are shown on both a main map and an inset map, more than one index key may be given for a single map page. Reference also may be made to more than a single map. In each case, however, the index key *letter and figure* precede the map *page number* to which reference is made. A lower case key letter indicates reference to an inset map which has been keyed separately.

All major and minor political divisions are followed by both a descriptive term (co., dist., reg., prov., dept., state, etc.), indicating political status, and by the country in which they are located. U.S. counties are listed with State locations; all others are given with country references.

PHYSICAL NAMES AND POINTS OF INTEREST

The more important physical names and points of interest that are shown on the maps are listed in the index. Each entry is followed by a descriptive term (*bay, hill, range, riv., tombs, nat. park, mtn., isl.*, etc.), to indicate its nature.

Country locations are given for each name, except for features entirely within States of the United States or provinces of Canada, in which case these divisions are also given.

Some names are included in the index that were omitted from the maps because of scale size or lack of space. These entries may be identified by an asterisk (*) and reference is given to the approximate location of the place.

A long name may appear on the map in a shortened form, with the full name given in the index. The part of the name not on the map then appears in brackets, thus: St. Gabriel [-de-Brandon].

In the index, when more than one name with the same spelling is shown, including both political and physical names, the order of precedence is as follows: *first*, place names, *second*, political divisions, and *third*, physical features.

Abbreviations

admin....administered
Afg....Afghanistan
Afr....Africa
Ala....Alabama
Alb....Albania
Alg....Algeria
Alsk....Alaska
Alta....Alberta
Am....American
Am. Sam....American Samoa
And....Andorra
Ang....Angola
Ant....Antarctica
Arc....Arctic
arch....archipelago
Arg....Argentina
Ariz....Arizona
Ark....Arkansas
Atl. O....Atlantic Ocean
Aus....Austria
Austl....Australia, Australian
auton....autonomous

Ba....Bahamas
Barb....Barbados
B.C....British Columbia
Bel....Belgium, Belgian
Bhu....Bhutan
Bis. Arch....Bismarck Archipelago
Bngl....Bangladesh
Bol....Bolivia
Bots....Botswana
Br....British
Braz....Brazil
Bru....Brunei
Bul....Bulgaria
Bur....Burma

Calif....California
Cam....Cameroon
Can....Canada
Can. Is....Canary Islands
Cen. Afr. Rep. ....Central African Republic
Cen. Am....Central America
C.H....Court House
chan....channel
co....county
Col....Colombia
Colo....Colorado
Con....Congo
Conn....Connecticut
cont....continent
C.R....Costa Rica
C.V....Cape Verde
Cyp....Cyprus
Czech....Czechoslovakia

Dan....Danish
D.C....District of Columbia
Del....Delaware
Den....Denmark
dept....department
dep.... dependency, dependencies
des....desert
dist....district
div....division
Dji....Djibouti
Dom. Rep....Dominican Republic

Ec....Ecuador
Eg....Egypt
Eng....England
Equat. Gui....Equatorial Guinea
est....estuary
Eth....Ethiopia
Eur....Europe

Falk. Is....Falkland Islands
Fed....Federation
Fin....Finland
Fla....Florida
Fr....France, French
F.R.G. ...Germany, Federal Republic of
Fr. Gu....French Guiana

Ga....Georgia
Gam....Gambia
G.D.R. ...German Democratic Republic
Gib....Gibraltar
Grc....Greece
Grnld....Greenland
Guad....Guadeloupe
Guat....Guatemala
Guy....Guyana

Hai....Haiti
Haw....Hawaii
hbr....harbor
Hond....Honduras
Hung....Hungary

I....island
I.C....Ivory Coast
Ice....Iceland
Ill....Illinois
incl....includes, including
Ind....Indiana
Indon....Indonesia
Indian res....Indian reservation
I. of Man....Isle of Man
Ire....Ireland
is....islands
isl....island

Isr....Israel
isth....isthmus
It....Italy

Jam....Jamaica
Jap....Japan

Kam....Kampuchea
Kans....Kansas
Ken....Kenya
Kir....Kiribati
Kor....Korea
Kuw....Kuwait
Ky....Kentucky

La....Louisiana
Leb....Lebanon
Le. Is....Leeward Islands
Leso....Lesotho
Lib....Liberia
Liech....Liechtenstein
Lux....Luxembourg

Mad....Madagascar
Mala....Malaysia
Man....Manitoba
Mart....Martinique
Mass....Massachusetts
Maur....Mauritania
Md....Maryland
Medit....Mediterranean
Mex....Mexico
Mich....Michigan
Minn....Minnesota
Miss....Mississippi
Mo....Missouri
Mong....Mongolia
Mont....Montana
Mor....Morocco
Moz....Mozambique
mtn....mount, mountain
mts....mountains
mun....municipality

N.A....North America
nat. mon....national monument
nat. park....national park
N.B....New Brunswick
N.C....North Carolina
N. Cal....New Caledonia
N. Dak....North Dakota
Nebr....Nebraska
Nep....Nepal
Neth....Netherlands
Nev....Nevada
Newf....Newfoundland

N.H....New Hampshire
Nic....Nicaragua
Nig....Nigeria
N. Ire....Northern Ireland
N.J....New Jersey
N. Mex....New Mexico
Nor....Norway, Norwegian
N.S....Nova Scotia
N.W. Ter....Northwest Territories
N.Y....New York
N.Z....New Zealand

occ....occupied area
Okla....Oklahoma
Om....Oman
Ont....Ontario
Oreg....Oregon

Pa....Pennsylvania
Pac. O....Pacific Ocean
Pak....Pakistan
Pan....Panama
Pap. N. Gui....Papua New Guinea
Par....Paraguay
par....parish
P.D.R. of Yemen..Yemen, People's Democratic Republic of
P.E.I....Prince Edward Island
pen....peninsula
Phil....Philippines
plat....plateau
Pol....Poland
pol. dist....political district
pop....population
Port....Portugal, Portuguese
poss....possession
P.R....Puerto Rico
pref....prefecture
prot....protectorate
prov....province, provincial
pt....point

Que....Quebec

reg....region, regions
rep....republic
res....reservation, reservoir
R.I....Rhode Island
riv....river
Rom....Romania

S.A....South America
S. Afr....South Africa
Sal....El Salvador

Sask....Saskatchewan
Sau. Ar....Saudi Arabia
S.C....South Carolina
Scot....Scotland
S. Dak....South Dakota
Sen....Senegal
S.L....Sierra Leone
Sol. Is....Solomon Islands
Som....Somalia
Sov. Un....Soviet Union
Sp....Spain, Spanish
St., Ste....Saint, Sainte
Sud....Sudan
Sur....Suriname
Swaz....Swaziland
Swe....Sweden
Switz....Switzerland
Syr....Syria

Tan....Tanzania
Tenn....Tennessee
ter....territories, territory
Tex....Texas
Thai....Thailand
Trin....Trinidad & Tobago
trust....trusteeship
Tun....Tunisia
Tur....Turkey

U.A.E....United Arab Emirates
Ug....Uganda
U.K....United Kingdom
Ur....Uruguay
U.S....United States

Va....Virginia
val....valley
Ven....Venezuela
Viet....Vietnam
Vir. Is....Virgin Islands
vol....volcano
Vt....Vermont

Wash....Washington
W.I....West Indies
Win. Is....Windward Islands
Wis....Wisconsin
W. Sahara....Western Sahara
W. Sam....Western Samoa
W. Va....West Virginia
Wyo....Wyoming

Yugo....Yugoslavia

Zimb....Zimbabwe

INDEX TO WORLD REFERENCE MAPS

Alagôas, state, Braz......C3, k5 57
Alagoinhas, Braz......D3 57
Alagón, Sp......B5 20
Alagón, riv., Sp......B2 20
Al 'Ajamīyīn, Eg......E2 32
Alajuela, C.R......E5 62
Alajuela, prov., C.R......*E5 62
Alajuela, see Madden, lake, Pan.
Alakanuk, Alsk......C7 79
Alakol, lake, Sov. Un......D10 29
Al'Alamayn (El Alamein), Eg......C5 43
Alalān, Iran......C4 41
Alalaú, riv., Braz......C2 59
Alamance, Alamance, N.C...B3 109
Alamance, co., N.C......B3 109
Al 'Amārah, Iraq......F3 41
Alameda, Alameda, Calif....h8 82
Alameda, Sask., Can......H4 70
Alameda, Bernalillo, N. Mex......B3, k7 107
Alameda, co., Calif......D3 82
Alaminos, Phil......n12 35
Al 'Āmirīyah, Eg......G7 31
Alamito, creek, Tex......p12 118
Alamo, Contra Costa, Calif.*D2 82
Alamo, Wheeler, Ga......D4 87
Alamo, Montgomery, Ind...E3 91
Alamo, Mex......m15 63
Alamo, Lincoln, Nev......F6 104
Alamo, Williams, N. Dak...A2 110
Alamo, Crockett, Tenn......B2 117
Alamo, Hidalgo, Tex......F3 118
Alamogordo, Otero, N. Mex.E4 107
Alamo Heights, Bexar, Tex......B4, k7 118
Alamo Hueco, mts., N. Mex...F1 107
Alamos, Mex......B3 63
Alamosa, Alamosa, Colo...D5 83
Alamosa, co., Colo......D5 83
Alamosa, creek, N. Mex...D2 107
Alamosa, riv., Colo......D4 83
Åland (Ahvenanmaa), dept., Fin......*G8 25
Alanreed, Gray, Tex......B2 118
Alanson, Emmet, Mich......C6 98
Alanya, Tur......D9 31
Alaotra, lake, Mad......g9 49
Alapah, mtn., Alsk......B9 79
Alapaha, Berrien, Ga......E3 87
Alapaha, riv., Ga......E3 87
Alapayevsk, Sov. Un......B6 29, D21 9
Al 'Aqabah, Jordan......E7 32
Al 'Arīsh, Eg......C6 43
Alarka, Swain, N.C......f9 109
Alasehir, Tur......C7 31
Alashantsochi (Payenhaote), China......E1 36
Alaska, state, U.S......E4 76, 79
Alaska, gulf, Alsk......D10 79
Alaska, pen., Alsk......D8 79
Alaska, range, Alsk......C9 79
Alassio, It......C2 21
Al 'Atrūn, Sud......B2 47
Alatyr, Sov. Un......C3 29
Alau, isl., Haw......C6 88
Alausí, Ec......B2 58
Alava, prov., Sp......*A4 20
Alava, cape, Wash......A1 122
Alaverdi, Sov. Un......B15 31
Al 'Aynā, Jordan......D7 32
Al 'Ayzarīyah (Bethany), Jordan......h12 32
Alba, It......B2 21
Alba, Antrim, Mich......D6 98
Alba, Jasper, Mo......D3 101
Alba, Bradford, Pa......C8 114
Alba, Wood, Tex......C5 118
Albacete, Sp......C5 20
Albacete, prov., Sp......*C5 20
Alba de Tormes, Sp......B3 20
Ålbaek, Den......A4 24
Ålbaek, bay, Den......A4 24
Alba Iulia, Rom......B6 22
Al Bājūr, Eg......C2 31
Albalate [del Arzobispo], Sp..B5 20
Al Ballah, Eg......D4 32
Albanel, lake, Que., Can......F18 67
Albania, country, Eur......G13 8, B3 23
Albano, lake, It......h9 21
Albano Laziale, It......D4, h9 21
Albany, Austl......F2 50
Albany, N.S., Can......E4 74
Albany, P.E.I., Can......C6 74
Albany, Dougherty, Ga......E2 87
Albany, Whiteside, Ill......B3 90
Albany, Delaware, Ind......D7 91
Albany, Clinton, Ky......D4 94
Albany, Livingston, La......g10 95
Albany, Stearns, Minn......E4 99
Albany, Gentry, Mo......A3 101
Albany, Albany, N.Y......C7 108
Albany, Athens, Ohio......C3 111
Albany, Bryan, Okla......D5 112
Albany, Linn, Oreg....C3, k11 113
Albany, Shackelford, Tex....C3 118
Albany, Orleans, Vt......B4 120
Albany, Green, Wis......F4 124
Albany, Albany, Wyo......E6 125
Albany, co., N.Y......C6 108
Albany, co., Wyo......E7 125
Albany, riv., Ont., Can......o18 72
Albany South, Dougherty, Ga......*E2 87
Al Barkāt, Libya......E2 43
Al Basrah, see Basra, Iraq
Al Batanūn, Eg......D2 32
Al Bawīti, Eg......D5 43
Albay, prov., Phil......*C6 35
Albee, Grant, S. Dak......B9 116
Albemarle, Stanly, N.C......B2 109
Albemarle, co., Va......C4 121
Albemarle, sound, N.C......A6 109
Albenga, It......B2 21
Alberche, riv., Sp......B3 20
Alberga, Swe......u34 25
Albergaria-a-Velha, Port...B1 20
Albers, Clinton, Ill......E4 90
Albersdorf, F.R.G......D4 18
Albert, Fr......B5 14
Albert, Barton, Kans......D5 93
Albert, Harding, N. Mex......B6 107
Albert, Caddo, Okla......B3 112
Albert, Tucker, W. Va......*B5 123
Albert, co., N.B., Can......D5 74
Albert, lake, Ug......A5 48
Alberta, Wilcox, Ala......C2 78
Alberta, Stevens, Minn......E2 99
Alberta, Brunswick, Va......D5 121
Alberta, prov., Can......F9 66, 69
Alberta, mtn., Alta., Can......C2 69
Alberta Beach, Alta., Can..*C3 69
Albert Canyon, B.C., Can...D8 68
Albert City, Buena Vista, Iowa......B3 92
Albert Edward, mtn., Pap. N. Gui......k12 50
Albert Lea, Freeborn, Minn.G5 99
Albert Markham, mtn., Ant...A28 5
Albert Nile, riv., Ug......A5 48
Alberton, P.E.I., Can......C5 74
Alberton, Mineral, Mont......C2 102
Albertson, Nassau, N.Y......h13 108
Albertville, Marshall, Ala...A3 78
Albertville, Sask., Can......D3 70
Albertville, Fr......E7 14
Albertville, Wright, Minn...E5 99
Albertville, Zaire......C4 48
Albeuve, Switz......C3 19
Albi, Fr......F5 14
Albia, Monroe, Iowa......C5 92
Albin, Tallahatchie, Miss...B3 100
Albin, Laramie, Wyo......E8 125
Albina, Sur......A4 59
Albion, Mendocino, Calif...C2 82
Albion, Cassia, Idaho......G5 89
Albion, Edwards, Ill......E5 90
Albion, Noble, Ind......B7 91
Albion, Marshall, Iowa......B5 92
Albion, Kennebec, Maine...D3 96
Albion, Calhoun, Mich......F6 98
Albion, Carter, Mont......E12 102
Albion, Boone, Nebr......C7 103
Albion, Orleans, N.Y......B2 108
Albion, Pushmataha, Okla..C6 112
Albion, Erie, Pa......C1 114
Albion, Providence, R.I......B11 84
Albion, Whitman, Wash......C8 122
Albion, Dane, Wis......F4 124
Al Bīrah, Jordan......h11 32
Alborán, isl., Sp......E4 20
Ålborg, Den......A3 24
Ålborg, bay, Den......B4 24
Alborn, St. Louis, Minn......D6 99
Albox, Sp......D4 20
Albreda, B.C., Can......C8 68
Albright, Preston, W. Va...*B5 123
Albrightsville, Carbon, Pa. D10 114
Al Bu'ayrāt, Libya.C3 43, I14 30
Albufeira, Port......D1 20
Albuñol, Sp......D4 20
Albuquerque, Bernalillo, N. Mex......B3, k7 107
Alburg, Grand Isle, Vt......B2 120
Alburnett, Linn, Iowa......B6 92
Alburquerque, Sp......C2 20
Alburtis, Lehigh, Pa......E10 114
Albury-Wodonga, Austl......H6 51
Al Busaylī, Eg......C2 31
Alca, Peru......E3 58
Alcabideche, Port......f9 20
Alcácer do Sal, Port......C1 20
Alcalá de Chisvert, Sp......B6 20
Alcalá [de Guadaira], Sp....D3 20
Alcalá de Henares, Sp..B4, p18 20
Alcalá de los Gazules, Sp....D3 20
Alcalá la Real, Sp......D4 20
Alcalde, Rio Arriba, N. Mex.A3 107
Alcaldedíaz, Pan......F8 62
Alcamo, It......F4 21
Alcanadre, riv., Sp......B5 20
Alcanar, Sp......B6 20
Alcañiz, Sp......B5 20
Alcántara, Braz......B2 57
Alcantarilla, Sp......D5 20
Alcaraz, Sp......C4 20
Alcaudete, Sp......D3 20
Alcázar de San Juan, Sp....C4 20
Alcester, Union, S.Dak......D9 116
Alcira, Sp......C5 20
Alco, Stone, Ark......B3 81
Alco, Vernon, La......C2 95
Alcoa, Blount, Tenn...D10, n14 117
Alcobendas, Sp......o17 20
Alcochete, Port......f10 20
Alcolu, Clarendon, S.C......D7 115
Alcomdale, Alta., Can......C4 69
Alcona, co., Mich......D7 98
Alcora, Sp......B5 20
Alcorcón, Sp......p17 20
Alcorisa, Sp......B5 20
Alcorn, Jackson, Ky......C5 94
Alcorn, Claiborne, Miss....D2 100
Alcorn, co., Miss......A5 100
Alcova, Natrona, Wyo......D6 125
Alcovy, mtn., Ga......C3 87
Alcoy, Sp......C5 20
Alda, Hall, Nebr......D7 103
Aldama, Mex......B3 63
Aldan, Delaware, Pa......*G11 114
Aldan, Sov. Un......D15 28
Aldan, plat., Sov. Un......D15 28
Aldan, riv., Sov. Un......C16 28
Aldeburgh, Eng......B9 12
Alden, McHenry, Ill......A5 90
Alden, Hardin, Iowa......B4 92
Alden, Rice, Kans......D5 93
Alden, Antrim, Mich......D5 98
Alden, Freeborn, Minn......G5 99
Alden, Erie, N.Y......C2 108
Alden, Luzerne, Pa......D9 114
Alden Bridge, Bossier, La...B2 95
Alder, Madison, Mont......E4 102
Alder, brook, Vt......B4 120
Alder, mtn., Scot......D4 13
Aldergrove, B.C., Can......*E6 68
Alderney, isl., Guernsey......F5 10
Aldershot, Eng......C7 12
Alderson, Pittsburg, Okla...C6 112
Alderson, Greenbrier and Monroe, W. Va......D4 123
Aldersyde, Alta., Can......D4 69
Aldie, Loudoun, Va......B5, g11 121
Aldine, Salem, N.J......D2 106
Aldora, Lamar, Ga......C2 87
Aldrich, Shelby, Ala......B3 78
Aldrich, Wadena, Minn......D4 99
Aldridge, Walker, Ala......B2 78
Aledo, Mercer, Ill......B3 90
Aledo, Parker, Tex......n9 118
Aleg, Maur......C2 45
Alegre, Braz......C4 56
Alegrete, Braz......D1 56
Alegria, Phil......*C6 35
Alegros, mtn., N. Mex......C1 107
Aleknagik, Alsk......D8 79
Aleksander, wadi, Isr......f10 32
Aleksandriya, Sov. Un......G9 27
Aleksandrov, Sov. Un......C12 27
Aleksandrov-Gay, Sov. Un...C3 29
Aleksandrovskoye, Sov. Un..A9 29
Aleksandrovsk [-Sakhalinskiy], Sov. Un......D17 28
Aleksandrow, Pol......B5 26
Aleksandrow, Pol......C5 26
Aleksin, Sov. Un......D11 27
Aleksinac, Yugo......D5 22
Alelai, pt., W. Sam...... 52
Alemania, Arg......E2 55
Alençon, Fr......C4 14
Alenquer, Braz......C4 59
Alenquer, Port......C1 20
Alentejo, reg., Port......C2 20
Alepokhori, Grc......g10 23
Aleppo (Halab), Syr......D11 31
Aleria, Fr......C2 21
Alert, N.W. Ter., Can......k39 67
Alert, Decatur, Ind......F6 95
Alert, Franklin, N.C......*A5 109
Alert Bay, B.C., Can......D4 68
Alès, Fr......E6 14
Alessandria, It......B2 21
Alestrup, Den......B3 24
Ålesund, Nor......F2 25
Alet, Fr......F5 14
Aleutian, is., Alsk......E3 79
Aleutian, range, Alsk......D9 79
Alex, Grady, Okla......C4 112
Alexander, Pulaski and Saline, Ark......C3, k10 81
Alexander, Man., Can......E1 71
Alexander, Burke, Ga......C5 87
Alexander, Morgan, Ill......D3 90
Alexander, Franklin, Iowa...B4 92
Alexander, Rush, Kans......D4 93
Alexander, Genesee, N.Y......C2 108
Alexander, Buncombe, N.C..f10 109
Alexander, McKenzie, N. Dak......B2 110
Alexander, Upshur, W. Va...C4 123
Alexander, co., Ill......F4 90
Alexander, co., N.C......B1 109
Alexander, arch., Alsk......D12 79
Alexander, isl., Ant......B5 5
Alexander, lake, Minn......D4 99
Alexander Bay, S. Afr......C2 49
Alexander City, Tallapoosa, Ala......C4 78
Alexander Humboldt, mts., Ant.B14 5
Alexander Mills, Rutherford, N.C......B1, f11 109
Alexandra, N.Z......P12 51
Alexandra, S. Afr......*C4 49
Alexandra, isl., Sov. Un......A10 4
Alexandretta, gulf, Tur......D10 31
Alexandria, Calhoun, Ala...B4 78
Alexandria, B.C., Can......C6 68
Alexandria, Ont., Can......B10 72
Alexandria (Al Iskandarīyah), Eg......C5 43
Alexandria, Madison, Ind...D6 91
Alexandria, Campbell, Ky......B5, k14 94
Alexandria, Rapides, La......C3 95
Alexandria, Douglas, Minn..E3 99
Alexandria, Clark, Mo......A6 101
Alexandria, Thayer, Nebr...D8 103
Alexandria, Grafton, N.H...C3 105
Alexandria, Licking, Ohio...B3 111
Alexandria, Huntingdon, Pa..E5 114
Alexandria, Rom......D7 22
Alexandria, Hanson, S. Dak..D8 116
Alexandria, DeKalb, Tenn..C7 117
Alexandria (Independent City), Va......B5, g12 121
Alexandria Bay, Jefferson, N.Y......A5, f9 108
Alexandria Southwest, Rapides, La......*C3 95
Alexandrina, lake, Austl......G2 51
Alexandroupolis, Grc......B5 23
Alexis, Warren and Mercer, Ill......B3 90
Alexis, riv., Newf., Can......B3 75
Alexis Creek, B.C., Can......C6 68
Aley, riv., Sov. Un......E25 9
Aleysk, Sov. Un......C10 29
Alfalfa, co., Okla......A3 112
Al Fandaqūmīyah, Jordan......B7, f11 32
Alfaro, Sp......A5 20
Al Fāshir, see El Fasher, Sud.
Al Fashn, Eg......D6 43
Alfatar, Bul......D8 22
Al Fāw, Iraq......G4 41
Al Fayyūm (El Faiyūm), Eg......E2 32
Alfeld, F.R.G......B4 17
Alfenas, Braz......C3, k9 56
Alfios (Alpheus), riv., Grc......D3 23
Alfonsine, It......E8 18
Alford, Eng......A8 12
Alford, Jackson, Fla......B1, u16 86
Alford, Pike, Ind......H3 91
Alford, Berkshire, Mass......B1 97
Alford, Scot......C6 13
Alfordsville, Daviess, Ind...C4 91
Alfortville, Fr......g10 14
Alfred, Ont., Can......B10 72
Alfred, York, Maine......E2 96
Alfred, Allegany, N.Y......C3 108
Alfred, La Moure, N. Dak...C6 110
Alfred Station, Allegany, N.Y.C3 108
Al Fuqahā', Libya......D3 43
Algarrobal, Chile......E1 55
Algarrobo, Chile......E1 55
Algarrobo del Aguilla, Arg..B3 54
Algarve, prov., Port......*D2 20
Algarve, reg., Port......D1 20
Algeciras, Sp......D3 20
Algemesí, Sp......C5 20
Alger, see Algiers, Alg.
Alger, Arenac, Mich......D6 98
Alger, Hardin, Ohio......B2 111
Alger, co., Mich......B4 98
Algeria, country, Afr......D5 42, D4 44
Algete, Sp......o18 20
Al Ghaydah, P.D.R. of Yemen......B7 47
Al Ghayatah, Eg......D2 32
Alghero, It......D2 21
Al Ghurdaqah, Eg......D6 43
Algiers (Alger), Alg..F8 30, B5 44
Algoa, bay, S. Afr......D4 49
Algodones, Sandoval, N. Mex......B3, k8 107
Algoma, Pontotoc, Miss......A4 100
Algoma, Kewaunee, Wis......D6 124
Algoma, dist., Ont., Can......A2 72
Algoma Mills, Ont., Can......A2 72
Algona, Kossuth, Iowa......A3 92
Algona, King, Wash......B3, f11 122
Algonac, St. Clair, Mich......F8 98
Algonquin, Ont., Can......C9 72
Algonquin, McHenry, Ill.A5, h8 90
Algonquin, prov. park, Ont., Can.B6 72
Algonquin Park, Ont., Can..B6 72
Algood, Putnam, Tenn......C8 117
Algorta, Ur......E1 56
Algrange, Fr......E6 15
Al Ḩāfir, Oasis, Sau. Ar......H13 31
Alhama, Sp......D4 20
Alhama, Sp......D5 20
Alhambra, Los Angeles, Calif......m12 82
Alhambra, Madison, Ill......f14 90
Al Hammār, Iraq......F3 41
Al Hāmūl, Eg......D3 32
Alhaurín el Grande, Sp......D3 20
Al Hawātah, Sud......C3 47
Al Ḩawrah, P.D.R. of Yem..C6 47
Al Ḩayy, Eg......E3 32
Al Hayy, Iraq......E3 41
Al Ḩayyānīyah, Sau. Ar...H14 31
Al Ḩillah (Hilla), Iraq......E2 41
Al Ḩişn, Jordan......B7 32
Al Hoceima, Mor......B4 44
Alhos Vedros, Port......f9 20
Al Hudaydah, Yemen......C5 47
Al Hufūf (Hofuf), Sau. Ar...I4 41
Al Ḩurqūş, isl., Sau. Ar......H4 41
Al Ḩuşayḩisaḩ, Sud......C3 47
Aliakom, riv., Grc......B3 23
'Alī al Gharbī, Iraq......E3 41
Alibāg, India......H4 40
Alicahue, Chile......A2 54
Alicante, Sp......C5 20
Alicante, prov., Sp......*C5 20
Alicante, gulf, Sp......C5 20
Alice, Ont., Can......B7 72
Alice, Cass, N. Dak......C8 110
Alice, Jim Wells, Tex......F3 118
Alice, lake, Minn......C7 99
Alicel, Union, Oreg......B9 113
Alice Southwest, Jim Wells, Tex......*F3 118
Alice Springs, Austl......D5 50
Aliceville, Pickens, Ala......B1 78
Aliceville, Coffey, Kans......D8 93
Alicia, Lawrence, Ark......B4 81
Alicudi, isl., It......E5 21
Alida, Sask., Can......H5 70
Alief, Harris, Tex......r14 118
Aligarh, India......C6 39
Alīgūdarz, Iran......E4 41
Alindao, Cen. Afr. Rep......E4 46
Aline, Chandler, Ga......D4 87
Aline, Alfalfa, Okla......A3 112
Alingsås, Swe......I5 25
Alīpur Duār, India......D12 40
Aliquippa, Beaver, Pa..E1, h13 114
Al Iskandarīyah, see Alexandria, Eg.
Al Ismā'īlīyah, Eg..G9 31, D4 32
Al Istiwā'īyah (Equatoria), prov., Sud......D3 47
Alistrati, Grc......B5 23
Aliwal North, S. Afr......D4 49
Alix, Franklin, Ark......B2 81
Alix, Alta., Can......C4 69
Al Jabalayn, Sud......C3 47
Al Jāfūrah, des., Sau. Ar......I4 41
Al Jaghbūb, Libya......D4 43
Al Jahrah, Kuw......G3 41
Al Jāniyah, Jordan......h11 32
Al Jawf, Sau. Ar......D7 43
Al Jawsh, Libya......C2 43
Aljezur, Port......D1 20
Al Jīzah (Giza), Eg......D3 32
Al Junaynah, Sud......C1 47
Aljustrel, Port......D1 20
Alkabo, Divide, N. Dak......A2 110
Al Kadhimain, Iraq......F15 31
Alkali, lake, Nev......B2 104
Alkali, lake, Oreg......E6 113
Alkaline, lake, N. Dak......C6 110
Al Karak, Jordan......C7 32
Al Kawm at Tawīl, Eg......C3 32
Al Khābūrah, Om......D2 39
Al Khalīl (Hebron), Jordan..C7 32
Al Khālis, Iraq......E2 41
Al Khandaq, Sud......B3 47
Al Khārijah, Eg......D6 43
Al Khartūm, see Khartoum, Sud.
Al Khartūm Bahrī, see Khartoum North, Sud.
Al Khasab, Om......H8 41
Al Khums, Libya......C2 43
Al Khurmah, Sau. Ar......A5 47
Al Khurtūm, prov., Sud......B3 47
Al Khushnīyah, Syr......B7 32
Alkionidhes, gulf, Grc......g10 23
Alkionidhes, is., Grc......g9 23
Alkmaar, Neth......B4 15
Alkol, Lincoln, W. Va......m12 123
Al Kubr, isl., Kuw......G4 41
Al Kūbrī, Eg......D4 32
Al Kufra (Cufra), oasis, Eg., Libya......E4 43
Al Kūh, cape, Iran......I8 41
Al Kuntillah, Eg......E6 32
Al Kūt, Iraq......E2 41
Allada, Benin......E5 45
Al Lādhiqīyah, see Latakia, Syr.
Allagash, lake, Maine......B3 96
Allagash, riv., Maine......B3 96
Allahābād, India....C7 39, E8 40
Allakaket, Alsk......B9 79
Allamakee, co., Iowa......A6 92
Allamuchy, Warren, N.J......B3 106
Allamuchy, mtn., N.J......B3 106
Allan, Sask., Can......F2 70
Allanmyo, Bur......E10 39
'Allaqi, wadi, Eg......E6 43
Allardt, Fentress, Tenn......C9 117
Allariz, Sp......A2 20
Allaykha, Sov. Un......B36 4
Alleene, Little River, Ark...D1 81
Allegan, Allegan, Mich......F5 98
Allegan, co., Mich......F4 98
Allegany, Cattaraugus, N.Y..C2 108
Allegany, Coos, Oreg......D2 113
Allegany, co., Md......A1 85
Allegany, co., N.Y......C2 108
Allegany, Indian res., N.Y......C2 108
Alleghany, Sierra, Calif......C3 82
Alleghany, Alleghany, Va...C2 121
Alleghany, co., N.C......A1 109
Alleghany, co., Va......C2 121
Allegheny, co., Pa......E2 114
Allegheny, mts., U.S......C11 77
Allegheny, plat., Pa., W. Va......E1 114, C3 123
Allegheny, res., N.Y......C2 108
Allegheny, riv., N.Y., Pa......E2 114
Allegheny Heights, mtn., Md....D1 85
Alleman, Polk, Iowa......e8 92
Allen, Clarke, Ala......D2 78
Allen, Lyons, Kans......D7 93
Allen, Floyd, Ky......C7 94
Allen, Wicomico, Md......D6 85
Allen, Dixon, Nebr......B9 103
Allen, Hughes and Pontotoc, Okla......C5 112
Allen, Cumberland, Pa......F7 114
Allen, Bennett, S. Dak......D4 116
Allen, co., Ind......B7 91
Allen, co., Kans......E8 93
Allen, co., Ky......D3 94
Allen, co., Ohio......B1 111
Allen, par., La......D3 95
Allen, lake, Ire......C3 11
Allen, mtn., N.Z......Q11 51
Allendale, Wabash, Ill......E6 90
Allendale, Worth, Mo......A3 101
Allendale, Bergen, N.J......A4 106
Allendale, Allendale, S.C...F5 115
Allendale, co., S.C......E5 115
Allende, Mex......B4 63
Allenford, Ont., Can......C3 72
Allenhurst, Liberty, Ga......E5 87
Allenhurst, Monmouth, N.J..C5 106
Allenhurst, Matagorda, Tex.G4 118
Allen Park, Wayne, Mich...p15 98
Allenport, Washington, Pa..*F2 114
Allenspark, Boulder, Colo...A5 83
Allenstein, see Olsztyn, Pol.
Allensville, Todd, Ky......D2 94
Allensville, Vinton, Ohio....C3 111
Allensville, Mifflin, Pa......E6 114
Allenton, Wilcox, Ala......B2 78
Allenton, St. Louis, Mo......g12 101
Allenton, Washington, R.I..C11 84
Allenton, Washington, Wis...E5 124
Allentown, Wilkinson, Ga...D3 87
Allentown, Monmouth, N.J..C3 106
Allentown, Allegany, N.Y...C2 108
Allentown, Lehigh, Pa......E11 114
Allenville, Moultrie, Ill......D5 90
Allenville, Mackinac, Mich..C6 98
Allenwood, Monmouth, N.J.C4 106
Allenwood, Union, Pa......D8 114
Alleppey, India......G6 39
Aller (Cabañaquinta), Sp....A3 20
Aller, riv., F.R.G......B4 16
Allerton, Champaign and Vermilion, Ill......D6 90
Allerton, Wayne, Iowa......D4 92
Allerton, pt., Mass......B6 97
Allgood, Blount, Ala......B3 78
Alliance, Alta., Can......C5 69
Alliance, Box Butte, Nebr...B3 103
Alliance, Pamlico, N.C......B6 109
Alliance, Stark, Ohio......B4 111
Allier, dept., Fr......*D5 14
Allier, riv., Fr......D5 14
Al Lifiyah, well, Sau. Ar......G14 31
Alligator, Bolivar, Miss......A3 100
Alligator, lake, Maine......D4 96
Alligator, riv., N.C......B6 109
Allihies, Ire......F1 11
Allimaso, creek, N. Mex......C5 107
Allingåbro, Den......B4 24
Allinge, Den......C8 24
Allingtown, New Haven, Conn. (part of West Haven)......D5 84
Allison, La Plata, Colo......D3 83
Allison, Butler, Iowa......B5 92
Allison, McKinley, N. Mex..B1 107
Allison, Fayette, Pa......G2 114
Allison Harbour, B.C., Can..D4 68
Allisonia, Pulaski, Va......D2 121
Allison Park, Allegheny, Pa.h14 114
Alliston, Ont., Can......C5 72
Al Līth, Sau. Ar......A5 47
Alloa, Scot......D5 13
Allons, Overton, Tenn......C8 117
Allouez, Keweenaw, Mich...A2 98
Allouez, Brown, Wis......h9 124
Alloway, Salem, N.J......D2 106
Alloway, creek, N.J......D2 106
All Pines, Belize......B3 62
Allred, Overton, Tenn......C8 117
All-Sabieh, A. & I......C5 47
Allsboro, Colbert, Ala......A1 78
Allschwil, Switz......A4 19
Al Luhayyah, Yemen......B5 47
Allumette, lake, Ont., Can......B7 72
Allyns Point, New London, Conn......D8 84
Alma, Crawford, Ark......B1 81
Alma, N.B., Can......D5 74
Alma, Ont., Can......D4 72
Alma, Que., Can......A6 73
Alma, Park, Colo......B4 83
Alma, Bacon, Ga......E4 87
Alma, Marion, Ill......E5 90
Alma, Wabaunsee, Kans......C7 93
Alma, Gratiot, Mich......E6 98
Alma, Lafayette, Mo......B4 101
Alma, Harlan, Nebr......D6 103
Alma, Robeson, N.C......C3 109
Alma, Stephens, Okla......C4 112
Alma, Tyler, W. Va......B4 123
Alma, Buffalo, Wis......D2 124
Alma, hill, N.Y......C2 108
Al Ma'ādī, Eg......E3 32
Alma-Ata, Sov. Un......E9 29
Alma Center, Jackson, Wis...D3 124
Almada, Port......C1, f9 20
Almadén, Sp......C3 20
Al Madīnah, see Medina, Sau. Ar.
Al-Mafraq, Jordan......F11 31
Almagro, Sp......C4 20
Al Mahallah al Kubrā, Eg...D3 32
Al Mahmūdīyah, Eg......C2 32
Al Mahsamah, Eg......D3 32
Al Mahtab, Sau. Ar......H11 31
Al Makīlī, Libya......F4 31
Almanor, lake, Calif......B3 82
Almansa, Sp......C5 20
Al Mansūrah, Eg....C3 32, C6 43
Al Manzilah, Eg......C3 32
Almanzora, riv., Sp......D4 20
Almargem [do Bispo], Port...f9 20
Al Marj (Barce), Libya......C4 43, F2 31
Almartha, Ozark, Mo......E5 101
Al Maşīrah, isl., Oman......D2 39
Al Maţarīyah, Eg......C4 32
Almaville, Rutherford, Tenn.B5 117
Al Mawşil, see Mosul, Iraq
Almazán, Sp......B4 20
Al Mazār, Jordan......C7 32
Al Mazār, Eg......C5 32
Almeirim, Braz......C4 56
Almeirim, Port......C1 25
Almelo, Neth......B6 15
Almelund, Chisago, Minn...E6 99
Almena, Norton, Kans......C4 93
Almena, Barron, Wis......C1 124
Almendralejo, Sp......C2 20
Almeria, Loup, Nebr......C6 103
Almería, Sp......D4 20
Almería, prov., Sp......*D4 20
Almería, gulf, Sp......D4 20
Almería, riv., Sp......D4 20
Älmhult, Swe......B8 24
Al Minyā, Eg......D6 43
Al Miqdādīyah, Iraq......E2 41
Almira, Lincoln, Wash......B7 122
Almirante, Pan......F6 62
Almirante Brown, Arg......g7 54
Almiros, Grc......C4 23
Almo, Cassia, Idaho......G5 89
Almo, Calloway, Ky......f9 94
Almodôvar, Port......D1 20
Almodóvar, Sp......C3 20
Almon, Newton, Ga......C3 87
Almonaster, Sp......D2 20
Almond, Randolph, Ala......B4 78
Almond, Allegany and Steuben, N.Y......C3 108
Almond, Swain, N.C......f9 109
Almond, Portage, Wis......D4 124
Almonesson, Gloucester, N.J......*D2 106
Almont, Lapeer, Mich......F7 98
Almont, Morton, N. Dak......C4 110
Almonte, Ont., Can......B8 72
Almonte, Sp......D2 20
Almonte, riv., Sp......C3 20
Almora, India......C6 39
Almoradí, Sp......C5 20
Al Mudawwarah, Jordan......E8 32
Al Mughaiyir, Jordan......g12 32
Al Muglad, Sud......C2 47
Al Mukallā, P.D.R. of Yemen......C6 47
Al Mukhā (Mocha) (Mokha), Yemen......C5 47
Almuñécar, Sp......D4 20
Al Musallamīyah, Sud......C3 47
Al Muwaylih, Sau. Ar......I10 31
Almy, Uinta, Wyo......*E2 125
Almyra, Arkansas, Ark......C4 81
Almyville, Windham, Conn.*C9 84
Alness, Scot......C4 13
Alnwick, Eng......C6 10
Aloha, Washington, Oreg...h12 113
Along, bay, Viet......B7 38
Alonsa, Man., Can......D2 71
Alor, isl., Indon......G6 35
Álora, Sp......D3 20
Alor Star, Mala......I4 38
Alorton (Fireworks), St. Clair, Ill......*E3 90
Alosno, Sp......D2 20
Alotai (Sharasume), China...B2 34
Alpachiri, Arg......B4 54
Alpaugh, Tulare, Calif......E4 82
Alpbach, Aus......E5 16
Alpena, Boone, Ark......A2 81
Alpena, Alpena, Mich......C7 98
Alpena, Jerauld, S. Dak......C7 116
Alpena, co., Mich......C7 98
Alpenrose, Switz......C8 19
Alpes-Maritimes, dept., Fr..*F7 14
Alpha, Henry, Ill......B3 90
Alpha, Fayette, Iowa......B5 92
Alpha, Clinton, Ky......D4 94
Alpha, Iron, Mich......B2 98
Alpha, Jackson, Minn......G4 99
Alpha, Warren, N.J......B2 106
Alpha, Greene, Ohio......C1 111
Alpharetta, Fulton, Ga......B2 87
Alphen aan den Rijn, Neth..B4 15
Alpheus, see Alfios, riv., Grc.
Alpiarça, Port......C1 20
Alpine, Talladega, Ala......B3 78
Alpine, Apache, Ariz......D6 80
Alpine, Clark, Ark......C2 81
Alpine, Bonneville, Idaho......F7 89
Alpine, Bergen, N.J......h9 106
Alpine, Benton, Oreg......C3 113
Alpine, Overton, Tenn......C8 117
Alpine, Brewster, Tex......o13 118
Alpine, Utah, Utah......C4 119
Alpine, co., Calif......C4 82
Alpoca, Wyoming, W. Va...D3 123
Alps, mts., Eur......F10 8
Al Qadārif, Sud......C4 47
Al Qaddāhīyah, Libya......I14 30
Al Qāhirah, see Cairo, Eg.
Al Qanāyāt, Eg......D3 32
Al Qantara, Eg......D4 32
Al Qaryah ash Sharqīyah, Libya......C2 43
Al Qasabāt, Libya......C2 43
Al Qasr, Eg......D5 43
Al Qatīf, Sau. Ar......H5 41
Al Qatrūn, Libya......E2 43
Al Qattā, Eg......D2 32
Al Qulayyibah, well, Sau. Ar..H14 31
Al Qunaytirah, see Kuneitra, Syr.
Al Qurnah, Iraq......F3 41
Al Qusaymah, Eg......D6 32
Al Qusayr, Eg......D6 43
Al Qutaynah, Sud......C3 47
Alright, isl., Que., Can......B8 74
Alrø, Den......C4 24
Als, Den......B4 24
Alsace, former prov., Fr......C7 14
Alsask, Sask., Can......F1 70
Alsasua, Sp......A4 20
Alsdorf, F.R.G......D6 15
Alsea, Benton, Oreg......C3 113
Alsek, riv., Alsk., B.C., Yukon, Can......D5 66
Alsen, Cavalier, N. Dak......A7 110
Alsenbrück-Langmeil, F.R.G......D2 17
Alsey, Scott, Ill......D3 90
Alsfeld, F.R.G......C4 18
Alsike, Swe......t35 25
Alsip, Cook, Ill......*B6 90
Alstead, Cheshire, N.H......D2 105
Alstead, riv., Sask., Can......B2 70
Alstead Center, Cheshire, N.H......D2 105
Alston, Eng......F6 13
Alston, Montgomery, Ga......D4 87
Alsuma, Tulsa, Okla......A6 112
Alta, Buena Vista, Iowa......B2 92
Alta, Teton, Wyo......C1 125
Altadena, Los Angeles, Calif......m12 82
Altaelv, riv., Nor......C10 25
Alta Gracia, Arg......A4 54
Altagracia, Ven......A3 60
Altagracia de Orituco, Ven..B4 60
Alta Hill, Nevada, Calif......*C3 82
Altai, mts., Asia......B3 34
Alta Loma, San Bernardino, Calif......*F5 82
Alta Loma, Galveston, Tex..r14 118
Altamaha, riv., Ga......E4 87
Altamaha, sound, Ga......E5 87
Altamahaw, Alamance, N.C..A3 109
Altamira, Braz......C4 59
Altamira, Chile......E2 55
Altamirano, Arg......g7 54
Altamont, Alameda, Calif......h9 82
Altamont, Man., Can......E2 71
Altamont, Effingham, Ill...D5 90
Altamont, Labetta, Kans...E8 93
Altamont, Daviess, Mo......B3 101
Altamont, Albany, N.Y......C6 108
Altamont, Klamath, Oreg...E5 113
Altamont, Deuel, S. Dak......C9 116
Altamont, Grundy, Tenn......D8 117
Altamont, Duchesne, Utah...C5 119
Altamonte Springs, Seminole, Fla......D5 86
Altamura, It......D6 21
Altamura, isl., Mex......C3 63
Altapass, Mitchell, N.C......f10 109
Altar, Mex......A2 63
Altario, Alta., Can......D5 69
Alta Vista, Chickasaw, Iowa.A5 92
Alta Vista, Wabaunsee, Kans......D7 93
Altavista, Jim Hogg, Tex......F3 118
Altavista, Campbell, Va......D3 121
Altdorf, F.R.G......D6 17
Altdorf, Switz......C6 19

Altefähr, G.D.R....D7 24
Altenberg, G.D.R....C8 17
Altenbruch, F.R.G....E2 24
Altenburg, G.D.R....C7 17
Altenburg, Perry, Mo....D8 101
Altenkirchen, F.R.G....C2 17
Altenkirchen, G.D.R....D7 24
Altenmarkt, F.R.G....A8 18
Altentreptow, G.D.R....E7 24
Alter do Chão, Port....C2 20
Altha, Calhoun, Fla....B1 86
Altheim, Aus....A9 18
Altheimer, Jefferson, Ark....C4 81
Altinho, Braz....C3, k6 57
Altkirch, Fr....B3 18
Altman, Screven, Ga....D5 87
Altmar, Oswego, N.Y....B4 108
Altnaharra, Scot....B4 13
Alto, Banks and Habersham, Ga....B3 87
Alto, Richland, La....F5 95
Alto, Kent, Mich....F5 98
Alto, Lincoln, N. Mex....D4 107
Alto, Franklin, Tenn....B6 117
Alto, Cherokee, Tex....D5 118
Alto Alentejo, prov., Port....*C2 20
Alto Araguaia, Braz....B2 56
Alto Cedro, Cuba....D5 64
Alto Longá, Braz....C2 57
Alto Molócuè, Moz....A6 49
Altomünster, F.R.G....A7 18
Alton, Jefferson, Ala....B3, f7 78
Alton, Ont., Can....D4 72
Alton, Eng....C7 12
Alton, Madison, Ill....C7, f13 90
Alton, Sioux, Iowa....B1 92
Alton, Osborne, Kans....C5 93
Alton, St. Tammany, La....h12 95
Alton, Oregon, Mo....E6 101
Alton, Belknap, N.H....D4 105
Alton, Franklin, Ohio....m10 111
Alton, Washington, R.I....D10 84
Alton, Kane, Utah....F3 119
Alton, Upshur, W. Va....C4 123
Altona, Man., Can....E3 71
Altona, Knox, Ill....B3 90
Altona, DeKalb, Ind....B7 91
Altona, Mecosta, Mich....E5 98
Altona, Clinton, N.Y....f11 108
Altonah, Duchesne, Utah....C5 119
Alton Bay, Belknap, N.H....D4 105
Altoona, Etowah, Ala....A3 78
Altoona, Lake, Fla....D5 86
Altoona, Polk, Iowa....C4, e9 92
Altoona, Wilson, Kans....E8 93
Altoona, Blair, Pa....E5 114
Altoona, Eau Claire, Wis....D2 124
Alto Paraná, dept., Par....E5 55
Alto Pass, Union, Ill....F4 90
Altötting, F.R.G....A8 18
Altrincham, Eng....A5 12
Altro, Breathitt, Ky....C6 94
Altstätten, Switz....B8 19
Altun Kopru, Iraq....E15 31
Altura, Winona, Minn....F7 99
Alturas, Modoc, Calif....B3 82
Altus, Franklin, Ark....B2 81
Altus, Jackson, Okla....C2 112
Altus Lake, res., Okla....C2 112
Alt Zachun, G.D.R....E5 24
Al Ubayyiḍ, see El Obeid, Sud.
Al Uḍayyah, Sud....C2 47
Alula, Som....C7 47
Alum Bank (Pleasantville), Bedford, Pa....F4 114
Alum Bridge, Lewis, W. Va....B4 123
Alum Creek, Kanawha, W. Va....m12 123
Aluminé, Arg....B2 54
Alupka, Sov. Un....I10 27
Al Uqaylah (Aghéila), Libya....C3 43
Al 'Uqayr, Sau. Ar....I5 41
Al Uqşur (Luxor), Eg....D6 43
Alutom, mtn., Guam.... 52
Al 'Uzayr, Iraq....F3 41
Alva, Lee, Fla....F5 86
Alva, Harlan, Ky....D6 94
Alva, Woods, Okla....A3 112
Alva, Scot....*D5 13
Alva, Crook, Wyo....B8 125
Alvand, mtn., Iran....D4 41
Alvarado, Mex....D5 63
Alvarado, Marshall, Minn....B2 99
Alvarado, Johnson, Tex....C4, n9 118
Alvaton, Meriwether, Ga....C2 87
Alvdalen, Swe....G6 25
Alvear, Arg....E4 55
Alvena, Sask., Can....E2 70
Alverca [do Ribatejo], Port....f9 20
Alverton, Westmoreland, Pa....F2 114
Alvesta, Swe....B8 24
Alvin, Vermilion, Ill....C6 90
Alvin, Berkeley, S.C....E8 115
Alvin, Brazoria, Tex....E5, r14 118
Alvinston, Ont., Can....E3 72
Alviso, Santa Clara, Calif....*D2 82
Alvo, Cass, Nebr....h12 103
Alvord, Lyon, Iowa....A1 92
Alvord, Wise, Tex....C4 118
Alvordton, Williams, Ohio....A1 111
Älvsborg, co., Swe....A6 24
Älvsered, Swe....A6 24
Alvsjö, Swe....t36 25
Al Wajh, Sau. Ar....D7 43
Alwar, India....C6 39
Al Wāsiţah, Eg....E3 32
Aly, Yell, Ark....C2 81
Alyaty-Pristan, Sov. Un....F3 29
Alyth, Scot....D5 13
Alytus, Sov. Un....A8 26
Alz, riv., F.R.G....D6 16
Alzada, Carter, Mont....E12 102
Alzey, F.R.G....D3 17
Ama, St. Charles, La....k11 95
Amadeus, lake, Austl....D5 50
Amadi, Sud....D3 47
Amadjuak, lake, N.W. Ter., Can....C18 67
Amado, Santa Cruz, Ariz....F4 80
Amador, co., Calif....C3 82
Amagansett, Suffolk, N.Y....n16 108
Amagasaki, Jap....o14 37
Amager, isl., Den....C6 24
Amagon, Jackson, Ark....B4 81
Amahai, Indon....F7 35
Amakusa, sea, Jap....J5 37
Amål, Swe....H5 25
Amalfi, It....D5 21
Amalga, Cache, Utah....B4 119
Amalia, Taos, N. Mex....A4 107
Amalias, Grc....D3 23
Amalner, India....G5 40
Amambay, dept., Par....D4 55
Amamio (Amami), isl., Jap....F10 34
Amana, Iowa, Iowa....C6 92
Amanã, lake, Braz....D5 60
Amanda, Fairfield, Ohio....C3 111
Amangeldy, Sov. Un....C7 29
Amantea, It....E6 21
Amantes, pt., Guam.... 52
Amapá, Braz....B4 59
Amapá, ter., Braz....B4 59
Amapala, Hond....D4 62
Amaraji, Braz....k6 57
Amarante, Braz....C2 57
Amaranth, Man., Can....D2 71
Amargosa, Braz....D3 57
Amargosa, range, Calif....D5 82
Amarillo, Potter and Randall, Tex....B2 118
Amaro, mtn., It....C5 21
Amarousion, Grc....g11 23
Amasa, Iron, Mich....B2 98
Amasra, Tur....B9 31
Amasya (Amasia), Tur....B10 31
Amawalk, res., N.Y....D2 84
Amazon, Sask., Can....F3 70
Amazon, see Solimões, riv., Braz., Peru
Amazon, see Amazonas, riv., S.A.
Amazonas, dept., Peru....B2 58
Amazonas, comisaría, Col....D3 60
Amazonas, state, Braz....B3 58
Amazonas, ter., Ven....C4 60
Amazonas (Amazon), riv., S.A....D5 47, C3 59
Amazonia, Andrew, Mo....B3 101
Ambāla, India....B6 40
Ambalavao, Mad....h9 49
Ambam, Cam....E2 46
Ambanja, Mad....f9 49
Ambarchik, Sov. Un....C19 28
Ambato, Ec....B2 58
Ambato-Boeni, Mad....g9 49
Ambatolampy, Mad....g9 49
Ambatosorata, Mad....g9 49
Amber, Grady, Okla....B4 112
Amberg, F.R.G....D6 17
Amberg, Marinette, Wis....C6 124
Ambérieu [-en-Bugey], Fr....E6 14
Amberley, Hamilton, Ohio....*C1 111
Amberson, Franklin, Pa....F6 114
Ambert, Fr....E5 14
Ambia, Benton, Ind....D2 91
Ambikāpur, India....F9 40
Ambilobe, Mad....f9 49
Amble, Eng....E7 13
Ambler, Alsk....B8 79
Ambler, Montgomery, Pa....F11, o21 114
Ambo, chan., Kwajalein.... 52
Ambo, Peru....D2 58
Amboear, Indon....F8 35
Amboina, Indon....F7 35
Amboina, isl., Indon....F7 35
Amboise, Fr....D4 14
Ambositra, Mad....h9 49
Ambovombe, Mad....k9 49
Amboy, San Bernardino, Calif....E6 82
Amboy, Lee, Ill....B4 90
Amboy, Miami, Ind....C6 91
Amboy, Blue Earth, Minn....G4 99
Amboy, Clark, Wash....D3 122
Ambridge, Beaver, Pa....E1, h13 114
Ambriz, Ang....C1 48
Ambrizete, Ang....C1 48
Ambrose, Coffee, Ga....E3 87
Ambrose, Divide, N. Dak....A2 110
Ambrosia Lake, McKinley, N. Mex....B2 107
Amchitka, isl., Alsk....E3 79
Amchitka, pass, Alsk....E4 79
Am Dam, Chad....C4 46
Amden, Switz....B7 19
Amderma, Sov. Un....C9 28
Ameagle, Raleigh, W. Va....D3, n13 123
Ameca, Mex....C4, m11 63
Amecameca, Mex....n14 63
Ameland, isl., Neth....A5 15
Amelia, St. Mary, La....E4, k9 95
Amelia, Holt, Nebr....B7 103
Amelia, Clermont, Ohio....C1 111
Amelia, co., Va....C4 121
Amelia City, Nassau, Fla....k9 86
Amelia Court House, Amelia, Va....C5 121
Amelinghausen, F.R.G....E4 24
Amendolara, It....E6 21
Amenia, Dutchess, N.Y....D7 108
Amenia, Cass, N. Dak....B8 110
American, highland, Ant....B21 5
American, riv., Calif....C3 82
American Bottom, valley, Oreg....C1 113
American Falls, Power, Idaho....G6 89
American Falls, dam, Idaho....G5 89
American Fork, Utah, Utah....C4 119
American Samoa, U.S. dep., Oceania.... 52
Americus, Sumter, Ga....D2 87
Americus, Lyon, Kans....D7 93
Amersfoort, Neth....B5 15
Amery, Man., Can....A4 71
Amery, Polk, Wis....C1 124
Amery, ice shelf, Ant....C20 5
Ames, Story, Iowa....B4 92
Ames, Cloud, Kans....C6 93
Ames, Dodge, Nebr....C9, g11 103
Ames, Major, Okla....A3 112
Amesbury, Essex, Mass....A6 97
Amfissa, Grc....C4 23
Amga, Sov. Un....C16 28
Amgu, Sov. Un....D8 37
Amgun, riv., Sov. Un....D16 28
Amhara, plat., Eth....D4 47
Amherst, N.S., Can....D5 74
Amherst, Phillips, Colo....A8 83
Amherst, Brevard, Fla....*D6 86
Amherst, Hancock, Maine....D4 96
Amherst, Hampshire, Mass....B2 97
Amherst, Buffalo, Nebr....D6 103
Amherst, Hillsboro, N.H....E3 105
Amherst (Eggertsville), Erie, N.Y....C2 108
Amherst, Lorain, Ohio....A3 111
Amherst, Marshall, S. Dak....B8 116
Amherst, Lamb, Tex....B1 118
Amherst, Amherst, Va....C3 121
Amherst, Portage, Wis....D4 124
Amherst, co., Va....C3 121
Amherst, isl., Que., Can....B7 74
Amherstburg, Ont., Can....E1 72
Amherstdale, Logan, W. Va....D3, n12 123
Amiata, mtn., It....C3 21
Amidon, Slope, N. Dak....C2 110
Amiens, Fr....C5 14
Aminuis, Namibia....B2 49
'Āmir, cape, Libya....C4 43
Amirante, is., Indian O....G24 3
Amiret, Lyon, Minn....F3 99
Amir Kabir, dam, Iran....C5 41
Amisk, Alta., Can....C5 69
Amisk, lake, Sask., Can....C4 70
Amistad, Union, N. Mex....B6 107
Amite, Tangipahoa, La....D5 95
Amite, co., Miss....D3 100
Amite, riv., La....h10 95
Amity, Clark, Ark....C2 81
Amity, De Kalb, Mo....B3 101
Amity, Yamhill, Oreg....B3, h11 113
Amity, Washington, Pa....F1 114
Amityville, Suffolk, N.Y....E7, n15 108
Amizmiz, Mor....I2 30
Amlekhganj, Nep....D10 40
Amlwch, Wales....A3 12
'Ammān, Jordan....G10 31
Ammanford, Wales....C3 12
Ammeloe, F.R.G....A1 17
Ammon, Bonneville, Idaho....F7 89
Ammonoosuc, riv., N.H....B3 105
Amne Machin, mts., China....E4 34
Amo, Hendricks, Ind....E4 91
Āmol, Iran....C6 41
Amonate, Tazewell, Va....e10 121
Amoret, Bates, Mo....C3 101
Amorgos, isl., Grc....D5 23
Amorita, Alfalfa, Okla....A3 112
Amory, Monroe, Miss....B5 100
Amos, Que., Can....k11 73
Amoy (Hsiamen), China....G8 34
Ampanihy, Mad....h8 49
Amparo, Braz....C3, m8 56
Amper, riv., F.R.G....E6 17
Ampezzo, It....C8 18
Amposta, Sp....B6 20
'Amrān, Yemen....B5 47
Amrāvati, India....G6 40
Amreli, India....G3 40
Amriswil, Switz....A7 19
Amritsar, India....B5 40
Amroha, India....C7 40
Amsteg, Switz....C6 19
Amsterdam, Decatur, Ga....F2 87
Amsterdam, Bates, Mo....C3 101
Amsterdam, Gallatin, Mont....E5 102
Amsterdam, Neth....B4 15
Amsterdam, Montgomery, N.Y....C6 108
Amsterdam, Jefferson, Ohio....B5 111
Amsterdam, isl., Indian O....I2 2
Amstetten, Aus....D7 16
Amston, Tolland, Conn....C7 84
Am Timan, Chad....C4 46
Amuchiakung, China....C11 40
Amukta, pass, Alsk....E5 79
Amulet, Sask., Can....H3 70
Amund Ringnes, isl., N.W. Ter., Can....m32 67
Amundsen, bay, Ant....C17 5
Amundsen, gulf, N.W. Ter., Can....B7 66
Amundsen, sea, Ant....B36 5
Amundsen-Scott Station, U.S. scientific station, Ant....A18 5
Amur, riv., Sov. Un....E16 28
'Ana, Iraq....E13 31
Anabar, riv., Sov. Un....B14 28
Anabta, Jordan....f11 32
Anacoco, Vernon, La....C2 95
Anaconda, Deer Lodge, Mont....D4 102
Anaconda, Valencia, N. Mex....B2 107
Anaconda, range, Mont....E3 102
Anacortes, Skagit, Wash....A3 122
Anacostia, riv., Md....C1 85
Anadarko, Caddo, Okla....B3 112
Anadia, Braz....C3, k5 57
Anadyr, Sov. Un....C20 28
Anadyr, gulf, Sov. Un....C21 28
Anadyr, range, Sov. Un....C20 28
Anadyr, riv., Sov. Un....C20 28
Anae, isl., Guam.... 52
Anafi (Anaphe), isl., Grc....D5 23
Anagance, N.B., Can....D4 74
'Ānah, Iraq....E13 31
Anaheim, Orange, Calif....F5, n13 82
Anahim Lake, B.C., Can....C5 68
Anahola, Kauai, Haw....A2 88
Anahuac, Chambers, Tex....E5, r15 118
Anajás, Braz....C5 59
Anakāpalle, India....I9 40
Anakie, Austl....A6 51
Anaklia, Sov. Un....A13 31
Analalava, Mad....f9 49
Anama Bay, Man., Can....D2 71
Ana María, gulf, Cuba....D4 64
Anambas, is., Indon....E3 35
Anamoose, McHenry, N. Dak....B5 110
Anamosa, Jones, Iowa....B6 92
Anamur, Tur....D9 31
Anamur, cape, Tur....D9 31
Anandale, Rapides, La....*C3 95
Anandpur, India....F10 40
Anantapur, India....F6 39
Anantnāg, India....B6 39
Ananyev, Sov. Un....H7 27
Anao, pt., Guam.... 52
Anapa, Sov. Un....I11 27
Anápolis, Braz....E1 57
Anapú, riv., Braz....C4 59
Anār, Iran....F7 41
Anārak, Iran....E6 41
Anār Darreh, Afg....E10 41
Añasco, mun., P.R....*B1 65
Añasco, bay, P.R.....B1 65
Anastasia, isl., Fla....C5 86
Anata, Jordan....h12 32
Anatahan (Anatajan) isl., Mariana Is....E8 7
Anatone, Asotin, Wash....C8 122
Añatuya, Arg....E3 55
Anauá, riv., Braz....C5 60
Anawalt, McDowell, W. Va....D3 123
Ancash, dept., Peru....C2 58
Ancaster, Ont., Can....D4 72
Anceney, Gallatin, Mont....E5 102
Ancenis, Fr....D3 14
Anchi, China....F8 34
Anchiang, see Chienyang, China
Anchieta, Braz....F2 57
Anching, China....I7 36
Ancho, Lincoln, N. Mex....D4 107
Anchor, Brazoria, Tex....G5 118
Anchorage, Alsk....C10, g17 79
Anchorage, Jefferson, Ky....g11 94
Anchor Bay Gardens, Macomb, Mich....*A8 98
Anchor Point, Alsk....D9, h16 79
Ancienne Lorette, Que., Can....C6, n17 73
Anclote, keys, Fla....D4 86
Anco, Knott, Ky....C6 94
Ancón, Peru....D2 58
Ancona, It....C4 21
Ancud, Chile....C2 54
Ancud, gulf, Chile....C2 54
Andacollo, Arg....B2 54
Andahuaylas, Peru....D3 58
Andale, Sedgwick, Kans....E6, g11 93
Andalgalá, Arg....E2 55
Åndalsnes, Nor....F2 25
Andalusia, Covington, Ala....D3 78
Andalusia, Rock Island, Ill....B3 90
Andalusia, reg., Sp....D3 20
Andaman, is., India....F9 39
Andaman, sea, Indian O....F10 39
Andaman and Nicobar Is., ter., India....*F9 39
Andamarca, Bol....C2 55
Andamarca, Peru....D3 58
Andapa, Mad....f9 49
Andavaka, cape, Mad....k9 49
Andebu, Nor....p28 25
Andeer, Switz....C7 19
Andenne, Bel....D5 15
Anderlecht, Bel....D4 15
Andermatt, Switz....C6 19
Andernach, F.R.G....C2 17
Anderslöv, Swe....C7 24
Anderson, Lauderdale, Ala....A2 78
Anderson, Alsk....C10 79
Anderson, Arg....g6 54
Anderson, Shasta, Calif....B2 82
Anderson, Madison, Ind....D6 91
Anderson, McDonald, Mo....E3 101
Anderson, Anderson, S.C....B2 115
Anderson, Franklin, Tenn....B6 117
Anderson, Grimes, Tex....D5 118
Anderson, co., Kans....D8 93
Anderson, co., Ky....C4 94
Anderson, co., S.C....B2 115
Anderson, co., Tenn....C9 117
Anderson, co., Tex....D5 118
Anderson, riv., N.W. Ter., Can....C7 66
Anderson Dam, Elmore, Idaho....F3 89
Anderson East Side, Madison, Ind....*D6 91
Anderson Ranch, res., Idaho....F3 89
Andersonville, Sumter, Ga....D2 87
Andersonville, Franklin, Ind....F7 91
Andes, Col....B2 60
Andes, Richland, Mont....C12 102
Andes, Delaware, N.Y....C6 108
Andes, lake, S. Dak....D7 116
Andes, mts., S.A....D3, H3 53
Andfjorden, fjord, Nor....C7 25
Andhra Pradesh, state, India....E6 39
Andikithira, isl., Grc....E4 23
Andilamena, Mad....g9 49
Andimeshk, Iran....E4 41
Anding, Yazoo, Miss....C3 100
Andizhan, Sov. Un....E8 29
Andkhvoy, Afg....C12 41
Andoas, Peru....B2 58
Andong, Kor....H4 37
Andorra, And....A6 20
Andorra, country, Eur....G9 8, A6 20
Andover, Tolland, Conn....C7 84
Andover, Eng....C6 12
Andover, Henry, Ill....B3 90
Andover, Butler, Kans....g12 93
Andover, Essex, Mass....A5 97
Andover, Anoka, Minn....m12 99
Andover, Merrimack, N.H....D3 105
Andover, Sussex, N.J....B3 106
Andover, Alleghany, N.Y....C3 108
Andover, Ashtabula, Ohio....A5 111
Andover, Day, S. Dak....B8 116
Andover, lake, Conn....C7 84
Andöya, isl., Nor....C6 25
Andraitx, Sp....C7 20
Andreanof, is., Alsk....E4 79
Andrelândia, Braz....g5 56
Andrew, Alta., Can....C4 69
Andrew, Jackson, Iowa....B7 92
Andrew, co., Mo....B3 101
Andrew, isl., N.S., Can....D9 74
Andrew Jackson, mtn., Ant....B6 5
Andrews, Huntington, Ind....C6 91
Andrews, Dorchester, Md....D5 85
Andrews, Cherokee, N.C....D2 109
Andrews, Georgetown and Williamsburg, S.C....E8 115
Andrews, Andrews, Tex....C1 118
Andrews, co., Tex....C1 118
Andreyevka, Sov. Un....G11 27
Andria, It....D6 21
Androka, Mad....h8 49
Andropov, Sov. Un....B1 29
Andros, Grc....D5 23
Andros, isl., Ba....B5 64
Andros, isl., Grc....D5 23
Androscoggin, co., Maine....D2 96
Androscoggin, lake, Maine....D2 96
Androscoggin, riv., Maine, N.H....f7 96, A4 105
Andrychow, Pol....h10 26
Andújar, Sp....C3 20
Andulo, Ang....D2 48
Anécho, Togo....E5 45
Anefis i-n-Darane, Mali....C5 45
Anegada, bay, Arg....C4 54
Anegada, isl., Vir. Is. (Br.)....G12 64
Anegada, passage, N.A....G12 64
Anegam, Pima, Ariz....E3 80
Añelo, Arg....B3 54
Anerley, Sask., Can....F2 70
Aneroid, Sask., Can....H2 70
Aneta, Nelson, N. Dak....B8 110
Aneth, San Juan, Utah....F6 119
Aneto, mtn., Sp....A6 20
Angadanan, Phil....n13 35
Angamos, pt., Chile....D1 55
Angangchi, China....B9 34
Angarsk, Sov. Un....A5 34
Angaur, isl., Palau Is.... 52
Angel, falls, Ven....B5 60
Angela, Rosebud, Mont....D10 102
Ángel de la Guarda, is., Mex....B2 63
Angeles, Phil....o13 35
Angeles, pt., Wash....A2 122
Angelholm, Swe....I5 25
Angelica, Allegany, N.Y....C2 108
Angelina, co., Tex....D5 118
Angelus, Sheridan, Kan....C3 93
Angelus, Chesterfield, S.C....B7 115
Ångermanälven, riv., Swe....F7 25
Angermünde, G.D.R....B7 16
Angers, Que., Can....D2 73
Angers, Fr....D3 14
Angicos, Braz....C3 57
Angie, Washington, La....D6 95
Angier, Hartnett, N.C....B4 109
Angikuni, lake, N.W. Ter., Can....D13 66
Angkor, ruins, Kam....F5 38
Anglem, mtn., N.Z....Q11 51
Anglesey, co., Wales....A3 12
Anglesey, is., Wales....A3 12
Anglet, Fr....F3 14
Angleton, Brazoria, Tex....E5, r14 118
Anglia, Sask., Can....F1 70
Angliers, Que., Can....G17 67
Angling, lake, Man., Can....C5 71
Angling, riv., Man., Can....A5 71
Anglo-Egyptian Sudan, see Sudan, country, Afr.
Angmagssalik, Grnld....C18 4
Ango, Zaire....A4 48
Angoche, isl., Moz....A6 49
Angol, Chile....B2 54
Angola, Steuben, Ind....A8 91
Angola, Labette, Kans....E8 93
Angola, Erie, N.Y....C1 108
Angola, country, Afr....H7 42, D2 48
Angola, swamp, N.C....C5 109
Angoon, Alsk....D13, m22 79
Angora, Morrill, Nebr....C2 103
Angostura, res., S. Dak....D2 116
Angoulême, Fr....E4 14
Angra do Heroismo, Port. (Azores)....g9 44
Angra dos Reis, Braz....C4, h5 56
Angren, Sov. Un....E7 29
Anguelhok, Mali....C5 45
Anguilla, Sharkey, Miss....B3 100
Anguilla, isl., St. Kitts-Nevis-Anguilla....G13 64
Anguillara Sabazia, It....g8 21
Anguille, cape, Newf., Can....E2 75
Angumu, Zaire....B4 48
Anguran, Iran....H8 41
Angus, Ont., Can....C5 72
Angus, Polk, Minn....B2 99
Angusville, Man., Can....D1 71
Angwin, Napa, Calif....*C2 82
Anhembi, Braz....m7 56
Anholt, Den....B5 24
Anholt, isl., Den....B5 24
Anhsi, China....C4 34
Anhua, China....J4 36
Anhwei, prov., China....E8 34
Aniak, Alsk....C8 79
Aniche, Fr....D3 15
Aniene, riv., It....h9 21
Animas, Hidalgo, N. Mex....F1 107
Animas, mts., N. Mex....F1 107
Animas, riv., Colo....D3 83
Animas, val., N. Mex....F1 107
Anina, Rom....C5 22
Anita, Cass, Iowa....C3 92
Anita, Jefferson, Pa....E4 114
Aniva (Rutaka), Sov. Un....C11 37
Aniva, bay, Sov. Un....C11 37
Aniva, cape, Sov. Un....C11 37
Aniwa, Shawano, Wis....C4 124
Anizy-le-Château, Fr....E3 15
Anjar, India....F3 40
Anjo, Jap....o16 37
Anjou, Que., Can....p19 73
Anjou, former prov., Fr....D3 14
Anjouan, isl., Comoros....f8 49
Anju, Kor....G2 37
Anjum, Neth....A6 15
Ankang, China....H3 36
Anka, Nig....D6 45
Ankara, Tur....C9 31
Ankavandra, Mad....g9 49
Ankazoabo, Mad....h8 49
Ankazobe, Mad....g9 49
Ankeny, Polk, Iowa....C4, e8 92
An Khe, Viet....F8 38
Anklam, G.D.R....B6 16
Ankober, Eth....D4 47
Ankona, St. Lucie, Fla....E6 86
Ankoro, Zaire....C4 48
Ankuang, China....D1 36
Anlung, China....F6 34
Ann, cape, Ant....C18 5
Ann, cape, Mass....A6 97
Anna, Union, Ill....F4 90
Anna, Shelby, Ohio....B1 111
Anna, Sov. Un....F13 27
Annaba (Bône), Alg....F10 30, B6 44
Annabella, Sevier, Utah....E3 119
Annaberg-Buchholz, G.D.R....C8 17
Annaburg, G.D.R....B8 17
Annada, Pike, Mo....B7 101
An Nafud, des., Sau. Ar....H13 31
An Najaf, Iraq....I17 9
Annalee Heights, Fairfax, Va....*B5 121
Annam, reg., Viet....D7 38
Anna Maria, Manatee, Fla....p10 86
Anna Maria, isl., Fla....q10 86
Annan, Scot....F5 13
Annan, riv., Scot....E5 13
Annandale, Wright, Minn....E4 99
Annandale, Hunterdon, N.J....B3 106
Annandale, Fairfax, Va....g12 121
Annapolis, Crawford, Ill....D6 90
Annapolis, Parke, Ind....E3 91
Annapolis, Anne Arundel, Md....C5 85
Annapolis, Iron, Mo....D7 101
Annapolis, Kitsap, Wash....D1 122
Annapolis, co., N.S., Can....E4 74
Annapolis, riv., N.S., Can....E4 74
Annapolis Junction, Howard, Md....B4 85
Annapolis Naval Academy, Md....C5 85
Annapolis Royal, N.S., Can....E4 74
Annapurna 1, peak, Nep....C9 40
An Nāqūrah, Leb....A7 32
Ann Arbor, Washtenaw, Mich....F7, p14 98
An Nārī, mtn., Libya....E4 43
An Nāşirīyah, Iraq....F3 41
Annawan, Henry, Ill....B4 90
An Nawfalīyah, Libya....C3 43
An Nazlah, Gaza Strip....C6 32
Anne Arundel, co., Md....B4 85
Annecy, Fr....E7 14
Annecy-le-Vieux, Fr....E1 19
Annemasse, Fr....D7 14
Annestown, Ire....E4 11
Annieopsquotch, mts., Newf., Can....D3 75
An Nīl Āl Azraq, (Blue Nile), prov., Sud....C3 47
Anniston, Calhoun, Ala....B4 78
Anniston, Mississippi, Mo....E8 101
Annobón, see Pagalu, isl., Equat. Gui.
Annonay, Fr....E6 14
Annotto Bay, Jam....E15 65
Annotto, bay, Jam....E15 65
Annsjon, lake, Swe....u33 25
An Nuhud, Sud....C2 47
An Nu'mānīyah, Iraq....E2 41
Annursnack, hill, Mass....g10 97
Annville, Jackson, Ky....C6 94
Annville, Lebanon, Pa....F8 114
An Oir, mtn., Scot....E3 13
Anoka, Anoka, Minn....E5, m12 99
Anoka, Boyd, Nebr....B7 103
Anoka, co., Minn....E5 99
Ano Theologos, Grc....B5 23
Ano Viannos, Grc....E5 23
Anoyia, Grc....E5 23
Anpei, China....D3 36
Anping, China....E6 36
Ansbach, F.R.G....D5 17
Anse-d'Hainault, Hai....E6 64
Anselmo, Custer, Nebr....C6 103
Anserma, Col....B2 60
Anshan, China....C9 34, D10 36
Anshun, China....F6 34
Ansley, Pike, Ala....D3 78
Ansley, Jackson, La....B3 95
Ansley, Hancock, Miss....E4 100
Ansley, Custer, Nebr....C6 103
Anson, Somerset, Maine....D3 96
Anson, Jones, Tex....C3 118
Anson, co., N.C....B2 109
Ansŏng, Kor....H3 37
Ansongo, Mali....C5 45
Ansonia, New Haven, Conn....D4 84
Ansonia, Darke, Ohio....B1 111
Ansonville, Anson, N.C....B2 109
Ansted, Fayette, W. Va....C3, m13 123
Anstruther, Scot....D6 13
Anta, China....C2 37
Anta, Peru....D3 58
Antabamba, Peru....D3 58
Antakya (Antioch), Tur....D11 31
Antalaha, Mad....f10 49
Antalāt, Libya....C4 43
Antalya, Tur....D8 31
Antananarivo, Mad....g9 49
Antarctic, pen., Ant....B6 5
Antarctica, cont.... 5
Antelope, Sask., Can....G1 70
Antelope, Marion, Kans....D7 93
Antelope, Sheridan, Mont....B12 102
Antelope, Wasco, Oreg....C6 113
Antelope, Todd, S. Dak....*D5 116
Antelope, co., Nebr....B7 103
Antelope, lake, Sask., Can....G1 70
Antelope, range, Nev....D7 104
Antelope, res., Oreg....E9 113
Antelope Mine, Zimb....B4 49
Antequera, Sp....D3 20
Antes Fort, Lycoming, Pa....D7 114
Anthon, Woodbury, Iowa....B2 92
Anthony, Hempstead, Ark....D2 81
Anthony, Marion, Fla....C4 86
Anthony, Harper, Kans....E5 93
Anthony, Dona Ana, N. Mex....F3 107
Anthony, Kent R.I....C10 84
Anthony, El Paso, Tex....o11 118
Anthony Wayne Village, Allen, Ind....*B7 91
Anti Atlas, mts., Mor....C3 44
Antibes, Fr....F7 14
Anticosti, isl., Que., Can....k14 73
Antietam, creek, Md....A2 85
Antietam, nat. battlefield site and cemetery, Md....B2 85
Antigo, Langlade, Wis....C4 124
Antigonish, N.S., Can....D8 74
Antigonish, co., N.S., Can....D7 74
Antigua, country, N.A....H14 64
Antigua, Guatemala, Guat....C2 62
Antilla, Cuba....D6 64
Antimony, Garfield, Utah....E4 119
Antioch, Contra Costa, Calif....h9 82
Antioch, Lake, Ill....A5, h8 90
Antioch, Clinton, Ind....D4 91
Antioch, Sheridan, Nebr....B3 103
Antioch, see Antakya, Tur.
Antionia, Jefferson, Mo....C7 101
Antioquia, Col....B2 60
Antioquia, dept., Col....B2 60
Antique, prov., Phil....*C6 35
Antiquity, Meigs, Ohio....D4 111
Antler, Sask., Can....H5 70
Antler, Bottineau, N. Dak....A4 110
Antler, riv., Man., Sask., Can....E1 71
Antlers, Pushmataha, Okla....C6 112
Antofagasta, Chile....D1 55
Antofagasta, prov., Chile....D1 55
Antofalla, vol., Arg....E2 55
Antoine, Pike, Ark....C2 81
Anton, Washington, Colo....B7 83
Antón, Pan....F7 62
Anton, Hockley, Tex....C1 118
Anton Chico, Guadalupe, N. Mex....B4 107
Antongil, bay, Mad....g9 49
Antonina, Braz....D3 56
Antonino, Ellis, Kans....D4 93
Antonio de Biedma, Arg....D3 54
Antônio Dias, Braz....E2 57
António Enes, Moz....A6 49
Antonito, Conejos, Colo....D5 83
Antony, Fr....g10 14
Antratsit, Sov. Un....q22 27
Antrim, Antrim, Mich....D5 98
Antrim, Hillsboro, N.H....D3 105
Antrim, N. Ire....C5 11
Antrim, Tioga, Pa....C7 114
Antrim, co., Mich....C5 98
Antrim, mts., N. Ire....C5 11
Antsalova, Mad....g8 49
Antsirabe, Mad....g9 49
Antsiranana, Mad....f9 49
Antsohihy, Mad....f9 49
Antung, see Tantung, China
Antwerp (Antwerpen), Bel....C4 15
Antwerp, Jefferson, N.Y....A5, f9 108
Antwerp, Paulding, Ohio....A1 111
Antwerp, prov., Bel....C4 15
Antwerpen, see Antwerp, Bel.
Anua, Am. Sam.... 52
An Uaimh, Ire....D5 11
Anuradhapura, Sri Lanka....G7 39
Anvers, isl., Ant....C6 5
Anvik, Alsk....C7 79
Anyama, I.C....*E4 45
Anyang, China....D7 34
Anyksciai, Sov. Un....A8 26
Anza, Riverside, Calif....F5 82
Anzá, Col....B2 60
Anzac, Alta., Can....A5 69
Anzhero-Sudzhensk, Sov. Un....B11 29
Anzin, Fr....D3 15
Anzio, It....D4, k9 21
Anzoátegui, state, Ven....B5 60
Aojidong, Kor....E5 37
Aomoen, isl., Bikini.... 52
Aomon, isl., Eniwetok.... 52
Aomori, Jap....F10 37
Aomori, pref., Jap....*F10 37
Aosta, It....B1 21
Aoûk, riv., Cen. Afr. Rep....D3 46
Aoukâr, reg., Maur....C2 45
Aoulef, Alg....D5 44
Apa, China....E5 34
Apa, riv., Par....D4 57
Apache, Caddo, Okla....C3 112
Apache, co., Ariz....B6 80
Apache, mts., Tex....o12 118
Apache, peak, Ariz....F5 80

Apache Creek, Catron, N. Mex....D1 107
Apache Junction, Pinal, Ariz...m9 80
Apalachee, Morgan, Ga....C3 87
Apalachee, bay, Fla....B2 86
Apalachicola, Franklin, Fla....C2 86
Apalachicola, bay, Fla....C2 86
Apalachicola, riv., Fla....B1 86
Apalachin, Tioga, N.Y....C4 108
Apalona, Perry, Ind....H4 91
Apan, Mex....n14 63
Apoporis, riv., Col....C3 60
Aparri, Phil....B6 35
Apatin, Yugo....C4 22
Apatity, Sov. Un....D15 25
Apatzingán, Mex....n12 63
Apeldoorn, Neth....B5 15
Apennines, mts., It....C4 21
Apex, Wake, N.C....B4 109
Apex, mtn., Yukon, Can....D5 66
Api, peak, Nep....C8 40
Apia, W. Sam.... 52
Apia, hbr., W. Sam.... 52
Apiacás, mts., Braz....E3 59
Apiaí, Braz....C3 56
Apiranthos, Grc....D5 23
Apishapa, riv., Colo....D6 83
Apison, Hamilton, Tenn....h11 117
Apizaco, Mex....n14 63
Aplao, Peru....E3 58
Aplin, Perry, Ark....C3 81
Aplington, Butler, Iowa....B5 92
Apo, vol., Phil....D6 35
Apodaca, Rio Arriba, N. Mex....A4 107
Apodi, Braz....C3 57
Apohaqui, N.B., Can....D4 74
Apolda, G.D.R....B6 17
Apolima, isl., W. Sam.... 52
Apolima, strait, W. Sam.... 52
Apollo, Armstrong, Pa....E2 114
Apolo, Bol....B2 55
Apopka, Orange, Fla....D5 86
Aporé, riv., Braz....B2 56
Apostle, is., Wis....A3 124
Apóstoles, Arg....E4 55
Apostólou Andréa, cape, Cyp....E10 31
Appalachia, Wise, Va....f9 121
Appalachian, mts., N.A....F12 61
Appam, Williams, N. Dak....A2 110
Appanoose, co., Iowa....D5 92
Appenzell, Switz....B7 19
Appenzell, canton, Switz....B7 19
Apperson, Osage, Okla....A5 112
Appingedam, Neth....A6 15
Apple, riv., Ill....F3 124
Apple, riv., Wis....C1 124
Appleby, Eng....F6 13
Appleby, Nacogdoches, Tex....D5 118
Apple Creek, Wayne, Ohio....B4 111
Applecross, Scot....C3 13
Applegate, Jackson, Oreg....E3 113
Applegate, Sanilac, Mich....E8 98
Applegate, butte, Oreg....E5 113
Applegate, riv., Oreg....E3 113
Apple Grove, Mason, W. Va....C2 123
Apple Hill, Ont., Can....B10 72
Apple River, N.S., Can....D5 74
Apple River, Jo Daviess, Ill....A3 90
Apple Springs, Trinity, Tex....D5 118
Appleton, Pope, Ark....B3 81
Appleton, Knox, Maine....D3 96
Appleton, Swift, Minn....E2 99
Appleton, Lawrence, Tenn....B4 117
Appleton, Klickitat, Wash....D4 122
Appleton, Outagamie, Wis....D5, h9 124
Appleton City, St. Clair, Mo....C3 101
Apple Valley, San Bernardino, Calif....E5 82
Apple Valley, Dakota, Minn....h12 99
Apple Valley, Burleigh, N. Dak....*C5 110
Appleyard, Chelan, Wash....B5 122
Appling, Columbia, Ga....C4 87
Appling, co., Ga....E4 87
Appomattox, Appomattox, Va....D4 121
Appomattox, co., Va....D4 121
Appomattox, riv., Va....n17 121
Apra, hbr., Guam.... 52
Aprelsk, Sov. Un....D14 28
Aprilia, It....D4, h9 21
Apsheron, pen., Sov. Un....G19 9
Apsley, Ont., Can....C6 72
Apt, Fr....F6 14
Apuai, riv., Braz....D5 60
Apulia, reg., It....D6 21
Apulyont, lake, Tur....B7 23
Apure, state, Ven....B3 60
Apure, riv., Ven....B4 60
Apurímac, dept., Peru....D3 58
Apurímac, riv., Peru....D3 58
Aqaba, gulf, Afr., Asia....H10 31
'Aqiq, Sud....B4 47
Aq Koprūk, Afg....C13 41
Aqraba, Jordan....B7, g12 32
'Aqrabā, Syr....A8 32
Aquarius, mts., Ariz....C2 80
Aquarius, plat., Utah....E4 119
Aquasco, Prince Georges, Md....C4 85
Aquashicola, creek, Pa....B2 106
Aquebogue, Suffolk, N.Y....n16 108
Aquidauana, Braz....C1 56
Aquileia, It....D9 18
Aquiles Serdán, Mex....B3 63
Aquin, Hai....E7 64
Aquone, Macon, N.C....f9 109
Arab, Marshall, Ala....A3 78
Arab, gulf, Eg....G7 31
'Arab, riv., Sud....D2 47
Arabela, Lincoln, N. Mex....D4 107
Arabi, Crisp, Ga....E3 87
Arabi, St. Bernard, La....k11 95
Arabia, see Saudi Arabia, Asia
Arabian, see Eastern, des., Eg.
Arabian, sea, Asia....H9 33
Araby, Yuma, Ariz....E1 80
Araçá, riv., Braz....B2 59
Aracaju, Braz....D3 57
Aracati, Braz....B3 57
Araçatuba, Braz....C2 56
Aracena, Sp....D2 20
Aracruz, Braz....E2 57
Araçuaí, Braz....E2 57
Arad, Rom....B5 22
Araduey, riv., Sp....B3 20
Arafura, sea, Indon....G8 35
Arago, Coos, Oreg....D2 113
Arago, cape, Oreg....D2 113
Aragon, Polk, Ga....B1 87
Aragon, Catron, N. Mex....D1 107
Aragon, reg., Sp....B5 20
Aragón, riv., Sp....A5 20
Aragua, state, Ven....A4 60
Araguaia, riv., Braz....D6 53
Aragua de Barcelona, Ven....B5 60
Araguao, riv. mouth, Ven....B5 60
Araguari, Braz....E1 57
Araguari, riv., Braz....B4 59
Arai, Jap....o16 37
Arāk (Sultanabad), Iran....D4 41
Arakabesan, isl., Palau Is.... 52
Arakan, range, Bur....E9 39
Arakhthos, riv., Grc....C3 23
Aral, sea, Sov. Un....D5 29
Aral Karkum, des., Sov. Un....D6 29
Aralsk, Sov. Un....D6 29
Aramac, Austl....D8 50
Aran, isl., Ire....C3 11
Aran, is., Ire....D2 11
Aranda de Duero, Sp....B4 20
Arandas, Mex....m12 63
Aranjuez, Sp....B4 20
Aranos, Namibia....B2 49
Aransas, co., Tex....E4 118
Aransas, bay, Tex....E4 118
Aransas Pass, San Patricio and Aransas, Tex....F4 118
Aranyaprathet, Thai....F5 38
Araouane, Mali....C4 45
Arapaho, Custer, Okla....B3 112
Arapaho, peak, Colo....A5 83
Arapahoe, Cheyenne, Colo....C8 83
Arapahoe, Furnas, Nebr....D6 103
Arapahoe, Pamlico, N.C....B6 109
Arapahoe, Fremont, Wyo....D4 125
Arapahoe, co., Colo....B6 83
Arapey, Ur....E1 56
Arapey Grande, riv., Ur....E1 56
Arapkir, Tur....C12 31
Arar, wadi, Sau. Ar....G13 31
Araranguá, Braz....D3 56
Araraquara, Braz....C3, k7 56
Araras, Braz....C3, m8 56
Araras, mts., Braz....B2 56
Ararat, Choctaw, Ala....D1 78
Ararat, Austl....H4 51
Ararat, Susquehanna, Pa....C10 114
Ararat, Patrick, Va....D2 121
Ararat, see Büyük Ağrı Dağı, mtn., Tur.
Arareh, Indon....F9 35
Araripe, mts., Braz....C2 57
Araruna, Braz....h6 57
Aras, riv., Asia....B3 41
Arauca, Col....B3 60
Arauca, intendencia, Col....B3 60
Arauca, riv., Ven....B4 60
Arauco, Chile....B2 54
Arauco, prov., Chile....B2 54
Aravalli, range, India....C5 39
Araxá, Braz....E1 57
Arayat, Phil....o13 35
Arba, Randolph, Ind....D8 91
Arba Minch, Eth....E4 74
Arbela, Scotland, Mo....A5 101
Arboga, Swe....t33 25
Arbois, Fr....D6 14
Arboles, Archuleta, Colo....D3 83
Arbon, Power, Idaho....G6 89
Arbon, Switz....A7 19
Arbor, Middlesex, N.J....*B4 106
Arborea, It....E2 21
Arborfield, Sask., Can....D4 70
Arborg, Man., Can....D3 71
Arbor Terrace, St. Louis, Mo....*C7 101
Arbor Vitae, Vilas, Wis....C4 124
Arbroath, Scot....D6 13
Arbuckle, Colusa, Calif....C2 28
Arbuckle, lake, Fla....E5 86
Arbuckle, mts., Okla....C4 112
Arcachon, Fr....E3 14
Arcade, Jackson, Ga....B3 87
Arcade, Wyoming, N.Y....C2 108
Arcadia, Los Angeles, Calif....m12 82
Arcadia, N.S., Can....F3 74
Arcadia, De Soto, Fla....E5 86
Arcadia, Hamilton, Ind....D5 91
Arcadia, Carroll, Iowa....B2 92
Arcadia, Crawford, Kans....E9 93
Arcadia, Bienville, La....B3 95
Arcadia, Manistee, Mich....D4 98
Arcadia, Iron, Mo....D7 101
Arcadia, Valley, Nebr....C6 103
Arcadia, Hancock, Ohio....A2 111
Arcadia, Oklahoma, Okla....B4 112
Arcadia, Indiana, Pa....E4 114
Arcadia, Washington, R.I....C10 84
Arcadia, Spartanburg, S.C....B4 115
Arcadia, Trempealeau, Wis....D2 124
Arcadia (Arkadhia), prov., Grc....*D4 23
Arcanum, Darke, Ohio....C1 111
Arcata, Humboldt, Calif....B1 82
Arc Dome, mtn., Nev....E4 104
Arcelia, Mex....n13 63
Arch, Roosevelt, N. Mex....C6 107
Archambault, lake, Que., Can....C3 73
Archbald, Lackawanna, Pa....m18 114
Archbold, Fulton, Ohio....A1 111
Archdale, Randolph, N.C....B3 109
Archer, Alachua, Fla....C4 86
Archer, Madison, Idaho....F7 89
Archer, O'Brien, Iowa....A2 92
Archer, Merrick, Nebr....C7 103
Archer, co., Tex....C3 118
Archer City, Archer, Tex....C3 118
Archer's Post, Ken....A6 48
Archerwill, Sask., Can....E4 70
Arches, nat. park, Utah....E6 119
Archidona, Sp....D3 20
Archie, Cass, Mo....C3 101
Archive, Sask., Can....G3 70
Archuleta, co., Colo....D3 83
Arcila, Mor....G3 30
Arcis-sur-Aube, Fr....C6 14
Arco, Butte, Idaho....F5 89
Arco, Lincoln, Minn....F2 99
Arcola, Sask., Can....H4 70
Arcola, Douglas, Ill....D5 90
Arcola, Allen, Ind....B7 91
Arcola, Washington, Miss....B3 100
Arcola, Dade, Mo....D4 101
Arcola, Loudoun, Va....g11 121
Arcos de la Frontera, Sp....D3 20
Arcot, India....F6 39
Arcoverde, Braz....C3, k5 57
Arctic, Alsk....B10 79
Arctic, ocean....B33 4
Arctic Bay, N.W. Ter., Can....B16 66
Arcueil, Fr....g10 14
Arda, riv., Bul....E7 22
Ardabīl, Iran....B4 41
Ardagh, Ire....E2 11
Ardahan, Tur....B14 31
Ardakān, Iran....F6 41
Ardara, Ire....C3 11
Ardath, Sask., Can....F2 70
Ardatov, Sov. Un....D16 27
Ardbeg, Ont. Can....B4 72
Ardea, It....h9 21
Ardèche, dept., Fr....*E6 14
Ardee, Ire....D5 11
Arden, Little River, Ark....D1 81
Arden, Sacramento, Calif....*C3 82
Arden, Man., Can....D2 71
Arden, Ont., Can....C8 72
Arden, New Castle, Del....A7 85
Arden, Den....B3 24
Arden, Buncombe, N.C....f10 109
Arden, Irion, Tex....D2 118
Arden Hills, Ramsey, Minn....*E7 99
Ardennes, dept., Fr....E4 15
Ardennes, mts., Bel....D5 15
Ardenno, It....C5 18
Ardenvoir, Chelan, Wash....B5 122
Arderin, mtn., Ire....D4 11
Ardestān, Iran....E6 41
Ardglass, N. Ire....C6 11
Ardgroom, Ire....F2 11
Ardila, riv., Port....C2 20
Ardill, Sask., Can....H3 70
Ardino, Bul....E7 28
Ardley, Alta., Can....C4 69
Ardmore, Limestone, Ala....A3 78
Ardmore, Alta., Can....B5 69
Ardmore, Ire....F4 11
Ardmore, Prince Georges, Md....C4 85
Ardmore, Carter, Okla....C4 112
Ardmore, Delaware and Montgomery, Pa....o20 114
Ardmore, Fall River, S. Dak....D2 116
Ardmore, Giles, Tenn....B5 117
Ardnamurchan, pt., Scot....D2 13
Ardnaree, Ire....C2 11
Ardnave, pt., Scot....E2 13
Ardoch, Walsh, N. Dak....A8 110
Ardpatrick, pt., Scot....E3 13
Ardres, Fr....D9 12
Ardrossan, Austl....G1 51
Ardrossan, Alta., Can....C4 69
Ardrossan, Scot....E4 13
Ardsley, Westchester, N.Y....g13 108
Arecibo, P.R....B2 65
Arecibo, mun., P.R....*B2 65
Aredale, Butler, Iowa....B4 92
Areia, Braz....h6 57
Areia Branca, Braz....B3 57
Arelee, Sask., Can....E2 70
Arena, Burleigh, N. Dak....B5 110
Arena, Iowa, Wis....E4 124
Arena, pt., Calif....C2 82
Arena, pt., Mex....C3 63
Arenac, co., Mich....D7 98
Arenas de San Pedro, Sp....B3 20
Arenas Valley, Grant, N. Mex....E1 107
Arendal, Nor....H3 25
Arendonk, Bel....C5 15
Arendsee, G.D.R....F5 24
Arendtsville, Adams, Pa....G7 114
Arenillas, Ec....B1 58
Arenzville, Cass., Ill....D3 90
Areopolis, Grc....D4 23
Arequipa, Peru....E3 58
Arequipa, dept., Peru....E3 58
Arezzo, It....C3 21
Arga, riv., Sp....A5 20
Argalasti, Grc....C4 23
Arganda, Sp....p18 20
Argelès-Gazost, Fr....F3 14
Argenta, Macon, Ill....D5 90
Argenta, It....B3 21
Argenta, Beaverhead, Mont....E4 102
Argentan, Fr....C4 14
Argentat, Fr....E5 14
Argenteuil, Fr....C5, g10 14
Argenteuil, co., Que., Can....D3 73
Argentina, country, S.A....G4 53, C3 54, E2 55
Argentino, lake, Arg....E2 54
Argenton-sur-Creuse, Fr....D4 14
Argesul, riv., Rom....C7 22
Arghandāb, res., Afg....F13 41
Arghandāb, riv., Afg....E13 41
Argo, Jefferson, Ala....f7 78
Argo, Cook, Ill....F2 90
Argo, Sud....B3 47
Agolís, prov., Grc....*D4 23
Argolis, gulf, Grc....D4 23
Argonia, Sumner, Kans....E6 93
Argonne, Forest, Wis....C5 124
Argonne, forest, Fr....E4 15
Argonne, plat., Fr....C6 14
Argos, Grc....D4 23
Argos, Marshall, Ind....B5 91
Argos Orestikon, Grc....B3 23
Argostolion, Grc....C3 23
Argun, riv., Sov. Un....D14 28
Argungu, Nig....D5 45
Argusville, Cass, N. Dak....B9 110
Argyle, N.S., Can....F4 74
Argyle, Walton, Fla....u15 86
Argyle, Clinch, Ga....E4 87
Argyle, Lee, Iowa....D6 92
Argyle, Sanilac, Mich....E8 98
Argyle, Marshall, Minn....B2 99
Argyle, Osage, Mo....C5 101
Argyle, Washington, N.Y....B7 108
Argyle, Lafayette, Wis....F4 124
Argyle Downs, Austl....C4 50
Århus, Den....B4 24
Århus, co., Den....B4 24
Århus, bay, Den....B4 24
Ariake, bay, Jap....K5 37
Ariano Irpino, It....D5 21
Ariano nel Polesine, It....E8 18
Ariari, riv., Col....C3 60
Arica, Chile....C1 55
Arichat, N.S., Can....D9 74
Ariège, dept., Fr....*F4 14
Ariège, riv., Fr....F4 14
Ariel, Lafourche, La....C6 95
Ariel, Cowlitz, Wash....D3 122
Ariesul, riv., Rom....B6 22
Arīhā (Jericho), Jordan....C7, h12 32
Arikaree, riv., Colo....B8 83
Arima, Trin....N23 65
Arimo, Bannock, Idaho....G6 89
Aringay, Phil....n13 35
Arinos, riv., Braz....E3 59
Ario de Rosales, Mex....D4, n13 63
Arion, Crawford, Iowa....C2 92
Aripeko, Pasco, Fla....D4 86
Aripo, mtn., Trin....N23 65
Aripuanã, riv., Braz....D2 59
Arisaig, Scot....D3 13
'Arīsh, wadi, Eg....E5 32
Arispe, Union, Iowa....D3 92
Aristazabal, isl., B.C., Can....C3 68
Ariton, Dale, Ala....D4 78
Arivaca, Pima, Ariz....F4 80
Arivonimamo, Mad....g9 49
Arizaro, salt flat, Arg....D2 55
Arizola, Pinal, Ariz....E4 80
Arizona, Arg....B3 54
Arizona, state, U.S....D5 76, 80
Arizona Sunsites, Cochise, Ariz....F6 80
Arizpe, Mex....A2 63
Arjay, Bell, Ky....D6 94
Arjeplog, Swe....D7 25
Arjona, Col....A2 60
Arjona, Sp....D3 20
Arkabutla, Tate, Miss....A3 100
Arkabutla, dam, Miss....A3 100
Arkabutla Lake, res., Miss....A4 100
Arkadelphia, Cullman, Ala....B3 78
Arkadelphia, Clark, Ark....C2 81
Arkadhia (Arcadia), prov., Grc....*D4 23
Arkaig, lake, Scot....D3 13
Arkalyk, Sov. Un....D7 29
Arkansas, state, U.S....C9 77, 81
Arkansas, co., Ark....C4 81
Arkansas, riv., U.S....C9 77
Arkansas City, Desha, Ark....D4 81
Arkansas City, Cowley, Kans....E6 93
Arkansaw, Pepin, Wis....D1 124
Arkelstorp, Swe....B8 24
Arkhangelsk, Sov. Un....C7 28
Arkhangelskoye, Sov Un....F13 27
Arkhara, Sov. Un....B5 37
Arkinda, Little River, Ark....D1 81
Arklow, Ire....E5 11
Arkoma, LeFlore, Okla....B7 112
Arkona, Ont., Can....D3 72
Arkonam, India....F6 39
Arkport, Steuben, N.Y....C3 108
Arkville, Delaware, N.Y....C6 108
Arkwright, Bibb, Ga....D3 87
Arkwright, Kent, R.I....C10 84
Arkwright, Spartanburg, S.C....*B4 115
Arlanza, riv., Sp....A4 20
Arlanza Village, Riverside, Calif....*F5 82
Arlanzón, riv., Sp....A4 20
Arlberg, tunnel, Aus....E5 16
Arlee, Lake, Mont....C2 102
Arles, Fr....F6 14
Arley, Winston, Ala....A2 78
Arline, Blount, Tenn....n13 117
Arlington, Maricopa, Ariz....D3 80
Arlington, Kiowa, Colo....C7 83
Arlington, Calhoun and Early, Ga....E2 87
Arlington, Bureau, Ill....A6, h9 90
Arlington, Rush, Ind....E6 91
Arlington, Fayette, Iowa....B6 92
Arlington, Reno, Kans....E5, g10 93
Arlington, Carlisle, Ky....f9 94
Arlington, East Baton Rouge, La....h9 95
Arlington, Middlesex, Mass....B5, g11 97
Arlington, Sibley, Minn....F4 99
Arlington, Washington, Nebr....C9, g12 103
Arlington, Dutchess, N.Y....D7 108
Arlington, Yadkin, N.C....A2 109
Arlington, Hancock, Ohio....B2 111
Arlington, Gilliam, Oreg....B6 113
Arlington, Spartanburg, S.C....B3 115
Arlington, Kingsbury S Dak....C8 116
Arlington, Shelby, Tenn....B2 117
Arlington, Tarrant, Tex....n9 118
Arlington, Bennington, Vt....E2 120
Arlington, Arlington, Va....C5, g12 121
Arlington, Snohomish, Wash....A3 122
Arlington, Columbia, Wis....E4 124
Arlington, co., Va....g12 121
Arlington Beach, Brookings, S. Dak....C8 116
Arlington Heights, Cook, Ill....A5, h9 90
Arlington Heights, Hamilton, Ohio....*C1 111
Arlon, Bel....E5 15
Arltunga, Austl....D5 50
Arly, riv., Fr....D2 18
Arm, Lawrence, Miss....D3 100
Arm, riv., Sask., Can....F3 70
Arma, Crawford, Kans....E9 93
Armada, Macomb, Mich....F8 98
Armadale, Scot....*E5 13
Armagh, Que., Can....C7 73
Armagh, Indiana, Pa....F3 114
Armathwaite, Fentress, Tenn....C9 117
Armavir, Sov. Un....G17 9, I13 27
Armenia, Col....C2 60
Armenia (S.S.R.) rep., Sov. Un....G17 9
Armentières, Fr....B5 14
Armeria, riv., Mex....n12 63
Armero, Col....C3 60
Armidale, Austl....E8 51
Armijo, Bernalillo, N. Mex....k7 107
Armington, Tazewell, Ill....C4 90
Armington, Cascade, Mont....C6 102
Arminto, Natrona, Wyo....C5 125
Armit, lake, Man., Can....C1 71
Armley, Sask., Can....D3 70
Armona, Kings, Calif....*D4 82
Armonk, Westchester, N.Y....*D6 108
Armorel, Mississippi, Ark....B6 81
Armour, Douglas, S. Dak....D7 116
Armstead, Blount, Ala....B3 78
Armstrong, B.C., Can....D8 68
Armstrong, St. Johns, Fla....C5 86
Armstrong, Vermilion, Ill....C6 90
Armstrong, Emmet, Iowa....A3 92
Armstrong, Howard, Mo....B5 101
Armstrong, Kenedy, Tex....F4 118
Armstrong, co., Pa....E3 114
Armstrong, co., Tex....B2 118
Armstrong, creek, W. Va....m13 123
Armstrong Creek, Forest, Wis....C5 124
Armstrong Station, Ont., Can....F15 67
Armuchee, Floyd, Ga....B1 87
Armyansk, Sov. Un....H9 27
Arnaud, Man., Can....*E3 71
Arnaud, riv., Que., Can....E18 67
Arnaudville, St. Landry and St. Martin, La....D4 95
Arneburg, G.D.R....F5 24
Arnedo, Sp....A4 20
Arnegard, McKenzie, N. Dak....B2 110
Arneiroz, Braz....C2 57
Arnett, Ellis, Okla....A2 112
Arnett, Raleigh, W. Va....D3, n13 123
Arney, riv., N. Ire....C4 11
Arnhem, Neth....C5 15
Arnhem, cape, Austl....B6 50
Arnhem Land, reg., Austl....B5 50
Arnissa, Grc....B3 23
Arno, riv., It....C3 21
Arnold, Calaveras, Calif....C3 82
Arnold, Ness, Kans....D3 93
Arnold, Marquette, Mich....B3 98
Arnold, St. Louis, Minn....D6 99
Arnold, Jefferson, Mo....C7 101
Arnold, Custer, Nebr....C5 103
Arnold, Westmoreland, Pa....h14 114
Arnold Mills, Providence, R.I....B11 84
Arnold Mills, res., R.I.....A11 84
Arnoldsburg, Calhoun, W. Va....C3 123
Arnolds Park, Dickinson, Iowa....A2 92
Arnoldsville, Oglethorpe, Ga....C3 87
Arnot, Tioga, Pa....C7 114
Arnouville [-lès-Gonesse], Fr....g10 14
Arnöya, isl., Nor....B9 25
Arnprior, Ont., Can....B8 72
Arnsberg, F.R.G....B3 17
Arnstadt, G.D.R....C5 17
Arnstein, Ont., Can....B5 72
Arnswalde, see Choszczno, Pol.
Årø, isl., Den....C3 24
Aroa, Ven....A4 60
Aroab, Namibia....C2 49
Arock, Malheur, Oreg....E9 113
Aroda, Madison, Va....B4 121
Arolsen, F.R.G....B4 17
Aroma, Sud....B4 47
Aroma, Hamilton, Ind....D6 91
Aroma Park, Kankakee, Ill....B6 90
Aroostook, co., Maine....B4 96
Aroostook, riv., Maine....B4 96
Aroostook Junction, N.B., Can....C2 74
Aroroy, Phil....*C6 35
Aros, Nor....p28 25
Arosa, Switz....C8 19
Arouca, Trin....N23 65
Aroya, Cheyenne, Colo....C8 83
Arp, Smith, Tex....C5 118
Arpajon, Fr....F2 15
Arpin, Wood, Wis....D3 124
Arques, Fr....D2 15
Arques-la-Bataille, Fr....E9 12
'Arrābah, Jordan....B7 32
Arrah, India....C7 39
Ar Rahad, Sud....C3 47
Arraias, Braz....D1 57
Arraiján, Pan....m11 62
Arraiolos, Port....C2 20
Ar Ramādī, Iraq....F14 31
Ar Ramthā, Jordan....B7 32
Arran, Sask., Can....F5 70
Arran, Wakulla, Fla....B2 86
Arran, isl., Scot....E3 13
Ar Rank, Sud....C3 47
Ar Raqqah, Syr....E12 31
Arras, Fr....B5 14
Ar Rawḑah, Eg....H8 31
Arrecife, Sp. (Can. Is.)....D2 44
Arrecifes, Arg....g6 54
Arrecifes, riv., Arg....f7 54
Arrey, Sierra, N. Mex....E2 107
Arriaga, Mex....m13 63
Arriba, Lincoln, Colo....B7 83
Arriikan, isl., Bikini.... 52
Arrington, Atchison, Kans....C8 93
Arrington, Nelson, Va....C4 121
Arriola, Montezuma, Colo....D2 83
Ar Riyāḑ, see Riyadh, Sau. Ar.
Arroio Grande, Braz....E2 56
Arroll, Texas, Mo....D6 101
Arrone, riv., It....h8 21
Arrow, creek, Mont....C6 102
Arrow, lake, Ont., Can....h9 99
Arrow, lake, Ire....C3 11
Arrow, riv., Ont., Can....h9 99
Arrowhead, B.C., Can....D9 68
Arrowhead Village, Ocean, N.J....C4 106
Arrow Rock, Saline, Mo....B5 101
Arrowsic, Sagadahoc, Maine....E3 96
Arrowsmith, McLean, Ill....C5 90
Arrowwood, Alta., Can....D4 69
Arroyo, P.R....C3 65
Arroyo, mun., P.R....*C3 65
Arroyo de la Luz, Sp....C2 20
Arroyo del Macho, riv., N. Mex....D5 107
Arroyo Grande, San Luis Obispo, Calif....E3 82
Arroyo Grande, Ur....f8 51
Arroyo Hondo, Taos, N. Mex....A4 107
Arroyo Seco, Taos, N. Mex....A4 107
Ar Rumaythah, Iraq....F2 41
Ar Rusayris, Sud....C3 47
Ar Ruwayḩī, ruins, Jordan....D7 32
Års, Den....B3 24
Arsenal, Jefferson, Ark....*C3 81
Arsenyev, Sov. Un....D6 37
Arta, Grc....C3 23
Arta, prov., Grc....*C3 23
Artaiyan, well, Sau. Ar....H13 31
Artas, Campbell, S. Dak....B6 116
Artashat, Sov. Un....B2 41
Artem, Sov. Un....E16 28
Artemisa, Cuba....C2 64
Artemovsk, Sov. Un....E27 9
Artemovsk, Sov. Un....G11, q21 27
Artemovskiy, Sov. Un....B6 29
Artemus, Knox, Ky....D6 94
Arter, mtn., Wyo....D4 125
Artern, G.D.R....B6 17
Artesia, Los Angeles, Calif....*F4 82
Artesia, Moffat, Colo....A1 83
Artesia, Lowndes, Miss....B5 100
Artesia, Eddy, N. Mex....E5 107
Artesian, Sanborn, S. Dak....C8 116
Artesia Wells, LaSalle, Tex....E3 118
Arth, Switz....B6 19
Arthabaska, Que., Can....C6 73
Arthabaska, co., Que, Can....C5 73
Arthur, Ont., Can....D4 72
Arthur, Douglas and Moultrie, Ill....D5 90
Arthur, Pike, Ind....H3 91
Arthur, Ida, Iowa....B2 92
Arthur, Arthur, Nebr....C4 103
Arthur, Cass, N. Dak....B8 110
Arthur, co., Nebr....C4 103
Arthur, kill, N.J....k8 106
Arthur, lake, La....D3 95
Arthur's Town, Ba....B6 64
Artibonite, riv., Hai....E7 64
Artigas, Ur....E1 56
Artigas, dept., Ur....*E1 56
Artland, Sask., Can....E1 70
Artois, former prov., Fr....B5 14
Artois, hills, Fr....D2 15
Artur de Paiva, Ang....D2 48
Artvin, Tur....B13 31
Aru, Zaire....A5 48
Aru, is., Indon....G8 35
Aru, pt., Ponape.... 52
Arua, Ug....A5 48
Aruanã, Braz....A2 56
Aruba, isl., Neth. Antilles....H17 65
Arucas, Sp. (Can. Is.)....m14 20
Arun, riv., Eng....D7 12
Arunachal Pradesh, ter., India....C9 39
Arundel, Que., Can....D3 73
Arundel, Eng....D7 12
Arundel Village, Anne Arundel, Md....*B4 85
Arusha, Tan....B6 48
Arusi, prov., Eth....D4 47
Aruwimi, riv., Zaire....A4 48
Arvada, Jefferson, Colo....B5 83
Arvada, Sheridan, Wyo....B6 125
Arvagh, Ire....D4 11
Arve, riv., Fr....D2 18
Arvida, Que., Can....A6 73
Arvidsjaur, Swe....E8 25
Arvigo, Switz....D7 19
Arvika, Swe....H5 25
Arvilla, Grand Forks, N. Dak....B8 110
Arvin, Kern, Calif....E4 82
Arvonia, Buckingham, Va....C4 121
Arys, Sov. Un....E7 29, C22 9
Arzamas, Sov. Un....B2 29
Arzew, Alg....G6 30
Arzgir, Sov. Un....I15 27
Arzúa, Sp....A1 20
As, Czech....C2 26
Aså, Den....A4 24
Asab, Namibia....C2 49
Asahigawa, Jap....E11 37
Asamankese, Ghana....*E4 45
Asan, Guam.... 52
Asan, pt., Guam.... 52
Asansol, India....D8 39
Asaph, Tioga, Pa....C7 114
Asbach, F.R.G....C2 17
Asbest, Sov. Un....B6 29
Asbestos, Que., Can....D6 73
Asbury, Jasper, Mo....D3 101
Asbury, Hunterdon and Warren, N.J....B2 106
Asbury Park, Monmouth, N.J....C4 106
Ascensión, Mex....A3 63
Ascension, par., La....D5 95
Ascension, isl., Atl. O....G9 6
Ascension Isl., Br. dep., Atl. O....G4 42
Aschaffenburg, F.R.G....D4 17
Aschersleben, G.D.R....B6 17
Ascoli Piceno, It....C4 21
Ascona, Switz....D6 19
Ascope, Peru....C2 58
Ascot Corner, Que., Can....D6 73
Ascutney, Windsor, Vt....E4 120
Ascutney, mtn., Vt....E4 120
Aseb, Eth....C5 47
Aselā, Eth....D4 47
Asele, Swe....E7 25
Asenovgrad, Bul....E7 22
Ash, Douglas, Oreg....D3 113
Asha, Sov. Un....B5 29
Ashanti, reg., Ghana....E4 45
Asharoken, Suffolk, N.Y....F3 84
Ashaway, Washington, R.I....D9 84
Ashbourne, Eng....A6 12
Ashburn, Turner, Ga....E3 87
Ashburn, Pike, Mo....B6 101
Ashburn, Loudoun, Va....B5 121
Ashburnham, Worcester, Mass....A4 97
Ashburton, Eng....D4 12
Ashburton, N.Z....O13 51
Ashburton, riv., Austl....D2 50
Ashby, Bibb, Ala....B3 78
Ashby, Middlesex, Mass....A4 97
Ashby, Grant, Minn....D3 99
Ashby, Grant, Nebr....B4 103
Ashbyburg, Hopkins, Ky....C2 94
Ashcroft, B.C., Can....D7 68
Ashdod, Isr....C6, h9 32
Ashdot Ya'aqov, Isr....B7 32
Ashdown, Little River, Ark....D1 81
Ashe, co., N.C....A1 109
Asheboro, Randolph, N.C....B3 109
Asheboro South, Randolph, N.C....*B3 109
Asheboro West, Randolph, N.C....*B3 109
Ashepoo, riv., S.C....F6 115
Asher, Yuma, Ariz....E1 80
Asher, Pottawatomie, Okla....C5 112
Ashern, Man., Can....D2 71
Asherton, Dimmit, Tex....E3 118
Asherville, Mitchell, Kans....C6 93
Asheville, Buncombe, N.C....f10 109
Ashfield, Franklin, Mass....A2 97
Ash Flat, Sharp, Ark....A4 81
Ashford, Houston, Ala....D4 78
Ashford, Eng....C8 12
Ashford, Windham, Conn....B8 84
Ashford, McDowell, N.C....B2, f11 109
Ashford, Boone, W. Va....m12 123
Ash Fork, Yavapai, Ariz....B3 80
Ash Grove, Greene, Mo....D4 101
Ashikaga, Jap....H9, m18 37
Ashington, Eng....E7 13
Ashio, Jap....H9 37
Ashkhabad, Sov. Un....H20 9
Ashkum, Iroquois, Ill....C6 90
Ash Lake, St. Louis, Minn....B6 99
Ashland, Clay, Ala....B4 78
Ashland, Cass, Ill....D3 90
Ashland, Clark, Kans....E4 93
Ashland, Boyd, Ky....B7 94
Ashland, Natchitoches, La....B2 95
Ashland, Aroostook, Maine....B4 96
Ashland, Middlesex, Mass....g10 97
Ashland, Benton, Miss....A4 100
Ashland, Boone, Mo....C5 101
Ashland, Rosebud, Mont....E10 102
Ashland, Saunders, Nebr....C9, g12 103
Ashland, Grafton, N.H....C3 105
Ashland, Ashland, Ohio....B3 111
Ashland, Jackson, Oreg....E4 113
Ashland, Schylkill and Columbia, Pa....E9 114
Ashland, Hanover, Va....C5 121
Ashland, Ashland, Wis....B3 124
Ashland, co., Ohio....B3 111
Ashland, co., Wis....B3 124
Ashland, mtn., Oreg....E4 113
Ashland, res., Mass....h10 97
Ashland City, Cheatham, Tenn....A4 117
Ashley, Washington, Ill....E4 90
Ashley, DeKalb and Steuben, Ind....A7 91
Ashley, Gratiot, Mich....E6 98
Ashley, Pike, Mo....B6 101
Ashley, McIntosh, N. Dak....C6 110
Ashley, Delaware, Ohio....B3 111
Ashley, Luzerne, Pa....n17 114
Ashley, co., Ark....D4 81
Ashley, creek, Utah....C6 119
Ashley, riv., S.C....F7 115
Ashley Falls, Berkshire, Mass....B1 97
Ashmont, Alta., Can....B5 69
Ashmore, Coles, Ill....D5 90
Ashmūn, Eg....D2 32
Ashnola, riv., Can., U.S....A5 122

Ashokan, Ulster, N.Y...D6 108
Ashokan, res., N.Y...D6 108
Ashport, Lauderdale, Tenn...B2 117
Ashqelon, Isr...C6 32
Ash Shabakah, Iraq...G14 31
Ash Shallāl, Eg...E6 43
Ash Shām, mtn., Om...D2 39
Ash Shamālīyah (Northern), prov., Sud...B2 47
Ash Shāriqah, U.A.E...I7 41
Ash Shaţrah, Iraq...F3 41
Ash Shawāshinah, Eg...E2 32
Ash Shawbak, Jordan...D7 32
Ash Shaykh Jarrāḩ, Jordan...m14 32
Ash Shaykh Miskīn, Syr...B8 32
Ash Shaykh Sa'd, Syr...B7 32
Ash Shiḩr, P.D.R. of Yem...C6 47
Ash Shurayk, Sud...B3 47
Ashtabula, Ashtabula, Ohio...A5 111
Ashtabula, co., Ohio...A5 111
Ashtabula, lake, N. Dak...B8 110
Ashton, Ont., Can...B8 72
Ashton, Fremont, Idaho...E7 89
Ashton, Lee, Ill...B4 90
Ashton, Osceola, Iowa...A2 92
Ashton, Montgomery, Md...B3 85
Ashton, Osceola, Mich...E5 98
Ashton, Sherman, Nebr...C7 103
Ashton, Providence, R.I...B11 84
Ashton, Spink, S. Dak...B7 116
Ashuanipi, lake, Newf., Can...h8 75
Ashuelot, Cheshire, N.H...E2 105
Ashuelot, riv., N.H...E2 105
Ashville, St. Clair, Ala...B3 78
Ashville, Man., Can...D1 71
Ashville, Pickaway, Ohio...C3 111
Ashwaubenon, Brown, Wis...g9 124
Ashwood, Jefferson, Oreg...C6 113
Ashwood, Maury, Tenn...B4 117
Asia, cont...C3 2, 33
Asiago, It...D7 18
Asifabad, India...H7 40
Asiga, pt., Guam...52
Asiga, pt. Tinian...52
Asinara, gulf, It...D2 21
Asinara, isl., It...D2 21
Asino, Sov. Un...B11 29
Asir, reg., Sau. Ar...B5 47
'Aşīrah ash Shamālīyah, Jordan...g12 32
Asker, Nor...p28 25
Askersund, Swe...H6 25
Askham, S. Afr...C3 49
Askew, Panola, Miss...A3 100
Askim, Nor...p29 25
Askim, Swe...A5 24
Askival, mtn., Scot...D2 13
Askö, isl., Swe...u35 25
Askov, Pine, Minn...D6 99
Asmantay Matay, lake, Sov. Un...F20 9
Āsmār, Afg...D15 41
Asmara (Asmera), Eth...B4 47
Asmera, see Asmara, Eth.
Asnaes, Den...C5 24
Asnebumskit, hill, Mass...B4 97
Asnen, lake, Swe...B8 24
Asnières [-sur-Seine], Fr...C5, g10 14, F2 15
Asopos, riv., Grc...g11 23
Asosa, Eth...C3 47
Asotin, Asotin, Wash...C8 122
Asotin, co., Wash...C8 122
Asotin, creek, Wash...C8 122
Aspe, Sp...C5 20
Aspen, Pitkin, Colo...B4 83
Aspen Hill, Giles, Tenn...B5 117
Asperg, F.R.G...E4 17
Aspermont, Stonewall, Tex...C2 118
Aspers, Adams, Pa...G7 114
Aspinwall, Crawford, Iowa...C2 92
Aspinwall, Allegheny, Pa...k14 114
Aspiring, mtn., N.Z...p12 51
Aspres [-sur-Buëch], Fr...E1 18
Aspropirgos, Grc...g11 23
Aspy, bay, N.S., Can...C9 74
Asquith, Sask., Can...E2 70
Assabet, riv., Mass...g9 97
Aş Şaff, Eg...E3 32
Aş Şāfī, Jordan...C7 32
Assatkwatamo, riv., Man., Can...A3 71
Aş Şāliḩīyah, Eg...D4 32
As Sallūm, Eg...C5 43
As Salman, Iraq...G15 31
As Salţ, Jordan...F10 31
Assam, state, India...C9 39
As Samū', Jordan...C7 32
Aş Şanamayan, Syr...A8 32
Assaria, Saline, Kans...D6 93
Assateague, isl., Md., Va...C7 121
Assateague Island, nat. seashore, Md., Va...D7 85
Assawompset, pond, Mass...C6 97
Assean, lake, Man., Can...A3 71
Assen, Neth...B6 15
Assens, Den...B4 24
As Sinbillāwayn, Eg...D3 32
Assiniboia, Sask., Can...H3 70
Assiniboine, mtn., Alta., B.C., Can...D3 69
Assiniboine, riv., Man., Sask., Can...F5 70
Assinica, prov. park, Que, Can...h11 73
Assinie, I.C...E4 45
Assinika, riv., Man., Can...C4 71
Assinippi, Plymouth, Mass...h12 97
Assis, Braz...C2 56
Assisi, It...C4 21
Assonet, Bristol, Mass...C5 97
As Sudd, swamp, Sud...D3 43
Aş Şūfiyah, Eg...D3 32
As Sulaymānīyāh, Iraq...E15 31
As Sulayyil, Sau. Ar...A6 47
As Sulţān, Libya...C3 43
Aş Şummān, des., Sau. Ar...H3 41
Assumption, Christian, Ill...D4 90
Assumption, par., La...E4 95
As Suwaydā', Syr...F11 31
As Suways, see Suez, Eg.
Astakos, Grc...C3 23
Āstārā, Iran...B4 41
Asten, Neth...C5 15
Asterābād, see Gorgan, Iran
Asti, It...B2 21
Astipalaia, isl., Grc...D6 23
Astola, isl., Pak...I11 41
Aston, Delaware, Pa...*G11 114
Aston-Junction, Que., Can...C5 73
Astor, Lake, Fla...C5 86
Astorga, Sp...A2 20
Astoria, Fulton, Ill...C3 90
Astoria, Clatsop, Oreg...A3 113
Astoria, Deuel, S. Dak...C9 116
Astor Park, Lake, Fla...C5 86
Astorville, Ont., Can...A5 72
Astrakhan, Sov. Un...D3 29
Astura, riv., It...h9 21
Asturias, reg., Sp...A2 20
Asuisui, cape, W. Sam...52
Asuke, Jap...n16 37
Asunción, Par...E4 55
Asuncion, isl., Mariana Is...E8 7
Asunción Mita, Guat...C3 62
Åsunden, lake, Swe...A7 24
Aswān, Eg...E6 43
Aswān High, dam, Eg...E6 43
Asyūţ, Eg...D6 43
Atacama, prov., Chile...E1 55
Atacama, des., Chile...D2 55
Atacama, salt flat, Chile...D2 55
'Aţā'itah, mtn., Jordan...D7 32
Atakpamé, Togo...E5 45
Atalaia, Braz...k6 57
Atalandi, Grc...C4 23
Atalissa, Muscatine, Iowa...C6 92
Atami, Jap...n18 37
Atar, Maur...B2 45
Atārūt, Jordan...h11 32
Atascadero, San Luis Obispo, Calif...E3 82
Atascosa, co., Tex...E3 118
Atasuskiy, Sov. Un...D8 29
Atatyn Hiid, Mong...A3 36
Ataúro, isl., Port. Timor...G7 35
'Atbarah, Sud...B3 47
Atbarah, riv., Sud...B4 47
Atbasar, Sov. Un...C7 29
Atchafalaya, bay, La...E4 95
Atchafalaya, riv., La...D4 95
Atchison, Atchison, Kans...C8 93
Atchison, co., Kans...C8 93
Atchison, co., Mo...A2 101
Atchugau, mtn., Saipan...52
Atco, Bartow, Ga. (part of Cartersville)...B2 87
Atco, Camden, N.J...D3 106
Atenango, riv., Mex...n14 63
Ath, Bel...D3 15
Athabasca, Alta., Can...B4, g8 69
Athabasca, lake, Alta., Sask., Can...m7 70
Athabasca, riv., Alta., Can...B4 69
Athalia, Lawrence, Ohio...D3 111
Athalmer, B.C., Can...D10 68
Athapapuskow, lake, Man., Can...B1 71
Atha Road, Ont., Can...k15 72
Athboy, Ire...D4 11
Athel, Wicomico, Md...D6 85
Athelstan, Que., Can...D3 73
Athelstan, Taylor, Iowa...D3 92
Athena, Umatilla, Oreg...B8 113
Athenry, Ire...D3 11
Athens, Limestone, Ala...A3 78
Athens, Howard, Ark...C2 81
Athens, Ont., Can...C9 72
Athens, Clarke, Ga...C3 87
Athens (Athinai), Grc...C4, h11 23
Athens, Menard, Ill...D4 90
Athens, Fulton, Ind...B5 91
Athens, Claiborne, La...B2 95
Athens, Somerset, Maine...D3 96
Athens, Calhoun, Mich...F5 98
Athens, Greene, N.Y...C7 108
Athens, Athens, Ohio...C3 111
Athens, Bradford, Pa...C8 114
Athens, McMinn, Tenn...D9 117
Athens, Henderson, Tex...C5 118
Athens, Windham, Vt...E3 120
Athens, Mercer, W. Va...D3 123
Athens, Marathon, Wis...C3 124
Athens, co., Ohio...C3 111
Athensville, Greene, Ill...D3 90
Atherley, Ont., Can...C5 72
Atherton, Austl...C8 50
Atherton, San Mateo, Calif...*D2 82
Athertonville, Larue, Ky...C4 94
Athi, riv., Ken...B6 48
Athiéme, Benin...E5 45
Athis-Mons, Fr...h10 14
Athleague, Ire...D3 11
Athlone, Ire...D4 11
Athok, Bur...E10 39
Athol, Kootenai, Idaho...B2 89
Athol, Smith, Kans...C5 93
Athol, Worcester, Mass...A3 97
Athol, Spink, S. Dak...B7 116
Athol, isl., Ba...m18 64
Athos, mtn., Grc...B5 23
Ath Thamad, Eg...D6 43
Athy, Ire...D5 11
Atibaia, Braz...m8 56
Atico, Peru...E3 58
Aticonipi, lake, Que., Can...C2 75
Atikameg, Alta., Can...B3 69
Atikokan, Ont., Can...o17 72
Atikonak, lake, Newf., Can...h8 75
Atimonan, Phil...p13 35
Atiquizaya, Sal...D3 62
Atizapán de Zaragoza, Mex...g9 63
Atka, Alsk...E5 79
Atka, isl., Alsk...E5 79
Atkarsk, Sov. Un...F15 27
Atkins, Pope, Ark...B3 81
Atkins, Benton, Iowa...B6 92
Atkins, Bossier, La...B2 95
Atkins, Smyth, Va...D1, f10 121
Atkinson, Brantley, Ga...E5 87
Atkinson, Henry, Ill...B3 90
Atkinson, Holt, Nebr...B7 103
Atkinson, Pender, N.C...C4 109
Atkinson, co., Ga...E4 87
Atkinson, lake, Man., Can...A4 71
Atkinson Depot (Atkinson), Rockingham, N.H...E4 105
Atlanta, Columbia, Ark...D2 81
Atlanta, Fulton and DeKalb, Ga...C2, h8 87
Atlanta, Elmore, Idaho...F3 89
Atlanta, Logan, Ill...C4 90
Atlanta, Hamilton, Ind...D5 91
Atlanta, Cowley, Kans...E7 93
Atlanta, Winn, La...C3 95
Atlanta, Montmorency, Mich...C6 98
Atlanta, Macon, Mo...B5 101
Atlanta, Phelps, Nebr...D6 103
Atlanta, Steuben, N.Y...C3 108
Atlanta, Pickaway, Ohio...C2 111
Atlanta, Cass, Tex...C5 118
Atlantic, Cass, Iowa...C2 92
Atlantic, Carteret, N.C...C6 109
Atlantic, co., N.J...E3 106
Atlantic, ocean...6
Atlantic, peak, Wyo...D3 125
Atlantic Beach, Duval, Fla...m9 86
Atlantic Beach, Nassau, N.Y...*G2 84
Atlantic City, Atlantic, N.J...E4 106
Atlantic City, Fremont, Wyo...D4 125
Atlantic Highlands, Monmouth, N.J...C4 106
Atlantic Mine, Houghton, Mich...A2 98
Atlántico, dept., Col...A2 60
Atlas, Northumberland, Pa...*E9 114
Atlas, mts., Afr...C5 42
Atlas Saharien, mts., Alg...C5 44
Atlee, Alta., Can...D5 69
Atlin, B.C., Can...m16 68
Atlin, lake, B.C., Can...E6 66
'Atlit, Isr...B6 32
Atlixco, Mex...n14 63
Atmore, Escambia, Ala...D2 78
Atna, peak, B.C., Can...C3 68
Atna, range, B.C., Can...B4 68
Atocha, Bol...D2 55
Atoka, Eddy, N. Mex...E5 107
Atoka, Atoka, Okla...C5 112
Atoka, Tipton, Tenn...B2 117
Atoka, co., Okla...C5 112
Atoka, res., Okla...C6 112
Atomic City, Bingham, Idaho...F6 89
Atotonilco el Alto, Mex...m12 63
Atoyac, Mex...m12 63
Atoyac, riv., Mex...n14 63
Atrak, riv., Iran...C8 41
Atrato, riv., Col...B2 60
Atrisco, Bernalillo, N. Mex...B3, k7 107
Atsugi, Jap...n18 37
Atsukeshi, bay, Jap...E12 37
Atsuma, Jap...E10 37
Atsumi, bay, Jap...o16 37
At Tabbīn, Eg...E3 32
Aţ Ţafīlah, Jordan...D7 32
Aţ Ţā'if, Sau. Ar...A5 47
Attala, co., Miss...B4 100
Attalla, Etowah, Ala...A3 78
Aţ Ţallāb, Libya...E4 43
At Tamīmī, Libya...C4 43
At Tannūrah, cape, Sau. Ar...H5 41
Attapulgus, Decatur, Ga...F2 87
Aţţarah, Jordan...g11 32
Attavyros, mtn., Grc...D6 23
Attawapiskat, Ont., Can...n19 72
Attawapiskat, riv., Ont., Can...n18 72
Attawaugan, Windham, Conn...B9 84
Aţ Ţayyibah, Jordan...C7, h12 32
Attean, pond, Maine...C2 96
Attica, Fountain, Ind...D3 91
Attica, Harper, Kans...E5 93
Attica, Lapeer, Mich...E7 98
Attica, Genesee and Wyoming, N.Y...C2 108
Attica, Seneca, Ohio...A3 111
Attica, reg., Grc...g11 23
Attica (Attiki), prov., Grc...*C4 23
Attigny, Fr...E4 15
Attikamagen, lake, Newf., Can...g8 75
Attiki (Attica), prov., Grc...*C4 23
Aţ Ţinah, Eg...C4 32
Attleboro, Bristol, Mass...C5 97
Attleborough, Eng...B9 12
Attopeu, Laos...E7 38
Attu, isl., Alsk...E2 79
Aţ Ţūr, Eg...D6 43
Aţ Ţūr, Jordan...m14 32
Attymon, Ire...D3 11
Atuel, riv., Arg...B3 54
Atu'u, Am. Sam...52
Åtvidaberg, Swe...H6 25
Atwater, Merced, Calif...D3 82
Atwater, Sask., Can...G4 70
Atwater, Kandiyohi, Minn...E4 99
Atwood, Ont., Can...D3 72
Atwood, Logan, Colo...A7 83
Atwood, Piatt and Douglas, Ill...D5 90
Atwood, Kosciusko, Ind...B6 91
Atwood, Rawlins, Kans...C2 93
Atwood, Hughes, Okla...C5 112
Atwood, Carroll, Tenn...B3 117
Atwood, res., Ohio...B4 111
Atwood Heights, Cook, Ill...*B6 90
Atzcapotzalco (Azcapotzalco), Mex...h9, n14 63
Aua, Am. Sam...52
Auau, chan., Haw...C5 88
Aubagne, Fr...F6 14
Aube, dept., Fr...F4 15
Aube, riv., Fr...F4 15
Aubenas, Fr...E6 14
Auberry, Fresno, Calif...D4 82
Aubervilliers Fr...g10 14
Aubière, Fr...E5 14
Aubigny-sur-Nère, Fr...D5 14
Aubin, Fr...E5 14
Aubrey, Lee, Ark...C5 81
Aubrey, Que., Can...D4 73
Auburn, Lee, Ala...C4 78
Auburn, Placer, Calif...C3 82
Auburn, Ont., Can...D3 72
Auburn, Barrow, Ga...B3 87
Auburn, Sangamon, Ill...D4 90
Auburn, DeKalb, Ind...B7 91
Auburn, Sac, Iowa...B3 92
Auburn, Shawnee, Kans...D8 93
Auburn, Logan, Ky...D3 94
Auburn, Androscoggin, Maine...D2, f7 96
Auburn, Worcester, Mass...B4 97
Auburn, Bay, Mich...E6 98
Auburn, Lincoln, Miss...D3 100
Auburn, Nemaha, Nebr...D10 103
Auburn, Rockingham, N.H...D4 105
Auburn, Salem, N.J...D2 106
Auburn, Cayuga, N.Y...C4 108
Auburn, Walsh, N. Dak...A8 110
Auburn, Schuylkill, Pa...E9 114
Auburn, King, Wash...B3, f11 122
Auburn, Ritchie, W. Va...B4 123
Auburn, Lincoln, Wyo...D1 125
Auburndale, Polk, Fla...D5 86
Auburndale, Wood, Wis...D3 124
Auburn Heights, Oakland, Mich...F7 98
Auburntown, Cannon, Tenn...B5 117
Aubusson, Fr...E5 14
Auch, Fr...F4 14
Auchel, Fr...D2 15
Auchterarder, Scot...D5 13
Auchtermuchty, Scot...*D5 13
Aucilla, Jefferson, Fla...B3 86
Aucilla, riv., Fla...B3 86
Auckland, N.Z...L15 51
Auckland, is., N.Z. (Pac. O.)...D29 5
Aude, dept., Fr...*F5 14
Aude, riv., Fr...F5 14
Audet, Que., Can...D7 73
Audierne, Fr...D1 14
Audincourt, Fr...D1 14
Audrain, co., Mo...B6 101
Audubon, Audubon, Iowa...C3 92
Audubon, Becker, Minn...D3 99
Audubon, Camden, N.J...D2 106
Audubon, co., Iowa...C3 92
Audubon Park, Jefferson, Ky...*B4 94
Audubon Park, Camden, N.J...*D3 106
Audun-le-Roman, Fr...E5 15
Aue, G.D.R...C7 17
Auerbach, G.D.R...C7 17
Au Fer, pt., La...E4 95
Augathella, Austl...B6 51
Aughnacloy, N. Ire...C5 11
Aughrim, Ire...E5 11
Auglaize, co., Ohio...B1 111
Auglaize, riv., Ohio...A1 111
Au Gres, Arenac, Mich...D7 98
Augsburg, F.R.G...E5 17
Augusta, Austl...F2 50
Augusta, Woodruff, Ark...B4 81
Augusta, Richmond, Ga...C5 87
Augusta, Hancock, Ill...C3 90
Augusta, Marion, Ind...k10 91
Augusta, It...F5 21
Augusta, Butler, Kans...E7, g13 93
Augusta, Bracken, Ky...B6 94
Augusta, Kennebec, Maine...D3 96
Augusta, Kalamazoo, Mich...F5 98
Augusta, St. Charles, Mo...C7 101
Augusta, Lewis and Clark, Mont...C4 102
Augusta, Sussex, N.J...A3 106
Augusta, Carroll, Ohio...B4 111
Augusta, Eau Claire, Wis...D2 124
Augusta, Hampshire, W. Va...B6 123
Augusta, co., Va...C3 121
Augusta Springs, Augusta, Va...C3 121
Augustenborg, Den...D3 24
Augustow, Pol...B7 26
Auineau, pen., Ont., Can...E4 71
Auja, see Yarkon, riv., Isr.
Aul, mtn., Switz...C7 19
Aulander, Bertie, N.C...A5 109
Aulendorf, F.R.G...B5 18
Aulnay-sous-Bois, Fr...g11 14
Aulne, riv., Fr...C1 14
Aulnoye [-Aymeries], Fr...D3 15
Ault, Weld, Colo...A6 83
Aumale, Alg...F8 30
Aumale, Fr...E9 12
Aumsville, Marion, Oreg...k12 113
Auneuil, Fr...E2 15
Auning, Den...B4 24
Aunis, former prov., Fr...*D3 14
Auno, Nig...D7 45
Aunuu, isl., Am. Sam...52
Aur, isl., Mala...K6 38
Aura, Baraga, Mich...B2 98
Auraiya, India...D7 40
Aurangābād, India...E6 39, G5 40
Auray, Fr...D2 14
Aurelia, Cherokee, Iowa...B2 92
Aurelian Springs, Halifax, N.C...A5 109
Aurich, F.R.G...B3 16
Aurillac, Fr...E5 14
Aurora, Ont., Can...D5 72
Aurora, Arapahoe and Adams, Colo...B6 83
Aurora, Guy...A3 59
Aurora, Kane, Ill...B5, k8 90
Aurora, Dearborn, Ind...F8 91
Aurora, Buchanan, Iowa...B6 92
Aurora, Cloud, Kans...C6 93
Aurora, Hancock, Maine...D4 96
Aurora, St. Louis, Minn...C6 99
Aurora, Lawrence, Mo...E4 101
Aurora, Hamilton, Nebr...D7 103
Aurora, Cayuga, N.Y...C4 108
Aurora, Beaufort, N.C...B6 109
Aurora, Portage, Ohio...A4 111
Aurora, Marion, Oreg...B4, h12 113
Aurora, Brookings, S. Dak...C9 116
Aurora, Sevier, Utah...E4 119
Aurora, Preston, W. Va...B5 123
Aurora, Florence, Wis...C5 124
Aurora, co., S. Dak...D7 116
Aurora Center, Brookings, S. Dak...D7 116
Aurskog, Nor...p29 25
Aus, Namibia...C2 49
Au Sable, Iosco, Mich...D7 98
Au Sable, pt., Mich...B4 98
Au Sable, pt., Mich...D7 98
Au Sable, riv., Mich...D6 98
Ausable, riv., N.Y...f11 108
Au Sable Forks, Clinton and Essex, N.Y...f11 108
Aussa, riv., It...D9 18
Ausser-Rhoden, sub canton, Switz...B7 19
Aust-Agder, co., Nor...*H3 25
Austell, Cobb, Ga...h7 87
Austin, Lonoke, Ark...C4 81
Austin, Man., Can...E2 71
Austin, Scott, Ind...G6 91
Austin, Barren, Ky...D3 94
Austin, Mower, Minn...G6 99
Austin, Lander, Nev...D4 104
Austin, Grant, Oreg...C8 113
Austin, Potter, Pa...C5 114
Austin, Travis, Tex...D4 118
Austin, co., Tex...E4 118
Austin, lake, Austl...E2 50
Austinburg, Ashtabula, Ohio...A5 111
Austin Lake, Kalamazoo, Mich...*F5 98
Austintown, Mahoning, Ohio...A5 111
Austinville, Butler, Iowa...B5 92
Austinville, Wythe, Va...E2 121
Australia, country, Oceania...H6 2, 50
Australian Alps, mts., Austl...G8 50
Australian Capital Territory, Austl...G7 51
Austria, country, Eur...F11 8, E6 16
Austwell, Refugio, Tex...E4 118
Autauga, co., Ala...C3 78
Autaugaville, Autauga, Ala...C3 78
Authie, riv., Fr...D2 15
Autlán de Navarro, Mex...D4, n11 63
Au Train, Alger, Mich...B4 98
Autreyville, Colquitt, Ga...E3 87
Autumn Hills, Douglas, Nebr...*C10 103
Autun, Fr...D6 14
Auvergne, Jackson, Ark...B4 81
Auvergane, Que., Can...C6 73
Auvergne, mts., Fr...E5 14
Auvergne, former prov., Fr...E5 14
Auvers [-sur-Oise], Fr...E2 15
Aux Barques, pt., Mich...D8 98
Aux Chene, riv., La...C7 95
Auxerre, Fr...D5 14
Auxier, Floyd, Ky...C7 94
Auxi-le-Château, Fr...D10 12
Auxonne, Fr...D6 14
Auxvasse, Callaway, Mo...B6 101
Ava, Jackson, Ill...F4 90
Ava, Douglas, Mo...E5 101
Ava, Noble, Ohio...C4 111
Avakubi, Zaire...A4 48
Avallon, Fr...D5 14
Avalon, Los Angeles, Calif...F4 82
Avalon, Stephens, Ga...B3 87
Avalon, Livingston, Mo...B4 101
Avalon, Cape May, N.J...E3 106
Avalon, Allegheny, Pa...h13 114
Avalon, pen., Newf., Can...E5 75
Avalon Lake, res., N. Mex...E5 107
Avanos, Tur...C10 31
Avant, Osage, Okla...A5 112
Avard, Woods, Okla...A3 112
Avaré, Braz...C3 56
Aveiro, Port...B1 20
Avella, Washington, Pa...F1 114
Avellaneda, Arg...A5, g7 54
Avellino, It...D5 21
Avenal, Kings, Calif...E3 82
Avenches, Switz...C3 19
Avenel, Middlesex, N.J...k7 106
Avening, Ont., Can...C4 72
Avenwedde, F.R.G...B3 17
Avera, Jefferson, Ga...C4 87
Averill, Clay, Minn...D2 99
Averill, lake, Vt...B5 120
Averill Park, Rensselaer, N.Y...C7 108
Aversa, It...D5 21
Avery, Shoshone, Idaho...B3 89
Avery, Monroe, Iowa...C5 92
Avery, Lincoln, Okla...B5 112
Avery, Red River, Tex...C5 118
Avery, co., N.C...e11 109
Avery Island, Iberia, La...E4 95
Aves, is., Ven...A4 60
Avesnes [-sur-Helpe], Fr...D3 15
Avesta, Swe...G7 25
Aveyron, dept., Fr...*E5 14
Avezzano, It...C4 21
Aviá Teraí, Arg...E3 55
Aviemore, Scot...C5 13
Avigliano, It...D5 21
Avignon, Fr...F6 14
Avila, San Luis Obispo, Calif...E3 82
Ávila, Sp...B3 20
Ávila, prov., Sp...*B3 20
Avilés, Sp...A3 20
Avilla, Noble, Ind...B7 91
Avilla, Jasper, Mo...D3 101
Avinger, Cass, Tex...C5 118
Avis, Clinton, Pa...D7 114
Avisio, riv., It...C7 18
Avize, Fr...F4 15
Avlon, Grc...g11 23
Avlum, Den...B2 24
Avoca, Lawrence, Ala...A2 78
Avoca, Benton, Ark...A1 81
Avoca, Lawrence, Ind...G4 91
Avoca, Pottawattamie, Iowa...C2 92
Avoca, Assumption, La...C5 95
Avoca, St. Clair, Mich...E8 98
Avoca, Murray, Minn...G3 99
Avoca, Cass, Nebr...h12 103
Avoca, Steuben, N.Y...C3 108
Avoca. Luzerne, Pa...m18 114
Avoca, Jones, Tex...C3 118
Avoca, Iowa, Wis...E3 124
Avola, It...F5 21
Avola, B.C., Can...D8 68
Avon, Ont., Can...E4 72
Avon, Hartford, Conn...B5 84
Avon, Fulton, Ill...C3 90
Avon, Polk, Iowa...e8 92
Avon, Franklin, Maine...D2 96
Avon, Norfolk, Mass...B5, h11 97
Avon, Stearns, Minn...E4 99
Avon, Washington, Miss...B2 100
Avon, Powell, Mont...D4 102
Avon, Livingston, N.Y...C3 108
Avon, Dare, N.C...B7 109
Avon, Lorain, Ohio...A3 111
Avon, Lebanon, Pa...*F9 114
Avon, Bon Homme, S. Dak...E7 116
Avon, Cache, Utah...B4 119
Avon, riv., Eng...E6 10, D6 12
Avon, riv., Eng...D6 10, B5 12
Avon, riv., Scot...C5 13
Avon by the Sea, Monmouth, N.J...*C4 106
Avondale, Maricopa, Ariz...m8 80
Avondale, Newf., Can...*E5 75
Avondale, Pueblo, Colo...C6 83
Avondale, Jefferson, La...*E5 95
Avondale, Prince Georges, Md...*C4 85
Avondale, Clay, Mo...h10 101
Avondale, Chester, Pa...G10 114
Avondale Estates, DeKalb, Ga...h8 87
Avondale, Washington, R.I...D9 84
Avon Lake, Polk, Iowa...e8 92
Avon Lake, Lorain, Ohio...A3 111
Avonlea, Sask., Can...G3 70
Avonmore, Westmoreland, Pa...E3 114
Avon Park, Highlands, Fla...E5 86
Avoyelles, par., La...C3 95
Avranches, Fr...C3 14
Awa, isl., Jap...G9 37
Awaji, isl., Jap...I7 37
'Awartā, Jordan...B7 32
Awasa, Eth...D4 47
Awash, Eth...D5 47
Awash, riv., Eth...C5 47
Awashi, Okinawa...52
Awbāri, Libya...D2 43
Awdeyle, Som...E5 47
Awe, lake, Scot...D3 13
Awjilah, Libya...D4 43
Axel, Neth...C3 15
Axel Heiberg, isl., N.W. Ter., Can...k33 67
Axial, basin, Colo...A2 83
Axim, Ghana...F4 45
Axios (Vardar), riv., Grc...B4 23
Axis, Mobile, Ala...E1 78
Ax-les-Thermes, Fr...F4 14
Axson, Atkinson, Ga...E4 87
Axtell, Marshall, Kans...C7 93
Axtell, Kearney, Nebr...D6 103
Axtell, Sanpete, Utah...D4 119
Ay, Fr...C6 14
Ay, riv., Sov. Un...B5 29
Ayabaca, Peru...B2 58
Ayabe, Jap...n14 37
Ayacucho, Arg...B5 54
Ayacucho, Peru...D3 58
Ayacucho, dept., Peru...D3 58
Ayaguz, Sov. Un...D10 29
Ayakhta, Sov. Un...D28 9
Ayamonte, Sp...D2 20
Ayan, Sov. Un...D16 28
Ayapel, Col...B2 60
Ayapel, mts., Col...B3 60
Ayas, Tur...B9 31
Ayaviri, Peru...D3 58
Aycliffe, Eng...F7 13
Aydar, riv., Sov. Un...G13 27
Ayden, Pitt., N.C...B5 109
Aydin (Aidin), Tur...D6 31
Aydlett, Currituck, N.C...A7 109
Ayer, Middlesex, Mass...A4, f9 97
Ayers, Washington, Maine...D5 96
Ayers Cliff, Que., Can...D5 73
Ayía, Grc...C4 23
Ayía Paraskeví, Grc...C6 23
Ayiassos, Grc...C6 23
Ayion Oros, see Mount Athos, prov., Grc.
Ayios Dhimitrios, Grc...g11 23
Ayios Nikolaos, Grc...E5 23
Aylen, lake, Ont., Can...B7 72
Aylesbury, Sask., Can...G3 70
Aylesbury, Eng...C7 12
Aylesford, N.S., Can...D5 74
Aylett, King William, Va...C5 121
Alymer, lake, N.W. Ter., Can...D11 66
Aylmer, mtn., Atla., Can...D3 69
Aylmer East, Que., Can...D2 73
Aylmer West, Ont., Can...E4 72
Aylsham, Sask., Can...D4 70
'Ayn al Bāghah, well, Eg...E5 32
Aynor, Horry, S.C...D9 115
'Ayn Sīdī Muḩammad, oasis, Libya...H3 31
'Ayn Sudr, well, Eg...E5 32
'Ayn Yabrūd, Jordan...h11 32
Ayon, isl., Sov. Un...C19 28
Ayora, Sp...C5 20
'Ayoûn el 'Atroûs, Maur...C3 45
Ayr, Ont., Can...D4 72
Ayr, Adams, Nebr...D7 103
Ayr, Cass, N. Dak...B8 110
Ayr, co., Scot...E4 13
Ayr, riv., Scot...E4 13
Ayrshire, Pike, Ind...H3 91
Ayrshire, Palo Alto, Iowa...A3 92
Aysary, Sov. Un...C8 29
Aysén, see Aisén, prov., Chile
Aysha, Eth...C5 47
Ayton, Ont., Can...C4 72
Aytos, Bul...D8 22
Aytre, Fr...D3 14
Ayu, isl., Indon...E8 35
Ayutla, Guat...C1 62
Ayutla [de los Libres], Mex...D5 63
Ayutthaya, Thai...E4 38
Ayvacik, Tur...C6 31
Ayvalik, Tur...C6 31
Azalea Park, Orange, Fla...*D5 86
Azalia, Bartholomew, Ind...F6 91
Azama, Okinawa...52
Azamgarh, India...D9 40
Azángaro, Peru...D3 58
Azaouâd, sand dunes, Mali...C4 45
Azare, Nig...D7 45
Azemmour, Mor...C3 44
Azerbaidzhan, (S.S.R.), rep., Sov. Un...G18 9
Azilal, Mor...I3 30
Aziscoos, lake, Maine...C1 96
Azle, Tarrant, Tex...n9 118
Azogues, Ec...B2 58
Azor, Isr...g10 32
Azores Islands, reg., Port. (Atl. O.)...h8 44
Azov, Sov. Un...H12 27
Azov, sea, Sov. Un...I11 27
Azrou, Mor...C3 44
Aztec, Yuma, Ariz...E2 80
Aztec, San Juan, N. Mex...A2 107
Aztec Ruins, nat. mon., N. Mex...A1 107
Azua, Dom. Rep...E8 64
Azuaga, Sp...C3 20
Azuay, prov., Ec...B2 58
Azuero, pen., Pan...G7 62
Azul, Arg...B5 54
Azul, range, Peru...C2 58
Azurdui, Bol...C3 55
Azusa, Los Angeles, Calif...m13 82
Az Ẓāhirīyah, Jordan...C6 32
Az Ẓahran, see Dhahran, Sau. Ar.
Az Zaqāzīq, Eg...D3 32
Az Zarqā', Jordan...B8 32
'Azzās, cape, Libya...C5 43
Az Zawiyah, Libya...C2 43
Az Zawr, cape, Sau. Ar...H4 41
Az Zaydāb, Sud...B3 47
Azzel Matti, lake, Alg...D5 44
Az Zubayr, Iraq...F3 41
Azzun, Jordan...g11 32

B

Baagö, isl., Den...C3 24
Baal, F.R.G...C6 15
Baar, Switz...B6 19
Baarle-Hertog, Bel...C4 15
Baba, cape, Tur...C6 23
Babadag, Rom...C9 22
Babaeski, Tur...B6 23
Babahoyo, Ec...B2 58
Babana, Nig...D5 45
Babanūsah, Sud...C2 47
Babati, Tan...B6 48
Babayevo, Sov. Un...B11 27
Babb, Glacier, Mont...B3 102
Babb, creek, Pa...C7 114
Babbie, Covington, Ala...D3 78
Babbit, Mineral, Nev...E3 104
Babbitt, St. Louis, Minn...C7 99
Babcock, Wood, Wis...D3 124
Bab el Mandeb, strait, Afr.-Asia...C5 47
Babelthuap, isl., Palau Is...52
Babenhausen, F.R.G...A6 18
Babi, is., Indon...K2 38
Babine, lake, B.C., Can...B5 68
Babine, range, B.C., Can...B4 68
Babine, riv., B.C., Can...B4 68
Babo, Indon...F8 35
Bābol, Iran...C6 41
Baboquivari, mts., Ariz...F4 80
Baboua, Cen. Afr. Rep...D2 46
Babson Park, Polk, Fla...E5 86
Babuna, mts., Yugo...E5 22
Babushkin, Sov. Un...A6 34
Babuyan, chan., Phil...*B6 35
Babuyan, is., Phil...B6 35
Babyak, Bul...E6 22
Babylon, Suffolk, N.Y...n15 108
Baca, co., Colo...D8 83
Bacabal, Braz...B2 57
Bacajá, riv., Braz...C4 59
Bacalar, Mex...D7 63
Bacarra, Phil...*B6 35
Bacău, Rom...B8 22
Baccalieu, isl., Newf., Can...D5 75
Baccarat, Fr...C7 14
Baccaro, pt., N.S., Can...F4 74
Baceras, Mex...A3 63
Bach, Huron, Mich...E7 98
Bach, Switz...C7 19

Bebra, F.R.G. C4 17
Becancour, Que., Can. C5 73
Becancour, riv., Que., Can. C6 73
Beccles, Eng. B9 12
Bečej, Yugo. C5 22
Becerreá, Sp. A2 20
Béchar, Alg. C4 44
Becharof, lake, Alsk. D8 79
Bechuanaland, see Botswana, country, Afr.
Bechyne, Czech. D9 17
Beckemeyer, Clinton, Ill. E4 90
Becker, Sherburne, Minn. E5 99
Becker, Monroe, Miss. B5 100
Becker, co., Minn. D3 99
Becket, Berkshire, Mass. B1 97
Beckham, co., Okla. B2 112
Beckley, Raleigh, W. Va. D3, n13 123
Beckum, F.R.G. B3 17
Beckville, Panola, Tex. C5 118
Beckwith, Lincoln, Wyo. E2 125
Beckwith, creek, La. D2 95
Bedale, Eng. F7 13
Bédarieux, Fr. F5 14
Bedburg, F.R.G. C1 17
Beddington, Washington, Maine D4 96
Bederkesa, F.R.G. E2 24
Bedford, N.S., Can. E6 74
Bedford, Que., Can. D5 73
Bedford, Eng. B7 12
Bedford, Lawrence, Ind. G5 91
Bedford, Taylor, Iowa D6 92
Bedford, Trimble, Ky. B4 94
Bedford, Middlesex, Mass. B5, g10 97
Bedford, Calhoun, Mich. F5 98
Bedford, Livingston, Mo. B4 101
Bedford, Hillsboro, N.H. E3 105
Bedford, Cuyahoga, Ohio A4, h9 111
Bedford, Bedford, Pa. F4 114
Bedford, Tarrant, Tex. *C4 118
Bedford (Independent City), Va. C3 121
Bedford, Lincoln, Wyo. D2 125
Bedford, co., Eng. B7 12
Bedford, co., Pa. G4 114
Bedford, co., Tenn. B5 117
Bedford, co., Va. C3 121
Bedford Heights, Cuyahoga, Ohio *A4 111
Bedford Hills, Westchester, N.Y. m15 108
Bedias, Grimes, Tex. D5 118
Bédja, prov., Tun. *B6 44
Bedlington[shire], Eng. C6 10
Bedminster, Somerset, N.J. B3 106
Bedourie, Austl. B2 51
Bedrock, Montrose, Colo. C2 83
Bedzin, Pol. g10 26
Bee, Seward, Nebr. C8 103
Bee, Johnston, Okla. C5 112
Bee, co., Tex. E4 118
Beebe, White, Ark. B4 81
Beebe, Que., Can. D5 73
Beebe Plain, Orleans, Vt. B4 120
Beebe River, Grafton, N.H. C3 105
Bee Branch, Van Buren, Ark. B3 81
Beech, fork, Ky. C4 94
Beech Bluff, Madison, Tenn. B3 117
Beechbottom, Brooke, W. Va. A4, f8 123
Beech Creek, Muhlenberg, Ky. C2 94
Beech Creek, Clinton, Pa. D6 114
Beecher, Will, Ill. B6 90
Beecher City, Effingham, Ill. D5 90
Beecher Falls, Essex, Vt. A5 120
Beechey, head, B.C., Can. h12 68
Beech Grove, Greene, Ark. A5 81
Beech Grove, Marion, Ind. E5, k10 91
Beech Grove, McLean, Ky. C2 94
Beechgrove, Coffee, Tenn. B5 117
Beech Island, Aiken, S.C. E4 115
Beechwood, N.B., Can. C2 74
Beechwood, Norfolk, Mass. h12 97
Beechwood Village, Jefferson, Ky. *B4 94
Beechy, Sask., Can. G2 70
Beecroft, head, Austl. G8 51
Beedeville, Jackson, Ark. B4 81
Beef, isl., Tenn. e8 117
Beef, isl., Vir. Is. (Br.) B7 65
Beek, Neth. D5 15
Beekman, Morehouse, La. B4 95
Beeler, Ness, Kans. D4 93
Beelitz, G.D.R. A7 17
Beemer, Cuming, Nebr. C9 103
Beenleigh, Austl. C9 51
Bee Ridge, Sarasota, Fla. q11 86
Beersheba, see Be'er Sheva', Isr.
Beersheba Springs, Grundy, Tenn. D8 117
Be'er Sheva' (Beersheba), Isr. C6 32
Beersville, N.B., Can. C4 74
Beeskow, G.D.R. A9 17
Beesleys Point, Cape May, N.J. E3 106
Beethoven, pen., Ant. B5 5
Beeton, Ont., Can. C5 72
Beetzendorf, G.D.R. F5 24
Beeville, Bee, Tex. E4 118
Befale, Zaire A3 48
Beg, lake, N. Ire. C5 11
Bega, Austl. H7 51
Begemdir & Simen, prov., Eth. C4 63
Beggs, Okmulgee, Okla. B5 112
Begi, Eth. D3 47
Begicheva, isl., Sov. Un. B3 4
Bègles, Fr. E3 14
Begovat, Sov. Un. G22 9
Béhague, pt., Fr. Gu. B4 59
Behbehān, Iran F5 41
Behm, canal, Alsk. n24 79
Beilngries, F.R.G. D6 17
Beira, Moz. A5 49
Beira, reg., Port. B2 20
Beira Alta, prov., Port. *B2 20
Beira Baixa, prov., Port. *C2 20
Beira Litoral, prov., Port. *B1 20
Beirne, Clark, Ark. D2 81
Beirut (Bayrūt), Leb. I16 9
Beiseker, Alta., Can. D4 69
Beitbridge, Zimb. B5 49
Beiuș, Rom. B6 22
Beja, Port. C2 20
Beja, Tun. B6 44
Bejaïa (Bougie), Alg. B6 44
Béjar, Sp. B3 20
Bejou, Mahnomen, Minn. C3 99
Bejuco, Pan. F8 62
Bekdash, Sov. Un. E4 29
Békés, Hung. B5 22
Békés, co., Hung. *B5 22
Bekescsaba, Hung. B5 22
Bekily, Mad. h9 49
Bela, India E8 40
Bela, Pak. C4 39
Bela Crkva, Yugo. C5 22
Belaga, Mala. E4 39
Bélair, Que., Can. n17 73
Bel Air, Harford, Md. A5 85
Bel Aire Estates, New London, Conn. *D9 84
Belalcázar, Sp. C3 20
Bel Alton, Charles, Md. D4 85
Bélanger, riv., Man., Can. C3 71
Bélanger, riv., Sask., Can. B2 70
Belas, Port. f9 20
Bela Vista, Braz. C1 56
Bela Vista, Moz. C5 49
Belawan, Indon. E1, m11 35
Belaya, riv., Sov. Un. B4 29
Belaya Glina, Sov. Un. H13 27
Belaya Tserkov, Sov. Un. G8 27
Belcamp, Harford, Md. B5 85
Belcher, Pike, Ky. C7 94
Belcher, Caddo, La. B2 95
Belcher, is., N.W. Ter., Can. E16 67
Belcherāgh, Afg. D12 41
Belchertown, Hampshire, Mass. B3 97
Belcourt, Rolette, N. Dak. A6 110
Belcoville, Atlantic, N.J. E3 106
Belden, Lee, Miss. A5 100
Belden, Cedar, Nebr. B8 103
Belden, Mountrail, N. Dak. A3 110
Belding, Ionia, Mich. E5 98
Belecke, F.R.G. B3 17
Beled Weyne, Som. E6 47
Belém (Pará), Braz. B1 57
Belém, Port. f9 20
Belén, Arg. E2 55
Belen, Quitman, Miss. A3 100
Belen, Valencia, N. Mex. C3 107
Belén, Par. D4 55
Belev, Sov. Un. E11 27
Belfair, Mason, Wash. B3 122
Belfast (Eldon), P.E.I., Can. C7 74
Belfast, Waldo, Maine D3 96
Belfast, Allegany, N.Y. C2 108
Belfast, N. Ire. C6 11
Belfast, Highland, Ohio C2 111
Belfast, Marshall, Tenn. B5 117
Belfast, bay, N. Ire. C6 11
Belfield, Stark, N. Dak. C2 110
Belford, Eng. E7 13
Belford, Monmouth, N.J. C4 106
Belfort, Fr. D7 14
Belfort, Lewis, N.Y. B5 108
Belfort, dept., Fr. B8 18
Belfry, Pike, Ky. C7 94
Belfry, Carbon, Mont. E7 102
Belgaum, India E5 39
Belgica, mts., Ant. B16 5
Belgium, Vermilion, Ill. C6 90
Belgium, Ozaukee, Wis. E6 124
Belgium, country, Eur. E9 8, D4 15
Belgorod, Sov. Un. F11 27
Belgorod-Dnestrovskiy, Sov. Un. H8 27
Belgrade, Kennebec, Maine D3 96
Belgrade, Stearns, Minn. E4 99
Belgrade, Washington, Mo. D7 101
Belgrade, Gallatin, Mont. E5 102
Belgrade, Nance, Nebr. C7 103
Belgrade (Beograd), Yugo. C5 22
Belgrade Lakes, Kennebec, Maine D3 96
Belgreen, Franklin, Ala. A2 78
Belhaven, Beaufort, N.C. B6 109
Belice, riv., It. F4 21
Beli Lom, riv., Bul. D8 22
Belington, Barbour, W. Va. B5 123
Belingwe, Zimb. B4 49
Belitung, isl., Indon. F3 35
Belize, Belize B3 62
Belize, country, N.A. H12 61, B3 62
Belize, riv., Belize B3 16
Belize City, see Belize, Belize
Belk, Fayette, Ala. B2 78
Belkino, Sov. Un. B11 37
Belknap, Johnson, Ill. F5 90
Belknap, Davis, Iowa D5 92
Belknap, co., N.H. C3 105
Belknap, crater, Oreg. C5 113
Belknap, mts., N.H. C4 105
Belkofski, Alsk. D7 79
Bel'kovski, isl., Sov. Un. B1 4
Bell, Los Angeles, Calif. *E4 82
Bell, Gilchrist, Fla. C4 86
Bell, Spokane, Wash. D8 122
Bell, co., Ky. D6 94
Bell, co., Tex. D4 118
Bell, isl., Newf., Can. C4 75
Bell, isl., Newf., Can. E5 75
Bella Bella, B.C., Can. C3 68
Bellac, Fr. D4 14
Bella Coola, B.C., Can. C4 68
Bella Coola, riv., B.C., Can. C4 68
Bell Acres, Allegheny, Pa. *E1 114
Bellagio, It. D5 18
Bellahy, Ire. D3 11
Bellaire, Sedgwick, Kans. g12 93
Bellaire, Smith, Kans. C5 93
Bellaire, Antrim, Mich. D5 98
Bellaire, Belmont, Ohio C5 111
Bellaire, Harris, Tex. r14 118
Bellamy, Sumter, Ala. C1 78
Bellary, India E6 39
Bella Unión, Ur. E1 56
Bella Vista, Arg. E2 55
Bella Vista, Arg. E4 55
Bella Vista, Benton, Ark. A1 81
Bella Vista, Par. D4 55
Bellbrook, Greene, Ohio C1 111
Bell Buckle, Bedford, Tenn. B5 117
Bellburn, Greenbrier, W. Va. C4 123
Bell City, Calcasieu, La. D3 95
Bell City, Stoddard, Mo. D8 101
Belle, Maries, Mo. C6 101
Belle, Kanawha, W. Va. C3, m12 123
Belle, bay, Newf., Can. E4 75
Belle, isl., Newf., Can. C4 75
Belle, isl., Fr. D2 14
Belle, riv., La. k9 95
Belleair, Pinellas, Fla. p10 86
Belle Center, Logan, Ohio B2 111
Belle Chasse, Plaquemines, La. E5, k12 95
Bellechasse, co., Que., Can. C7 73
Belle Creek, Powder River, Mont. E11 102
Belledune, N.B., Can. B4 74
Belleek, N. Ire. C3 11
Bellefleur, N.B., Can. B2 74
Bellefontaine, Webster, Miss. B4 100
Bellefontaine, Logan, Ohio B2 111
Bellefontaine Neighbors, St. Louis, Mo. *C7 101
Bellefonte, Boone, Ark. A2 81
Bellefonte, New Castle, Del. A7 85
Bellefonte, Centre, Pa. E6 114
Belle Fourche, Butte, S. Dak. C2 116
Belle Fourche, res., S. Dak. C2 116
Belle Fourche, riv., S. Dak., Wyo. C2 110, B8 125
Bellegarde-sur-Valserine, Fr. C1 18
Belle Glade, Palm Beach, Fla. F6 86
Belle Haven, Accomack, Va. C7 121
Belle Helene, Ascension, La. B5 95
Belle Hôtesse, mtn., Guad. Q8 65
Belle Isle, Orange, Fla. D5 86
Belle Isle, strait, Newf., Can. C3 75
Belleisle Creek, N.B., Can. D4 74
Bellemead, Prince Georges, Md. *C4 85
Belle Mead, Somerset, N.J. C3 106
Belle Meade, Davidson, Tenn. g10 117
Belle Mina, Limestone, Ala. A3 78
Belleoram, Newf., Can. E4 75
Belleplain, Cape May, N.J. E3 106
Belle-Plaine, Sask., Can. G3 70
Belle Plaine, Benton, Iowa C5 92
Belle Plaine, Sumner, Kans. E6 93
Belle Plaine, Scott, Minn. F5 99
Belle Rive, Jefferson, Ill. E5 90
Belle River, Ont., Can. E2 72
Bellerive Station, Que., Can. C3 73
Belle Rose, Assumption, La. D4, h9 95
Bellerose, Nassau, N.Y. *n15 108
Belleterre, Que., Can. *h11 73
Belleu, Fr. E3 15
Belle Valley, Noble, Ohio C4 111
Belle Vernon, Fayette, Pa. F2 114
Belleview, Marion, Fla. C4 86
Belleview, Iron, Mo. D7 101
Belleview, Jackson, Oreg. E4 113
Belle View, Fairfax, Va. g12 121
Belleville, Yell, Ark. B2 81
Belleville, N.S., Can. F4 74
Belleville, Ont., Can. C7 72
Belleville, Fr. E5 15
Belleville, St. Clair, Ill. E4 90
Belleville, Republic, Kans. C6 93
Belleville, Wayne, Mich. p14 98
Belleville, Essex, N.J. B4, h8 106
Belleville, Jefferson, N.Y. B4 108
Belleville, Mifflin, Pa. E6 114
Belleville, Washington, R.I. C11 84
Belleville, Wood, W. Va. B3 123
Belleville, Dane and Green, Wis. F4 124
Belleville North, Wayne, Mich. *p15 98
Belleville [-sur-Saône], Fr. D6 14
Bellevue, Alta., Can. E3 69
Bellevue, Blaine, Idaho F4 89
Bellevue, Peoria, Ill. *C4 90
Bellevue, Jackson, Iowa B7 92
Bellevue, Campbell, Ky. h13 94
Bellevue, Talbot, Md. C5 85
Bellevue, Eaton, Mich. F5 98
Bellevue, Sarpy, Nebr. C10, g13 103
Bellevue, Huron and Sandusky, Ohio A3 111
Bellevue, Allegheny, Pa. F1, k13 114
Bellevue, Clay, Tex. C3 118
Bellevue, King, Wash. e11 122
Belley, Fr. E6 14
Bellflower, Los Angeles, Calif. n12 82
Bellflower, McLean, Ill. C5 90
Bellflower, Montgomery, Mo. B6 101
Bellin, Que., Can. f12 73
Bellingham, Eng. E6 13
Bellingham, Norfolk, Mass. B5, h10 97
Bellingham, Lac qui Parle, Minn. E2 99
Bellingham, Whatcom, Wash. A3 122
Bellingshausen, sea, Ant. C3 5
Bellinzona, Switz. D7 19
Bell-Irving, riv., B.C., Can. A3 68
Bellis, Alta., Can. B4 69
Bellivela, Lib. E3 45
Bellmawr, Camden, N.J. D2 106
Bellmead, McLennan, Tex. *D4 118
Bellmont, Wabash, Ill. E6 90
Bellmore, Parke, Ind. E3 91
Bellmore, Nassau, N.Y. G2 84
Bello, Col. B2 60
Bellows Falls, Windham, Vt. E4 120
Bellpat, Pak. C4 39
Bellport, Suffolk, N.Y. n16 108
Bell Ranch, San Miguel, N. Mex. B5 107
Bell River, Ont., Can. *E2 72
Bells, Crockett, Tenn. B2 117
Bells, creek, W. Va. m13 123
Bellsburg, Dickson, Tenn. A4 117
Bells Corners, Ont., Can. h12 72
Bellton, Hall and Banks, Ga. (part of Lula) B3 87
Belltown, Sussex, Del. C7 85
Belluno, It. A4 21
Bellview, Curry, N. Mex. C6 107
Bell Ville, Arg. A4 54
Bellville, Evans, Ga. D5 87
Bellville, Richland, Ohio B3 111
Bellville, S. Afr. *D2 49
Bellville, Austin, Tex. E4 118
Bellvue, Larimer, Colo. A5 83
Bellwood, Geneva, Ala. D4 78
Bellwood, Cook, Ill. k9 90
Bellwood, Butler, Nebr. C8 103
Bellwood, Blair, Pa. E5 114
Belly, riv., Alta., Can. E4 69
Belmar, Monmouth, N.J. C4 106
Bélmez, Sp. C3 20
Belmond, Wright, Iowa B4 92
Belmont, San Mateo, Calif. h8 82
Belmont, Man., Can. E2 71
Belmont, N.S., Can. D6 74
Belmont, Ont., Can. E3 72
Belmont, Pinellas, Fla. *E4 86
Belmont, Kingman, Kans. E6, g11 93
Belmont, Pointe Coupee, La. C2 95
Belmont, Middlesex, Mass. g11 97
Belmont, Tishomingo, Miss. A5 100
Belmont, Golden Valley, Mont. D7 102
Belmont, Dawes, Nebr. B2 103
Belmont, Belknap, N.H. D4 105
Belmont, Allegany, N.Y. C2 108
Belmont, Gaston, N.C. B1 109
Belmont, Belmont, Ohio B4 111
Belmont, Gonzales, Tex. h8 118
Belmont, Rutland, Vt. E3 120
Belmont, Whitman, Wash. B8 122
Belmont, Pleasants, W. Va. B3 123
Belmont, Lafayette, Wis. F3 124
Belmont, co., Ohio C4 111
Belmonte, Braz. E3 57
Belmont Heights, Salt Lake, Utah *C4 119
Belmopan, Belize B3 62
Belmore, Putnam, Ohio A2 111
Belmullet, Ire. C2 11
Bel-Nor, St. Louis, Mo. f13 101
Belo, Mad. g8 49
Beloeil, Que., Can. D4 73
Belogorsk, Sov. Un. D15 28
Belo Horizonte, Braz. E2 57
Beloit, Lyon, Iowa A1 92
Beloit, Mitchell, Kans. C5 93
Beloit, Mahoning, Ohio B5 111
Beloit, Rock, Wis. F4 124
Beloit North (Perrygo Place), Rock, Wis. *F4 124
Beloit West, Rock, Wis. *F4 124
Belokany, Sov. Un. B16 31
Belomorsk, Sov. Un. E16 25
Belopolye, Sov. Un. F10 27
Beloretsk, Sov. Un. C5 29
Belovo, Sov. Un. E26 9
Beloye, lake, Sov. Un. A11 27
Belozersk, Sov. Un. A11 27
Belp, Switz. C4 19
Belper, Eng. A6 12
Belpre, Edwards, Kans. E4 93
Belpre, Washington, Ohio C4 111
Bel-Ridge, St. Louis, Mo. *C7 101
Belspring, Pulaski, Va. C2 121
Belt, Cascade, Mont. C6 102
Belt, creek, Mont. C6 102
Belted, range, Nev. F5 104
Belterra, Braz. C4 59
Belton, Cass, Mo. C3 101
Belton, Anderson, S.C. B3 115
Belton, Bell, Tex. D4 118
Belton Lake, res., Tex. D4 118
Beltra, Ire. C3 11
Beltrami, Polk, Minn. C2 99
Beltrami, co., Minn. B3 99
Beltsville, Prince Georges, Md. B4 85
Beltsy, Sov. Un. H6 27
Belturbet, Ire. C4 11
Belukha, mtn., Sov. Un. E11 28
Beluran, Mala. D5 35
Belva, Woodward, Okla. A2 112
Belvedere, Marin, Calif. *C2 82
Belvedere, Aiken, S.C. D4 115
Belvedere, Fairfax, Va. *B5 121
Belvedere Marittimo, It. E5 21
Belvidere, New Castle, Del. A6 85
Belvidere, Boone, Ill. A5 90
Belvidere, Kiowa, Kans. E4 93
Belvidere, Thayer, Nebr. D8 103
Belvidere, Warren, N.J. B2 106
Belvidere, Perquimans, N.C. A6 109
Belvidere, Jackson, S. Dak. D4 116
Belvidere, Franklin, Tenn. B5 117
Belvidere, mtn., Vt. B3 120
Belvidere Center, Lamoille, Vt. B3 120
Belview, Redwood, Minn. F3 99
Belvue, Pottawatomie, Kans. C7 93
Belwood, Ont., Can. D4 72
Belyando, riv., Austl. D8 50
Belyy, Sov. Un. D9 27
Belyy, isl., Sov. Un. B9 28
Belyy Bom, Sov. Un. E26 9
Belyy Yar, Sov. Un. B11 29
Belzig, G.D.R. A7 17
Belzoni, Humphreys, Miss. B3 100
Bembezar, riv., Sp. D3 20
Bement, Piatt, Ill. D5 90
Bemidji, Beltrami, Minn. C4 99
Bemidji, lake, Minn. C4 99
Bemis, Deuel, S. Dak. C9 116
Bemis, Madison, Tenn. B3 117
Bemis, Randolph, W. Va. C5 123
Bemiss, Lowndes, Ga. F3 87
Bemus Point, Chautauqua, N.Y. C1 108
Bena, Cass, Minn. C4 99
Benabarre, Sp. A6 20
Bena Dibele, Zaire B3 48
Benadir, reg., Som. E5 47
Benalla, Austl. H5 51
Benalto, Alta., Can. C3 69
Benares, see Varānasi, India
Benatky nad Jizerou, Czech. n18 26
Benavente, Sp. A3 20
Benavides, Duval, Tex. F3 118
Ben Avon, Allegheny, Pa. *E1 114
Benbane, head, Ire. B5 11
Benbecula, isl., Scot. C1 13
Ben Bolt, Jim Wells, Tex. F3 118
Benbrook, Tarrant, Tex. *C4 118
Benbrook Lake, res., Tex. n9 118
Benbush, Tucker, W. Va. B5 123
Ben Cat, Viet. G7 38
Benchland, Judith Basin, Mont. C6 102
Bend, Deschutes, Oreg. C5 113
Bend, San Saba, Tex. D3 118
Ben Davis, pt., N.J. E2 106
Bendeleben, mtn., Alsk. B7 79
Bender Beila, Som. D7 47
Bendersville, Adams, Pa. G7 114
Bendery, Sov. Un. H7 27
Bendigo, Austl. H5 51
Bendorf, F.R.G. C2 17
Bene Berit, Isr. B7 32
Benedict, Wilson, Kans. E8 93
Benedict, Charles, Md. C4 85
Benedict, York, Nebr. C8 103
Benedict, McLean, N. Dak. B4 110
Benedict, mtn., Newf., Can. g10 75
Benedicta, Aroostook, Maine C4 96
Benenitra, Mad. E9 49
Beneraird, mtn., Scot. E4 13
Benešov, Czech. D3, o18 26
Bénestroff, Fr. F6 15
Benevento, It. D5 21
Benevolence, Randolph, Ga. E2 87
Benewah, co., Idaho B2 89
Benezett, Elk, Pa. D5 114
Benfeld, Fr. A3 18
Bengal, Latimer, Okla. C6 112
Bengal, reg., Bngl., India D8 39
Bengal, bay, India F8 39
Ben Gardane, Tun. C7 44
Bengasi (Banghāzī), Libya C4 43
Bengkalis, Indon. E2 35
Bengkulu, Indon. F2 35
Ben Goi, bay, Viet. F8 38
Bengough, Sask., Can. H3 70
Benguela, Ang. D1 48
Benguela, dist., Ang. D1 48
Benguerir, Mor. H3 30
Benham, Harlan, Ky. D7 94
Ben Hill, co., Ga. E3 87
Beni, Zaire A4 48
Beni, Nig. D7 45
Beni, dept., Bol. B3 55
Beni, riv., Bol. B2 55
Beni Abbès, Alg. C4 44
Benicarló, Sp. B6 20
Benicia, Solano, Calif. C2, g8 82
Benicito, riv., Bol. B2 55
Beni Mellal, Mor. C3 44
Benin, Nig. E6 45
Benin, country, Afr. F6 42, E5 45
Benin, bight, Afr. E5 45
Beni Ounif, Alg. C4 44
Benisa, Sp. C6 20
Beni Saf, Alg. B4 44
Benito, Man., Can. D1 71
Benjamin, Knox, Tex. C3 118
Benjamin, Utah, Utah *C4 119
Benjamin Constant, Braz. B3 58
Benkelman, Dundy, Nebr. D4 103
Benkovac, Yugo. C2 22
Benld, Macoupin, Ill. D4 90
Ben Lomond, Sevier, Ark. D1 81
Benmore, head, Ire. B5 11
Benndale, George, Miss. E5 100
Bennet, Lancaster, Nebr. D9, h11 103
Bennett, Adams, Colo. B6 83
Bennett, Cedar, Iowa C7 92
Bennett, Lea., N. Mex. E6 107
Bennett, Chatham, N.C. B3 109
Bennett, Douglas, Wis. B2 124
Bennett, co., S. Dak. D4 116
Bennett, creek, Md. B3 85
Bennett, isl., Sov. Un. B17 28
Bennett, lake, Man., Can. C3 71
Bennette, butte, Oreg. E2 113
Bennetts, Miami, Ind. C5 91
Bennettsbridge, Ire. E4 11
Bennettsville, Marlboro, S.C. B8 115
Bennettsville Southwest, Marlboro, S.C. *B8 115
Benningen, Switz. A4 19
Bennington, Bear Lake, Idaho G7 89
Bennington, Ottawa, Kans. C6 93
Bennington, Douglas, Nebr. g12 103
Bennington, Hillsboro, N.H. D3 105
Bennington, Bryan, Okla. D5 112
Bennington, Bennington, Vt. F2 120
Bennington, co., Vt. E2 120
Bennion, Salt Lake, Utah *C4 119
Benns Church, Isle of Wight, Va. k14 121
Benoit, Bolivar, Miss. B2 100
Benoit, Bayfield, Wis. B2 124
Benoit's Cove, Newf., Can. *D2 75
Benoni, S. Afr. *C4 49
Benoud, Alg. C5 44
Bénoué, riv., Cam. D2 46
Benque Viejo, Belize B3 62
Bens, pt., N.Y. E8 84
Bensané, Guinea D2 45
Bensberg, F.R.G. C2 17
Bensenville, Du Page, Ill. B6, k9 90
Bensheim, F.R.G. D3 17
Bensley, Chesterfield, Va. C5, n18 121
Benson, Cochise, Ariz. F5 80
Benson, Sask., Can. H4 70
Benson, Woodford, Ill. C4 90
Benson, De Soto, La. C2 95
Benson, Harford, Md. A5 85
Benson, Swift, Minn. E3 99
Benson, Johnston, N.C. B4 109
Benson, Somerset, Pa. *F4 114
Benson, Rutland, Vt. D2 120
Benson, co., N. Dak. A6 110
Bens Run, Tyler, W. Va. B3 123
Bensted Corner, Hartford, Conn. *C5 84
Bent, Otero, N. Mex. D4 107
Bent, co., Colo. D7 83
Bentheim, F.R.G. A2 17
Bentiu, Sud. D2 47
Bentley, Alta., Can. C3 69
Bentley, Sedgwick, Kans. E6, g11 93
Bentley, Grant, La. C3 95
Bentley, Bay, Mich. E6 98
Bentley, Hettinger, N. Dak. C3 110
Bentley Creek, Bradford, Pa. C8 114
Bentley Springs, Baltimore, Md. A4 85
Bentleyville, Washington, Pa. F1 114
Benton, Saline, Ark. k9 81
Benton, Mono, Calif. D4 82
Benton, N.B., Can. D2 74
Benton, Franklin, Ill. E5 90
Benton, Elkhart, Ind. A6 91
Benton, Ringgold, Iowa D3 92
Benton, Butler, Kans. E6, g12 93
Benton, Marshall, Ky. f9 94
Benton, Bossier, La. B2 95
Benton, Kennebec, Maine D3 96
Benton, Yazoo, Miss. C3 100
Benton, Scott, Mo. D8 101
Benton, Grafton, N.H. C3 105
Benton, Columbia, Pa. D9 114
Benton, Polk, Tenn. D9 117
Benton, Atascosa, Tex. E3 118
Benton, Lafayette, Wis. F3 124
Benton, co., Ark. A1 81
Benton, co., Ind. C3 91
Benton, co., Iowa B5 92
Benton, co., Minn. E4 99
Benton, co., Miss. A4 100
Benton, co., Mo. C4 101
Benton, co., Oreg. C3 113
Benton, co., Tenn. A3 117
Benton, co., Wash. C6 122
Benton City, Audrain, Mo. B6 101
Benton City, Benton, Wash. C6 122
Benton Harbor, Berrien, Mich. F4 98
Benton Heights, Berrien, Mich. F4 98
Bentonia, Yazoo, Miss. C3 100
Benton Ridge, Hancock, Ohio A2 111
Benton Station, Alta., Can. D5 69
Bentonville, Benton, Ark. A1 81
Bentonville, Adams, Ohio D2 111
Bentonville, Warren, Va. B4 121
Bentree, Nicholas, W. Va. m13 123
Benue, riv., Nig. E6 45
Benwee, head, Ire. C2 11
Benwood, Marshall, W. Va. A4, f8 123
Benzie, co., Mich. D4 98
Benzonia, Benzie, Mich. D4 98
Beo, Indon. E7 35
Beograd, see Belgrade, Yugo.
Béoumi, I.C. E3 45
Beowawe, Eureka, Nev. C5 104
Beppu, Jap. J5 37
Bequia, isl., St. Vincent U26 65
Berach, riv., India E5 40
Berat, Alb. B2 23
Berat, pref., Alb. *B2 23
Berbera, Som. C6 47
Berbérati, Cen. Afr. Rep. E3 46
Berbice, riv., Guy. A3 59
Berceto, It. E6 18
Bercher, Switz. C2 19
Berchogur, Sov. Un. D5 29
Berchtesgaden, F.R.G. E6 16
Berck-sur-Mer, Fr. B4 14
Berclair, Leflore, Miss. B3 100
Berclair, Goliad, Tex. E4 118
Berdichev, Sov. Un. G7 27
Berdsk, Sov. Un. E25 9
Berdyansk, Sov. Un. H11 27
Berea, Madison, Ky. C5 94
Berea, Box Butte, Nebr. B3 103
Berea, Cuyahoga, Ohio A4, h9 111
Berea, Greenville, S.C. B3 115
Berebere, Indon. E7 35
Beregovo, Sov. Un. G4 27
Bereku, Tan. B6 48
Berenice, Butte, Idaho F6 89
Berenice, ruins, Eg. E7 43
Berens, isl., Man., Can. C3 71
Berens, riv., Man., Can. C3 71
Berens River, Man., Can. C3, g8 71
Beresford, Man., Can. E1 71
Beresford, Lincoln and Union, S. Dak. D9 116
Berettyoujfalu, Hung. B5 22
Berezhany, Sov. Un. G5 27
Berezina, riv., Sov. Un. E7 27
Berezna, Sov. Un. F8 27
Berezniki, Sov. Un. B5 29
Berezovo, Sov. Un. C21 9
Berezovskiy, Sov. Un. D21 9
Berg, Nor. q27 25
Berga, Sp. A6 20
Berga, Swe. B8 24
Bergama, Tur. C6 23
Bergamasque Alps, mts., It. C5 18
Bergamo, It. B2 21
Bergedorf, Ger. (part of Hamburg) B5 16
Bergen, see Mons, Bel.
Bergen, G.D.R. A6 16
Bergen, Genesee, N.Y. B3 108
Bergen, McHenry, N. Dak. B5 110
Bergen, Nor. G1 25
Bergen, co., N.J. A4 106
Bergen aan Zee, Neth. B4 15
Bergen [bei Celle] (Bergen-Belsen), F.R.G. F3 24
Bergenfield, Bergen, N.J. B4, h8 106
Bergen op Zoom, Neth. C4 15
Berger, Franklin, Mo. C6 101
Bergerac, Fr. E4 14
Bergheim, Kendall, Tex. h7 118
Bergholz, Jefferson, Ohio B5 111
Bergisch, Gladbach, F.R.G. C2 17
Bergkamen, F.R.G. B2 17
Bergland, Ontonagon, Mich. m12 98
Bergman, Boone, Ark. A2 81
Bergoo, Webster, W. Va. C4 123
Bergton, Rockingham, Va. B4 121
Berguent, Mor. C4 44
Bergün, Switz. C8 19
Berhampore, India E12 40
Berhampur, India H10 40
Bering, sea, Alsk., Sov. Un. D3 79
Bering, strait, Alsk. C5 79
Berino, Dona Ana, N. Mex. E3 107
Berislav, Sov. Un. H9 27
Berja, Sp. D4 20
Berkane, Mor. C4 44
Berkeley, Alameda, Calif. D2, h8 82
Berkeley, Ont., Can. C4 72
Berkeley, Cook, Ill. *k9 90
Berkeley, St. Louis, Mo. f13 101
Berkeley, Providence, R.I. B11 84
Berkeley, co., S.C. E8 115
Berkeley, co., W. Va. B6 123
Berkeley, cape, Ec. g5 58
Berkeley Heights, Union, N.J. B4 106
Berkeley Springs (Bath), Morgan, W. Va. B6 123
Berkey, Lucas, Ohio A2, e6 111
Berkley, Boone, Iowa C3 92
Berkley, Harford, Md. A5 85
Berkley, Bristol, Mass. C5 97
Berkley, Oakland, Mich. F7, p15 98
Berkner, isl., Ant. B7 5
Berkovitsa, Bul. D6 22
Berks, co., Pa. F9 114
Berkshire, Prince Georges, Md. *C4 85
Berkshire, Berkshire, Mass. A1 97
Berkshire, Tioga, N.Y. C4 108
Berkshire, Franklin, Vt. B3 120
Berkshire, co., Eng. C6 12
Berkshire, co., Mass. B1 97
Berkshire, hills, Mass. B1 97
Berland, riv., Alta., Can. C1 69
Berleburg, F.R.G. B3 17
Berlengas, is., Port. C1 20
Berlin, Hartford, Conn. C5 84
Berlin, Colquitt, Ga. E3 87
Berlin, East, G.D.R. B6 16
Berlin, West, F.R.G. B6 16
Berlin, West, state, F.R.G. A8 17
Berlin, Worcester, Md. D7 85
Berlin, Worcester, Mass. B4 97
Berlin, Coos, N.H. B4 105
Berlin, Camden, N.J. D3 106
Berlin, Rensselaer, N.Y. C7 108
Berlin, La Moure, N. Dak. C7 110
Berlin, Holmes, Ohio B4 111
Berlin, Roger Mills, Okla. B2 112
Berlin, Somerset, Pa. G4 114
Berlin, Washington, Vt. C3 120
Berlin, Green Lake and Waushara, Wis. E5 124
Berlin, mtn., Ant. B35 1
Berlin, mtn., Nev. E4 105
Berlin Heights, Erie, Ohio A3 111
Berlin Lake, res., Ohio A4 114
Bermejo, riv., Arg., Par. E4 55
Bermeo, Sp. A4 20
Bermuda, Br. dep., N.A. F14 61, p20 64
Bermuda Hundred, Chesterfield, Va. n18 121
Bern, Nemaha, Kans. C8 93
Bern, Switz. C3 19
Bern, canton, Switz. C3 19
Bernalillo, Sandoval, N. Mex. B3, k7 107
Bernalillo, co., N. Mex. C3 107
Bernard, Sask., Can. G2 70
Bernard, Dubuque, Iowa B7 92
Bernard, Hancock, Maine D4 96
Bernard, isl., Truk 52
Bernard, lake, Ont., Can. B5 72
Bernardston, Franklin, Mass. A2 97
Bernardsville, Somerset, N.J. B3 106
Bernasconi, Arg. B4 54
Bernau, F.R.G. B8 18
Bernau, G.D.R. B6 16
Bernay, Fr. C4 14
Bernburg, G.D.R. B6 17
Berndorf, Aus. E8 16
Berne, Adams, Ind. C8 91
Berne, Albany, N.Y. C6 108
Berneray, isl., Scot. C1 13
Bernese Alps, mts., Switz. D3 19
Bernice, Union, La. B3 95
Bernice, Delaware, Okla. A7 112
Bernie, Stoddard, Mo. E8 101
Bernina, pass, Switz. D8 19
Bernina, peak, Switz. D8 19

Bonnie, Jefferson, Ill E5 90
Bonnie Doone, Cumberland, N.C. B4 109
Bonnieville, Hart, Ky C4 94
Bonnots Mill, Osage, Mo C6 101
Bonny, Nig F6 45
Bonny, res., Colo B8 83
Bonny Blue, Lee, Va f8 121
Bonnyrigg & Lasswade, Scot *E5 13
Bonnyview, Shasta, Calif B2 82
Bonnyville, Alta., Can B5 69
Bono, Craighead, Ark B5 81
Bono, Lawrence, Ind G5 91
Bonorva, It D2 21
Bonsal, Wake, N.C B4 109
Bon Secour, Baldwin, Ala E2 78
Bonshaw, P.E.I., Can C6 74
Bonsucesso, Braz m7 56
Bontang, Indon E5 35
Bonthain, Indon G5 35
Bonthe, S.L E2 45
Bontoc, Phil *B6 35
Bon Wier, Newton, Tex D6 118
Book, Catahoula, La C4 95
Book, cliffs, Colo B1 83
Book, cliffs, Utah D5 119
Booker, Lipscomb and Ochiltree, Tex A2 118
Booker T. Washington, nat. mon., Va C3 121
Booligal, Austl F5 51
Boolyglass, Ire E4 11
Boomer, Fayette, W. Va C3, m13 123
Boon, Wexford, Mich D5 98
Boone, Pueblo, Colo C6 83
Boone, Boone, Iowa B4 92
Boone, Boone, Nebr C8 103
Boone, Watauga, N.C A1 109
Boone, co., Ark A2 81
Boone, co., Ill A5 90
Boone, co., Ind D4 91
Boone, co., Iowa B9 92
Boone, co., Ky B5 94
Boone, co., Mo B5 101
Boone, co., Nebr C7 103
Boone, co., W. Va C3 123
Boone, riv., Iowa B4 92
Boone Grove, Porter, Ind B3 91
Boones Mill, Franklin, Va D3 121
Booneville, Logan, Ark B2 75
Booneville, Owsley, Ky C6 94
Booneville, Prentiss, Miss A5 100
Boons, pond, Mass g10 97
Boonsboro, Washington, Md A2 85
Boon Terrace, Washington, Pa *F1 114
Boonton, Morris, N.J B4 106
Boonville, Mendocino, Calif C2 82
Boonville, Warrick, Ind H3 91
Boonville, Copper, Mo C5 101
Boonville, Oneida, N.Y B5 108
Boonville, Yadkin, N.C A2 109
Booth, Autauga, Ala C3 78
Boothbay, Lincoln, Maine E3 96
Boothbay Harbor, Lincoln, Maine E3 96
Boothby, cape, Ant C18 5
Boothia, gulf, N.W. Ter., Can B14 66
Boothia, pen., N.W. Ter., Can B13 66
Booths, creek, W. Va h11 123
Boothville, Plaquemines, La E6 95
Boothwyn, Delaware, Pa *G11 114
Bootle, Eng A4 12
Booué, Gabon E2 46
Boporo, Lib E2 45
Boppard, F.R.G C2 17
Boque, inlet, N.C C5 109
Boqueron, dept., Par D3 55
Boquerõn, bay, P.R. B1 65
Boqueron, pass, Peru C2 58
Boqueron, riv., Pan k11 62
Boquete, Pan F6 62
Bor, Sov. Un D17 9
Bor, Sud D3 47
Bor, Yugo C6 22
Borah, peak, Idaho E5 89
Borama, Som C5 47
Borama, dist., Som C5 47
Borås, Swe A6 24, I5 25
Borāzjān, Iran G5 46
Borba, Braz C3 59
Borborema, plat., Braz h5 57
Borculo, Neth B6 15
Bordeaux, Fr E3 14
Bordeaux, Thurston, Wash C2 122
Borden, Sask., Can E2 70
Borden (New Providence), Clark, Ind H6 91
Borden, co., Tex C2 118
Borden, isl., N.W. Ter., Can m29 67
Borden, pen., N.W. Ter., Can B16 66
Borden Springs, Cleburne, Ala B4 78
Bordentown, Burlington, N.J C3 106
Border, Lincoln, Wyo D2 125
Borderland, Mingo, W. Va D2 123
Borders, reg., Scot E5 13
Bordertown, Austl H3 51
Bordighera, It C1 21
Bordj Amguid, Alg D6 44
Bordj Bou Arreridj, Alg B5 44
Bordj-Ménaïel, Alg *B5 44
Bordj Ouallen, Alg E5 44
Bordj Viollette, Alg D4 44
Bordley, Union, Ky C2 94
Bordulac, Foster, N. Dak B7 110
Bordzon, Mong C1 36
Boré, Mali C4 45
Boren, lake, Swe u33 25
Borensberg, Swe u33 25
Borg, mtn., Ant B12 5
Borgå, Fin G11 25
Börger, F.R.G B7 15
Borger, Neth B6 15
Borger, Hutchinson, Tex B2 118
Borgholm, Swe I7 25
Borghorst, F.R.G A2 17
Borgne, lake, La k12 95
Borgne, riv., Switz D3 19
Borgomanero, It B2 21
Borgo Piave, It k9 21
Borgo Val di Taro, It B2 21
Borgo Valsugana, It C7 18
Borikhane, Laos C5 38
Borislav, Sov. Un G4 27
Borisoglebsk, Sov. Un C2 29
Borisov, Sov. Un D7 27
Borispol, Sov. Un F8 27
Borja, Sp B5 20
Borjas Blancas, Sp B6 20
Borken, F.R.G B1 17
Borken, F.R.G B4 17
Børkop, Den C3 24
Borkou, reg., Chad B3 46
Borkum, F.R.G A6 15
Borkum, isl., F.R.G B3 16
Borlänge, Swe G6 25
Bormes, Fr F7 14
Bormida, riv., It E4 18
Bormio, It C6 18
Borna, G.D.R B7 17
Borne, Neth B6 15
Borneo, North, see Sabah, state, Mala.
Borneo (Kalimantan), isl., Asia E4 35
Bornheim, F.R.G C2 17
Bornholm, co., Den C8 24
Bornholm, isl., Den C8 24
Bornholmsgat, chan., Den C8 24
Bornos, Sp D3 20
Boromlya, Sov. Un F10 27
Boromo, Upper Volta D4 45
Boron, Kern, Calif E5 82
Borongan, Phil *C7 35
Borovan, Bul D6 22
Borovichi, Sov. Un B9 27
Borovsk, Sov. Un D20 9
Borovskoye, Sov. Un q21 27
Borrby, Swe C8 24
Borre, Den D6 24
Borrego Springs, San Diego, Calif F5 82
Borris, Ire E5 11
Borrisokane, Ire E3 11
Borrisoleigh, Ire E4 11
Borsod-Abauj-Zemplen, co., Hung *A5 22
Bort-les-Orgues, Fr E5 14
Borūjerd, Iran E4 41
Borup, Norman, Minn C2 99
Borzhomi, Sov. Un B14 25
Borzna, Sov. Un F9 27
Borzonasca, It E5 18
Bosa, It D2 21
Bosanska Dubica, Yugo C3 22
Bosanska Gradiska, Yugo C3 22
Bosanska Kostajnica, Yugo C3 22
Bosanski Novi, Yugo C3 22
Bosanski Petrovac, Yugo C3 22
Bosanski Samac, Yugo C4 22
Bosaso, Som C6 47
Boscawen, Merrimack, N.H D3 105
Boscobel, Grant, Wis E3 124
Bosdagan, Tur D7 23
Boshrūyeh, Iran, E8 41
Boskovice, Czech D4 26
Bosler, Albany, Wyo E7 125
Bosna, riv., Yugo C3 22
Bosnek, Indon F9 35
Bosnia, reg., Yugo C3 22
Bosnia-Hercegovina, rep., Yugo *C3 22
Bosobolo, Zaire A2 48
Bosporus, strait, Tur B7 31
Bosque, Valencia, N. Mex C3 107
Bosque, co., Tex D4 118
Bossangoa, Cen. Afr. Rep D3 46
Bossembélé, Cen. Afr. Rep D3 46
Bossert Estates, Burlington, N.J C3 106
Bossier, Bossier, La B2 95
Bossier, par., La B2 95
Bosso, Niger D7 45
Boston, Eng B7 12
Boston, Thomas, Ga F3 87
Boston, Wayne, Ind E8 91
Boston, Suffolk, Mass B5, g11 97
Boston, Summit, Ohio *A4 111
Boston, Allegheny, Pa *F2 114
Boston, bay, Mass B6 97
Boston, mts., Ark B2 81
Boston, mts., Okla B7 112
Boston Bar, B.C., Can E7 68
Boston Heights, Summit, Ohio h9 111
Bostonnais, riv., Que., Can B5 73
Bostwick, Putnam, Fla C5 86
Bostwick, Morgan, Ga C3 87
Boswarlos, Newf., Can D2 75
Boswell, Izard, Ark A3 81
Boswell, B.C., Can E9 68
Boswell, Benton, Ind C3 91
Boswell, Choctaw, Okla C6 112
Boswell, Somerset, Pa F3 114
Bosworth, Carroll, Mo B4 101
Botany, bay, Austl F9 50
Boteti, riv., Bots B3 49
Botetourt, co., Va C3 121
Botev, peak, Bul D7 22
Botevgrad, Bul D6 22
Botha, Alta., Can C4 69
Bothell, King, Wash B3 122
Bothnia, gulf, Eur F9 25
Bothwell, Ont., Can E3 72
Bothwell, P.E.I., Can C7 74
Bothwell, Box Elder, Utah B3 119
Botijas, P.R C5 65
Botkinburg, Van Buren, Ark B3 81
Botkins, Shelby, Ohio B1 111
Botkyrka, Swe t35 25
Botolan, Phil o13 35
Botoşani, Rom B8 22
Botsford, Fairfield, Conn D3 84
Botswana, country, Afr I8 42, B3 49
Bottineau, Bottineau, N. Dak A5 110
Bottineau, co., N. Dak A4 110
Bottrop, F.R.G B1 17
Botucatu, Braz C3, m7 56
Botwood, Newf., Can D4 75
Bouaflé, I.C E3 45
Bouaké, I.C E3 45
Bouar, Cen. Afr. Rep D3 46
Boucau, Fr F3 14
Boucher, lake, Que., Can C2 75
Boucherville, Que., Can D4, p20 73
Bouches-du-Rhône, dept., Fr *F6 14
Bouchette, Que., Can C2 73
Boudenib, Mor C4 44
Boû Djébéha, well, Mali C4 45
Boudreaux, lake, La E5 95
Boudry, Switz C2 19
Boufarik, Alg *B5 44
Bougainville, isl., Pap. N. Gui G9 7
Bougaroun, cape, Alg F10 30
Bougie, see Bejaïa, Alg.
Bougival, Fr g9 14
Bougouni, Mali D3 45
Bouillon, Bel E5 15
Boulder, Boulder, Colo A5 83
Boulder, Jefferson, Mont D4 102
Boulder, Garfield, Utah F4 119
Boulder, Sublette, Wyo D3 125
Boulder, co., Colo A5 83
Boulder City, Clark, Nev H7 104
Boulder Creek, Santa Cruz, Calif C5 82
Boulevard, San Diego, Calif F5 82
Boulevard Heights, Prince Georges, Md f9 85
Boulogne-Billancourt, Fr C5, g9 14
Boulogne-sur-Mer., Fr D9 12, B4 14
Boulsa, Upper Volta D4 45
Boumalne, Mor C3 44
Boumerdas, Alg B5 44
Bouna, I.C E4 45
Boundary, Alsk C11 79
Boundary, co., Idaho A2 89
Boundary, peak, Nev F3 104
Boundary Bend, Austl G4 51
Bound Brook, Somerset, N.J B3 106
Boundiali, I.C E3 45
Bountiful, Davis, Utah C4 119
Bounty, Sask., Can F2 70
Bounty, is., Pac. O J11 7
Bourbeuse, riv., Mo C6 101
Bourbon, Marshall, Ind B5 91
Bourbon, Crawford, Mo C6 101
Bourbon, co., Kans E9 93
Bourbon, co., Ky B5 94
Bourbonnais, Kankakee, Ill B6 90
Bourbonnais, former prov., Fr D5 14
Bourbonne-les-Bains, Fr A1 18
Bourem, Mali C4 45
Bourg, Terrebonne, La E5 95
Bourg-Bruche, Fr A3 18
Bourg-de-Péage, Fr E6 14
Bourg [-en-Bresse], Fr D6 14
Bourges, Fr D5 14
Bourget, Ont., Can B9 72
Bourget, lake, Fr D1 18
Bourg-la-Reine, Fr g10 14
Bourgoin, Fr E6 14
Bourg-St.-Andéol, Fr E6 14
Bourg-St. Maurice, Fr D2 18
Bou Rjeïmât, well, Maur C1 45
Bourke, Austl E5 51
Bourlamaque, Que., Can *k11 73
Bourne, Eng B7 12
Bourne, Barnstable, Mass C6 97
Bournemouth, Eng D6 12
Bourneville, Ross, Ohio C2 111
Bou Saâda, Alg B5 44
Bouse, Yuma, Ariz D2 80
Bousso, Chad C3 46
Boutilimit, Maur C2 45
Boutte, St. Charles, La k11 95
Bouvet, isl., Nor. (Atl. O.) D13 5
Bovey, Itasca, Minn C5 99
Bovill, Latah, Idaho C2 89
Bovina, Lincoln, Colo B7 85
Bovina, Warren, Miss C3 100
Bovina, Parmer, Tex B1 181
Bovina Center, Delaware, N.Y C6 108
Bow, Merrimack, N.H D3 105
Bow, lake, N.H D4 105
Bow, riv., Alta., Can D4 69
Bowbells, Burke, N. Dak A3 110
Bowden, Alta., Can D4 69
Bowden, Creek, Okla A5 112
Bowdens, Duplin, N.C B4 109
Bowdle, Emunds, S. Dak B6 116
Bowdoin, Sagadahoc, Maine f8 96
Bowdoinham, Sagadahoc, Maine D3, f8 96
Bowdon, Carroll, Ga C1 87
Bowdon, Wells, N. Dak B6 110
Bowen, Austl C8 50
Bowen, Hancock, Ill C2 90
Bowers, Kent, Del B7 85
Bowerston, Harrison, Ohio B4 111
Bowersville, Hart, Ga B3 87
Bowersville, Greene, Ohio C2 111
Bowesmont, Pembina, N. Dak A8 110
Bowie, Cochise, Ariz E6 80
Bowie, Delta, Colo C3 83
Bowie, Prince Georges, Md B4 85
Bowie, Montague, Tex C4 118
Bowie, co., Tex C5 118
Bowie, creek, Miss D4 100
Bow Island, Alta., Can E5 69
Bowlegs, Seminole, Okla B5 112
Bowler, Shawano, Wis D5 124
Bowling Green, Hardee, Fla E5 86
Bowling Green, Clay, Ind F3 91
Bowling Green, Warren, Ky D3 94
Bowling Green, Pike, Mo B6 101
Bowling Green, Wood, Ohio A2, f6 111
Bowling Green, York, S.C A5 115
Bowling Green, Caroline, Va B5 121
Bowlus, Morrison, Minn E4 99
Bowman, Elbert, Ga B3 87
Bowman, Bowman, N. Dak C2 110
Bowman, Orangeburg, S.C E6 115
Bowman, co., N. Dak C2 110
Bowman, creek, Pa m16 114
Bowman, isl., Ant C23 5
Bowman-Haley Lake, res., N. Dak C2 110
Bowmanville, Ont., Can D6 72
Bowmont, Canyon, Idaho F2 89
Bowmore, Scot E2 13
Bowness, Alta., Can D3 69
Bowokan, is., Indon F6 35
Bowral, Austl G8 51
Bowring, Osage, Okla A5 112
Bowron, riv., B.C., Can C7 68
Bowron Lake, prov. park, B.C., Can C7 68
Bowser, lake, B.C., Can A3 68
Bowsman, Man., Can C1 71
Bowstring, lake, Minn C5 99
Bowstring, riv., Minn C5 99
Bow Valley, Cedar, Nebr B8 103
Boxborough, Middlesex, Mass A5, f10 97
Box Butte, co., Nebr B2 103
Box Butte, creek, Nebr B3 103
Box Butte Table, plat., Nebr B2 103
Box Elder, Hill, Mont B6 102
Box Elder, Pennington, S. Dak C2 116
Box Elder, co., Utah B2 119
Box Elder, creek, Colo A6 83
Boxelder, creek, Mont E12 102
Box Elder, creek, Mont C8 102
Boxford, Essex, Mass A6 97
Boxholm, Boone, Iowa B3 92
Boxmeer, Neth C5 15
Boxtel, Neth C5 15
Boyacá, dept., Col B3 60
Boyce, Rapides, La C3 95
Boyce, Ellis, Tex n10 118
Boyce, Clarke, Va A4 121
Boyceville, Dunn, Wis C1 124
Boyd, Lac qui Parle, Minn F3 99
Boyd, Carbon, Mont E7 102
Boyd, Wise, Tex C4, m9 118
Boyd, Chippawa, Wis D2 124
Boyd, co., Ky B7 94
Boyd, co., Nebr B7 103
Boyd, glacier, Ant B34 5
Boyd, lake, Maine C4 96
Boydell, Ashley, Ark D4 81
Boyden, Sioux, Iowa A2 92
Boyds, Montgomery, Md B3 85
Boyd's Cove, Newf., Can D4 75
Boyds Creek, Sevier, Tenn D10 117
Boydsville, Clay, Ark A5 81
Boydton, Mecklenburg, Va D4 121
Boyer, riv., Iowa C2 92
Boyera, Zaire C2 48
Boyer Knob, mtn., Md k13 85
Boyero, Lincoln, Colo C7 83
Boyers, Butler, Pa D2 114
Boyertown, Berks, Pa F10 114
Boyes, Carter, Mont E11 102
Boykin, Miller, Ga E2 87
Boykins, Southampton, Va D5 121
Boyle, Alta., Can B4 69
Boyle, Ire D3 11
Boyle, Bolivar, Miss B3 100
Boyle, co., Ky C5 94
Boylston, N.S., Can D8 74
Boylston, Worcester, Mass B4 97
Boyne, riv., Ire D5 11
Boyne City, Charlevoix, Mich C5 98
Boyne Falls, Charlevoix, Mich C6 98
Boynton, Muskogee, Okla B6 112
Boynton, Somerset, Pa G3 114
Boynton Beach, Palm Beach, Fla F6 86
Boyoma (Stanley), falls, Zaire A3 48
Boy River, Cass, Minn C4 99
Boysen, res., Wyo C4 125
Boys Ranch, Oldham, Tex B1 118
Boys Town, Douglas, Nebr g12 103
Boz, cape, Tur B7 23
Bozcaada, Tur C6 23
Bozcaada (Tenedos), isl., Tur C6 23
Bozeman, Gallatin, Mont E5 102
Bozeman, pass, Mont E6 102
Bozman, Talbot, Md C5 85
Bozoum, Cen. Afr. Rep D3 46
Bozovici, Rom C6 22
Bozqūsh, mts., Iran C3 41
Bozrah (Town of), New London, Conn *C8 84
Bozuyuk, Tur C8 31
Bra., It B1 21
Brabant, isl., Ant C6 5
Brabant, lake, Sask., Can A4 70
Brabant, prov., Bel D4 15
Brac, isl., Yugo D3 22
Bracadale, Scot C2 13
Bracadale, inlet, Scot C2 13
Bracciano, It g8 21
Bracciano, lake, It C4 21
Bracebridge, Ont., Can B5 72
Braceville, Grundy, Ill B5 90
Brach, Libya D2 43
Bracken, Sask., Can H1 70
Bracken, co., Ky B5 94
Bracken, lake, Man., Can C2 71
Brackenridge, Allegheny, Pa h15 114
Brackett, Eau Claire, Wis D2 124
Brackettville, Kinney, Tex E2 118
Brackley, Eng B6 12
Bracknell, Eng C7 12
Brackwede, F.R.G B3 17
Brad, Rom B6 22
Bradano, riv., It D6 21
Bradbury Heights, Prince Georges, Md *C3 85
Braddock, Camden, N.J D3 106
Braddock, Emmons, N. Dak C5 110
Braddock, Allegheny, Pa k14 114
Braddock, pt., S.C G6 115
Braddock Heights, Frederick, Md B2 85
Braddock Hills, Allegheny, Pa *F2 114
Braddyville, Page, Iowa D2 92
Braden, Fayette, Tenn B2 117
Bradenton, Manatee, Fla E4, q10 86
Bradenton Beach, Manatee, Fla *E4 86
Bradenville, Westmoreland, Pa F3 114
Bradford, White, Ark B4 81
Bradford, Ont., Can C5 72
Bradford, Eng A6 12
Bradford, Stark, Ill B4 90
Bradford, Franklin, Iowa B4 92
Bradford, Penobscot, Maine C4 96
Bradford, Merrimack, N.H D6 105
Bradford, Darke and Miami, Ohio B1 111
Bradford, McKean, Pa C4 114
Bradford, Washington, R.I D10 84
Bradford, Gibson, Tenn A3 117
Bradford, Orange, Vt D4 120
Bradford, co., Fla C4 88
Bradford, co., Pa C8 114
Bradford, mtn., Conn B3 84
Bradfordsville, Marion, Ky C4 94
Bradfordwoods, Allegheny, Pa h13 114
Bradgate, Humboldt, Iowa B3 92
Bradley, Escambia, Ala D3 78
Bradley, Lafayette, Ark D2 81
Bradley, Monterey, Calif E3 82
Bradley, Polk, Fla E5 86
Bradley, Kankakee, Ill B6 90
Bradley, Penobscot, Maine D4 96
Bradley, Jefferson, Ohio B5 111
Bradley, Grady, Okla C4 112
Bradley, Greenwood, S.C C3 115
Bradley, Clark, S. Dak B8 116
Bradley, Raleigh, W. Va D3, n13 123
Bradley, co., Ark D3 81
Bradley, co., Tenn D9 117
Bradley Beach, Monmouth, N.J C4 106
Bradley Gardens, Somerset, N.J *B3 106
Bradleyton, Crenshaw, Ala D3 78
Bradleyville, New Haven, Conn *C4 84
Bradner, Wood, Ohio A2 111
Brador, bay, Que., Can C3 75
Bradshaw, Baltimore, Md B5 85
Bradshaw, York, Nebr D8 103
Bradshaw, Taylor, Tex C3 118
Bradshaw, McDowell, W. Va D3 123
Bradshaw, mts., Ariz C3 80
Bradstreet, Hampshire, Mass B2 97
Bradwardine, Man., Can D1 71
Bradwell, Sask., Can F2 70
Brady, Pondera, Mont B5 102
Brady, Lincoln, Nebr C5 103
Brady, McCulloch, Tex D3 118
Brady, mts., Tex D3 118
Bradyville, Cannon, Tenn B5 117
Braedstrup, Den C3 24
Braemar, Scot D5 13
Braeside, Ont., Can B8 72
Braga, Port B1 20
Bragado, Arg B4, g6 54
Bragança, Braz B1 57
Bragança, Port B2 20
Bragança Paulista, Braz C3, m8 56
Braggadocio, Pemiscot, Mo E8 101
Braggs, Muskogee, Okla B6 112
Braham, Isanti, Minn E5 99
Brāhmani, riv., India G10 40
Brahmaputra (Yalutsangpu), riv., Asia C11 40
Braidwood, Will, Ill B5 90
Brail, Switz C9 19
Brăila, Rom C8 22
Brainard, Butler, Nebr C9 103
Braine-le-Comte, Bel D4 15
Brainerd, Butler, Kans g12 93
Brainerd, Crow Wing, Minn D4 99
Braintree, Eng C8 12
Braintree, Norfolk, Mass B5, h11 97
Braintree, Orange, Vt D3 120
Braithwaite, Plaquemines, La k12 95
Brake, F.R.G E2 24
Brakel, F.R.G B4 17
Brakpan, S. Afr C4 49
Bralorne, B.C., Can D6 68
Braman, Kay, Okla A4 112
Bramche, F.R.G B7 15
Bramhapuri, India G7 40
Bramming, Den C2 24
Brampton, Ont., Can D5, m14 72
Brampton, Eng F6 13
Bramtpon, Sargent, N. Dak D8 110
Bramwell, Mercer, W. Va D3 123
Branch, Franklin, Ark B2 81
Branch, Newf., Can E5 75
Branch, Acadia, La D3 95
Branch, Scott, Miss C4 100
Branch, Manitowoc, Wis h10 124
Branch, co., Mich G5 98
Branch, pond, Maine D4 96
Branch, riv., Wis h10 124
Branchland, Lincoln, W. Va C2 123
Branchport, Yates, N.Y C3 108
Branch Village, Providence, R.I *A10 84
Branchville, St. Clair, Ala B3 78
Branchville, Fairfield, Conn D3 84
Branchville, Sussex, N.J A3 106
Branchville, Orangeburg, S.C E6 115
Branchville, Southampton, Va D5 121
Branco, riv., Braz C5 60
Branco, riv., Braz E2 59
Brandberg, mtn., Namibia B1 49
Brande, Den C3 24
Brandenburg, G.D.R A7 17
Brandenburg, Meade, Ky C3 94
Brandenburg, reg., G.D.R B6 16
Brandon, Man., Can E2, h7 71
Brandon, Kiowa, Colo C8 83
Brandon, Hillsborough, Fla E4 86
Brandon, Buchanan, Iowa B6 92
Brandon, Douglas, Minn E3 99
Brandon, Rankin, Miss C4 100
Brandon, Perkins, Nebr D4 103
Brandon, Greenville, S.C B3 115
Brandon, Minnehaha, S. Dak D9 116
Brandon, Rutland, Vt D2 120
Brandon, Fond du Lac, Wis E5 124
Brandon, head, Ire E1 11
Brandon, hill, Ire E1 11
Brandsville, Howell, Mo E6 101
Brandt, Miami, Ohio C1 111
Brandt, Susquehanna, Pa C10 114
Brandt, Deuel, S. Dak C9 116
Brandvlei, S. Afr D3 49
Brandys nad Labem, Czech n18 26
Brandy Station, Culpeper, Va B5 121
Brandywine, Prince Georges, Md C4 85
Brandywine, Pendleton, W. Va C5 123
Brandywine, creek, Del A6 85
Branford, New Haven, Conn D5 84
Branford, Suwannee, Fla C4 86
Branford Hills, New Haven, Conn *D5 84
Branford Point, New Haven, Conn D5 84
Braniewo, Pol A5 26
Bransfield, strait, Ant C6 5
Bransk, Pol B7 26
Branson, Las Animas, Colo D7 83
Branson, Taney, Mo E4 101
Brant, Alta., Can D4 69
Brant, co., Ont., Can D4 72
Brantford, Ont., Can D4 72
Brantford, Eddy, N. Dak B7 110
Brant Lake, Warren, N.Y B7 108
Brantley, Crenshaw, Ala D3 78
Brantley, co., Ga E4 87
Brant Rock, Plymouth, Mass B6 97
Brantville, N.B., Can B5 74
Brantwood, Price, Wis C3 124
Bras-d'Apic, Que., Can C7 73
Bras-d'Or., N.S., Can C9 74
Bras d'Or, lake, N.S., Can D9 74
Brasfield, Prairie, Ark C4 81
Brashear, Adiar, Mo A5 101
Brasiléia, Braz D4 58
Brasília, Braz B3 56, E1 57
Brasília, Braz E2 57
Braşov, Rom C7 22
Brass, is., Vir. Is. (U.S.) f15 65
Brasstown, Clay, N.C f9 109
Brasstown Bald, mtn., Ga B3 87
Brassua, lake, Maine C3 96
Bratenahl, Cuyahoga, Ohio g9 111
Bratislava, Czech D4 26
Bratsk, Sov. Un D29 9
Bratsk, res., Sov. Un D13 28
Bratslav, Sov. Un G7 27
Bratt, Escambia, Fla u14 86
Brattleboro, Windham, Vt F3 120
Braunau [am Inn], Aus D6 16
Braunfels, F.R.G C3 17
Braunschweig, F.R.G A5 17
Brava, Som E5 47
Brave, Greene, Pa G1 114
Bråviken, lake, Swe u34 25
Bravo, riv., Chile D2 54
Brawley, Imperial, Calif F6 82
Braxton, Simpson, Miss C4 100
Braxton, co., W. Va C4 123
Bray, Ire D5 11
Bray, head, Ire D5 11
Bray, head, Ire F1 11
Braymer, Caldwell, Mo B4 101
Brayton, Audubon, Iowa C3 92
Brazeau, mtn., Alta., Can C2 69
Brazeau, riv., Alta., Can C2 69
Brazil, Clay, Ind E3 91
Brazil, Appanoose, Iowa D5 92
Brazil, Gibson, Tenn B2 117
Brazil, country, S.A D5 53, B2 56, 57
Brazil Lake, N.S., Can F4 74
Brazilton, Crawford, Kans E9 93
Brazoria, Brazoria, Tex E5, r14 118
Brazoria, co., Tex E5 118
Brazos, co., Tex D4 118
Brazox, riv., Tex r14 118
Brazzaville, Con F3 46
Brčko, Yugo C4 22
Brda, riv., Pol B4 26
Brea, Orange, Calif n13 82
Brea, pt., P.R C2 65
Breaden, lake, Austl E4 51
Bread Loaf, mtn., Vt C3 120
Breakenridge, mtn., B.C., Can E7 68
Breakers, pt., Am. Sam 52
Breakeyville, Que., Can o17 73
Breakneck, hill, Md D2 85
Breared, Swe B7 24
Breathitt, co., Ky C6 94
Breaux Bridge, St. Martin, La D4 95
Brechin, Scot D6 13
Brechin, Ont., Can C5 72
Breckenridge, Que., Can h12 72
Breckenridge, Summit, Colo B4 83
Breckenridge, Gratiot, Mich E6 98
Breckenridge, Wilkin, Minn D2 99
Breckenridge, Caldwell, Mo B4 101
Breckenridge, Stephens, Tex C3 118
Breckenridge Hills, St. Louis, Mo *C7 101
Breckinridge, Garfield, Okla A4 112
Breckinridge, co., Ky C3 94
Breckinridge, mtn., Calif E4 84
Brecksville, Cuyahoga, Ohio A4, h9 111
Breclav, Czech D4 26
Brecon, Wales C4 12
Brecon, co., Wales C4 12
Brecon Beacons, mts., Wales C4 12
Breda, Carroll, Iowa B3 92
Breda, Neth C4 15
Bredasdorp, S. Afr D3 49
Bredenbury, Sask., Can G4 70
Bredstedt, F.R.G D2 24
Bredy, Sov. Un E21 9
Bree, Bel C5 15
Breese, Clinton, Ill E4 90
Bregalnica, riv., Yugo E6 22
Bregenz, Aus E4 16
Bregovo, Bul C6 22
Breid, bay, Ant B15 5
Breien, Morton, N. Dak C5 110
Breil [sur Roya], Fr F7 14
Breisach, F.R.G A3 18
Breitenbush, Marion, Oreg C5 113
Brejo, Braz B2 57
Bremen, Cullman, Ala B2 78
Bremen, Haralson, Ga C1 87
Bremen, F.R.G B4 16, E2 24
Bremen, Marshall, Ind B5 91
Bremen, Muhlenberg, Ky C2 94
Bremen, Wells, N. Dak B6 110
Bremen, Fairfield, Ohio C3 111
Bremen, state, F.R.G E2 24
Bremer, co., Iowa B5 92
Bremerhaven, F.R.G B4 16, E2 24
Bremerton, Kitsap, Wash B3, e10 122
Bremerton East (Enetai), Kitsap, Wash *B3 122
Bremervörde, F.R.G E3 24
Bremgarten, Switz *B5 19
Bremo Bluff, Fluvanna, Va C4 121
Bremond, Robertson, Tex D4 118
Brenham, Washington, Tex D4 118
Brenish, Scot B1 13
Brenner, pass, Aus., It C7 18
Brent, Bibb, Ala C2 78
Brent, Ont., Can A6 72
Brent, Escambia, Fla u14 86
Brenta, riv., It D7 18
Brentford, Spink, S. Dak B7 116
Brenton, Wyoming, W. Va *D3 123
Brenton, pt., R.I D11 84
Brentwood, Contra Costa, Calif h9 82
Brentwood, Eng k13 10
Brentwood, Prince Georges, Md C1 85
Brentwood, St. Louis, Mo f12 101
Brentwood, Rockingham, N.H E4 105
Brentwood, Suffolk, N.Y F3 84
Brentwood, Allegheny, Pa k14 114
Brentwood, Charleston, S.C k11 115
Brentwood, Williamson, Tenn A5, g10 117
Brescia, It D6 18, B3 21
Breskens, Neth C3 15
Breslau, see Wrocław, Pol.
Bressanone, It A3 21
Bressler, Dauphin, Pa *F8 114
Bressuire, Fr D3 14
Brest, Fr C1 14
Brest, Sov. Un E4 27
Breteuil, Fr E2 15
Brétigny [-sur-Orge], Fr F2 15
Breton, Alta., Can C3 69
Breton, is., La E6 95
Breton, sound, La E6 95
Breton, strait, Fr D3 14
Breton Woods, Ocean, N.J C4 106
Bretton Woods, Eaton, Mich *F6 98
Bretton Woods, Coos, N.H B4 105
Breuil, It D3 18
Brevard, Transylvania, N.C f10 109
Brevard, co., Fla D6 86
Breves, Braz C4 59
Brevik, Nor p27 25
Brevnov, Czech. (part of Prague) n17 26
Brevoort, lake, Mich B6 98
Brewarrina, Austl D6 51
Brewer, Penobscot, Maine D4 96
Brewer, Perry, Mo D8 101
Brewster, Thomas, Kans C2 93
Brewster, Barnstable, Mass C7 97
Brewster, Nobles, Minn G3 99
Brewster, Blaine, Nebr C6 103
Brewster, Putnam, N.Y D7, m15 108
Brewster, Stark, Ohio B4 111
Brewster, Okanogan, Wash A6 122
Brewster, co., Tex p13 118
Brewster, cape, Grnld C17 4
Brewster, isl., Mass g12 97
Brewton, Escambia, Ala D2 78
Brewton, Laurens, Ga D4 87
Brežice, Yugo C2 22
Breznice, Czech D8 17
Breznik, Bul D6 22
Brezno [nad Hronom], Czech D5 26
Bria, Cen. Afr. Rep D4 46
Brian Boru, peak, B.C., Can B4 68
Briançon, Fr E7 14
Brian Head, mtn., Utah F3 119
Briar Bluff, Henry, Ill D7 92

Briarcliff, Delaware, Pa...*G11 114
Briare, Fr...D5 14
Brice, Franklin, Ohio...m11 111
Bricelyn, Fairbault, Minn...G5 99
Briceville, Anderson, Tenn...C9 117
Brickaville, Mad...g9 49
Brickeys, Lee, Ark...C5 81
Brick Town, Ocean, N.J...C4 106
Bridal Veil, Multnomah, Oreg...B4 113
Bridal Veil, falls, Utah...C4 119
Bride, riv., Ire...E3 11
Bridesville, B.C., Can...E8 68
Bridge, Cassia, Idaho...G5 89
Bridge, Coos, Oreg...D3 113
Bridge, creek, Sask., Can...H1 70
Bridge, riv., B.C., Can...D6 68
Bridgeboro, Worth, Ga...E3 87
Bridge City, Jefferson, La...*E5 95
Bridge City, Orange, Tex...*D6 118
Bridgedale, Jefferson, La...*E5 95
Bridgeford, Sask., Can...G2 70
Bridgehampton, Suffolk, N.Y...n16 108
Bridge Lake, B.C., Can...D7 68
Bridgeland, Duchesne, Utah...C5 119
Bridgend, Wales...C4 12
Bridgeport, Jackson, Ala...A4 78
Bridgeport, Mono, Calif...C4 82
Bridgeport, Ont., Can...D4 72
Bridgeport, Fairfield, Conn...E4 84
Bridgeport, Lawrence, Ill...E6 90
Bridgeport, Marion, Ind...m9 91
Bridgeport, Saginaw, Mich...E7 98
Bridgeport, Morrill, Nebr...C2 103
Bridgeport, Gloucester, N.J...D2 106
Bridgeport, Belmont, Ohio...B5 111
Bridgeport, Caddo, Okla...B3 112
Bridgeport, Baker, Oreg...C9 113
Bridgeport, Wise, Tex...C4 118
Bridgeport, Douglas, Wash...B6 122
Bridgeport, Harrison, W. Va...B4, k10 123
Bridger, Carbon, Mont...E8 102
Bridger, Ziebach, S. Dak...C4 116
Bridger, mts., Wyo...C4 125
Bridger, peak, Wyo...E5 125
Bridger, range, Mont...E6 102
Bridgeton, Parke, Ind...E3 91
Bridgeton, St. Louis, Mo...C7, f13 101
Bridgeton, Cumberland, N.J...E2 106
Bridgeton, Craven, N.C...B5 109
Bridgeton, Multnomah, Oreg...g12 113
Bridgetown, Barb...K20 65
Bridgetown, N.S., Can...E4 74
Bridgetown, Hamilton, Ohio...*C1 111
Bridgeview, Cook, Ill...*B6 90
Bridgeville, N.S., Can...D7 74
Bridgeville, Sussex, Del...C6 85
Bridgeville, Allegheny, Pa...k13 114
Bridgewater, Austl...o15 50
Bridgewater, N.S., Can...E5 74
Bridgewater, Litchfield, Conn...C3 84
Bridgewater, Adair, Iowa...C3 92
Bridgewater, Aroostook, Maine...B5 96
Bridgewater, Plymouth, Mass...C6 97
Bridgewater, Grafton, N.H...C3 105
Bridgewater, Somerset, N.J...B3 106
Bridgewater, McCook, S. Dak...D8 116
Bridgewater, Windsor, Vt...D3 120
Bridgewater, Rockingham, Va...B4 121
Bridgewater Corners, Windsor, Vt...D3 120
Bridgman, Berrien, Mich...G4 98
Bridgnorth, Eng...B5 12
Bridgton, Cumberland, Maine...D2 96
Bridgwater, Eng...C4 12
Bridgwater, bay, Eng...C4 12
Bridlington, Eng...C6 10
Bridport, Eng...D5 12
Bridport, Addison, Vt...D2 120
Brielle, Monmouth, N.J...C4 106
Brienz, Switz...C5 19
Brienz, lake, Switz...C5 19
Brier, creek, Ga...C5 87
Briercrest, Sask., Can...G3 70
Brièreville, Alta., Can...B5 69
Brierfield, Bibb, Ala...B3 78
Brier Hill, St. Lawrence, N.Y...f9 108
Brig. Switz...D4 19
Brigantine, Atlantic, N.J...E4 106
Brigantine, beach, N.J...E4 106
Brig Bay, Newf., Can...C3 75
Brigden, Ont., Can...E2 72
Brigg, Eng...A7 12
Briggs, Douglas, Nebr...*C10 103
Briggs, Burnet, Tex...D4 118
Briggs, Windsor, Vt...D3 120
Briggsdale, Weld, Colo...A6 83
Briggsville, Yell, Ark...C2 81
Briggsville, Berkshire, Mass...A1 97
Briggsville, Marquette, Wis...E4 124
Brigham City, Box Elder, Utah...B3 119
Brig Harbour, isl., Newf., Can...A3 75
Bright, Ont., Can...D4 72
Bright, lake, Ont., Can...B7 98
Brighton, Jefferson, Ala...B3, g7 78
Brighton, Ont., Can...C7 72
Brighton, Adams, Colo...B6 83
Brighton, Eng...D7 12
Brighton, Highlands, Fla...E5 86
Brighton, Macoupin and Jersey, Ill...D3 90
Brighton, Washington, Iowa...C6 92
Brighton, Somerset, Maine...C3 96
Brighton, Livingston, Mich...F7 98
Brighton, Monroe, N.Y...B3 108
Brighton, Tillamook, Oreg...B3 113
Brighton, Tipton, Tenn...B2 117
Brighton, Salt Lake, Utah...*C4 119
Brighton (Town of), Essex, Vt...*B5 120
Brighton, Kenosha, Wis...F1 124
Brightsand, lake, Sask., Can...D1 70
Brightshade, Clay, Ky...C6 94
Brightwater, lake, Sask., Can...F2 70
Brightwood, Guilford, N.C...A3 109
Brignac, Ascension, La...B6 95
Brignoles, Fr...F7 14
Brigus, Newf., Can...E5 75
Brihuega, Sp...B4 20
Brijnagar, India...E6 40
Brilhante, riv., Braz...C2 56
Brilliant, Marion, Ala...A2 78
Brilliant, B.C., Can...E9 68
Brilliant, Jefferson, Ohio...B5 111
Brillion, Calumet, Wis...D5, h9 124
Brilon, F.R.G...B3 17
Brimfield, Peoria, Ill...C4 90
Brimfield, Hampden, Mass...*B3 97
Brimhall, McKinley, N. Mex...B1 107
Brimley, Chippewa, Mich...B6 98
Brimson, Grundy, Mo...A4 101
Brimson, St. Louis, Minn...C7 99
Brindisi, It...D6 21
Bringhurst, Carroll, Ind...C4 91
Brinje, Yugo...C2 22
Brinkhaven (Gann), Knox, Ohio...B3 111
Brinkley, Monroe, Ark...C4 81
Brinkman, Greer, Okla...B2 112
Brinkworth, Austl...F2 51
Brinnon, Jefferson, Wash...B3 122
Brinsmade, Benson, N. Dak...A6 110
Brinson, Decatur. Ga...F2 87
Brion, isl., Que., Can...B8 74
Brione-Verzasca, Switz...D6 19
Brioude, Fr...E5 14
Brisbane, Austl...C9 51
Brisbane, San Mateo, Calif...*B5 82
Briscoe, Wheeler, Tex...B2 118
Briscoe, co., Tex...B2 118
Brissago, Switz...D6 19
Bristol, N.B., Can...C2 74
Bristol, Prowers, Colo...C8 83
Bristol, Hartford, Conn...C5 84
Bristol, Eng...C5 12
Bristol, Liberty, Fla...B2 86
Bristol, Elkhart, Ind...A6 91
Bristol, Grafton, N.H...C3 105
Bristol, Bucks, Pa...F12 114
Bristol, Bristol, R.I...C12 84
Bristol, Day, S. Dak...B8 116
Bristol, Sullivan, Tenn...C11 117
Bristol, Addison, Vt...C2 120
Bristol (Independent City), Va...f9 121
Bristol, Harrison, W. Va...k9 123
Bristol, Kenosha, Wis...F5, n11 124
Bristol, co., Mass...C5 97
Bristol, co., R.I...C11 84
Bristol, bay, Alsk...D7 79
Bristol, chan., Eng., Wales...C4 12
Bristol Ferry, Newport, R.I...C12 84
Bristol Terrace No. 2, Bucks, Pa...*F12 114
Bristolville, Trumbull, Ohio...A5 111
Bristow, Perry, Ind...H4 91
Bristow, Butler, Iowa...B5 92
Bristow, Boyd, Nebr...B7 103
Bristow, Creek, Okla...B5 112
Britannia, range, Ant...B28 5
Britannia Bay, Ont., Can...h12 72
Britannia Beach, B.C., Can...E6 68
British, mts., Yukon, Can...C4 66
British Columbia, prov., Can...E7 66, 68
British Honduras, see Belize, Br. dep., N.A.
British North Borneo, see Sabah, state, Mala.
Britstown, S. Afr...D3 49
Britt, Ont., Can...B4 72
Britt, Hancock, Iowa...A4 92
Britt, St. Louis, Minn...C6 99
Brittany (Bretagne), former prov., Fr...C2 14
Britton, Lenawee, Mich...G7 98
Britton, Oklahoma, Okla. (part of Oklahoma City)...B4 112
Britton, Marshall, S. Dak...B8 116
Brive [-la-Gaillarde], Fr...E4 14
Briviesca, Sp...A4 20
Brixham, Eng...D4 12
Brno, Czech...D4 26
Broa, bay, Cuba...C3 64
Broach, India...G4 40
Broad, bay, Scot...B2 13
Broad, riv., Ga...B4 87
Broad, riv., S.C...C5 115
Broad, run., Va...g11 121
Broadacres, Sask., Can...E1 70
Broadalbin, Fulton, N.Y...B6 108
Broadback, riv., Que., Can...F17 67
Broadbent, Coos, Oreg...D2 113
Broad Brook, Hartford, Conn...B6 84
Broaddus, San Augustine, Tex...D5 118
Broadford, Scot...C3 13
Broadford, Smyth, Va...f10 121
Broad Haven, bay, Ire...C2 11
Broadhead, creek, Pa...A2 106
Broadkill, riv., Del...C7 85
Broadkill Beach, Sussex, Del...C7 85
Broadland, Beadle, S. Dak...C7 116
Broadlands, Champaign, Ill...D5 90
Broadmead, Polk and Yamhill, Oreg...h11 113
Broadmoor, El Paso, Colo...C6 83
Broad Top, Huntingdon, Pa...F5 114
Broadus, Powder River, Mont...E11 102
Broadview, Sask., Can...G4 70
Broadview, Cook, Ill...*B6 90
Broadview, Monroe, Ind...*F4 91
Broadview, Yellowstone, Mont...D8 102
Broadview, Curry, N. Mex...C6 107
Broadview Heights, Cuyahoga, Ohio...h9 111
Broadwater, Morrill, Nebr...C3 103
Broadwater, co., Mont...D5 102
Broadway, Warren, N.J...B2 106
Broadway, Lee, N.C...B3 109
Broadway, Union, Ohio...B2 111
Broadway, Rockingham, Va...B4 121
Broager, Den...D3 24
Brochet, Man., Can...E12 66
Brock, Sask., Can...F1 70
Brock, Nemaha, Nebr...D10 103
Brock, isl., N.W. Ter., Can...m28 67
Brocken, mtn., G.D.R...B5 17
Brocket, Alta., Can...E4 69
Brocket, Ramsey, N. Dak...A7 110
Brockport, Monroe, N.Y...B3 108
Brockport, Elk., Pa...D4 114
Brocksburg, Keya Paha, Nebr...B6 103
Brockton, Plymouth, Mass...B5, h11 97
Brockton, Roosevelt, Mont...B12 102
Brockton, res., Mass...h11 97
Brockville, Ont., Can...C9 72
Brockway, McCone, Mont...C11 102
Brockway, Jefferson, Pa...D4 114
Brockwell, Izard, Ark...A4 81
Brocton, Edward, Ill...D6 90
Brocton, Chautauqua, N.Y...C1 108
Brod, Yugo...C4 22
Broderick, Sask., Can...F2 70
Brodeur, pen., N.W., Ter., Can...B15 66
Brodhead, Rockcastle, Ky...C5 94
Brodhead, Green, Wis...F4 124
Brodheadsville, Monroe, Pa...E11 114
Brodick, Scot...E3 13
Brodnax, Brunswick and Mecklenburg, Va...D4 121
Brodnica, Pol...B5 26
Brody, Sov. Un...F5 27
Brogado, Reeves, Tex...o13 118
Brogan, Malheur, Oreg...C9 113
Brokaw, Marathon, Wis...C4 124
Broken Arrow, Tulsa, Okla...A6 112
Broken Bow, Custer, Nebr...C6 103
Broken Bow, McCurtain, Okla...C7 112
Broken Hill, Austl...E3 51
Brome, Que., Can...D5 73
Brome, F.R.G...F4 24
Brome, co., Que., Can...D5 73
Brome, lake, Que., Can...D5 73
Bromhead, Sask., Can...H4 70
Bromide, Coal and Johnston, Okla...C5 112
Bromley, Eng. (part of London)...m13 10
Bromley, mtn., Vt...E3 120
Bromptonville, Que., Can...D6 73
Bromsgrove, Eng...B5 12
Bromyard, Eng...B5 12
Bronaugh, Vernon, Mo...D3 101
Bronco, Yoakum, Tex...C1 118
Brønderslev, Den...A3 24
Brong-Ahafo, reg., Ghana...E4 45
Bronlund, peak, B.C., Can...E7 66
Bronnitsy, Sov. Un...n18 27
Brönnöysund, Nor...E5 25
Bronson, Levy, Fla...C4 86
Bronson, Woodbury, Iowa...B1 92
Bronson, Bourbon, Kans...E8 93
Bronson, Branch, Mich...G5 98
Bronson, Sabine, Tex...D5 118
Bronte, Coke, Tex...D2 118
Bronwood, Terrell, Ga...E2 87
Bronxville, Westchester, N.Y...h13 108
Brook, Newton, Ind...C3 91
Brookdale, Man., Can...D2 71
Brookdale, Pierce, Wash. (part of Parkland)...B3 122
Brooke, Stafford, Va...B5 121
Brooke, co., W. Va...A4 123
Brooker, Bradford, Fla...C4 86
Brookeville, Montgomery, Md...B3 85
Brookfield, N.S., Can...D6 74
Brookfield, Fairfield, Conn...D3 84
Brookfield, Tift, Ga...E3 87
Brookfield, Cook, Ill...k9 90
Brookfield, Worcester, Mass...B3 97
Brookfield, Linn, Mo...B4 101
Brookfield, Carroll, N.H...C4 105
Brookfield, Madison, N.Y...C5 108
Brookfield, Orange, Vt...C3 120
Brookfield, Fairfax, Va...*B5 121
Brookfield, Waukesha, Wis...m11 124
Brookfield Center, Fairfield, Conn...D3 84
Brookfield Mines, N.S., Can...E5 74
Brookford, Catawba, N.C...B1 109
Brookhaven, Lincoln, Miss...D3 100
Brookhaven, Suffolk, N.Y...F5 84
Brookhaven, Delaware, Pa...*G11 114
Brookhaven, Monongalia, W. Va...h11 123
Brooking, Sask., Can...H3 70
Brookings, Curry, Oreg...E2 113
Brookings, Brookings, S. Dak...C9 116
Brookings, co., S. Dak...C9 116
Brookland, Craighead, Ark...B5 81
Brooklands, Man., Can...*E3 71
Brooklands, Oakland, Mich...*F7 98
Brooklandville, Baltimore, Md...g10 85
Brooklawn, Camden, N.J...D2 106
Brooklet, Bulloch, Ga...D5 87
Brooklin, Hancock, Maine...D4 96
Brookline, Norfolk, Mass...B5, g11 97
Brookline, Jackson, Mich...*F6 98
Brookline, Hillsboro, N.H...E3 105
Brookline (Town of), Windham, Vt...*E3 120
Brooklyn, Conecuh, Ala...D3 78
Brooklyn, N.S., Can...E5 74
Brooklyn, Windham, Conn...*B9 84
Brooklyn, Stewart, Ga...D2 87
Brooklyn (Lovejoy), St. Clair, Ill...B8 101
Brooklyn, Schuyler, Ill...C3 90
Brooklyn, Morgan, Ind...E5 91
Brooklyn, Poweshiek, Iowa...C5 92
Brooklyn, Jackson, Mich...F6 98
Brooklyn, Forrest, Miss...D4 100
Brooklyn, Cuyahoga, Ohio...h9 111
Brooklyn, Susquehanna, Pa...C10 114
Brooklyn, Lancaster, S.C...B6 115
Brooklyn, Pacific, Wash...C2 122
Brooklyn, Dane and Green, Wis...F4 124
Brooklyn Center, Hennepin, Minn...m12 99
Brooklyn Park, Anne Arundel, Md...h11 85
Brooklyn Park, Hennepin, Minn...m12 99
Brookmere, B.C., Can...E7 68
Brookneal, Campbell, Va...C4 121
Brook Park, Pine, Minn...E5 99
Brook Park, Cuyahoga, Ohio...h9 111
Brookport, Massac, Ill...F5 90
Brooks, Covington, Ala...D3 78
Brooks, Alta., Can...D5 69
Brooks, Adams, Iowa...D3 92
Brooks, Bullitt, Ky...g11 94
Brooks, Waldo, Maine...D3 96
Brooks, Red Lake, Minn...C3 99
Brooks, Marion, Oreg...h12 113
Brooks, Adams, Wis...E4 124
Brooks, co., Ga...F3 89
Brooks, co., Tex...F3 118
Brooks, pen., B.C., Can...D4 68
Brooks, range, Alsk...B8 79
Brooksburg, Jefferson, Ind...G7 91
Brooksby, Sask., Can...E3 70
Brookshire, Waller, Tex...E5, r14 118
Brookside, Jefferson, Ala...f7 78
Brookside, Fremont, Colo...C5 83
Brookside, New Castle, Del...A6 85
Brooks Place, Plymouth, Mass...*B5 97
Brookston, White, Ind...C4 91
Brookston, St. Louis, Minn...D6 99
Brooksvale, New Haven, Conn...*D5 84
Brooksville, Hernando, Fla...D4 86
Brooksville, Bracken, Ky...B5 94
Brooksville, Pottawatomie, Okla...B5 112
Brooksville, Noxubee, Miss...B5 100
Brookton, Washington, Maine...C5 96
Brooktondale, Tompkins, N.Y...C4 108
Brookvale, Clear Creek, Colo...B5 83
Brookview, Duval, Fla...*B5 86
Brookview, Dorchester, Md...C6 85
Brookville, Ogle, Ill...A4 90
Brookville, Franklin, Ind...F7 91
Brookville, Saline, Kans...D6 93
Brookville, Norfolk, Mass...h11 97
Brookville, Nassau, N.Y...*F2 84
Brookville, Montgomery, Ohio...C1 111
Brookville, Jefferson, Pa...D3 114
Brookwood, Tuscaloosa, Ala...B2 78
Brookwood, Ocean, N.J...C4 106
Broom, inlet, Scot...B4 10
Broomall, Delaware, Pa...p20 114
Broome, Austl...C3 50
Broome, co., N.Y...C5 108
Broomes Island, Calvert, Md...D4 85
Broomfield, Boulder and Jefferson, Colo...B5 83
Broomtown, val., Ala...A4 78
Brooten, Stearns, Minn...E3 99
Brora, Scot...B5 13
Brora, riv., Scot...B4 13
Brösarp, Swe...C8 24
Broseley, Butler, Mo...E7 101
Brosna, riv., Ire...D4 11
Brossard, Que., Can...q20 73
Brotas de Macaubas, Braz...D2 57
Brothers, Deschutes, Oreg...D6 113
Brothers, is., Thai...I3 38
Brotherton, Putnam, Tenn...C8 117
Brothertown, Calumet, Wis...k9 124
Brotmanville, Salem, N.J...D2 106
Brou, Fr...C4 14
Brough, Eng...F6 13
Brough, head, Scot...A5 13
Broughton, Hamilton, Ill...F5 90
Broughton Station, Que., Can...C6 73
Broughty Ferry, Scot. (part of Dundee)...B5 10
Broussard, Lafayette, La...D4 95
Brovst, Den...A3 24
Broward, co., Fla...F6 86
Browerville, Todd, Minn...D4 99
Brown, co., Ill...D3 90
Brown, co., Ind...F5 91
Brown, co., Kans...C8 93
Brown, co., Minn...F4 99
Brown, co., Nebr...B6 103
Brown, co., Ohio...D2 111
Brown, co., S. Dak...B7 116
Brown, co., Tex...D3 118
Brown, co., Wis...D6 124
Brown or Roan, cliffs, Utah...D6 119
Brown, pt., Wash...C1 122
Brown City, Sanilac, Mich...E8 98
Brown Deer, Milwaukee, Wis...m12 124
Brownell, Ness, Kans...D4 93
Brownfield, Pope, Ill...F5 90
Brownfield, Terry, Tex...C1 118
Brownfields, East Baton Rouge, La...*D4 95
Browning, Sask., Can...H4 70
Browning, Schuyler, Ill...C3 90
Browning, Linn and Sullivan, Mo...A4 101
Browning, Glacier, Mont...B3 102
Browning, entrance, B.C., Can...C2 68
Brownington, Henry, Mo...C4 101
Brownington, Orleans, Vt...B4 120
Brownington Center, Orleans, Vt...B4 120
Brownlee, Sask., Can...G2 70
Brownlee, Cherry, Nebr...B5 103
Brownlee, Baker, Oreg...C10 113
Brownlee, dam, Idaho...D2 89
Brownlee, res., Idaho, Oreg...C10 113
Brown Lee Park, Calhoun, Mich...*F5 98
Browns, Edwards, Ill...E6 90
Browns, inlet, N.C...C5 109
Browns, riv., Vt...B2 120
Browns, val., Ala...B3 78
Brownsboro, Oldham, Ky...A4 94
Brownsboro, Jackson, Oreg...E4 113
Brownsburg, Que., Can...D3 73
Brownsburg, Hendricks, Ind...E5 91
Brownsburg, Rockbridge, Va...C3 121
Brownsdale, Mower, Minn...G6 99
Brownsmead, Clatsop, Oreg...A3 113
Browns Mills, Burlington, N.J...D3 106
Brownstown, Sevier, Ark...D1 81
Brownstown, Fayette, Ill...D5 90
Brownstown, Jackson, Ind...G5 91
Browns Town, Jam...E14 65
Brownstown, Cambria, Pa...*F4 114
Brownstown, Lancaster, Pa...F9 114
Brownstown, Yakima, Wash...C5 122
Brownstown, head, Ire...E4 11
Browns Valley, Montgomery, Ind...E4 91
Browns Valley, Traverse, Minn...E2 99
Brownsville, Dade, Fla...s13 86
Brownsville, Union, Ind...E8 91
Brownsville, Edmonson, Ky...C3 94
Brownsville, Ouachita, La...*B3 95
Brownsville, Houston, Minn...G7 99
Brownsville, Linn Oreg...C4 113
Brownsville, Fayette, Pa...F2 114
Brownsville, Haywood, Tenn...B2 117
Brownsville, Cameron, Tex...G4 118
Brownsville, Windsor, Vt...E4 120
Brownton, McLeod, Minn...F4 99
Brownton, Barbour, W. Va...B4 123
Browntown, Green, Wis...F4 124
Brownvale, Alta., Can...A2 69
Brownville, Jefferson, Ala...E4 78
Brownville, Tuscaloosa, Ala...B2 78
Brownville, Piscataquis, Maine...C3 96
Brownville, Nemaha, Nebr...D10 103
Brownville, Jefferson, N.Y...A5 108
Brownville Junction, Piscataquis, Maine...C3 96
Brown Willy, mtn., Eng...D3 12
Brownwood, Stoddard, Mo...D8 101
Brownwood, Brown, Tex...D3 118
Brownwood, Orange, Tex...*D6 118
Brownwood, lake, Tex...D3 118
Broxton, Coffee, Ga...E4 87
Broye, riv., Switz...C2 19
Broyhill Park, Fairfax, Va...*B5 121
Brozas, Sp...C2 20
Bruay-en-Artois, Fr...B5 14, D2 15
Bruce, Alta., Can...C4 69
Bruce, Walton, Fla...u16 86
Bruce, Calhoun, Miss...B4 100
Bruce, Brookings, S. Dak...C9 116
Bruce, Rusk., Wis...C2 124
Bruce, co., Ont., Can...C3 72
Bruce, mtn., Austl...D2 50
Bruce, pen., Ont., Can...B3 72
Bruce, pt., P.E.I., Can...C7 74
Bruce Crossing, Ontonagon, Mich...m12 98
Brucefield, Ont., Can...D3 72
Bruceton, Carroll, Tenn...A3 117
Bruceton Mills, Preston, W. Va...B5 123
Brucetown, Frederick, Va...A4 121
Bruceville, Knox, Ind...G3 91
Bruchsal, F.R.G...D3 17
Bruck, Aus...E7 16
Bruck, Aus...E8 16
Brück, G.D.R...A7 17
Brückenau, F.R.G...C4 17
Bruck-Fusch (Bruck an der Grossglocknerstrasse), Aus...B8 18
Bruderheim, Alta., Can...C4 69
Bruff, Ire...E3 11
Brugg, Switz...B5 19
Brugge (Bruges), Bel...C3 15
Brühl, F.R.G...C1 17
Bruin, Butler, Pa...D2 114
Bruin, pt., Utah...D5 119
Bruins, Crittenden, Ark...C5 81
Bruja, mtn., Pan...k11 62
Brule, Keith, Nebr...C4 103
Brule, Douglas, Wis...B2 124
Brule, co., S. Dak...D6 116
Brûlé, lake, Alta., Can...C2 69
Brule, lake, Minn...k9 99
Brule, riv., Mich...C2 98
Brule, riv., Wis...B2 124
Brûlé Lake Station, Ont., Can...B6 72
Brumath, Fr...C7 14
Brumley, Miller, Mo...C5 101
Brundidge, Pike, Ala...D4 78
Bruneau, Owyhee, Idaho...G3 89
Bruneau, riv., Idaho...G3 89
Bruneau, riv., Nev...B6 104
Brunei, see Banda Seri Begawan, Bru.
Brunei, country, Asia...I14 33, E4 35
Brunete, Sp...p16 20
Brunette, isl., Newf., Can...E4 75
Bruni, Webb, Tex...F3 118
Brunico, It...C7 18
Brünig-Hasliberg, Switz...C5 19
Bruning, Thayer, Nebr...D8 103
Brunkild, Man., Can...E3 71
Brunnen, Switz...C6 19
Bruno, Sask., Can...E3 70
Bruno, Pine, Minn...D6 99
Bruno, Butler, Nebr...C9 103
Brunsbüttel, F.R.G...E3 24
Brunson, Hampton, S.C...F5 115
Brunsville, Plymouth, Iowa...B1 92
Brunswick, Glynn, Ga...E5 87
Brunswick, Lake, Ind...B2 91
Brunswick, Cumberland, Maine...E2, g8 96
Brunswick, Frederick, Md...B2 85
Brunswick, Chariton, Mo...B4 101
Brunswick, Antelope, Nebr...B8 103
Brunswick, Columbus, N.C...C4 109
Brunswick, Medina, Ohio...A4 111
Brunswick (Town of), Essex, Vt...*B5 120
Brunswick, co., N.C...C4 109
Brunswick, co., Va...E5 121
Brunswick, pen., Chile...h11 54
Bruny, isl., Austl...o15 50
Bruree, Ire...E3 11
Brusett, Garfield, Mont...C9 102
Brush, Morgan, Colo...A7 83
Brush, mtn., Va...D1 121
Brushy, mts., N.C...B1 109
Brus Laguna, Hond...C5 62
Brusly, East Baton Rouge, La...h9 95
Brusque, Braz...D3 56
Brussels (Bruxelles), Bel...D4 15
Brussels, Ont., Can...D3 72
Brussels, Calhoun, Ill...E3 90
Brussels, Door, Wis...D6 124
Bruton, Eng...C5 12
Brutus, Emmet, Mich...C6 98
Bruyères-en-Vosges, Fr...A2 18
Bryan, Williams, Ohio...A1 111
Bryan, Brazos, Tex...D4 118
Bryan, co., Ga...D5 87
Bryan, co., Okla...D5 112
Bryanka, Sov. Un...q21 27
Bryansk, Sov. Un...E10 27
Bryans Road, Charles, Md...C3 85
Bryant, Saline, Ark...C3, k10 81
Bryant, Palm Beach, Fla...F6 86
Bryant, Fulton, Ill...C3 90
Bryant, Jay, Ind...C8 91
Bryant, Clackamas, Oreg. (part of Oswego)...B2 113
Bryant, Hamlin, S. Dak...C8 116
Bryant, Langlade, Wis...C4 124
Bryant, creek, Mo...D5 101
Bryant, mtn, Mass...B2 97
Bryantown, Charles, Md...C4 85
Bryant Pond, Oxford, Maine...D2 96
Bryantsville, Garrard, Ky...C5 94
Bryantville, Plymouth, Mass...B6 97
Bryce Canyon, Garfield, Utah...F3 119
Bryce Canyon, nat. park, Utah...F3 119
Bryceland, Bienville, La...B3 95
Bryceville, Nassau, Fla...B5 86
Brynica, riv., Pol...g9 26
Bryn Mawr, Delaware and Montgomery, Pa...o20 114
Bryn Mawr, King, Wash...e11 122
Bryson, Jack, Tex...C3 118
Bryson City, Swain, N.C...f9 109
Brzeg, Pol...C4 26
Brzesko, Pol...D6 26
Brzezinka, Pol...g10 26
Brzeziny, Pol...C5 26
Brzozow, Pol...D7 26
B-Say-Tah, Sask., Can...G4 70
Buayan, Phil...*D7 35
Buba, Guinea-Bissau...D2 45
Bubiyan, isl., Kuw...G4 41
Bucaramanga, Col...B3 60
Buccaneer, arch., Austl...C3 50
Buchach, Sov. Un...G5 27
Buchanan, Sask., Can...F4 70
Buchanan, Haralson, Ga...C1 87
Buchanan, Lib...E2 45
Buchanan, Berrien, Mich...G4 98
Buchanan, Westchester, N.Y...*D7 108
Buchanan, Stutsman, N. Dak...B7 110
Buchanan, Henry, Tenn...A3 117
Buchanan, Botetourt, Va...C3 121
Buchanan, co., Iowa...B6 92
Buchanan, co., Mo...B3 101
Buchanan, co., Va...e9 121
Buchan Ness, cape, Scot...C7 13
Buchans, Newf., Can...D3 75
Buchardo, Arg...A4 54
Bucharest (București), Rom...C8 22
Buchen, F.R.G...D4 17
Buchholz, F.R.G...E3 24
Buchloe, F.R.G...D5 16
Buchs, Switz...B7 19
Buchtel, Athens, Ohio...C3 111
Buck, creek, Ind...m11 91
Buck, creek, Ky...C5 94
Buck, lake, Alta., Can...C3 69
Buck, mtn., Wash...A6 122
Buckatunna, Wayne, Miss...D5 100
Buck Creek, Tippecanoe, Ind...D4 91
Bückeburg, F.R.G...A4 17
Buckeye, Maricopa, Ariz...D3, m7 80
Buckeye, Hardin, Iowa...B4 92
Buckeye, Lea, N. Mex...E6 107
Buckeye, Pocahontas, W. Va...C4 123
Buckeye Lake, Licking, Ohio...C3 111
Buckeystown, Frederick, Md...B3 85
Buckfield, Oxford, Maine...D2 96
Buckhannon, Upshur, W. Va...C4 123
Buckhaven [& Methil], Scot...D5 13
Buckhead, Morgan, Ga...C3 87
Buck Hill Falls, Monroe, Pa...D11 114
Buckhorn, Maricopa, Ariz...D4, m9 80
Buckhorn, Grant, N. Mex...D1 107
Buckhorn Knob, mtn., W. Va...D4 123
Buckhorn Lake, res., Ky...C6 94
Buckie, Scot...C6 13
Buckingham, Que., Can...D2 73
Buckingham, Eng...C6 12
Buckingham, Buckingham, Va...C4 121
Buckingham, co., Eng...C7 12
Buckingham, co., Va...C4 121
Buckland (Elephant Point), Alsk...B7 79
Buckland, Que., Can...C7 73
Buckland, Hartford, Conn. (part of Manchester)...B6 84
Buckland, Franklin, Mass...A2 97
Buckland, Auglaize, Ohio...B1 111
Buckley, Iroquois, Ill...C5 90
Buckley, Wexford, Mich...D5 98
Buckley, Pierce, Wash...B3, f11 122
Bucklin, Ford, Kans...E4 93
Bucklin, Linn, Mo...B5 101
Buckman, Morrison, Minn...E4 99
Bucknell Manor, Fairfax, Va...*B5 121
Buckner, Lafayette, Ark...D2 81
Buckner, Franklin, Ill...F4 90
Buckner, Oldham, Ky...g12 94
Buckner, Jackson, Mo...h11 101
Buckner, creek, Kans...D4 93
Bucknum, Natrona, Wyo...C6 125
Bucks, Mobile, Ala...E1 78
Bucks, co., Pa...F11 114
Bucks Harbor, Washington, Maine...D5 96
Buckskin, Gibson, Ind...H3 91
Buckskin, mts., Ariz...C2 80
Bucksport, Hancock, Maine...D4 96
Bucksport, Horry, S.C...D9 115
Buckville, Garland, Ark...C2 81
Bucoda, Thurston, Wash...C3 122
Bucovina, see Bukovina, prov., Rom.
Bucovina, reg., Rom., Sov. Un...B7 22
Buco Zau, Ang...B1 48
Buctouche, N.B., Can...C5 74
Bucyrus, Miami, Kans...D9 93
Bucyrus, Adams, N. Dak...C3 110
Bucyrus, Crawford, Ohio...B3 111
Bud, Wyoming, W. Va...D3 123
Buda, Bureau, Ill...B4 90
Buda, Hays, Tex...D4 118
Budapest, Hung...B4 22
Budaun, India...C7 40
Budd, coast, Ant...C24 5
Budd, lake, N.J...B3 106
Budd Lake, Morris, N.J...B3 106
Buddon Ness, cape, Scot...D6 13
Buddtown, Burlington, N.J...D3 106
Bude, Eng...D3 12
Bude, Franklin, Miss...D3 100
Bude, bay. Eng...D3 12
Budennovsk, Sov. Un...G17 9
Budjala, Zaire...A2 48
Budnany, Czech...o17 26
Budrio, It...B3 21
Budyne, Czech...n17 26
Buechel, Jefferson, Ky...B4, g11 94
Buena, Atlantic, N.J...D3 106
Buena, Yakima, Wash...C5 122
Buena, riv., Chile...C2 54
Buena Park, Orange, Calif...n13 82
Buenave tura Col...C2 60
Buenaventura, Mex...B3 63
Buena Vista, Monroe, Ala...D2 78
Buena Vista, Bol...C3 55
Buena Vista, Chaffee, Colo...C4 83
Buena Vista, Pasco, Fla...D4 86
Buena Vista, Marion, Ga...D2 87
Buena Vista, Chickasaw, Miss...B5 100
Buena Vista, Mora, N. Mex...B4 107
Buena Vista, Taos, N. Mex...*A4 107
Buena Vista, Scioto, Ohio...D2 111
Buena Vista, Carroll, Tenn...B3 117
Buena Vista (Independent City) Va...C3 121
Buena Vista, co., Iowa...B2 92
Buenos Aires, Arg...A5, g7 54
Buenos Aires, C.R...F6 62
Buenos Aires, Pan...k11 62
Buenos Aires, prov., Arg...B4 54
Buenos Aires, lake, Arg...D2 54
Bueyeros, Harding, N. Mex...B6 107
Buffalo, Chambers, Ala...C4 78
Buffalo, Alta., Can...D5 69
Buffalo, Sangamon, Ill...D4 90
Buffalo, White, Ind...C4 91
Buffalo, Scott, Iowa...C7, h10 92
Buffalo, Wilson, Kans...E8 93
Buffalo, Wright, Minn...E5 99
Buffalo, Dallas, Mo...D4 101
Buffalo, Fergus, Mont...D7 102
Buffalo, Erie, N.Y...C2 108
Buffalo, Cass, N. Dak...C8 110
Buffalo, Guernsey, Ohio...C4 111
Buffalo, Harper, Okla...A2 112
Buffalo, Union, S.C...B4 115
Buffalo, Harding, S. Dak...B2 116
Buffalo, Leon, Tex...D4 118
Buffalo, Putnam, W. Va...C3 123
Buffalo, Buffalo, Wis...D2 124
Buffalo, Johnson, Wyo...B6 125
Buffalo, co., Nebr...D6 103
Buffalo, co., S. Dak...C6 116
Buffalo, co., Wis...D2 124
Buffalo, creek, Kans...C5 93
Buffalo, creek, W. Va...h10 123
Buffalo, creek, W. Va...f8 123
Buffalo, creek, W. Va...n12 123

Calcutta, Columbiana, Ohio ... B5 111
Calcutta, lake, Nev ... B2 104
Caldaro, It ... C7 18
Caldas, dept., Col ... B2 60
Caldas da Rainha, Port ... C1 20
Calder, Sask., Can ... F5 70
Calder, Shoshone, Idaho ... B2 89
Calder, lake, Scot ... B5 13
Calder, riv., Eng ... A6 12
Caldera, Chile ... E1 55
Calderwood, Blount, Tenn ... D10 117
Caldron Falls, res., Wis ... C5 124
Caldwell, Canyon, Idaho ... F2 89
Caldwell, Sumner, Kans ... E6 93
Caldwell, Essex, N.J. ... B4 106
Caldwell, Noble, Ohio ... C4 111
Caldwell, Burleson, Tex ... D4 118
Caldwell, Greenbrier, W. Va ... D4 123
Caldwell, co., Ky ... C2 94
Caldwell, co., Mo ... B3 101
Caldwell, co., N.C. ... B1 109
Caldwell, co., Tex ... E4 118
Caldwell, par., La ... B3 95
Cale, Nevada, Ark ... D2 81
Caledon, N. Ire ... C5 11
Caledonia, N.S., Can ... E4 74
Caledonia, Ont., Can ... D5 72
Caledonia, Boone, Ill ... A5 90
Caledonia, Kent, Mich ... F5 98
Caledonia, Huston, Minn ... G7 99
Caledonia, Lowndes, Miss ... B5 100
Caledonia, Livingston, N.Y. ... C3 108
Caledonia, Traill, N. Dak ... B9 110
Caledonia, Marion, Ohio ... B3 111
Caledonia, Elk, Pa ... D5 115
Caledonia, Racine, Wis ... F2 124
Caledonia, co., Vt ... C4 120
Caledonian, canal, Scot ... C4 13
Calella, Sp ... B7 20
Calenzana, Fr ... C2 21
Calera, Shelby, Ala ... B3 78
Calera, Chile ... A2 54
Calera, Bryan, Okla ... D5 112
Caleta Buena, Chile ... C2 55
Caleta Olivia, Arg ... D3 54
Calexico, Imperial, Calif ... F6 82
Calf of Man, isl., I. of Man ... C4 10
Calgary, Alta., Can ... D3, g8 69
Calha, pt., Port ... F9 20
Calhan, El Paso, Colo ... B6 83
Calheta, Port. (Madeira Is.) ... h11 20
Calhoun, Lowndes, Ala ... C3 78
Calhoun, N.B., Can ... C5 74
Calhoun, Gordon, Ga ... B2 87
Calhoun, Richland, Ill ... E5 90
Calhoun, McLean, Ky ... C2 94
Calhoun, Ouachita, La ... B3 95
Calhoun, Henry, Mo ... C4 101
Calhoun, McMinn, Tenn ... D9 117
Calhoun, co., Ala ... B4 78
Calhoun, co., Ark ... D3 81
Calhoun, co., Fla ... B1 86
Calhoun, co., Ga ... E2 87
Calhoun, co., Ill ... D3 90
Calhoun, co., Iowa ... B3 92
Calhoun, co., Mich ... F5 98
Calhoun, co., Miss ... B4 100
Calhoun, co., S.C ... D6 115
Calhoun, co., Tex ... E4 118
Calhoun, co., W. Va ... C3 123
Calhoun City, Calhoun, Miss ... B4 100
Calhoun Falls, Abbeville, S.C ... C3 115
Cali, Col ... C2 60
Calico Rock, Izard, Ark ... A3 81
Calicut, India ... F6 39
Caliente, Kern, Calif ... E4 82
Caliente, Lincoln, Nev ... F7 104
Califon, Hunterdon, N.J ... B3 106
California, Harrison, Iowa ... C2 92
California, Campbell, Ky ... k14 94
California, Moniteau, Mo ... C5 101
California, Washington, Pa ... F2 114
California, state, U.S ... C3 76, 82
California, gulf, Mex ... B2 63
California Oil Camp, Rio Blanco, Colo ... A2 83
Caliman, mts., Rom ... B7 22
Calingasta, Arg ... A3 54
Calio, Cavalier, N. Dak ... A7 110
Calion, Union, Ark ... D3 81
Calipatria, Imperial, Calif ... F6 82
Calistoga, Napa, Calif ... C2 82
Call, Newton, Tex ... D6 118
Callabonna, lake, Austl ... D3 51
Callabonna, riv., Austl ... D3 51
Callahan, mtn., Nev ... D5 104
Callahan, Siskiyou, Calif ... B2 82
Callahan, Nassau, Fla ... B5, k8 86
Callahan, Sedgwick, Kans ... g12 93
Callahan, Webb, Tex ... C3 118
Callahan, co., Tex ... C3 118
Callan, Ire ... E4 11
Callan, Menard, Tex ... D3 118
Callander, Ont., Can ... A5 72
Callander, Scot ... D4 13
Callands, Pittsylvania, Va ... D3 121
Callao, Macon, Mo ... B5 101
Callao, Peru ... D2 58
Callao, Northumberland, Va ... C6 121
Callao, dept., Peru ... *D2 58
Callaway, St. Marys, Md ... D4 85
Callaway, Becker, Minn ... D3 99
Callaway, Custer, Nebr ... C6 103
Callaway, Franklin, Va ... C2 121
Callaway, co., Mo ... C6 101
Calle Blancos, C.R ... *F5 62
Callender, Webster, Iowa ... B3 92
Callensburg, Clarion, Pa ... D2 114
Callery, Butler, Pa ... E1 114
Callicoon, Sullivan, N.Y ... D5 108
Callicoon Center, Sullivan, N.Y ... D6 108
Calliham, McMullen, Tex ... E3 118
Calling, lake, Alta., Can ... B4 69
Calling Lake, Alta., Can ... B4 69
Calloway, co., Ky ... f9 94
Calmar, Alta., Can ... C4 69
Calmar, Winneshiek, Iowa ... A6 92
Calne, Eng ... C6 12
Caloocan, Phil ... o13 35
Caloosahatchee, riv., Fla ... F5 86
Caloundra, Austl ... C9 51
Calpella, Mendocino, Calif ... C2 82
Calpet, Sublette, Wyo ... D2 125
Caltagirone, It ... F5 21
Caltanissetta, It ... F5 21
Caltra, Ire ... D3 11
Caluire [-et-Cuire], Fr ... E6 14
Calulo, Ang ... D1 48
Calumet, Walker, Ala ... B2 78
Calumet, Que., Can ... D3 73
Calumet, O'Brien, Iowa ... B2 92
Calumet, Houghton, Mich ... A2 98
Calumet, Itasca, Minn ... C5 99
Calumet, Canadian, Okla ... B3 112
Calumet, Westmoreland, Pa ... *F3 114
Calumet, co., Wis ... D5 124
Calumet, lake, Ill ... k9 90
Calumet City, Cook, Ill ... B6, k9 90
Calumet Park, Cook, Ill ... *B6 90
Calumet Sag, chan., Ill ... k9 90
Calumetville, Fond du Lac, Wis ... k9 124
Calva, Graham, Ariz ... D5 80
Calvados, dept., Fr ... *C3 14
Calvary, Grady, Ga ... F2 87
Calvary, Fond du Lac, Wis ... k9 124
Calvert, Washington, Ala ... D1 78
Calvert, Robertson, Tex ... D4 118
Calvert, co., Md ... C4 85
Calvert, isl., B.C., Can ... D3 68
Calvert City, Marshall, Ky ... e9 94
Calverton, Fauquier, Va ... B5 121
Calverton Park, St. Louis, Mo ... f13 101
Calvi, Fr ... C2 21
Calvillo, Mex ... m12 63
Calvin, Winn, La ... C3 95
Calvin, Cavalier, N. Dak ... A7 110
Calvin, Hughes, Okla ... C5 112
Calvin, Lee, Va ... f9 121
Calvinia, S. Afr ... D2 49
Calvörde, G.D.R ... A6 17
Calw, F.R.G ... E3 17
Calwa, Fresno, Calif ... *D4 82
Calypso, Duplin, N.C ... B4 109
Calzada de Calatrava, Sp ... C4 20
Cam, riv., Eng ... B8 12
Camabatela, Ang ... C2 48
Camacho, Mex ... C4 63
Camagüey, Cuba ... D5 64
Camagüey, prov., Cuba ... D4 64
Camajuaní, Cuba ... C4 64
Camak, Warren, Ga ... C4 87
Camamu, Braz ... D3 57
Camaná, Peru ... E3 58
Camanche, Clinton, Iowa ... C7 92
Camano, isl., Wash ... A3 122
Camaquã, riv., Braz ... E2 56
Camaquã, Braz ... E2 56
Camargo, Bol ... D2 55
Camargo, Douglas, Ill ... D5 90
Camargo, see Ciudad Camargo, Mex.
Camargo, Dewey, Okla ... A2 112
Camarillo, Ventura, Calif ... *E4 82
Camarines Norte, prov., Phil ... *C6 35
Camarines Sur, prov., Phil ... *C6 35
Camarón, cape, Hond ... C5 62
Camarones, Arg ... C3 54
Camarones, bay, Arg ... C3 54
Camas, Jefferson, Idaho ... E6 89
Camas, Clark, Wash ... D3 122
Camas, co., Idaho ... F4 89
Camas Valley, Douglas, Oreg ... D3 113
Camataquí, Bol ... D2 55
Camau, pt., Viet ... H6 38
Cambalache Central, P.R ... B4 65
Cambay, India ... F4 40
Cambodia, see Kampuchea, country, Asia
Camborne [-Redruth], Eng ... D2 12
Cambra, Luzerne, Pa ... D9 114
Cambrai, Fr ... B5 14
Cambria, San Luis Obispo, Calif ... E3 82
Cambria, Wayne, Iowa ... D4 92
Cambria, Hillsdale, Mich ... G6 98
Cambria, Columbia, Wis ... E4 124
Cambria, co., Pa ... E4 114
Cambrian, mts., Wales ... B4 12
Cambrian Park, Santa Clara, Calif ... *D3 82
Cambridge, Ont., Can ... D4 41
Cambridge, Eng ... B8 12
Cambridge, Washington, Idaho ... E2 89
Cambridge, Henry, Ill ... B3 90
Cambridge, Story, Iowa ... C4, e9 92
Cambridge, Cowley, Kans ... E7 93
Cambridge, Somerset, Maine ... C3 96
Cambridge, Dorchester, Md ... C5 85
Cambridge, Middlesex, Mass ... B5, g11 97
Cambridge, Isanti, Minn ... E5 99
Cambridge, Furnas, Nebr ... D5 103
Cambridge, Burlington, N.J. ... *D3 106
Cambridge, Washington, N.Y ... B7 108
Cambridge, Guernsey, Ohio ... B4 111
Cambridge, Lamoille, Vt ... B3 120
Cambridge, Dane, Wis ... F4 124
Cambridge, res., Mass ... g10 97
Cambridge [& Isle of Ely], co., Eng ... B8 12
Cambridge Bay, N.W. Ter., Can ... C12 66
Cambridge City, Wayne, Ind ... E7 91
Cambridge Junction, Lamoille, Vt ... B3 120
Cambridgeport, Windham, Vt ... E3 120
Cambridge Springs, Crawford, Pa ... C1 114
Cambuí, Braz ... m8 56
Camby, Marion, Ind ... E5, m9 91
Camden, Wilcox, Ala ... D2 78
Camden, Ouachita, Ark ... D3 81
Camden, Kent, Del ... B6 85
Camden, Schuyler, Ill ... C3 90
Camden, Carroll, Ind ... C4 91
Camden, Knox, Maine ... D3 96
Camden, Hillsdale, Mich ... G6 98
Camden, Madison, Miss ... C4 100
Camden, Ray, Mo ... B3 101
Camden, Camden, N.J ... D2 106
Camden, Oneida, N.Y ... B5 108
Camden, Camden, N.C ... A6 109
Camden, Preble, Ohio ... C1 111
Camden, Kershaw, S.C ... C6 115
Camden, Benton, Tenn ... A3 117
Camden, Polk, Tex ... D5 118
Camden, Lewis, W. Va ... B4 123
Camden, co., Ga ... F5 87
Camden, co., Mo ... C5 101
Camden, co., N.J ... D3 106
Camden, co., N.C ... A6 109
Camden on Gauley, Webster, W. Va ... C4 123
Camdenton, Camden, Mo ... D5 101
Camelback, mtn., Ariz ... k9 80
Camelback, mtn., Pa ... A2 106
Camels Hump, mtn., Vt ... C3 120
Camerino, It ... C4 21
Cameron, Coconino, Ariz ... B4 80
Cameron, Warren, Ill ... C3 90
Cameron, Cameron, La ... E2 95
Cameron, Clinton and De Kalb, Mo ... B3 101
Cameron, Madison, Mont ... E5 102
Cameron, Quay, N. Mex ... C6 107
Cameron, Moore, N.C ... B3 109
Cameron, LeFlore, Okla ... B7 112
Cameron, Cameron, Pa ... D5 114
Cameron, Calhoun, S.C ... D6 115
Cameron, Milam, Tex ... D4 118
Cameron, Marshall, W. Va ... B4, g8 123
Cameron, Barron, Wis ... C2 124
Cameron, co., Pa ... D5 114
Cameron, co., Tex ... F4 118
Cameron, par., La ... E2 95
Cameron, hills, Alta., N.W. Ter., Can ... E9 66
Cameron, isl., N.W. Ter., Can ... m31 67
Cameroon, country, Afr ... F7 42, D2 46
Cameroon, mtn., Cam ... F6 45
Cametá, Braz ... C5 59
Cameta, Sharkey, Miss ... B3 100
Camiling, Phil ... o13 35
Camilla, Mitchell, Ga ... E2 87
Camillus, Onondaga, N.Y ... *B4 108
Caminha, Port ... B1 20
Camino, El Dorado, Calif ... C3 82
Camlachie, Ont., Can ... D2 72
Cammack (Cammack Village), Pulaski, Ark ... C3, h10 81
Cammal, Lycoming, Pa ... D7 114
Cammin, see Kamien Pomorski, Pol.
Camocim, Braz ... B2 57
Camooweal, Austl ... C6 50
Camp, co., Tex ... C5 118
Campagna di Roma, reg., It ... h9 21
Campaign, Warren, Tenn ... D8 117
Camp Allison, Sutton, Tex ... D2 118
Campana, Arg ... g7 54
Campana, isl., Chile ... D1 54
Campanario, Sp ... C3 20
Campania, pol. dist., It ... *D5 21
Campania, reg., It ... D5 21
Campania, isl., B.C., Can ... C3 68
Campanquiz, mts., Peru ... B2 58
Campbell, Clarke, Ala ... D2 78
Campbell, Searcy, Ark ... B3 81
Campbell, Santa Clara, Calif ... k8 82
Campbell, Osceola, Fla ... D5 86
Campbell, Wilkin, Minn ... D2 99
Campbell, Dunklin, Mo ... E7 101
Campbell, Franklin, Nebr ... D7 103
Campbell, Steuben, N.Y ... C3 108
Campbell, Mahoning, Ohio ... A5 111
Campbell, co., Ky ... B5 94
Campbell, co., S. Dak ... B5 116
Campbell, co., Tenn ... C9 117
Campbell, co., Va ... C3 121
Campbell, co., Wyo ... B7 125
Campbell, cape, N.Z ... N15 51
Campbell, creek, W. Va ... m12 123
Campbell, hill, Ohio ... B2 111
Campbell, isl., B.C., Can ... C3 68
Campbell, isl., Oceania ... J8 2
Campbell, lake, Oreg ... E7 113
Campbellford, Ont., Can ... C7 72
Campbell Hill, Jackson, Ill ... F4 90
Campbell Island, B.C., Can ... C3 68
Campbellpore, Pak ... B5 39
Campbell River, B.C., Can ... D5 68
Campbells Bay, Que., Can ... B8 72
Campbellsburg, Washington, Ind ... G5 91
Campbellsburg, Henry, Ky ... C4 94
Campbellsport, Fond du Lac, Wis ... E5 124
Campbell Station, Jackson, Ark ... *B4 81
Campbellsville, Taylor, Ky ... C4 94
Campbellsville, Giles, Tenn ... B4 117
Campbellton, N.B., Can ... A3 74
Campbellton, Newf., Can ... D4 75
Campbellton, P.E.I., Can ... C5 75
Campbellton, Jackson, Fla ... B1, u16 86
Campbelltown, Lebanon, Pa ... *F9 114
Campbeltown, Scot ... E3 13
Campcreek, Greene, Tenn ... C11 117
Camp Crook, Harding S. Dak ... B2 116
Camp Douglas, Juneau, Wis ... E3 124
Campeche, Mex ... D6 63
Campeche, state, Mex ... D6 63
Campeche, bay, Mex ... C6 63
Campechuela, Cuba ... D5 64
Camperdown, Austl ... I4 51
Camperville, Man., Can ... C1 71
Camp Grove, Marshall, Ill ... B4 90
Camp Hill, Tallapoosa, Ala ... C4 78
Camp Hill, Cumberland, Pa ... F8 114
Campiglia, Marittima, It ... C3 21
Campina Grande, Braz ... C3, h6 57
Campinas, Braz ... C3, m8 56
Campion, Larimer, Colo ... A5 83
Campione d'Italia, It ... D4 18
Camp Namanu, Clackamas, Oreg ... B4 113
Campo, San Diego, Calif ... F5 82
Campo, Cam ... E1 46
Campo, Baca, Colo ... D8 83
Campoalegre, Col ... C2 60
Campobasso, It ... D5 21
Campobello, Spartanburg, S.C ... A3 115
Campobello, isl., N.B., Can ... E3 74
Campo Belo, Braz ... F1 57
Campo de Criptana, Sp ... C4 20
Campo Gallo, Arg ... E3 55
Campo Grande, Braz ... C2 56
Campo Maior, Braz ... B2 57
Campo Maior, Port ... C2 20
Campo Real, Sp ... p18 20
Campos, Braz ... C4 56
Camposampiero, It ... D7 18
Campos Novos, Braz ... D2 56
Campos Sales, Braz ... C2 57
Campo Tencia, mtn., Switz ... D6 19
Campo Tures, It ... C7 18
Camp Point, Adams, Ill ... C2 90
Camp San Saba, McCulloch, Tex ... D3 118
Camp Sealth, King, Wash ... D1 122
Camp Sherman, Jefferson, Oreg ... C5 113
Camp Springs, Prince Georges, Md ... f9 85
Campti, Natchitoches, La ... C2 95
Campton, Okaloosa, Fla ... u15 86
Campton, Walton, Ga ... C3 87
Campton, Wolfe, Ky ... C6 94
Campton, Grafton, N.H ... C3 105
Camptown, Bradford, Pa ... C9 114
Campus, Livingston, Ill ... B5 90
Camp Verde, Yavapai, Ariz ... C4 80
Campville, Alachua, Fla ... C4 86
Camp Wood, Real, Tex ... E2 118
Camrose, Alta., Can ... C4 69
Camuy, mun., P.R ... *B2 65
Canaan, Searcy, Ark ... B3 81
Canaan, Litchfield, Conn ... A3 84
Canaan, Jefferson, Ind ... G7 91
Canaan, Benton, Miss ... A4 100
Canaan, Grafton, N.H ... C2 105
Canaan, Columbia, N.Y ... C7 108
Canaan, Essex, Vt ... B5 120
Canaan, riv., N.B., Can ... C4 74
Canaan Center, Grafton, N.H ... C2 105
Canaan Station, N.B., Can ... C4 74
Canaan Street, Grafton, N.H ... C2 105
Canada, Pike, Ky ... C7 94
Canada, country, N.A ... D10 61, 66
Canada, bay, Newf., Can ... C3 75
Cañada de Gómez, Arg ... A4 54
Canada Falls Deadwater, lake, Maine ... C2 96
Canadensis, Monroe, Pa ... D11 114
Canadian, Pittsburg, Okla ... B6 112
Canadian, Hemphill, Tex ... B2 118
Canadian, co., Okla ... B4 112
Canadian, riv., U.S ... C7 76
Cañadon León, Arg ... D2 54
Canadys, Colleton, S.C ... E6 115
Canajoharie, Montgomery, N.Y ... C6 108
Çanakkale, Tur ... B6 23
Canal [Township], Venango, Pa ... D2 114
Canal, riv., Ven ... C4 60
Canale, It ... E3 18
Canal Fulton, Stark, Ohio ... B4 111
Canalou, New Madrid, Mo ... E8 101
Canal Point, Palm Beach, Fla ... F6 86
Canal Winchester, Franklin, Ohio ... C3, m11 111
Canandaigua, Ontario, N.Y ... C3 108
Canandaigua, lake, N.Y ... C3 108
Cananea, Mex ... A2 63
Cananéia, Braz ... D3 56
Cañar, Ec ... B2 58
Cañar, prov., Ec ... B2 58
Canary Islands, reg., Sp. (Atl. O.) ... D1 44
Cañas, C.R ... E5 62
Canaseraga, Allegany, N.Y ... C3 108
Canastota, Madison, N.Y ... B5 108
Canaveral, cape, Fla ... D6 86
Canavieiras, Braz ... E3 57
Cañazas, Pan ... F7 62
Canazei, It ... C7 18
Canbelego, Austl ... E6 51
Canberra, Austl ... G8 45, G7 51
Canby, Modoc, Calif ... B3 82
Canby, Yellow Medicine, Minn ... F2 99
Canby, Clackamas, Oreg ... B4, h12 113
Cancale, Fr ... C3 14
Canche, riv., Fr ... D1 15
Candelaria, Cuba ... C2 64
Candelaria, Phil ... o12 35
Candelaria, Presidio, Tex ... F2 118
Candeleda, Sp ... B3 20
Candia, see Iraklion, Grc.
Candia, Rockingham, N.H ... D4 105
Candiac, Que., Can ... q19 73
Candia Village, Rockingham, N.H ... D4 105
Candle, Alsk ... B7 79
Candle, lake, Sask., Can ... D3 70
Candler, Marion, Fla ... C5 86
Candler, co., Ga ... D4 87
Candlestick, Hinds, Miss ... C3 100
Candlewood, lake, Conn ... D3 84
Candlewood Lake, res., N.Y ... D7 108
Candlewood Shores, Fairfield, Conn ... *D3 84
Cando, Sask., Can ... E1 70
Cando, Towner, N. Dak ... A6 110
Candor, Tioga, N.Y ... C4 108
Candor, Montgomery, N.C ... B3 109
Cane, riv., La ... C2 95
Canea, see Khaniá, Grc.
Cane Beds, Mohave, Ariz ... A3 80
Caneel, bay, Vir. Is. (U.S.) ... f15 65
Canela, Braz ... D2 56
Canelones, Ur ... E1 56
Canelones, dept., Ur ... *E1 56
Cañete, Chile ... B2 54
Cañete, Peru ... D2 58
Cane Valley, Adair, Ky ... C4 94
Caney, Montgomery, Kans ... E8 93
Caney, Morgan, Ky ... C6 94
Caney, Atoka, Okla ... C5 112
Caney, creek, Tex ... r14 118
Caney, fork, Tenn ... C8 117
Caney, riv., Okla ... A5 112
Caneyville, Grayson, Ky ... C3 94
Canfield, Lafayette, Ark ... D2 81
Canfield, Mahoning, Ohio ... A5 111
Cangallo, Peru ... D3 58
Cangamba, Ang ... D3 48
Cangombe, Ang ... D3 48
Cangas, Sp ... A1 20
Cangas de Narcea, Sp ... A2 20
Cangas de Onís, Sp ... A3 20
Canguaretama, Braz ... C3, h6 57
Canguçu, Braz ... E2 56
Canhotinho, Braz ... k5 57
Canicanian, Phil ... o13 35
Canicatti, It ... F4 21
Caniles, Sp ... D4 20
Canim, lake, B.C., Can ... D7 68
Canim Lake, B.C., Can ... D7 68
Canindé, Braz ... B3 57
Canistear, res., N.J ... A4 106
Canisteo, Steuben, N.Y ... C3 108
Canisteo, riv., N.Y ... C3 108
Canistota, McCook, S. Dak ... D8 116
Canje, riv., Guy ... A3 59
Canjilon, Rio Arriba, N. Mex ... A3 107
Çankiri (Changra), Tur ... B9 31
Canmer, Hart, Ky ... C4 94
Canmore, Alta., Can ... D3 69
Canna, isl., Scot ... C2 13
Canna, sound, Scot ... C2 13
Cannelburg, Daviess, Ind ... G4 91
Cannel City, Morgan, Ky ... C6 94
Cannelton, Perry, Ind ... I4 91
Cannelton, Fayette, W. Va ... m13 123
Cannes, Fr ... F7 14
Cannes, bayou, La ... D3 95
Canneto sull'Oglio, It ... D6 18
Cannich, Scot ... C4 13
Canning, N.S., Can ... D5 74
Cannington, Ont., Can ... C5 72
Cannock, Eng ... B5 12
Cannon, Sussex, Del ... C6 85
Cannon, co., Tenn ... B5 117
Cannon, bay, Fla ... G5 86
Cannon, riv., Minn ... F6 99
Cannon Ball, Sioux, N. Dak ... C5 110
Cannonball, riv., N. Dak ... C3 110
Cannon Beach, Clatsop, Oreg ... B3 113
Cannondale, Fairfield, Conn ... E3 84
Cannon Falls, Goodhue, Minn ... F6 99
Cannonsburg, Boyd, Ky ... B7 94
Cannonsburg, Jefferson, Miss ... D2 100
Cannonsville, res., N.Y ... C5 108
Cannonville, Garfield, Utah ... F3 119
Cannouan, isl., St. Vincent ... V26 65
Canobie Lake, Rockingham, N.H ... E4 105
Canoe, Escambia, Ala ... D2 78
Canoe, B.C., Can ... D8 68
Canoe, riv., B.C., Can ... C8 68
Canoe Lake, Ont., Can ... B6 72
Canoe Lake, Sask., Can ... *m7 70
Canoinhas, Braz ... D2 56
Canon, Franklin and Hart, Ga ... B3 87
Canon, Taos, N. Mex ... A4 107
Canonchet, Washington, R.I ... D10 84
Canon City, Fremont, Colo ... C5 83
Canones, Rio Arriba, N. Mex ... A3 107
Canon Plaza, Rio Arriba, N. Mex ... A3 107
Canonsburg, Washington, Pa ... F1 114
Canoochee, riv., Ga ... D5 87
Canora, Sask., Can ... F4 70
Canosa, It ... D6 21
Canova, Miner, S. Dak ... D8 116
Canso, N.S., Can ... D8 74
Cantabrian, mts., Sp ... A3 20
Cantal, dept., Fr ... *E5 14
Cantanhede, Port ... B1 20
Cantaura, Ven ... B5 60
Canterbury, Austl ... B3 51
Canterbury, N.B., Can ... D2 74
Canterbury, Windham, Conn ... C9 84
Canterbury, Eng ... C9 12
Canterbury, Merrimack, N.H ... D3 105
Canterbury, bight, N.Z ... P13 51
Can Tho, Viet ... G6 38
Cantilan, Phil ... *D7 35
Cantley, Que., Can ... D2 73
Canton, China ... G7 34
Canton, Hartford, Conn ... B5 84
Canton, Cherokee, Ga ... B2 87
Canton, Fulton, Ill ... C3 90
Canton, McPherson, Kans ... D6 93
Canton, Trigg, Ky ... D2 94
Canton, Oxford, Maine ... D2 96
Canton, Norfolk, Mass ... B5, h11 97
Canton, Fillmore, Minn ... G7 99
Canton, Madison, Miss ... C3 100
Canton, Lewis, Mo ... A6 101
Canton, Salem, N.J ... E2 106
Canton, St. Lawrence, N.Y ... f9 108
Canton, Haywood, N.C ... f10 109
Canton, Stark, Ohio ... B4 111
Canton, Blaine, Okla ... A3 112
Canton, Bradford, Pa ... C8 114
Canton, Lincoln, S. Dak ... D9 116
Canton, Van Zandt, Tex ... C5 118
Canton, Barron, Wis ... C2 124
Canton, isl., Kir ... G11 7
Canton Center, Hartford, Conn ... B5 84
Canton Lake, res., Okla ... A3 112
Cantonment, Escambia, Fla ... u14 86
Canton Point, Oxford, Maine ... D2 96
Cantril, Van Buren, Iowa ... D5 92
Cantuar, Sask., Can ... G1 70
Cantwell, Choctaw, Ala ... D1 78
Cantwell, Alsk ... C10 79
Cañuelas, Arg ... B5, g7 54
Canutama, Braz ... D2 59
Canute, Washita, Okla ... B2 112
Canutillo, El Paso, Tex ... o11 118
Canwood, Sask., Can ... D2 70
Cany-Barville, Fr ... E8 12
Canyon, Randall, Tex ... B2 118
Canyon, Park, Wyo ... *B2 125
Canyon, co., Idaho ... F2 89
Canyoncito, Santa Fe, N. Mex ... h9 107
Canyon City, Grant, Ore ... C8 113
Canyon Creek, Alta., Can ... B3 69
Canyon Creek, Lewis and Clark, Mont ... D4 102
Canyon De Chelly, nat. mon., Ariz ... A6 80
Canyon Ferry Lake, res., Mont ... D5 102
Canyonlands, nat. park, Utah ... E6 119
Canyonville, Douglas, Ore ... E3 113
Cao Bang, Viet ... A7 38
Caonao, riv., Cuba ... D4 64
Caorle, It ... D8 18
Cap, mtn., N.W. Ter., Can ... D8 66
Capa, Jones, S. Dak ... C5 116
Capac, St. Clair, Mich ... F8 98
Cap-à-l'Aigle, Que., Can ... B7 73
Capalonga, Phil ... o14 35
Capanaparo, riv., Ven ... B4 60
Capanema, Braz ... B1 57
Capão Bonito, Braz ... C3, m7 56
Caparica, Port ... f9 20
Capasin, Sask., Can ... D2 70
Capatárida, Ven ... A3 60
Cap Bon, prov., Tun ... *B7 44
Capbreton, Fr ... F3 14
Cap Chat, Que., Can ... G19 67
Cap-de-la-Madeleine, Que., Can ... C5 73
Capdenac-Gare, Fr ... E5 14
Cape, see Cape of Good Hope, prov., S. Afr.
Cape, isl., S.C ... E9 115
Cape Breton, co., N.S., Can ... C9 74
Cape Breton, isl., N.S., Can ... C9 74
Cape Breton Highlands, nat. park, N.S., Can ... C9 74
Cape Broyle, Newf., Can ... E5 75
Cape Canaveral, Fla ... D6 86
Cape Charles, Newf., Can ... B4 75
Cape Charles, Northampton, Va ... C6 121
Cape Coast, Ghana ... E4 45
Cape Cod, bay, Mass ... C7 97
Cape Cod, canal, Mass ... C6 97
Cape Cod, reg., Mass ... C7 97
Cape Coral, Lee, Fla ... F5 86
Cape Dorset, N.W. Ter., Can ... D17 67
Cape Elizabeth (The Cape), Cumberland, Maine ... E2, g7 96
Cape Fair, Stone, Mo ... E4 101
Cape Fear, riv., N.C ... C4 109
Cape Girardeau, Cape Girardeau, Mo ... D8 101
Cape Girardeau, co., Mo ... D8 101
Cape Hatteras, nat. seashore recreational area, N.C ... B7 109
Cape Horn, Skamania, Wash ... D3 122
Cape la Hune, Newf., Can ... E3 75
Capelinha, Braz ... E3 57
Capels, McDowell, W. Va ... D3 123
Cape May, Cape May, N.J ... F3 106
Cape May, co., N.J ... E3 106
Cape May Court House, Cape May, N.J ... E3 106
Cape May Point, Cape May, N.J ... F3 106
Cape Neddick, York, Maine ... E2 96
Cape of Good Hope, prov., S. Afr ... D3 49
Cape Pole, Alsk ... m23 79
Cape Porpoise, York, Maine ... E2 96
Cape Ray, Newf., Can ... E2 75
Capers, Pueblo, Colo ... D6 83
Capers, inlet, S.C ... k12 115
Capers, is., S.C ... F8 115
Capers, is., S.C ... G6 115
Cape Sable, isl., N.S., Can ... F4 74
Capesterre, Guad ... Q8 65
Capeto, Chile ... D2 55
Cape Tormentine, N.B., Can ... C6 74
Cape Town (Kaapstad), S. Afr ... D2 49
Cape Verde, country, Afr ... E3 42
Cape Verde, is., Atl. O ... E3 42
Capeville, Northampton, Va ... h16 121
Cape Vincent, Jefferson, N.Y ... A4 108
Cape York, pen., Austl ... B7 50
Cap-Haïtien, Hai ... E7 64
Capilla del Monte, Arg ... A4 54
Capilla del Señor, Arg ... g7 54
Capinota, Bol ... C2 55
Capistrano Beach, Orange, Calif ... *F5 82
Capital Federal, fed. dist., Arg ... *A5 54
Capitan, Lincoln, N. Mex ... D4 107
Capitan, mts., N. Mex ... D4 107
Capitan, peak, N. Mex ... D4 107
Capitán Bado, Par ... D4 55
Capitol, Carter, Mont ... E12 104
Capitol, peak, Nev ... B4 102
Capitola, Leon, Fla ... B2 86
Capitol Heights, Polk, Iowa ... e8 92
Capitol Heights, Prince Georges, Md ... C4, f9 85
Capitol Reef, nat. mon., Utah ... E4 119
Capivarí, Braz ... m8 56
Capiz, see Roxas, Phil.
Capiz, prov., Phil ... *C6 35
Capleville, Shelby, Tenn ... e9 117
Capon Bridge, Hampshire, W. Va ... B6 123
Capon Springs, Hampshire, W. Va ... B6 123
Cap-Pelé, N.B., Can ... C5 74
Cappoquin, Ire ... E4 11
Capps, Henry, Ala ... D4 78
Cappstown, Miller, Ark ... D2 81
Capraia, isl., It ... C2 21
Caprara, pt., It ... D2 21
Capreol, Ont., Can ... p19 72
Caprera, isl., It ... D2 21
Capri, isl., It ... D5 21
Capricorn, is., Austl ... J9 51
Caprock, Lea, N. Mex ... D6 107
Capron, Boone, Ill ... A5 90
Capron, Woods, Okla ... A3 112
Capron, Southampton, Va ... D5 121
Cap-Rouge, Que., Can ... n17 73
Cap-St. Ignace, Que., Can ... B7 73
Cap-Santé, Que., Can ... C6 73
Capshaw, Limestone, Ala ... A3 78
Captain Cook, Hawaii, Haw ... D6 88
Captiva, Lee, Fla ... F4 86
Captiva, isl., Fla ... F4 86
Capua, It ... D5 21
Capulin, Conejos, Colo ... D4 83
Capulin, Union, N. Mex ... A6 107
Capulin Mountain, nat. mon., N. Mex ... A6 107
Caputa, Pennington, S. Dak ... D2 116
Caquetá, intendencia, Col ... C3 60
Caquetá, riv., Col ... D3 60
Carabaña, Sp ... p18 20
Carabobo, state, Ven ... A4 60
Caracal, Rom ... C7 22
Caracas, Ven ... A4 60
Carajás, mts., Braz ... D4 59
Carangola, Braz ... F2 57
Caransebes, Rom ... C6 22
Carapari, Bol ... D3 55
Carapeguá, Par ... E4 55
Caraquet, N.B., Can ... B5 74
Caratasca, lagoon, Hond ... C6 62
Caratinga, Braz ... E2 57
Caratunk, Somerset, Maine ... C3 96
Caraúbas, Braz ... C3 57
Caraúbas, Braz ... h5 57
Caravaca, Sp ... C5 20
Caravelas, Braz ... E3 57
Caraveli, Peru ... E3 58
Caraway, Craighead, Ark ... B5 81
Caraz, Peru ... C2 58
Caràzinho, Braz ... D2 56
Carballino, Sp ... A1 20
Carballo, Sp ... A1 20
Carberry, Man., Can ... E2 71
Carbó, Mex ... B2 63
Carbon, Alta., Can ... D4 69
Carbon, Clay, Ind ... E3 91
Carbon, Adams, Iowa ... C3 92
Carbon, Kanawha, W. Va ... m13 123
Carbon, co., Mont ... E7 102
Carbon, co., Pa ... E10 114
Carbon, co., Utah ... D5 119
Carbon, co., Wyo ... E5 125
Carbonado, Pierce, Wash ... B3 122
Carbonara, cape, It ... E2 21
Carbon Cliff, Rock Island, Ill ... *B3 90
Carbondale, Alta., Can ... C4 69
Carbondale, Garfield, Colo ... B3 83
Carbondale, Jackson, Ill ... F4 90
Carbondale, Osage, Kans ... D8 93
Carbondale, Athens, Ohio ... C3 111
Carbondale, Lackawanna, Pa ... C10 114
Carbonear, Newf., Can ... E5 75
Carbon Hill, Walker, Ala ... B2 78
Carbon Hill, Grundy, Ill ... B5 90
Carbonia, It ... E2 21
Carbonville, Carbon, Utah ... D5 119
Carbury, Bottineau, N. Dak ... A5 110
Carcagente, Sp ... C5 20
Carcans, lagoon, Fr ... E3 14
Carcar, Phil ... *C6 35
Carcassonne, Fr ... F5 14
Carchi, prov., Ec ... A2 58
Carcross, Yukon, Can ... D6 66
Cardak, Tur ... D7 23
Cardale, Man., Can ... D1 71
Cardale, Fayette, Pa ... *G2 114
Cárdenas, Cuba ... C3 64
Cárdenas, Mex ... k14 63
Cárdenas, Mex ... D6 63
Carderview, Johnson, Tenn ... C12 117

Cardiel, lake, Arg D2 54
Cardiff, Jefferson, Ala f7 78
Cardiff, Harford, Md A5 85
Cardiff, Atlantic, N.J E3 106
Cardiff, Wales C4 12
Cardigan, P.E.I., Can C7 74
Cardigan, Wales B3 12
Cardigan, co., Wales B3 12
Cardigan, bay, P.E.I., Can C7 74
Cardigan, bay, Wales B3 12
Cardinal, Man., Can E2 71
Cardinal, Ont., Can C9 72
Cardinal, lake, Alta., Can A2 69
Cardington, Morrow, Ohio B3 111
Cardona, Ur E1 56
Cardross, Sask., Can H3 70
Cardston, Alta., Can E4 69
Cardville, Penobscot, Maine C4 96
Cardwell, Dunklin, Mo E7 101
Cardwell, Jefferson, Mont E5 102
Cardwell, mtn., Tenn D8 117
Carega, mtn., It D7 18
Carei, Rom B6 22
Carencro, Lafayette, La D3 95
Carenero, Ven A4 60
Carentan, Fr C3 14
Caretta, McDowell, W. Va D3 123
Carey, Blaine, Idaho F5 89
Carey, Wyandot, Ohio B2 111
Carey, Childress, Tex B2 118
Careysburg, Lib E2 45
Careywood, Bonner, Idaho A2 89
Carhaix, Fr C2 14
Carhuaz, Peru C2 58
Cariamanga, Ec B2 58
Cariati, It E6 21
Caribana, pt., Col B2 60
Caribbean, sea, N.A H13 61
Cariboo, mts., B.C., Can C7 68
Caribou, Man., Can f8 71
Caribou, Aroostook, Maine B5 96
Caribou, co., Idaho G7 89
Caribou, isl., N.S., Can D7 74
Caribou, lake, Maine C3 96
Caribou, mts., Alta., Can f7 69
Caribou, mtn., Idaho F7 89
Caribou, mtn., Maine C2 96
Caribou, range, Idaho F7 89
Carichic, Mex B3 63
Carievale, Sask., Can H5 70
Carignan, Fr E5 15
Carinhanha, Braz D2 57
Carini, It E4 21
Carinish, Scot C1 13
Carinthia, reg., Aus E6 16
Caripe, Ven A5 60
Caripito, Ven A5 60
Cariris Velhos, mts., Braz h5 57
Cariús, Braz C3 57
Carl Blackwell, lake, Okla A4 112
Carle Place, Nassau, N.Y *G2 84
Carleton, Monroe, Mich F7 98
Carleton, Thayer, Nebr D8 103
Carleton, co., N.B., Can C2 74
Carleton, mtn., N.B., Can B3 74
Carleton Place, Ont., Can B8 72
Carletonville, S. Afr C4 49
Carlile, Crook, Wyo B8 125
Carlin, Elko, Nev C5 104
Carlin Bay, Kootenai, Idaho B2 89
Carlingford, Ire C5 11
Carlingford, bay, Ire., N. Ire C5 11
Carlinville, Macoupin, Ill D4 90
Carlisle, Lonoke, Ark C4 81
Carlisle, Eng C5 10
Carlisle, Sullivan, Ind G3 91
Carlisle, Warren, Iowa C4, f8 92
Carlisle, Nicholas, Ky B5 94
Carlisle, Middlesex, Mass f10 97
Carlisle, Warren, Ohio C1 111
Carlisle, Cumberland, Pa F7 114
Carlisle, Union, S.C B5 115
Carlisle, Stewart, Tenn A4 117
Carlisle, co., Ky f8 94
Carl Junction, Jasper, Mo D3 101
Carlock, McLean, Ill C4 90
Carloforte, It E2 21
Carlos, Allegany, Md k13 85
Carlos, Douglas, Minn E3 99
Carlos Casares, Arg B4 54
Carlos Chagas, Braz E2 57
Carlos Tejedor, Arg B4 54
Carlow, Ire E5 11
Carlow, co., Ire E4 11
Carloway, Scot B2 13
Carlowville, Dallas, Ala C2 78
Carlsbad, San Diego, Calif F5 82
Carlsbad, Eddy, N. Mex E5 107
Carlsbad, Tom Green, Tex D2 118
Carlsbad Caverns, nat. park, N. Mex E5 107
Carlsbad Springs, Ont., Can h13 72
Carlsborg, Clallam, Wash A2 122
Carlstadt, Bergen, N.J h8 106
Carlton, Clarke, Ala D2 78
Carlton, Sask., Can E2 70
Carlton, Eng B6 12
Carlton, Madison, Ga B3 87
Carlton, Dickinson, Kans D6 93
Carlton, Carlton, Minn D6 99
Carlton, Yamhill, Oreg B3, h11 113
Carlton, Hamilton, Tex D3 118
Carlton, co., Minn D6 99
Carluke, Scot E5 13
Carlyle, Sask., Can H4 70
Carlyle, Clinton, Ill E4 90
Carlyle, Wibaux, Mont D12 102
Carlyle, res., Ill C8 101
Carmacks, Yukon, Can D5 66
Carmagnola, It B1 21
Carman, Man., Can E2 71
Carman, hill, Pa C6 114
Carmangay, Alta., Can D4 69
Carmans, riv., N.Y F5 84
Carmanville, Newf., Can D4 75
Carmarthen, Wales C3 12
Carmarthen, co., Wales C3 12
Carmarthen, bay, Wales C3 12
Carmaux, Fr E5 14
Carmel, Monterey, Calif C6, D3 82
Carmel, Sask., Can E3 70
Carmel, Hamilton, Ind E5 91
Carmel, Penobscot, Maine D3 96
Carmel, Cumberland, N.J E2 106
Carmel, Putnam, N.Y D7 108
Carmel, head, Wales A3 12
Carmel, see Hakarmel, mtn., Isr.
Carmelo, Ur E1 56
Carmel Valley, Monterey, Calif *D3 82
Carmel Woods, Monterey, Calif *D3 82
Carmen, Santa Cruz, Ariz F4 80
Carmen, Lemhi, Idaho D5 89
Carmen, Alfalfa, Okla A3 112
Carmen, isl., Mex B2 63
Carmen, riv., Mex G3 107
Carmen Alto, Chile D2 55
Carmen de Areco, Arg A5, g7 54
Carmen del Paraná, Par E4 55
Carmen de Patagones, Arg C4 54
Carmi, White, Ill E5 90
Carmi, lake, Vt B3 120
Carmichael, Ba m17 64
Carmichael, Sask., Can G1 70
Carmichaels, Greene, Pa G2 114
Carmine, Fayette, Tex E4 118
Carmona, Sp D3 20
Carnarvon, Austl D1 50
Carnarvon, Sac, Iowa B2 92
Carnarvon, S. Afr D3 49
Carnation, King, Wash B4 122
Carnaxide, Port f9 20
Càrn Bàn, mtn., Scot C4 13
Carncastle, N. Ire C6 11
Carndonagh, Ire B4 11
Carnduff, Sask., Can H5 70
Carnegie, Randolph, Ga E2 86
Carnegie, Caddo, Okla B3 112
Carnegie, Allegheny, Pa F1, k13 114
Càrn Eige, mtn., Scot C3 13
Carnes, Forrest, Miss E4 100
Carnesville, Franklin, Ga B3 87
Carnew, Ire E5 11
Carney, Menominee, Mich C3 98
Carney, Lincoln, Okla B4 112
Carneys Point, Salem, N.J D2 106
Carnforth, Eng F6 13
Carnic Alps, mts., Aus E6 16
Car Nicobar, isl., India G9 39
Carnlough, N. Ire C6 11
Carnot, Cen. Afr. Rep D3 46
Carnoustie, Scot D6 13
Carnsore, pt., Ire E5 11
Carnuel, Bernalillo, N. Mex B3, k8 107
Caro, Tuscola, Mich E7 98
Carol City, Dade, Fla s13 86
Caroleen, Rutherford, N.C B1 109
Carolina, Braz C1 57
Carolina, mun., P.R *B4 65
Carolina, Washington, R.I D10 84
Carolina, S. Afr C5 49
Carolina, Marion, W. Va k10 123
Carolina Beach, New Hanover, N.C C5 109
Caroline, Alta., Can C3 69
Caroline, Shawano, Wis D5 124
Caroline, co., Md C6 85
Caroline, co., Va C5 121
Caroline, atoll, Kir G13 7
Caroline, is., Kir F8 7
Caron, Sask., Can G3 70
Carona, Cherokee, Kans E9 93
Caron Brook, N.B., Can A4 96
Caroni, riv., Trin N23 65
Caroní, riv., Ven B5 60
Carora, Ven A3 60
Carouge, Switz D1 19
Carp, Ont., Can B8, h11 72
Carp, Lincoln, Nev F7 104
Carp, lake, B.C., Can B6 68
Carpathians, mts., Czech., Pol., Rom D6 26, H5 27
Carpentaria, gulf, Austl B6 50
Carpenter, Madison, Ill f14 101
Carpenter, Mitchell, Iowa A4 92
Carpenter, Copiah, Miss C3 100
Carpenter, Roger Mills, Okla B2 112
Carpenter, Clark, S. Dak C8 116
Carpenter, Laramie, Wyo E8 125
Carpenter, dam, Ark g7 81
Carpentersville, Kane, Ill A5, h8 90
Carpentras, Fr E6 14
Carpi, It B3 21
Carpinteria, Santa Barbara, Calif E4 82
Carpio, Ward, N. Dak A4 110
Carp Lake, Emmet, Mich C6 98
Carr, Weld, Colo A6 83
Carr, lake, Ind G4 91
Carrabasset Valley, Franklin, Maine C2 96
Carrabelle, Franklin, Fla C2 86
Carradale, Scot E3 13
Carragana, Sask., Can E4 70
Carrantuohill, mtn., Ire E2 11
Carranza, cape, Chile B2 54
Carrara, It B3 21
Carrboro, Orange, N.C B3 109
Carr Bridge, Scot C5 13
Carriacou, isl., Grenada W26 65
Carrickfergus, N. Ire C6 11
Carrickmacross, Ire D5 11
Carrick-on-Shannon, Ire D4 11
Carrick-on-Suir, Ire E4 11
Carrie, mtn., Wash B2 122
Carrier, Que., Can o17 73
Carrier, Garfield, Okla A3 112
Carriere, Pearl River, Miss E4 100
Carriers Mills, Saline, Ill F5 90
Carrigahorig, Ire D3 11
Carrigain, mtn., N.H B4 105
Carrigaline, Ire F3 11
Carrigan, head, Ire C3 11
Carrington, Foster, N. Dak B6 110
Carrión, riv., Sp A3 20
Carrión de los Condes, Sp A3 20
Carrizal Bajo, Chile E1 55
Carrizo, Navajo, Ariz C5 80
Carrizo, creek, Ariz., N. Mex C6 80
Carrizo, creek, N. Mex., Tex A6 107
Carrizo, mts., N. Mex D4 107
Carrizo, mts., Ariz., N. Mex A1 107
Carrizo Springs, Dimmit, Tex E3 118
Carrizozo, Lincoln, N. Mex D4 107
Carroll, Man., Can E1 71
Carroll, Carroll, Iowa B3 92
Carroll, Penobscot, Maine C4 96
Carroll, Wayne, Nebr B8 103
Carroll, Fairfield, Ohio C3 111
Carroll, co., Ark A2 81
Carroll, co., Ga C1 87
Carroll, co., Ill A4 90
Carroll, co., Ind C4 91
Carroll, co., Iowa B3 92
Carroll, co., Ky B4 94
Carroll, co., Md A3 85
Carroll, co., Miss B4 100
Carroll, co., Mo B4 101
Carroll, co., N.H C4 105
Carroll, co., Ohio B4 111
Carroll, co., Tenn B3 117
Carroll, co., Va D2 121
Carroll, lake, Man., Ont., Can D4 71
Carrolls, Cowlitz, Wash C3 122
Carrollton, Pickens, Ala B1 78
Carrollton, Carroll, Ga C1 87
Carrollton, Greene, Ill D3 90
Carrollton, Carroll, Ky B4 94
Carrollton, Prince Georges, Md *C4 85
Carrollton, Saginaw, Mich E7 98
Carrollton, Carroll, Miss B4 100
Carrollton, Carroll, Mo B4 101
Carrollton, Carroll, Ohio B4 111
Carrollton, Dallas, Tex B5 118
Carrolltown, Cambria, Pa E4 114
Carron, riv., Scot C3 13
Carrot, riv., Man., Sask., Can D4 70
Carrot River, Sask., Can D4 70
Carrowkeel, Ire B4 11
Carrowmore, lake, Ire C2 11
Carrsville, Ky e9 94
Carruthers, Sask., Can E1 70
Carrville, Tallapoosa, Ala C4 78
Carry Falls, res., N.Y f10 108
Carrying Place, Ont., Can C7 72
Çarşamba, Tur B11 31
Carseland, Alta., Can D4 69
Carson, Washington, Ala D2 78
Carson, Los Angeles, Calif *E4 82
Carson, Pottawattamie, Iowa C2 92
Carson, Jefferson Davis, Miss D4 100
Carson, Taos, N. Mex A4 107
Carson, Grant, N. Dak C4 110
Carson, Dinwiddie, Va C5 121
Carson, Skamania, Wash D4 122
Carson, co., Tex B2 118
Carson, intermittent lake, Nev D3 104
Carson, riv., Nev D3 104
Carson City, Montcalm, Mich E5 98
Carson City, Ormsby, Nev D2 104
Carsonville, Sanilac, Mich E8 98
Carsonville, St. Louis, Mo *C7 101
Carstairs, Alta., Can D3 69
Carswell, McDowell, W. Va *D3 123
Cartagena, Chile A2 54
Cartagena, Col A2 60
Cartagena, Sp D5 20
Cartago, Col C2 60
Cartago, C.R F6 62
Cartago, prov., C.R *F6 62
Carta Valley, Edwards, Tex E2 118
Cartaxo, Port C1 20
Cartaya, Sp D2 20
Carter, Carter, Ky B6 94
Carter, Chouteau, Mont C6 102
Carter, Beckham, Okla B2 112
Carter, Tripp, S. Dak D5 116
Carter, Carter, Tenn C11 117
Carter, Forest, Wis C5 124
Carter, Uinta, Wyo E2 125
Carter, co., Ky B6 94
Carter, co., Mo E7 101
Carter, co., Mont E12 102
Carter, co., Okla C4 112
Carter, co., Tenn C11 117
Carter, caves and natural bridge, Ky B6 94
Carteret, Middlesex, N.J B4, k8 106
Carteret, co., N.C C6 109
Carter Lake, Pottawattamie, Iowa C2 92
Carters, Murray, Ga B2 87
Cartersburg, Hendricks, Ind E5 91
Cartersville, Bartow, Ga B2 87
Cartersville, Florence, S.C C7 115
Cartersville, Cumberland, Va D4 121
Carterville, Williamson, Ill F4 90
Carterville, Jasper, Mo D3 101
Carthage, Dallas, Ark C3 81
Carthage, Hancock, Ill C2 90
Carthage, Rush, Ind E6 91
Carthage, Leake, Miss C4 100
Carthage, Jasper, Mo D3 101
Carthage, Jefferson, N.Y B5 108
Carthage, Moore, N.C B3 109
Carthage, Miner, S. Dak C8 116
Carthage, Smith, Tenn C8 117
Carthage, Panola, Tex C5 118
Carthage, Tun *F12 30
Carthage, ruins, Tun F12 30
Cartwright, Man., Can E2 71
Cartwright, Newf., Can B3, h10 75
Cartwright, McKenzie, N. Dak B2 110
Cartwright, Bryan, Okla D5 112
Caruaru, Braz C3, k6 57
Carúpano, Ven A5 60
Caruthersville, Pemiscot, Mo E8 101
Carver, Plymouth, Mass C6 97
Carver, Carver, Minn n11 99
Carver, co., Minn F5 99
Carville, Iberville, La h9 95
Carvin, Fr D3 15
Cary, Bleckley, Ga D3 87
Cary, McHenry, Ill A5, h8 90
Cary, Sharkey, Miss C3 100
Cary, Wake, N.C B4 109
Cary, mts., Ant B1 5
Caryville, Washington, Fla u16 86
Caryville, Campbell, Tenn C9 117
Casa, Perry, Ark B2 81
Casa Blanca, Valencia, N. Mex B2 107
Casablanca, Mor C3 44, H3 30
Casa Branca, Braz C3, k8 56
Casa de Oro, San Diego, Calif *F5 82
Casa de Piedra, P.R B3 65
Casa Grande, Pinal, Ariz E4 80
Casa Grande, nat. mon., Ariz E4 80
Casale Monferrato, It B2 21
Casanare, intendencia, Col B3 60
Casanova, Fauquier, Va B5 121
Casape, It h9 21
Casa Piedra, Presidio, Tex p12 118
Casar, Cleveland, N.C B1 109
Casarano, It D7 21
Casas Adobes, Pima, Ariz E5 80
Casas Grandes, riv., Mex F1 107
Cascade, B.C., Can E8 68
Cascade, El Paso, Colo C6 83
Cascade, Valley, Idaho E2 89
Cascade, Dubuque and Jones, Iowa B6 92
Cascade, Wayne, Mo D7 101
Cascade, Cascade, Mont C5 102
Cascade, Coos, N.H B4 105
Cascade, Pittsylvania, Va D3 121
Cascade, Preston, W. Va B5 123
Cascade, Sheboygan, Wis E5 124
Cascade, co., Mont C5 102
Cascade, range, Can., U.S B3 76
Cascade, tunnel, Wash B5 122
Cascade Locks, Hood River, Oreg B5 113
Cascade Summit, Klamath, Oreg D4 113
Cascadia, Linn, Oreg C4 113
Cascais, Port C1, f9 20
Cascajal, riv., Pan h11 62
Cascavel, Braz B3 57
Cascilla, Tallahatchie, Miss B3 100
Casco, Cumberland, Maine D2 96
Casco, Kewaunee, Wis D6 124
Casco, bay, Maine E3 96
Caselton, Lincoln, Nev F7 104
Caserta, It D5 21
Caseville, Huron, Mich E7 98
Casey, Clark, Ill D6 90
Casey, Guthrie and Adair, Iowa C3 92
Casey, co., Ky C5 94
Casey, bay, Ant C17 5
Casey, key, Fla E4 86
Casey, mtn., Idaho A2 89
Caseyville, St. Clair, Ill *E9 90
Cash, Craighead, Ark B5 81
Cashel, Ire D2 11
Cashel, Ire E4 11
Cashiers, Jackson, N.C f9 109
Cashion, Maricopa, Ariz m8 80
Cashion, Kingfisher, Okla B4 112
Cashmere, Chelan, Wash B5 122
Cashton, Monroe, Wis E3 124
Cashtown, Adams, Pa G7 114
Casiguran, Phil n14 35
Casilda, Arg A4 54
Casilda, Cuba D3 64
Casino, Austl D9 51
Casiquiare, riv., Ven C4 60
Casky, Christian, Ky D2 94
Caslav, Czech D3 26
Casma, Peru C2 58
Casmalia, Santa Barbara, Calif E3 82
Caspar, Mendocino, Calif C2 82
Caspe, Sp B5 20
Casper, Natrona, Wyo D6 125
Caspian, Iron, Mich B2 98
Caspian, depression, Sov. Un F19 9
Caspian, lake, Vt B4 120
Caspian, sea, Iran, Sov. Un G19 9
Caspiana, Caddo, La B2 95
Cass, Sullivan, Ind F3 91
Cass, Pocahontas, W. Va C5 123
Cass, co., Ill D3 90
Cass, co., Ind C5 91
Cass, co., Iowa C3 92
Cass, co., Mich G4 98
Cass, co., Minn D4 99
Cass, co., Mo C3 101
Cass, co., Nebr D9 103
Cass, co., N. Dak C8 110
Cass, co., Tex C5 118
Cass, lake, Minn C4 99
Cass, riv., Mich E7 98
Cassá, Sp B7 20
Cassa, Platte, Wyo D8 125
Cassadaga, Chautauqua, N.Y C1 108
Cassandra, see Kassandra gulf, Grc.
Cass City, Tuscola, Mich E7 98
Cassel, Fr D2 15
Casselberry, Seminole, Fla D5 86
Casselman, Ont., Can B9 72
Casselman, Somerset, Pa G3 114
Casselman, riv., Md k12 85
Casselton, Cass, N. Dak C8 110
Cassia, co., Idaho G5 89
Cassiar, mts., B.C., Can E6 66
Cassidy, B.C., Can f12 68
Cassino, It D4 21
Cassiporé, riv., Braz B4 59
Cass Lake, Cass, Minn C4 99
Cassoday, Butler, Kans D7 93
Cassopolis, Cass, Mich G4 98
Casstown, Miami, Ohio B1 111
Cassville, Bartow, Ga B2 87
Cassville, Barry, Mo E4 101
Cassville, Grant, Wis F3 124
Castalia, Winneshiek, Iowa A6 92
Castalia, Nash, N.C A4 109
Castalia, Erie, Ohio A3 111
Castalian Springs, Sumner, Tenn A5 117
Castana, Monona, Iowa B2 92
Castanea, Clinton, Pa D7 114
Castanheira de Pêra, Port B1 20
Castaños, Mex B4 63
Castelfranco Emilia, It E7 18
Castelfranco Veneto, It D7 18
Castel Gandolfo, It h9 21
Castel Giuliano, It g8 21
Casteljaloux, Fr E3 14
Castella, Shasta, Calif B2 82
Castellamonte, It E3 18
Castelli, Arg B5 54
Castelli, Arg E3 55
Castellón (Castellón de la Plana), prov., Sp *C5 20
Castellón de la Plana, Sp C5 20
Castel Madama, It h9 21
Castelnaudary, Fr F4 14
Castelo, Braz F2 57
Castelo Branco, Port C2 20
Castelo de Vide, Port C2 20
Castel San Pietro dell'Emilia, It E7 18
Castelsarrasin, Fr E4 14
Castelvetrano, It F4 21
Casterton, Austl H3 51
Castile, Wyoming, N.Y C2 108
Castilla, Peru C1 58
Castillo de San Marcos, nat. mon., Fla C5 86
Castillos, Ur E2 56
Castine, Hancock, Maine D4 96
Castle, Okfuskee, Okla B5 112
Castle, butte, Idaho G3 89
Castle, hbr., Bermuda o20 64
Castle, mtn., Yukon, Can D5 66
Castle, mts., Mont D6 102
Castle, rock, Oreg C8 113
Castlebar, Ire D2 11
Castlebay, Scot D1 13
Castlebellingham, Ire D5 11
Castleberry, Conecuh, Ala D2 78
Castleblayney, Ire C5 11
Castlecomer, Ire D4 11
Castle Dale, Emery, Utah D5 119
Castlederg, N. Ire C4 11
Castledome, mts., Ariz D1 80
Castle Douglas, Scot F5 13
Castlefinn, Ire C4 11
Castleford, Twin Falls, Idaho G4 89
Castlegar, B.C., Can E9 68
Castle Gate, Carbon, Utah D5 119
Castlegregory, Ire E1 11
Castle Hayne, New Hanover, N.C C5 109
Castle Hill, Black Hawk, Iowa B5 92
Castle Hills, Bexar, Tex *E3 118
Castle Hot Springs, Yavapai, Ariz D3 80
Castleisland, Ire E2 11
Castlemaine, Austl H5 51
Castlemaine, Ire E2 11
Castlemartyr, Ire F3 11
Castlepollard, Ire D4 11
Castlerea, Ire D3 11
Castle Rock, Douglas, Colo B6 83
Castle Rock, Dakota, Minn F5 99
Castle Rock, Summit, Utah B4 119
Castle Rock, Cowlitz, Wash C3 122
Castle Rock, butte, S. Dak B2 116
Castle Rock, mtn., Va C4 121
Castle Rock Lake, res., Wis E4 124
Castleton, Ont., Can C7 72
Castleton, Stark, Ill B4 90
Castleton, Marion, Ind k10 91
Castleton, Jam E15 65
Castleton, Reno, Kans g11 93
Castleton, Rutland, Vt D2 120
Castleton-on-Hudson, Rensselaer, N.Y C7 108
Castletown, Ire D4 11
Castletown, I. of Man F4 13
Castletownroche, Ire E3 11
Castlewellan, N. Ire C6 11
Castlewood, Hamlin, S. Dak C8 116
Castlewood, Russell, Va f9 121
Castolon, Brewster, Tex E1 118
Castor, Alta., Can C5 69
Castor, Bienville, La B2 95
Castor, riv., Mo D7 101
Castorland, Lewis, N.Y B5 108
Castres, Fr F5 14
Castries, St. Lucia J14 64
Castro, Braz C3 56
Castro, Chile C2 54
Castro, Sp D3 20
Castro, co., Tex B1 118
Castro Alves, Braz D3 57
Castro Daire, Port B2 20
Castro Marim, Port D2 20
Castropol, Sp A2 20
Castrop-Rauxel, F.R.G *B2 17
Castro Urdiales, Sp A4 20
Castro Valley, Alameda, Calif h8 82
Castro Verde, Port D1 20
Castrovillari, It E6 21
Castroville, Monterey, Calif D3 82
Castroville, Medina, Tex E3 118
Castrovirreyna, Peru D2 58
Castuera, Sp C3 20
Caswell, co., N.C A3 109
Cat, isl., Ba B6 64
Cat, isl., Mass f12 97
Cat, isl., Miss g7 100
Cat, isl., S.C E9 115
Catacamas, Hond C5 62
Catacaos, Peru C1 58
Catacocha, Ec B2 58
Catacombs, tombs, It h9 21
Cataguases, Braz C4, g6 57
Catahoula, par., La C4 95
Catahoula, lake, La C3 95
Cataiñgan, Phil *C6 35
Catalão, Braz E1 57
Catalca, Tur B3 29
Catalina, Newf., Can D5 75
Catalina, pt., Guam 52
Catalonia, reg., Sp B6 20
Catamarca, Arg E2 55
Catamarca, prov., Arg E2 55
Catanauan, Phil p14 35
Catanduanes, prov., Phil *C6 35
Catanduanes, isl., Phil C6 35
Catanduva, Braz C3 56
Catania, It F5 21
Catania, gulf, It F5 21
Cataño, P.R B3 65
Cataño, mun., P.R *B3 65
Catanzaro, It E6 21
Cataouatche, lake, La k11 95
Cataract, Owen, Ind F4 91
Cataract, Monroe, Wis D3 124
Catarina, Dimmit, Tex E3 118
Catarman, Phil *C6 35
Catarroja, Sp C5 20
Catasauqua, Lehigh, Pa E11 114
Cataula, Harris, Ga D2 87
Cataumet, Barnstable, Mass C6 97
Catawba, Catawba, N.C B1 109
Catawba, York, S.C B6 115
Catawba, Roanoke, Va C2 121
Catawba, Marion, W. Va h10 123
Catawba, Price, Wis C3 124
Catawba, co., N.C B1 109
Catawba, riv., N.C B2 109
Catawba Island, Ottawa, Ohio A3 111
Catawissa, Columbia, Pa E9 114
Catbalogan, Phil C6 35
Cat Creek, Petroleum, Mont C8 102
Catechee, Pickens, S.C B2 115
Cateel, Phil *D7 35
Cater, Sask., Can D1 70
Cates, Fountain, Ind E3 91
Catete, Ang C1 48
Cathance, Sagadahoc, Maine D5 96
Cathance, lake, Maine D5 96
Catharine, Ellis, Kans D4 93
Cathay, Wells, N. Dak B6 110
Cathedral, bluffs, Colo B2 83
Cathedral, mtn., Tex o13 118
Cathedral City, Riverside, Calif F5 82
Catherine, Wilcox, Ala C2 78
Catherine, lake, Ark g8 81
Cathlamet, Wahkiakum, Wash C2 122
Cathro, Alpena, Mich C7 98
Cativá, Pan k11 62
Catlettsburg, Boyd, Ky B7 94
Catlin, Vermilion, Ill C6 90
Catlin, Parke, Ind E3 91
Cato, Faulkner, Ark C3 81
Cato, Cayuga, N.Y B4 108
Catoche, cape, Mex C7 63
Catoctin, mtn., Md B2 85
Catonsville, Baltimore, Md B4, g10 85
Catoosa, Rogers, Okla A6 112
Catoosa, co., Ga B1 87
Catriló, Arg B4 54
Catrimani, riv., Braz C5 60
Catron, New Madrid, Mo E8 101
Catron, co., N. Mex D1 107
Catskill, Greene, N.Y C7 108
Catskill, mts., N.Y C6 108
Catt, mtn., B.C., Can B3 68
Cattaraugus, Cattaraugus, N.Y C2 108
Cattaraugus, co., N.Y C2 108
Cattaraugus, Indian res., N.Y C2 108
Cattolica, It C4 21
Catuá, riv., Braz D4 60
Catumbela, riv., Ang D1 48
Cauayan, Phil *D6 35
Cauca, dept., Col C2 60
Cauca, riv., Col B2 60
Cauca, val., Col C2 60
Caucasia, Col B2 60
Caucasus, mts., Sov. Un G17 9
Cauchon, lake, Man., Can B3 71
Caucomgomac, lake, Maine B3 96
Caudebec [-lès-Elbeuf], Fr C4 14
Caudéran, Fr E3 14
Caudete, Sp C5 20
Caudry, Fr B5 14
Caughnawaga, Que., Can D4, q19 73
Caúngula, Ang C2 48
Cauquenes, Chile B2 54
Caura, riv., Ven B5 60
Causapscal, Que., Can *h14 73
Causey, Roosevelt, N. Mex D6 107
Caussade, Fr E4 14
Cauthron, Scott, Ark C1 81
Cautín, prov., Chile B2 54
Caution, cape, B.C., Can D4 68
Cauto, riv., Cuba D5 64
Cauvery, riv., India F6 39
Cavado, riv., Port B1 20
Cavaillon, Fr F6 14
Cavalier, Pembina, N. Dak A8 110
Cavalier, co., N. Dak A7 110
Cavalla, riv., I.C E3 45
Cavallo, mtn., It C8 18
Cavan, Ire D4 11
Cavan, co., Ire D4 11
Cavanal, mtn., Okla B7 112
Cavarzere, It B4 21
Cave, It h9 21
Cave City, Sharp, Ark B4 81
Cave City, Barren, Ky C4 94
Cavecreek, Maricopa, Ariz D4, k9 80
Cave in Rock, Hardin, Ill F5 90
Cave Junction, Josephine, Oreg E3 113
Cavell, Sask., Can E1 70
Cavendish, Alta., Can D5 69
Cavendish, Clearwater, Idaho C2 89
Cavendish, Windsor, Vt E3 120
Cave Spring, Floyd, Ga B1 87
Cave Spring, Roanoke, Va C2 121
Cave Spring Onyx, caverns, Mo E6 101
Cave Springs, Benton, Ark A1 81
Cave Springs, cave, Ga B1 87
Cavetown, Washington, Md A2 85
Cavite, Phil o13 35
Cavite, prov., Phil *C6 35
Cavour, Beadle, S. Dak C7 116
Cavour, Forest, Wis C5 124
Cawdor, Scot C5 13
Cawker City, Mitchell, Kans C5 93
Cawnpore, see Kanpur, India.
Cawood, Harlan, Ky D6 94
Cawston, B.C., Can E8 68
Caxias, Braz B2 57
Caxias do Sul, Braz D2 56
Caxito, Ang C1 48
Cay, pt., Ba n17 64
Cayambe, Ec A2 58
Cayce, Fulton, Ky f8 94
Cayce, Lexington, S.C D5 115
Cayenne, Fr. Gu B4 59
Cayeux-sur-Mer, Fr D9 12
Cayey, P.R B3 65
Cayey, mun., P.R *B3 65
Cayey, mts., P.R B3 65
Cayley, Alta., Can D4 69
Cayman Brac, isl., Cayman Is E4 64
Cayman Islands, Br. dep., N.A E4 64
Cayo, Belize B3 62
Cayo, isl., Cuba C4 64
Cayuga, Ont., Can E5 72
Cayuga, Vermillion, Ind E3 91
Cayuga, Hinds, Miss C3 100
Cayuga, Sargent, N. Dak C8 110
Cayuga, Ashland, Wis B3 124
Cayuga, co., N.Y C4 108
Cayuga, lake, N.Y C4 108
Cayuga Heights, Tompkins, N.Y C4 108
Cayuse, Umatilla, Oreg B8 113
Cazalla de la Sierra, Sp D3 20
Cazaux, lagoon, Fr E3 14
Cazenovia, Madison, N.Y C5 108
Cazenovia, Richland, Wis E3 124
Cazombo, Ang D3 48
Cazorla, Sp D4 20
Cea, riv., Sp A3 20
Ceanannas, Ire D5 11
Ceará, state, Braz C3 57
Ceará Mirim, Braz C3, g6 57
Ceará Mirim, riv., Braz g6 57
Cebolla, Rio Arriba, N. Mex A3 107
Cebollar, Arg E2 55
Cebollati, riv., Ur E2 56
Cebreros, Sp B3 20
Cebu, Phil C6 35
Cebu, prov., Phil *C6 35
Cebu, isl., Phil C6 35
Cecil, Montgomery, Ala C3 78
Cecil, Cook, Ga E3 87
Cecil, Paulding, Ohio A1 111
Cecil, Morrow, Oreg B7 113
Cecil, Washington, Pa F1 114
Cecil, Shawano, Wis D5 124
Cecil, co., Md A6 85
Cecil M. Harden Lake, res., Ind E3 91
Cecile, Caddo, La B2 95
Cecilia, Hardin, Ky C4 94
Cecilton, Cecil, Md B6 85
Cecina, It C3 21
Cedar, Smith, Kans C5 93
Cedar, Washington, Maine C5 96
Cedar, Leelanau, Mich D5 98
Cedar, Anoka, Minn E5 99
Cedar, co., Iowa C6 92
Cedar, co., Mo D4 101
Cedar, co., Nebr B8 103
Cedar, creek, Ind B7 91
Cedar, creek, Iowa C6 92
Cedar, creek, Mo C5 101
Cedar, creek, N.J D4 106
Cedar, creek, N. Dak C3 110
Cedar, creek, Ohio e7 111
Cedar, isl., N.C C6 109
Cedar, isl., S.C E9 115
Cedar, isl., Va C7 121
Cedar, keys, Fla C3 86
Cedar, lake, Man., Can C1 71
Cedar, lake, Ont., Can A6 72
Cedar, mtn., Calif B3 82
Cedar, mts., Nev E4 104
Cedar, mts., Oreg D9 113
Cedar, mts., Utah C2 119
Cedar, pt., Fla D4 86
Cedar, pt., Md D5 85
Cedar, pt., Ohio A3 111
Cedar, riv., Iowa, Minn C6 92
Cedar, riv., Nebr C7 103
Cedar, riv., Wash B4 122
Cedar, swamp, Mass f11 97
Cedar, val., Wash C4 122
Cedar Bluff, Cherokee, Ala A4 78
Cedar Bluff, Caldwell, Ky C2 94
Cedarbluff, Clay, Miss B5 100
Cedar Bluff, Tazewell, Va *e10 121
Cedar Bluff, res., Kans D4 93

Chocolate Bayou, Brazoria, Tex r14 118
Chocontá, Col B3 60
Choconut [Township], Susquehanna, Pa C9 114
Chocorua, Carroll, N.H C4 105
Chocorua, mtn., N.H C4 105
Chocowinity, Beaufort, N.C B5 109
Choctaw, Oklahoma, Okla B4 112
Choctaw, co., Ala C1 78
Choctaw, co., Miss B4 100
Choctaw, co., Okla C6 112
Choctaw, Indian res., Miss C4 100
Choctaw Bluff, Clarke, Ala D2 78
Choctaw City, Choctaw, Ala C1 78
Choctawhatchee, bay, Fla u15 86
Choctawhatchee, riv., Ala., Fla D4 78
Chodziez, Pol B4 26
Choele Choel, Arg B3 54
Choerh, riv., China C1 37
Choibalsan, Mong B7 34
Choiceland, Sask., Can D3 70
Choiseul, isl., Sol. Is G9 7
Choisy-le-Roi, Fr g10 14
Choix, Mex B3 63
Chojna, Pol B3 26
Chojnice, Pol B4 26
Chojnow, Pol C3 26
Chokai-San, peak, Jap G10 37
Choke, mts., Eth C4 47
Chokio, Stevens. Minn E2 99
Chokoloskee, Collier, Fla G8 86
Cholame, San Luis Obispo, Calif E3 82
Cholet, Fr D3 14
Cholo, Malawi A6 49
Choluteca, Hond D4 62
Choluteca, riv., Hond D4 62
Choma, Zambia E4 48
Chomedey, Que., Can D4, p19 73
Chomo Lhāri, peak, Bhu D12 40
Chomutov, Czech C2 26
Chonan, Kor H3 37
Chon Buri, Thai F4 38
Chone, Ec B1 58
Chŏngjin, Kor F4 37
Chŏngju, Kor H3 37
Chongsong, Kor E4 37
Chonju, Kor I3 37
Chonos, arch., Chile C2 54
Chonzie, mtn., Scot D5 13
Chopin, riv., Braz D2 57
Choptank, Caroline, Md C6 85
Choptank, riv., Md C6 85
Chorrillos, Peru D2 58
Chortkov, Sov. Un I9 27
Chorum (Corum), Tur B10 31
Chorwon, Kor G3 37
Chorzów, Pol C5, g9 26
Chosan, Kor F2 37
Chosen, see Korea, Asia
Chosen, Palm Beach, Fla F6 86
Chōshi, Jap I10, n19 37
Chosica, Peru D2 58
Chos Malal, Arg B2 54
Choszczno, Pol B3 26
Chota, Peru C2 58
Choteau, Teton, Mont C4 102
Chotetov, Czech n18 26
Choudrant, Lincoln, La B3 95
Choum, Maur B2 45
Choushan, is., China I10 36
Chouteau, Mayes, Okla A6 12
Chouteau, co., Mont C6 102
Choutsun, China F7 36
Chowan, co., N.C A6 109
Chowan, riv., N.C A6 109
Chowchilla, Madera, Calif D3 82
Choyren, Mong B6 34
Chrisman, Edgar, Ill D6 90
Chrisney, Spencer, Ind H3 91
Christchurch, Eng D6 12
Christchurch, N.Z O14 51
Christian, co., Ill D4 90
Christian, co., Ky D2 94
Christian, co., Mo E2 101
Christian, isl., Ont., Can C4 72
Christian, sound, Alsk m22 79
Christiana, New Castle, Del A6 85
Christiana, Jam E14 65
Christiana, Lancaster, Pa G6 114
Christiana, S. Afr C4 49
Christiana, Rutherford, Tenn B5 117
Christiansburg, Champaign, Ohio B1 111
Christiansburg, Montgomery, Va C2 121
Christiansfeld, Den C3 24
Christiansted, Vir. Is. (U.S.) C6 65
Christina, Fergus, Mont C 102
Christina, lake, Alta., Can B5 69
Christina, lake, B.C., Can A7 122
Christina, lake, Minn D3 99
Christina, riv., Alta., Can A5 69
Christine, Richland, N. Dak C9 110
Christine, Atascosa, Tex E3 118
Christmas, Gila, Ariz E5 80
Christmas, Orange, Fla D5 86
Christmas, isl., Kir F12 7
Christmas, lake, Oreg D6 113
Christmas Island, Austl. dep., Ind. O G5 7
Christmas Valley, Lake, Oreg D6 113
Christopher, Franklin, Ill F4 90
Christopher, King, Wash D2 122
Christoval, Tom Green, Tex D2 118
Chromo, Archuleta, Colo D4 83
Chronister, Cherokee, Okla B7 112
Chrudim, Czech D3 26
Chrysler, Monroe, Ala D2 78
Chrzanow, Pol g10 26
Chu, China H8 36
Chu, Sov. Un E8 29
Chu, riv., Sov. Un G23 9
Chualar, Monterey, Calif C6 82
Chüanchou, China F7 34
Chüanchou, China G8 34
Chuangho, China E10 36
Chubbuck, Bannock, Idaho G6 89
Chubut, prov., Arg C3 54
Chucheng, China G8 36
Chuchi, China J9 36
Chuchou, China K5 36
Chu Chua, B.C., Can D7 68
Chuckey, Greene, Tenn C11 117
Chudovo, Sov. Un G8 27
Chuehshan, China H6 36
Chüfou, China *D8 34
Chugach, is., Alsk h16 79
Chugach, mts., Alsk g17 79
Chugiak, Alsk C10, g17 79
Chuguyev, Sov. Un G11 27
Chugwater, Platte, Wyo E8 125
Chugwater, creek, Wyo E8 125
Chuho, China D3 37
Chühsien, China J8 36
Chühsien, China G8 36
Chuhsiung, China F5 34
Chui Chuischu, Pinal, Ariz E4 80
Chuius, mtn., B.C., Can B5 68
Chukai, Mala J5 38
Chukchi, sea, Sov. Un C32 4
Chukotsk, pen., Sov. Un C32 4
Chula, Tift, Ga E3 87
Chula, Livingston, Mo B3 101
Chula, Amelia, Va C5 121
Chulahoma, Marshall, Miss A4 100
Chula Vista, San Diego, Calif F5, o15 82
Chulu, China F6 36
Chulucanas, Peru B1 58
Chulumani, Bol C2 55
Chulym, Sov. Un B10 29
Chulym, riv., Sov. Un D11 28
Chumar, India A7 40
Chumatien, China H6 36
Chumbicha, Arg E2 55
Chumikan, Sov. Un D16 28
Chumphon, Thai G3 38
Chumysh, riv., Sov. Un C10 29
Chunchŏn, Kor H3 37
Chunchula, Mobile, Ala E1 78
Chungan, China K7 36
Chunghsiang, China I5 36
Chunghsien, China E6 34
Chungju, Kor H3 37
Chungking (Chungching), China G13 33, J2 36
Chungpa, China C7 39
Chungtien, China F4 34
Chungwei, China D6 34
Chunky, Newton, Miss C5 100
Chunya, Tan C5 48
Chupaca, Peru D2 58
Chupadera, mesa, N. Mex D3 107
Chupadero, Santa Fe, N. Mex *B4 107
Chupara, pt., Trin N23 65
Chuquibamba, Peru E3 58
Chuquicamata, Chile D2 55
Chuquisaca, dept., Bol C2 55
Chur, Switz C8 19
Church, mtn., B.C., Can f14 68
Churchbridge, Sask., Can G5 70
Church Creek, Dorchester, Md C5 85
Church Hill, Queen Annes, Md B6 85
Church Hill, Hawkins, Tenn C11 117
Churchill, Man., Can f9 71
Churchill, Cassia, Idaho G5 89
Church Hill, Jefferson, Miss D2 100
Churchill, co., Nev D3 104
Churchill, cape, Man., Can f9 71
Churchill, lake, Sask., Can m7 70
Churchill, lake, Maine B3 96
Churchill, mtn., B.C., Can E6 68
Churchill, riv., Man., Sask., Can E11 66
Church Point, Acadia, La D3 95
Church Point, N.S., Can E3 74
Church Rock, McKinley, N. Mex B1 107
Churchs Ferry, Ramsey, N. Dak A6 110
Church Stretton, Eng B5 12
Churchton, Anne Arundel, Md C4 85
Churchville, Harford, Md A5 85
Churchville, Monroe, N.Y B3 108
Churchville, Bucks, Pa *F11 114
Churchville, Augusta, Va B3 121
Churdan, Greene, Iowa B3 92
Churu, India C5 40
Churubusco, Whitley, Ind B7 91
Churubusco, Clinton, N.Y f11 108
Churuguara, Ven A4 60
Churumuco, Mex n13 63
Chushan, China E7 34
Chuska, mts., N. Mex A1 107
Chusovaya, riv., Sov. Un D20 9
Chusovoy, Sov. Un B5 29
Chust, Sov. Un G23 9
Chybie, Pol h9 26
Ciales, mun., P.R *B2 65
Ciano d'Enza, It E6 18
Cibecue, Navajo, Ariz. C5 80
Cibola, co., N. Mex. C1 107
Cibolo, creek, Tex. h7 118
Cicekdag, Tur C10 31
Cicero, Cook, Ill B6, k9 90
Cicero, Hamilton, Ind D5 91
Cícero Dantas, Braz D3 57
Cide, Tur B9 31
Cidra, mun., P.R *B3 65
Cidra, res., P.R B3 65
Ciechanow. Pol B6 26
Ciego de Avila, Cuba D4 64
Ciempozuelos, Sp B4 20
Ciénaga, Col A3 60
Ciénaga de Oro, Col B2 60
Cienfuegos, Cuba C3 64
Cieszyn, Pol D5 26
Cieza, Sp C5 20
Ciezkowice, Pol g10 26
Cihanbeyli, Tur C9 31
Cihuatlán, Mex n11 63
Cilacap, Indon G3 35
Cima, San Bernardino, Calif E6 82
Cimarron, Gray, Kans E3 93
Cimarron, Colfax, N. Mex A5 107
Cimarron, co., Okla e8 112
Cimarron, riv., U.S. C8 76
Cîmpina, Rom C7 22
Cîmpulung, Rom C7 22
Cîmpulung Moldovenesc, Rom B7 22
Cincinnati, Appanoose Iowa D5 92
Cincinnati, Hamilton, Ohio C1, o12 111
Cincinnatus, Cortland, N.Y C5 108
Cinco Bayou, Okaloosa, Fla u15 86
Cinconsine, lake, Que., Can B4 73
Cine, Tur D7 23
Cinnaminson, Burlington, N.J D3 106
Cinto, mtn., Fr C2 21
Cipolletti, Arg B3 54
Cipres, Hidalgo, Tex F3 118
Circle, Alsk B11 79
Circle, McCone, Mont C11 102
Circle Hot Springs, Alsk B11 79
Circle Pines, Anoka, Minn m12 99
Circleville, Jackson, Kans C8 93
Circleville, Pickaway, Ohio C3 111
Circleville, Piute, Utah E3 119
Circleville, Pendleton, W. Va C5 123
Cirencester, Eng C6 12
Ciri, riv., Pan m10 62
Cirrik, Alb E4 22
Cisco, Piatt, Ill C5 90
Cisco, Magoffin, Ky C6 94
Cisco, Eastland, Tex C3 118
Cisco, Grand, Utah E6 119
Cisne, Wayne, Ill E5 90
Cisneros, Col B2 60
Ciso, Murray, Ga B2 87
Cispus, riv., Wash C4 122
Cissna Park, Iroquois, Ill C6 90
Cistern, Fayette, Tex E4 118
Cisterna di Latina, It h9 21
Cistierna, Sp A3 20
Citra, Marion, Fla C4 86
Citronelle, Mobile, Ala D1 78
Citrus, co., Fla D4 86
Citrus Heights, Sacramento, Calif *C3 82
Cittadella, It B3 21
Città di Castello, It C4 21
City, isl., N.Y B5 106
City Mills, Norfolk, Mass h10 97
City of London, Eng. (part of London) k12 10
City Park, Christian, Ill *D4 90
City Point, Brevard, Fla D6 86
City Terrace, Los Angeles, Calif *F4 82
City View, Greenville, S.C B2 115
Ciucul, mts., Rom B7 22
Ciudad Altamirano, Mex n13 63
Ciudad Bolívar, Ven B5 60
Ciudad Bolivia, Ven B3 60
Ciudad Camargo, Mex B3 63
Ciudad Camargo, Mex F3 118
Ciudad Chetumal, Mex D7 63
Ciudad del Carmen, Mex D6 63
Ciudad del Maíz, Mex C5 63
Ciudad de Valles, Mex C5, m14 63
Ciudad Dr. Hernández Alvarez, Mex m13 63
Ciudadela, Sp B7 20
Ciudad García [Salinas], Mex C4 63
Ciudad Guayana, Ven B5 60
Ciudad Guzmán, Mex D4, n12 63
Ciudad Hidalgo, Mex n13 63
Ciudad Juárez, Mex A3 63
Ciudad Lerdo, Mex B4 63
Ciudad Madero, Mex C5 63
Ciudad Mante, Mex C5 63
Ciudad Melchor Múzquiz, Mex B4 63
Ciudad Obregón, Mex B3 63
Ciudad Real, Sp C4 20
Ciudad Real, prov., Sp *C4 20
Ciudad Rodrigo, Sp B2 20
Ciudad Serdán, Mex n15 63
Ciudad Victoria, Mex C5 63
Cividale del Friuli, It A4 21
Civitanova Marche, It C4 21
Civitavecchia, It C3 21
Civray, Fr D4 14
Civril, Tur C7 23
Cizre, Tur D14 31
C. J. Strike, res., Idaho G3 89
Clackamas, Clackamas, Oreg h12 113
Clackamas, co., Oreg B4 113
Clacton-on-Sea, Eng C9 12
Claflin, Barton, Kans D5 93
Claiborne, Monroe, Ala D2 78
Claiborne, Ouachita, La *B3 95
Claiborne, Talbot, Md C5 85
Claiborne, co., Miss D3 100
Claiborne, co., Tenn C10 117
Claiborne, par., La B2 95
Clair, N.B., Can B1 74
Clair, Sask., Can E3 70
Claire, lake, Alta., Can f8 69
Claire, riv., Viet B6 38
Claire City, Roberts, S. Dak B8 116
Clairemont, Kent, Tex C2 118
Clair Engle, lake, Calif B2 82
Clairfield, Claiborne, Tenn C10 117
Clair Haven, Macomb, Mich *F8 98
Clairmont, Alta., Can B1 69
Clairmont Springs, Clay, Ala B4 78
Clairton, Allegheny, Pa F2 114
Clallam, co., Wash B2 122
Clallam Bay, Clallam, Wash A1 122
Clam, lake, Sask., Can B3 70
Clam, lake, Wis C1 124
Clamart, Fr g10 14
Clamecy, Fr D5 14
Clan Alpine, mts., Nev D4 104
Clancy, Jefferson, Mont D5 102
Clandeboye, Ont., Can D3 72
Clandonald, Alta., Can C5 69
Clanton, Chilton, Ala C3 78
Clanwilliam, Man., Can D2 71
Clanwilliam, S. Afr D2 49
Clapperton, isl., Ont., Can A2 72
Clara, Ire D4 11
Clara, Wayne, Miss D5 100
Clara Barton, Middlesex, N.J *B4 106
Clara City, Chippewa, Minn F3 99
Clare, Austl F2 51
Clare, Hamilton, Ind D6 91
Clare, Webster, Iowa B3 92
Clare, Clare, Mich E6 98
Clare, co., Ire E2 11
Clare, co., Mich E6 98
Clare, isl., Ire D1 11
Clare, riv., Ire D3 11
Clarecastle, Ire E3 11
Claregalway, Ire D3 11
Claremont, Los Angeles, Calif m13 82
Claremont, Dodge, Minn F6 99
Claremont, Sullivan, N.H D2 105
Claremont, Catawba, N.C B1 109
Claremont, Brown, S. Dak B7 116
Claremont, Surry, Va C6 121
Claremont, mtn., Calif C3 82
Claremore, Rogers, Okla A6 112
Claremorris, Ire D2 11
Clarence, Cedar, Iowa C6 92
Clarence, Natchitoches, La C2 95
Clarence, Shelby, Mo B5 101
Clarence, Erie, N.Y *C2 108
Clarence, Centre, Pa D6 114
Clarence, isl., Ant C7 5
Clarence, strait, Austl B5 50
Clarence Town, Ba C6 64
Clarenceville, Que., Can D4 73
Clarendon, Monroe, Ark C4 81
Clarendon, Warren, Pa C3 114
Clarendon, Donley, Tex B2 118
Clarendon, Rutland, Vt D3 120
Clarendon, co., S.C D7 115
Clarendon, riv., Vt E2 120
Clarendon Hills, Du Page, Ill k9 90
Clarendon Springs, Rutland, Vt D2 120
Clarendon Station, Ont., Can C8 72
Clarenville, Newf., Can D5 75
Claresholm, Alta., Can D4 69
Clareville, Bee, Tex E4 118
Claridge, Westmoreland, Pa F2 114
Clarie, coast, Ant C26 5
Clarinda, Page, Iowa D2 92
Clarington, Monroe, Ohio C5 111
Clarington, Forest, Pa D3 114
Clarion, Wright, Iowa B4 92
Clarion, Clarion, Pa D3 114
Clarion, co., Pa D3 114
Clarion, riv., Pa D3 114
Clarissa, Todd, Minn D4 96
Clarita, Coal, Okla C5 112
Clark, Routt, Colo A4 83
Clark, Randolph, Mo B5 101
Clark, Union, N.J B4 106
Clark, Coshocton and Holmes, Ohio B4 111
Clark, Mercer, Pa *D1 114
Clark, Clark, S. Dak C8 116
Clark, co., Ark C2 81
Clark, co., Idaho E6 89
Clark, co., Ill D6 90
Clark, co., Ind H6 91
Clark, co., Kans E4 93
Clark, co., Ky C5 94
Clark, co., Mo A6 101
Clark, co., Nev G6 104
Clark, co., Ohio C2 111
Clark, co., S. Dak C8 116
Clark, co., Wash D3 122
Clark, co., Wis D3 124
Clark (Blackfoot, riv.), fork, Mont D3 102
Clark, lake, Alsk C9 79
Clark, pt., Ont., Can C3 72
Clark Colony, Spink, S. Dak *C7 116
Clarkdale, Yavapai, Ariz C5 80
Clarkdale, Cobb, Ga h7 87
Clarke, co., Ala D2 78
Clarke, co., Ga C3 87
Clarke, co., Iowa D4 92
Clarke, co., Miss C5 100
Clarke, co., Va A4 121
Clarke, lake, Sask., Can C2 70
Clarke City, Que., Can F19 67
Clarkedale, Crittenden, Ark e8 117
Clarke's Beach, Newf., Can *E5 75
Clarkesville, Habersham, Ga B3 87
Clarkfield, Yellow Medicine, Minn F3 99
Clark Fork, Bonner, Idaho A2 89
Clark Fork, riv., Idaho, Mont B3 89
Clark Hill, res., Ga C4 88
Clarkia, Shoshone, Idaho C2 89
Clark Mills, Oneida, N.Y *B5 108
Clarkrange, Fentress, Tenn C8 117
Clarks, Caldwell, La B3 95
Clarks, Merrick, Nebr C8 103
Clarks, riv., Ky e9 94
Clarksboro, Gloucester, N.J D2 106
Clarksburg, Ont., Can C4 72
Clarksburg, Decatur, Ind F7 91
Clarksburg, Montgomery, Md B3 85
Clarksburg (Town of), Berkshire, Mass *A1 97
Clarksburg, Moniteau, Mo C5 101
Clarksburg, Monmouth, N.J C4 106
Clarksburg, Ross, Ohio C2 111
Clarksburg, Carroll, Tenn B3 117
Clarksburg, Harrison, W. Va B4, k10 123
Clarks Corners, Windham, Conn B8 84
Clarksdale, Coahoma, Miss A3 100
Clarksdale, De Kalb, Mo B3 101
Clarks Falls, New London, Conn D9 84
Clarks (Yellowstone, riv.), fork, Mont., Wyo F7 102
Clarks Green, Lackawanna, Pa *D10 114
Clarks Grove, Freeborn, Minn G5 99
Clark's Harbour, N.S., Can F4 74
Clarks Hill, Tippecanoe, Ind D4 91
Clarkson, Ont., Can D5 72
Clarkson, Grayson, Ky C3 94
Clarkson, Webster, Miss B4 100
Clarkson, Colfax, Nebr C8 103
Clarks Point, Alsk D8 79
Clarks Summit, Lackawanna, Pa m18 114
Clarkston, De Kalb, Ga h8 87
Clarkston, Oakland, Mich F7 98
Clarkston, Cache, Utah B3 119
Clarkston, Asotin, Wash C8 122
Clarksville, Johnson, Ark B2 81
Clarksville, N.S., Can D6 74
Clarksville, Sussex, Del C7 85
Clarksville, Kootenai, Idaho B2 89
Clarksville, Clark, Ind H6 91
Clarksville, Butler, Iowa B5 92
Clarksville, Howard, Md B4 85
Clarksville, Ionia, Mich F5 98
Clarksville, Pike, Mo B7 101
Clarksville, Clinton, Ohio C2 111
Clarksville, Montgomery, Tenn A4 117
Clarksville, Red River, Tex C5 118
Clarksville, Mecklenburg, Va D4 121
Clarkton, Dunklin, Mo E8 101
Clarkton, Bladen, N.C C4 109
Clarno, Wheeler, Oreg C6 113
Claryville, Campbell, Ky k14 94
Claryville, Perry, Mo D8 101
Clashmore, Ire E4 11
Clatonia, Gage, Nebr D9 103
Clatskanie, Columbia, Oreg A3 113
Clatsop, co., Oreg A3 113
Claude, Armstrong, Tex B2 118
Claudy, N. Ire C4 11
Claunch, Socorro, N. Mex C3 107
Clausthal-Zellerfeld, F.R.G B5 17
Claveria, Phil *B6 35
Clavet, Sask., Can F2 70
Clawson, Oakland, Mich o15 98
Clawson, Emery, Utah D4 119
Claxton, Evans, Ga D5 87
Clay, Webster, Ky C2 94
Clay, Onondaga, N.Y B4 108
Clay, Burleson, Tex D4 118
Clay, Clay, W. Va C3, m13 123
Clay, Weston, Wyo B8 125
Clay, co., Ala B4 78
Clay, co., Ark A5 81
Clay, co., Fla B5 86
Clay, co., Ga E2 87
Clay, co., Ill E5 90
Clay, co., Ind F3 91
Clay, co., Iowa A2 92
Clay, co., Kans C6 93
Clay, co., Ky C6 94
Clay, co., Minn D2 99
Clay, co., Miss B5 100
Clay, co., Mo B3 101
Clay, co., Nebr D7 103
Clay, co., N.C f9 109
Clay, co., S. Dak E8 116
Clay, co., Tenn C8 117
Clay, co., Tex C3 118
Clay, co., W. Va C3 123
Clay Center, Clay, Kans C6 93
Clay Center, Clay, Nebr D7 103
Clay Center, Ottawa, Ohio A2, e7 111
Clay City, Clay, Ill E5 90
Clay City, Clay, Ind F3 91
Clay City, Powell, Ky C6 94
Claycomo, Clay, Mo *B3 101
Clay Cross, Eng *A6 12
Claydon, Sask., Can H1 70
Clayhatchee, Dale, Ala D4 78
Clayhole, wash, Utah G2 119
Claymont, New Castle, Del A7 85
Clayoquot, sound, B.C., Can E4 68
Claypool, Gila, Ariz D5 80
Claypool, Kosciusko, Ind B6 91
Claysburg, Blair, Pa F5 114
Clay Springs, Navajo, Ariz C5 80
Claysville, Washington, Pa F1 114
Clayton, Barbour, Ala D4 78
Clayton, Ont., Can B8 72
Clayton, Kent, Del B6 85
Clayton, Rabun, Ga B3 87
Clayton, Custer, Idaho E3 89
Clayton, Adams, Ill C3 90
Clayton, Hendricks, Ind E4 91
Clayton, Clayton, Iowa B6 92
Clayton, Norton and Decatur, Kans C3 93
Clayton, Concordia, La C4 95
Clayton, St. Louis, Mo C7, f13 101
Clayton, Gloucester, N.J D2 106
Clayton, Union, N. Mex A6 107
Clayton, Jefferson, N.Y A4, f8 108
Clayton, Johnston, N.C B4 109
Clayton, Pushmataha, Okla C6 112
Clayton, Obion, Tenn A2 117
Clayton, Stevens, Wash B8 122
Clayton, Polk, Wis C1 124
Clayton, co., Ga C2 87
Clayton, co., Iowa B6 92
Clayton Lake, Aroostook, Maine B3 96
Clayville, Providence, R.I B10 84
Clear, cape, Ire F2 11
Clear, creek, Ariz C4 80
Clear, creek, Tenn C9 117
Clear, creek, Wyo B6 125
Clear, fork, Ohio B3 111
Clear, fork, Tenn C9 117
Clear, fork, W. Va D3 123
Clear, fork, W. Va n13 123
Clear, isl., Ire F2 11
Clear, lake, Calif C2 82
Clear, lake, Man., Can D1 71
Clear, lake, Ont., Can B7 72
Clear, lake, Iowa A4 92
Clear, lake, Utah D3 119
Clear, riv., Alta., Can A1 69
Clear, stream, N.H A4 105
Clear Boggy, creek, Okla C5 112
Clearbrook, B.C., Can f13 68
Clearbrook, Clearwater, Minn C3 99
Clear Creek, Monroe, Ind F4 91
Clear Creek, Carbon, Utah D4 119
Clear Creek, Raleigh, W. Va n13 123
Clear Creek, co., Colo B5 83
Cleare, cape, Alsk D10 79
Clearfield, Taylor and Ringgold, Iowa D3 92
Clearfield, Rowan, Ky B6 94
Clearfield, Clearfield, Pa D5 114
Clearfield, Davis, Utah B3 119
Clearfield, co., Pa D5 114
Clear Fork, Wyoming, W. Va D3 123
Clear Lake, Cerro Gordo, Iowa A4 92
Clear Lake, Sherburne, Minn E5 99
Clear Lake, Deuel, S. Dak C9 116
Clearlake, Skagit, Wash A3 122
Clear Lake, Polk, Wis C1 124
Clear Lake, res., Calif B3 82
Clear Lake Shores, Tex r14 118
Clearmont, Nodaway, Mo A2 101
Clearmont, Sheridan, Wyo B6 125
Clear Spring, Washington, Md A2 85
Clearview, Okfuskee, Okla B5 112
Clearville, Bedford, Pa G5 114
Clearwater, B.C., Can D7 68
Clearwater, Man., Can E2 71
Clearwater, Pinellas, Fla E4, p10 86
Clearwater, Idaho, Idaho C3 89
Clearwater, Sedgwick, Kans E6, h11 93
Clearwater, Wright, Minn E4 99
Clearwater, Antelope, Nebr B7 103
Clearwater, Aiken, S.C E4 115
Clearwater, Jefferson, Wash B1 122
Clearwater, co., Idaho C3 89
Clearwater, co., Minn C3 99
Clearwater, creek, Kans B4 93
Clearwater, lake, B.C., Can C7 68
Clearwater, lake, Man., Can B1 71
Clearwater, lake, Que., Can g11 73
Clearwater, mts., Idaho C2 89
Clearwater, prov. park, Man., Can C1 71
Clearwater, riv., Alta., Can A5 69
Clearwater, riv., Alta., Can D3 69
Clearwater, riv., B.C., Can C7 68
Clearwater, riv., Idaho C2 89
Clearwater, riv., Minn C3 99
Clearwater Lake, Oneida, Wis C4 124
Clearwater Lake, res., Mo D7 101
Cleaton, Muhlenberg, Ky C2 94
Cleator Moor, Eng F5 13
Clebit, McCurtain, Okla C7 112
Cleburne, Johnson, Tex C4 118
Cleburne, co., Ala B4 78
Cleburne, co., Ark B3 81
Cle Elum, Kittitas, Wash B5 122
Cle Elum, riv., Wash B4 122
Cle Elum Lake, res., Wash B4 122
Cleethorpes, Eng A7 12
Cleeves, Sask., Can D1 70
Clegg, Live Oak, Tex E3 118
Cleggan, Ire D1 11
Cleghorn, Cherokee, Iowa B2 92
Cleghorn, Eau Claire, Wis D2 124
Clem, Carroll, Ga C1 87
Clementon, Camden, N.J D3 106
Clements, Chase, Kans D7 93
Clements, St. Marys, Md D4 85
Clements, Redwood, Minn F3 99
Clementsport, N.S., Can E4 74
Clementsvale, N.S., Can E4 74
Clemmons, Forsyth, N.C A2 109
Clemons, Marshall, Iowa B4 92
Clemons, Washington, N.Y B7 108
Clemscot, Carter, Okla C4 112
Clemson, Pickens, S.C B2 115
Clendenin, Kanawha, W. Va C3, m13 123
Clendening Lake, res., Ohio B4 111
Cleona, Lebanon, Pa F9 114
Cleo Springs, Major, Okla A3 112
Clermont, Austl D8 51
Clermont, Que., Can B7 73
Clermont, Lake, Fla D5 86
Clermont, Fr E2 15
Clermont, Hall, Ga B3 87
Clermont, Marion, Ind k9 91
Clermont, Fayette, Iowa A6 92
Clermont, Bullitt, Ky C4 94
Clermont, McKean, Pa C5 114
Clermont, co., Ohio C1 111
Clermont-Ferrand, Fr E5 14
Clermont-l'Hérault, Fr F5 14
Clervaux, Lux D6 15
Cleve, see Kleve, F.R.G.
Clevedon, Eng C5 12
Cleveland, Blount, Ala A3 78
Cleveland, Conway, Ark B3 81
Cleveland, Charlotte, Fla F5 86
Cleveland, White, Ga B3 87
Cleveland, Le Sueur, Minn F5 99
Cleveland, Bolivar, Miss B3 100
Cleveland, Cass, Mo C3 101
Cleveland, Mora, N. Mex A4 107
Cleveland, Oswego, N.Y B5 108
Cleveland, Rowan, N.C. B2 109
Cleveland, Stutsman, N. Dak C6 110
Cleveland, Cuyahoga, Ohio A4, h9 111
Cleveland, Pawnee, Okla A5 112
Cleveland, Greenville, S.C A2 115
Cleveland, Bradley, Tenn D9 117
Cleveland, Liberty, Tex D5 118
Cleveland, Emery, Utah D5 119
Cleveland, Russell, Va f9 121
Cleveland, Manitowoc, Wis k10 124
Cleveland, co., Ark D3 81
Cleveland, co., Eng F7 13
Cleveland, co., N.C B1 109
Cleveland, co., Okla B4 112
Cleveland, hills, Eng F7 13
Cleveland, mtn., Mont B3 102
Cleveland Heights, Cuyahoga, Ohio A4, g9 111
Clevelãndia, Braz D2 56
Clever, Christian, Mo D4 101
Cleves, Hamilton, Ohio o11 111
Clew, bay, Ire D2 11
Clewiston, Hendry, Fla F6 86
Clichy [-la-Garenne], Fr g10 14
Clifden, Ire D1 11
Cliff, Grant, N. Mex E1 107
Clifford, Ont., Can D4 72
Clifford, Bartholomew, Ind F6 91
Clifford, Lapeer, Mich E7 98
Clifford, Traill, N. Dak B8 110
Clifford, Susquehanna, Pa C10 114
Clifford, Amherst, Va C3 121
Cliffside, B.C., Can g12 68
Cliffside, Rutherford, N.C B1, f11 109
Cliffside Park, Bergen, N.J h9 106
Clifftop, Fayette, W. Va m14 123
Cliffwood, Monmouth, N.J *C4 106
Cliffwood Beach, Middlesex and Monmouth, N.J *C4 106
Clifton, Greenlee, Ariz D6 80
Clifton, Mesa, Colo B2 83
Clifton, Franklin, Idaho G7 89
Clifton, Iroquois, Ill C6 90
Clifton, Washington and Clay, Kans C6 93
Clifton, Passaic, N.J B4, h8 106
Clifton, Spartanburg, S.C B4 115
Clifton, Wayne, Tenn B4 117
Clifton, Bosque, Tex D4 118
Clifton, Weston, Wyo C8 125
Clifton City, Cooper, Mo C4 101
Clifton Forge (Independent City), Va C3 121
Clifton Hill, Randolph, Mo B5 101
Clifton Knolls, Saratoga, N.Y C7 108
Clifton Springs, Ontario, N.Y C3 108
Cliftonville, Noxubee, Miss B5 100
Clifty, Decatur, Ind F6 91
Climax, Sask., Can H1 70
Climax, Lake, Colo B4 83
Climax, Decatur, Ga F2 87
Climax, Greenwood, Kans E7 93
Climax, Kalamazoo, Mich F5 98
Climax, Polk, Minn C2 99
Climax Springs, Camden, Mo C4 101
Climbing Hill, Woodbury, Iowa B1 92
Clinch, co., Ga F4 87
Clinch, mtn., Va f9 121
Clinch, mts., Tenn C10 117
Clinch, riv., Tenn D9 117
Clinch, riv., Va f9 121
Clinchburg, Washington, Va f10 121
Clincho, Dickenson, Va e9 121
Clinchfield, Houston, Ga D3 87
Clinchfield, McDowell, N.C *f10 109
Clinchport, Scott, Va f9 121
Cline, Uvalde, Tex E2 118
Clingmans Dome, mtn., Tenn D10 117
Clint, El Paso, Tex o11 118
Clinton, Greene, Ala C1 78
Clinton, Van Buren, Ark B3 81
Clinton, B.C., Can D7 68
Clinton, Ont., Can D3 72
Clinton, Middlesex, Conn D6 84
Clinton, Jones, Ga C3 87
Clinton, DeWitt, Ill C5 90
Clinton, Vermillion, Ind E3 91
Clinton, Clinton, Iowa C7 92
Clinton, Hickman, Ky f9 94
Clinton, East Feliciana, La D4 95
Clinton, Kennebec, Maine D3 96
Clinton, Prince Georges, Md C4 85
Clinton, Worcester, Mass B4 97
Clinton, Lenawee, Mich F7 98
Clinton, Big Stone, Minn E2 98
Clinton, Hinds, Miss C3 100
Clinton, Henry, Mo C4 101
Clinton, Missoula, Mont D3 102
Clinton, Sheridan, Nebr B3 103
Clinton, Hunterdon, N.J B3 106
Clinton, Oneida, N.Y B5 108
Clinton, Sampson, N.C C4 109
Clinton, Summit, Ohio *B4 111
Clinton, Custer, Okla B3 112
Clinton, Laurens, S.C C4 115
Clinton Anderson, Tenn C9, m13 117
Clinton, Davis, Utah B3 119
Clinton, Rock, Wis F5 124

80X CLIN-CONC

Clinton, co., Ill E4 90
Clinton, co., Ind D4 91
Clinton, co., Iowa C7 92
Clinton, co., Ky D4 94
Clinton, co., Mich F6 98
Clinton, co., Mo B3 101
Clinton, co., N.Y f11 108
Clinton, co., Ohio C2 111
Clinton, co., Pa D6 114
Clinton, res., N.J. A4 106
Clinton-Colden, lake, N.W. Ter., Can D11 66
Clintonville, New Haven, Conn. (part of North Haven) D5 84
Clintonville, Bourbon, Ky B5 94
Clintonville, Venango, Pa D2 114
Clintonville, Greenbrier, W. Va D4 123
Clintonville, Waupaca, Wis D5 124
Clintwood, Dickenson, Va e9 121
Clio, Barbour, Ala D4 78
Clio, Wayne, Iowa D4 92
Clio, Livingston, La h10 95
Clio, Genesee, Mich E7 98
Clio, Marlboro, S.C B8 115
Clio, Roane, W. Va C3 123
Clipper, Whatcom, Wash A3 122
Clipperton, isl., Pac. O F15 7
Clisham, mtn., Scot C2 13
Clitherall, Ottertail, Minn D3 99
Clive, Alta., Can C4 69
Clive, Polk, Iowa e8 92
Cliza, Bol C2 55
Cloan, Sask., Can E1 70
Cloe, Jefferson, Pa E4 114
Cloghan, Ire C4 11
Cloghan, Ire D4 11
Cloghane, Ire E1 11
Clogheen, Ire E3 11
Clogher, head, Ire D5 11
Clonakilty, Ire F3 11
Clonakilty, bay, Ire F3 11
Cloncurry, Austl D7 50
Clones, Ire C4 11
Clonmany, Ire B4 11
Clonmel, Ire E4 11
Clonmellon, Ire D4 11
Clontarf, Swift, Minn E3 99
Cloone, Ire D4 11
Clo-oose, B.C., Can E5 68
Cloppenburg, F.R.G F2 24
Clopton, Dale, Ala D4 78
Cloquet, Carlton, Minn D6 99
Cloquet, riv., Minn C6 99
Closter, Bergen, N.J B5, h9 106
Clothier, Logan, W. Va n12 123
Cloud, co., Kans C6 93
Cloud, peak, Wyo B5 125
Cloud Chief, Washita, Okla B3 112
Cloudcroft, Otero, N. Mex E4 107
Cloud Lake, Palm Beach, Fla *F6 86
Cloudy, bay, N.Z N15 51
Clover, York, S.C A5 115
Clover, Halifax, Va D4 121
Clover Bottom, Jackson, Ky C5 94
Cloverdale, Lauderdale, Ala A2 78
Cloverdale, Sonoma, Calif C2 82
Cloverdale, B.C., Can f13 68
Cloverdale, Du Page, Ill F2 90
Cloverdale, Putnam, Ind E4 91
Cloverdale, Wake, N.C B4 109
Cloverdale, Tillamook, Oreg B3 113
Cloverleaf, Harris, Tex *E5 118
Cloverport, Breckinridge, Ky C3 94
Clovis, Fresno, Calif D4 82
Clovis, Curry, N. Mex C6 107
Cloyne, Ire F3 11
Claunie, lake, Scot. C3 13
Cluj-Napoca, Rom B6 22
Clune, Indiana, Pa E3 114
Cluny, Alta., Can D4 69
Cluny, Fr D6 14
Clusone, It B2 18
Cluster Springs, Halifax, Va D4 121
Clute, Brazoria, Tex r14 116
Clutier, Tama, Iowa B5 92
Clyattville, Lowndes, Ga F3 87
Clyde, Alta., Can B4 69
Clyde, N.W. Ter., Can B19 67
Clyde, Cloud, Kans C6 93
Clyde, Nodaway, Mo A3 101
Clyde, Wayne, N.Y B4 108
Clyde, Haywood, N.C f10 109
Clyde, Cavalier, N. Dak A7 110
Clyde, Sandusky, Ohio A3 111
Clyde, Callahan, Tex C3 118
Clyde, firth, Scot E4 13
Clyde, riv., N.S., Can E4 74
Clyde, riv., Scot E4 13
Clydebank, Scot E4 13
Clyde Hill, King, Wash *B3 122
Clyde Park, Park, Mont E6 102
Clymer, Chautauqua, N.Y C1 108
Clymer, Indiana, Pa E3 114
Clyo, Effingham, Ga D5 87
Cnoc Moy, mtn., Scot E3 13
Cnossus, ruins, Grc E5 23
Coachella, Riverside, Calif F5 82
Coachella, canal, Calif F6 82
Coachford, Ire F3 11
Coahoma, Coahoma, Miss A3 100
Coahoma, Howard, Tex C2 118
Coahoma, co., Miss A3 100
Coahuila, state, Mex B4 63
Coal, co., Okla C5 112
Coal, creek, Ind D3 91
Coal, creek, Okla B6 112
Coal, fork, W. Va m12 123
Coal, riv., W. Va E3 123
Coal Bluff, Vigo, Ind E3 91
Coal Branch, N.B., Can C4 74
Coal City, Grundy, Ill B5 90
Coal City, Owen, Ind F3 91
Coalcoman, Mex D4, h12 63
Coal Creek, Fremont, Colo C5 83
Coaldale, Alta., Can E4 69
Coaldale, Fremont, Colo C5 83
Coaldale, Schuylkill, Pa E10 114
Coalfield, Morgan, Tenn C9 117
Coal Fork, Kanawha, W. Va C3, m12 123
Coalgate, Coal, Okla C5 112
Coalgood, Harlan, Ky D6 94
Coal Grove, Lawrence, Ohio D3 111
Coal Harbour, B.C., Can D4 68
Coal Hill, Johnson, Ark B2 81
Coalhurst, Alta., Can E4 69
Coaling, Tuscaloosa, Ala B2 78
Coalinga, Fresno, Calif D3 82
Coalmont, B.C., Can E7 68
Coalmont, Jackson, Colo A4 83
Coalmont, Clay, Ind F3 91
Coalmont, Grundy, Tenn D8 117
Coalport, Clearfield, Pa E4 114
Coalridge, Noble, Ohio C4 111
Coalspur, Alta., Can C2 69
Coalton, Montgomery, Ill D4 90
Coalton, Jackson, Ohio C3 111
Coalton, Okmulgee, Okla B6 112
Coaltown, Lawrence, Pa *D1 114
Coal Valley, Walker, Ala B2 78
Coal Valley, Rock Island, Ill h11 92
Coalville, Eng B6 12
Coalville, Webster, Iowa B3 92
Coalville, Summit, Utah C4 119
Coalwood, Powder River, Mont E11 102
Coalwood, McDowell, W. Va D3 123
Coamo, P.R B3 65
Coamo, mun., P.R *B3 65
Coari, Braz D5 60
Coast, reg., Ken B6 48
Coast, mts., Alsk., B.C., Can E6 66
Coast, ranges, U.S B3 76
Coastal, plain, U.S E2 106, C5 109
Coatbridge, Scot E5 13
Coatepec, Mex n15 63
Coatepeque, Guat C2 62
Coatesville, Hendricks, Ind E4 91
Coatesville, Chester, Pa G10 114
Coaticook, Que., Can D6 73
Coatopa, Sumter, Ala C1 78
Coats, Pratt, Kans E5 93
Coats, Harnett, N.C B4 109
Coats, isl., N.W. Ter., Can D16 67
Coats Land, reg., Ant B9 5
Coatsville, Schuyler, Mo A5 101
Coatzacoalcos (Puerto México), Mex D6 63
Cobalt, Ont., Can p19 72
Cobalt, Middlesex, Conn C6 84
Cobalt, Lemhi, Idaho E4 89
Cobán, Guat C2 62
Cobar, Austl E5 51
Cobb, Sumter, Ga E3 87
Cobb, Caldwell, Ky C2 94
Cobb, Iowa, Wis F3 124
Cobb, co., Ga C2 87
Cobb, isl., Md D4 85
Cobb, riv., Minn G5 99
Cobb Island, Charles, Md D4 85
Cobble Hill, B.C., Can g12 68
Cobble Mountain, res., Mass B2 84
Cobbosseecontee, lake, Maine D3 96
Cobbtown, Tattnall, Ga D4 87
Cobbville, Telfair, Ga E4 87
Cobden, Ont., Can B8 72
Cobden, Union, Ill F4 90
Cobequid, mts., N.S., Can D5 74
Cobh, Ire F3 11
Cobham, riv., Man., Can C4 71
Cobija, Bol B2 55
Cobija, Chile D1 55
Coble, Hickman, Tenn B4 117
Cobleskill, Schoharie, N.Y C6 108
Coboconk, Ont., Can C6 72
Cobourg, Ont., Can D6 72
Cobourg, pen., Austl B5 50
Cobre, Elko, Nev B7 105
Cobun, creek, W. Va h11 123
Coburg, F.R.G C5 17
Coburg, Montgomery, Iowa D2 92
Coburg, Lane, Oreg C3 113
Coburg, isl., N.W. Ter., Can m36 67
Coburn, Centre, Pa E7 114
Coburn, Wetzel, W. Va B4, h10 123
Coburn, mtn., Maine C2 96
Coburn Gore, Franklin, Maine C2 96
Coca, Ec B2 58
Cocanada, see Kakinada, India
Cocentaina, Sp C5 20
Cochabamba, Bol C2 55
Cochabamba, dept., Bol C2 55
Coche, isl., Ven A5 60
Cocheco, riv., N.H D4 105
Cochem, F.R.G C3 17
Cochesett, Plymouth, Mass B5 97
Cochetopa, creek, Colo C4 83
Cochetopa, hills, Colo C4 83
Cochin, India G6 39
Cochin China, reg., Viet G7 38
Cochise, Cochise, Ariz E6 80
Cochise, co., Ariz F5 80
Cochise Head, mtn., Ariz E6 80
Cochiti, Sandoval, N. Mex h8 107
Cochiti, Indian res., N. Mex h8 107
Cochituate, Middlesex, Mass g10 97
Cochituate, lake, Mass g10 97
Cochran, Bleckley, Ga D3 87
Cochran, co., Tex C1 118
Cochrane, Alta., Can D3 69
Cochrane, Ont., Can o19 72
Cochrane, Buffalo, Wis D2 124
Cochrane, dist., Ont., Can o18 72
Cochrane, mtn., Arg D2 54
Cochranton, Crawford, Pa C1 114
Cochranville, Chester, Pa G10 114
Cockburn, Austl F3 51
Cockburn, isl., Ont., Can C7 98
Cocke, co., Tenn D10 117
Cockenzie & Port Seton, Scot *E6 13
Cockermouth, Eng F5 13
Cockeysville, Baltimore, Md B4 85
Cockrell Hill, Dallas, Tex n10 118
Cockrum, De Soto, Miss A4 100
Coco, riv., Hond., Nic C6 62
Cocoa, Brevard, Fla D6 86
Cocoa Beach, Brevard, Fla D6 86
Cocoa West, Brevard, Fla *D6 86
Cocobeach, Gabon E2 46
Cocolalla, Bonner, Idaho A2 89
Coconino, co., Ariz B3 80
Coconino, plat., Ariz B3 80
Cocos, bay, Trin O23 65
Cocos, isl., Guam 52
Cocos, lagoon, Guam 52
Cocos, lake, Ont., Can C5 71
Cocos (Keeling) Is., Austl. dep., Oceania G3 2
Coco Solo, Pan k11 62
Cocula, Mex C4, m12 63
Cocuy, Col B3 60
Cod, cape, Mass B7 97
Cod, isl., Newf., Can g9 75
Codajás, Braz D5 60
Codajás, lake, Braz D5 60
Codell, Rooks, Kans C4 93
Coden, Mobile, Ala E1 78
Coderre, Sask., Can G2 70
Codesa, Alta., Can B1 69
Codette, Sask., Can D3 70
Codigoro, It E8 18
Codington, co., S. Dak C8 116
Codó, Braz B2 57
Codogno, It B2 21
Codpa, Chile C2 55
Codroipo, It D8 15
Codroy, Newf., Can E2 75
Codroy Pond, Newf., Can D2 75
Codrul, mts., Rom B6 22
Cody, Cherry, Nebr B4 103
Cody, Park, Wyo B3 125
Codys, N.B., Can D4 74
Coeburn, Wise, Va f9 121
Coe Hill, Ont., Can C7 72
Coesfeld, F.R.G B2 17
Coesse, Whitley, Ind B7 91
Coeur d'Alene, Kootenai, Idaho B2 89
Coeur d'Alene, lake, Idaho B2 89
Coeur d'Alene, mtn., Idaho g15 122
Coeur d'Alene, mts., Idaho B2 89
Coevorden, Neth B6 15
Coffee, co., Ala D3 78
Coffee, co., Ga E4 87
Coffee, co., Tenn B5 117
Coffee Creek, Fergus, Mont C6 102
Coffeen, Montgomery, Ill D4 90
Coffee Springs, Geneva, Ala D4 78
Coffeeville, Clarke, Ala D1 78
Coffeeville, Yalobusha, Miss B4 100
Coffey, Daviess, Mo A3 101
Coffey, co., Kans D8 93
Coffeyville, Montgomery, Kans E8 93
Coffin, isl., Que., Can B8 74
Coff's Harbour, Austl E9 51
Cofield, Hertford, N.C A6 109
Cogdell, Clinch, Ga E4 87
Coggon, Linn, Iowa B6 92
Coghinas, riv., It D2 21
Coglar, buttes, Oreg E6 113
Cognac, Fr E3 14
Cogswell, Sargent, N. Dak C8 110
Cohagen, Garfield, Mont C10 102
Cohansey, riv., N.J E2 106
Cohasset, Norfolk, Mass B6, h12 97
Cohasset, Itasca, Minn C5 99
Cohay, Smith, Miss D4 100
Cohocton, Steuben, N.Y C3 108
Cohocton, riv., N.Y C3 108
Cohoes, Albany, N.Y C7 108
Cohutta, Whitfield, Ga B2 87
Cohutta, mtn., Ga B2 87
Coiba, isl., Pan G7 62
Coila, Carroll, Miss B4 100
Coimbatore, India F6 39
Coimbra, Port B1 20
Coin, Page, Iowa D2 92
Coín, Sp D3 20
Coinjock, Currituck, N.C A7 109
Coipasa, lake, Bol C2 55
Coipasa, salt flat, Bol C2 55
Coire, lake, Scot B4 13
Cojedes, state, Ven B4 60
Cojutepeque, Sal D3 62
Cokato, Wright, Minn E4 99
Coke, co., Tex D2 118
Cokeburg, Washington, Pa *F1 114
Coker, Tuscaloosa, Ala B2 78
Cokesbury, Greenwood, S.C C3 115
Coketon, Brooke, W. Va f8 123
Coketon, Tucker, W. Va B5 123
Cokeville, Lincoln, Wyo D2 125
Colac, Austl I4 51
Colares, Port f9 20
Colatina, Braz E2 57
Colbeck, cape, Ant B33 5
Colbert, Madison, Ga B3 87
Colbert, Bryan, Okla D5 112
Colbert, co., Ala A2 78
Colborne, Ont., Can D7 72
Colbún, Chile B2 54
Colburn, Bonner, Idaho A2 89
Colburn, Tippecanoe, Ind C4 91
Colby, Thomas, Kans C2 93
Colby, Aroostook, Maine B4 96
Colby, Marathon and Clark, Wis D3 124
Colbyville, Washington, Vt C3 120
Colchagua, prov., Chile A2 54
Colchester, New London, Conn C7 84
Colchester, Eng C8 12
Colchester, McDonough, Ill C3 90
Colchester, Chittenden, Vt B2 120
Colchester, co., N.S., Can D6 74
Colcord, Delaware, Okla A7 112
Cold, lake, Alta., Sask., Can B5 69
Cold, riv., N.H C4 105
Cold, riv., N.H D2 105
Cold Bay, Alsk E7 79
Cold Fell, mtn., Eng F6 13
Cold Hollow, mts., Vt B3 120
Colditz, G.D.R B7 17
Cold Lake, Alta., Can B5 69
Cold River, Cheshire, N.H D2 105
Cold Spring, Campbell, Ky A5, h14 94
Cold Spring, Stearns, Minn E4 99
Cold Spring, Cape May, N.J F3 106
Cold Spring, Putnam, N.Y *D7 108
Coldspring, San Jacinto, Tex D5 118
Cold Spring, hbr., N.Y F3 84
Cold Spring Harbor, Suffolk, N.Y F3 84
Cold Springs, Kiowa, Okla C3 112
Coldstream, Scot E6 13
Cold Stream, pond, Maine C4 96
Coldwater, Ont., Can C5 72
Coldwater, Comanche, Kans E4 93
Coldwater, Branch, Mich G5 98
Coldwater, Tate, Miss A4 100
Coldwater, Mercer, Ohio B1 111
Coldwater, creek, Okla e9 112
Coldwater, creek, Tex A1 118
Coldwater, riv., Miss A3 100
Cole, McClain, Okla B4 112
Cole, co., Mo C5 101
Colebrook, Litchfield, Conn B4 84
Colebrook, Coos, N.H g6 105
Cole Camp, Benton, Mo C4 101
Coleharbor, McLean, N. Dak B4 110
Cole Lake, Ont., Can C8 72
Coleman, Alta., Can E3 69
Coleman, P.E.I., Can C5 74
Coleman, Sumter, Fla D4 86
Coleman, Randolph, Ga E2 87
Coleman, Hancock, Ga C4 87
Coleman, Kent, Md B5 85
Coleman, Midland, Mich E6 98
Coleman, Johnston, Okla C5 112
Coleman, Coleman, Tex D3 118
Coleman, Marinette, Wis C5 124
Coleman, co., Tex D3 118
Coleman, riv., Austl B7 50
Coleman Falls, Bedford, Va C3 121
Colen, lakes, Man., Can B4 71
Colerain, Bertie, N.C A6 109
Coleraine, Austl H3 51
Coleraine, N. Ire B5 11
Coleraine, Itasca, Minn C5 99
Coleridge, Cedar, Nebr B8 103
Coleridge, Randolph, N.C B3 109
Coles, Amite, Miss D2 100
Coles, co., Ill D5 90
Colesberg, S. Afr D4 49
Colesburg, Camden, Ga F5 87
Colesburg, Delaware, Iowa B6 92
Colesburg, Hardin, Ky C4 94
Colestin, Jackson, Oreg E4 113
Coleta, Whiteside, Ill B4 90
Coleville, Sask., Can F1 70
Coleville, Mono, Calif C4 82
Coley's Point South, Newf., Can *E5 75
Coleyville, Cottle, Tex B2 118
Colfax, Placer, Calif C3 82
Colfax, Sask., Can H4 70
Colfax, McLean, Ill C5 90
Colfax, Clinton, Ind D4 91
Colfax, Jasper, Iowa C4 92
Colfax, Grant, La C3 95
Colfax, Richland, N. Dak C9 110
Colfax, Whitman, Wash C8 122
Colfax, Dunn, Wis D2 124
Colfax, co., Nebr C8 103
Colfax, co., N. Mex A5 107
Colgate, Sask., Can H4 70
Colgate, Washington, Wis E1 124
Colibris, pt., Guad Q9 65
Colico, It C5 18
Colijnsplaat, Neth C3 15
Colima, Mex D4, n12 63
Colima, state, Mex D4, n12 63
Colinas, Braz C2 57
Colinet, Newf., Can E5 75
Colington, Dare, N.C A7 109
Colinton, Alta., Can B4 69
Coll, isl., Scot D3 13
Collbran, Mesa, Colo B3 83
College, Alsk C10 79
College Corner, Preble and Butler, Ohio C1 111
Collegedale, Hamilton, Tenn h11 117
College Gardens, Stanislaus, Calif *D3 82
College Grove, Williamson, Tenn B5 117
College Park, Fulton and Clayton, Ga C2, h8 87
College Park, Prince Georges, Md C4, f9 85
College Place, Richland, S.C C5 115
College Place, Walla Walla, Wash C7 122
College Springs, Page, Iowa D2 92
College Station, Brazos, Tex D4 118
College View, Arapahoe, Colo *B6 83
Collegeville, Saline, Ark D5 81
Collegeville, Jasper, Ind C3 91
Collegeville (P.O.), Stearns, Minn *E4 99
Collegeville, Montgomery, Pa F11 114
College Ward, Cache, Utah *B4 119
Colleton, co., S.C F6 115
Collie, Austl F2 50
Collier, co., Fla F5 86
Collier, bay, Austl C3 50
Colliers, Brooke, W. Va f8 123
Collierville, Shelby, Tenn B2 117
Collin, co., Tex C4 118
Collingdale, Delaware, Pa p20 114
Collingswood, Camden, N.J D2 106
Collingsworth, co., Tex B2 118
Collingwood, Ont., Can C4 72
Collins, Drew, Ark D4 81
Collins, Tattnall, Ga D4 87
Collins, Whitley, Ind B7 91
Collins, Story, Iowa C4 92
Collins, Covington, Miss D4 100
Collins, St. Clair, Mo D4 101
Collins, Manitowoc, Wis h10 124
Collins Park, New Castle, Del *A6 85
Collinston, Morehouse, La B4 95
Collinston, Box Elder, Utah B3 119
Collins View, Multnomah, Oreg *B4 113
Collinsville, DeKalb, Ala A4 78
Collinsville, Hartford, Conn B5 84
Collinsville, DeKalb, Ga h8 87
Collinsville, Madison and St. Clair, Ill E4 90
Collinsville, Lauderdale, Miss C5 100
Collinsville, Tulsa, Okla A6 112
Collinsville, Henry, Va D3 121
Collinwood, Wayne, Tenn B4 117
Collipulli, Chile B2 54
Collis, Traverse, Minn E2 99
Collister, Ada, Idaho F2 89
Collo, Alg B6 44
Collooney, Ire C3 11
Collyer, Trego, Kans C3 93
Colman, Moody, S. Dak D9 116
Colmar, Fr C7 14, A3 18
Colmar, Bell, Ky D6 94
Colmar Manor, Prince Georges, Md f9 85
Colmenar de Oreja, Sp B4 20
Colmenar Viejo, Sp B4, o17 20
Colmesneil, Tyler, Tex D5 118
Colo, Story, Iowa B4 92
Cologne (Köln), F.R.G C3 16
Cologne, Carver, Minn F5 99
Cologne, Atlantic, N.J D3 106
Cologne, King and Queen, Va C6 121
Coloma, Berrien, Mich F4 98
Coloma, Waushara, Wis D4 124
Colombes, Fr g10 14
Colombia, Col C3 60
Colombia, country, S.A C3 53, C3 60
Colombier, Switz C2 19
Colombo, Sri Lanka G6 39
Colome, Tripp, S. Dak D6 116
Colón, Arg A5 54
Colón, Cuba C3 64
Colon, St. Joseph, Mich G5 98
Colon, Saunders, Nebr g11 103
Colon, Lee, N.C B3 109
Colón, Pan F8, k11 62
Colón, Archipiélago de (Galápagos Is.), prov., Ec g5 58
Colona, Ouray, Colo C3 83
Colonia, Middlesex, N.J k7 106
Colonia, Ur E1 56
Colonia, dept., Ur *E1 56
Colonia, Yap 52
Colonia Dora, Arg E3 55
Colonia Gustavo A. Madero, Mex h9 63
Colonia Las Heras, Arg D3 54
Colonial Beach, Westmoreland, Va C6 121
Colônia Leopoldina, Braz k6 57
Colonial Heights, Sullivan, Tenn C11 117
Colonial Heights (Independent City), Va C5, n18 121
Colonial Manor, Gloucester, N.J *D2 106
Colonial Park, Dauphin, Pa *F8 114
Colonia Mennonita, Par D4 55
Colonia Sarmiento, Arg D3 54
Colonia Suiza, Ur g8 54
Colonie, Albany, N.Y C7 108
Colonna, It h9 21
Colonne, cape, It E6 21
Colonsay, Sask., Can F3 70
Colonsay, isl., Scot D2 13
Colony, Anderson, Kans D8 93
Colony, Washita, Okla B3 112
Colorado, C.R E6 62
Colorado, state, U.S C6, 76 83
Colorado, co., Tex E4 118
Colorado, nat. mon., Colo B2 83
Colorado, plat., Ariz A3 80
Colorado, plat., N. Mex B1 107
Colorado, riv., Arg B3 54
Colorado, riv., Tex D3 118
Colorado, riv., U.S D5 76
Colorado City, Mohave, Ariz A3 80
Colorado City, Pueblo, Colo D6 83
Colorado City, Mitchell, Tex C2 118
Colorado River, Indian res., Ariz D1 80
Colorados, arch., Cuba C1 64
Colorado Springs, El Paso, Colo C6 83
Colored Hill, Mercer, W. Va *D3 123
Coloso, Chile D1 55
Colotepec, Mex D5 63
Colotlán, Mex C4, k12 63
Colquechaca, Bol C2 55
Colquitt, Miller, Ga E2 87
Colquitt, Claiborne, La B3 95
Colquitt, co., Ga E3 87
Colrain, Franklin, Mass A2 97
Colstrip, Rosebud, Mont E10 102
Colt, St. Francis, Ark B5 81
Coltauco, Chile A2 54
Colton, San Bernardino, Calif *E5 82
Colton, St. Lawrence, N.Y f10 108
Colton, Clackamas, Oreg B4 113
Colton, Minnehaha, S. Dak D9 116
Colton, Utah, Utah D5 119
Colton, Whitman, Wash C8 122
Colton, hill, Vt D4 120
Coltons Point, St. Marys, Md D4 85
Colts Neck, Monmouth, N.J C4 106
Columbia, Houston, Ala D4 78
Columbia, Tolland, Conn C7 84
Columbia, Monroe, Ill E3 90
Columbia, Adair, Ky C4 94
Columbia, Caldwell, La B3 95
Columbia, Howard, Md B4 85
Columbia, Marion, Miss D4 100
Columbia, Boone, Mo C5 101
Columbia, Warren, N.J B2 106
Columbia, Tyrrell, N.C B7 109
Columbia, Lancaster, Pa F9 114
Columbia, Richland, S.C D5 115
Columbia, Brown, S. Dak B7 116
Columbia, Maury, Tenn B4 117
Columbia, Fluvanna, Va C4 121
Columbia, co., Ark D2 81
Columbia, co., Fla B4 86
Columbia, co., Ga C4 87
Columbia, co., N.Y C7 108
Columbia, co., Oreg B3 113
Columbia, co., Pa D9 114
Columbia, co., Wash C7 122
Columbia, co., Wis E4 124
Columbia, basin, Wash C6 122
Columbia, cape, N.W. Ter., Can A22 4
Columbia, dam, Ala., Ga E1 87
Columbia, lake, B.C., Can D10 68
Columbia, lake, Conn C7 84
Columbia, mtn., Alta., Can C2 69
Columbia, mts., Mex B2 63
Columbia, riv., Can., U.S G9 66
Columbia Bridge, Coos, N.H B1 105
Columbia City, Whitley, Ind B7 91
Columbia City, Columbia, Oreg B4 113
Columbia Cross Roads, Bradford, Pa C8 114
Columbia Falls, Washington, Maine D5 96
Columbia Falls, Flathead, Mont B2 102
Columbia Heights, Anoka, Minn m12 99
Columbia Heights, Cowlitz, Wash *C3 122
Columbiana, Shelby, Ala B3 78
Columbiana, Columbiana, Ohio B5 111
Columbiana, co., Ohio B5 111
Columbia Park (Pittsburg East), Contra Costa, Calif *h8 82
Columbia Station, Lorain, Ohio *A3 111
Columbiaville, Lapeer, Mich E7 98
Columbus, Hempstead, Ark D2 81
Columbus, Muscogee, Ga D2 87
Columbus, Bartholomew, Ind F6 91
Columbus, Cherokee, Kans E9 93
Columbus, Hickman, Ky f8 94
Columbus, Lowndes, Miss B5 100
Columbus, Stillwater, Mont E7 102
Columbus, Platte, Nebr C8 103
Columbus, Burlington, N.J C3 106
Columbus, Luna, N. Mex F2 107
Columbus, Polk, N.C f10 109
Columbus, Burke, N. Dak A3 110
Columbus, Franklin, Ohio C3, m11 111
Columbus, Warren, Pa C2 114
Columbus, Colorado, Tex E4 118
Columbus, Columbus, Wis E4 124
Columbus, co., N.C C4 109
Columbus City, Louisa, Iowa C6 92
Columbus Grove, Putnam, Ohio B1 111
Columbus Junction, Louisa, Iowa C6 92
Columbus Manor, Cook, Ill *B6 90
Colusa, Colusa, Calif C2 82
Colusa, co., Calif C2 82
Colver, Cambria, Pa E4 114
Colville, Stevens, Wash A8 122
Colville, isl., N.W. Ter., Can C7 66
Colville, lake, Wash B7 122
Colville, riv., Alsk B9 79
Colville, riv., Wash A8 122
Colvin, mtn., Ala B4 78
Colvos, chan., Wash f10 122
Colwich, Sedgwick, Kans E6, g11 93
Colwood, B.C., Can h12 68
Colwyn, Delaware, Pa *G11 114
Colwyn Bay, Wales A4 12
Colyell, creek, La h10 95
Comacchio, It B4 21
Comal, co., Tex E3 118
Comalapa, Guat C2 62
Coman, mtn., Ant B6 6
Comanche, Stephens, Okla C4 112
Comanche, Comanche, Tex D3 118
Comanche, co., Kans E4 93
Comanche, co., Okla C3 112
Comanche, co., Tex C3 118
Comarapa, Bol C3 55
Comayagua, Hond C4 62
Combahee, riv., S.C F6 115
Combarbalá, Chile A2 54
Combeaufontaine, Fr B1 18
Comber, Ont., Can E2 72
Comber, N. Ire C6 11
Combermere, Ont., Can B7 72
Combined Locks, Outagamie, Wis h9 124
Combs, Madison, Ark B2 81
Combs, Perry, Ky C6 94
Comer, Barbour, Ala C4 78
Comer, Madison, Ga B3 87
Comeragh, mts., Ire E4 11
Comerio, P.R B3 65
Comerío, mun., P.R *B3 65
Comertown, Sheridan, Mont B12 102
Comfort, Jones, N.C C5 109
Comfort, Kendall, Tex E3 118
Comfort, Boone, W. Va m12 123
Comfrey, Brown, Minn F4 99
Comilla, Bngl D9 39
Comines, Bel D2 15
Comins, Oscoda, Mich D6 98
Comiso, It F5 21
Comitán, Mex D6 63
Comite, riv., La D4 95
Commack, Suffolk, N.Y F3 84
Commentry, Fr D5 14
Commerce, Conecuh, Ala D3 78
Commerce, Los Angeles, Calif *F5 82
Commerce, Jackson, Ga B3 87
Commerce, Oakland, Mich *F7 98
Commerce, Scott, Mo D8 101
Commerce, Ottawa, Okla A7 112
Commerce, Hunt, Tex C5 118
Commerce City, Adams, Colo B6 83
Commercial Point, Pickaway, Ohio C2 111
Commercy, Fr C6 14
Commiskey, Jennings, Ind G6 91
Committee, bay, N.W. Ter., Can C15 66
Common Fence Point, Newport, R.I *C12 84
Commonwealth, bay, Ant C27 5
Commonwealth, range, Ant A30 5
Communism, peak, Sov. Un H23 9
Como, Que., Can q18 73
Como, It B2 21
Como, Panola, Miss A4 100
Como, Hertford, N.C A5 109
Como, Henry, Tenn A3 117
Como, lake, It B2 21
Comobabi, Pima, Ariz E4 80
Comodoro Rivadavia, Arg D3 54
Comoros, country, Afr H10 42, f9 49
Comox, B.C., Can E5 68
Compass Lake, Jackson, Fla B1, u16 86
Compeer, Alta., Can D5 69
Competition, Laclede, Mo D5 101
Compiègne, Fr C5 14
Comptche, Mendocino, Calif C2 82
Compton, Los Angeles, Calif n12 82
Compton, Que., Can D6 73
Compton, co., Que., Can D6 73
Compton, Lee, Ill B4 90
Comstock, Kalamazoo, Mich F5 98
Comstock, Clay, Minn D2 99
Comstock, Custer, Nebr C6 103
Comstock, Val Verde, Tex E2 118
Comstock, Barron, Wis C1 124
Comstock Park, Kent, Mich *E5 98
Conakry, Guinea E2 45
Conanicut, isl., R.I C11 84
Conasauga, Polk, Tenn D9 117
Concarneau, Fr D2 14
Conceição do Norte, Braz D1 57
Concepción, Arg E2 55
Concepción, Bol C3 55
Concepción, Bol D3 55
Concepción, Chile B2 54
Concepción, Guat C2 62
Concepción, Pan F6 62
Concepción, Par D4 55
Concepcion, Phil o13 35
Concepcion, Duval, Tex F3 118
Concepción, dept., Par D4 55
Concepción, prov., Chile B2 54
Concepción del Oro, Mex C4 63
Concepción del Uruguay, Arg A5 54
Conception, Nodaway, Mo A3 101
Conception, bay, Newf., Can E5 75
Conception, isl., Ba C6 64
Conception, pt., Calif E3 82
Conception Harbour, Newf., Can *E5 75
Conception Junction, Nodaway, Mo A3 101
Conchas, Braz m7 56
Conchas Dam, San Miguel, N. Mex B5 107
Conchas Lake, res., N. Mex B5 107
Conche, Newf., Can C4 75
Conchi, Chile D2 55
Conchillas, Ur g7 54
Concho, Apache, Ariz C6 80
Concho, Canadian, Okla B4 112
Concho, co., Tex D3 118
Conconully, Okanogan, Wash A6 122
Concord, Contra Costa, Calif h8 82
Concord, Gadsden, Fla B2 86
Concord, Pike, Ga C2 87
Concord, Morgan, Ill D3 90
Concord, Lewis, Ky B6 94
Concord, Middlesex, Mass B5, g10 97
Concord, Jackson, Mich F6 98
Concord, St. Louis, Mo f13 101
Concord, Dixon, Nebr B9 103
Concord, Merrimack, N.H D3 105
Concord, Cabarrus, N.C B2 109
Concord, Franklin, Pa F6 114
Concord, Knox, Tenn D9, n13 117
Concord, Essex, Vt C5 120
Concord, Campbell, Va C4 121
Concord, riv., Mass A5 97
Concordia, Arg A5 54
Concordia, Col B2 60
Concordia, Cloud, Kans C6 93
Concordia, Lafayette, Mo C4 101
Concordia, par., La C4 95

Concrete, Pembina, N. Dak...A8 110
Concrete, Skagit, Wash....A4 122
Conda, Caribou, Idaho....G7 89
Conde, Braz....D3 57
Conde, Spink, S. Dak....B7 116
Condé [-sur-l'Escaut], Fr....D3 15
Condé-sur-Marne, Fr....E4 15
Condé-sur-Noireau, Fr....C3 14
Condeúba, Braz....D2 57
Condino, It....D6 18
Condobolin, Austl....F6 51
Condom, Fr....F4 14
Condon, Missoula, Mont....C3 102
Condon, Gilliam, Oreg....B6 113
Condor, range, Peru....B2 58
Cone, Crosby, Tex....C2 118
Conecuh, co., Ala....D2 78
Conecuh, riv., Ala....D3 78
Conegliano, It....B4 21
Conehatta, Newton, Miss....C4 100
Conejos, Conejos, Colo....D4 83
Conejos, co., Colo....D4 83
Conejos, peak, Colo....D4 83
Conejos, riv., Colo....D4 83
Conemaugh, Cambria, Pa....F4 114
Conemaugh River Lake, res., Pa.F3 114
Cones, Coos, N.H....B1 105
Conestee, Greenville, S.C....B3 115
Conesville, Muscatine, Iowa.C6 92
Conesville, Coshocton, Ohio.B4 111
Conetoe, Edgecomb, N.C....B5 109
Coney, isl., N.Y.....k13 108
Conflans-en-Jarnisy, Fr....E5 15
Conflans-Ste. Honorine, Fr...g9 14
Confluence, Leslie, Ky....C6 94
Confluence, Somerset, Pa....G3 114
Confolens, Fr....D4 14
Confusion, bay, Newf., Can....C4 75
Confusion, range, Utah....D2 119
Cong, Ire....D2 11
Congamond, Hampden, Mass....B2 97
Congamond, lakes, Conn., Mass.B2 97
Congaree, riv., S.C.....D6 115
Conger, Freeborn, Minn....G5 99
Congers, Rockland, N.Y...*D7 108
Congleton, Eng....A5 12
Congo, Perry, Ohio....C3 111
Congo, Hancock, W. Va....e8 123
Congo, country, Afr....G7 42, B2 48
Congo, The, see Zaire, country, Afr.
Congo (Zaire), riv., Afr....G7 42
Congress, Yavapai, Ariz....C3 80
Congress, Sask., Can....H2 70
Conifer, St. Lawrence, N.Y....A6, f10 108
Conil, Sp....D2 20
Coniston, Ont., Can....A4, p19 72
Coniston Water, lake, Eng....F5 13
Conklin, Alta., Can....B5 69
Conklin, Ottawa, Mich....E5 98
Conklin, Broome, N.Y....C5 108
Conklin, pt., N.Y.....G3 84
Conlen, Dallam, Tex....A1 118
Conn, lake, Ire....C2 11
Connacht, prov., Ire....D2 11
Conneaut, Ashtabula, Ohio..A5 111
Conneaut, creek, Ohio....A5 111
Conneaut Lake, Crawford, Pa....C1 114
Conneautville, Crawford, Pa.C1 114
Connecticut, state, U.S..B13 77, 84
Connecticut, lake, N.H.....A2 105
Connecticut, riv., U.S.....B2 97
Connell, Franklin, Wash....C7 122
Connell, mtn., B.C., Can....A1 102
Connellsville, Fayette, Pa....F2 114
Connelsville, Adair, Mo....A5 101
Connemara, mts., Ire....D2 11
Conner, Ravalli, Mont....E2 102
Connersville, Fayette, Ind....E7 91
Connerville, Johnston, Okla..C5 112
Connoire, bay, Newf., Can....E3 75
Connor, N.B., Can....B1 74
Conococheague, creek, Md....A2 85
Conover, Catawba, N.C....B1 109
Conowingo, Cecil, Md....A5 85
Conowingo, dam, Md....A5 85
Conquest, Sask., Can....F2 70
Conrad, Grundy, Iowa....B5 92
Conrad, Pondera, Mont....B5 102
Conrad, Potter, Pa....C5 114
Conran, New Madrid, Mo....E8 101
Conrath, Rusk, Wis....C2 124
Conroe, Montgomery, Tex...D5 118
Conroy, Iowa, Iowa....C6 92
Consecon, Ont., Can....D7 72
Conselheiro Lafaiete, Braz...F2 57
Consett, Eng....F7 13
Conshohocken, Montgomery, Pa....F11, o20 114
Consolación del Sur, Cuba...C2 64
Consort, Alta., Can....C5 69
Constable, Franklin, N.Y....f10 108
Constableville, Lewis, N.Y...B5 108
Constance, Boone, Ky....*A5 94
Constance, mtn., Wash....B2 122
Constanța, Rom....C9 22
Constantia, Oswego, N.Y....B5 108
Constantina, Sp....D3 20
Constantine, Alg...B6 44, F10 30
Constantine, St. Joseph, Mich....G5 98
Constantine, dept., Alg....*F10 30
Constantinople, see İstanbul, Tur.
Constitución, Chile....B2 54
Constitution, De Kalb, Ga..*C2 88
Consuegra, Sp....C4 20
Consul, Marengo, Ala....C2 78
Consul, Sask., Can....H1 70
Contact, Elko, Nev....B7 104
Contai, India....G11 40
Contamana, Peru....C3 58
Contendas, Braz....D2 57
Content, keys, Fla....H5 86
Continental, Putnam, Ohio..A1 111
Continental, divide, Can., U.S.....E6 66, B6 76
Continental, res., Colo....D3 83
Continental Divide, McKinley, N. Mex....B1 107
Contoocook, Merrimack, N.H....D3 105
Contoocook, riv., N.H.....D3 105
Contraalmirante Cordero, Arg....B3 54
Contra Costa, co., Calif....D2 82
Contratación, Col....B3 60
Contrecoeur, Que., Can....D4 73
Contreras, Mex....h9 53
Contreras, Socorro, N. Mex..C3 107
Contrexéville, Fr....A1 18
Contumaza, Peru....C2 58
Contwoyto, lake, N.W. Ter., Can....C10 66
Convent, St. James, La.D5, h10 95
Converse, Miami, Ind....C6 91
Converse, Sabine, La....C2 95
Converse, Spartanburg, S.C..B4 115
Converse, co., Wyo....C7 125
Converse, lake, Ala....E1 78
Convoy, Van Wert, Ohio....B1 111
Conway, Faulkner, Ark....B3 81
Conway, P.E.I., Can....C6 74
Conway, Orange, Fla....D5 86
Conway, Taylor, Iowa....D3 92
Conway, McPherson, Kans...D6 93
Conway, Franklin, Mass....A2 97
Conway, Leake, Miss....C4 100
Conway, Laclede, Mo....D5 101
Conway, Carroll, N.H....C4 105
Conway, Northampton, N.C.A5 109
Conway, Walsh, N. Dak....A8 110
Conway, Beaver, Pa....E1 114
Conway, Horry, S.C....D9 115
Conway, Carson, Tex....B2 118
Conway, Wales....A4 12
Conway, co., Ark....B3 81
Conway, lake, N.H....C4 105
Conway Springs, Sumner, Kans....E6 93
Conyers, Rockdale, Ga..C2, h8 87
Cooch Behār, India....D12 40
Cook, Austl....F5 50
Cook, St. Louis, Minn....C6 99
Cook, Johnson, Nebr....D9 103
Cook, co., Ga....E3 87
Cook, co., Ill....B6 90
Cook, co., Minn....A6 99
Cook, cape, B.C., Can....D4 68
Cook, inlet, Alsk....D9 79
Cook, mtn., W. Va....n12 123
Cook, pt., Md....C5 85
Cook, strait, N.Z.....N15 51
Cooke, co., Tex....C4 118
Cooke City, Park, Mont....E7 102
Cookes, peak, N. Mex....E2 107
Cookeville, Putnam, Tenn....C8 117
Cooking, lake, Alta., Can....C4 69
Cook Islands, N.Z. dep., Oceania....H12 7
Cooks, Schoolcraft, Mich....C4 98
Cooksburg, Forest, Pa....D3 114
Cooks Falls, Delaware, N.Y..D5 108
Cook's Harbour, Newf., Can.C4 75
Cookshire, Que., Can....D6 73
Cooks Knob, mtn., Mo....C4 101
Cookstown, Ont., Can....C5 72
Cookstown, Burlington, N.J..C3 106
Cookstown, N. Ire....C5 11
Cooksville, Ont., Can..D5, m14 72
Cooksville, McLean, Ill....C5 90
Cooktown, Austl....C8 50
Cookville, Titus, Tex....C5 118
Coolaney, Ire....C3 11
Cooleemee, Davie, N.C....B2 109
Coolgardie, Austl....F3 50
Coolidge, Pinal, Ariz....E4 80
Coolidge, Thomas, Ga....E3 87
Coolidge, Hamilton, Kans...D2 93
Coolidge, Limestone, Tex....D4 118
Coolin, Bonner, Idaho....A2 89
Cool Ridge, Raleigh, W. Va.D3 123
Coolspring, Jefferson, Pa....D3 114
Cool Valley, St. Louis, Mo.*C7 101
Coolville, Athens, Ohio....C4 111
Cooma, Austl....H7 51
Coonabarabran, Austl....E7 51
Coonamble, Austl....E7 51
Coon Rapids, Carroll, Iowa..C3 92
Coon Rapids, Anoka, Minn.m12 99
Coon Valley, Vernon, Wis...E3 124
Cooper, Chilton, Ala....C3 78
Cooper, Greene, Iowa....C3 92
Cooper, Wayne, Ky....D5 94
Cooper, Washington, Maine.D5 96
Cooper, Osage, Okla....A5 112
Cooper, Delta, Tex....C5 118
Cooper, co., Mo....C5 101
Cooper, mtn., Wyo....C5 125
Cooper, riv., S.C.....E8 115
Co-Operative, McCreary, Ky....D5 94
Cooper Lake, Albany, Wyo..E7 125
Cooper Road, Caddo, La....*B2 95
Coopersburg, Lehigh, Pa....E10 114
Coopers Mills, Lincoln, Maine....D3 96
Cooperstown, Otsego, N.Y...C6 108
Cooperstown, Griggs, N. Dak.B7 110
Cooperstown, Venango, Pa....D2 114
Cooperstown, Manitowoc, Wis....h10 124
Coopersville, Ottawa, Mich...E5 98
Cooperton, Kiowa, Okla....C3 112
Coopertown, Robertson, Tenn....A5 117
Coorg, state, India....*F6 39
Coos, co., N.H....A4 105
Coos, co., Oreg....D2 113
Coos, riv., Oreg....D2 113
Coosa, co., Ala....C3 78
Coosa, riv., Ala., Ga....A4 78
Coosada, Elmore, Ala....C3 78
Coosawattee, riv., Ga....B2 87
Coosawhatchie, Jasper, S.C..F6 115
Coosawhatchie, riv., S.C.....F5 115
Coos Bay, Coos, Oreg....D2 113
Coos Junction, Coos, N.H....A3 105
Cootamundra, Austl....G7 51
Cootehill, Ire....C4 11
Cooter, Pemiscot, Mo....E7 101
Copacabana, Arg....E2 55
Copacabana, Bol....C2 55
Copainalá, Mex....D6 63
Copake, Columbia, N.Y....C7 108
Copalis Beach, Grays Harbor, Wash....B1 122
Copalis Crossing, Grays Harbor, Wash....B1 122
Copán, Hond....C3 62
Copan, Washington, Okla...A6 112
Cope, Washington, Colo....B8 83
Cope, Orangeburg, S.C....E5 115
Copeland, Collier, Fla....G5 86
Copeland, Boundary, Idaho..A2 89
Copeland, Gray, Kans....E3 93
Copemish, Manistee, Mich...D5 98
Copen, Braxton, W. Va....C4 123
Copenhagen (København), Den....C6 24
Copenhagen, Lewis, N.Y....B5 108
Copenhagen (København), co., Den....C6 24
Copetonas, Arg....B4 54
Copeville, Collin, Tex....m10 118
Copiague, Suffolk, N.Y....G3 84
Copiah, co., Miss....D3 100
Copiapó, Chile....E1 55
Copinsay, isl., Scot....B6 13
Coplay, Lehigh, Pa....E10 114
Copley, Summit, Ohio....*A4 111
Copparo, It....B3 21
Copper, mts., Ariz....E2 80
Copper, ridge, Tenn....m13 117
Copper, riv., Alsk....C11 79
Copperas Cove, Coryell, Tex.D4 118
Copperbelt, prov., Zambia...D4 48
Copper Center, Alsk...C10, g19 79
Copper Cliff, Ont., Can....A3 72
Copper Harbor, Keweenaw, Mich....A3 98
Copperhill, Polk, Tenn....D9 117
Copper Hill, Floyd, Va....C2 121
Coppermine, N.W. Ter., Can....C9 66
Coppermine, riv., N.W. Ter., Can....C10 66
Copper Mountain, B.C., Can.E7 68
Copperton, Salt Lake, Utah.*C3 119
Coppet, Switz....D1 19
Copton, creek, Alta., Can....B1 69
Coquet, riv., Eng....E7 13
Coquilhatville, see Mbandaka, Zaire
Coquille, Coos, Oreg....D2 113
Coquimbana, Chile....E1 55
Coquimbo, Chile....E1 55
Coquimbo, prov., Chile....A2 54
Cora, Iberville, La....B5 95
Cora, Logan, W. Va....*D2 123
Cora, Sublette, Wyo....D3 125
Corabia, Rom....D7 22
Coracora, Peru....E3 58
Coral, Montcalm, Mich....E5 98
Coral, Indiana, Pa....F3 114
Coral, sea, Pac. O....G9 7
Coral Gables, Dade, Fla.G6, s13 86
Coral Rapids, Ont., Can....o19 72
Coralville, Johnson, Iowa....C6 92
Coram, Flathead, Mont....B2 102
Coraopolis, Allegheny, Pa....E1, h13 114
Corato, It....D6 21
Corazón, Ec....B2 58
Corbeil, Fr....C5 14
Corbeny, Fr....E3 15
Corbett, Delaware, N.Y....C5 108
Corbetton, Ont., Can....C4 72
Corbie, Fr....C5 14
Corbin, Sumner, Kans....E6 93
Corbin, Whitley and Knox, Ky....D5 94
Corbin, Livingston, La....h10 95
Corbin, Jefferson, Mont....D4 102
Corbin City, Atlantic, N.J...E3 106
Corby, Eng....B7 12
Corcoran, Kings, Calif....D4 82
Corcoran, Hennepin, Minn.m11 99
Corcovado, gulf, Chile....C2 54
Cord, Independence, Ark....B4 81
Cordaville, Worcester, Mass..g9 97
Cordele, Crisp, Ga....E3 87
Cordell (New Cordell), Washita, Okla....B3 112
Cordell Hull, glacier, Ant....B35 5
Corder, Lafayette, Mo....B4 101
Cordesville, Berkeley, S.C....E8 115
Cordillera, dept., Par....D4 55
Cordillera Central, range, Bol., Col....C2 55, C2 60
Cordillera Occidental, range, Bol., Col....C2 55, C2 60
Cordillera Occidental o de la Costa, range, Peru....D3 58
Cordillera Oriental, range, Bol., Col....C3 55, B3 60
Córdoba, Arg....A4 54
Córdoba, Mex....n15 63
Córdoba, Sp....D3 20
Córdoba, prov., Arg....A4 54
Córdoba, dept., Col....B2 60
Córdoba, prov., Sp....*D3 20
Cordon, Phil....n13 35
Cordova, Walker, Ala....B2 78
Cordova, Alsk....C10, g19 79
Cordova, Rock Island, Ill....B3 90
Cordova, Talbot, Md....C6 85
Cordova, Seward, Nebr....D8 103
Cordova, Rio Arriba, N. Mex....B4 107
Cordova, Richmond, N.C....C3 109
Córdova, Peru....D2 58
Cordova, Orangeburg, S.C...E6 115
Cordova, see Córdoba, prov. and city, Sp.
Cordova, Shelby, Tenn....B2 117
Cordova, peak, Alsk....g19 79
Cordova Mines, Ont., Can...C7 72
Corea, Hancock, Maine....D5 96
Coreaú, Braz....B2 57
Corella, Sp....A5 20
Corfu, Genesee, N.Y....C2 108
Corfu, see Kerkira, isl., Grc.
Cori, It....h9 21
Coria, Sp....C2 20
Corigliano, Calabro, It....E6 21
Corine, key, Fla....G6 86
Corinna, Penobscot, Maine..D3 96
Corinne, Box Elder, Utah....B3 119
Corinne, Wyoming, W. Va..*D3 123
Corinth, see Kórinthos, Grc.
Corinth, Heard, Ga....C2 87
Corinth, Grant, Ky....B5 94
Corinth, Alcorn, Miss....A5 100
Corinth, Saratoga, N.Y....B7 108
Corinth, Orange, Vt....C4 120
Corinth, Preston, W. Va....B5 123
Corinth, bay, Grc....h9 23
Corinth, canal, Grc....h10 23
Corinth, gulf, Grc....C4 23
Corinthia (Korinthia), prov., Grc....*D4 23
Corinto, Braz....E2 57
Corinto, Nic....D4 62
Corisco, isl., Equat. Gui....E1 46
Cork, Ire....F3 11
Cork, co., Ire....F3 11
Cork, hbr., Ire....E2 10
Cork Station, N.B., Can....D3 74
Corleone, It....F4 21
Çorlu, Tur....B6 31
Cormeilles-en-Parisis, Fr....g9 14
Cormoran, reef, Palau Is.... 52
Cormorant, Man., Can....B1 71
Cormorant, lake, Man., Can....B1 71
Corn, Washita, Okla....B3 112
Corn, is., Cen. Am....D6 62
Cornelia, Habersham, Ga....B3 87
Cornelius, Mecklenburg, N.C.B2 109
Cornelius, Washington, Oreg....g11 113
Cornell, Livingston, Ill....C5 90
Cornell, Chippewa, Wis....C2 124
Corner Brook, Newf., Can...D3 75
Cornersville, Marshall, Tenn.B5 117
Cornerville, Lincoln, Ark....D4 81
Cornfield, pt., Conn....D7 84
Cornhill, N.B., Can....D4 74
Cornimont, Fr....B2 18
Corning, Clay, Ark....A5 81
Corning, Tehama, Calif....C2 82
Corning, Sask., Can....H4 70
Corning, Adams, Iowa....D3 92
Corning, Nemaha, Kans....C7 93
Corning, Holt, Mo....A2 101
Corning, Steuben, N.Y....C3 108
Corning, Perry, Ohio....C3 111
Corning, Lincoln, Wis....C4 124
Cornish, Weld, Colo....A5 83
Cornish, York, Maine....E2 96
Cornish, Jefferson, Okla....C4 112
Cornish, Cache, Utah....B4 119
Cornish Flat, Sullivan, N.H..D2 105
Cornishville, Mercer, Ky....C5 94
Corno, mtn., It....C4 21
Cornucopia, Baker, Oreg....C9 113
Cornucopia, Bayfield, Wis...B2 124
Cornudas, Hudspeth, Tex....F1 118
Cornville, Yavapai, Ariz....C4 80
Cornville, Somerset, Maine..D3 96
Cornwall, Ont., Can....B10 72
Cornwall, Litchfield, Conn...B3 84
Cornwall, Lebanon, Pa....F9 114
Cornwall, Addison, Vt....D2 120
Cornwall, Rockbridge, Va....C3 121
Cornwall, co., Eng....D3 12
Cornwall, isl., N.W. Ter., Can....m32 67
Cornwall Bridge, Litchfield, Conn....B3 84
Cornwallis, isl., N.W. Ter., Can....m32 67
Cornwall-on-the-Hudson, Orange, N.Y....D6 108
Cornwells Heights, Bucks, Pa....o22 114
Coro, Ven....A4 60
Coroatá, Braz....B2 57
Corocoro, Bol....C2 55
Coroico, Bol....C2 55
Corolla, Currituck, N.C....A7 109
Coromandel, N.Z....L15 51
Coromandel, coast, India....F7 39
Corona, Walker, Ala....B2 78
Corona, Riverside, Calif.F5, n13 82
Corona, Lincoln, N. Mex....C4 107
Corona, Roberts, S. Dak....B9 116
Coronaca, Greenwood, S.C..C3 115
Coronach, Sask., Can....H3 70
Coronado, San Diego, Calif....F5, o15 82
Coronado, bay, C.R....F6 62
Coronation, Alta., Can....C5 69
Coronation, gulf, N.W. Ter., Can....C10 66
Coronation, isl., Ant....C8 5
Coronda, Arg....A4 54
Coronel, Chile....B2 54
Coronel Brandsen, Arg...B5, g7 54
Coronel Dorrego, Arg....B4 54
Coronel Oviedo, Par....E4 55
Coronel Pringles, Arg....B4 54
Coronel Pringles, Arg....C4 54
Coronel Suárez, Arg....B4 54
Corowa, Austl....G6 51
Corozal, Belize....A3 62
Corozal, Col....B2 60
Corozal, mun., P.R....*B3 65
Corpataux, Switz....C3 19
Corpen, Arg....D3 54
Corps, Fr....E1 18
Corpus Christi, Nueces, Tex..F4 118
Corral, Chile....B2 54
Corral, Camas, Idaho....F4 89
Corral de Almaguer, Sp....C4 20
Corrales, Col....B3 60
Corralillo, Cuba....C3 64
Corraun, Ire....D2 11
Corravillers, Fr....B2 18
Correctionville, Woodbury, Iowa....B2 92
Corregidor, isl., Phil....o13 35
Correll, Big Stone, Minn....E2 99
Corrente, Braz....D2 57
Correntes, Braz....k5 57
Correntina, Braz....D2 57
Corrèze, dept., Fr....*E4 14
Corrib, lake, Ire....D2 11
Corrientes, Arg....E4 55
Corrientes, prov., Arg....E4 55
Corrientes, bay, Cuba....D1 64
Corrientes, cape, Cuba....D1 64
Corrientes, cape, Mex....C3 63
Corrientes, riv., Arg....E4 55
Corrientes, riv., Peru....B3 58
Corrigan, Polk, Tex....D5 118
Corriganville, Allegany, Md.k13 85
Corro, isl., Az. Is....g8 44
Corrofin, Ire....E2 11
Corry, Erie, Pa....C2 114
Corryton, Knox, Tenn....C10 117
Corse, cape, Fr....C2 21
Corse (Corsica), dept., Fr..*C2 21
Corsica, Jefferson, Pa....D3 114
Corsica, Douglas, S. Dak....D7 116
Corsica (Corse), dept., Fr..*C2 21
Corsicana, Navarro, Tex....C4 118
Corson, Minnehaha, S. Dak.D9 116
Corson, co., S. Dak....B4 116
Corson, inlet, N.J....E3 106
Corte, Fr....C2 21
Corte Alto, Chile....C2 54
Cortegana, Sp....D2 20
Corte Madera, Marin, Calif..*h7 82
Cortemilia, It....E4 18
Cortes, Sp....D3 20
Cortez, Montezuma, Colo....D1 83
Cortez, Manatee, Fla....q10 86
Cortez, mts., Nev....C5 104
Cortina d'Ampezzo, It....C8 18
Cortland, DeKalb., Ill....B5 90
Cortland, Jackson, Ind....G6 91
Cortland, Gage, Nebr....D9 103
Cortland, Cortland, N.Y....C4 108
Cortland, Trumbull, Ohio....A5 111
Cortland, co., N.Y....C4 108
Cortona, It....C3 21
Coruche, Port....C1 20
Coruh, riv., Tur....G17 9
Çorum (Chorum), Tur....B10 31
Corumbá, Braz....B1 56
Corunba, riv., Braz....E1 57
Corunna, Ont., Can....E2 72
Corunna, DeKalb, Ind....B7 91
Corunna, Shiawassee, Mich..F6 98
Corvallis, Ravalli, Mont....D2 102
Corvallis, Benton, Oreg.C3, k11 113
Corvo, isl., Port. (Azores)....g8 44
Corwin, Harper, Kans....E5 93
Corwin Springs, Park, Mont.E6 102
Corwith, Hancock, Iowa....B4 92
Cory, Clay, Ind....F3 91
Corydon, Harrison, Ind....H5 91
Corydon, Wayne, Iowa....D4 92
Corydon, Henderson, Ky....C2 94
Corydon, Warren, Pa....C4 114
Coryell, co., Tex....D4 118
Coryville, McKean, Pa....C5 114
Cosalá, Mex....C3 63
Cosby, Andrew, Mo....B3 101
Cosby, Cocke, Tenn....D10 117
Cos Cob, Fairfield, Conn. (part of Greenwich)....E2 84
Coscomatepec, Mex....n15 63
Cosegüina, pt., Nic....D4 62
Cosenza, It....E6 21
Coshocton, Coshocton, Ohio.B4 111
Coshocton, co., Ohio....B3 111
Cosmopolis, Grays Harbor, Wash....C2 122
Cosmos, Meeker, Minn....F4 99
Cosne [-sur-Loire], Fr....D5 14
Cossatot, mts., Ark....C2 81
Cossatot, riv., Ark....C1 81
Cossonay, Switz....C2 19
Costa Mesa, Orange, Calif..n13 82
Costa Rica, country, N.A....H12 61, E5 62
Costello, Potter, Pa....C5 114
Costelloe, Ire....D2 11
Costigan, Penobscot, Maine..C4 96
Costilla, Taos, N. Mex....A4 107
Costilla, co., Colo....D5 83
Coswig, G.D.R....B7 17
Coswig, G.D.R....B8 17
Cotabato, Phil....D6 35
Cotabato, prov., Phil....*D6 35
Cotagaita, Bol....D2 55
Cotahuasi, Peru....D2 58
Cotati, Sonoma, Calif....B5 83
Coteau, Burke, N. Dak....A3 110
Coteau, The, hills, Sask., Can...F2 70
Coteau-Landing, Que., Can.D3 73
Coteau-Station, Que., Can.*D3 73
Coteaux, Hai....E6 64
Côte-d'Or, dept., Fr....*D6 14
Côte d'Or, ridge, Fr....D6 14
Cote St. Luc, Que., Can...*D4 73
Côtes de Fer, Hai....E7 64
Côtes de L'ile de France, mts., Fr.F3 15
Côtes de Meuse, mts., Fr....E5 15
Côtes-du-Nord, dept., Fr...*C2 14
Cotesfield, Howard, Nebr....C7 103
Cotija, Mex....n12 63
Cotingo, riv., Braz....C5 60
Cotonou, Benin....E5 45
Cotopaxi, Fremont, Colo....C5 83
Cotopaxi, prov., Ec....B2 58
Cotopaxi, vol., Ec....B2 58
Cotswold, hills, Eng....C5 12
Cottage, Aroostook, Maine..A4 96
Cottage City, Prince Georges, Md....*f9 85
Cottage Grove, Washington, Minn....n13 99
Cottage Grove, Lane Oreg..D3 113
Cottage Grove, Henry, Tenn.A3 117
Cottage Grove, Dane, Wis..*E4 124
Cottage Grove, res., Oreg....D3 113
Cottage Hills, Madison, Ill..*E3 90
Cottageville, Colleton, S.C...F7 115
Cottageville, Jackson, W. Va.C3 123
Cottam, Ont., Can....E2 72
Cottbus, G.D.R....B9 17
Cottel, isl., Newf., Can....D5 75
Cotter, Baxter, Ark....A3 81
Cottian Alps, mts., Fr....E7 14
Cottingham, Eng....G8 13
Cottle, co., Tex....B2 118
Cottle Knob, mtn., W. Va....C4 123
Cottleville, St. Charles, Mo..f12 101
Cotton, Mitchell, Ga....E2 87
Cotton, St. Louis, Minn....C6 99
Cotton, co., Okla....C3 112
Cotton Center, Hale, Tex....B2 118
Cottondale, Tuscaloosa, Ala..B2 78
Cottondale, Jackson, Fla....B1, u16 86
Cotton Mills, Grayson, Tex.*C4 118
Cotton Plant, Woodruff, Ark.B4 81
Cottonport, Avoyelles, La...D3 95
Cottonton, Russell, Ala....C4 78
Cotton Town, Yell, Ark....B2 81
Cottontown, Sumner, Tenn..A5 117
Cotton Valley, Webster, La...B2 95
Cottonwood, Houston, Ala..D4 78
Cottonwood, Yavapai, Ariz...C3 80
Cottonwood, Shasta, Calif...B2 82
Cottonwood, Idaho, Idaho...C2 89
Cottonwood, Lyon, Minn....F3 99
Cottonwood, Coal, Okla....C5 112
Cottonwood, Jackson, S. Dak....D4 116
Cottonwood, Callahan, Tex..C3 118
Cottonwood, co., Minn....F3 99
Cottonwood, creek, Utah....F6 119
Cottonwood, creek, Wyo....C4 125
Cottonwood, creek, Wyo....D2 125
Cottonwood, riv., Kans....D7 93
Cottonwood, riv., Minn....F3 99
Cottonwood Falls, Chase, Kans....D7 93
Cottonwood Heights, Salt Lake, Utah....*C4 119
Cotuit, Barnstable, Mass....C7 97
Cotulla, La Salle, Tex....E3 118
Couchiching, lake, Ont., Can...C5 72
Couchville, Davidson, Tenn.g10 117
Couchwood, Webster, La....B2 95
Coudekerque-Branche, Fr....B5 14
Couderay, Sawyer, Wis....C2 124
Coudersport, Potter, Pa....C5 114
Couëron, Fr....D3 14
Cougar, peak, Oreg....E6 113
Cougar, rock, Oreg....C4 113
Coulee, Mountrail, N. Dak..A3 110
Coulee, creek, Wash....g13 122
Coulee City, Grant, Wash...B6 122
Coulee Dam, Douglas, Grant, and Okanogan, Wash....B7 122
Coulman, isl., Ant....B29 5
Coulommiers, Fr....C5 14
Coulonge, riv., Que., Can....A8 72
Coulsdon, Eng. (part of London)....m12 10
Coulter, Man., Can....E1 71
Coulter, Franklin, Iowa....B4 92
Coulterville, Mariposa, Calif.D3 82
Coulterville, Randolph, Ill...E4 90
Coulwood, Russell, Va....f9 121
Counce, Hardin, Tenn....B3 117
Council, Clinch, Ga....F4 87
Council, Adams, Idaho....E2 89
Council, Buchanan, Va....e9 121
Council Bluffs, Pottawattamie, Iowa....C2 92
Council Grove, Morris, Kans.D7 93
Council Hill, Muskogee, Okla....B6 112
Country Club Hills, Cook, Ill....*B6 90
Country Club Hills, St. Louis, Mo....*C7 101
Country Homes, Spokane, Wash....B8, g14 122
Countyline, Carter and Stephens, Okla....C4 112
Coupar Angus, Scot....D5 13
Coupeville, Island, Wash....A3 122
Coupon, Cambria, Pa....E4 114
Courantyne, riv., Fr., Guy, Sur....A3 59
Courbevoie, Fr....g10 14
Courcelles, Que., Can....D7 73
Courland (Kurisches Haff), lagoon, Sov. Un....A6 26
Courmayeur, It....D2 18
Coursan, Fr....F5 14
Courtenay, B.C., Can....E5 68
Courtenay, Stutsman, N. Dak....B7 110
Courtland, Lawrence, Ala....A2 78
Courtland, Ont., Can....E4 72
Courtland, Republic, Kans...C6 93
Courtland, Nicollet, Minn....F4 99
Courtland, Panola, Miss....A4 100
Courtland, Southampton, Va....D5 121
Courtmacsherry, Ire....F3 11
Courtrai, see Kortrijk, Bel.
Courtright, Ont., Can....E2 72
Courtrock, Grant, Oreg....C7 113
Courval, Sask., Can....G2 70
Coushatta, Red River, La...B2 95
Coutances, Fr....C3 14
Coutras, Fr....E3 14
Coutts, Alta., Can....E5 69
Couvin, Bel....D4 15
Covada, Ferry, Wash....A7 122
Cove, Polk, Ark....C1 81
Cove, Garrett, Md....D1 85
Cove, Mille Lacs, Minn....D5 99
Cove, Union, Oreg....B9 113
Cove, Scot....C3 13
Cove, Chambers, Tex....r15 118
Cove, isl., Ont., Can....B3 72
Cove, pt., Md....D5 85
Cove & Kilcreggan, Scot....*E4 13
Cove City, Craven, N.C....B5 109
Cove City, Orange, Tex....*D6 118
Covedale, Hamilton, Ohio...o12 111
Covelo, Mendocino, Calif....C2 82
Coventry, Tolland, Conn....B7 84
Coventry, Eng....B6 12
Coventry, Kent, R.I....C10 84
Coventry, Orleans, Vt....B4 120
Coventry Center, Kent, R.I.C10 84
Covered Bridge, N.H....B2 105
Covert, Osborne, Kans....C5 93
Covert, Van Buren, Mich....F4 98
Covesville, Albemarle, Va...C4 121
Covilhã, Port....B2 20
Covin, Fayette, Ala....B2 78
Covina, Los Angeles, Calif..m13 82
Covington, Newton, Ga....C3 87
Covington, Fountain, Ind...D3 91
Covington, Kenton, Ky.A5, h13 94
Covington, St. Tammany, La....D5, h11 95
Covington, Baraga, Mich....B2 98
Covington, Miami, Ohio....B1 111
Covington, Garfield, Okla....A4 112
Covington, Tioga, Pa....C7 114
Covington, Tipton, Tenn....B2 117
Covington (Independent City), Va....C3 121
Covington, King, Wash....f11 122
Covington, co., Ala....D3 78
Covington, co., Miss....D4 100
Cow, creek, Kans....D5 93
Cow, creek, Wash....C7 122
Cow, lakes, Oreg....D9 113
Cowal, lake, Austl....F6 51
Cowan, Delaware, Ind....D7 91
Cowan, Franklin, Tenn....B5 117
Cowan, lake, Austl....F3 50
Cowan, lake, Sask., Can....C2 70
Cowan, riv., Sask., Can....C2 70
Cowangie, Austl....G3 51
Cowan Knob, mtn., Ark....B2 81
Cowansville, Que., Can....D5 73
Cowansville, Armstrong, Pa..E2 114
Coward, Florence, S.C....D8 115
Coward Springs, Austl....E6 50
Cowarts, Houston, Ala....D4 78
Cowcreek, Owsley, Ky....*C6 94
Cow Creek, Rosebud, Mont.E10 102
Cowden, Shelby, Ill....D5 90
Cowdenbeath, Scot....D5 13
Cowdrey, Jackson, Colo....A4 83
Cowell, Newton, Ark....B2 81
Cowen, Webster, W. Va....C4 123
Cowen, mtn., Mont....E6 102
Cowes, Eng....D6 12
Coweta, Wagoner, Okla....B6 112
Coweta, co., Ga....C2 87
Cowgill, Caldwell, Mo....B4 101
Cow Head, Newf., Can.D3, k10 75
Cowichan, lake, B.C., Can....E5 68
Cowichan Bay, B.C., Can...g12 68
Cowiche, Kakima, Wash....C5 122
Cowles, Webster, Neb....D7 103
Cowley, Alta., Can....E3 69
Cowley, Big Horn, Wyo....B4 125
Cowley, co., Kans....E7 93
Cowlic, Pima, Ariz....F4 80
Cowlington, LeFlore, Okla...B7 112
Cowlitz, co., Wash....C3 122
Cowlitz, riv., Wash....C3 122
Cowpasture, riv., Va....B3 121
Cowpen mtn., Ga....B2 87
Cowpens, Spartanburg, S.C.A4 115
Cowra, Austl....F7 51
Cowskin, riv., Kans....g11 93
Cow Springs, Coconino, Ariz.A5 80
Coxburg, Holmes, Miss....B3 100
Cox City, Grady, Okla....C4 112
Coxim, Braz....B2 56
Coxipi, riv., Que., Can....C2 75
Coxsackie, Greene, N.Y....C7 108
Cox's Cove, Newf., Can....D2 75
Coxs Mills, Gilmer, W. Va..B4 123
Coy, Wilcox, Ala....D2 78
Coy, Lonoke, Ark....C4 81
Coya, Chile....D2 55
Coyame, Mex....B3 63
Coyanosa, draw, Tex....D1 118
Coyle, Logan, Okla....B4 112
Coyoacán, Mex....h9, n14 63
Coyote, Rio Arriba, N. Mex.A3 107
Coyote, basin, Colo....A2 83
Coyville, Wilson, Kans....E8 93
Cozad, Dawson, Nebr....D6 103
Cozahome, Searcy, Ark....A3 81
Cozumel, Mex....C7 63
Cozumel, isl., Mex....C7 63
Crab, creek, Wash....B7 122
Crab, creek, Wash....C6 122
Crab Orchard, Lincoln, Ky...C5 94
Crab Orchard, Johnson, Nebr....D9 103
Crab Orchard, Cumberland, Tenn....D9 117
Crab Orchard, Raleigh, W. Va....n13 123

Crab Orchard, lake, Ill ... F5 90
Crab Orchard, mts., Tenn ... D9 117
Crabtree, Van Buren, Ark ... B3 81
Crabtree, Linn, Oreg ... C4, k12 113
Crabtree, Westmoreland, Pa ... F3 114
Crabtree Mills, Que., Can ... D4 73
Cracking, riv., Sask., Can ... D4 70
Cracow, Austl ... B8 51
Cracow (Kraków), Pol ... C5 26
Cradock, S. Afr ... D4 49
Crafton, Allegheny, Pa ... k13 114
Craftsbury, Orleans, Vt ... B4 120
Craftsbury Common, Orleans, Vt ... B4 120
Cragford, Clay, Ala ... B4 78
Cragged, mtn., N.H ... C4 105
Crags, mts., Idaho ... C3 89
Craig, Alsk ... D13, n23 79
Craig, Moffat, Colo ... A3 83
Craig, Monroe, Fla ... H6 86
Craig, Plymouth, Iowa ... B1 92
Craig, Holt, Mo ... A2 101
Craig, Lewis and Clark, Mont ... C4 102
Craig, Burt, Nebr ... C9 103
Craig, co., Okla ... A6 112
Craig, co., Va ... C2 121
Craig, creek, Va ... C2 121
Craig Beach, Mahoning, Ohio ... *A5 111
Craigellachie, B.C., Can ... D8 68
Craighead, co., Ark ... B5 81
Craighouse, Scot ... E3 13
Craighurst, Ont., Can ... C5 72
Craigmont, Lewis, Idaho ... C2 89
Craigmyle, Alta., Can ... D4 69
Craigs Road, Que., Can ... o17 73
Craigsville, Augusta, Va ... B3 121
Craigsville, Nicholas, W. Va ... C4 123
Craigville, Wells, Ind ... C7 91
Craik, Sask., Can ... F3 70
Crail, Scot ... D6 13
Crailsheim, F.R.G ... D5 17
Craiova, Rom ... C6 22
Cramerton, Gaston, N.C ... B1 109
Crampton, Henry, Ill ... D7 92
Cranberry, Venango, Pa ... D2 114
Cranberry, lake, N.Y ... A6 108
Cranberry Isles, Hancock, Maine ... D4 96
Cranberry Lake, Sussex, N.J ... B3 106
Cranberry Lake, St. Lawrence, N.Y ... A6, f10 108
Cranberry Portage, Man., Can ... B1 71
Cranbrook, B.C., Can ... E10 68
Cranbury, Middlesex, N.J ... C3 106
Crandall, Man., Can ... D1 71
Crandall, Murray, Ga ... B2 87
Crandall, Clarke, Miss ... D5 100
Crandall, Day, S. Dak ... B8 116
Crandall, Kaufman, Tex ... n10 118
Crandon, Forest, Wis ... C5 124
Crane, Stone, Mo ... E4 101
Crane, Richland, Mont ... C12 102
Crane, Harney, Oreg ... D8 113
Crane, Crane, Tex ... D1 118
Crane, co., Tex ... D1 118
Crane, creek, Ohio ... e7 111
Crane, lake, Sask., Can ... G1 70
Crane, lake, Ill ... C3 90
Crane, lake, Minn ... B6 99
Crane, mtn., Oreg ... E6 113
Crane Creek, res., Idaho ... E2 89
Crane Hill, Cullman, Ala ... A2 78
Crane Lake, St. Louis, Minn ... B6 99
Crane Neck, pt., N.Y ... F4 84
Crane Prairie, res., Oreg ... D5 113
Cranesville, Erie, Pa ... C1 114
Crane Valley, Sask., Can ... H3 70
Cranfield, Adams, Miss ... D2 100
Cranford, Union, N.J ... B4 106
Cransac, Fr ... E5 14
Cranston, Providence, R.I ... B11 84
Cranstown, cape, Grnld ... B20 4
Crapaud, P.E.I., Can ... C6 74
Crapo, Dorchester, Md ... D5 85
Crary, Ramsey, N. Dak ... A7 110
Craryville, Columbia, N.Y ... C7 108
Crasna, riv., Rom ... B6 22
Crater, lake, Oreg ... E4 113
Crater, lake, St. Vincent ... U26 65
Crater Lake, Klamath, Oreg ... E4 113
Crater Lake, nat. park, Oreg ... E4 113
Craters of the Moon, nat. mon., Idaho ... F5 89
Crateús, Braz ... C2 57
Crato, Braz ... C3 57
Craughwell, Ire ... D3 11
Craven, Sask., Can ... G3 70
Craven, co., N.C ... B5 109
Cravinhos, Braz ... k8 56
Crawford, Delta, Colo ... C3 83
Crawford, Oglethorpe, Ga ... C3 87
Crawford, Washington, Maine ... C5 96
Crawford, Lowndes, Miss ... B5 100
Crawford, Dawes, Nebr ... B2 103
Crawford, Roger Mills, Okla ... B2 112
Crawford, co., Ark ... B1 81
Crawford, co., Ga ... D3 87
Crawford, co., Ill ... D6 90
Crawford, co., Ind ... H4 91
Crawford, co., Iowa ... B2 92
Crawford, co., Kans ... E9 93
Crawford, co., Mich ... D6 98
Crawford, co., Mo ... D6 101
Crawford, co., Ohio ... B2 111
Crawford, co., Pa ... C1 114
Crawford, co., Wis ... E3 124
Crawford, lake, Maine ... C5 96
Crawford Bay, B.C., Can ... E9 68
Crawfordsville, Crittenden, Ark ... B5 81
Crawfordsville, Montgomery, Ind ... D4 91
Crawfordsville, Washington, Iowa ... C6 92
Crawfordsville, Linn, Oreg ... C4 113
Crawfordville, Wakulla, Fla ... B2 86
Crawfordville, Taliaferro, Ga ... C4 87
Crawley, Eng ... C7 12
Crayne, Crittenden, Ky ... e9 94
Crazy, mts., Mont ... D6 102
Crazy, peak, Mont ... D6 102
Crazy Woman, creek, Wyo ... B6 125
Creal Springs, Williamson and Marion, Ill ... F5 90
Creamridge, Monmouth, N.J ... C3 106
Crean, lake, Sask., Can ... C2 70
Crediton, Eng ... D4 12
Cree lake, Sask., Can ... m7 70
Cree, riv., Sask., Can ... E11 66
Creede, Mineral, Colo ... D4 83
Creedmoor, Granville, N.C ... A4 109
Creek, co., Okla ... B5 112
Creekside, Indiana, Pa ... E3 114
Creek Village, Ba ... m18 64
Creelman, Sask., Can ... H4 70
Creemore, Ont., Can ... C4 72
Creggan, N. Ire ... C4 11
Cregganbaun, Ire ... D2 11
Creighton, Sask., Can ... C5 70
Creighton, Cass, Mo ... C3 101
Creighton, Knox, Nebr ... B8 103
Creighton, Allegheny, Pa ... h14 114
Creighton Mine, Ont., Can ... A3, p19 72
Creil, Fr ... C5 14
Crellin, Garrett, Md ... m12 85
Crema, It ... B2 21
Cremona, Alta., Can ... D3 69
Cremona, It ... B3 21
Crenshaw, Panola, Miss ... A3 100
Crenshaw, Jefferson, Pa ... D4 114
Crenshaw, co., Ala ... D3 78
Creola, Mobile, Ala ... E1 78
Creole, Cameron, La ... E2 95
Crépy-en-Valois, Fr ... E2 15
Cres, isl., Yugo ... C2 22
Cresaptown, Allegany, Md ... k13 85
Cresbard, Faulk, S. Dak ... B7 116
Crescent, McIntosh, Ga ... E5 87
Crescent, Pottawattamie, Iowa ... C2 92
Crescent, St. Louis, Mo ... g12 101
Crescent, Logan, Okla ... B4 112
Crescent, Klamath, Oreg ... D5 113
Crescent, lake, Fla ... C5 86
Crescent, lake, Oreg ... D5 113
Crescent, lake, Wash ... A2 122
Crescent, range, N.H ... B4 105
Crescent Beach, New London, Conn. (part of Niantic) ... D8 84
Crescent Beach, Cumberland, Maine (part of Cape Elizabeth) ... E5 96
Crescent City, Del Norte, Calif ... B1 82
Crescent City, Putnam, Fla ... C5 86
Crescent City, Iroquois, Ill ... C6 90
Crescent City Northwest, Del Norte, Calif ... *B1 82
Crescent Lake, Klamath, Oreg ... D5 113
Crescent Springs, Kenton, Ky ... h13 94
Cresco, Howard, Iowa ... A5 92
Cresco, Monroe, Pa ... D11 114
Cresent Spur, B.C., Can ... C7 68
Crespo, see Villa Crespo, Arg.
Cresskill, Bergen, N.J ... h9 106
Cresson, Cambria, Pa ... F4 114
Cresson, Hood, Tex ... n9 118
Cressona, Schuylkill, Pa ... E9 114
Crest, Fr ... E6 14
Cresta, Switz ... D8 19
Crested Butte, Gunnison, Colo ... C4 83
Crest Hill, Will, Ill ... k8 90
Cresthill, Fauquier, Va ... B5 121
Crestline, Crawford, Ohio ... B3 111
Crestmont, Montgomery, Pa ... *F11 114
Crestmore, San Bernardino and Riverside, Calif ... *E5 82
Creston, B.C., Can ... E9 68
Creston, Newf., Can ... E4 75
Creston, Ogle, Ill ... B5 90
Creston, Union, Iowa ... C3 92
Creston, Flathead, Mont ... B2 102
Creston, Platte, Nebr ... C8 103
Creston, Wayne, Ohio ... B4 111
Creston, Malheur, Oreg ... D8 113
Creston, Calhoun, S.C ... D6 115
Creston, Cumberland, Tenn ... C8 117
Creston, Lincoln, Wash ... B7 122
Creston, Wirt, W. Va ... C3 123
Crestone, Saguache, Colo ... D5 83
Crestone, peak, Colo ... D5 83
Crestview, Okaloosa, Fla ... u15 86
Crestview, Honolulu, Haw ... g9 88
Crestwood, Cook, Ill ... *B6 90
Crestwood, Oldham, Ky ... B4, g12 94
Crestwood, St. Louis, Mo ... *C7 101
Crestwood Village, Ocean, N.J ... D4 106
Crestwynd, Sask., Can ... G3 70
Creswell, Washington, N.C ... B6 109
Creswell, Lane, Oreg ... D3 113
Crete, Will, Ill ... B6, m9 90
Crete, Saline, Nebr ... D9 103
Crete, Sargent, N. Dak ... C8 110
Crete, isl., Grc ... E5 23
Crete, sea, Grc ... D5 23
Cretone, It ... g9 21
Creuse, dept., Fr ... *D4 14
Creuse, riv., Fr ... D4 14
Creutzwald, Fr ... C7 14
Crevasse Valley, glacier, Ant ... B34 5
Creve Coeur, Tazewell, Ill ... C4 90
Creve Coeur, St. Louis, Mo ... *C7 101
Crevillente, Sp ... C5 20
Crewe, Eng ... A5 12
Crewe, Nottoway, Va ... C4 121
Crewkerne, Eng ... D5 12
Cricket, Wilkes, N.C ... A1 109
Cricket, mts., Utah ... E3 119
Cridersville, Auglaize, Ohio ... B1 111
Crieff, Scot ... D5 13
Criffell, mtn., Scot ... F5 13
Criglersville, Madison, Va ... B4 121
Crikvenica, Yugo ... C2 22
Crimea, see Krym, pen., Sov. Un.
Crimmitschau, G.D.R ... C7 17
Crimson Lake, prov. park, Alta., Can ... C3 69
Crinan, Scot ... D3 13
Cripple Creek, Teller, Colo ... C5 83
Cripple Creek, Wythe, Va ... D1 121
Crisana-Maramures, prov., Rom ... *B6 22
Crisfield, Somerset, Md ... E6 85
Crisman, Porter, Ind. (part of Portage) ... A3 91
Crisp, Ellis, Tex ... B6 118
Crisp, co., Ga ... E3 87
Criss Creek, B.C., Can ... D7 68
Crissolo, It ... E3 18
Cristal, mts., Gabon ... E2 46
Cristalina, Braz ... E1 57
Cristóbal, Pan ... k11 62
Cristobal, dist., Pan ... *k11 62
Cristóbal Colón, mtn., Col ... A3 60
Crisul Alb, riv., Rom ... B5 22
Crittenden, Grant, Ky ... B5, k13 94
Crittenden, co., Ark ... B5 81
Crittenden, co., Ky ... e9 94
Crivitz, G.D.R ... E5 24
Crivitz, Marinette, Wis ... C6 124
Crna, riv., Yugo ... E5 22
Crna Gora (Montenegro), rep., Yugo ... *D4 22
Črnomelj, Yugo ... C2 22
Croatia, rep., Yugo ... *C2 22
Croatia, reg., Yugo ... C2 22
Croche, riv., Que., Can ... A5 73
Crocheron, Dorchester, Md ... D5 85
Crocker, Pulaski, Mo ... D5 101
Crocker, Clark, S. Dak ... B8 116
Crockett, Contra Costa, Calif ... g8 82
Crockett, Houston, Tex ... D5 118
Crockett, co., Tenn ... B2 117
Crockett, co., Tex ... D2 118
Crockett Mills, Crockett, Tenn ... B2 117
Crocketville, Hampton, S.C ... F5 115
Crofton, Christian, Ky ... C2 94
Crofton, Anne Arudel, Md ... B4 85
Crofton, Knox, Nebr ... B8 103
Croghan, Lewis, N.Y ... B5 108
Crohy, head, Ire ... C3 11
Croix, Fr ... D3 15
Croker, cape, Ont., Can ... C4 72
Croker, isl., Austl ... B5 50
Crolly, Ire ... B3 11
Cromarty, Scot ... C4 13
Cromer, Man., Can ... E1 71
Cromer, Eng ... B9 12
Cromona (Haymond), Letcher, Ky ... C7 94
Cromwell, Choctaw, Ala ... C1 78
Cromwell, Middlesex, Conn ... C6 84
Cromwell, Noble, Ind ... B6 91
Cromwell, Union, Iowa ... C3 92
Cromwell, Ohio, Ky ... C3 94
Cromwell, Carlton, Minn ... D6 99
Cromwell, N.Z ... P12 51
Cromwell, Seminole, Okla ... B5 112
Cromwell, Pierce, Wash ... D1 122
Crook, Logan, Colo ... A8 83
Crook, Eng ... F7 13
Crook, co., Oreg ... C6 113
Crook, co., Wyo ... B8 125
Crooked, creek, Ark ... A3 81
Crooked, creek, Kans ... B7 93
Crooked, creek, Kans ... E3 93
Crooked, creek, Pa ... C7 114
Crooked, isl., Ba ... C6 64
Crooked, lake, Newf., Can ... D3 75
Crooked, lake, Sask., Can ... G4 70
Crooked, lake, Fla ... E5 86
Crooked, lake, Minn ... B7 99
Crooked, riv., B.C., Can ... B6 68
Crooked, riv., Oreg ... C6 113
Crooked Creek, Alsk ... C8 79
Crooked Creek, res., Pa ... E3 114
Crooked Island, passage, Ba ... C6 64
Crooked River, Sask., Can ... E4 70
Crooks, Minnehaha, S. Dak ... D9 116
Crooks, lake, Nev ... B2 104
Crookston, Polk, Minn ... C2 99
Crookston, Cherry, Nebr ... B5 103
Crookstown, Ire ... F3 11
Crooksville, Perry, Ohio ... C3 111
Crookwell, Austl ... G7 51
Croom, Ire ... E3 11
Croom Station, Prince Georges, Md ... C4 85
Cropper, Shelby, Ky ... B4 94
Cropsey, McLean, Ill ... C5 90
Croque, hbr., Newf., Can ... C4 75
Crosby, Crow Wing, Minn ... D5 99
Crosby, Amite and Wilkinson, Miss ... D2 100
Crosby, Divide, N. Dak ... A2 110
Crosby, McKean, Pa ... C5 114
Crosby, Harris, Tex ... r14 118
Crosby, co., Tex ... C2 118
Crosby, mtn., Wyo ... C3 125
Crosbyton, Crosby, Tex ... C2 118
Crosland, Colquitt, Ga ... E3 87
Cross, Berkeley, S.C ... E7 115
Cross, co., Ark ... B5 81
Cross, bay, Man., Can ... C2 71
Cross, cape, Namibia ... B1 49
Cross, creek, W. Va ... f8 123
Cross, isl., Maine ... D5 96
Cross, lake, Man., Can ... B3 71
Cross, lake, La ... B2 95
Cross, lake, Maine ... A4 96
Cross, mtn., Tenn ... C9 117
Cross, mts., Ark ... C1 81
Cross, riv., Nig ... E6 45
Cross, sound, Alsk ... k21 79
Cross Anchor, Spartanburg, S.C ... B4 115
Crossbost, Scot ... B2 13
Cross City, Dixie, Fla ... C3 86
Cross Creek, N.B., Can ... C3 74
Cross Creek, Brooke, W. Va ... *A4 123
Crossdoney, Ire ... D4 11
Crosses, Madison, Ark ... B2 81
Crossett, Ashley, Ark ... D4 81
Cross Fell, mtn., Eng ... F6 13
Crossfield, Alta., Can ... D3 69
Crossgar, N. Ire ... C6 11
Crosshaven, Ire ... F3 11
Cross Hill, Laurens, S.C ... C4 115
Cross Keys, Bibb, Ga ... *D3 87
Cross Keys, Gloucester, N.J ... D2 106
Cross Lake, Man., Can ... B3 71
Crosslake, Crow Wing, Minn ... D4 99
Cross Lanes, Kanawha, W.Va ... C3 123
Crossmaglen, N. Ire ... C5 11
Cross Mill, McDowell, N.C ... f10 109
Crossmolina, Ire ... C2 11
Cross Plains, Ripley, Ind ... G7 91
Cross Plains, Robertson, Tenn ... A5 117
Cross Plains, Callahan, Tex ... C3 118
Cross Plains, Dane, Wis ... E4 124
Cross Roads, San Bernardino, Calif ... E6 82
Crossroads, Lea, N. Mex ... D6 107
Cross Roads Ohio, N.S., Can ... D7 74
Cross Timbers, Hickory, Mo ... C4 101
Crosstown, Perry, Mo ... D8 101
Cross Village, Emmet, Mich ... C5 98
Crossville, DeKalb, Ala ... A4 78
Crossville, White, Ill ... E5 90
Crossville, Cumberland, Tenn ... D8 117
Crosswicks, Burlington, N.J ... C3 106
Croswell, Sanilac, Mich ... E8 98
Crothersville, Jackson, Ind ... G6 91
Croton, Lee, Iowa ... D6 92
Croton, Newaygo, Mich ... E5 98
Croton, Hunterdon, N.J ... B3 106
Croton (Hartford), Licking, Ohio ... B3 111
Crotone, It ... E6 21
Croton Falls, Westchester, N.Y ... *D7 108
Croton Falls, res., N.Y ... D2 84
Croton-on-Hudson, Westchester, N.Y ... D7, m15 108
Crottendorf, G.D.R ... C7 17
Crouch, Boise, Idaho ... E3 89
Crouse, Lincoln, N.C ... B1 109
Crouseville, Aroostook, Maine ... B4 96
Crow, creek, Colo ... A6 83
Crow, creek, Wyo ... E8 125
Crow, Indian res., Mont ... E9 102
Crow, peak, Mont ... D5 102
Crow, riv., Minn ... F5 99
Crow Agency, Big Horn, Mont ... E9 102
Crowder, Panola and Quitman, Miss ... A3 100
Crowder, Pittsburg, Okla ... B6 112
Crowduck, lake, Man., Can ... D4 71
Crowell, Foard, Tex ... C3 118
Crowheart, Fremont, Wyo ... C3 125
Crowley, Crowley, Colo ... C7 83
Crowley, Acadia, La ... D3 95
Crowley, Tarrant, Tex ... n9 118
Crowley, co., Colo ... C7 83
Crowley, lake, Calif ... D4 82
Crowleys, ridge, Ark., Mo ... E7 101
Crown City, Gallia, Ohio ... D3 111
Crown King, Yavapai, Ariz ... C3 80
Crown Point, Lake, Ind ... B3 91
Crown Point, Jefferson, La ... k11 95
Crown Point, Douglas, Nebr ... *C10 103
Crownpoint, McKinley, N. Mex ... B1 107
Crown Point, Essex, N.Y ... B7 108
Crowsnest, B.C., Can ... E10 68
Crows Nest, Marion, Ind ... k10 91
Crows Nest, mtn., S. Dak ... C2 116
Crowsnest, pass, Alta., B.C., Can ... E3 69
Crow Wing, co., Minn ... D4 99
Crow Wing, riv., Minn ... D4 99
Croydon, Austl ... C7 50
Croydon, Eng. (part of London) ... C7 12, E6, m12 10
Croydon, Sullivan, N.H ... D2 105
Croydon, Bucks, Pa ... F12 114
Croydon, Morgan, Utah ... B4 119
Croydon, mtn., N.H ... D2 105
Croydon, peak, N.H ... D2 105
Croydon Flat, Sullivan, N.H ... D2 105
Crozet, Albemarle, Va ... B4 121
Crozet, is., Indian O ... J24 3
Crozier, Goochland, Va ... C5 121
Crozon, Fr ... C1 14
Cruachan, mtn., Scot ... D3 13
Cruagh, isl., Ire ... D1 11
Crucero, Peru ... D3 58
Cruces, Cuba ... C3 64
Crucible, Greene, Pa ... G1 114
Cruden Bay, Scot ... C7 13
Cruger, Holmes, Miss ... B3 100
Crum, Wayne, W. Va ... D2 123
Crumlin, N. Ire ... C5 11
Crum Lynne, Delaware, Pa ... *G11 114
Crummock Water, lake, Eng ... F5 13
Crump, lake, Oreg ... E7 113
Crumpton, Queen Annes, Md ... B6 85
Crumstown, St. Joseph, Ind ... A5 91
Cruseilles, Fr ... C2 18
Crusheen, Ire ... E3 11
Cruso, Haywood, N.C ... f10 109
Crutwell, Sask., Can ... D2 70
Cruz, cape, Cuba ... E5 64
Cruz Alta, Arg ... A4 54
Cruz Alta, Braz ... D2 56
Cruz Bay, Vir. Is. (U.S.) ... B6 65
Cruz del Eje, Arg ... A4 54
Cruzeiro, Braz ... C4 56
Cruzeiro do Sul, Braz ... C3 58
Cruz Grande, Chile ... E1 55
Crysler, Ont., Can ... B9 72
Crystal, Montcalm, Mich ... E6 98
Crystal, Hennepin, Minn ... m12 99
Crystal, Coos, N.H ... A4 105
Crystal, San Juan, N. Mex ... A1 107
Crystal, Pembina, N. Dak ... A8 110
Crystal, Klamath, Oreg ... E4 113
Crystal, bay, Fla ... D4 86
Crystal, caverns, Mo ... E4 101
Crystal, lake, Conn ... B7 84
Crystal, lake, Mich ... D4 98
Crystal, lake, N.H ... D4 105
Crystal, lake, Vt ... B4 120
Crystal, mtn., N.H ... g7 105
Crystal, pond, Conn ... B8 84
Crystal, riv., Colo ... B3 83
Crystal Bay, Washoe, Nev ... D2 104
Crystal Beach, Pinellas, Fla ... D4 86
Crystal City, Man., Can ... E2 71
Crystal City, Jefferson, Mo ... C7, g13 101
Crystal City, Zavala, Tex ... E3 118
Crystal Falls, Iron, Mich ... B2 98
Crystal Hill, Halifax, Va ... D4 121
Crystal Lake, Tolland, Conn ... B7 84
Crystal Lake, Washington, Fla ... u16 86
Crystal Lake, McHenry, Ill ... A5, h8 90
Crystal Lake, Hancock, Iowa ... A4 92
Crystal Lake, cave, Iowa ... B7 92
Crystal Lawn, Will, Ill ... k8 90
Crystal River, Citrus, Fla ... D4 86
Crystal Springs, Garland, Ark ... C2, f7 81
Crystal Springs, Sask, Can ... E3 70
Crystal Springs, Pasco, Fla ... D4 86
Crystal Springs, Copiah, Miss ... D3 100
Crystal Springs, Kidder, N. Dak ... C6 110
Crystal Valley, Oceana, Mich ... E4 98
Csongrad, Hung ... B5 22
Csongrad, co., Hung ... *B5 22
Csorna, Hung ... B3 22
Cuajimalpa, Mex ... h9 63
Cuando, riv., Ang., Zambia ... E3 48
Cuando Cubango, dist., Ang ... E2 48
Cuangar, Ang ... E2 48
Cuango, riv., Ang ... C2 48
Cuanza, riv., Ang ... C2 48
Cuanza Norte, dist., Ang ... C1 48
Cuanza Sul, dist., Ang ... D1 48
Cua Rao, Viet ... C6 38
Cuarto, riv., Arg ... A4 54
Cuauhtémoc, Mex ... B3 63
Cuautepec, Mex ... g9 63
Cuautla [Morelos], Mex ... n14 63
Cuba, Sumter, Ala ... C1 78
Cuba, Fulton, Ill ... C3 90
Cuba, Republic, Kans ... C6 93
Cuba, Crawford, Mo ... C6 101
Cuba, Sandoval, N. Mex ... A3 107
Cuba, Allegany, N.Y ... C2 108
Cuba, Clinton, Ohio ... C2 111
Cuba, Port ... C2 20
Cuba, country, N.A ... G12 61, C3 64
Cuba City, Grant, Wis ... F3 124
Cubal, Ang ... D1 48
Cubango, riv., Ang ... E2 48
Cubero, Valencia, N. Mex ... B2 107
Cub Run, Hart, Ky ... C4 94
Cuchara, Huerfano, Colo ... D6 83
Cucharas, riv., Colo ... D6 83
Cuchillo, Sierra, N. Mex ... D2 107
Cuchivero, riv., Ven ... B4 60
Cuchumatanes, mts., Guat ... C2 62
Cuckfield, Eng ... C7 12
Cúcuta, Col ... B3 60
Cudahy, Los Angeles, Calif ... *E4 82
Cudahy, Milwaukee, Wis ... F6, n12 124
Cuddalore, India ... F6 39
Cuddapah, India ... F6 39
Cuddy, Allegheny, Pa ... *F2 114
Cudgewa, Austl ... H6 51
Cudjos, cave, Ky., Va ... *D6 94
Cudworth, Sask., Can ... E3 70
Cue, Austl ... E2 50
Cuéllar, Sp ... B3 20
Cuenca, Ec ... B2 58
Cuenca, Sp ... B4 20
Cuenca, prov., Sp ... *B4 20
Cuenca, mts., Sp ... B4 20
Cuencamé [de Ceniceros], Mex ... C4 63
Cuernavaca, Mex ... D5, n14 63
Cuero, DeWitt, Tex ... E4 118
Cuervo, Cuba ... k12 64
Cuervo, Guadalupe, N. Mex ... B5 107
Cuetzalan [del Progreso], Mex ... m15 63
Cuevas, Harrison, Miss ... f7 100
Cuevas, Sp ... D5 20
Cuglieri, It ... D2 21
Cuiabá, Braz ... B1 56
Cuiabá, riv., Braz ... B1 56
Cuicas, Ven ... B3 60
Cuicatlán, Mex ... o15 63
Cuilapa, Guat ... C2 62
Cuilcagh, mtn., Ire ... C4 11
Cuilco, Guat ... C2 62
Cuillin, hills, Scot ... C2 13
Cuillin, sound, Scot ... B3 10
Cuipo, Pan ... k10 62
Cuito, riv., Ang ... E2 48
Cuito-Cuanavale, Ang ... E2 48
Cuitzéo, lake, Mex ... n13 63
Cuivre, riv., Mo ... B6 101
Culberson, co., Tex ... o12 118
Culbertson, Roosevelt, Mont ... B12 102
Culbertson, Hitchcock, Nebr ... D5 103
Culcairn, Austl. ... G6 51
Culdaff, bay, Ire ... B4 11
Culdesac, Nez Perce, Idaho ... C2 89
Culebra, P.R ... B5 65
Culebra, mun., P.R ... *B5 65
Culebra, isl., P.R ... B5 65
Culebra, peak, Colo ... D5 83
Culhuacán, Mex ... h9 63
Culiacán, Mex ... C3 63
Culion, Phil ... C6 35
Cúllar de Baza, Sp ... D4 20
Cullen, Webster, La ... B2 95
Cullen, Frederick, Md ... A3 85
Cullen, Scot ... C6 13
Culleoka, Maury, Tenn ... B4 117
Cullera, Sp ... C5 20
Cullion, N. Ire ... C4 11
Cullison, Pratt, Kans ... E5 93
Cullman, Cullman, Ala ... A3 78
Cullman, co., Ala ... A3 78
Culloden, Monroe, Ga ... D2 87
Culloden, Cabell, W. Va ... C2 123
Culloden, pt., N.Y ... E9 84
Cullom, Livingston, Ill ... C5 90
Cullowhee, Jackson, N.C ... f9 109
Culmore, Fairfax, Va ... *B5 121
Culoz, Fr ... D1 18
Culp Creek, Lane, Oreg ... D4 113
Culpeper, Van Buren, Ark ... B3 81
Culpeper, Culpeper, Va ... B4 121
Culpeper, co., Va ... B5 121
Culross, Scot ... *D5 13
Cultus Lake, B.C., Can ... f14 68
Culuene, riv., Braz ... A2 56
Culver, Marshall, Ind ... B5 91
Culver, Ottawa, Kans ... D6 93
Culver, St. Louis, Minn ... D6 99
Culver, Jefferson, Oreg ... C5 113
Culver City, Los Angeles, Calif ... m12 82
Culvers, lake, N.J ... A3 106
Culverton, Hancock, Ga ... C4 87
Culzean, bay, Scot ... E4 13
Cumaná, Ven ... A5 60
Cumberland, B.C., Can ... E5 68
Cumberland, Ont., Can ... g13 72
Cumberland, Marion, Ind ... E6, k11 91
Cumberland, Cass, Iowa ... C3 92
Cumberland, Harlan, Ky ... D7 94
Cumberland Foreside, Cumberland, Maine ... E2, g7 96
Cumberland, Allegany, Md ... k13 85
Cumberland, Webster, Miss ... B4 100
Cumberland, Cumberland, N.J ... E3 106
Cumberland, Cumberland, N.C ... C4 109
Cumberland, Guernsey, Ohio ... C4 111
Cumberland, Marshall, Okla ... C5 112
Cumberland, Cumberland, Va ... D4 121
Cumberland, King, Wash ... f12 122
Cumberland, Barron, Wis ... C1 124
Cumberland, co., N.S., Can ... D5 74
Cumberland, co., Ill ... D5 90
Cumberland, co., Ky ... D4 94
Cumberland, co., Maine ... E2 96
Cumberland, co., N.J ... E2 106
Cumberland, co., N.C ... C4 109
Cumberland, co., Pa ... F7 114
Cumberland, co., Tenn ... D8 117
Cumberland, co., Va ... C4 121
Cumberland, lake, Sask., Can ... C4 70
Cumberland, lake, Ky ... D5 94
Cumberland, mtn., Ky., Tenn ... C9 117
Cumberland, pen., N.W. Ter., Can ... C19 67
Cumberland, plat., Ala., Ky., Tenn ... A3 78, C6 94, D7 117
Cumberland, riv., U.S ... C11 77
Cumberland, sound, N.W. Ter., Can ... C19 67
Cumberland Center, Cumberland, Maine ... g7 96
Cumberland City, Stewart, Tenn ... A4 117
Cumberland Furnace, Dickson, Tenn ... A4 117
Cumberland Gap, Claiborne, Tenn ... C10 117
Cumberland Hill, Providence, R.I ... B11 84
Cumberland House, Sask., Can ... D4 70
Cumbres, pass, Colo ... D4 83
Cumbria, co., Eng ... F5 13
Cuming, co., Nebr ... C9 103
Cumming, Forsyth, Ga ... B2 87
Cumming, Warren, Iowa ... f8 92
Cummings, Atchison, Kans ... A7 93
Cummings, Traill, N. Dak ... B8 110
Cummington, Hampshire, Mass ... B2 97
Cumnock, Lee, N C ... B3 109
Cumnock [& Holmhead], Scot ... E4 13
Cumpas, Mex ... A3 63
Cumra, Tur ... D9 31
Cunard, Fayette, W. Va ... m13 123
Cunco, Chile ... B2 54
Cuncumen, Chile ... A2 54
Cundiff, Adair, Ky ... D4 94
Cundinamarca, dept., Col ... C3 60
Cundiyo, Santa Fe, N. Mex ... *B4 107
Cundys Harbor, Cumberland, Maine ... g8 96
Cunene, dist., Ang ... E1 48
Cunene, riv., Ang., S.W. Afr ... A1 49
Cuneo, It ... B1 21
Cunnamulla, Austl ... D5 52
Cunningham, Kingman, Kans ... E5 93
Cunningham, Carlisle, Ky ... f9 94
Cunningham, Montgomery, Tenn ... A4 117
Cupar, Sask., Can ... G3 70
Cupar, Scot ... D5 13
Cuprum, Adams, Idaho ... D2 89
Curacá, Braz ... C3 57
Curaçao, isl., Neth. Antilles ... H18 65
Curacautín, Chile ... B2 54
Curacó, riv., Arg ... B3 54
Curañilahue, Chile ... B2 54
Curaray, riv., Ec., Peru ... B2 58
Curdsville, Daviess, Ky ... C2 94
Curepto, Chile ... B2 54
Curiapo, Ven ... B5 60
Curicó, Chile ... A2 54
Curicó, prov., Chile ... A2 54
Curicuriari, riv., Braz ... D4 60
Curimata, riv., Braz ... h6 57
Curitiba, Braz ... D3 56
Curitibanos, Braz ... D2 56
Curlew, Palo Alto, Iowa ... B3 92
Curlew, Ferry, Wash ... A7 122
Curlew, lake, Wash ... A7 122
Curlew, riv., Wash ... A5 122
Curon Venosta, It ... C6 18
Currais Novos, Braz ... C3, h5 57
Curralinho, Braz ... C5 59
Curran, Ont., Can ... B10 72
Curran, Alcona, Mich ... D7 98
Currans, Ire ... E2 11
Currant, creek, Colo ... C5 83
Curreeny, Ire ... E3 11
Current, riv., Ark., Mo ... D6 101
Currie, Murray, Minn ... F3 99
Currituck, Currituck, N.C ... A6 109
Currituck, co., N.C ... A6 109
Curry, Alsk ... C10, f17 79
Curry, co., N. Mex ... C6 107
Curry, co., Oreg ... E2 113
Curryville, Pike, Mo ... B6 101
Curtea-de-Arges, Rom ... C7 22
Curtice, Lucas and Ottawa, Ohio ... A2, e7 111
Curtici, Rom ... B5 22
Curtin, Douglas, Oreg ... D3 113
Curtis, Clark, Ark ... D2 81
Curtis, Mackinac, Mich ... B5 98
Curtis, Frontier, Nebr ... D5 103
Curtis, Woodward, Okla ... A2 112
Curtis, isl., Austl ... A8 51
Curtiss, Clark, Wis ... D3 124
Curtisville, Allegheny, Pa ... E2, h14 114
Curuá, riv., Braz ... D4 59
Curuá do Sul, riv., Braz ... C4 59
Curuçá, Braz ... B1 57
Curug, Yugo ... C5 22
Curuguaty, Par ... D4 55
Curundu, Pan ... m11 62
Curupira, mts., Ven ... C5 60
Curuzú Cuatia, Arg ... E4 55
Curve, Lauderdale, Tenn ... B2 117
Curvelo, Braz ... E2 57
Curver, mtn., Switz ... C7 19
Curwensville, Clearfield, Pa ... E4 114
Curwood, mtn., Mich ... B2 98
Cushendall, N. Ire ... B5 11
Cushendunn, N. Ire ... B5 11
Cushing, Woodbury, Iowa ... B2 92
Cushing, Knox, Maine ... D3 96
Cushing, Howard, Nebr ... C7 103
Cushing, Payne, Okla ... B5 112
Cushing, Nacogdoches, Tex ... D5 118
Cushman, Independence, Ark ... B4 81
Cushman, Hampshire, Mass ... B3 97
Cushman, Golden Valley, Mont ... D7 102
Cushman, Lane, Oreg ... D2 113
Cushman, mtn., N.H ... C3 105
Cushman Lake, res., Wash ... B2 122
Cusick, Pend Oreille, Wash ... A8 122
Cusihuiriachic, Mex ... B3 63
Cusset, Fr ... D5 14
Cusseta, Chambers, Ala ... C4 78
Cusseta, Chattahoochee, Ga ... D2 87
Custar, Wood, Ohio ... A2 111
Custer, Mason, Mich ... E4 98
Custer, Yellowstone, Mont ... D9 102
Custer, Custer, Okla ... B3 112
Custer, Custer, S. Dak ... D2 116
Custer, Whatcom, Wash ... A3 122
Custer, co., Colo ... C5 83
Custer, co., Idaho ... E4 89
Custer, co., Mont ... D11 102
Custer, co., Nebr ... C6 103
Custer, co., Okla ... B2 112
Custer, co., S. Dak ... D2 116
Custer, peak, S. Dak ... C2 116
Custer Battlefield, nat. mon., Mont ... E9 102
Custer City, McKean, Pa ... C4 114
Cut Bank, Glacier, Mont ... B4 102
Cutbank, riv., Alta., Can ... B1 69
Cut Beaver, lake, Sask., Can ... D4 70
Cutchogue, Suffolk, N.Y ... m16 108
Cutervo, Peru ... C2 58
Cuthbert, Randolph, Ga ... E2 87
Cut Knife, Sask., Can ... E1 70
Cutler, Tulare, Calif ... *D4 82
Cutler, Ont., Can. ... A2 72
Cutler, Carroll, Ind ... D4 91
Cutler, Washington, Maine ... D5 96
Cutler City, Lincoln, Oreg ... C3 113
Cutler Ridge, Dade, Fla ... s13 86
Cut Off, Lafourche, La ... E5 95
Cutshin, Leslie, Ky ... C6 94
Cuttack, India ... D8 38, G10 40
Cutten, Humboldt, Calif ... *B1 82

Defiance, co., Ohio ... A1 111
Defiance, mtn., Oreg ... B5 113
Deford, Tuscola, Mich ... E7 98
De Forest, Dane, Wis ... E4 124
De Funiak Springs, Walton, Fla ... u15 86
Degeberga, Swe ... C8 24
Degeh Bur, Eth ... D5 47
Degerön, Swe ... u33 25
Degersheim, Switz ... B7 19
Deggendorf, Ger ... E7 17
De Graff, Swift, Minn ... E3 99
DeGraff, Logan, Ohio ... B2 111
Deh Bid, Iran ... F6 41
Dehibat, Tun ... C7 44
Dehiwala-Mount Lavinia, Sri Lanka ... *G6 39
Dehra Dūn, India ... B6 39, B6 40
Deh Shū, Afg ... F11 41
Deinze, Bel ... D3 15
Dej, Rom ... B6 22
Dejvice, Czech. (part of Prague) ... n17 26
De Kalb, De Kalb, Ill ... B5 90
De Kalb, Kemper, Miss ... C5 100
De Kalb, Buchanan, Mo ... B3 101
De Kalb, St. Lawrence, N.Y ... f9 108
De Kalb, Bowie, Tex ... C5 118
De Kalb, co., Ala ... A4 78
De Kalb, co., Ga ... C2 87
De Kalb, co., Ill ... B5 90
De Kalb, co., Ind ... B7 91
De Kalb, co., Mo ... B3 101
De Kalb, co., Tenn ... D8 117
De Kalb Junction, St. Lawrence, N.Y ... f9 108
Dekehare, Eth ... B4 47
Dekese, Zaire ... B3 48
Dekoa, Cen. Afr. Rep ... D3 46
Delacroix, St. Bernard, La ... k12 95
Delafield, Waukesha, Wis ... *E5 124
Delagua, Las Animas, Colo ... D6 83
Del Aire, Los Angeles, Calif ... *n12 82
Delake, Lincoln, Oreg ... C3 113
De Lamere, Sargent, N. Dak ... C8 110
Delanco, Burlington, N.J ... C3 106
De Land, Volusia, Fla ... C5 86
De Land, Piatt, Ill ... C5 90
Delaney, Madison, Ark ... B2 81
Delano, Kern, Calif ... E4 82
Delano, Wright, Minn ... E5 99
Delano, Polk, Tenn ... D9 117
Delano, peak, Utah ... E3 119
Delanson, Schenectady, N.Y ... C6 108
Delaplaine, Greene, Ark ... A5 81
Delārām, Afg ... E11 41
Delaronde, lake, Sask., Can ... C2 70
Delavan, Tazewell, Ill ... C4 90
Delavan, Morris, Kans ... D7 93
Delavan, Faribault, Minn ... G4 99
Delavan, Walworth, Wis ... F5 124
Delavan Lake, Walworth, Wis ... *F5 124
Delaware, Logan, Ark ... B2 81
Delaware, Ont., Can ... E3 72
Delaware, Delaware, Iowa ... B6 92
Delaware, Warren, N.J ... B2 106
Delaware, Delaware, Ohio ... B2 111
Delaware, Nowata, Okla ... A6 112
Delaware, co., Ind ... D7 91
Delaware, co., Iowa ... B6 92
Delaware, co., N.Y ... C5 108
Delaware, co., Ohio ... B2 111
Delaware, co., Okla ... A7 112
Delaware, co., Pa ... G11 114
Delaware, state, U.S ... C12 77, 85
Delaware, bay, Del ... C7 85
Delaware, bay, N.J ... E2 106
Delaware, mts., Tex ... o12 118
Delaware, riv., U.S ... C3 106
Delaware, riv., Kans ... A7 93
Delaware City, New Castle, Del ... A6 85
Delaware Lake, res., Ohio ... B2 111
Delaware Water Gap, Monroe, Pa ... E11 114
Delaware Water Gap, N.J., Pa ... B2 106
Delbarton, Mingo, W. Va ... D2 123
Delburne, Alta., Can ... C4 69
Delcambre, Vermilion and Iberia, La ... E4 95
Del City, Oklahoma, Okla ... B4 112
Delco, Columbus, N.C ... C4 109
Deleau, Man., Can ... E1 71
Delémont, Switz ... B3 19
De Leon, Comanche, Tex ... C3 118
De Leon Springs, Volusia, Fla ... C5 86
Delevan, Cattaraugus, N.Y ... C2 108
Delfore, Craighead, Ark ... B5 81
Delft, Cottonwood, Minn ... G3 99
Delft, Neth ... B4 15
Delfzijl, Neth ... A6 15
Delgado, Sal ... *D3 62
Delgado, cape, Moz ... D7 48
Delger Tsogtuin Huryee, Mong ... A2 36
Delhi, Merced, Calif ... *D3 82
Delhi, Ont., Can ... E4 72
Delhi, India ... C6 39, C6 40
Delhi, Delaware, Iowa ... B6 92
Delhi, Richland, La ... B4 95
Delhi, Redwood, Minn ... F3 99
Delhi, Delaware, N.Y ... C6 108
Delhi, Beckham, Okla ... B2 112
Delhi, ter., India ... *C6 40
Delhi Hills, Hamilton, Ohio ... *D1 111
Delia, Alta., Can ... D4 69
Delia, Jackson, Kans ... C8 93
Delight, Pike, Ark ... C2 81
Delikli, cape, Tur ... B8 31
Delisle, Que., Can ... A6 73
Delisle, Sask., Can ... F2 70
De Lisle, Harrison, Miss ... E4, f7 100
Delitzsch, G.D.R ... B7 17
Dell, Mississippi, Ark ... B5 81
Dell, Beaverhead, Mont ... F4 102
Delle, Fr ... B3 18
Dellenbaugh, mtn., Ariz ... A2 80
Dell Rapids, Minnehaha, S. Dak ... D9 116
Dellrose, Lincoln, Tenn ... B5 117
Dellroy, Carroll, Ohio ... B4 111
Dells, gorge, Wis ... E4 124
Dellslow, Monongalia, W. Va ... h11 123
Dellwood, Jackson, Fla ... B1 86
Dellwood, St. Louis, Mo ... *C7 101
Dellwood, Yamhill, Oreg ... B1 113
Dellys, Alg ... B5 44
Delmar, Winston, Ala ... A2 78
Del Mar, San Diego, Calif ... o15 82
Delmar, Sussex, Del ... D6 85
Delmar, Clinton, Iowa ... C7 92
Delmar, Wicomico, Md ... D6 85
Delmar, Albany, N.Y ... C7 108
Del Mar-Heights, San Luis Obispo, Calif ... *E3 82
Delmas, Sask., Can ... E1 70
Delmenhorst, F.R.G ... B4 16
Delmita, Starr, Tex ... F3 118
Delmont, Cumberland, N.J ... E3 106
Delmont, Westmoreland, Pa ... *F2 114
Delmont, Douglas, S. Dak ... D7 116
Del Monte Heights, Monterey, Calif ... *D3 82
Del Monte Park, Monterey, Calif ... *D3 82
Del Norte, Rio Grande, Colo ... D4 83
Del Norte, co., Calif ... B2 82
Deloit, Crawford, Iowa ... B2 92
Delong, Fulton, Ind ... B5 91
De Long, is., Sov. Un ... B35 4
Deloraine, Man., Can ... E1 71
Delorme, lake, Que., Can ... F18 67
Deloro, Ont., Can ... C7 72
De Loutre, bayou, La ... B3 95
Del Paso Heights, Sacramento, Calif ... *C3 82
Delphi, Carroll, Ind ... C4 91
Delphia, Musselshell, Mont ... D8 102
Delphos, Ottawa, Kans ... C6 93
Delphos, Allen, Ohio ... B1 111
Delran, Burlington, N.J ... C3 106
Delray Beach, Palm Beach, Fla ... F6 86
Del Ray Oaks, Monterey, Calif ... *D3 82
Del Rio, Cocke, Tenn ... D10 117
Del Rio, Val Verde, Tex ... E2 118
Del Rosa, San Bernardino, Calif ... *E5 82
Delson, Que., Can ... q19 73
Delta, Clay, Ala ... B4 78
Delta, Ont., Can ... C8 72
Delta, Delta, Colo ... C2 83
Delta, Keokuk, Iowa ... C5 92
Delta, Madison, La ... B5 95
Delta Cape Girardeau, Mo ... D8 101
Delta, Fulton, Ohio ... A2 111
Delta, York, Pa ... G9 114
Delta, Millard, Utah ... D3 119
Delta, co., Colo ... C3 83
Delta, co., Mich ... C4 98
Delta, co., Tex ... C5 118
Delta, peak, B.C., Can ... A3 68
Delta, res., N.Y ... B5 108
Delta Amacuro, ter., Ven ... B5 60
Delta Beach, Man., Can ... D2 71
Delta City, Sharkey, Miss ... B3 100
Delta Farms, Lafourche, La ... E5 95
Delta Junction, Alsk ... C10 79
Deltaville, Middlesex, Va ... C6 121
Delton, Barry, Mich ... F5 98
Deltona, Volusia, Fla ... D5 86
Delungra, Austl ... D8 51
Delvin, Ire ... D4 11
Delvine, Alb ... C3 23
Delyatin, Sov. Un ... G5 27
Demaine, Sask., Can ... G2 70
Demarcation, bay, Alsk ... B11 79
Demarest, Bergen, N.J ... h9 106
Demavend, mtn., Iran ... D6 41
Demba, Zaire ... C3 44
Dembidolo, Eth ... D3 47
Demchok, China ... A7 40
Demerara, riv., Guy ... A3 59
Demidov, Sov. Un ... D8 27
Deming, Hamilton, Ind ... D5 91
Deming, Luna, N. Mex ... E2 107
Deming, Whatcom, Wash ... A3 122
Demirci, Tur ... C7 23
Demir Kapija, Yugo ... E6 22
Demmin, G.D.R ... B6 16
Demmitt, Alta., Can ... B1 69
Demnate, Mor ... C3 44
Demopolis, Marengo, Ala ... C2 78
Demorest, Habersham, Ga ... B3 87
Demorestville, Ont., Can ... C7 72
DeMossville, Pendleton, Ky ... k14 94
Demotte, Jasper, Ind ... B3 91
Dempster, Hamlin, S. Dak ... C9 116
Demyanka, riv., Sov. Un ... B8 29
Demyanovka, Sov. Un ... C7 29
Denain, Fr ... D3 15
Denali, nat. park, Alsk ... C9 79
Denare Beach, Sask., Can ... C4 70
Denau, Sov. Un ... B13 41
Denaud, Hendry, Fla ... F5 86
Denbigh, McHenry, N. Dak ... A5 110
Denbigh, Wales ... A4 12
Denbigh, co., Wales ... A4 12
Den Burg, Neth ... A4 15
Dendermonde, Bel ... C4 15
Dendron, Sask., Can ... G2 70
Dendron, Surry, Va ... C6 121
Denezhkin Kamen, mtn., Sov. Un ... A5 29
Denham, Pulaski, Ind ... B4 91
Denham, mtn., Jam ... E13 65
Denham, Pine, Minn ... D6 99
Denham Springs, Livingston, La ... D5, h10 95
Den Helder, Neth ... B4 15
Denhoff, Sheridan, N. Dak ... B5 110
Denholm, Sask., Can ... E1 70
Den Hoorn, Neth ... A4 15
Denia, Sp ... C6 20
Deniau, Que., Can ... B8 73
Deniliquin, Austl ... G5 51
Denio, Humboldt, Nev ... B3 104
Denison, Crawford, Iowa ... B2 92
Denison, Jackson, Kans ... k14 93
Denison, Grayson, Tex ... C4 118
Denison, dam, Okla ... D5 112
Denizli, Tur ... D7 23
Denman, glacier, Ant ... C22 5
Denmark, Jackson, Ark ... B4 81
Denmark, N.S., Can ... D6 74
Denmark, Lee. Iowa ... D6 92
Denmark, Oxford, Maine ... E2 96
Denmark, Curry, Oreg ... E2 113
Denmark, Bamberg, S.C ... E5 115
Denmark, Madison, Tenn ... B2 117
Denmark, Brown, Wis ... D6, h10 124
Denmark, country, Eur ... D10 8, 24
Denmark, strait, Grnld., Ice ... C17 4
Dennard, Van Buren, Ark ... B3 81
Dennehotso, Apache, Ariz ... A6 80
Denning, Franklin, Ark ... B2 81
Denning, San Augustine, Tex ... D5 118
Dennis, Labette, Kans ... E8 93
Dennis, Barnstable, Mass ... C7 97
Dennis, Tishomingo, Miss ... A5 100
Dennis, hill, Conn ... B4 84
Dennis Port, Barnstable, Mass ... C7 97
Dennison, Goodhue and Rice, Minn ... F5 99
Dennison, Tuscarawas, Ohio ... B4 111
Denniston, Halifax, Va ... D4 121
Dennisville, Cape May, N.J ... E3 106
Denny & Dunipace, Scot ... *D5 13
Dennysville, Washington, Maine ... D5 96
Denny Terrace, Richland, S.C ... C5 115
Den Oever, Neth ... B5 15
Denoya, Osage, Okla ... A5 112
Denpasar, Indon ... G5 35
Dent, Otter Tail, Minn ... D3 99
Dent, co., Mo ... D6 101
Dent du Midi, mtn., Switz ... D2 19
Denton, Jeff Davis, Ga ... E4 87
Denton, Doniphan, Kans ... C8 93
Denton, Caroline, Md ... C6 85
Denton, Wayne, Mich ... p14 98
Denton, Fergus, Mont ... C7 102
Denton, Lancaster, Nebr ... D9 103
Denton, Davidson, N.C ... B2 109
Denton, Denton, Tex ... C4 118
Denton, co., Tex ... C4 118
Denton, creek, Tex ... A5 118
D'Entrecasteaux, pt., Austl ... F2 50
D'Entrecasteaux, is., Pap. N. Gui ... k13 50
D'Entrée, isl., Que., Can ... B8 74
Dentsville, Richland, S.C ... C6 115
Denver, Denver, Colo ... B6 83
Denver, Hancock, Ill ... C2 90
Denver, Miami, Ind ... C5 91
Denver, Bremer, Iowa ... B5 92
Denver, Worth, Mo ... A3 101
Denver, Lincoln, N.C ... B1 109
Denver, Lancaster, Pa ... F9 114
Denver, Humphreys, Tenn ... A4 117
Denver, Preston, W. Va ... B5 123
Denver, co., Colo ... B6 83
Denver City, Yoakum, Tex ... C1 118
Denville, Morris, N.J ... B4 106
Denzil, Sask., Can ... E1 70
Deoghar, India ... E11 40
Deora, Baca, Colo ... D8 83
De Panne, Bel ... C2 15
Departure Bay, B.C., Can ... f12 68
Depauville, Jefferson, N.Y ... A4 108
Depauw, Harrison, Ind ... H5 91
De Pere, Brown, Wis ... D5, h9 124
Depew, Erie, N.Y ... C2 108
Depew, Creek, Okla ... B5 112
Depoe Bay, Lincoln, Oreg ... C3 113
Deport, Lamar and Red River, Tex ... C5 118
Deposit, Broome and Delaware, N.Y ... C5 108
Depot Harbour, Ont., Can ... B4 72
Depue, Bureau, Ill ... B4 90
Deputy, Jefferson, Ind ... G6 91
DeQueen, Sevier, Ark ... C1 81
Dequen, Que., Can ... A5 73
DeQuincy, Calcasieu, La ... D2 95
Dera Ghāzi Khān, Pak ... B5 39, B3 40
Dera Ismāil Khān, Pak ... B3 40
Derbent, Sov. Un ... E3 29, G18 9
Derbetovka, Sov. Un ... I14 27
Derby, Austl ... C3 50
Derby, N.B., Can ... C4 74
Derby, Adams, Colo ... *B6 83
Derby, New Haven, Conn ... D4 84
Derby, Eng ... B6 12
Derby, Perry, Ind ... H4 91
Derby, Lucas, Iowa ... D4 92
Derby, Sedgwick, Kans ... E6, g12 93
Derby, Piscataquis, Maine ... C4 96
Derby, Pearl River, Miss ... E4 100
Derby, Erie, N.Y ... C2 108
Derby, Pickaway, Ohio ... C2 111
Derby, Orleans, Vt ... B4 120
Derby, Wise, Va ... f9 121
Derby, co., Eng ... A6 12
Derby Junction, N.B., Can ... C4 74
Derby Line, Orleans, Vt ... B4 120
Derecske, Hung ... B5 22
Derg, lake, Ire ... E3 11
De Ridder, Beauregard, La ... D2 95
Derik, Tur ... D13 31
Derma, Calhoun, Miss ... B4 100
Dermott, Chicot, Ark ... D4 81
Dermott, Scurry, Tex ... C2 118
Derna, see Darnah, Libya
Derniere, isl., La ... E5 95
Derravaragh, lake, Ire ... D4 11
Derry, Natchitoches, La ... C3 95
Derry, Rockingham, N.H ... E4 105
Derry, Sierra, N. Mex ... E2 107
Derry, Westmoreland, Pa ... F3 114
Derrybrien, Ire ... D3 11
Derudeb, Sud ... B4 47
De Ruyter, Madison, N.Y ... C5 108
Derventa, Yugo ... C3 22
Derwent, Alta., Can ... C5 69
Derwent, Guernsey, Ohio ... C4 111
Derwent, riv., Eng ... F5 13
Derwent, riv., Eng ... F6 13
Derwent, riv., Eng ... F8 13
Derwood, Montgomery, Md ... B3 85
Derzhavinskoye, Sov. Un ... E22 9
Desaguadero, riv., Arg ... A3 54
Desaguadero, riv., Bol ... C2 55
Des Allemands, St. Charles, La ... E5, k11 95
Des Allemands, bayou, La ... k11 95
Des Allemands, lake, La ... E5 95
Des Arc, Prairie, Ark ... C4 81
Des Arc, Iron, Mo ... D7 101
Des Arc, bayou, Ark ... B4 81
Des Arc, mtn., Mo ... D7 101
Desatoya, mts., Nev ... D4 104
Desatoya, peak, Nev ... D4 104
Desbiens, Que., Can ... A6 73
Desboro, Ont., Can ... C3 72
Descalvado, Braz ... k8 56
Deschaillons, Que., Can ... C5 73
Deschaillons sur St. Laurent, Que., Can ... *C5 73
Deschambault, Que., Can ... C6 73
Deschambault, lake, Sask., Can ... C4 70
Deschambault Lake, Sask., Can ... C4 70
Deschênes, Que., Can ... D2 73
Deschutes, co., Oreg ... D5 113
Deschutes, peak, Wash ... C3 122
Deschutes, riv., Oreg ... B6 113
Dese, Eth ... C4 47
Desengaño, cape, Arg ... D3 54
Desenzano del Garda, It ... D6 18
Deseret, Millard, Utah ... D3 119
Deseret, peak, Utah ... C3 119
Deseronto, Ont., Can ... C7 72
Desert, game range, Nev ... G6 104
Desert, mtn., W. Va ... m13 123
Desert, peak, Utah ... B2 119
Desert, val., Nev ... B3 104
Deserta Grande, isl., Port. (Madeira Is.) ... h12 20
Desert Center, Riverside, Calif ... F6 82
Desert Hot Springs, Riverside, Calif ... F5 82
Desha, Independence, Ark ... B4 81
Desha, co., Ark ... D4 81
Deshler, Thayer, Nebr ... D8 103
Deshler, Henry, Ohio ... A2 111
Desio, It ... D5 18
Des Lacs, Ward, N. Dak ... A4 110
Des Lacs, riv., N. Dak ... A4 110
Desloge, St. Francois, Mo ... D7 101
Desmarais, Alta., Can ... B4 69
Desmet, Benewah, Idaho ... B2 89
De Smet, Kingsbury, S. Dak ... C8 116
Desmochado, Par ... E4 55
Des Moines, Polk, Iowa ... C4, e8 92
Des Moines, Union, N. Mex ... A6 107
Des Moines, King, Wash ... B3, f11 122
Des Moines, co., Iowa ... D6 92
Des Moines, riv., U.S ... B9 77
Desna, riv., Sov. Un ... F8 27
Desolation, canyon, Utah ... D5 119
Desolacion, isl., Chile ... h11 54
De Soto, Sumter, Ga ... E2 87
De Soto, Jackson, Ill ... F4 90
De Soto, Dallas, Iowa ... C3 92
De Soto, Johnson, Kans ... D9, m16 93
De Soto, Clarke, Miss ... D5 100
De Soto, Jefferson, Mo ... C7 101
De Soto, Dallas, Tex ... *C4 118
De Soto, Crawford and Vernon, Wis ... E2 124
De Soto, co., Fla ... E5 86
De Soto, co., Miss ... A3 100
De Soto, par., La ... B2 95
De Soto City, Highlands, Fla ... E5 86
Despard, Harrison, W. Va ... k10 123
Des Peres, St. Louis, Mo ... f13 101
Des Plaines, Cook, Ill ... A6, h9 90
Des Plaines, riv., Ill., Wis ... k8 90, n11 124
Dessau, G.D.R ... B7 17
Destin, Okaloosa, Fla ... u15 86
Destrehan, St. Charles, La ... E5, k11 95
Desvres, Fr ... D9 12
Detlor, Ont., Can ... B7 72
Detmold, F.R.G ... B3 17
De Tour, Chippewa, Mich ... C7 98
Detour, pt., Mich ... C4 98
Detroit, Lamar, Ala ... A1 78
Detroit, Dickinson, Kans ... D6 93
Detroit, Somerset, Maine ... D3 96
Detroit, Wayne, Mich ... F7, p15 98
Detroit, Marion, Oreg ... C4 113
Detroit, Red River, Tex ... C5 118
Detroit, riv., Ont., Can., Mich ... F7 98
Detroit Beach, Monroe, Mich ... *G7 98
Detroit Lake, res., Oreg ... C4 113
Detroit Lakes, Becker, Minn ... D3 99
Dett, Zimb ... A4 49
Detva, Czech ... D5 26
Deuel, co., Nebr ... C3 103
Deuel, co., S. Dak ... C9 116
Deurne, Bel ... C4 15
Deux Frères, isl., Viet ... H7 38
Deux-Montagnes, Que., Can ... p19 73
Deux-Montagnes, co., Que., Can ... D3 73
Deux-Rivières, Ont., Can ... A6 72
Deux Rivières, Que., Can ... C5 73
Deux-Sèvres, dept., Fr ... *D3 14
Deva, Rom ... C6 22
De Valls Bluff, Prairie, Ark ... C4 81
Devavanya, Hung ... B5 22
Deventer, Neth ... B6 15
Devereux, Hancock, Ga ... C3 87
Deveron, riv., Scot ... C6 13
De View, bayou, Ark ... B4 81
Devil River, peak, N.Z ... N14 51
Devils, isl., Fr. Gu ... A4 59
Devils, lake, N. Dak ... A6 110
Devils, riv., Tex ... E2 118
Devils Elbow, Pulaski, Mo ... D5 101
Devils Lake, Ramsey, N. Dak ... B7 110
Devils Postpile, nat. mon., Calif ... D4 82
Devils Slide, Morgan, Utah ... B4 119
Devils Thumb, mtn., Alsk., B.C., Can ... E6 66
Devils Tower, Crook, Wyo ... B8 125
Devils Tower, nat. mon., Wyo ... B8 125
Devils Track, lake, Minn ... k9 99
Devin, Bul ... E7 22
Devine, Medina, Tex ... E3 118
Devizes, Eng ... C6 12
Devol, Cotton, Okla ... C3 112
DeVola, Washington, Ohio ... C4 111
Devoll, riv., Alb ... B3 23
Devon, Alta., Can ... C4 69
Devon, Bourbon, Kans ... E9 93
Devon, Toole, Mont ... B5 102
Devon, Chester, Pa ... *G11 114
Devon, co., Eng ... D4 12
Devon, isl., N.W. Ter., Can ... A15 66
Devonia, Anderson, Tenn ... C9 117
Devonport, Austl ... o15 50
Devonport, N.Z ... L15 51
Dewalt, Fort Bend, Tex ... r14 118
Dewar, Okmulgee, Okla ... B6 112
Dewar Lake, Sask., Can ... F1 70
Dewberry, Alta., Can ... C5 69
Dewdney, B.C., Can ... E6 68
Dewees, inlet, S.C ... k12 115
Dewees, isl., S.C ... F8 115
Deweese, Clay, Nebr ... D7 103
Dewey, Yavapai, Ariz ... C3 80
Dewey, Beaverhead, Mont ... E4 102
Dewey, Washington, Okla ... A6 112
Dewey, co., Okla ... B2 112
Dewey, co., S. Dak ... B4 116
Dewey Beach, Sussex, Del ... C7 85
Dewey Lake, res., Ky ... C7 94
Deweyville, Newton, Tex ... D6 118
Deweyville, Box Elder, Utah ... B3 119
De Winton, Alta., Can ... D3 69
DeWitt, Arkansas, Ark ... C4 81
DeWitt, DeWitt, Ill ... C5 90
DeWitt, Clinton, Iowa ... C7 92
DeWitt, Clinton, Mich ... F6 98
DeWitt, Carroll, Mo ... B4 101
DeWitt, Saline, Nebr ... D9 103
De Witt, Onondaga, N.Y ... B4 108
Dewitt, Dinwiddie, Va ... C5 121
DeWitt, co., Ill ... C5 90
DeWitt, co., Tex ... E4 118
Dewsbury, Eng ... A6 12
Dexter, Laurens, Ga ... D3 87
Dexter, Dallas, Iowa ... C3 92
Dexter, Cowley, Kans ... E7 93
Dexter, Calloway, Ky ... f10 94
Dexter, Penobscot, Maine ... C3 96
Dexter, Washtenaw, Mich ... F7 98
Dexter, Mower, Minn ... G6 99
Dexter, Stoddard, Mo ... E8 101
Dexter, Chaves, N. Mex ... D5 107
Dexter, Jefferson, N.Y ... A4 108
Dexter, Lane, Oreg ... D4 113
Dexter, lake, Fla ... C5 86
Deyhuk, Iran ... E8 41
Deyyer, Iran ... H5 41
Dez, riv., Iran ... E4 41
Dezfūl, Iran ... E4 41
Dezhnev, cape, Sov. Un ... C21 28
Dhahran (Aẓ Ẓahrān), Sau. Ar ... H5 41
Dhamtari, India ... G8 40
Dhānbād, India ... F11 40
Dhangarhi, Nep ... C8 40
Dhankuta, Nep ... D11 40
D'Hanis, Medina, Tex ... E3 118
Dhār, India ... F5 40
Dharamjaygarh, India ... F9 40
Dharmapuri, India ... F6 39
Dharmsāla, India ... A6 40
Dhārwār, India ... E6 39
Dhāt al Ḩajj, Sau. Ar ... H11 31
Dhaulāgiri, peak, Nep ... C9 40
Dhekelia, Grc ... g11 23
Dhenousa, isl., Grc ... D5 23
Dhībān, Jordan ... G10 31
Dhidhimotikhon, Grc ... B6 23
Dhílos (Delos), isl., Grc ... D5 23
Dhimitsana, Grc ... D4 23
Dhodekanisos, prov., Grc ... *D6 23
Dholpur, India ... D6 40
Dhoraji, India ... G3 40
Dhritsa, Grc ... g11 23
Dhubri, India ... E12 40
Dhule, India ... G5 40
Dia, isl., Grc ... E5 23
Diable, pt., Mart ... S11 65
Diablerets, mtn., Switz ... D3 19
Diablo, Contra Costa, Calif ... *D2 82
Diablo, canyon, Ariz ... C4 80
Diablo, dam, Wash ... A4 122
Diablo, mtn., Calif ... h9 82
Diablo, mtn., Oreg ... E6 113
Diablo, range, Calif ... D3 82
Diablo Heights, Pan ... m11 62
Diafarabé, Mali ... *D3 45
Diagonal, Ringgold, Iowa ... D3 92
Diamante, Arg ... A4 54
Diamantina, Braz ... E2 57
Diamantina, riv., Austl ... D7 50
Diamond, Ont., Can ... h11 72
Diamond, Parke, Ind ... E3 91
Diamond, Newton, Mo ... E3 101
Diamond, Portage, Ohio ... A4 111
Diamond, Harney, Oreg ... D8 113
Diamond, Kanawha, W. Va ... m12 123
Diamond, cave, Ark ... B2 81
Diamond, head, Haw ... g10 88
Diamond, lake, Oreg ... D4 113
Diamond, mts., Nev ... D6 104
Diamond, peak, Oreg ... D4 113
Diamond, pt., Indon ... k11 35
Diamond Bluff, Pierce, Wis ... D1 124
Diamond City, Alta, Can ... E4 69
Diamond Harbour, India ... F12 40
Diamond Hill, Providence, R.I ... *B11 84
Diamond Lake, Lake, Ill ... h9 90
Diamond Point, Warren, N.Y ... B7 108
Diamond Springs, Eldorado, Calif ... C3 82
Diamondville, Lincoln, Wyo ... E2 125
Diana, Giles, Tenn ... B5 117
Diana, Webster, W. Va ... C4 123
Dianalund, Den ... C5 24
Dianópolis, Braz ... D1 57
Díapaga, Upper Volta ... D5 45
Diapitan, bay, Phil ... n14 35
Diarbekr (Diyarbakir), Tur ... D3 31
Diaz, Jackson, Ark ... B4 81
Dibaya, Zaire ... C3 48
Dibble, iceberg tongue, Ant ... C26 5
Diber (Dibra), pref., Alb ... *B3 23
D'Iberville, Harrison and Jackson, Miss ... E5, f2 100
D'Iberville, lake, Que., Can ... g12 73
Diboll, Angelina, Tex ... D5 118
Dibra (Diber), pref., Alb ... *B3 23
Dibrell, Warren, Tenn ... D8 117
Dibrugarh, India ... C9 39
Dickens, Clay, Iowa ... A2 92
Dickens, Lincoln, Nebr ... D5 103
Dickens, Dickens, Tex ... C2 118
Dickens, co., Tex ... C2 118
Dickenson, co., Va ... e9 121
Dickerson, Montgomery, Md ... B3 85
Dickey, Aroostook, Maine ... A4 96
Dickey, LaMoure, N. Dak ... C7 110
Dickey, co., N. Dak ... C7 110
Dickeyville, Grant, Wis ... F3 124
Dickinson, Clarke, Ala ... D2 78
Dickinson, Stark, N. Dak ... C3 110
Dickinson, Galveston, Tex ... *E5 118
Dickinson, co., Iowa ... A2 92
Dickinson, co., Kans ... D6 93
Dickinson, co., Mich ... B3 98
Dickinson, dam, N. Dak ... C3 110
Dickinson Center, Franklin, N.Y ... f10 108
Dickson, Carter, Okla ... C5 112
Dickson, Dickson, Tenn ... A4 117
Dickson, co., Tenn ... A4 117
Dickson City, Lackawanna, Pa ... D10, m18 114
Dicle, riv., Tur ... D13 31
Didsbury, Alta., Can ... D3 69
Didwana, India ... D5 40
Die, Fr ... E6 14
Diébougou, Upper Volta ... D4 45
Dieburg, F.R.G ... D3 17
Diégo-Suarez, see Antsiranana, Mad.
Diégo-Suarez, prov., Mad ... f9 49
Diekirch, Lux ... E6 15
Diemel, riv., F.R.G ... B3 17
Dien Bien Phu, Viet ... B5 38
Diepholz, F.R.G ... B4 16
Dieppe, N.B., Can ... C5 74
Dieppe, Fr ... C4 14
Dierks, Howard, Ark ... C1 81
Diessen, F.R.G ... B7 18
Diest, Bel ... D5 15
Dieterich, Effingham, Ill ... D5 90
Dietikon, Switz ... B5 19
Dietrich, Lincoln, Idaho ... G4 89
Dieuze, Fr ... F6 15
Diever, Neth ... B6 15
Diez, F.R.G ... C3 17
Dif, Som ... E5 47
Differdange, Lux ... E5 15
Difficult, Smith, Tenn ... C8 117
Digby, N.S., Can ... E4 74
Digby, co., N.S., Can ... E4 74
Dighton, Lane, Kans ... D3 93
Dighton, Bristol, Mass ... C5 97
Dighton, Osceola, Mich ... D5 98
Digne, Fr ... E7 14
Digoel, riv., Indon ... G10 35
Digoin, Fr ... D5 14
Digos, Phil ... *D7 35
Dijon, Fr ... D6 14
Dike, Grundy, Iowa ... B5 92
Dikhil, Dji ... C5 47
Dikili, Tur ... C6 23
Dikirnis, Eg ... C3 32
Diksmuide, Bel ... C2 15
Dikson, Sov. Un ... B10 28
Dikwa, Nig ... D7 45
Dila, Eth ... D4 47
Dildo, Newf., Can ... *D5 75
Dili (Dilli), Indon ... G7 35
Dilia, Guadalupe, N. Mex ... B4 107
Dilke, Sask., Can ... G3 70
Dilkon, Navajo, Ariz ... B5 80
Dillard, Rabun, Ga ... B3 87
Dillard, Carter, Okla ... C4 112
Dill City, Washita, Okla ... B2 112
Dille, Clay, W. Va ... C4 123
Dillen, Johnson, Ark ... B2 81
Dillenburg, F.R.G ... C3 17
Diller, Jefferson, Nebr ... D9 103
Dilley, Frio, Tex ... E3 118
Dilliner, Greene, Pa ... F2 114
Dilling, Sud ... C2 47
Dillingen [an der Donau], F.R.G ... E5 17
Dillingen, F.R.G ... D1 17
Dillingham, Alsk ... D8 79
Dillon, Summit, Colo ... B4 83
Dillon, Beaverhead, Mont ... E4 102
Dillon, Dillon, S.C ... C9 115
Dillon, co., S.C ... C9 115
Dillon, lake, Sask., Can ... B6 69
Dillon, riv., Alta., Can ... B5 69
Dillon Lake, res., Ohio ... B3 111
Dillonvale, Jefferson, Ohio ... B5 111
Dillsboro, Dearborn, Ind ... F7 91
Dillsboro, Jackson, N.C ... f9 109
Dillsburg, York, Pa ... F7 114
Dillwyn, Buckingham, Va ... C4 121
Dilolo, Zaire ... D3 48
Dilworth, Clay, Minn ... D2 99
Dimashq, see Damascus, Syr.
Dimbelenge, Zaire ... C3 48
Dimbokro, I.C ... E4 45
Dîmbovița, riv., Rom ... C7 22
Dimitrovgrad, Bul ... D7 22
Dimitrovgrad, Yugo ... D6 22
Dimmit, co., Tex ... E3 118
Dimmitt, Castro, Tex ... B1 118
Dimock, Hutchinson, S. Dak ... D8 116
Dimona, Isr ... C7 32
Dimondale, Eaton, Mich ... F6 98
Di Monte Santu, cape, It ... D2 21
Dinagat, isl., Phil ... C7 35
Dinajpur, Bngl ... E12 40
Dinan, Fr ... C3 14
Dinant, Bel ... D4 15
Dinar, Tur ... C8 23
Dinard [-St. Enogat], Fr ... C2 14
Dinaric Alps, mts., Yugo ... D3 22
Dindigul, India ... F6 39
Dinero, Live Oak, Tex ... E4 118
Dingalan, bay, Phil ... o13 35
Dingelstädt, G.D.R ... B5 17
Dingess, Mingo, W. Va ... D2 123
Dingle, Bear Lake, Idaho ... G7 89
Dingle, Ire ... E1 11
Dingle, Phil ... *C6 35
Dingle, bay, Ire ... E1 11
Dingmans Ferry, Pike, Pa ... D12 114
Dingo, Austl ... A7 51
Dingolfing, F.R.G ... E7 17
Dinguiraye, Guinea ... D2 45
Dingwall, N.S., Can ... C9 74
Dingwall, Scot ... C4 13
Dinh Lap, Viet ... B7 38
Dinkelsbühl, F.R.G ... D5 17
Dinkey Creek, Fresno, Calif ... D4 82
Dinklage, F.R.G ... F2 24
Dinorwic, lake, Ont., Can ... E5 71
Dinosaur, nat. mon., Colo., Utah ... A1 83
Dinosaur, prov. park, Alta., Can ... D5 69
Dinsdale, Tama, Iowa ... B5 92
Dinslaken, F.R.G ... B1 17
Dinsmore, Sask., Can ... F2 70
Dinuba, Tulare, Calif ... D4 82
Dinwiddie, Dinwiddie, Va ... C5 121
Dinwiddie, co., Va ... C5 121
Dioïla, Mali ... D3 45
Diomede, is., Alsk ... C31 4
Diourbel, Sen ... D1 45
Diphu, pass, China, India ... C10 39
Diplo, Pak ... E2 40
Dipolog, Phil ... *D6 35
Dipper Harbour, N.B., Can ... D3 74
Dippoldiswalde, G.D.R ... C8 17
Diré, Mali ... C4 45
Dire Dawa, Eth ... D5 47
Diriamba, Nic ... E4 62
Dirico, Ang ... E3 48
Dirk Hartog, isl., Austl ... E1 50
Dirkou, Niger ... C7 45
Dirmil, Tur ... D7 23
Dirranbandi, Austl ... D7 51
Dirty Devil, riv., Utah ... E5 119
Disappointment, cape, Ant ... D9 5
Disappointment, cape, Wash ... C1 122
Disappointment, lake, Austl ... D3 50
Disautel, Okanogan, Wash ... A6 122
Discovery, mtn., Ant ... f39 5
Disentis (Mustèr), Switz ... C6 19
Dishman, Spokane, Wash ... g14 122
Dishnā, Eg ... D6 43
Disko, Fulton, Ind ... B6 91
Disko, isl., Grnld ... C20 4
Disley, Sask., Can ... G3 70
Disney, Mayes, Okla ... A6 112
Disputanta, Prince George, Va ... C5 121
Disraëli, Que., Can ... D6 73
Diss, Eng ... B9 12
Distant, Armstrong, Pa ... E3 114
District of Columbia, U.S ... C12 77, f8 85
Distrito Federal, fed. dist., Braz ... *B3 56
Distrito Federal, fed. dist., Mex ... D5 63
Distrito Federal, fed. dist., Ven ... A4 60
Disūq, Eg ... C2 32
Dittlinger, Comal, Tex ... h7 118
Ditzum, F.R.G ... A7 15
Diu, India ... G3 40
Divenié, Con ... F2 46
Divernon, Sangamon, Ill ... D4 90
Dives-sur-Mer, Fr ... C4 14
Divide, Silver Bow, Mont ... E4 102
Divide, co., N. Dak ... A2 110
Divide, peak, Wyo ... E5 125
Dividing, creek, Md ... D6 85
Dividing Creek, Cumberland, N.J ... E2 106
Divinópolis, Braz ... F2 57
Divion, Fr ... D2 15
Divisov, Czech ... o18 26
Divnoye, Sov. Un ... D2 29
Divo, I.C ... E3 45
Divrigi, Tur ... C12 31

Dix, Jefferson, Ill E5 90
Dix, Kimball, Nebr C2 103
Dix, dam, Ky C5 94
Dix, hills, N.Y. F3 84
Dix, mtn., N.Y. A7 108
Dix, riv., Ky C5 94
Dixence, riv., Switz D3 19
Dixfield, Oxford, Maine D2 96
Dixiana, Jefferson, Ala B3 78
Dixie, Escambia, Ala D3 78
Dixie, Woodruff, Ark B4 81
Dixie, Ont., Can m14 72
Dixie, Brooks, Ga F3 87
Dixie, Idaho, Idaho D3 89
Dixie, Caddo, La B2 95
Dixie, Stephens, Okla C4 112
Dixie, Walla Walla, Wash C7 122
Dixie, Nicholas, W. Va C3, m13 123
Dixie, co., Fla C3 86
Dixie, butte, Oreg C8 113
Dixie Union, Ware, Ga E4 87
Dixmoor, Cook, Ill *B6 90
Dixon, Solano, Calif C3 82
Dixon, Lee, Ill B4 90
Dixon, Scott, Iowa C7 92
Dixon, Webster, Ky C2 94
Dixon, Pulaski, Mo D5 101
Dixon, Sanders, Mont C2 102
Dixon, Dixon, Nebr B9 103
Dixon, Rio Arriba, N. Mex A4 107
Dixon, Van Wert, Ohio B1 111
Dixon, Gregory, S. Dak D6 116
Dixon, Carbon, Wyo E5 125
Dixon, co., Nebr B9 103
Dixon, entrance, Alsk., B.C., Can B1 68
Dixons Mills, Marengo, Ala C2 78
Dixon Springs, Pope, Ill F5 90
Dixonville, Escambia, Ala D2 78
Dixonville, Alta., Can A2 69
Dixonville, Indiana, Pa E4 114
Dixville, Que., Can D6 74
Dixville, peak, N.H g7 105
Dixville Notch, Coos, N.H g7 105
Diyarbakir, Tur D13 31
Dizy-le-Gros, Fr E4 15
Dizy-Magenta, Fr E3 15
Dja, riv., Cam E2 46
Djado, Niger B7 45
Djafou, Alg D5 44
Djakarta, see Jakarta, Indon.
Djakovica, Yugo D5 22
Djakovo, Yugo C4 22
Djambala, Con F2 46
Djanet, Alg E6 44
Djaravica, peak, Yugo D5 22
Djedeida, Tun F11 30
Djelfa, Alg C5 44
Djema, Cen. Afr. Rep D5 46
Djénné, Mali D4 45
Djerba, isl., Tun C7 44, H12 30
Djerid, salt lake, Tun C6 44
Djibo, Upper Volta D4 45
Djibouti, Dji C5 47
Djibouti, country E10 42, C5 47
Djidjelli, Alg B6 44
Djiring, Viet G8 38
Djokupunda, see Charlesville, Zaire
Djolu, Zaire A3 48
Djoua, riv., Con., Gabon E2 46
Djouf, basin, Maur B3 45
Djougou, Benin E5 45
Djugu, Zaire A5 48
Djurdjevac, Yugo B3 22
Djursholm, Swe t36 25
D'Lo, Simpson, Miss D4 100
Dmitriyevka, Sov. Un H12, q21 27
Dmitriyev-Lgovskiy, Sov. Un E10 27
Dmitrov, Sov. Un C11 27
Dmitrovsk-Orlovskiy, Sov. Un E10 27
Dnepr, riv., Sov. Un H9 27
Dneprodzerzhinsk, Sov. Un G10 27
Dnepropetrovsk, Sov. Un G10 27
Dnestr, riv., Sov. Un H7 27
Dno, Sov. Un C7 27
Doaktown, N.B., Can C3 74
Doba, Chad D3 46
Dobbinton, Ont., Can C3 72
Dobbs Ferry, Westchester, N.Y g13 108
Dobbyn, Austl C6 50
Döbeln, G.D.R B6 17
Doberlug-Kirchhain, G.D.R B8 17
Doblas, Arg B4 54
Dobo, Indon G8 35
Doboj, Yugo C4 22
Doboy, sound, Ga E5 87
Dobrejovice, Czech o18 26
Dobrich, see Tolbukhin, Bul.
Dobris, Czech o17 26
Dobrogea, prov., Rom *C9 22
Dobrovice, Czech n18 26
Dobrovolsk, Sov. Un A7 26
Dobruja, reg., Bul., Rom C9 22
Dobsina, Czech D6 26
Dobson, Surry, N.C. A2 109
Doce, riv., Braz E2 55
Docena, Jefferson, Ala f7 78
Dock Junction, Glynn, Ga *E5 87
Dockton, King, Wash f11 122
Doctor Arroyo, Mex C4 63
Dr. B. T. Diefenbaker, lake, Sask., Can F2 70
Doctors, lake, Fla m8 86
Doctors Inlet, Clay, Fla m8 86
Doctortown, Wayne, Ga E5 87
Doddridge, Miller, Ark D2 81
Doddridge, co., W. Va B4 123
Dodds, Alta., Can C4 69
Doddsville, Sunflower, Miss D3 100
Dodecanese, prov., Grc D6 23
Dodecanese, is., Grc D6 23
Dodge, Worcester, Mass B4 97
Dodge, Dodge, Nebr C9 103
Dodge, Dunn, N. Dak B3 110
Dodge, Trempealeau, Wis D2 124
Dodge, co., Ga D3 87
Dodge, co., Minn G6 99
Dodge, co., Nebr C9 103
Dodge, co., Wis E5 124
Dodge Center, Dodge, Minn F6 99
Dodge City, Ford, Kans E3 93
Dodgeville, Ashtabula, Ohio A5 111
Dodgeville, Iowa, Wis F3 124
Dodoma, Tan C6 48
Dodsland, Sask., Can F1 70
Dodson, Winn, La B3 95
Dodson, Phillips, Mont B8 102
Dodson, Collingsworth, Tex B2 118
Dodson, pen., Ant B6 5
Doebay, San Juan, Wash A3 122
Doe River, B.C., Can A7 68
Doerun, Colquitt, Ga E3 87
Doe Run, St. Francois, Mo D7 101
Doetinchem, Neth C6 15
Dog, isl., Fla C2 86
Dog, lake, Man., Can D2 71
Dog, riv., Vt C3 120
Dog Creek, B.C., Can D6 68
Dog Keys, pass, Miss g8 100
Dogondoutchi, Niger D5 45
Dogubayazit, Tur C15 31
Doha (Ad Dawḥah), Qatar I5 41
Dohad, India F5 40
Doheny, Que., Can B5 73
Doi Angka, mtn., Thai C3 38
Dois Irmãos, mts., Braz C2 57
Dojran, lake, Yugo E6 22
Dokkum, Neth A6 15
Doksy, Czech C9 17
Doland, Spink, S. Dak C7 116
Dolavón, Arg C3 54
Dolbeau, Que., Can G18 66
Dolchburg, Maverick, Tex E2 118
Dol [-de-Bretagne], Fr C3 14
Dôle, Fr D6 14
Dolega, Pan F6 62
Doleib Hill, Sud D3 47
Doles, Worth, Ga E3 87
Dolgellau, Wales B4 12
Dolgeville, Fulton and Herkimer, N.Y. B6 108
Dolina, Sov. Un D8 26
Dolinsk, Sov. Un C11 37
Dolinskoye, Sov. Un B9 22
Dolisie, Con F2 46
Dollar, Scot *D5 13
Dollar Bay, Houghton, Mich A2 98
Dollard, Sask., Can H1 70
Dollart, bay, Neth A7 15
Dollarville, Luce, Mich B5 98
Dolliver, Emmet, Iowa A3 92
Dolo, Eth E5 47
Dolomite, Jefferson, Ala B3, g7 78
Dolomites, mts., It C7 18
Dolores, Arg B5 54
Dolores, Montezuma, Colo D2 83
Dolores, Guat B3 62
Dolores, Mex B3 63
Dolores, Webb, Tex F3 118
Dolores, Ur E1 56
Dolores, co., Colo D2 83
Dolores, riv., Colo., Utah E7 119
Dolores Hidalgo, Mex m13 63
Dolphin and Union, straits, N.W. Ter., Can C9 66
Dolphin Head, mtn., Jam E12 65
Dolton, Cook, Ill k9 90
Dolton, Turner, S. Dak D8 116
Dolzhanskaya, Sov. Un q22 27
Dom, mtn., Switz D4 19
Domadare, Som E5 47
Domanovici, Yugo D3 22
Domažlice, Czech D6 26
Dombarovskiy, Sov. Un C5 29
Dombås, Nor F3 25
Dombasle [-sur-Meurthe], Fr F6 15
Dombe Grande, Ang D1 48
Dombey, Beaver, Okla D3 112
Dombóvár, Hung B4 22
Domburg, Neth C3 15
Dome, Yuma, Ariz E1 80
Dome, mts., Ariz D1 80
Dome, The, mtn., Vt F2 120
Domeyko, Chile D2 55
Domeyko, range, Chile D2 55
Domfront, Fr C3 14
Dominguez, Los Angeles, Calif *F4 82
Dominica, country, N.A I14 64
Dominica, passage, N.A I14 64
Dominican Republic, country, N.A H13 61, E8 64
Dominion, N.S., Can C9 74
Dominion, cape, N.W. Ter., Can C18 67
Dominion, lake, Newf., Can h9 75
Dominion City, Man., Can E3 71
Domino, Cass, Tex C5 118
Dömitz, G.D.R B5 16
Dommel, riv., Neth C5 15
Domo, Eth D6 47
Domodedovo, Sov. Un n17 27
Domodossola, It C4 18
Dom Pedrito, Braz E2 56
Dompierre [-sur-Authie], Fr D9 12
Domremy, Sask., Can E3 70
Domuyo, mtn., Arg B2 54
Domvraina, Grc g9 23
Don, pen., B.C., Can C3 68
Don, riv., Sov. Un C11 29
Dona Ana, Dona Ana, N. Mex E3 107
Dona Ana, co., N. Mex E2 107
Donaghadee, N. Ire C6 11
Donald, Ont., Can C6 72
Donald, Marion, Oreg h12 113
Donald, Taylor, Wis C3 124
Donalda, Alta., Can C4 69
Donalds, Abbeville, S.C. C3 115
Donaldson, Hot Springs, Ark C3 81
Donaldson, Marshall, Ind B5 91
Donaldson, Kittson, Minn B2 99
Donaldson, Schuylkill, Pa E9 114
Donaldsonville, Ascension, La D4, h10 95
Donaldsonville, Seminole, Ga E2 87
Donard, Ire D5 11
Donat-Ems, Switz C7 19
Donau (Danube), riv., Aus A2 22
Donaueschingen, F.R.G E4 16
Donauwörth, F.R.G B5 17
Donavon, Sask., Can E2 70
Don Benito, Sp C3 20
Doncaster, Eng A6 12
Dondo, Ang C1 48
Dondo, Moz A5 49
Donegal, Ire C3 11
Donegal, co., Ire C3 11
Donegal, bay, Ire C3 11
Donegal, pt., Ire D2 11
Doneraile, Darlington, S.C. C8 115
Donets, riv., Sov. Un G13 27
Donetsk, Sov. Un H11, q20 27
Dongara, Austl E1 50
Donggala, Indon F5 35
Dong Hoi, Viet D7 38
Dongo, Zaire A2 48
Dongola, Union, Ill F4 90
Dongou, Con E3 46
Donington, Eng B7 12
Doniphan, Ripley, Mo E7 101
Doniphan, Hall, Nebr D7 103
Doniphan, co., Kans C8 93
Donji Vakuf, Yugo C3 22
Donkey, creek, Wyo B7 125
Donkin, N.S., Can C10 74
Donley, co., Tex B2 118
Donna, Hidalgo, Tex F3 118
Donnacona, Que., Can C6, o16 73
Donnellson, Montgomery and Bond, Ill D4 90
Donnellson, Lee, Iowa D6 92
Donnelly, Alta., Can B2 69
Donnelly, Valley, Idaho E2 89
Donnelly, Stevens, Minn E2 99
Donner, Terrebonne, La E5, k10 95
Donnybrook, Ward, N. Dak A4 110
Donora, Washington, Pa F2 114
Donovan, Iroquois, Ill C6 90
Donzère, Fr E6 14
Dooagh, Ire D1 11
Doogort, Ire C1 11
Doole, McCulloch, Tex D3 118
Dooling, Dooly, Ga D3 87
Doolittle, Phelps, Mo D6 101
Dooly, co., Ga D3 87
Doon, Lyon, Iowa A1 92
Doon, lake, Scot E4 13
Doonbeg, Ire E2 11
Door, co., Wis D6 124
Dora, Walker, Ala B2 78
Dora, Ozark, Mo E5 101
Dora, Roosevelt, N. Mex D6 107
Dora, Coos, Oreg D3 113
Dorado, mun., P.R *B3 65
Doran, Wilkin, Minn D2 99
Doraville, DeKalb, Ga h8 87
Dorcas, Okaloosa, Fla u15 86
Dorchester, N.B., Can D5 74
Dorchester, Eng D5 12
Dorchester, Liberty, Ga E2 87
Dorchester, Allamakee, Iowa A6 92
Dorchester, Saline, Nebr D8 103
Dorchester, Cumberland, N.J E3 106
Dorchester, Dorchester, S.C. E7 115
Dorchester, Clark, Wis D3 124
Dorchester, co., Que., Can C7 73
Dorchester, co., Md D5 85
Dorchester, co., S.C E7 115
Dorchester, cape, N.W. Ter., Can C17 67
Dorchester Crossing, N.B., Can C5 74
Dorcyville, Iberville, La h9 95
Dordogne, dept., Fr *E4 14
Dordogne, riv., Fr E3 14
Dordrecht, Neth C4 15
Dordrecht, S. Afr D4 49
Doré, lake, Ont., Can B7 72
Doré, lake, Sask., Can C2 70
Doré Lake, Sask., Can C2 70
Dorena, Lane, Oreg D4 113
Dorenlee, Alta., Can C4 69
Dores, Scot C4 13
Dores do Indaiá, Braz E1 57
Dorfen, F.R.G A8 18
Dorgali, It D2 21
Dori, Upper Volta D4 45
Dorion-Vaudreuil, Que., Can q18 73
Dorking, Eng m12 10
Dormans, Fr E3 15
Dormont, Allegheny, Pa k13 114
Dornbirn, Aus B5 18
Dornie, Scot C3 13
Dornoch, Scot C4 13
Dornoch, firth, Scot C5 13
Dorogobuzh, Sov. Un D9 27
Dorohoi, Rom B8 22
Dorothy, Alta., Can D4 69
Dorothy, Red Lake, Minn C2 99
Dorothy, Atlantic, N.J E3 106
Dorothy, Raleigh, W. Va n13 123
Dorothy Pond, Worcester, Mass B4 97
Dorr, Allegan, Mich F5 98
Dorrance, Russell, Kans D5 93
Dorrigo, Austl E9 51
Dorris, Siskiyou, Calif B3 82
Dorset, Ont., Can B6 72
Dorset, Hubbard, Minn D4 99
Dorset, Ashtabula, Ohio A7 111
Dorset, Bennington, Vt E2 120
Dorset, co., Eng D5 12
Dorset, peak, Vt E2 120
Dorsey, Madison, Ill f13 101
Dorsey, Anne Arundel and Howard, Md B4 85
Dorsey, Itawamba, Miss A5 100
Dorsten, F.R.G B1 17
Dortmund, F.R.G B2 17
Dortmund-Ems, canal, F.R.G B2 17
Dorton, Pike, Ky C7 94
Dortyol, Tur D11 31
Dorum, F.R.G E2 24
Doruma, Zaire A4 48
Dorval, Que., Can q19 73
Dorya, riv., Eth D5 47
Dos Bahias, cape, Arg C3 54
Dos Bocas, res., P.R B2 65
Dos Hermanas, Sp D3 20
Dosquet, Que., Can C6 73
Dos Rios, Mendocino, Calif C2 82
Dosse, riv., G.D.R E6 24
Dosso, Niger D5 45
Dothan, Houston, Ala D4 78
Dothan, Fayette, W. Va n13 123
Doting Cove, Newf., Can D5 75
Dott, Mercer, W. Va D3 123
Doty, Lewis, Wash C2 122
Doty, isl., Wis h9 124
Douai, Fr B5 14
Douala (Duala), Cam E1 46
Douarnenez, Fr C1 14
Doub, Frederick, Md B3 85
Double, mtn., Ala g7 78
Double Bayou, Chambers, Tex r15 118
Double Mer, lake, Newf., Can A2 75
Double Oak, mtn., Ala g7 78
Double Springs, Winston, Ala A2 78
Doubletop, peak, Wyo C2 125
Doubs, dept., Fr B2 19
Doubs, riv., Fr., Switz B2 19, D7 14
Doubtful, sound, N.Z P11 51
Doucette, Tyler, Tex D5 118
Douds, Van Buren, Iowa D5 92
Doué [-la-Fontaine], Fr D3 14
Douentza, Mali D4 45
Dougherty, Cerro Gordo, Iowa B4 92
Dougherty, Murray, Okla C4 112
Dougherty, co., Ga E2 87
Douglas, Alsk D13, k22 79
Douglas, Cochise, Ariz F6 80
Douglas, Ont., Can B8 72
Douglas, Coffee, Ga E4 87
Douglas, I. of Man C4 10
Douglas, Worcester, Mass B4 97
Douglas, Allegan, Mich F4 98
Douglas, Olmsted, Minn F6 99
Douglas, Otoe, Nebr D9 103
Douglas, Ward, N. Dak B4 110
Douglas, Garfield, Okla A4 112
Douglas, Scot E5 13
Douglas, S. Afr C3 49
Douglas, Converse, Wyo D7 125
Douglas, co., Colo B6 83
Douglas, co., Ga C2 87
Douglas, co., Ill D5 90
Douglas, co., Kans D8 93
Douglas, co., Minn E3 99
Douglas, co., Mo E5 101
Douglas, co., Nebr C9 103
Douglas, co., Nev E2 104
Douglas, co., Oreg D3 113
Douglas, co., S. Dak D7 116
Douglas, co., Wash B6 122
Douglas, co., Wis B2 124
Douglas, chan., B.C., Can C3 68
Douglas, lake, Mich C6 98
Douglas, lake, Tenn D10 117
Douglas, pt., Ont., Can C3 72
Douglas Lake, B.C., Can D7 68
Douglass, Butler, Kans E7, h12 93
Douglas Station, Man., Can E2 71
Douglastown, N.B., Can B4 74
Douglasville, Baldwin, Ala E2 78
Douglasville, Douglas, Ga C2 87
Doullens, Fr B5 14
Doulus, head, Ire F1 11
Doumé, Cam E2 46
Doune, Scot *D5 13
Dounreay, Scot B5 13
Dour, Bel D3 15
Doura, Mali D3 45
Dourada, mts., Braz D1 57
Dourado, Braz m7 56
Dourdan, Fr F2 15
Douro (Duero), riv., Port B1 20
Douro Litoral, prov., Port *B1 20
Dousman, Waukesha, Wis E5 124
Douz, Tun C6 44
Dove Creek, Dolores, Colo D2 83
Dover, Pope, Ark B2 81
Dover, Kent, Del B6 85
Dover, Eng C9 12
Dover, Hillsborough, Fla D4 86
Dover, Screven, Ga D5 87
Dover, Bonner, Idaho A2 89
Dover, Shawnee, Kans D8 93
Dover, Mason, Ky B6 94
Dover, Norfolk, Mass h10 97
Dover, Olmsted, Minn G6 99
Dover, Lafayette, Mo B4 101
Dover, Stafford, N.H D5 105
Dover, Morris, N.J B3 106
Dover, Craven, N.C B5 109
Dover, Tuscarawas, Ohio B4 111
Dover, Kingfisher, Okla B4 112
Dover, York, Pa F8 114
Dover, Stewart, Tenn A4 117
Dover, riv., Alta., Can A4 69
Dover, strait, Eng., Fr E7 10
Dover-Foxcroft, Piscataquis, Maine C3 96
Doverhill, Martin, Ind G4 91
Dover Plains, Dutchess, N.Y D7 108
Dover South Mills, Piscataquis, Maine C3 96
Dovesville, Darlington, S.C C8 115
Dovray, Murray, Minn F3 99
Dovrefjell, mts., Nor F3 25
Dow, Pittsburg, Okla C6 112
Dow, Jersey, Ill D3 90
Dowa, Malawi D5 48
Dowagiac, Cass, Mich G4 98
Dow City, Crawford, Iowa C2 87
Dowdell Knob, mtn., Ga D2 87
Dowell, Jackson, Ill F4 90
Dowell, Calvert, Md D5 85
Dowelltown, De Kalb, Tenn C8 117
Dowlat Yār, Afg D12 41
Dowlatābād, Afg C13 41
Dowling, lake, Alta., Can D4 69
Dowling Park, Suwannee, Fla B3 86
Downer, Clay, Minn D2 99
Downer, Sheridan, Wyo *B6 125
Downers Grove, Du Page, Ill B5, k8 90
Downey, Los Angeles, Calif n12 82
Downey, Bannock, Idaho G6 89
Downham Market, Eng B8 12
Downhill, N. Ire B5 11
Downieville, Sierra, Calif C3 82
Downing, Schuyler, Mo A5 101
Downing, Dunn, Wis C1 124
Downingtown, Chester, Pa F10 114
Downpatrick, N. Ire C6 11
Downpatrick, head, Ire C2 11
Downs, McLean, Ill C5 90
Downs, Osborne, Kans C5 93
Downs, mtn., Wyo C3 125
Downsville, Union, La B3 95
Downsville, Delaware, N.Y C5 108
Downsville, Dunn, Wis D2 124
Downton, mtn., B.C., Can C5 68
Dows, Wright and Franklin, Iowa B4 92
Dowshi, Afg D14 41
Doyle, Lassen, Calif B3 82
Doyle, Livingston, La. (part of Livingston) A6 95
Doyle, White, Tenn D8 117
Doyle, creek, Kans A6 93
Doyles, Newf., Can E2 75
Doylestown, Wayne, Ohio B4 111
Doylestown, Bucks, Pa F11 114
Doyline, Webster, La B2 95
Doyon, Ramsey, N. Dak A7 110
Dozier, Crenshaw, Ala D3 78
Dra, plat., Alg D3 44
Drâa, wadi, Alg., Mor D3 44
Drabenderhöhe, F.R.G C2 17
Drachten, Neth A6 15
Dracut, Middlesex, Mass A5 97
Drăgăneşti, Rom C7 22
Draganovo, Bul D7 22
Drăgăşani, Rom C7 22
Dragons Mouth, strait, Trin N22 65
Dragoon, Cochise, Ariz E5 80
Dragoon, creek, Kans D8 93
Dragør, Den C6 24
Draguignan, Fr F7 14
Drain, Douglas, Oreg D3 113
Drake, Yavapai, Ariz C3 80
Drake, Sask., Can E3 70
Drake, Larimer, Colo A5 83
Drake, McHenry, N. Dak B5 110
Drake, creek, Ky D3 94
Drake, passage, Ant D6 5
Drakensberg, mts., S. Afr J8 42
Drakesboro, Muhlenberg, Ky C2 94
Drakes Branch, Charlotte, Va D4 121
Drakesville, Davis, Iowa D5 92
Draketown, Haralson, Ga C1 87
Drama, Grc B5 23
Drama, prov., Grc *B5 23
Drama, riv., Pol g9 26
Drammen, Nor H4, p28 25
Dramselva, riv., Nor p27 25
Drance, riv., Fr C2 14
Drancy, Fr g10 14
Draper, Jones, S. Dak D5 116
Draper, Salt Lake, Utah C4 119
Draperstown, N. Ire C5 11
Drasco, Cleburne, Ark B4 81
Drau, riv., Aus E6 16
Drava, riv., Yugo B2 22
Draveil, Fr F2 15
Dravograd, Yugo B2 22
Drawenburg, see Drawsko, Pol.
Drawsko, Pol B3 26
Drayton, Ont., Can D4 72
Drayton, Pembina, N. Dak A8 110
Drayton, Spartanburg, S.C. B4 115
Drayton Plains, Oakland, Mich F7 98
Drayton Valley, Alta., Can C3 69
Drebkau, G.D.R B9 17
Drelsdorf, F.R.G D3 24
Drenthe, prov., Neth B6 15
Dresbach, Winona, Minn G7 99
Dresden, Ont., Can E2 72
Dresden, G.D.R B8 17
Dresden, Decatur, Kans C3 93
Dresden, Sagadahoc, Maine D3 96
Dresden, Cavalier, N. Dak A7 110
Dresden, Muskingum, Ohio B3 111
Dresden, Weakley, Tenn A3 117
Dresden Village, Macomb, Mich *F7 98
Dresser, Polk, Wis C1 124
Dresslerville, Douglas, Nev E2 104
Dreux, Fr C4 14
Drew, Penobscot, Maine C4 96
Drew, Sunflower, Miss B3 100
Drew, Douglas, Oreg E4 113
Drew, co., Ark D4 81
Drewryville, Southampton, Va D5 121
Drews, res., Oreg E6 113
Drewsey, Harney, Oreg D8 113
Drewsville, Cheshire, N.H D2 105
Drexel, Cass, Mo C3 101
Drexel, Burke, N.C B1 109
Drexel, Montgomery, Ohio C1 111
Drexel Hill, Delaware, Pa p20 114
Drezna, Sov. Un n18 27
Driffield, Eng F8 13
Drift, Floyd, Ky C7 94
Drifton, Luzerne, Pa D10 114
Driftpile, Alta., Can B3 69
Driftpile, riv., Alta., Can B3 69
Driftwood, Alfalfa, Okla A3 112
Driftwood, Cameron, Pa D5 114
Driggs, Teton, Idaho F7 89
Drimoleague, Ire F2 11
Drin, gulf, Alb B2 23
Drina, riv., Yugo C4 22
Drinkwater, Sask., Can G3 70
Dripping Springs, Hays, Tex D3 118
Driscoll, Burleigh, N. Dak C5 110
Driscoll, Nueces, Tex F4 118
Driskill, mtn., La B3 95
Drissa, Sov. Un D6 27
Driver, Mississippi, Ark B5 81
Dröbak, Nor H4, p28 25
Drogheda, Ire D5 11
Drogobych, Sov. Un G4 27
Droitwich, Eng B5 12
Dromahair, Ire C3 11
Drôme, dept., Fr *E6 14
Drôme, riv, Fr E6 14
Dromore, N. Ire C4 11
Dromore West, Ire C3 11
Dronero, It E3 18
Dronfield, Eng A6 12
Dronninglund, Den A4 24
Dropmore, Man., Can D1 71
Druid, Sask., Can F1 70
Druid Hills, DeKalb, Ga *C2 87
Drum, isl., S.C k12 115
Drumahoe, N. Ire C4 11
Drumbeg, Scot B3 13
Drumbo, Ont., Can D4 72
Drumcliffe, Ire C3 11
Drumheller, Alta., Can D4 69
Drumlish, Ire D4 11
Drummond, Fremont, Idaho E7 89
Drummond, Granite, Mont D3 102
Drummond, Garfield, Okla A3 112
Drummond, Bayfield, Wis B2 124
Drummond, co., Que., Can D5 73
Drummond, isl., Mich B7 98
Drummond, lake, Va D6 121
Drummond Island, Chippewa, Mich B7 98
Drummondville, Que., Can D5 73
Drummore, Scot F4 13
Drumod, Ire D4 11
Drumquin, N. Ire C4 11
Drumright, Creek, Okla B5 112
Drumshanbo, Ire C3 11
Druzhina, Sov. Un C36 4
Druzhkovka, Sov. Un q20 27
Drweca, riv., Pol B5 26
Dry, creek, Kans g12 93
Dry, fork, Mo D3 101
Dry, fork, Mo D6 101
Dry, fork, W. Va B5 123
Dry, fork, W. Va D3 123
Dryad, Lewis, Wash C2 122
Dryberry, lake, Ont., Can E5 71
Dry Branch, Bibb, Ga D3 87
Drybranch, Kanawha, W. Va m13 123
Dry Creek, Beauregard, La D2 95
Dryden, Ont., Can o16 72
Dryden, Franklin, Maine D2 96
Dryden, Lapeer, Mich F7 98
Dryden, Tompkins, N.Y C4 108
Dryden, Josephine, Oreg E3 113
Dryden, Terrell, Tex D1 118
Dryden, Chelan, Wash B5 122
Dryfork, Carroll, Ark A2 81
Dry Fork, Pittsylvania, Va D3 121
Dryfork, Randolph, W. Va C5 123
Drygalski, isl., Ant C22 5
Dry Harbour, mts., Jam E13 65
Drymen, Scot D4 13
Dry Mills, Cumberland, Maine E2, g7 96
Dry Prong, Grant, La C3 95
Dry Ridge, Grant, Ky B5 94
Dry Run, Franklin, Pa F6 114
Dry Tortugas, is., Fla H4 86
Drywood, Alta., Can E4 69
Dsalatu, Mong B6 36
Dschang, Cam D2 46
Duala (Douala), Cam E1 46
Duaringa, Austl D8 51
Duart, pt., Scot D3 13
Duarte, Los Angeles, Calif *E4 82
Duarte, peak, Dom. Rep E8 64
Dubach, Lincoln, La B3 95
Dubai (Dubayy), U.A.E I7 4
Dubawnt, lake, N.W. Ter., Can D12 66
Dubawnt, riv., N.W. Ter., Can D12 66
Du Bay Lake, res., Wis D4 124
Dubberly, Webster, La B2 95
Dubbo, Austl F7 51
Dubbs, Tunica, Miss A3 100
Dübendorf, Switz B6 19
Dublin, Montgomery, Ala C3 78
Dublin, Alameda, Calif *D3 82
Dublin, Ont., Can D3 72
Dublin, Laurens, Ga D4 87
Dublin, Wayne, Ind E7 91
Dublin (Baile Átha Cliath), Ire D5 11
Dublin, Harford, Md A5 85
Dublin, Coahoma, Miss A3 100
Dublin, Cheshire, N.H E2 105
Dublin, Bladen, N.C C4 109
Dublin, Franklin, Ohio k10 111
Dublin, Bucks, Pa F11 114
Dublin, Erath, Tex C3 118
Dublin, Pulaski, Va C2 121
Dublin, co., Ire D5 11
Dublin, bay, Ire D5 11
Dublin Shore, N.S., Can E5 74
Dublon, isl., Truk 52
Dubois, Clark, Idaho E6 89
Dubois, Washington, Ill E4 90
Dubois, Dubois, Ind H4 91
Du Bois, Pawnee, Nebr D9 103
Du Bois, Clearfield, Pa D4 114
Dubois, Fremont, Wyo C3 125
Dubois, co., Ind H4 91
Duboistown, Lycoming, Pa D7 114
Du Bose Park, Kershaw, S.C *C6 115
Dubossary, Sov. Un H7 27
Dubossary, res., Sov. Un B8 28
Dubovka, Sov. Un D2 29
Dubrovka, Sov. Un s31 25
Dubrovnik, Yugo D4 22
Dubsdread, Orange, Fla *D5 86
Dubuc, Sask., Can G4 70
Dubulu, Zaire A3 48
Dubuque, Dubuque, Iowa B7 92
Dubuque, co., Iowa B7 92
Du Chein, bayou, Ky f9 94
Duchesne, Duchesne, Utah C5 119
Duchesne, co., Utah C5 119
Duchesne, riv., Utah C5 119
Duchess, Alta., Can D5 69
Duchov, Czech C2 26
Ducie, isl., Pac. O H14 7
Duck, Dare, N.C A7 109
Duck, creek, Del B7 85
Duck, creek, Nev D7 104
Duck, creek, Ohio C4 111
Duck, creek, Wis h9 124
Duck, lake, Man., Can B2 71
Duck, lake, Maine C4 96
Duck, mtn., Man., Can D1 71
Duck, riv., Tenn B4 117
Duck Bay, Man., Can C1 71
Duck Hill, Montgomery, Miss B4 100
Duck Lake, Sask., Can E2 70
Duck Mountain, prov. park, Man., Sask., Can C1 71
Duck Pond, pt., N.Y. E6 84
Duck River, Hickman, Tenn B4 117
Ducktown, Polk, Tenn D9 117
Duckwater, Nye, Nev E6 104
Duckwater, peak, Nev E6 104
Ducor, Tulare, Calif E4 82
Dudelange, Lux E6 15
Duderstadt, F.R.G B5 17
Dudhi, India E9 40
Dudinka, Sov. Un C11 28
Dudley, Eng B5 12
Dudley, Laurens, Ga D3 87
Dudley, Worcester, Mass B4 97
Dudley, Stoddard, Mo E7 101
Dudley, Wayne, N.C B4 109
Dudley, Huntingdon, Pa F5 114
Dudweiler, F.R.G D2 17
Duékoué, I.C E3 45
Duenweg, Jasper, Mo D3 101
Duero (Douro), riv., Sp B3 20
Due West, Abbeville, S.C C3 115
Duff, Sask., Can G4 70
Duff, Dubois, Ind H3 91
Duff, Campbell, Tenn C9 117
Duff, reef, Fiji 52
Duffee, Newton, Miss C5 100
Duffer, peak, Nev B3 104
Dufferin, co., Ont., Can C4 72
Duffield, Alta., Can C3 69
Dufftown, Scot C5 13
Duffy, Monroe, Ohio C5 111
Dufrost, Man., Can E3 71
Dufur, Wasco, Oreg B5 113
Dugdemona, bayou, La B3 95
Dugdown, mtn., Ga C1 87
Dugger, Sullivan, Ind F3 91
Dug Hill, ridge, Md A4 85
Dugi Otok, isl., Yugo C2 22
Duhamel, Que., Can D2 73
Duich, inlet, Scot C3 13
Duisburg, F.R.G B1 17, C3 16
Duitama, Col B3 60
Duiwelskloof, S. Afr B5 49
Dujuma, Som E5 47
Dukān, dam, Iraq C2 41
Duke, Calhoun, Ala B4 78
Duke, Phelps, Mo D5 101
Duke, Jackson, Okla C2 112
Duke, isl., Alsk n24 79
Duke, Center, McKean, Pa C5 114
Dukedom, Weakley, Tenn A2 117
Duke Ernst, bay, Ant B9 5
Dukes, co., Mass D6 97
Duk Fadiat, Sud D3 47
Duki, Pak B4 39
Dukla, pass, Czech., Pol D6 26
Dulawan, Phil *D6 35
Dulce, Rio Arriba, N. Mex A2 107
Dulce, riv., Arg E3 55
Dülken, F.R.G C6 15
Dülmen, F.R.G B2 17
Dulowa, Pol g11 26
Duluth, Gwinnett, Ga B2, g8 87
Duluth, St. Louis, Minn D6 99
Dūmā, Jordan g12 32
Dumaguete, Phil D6 35
Dumaran, isl., Phil C5 35
Dumas, Desha, Ark D4 81
Dumas, Webster, Ga D2 87
Dumas, Tippah, Miss A5 100
Dumas, Moore, Tex B2 118
Dumba, Zaire B3 48
Dumbarton, Scot E4 13
Dumboa, Nig D7 45
Dumfries, Scot E5 13
Dumfries, Prince William, Va B5 121
Dumfries and Galloway, reg., Scot E4 13

EAST-ELKL 87X

East Peru, Oxford, Maine...D2 96
East Petersburg, Lancaster, Pa....F9 114
East Pine, B.C., Can....B7 68
East Pines, Prince Georges, Md....*C4 85
East Pittsburgh, Allegheny, Pa....k14 114
Eastpoint, Franklin, Fla....C2 86
East Point, Fulton, Ga...C2, h8 87
East Point, Red River, La...B2 95
East Poland, Androscoggin, Maine....D2 96
East Poplar, Sask., Can....H3 70
Eastport, Newf., Can....D5 75
Eastport, Boundary, Idaho...A2 89
Eastport, Washington, Maine....D6 96
Eastport, Suffolk, N.Y....n16 108
East Portal, Gilpin, Colo....B5 83
East Porterville, Tulare, Calif....*D4 82
East Poultney, Rutland, Vt..D2 120
East Prairie, Mississippi, Mo.E8 101
East Princeton, Worcester, Mass....B4 97
East Prospect, York, Pa....G8 114
East Providence, Providence, R.I....B11 84
East Pryor, mtn., Mont....E8 102
East Putney, Windham, Vt..F4 120
East Quincy, Plumas, Calif.*C3 82
East Quogue, Suffolk, N.Y..n16 108
East Randolph, Cattaraugus, N.Y....C2 108
East Randolph, Orange, Vt..D3 120
East Retford, Eng....A7 12
East Richmond, Contra Costa, Calif....*C3 82
East Ridge, Hamilton, Tenn....h11 117
East Riding (York), co. part, Eng....*A6 12
East Rindge, Cheshire, N.H..E3 105
East River, New Haven, Conn....D6 84
East River, mtn., Va....C1 121
East River Sheet Harbour, N.S., Can....E7 74
East Rochester, Monroe, N.Y.B3 108
East Rockaway, Nassau, N.Y.G2 84
East Rockingham, Richmond, N.C....C3 109
East Rockwood, Wayne, Mich....*F7 98
East Rutherford, Bergen, N.J.h8 106
East Ryegate, Caledonia, Vt..C4 120
East Saint John, N.B., Can..D4 74
East St. Johnsbury, Caledonia, Vt....C5 120
East St. Louis, St. Clair, Ill..E3 90
East Salt, creek, Colo....B2 83
East Sandwich, Barnstable, Mass....C7 97
East Sebago, Cumberland, Maine....E2 96
East Selkirk, Man., Can....D3 71
East Setauket, Suffolk, N.Y..F4 84
East Siberian, sea, Sov. Un....B18 28
Eastside, Coos, Oreg....D2 113
Eastside Galesburg, Knox, Ill....*C3 90
East Sioux Falls, Minnehaha, S. Dak....D9 116
East Smithfield, Bradford, Pa....C8 114
Eastsound, San Juan, Wash..A3 122
East Sparta, Stark, Ohio....B4 111
East Spencer, Rowan, N.C...B2 109
East Springfield, Otsego, N.Y....C6 108
East Springfield, Erie, Pa....C1 114
East Stoneham, Oxford, Maine....D2 96
East Stroudsburg, Monroe, Pa....D11 114
East Sudbury, Middlesex, Mass....g10 97
East Suffolk (Suffolk), co. part, Eng....B9 12
East Sullivan, Hancock, Maine....D4 96
East Sullivan, Cheshire, N.H....E2 105
East Sumner, Oxford, Maine....D2 96
East Sussex (Sussex), co. part, Eng....C8 12
East Swamp, creek, Pa....C2 106
East Swanzey, Cheshire, N.H....E2 105
East Tawas, Iosco, Mich....D7 98
East Templeton, Worcester, Mass....A3 97
East Thermopolis, Hot Springs, Wyo....*C4 125
East Thetford, Orange, Vt...D4 120
East Tirol, reg., Aus....C8 18
East Tohopekaliga, lake, Fla...D5 86
East Towanda, Bradford, Pa.C9 114
East Trout, lake, Sask., Can...C3 70
East Troy, Walworth, Wis...F5 114
East Tulare, Tulare, Calif..*D4 82
East Uniontown, Fayette, Pa....*G2 114
East Vandergrift, Westmoreland, Pa....*E2 114
East View, Harrison, W. Va....k10 123
Eastville, Northampton, Va..C7 121
East Wakefield, Carroll, N.H....C4 105
East Walker, riv., Nev....E2 104
East Wallingford, Rutland, Vt....E3 120
East Walpole, Norfolk, Mass....h11 97
East Wareham, Plymouth, Mass....C6 97
East Washington, Sullivan, N.H....D2 105
East Washington, Washington, Pa....F1 114
East Waterboro, York, Maine....E2 96
East Waterford, Oxford, Maine....D2 96
East Waterford, Juniata, Pa..F6 114
East Wellington, B.C., Can..f11 68
East Wenatchee, Douglas, Wash....B5 122
East Wenatchee Beach, Douglas, Wash....*B5 122
East Whittier, Los Angeles, Calif....*F4 82
East Willington, Tolland, Conn....B7 84
East Williston, Nassau, N.Y..G2 84
East Wilmington, New Hanover, N.C....*C5 109
East Wilton, Franklin, Maine....D2 96
East Windsor (Town of), Hartford, Conn....*B6 84
East Windsor, Mercer, N.J...C3 106
East Windsor Hill, Hartford, Conn....B6 84
East Wolfeboro, Carroll, N.H....C4 105
Eastwood, Jefferson, Ky....A4 94
Eastwood, Kalamazoo, Mich....*E5 98
Eastwood Hills, Salt Lake, Utah....*C4 119
East Woodstock, Windham, Conn....B9 84
East Worcester, Otsego, N.Y.C6 108
East York, York, Pa....*G8 114
Eaton, Weld, Colo....A6 83
Eaton, Crawford, Ill....D6 90
Eaton, Delaware, Ind....D7 91
Eaton, Washington, Maine...C5 96
Eaton, Madison, N.Y....C5 108
Eaton, Preble, Ohio....C1 111
Eaton, Gibson, Tenn....B2 117
Eaton, co., Mich....F6 98
Eaton Center, Carroll, N.H..C4 105
Eatonia, Sask., Can....F1 70
Eaton Rapids, Eaton, Mich..F6 98
Eatons, neck, N.Y....F3 84
Eatons Neck, pt., N.Y....F3 84
Eatonton, Putnam, Ga....C3 87
Eatontown, Monmouth, N.J.C4 106
Eatonville, Pierce, Wash....C3 122
Eau Claire, Berrien, Mich...G4 98
Eau Claire, Chippewa and Eau Claire, Wis....D2 124
Eau Claire, co., Wis....D2 124
Eau Claire, riv., Wis....D3 124
Eau Claire Southeast, Eau Claire, Wis....*D2 124
Eau Galle, Dunn, Wis....D2 124
Eau Pleine, riv., Wis....D3 124
Eauze, Fr....F4 14
Ebadon, isl., Kwajalein.... 52
Ebb, Madison, Fla....B3 86
Ebb and Flow, lake, Man., Can....D2 71
Ebbw Vale, Wales....C4 12
Ebeleben, G.D.R....B5 17
Ebeltoft, Den....B4 24
Ebenezer, Sask., Can....F4 70
Ebenezer, Holmes, Miss....C3 100
Eben Junction, Alger, Mich..B4 98
Ebensburg, Cambria, Pa....F4 114
Ebermannstadt, F.R.G....D6 17
Ebersbach, F.R.G....E6 17
Ebersbach, G.D.R....B9 17
Eberswalde, G.D.R....B6 16
Ebeye, Kwajalein.... 52
Ebingen, F.R.G....D4 16
Eboli, It....D5 21
Ebolowa, Cam....E2 46
Ebony, Crittenden, Ark....E8 81
Ebro, Washington, Fla....u16 86
Ebro, Clearwater, Minn....C3 99
Ebro, riv., Sp....B6 20
Eccles, Raleigh, W. Va....D3, n13 123
Eceabat (Maydos), Tur....B6 23
Echague, Phil....n13 35
Echallens, Switz....C2 19
Echeconnee, creek, Ga....D3 87
Echigawa, Jap....n15 37
Echo, Dale, Ala....D4 78
Echo, Rapides, La....C3 95
Echo, Yellow Medicine, Minn....F3 99
Echo, Umatilla, Oreg....B7 113
Echo, Summit, Utah....C4 119
Echo, lake, Ont., Can....B7 98
Echo, lake, Maine....D2 96
Echo, pond, Vt....B5 120
Echo Bay, Clark, Nev....G7 104
Echoing, lake, Ont., Can....B5 71
Echoing, riv., Man., Ont., Can....B6 71
Echola, Tuscaloosa, Ala....B2 78
Echols, co., Ga....F4 87
Echt, Neth....C5 15
Echt, Scot....C6 13
Echternach, Lux....E6 15
Echuca, Austl....H5 51
Écija, Sp....D3 20
Eckelson, Barnes, N. Dak...C7 110
Eckerman, Chippewa, Mich.B5 98
Eckernförde, F.R.G....A4 16
Eckernförder Bucht, bay, F.R.G.D4 24
Eckerty, Crawford, Ind....H4 91
Eckhart, Allegany, Md....k13 85
Eckley, Yuma, Colo....A8 83
Eckley, Luzerne, Pa....E10 114
Eckman, Bottineau, N. Dak..A4 110
Eckman, McDowell, W. Va.*D3 123
Eckville, Alta., Can....C3 69
Eclectic, Elmore, Ala....C3 78
Eclipse, sound, N.W. Ter. Can....B17 67
E. C. Manning, prov. park, B.C., Can....E7 68
Econfina, riv., Fla....B3 86
Economy, N.S., Can....D6 74
Economy, Wayne, Ind....E7 91
Economy, Beaver, Pa....*E1 114
Écorces, riv., Que., Can....A6 73
Ecorse, Wayne, Mich....p15 98
Ecru, Pontotoc, Miss....A4 100
Ector, co., Tex....D1 118
Ecuador, country, S.A....D3 53, 58
Ecum Secum, N.S., Can....E7 74
Ecum Secum Bridge, N.S., Can....E7 74
Ed, Eth....C5 47
Eda, Swe....H5 25
Edam, Sask., Can....D1 70
Edam, Neth....B5 15
Eday, isl., Scot....A6 13
Edberg, Alta., Can....C4 69
Edcouch, Hidalgo, Tex....F4 118
Eddiceton, Franklin, Miss...D3 100
Eddington, Penobscot, Maine....D4 96
Eddrachillis, bay, Scot....B3 13
Eddy, co., N. Mex....E5 107
Eddy, co., N. Dak....B7 110
Eddystone, Delaware, Pa...p20 114
Eddystone, rocks, English Chan..E4 10
Eddyville, Pope, Ill....F5 90
Eddyville, Wapello and Mahaska, Iowa....C5 92
Eddyville, Lyon, Ky....e9 94
Eddyville, Dawson, Nebr....C6 103
Ed Dzong, see Aitetsung, China
Ede, Neth....B5 15
Ede, Nig....*E5 45
Edéa, Cam....E2 46
Eden, Graham, Ariz....E6 80
Eden, Austl....H7 51
Eden, Man., Can....D2 71
Eden, Effingham, Ga....D5 87
Eden, Jerome, Idaho....G4 89
Eden, Hancock, Maine....D4 96
Eden, Somerset, Md....D6 85
Eden, Yazoo, Miss....C3 100
Eden, Erie, N.Y....C2 108
Eden, Rockingham, N. Car..A3 109
Eden, Marshall, S. Dak....B8 116
Eden, Concho, Tex....D3 118
Eden, Weber, Utah....B4 119
Eden, Lamoille, Vt....B3 120
Eden, Fond du Lac, Wis....E5 124
Eden, Sweetwater, Wyo....D3 125
Eden, hill, Conn....D3 84
Eden, lake, Man., Can....A1 71
Eden, riv., Eng....C5 10
Eden, riv., Scot....D5 13
Edenborn, Fayette, Pa....G2 114
Edenderry, Ire....D4 11
Eden Mills, Lamoille, Vt....B3 120
Eden Prairie, Hennepin, Minn....n12 99
Edenton, Chowan, N.C....A6 109
Eden Valley, Meeker and Stearns, Minn....E4 99
Edenwold, Sask., Can....G3 70
Eder, riv., F.R.G....B4 17
Edesville, Kent, Md....B5 85
Edgar, Carbon, Mont....E8 102
Edgar, Clay, Nebr....D8 103
Edgar, Marathon, Wis....D4 120
Edgar, co., Ill....D6 90
Edgard, St. John the Baptist, La....D5, h10 95
Edgar Springs, Phelps, Mo..D6 101
Edgartown, Dukes, Mass....D6 97
Edge, isl., Nor....B12 4
Edgecombe, co., N.C....B5 109
Edgecumbe, ape, Alsk....m22 79
Edgefield, Edgefield, S.C....D4 115
Edgefield, co., S.C....D4 115
Edgeley, Sask., Can....G4 70
Edgeley, La Moure, N. Dak .C7 110
Edgely, Bucks, Pa....*F12 114
Edgemere, Baltimore, Md..*B5 85
Edgemont, Cleburne, Ark....B3 81
Edgemont, Riverside, Calif.*F5 82
Edgemont, Fall River, S. Dak....D2 116
Edgemont, chan., Fla....F1 86
Edgemont, key, Fla....F1 86
Edgemoor, Chester, S.C....B5 115
Edgemoor, Anderson, Tenn....m13 117
Edgerly, Calcasieu, La....D2 95
Edgerton, Alta., Can....C5 69
Edgerton, Johnson, Kans....D8 93
Edgerton, Pipestone, Minn..G2 99
Edgerton, Platte, Mo....B3 101
Edgerton, Williams, Ohio....A1 111
Edgerton, Rock, Wis....F4 124
Edgerton, Natrona, Wyo....C6 125
Edgewater, Jefferson, Ala....f7 78
Edgewater, Jefferson, Colo..B5 83
Edgewater, Volusia, Fla....D6 86
Edgewater, Anne Arundel, Md....C4 85
Edgewater, Bergen, N.J....h9 106
Edgewater Park, Burlington, N.J....C3 106
Edgewood, B.C., Can....E8 68
Edgewood, Effingham, Ill....E5 90
Edgewood, Madison, Ind...m10 91
Edgewood, Clayton and Delaware, Iowa....B6 92
Edgewood, Kenton, Ky....h13 94
Edgewood, Harford, Md....B5 85
Edgewood, Santa Fe, N. Mex....B3, k8 107
Edgewood, Ashtabula, Ohio..A5 111
Edgewood, Allegheny, Pa....F2 114
Edgewood, Northumberland, Pa....*E8 114
Edgewood, Pierce, Wash....f11 122
Edgeworth, Allegheny, Pa...h13 114
Edgigen, isl., Kwajalein.... 52
Edgin, Briscoe, Tex....B2 118
Edgmoor, Chester, S.C....B5 115
Edhessa, Grc....B4 23
Edina, Hennepin, Minn....n12 99
Edina, Knox, Mo....A5 101
Edinboro, Erie, Pa....C1 114
Edinburg, Christian, Ill....D4 90
Edinburg, Johnson, Ind....F6 91
Edinburg, Leake, Miss....C4 100
Edinburg, Mercer, N.J....*C3 106
Edinburg, Saratoga, N.Y....B6 108
Edinburg, Walsh, N. Dak....A8 110
Edinburg, Hidalgo, Tex....F3 118
Edinburg, Shenandoah, Va..B4 121
Edinburgh, Scot....E5 13
Edirne, Tur....B6 23
Edison, Calhoun, Ga....E2 87
Edison, Furnas, Nebr....D6 103
Edison, Middlesex, N.J....B4 106
Edison, Morrow, Ohio....B3 111
Edison, Skagit, Wash....A3 122
Edisto, isl., S.C....F7 115
Edisto, riv., S.C....E6 115
Edisto Island, Charleston, S.C....F7, k11 115
Edith, Woods, Okla....A2 112
Edith, mtn., Mont....D5 102
Edithburgh, Austl....G1 51
Edith Ronne Land, reg., Ant....A5 5
Edmeston, Otsego, N.Y....C5 108
Edmond, Norton, Kans....C4 93
Edmond, Oklahoma, Okla...B4 112
Edmonds, Snohomish, Wash.B3 122
Edmondson, Crittenden, Ark.B5 81
Edmonson, co., Ky....C3 94
Edmonston, Prince Georges, Md....*C4 85
Edmonton, Alta., Can...C4, g8 69
Edmonton, Metcalfe, Ky....C4 94
Edmore, Montcalm, Mich....E5 98
Edmore, Ramsey, N. Dak...A7 110
Edmund, lake, Man., Can....B5 71
Edmunds, co., S. Dak....B6 116
Edmundson, St. Louis, Mo.*C7 101
Edmundston, N.B., Can....B1 74
Edna, Labette, Kans....E8 93
Edna, Jackson, Tex....E4 118
Edna, Monongalia, W. Va...h10 123
Edon, Williams, Ohio....A1 111
Edouard, lake, Que., Can....B5 73
Edremit, Tur....C6 23
Edsel Ford, ranges, Ant....B34 5
Edson, Alta., Can....C2, g7 69
Edson, Sherman, Kans....C2 93
Eduardo Castex, Arg....B4 54
Eduni, mtn., N.W. Ter., Can...D7 66
Edwall, Lincoln, Wash....B8 122
Edwand, Alta., Can....B4 69
Edward, lake, Zaire....B4 48
Edward VII, pen., Ant....B33 5
Edward VIII, bay, Ant....C18 5
Edwards, Ont., Can....h13 72
Edwards, Eagle, Colo....B4 83
Edwards, Peoria, Ill....C4 90
Edwards, Hinds, Miss....C3 100
Edwards, St. Lawrence, N.Y....A5, f9 108
Edwards, co., Ill....E5 90
Edwards, co., Kans....E4 93
Edwards, co., Tex....E2 118
Edwards, butte, Oreg....B3 113
Edwards, plat., Tex....D2 118
Edwardsburg, Cass, Mich..G4 98
Edwardsport, Knox, Ind....G3 91
Edwardsville, Cleburne, Ala..B4 78
Edwardsville, Madison, Ill...E4 90
Edwardsville, Wyandotte, Kans....k16 93
Edwardsville, Luzerne, Pa..n17 114
Edwin, Henry, Ala....D4 78
Edzell, Scot....D6 13
Eek, Alsk....C7 79
Eekloo, Bel....C3 15
Eel, riv., Calif....B2 82
Eel, riv., Ind....C5 91
Eel, riv., Ind....F3 91
Eferding, Aus....D7 16
Efestiniog, Wales....B4 12
Effie, Avoyelles, La....C3 95
Effie, Itasca, Minn....C5 99
Effingham, Effingham, Ill...D5 90
Effingham, Atchison, Kans..C8 93
Effingham, Carroll, N.H....C4 105
Effingham, Florence, S.C....C8 115
Effingham, co., Ga....D5 87
Effingham, co., Ill....D5 90
Efland, Orange, N.C....A3 109
Eforie, Rom....C9 22
Ega, riv., Sp....A4 20
Egadi, is., It....F4 21
Egan, Fulton, Ga. (part of East Point)....B5 87
Egan, Moody, S. Dak....D9 116
Egan, range, Nev....E7 104
Eganville, Ont., Can....B7 72
Egbert, Laramie, Wyo....E8 125
Egegik, Alsk....D8 79
Egeland, Towner, N. Dak...A6 110
Egeln, G.D.R....B6 17
Eger, Hung....B5 22
Egersund, Nor....H2 25
Egerton, mtn., Ant....A28 5
Egg, lake, Sask., Can....B3 70
Eggebek, F.R.G....D3 24
Eggenfelden, F.R.G....E7 17
Egg Harbor, Door, Wis....C6 124
Egg Harbor City, Atlantic, N.J....D3 106
Egg Island, pt., N.J....E2 106
Egilsstadir, Ice....n25 25
Égletons, Fr....E4 14
Eglinton, isl., N.W. Ter., Can....m28 67
Eglisau, Switz....A6 19
Egmond aan Zee, Neth....B4 15
Egmont, bay, P.E.I., Can....C5 74
Egmont, cape, N.Z....M14 51
Egmont, mtn., N.Z....M15 51
Egnar, San Miguel, Colo....D2 83
Egremont, Alta., Can....B4 69
Egremont, Eng....F5 13
Egremont (Town of), Berkshire, Mass....*B1 97
Egridir, Tur....D8 31
Eğridir, lake, Tur....C8 31
Egtved, Den....C3 24
Egypt, Craighead, Ark....B5 81
Egypt, Effingham, Ga....D5 87
Egypt, Plymouth, Mass....B6, h12 97
Egypt, Chickasaw, Miss....B5 100
Egypt, country, Afr..D8 42, D5 43
Ehime, pref., Jap....*J6 37
Ehrenberg, Yuma, Ariz....D1 80
Ehrenfeld, Cambria, Pa....F4 114
Ehrhardt, Bamberg, S.C....E5 115
Éibar, Sp....A4 20
Eibau, G.D.R....C9 17
Eibenstock, G.D.R....C7 17
Eichstätt, F.R.G....E6 17
Eider, riv., F.R.G....A4 16
Eidsberg, Nor....H4, p29 25
Eidson, Hawkins, Tenn....C10 117
Eidsvold, Austl....B8 51
Eidsvoll, Nor....G4 25
Eifel, mts., F.R.G....C1 17
Eigg, isl., Scot....D2 13
Eigg, sound, Scot....D2 13
Eightmile, Morrow, Oreg....B7 113
Eights, coast, Ant....B3 5
Eighty Eight, Barren, Ky....D4 94
Eighty Mile, beach, Austl....C3 50
Eikeren, lake, Nor....p27 25
Eil, Som....D6 47
Eildon, res., Austl....H6 51
Eileen, lake, N.W. Ter., Can..D11 66
Eilenburg, G.D.R....B7 17
Eiler Rasmussen, cape, Grnld..A16 4
Eil Malk, isl., Palau Is.... 52
Einbeck, F.R.G....B4 17
Eindhoven, Neth....C5 15
Ein Scilleme, mtn., Libya....E4 43
Einsiedeln, Switz....B6 19
Eirunepé, Braz....C4 58
Eisenach, G.D.R....C5 17
Eisenberg, G.D.R....C6 17
Eisenhüttenstadt, G.D.R....A9 17
Eiserfeld, F.R.G....C3 17
Eisfeld, F.R.G....C5 17
Eisleben, G.D.R....B6 17
Eita, isl., Tarawa.... 52
Eitorf, F.R.G....C2 17
Eitzen, Houston, Minn....G7 99
Ejby, Den....C3 24
Ejea de los Caballeros, Sp...A5 20
Ejeda, Mad....h8 49
Ejstrup, Den....C3 24
Ejutla de Crespo, Mex....D5 63
Ekalaka, Carter, Mont....E12 102
Ekenäs, Fin....G10 25
Ekeren, Bel....C4 15
Ekhinos, Grc....B5 23
Ekimchan, Sov. Un....D16 28
Eklutna, Alsk....C10, g17 79
Ekoln, lake, Swe....t35 25
Ekron, Meade, Ky....C3 94
Eksjö, Swe....I6 25
Ekumakoko, Zaire....B3 48
Ekwan, riv., Ont., Can....F15 67
Ekwok, Alsk....D8 79
El Aaiún, W. Sahara....D2 44
El-Abiod Sidi Cheikh, Alg..H7 30
Elaine, Phillips, Ark....C5 81
El Alamein, see Al 'Alamayn, Eg.
El Alia, Alg....C6 44
El Alto, P.R....B5 65
Elamanchili, India....I9 40
Elamton, Morgan, Ky....C6 94
Elamville, Barbour, Ala....D4 78
Eland, Shawano, Wis....D4 124
El Arahal, Sp....D3 20
El Aricha, Alg....G6 30
El Asnam (Orléansville), Alg.B5 44
Elasson, Grc....C4 23
Elat (Elath), Isr....E6 32
Elath, see Elat, Isr.
Elâzığ, Tur....C12 31
El Azucar, res., Mex....F3 118
Elba, Coffee, Ala....D3 78
Elba, Van Buren, Ark....B3 81
Elba, Cassia, Idaho....G5 89
Elba, Lapeer, Mich....E7 98
Elba, Winona, Minn....F6 99
Elba, Howard, Nebr....C7 103
Elba, Genesee, N.Y....B2 108
Elba, dam, Ala....D3 78
Elba, isl., It....C3 21
El Banco, Col....B3 60
El Barco, Sp....A2 20
Elbasan, Alb....B3 23
Elbasan, pref., Alb....*B3 23
El Baúl, Ven....B4 60
El Bayadh, Alg....C5 44
Elbe, riv., F.R.G., G.D.R....B5 16
Elberfeld, Warrick, Ind....H3 91
Elberon, Tama, Iowa....B5 92
Elbert, Elbert, Colo....B6 83
Elbert, Throckmorton, Tex..C3 118
Elbert, co., Colo....B6 83
Elbert, co., Ga....B4 87
Elbert, mtn., Colo....B4 83
Elberta, Baldwin, Ala....E2 78
Elberta, Houston, Ga....D3 87
Elberta, Benzie, Mich....D4 98
Elberta, Utah, Utah....D4 119
Elberton, Elbert, Ga....B4 87
Elberton, Whitman, Wash...C8 122
Elbeuf, Fr....C4 14
Elbigenalp, Aus....B6 18
Elbing, Butler, Kans....f12 93
Elbistan, Tur....C11 31
Elbląg, Pol....A5 26
El Bluff, Nic....D6 62
El Bolsón, Arg....C2 54
El Bonillo, Sp....C4 20
El Bordo, Col....C2 60
El Borouj, Mor....H3 30
Elbow, Sask., Can....F2 70
Elbow, lake, Man., Can....B1 71
Elbow, riv., Alta., Can....D3 69
Elbow Lake, Grant, Minn...E3 99
Elbridge, Obion, Tenn....A2 117
Elbrus, mtn., Sov. Un....G17 9
El Bur, Som....E6 47
Elburg, Neth....B5 15
El Burgo de Osma, Sp....B4 20
Elburn, Kane, Ill....B5 90
Elburz, mts., Iran....C5 41
El Cajon, San Diego, Calif....F5, o16 82
El Callao, Ven....B5 60
El Campo, Wharton, Tex....E4 118
El Campo North, Wharton, Tex....*E4 118
El Campo South, Wharton, Tex....*E4 118
El Capitan, mtn., Mont....D2 102
El Capitan, res., Calif....o16 82
El Carmen, Bol....C4 55
El Carmen, Col....B2 60
El Carrizo, Mex....B3 63
El Centro, Imperial, Calif..F6 82
El Cerrito, Contra Costa, Calif....h8 82
El Cerro, Bol....C3 55
El Cesar, dept., Col....B3 60
El Chaparro, Ven....B4 60
Elche, Sp....C5 20
Elcho, Langlade, Wis....C4 124
Elco, Alexander, Ill....F4 90
El Cuervo, butte, N. Mex....k9 107
Elda, Sp....C5 20
Elde, riv., G.D.R....B5 16
Elderon, Marathon, Wis....D4 124
Eldersley, Sask., Can....E4 70
Elderton, Armstrong, Pa....E3 114
El Diviso, Col....C2 60
El Djem, Tun....G12 30
Eldon, Wapello, Iowa....D5 92
Eldon, Miller, Mo....C5 101
Eldora, Hardin, Iowa....B4 92
El Dorado, Union, Ark....D3 81
Eldorado, Braz....C3 56
Eldorado, Ont., Can....C7 72
Eldorado, Sask., Can....m7 70
Eldorado, Saline, Ill....F5 90
El Dorado, Butler, Kans .E7, g13 93
Eldorado, Dorchester, Md...C6 85
Eldorado, Montgomery, N.C .B3 109
Eldorado, Preble, Ohio....C1 111
Eldorado, Jackson, Okla....C2 112
Eldorado, Schleicher, Tex...D2 118
El Dorado, co., Calif....C3 82
Eldorado, mtn., Wash....A4 122
Eldorado Springs, Boulder, Colo....B5 83
El Dorado Springs, Cedar, Mo....D3 101
Eldoret, Ken....A6 48
Eldred, Greene, Ill....D3 9
Eldred, Polk, Minn....C2 99
Eldred, McKean, Pa....C5 114
Eldridge, Walker, Ala....B2 78
Eldridge, Scott, Iowa...C7, g10 92
Eldridge, Laclede, Mo....D5 101
Eldridge, Stutsman, N. Dak..C7 110
Eleanor, Putnam, W. Va....C3 123
Electra, Wichita, Tex....B3 118
Electra, lake, Colo....D3 83
Electric, peak, Mont., Wyo...E2 102
Electric City, Grant, Wash..B6 122
Electric Mills, Kemper, Miss.C5 100
Eleele, Kauai, Haw....B2 88
Elektrogorsk, Sov. Un....n18 27
Elektrostal, Sov. Un....n18 27
Elephant, butte, N. Mex....D2 107
Elephant, isl., Ant....C7 5
Elephant, mtn., Maine....D2 96
Elephant, range, Camb....G5 38
Elephant Butte, res., N. Mex..D2 107
El Escorial, Sp....o16 20
El Eulma, Alg....B6 44
Eleuthera, isl., Ba....B5 64
Eleva, Trempealeau, Wis....D2 124
Eleven Mile Canyon, res., Colo..C5 83
Eleven Point, riv., Mo....F6 101
Elevsis (Eleusis), Grc....g11 23
Elevsis, gulf, Grc....g11 23
El Faiyûm (Al Fayyūm), Eg..E2 32
El Fasher (Al Fāshir), Sud...C2 47
El Ferrol, Sp....A1 20
Elfin Cove, Alsk....k21 79
Elfrida, Cochise, Ariz....F6 80
Elfros, Sask., Can....F4 70
El Fud, Eth....D5 47
El Fuerte, Mex....B3 63
El Galhak, Sud....C3 47
Elgin, Lauderdale, Ala....A2 78
Elgin, Santa Cruz, Ariz....F5 80
Elgin, Man., Can....E1 71
Elgin, N.B., Can....D4 74
Elgin, Cook and Kane, Ill....A5, h8 90
Elgin, Fayette, Iowa....B6 92
Elgin, Chautauqua, Kans....E7 93
Elgin, Wabasha, Minn....F6 99
Elgin, Antelope, Nebr....C7 103
Elgin, Lincoln, Nev....F7 104
Elgin, Grant, N. Dak....C4 110
Elgin, Comanche, Okla....C3 112
Elgin, Union, Oreg....B7 113
Elgin, Erie, Pa....C2 114
Elgin, Scot....C5 13
Elgin, Lancaster, S.C....B6 115
Elgin, Bastrop, Tex....D4 118
Elgin, co., Ont., Can....E3 72
Elgol, Scot....C2 13
El Goléa, Alg....C5 44
Elgon, mtn., Ug....A5 48
El Grullo, Mex....n11 63
El Hamurre, Som....D6 47
El Haseke, Syr....D13 31
El Huecu, Arg....B2 54
Eli, Cherry, Nebr....B4 103
Eliasville, Young, Tex....C3 118
Elida, Roosevelt, N. Mex....D6 107
Elida, Allen, Ohio....B1 111
Elie & Earlsferry, Scot....*D6 13
Elikon (Helicon), mtn., Grc....g9 23
Elila, riv., Zaire....B4 48
Elim, Alsk....C7 79
Elim, Cambria, Pa....*F4 114
El Indio, Maverick, Tex....E2 118
Eliot, York, Maine....E2 96
Eliot, riv., P.E.I., Can....C6 74
Elis, (Ilia), prov., Grc....*D3 23
Élisabethville, see Lubumbashi, Zaire
Elista, Sov. Un....D2 29
E izabeth, Fulton, Ark....A3 81
Elizabeth, Austl....F6 50
Elizabeth, Elbert, Colo....B6 83
Elizabeth, Cobb, Ga....C2, h7 87
Elizabeth, Jo Daviess, Ill....A3 90
Elizabeth, Harrison, Ind....H6 91
Elizabeth, Allen, La....D3 95
Elizabeth, Otter Tail, Minn .D2 99
Elizabeth, Washington, Miss .B3 100
Elizabeth, Union, N.J....B4, k8 106
Elizabeth, Alleghany, Pa....*F2 114
Elizabeth, Wirt, W. Va....B3 123
Elizabeth, bay, Ec....g5 58
Elizabeth, cape, Maine....g7 96
Elizabeth, cape, Wash....B1 122
Elizabeth, is., Mass....D6 97
Elizabeth City, Pasquotank, N.C....A6 109
Elizabeth Lake Estates, Oakland, Mich....*F7 98
Elizabethton, Carter, Tenn.C11 117
Elizabethtown, Hardin, Ill...F5 90
Elizabethtown, Bartholomew, Ind....F6 91
Elizabethtown, Hardin, Ky..C4 94
Elizabethtown, Essex, N.Y....A7, f11 108
Elizabethtown, Bladen, N.C..C4 109
Elizabethtown, Lancaster, Pa....F8 114
Elizabethville, Dauphin, Pa..E8 114
El Jadida, Mor....C3 44
El Jebel, Eagle, Colo....B3 83
El Jeib, wadi, Jordan....D7 32
Elk, Mendocino, Calif....C2 82
Elk, Pol....B7 26
Elk, Spokane, Wash....A8 122
Elk, co., Kans....E7 93
Elk, co., Pa....D4 114
Elk, creek, Okla....B2 112
Elk, creek, S. Dak....C3 116
Elk, isl., Man., Can....D3 71
Elk, mtn., N. Mex....D1 107
Elk, mtn., Okla....C3 112
Elk, mtn., S. Dak....D1 116
Elk, mtn., Wyo....E6 125
Elk, mts., Colo....B3 83
Elk, peak, Mont....D6 102
Elk, riv., B.C., Can....D10 68
Elk, riv., Colo....A4 83
Elk, riv., Kans....E7 93
Elk, riv., Md....A6 85
Elk, riv., Tenn....B5 117
Elk, riv., W. Va....C3 123
Elk, riv., Wis....C3 124
Elkader, Clayton, Iowa....B6 92
El Kairouan, Tun....B7 44
El Kasserine, Tun....B6 44
Elkatawa, Breathitt, Ky....C6 94
Elk City, Idaho, Idaho....D3 89
Elk City, Montgomery, Kans .E8 93
Elk City, Douglas, Nebr....g12 103
Elk City, Beckham, Okla....B2 112
Elk Creek, Glenn, Calif....C2 82
Elk Creek, Johnson, Nebr...D9 103
Elk Creek, Grayson, Va....D1 121
El Kef, Tun....B6 44
El Kere, Eth....D5 47
Elk Falls, Elk, Kans....E7 93
Elk Garden, Mineral, W. Va.B5 123
Elk Grove, Sacramento, Calif....C3 82
Elk Grove Village, Cook, Ill..h9 90
Elkhart, Logan, Ill....C4 90
Elkhart, Elkhart, Ind....A6 91
Elkhart, Polk, Iowa....e8 92
Elkhart, Morton, Kans....E2 93
Elkhart, Anderson, Tex....D5 118
Elkhart, co., Ind....A6 91
Elkhart Lake, Sheboygan, Wis....E5, k9 124
Elk Head, mts., Colo....A3 83
Elkhorn, Man., Can....E1 71
Elk Horn, Shelby, Iowa....C2 92
Elkhorn, Douglas, Nebr....g12 103
Elkhorn, McDowell, W. Va.*D3 123
Elkhorn, Walworth, Wis....F5 124
Elkhorn, peaks, Idaho....F7 89
Elkhorn, riv., Nebr....B7 103
Elkhorn City, Pike, Ky....C7 94
Elkhovo, Bul....D8 22
Elkin, Surry, N.C....A2 109
Elkins, Washington, Ark....B1 81
Elkins, Merrimack, N.H....D3 105
Elkins, Chaves, N. Mex....D5 107
Elkins, Randolph, W. Va....C5 123
Elkins Park, Montgomery, Pa....o21 114
Elkinsville, Brown, Ind....F5 91
Elk Island, nat. park, Alta., Can.C4 69
Elk Lake, Deschutes, Oreg...D5 113
Elkland, Webster, Mo....D4 101
Elkland, Tioga, Pa....C7 114

Elk Mills, Cecil, Md ... A6 85
Elkmont, Limestone, Ala ... A3 78
Elkmont, Sevier, Tenn ... D10 117
Elk Mound, Dunn, Wis ... D2 124
Elk Mountain, Buncombe, N.C ... f10 109
Elk Mountain, Carbon, Wyo ... E6 125
Elko, B.C., Can ... E10 68
Elko, Houston, Ga ... D3 87
Elko, Elko, Nev ... C6 104
Elko, Barnwell, S.C ... E5 115
Elko, co., Nev ... B6 104
Elkol, Lincoln, Wyo ... E2 125
Elk Park, Avery, N.C ... A1, e11 109
Elk Point, Alta., Can ... C5 69
Elk Point, Union, S. Dak ... E9 116
Elk Ranch, Carroll, Ark ... A2 81
Elk Rapids, Antrim, Mich ... D5 98
Elkridge, Howard, Md ... B4, h10 85
Elkridge, Fayette, W. Va ... m13 123
Elk River, Clearwater, Idaho ... C2 89
Elk River, Sherburne, Minn ... E5 99
Elk Run Heights, Black Hawk, Iowa ... *B5 92
Elk Springs, Moffat, Colo ... A2 83
Elkton, St. Johns, Fla ... C5 86
Elkton, Todd, Ky ... D2 94
Elkton, Cecil, Md ... A6 85
Elkton, Huron, Mich ... E7 98
Elkton, Mower, Minn ... G6 99
Elkton, Douglas, Oreg ... D3 113
Elkton, Brookings, S. Dak ... C9 116
Elkton, Giles, Tenn ... B5 117
Elkton, Rockingham, Va ... B4 121
Elk Valley, Campbell, Tenn ... C9 117
Elkview, Kanawha, W. Va ... m13 123
Elkville, Jackson, Ill ... F4 90
Ellabell, Bryan, Ga ... D5 87
Ellamore, Randolph, W. Va ... C4 123
Ellaville, Schley, Ga ... D2 87
Ellef Ringnes, isl., N.W. Ter., Can ... m31 67
Ellen, mtn., Utah ... E5 119
Ellen, mtn., Vt ... C3 120
Ellenboro, Rutherford, N.C ... B1 109
Ellenboro, Ritchie, W. Va ... B3 123
Ellenburg Center, Clinton, N.Y ... f11 108
Ellendale, Sussex, Del ... C7 85
Ellendale, Steele, Minn ... G5 99
Ellendale, Dickey, N. Dak ... C7 110
Ellendale, Shelby, Tenn ... *B1 117
Ellensburg, Kittitas, Wash ... C5 122
Ellenton, Manatee, Fla ... E4, p10 86
Ellenton, Colquitt, Ga ... E3 87
Ellenville, Ulster, N.Y ... D6 108
Ellenwood, Clayton, Ga ... h8 87
Eller, isl., Kwajalein ... 52
Ellerbe, Richmond, N.C ... B3 109
Ellershouse, N.S., Can ... E6 74
Ellerslie, Harris, Ga ... D2 87
Ellerslie, Allegany, Md ... k13 85
Ellesmere, isl., N.W. Ter., Can ... m35 67
Ellesmere Port, Eng ... A5 12
Ellettsville, Monroe, Ind ... F4 91
Ellichpur, India ... G6 40
Ellicott City, Howard and Baltimore, Md ... B4 85
Ellicottville, Cattaraugus, N.Y ... C2 108
Ellijay, Gilmer, Ga ... B2 87
Ellington, Tolland, Conn ... B7 84
Ellington, Reynolds, Mo ... D7 101
Ellinwood, Barton, Kans ... D5 93
Elliot, Windham, Conn ... B8 84
Elliot, lake, Man., Can ... C4 71
Elliot Lake, Ont., Can ... A2 72
Elliott, Ford, Ill ... C5 90
Elliott, Montgomery, Iowa ... C2 92
Elliott, Grenada, Miss ... B4 100
Elliott, Ransom, N. Dak ... C8 110
Elliott, Lee, S.C ... C7 115
Elliott, co., Ky ... B6 94
Elliott, bay, Wash ... e11 122
Elliott, key, Fla ... G6 86
Ellis, Baxter, Ark ... A3 81
Ellis, Lemhi, Idaho ... E4 89
Ellis, Ellis, Kans ... D4 93
Ellis, Gage, Nebr ... D9 103
Ellis, Minnehaha, S. Dak ... D9 116
Ellis, co., Kans ... D4 93
Ellis, co., Okla ... A2 112
Ellis, co., Tex ... C4 118
Ellis, pond, Maine ... D2 96
Ellis, riv., N.H ... B4 105
Ellisburg, Jefferson, N.Y ... B4 108
Ellisdale, Burlington and Monmouth, N.J ... C3 106
Ellisgrove, Randolph, Ill ... E4 90
Ellison Bay, Door, Wis ... C5 124
Elliston, Austl ... F5 50
Elliston, Newf., Can ... D5 75
Elliston, Powell, Mont ... D4 102
Elliston, Montgomery, Va ... C2 121
Ellisville, Jones, Miss ... D4 100
Ellisville, St. Louis, Mo ... f12 101
El Llanito, Sandoval, N. Mex ... B3, k7 107
Ellon, Scot ... C6 13
Ellore, see Elūru, India
Elloree, Orangeburg, S.C ... D6 115
Ellport, Lawrence, Pa ... E1 114
Ellrich, F.R.G ... B5 17
Ells, riv., Alta., Can ... A4 69
Ellscott, Alta., Can ... B4 69
Ellsinore, Carter, Mo ... E7 101
Ellston, Ringgold, Iowa ... D3 92
Ellsworth, McLean, Ill ... C5 90
Ellsworth, Hamilton, Iowa ... B4 92
Ellsworth, Ellsworth, Kans ... D5 93
Ellsworth, Hancock, Maine ... D4 96
Ellsworth, Antrim, Mich ... C5 98
Ellsworth, Nobles, Minn ... G3 99
Ellsworth, Sheridan, Nebr ... B3 103
Ellsworth, Grafton, N.H ... C3 105
Ellsworth, Washington, Pa ... F1 114
Ellsworth, Pierce, Wis ... D1 124
Ellsworth, co., Kans ... D5 93
Ellsworth, hill, Conn ... B3 84
Ellsworth, mtn., Ant ... B4 5
Ellwangen, F.R.G ... E5 17
Ellwood City, Beaver and Lawrence, Pa ... E1 114
Ellzey, Levy, Fla ... C4 86
Elm, riv., N. Dak ... B8 110
Elma, Howard, Iowa ... A5 92
Elma, Erie, N.Y ... *C2 108
Elma, Grays Harbor, Wash ... B2 122
El Mahdia, Tun ... B7 44
Elmali, Tur ... D7 31
El Manteco, Ven ... B5 60
Elm City, Wilson, N.C ... B5 109
Elm Creek, Man., Can ... E3 71
Elm Creek, Buffalo, Nebr ... D6 103
Elmcrest, Genesee, Mich ... *E7 98
Elmdale, Chase, Kans ... D7 93
El Meghaïer, Alg ... C6 44
Elmendorf, Bexar, Tex ... k7 118
El Mene, Ven ... A3 60
Elmer, Macon, Mo ... B5 101
Elmer, Salem, N.J ... D2 106
Elmer, Jackson, Okla ... C2 112
Elmer City, Okanogan, Wash ... B7 122
El Metlaoui, Tun ... C6 44
Elm Grove, Waukesha, Wis ... m11 124
Elmhurst, DuPage, Ill ... B6, k9 90
Elmhurst, Lakawanna, Pa ... D10, m18 114
Elmira, Solano, Calif ... B6 82
Elmira, P.E.I., Can ... C7 74
Elmira, Ont., Can ... D4 72
Elmira, Bonner, Idaho ... A2 89
Elmira, Otsego, Mich ... C6 98
Elmira, Ray, Mo ... B3 101
Elmira, Chemung, N.Y ... C4 108
Elmira, Lane, Oreg ... C3 113
Elmira, Braxton, W. Va ... C4 123
Elmira Heights, Chemung, N.Y ... C4 108
El Mirage, Maricopa, Ariz ... k8 80
Elmo, Dickinson, Kans ... D6 93
Elmo, Nodaway, Mo ... A2 101
Elmo, Lake, Mont ... C2 102
Elmo, Emery, Utah ... D5 119
Elmo, Carbon, Wyo ... E6 125
Elmodel, Baker, Ga ... E2 87
El Modeno, Orange, Calif ... *F5 82
El Moknine, Tun ... B7 44
Elmont, Shawnee, Kans ... k14 93
Elmont, Nassau, N.Y ... k13 108
Elmont, Hanover, Va ... C5 121
El Monte, Los Angeles, Calif ... *E4 82
Elmora (Bakerton), Cambria, Pa ... E4 114
Elmore, Elmore, Ala ... C3 78
Elmore, Faribault, Minn ... G4 99
Elmore, Ottawa, Ohio ... A2 111
Elmore (Town of), Lamoille, Vt ... *B3 120
Elmore, co., Ala ... C3 78
Elmore, co., Idaho ... F3 89
Elmore City, Garvin, Okla ... C4 112
El Moro, Las Animas, Colo ... D6 83
El Morro, nat. mon., N. Mex ... B1 107
Elm Park, West Feliciana, La ... D4 95
El Mreiti, well, Maur ... B3 45
Elms, York, Maine ... E2 96
Elmsdale, N.S., Can ... E6 74
Elmshorn, F.R.G ... B4 17
Elm Springs, Washington, Ark ... A1 81
Elm Springs, Meade, S. Dak ... C3 116
Elmsville, N.B., Can ... D3 73
Elmvale, Ont., Can ... C5 72
Elmville, Windham, Conn ... B9 84
Elmwood, Ont., Can ... C3 72
Elmwood, Hartford, Conn. (part of West Hartford) ... C6 84
Elmwood, Peoria, Ill ... C4 90
Elmwood, Plymouth, Mass ... B6 98
Elmwood, Cass, Nebr ... D9, h12 103
Elmwood, Pierce, Wis ... D1 124
Elmwood Park, Cook, Ill ... k9 90
Elmwood Park, Bergen, N.J ... h8 106
Elmwood Place, Hamilton, Ohio ... o13 111
Elna, Johnson and Morgan, Ky ... C7 94
Elne, Fr ... F5 14
Elnora, Alta., Can ... D4 69
Elnora, Daviess, Ind ... G3 91
El Obeid (Al Ubayyiḑ), Sud ... C3 47
Eloise, Polk, Fla ... E5 86
Eloise, Wayne, Mich ... A7 98
Elon College, Alamance, N.C ... A3 109
Elora, Ont., Can ... D4 72
Elora, Lincoln, Tenn ... B5 117
El Oro, prov., Ec ... B2 58
El Oued, Alg ... C6 44
Eloy, Pinal, Ariz ... E4 80
El Palmito, Mex ... B3 63
El Pao, Ven ... B5 60
El Paraíso, Hond ... D4 62
El Paso, White, Ark ... B3 81
El Paso, Woodford, Ill ... C4 90
El Paso, El Paso, Tex ... o11 118
El Paso, co., Colo ... C6 83
El Paso, co., Tex ... o11 118
Elphin, Ire ... D3 11
Elphinstone, Man., Can ... D1 71
El Portal, Mariposa, Calif ... D4 82
El Portal, Dade, Fla ... s13 86
El Porvenir, San Miguel, N. Mex ... B4 107
El Prado, Taos, N. Mex ... A4 107
El Progreso, Hond ... C4 62
El Pueblo, San Miguel, N. Mex ... B4 107
El Puerto de Santa María, Sp ... D2 20
El Qaryatein, Syr ... E11 31
Elqui, riv., Chile ... F1 55
Elrama, Washington, Pa ... F2 114
El Real, Pan ... F9 62
El Reno, Canadian, Okla ... B4 112
El Rio, Ventura, Calif ... E4 82
El Rito, Rio Arriba, N. Mex ... A3 107
El Roboré, Bol ... C4 55
Elrod, Tuscaloosa, Ala ... B2 78
Elrosa, Stearns, Minn ... E4 99
Elrose, Sask., Can ... F1 70
Elroy, Juneau, Wis ... E3 124
Elsa, Hidalgo, Tex ... F3 118
Elsa, Yukon, Can ... D5 66
Elsah, Jersey, Ill ... f13 101
El Salto, Mex ... C3 63
El Salvador, country, N.A ... H12 61, D3 62
El Samán, Ven ... B4 60
El Sauce, Nic ... D4 62
Elsberry, Lincoln, Mo ... B6 101
El Seibo, Dom. Rep ... E9 64
Elsie, Clinton, Mich ... E6 98
Elsie, Perkins, Nebr ... D4 103
Elsinore, Sevier, Utah ... E3 119
Elsmere, New Castle, Del ... A6 85
Elsmere, Kenton, Ky ... B5, k13 94
Elsmere, Cherry, Nebr ... B5 103
Elsmore, Allen, Kans ... E8 93
El Sobrante, Contra Costa, Calif ... *D3 82
El Sombrero, Ven ... B4 60
Elsterwerda, G.D.R ... B8 17
Elstow, Sask., Can ... F2 70
El Tigre, Ven ... B5 60
El Tocuyo, Ven ... B4 60
Elton, Jefferson Davis, La ... D3 95
Elton, Langlade, Wis ... C5 124
Eltopia, Franklin, Wash ... C6 122
El Transito, Chile ... E1 55
El Triunfo, Hond ... D4 62
El Triunfo, Mex ... C2 63
El Tucuche, mtn., Trin ... N23 65
Eltville, F.R.G ... C3 17
Elūru (Ellore), India ... I8 40
Elva, Man., Can ... E1 71
El Vado, res., N. Mex ... A3 107
El Valle, Taos, N. Mex ... *A4 107
El Valle, Pan ... F7 62
Elvas, Port ... C2 20
Elvaston, Hancock, Ill ... C2 90
El Verano, Sonoma, Calif ... *C2 82
Elverson, Chester, Pa ... F10 114
Elverum, Nor ... G4 25
El Viejo, Nic ... E4 62
El Vigía, Ven ... B3 60
Elvins, Francois, Mo ... D7 101
El Vista, Peoria, Ill ... *C4 90
El Volcán, Chile ... A2 54
El Wak, Ken ... A7 48
Elwell Lake, res., Mont ... B5 102
Elwha, riv., Wash ... A2 122
Elwood, Will, Ill ... B5 90
Elwood, Madison, Ind ... D6 91
Elwood, Doniphan, Kans ... C9 93
Elwood, Gosper, Nebr ... D6 103
Elwood, Atlantic, N.J ... D3 106
Elwood, Suffolk, N.Y ... *n15 84
Elwood, Box Elder, Utah ... B3 119
Elwood Park, Manatee, Fla ... E4, q11 86
Elwyn, Delaware, Pa ... *G10 114
Ely, Eng ... B8 12
Ely, Linn, Iowa ... C6 92
Ely, St. Louis, Minn ... C7 99
Ely, White Pine, Nev ... D7 104
Ely, Orange, Vt ... D4 120
Elyria, McPherson, Kans ... D6 93
Elyria, Valley, Nebr ... C6 103
Elyria, Lorain, Ohio ... A3 111
Elysburg, Northumberland, Pa ... E8 114
Elysian, Le Sueur, Minn ... F5 99
El Yungue, mtn., P.R ... B4 65
Elzach, F.R.G ... A4 18
Emāmshahr, Iran ... C7 41
Emanuel, co., Ga ... D4 87
Emba, Sov. Un ... D5 29
Emba, riv., Sov. Un ... F20 9
Embalse Guri, res., Ven ... A2 59
Embarcación, Arg ... D3 55
Embarras, riv., Ill ... E6 90
Embarrass, St. Louis, Minn ... C6 99
Embarrass, Waupaca, Wis ... D5 124
Embarrass, riv., Wis ... D5 124
Embden, pond, Maine ... E3 96
Embden, Cass, N. Dak ... C8 110
Embetsu, Jap ... D10 37
Embira, riv., Braz ... C3 58
Emblem, Big Horn, Wyo ... A4 125
Embree, Newf., Can ... *D4 75
Embreeville, Washington, Tenn ... C11 117
Embro, Ont., Can ... D4 72
Embrun, Ont., Can ... B9 72
Embrun, Fr ... E7 14
Embu, Ken ... B6 48
Embudo, Rio Arriba, N. Mex ... A4 107
Emden, F.R.G ... B3 16
Emden, Logan, Ill ... C4 90
Emden, Shelby, Mo ... B6 101
Emelle, Sumter, Ala ... C1 78
Emerado, Grand Forks, N. Dak ... B8 110
Emerald, Austl ... A7 51
Emerald, Lancaster, Nebr ... *D9 103
Emerson, Columbia, Ark ... D2 81
Emerson, Man., Can ... E3 71
Emerson, Bartow, Ga ... B2 87
Emerson, Mills, Iowa ... C2 92
Emerson, D'kota, Nebr ... B9 103
Emerson, Bergen, N.J ... h8 106
Emery, Hanson, S. Dak ... D8 116
Emery, Emery, Utah ... E4 119
Emery, co., Utah ... E5 119
Emery Mills, York, Maine ... E2 96
Emeryville, Alameda, Calif ... *D2 82
Emet, Tur ... C7 23
Emida, Benewah, Idaho ... B2 89
Emigrant, Park, Mont ... E6 102
Emigrant Gap, Placer, Calif ... C3 82
Emi Koussi, vol., Chad ... B3 46
Emilia-Romagna, pol. dist., It ... E6 18
Emilia, reg., It ... B3 21
Emiliano Zapata, Mex ... D6 63
Emílio Meyer, Braz ... E2 56
Emily, Crow Wing, Minn ... D5 99
Emily, lake, Minn ... E3 99
Emine, cape, Bul ... D9 22
Eminence, Morgan, Ind ... E4 91
Eminence, Henry, Ky ... B4 94
Eminence, Shannon, Mo ... D6 101
Emington, Livingston, Ill ... C5 90
Emirau, isl., Pap. N. Gui ... h13 50
Emirdag, Tur ... C8 31
Emlenton, Venango, Pa ... D2 114
Emlyn, Whitley, Ky ... D5 94
Emma, Lafayette and Saline, Mo ... C4 101
Emma, lake, Sask., Can ... D3 70
Emmaus, Lehigh, Pa ... E11 114
Emme, riv., Switz ... B3 19
Emmeline, lake, Sask., Can ... C2 70
Emmen, Neth ... B6 15
Emmen, Switz ... B5 19
Emmendingen, F.R.G ... A3 18
Emmerich, F.R.G ... C3 17
Emmet, Nevada, Ark ... D2 81
Emmet, Holt, Nebr ... B7 103
Emmet, McLean, N. Dak ... B4 110
Emmet, co., Iowa ... A3 92
Emmet, co., Mich ... C6 98
Emmett, Gem, Idaho ... F2 89
Emmett, Pottawatomie, Kans ... C7 93
Emmett, St. Clair, Mich ... F8 98
Emmetsburg, Palo Alto, Iowa ... A3 92
Emmitsburg, Frederick, Md ... A3 85
Emmonak, Alsk ... C7 79
Emmons, Freeborn, Minn ... G5 99
Emmons, co., N. Dak ... C5 110
Emory, Rains, Tex ... C5 118
Emory, Summit, Utah ... B4 119
Emory, peak, Tex ... p13 118
Emory University, De Kalb, Ga ... *C2 87
Empangeni, S. Afr ... C5 49
Empedrado, Arg ... E4 55
Empire, Walker, Ala ... B2 78
Empire, Stanislaus, Calif ... *D3 82
Empire, Clear Creek, Colo ... B5 83
Empire, Dodge, Ga ... D3 87
Empire, Plaquemines, La ... E6 95
Empire, Leelanau, Mich ... D4 98
Empire, Washoe, Nev ... C2 104
Empire, Jefferson, Ohio ... B5 111
Empire, Coos, Oreg ... D2 113
Empoli, It ... C3 21
Emporia, Lyon, Kans ... D7 93
Emporia (Independent City), Va ... D5 121
Emporium, Cameron, Pa ... C5 114
Empress, Alta, Can ... D5 69
Emptinne, Bel ... D5 15
Ems, riv., F.R.G ... A2 17
Emsdale, Ont., Can ... B5 72
Emsdetten, F.R.G ... A2 17
Ems-Jade, canal, F.R.G ... A7 15
Emsworth, Allegheny, Pa ... h13 114
Emyvale, Ire ... C5 11
Ena (Nakatsu), Jap ... n16 37
Enard, bay, Scot ... B3 13
Ena-San, peak, Jap ... n16 37
Encampment, Carbon, Wyo ... D6 125
Encanto, cape, Phil ... o13 35
Encarnación, Par ... E4 55
Encarnación de Díaz, Mex ... m12 63
Enchant, Alta., Can ... D4 69
Enchi, Ghana ... E4 45
Encinal, Valencia, N. Mex ... *C2 107
Encinal, LaSalle, Tex ... E3 118
Encinitas, San Diego, Calif ... F5 82
Encino, Torrance, N. Mex ... C4 107
Encino, Brooks, Tex ... F3 118
Encontrados, Ven ... B3 60
Encounter, bay, Austl ... G2 51
Endako, B.C., Can ... B5 68
Endako, riv., B.C., Can ... B5 68
Ende, Indon ... G6 35
Endeavor, Forest, Pa ... C3 114
Endeavor, Marquette, Wis ... E4 124
Endeavour, Sask., Can ... E4 70
Endelave, Den ... C4 24
Endelave, isl., Den ... C4 24
Enderby, B.C., Can ... D8 68
Enderby Land, reg., Ant ... C18 5
Enderlin, Ransom, N. Dak ... C8 110
Enders, Chase, Nebr ... D4 103
Enders, res., Kans ... B2 93
Endiang, Alta., Can ... D4 69
Endicott, Jefferson, Nebr ... D8 103
Endicott, Broome, N.Y ... C4 108
Endicott, Whitman, Wash ... C8 122
Endicott, mts., Alsk ... B9 79
Endless, lake, Maine ... C4 96
Endwell, Tioga, N.Y ... C4 108
Ene, riv., Peru ... D3 58
Enebakk, Nor ... p29 25
Energetik, Sov. Un ... C5 29
Enez, Tur ... B6 23
Enfield, N.S., Can ... E6 74
Enfield, Hartford, Conn ... B6 84
Enfield, Eng. (part of London) ... C7 12
Enfield, White, Ill ... E5 90
Enfield, Grafton, N.H ... C2 105
Enfield, Tompkins, N.Y ... *C4 108
Enfield, Halifax, N.C ... A6 109
Enfield Center, Grafton, N.H ... C2 105
Engadine, Mackinac, Mich ... B5 98
Engaño cape, Dom. Rep ... E9 64
Engaru, Jap ... D11 37
Engebi, isl., Eniwetok ... 52
Engelberg, Switz ... C5 19
Engelhard, Hyde, N.C ... B8 109
Engels, Sov. Un ... C3 29
Enghien, Bel ... D4 15
Enghien, Fr ... g10 14
'En Gedi, Isr ... C7 32
'En Gev, Isr ... B7 32
England, Lonoke, Ark ... C4, k11 81
England, reg., U.K ... D6 10, B6 12
Engle, Sierra, N. Mex ... D3 107
Englee, Newf., Can ... C3, h10 75
Englefeld, Sask., Can ... E3 70
Engleside, Fairfax, Va ... g12 121
Englevale, Ransom, N. Dak ... C8 110
Englewood, B.C., Can ... D4 68
Englewood, Arapahoe, Colo ... B6 83
Englewood, Duval, Fla ... *B5 86
Englewood, Sarasota, Fla ... F4 86
Englewood, Lawrence, Ind ... *G5 91
Englewood, Clark, Kans ... E4 93
Englewood, Bergen, N.J ... h9 106
Englewood, Montgomery, Ohio ... C1 111
Englewood, Coos, Oreg ... *D2 113
Englewood, McMinn, Tenn ... D9 117
Englewood Cliffs, Bergen, N.J ... h9 106
English, Crawford, Ind ... H5 91
English, chan., Eng., Fr ... C11 10
English, riv., Iowa ... C5 92
English Bazar, India ... E12 40
English Bay, Alsk ... h16, D9 79
English Center, Lycoming, Pa ... D7 114
English Creek, Atlantic, N.J ... E3 106
English Harbour West, Newf., Can ... E4 75
English Lake, Starke, Ind ... B4 91
Englishtown, Monmouth, N.J ... C4 106
Enguera, Sp ... C5 20
'En Harod, Isr ... B7 32
Enhaut, Dauphin, Pa ... *F8 114
Enid, Tallahatchie, Miss ... A4 100
Enid, Richland, Mont ... C12 102
Enid, Garfield, Okla ... A4 112
Enid, res., Miss ... A4 100
Enigma, Berrien, Ga ... E3 87
Enilda, Alta., Can ... B2 69
Enirik, isl., Bikini ... 52
Eniwetok, isl., Marshall Is ... 52
Enka, Buncombe, N.C ... f10 109
Enkeldoorn, Zimb ... A5 49
'En Kerem, Isr. (part of Jerusalem) ... h11 32
Enkhuizen, Neth ... B5 15
Enköping, Swe ... H7, t35 25
Enna, It ... F5 21
En Naqura, Leb ... A7 32
En Nebk, Syr ... E11 31
Ennadai, lake, N.W. Ter., Can ... D12 66
Ennedi, plat., Chad ... B4 46
Ennell, lake, Ire ... D4 11
Enngonia, Austl ... D5 51
Ennigerloh, F.R.G ... B3 17
Enning, Meade, S. Dak ... C3 116
Ennis, Ire ... E3 11
Ennis, Madison, Mont ... E5 102
Ennis, Ellis, Tex ... C4, n10 118
Enniscorthy, Ire ... E5 11
Ennis Creek, Clallam, Wash ... A2 122
Enniskillen, N. Ire ... C4 11
Ennistymon, Ire ... E2 11
Enns, Aus ... D7 16
Enns, riv., Aus ... D7 16
Ennylabegan, isl., Kwajalein ... 52
Enoch, Iron, Utah ... F3 119
Enochs, Bailey, Tex ... C1 118
Enochsburg, Franklin, Ind ... F7 91
Enola, Faulkner, Ark ... B3 81
Enola, Madison, Nebr ... C8 103
Enola, Cumberland, Pa ... F8 114
Enon, Bullock, Ala ... C4 78
Enon, Clark, Ohio ... C2 111
Enoree, Spartanburg, S.C ... B4 115
Enoree, riv., S.C ... B3 115
Enos, Newton, Ind ... B3 91
Enosburg (Town of), Franklin, Vt ... *B3 120
Enosburg Falls, Franklin, Vt ... B3 120
Enriquillo, Dom. Rep ... F8 64
Enriquillo, lake, Dom. Rep ... E8 64
Enschede, Neth ... B6 15
Ensenada, Arg ... g8 54
Ensenada, Mex ... A1 63
Ensenada, Rio Arriba, N. Mex ... A3 107
Enshih, China ... E6 34
Ensign, Alta., Can ... D4 69
Ensign, Gray, Kans ... E3 93
Ensign, Delta, Mich ... C4 98
Ensisheim, Fr ... B3 18
Ensley, Escambia, Fla ... u14 86
Entebbe, Ug ... A5 48
Enterprise, Coffee, Ala ... D4 78
Enterprise, Shasta, Calif ... *B2 82
Enterprise, Ont., Can ... C8 72
Enterprise, Polk, Iowa ... e8 92
Enterprise, Dickinson, Kans ... D6 93
Enterprise, Clarke, Miss ... C5 100
Enterprise, Wallowa, Oreg ... B9 113
Enterprise, Washington, Utah ... F2 119
Enterprise, Harrison, W. Va ... B4, k10 123
Entiat, Chelan, Wash ... B5 122
Entiat, mts., Wash ... B5 122
Entiat, riv., Wash ... B5 122
Entrance, Alta., Can ... C2 69
Entraygues, Fr ... E5 14
Entre Minho e Douro, reg., Port ... B1 20
Entre Rios, Moz ... D6 48
Entre Ríos, prov., Arg ... A5, f7 54
Entwistle, Alta., Can ... C3 69
Enugu, Nig ... E6 45
Enumclaw, King, Wash ... B3, f12 122
Envermeu, Fr ... E9 12
Enville, Chester, Tenn ... B3 117
Enyu, chan., Bikini ... 52
Enyu, isl., Bikini ... 52
Enz, riv., F.R.G ... E3 17
Enza, riv., It ... E6 18
Enzan, Jap ... n17 37
Eola, Avoyelles, La ... D3 95
Eola, hills, Oreg ... h11 113
Eolia, Pike, Mo ... B6 101
Eoline, Bibb, Ala ... C2 78
Epe, Neth ... B5 15
Epéna, Con ... E3 46
Épernay, Fr ... C5 14
Epes, Sumter, Ala ... C1 78
Ephesus, Heard, Ga ... C1 87
Ephesus, ruins, Tur ... D6 23
Ephraim, Sanpete, Utah ... D4 119
Ephraim, Door, Wis ... C6 124
Ephrata, Lancaster, Pa ... F9 114
Ephrata, Grant, Wash ... B6 122
Épila, Sp ... B5 20
Epileptic Village, Henry, Ind ... E7 91
Épinal, Fr ... A2 18, C7 14
Épinay [-sur-Seine], Fr ... g10 14
Epirus, reg., Grc ... C3 23
Epoufette, Mackinac, Mich ... B5 98
Epping, Eng ... k13 10
Epping, Rockingham, N.H ... D4 105
Epping, Williams, N. Dak ... A2 110
Eppingen, F.R.G ... D3 17
Epps, West Carroll, La ... B4 95
Epsie, Powder River, Mont ... E11 102
Epsom, Daviess, Ind ... G3 91
Epsom, Merrimack, N.H ... D4 105
Epsom [& Ewell], Eng ... C7 12
Epworth, Dubuque, Iowa ... B7 92
Equality, Coosa, Ala ... C3 78
Equality, Gallatin, Ill ... F5 90
Equatorial Guinea, country, Afr ... F6 42, E2 46
Équeurdreville, Fr ... C3 14
Equinunk, Wayne, Pa ... C11 114
Erath, Vermilion, La ... E3 95
Erath, co., Tex ... C3 118
Erba, mtn., Sud ... A4 47
Erbach, F.R.G ... D3 17
Erbacon, Webster, W. Va ... C4 123
Erbendorf, F.R.G ... D7 17
Erciş, Tur ... C10 31
Erciyeş, mtn., Tur ... C10 31
Ercsi, Hung ... B4 22
Érd, Hung ... B4 22
Erdek, Tur ... B6 23
Erdenheim, Montgomery, Pa ... o21 114
Erdeni Dzuu, Mong ... B5 34
Erding, F.R.G ... D5 18
Erebus, mtn., Ant ... B29 5
Erechim, Braz ... D2 56
Eregli, Tur ... B8 31
Eregli, Tur ... D10 31
Erepecurú, riv., Braz ... C3 59
Eressós, Grc ... C5 23
Eretria, see Nea Psara, Grc.
Erft, riv., F.R.G ... D6 15
Erfurt, G.D.R ... C6 17
Ergene, riv., Tur ... B6 23
Erhard, Otter Tail, Minn ... D2 99
Eria, riv., Sp ... A3 20
Erial, Camden, N.J ... D2 106
Eriboll, inlet, Scot ... B4 13
Erice, It ... E4 21
Ericht, lake, Scot ... D4 13
Erick, Beckham, Okla ... B2 112
Erickson, B.C., Can ... E9 68
Erickson, Man., Can ... D2 71
Ericsburg, Koochiching, Minn ... B5 99
Ericson, Wheeler, Nebr ... C7 103
Erie, Weld, Colo ... A5 83
Erie, Whiteside, Ill ... B3 90
Erie, Neosho, Kans ... E8 93
Erie, Monroe, Mich ... G7 98
Erie, Cass, N. Dak ... B8 110
Erie, Erie, Pa ... B1 114
Erie, co., N.Y ... C2 108
Erie, co., Ohio ... A3 111
Erie, co., Pa ... C1 114
Erie, lake, U.S. and Can ... B11 77
Erieau, Ont., Can ... E3 72
Erigavo, Som ... C6 47
Erigavo, dist., Som ... C6 47
Eriksdale, Man., Can ... D2 71
Erimanthos, mtn., Grc ... D3 23
Erimo, cape, Jap ... F11 37
Erin, Ont., Can ... D4 72
Erin, Houston, Tenn ... A4 117
Erin, pt., Trin ... O22 65
Eriskay, isl., Scot ... C1 13
Erisort, inlet, Scot ... B2 13
Erithraí, Grc ... C4, g10 23
Eritrea, prov., Eth ... B4 47
Erkelenz, F.R.G ... C6 15
Erken, lake, Swe ... t36 25
Erlangen, F.R.G ... D6 17
Erlanger, Kenton, Ky ... A5, h13 94
Erma, Cape May, N.J ... F3 106
Ermelo, Neth ... B5 15
Ermelo, S. Afr ... C5 49
Ermenak, Tur ... D9 31
Ermont, Fr ... g10 14
Ernakulam, India ... *G6 40
Erne, lake, N. Ire ... C4 11
Ernée, Fr ... C3 14
Ernest, Indiana, Pa ... E3 114
Ernestina, Arg ... g7 54
Ernestville, Unicoi, Tenn ... C11 117
Ernfold, Sask., Can ... G2 70
Eromanga, Austl ... C4 51
Eros, Jackson, La ... B3 95
Errigal, mtn., Ire ... B3 11
Erris, head, Ire ... C1 11
Errol, Coos, N.H ... g7 105
Errol Heights, Multnomah, Oreg ... *B4 113
Erskine, Alta., Can ... C4 69
Erskine, Polk, Minn ... C3 99
Erstein, Fr ... C7 14
Erstfeld, Switz ... C6 19
Erving, Franklin, Mass ... A3 97
Erwin, Harnett, N.C ... B4 109
Erwin, Kingsbury, S. Dak ... C8 116
Erwin, Unicoi, Tenn ... C11 117
Erwin, Preston, W. Va ... B5 123
Erwood, Sask., Can ... E4 70
Erzincan (Erzinjan), Tur ... C12 31
Erzurum, Tur ... C13 31
Esan, cape, Jap ... F10 37
Esashi, Jap ... D11 37
Esashi, Jap ... F10 37
Esbjerg, Den ... C2 24
Esbon, Jewell, Kans ... C5 93
Escabosa, Bernalillo, N. Mex ... m8 107
Escada, Braz ... k6 57
Escalante, Garfield, Utah ... F4 119
Escalante, des., Utah ... F2 119
Escalante, hills, Colo ... A2 83
Escalante, riv., Utah ... F4 119
Escalon, San Joaquin, Calif ... D3 82
Escalón, Mex ... B4 63
Escambia, co., Ala ... D2 78
Escambia, co., Fla ... u14 86
Escambia, riv., Ala., Fla ... D2 78
Escanaba, Delta, Mich ... C3 98
Escanaba, riv., Mich ... B3 98
Escatawpa, Jackson, Miss ... E5, f8 100
Escatawpa, riv., Ala., Miss ... E5 100
Eschede, F.R.G ... B5 17
Eschenbach, F.R.G ... D6 17
Escholzmatt, Switz ... C4 19
Esch-sur-Alzette, Lux ... E5 15
Eschwege, F.R.G ... B5 17
Eschweiler, F.R.G ... C6 15
Escobal, Pan ... k11 62
Escobar, Arg ... g7 54
Escocesa, bay, Dom. Rep ... E9 64
Escoheag, Kent, R.I ... C9 84
Escondida, Socorro, N. Mex ... C3 107
Escondida, pt., Mex ... D5 63
Escondido, San Diego, Calif ... F5 82
Escondido, riv., Nic ... D5 62
Escoublac-La-Baule, Fr ... D2 14
Escoumains, riv., Que., Can ... A8 73
Escuinapa, Mex ... C3 63
Escuintla, Guat ... C2 62
Escuminac, pt., N.B., Can ... B5 74
Eséka, Cam ... E2 46
Esens, F.R.G ... A7 15
Eşfahan (Isfahan), Iran ... E5 41
Esgueva, riv., Sp ... B3 20
Esher, Eng ... m12 10
Eshimba, Zaire ... C3 48
Eshkāshem, Afg ... C15 41
Eshowe, S. Afr ... C5 49
Esh Shobek, Jordan ... D7 32
Esk, riv., Eng ... F5 13
Esk, riv., Scot ... E6 13
Eskbank, Sask., Can ... G2 70
Eskdale, Kanawha, W. Va ... C3, m13 123
Eske, lake, Ire ... C3 11
Eskifoca, Tur ... C6 23
Eskilstuna, Swe ... H7, t34 25
Eskimo, lakes, N.W. Ter., Can ... C6 66
Eskimo Point, N.W. Ter., Can ... D14 66
Eskişehir, Tur ... C8 23
Esko, Carlton, Minn ... D6 99
Eskridge, Wabaunsee, Kans ... D7 93
Esla, riv., Sp ... B3 20
Eslarn, F.R.G ... D7 17
Eslava, riv., Mex ... h9 63
Eslöv, Swe ... C7 24
Esme, Tur ... C7 23
Esmeralda, Ven ... C4 60
Esmeralda, co., Nev ... F4 104
Esmeraldas, Ec ... A2 58
Esmeraldas, prov., Ec ... A2 58
Esmeraldas, riv., Ec ... A2 58
Esmond, DeKalb, Ill ... A5 90
Esmond, Benson, N. Dak ... A6 110
Esmond, Providence, R.I ... B10 84
Esmond, Kingbury, S. Dak ... C8 116
Esmont, Albemarle, Va ... C4 121
Esom Hill, Polk, Ga ... C1 87
Esopus, Ulster, N.Y ... *D7 108
Espada, pt., Col ... A3 60
Espanola, Ont., Can ... A3 72
Espanola, Flagler, Fla ... C5 86
Espanola, Rio Arriba and Santa Fe, N. Mex ... B3 107
Espanola, Spokane, Wash ... g13 122
Española, isl., Ec ... g6 58
Esparto, Yolo, Calif ... C2 82
Esperance, Austl ... F3 50
Esperanza, Arg ... A4 54
Esperanza, Pontotoc, Miss ... A4 100
Esperanza, Hudspeth, Tex ... o12 118
Esperanza, riv., Pan ... k12 62
Espichel, cape, Port ... C1 20
Espinhaço, mts., Braz ... E2 57
Espírito Santo, Braz ... F2 57
Espírito Santo, state, Braz ... C4 56
Espíritu Santo, isl., New Hebr ... H10 7
Espita, Mex ... C7 63
Esposende, Port ... B1 20
Espungabera, Moz ... B5 49
Espy, Columbia, Pa ... D9 114
Espyville Station, Crawford, Pa ... C1 114
Esquatzel Coulee, creek, Wash ... C6 122
Esquel, Arg ... C2 54

Esquimalt, B.C., Can...E6, h12 68
Esquina, Arg...F4 55
Essaouira (Mogador), Mor...C3 44
Essen, Bel...C4 15
Essen, F.R.G...B2 17
Essequibo, riv., Guy...B3 59
Essex, San Bernardino, Calif.E6 82
Essex, Ont., Can...E2 72
Essex, Middlesex, Conn...D7 84
Essex, Kankakee, Ill...B5 90
Essex, Page, Iowa...D2 92
Essex, Baltimore, Md...B5 85
Essex, Essex, Mass...A6 97
Essex, Stoddard, Mo...E8 101
Essex, Flathead, Mont...B3 102
Essex, Essex, N.Y...f11 108
Essex, Chittenden, Vt...B2 120
Essex, co., Ont., Can...E2 72
Essex, co., Eng...C8 12
Essex, co., Mass...A5 97
Essex, co., N.J...B4 106
Essex, co., N.Y...B7 108
Essex, co., Vt...B5 120
Essex, co., Va...B5 121
Essex Fells, Essex, N.J...*B4 106
Essex Junction, Chittenden,
Vt...C2 120
Essexvale, Zimb...B4 49
Essexville, Bay, Mich...E7 98
Essington, Delaware, Pa...*G11 114
Esslingen, F.R.G...E4 17
Es Suki, Sud...C3 47
Est, isl., Que., Can...B8 74
Est, pt., Que., Can...B8 74
Estacada, Clackamas, Oreg..B4 113
Estación Superi, Arg...E2 55
Estados, isl., Arg...h13 54
Estaire, Ont., Can...A4 72
Estância, Braz...D3 57
Estancia, Torrance, N. Mex.C3 107
Estand, mtn., Iran...F9 41
Estarreja, Port...B1 20
Estcourt, Que., Can...B8 73
Estcourt, S. Afr...C4 49
Este, It...B3 21
Este, pt., P.R....B5 65
Estelí, Nic...D4 62
Estella, Craig, Okla...A6 112
Estella, Sp...A4 20
Estell Manor, Atlantic, N.J..E3 106
Estelline, Hamlin, S. Dak...C9 116
Estelline, Hall, Tex...B2 118
Estepa, Sp...D3 20
Estepona, Sp...D3 20
Esterbrook, Converse, Wyo..D7 125
Esterhazy, Sask., Can...G4 70
Esternay, Fr...F3 15
Esternberg, Aus...E8 17
Estero, Lee, Fla...F5 86
Estero, bay, Calif...E3 82
Estero, isl., Fla...F5 86
Estes Park, Larimer, Colo...A5 83
Estevan, Sask., Can...H4 70
Estevan, is., B.C., Can...C3 68
Estevan Point, B.C., Can...E4 68
Esther, Alta., Can...D5 69
Esther, St. Francois, Mo...*D7 101
Estherville, Emmet, Iowa...A3 92
Estherwood, Acadia, La...D3 95
Estill, Washington, Miss...B3 100
Estill, Hampton, S.C...F5 115
Estill, co., Ky...C6 94
Estillfork, Jackson, Ala...A3 78
Estill Springs, Franklin,
Tenn...B5 117
Estlin, Sask., Can...G3 70
Esto, Holmes, Fla...u16 86
Eston, Sask., Can...F1 70
Eston, Eng...*F7 13
Estonia (S.S.R.), rep.,
Sov. Un...D5 28
Estrées-St.-Denis, Fr...E5 14
Estrêla, Braz...D2 56
Estrêla, mts., Port...B2 20
Estremadura, prov., Port...*C1 20
Estremadura, reg., Port...C1 20
Estremadura, reg., Sp...C2 20
Estremoz, Port...C2 20
Estrondo, mts., Braz..C1 57, D5 59
Estuary, Sask., Can...G1 70
Esztergom, Hung...B4 22
Etah, Grnld...B22 4
Étain, Fr...E5 15
Etamamiou, riv., Que., Can...C1 75
Étampes, Fr...C5 14
Étang-du-Nord, Que., Can...B8 74
Étang Saumatre, lake, Hai...E7 64
Étaples, Fr...B4 14
Etawa, India...D7 40
Etāwah, India...C6 39, D7 40
Eten, isl., Truk...52
Eternity, range, Ant...C6 5
Ethan, Davison, S. Dak...D8 116
Ethel, Ont., Can...D3 72
Ethel, Attala, Miss...B4 100
Ethel, Macon, Mo...B5 101
Ethel, Lewis, Wash...C3 122
Ethel, Logan, W. Va...n12 123
Ethel, mtn., Colo...A4 83
Ethelbert, Man., Can...D1 71
Ethelsville, Pickens, Ala...B1 78
Ethelton, Sask., Can...E3 70
Ether, Montgomery, N.C...B3 109
Ethete, Fremont, Wyo...D4 125
Ethiopia (Abyssinia), country,
Afr...F9 42, D4 47
Ethridge, Toole, Mont...B5 102
Ethridge, Lawrence, Tenn...B4 117
Etive, inlet, Scot...D3 13
Etlan, Madison, Va...B4 121
Etna, Penobscot, Maine...D3 96
Etna, Grafton, N.H...C2 105
Etna, Tompkins, N.Y...C4 108
Etna, Licking, Ohio...C3 111
Etna, Allegheny, Pa...k14 114
Etna, Lincoln, Wyo...C2 125
Etna, vol., It...F5 21
Etna Green, Kosciusko, Ind..B5 91
Etolin, isl., Alsk...m23 79
Etolin, strait, Alsk...C6 79
Eton, Murray, Ga...B2 87
Etoshapan, lake, Namibia...A2 49
Etowah, Mississippi, Ark...B5 81
Etowah, McMinn, Tenn...D9 117
Etowah, co., Ala...A3 78
Etowah, riv., Ga...B2 87
Etra, Mercer, N.J...C3 106
Etretat, Fr...C4 14
Etta, Union, Miss...A4 100
Eṭ Ṭaiyiba, Jordan...B7, f11 32
Ettelbruck, Lux...E6 15
Etter, Moore, Tex...A1 118
Etters (Goldsboro), York, Pa.F8 114
Ettington, Sask., Can...H2 70
Eṭ Ṭira, Isr...B6, g10 33
Ettlingen, F.R.G...E3 17
Ettrick, Chesterfield,
Va...C5, n18 121
Ettrick, Trempealeau, Wis...D2 124
Etzatlán, Mex...m11 63
Etzikom, Alta., Can...E5 69
Etzikom Coulee, riv., Alta., Can..E5 69
Eu, Fr...B4 14
Euboea (Evvoia), prov.,
Grc...*C4 23
Eucha, Delaware, Okla...A7 112
Euclid, Polk, Minn...C2 99
Euclid, Cuyahoga, Ohio.A4, g9 111
Euclid, Butler, Pa...E2 114
Euclid Center, Berrien,
Mich...*F4 98
Euclid Heights, Garland,
Ark...*C2 81
Eucumbene, lake, Austl...H7 51
Eudora, Chicot, Ark...D4 81
Eudora, Douglas, Kans.D8, m15 93
Eudora, De Soto, Miss...A3 100
Eudunda, Austl...G2 51
Eufaula, Barbour, Ala...D4 78
Eufaula, McIntosh, Okla...B6 112
Eugene, Vermillion, Ind...E3 91
Eugene, Cole, Mo...C5 101
Eugene, Lane, Oreg...C3 113
Eugenia, pt., Mex...B1 63
Euless, Tarrant, Tex...*C4 118
Eulonia, McIntosh, Ga...E5 87
Eunice, St. Landry, La...D3 95
Eunice, Lea, N. Mex...E6 107
Eupen, Bel...D6 15
Euphrates, riv., Asia...H16 9
Eupora, Webster, Miss...B4 100
Eure, Gates, N.C...A6 109
Eure, dept., Fr...*C4 14
Eure, riv., Fr...C4 14
Eure-et-Loir, dept., Fr...*C4 14
Eureka, Humboldt, Calif...B2 82
Eureka, N.W. Ter., Can...m35 67
Eureka, Marion, Fla...C5 86
Eureka, Woodford, Ill...C4 90
Eureka, Greenwood, Kans...E7 93
Eureka, St. Louis, Mo...f12 101
Eureka, Lincoln, Mont...B1 102
Eureka, Eureka, Nev...D6 104
Eureka, Wayne, N.C...B5 109
Eureka (Chambersburg),
Gallia, Ohio...D3 111
Eureka, Aiken, S.C...D4 115
Eureka, McPherson, S. Dak..B6 116
Eureka, Juab, Utah...D3 119
Eureka, Pleasants, W. Va...B3 123
Eureka, Winnebago, Wis...D5 124
Eureka, co., Nev...D5 104
*Eureka, sound, N.W. Ter.,
Can*...m34 67
Eureka Springs, Carroll, Ark.A2 81
Euroa, Austl...H5 51
Europa, isl., Afr...B7 49
Europe, cont...C22 3, 8
Euros, riv., Tur...B6 31
Euskirchen, F.R.G...C1 17
Eustis, Lake, Fla...D5 86
Eustis, Franklin, Maine...C2 96
Eustis, Frontier, Nebr...D5 103
Eutaw, Greene, Ala...C2 78
Eutawville, Orangeburg, S.C.E7 115
Eutin, F.R.G...D4 24
Eutsuk, lake, B.C., Can...C4 68
Eva, Morgan, Ala...A3 78
Eva, Texas, Okla...e9 112
Eva, Benton, Tenn...A3 117
Evadale, Jasper, Texas...*D5 118
Evale, Ang...E2 48
Evan, Brown, Minn...F4 99
Evangeline, par., La...D3 95
Evans, Weld, Colo...A6 83
Evans, Columbia, Ga...C4 87
Evans, Vernon, La...D2 95
Evans, Jackson, W. Va...C3 123
Evans, co., Ga...D5 87
Evans, lake, Que., Can...o20 72
Evans, mtn., Colo...B5 83
Evans, mtn., N.Z...O13 51
Evans, strait, N.W. Ter., Can.D16 67
Evansburg, Alta., Can...C3 69
Evans City, Butler, Pa...E1 114
Evansdale, Black Hawk,
Iowa...B5 92
Evans Landing, Harrison,
Ind...H6 91
Evans Mills, Jefferson, N.Y..A5 108
Evansport, Defiance, Ohio...A1 111
Evanston, Weld, Colo...A6 83
Evanston, Cook, Ill...A6, h9 90
Evanston, Breathitt, Ky...C6 94
Evanston, Uinta, Wyo...D2 125
Evansville, Washington, Ark.B1 81
Evansville, Randolph, Ill...E4 90
Evansville, Vanderburgh, Ind.I2 91
Evansville, Douglas, Minn...D3 99
Evansville, Tunica, Miss...A3 100
Evansville, Orleans, Vt...B4 120
Evansville, Rock, Wis...F4 124
Evansville, Natrona, Wyo...D6 125
Evant, Coryell, Tex...D3 118
Evanton, Scot...C4 13
Evart, Osceola, Mich...E5 98
Evarts, Harlan, Ky...D6 94
Eveleth, St. Louis, Minn...C6 99
Evening Shade, Sharp, Ark..A4 81
Even Yehuda, Isr...f10 32
Everard, lake, Austl...F5 50
Everard, mtn., B.C., Can...D5 68
Everard, ranges, Austl...E5 50
Everest, Brown, Kans...C8 93
Everest, peak, Nep...D11 40
Everett, Ont., Can...C5 72
Everett, Middlesex, Mass...g11 97
Everett, Bedford, Pa...F5 114
Everett, Snohomish, Wash..B3 122
Everett, mtn., Mass...B1 97
Everett, mts., N.W. Ter., Can..D19 67
Everitt, Glynn, Ga...E5 87
Everettville, Monongalia,
W. Va...h10 123
Evergem, Bel...C3 15
Everglades, nat. park, Fla...G6 86
Everglades, swamp, Fla...G6 86
Evergreen, Conecuh, Ala...D3 78
Evergreen, Jefferson, Colo..B5 83
Evergreen, Avoyelles, La...D3 95
Evergreen, Itawamba, Miss..A5 100
Evergreen, Columbus, N.C...C4 109
Evergreen Appomattox, Va..C4 121
Evergreen Park, Cook, Ill...k9 90
Everly, Clay, Iowa...A2 92
Everman, Tarrant, Tex...*C4 118
Everson, Fayette, Pa...F2 114
Everson, Whatcom, Wash...A3 122
Everton, Boone, Ark...A3 81
Everton, Dade, Mo...D4 101
Evesham, Sask., Can...E1 70
Evesham, Eng...B6 12
Évian-les-Bains, Fr...C2 18
Evinayong, Equat. Gui...E2 46
Evington, Campbell, Va...C3 121
Evolène, Switz...D3 19
Evora, Port...C2 20
Évreux, Fr...C4 14
Evritania, prov., Grc...*C3 23
Évron, Fr...C3 14
Évros, prov., Grc...*B5 23
Évros, riv., Grc...B6 23
Evrotas, riv., Grc...D4 23
Evstratios, isl., Grc...C5 23
Evvoia (Euboea), prov.,
Grc...*C4 23
Evvoia (Northern), gulf, Grc...C4 23
Evvoia (Southern), gulf, Grc...g11 23
Evvoia (Eugoea), isl., Grc...C4 23
Ewa, Honolulu, Haw...B3, g9 88
Ewa, beach, Haw...g9 87
Ewab, is., Indon...G8 35
Ewa Beach, Honolulu, Haw..g9 88
Ewan, Whitman, Wash...B8 122
Ewarton, Jam...E14 65
Ewe, inlet, Scot...C3 13
Ewell, Somerset, Md...E5 85
Ewen, Ontonagon, Mich...m12 98
Ewing, Franklin, Ill...E5 90
Ewing, Jackson, Ind...G5 91
Ewing, Fleming, Ky...B6 94
Ewing, Lewis, Mo...A5 101
Ewing, Holt, Nebr...B7 103
Ewing, Lee, Va...f8 121
Ewing Township, Mercer,
N.J...C3 106
Ewo, Con...F2 46
Exaltación, Bol...B2 55
Excel, Monroe, Ala...D2 78
Excel, Alta., Can...D5 69
Excello, Macon, Mo...B5 101
Excelsior, Hennepin,
Minn...*F5 99
Excelsior, mtn., Calif...C4 82
Excelsior, mts., Nev...E3 104
Excelsior Springs, Clay and
Ray, Mo...B3, h11 101
Exchange, Montour, Pa...D8 144
Exchange, Braxton, W. Va..C4 123
Excursion Inlet, Alsk...k22 79
Exe, riv., Eng...D4 12
*Executive Committee, range,
Ant*...B36 5
Exeland, Sawyer, Wis...C4 124
Exeter, Tulare, Calif...D4 82
Exeter, Ont., Can...D3 72
Exeter, Eng...D4 12
Exeter, Penobscot, Maine...D3 96
Exeter, Barry, Mo...E4 101
Exeter, Fillmore, Nebr...D8 103
Exeter, Rockingham, N.H...E5 105
Exeter, Luzerne, Pa...D10, n17 114
Exeter, Washington, R.I...C10 84
Exeter, riv., N.H....E5 105
Exira, Audubon, Iowa...C3 92
Exline, Appanoose, Iowa...D5 92
Exmoor, moor, Eng...C4 12
Exmore, Northampton, Va...C7 121
Exmouth, Austl...D1 50
Exmouth, Eng...D4 12
Exmouth, gulf, Austl...D1 50
Expanse, Sask., Can...H3 70
Experiment, Spalding, Ga...C2 87
Exploits, bay, Newf., Can...D4 75
Exploits, riv., Newf., Can...D3 75
Export, Westmoreland, Pa...F2 114
Exshaw, Alta., Can...D3 69
Extension, B.C., Can...f12 68
*Extinct Volcanoes and Lava Beds,
Ariz*...C6 80
Exuma, sound, Ba...B5 64
Eya, riv., Sov. Un...H12 27
Eyasi, lake, Tan...B5 48
Eye, pen., Scot...B2 13
Eyebrow, Sask., Can...G2 70
Eyehill, creek, Alta., Sask., Can..C5 69
Eyemouth, Scot...E6 13
Eynort, inlet, Scot...C1 13
Eyota, Olmsted, Minn...G6 99
Eyre, Sask., Can...F1 70
Eyre, lake, Austl...E6 50
Eyre, pen., Austl...F6 50
Eyrecourt, Ire...D3 11
Ezeiza, Arg...g7 56
Ezine, Tur...C6 23

F

Faaborg, Den...C4 24
Fabens, El Paso, Tex...o11 118
Faber, Nelson, Va...C4 121
Faber, lake, N.W. Ter., Can...D9 66
Fabius, Onondaga, N.Y...C5 108
Fabius San Hilo, pt., Tinian...52
Fabriano, It...C4 21
Fabrica, Phil...*C6 35
Fabyan, Windham, Conn...A9 84
Facatativá, Col...C3 60
Fachi, Niger...C7 45
Fackler, Jackson, Ala...A4 78
Facpi, pt., Guam...52
Factoryville, Wyoming, Pa..C10 114
Fada, Chad...B4 46
Fada Ngourma,
Upper Volta...D5 45
Faddeya, gulf, Sov. Un...B3 4
Faddeyev, isl., Sov. Un...B17 28
Fadian, pt., Guam...52
Faenza, It...B3 21
Faeroe Islands, Dan. dep.,
Eur...C7 8
Fafa, Mali...C5 45
Fafe, Port...B1 20
Fafen, riv., Eth...D5 47
Faga'alu, Am. Sam...52
Fagaloa, bay, W. Sam...52
Făgăras, Rom...C7 22
Fagatogo, Am. Sam...52
Fågelbro, Swe...t36 25
Fagernes, Nor...G3 25
Fagersta, Swe...G6 25
Faggo, Nig...D6 45
Fagnano, lake, Arg...h12 54
Faguibine, lake, Mali...C4 45
Fagus, Butler, Mo...E7 101
Fahan, Ire...B4 11
Fahan, inlet, Saipan...52
Fahraj, Iran...H10 41
Faial, isl., Port. (Azores)...g8 44
Fā'id, Eg...D3 41
Faido, Switz...D6 19
Faifo, Viet...E8 38
Fairacres, Dona Ana,
N. Mex...E3 107
Fairbank, Cochise, Ariz...F5 80
Fairbank, Buchanan and
Fayette, Iowa...B5 92
Fairbanks, Alsk...C10 79
Fairbanks, Alachua, Fla...C4 86
Fairbanks, Franklin, Maine..D2 96
Fair Bluff, Columbus, N.C...C3 109
Fairborn, Greene, Ohio...C1 111
Fairburn, Fulton, Ga...C2, h7 87
Fairburn, Custer, S. Dak...D2 116
Fairbury, Livingston, Ill...C5 90
Fairbury, Jefferson, Nebr...D8 103
Fairchance, Fayette, Pa...G2 114
Fairchild, Eau Claire, Wis..D3 124
Fairdale, Jefferson, Ky..B4, g11 94
Fairdale, Walsh, N. Dak...A7 110
Fairfax, Chambers, Ala...C4 78
Fairfax, Marin, Calif...C2, h7 82
Fairfax, Man., Can...E1 71
Fairfax, New Castle, Del...*A6 85
Fairfax, Linn, Iowa...C6 92
Fairfax, Renville, Minn...F4 99
Fairfax, Atchison, Mo...A2 101
Fairfax, Hamilton, Ohio...*C1 111
Fairfax, Osage, Okla...A5 112
Fairfax, Allendale, S.C...F5 115
Fairfax, Gregory, S. Dak...D7 116
Fairfax, Franklin, Vt...B2 120
Fairfax (Independent City),
Va...B5, g12 121
Fairfax, co., Va...B5 121
Fairfax Station, Fairfax, Va.g12 121
Fairfield, Jefferson, Ala..B3, f7 78
Fairfield, Solano, Calif...C2, h7 82
Fairfield, Fairfield, Conn...E3 84
Fairfield, Camas, Idaho...F4 89
Fairfield, Wayne, Ill...E5 90
Fairfield, Jefferson, Iowa...C6 92
Fairfield, Nelson, Ky...C4 94
Fairfield, Somerset, Maine..D3 96
Fairfield, Teton, Mont...C5 102
Fairfield, Clay, Nebr...D7 103
Fairfield, Essex, N.J...*B4 106
Fairfield, Hyde, N.C...B6 109
Fairfield, Billings, N. Dak...B2 110
Fairfield, Butler, Ohio...n12 111
Fairfield, Lane, Oreg...*C3 113
Fairfield, Adams, Pa...G7 114
Fairfield, Freestone, Tex...D4 118
Fairfield, Utah, Utah...C3 119
Fairfield, Franklin, Vt...B3 120
Fairfield, Spokane,
Wash...B8, h14 122
Fairfield, co., Conn...D3 84
Fairfield, co., Ohio...C3 111
Fairfield, co., S.C...C5 115
Fairfield, pond, Vt...B2 120
Fairford, Washington, Ala...D1 78
Fairford, Eng...*C6 12
Fairgrove, Tuscola, Mich...E7 98
Fair Grove, Greene, Mo...D4 101
Fair Grove, Davidson, N.C...B2 109
Fairhaven, Bristol, Mass...C6 97
Fair Haven, St. Clair, Mich..F8 98
Fairhaven, Stearns, Minn...E4 99
Fair Haven, Monmouth, N.J.C4 106
Fair Haven, Cayuga. N.Y...B4 108
Fair Haven, Rutla.. , Vt...D2 120
Fairholme, Sask., Can...D1 70
Fairhope, Baldwin, Ala...E2 78
Fairhope, Fayette, Pa...*F2 114
Fairland, Shelby, Ind...E6 91
Fairland, Ottawa, Okla...A7 112
Fair Lawn, Bergen, N.J...h8 106
Fairlawn, Pulaski, Va...C2 121
Fair Lawn Heights, Summit,
Ohio...*A4 111
Fairlea, Greenbrier, W. Va..D4 123
Fairlee, Kent, Md...B5 85
Fairlee, Orange, Vt...D4 120
Fairless Hills, Bucks, Pa...*F12 114
Fairlight, Sask., Can...H5 70
Fairmont, Will, Ill...k8 90
Fairmont, Martin, Minn...G4 99
Fairmont, Fillmore, Nebr...D8 103
Fairmont, Robeson, N.C...C3 109
Fairmont, Garfield, Okla...A4 112
Fairmont, Spartanburg, S.C..B3 115
Fairmont, Snohomish,
Wash...*B3 122
Fairmont, Marion,
W. Va...B4, k10 123
Fairmont City, St. Clair, Ill..f13 101
Fairmont Heights, Prince
Georges, Md...f9 85
Fairmount, Gordon, Ga...B2 87
Fairmount, Vermilion, Ill...C6 90
Fairmount, Grant, Ind...D6 91
Fairmount, Leavenworth,
Kans...B8 93
Fairmount, Somerset, Md...D6 85
Fairmount, Onondaga, N.Y..*B4 108
Fairmount, Richland,
N. Dak...C9 110
Fairoaks, Cross, Ark...B4 81
Fair Oaks, Sacramento,
Calif...*C3 82
Fair Oaks, San Luis Obispo,
Calif...*E3 82
Fair Oaks, Cobb, Ga...h7 87
Fair Oaks, Jasper, Ind...B3 91
Fairoaks, Allegheny, Pa...h13 114
Fair Plain, Berrien, Mich...*F4 98
Fairplay, Park, Colo...B5 83
Fair Play, Washington, Md..A2 85
Fair Play, Polk, Mo...D4 101
Fair Play, Oconee, S.C...B2 115
Fairpoint, Belmont, Ohio...B5 111
Fairport, Muscatine, Iowa...C7 92
Fairport, Delta, Mich...C4 98
Fairport, De Kalb, Mo...B3 101
Fairport, Monroe, N.Y...B3 108
Fair Port, Northumberland,
Va...C6 121
Fairport Harbor, Lake Ohio.A4 111
Fairton, Cumberland, N.J...E2 106
Fairvale, N.B., Can...D4 74
Fairvalley, Woods, Okla...A2 112
Fairview, Atla., Can...A1 69
Fairview, Walker, Ga...*B1 87
Fairview, Fulton, Ill...C3 90
Fairview, St. Clair, Ill...*E3 90
Fairview, Switzerland, Ind..G7 91
Fairview, Brown, Kans...C8 93
Fairview, Christian & Todd,
Ky...D2 94
Fairview, Concordia, La...C4 95
Fairview, Oscoda, Mich...D6 98
Fairview, Newton, Mo...E3 101
Fairview, Richland, Mont..C12 102
Fairview, Bergen, N.J...h8 106
Fairview, Monmouth, N.J...*C4 106
Fairview, Dutchess, N.Y...*D7 108
Fairview, Belmont and Guern-
sey, Ohio...B4 111
Fairview, Major, Okla...A3 112
Fairview, Multnomah,
Oreg...B4, g12 113
Fairview, Erie, Pa...B1 114
Fairview, Northampton,
Pa...*E11 114
Fairview, Northumberland,
Pa...*E8 114
Fairview, Lincoln, S. Dak...D9 116
Fairview, Williamson, Tenn..B4 117
Fairview, Sanpete, Utah...D4 119
Fairview, Yakima, Wash...*C5 122
Fairview, Marion,
W. Va...B4, h10 123
Fairview, Lincoln, Wyo...D2 125
Fairview, peak, Nev...D3 104
Fairview Heights, St. Clair,
Ill...E3 90
Fairview Park, Vermillion,
Ind...E3 91
Fairview Park, Cuyahoga,
Ohio...h9 111
Fairview Shores, Orange,
Fla...*D5 86
Fairvilla, Orange, Fla...*D5 86
Fair Water, Fond du Lac,
Wis...E5 124
Fairway, Johnson, Kans...k16 93
*Fairweather, mtn., Alsk., B.C.,
Can*...D12 79
Fairy Glen, Sask., Can...D3 70
Fairyland, Walker, Ga...*B1 87
Faisalbad, Pak...B5 39, B4 40
Faison, Duplin, N.C...B4 109
Faith, Rowan, N.C...B2 109
Faith, Meade, S. Dak...B3 116
Faithorn, Menominee, Mich.C3 98
Faizābād, India...C7 39, D9 40
Fajardo, P.R...B4 65
Fajardo, mun., P.R...*B4 65
Fakenham, Eng...B8 12
Fakfak, Indon...F8 35
Fakse, Den...C6 24
Fakse, bay, Den...C6 24
Fakse Ladeplads, Den...C6 24
Faku, China...C10 36
Fal, Vernon, La...D2 95
Fal, riv., Eng...D3 12
Falaba, S.L...E2 45
Falabequets, isl., Truk...52
Falaise, Fr...C3 14
Falalu, isl., Truk...52
Falas, isl., Truk...52
Fălciu, Rom...B9 22
Falcon, Nevada, Ark...D2 81
Falcon, Quitman, Miss...A3 100
Falcon, El Paso, Colo...C6 83
Falcon, Cumberland, N.C...B4 109
Falcon, Zapata, Tex...F3 118
Falcón, state, Ven...A3 60
Falconer, Chautauqua, N.Y..C1 108
Falcon Heights, Ramsey,
Minn...n12 99
Falcon Heights, Klamath,
Oreg...E5 113
Falconwood, Erie, N.Y...*C2 108
Falealili, hbr., W. Sam...52
Falefa, hbr., W. Sam...52
Falémé, riv., Mali, Sen...D2 45
Faleshty, Sov. Un...B8 22
Falfurrias, Brooks, Tex...F3 118
Falher, Alta., Can...B2 69
Falkenberg, G.D.R...B8 17
Falkenberg, Swe...B6 24
Falkenburg Station, Ont.,
Can...B5 72
Falkenstein, G.D.R...C7 17
Falkirk, McLean, N. Dak...B4 110
Fallkirk, Scot...E5 13
Falkland, B.C., Can...D8 68
Falkland, Scot...*D5 13
Falkland Islands, Br. dep.,
S.A...I4 53
Falkner, Tippah, Miss...A5 100
Falköping, Swe...H5 25
Falkville, Morgan, Ala...A3 78
Fall, F.R.G...B7 18
Fall, riv., Kans...E7 93
Fall Branch, Washington,
Tenn...C11 117
Fallbrook, San Diego, Calif..F5 82
Fall City, King, Wash..B4, e12 122
Fall Creek, Eau Claire, Wis..D2 124
Fallentimber, Cambria, Pa..E5 114
Falling, creek, Va...n17 121
Falling, ıeek, W. Va...m13 123
Falling Creek, Chesterfield,
Va...*C5 121
Falling Water, Hamilton,
Tenn...h11 117
Falling Waters, Berkeley,
W. Va...B6 123
Fallis, Lincoln, Okla...B4 112
Fall Mountain Lake, Litchfield,
Conn...*C4 84
Fållnäs, Swe...u35 25
Fallon, Prairie, Mont...D11 102
Fallon, Churchill, Nev...D3 104
Fallon, co., Mont...D12 102
Fall River, Greenwood, Kans.E7 93
Fall River, Bristol, Mass...C5 97
Fallriver, Lawrence, Tenn...B4 117
Fall River, Columbia, Wis...E4 124
Fall River, co., S. Dak...D2 116
Fall River Lake, res., Kans...E7 93
Fall River Mills, Shasta,
Calif...B3 82
Fall Rock, Clay, Ky...C6 94
Falls, Wyoming, Pa...D10, m17 114
Falls, co., Tex...D4 118
Falls, riv., Wyo...B2 125
Fallsburg, Lawrence, Ky...B7 94
Falls Church (Independent
City), Va...g12 121
Falls City, Richardson,
Nebr...D10 103
Falls City, Polk, Oreg...C3 113
Falls Creek, Clearfield and
Jefferson, Pa...D4 114
Fallsington, Bucks, Pa...*F12 114
Falls of Rough, Grayson, Ky.C3 94
Fallston, Harford, Md...A5 85
Fallston, Cleveland, N.C...B1 109
Falls Village, Litchfield,
Conn...B3 84
Falmouth, N.S., Can...E5 74
Falmouth, Eng...D2 12
Falmouth, Suwannee, Fla...B3 86
Falmouth, Jam...E5 64, E13 65
Falmouth, Pendleton, Ky...B5 94
Falmouth, Cumberland,
Maine...E2, g7 96
Falmouth, Barnstable, Mass..C6 97
Falmouth, Missaukee, Mich..D5 98
Falmouth, Stafford, Va...B5 121
Falmouth, bay, Eng...D2 12
Falmouth Foreside, Cumberland,
Maine (part of Falmouth).E5 96
Falo, isl., Truk...52
Falsa Chipana, pt., Chile...D1 55
False, bay, S. Afr...D2 49
False, cape, Fla...D6 86
False, cape, Va...D7 121
Falso, cape, Hond...C6 62
Falster, isl., Den...D5 24
Falsterbo, Swe...C6 24
Fălticeni, Rom...B8 22
Falun, Saline, Kans...D6 93
Falun, Swe...G6 25
Famagusta, Cyp...E9 31
Famatina, mts., Arg...E2 55
Fame, McIntosh, Okla...B6 112
Family, lake, Man., Can...D4 71
Fancy Farm, Graves, Ky...f9 94
Fangcheng, China...H5 36
Fanghsien, China...E7 34
Fangshen, China...C8 36
Fannettsburg, Franklin, Pa..F6 114
Fannin, Rankin, Miss...C4 100
Fannin, Goliad, Texas...E4 118
Fannin, co., Ga...B2 87
Fannin, co., Tex...C4 118
Fanning, isl., Kir...F12 7
Fannūj, Iran...H9 41
Fanny Bay, B.C., Can...E5 68
Fannystelle, Man., Can...E3 71
Fano, It...C4 21
Fanø, bay, Den...C2 24
Fanø, isl., Den...C2 24
Faqūs, Eg...D3 32
Faradje, Zaire...A4 48
Faradofay, Mad...i9 49
Farafangana, Mad...h9 49
Farāfirah, oasis, Eg...D5 43
Farāh, Afg...E11 41
Farāh, riv., Afg...E11 41
Farallón, pt., Mex...n11 63
Faramana, Upper Volta...D4 45
Faranah, Guinea...D2 45
Farber, Audrain, Mo...B6 101
Fareham, Eng...D6 12
Farewell, cape, Grnld...D19 4
Farewell, cape, N.Z...N14 51
Fargo, Monroe, Ark...C4 81
Fargo, Clinch, Ga...F4 87
Fargo, Cass, N. Dak...C9 110
Fargo, Ellis, Okla...A2 112
Far Hills, Somerset, N.J...B3 106
Fāri'ah, wadi, Jordan...g12 32
Faribault, Rice, Minn...F5 99
Faribault, co., Minn...G5 99
Faridpur, Bngl...F12 40
Fārigh, wadi, Libya...G3 31
Farilhoes, is., Port...C1 20
Farina, Austl...E2 51
Farina, Fayette, Ill...E5 90
Farisita, Huerfano, Colo...D5 83
Fāriskūr, Eg...C3 32
Farley, Dubuque, Iowa...B6 92
Farley, Franklin, Mass...A3 97
Farley, Platte, Mo...h10 101
Farley, Colfax, N. Mex...A5 107
Farm, pond, Mass...h10 97
Farmer, Defiance, Ohio...A1 111
Farmer, Hanson, S. Dak...D8 116
Farmer City, De Witt, Ill...C5 90
Farmers, Rowan, Ky...B6 94
Farmersburg, Sullivan, Ind..F3 91
Farmersburg, Clayton, Iowa..B6 92
Farmersville, Lowndes, Ala..C3 78
Farmersville, Tulare, Calif..*D4 82
Farmersville, Montgomery,
Ill...D4 90
Farmersville, Collins, Tex...C4 118
Farmerville, Union, La...B3 95
Farmingdale, Pennington,
S. Dak...D3 116
Farmington, Washington,
Ark...A1 81
Farmington, Hartford, Conn.C5 84
Farmington, Kent, Del...C6 85
Farmington, Fulton, Ill...C3 90
Farmington, Van Buren,
Iowa...D6 92
Farmington, Franklin,
Maine...D2 96
Farmington, Oakland, Mich.p15 98
Farmington, Dakota, Minn..F5 99
Farmington, St. Francois,
Mo...D7 101
Farmington, Stafford, N.H..D4 105
Farmington, San Juan,
N. Mex...A1 107
Farmington, Davie, N.C...A2 109
Farmington, Fayette, Pa...G2 114
Farmington, Marshall, Tenn.B5 117
Farmington, Davis, Utah...C4 119
Farmington, Whitman, Wash.B8 122
Farmington, Marion,
W. Va...h10 123
Farmington, riv., Conn...B5 84
Farmington Hills, Oakland,
Mich...o15 98
Farmingville, Suffolk, N.Y.*n16 108
Farmland, Randolph, Ind...D7 91
Farmville, Pitt, N.C...B5 109
Farmville, Prince Edward,
Va...C4 121
Farnam, Dawson, Nebr...D5 103
Farnborough, Eng...C7 12
Farne, is., Eng...C6 10
Farner, Polk, Tenn...D9 117
Farnham, Que., Can...D5 73
Farnham, Erie, N.Y...C1 108
Farnham, mtn., B.C., Can...D9 68
Farnhamville, Calhoun,
Iowa...B3 92
Farnham, Richmond, Va...C6 121
Farnhurst, New Castle, Del..A6 85
Farnigen, Switz...C6 19
Faro, Braz...C3 59
Faro, Port...D2 20
Farragut, Fremont, Iowa...D2 92
Farrar, Polk, Iowa...e9 92
Farrar, riv., Scot...C4 13
Farrāshband, Iran...G6 41
Farrell, Coahoma, Miss...A3 100
Farrell, Mercer, Pa...D1 114
Farrellton, Quebec, Can...D2 73
Farrerdale, Sask., Can...F3 70
Farrington, Chatham, N.C..*B3 109
Farris, Atoka, Okla...C6 112
Farris, lake, Nor...p27 25
Farrukhābād, India.C6 39, D7 40
Farry, Woods, Okla...A2 112
Farsala, Grc...C4 23
Fārsi, Afg...E11 41
Farsø, Den...B3 24
Farson, Wapello, Iowa...C5 92
Farson, Sweetwater, Wyo...D3 125
Farsund, Nor...H2 25
Fårup, Den...B3 24
Farwell, Clare, Mich...E6 98
Farwell, Pope, Minn...E3 99
Farwell (Fardale), Howard,
Nebr...C7 103
Farwell, Parmer, Tex...B1 118
Fasā, Iran...G6 41
Fasano, It...D6 21
Fashoda, see Kodok, Sud.
Fassett, Que., Can...D3 73

Fastov, Sov. Un F7 27
Fatehpur, India C7 39
Fatick, Sen *D1 45
Fatsa, Tur B11 31
Fatu, rock, Am. Sam 52
Fatumafuti, Am. Sam 52
Fatuosofia, cape, W. Sam 52
Fatuvalu, W. Sam 52
Faucett, Buchanan, Mo B3 101
Faulk, co., S. Dak B6 116
Faulkner, co., Ark B3 81
Faulkton, Faulk, S. Dak B6 116
Fault, bluff, Ant f41 5
Faunsdale, Marengo, Ala C2 78
Fauquembergues, Fr D10 12
Fauquier, B.C., Can E8 68
Fauquier, co., Va B5 121
Faussepoint, lake, La D4 95
Faust, Alta., Can B3 69
Faust, Tooele, Utah C3 119
Favara, It F4 21
Faverges, Fr D1 18
Faversham, Eng C8 12
Favorita, Flagler, Fla C5 86
Fawcett, Alta., Can B3 69
Fawcett, lake, Alta., Can B4 69
Fawn, hbr., Fiji 52
Fawn, lake, Ont., Can F15 67
Fawnie, range, B.C., Can C5 68
Fawnie Nose, mtn., B.C., Can C5 68
Faxaflói, bay, Ice n21 25
Faxon, Comanche, Okla C3 112
Faxon, Lycoming, Pa *D8 114
Faxon, Benton, Tenn A3 117
Fay, Dewey, Okla B3 112
Fayd, Sau. Ar I14 31
Fayette, Fayette, Ala B2 78
Fayette, Boone, Ind E5 91
Fayette, Fayette, Iowa B6 92
Fayette, Jefferson, Miss D2 100
Fayette, Howard, Mo B5 101
Fayette, Fulton, Ohio A1 111
Fayette, Sanpete, Utah D4 119
Fayette, co., Ala B2 78
Fayette, co., Ga C2 87
Fayette, co., Ill E5 90
Fayette, co., Ind E7 91
Fayette, co., Iowa B6 92
Fayette, co., Ky B5 94
Fayette, co., Ohio C2 111
Fayette, co., Pa G2 114
Fayette, co., Tenn B2 117
Fayette, co., Tex E4 118
Fayette, co., W. Va C3 123
Fayette City, Fayette, Pa *G2 114
Fayetteville, Talladega, Ala B3 78
Fayetteville, Washington, Ark A1 81
Fayetteville, Fayette, Ga C2 87
Fayetteville, St. Clair, Ill g14 101
Fayetteville, Lawrence, Ind G4 91
Fayetteville, Cumberland, N.C B4 109
Fayetteville, Brown, Ohio C2 111
Fayetteville, Franklin, Pa G6 114
Fayetteville, Lincoln, Tenn B5 117
Fayetteville, Fayette, W. Va C3, m13 123
Fayetteville North, Cumberland, N.C *B4 109
Faylakah, isl., Kuw G4 41
Fays-Billot, Fr B1 18
Fayston (Town of), Washington, Vt *C3 120
Fayville, Worcester, Mass g9 97
Faywood, Grant, N. Mex E1 107
Fdérik, Maur B2 45
Fear, cape, N.C D5 109
Feasterville, Bucks, Pa o21 114
Feather, mtn., Ant e40 5
Feather, riv., Calif C3 82
Feather Falls, Butte, Calif C3 82
Featherston, Pittsburg, Okla B6 112
Fécamp, Fr C4 14
Federal, Ont., Can h12 72
Federal, Laramie, Wyo E7 125
Federal Dam, Cass, Minn C4 99
Federal Point, Putnam, Fla C5 86
Federalsburg, Caroline, Md C6 85
Federal Way, King, Wash *B3 122
Fedora, Miner, S. Dak C8 116
Fedscreek, Pike, Ky C7 94
Feeding Hills, Hampden, Mass B2 97
Fefan, isl., Truk 52
Fegen, Swe A7 24
Fehmarn, isl., F.R.G D5 24
Feijó, Braz C3 58
Feilding, N.Z N15 51
Feira, Zambia E5 48
Feira de Santana, Braz D3 57
Fejer, co., Hung *B4 22
Fejø, isl., Den D5 24
Felanitx, Sp C7 20
Felch, Dickinson, Mich B3 98
Felda, Hendry, Fla F5 86
Feldbach, Aus E7 16
Feldberg, G.D.R E7 24
Feldberg, mtn., F.R.G B3 18
Feldkirch, Aus E4 16
Felicity, Clermont, Ohio D1 111
Felipe Carrillo Puerto, Mex D7 63
Felix, cape, N.W. Ter., Can B13 66
Felixstowe, Eng C9 12
Félix U Gómez, Mex G4 107
Felixville, East Feliciana, La D5 95
Fellbach, F.R.G E4 17
Fellingsbro, Swe *t33 25
Fellows, Kern, Calif *E4 82
Fellowship, Burlington, N.J *D3 106
Fellsmere, Indian River, Fla E6 86
Felsenthal, Union, Ark D3 81
Felt, Teton, Idaho F7 89
Felt, Cimarron, Okla e8 112
Felton, Santa Cruz, Calif D2 82
Felton, Kent, Del D6 85
Felton, Haralson, Ga C1 87
Felton, Clay, Minn C2 99
Felton, York, Pa G8 114
Feltre, It A3 21
Femø, isl., Den C5 24
Femunden, lake, Nor F4 25
Fena Valley, res., Guam 52
Fence, Florence, Wis C5 124
Fence, lake, Wis C4 124
Fence, riv., Mich B2 98
Fence Lake, Valencia, N. Mex C1 107
Fender, Tift, Ga E3 87
Fenelon Falls, Ont., Can C6 72
Fener, cape, Tur D10 31
Fénérive, Mad g9 49
Fengchen, China D5 36
Fengcheng, China J6 36
Fengchieh, China I3 36
Fengching, China G4 34
Fenghsiang, China G2 36
Fengning, China D7 36
Fengshan, China C4 37
Fengshan, Taiwan *G9 34
Fengtu, China J2 36
Fenick, isl., S.C G1 115
Fenn, Idaho, Idaho D2 89
Fennimore, Grant, Wis F3 124
Fennville, Allegan, Mich F4 98
Fens, The, reg., Eng B8 12
Fenton, Sask., Can D3 70
Fenton, Kossuth, Iowa A3 90
Fenton, Jefferson Davis, La D3 95
Fenton, Genesee, Mich F7 98
Fentress, Caldwell, Tex h8 118
Fentress, co., Tenn C9 117
Fenwick, Nicholas, W. Va C4 123
Fenwood, Sask., Can F4 70
Fenyang, China D7 34, F4 36
Feodosiya, Sov. Un I10 27
Ferbane, Ire D4 11
Ferdig, Toole, Mont B5 102
Ferdinand, Idaho, Idaho C2 89
Ferdinand, Dubois, Ind H4 91
Ferdinand (Town of), Essex, Vt *B5 120
Ferdinandshof, G.D.R E7 24
Ferdows, Iran E9 41
Fère-Champenoise, Fr F4 15
Ferentino, It D4 21
Fergana, Sov. Un E8 29
Fergana, mts., Sov. Un E8 29
Fergus, Ont., Can D4 72
Fergus, Fergus, Mont C7 102
Fergus, co., Mont C7 102
Fergus Falls, Otter Tail, Minn D2 99
Ferguson, B.C., Can. D9 68
Ferguson, Marshall, Iowa C5 92
Ferguson, Pulaski, Ky C5 94
Ferguson, St. Louis, Mo C7, f13 101
Ferguson, Wayne, W. Va C2 123
Ferguson Creek, Pike, Ky *C7 94
Fériana, Tun G11 30
Ferintosh, Alta., Can C4 69
Ferme-Neuve, Que., Can C2 73
Fermeuse, Newf., Can E5 75
Fermo, It C4 21
Fermoselle, Sp B2 20
Fermoy, Ire E3 11
Fern, creek, Ky g11 94
Fernandina Beach, Nassau, Fla B5, k9 86
Fernandina (Narborough), isl., Ec g5 58
Fernando de Noronha, ter., Braz B4 57
Fernando de Noronha, isl., Braz B4 57
Fernando Póo, prov., Equat. Gui F6 42, E1 46
Fernán-Núñez, Sp D3 20
Fernbank, Lamar, Ala B1 78
Fern Creek, Jefferson, Ky g11 94
Fern Crest Village, Broward, Fla *F6 86
Ferndale, Pulaski, Ark h9 81
Ferndale, Humboldt, Calif B1 82
Ferndale, Bell, Ky D6 94
Ferndale, Anne Arundel, Md B4 85
Ferndale, Oakland, Mich p15 98
Ferndale, Cambria, Pa F4 114
Ferndale, Northumberland, Pa *D8 114
Ferndale, Schuylkill, Pa E9 114
Ferndale, Whatcom, Wash A3 122
Ferney, Brown, S. Dak B7 116
Fernie, B.C., Can E10 68
Fernley, Lyon, Nev D2 104
Fern Ridge, res., Oreg C3 113
Ferns, Ire E5 11
Fernwood, Benewah, Idaho B2 89
Fernwood, Pike, Miss D3 100
Fernwood, Oswego, N.Y B4 108
Ferrara, It E7 18, B3 21
Ferreira do Alentejo, Port C1 20
Ferreira do Zêzere, Port C1 20
Ferrellsburg, Lincoln, W. Va C2 123
Ferrelo, cape, Oreg E2 113
Ferreñafe, Peru C2 58
Ferriday, Concordia, La C4 95
Ferriere, It E5 18
Ferris, Ont., Can *A5 72
Ferris, Hancock, Ill C2 90
Ferris, Ellis, Tex C4, n10 118
Ferris, mts., Wyo D5 125
Ferrisburg, Addison, Vt C2 120
Ferron, Emery, Utah D4 119
Ferros, Braz E2 57
Ferrum, Franklin, Va D2 121
Ferry, Oceana, Mich E4 98
Ferry, co., Wash A7 122
Ferry, pt., N.J k7 106
Ferry Farms, Stafford, Va B5 121
Ferryland, Newf., Can E5 75
Ferrysburg, Ottawa, Mich *E4 98
Ferryville, Tun F11 30
Ferryville, Crawford, Wis E2 124
Fertile, Worth, Iowa A4 92
Fertile, Polk, Minn C2 99
Fertilia, It D2 21
Fès (Fez), Mor C3 44, G4 30
Feshi, Zaire C2 48
Fessenden, Wells, N. Dak B6 110
Festina, Winneshiek, Iowa A6 92
Festus, Jefferson, Mo C7, g13 101
Feteşti, Rom C8 22
Fethard, Ire E4 11
Fethiye, Tur D7 23
Fetisovo, Sov. Un E4 29
Fettercairn, Scot D6 13
Feucht, F.R.G D6 17
Feuchtwangen, F.R.G D5 17
Feudal, Sask., Can F2 70
Feurs, Fr E6 14
Feversham, Ont., Can C4 72
Feyzābād, Afg C15 41
Fezzan (Fazzān), prov., Libya D2 43
Ffestiniog, Wales B4 12
Fhada, mtn., Scot C3 13
Fiambala, Arg E2 55
Fianarantsoa, Mad h9 49
Fianarantsoa, prov., Mad h9 49
Fianga, Chad D3 46
Fibre, Chippewa, Mich B6 98
Ficarolo, It E7 18
Fiche, Eth D5 47
Fichtel Gebirge, mts., F.R.G C6 17
Ficklin, Wilkes, Ga C4 87
Ficksburg, S. Afr C4 49
Fidalgo, isl., Wash A3 122
Fidenza, It B3 21
Fidler, lake, Man., Can A3 71
Field, B.C., Can D9 68
Field, lake, La E5 95
Fieldale, Henry, Va E3 121
Field Crest Estates, New London, Conn *D9 84
Fielding, Sask., Can E2 70
Fielding, Box Elder, Utah B3 119
Fieldon, Jersey, Ill D3 90
Fields, Harney, Oreg E8 113
Fieldsboro, Burlington, N.J C3 106
Fier, Alb B2 23
Fierro, Grant, N. Mex E1 107
Fiesch, Switz D5 19
Fiesole, It C3 21
Fife, Pierce, Wash *B3 122
Fife, co., Scot D5 13
Fife, lake, Sask., Can H3 70
Fife Lake, Sask., Can H3 70
Fife Lake, Grand Traverse, Mich D5 98
Fife Ness, cape, Scot D6 13
Fifield, Price, Wis C3 124
Fifteenmile, creek, Wyo B4 125
Fifty Lakes, Crow Wing, Minn D4 99
Figeac, Fr E4 14
Figtree, Zimb B4 49
Figueira da Foz, Port B1 20
Figueras, Sp A7 20
Figuig, Mor C4 44
Figure Five, Crawford, Ark B1 81
Fiji, country, Oceania H11, 7 52
Fik, Eth D5 47
Filchner, ice shelf, Ant B6 5
File, lake, Man., Can B1 71
File, riv., Man., Can B1 71
Filer, Twin Falls, Idaho G4 89
Filer City, Manistee, Mich D4 98
Filey, Eng F8 13
Fili, Grc g11 23
Filiatra, Grc D3 23
Filicudi, isl., It E5 21
Filingué, Niger D5 45
Filisur, Switz C8 19
Filley, Gage, Nebr D9 103
Fillmore, Ventura, Calif E4 82
Fillmore, Sask., Can H4 70
Fillmore, Montgomery, Ill D4 90
Fillmore, Putnam, Ind E4 91
Fillmore, Andrew, Mo A3 101
Fillmore, Allegany, N.Y C2 108
Fillmore, Benson, N. Dak A6 110
Fillmore, Johnston, Okla C5 112
Fillmore, Millard, Utah E3 119
Fillmore, co., Minn G6 99
Fillmore, co., Nebr D8 103
Fimi, riv., Zaire B2 48
Finale Emilia, It E7 18
Fina Susu, mtn., Saipan 52
Fincastle, Botetourt, Va C3 121
Finch, Ont., Can B9 72
Finderne, Somerset, N.J *B3 106
Findhorn, Scot C5 13
Findhorn, riv., Scot C5 13
Findlater, Sask., Can G3 70
Findlay, Shelby, Ill D5 90
Findlay, Hancock, Ohio A2 111
Findlay, mtn., B.C., Can D9 68
Findochty, Scot *C6 13
Fine, St. Lawrence, N.Y A5, f9 108
Finesville, Warren, N.J B2 106
Fingal, Barnes, N. Dak C8 110
Finger, McNairy, Tenn B3 117
Fingerville, Spartanburg, S.C A3 115
Finges, lake, Ont., Can C4 71
Fíngoè, Moz A5 49
Finike, Tur D8 23
Finistère, dept., Fr *C2 14
Finisterre, cape, Sp A1 20
Finjasjon, lake, Swe B7 24
Finke, riv., Austl E5 50
Finksburg, Carroll, Md B4 85
Finland, Lake, Minn C7 99
Finland, country, Eur C14 8, E12 25
Finland, gulf, Fin., Sov. Un H11 25
Finlay, riv., B.C., Can A5 68
Finlay Forks, B.C., Can m17 68
Finlayson, Pine, Minn D6 99
Finley, Steele, N. Dak B8 110
Finley, Pushmataha, Okla C6 112
Finley, Dyer, Tenn A2 117
Finleyson, Pulaski, Ga D3 87
Finmoore, B.C., Can C6 68
Finnegan, Alta., Can D4 69
Finney, co., Kans D3 93
Finneytown, Hamilton, Ohio *C1 111
Finnmark, co., Nor *B13 25
Finschhafen, Pap. N. Gui k12 50
Finspång, Swe u33 25
Finsteraarhorn, mtn., Switz C5 19
Finsterwalde, G.D.R B8 17
Fintona, N. Ire C4 11
Fintown, Ire C3 11
Finvoy, N. Ire B5 11
Finzel, Garrett, Md k13 85
Fionn, lake, Scot C3 13
Fiq, Syr F10 31
Fir, riv., Sask., Can D4 70
Firecrest, Pierce, Wash f10 122
Fire, isl., N.Y G4 84
Fire, is., N.Y G4 84
Firebaugh, Fresno, Calif D3 82
Fire Island, inlet, N.Y G3 84
Firenze, see Florence, It.
Firenzuola, It B3 21
Firesteel, Dewey, S. Dak B4 116
Firestone, Weld, Colo A6 83
Firmat, Arg A4 54
Firminy, Fr E6 14
Fir Mountain, Sask., Can H2 70
Fīrozābād, India D7 40
Fīrozpur, India B5 40
Firsby, Eng A8 12
Firsovo, Sov. Un C11 37
Firth, Bingham, Idaho F6 89
Firth, Lancaster, Nebr D9 103
Fīrūzābād, Iran G6 41
Fīrūz Kūh, Iran D6 41
Fischot, is., Newf., Can C4 75
Fish, lake, Utah E4 119
Fish, mtn., Oreg D4 131
Fish, riv., Maine A4 96
Fish, riv., Namibia C2 49
Fish Cove, pt., Newf., Can A3 75
Fish Creek, Door, Wis C5 124
Fisheating, creek, Fla F5 86
Fisher, Poinsett, Ark B5 81
Fisher, Champaign, Ill C5 90
Fisher, Polk, Minn C2 99
Fisher, Clarion, Pa D3 114
Fisher, Hardy, W. Va B5 123
Fisher, co., Tex C2 118
Fisher, bay, Man., Can D3 71
Fisher, glacier, Ant B19 5
Fisher, lake, N.S., Can E4 74
Fisher, peak, Va D2 121
Fisher, riv., Man., Can D3 71
Fisher, strait, N.W. Ter., Can D16 67
Fisher Branch, Man., Can D3 71
Fisherman, isl., Va h16 121
Fishers, Hamilton, Ind E5, k10 91
Fishers, isl., N.Y m16 108
Fishers, peak, Colo D6 83
Fishers Island, sound, Conn D8 84
Fishersville, Augusta, Va B4 121
Fishertown, Bedford, Pa F4 114
Fisherville, Ont., Can E5 72
Fishguard [& Goodwick], Wales C3 12
Fish Haven, Bear Lake, Idaho G7 89
Fishing, bay, Md D5 85
Fishing, creek, N.C A5 109
Fishing, creek, S.C B5 115
Fishing, creek, W. Va B4 123
Fishing, lake, Man., Can C4 71
Fishing, lake, Sask., Can F4 70
Fishing, The, lakes, Sask., Can G3 70
Fishing Creek, Dorchester, Md D5 81
Fishing Creek, res., S.C B6 115
Fishkill, Dutchess, N.Y D7 108
Fishkill, creek, N.Y C2 84
Fish River, lake, Maine B4 96
Fish Springs, range, Utah D2 119
Fishtail, Stillwater, Mont E7 102
Fishtail, pt., Ant f39 5
Fishtrap, Lincoln, Wash B8 122
Fishville, Grant, La C3 95
Fisk Butler, Mo E7 101
Fiskburg, Kenton, Ky B5, k13 94
Fiskdale, Worcester, Mass B3 97
Fiske, Sask., Can F1 70
Fiskeville, Providence, R.I. (part of Cranston) C10 84
Fismes, Fr E3 15
Fitch Bay, Que., Can D5 73
Fitchburg, Worcester, Mass A4 97
Fitchville, New London, Conn C8 84
Fithian, Vermilion, Ill C6 90
Fitler, Issaquena, Miss C2 100
Fittstown, Pontotoc, Okla B5 112
Fitzgerald, Ben Hill, Ga E3 87
Fitzhugh, Pontotoc, Okla C5 112
Fitz Hugh, sound, B.C., Can D4 68
Fitzpatrick, Que., Can B5 73
Fitz Roy, Arg D3 54
Fitzroy, Austl C4 50
Fitz Roy, mtn., Arg D2 54
Fitzroy, riv., Austl C3 50
Fitzroy, riv., Austl D8 50
Fitzroy Harbour, Ont., Can B8 72
Fitzwilliam, Cheshire, N.H E2 105
Fitzwilliam, isl., Ont., Can B3 72
Fitzwilliam Depot, Cheshire, N.H E2 105
Fiume, see Rijeka, Yugo.
Fiumicino, It h8 21
Five Islands, N.S., Can D5 74
Fivemile, creek, Wyo C4 125
Fivemiletown, N. Ire C4 11
Five Points, Chambers, Ala B4 78
Five Points, Marion, Ind m10 91
Five Points, Bernalillo, N. Mex B3, k7 107
Fizi, Zaire B4 48
Fjärås Kyrkby, Swe A6 24
Fjärdhundra, Swe t34 25
Fjerritslev, Den A3 24
Flagg, Castro, Tex B1 118
Flagg, mtn., Ala C3 78
Flagler, Kit Carson, Colo B7 83
Flagler, co., Fla C5 86
Flagler Beach, Flagler, Fla C5 86
Flag Pond, Unicoi, Tenn C11 117
Flagstaff, Coconino, Ariz B4 80
Flagstaff, lake, Oreg E7 113
Flagtown, Somerset, N.J B3 106
Flamand, lake, Que., Can B4 73
Flambeau, riv., Wis C2 124
Flamborough, head, Eng C6 10
Flaming Gorge, dam, Utah C6 119
Flaming Gorge, res., Utah, Wyo B6 119
Flanagan, Livingston, Ill C5 90
Flanders, Ont., Can E5 71
Flanders, Litchfield, Conn B3 84
Flanders, Suffolk, N.Y F6 84
Flanders (Flandre), former prov., Fr B5 14
Flanders, bay, N.Y F6 84
Flandreau, Moody, S. Dak C9 116
Flannan, is., Scot A3 10
Flasher, Morton, N. Dak C4 110
Flat, Alsk C8 79
Flat, Wolfe, Ky C6 94
Flat, Phelps, Mo D6 101
Flat, brook, N.J A3 106
Flat, isl., Newf., Can C3 75
Flat, lake, Alta., Can B4 69
Flat, lake, La k9 95
Flat, riv., Mich E5 98
Flat Bay, Newf., Can D2 75
Flatbrookville, Sussex, N.J A3 106
Flatbush, Alta., Can B3 69
Flat Creek, Walker, Ala B2, f6 78
Flatcreek, Bedford, Tenn B5 117
Flathead, co., Mont B2 102
Flathead, lake, Mont C2 102
Flathead, riv., B.C., Can., Mont E10 68
Flathead, val., Mont C2 102
Flatlands, N.B., Can B3 74
Flat Lick, Knox, Ky D6 94
Flatonia, Fayette, Tex E4 118
Flat River, P.E.I., Can C7 74
Flat River, St. Francois, Mo D7 101
Flat River, res., R.I C10 84
Flat Rock, Jackson, Ala A4 78
Flat Rock, Newf., Can *E5 75
Flat Rock, Crawford, Ill E6 90
Flat Rock, Shelby, Ind F6 91
Flat Rock, Wayne, Mich F7 98
Flat Rock, Henderson, N.C f10 109
Flat Rock, Seneca, Ohio A5 111
Flatrock, lake, Man., Can B1 71
Flatrock, riv., Ind F6 91
Flattery, cape, Wash A1 122
Flattop, Platte, Wyo *D8 125
Flat Tops, plat., Colo B3 83
Flatts, Bermuda p20 64
Flatwillow, creek, Mont D8 102
Flatwood, Wilcox, Ala C2 78
Flatwoods, Greenup, Ky B7 94
Flatwoods, Rapides, La C3 95
Flat Woods, Perry, Tenn B4 117
Flawil, Switz B7 19
Flaxcombe, Sask., Can F1 70
Flaxton, Burke, N. Dak A3 110
Flaxville, Daniels, Mont B11 102
Fleet, Alta., Can C5 69
Fleet, Eng C7 12
Fleetwing Estates, Bucks, Pa *F12 114
Fleetwood, Eng G5 13
Fleetwood, Ashe, N.C A1 109
Fleetwood, Berks, Pa F10 114
Fleischmanns, Delaware, N.Y C6 108
Flekkefjord, Nor H2 25
Fleming, Sask., Can G5 70
Fleming, Logan, Colo A8 83
Fleming, Liberty, Ga E5 87
Fleming (Unionville), Centre, Pa E6 114
Fleming, co., Ky B6 94
Flemingsburg, Fleming, Ky B6 94
Flemington, Liberty, Ga E5 87
Flemington, Polk, Mo D4 101
Flemington, Hunterdon, N.J B3 106
Flemington, Clinton, Pa D7 114
Flemington, Taylor, W. Va k10 123
Flen, Swe t34 25
Flensburg, F.R.G A4 16, D3 24
Flensburg, Morrison, Minn E4 99
Flensburg, fjord, Den D3 24
Flers, Fr C3 14
Flesherton, Ont., Can C4 72
Fletcher, Ont., Can E2 72
Fletcher, Henderson, N.C f10 109
Fletcher, Miami, Ohio B1 111
Fletcher, Comanche, Okla C3 112
Fletcher, Franklin, Vt B3 120
Fletcher, is., Ant B3 5
Fletcher Park, Albany, Wyo *D7 125
Fleur-de-Lys, Newf., Can C3, h10 75
Fleurier, Switz C2 19
Flieden, F.R.G C4 17
Flims, Switz C7 19
Flinders, is., Austl F5 50
Flinders, isl., Austl n15 50
Flinders, range, Austl F6 50
Flinders, riv., Austl C7 50
Flin Flon, Man., Can B1, g7 71
Flint, Morgan, Ala A3 78
Flint, Steuben, Ind A7 91
Flint, Genesee, Mich E7 98
Flint, Wales A4 12
Flint, co., Wales A4 12
Flint, isl., Kir G12 7
Flint, riv., Ga D2 87
Flint, riv., Mich E5 98
Flint, run, W. Va k9 123
Flint Creek, range, Mont D3 102
Flinthill, St. Charles, Mo C7 101
Flint Hill, Rappahannock, Va B4 121
Flintridge, Los Angeles, Calif *E4 82
Flintoft, Sask., Can H2 70
Flinton, Ont., Can C7 72
Flintstone, Allegany, Md k13 85
Flintville, Lincoln, Tenn B5 117
Flipper, pt., Wake Isl 52
Flippin, Marion, Ark A3 81
Flippin, Monroe, Ky D4 94
Flixecourt, Fr D2 15
Flöha, G.D.R C8 17
Flom, Norman, Minn C2 99
Flomaton, Escambia, Ala D2 78
Flomot, Motley, Tex B2 118
Floodwood, Dickinson, Mich B2 98
Floodwood, St. Louis, Minn D6 99
Flora, Clay, Ill E5 90
Flora, Carroll, Ind C4 91
Flora, Madison, Miss C3 100
Flora, Benson, N. Dak B6 110
Flora, Wallowa, Oreg B9 113
Florahome, Putnam, Fla C5 86
Florala, Covington, Ala D3 78
Floral City, Citrus, Fla D4 86
Floral Park, Silver Bow, Mont *D4 102
Flora Vista, San Juan, N. Mex A1 107
Florence, Lauderdale, Ala A2 78
Florence, Pinal, Ariz E4 80
Florence, Los Angeles, Calif *E4 82
Florence, Fremont, Colo C5 83
Florence, Switzerland, Ind G8 91
Florence (Firenze), It C3 21
Florence, Marion, Kans D7 93
Florence, Boone, Ky A5, k13 94
Florence, Rankin, Miss C3 100
Florence, Morgan, Mo C5 101
Florence, Ravalli, Mont D2 102
Florence, Burlington, N.J C3 106
Florence, Lane, Oreg D2 113
Florence, Florence, S.C C8 115
Florence, Codington, S. Dak B8 116
Florence, Williamson, Tex D4 118
Florence, Rutland, Vt D2 120
Florence, Snohomish, Wash A3 122
Florence, Florence, Wis C5 124
Florence, co., S.C C8 115
Florence, co., Wis C5 124
Florence Junction, Pinal, Ariz D4 80
Florenceville, N.B., Can C2 74
Florencia, Col C2 60
Florenville, Bel E5 15
Florenville, St. Tammany, La B8 95
Flores, Guat B3 62
Flores, dept., Ur *E1 56
Flores, isl., B.C., Can E4 68
Flores, isl., Indon G6 35
Flores, isl., Port. (Azores) g8 44
Flores, sea, Indon G6 35
Floresta, Braz C3 57
Floresville, Wilson, Tex E3, k7 118
Florey, Andrews, Tex C1 118
Florham Park, Morris, N.J B4 106
Floriano, Braz C2 57
Florianópolis, Braz D3 56
Florida, Cuba D4 64
Florida, Berkshire, Mass A1 97
Florida, Socorro, N. Mex C3 107
Florida, Orange, N.Y D6, m14 108
Florida, Henry, Ohio A1 111
Florida, Ur E1 56
Florida, dept., Ur *E1 56
Florida, state, U.S E11, 77 86
Florida, bay, Fla H6 86
Florida, cape, Fla G6 86
Florida, keys, Fla H6 86
Florida, mts., N. Mex E2 107
Florida, straits, Fla H6 86
Florida City, Dade, Fla G6, t13 86
Florien, Sabine, La C2 95
Florin, Lancaster, Pa F8 114
Florina, Grc B3 23
Florina, prov., Grc *B3 23
Floris, Davis, Iowa D5 92
Florissant, Teller, Colo C5 83
Florissant, St. Louis, Mo f13 101
Florosa, Okaloosa, Fla G2 86
Flossmoor, Cook, Ill k9 90
Flour Bluff, Nueces, Tex *F4 118
Flournoy, Tehama, Calif C2 82
Flourtown, Montgomery, Pa o21 114
Flovilla, Butts, Ga C3 87
Flower, brook, Vt E2 120
Floweree, Chouteau, Mont C5 102
Flower Hill, Nassau, N.Y *E7 108
Flower's Cove, Newf., Can C3 75
Flower Station, Ont., Can B8 72
Flower Village, Kern, Calif *E4 82
Flowery Branch, Hall, Ga B3 87
Flowood, Rankin, Miss C3 100
Floyd, Floyd, Iowa A5 92
Floyd, Roosevelt, N. Mex C6 107
Floyd, Floyd, Va D2 121
Floyd, co., Ga B1 87
Floyd, co., Ind H6 91
Floyd, co., Iowa A5 92
Floyd, co., Ky C7 94
Floyd, co., Tex B2 118
Floyd, co., Va D2 121
Floyd, mtn., Ariz B3 80
Floyd, riv., Iowa B1 92
Floydada, Floyd, Tex C2 118
Floyd Dale, Dillon, S.C C9 115
Floyds, canyon, Nev C4 104
Floydsburg, Oldham, Ky g12 94
Floyds Knobs, Floyd, Ind H6 91
Fluchthorn, mtn., Aus., Switz C9 19
Fluessen, lake, Neth B5 15
Flumendosa, riv., It E2 21
Flums, Switz B7 19
Flushing, Genesee, Mich E7 98
Flushing, Belmont, Ohio B4 111
Fluvanna, Scurry, Tex C2 118
Fluvanna, co., Va C4 121
Fly Creek, Otsego, N.Y C6 108
Flyinge, Swe C7 24
Flying H. Chaves, N. Mex D4 107
Foam, lake, Sask., Can F4 70
Foam Lake, Sask., Can F4 70
Foard, co., Tex B3 118
Foard City, Foard, Tex C3 118
Foča, Yugo D4 22
Fochabers, Scot C5 13
Focşani, Rom C8 22
Fogauso, cape, Am. Sam 52
Foggia, It D5 21
Fogliano, It k9 21
Fogo, Newf., Can D4 75
Fogo, cape, Newf., Can D5 75
Fogo, isl., Newf., Can D4 75
Fohnsdorf, Aus E7 16
Föhr, isl., F.R.G A4 16
Foix, Fr F4 14
Foix, former prov., Fr *F4 14
Fokis (Phocis), prov., Grc *C4 23
Folcroft, Delaware, Pa *G11 114
Foley, Baldwin, Ala E2 78
Foley, Benton, Minn E5 99
Foley, Lincoln, Mo B7 101
Foley, isl., N.W. Ter., Can C17 67
Foligno, It C4 21
Folkestone, Eng C9 12
Folkston, Charlton, Ga F4 87
Folkstone, Onslow, N.C C5 109
Follansbee, Brooke, W. Va A4, f8 123
Follett, Lipscomb, Tex A2 118
Follonica, It C3 21
Folly, isl., S.C F8 115
Folly Beach, Charleston, S.C F8, k12 115
Follyfarm, Malheur, Oreg D8 113
Folly Lake, N.S., Can D6 74
Folsom, Sacramento, Calif C3 82
Folsom, St. Tammany, La D5 95
Folsom, Atlantic, N.J D3 106
Folsom, Union, N. Mex A6 107
Folsom, Delaware, Pa *G11 114
Folsom, Wetzel, W. Va B4, k9 123
Folsomville, Warrick, Ind H3 91
Fomento, Cuba C4 64
Fonda, Pocahontas, Iowa B3 92
Fonda, Montgomery, N.Y C6 108
Fond-du-Lac, Sask., Can m7 70
Fond du Lac, Fond du Lac, Wis E5, k9 124
Fond du Lac, co., Wis E5 124
Fond du Lac, Indian res., Minn D6 99
Fonde, Bell, Ky D6 94
Fondi, It D4 21
Fonsagrada, Sp A2 20
Fonseca, gulf, Cen. Am D4 62
Fontainebleau, Fr C5 14
Fontana, San Bernardino, Calif m14 82
Fontana, Miami, Kans D9 93
Fontana, Walworth, Wis F5 124
Fontana Dam, Graham, N.C f9 109
Fontanelle, Adair, Iowa C3 92
Fontanet, Vigo, Ind E3 91
Fonte Boa, Braz D4 60
Fontenay-le-Comte, Fr D3 14
Fontenay [-sous-Bois], Fr g10 14
Fontenelle, Lincoln, Wyo E2 125
Fontenelle, res., Wyo A5 119
Foochow, see Fuchou, China
Foosland, Champaign, Ill C5 90
Foothill, Spokane, Wash D8 122
Foothills, Alta., Can C2 69
Footville, Rock, Wis F4 124
Foping, China H2 36
Forada, Douglas, Minn E3 99
Foraker, Hardin, Ohio B2 111
Foraker, Osage, Okla A5 112
Forbach, Fr C7 14
Forbes, Austl F7 51
Forbes, St. Louis, Minn C6 99
Forbes, Holt, Mo B2 101
Forbes, Mitchell, N.C e10 109
Forbes, Dickey, N. Dak D7 110
Forbes, mtn., Alta., Can D2 69
Forbing Park, Yavapai, Ariz C3 80
Forcados, Nig E6 45
Forcalquier, Fr F6 14
Force, Elk, Pa D4 114
Forchheim, F.R.G D6 17
Ford, Kootenai, Idaho E8 89
Ford, Ford, Kans E4 93
Ford, Clark, Ky C5 94
Ford, Scot D3 13
Ford, co., Ill C5 90
Ford, co., Kans E4 93
Ford, riv., Mich C3 98
Ford City, Kern, Calif E4 82
Ford City, Armstrong, Pa E2 114
Fordland, Webster, Mo D5 101
Fordlândia, Braz C3 59
Ford River, Delta, Mich C3 98
Fords, Middlesex, N.J B4 106
Fords Prairie, Lewis, Wash C2 122
Fordsville, Ohio, Ky C3 94
Fordville, Walsh, N. Dak A8 110
Fordwich, Ont., Can D3 72
Fordyce, Dallas, Ark D3 81
Fordyce, Cedar, Nebr B8 103
Forécariah, Guinea E2 45
Foreman (New Rocky Comfort), Little River, Ark D1 81
Foremost, Alta., Can E5 69
Forest, Bel D4 15
Forest, Ont., Can D2 72
Forest, Livingston, Ill C5 90
Forest, Clinton, Ind D5 91
Forest, Scott, Miss C4 100
Forest, Hardin, Ohio B2 111
Forest, Cherokee, Tex D5 118

Forest, Bedford, Va.....C3 121
Forest, co., Pa.....C3 114
Forest, co., Wis.....C5 124
Forest, riv., N. Dak.....A8 110
Forest Acres, Richland, S.C.*D6 115
Forestburg, Alta., Can.....C4 69
Forestburg, Sanborn, S. Dak.C8 116
Forest City, Mason, Ill.....C4 90
Forest City, Winnebago, Iowa.....A4 92
Forest City, Washington, Maine.....C5 96
Forest City, Holt, Mo.....B2 101
Forest City, Rutherford, N.C.....B1, f11 109
Forest City, Susquehanna, Pa.....C11 114
Forestdale, Clarke, Ala.....D2 78
Forestdale, Providence, R.I. B10 84
Forest Dale, Rutland, Vt.....D2 120
Forester, Scott, Ark.....C2 81
Forest Glen, St. Tammany, La.....h12 95
Forest Glen, Montgomery, Md.....B3 85
Forest Green, Chariton, Mo..B5 101
Forestgrove, Fergus, Mont...D7 102
Forest Grove, Washington, Oreg.....B3, g11 113
Forest Hill, Ont., Can.....m15 72
Forest Hill, Rapides, La.....C3 95
Forest Hill, Harford, Md.....A5 85
Forest Hill, Tarrant, Tex...*C4 118
Forest Hills, N.B., Can.....*D4 74
Forest Hills, Allegheny, Pa..k14 114
Forest Hills, Davidson, Tenn.....*A5 117
Forest Home, Butler, Ala.....D3 78
Forest Homes, Madison, Ill.*E3 90
Forest Junction, Calumet, Wis.....h9 124
Forest Knolls, Marin, Calif...g7 82
Forest Lake, Alger, Mich.....B4 98
Forest Lake, Washington, Minn.....E6 99
Forest Lawn, Alta., Can.....D4 69
Foreston, Mille Lacs, Minn..E5 99
Foreston, Clarendon, S.C.....D7 115
Forest Park, Clayton, Ga.C2, h8 87
Forest Park, Cook, Ill.....k9 90
Forest Park, Ouachita, La..*B3 95
Forestport, Oneida, N.Y.....B5 108
Forest River, Walsh, N. Dak.A8 110
Forest View, Cook, Ill.....*B6 90
Forest View, Greenville, S.C.....*B3 115
Forestville, Que., Can.....*B2 73
Forestville, Hartford, Conn. (part of Bristol).....C5 84
Forestville, Prince Georges, Md.....*C4 85
Forestville, Chautauqua, N.Y.....C1 108
Forestville, Butler, Pa.....D1 114
Forestville, Door, Wis.....D6 124
Forfar, Scot.....D6 13
Forgan, Sask., Can.....F2 70
Forgan, Beaver, Okla....A1, e10 112
Forges-les-Eaux, Fr.....C4 14
Forget, Sask., Can.....H4 70
Forge Village, Middlesex, Mass.....A5, f10 97
Forillon, nat. park, Que., Can..k13 73
Fork, Davie, N.C.....B3 109
Fork, Dillon, S.C.....C9 115
Fork, creek, W. Va.....m12 123
Forked Deer, riv., Tenn.....B2 117
Forked River, Ocean, N.J.....D4 106
Forkland, Greene, Ala.....C2 78
Fork Mountain, Anderson, Tenn.....C9 117
Fork River, Man., Can.....D1 71
Forks, Clallam, Wash.....B1 122
Fork Shoals, Greenville, S.C.B3 115
Forksville, Sullivan, Pa.....D8 114
Fork Union, Fluvanna, Va...C4 121
Forkville, Scott, Miss.....*C4 100
Forlì, It.....B4 21
Forman, Sargent, N. Dak.....C8 110
Formazza, It.....C4 18
Formby, Eng.....A4 12
Formello, It.....g8 21
Formentera, isl., Sp.....C6 20
Formiga, Braz.....F1 57
Formosa, Arg.....E4 55
Formosa, Van Buren, Ark.....B3 81
Formosa, Braz.....E1 57
Formosa, Ont., Can.....C3 72
Formosa, prov., Arg.....E4 55
Formosa, see Taiwan, country, Asia.
Formosa, bay, Ken.....B7 48
Formosa, strait, China.....G8 34
Formoso, Jewell, Kans.....C6 93
Forney, Kaufman, Tex...C4, n10 118
Fornovo di Taro, It.....E6 18
Forres, Scot.....C5 13
Forrest, Austl.....F4 50
Forrest, Livingston, Ill.....C5 90
Forrest, Quay, N. Mex.....C6 107
Forrest, co., Miss.....D4 100
Forrest City, St. Francis, Ark.B5 81
Forreston, Ogle, Ill.....A4 90
Forrest Station, Man., Can..E2 71
Forsan, Howard, Tex.....C2 118
Forsayth, Austl.....C7 50
Forserum, Swe.....A8 24
Förslövsholm, Swe.....B6 24
Forst, G.D.R.....B9 17
Forster-Tuncurry, Austl.....F9 51
Forsyth, Monroe, Ga.....C3 87
Forsyth, Macon, Ill.....D5 90
Forsyth, Taney, Mo.....E4 101
Forsyth, Rosebud, Mont...D10 102
Forsyth, co., Ga.....B2 87
Forsyth, co., N.C.....A2 109
Fort Adams, Wilkinson, Miss.....D2 100
Fort Albany, Ont., Can.....n19 72
Fortaleza, Braz.....B3 57
Fort Ann, Washington, N.Y..B7 108
Fort Apache, Navajo, Ariz..D6 80
Fort Apache, Indian res., Ariz..C5 80
Fort Archambault, see Sarh, Chad
Fort Ashby, Mineral, W. Va.B6 123
Fort Assiniboine, Alta., Can..B3 69
Fort Atkinson, Winneshiek, Iowa.....A6 92
Fort Atkinson, Jefferson, Wis.F5 124
Fort Augustus, Scot.....C4 13
Fort Barnwell, Craven, N.C..B5 109
Fort Beaufort, S. Afr.....D4 49
Fort Belknap, Indian res., Mont.....B8 102
Fort Belknap Agency, Blaine, Mont.....B8 102
Fort Bellefontaine, St. Louis, Mo.....f13 101
Fort Bend, co., Tex.....E5 118
Fort Benning, Chattahoochee, Ga.....D2 87
Fort Benton, Chouteau, Mont.....C6 102
Fort Berthold, Indian res., N. Dak.....B3 110
Fort Bidwell, Modoc, Calif...B3 82
Fort Bidwell, Indian res., Calif..B3 82
Fort Blackmore, Scott, Va.....f9 121
Fort Bragg, Mendocino, Calif.....C2 82
Fort Branch, Gibson, Ind.....H2 91
Fort Bridger, Uinta, Wyo...E2 125
Fort Calhoun, Washington, Nebr.....C9, g12 103
Fort Chambly, Que., Can..*D4 73
Fort-Chimo, Que., Can.....g13 73
Fort Chipewyan, Alta., Can..f8 69
Fort Clark, Oliver, N. Dak..B4 110
Fort Cobb, Caddo, Okla.....B3 112
Fort Cobb, res., Okla.....B3 112
Fort Collins, Larimer, Colo..A5 83
Fort Coulonge, Que., Can...B8 72
Fort Covington, Franklin, N.Y.....f10 108
Fort Crampel, Cen. Afr. Rep.D3 46
Fort Davis, Macon, Ala.....C4 78
Fort Davis, Jeff Davis, Tex..o13 118
Fort Defiance, Apache, Ariz..B6 80
Fort-de-France, Mart.....S10 65
Fort-de-France, bay, Mart.....S10 65
Fort Deposit, Lowndes, Ala..D3 78
Fort Dodge, Webster, Iowa..B3 92
Fort Dodge, Ford, Kans.....E4 93
Fort Donelson, nat. military park, Tenn.....A4 117
Fort Duchesne, Uintah, Utah.....C6 119
Forteau, Newf., Can.....C3 75
Fort Edward, Washington, N.Y.....B7 108
Fort Erie, Ont., Can.....E6 72
Fortescue, Holt, Mo.....A2 101
Fortescue, Cumberland, N.J..E2 106
Fortescue, riv., Austl.....D2 50
Fort Fairfield, Aroostook, Maine.....B5 96
Fort Fitzgerald, Alta., Can.....f8 69
Fort Foureau, Cam.....C2 46
Fort Frances, Ont., Can.....o16 72
Fort Fraser, B.C., Can.....C5 68
Fort Gaines, Clay, Ga.....E1 87
Fort Garland, Costilla, Colo.....D5 83
Fort Gay, Wayne, W. Va.....C2 123
Fort-George, Que., Can.....h11 73
Fort George, riv., Que., Can...h11 73
Fort Gibson, Muskogee, Okla.....B6 112
Fort Good Hope, N.W. Ter., Can.....C7 66
Fort Grahame, B.C., Can.....A5 68
Fort Green, Hardee, Fla.....E5 86
Fort Griffin, Shackelford, Tex.C3 118
Forth, firth, Scot.....D6 13
Forth, riv., Scot.....D4 13
Fort Hall, Bingham, Idaho...F6 89
Fort Hall, Ken.....B6 48
Fort Hall, Indian res., Idaho....F6 89
Fort Hancock, Hudspeth, Tex.....o12 118
Fort Hill, Somerset, Pa.....G3 114
Fort Howard, Baltimore, Md.B5 85
Fort Huachuca, Cochise, Ariz.....F5 80
Fortierville, Que., Can.....C5 73
Fortín Uno, Arg.....B3 54
Fortine, Lincoln, Mont.....B2 102
Fort Jefferson, nat. mon., Fla...H4 86
Fort Jennings, Putnam, Ohio.B1 111
Fort Jones, Siskiyou, Calif...B2 82
Fort Kent, Aroostook, Maine.A4 96
Fort Kent, Alta., Can.....B5 69
Fort Kent Village, Aroostook, Maine (part of Fort Kent).A4 96
Fort Klamath, Klamath, Oreg.....E5 113
Fort Knox, Hardin, Ky.....C4 94
Fort Lallemand, Alg.....C6 44
Fort-Lamy, see Ndjamena, Chad.
Fort Langley, B.C., Can.....f13 68
Fort Laramie, Goshen, Wyo.D8 125
Fort Laramie, nat. historic site, Wyo.....D8 125
Fort Lauderdale, Broward, Fla.....F6, r13 86
Fort Lawn, Chester, S.C.....B6 115
Fort Lee, Bergen, N.J.....h9 106
Fort Liard, N.W., Ter., Can.D8 66
Fort-Liberté, Hai.....E8 64
Fort Lincoln Estates, Burleigh, N. Dak.....*C5 110
Fort Littleton, Fulton, Pa.....F6 114
Fort Loramie, Shelby, Ohio..B1 111
Fort Loudon, Franklin, Pa...G6 114
Fort Loudon, lake, Tenn.....D9 117
Fort Lupton, Weld, Colo.....A6 83
Fort Lyon, Bent, Colo.....C7 83
Fort McDermitt, Indian res., Nev.....B4 104
Fort McDowell, Maricopa, Ariz.....k9 80
Fort McDowell, Indian res., Ariz.....D4, k9 80
Fort McHenry, nat. mon. and historical shrine, Md.....C2 85
Fort McIntosh, Webb, Tex. (part of Laredo).....F3 118
Fort McKavett, Menard, Tex.....D2 118
Fort McKay, Alta., Can.....f8 69
Fort McKenzie, Que., Can..g13 73
Fort McKinley, Montgomery, Ohio.....*C1 111
Fort Macleod, Alta., Can.....E4 69
Fort Mac Mahon, Alg.....D5 44
Fort McMurray, Alta., Can.....A5, f8 69
Fort McPherson, N.W. Ter., Can.....C6 66
Fort Madison, Lee, Iowa.....D6 92
Fort Matanzas, nat. mon., Fla..C5 86
Fort Meade, Polk, Fla.....E5 86
Fort Meade, Meade, S. Dak..C2 116
Fort Meadow, res., Mass.....g9 97
Fort Mill, York, S.C.....A6 115
Fort Miller, Washington, N.Y.....B7 108
Fort Mitchell, Russell, Ala...C4 78
Fort Mitchell, Lunenburg, Va.....D4 121
Fort Mohave, Indian res., Ariz..C1 80
Fort Morgan, Baldwin, Ala..E1 78
Fort Morgan, Morgan, Colo..A7 83
Fort Motte, Calhoun, S.C.....D6 115
Fort Munro, Pak.....C2 40
Fort Myers, Lee, Fla.....F5 86
Fort Myers Beach, Lee, Fla..F5 86
Fort Nelson, B.C., Can.....m18 68
Fort Norman, N.W. Ter., Can.....D7 66
Fort Ogden, DeSoto, Fla.....E5 86
Fort Oglethorpe, Catoosa and Walker, Ga.....B1 87
Fort Payne, DeKalb, Ala.....A4 78
Fort Peck, Valley, Mont.....B10 102
Fort Peck, dam, Mont.....B10 102
Fort Peck, Indian res., Mont...B11 102
Fort Peck Lake, res., Mont....C10 102
Fort Pierce, St. Lucie, Fla...E6 86
Fort Pierce, inlet, Fla.....E6 86
Fort Pierre, Stanley, S. Dak..C5 116
Fort Plain, Montgomery, N.Y.....C6 108
Fort Portal, Ug.....A5 48
Fort Providence, N.W. Ter., Can.....D9 66
Fort Pulaski, nat. mon., Ga.....D6 87, G6 115
Fort Qu'Appelle, Sask., Can.....G4 70
Fort Randall, dam., S. Dak....D7 116
Fort Ransom, Ransom, N. Dak.....C8 110
Fort Recovery, Mercer, Ohio.B1 111
Fort Reliance, N.W. Ter., Can.....D11 66
Fort Reno, Canadian, Okla..B3 112
Fort Resolution, N.W. Ter., Can.....D10 66
Fort Rice, Morton, N. Dak..C5 110
Fort Ripley, Crow Wing, Minn.....D4 99
Fort Ritner, Lawrence, Ind..G5 91
Fort Robinson, Dawes, Nebr.....B2 103
Fort Robinson, Sullivan, Tenn.....*C11 117
Fort Rock, Lake, Oreg.....D5 113
Fortrose, N.Z.....Q12 51
Fortrose, Scot.....C4 13
Fort Ross, N.W. Ter., Can..B14 66
Fort Rousset, Con.....F3 46
Fort St. James, B.C., Can.....B5 68
Fort St. John, B.C., Can.....A7, m18 68
Fort Sandeman, Pak.....B4 39
Fort Saskatchewan, Alta., Can.....C4 69
Fort Scott, Bourbon, Kans...E9 93
Fort Severn, Ont., Can.....n18 72
Fort Shaw, Cascade, Mont..C5 102
Fort Shawnee, Allen, Ohio...B1 111
Fort Sheridan, Lake, Ill.....h9 90
Fort Shevchenko, Sov. Un....E4 29
Fort Sibut, Cen. Afr. Rep....D3 46
Fort Simpson, N.W. Ter., Can.....D8 66
Fort Smith, Sebastian, Ark...B1 81
Fort Smith, N.W. Ter., Can.....D10 66
Fort Stanton, Lincoln, N. Mex.....D4 107
Fort Steele, B.C., Can.....E10 68
Fort Steilacoom, Pierce, Wash.....D1 122
Fort Stockton, Pecos, Tex...D1 118
Fort Sumner, De Baca, N. Mex.....C5 107
Fort Sumter, nat. mon., S.C.....F3 115
Fort Supply, Woodward, Okla.....A2 112
Fort Supply Lake, res., Okla....A2 112
Fort Thomas, Graham, Ariz.D6 80
Fort Thomas, Campbell, Ky.....h14 94
Fort Thompson, Buffalo, S. Dak.....C6 116
Fort Totten, Benson, N. Dak.B6 110
Fort Totten, Indian res., N. Dak.B7 110
Fort Towson, Choctaw, Okla.....C6 112
Fort Trinquet, see Bir Mogreïn, Maur.
Fortuna, Humboldt, Calif.....B1 82
Fortuna, Moniteau, Mo.....C5 101
Fortuna, Divide, N. Dak.....A2 110
Fortuna Ledge, Alsk.....C7 79
Fortune, Newf., Can.....E4 75
Fortune, bay, Newf., Can.....E4 75
Fortune Harbour, Newf., Can.....D4 75
Fort Valley, Peach, Ga.....D3 87
Fort Vermilion, Alta., Can.....f7 69
Fortville, Hancock, Ind.....E6 91
Fort Walton Beach, Okaloosa, Fla.....u15 86
Fort Washakie, Fremont, Wyo.....C4 125
Fort Washington, Prince Georges, Md.....C3 85
Fort Washington Montgomery, Pa.....o21 114
Fort Wayne, Allen, Ind.....B7 91
Fort White, Columbia, Fla..C4 86
Fort William, Scot.....D3 13
Fort William, mtn., Austl.....B8 51
Fort Wingate, McKinley, N. Mex.....B1 107
Fort Worth, Tarrant, Tex.....C4, n9 118
Fort Wright, Kenton, Ky.....h13 94
Fort Yates, Sioux, N. Dak...C5 110
Forty Fort, Luzerne, Pa.....D10, n17 114
Fort Yukon, Alsk.....B10 79
Fort Yuma, Indian res., Calif...F6 82
Foshee, Escambia, Ala.....D2 78
Foss, Washita, Okla.....B2 112
Fossano, It.....B1 21
Fosser, Nor.....p29 25
Fossil, Wheeler, Oreg.....B6 113
Fossil, lake, Oreg.....D6 113
Fossil, ridge, Colo.....C4 83
Fossombrone, It.....C4 21
Fosston, Sask., Can.....E4 70
Fosston, Polk, Minn.....C3 99
Foster, Que., Can.....D5 73
Foster, Bracken, Ky.....B5 94
Foster, Bates, Mo.....C3 101
Foster, Pierce, Nebr.....B8 103
Foster, Garvin, Okla.....C4 112
Foster, Linn, Oreg.....C4 113
Foster, Providence, R.I.....B10 84
Foster, Eau Claire, Wis.....D2 124
Foster, co., N. Dak.....B6 110
Foster, riv., Sask., Can.....A3 70
Foster Brook, McKean, Pa...C4 114
Fosterburg, Madison, Ill.....A8 90
Foster City, Dickinson, Mich.C3 98
Fosters, Tuscaloosa, Ala.....B2 78
Fosters, pond, Mass.....f11 97
Fosters Falls, Wythe, Va.....D2 121
Foster Village, Honolulu, Haw.....g10 88
Fosterville, Rutherford, Tenn.....B5 117
Fostoria, Lowndes, Ala.....C3 78
Fostoria, Clay, Iowa.....A2 92
Fostoria, Pottawatomie, Kans.....C7 93
Fostoria, Tuscola, Mich.....E7 98
Fostoria, Seneca and Hancock, Ohio.....A2 111
Fostoria, Montgomery, Tex..D5 118
Fougamou, Gabon.....F2 46
Fougères, Fr.....C3 14
Fouhsin, China.....C9 34
Fouke, Miller, Ark.....D2 81
Foula, isl., Scot.....g9 10
Fouling, China.....F6 34
Foulness, isl., Eng.....C8 12
Foulwind, cape, N.Z.....N13 51
Foumban, Cam.....D2 46
Foum el Hassane, Mor.....D3 44
Fount, Knox, Ky.....D6 94
Fountain, Monroe, Ala.....D2 78
Fountain, El Paso, Colo.....C6 83
Fountain, Bay, Fla.....B1, u16 86
Fountain, Mason, Mich.....D4 98
Fountain, Fillmore, Minn...G6 99
Fountain, co., Ind.....D3 91
Fountain, creek, Colo.....C6 83
Fountain City, Wayne, Ind..E8 91
Fountain City, Buffalo, Wis..D2 124
Fountain Green, Sanpete, Utah.....D4 119
Fountain Hill, Ashley, Ark..D4 81
Fountain Hill, Lehigh, Pa..E11 114
Fountain Inn, Greenville, S.C.....B3 115
Fountain Place East Baton Rouge, La.....*D4 95
Fountain Run, Monroe, Ky.D4 94
Fountain, Pitt, N.C.....B5 109
Fountaintown, Shelby, Ind...E6 91
Fountain Valley, Orange, Calif.....*F5 82
Fouping, China.....E6 36
Four Buttes, Daniels, Mont.B11 102
Fourchambault, Fr.....D5 14
Fourche, creek, Ark.....k10 81
Fourche LaFave, riv., Ark.....C2 81
Fourche Maline, riv., Okla.....C6 112
Fourchu, N.S., Can.....D9 74
Four Corners, Marion, Oreg.....*C4 113
Four Corners, Weston, Wyo..B8 125
Four Holes, Orangeburg, S.C.....E7 115
Four Lakes, Spokane, Wash.....B8, g13 122
Fourmies, Fr.....B6 14
Fourmile, Bell, Ky.....D6 94
Fourmile, creek, Iowa.....e8 92
Four Mountains, isl., Alsk.....E6 79
Fournier, Ont., Can.....B10 72
Fournier, Aroostook, Maine..A4 96
Four Oaks, Johnston, N.C...B4 109
Fourup, isl., Truk..... 52
Fouta Djallon, mts., Guinea....D2 45
Fouyang, China.....H6 36
Foveaux, strait, N.Z.....O12 51
Fowey, Eng.....D3 12
Fowler, Conecuh, Ala.....D2 78
Fowler, Fresno, Calif.....D4 82
Fowler, Otero, Colo.....C6 83
Fowler, Adams, Ill.....C2 90
Fowler, Benton, Ind.....C3 91
Fowler, Meade, Kans.....E3 93
Fowler, Clinton, Mich.....E6 98
Fowlerton, Grant, Ind.....D6 91
Fowlerton, LaSalle, Tex.....E3 118
Fowlerville, Livingston, Mich.....F6 98
Fowlkes, Dyer, Tenn.....B2 117
Fowlstown, Decatur, Ga.....F2 87
Fox, Stone, Ark.....B3 81
Fox, Carter, Okla.....C4 112
Fox, Grant, Oreg.....C7 113
Fox, isl., Wash.....f10 122
Fox, is., Alsk.....E5 79
Fox, lake, Ill.....h8 90
Fox, mtn., Yukon, Can.....D6 66
Fox, riv., Man., Can.....B4 71
Fox, riv., Ill.....h8 90
Fox, riv., Iowa.....D6 92
Fox, riv., Mich.....B5 98
Fox, riv., Mo.....A6 101
Fox, riv., Wis.....D5 124
Foxboro, Ont., Can.....C7 72
Foxboro, Norfolk, Mass.....B5 97
Foxboro, Douglas, Wis.....B1 124
Foxburg, Clarion, Pa.....D2 114
Fox Chapel, Allegheny, Pa..*F2 114
Fox Creek, see Iosegun Lake, Alta., Can.
Foxdale, I. of Man.....F4 13
Foxe, basin, N.W. Ter., Can...C17 67
Foxe, chan., N.W. Ter., Can..D16 67
Foxe, pen., N.W., Ter., Can...C17 67
Fox Farm, Laramie, Wyo..*D8 124
Foxford, Sask., Can.....D3 70
Foxford, Ire.....D2 11
Fox Harbour, Newf., Can.....B4 75
Fox Harbour, Newf., Can.....E5 75
Foxholm, Ward, N. Dak.....A4 110
Fox Lake, Lake, Ill.....A5, h8 90
Fox Lake, Dodge, Wis.....E5 124
Foxon, New Haven, Conn. (part of East Haven).....D5 84
Foxpark, Albany, Wyo.....E6 125
Fox Point, Miwaukee, Wis.....E6, m12 124
Fox River Grove, McHenry, Ill.....h8 90
Foxton, N.Z.....N15 51
Foxvale, Norfolk, Mass.....B5 97
Fox Valley, Sask., Can.....G1 70
Foxville, Orange, Vt.....C4 120
Foxwarren, Man., Can.....D1 71
Foxworth, Marion, Miss.....D4 100
Foyil, Rogers, Okla.....A6 112
Foyle, bay, N. Ire.....B4 11
Foyle, riv., N. Ire.....C4 11
Foynes, Ire.....E2 11
Foz do Iguaçu, Braz.....D2 56
Frackville, Schuylkill, Pa.....E9 114
Fraga, Sp.....B6 20
Fraile Muerto, Ur.....E2 56
Frametown, Braxton, W. Va.C4 123
Framingham, Middlesex, Mass.....B5, g10 97
Framnes, mts., Ant.....C19 5
França, Braz.....D2 57
Franca, Braz.....F1 57
Francavilla Fontana, It.....D6 21
France, country, Eur.....F9 8, 14
Frances, Crittenden, Ky.....e9 94
Frances, Pacific, Wash.....C2 122
Francés, cape, Cuba.....D2 64
Francestown, Hillsboro, N.H..E3 105
Francesville, Pulaski, Ind.....C4 91
Franceville, Gabon.....F2 46
Franche-Comté, former prov., Fr.....D6 14
Francis, Sask., Can.....G4 70
Francis, Pontotoc, Okla.....C5 112
Francis, Summit, Utah.....C4 119
Francis, Harrison, W. Va...k10 123
Francis, lake, N.H.....f7 105
Francis Case, lake, S. Dak.....D6 116
Francisco, Gibson, Ind.....H3 91
Francis Creek, Manitowoc, Wis.....h10 124
Francistown, Bots.....B4 49
François, Newf., Can.....E3 75
Francois, lake, B.C., Can.....C5 68
Franconia, Grafton, N.H.....B3 105
Franconia, Fairfax, Va.....*B5 121
Franconville, Fr.....g9 14
Francs, peak, Wyo.....C3 125
Franeker, Neth.....A5 15
Frank, Alta., Can.....*E3 69
Frank, Pocahontas, W. Va...C5 123
Frank, lake, Alta., Can.....D4 69
Frankenberg, F.R.G.....B3 17
Frankenberg, G.D.R.....C8 17
Frankenmuth, Saginaw, Mich.....E7 98
Frankenthal, F.R.G.....D3 17
Frankewing, Giles, Tenn.....B5 117
Frankfield, Jam.....E14 65
Frankford, Ont., Can.....C7 72
Frankford, Sussex, Del.....C7 85
Frankford, Pike, Mo.....B6 101
Frankford, Greenbrier, W. Va.....D4 123
Frankfort, Will, Ill.....m9 90
Frankfort, Clinton, Ind.....D4 91
Frankfort, Marshall, Kans...C7 93
Frankfort, Franklin, Ky.....B5 94
Frankfort, Waldo, Maine.....D4 96
Frankfort, Benzie, Mich.....D4 98
Frankfort, Herkimer, N.Y...B5 108
Frankfort, Ross, Ohio.....C2 111
Frankfort, Spink, S. Dak.....C7 116
Frankfort, S. Afr.....C4 49
Frankfurt [am Main], F.R.G.....C4 16, C3 17
Frankfurt [an der Oder], G.D.R.....A9 17
Frankische Saale, riv., F.R.G...C4 17
Franklin, Macon, Ala.....C4 78
Franklin, Monroe, Ala.....D2 78
Franklin, Izard, Ark.....A4 80
Franklin, Man., Can.....D2 71
Franklin, New London, Conn.....C8 84
Frank in, Heard, Ga.....C1 87
Franklin, Ada, Idaho.....*F2 89
Franklin, Franklin, Idaho...G7 89
Franklin, Morgan, Ill.....D3 90
Franklin, Johnson, Ind.....F5 91
Franklin, Lee, Iowa.....D6 92
Franklin, Crawford, Kans...E9 93
Franklin, Simpson, Ky.....D3 94
Franklin, St. Mary, La.....E4 95
Franklin, Hancock, Maine...D4 96
Franklin, Allegany, Md.....D1 85
Franklin, Norfolk, Mass.....B5 97
Franklin, Oakland, Mich.....*F7 98
Franklin, Renville, Minn.....F4 99
Franklin, Howard, Mo.....B5 101
Franklin, Franklin, Nebr.....D7 103
Franklin, Merrimack, N.H...D3 105
Franklin, Sussex, N.J.....A3 106
Franklin, Delaware, N.Y.....C5 108
Franklin, Macon, N.C.....f9 109
Franklin, Warren, Ohio.....C1 111
Franklin, Cambria, Pa.....*F4 114
Franklin, Venango, Pa.....D2 114
Franklin, Williamson, Tenn..B5 117
Franklin, Robertson, Tex.....D4 118
Franklin, Franklin, Vt.....B3 120
Franklin (Independent City), Va.....D6 121
Franklin, Pendleton, W. Va..C5 123
Franklin, Milwaukee, Wis...n11 124
Franklin, co., Ala.....A4 78
Franklin, co., Ark.....B2 81
Franklin, co., Fla.....C2 86
Franklin, co., Ga.....B3 87
Franklin, co., Idaho.....G7 89
Franklin, co., Ill.....E5 90
Franklin, co., Ind.....F7 91
Franklin, co., Iowa.....B4 92
Franklin, co., Kans.....D8 93
Franklin, co., Ky.....B5 94
Franklin, co., Maine.....C2 96
Franklin, co., Mass.....A2 97
Franklin, co., Miss.....D3 100
Franklin, co., Mo.....C6 101
Franklin, co., Nebr.....D7 103
Franklin, co., N.Y.....A6 108
Franklin, co., N.C.....A4 109
Franklin, co., Ohio.....B2 111
Franklin, co., Pa.....G6 114
Franklin, co., Tenn.....B5 117
Franklin, co, Tex.....C5 118
Franklin, co., Vt.....B2 120
Franklin, co., Va.....D3 121
Franklin, co., Wash.....C7 122
Franklin, dist., N.W. Ter., Can.....B9 66
Franklin, par., La.....B4 95
Franklin, isl., Ont., Can.....B4 72
Franklin, lake, N.W. Ter., Can.....C13 66
Franklin, lake, Nev.....C6 104
Franklin, mts., N.W. Ter., Can..C7 66
Franklin, pt., Alsk.....A8 79
Franklin, strait, N.W. Ter., Can.....B13 66
Franklin D. Roosevelt, lake, Wash.....A7 122
Franklin Furnace, Scioto, Ohio.....D3 111
Franklin Grove, Lee, Ill.....B4 90
Franklin, Hartsell, Brown and Norcot Mills (West Concord), Cabarrus, N.C.....*B2 109
Franklin Lakes, Bergen, N.J.*B4 106
Franklin Mine, Houghton, Mich.....A2 98
Franklin Park, Cook, Ill.....k9 90
Franklin Park, Fairfax, Va..*B5 121
Franklin Square, Nassau, N.Y.....G2 84
Franklinton, Washington, La.....D5 95
Franklinton, Franklin, N.C..A4 109
Franklinville, Gloucester, N.J.....D2 106
Franklinville, Cattaraugus, N.Y.....C2 108
Franklinville, Randolph, N.C.....B3 109
Frankston, Anderson, Tex.....C5 118
Franksville, Racine, Wis.....n12 124
Frankton, Madison, Ind.....D6 91
Franktown, Douglas, Colo...B6 83
Frankville, Washington, Ala.D1 78
Frankville, Garrett, Md.....D1 85
Frankville, N.S., Can.....D8 74
Frannie, Park, Wyo.....B4 125
Franz Josef Land, arch., Sov. Un.....A8 4
Frascati, It.....D4, h9 21
Fraser, Grand, Colo.....B5 83
Fraser, Boone, Iowa.....B4 92
Fraser, Macomb, Mich.....*F8 98
Fraser (Great Sandy), isl., Austl.B9 51
Fraser, lake, B.C., Can.....B5 68
Fraser, mtn., B.C., Can.....C8 68
Fraser, plat., B.C., Can.....D6 68
Fraser, riv., B.C., Can.....C6 68
Fraser, riv., Newf., Can.....g9 75
Fraserburg, S. Afr.....D3 49
Fraserburgh, Scot.....C7 13
Fraserdale, Ont., Can.....o19 72
Fraser Lake, B.C., Can.....B5 68
Fraser Mills, B.C., Can.....*E6 68
Fraser Reach, chan., B.C., Can..C3 68
Fraserwood, Man., Can.....D3 71
Frasne, Fr.....C2 18
Frauenfeld, Switz.....A6 19
Fray Bentos, Ur.....E1 56
Frazee, Becker, Minn.....D3 99
Frazer, Valley, Mont.....B10 102
Frazeysburg, Muskingum, Ohio.....B3 111
Frazier Park, Kern, Calif.....E4 82
Frederic, Crawford, Mich.....D6 98
Frederic, Polk, Wis.....C1 124
Frederica, Kent, Del.....B7 85
Fredericia, Den.....C3 24
Frederick, Weld, Colo.....A6 83
Frederick, Schuyler, Ill.....C3 90
Frederick, Frederick, Md.....B3 85
Frederick, Tillman, Okla.....C2 112
Frederick, Brown, S. Dak...B7 116
Frederick, co., Md.....B3 85
Frederick, co., Va.....A4 121
Frederick, sound, Alsk.....m23 79
Frederick Hall, Louisa, Va...C5 121
Frederick Junction, Frederick, Md.....B3 85
Fredericksburg, Washington, Ind.....H5 91
Fredericksburg, Chickasaw, Iowa.....B5 92
Fredericksburg, Wayne, Ohio.....B4 111
Fredericksburg, Lebanon, Pa.F9 114
Fredericksburg, Gillespie, Tex.....D3 118
Fredericksburg (Independent City), Va.....B5 121
Fredericktown, Cecil, Md.....B6 85
Fredericktown, Madison, Mo.....D7 101
Fredericktown, Knox, Ohio..B3 111
Fredericktown, Washington, Pa.....F1 114
Fredericton, N.B., Can.....D3 74
Fredericton Junction, N.B., Can.....D3 74
Frederika, Bremer, Iowa.....B5 92
Frederiksborg, co., Den.....C6 24
Frederikshavn, Den.....A4 24
Frederikssund, Den.....C6 24
Frederiksted, Vir. Is. (U.S.).H12 64
Frederiksvaerk, Den.....C6 24
Frederik Willem IV, falls, Guy..B3 59
Fredonia, Chambers, Ala.....C4 78
Fredonia, Coconino, Ariz.....A3 80
Fredonia (Biscoe), Prairie, Ark.....C4 81
Fredonia, Louisa, Iowa.....C6 92
Fredonia, Wilson, Kans.....E8 93
Fredonia, Caldwell, Ky.....C1 94
Fredonia, Chautauqua, N.Y.C1 108
Fredonia, Logan, N. Dak.....C6 110
Fredonia, Mercer, Pa.....D1 114
Fredonia, Mason, Tex.....D3 118
Fredonia, Ozaukee, Wis.....E6 124
Fredrikstad, Nor.....H4, p28 25
Freeborn, Freeborn, Minn...G5 99
Freeborn, co., Minn.....G5 99
Freeburg, St. Clair, Ill.....E4 90
Freeburg, Osage, Mo.....C6 101
Freeburg, Houston, Minn.....G7 99
Freeburg, Snyder, Pa.....E8 114
Freedom, Santa Cruz, Calif.*D2 82
Freedom, Owen, Ind.....F4 91
Freedom, Carroll, N.H.....C4 105
Freedom, Woods, Okla.....A2 112
Freedom, Beaver, Pa.....E1 114
Freedom, Outagamie, Wis.....h9 124
Freedom, Lincoln, Wyo.....D2 125
Freehold, Monmouth, N.J...C4 106
Freeland, Saginaw, Mich.....E6 98
Freeland, Brunswick, N.C.....C4 109
Freeland, Luzerne, Pa.....D10 114
Freeland, Park, Benton, Ind.C3 91
Freelandville, Knox, Ind.....G3 91
Freels, cape, Newf., Can.....D5 75
Freels, cape, Newf., Can.....E5 75
Freelton, Ont., Can.....*D4 72
Freeman, Cass, Mo.....C3 101
Freeman, Hutchinson, S. Dak.....D8 116
Freeman, Spokane, Wash.....g14 122
Freeman, lake, Ind.....C4 91
Freeman, riv., Alta., Can.....B3 69
Freemansburg, Northampton, Pa.....E11 114
Freemanville, Escambia, Ala.....D2 78
Freemason, is., La.....E7 95
Freemount, Ire.....E3 11
Freeport, Ba.....*A4 64
Freeport, N.S., Can.....E3 74
Freeport, Walton, Fla.....u15 86
Freeport, Stephenson, Ill.....A4 90
Freeport, Winneshiek, Iowa..A6 92
Freeport, Harper, Kans.....E6 93
Freeport, Cumberland, Maine.....E2, g7 96
Freeport, Barry, Mich.....F5 98
Freeport, Stearns, Minn.....E4 99
Freeport, Nassau, N.Y.....G2 84
Freeport, Harrison, Ohio.....B4 111
Freeport, Armstrong, Pa.....E2 114
Freeport, Brazoria, Tex..E5, s14 118
Freer, Duval, Tex.....F3 118
Free Soil, Mason, Mich.....D4 98
Freestone, co., Tex.....D4 118
Freetown, P.E.I., Can.....C6 74
Freetown, S.L.....E2 45
Freetown, Jackson, Ind.....G5 91
Freetown (Town of), Bristol, Mass.....*C5 97
Freetown, Suffolk, N.Y.....*n16 108
Free Union, Albemarle, Va...B4 121
Freeville, Tompkins, N.Y.....C4 108
Freewater, see Milton-Freewater, Oreg.
Freezeout, mts., Wyo.....D6 125
Fregenal de la Sierra, Sp.....C2 20
Fregene, It.....h8 21

Garrett, Floyd, Ky...C7 94
Garrett, Somerset, Pa...G3 114
Garrett, Albany, Wyo...D7 125
Garrett, co., Md...k12 85
Garrett Park, Montgomery, Md...B3 85
Garrettsville, Portage, Ohio...A4 111
Garrick, Sask., Can...D3 70
Garrison, Benton, Iowa...B5 92
Garrison, Lewis, Ky...B6 94
Garrison, Baltimore, Md...B4 85
Garrison, Crow Wing, Minn...D5 99
Garrison, Powell, Mont...D4 102
Garrison, Putnam, N.Y...D7, m15 108
Garrison, McLean, N. Dak...B4 110
Garrison, Nacogdoches, Tex...D5 118
Garrison, Millard, Utah...E1 119
Garrison, dam, N. Dak...B4 110
Garrisonville, Stafford, Va...C5 121
Garristown, Ire...D5 11
Garrote, Pan...h11 62
Garrovillas, Sp...C2 20
Garruk, Pak...C4 39
Garry, lake, N.W., Ter., Can...C13 66
Garry, riv., Scot...D5 13
Garryowen, Big Horn, Mont...E9 102
Garson, Ont., Can...*p19 72
Garson, lake, Alta., Sask., Can...A5 69
Garson Quarry, Man., Can...D3 71
Garstang, Eng...G6 13
Garth, Jackson, Ala...A3 78
Garthby Station, Que., Can...D6 73
Gartok, see Kaerh, China
Gartz, G.D.R...E8 24
Garvagh, N. Ire...C5 11
Garve, Scot...C4 13
Garvin, Lyon, Minn...F3 99
Garvin, McCurtain, Okla...D7 112
Garvin, co., Okla...C4 112
Garwin, Tama, Iowa...B5 92
Garwolin, Pol...C6 26
Garwood, Union, N.J...*B4 106
Garwood, Colorado, Tex...E4 118
Gary, Lake, Ind...A3 91
Gary, Norman, Minn...C2 99
Gary, Deuel, S. Dak...C9 116
Gary, Panola, Tex...C5 118
Gary, McDowell, W. Va...D3 123
Garysburg, Northampton, N.C...A6 109
Garyville, St. John the Baptist, La...D5, h10 95
Garza, co., Tex...C2 118
Garza Little Elm, res., Tex...m9 118
Garzón, Col...C2 60
Gas, Allen, Kans...E8 93
Gas City, Grant, Ind...D6 91
Gascon, Mora, N. Mex...B4 107
Gasconade, Gasconade, Mo...C6 101
Gasconade, co., Mo...C6 101
Gasconade, riv., Mo...C6 101
Gascons, Que., Can...*k13 73
Gascony (Gascogne), former prov., Fr...E3 14
Gascoyne, Bowman, N. Dak...C2 110
Gashaka, Cam...E7 45
Gas Hills, Fremont, Wyo...D5 125
Gashua, Nig...D7 45
Gasmata, Pap. N. Gui...k13 50
Gasparilla, pass, Fla...F4 86
Gaspé, Que., Can...k14 73
Gaspé, cape, Que., Can...G20 67
Gaspé, pen., Que., Can...k13 73
Gaspe East, co., Que., Can...*k14 73
Gaspe West, co., Que., Can...*k13 73
Gasport, Niagara, N.Y...B2 108
Gasque, Baldwin, Ala...E2 78
Gassaway, Cannon, Tenn...B5 117
Gassaway, Braxton, W. Va...*C4 123
Gassetts, Windsor, Vt...E3 120
Gassol, Nig...E7 45
Gassville, Baxter, Ark...A3 81
Gaston, Delaware, Ind...D6 91
Gaston, Northampton, N.C...A5 109
Gaston, Washington, Oreg...h11 113
Gaston, Lexington, S.C...D5 115
Gaston, co., N.C...B1 109
Gastonia, Gaston, N.C...B1 109
Gastre, Arg...C3 54
Gata, cape, Sp...D4 20
Gata, mts., Sp...B2 20
Gátas, cape, Cyp...E9 31
Gatchel, Perry, Ind...H4 91
Gatchina, Sov. Un...B8 27, s31 25
Gate, Beaver, Okla...A1, e10 112
Gate City, Scott, Va...f9 121
Gatehouse-of-Fleet, Scot...F4 13
Gates, Custer, Nebr...C6 103
Gates, Monroe, N.Y...*B3 108
Gates, Gates, N.C...A6 109
Gates, Lauderdale, Tenn...B2 117
Gates, co., N.C...A6 109
Gateshead, Eng...C6 10
Gates Mills, Cuyahoga, Ohio...*A4 111
Gatesville, Gates, N.C...A6 109
Gatesville, Coryell, Tex...D4 118
Gateway, Mesa, Colo...C2 83
Gateway, Jefferson, Oreg...C5 113
Gatineau, Que., Can...D2 73
Gatineau, co., Que., Can...C2 73
Gatineau, nat. park, Que., Can...D2 73
Gatineau, riv., Que., Can...D2 73
Gatliff, Whitely, Ky...D5 94
Gatlinburg, Sevier, Tenn...D10 117
Gato, Archuleta, Colo...D3 83
Gattman, Monroe, Miss...B5 100
Gatton, Austl...C9 51
Gatún, Pan...k11 62
Gatun, lake, Pan...k11 62
Gatzke, Marshall, Minn...B3 99
Gauer, lake, Man., Can...A3 71
Gauhāti, India...C9 39
Gauja, riv., Sov. Un...C5 27
Gaula, riv., Nor...F4 25
Gauley, riv., W. Va...C4 123
Gauley Bridge, Fayette, W. Va...C3, m13 123
Gauley Mills, Webster, W. Va...C4 123
Gause, Milam, Tex...D4 118
Gautier, Jackson, Miss...f8 100
Gavdhos, isl., Grc...E5 23
Gave de Pau, riv., Fr...F3 14
Gave d'Oloron, riv., Fr...F3 14
Gaviota, Santa Barbara, Calif...E3 82
Gavins Point, dam, Nebr...B8 103
Gävle, Swe...G7 25
Gävleborg, co., Swe...*G7 25
Gävlebukten, bay, Swe...G7 25
Gavrilov Posad, Sov. Un...C13 27
Gavrilovka, Sov. Un...G11 27
Gawler, Austl...G2 51
Gawler, ranges, Austl...F6 50
Gay, Meriwether, Ga...C2 87
Gay, Keweenaw, Mich...A2 98
Gay, head, Mass...D6 97
Gaya, Niger...D5 45
Gaya, India...D7 39, E10 40
Gaya, Nig...F6 45
Gay Head, Dukes, Mass...D6 97
Gaylesville, Cherokee, Ala...A4 78
Gaylord, Smith, Kans...C5 93
Gaylord, Otsego, Mich...C6 98
Gaylord, Sibley, Minn...F4 99
Gaylord, Coos, Oreg...E2 113
Gaylordsville, Litchfield, Conn...C3 84
Gayndah, Austl...B8 51
Gays, Moultrie, Ill...D5 90
Gaysin, Sov. Un...G7 27
Gays Mills, Crawford, Wis...E3 118
Gaysville, Windsor, Vt...D3 120
Gayville, Yankton, S. Dak...E8 116
Gaza, O'Brien, Iowa...A2 92
Gaza (Ghazzah), Gaza Strip...C6 32
Gaza, prov., Moz...B5 49
Gaza Strip, Isr. occ., Asia...C6 32
Gaziantep, Tur...D11 31
Gboko, Nig...E6 45
Gdańsk (Danzig), Pol...A5 26
Gdov, Sov. Un...B6 27
Gdynia, Pol...A5 26
Gearhart, Clatsop, Oreg...A3 113
Gearhart, mtn., Oreg...E6 113
Geary, N.B., Can...D3 74
Geary, Canadian and Blaine, Okla...B3 112
Geary, co., Kans...D7 93
Geauga, co., Ohio...A4 111
Gebeit Mine, Sud...A4 47
Gebo, Hot Springs, Wyo...C4 125
Gebze, Tur...B7 23
Ged, Calcasieu, La...D2 95
Geddes, Charles Mix, S. Dak...D7 116
Gedera, Isr...h10 32
Gedern, F.R.G...C4 17
Gedinne, Bel...E4 15
Gediz, Tur...C7 23
Gediz (Hermus), riv., Tur...C6 23
Gedser, Den...D5 24
Geel, Bel...C5 15
Geelong, Austl...I5 51
Geelvink, bay, Indon...F9 35
Geeraardsbergen, Bel...D3 15
Geetbets, Bel...D5 15
Geff (Jeffersonville), Wayne, Ill...E5 90
Geidam, Nig...D7 45
Geiger, Sumter, Ala...C1 78
Geisenfeld, F.R.G...E6 17
Geislingen, F.R.G...E4 17
Geismar, Ascension, La...h9 95
Geist, res., Ind...E6 91
Geistown, Cambria, Pa...F4 114
Geita, Tan...B5 48
Gela, It...F5 21
Gelderland, prov., Neth...B5 15
Geldermalsen, Neth...C5 15
Geldern, F.R.G...C3 17
Geldrop, Neth...C5 15
Geleen, Neth...D5 15
Gelert, Ont., Can...C6 72
Gelfingen, Switz...B5 19
Gelibolu (Gallipoli), Tur...B6 23
Gelligaer, Wales...C5 12
Gellinam, isl., Kwajalein... 52
Gelnhausen, F.R.G...C4 17
Gelsenkirchen, F.R.G...B2 17
Gelting, F.R.G...D3 24
Gem, Alta., Can...D4 69
Gem, Shoshone, Idaho...B3 89
Gem, Thomas, Kans...C3 93
Gem, Braxton, W. Va...C4 123
Gem, co., Idaho...E2 89
Gemas, Mala...k5 38
Gembloux, Bel...D4 15
Gemena, Zaire...A2 48
Gemert, Neth...C5 15
Gemla, Swe...B8 24
Gemlik, Tur...B7 23
Gemona del Friuli, It...C9 18
Gemu Gofa, prov., Eth...D4 47
Gemünden, F.R.G...C4 17
Gem Village, La Plata, Colo...D3 83
Genale, riv., Eth...D5 47
Genarp, Swe...C7 24
Gene Autry, Carter, Okla...C4 112
General Acha, Arg...B4 54
General Alvarado, Arg...B5 54
General Alvear, Arg...B5 54
General Alvear, Arg...A3 54
General Belgrano, Arg...B5 54
General Bravo, Mex...G3 118
General Conesa, Arg...C4 54
General La Madrid, Arg...B4 54
General Lavalle, Arg...B5 54
General Machado, Ang...D2 48
General Madariaga, Arg...B5 54
General Paz, Arg...E4 55
General Pico, Arg...B4 54
General Pinedo, Arg...E3 55
General Roca, Arg...B3 54
General San Martín (San Martín), Arg...g7 54
General Sarmiento, Arg...g7 54
General Toshevo, Bul...D9 22
General Viamonte, Arg...B4 54
General Villegas, Arg...A4 54
Genesee, Latah, Idaho...C2 89
Genesee, Genesee, Mich...E7 98
Genesee, Potter, Pa...C6 114
Genesee, co., Mich...E7 98
Genesee, co., N.Y...B2 108
Genesee, riv., N.Y...C2 108
Genesee Depot, Waukesha, Wis...n11 124
Geneseo, Henry, Ill...B3 90
Geneseo, Rice, Kans...D5 93
Geneseo, Livingston, N.Y...C3 108
Geneseo, Sargent, N. Dak...C8 110
Geneva, Geneva, Ala...D4 78
Geneva, Talbot, Ga...D2 87
Geneva, Bear Lake, Idaho...G7 89
Geneva, Kane, Ill...B5, k8 90
Geneva, Adams, Ind...C8 91
Geneva, Franklin, Iowa...B4 92
Geneva, Henderson, Ky...C2 94
Geneva, Fillmore, Nebr...D8 103
Geneva, Ontario, N.Y...C4 108
Geneva, Ashtabula, Ohio...A7 111
Geneva, Crawford, Pa...C1 114
Geneva, co., Ala...D4 78
Geneva, see Léman, lake, Switz.
Geneva, lake, Wis...F5 124
Genève (Geneva), Switz...D1 19
Genève, canton, Switz...D1 19
Genevia, Pulaski, Ark...C3, k10 81
Genichesk, Sov. Un...H10 27
Genil, riv., Sp...D3 20
Génissiat, Fr...C1 18
Genk, Bel...D5 15
Gennep, Neth...C5 15
Gennevilliers, Fr...g10 14
Genoa, Miller, Ark...D2 81
Genoa, Lincoln, Colo...B7 83
Genoa, DeKalb, Ill...A5 90
Genoa (Genova), It...B2 21
Genoa, Nance, Nebr...C8 103
Genoa, Douglas, Nev...E2 104
Genoa, Cayuga, N.Y...C4 108
Genoa, Ottawa, Ohio...A2, e7 111
Genoa, Harris, Tex. (part of Houston)...*E5 118
Genoa, Vernon, Wis...E2 124
Genoa gulf, It...B2 21
Genoa City, Walworth, Wis...F5, n11 124
Genola, Morrison, Minn...E4 99
Genola, Utah, Utah...D4 119
Genolier, Switz...D1 19
Genova, see Genoa, It.
Genovesa, isl., Ec...f6 58
Gent (Gand) (Ghent), Bel...C3 15
Gentbrugge, Bel...C3 15
Genthin, G.D.R...A7 17
Gentilly, Fr...g10 14
Gentilly, Polk, Minn...C2 99
Gentry, Benton, Ark...A1 81
Gentry, Gentry, Mo...A3 101
Gentry, co., Mo...A3 101
Gentryville, Spencer, Ind...H3 91
Gentryville, Gentry, Mo...A3 101
Genzano di Roma, It...h9 21
Geographe, bay, Austl...F2 50
Geographe, chan., Austl...D1 50
Geographical Society, isl., Grnld...B17 4
Geographic Center of North America, N. Dak...A5 110
Geographic Center of United States, S. Dak...B7 76
Geokchay, Sov. Un...G18 9
George, Lyon, Iowa...A2 92
George, Northampton, N.C...A5 109
George, S. Afr...D3 49
George, co., Miss...E5 100
George, cape, N.S., Can...D8 74
George, hill, Md...k12 85
George, isl., Newf., Can...A3 75
George, isl., Sov. Un...B10 4
George, lake, Austl...G7 51
George, lake, N.S., Can...E3 74
George, lake, Ont., Can...B6 98
George, lake, Fla...C5 86
George, lake, N.Y...B7 108
George, peak, Utah...B2 119
George, riv., Que., Can...E19 67
George B. Stevenson, flood control res., Pa...D5 114
George V, coast, Ant...C28 5
George VI, sound, Ant...B6 5
Georges, Mills, Sullivan, N.H...B1 105
Georgesville, Franklin, Ohio...m10 111
Georgetown, White, Ark...B4 81
George Town, Austl...o15 50
George Town, Ba...C6 64
Georgetown, El Dorado, Calif...C3 82
Georgetown, Ont., Can...D5 72
Georgetown, P.E.I., Can...C7 74
Georgetown, Clear Creek, Colo...B5 83
Georgetown, Fairfield, Conn...E3 84
Georgetown, Sussex, Del...C7 85
Georgetown, Putnam, Fla...C5 86
Georgetown, Gam...D2 45
Georgetown, Quitman, Ga...E1 87
Georgetown, Guy...A3 59
Georgetown, Bear Lake, Idaho...G7 89
Georgetown, Vermilion, Ill...D6 90
Georgetown, Floyd, Ind...H6 91
Georgetown, Scott, Ky...B5 94
Georgetown, Grant, La...C3 95
George Town (Pinang), Mala...J4 38
Georgetown, Kent, Md...B6 85
Georgetown, Essex, Mass...A6 97
Georgetown, Clay, Minn...C2 99
Georgetown, Copiah, Miss...D3 100
Georgetown, Burlington, N.J...C3 106
Georgetown, Madison, N.Y...C5 108
Georgetown, Brown, Ohio...D2 111
Georgetown, Beaver, Pa...*E1 114
Georgetown, St. Vincent...U26 65
Georgetown, Georgetown, S.C...E9 115
Georgetown, Hamilton, Tenn...D9 117
Georgetown, Williamson, Tex...D4 118
Georgetown, co., S.C...D9 115
Georgeville, Que., Can...D5 73
George Washington Birthplace, nat. mon., Va...B6 121
George West, Live Oak, Tex...E3 118
Georgia (Georgian S.S.R.), rep., Sov. Un...G17 9
Georgia, state, U.S...D11 77, 87
Georgia, strait, B.C., Can...E5 68
Georgia Center, Franklin, Vt...B2 120
Georgian S.S.R., see Georgia rep., Sov. Un.
Georgian, bay, Ont., Can...B3 72
Georgiana, Butler, Ala...D3 78
Georgian Bay Islands, nat. park, Ont., Can...B3, C5 72
Georgina, riv., Austl...D6 50
Georgiu-Dez (Liski), Sov. Un...F12 27
Georgiyevsk, Sov. Un...G17 9
Gera, G.D.R...C7 17
Gerald, Sask., Can...G5 70
Gerald, Franklin, Mo...C6 101
Geraldine, De Kalb, Ala...A4 78
Geraldine, Chouteau, Mont...C6 102
Geraldton, Austl...E1 50
Geraldton, Ont., Can...o18 72
Gerard, Somerset, Maine...C2 96
Gérardmer, Fr...A2 18
Gerber, Tehama, Calif...B2 82
Gerbstedt, G.D.R...B6 17
Gercüs, Tur...D13 31
Gerdau, riv., F.R.G...F4 24
Gerdine, mtn., Alsk...g15 79
Gerede, Tur...B9 31
Gereh, mtn., Iran...F5 41
Gereshk, Afg...F12 41
Gérgal, Sp...D4 20
Gering, Scotts Bluff, Nebr...C2 103
Gerlach, Washoe, Nev...C2 104
Gerlachovka, mtn., Czech...D6 26
German Democratic Republic (East Germany), country, Eur...E11 8, B5 16
Germania, Atlantic, N.J...D3 106
Germania, Potter, Pa...C6 114
Germansen, lake, B.C., Can...B5 68
Germantown, N.B., Can...C5 74
Germantown, Fairfield, Conn...*D3 84
Germantown, Clinton, Ill...E4 90
Germantown, Bracken and Mason, Ky...B6 94
Germantown, Montgomery, Md...B3 85
Germantown, Montgomery, Ohio...C1 111
Germantown, Shelby, Tenn...B2 117
Germantown, Washington, Wis...E5, m11 124
Germany, Federal Republic of (West Germany), country, Eur...E10 8, B3 16
Germersheim, F.R.G...D3 17
Germfask, Schoolcraft, Mich...B5 98
Germiston, S. Afr...C4 49
Gernrode, G.D.R...B6 17
Gernsheim, F.R.G...D3 17
Gero, Jap...n16 37
Gerolzhofen, F.R.G...D5 17
Gerona, Phil...o13 35
Gerona, Sp...B7 20
Gerona, prov., Sp...*B7 20
Geronimo, Comanche, Okla...C3 112
Geronimo, Guadalupe, Tex...h8 118
Gerrardstown, Berkeley, W. Va...B6 123
Gers, dept., Fr...*F4 14
Gersfeld, F.R.G...C4 17
Gersthofen, F.R.G...E5 17
Gerty, Hughes, Okla...C5 112
Gervais, Marion, Oreg...B4, h12 113
Gerze, Tur...B10 31
Geseke, F.R.G...B3 17
Gesher, HaZiw, Isr...A7 32
Gessie, Vermillion, Ind...D3 91
Getafe, Sp...B4, p17 20
Gethsémani, Que., Can...h9 75
Gettysburg, Darke, Ohio...B1 111
Gettysburg, Adams, Pa...G7 114
Gettysburg, Potter, S. Dak...C6 116
Getúlio Vargas, Braz...D2 56
Getz, ice shelf, Ant...B36 5
Geuda Springs, Sumner and Cowley, Kans...E6 93
Gevelsberg, F.R.G...B2 17
Gex, Fr...C2 18
Geyser, Judith Basin, Mont...C6 102
Geyserville, Sonoma, Calif...C2 82
Geyve, Tur...B8 23
Gézenti, Chad...A3 46
Ghadir as Sufi (Oasis), Iraq...F13 31
Ghagar, res., India...E9 40
Ghaggar, riv., India...C5 40
Ghāghra, riv., India...C7 39
Ghana, country, Afr...F5 42, E4 45
Ghanzi, Bots...B3 49
Ghardaïa, Alg...C5 44
Ghardaïa, reg., Alg...C5 44
Gharyān, Libya...C2 43
Ghāt, Libya...E2 43
Ghazal, riv., Chad...C3 46
Ghazal, riv., Sud...D2 47
Ghazaouet, Alg...B4 44
Ghāzīpur, India...E9 40
Ghaznī, Afg...E14 41
Ghazzah, see Gaza, Gaza Strip
Gheen, St. Louis, Minn...C6 99
Gheens, Lafourche, La...E5, k11 95
Ghent, see Gent, Bel.
Ghent, Carroll, Ky...B4 94
Ghent, Lyon, Minn...F3 99
Ghent, Columbia, N.Y...C7 108
Gheorgheni, Rom...B7 22
Gherla, Rom...B6 22
Ghimir, see Ginir, Eth.
Gholson, Noxubee, Miss...C5 100
Ghudāmis, Libya...C1 43
Ghūriān, Afg...D10 41
Giamda, see Taichao, China
Giannutri, isl., It...C3 21
Giant, mtn., N.Y...A7 108
Giants Neck, New London, Conn...*D8 84
Giaveno, It...D3 18
Gibara, Cuba...D5 64
Gibbon, Sibley, Minn...F4 99
Gibbon, Buffalo, Nebr...D7 103
Gibbon, Umatilla, Oreg...B8 113
Gibbons, Alta., Can...C4 69
Gibbonsville, Lemhi, Idaho...D5 89
Gibbs, Adair, Mo...A5 101
Gibbs City, Iron, Mich...B2 98
Gibbstown, Gloucester, N.J...D2 106
Gibeon, Namibia...C2 49
Gibraleón, Sp...D2 20
Gibraltar, Gib...D3 20
Gibraltar, Br. dep., Eur...*D3 20
Gibraltar, Wayne, Mich...*F7 98
Gibraltar, bay, Sp...D3 20
Gibraltar, pt., Eng...A8 12
Gibraltar, strait, Afr., Eur...G4 30
Gibsland, Bienville, La...B2 95
Gibson, Glascock, Ga...C4 87
Gibson, Terrebonne, La...E5, k10 95
Gibson, Monroe, Miss...B5 100
Gibson, Dunklin, Mo...E8 101
Gibson, Scotland, N.C...C3 109
Gibson, Susquehanna, Pa...C10 114
Gibson, Gibson, Tenn...B3 117
Gibson, co., Ind...H2 91
Gibson, co., Tenn...A3 117
Gibson, des., Austl...D3 50
Gibson, isl., Md...B5 85
Gibsonburg, Sandusky, Ohio...A2, e7 111
Gibson City, Ford, Ill...C5 90
Gibsonia, Allegheny, Pa...h14 114
Gibsons, B.C., Can...E6 68
Gibsonton, Hillsborough, Fla...p11 86
Gibsonville, Guilford and Alamance, N.C...A3 109
Gidam, India...H8 40
Giddings, Lee, Tex...D4 118
Gideon, New Madrid, Mo...E8 101
Gidole, Eth...D4 47
Gien, Fr...D5 14
Giessen, F.R.G...C3 17
Gifford, Hot Spring, Ark...g8 81
Gifford, Indian River, Fla...E6 86
Gifford, Nez Perce, Idaho...C2 89
Gifford, Champaign, Ill...C5 90
Gifford, McKean, Pa...C4 114
Gifhorn, F.R.G...B5 17
Gift, Tipton, Tenn...B2 117
Gifu, Jap...I8, n15 37
Gifu, pref., Jap...*I8 37
Giganta, mts., Mex...B2 63
Gigante, Col...C2 60
Gigha, isl., Scot...E3 13
Gig Harbor, Pierce, Wash...B3, f10 122
Giglio, isl., It...C3 21
Giguela, riv., Sp...C4 20
Gihon, riv., Vt...B3 120
Gijón, Sp...A3 20
Gil, isl., B.C., Can...C3 68
Gila, Grant, N. Mex...E1 107
Gila, co., Ariz...D5 80
Gila, mts., Ariz...D6 80
Gila, riv., Ariz., N. Mex...E2 80
Gila Bend, Maricopa, Ariz...E3 80
Gila Bend, Indian res., Ariz...D2 80
Gila Bend, mts., Ariz...D2 80
Gila Center, Yuma, Ariz...E1 80
Gila Cliff Dwellings, nat. mon., N. Mex...D1 107
Gila River, Indian res., Ariz...D4 80
Gilbert, Maricopa, Ariz...D4, m9 80
Gilbert, Searcy, Ark...B3 81
Gilbert, Story, Iowa...B4 92
Gilbert, Franklin, La...B4 95
Gilbert, St. Louis, Minn...C6 99
Gilbert, Multnomah, Oreg...*B4 113
Gilbert, Lexington, S.C...D5 115
Gilbert, Mingo, W. Va...D3 123
Gilbert, riv., Austl...C7 50
Gilbert, riv., Newf., Can...B3 75
Gilbert Plains, Man., Can...D1 71
Gilberton, Schuylkill, Pa...*E9 114
Gilbertown, Choctaw, Ala...D1 78
Gilbertsville, Marshall, Ky...A3 94
Gilbertsville, Otsego, N.Y...C5 108
Gilbertsville, Montgomery, Pa...F10 114
Gilbertville, Black Hawk, Iowa...B5 92
Gilbertville, Worcester, Mass...B3 97
Gilboa, Cheshire, N.H...E2 105
Gilboa, Putnam, Ohio...A2 111
Gilby, Grand Forks, N. Dak...A8 110
Gilchrist, Klamath, Oreg...D5 113
Gilchrist, co., Fla...C4 86
Gilcrest, Weld, Colo...A6 83
Gildford, Hill, Mont...B6 102
Gilead, Tolland, Conn...C7 84
Gilead, Oxford, Maine...D2 96
Gilead, Thayer, Nebr...D8 103
Giles, co., Tenn...B4 117
Giles, co., Va...C2 121
Gilford, Balknap, N.H...C4 105
Gilford, N. Ire...C5 11
Gilford, isl., B.C., Can...D4 68
Gilford Park, Ocean, N.J...*D4 106
Gilgandra, Austl...F8 51
Gilgit, Pak...A5 39
Gill, Weld, Colo...A6 83
Gill (Town of), Franklin, Mass...*A2 97
Gill, lake, Ire...C3 11
Gillam, Man., Can...A4 71
Gilleleje, Den...B6 24
Gillen, lake, Austl...E3 50
Gillespie, Macoupin, Ill...D4 90
Gillespie, co., Tex...D3 118
Gillespie, dam, Ariz...D3 80
Gillet, Manatee, Fla...p10 86
Gillett, Arkansas, Ark...C4 81
Gillett, Bradford, Pa...C8 114
Gillett, Karnes, Tex...k8 118
Gillett, Oconto, Wis...D5 124
Gillette, Campbell, Wyo...B7 125
Gillett Grove, Clay, Iowa...A2 92
Gillham, Sevier, Ark...C1 81
Gilliam, Caddo, La...B2 95
Gilliam, Saline, Mo...B4 101
Gilliam, co., Oreg...B6 113
Gillingham, Eng...E7 12
Gillsburg, Amite, Miss...D3 100
Gillis Point, N.S., Can...C9 74
Gilly, Bel...D4 15
Gilman, Eagle, Colo...B4 83
Gilman, New London, Conn...C8 84
Gilman, Iroquois, Ill...C5 90
Gilman, Marshall, Iowa...C5 92
Gilman, Benton, Minn...E5 99
Gilman, Essex, Vt...C5 120
Gilman, Taylor, Wis...C3 124
Gilman City, Harrison, Mo...A4 101
Gilmanton, Belknap, N.H...D4 105
Gilmanton, Buffalo, Wis...D2 124
Gilmanton Iron Works, Belknap, N.H...D4 105
Gilmer, Upshur, Tex...C5 118
Gilmer, Gilmer, W. Va...C4 123
Gilmer, co., Ga...B2 87
Gilmer, co., W. Va...C4 123
Gilmore, Crittenden, Ark...B5 81
Gilmore City, Humboldt, Iowa...B3 92
Gilmour, Ont., Can...C7 72
Gilo, riv., Eth...D3 47
Gilpin, Casly, Ky...C5 94
Gilpin, co., Colo...B5 83
Gilroy, Santa Clara, Calif...D3 82
Gilroy, Sask., Can...G2 70
Gilson, Knox, Ill...C3 90
Gilsum, Cheshire, N.H...D2 105
Giltner, Hamilton, Nebr...D7 103
Gima, Okinawa... 52
Gimli, Man., Can...D3 71
Gingoog, Phil...*D6 35
Ginir, Eth...D5 47
Ginosa, It...D6 21
Ginzo, Sp...A2 20
Gioia del Colle, It...D6 21
Gioiosa Ionica, It...E6 21
Gi-Paraná, riv., Braz...E2 59
Gipsera, Switz...C3 19
Girard, Burke, Ga...C5 87
Girard, Macoupin, Ill...D4 90
Girard, Crawford, Kans...E9 93
Girard, Richland, La...B4 95
Girard, Trumbull, Ohio...A5 111
Girard, Erie, Pa...C1 114
Girard, Kent, Tex...C2 118
Girardot, Col...C3 60
Girardville, Schuylkill, Pa...E9 114
Girdletree, Worcester, Md...D7 85
Gireh, mtn., Iran...H8 41
Giresun (Kerasund), Tur...B12 31
Giri, riv., Zaire...A2 48
Giridih, India...E11 40
Girna, riv., India...G5 40
Giromagny, Fr...D7 14
Girón, Ec...B2 58
Gironde, dept., Fr...*E3 14
Gironde, riv., Fr...E3 14
Giroux, Man., Can...E3 71
Girouxville, Alta., Can...B2 69
Girvan, Scot...E4 13
Girvin, Sask., Can...F3 70
Girvin, Pecos, Tex...D1 118
Gisborne, N.Z...M17 51
Gisborne, lake, Newf., Can...E4 75
Giscome, B.C., Can...B6 68
Gisenyi, Rwanda...B4 48
Gislaved, Swe...A7 24
Gisors, Fr...C4 14
Gitano, Jones, Miss...D4 100
Gitega, Burundi...B4 48
Giulianova, It...C4 21
Giurgiu, Rom...D7 22
Giv'atayim, Isr...g10 32
Give, Den...C3 24
Givet, Fr...B6 14
Givhans, Dorchester, S.C...E7, h11 115
Givors, Fr...E6 14
Givry, isl., Turk... 52
Gizāb, Afg...E13 41
Gizhduvan, Sov. Un...A12 41
Gizhiga, Sov. Un...C19 28
Gizycko, Pol...A6 26
Gjinokaster, Alb...B3 23
Gjinokaster, pref., Alb...*B3 23
Gjoa Haven, N.W. Ter., Can...C13 66
Gjövik, Nor...G4 25
Glace Bay, N.S., Can...C10 74
Glacier, B.C., Can...D9 68
Glacier, Whatcom, Wash...A4 122
Glacier, co., Mont...B2 102
Glacier, bay, Alsk...k21 79
Glacier, nat. park, B.C., Can...D9 68
Glacier, nat. park, Mont...B2 102
Glacier, peak, Wash...A4 122
Glacier Bay, nat. park, Alsk...D12 79
Gladbeck, F.R.G...B1 17
Gladbrook, Tama, Iowa...B5 92
Glade, Phillips, Kans...C4 93
Glade, Catahoula, La...C4 95
Glade, creek, W. Va...n14 123
Glade Park, Mesa, Colo...B2 83
Glades, co., Fla...F5 86
Glade Spring, Washington, Va...f10 121
Glade Valley, Alleghany, N.C...A1 109
Gladeville, Wilson, Tenn...A5 117
Gladewater, Gregg and Upshur, Tex...C5 118
Gladmar, Sask., Can...H3 70
Gladsakse, Den...*C6 24
Gladstone, Austl...A8 51
Gladstone, Man., Can...D2 71
Gladstone, Henderson, Ill...C3 90
Gladstone, Delta, Mich...C3 98
Gladstone, Clay, Mo...h10 101
Gladstone, Jefferson, Nebr...D8 103
Gladstone (Peapack-Gladstone), Somerset, N.J...B3 106
Gladstone, Union, N. Mex...A6 107
Gladstone, Stark, N. Dak...C3 110
Gladstone, Clackamas, Oreg...B4, h12 113
Gladstone, Nelson, Va...C4 121
Glad Valley, Ziebach, S. Dak...B4 116
Gladwin, Gladwin, Mich...E6 98
Gladwin, co., Mich...D6 98
Gladwyne, Montgomery, Pa...*F11 114
Glady, Randolph, W. Va...C5 123
Gladys, Campbell, Va...C3 121
Glåma, riv., Nor...G5, p29 25
Glamis, Sask., Can...F2 70
Glamoč, Yugo...C3 22
Glamorgan, co., Wales...C4 12
Glan, Phil...*D7 35
Glan, lake, Swe...u33 25
Glan, riv., F.R.G...D2 17
Glancy, Copiah, Miss...D3 100
Gland, Switz...D1 19
Glandorf, Putnam, Ohio...A1 111
Glanshammar, Swe...t33 25
Glarnisch, mtn., Switz...C6 19
Glarus, Switz...B7 19
Glarus, canton, Switz...C7 19
Glarus Alps, mts., Switz...C6 19
Glasco, Cloud, Kans...C6 93
Glasco, Ulster, N.Y...C7 108
Glascock, co., Ga...C4 87
Glasford, Peoria, Ill...C4 90
Glasgo, New London, Conn...C9 84
Glasgow, Barren Ky...C4 94
Glasgow, Howard, Mo...B5 101
Glasgow, Valley, Mont...B10 102
Glasgow, Scot...E4 13
Glasgow, Rockbridge, Va...C3 121
Glasgow, Kanawha, W. Va...m13 123
Glaslyn, Sask., Can...D1 70
Glasnevin, Sask., Can...H3 70
Glass, butte, Oreg...D6 113
Glass, Obion, Tenn...A2 117
Glass, mts., Tex...o13 118
Glassboro, Gloucester, N.J...D2 106
Glasscock, co., Tex...D2 118
Glassport, Allegheny, Pa...F2 114
Glasston, Pembina, N. Dak...A8 110
Glastenbury, mtn., Vt...F2 120
Glastonbury, Hartford, Conn...C6 84
Glastonbury, Eng...E5 12
Glauchau, G.D.R...C7 17
Glazier, Hemphill, Tex...A2 118
Glazier, lake, Maine...A3 96
Glazov, Sov. Un...B4 29
Glazypeau, mtn., Ark...f7 81
Gleason, Weakley, Tenn...A3 117
Gleason, Lincoln, Wis...C4 124
Gleasondale, Middlesex, Mass...g9 97
Gleichen, Alta., Can...D4 69
Glen, Beaverhead, Mont...E4 102
Glen, Sioux, Nebr...B2 103
Glen, Carroll, N.H...B4 105
Glen, canyon, Utah...G4 119
Glen, lake, Mich...D5 98
Glenada, Lane, Oreg...D2 113
Glenade, Ire...C3 11
Glen Alice, Roane, Tenn...D9 117
Glen Allan, Washington, Miss...B2 100
Glen Allen, Fayette, Ala...B2 78
Glenallen, Bollinger, Mo...D7 101
Glenallen, Henrico, Va...D5 121
Glen Almond, Que., Can...D2 73
Glen Alpine, Burke, N.C...B1, f11 109
Glenamoy, Ire...C2 11
Glénans, is., Fr...D1 14
Glen Arbor, Leelanau, Mich...D4 98
Glenarden, Prince Georges, Md...*C4 85
Glenarm, N. Ire...C6 11
Glenavon, Sask., Can...G4 70
Glen Avon Heights, Riverside, Calif...*F5 82
Glenbain, Sask., Can...H2 70
Glenbarr, Scot...E3 13
Glenbeigh, Ire...E2 11
Glenbeulah, Sheboygan, Wis...k9 124
Glenboro, Man., Can...E2 71
Glenbrook, Douglas, Nev...D2 104
Glenburn, Renville, N. Dak...A4 110

GRAN-GREI 95X

Grand Bay, N.B., Can......D3 74
Grand Bayou, Red River, La......B2 95
Grand Beach, Man., Can....D3 71
Grand Bend, Ont., Can.....D3 72
Grand Blanc, Genesee, Mich.F7 98
Grand Bonhomme, mtn., St. Vincent......U26 65
Grand Bostonnais, lake, Que., Can......B5 73
Grand-Bourg, Guad.......R9 65
Grand Bruit, Newf., Can....E2 75
Grand Cane, De Soto, La....B2 95
Grand Canyon, Coconino, Ariz......A3 80
Grand Canyon, nat. park, Ariz......B3 80
Grand Centre, Alta., Can....B5 69
Grand Cess, Lib.........F3 45
Grand Chenier, Cameron, La......E3 95
Grand Combin, mtn., Switz....E3 19
Grand Coteau, St. Landry, La......D3 95
Grand Coulee, Grant, Wash..B6 122
Grand Coulee, canyon, Wash...B6 122
Grand Coulee, dam, Wash.....B6 122
Grande, bay, Arg.........E3 54
Grande, hills, Ur.........f8 54
Grande, isl., Braz.........h5 56
Grande, mts., Mex........G2 118
Grande, riv., Arg.........B3 54
Grande, riv., Bol.........C3 55
Grande, riv., Braz.........B2 56
Grande, riv., Braz.........D2 57
Grande, riv., Braz.........D2 55
Grande, riv., Chile.........D2 55
Grande, riv., Nic.........D6 62
Grande, riv., Pan.........k11 62
Grande, riv. mouth, Ven......B5 60
Grande-Anse, N.B., Can.....B4 74
Grande Cache, Alta., Can....C1 69
Grande Catwick, is., Viet.....G8 38
Grande de Arecibo, riv., P.R....B2 65
Grande de Santiago, riv., Mex.m11 63
Grande-Digue, N.B., Can....C5 74
Grand-Entrée, Que., Can.....B8 74
Grande-Greve, Que., Can....A4 73
Grande-Ligne, Que., Can....D4 73
Grande Prairie, Alta., Can......B1, f7 69
Grand Erg Occidental, sand dunes, Alg......C5 44
Grand Erg Oriental, sand dunes, Alg......D6 44
Grande Rivière, Que., Can.*k14 73
Grande Ronde, riv., Oreg., Wash......B9 113
Grandes-Bergeronnes, Que., Can......A8 73
Grandes Piles, Que., Can....C5 73
Grand-Étang, N.S., Can.....C8 74
Grande-Terre, isl., Guad.....Q9 65
Grande Vigie, pt., Guad.......P9 65
Grand Falls, N.B., Can......B2 74
Grand Falls, Newf., Can.....D4 75
Grandfalls, Ward, Tex.......D1 118
Grand Falls, lake, Maine.....C5 96
Grandfather, mtn., N.C.......A1 109
Grandfield, Tillman, Okla....C3 112
Grand Forks, B.C., Can.....E8 68
Grand Forks, Grand Forks, N. Dak......B8 110
Grand Forks, co., N. Dak....B8 110
Grand Gorge, Delaware, N.Y......C6 108
Grand Gulf, Claiborne, Miss.C2 100
Grand Harbour, N.B., Can..E3 74
Grand Haven, Ottawa, Mich.E4 98
Grand Hogback, mtn., Colo....B3 83
Grandin, Putnam, Fla......C5 86
Grandin, Carter, Mo.......E7 101
Grandin, Cass, N. Dak.....B9 110
Grand Island, Hall, Nebr....D7 103
Grand Isle, Jefferson, La....E6 95
Grand Isle, Aroostook, Maine......A4 96
Grand Isle, Grand Isle, Vt...B2 120
Grand Isle, co., Vt.........B2 120
Grand Junction, Mesa, Colo.B2 83
Grand Junction, Kootenai, Idaho......D8 122
Grand Junction, Greene, Iowa......B3 92
Grand Junction, Van Buren, Mich......F4 98
Grand Junction, Hardeman, Tenn......B2 117
Grand lac Bostonnais, lake, Que., Can......B5 73
Grand-Lahou, I.C.........E3 45
Grand Lake, Grand, Colo....A5 83
Grand Lake, Cameron, La....D2 95
Grand Lake Stream, Washington, Maine......C5 96
Grand Ledge, Eaton, Mich..F6 98
Grand-Lieu, lake, Fr........D3 14
Grand Manan, chan., Can., U.S......E3 74
Grand Manan, isl., N.B., Can...E3 74
Grand Marais, Alger, Mich..B5 98
Grand Marais, Cook, Minn..k9 99
Grand Marsh, Adams, Wis..E4 124
Grand Meadow, Mower, Minn......G6 99
Grand'Mère, Que., Can.....C5 73
Grand Mound, Clinton, Iowa......C7 92
Grândola, Port............C1 20
Grand Pass, Saline, Mo......B4 101
Grand Portage, Cook, Minn.k10 99
Grand Portage, Indian res., Minn......k10 99
Grand Prairie, Dallas, Tex..n10 118
Grand-Pré, N.S., Can......D5 74
Grand Rapids, Man., Can...C2 71
Grand Rapids, Kent, Mich..F5 98
Grand Rapids, Itasca, Minn.C5 99
Grand Rapids, La Moure, N. Dak......C7 110
Grand Rapids, Wood, Ohio......A2, f6 111
Grand Ridge, Jackson, Fla...B1 86
Grand Ridge, LaSalle, Ill....B5 90
Grand River, N.S., Can......D9 74
Grand River, Decatur, Iowa.D4 92
Grand River, val., Colo., Utah......B2 83
Grand Rivers, Livingston, Ky.f9 94
Grand' Rivière, Mart........S10 65
Grand St. Bernard, pass, Switz., It......D3 18
Grand Saline, Van Zandt, Tex......C5 118
Grand Seboeis, lake, Maine....B4 96
Grandson, Switz...........E3 19
Grand Terrace, San Bernardino, Calif......*E5 82
Grand Terre, is., La.........E6 95
Grand Teton, mtn., Wyo.....C2 125
Grand Teton, nat. park, Wyo...C2 125
Grand Tower, Jackson, Ill...F4 90
Grand Traverse, co., Mich..D5 98
Grand Traverse, bay, Mich.....C5 98
Grand Valley, Ont., Can.....D4 72
Grand Valley, Garfield, Colo.B2 83
Grand Valley Warren Pa...C2 114
Grandview, Man., Can......D1 71
Grand View, Owyhee, Idaho......G2 89
Grandview, Edgar, Ill.......D6 90
Grandview, Sangamon, Ill..*D4 90
Grand View, Spencer, Ind....I4 91
Grandview, Louisa, Iowa....C6 92
Grandview, Jackson, Mo......C3, k10 101
Grandview, Cherokee, N.C....f8 109
Grandview, Washington, Ohio......C4 111
Grandview, Jefferson, Oreg..C5 113
Grandview, Rhea, Tenn......D9 117
Grandview, Johnson, Tex...*C4 118
Grandview, Yakima, Wash..C6 122
Grandview, Bayfield, Wis....B2 124
Grandview Heights, Franklin, Ohio......m10 111
Grandview Heights, Lancaster, Pa......*F9 114
Grandville, Kent, Mich......F5 98
Grandvilliers, Fr...........E1 15
Grand Vu, Grand, Utah....*E6 119
Grand Wash, cliffs, Ariz......A2 80
Grandy, Isanti, Minn.......E5 99
Grandy, Currituck, N.C.....A7 109
Grangärde, Swe...........G6 25
Grange, Sharp, Ark........B4 81
Grange, Eng..............F6 13
Grangeburg, Houston, Ala...D4 78
Grangemont, Clearwater, Idaho......C2 89
Grangemouth, Scot.........D5 13
Granger, St. Joseph, Ind....A5 91
Granger, Dallas, Iowa....C4, e8 92
Granger, Scotland, Mo......A6 101
Granger, Williamson, Tex...D4 118
Granger, Salt Lake, Utah..*C4 119
Granger, Yakima, Wash.....C5 122
Granger, Sweetwater, Wyo...E3 125
Granges, Fr...............A2 18
Grangeville, Idaho, Idaho...D2 89
Grangeville, St. Helena, La..D5 95
Grangeville, York, Pa.......*G8 114
Granite, Chaffee, Colo......B4 83
Granite, Greer, Okla........C2 112
Granite, Salt Lake, Utah...*C4 119
Granite, co., Mont.........D3 102
Granite, hbr., Ant..........e39 5
Granite, mtn., Ark..........k10 81
Granite, mts., Ariz.........E2 80
Granite, pass, Wyo.........B5 125
Granite, peak, Mont........E7 102
Granite, peak, Nev.........C2 104
Granite, peak, Utah........C2 119
Granite, peak, Utah........E3 119
Granite, peak, Wyo.........D4 125
Granite, pt., Newf., Can.....C3 75
Granite, range, Nev.........C2 104
Granite Canon, Laramie, Wyo......E7 125
Granite City, Madison, Ill...E3 90
Granite Falls, Yellow Medicine and Chippewa, Minn......F3 99
Granite Falls, Caldwell, N.C.B1 109
Granite Falls, Snohomish, Wash......A4 122
Granite Park, Salt Lake, Utah......*C4 119
Granite Quarry, Rowan, N.C......B2 109
Graniteville, Middlesex, Mass......f10 97
Graniteville, Iron, Mo......D7 101
Graniteville, Aiken, S.C.....D4 115
Graniteville, Washington, Vt.C4 120
Granja, Braz.............B2 57
Granja de Torrehermosa, Sp.C3 20
Grannis, Polk, Ark.........C1 81
Grano, Renville, N. Dak....A4 110
Granollers, Sp.............B7 20
Gran Quivira, nat. mon., N. Mex......C3 107
Gran Sabana, plat., Ven......B5 60
Gransee, G.D.R............F7 24
Grant, Marshall, Ala........A3 78
Grant, Park, Colo..........B5 83
Grant, Brevard, Fla.........E6 86
Grant, Montgomery, Iowa...C3 92
Grant, Allen, La...........D3 95
Grant, Newaygo, Mich.......E5 98
Grant, Beaverhead, Mont....F3 102
Grant, Perkins, Nebr.......D4 103
Grant, Choctaw, Okla.......D6 112
Grant, co., Ark............C3 81
Grant, co., Ind............C6 91
Grant, co., Kans...........E2 93
Grant, co., Ky.............B5 94
Grant, co., Minn...........E2 99
Grant, co., Nebr...........C4 103
Grant, co., N. Mex.........E1 107
Grant, co., N. Dak.........C4 110
Grant, co., Okla...........A4 112
Grant, co., Oreg...........C7 113
Grant, co., S. Dak.........B8 116
Grant, co., Wash..........B6 122
Grant, co., W. Va..........B5 123
Grant, co., Wis............F3 124
Grant, par., La............C3 95
Grant, mtn., Nev...........D4 104
Grant, mtn., Nev...........E3 104
Grant, range, Nev..........E6 104
Grant City, Worth, Mo......A3 101
Grantham, Eng.............B7 12
Grantham, Sullivan, N.H....D2 105
Granton, Ont., Can.........D3 72
Granton, Clark, Wis........D3 124
Grant Orchards, Grant, Wash......B6 122
Grantown-on-Spey, Scot......C5 13
Grant Park, Kankakee, Ill...B6 90
Grants, Valencia, N. Mex....B2 107
Grantsboro, Pamlico, N.C....B6 109
Grantsburg, Crawford, Ind...H5 91
Grantsburg, Burnett, Wis....C1 124
Grantsdale, Ravalli, Mont....D2 102
Grants Lick, Campbell, Ky.k14 94
Grants Pass, Josephine, Oreg.E3 113
Grants Pass Southwest, Josephine, Oreg......*E3 113
Grantsville, Garrett, Md.....k12 85
Grantsville, Tooele, Utah....C3 119
Grantsville, Calhoun, W. Va.C3 123
Grant Town, Marion, W. Va......B4, h10 123
Grantville Coweta, Ga.......C2 87
Grantville, Jefferson, Kans..k14 93
Grantville, Dauphin, Pa.....F8 114
Granum, Alta., Can.........E4 69
Granville, Greenlee, Ariz...*D6 80
Granville, Fr...............C3 14
Granville, Putnam, Ill.......B4 90
Granville, Sioux, Iowa.......B2 92
Granville, Hampden, Mass..B2 97
Granville, Washington, N.Y..B7 108
Granville, McHenry, N. Dak.A5 110
Granville, Licking, Ohio.....B3 111
Granville, Jackson, Tenn....C8 117
Granville, Addison, Vt......D3 120
Granville, co., N.C.........A4 109
Granville, lake, Man., Can.....A1 71
Granville Centre, N.S., Can..E4 74
Granville Ferry, N.S., Can...E4 74
Grão Mogol, Braz..........E2 57
Grapeland, Houston, Tex....D5 118
Grapeview, Mason, Wash....B3 122
Grapeville, Westmoreland, Pa......*F2 114
Grapevine, Hopkins, Ky.....C2 94
Grapevine, Tarrant, Tex.C4, n9 118
Grapevine Lake, res., Tex.......n9 118
Grasmere, Owyhee, Idaho...G3 89
Grasonville, Queen Annes, Md......C5 85
Grass, isl., Fla.............C3 86
Grass, lake, Ill.............h8 90
Grass, riv., Man., Can.......B2 71
Grass, riv., N.Y............f9 108
Grasscreek, Fulton, Ind.....C5 91
Grass Creek, Hot Springs, Wyo......C4 125
Grasse, Fr................F7 16
Grasselli, Jefferson, Ala...B3, g7 78
Grassflat, Clearfield, Pa.....D5 114
Grassington, Eng...........F7 13
Grass Lake, Lake, Ill........h8 90
Grass Lake, Jackson, Mich...F6 98
Grassrange, Fergus, Mont....C8 102
Grass River, prov. park, Man., Can......B1 71
Grasston, Kanabec, Minn....E5 99
Grass Valley, Nevada, Calif..C3 82
Grass Valley, Sherman, Oreg.B6 113
Grassy, brook, Vt...........E3 120
Grassy, lake, La............k9 95
Grassy, mtn., Oreg.........D2 113
Grassy Butte, McKenzie, N. Dak......B2 110
Grassy Creek, Ashe, N.C....A1 109
Grassy Knob, mtn., Mo.......D8 101
Grassy Lake, Alta., Can.....E5 69
Grates, pt., Newf., Can......D5 75
Grates Cove, Newf., Can....D5 75
Gratiot, Licking and Muskingum, Ohio......C3 111
Gratiot, Lafayette, Wis.....F3 124
Gratiot, co., Mich..........E6 98
Gratis, Preble, Ohio........C1 111
Graton, Sonoma, Calif......*C2 82
Gratz, Dauphin, Pa.........E8 114
Graubünden, canton, Switz...C7 19
Graue Hörner, mtn., Switz......C7 19
Graulhet, Fr...............F5 14
Gravatá, Braz..........C3, k6 57
Grave, creek, W. Va.........g8 123
Grave, peak, Idaho.........C4 89
Gravelbourg, Sask., Can....H2 70
Gravelines, Fr.............D10 12
Gravelly, Yell, Ark.........C2 81
Gravelly, range, Mont.......E4 102
Gravelridge, Bradley, Ark...D3 81
Gravenhurst, Ont., Can.....C5 72
Graves, Terrell, Ga........E2 87
Graves, Georgetown, S.C.....E9 115
Graves, co., Ky............f9 94
Graves, The, is., Mass.......g12 97
Gravesend, Eng............C8 12
Gravesend, bay, N.Y.........k8 106
Gravesville, Calumet, Wis....h9 124
Gravette, Benton, Ark.......A1 81
Gravina [in Puglia], It......D6 21
Gravity, Taylor, Iowa.......D3 92
Gravois, pt., Hai............E7 64
Gravois Mills, Morgan, Mo..C5 101
Grawn, Grand Traverse, Mich......D5 98
Gray, Sask., Can...........G3 70
Gray, Fr..................D6 14
Gray, Jones, Ga............C3 87
Gray, Audubon, Iowa.......C3 92
Gray, Knox, Ky.............D5 94
Gray, Terrebonne, La.......k10 95
Gray, Cumberland, Maine....g7 96
Gray, Somerset, Pa.........f3 114
Gray, co., Kans............E3 93
Gray, co., Tex.............B2 118
Gray Court, Laurens, S.C....B3 115
Gray Horse, Osage, Okla....A5 112
Grayland, Grays Harbor, Wash......C1 122
Grayling, Alsk.............C7 79
Grayling, Crawford, Mich...D6 98
Grayridge, Stoddard, Mo....E8 101
Grays, Eng................m13 10
Grays, Jasper, S.C..........F5 115
Grays, harbor, Wash.........C1 122
Grays, lake, Idaho..........F7 89
Grays, peak, Colo...........B5 83
Grays Branch, Greenup, Ky..B7 94
Grays Harbor, co., Wash....B2 122
Grayslake, Lake, Ill.....A5, h8 90
Grayson, Winston, Ala.......A2 78
Grayson, Sask., Can........G4 70
Grayson, Gwinnett, Ga...C3, h9 87
Grayson, Carter, Ky........B7 94
Grayson, Caldwell, La......B3 95
Grayson, Okmulgee, Okla...B6 112
Grayson, co., Ky...........C3 94
Grayson, co., Tex..........C4 118
Grayson, co., Va...........D1 121
Grays River, Wahkiakum, Wash......C2 122
Gray Station, Cumberland, Maine......E5 96
Gray Summit, Franklin, Mo..f12 101
Graysville, Jefferson, Ala....f7 78
Graysville, Monroe, Ohio....C4 111
Graysville, Greene, Pa......G1 114
Graysville, Rhea, Tenn......D8 117
Grayville, White and Edwards, Ill......E5 90
Graz, Aus.................E7 16
Greasewood, Navajo, Ariz...B6 80
Great, basin, U.S...........C4 76
Great, bay, N.H............D5 105
Great, bay, N.J............D4 106
Great, chan., India..........G9 39
Great, isl., Mass............D7 97
Great, isl., N.C............B6 109
Great, lake, Austl..........o15 50
Great, pt., Mass............D7 97
Great, pond, Maine..........D3 96
Great, pond, Mass...........h11 97
Great, pond, Mass...........h12 97
Great, riv., Jam............E13 65
Great, sound, Bermuda......p19 64
Great, swamp, N.C..........C4 109
Great, val., U.S.......B3 106, f9 117
Great Abaco, isl., Ba........A5 64
Great Alföld, reg., Hung.....B5 22
Great Artesian, basin, Austl...D7 50
Great Australian, bight, Austl...F5 50
Great Barrier, isl., N.Z.......L15 51
Great Barrier, reef, Austl.....C8 50
Great Barrington, Berkshire, Mass......B1 97
Great Basin, boundary, Nev..B4, E7 104
Great Basin, boundary, Oreg......D7, E5, E8 113
Great Basin, reg., Nev......C3, E3 104
Great Bear, lake, N.W. Ter., Can......C8 66
Great Bend, Barton, Kans...D5 93
Great Bend, Richland, N. Dak......C9 110
Great Bend, Susquehanna, Pa......C10 114
Great Bitter, lake, Eg........D4 32
Great Blasket, isl., Ire.......E1 11
Great Blue, hill, Mass........B5 97
Great Britain & Northern Ireland, see United Kingdom, country, Eur.
Great Burnt, lake, Newf., Can..D3 75
Great Cacapon, Morgan, W. Va......B6 123
Great Camanoe, isl., Vir. Is. (Br.).A7 65
Great Captain, isl., Conn......F2 84
Great Deer, Sask., Can......E2 70
Great Dismal, swamp, N.C., Va.A6 109
Great Divide, basin, Wyo......E4 125
Great Dividing, range, Austl......C7 50, E8 51
Great Duck, isl., Ont., Can....B2 72
Great East, pond, Maine.......E2 96
Great Egg Harbor, riv., N.J....D3 106
Greater Antilles, is., W.I.......B3 53
Greater Khingan, range, Asia..E14 33
Greater Leech Lake, Indian res., Minn......C4 99
Greater London (Metropolis), co., Eng......C7 12
Great Exuma, isl., Ba.........C6 64
Great Falls, Man., Can......D3 71
Great Falls, Cascade, Mont..C5 102
Great Falls, Chester, S.C....B6 115
Great Falls, dam, Tenn.......D8 117
Great Guana, isl., Ba.........B5 64
Great Harbour Deep, bay, Newf., Can......C3 75
Great Hog, neck, N.Y.........E7 84
Greathouse, peak, Mont.......D7 102
Great Inagua, isl., Ba.........D7 64
Great Indian, des., India......D3 40
Great Karroo, plat., S. Afr.....D3 49
Great Lakes, Lake, Ill.......E2 90
Great Meadows, Warren, N.J......B3 106
Great Mercury, isl., N.Z.......L15 51
Great Miami, riv., Ohio.......C1 111
Great Misery, isl., Mass.......f12 97
Great Natuna, isl., Indon......E3 35
Great Neck, Nassau, N.Y...h13 108
Great Neck, Nassau, N.Y...h13 108
Great Nicobar, isl., India......G9 39
Great North, mtn., Va.........B4 121
Great Paternoster, isl., Indon...G5 35
Great Peconic, bay, N.Y.......F6 84
Great Pedro Bluff, pt., Jam...F13 65
Great Pee Dee, riv., N.C., S.C..D9 115
Great Pond, Hancock, Maine......D4 96
Great Quittacas, pond, Mass....C6 97
Great Rann of Kutch, salt flat, India......F2 40
Great River, Suffolk, N.Y....G4 84
Great St. Bernard, pass, Switz...E3 19
Great Salt, lake, Utah........B3 119
Great Salt, pond, Jam.........F15 65
Great Salt, pond, R.I.........E10 84
Great Salt Lake, des., Utah....C2 119
Great Salt Plains Lake, res., Okla......A3 112
Great Sand, hills, Sask., Can...G1 70
Great Sand Dunes, nat. mon., Colo......D5 83
Great Sandy, des., Austl.......D3 50
Great Scandaga Lake, res., N.Y.B6 108
Great Sea, reef, Fiji.........I14 52
Great Seneca, creek, Md.......B3 85
Great Skellig, isl., Ire........F1 11
Great Slave, lake, N.W. Ter., Can......D10 66
Great Smoky, mts., N.C., Tenn......D2 109, D10 117
Great Smoky Mountains, nat. park, N.C., Tenn......D2 109, D10 117
Great South, bay, N.Y.........G4 84
Great South, beach, N.Y.......G5 84
Great Stone Face (Old Man of the Mountain), mtn., N.H......B3 105
Great Victoria, des., Austl......E4 50
Great Village, N.S., Can.....D6 74
Great Wall, wall, China.......B7 34
Great Wass, isl., Maine.......D5 96
Great Whale, riv., Que., Can...g11 73
Great Works, Somerset, Maine (part of Old Town)......D4 96
Great Yarmouth, Eng.........B9 12
Great Zab, riv., Iraq.........D14 31
Gredos, mts., Sp.............B3 20
Greece, Monroe, N.Y........B3 108
Greece, country, Eur......H13 8, C4 23
Greeley, Weld, Colo.........A6 83
Greeley, Delaware, Iowa....B6 92
Greeley, Anderson, Kans....D8 93
Greeley, Greeley, Nebr......C7 103
Greeley, Pike, Pa...........D12 114
Greeley, co., Kans.........D2 93
Greeley, co., Nebr..........C7 103
Greeleyville, Williamsburg, S.C......D8 115
Greely, fjord, N.W. Ter., Can..k34 67
Green, Clay, Kans...........C6 93
Green, Ontonagon, Mich...m12 98
Green, Douglas, Oreg........D3 113
Green, co., Ky..............C4 94
Green, co., Wis.............F4 124
Green, bay, Mich., Wis.......C3 98
Green, lake, B.C., Can.......D7 68
Green, lake, Sask., Can.......C2 70
Green, lake, Maine..........D4 96
Green, lake, Minn...........E4 99
Green, lake, Wis............E5 124
Green, mts., Vt.............F2 120
Green, mts., Wyo............D5 125
Green, pond, N.J............A4 106
Green, ridge, Colo...........A5 83
Green, riv., N.B., Can........B1 74
Green, riv., Ill.............B4 90
Green, riv., Ky..............C2 94
Green, riv., U.S.............D6 119
Green, riv., Vt..............F3 120
Green, riv., Wash...........B2 122
Green, swamp, N.C..........C4 109
Green, val., Tex............p13 118
Greenacres, Kern, Calif....*E4 82
Green Acres, Montgomery, Md......*C3 85
Green Acres, Coos, Oreg....D2 113
Greenacres, Spokane, Wash......B8, g14 122
Greenacres City, Palm Beach, Fla......F6 86
Greenback, Loudon, Tenn...D9 117
Green Bank, Burlington, N.J.D3 106
Green Bank, Pocahontas, W. Va......C5 123
Green Bay, Prince Edward, Va......C4 121
Green Bay, Brown, Wis D6, g10 124
Greenbelt, Prince Georges, Md......B4 85
Greenbrae, Marin, Calif...*D2 82
Greenbriar, Fairfax, Va....g12 121
Greenbrier, Limestone, Ala..A3 78
Greenbrier, Faulkner, Ark...B3 81
Greenbrier, Robertson, Tenn......A5 117
Greenbrier, co., W. Va......D4 123
Greenbrier, riv., W. Va.......D4 123
Green Brook, Somerset, N.J.*B4 106
Greenburr, Clinton, Pa......D7 114
Greenbush, Alcona, Mich...D7 98
Greenbush, Roseau, Minn...B2 99
Greenbush, Sheboygan, Wis..k9 124
Green Camp, Marion, Ohio..B2 111
Greencastle, Putnam, Ind....E4 91
Green Castle, Sullivan, Mo..A5 101
Greencastle, Franklin, Pa....G6 114
Green City, Sullivan, Mo....A5 101
Green Court, Alta., Can.....B3 69
Green Cove Springs, Clay, Fla......C5, n8 86
Greencreek, Idaho, Idaho....C2 89
Green Creek, Cape May, N.J.E3 106
Greendale, Dearborn, Ind...F8 91
Greendale, Milwaukee, Wis......F5, n11 124
Greendell, Sussex, N.J......B3 106
Greene, Butler, Iowa........B5 92
Greene, Androscoggin, Maine......D2 96
Greene, Chenango, N.Y......C5 108
Greene, Renville, N. Dak., 15.A4 110
Greene, Kent, R.I..........C10 84
Greene, co., Ala............C1 78
Greene, co., Ark............A5 81
Greene, co., Ga.............C3 87
Greene, co., Ill.............D3 90
Greene, co., Ind............F3 91
Greene, co., Iowa...........B3 92
Greene, co., Miss...........D5 100
Greene, co., Mo............D4 101
Greene, co., N.Y...........C6 108
Greene, co., N.C...........B5 109
Greene, co., Ohio...........C2 111
Greene, co., Pa.............G1 114
Greene, co., Tenn..........C11 117
Greene, co., Va.............B4 121
Greeneville, Greene, Tenn..C11 117
Greenfield, Monterey, Calif..D3 82
Greenfield, Greene, Ill......D3 90
Greenfield, Hancock, Ind....E6 91
Greenfield, Adair, Iowa.....C3 92
Greenfield, Penobscot, Maine......C4 96
Greenfield, Franklin, Mass...A2 97
Greenfield, Dade, Mo........D4 101
Greenfield, Hillsboro, N.H...E3 105
Greenfield, Chaves, N. Mex..D5 107
Greenfield, Highland, Ohio..C2 111
Greenfield, Blaine, Okla.....B3 112
Greenfield, Weakley, Tenn...A3 117
Greenfield, Nelson, Va......C4 121
Greenfield, Milwaukee, Wis.n12 124
Greenfield Hill, Fairfield, Conn......E3 84
Greenfield Park, Que., Can.q20 73
Greenfield Plaza, Warren, Iowa......e8 92
Green Forest, Carroll, Ark...A2 81
Green Garden, Marquette, Mich......B3 98
Green Grass, Dewey, S. Dak......B4 116
Green Harbor, Plymouth, Mass......B6 97
Green Haven, Anne Arundel, Md......*B4 85
Greenhill, Lauderdale, Ala..A2 78
Greenhill, Warren, Ind......D3 91
Green Hill, Washington, R.I......D10 84
Greenhills, Hamilton, Ohio.n12 111
Green Hills, Davidson, Tenn......*A5 117
Greenhorn, mtn., Colo.......D6 83
Green Island, Jackson, Iowa.B7 92
Green Island, Albany, N.Y.*C7 108
Green Isle, Sibley, Minn.....F4 99
Green Lake, Sask., Can......C2 70
Green Lake, Green Lake, Wis......E5 124
Green Lake, co., Wis.......E4 124
Greenland, Washington, Ark.B1 81
Greenland, Duval, Fla.......C6 86
Greenland, Ontonagon, Mich......m12 98
Greenland, Rockingham, N.H......D5 105
Greenland, Dan. dep., N.A......B20 4, B16 61
Greenland, sea, Eur..........B15 4
Greenlaw, Scot.............E6 13
Greenlawn, Suffolk, N.Y....F3 84
Greenleaf, Washington, Kans......C7 93
Greenleaf, Brown, Wis......h9 124
Greenlee, co., Ariz.........D6 80
Green Lowther, mtn., Scot......E5 13
Green Manorville, Hartford, Conn......*B6 84
Green Meadows, Prince Georges, Md......*C4 85
Greenmount, Carroll, Md....A4 85
Green Mountain, Marshall, Iowa......B5 92
Greenmountain, Yancey, N.C......f10 109
Green Mountain, res., Colo......B4 83
Greenock, Allegheny, Pa.....F2 114
Greenock, Scot.............C3 13
Greenough, Missoula, Mont.D3 102
Greenough, pt., Ont., Can.....C3 72
Green Peter Lake, res., Oreg...C4 113
Green Pond, Bibb, Ala.......B2 78
Green Pond, Colleton, S.C...F6 115
Green Pond, mtn., N.J.........B3 106
Greenport, Suffolk, N.Y....m16 108
Green Ridge, Pettis, Mo.....C4 101
Green River, Emery and Grand, Utah......D5 119
Green River, Windham, Vt..F3 120
Green River, Sweetwater, Wyo......E3 125
Green River, res., Vt.........B3 120
Green Rock, Henry, Ill......*B3 90
Greens, peak, Ariz..........C6 80
Greensboro, Hale, Ala......C2 78
Greensboro, Gadsden, Fla...B2 86
Greensboro, Greene, Ga.....C3 87
Greensboro, Henry, Ind.....E7 91
Greensboro, Caroline, Md...C6 85
Greensboro, Guilford, N.C..A3 109
Greensboro, Greene, Pa......F2 114
Greensboro, Orleans, Vt.....B4 120
Greensboro Bend, Orleans, Vt......B4 120
Greensburg, Decatur, Ind....F7 91
Greensburg, Kiowa, Kans....E4 93
Greensburg, Green, Ky......C4 94
Greensburg, St. Helena, La..D5 95
Greensburg, Westmoreland, Pa......F2 114
Greens Creek, Jackson, N.C...f9 109
Green Sea, Horry, S.C.....C10 115
Greens Farms, Fairfield, Conn......E3 84
Greens Fork, Wayne, Ind....E7 91
Green's Harbour, Newf., Can......*E5 75
Greenspond, Newf., Can....D5 75
Green Spring, Hampshire, W. Va......B6 123
Green Springs, Sandusky and Seneca, Ohio......A2 111
Greenstone, pt., Scot.........C3 13
Green Sulphur Springs, Summers, W. Va......D4 123
Greensville, co., Va.........D5 121
Greentop, Schuyler, Mo.....A5 101
Greentown, Howard, Ind....D6 91
Green Tree, Allegheny, Pa..*F1 114
Greenup, Cumberland, Ill...D5 90
Greenup, Greenup, Ky......B7 94
Greenup, co., Ky...........B7 94
Greenvale, Nassau, N.Y.....*F2 84
Green Valley, Tazewell, Ill..C4 90
Green Valley, Lyon, Minn...F3 99
Greenvalley, Shawano, Wis..D5 124
Greenview, Menard, Ill......C4 90
Greenview, Boone, W. Va...n12 123
Greenville, Butler, Ala......D3 78
Greenville, Plumas, Calif....B3 82
Greenville, Madison, Fla....B3 86
Greenville, Meriwether, Ga..C2 87
Greenville, Bond, Ill........E4 90
Greenville, Floyd, Ind.......H6 91
Greenville, Clay, Iowa.......A2 92
Greenville, Muhlenberg, Ky.C2 94
Greenville, Lib.............F3 45
Greenville, Piscataquis, Maine......C3 96
Greenville, Montcalm, Mich.E5 98
Greenville, Washington, Miss.B2 100
Greenville, Wayne, Mo.......D7 101
Greenville, Hillsboro, N.H...E3 105
Greenville, Greene, N.Y.....C6 108
Greenville, Westchester, N.Y......*D7 108
Greenville, Pitt, N.C........B5 109
Greenville, Darke, Ohio......B1 111
Greenville, Mercer, Pa.......D1 114
Greenville, Providence, R.I.B10 84
Greenville, Greenville, S.C..B3 115
Greenville, Hunt, Tex.......C4 118
Greenville, Beaver, Utah....E3 119
Greenville, Monroe, W. Va..D4 123
Greenville, Outagamie, Wis..h8 124
Greenville, co., S.C.........B3 115
Greenville, creek, Ohio........B1 111
Greenville Junction, Piscataquis, Maine......C3 96
Greenwald, Stearns, Minn...E4 99
Greenwater Lake, prov. park, Sask., Can......E4 70
Greenway, Clay, Ark........A5 81
Greenway, Man., Can.......E2 71
Greenway, McPherson, S. Dak......B6 116
Greenwich, Fairfield, Conn..E2 84
Greenwich, Eng. (part of London)......C7 12, m13 10
Greenwich, Sedgwick, Kans.g12 93
Greenwich, Cumberland, N.J......E2 106
Greenwich, Washington, N.Y......B7 108
Greenwich, Huron, Ohio.....A3 111
Greenwich, Piute, Utah.....E4 119
Greenwich, pt., Conn.........E2 84
Greenwich Hill, N.B., Can...D3 74
Greenwood, Jefferson, Ala...B3 78
Greenwood, Sebastian, Ark..B1 81
Greenwood, B.C., Can.......E8 68
Greenwood, Sussex, Del.....C6 85
Greenwood, Jackson, Fla.....B1 86
Greenwood, Johnson, Ind......E5, m10 91
Greenwood, McCreary, Ky..D5 94
Greenwood, Caddo, La.......B2 95
Greenwood, Leflore, Miss...B3 100
Greenwood, Jackson, Mo....k11 101
Greenwood, Cass, Nebr.D9, h12 103
Greenwood, Steuben, N.Y...C3 108
Greenwood, Blair, Pa........F5 114
Greenwood, Greenwood, S.C......C3 115
Greenwood, Charles Mix, S. Dak......E7 116
Greenwood, Clark, Wis......D3 124
Greenwood, co., Kans.......E7 93
Greenwood, co., S.C........C3 115
Greenwood, lake, Minn........C7 99
Greenwood, lake, N.J., N.Y....A4 106
Greenwood, lake, S.C.........C4 115
Greenwood Lake, Orange, N.Y......D6 108
Greenwood Mountain, Oxford, Maine......D2 96
Greer, Clearwater, Idaho....C2 89
Greer, Oregon, Mo..........E6 101
Greer, Greenville and Spartanburg, S.C......B3 115
Greer, co., Okla............C2 112
Greetsiel, F.R.G...........A7 15
Gregg, co., Tex.............C5 118
Gregoire, lake, Alta., Can......A5 69
Gregory, Livingston, Mich...F6 98
Gregory, Currituck, N.C.....A6 109
Gregory, Gregory, S. Dak...D6 116
Gregory, San Patricio, Tex.*F4 118
Gregory, co., S. Dak........D6 116
Gregory, lake, Austl.........E6 50
Gregory, range, Austl.........C6 50
Gregory, riv., Austl..........C6 50
Greifenhagen, see Gryfino, Pol.
Greifswald, G.D.R..........A6 16
Greifswalder, bay, G.D.R......D7 24
Gregory Bald, mtn., Tenn.....D10 117
Greig, Lewis, N.Y..........B5 108

H

Halifax, co., N.C. A5 109
Halifax, co., Va D4 121
Halifax, bay, Austl C8 50
Haliimaile, Maui, Haw C5 88
Halileh, cape, Iran G5 41
Halin (Oasis), Som D6 47
Haliri, riv., Iran H9 41
Halkirk, Alta., Can C4 69
Hall, Aus E5 16
Hall, Morgan, Ind E4 91
Hall, Granite, Mont D3 102
Hall, Ontario, N.Y C3 108
Hall, co., Ga B3 87
Hall, co., Nebr D7 103
Hall, co., Tex B2 118
Hall, basin, N.W. Ter., Can. . . k39 67
Hall, mtn., Wash A8 122
Hall, pen., N.W. Ter., Can. . . D19 67
Halladale, riv., Scot B5 13
Hallam, Lancaster, Nebr D9 103
Hallam, peak, B.C., Can C8 68
Halland, co., Swe B6 24
Hallandale, Broward, Fla G6, s13 86
Hallands Väderö, isl., Swe B6 24
Halla San, peak, Kor J3 37
Hallboro, Man., Can D2 71
Halldale, Waldo, Maine D3 96
Halle, Bel D4 15
Halle, F.R.G A3 17
Halle, G.D.R B6 17
Halleck, Elko, Nev C6 104
Hallein, Aus E6 16
Hällestad, Swe u33 25
Hallett, Pawnee, Okla A5 112
Hallett, cape, Ant B30 5
Hallettsville, Lavaca, Tex E4 118
Halley, Desha, Ark D4 81
Halley Bay, Br. scientific station, Ant B10 5
Halliday, Dunn, N. Dak B3 110
Hallie, Chippewa, Wis D2 124
Hall Meadow, brook, Conn B4 84
Hall Meadow Brook, res., Conn . B4 84
Hallock, Kittson, Minn B2 99
Hallowell, Cherokee, Kans . . . E9 93
Hallowell, Kennebeck, Maine D3 96
Halls, Lauderdale, Tenn B2 117
Halls, creek, Utah F5 119
Halls, stream, N.H f6 105
Hallsberg, Swe t33 25
Hallsboro, Columbus, N.C . . . C4 109
Halls Creek, Sumter, Ala C2 78
Hall's Creek, Austl C4 50
Halls Crossroads, Knox, Tenn n14 117
Halls Harbour, N.S., Can . . . D5 74
Halls Summit, Coffey, Kans . D8 93
Hallstead, Susquehanna, Pa . C10 114
Hall Summit, Red River, La . B2 95
Hallsville, Boone, Mo B5 101
Hallsville, Ross, Ohio C3 111
Hallsville, Harrison, Tex C5 118
Hallton, Elk, Pa D4 114
Halltown, Lawrence, Mo D4 101
Hallville, New London, Conn . D8 84
Hallwil, lake, Switz B5 19
Hallwood, Accomack, Va C7 121
Halma, Kittson, Minn B2 99
Halmahera, isl., Indon E7 35
Halmstad, Swe B6 24
Hals, Den B4 24
Halsell, Choctaw, Ala C1 78
Halsey, Thomas, Nebr C5 103
Halsey, Sussex, N.J A3 106
Halsey, Linn, Oreg C3 113
Halsö, isl., Swe A5 24
Halstad, Norman, Minn C2 99
Halstead, Eng C8 12
Halstead, Harvey, Kans . E6, g11 93
Haltern, F.R.G B2 17
Haltia, mtn., Fin., Nor C9 25
Halton, co., Ont., Can D4 72
Halton City, Tarrant, Tex . . *C4 118
Haltwhistle, Eng F6 13
Ham, Fr E3 15
Hama, Okinawa 52
Hamada, Jap I6 37
Hamadān, Iran D4 41
Hamāh, Syr E11 31
Hamahiga, isl., Okinawa 52
Hamamatsu, Jap I8, o16 37
Hamar, Eddy, N. Dak B7 110
Hamar, Nor G4 25
Hamatombetsu, Jap D11 37
Hambantota, Sri Lanka G7 39
Hamber, prov. park, B.C., Can . C8 68
Hamberg, Wells, N. Dak B6 110
Hamblen, co., Tenn C10 117
Hamburg, Ashley, Ark D4 81
Hamburg, New London, Conn D7 84
Hamburg, F.R.G . . . B5 16, E4 24
Hamburg, Calhoun, Ill D3 90
Hamburg, Fremont, Iowa D2 92
Hamburg, Franklin, Miss D2 100
Hamburg, Sussex, N.J A3 106
Hamburg, Erie, N.Y C2 108
Hamburg, Berks, Pa E10 114
Hamburg, Aiken, S.C E4 115
Hamburg, Marathon, Wis . . . C4 124
Hamburg, state, F.R.G E3 24
Hamburg, mts., N.J A3 106
Hamden, New Haven, Conn . D5 84
Hamden, Delaware, N.Y C6 108
Hamden, Vinton, Ohio C3 111
Häme, dept., Fin *G11 25
Hämeenlinna, Fin G11 25
Hamel, Madison, Ill f14 101
Hamel, Hennepin, Minn m11 99
Hameln, F.R.G A4 17
Hamer, Jefferson, Idaho F6 89
Hamer, Dillon, S.C C9 115
Hamersley, plat., Austl D2 50
Hamersville, Brown, Ohio . . . D2 111
Hamhŭng, Kor G3 37
Hami (Kumul) (Qomul), China C3 34
Hamill, Tripp, S. Dak D6 116
Hamilton, Marion, Ala A2 78
Hamilton, Alsk C7 79
Hamilton, Austl H4 51
Hamilton, Bermuda p20 64
Hamilton, Glenn, Calif C2 82
Hamilton, Ont., Can D5 72
Hamilton, Moffat, Colo A3 83
Hamilton, Harris, Ga D2 87
Hamilton, Hancock, Ill C2 90
Hamilton, Steuben, Ind A8 91
Hamilton, Marion, Iowa C5 92
Hamilton, Greenwood, Kans . E7 93
Hamilton, Boone, Ky k13 94
Hamilton, Essex, Mass . . A6, f12 97
Hamilton, Allegan, Mich F4 98
Hamilton, Monroe, Miss B5 100
Hamilton, Caldwell, Mo B3 101
Hamilton, Ravalli, Mont D2 102
Hamilton, Mercer, N.J *C3 106
Hamilton, Madison, N.Y C5 108
Hamilton, N.Z L15 51
Hamilton, Martin, N.C B5 109
Hamilton, Pembina, N. Dak . A8 110
Hamilton, Butler, Ohio . C1, n12 111
Hamilton, Grant, Oreg C7 113
Hamilton, Washington, R.I . C11 84
Hamilton, Scot E4 13
Hamilton, Hamilton, Tex D3 118
Hamilton, Loudoun, Va A5 121
Hamilton, Skagit, Wash A4 122
Hamilton, co., Fla B3 86
Hamilton, co., Ill E5 90
Hamilton, co., Ind D5 91
Hamilton, co., Iowa B4 92
Hamilton, co., Kans E2 93
Hamilton, co., Nebr D7 103
Hamilton, co., N.Y B6 108
Hamilton, co., Ohio C1 111
Hamilton, co., Tenn D8 117
Hamilton, co., Tex D3 118
Hamilton, inlet, Newf., Can . . . A2 75
Hamilton, lake, Ark g7 81
Hamilton, mtn., Alsk C8 79
Hamilton, mtn., Calif k9 82
Hamilton, mtn., Nev D6 104
Hamilton, mtn., N.Y B6 108
Hamilton, res., Mass B3 97
Hamilton, riv., Newf., Can h9 75
Hamilton, sound, Newf., Can . . D4 75
Hamilton Acres, Alsk *C7 79
Hamilton Dome, Hot Springs, Wyo C4 125
Hamilton Park, Lancaster, Pa *F9 114
Hamilton Square, Mercer, N.J C3 106
Hamina, Fin G12 25
Hamiota, Man., Can D1 71
Hamirpur, India C7 39
Hamirpur, India B6 40
Hamler, Henry, Ohio A1 111
Hamlet, Starke, Ind B4 91
Hamlet, Hayes, Nebr D4 103
Hamlet, Richmond, N.C C3 109
Hamletsburg, Pope, Ill F5 90
Hamlin, Audubon, Iowa C3 92
Hamlin, Brown, Kans C8 93
Hamlin, Wayne, Pa D11 114
Hamlin, Jones and Fisher, Tex C2 118
Hamlin, Lincoln, W. Va C2 123
Hamlin, co., S. Dak C8 116
Hamlin, lake, Mich D4 98
Hammamet, gulf, Tun F12 30
Hammam Lif, Tun B7 44
Ḩammār, lake, Iraq F3 41
Hammarby, Swe t35 25
Hammarsjön, lake, Swe C8 24
Hamme, Bel C4 15
Hammel, Den B3 24
Hammelburg, F.R.G C4 17
Hammer, Roberts, S. Dak . . . B8 116
Hammerfest, Nor B10 25
Hammett, Elmore, Idaho G3 89
Hamm [in Westfalen], F.R.G B2 17
Hammon, Roger Mills, Okla . B2 112
Hammonasset, pt., Conn E6 84
Hammonasset, riv., Conn D5 84
Hammond, Piatt, Ill D5 90
Hammond, Lake, Ind A2 91
Hammond, Tangipahoa, La D5, g11 95
Hammond, Wabasha, Minn . F6 99
Hammond, Carter, Mont . . . E12 102
Hammond, St. Lawrence, N.Y f9 108
Hammond, Clatsop, Oreg . . . A3 113
Hammond, St. Croix, Wis . . . D1 124
Hammond, bay, Mich C6 98
Hammond East, Tangipahoa, La *D5 95
Hammondsport, Steuben, N.Y C3 108
Hammondsville, Jefferson, Ohio e8 123
Hammonton, Atlantic, N.J . . D3 106
Hammeda, Swe B7 24
Ham-Nord, Que., Can D6 73
Hamoyet, mtn., Eth B4 47
Hampden, Newf., Can D3 75
Hampden, Penobscot, Maine . D4 96
Hampden, Hampden, Mass . . B3 97
Hampden, N.Z P13 51
Hampden, Ramsey, N. Dak . . A7 110
Hampden, co., Mass B2 97
Hampden Highlands, Penobscot, Maine D4 96
Hampshire, Kane, Ill A5 90
Hampshire, Maury, Tenn . . . B11 117
Hampshire, co., Eng C6 12
Hampshire (Hampshire), co., part, Eng *C6 12
Hampshire, co., Mass B2 97
Hampshire, co., W. Va B6 123
Hampshire Road, Rockingham, N.H E4 105
Hampstead, N.B., Can D3 74
Hampstead, Que., Can *D8 73
Hampstead, Eng. (part of London) k12 10
Hampstead, Carroll, Md A4 85
Hampstead, Rockingham, N.H E4 105
Hampstead, Pender, N.C C5 109
Hampton, Calhoun, Ark D3 81
Hampton, N.B., Can D4 74
Hampton, Windham, Conn . . B8 84
Hampton, Bradford, Fla C4 86
Hampton, Henry, Ga C2 87
Hampton, Rock Island, Ill . . g11 92
Hampton, Franklin, Iowa B4 92
Hampton, Livingston, Ky . . . A3 94
Hampton, Dakota, Minn F6 99
Hampton, Washington, Miss . B2 100
Hampton, Hamilton, Nebr . . D8 103
Hampton, Rockingham, N.H . E5 105
Hampton, Hunterdon, N.J . . . B3 106
Hampton, Washington, N.Y . B7 108
Hampton, Deschutes, Oreg . . D6 113
Hampton, Hampton, S.C F5 115
Hampton, Carter, Tenn C11 117
Hampton (Independent City), Va C6, h15 121
Hampton, Uinta, Wyo E2 125
Hampton, co., S.C F5 115
Hampton, butte, Oreg D6 113
Hampton Bays, Suffolk, N.Y n16 108
Hampton Beach, Rockingham, N.H E2 105
Hampton Falls, Rockingham, N.H E5 105
Hampton Roads, harbor, Va . . . k15 121
Hamrā, plat., Libya D2 43
Hams, fork, Wyo E2 125
Hamsfork, Lincoln, Wyo . . . *D2 125
Ham-Sud, Que., Can D6 73
Hamtramck, Wayne, Mich . . p15 98
Hāmūn-i-Māshkel, lake, Pak . . G11 41
Hāmūn-i-Mūrgho, lake, Pak . . H12 41
Hamyang, Kor I3 37
Hana, Maui, Haw C2 88
Hanahan, Berkeley, S.C . F7, k11 115
Hanalei, Kauai, Haw A2 88
Hanalei, bay, Haw A2 88
Hanamaulu, Kauai, Haw B2 88
Hanapepe, Kauai, Haw B2 88
Hanau, F.R.G C3 17
Hanceville, Cullman, Ala A3 77
Hanceville, B.C., Can D6 68
Hanchung, China H2 36
Hancock, Pottawattamie, Iowa C2 92
Hancock, Hancock, Maine . . . D4 96
Hancock, Washington, Md . . . A1 85
Hancock, Berkshire, Mass . . . A1 97
Hancock, Houghton, Mich . . . A2 98
Hancock, Stevens, Minn E3 99
Hancock, Hillsboro, N.H E3 105
Hancock, Delaware, N.Y D5 108
Hancock, Addison, Vt D3 120
Hancock, Morgan, W. Va B6 123
Hancock, Waushara, Wis D4 124
Hancock, co., Ga C3 87
Hancock, co., Ill C2 90
Hancock, co., Ind E6 91
Hancock, co., Iowa A4 92
Hancock, co., Ky C3 94
Hancock, co., Maine D4 96
Hancock, co., Miss E4 100
Hancock, co., Ohio A2 111
Hancock, co., Tenn C10 117
Hancock, co., W. Va A4 123
Hancock, mtn., N.H B3 105
Hancock, pond, Maine E2 96
Hancocks Bridge, Salem, N.J D2 106
Hand, co., S. Dak C6 116
Handa, Jap o15 37
Handa, isl., Scot B3 13
Handel, Sask., Can E1 70
Handeni, Tan C6 48
Handley, Kanawha, W. Va . m13 123
Hando, Som C7 47
Handsworth, Sask., Can H4 70
Hanegev, reg., Isr D6 32
Haney, B.C., Can E6, f13 68
Hanford, Kings, Calif D4 82
Hanford, Benton, Wash C6 122
Hanford Northwest, Kings, Calif *D4 82
Hangchou, China E8 34, I9 36
Hangchow, bay, China I9 36
Hangelsberg, G.D.R F7 24
Hanging Rock, Lawrence, Ohio D3 111
Hangingstone, riv., Alta., Can . . A5 69
Hangman, creek, Wash B8 122
Hangö, Fin H10 25
Haniqra, cape, Isr., Leb A7 32
Ḩanita, Isr A7 32
Hankinson, Claiborne, Miss . . C3 100
Hankinson, Richland, N. Dak C9 110
Hanks, Williams, N. Dak . . . A2 110
Hanksville, Wayne, Utah . . . E5 119
Hanley, Sask., Can F2 70
Hanley Falls, Yellow Medicine, Minn F3 99
Hanley Hills, St. Louis, Mo . *C7 101
Hanlontown, Worth, Iowa . . . A4 92
Hann, mtn., Austl C4 50
Hanna, Alta., Can D5 69
Hanna, LaPorte, Ind B4 91
Hanna, McIntosh, Okla B6 112
Hanna, Duchesne, Utah C5 119
Hanna, Carbon, Wyo E6 125
Hanna City, Peoria, Ill C4 90
Hannaford, Griggs, N. Dak . . B7 110
Hannagan, Greenlee, Ariz . . D6 80
Hannah, Cavalier, N. Dak . . A7 110
Hannawa Falls, St. Lawrence, N.Y f10 108
Hannibal, Marion and Ralls, Mo B6 101
Hannibal, Oswego, N.Y B4 108
Hannibal, Monroe, Ohio C5 111
Hannon, Macon, Ala C4 77
Hannover (Hanover), F.R.G A4 17
Hannover, Oliver, N. Dak . . B4 110
Hannoversch Münden, see Münden, F.R.G.
Hanöbukten, bay, Swe J6 25
Hanoi, Viet B6 38
Hanover, Stone, Ark B3 81
Hanover, Ont., Can C3 72
Hanover, New London, Conn C8 84
Hanover (Hannover), F.R.G A4 17
Hanover, Jo Daviess, Ill A3 90
Hanover, Jefferson, Ind G7 91
Hanover, Washington, Kans . C7 93
Hanover, Oxford, Maine D2 96
Hanover, Plymouth, Mass B6, h12 97
Hanover, Jackson, Mich F6 98
Hanover, Hennepin and Wright, Minn m11 99
Hanover, Fergus, Mont C7 102
Hanover, Grafton, N.H C2 105
Hanover, Grant, N. Mex E1 107
Hanover, Licking, Ohio B3 111
Hanover, York, Pa G8 114
Hanover, Hanover, Va C5 121
Hanover, Wyoming, W. Va . D3 123
Hanover, co., Va C5 121
Hanover, reg., F.R.G B4 16
Hanover, isl., Chile E2 54
Hanover Center, Plymouth, Mass h12 97
Hanover Green, Luzerne, Pa *D10 114
Hanover Park, Lake, Ill k8 90
Hanoverton, Columbiana, Ohio B5 111
Hansard, B.C., Can B7 68
Hansboro, Towner, N. Dak . A6 110
Hansell, Franklin, Iowa B4 92
Hansen, Twin Falls, Idaho . . G4 89
Hansford, co., Tex A2 118
Han Shui, riv., China E7 34
Hanska, Brown, Minn F4 99
Hanson, Madison, Fla B3 86
Hanson, Hopkins, Ky C2 94
Hanson, Plymouth, Mass B6 97
Hanson, Sequoyah, Okla B7 112
Hanson, co., S. Dak D8 116
Hanson, lake, Sask., Can C4 70
Hansted, see Hanstholm, Den.
Hanstholm (Hansted), Den . . A2 24
Hanston, Hodgeman, Kans . . D4 93
Hantachi, China A3 37
Hantan, China D7 34
Hants, co., N.S., Can D6 74
Hant's Harbour, Newf., Can . D5 75
Hantsport, N.S., Can D5 74
Haoching, China F5 34
Haparanda, Swe E11 25
Hapeville, Fulton, Ga . . . C2, h8 87
Happy, Randall and Swisher, Tex B2 118
Happy Camp, Siskiyou, Calif . B2 82
Happy Jack, Coconino, Ariz . C4 80
Happy Valley, Newf., Can B1, h9 75
Happy Valley, Eddy, N. Mex E5 107
Happy Valley, Clackamas, Oreg *B4 113
Hapsu, Kor F4 37
Ḩaql, Sau. Ar H10 31
Haque, Alachua, Fla C4 86
Häradsback, Swe B8 24
Harahan, Jefferson, La k11 95
Harald, isl., Sov. Un B32 4
Haralson, co., Ga C1 87
Harar (Harer), Eth D5 47
Harardera, Som E6 47
Hara Usa, lake, Mong B3 34
Haraze, Chad D4 46
Harbeson, Sussex, Del C7 85
Harbin (Haerhpin), China B10 34, D3 37
Harbinger, Currituck, N.C . . A7 109
Harbøør, Den B2 42
Harbor, Curry, Oreg E2 113
Harbor Beach, Huron, Mich . E7 98
Harborcreek, Erie, Pa B2 114
Harbor Isle, Nassau, N.Y . . *n15 108
Harbor Springs, Emmet, Mich C5 98
Harborton, Accomack, Va . . . C7 121
Harbor View, Lucas, Ohio . . . e7 111
Harbour Breton, Newf., Can . E4 75
Harbour Buffet, Newf., Can . E4 75
Harbour Deep, Newf., Can . . C3 75
Harbour Grace, Newf., Can . E5 75
Harbour Main, Newf., Can . . E5 75
Harbour Mille, Newf., Can . . E4 75
Harbourton, Mercer, N.J . . . C3 106
Harbourville, N.S., Can D5 74
Hårby, Den C4 24
Harcourt, N.B., Can C4 74
Harcourt, Webster, Iowa B3 92
Harcuvar, mts., Ariz D2 80
Harda, India F6 40
Hardangerfjorden, fjord, Nor . . H1 25
Hardangerjökelen, mtn., Nor . . G2 25
Hardangervidda, mts., Nor G2 25
Hardaway, Macon, Ala C4 78
Hardburly, Perry, Ky C6 94
Hardee, Issaquena, Miss C3 100
Hardee, co., Fla E5 86
Hardeeville, Beaufort and Jasper, S.C G5 115
Hardeman, co., Tenn B2 117
Hardeman, co., Tex B3 118
Hardenberg, Neth B6 15
Harden City, Pontotoc, Okla C5 112
Harderwijk, Neth B5 15
Hardesty, Texas, Okla e9 112
Hardin, Calhoun, Ill D3 90
Hardin, Marshall, Ky f9 94
Hardin, Ray, Mo B4 101
Hardin, Big Horn, Mont E9 102
Hardin, co., Ill F5 90
Hardin, co., Iowa B4 92
Hardin, co., Ky C4 94
Hardin, co., Ohio B2 111
Hardin, co., Tenn B3 117
Hardin, co., Tex D5 118
Harding, Randolph, W. Va . . C5 123
Harding, co., N. Mex B5 107
Harding, co., S. Dak B2 116
Harding, lake, Ala., Ga C4 78
Harding, lake, Man., Can A2 71
Hardinsburg, Washington, Ind H5 91
Hardinsburg, Breckinridge, Ky C3 94
Hardisty, Alta., Can C5 69
Hardisty, lake, N.W. Ter., Can D9 66
Hardman, Morrow, Oreg B7 113
Hardoi, India D8 40
Hardtner, Barber, Kans E5 93
Hardwār, India C7 40
Hardwick, Baldwin, Ga C3 87
Hardwick, Worcester, Mass . . B3 97
Hardwick, Rock, Minn G2 99
Hardwick, Caledonia, Vt B4 120
Hardwicke, N.B., Can B5 74
Hardy, Alg B5 44
Hardy, Sharp, Ark A4 81
Hardy, Sask., Can H3 70
Hardy, Pike, Ky C7 94
Hardy, Grenada, Miss B4 100
Hardy, Nuckolls, Nebr D8 103
Hardy, Kay, Okla A5 112
Hardy, co., W. Va B6 123
Hare, bay, Newf., Can C4 75
Hare Bay, Newf., Can D4 75
Hareford, inlet, N.J E3 106
Haren, Neth A6 11
Harer, see Harar, Eth.
Harerge, prov., Eth D5 47
Harfleur, Fr C4 14
Harford, Susquehanna, Pa . C10 114
Harford, co., Md A5 85
Hargeisa (Hargeysa), Som . . . D6 47
Hargeisa, dist., Som D5 47
Hargeysa, reg., Som D5 47
Hargeysa, see Hargeisa, Som.
Harghitei, mts., Rom B7 22
Hargill, Hidalgo, Tex F3 118
Hargrave, Man., Can E1 71
Hargrave, lake, Man., Can B2 71
Hargrave, riv., Man., Can B2 71
Harihar, India F6 39
Harir, wadi, Syria B7 32
Harirūd, riv., Afg D10 41
Harkers Island, Carteret, N.C C6 109
Harlan, Allen, Ind B8 91
Harlan, Shelby, Iowa C2 92
Harlan, Smith, Kans C5 93
Harlan, Harlan, Ky D6 94
Harlan, co., Ky D6 94
Harlan, co., Nebr D6 103
Harlan County Lake, res., Nebr . D6 103
Harlech, Wales B3 12
Harlem, Hendry, Fla *F6 86
Harlem, Columbia, Ga C4 87
Harlem, Blaine, Mont B8 102
Harlem, riv., N.Y D5 106
Harleton, Harrison, Tex C5 118
Harleyville, Dorchester, S.C . . E7 115
Harlingen, Neth A5 15
Harlingen, Cameron, Tex . . . F4 118
Harlow, Eng C8 12
Harlow, Benson, N. Dak A6 110
Harlowton, Wheatland, Mont D7 102
Harman, Randolph, W. Va . . C5 123
Harmans, Anne Arundel, Md B4 103
Harmon, Lee, Ill B4 90
Harmon, Red River, La B2 95
Harmon, Ellis, Okla A2 112
Harmon, co., Okla C2 112
Harmon, creek, W. Va f8 123
Harmonsburg, Crawford, Pa . C1 114
Harmony, Clay, Ind E3 91
Harmony, Somerset, Maine . . D3 96
Harmony, Fillmore, Minn . . . G6 99
Harmony, Warren, N.J B2 106
Harmony, Iredell, N.C B2 109
Harmony, Butler, Pa E1 114
Harmony, Providence, R.I . . B10 84
Harmony, Halifax, Va D4 121
Harmonyville, Windham, Vt E3 120
Harms, Lincoln, Tenn B5 117
Harned, Breckinridge, Ky . . . C3 94
Harnett, co., N.C B4 109
Harney, Carroll, Md B3 85
Harney, co., Oreg D7 113
Harney, lake, Fla D6 86
Harney, lake, Oreg D7 113
Harney, peak, S. Dak D2 116
Harney, valley, Oreg D8 113
Härnösand, Swe F8 25
Haro, Sp A4 20
Haro, cape, Mex B2 63
Haro, strait, B.C., Can g12 68
Harold, Santa Rosa, Fla u15 86
Harold, pond, Ba m17 64
Harper, Keokuk, Iowa C5 92
Harper, Harper, Kans E5 93
Harper, Lib H3 45
Harper, Malheur, Oreg D9 113
Harper, Gillespie, Tex D3 118
Harper, Kitsap, Wash e10 122
Harper, co., Kans E5 93
Harper, co., Okla A2 112
Harpers Ferry, Allamakee, Iowa A6 92
Harpers Ferry, Jefferson, W. Va B7 123
Harpersville, Shelby, Ala B3 78
Harperville, Scott, Miss C4 100
Harper Woods, Wayne, Mich *F7 98
Harpeth, riv., Tenn A5 117
Harpster, Idaho, Idaho D3 89
Harpster, Wyandot, Ohio . . . B2 111
Harptree, Sask., Can H3 70
Harquahala, mts., Ariz D2 80
Harrah, Oklahoma, Okla B4 112
Harrah, Yakima, Wash C5 122
Harray, lake, Scot A5 13
Harrell, Calhoun, Ark D3 81
Harricana, riv., Ont., Que., Can F17 67
Harrietta, Wexford, Mich . . . D5 98
Harriettsville, Noble, Ohio . . C4 111
Harriman, Klamath, Oreg . . . E4 113
Harriman, Roane, Tenn D9 117
Harriman, res., Vt A2 97
Harrington, Kent, Del C6 85
Harrington, Washington, Maine D5 96
Harrington, Lincoln, Wash . B7 122
Harrington, lake, Maine C3 96
Harrington, sound, Bermuda . . o20 64
Harrington Park, Bergen, N.J h9 106
Harriott, lake, Sask., Can A4 70
Harris, Sask., Can F2 70
Harris, Osceola, Iowa A2 92
Harris, Anderson, Kans D8 93
Harris, Chisago, Minn E6 99
Harris, Sullivan, Mo A4 101
Harris, McCurtain, Okla D7 112
Harris, Kent, R.I *C10 84
Harris, Scot D2 13
Harris, Obion, Tenn A3 117
Harris, co., Ga D2 87
Harris, co., Tex E5 118
Harris, hill, Mass A3 97
Harris, lake, Fla D5 86
Harris, sound, Scot C1 13
Harrisburg, Poinsett, Ark . . . B5 81
Harrisburg, Saline, Ill F5 90
Harrisburg, Boone, Mo B5 101
Harrisburg, Banner, Nebr . . . C2 103
Harrisburg, Pickaway and Franklin, Ohio m10 111
Harrisburg, Linn, Oreg C3 113
Harrisburg, Dauphin, Pa . . . F8 114
Harrisburg, Lincoln, S. Dak . G9 116
Harris Grove, York, Va h15 121
Harris Hill, Erie, N.Y *C2 108
Harrismith, S. Afr C4 49
Harrison, Boone, Ark A2 81
Harrison, Washington, Ga . . D4 87
Harrison, Kootenai, Idaho . . B2 89
Harrison, Cumberland, Maine D2 96
Harrison, Clare, Mich D6 98
Harrison, Madison, Mont . . . E5 102
Harrison, Sioux, Nebr B2 103
Harrison, Hudson, N.J k8 106
Harrison, Westchester, N.Y . h13 108
Harrison, Hamilton, Ohio . . . C1 111
Harrison, Douglas, S. Dak . . D7 116
Harrison, Hamilton, Tenn . . h11 117
Harrison, co., Ind H5 91
Harrison, co., Iowa C2 92
Harrison, co., Ky B5 94
Harrison, co., Miss E4 100
Harrison, co., Mo A3 101
Harrison, co., Ohio B4 111
Harrison, co., Tex C5 118
Harrison, co., W. Va B4 123
Harrison, bay, Alsk A9 79
Harrison, cape, Newf., Can . . . g10 75
Harrison, lake, B.C., Can E7 68
Harrisonburg, Catahoula, La C4 95
Harrisonburg (Independent City), Va B4 121
Harrison Hot Springs, B.C., Can f14 68
Harrison Valley, Potter, Pa . C6 114
Harrisonville, Monroe, Ill . . E3 90
Harrisonville, Cass, Mo C3 101
Harrisonville, Gloucester, N.J D2 106
Harrisonville, Fulton, Pa . . . G5 114
Harriston, Ont., Can D4 72
Harriston, Jefferson, Miss . . D2 100
Harristown, Macon, Ill D4 90
Harrisville, Alcona, Mich . . . D7 98
Harrisville, Simpson, Miss . . D3 100
Harrisville, Cheshire, N.H . . E2 105
Harrisville, Lewis, N.Y A5 108
Harrisville, Harrison, Ohio . . B1 123
Harrisville, Butler, Pa D1 114
Harrisville, Providence, R.I . B10 84
Harrisville, Weber, Utah . . . B4 119
Harrisville, Ritchie, W. Va . . B3 123
Harrisville, Marquette, Wis . . E4 124
Harrisville Heights, Weber, Utah *B3 119
Harrod, Allen, Ohio B2 111
Harrods, creek, Ky g11 94
Harrodsburg, Monroe, Ind . . F4 91
Harrodsburg, Mercer, Ky . . . C5 94
Harrogate, Eng C6 10
Harrold, Hughes, S. Dak . . . C6 116
Harrold, Wilbarger, Tex B3 118
Harrop, lake, Man., Can C4 71
Harrow, Ont., Can E2 72
Harrow, Eng. (part of London) C7 12
Harrowby, Man., Can D1 71
Harrowsmith, Ont., Can C8 72
Harrys, riv., Newf., Can D2 75
Harstad, Nor C7 25
Hart, Oceana, Mich E4 98
Hart, Castro, Tex B1 118
Hart, co., Ga B4 87
Hart, co., Ky C4 94
Hart, isl., Md B5 85
Hart, isl., N.Y B5 106
Hart, lake, Fla D5 86
Hart, lake, Oreg E7 113
Hart, mtn., Man., Can C1 71
Hartell, Alta., Can D3 69
Hartfield, Middlesex, Va C6 121
Hartford, Geneva, Ala D4 78
Hartford, Sebastian, Ark B1 81
Hartford, Hartford, Conn . . . B6 84
Hartford, Madison, Ill E3 90
Hartford, Warren, Iowa . . C4, f9 92
Hartford, Lyon, Kans D8 93
Hartford, Ohio, Ky C3 94
Hartford, Oxford, Maine D2 96
Hartford, Van Buren, Mich . . F4 98
Hartford, Burlington, N.J . . . D3 106
Hartford, Washington, N.Y . . B7 108
Hartford, Minnehaha, S. Dak D9 116
Hartford, Cocke, Tenn D10 117
Hartford, Windsor, Vt D4 120
Hartford, Mason, W. Va C3 123
Hartford, Washington, Wis E5, m11 124
Hartford, co., Conn B5 84
Hartford City, Blackford, Ind D7 91
Hartha, G.D.R B7 17
Hartington, Cedar, Nebr B8 103
Hartland, N.B., Can C2 74
Hartland (Town of), Hartford, Conn *B5 84
Hartland, Somerset, Maine . . D3 96
Hartland, Livingston, Mich . . F7 98
Hartland, Freeborn, Minn . . . G5 99
Hartland, Windsor, Vt D4 120
Hartland, Waukesha, Wis E6, m11 124
Hartland, pt., Eng C3 12
Hartland Four Corners, Windsor, Vt D4 120
Hartlepool, Eng C6 10
Hartley, O'Brien, Iowa A2 92
Hartley, Rh A5 49
Hartley, Hartley, Tex B1 118
Hartley, co., Tex B1 118
Hartline, Grant, Wash B6 122
Hartly, Kent, Del B6 85
Hartman, Johnson, Ark B2 81
Hartman, Prowers, Colo C8 83
Hartney, Man., Can E1 71
Hartsburg, Logan, Ill C4 90
Hartsburg, Boone, Mo C5 101
Hartsdale, Westchester, N.Y *D7 108
Hartsel, Park, Colo B5 83
Hartselle, Morgan, Ala A3 78
Hartsfield, Colquitt, Ga E3 87
Hartshorn, Texas, Mo D6 101
Hartshorne, Pittsburg, Okla . C6 112
Hartsville, Bartholomew, Ind . F6 91
Hartsville, Berkshire, Mass . . *B1 97
Hartsville, Darlington, S.C . . C7 115
Hartsville, Trousdale, Tenn . . A5 117
Hartuv, Isr h11 32
Hartville, Stark, Ohio B4 111
Hartville, Wright, Mo D5 101
Hartville, Platte, Wyo D8 125
Hartwell, Hart, Ga B4 87
Hartwell, res., Ga., S.C B3 87, B1 115
Hartwick, Poweshiek, Iowa . . C5 92
Hartwick, Otsego, N.Y C5 108
Harty, Ont., Can *o17 72
Harūt, riv., Afg E10 41
Harvard, McHenry, Ill A5 90
Harvard, Wayne, Iowa D4 92
Harvard, Worcester, Mass B4, f9 97
Harvard, Clay, Nebr D7 103
Harvard, mtn., Colo C4 83
Harvel, Montgomery and Christian, Ill D4 90
Harvest, Madison, Ala A3 78
Harvey, N.B., Can D3 74
Harvey, Cook, Ill B6, k9 90
Harvey, Marion, Iowa C5 92
Harvey, Jefferson, La E5, k11 95
Harvey, Marquette, Mich B3 98
Harvey, Wells, N. Dak B3 98
Harvey, Fayette, W. Va n13 123
Harvey, co., Kans D6 93
Harvey, lake, Pa m17 114
Harvey, mtn., Mass B1 97
Harveys, creek, Pa n16 114
Harveysburg, Warren, Ohio . C1 111
Harvey Station, N.B., Can . . . D3 74
Harveyton, Perry, Ky C6 94
Harveyville, Wabaunsee, Kans D8 93
Harviell, Butler, Mo E7 101
Harwich, Eng C9 12
Harwich, Barnstable, Mass . . C7 97
Harwich Port, Barnstable, Mass C7 97
Harwick, Allegheny, Pa *E2 114
Harwinton, Litchfield, Conn . B4 84
Harwood, Ont., Can C6 72
Harwood, Anne Arundel, Md C4 85
Harwood, Middlesex, Mass . . f9 97
Harwood, Vernon, Mo D3 101
Harwood, Cass, N. Dak C9 110
Harwood Heights, Cook, Ill . *B6 90
Haryana, state, India C5 40
Harz, mts., G.D.R B5 17
Harzgerode, G.D.R B6 17
Hasa, reg., Sau. Ar *H4 41
Ḩasan Kiādeh, Iran C4 41
Hasbrouck Heights, Bergen, N.J h8 106
Hasdo, riv., India F9 40

Hickman, co., Tenn B4 117
Hickman's Harbour, Newf., Can D5 75
Hickok, Grant, Kans E2 93
Hickory, Graves, Ky f9 94
Hickory, Newton, Miss C4 100
Hickory, Catawba, N.C B1 109
Hickory, Murray, Okla C5 112
Hickory, co., Mo D4 101
Hickory Corners, Barry, Mich F5 98
Hickory East, Catawba, N.C *B1 109
Hickory Flat, Benton, Miss . . A4 100
Hickory Grove, York, S.C . . B5 115
Hickory Hills, Cook, Ill *B6 90
Hickory Plains, Prairie, Ark . . C4 81
Hickory Ridge, Cross, Ark . . . B5 81
Hickory Valley, Hardeman, Tenn B2 117
Hickory Withe, Fayette, Tenn B2 117
Hickox, Brantley, Ga E4 87
Hickson, Ont., Can D4 72
Hickson, Cass, N. Dak C9 110
Hickson, lake, Sask., Can A3 70
Hicksville, Nassau, N.Y . E7, n15 108
Hicksville, Defiance, Ohio . . . A1 111
Hico, Hamilton, Tex C4 118
Hico, Fayette, W. Va . . C4, m13 123
Hicoria, Highlands, Fla E5 86
Hidalgo, Jasper, Ill D5 90
Hidalgo, Hidalgo, Tex *F3 118
Hidalgo, co., N. Mex F1 107
Hidalgo, co., Tex F3 118
Hidalgo, state, Mex . . . C5, m14 63
Hidalgo del Parral, Mex B3 63
Hiddenite, Alexander, N.C . . B1 109
Hiddensee, isl., G.D.R D7 24
Hidden Valley, Washoe, Nev *D2 104
Hideaway Park, Grand, Colo B5 83
Hierro, isl., Sp. (Can. Is.) n13 20
Higashi (Dōgo), isl., Jap H6 37
Higbee, Randolph, Mo B5 101
Higden, Cleburne, Ark B3 81
Higdon, Jackson, Ala A4 78
Higganum, Middlesex, Conn D6 84
Higgins, Lipscomb, Tex A2 118
Higgins, pond, Md C6 85
Higgins Lake, Roscommon, Mich D6 98
Higginson, White, Ark B4 81
Higginsport, Brown, Ohio . . . D2 111
Higginsville, Lafayette, Mo . . B4 101
High, Carroll, Ark A2 81
High, des, Oreg D6 113
High, hill, N.Y F3 84
High, isl., Mich C5 98
High, peak, Phil o13 35
High Bluff, Man., Can D2 71
High Bridge, Jessamine, Ky . . C5 94
High Bridge, Hillsboro, N.H . E2 105
High Bridge, Hunterdon, N.J B3 106
Highest Point in Ala B4 78
Highest Point in Alsk C9 79
Highest Point in Ariz B4 80
Highest Point in Ark B2 81
Highest Point in Calif D4 82
Highest Point in Can D4 66
Highest Point in Colo B4 83
Highest Point in Conn A3 84
Highest Point in Del A6 85
Highest Point in Fla u15 86
Highest Point in Ga B3 87
Highest Point in Haw D6 88
Highest Point in Idaho E5 89
Highest Point in Ill A3 90
Highest Point in Ind D8 91
Highest Point in Iowa A2 92
Highest Point in Kans D1 93
Highest Point in Ky D7 94
Highest Point in La B3 95
Highest Point in Maine C4 96
Highest Point in Md m12 85
Highest Point in Mass A1 97
Highest Point in Mich B2 98
Highest Point in Minn k9 99
Highest Point in Miss A5 100
Highest Point in Mo D7 101
Highest Point in Mont E7 102
Highest Point in Nebr C1 103
Highest Point in Nev F3 104
Highest Point in N.H B4 105
Highest Point in N.J A3 106
Highest Point in N. Mex A4 107
Highest Point in N.Y A7 108
Highest Point in N.A C9 79
Highest Point in N.C f10 109
Highest Point in N. Dak C2 110
Highest Point in Ohio B2 111
Highest Point in Okla D1 112
Highest Point in Oreg B5 113
Highest Point in Pa G3 114
Highest Point in R.I B9 84
Highest Point in S.C A2 115
Highest Point in S. Dak D2 116
Highest Point in Tenn D10 117
Highest Point in Tex E2 118
Highest Point in U.S C9 79
Highest Point in Utah C5 119
Highest Point in Vt B3 120
Highest Point in Va f10 121
Highest Point in Wash C4 122
Highest Point in W. Va C5 123
Highest Point in Wis D4 124
Highest Point in Wyo C3 125
Highfalls, Moore, N.C B3 109
High Falls, res., Wis C5 124
Highfield, Washington, Md . . A3 85
Highfield, Zimb D5 49
Highgate, Ont., Can E3 72
Highgate Center (Highgate), Franklin, Vt B2 120
Highgate Falls, Franklin, Vt . B2 120
Highgate Springs, Franklin, Vt . B2 120
Highgrove, Riverside, Calif *F5 82
High Hill, Montgomery, Mo C6 101
High Hill, lake, Man., Can B4 71
High Hill, riv., Alta., Can A5 69
High Island, Galveston, Tex E5 118
High Knob, mtn., Md B3 85
High Knob, mtn., Va A4 121
High Knob, mtn., W. Va B6 123
High Knob, mtn., W. Va C5 123
Highland, Madison, Ill E4 90
Highland, Lake, Ind A3 91
Highland, Doniphan, Kans . . C8 93
Highland, Oakland, Mich . . . o14 98
Highland, Ulster, N.Y D7 108
Highland, Highland, Ohio . . . C2 111
Highland, Utah, Utah *C4 119
Highland, Iowa, Wis E3 124
Highland, co., Ohio C2 111
Highland, co., Va B3 121
Highland, reg., Scot B4 13
Highland, lake, Maine g7 96
Highland, peak, Calif C4 82
Highland, pt., Fla G5 86
Highland Beach, Palm Beach, Fla *F6 86
Highlandale, Leflore, Miss . . B3 100
Highland City, Polk, Fla . . . *E5 86
Highland Crest, Wyandotte, Kans *C9 93
Highland Falls, Orange, N.Y *D6 108
Highland Grove, Ont., Can . . B6 72
Highland Heights, Cuyahoga, Ohio *A4 111
Highland Home, Crenshaw, Ala D3 78
Highland Lake, Cumberland, Maine (part of Westbrook) . E5 96
Highland Lakes, Sussex, N.J A4 106
Highland Park, Lake, Ill A6, h9 90
Highland Park, Wayne, Mich p15 98
Highland Park, Middlesex, N.J *C4 106
Highland Park, Mifflin, Pa . *E6 114
Highland Park, Dallas, Tex . n10 118
Highland Park, Norfolk, Va *D6 121
Highlands, Broward, Fla . . . *F6 86
Highlands, Coos, N.H B4 105
Highlands, Monmouth, N.J . . C5 106
Highlands, Macon, N.C f9 109
Highlands, Harris, Tex r14 118
Highlands, Morgan, Utah . . *B4 119
Highlands, co., Fla E5 86
Highland Springs, Henrico, Va C5, m18 121
Highlandville, Winneshiek, Iowa A6 92
Highmore, Hyde, S. Dak . . . C6 116
Highpine, York, Maine E2 96
High Point, Garland, Ark . . . C6 81
Highpoint, Winston, Miss . . . B4 100
High Point, Guilford, N.C . . . B2 109
High Point, King, Wash e11 122
High Point, mtn., N.J A3 106
High Prairie, Alta., Can B2 69
High Ridge, Fairfield, Conn. (part of Stamford) E2 84
High Ridge, Jefferson, Mo . . g12 101
High River, Alta., Can D4 69
Highrock, York, Pa G9 114
Highrock, lake, Man., Can B1 71
High Rock, lake, N.C B2 109
High Rock, mtn., Md k12 85
High Rolls-Mountain Park, Otero, N. Mex E4 107
High Shoals, Morgan and Oconee, Ga C3 87
Highshoals, Gaston, N C B1 109
Highspire, Dauphin, Pa F8 114
High Springs, Alachua, Fla . C4 86
Hightstown, Mercer, N.J C3 106
Highway City, Fresno, Calif *D4 82
Highway Village, Nucces, Tex *F4 118
High Willhays, mtn., Eng D3 12
Highwood, Lake, Ill A6, h9 90
Highwood, Gladwin, Mich . . E6 98
Highwood, Chouteau, Mont C6 102
Highwood, mts., Mont C6 102
Highwood Baldy, peak, Mont . C6 102
High Wycombe, Eng E6 10, C7 12
Higley, Maricopa, Ariz . D4, m9 80
Higuero, pt., P.R B1 65
Higüey, Dom. Rep E9 64
Hiiumaa, isl., Sov. Un B4 27
Hijo, Phil *D7 35
Hika, Manitowoc, Wis B6 124
Hiko, Lincoln, Nev F6 104
Hikone, Jap n15 37
Hikurangi, mtn., N.Z L17 51
Hilāl, mtn., Eg D5 32
Hiland, Natrona, Wyo C5 125
Hilbert, Calumet, Wis . . D5, h9 124
Hilda, Alta., Can D5 69
Hilda, Barnwell, S.C E5 115
Hildale, Washington, Utah . . F3 119
Hildburghausen, G.D.R C5 17
Hildebrand, Klamath, Oreg . E5 113
Hilden, N.S., Can D6 74
Hilden, F.R.G B1 17
Hildesheim, F.R.G A4 17
Hildreth, Franklin, Nebr . . . D6 103
Hiles, Forest, Wis C5 124
Hilger, Fergus, Mont C7 102
Hill, Merrimack, N.H C3 105
Hill, co., Mont B6 102
Hill, co., Tex D4 118
Hill, lake, Ark h10 81
Hilla, see Al Hillah, Iraq
Hillaby, mtn., Barb K20 65
Hillared, Swe A7 24
Hillburn, Rockland, N.Y . . *D6 108
Hill Center, Merrimack, N.H C3 105
Hill City, Camas, Idaho F3 89
Hill City, Graham, Kans C4 93
Hill City, Aitkin, Minn D5 99
Hill City, Pennington, S. Dak D2 116
Hillcrest, Gogebic, Mich . . . m11 98
Hillcrest, Warren, N.J *B2 106
Hillcrest, Broome, N.Y *C5 108
Hillcrest, Rockland, N.Y . . . *g12 108
Hillcrest Center, Kern, Calif *E4 82
Hillcrest Heights, Prince Georges, Md f9 85
Hillcrest Mines, Alta., Can E3 69
Hillegom, Neth B4 15
Hiller, Fayette, Pa *F2 114
Hillerage, Scotts Bluff, Nebr . *C2 103
Hillerød, Den C6 24
Hillesheim, F.R.G C1 17
Hillhead, Marshall, S. Dak B8 116
Hilliard, Alta., Can C4 69
Hilliard, Nassau, Fla B5 86
Hilliard, Franklin, Ohio . . . k10 111
Hilliards, Butler, Pa D2 114
Hilliers, Ont., Can D7 72
Hillisburg, Clinton, Ind D5 91
Hillman, Montmorency, Mich C7 98
Hillman, Morrison, Minn . . . D5 99
Hillmond, Sask., Can D1 70
Hillrose, Morgan, Colo A7 83
Hills, Johnson, Iowa C6 92
Hills, Rock, Minn G2 99
Hillsboro, Lawrence, Ala A2 78
Hillsboro, Jasper, Ga C3 87
Hillsboro, Montgomery, Ill . . D4 90
Hillsboro, Fountain, Ind D3 91
Hillsboro, Henry, Iowa D6 92
Hillsboro, Marion, Kans D6 93
Hillsboro, Caroline, Md C6 85
Hillsboro, Scott, Miss C4 100
Hillsboro, Jefferson, Mo . C7, g12 101
Hillsboro, Hillsboro, N.H D3 105
Hillsboro, Sierra, N. Mex E2 107
Hillsboro, Orange, N.C A3 109
Hillsboro, Traill, N. Dak B8 110
Hillsboro, Highland, Ohio . . . C2 111
Hillsboro, Washington, Oreg B4, g12 113
Hillsboro, Coffee, Tenn B6 117
Hillsboro, Hill, Tex C4 118
Hillsboro, Pocahontas, W. Va C4 123
Hillsboro, Vernon, Wis E3 124
Hillsboro, co., N.H E3 105
Hillsboro, canal, Fla F6 86
Hillsboro Beach, Broward, Fla *F6 86
Hillsboro Lower Village, Hillsboro, N.H D3 105
Hillsboro Upper Village, Hillsboro, N.H D3 105
Hillsborough, N.B., Can D5 74
Hillsborough, Grenada W25 65
Hillsborough, co., Fla E4 86
Hillsborough, bay, P.E.I., Can . C6 74
Hillsborough, bay, Fla E2 86
Hillsburgh, Ont., Can D4 72
Hills Creek Lake, res., Oreg . . D4 113
Hillsdale, Ont., Can C5 72
Hillsdale, Rock Island, Ill . . . B3 90
Hillsdale, Vermillion, Ind . . . E3 91
Hillsdale, Miami, Kans D9 93
Hillsdale, Hillsdale, Mich . . . G6 98
Hillsdale, St. Louis, Mo *C7 101
Hillsdale, Pearl River, Miss . E4 100
Hillsdale, Bergen, N.J g8 106
Hillsdale, Columbia, N.Y C7 108
Hillsdale, Garfield, Okla A4 112
Hillsdale, Macon, Tenn C7 117
Hillsdale, Barron, Wis C2 124
Hillsdale, Laramie, Wyo E8 125
Hillsdale, co., Mich G6 98
Hillsgrove, Sullivan, Pa D8 114
Hillside, Fremont, Colo C5 83
Hillside, Cook, Ill *B6 90
Hillside, Union, N.J k8 106
Hillside Manor, Nassau, N.Y *G2 84
Hill Spring, Alta., Can E4 69
Hillston, Austl F5 51
Hillsview, McPherson, S. Dak B6 116
Hillsville, Lawrence, Pa D1 114
Hillsville, Carroll, Va D2 121
Hilltonia, Screven, Ga D5 87
Hilltop, Cochise, Ariz F6 80
Hilltop, Camden, N.J *D2 106
Hilltown, N. Ire C5 11
Hillview, Greene, Ill D3 90
Hillville, Haywood, Tenn . . . B2 117
Hillwood, Coosa, Ala C3 78
Hillwood, Fairfax, Va *B5 121
Hilly, Lincoln, La B3 95
Hilo, Hawaii, Haw D6, n16 88
Hilo, bay, Haw D6 88
Hilpoltstein, F.R.G D6 17
Hilt, Siskiyou, Calif B2 82
Hilton, Early, Ga E1 87
Hilton, Monroe, N.Y B3 108
Hiltonhead, Beaufort, S.C . . . G6 115
Hilton Head, isl., S.C G6 115
Hiltons, Scott, Va f9 121
Hilversum, Neth B5 15
Hima, Clay, Ky C6 94
Himachal Pradesh, state, India B6 40
Himalaya, mts., Asia G11 33
Himeji, Jap I7 37
Himes, Big Horn, Wyo B4 125
Himrod, Yates, N.Y C4 108
Hinch, mtn., Tenn D9 117
Hinche, Hai E7 64
Hinchinbrook, isl., Alsk g18 79
Hinchinbrook, isl., Austl C8 50
Hinchliffe, Sask., Can E4 70
Hinckley, Eng B6 12
Hinckley, DeKalb, Ill B5 90
Hinckley, Somerset, Maine . . D3 96
Hinckley, Pine, Minn D6 99
Hinckley, Medina, Ohio A4 111
Hinckley, Millard, Utah D3 119
Hinckley, res., N.Y B5 108
Hindarabi, isl., Iran H6 41
Hindian, Iran F7 41
Hindman, Knott, Ky C7 94
Hindmarsh, lake, Austl G7 51
Hinds, co., Miss C3 100
Hinds, lake, Newf., Can D3 75
Hindsboro, Douglas, Ill D5 90
Hindsville, Madison, Ark . . . A2 81
Hindubāgh, Pak B4 39
Hindu Kush, mts., Afg D14 41
Hines, Beltrami, Minn C4 99
Hines, Harney, Oreg D7 113
Hines, creek, Alta., Can A1 69
Hinesburg, Chittenden, Vt . . C2 120
Hines Creek, Alta., Can A1 69
Hinesville, Liberty, Ga E5 87
Hingham, Plymouth, Mass B6, h12 97
Hingham, Hill, Mont B6 102
Hingham, bay, Mass g12 97
Hingham Center, Plymouth, Mass D3 97
Hingoli, India H6 40
Hinis, Tur C13 31
Hinkle, Alcorn, Miss A5 100
Hinkley, San Bernardino, Calif E5 82
Hinnom, val., Isr., Jordan m14 32
Hinnöya, isl., Nor C6 25
Hinojosa [del Duque], Sp C3 20
Hinsdale, Du Page and Cook, Ill k9 90
Hinsdale, Berkshire, Mass . . . B1 97
Hinsdale, Valley, Mont B9 102
Hinsdale, Cheshire, N.H E2 105
Hinsdale, Cattaraugus, N.Y . . C2 108
Hinsdale, co., Colo D3 83
Hinterrhein, Switz C7 21
Hinton, Alta., Can C2 69
Hinton, Plymouth, Iowa B1 92
Hinton, Caddo, Okla B3 112
Hinton, Summers, W. Va . . . D4 123
Hintonville, Perry, Miss D5 100
Hinze, Winston, Miss B4 100
Hirado, isl., Jap J4 37
Hiraiwa, cape, Iwo 52
Hiram, Paulding, Ga C2 87
Hiram, Oxford, Maine E2 96
Hiram, Portage, Ohio A4 111
Hiran, reg., Som E6 47
Hiratsuka, Jap n17 37
Hiraya, Jap n14 37
Hîrlău, Rom B8 22
Hirosaki, Jap F10 37
Hiroshima, Jap I6 37
Hiroshima, pref., Jap *I6 37
Hirson, Fr C5 14
Hîrşova, Rom C8 22
Hirtshals, Den A3 24
Hisār, India C5 40
Hisarönu, Tur B9 31
Hiseville, Barren, Ky C4 94
Hispaniola, isl., N.A D8 64
Hit, Iraq F14 31
Hita, Jap *J5 37
Hitachi, Jap H10 37
Hitchcock, Sask., Can H4 70
Hitchcock, Blaine, Okla B3 112
Hitchcock, Beadle, S. Dak . . . C7 116
Hitchcock, Galveston, Tex . . r14 118
Hitchcock, co., Nebr D4 103
Hitchcock Lake, New Haven, Conn *C5 84
Hitchin, Eng C7 12
Hitchins, Carter, Ky B7 94
Hitchita, McIntosh, Okla B6 112
Hiteman, Monroe, Iowa C5 92
Hitoyoshi, Jap J5 37
Hitra, isl., Nor F3 25
Hitterdal, Clay, Minn D2 99
Hitzacker, F.R.G E5 18
Hivonnait, Arg E4 55
Hiwassee, Pulaski, Va D2 121
Hiwassee, riv., Tenn D9 117
Hixon, B.C., Can C6 68
Hixson, Hamilton, Tenn D8 117
Hixton, Jackson, Wis D2 124
Hjallerup, Den A4 24
Hjälmaren (Hjalmar), lake, Swe . H7 25
Hjälmseryd, Swe A8 24
Hjo, Swe H6 25
Hjørring, Den A3 24
Hkakabo Razi, mtn., Bur C10 39
Hlohovec, Czech D4 26
Hlomsak, Thai D4 38
Ho, China F4 36
Hoa Binh, Viet B6 38
Hoagland, Allen, Ind C8 91
Hoagland, Logan, Nebr C5 103
Hoback, riv., Wyo C2 125
Hoban Heights, Wyoming, Pa D10 114
Hobart, Austl o15 50
Hobart, Lake, Ind A3 91
Hobart, Delaware, N.Y C6 108
Hobart, Kiowa, Okla B2 112
Hobbema, Alta., Can C4 69
Hobbies, Bernalillo, N. Mex . *B3 107
Hobbieville, Greene, Ind G4 91
Hobbs, Tipton, Ind D6 91
Hobbs, Lea, N. Mex E6 107
Hobbs Island, Madison, Ala . . A3 78
Hobe Sound, Martin, Fla E6 86
Hobgood, Halifax, N.C A5 109
Hoboken, Bel C4 15
Hoboken, Brantley, Ga E4 87
Hoboken, Hudson, N.J k8 106
Hobro, Den B3 24
Hobsogol Dalay, lake, Mong . . . A5 34
Hobson, Judith Basin, Mont . D7 102
Hobson, White Pine, Nev C6 104
Hobson, lake, B.C., Can C7 68
Hobson City, Calhoun, Ala . . B4 78
Hobucken, Pamlico, N.C B6 109
Hochatown, McCurtain, Okla C7 112
Hochfeld, Namibia B2 49
Hochfelden, Fr F7 15
Hochien, China E7 36
Ho Chi Minh City (Saigon), Viet G7 38
Höchstadt, F.R.G D5 17
Hochuan, China I2 36
Hockenheim, F.R.G D3 17
Hockerville, Ottawa, Okla . . . A7 112
Hockessin, New Castle, Del . . A6 85
Hocking, co., Ohio C3 111
Hocking, riv., Ohio C3 111
Hockingport, Athens, Ohio . . C4 111
Hockinson, Clark, Wash D3 122
Hockley, Harris, Tex q14 118
Hockley, co., Tex C1 118
Hoddesdon, Eng k13 10
Hodgdon, Aroostook, Maine . . B5 96
Hodge, Jackson, La B3 95
Hodgeman, co., Kans D4 93
Hodgenville, Larue, Ky C4 94
Hodges, Franklin, Ala A2 78
Hodges, Dawson, Mont D12 102
Hodges, Greenwood, S.C C3 115
Hodges, hill, Newf., Can D4 75
Hodges Village, res., Mass B4 97
Hodgeville, Sask., Can G2 70
Hodgkins, Cook, Ill *B6 90
Hodgson, Man., Can D3 71
Hódmezővásárhely, Hung . . . B5 22
Hodna, lake, Alg G9 30
Hodonin, Czech D4 26
Hoehne, Las Animas, Colo . . D6 83
Hoek Nederburgh, pt., Indon . . . F6 35
Hoek van Holland, Neth., (part of Rotterdam) C4 15
Hoensbroek, Neth D5 15
Hoeryong, Kor E4 37
Hoey, Sask., Can E3 70
Hof, F.R.G C6 17
Hof, Nor p28 25
Hofei, China I7 36
Hoffman, Grant, Minn E3 99
Hoffman, Richmond, N.C B3 109
Hoffman, Okmulgee, Okla . . . B6 112
Hoffman Estates, Cook, Ill . . . h8 90
Hofgeismar, F.R.G B4 17
Hofn, Ice n25 25
Hofsjökull, glacier, Ice n23 25
Hofu, Jap I5 37
Hog, isl., Ba m18 64
Hog, isl., Fla C3 86
Hog, isl., Mich C5 98
Hog, isl., N.C B6 109
Hog, isl., Va C7 121
Hogan, Duval, Fla B5 86
Höganäs, Swe B6 24
Hogansburg, Franklin, N.Y . . f10 108
Hogansville, Troup, Ga C2 87
Hogback, mtn., Mont F4 102
Hog Back, mtn., Nebr C2 103
Hog Creek, pt., N.Y E8 84
Hogeland, Blaine, Mont B8 102
Hogglesville, Hale, Ala C2 78
Hogup, mts., Utah B2 119
Hoh, head, Wash B1 122
Hoh, riv., Wash B1 122
Hohenlinden, Webster, Miss . B4 100
Hohen Solms, Ascension, La h9 95
Hohenwald, Lewis, Tenn B4 117
Hohe Tauern, mts., Aus E6 16
Hohoe, Ghana E5 45
Ho-Ho-Kus, Bergen, N.J h8 106
Hohsien, China G7 34
Hohwachter, bay, F.R.G D4 24
Hoihong, see Haikang, China
Hoihow, see Haikou, China
Hoima, Ug A5 48
Hoisington, Barton, Kans . . . D5 93
Hoi Xuan, Viet B6 38
Højer, Den D2 24
Hokah, Houston, Minn G7 99
Hokang, China B11 34
Hoke, co., N.C B3 109
Hokendauqua, Lehigh, Pa . *E11 114
Hokes Bluff, Etowah, Ala . . . B4 78
Hokitika, N.Z O13 51
Hokkaidō, isl., Jap E10 37
Hokkaido, ter., Jap *E10 37
Hokoda, Jap m19 37
Holabird, Hyde, S. Dak C6 116
Holan Shan, mts., China D6 34
Holap, isl., Truk 52
Holbaek, Den C5 24
Holbeach, Eng B8 12
Holbrook, Navajo, Ariz C5 80
Holbrook, Oneida, Idaho . . . G6 89
Holbrook, Norfolk, Mass B5, h11 97
Holbrook, Furnas, Nebr D5 103
Holbrook, Suffolk, N.Y *F4 84
Holcomb, Finney, Kans E3 93
Holcomb, Grenada, Miss B4 100
Holcomb, Dunklin, Mo E7 101
Holcomb, Pacific, Wash C2 122
Holcombe, Chippewa, Wis . . C2 124
Holcut, Tishomingo, Miss . . . A5 100
Holden, Alta., Can C4 69
Holden, Livingston, La g10 95
Holden, Worcester, Mass B4 97
Holden, Johnson, Mo C4 101
Holden, Millard, Utah D3 119
Holden, Rutland, Vt D3 120
Holden, Chelan, Wash A5 122
Holden, Logan, W. Va D2 123
Holdenville, Hughes, Okla . . B5 112
Holderness, Grafton, N.H . . . C3 105
Holdfast, Sask., Can G3 70
Holdingford, Stearns, Minn . E4 99
Holdman, Umatilla, Oreg . . . B8 113
Holdrege, Phelps, Nebr D6 103
Holeb, Somerset, Maine C2 96
Hole in the Mountain, peak, Nev . C6 104
Hölen, Nor p28 25
Holetown, Barb K20 65
Holgate, Henry, Ohio A1 111
Holguín, Cuba D5 64
Holikachuk, Alsk C8 79
Hollabrunn, Aus D8 16
Holladay, Benton, Tenn B3 117
Holladay, Salt Lake, Utah . . . C4 119
Holladay, Spotsylvania, Va . . C5 115
Holland, Fulkner, Ark B3 81
Holland, Man., Can E2 71
Holland, Dubois, Ind H3 91
Holland, Grundy, Iowa B5 92
Holland, Allen, Ky D3 94
Holland, Hampden, Mass B3 97
Holland, Ottawa, Mich F4 98
Holland, Pipestone, Minn . . . F2 99
Holland, Pemiscot, Mo E8 101
Holland, Erie, N.Y C2 108
Holland, Lucas, Ohio A2, e6 111
Holland, Bell, Tex D4 118
Holland, Brown, Wis h9 124
Holland (Lincoln), co. part, Eng B7 12
Holland, isl., Md D5 85
Holland, pt., Md C4 85
Holland, straits, Md D5 85
Hollandale, Washington, Miss B3 100
Hollandale, Iowa, Wis F4 124
Holland Centre, Ont., Can . . C4 72
Holland Patent, Oneida, N.Y . B5 108
Hollansburg, Darke, Ohio . . . B1 111
Hollenberg, Washington, Kans C7 93
Holley, Orleans, N.Y B2 108
Hollick-Kenyon, plat., Ant B2 5
Holliday, Johnson, Kans B8 93
Holliday, Monroe, Mo B5 101
Holliday, Archer, Tex C3 118
Hollidaysburg, Blair, Pa F5 114
Hollins, Clay, Ala B3 78
Hollins, Baltimore, Md C2 85
Hollins, Roanoke, Va C3 121
Hollis, Alsk n23 79
Hollis, Perry, Ark C2 81
Hollis, Hillsboro, N.H E3 105
Hollis, Harmon, Okla C2 112
Hollis, res., Trin N23 65
Hollis Center, York, Maine . . E2 96
Hollister, San Benito, Calif . . D3 82
Hollister, Twin Falls, Idaho . G4 89
Hollister, Taney, Mo E4 101
Hollister, Halifax, N.C A5 109
Hollister, Tillman, Okla C3 112
Hollister, Langdale, Wis C5 124
Hollisterville, Wayne, Pa . . . D11 114
Holliston, Middlesex, Mass . . h10 97
Holloway, Swift, Minn E3 99
Holloway Terrace, New Castle, Del *A6 85
Hollow Rock, Carroll, Tenn . A3 117
Hollowtop, mtn., Mont E4 102
Hollsopple (P.O.), Somerset, Pa F4 114
Hollum, Neth A5 15
Holly, Prowers, Colo C8 83
Holly, Oakland, Mich F7 98
Holly Beach, Cameron, La . . . E2 95
Holly Bluff, Yazoo, Miss C3 100
Holly Grove, Monroe, Ark . . . C4 81
Holly Hill, Volusia, Fla C5 86
Holly Hill, Orangeburg, S.C . E7 115
Holly Oak, New Castle, Del . A7 85
Holly Pond, Cullman, Ala . . . A3 78
Holly Ridge, Richland, La . . . B4 95
Holly Ridge, Onslow, N.C . . . C5 109
Holly Shelter, swamp, N.C C5 109
Holly Springs, Dallas, Ark . . . D3 81
Holly Springs, Cherokee, Ga . B2 87
Holly Springs, Marshall, Miss A4 100
Holly Springs, Wake, N.C . . . B4 109
Hollywood, Jackson, Ala A4 78
Hollywood, Graham, Ariz . . . E6 80
Hollywood, Clark, Ark C2 81
Hollywood, Los Angeles, Calif. (part of Los Angeles) . . . m12 82
Hollywood, Broward, Fla F6, r13 86
Hollywood, Habersham, Ga . . B3 87
Hollywood, Calcasieu, La . . . *D2 95
Hollywood, St. Marys, Md . . D4 85
Hollywood, Montgomery, Pa *F12 114
Hollywood, Charleston, S.C . k11 115
Hollywood Heights, St. Clair, Ill *E3 90
Hollywood Ridge Farms, Broward, Fla *F6 86
Holman, Mora, N. Mex A4 107
Holman Island, N.W. Ter., Can B9 66
Holmdel, Monmouth, N.J . . . C4 106
Holmen, LaCrosse, Wis E2 124
Holmes, Delaware, Pa *G11 114
Holmes, co., Fla u16 86
Holmes, co., Miss B3 100
Holmes, co., Ohio B4 111
Holmes, lake, Man., Can A3 71
Holmes, mtn., Wyo B2 125
Holmes Beach, Mantee, Fla . *E4 86
Holmes Run Acres, Fairfax, Va *B5 121
Holmes Run Park, Fairfax, Va *B5 121
Holmestrand, Nor p28 25
Holmesville, Holmes, Ohio . . B4 111
Holmfield, Man., Can E2 71
Holmsbu, Nor p28 25
Holmsund, Swe F9 25
Holon, Isr B6, g10 32
Holopaw, Osceola, Fla D5 86
Holstebro, Den B2 24
Holsted, Den C2 24
Holstein, Ont., Can C4 72
Holstein, Ida, Iowa B2 92
Holstein, Warren, Mo C6 101
Holstein, Adams, Nebr D7 103
Holston, riv., Tenn C11 117
Holston, riv., Va f9 121
Holston High Knob, mtn., Tenn . C11 117
Holsworthy, Eng D3 12
Holt, Tuscaloosa, Ala B2 78
Holt, Okaloosa, Fla u15 86
Holt, Ingham, Mich F6 98
Holt, Marshall, Minn B2 99
Holt, Clay and Clinton, Mo . . B3 101
Holt, co., Mo A2 101
Holt, co., Nebr B7 103
Holter Dam, Lewis and Clark, Mont D4 102
Holtland, Marshall, Tenn . . . B5 117
Holton, Ripley, Ind F7 91
Holton, Jackson, Kans C8 93
Holton, Tangipahoa, La D5 95
Holton, Muskegon, Mich E4 98
Holtville, Imperial, Calif F6 82
Holtwood, Lancaster, Pa G9 114
Holualoa, Hawaii, Haw D6 88
Holy, isl., Eng C6 10
Holy, isl., Wales A3 12
Holy Cross, Alsk C8 79
Holy Cross, Dubuque, Iowa . B7 92
Holycross, Ire E4 11
Holy Cross, mtn., Colo B4 83
Holy Cross, nat. mon., Colo B4 83
Holyhead, Wales A3 12
Holyoke, Phillips, Colo A8 83
Holyoke, Hampden, Mass B2 97
Holyoke, Carlton, Minn D6 99
Holyoke, range, Mass B2 97
Holyrood, Ellsworth, Kans . . D5 93
Holy Trinity, Russell, Ala . . . C4 78
Holzkirchen, F.R.G B7 18
Holzminden, F.R.G B4 17
Homalin, Bur D9 39
Homathko, riv., B.C., Can D5 68
Homāyūnshahr, Iran E5 41
Homberg, F.R.G B1 17
Homberg, F.R.G B4 17
Hombori, Mali C4 45
Homburg, F.R.G D2 17
Home, Marshall, Kans C7 93
Home, Baker, Oreg C9 113
Home, bay, N.W. Ter., Can C19 67
Homeacre, Butler, Pa *E2 114
Home Corner, Grant, Ind . . *C6 91
Homécourt, Fr C6 14
Homedale, Owyhee, Idaho . . F2 89
Homedale, Franklin, Ohio . . *C2 111
Home Gardens, Riverside, Calif *F5 82
Home Hill, Austl C8 50
Homelake, Rio Grande, Colo D4 83
Homeland, Polk, Fla E5 86
Homeland, Charlton, Ga F4 87
Home Place, Hamilton, Ind E5, k10 91
Homer, Alsk D9 79
Homer, Banks, Ga B3 87
Homer, Champaign, Ill C6 90
Homer, Claiborne, La B2 95
Homer, Calhoun, Mich F6 98
Homer, Dakota, Nebr B9 103
Homer, Cortland, N.Y C4 108
Homer, Licking, Ohio B3 111
Homer City, Indiana, Pa E3 114
Homerville, Clinch, Ga E4 87
Homer Youngs, peak, Mont . . . E3 102
Homestead, Dade, Fla . . G6, t13 86
Homestead, Iowa, Iowa C6 92
Homestead, Sheridan, Mont B12 102
Homestead, Blaine, Okla A3 112
Homestead, Allegheny, Pa . . k14 114
Homestead, nat. mon., Nebr . . . D9 103
Homestead Valley, Marin, Calif C2 82
Hometown, Cook, Ill *B6 90
Homewood, Jefferson, Ala . . . g7 78
Homewood Placer, Calif C3 82
Homewood, Cook, Ill B6, k9 90
Homewood, Scott, Miss C4 100
Homewood, Butler, Ohio C1, n12 111
Homewood, Horry, S.C D9 115
Homeworth, Columbiana, Ohio B4 111
Hominy, Osage, Okla A5 112
Hominy, creek, Okla A5 112
Homme, dam, N. Dak A8 110
Homochitto, riv., Miss D2 100
Homosassa, Citrus, Fla D4 86
Homosassa, pt., Fla D4 86
Homs, Syr E11 31
Hon, Scott, Ark C1 81
Honaker, Russell, Va e10 121
Honan, prov., China E7 34
Honaunau, Hawaii, Haw D6 88
Hon Chuoi, isl., Viet H6 38
Honda, Col B3 60
Honda, bay, Phil D5 35
Hondo, Alta., Can B4 69
Hondo, Lincoln, N. Mex D4 107
Hondo, Medina, Tex E3 118
Hondo, riv., Belize A3 62
Hondo, riv., Mex h9 63
Honduras, country, N.A H12 61, C4 62
Honduras, cape, Hond B4 62
Honduras, gulf, N.A B4 62
Honea Path, Anderson, S.C . C3 115
Hönefoss, Nor G4 25
Honeoye Falls, Monroe, N.Y . C3 108
Honesdale, Wayne, Pa C11 114
Honey, lake, Calif B3 82
Honey Brook, Chester, Pa . . F10 114

Huntsville, Madison, Ala....A3 78
Huntsville, Madison, Ark....A2 81
Huntsville, Ont., Can....B5 72
Huntsville, Madison, Ind....E6 91
Huntsville, Butler, Ky....C3 94
Huntsville, Randolph, Mo....B5 101
Huntsville, Scott, Tenn....C9 117
Huntsville, Walker, Tex....D5 118
Huntsville, Weber, Utah....B4 119
Huntsville, Columbia, Wash....C7 122
Hunucmá, Mex....C7 63
Hunyüan, China....D7 34
Huon, gulf, Pap. N. Gui....k12 50
Hupeh, prov., China....E7 34
Hurd, cape, Ont., Can....B3 72
Hurdland, Knox, Mo....A5 101
Hurdsfield, Wells, N. Dak....B6 110
Hurley, Jackson, Miss....E5 100
Hurley, Stone Mo....E4 101
Hurley, Grant, N. Mex....E1 107
Hurley, Ulster, N.Y....D6 108
Hurley, Turner, S. Dak....D8 116
Hurley, Buchanan, Va....e9 121
Hurley, Iron, Wis....B3 124
Hurleyville, Sullivan, N.Y....D6 108
Hurliness, Scot....B5 13
Hurlock, Dorchester, Md....C6 85
Hurmāgai, Pak....G12 41
Huron, Fresno, Calif....*D3 82
Huron, Lawrence, Ind....G4 91
Huron, Atchison, Kans....C8 93
Huron, Erie, Ohio....A3 111
Huron, Beadle, S. Dak....C7 116
Huron, co., Ont., Can....D3 72
Huron, co., Mich....E7 98
Huron, co., Ohio....A3 111
Huron, lake, Can., U.S....B11 77
Huron, mts., Mich....B3 98
Huron, riv., Mich....p14 98
Hurricane, Washington, Utah....F2 119
Hurricane, Putnam, W. Va....C2 123
Hurricane, cliffs, Ariz., Utah....F2 119
Hurricane, creek, Ark....C3 81
Hurricane, creek, Ga....E4 87
Hurricane, mtn., Tenn....C9 117
Hurricane Mills, Humphreys, Tenn....B4 117
Hurst, Williamson, Ill....F4 90
Hurst, Tarrant, Tex....*C4 118
Hurt, Pittsylvania, Va....C3 121
Hurth, F.R.G....C1 17
Hurtsboro, Russell, Ala....C4 78
Hurup, Den....B2 24
Huşi, Rom....B9 22
Huskvarna, Swe....I6 25
Huson, Missoula, Mont....C2 102
Hussar, Alta., Can....D4 69
Husser, Tangipahoa, La....D5 95
Hussein-Dey, Alg....*B5 44
Hustburg, Humphreys, Tenn....B4 117
Hustisford, Dodge, Wis....E5 124
Hustle, Essex, Va....B5 121
Hustontown, Fulton, Pa....F5 114
Hustonville, Lincoln, Ky....C5 94
Husum, F.R.G....A4 16
Husum, Klickitat, Wash....D4 122
Hutch, isl., S.C....G1 115
Hutch, mtn., Ariz....C4 80
Hutchins, Dallas, Tex....n10 118
Hutchinson, Reno, Kans....D6, f11 93
Hutchinson, McLeod, Minn....F4 99
Hutchinson, Warren, N.J....B2 106
Hutchinson, co., S. Dak....D8 116
Hutchinson, co., Tex....B2 118
Hutchinson, isl., Fla....E6 86
Hutsonville, Crawford, Ill....D6 90
Hottental, F.R.G....C3 17
Huttig, Union, Ark....D3 81
Hutto, Williamson, Tex....D4 118
Hutton, Garrett, Md....m12 85
Huttonsville, Randolph, W. Va....C5 123
Huttwil, Switz....B4 19
Huu, Indon....G5 35
Huwwarah, Jordan....g12 32
Huxford, Escambia, Ala....D2 78
Huxley, Alta., Can....D4 69
Huxley, Story, Iowa....C4, e8 92
Huy, Bel....D5 15
Huyett, Washington, Md....A2 85
Hvalpsund, Den....B3 24
Hvannadalshnukúr, mtn., Ice....C3 8
Hvidbjerg, Den....B2 24
Hvide Sande, Den....C2 24
Hvidovre, Den....*C6 24
Hvitstein, Nor....p28 25
Hvittingfoss, Nor....p28 25
Hwange, Zimb....A4 49
Hyak, Kittitas, Wash....B4 122
Hyampom, Trinity, Calif....B2 82
Hyannis, Barnstable, Mass....C7 97
Hyannis, Grant, Nebr....B4 103
Hyannis Port, Barnstable, Mass....C7 97
Hyas, Sask., Can....F4 70
Hyatts, Delaware, Ohio....B2 111
Hyattstown, Montgomery, Md....B3 85
Hyattsville, Prince Georges, Md....C4, f9 85
Hyattsville, Big Horn, Wyo....B5 125
Hybart, Monroe, Ala....D2 78
Hybla Valley, Fairfax, Va....g12 121
Hyco, riv., Va....E3 121
Hydaburg, Alsk....D13, n23 79
Hyde, co., N.C....B7 109
Hyde, co., S. Dak....C6 116
Hyden, Austl....F2 50
Hyden, Leslie, Ky....C6 94
Hyde Park, Guy....A3 59
Hyde Park, Dutchess, N.Y....D7 108
Hyde Park, Cache, Utah....B4 119
Hyde Park, Lamoille, Vt....B3 120
Hyder, Alsk....D13, n24 79
Hyderābād, India....E6 39, I7 40
Hyderābād, Pak....C4 39, E2 40
Hydetown, Crawford, Pa....C2 114
Hyde Villa, Berks, Pa....*F10 114
Hydeville, Rutland, Vt....D2 120
Hydraulic, B.C., Can....C7 68
Hydro, Caddo, Okla....B3 112
Hyères, Fr....F7 14
Hyères, is., Fr....F7 14
Hyesanjin, Kor....F4 37
Hygiene, Boulder, Colo....A5 83
Hylo, Alta., Can....B4 69
Hyman, Florence, S.C....D8 115
Hymera, Sullivan, Ind....F3 91
Hyndman, Bedford, Pa....G4 114
Hyndman, peak, Idaho....F4 89
Hyner, Clinton, Pa....D6 114
Hyogo, pref., Jap....*I7 37
Hyopchon, Kor....I4 37
Hyrum, Cache, Utah....B4 119
Hyrynsalmi, Fin....E13 25
Hysham, Treasure, Mont....D9 102
Hythe, Alta., Can....B1 69
Hythe, Eng....C9 12

I

Iaeger, McDowell, W. Va....D3 123
Ialomita, riv., Rom....C8 22
Iamonia, lake, Fla....B2 86
Iantha, Barton, Mo....D3 101
Iaşi (Jassy), Rom....B8 22
Iatan, Platte, Mo....B3 101
Iates, pt., Guam.... 52
Iatt, lake, La....C3 95
Iba, Phil....o12 35
Ibadan, Nig....E5 45
Ibagué, Col....C2 60
Ibanda, Ug....B5 48
Ibapah, Tooele, Utah....C2 119
Ibapah, peak, Utah....D2 119
Ibar, riv., Yugo....D5 22
Ibaraki, pref., Jap....*H10 37
Ibarra, Ec....A2 58
Ibbenbüren, F.R.G....A2 17
Ibera, lake, Arg....E4 55
Iberia, Miller, Mo....C5 101
Iberia, Morrow, Ohio....B3 111
Iberia, par., La....E4 95
Iberville, Que., Can....D4 73
Iberville, Iberville, La....D4, h9 95
Iberville, co., Que., Can....D4 73
Iberville, par., La....D4 95
Iberville, mtn., Newf., Can....f9 75
Ibi, Nig....E6 45
Ibiá, Braz....E1 57
Ibiapaba, mts., Braz....B2 57
Ibicuí, riv., Braz....D2 56
Ibicuy, Arg....A5, f7 54
Ibiraputa, riv., Braz....E1 56
Ibitinga, Braz....C3 56
Ibiza, Sp....C6 20
Ibiza, isl., Sp....C6 20
Ibo, Moz....D7 48
Ibu, Okinawa.... 52
Iburg, F.R.G....A3 17
Ica, Peru....D2 58
Ica, dept., Peru....D2 58
Içá, riv., Braz....D4 60
Icacos, pt., Trin....O22 65
Içana, riv., Braz....C4 60
Ice, cave, Iowa....A6 92
Ice, mtn., B.C., Can....B7 68
Ice, mtn., W. Va....B6 123
Ice, pond, Pa....A1 106
Ice Harbor, dam, Wash....C7 122
Iceland country, Eur....C5 8, n23 25
Ichang, China....I4 36
Icheng, China....I5 36
Ichikawa, Jap....n18 37
Ichinomiya, Jap....n15 37
Ichinoseki, Jap....G10 37
Ichitai, lake, China....A8 39
Ichnya, Sov. Un....F9 27
Ichuan, China....F4 36
Ichun, China....B10 34
Ichun, China....K6 36
Icicle, creek, Wash....B5 122
Ickesburg, Perry, Pa....F7 114
Icó, Braz....C3 57
Icy, cape, Alsk....A7 79
Icy, strait, Alsk....k22 79
Ida, Caddo, La....A2 95
Ida, Monroe, Mich....G7 98
Ida, co., Iowa....B2 72
Ida, lake, Minn....E3 99
Ida, mtn., Grc....E5 29
Idabel, McCurtain, Okla....D7 112
Ida Grove, Ida, Iowa....B2 92
Idah, Nig....E6 45
Idaho, co., Idaho....D3 89
Idaho, state, U.S....B5, 76 89
Idaho City, Boise, Idaho....F3 89
Idaho Falls, Bonneville, Idaho....F6 89
Idaho Springs, Clear Creek, Colo....B5 83
Idalia, Yuma, Colo....B8 83
Idalou, Lubbock, Tex....C2 118
Idana, Clay, Kans....C6 93
Idanha, Marion, Oreg....C4 113
Idanha-a-Nova, Port....C2 20
Idar-Oberstein, F.R.G....D2 17
Idaville, White, Ind....C4 91
'Idd Abū Sufyān, well, Sud....B2 47
Iddan, Som....D6 47
'Iddel Ghanam, Sud....C1 47
Iddesleigh, Alta., Can....D5 69
Ideal, Macon, Ga....D2 87
Ideal, Tripp, S. Dak....D6 116
Idehan, des., Libya....D2 43
Idehan Marzūq, dunes, Libya....E2 43
Ider, DeKalb, Ala....A4 78
Idfīnā, Eg....C2 32
Idfū, Eg....E6 43
Idhra, Grc....D7 23
Ídhra (Hydra), isl., Grc....D4 23
Idi, Indon....E1, m11 35
Idiofa, Zaire....C2 48
Idkū, Eg....C2 32
Idlewild, Gibson, Tenn....A3 117
Idleyld Park, Douglas, Oreg....D4 113
Idlib, Syr....E11 31
Idnah, Jordan....C6 32
Idrigill, pt., Scot....C2 13
Idrija, Yugo....B2 22
Idrinskoye, Sov. Un....E27 9
Idritsa, Sov. Un....C7 27
Idro, lake, It....D6 18
Ie, isl., Okinawa.... 52
Ieper (Ypres), Bel....D2 15
Ierapetra, Grc....E5 23
Ierissos, Grc....B4 23
Iesi, It....C4 21
Ifakara, Tan....C4 48
Ife, Nig....E5 45
Iferouâne, Niger....C6 45
Iganga, Ug....A5 48
Igaraçu, Braz....h6 57
Igara Paraná, riv., Col....D3 60
Igarapava, Braz....F1 57
Igarape Açu, Braz....B1 57
Igarapé Água Preta, riv., Braz....C2 59
Igarapé-Mirí, Braz....C5 59
Igarka, Sov. Un....C11 28
Igdir, Tur....C15 31
Ighil Izane, Alg....B5 44
Iglesias, It....E2 21
Igloolik, N.W. Ter., Can....C23 4
Ignace, Ont., Can....*E7 72
Ignacio, LaPlata, Colo....D3 83
Igneada, Tur....B6 23
Igny, Fr....h9 14
Igoumenitsa, Grc....C3 23
Igra, Sov. Un....B4 29
Iguaçu, cataracts, Braz....D2 56
Iguaçu, riv., Braz....D2 56
Iguala, Mex....D4, n14 63
Igualada, Sp....B6 20
Iguape, Braz....C3 56
Iguatemi, riv., Braz....C2 56
Iguatu, Braz....C3 57
Iguéla, Gabon....F1 46
Iguidi, sand dunes, Alg., Maur....D3 44
Igurin, isl., Eniwetok.... 52
Iha, Okinawa.... 52
Ihiala, Nig....E6 45
Ihlen, Pipestone, Minn....G2 99
Ihosy, Mad....L7 49
Ihsien, China....D9 36
Ihsien, China....F8 36
Ihsien, China....G7 36
Ihsing, China....I8 36
Iida, Jap....I8, n16 37
Iide-San, peak, Jap....H9 37
Iijima, Jap....n16 37
Iisalmi, Fin....F12 25
Iizuka, Jap....*J5 37
Ijamsville, Frederick, Md....B3 85
Ijebu Ode, Nig....E5 45
IJmuiden, Neth....B4 15
IJssel, riv., Neth....B6 15
IJsselmeer (Zuider Zee), sea, Neth....B5 15
Ijuí, Braz....D2 56
Ijuí, riv., Braz....D2 56
Ikaalinen, Fin....G10 25
Ikaria, isl., Grc....D6 23
Ikast, Den....B3 24
Ike, isl., Okinawa.... 52
Ikeda, Jap....o14 37
Ikela, Zaire....B3 48
Ikerre, Nig....*E6 45
Ikhtiman, Bul....D6 22
Iki, isl., Jap....J4 37
Ila, Madison, Ga....B3 87
Ilagan, Phil....B6 35
Ilan, Taiwan....*G9 34
Ilan, China....B10 34
Ilanz, Switz....C7 19
Ilawa, Pol....B5 26
Ilbunga, Austl....E6 51
Ilchester, Howard, Md....B4 85
Ilderton, Ont., Can....D3 72
Île-à-la-Crosse, Sask., Can....m7 70
Île-à-la-Crosse, lake, Sask., Can....B2 70
Île aux Coudres, isl., Que., Can....B7 73
Île aux Grues, isl., Que., Can....B7 73
Île aux Lièvres, isl., Que., Can....B8 73
Île aux Oies, isl., Que., Can....B7 73
Ilebo (Port-Francqui), Zaire....B3 48
Ile-de-France, former prov., Fr....C5 14
Ile de France, hills, Fr....F3 15
Île d' Orléans, isl., Que., Can....C6 73
Île du Bic, isl., Que., Can....A9 73
Île-Perrot, Que., Can....q19 73
Ilesha, Nig....E5 45
Ilfeld, San Miguel, N. Mex....B4 107
Ilford, Man., Can....A4 71
Ilfracombe, Eng....C3 12
Ilgin, Tur....C8 31
Ilhavo, Port....B1 20
Ilhéus, Braz....D3 57
Ili, Sov. Un....E9 29
Ili, riv., Sov. Un....G24 9
Ilia (Elis), prov., Grc....*D3 23
Iliamna, (Newhalen), Alsk....D8 79
Iliamna, lake, Alsk....D8 79
Iliamna, vol., Alsk....g15 79
Iliang, China....D11 39
Iliff, Logan, Colo....A7 83
Iligan, Phil....*D6 35
Iliki, lake, Grc....g10 23
Ilinskaya, Sov. Un....I13 27
Iliodhromia, isl., Grc....C4 23
Ilion, Herkimer, N.Y....B5 108
Ilkeston, Eng....B6 12
Ilkley, Eng....G7 13
Ill, riv., Aus....E4 16
Illampu, mtn., Bol....C2 55
Illana, bay, Phil....D6 35
Illapel, Chile....A2 54
Ille-et-Vilaine, dept., Fr....*C3 14
Iller, riv., F.R.G....D5 16
Ille [-sur-la-Têt], Fr....F5 14
Iliang, China....G5 34
Illianna, lake, Alsk....D8 79
Illiers, Fr....C4 14
Illinois, state, U.S....B10, 77 90
Illinois, bayou, Ark....B2 81
Illinois, peak, Idaho, Mont....B3 89
Illinois, riv., Ark., Okla....B6 112
Illinois, riv., Ill....B5 90
Illinois, riv., Oreg....E3 113
Illinois City, Rock Island, Ill....B3 90
Illiopolis, Sangamon, Ill....D4 90
Illizi, Alg....D6 44
Illkirch-Graffenstaden, Fr....F7 15
Illmo, Scott, Mo....D8 101
Illo, Nig....D5 45
Illora, Sp....D4 20
Ilmen, lake, Sov. Un....B8 27
Ilmenau, G.D.R....C5 17
Ilmenau, riv., F.R.G....B5 24
Ilo, Peru....E3 58
Ilobu, Nig....*E5 45
Ilocos Norte, prov., Phil....*B6 35
Ilocos Sur, prov., Phil....*B6 35
Iloilo, Phil....C6 35
Iloilo, prov., Phil....*C6 35
Ilorin, Nig....E5 45
Ilovaysk, Sov. Un....q21 27
Ilovlinskaya, Sov. Un....D2 29
Ilsenburg, G.D.R....B5 17
Ilubabor, prov., Eth....D3 47
Ilwaco, Pacific, Wash....C1 122
Ilwaki, Indon....G7 35
Ilza, Pol....C6 26
Imabari, Jap....I6 37
Imambaba, Sov. Un....C11 41
Iman, riv., Sov. Un....D7 37
Imathia, prov., Grc....*B4 23
Imazu, Jap....n15 37
Imbābah, Eg....*C6 43
Imbabura, prov., Ec....A2 58
Imbler, Union, Oreg....B9 113
Imboden, Lawrence, Ark....A4 81
Ime, mtn., Scot....D4 13
Imgyt, marsh, Sov. Un....B8 29
Imi, Eth....D5 47
Imienpo, China....D4 37
Imilac, Chile....D2 55
Imlay, Pershing, Nev....C3 104
Imlay City, Lapeer, Mich....E7 98
Imlaystown, Monmouth....C3 106
Immeln, lake, Swe....B8 24
Immenstadt, F.R.G....E5 16
Immokalee, Collier, Fla....F5 86
Imnaha, Wallowa, Oreg....B10 113
Imnaha, riv., Oreg....B10 113
Imogene, Fremont, Iowa....D2 92
Imola, It....B3 21
Imotski, Yugo....D3 22
Imperatriz, Braz....C1 57
Imperia, It....C2 21
Imperial, Imperial, Calif....F6 82
Imperial, Sask., Can....F3 70
Imperial, Jefferson, Mo....C7, g13 101
Imperial, Chase, Nebr....D4 103
Imperial, Allegheny, Pa....k13 114
Imperial, Pecos, Tex....D1 118
Imperial, co., Calif....F6 82
Imperial, diversion dam, Ariz....E1 80
Imperial, val., Calif....F6 82
Imperial Beach, San Diego, Calif....o15 82
Imperial Mills, Alta., Can....B5 69
Imphāl, India....D9 39
Imst, Aus....E5 16
Imus, Phil....o13 35
'Imwās, Jordan....h10 32
Ina, Jap....n16 37
Ina, Jefferson, Ill....E5 90
Ina, riv., Pol....B3 26
Inajá, Braz....C3 57
I-n-Aleï, well, Mali....C4 45
In Amguel, Alg....E6 44
Inanwatan, Indon....F8 35
Iñapari, Peru....D4 58
Inarajan, Guam.... 52
Inarajan, bay, Guam.... 52
Inari, Fin....C12 25
Inari, lake, Fin....C12 25
Inatori, Jap....o18 37
Inavale, Webster, Nebr....D7 103
Inawashiro, lake, Jap....H10 37
In Azaoua (Oasis), Niger....B6 45
In Belbel, Alg....D5 44
In Beriem (Well), Mali....C4 45
Inca, Sp....C7 20
Incastro, riv., It....h9 21
Ince, cape, Tur....A10 31
Incesu, Tur....C10 31
Inch, Ire....E2 11
Inchard, inlet, Scot....B3 13
Inchelium, Ferry, Wash....A7 122
Inchŏn, Kor....H3 37
Indalsälven, riv., Swe....F7 25
Indan, Phil....o14 35
Indang, Phil....o13 35
Indaw, Bur....D10 39
Independence, Inyo, Calif....D4 82
Independence, Warren, Ind....D3 91
Independence, Buchanan, Iowa....B6 92
Independence, Montgomery, Kans....E8 93
Independence, Kenton, Ky....B5, k13 94
Independence, Tangipahoa, La....D5 95
Independence, Hennepin, Minn....*F5 99
Independence, Tate, Miss....A4 100
Independence, Jackson, Mo....B3, h11 101
Independence, Polk, Oreg....C3, k11 113
Independence, Grayson, Va....D1 121
Independence, Trempealeau, Wis....D2 124
Independence, co., Ark....B4 81
Independence, mts., Nev....C5 104
Independence, riv., N.Y....B5 108
Independence, rock, Wyo....D5 125
Independence Hill, Lake, Ind....*B3 91
Independencia, Bol....C2 55
Inderagiri, riv., Indon....F2 35
Inderborskiy, Sov. Un....D4 29
India, country, Asia....G10 33, D6 39
India, Portuguese, see Goa, Daman, and Diu, ter., India
Indiahoma, Comanche, Okla....C3 112
Indialantic, Brevard, Fla....*D6 86
Indian, bay, Fla....D4 86
Indian, creek, Ind....H5 91
Indian, creek, Md....C4 85
Indian, creek, Ohio....C1 111
Indian, creek, S. Dak....B2 116
Indian, creek, Tenn....B3 117
Indian, creek, W. Va....D4 123
Indian, isl., N.C....B6 109
Indian, lake, Mich....C4 98
Indian, lake, N.Y....B6 108
Indian, lake, Ohio....B2 111
Indian, mtn., Conn....B3 84
Indian, ocean, World....G2 2
Indian, peak, Utah....E2 119
Indian, peak, Wyo....B3 125
Indian, pond, Maine....B3 96
Indian, pond, Maine....C3 96
Indian, pond, Maine....D3 96
Indian, riv., Ont., Can....B7 72
Indian, riv., Del....C7 85
Indian, riv., Fla....D6 86
Indian, riv., N.Y....A5 108
Indian, rock, Oreg....C8 113
Indian, stream, N.H....f7 105
Indiana, Indiana, Pa....E3 114
Indiana, co., Pa....E3 114
Indiana, state, U.S....B10 77, 91
Indian Agency, La Plata, Colo....D3 83
Indianapolis, Marion, Ind....E5, k10 91
Indianapolis, Custer, Okla....B3 112
Indian Bay, Man., Can....E4 71
Indian Bayou, Vermilion, La....D3 95
Indian Brook, N.S., Can....C9 74
Indian Cove, Owyhee, Idaho....G3 89
Indian Creek, Dade, Fla....*G6 86
Indian Grave, mtn., Ga....C2 87
Indian Head, Sask., Can....G4 70
Indian Head, Charles, Md....C3 85
Indian Lake, Hamilton, N.Y....B6 108
Indian Mound, Stewart, Tenn....A4 117
Indian Mound Beach, Plymouth, Mass....*C6 97
Indianola, Vermilion, Ill....D6 90
Indianola, Warren, Iowa....C4 92
Indianola, Sunflower, Miss....B3 100
Indianola, Red Willow, Nebr....D5 103
Indianola, Pittsburg, Okla....B6 112
Indianola, Allegheny, Pa....*E2 114
Indian Pass, Gulf, Fla....C1 86
Indian Prairie, canal, Fla....E5 86
Indian River, Ont., Can....C6 72
Indian River (village), Washington, Maine....D5 96
Indian River, Cheboygan, Mich....C6 98
Indian River, co., Fla....E6 86
Indian Rocks Beach, Pinellas, Fla....p10 86
Indian Springs, Butts, Ga....C3 87
Indian Springs, Martin, Ind....G4 91
Indian Springs, Clark, Nev....G6 104
Indiantown, Martin, Fla....E6 86
Indian Trail, Union, N.C....B2 109
Indian Valley, Adams, Idaho....E2 89
Indian Valley, Floyd, Va....D2 121
Indian Wells, Navajo, Ariz....B5 80
Indiga, Sov. Un....B18 9
Indigirka, riv., Sov. Un....C17 28
Indio, Riverside, Calif....F5 82
Indio, riv., Pan....k10 62
Indio, riv., Pan....k12 62
Indochina, reg., Asia....D6 38, H13 33
Indonesia, country, Asia....J15 33, F6 35
Indore, India....D6 39, F5 40
Indrāvati, riv., India....H8 40
Indre, dept., Fr....*D4 14
Indre-et-Loire, dept., Fr....*D4 14
Indus, Koochiching, Minn....B5 99
Indus, riv., Pak....C4 39
Industrial, York, S.C....B6 115
Industrial City, Jefferson, Ala....*B3 78
Industry, McDonough, Ill....C3 90
Industry, Beaver, Pa....*E1 114
Ine, Jap....n14 37
Inebolu, Tur....B9 31
Inez, Martin, Ky....C7 94
Inez, Victoria, Tex....E4 118
Infanta, Phil....o12 35
Infanta, Phil....o13 35
Infantas, Col....B3 60
Infantes, Sp....C4 20
Infiesto, Sp....A3 20
Ingá, Braz....h6 57
I-n-Gall, Niger....C6 45
Ingalls, Bradley, Ark....D3 81
Ingalls, Madison, Ind....E6 91
Ingalls, Gray, Kans....E3 93
Ingalls, Menominee, Mich....C3 98
Ingalls Park, Will, Ill....B5 90
Ingallston, Menominee, Mich....C3 98
Ingelheim, F.R.G....D3 17
Ingende, Zaire....B2 48
Ingeniero Jacobacci, Arg....C3 54
Ingeniero Luiggi, Arg....B4 54
Ingenika, riv., B.C., Can....A5 68
Inger, Itasca, Minn....C5 99
Ingersheim, Fr....A3 18
Ingersoll, Ont., Can....D4 72
Ingersoll, Alfalfa, Okla....A3 112
Ingham, Austl....C8 50
Ingham, Lincoln, Nebr....D5 103
Ingham, co., Mich....F6 98
Ingleford, Spokane, Wash....D7 122
Ingleside, Queen Annes, Md....B6 85
Ingleside, San Patricio, Tex....F4 118
Inglewood, Austl....D8 51
Inglewood, Los Angeles, Calif....n12 82
Inglewood, Ont., Can....D5 72
Inglewood, N.Z....M15 51
Inglis, Man., Can....D1 71
Ingold, Sampson, N.C....C4 109
Ingoldsby, Ont., Can....C6 72
Ingolf, Ont., Can....E4 71
Ingolstadt, F.R.G....E6 17
Ingomar, Union, Miss....A4 100
Ingomar, Rosebud, Mont....D9 102
Ingomar, Allegheny, Pa....h13 114
Ingonish, N.S., Can....C9 74
Ingonish Beach, N.S., Can....C9 74
Ingornachoix, bay, Newf., Can....C3 75
Ingraham, lake, Fla....G5 86
Ingram, Randolph, Ark....A4 81
Ingram, Allegheny, Pa....k13 114
Ingram, Kerr, Tex....*D3 118
Ingram, Rusk, Wis....C3 124
Ingramport, N.S., Can....*E6 74
Ingrid Christensen, coast, Ant....C20 5
In Guezzam, Alg....F6 44
Ingul, riv., Sov. Un....H9 27
Ingulets, riv., Sov. Un....H9 27
Inhambane, Moz....B6 49
Inhambane, prov., Moz....B5 49
Inhambane, bay, Moz....B6 49
Inhambupe, Braz....D3 57
Inhaminga, Moz....A6 49
Inharrime, Moz....B6 49
Inhuçu, Braz....B2 57
Inhumas, Braz....B3 56
Iniesta, Sp....C5 20
Ining (Kuldja), China....E10 29
Inírida, riv., Col....C4 60
Inishark, isl., Ire....D1 11
Inishbofin, isl., Ire....D1 11
Inishcrone, Ire....C2 11
Inisheer, isl., Ire....D2 11
Inishkea, is., Ire....C1 11
Inishmaan, isl., Ire....D2 11
Inishmore, isl., Ire....D2 11
Inishmurray, isl., Ire....C3 11
Inishowen, head, Ire....B5 11
Inishtioge, Ire....E4 11
Inishtooskert, isl., Ire....E1 11
Inishtrahull, isl., Ire....B4 11
Inishturk, isl., Ire....D1 11
Inishvickillane, isl., Ire....E1 11
Injasuti, mtn., Leso., S. Afr....C4 49
Injune, Austl....B7 51
Inkerman, N.B., Can....B5 74
Inkerman, Luzerne, Pa....*D10 114
Inkom, Bannock, Idaho....G6 89
Inkster, Wayne, Mich....p15 98
Inkster, Grand Forks, N. Dak....A8 110
Inland, sea, Jap....I6 37
Inlet, Hamilton, N.Y....B6 108
Inlet, pt., N.Y....E7 84
Inman, Fayette, Ga....C2 87
Inman, McPherson, Kans....D6 93
Inman, Holt, Nebr....B7 103
Inman, Spartanburg, S.C....A3 115
Inman Mills, Spartanburg, S.C....*A3 115
Inn, riv., Aus., F.R.G., Switz....E8 17, D6 16
Inner, sound, Scot....C3 13
Inner Hebrides, is., Scot....D2 13
Innerleithen, Scot....E5 13
Inner Mongolia, auton. reg., China....C7 34
Inner-Rhoden, sub canton, Switz....B7 19
Innerthaler, lake, Switz....B6 19
Innisfail, Austl....C8 50
Innisfail, Alta., Can....C4 69
Innisfree, Alta., Can....C5 69
Inniswold, East Baton Rouge, La....*D4 95
Innokentyevskiy, Sov. Un....B10 37
Innsbruck, Aus....E5 16
Inny, riv., Ire....D4 11
Inola, Rogers, Okla....A6 112
Inongo, Zaire....B2 48
Inoucdjouac, Que., Can....g11 73
Inowroclaw, Pol....B5 26
Ins, Switz....B3 19
In Salah, Alg....D5 44
Insch, Scot....C6 13
Insein, Bur....E10 39
Insinger, Sask., Can....F4 70
Inspiration, Gila, Ariz....D5 80
Institute, Kanawha, W. Va....m12 123
Instow, Sask., Can....H1 70
Intake, Dawson, Mont....C12 102
Intercession City, Osceola, Fla....D5 86
Intercity, Snohomish, Wash....*B3 122
Interior, Jackson, S. Dak....D4 116
Interlachen, Putnam, Fla....C5 86
Interlaken, Berkshire, Mass....*B1 97
Interlaken, Monmouth, N.J....*C4 106
Interlaken, Seneca, N.Y....C4 108
Interlaken, Switz....C4 19
International Falls, Koochiching, Minn....B5 99
International Peace Garden, park, Man., Can., N. Dak....E1 71
Intersection, mtn., B.C., Can....C7 68
Intervale, Carroll, N.H....B4 105
Intiyaco, Arg....E3 55
Intracoastal, waterway, La....k11 95
Intracoastal City, Vermilion, La....E3 95
Inubo, cape, Jap....I10 37
Inútil, bay, Chile....h12 54
Inuvik, N.W. Ter., Can....C6 66
Inver, bay, Ire....C3 11
Inveraray, Scot....D3 13
Inverbervie, Scot....D6 13
Invercargill, N.Z....Q12 51
Inverell, Austl....D8 51
Invergarry, Scot....C4 13
Invergordon, Scot....C4 13
Inver Grove Heights, Dakota, Minn....n12 99
Inverkeithing, Scot....*D5 13
Invermay, Sask., Can....F4 70
Invermere, B.C., Can....D9 68
Inverness, Bullock, Ala....D4 78
Inverness, Marin, Calif....C2 82
Inverness, N.S., Can....C8 74
Inverness, Que., Can....C6 73
Inverness, Citrus, Fla....D4 86
Inverness, Cook, Ill....*B6 90
Inverness, Sunflower, Miss....B3 100
Inverness, Hill, Mont....B6 102
Inverness, Scot....C4 13
Inverness, co., N.S., Can....C8 74
Inverurie, Scot....C6 13
Inwood, Ont., Can....E3 72
Inwood, Man., Can....D3 71
Inwood, Marshall, Ind....B5 91
Inwood, Lyons, Iowa....A1 92
Inwood, Nassau, N.Y....k13 108
Inwood, Caledonia, Vt....C4 120
Inwood, Berkeley, W. Va....*B6 123
Inyanga, Zimb....A5 49
Inyankara, mtn., Wyo....B8 125
Inyo, co., Calif....D5 82
Inyokern, Kern, Calif....E5 82
Inyonga, Tan....C5 48
Inza, Sov. Un....E16 27
Inzana, lake, B.C., Can....B5 68
Ioannina, Grc....C3 23
Ioannina, prov., Grc....*C3 23
Iola, Clay, Ill....E5 90
Iola, Allen, Kans....E8 93
Iola, Waupaca, Wis....D4 124
Iona, N.S., Can....D9 74
Iona, Bonneville, Idaho....F7 89
Iona, Murray, Minn....G3 99
Iona, Gloucester, N.J....D2 106
Iona, Lyman, S. Dak....D6 116
Iona, isl., Scot....D2 13
Ione, Amador, Calif....C3 82
Ione, Weld, Colo....A6 83
Ione, Nye, Nev....E4 104
Ione, Morrow, Oreg....B7 113
Ione, Pend Oreille, Wash....A8 122
Ionia, Chickasaw, Iowa....A5 92
Ionia, Jewell, Kans....C5 93
Ionia, Ionia, Mich....F5 98
Ionia, Benton, Mo....G4 101
Ionia, co., Mich....F5 98
Ionian, is., Grc....C3 23
Ionian, sea, Grc....C2 23
Ios, isl., Grc....D5 23
Iosco, co., Mich....D7 98
Iosegun riv., Alta., Can....B2 69
Iosegun Lake (Fox Creek), Alta., Can....B2 69
Iota, Acadia, La....D3 95
Iowa, Calcasieu, La....D2 95
Iowa, co., Iowa....C5 92
Iowa, co., Wis....E3 124
Iowa, state, U.S....B9, 77 92
Iowa, lake, Iowa....A3 92
Iowa, riv., Iowa....C5 92
Iowa City, Johnson, Iowa....C6 92
Iowa Falls, Hardin, Iowa....B4 92
Iowa Park, Wichita, Tex....C3 118
Ipameri, Braz....E1 57
Ipava, Fulton, Ill....C3 90
Ipel, riv., Czech....D5 26
Iphigenia, sound, Alsk....n23 79
Ipiales, Col....C2 60
Ipin, China....F5 34
Ipirá, Braz....D3 57
Ipoh, Mala....J4 38
Ipoly, riv., Hung....B4 22
Ippy, Cen. Afr. Rep....D4 46
Ipsala, Tur....B6 23
Ipswich, Austl....C9 51
Ipswich, Eng....B9 12
Ipswich, Essex, Mass....A6 97
Ipswich, Edmunds, S. Dak....B6 116
Ipswich, riv., Mass....A5 97
Ipu, Braz....B2 57
Ipueiras, Braz....B2 57
Iquique, Chile....D1 55
Iquitos, Peru....B3 58
Ira, Jasper, Iowa....C4 92
Ira, Scurry, Tex....C2 118
Ira, Rutland, Vt....D2 120
Iraan, Pecos, Tex....D2 118
Iracoubo, Fr., Gu....A4 59
Iraklion, Grc....E5 23
Iraklion, prov., Grc....*E5 23
Irala, Par....E5 55
Iran (Persia), country, Asia....F8 33 41
Iran, mts., Indon., Mala....E4 35
Iran, plat., Iran....E7 41
Irapa, Ven....A5 60
Irapuato, Mex....C4, m13 63

Iraq, country, Asia .F14 31, E2 41
Irasburg, Orleans, Vt ...B4 120
Irasville, Washington, Vt ...C3 120
Irazú, vol., C.R. ...F6 62
Irbid, Jordan ...B7 32
Irbil, Iraq ...D15 31
Irbit, Sov. Un ...D21 9
Irebu, Zaire ...B2 48
Iredell, co., N.C ...B2 109
Ireland, Dubois, Ind ...H3 91
Ireland (Eire), country, Eur ...E7 8, D3 10
Ireland, isl., Bermuda ...p19 64
Irene, Clay, S. Dak ...D8 116
Ireton, Sioux, Iowa ...B1 92
Irgiz, Sov. Un ...D6 29
Irgiz, riv., Sov. Un ...F21 9
Irharrhar, riv., Alg ...D6 44
Irharrhar, riv., Alg ...E6 44
Iri, Kor ...I3 37
Irian Jaya, reg., Indon ...F9 35
Iriklinskoye, res., Sov. Un ...C5 29
Iringa, Tan ...C6 48
Iriomote, isl., Jap ...G9 34
Irion, co., Tex ...D2 118
Iriona, Hond ...C5 62
Iriri, riv., Braz ...C4 59
Irish, sea, Eur ...D4 10
Irkutsk, Sov. Un ...D13 28
Irma, Alta., Can ...C5 69
Irmo, Lexington, S.C ...C5 115
Iron, St. Louis, Minn ...C6 99
Iron, co., Mich ...B2 98
Iron, co., Mo ...D7 101
Iron, co., Utah ...F2 119
Iron, co., Wis ...B3 124
Iron, mtn., Ariz ...D4 80
Iron, mtn., Fla ...E5 86
Iron, mts., Ire ...C4 11
Iron, mts., Va ...f10 121
Iron Belt, Iron, Wis ...B3 124
Iron City, Seminole, Ga ...F2 87
Iron City, Lawrence, Tenn ...B4 117
Irondale, Jefferson, Ala ...f7 78
Irondale, Washington, Mo ...D7 101
Irondale, Jefferson, Ohio ...B5 111
Irondequoit, Monroe, N.Y ...B3 108
Iron Gate, Alleghany, Va ...C3 121
Iron Gate, gorge, Rom., Yugo ...C6 22
Ironia, Morris, N.J ...B3 106
Iron Lightning, Ziebach, S. Dak ...B4 116
Iron Mountain, Dickinson, Mich ...C2 98
Iron Mountain, St. Francois, Mo ...D7 101
Iron Mountain, Iron, Utah ...F2 119
Iron Mountain, Laramie, Wyo ...E7 125
Iron Ridge, Dodge, Wis ...E5 124
Iron River, Iron, Mich ...B2 98
Iron River, Bayfield, Wis ...B2 124
Irons, Lake, Mich ...D5 98
Irons, mtn., Ark ...B3 81
Ironside, Que., Can ...h12 72
Ironside, Malheur, Oreg ...C9 113
Ironspot, Muskingum, Ohio .C3 111
Iron Springs, Yavapai, Ariz .C3 80
Ironton, Crow Wing, Minn .D5 99
Ironton, Iron, Mo ...D7 101
Ironton, Lawrence, Ohio ...D3 111
Ironwood, Gogebic, Mich ...n11 98
Iroquois, N.B., Can ...*B1 74
Iroquois, Ont., Can ...C9 72
Iroquois, Iroquois, Ill ...C6 90
Iroquois, Beadle and Kingsbury, S. Dak ...C8 116
Iroquois, co., Ill ...C3 90
Iroquois, lake, Vt ...C2 120
Iroquois, riv., Ind ...C3 91
Iroquois Falls, Ont., Can ...G16 67
Irosin, Phil ...*C6 35
Irrawaddy, riv., Bur ...D10 39
Irricana, Alta., Can ...D4 69
Irrigon, Morrow, Oreg ...B7 113
Irt, riv., Eng ...F5 13
Irthing, riv., Eng ...F5 13
Irtysh, Sov. Un ...C8 29
Irtysh, riv., Sov. Un ...E24 9
Irumu, Zaire ...A4 48
Irún, Sp ...A5 20
Irvine, Orange, Calif ...n6 82
Irvine, Alta., Can ...E5 69
Irvine, Marion, Fla ...C4 86
Irvine, Estill, Ky ...C6 94
Irvine, Warren, Pa ...C3 114
Irvine, Scot ...E4 13
Irvine, riv., Scot ...E4 13
Irvines Landing, B.C., Can .E5 68
Irving, Montgomery, Ill ...D4 90
Irving, Dallas, Tex ...n10 118
Irvington, Mobile, Ala ...E1 78
Irvington, Washington, Ill ...E4 90
Irvington, Breckinridge, Ky .C3 94
Irvington, Douglas, Nebr ...g12 103
Irvington, Essex, N.J ...k8 106
Irvington, Westchester, N.Y.g13 108
Irvington, Lancaster, Va ...C6 121
Irvona, Clearfield, Pa ...E4 114
Irwin, Bonneville, Idaho ...F7 89
Irwin, Shelby, Iowa ...C2 92
Irwin, Cherry, Nebr ...B4 103
Irwin, Westmoreland, Pa ...F2 114
Irwin, Lancaster, S.C ...*B6 115
Irwin, co., Ga ...E3 87
Irwindale, Los Angeles, Calif ...*E4 82
Irwinton, Wilkinson, Ga ...D3 87
Irwinville, Irwin, Ga ...E3 87
Isa, Nig ...D6 45
Isa, Okinawa ... 52
Isaac, lake, B.C., Can ...C7 68
Isaac's Harbour, N.S., Can .D8 74
Isabel, Barber, Kans ...E5 93
Isabel, Dewey, S. Dak ...B4 116
Isabel, mtn., Wyo ...D2 125
Isabela (Basilan), Phil ...D6 35
Isabela, P.R ...A1 65
Isabela, mun., P.R ...*B1 65
Isabela, prov., Phil ...*B6 35
Isabela (Albemarle), isl., Ec ...g5 58
Isabella, Man., Can ...D1 71
Isabella, Worth, Ga ...E3 87
Isabella, Delta, Mich ...C4 98
Isabella, Lake, Minn ...C7 99
Isabella, Ozark, Mo ...E5 101
Isabella, Major, Okla ...A3 112
Isabella, Fayette, Pa ...G2 114
Isabella, Polk, Tenn ...D9 117
Isabella, co., Mich ...E6 98
Isabella, lake, Minn ...C7 99
Isabella, mts., Nic ...D5 62
Isaccea, Rom ...C9 22
Isachsen, N.W. Ter., Can ...m31 67
Ísafjördur, Ice ...m21 25
Isahaya, Jap ...J5 37
Isaka, Zaire ...B3 48
Isanga, Zaire ...B3 48
Isangi, Zaire ...A3 48
Isanti, Isanti, Minn ...E5 99
Isanti, co., Minn ...E5 99
Isar, riv., F.R.G ...E7 17
Isarco, riv., It ...A3 21
'Isāwīyah, Jordan ...m14 32
Isbergues, Fr ...D2 15
Isbister, riv., Man., Can ...C4 71
Ischia, isl., It ...D4 21
Ischua, Cattaraugus, N.Y ...C2 108
Ise, riv., F.R.G ...F4 24
Isel, riv., Aus ...E6 16
Iselin, Middlesex, N.J ...B4 106
Iselin, Indiana, Pa ...E3 114
Isen, riv., F.R.G ...A8 18
Isenthal, Switz ...C6 19
Iseo, lake, It ...B3 21
Isère, dept., Fr ...D1 18
Isère, riv., Fr ...E6 14
Iserlohn, F.R.G ...B2 17
Isernia, It ...D5 21
Iseyin, Nig ...E5 45
Isezaki, Jap ...H9, m18 37
Isfahan, see Eşfahān, Iran
Ishan, China ...G6 38
Ishikawa, Okinawa ... 52
Ishikawa, pref., Jap ...*H8 37
Ishim, Sov. Un ...B7 29
Ishim, riv., Sov. Un ...D23 9
Ishimbay, Sov. Un ...C5 29
Ishinomaki, Jap ...G10 37
Ishioka, Jap ...m19 37
Ishpeming, Marquette, Mich .B3 98
Isigny-sur-Mer, Fr ...C3 14
Isil-Kul, Sov. Un ...C8 29
Isiolo, Ken ...A6 48
Isiro (Paulis), Zaire ...A4 48
Isisford, Austl ...B5 51
Iskenderun (Alexandretta), Tur ...D11 31
Isker, riv., Bul ...D6 22
Iskilip, Tur ...B10 31
Iskitim, Sov. Un ...E25 9
Iskushuban, Som ...C7 47
Iskwatikan, lake, Sask., Can ...B3 70
Isla Cabellos, Ur ...E1 56
Isla Cristina, Sp ...D2 20
Islāmābād, Pak ...B5 39
Islamorada, Monroe, Fla ...H6 86
Island, McLean, Ky ...C2 94
Island, co., Wash ...A3 122
Island, beach, N.J ...D4 106
Island, dam, Ala ...B3 78
Island, lake, Man., Can ...C4 71
Island, pond, N.H ...E4 105
Island, pond, Vt ...B5 120
Island Brook, Que., Can ...D6 73
Island City, Union, Oreg ...B8 113
Island Creek, Plymouth, Mass ...*B6 97
Island Falls, Sask., Can ...B4 70
Island Falls, Aroostook, Maine ...B4 96
Island Grove, Alachua, Fla ..C4 86
Island Heights, Ocean, N.J ..D4 106
Island Lake, Man., Can ...C4 71
Island Lake, Lake and McHenry, Ill ...*A5 90
Island Lake, riv., Man., Can ...B4 71
Island Park, Fremont, Idaho .E7 89
Island Park, Nassau, N.Y ..*E7 108
Island Park, Newport, R.I ..C12 84
Island Park, res., Idaho ...E7 89
Island Pond, Essex, Vt ...B5 120
Islands, bay, Newf., Can ...D2 75
Isla Vista, Santa Barbara, Calif ...E4 82
Islay, Alta., Can ...C5 69
Islay, isl., Scot ...E2 13
Islay, sound, Scot ...E3 13
Isle, Mille Lacs, Minn ...D5 99
Isle, riv., Fr ...E4 14
Isle au Haut, Knox, Maine ..D4 96
Isle-aux-Morts, Newf., Can ..E2 75
Isle La Motte, Grand Isle, Vt.B2 120
Isle Maligne (part of Alma), Que., Can ...A6 73
Isle of Hope, Chatham, Ga ...*D6 87
Isle of Man, Br. dep., Eur ..C7 11
Isle of Palms, Charleston, S.C ...k12 115
Isle of Wight, Isle of Wight, Va ...D6, k14 121
Isle of Wight (Hampshire), co. part, Eng ...D6 12
Isle of Wight, co., Va ...D6 121
Isle of Wight, isl., Eng ...E6 10
Isle Pierre, B.C., Can ...C6 68
Isle Royale, isl., Mich ...h9 98
Isle Royale, nat. park, Mich ...h9 98
Islesboro, Waldo, Maine ...D4 96
Islesford, Hancock, Maine ..D4 96
Isleta, Bernalillo, N. Mex ...C3, m7 107
Isleta, Indian res., N. Mex ...C3 107
Isleton, Sacramento, Calif ..C3 82
Isle-Verte, Que., Can ...A8 73
Islington, Norfolk, Mass ...h11 97
Islip, Suffolk, N.Y ...*G4 84
Islip Terrace, Suffolk, N.Y .*G4 84
Islitas, Webb, Tex ...F3 118
Ismā'ilīyah, canal, Eg ...D3 32
Ismay, Custer, Mont ...D12 102
Isnā, Eg ...D6 43
Isoka, Zambia ...D5 48
Isola, Humphreys, Miss ...B3 100
Isola Capo Rizzuto, It ...E6 21
Isola della Scala, It ...D7 18
Isparta, Tur ...D8 31
Ispir, Tur ...B13 31
Israel, country, Asia ...F6, 33 32
Israel, riv., N.H ...B3 105
Issano Landing, Guy ...A3 59
Issaquah, King, Wash ...B3, e11 122
Issaquena, co., Miss ...C2 100
Issia, I.C ...E3 45
Issoire, Fr ...E5 14
Issoudun, Fr ...D4 14
Issuna, Tan ...C5 48
Issyk-kul, lake, Sov. Un ...G24 9
Issy [-les-Moulineaux], Fr ...g10 14
Istachatta, Hernando, Fla ...D4 86
Istādeh-ye Moqor, lake, Afg ...E13 41
Istanbul (Constantinople), Tur ...B7 23, B7 31
Istiaia, Grc ...C4 23
Istokpoga, lake, Fla ...E5 86
Istonio, see Vasto, It.
Istranca, mts., Tur ...B6 23
Istres, Fr ...F6 14
Istrian, pen., Yugo ...C2 22
Itá, Par ...E4 55
Itabaiana, Braz ...C3, h6 57
Itabaiana, Braz ...D3 57
Itabaianinha, Braz ...D3 57
Itabapoana, riv., Braz ...C4 56
Itaberaba, Braz ...D2 57
Itaberaí, Braz ...B3 56
Itabira, Braz ...E2 57
Itaboraí, Braz ...C4, h6 56
Itabuna, Braz ...D3 57
Itacaiunas, riv., Braz ...D4 59
Itacoatiara, Braz ...C3 59
Itaetê, Braz ...D2 57
Itaguaçu, Braz ...E2 57
Itaituba, Braz ...C3 59
Itajaí, Braz ...D3 57
Itajubá, Braz ...C3 57
Itale, Som ...E6 47
Italia, Nassau, Fla ...B6 86
Italy, Ellis, Tex ...C4 118
Italy, country, Eur ...G11, 8 21
Italy Cross, N.S., Can ...E5 74
Itamaraca, isl., Braz ...h6 57
Itami, Jap ...o14 37
Itanhaém, Braz ...n8 56
Itapecurú, riv., Braz ...B2 57
Itapecuru-Mirim, Braz ...B2 57
Itapemirim, Braz ...C4 56
Itaperuna, Braz ...C4 56
Itapetininga, Braz ...C3, m7 56
Itapeva, Braz ...C3 56
Itapi, riv., Braz ...C3 59
Itapicurú, riv., Braz ...D3 57
Itapipoca, Braz ...B3 57
Itápolis, Braz ...k7 56
Itaporanga, Braz ...C3 57
Itapúa, dept., Par ...E4 55
Itaqui, Braz ...D1 56
Itararé, Braz ...C3 56
Itararé, riv., Braz ...C3 56
Itaretama, Braz ...C3, g5 57
Itarsi, India ...F6 40
Itasca, DuPage, Ill ...k8 90
Itasca, Hill, Tex ...C4 118
Itasca, co., Minn ...C5 99
Itasca, lake, Minn ...C3 99
Itatiaya, peak, Braz ...h5 56
Itatiba, Braz ...m8 56
Itatinga, Braz ...m7 56
Itaúna, Braz ...F2 57
Itawamba, co., Miss ...A5 100
Itea, Grc ...C4 23
Itecoaí, riv., Braz ...C3 58
Itezehoe, F.R.G ...E4 15
Ithaca, Gratiot, Mich ...E6 98
Ithaca, Saunders, Nebr ...g11 103
Ithaca, Tompkins, N.Y ...C4 108
Ithaki, Grc ...C3 23
Ithákí (Ithaca), isl., Grc ...C3 23
Itigi, Tan ...C5 48
Itimbiri, riv., Zaire ...A3 48
Itirapina, Braz ...m8 56
Itō, Jap ...o18 37
Itoko, Zaire ...B3 48
Itoman, Okinawa ... 52
Itsmina, Col ...B2 60
Itta Bena, Leflore, Miss ...B3 100
Itu, Braz ...C3, m8 56
Itu, China ...F8 36
Ituango, Col ...B2 60
Ituiutaba, Braz ...B3 56
Itumbiara, Braz ...B3 56
Ituna, Sask., Can ...F4 70
Ituxi, riv., Braz ...D4 58
Ityāy al Bārūd, Eg ...D2 32
Itzehoe, F.R.G ...E4 16
Iuka, Marion, Ill ...E5 90
Iuka, Pratt, Kans ...E5 93
Iuka, Tishomingo, Miss ...A5 100
Iva, W. Sam ... 52
Iva, Anderson, S.C ...C2 115
Ivaí, riv., Braz ...C2 56
Ivalo, Fin ...C12 25
Ivangrad, Yugo ...D4 22
Ivanhoe, Austl ...F5 51
Ivanhoe, Tulare, Calif ...*D4 82
Ivanhoe, Lincoln, Minn ...F2 99
Ivanhoe, Sampson, N.C ...C4 109
Ivanhoe, Wythe, Va ...D2 121
Ivanić Grad, Yugo ...C3 22
Ivanovichi, Sov. Un ...D7 27
Ivano-Frankovsk, Sov. Un ..G5 27
Ivanovka, Sov. Un ...p21 27
Ivanovka, Sov. Un ...A4 37
Ivanovo, Sov. Un ...B2 29
Ivanteyevka, Sov. Un ...n17 27
Ivato, Mad ...g9 49
Ivaylovgrad, Bul ...E8 22
Ivdel, Sov. Un ...A6 29
Ivesdale, Champaign and Piatt, Ill ...D5 90
Ivigtut, Grnld ...C19 4
Ivinheima, riv., Braz ...C2 57
Ivins, Washington, Utah ...F2 119
Ivohibe, Mad ...h9 49
Ivor, Southampton, Va ...D6 121
Ivory Coast, country, Afr ...F5 42, E3 45
Ivoryton, Middlesex, Conn .D7 84
Ivösjön, lake, Swe ...B8 24
Ivrea, It ...B1 21
Ivry-Nord, Que., Can ...C3 73
Ivry-sur-Seine, Fr ...g10 14
Ivujivik, Que., Can ...D17 67
Ivy, Dallas, Ark ...C3 81
Ivy, Albemarle, Va ...B4 121
Ivy, mtn., Conn ...B4 84
Ivydale, Clay, W. Va ...C3 123
Ivyton, Magoffin, Ky ...C7 94
Ivywild, El Paso, Colo ...C6 83
Iwakuni, Jap ...I6 37
Iwamisawa, Jap ...E10 37
Iwamurada, Jap ...m17 37
Iwanai, Jap ...E10 37
Iwate, pref., Jap ...*G10 37
Iwaya, Jap ...o14 37
Iwo, Nig ...E5 45
Iwo (Iō), isl., Pac. O ... 52
Iwon, Kor ...F4 37
Ixiamas, Bol ...B2 55
Ixmiquilpan, Mex ...m14 63
Ixmiquilpan, lake, Mex ...m14 63
Ixtacalco, Mex ...h9 63
Ixtapalapa, Mex ...h9 63
Ixtlán de Juárez, Mex ...o15 63
Ixtlán del Río, Mex ...C4, m11 63
Iyang, China ...J5 36
Izabal, lake, Guat ...C3 62
Izad Khvāst, Iran ...F6 41
Izamal, Mex ...C7 63
Izard, co., Ark ...A4 81
Izberbash, Sov. Un ...G18 9
Izee, Grant, Oreg ...C7 113
Izegem, Bel ...D3 15
Izhevsk, Sov. Un ...B4 29
Izhma, riv., Sov. Un ...C19 9
Izmail, Sov. Un ...I7 27
Izmir (Smyrna), Tur ...C6 23, C6 31
Izmir, bay, Tur ...C6 23
Izmit (Kocaeli), Tur ...B7 23
Iznik, Tur ...B7 23
Iznik, lake, Tur ...B7 23
Izra', Syr ...B8 32
Izu, isl., Pac. O ...D8 7
Izúcar de Matamoros, Mex .n14 63
Izuhara, Jap ...I4 37
Izumo, Jap ...I6 37
Izyum, Sov. Un ...G11 27

J

Jabal, see Mountain Nile, riv., Sud.
Jabal al Awliyā', Sud ...B3 47
Jabalón, riv., Sp ...C4 20
Jabalpur, India ...D6 39, F7 40
Jabālyah, Gaza Strip ...C6 32
Jablonec [nad Nisou], Czech ...C3 26
Jablonna, Czech ...o17 26
Jablonna, Pol ...k13 26
Jablunkov, pass, Czech ...D5 26
Jaboatão, Braz ...C4, k6 57
Jaboticabal, Braz ...C3, k7 56
Jabrin, isl., Iran ...H5 41
Jaca, Sp ...A5 20
Jacala [de Ledesma], Mex ..m14 63
Jacaraci, Braz ...D2 57
Jacaré, riv., Braz ...D2 57
Jacareí, Braz ...m9 56
Jacarèzinho, Braz ...C3 56
Jachal, Arg ...F2 55
Jachymov, Czech ...C2 26
Jacinto, Dallas, Ark ...D3 81
Jacinto, Alcorn, Miss ...A5 100
Jacinto City, Harris, Tex ...r14 118
Jack, co., Tex ...C3 118
Jack, mtn., Mont ...D4 102
Jack, mtn., Va ...B3 121
Jack, mtn., Wash ...A5 122
Jackfish, lake, Sask., Can ...D1 70
Jackhead Harbour, Man., Can ...D3 71
Jackman, Somerset, Maine ..C2 96
Jackpot, Elko, Nev ...B7 104
Jacks, peak, Utah ...E3 119
Jacksboro, Campbell, Tenn ..C9 117
Jacksboro, Jack, Tex ...C3 118
Jacks Creek, Chester, Tenn ..B3 117
Jackson, Clarke, Ala ...D2 78
Jackson, Amador, Calif ...C3 82
Jackson, Butts, Ga ...C3 87
Jackson, Breathitt, Ky ...C6 94
Jackson, Calcasieu, La ...D4 95
Jackson, Waldo, Maine ...D3 96
Jackson, Jackson, Mich ...F6 98
Jackson, Jackson, Minn ...G4 99
Jackson, Hinds, Miss ...C3 100
Jackson, Cape Girardeau, Mo ...D8 101
Jackson, Beaverhead, Mont ..E3 102
Jackson, Dakota, Nebr ...B9 103
Jackson, Carroll, N.H ...B4 105
Jackson, Ocean, N.J ...C4 106
Jackson, Northampton, N.C.A5 109
Jackson, Jackson, Ohio ...C3 111
Jackson, Providence, R.I ...C10 84
Jackson, Aiken, S.C ...E4 115
Jackson, Madison, Tenn ...B3 117
Jackson, Washington, Wis ...E5, m11 124
Jackson, Teton, Wyo ...C2 125
Jackson, co., Ala ...A3 78
Jackson, co., Ark ...B4 81
Jackson, co., Colo ...A4 83
Jackson, co., Fla ...u16 86
Jackson, co., Ga ...B3 87
Jackson, co., Ill ...F4 90
Jackson, co., Ind ...G5 91
Jackson, co., Iowa ...B7 92
Jackson, co., Kans ...C8 93
Jackson, co., Ky ...C5 94
Jackson, co., Mich ...F6 98
Jackson, co., Minn ...G3 99
Jackson, co., Miss ...E5 100
Jackson, co., Mo ...C3 101
Jackson, co., N.C ...f9 109
Jackson, co., Ohio ...C3 111
Jackson, co., Okla ...C2 112
Jackson, co., Oreg ...E4 113
Jackson, co., S. Dak ...D4 116
Jackson, co., Tenn ...C8 117
Jackson, co., Tex ...E4 118
Jackson, co., W. Va ...C3 123
Jackson, co., Wis ...D3 124
Jackson, par., La ...B3 95
Jackson, lake, Fla ...B2 86
Jackson, lake, Fla ...E5 86
Jackson, lake, Ga ...C3 87
Jackson, lake, Wyo ...C2 125
Jackson, mtn., Maine ...D2 96
Jackson, mts., Nev ...B3 104
Jackson, riv., Va ...C3 121
Jacksonboro, Colleton, S.C ...F7, k11 115
Jacksonburg, Wetzel, W. Va ...B4, h9 123
Jackson Center, Shelby, Ohio ...B1 111
Jackson Center, Mercer, Pa ..D1 114
Jackson Hill, Sullivan, Ind ..F3 91
Jackson Junction, Winneshiek, Iowa ...A5 92
Jacksonport, Jackson, Ark ...B4 81
Jackson's Arm, Newf., Can ..D3 75
Jacksons Gap, Tallapoosa, Ala ...C4 78
Jacksonville, Calhoun, Ala ...B4 78
Jacksonville, Pulaski, Ark ...C3, h10 81
Jacksonville, Duval, Fla .B5, m8 86
Jacksonville, Telfair, Ga ...E3 87
Jacksonville, Morgan, Ill ...D3 90
Jacksonville, Shelby, Iowa ...C2 92
Jacksonville, Washington, Maine ...D5 96
Jacksonville, Randolph, Mo ..B5 101
Jacksonville, Onslow, N.C ...C5 109
Jacksonville, Athens, Ohio ...C3 111
Jacksonville, Jackson, Oreg ..E4 113
Jacksonville, Cherokee, Tex .D5 118
Jacksonville, Windham, Vt ..F3 120
Jacksonville Beach, Duval, Fla ...B5, m9 86
Jacmel, Hai ...E7 64
Jacob, Con ...B1 48
Jacob Lake, Coconino, Ariz ..A3 80
Jacobābād, Pak ...C4 39
Jacobina, Braz ...D2 57
Jacobson, Aitkin, Minn ...C5 99
Jacobstown, Burlington, N.J ..C3 106
Jacobsville, Houghton, Mich .B2 98
Jacques Cartier, mtn., Que., Can ...G19 67
Jacques-Cartier, strait, Que., Can ...h8 75
Jacquet, riv., N.B., Can ...B3 74
Jacquet River, N.B., Can ...B4 74
Jacquinot, bay, Pap. N. Gui ...k13 50
Jacuí, Braz ...k8 56
Jacuí, riv., Braz ...D2 56
Jacuípe, riv., Braz ...D3 57
Jacuitiba, Braz ...m8 57
Jacumba, San Diego, Calif ...F5 82
Jacundá, riv., Braz ...C4 59
Jaddi, cape, Pak ...I11 41
Jade, F.R.G ...A8 15
Jade, bay, F.R.G ...E4 16
Jadhamiyah, Sau. Ar ...I14 31
Jadotville, Zaire ...D4 48
Jādū, Libya ...C2 43
Jaegerspris, Den ...C5 24
Jaén, Peru ...C2 58
Jaén, Sp ...D4 20
Jaén, prov., Sp ...*D4 20
Jaffa, see Tel Aviv-Yafo, Isr.
Jaffa, cape, Austl ...H2 51
Jaffna, Sri Lanka ...G7 39
Jaffrey, Cheshire, N.H ...E2 105
Jaffrey Center, Cheshire, N.H ...E2 105
Jagadhri, India ...B6 40
Jagdalpur, India ...H9 40
Jagin, riv., Iran ...H9 41
Jagok, lake, China ...B12 40
Jagst, riv., F.R.G ...D4 17
Jaguarão, Braz ...E2 56
Jaguariaíva, Braz ...C3 56
Jagüey Grande, Cuba ...C3 64
Jahrom, Iran ...G6 41
Jaicós, Braz ...C2 57
Jailolo, Indon ...E7 35
Jaipur, India ...C6 39, D5 40
Jaisalmer, India ...C5 40
Jajce, Yugo ...C3 22
Jājpur, India ...G11 40
Jakarta (Djakarta), Indon ..G3 35
Jakes Corner, Gila, Ariz ...C4 80
Jakestown, Putnam, Tenn ...C8 117
Jakin, Early, Ga ...E2 87
Jakobstad, Fin ...F10 25
Jal, Lea, N. Mex ...E6 107
Jalaiha, pt., Guam ... 52
Jalālābād, Afg ...D15 41
Jalālah al Baḩrīyah, mts., Eg ...E4 32
Jalapa, Guat ...C2 62
Jalapa Enríquez (Jalapa), Mex ...D5, n15 63
Jālaun, India ...D7 40
Jalca Grande Amazonas, Peru ...C2 58
Jaleshwar, Nep ...D10 40
Jālgaon, India ...G5 40
Jalisco, Mex ...m11 63
Jalisco, state, Mex ...C4, m12 63
Jālna, India ...H5 40
Jalón, riv., Sp ...B5 20
Jālor, India ...E4 40
Jalpa, Mex ...C4, m12 63
Jalpaiguri, India ...D12 40
Jalpan, Mex ...C5, m14 63
Jālū, oasis, Libya ...D4 43
Jalūlā, Iraq ...E15 31
Jamachim, riv., Braz ...D3 59
Jamaica, Guthrie, Iowa ...C3 92
Jamaica, Windham, Vt ...E3 120
Jamaica, country, N.A ...E13 65
Jamaica, bay, N.Y ...k13 108
Jamaica, chan., W.I ...F6 64
Jamālpur, Bngl ...E12 40
Jamame (Margherita), Som ..E5 47
Jambi, Indon ...F2 35
James, Jones, Ga ...D3 87
James, bay, Ont., Can ...F16 67
James, isl., B.C., Can ...C3 68
James, isl., Md ...C5 85
James, isl., S.C ...F8 115
James, lake, Ind ...A7 91
James, lake, N.C ...B1 109
James, pt., Md ...C5 85
James, range, Austl ...D5 50
James, riv., Alta., Can ...D3 69
James, riv., Mo ...E4 101
James, riv., N. Dak ...C7 110
James, riv., S. Dak ...C7 116
James, riv., Va ...C5 121
Jamesburg, Middlesex, N.J ..C4 106
James City, Craven, N.C ...B5 109
James City, Elk, Pa ...C4 114
James City, co., Va ...C6 121
James Craik, Arg ...A4 54
James Creek (Marklesburg), Huntingdon, Pa ...E5 114
James Island, B.C., Can ...g12 68
James Island, Charleston, S.C ...k12 115
Jamesport, Daviess, Mo ...A3 101
Jamesport, Daviess, Mo ...B4 101
Jamesport, Suffolk, N.Y ...F6 84
James Ross, isl., Ant ...C7 5
James Ross, strait, N.W. Ter., Can ...C13 66
Jamestown, Cherokee, Ala ...A4 78
Jamestown, Austl ...F2 51
Jamestown, Tuolumne, Calif.D3 82
Jamestown, Boulder, Colo ...A5 83
Jamestown, Clinton, Ill ...E4 90
Jamestown, Boone, Ind ...E4 91
Jamestown, Ire ...D3 11
Jamestown, Cloud, Kans ...C6 93
Jamestown, Russell, Ky ...D4 94
Jamestown, Bienville, La ...B2 95
Jamestown, Montieau, Mo ...C5 101
Jamestown, Chautauqua, N.Y ...C1 108
Jamestown, Guilford, N.C ...B3 109
Jamestown, Stutsman, N. Dak ...C7 110
Jamestown, Greene, Ohio ...C2 111
Jamestown, Mercer, Pa ...D1 114
Jamestown, Newport, R.I ..D11 84
Jamestown, Berkeley, S.C ...E8 115
Jamestown, Fentress, Tenn ..C9 117
Jamestown, James City, Va .h14 121
James Town, Sweetwater, Wyo ...E3 125
Jamestown, dam, N. Dak ...C7 110
Jamestown, res., N. Dak ...B7 110
Jamesville, Onondaga, N.Y .*C4 108
Jamesville, Martin, N.C ...B6 109
Jamesville, Northampton, Va ...C7 121
Jamieson, Maheur, Oreg ...C9 113
Jamiltepec, Mex ...D5 63
Jamison, Keya Paha, Nebr ..B6 103
Jammain, Jordan ...g11 32
Jammerbugten, bay, Den ...A3 24
Jammu, India ...B5 39, A5 40
Jammu and Kashmir, disputed reg., India, Pak ...B6 39
Jāmnagar, India ...D5 39, F3 40
Jampur, Pak ...C3 40
Jamsah, Eg ...D6 43
Jamshedpur, India .D8 39, F11 40
Jämshög, Swe ...B8 24
Jämtland, co., Swe ...*F6 25
Jamul, San Diego, Calif ...F5 82
Jamuna, riv., Bngl ...E12 40
Jamundá, riv., Braz ...C3 59
Jan, lake, Sask., Can ...C4 70
Jándula, riv., Sp ...C4 20
Jane, McDonald, Mo ...E3 101
Jane Lew, Lewis, W. Va ...B4 123
Janesville, Lassen, Calif ...B3 82
Janesville, Bremer and Black Hawk, Iowa ...B5 92
Janesville, Waseca, Minn ...F5 99
Janesville, Rock, Wis ...F4 124
Janesville, N.B., Can ...B4 74
Jangipur, India ...E12 40
Janīn, Jordan ...B7 32
Jan Mayen, isl., Nor. (Atl. O.) ...B15 4
Janos, Mex ...A3 63
Janoshalma, Hung ...B4 22
Janow, Man., Can ...E4 71
Janow Lubelski, Pol ...C7 26
Jansen, Sask., Can ...F3 70
Jansen, Las Animas, Colo ...D6 83
Jansen, Jefferson, Nebr ...D8 103
Januária, Braz ...E2 57
Jaoho (Tuanshantzu), China ...B11 34
Japan, country, Asia ...F16, 33 37
Japan, sea, Asia ...G7 37
Japaratuba, Braz ...D3 57
Japurá, riv., Braz ...D4 60
Japvo, peak, India ...C9 39
Jaqué, Pan ...G8 62
Jarablus, Syr ...D11 31
Jaraguá, Braz ...B3 56
Jaraguá do Sul, Braz ...D3 56
Jaral [del Progreso], Mex ...m13 63
Jarales, Valencia, N. Mex ...C3 107
Jarama, riv., Sp ...B4 20
Jarash, Jordan ...B7 32
Jarbalo, Leavenworth, Kans ...k15 93
Jarbidge, Elko, Nev ...B6 104
Jardim de Angicos, Braz ...g6 57
Jardim do Seridó, Braz ...C3 57
Jardine, Park, Mont ...E6 102
Jardines de la Reina, is., Cuba ...D4 64
Jardinópolis, Braz ...k8 56
Jari, riv., Braz ...B4 59
Järlåsa, Swe ...t35 25
Järna, Swe ...t35 25
Jarnac, Fr ...E3 14
Jarny, Fr ...E5 15
Jarocin, Pol ...C4 26
Jaroslaw, Pol ...C7 26
Jaroso, Costilla, Colo ...D5 83
Jarrahi, riv., Iran ...F4 41
Jarratt, Sussex, Va ...D5 121
Jarrettsville, Harford, Md ..A5 85
Jarrow, Alta., Can ...C5 69
Jarvie, Alta., Can ...B3 69
Jarvis, Ont., Can ...E4 72
Jarvis, isl., Pac. O ...G12 7
Jarvisburg, Currituck, N.C ..A7 109
Jarvisville, Harrison, W. Va .*B4 123
Jasien, Pol ...B10 17
Jāsk, Iran ...I8 41
Jask, bay, Iran ...I8 41
Jaslo, Pol ...D6 26
Jasmin, Sask., Can ...F4 70
Jasmine, White, Ark ...B4 81
Jasmine Estates, Pasco, Fla .D4 86
Jason, pen., Ant ...C6 5
Jasonville, Greene, Ind ...F3 91
Jasper, Walker, Ala ...B2 78
Jasper, Newton, Ark ...B2 81
Jasper, Alta., Can ...C1, g7 69
Jasper, Ont., Can ...C9 72
Jasper, Hamilton, Fla ...B4 86
Jasper, Pickens, Ga ...B2 87
Jasper, Dubois, Ind ...H4 91
Jasper, Pipestone and Rock, Minn ...G2 99
Jasper, Jasper, Mo ...D3 101
Jasper, Steuben, N.Y ...C3 108
Jasper, Pike, Ohio ...C2 111
Jasper, Lane, Oreg ...D4 113
Jasper, Marion, Tenn ...D8 117
Jasper, Jasper, Tex ...D6 118
Jasper, co., Ga ...C3 87
Jasper, co., Ill ...E5 90
Jasper, co., Ind ...B3 91
Jasper, co., Iowa ...C4 92
Jasper, co., Miss ...C4 100
Jasper, co., Mo ...D3 101
Jasper, co., S.C ...G5 115
Jasper, co., Tex ...D6 118
Jasper, nat. park, Alta., Can ...C1 69
Jasper Place, Alta., Can ...C4 69
Jastarnia, Pol ...A5 26
Jastrzebia Gora, Pol ...A5 26
Jastrzebie, Pol ...h9 26
Jaszapati, Hung ...B5 22
Jaszbereny, Hung ...B4 22
Jāti, Pak ...E2 40
Jatibonico, Cuba ...D4 64
Játiva, Sp ...C5 20
Jaú, Braz ...C3, m7 56
Jaú, riv., Braz ...D5 60
Jauaperi, riv., Braz ...C5 60
Jauja, Peru ...D2 58
Jaumave, Mex ...C5 63
Jaunpur, India ...E9 40
Java, Walworth, S. Dak ...B6 116
Java, Pittsylvania, Va ...D3 121
Java, isl., Indon ...G4 35
Java, sea, Indon ...G4 35
Javaés, riv., Braz ...E5 59
Jávea, Sp ...C6 20
Jawhār, India ...H4 40
Jawor, Pol ...C4 26
Jaworzno, Pol ...g10 26
Jay, Santa Rosa, Fla ...u14 86
Jay, Franklin, Maine ...D2 96
Jay, Essex, N.Y ...f11 108
Jay, Delaware, Okla ...A7 112
Jay, co., Ind ...D7 91
Jay, peak, Vt ...B3 120
Jaya, peak, Indon ...F9 35
Jayanga, Peru ...C2 58
Jayapura (Sukarnapura), Indon ...F10 35
Jay Em, Goshen, Wyo ...D8 125
Jayess, Lawrence, Miss ...D3 100
Jaynes, Pima, Ariz ...E4 80
Jayton, Kent, Tex ...C2 118
Jayuya, mun., P.R ...*B2 65
Jean, Clark, Nev ...H6 104
Jeanerette, Iberia, La ...E4 95
Jeannette, Westmoreland, Pa.F2 114
Jeannette, isl., Sov. Un ...B35 4
Jebba, Nig ...E5 45
Jebel Akhdhar, mtn., Om ...D2 39
Jebel ed Druz, mtn., Syr ...F11 31

Kirkcaldy, Alta., Can D4 69
Kirkcaldy, Scot D5 13
Kirkcolm, Scot F3 13
Kirkcudbright, Scot F4 13
Kirkcudbright, bay, Scot F4 13
Kirkella, Man., Can D1 71
Kirkella, Sask., Can G5 70
Kirkenes, Nor C14 25
Kirkersville, Licking, Ohio C3 111
Kirkfield, Ont., Can C5 72
Kirkintilloch, Scot E4 13
Kirkland, Escambia, Ala D2 78
Kirkland, Yavapai, Ariz C3 80
Kirkland, Atkinson, Ga E4 87
Kirkland, DeKalb, Ill A5 90
Kirkland, Oneida, N.Y *B5 108
Kirkland, Williamson, Tenn B5 117
Kirkland, Childress, Tex B2 118
Kirkland, King, Wash B3, e11 122
Kirkland Junction, Yavapai, Ariz C3 80
Kirkland Lake, Ont., Can o19 72
Kirklareli, Tur B6 23
Kirklin, Clinton, Ind D5 91
Kirkman, Shelby, Iowa C2 92
Kirkmansville, Todd, Ky D2 94
Kirkoswald, Eng F6 13
Kirkpatrick, lake, Alta., Can D5 69
Kirkpatrick, mtn., Ant A29 5
Kirksey, Calloway, Ky f9 94
Kirksey, Greenwood, S.C C3 115
Kirksville, Monroe, Ind F4 91
Kirksville, Madison, Ky C5 94
Kirksville, Adair, Mo A5 101
Kirkton, Ont., Can D3 72
Kirkton of Glenisla, Scot D5 13
Kirkūk, Iraq D2 41
Kirkville, Wapello, Iowa C5 92
Kirkwall, Scot B6 13
Kirkwood, New Castle, Del A6 85
Kirkwood, Warren, Ill C3 90
Kirkwood, Prince Georges, Md *C4 85
Kirkwood, St. Louis, Mo f13 101
Kirkwood, S. Afr D4 49
Kirn, F.R.G D2 17
Kiron, Crawford, Iowa B2 92
Kirov, Sov. Un B3 29
Kirova, bay, Sov. Un B4 41
Kirovabad, Sov. Un E3 29
Kirovabad (Pyandzh), Sov. Un H22 9
Kirovakan, Sov. Un B15 31
Kirovgrad, Sov. Un B6 29
Kirovograd, Sov. Un G9 27
Kirovsk, Sov. Un D15 25
Kirriemuir, Alta., Can D5 69
Kirriemuir, Scot D5 13
Kirsanov, Sov. Un E14 27
Kirsehir (Kir-Shehr), Tur C10 31
Kīrthar, range, Pak C4 39
Kirtland, San Juan, N. Mex A1 107
Kirtland, Lake, Ohio *A4 111
Kiruna, Swe D9 25
Kirundu, Zaire B4 48
Kirwin, Phillips, Kans C4 93
Kirwin, res., Kans C4 93
Kiryū, Jap H9, m18 37
Kisaki, Tan C6 48
Kisanga, Zaire C4 48
Kisangani (Stanleyville), Zaire A4 48
Kisarazu, Jap n18 37
Kisbey, Sask., Can H4 70
Kiselevsk, Sov. Un C11 29
Kisengi, Zaire D3 48
Kisengwa, Zaire C4 48
Kishanganj, India D11 40
Kishangarh, India C5 39
Kishi, Nig E5 45
Kishinev, Sov. Un B9 22, H7 27
Kishiwada, Jap o14 37
Kishorganj, Bngl D9 39
Kisii, Ken B5 48
Kisiju, Tan C6 48
Kisiwa, creek, Kans g11 93
Kisiwani, Tan B6 48
Kiska, isl., Alsk E3 79
Kiskatinaw, riv., B.C., Can B7 68
Kiskitto, lake, Man., Can B2 71
Kiskittogis, lake, Man., Can B2 71
Kiskoros, Hung B4 22
Kiskundorozsma, Hung B5 22
Kiskunfelegyhaza, Hung B4 22
Kiskunhalas, Hung B4 22
Kiskunmajsa, Hung B4 22
Kislovodsk, Sov. Un E2 29
Kismayu, Som F5 47
Kismet, Seward, Kans E3 93
Kiso-Sammyaku, mts., Jap n16 37
Kissee Mills, Taney, Mo E4 101
Kisseynew, lake, Man., Can B1 71
Kissidougou, Guinea E2 45
Kissimmee, Osceola, Fla D5 86
Kisimmee, lake, Fla E5 86
Kissimmee, riv., Fla E5 86
Kissimmee Park, Osceola, Fla D5 86
Kississing, Man., Can B1 71
Kississing, lake, Man., Can B1 71
Kississing, riv., Man., Can B1 71
Kistefjellet, mtn., Nor C8 25
Kistigan, lake, Man., Can B5 71
Kistler, Logan, W. Va D3, n12 123
Kistna, riv., India E6 39
Kistrand, Nor B11 25
Kisujszallas, Hung B5 22
Kisumu, Ken B5 48
Kisvarda, Hung A6 22
Kita, Iwo 52
Kita, Mali D3 45
Kita Iwo, isl., Pac. O E8 7
Kitakyūshū, Jap J5 37
Kitale, Ken A5 48
Kitamaki, Jap m17 37
Kitami, Jap E11 37
Kitangari, Tan D6 48
Kitano, pt., Iwo 52
Kita-Shiretoko, cape, Sov. Un B12 37
Kit Carson, Cheyenne, Colo C8 83
Kit Carson, co., Colo B8 83
Kitchener, Ont., Can D4 72
Kitchen's Creek, falls, Pa D9 114
Kite, Johnson, Ga D4 87
Kitgum, Ug A5 48
Kithira, Grc D4 23
Kíthira (Cythera), isl., Grc D4 23
Kithnos, isl., Grc D5 23
Kiti, pt., Ponape 52
Kitimat, B.C., Can B3 68
Kitsap, co., Wash B3 122
Kitscoty, Alta., Can C5 69
Kittanning, Armstrong, Pa E2 114
Kittatinny, mts., N.J B2 106
Kittery, York, Maine E2 96
Kittery Point, York, Maine E2 96
Kittilä, Fin D11 25
Kittitas, Kittitas, Wash C5 122
Kittitas, co., Wash B5 122
Kittitas, val., Wash B5 122
Kittrell, Vance, N.C A4 109
Kitts, Harlan, Ky D6 94
Kittson, co., Minn B2 99
Kitty Hawk, Dare, N.C A7 109
Kitty Hawk, bay, N.C A7 109
Kitui, Ken B6 48
Kitwanga, B.C., Can B3 68
Kitwe, Zambia D4 48
Kitzbühel, Aus E6 16
Kitzingen, F.R.G D5 17
Kitzmiller, Garrett, Md m12 85
Kivalina, Alsk B7 79
Kivu, reg., Zaire B4 48
Kivu, lake, Zaire B4 48
Kiya, riv., Sov. Un D26 9
Kiyan, Okinawa 52
Kıyıköy, Tur B7 31
Kiyiu, lake, Sask., Can F1 70
Kizel, Sov. Un B5 29
Kızıl, riv., Tur B10 31
Kizilirmak, riv., Tur H15 9
Kizlyar, Sov. Un E3 29
Kizyl-Arvat, Sov. Un H20 9
Kjakan, Nor C10 25
Kjelvik, Nor B12 25
Kjellerup, Den B3 24
Kladno, Czech C3, n17 26
Klagenfurt, Aus E7 16
Klagetoh, Apache, Ariz B6 80
Klaipeda (Memel), Sov. Un D3 27
Klamath, Del Norte, Calif B1 82
Klamath, co., Oreg E5 113
Klamath, Indian res., Oreg E5 113
Klamath, mts., Oreg E2 113
Klamath, riv., Calif., Oreg B2 82
Klamath Falls, Klamath, Oreg E5 113
Klang, Mala K4 38
Klanxbüll, F.R.G D2 24
Klarälven, riv., Swe G5 25
Klatovy, Czech D2 26
Klawock, Alsk D13, n23 79
Kleberg, Dallas, Tex *C4 118
Kleberg, co., Tex F4 118
Klecany, Czech n17 26
Kleena Kleene, B.C., Can D5 68
Klein, Musselshell, Mont D8 102
Kleinburg, Ont., Can k14 72
Klemme, Hancock, Iowa A4 92
Klerksdorp, S. Afr C4 49
Kletnya, Sov. Un E9 27
Kletsk, Sov. Un E6 27
Kleve, F.R.G C6 15
Klibreck, mtn., Scot B4 13
Klickitat, Klickitat, Wash D4 122
Klickitat, co., Wash D5 122
Klickitat, creek, Wash D5 122
Klickitat, riv., Wash C4 122
Klimovsk, Sov. Un n17 27
Klin, Sov. Un C11 27
Klinaklini, riv., B.C., Can D5 68
Kline, Barnwell, S.C E5 115
Klingenthal, G.D.R C7 17
Klintsy, Sov. Un E9 27
Klippan, Swe B7 24
Klitmøller, Den A2 24
Ključ, Yugo C3 22
Klobuck, Pol C5 26
Kloch, lake, B.C., Can B5 68
Klock, Ont., Can A6 72
Klodnica, riv., Pol g9 26
Klodzko, Pol C4 26
Klondike, DeKalb, Ga B5 87
Klondike, Lake, Ill A5 90
Klondike, Delta, Tex C5 118
Klondike, Milwaukee, Wis F2 124
Klondike, reg., Yukon, Can D4 66
Klostermansfeld, G.D.R B6 17
Klosterneuburg, Aus D8 16
Klosters, Switz C8 19
Kloten, Nelson, N. Dak B7 110
Kloten, Switz B6 19
Klötze, G.D.R F5 24
Klotzsche, G.D.R B8 17
Klotzville, Assumption, La h9 95
Kluane, lake, Yukon, Can D5 66
Kluane, nat. park, Yukon, Can D4 66
Kluczbork, Pol C5 26
Klucze, Pol g11 26
Klukwan, Alsk k22 79
Klütz, G.D.R E5 24
Klyazma, riv., Sov. Un B2 29
Klyuchevskaya, vol., Sov. Un D18 28
Knapp, Dunn, Wis D1 124
Knaresborough, Eng F7 13
Knee, lake, Man., Can B4 71
Knee, lake, Sask., Can B2 70
Knesebeck, F.R.G F4 24
Knezha, Bul D7 22
Knickerbocker, Tom Green, Tex D2 118
Knierim, Calhoun, Iowa B3 92
Knife, riv., N. Dak B3 110
Knife River, Lake, Minn D7 99
Knifley, Adair, Ky C4 94
Knight, inlet, B.C., Can D5 68
Knightdale, Wake, N.C B4 109
Knighton, Wales B4 12
Knights Landing, Yolo, Calif C3 82
Knightstown, Henry, Ind E6 91
Knight's Town, Ire F1 11
Knightsville, Clay, Ind E3 91
Knightsville, res., Mass B2 97
Knik, Alsk C10, g17 79
Knin, Yugo C3 22
Knippa, Uvalde, Tex E3 118
Knislinge, Swe B8 24
Knittlefeld, Aus E7 16
Knob, creek, Ky g11 94
Knobel, Clay, Ark A5 81
Knobley, mtn., W. Va B5 123
Knob Lick, Metcalfe, Ky C4 94
Knob Lick, St. Francois, Mo D7 101
Knob Noster, Johnson, Mo C4 101
Knobs, mtn., Pa D5 114
Knobsville, Fulton, Pa F6 114
Knock, Ire E2 11
Knockadoon, head, Ire F4 11
Knockanefune, mtn., Ire E2 11
Knocklong, Ire E3 11
Knockmealdown, mts., Ire D2 10
Knokke, Bel C3 15
Knollwood, Middlesex, Conn *D7 84
Knollwood, Greene, Ohio *C1 111
Knollwood, Kanawha, W. Va m12 123
Knollwood Park, Jackson, Mich *F6 98
Knops, pond, Mass f9 97
Knott, Howard, Tex C2 118
Knott, co., Ky C6 94
Knotts Island, Currituck, N.C A7 109
Knottsville, Daviess, Ky C3 94
Knowles, Beaver, Okla A1, e10 112
Knowlton, Marathon, Wis D4 124
Knox, Knox, Ill C3 90
Knox, Starke, Ind B4 91
Knox, Benson, N. Dak A6 110
Knox, Clarion, Pa D2 114
Knox, co., Ill B3 90
Knox, co., Ind G3 91
Knox, co., Ky D6 94
Knox, co., Maine D4 96
Knox, co., Mo A5 101
Knox, co., Nebr B8 103
Knox, co., Ohio B3 111
Knox, co., Tenn C10 117
Knox, co., Tex C3 118
Knox, cape, B.C., Can B1 68
Knox, coast, Ant C23 5
Knox, creek, Ky., Va., W. Va D2 123
Knox City, Knox, Mo A5 101
Knox City, Knox, Tex C3 118
Knox Dale, Jefferson, Pa D3 114
Knoxville, Greene, Ala C2 78
Knoxville, Johnson, Ark B2 81
Knoxville, Crawford, Ga D3 87
Knoxville, Knox, Ill C3 90
Knoxville, Marion, Iowa C4 92
Knoxville, Frederick, Md B2 85
Knoxville, Franklin, Miss D2 100
Knoxville, Ray, Mo B3 101
Knoxville, Tioga, Pa C7 114
Knoxville, Knox, Tenn D10, n14 117
Knysna, S. Afr D3 49
Knyszyn, Pol B7 26
Kobdo, riv., Mong B3 34
Kobe, Jap I7, o14 37
Kobelyaki, Sov. Un G10 27
København (Copenhagen), co., Den C6 24
Koblenz, F.R.G C2 17
Kobona, Sov. Un r32 25
Kobrin, Sov. Un E5 27
Kobroor, isl., Indon G8 35
Kobuk, Alsk B8 79
Kobuk, riv., Alsk B8 79
Kobuleti, Sov. Un B13 31
Koca (Xanthus), riv., Tur D7 23
Kocaba, riv., Czech o17 26
Kočani, Yugo E6 22
Kočevje, Yugo C2 22
Koch, peak, Mont E5 102
Kochel, F.R.G B7 18
Kochel, lake, F.R.G B7 18
Kōchi, Jap J6 37
Kōchi, pref., Jap *J6 37
Kochiu, China G5 34
Kock, Pol C7 26
Kodak, Perry, Ky C6 94
Kodiak, Alsk D9 79
Kodiak, isl., Alsk D9 79
Kodok (Fashoda), Sud D3 47
Koepang, Indon H6 35
Koerhchinyuichienchi (Ulanhot), China A10 36
Koerhmu, China D3 34
Koes, Namibia C2 49
Koetaradja, Indon k11 35
Koetatjane, Indon K2 38
Koettlitz, glacier, Ant f39 5
Kofa, mts., Ariz D2 80
Koffiefontein, S. Afr C4 49
Koforidua, Ghana E4 45
Kōfu, Jap I9, n17 37
Koga, Jap m18 37
Kogaluk, riv., Newf., Can g9 75
Køge, Den C6 24
Køge, bay, Den C6 24
Kogilnik, riv., Sov. Un B9 22
Kohāt, Pak B5 39
Kohatk, Pinal, Ariz E3 80
Kohīma, India C9 39
Kohler, Sheboygan, Wis E6, k10 124
Kohls Ranch, Gila, Ariz C4 80
Kohlu, Pak C4 39
Kohtla-Järve, Sov. Un B6 27
Köinge, Swe A6 24
Koje, isl., Kor I4 37
Kokadjo, Piscataquis, Maine C3 96
Kokadjo, lake, Maine C3 96
Kokai, see Kanggye, Kor.
Kokand, Sov. Un E8 29
Kokanee Glacier, prov. park, B.C., Can E9 68
Kokchetav, Sov. Un C7 29
Kokkola, Fin F10 25
Koko, Nig D5 45
Koko, head, Haw B4 88
Kokohsili, China D3 34
Kokomo, Maui, Haw C5 88
Kokomo, Howard, Ind D5 91
Kokomo, Marion, Miss D3 100
Koko-Nor (Tsinghai), lake, China D4 34
Kokopo, Pap. N. Gui h13 50
Kokos, is., Indon K1 38
Kokosing, riv., Ohio B3 111
Kokrines, Alsk C9 79
Koksilah, B.C., Can g12 68
Koksoak, riv., Que., Can E19 67
Kokstad, S. Afr D4 49
Kol, riv., Iran H7 41
Kola, Sov. Un C15 25
Kola, pen., Sov. Un D17 25
Kolamai (Karamai), China B1 34
Kolan, China E4 36
Kolār Gold Fields, India F6 39
Kolari, Fin D10 25
Kolarovo, Bul D8 22
Kolarovo, Czech E4 26
Kolbäck, Swe t34 25
Kolbano, Indon H6 35
Kolbio, Som F5 47
Kolbuszowa, Pol C6 26
Kolchugino, Sov. Un C12 27
Kołczewo, Pol E8 24
Kolda, Sen D2 45
Koldewey, isl., Grnld B16 4
Kolding, Den C3 24
Kole, Zaire B3 48
Kolec, Czech n17 26
Koleno, Sov. Un F13 27
Kolezhma, Sov. Un E16 25
Kolgueyv, isl., Sov. Un B18 9
Kolhāpur, India E5 39, I5 40
Koliganek Alsk D8 79
Kolimbine, riv., Maur C2 45
Kolin, Czech C3 26
Kolin, Rapides, La C3 95
Kolin, Judith Basin, Mont C7 102
Kölleda, G.D.R B6 17
Köln, see Cologne, F.R.G.
Kolno, Pol B6 26
Kolo, Pol B5 26
Koloa, Kauai, Haw B2 88
Kolob, canyon, Utah F2 119
Kolobrzeg, Pol A3 26
Kolokani, Mali D3 45
Kolola Springs, Lowndes, Miss B5 100
Kolomna, Sov. Un B1 29
Kolomyya, Sov. Un G5 27
Kolonia, Ponape 52
Kolonodale, Indon F6 35
Kolp, riv., Sov. Un B11 27
Kolpashevo, Sov. Un B10 29
Kolpino, Sov. Un s31 25
Kolva, riv., Sov. Un A5 29
Kolwa, Pak C3 39
Kolwezi, Zaire D4 48
Kolyberovo, Sov. Un n18 27
Kolyma, riv., Sov. Un C18 28
Komádi, Hung B5 22
Komandorski Village, Alameda, Calif *D3 82
Komandorskiye, is., Sov. Un D19 28
Komarno, Man., Can D3 71
Komarno, Czech E5 26
Komarno, Sov. Un D7 26
Komarno, marsh, Sov. Un B10 29
Komarom, Hung B4 22
Komárom, co., Hung *B4 22
Komatipoort, S. Afr C5 49
Komatsu, Jap H8 37
Komatsushima, Jap I7 37
Komelik, Pima, Ariz F4 80
Komlo, Hung B4 22
Kommunarsk, Sov. Un G12, q21 27
Kominato, Jap n19 37
Komodo, isl., Indon G5 35
Komoé, riv., I.C E4 45
Komono, Con F2 46
Komoran, isl., Indon G9 35
Komotiní (Komotine), Grc B5 23
Kompong Cham, Kam F6 38
Kompong Chhnang, Kam F6 38
Kompong Kleang, Kam F6 38
Kompong Som (Sihanoukville), Kam G5 38
Kompong Som, bay, Kam G5 38
Kompong Speu, Kam G6 38
Kompong Thom, Kam F6 38
Komrat, Sov. Un H7 27
Komsomolets, isl., Sov. Un A4 4
Komsomolsk [-na Amure], Sov. Un D16 28
Kom Vo, Pima, Ariz F3 80
Konar, riv., Afg., Pak A5 39, D15 41
Konar-e Khāş, Afg D15 41
Konawa, Seminole, Okla C5 112
Kondoa, Tan B6 48
Kondopoga, Sov. Un F16 25
Konechnaya, Sov. Un C9 29
Kong, reg., I.C E4 45
Kong, isl., Kam G5 38
Kongeå, riv., Den C2 24
Kongju, Kor H3 37
Kongolo, Zaire C4 48
Kongsberg, Nor H3, p27 25
Kongsmark, Den C2 24
Kongsvinger, Nor G5 25
Königsbrück, G.D.R B8 17
Königshofen, F.R.G C5 17
Königslutter, F.R.G A5 17
Königstein, G.D.R C9 17
Königs Wusterhausen, G.D.R A8 17
Konin, Pol B5 26
Konispol, Alb C3 23
Konitsa, Grc B3 23
Köniz, Switz C3 19
Konjic, Yugo D3 22
Könnern, G.D.R B6 17
Konolfingen, Switz C4 19
Konomoc, lake, Conn D8 84
Konosha, Sov. Un A13 27
Konotop, Sov. Un F9 27
Konskie, Pol C6 26
Konstantinovka, Sov. Un q20 27
Konstanz, F.R.G E4 16
Konta, India I8 40
Kontagora, Nig D6 45
Kontcha, Cam D2 46
Kontich, Bel C4 15
Kontiomäki, Fin E13 25
Kontum, Viet E8 38
Konya, Tur D9 31
Konyang, Kor I3 37
Konzhakovskiy Kamen, mtn., Sov. Un B5 29
Koochiching, co., Minn B4 99
Koolau, range, Haw g10 88
Koontz Lake, Starke, Ind B5 91
Koosharem Sevier, Utah E4 119
Kooskia, Idaho, Idaho C3 89
Kootenai, Bonner, Idaho A2 89
Kootenai, co., Idaho B2 89
Kootenai, riv., Mont B1 102
Kootenay, lake, B.C., Can E9 68
Kootenay, nat. park, B.C., Can D9 68
Kootenay, riv., B.C., Can D10 68
Kópasker, Ice m24 25
Kopervik, Nor H1 25
Kopet, mts., Sov. Un B7 41
Kopeysk, Sov. Un B6 29
Köping, Swe H6, t33 25
Koppany, riv., Hung B4 22
Kopparberg, co., Swe *G6 25
Koppel, Beaver, Pa E1 114
Koprivnica, Yugo B3 22
Kopychintsy, Sov. Un G5 27
Korahe, Eth D5 17
Korarou, lake, Mali C4 45
Korba, Tun F12 30
Korbach, F.R.G B3 17
Korbu, mtn., Mala J4 38
Korçë, Alb B3 23
Korçë, pref., Alb *B3 23
Korcula, isl., Yugo D3 22
Korea, reg., Asia F15 33, 37
Korea, North, country, Asia F4 37
Korea, South, country, Asia H3 37
Korea, bay, China D9 34
Korea, strait, Kor I4 37
Korea Joeri, Neth. Antilles H18 65
Korets, Sov. Un F6 27
Korhogo, I.C E3 45
Kori, creek, Pak D4 39, F2 40
Korinthía (Corinthia), prov., Grc *D4 23
Kórinthos (Corinth), Grc D4, h9 23
Kóriyama, Jap H10 37
Korkino, Sov. Un D21 9
Kormakíti, cape, Cyp E9 31
Kormend, Hung B3 22
Kornat, isl., Yugo D2 22
Korneuburg, Aus D8 16
Kornwestheim, F.R.G E4 17
Koro, isl., Fiji 52
Korogwe, Tan C6 48
Koromo, Jap n16 37
Koronis, lake, Minn E4 99
Koropi, Grc h11 23
Koro, Palau Is 52
Koror, isl., Palau Is 52
Korosten, Sov. Un F7 27
Korotoyak, Sov. Un F12 27
Korovin, vol., Alsk E5 79
Korsakov (Otomari), Sov C11 37
Korsør, Den C5 24
Kortrijk, Bel D3 15
Korumburra, Austl I5 51
Korville, Harris, Tex F4 118
Koryak, mts., Sov. Un C19 28
Kos, Grc D6 23
Kos, isl., Grc D6 23
Koschagyl, Sov. Un D4 29
Koscian, Pol B4 26
Koscierzyna, Pol A4 26
Kosciusko, Attala, Miss B4 100
Kosciusko, co., Ind B6 91
Kosciusko, mtn., Austl H7 51
Koshan, China B10 34
Koshiki, isl., Jap K4 37
Koshkonong, Oregon, Mo E6 101
Koshkonong, lake, Wis F5 124
Košice, Czech D6 26
Koskaecodde, lake, Newf., Can D4 75
Koslan, Sov. Un C18 9
Kosong, Kor G4 37
Kosove (Kosovo), pref., Alb *A3 23
Kosovska Mitrovica, Yugo D5 22
Kosse, Limestone, Tex D4 118
Kösslarn, F.R.G A9 18
Kossol, reef, Palau Is 52
Kossuth, Alcorn, Miss A5 100
Kossuth, co., Iowa A3 92
Kostelec, Czech n18 26
Kostelec nad Cernymi Lesy, Czech o18 26
Kostroma, Sov. Un B2 29
Kostrzyn, Pol B3 26
Koszalin, Pol A4 26
Koszeg, Hung B3 22
Kotabaru, Indon F5 35
Kota Baharu, Mala I5 38
Kota, India E5 40
Kotatengah, Indon L4 38
Kotel, Bul D8 22
Kotelnich, Sov. Un B3 29
Kotelnikovskiy, Sov. Un D2 29
Kotelny, isl., Sov. Un B16 28
Köthen, G.D.R B7 17
Kotido, Ug A5 48
Kotka, Fin G12 25
Kotlas, Sov. Un C18 9
Kotlik, Alsk C7 79
Kotonkoro, Nig D6 45
Kotor, Yugo D4 22
Kotor, bay, Yugo D4 22
Kotor Varos, Yugo C3 22
Kotovsk, Sov. Un E13 27
Kotovsk, Sov. Un H7 27
Kotovskoye, Sov. Un B9 22
Kotri, Pak E2 40
Kottas, mts., Ant B11 5
Kotung, China B3 37
Kotzebue, Alsk B7 79
Kotzebue, sound, Alsk B7 79
Kötzting, F.R.G D7 17
Kouango, Cen. Afr. Rep D3 46
Kouba, Alg *B5 44
Kouchibouguac, nat. park, N.B., Can C5 74
Kouchibouguacis, riv., N.B., Can C4 74
Koudougou, Upper Volta D4 45
Koula-Moutou, Gabon F2 46
Koulikoro, Mali D3 45
Koumra, Chad D3 46
Kounradskiy, Sov. Un D9 29
Kountze, Hardin, Tex D5 118
Koupangtzu, China D9 36
Kouri, isl., Okinawa 52
Kourou, Fr. Gu A4 59
Kouroussa, Guinea D3 45
Koutiala, Mali D3 45
Kouts, Porter, Ind B3 91
Kouvola, Fin G12 25
Ko Vayo, Pima, Ariz E3 80
Kovel, Sov. Un F5 27
Kovik, Que., Can f11 73
Kovrov, Sov. Un B2 29
Kowa, Jap o15 37
Kowie, see Port Alfred, S. Afr.
Kowloon, Hong Kong G7 34
Kowon, Kor G3 37
Koyuk, Alsk C7 79
Koyukuk, Alsk C8 79
Koyukuk, riv., Alsk B9 79
Koza, Okinawa 52
Kozan, Tur D10 31
Kozani, Grc B3 23
Kozani, prov., Grc *B3 23
Kozelsk, Sov. Un D10 27
Kozhva, Sov. Un B20 9
Kozienice, Pol C6 26
Kozle, Pol C5 26
Kozloduy, Bul D6 22
Kozu, isl., Jap I9 37
Kozuchow, Pol C3 26
Kpandu, Ghana E5 45
Kra, isth., Thai G3 38
Kraemer, La Fourche, La k10 95
Kragerö, Nor H3 25
Kragujevac, Yugo D5 22
Krakow, G.D.R E6 24
Kraków (Cracow), Pol C5 26
Krakower, lake, G.D.R E6 24
Kraljevo, Yugo D5 22
Kralupy [nad Vltavou], Czech n17 26
Kraluv, Dvur, Czech o17 26
Kramatorsk, Sov. Un G11, q20 27
Kramer, Warren, Ind D3 91
Kramer, Bottineau, N. Dak A5 110
Kramer Junction, San Bernardino, Calif E5 82
Kranidhion, Grc D4 23
Kranj, Yugo B2 22
Kranzburg, Codington, S. Dak C9 116
Kraslice, Czech C2 26
Krasnaya Sloboda, Sov. Un D2 29
Krasnik Lubelski, Pol C7 26
Krasnoarmeysk, Sov. Un F15 27
Krasnoarmeysk, Sov. Un G15 27
Krasnodar, Sov. Un I12 27
Krasnodon, Sov. Un q22 27
Krasnogorsk, Sov. Un B11 37
Krasnograd, Sov. Un G10 27
Krasnokamsk, Sov. Un B5 29
Krasnoselkup, Sov. Un B25 9
Krasnoselye, Sov. Un G9 27
Krasnoslobodsk, Sov. Un D14 27
Krasnoturinsk, Sov. Un B6 29
Krasnoufimsk, Sov. Un B5 29
Krasnouralsk, Sov. Un D21 9
Krasnovishersk, Sov. Un A5 29
Krasnovodsk, Sov. Un E4 29
Krasnoyarsk, Sov. Un D27 9, D12 28
Krasnoye Selo, Sov. Un s31 25
Krasnoznamenskiy, Sov. Un C7 29
Krasnystaw, Pol C7 26
Krasnyy Kholm, Sov. Un B11 27
Krasnyy Kut, Sov. Un C3 29
Krasnyy Liman, Sov. Un q20 27
Krasnyy Luch, Sov. Un q21 27
Krasnyy Sulin, Sov. Un H13 27
Krasnyy Yar, Sov. Un F15 27
Kratie, Camb F7 38
Kratovo, Yugo D6 22
Kraul, mts., Ant B11 5
Krebs, Pittsburg, Okla C6 112
Krefeld, F.R.G B1 17
Kremenchug, Sov. Un G9 27
Kremenchug, res., Sov. Un G9 27
Kremenets, Sov. Un F5 27
Kremennaya, Sov. Un p21 27
Kremlin, Hill, Mont B6 102
Kremlin, Garfield, Okla A4 112
Kremmling, Grand, Colo A4 83
Krems, Aus D7 16
Kresgeville, Monroe, Pa E10 114
Kress, Swisher, Tex B2 118
Kreuzlingen, Switz A7 19
Kribi, Cam E1 46
Krichev, Sov. Un E8 27
Kriens, Switz B5 19
Krilon, cape, Sov. Un D11 37
Krilon, pen., Sov. Un C11 37
Krishnagiri, India F6 39
Krishnanagar, India F12 40
Kristiansand, Nor H2 25
Kristianstad, Swe I6 25
Kristianstad, co., Swe B7 24
Kristiansund, Nor F2 25
Kristinestad, Fin F9 25
Kriva Palanka, Yugo D6 22
Krivoy Rog, Sov. Un H9 27
Križevci, Yugo B3 22
Krk, isl., Yugo C2 22
Krka, riv., Yugo D2 22
Krnov, Czech C4 26
Krokeai, Grc D4 23
Krokstadelva, Nor p28 25
Krolevets, Sov. Un F9 27
Kromeriz, Czech D4 26
Kromy, Sov. Un E10 27
Kronach, F.R.G C6 17
Kronau, Sask., Can G3 70
Kronoberg, co., Swe B8 24
Kronshtadt, Sov. Un B7 27
Kroonstad, S. Afr C4 49
Kröpelin, G.D.R D5 24
Kropotkin, Sov. Un I13 27
Krosno, Pol D6 26
Krosno Odrzanskie, Pol B3 26
Krotoszyn, Pol C4 26
Krotz Springs, St. Landry, La D4 95
Krsko, Yugo C2 22
Kruger, nat. park, S. Afr B5 49
Krugersdorp, S. Afr C4 49
Krujë, Alb B2 23
Krumbach, F.R.G A6 18
Krumovgrad, Bul E7 22
Krumroy, Summit, Ohio *A4 111
Krusenstern Rock, reef, Haw m12 88
Kruševac, Yugo D5 22
Kruševo, Yugo E6 22
Kruszwica, Pol B5 26
Krydor, Sask., Can E2 70
Krym (Crimea), pen., Sov. Un I10 27
Krymskaya, Sov.Un I11 27
Krynica, Pol D6 26
Krynki, Pol B7 26
Ksar el Boukhari, Alg B5 44
Ksar el Kebir, Mor B3 44
Ksar es Souk, Mor C4 44
Ktipas, mtn., Grc g10 23
Kuala Dungun, Mala J5 38
Kuala Kerau, Mala K5 38
Kualakurun, Indon F4 35
Kuala Lipis, Mala J5 38
Kuala Lumpur, Mala K4 38
Kualapuu, Maui, Haw B4 88
Kuala Terengganu, Mala J5 38
Kuan, China F6 36
Kuandang, Indon E6 35
Kuangan, China I2 36
Kuangchang, China K7 36
Kuanghua, China H4 36
Kuangnan, China G6 34
Kuangte, China I8 36
Kuangyüan, China H1 36
Kuantan, Mala K5 38
Kuanti, China E4 37
Kuantien, China F2 37
Kuanyün, China G8 36
Kuba, Sov. Un E3 29
Kuban, riv., Sov. Un F16 9
Kubitzer, bay, G.D.R D7 24
Kuchen, China H7 36
Kucheng, China H4 36
Kuching, Mala E4 35
Kuchino, isl., Jap L4 37
Kuchino Erabu, isl., Jap K5 37
Kudaka, isl., Okinawa 52
Kudat, Mala D5 35
Kudymkar, Sov. Un B4 29
Kueichi, China J7 36
Kueichih, China I7 36
Kueihsien, China G6 34
Kueilin, China F7 34
Kueisui, see Huhehot, China
Kueite, China D5 34
Kueiyang, China F6 34
Kuerhlo (Korla), China C2 34
Kufstein, Aus E6 16
Kuge, Jap n14 37
Kuh, cape, Iran I8 41
Kuhaylī, Sud B3 47
Kuh-e-Sahand, mtn., Iran C3 41
Kūhestan, Afg D10 41
Kuh-i-Gugird, mts., Iran D6 41
Kuh-i-Rahmand, mtn., Iran D4 41
Kuh-i-Surkh, mts., Iran D9 41
Kūhpāyeh, Iran E6 41
Kūhrān, mtn., Iran H9 41
Kuito, see Bié, Ang.
Kuji, Jap F10 37
Kuju-San, peak, Jap J5 37
Kukaiau, Hawaii, Haw C6 88
Kukawa, Nig D7 45
Kukës, Alb A3 23
Kuki, Jap m18 37
Kuku, pt., Wake Isl 52
Kukuihaele, Hawaii, Haw C6 88
Kukuiula, Kaua, Haw B2 88
Kula, Bul D6 22
Kula, Tur C7 23
Kula, Yugo C4 22
Kula Kangri, peak, China C13 40
Ku Lao Cham, isl., Viet E8 38
Ku Lao Re, isl., Viet E8 38
Kulebaki, Sov. Un D14 27
Kuling, see Lushan, China
Kulltorp, Swe A7 24
Kulm, La Moure, N. Dak C7 110
Kulmbach, F.R.G C6 17

Kulpmont, Northumberland, Pa ... E9 114
Kulu, isl., Alsk ... m22 79
Kulun, China ... C9 36
Kulunda, Sov. Un ... C9 29
Kulunda, lake, Sov. Un ... C9 29
Kulyab, Sov. Un ... H22 9
Kuma, riv., Sov. Un ... F18 9
Kumagaya, Jap ... m18 37
Kumai, Indon ... F4 35
Kumamoto, Jap ... J5 37
Kumamoto, pref., Jap ... *J5 37
Kumanovo, Yugo ... D5 22
Kumasi, Ghana ... E4 45
Kumba, Cam ... E1 46
Kumbakonam, India ... F6 39
Kumhwa, Kor ... G3 37
Kumi, Ug ... A5 48
Kumihama, Jap ... n14 37
Kumkale, Tur ... C6 23
Kumla, Swe ... H6, t33 25
Kummerower, lake, G.D.R ... E6 24
Kumsong, Kor ... G3 37
Kumukahi, cape, Haw ... D7 88
Kuna, Ada, Idaho ... F2 89
Kundar, riv., Pak ... B2 40
Kuneitra (Al Qunayṭirah), Syr ... F10 31
Kungchuling, see Huaite, China
Kunghit, isl., B.C., Can ... C2 68
Kungrad, Sov. Un ... E5 29
Kungsbacka, Swe ... A6 24
Kungsör, Swe ... t34 25
Kungu, Zaire ... A2 48
Kungur, Sov. Un ... D20 9
Kunia, Honolulu, Haw ... g9 88
Kunkle, Luzerne, Pa ... m17 114
Kunkletown, Monroe, Pa ... B2 106
Kunlun, mts., China ... D3 34
Kunming (Yunnanfu), China ... F5 34, C11 39
Kunsan, Kor ... I3 37
Kunszentmarton, Hung ... B5 22
Kuntu, China ... B9 36
Künzelsau, F.R.G ... D4 17
Kuohsien, China ... D7 34
Kuolayarvi, Sov. Un ... D13 25
Kuop (Royalist), is., Truk ... 52
Kuopio, Fin ... F12 25
Kuopio, dept., Fin ... *F12 25
Kuoyang, China ... H7 36
Kupa, riv., Yugo ... C2 22
Kupang, Indon ... H6 35
Kupino, Sov. Un ... C9 29
Kupk, Pima, Ariz ... F3 80
Kupreanof, Alsk ... m23 79
Kupreanof, isl., Alsk ... m23 79
Kupyansk, Sov. Un ... G11 27
Kur, riv., Sov. Un ... B7 37
Kura, riv., Sov. Un ... G17 9
Kurakhovka, Sov. Un ... q20 27
Kurashiki, Jap ... I6 37
Kuray, Sov. Un ... E26 9
Kuraymah, Sud ... B3 47
Kurdikos-Naumiestis, Sov. Un ... A7 26
Kurdufān, prov., Sud ... C2 47
Kurdzhali, Bul ... E7 22
Kure, Jap ... I6 37
Kure, isl., Haw ... k12 88
Kuressaare, Sov. Un ... B4 27
Kureyka, riv., Sov. Un ... C12 28
Kurgaldzhina, Sov. Un ... C8 29
Kurgan, Sov. Un ... B7 29
Kurgannaya, Sov. Un ... G17 9
Kurgan-Tyube, Sov. Un ... H22 9
Kurigram, Bngl ... E12 40
Kuril, is., Sov. Un ... E17 28
Kuril, strait, Sov. Un ... D18 28
Kurinskaya, cape, Sov. Un ... H18 9
Kurkhera, India ... G8 40
Kurmuk, Sud ... C3 47
Kurnool, India ... E6 38
Kuro, isl., Jap ... K4 37
Kuroki, Sask., Can ... F4 70
Kurovskoye, Sov. Un ... n18 27
Kurow, N.Z ... P13 51
Kurri Kurri-Weston, Austl ... F8 51
Kursk, Sov. Un ... F11 27
Kuršumlija, Yugo ... D5 22
Kurtalan, Tur ... D13 31
Kurthwood, Vernon, La ... C2 95
Kūrtī, Sud ... B3 47
Kurtistown, Hawaii, Haw ... D6 88
Kurtz, Jackson, Ind ... G5 91
Kuruman, S. Afr ... C3 49
Kurume, Jap ... J5 37
Kurunegala, Sri Lanka ... G7 39
Kusadasi, Tur ... D6 23
Kusakaki, isl., Jap ... K4 37
Kusatsu, Jap ... n14 37
Kusel, F.R.G ... D2 17
Kushchevskaya, Sov. Un ... H12 27
Kushevat, Sov. Un ... B22 9
Kushih, China ... E8 34
Kushiro, Jap ... E12 37
Kushka, Sov. Un ... H21 9
Kushmurun, Sov. Un ... C6 29
Kushmurun, lake, Sov. Un ... C6 29
Kuskokwim, bay, Alsk ... D7 79
Kuskokwim, mts., Alsk ... C8 79
Kuskokwim, riv., Alsk ... C8 79
Küsnacht, Switz ... B6 19
Küssnacht, Switz ... B5 19
Kustanay, Sov. Un ... C6 29
Kusten, canal, F.R.G ... A7 15
Kūstī, Sud ... C3 47
Küstrin, see Kostrzyn, Pol.
Kut, isl., Thai ... G5 38
Kutacane, Indon ... K2 38
Kutahya (Kutaiah), Tur ... C7 23
Kutaisi, Sov. Un ... A14 31
Kutawagan, lake, Sask., Can ... F3 70
Kutch, gulf, India ... D4 39
Kute, Alb ... B2 23
Kutina, Yugo ... C3 22
Kutlay, Sov. Un ... D4 29
Kutna Hora, Czech ... D3 26
Kutno, Pol ... B5 26
Kuttawa, Lyon, Ky ... A3 94
Kutu, Zaire ... B2 48
Kutua, pt., Truk ... 52
Kutum, Sud ... C1 47
Kuty, Sov. Un ... A7 22
Kutztown, Berks, Pa ... E10 114
Kuusamo, Fin ... E13 25
Kuvandyk, Sov. Un ... E20 9
Kuwait, Kuw ... G4 41
Kuwait, country, Asia ... G7 33, G3 41
Kuwana, Jap ... I8, n15 37
Kuyang, Mong ... D4 36
Kuybyshev, Sov. Un ... B9 29
Kuybyshev, Sov. Un ... C4 29
Kuybyshev, res., Sov. Un ... D8 28
Kūysanjaq, Iraq ... C2 41
Kuyto Ozero, lake, Sov. Un ... E14 25
Kuyuan, China ... G2 36
Kuznetsk, Sov. Un ... C3 29
Kuznetsk Alatau, mts., Sov. Un ... B11 29
Kuznetsk Basin, reg., Sov. Un ... E26 9
Kuznetsova, Sov. Un ... C10 37
Kuzomen, Sov. Un ... D17 25
Kvarner, gulf, Yugo ... C2 22
Kvismare, can., Swe ... t33 25
Kvitoya, isl., Nor ... A11 4
Kwajalein, atoll, Marshall Is. ... 52
Kwajalein, isl., Kwajalein ... 52
Kwakoegron, Sur ... A3 59
Kwale, Ken ... B6 48
Kwamouth, Zaire ... B2 48
Kwa Mtoro, Tan ... C6 48
Kwangchow, bay, China ... B9 38
Kwangju, Kor ... I3 37
Kwango, riv., Zaire ... C 48
Kwangsi Chuang, auton. reg., China ... F7 34
Kwangtung, prov., China ... G7 34
Kwatisore, Indon ... F8 35
Kweichow, prov., China ... F6 34
Kwekwe, Zimb ... A4 49
Kwenge, riv., Zaire ... C2 48
Kwethluck, Alsk ... C7 79
Kwidzyn, Pol ... B5 26
Kwigillingok, Alsk ... D7 99
Kwilu, riv., Zaire ... B2 48
Kwinana, Austl ... F2 50
Kyabé, Chad ... D3 46
Kyabra Creek, riv., Austl ... B4 51
Kyabram, Austl ... H5 51
Kyaiklat, Bur ... E10 39
Kyaikto, Bur ... D2 38
Kyakhta, Sov. Un ... D13 28
Kyan, pt., Okinawa ... 52
Kyaukpadaung, Bur ... C1 38
Kyaukpyu, Bur ... E9 39
Kyaukse, Bur ... B2 38
Kybartai, Sov. Un ... A7 26
Kyelang, India ... A6 40
Kyje, Czech ... D9, n18 26
Kyle, Sask., Can ... G1 70
Kyle, Shannon, S. Dak ... D3 116
Kyle, Hays, Tex ... E4 118
Kyle of Durness, inlet, Scot ... B4 13
Kyle [of Lochalsh], Scot ... C3 13
Kyle of Tongue, inlet, Scot ... B4 13
Kyles Ford, Hancock, Tenn ... C10 117
Kylestrome, Scot ... B3 13
Kyll, riv., F.R.G ... D1 17
Kyllburg, F.R.G ... D6 15
Kymes, mtn., Ark ... B1 81
Kymi, dept., Fin ... *G12 25
Kymulga, cove, Ala ... B3 78
Kynlyn, New Castle, Del ... *A6 85
Kynuna, Austl ... D7 50
Kyoga, cape, Jap ... I7 37
Kyoga, lake, Ug ... A5 48
Kyŏngju, Kor ... I4 37
Kyongsong, Kor ... F4 37
Kyōto, Jap ... I7, n14 37
Kyōto, pref., Jap ... *I7 37
Kyrenia, Cyp ... E9 31
Kyritz, G.D.R ... B6 16
Kyrkjebö, Nor ... G1 25
Kyrock, Edmonson, Ky ... C3 94
Kyshtovka, Sov. Un ... D24 9
Kyshtym, Sov. Un ... B6 29
Kyuquot, B.C., Can ... D4 68
Kyuquot, sound, B.C., Can ... E4 68
Kyuroku, isl., Jap ... F9 37
Kyūshū, isl., Jap ... J5 37
Kyustendil, Bul ... D6 22
Kyzyl, Sov. Un ... D12 28
Kyzyl-Kiya, Sov. Un ... E8 29
Kyzyl-Kum, des., Sov. Un ... E6 29
Kzyl-Orda, Sov. Un ... E7 29

L

Laa, Aus ... D8 16
Laage, G.D.R ... E6 24
Laager, Grundy, Tenn ... D8 117
La Almunia de Doña Godina, Sp ... B5 20
La Asunción, Ven ... A5 60
Laau, pt., Haw ... B4 88
Labadie, Franklin, Mo ... C7 101
Labadieville, Assumption, La ... E5, k10 95
La Baie, Que., Can ... A7 73
La Banda, Arg ... E3 55
La Barca, Mex ... C4, m12 63
La Barge, Lincoln, Wyo ... D2 125
La Barge, creek, Wyo ... D2 125
Labé, Guinea ... D2 45
Labe (Elbe), riv., Czech ... C3 26
Labelle, Que., Can ... C3 73
Labelle, co., Que., Can ... C2 73
La Belle, Hendry, Fla ... F5 86
La Belle, Lewis, Mo ... A6 101
Laberge, lake, Yukon, Can ... D5 66
Labette, Labette, Kans ... E8 93
Labette, co., Kans ... E8 93
Labette, creek, Kans ... E8 93
Labin, Yugo ... C2 22
La Bisbal, Sp ... B7 20
Labo, Phil ... o14 35
Labo, mtn., Phil ... p14 35
La Boca, Pan ... m11 62
Laboe, F.R.G ... D4 24
Labouheyre, Fr ... E3 14
Laboulaye, Arg ... A4 54
Labrador, reg., Newf., Can ... g8 75
Labrador, sea, Newf., Can ... A3 75
Labrador City, Newf., Can ... h8 75
Lábrea, Braz ... D2 59
LaBrea, Trin ... O22 65
La Broquerie, Man., Can ... E3 71
Labuan, isl., Mala ... D5 35
Labuco, Jefferson, Ala ... E4 78
Labuha, Indon ... F7 35
Labuhanbilik, Indon ... K4 38
Labuk, bay, Mala ... D5 35
Laburnum Manor, Henrico, Va ... *C5 121
Lac-à-Beauce, Que., Can ... B5 63
Lacadena, Sask., Can ... G1 70
L'Acadie, Que., Can ... D4 73
Lacamp, Vernon, La ... C3 92
La Canada, Los Angeles, Calif ... m12 82
La Capelle, Fr ... E3 15
La Carlota, Arg ... A4 54
La Carlota, Phil ... *C6 35
La Carolina, Sp ... C4 20
Lac au Saumon, Que., Can ... *k13 73
Lac-aux-Brochets, Que., Can ... B5 73
Lac-aux-Sables, Que., Can ... C5 73
Lac-Baker, N.B., Can ... B1 74
Lac-Beauport, Que., Can ... n17 73
Lac-Bouchette, Que., Can ... A5 73
Lac-Brome, Que., Can ... D5 73
Laccadive, is., India ... F5 39
Lac-Carré, Que., Can ... C3 73
Lac Champdoré, lake, Que., Can ... g8 75
Lac Chat, Que., Can ... B5 73
Lac Courte Oreilles, lake, Wis ... C2 124
Lac Courte Oreilles, Indian res., Wis ... C2 124
Lac de Gras, lake, N.W. Ter., Can ... D10 66
Lac des Bois, lake, N.W. Ter., Can ... C8 66
Lac des Commissaires, lake, Que., Can ... A5 73
Lac des Duex-Montagnes, lake, Que., Can ... q18 73
Lac-des-Écorces, Que., Can ... C2 73
Lac des Iles, lake, Sask., Can ... B6 69
Lac du Bonnet, Man., Can ... D3 71
Lae du Bonnet, lake, Man., Can ... D4 71
Lac Du Flambeau, Vilas, Wis ... C4 124
Lac Du Flambeau, Indian res., Wis ... C3 124
Lac-Édouard, Que., Can ... B5 73
La Ceiba, Ven ... B3 60
La Ceiba, Hond ... C4 62
La Ceja, Col ... B2 60
La Center, Ballard, Ky ... e9 94
Lac-Etchemin, Que., Can ... C7 73
Lacey, Thurston, Wash ... B3 122
Lacey Park, Bucks, Pa ... *F11 114
Laceys Spring, Morgan, Ala ... A3 78
Lac-Frontière, Que., Can ... C7 73
La Chambre, Fr ... D2 18
La Charité, Fr ... D5 14
La Charqueada, Ur ... E2 56
La Châtre, Fr ... D5 14
La Chaux-de-Fonds, Switz ... B2 19
Lachen, Switz ... B6 19
Lachine, Que., Can ... D4, q19 73
Lachine, Alpena, Mich ... C7 98
Lachlan, riv., Austl ... F6 51
La Chorrera, Pan ... F8, m11 62
Lachute, Que., Can ... D3 73
La Cienega, Santa Fe, N. Mex ... h8 107
La Ciotat, Fr ... F6 14
La Cisa, pass., It ... B3 21
Lackawanna, Erie, N.Y ... C2 108
Lackawanna, co., Pa ... D10 114
Lackawaxen, Pike, Pa ... D12 114
Lac la Biche, Alta., Can ... B5 69
Lac la Biche, lake, Alta., Can ... B4 69
Lac la Croix, lake, Minn ... B6 99
Lac la Hache, B.C., Can ... D7 68
Lac la Loche, lake, Sask., Can ... A6 69
Lac la Martre, lake, N.W. Ter., Can ... D9 66
Lac la Plonge, lake, Sask., Can ... B2 70
Lac la Ronge, lake, Sask., Can ... B3 70
Lac la Ronge, prov. park, Sask., Can ... B3 70
Laclede, Bonner, Idaho ... A2 89
La Clede, Fayette, Ill ... E5 90
Laclede, Linn, Mo ... B4 101
Laclede, co., Mo ... D4 101
Lac Masson, Que., Can ... C3 73
Lac-Mégantic, Que., Can ... D7 73
Lacolle, Que., Can ... D4 73
La Colorado, Mex ... B2 63
Lacomb, Linn, Oreg ... C4, k12 113
Lacombe, Alta., Can ... C4 69
Lacombe, St. Tammany, La ... D6, h12 95
Lacombe, bayou, La ... h12 95
Lacon, Marshall, Ill ... B4 90
Lacona, Warren, Iowa ... C4 92
Lacona, Oswego, N.Y ... B4 108
La Conception, Que., Can ... C3 73
Laconia, Belknap, N.H ... C4 105
Laconia, Fayette, Tenn ... B2 117
Laconia, see Lakonia, prov., Grc.
Laconia, gulf, Grc ... D4 23
La Conner, Skagit, Wash ... A3 122
Lacoochee, Pasco, Fla ... D4 86
La Coruña, Sp ... A1 20
La Coruña, prov., Sp ... *A1 20
Lacota, Van Buren, Mich ... F4 98
La Courneuve, Fr ... g10 14
Lac Privert, lake, Que., Can ... g8 75
Lac qui Parle, co., Minn ... F2 99
Lac qui Parle, lake, Minn ... E2 99
Lac qui Parle, riv., Minn ... F2 99
Lacreek, lake, S. Dak ... D4 116
La Crescent, Houston, Minn ... G7 99
La Crescenta, Los Angeles, Calif ... *E4 82
La Cresta Village, Kern, Calif ... *E4 82
La Crête, Alta., Can ... f7 69
La Crosse, Izard, Ark ... A4 81
La Crosse, Alachua, Fla ... C4 86
La Crosse, La Porte, Ind ... B4 91
La Crosse, Rush, Kans ... D4 93
La Crosse, Mecklenburg, Va ... D4 121
Lacrosse, Whitman, Wash ... C8 122
La Crosse, La Crosse, Wis ... E2 124
La Crosse, co., Wis ... E2 124
La Crosse, riv., Wis ... E3 124
La Cruz, Col ... C2 60
La Cruz, C.R ... E5 62
La Cruz, Mex ... C3 63
La Cruz [de Rió Grande], Nic ... D5 62
Lac-Saguay, Que., Can ... C2 73
Lac-St. Jean-Est, co., Que., Can ... A6 73
Lac-St. Jean-Ouest, co., Que., Can ... A5 73
Lac Seul, lake, Ont., Can ... g9 71
La Cueva, Mora, N. Mex ... B4 107
Lac Vert, Sask., Can ... E3 70
Lac Whitegull, lake, Que., Can ... g8 75
La Cygne, Linn, Kans ... D9 93
Lacy-Lakeview, McLennan, Tex ... *D4 118
Ladd, Bureau, Ill ... B4 90
Ladder, creek, Kans ... D2 93
Laddonia, Audrain, Mo ... B6 101
Ladera Heights, Los Angeles, Calif ... *E4 82
La Désirade, isl., Guad ... Q9 65
Ladies, isl., S.C ... G6 115
Ladispoli, It ... h8 21
Lādīz, Iran ... G10 41
Ladner, B.C., Can ... E6, f12 68
Ladner, Harding, S. Dak ... B2 116
Ladoga, Montgomery, Ind ... E4 91
Ladoga, lake, Sov. Un ... A8 27
Ladonia, Fannin, Tex ... C5 118
Ladora, Iowa, Iowa ... C5 92
La Dorado, Col ... B3 60
Ladson, Charleston and Berkeley, S.C ... F7, k11 115
La Due, Henry, Mo ... C4 101
Ladue, St. Louis, Mo ... *C7 101
Ladybank, Scot ... D5 13
Ladybrand, S. Afr ... C4 49
Lady Lake, Lake, Fla ... D5 86
Lady Laurier, mtn., B.C., Can ... A6 68
Ladysmith, B.C., Can ... E6, g12 68
Ladysmith, S. Afr ... C4 49
Ladysmith, Rusk, Wis ... C2 124
Lae, Pap. N. Gui ... k12 50
Laerdal, Nor ... G2 25
Laesø, isl., Den ... A4 24
La Esperanza, Cuba ... C2 64
La Esperanza, Hond ... C3 62
La Estrada, Sp ... A1 20
La Estrella, Bol ... C3 55
La Farge, Vernon, Wis ... E3 124
La Fargeville, Jefferson, N.Y ... A5, f9 108
Lafayette, Chambers, Ala ... C4 78
Lafayette, Boulder, Colo ... B5 83
La Fayette, Walker, Ga ... B1 87
La Fayette, Stark, Ill ... B4 90
Lafayette, Tippecanoe, Ind ... D4 91
La Fayette, Christian, Ky ... D2 94
Lafayette, Lafayette, La ... D3 95
Lafayette, Nicollet, Minn ... F4 99
Lafayette, Sussex, N.J ... A3 106
Lafayette, Onondaga, N.Y ... C4 108
Lafayette, Cumberland, N.C ... B3 109
Lafayette, Madison, Ohio ... C2 111
Lafayette, Yamhill, Oreg ... B3, h11 113
La Fayette, Washington, R.I ... C11 84
Lafayette, Macon, Tenn ... C7 117
Lafayette, co., Ark ... D2 81
Lafayette, co., Fla ... C3 86
Lafayette, co., Miss ... A4 100
Lafayette, co., Mo ... B4 101
Lafayette, co., Wis ... F3 124
Lafayette, par., La ... D3 95
Lafayette, mtn., N.H ... B3 105
Lafayette Hill, Montgomery, Pa ... *F11 114
Lafayette Southwest, Lafayette, La ... *D3 95
Lafayette Springs, Lafayette, Miss ... A4 100
Lafe, Greene, Ark ... A5 81
La Fère, Fr ... E3 15
La Feria, Cameron, Tex ... F4 118
La Ferté-Bernard, Fr ... C4 14
La Ferté-Macé, Fr ... C3 14
La Ferté-sous-Jouarre, Fr ... C5 14
Lafferty, Izard, Ark ... B4 81
Lafferty, Belmont, Ohio ... B4 111
Lafia, Nig ... E6 45
Lafiagi, Nig ... E6 45
Lafitte, Jefferson, La ... k11 95
Laflèche (Mackayville), Que., Can ... *D4 73
Laflèche, Sask., Can ... H2 70
La Flèche, Fr ... D3 14
La Follette, Campbell, Tenn ... C9 117
La Fontaine, Wabash, Ind ... C6 91
Lafontaine, Wilson, Kans ... E8 93
Lafourche, Lafourche, La ... E5, k10 95
Lafourche, par., La ... E3 95
Lafourche, bayou, La ... E5 95
La France, Anderson, S.C ... B2 115
Lafrenais, lake, Que., Can ... A4 73
La Garita, Saguache, Colo ... D4 83
Lage, F.R.G ... B3 17
Lågen, riv., Nor ... G3, p27 25
Lagg, Scot ... E3 13
Laggan, bay, Scot ... E2 13
Laggan, lake, Scot ... D4 13
Laghouat, Alg ... C5 44
La Gloria, Col ... B3 60
Lagny, Fr ... C5 14
Lago, mtn., Wash ... A5 122
Lagoa, Port ... D1 20
Lago Argentino, Arg ... E2 54
Lago Buenos Aires, Arg ... D2 54
Lago de Tefé, lake, Braz ... C1 59
Lago Posadsa, Arg ... D2 54
Lagos, Chile ... B2 54
Lagos, Nig ... E5 45
Lagos, fed. reg., Nig ... *E5 45
Lagos, Port ... D1 20
Lagos de Moreno, Mex ... C4, m13 63
Lago Viedma, Arg ... D2 54
La Grand' Combe, Fr ... E5 14
La Grande, Union, Oreg ... B8 113
La Grange, Lee, Ark ... C5 81
La Grange, Austl ... C3 50
La Grange, Brevard, Fla ... D6 86
La Grange, Troup, Ga ... C1 87
La Grange, Cook, Ill ... B6, k9 90
Lagrange, Lagrange, Ind ... A7 91
La Grange, Oldham, Ky ... B4 94
La Grange, Penobscot, Maine ... C4 96
La Grange, Lewis, Mo ... A6 101
La Grange, Lenoir, N.C ... B5 109
Lagrange, Lorain, Ohio ... A3 111
La Grange, Fayette, Tenn ... B2 117
La Grange, Fayette, Tex ... E4 118
Lagrange, Goshen, Wyo ... E8 125
Lagrange, co., Ind ... A7 91
La Grange Highlands, Cook, Ill ... *B6 90
La Grange Park, Cook, Ill ... k9 90
La Guadeloupe, Que., Can ... D7 73
La Guaira, Ven ... A4 60
La Guajira, dept., Col ... A3 60
La Guardia, Sp ... B1 20
Laguna, Yuma, Ariz ... E1 80
Laguna, Braz ... D3 56
Laguna, Valencia, N. Mex ... B2 107
Laguna, prov., Phil ... *C6 35
Laguna, dam, Ariz ... E1 80
Laguna, Indian res., N. Mex ... C2 107
Laguna Beach, Orange, Calif ... F5, n13 82
Laguna del Perro, lake, N. Mex ... C4 107
Laguna Madre, lagoon, Tex ... F4 118
Laguna Shores, Nueces, Tex ... *F4 118
Lagunillas, Bol ... C3 55
Lagunillas, Ven ... A3 60
Lagrue, bayou, Ark ... C4 81
La Habana, see Havana, Cuba
La Habana, prov., Cuba ... C2 64
La Habra, Orange, Calif ... n13 82
Lahad Datu, Mala ... L5 35
Lahaina, Maui, Haw ... C5 88
La Harpe, Hancock, Ill ... C3 90
La Harpe, Allen, Kans ... E8 93
Lahat, Indon ... F2 35
La Have, N.S., Can ... E5 74
La Have, riv., N.S., Can ... E5 74
La Have Island, N.S., Can ... E5 74
La Haye-Descartes, Fr ... D4 14
Laheria Sarai, India ... D10 40
Laḥij, P. D. R. of Yem ... C5 47
Lahinch, Ire ... E2 11
Lahn, riv., F.R.G ... C3 17
Laholm, Swe ... B7 24
Laholmsbukten, bay, Swe ... B6 24
Lahoma, Garfield, Okla ... A3 112
Lahontan, res., Nev ... D2 104
Lahore, Pak ... B5 39, B5 40
Lahr, F.R.G ... D3 16
Lahri, Pak ... C2 40
Lahti, Fin ... G11 25
La Huaca, Peru ... B1 58
Laï, Chad ... D3 46
Lai Chau, Viet ... A5 38
Laichow, bay, China ... F8 36
Laide, Scot ... C3 13
Laidon, lake, Scot ... D4 13
Laie, Honolulu, Haw ... B4, f10 88
Laifeng, China ... J3 36
Laigle, Fr ... C4 14
Laihka, Bur ... B2 38
Laingsburg, Shiawassee, Mich ... F6 98
Laingsburg, S. Afr ... D3 49
Lair, Harrison, Ky ... B5 94
Laird, Sask., Can ... E2 70
Laird, Yuma, Colo ... A8 83
Lairg, Scot ... B4 13
Laiwui, Indon ... F7 35
Laiyang, China ... F9 36
Laiyuan, China ... E6 36
La Jara, Conejos, Colo ... D5 83
La Jara, Sandoval, N. Mex ... A3 107
Lajas, mun., P.R ... *B1 65
Lajes, Braz ... D2 56
La Jolla, pt., Calif ... o15 82
Lajord, Sask., Can ... G3 70
La Jose (Newburg), Clearfield, Pa ... E8 114
Lajosmizse, Hung ... B4 22
Lajoya, Socorro, N. Mex ... C3 107
La Joya, Peru ... E3 58
La Junta, Otera, Colo ... D7 83
Lak, riv., Ken ... A7 48
Laka, lake, China ... B8 40
Lake, Clare, Mich ... E5 98
Lake, Scott, Miss ... C4 100
Lake, co., Calif ... C2 82
Lake, co., Colo ... B4 83
Lake, co., Fla ... D5 86
Lake, co., Ill ... A6 90
Lake, co., Ind ... B3 91
Lake, co., Mich ... E5 98
Lake, co., Minn ... C7 99
Lake, co., Mont ... C2 102
Lake, co., Ohio ... A4 111
Lake, co., Oreg ... E6 113
Lake, co., S. Dak ... C8 116
Lake, co., Tenn ... A2 117
Lake, reg., Tan ... B5 48
Lake, creek, Wash ... B7 122
Lake, fork, Colo ... C3 83
Lake, mtn., Wyo ... E6 125
Lake, range, Nev ... C2 104
Lake, swamp, S.C ... D8 115
Lake Alfred, Polk, Fla ... D5 86
Lake Alma, Sask., Can ... H3 70
Lake Andes, Charles Mix, S. Dak ... D7 116
Lake Annis, N.S., Can ... E4 74
Lake Ariel, Wayne, Pa ... D11 114
Lake Arrowhead, San Bernardino, Calif ... E5 82
Lake Arthur, Jefferson Davis, La ... D3 95
Lake Arthur, Chaves, N. Mex ... D5 107
Lake Barcroft, Fairfax, Va ... *B5 121
Lake Benton, Lincoln, Minn ... F2 99
Lake Beseck, Middlesex, Conn ... *B6 84
Lake Beulah, Walworth, Wis ... n11 124
Lake Bluff, Lake, Ill ... A6, h9 90
Lake Bonaparte, Lewis, N.Y ... A5 108
Lake Bronson, Kittson, Minn ... B2 99
Lake Brown, Austl ... F2 50
Lake Bruce, Pulaski, Ind ... B5 91
Lake Burien Heights, King, Wash ... *B3 122
Lake Butler, Union, Fla ... B4 86
Lake Butte des Morts, Winnebago, Wis ... *D5 124
Lake Cargelliga, Austl ... F6 51
Lake Chance, creek, Utah ... F4 119
Lake Charles, Calcasieu, La ... D2 95
Lake Chelan, nat. recreation area, Wash ... A5 122
Lake City, Craighead, Ark ... B5 81
Lake City, Modoc, Calif ... B3 82
Lake City, Hinsdale, Colo ... C3 83
Lake City, Columbia, Fla ... B4 86
Lake City, Clayton, Ga ... *C2 87
Lake City, Calhoun, Iowa ... B3 92
Lake City, Barber, Kans ... E5 93
Lake City, Missaukee, Mich ... D5 98
Lake City, Wabasha, Minn ... F6 99
Lake City, Erie, Pa ... B1 114
Lake City, Florence, S.C ... D8 115
Lake City, Marshall, S. Dak ... B8 116
Lake City, Anderson, Tenn ... C9 117
Lake Como, Jasper, Miss ... D4 100
Lake Como, Wayne, Pa ... C11 114
Lake Cormorant, De Soto, Miss ... A3 100
Lake Cowichan, B.C., Can ... g11 68
Lakecreek, Jackson, Oreg ... E5 113
Lake Crystal, Blue Earth, Minn ... F4 99
Lakedale, Cumberland, N.C. (part of Fayetteville) ... B5 109
Lake Delta, Oneida, N.Y ... B5 108
Lake Delton, Sauk, Wis ... E4 124
Lake Dick, Jefferson, Ark ... C4 81
Lake District, reg., Eng ... C5 10
Lake Elmo, Washington, Minn ... E7 99
Lake Elmore, Lamoille, Vt ... B3 120
Lake Entiat, res., Wash ... B5 122
Lake Erie Beach, Erie, N.Y ... C1 108
Lake Fenton, Genesee, Mich ... *F7 98
Lakefield, Ont., Can ... C6 72
Lakefield, Jackson, Minn ... G3 99
Lake Forest, Lake, Ill ... A6, h9 90
Lake Forest, Greenville, S.C ... *B3 115
Lake Forest Park, King, Wash ... *B3 122
Lake Fork, Logan, Ill ... D4 90
Lake Fork, riv., Utah ... C5 119
Lake Fork Valley, Idaho ... E2 89
Lake Fort Gibson, res., Okla ... A6 112
Lake Geneva, Walworth, Wis ... F5 124
Lake George, Park, Colo ... C5 83
Lake George, Claire, Mich ... E6 98
Lake George, Warren, N.Y ... B7 108
Lake Greeson, res., Ark ... C2 81
Lake Hamilton, Polk, Fla ... *D5 86
Lake Harbor, Palm Beach, Fla ... F6 86
Lake Harbour, N.W. Ter., Can ... D19 67
Lake Helen, Volusia, Fla ... D5 86
Lake Hiawatha, Morris, N.J ... B4 106
Lake Hills, King, Wash ... *D2 122
Lake Holloway, Polk, Fla ... *D5 86
Lake Hopatcong (Espanong) Morris, N.J ... *B3 106
Lake Hubert, Crow Wing, Minn ... D4 99
Lake Hughes, Los Angeles, Calif ... E4 82
Lake Huntington, Sullivan, N.Y ... D5 108
Lakehurst, Ocean, N.J ... C4 106
Lake in the Hills, McHenry, Ill ... h8 90
Lake Itasca, Clearwater, Minn ... C3 99
Lake Jackson, Brazoria, Tex ... r14 118
Lake June, Dallas, Tex. (part of Dallas) ... *C4 118
Lake Katrine, Ulster, N.Y ... D7 108
Lakeland, Polk, Fla ... D5 86
Lakeland, Lanier, Ga ... E3 87
Lakeland, La Porte, Ind. (part of Michigan City) ... A4 91
Lakeland, Ranklin, Miss ... C3 100
Lakeland Village, Riverside, Calif ... *F5 82
Lake Lemon, res., Ind ... F5 91
Lake Lenore, Sask., Can ... E3 70
Lake Lillian, Kandiyohi, Minn ... F4 99
Lake Linden, Houghton, Mich ... A2 98
Lake Lindsey, Hernando, Fla ... D4 86
Lake Lotawana, Jackson, Mo ... *C3 101
Lake Louise, Alta., Can ... D2 69
Lake Luzerne, Warren, N.Y ... B7 108
Lake McDonald, Flathead, Mont ... B3 102
Lake Magdalene, Hillsborough, Fla ... o11 86
Lake Mary, Seminole, Fla ... D5 86
Lakemba, isl., Fiji ... 52
Lakemba, passage, Fiji ... 52
Lake Mead, nat. recreation area, Ariz., Nev ... A1 80, H6 104
Lake Merwin, res., Wash ... D3 122
Lake Metigoshe, Bottineau, N. Dak ... A5 110
Lake Mills, Winnebago, Iowa ... A4 92
Lake Mills, Jefferson, Wis ... E5 124
Lake Minchumina, Alsk ... C9 79
Lakemont, Blair, Pa ... F5 114
Lakemore, Summit, Ohio ... A4 111
Lakenan, Shelby, Mo ... B6 101
Lake Nasser, res., Eg. Sud ... E6 43, D4 47
Lake Nebagamon, Douglas, Wis ... B2 124
Lake Norden, Hamlin, S. Dak ... C8 116
Lake Odessa, Ionia, Mich ... F5 98
Lake of the Rivers, lake, Sask., Can ... H3 70
Lake of the Woods, co., Minn ... B4 99
Lake of the Woods, lake, Can., Minn ... G14 66
Lake Orion, Oakland, Mich ... F7 98
Lake Oswego, Clackamas and Multnomah, Oreg ... B4, h12 113
Lake O'the Pines, res., Tex ... C5 118
Lake Ouachita, res., Ark ... C2 81
Lake Ozark, Miller, Mo ... C5 101
Lake Park, Palm Beach, Fla ... F6 86
Lake Park, Lowndes, Ga ... F3 87
Lake Park, Dickinson, Iowa ... A2 92
Lake Park, Becker, Minn ... D2 99
Lake Placid, Highlands, Fla ... E2 86
Lake Placid, Essex, N.Y ... A7, f10 108
Lake Pleasant, Hamilton, N.Y ... B6 108
Lakeport, Lake, Calif ... C2 82
Lake Preston, Kingsbury, S. Dak ... C8 116
Lake Providence, East Carroll, La ... B4 95
Lakeridge, Douglas, Nev ... *E2 104
Lake River, Ont., Can ... n19 72
Lake Ronkonkoma, Suffolk, N.Y ... F4 84
Lake St. John, Concordia, La ... C4 95
Lakesfjorden, fjord, Nor ... B12 25
Lake Shore, Anne Arundel, Md ... B4 85
Lake Shore, Ramsey, Minn ... E7 99
Lakeshore, Hancock, Miss ... E4 100
Lakeside, Navajo, Ariz ... C6 80
Lakeside, San Diego, Calif ... F5, o16 82
Lakeside, N.S., Can ... E6 74
Lakeside, New Haven, Conn ... *D4 84
Lakeside, Buena Vista, Iowa ... B2 92
Lakeside (Pineville Junction), Rapides, La ... *C3 95
Lakeside, Flathead, Mont ... B2 102
Lakeside, Sheridan, Nebr ... B3 103
Lakeside, Passaic, N.J ... A4 106
Lakeside, Ottawa, Ohio ... A3 111
Lakeside, Coos, Oreg ... D2 113
Lakeside, Henrico, Va ... *C5 121
Lakeside, Chelan, Wash. (part of Chelan) ... B5 122
Lakeside, mts., Utah ... B3 119
Lakeside Park, Kenton, Ky ... h13 94
Lake Station, Lake, Ind ... A3 91
Lake Station, Tulsa, Okla ... A5 112
Lake Stevens, Snohomish, Wash ... A3 122
Lake Superior, prov. park, Ont., Can ... p18 72
Lake Tansi, Cumberland, Tenn ... D8 111
Lake Tawakoni, res., Tex ... C4 118
Lake Telemark, Morris, N.J ... B4 106
Lake Tomahawk, Oneida, Wis ... C4 124
Laketon, Wabash, Ind ... C6 91
Laketown, Rich, Utah ... B4 119
Lake Toxaway, Transylvania, N.C ... f10 109
Lake Traverse, Ont., Can ... B6 72
Lake Valley, Sask., Can ... G2 70
Lakeview, Ont., Can ... m14 72
Lakeview, Catoosa, Ga ... *B1 87
Lakeview, Bonner, Idaho ... B2 89
Lake View, Sac, Iowa ... B2 92
Lakeview, Calhoun, Mich ... *F5 98

Lakeview, Montcalm, Mich..E5 98
Lake View, De Soto, Miss..f8 117
Lakeview, Beaverhead, Mont..F5 102
Lake View, Erie, N.Y..C2 108
Lakeview, Logan, Ohio..B2 111
Lakeview, Lake, Oreg..E6 113
Lake View, Dillon, S.C..C9 115
Lakeview, Dallas, Tex..*B6 118
Lakeview, Hall, Tex..B2 118
Lakeview, Jefferson, Tex..*E6 118
Lake Villa, Lake, Ill..h8 90
Lake Village, Chicot, Ark..D4 81
Lake Village, Newton, Ind..B3 91
Lakeville, Litchfield, Conn..B3 84
Lakeville, St. Joseph, Ind..A5 91
Lakeville, Plymouth, Mass..C6 97
Lakeville, Dakota, Minn..F5 99
Lakeville, Livingston, N.Y..C3 108
Lakeville, Ashtabula, Ohio..*A5 111
Lake Waccamaw, Columbus, N.C..C4 109
Lake Wales, Polk, Fla..E5 86
Lake Wazeecha, Wood, Wis..*D4 124
Lake Williams, Kidder, N. Dak..B6 110
Lake Wilson, Murray, Minn..G3 99
Lake Winola, Wyoming, Pa..m17 114
Lake Wissota, Chippewa, Wis..*D2 124
Lakewood, Los Angeles, Calif..n12 82
Lakewood, N.B., Can..*C2 74
Lakewood, Jefferson, Colo..B5 83
Lakewood, Duval, Fla..*B6 86
Lakewood, Walton, Fla..G3 86
Lakewood, Warren, Iowa..f8 92
Lakewood, Somerset, Maine..D3 96
Lakewood, Ocean, N.J..C4 106
Lakewood, Eddy, N. Mex..E5 107
Lakewood, Chautauqua, N.Y..C1 108
Lakewood, Cuyahoga, Ohio..A4, h9 111
Lakewood, Wayne, Pa..C11 114
Lakewood, Harris, Tex..*E5 118
Lakewood, Snohomish, Wash..A3 122
Lakewood, Oconto, Wis..C5 124
Lakewood Center, Pierce, Wash..B3, f10 122
Lake Worth, Palm Beach, Fla..F6 86
Lake Worth Village, Tarrant, Tex..*B5 112
Lake Worth, inlet, Fla..F6 86
Lake Zurich, Lake, Ill..h8 90
Lakhī, Afg..F12 41
Lakhīmpur, India..D8 40
Lakhpat, India..F2 40
Lakhta, Sov. Un..r31 25
Lakin, Kearney, Kans..E2 93
Lakonia (Laconia), prov., Grc..*D4 23
Lakota, Kossuth, Iowa..A3 92
Lakota, I.C..E3 45
Lakota, Nelson, N. Dak..A7 110
Lakshadweep (Laccadive, Minicoy & Amindivi Islands), ter., India..*F5 39
La Laguna, Sp. (Can. Is.)..m13 20
Lālī, Iran..E4 41
La Libertad, Guat..B2 62
La Libertad, Sal..D3 62
La Libertad, dept., Peru..C2 58
La Ligua, Chile..A2 54
Lalín, Sp..A1 20
La Línea, Sp..D3 20
Lalitpur, India..E7 40
Lalitpur (Patan), Nep..D10 40
Lalo, pt., Tinian.. 52
La Loche, Sask., Can..m7 70
La Loma, Stánislaus, Calif..*D3 82
La Loma, Guadalupe, N. Mex..B4 107
La Louvière, Bel..D4 15
La Luz, Otero, N. Mex..E4 107
La Machine, Fr..D5 14
La Maddalena, It..D2 21
La Madeleine, Fr..D5 14
La Madera, Rio Arriba, N. Mex..A3 107
Lama-kara, Togo..E5 45
La Malbaie, Que., Can..B7 73
Lamaline, Newf., Can..E4 75
Lamar, Johnson, Ark..B2 81
Lamar, Prowers, Colo..C8 83
Lamar, Benton, Miss..A4 100
Lamar, Barton, Mo..D3 101
Lamar, Chase, Nebr..D4 103
Lamar, Hughes, Okla..B5 112
Lamar, Clinton, Pa..D6 114
Lamar, Darlington, S.C..C7 115
Lamar, co., Ala..B1 78
Lamar, co., Ga..C2 87
Lamar, co., Miss..D4 100
Lamar, co., Tex..C5 118
Lamar, riv., Wyo..B2 125
Lamarche, Fr..A1 18
La Marque, Galveston, Tex..r15 118
Lamartine, Que., Can..B7 73
Lamas, Peru..C2 58
Lamasco, Lyon, Ky..f10 94
Lamb, co., Tex..B1 118
Lamballe, Fr..C2 14
Lambaréné, Gabon..F2 46
Lambasa, Fiji.. 52
Lambay, isl., Ire..D5 11
Lambayeque, Peru..C2 58
Lambayeque, dept., Peru..C2 58
Lambert, Cook, Ill..F2 90
Lambert, Quitman, Miss..A3 100
Lambert, Richland, Mont..C12 102
Lambert, Alfalfa, Okla..A3 112
Lambert, glacier, Ant..B19 5
Lambert Lake, Washington, Maine..C5 96
Lamberton, Redwood, Minn..F3 99
Lambert's Bay, S. Afr..D2 49
Lambertville, Monroe, Mich..G7 98
Lambertville, Hunterdon, N.J..C3 106
Lambeth, Ont., Can..E3 72
Lambeth, Eng. (part of London)..m12 10
Lambourn, Eng..C6 12
Lambrecht, F.R.G..D3 17
Lambro, riv., It..D5 18
Lambrook, Phillips, Ark..C5 81
Lambs, ferry, Ala..B2 78
Lamb's head, Ire..F1 11
Lambsburg, Carroll, Va..D2 121
Lambton, Que., Can..D6 73
Lambton, co., Ont., Can..E2 72
Lambton, cape, N.W. Ter., Can..B8 66
Lamdessar Timur, Indon..G8 35
Lame Deer, Rosebud, Mont..E10 102
Lamego, Port..B2 20
Lamèque, N.B., Can..B5 74
La Mère et L'Enfant, mtn., Viet..F8 38
La Mesa, San Diego, Calif..o15 82
La Mesa, Dona Ana, N. Mex..E3 107
Lamesa, Dawson, Tex..C2 118
Lamezia Terme, see Nicastro, It.
Lamia, Grc..C4 23
La Minerve, Que., Can..C3 73
La Mirada, Los Angeles, Calif..*E4 82
Lamlash, Scot..E3 13
Lammermuir, hills, Scot..E6 13
Lammhult, Swe..A8 24
Lamoil, isl., Truk.. 52
La Moille, Bureau, Ill..B4 90
Lamoille, Elko, Nev..C6 104
Lamoille, co., Vt..B3 120
Lamoille, riv., Vt..B3 120
Lamoine, Hancock, Maine..D4 96
La Moine, riv., Ill..C3 90
Lamon, bay, Phil..C6, o13 35
Lamona, Lincoln, Wash..B7 122
Lamoni, Decatur, Iowa..D4 92
Lamont, Kern, Calif..E4 82
Lamont, Alta., Can..C4 69
Lamont, Jefferson, Fla..B3 86
Lamont, Fremont, Idaho..F7 89
Lamont, Buchanan, Iowa..B6 92
Lamont, Greenwood, Kans..D7 93
Lamont, Grant, Okla..A4 112
Lamont, Whitman, Wash..B8 122
Lamont, Carbon, Wyo..D5 125
LaMonte, Pettis, Mo..C4 97
La Motte, Jackson, Iowa..B7 92
La Motte, isl., Vt..B2 120
La Moure, La Moure, N. Dak..C7 110
La Moure, co., N. Dak..C7 110
Lampa, Peru..E3 58
Lampang, Thai..C3 38
Lampasas, Lampasas, Tex..D3 118
Lampasas, co., Tex..D3 118
Lampedusa, isl., It..G13 30
Lampertheim, F.R.G..D3 17
Lampeter, Wales..B3 12
Lamphun, Thai..C3 38
Lampman, Sask., Can..H4 70
Lamu, Ken..B7 48
La Mure, Fr..E6 14
Lamy, Santa Fe., N. Mex..B4, k9 107
L'Anacoco, bayou, La..C2 95
Lanagan, McDonald, Mo..E3 101
Lanai, isl., Haw..C5 88
Lanai City, Maui, Haw..C5 88
Lanak La, pass, China, India..B6 39
Lanao del Norte, prov., Phil..*D6 35
Lanao del Sur, prov., Phil..*D6 35
Lanark, Ont., Can..C8 72
Lanark, Carroll, Ill..A4 90
Lanark, Scot..E5 13
Lanark, Raleigh, W. Va..D3, n13 123
Lanark, co., Ont., Can..B8 72
Lanark, co., Scot..E5 13
Lancashire, co., Eng..A5 12
Lancaster, Los Angeles, Calif..E4 82
Lancaster, N.B., Can..D3 74
Lancaster, Ont., Can..B10 72
Lancaster, Eng..C5 10
Lancaster, Atchison, Kans..C8 93
Lancaster, Garrard, Ky..C5 94
Lancaster, Worcester, Mass..B4 97
Lancaster, Kittson, Minn..B2 99
Lancaster, Schuyler, Mo..A5 101
Lancaster, Coos., N.H..B3 105
Lancaster, Erie, N.Y..C2 108
Lancaster, Fairfield, Ohio..C3 111
Lancaster, Lancaster, Pa..F9 114
Lancaster, Lancaster, S.C..B6 115
Lancaster, Smith, Tenn..C8 117
Lancaster, Dallas, Tex..n10 118
Lancaster, Lancaster, Va..C6 121
Lancaster, Grant, Wis..F3 124
Lancaster, co., Nebr..D9 103
Lancaster, co., Pa..G9 114
Lancaster, co., S.C..B6 115
Lancaster, co., Va..C6 121
Lancaster, sound, N.W. Ter., Can..B15 66
Lance, creek, Wyo..C8 125
Lance, pt., Newf., Can..E4 75
Lance Creek, Niobrara, Wyo..C8 125
Lancer, Sask., Can..G1 70
Lancer, Floyd, Ky..C7 94
Lanchi, China..J8 36
Lanchou, China..D5 34
Lanciano, It..C5 21
Lancing, Morgan, Tenn..C9 117
Lancut, Pol..C7 26
Landa, Bottineau, N. Dak..A5 110
Landaff, Grafton, N.H..B3 105
Landau [an der Isar], F.R.G..E7 17
Landau [in der Pfalz], F.R.G..D3 17
Landeck, Aus..E5 15
Landen, Bel..D5 15
Lander, Fremont, Wyo..D4 125
Lander, co., Nev..C4 104
Landerneau, Fr..C1 14
Landes, dept., Fr..*F3 14
Landes, heath, Fr..E3 14
Landess, Grant, Ind..C6 91
Landing, Morris, N.J..*B3 106
Landing, lake, Man., Can..B3 71
Landis, Sask., Can..E1 70
Landis, Rowan, N.C..B2 109
Landisburg, Perry, Pa..F7 114
Landisville, Bucks, Pa..*F11 114
Landivisiau, Fr..C2 14
Lando, Chester, S.C..B5 115
Land O'Lakes, Vilas, Wis..B4 124
Landover Hills, Prince Georges, Md..*C1 85
Landquart, Switz..C8 19
Landquart, riv., Switz..C8 19
Landrum, Spartanburg, S.C..A3 115
Landsberg, F.R.G..D5 16
Land's End, cape, Eng..D2 10
Landshut, F.R.G..E7 17
Landskrona, Swe..C6 24
Landsman, creek, Colo..B8 83
Landsort, Swe..u35 25
Landusky, Phillips, Mont..C8 102
Landwasser, riv., Switz..C8 19
Lane, DeWitt, Ill..C5 90
Lane, Franklin, Kans..D8 93
Lane, White Pines, Nev..D7 104
Lane, Williamsburg, S.C..D8 115
Lane, Jerauld, S. Dak..C7 116
Lane, Dyer, Tenn..A2 117
Lane, co., Kans..D3 93
Lane, co., Oreg..D4 113
Laneburg, Nevada, Ark..D2 81
La Negra, Chile..D2 55
Lanesboro, Carroll, Iowa..B3 92
Lanesboro, Berkshire, Mass..A1 97
Lanesboro, Fillmore, Minn..G7 99
Lanesboro, Susquehanna, Pa..C10 114
Lanesville, Litchfield, Conn..*C3 84
Lanesville, Harrison, Ind..H6 91
Lanett, Chambers, Ala..C4 78
Lanfine, Alta., Can..D5 69
Lang, Sask., Can..H3 70
Langaa, Den..B3 24
Langadhas, Grc..B4 23
Langa Langa, Zaire..B2 48
Långås, Swe..B6 24
Langbank, Sask., Can..G4 70
Lang Bay, B.C., Can..E5 68
Langchung, China..I2 36
Langdale, Chambers, Ala..C4 78
Langdon, Alta., Can..D4 69
Langdon, Clay, Iowa..A2 92
Langdon, Reno, Kans..E5 93
Langdon, Atchison, Mo..A2 101
Langdon, Sullivan, N.H..D2 105
Langdon, Cavalier, N. Dak..A7 110
Langeac, Fr..E5 14
L'Ange-Gardien, Que., Can..n17 73
Langeland, isl., Den..D4 24
Langelandsbaelt, strait, Den..D4 24
Langell, valley, Oreg..E5 113
Langeloth, Washington, Pa..F1 114
Langen, F.R.G..D3 17
Langenau, F.R.G..E5 17
Langenburg, Sask., Can..G5 70
Langenselbold, F.R.G..C4 17
Langenthal, Switz..B4 19
Langenzenn, F.R.G..D5 17
Langeoog, F.R.G..A7 15
Langeoog, isl., F.R.G..B3 16
Langesund, Nor..H3, p27 25
Langevin, Que., Can..C7 73
Langford, B.C., Can..h12 68
Langford, Marshall, S. Dak..B8 116
Långhalsen, lake, Swe..u34 25
Langham, Sask., Can..E2 70
Långhem, Swe..A7 24
Langholm, Scot..E5 13
Langhorne, Bucks, Pa..F12 114
Langhorne Manor, Bucks, Pa..*F12 114
Langjokull, glacier, Ice..n22 25
Langkawi, isl., Mala..I3 38
Langkha Tuk, mtn., Thai..H3 38
Langlade, co., Wis..C4 124
Langlade, isl., St. Pierre & Miquelon..E3 75
Langley, Pike, Ark..C2 81
Langley, B.C., Can..f13 68
Langley, Floyd, Ky..C7 94
Langley, Mayes, Okla..A6 112
Langley, Aiken, S.C..D4 115
Langley, Island, Wash..A3 122
Langley Park, Prince Georges, Md..f9 85
Langleyville, Christian, Ill..D4 90
Langlois, Curry, Oreg..E2 113
Langnau in Emmental, Switz..C4 19
Langogne, Fr..E5 14
Langon, Fr..E3 14
Langöya, isl., Nor..C6 25
Langreo, Sp..A3 20
Langres, Fr..D6 14
Langres, plat., Fr..D6 14
Langruth, Man., Can..D2 71
Langsa, Indon..E1, m11 35
Lang Son, Viet..B7 38
Langstaff, Ont., Can..k15 72
Langston, Jackson, Ala..A3 78
Langston, Logan, Okla..B4 112
Langton, Ont., Can..E4 72
Langtry, Val Verde, Tex..E2 118
Languedoc, former prov., Fr..F5 14
L'Anguille, riv., Ark..B5 81
Lanham, Prince Georges, Md..C4 85
Lanham, Gage, Nebr..D9 103
Lanhsi, China..C3 37
Lanier, co., Ga..E3 87
Lanigan, Sask., Can..F3 70
Lanigan, creek, Sask., Can..F3 70
Lanín, vol., Arg..B2 54
Lankin, Walsh, N. Dak..A8 110
Lanklaar, Bel..C5 15
Lannion, Fr..C2 14
Lannon, Waukesha, Wis..m11 124
L'Annonciation, Que., Can..C3 73
Lanoka Harbor, Ocean, N.J..D4 106
Lanoraie, Que., Can..D4 73
Lansdale, Montgomery, Pa..F11 114
Lansdowne, Ont., Can..C8 72
Lansdowne, Baltimore, Md..B4, h11 85
Lansdowne House, Ont., Can..n18 72
L'Anse, Baraga, Mich..B2 98
L'Anse, Indian res., Mich..B2 98
L'Anse-au-Clair, Newf., Can..C3 75
L'Anse-au-Loup, Newf., Can..C3 75
L'Anse-au-Meadow, Newf., Can..C4 75
L'Anse-Saint Jean, Que., Can..A7 73
Lansford, Bottineau, N. Dak..A4 110
Lansford, Carbon, Pa..E10 114
Lansing, Ont., Can..m15 72
Lansing, Cook, Ill..B6, k9 90
Lansing, Allamakee, Iowa..A6 92
Lansing, Leavenworth, Kans..C9, k16 93
Lansing, Ingham, Mich..F6 98
Lansing, Ashe, N.C..A1 109
Lansing, Fayette, W. Va..m13 123
Lanslebourg, Fr..D2 18
Lanta, isl., Thai..I3 38
Lantana, Palm Beach, Fla..F6 86
Lantern, hill, Conn..D9 84
Lantry, Dewey, S. Dak..B4 116
Lantsang, China..G4 34
Lanús, Arg..*g7 54
Lanusei, It..E2 21
Lanuvio, It..h9 21
Lanzarote, isl., Sp. (Can. Is.)..D2 44
Laoag, Phil..B6 35
Laoighis, co., Ire..D4 11
Lao Kay, Viet..A6 38
Laon, Fr..C5 14
Laona, Forest, Wis..C5 124
La Oroya, Peru..D2 58
Laos, country, Asia..G13 33, C5 38
Laotto, Noble, Ind..B7 91
Lap, isl., Truk.. 52
Lapa, Braz..D3 56
La Palma, Pinal, Ariz..E4 80
La Palma, Pan..F8 62
La Palma, Sp..D2 20
La Pampa, prov., Arg..B3 54
La Paragua, Ven..B5 60
La Passe, Ont., Can..B8 72
La Patrie, Que., Can..D6 73
La Paz, Arg..A5 54
La Paz., Arg..A3 54
La Paz, Bol..C2 55
La Paz, Col..A3 60
La Paz, Hond..C4 62
Lapaz, Marshall, Ind..B5 91
La Paz, Mex..C2 63
La Paz, Mex..C4 63
La Paz, co., Ariz..D1 80
La Paz, dept., Bol..C2 55
La Pedrera, Col..D4 60
Lapeer, Lapeer, Mich..E7 98
Lapeer, co., Mich..E7 98
Lapel, Madison, Ind..D6 91
Lapi (Lappi), dept., Fin..*D11 25
La Pice, St. James, La..B5 95
La Piedad, Mex..m12 63
Lapine, Montgomery, Ala..D3 78
La Pine, Deschutes, Oreg..D5 113
La Place, St. John the Baptist, La..h11 95
Lapland, reg., Eur..C12 25
La Plant, Dewey, S. Dak..B5 116
La Plata, Arg..A5, g8 54
La Plata, Col..C2 60
La Plata, Charles, Md..C4 85
La Plata, Macon, Mo..A5 101
Laplata, San Juan, N. Mex..A1 107
La Plata, co., Colo..D3 83
La Plata, mts., Colo..D2 83
La Plata, peak, Colo..B4 83
La Plata, riv., Arg..B5 54
La Platte, Sarpy, Nebr..g13 103
La Platte, riv., Vt..C2 120
La Pobla de Lillet, Sp..A6 20
La Pocatière, Que., Can..B7 73
La Poile, bay, Newf., Can..E2 75
Lapoint, Unitah, Utah..C6 119
Lapointe, Que., Can..B8 73
La Pointe, Ashland, Wis..B3 124
La Pola, Sp..A3 20
La Porte, Plumas, Calif..C3 82
Laporte, Sask., Can..F1 70
Laporte, Larimer, Colo..A5 83
La Porte, La Porte, Ind..A4 91
Laporte, Hubbard, Minn..C4 99
Laporte, Sullivan, Pa..D9 114
La Porte, Harris, Tex..r14 118
La Porte, co., Ind..A4 91
La Porte City, Black Hawk, Iowa..B5 92
Läppe, Swe..t33 25
Lappeenranta, Fin..G13 25
Lappi (Lapi), dept. Fin..*D11 25
La Prairie, Que., Can..D4, q20 73
La Prairie, Itasca, Minn..C5 99
Laprairie, co., Que., Can..D4 73
La Presa, San Diego, Calif..*F5 82
Laprida, Arg..B4 54
La Providence, Que., Can..*D5 73
La Pryor, Zavala, Tex..E3 118
Lâpseki, Tur..B6 31
Laptev, sea, Sov. Un..B15 28
La Puebla, Sp..C7 20
La Puebla de Montalbán, Sp..C3 20
La Puente, Rio Arriba, N. Mex..A3 107
La Purísima, Mex..B2 63
La Push, Clallam, Wash..B1 122
Lapwai, Nez Perce, Idaho..C2 89
Laqiyat al Arab 'in, Sud..B2 47
La Quiaca, Arg..D2 55
L'Aquila, It..C4 21
Lār, Iran..H7 41
Lara, state, Ven..A3 60
Larache, Mor..G3 30, B3 44
Larak, isl., Iran..H8 41
Laramie, Albany, Wyo..E7 125
Laramie, co., Wyo..E8 125
Laramie, mts., Colo., Wyo..A5 83, D7 125
Laramie, peak, Wyo..D7 125
Laramie, riv., Wyo..E7 125
Laranjeiras, Braz..D3 57
Laranjeiras do Sul, Braz..D2 56
Larantuka, Indon..G6 35
Larche, pass, Fr., It..E2 18
Larchmont, Westchester, N.Y..h13 108
Larchmont North, Westchester, N.Y..*D7 108
Larchwood, Lyon, Iowa..A1 92
Lardeau, B.C., Can..D9 68
L'Ardoise, N.S., Can..D9 74
Laredo, Grundy, Mo..A4 101
Laredo, Hill, Mont..B7 102
Laredo, Sp..A4 20
Laredo, Webb, Tex..F3 118
Laredo, sound, B.C., Can..C3 68
La Réole, Fr..E4 14
Lares, P.R..B2 65
Lares, mun., P.R..*B2 65
Largeau, Chad..B3 46
Largentière, Fr..E6 14
Largo, Pinellas, Fla..E4, p10 86
Largo, isl., Cuba..D3 64
Largo, key, Fla..G6 86
Largs, Scot..E4 13
Lariat, Parmer, Tex..B1 118
La Ricamarie, Fr..E6 14
Larimer, co., Colo..A5 83
Larimore, Grand Forks, N. Dak..B8 110
Larino, It..D5 21
La Rioja, Arg..E2 55
La Rioja, Cuba..D5 64
La Rioja, prov., Arg..E2 55
Lárisa (Larissa), Grc..C4 23
Larisa (Larissa), prov., Grc..*C4 23
La Rivière, Man., Can..E2 71
Lark, Grant, N. Dak..C4 110
Lark, Salt Lake, Utah..C3 119
Lārkāna, Pak..D2 40
Lark Harbour, Newf., Can..D2 75
Larkinburg, Jackson, Kans..A7 93
Larkinsville, Jackson, Ala..A3 78
Larkspur, Marin, Calif..h7 82
Larkspur, Douglas, Colo..B6 83
Larksville, Luzerne, Pa..n17 114
Larne, N. Ire..C6 11
Larned, Pawnee, Kans..D4 93
La Robla, Sp..A3 20
La Rochelle, Fr..D3 14
La Roche-sur-Foron, Fr..C2 18
La Roche-sur-Yon, Fr..D3 14
La Roda, Sp..C4 20
La Romana, Dom. Rep..E9 64
LaRonge, Sask., Can..B3 70
Larose, Lafourche, La..E5 95
Larrabee, Cherokee, Iowa..B2 92
Larrys River, N.S., Can..D8 74
Larsen, ice shelf, Ant..C6 5
Larsen Bay, Alsk..D9 79
Larslan, Valley, Mont..B10 102
Larsmont, Lake, Minn..D7 99
Larson, Burke, N. Dak..A3 110
Larto, Catahoula, La..C4 95
La Rue, Marion, Ohio..B2 111
Larue, co., Ky..C4 94
Laruns, Fr..F3 14
Larvik, Nor..H4, p28 25
Larwill, Whitley, Ind..B6 91
Laryak, Sov. Un..C25 9
Lasa, see Lhasa, China
La Sal, San Juan, Utah..E6 119
La Sal, mts., Utah..E6 119
La Salle, Man., Can..E3 71
La Salle, Que., Can..q19 73
La Salle, Weld, Colo..A6 83
La Salle, LaSalle, Ill..B4 90
La Salle, Watonwan, Minn..F4 99
La Salle, co., Ill..B5 90
La Salle, co., Tex..E3 118
La Salle, par., La..C3 95
Las Animas, Bent, Colo..C7 83
Las Animas, co., Colo..D6 83
Las Anod, Som..D6 47
Las Anod, dist., Som..D6 47
La Sarre, Que., Can..k11 73
Lasauses, Conejos, Colo..D5 83
Lasberg, Aus..E9 17
Las Cabras, Chile..A2 54
Lascahobas, Hai..E8 64
Lascano, Ur..E2 56
Lascassas, Rutherford, Tenn..B5 117
L'Ascension, Que., Can..A6 73
La Scie, Newf., Can..D4 75
Las Coloradas, Arg..B2 54
Las Conchas, Arg..g7 54
Las Cordilleras, dept., Par..*E4 55
Las Cruces, Dona Ana, N. Mex..E3 107
La Selle, peak, Hai..E8 64
La Serena, Chile..E1 55
La Seyne [-sur-Mer], Fr..F6 14
Las Flores, Arg..B5 54
Lashburn, Sask., Can..D1 70
Lāsh-e Joveyn, Afg..F10 41
Lashio, Bur..D10 39
Lashkar, see Gwalior, India
La Sierra, Riverside, Calif..n14 82
Lasithi (Lasithion), prov., Grc..*E5 23
Lask, Pol..C5 26
Las Lajas, Arg..B2 54
Las Lajas, Pan..F7 62
Las Lomitas, Arg..D3 55
Las Marías, mun., P.R..*B1 65
Las Nutrias, Socorro, N. Mex..C3 107
La Solana, Sp..C4 20
Las Palmas, Pan..F7 62
Las Palmas [de Gran Canaria], Sp. (Can. Is.)..D1 44
Las Palmas, prov., Sp..*m14 20
Las Palomas, Sierra, N. Mex..D2 107
La Spezia, It..B2 21
Las Piedras, Ur..E1 56
Las Piedras, mun., P.R..*B4 65
Las Pipinas, Arg..B5 54
Las Plumas, Arg..C3 54
Las Rosas, Arg..A4 54
Las Rozas de Madrid, Sp..D6, p17 20
Lassen, co., Calif..B3 82
Lassen, peak, Calif..B3 82
Lassen Volcanic, nat. park, Calif..B3 82
Lasso, mtn., Tinian.. 52
L'Assomption, Que., Can..D4 73
L'Assomption, co., Que., Can..D4 73
Las Tablas, Rio Arriba, N. Mex..A3 107
Las Tablas, Pan..G7 62
Las Termas, Arg..E3 55
Last Mountain, lake, Sask., Can..F3 70
Lastourville, Gabon..F2 46
Lastrup, F.R.G..B7 15
Lastrup, Morrison, Minn..D4 99
Las Varillas, Arg..A4 54
Las Vegas, Clark, Nev..G6 104
Las Vegas (city), San Miguel, N. Mex..B4 107
Las Vigas, Mex..n15 63
Las Villas, prov., Cuba..C3 64
La Tabatière, Que., Can..C2 75
Latacunga, Ec..B2 58
Latady, isl., Ant..B5 5
La Tagua, Col..D3 60
Latah, Spokane, Wash..B8 122
Latah, co., Idaho..C2 89
Latakia (Al Lādhiqīyah), Syr..E10 31
Laterrière, Que., Can..A6 73
La Teste-de-Buch, Fr..E3 14
Latexo, Houston, Tex..D5 118
Latham, Baldwin, Ala..D2 78
Latham, Logan, Ill..D4 90
Latham, Butler, Kans..E7 93
Latham, Albany, N.Y..*C7 108
Lathrop, San Joaquin, Calif..*D3 82
Lathrop, Delta, Mich..B3 98
Lathrop, Clinton, Mo..B3 101
Lathrop Wells, Nye, Nev..G5 104
Lathrup Village, Oakland, Mich..*F7 98
Latimer, Franklin, Iowa..B4 92
Latimer, Morris, Kans..D7 93
Latimer, co., Okla..C6 112
Latina, It..D4, k9 21
Latium, reg., It..C4 21
La Toma, Ec..B2 58
Laton, Fresno, Calif..D4 82
Latour, Johnson, Mo..C3 101
La Tour-du-Pin, Fr..E6 14
La Tremblade, Fr..E3 14
La Trinité, Mart..S11 65
Latrobe, Westmoreland, Pa..F3 114
Laṭrūn, Jordan..C6, h10 32
Latta, Dillon, S.C..C9 115
Lattimer Mines, Luzerne, Pa..E10 114
Lattimore, Cleveland, N.C..B1 109
Lattingtown, Nassau, N.Y..*F2 84
Latty, Paulding, Ohio..A1 111
La Tuque, Que., Can..B5 73
Latvia (S.S.R.), rep., Sov. Un..D5 28
Latzu (Lhatse Dzong), China..C11 40
Lau, Nig..E7 45
Lau, is., Fiji.. 52
Lauchhammer, G.D.R..B8 17
Laud, Whitley, Ind..B7 91
Lauda, F.R.G..D4 17
Lauder, Man., Can..E1 71
Lauder, Scot..E6 13
Lauderdale, St. James, La..B5 95
Lauderdale, Ramsey, Minn..*F5 99
Lauderdale, Lauderdale, Miss..C5 100
Lauderdale, co., Ala..A2 78
Lauderdale, co., Miss..C5 100
Lauderdale, co., Tenn..B2 117
Lauderdale-by-the-Sea, Broward, Fla..*F6 86
Lauderdale Lakes, Broward, Fla..r13 86
Lauenburg, F.R.G..E4 24
Lauf, F.R.G..D6 17
Laufen, F.R.G..B8 18
Laufen, Switz..B4 19
Lauffen, F.R.G..D4 17
Laughery, creek, Ind..F7 91
Laughlin, Clark, Nev..H7 104
Laughlin, peak, N. Mex..A5 107
Laughlintown, Westmoreland, Pa..F3 114
Lauingen, F.R.G..E5 17
Laulau, Saipan.. 52
Lauliifou, Am. Sam.. 52
Launceston, Austl..o15 50
Launceston, Eng..D3 12
La Unión, Arg..B3 54
La Unión, Chile..C2 54
La Unión, Col..C2 60
La Unión, Mex..D4, o13 63
La Union, Dona Ana, N. Mex..F3 107
La Unión, Peru..C2 58
La Unión, Sal..D4 62
La Unión, Sp..D5 20
La Union, prov., Phil..*B6 35
Laupahoehoe, Hawaii, Haw..D6 89
Laupheim, F.R.G..D4 16
Laura, Sask., Can..F2 70
Laura, Miami, Ohio..C1 111
Laurbjerg, Den..B3 24
Laurel, Ont., Can..D4 72
Laurel, Sussex, Del..C6 85
Laurel, Sarasota, Fla..E4 86
Laurel, Franklin, Ind..E7 91
Laurel, Marshall, Iowa..C5 92
Laurel, Prince Georges, Md..B4 85
Laurel, Jones, Miss..D4 100
Laurel, Yellowstone, Mont..E8 102
Laurel, Cedar, Nebr..B8 103
Laurel, Suffolk, N.Y..F6 84
Laurel, Washington, Oreg..B1 113
Laurel, Henrico, Va..C5 121
Laurel, Whatcom, Wash..A3 122
Laurel, Klickitat, Wash..D4 122
Laurel, co., Ky..C5 94
Laurel, creek, W. Va..m12 123
Laurel, creek, W. Va..n14 123
Laurel, fork, W. Va..C5 123
Laurel, mtn., W. Va..B5 123
Laurel, riv., Del..C6 85
Laurel, riv., Ky..D5 94
Laurel Bloomery, Johnson, Tenn..C12 117
Laureldale, Atlantic, N.J..D3 106
Laureldale, Berks, Pa..F10 114
Laureles, Ur..E1 56
Laurel Fork, Carroll, Va..D2 121
Laurel Gardens, Alleghany, Pa..*F2 114
Laurel Heights, Snohomish, Wash..*B3 122
Laurel Hill, Okaloosa, Fla..u15 86
Laurel Hill, Scotland, N.C..C3 109
Laurel Run, Luzerne, Pa..n17 114
Laurel Springs, Camden, N.J..*D3 106
Laurelton, Union, Pa..E7 114
Laurelville, Hocking, Ohio..C3 111
Laurence Harbor, Middlesex, N.J..C4 106
Laurencekirk, Scot..D6 13
Laurens, Pocahontas, Iowa..B3 92
Laurens, Laurens, S.C..B3 115
Laurens, co., Ga..D4 87
Laurens, co., S.C..C4 115
Laurentides, Que., Can..D4 73
Laurentides, prov. park, Que., Can..B6 73
Laurie, isl., Ant..C8 5
Laurie, lake, Man., Can..A1 71
Laurie, riv., Man., Can..A1 71
Laurier, Man., Can..D2 71
Laurier, Que., Can..C6 73
Laurierville, Que., Can..C6 73
Laurin, Madison, Mont..E4 102
Laurinburg, Scotland, N.C..C3 109
Lauritzen, bay, Ant..C28 5
Laurium, Houghton, Mich..A2 98
Laurot, is., Indon..F5 35
Lausanne, Switz..C2 19
Lauscha, G.D.R..C6 17
Laut, isl., Indon..F5 35
Lautaro, Chile..B2 54
Lauterbach, F.R.G..C4 17
Lauterbrunnen, Switz..C4 19
Lauterecken, F.R.G..D2 17
Lauthala, is., Fiji.. 52
Lautoka, Fiji.. 52
Lauwers Zee, riv., Neth..A6 15
Lauzon, Que., Can..C6, n17 73
Lava Beds, Idaho..F4 89
Lava Beds, Nev..C3 104
Lava Beds, nat. mon., Calif..B3 82
Lavaca, Choctaw, Ala..C1 78
Lavaca, Sebastian, Ark..B1 81
Lavaca, co., Tex..E4 118
Lava Hot Springs, Bannock, Idaho..G6 89
Laval, Fr..C3 14
La Vale, Allegany, Md..k13 85
Laval-des-Rapides, Que., Can..p19 73
Lavalle Arg..A3 54
La Valle, Sauk, Wis..E3 124
Lavalleja, dept., Ur..*E1 56
Lavallette, Ocean, N.J..D4 106
La Valley, Costilla, Colo..D5 83
Laval-Ouest, Que., Can..*D4 73
Lavaltrie, Que., Can..C4 73
Lāvān, isl., Iran..H6 41
Lavant, riv., Aus..E7 16
Lavant Station, Ont., Can..B8 72
Lavaur, Fr..F4 14
Lavaveix-les-Mines, Fr..D5 14
Laveen, Maricopa, Ariz..m8 80
La Vega, Dom. Rep..E8 64
La Vela, Ven..A4 60
Lavelanet, Fr..F4 14
Lavello, It..D5 21
L'Avenir, Que., Can..D5 73
La Vérendrye, prov. park, Que., Can..k11 73
La Vergne, Rutherford, Tenn..A5, g10 117
La Verkin, Washington, Utah..F2 119
La Verne, Los Angeles, Calif..m13 82
Laverne, Harper, Okla..A2 112
La Vernia, Wilson, Tex..E3, k7 118
Laverton, Austl..E3 50
La Veta, Huerfano, Colo..D5 83
Laviana, Sp..A3 20
La Victoria, Ven..A4 60

Livny, Sov. Un. E11 27
Livona, Emmons, N. Dak C5 110
Livonia, Washington, Ind G5 91
Livonia, Pointe Coupee, La D4 95
Livonia, Wayne, Mich F7, p15 98
Livonia, Putnam, Mo A5 101
Livonia, Livingston, N.Y C3 108
Livorno (Leghorn), It C3 21
Livramento, Braz E1 56
Livry-Gargan, Fr g11 14
Liwale, Tan C6 48
Liyang, China E8 36
Lizard, creek, Iowa B3 92
Lizard, pt., Eng D2 12
Lizard Head, pass, Colo D3 83
Lizard Head, peak, Wyo D3 125
Lizella, Bibb, Ga D3 87
Lizemores, Clay, W. Va C3, m13 123
Lizotte, Que., Can A5 73
Lizton, Hendricks, Ind E4 91
Ljubljana, Yugo B2 22
Ljubuski, Yugo D3 22
Ljungby, Swe I5 25
Ljusdal, Swe G7 25
Ljusterö, Swe t36 25
Llandeilo, Wales C4 12
Llandovery, Wales C4 12
Llandrindod Wells, Wales B4 12
Llandudno, Wales A4 12
Llanelli, Wales C3 12
Llanes, Sp A3 20
Llanfyllin, Wales B4 12
Llangefni, Wales A3 12
Llangollen, Wales B4 12
Llangynog, Wales B4 12
Llanidloes, Wales B4 12
Llano, Llano, Tex D3 118
Llano, Taos, N. Mex A4 107
Llano, co., Tex D3 118
Llano Estacado, plain, N. Mex., Tex C1 118
Llanos, plains, Col., Ven C4 53
Llanquihue, lake, Chile C2 54
Llanquihue, prov., Chile C2 54
Llanrwst, Wales A4 12
Llata, Peru C2 58
Llaves, Rio Arriba, N. Mex A3 107
Llerena, Sp C2 20
Lleyn, pen., Wales B3 12
Llico, Chile A2 54
Llivia, Sp F4 14
Llobregat, riv., Sp B6 20
Llorona, pt., C.R F6 62
Lloyd, Jefferson, Fla B2 86
Lloyd, Greenup, Ky B7 94
Lloyd, Blaine, Mont B7 102
Lloyd, neck, N.Y F3 84
Lloyd, pt., N.Y F3 84
Lloyd Harbor, Suffolk, N.Y *F3 84
Lloydminster, Alta. and Sask., Can D1 70
Lloyd Place, Nansemond, Va *D6 121
Lloyds, riv., Newf., Can D3 75
Lluchmayor, Sp C7 20
Llullaillaco, vol., Chile D2 55
Llyswen, Blair, Pa. (part of Altoona) F5 114
Loa, riv., Chile D2 55
Loa, Wayne, Utah E4 119
Loachapoka, Lee, Ala C4 78
Loami, Sangamon, Ill D4 90
Loan, lake, Maine B3 96
Loange, riv., Zaire C3 48
Loanhead, Scot *E5 13
Lobatse, Bots C4 49
Löbau, G.D.R B9 17
Lobaye, riv., Cen. Afr. Rep E3 46
Lobelville, Perry, Tenn B4 117
Lobenstein, G.D.R C6 17
Lobería, Arg B5 54
Lobito, Ang D1 48
Lobnya, Sov. Un m17 27
Lobo, Phil p13 35
Lobos, Arg B5, g7 54
Lobos de Tierra, isl., Peru C1 58
Lobster, lake, Maine C3 96
Lobstick, lake, Newf., Can g8 75
Loburg, G.D.R A7 17
Locarno, Switz D6 19
Lochaber, N.S., Can D7 74
Lochaline, Scot D3 13
Lochbroom, Scot B4 13
Lochcarron, Scot C3 13
Lochdonhead, Scot C3 13
Lochearn, Baltimore, Md *B4 85
Lochearnhead, Scot D4 13
Lochem, Neth B6 15
Locheng (Lokwei), China C9 38
Loches, Fr D4 14
Lochgelly, Scot *D5 13
Lochgilphead, Scot D3 13
Lochiel, Santa Cruz, Ariz F5 80
Loching, China J9 36
Lochinver, Scot B3 13
Loch Lomond, Prince William, Va *B5 121
Loch Lynn Heights, Garrett, Md m12 85
Lochmaben, Scot E5 13
Lochmere, Belknap, N.H D3 105
Lochnagar, mtn., Scot D5 13
Lochranza, Scot E3 13
Loch Raven, Baltimore, Md *B4 85
Loch Raven, res., Md B4 85
Lochsa, riv., Idaho C3 89
Lochuan, China G3 36
Lochy, lake, Scot D4 13
Lockbourne, Franklin, Ohio m11 111
Locke, Elkhart, Ind B5 91
Locke, Cayuga, N.Y C4 108
Locke, Shelby, Tenn B1, e8 117
Locke, Pend Oreille, Wash A8 122
Lockeford, San Joaquin, Calif *C3 82
Locke Mills, Oxford, Maine D2 96
Lockeport, N.S., Can F4 74
Lockerbie, Scot E5 13
Lockesburg, Sevier, Ark D1 81
Lockhart, Covington, Ala D3 78
Lockhart, Orange, Fla *D5 86
Lockhart, Norman, Minn C2 99
Lockhart, Union, S.C B5 115
Lockhart, Caldwell, Tex E4, h8 118
Lock Haven, Clinton, Pa D7 114
Lockland, Hamilton, Ohio h14 94
Lockney, Floyd, Tex B2 118
Lockport, Man., Can D3 71
Lockport, Will, Ill B5, k8 90
Lockport, Henry, Ky B5 94
Lockport, Lafourche, La E5, k10 95
Lockport, Niagara, N.Y B2 108
Lockport Station, Lafourche, La k10 95
Lockridge, Jefferson, Iowa C6 92
Lock Springs, Daviess, Mo B4 101
Lockwood, Sask., Can F3 70
Lockwood, Dade, Mo D4 101
Lockwood, Yellowstone, Mont E8 102
Lockwood, Nicholas, W. Va C3, m13 123
Locminé, Fr D2 14
Loc Ninh, Viet G7 38
Loco, Stephens, Okla C4 112
Loco Hills, Eddy, N. Mex E6 107
Locumba, Peru E3 58
Locust, Monmouth, N.J C4 106
Locust, Stanly, N.C B2 109
Locust, creek, Mo B4 101
Locust, fork, Ala f6 78
Locust, pt., Md B5 85
Locust Bayou, Calhoun, Ark D3 81
Locust Grove, Henry, Ga C2 87
Locust Grove, Washington, Md B2 85
Locust Grove, Mayes, Okla A6 112
Locust Hill, Ont., Can k15 72
Locust Valley, Nassau, N.Y F2 84
Lod (Lydda), Isr C6, h10 32
Loda, Iroquois, Ill C5 90
Löderup, Swe C8 24
Lodève, Fr F5 14
Lodeynoye Pole, Sov. Un A9 27
Lodge, Colleton, S.C E6 115
Lodge, creek, Can., Mont B7 102
Lodge Grass, Big Horn, Mont E9 102
Lodgepole, Alta., Can C3 69
Lodgepole, Cheyenne, Nebr C3 103
Lodgepole, Perkins, S. Dak B3 116
Lodgepole, creek, Nebr., Wyo C3 103, E8 125
Lodhran, Pak C3 40
Lodi, San Joaquin, Calif C3 82
Lodi, It D5 18
Lodi, Bergen, N.J h8 106
Lodi, Seneca, N.Y C4 108
Lodi, Medina, Ohio A3 111
Lodi, Washington, Va f10 121
Lodi, Columbia, Wis E4 124
Lodi, Zaire B3 48
Lodja, Zaire B3 48
Lodore, canyon, Colo A2 83
Lods, Fr B2 18
Lodwar, Ken A6 48
Łódź, Pol C5 26
Loeches, Sp p18 20
Loei, Thai D4 38
Loelli (well), Sud D3 47
Loeriesfontein, S. Afr D2 49
Lofer, Aus B8 18
Lofgreen, Tooele, Utah C5 119
Lofoten, is., Nor C5 25
Loftus, Eng F8 13
Logan (Hanaford), Franklin, Ill F5 90
Logan, Harrison, Iowa C2 92
Logan, Phillips, Kans C4 93
Logan, Gallatin, Mont E5 102
Logan, Quay, N. Mex B7 107
Logan, Ward, N. Dak A4 110
Logan, Hocking, Ohio C3 111
Logan, Beaver, Okla A1, e10 112
Logan, Cache, Utah B4 119
Logan, Logan, W. Va D3, n12 123
Logan, co., Ark B2 81
Logan, co., Colo A7 83
Logan, co., Ill C4 90
Logan, co., Kans D2 93
Logan, co., Ky D3 94
Logan, co., Nebr C5 103
Logan, co., N. Dak C6 110
Logan, co., Ohio B2 111
Logan, co., Okla B4 112
Logan, co., W. Va D3 123
Logan, creek, Nebr B9 103
Logan, mtn., Yukon, Can D4 66
Logan, mtn., Wash A5 122
Logan, mts., Yukon, Can D7 66
Logan, pass, Mont B3 102
Logan, peak, Ala A3 78
Logandale, Clark, Nev G7 104
Logansport, Cass, Ind C5 91
Logansport, Butler, Ky C3 94
Logansport, De Soto, La C2 95
Loganton, Clinton, Pa D7 114
Loganville, Gwinnett and Walton, Ga C3 87
Loganville, York, Pa G8 114
Loganville, Sauk, Wis E3 124
Logdell, Grant, Oreg C7 113
Loge, riv., Ang C1 48
Loggieville, N.B., Can B4 74
Log Lane Village, Morgan, Colo A7 83
Logone, riv., Chad C3 46
Logroño, Sp A4 20
Logroño, prov., Sp *A4 20
Løgstør, Den B3 24
Logtown, Hancock, Miss E4 100
Løgumkloster, Den C2 24
Lohals, Den C4 24
Lohārdaga, India F10 40
Loho, China E7 34
Lohr, F.R.G D4 17
Lohrville, Calhoun, Iowa B3 92
Loi Mai, mtn., Bur B2 38
Loire, dept., Fr *E6 14
Loire, riv., Fr D3 14
Loire-Atlantique, dept., Fr *D3 14
Loiret, dept., Fr *D4 14
Loir-et-Cher, dept., Fr *D4 14
Loíza, P.R B4 65
Loíza, mun., P.R *B4 65
Loíza, res., P.R B4 65
Loja, Ec B2 58
Loja, Sp D3 20
Loja, prov., Ec B2 58
Lokan, res., Fin C13 25
Lokandu, Zaire B4 48
Lokeren, Bel C3 15
Lokhvitsa, Sov. Un F9 27
Lokichar, Ken A5 48
Lokichokio, Ken A5 48
Lokitaung, Ken A6 48
Løkken, Den A3 24
Lokoja, Nig E6 45
Lokoro, riv., Zaire B3 48
Lokossa, Benin E5 45
Lokwei, see Locheng, China
Lol, riv., Sud D2 47
Lola, Livingston, Ky A3 94
Lolland, isl., Den D5 24
Lollar, F.R.G C3 17
Lollie (Minter), Laurens, Ga D4 87
Lolo, Missoula, Mont D2 102
Lolo, pass, Idaho, Mont C4 89
Lolo Hot Springs, Missoula, Mont D2 102
Lom, Bul D6 22
Loma, Mesa, Colo B2 83
Loma, Chouteau, Mont C6 102
Loma, Butler, Nebr C9 103
Loma, Cavalier, N. Dak A7 110
Loma, mts., Guinea, S.L E2 45
Loma Linda, San Bernardino, Calif *E5 82
Lomami, riv., Zaire B3 48
Loman, Koochiching, Minn B5 99
Lomas, Peru E3 58
Lomas de Zamora, Arg A5, g7 54
Lomax, Chilton, Ala C3 78
Lomax, Henderson, Ill C2 90
Lombard, Du Page, Ill k8 90
Lombardia, pol. dist., It *B2 21
Lombardy, reg., It B2 21
Lomblen, isl., Indon G6 35
Lombok, isl., Indon G5 35
Lombok strait, Indon G5 35
Lomé, Togo E5 45
Lomela, Zaire B3 48
Lomela, riv., Zaire B3 48
Lometa, Lampasas, Tex D3 118
Lomié, Cam E2 46
Lomira, Dodge, Wis E5 124
Lomita, Los Angeles, Calif *E4 82
Lommel, Bel C5 15
Lomond, Alta., Can D4 69
Lomond, Newf., Can D3 75
Lomond, lake, Scot D4 13
Lomonosov, Sov. Un s30 25
Lomonosovskaya, Sov. Un C7 29
Lompoc, Santa Barbara, Calif E3 82
Lomza, Pol B7 26
Lonaconing, Allegany, Md k12 85
Loncoche, Chile B2 54
Londesborough, Ont., Can D3 72
London, Pope, Ark B2 81
London, Ont., Can E3 72
London, Eng E6 10, C7 12
London, Laurel, Ky C5 94
London, Madison, Ohio C2 111
London, Kimble, Tex D3 118
London, Kanawha, W. Va *C3 123
London, co., Eng *E6 10
Londonbridge, Princess Anne, Va *E6 121
Londonderry, N.S., Can D6 74
Londonderry, N. Ire B4 11
Londonderry, Rockingham, N.H E4 105
Londonderry, Ross, Ohio C3 111
Londonderry, Windham, Vt E3 120
Londonderry, cape, Austl B4 50
Londonderry, isl., Chile k11 54
London Mills, Fulton and Knox, Ill C3 90
Londontowne, Anne Arundel, Md C4 85
Londrina, Braz C2 56
Lone, plat., Colo D2 83
Lone Elm, Anderson, Kans D8 93
Lone Grove, Carter, Okla C4 112
Lone Jack, Jackson, Mo C3 101
Lonely, isl., Ont., Can B3 72
Lone Mountain, Claiborne, Tenn C10 117
Loneoak, McCracken, Ky A2 94
Lone Oak, Hunt, Tex C5 118
Lone Pine, Inyo, Calif D4 82
Lonepine, Evangeline, La D3 95
Lonepine, Sanders, Mont C2 102
Lone Rock, Sask., Can D1 70
Lone Rock, Kossuth, Iowa A3 92
Lonerock, Gilliam, Oreg B7 113
Lone Rock, Richland, Wis E3 124
Lone Star, Calhoun, S.C D6 115
Lone Star, Morris, Tex *C5 118
Lone Tree, Johnson, Iowa C6 92
Lonetree, Uinta, Wyo E2 125
Lone Tree, creek, Colo A6 83
Lone Wolf, Kiowa, Okla C2 112
Long, co., Ga E5 87
Long, bay, Jam E12 65
Long, bay, Jam F14 65
Long, bay, N.C D4 109
Long, beach, N.Y E7 84
Long, beach, N.Y G2 84
Long, creek, Sask., Can H3 70
Long, creek, N. Dak A2 110
Long, isl., Ba C6 64
Long, isl., Ba m17 64
Long, isl., N.S., Can E3 74
Long, isl., Fla H6 86
Long, isl., Maine g8 96
Long, isl., Mass g12 97
Long, isl., Pap. N. Gui *k12 50
Long, isl., N.Y G3 84
Long, key, Fla E4 86
Long, key, Fla H6 86
Long, lake, N.B., Can B3 74
Long, lake, Maine A4 96
Long, lake, Maine D2 96
Long, lake, Mich C7 98
Long, lake, Mich D5 98
Long, lake, Minn D4 99
Long, lake, N.Y B6 108
Long, lake, N. Dak C6 110
Long, lake, Wash f10 122
Long, lake, Wis C2 124
Long, mtn., N.H A4 105
Long, pt., Man., Can C2 71
Long, pt., Newf., Can D2 75
Long, pt., Ont., Can E4 72
Long, pond, Fla C4 86
Long, pond, Maine C2 96
Long, pond, Maine C3 96
Long, pond, Mass C6 97
Long, pond, Mass C6 97
Long, strait, Sov. Un B20 28
Longa, riv., Ang D1 48
Longá, riv., Braz B2 56
Longacre, Fayette, W. Va m13 123
Longarone, It C8 18
Long Bar Harbor, Harford, Md B5 85
Long Beach, Los Angeles, Calif F4, n12 82
Longbeach, Manatee, Fla F2 86
Long Beach, La Porte, Ind A4 91
Long Beach, Pope, Minn E3 99
Long Beach, Harrison, Miss E4, f7 100
Long Beach, Nassau, N.Y E7, n15 108
Long Beach, Pacific, Wash C1 122
Long Beach Resort, Bay, Fla *G3 86
Longbenton, Eng *E7 13
Longboat, key, Fla E4 86
Longboat, pass, Fla q10 86
Longboat Key, Manatee and Sarasota, Fla q10 86
Long Bottom, Meigs, Ohio C4 111
Long Branch, Ont., Can m14 72
Long Branch, Monmouth, N.J C5 106
Long Branch, Panola, Tex C5 118
Longbranch, Pierce, Wash B3 122
Long Cliff, Cass, Ind C5 91
Long Corner, Howard, Md B3 85
Long Creek, Grant, Oreg C7 113
Longcreek, Oconee, S.C B1 115
Longdale, Blaine, Okla A3 112
Long Eaton, Eng B6 12
Long Eddy, Sullivan, N.Y D5 108
Longeten, riv., Switz B4 19
Longford, Ire D4 11
Longford, Clay, Kans C6 93
Longford, co., Ire D4 11
Longford Mills, Ont., Can C5 72
Long Grove, Scott, Iowa C7 92
Long Harbour, Newf., Can E5 75
Long Hill, Fairfield, Conn. (part of Trumbull) D4 84
Longhorn, Bexar, Tex B4 118
Longiram, Indon F5 35
Long Island, Jackson, Ala A4 78
Long Island, Phillips, Kans C4 93
Long Island, Cumberland, Maine (part of Portland) E5 96
Longisland, Catawba, N.C B2 109
Long Island, Campbell, Va C3 121
Long Island, sound, Conn., N.Y E4 84
Longlac, Ont., Can G15 67
Long Lake, Lake, Ill h8 90
Long Lake, Iosco, Mich D7 98
Long Lake, Hennepin, Minn *F5 99
Long Lake, Hamilton, N.Y B6 108
Long Lake, McPherson, S. Dak B6 116
Long Lake, Florence, Wis C5 124
Long Lake Colony, McPherson, S. Dak *B7 116
Long Lane, Dallas, Mo D5 101
Longleaf, Rapides, La C3 95
Long Leaf Park (South Wilmington), New Hanover, N.C *C5 109
Longmeadow, Hampden, Mass B2 97
Longmont, Boulder, Colo A5 83
Long Pine, Brown, Nebr B6 103
Long Point, N.S., Can D8 74
Long Point, Livingston, Ill B5 90
Long Point Beach, Ont., Can E4 72
Long Pond, Newf., Can E5 75
Long Pond, Somerset, Maine C2 96
Longport, Atlantic, N.J E3 106
Long Prairie, Todd, Minn E4 99
Long Range, mts., Newf., Can E2 75
Longreach, Austl D7 51
Long Ridge, Fairfield, Conn. (part of Stamford) E2 84
Longridge, Eng G6 13
Long Run, Doddridge, W. Va k9 123
Longs, creek, Ark A2 81
Longs, peak, Colo A5 83
Longstreet, DeSoto, La B2 95
Longton, Elk, Kans E7 93
Longtown, Eng E6 13
Longtown, Perry, Mo D8 101
Longueau, Fr E2 15
Longueuil, Que., Can D4, p19 73
Longuyon, Fr C6 14
Longvale, Mendocino, Calif C2 82
Long Valley, Coconino, Ariz C4 80
Long Valley, Morris, N.J B3 106
Longvalley, Jackson, S. Dak D4 116
Longview, Alta., Can D3 69
Longview, Champaign, Ill D5 90
Long View, Hardin, Ky C4 94
Longview, Oktibbeha, Miss B5 100
Longview, Catawba, N.C B1 109
Longview, Gregg, Tex C5 118
Longview, Cowlitz, Wash C3 122
Longville, Beauregard, La D2 95
Longville, Cass, Minn C4 99
Longwood, Seminole, Fla *D5 86
Longwood, Brunswick, N.C C4 109
Longwoods, Talbot, Md C5 85
Longwy, Fr C6 14
Long Xuyen, Viet G6 38
Loning, China G4 36
Lonkin, Bur C10 39
Lonoke, Lonoke, Ark C4, h11 81
Lonoke, co., Ark C4 81
Lönsdal, Nor D6 25
Lonsdale, Garland, Ark C3, f8 81
Lonsdale, Ont., Can C7 72
Lonsdale, Rice, Minn F5 99
Lonsdale, Providence, R.I B11 84
Lons-le-Saunier, Fr D6 14
Loogootee, Martin, Ind G4 91
Lookeba, Caddo, Okla B3 112
Lookout, Modoc, Calif B3 82
Lookout, Pike, Ky C7 94
Lookout, Woods, Okla A2 112
Lookout, Fayette, W. Va C4, m14 123
Lookout, Albany, Wyo E7 125
Lookout, cape, N.C C6 109
Lookout, mtn., Oreg C6 113
Lookout, mtn., Tenn D8 117
Lookout, mtn., Wash C3 122
Lookout, pass, Mont C1 102
Lookout, pt., Mich D7 98
Lookout Mountain, Hamilton, Tenn h11 117
Lookout Mountain, ridge, U.S A4 78
Lookout Point Lake, res., Oreg D4 113
Looma, Alta., Can C4 69
Loomis, Sask., Can H1 70
Loomis, Phelps, Nebr D6 103
Loomis, Davison, S. Dak D7 116
Loomis, Okanogan, Wash A6 122
Loon, creek, Sask., Can F3 70
Loon, lake, Alta., Can A3 69
Loon, lake, Man., Can B1 71
Loon, riv., Alta., Can A3 69
Loon, riv., Man., Can A1 71
Loon Bay, Newf., Can D4 75
Loonhaunt, lake, Ont., Can B5 99
Loon Lake, Sask., Can *n7 70
Loon Lake, Stevens, Wash A8 122
Loon Lake, mts., N.Y f10 108
Loon Straits, Man., Can D3 71
Loop, Gaines, Tex C1 118
Loop, creek, W. Va m13 123
Loop, head, Ire E2 11
Loos, Fr D3 15
Loosahatchie, riv., Tenn e9 117
Loose Creek, Osage, Mo C6 101
Looxahoma, Tate, Miss A4 100
Lopatka, cape, Sov. Un D18 28
Lopei, China C5 37
Lopeno, Zapata, Tex F3 118
Lopez, Sullivan, Pa F9 114
Lopez, Phil p14 35
Lopez, cape, Gabon F1 46
Lopez, isl., Wash A3 122
Loping, China J7 36
Lop Nor, lake, China D3 34
Lopori, riv., Zaire A3 48
Loppheavet, sea, Nor B9 25
Lora, Sp D3 20
Lorado, Logan, W. Va D3, n12 123
Lorain, Lorain, Ohio A3 111
Lorain, co., Ohio A3 111
Lorain, Cambria, Pa *F4 114
Loraine, Adams, Ill C2 90
Loraine, Renville, N. Dak A4 110
Loraine, Mitchell, Tex C2 118
Loralai, Pak B2 40
Loramie, lake, res., Ohio B1 111
Loranger, Tangipahoa, La D5 95
Lorca, Sp D5 20
Lord Howe, is., Pac. O I9 7
Lordsburg, Hidalgo, N. Mex E1 107
Loreauville, Iberia, La D4 95
Loreburn, Sask., Can F2 70
Lore City, Guernsey, Ohio C4 111
Lorena, Braz C3 56
Lorentz, Upshur, W. Va B4 123
Lorenzo, Jefferson, Idaho F7 89
Lorenzo, Cheyenne, Nebr C2 103
Lorenzo, Crosby, Tex C2 118
Loreto, Arg E3 55
Loreto, Braz C1 57
Loreto, Col D3 60
Loreto, It C4 21
Loreto, Mex B2 63
Loreto, Par D4 55
Loreto, dept., Peru C3 58
Loretta, Rush, Kans D4 93
Loretta, Sawyer, Wis C3 124
Lorette, Man., Can E3 71
Loretteville, Que., Can C6, n17 73
Loretto, Marion, Ky C4 94
Loretto, Dickinson, Mich C3 98
Loretto, Boone, Nebr C7 103
Loretto, Cambria, Pa E4 114
Loretto, Lawrence, Tenn B4 117
Lorica, Col B2 60
Lorida, Highlands, Fla E5 86
Lorient, Fr D2 14
L'Orignal, Ont., Can B10 72
Lorimor, Union, Iowa C3 92
Loring, Phillips, Mont B9 102
Loris, Horry, S.C C10 115
Lorlie, Sask., Can G4 70
Lorman, Jefferson, Miss D2 100
Lorne, N.B., Can B3 74
Lorne, firth, Scot D3 13
Lorne Park, Ont., Can m14 72
Lorneville, N.B., Can D3 74
Lorneville, Ont., Can C5 72
Lörrach, F.R.G E3 16
Lorraine, Ellsworth, Kans D5 93
Lorraine, Jefferson, N.Y B5 108
Lorraine, plat., Fr F6 16
Lorraine, former prov., Fr C6 14
Lorsch, F.R.G D3 17
Lorton, Otoe, Nebr D9 103
Lorup, F.R.G B3 17
Los Alamitos, Orange, Calif *F5 82
Los Alamos, Santa Barbara, Calif E3 82
Los Alamos, Los Alamos, N. Mex B3 107
Los Alamos, co., N. Mex B3 107
Los Altos, Santa Clara, Calif k8 82
Los Amates, Guat C3 62
Los Andes, Chile A2 54
Los Angeles, Los Angeles, Calif F4, m12 82
Los Angeles, Chile B2 54
Los Angeles, co., Calif E4 82
Los Angeles, aqueduct, Calif E4 82
Losantville, Randolph, Ind D7 91
Los Banos, Merced, Calif D3 82
Los Barrios, Sp D3 20
Los Blancos, Arg D3 55
Los Cerrillos, Arg A3 54
Los Ebanos, Hidalgo, Tex F3 118
Los Fresnos, Cameron, Tex F4 118
Los Gatos, Santa Clara, Calif D2 82
Loshan, China F5 34
Loshan, China H6 36
Los Herreras, Mex G3 118
Lošinj, isl., Yugo C2 22
Los Lunas, Valencia, N. Mex C3 107
Los Mochis, Mex B3 63
Los Molinos, Tehama, Calif B2 82
Los Nietos, Los Angeles, Calif *E4 82
Losombo, Zaire A2 48
Los Padillas, Bernalillo, N. Mex *B3 107
Los Palacios, Cuba C2 64
Los Palacios, Sp D3 20
Los Pinos, Rio Arriba, N. Mex A3 107
Los Pinos, riv., Colo D3 83
Los Pozos, Chile E1 55
Los Ranchos de Albuquerque, Bernalillo, N. Mex B3, k7 107
Los Reyes, Mex D4, n12 63
Los Reyes [la Paz], Mex h10 63
Los Ríos, prov., Ec B2 58
Los Santos, Pan G7 62
Los Santos, Sp C2 20
Los Sarmientos, Arg E2 55
Los Sauces, Chile B2 54
Lossiemouth [& Brandenburgh], Scot C5 13
Lössnitz, G.D.R C7 17
Lost, creek, Wyo D4 125
Lost, peak, Utah F2 119
Lost, riv., Ind G4 91
Lost, riv., Minn C3 99
Lost, riv., Wash A5 122
Lost, riv., W. Va B6 123
Lostant, La Salle, Ill B4 90
Los Taques, Ven A3 60
Lost Cabin, Fremont, Wyo C5 125
Lost City, Hardy, W. Va C6 123
Lost Creek, Harrison, W. Va B4 123
Los Teques, Ven A4 60
Lost Hills, Kern, Calif E4 82
Lost Horse, plat., Wash C4 122
Lostine, Wallowa, Oreg B9 113
Lost Nation, Clinton, Iowa C7 92
Lost River, Hardy, W. Va C6 123
Lost River, cave, Ky D3 94
Lost River, range, Idaho E5 89
Lost River Glacial, caverns, N.H B3 105
Lost Springs, Marion, Kans D7 93
Lost Springs, Converse, Wyo D8 125
Lost Trail, pass, Mont E3 102
Los Trujillos, Valencia, N. Mex C3 107
Los Vigiles, San Miguel, N. Mex *B5 107
Los Vilos, Chile A2 54
Lot, Ponape 52
Lot, dept., Fr *E4 14
Lot, hbr., Ponape 52
Lot, riv., Fr E4 14
Lota, Chile B2 54
Lotawana, lake, Mo k11 101
Lotbinière, Que., Can C6 73
Lotbinière, co., Que., Can C6 73
Lot-et-Garonne, dept., Fr *E4 14
Lothair, Perry, Ky C6 94
Lothair, Liberty, Mont B5 102
Lothian, reg., Scot E5 13
Loting, China A9 38
Loto, Zaire B3 48
Lotofaga, W. Sam 52
Lötschberg, tunnel, Switz D4 19
Lott, Falls, Tex D4 118
Lotung, Taiwan G9 34
Lotus Point, Lake, Ill *A5 90
Louann, Ouachita, Ark D3 81
Loudon, Merrimack, N.H D4 105
Loudon, Loudon, Tenn D9 117
Loudon, co., Tenn D9 117
Loudonville, Albany, N.Y *C7 108
Loudonville, Ashland, Ohio B3 111
Loudoun, co., Va A5 121
Loudun, Fr D4 14
Louetta, Harris, Tex F5 118
Louga, Sen C1 45
Loughborough, Eng B6 12
Lougheed, Alta., Can C5 69
Lougheed, isl., N.W. Ter., Can m31 67
Loughman, Polk, Fla D5 86
Loughrea, Ire D3 11
Loughros More, bay, Ire C3 11
Louin, Jasper, Miss C4 100
Louisa, Lawrence, Ky B7 94
Louisa, Louisa, Va B4 121
Louisa, co., Iowa C6 92
Louisa, co., Va C5 121
Louisa, lake, Fla D5 86
Louisbourg, N.S., Can D10 74
Louisburg, Miami, Kans D9 93
Louisburg, Lac qui Parle, Minn E2 99
Louisburg, Dallas, Mo D4 101
Louisburg, Franklin, N.C A4 109
Louisburgh, Ire D2 11
Louisdale, N.S., Can D8 74
Louise, Humphreys, Miss B3 100
Louise, Wharton, Tex E4 118
Louise, Brooke, W. Va f8 123
Louise, isl., B.C., Can C2 68
Louise, lake, Alsk f18 79
Louisiade, arch., Sol. Is G9 7
Louisiana, Pike, Mo B6 101
Louisiana, state, U.S D9 77, 95
Louisiana, pt., La E2 95
Louis Trichardt, S. Afr B4 49
Louisville, Barbour, Ala D4 78
Louisville, Que., Can C5 73
Louisville, Boulder, Colo B5 83
Louisville, Jefferson, Ga C4 87
Louisville, Clay, Ill E5 90
Louisville, Pottawatomie, Kans C7 93
Louisville, Jefferson, Ky B4, g11 94
Louisville, Winston, Miss B4 100
Louisville, Cass, Nebr D9, h12 103
Louisville, St. Lawrence, N.Y f9 108
Louisville, Stark, Ohio B4 111
Louisville, Blount, Tenn D9, n13 117
Loukhi, Sov. Un D15 25
Loulé, Port D1 20
Louny, Czech C2 26
Loup, co., Nebr C6 103
Loup, isl., Que., Can B8 74
Loup, riv., Que., Can C4 73
Loup, riv., Nebr C8 103
Loup City, Sherman, Nebr C7 103
Lourdes, Newf., Can D2 75
Lourdes, Que., Can C4 73
Lourdes, Que., Can C6 73
Lourdes, Fr F4 14
Lourenço Marques, see Maputo, Moz.
Loures, Port f9 20
Lousã, Port B1 20
Lousana, Alta., Can C4 69
Louth, Eng A8 12
Louth, Ire D5 11
Louth, co., Ire D5 11
Loutrá Aidhipsoú, Grc C4 23
Louvain, see Leuven, Bel.
Louvale, Stewart, Ga D2 87
Louviers, Douglas, Colo B6 83
Louviers, Fr C4 14
Lovat, riv., Sov. Un C8 27
Love, Sask., Can D3 70
Love, co., Okla D4 112
Love, pt., Md B5 85
Lovech, Bul D7 22
Lovejoy, St. Clair, Ill *E3 90
Lovelaceville, Ballard, Ky f9 94
Loveladies, Ocean, N.J D4 106
Lovelady, Houston, Tex D5 118
Loveland, Larimer, Colo A5 83
Loveland, Pottawattamie, Iowa C2 92
Loveland, Hamilton, Warren and Clermont, Ohio C1, n13 111
Loveland, Tillman, Okla C3 112
Loveland, pass, Colo B5 83
Loveland Park, Warren, Ohio C1, n13 111
Lovell, Oxford, Maine D2 96
Lovell, Logan, Okla A4 112
Lovell, Big Horn, Wyo B4 125
Lovelock, Pershing, Nev C3 104
Lovely, Martin, Ky C7 94
Loverna, Sask., Can F1 70
Loves Park, Winnebago, Ill A4 90
Lovett, Laurens, Ga D4 87
Lovett, Jennings, Ind G6 91
Lovettsville, Loudoun, Va A5 121
Lovewell, pond, Maine D2 96
Lovick, Jefferson, Ala f7 78
Lovilia, Monroe, Iowa C5 92
Loving, Eddy, N. Mex E5 107
Loving, co., Tex o13 118
Lovingston, Nelson, Va C4 121
Lovington, Moultrie, Ill D5 90
Lovington, Polk, Iowa e8 92
Lovington, Lea, N. Mex E6 107
Lovisa, Fin G12 25
Lovosice, Czech C9 17
Low, Que., Can D2 73
Low, cape, N.W. Ter., Can D15 67
Lowa, Zaire B4 48
Lowa, riv., Zaire B4 48
Lowden, Cedar, Iowa C7 92
Lowe Farm, Man., Can E3 71
Lowell, Benton, Ark A1 81
Lowell, Lake, Ind B3 91
Lowell, Middlesex, Mass A5, f10 97
Lowell, Kent, Mich F5 98
Lowell, Gaston, N.C B1 109
Lowell, Washington, Ohio C4 111
Lowell, Lane, Oreg D4 113
Lowell, Orleans, Vt B4 120
Lowell, Snohomish, Wash *B3 122

Lowell, Summers, W. Va....D4 123
Lowell, Dodge, Wis........E5 124
Lowell, mts., Vt..........B4 120
Lowell Lake, res., Idaho........F2 89
Lowell Thomas, mts., Ant.......B5 5
Lowellville, Mahoning, Ohio.A5 111
Lower, lake, Nev............B2 104
Lower Arrow, lake, B.C., Can..E8 68
Lower Bank, Burlington, N.J.............D3 106
Lower Brule, Lyman, S. Dak............C6 116
Lower Burrell, Westmoreland, Pa...........*E2 114
Lower Cabot, Washington, Vt.............C4 120
Lower California, pen., Mex...B2 63
Lower Caraquet, N.B., Can.*B5 74
Lower East Pubnico, N.S., Can............F4 74
Lower Gilmanton, Belknap, N.H............D4 105
Lower Hutt, N.Z........*N15 51
Lower Island Cove, Newf., Can...........D5 75
Lower Juba, reg., Som........E5 47
Lower Marlboro, Calvert, Md.............C4 85
Lower Matecumbe, key, Fla....H6 86
Lower New York, bay, N.Y....k12 106
Lower Paia, Maui, Haw.....C5 88
Lower Peach Tree, Wilcox, Ala.............D2 78
Lower Red, lake, Minn........C3 99
Lower Rice, lake, Minn........C3 99
Lower Rociada, San Miguel, N. Mex..........B4 107
Lower Salem, Washington, Ohio............C4 111
Lower Salmon, dam, Idaho....G4 89
Lower Saxony, see Niedersachsen, state, F.R.G.
Lower Southampton, N.B., Can............D2 74
Lower Village, Lamoille, Vt .C3 120
Lower West Pubnico, N.S., Can............F4 74
Lower Wood's Harbour, N.S., Can............F4 74
Lowes, Graves, Ky........A2 88
Lowestoft, Eng...........B9 12
Lowgap, Newton, Ark.......A2 81
Lowgap, Surry, N.C........A2 109
Lowicz, Pol..............B5 26
Lowland, Pamlico, N.C.....B6 109
Lowman, Boise, Idaho......E3 89
Lowmansville, Lawrence, Ky.............C7 94
Low Moor, Clinton, Iowa....C7 92
Lowmoor, Alleghany, Va....C3 121
Lowndes, Wayne, Mo........D7 101
Lowndes, co., Ala.........C3 78
Lowndes, co., Ga..........F3 87
Lowndes, co., Miss........B5 100
Lowndesboro, Lowndes, Ala.C3 78
Lowndesville, Abbeville, S.C.C2 115
Lowry, Pope, Minn.........E3 99
Lowry, Walworth, S. Dak...B6 116
Lowry City, St. Clair, Mo..C4 101
Lowrys, Chester, S.C.......B5 115
Low Tatra, mts., Czech......D5 26
Lowville, Lewis, N.Y.......B5 108
Low Water, lake, Alta., Can...C3 69
Loxley, Baldwin, Ala........E2 78
Loxton, Austl.............G3 51
Loyal, Kingfisher, Okla.....B3 112
Loyal, Clark, Wis..........D3 124
Loyalhanna, Westmoreland, Pa...........*F3 114
Loyalist, Alta., Can........D5 69
Loyall, Harlan, Ky.........D6 94
Loyalsock, creek, Pa........D8 114
Loyalton, Sierra, Calif......C3 82
Loyalty, is., Pac. O........H10 7
Loyang, China.............G5 36
Loysburg, Bedford, Pa......F5 114
Loysville, Perry, Pa........F7 114
Lozère, dept., Fr..........*E5 14
Loznica, Yugo.............C4 22
Lozva, riv., Sov. Un........C21 9
Lozovatka, Sov. Un.........G9 27
Lozovaya, Sov. Un..........G11 27
Lozoya, canal, Sp..........o17 20
Lualaba, riv., Zaire........B4 48
Luama, riv., Zaire.........B4 48
Luampa, Zambia............D4 48
Luan, riv., China..........C8 34
Luana, Clayton, Iowa.......A6 92
Luanda, Ang...............C1 48
Luanda, dist., Ang.........C1 48
Luang Prabang, Laos........C5 38
Luanginga, riv., Ang., Zambia..........D3 48
Luangwa, riv., Zambia.......D5 48
Luanhsien, China...........E8 36
Luanshya, Zambia..........D4 48
Luarca, Sp................A2 20
Luashi, Zaire.............D3 48
Lubaczow, Pol.............C7 26
Luban, Pol................C3 26
Lubang, Phil..............p13 35
Lubang, is., Phil...........C6 35
Lubango, Ang..............D1 48
Lubao, Phil...............o13 35
Lubartow, Pol.............C7 26
Lubawa, Pol...............B5 26
Lübbecke, F.R.G...........A3 17
Lübben, F.R.G.............B8 17
Lübbenau, G.D.R...........B8 17
Lubbock, Lubbock, Tex.....C2 118
Lubbock, co., Tex.........C2 118
Lubec, Washington, Maine.D6 96
Lübeck, F.R.G......B5 16, E4 8
Lübeck, bay, F.R.G., G.D.R....B5 16
Lubefu, Zaire..............B3 48
Lubero, Zaire..............B4 48
Lubicon, lake, Alta., Can.....A3 69
Lubilash, riv., Zaire........C3 48
Lubin, Pol................C4 26
Lublin, Pol...............C7 26
Lublin, Taylor, Wis........C3 124
Lubliniec, Pol.............C5 26
Lubny, Sov. Un............F9 27
Lubrín, Sp................D4 20
Lubsko, Pol...............C3 26
Lübtheen, G.D.R...........E5 24
Lubudi, Zaire..............C4 48
Lubudi, riv., Zaire.........C3 48
Lubue, Zaire..............B2 48
Lubumbashi (Élisabethville), Zaire...........D4 48
Lubutu, Zaire..............B4 48
Lucama, Wilson, N.C.......B4 109
Lucan, Ont., Can..........D3 72
Lucan, Ire................D5 11
Lucan, Redwood, Minn.....F3 99
Lucania, see Basilicata, reg., It.
Lucania, mtn., Yukon, Can.....D4 66
Lucas, Lucas, Iowa........C4 92
Lucas, Russell, Kans.......C5 93
Lucas, Barren, Ky.........D4 94
Lucas, Missaukee, Mich.....D5 98
Lucas, Richland, Ohio......B3 111
Lucas, Gregory, S. Dak......D6 116
Lucas, co., Iowa...........C4 92
Lucas, co., Ohio...........A2 111
Lucasville, Scioto, Ohio....D3 111
Lucca, It..................C3 21
Lucé, Fr..................C4 14
Luce, co., Mich............B5 98
Luce, bay, Scot...........F4 13
Lucea, Jam................E12 65
Lucedale, George, Miss.....E5 100
Lucena, Phil..........C6, p13 35
Lucena, Sp................D3 20
Lucena del Cid, Sp.........B5 20
Lučenec, Czech.............D5 26
Lucera, It.................D5 21
Lucerne, Weld, Colo........A6 83
Lucerne, Cass, Ind.........C5 91
Lucerne, Putnam, Mo.......A4 101
Lucerne, see Luzern, Switz.
Lucerne, lake, Switz........B5 19
Lucernemines, Indiana, Pa..E3 114
Lucerne Valley, San Bernardino, Calif..............E5 82
Luceville, Que., Can........A9 73
Luchi, China...............J4 36
Luchou (Luhsien), China....F6 34
Lüchow, F.R.G.............F5 24
Lucien, Franklin, Miss.....D3 100
Lucien, Noble, Okla........A4 112
Lucile, Idaho, Idaho.......D2 89
Lucin, Box Elder, Utah.....B2 119
Lucinda, Clarion, Pa.......D3 114
Lucipara, is., Indon........G7 35
Lucira, Ang................D1 48
Luck, Madison, N.C........f10 109
Luck, Polk, Wis............C1 124
Luck, lake, Sask., Can......F2 70
Luckau, G.D.R.............C7 16
Luckenwalde, G.D.R........A8 17
Luckey, Wood, Ohio.....A2, f7 111
Lucknow, Ont., Can........D3 72
Lucknow, India.....C7 39, D8 40
Lucknow, Dauphin, Pa.....*F8 114
Lucky Lake, Sask., Can.....G2 70
Lucky MacCamp, Fremont, Wyo..............*D4 125
Lucky Peak Lake, res., Idaho...F3 89
Lucky Strike, Alta., Can.....E5 69
Luçon, Fr..................D3 14
Lucrecia, cape, Cuba........D6 64
Lucy, St. John the Baptist, La................h10 95
Lucy, Shelby, Tenn......B2, e9 117
Luda Kamchiya, riv., Bul.....D8 22
Ludden, Dickey, N. Dak....D7 110
Ludell, Rawlins, Kans......C3 93
Lüdenscheid, F.R.G........B2 17
Lüderitz, Namibia..........F3 49
Ludgate, Ont., Can.........B4 72
Ludhiāna, India.....B6 39, B5 40
Lüdinghausen, F.R.G.......B2 17
Ludington, Mason, Mich.....E4 98
Ludlam, Dade, Fla.........*G6 86
Ludlow, San Bernardino, Calif.............E5 82
Ludlow, N.B., Can.........C3 74
Ludlow, Eng...............B5 12
Ludlow, Champaign, Ill.....C5 90
Ludlow, Kenton, Ky........h13 94
Ludlow, Aroostook, Maine..B4 96
Ludlow, Hampden, Mass....B3 97
Ludlow, Scott, Miss........C4 100
Ludlow, Livingston, Mo.....B4 101
Ludlow, McKean, Pa........C4 114
Ludlow, Harding, S. Dak....B2 116
Ludlow, Windsor, Vt........E3 120
Ludlow, mtn., Vt...........E3 120
Ludlow Falls, Miami, Ohio..B1 111
Ludowici, Long, Ga.........E5 87
Ludvika, Swe...............G6 25
Ludwigsburg, F.R.G.........E4 17
Ludwigshafen, F.R.G........D3 17
Ludwigslust, G.D.R.........B5 16
Luebo, Zaire...............C3 48
Lueders, Jones, Tex........C3 118
Luepa, Ven.................B5 60
Lufkin, Angelina, Tex......D5 118
Lufuna, Zaire..............C2 48
Luga, Sov. Un..............B7 27
Luga, riv., Sov. Un.........B7 27
Lugagnano Val d'Arda, It...E5 18
Lugan, riv., Sov. Un.........q22 27
Luganchik, riv., Sov. Un.....q22 27
Lugano, Switz..............D6 19
Lugano, lake, Switz.........E6 19
Lugansk, see Voroshilovgrad, Sov. Un.
Lugau, G.D.R..............C7 17
Lugenda, riv., Moz.........D6 48
Lugh Ganane, Som..........E5 47
Lugnaquilla, mtn., Ire.......E5 11
Lugo, It...................B3 21
Lugo, Sp..................A2 20
Lugo, prov., Sp...........*A2 20
Lugoff, Kershaw, S.C.......C6 115
Lugoj, Rom................C5 22
Lugovoy, Sov. Un..........E8 29
Luhosien, China............E5 37
Luhsien, see Luchou, China
Luichow, pen., China........G6 34
Luing, isl., Scot...........D3 13
Luís Correia, Braz..........B2 57
Luís Gomes, Braz...........C3 57
Luis Lopez, Socorro, N. Mex............D3 107
Luiza, Zaire...............C3 48
Luján, Arg.................g7 54
Luján [de Cuyo], Arg.......A3 54
Lukachukai, Apache, Ariz...............A6 80
Luke, Allegany, Md.........m12 85
Lukenie, riv., Zaire........B2 48
Lukeville, Pima, Ariz.......F3 80
Lukolela, Zaire............B2 48
Lukovit, Bul...............D7 22
Lukow, Pol.................C7 26
Lukoyanov, Sov. Un........D15 27
Lukuga, riv., Zaire.........C4 48
Lukulu, Zambia............D3 48
Lula, Hall, Ga.............B3 87
Lula, Coahoma, Miss.......A3 100
Lula, Pontotoc, Okla.......C5 112
Luleå, Swe................E10 25
Luleälven, riv., Swe........D9 25
Luling, St. Charles, La.....k11 95
Luling, Caldwell, Tex....E4, h8 118
Lulu, Columbia, Fla........B4 86
Lulua, riv., Zaire..........C3 48
Luluabourg, see Kananga, Zaire
Lulung, China.............E8 36
Lum, Lapeer, Mich.........E7 98
Lumba, Zaire..............A2 48
Lumber, Darlington, S.C....C8 115
Lumber, riv., N.C..........C4 109
Lumber Bridge, Robeson, N.C.............C3 109
Lumber City, Telfair, Ga....E4 87
Lumberport, Harrison, W. Va..........A6, B4, k10 123
Lumberton, Lamar, Miss....D4 100
Lumberton, Burlington, N.J.D3 106
Lumberton, Rio Arriba, N. Mex.............A3 107
Lumberton, Robeson, N.C...C4 109
Lumbo, Moz...............D7 48
Lumby, B.C., Can..........D8 68
Luminao, reef, Guam.............. 52
Lummi, Indian res., Wash.....A3 122
Lumpkin, Stewart, Ga......D2 87
Lumpkin, co., Ga..........B2 87
Lumsden, Newf., Can.......D5 75
Lumsden, Sask., Can.......G3 70
Lumsden, N.Z..............P12 51
Lumsden, Scot.............C6 13
Lumsden Beach, Sask., Can.G3 70
Lumut, mtn., Indon..........F6 35
Lumut, pt., Indon..........F3 35
Luna, Catron, N. Mex......D1 107
Luna, co., N. Mex.........E2 107
Luna Pier, Monroe, Mich....G7 98
Lund, B.C., Can...........D5 68
Lund, White Pine, Nev.....E6 104
Lund, Swe.................J5 25
Lund, Iron, Utah...........E2 119
Lunda, dist., Ang..........C2 48
Lundale, Logan, W. Va....n12 123
Lundar, Man., Can.........D2 71
Lundazi, Zambia...........D5 48
Lundbreck, Alta., Can......E3 69
Lundby, Den...............C5 24
Lundby, Swe...............t34 25
Lundell, Phillips, Ark......C5 81
Lunderskov, Den...........C3 24
Lundu, Mala...............E3 35
Lundy, isl., Eng............C3 12
Lune, riv., Eng............F6 13
Lüneburg, F.R.G...........B5 16
Lunel, Fr..................F6 14
Lünen, F.R.G..............B2 17
Lunenburg, N.S., Can......E5 74
Lunenburg, Worcester, Mass.A4 97
Lunenburg, Essex, Vt.......C5 120
Lunenburg, Lunenburg, Va..D4 121
Lunenburg, co., N.S., Can..E5 74
Lunenburg, co., Va.........D4 121
Lunéville, Fr..............C7 14
Lung, China...............G2 36
Lungchen, China...........B3 37
Lungchou, China...........G6 34
Lungchuan, China..........J8 36
Lungchuchai, China........H4 36
Lungkou, China............F9 36
Lunglin, China.............G6 34
Lungping, China...........F6 36
Lungué-Bungo, riv., Ang., Zambia...........D3 48
Lungyen, China............F8 34
Lūni, riv., India...........E3 40
Lunino, Sov. Un...........E15 27
Lunining, Mineral, Nev.....E3 104
Lunsar, S.L................E2 45
Lunyama, Zaire............C4 48
Luozi, Zaire...............B1 48
Lup, Thai..................D5 38
Lupani, Zimb...............E4 48
Lupeni, Rom...............C6 22
Lupin, see Manchouli, China.
Lupton, Apache, Ariz.......B6 80
Lupton, Ogemaw, Mich......D6 98
Lupus, Moniteau, Mo........C5 101
Luque, Par.................E4 55
Luquillo, mun., P.R........*B4 65
Luquillo, mts., P.R.........B4 65
Lūrah, riv., Afg...........B4 39
Luray, Russell, Kans........C5 93
Luray, Clark, Mo...........A6 101
Luray, Hampton, S.C.......F5 115
Luray, Henderson, Tenn....B3 117
Luray, Page, Va............B4 121
Lure, Fr...................D7 14
Lurgan, N. Ire..............C5 11
Luribay, Bol...............C2 55
Lurín, Peru................D2 58
Lúrio, Moz.................D7 48
Lurio, riv., Moz...........D6 48
Lurton, Newton, Ark........B2 81
Lusaka, Zambia............D4 48
Lusambo, Zaire............B3 48
Lusby, Calvert, Md.........D5 85
Luscar, Alta., Can.........C2 69
Luseland, Sask., Can.......E1 70
Lushan, China.............H5 36
Lushan (Kuling), China.....J6 36
Lushnjë, Alb...............B2 23
Lushoto, Tan...............B6 48
Lushton, York, Nebr........D8 103
Lüshun (Port Arthur), China...............D9 34
Lusignan, Fr...............D4 14
Lusk, Niobrara, Wyo.......D8 125
Luso, Ang.................D2 48
Lustre, Valley, Mont......B11 102
Lüta (Dairen), China.......D9 34
Lutcher, St. James, La..D5, h10 95
Lutesville, Bollinger, Mo....D8 101
Luther, Lake, Mich.........D5 98
Luther, Carbon, Mont.......E7 102
Luther, Oklahoma, Okla.....B4 112
Luthersville, Meriwether, Ga.C2 87
Lutherville, Baltimore, Md..B4 85
Luting, China..............F5 34
Lütjenburg, F.R.G..........D4 24
Luton, Eng.................C7 12
Luton, Woodbury, Iowa.....B1 92
Lutsen, Cook, Minn.........k9 99
Lutsk, Sov. Un.............F5 27
Luttrell, Union, Tenn......C10 117
Lutts, Wayne, Tenn........B4 117
Lutugino, Sov. Un..........q22 27
Lutz, Hillsborough, Fla.....D4 86
Lützow-Holm, bay, Ant......C16 5
Luverne, Crenshaw, Ala.....D3 78
Lu Verne, Kossuth and Humboldt, Iowa.............B3 92
Luverne, Rock, Minn.......G2 99
Luverne, Steele, N. Dak....B8 110
Luvua, riv., Zaire..........C4 48
Luwingu, Zambia...........D4 48
Luwuk, Indon..............F6 35
Luxapallila, creek, Ala., Miss..B2 78
Luxembourg, Lux...........E6 15
Luxembourg, country, Eur..............F10 8, E6 15
Luxembourg, prov., Bel.....E5 15
Luxemburg, Dubuque, Iowa.B6 92
Luxemburg, Kewaunee, Wis.D6 124
Luxeuil-les-Bains, Fr.......D7 14
Luxomni, Gwinnett, Ga......h8 87
Luxor, see Al Uqşur Eg.
Luxora, Mississippi, Ark....B6 81
Luz, Braz..................E1 57
Luza, riv., Sov. Un.........A3 29
Luzern, Switz..............B5 19
Luzern, canton, Switz......B5 19
Luzerne, Oscoda, Mich......D6 98
Luzerne, Luzerne, Pa......n17 114
Luzerne, co., Pa...........D9 114
Luznice, riv., Czech.........D3 26
Luzon, isl., Phil.........B6, o13 35
Lvov, Sov. Un........D8 24, G5 27
Lwow, see Lvov, Sov. Un.
Lwowek Slaskie, Pol........C3 26
Lyakhov, is., Sov. Un.......B36 4
Lyall, mtn., N.Z...........P11 51
Lyaskovets, Bul............D7 22
Lybster, Scot..............B5 13
Lychen, G.D.R.............E7 24
Lycksele, Swe..............E8 25
Lycoming, Oswego, N.Y.....B4 108
Lycoming, co., Pa..........D7 114
Lycoming, creek, Pa.........D7 114
Lydenburg, S. Afr..........C5 49
Lydia, Washington, Md.....A2 85
Lydia, Darlington, S.C......C7 115
Lydia Mills, Laurens, S.C..*C4 115
Lydick, St. Joseph, Ind.....A5 91
Lyell, isl., B.C., Can.......C2 68
Lyell, mtn., Alta., B.C., Can..D2 69
Lyerly, Chattooga, Ga......B1 87
Lyford, Parke, Ind.........E3 91
Lyford, Willacy, Tex.......F4 118
Lygnern, lake, Swe.........A6 24
Lykens, Dauphin, Pa.......E8 114
Lyle, Mower, Minn.........G6 99
Lyle, Klickitat, Wash......D4 122
Lyles, Hickman, Tenn......B4 117
Lyleton, Man., Can.........E1 71
Lyman, Harrison, Miss...E4, f7 100
Lyman, Scotts Bluff, Nebr..C1 103
Lyman, Grafton, N.H.......B3 105
Lyman, Spartanburg, S.C....B3 115
Lyman, Wayne, Utah........E4 119
Lyman, Skagit, Wash.......A3 122
Lyman, Uinta, Wyo.........E2 125
Lyman, co., S. Dak.........D6 116
Lyman Lake, res., Ariz.......C6 80
Lyme, New London, Conn...D7 84
Lyme (Town of), New London, Conn...............*D7 84
Lyme, Grafton, N.H........C2 105
Lyme, bay, Eng............D4 12
Lyme Center, Grafton, N.H.C2 105
Lymington, Eng............D6 12
Lyna, riv., Pol., Sov. Un......B6 26
Lynbrook, Nassau, N.Y.....G2 52
Lynch, Harlan, Ky.........D7 94
Lynch, Kent, Md...........B5 85
Lynch, Boyd, Nebr.........B7 103
Lynchburg, Cass, N. Dak....C8 110
Lynchburg, Highland, Ohio..C2 111
Lynchburg, Lee, S.C........C7 115
Lynchburg, Moore, Tenn....B5 117
Lynchburg (Independent City), Va...............C3 121
Lynches, riv., S.C.........D8 115
Lynch Station, Campbell, Va...............C3 121
Lynd, Lyon, Minn..........F3 99
Lynde, pt., Conn...........D7 84
Lyndeboro, Hillsboro, N.H..E3 105
Lynden, Ont., Can.........*D4 72
Lynden, Whatcom, Wash....A3 122
Lyndhurst, Ont., Can.......C8 72
Lyndhurst, Bergen, N.J.....h8 106
Lyndhurst, Cuyahoga, Ohio..g9 111
Lyndon, Whiteside, Ill......B4 90
Lyndon, Osage, Kans........D8 93
Lyndon, Jefferson, Ky......g11 94
Lyndon, Caledonia, Vt......B4 120
Lyndon B. Johnson, space center, Tex..............r14 118
Lyndon Center, Caledonia, Vt...............B4 120
Lyndon Station, Juneau, Wis.E4 124
Lyndonville, Orleans, N.Y...B2 108
Lyndonville, Caledonia, Vt..B5 120
Lyndora, Butler, Pa.........E2 114
Lyngby, Den................C6 24
Lynhurst, Marion, Ind......k10 91
Lynn, Winston, Ala.........A2 78
Lynn, Lawrence, Ark.......A4 81
Lynn, Randolph, Ind........D8 91
Lynn, Essex, Mass.....B6, g12 97
Lynn, Susquehanna, Pa.....C10 114
Lynn, co., Tex.............C2 118
Lynn, canal, Alsk..........k22 79
Lynn, lake, W. Va..........B5 123
Lynn Creek, B.C., Can......f12 68
Lynndyl, Millard, Utah.....D3 119
Lynne, Marion, Fla.........C5 86
Lynnfield, Essex, Mass.....f11 97
Lynn Garden, Sullivan, Tenn...............C11 117
Lynn Grove, Calloway, Ky..B3 94
Lynn Haven, Bay, Fla.......u16 86
Lynnhaven Roads, hbr., Va....k15 121
Lynn Lake, Man., Can....A1, f7 71
Lynnport, Lehigh, Pa.......E10 114
Lynnview, Jefferson, Ky....*B4 94
Lynnville, Warrick, Ind.....H3 91
Lynnville, Jasper, Iowa.....C5 92
Lynnville, Graves, Ky.......f9 94
Lynnville, Giles, Tenn......B5 117
Lynnwood, Fayette, Pa.....*F2 114
Lynnwood, Luzerne, Pa....*D10 114
Lynnwood, Snohomish, Wash...............B3 122
Lynton, Eng................C4 12
Lynwood, Los Angeles, Calif...............n12 82
Lynxville, Crawford, Wis....E2 124
Lyø, isl., Den............C4 24
Lyon (Lyons), Fr...........E6 14
Lyon, Coahoma, Miss.......A3 100
Lyon, co., Iowa............A1 92
Lyon, co., Kans............D7 93
Lyon, co., Ky..............C1 94
Lyon, co., Minn............F3 99
Lyon, co., Nev.............D2 104
Lyon, creek, Kans..........D7 93
Lyon, mtn., N.Y...........f11 108
Lyon, riv., Scot...........D4 13
Lyon Mountain, Clinton, N.Y...............f11 108
Lyonnais, former prov., Fr..E6 14
Lyons, Boulder, Colo.......A5 83
Lyons (Lyon), Fr...........E6 14
Lyons, Toombs, Ga.........D4 87
Lyons, Cook, Ill............k9 90
Lyons, Greene, Ind.........G3 91
Lyons, Rice, Kans..........D5 93
Lyons, Ionia, Mich.........F6 98
Lyons, Burt, Nebr..........C9 103
Lyons, Wayne, N.Y..........B3 108
Lyons, Fulton, Ohio........A1 111
Lyons, Linn, Oreg..........C4 113
Lyons, Minnehaha, S. Dak..D9 116
Lyons, Burleson, Tex.......D4 118
Lyons, Walworth, Wis.....n11 124
Lyons Falls, Lewis, N.Y.....B5 108
Lyons Plains, Fairfield, Conn...............*E3 84
Lyracrompane, Ire..........E2 11
Lys, riv., Bel., Fr..........D3 15
Lysa, Czech...............n18 26
Lysaya Gora, Sov. Un......G8 27
Lysekil, Swe...............H4 25
Lysite, Fremont, Wyo......C5 125
Lysogory, mts., Pol.........C6 26
Lyss, Switz................B3 19
Lyster Station, Que., Can...C6 73
Lysva, Sov. Un.............C5 29
Lytham, St. Annes, Eng....A5 12
Lytle, Atascosa, Tex.......E3 118
Lytton, B.C., Can..........D7 68
Lytton, Sac and Calhoun, Iowa...............B3 92
Lyubar, Sov. Un............G6 27
Lyubertsy, Sov. Un........n17 27

M

Ma'ād, Jordan.............B7 32
Maalaea, Maui, Haw........*C5 88
Maalaea, bay, Haw.........C5 88
Ma'alot-Tarshiha, Isr......A7 32
Maam Cross, Ire...........D2 11
Ma'ān, Jordan............G10 31
Maas, Ire.................C3 11
Maas, riv., Neth...........C5 15
Maaseik, Bel...............C5 15
Maastricht, Neth...........D5 15
Mab, Allen, La.............D3 95
Mabana, Island, Wash......A3 122
Mabank, Kaufman, Tex......C4 118
Mabber, cape, Som.........D6 47
Mabel, Fillmore, Minn......G7 99
Mabel, lake, B.C., Can.....D8 68
Mabelvale, Pulaski, Ark....k10 81
Maben, Oktibbeha and Webster, Miss.........B4 100
Maberly, Ont., Can.........C8 72
Mabie, Randolph, W. Va....C5 123
Mablethorpe, Eng..........A8 12
Mableton, Cobb, Ga.........h7 87
Mabote, Moz...............B5 49
Mabou, N.S., Can...........C8 74
Mabrous Tafidinga, well, Niger.B7 45
Mabscott, Raleigh, W. Va...............n13 123
Mabton, Yakima, Wash......C5 122
Macachín, Arg..............B4 54
McAdam, N.B., Can........D2 74
McAdams, Attala, Miss.....B4 100
McAdenville, Gaston, N.C..*B2 109
McAdoo, Schuylkill, Pa.....E9 114
McAdoo, Dickens, Tex......C2 118
Macaé, Braz...............C4 56
McAfee, De Kalb, Ga.......*C2 87
McAfee, Leake, Miss........C4 100
McAfee, Sussex, N.J........A3 106
Macaíba, Braz..............g6 57
Macalelon, Phil.............p14 35
McAlester, Pittsburg, Okla..C6 112
McAlester, lake, Okla........B6 112
Macalister, B.C., Can.......C6 68
McAlister, Quay, N. Mex....C6 107
McAlisterville, Juniata, Pa..E7 114
McAllen, Hidalgo, Tex......F3 118
McAllister, Madison, Mont..E5 102
McAlmont, Pulaski, Ark.....h10 81
McAlpin, Suwannee, Fla.....B4 86
McAlpine, Howard, Md......B4 85
MacAlpine, lake, N.W. Ter., Can..............C12 66
Macamic, Que., Can.......*h12 73
McAndrews, Pike, Ky.......C7 94
Macao, Macao..............G7 34
Macao, Port. dep., Asia....G7 34
Macapá, Braz...............B4 59
Macará, Ec.................B2 58
McArthur, Vinton, Ohio....C3 111
Macas, Ec..................B2 58
Macau, Braz................C3 57
McAuley, Man., Can........D1 71
McBain, Missaukee, Mich...D5 98
McBaine, Boone, Mo........C5 101
McBee, Chesterfield, S.C....C7 115
Mcbeth, Berkeley, S.C.......E8 115
McBride, B.C., Can.........C7 68
McBride, Perry, Mo.........D8 101
McCabe, Roosevelt, Mont..B12 102
McCall, Valley, Idaho......E2 89
McCalla, Jefferson, Ala.....g6 78
McCall Creek, Franklin, Miss...............D3 100
McCallsburg, Story, Iowa...B4 92
McCamey, Upton, Tex.......D1 118
McCammon, Bannock, Idaho...............G6 89
Maccan, N.S., Can..........D5 74
McCanna, Grand Forks, N. Dak...............A8 110
Maccarese, It...............h8 21
McCarthy, Alsk.............C11 79
McCartney, mtn., Mont......E4 102
McCartys, Valencia, N. Mex.B2 107
McCaskill, Hempstead, Ark..D2 81
McCauley, isl., B.C., Can....C2 68
McCauley, Fisher, Tex......C2 118
McCaysville, Fannin, Ga....B2 87
McChesneytown, Westmoreland, Pa...............*F3 114
McClain, co., Okla..........B4 112
McClave, Bent, Colo........C8 83
McCleary, Grays Harbor, Wash...............B2 122
McClelland, Woodruff, Ark..B4 81
McClelland, Pottawattamie, Iowa...............C2 92
McClellanville, Charleston, S.C...............F9 115
Macclenny, Baker, Fla......B4 86
Macclesfield, Eng...........A5 12
Macclesfield, Edgecombe, N.C...............B5 109
M'Clintock, chan., N.W. Ter., Can...............B12 66
McClintock, mtn., Ant......A28 5
McCloud, Siskiyou, Calif....B2 82
Macclure, gulf, Indon.......F8 35
McClure, Alexander, Ill.....F4 90
McClure, Henry, Ohio......A2 111
McClure, Snyder, Pa........E7 114
McClure, Dickenson, Va.....e9 121
M'Clure, cape, N.W. Ter., Can.B8 66
M'Clure, strait, N.W. Ter., Can.B9 66
McClusky, Sheridan, N. Dak...............B5 110
McColl, Marlboro, S.C......B8 115
McComas, Mercer, W. Va..D3 123
McComb, Pike, Miss........D3 100
McComb, Hancock, Ohio...A2 111
McConaughy, lake, Nebr......C4 103
McCondy, Chickasaw, Miss..B5 100
McCone, co., Mont.........C11 102
McConnell, Stephenson, Ill..A4 90
McConnell, Obion, Tenn....A3 117
McConnells, York, S.C......B5 115
McConnellsburg, Fulton, Pa.G6 114
McConnellstown, Huntington, Pa...............F5 114
McConnelsville, Morgan, Ohio..............C4 111
McCook, Red Willow, Nebr..D5 103
McCook, co., S. Dak........D8 116
McCook Lake, Union, S. Dak..............E9 116
McCool, Attala, Miss.......B4 100
McCoole, Allegany, Md.....D2 85
McCool Junction, York, Nebr..............D8 103
McCord, Sask., Can.........H2 70
McCordsville, Hancock, Ind.E6 91
McCormick, McCormick, S.C...............D3 115
McCormick, co., S.C........D3 115
McCoy, Eagle, Colo.........B4 83
McCracken, Rush, Kans.....D4 93
McCracken, co., Ky.........e9 94
McCreary, Man., Can........D2 71
McCreary, co., Ky..........D5 94
McCrory, Woodruff, Ark.....B4 81
McCulloch, co., Tex........D3 118
MacCulloch, cape, N.W. Ter., Can..............B18 67
McCullom Lake, McHenry, Ill...............*A5 90
McCullough, Escambia, Ala.D2 78
McCullough, mtn., Nev.......H6 104
McCullum, Walker, Ala......B2 78
McCune, Crawford, Kans....E8 93
McCurtain, Haskell, Okla...B7 112
McCurtain, co., Okla........C7 112
McCutchenville, Wyandot and Seneca, Ohio.........A2 111
McDade, Bastrop, Tex.......D4 118
McDaniel, Talbot, Md.......C5 85
McDavid, Escambia, Fla.....u14 86
McDermitt, Humboldt, Nev..B4 104
McDermott, Scioto, Ohio....C2 111
Macdhui, mtn., Scot........C5 13
Macdona, Bexar, Tex.......B3 118
Macdonald, Man., Can......D2 71
McDonald, Rawlins, Kans...C2 93
McDonald, Neshoba, Miss...C4 100
McDonald, Lea, N. Mex......D6 107
McDonald, Washington and Allegheny, Pa.........*F1 114
McDonald, Bradley, Tenn..h12 117
MacDonald, Fayette, W. Va...........D3, n13 123
McDonald, co., Mo.........E3 101
McDonald, creek, Mont.......C8 102
McDonald, isl., Indian O.......J1 2
Macdonald, lake, Austl.......D4 50
MacDonald, range, B.C., Can..E10 68
Macdonaldton, Somerset, Pa...............G4 114
MacDonnell, ranges, Austl....D5 50
McDonough, Henry, Ga.....C2 87
McDonough, Chenango, N.Y...............C5 108
McDonough, co., Ill.........C3 90
McDougal, Clay, Ark.........A5 81
McDougal, mtn., Wyo........H2 125
McDowell, Floyd, Ky........C7 94
McDowell, Highland, Va.....B3 121
McDowell, co., N.C..........f10 109
McDowell, co., W. Va.......D3 123
McDowell, mtn., Ariz........k9 80
Macduff, Scot..............C6 13
McDuffie, co., Ga...........C4 87
Macedon, Wayne, N.Y.......B3 108
Macedonia, Litchfield, Conn...............C3 84
Macedonia, Pottawattamie, Iowa...............C2 92
Macedonia, Summit, Ohio..........A4, h10 111
Macedonia, reg., Eur........B4 23
Macedonia, rep., Yugo......*D5 22
Maceió, Braz...........C3, k6 57
McElhattan, Clinton, Pa....D7 114
McElroy, creek, W. Va......k9 123
Macenta, Guinea............E3 45
Maceo, Daviess, Ky.........C2 94
Macerata, It................C4 21
Maces, bay, N.B., Can.......D3 74
McEwen, Baker, Oreg......C8 113
McEwen, Humphreys, Tenn.A4 117
McFadden, Jackson, Ark....B4 81
McFadden, Carbon, Wyo....E6 125
McFaddin, Victoria, Tex.....E4 118
McFall, Gentry, Mo..........A3 101
McFarlan, Anson, N.C.......C2 109
Macfarlan, Ritchie, W. Va..B3 123
McFarland, Kern, Calif......E4 82
McFarland, Wabaunsee, Kans...............C7 93
McFarland, Marquette, Mich...............B3 98
McFarland, Dane, Wis.......E4 124
McGaheysville, Rockingham, Va...............B4 121
McGee, Sask., Can..........F1 70
McGehee, Desha, Ark.......D4 81
McGill, White Pine, Nev....D7 104
MacGillicuddy's Reeks, mts., Ire.F2 11
McGillivray, B.C., Can......D6 68
McGillivray, lake, Ont., Can....A7 72
McGiverin, lake, Ont., Can.....B8 98
McGivney, N.B., Can........C3 74
McGrady, Wilkes, N.C.......A1 109
McGrann, Armstrong, Pa....*E2 114
McGrath, Alsk..............C8 79
McGrath, Aitkin, Minn......D5 99
McGraw, Cortland, N.Y.....C4 108
McGraws, Wyoming, W. Va.D3 123
Mac Gregor, Man., Can......E2 71
McGregor, Clayton, Iowa....A6 92
McGregor, Aitkin, Minn.....D5 99
McGregor, Williams, N. Dak...............A3 110
McGregor, McLennan, Tex...............D4 118
McGregor, lake, Alta., Can....D4 69
McGregor, riv., B.C., Can.....B7 68
McGrew, Scotts Bluff, Nebr..C2 103
McGuffey, Hardin, Ohio....B2 111
McGuire, mtn., Idaho.........D4 89
McGuires, Kootenai, Idaho..B2 89
Mach, Pak..................C1 40
Machachi, Ec...............B2 58
Machado, Braz..........C3, k9 56
Machakos, Ken.............B6 48
Machala, Ec................B2 58
Machanao, mtn., Guam.............. 52
Macheng, China............I6 36

McHenry, McHenry, Ill ... A5, h8 90
McHenry, Ohio, Ky ... C3 94
McHenry, Garrett, Md ... k12 85
McHenry, Stone, Miss ... E4 100
McHenry, Foster, N. Dak ... B7 110
McHenry, co., Ill ... A5 90
McHenry, co., N. Dak ... A5 110
Machens, St. Charles, Mo ... A8 101
Machias, Washington, Maine ... D5 96
Machias, Cattaraugus, N.Y ... C2 108
Machias, bay, Maine ... D5 96
Machias, lakes, Maine ... C4 96
Machias, riv., Maine ... B4 96
Machias, riv., Maine ... D5 96
Machiasport, Washington, Maine ... D5 96
Machichi, riv., Man., Can ... A6 71
Machico, Port. (Madeira Is.), ... h12 20
Machida, Jap ... *I9 37
Machilīpatnam (Bandar), India ... E7 39
Machiques, Ven ... A3 60
Machrihanish, Scot ... E3 13
McHue, Independence, Ark ... B4 81
Machu Picchu, Peru ... D3 58
Machynlleth, Wales ... B4 12
Macia, Moz ... C5 49
Măcin, Rom ... C9 22
Macina, reg., Mali ... D4 45
McIndoe Falls, Caledonia, Vt ... C4 120
McIntire, Mitchell, Iowa ... A5 92
McIntosh, Washington, Ala ... D1 78
McIntosh, Ont., Can ... E5 71
McIntosh, Marion, Fla ... C4 86
McIntosh, Liberty, Ga ... E5 87
McIntosh, Polk, Minn ... C3 99
McIntosh, Torrance, N. Mex ... C3 107
McIntosh, Corson, S. Dak ... B4 116
McIntosh, co., Ga ... E5 87
McIntosh, co., N. Dak ... C6 110
McIntosh, co., Okla ... B6 112
McIntosh, lake, Sask., Can ... B3 70
McIntosh, run, Md ... D4 85
McIntyre, Wilkinson, Ga ... D3 87
McIntyre, Indiana, Pa ... E3 114
McIntyre, creek, Ohio ... f8 123
Mack, Mesa Colo ... B2 83
Mack, Hamilton, Ohio ... o12 111
McKague, Sask., Can ... E4 70
Mackay, Austl ... D8 50
Mackay, Custer, Idaho ... F5 89
Mackay, lake, Austl ... D4 50
MacKay, lake, N.W. Ter., Can ... D10 66
MacKay, riv., Alta., Can ... A4 69
McKean, Erie, Pa ... C1 114
McKean, co., Pa ... C4 114
McKee, Jackson, Ky ... C6 94
McKee City, Atlantic, N.J ... E3 106
McKeesport, Allegheny, Pa ... F2, k14 114
McKees Rocks, Allegheny, Pa ... F1, k13 114
Mackenna, Arg ... A4 54
McKenney, Dinwiddie, Va ... D5 121
McKenzie, Butler, Ala ... D3 78
Mackenzie, Guy ... A3 59
McKenzie, Burleigh, N. Dak ... C5 110
McKenzie, Carroll and Weakley, Tenn ... A3 117
McKenzie, co., N. Dak ... B2 110
Mackenzie, dist., N.W. Ter., Can ... D8 66
MacKenzie, bay, Ant ... C20 5
Mackenzie, bay, N.W. Ter., Yukon, Can ... C5 66
Mackenzie, mts., N.W. Ter., Can ... D7 66
McKenzie, pass, Oreg ... C4 113
Mackenzie, riv., N.W. Ter., Can ... C6 66
McKenzie Bridge, Lane, Oreg ... C4 113
Mackenzie King, isl., N.W. Ter., Can ... m30 67
McKerrow, Ont., Can ... A3 72
Mackey, Gibson, Ind ... H3 91
Mackeys, Washington, N.C ... B6 109
Mackeys Station, Ont., Can ... A7 72
Mackeyville, Clinton, Pa ... D7 114
Mackinac, co., Mich ... B5 98
Mackinac, isl., Mich ... C6 98
Mackinac, straits, Mich ... C6 98
Mackinac Island, Mackinac, Mich ... C6 98
Mackinaw, Tazewell, Ill ... C4 90
Mackinaw, riv., Ill ... C4 90
Mackinaw City, Cheboygan and Emmet, Mich ... C6 98
McKinley, Marengo, Ala ... C2 78
McKinley, St. Louis, Minn ... C6 99
McKinley, co., N. Mex ... B1 107
McKinley, mtn., Alsk ... C9 79
McKinley Heights, Trumbull, Ohio ... *A5 111
McKinley Park, Alsk ... C10 79
McKinleyville, Humboldt, Calif ... B1 82
McKinney, Lincoln, Ky ... C5 94
McKinney, Collins, Tex ... C4 118
McKinney, lake, Kans ... E2 93
McKinnon, Sweetwater, Wyo ... E3 125
Mackinnon Road, Ken ... B6 48
McKittrick, Kern, Calif ... E4 82
McKittrick, Montgomery, Mo ... C6 101
McKittrick Summit, mtn., Calif ... E4 82
Macklin, Sask., Can ... E1 70
McKnight, Allegheny, Pa ... A5 114
McKnight, lake, Man., Can ... A1 71
McKownville, Albany, N.Y ... *C7 108
Macksburg, Madison, Iowa ... C3 92
Macksburg, Washington, Ohio ... C4 111
Macks Creek, Camden, Mo ... D5 101
Macksville, Stafford, Kans ... E5 93
Mackville, Washington, Ky ... C4 94
Mackville, Caledonia, Vt ... C4 120
Mackville, Outagamie, Wis ... h9 124
McLain, Greene, Miss ... D5 100
McLaughlin, Alta., Can ... C5 69
McLaughlin, Corson, S. Dak ... B5 116
McLaughlin, mtn., Oreg ... E4 113
McLaughlin, riv., Man., Can ... C3 71
McLaurin, Forrest, Miss ... D4 100
Maclean, Austl ... D9 51
McLean, Sask., Can ... G3 70
McLean, McLean, Ill ... C4 90
McLean, Pierce, Nebr ... B8 103
McLean, Gray, Tex ... B2 124
McLean, Fairfax, Va ... g12 121
McLean, co., Ill ... C5 90
McLean, co., Ky ... C2 94
McLean, co., N. Dak ... B4 110
McLean, lake, Sask., Can ... A6 69
McLean, mtn., Maine ... A4 96
Maclean, strait, N.W. Ter., Can ... m31 67
McLeansboro, Hamilton, Ill ... E5 90
Maclear, S. Afr ... D4 49
McLemoresville, Carroll, Tenn ... B3 117
McLennan, Alta., Can ... B2 69
McLennan, co., Tex ... D4 118
McLennan, lake, Sask., Can ... B3 70
McLeod, Sweet Grass, Mont ... E6 102
McLeod, Ransom, N. Dak ... C8 110
McLeod, co., Minn ... F4 99
McLeod, lake, B.C., Can ... B6 68
McLeod, riv., Alta., Can ... C2 69
MacLeod Lake, B.C., Can ... B6, n18 68
McLoud, Pottawatomie, Okla ... B4 112
McLoughlin, mtn., Oreg ... E4 113
McLouth, Jefferson, Kans ... C8, k15 93
McMahon, Sask., Can ... G2 70
McMasterville, Que., Can ... *D4 73
McMechen, Marshall, W. Va ... B4, g8 123
McMichael, creek, Pa ... B2 106
McMillan, Luce, Mich ... B5 98
McMillan, Knox, Tenn ... m14 117
McMillan, lake, N. Mex ... E5 107
McMillan Manor, Ventura, Calif ... *E4 82
McMinn, co., Tenn ... D9 117
McMinnville, Yamhill, Oreg ... B3, h11 113
McMinnville, Warren, Tenn ... D8 117
McMorran, Sask., Can ... F1 70
McMullen, co., Tex ... E3 118
McMurdo, sound, Ant ... B29 5
McMurdo, U.S. scientific station, Ant ... B29 5
McMurray, Skagit, Wash ... A3 122
McNab, Hempstead, Ark ... D2 81
McNair, Jefferson, Miss ... D2 100
McNairy, McNairy, Tenn ... B3 117
McNairy, co., Tenn ... B3 117
McNary, Apache, Ariz ... C6 80
McNary, Rapides, La ... D3 95
McNary, Umatilla, Oreg ... B7 113
McNary, Hudspeth, Tex ... o12 124
McNeal, Cochise, Ariz ... F6 80
McNeil, Columbia, Ark ... D2 81
McNeil, Travis, Tex ... D4 124
McNeil, isl., Wash ... f10 122
McNeil, mtn., B.C., Can ... B2 68
McNeill, Pearl River, Miss ... E4 100
McNulty, Columbia, Oreg ... *B4 113
MacNutt, Sask., Can ... F5 70
McNutt, isl., N.S., Can ... F4 74
Maco, Bol ... B2 55
Macocolo, Ang ... C2 48
Macomb, McDonough, Ill ... C3 90
Macomb, Pottawatomie, Okla ... B4 112
Macomb, co., Mich ... F8 98
Mâcon, Fr ... D6 14
Macon, Bibb, Ga ... D3 87
Macon, Macon, Ill ... D5 90
Macon, Noxubee, Miss ... B5 100
Macon, Macon, Mo ... B5 101
Macon, Franklin, Nebr ... D7 103
Macon, Warren, N.C ... A4 109
Macon, Fayette, Tenn ... B2 117
Macon, co., Ala ... C4 78
Macon, co., Ga ... D2 87
Macon, co., Ill ... D5 90
Macon, co., Mo ... B5 101
Macon, co., N.C ... f9 109
Macon, co., Tenn ... C7 117
Macon, bayou, La ... B4 95
Macoun, Sask., Can ... H4 70
Macoun, lake, Sask., Can ... A4 70
Macoupin, co., Ill ... D4 90
Macouria, Fr. Gu ... B4 59
Macovane, Moz ... B6 49
McPhail, riv., Man., Can ... C3 71
McPherson, McPherson, Kans ... D6 93
McPherson, co., Kans ... D6 93
McPherson, co., Nebr ... C4 103
McPherson, co., S. Dak ... B6 116
McQuady, Breckinridge, Ky ... C3 94
Macquarie, isl., Oceania ... J7 2
Macquarie, riv., Austl ... E6 51
McQueeney, Guadalupe, Tex ... h7 118
McRae, White, Ark ... B4 81
McRae, Telfair, Ga ... D4 87
McRoberts, Letcher, Ky ... C7 94
Mac-Robertson, coast, Ant ... C19 5
Macroom, Ire ... F3 11
Macrorie, Sask., Can ... F2 70
McSherrystown, Adams, Pa ... G7 114
McTaggart, Sask., Can ... H3 70
McTavish, Man., Can ... E3 71
MacTier, Ont., Can ... B5 72
Macuelizo, Hond ... C3 62
Macungie, Lehigh, Pa ... E10 114
McVeigh, Pike, Ky ... C7 94
McVeytown, Mifflin, Pa ... F6 114
McVille, Nelson, N. Dak ... B7 110
Macwahoc, Aroostook, Maine ... C4 96
McWilliams, Wilcox, Ala ... D2 78
Macy, Miami, Ind ... C5 91
Macy, Thurston, Nebr ... B2 103
Mad, creek, Ga ... B5 87
Mad, lake, Idaho ... D8 122
Mad, riv., Calif ... B2 82
Mad, riv., N.H ... C3 105
Mad, riv., Ohio ... C2 111
Mad, riv., Vt ... C3 120
Ma'dabā, Jordan ... C7 32
Madaba, Tan ... C6 48
Madagascar (Malagasy Republic), country, Afr ... I10 42, h9 49
Madagascar, isl., Afr ... I10 42
Madame, isl., N.S., Can ... D9 74
Madang, Pap. N. Gui ... k12 50
Madaoua, Niger ... D6 45
Mādārīpur, Bngl ... F13 40
Madawaska, Ont., Can ... B7 72
Madawaska, Aroostook, Maine ... A4 96
Madawaska, co., N.B., Can ... B1 74
Madawaska, lake, Maine ... B4 96
Madawaska, riv., N.B., Que., Can ... B1 74
Madawaska, riv., Ont., Can ... B7 72
Madaya, Bur ... A2 38
Madbury, Strafford, N.H ... D5 105
Madden, Leake, Miss ... C4 100
Madden, lake, Pan ... k11 62
Maddock, Benson, N. Dak ... B6 110
Maddox, St. Marys, Md ... D4 85
Madeira, Hamilton, Ohio ... o13 111
Madeira, riv., Braz ... D2 59
Madeira Islands, reg., Port. (Atl. O.) ... h11 20, C1 44
Madeleine, co., Que., Can ... B8 74
Madeleine, is., Que., Can ... B8 74
Madelia, Watonwan, Minn ... F4 99
Madeline, Lassen, Calif ... B3 82
Madeline, isl., Wis ... B3 124
Madera, Madera, Calif ... D3 82
Madera, Mex ... B3 63
Madera, Clearfield, Pa ... E4 114
Madera, co., Calif ... D4 82
Madgaon, India ... E5 39
Madge, lake, Sask., Can ... D1 71
Madhupur, India ... E11 40
Madhya Pradesh, state, India ... D6 39
Madill, Marshall, Okla ... C5 112
Madimba, Zaire ... C2 48
Madīnat ash Sha'b, P.D.R. of Yem ... C5 47
Madingou, Con ... F2 46
Madison, Madison, Ala ... A3 78
Madison, Montgomery, Ala ... C3 78
Madison, St. Francis, Ark ... B5 81
Madison, Sask., Can ... F1 70
Madison, New Haven, Conn ... D6 84
Madison, Madison, Fla ... B3 86
Madison, Morgan, Ga ... C3 87
Madison, Madison, Ill ... E3 90
Madison, Jefferson, Ind ... G7 91
Madison, Greenwood, Kans ... D7 93
Madison, Somerset, Maine ... D3 96
Madison, Dorchester, Md ... C5 85
Madison, Lac qui Parle, Minn ... E2 99
Madison, Madison, Miss ... C3 100
Madison, Monroe, Mo ... f13 101
Madison, Madison, Nebr ... C8 103
Madison, Carroll, N.H ... C4 105
Madison, Morris, N.J ... B4 106
Madison, Madison, N.Y ... C5 108
Madison, Rockingham, N.C ... A3 109
Madison, Lake, Ohio ... A4 111
Madison, Oconee, S.C ... B1 115
Madison, Lake, S. Dak ... C8 116
Madison, Madison, Va ... B4 121
Madison, Boone, W. Va ... C3, m12 123
Madison, Dane, Wis ... E4 124
Madison, co., Ala ... A3 78
Madison, co., Ark ... B2 81
Madison, co., Fla ... B3 86
Madison, co., Ga ... B3 87
Madison, co., Idaho ... F7 89
Madison, co., Ill ... E4 90
Madison, co., Ind ... D6 91
Madison, co., Iowa ... C3 92
Madison, co., Ky ... C5 94
Madison, co., Miss ... C4 100
Madison, co., Mo ... D7 101
Madison, co., Mont ... E4 102
Madison, co., Nebr ... C8 103
Madison, co., N.Y ... C5 108
Madison, co., N.C ... f10 109
Madison, co., Ohio ... C2 111
Madison, co., Tenn ... B3 117
Madison, co., Tex ... D5 118
Madison, co., Va ... B4 121
Madison, par., La ... B4 95
Madison, range, Mont ... E5 102
Madison, riv., Mont ... E5 102
Madisonburg, Centre, Pa ... E6 114
Madison Heights, Oakland, Mich ... o15 98
Madison Heights, Amherst, Va ... C3 121
Madison Lake, Blue Earth, Minn ... F5 99
Madisonville, Hopkins, Ky ... C2 94
Madisonville, St. Tammany, La ... D5, h11 95
Madisonville, Monroe, Tenn ... D9 117
Madisonville, Madison, Tex ... D5 118
Madiun, Indon ... *G4 35
Madoc, Ont., Can ... C7 72
Madoc, Daniels, Mont ... B11 102
Mado Gashi, Ken ... A6 48
Madon, riv., Fr ... A2 18
Madona, Sov. Un ... C6 27
Madonna di Campiglio, It ... C6 18
Madras, India ... F7 39
Madras, Jefferson, Oreg ... C5 113
Madras, state, India ... F6 39
Madre, mts., Guat ... C2 62
Madre, mts., Mex ... D6 63
Madre, mts., Phil ... B6 35
Madre de Dios, dept., Peru ... D3 58
Madre de Dios, isl., Chile ... E1 54
Madre de Dios, riv., Bol., Peru ... B2 55
Madre del Sur, mts., Mex ... o13 63
Madre Occidental, mts., Mex ... C3 63
Madre Oriental, mts., Mex ... C5 63
Madrid, Houston, Ala ... D4 78
Madrid, Boone, Iowa ... C4, e8 92
Madrid, Perkins, Nebr ... D4 103
Madrid, Santa Fe, N. Mex ... B3, k8 107
Madrid, St. Lawrence, N.Y ... f9 108
Madrid, Sp ... B4, p17 20
Madrid, prov., Sp ... *B4, p17 20
Madridejos, Phil ... *C6 35
Madridejos, Sp ... C4 20
Madrūsah, Libya ... E2 43
Mādugula, India ... I9 40
Madura, isl., Indon ... G4 35
Madurai, India ... G6 39
Mae, Grant, Wash ... B6 122
Maebashi, Jap ... H9, m18 37
Mae Hong Son, Thai ... C3 38
Maelamun, mtn., Thai ... E3 38
Maella, Sp ... B6 20
Maengsan, Kor ... G3 37
Maes, San Miguel, N. Mex ... B5 107
Maeser, Uintah, Utah ... C6 119
Maesteg, Wales ... C4 12
Maestra, mts., Cuba ... D5 64
Maevatanana, Mad ... g9 49
Ma'fan, Libya ... D2 43
Mafeking, Man., Can ... C1 71
Mafeking, S. Afr ... C4 49
Maffra, Austl ... H6 51
Mafra, Braz ... D3 56
Mafra, Port ... C1 20
Maga, mtn., Tinian ... 52
Magadan, Sov. Un ... D18 28
Magadi, Ken ... B6 48
Magadi, lake, Ken ... B6 48
Magaguadavic, lake, N.B., Can ... D2 74
Magalia, Butte, Calif ... C3 82
Magallanes, see Punta Arenas, Chile
Magallanes, prov., Chile ... E2, h11 54
Magallanes, strait, Chile ... h11 54
Maganga, Zaire ... A4 48
Magangué, Col ... B3 60
Magaria, Niger ... D6 45
Magat, riv., Phil ... n13 35
Magazine, Logan, Ark ... B2 81
Magazine, mtn., Ark ... B2 81
Magdalena, Arg ... B5, g8 54
Magdalena, Bol ... B3 55
Magdalena, Mex ... A2 63
Magdalena, Socorro, N. Mex ... C2 107
Magdalena, dept., Col ... A3 60
Magdalena, isl., Chile ... C2 54
Magdalena, isl., Mex ... C2 63
Magdalena, lake, Mex ... m11 63
Magdalena, mts., N. Mex ... D2 107
Magdalena, plain, Mex ... C2 63
Magdalena, riv., Col ... B3 60
Magdalena, riv., Mex ... h9 63
Magdalo, Phil ... o13 35
Magdeburg, G.D.R ... A6 17
Magdi'el, Isr ... g10 32
Magé, Braz ... h6 56
Magee, Simpson, Miss ... D4 100
Magelang, Indon ... G4 39
Mageney, Ire ... E5 11
Magenta, It ... B2 21
Maggia, riv., Switz ... D6 19
Maggie, creek, Nev ... C5 104
Maggiore, lake, It. and Switz ... C4 18
Maghāghah, Eg ... D6 43
Maghama, Maur ... C2 45
Maghera, N. Ire ... C5 11
Magherafelt, N. Ire ... C5 11
Maghery, Ire ... C3 11
Magic, res., Idaho ... F4 89
Magicienne, bay, Saipan ... 52
Magilligan, pt., Ire ... B5 11
Maglaj, Yugo ... C4 22
Maglic, Yugo ... D5 22
Maglie, It ... D7 21
Magna, Salt Lake, Utah ... C3 119
Magness, Independence, Ark ... B4 81
Magnet, Man., Can ... D2 71
Magnet, Cedar, Nebr ... B8 103
Magnetawan, Ont., Can ... B5 72
Magnetawan, riv., Ont., Can ... B4 72
Magnet Cove, Hot Spring, Ark ... C3, g8 81
Magnetic Springs, Union, Ohio ... B2 111
Magnisia, prov., Grc ... *C4 23
Magnitogorsk, Sov. Un ... C5 29
Magnolia, Columbia, Ark ... D2 81
Magnolia, Kent, Del ... B7 85
Magnolia, Putnam, Ill ... B4 90
Magnolia, Harrison, Iowa ... C2 92
Magnolia, Larue, Ky ... C4 94
Magnolia, Harford, Md ... B5 85
Magnolia, Rock, Minn ... G2 99
Magnolia, Pike, Miss ... D3 100
Magnolia, Camden, N.J ... *D2 106
Magnolia, Duplin, N.C ... C4 109
Magnolia, Carroll and Stark, Ohio ... B4 111
Magnolia, Montgomery, Tex ... D5 118
Magnolia Springs, Baldwin, Ala ... E2 78
Magoari, cape, Braz ... B1 57
Magoffin, co., Ky ... C6 94
Magog, Que., Can ... D5 73
Magothy, riv., Md ... B4 85
Magoula, Grc ... g11 23
Magpie, Que., Can ... h8 75
Magpie, riv., Que., Can ... h8 75
Magrath, Alta., Can ... E4 69
Magruder, mtn., Nev ... F4 104
Magude, Moz ... B5 49
Magwe, Bur ... D9 39
Mahābād, Iran ... C2 41
Mahaffey, Clearfield, Pa ... E4 114
Mahagi, Zaire ... A5 48
Mahaicony, Guy ... A3 59
Mahajanga, Mong ... g9 49
Mahakam, riv., Indon ... F5 35
Mahalatswe, Bots ... B4 49
Mahameru, mtn., Indon ... G4 35
Mahānadī, riv., India ... G10 40
Mahanoro, Mad ... g9 49
Mahanoy City, Schuylkill, Pa ... E9 114
Maharashtra, state, India ... D5 39
Maha Sarakham, Thai ... D5 38
Mahaska, Washington, Kans ... C6 93
Mahaska, co., Iowa ... C5 92
Maḩaţţat al Ḩasā, Jordan ... D7 32
Maḩaţţat al Manzil, Jordan ... C8 32
Maḩaţţat al Qaţrānah, Jordan ... G11 31
Maḩaţţat Dab'ah, Jordan ... C8 32
Maḩaţţat Jurf ad Darāwīsh, Jordan ... D7 32
Mahbūbnagar, India ... I7 40
Mahe, India ... F6 39
Mahenge, Tan ... C6 48
Mahi, riv., India ... F4 40
Mahia, pen., N.Z ... M16 51
Mahitahi, N.Z ... O12 51
Mahned, Perry, Miss ... D4 100
Mahnomen, Mahnomen, Minn ... C3 99
Mahnomen, co., Minn ... C3 99
Mahomet, Champaign, Ill ... C5 90
Mahón, Sp ... C8 20
Mahone Bay, N.S., Can ... E5 74
Mahoning, co., Ohio ... B5 111
Mahoning, riv., Ohio ... A5 111
Mahoosuc, range, Maine, N.H ... D1 96, B4 105
Mahopac, Putnam, N.Y ... D7, m15 108
Mahopac, lake, N.Y ... D1 84
Mahto, Corson, S. Dak ... B5 116
Mahtomedi, Washington, Minn ... E7 99
Mahtowa, Carlton, Minn ... D6 99
Mahuta, Tan ... D6 48
Mahuva, India ... G3 40
Mahwah, Bergen, N.J ... A4 106
Maîche, Fr ... B2 18
Maicurú, riv., Braz ... C4 59
Maida, Cavalier, N. Dak ... A7 110
Maiden, Catawba, N.C ... B1 109
Maidenhead, Eng ... C7 12
Maiden Rock, Pierce, Wis ... D1 124
Maidens, isl., Ire ... C6 11
Maidstone, Sask., Can ... D1 70
Maidstone, Eng ... C8 12
Maidstone (Town of), Essex, Vt ... *B5 120
Maidstone, lake, Vt ... B5 120
Maidsville, Monongalia, W. Va ... B5 123
Maiduguri, Nig ... D7 45
Maihar, India ... E8 40
Maikala, range, India ... F8 40
Maiko, riv., Zaire ... B4 48
Maikoor, isl., Indon ... G8 35
Maili, pt., Haw ... g9 88
Maillard, Que., Can ... B7 73
Maillot, Alg ... F9 30
Main, chan., Ont., Can ... B3 72
Main, pass, La ... E6 95
Main, riv., F.R.G ... C3 17
Main, riv., Ire ... C5 11
Main-a-Dieu, N.S., Can ... C10 74
Mainburg, F.R.G ... E6 17
Main Centre, Sask., Can ... G2 70
Mai-Ndombe, lake, Zaire ... B2 48
Maine, Broome, N.Y ... C4 108
Maine, former prov., Fr ... C3 14
Maine, state, U.S ... A14 77, 96
Maine-et-Loire, dept., Fr ... *D3 14
Mainesburg, Tioga, Pa ... C7 114
Maïné-Soroa, Niger ... D7 45
Mainland, see Pomona, isl., Scot.
Mainland, isl., Scot ... g10 10
Mainland, riv., Man., Can ... C4 71
Maintirano, Mad ... g8 49
Main Topsail, mtn., Newf., Can ... D3 75
Mainz, F.R.G ... D3 17
Maipó, vol., Arg., Chile ... A2 54
Maipú, Arg ... B5 54
Maiquetía, Ven ... A4 60
Maira, riv., It ... E3 18
Maire, strait, Arg ... h12 54
Mairhofen, Aus ... B7 18
Mairiporã, Braz ... m8 56
Mairum, Pak ... G11 46
Maisi, cape, Cuba ... D6 64
Maison-Carrée, Alg ... *B5 44
Maisonette, N.B., Can ... B4 74
Maisons-Alfort, Fr ... g10 14
Maisons-Laffitte, Fr ... g9 14
Mait, Som ... C6 47
Maitland, Austl ... F8 51
Maitland, N.S., Can ... D6 74
Maitland, Ont., Can ... C9 72
Maitland (Lake Maitland), Orange, Fla ... *D5 86
Maitland, Holt, Mo ... A2 101
Maize, Sedgwick, Kans ... g12 93
Maizuru, Jap ... I7, n14 37
Majagual, Col ... B3 60
Majé, see Magé, Braz.
Majene, Indon ... F5 35
Majestic, Pike, Ky ... C7 94
Maji, Eth ... D4 47
Majijo, peak, Ponape ... 52
Major, Sask., Can ... F1 70
Major, co., Okla ... A3 112
Majunga, prov., Mad ... g9 49
Makah, Indian res., Wash ... A1 122
Makaha, Honolulu, Haw ... G9 88
Makakilo, Honolulu, Haw ... g9 88
Makalado, Zaire ... B4 48
Makanda, Jackson, Ill ... F4 90
Makanza, see Nouvelle-Anvers, Zaire
Makapala, Hawaii, Haw ... C6 88
Makapuu, pt., Haw ... B4 88
Makarov, Sov. Un ... B11 37
Makarska, Yugo ... D3 22
Makassar (Macassar), strait, Indon ... F5 35
Makat, Sov. Un ... D4 29
Makatea, isl., Fr. Polynesia ... *H13 7
Makati, Phil ... *C6 35
Makawao, Maui, Haw ... C5 88
Makaweli, Kauai, Haw ... B2 88
Makena, Maui, Haw ... C5 88
Makeni, S.L ... E2 45
Makenzen, see Orlyak, Bul.
Makeyevka, Sov. Un ... G11 27
Makgadikgadi, lake, Bots ... B4 49
Makhachkala, Sov. Un ... E3 29
Makharadze, Sov. Un ... B14 31
Makhfah al Quwayrah, Jordan ... E7 32
Makhlata, Bul ... D7 22
Makin, isl., Gilbert & Ellice Is ... F10 7
Makinak, Man., Can ... D2 71
Makinsk, Sov. Un ... C8 29
Makkah, see Mecca, Sau. Ar.
Makkinga, Neth ... B6 15
Makkovik, Newf., Can ... g10 75
Makkum, Neth ... A5 15
Mako, Hung ... B5 22
Makokou, Gabon ... E2 46
Makongai, isl., Fiji ... 52
Makoti, Ward, N. Dak ... B4 110
Makoua, Con ... F3 46
Makow, Pol ... B6 26
Maktar, Tun ... G11 30
Makteïr, sand dunes, Maur ... B2 45
Mākū, Iran ... B2 41
Makumbi, Zaire ... C3 48
Makurazaki, Jap ... K5 37
Makurdi, Nig ... E6 45
Makushin, vol., Alsk ... E6 79
Mal, bay, Ire ... E2 11
Mala, pt., Pan ... G8 62
Malabang, Phil ... *D6 35
Malabar, Brevard, Fla ... E6 86
Malabar, coast, India ... F5 39
Malabo, Equat. Gui ... E1 46
Malabon, Phil ... *C6 35
Mal Abrigo, Ur ... E1 56
Malacca, see Melaka, Mala.
Malacca, strait, Asia ... K4 38
Malad City, Oneida, Idaho ... G6 89
Malafede, riv., It ... h8 21
Málaga, Col ... B3 60
Malaga, Gloucester, N.J ... D2 106
Malaga, Eddy, N. Mex ... E5 107
Málaga, Sp ... D3 20
Málaga, prov., Sp ... *D3 20
Málaga, bay, Sp ... D3 20
Malagash, N.S., Can ... D6 74
Malagasy Republic, see Madagascar, country, Afr.
Malagón, Sp ... C4 20
Malaimbandy, Mad ... h9 49
Malaita, is., Solomon Is ... G9 7
Malakāl, Sud ... D3 47
Malakoff, Fr ... g10 14
Malakoff, Henderson, Tex ... C4 118
Malalbergo, It ... E7 18
Malang, Indon ... G4 35
Malanje, Ang ... C2 48
Malanje, dist., Ang ... C2 48
Malanzán, Arg ... A3 54
Mälaren, lake, Swe ... t34 25
Malargüe, Arg ... B3 54
Malartic, Que., Can ... k11 73
Malaspina, glacier, Alsk ... D11 79
Malaspina, Arg ... C3 54
Malatya, Tur ... C12 31
Malawi (Nyasaland), country, Afr ... H9 42, D5 48
Malay, pen., Asia ... I13 33
Malaya Uzen', riv., Sov. Un ... F18 9
Malaya Vishera, Sov. Un ... B9 27
Malaybalay, Phil ... D7 35
Malāyer, Iran ... D4 41
Malaysia, country, Asia ... E4 35, J5 38
Malazgirt, Tur ... C14 31
Malbaie, riv., Que., Can ... B7 73
Malbon, Austl ... D7 50
Malbork, Pol ... A5 26
Malchin, G.D.R ... B6 16
Malchow, G.D.R ... E6 24
Malcolm, Austl ... E3 50
Malcolm, Lancaster, Nebr ... D9 103
Malcomb, Poweshiek, Iowa ... C5 92
Malden, Bureau, Ill ... B4 90
Malden, Middlesex, Mass ... B5, g11 97
Malden, Dunklin, Mo ... E8 101
Malden, Whitman, Wash ... B8 122
Malden, Kanaswa, W. Va ... m12 123
Malden, isl., Kir ... G12 7
Maldives, country, Asia ... I10 33, G5 39
Maldon, Eng ... C8 12
Maldonado, Ur ... E2 56
Maldonado, dept., Ur ... *E2 56
Malè, It ... C6 18
Malé, Maldives ... *I10 33
Malea, cape, Grc ... D4 23
Mālegaon, India ... G5 40
Malemba-Nkulu, Zaire ... C4 48
Māler Kotla, India ... B5 40
Malesherbes, Fr ... C5 14
Malesus, Madison, Tenn ... B3 117
Malha Wells, Sud ... B2 47
Malheur, Malheur, Oreg ... C9 113
Malheur, co., Oreg ... D9 113
Malheur, lake, Oreg ... D8 113
Malheur, riv., Oreg ... D9 113
Mali, Guinea ... D2 45
Mali, country, Afr ... E5 42, C4 45
Mali, isl., Fiji ... 52
Malibu, Los Angeles, Calif ... m11 82
Maligne, lake, Alta., Can ... C2 69
Malin, Ire ... B4 11
Malin, Klamath, Oreg ... E5 113
Malin, Sov. Un ... F7 27
Malin, head, Ire ... B4 11
Malinau, Indon ... E5 35
Malin Beg, Ire ... C3 11
Malindi, Ken ... B7 48
Malinec, Czech ... D5 26
Malinmore, head, Ire ... C3 11
Malino, Sov. Un ... n18 27
Malinta, Henry, Ohio ... A1 111
Malita, Phil ... *D7 35
Maliwun, Bur ... G3 38
Maljamar, Lea, N. Mex ... E6 107
Malkangiri, India ... H8 40
Malkara, Tur ... B6 23
Malko Turnovo, Bul ... E8 22
Mallaig, Alta., Can ... B5 69
Mallaig, Scot ... D3 13
Mallard, Palo Alto, Iowa ... B3 92
Malawī, Eg ... D6 43
Malleco, prov., Chile ... B2 54
Mallersdorf, F.R.G ... E7 17
Malles Venosta, It ... C6 18
Mallet Creek, Medina, Ohio ... A4 111
Malletts, bay, Vt ... B2 120
Mallorca, is., Sp ... C7 20
Mallory, Logan, W. Va ... *D3 123
Mallorytown, Ont., Can ... C9 72
Mallow, Ire ... E3 11
Malmbäck, Swe ... A4 24
Malmberget, Swe ... D9 25
Malmédy, Bel ... D6 15
Malmköping, Swe ... t34 25
Malmo, Saunders, Nebr ... C9, g11 103
Malmö, Swe ... C7 24, J5 25
Malmöhus, co., Swe ... C7 24
Maloarkhangelsk, Sov. Un ... E11 27
Maloja, Switz ... D8 19
Maloja, pass, Switz ... D8 19
Maloloi, isl., Fiji ... 52
Malolos, Phil ... o13 35
Malone, Ont., Can ... C7 72
Malone, Jackson, Fla ... B1 86
Malone, Franklin, N.Y ... f10 108
Malone, Grays Harbor, Wash ... C2 122
Malone, Fond du Lac, Wis ... B5 124
Maloney Lake, res., Nebr ... C5 103
Maloneyville, Knox, Tenn ... m14 117
Malonton, Man., Can ... D3 71
Malott, Okanogan, Wash ... A6 122
Maloy, Ringgold, Iowa ... D3 92
Maloyaroslavets, Sov. Un ... D11 27
Malpeque, bay, P.E.I., Can ... C6 74
Malpura, India ... D5 40
Malsch, F.R.G ... E3 17
Malshaya Uzen, riv., Sov. Un ... D3 29
Malta, Cassia, Idaho ... G5 89
Malta, De Kalb, Ill ... B5 90
Malta, Phillips, Mont ... B9 102
Malta, Morgan, Ohio ... C4 111
Malta, country, Eur ... G14 30
Malta Bend, Saline, Mo ... B4 101
Maltahöhe, Namibia ... B2 49
Malton, Ont., Can ... m14 72
Malton, Eng ... C6 10
Malung, Swe ... G5 25
Malvern, Geneva, Ala ... D4 78
Malvern, Hot Springs, Ark ... C3, g8 81
Malvern, Eng ... B5 12
Malvern, Mills, Iowa ... C2 92
Malvern, Carroll, Ohio ... B4 111
Malvern, Chester, Pa ... o19 114
Malverne, Nassau, N.Y ... G2 84
Malwood, Ont., Can ... h11 72
Malyye Karmakuly, Sov. Un ... B9 4
Mamala, bay, Haw ... g10 88
Mamanguape, Braz ... C3, h6 57
Mamantel, Mex ... D6 63
Mamaroneck, Westchester, N.Y ... h13 108
Mamba, Jap ... m17 37
Mambasa, Zaire ... A4 48
Mamberamo, riv., Indon ... F9 35
Ma-Me-O Beach, Alta., Can ... C4 69
Mamers, Fr ... C4 14
Mamers, Harnett, N.C ... B4 109
Mamfe, Cam ... E6 45
Mamie, Currituck, N.C ... A7 109
Mamiña, Chile ... D2 55
Mammern, Switz ... A6 19
Mammoth, Pinal, Ariz ... E5 80
Mammoth, Juab, Utah ... D3 119
Mammoth, Kanawha, W. Va ... C3, m13 123
Mammoth Cave, nat. park, Ky ... C4 94
Mammoth Lakes, Mono, Calif ... D4 82
Mammoth Spring, Fulton, Ark ... A4 81
Mamoré, riv., Bol., Braz ... B2 55
Mamou, Guinea ... D2 45
Mamou, Evangeline, La ... D3 95
Mampawah, Indon ... E3 35
Mampong, Ghana ... E4 45
Mamry, lake, Pol ... A6 26
Mamudju, Indon ... F5 35
Man, I.C ... E3 45
Man, Logan, W. Va ... D3, n12 123

114X MAN-MARR

Man, Isle of, see Isle of Man, Br. dep., Eur.
Man, riv., Sask., Can....D4 70
Mana, Fr. Gu....A4 59
Mana, Kauai, Haw....A2 88
Manabí, prov., Ec....B1 58
Manabo, Malag....h8 49
Manacapuru, Braz....D5 60
Manacor, Sp....C7 20
Manado, Indon....E6 35
Managua, Nic....D4 62
Managua, lake, Nic....D4 62
Manahawkin, Ocean, N.J....D4 106
Manakara, Mad....h9 49
Manakin, Goochland, Va....C5 121
Manalapan, Monmouth, N.J....C4 106
Manam, isl., Pap. N. Gui....h12 50
Manama, Bahrain....G8 33
Manana, isl., Haw....g11 88
Mananara, Mad....g9 49
Mananara, riv., Mad....h9 49
Mananjary, Mad....h9 49
Manantenina, Mad....h9 49
Manantico, creek, N.J....E3 106
Manapire, riv., Ven....B4 60
Manasarowar, lake, China....B9 40
Manasquan, Monmouth, N.J....C4 106
Manasquan, riv., N.J....C4 106
Manassa, Conejos, Colo....D5 83
Manassas, Tattnall, Ga....D4 87
Manassas, Prince William, Va....B5, g12 121
Manassas Park, Prince William, Va....B5, g12 121
Manassu (Suilai), China....C2 34
Manassu, riv., China....C2 34
Manatee, co., Fla....E4 86
Manatee, riv., Fla....E4 86
Manatí, P.R....B3 65
Manatí, mun., P.R....*B3 65
Manaus, Braz....C2 59
Manavgat, Tur....D8 31
Manawa, Waupaca, Wis....D5 124
Manawan. lake, Sask., Can....B4 70
Mancelona, Antrim, Mich....D5 98
Mancha, reg., Sp....C4 20
Manchac, bayou, La....h10 95
Mancha Real, Sp....D4 20
Manchaug, Worcester, Mass....B4 97
Manche, dept., Fr....*C3 14
Manchester, Hartford, Conn....B6 84
Manchester, Eng....D6 10, A5 12
Manchester, Meriwether and Talbot, Ga....D2 87
Manchester, Scott, Ill....D3 90
Manchester, Delaware, Iowa....B6 92
Manchester, Dickinson, Kans....C6 93
Manchester, Clay, Ky....C6 94
Manchester, Kennebec, Maine....D3 96
Manchester, Carroll, Md....A4 85
Manchester, Essex, Mass....A6, f12 97
Manchester, Washtenaw, Mich....F6 98
Manchester, St. Louis, Mo....f12 101
Manchester, Hillsboro, N.H....E4 105
Manchester, Ontario, N.Y....C3 108
Manchester, Adams, Ohio....D2 111
Manchester, Grant, Okla....A3 112
Manchester, York, Pa....F8 114
Manchester, Kingsbury, S. Dak....C8 116
Manchester, Coffee, Tenn....B5 117
Manchester, Bennington, Vt....E2 120
Manchester Center, Bennington, Vt....E2 120
Manchester Depot, Bennington, Vt....E2 120
Manchouli (Lupin), China....B8 34
Manchuria, reg., China....B10 34
Mancos, Montezuma, Colo....D2 83
Mancos, riv., Colo....D2 83
Mandabe, Mad....h8 49
Mandaguari, Braz....C2 56
Mandal, Nor....H2 25
Mandalay, Bur....B2 38, D10 39
Mandalaya, gulf, Tur....D6 23
Mandalī, Iraq....E2 41
Mandaluyong, Phil....*C6 35
Mandan, Morton, N. Dak....C5 110
Mandar, gulf, Indon....F5 35
Mandara, mts., Cam....C2 46
Mandaree, McKenzie, N. Dak....B3 110
Mandasor, India....E5 40
Mandel, Afg....E10 41
Mandera, Ken....A7 48
Manderfeld, Bel....D6 15
Manderson, Shannon, S. Dak....D3 116
Manderson, Big Horn, Wyo....B5 125
Mandeville, Miller, Ark....D2 81
Mandeville, Que., Can....C4 73
Mandeville, Jam....E13 65
Mandeville, St. Tammany, La....D5, h11 95
Mandimba, Moz....D6 48
Mandla, India....F8 40
Mandø, isl., Den....C2 24
Mandra, Grc....C4, g11 23
Mandritsara, Mad....g9 49
Mandurah, Austl....F2 50
Manduria, It....D6 21
Māndvi, India....F2 40
Manes, Wright, Mo....D5 71
Manfalūţ, Eg....D6 43
Manfred, Wells, N. Dak....B6 110
Manfredonia, It....D5 21
Manfredonia, gulf, It....D6 21
Manga, Braz....D2 57
Mangalia, Rom....D9 22
Mangalore, India....F5 39
Mangaratiba, Braz....h5 56
Mangatarem, Phil....o13 35
Mañgero, Phil....*C6 35
Mangerton, mtn., Ire....F2 11
Mangham, Richland, La....B4 95
Mango, isl., Fiji....52
Mangoche, Malawi....D6 48
Mangoky, riv., Mad....h8 49
Mangole, isl., Indon....F7 35
Mangonia Park, Palm Beach, Fla....*F6 86
Mangotsfield, Eng....*C5 12
Mangrove, pt., Fla....F2 86
Mangrove, swamp, Fla....G6 86
Mangualde, Port....B2 20
Mangueni, plat., Niger....B7 45
Mangum, Greer, Okla....C2 112
Mangyshlak, pen., Sov. Un....E4 29
Manhasset, Nassau, N.Y....F2 84
Manhattan, Will, Ill....*B6 90
Manhattan, Putnam, Ind....E4 91
Manhattan, Riley, Kans....C7 93
Manhattan, Gallatin, Mont....E5 102
Manhattan, Nye, Nev....E4 104
Manhattan, borough, New York, N.Y. (Part of New York City)....*k8 106
Manhattan, isl., N.Y....k8 106
Manhattan Beach, Los Angeles, Calif....n12 82
Manheim, Lancaster, Pa....F9 114
Manheim, Preston, W. Va....B5 123
Manhiça, Moz....C5 49
Manhuaçu, Braz....F2 57
Maniagassa, isl., Saipan....52
Maniago, It....C8 18
Manica E Sofala, prov., Moz....A5 49
Manicoré, Braz....D2 59
Manicouagan, riv., Que., Can....h13 73
Manigotagan, Man., Can....D3, g8 71
Manigotagan, lake, Man., Can....D4 71
Manigotagan, riv., Man., Can....D3 71
Manihiki, is., Pac. O....G12 7
Manila, Mississippi, Ark....B5 81
Manila, Phil....C6, o13 35
Manila, Daggett, Utah....C6 119
Manila, bay, Phil....C6, o13 35
Manilla, Austl....E8 51
Manilla, Rush, Ind....E6 91
Manilla, Crawford, Iowa....C2 92
Manipur, state, India....D9 39
Manisa, Tur....C6 23
Manistee, Manistee, Mich....D4 98
Manistee, co., Mich....D4 98
Manistee, riv., Mich....D5 98
Manistique, Schoolcraft, Mich....C4 98
Manistique, lake, Mich....B5 98
Manistique, riv., Mich....B4 98
Manito, Mason, Ill....C4 90
Manito, lake, Sask., Can....E1 70
Manitoba, prov., Can....E13 66, 71
Manitoba, lake, Man., Can....D2 71
Manitou, Man., Can....E2 71
Manitou, Tillman, Okla....C3 112
Manitou, isl., Mich....A3 98
Manitou, lake, Ont., Can....B3 72
Manitou, lakes, Ont., Can....E5 71
Manitou, riv., Ont., Can....E5 71
Manitou Beach, Sask., Can....F3 70
Manitou Beach, Lenawee, Mich....*G6 98
Manitoulin, dist., Ont., Can....B2 72
Manitoulin, isl., Ont., Can....B2 72
Manitou Springs, El Paso, Colo....C6 83
Manitowaning, Ont., Can....B3 72
Manitowoc, Manitowoc, Wis....D6, h10 124
Manitowoc, co., Wis....D6 124
Manitowoc, riv., Wis....h10 124
Manitowoc Rapids, Manitowoc, Wis....B6 124
Maniwaki, Que., Can....C2 73
Maniya (Oasis), Iraq....G14 31
Manizales, Col....B2 60
Manja, Mad....h8 49
Manjimup, Austl....F2 50
Mānjra, riv., India....E6 39
Mankato, Jewell, Kans....C5 93
Mankato, Blue Earth, Minn....F5 99
Mankono, I.C....E3 45
Mankota, Sask., Can....H2 70
Mankoya, Zambia....D3 48
Manley, Cass, Nebr....h12 103
Manley Hot Springs, Alsk....B9 79
Manlius, Bureau, Ill....B4 90
Manlius, Onondaga, N.Y....C5 108
Manlléu, Sp....A7 20
Manly, Worth, Iowa....A4 92
Manly, Moore, N.C....B3 109
Manlyville, Henry, Tenn....A3 117
Manmad, India....G5 40
Mann, ranges, Austl....E5 50
Mannar, Sri Lanka....G6 39
Mannar, gulf, Sri Lanka....G6 39
Mannboro, Amelia, Va....C5 121
Mannford, Creek, Okla....A5 112
Mannheim, F.R.G....D3 17
Manning, Dallas, Ark....C3 81
Manning, Alta., Can....A2 69
Manning, Carroll, Iowa....C2 92
Manning, Dunn, N. Dak....B3 110
Manning, Washington, Oreg....g11 113
Manning, Clarendon, S.C....D7 115
Mannington, Christian, Ky....C2 94
Mannington, Marion, W. Va....B4, h10 123
Manns, creek, W. Va....n14 123
Manns Choice, Bedford, Pa....G4 114
Manns Harbor, Dare, N.C....B7 109
Mannsville, Jefferson, N.Y....B4 108
Mannsville, Johnston, Okla....C5 112
Mannu, riv., It....E2 21
Mannum, Austl....G2 51
Mannville, Alta., Can....C5 69
Man of War, bay, Trin....M24 65
Manokin, Somerset, Md....D6 85
Manokin, riv., Md....D6 85
Manokotak, Alsk....D8 79
Manokwari, Indon....F8 35
Manombo, Mad....h8 49
Manomet, Plymouth, Mass....C6 97
Manomet, hill, Mass....C6 97
Manomet, pt., Mass....C6 97
Manono, Zaire....C4 48
Manono, isl., W. Sam....52
Manor, Sask., Can....H4 70
Manor, Ware, Ga....E4 87
Manor, Westmoreland, Pa....*F2 114
Manor, Travis, Tex....D4 118
Manorhamilton, Ire....C3 11
Manorhaven, Nassau, N.Y....*G2 84
Manorville, Armstrong, Pa....E2 114
Manosque, Fr....F6 14
Manotick, Ont., Can....B9 72
Manouane, lake, Que., Can....h12 73
Manpojin, Kor....F3 37
Manresa, Sp....B6 20
Mansa (Fort Rosebery), Zambia....D4 48
Mansalay, Phil....*C6 35
Månsarp, Swe....A8 24
Manseau, Que., Can....C5 73
Mansel, isl., N.W. Ter., Can....D16 67
Mansfield, Scott and Sebastian, Ark....B1 81
Mansfield, Austl....H6 51
Mansfield, Eng....A6 12
Mansfield, Newton, Ga....C3 87
Mansfield, Piatt, Ill....C5 90
Mansfield, De Soto, La....B2 95
Mansfield, Bristol, Mass....B5 97
Mansfield, Wright, Mo....D5 101
Mansfield, Richland, Ohio....B3 111
Mansfield, Tioga, Pa....C7 114
Mansfield, Spink, S. Dak....B7 116
Mansfield, Henry, Tenn....A3 117
Mansfield, Tarrant, Tex....n9 118
Mansfield, Douglas, Wash....B6 112
Mansfield, mtn., Vt....B3 120
Mansfield Center, Tolland, Conn....B8 84
Mansfield City, Tolland, Conn....B7 84
Mansfield Depot, Tolland, Conn....B7 84
Mansfield Hallow, res., Conn....B8 84
Mansfield Southeast, Richland, Ohio....*B3 111
Manson, Calhoun, Iowa....B3 92
Manson, Chelan, Wash....B5 122
Manson, riv., B.C., Can....B5 68
Manson Creek, B.C., Can....B5 68
Mansonville, Que., Can....D5 73
Manso ou das Mortes, riv., Braz....A2 56
Mansura, Avoyelles, La....C3 95
Mant, hbr., Ponape....52
Mant, is., Ponape....52
Manta, Ec....B1 58
Mantachie, Itawamba, Miss....A5 100
Mantador, Richland, N. Dak....C9 110
Mantagao, riv., Man., Can....D3 71
Mantario, Sask., Can....F1 70
Mantaro, riv., Peru....D3 58
Manteca, San Joaquin, Calif....D3 82
Mantee, Webster, Miss....B4 100
Manteno, Kankakee, Ill....B6 90
Manteo, Dare, N.C....B7 109
Manter, Stanton, Kans....E2 93
Mantes [-la-Jolie], Fr....C4 14
Manthani, India....H7 40
Manti, Sanpete, Utah....D4 119
Mantiqueira, mts., Braz....C4 56
Manton, Wexford, Mich....D5 98
Mantorville, Dodge, Minn....F6 99
Mantova, It....D6 18, B3 21
Mantua, Gloucester, N.J....D2 106
Mantua, Portage, Ohio....A4 111
Mantua, Box Elder, Utah....B4 119
Mantua Hills, Fairfax, Va....*B5 121
Manú, Peru....D3 58
Manucan, Phil....*D6 35
Manuel Alves, riv., Braz....C1 57
Manuel Benavides, Mex....B4 63
Manuelito, McKinley, N. Mex....B1 107
Manuels, Newf., Can....*E5 75
Manui, isl., Indon....F6 35
Manukau, hbr., N.Z....L15 51
Manulla, riv., Ire....D2 11
Manumuskin, riv., N.J....E3 106
Manvel, Grand Forks, N. Dak....A8 110
Manvel, Brazoria, Tex....r14 118
Manville, Somerset, N.J....B3 106
Manville, Providence, R.I....B11 84
Manville, Niobrara, Wyo....D8 125
Many, Sabine, La....C2 95
Manyara, lake, Tan....B6 48
Manyas, lake, Tur....B6 23
Manyberries, Alta., Can....E5 69
Manych, canal, Sov. Un....H14 27
Manych, lake, Sov. Un....H14 27
Manych, riv., Sov. Un....F17 9
Many Farms, Apache, Ariz....A6 80
Many Island, lake, Alta., Can....D5 69
Manyoni, Tan....C5 48
Manzanares, Sp....C4 20
Manzanares, canal, Sp....p17 20
Manzanares, riv., Sp....o17 20
Manzanillo, Cuba....D5 64
Manzanillo, Mex....D4, n11 63
Manzanita, Tillamook, Oreg....B3 113
Manzano, Torrance, N. Mex....C3 107
Manzano, mts., N. Mex....C3 107
Manzano, peak, N. Mex....C3 107
Manzanola, Otero, Colo....C7 83
Manziana, It....g8 21
Manzilah, lake, Eg....C3 32
Mao, Chad....C3 46
Maoming, China....G7 34
Maomu (Tinghsin), China....C4 34
Mapai, Moz....B5 49
Mapastepec, Mex....D6 63
Mapaville, Jefferson, Mo....C7 101
Mapes, Nelson, N. Dak....A7 110
Mapia, is., Indon....E8 35
Mapiri, Bol....C2 55
Maple, Ont., Can....k14 72
Maple, Bailey, Tex....C1 118
Maple, Douglas, Wis....B2 124
Maple, riv., Iowa....B2 92
Maple, riv., N. Dak....C7 110
Maple, riv., N. Dak....C8 110
Maple Bay, Polk, Minn....C2 99
Maple Bluff, Dane, Wis....*E4 124
Maple Creek, Sask., Can....H1 70
Maple Grove, Hennepin, Minn....m12 99
Maple Heights, Cuyahoga, Ohio....h9 111
Maple Hill, Wabaunsee, Kans....C7 93
Maple Hill, Douglas, Nebr....*C10 103
Maple Hill, Pender, N.C....C5 109
Maple Lake, Wright, Minn....E5 99
Maple Lane, St. Joseph, Ind....*A5 91
Maple Mount, Daviess, Ky....C2 94
Maple Rapids, Clinton, Mich....E6 98
Maples, Allen, Ind....B8 91
Maple Shade, Burlington, N.J....D2 106
Maplesville, Clinton, Ala....C3 78
Mapleton, Monona, Iowa....B2 92
Mapleton, Bourbon, Kans....D9 93
Mapleton, Aroostook, Maine....B4 96
Mapleton, Blue Earth, Minn....G5 99
Mapleton, Cass, N. Dak....C8 110
Mapleton, Lane, Oreg....C3 113
Mapleton, Utah, Utah....C4 119
Mapleton Depot, Huntingdon, Pa....E6 114
Maple Valley, King, Wash....f11 122
Mapleville, Providence, R.I....B10 84
Maplewood, Calcasieu, La....D2 95
Maplewood, York, Maine....E2 96
Maplewood, Ramsey, Minn....n12 99
Maplewood, St. Louis, Mo....f12 101
Maplewood, Essex, N.J....B4 106
Maplewood, Albany, N.Y....*C7 108
Maplewood, Multnomah, Oreg....*B4 113
Maplewood Park, Delaware, Pa....*G11 114
Mapuera, riv., Braz....C3 53
Maputo (Lourenço Marques), Moz....C5 49
Maputo, prov., Moz....C5 49
Ma'qalā', Sau. Ar....H3 41
Maqnāh, Sau. Ar....H10 31
Maquela do Zombo, Ang....C2 48
Maquinchao, Arg....C3 54
Maquoketa, Jackson, Iowa....B7 92
Maquoketa, riv., Iowa....B7 92
Maquon, Knox, Ill....C3 90
Mar, mts., Braz....D3 56
Marabá, Braz....D5 59
Maracá, isl., Braz....B4 59
Maracai, lake, Braz....D4 60
Maracaibo, Ven....A3 60
Maracaibo, lake, Ven....B3 60
Maracaju Braz....C1 56
Maracay, Ven....A4 60
Marādah, Libya....D3 43
Maradi, Niger....D6 45
Marāgheh, Iran....C3 41
Maragogi, Braz....k6 57
Maragogipe, Braz....D3 57
Marais des Cygnes (Osage), riv., Kans....D8 93
Marajó, isl., Braz....C5 60
Maralal, Ken....A6 48
Maramec, Pawnee, Okla....A5 112
Marana, Pima, Ariz....E4 80
Marand, Iran....B2 41
Marandellas, Zimb....A5 49
Maranguape, Braz....B3 57
Maranhão, state, Braz....B1 57
Marano, lagoon, It....D9 18
Maranoa, riv., Austl....C7 51
Marañón, riv., Peru....B2 58
Marans, Fr....D3 14
Maraş (Marash), Tur....D11 31
Mărăşeşti, Rom....C8 22
Marash (Maras), Tur....D11 31
Marathon, Ont., Can....o18 72
Marathon, Monroe, Fla....H5 86
Marathon, Grc....g11 23
Marathon, Buena Vista, Iowa....B3 92
Marathon, Cortland, N.Y....C4 108
Marathon, Brewster, Tex....D1, o13 118
Marathon, Marathon, Wis....D4 124
Marathon, co., Wis....D4 124
Maratua, isl., Indon....E5 35
Maravatío, Mex....n13 63
Marāwah, Libya....F3 31
Marawī, Sud....B3 47
Marbach, F.R.G....E4 11
Marbella, Sp....D3 20
Marble, Madison, Ark....A2 81
Marble, Gunnison, Colo....B3 83
Marble, Itasca, Minn....C5 99
Marble, Cherokee, N.C....f9 109
Marble Bar, Austl....D2 50
Marble Canyon, Coconino, Ariz....A4 80
Marble City, Sequoyah, Okla....B7 112
Marble Cliff, Franklin, Ohio....m10 111
Marble Dale, Litchfield Conn....C3 84
Marbledale, Knox, Tenn....n14 117
Marble Falls, Burnet, Tex....D3 118
Marble Hall, S. Afr....B4 49
Marblehead, Adams, Ill....D2 90
Marblehead, Essex, Mass....B6, f12 97
Marblehead, Ottawa, Ohio....A3 111
Marblehill, Pickens, Ga....B2 87
Marble Hill, Bollinger, Mo....D8 101
Marblemount, Skagit, Wash....A4 122
Marble Mountain, N.S., Can....D8 74
Marble Rock, Floyd, Iowa....B5 92
Marbleton, Que., Can....D6 73
Marbleton, Sublette, Wyo....D2 125
Marburg, F.R.G....C3 17
Marbury, Autauga, Ala....C3 78
Marbury, Charles, Md....C3 85
Marcala, Hond....C4 62
Marcaria, It....D6 18
Marcelin, Sask., Can....E2 70
Marceline, Adams, Ill....C2 90
Marceline, Linn, Mo....B5 101
Marcella, Stone, Ark....B4 81
Marcellus, Cass, Mich....F5 98
Marcellus, cave, Mo.....D6 101
March, Eng....B8 12
Marchand, Man., Can....E3 71
Marchand, Mor....H3 30
Marche, Pulaski, Ark....h10 81
Marche, pol, dist., It....*C4 21
Marche, former prov., Fr....D4 14
Marche-en-Famenne, Bel....D5 15
Marchena, Sp....D3 20
Marchena, isl., Ec....f5 58
Marches, reg., It....C4 21
Marchwell, Sask., Can....G5 70
Marco, Collier, Fla....G5 86
Marco, Greene, Ind....G3 91
Marcola, Lane, Oreg....C4 113
Marcos Juárez, Arg....A4 54
Marcus, Cherokee, Iowa....B2 92
Marcus, Stevens, Wash....A7 122
Marcus Baker, mtn., Alsk....g18 79
Marcus Hook, Delaware, Pa....G11 114
Marcy Colony, Hutchinson, S. Dak....D8 116
Marcy, mtn., N.Y....A7 108
Mardān, Pak....B5 39
Mar de Espanha, Braz....g6 56
Mardela Springs, Wicomico, Md....D6 85
Mar del Plata, Arg....B5 54
Mardin, Tur....D13 31
Marechal Deodoro, Braz....C3, k6 57
Maree, Austl....E6 50
Maree, lake, Scot....C3 13
Mareg, Som....E6 47
Marengo, Sask., Can....F1 70
Marengo, McHenry, Ill....A5 90
Marengo, Crawford, Ind....H5 91
Marengo, Iowa, Iowa....C5 92
Marengo, Morrow, Ohio....B3 111
Marengo, Ashland, Wis....B3 124
Marengo, co., Ala....C2 78
Marengo, cave, Ind....H5 91
Marenisco, Gogebic, Mich....n12 98
Marennes, Fr....E3 14
Maretz, Fr....D3 15
Mareuil-sur-Ourcq, Fr....E3 15
Mareyevka, Sov. Un....C7 29
Marfa, Presidio, Tex....o12 118
Marfrance, Greenbrier, W. Va....C4 123
Marganets, Sov. Un....H10 27
Margaree, N.S., Can....C8 74
Margaree Harbour, N.S., Can....C8 74
Margaret, St. Clair, Ala....B3 78
Margaret, Man., Can....E2 71
Margaret, Foard, Tex....B3 118
Margaretsville, N.S., Can....D4 74
Margaretville, Delaware, N.Y....C6 108
Margarita, isl., Ven....A5 60
Margate, Eng....C9 12
Margate, Broward, Fla....F6 86
Margate City, Atlantic, N.J....E3 106
Margelan, Sov. Un....E8 29
Margerum, Colbert, Ala....A1 78
Marggrabowa, see Olecko, Pol.
Margherita, see Jamame, Som.
Margherita, mtn., Ug., Zaire....A5 48
Marghī, Afg....D13 41
Marghub, mtn., Iran....E8 41
Margie, Koochiching, Minn....B5 99
Margny-lès-Compiègne, Fr....E2 15
Margo, Sask., Can....F4 70
Margrethe, lake, Mich....D6 98
Marguerite, bay, Ant....C6 5
Mari, lake, Sask., Can....B4 70
Maria, Que., Can....A3 74
Maria, isl., Austl....o15 50
Maria, riv., Arg....E2 55
María Chiquita, Pan....k11 62
Mariager, Den....B3 24
Mariager, fjord, Den....B4 24
María Grande, Arg....A5 54
María la Baja, Col....A2 60
Marian, lake, Fla....E5 86
Mariana, is., Pac. O....E8 7
Marianao, Cuba....C2 64
Marianna, Lee, Ark....C5 81
Marianna, Jackson, Fla....B1 86
Marianna, Washington, Pa....*F1 114
Mariano Machado, Ang....D1 48
Marianske Lazne, Czech....D2 26
Mariapolis, Man., Can....E2 71
Marias, pass, Mont....B3 102
Marias, riv., Mont....B4 102
Maria Stein, Mercer, Ohio....B1 111
Maria Van Diemen, cape, N.Z....K14 51
Mariaville, Hancock, Maine....D4 96
Maribel, Pamlico, N.C....B6 109
Maribel, Manitowoc, Wis....h10 124
Maribo, Den....D5 24
Maribor, Yugo....B2 22
Maricá, Braz....h6 56
Maricaban, isl., Phil....p13 35
Maricao, mun., P.R....*B2 65
Maricopa, Pinal, Ariz....E3 80
Maricopa, Kern, Calif....E4 82
Maricopa, co., Ariz....D3 80
Maricourt, Que., Can....f12 73
Marīdī, Sud....E2 47
Marie, lake, Alta., Can....B5 69
Marié, riv., Braz....D4 60
Marie Byrd Land, reg., Ant....B36 5
Mariedamm, Swe....u33 25
Mariefred, Swe....t35 25
Marie-Galante, isl., Guad....R9 65
Mariehamn, Fin....G8 25
Mariembourg, Bel....D4 15
Mariemont, Hamilton, Ohio....o13 111
Marienberg, G.D.R....C8 17
Mariental, Namibia....B2 49
Marienville, Forest, Pa....D3 114
Marie-Reine, Alta., Can....A2 69
Maries, co., Mo....C6 101
Mariestad, Swe....H5 25
Marietta, Cobb, Ga....C2, h7 87
Marietta, Shelby, Ind....F6 91
Marietta, Lac qui Parle, Minn....E2 99
Marietta, Prentiss, Miss....A5 100
Marietta, Washington, Ohio....C4 111
Marietta, Love, Okla....D4 112
Marietta, Lancaster, Pa....F8 114
Marietta, Greenville, S.C....A2 115
Marietta, Whatcom, Wash....A3 122
Marietta East, Cobb, Ga....*C2 87
Marieville, Que., Can....D4 73
Mariinsk, Sov. Un....B11 29
Mariinskiy, Sov. Un....E23 9
Marijampole, Sov. Un....A7 26
Marília, Braz....C3 56
Marín, Sp....A1 20
Marin, co., Calif....C2 82
Marina, Monterey, Calif....*D3 82
Marina de Ravenna, It....E8 18
Marin City, Marin, Calif....*C2 82
Marinduque, prov., Phil....*C6 35
Marine, Madison, Ill....E4 90
Marine City, St. Clair, Mich....F8 98
Marine on St. Croix, Washington, Minn....E6 99
Marinette, Marinette, Wis....C6 124
Marinette, co., Wis....C5 124
Maringa, riv., Zaire....A3 48
Maringouin, Iberville, La....D4 95
Marinha Grande, Port....C1 20
Marino, It....h9 21
Marinovka, Sov. Un....q21 27
Marion, Perry, Ala....C2 78
Marion, Crittenden, Ark....B5 81
Marion, Austl....*G2 51
Marion, Hartford, Conn....C5 84
Marion, Williamson, Ill....F5 90
Marion, Grant, Ind....C6 91
Marion, Linn, Iowa....B6 92
Marion, Marion, Kans....D6 93
Marion, Crittenden, Ky....e9 94
Marion, Union, La....B3 95
Marion, Plymouth, Mass....C6 97
Marion, Osceola, Mich....D5 98
Marion, Lauderdale, Miss....C5 100
Marion, Flathead, Mont....B2 102
Marion, Red Willow, Nebr....D5 103
Marion, Wayne, N.Y....B3 108
Marion, McDowell, N.C....B1, f10 109
Marion, LaMoure, N. Dak....C7 110
Marion, Marion, Ohio....B2 111
Marion, Marion, Oreg....k12 113
Marion, Franklin, Pa....G6 114
Marion, Marion, S.C....C9 115
Marion, Turner, S. Dak....D8 116
Marion, Summit, Utah....C4 119
Marion, Smyth, Va....f10 121
Marion, Waupaca, Wis....D5 124
Marion, co., Ala....A2 78
Marion, co., Ark....A3 81
Marion, co., Fla....C4 86
Marion, co., Ga....D2 87
Marion, co., Ill....E5 90
Marion, co., Ind....E5 91
Marion, co., Iowa....C4 92
Marion, co., Kans....D6 93
Marion, co., Ky....C4 94
Marion, co., Miss....D4 100
Marion, co., Mo....B6 101
Marion, co., Ohio....B2 111
Marion, co., Oreg....C4 113
Marion, co., S.C....C9 115
Marion co., Tenn....D8 117
Marion, co., Tex....C5 118
Marion, co., W. Va....B4 123
Marion, lake, S.C....E7 115
Marion Center, Indiana, Pa....E3 114
Marion Junction, Dallas, Ala....B2 78
Marion Station, Somerset, Md....D6 85
Marionville, Lawrence, Mo....D4 101
Mariposa, Mariposa, Calif....D4 82
Mariposa, co., Calif....D3 82
Mariposas, Chile....B2 54
Marismas, marshes, Sp....D2 20
Marissa, St. Clair, Ill....E4 90
Mariscal Estigarribia, Par....D3 55
Maritime Alps, mts., Fr., It....E7 14
Maritsa, riv., Bul....D7 22
Marivales, Phil....o13 35
Marīvān, Iran....D3 41
Mark, Putnam, Ill....B4 90
Marka, Som....E5 47
Markala, Mali....D3 45
Markaryd, Swe....I5 25
Markdale, Ont., Can....C4 72
Marked Tree, Poinsett, Ark....B5 101
Markerwaard Polder, reg., Neth....B5 15
Markesan, Green Lake, Wis....E5 124
Market Drayton, Eng....B5 12
Market Harborough, Eng....B7 12
Markethill, N. Ire....C5 11
Market Rasen, Eng....A7 12
Market Weighton, Eng....G8 13
Markham, Ont., Can....D5, k15 72
Markham, Cook, Ill....k9 90
Markham, Matagorda, Tex....E4 118
Markham, Fauquier, Va....B5 121
Markham, Grays Harbor, Wash....C2 122
Markham, mtn., Ant....A29 5
Marki, Pol....k14 26
Markinch, Sask., Can....G3 70
Markinch, Scot....*D5 13
Markkleeberg, G.D.R....B7 17
Markland, Switzerland, Ind....G8 91
Markle, Huntington and Wells, Ind....C7 91
Markleeville, Alpine, Calif....C4 82
Markleville, Madison, Ind....E6 91
Markleysburg, Fayette, Pa....G3 114
Markneukirchen, G.D.R....C7 17
Markopoulon, Grc....h11 23
Markovka, Sov. Un....G12 27
Markovo, Sov. Un....C20 28
Markovo, Sov. Un....C6 4
Markranstädt, G.D.R....B7 17
Marks, Quitman, Miss....A3 100
Marksboro, Warren, N.J....B3 106
Markstay, Ont., Can....*p19 72
Marksville, Avoyelles, La....C3 95
Marktheidenfeld, F.R.G....D4 17
Marktredwitz, F.R.G....D7 17
Markville, Pine, Minn....D6 99
Marl, F.R.G....*C3 16
Marland, Noble, Okla....A4 112
Marlbank, Ont., Can....C7 72
Marlboro, Alta., Can....C2 69
Marlboro, Cheshire, N.H....E2 105
Marlboro, Monmouth, N.J....C4 106
Marlboro, Ulster, N.Y....D6 108
Marlboro, Windham, Vt....F3 120
Marlboro, Chesterfield, Va....n17 121
Marlboro, co., S.C....B8 115
Marlborough, Hartford, Conn....C7 84
Marlborough, Eng....C6 12
Marlborough, Guy....A3 59
Marlborough, Middlesex, Mass....B4, g9 97
Marle, Fr....E3 15
Marlene Village, Washington, Oreg....*B3 113
Marlette Sanilac, Mich....E7 98
Marley, Anne Arundel, Md....B4 85
Marlin, Falls, Tex....D4 118
Marlin (Krupp), Grant, Wash....B7 122
Marlinton, Pocahontas, W. Va....C4 123
Marlow, Baldwin, Ala....E2 78
Marlow, Effingham, Ga....D5 87
Marlow, G.D.R....D6 24
Marlow, Cheshire, N.H....D2 105
Marlow, Stephens, Okla....C4 112
Marlowe, Berkeley, W. Va....B7 123
Marlton, Burlington, N.J....D3 106
Marly-le-Roi, Fr....g9 14
Marmaduke, Greene, Ark....A5 81
Marmagoa, India....E5 39
Marmande, Fr....E4 14
Marmara, isl., Tur....B6 23
Marmara, sea, Tur....B7 23
Marmaris, Tur....D7 23
Marmarth, Slope, N. Dak....C2 110
Mar Menor, lagoon, Sp....D5 20
Marmet, Kanawha, W. Va....C3, m12 123
Marmolada, mtn., It....C7 18
Marmora, Ont., Can....C7 72
Marmora, Cape May, N.J....E3 106
Marmora, peak, It....D2 21
Marnay, Fr....B1 18
Marne, F.R.G....E3 24
Marne, Cass, Iowa....C2 92
Marne, Ottawa, Mich....E5 98
Marne, canal, Fr....F4 15
Marne, dept., Fr....F4 15
Marne, riv., Fr....C5 14
Marne au Rhin, canal, Fr....F6 15
Maro, reef, Haw....k13 89
Maroa, Macon, Ill....C5 90
Maroantsetra, Mad....g9 49
Maromokotro, mtn., Mad....f9 49
Maroni, riv., Sur....B4 60
Maroochydore-Mooloolaba, Austl....C9 51
Maroua, Cam....C2 46
Marovoay, Mad....g9 49
Marpi, mtn., Saipan....52
Marpi, pt., Saipan....52
Marpo, pt., Tinian....52
Marquam, Clackamas, Oreg....B4, h12 113
Marquand, Madison, Mo....D7 101
Marquesas, is., Fr. Polynesia....G13 7
Marquesas, keys, Fla....H4 86
Marquês de Valença, Braz....C4, h6 56
Marquette, Man., Can....D3 71
Marquette, Clayton, Iowa....A6 92
Marquette, McPherson, Kans....D6 93
Marquette, Marquette, Mich....B3 98
Marquette, Hamilton, Nebr....D8 103
Marquette, co., Mich....B3 98
Marquette, co., Wis....E4 124
Marquette Heights, Tazewell, Ill....*C4 90
Marquez, Leon, Tex....D4 118
Marquis, Sask., Can....G3 70
Marquise, Fr....D9 12
Marrah, mtn., Sud....C1 47
Marrakech, Mor....C3 44, I3 30
Marrero, Jefferson, La....k11 95
Marrickville, Austl....*F8 51
Marriott, Weber, Utah....*B3 119
Marromeu, Moz....A6 49
Marroqui, pt., Sp....D3 20
Marrowbone, Cumberland, Ky....D4 94
Marrtown, Wood, W. Va....B3 123

Medicine, creek, Mo....A4 101
Medicine, creek, Nebr....D5 103
Medicine Bow, Carbon, Wyo....E6 125
Medicine Bow, mts., Colo., Wyo....E6 125
Medicine Bow, peak, Wyo....E6 125
Medicine Bow, riv., Wyo....E6 125
Medicine Hat, Alta., Can.D5, g8 69
Medicine Lake, Sheridan, Mont....B12 102
Medicine Lodge, Barber, Kans....E5 93
Medicine Lodge, riv., Kans....E5 93
Medicine Park, Comanche, Okla....C3 112
Medill, Clark, Mo....A6 101
Medimont, Kootenai, Idaho .B2 89
Medina, Orleans, N.Y....B2 108
Medina, Stutsman, N. Dak..C6 110
Medina, Medina, Ohio....A4 111
Medina (Al Madīnah), Sau. Ar....E7 43
Medina, Gibson, Tenn....B3 117
Medina, Bandera, Tex....F3 118
Medina, King, Wash....e11 122
Medina, co., Ohio....A4 111
Medina, co., Tex....E3 118
Medina, riv., Tex....k7 118
Medina del Campo, Sp....B3 20
Medina de Rioseco, Sp....B3 20
Medinah, Du Page, Ill....*B5 90
Medina Sidonia, Sp....D3 20
Mediterranean, sea....H10 8
Medium, lake, Iowa....A3 92
Medjerda, riv., Tun.; Alg....F11 30
Medjez-el-Bab, Tun....F11 30
Medley, Dade, Fla....*G6 86
Mednogorsk, Sov. Un....C5 29
Medomak, Lincoln, Maine...D3 96
Medon, Madison, Tenn....B3 117
Medora, Man., Can....E1 71
Medora, Macoupin, Ill....D3 90
Medora, Jackson, Ind....G5 91
Medora, Reno, Kans....D6 93
Medora, Billings, N. Dak....C2 110
Médouneu, Gabon....E2 46
Medstead, Sask., Can....D1 70
Meductic, N.B., Can....D2 74
Meduxnekeag, riv., Maine....B5 96
Medveditsa, riv., Sov. Un....C2 29
Medvedovskaya, Sov. Un...F16 9
Medvezhi, is., Sov. Un....B19 28
Medvezhyegorsk, Sov. Un..F16 25
Medway, Penobscot, Maine..C4 96
Medway, Norfolk, Mass.B5, h10 97
Medway, riv., N.S., Can....E5 74
Medzhibozh, Sov. Un....G6 27
Meehan, Lauderdale, Miss...C5 100
Meekatharra, Austl....E2 50
Meeker, Rio Blanco, Colo...A3 83
Meeker, Lincoln, Okla....B5 112
Meeker, co., Minn....E4 99
Meelpaeg, lake, Newf., Can....E3 75
Meeme, Manitowoc, Wis....B6 124
Meerane, G.D.R....C7 17
Meerle, Bel....C4 15
Meerut, India....C6 40
Meerut Cantonment, India.*C6 40
Meeteetse, Park, Wyo....B4 125
Meeting, lake, Sask., Can....D2 70
Meeting Creek, Alta., Can...C4 69
Meeyomoot, lake, Sask., Can....D3 70
Megali, canal, Grc....g10 23
Megalopolis, Grc....D4 23
Mégantic, co., Que., Can....C6 73
Mégantic, lake, Que., Can....D7 73
Mégantic, mtn., Que., Can....D6 73
Megara, Grc....C4, g10 23
Megargel, Monroe, Ala....D2 78
Megargel, Archer, Tex....C3 118
Meggett, Charleston, S.C....F7, k11 115
Meghalaya, state, India....C9 39
Mehan, Payne, Okla....A5 112
Mehar, Pak....C4 39
Mehekar, India....G6 40
Meherpur, Bngl....F12 40
Meherrin, Lunenburg, Va....C4 121
Meherrin, riv., Va....D4 121
Mehlville, St. Louis, Mo....f13 101
Mehoopany, Wyoming, Pa..C9 114
Mehsāna, India....F4 40
Mehun-sur-Yèvre, Fr....D5 14
Meiganga, Cam....D2 46
Meighen, isl., N.W. Ter., Can.k32 67
Meigs, Thomas and Mitchell, Ga....F2 87
Meigs, co., Ohio....C3 111
Meigs, co., Tenn....D9 117
Meihsien, China....G8 34
Meiktila, Bur....D10 39
Meilap, Ponape.... 52
Meilen, Switz....*B6 19
Meilleur, lake, Que., Can....A4 74
Meiners Oaks, Ventura, Calif....*E4 82
Meiningen, G.D.R....C5 17
Meiringen, Switz....C5 19
Meissen, G.D.R....B8 17
Meitan, China....K2 36
Mejicana, mtn., Arg....E2 55
Mejicanos, Sal....*D3 62
Mejillones, Chile....D1 55
Mekambo, Gabon....E2 46
Mekdela, Eth....C4 47
Mekele, Eth....C4 47
Mékhé, Sen....C1 45
Mekhtar, Pak....B2 40
Mekinac, lake, Que., Can....B5 75
Mekinock, Grand Forks, N. Dak....A8 110
Meknès, Mor....C3 44, H4 30
Mekong, riv., Asia...E6 38, B10 39
Mekoryuk, Alsk....C6 79
Melaka (Malacca), Mala....K5 38
Melaka, state, Mala....K5 38
Melambes, Grc....E5 23
Melaval, Sask., Can....H2 70
Melba, Canyon, Idaho....F2 89
Melber, McCracken, Ky....f9 94
Melbern, Williams, Ohio....A1 111
Melbeta, Scotts Bluff, Nebr..C2 103
Melbourne, Izard, Ark....A4 81
Melbourne, Austl....H5 51
Melbourne, Ont., Can....E3 72
Melbourne, Brevard, Fla....D6 86
Melbourne, Marshall, Iowa..C4 92
Melbourne, Campbell, Ky..h14 94
Melbourne, Harrison, Mo....A4 101
Melbourne Beach, Brevard, Fla....D6 86
Melcher, Marion, Iowa....C4 92
Meldorf, F.R.G....D3 24
Meldrim, Effingham, Ga....D5 87
Meldrum Bay, Ont., Can....B1 72
Meleb, Man., Can....D3 71
Melekeiok, Palau.... 52
Melekess, Sov. Un....E18 9
Melenki, Sov. Un....D13 27
Mélèzes, riv., Que., Can....g12 73
Melfi, Chad....C3 46
Melfi, It....D5 21
Melfort, Sask., Can....E3 70
Melilla, Sp. dep., Afr....B4 44
Melipilla, Chile....A2 54
Melita, Man., Can....E1 71
Melito di Porto Salvo, It....F5 21
Melitopol, Sov. Un....H10 27
Mella, riv., It....D6 18
Melle, Fr....D3 14
Melle, F.R.G....A3 17
Mellen, Ashland, Wis....B3 124
Mellette, Spink, S. Dak....B7 116
Mellette, co., S. Dak....D4 116
Mellit, Sud....C2 47
Mellor, glacier, Ant....B19 5
Mellott, Fountain, Ind....D3 91
Mellow Valley, Clay, Ala....B4 78
Mellrichstadt, F.R.G....C5 17
Mellum, isl., F.R.G....E2 24
Mellwood, Phillips, Ark....C5 81
Melmore, Seneca, Ohio....A2 111
Melnik, Czech....n18 26
Melo, Ur....E2 56
Melocheville, Que., Can....q19 73
Melouprey, Camb....F6 38
Melrose, N.B., Can....C6 74
Melrose, N.S., Can....D7 74
Melrose, Hartford, Conn....B6 84
Melrose, Alachua, Fla....C4 86
Melrose, Monroe, Iowa....D4 92
Melrose, Natchitoches, La...C3 95
Melrose, Middlesex, Mass....B5, g11 97
Melrose, Stearns, Minn....E4 99
Melrose, Silver Bow, Mont...E4 102
Melrose, Curry, N. Mex....C6 107
Melrose, Paulding, Ohio....A1 111
Melrose, Douglas, Oreg....D3 113
Melrose, Scot....*E6 13
Melrose, Jackson, Wis....D2 124
Melrose Park, Broward, Fla.*F6 86
Melrose Park, Cook, Ill....F2 90
Melrose Park, Montgomery, Pa....*G11 114
Mels, Switz....B7 19
Melsetter, Zimb....A5 49
Melstone, Musselshell, Mont.D9 102
Melstrand, Alger, Mich....B4 98
Melsungen, F.R.G....B4 17
Melton Hill Lake, res., Tenn....D9, n13 117
Melton Mowbray, Eng....B7 12
Melun, Fr....C5 14
Melvaig, Scot....C3 13
Melvern, Osage, Kans....D8 93
Melville, Sask., Can....G4 70
Melville, St. Landry, La....D4 95
Melville, Sweet Grass, Mont.D7 102
Melville, bay, Grnld....B21 4
Melville, cape, Austl....B7 50
Melville, hills, N.W. Ter., Can.C8 66
Melville, isl., Austl....B5 50
Melville, isl., N.W. Ter., Can....m29 67
Melville, lake, Newf., Can....B2 75
Melville, pen., N.W. Ter., Can....C16 66
Melvin, Choctaw, Ala....D1 78
Melvin, Ford, Ill....C5 90
Melvin, Osceola, Iowa....A2 92
Melvin, Floyd, Ky....C7 94
Melvin, McCulloch, Tex....D3 118
Melvin, lake, Ire....C3 11
Melvindale, Wayne, Mich....A7 98
Melvine, Bledsoe, Tenn....D8 117
Melvin Village, Carroll, N.H....C4 105
Melykut, Hung....B4 22
Memba, Moz....D7 48
Memel, see Klaipeda, Sov. Un.
Memmingen, F.R.G....E5 16
Memphis, Manatee, Fla....p10 86
Memphis, Clark, Ind....H6 91
Memphis, Macomb and St. Clair, Mich....F8 98
Memphis, Scotland, Mo....A5 101
Memphis, Saunders, Nebr...g12 103
Memphis, Shelby, Tenn..B1, e9 117
Memphis, Hall, Tex....B2 118
Memphis, ruins, Eg....D6 43
Memphremagog, lake, Que., Can., Vt....B4 120
Memramcook, N.B., Can....C5 74
Memramcook East, N.B., Can....*C5 74
Mena, Polk, Ark....C1 81
Menahga, Wadena, Minn....D3 99
Menai, strait, Wales....A3 12
Ménaka, Mali....C5 45
Menam, see Chao Phraya, riv., Thai.
Menan, Jefferson, Idaho....F7 89
Menands, Albany, N.Y....C7 108
Menard, Menard, Tex....D3 118
Menard, co., Ill....C4 90
Menard, co., Tex....D3 118
Menasha, Winnebago, Wis....D5, h9 124
Mendawi, riv., Indon....F4 35
Mende, Fr....E5 14
Menden, F.R.G....B2 17
Mendenhall, Simpson, Miss..D4 100
Menderes (Scamander), riv., Tur....C6 23
Mendes, Tattnall, Ga....F5 87
Méndez, Mex....E5 63
Mendham, Sask., Can....G1 70
Mendham, Morris, N.J....B3 106
Mendi, Eth....D4 47
Mendip, hills, Eng....C5 12
Mendocino, Mendocino, Calif....C2 82
Mendocino, co., Calif....C2 82
Mendon, Adams, Ill....C2 90
Mendon, Worcester, Mass....h9 97
Mendon, St. Joseph, Mich....F5 98
Mendon, Chariton, Mo....B4 101
Mendon, Mercer, Ohio....B1 111
Mendon, Cache, Utah....B4 119
Mendon, Rutland, Vt....D3 120
Mendota, Fresno, Calif....D3 82
Mendota, La Salle, Ill....B4 90
Mendota, lake, Wis....E4 124
Mendota Heights, Dakota, Minn....*F5 99
Mendoza, Arg....A3 54
Mendoza, prov., Arg....A3 54
Mendoza, Pan....k11 62
Mendrisio, Switz....E6 19
Menemen, Tur....C6 23
Menen, Bel....D3 15
Menfi, It....F4 21
Mengcheng, China....H7 36
Menggala, Indon....F2 35
Menglien, China....G4 34
Mengtzu, China....G5 34
Menifee, Conway, Ark....B3 81
Menifee, co., Ky....C6 94
Menihek, lakes, Newf., Can....g8 75
Menindee, Austl....F4 51
Menindee, lake, Austl....F4 51
Menlo, Chattooga, Ga....B1 87
Menlo, Guthrie, Iowa....C3 92
Menlo, Thomas, Kans....C3 93
Menlo, Pacific, Wash....C2 122
Menlo Park, San Mateo, Calif....k8 82
Menlo Park Terrace, Middlesex, N.J....*B4 106
Menno, Hutchinson, S. Dak.D8 116
Meno, Major, Okla....A3 112
Menoken, Burleigh, N. Dak..C5 110
Menola, Hertford, N.C....A5 109
Menominee, Menominee, Mich....C3 98
Menominee, co., Mich....C3 98
Menominee, co., Wis....C5 124
Menominee, Indian res., Wis...C5 124
Menominee, riv., Mich., Wis....C3 92, C6 124
Menomonee, riv., Wis....m11 124
Menomonee Falls, Waukesha, Wis....E5, m11 124
Menomonie, Dunn, Wis....D2 124
Menongue, Ang....D2 48
Menorca, isl., Sp....B7 20
Mentana, It....g9 21
Mentawai, is., Indon....F1 35
Mentmore, McKinley, N. Mex....B1 107
Menton, Fr....F7 14
Mentone, DeKalb, Ala....A4 78
Mentone, San Bernardino, Calif....E5 82
Mentone, Kosciusko, Ind....B5 91
Mentone, Loving, Tex..D1, o13 118
Mentor, Campbell, Ky....k14 94
Mentor, Polk, Minn....C2 99
Mentor, Lake, Ohio....A4 111
Mentor, Blount, Tenn....E11 117
Mentor Headlands, Lake, Ohio....*A4 111
Mentor-on-the-Lake, Lake, Ohio....A4 111
Menzel Bourguiba, Tun....B6 44
Menzies, mtn., Ant....B19 5
Menziken, Switz....B5 19
Meoqui, Mex....B3 63
Meota, Sask., Can....D1 70
Meppel, Neth....B6 15
Meppen, F.R.G....B3 16
Meqa, Eth....E4 47
Mequellarë, Alb....B3 23
Mequon, Ozaukee, Wis.E6, m12 124
Merabello, gulf, Grc....E5 23
Meramec, caverns, Mo....C6 101
Meramec, riv., Mo....C7 101
Merano, It....A3 21
Merasheen, Newf., Can....E4 75
Merasheen, isl., Newf., Can....E4 75
Merauke, Indon....G10 35
Meraux, St. Bernard, La....k12 95
Mercāra, India....F6 39
Merced, Merced, Calif....D3 82
Merced, co., Calif....D3 82
Merced, riv., Calif....D3 82
Mercedes, Arg....A3 54
Mercedes, Arg....A5, g7 54
Mercedes, Arg....E4 55
Mercedes, Hidalgo, Tex....F4 118
Mercedes, Ur....E1 56
Mercer, Somerset, Maine....D3 96
Mercer, Mercer, Mo....A4 101
Mercer, McLean, N. Dak....B5 110
Mercer, Mercer, Ohio....B1 111
Mercer, Mercer, Pa....D1 114
Mercer, Madison, Tenn....B2 117
Mercer, Iron, Wis....B3 124
Mercer, co., Ill....B3 90
Mercer, co., Ky....C5 94
Mercer, co., Mo....A4 101
Mercer, co., N.J....C3 106
Mercer, co., N. Dak....B4 110
Mercer, co., Ohio....B1 111
Mercer, co., Pa....D1 114
Mercer, co., W. Va....D3 123
Mercer, isl., Wash....e11 122
Mercer Island, King, Wash....B3, e11 122
Mercersburg, Franklin, Pa...G6 114
Mercerville, Mercer, N.J....C3 106
Mercês, Braz....g6 56
Merchantville, Camden, N.J....*D2 106
Mercier, Que., Can....D4, q19 73
Mercier, Brown, Kans....C8 93
Mercoal, Alta., Can....C2 69
Mercury, McCulloch, Tex....D3 118
Mercury, bay, N.Z....L15 51
Mercy, cape, N.W. Ter., Can.D20 67
Merdjayoun, Leb....F1 31
Meredith, Pitkin, Colo....B4 83
Meredith, Belknap, N.H....C3 105
Meredith, King, Wash....D2 122
Meredith, lake, Colo....C7 83
Meredith Center, Belknap, N.H....C3 105
Meredosia, Morgan, Ill....D3 90
Merefa, Sov. Un....G11 31
Mergui, Bur....F10 39
Mergui, arch., Bur....F10 39
Mérida, Sask., Can....F1 70
Mérida, Mex....C7 63
Mérida, Sp....C2 20
Mérida, Ven....B3 60
Mérida, state, Ven....B3 60
Meriden, New Haven, Conn.C5 84
Meriden, Cherokee, Iowa....B2 92
Meriden, Jefferson, Kans....C8, k14 93
Meriden, Steele, Minn....F5 99
Meriden, Sullivan, N.H....C2 105
Meriden, Laramie, Wyo....E8 125
Meridian, McIntosh, Ga....E5 87
Meridian, Ada, Idaho....F2 89
Meridian, Lauderdale, Miss.C5 100
Meridian, Cayuga, N.Y....B4 108
Meridian, Logan, Okla....B4 112
Meridian, Butler, Pa....*E2 114
Meridian, Bosque, Tex....D4 118
Meridian Hills, Marion, Ind....*E5 91
Meridiano, Arg....B4 54
Meridianville, Madison, Ala.A3 78
Mérignac, Fr....E3 14
Merigold, Bolivar, Miss....B3 100
Merigomish, N.S., Can....D7 74
Merino, Logan, Colo....A7 83
Merioneth, co., Wales....B4 11
Merion Park, Montgomery, Pa....*F11 114
Merion Station, Montgomery, Pa....*F11 114
Merir, salt lake, Alg....C6 44
Meriwether, co., Ga....C2 87
Merizo, Guam.... 52
Merkarvia, Fin....G9 25
Merkel, Taylor, Tex....C2 118
Merkine, Sov. Un....A8 26
Merkis, riv., Sov. Un....D5 27
Merksem, Bel....C4 15
Merksplas, Bel....C4 15
Merlin, Ont., Can....E2 72
Merlin, Josephine, Oreg....E3 113
Merlo, Arg....g7 54
Mermentau, Acadia, La....D3 95
Mermentau, riv., La....E2 95
Mern, Den....C6 24
Merna, Custer, Nebr....C6 103
Merom, Sullivan, Ind....F2 91
Meron, mtn., Isr....A7 32
Merriam, Johnson, Kans....k6 93
Merrick, Nassau, N.Y....G2 84
Merrick, co., Nebr....C7 103
Merrick, mtn., Scot....E4 13
Merrickville, Ont., Can....C9 72
Merricourt, Dickey, N. Dak..C7 110
Merrifield, Crow Wings, Minn....D4 99
Merrifield, Fairfax, Va....*B5 121
Merrill, Plymouth, Iowa....B1 92
Merrill, Saginaw, Mich....E6 98
Merrill, George, Miss....E5 100
Merrill, Klamath, Oreg....E5 113
Merrill, Lincoln, Wis....C4 124
Merrillan, Jackson, Wis....D3 124
Merrillville, Lake, Ind....B3 91
Merrimac, Taylor, Ky....C4 94
Merrimac, Essex, Mass....A5 97
Merrimac, Sauk, Wis....E4 124
Merrimack, Hillsboro, N.H..E4 105
Merrimack, co., N.H....D3 101
Merrimack, riv., Mass., N.H...A5 97
Merrimacport, Essex, Mass..A6 97
Merriman, Cherry, Nebr....B4 103
Merrimon, Carteret, N.C....C6 109
Merrionette Park, Cook, Ill. *B6 90
Merritt, B.C., Can....D7 68
Merritt, Pamlico, N.C....B6 109
Merritt Island, Brevard, Fla .D6 86
Merritt-Peck Colonies, Fresno, Calif....*D4 82
Merriwa, Austl....F8 51
Merriweather, Ontonagon, Mich....m12 98
Mer Rouge, Morehouse, La..B4 95
Merrow, Tolland, Conn....B7 84
Merry Hills, Bertie, N.C....A6 109
Merrymeeting, lake, N.H....D4 105
Merry Oaks, Chatham, N.C..B3 109
Merryville, Beauregard, La..D2 95
Mersa Fatma, Eth....B5 47
Merseburg, G.D.R....B6 17
Mers-el-Kebir, Alg....C6 30
Mersey, riv., Eng....A5 12
Mershon, Pierce, Ga....E4 87
Mersin, Tur....D10 31
Mersing, Mala....K5 38
Merthyr Tydfil, Wales....C4 12
Merti, Ken....A6 48
Mértola, Port....D2 20
Merton, Waukesha, Wis....m11 124
Mertz, glacier, Ant....C27 5
Mertzon, Irion, Tex....D2 118
Méru, Fr....C5 14
Meru, Ken....A6 48
Meru, mtn., Tan....B6 48
Merundung, isl., Indon....K8 38
Mervelier, Switz....B4 19
Merville, Fr....D2 15
Mervin, Sask., Can....D1 70
Merwin, Bates, Mo....C3 101
Méry [-sur-Seine], Fr....F3 15
Merzifon, Tur....B10 31
Merzig, F.R.G....E6 15
Mesa, Maricopa, Ariz....D4, m9 80
Mesa, Mesa, Colo....B2 83
Mesa, Adams, Idaho....E2 89
Mesa, co., Colo....B2 83
Mesa, mts., Colo....D3 83
Mesa, peak, Colo....D4 83
Mesabi, iron range, Minn....C5 99
Mesa De Maya, plat., Colo....D7 83
Mesagne, It....D6 21
Mesa Verde, nat. park, Colo....D2 83
Mesa Verde, plat., Colo....D2 83
Mescalero, Otero, N. Mex...D4 107
Mescalero, Indian res., N. Mex.D4 107
Meschede, F.R.G....B3 17
Mesegon, isl., Truk.... 52
Mesena, Warren, Ga....C4 87
Meservey, Cerro Gordo, Iowa....B4 92
Mesewa, see Massawa, Eth.
Meshcherskoye, Sov. Un....n17 27
Meshchovsk, Sov. Un....D10 27
Meshed, see Mashhad, Iran
Meshkovskaya, Sov. Un....G13 27
Meshomasic, mtn., Conn....C6 84
Meshoppen, Wyoming, Pa...C9 114
Mesic, Pamlico, N.C....B6 109
Mesick, Wexford, Mich....D5 98
Mesilinka, riv., B.C., Can....A5 68
Mesilla, Dona Ana, N. Mex..E3 107
Mesita, Costilla, Colo....D5 83
Mesita, Valencia, N. Mex....C2 107
Meskéné, Syr....D12 31
Mesocco, Switz....D7 19
Mesologion, Grc....C3 23
Mesquita, Braz....*C4 56
Mesquite, Clark, Nev....G7 104
Mesquite, Dona Ana, N. Mex....E3 107
Mesquite, Dallas, Tex....n10 118
Messalonskee, lake, Maine....D3 96
Messen, Switz....B3 19
Messenia (Messinia), prov., Grc....*D4 23
Messex, Washington, Colo...A7 83
Messina, It....E5 21
Messina, S. Afr....B5 49
Messina, strait, It....E5 21
Messini, Grc....D3 23
Messini, gulf, Grc....D4 23
Messinia (Messenia), prov., Grc....*D4 23
Messkirch, F.R.G....B5 18
Mesta, riv., Bul....E6 22
Mestre, It....B4 21
Mesudiye, Tur....B11 31
Meta, Osage, Mo....C5 101
Meta, dept., Col....C3 60
Meta, pond, Newf., Can....D4 75
Meta, riv., Ven....B4 60
Métabetchouan, Que., Can..A6 73
Métabetchouan, riv., Que., Can...A5 73
Metairie, Jefferson, La....k11 95
Metaline, Pend Oreille, Wash....A8 122
Metaline Falls, Pend Oreille, Wash....A8 122
Metalton, Carroll, Ark....A2 81
Metamora, Woodford, Ill....C4 90
Metamora, Franklin, Ind....F7 91
Metamora, Lapeer, Mich....F9 98
Metamora, Fulton, Ohio....A2 111
Metán, Arg....E3 55
Metangula, Moz....D5 48
Metapán, Sal....C3 62
Metaponto, It....D6 21
Metarica, Moz....D6 48
Métascouac, lake, Que., Can....B6 73
Metasville, Wilkes, Ga....C4 87
Metcalf, Thomas, Ga....F3 87
Metcalf, Edgar, Ill....D6 90
Metcalfe, Ont., Can....B9 72
Metcalfe, Washington, Miss..B2 100
Metcalfe, co., Ky....D4 94
Metchosin, B.C., Can....h12 68
Metedeconk, riv., N.J....C4 106
Meteghan, N.S., Can....E3 74
Meteghan River, N.S., Can....E3 74
Meteghan Station, N.S., Can.E3 74
Metema, Eth....C4 47
Meteor, crater, Ariz....C4 80
Methoni, Grc....D3 23
Methow, Okanogan, Wash...A5 122
Methuen, Essex, Mass....A5 97
Metiskow, Alta., Can....C5 69
Metković, Yugo....D3 22
Metlakatla, Alsk....D13, n14 79
Meto, bayou, Ark....C4 81
Metolius, Jefferson, Oreg....C5 113
Metolius, bench, Oreg....C5 113
Metonga, lake, Wis....C4 124
Metropolis, Massac, Ill....F5 90
Metropolitan, Dickinson, Mich....C3 98
Metsovon, Grc....C3 23
Mettawee, riv., Vt....E2 120
Metten, F.R.G....E7 17
Metter, Candler, Ga....D4 87
Mettet, Bel....D4 15
Mettingen, F.R.G....A2 17
Mettmann, F.R.G....B1 17
Metuchen, Middlesex, N.J...B4 106
Metulla, Isr....A7 32
Metz, Fr....C7 14
Metz, Steuben, Ind....A8 91
Metz, Presque Isle, Mich....C7 98
Metz, Vernon, Mo....C3 101
Metzeral, Fr....A3 18
Metzger, Washington, Oreg. (part of Tigard)....h12 113
Meudon, Fr....g9 14
Meulaboh, Indon....J2 38
Meung [-sur-Loire], Fr....D4 14
Meureudoe, Indon....J2 38
Meurthe, riv., Fr....F6 15
Meurthe-et-Moselle, dept., Fr....F6 15
Meuse, dept., Fr....F5 15
Meuse, hills, Fr....C6 14
Meuse, riv., Bel., Fr....C6 14, D5 15, A1 18
Meuselwitz, G.D.R....B7 17
Mew, isl., Ire....C6 11
Mexcala, riv., Mex....n12 63
Mexhoma, Cimarron, Okla..D1 112
Mexia, Monroe, Ala....D2 78
Mexia, Limestone, Tex....D4 118
Mexicali, Mex....A1 63
Mexican Hat, San Juan, Utah....*F6 119
Mexican Springs, McKinley, N. Mex....B1 107
Mexico, Miami, Ind....C5 91
Mexico, Crittenden, Ky....e9 94
Mexico, Oxford, Maine....D2 96
Mexico, Audrain, Mo....B6 101
Mexico, Oswego, N.Y....B4 108
Mexico, Juniata, Pa....E7 114
Mexico, country, N.A...G10 61, 63
Mexico, state, Mex....D5, n14 63
Mexico, gulf, N.A....G12 61
Mexico City, Mex....D5 63
Meyādīn, Syr....E13 31
Meydani, cape, Iran....I9 41
Meyers Chuck, Alsk....n23 79
Meyersdale, Somerset, Pa...G3 114
Meymaneh, Afg....D12 41
Meyronne, Sask., Can....H2 70
Mèze, Fr....F5 14
Mezen, Sov. Un....B17 9
Mézenc, mtn., Fr....E6 14
Mezenskaya, bay, Sov. Un....B17 9
Mezhdurechenskij, Sov. Un..B7 29
Meziadin, lake, B.C., Can....A3 68
Mézières, Fr....C6 14
Mézières, Switz....C2 19
Mezokovesd, Hung....B5 22
Mezotur, Hung....B5 22
Mezotur, Hung....B5 22
Mezquital, Mex....C4 63
Mezzana, It....C6 18
Mezzolombardo, It....C7 18
Mga, Sov. Un....s32 25
Mga, riv., Sov. Un....s32 25
Mglin, Sov. Un....E9 27
Mhor, lake, Scot....C4 13
Mhòr, mtn., Scot....C1 13
Mhow, India....F5 40
Miahuatlán, Mex....D5 63
Miajadas, Sp....C3 20
Miājlar, India....D3 40
Miami, Gila, Ariz....D5 80
Miami, Man., Can....E2 71
Miami, Dade, Fla....G6, s13 86
Miami, Miami, Ind....C5 91
Miami, Saline, Mo....B4 101
Miami, Colfax, N. Mex....A5 107
Miami, Ottawa, Okla....A7 112
Miami, Zimb....A4 49
Miami, Roberts, Tex....B2 118
Miami, Kanawha, W. Va...m13 123
Miami, co., Ind....C5 91
Miami, co., Kans....D9 93
Miami, co., Ohio....B1 111
Miami, canal, Fla....F6 86
Miami Beach, Dade, Fla....G6, s13 86
Miamisburg, Montgomery, Ohio....C1 111
Miami Shores, Dade, Fla....G6, s13 86
Miami Shores, Montgomery, Ohio....*C1 111
Miami Springs, Dade, Fla....G6, s13 86
Miamitown, Hamilton, Ohio....o12 111
Miāndasht, Iran....C8 41
Miāndowāb, Iran....C3 41
Miandrivazo, Mad....g9 49
Miāneh, Iran....C3 41
Miān Kāleh, pen., Iran....C6 41
Mianus, res., Conn....E2 84
Miānwāli, Pak....A3 40
Miaoli, Taiwan....*G9 34
Miarinarivo, Mad....g9 49
Miass, Sov. Un....C6 29
Miass, riv., Sov. Un....B6 29
Miasteczko Slaskie, Pol....f9 26
Miastko, Pol....A4 26
Mica, Spokane, Wash....g14 122
Mica, mtn., Ariz....E5 80
Micanopy, Alachua, Fla....C4 86
Micay, Col....C2 60
Micco, Brevard, Fla....E6 86
Miccosukee, Leon, Fla....B2 86
Miccosukee, lake, Fla....B2 86
Michael, lake, Newf., Can....A2 75
Michalovce, Czech....D6 26
Michalow, Pol....k13 26
Michaud, pt., N.S., Can....D9 74
Michaudville, Que., Can...*D4 73
Michel, B.C., Can....E10 68
Michelson, mtn., Alsk....B11 79
Michendorf, G.D.R....A8 17
Michiana Shores, La Porte, Ind....*A4 91
Michichi, Alta., Can....D4 69
Michie, McNairy, Tenn....B3 117
Michigamme, Marquette, Mich....B2 98
Michigamme, lake, Mich....B2 98
Michigan, Nelson, N. Dak....A7 110
Michigan, state, U.S....A10 77, 98
Michigan, creek, Colo....A4 83
Michigan, isl., Wis....B3 124
Michigan, lake, U.S....B10 77
Michigan, prairie, Wash....C7 122
Michigan Center, Jackson, Mich....F6 98
Michigan City, La Porte, Ind....A4 91
Michigan City, Benton, Miss....A4 100
Michigantown, Clinton, Ind.D5 91
Michikamau, lake, Newf., Can..g8 75
Michoacán, state, Mex.D4, n13 63
Michurin, Bul....D8 22
Michurinsk, Sov. Un....C2 29
Mico, pt., Nic....E6 62
Micoud, St. Lucia....I14 64
Micro, Johnston, N.C....B4 109
Midai, isl., Indon....K7 38
Midale, Sask., Can....H4 70
Midas, Bonner, Idaho....A2 89
Middelburg, Neth....C3 15
Middelburg, S. Afr....B4 49
Middelfart, Den....C3 24
Middelharnis, Neth....C4 15
Middelkerke, Bel....C2 15
Middle, riv., B.C., Can....B5 68
Middle, riv., Iowa....C3 92
Middle, riv., Minn....B2 99
Middle Amana, Iowa, Iowa.C6 92
Middle Andaman, isl., India....F9 39
Middleboro, Plymouth, Mass....C6 97
Middlebourne, Tyler, W. Va.B4 123
Middlebranch, Holt, Nebr...B7 103
Middlebranch, Stark, Ohio..B4 111
Middlebro, Man., Can....E4 71
Middle Brook, Newf., Can...D4 75
Middlebrook, Augusta, Va...B3 121
Middleburg, Clay, Fla....B5 86
Middleburg, Casey, Ky....C5 94
Middleburg, Carroll, Md....A3 85
Middleburg, Schoharie, N.Y.C6 108
Middleburg, Vance, N.C....A4 109
Middleburg, Logan, Ohio....B2 111
Middleburg, Snyder, Pa....E7 114
Middleburg, Hardeman, Tenn....B2 117
Middleburg, Loudoun, Va...B5 121
Middleburgh Heights, Cuyahoga, Ohio....h9 111
Middlebury, New Haven, Conn....C4 84
Middlebury, Elkhart, Ind....A6 91
Middlebury, Addison, Vt....C2 120
Middle Bushkill, creek, Pa....A2 106
Middle Caraquet, N.B., Can....*B5 74
Middlefield, Middlesex, Conn....C6 84
Middlefield, Hampshire, Mass....B1 97
Middlefield, Geauga, Ohio..A4 111
Middle Granville, Washington, N.Y....B7 108
Middle Ground, isl., Midway Is.... 52
Middle Haddam, Middlesex, Conn....C6 84
Middle Island, Suffolk, N.Y..F5 84
Middle Island, creek, W. Va....B3 123
Middle Lake, Sask., Can....E3 70
Middle Loup, riv., Nebr....C6 103
Middle Musquodoboit, N.S., Can....D6 74
Middle Nodaway, riv., Iowa....C3 92
Middle Park, basin, Colo....A4 83
Middle Patuxent, riv., Md....B4 85
Middle Point, Van Wert, Ohio....B1 111
Middleport, Niagara, N.Y...B2 108
Middleport, Meigs, Ohio....C3 111
Middle Raccoon, riv., Iowa....C3 92
Middle River, Baltimore, Md....*B5 85
Middle River, Marshall, Minn....B2 99
Middlesboro, Bell, Ky....D6 94
Middlesbrough, Eng....C6 10
Middlesex, Belize....E3 62
Middlesex, Middlesex, N.J...B4 106
Middlesex, Yates, N.Y....C3 108
Middlesex, Nash, N.C....B4 109
Middlesex, Washington, Vt..C3 120
Middlesex, co., Ont., Can...D3 72
Middlesex, co., Conn....D6 84
Middlesex, co., Mass....A5 97
Middlesex, co., N.J....C4 106
Middlesex, co., Va....C6 121
Middlesex Fells, res., Mass....g11 97
Middle Stewiacke, N.S., Can....D6 74
Middleton, N.S., Can....E4 74
Middleton, Eng....*A5 12
Middleton, Canyon, Idaho...F2 89
Middleton, Essex, Mass..A5, f11 97
Middleton, Gratiot, Mich....E6 98
Middleton, Strafford, N.H...D4 105
Middleton, Hardeman, Tenn....B3 117
Middleton, Dane, Wis....E4 124
Middletown, Lake, Calif....C2 82
Middletown, Middlesex, Conn....C6 84
Middletown, New Castle, Del....B6 85
Middletown, Logan and Menard, Ill....C4 90
Middletown, Henry, Ind....D6 91
Middletown, Des Moines, Iowa....D6 92
Middletown, Jefferson, Ky...g11 94
Middletown, Frederick, Md.B2 85

Middletown, Montgomery, Mo. B6 101
Middletown, Monmouth, N.J. C4 106
Middletown, Orange, N.Y. D6 108
Middletown, Hyde, N.C. B6 109
Middletown, Butler, Ohio C1 111
Middletown, Dauphin, Pa. F8 114
Middletown, Newport, R.I. C12 84
Middletown, Frederick, Va. A4 121
Middletown Heights, Delaware, Pa. *G11 114
Middletown Springs, Rutland, Vt. E2 120
Middle Valley, Morris, N.J. B3 106
Middleville, Ont., Can. B8 72
Middleville, Barry, Mich. F6 98
Middleville, Sussex, N.J. A3 106
Middleville, Herkimer, N.Y. B6 108
Middle Water, Hartley, Tex. B1 118
Midelt, Mor. H4 30
Midfield, Jefferson, Ala. g7 78
Midgic, N.B., Can. D5 74
Midhurst, Ont., Can. C5 72
Midkiff, Lincoln, W. Va. C2 123
Midland, Sebastian, Ark. B1 75
Midland, Riverside, Calif. F6 82
Midland, Ont., Can. C5 72
Midland, Greene, Ind. F3 91
Midland, Acadia, La. D3 95
Midland, Allegany, Md. k13 85
Midland, Midland, Mich. E6 98
Midland, Cabarrus, N.C. B2 109
Midland, Clinton, Ohio C2 111
Midland, Beaver, Pa. E1 114
Midland, Washington, Pa. *F1 108
Midland, Haakon, S. Dak. C4 116
Midland, Midland, Tex. D1 118
Midland, Fauquier, Va. B5 121
Midland, Clark, Wash. *D3 122
Midland, Pierce, Wash. *B3 122
Midland, co., Mich. E6 98
Midland, co., Tex. D1 118
Midland, basin, Colo. A2 83
Midland City, Dale, Ala. D4 78
Midland Park, Bergen, N.J. B4 106
Midland Park, Charleston, S.C. k11 115
Midlandvale, Alta., Can. D4 69
Midleton, Ire. F3 11
Midlothian, Cook, Ill. k9 90
Midlothian, Allegany, Md. k13 85
Midlothian, Ellis, Tex. C4, n9 118
Midlothian, Chesterfield, Va. *C5 121
Midnapore, Alta., Can. D3 69
Midnapore, India F11 40
Midnight, Humphreys, Miss. B3 100
Midongy Sud, Mad. h9 49
Midpines, Mariposa, Calif. D4 82
Midstate Mill (Amerotron Mill), Robeson, N.C. *C3 109
Midvale, Washington, Idaho E2 89
Midvale, Tuscarawas, Ohio B4 111
Midvale, Salt Lake, Utah C4 119
Midville, Burke, Ga. D4 87
Midway, Bullock, Ala. C4 78
Midway, B.C., Can. E8 68
Midway, Gadsden, Fla. B2 86
Midway, Woodford, Ky. B5 94
Midway, Multnomah, Oreg. *B4 113
Midway, Adams, Pa. G7 114
Midway, Greene, Tenn. C11 117
Midway, Wasatch, Utah C4 119
Midway, King, Wash. D2 122
Midway, range, B.C., Can. E8 68
Midway City, Orange, Calif. *F5 82
Midway Islands, U.S. dep., Oceania 52
Midway Village, Oklahoma, Okla. *B4 112
Midwest, Natrona, Wyo. C6 125
Midwest City, Oklahoma, Okla. B4 112
Mid-Western, reg., Nig. E6 45
Midyat, Tur. D13 31
Mie, pref., Jap. *I8 37
Miechow, Pol. C6 26
Miechowice, Pol. g9 26
Miedzychod, Pol. B3 26
Miedzyrzec, Pol. C7 26
Miedzyrzecz, Pol. B3 26
Miedzyrzecz, Pol. g10 26
Miedzyzdroje, Pol. A3 26
Mielec, Pol. C6 26
Mien, lake, Swe. B8 24
Mienia, riv., Pol. m14 26
Mienning, China C11 39
Mienyang, China I5 36
Mieres, Sp. A3 20
Miesbach, F.R.G. B7 18
Miēso, Eth. D5 47
Mifflin, Juniata, Pa. E7 114
Mifflin, Chester, Tenn. B3 117
Mifflin, Kenedy, Tex. F4 118
Mifflin, co., Pa. E6 114
Mifflinburg, Union, Pa. E7 114
Mifflintown, Juniata, Pa. E7 114
Mifflinville, Columbia, Pa. D7 114
Migdal, Isr. B7 32
Migennes, Fr. D5 14
Migiurtinia, reg., Som. D6 47
Migliarino, It. E7 18
Miguel Alemán, res., Mex. D5 63
Miguel Alves, Braz. B2 57
Miguel Auza, Mex. C4 63
Mihai-Viteazu, Rom. C9 22
Mihara, Jap. *I6 37
Mijares, riv., Sp. B5 20
Mijdaḥah, P.D.R. of Yem. C6 47
Mikado, Sask., Can. F4 70
Mikado, Alcona, Mich. D7 92
Mikana, Barron, Wis. C2 118
Mikasa, Jap. *E10 37
Mikha Tskhakaya, Sov. Un. A13 31
Mikhaylov, Sov. Un. D12 27
Mikhaylov, cape, Ant. C24 5
Mikhaylovgrad, Bul. D6 22
Mikhaylovka, Sov. Un. C2 29
Mikhaylovka, Sov. Un. H10 27
Mikhaylovskiy, Sov. Un. C9 29
Mikindani, Tan. D7 48
Mikkalo, Gilliam, Oreg. B6 113
Mikkeli, Fin. G12 25
Mikkeli, dept., Fin. *G12 25
Mikolow, Pol. g9 26
Mikonos, isl., Grc. D5 23
Mikope, Zaire C3 48
Mikulczyce, Pol. g9 26
Mikulov, Czech. D4 26
Mikura, isl., Jap. J9 37
Milaca, Mille Lacs, Minn. E5 99
Milagro, Arg. A3 54
Milam, Hardy, W. Va. C5 123
Milam, co., Texas D4 118
Milan, Que., Can. D6 73
Milan, Telfair and Dodge, Ga. D3 87
Milan, Rock Island, Ill. B3 90
Milan, Ripley, Ind. F7 91
Milan (Milano), It. B2 21
Milan, Sumner, Kans. E7 93
Milan, Monroe and Washtenaw, Mich. F7 98
Milan, Chippewa, Minn. E3 99
Milan, Sullivan, Mo. A4 101
Milan, Coos, N.H. A4 104
Milan, Valencia, N. Mex. B2 107
Milan, Erie, Ohio A3 111
Milan, Bradford, Pa. C8 114
Milan, Gibson, Tenn. B3 117
Milan, Spokane, Wash. B8 122
Milan, Marathon, Wis. D3 124
Milano, see Milan, It.
Milano, Milam, Tex. D4 118
Milas, Tur. D5 23
Milazzo, It. E5 21
Milbank, Grant, S. Dak. B9 116
Milbanke, sound, B.C., Can. C3 68
Milbridge, Washington, Maine D5 96
Milburn, Carlisle, Ky. f9 94
Milburn, Custer, Nebr. C6 103
Milburn, Johnston, Okla. C5 112
Milden, Sask., Can. F2 70
Mildenhall, Eng. B8 12
Mildmay, Ont., Can. C3 72
Mildred, Sask., Can. D2 70
Mildred, Allen, Kans. D8 93
Mildred, Prairie, Mont. D12 102
Mildred, Sullivan, Pa. D9 114
Mildura, Austl. G4 51
Milea, Grc. C4 23
Miles, Austl. C8 51
Miles, Jackson, Iowa B7 92
Miles, Runnels, Tex. D2 118
Miles, mtn., Vt. C5 120
Milesburg, Centre, Pa. E6 114
Miles City, Custer, Mont. D11 102
Milestone, Sask., Can. G3 70
Milesville, Haakon, S. Dak. C4 116
Miletus, ruins, Tur. D6 23
Milevsko, Czech. D9 17
Miley, Hampton, S.C. F5 115
Milfay, Creek, Okla. B5 112
Milford, New Haven, Conn. E4 84
Milford, Sussex and Kent, Del. C7 85
Milford, Iroquois, Ill. C6 90
Milford, Kosciusko, Ind. B6 91
Milford, Dickinson, Iowa A2 92
Milford, Geary, Kans. C7 93
Milford, Bracken, Ky. B5 94
Milford, Penobscot, Maine D4 96
Milford, Worcester, Mass. B4, h9 97
Milford, Oakland, Mich. F7, o14 98
Milford, Seward, Nebr. D8 103
Milford, Hillsboro, N.H. E3 105
Milford, Hunterdon, N.J. B2 106
Milford, Otsego, N.Y. C6 108
Milford, Hamilton and Clermont, Ohio C1 111
Milford, Pike, Pa. D12 114
Milford, Beaver, Utah E2 119
Milford, Caroline, Va. B5 121
Milford Center, Union, Ohio B2 111
Milford Haven, Wales C2 12
Milford Mills, Baltimore, Md. *B4 85
Milford Station, N.S., Can. D6 74
Miliana, Alg. B5 44
Milicz, Pol. C4 26
Mililani Town, Honolulu, Haw. g9 88
Miling, Austl. F2 50
Milk, riv., Alta., Can., Mont. G11 66
Milk River, Alta., Can. E4 69
Milk River Ridge, res., Alta., Can. E4 69
Mill, brook, Vt. B5 120
Mill, creek, Ind. F4 91
Mill, creek, Kans. C6 93
Mill, creek, Kans. D7 93
Mill, creek, N.J. D4 106
Mill, creek, Ohio B2 111
Mill creek, Tenn. g10 117
Mill, creek, W. Va. C3 91
Mill, isl., Ant. C23 5
Mill, riv., Mass. h9 97
Milladore, Wood, Wis. D4 124
Millard, Pike, Ky. *C7 94
Millard, Adair, Mo. A5 101
Millard, co., Utah D2 119
Millarton, Stutsman, N. Dak. C7 110
Millau, Fr. E5 14
Millbank, Ont., Can. D4 72
Millboro, Tripp, S. Dak. D6 116
Millboro, Bath, Va. C3 121
Millbrae, San Mateo, Calif. h8 82
Mill Bridge, Ont., Can. C7 72
Millbrook, Elmore, Ala. C3 78
Millbrook, Ont., Can. C6 72
Millbrook, Mecosta, Mich. E5 98
Millbrook, Morris, N.J. *B3 106
Millbrook, Dutchess, N.Y. D7 108
Millbrook, Wake, N.C. B4 109
Millburn, Lake, Ill. D2 90
Millburn, Essex, N.J. B4 106
Millbury, Worcester, Mass. B4 97
Millbury, Wood, Ohio e7 111
Mill City, Pershing, Nev. C3 104
Mill City, Marion, Oreg. C4 113
Mill City, Wyoming, Pa. m17 114
Millcreek, Union, Ill. F4 90
Mill Creek, La Porte, Ind. A4 91
Millcreek, Madison, Mo. D7 101
Mill Creek, Deer Lodge, Mont. D4 102
Mill Creek, Johnston, Okla. C5 112
Mill Creek, Huntingdon, Pa. E6 114
Mill Creek, Randolph, W. Va. C5 123
Millcreek, Salt Lake, Utah C4 119
Millcreek Township, Erie, Pa. B1 114
Milldale, Hartford, Conn. C5 84
Milledgeville, Baldwin, Ga. C3 87
Milledgeville, Carroll, Ill. B4 90
Milledgeville, McNairy, Tenn. B3 117
Mille Îles, riv., Que., Can. p19 73
Mille Lacs, co., Minn. E5 99
Mille Lacs, Indian res., Minn. D5 99
Mille Lacs, lake, Minn. D5 99
Millen, Jenkins, Ga. D5 87
Miller, De Soto, Miss. A4 100
Miller, Buffalo, Nebr. D6 103
Miller, Lawrence, Ohio D3 111
Miller, Sherman, Oreg. B6 113
Miller, Hand, S. Dak. C7 116
Miller, co., Ark. D2 81
Miller, co., Ga. E2 87
Miller, co., Mo. C5 101
Miller, flat, Oreg. C5 113
Miller, isl., Md. B5 86
Miller, peak, Alsk. C11 79
Miller, peak, Ariz. F5 80
Miller, run, Vt. B4 120
Miller, sound, Ba. n17 64
Miller Dale Colony, Hand, S. Dak. C6 116
Miller Heights, Northampton, Pa. *E11 114
Millerovo, Sov. Un. D2 29
Miller Place, Suffolk, N.Y. F5 84
Millers, Carroll, Md. A4 85
Millers, riv., Mass. A3 97
Millersburg, Elkhart, Ind. A6 91
Millersburg, Iowa, Iowa C5 92
Millersburg, Bourbon, Ky. B5 94
Millersburg, Presque Isle, Mich. C6 98
Millersburg, Holmes, Ohio B4 111
Millersburg, Linn, Oreg. C1 113
Millersburg, Dauphin, Pa. E8 114
Millers Falls, Franklin, Mass. A3 97
Millers Ferry, Wilcox, Ala. C2 78
Millersport, Fairfield, Ohio C3 111
Millersview, Concho, Tex. D3 118
Millersville, Marion, Ind. k10 91
Millersville, Lancaster, Pa. F9 114
Millerton, N.B., Can. C4 74
Millerton, Wayne, Iowa D4 92
Millerton, Dutchess, N.Y. D7 108
Millerton, McCurtain, Okla. D6 112
Millerton, Tioga, Pa. C8 114
Millertown, Newf., Can. D3 75
Millertown Junction, Newf., Can. D3 75
Millerville, Clay, Ala. B4 78
Millerville, Douglas, Minn. D3 99
Millet, Alta., Can. C4 69
Millett, Allendale, S.C. E4 115
Millett, La Salle, Tex. E3 118
Millgrove, Blackford, Ind. D7 91
Mill Grove, Mercer, Mo. A4 101
Mill Hall, Clinton, Pa. D7 114
Millheim, Centre, Pa. E7 114
Millhousen, Decatur, Ind. F7 91
Millhurst, Monmouth, N.J. C4 106
Millicent, Austl. H3 51
Millicent, Alta., Can. D5 69
Milligan, Okaloosa, Fla. u15 86
Milligan, Fillmore, Nebr. D8 103
Milligan College, Carter, Tenn. C11 117
Milliken, Weld, Colo. A6 83
Millington, Kent and Queen Annes, Md. B6 85
Millington, Tuscola, Mich. E7 98
Millington, Morris, N.J. *B3 106
Millington, Coos, Oreg. D2 113
Millington, Shelby, Tenn. B2 117
Millinocket, Penobscot, Maine C4 96
Millinocket, lake, Maine B4 96
Millinocket, lake, Maine C4 96
Mill Iron, Carter, Mont. E12 102
Millis, Norfolk, Mass. B5, h10 97
Millom, Eng. F5 13
Mill Plain, Fairfield, Conn. (part of Danbury) D2 84
Mill Point, Pocahontas, W. Va. C4 123
Millport, Lamar, Ala. B1 78
Millport, Potter, Pa. C5 114
Millport, Scot. E4 13
Millrift, Pike, Pa. D12 114
Mill River, Berkshire, Mass. B1 97
Mill Run, Fayette, Pa. G3 114
Millry, Washington, Ala. D1 78
Mills, Keya Paha, Nebr. B6 103
Mills, Harding, N. Mex. A5 107
Mills, Potter, Pa. C6 114
Mills, Natrona, Wyo. D6 125
Mills, co., Iowa C2 92
Mills, co., Tex. D3 118
Mills, lake, N.W. Ter., Can. D9 66
Millsboro, Sussex, Del. C6 85
Millsboro, Washington, Pa. G1 114
Mill Shoals, White, Ill. E5 90
Millside, New Castle, Del. *A6 85
Mill Spring, Wayne, Mo. D7 101
Millstadt, St. Clair, Ill. E3 90
Millston, Jackson, Wis. D3 124
Millstone, New London, Conn. D8 84
Millstone, Somerset, N.J. B3 106
Millstone, riv., N.J. C3 106
Mill Stream, Austl. D2 50
Millstreet, Ire. E2 11
Milltown, Chambers, Ala. B4 78
Milltown, N.B., Can. D2 74
Milltown, Newf., Can. E4 75
Milltown, Crawford and Harrison, Ind. H5 91
Milltown, Adair, Ky. C4 94
Mill Town, Madison, Miss. *C3 100
Milltown, Missoula, Mont. D3 102
Milltown, Middlesex, N.J. C4 106
Milltown, Hutchinson, S. Dak. D8 116
Milltown, Polk, Wis. C1 124
Millvale, Allegheny, Pa. B6 114
Mill Valley, Marin, Calif. D2, h7 82
Mill Village, N.S., Can. E5 74
Mill Village, Erie, Pa. C2 114
Millville, N.B., Can. C2 74
Millville, Sussex, Del. C7 85
Millville, Woodford, Ky. B5 94
Millville, Worcester, Mass. B4 97
Millville, Cumberland, N.J. E2 106
Millville, Butler, Ohio n12 111
Millville, Columbia, Pa. D9 114
Millville, Cache, Utah B4 119
Millville, Jefferson, W. Va. B7 123
Millwood, Clarke, Va. A4 121
Millwood, Spokane, Wash. g14 122
Milmay, Atlantic, N.J. E3 106
Milmont Park, Delaware, Pa. *G11 114
Milner, B.C., Can. f13 68
Milner, Routt, Colo. A3 83
Milner, Lamar, Ga. C2 87
Milner, dam, Idaho G5 89
Milner Ridge, Man., Can. D3 71
Milnesand, Roosevelt, N. Mex. D6 107
Milngavie, Scot. *E4 13
Milnor, Sargent, N. Dak. C8 110
Milo, Alta., Can. D4 69
Milo, Warren, Iowa C4 92
Milo, Piscataquis, Maine C4 96
Milo, Vernon, Mo. D3 101
Milolii, Hawaii, Haw. D6 88
Milos, isl., Grc. D5 23
Milparinka, Austl. D3 51
Milpitas, Santa Clara, Calif. *D3 82
Milroy, Rush, Ind. F7 91
Milroy, Redwood, Minn. F3 99
Milroy, Mifflin, Pa. E6 114
Milstead, Rockdale, Ga. C3, h8 87
Miltenberg, F.R.G. D4 17
Milton, N.S., Can. E5 74
Milton, Ont., Can. D5 72
Milton, Litchfield, Conn. B3 84
Milton, Sussex, Del. C7 85
Milton, Santa Rosa, Fla. u14 86
Milton, Madison, Ill. (part of Alton) A8 101
Milton, Pike, Ill. D3 90
Milton, Wayne, Ind. E7 91
Milton, Van Buren, Iowa D5 92
Milton, Sumner, Kans. E6 93
Milton, Trimble, Ky. B4 94
Milton, Lafayette, La. D3 95
Milton, Norfolk, Mass. B5, g11 97
Milton, Strafford, N.H. D5 105
Milton, Ulster, N.Y. D7 108
Milton, N.Z. Q12 51
Milton, Caswell, N.C. A3 109
Milton, Cavalier, N. Dak. A7 110
Milton, Northumberland, Pa. D8 114
Milton, Chittenden, Vt. B2 120
Milton, Pierce, Wash. f11 122
Milton, Cabell, W. Va. C2 123
Milton, Rock, Wis. F5 124
Milton, res., Colo. A6 83
Milton Lake, res., Ohio A4 111
Miltona, Douglas, Minn. D3 99
Miltona, lake, Minn. D3 99
Milton-Freewater, Umatilla, Oreg. B8 113
Milton Mills, Strafford, N.H. D5 105
Milton Station, P.E.I., Can. *C6 74
Miltonvale, Cloud, Kans. C6 93
Miltown Malbay, Ire. E2 11
Milverton, Ont., Can. D4 72
Milwaukee, Northampton, N.C. A5 109
Milwaukee, Milwaukee, Wis. E6, m12 124
Milwaukee, co., Wis. E5 124
Milwaukee, riv., Wis. m12 124
Milwaukie, Clackamas, Oreg. B4, h12 113
Mimbres, Grant, N. Mex. E1 107
Mimbres, mts., N. Mex. D2 107
Mimico, Ont., Can. m15 72
Mimizan, Fr. E3 14
Mimon, Czech. C9 17
Mimongo, Gabon F2 46
Mimosa Park, St. Charles, La. *E5 95
Mims, Brevard, Fla. D6 86
Min, riv., China F8 34
Mina, Mineral, Nev. E3 104
Mina, Edmunds, S. Dak. B7 116
Mināb, Iran H8 41
Minago, riv., Man., Can. B2 71
Minaki, Ont., Can. E4 71
Minam, Wallowa, Oreg. B9 113
Minamata, Jap. J5 37
Minami, Iwo 52
Minami-Iwo, isl., Pac. O. E8 7
Minas, Cuba D5 64
Minas, Ur. E1 56
Minas, basin, N.S., Can. D5 74
Minas, chan., N.S., Can. D5 74
Minas de Oro, Hond. C4 62
Minas de Ríotinto, Sp. D2 20
Minas Gerais, state, Braz. B4 56
Minatare, Scotts Bluff, Nebr. C2 103
Minatitlán, Mex. D6 63
Minato, see Nakaminato, Jap.
Minato, Jap. n18 37
Minbu, Bur. D9 39
Minburn, Alta., Can. C5 69
Minburn, Dallas, Iowa C3 92
Minch, The, strait, Scot. B3 13
Minchin, China D3 34
Mincio, riv., It. B3 21
Minco, Grady, Okla. B4 112
Mindanao, isl., Phil. D7 35
Mindanao, sea, Phil. D6 35
Mindel, riv., F.R.G. A6 18
Mindelheim, F.R.G. A6 18
Mindelo, C.V. Is. *E3 42
Mindemoya, Ont., Can. B2 72
Minden, Ont., Can. C6 72
Minden, F.R.G. A3 17
Minden, Pottawattamie, Iowa C2 92
Minden, Webster, La. B2 95
Minden, Kearney, Nebr. D7 103
Minden, Douglas, Nev. E2 104
Minden, Fayette, W. Va. D3, n13 123
Minden City, Sanilac, Mich. E8 98
Mindenmines, Barton, Mo. D3 101
Mindi, Pan. k11 62
Mindoro, La Crosse, Wis. D2 124
Mindoro, isl., Phil. C6 35
Mindoro, strait, Phil. C6 35
Mine Centre, Ont., Can. E5 71
Minechoag, mtn., Mass. B3 97
Minehead, Eng. C4 12
Mine Hill, Morris, N.J. B3 106
Mineiros, Braz. B2 56
Mine La Motte, Madison, Mo. D7 101
Mineola, Mills, Iowa C2 92
Mineola, Clark, Kans. E3 93
Mineola, Nassau, N.Y. E7, n15 108
Mineola, Wood, Tex. C5 118
Miner, Scott, Mo. E8 101
Miner, co., S. Dak. D8 116
Mineral, Tehama, Calif. B3 82
Mineral, Bureau, Ill. B4 90
Mineral, Louisa, Va. B5 121
Mineral, Lewis, Wash. C3 122
Mineral, co., Colo. D4 83
Mineral, co., Mont. C1 102
Mineral, co., Nev. E3 104
Mineral co., W. Va. B6 123
Mineral, mtn., Ariz. D2 80
Mineral, mts., Utah E3 119
Mineral City, Tuscarawas, Ohio B4 111
Mineral del Oro, Mex. n13 63
Mineral Hills, Iron, Mich. B2 98
Mineral Park, Bradley, Tenn. h11 117
Mineral Point, Washington, Mo. D7 101
Mineral Point, Iowa, Wis. F3 124
Mineral Ridge, Mahoning and Trumbull, Ohio *A5 111
Mineral Springs, Howard, Ark. D2 81
Mineral Wells, De Soto, Miss. A4 100
Mineral Wells, Palo Pinto, Tex. C3 118
Minersville, Meigs, Ohio C4 111
Minersville, Schuylkill, Pa. E9 114
Minersville, Beaver, Utah E3 119
Minerva, Terrebonne, La. C6 95
Minerva, Essex, N.Y. B7 108
Minerva, Carroll and Stark, Ohio B4 111
Minerva Park, Franklin, Ohio *C3 111
Minervino, Murge, It. D6 21
Minetto, Oswego, N.Y. B4 108
Mineville, Essex, N.Y. A7 108
Mingan, Que., Can. h8 75
Mingchiang, China A7 38
Mingechaur, Sov. Un. G18 9
Mingechaur, res., Sov. Un. E3 29
Mingenew, Austl. E2 50
Mingo, Jasper, Iowa C4 92
Mingo, Thomas, Kans. C3 93
Mingo, co., W. Va. D2 123
Mingo Junction, Jefferson, Ohio B5 111
Mingoyo, Tan. D6 48
Mingshui, China C2 37
Mingshui, China C4 34
Minho, prov., Port. *B1 20
Minho, riv., Jam. E14 65
Minho, riv., Port. B1 20
Minhou, China L8 36
Minicoy, isl., India G5 39
Minidoka, Minidoka, Idaho G5 89
Minidoka, co., Idaho G5 89
Minidoka, dam, Idaho G5 89
Minier, Tazewell, Ill. C4 90
Miniota, Man., Can. D1 71
Minipi, lake, Newf., Can. h9 75
Minisink, isl., N.J. A3 106
Minitonas, Man., Can. C1 71
Mink Creek, Franklin, Idaho G7 89
Minna, Nig. E6 45
Minna, bluff, Ant. B29 5
Minneapolis, Ottawa, Kans. C6 93
Minneapolis, Hennepin, Minn. F5, n12 99
Minneapolis, Avery, N.C. C4 103
Minnedosa, Man., Can. D2 71
Minnedosa, riv., Man., Can. D1 71
Minnehaha, Clark, Wash. *D3 122
Minnehaha, co., S. Dak. D6 116
Minneiska, Wabasha, Minn. F7 99
Minneota, Lyon, Minn. F3 99
Minnesota, state, U.S. A9 77, 99
Minnesota, riv., Minn. F3 99
Minnesota Lake, Faribault, Minn. G5 99
Minnetonka, Hennepin, Minn. n12 99
Minnetonka, lake, Minn. n11 99
Minnetrista, Hennepin, Minn. *E5 99
Minnewanka, lake, Alta., Can. D3 69
Minnewaska, lake, Minn. E3 99
Minnewaukan, Benson, N. Dak. A6 110
Mino, Jap. n15 37
Miño, riv., Sp. A1 20
Minoa, Onondaga, N.Y. *B4 108
Minocqua, Oneida, Wis. C4 124
Minokamo [Ota], Jap. n15 37
Minong, Washburn, Wis. B2 124
Minonk, Woodford, Ill. C4 90
Minooka, Grundy, Ill. B5 90
Minor Hill, Giles, Tenn. B11 117
Minot, Plymouth, Mass. h12 97
Minot, Ward, N. Dak. A4 110
Minquadale, New Castle, Del. *A6 85
Minsen, F.R.G. A7 15
Minsk, Sov. Un. E6 27
Minsk Mazowiecki, Pol. B6, m15 26
Minster, Auglaize, Ohio B1 111
Minstra, mts., Sp. B4 20
Minster, Dallas, Ala. C2 78
Minter City, Leflore, Miss. B3 100
Mint Hill, Mecklenburg, N.C. B2 109
Minto, Alsk. C10 79
Minto, Man., Can. E1 71
Minto, N.B., Can. C3 74
Minto, Walsh, N. Dak. A8 110
Minto, lake, Que., Can. g11 73
Minto, pass, Oreg. C5 113
Minton, Sask., Can. H3 70
Mintons Corner, Brevard, Fla. *D6 86
Minturn, Lawrence, Ark. B4 81
Minturn, Eagle, Colo. B4 83
Minturn, Hancock, Maine D4 96
Minturno, It. D4 21
Minūf, Eg. D2 32
Minusinsk, Sov. Un. E27 9
Minute Man, nat. historical park, Mass. g10 97
Minvoul, Gabon E2 46
Minyā al Qamḥ, Eg. D3 32
Minya Konka, peak, China F5 34
Mio, Oscoda, Mich. D6 98
Miquelon, isl., St. Pierre & Miquelon E3 75
Mira, N.S., Can. C10 74
Mira, Caddo, La. B2 95
Mira, Port. B1 20
Mira, riv., Port. D1 20
Miracle Hot Springs, Kern, Calif. E4 82
Mirador, Braz. C2 57
Miraflores, Col. C3 60
Miraflores, Peru E3 58
Miraflores, locks, C.Z. m11 62
Miragoâne, Hai. E7 64
Miraj, India I5 40
Miraleste, Los Angeles, Calif. *E4 82
Mira Loma, Riverside, Calif. *F5 82
Miramar, San Diego, Calif. *F5 82
Miramar, Broward, Fla. s13 86
Miramichi, bay, N.B., Can. B4 74
Miranda, Braz. C1 56
Miranda, Col. C2 60
Miranda, Faulk, S. Dak. C7 116
Miranda, state, Ven. A4 60
Miranda, riv., Braz. C1 56
Miranda de Ebro, Sp. A4 20
Miranda do Douro, Port. B2 20
Mirande, Fr. F4 14
Mirandela, Port. B2 20
Mirando City, Webb, Tex. F3 118
Mirandola, It. E7 18
Mirassol, Braz. C3 56
Mirebalais, Hai. E7 64
Mirecourt, Fr. C7 14
Mirepoix, Fr. F4 14
Mirgorod, Sov. Un. G9 27
Miri, Mala. E4 35
Mirialguda, India I7 40
Miriam Vale, Austl. B8 51
Mirnyy, U.S.S.R. scientific station, Ant. C22 5
Mirond, lake, Sask., Can. B4 70
Mirow, G.D.R. E6 24
Mirpur Khās, Pak. E2 40
Mirpur Mathelo, Pak. D2 40
Mirror, Alta., Can. C4 69
Mirror Lake, Carroll, N.H. C4 105
Mirzāpur, India C7 39, E9 40
Misakubo, Jap. n16 37
Misamis Occidental, prov., Phil. *D6 35
Misamis Oriental, prov., Phil. *D6 35
Misantla, Mex. D5, n15 63
Misawa, Jap. *F10 37
Misburg, F.R.G. A4 17
Miscoe, hill, Mass. h9 97
Miscou, isl., N.B., Can. B5 74
Miscou, pt., N.B., Can. A5 74
Miscou Centre, N.B., Can. B5 74
Miscouche, P.E.I., Can. C6 74
Misenheimer, Stanly, N.C. B2 109
Mishan, China D6 37
Mishawaka, St. Joseph, Ind. A5 91
Mishicot, Manitowoc, Wis. D6, h10 124
Mishima, Jap. I9, n17 37
Misiones, prov., Arg. E4 55
Misiones, dept., Par. E4 55
Miskitos, is., Nic. C6 62
Miskolc, Hung. A5 22
Mismār, Sud. B4 47
Misoöl, isl., Indon. F7 35
Mispillion, riv., Del. C7 85
Misquah, hills, Minn. B7 99
Misquamicut, Washington, R.I. D9 84
Misr al Jadidah (Heliopolis), Eg. D3 32
Misrātah, Libya C3 43
Misratah, cape, Libya H14 30
Missaukee, co., Mich. D5 98
Missaukee, lake, Mich. D5 98
Missinaibi, riv., Ont., Can. G16 67
Mission, Johnson, Kans. m16 93
Mission, Todd, S. Dak. D5 116
Mission, Hidalgo, Tex. F3 118
Mission, range, Mont. C3 102
Mission City, B.C., Can. E6, f13 68
Mission Hill, Yankton, S. Dak. E8 116
Mission Viejo, Orange, Calif. n13 82
Missipuskiow, riv., Sask., Can. D4 70
Missisquoi, co., Que., Can. D4 73
Missisquoi, bay, Vt. A2 120
Missisquoi, riv., Vt. B3 120
Mississagi, riv., Ont., Can. B7 98
Mississagi, strait, Ont., Can. C7 98
Mississinewa, riv., Ind. C6 91
Mississippi, co., Ark. B5 81
Mississippi, co., Mo. E8 101
Mississippi, state, U.S. D10 77, 100
Mississippi, delta, La. E6 95
Mississippi, lake, Ont., Can. B8 72
Mississippi, riv., U.S. D9 77
Mississippi, sound, Miss. E5 100
Missoula, Missoula, Mont. D2 102
Missoula, co., Mont. D2 102
Missoula Southwest, Missoula, Mont. *D2 102
Missour, Mor. C4 44
Missouri, state, U.S. C9 77, 101
Missouri, buttes, Wyo. B8 125
Missouri, caverns, Mo. C6 101
Missouri, riv., U.S. B8 77
Missouri City, Clay, Mo. h11 101
Missouri City, Fort Bend, Tex. r14 118
Missouri Valley, Harrison, Iowa C2 92
Mistaken, pt., Newf., Can. E5 75
Mistassini, lake, Que., Can. h12 73
Mistastin, lake, Newf., Can. g9 75
Mistatim, Sask., Can. E4 70
Mistelbach [an der Zaya], Aus. D8 16
Misti, vol., Peru E3 58
Miston, Dyer, Tenn. A2 117
Mistretta, It. F5 21
Mita, pt., Mex. C3 63
Mitaka, Jap. *I9 37
Mitake, Jap. I8, n16 37
Mitchell, Bullock, Ala. C4 78
Mitchell, Austl. C6 51
Mitchell, Ont., Can. D3 72
Mitchell, Glascock, Ga. C4 87
Mitchell, Madison, Ill. F13 101
Mitchell, Lawrence, Ind. G5 91
Mitchell, Mitchell, Iowa A5 92
Mitchell, Sabine, La. C2 95
Mitchell, Scotts Bluff, Nebr. C2 103
Mitchell, Wheeler, Oreg. C6 113
Mitchell, Davison, S. Dak. D7 116
Mitchell, co., Ga. E2 87
Mitchell, co., Iowa A5 92
Mitchell, co., Kans. C5 93
Mitchell, co., N.C. e10 109
Mitchell, co., Tex. C2 118
Mitchell, isl., La. E6 95
Mitchell, lake, Ala. C3 78
Mitchell, lake, Mich. D5 98
Mitchell, mtn., N.C. f10 109
Mitchell, riv., Austl. C7 50
Mitchellsberg, Boyle, Ky. C5 94
Mitchellville, Polk, Iowa C4, e9 92
Mitchellville, Sumner, Tenn. A5 117
Mitchelstown, Ire. E3 11
Mit Fāris, Eg. C3 32
Mit Ghamr, Eg. D3 32
Mitilini (Mytilene), Grc. C6 23
Mitishto, riv., Man., Can. B2 71
Mitla, pass, Eg. D4 32
Mito, Jap. H10, m19 37
Mitre, mtn., N.Z. N15 51
Mitsinjo, Mad. g9 49
Mittagong, Austl. *F9 50
Mittelland, canal, F.R.G., G.D.R. B5 16
Mittenwald, F.R.G. B7 18
Mittersill, Aus. B8 18
Mitterteich, F.R.G. D7 17
Mittl Isar, canal, F.R.G. A7 18
Mittweida, G.D.R. C7 17
Mitú, Col. C3 60
Mitumba, mts., Zaire C4 48
Mitwaba, Zaire C4 48
Mitzic, Gabon E2 46
Miura (Misaki), Jap. n18 37
Mixcoac, Mex. (part of Mexico City) h9 63
Mixquiahuala, Mex. m14 63
Mixteco, riv., Mex. o14 63
Miyagi, pref., Jap. *G10 37
Miyagusuku, isl., Okinawa 52
Miyake, isl., Jap. I9 37
Miyako, Jap. G10 37
Miyakonojo, Jap. K5 37
Miyata, Jap. *J5 37
Miyazaki, Jap. K5 37
Miyazaki, pref., Jap. *K5 37
Miyazu, Jap. n14 37
Mizdah, Libya C2 43
Mize, Smith, Miss. D4 100
Mizen, head, Ire. F2 11
Mizil, Rom. C8 22
Mizoram, ter., India D9 39
Mizpah, Koochiching, Minn. C4 99

Mizpah, Custer, Mont...D11 102
Mizpah, Atlantic, N.J...E3 106
Mizpah, creek, Mont...E11 102
Mizpe Ramon, Isr...D6 32
Mizque, Bol...C2 55
Mjölby, Swe...H6 25
Mjösa, lake, Nor...G4 25
Mkalama, Tan...B5 48
M. Kemalpasa, see Mustafa Kemalpasa, Tur.
Mlada Boleslav, Czech...C3, n18 26
Mlanje, Malawi...E6 48
Mlawa, Pol...B6 26
Mljet, isl., Yugo...D3 22
Mnichovo Hradiste, Czech...C9 17
Mo, Nor...D6 25
Moa, isl., Indon...G7 35
Moab, Grand, Utah...E6 119
Moala, isl., Fiji...52
Moamba, Moz...C5 49
Moanda, Gabon...F2 46
Moapa, Clark, Nev...G7 104
Moapa River, Indian res., Nev...G7 104
Moar, lake, Man., Can...C4 71
Moark, Clay, Ark...A5 81
Moate, Ire...D4 11
Moba, Zaire...C4 48
Mobara, Jap...n19 37
Mobaye, Cen. Afr. Rep...E4 46
Mobayi-Mbongo, see Banzyville, Zaire
Mobeetie, Wheeler, Tex...B2 118
Moberly, Randolph, Mo...B5 101
Moberly, lake, B.C., Can...B7 68
Moberly Lake, B.C., Can...B7 68
Mobile, Mobile, Ala...E1 78
Mobile, Maricopa, Ariz...D3 80
Mobile, Newf., Can...E5 75
Mobile, co., Ala...E1 78
Mobile, bay, Ala...E1 78
Mobile, riv., Ala...E1 78
Mobridge, Walworth, S. Dak...B5 116
Mobula, Zaire...A4 48
Moca, Dom. Rep...E8 64
Moca, mun., P.R...*B1 65
Mocajuba, Braz...C5 59
Moçambique, Moz...E7 48
Mocambique, prov., Moz...D6 48
Moçâmedes, Ang...E1 48
Moçâmedes, dist., Ang...E1 48
Mocanaqua, Luzerne, Pa...D9 114
Moccasin, Mohave, Ariz...A3 80
Moccasin, Judith Basin, Mont...C7 102
Mocha (Mokha) (Al Mukhā), Yemen...C5 47
Mocha, isl., Chile...B2 54
Möcheln, lake, Swe...B8 24
Mocho, mts., Jam...E14 65
Mochudi, Bots...B4 49
Mocímboa da Praia, Moz...D7 48
Mocksville, Davie, N.C...B2 109
Moclips, Grays Harbor, Wash...B1 122
Mocoa, Col...C2 60
Mococa, Braz...C3, k8 56
Mocomoco, Bol...C2 55
Mocorito, Mex...B3 63
Moctezuma, Mex...B3 63
Moctezuma, riv., Mex...m14 63
Mocuba, Moz...A6 49
Mocubúri, Moz...D6 48
Modale, Harrison, Iowa...C2 92
Modane, Fr...D2 18
Mode, Shelby, Ill...D5 90
Model, Las Animas, Colo...D6 83
Model, res., Colo...D6 83
Modena, It...E6 19, B3 21
Modena, Mercer, Mo...A4 101
Modena, Ulster, N.Y...D6 108
Modena, Iron, Utah...F2 119
Modena, Buffalo, Wis...D2 124
Modeste, Ascension, La...h9 95
Modesto, Stanislaus, Calif...D3 82
Modesto, Macoupin, Ill...D4 90
Modica, It...F5 21
Modjokerto, Indon...*G4 35
Modlin, Pol...B6, k13 26
Mödling, Aus...D8 16
Modoc, Emanuel, Ga...D4 87
Modoc, Randolph, Ind...D7 91
Modoc, Scott, Kans...D2 93
Modoc, co., Calif...B3 82
Modoc Point, Klamath, Oreg...E5 113
Modřany, Czech...o17 26
Moecherville, Kane, Ill...*B5 90
Moen, Truk...52
Moen, isl., Truk...52
Moengo, Sur...A4 59
Moenkopi, Coconino, Ariz...A4 80
Moenkopi, wash, Ariz...A5 80
Moerbeke, Bel...C3 15
Moers, F.R.G...B1 17
Moesa, riv., Switz...D7 19
Moeskroen, see Mouscron, Bel.
Moe-Yallourn, Austl...I6 51
Moffat, Saguache, Colo...C5 83
Moffat, co., Colo...A2 83
Moffat, Scot...E5 13
Moffat, railroad tunnel, Colo...B5 83
Moffett, Sequoyah, Okla...B7 112
Moffit, Burleigh, N. Dak...C5 110
Moga, Zaire...B4 48
Mogadisho (Mogadishu), Som...E6 47
Mogadishu, see Mogadisho, Som.
Mogador, see Essaouira, Mor.
Mogadore, Portage and Summit, Ohio...A4 111
Mogaung, Bur...C10 39
Mogi das Cruzes, Braz...C3, m8 56
Mogielnica, Pol...C6 26
Mogi Guaçu, riv., Braz...k8 56
Mogilev, Sov. Un...E8 27
Mogilev-Podolskiy, Sov. Un...G6 27
Mogilno, Pol...B4 26
Mogí Mirim, Braz...m8 56
Mogincual, Moz...A7 49
Mogocha, Sov. Un...D14 28
Mogochin, Sov. Un...B10 29
Mogok, Bur...D10 39
Mogollon, Carton, N. Mex...D1 107
Mogollon, mts., N. Mex...D1 107
Mogollon, mesa, Ariz...C4 80
Mogollon, rim, Ariz...C4 80
Mogote, Conejos, Colo...D4 83
Mogotes, pt., Arg...B5 54
Mogpog, Phil...p13 35
Moguer, Sp...D2 20
Mohacs, Hung...C4 24
Mohale's Hoek, Leso...D4 49
Mohall, Renville, N. Dak...A4 110
Mohammed, cape, Eg...I10 31
Mohammedia, Mor...C3 44
Mohave, co., Ariz...B1 80
Mohave, lake, Ariz...B1 80
Mohave, mts., Ariz...C1 80
Mohave Valley, Mohave, Ariz...C1 80
Mohawk, Yuma, Ariz...E2 80
Mohawk, Keweenaw, Mich...A2 98
Mohawk, Herkimer, N.Y...C5 108
Mohawk, Lane, Oreg...C4 113
Mohawk, lake, N.J...A3 106
Mohawk, mtn., Conn...B3 84
Mohawk, riv., N.H...g7 105
Mohawk, riv., N.Y...C6 108
Mohegan, New London, Conn...D8 84
Mohegan Lake, Westchester, N.Y...*D7 108
Mohican, riv., Ohio...B3 111
Mohill, Ire...D4 11
Mohler, Lewis, Idaho...C2 89
Mohler, Lincoln, Wash...B7 122
Mohnton, Berks, Pa...F10 114
Moho, China...A9 34
Mohoro, Tan...C6 48
Moiese, Lake, Mont...C2 102
Moinesti, Rom...B8 22
Mointy, Sov. Un...D8 29
Moio, Eth...D4 47
Moira, Franklin, N.Y...f10 108
Moisie, Que., Can...h8 75
Moisie, riv., Que., Can...h8 75
Moissac, Fr...E4 14
Moïssala, Chad...D3 46
Moita, Port...f10 20
Mojave, Kern, Calif...E4 82
Mojave, desert, Calif...E5 82
Mojave, riv., Calif...E5 82
Mokameh, India...E10 40
Mokane, Callaway, Mo...C6 101
Mokapu, pt., Haw...g11 88
Mokelumne, riv., Calif...C3 82
Mokelumne Hill, Calaveras, Calif...C3 82
Mokena, Will, Ill...k9 90
Mokepa, Zaire...A4 48
Mokha (Mocha) (Al Mukhā), Yemen...C5 47
Mokhotlong, Leso...C4 49
Moknine, Tun...*B7 44
Mokolo, Cam...C2 46
Mokolo, Zaire...A2 48
Mokpo, Kor...I3 37
Moksha, riv., Sov. Un...C2 29
Mokuaweoweo, crater, Haw...D6 88
Moku Manu, isl., Haw...g11 88
Mol, Bel...C5 15
Mol, Yugo...C5 22
Mola di Bari, It...D6 21
Molalla, Clackamas, Oreg...B4 113
Molanosa, Sask., Can...C3 70
Moláoi, Grc...D4 23
Molasses, pond, Maine...D4 96
Mold, Wales...A4 12
Moldavia (Moldova), prov., Rom...*B8 22
Moldavia, reg., Rom...B8 22
Moldavia (S.S.R.), rep., Sov. Un...E5 28
Molde, Nor...F2 25
Moldova (Moldavia), prov., Rom...*B8 22
Moldova, riv., Rom...B8 22
Moldoveanu, mtn., Rom...C7 22
Molega, lake, N.S., Can...E5 74
Molena, Pike, Ga...D2 87
Molenbeek-St. Jean, Bel...*D4 15
Molengraaff, mts., Indon...F5 35
Molepolole, Bots...B4 49
Môle St. Nicolas, Hai...E7 64
Molfetta, It...D6 21
Molina, Chile...B2 54
Molina de Aragón, Sp...B5 20
Molina de Segura, Sp...C5 20
Moline, Rock Island, Ill...B3 90
Moline, Elk, Kans...E7 93
Moline, Allegan, Mich...F5 98
Moline, Wood, Ohio...e6 111
Moline Acres, St. Louis, Mo...*C7 101
Molinella, It...E7 18
Molino, Escambia, Fla...u14 86
Molinos, Arg...E2 55
Moliro, Zaire...C5 48
Moliterno, It...D5 21
Mill, riv., Aus...C9 18
Mölle, Swe...B6 24
Mollendo, Peru...E3 58
Mollusk, Lancaster, Va...C6 121
Mölndal, Swe...I5 25
Molochansk, Sov. Un...H10 27
Molodechno, Sov. Un...D6 27
Molokai, isl., Haw...B5 88
Molokini, isl., Haw...C5 88
Molopo, riv., Bots., S. Afr...C3 49
Molotovskoye, Sov. Un...I13 27
Moloundou, Cam...E3 46
Mols, isl., Den...B4 24
Molsheim, Fr...F7 15
Molson, Man., Can...D3 71
Molson, Okanogan, Wash...A6 122
Molson, lake, Man., Can...B3 71
Molson, riv., Man., Can...B3 71
Molt, Stillwater, Mont...E8 102
Molteno, S. Afr...D4 49
Molucca, passage, Indon...E7 35
Molucca, sea, Indon...E7 35
Moluccas, is., Indon...F7 35
Molus, Harlan, Ky...D6 94
Moma, Moz...A6 49
Momauguin, New Haven, Conn. (part of East Haven)...E5 84
Mombasa, Ken...B6 48
Mombetsu, Jap...D11 37
Mombongo, Zaire...A3 48
Momboyo, riv., Zaire...B2 48
Momchilgrad, Bul...E7 22
Momence, Kankakee, Ill...B6 90
Momi, Fiji...52
Momostenango, Guat...C2 62
Mompono, Zaire...A3 48
Mompog, pass, Phil...p14 37
Mompós, Col...B3 60
Møn, isl., Den...D6 24
Mona, Richland, Mont...B12 102
Mona, Juab, Utah...D4 119
Mona (Granville), Monongalia, W. Va...h11 123
Mona, isl., P.R...E10 64
Mona, passage, W.I...E9 64
Mona, pt., C.R...F6 62
Monaca, Beaver, Pa...E1 114
Monaco, Monaco...F7 14
Monaco, country, Eur...F7 14
Monadhliath, mts., Scot...C4 13
Monadnock, mtn., N.H...E2 105
Monadnock, mtn., Vt...B5 120
Monagas, state, Ven...B5 60
Monaghan, Ire...C5 11
Monaghan, co., Ire...C4 11
Monahans, Ward, Tex...D1 118
Monamolin, Ire...E5 11
Monango, Dickey, N. Dak...C7 110
Monarch, Alta., Can...E4 69
Monarch, Cascade, Mont...C6 102
Monarch (Monarch Mills), Union, S.C...B4 115
Monarch, mtn., B.C., Can...D5 68
Monarda, Aroostook, Maine...C4 96
Monashee, mts., B.C., Can...D8 68
Monastir, Tun...B7 44
Monastyrshchina, Sov. Un...D8 27
Mona Vatu, mtn., Fiji...52
Monaville, Logan, W. Va...*D3 123
Monção, Braz...B1 57
Moncayo, mtn., Sp...B5 20
Monchegorsk, Sov. Un...D15 25
Mönchengladbach, F.R.G...C3 16, C6 15
Monchique, Port...D1 20
Monchique, mts., Port...D1 20
Moncks Corner, Berkeley, S.C...E7 115
Monclo, Logan, W. Va...D3, n12 123
Monclova, Mex...B4 63
Monclova, Lucas, Ohio...e6 111
Moncton, N.B., Can...C5 74
Moncure, Chatham, N.C...B3 109
Mond, lake, F.R.G...B9 18
Mondamin, Harrison, Iowa...C1 92
Mondego, cape, Port...B1 20
Mondego, riv., Port...B1 20
Mondoñedo, Sp...A2 20
Mondorf-les-Bains, Lux...E6 15
Mondovi, It...B1 21
Mondovi, Buffalo, Wis...D2 124
Monee, Will, Ill...B6 90
Monegaw Springs, St. Clair, Mo...C4 101
Monemvasia, Grc...D4 23
Monero, Rio Arriba, N. Mex...A3 107
Monessen, Westmoreland, Pa...F2 114
Moneta, Bedford, Va...C3 121
Moneta, Fremont, Wyo...C5 125
Monett, Barry and Lawrence, Mo...E4 100
Monetta, Aiken and Saluda, S.C...D4 115
Monette, Craighead, Ark...B5 81
Money, Leflore, Miss...B3 100
Moneymore, N. Ire...C5 11
Monfalcone, It...B4 21
Monforte de Lemos, Sp...A2 20
Monfort Heights, Hamilton, Ohio...*C1 111
Monga, Zaire...A3 48
Mongala, riv., Zaire...A3 48
Mongalla, Sud...D3 47
Monges, is., Ven...A3 60
Mong Hpayak, Bur...B3 38
Mong Hsat, Bur...B3 38
Monghyr, India...C8 38, E11 40
Mong Mit, Bur...D10 39
Mong Nai, Bur...A3 38
Mongo, Chad...C3 46
Mongo, Lagrange, Ind...A7 91
Mongolia, Ont., Can...k15 72
Mongolia, country, Asia...E13 33, B5 34
Mongolia, plat, Mong...B6 34
Mong Pan, Bur...B3 38
Mongu, Zambia...E3 48
Monhegan, isl., Maine...E3 96
Moniaive, Scot...E5 13
Monico, Oneida, Wis...C4 120
Monida, Beaverhead, Mont...F4 102
Monida, pass, Idaho, Mont...F4 102
Monie, Somerset, Md...D6 85
Monifieth, Scot...*D6 13
Moniquirá, Col...B3 60
Moniteau, co., Mo...C5 101
Monitor, Alta., Can...D5 69
Monitor, Marion, Oreg...h12 113
Monitor, Chelan, Wash...B5 122
Monitor, range, Nev...E5 104
Monitor, val., Nev...E5 104
Monivea, Ire...D3 11
Monkey River, Belize...B3 62
Monkira, Austl...B3 51
Monkoto, Zaire...B3 48
Monkton, Ont., Can...D3 72
Monkton, Addison, Vt...C2 120
MonLouis, Mobile, Ala...E1 78
Monmouth, Warren, Ill...C3 90
Monmouth, Jackson, Iowa...B7 92
Monmouth, Kennebec, Maine...D2 96
Monmouth, Polk, Oreg...C3, k11 113
Monmouth, Wales...C5 12
Monmouth, co., Wales...C4 12
Monmouth, co., N.J...C4 106
Monmouth, mtn., B.C., Can...D6 68
Monmouth Beach, Monmouth, N.J...C5 106
Monmouth Junction, Middlesex, N.J...C3 106
Monnikendam, Neth...B5 15
Monnow, riv., Eng., Wales...C5 12
Mono, co., Calif...D4 82
Mono, lake, Calif...D4 82
Monocacy, riv., Md...B3 85
Monomonac, lake, Mass...A3 97
Monomoy, isl., Mass...C8 97
Monomoy, pt., Mass...C7 97
Monon, White, Ind...C4 91
Monona, Clayton, Iowa...A6 92
Monona, Dane, Wis...E4 118
Monona, co., Iowa...B1 92
Monona, lake, Wis...E4 124
Monongah, Marion, W. Va...B4, k10 123
Monongahela, Washington, Pa...F2 114
Monongahela, riv., Pa. W. Va...h10 123
Monongalia, co., W. Va...B4 123
Monopoli, It...D6 21
Monor, Hung...B4 24
Monos, isl., Trin...N22 65
Monóvar, Sp...C5 20
Monoville, Smith, Tenn...C8 117
Monowi, Boyd, Nebr...B7 103
Monowice, Pol...g10 26
Monponsett, Plymouth, Mass...B6 97
Monreale, It...E4 21
Monroe, Monroe, Ark...C4 81
Monroe, Fairfield, Conn...D4 84
Monroe, Walton, Ga...C3 87
Monroe, Adams, Ind...C8 91
Monroe, Tippecanoe, Ind...D4 91
Monroe, Jasper, Iowa...C4 92
Monroe, Ouachita, La...B3 95
Monroe, Waldo, Maine...D3 96
Monroe (Town of), Franklin, Mass...*A2 97
Monroe, Monroe, Mich...G7 98
Monroe, Platte, Nebr...C8 103
Monroe, Grafton, N.H...B2 105
Monroe, Sussex, N.J...A3 106
Monroe, Orange, N.Y...D6, m14 108
Monroe, Union, N.C...C2 109
Monroe, Butler and Warren, Ohio...C1, n13 111
Monroe, Le Flore, Okla...C7 112
Monroe, Benton, Oreg...C3 113
Monroe, Turner, S. Dak...D8 116
Monroe, Overton, Tenn...G8 117
Monroe, Sevier, Utah...E3 119
Monroe, Amherst, Va...C3 121
Monroe, Snohomish, Wash...B4 122
Monroe, Greene, Wis...F4 124
Monroe, co., Ala...D2 78
Monroe, co., Ark...C4 81
Monroe, co., Fla...H5 86
Monroe, co., Ga...D3 87
Monroe, co., Ill...E4 90
Monroe, co., Ind...F4 91
Monroe, co., Iowa...C5 92
Monroe, co., Ky...D4 94
Monroe, co., Mich...G7 98
Monroe, co., Miss...B5 100
Monroe, co., Mo...B5 101
Monroe, co., N.Y...B3 108
Monroe, co., Ohio...C4 111
Monroe, co., Pa...D11 114
Monroe, co., Tenn...D9 117
Monroe, co., W. Va...D4 123
Monroe, co., Wis...E3 124
Monroe Bridge, Franklin, Mass...A2 97
Monroe Center, Fairfield, Conn...D4 84
Monroe Center, Ogle, Ill...A5 90
Monroe City, Knox, Ind...G3 91
Monroe City, Monroe and Marion, Mo...B6 101
Monroe Lake, res., Ind...F5 91
Monroeton, Bradford, Pa...C9 114
Monroeville, Monroe, Ala...D2 78
Monroeville, Allen, Ind...C8 91
Monroeville, Salem, N.J...D2 106
Monroeville, Huron, Ohio...A3 111
Monroeville, Allegheny, Pa...k14 114
Monrovia, Los Angeles, Calif...m13 82
Monrovia, Morgan, Ind...E5 91
Monrovia, Atchison, Kans...A7 93
Monrovia, Lib...E2 45
Mons, Bel...D3 15
Monsanto, St. Clair, Ill...f13 101
Monschau, F.R.G...D6 15
Monselice, It...D7 18
Monsey, Rockland, N.Y...*D6 108
Møns Klint, isl., Den...D6 24
Monson, Piscataquis, Maine...C3 96
Monson, Hampden, Mass...B3 97
Monson Junction, Piscataquis, Maine...C3 96
Montabaur, F.R.G...C2 17
Montagnais, pt., Newf., Can...B2 75
Montagnana, It...D7 18
Montague, Siskiyou, Calif...B2 82
Montague, P.E.I., Can...C7 74
Montague, Franklin, Mass...A2 97
Montague, Muskegon, Mich...E4 98
Montague, Montague, Tex...C4 118
Montague, co., Tex...C4 118
Montague, isl., Alsk...D10 79
Montague, isl., Mex...A2 63
Montague, lake, Sask., Can...H3 70
Montalbán, Sp...B5 20
Montalegre, Port...B2 20
Montalto, Franklin, Pa...G6 114
Montalto, mtn., It...E5 20
Montalvo, Ventura, Calif...*E4 82
Montana, Alsk...f17 76
Montana, Johnson, Ark...B2 81
Montana, state, U.S...A5 76, 102
Montana-Vermala, Switz...D3 19
Montánchez, Sp...C2 20
Montandon, Northumberland, Pa...E8 114
Montargis, Fr...D5 14
Montataire, Fr...E2 15
Montauban, Que., Can...C5 73
Montauban, Fr...E4 14
Montauban-les-Mines, Que., Can...C5 73
Montauk, Suffolk, N.Y...m17 108
Montauk, hbr., N.Y...E9 84
Montauk, pt., N.Y...E9 84
Monta Vista, Santa Clara, Calif...*D2 82
Montbard, Fr...D6 14
Montbéliard, Fr...D7 14
Mont Belvieu, Chambers, Tex...E5, r15 118
Montblanch, Sp...B6 20
Montbrison, Fr...E5 14
Montcalm, co., Que., Can...C3 73
Montcalm, co., Mich...E5 98
Montcalm, peak, Fr...F4 14
Mont-Carmel, Que., Can...B8 73
Montceau-les-Mines, Fr...D6 14
Mont Cenis, pass, Fr., It...D2 18
Mont Cenis, tunnel, Fr., It...D2 18
Montcerf, Que., Can...C1 73
Montchanin [-les-Mines], Fr...D6 14
Montclair (Monte Vista), San Bernardino, Calif...m13 82
Montclair, Essex, N.J...B4 106
Mont Clare, Montgomery, Pa...o19 114
Montcoal, Raleigh, W. Va...D3, n12 123
Montcornet, Fr...E4 15
Mont-de-Marsan, Fr...F3 14
Montdidier, Fr...C5 14
Monteagle, Grundy and Marion, Tenn...D8 117
Monteagudo, Arg...D2 56
Monte Alegre, Braz...C2 56
Monte Alegre, Braz...C4 59
Monte Azul, Braz...E2 57
Montebello, Los Angeles, Calif...m12 82
Montebello, Que., Can...D3 73
Montebello, P.R...B4 65
Montebello, Nelson, Va...C3 121
Monte Bello, is., Austl...D2 50
Montebelluna, It...D8 18
Monte Carlo, Monaco (part of Monaco)...*F7 14
Monte Carmelo, Braz...E1 57
Monte Caseros, Arg...A5 54
Montecatini Terme, It...C3 21
Montecito, It...g9 21
Montecito, Santa Barbara, Calif...*E4 82
Monte Coman, Arg...A3 54
Monte Creek, B.C., Can...D8 68
Montecristi, Dom. Rep...E8 64
Montecristi, Ec...B1 58
Monte Cristo, Bol...B3 55
Montecristo, isl., It...C3 21
Montefrío, Sp...D3 20
Monte Gargano, pen., It...D5 20
Montego, bay, Jam...D12 65
Montego Bay, Jam...E13 65
Montegut, Terrebonne, La...E5 95
Monteiro, Braz...C3 57
Monteith, mtn., B.C., Can...B6 68
Montelavar, Port...F9 20
Montélimar, Fr...E6 14
Montellano, Sp...D3 20
Montello, Elko, Nev...B7 104
Montello, Marquette, Wis...E4 124
Montemorelos, Mex...B5 63
Montemor-o-Novo, Port...C1 20
Montenegro, Braz...D2 56
Montenegro, reg., Yugo...D4 22
Montenegro (Crna Gora), rep., Yugo...*D4 22
Monte Patria, Chile...A2 54
Monte Plata, Dom. Rep...E9 64
Montepuez, Moz...D6 48
Montepulciano, It...C3 21
Monte Quemado, Arg...E3 55
Montereau, Fr...C5 14
Monterey, Butler, Ala...D3 78
Monterey, Monterey, Calif...D3 82
Monterey, Pulaski, Ind...B4 91
Monterey, Owen, Ky...B5 94
Monterey, Berkshire, Mass...B1 97
Monterey, Hamilton, Ohio...*C1 111
Monterey, Putnam, Tenn...C8 117
Monterey, Highland, Va...B3 121
Monterey, co., Calif...D3 82
Monterey, bay, Calif...D3 82
Monterey Park, Los Angeles, Calif...m12 82
Montería, Col...B2 60
Monteros, Arg...E2 55
Monterotondo, It...g9 21
Monterrey, Mex...B4 63
Montesano, Grays Harbor, Wash...C2 122
Monte Sano, mts., Ala...A3 78
Monte Sant'Angelo, It...D5 21
Monte Santo, Braz...D3 57
Montes Claros, Braz...E2 57
Monte Sereno, Santa Clara, Calif...*D3 82
Montevallo, Shelby, Ala...B3 78
Montevarchi, It...C3 21
Montevideo, Chippewa, Minn...F3 99
Montevideo, Ur...E1 56
Montevideo, dept., Ur...*E1 56
Monteview, Jefferson, Idaho...F6 89
Monte Vista, Rio Grande, Colo...D4 83
Monte Vista, Webster, Miss...B4 100
Monte Vista, Pierce, Wash...*B3 122
Montevue, Frederick, Md...B3 85
Montezuma, Macon, Ga...D2 87
Montezuma, Parke, Ind...E3 91
Montezuma, Poweshiek, Iowa...C5 92
Montezuma, Gray, Kans...E3 93
Montezuma, San Miguel, N. Mex...B4 107
Montezuma, Mercer, Ohio...B1 111
Montezuma, Chester, Tenn...B3 117
Montezuma, co., Colo...D2 83
Montezuma Castle, nat. mon., Ariz...C4 80
Montezuma Creek, San Juan, Utah...F6 119
Montfaucon, Switz...B3 19
Montfort, Que., Can...D3 73
Montfort, Grant, Wis...F3 124
Montfort-sur-Meu, Fr...C3 14
Montgomery, Montgomery, Ala...C3 78
Montgomery, Alta., Can...D3 69
Montgomery, Chatham, Ga...E5 87
Montgomery, Kane, Ill...B5, k8 90
Montgomery, Daviess, Ind...G3 91
Montgomery, Grant, La...C3 95
Montgomery, Hampden, Mass...B2 97
Montgomery, Hillsdale, Mich...G6 98
Montgomery, Le Sueur, Minn...F5 99
Montgomery, Orange, N.Y...D6 108
Montgomery, Hamilton, Ohio...o13 111
Montgomery, see Sāhiwāl, Pak
Montgomery, Lycoming, Pa...D8 114
Montgomery, Franklin, Vt...B3 120
Montgomery, Wales...B4 12
Montgomery, Fayette and Kanawha, W. Va...C3, m13 123
Montgomery, co., Ala...C3 78
Montgomery, co., Ark...C2 81
Montgomery, co., Ga...D4 87
Montgomery, co., Ill...D4 90
Montgomery, co., Ind...D4 91
Montgomery, co., Iowa...C2 92
Montgomery, co., Kans...E8 93
Montgomery, co., Ky...B6 94
Montgomery, co., Md...B3 85
Montgomery, co., Miss...B4 100
Montgomery, co., Mo...C6 101
Montgomery, co., N.Y...C6 108
Montgomery, co., N.C...B3 109
Montgomery, co., Ohio...C1 111
Montgomery, co., Pa...F10 114
Montgomery, co., Tenn...A4 117
Montgomery, co., Tex...D5 118
Montgomery, co., Va...C2 121
Montgomery, co., Wales...B4 12
Montgomery Center, Franklin, Vt...B3 120
Montgomery City, Montgomery, Mo...C4 101
Montgomery Creek, Shasta, Calif...B3 82
Monthermé, Fr...E4 15
Monthey, Switz...D2 19
Monticello, Drew, Ark...D4 81
Monticello, P.E.I., Can...C7 74
Monticello, Jefferson, Fla...B3 86
Monticello, Jasper, Ga...C3 87
Monticello, Piatt, Ill...C5 90
Monticello, White, Ind...C4 91
Monticello, Jones, Iowa...B6 92
Monticello, Wayne, Ky...D5 94
Monticello, Aroostook, Maine...B5 96
Monticello, Wright, Minn...E5 99
Monticello, Lawrence, Miss...D3 100
Monticello, Lewis, Mo...A6 101
Monticello, Sierra, N. Mex...D2 107
Monticello, Sullivan, N.Y...D6 108
Monticello, San Juan, Utah...F6 119
Monticello, Green, Wis...F4 124
Mont Ida, Anderson, Kans...D8 93
Montier-en-Der, Fr...F4 15
Montiers-sur-Saulx, Fr...F5 15
Montigny-lès-Metz, Fr...F6 15
Montijo, Port...C1, f10 20
Montijo, Sp...C2 20
Montilla, Sp...D3 20
Monti Verdi, Morgan, Utah...*B4 119
Montivilliers, Fr...C3 14
Mont-Joli, Que., Can...A9 73
Mont-Laurier, Que., Can...C2 73
Montluçon, Fr...D5 14
Montmagny, Que., Can...C7 73
Montmagny, co., Que., Can...C7 73
Montmartre, Sask., Can...G4 70
Montmédy, Fr...E5 15
Montmélian, Fr...D2 18
Montmirail, Fr...F3 15
Montmorenci, Tippecanoe, Ind...D3 91
Montmorenci, Aiken, S.C...D4 115
Montmorency, Fr...g10 14
Montmorency, co., Mich...C6 98
Montmorency No. 1, co., Que., Can...B6 73
Montmorency No. 2, co., Que., Can...C6 73
Montmorency, riv., Que., Can...B6 73
Montmorillon, Fr...D4 14
Montney, B.C., Can...A7 68
Monto, Austl...B8 51
Montone, riv., It...B3 21
Montoro, Sp...C3 20
Montour, Gem, Idaho...F2 89
Montour, Tama, Iowa...C5 92
Montour, co., Pa...D8 114
Montour Falls, Schuyler, N.Y...C4 108
Montoursville, Lycoming, Pa...D8 114
Montowese, New Haven, Conn. (part of North Haven)...D5 84
Montoya, Quay, N. Mex...B5 107
Montpelier, Bear Lake, Idaho...G7 89
Montpelier, Blackford, Ind...C7 91
Montpelier, Muscatine, Iowa...C7 92
Montpelier, St. Helena, La...D5 95
Montpelier, Clay, Miss...B4 100
Montpelier, Stutsman, N. Dak...C7 110
Montpelier, Williams, Ohio...A1 111
Montpelier, Washington, Vt...C3 120
Montpelier Station, Orange, Va...B4 121
Montpellier, Que., Can...D2 73
Montpellier, Fr...F5 14
Montréal, Que., Can...D4, q19 73
Montreal, Iron, Wis...B3 124
Montreal, lake, Sask., Can...C3 70
Montreal, riv., Sask., Can...C3 70
Montréal-Est, Que., Can...*D4 73
Montreal Lake, Sask., Can...C3 70
Montréal-Nord, Que., Can...p19 73
Montréal West, Que., Can...*D4 73
Montreat, Buncombe, N.C...f10 109
Montreuil, Fr...C5, g10 14, F2 15
Montreuil-sur-Mer, Fr...B4 14
Montreux, Switz...D2 19
Montricher, Switz...C1 19
Mont-Rolland, Que., Can...D3 73
Montrose, Baldwin, Ala...E2 78
Montrose, Ashley, Ark...D4 81
Montrose, Los Angeles, Calif...*E4 82
Montrose, B.C., Can...E9 68
Montrose, Montrose, Colo...C3 83
Montrose, Laurens, Ga...D3 87
Montrose, Effingham, Ill...D5 90
Montrose, Lee, Iowa...D6 92
Montrose, Jewell, Kans...C5 93
Montrose, Natchitoches, La...C2 95
Montrose, Genesee, Mich...E7 98
Montrose, Jasper, Miss...C4 100
Montrose, Henry, Mo...C4 101
Montrose, Westchester, N.Y...*D7 108
Montrose, Berks, Pa...*F10 114
Montrose, Susquehanna, Pa...C10 114
Montrose, Scot...D6 13
Montrose, McCook, S. Dak...D8 116
Montrose, Henrico, Va...m18 121
Montrose, co., Colo...C2 83
Montrose Hill, Allegheny, Pa...*E2 114
Montross, Westmoreland, Va...B6 121
Mont-Royal, Que., Can...p19 73
Montrouge, Fr...g10 14
Mont-St. Martin, Fr...C6 14
Mont-St. Michel, Fr...C3 14
Montserrat, Johnson, Mo...C4 101
Montserrat, Br. dep., N.A...H13 64
Montserrat, peak, Sp...B6 20
Mont-Tremblant, Que., Can...C3 73
Mont Tremblant, prov. park, Que., Can...C3 73
Montvale, Bergen, N.J...g8 106
Montvale, Bedford, Va...C3 121
Mont Vernon, Hillsboro, N.H...E3 105
Montville, New London, Conn...D8 84
Montville, Berkshire, Mass...B1 97
Montville, Morris, N.J...B4 106
Montz, St. Charles, La...h11 95
Montzen, Bel...D5 15
Monument, El Paso, Colo...B6 83
Monument, Logan, Kans...C2 93
Monument, Lea, N. Mex...E6 107
Monument, Grant, Oreg...C7 113
Monument, Centre, Pa...D6 114
Monument, peak, Colo...B3 83
Monument, peak, Idaho...D2 89
Monument, peak, Oreg...C4 113
Monumental, buttes, Idaho...B3 89
Monument Beach, Barnstable, Mass...C6 97
Monument Heights, Henrico, Va...*C5 121
Monument Valley, San Juan, Utah...*F6 119
Monument Valley, ruins, Ariz...A5 80
Monywa, Bur...D10 39
Monza, It...D5 18, B2 21
Monze, Zambia...E4 48
Monze, cape, Pak...I13 41
Monzón, Peru...C2 58
Monzón, Sp...B6 20
Moodus, Middlesex, Conn...D7 84
Moodus, res., Conn...C7 84
Moody, York, Maine...E2 96
Moody, Howell, Mo...E6 101
Moody, McLennan, Tex...D4 118
Moody, co., S. Dak...C9 116
Mooers, Clinton, N.Y...f11 108
Mooers Forks, Clinton, N.Y...f11 108
Moon, McCurtain, Okla...D7 112
Moon, lake, Miss...A3 100
Moonachie, Bergen, N.J...*B4 106
Moon Crest, Allegheny, Pa...*E1 114
Moon Run, Allegheny, Pa...k13 114
Moonta, Austl...F6 50
Moora, Austl...F2 50
Moorabbin, Austl...*H5 51

Moorcroft, Crook, Wyo B8 125
Moore, Butte, Idaho F5 89
Moore, Fergus, Mont D7 102
Moore, Cleveland, Okla B4 112
Moore, Spartanburg, S.C. B4 115
Moore, Frio, Tex E3 118
Moore, Tucker, W. Va. B5 123
Moore, co., N.C. B3 109
Moore, co., Tenn B5 117
Moore, co., Tex B2 118
Moore, res., N.H., Vt C5 120
Moorefield, Ont., Can D4 72
Moorefield, Nicholas, Ky B6 94
Moorefield, Frontier, Nebr D7 103
Moorefield, Hardy, W. Va B6 123
Moore Haven, Glades, Fla F5 86
Moorehead, Monona, Iowa C2 92
Mooreland, Henry, Ind E7 91
Mooreland, Woodward, Okla A2 112
Mooreland Heights, Knox, Tenn *D10 117
Moorepark, Man., Can D2 71
Mooresburg, Hawkins, Tenn C10 117
Moores Corner, Franklin, Mass A2 97
Moores Hill, Dearborn, Ind F7 91
Moore's Mills, N.B., Can D2 74
Moorestown, Missaukee, Mich D5 98
Moorestown, Burlington, N.J D3 106
Mooresville, Morgan, Ind E5 91
Mooresville, Livingston, Mo B4 101
Mooresville, Iredell, N.C B2 109
Mooresville, Marshall, Tenn B5 117
Mooreton, Richland, N. Dak C9 110
Mooreville, Lee, Miss A5 100
Moorhead, Clay, Minn D2 99
Moorhead, Sunflower, Miss B3 100
Mooring, Lake, Tenn A2 117
Mooringsport, Caddo, La B2 95
Moor Lake Station, Ont., Can A7 72
Moorland, Webster, Iowa B3 92
Moorman, Muhlenberg, Ky C2 94
Moosburg, F.R.G E6 17
Moose, Teton, Wyo C2 125
Moose, hill, Mass h11 97
Moose, isl., Man., Can D3 71
Moose, lake, B.C., Can C1 69
Moose, lake, Man., Can A4 71
Moose, mtn., Sask., Can H4 70
Moose, mtn., N.H C2 105
Moose, pond, Maine D3 96
Moose, riv., Maine C2 96
Moose, riv., N.H B4 105
Moose, riv., N.Y B5 108
Moose, riv., Vt B5 120
Moose Creek, Ont., Can B10 72
Moose Creek, buttes, Idaho C3 89
Moose Factory, Ont., Can F16 67
Moosehead, Piscataquis, Maine C3 96
Moosehead, lake, Maine C3 96
Mooseheart, Kane, Ill B5, k8 90
Moose Heights, B.C., Can C6 68
Moosehorn, Man., Can D2 71
Moosehorn, Franklin, Maine C2 96
Moose Jaw, Sask., Can G3, n7 70
Moose Jaw, riv., Sask., Can G3 70
Moose Lake, Man., Can C1 71
Moose Lake, Carlton, Minn D6 99
Moose Lake, res., Wis B3 124
Mooseleuk, stream, Maine B4 96
Mooselookmeguntic, lake, Maine D2 96
Moose Mountain, creek, Sask., Can H4 70
Moose Mountain, prov. park, Sask., Can H4 70
Moose Pass, Alsk C10, g17 79
Moose River, Somerset, Maine C2 96
Moosic, Lackawanna, Pa m18 114
Moosic, mts., Pa m18 114
Moosilauke, mtn., N.H B3 105
Moosomin, Sask., Can G5 70
Moosonee, Ont., Can o19 72
Moosup, Windham, Conn C9 84
Moosup Valley, Providence, R.I C9 84
Mopang, lakes, Maine D5 96
Mopeia Velha, Moz A6 49
Mopti, Mali D4 45
Moquegua, Peru E3 58
Moquegua, dept., Peru E3 58
Mor, Hung B4 22
Mor, isl., Truk 52
Mora, Cam C2 46
Mora, Atkinson, Ga E4 87
Mora, Kanabec, Minn E5 99
Mora, Mora, N. Mex B4 107
Mora, Sp C4 20
Mora, Swe G6 52
Mora, co., N. Mex A5 107
Mora, riv., N. Mex B5 107
Morača, riv., Yugo D4 22
Morada, San Joaquin, Calif *D3 82
Morādābād, India C6 39, C7 40
Morada Nova, Braz D3 57
Mora de Ebro, Sp B6 20
Morafenobe, Mad g8 49
Morag, Pol B5 26
Moraga, Contra Costa, Calif *D2 82
Moraine, Montgomery, Ohio *C1 111
Morales, Guat C3 62
Morales, Mex k13 63
Moramanga, Mad g9 49
Moran, Clinton, Ind D4 91
Moran, Allen, Kans E8 93
Moran, Mackinac, Mich B6 98
Moran, Shackelford, Tex C3 118
Moran, Teton, Wyo C2 125
Morann, Clearfield, Pa E5 114
Morant, pt., Jam F16 65
Morant Bay, Jam F16 65
Morar, lake, Scot D3 13
Morat, lake, Switz C3 18
Morata de Tajuña, Sp p18 20
Moratalla, Sp C5 20
Morattico, Lancaster, Va D6 121
Moratuwa, Sri Lanka *G6 39
Morava, riv., Czech D4 26
Morava, riv., Yugo C5 22
Moravia (Morava), reg., Czech D4 26
Moravia, Appanoose, Iowa D5 92
Moravia, Cayuga, N.Y C4 108
Morawhanna, Guy A3 59
Moraya, Bol D2 55
Moray, firth, Scot C5 13
Morbach, F.R.G D2 17
Morbihan, dept., Fr *D2 14
Morcenx, Fr E3 14
Morco, Anderson, Tenn C9 117
Morden, Man., Can E2 71
Morden, N.S., Can D5 74
More, mtn., Scot D3 13
More, mtn., Scot D4 13
More Assynt, mtn., Scot B4 13
Moreau, riv., S. Dak B3 116
Moreauville, Avoyelles, La C4 95
Morecambe, Eng F6 13
Morecambe, bay, Eng D5 10
Moree, Austl D7 51
Morehead, Rowan, Ky B6 94
Morehead City, Carteret, N.C C6 109
Morehouse, New Madrid, Mo E8 101
Morehouse, par., La B4 95
Mörel, Switz D5 19
Moreland, Pope, Ark B3 81
Moreland, Coweta, Ga C2 87
Moreland, Bingham, Idaho F6 89
Moreland, Lincoln, Ky C5 94
Moreland, Lycoming, Pa D8 114
Moreland Hills, Cuyahoga, Ohio *A4 111
Morelia, Mex D4, n13 63
Morell, P.E.I., Can C7 74
Morella, Sp B5 20
Morelos, state, Mex D5, n14 63
Morelos, dam, Ariz E1 80
Morena, mts., Sp C3 20
Morenci, Greenlee, Ariz D6 80
Morenci, Lenawee, Mich G6 98
Moreno, pt., Fla G2 86
Möre og Romsdal, co., Nor *F2 25
Moresby, isl., B.C., Can C1 68
Moreton, bay, Austl C9 51
Moreton, isl., Austl C9 51
Moreton-in-Marsh, Eng C6 12
Moretown, Washington, Vt C3 120
Moreuil, Fr E2 15
Morewood, Ont., Can B9 72
Morey, lake, Vt D4 120
Morez, Fr D7 14
Morgan, Austl G2 51
Morgan, Calhoun, Ga E2 87
Morgan, Pendleton, Ky B5 94
Morgan, Redwood, Minn F4 99
Morgan, Phillips, Mont B9 102
Morgan, Morrow, Oreg B7 113
Morgan, Bosque, Texas C4 118
Morgan, Morgan, Utah B4 119
Morgan, Orleans, Vt B4 120
Morgan, co., Ala A3 78
Morgan, co., Colo A7 83
Morgan, co., Ga C3 87
Morgan, co., Ill D3 90
Morgan, co., Ind F5 91
Morgan, co., Ky C6 94
Morgan, co., Mo C5 101
Morgan, co., Ohio C4 111
Morgan, co., Tenn C9 117
Morgan, co., Utah B4 119
Morgan, co., W. Va B6 123
Morgan, isl., S.C G6 115
Morgan, pt., Conn E5 84
Morgan Center, Orleans, Vt B5 120
Morgan City, St. Mary, La E4, k9 95
Morgan City, Leflore, Miss B3 100
Morganfield, Union, Ky C2 94
Morgan Hill, Santa Clara, Calif D3 82
Morganton, Van Buren, Ark B3 81
Morganton, Fannin, Ga B2 87
Morganton, Burke, N.C B1 109
Morgantown, Morgan, Ind F5 91
Morgantown, Butler, Ky C3 94
Morgantown, Adams, Miss D2 100
Morgantown, Marion, Miss D4 100
Morgantown, Berks, Pa F10 114
Morgantown, Bledsoe, Tenn D8 117
Morgantown, Monongalia, W. Va B5, h11 123
Morganville, Dade, Ga B1 87
Morganville, Clay, Kans C6 93
Morganville, Monmouth, N.J C4 106
Morganza, Pointe Coupee, La D4 95
Morges, Switz C1 19
Morgex, It D3 18
Morghāb, riv., Afg D12 41
Morhange, Fr F6 15
Mori, Jap E10 37
Moriah, Essex, N.Y A7 108
Moriah, Trin M24 65
Moriah, mtn., Nev D7 104
Moriah, mtn., N.H B4 105
Moriarty, Torrance, N. Mex C3, m8 107
Morice, lake, B.C., Can B4 68
Morice, riv., B.C., Can B4 68
Moriches, bay, N.Y G5 84
Moriguchi, Jap *o14 37
Morin Heights, Que., Can D3 73
Morinville, Alta., Can C4 69
Morioka, Jap G10 37
Morisset Station, Que., Can C7 73
Moriyama, Jap *I9 37
Morjärv, Swe D10 25
Morkill, riv., B.C., Can C7 68
Morlaix, Fr C2 14
Morland, Graham, Kans C3 93
Morley, Alta., Can D3 69
Morley, Eng *A6 12
Morley, Mecosta, Mich E5 98
Morley, Scott, Mo D8 101
Morley, St. Lawrence, N.Y f9 108
Mormon, range, Nev G7 104
Mormon Lake, Coconino, Ariz C4 80
Morne-à-l'Eau, Guad Q8 65
Morningdale, Worcester, Mass B4 97
Morningside, Prince Georges, Md *C4 85
Morningside, Hennepin, Minn *F5 99
Morningside, Beadle, S. Dak C7 116
Morning Sun, Louisa, Iowa C6 92
Mornington, isl., Chile D1 54
Morning View, Kenton, Ky k14 94
Moro, Lee, Ark C5 81
Moro, Madison, Ill f13 101
Moro, Sherman, Oreg B6 113
Moro, creek, Ark D3 81
Moro, gulf, Phil D6 35
Morobay, Bradley, Ark D3 81
Morobe, Pap. N. Gui k12 50
Morocco, Newton, Ind C3 91
Morocco, country, Afr C5 42, C3 44
Morococha, Peru D2 58
Morogoro, Tan C6 48
Moroleón, Mex m13 63
Morombe, Mad h8 49
Morón, Cuba C4 64
Morona, riv., Peru B2 58
Morondava, Mad h8 49
Morón de la Frontera, Sp D3 20
Moroni, Comoro Is *f8 49
Moroni, Sanpete, Utah D4 119
Morong, Phil o13 35
Morotai, isl., Indon E7 35
Moroto, Ug A5 48
Morovis, mun., P.R *B3 65
Morozovsk, Sov. Un D2 29
Morpeth, Ont., Can E3 73
Morpeth, Eng E7 13
Morphou, Cyp E9 31
Morral, Marion, Ohio B2 111
Morrill, Brown, Kans C8 93
Morrill, Scotts Bluff, Nebr C2 103
Morrill, co., Nebr C2 103
Morrilton, Conway, Ark B3 81
Morrin, Alta., Can D4 69
Morrinhos, Braz E1 57
Morrinsville, N.Z L15 51
Morris, Jefferson, Ala B3 78
Morris, Man., Can E3 71
Morris, Litchfield, Conn C4 84
Morris, Quitman, Ga E2 87
Morris, Grundy, Ill B5 90
Morris, Ripley, Ind F7 91
Morris, Stevens, Minn E3 99
Morris, Otsego, N.Y C5 108
Morris, Okmulgee, Okla B6 112
Morris, co., Kans D7 93
Morris, co., N.J B3 106
Morris, co., Tex C5 118
Morris, isl., S.C F8 115
Morris, mtn., N.Y A6 108
Morrisburg, Ont., Can C9 72
Morris Chapel, Hardin, Tenn B3 117
Morrisdale, Clearfield, Pa E5 114
Morris Jesup, cape, Grnld A18 4
Morrison, Jefferson, Colo B5 83
Morrison, Whiteside, Ill B4 90
Morrison, Gasconade, Mo C6 101
Morrison, Noble, Okla A6 112
Morrison, Warren, Tenn D8 117
Morrison, Brown, Wis h10 124
Morrison, co., Minn D4 99
Morrison City, Sullivan, Tenn C11 117
Morrisonville, Christian, Ill D4 90
Morrisonville, Clinton, N.Y f11 108
Morris Plains, Morris, N.J B4 106
Morris Run, Tioga, Pa C7 114
Morriston, Levy, Fla C4 86
Morristown, Maricopa, Ariz D3, k7 80
Morristown, Shelby, Ind E6 91
Morristown, Rice, Minn F5 99
Morristown, Morris, N.J B4 106
Morristown, St. Lawrence, N.Y f9 108
Morristown, Corson, S. Dak B4 116
Morristown, Hamblen, Tenn C10 117
Morristown, Lamoille, Vt B3 120
Morristown, nat. historical park, N.J B3 106
Morrisville, Polk, Mo D4 101
Morrisville, Madison, N.Y C5 108
Morrisville, Bucks, Pa F12 114
Morrisville, Lamoille, Vt B3 120
Morrito, Nic E5 62
Morro, Ec B1 58
Morro Bay, San Luis Obispo, Calif E3 82
Morro do Chapéu, Braz D2 57
Morropón, Peru C2 58
Morrosquillo, gulf, Col B2 60
Morrow, Clayton, Ga C2, h8 87
Morrow, St. Landry, La D3 95
Morrow, Warren, Ohio C1 111
Morrow, co., Ohio B3 111
Morrow, co., Oreg B7 113
Morrowville, Washington, Kans C6 93
Morse, Sask., Can G2 70
Morse, Acadia, La D3 95
Morse, Hansford, Tex A2 118
Morse, Ashland, Wis B3 124
Morse, res., Ind D5 91
Morse Bluff, Saunders, Nebr C9 103
Morse Mill, Jefferson, Mo g12 101
Morses, creek, N.J k8 106
Morshansk, Sov. Un C2 29
Mortagne [-au-Perche], Fr C4 14
Mortara, It B2 21
Morteau, Fr D7 14
Morteros, Arg A4 54
Mortlach, Sask., Can G2 70
Morton, Tazewell, Ill C4 90
Morton, Renville, Minn F4 99
Morton, Scott, Miss C4 100
Morton, Delaware, Pa *G11 114
Morton, Cochran, Tex C1 118
Morton, Lewis, Wash C3 122
Morton, Freemont, Wyo C4 125
Morton, co., Kans E2 93
Morton, co., N. Dak C4 110
Morton Grove, Cook, Ill h9 90
Mortons Gap, Hopkins, Ky C2 94
Moruga, Trin O23 65
Moruya, Austl G8 51
Morvan, mts., Fr D6 14
Morven, Brooks, Ga F3 87
Morven, Anson, N.C C2 109
Morven, mtn., Scot B5 13
Morvi, India F3 40
Moryakovskiy Zaton, Sov. Un B10 29
Morye, Sov. Un r32 25
Mosalsk, Sov. Un D10 27
Mosbach, F.R.G D4 17
Mosby, Clay, Mo h11 101
Mosby, Garfield, Mont D9 102
Mosca, Alamosa, Colo D5 83
Moscarello, riv., It k9 21
Moscos, is., Bur E2 38
Moscow, Jefferson, Ark C4 81
Moscow, Latah, Idaho C2 89
Moscow, Rush, Ind F6 91
Moscow, Muscatine, Iowa C6 92
Moscow, Stevens, Kans E2 93
Moscow, Clermont, Ohio D1 111
Moscow, Lackawanna, Pa m18 114
Moscow (Moskva), Sov. Un D11, n17 27
Moscow, Fayette, Tenn B2 117
Moscow, Lamoille, Vt C3 120
Moscow Mills, Lincoln, Mo C7 101
Mosel, riv., F.R.G C2 17
Moseley, Powhatan, Va C5 121
Moselle, Jones, Miss D4 100
Moselle, dept., Fr E6 15
Moselle, riv., Fr C7 14
Mosers River, N.S., Can E7 74
Moses, lake, Wash B6 122
Moses Coulee, canyon, Wash B6 122
Moses Lake, Grant, Wash B6 122
Mosgiel, N.Z P13 51
Mosheim, Greene, Tenn C11 117
Mosher, Mellette, S. Dak D5 116
Mosherville, N.S., Can D6 74
Moshi, Tan B6 48
Moshupa, Bots B4 49
Mosier, Wasco, Oreg B5 113
Mosinee, Marathon, Wis D4 124
Mosjöen, Nor E5 25
Moskva, see Moscow, Sov. Un.
Moskva, riv., Sov. Un n17 27
Mosley, creek, B.C., Can D5 68
Mosonmagyaróvár, Hung B3 22
Mosquera, Col C2 60
Mosquero, Harding and San Miguel, N. Mex B6 107
Mosquito, Newf., Can E5 75
Mosquito, creek, Iowa D5 92
Mosquito, lagoon, Fla D6 86
Mosquito Coast, reg., Hond., Nic D6 62
Mosquito Creek Lake, res., Ohio A5 111
Mosquitos, gulf, Pan F7 62
Moss, Jasper, Miss D4 100
Moss, Nor H4, p28 25
Moss, Clay, Tenn C8 117
Moss, mtn., Ark C3 81
Mossaka, Con F3 46
Mossbank, Sask., Can H3 70
Moss Bluff, Calcasieu, La D2 95
Moss Bluff, Liberty, Tex F5 118
Mosselbaai (Mossel Bay), S. Afr D3 49
Mossendjo, Con F2 46
Moss Landing, Monterey, Calif *D3 82
Mossleigh, Alta., Can D4 69
Mossoro, Braz C3 56
Moss Point, Jackson, Miss E5, f8 100
Moss Vale, Austl G8 51
Mossville, Newton, Ark B2 81
Mossville, Calcasieu, La *D2 95
Mossy, riv., Man., Can D2 71
Mossy, riv., Sask., Can C4 70
Mossy Head, Walton, Fla u15 86
Mossyrock, Lewis, Wash C3 122
Most, Czech C2 24
Mostaganem, Alg B5 44
Mostar, Yugo D3 22
Móstoles, Sp p17 20
Mosul (Al Mawşil), Iraq D14 31
Motagua, riv., Guat C3 62
Motala, Swe H6 25
Motatán, Ven B3 60
Mothe, isl., Fiji Is 52
Motherwell [& Wishaw], Scot E5 13
Motihari, India D10 40
Motilla del Palancar, Sp C5 20
Motley, Morrison, Minn D4 99
Motley, co., Tex B2 118
Moto, see Ōshima, Jap.
Moto, mtn., Iwo 52
Motombo-Mukulu, Zaire C3 48
Motoyoshi, Jap G10 37
Motril, Sp D4 20
Motrul, riv., Rom C6 22
Mott, Hettinger, N. Dak C3 110
Motta di Livenza, It D8 19
Motueka, N.Z N14 51
Motuhora, N.Z M16 51
Motul [de Felipe Carrillo Puerto], Mex C7 63
Motupe, Peru C2 58
Moturiki, isl., Fiji 52
Mouat Mine, Stillwater, Mont *E7 102
Moudhros (Mudros), Grc C5 23
Moudjéria, Maur C2 45
Moudon, Switz C2 19
Mouila, Gabon F2 46
Moulde Bay, N.W., Ter., Can m28 67
Moule, see Le Moule, Guad.
Moulins, Fr D5 14
Moúlki, Grc g10 23
Moulmein, Bur D2 38, E10 39
Moulouya, riv., Mor C4 44
Moulton, Lawrence, Ala A2 78
Moulton, Appanoose, Iowa D5 92
Moulton, valley, Ala A2 78
Moultonboro, Carroll, N.H C4 105
Moultonville, Carroll, N.H C4 105
Moultrie, Colquitt, Ga E3 87
Moultrie, co., Ill D5 90
Moultrie, lake, S.C E7 115
Mound, Hennepin, Minn n11 99
Mound Bayou, Bolivar, Miss B3 100
Mound City, Pulaski, Ill F4 90
Mound City, Linn, Kans D9 93
Mound City, Holt, Mo A2 101
Mound City, Campbell, S. Dak B5 116
Mound City Group, nat. mon., Ohio C2 111
Moundou, Chad D3 46
Moundridge, McPherson, Kans D6 93
Mounds, Pulaski, Ill F4 90
Mounds, Creek, Okla B5 112
Mounds View, Ramsey, Minn m12 99
Moundsville, Marshall, W. Va B4, g8 123
Mound Valley, Labette, Kans E8 93
Moundville, Hale, Ala C2 78
Moundville, Vernon, Mo D3 101
Mounier, mtn., Fr E7 14
Mountain, Pembina, N. Dak A8 110
Mountain, Ritchie, W. Va B4 123
Mountain, Oconto, Wis C5 124
Mountain, prov., Phil *B6 35
Mountain, lake, Sask., Can B3 70
Mountainair, Torrance, N. Mex C3 107
Mountainaire, Coconino, Ariz B4 80
Mountain Ash, Whitley, Ky D5 94
Mountain Brook, Jefferson, Ala g7 78
Mountainburg, Crawford, Ark B1 81
Mountain City, Rabun, Ga B3 87
Mountain City, Elko, Nev B6 104
Mountain City, Johnson, Tenn C12 117
Mountain Creek, Chilton, Ala C3 78
Mountain Dale, Sullivan, N.Y D6 108
Mountain Fork, riv., Okla C7 112
Mountain Grove, Ont., Can C8 72
Mountain Grove, Wright, Mo D5 101
Mountain Home, Baxter, Ark A3 81
Mountain Home, Elmore, Idaho F3 89
Mountainhome, Monroe, Pa D11 114
Mountain Home, Kerr, Tex D3 118
Mountain Home, Duchesne, Utah C5 119
Mountain Iron, St. Louis, Minn C6 99
Mountain Lake, Cottonwood, Minn G4 99
Mountain Lake Park, Garrett, Md m12 85
Mountain Lakes, Morris, N.J B4 106
Mountain Nile, riv., Sud D3 47
Mountain Park, Alta., Can C2 69
Mountain Park, Kiowa, Okla C3 112
Mountain Pine, Garland, Ark C2, f7 81
Mountainside, Union, N.J B4 106
Mountain Valley, Garland, Ark C2 81
Mountain View, Stone, Ark B3 81
Mountain View, Santa Clara, Calif k8 82
Mountain View, Alta., Can E4 69
Mountain View, Larimer, Colo *A5 83
Mountain View, Clayton, Ga *C2 87
Mountainview, Hawaii, Haw D6 88
Mountain View, Ada, Idaho *F2 89
Mountain View, Howell, Mo D6 101
Mountain View, Bernalillo, N. Mex C3 107
Mountain View, Kiowa, Okla B3 112
Mountain View, Asotin, Wash C8 122
Mountain View, Natrona, Wyo *D6 125
Mountain View, Uinta, Wyo E2 125
Mountain Village, Alsk C7 79
Mount Airy, Habersham, Ga B3 87
Mount Airy, Carroll and Frederick, Md B3 85
Mount Airy, Surry, N.C A2 109
Mount Albert, Ont., Can C5 72
Mount Andrew, Barbour, Ala D4 78
Mount Angel, Marion, Oreg B4, h12 113
Mount Arlington, Morris, N.J B3 106
Mount Assiniboine, prov. park, B.C., Can D10 68
Mount Athos (Ayion Oros), prov., Grc B5 23
Mount Auburn, Christian, Ill D4 90
Mount Auburn, Benton, Iowa B5 92
Mount Ayr, Newton, Ind C3 91
Mount Ayr, Ringgold, Iowa D3 92
Mount Barker, Austl G2 51
Mount Bellew, Ire D3 11
Mount Berry, Floyd, Ga B1 87
Mount Blanchard, Hancock, Ohio B2 111
Mount Blanc, tunnel, Fr., It D2 18
Mount Brydges, Ont., Can E3 72
Mount Calvary, Fond du Lac, Wis E5, k9 124
Mount Carmel, Montgomery, Ala C3 78
Mount Carmel, Newf., Can E5 75
Mount Carmel, Wabash, Ill E6 90
Mount Carmel, Franklin, Ind F8 91
Mount Carmel, Cavalier, N. Dak A7 110
Mount Carmel, Clermont, Ohio o13 111
Mount Carmel, Northumberland, Pa E9 114
Mount Carmel, McCormick, S.C C3 115
Mount Carmel, Kane, Utah F3 119
Mount Carmel Junction, Kane, Utah F3 119
Mount Carroll, Carroll, Ill A4 90
Mount Clare, Harrison, W. Va B4 123
Mount Clemens, Macomb, Mich F8, o16 98
Mount Clinton, Rockingham, Va B4 121
Mount Cory, Hancock, Ohio B2 111
Mount Croghan, Chesterfield, S.C B7 115
Mount Darwin, Zimb A5 49
Mount Desert, isl., Maine D4 96
Mount Dora, Lake, Fla D5 86
Mount Dora, Union, N. Mex A6 107
Mount Eaton, Wayne, Ohio B4 111
Mount Eden, Spencer, Ky B4 94
Mount Edgecumbe, Alsk m22 79
Mount Elgin, Ont., Can E4 72
Mount Emmons, Duchesne, Utah *C5 119
Mount Enterprise, Rusk, Tex D5 118
Mount Ephraim, Camden, N.J *D2 106
Mount Erie, Wayne, Ill E5 90
Mount Etna, Huntington, Ind C6 91
Mount Etna, Adams, Iowa C3 92
Mount Forest, Ont., Can D4 72
Mount Forest, Bay, Mich E6 98
Mount Freedom, Morris, N.J B3 106
Mount Gambier, Austl H3 51
Mount Gay, Logan, W. Va D2 123
Mount Gilead, Montgomery, N.C B3 109
Mount Gilead, Morrow, Ohio B3 111
Mount Hagen, Pap. N. Gui k11 50
Mount Healthy, Hamilton, Ohio o12 111
Mount Hebron, Greene, Ala C1 78
Mount Hebron, Siskiyou, Calif B3 82
Mount Hermon, Washington, La D5 95
Mount Hermon, Franklin, Mass A3 97
Mount Heron, Buchanan, Va e9 121
Mount Holly, Union, Ark D3 81
Mount Holly, Burlington, N.J C3 106
Mount Holly, Berkeley, S.C E7, h11 115
Mount Holly, Rutland, Vt E3 120
Mount Holly Springs, Cumberland, Pa F7 114
Mount Hood, Hood River, Oreg B5 113
Mount Hope, Lawrence, Ala A2 78
Mount Hope, Austl F5 51
Mount Hope, Ont., Can D5 72
Mount Hope, Tolland, Conn B8 84
Mount Hope, Sedgwick, Kans E6, g11 93
Mount Hope, Spokane, Wash D8 122
Mount Hope, Fayette, W. Va D3, n13 123
Mount Hope, Grant, Wis F3 124
Mount Hope, riv., Conn B8 84
Mount Horeb, Dane, Wis F4 124
Mount Ida, Montgomery, Ark C2 81
Mount Idaho, Idaho, Idaho D2 89
Mount Isa, Austl D6 50
Mount Jackson, Shenandoah, Va B4 121
Mount Jewett, McKean, Pa C4 114
Mount Joy, Scott, Iowa g10 92
Mount Joy, Lancaster, Pa F9 114
Mount Judea, Newton, Ark B2 81
Mount Juliet, Wilson, Tenn A5 117
Mount Kisco, Westchester, N.Y D7, m15 108
Mount-Laurier, Que., Can p20 72
Mount Lebanon, Allegheny, Pa k13 114
Mount Lookout, Nicholas, W. Va m14 123
Mount Magnet, Austl E2 50
Mount Meigs, Montgomery, Ala C3 78
Mountmellick, Ire D4 11
Mount Misery, pt., N.Y F4 84
Mount Montgomery, Mineral, Nev F3 104
Mount Morgan, Austl A8 51
Mount Moriah, Newf., Can *D2 75
Mount Moriah, Harrison, Mo A4 101
Mount Morris, Ogle, Ill A4 90
Mount Morris, Genesee, Mich E7 98
Mount Morris, Livingston, N.Y C3 108
Mount Morris, Greene, Pa G1 114
Mount Olive, Jefferson, Ala B3, f7 78
Mount Olive, Macoupin, Ill D4 90
Mount Olive, Covington, Miss D4 100
Mount Olive, Wayne, N.C B4 109
Mount Olive, Knox, Tenn h14 117
Mount Olivet, Robertson, Ky B5 94
Mount Orab, Brown, Ohio C2 111
Mount Pearl Park, Newf., Can *f9 75
Mount Penn, Berks, Pa F10 114
Mount Perry, Marion, Ind I8 91
Mount Pisgah, Augusta, Va B3 121
Mount Pleasant, Izard, Ark B4 81
Mount Pleasant, Gadsden, Fla B2 86
Mount Pleasant, Henry, Iowa D6 92
Mount Pleasant, Frederick, Md B3 85
Mount Pleasant, Isabella, Mich E6 98
Mount Pleasant, Marshall, Miss A4 100
Mount Pleasant, Hunterdon, N.J B2 106
Mount Pleasant, Cabarrus, N.C B2 109
Mount Pleasant, Jefferson, Ohio f8 123
Mount Pleasant, Westmoreland, Pa F2 114
Mount Pleasant, Charleston, S.C F8, k12 115
Mount Pleasant, Maury, Tenn B5 117
Mount Pleasant, Titus, Tex C5 118
Mount Pleasant, Sanpete, Utah D4 119
Mount Pocono, Monroe, Pa D11 114
Mount Prospect, Cook, Ill A6, h9 90
Mountrail, co., N. Dak A3 110
Mount Rainier, nat. park, Wash C4 122
Mount Rainier, Prince Georges, Md C1 85
Mount Revelstoke, nat. park, B.C., Can D8 68
Mount Robson, prov. park, B.C., Can C8 68
Mount Rushmore, nat. memorial, S. Dak D2 106
Mounts, bay, Eng D2 12
Mount Savage, Allegany, Md k13 85
Mount Shasta, Siskiyou, Calif B2 82
Mount Sherman, Newton, Ark A2 81
Mount Sidney, Augusta, Va B4 121
Mount Solon, Augusta, Va B3 121
Mount Sterling, Choctaw, Ala C1 78
Mount Sterling, Brown, Ill D3 90
Mount Sterling, Montgomery, Ky B6 94
Mount Sterling, Madison, Ohio C2 111
Mount Stewart, P.E.I., Can C7 74
Mount Storm, Grant, W. Va B5 123
Mount Summit, Henry, Ind D7 91
Mount Tabor, Rutland, Vt E3 120
Mount Uniacke, N.S., Can E6 74
Mount Union, Henry, Iowa C6 92
Mount Union, Huntingdon, Pa E6 114
Mount Upton, Chenango, N.Y C5 108
Mount Vernon, Mobile, Ala D1 78
Mount Vernon, Faulkner, Ark B3 81
Mount Vernon, Montgomery, Ga D4 87
Mount Vernon, Jefferson, Ill E5 90
Mount Vernon, Posey, Ind I2 91
Mount Vernon, Linn, Iowa C6 92
Mount Vernon, Rockcastle, Ky C5 94

Mount Vernon, Kennebec, Maine D3 96
Mount Vernon, Somerset, Md D6 85
Mount Vernon, Lawrence, Mo D4 101
Mount Vernon, Westchester, N.Y h13 108
Mount Vernon, Knox, Ohio B3 111
Mount Vernon, Lucas, Ohio e6 111
Mount Vernon, Grant, Oreg C7 113
Mount Vernon, Davison, S. Dak D7 116
Mount Vernon, Monroe, Tenn D9 117
Mount Vernon, Franklin, Tex C5 118
Mount Vernon, Fairfax, Va *B5 121
Mount Vernon, Skagit, Wash A3 122
Mount Victory, Hardin, Ohio B2 111
Mount View, Washington, R.I *C11 84
Mountville, Troup, Ga C2 87
Mountville, Lancaster, Pa *F9 114
Mountville, Laurens, S.C C4 115
Mount Viso, mtn., It E3 18
Mount Washington, Bullitt, Ky B4, g11 94
Mount Washington, Berkshire, Mass B1 97
Mount Washington, Coos, N.H B4 105
Mount Wolf, York, Pa F8 114
Mount Zion, Carroll, Ga C1 87
Mount Zion, Macon, Ill D5 90
Moura, Braz D5 60
Moura, Port C2 20
Mourdi, depression, Chad B4 46
Mourmelon-le-Grand, Fr E4 15
Mourne, mts., N. Ire C5 11
Mouscron, Bel D3 15
Mouse Island, Newf., Can E2 75
Mousie, Knott, Ky C7 94
Moussoro, Chad C3 46
Moutiers [-Tarentaise], Fr E7 14
Moutier, Switz B3 19
Mouton, isl., N.S., Can F5 74
Mouy, Fr E2 15
Movico, Mobile, Ala. (part of Mount Vernon) D1 78
Moville, Woodbury, Iowa B1 92
Moville, Ire B4 11
Mowbullan, mtn., Austl C8 51
Moweaqua, Shelby, Ill D4 90
Mower, co., Minn G6 99
Mowich, Klamath, Oreg D5 113
Mowrystown, Highland, Ohio C2 111
Moxahala, Perry, Ohio C3 111
Moxee City, Yakima, Wash C5 122
Moxico, dist., Ang D3 48
Moxie, mtn., Maine C3 96
Moxie, pond, Maine C3 96
Moxley, Jefferson, Ga D4 87
Moy, Scot C4 13
Moy, riv., Ire C2 11
Moyale, Eth E4 47
Moyale, Ken A6 48
Moyamba, S.L E2 45
Moycullen, Ire D2 11
Moyers, Pushmataha, Okla C6 112
Moyeuvre-Grande, Fr E6 15
Moyie, B.C., Can E10 68
Moyie, range, B.C., Can E2 69
Moyie Springs, Boundary, Idaho A2 89
Moylan, Delaware, Pa *G10 114
Moynalty, Ire D5 11
Moyo, Ug A5 48
Moyobamba, Peru C2 58
Moyock, Currituck, N.C A6 109
Moyuta, Guat C2 62
Moza, Isr h11 32
Mozambique, country, Afr I9 42, B5 49
Mozambique, chan., Afr g9 49
Mozart, Sask., Can F3 70
Mozdok, Sov. Un E2 29
Mozhaysk, Sov. Un D11 27
Mozhga, Sov. Un D19 9
Mozyr, Sov. Un E7 27
Mpanda, Tan C5 48
Mpika, Zambia D5 48
Mporokoso, Zambia C5 48
Mpouya, Con F3 46
Mpraeso, Ghana E4 45
Mpulungu, Zambia C5 48
Mpwapwa, Tan C6 48
Mrągowo, Pol B6 26
Mrewa, Zimb A5 49
Msec, Czech n16 26
Msene, Czech n17 26
M'Sila, Alg B5 44
Msta, riv., Sov. Un B9 27
Mstislavl, Sov. Un D8 27
Mtakuja, Tan C5 48
Mtoko, Zimb A5 49
Mtorashanga, Zimb A5 49
Mtsensk, Sov. Un E11 27
Mtubatuba, S. Afr C5 49
Mtwara, Tan D7 48
Muang Fang, Thai C3 38
Muang Hot, Thai C3 38
Muang Nan, Thai C4 38
Mubende, Ug A5 48
Mubi, Nig D7 45
Mucajaí, riv., Braz C5 60
Mücheln, G.D.R B6 17
Muchkap, Sov. Un F14 27
Much Wenlock, Eng B5 12
Muck, isl., Scot D2 13
Muckalee, creek, Ga D2 87
Muckleshoot, Indian res., Wash f11 122
Mucuri, Braz B5 57
Mucuri, riv., Braz E2 57
Mucusso, Ang E3 48
Mud, creek, Ala g6 78
Mud, creek, Ga B5 87
Mud, creek, Iowa e9 92
Mud, creek, Okla C4 112
Mud, lake, Maine A5 96
Mud, lake, Minn C5 99
Mud, riv., Minn B3 99
Mud, riv., W. Va C2 123
Mudanya, Tur B7 23
Mud Butte, Meade, S. Dak C3 116
Muddy, Saline, Ill F5 90
Muddy, creek, Colo A4 83
Muddy, creek, Kans k14 93
Muddy, creek, Utah E4 119
Muddy, creek, Wyo C4 125
Muddy, creek, Wyo D6 125
Muddy, creek, Wyo E2 125
Muddy, creek, Wyo E5 125
Muddy, fork, Ind g11 94
Muddy, lake, Sask., Can E1 70
Muddy, mts., Nev G7 104
Muddy, peak, Nev G7 104
Muddy Boggy, creek, Okla C6 112
Muddy Creek, mtn., Ark C2 81
Müden, F.R.G F4 24
Mudgee, Austl F7 51
Mudjatik, riv., Sask., Can A2 70
Mud Lake, Jefferson, Idaho F6 89
Mud Lick, creek, Ky k13 94
Mudon, Bur E10 39
Mudros, see Moudhros, Grc.
Mudugh, reg., Som D6 47
Mueda, Mos D6 48
Muenster, Sask., Can E3 70
Muenster, Cooke, Tex C4 118
Muff, Ire B4 11
Mufulira, Zambia D4 48
Mugía, Sp A1 20
Mugla, Tur D7 23
Mugodzhary, mts., Sov. Un D5 29
Muhammad Qawl, Sud A4 47
Muhinga, Burundi B5 48
Mühlacker, F.R.G E3 17
Mühldorf, F.R.G D6 16
Muhlenberg, co., Ky C2 94
Muhlenberg Park, Berks, Pa *F10 114
Mühlhausen, G.D.R B5 17
Mühlig-Hofmann, mts., Ant B13 5
Muhulu, Zaire B4 48
Muhutwe, Tan B5 48
Mui, isl., Eniwetok 52
Muir, Ionia, Mich E6 98
Muirkirk, Prince Georges, Md B4 85
Muirkirk, Scot E4 13
Mui Ron, cape, Viet C7 38
Muir Woods, nat. mon., Calif h7 82
Mukachevo, Sov. Un G4 27
Mukah, Mala E4 35
Mukden, see Shenyang, China
Mukeru, Palau 52
Mukilteo, Snohomish, Wash B3 122
Mukutawa, riv., Man., Can C3 71
Mukwonago, Waukesha, Wis F5, n11 124
Mula, Sp C5 20
Mulanje, Malawi E6 48
Mulat, isl., Yugo C2 22
Mulberry, Crawford, Ark B1 81
Mulberry, Butte, Calif *C3 82
Mulberry, Polk, Fla E5 86
Mulberry, Clinton, Ind D4 91
Mulberry, Crawford, Kans E9 93
Mulberry, Wilkes, N.C A1 109
Mulberry, Clermont, Ohio C1 111
Mulberry, Lincoln, Tenn B5 117
Mulberry, fork, Ala B3 78
Mulberry, mtn., Ark B3 81
Mulberry, riv., Ark B2 81
Mulberry Grove, Bond, Ill E4 90
Mulchén, Chile B2 54
Mulde, riv., G.D.R C6 16
Muldoon, Fayette, Tex E4 118
Muldraugh, Meade, Ky C4 94
Muldrow, Sequoyah, Okla B7 112
Mule, creek, Kans E4 93
Mule Creek, Grant, N. Mex D1 107
Mulegé, Mex B2 63
Muleng, China D5 37
Muleng, riv., China D6 37
Muleshoe, Bailey, Tex B1 118
Mulga, Jefferson, Ala B3, f7 78
Mulga Mine, Jefferson, Ala *B2 78
Mulgrave, N.S., Can D8 74
Mulgrave, isl., Austl B7 51
Mulhacén, mtn., Sp D4 20
Mulhall, Logan, Okla A4 112
Mülheim [an der Ruhr], F.R.G B1 17
Mulhouse, Fr D7 14, B3 18
Mulino, Clackamas, Oreg B4, h12 113
Mulitapuili, cape, W. Sam 52
Mull, head, Scot B6 13
Mull, isl., Scot D3 13
Mull, sound, Scot D3 13
Mullaghareirk, mts., Ire E2 11
Mullaghcleevaun, mtn., Ire D5 11
Mullan, Shoshone, Idaho B3 89
Mullan, pass, Mont D4 102
Mullen, Hooker, Nebr B4 103
Mullens, Wyoming, W. Va D3 123
Müller, mts., Indon E4 35
Mullet, key, Fla p10 86
Mullet, pen., Ire C1 11
Mullett, lake, Mich C6 98
Mullewa, Austl E2 50
Müllheim, F.R.G E2 16
Mullica, riv., N.J D3 106
Mullica Hill, Gloucester, N.J D2 106
Mulliken, Eaton, Mich F6 98
Mullin, Mills, Tex D3 118
Mullinavat, Ire E4 11
Mullingar, Ire D4 11
Mullins, Marion, S.C C9 115
Mullinville, Kiowa, Kans E4 93
Mull of Galloway, head, Scot F4 13
Mull of Kintyre, head, Scot E3 13
Müllrose, G.D.R A9 17
Mulobezi, Zambia E4 48
Mulrany, Ire D2 11
Mulroy, bay, Ire B4 11
Multān, Pak B5 39, B3 40
Multnomah, co., Oreg B4 113
Mulvane, Sumner and Sedgwick, Kans E6, h12 93
Mulvihill, Man., Can D2 71
Mumbwa, Zambia D4 48
Mummy, range, Colo A5 83
Mumper, Garden, Nebr C3 103
Mun, riv., Thai D5 38
Muna, Mex C7 63
Munascong, lake, Mich B6 98
Münchberg, F.R.G C6 17
München, see Munich, F.R.G.
Münchenstein, Switz A4 19
Muncie, Delaware, Ind D7 91
Muncie, Wyandotte, Kans *C9 93
Muncy, Lycoming, Pa D8 114
Muncy Valley, Sullivan, Pa D8 114
Mundare, Alta., Can C4 69
Munday, Knox, Tex C3 118
Mundelein, Lake, Ill A5, h9 90
Münden, F.R.G B4 17
Munden, Republic, Kans C6 93
Munford, Talladega, Ala B4 78
Munford, Tipton, Tenn B2 117
Munfordville, Hart, Ky C4 94
Mungallala, creek, Austl D6 51
Mungana, Austl C7 50
Mungári, Moz A5 49
Mungbere, Zaire A4 48
Munger, Bay, Mich E7 98
Mungindi, Austl D7 51
Munhall, Allegheny, Pa k14 114
Munich (München), F.R.G D5 16
Munich, Cavalier, N. Dak A7 110
Munising, Alger, Mich B4 98
Munith, Jackson, Mich F6 98
Munjor, Ellis, Kans D4 93
Munnsville, Madison, N.Y C5 108
Munoz, Phil o13 35
Munoz Gamero, pen., Chile h11 54
Munro, lake, Man., Can B4 71
Munsan, Kor H3 37
Munsey Park, Nassau, N.Y *F2 84
Münsingen, F.R.G E4 17
Münsingen, Switz C4 19
Munson, Alta., Can D4 69
Munson, Santa Rosa, Fla u15 86
Munson, Clearfield, Pa E5 114
Munsonville, Cheshire, N.H D2 105
Munster, F.R.G B5 16
Munster, Fr C7 14
Munster, Lake, Ind A2 91
Munster, prov., Ire E2 11
Münster [in Westfalen], F.R.G B2 17
Munsungan, lake, Maine B3 96
Muntenia, prov., Rom *C8 22
Muntenia, reg., Rom C7 22
Muntok, Indon F3 35
Muong Hou Nua, Laos A4 38
Muong Hou Tai, Laos A4 38
Muong Hun Xieng Hung, Laos B5 38
Muong Lane, Laos C5 38
Muong May, Laos E7 38
Muong Phalane, Laos D6 38
Muong Sing, Laos B4 38
Muong Soui, Laos C5 38
Muong Sung, Laos B5 38
Muonio, Fin D10 25
Muonio, riv., Fin D10 25
Muotathal, Switz C6 19
Mur, riv., Aus E7 16
Mura, riv., Yugo B3 22
Murakami, Jap G9 37
Murano, It D8 18
Murashi, Sov. Un B3 29
Murat, Fr E5 14
Murat, mtn., Tur C7 23
Murat, riv., Tur C13 31
Murau, Aus E7 16
Muravera, It E2 21
Muravyevo, Sov. Un C11 37
Mürcheh Khvort, Iran E5 41
Murchison, N.Z N14 51
Murchison, see Kabarega, falls, Ug.
Murchison, riv., Austl E2 50
Murcia, Sp D5 20
Murcia, prov., Sp *D5 20
Murcia, reg., Sp C5 20
Murcki, Pol g10 26
Murdab, bay, Iran C4 41
Murderkill, riv., Del B7 85
Murdo, Jones, S. Dak D5 116
Murdoch, Charlotte, Fla E4 86
Murdock, Kingman, Kans E6, g11 93
Murdock, Swift, Minn E3 99
Murdock, Cass, Nebr h12 103
Muresul, riv., Rom B7 22
Muret, Fr F4 14
Murfreesboro, Pike, Ark C2 81
Murfreesboro, Hertford, N.C A5 109
Murfreesboro, Rutherford, Tenn B5 117
Murgha Kibzai, Pak B4 39, B2 40
Murgon, Austl C8 51
Muri, Nig E7 45
Muri, Switz C4 19
Muriaé, Braz C4 56
Murici, Braz k6 57
Muriel, lake, Alta., Can B5 69
Muritz, lake, G.D.R B6 16
Murmansk, Sov. Un C15 25
Murnau, F.R.G B7 18
Murom, Sov. Un B2 28
Muroran, Jap E10 37
Muros, Sp A1 20
Muroto, cape, Jap J7 37
Murphy, Owyhee, Idaho F2 89
Murphy, Jefferson, Mo g12 101
Murphy, Cherokee, N.C f8 109
Murphy, Mayes, Okla A6 112
Murphy, Josephine, Oreg E3 113
Murphy, isl., S.C E9 115
Murphy, lake, B.C., Can C7 68
Murphys, Calaveras, Calif C3 82
Murphysboro, Jackson, Ill F4 90
Murphytown, Wood, W. Va B3 123
Murray, Shoshone, Idaho B3 89
Murray, Clarke, Iowa C4 92
Murray, Calloway, Ky f9 94
Murray, Cass, Nebr D10, h13 103
Murray, Salt Lake, Utah C4 119
Murray, co., Ga B2 87
Murray, co., Minn F3 99
Murray, co., Okla C4 112
Murray, cape, Ant f40 5
Murray, head, P.E.I., Can C7 74
Murray, lake, Alta., Can E5 69
Murray, lake, Okla C4 112
Murray, lake, S.C C5 115
Murray, riv., Austl G2 51
Murray, riv., B.C., Can B7 68
Murray Bridge, Austl G2 51
Murray City, Hocking, Ohio C3 111
Murray Harbour, P.E.I., Can C7 74
Murray River, P.E.I., Can C7 74
Murraysburg, S. Afr D3 49
Murraysville, Jackson, W. Va D3 123
Murrayville, B.C., Can f13 68
Murrayville, Hall, Ga B3 87
Murrayville, Morgan, Ill D3 90
Murrells Inlet, Georgetown, S.C D9 115
Murrells, inlet, S.C D10 115
Mürren, Switz C4 19
Murrhardt, F.R.G E4 17
Murrieta, Riverside, Calif F5 82
Murrumbidgee, riv., Austl G5 51
Murrupula, Moz A6 49
Murrysville, Westmoreland, Pa B7 114
Mursala, isl., Indon L3 38
Murska Sobota, Yugo B3 22
Murtaugh, Twin Falls, Idaho G4 89
Murten, Switz C3 19
Murtle, lake, B.C., Can C8 68
Murud, India H4 40
Murwāra, (Katni), India E8 40
Murwillumbah, Austl D9 51
Mürz, riv., Aus E7 16
Mürzzuschlag, Aus E7 16
Mus, Tur C13 31
Musaid, Libya C4 43
Musala, peak, Bul D6 22
Musan, Kor E4 37
Musangoi, Zaire C3 48
Mūsā Qal'eh, Afg E12 41
Musāsh as Sirr, Eg D5 32
Muscat, Om D2 39
Muscatatuck, riv., Ind G5 91
Muscatine, Muscatine, Iowa C6 92
Muscatine, co., Iowa C6 92
Muscle Shoals, Colbert, Ala A2 78
Muscow, mtn., B.C., Can C4 68
Muscoda, Grant, Wis E3 124
Muscogee, co., Ga D2 87
Musconetcong, mtn., N.J B2 106
Musconetcong, riv., N.J B3 106
Muscotah, Atchison, Kans C8 93
Muscoy, San Bernardino, Calif *E5 82
Muse, LeFlore, Okla C7 113
Muse, Washington, Pa F1 114
Musgrave, ranges, Austl E5 51
Musgrave Harbour, Newf., Can D5 75
Musgravetown, Newf., Can D5 75
Mushāsh Abū Khawf, well, Eg E6 32
Mushāsh as Sirr, well, Eg D5 32
Mushie, Zaire B2 48
Mushketovo, Sov. Un q20 27
Musi, riv., Indon F2 35
Muskeget, chan., Mass D7 97
Muskeget, isl., Mass D7 97
Muskego, Waukesha, Wis F5, n11 124
Muskego, lake, Wis F1 124
Muskegon, Muskegon, Mich E4 98
Muskegon, co., Mich E4 98
Muskegon, lake, Mich E4 98
Muskegon, riv., Mich D4 98
Muskegon Heights, Mich E4 98
Muskingum, co., Ohio B3 111
Muskingum, riv., Ohio C4 111
Muskö, Swe u36 25
Muskogee, Muskogee, Okla B6 112
Muskogee, co., Okla B6 112
Muskoka, dist., Ont., Can B5 72
Muskoka, lake, Ont., Can C5 72
Muskratdam, lake, Ont., Can C6 71
Muskwa, lake, Alta., Can A3 69
Muskwa, riv., Alta., Can A3 69
Musoma, Tan B5 48
Musquacook, lakes, Maine B3 96
Musquaro, lake, Que., Can h14 73
Musquash, N.B., Can D3 74
Musquash, mtn., Maine C5 96
Musquodoboit Harbour, N.S., Can E6 74
Musselburgh, Scot E5 13
Musselshell, Musselshell, Mont D8 102
Musselshell, co., Mont D8 102
Musselshell, riv., Mont D9 102
Mussende, Ang D2 48
Mussidan, Fr E4 14
Mussoorie, India B7 40
Mustafa Kemalpasa, Tur B7 31
Mustang, Canadian, Okla B4 112
Musters, lake, Arg D3 54
Mustinka, riv., Minn E2 99
Mustique, isl., St. Vincent V26 65
Mustvee, Sov. Un B6 27
Musumusu, W. Sam 52
Muswellbrook, Austl F8 51
Müt, Eg D5 43
Mut, Tur D9 31
Mutá, pt., Braz D3 57
Mutan, riv., China D4 37
Mutanchiang, China C10 34, D4 37
Mutare, Zimb A5 49
Mutayyin, Yemen B5 47
Mutcho, pt., Saipan 52
Mutena, Zaire C3 48
Muti, isl., Eniwetok 52
Mutok, hbr., Ponape 52
Mutsu, bay, Jap F10 37
Mutton, mts., Oreg C5 113
Mutton Bay, Que., Can C2, h10 75
Muttontown, Nassau, N.Y *F2 84
Muttra, see Mathura, India
Mutual, Woodward, Okla A2 112
Muṭūbis, Eg C2 32
Mutzig, Fr F7 15
Muxima, Ang C1 48
Muynak, Sov. Un E5 29
Muyunkum, des., Sov. Un E7 29
Muzaffargarh, Pak B3 40
Muzaffarnagar, India *C6 40
Muzaffarpur, India C8 39, D10 40
Muzambinho, Braz k8 56
Muzhi, Sov. Un B21 9
Muzon, cape, Alsk n23 79
Muztagh, mtn., China F11 28
Muztagh Ata, mtn., China H24 9
Mwanza, Tan B5 48
Mwaya, Tan C5 48
Mweelrea, mtn., Ire D2 11
Mweka, Zaire B3 48
Mwene-Ditu, Zaire C3 48
Mwenga, Zaire B4 48
Mweru, lake, Zaire, Zambia C4 48
Mwimba, Zaire C3 48
Mwinilunga, Zambia D3 48
Myakka, riv., Fla E4 86
Myakka City, Manatee, Fla E4 86
Myaungmya, Bur D1 38
Mycenae, ruins, Grc D4 23
Myers, Treasure, Mont D9 102
Myers, Charleston, S.C k12 115
Myerstown, Lebanon, Pa F9 114
Myersville, Frederick, Md A2 85
Myingyan, Bur D10 39
Myitkyina, Bur C10 39
Myitnge, riv., Bur B2 38
Myjava, Czech D4 26
Mylo, Rolette, N. Dak A6 110
Myn-Aral, Sov. Un D8 29
Mynard, Cass, Nebr E3 103
Myrick, Jones, Miss D5 100
Myrnam, Alta., Can C5 69
Myrtle, Man., Can E3 71
Myrtle, Ont., Can C6 72
Myrtle, Freeborn, Minn G5 99
Myrtle, Union, Miss A4 100
Myrtle, Oregon, Mo E6 101
Myrtle Beach, New Haven, Conn. (part of Milford) E4 84
Myrtle Beach, Horry, S.C D10 115
Myrtle Creek, Douglas, Oreg D3 113
Myrtle Grove, Escambia, Fla u14 86
Myrtle Point, Coos, Oreg D2 113
Myrtlewood, Marengo, Ala C2 78
Mysen, Nor p29 25
Myslenice, Pol D5 26
Myślibórz, Pol B3 26
Myslowice, Pol g10 26
Mysore, India F6 39
Mystic, New London, Conn D9 84
Mystic, Irwin, Ga E3 87
Mystic, Appanoose, Iowa D5 91
Mystic, Pennington, S. Dak C2 116
Mystic, cavern, Ark A2 81
Mystic, lakes, Mass g11 97
My Tho, Viet G7 38
Mytilene, see Mitilini, Grc.
Mytishchi, Sov. Un n17 27
Myton, Duchesne, Utah C5 119
Mže, riv., Czech D8 17
Mzimba, Malawi D5 48
Mzuzu, Malawi D5 48

N

Naalehu, Hawaii, Haw D6 88
Na'an, Isr h10 32
Naantali, Fin G10 25
Naas, Ire D5 11
Nabadwip, India *F12 40
Nabberu, lake, Austl E3 50
Nabburg, F.R.G D7 17
Nabeul, Tun B7 44
Naboomspruit, S. Afr B4 49
Nabnasset, Middlesex, Mass A5 97
Nabq, Eg H10 31
Nābulus, Jordan B7, g12 32
Nacala-Velha, Moz D7 48
Nacaome, Hond D4 62
Na Cham, Viet A7 38
Naches, Yakima, Wash C5 122
Naches, riv., Wash C5 122
Nachingwea, Tan D6 48
Náchod, Czech C4 26
Nacimiento, Chile B2 54
Nacimiento, res., Calif E3 82
Nacmine, Alta., Can D4 69
Naco, Cochise, Ariz F6 80
Nacogdoches, Nacogdoches, Tex D5 118
Nacogdoches, co., Tex D5 118
Nacozari, Mex A3 63
Nadarzyn, Pol m13 26
Nadeau, Menominee, Mich C3 98
Naden, hbr., B.C., Can B1 68
Nadiād, India F4 40
Nădlac, Rom B5 22
Nador, Mor B4 44
Nadvornaya, Sov. Un G5 27
Nadym, riv., Sov. Un B23 9
Naesong, Kor H4 37
Naestved, Den C5 25
Naf, Cassia, Idaho G5 89
Nafada, Nig D7 45
Nafishah, Eg D4 32
Nafutan, mtn., Saipan 52
Nafutan, pt., Saipan 52
Naga, Phil C6 35
Naga, hills, India, Bur C10 39
Nagahama, Jap *n15 37
Nagaland, state, India *C9 39
Naga-Naga, Phil *D6 35
Nagano, Jap H9 37
Nagano, pref., Jap *H9 37
Nagaoka, Jap H9 37
Nāgappattinam, India F6 39
Nagar, India A6 40
Nagarote, Nic D4 62
Nagar-Pārkar, Pak E3 40
Nagasaki, Jap J4 37
Nagasaki, pref., Jap *J4 37
Nāgaur, India D4 40
Nagcarlan, Phil o13 35
Nageezi, San Juan A2 107
Nagele, Eth D4 47
Nāgercoil, India G6 39
Nagles, mts., Ire E3 11
Nago, Okinawa 52
Nago, bay, Okinawa 52
Nagog, pond, Mass f10 97
Nagold, F.R.G E3 17
Nagoya, Jap I8, n15 37
Nāgpur, India D6 39, G7 40
Nags Head, Dare, N.C B7 109
Nagua, Dom. Rep E9 64
Naguabo, P.R B4 65
Naguabo, mun., P.R *B4 65
Naguilian, Phil n13 35
Nagykanizsa, Hung B3 22
Nagykoros, Hung B4 22
Naha, Okinawa 52
Naḥalat Yehuda, Isr h10 32
Nahanni, nat. park, N.W. Ter., Can D7 66
Nahant, Essex, Mass g12 97
Nahariyya, Isr B7 32
Nahe, riv., F.R.G D2 17
Nahma, Delta, Mich C4 98
Nahmakanta, lake, Maine C3 96
Nahr al Khābūr, riv., Syr E13 31
Nahuel Huapí, Arg C2 54
Nahuel Huapí, lake, Arg C2 54
Nahuel Niyeu, Arg C3 54
Nahuelquir, Arg C3 54
Nahunta, Brantley, Ga E5 87
Naic, Phil o13 35
Naicam, Sask., Can E3 70
Naihāti, India *F12 40
Naikorokoro, pt., Fiji 52
Naila, F.R.G C6 17
Nailanga, Fiji 52
Nain, Newf., Can g9 75
Nā'īn, Iran E6 41
Naingoro, pass, Fiji 52
Naini-Tal, India C7 40
Nairai, isl., Fiji 52
Nairn, Scot C5 13
Nairn, riv., Scot C4 13
Nairobi, Ken B6 48
Nairobi, prov. dist., Ken *B6 48
Naitonitoni, Fiji 52
Naivasha, Ken B6 48
Najd, reg., Sau. Ar I3 31
Najibabad, India C7 40
Najin, Kor E5 37
Nakadori, isl., Jap J4 37
Nakagusuku, bay, Okinawa 52
Nakaminto, Jap m19 37
Nakamura, Jap J6 37
Nakano, isl., Jap L4 37
Nakaosu, Okinawa 52
Nakatsu, Jap J5 37
Nakatsu, see Ena, Jap.
Nakaushi, Okinawa 52
Nakfa, Eth B4 47
Nakhichevan na Arakse, Sov. Un F3 29
Nakhodka, Sov. Un E6 37
Nakhon Pathom, Thai F4 38
Nakhon Ratchasima, Thai E5 38
Nakhon Sawan, Thai E4 38
Nakhon Si Thammarat, Thai H3 38
Nakhrachi, Sov. Un B7 29
Nakina, Ont., Can o18 72
Nakina, Columbus, N.C C4 109
Nakiri, Jap o15 37
Naklo, Pol B4 26
Naknek, Alsk D8 79
Naknek, lake, Alsk D8 79
Nakochak, China B9 40
Nakskov, Den D5 24
Nakuru, Ken B6 48
Nakusp, B.C., Can D9 68
Nāl, riv., Pak H12 41
Nalchik, Sov. Un E2 29
Nallen, Fayette, W. Va m14 123
Nalón, riv., Sp A2 20
Nālūt, Libya C2 43
Namai, bay, Palau Is 52
Namak, salt lake, Iran D5 41
Namaka, Alta., Can D4 69
Namakan, lake, Minn B6 99
Namakzār, salt lake, Iran D10 41
Namangan, Sov. Un E8 29
Namanock, isl., N.J A3 106
Namanyere, Tan C5 48
Namapa, Moz D6 48
Namasagali, Ug A5 48
Namatanai, Pap. N. Gui h13 50
Nambekavu, Fiji 52
Nambe Pueblo, Santa Fe, N. Mex B4 107
Nambour, Austl C9 51
Nambouwalu, Fiji 52
Namcha Barwa, mtn., China F4 34
Nam Dinh, Viet B7 38
Nāmdö, isl., Swe t36 25
Namekagon, lake, Wis B2 124
Namekagon, riv., Wis B2 124
Nametil, Moz A6 49
Namew, lake, Man., Sask., Can C5 70
Namib, des., Namibia B1 49
Namibia (South West Africa) country, Afr I7 42, B2 49
Namiquipa, Mex B3 63
Namlea, Indon F7 35
Namoi, riv., Austl E7 51
Nampa, Alta., Can A2 69
Nampa, Canyon, Idaho F2 89
Nampala, Mali C3 45
Nampo, see Chinnampo, Kor.
Nampula, Moz A6 49
Namsen, riv., Nor E4 25
Namsos, Nor E4 25
Namu, B.C., Can D4 68
Namu, isl., Bikini 52
Namu (Tengri), lake, China E3 34
Namua, isl., W. Sam 52
Namur, Bel D4 15
Namur, Que., Can D3 73
Namur, prov., Bel D4 15
Namur, isl., Kwajalein 52
Namutoni, Namibia A2 49
Namwala, Zambia E4 48
Namwŏn, Kor I3 37
Namyslow, Pol C4 26
Nan, riv., Thai C4 38
Nana, riv., Cen. Afr. Rep D3 46
Nanafalia, Marengo, Ala C2 78
Nanaimo, B.C., Can E5, f12 68
Nanakuli, Honolulu, Haw B3, g9 88
Nanam, Kor F4 37
Nanao, Jap H8 37
Nanatsu, isl., Jap H8 37
Nanawan, riv., Man., Can C3 71
Nance, co., Nebr C7 103
Nanchang, China I4 36
Nancheng, China J6 36
Nancheng, China K7 36
Nanchuan, China J2 36
Nanchung, China I2 36
Nancy, Fr C7 14, F6 15
Nancy, Pulaski, Ky C5 94
Nancy, creek, Ga h8 87
Nanda Devi, peak, India B7 40
Nānded, India H6 40
Nandi, Fiji 52
Nandurbār, India G5 40
Nanduri, Fiji 52
Nanfeng, China K7 36
Nanga-Eboko, Cam E2 46
Nānga Parbat, peak, India A5 39
Nangis, Fr F3 15
Nang Rong, Thai E5 38
Nanhai (Fatshan), China *G7 34
Nanhua, China F5 34
Nanjemoy, Charles, Md D3 85
Nankapenparam, reef, Ponape 52
Nankin, Ashland, Ohio B3 111
Nanking, China E8 34, H8 36
Nankou, pass, China D7 36
Nankung, China F6 36
Nannine, Austl E2 50
Nanning (Yungning), China G6 34
Nanoose Bay, B.C., Can f11 68
Nanping, China K8 36
Nansemond, Nansemond, Va k14 121
Nansemond, riv., Va k14 121
Nansen, sound, N.W. Ter., Can k33 67
Nan Shan, mts., China D4 34
Nansio, Tan B5 48
Nanson, Rolette, N. Dak A6 110
Nantel, Que., Can C3 73
Nanterre, Fr g9 14
Nantes, Fr D3 14
Nanteuil-le-Haudouin, Fr E2 15
Nanticoke, Ont., Can E4 72
Nanticoke, Wicomico, Md D6 85
Nanticoke, Luzerne, Pa D10, n16 114
Nanticoke, riv., Del., Md D6 85
Nantien, China J9 36
Nanton, Alta., Can D4 69
Nantua, Fr D6 14
Nantucket, Nantucket, Mass D7 97
Nantucket, co., Mass D7 97
Nantucket, isl., Mass D7 97
Nantucket, sound, Mass C7 97
Nantung, China H9 36
Nantuxent, pt., N.J E2 106
Nantwich, Eng A5 12
Nanty Glo, Cambria, Pa F4 114
Nanuet, Rockland, N.Y g12 108
Nanuku, passage, Fiji 52
Nanuku, reef, Fiji 52
Nanukuloa, Fiji 52
Nanyang, China H5 36
Nanyuki, Ken A6 48
Nao, cape, Sp C6 20
Naoli, riv., China C6 37

Naoma, Raleigh, W. Va....n13 123
Naomi, lake, Pa....A2 106
Naomi, peak, Utah....B4 119
Naousa, Grc....B4 23
Napa, Napa, Calif....C2 82
Napa, co., Calif....C2 82
Napadogan, N.B., Can....C3 74
Napakiak, Alsk....C7 79
Napaktok, bay, Newf., Can....f9 75
Napanee, Ont., Can....C8 72
Napanoch, Ulster, N.Y....D6 108
Napatree, pt., R.I.....D9 84
Napavine, Lewis, Wash....C3 122
Nape, Laos....C6 38
Napeague, bay, N.Y.....E8 84
Napeague, beach, N.Y.....F8 84
Naper, Boyd, Nebr....B6 103
Naperville, Du Page, Ill..B5, k8 90
Napetipi, riv., Que., Can....C2 75
Napf, mtn., Switz....C4 19
Napier, N.Z....M16 51
Napier, mts., Ant....C18 5
Napierville, Que., Can....D4 73
Napierville, co., Que., Can..D4 73
Napinka, Man., Can....E1 71
Naples, Collier, Fla....F5 86
Naples, Boundary, Idaho....A2 89
Naples, Scott, Ill....D3 90
Naples (Napoli), It....D5 21
Naples, Cumberland, Maine..E2 96
Naples, Ontario, N.Y....C3 108
Naples, Clark, S. Dak....C8 116
Naples, Morris, Tex....C5 118
Naples, Uintah, Utah....C6 119
Naples, bay, It....D5 21
Napo, prov., Ec....B2 58
Napo, riv., Ec....B2 58
Napoleon, Ripley, Ind....F7 91
Napoleon, Lafayette, Mo....B3 101
Napoleon, Logan, N. Dak....C6 110
Napoleon, Henry, Ohio....A1 111
Napoleonville, Assumption,
La....E4, k9 95
Napoli, see Naples, It.
Naponee, Franklin, Nebr....D6 103
Napoopoo, Hawaii, Haw....D6 88
Nappanee, Elkhart, Ind....B5 91
Napton, Saline, Mo....B4 101
Nara, Jap....o14 37
Nara, Mali....C3 45
Nara, pref., Jap....*I7 37
Nāra, canal, Pak....E2 40
Naracoorte, Austl....H3 51
Narai, Jap....n16 37
Naramata, B.C., Can....E8 68
Na'rān, Syr....A7 32
Naranja, Dade, Fla....G6 86
Naranjas, pt., Pan....G7 62
Naranjito, mun., P.R....*B3 65
Nararu, mtn., Fiji.... 52
Nara Visa, Quay, N. Mex....B6 107
Nārāyanganj, Bngl....F13 40
Nārāyanpet, India....I6 40
Narberth, Montgomery, Pa.p20 114
Narberth, Wales....C3 12
Narbonne, Fr....F5 14
Narcisse, Man., Can....D3 71
Narcoossee, Osceola, Fla....D5 86
Nardin, Kay, Okla....A4 112
Nardò, It....D7 21
Nares, strait, Can., Grnld....B22 4
Narew, riv., Pol....B6 26
Nariño, dept., Col....C2 60
Narita, Jap....n19 37
Narka, Republic, Kans....C6 93
Narmada, riv., India....F7 40
Narodnaya, mtn., Sov. Un....B21 9
Naro-Fominsk, Sov. Un....D11 27
Narok, Ken....B6 48
Narol, Man., Can....D3 71
Narrabri, Austl....F8 51
Narragansett, Washington
R.I....D11 84
Narragansett, bay, R.I.....C11 84
Narraguagus, riv., Maine....D5 96
Narran, riv., Austl....D6 51
Narrandera, Austl....G6 51
*Narraway, riv., Alta., B.C.,
Can*....B7 68
Narrogin, Austl....F2 50
Narromine, Austl....F7 51
Narrows, Giles, Va....C2 121
Narrows, The, strait, N.Y.....E5 106
Narrowsburg, Sullivan, N.Y.D5 108
Narsimhapur, India....F7 40
Naruna, Campbell, Va....C3 121
Narva, Sov. Un....B7 27
Narvik, Nor....C7 25
Naryan-Mar, Sov. Un....B19 9
Naryilco, Austl....D3 51
Narym, Sov. Un....D25 9
Naryn, Sov. Un....E9 29
Naryn, riv., Sov. Un....E9 29
Nasarawa, Nig....E6 45
Nasca, Peru....D3 58
Naschitti, San Juan,
N. Mex....A1 107
Nase, Jap....F10 34
Naseby, N.Z....P13 51
Nash, Walsh, N. Dak....A8 110
Nash, Grant, Okla....A3 112
Nash, Bowie, Tex....C5 118
Nash, co., N.C....A4 109
Nash, stream, N.H....A4 105
Nashawena, isl., Mass....D6 97
Nash Creek, N.B., Can....B3 74
Nashoba, Pushmataha, Okla C6 112
Nashoba, hill, Mass....f10 97
Nāshua, Chickasaw, Iowa....B5 92
Nashua, Wilkin Minn....D2 99
Nashua, Valley, Mont....B10 102
Nashua, Hillsboro, N.H....E4 105
*Nashua, riv., Mass.,
N.H*....A4 97
Nashville, Howard, Ark....D2 81
Nashville, Berrien, Ga....E3 87
Nashville, Washington, Ill...E4 90
Nashville, Brown, Ind....F5 91
Nashville, Kingman, Kans....E5 93
Nashville, Barry, Mich....F5 98
Nashville, Nash., N.C....B5 109
Nashville, Holmes, Ohio....B3 111
Nashville, Davidson,
Tenn....A5, g10 117
Nashwaak, riv., N.B., Can....C3 74
Nashwaaksis, N.B., Can....D3 74
Nashwauk, Itasca, Minn....C5 99
Našice, Yugo....C4 24
Nasielsk, Pol....B6 26
Nasijarvi, lake, Fin....G10 25
Nāsik, India....E5 39, G4 40
Nāşir, Sud....D4 47
Nasirābād, Bngl....D9 39
Naskaupi, riv., Newf., Can....g9 75
Nason, Jefferson, Ill....E4 90
Nasonville, Providence, R.I.B10 84
Nass, riv., B.C., Can....B3 68
Nassau, Ba....B5, m17 64
Nassau, Lac qui Parle, Minn.E2 99
Nassau, Rensselaer, N.Y....C7 108
Nassau, co., Fla....B5 86
Nassau, co., N.Y....E7 108
Nassau, gulf, Chile....k12 54
Nassau, pt., N.Y.....F7 84
Nassau, range, Indon....F9 35
Nassau, riv., Fla....k8 86
Nassau, sound, Fla....k8 86
Nassauville, Nassau, Fla..B5, k8 86
Nassawadox, Northampton,
Va....C7 121
Nässjö, Swe....I6 25
Nasugbu, Phil....o13 35
Nasukoin, mtn., Mont....B2 102
Natá, Pan....F7 62
Natagaima, Col....C2 60
Natal, Braz....C3, g6 57
Natal, B.C., Can....E10 68
Natal, prov., S. Afr....C5 49
Natalbany, Tangipahoa, La..D5 95
Natalia, Medina, Tex....E3 118
Natanes, plat., Ariz....D5 80
Natashquan, Que., Can....h9 75
Natashquan, riv., Que., Can....h9 75
Natawahunan, lake, Man., Can..B3 71
Natchaug, riv., Conn....B8 84
Natchez, Adams, Miss....D2 100
Natchitoches, Natchitoches,
La....C2 95
Natchitoches, par., La....C2 95
Natewa, bay, Fiji.... 52
Nathalie, Halifax, Va....D4 121
Nathilau, pt., Fiji.... 52
Nathrop, Chaffee, Colo....C4 83
Nathula, isl., Fiji.... 52
Natick, Middlesex,
Mass....B5, g10 97
Natimuk, Austl....H3 51
Nation, lakes, B.C., Can....B5 68
Nation, riv., B.C., Can....B6 68
National, Pierce, Wash....C3 122
National, Monongalia,
W. Va....B4, h10 123
National City, San Diego,
Calif....F5, o15 82
National City, Iosco, Mich..D7 98
National Garden, Volusia,
Fla....C5 86
National Park, Gloucester,
N.J....*D2 106
Natitingou, Benin....D5 45
Natividade, Braz....D1 57
Natívitas, Mex....h9 63
Natoena, isl., Indon....E3 34
Natoma, Osborne, Kans....C4 93
Natron, lake, Tan....B6 48
Natrona, co., Wyo....D6 125
Natrona Heights, Allegheny,
Pa....E2, h15 114
Nåttarö, isl., Swe....u36 25
Nattaung, mtn., Bur....C2 38
Natuna, isl., Indon....E3 35
Natural, bridge, Va....C3 121
Natural Bridge, Winston,
Ala....A2 78
Natural Bridge, Jefferson,
N.Y....A5 108
Natural Bridge, Rockbridge,
Va....C3 121
Natural, bridge, Utah....F3 119
*Natural Bridges, nat. mon.,
Utah*....F6 119
Naturaliste, cape, Austl....F2 50
Natural Steps, Pulaski, Ark..h10 81
Naturita, Montrose, Colo....C2 83
Naubinway, Mackinac,
Mich....B5 98
Naucalpan de Juárez, Mex..h9 63
Nauders, Aus....E5 16
Nauen, G.D.R....B6 16
Naugatuck, New Haven,
Conn....D4 84
Naugatuck, riv., Conn....B4 84
Naughton, Ont., Can....A3 72
Naumburg [an der Saale],
G.D.R....C5 16
Naumburg [in Hessen],
F.R.G....B4 17
Naunhof, G.D.R....B7 17
Naupe, Peru....C2 58
Nauru, country, Oceania...G10 7
Naushon, isl., Mass....D6 97
Nautla, Mex....C5, m15 63
Nauvoo, Walker, Ala....B2 78
Nauvoo, Hancock, Ill....C2 90
Nauwigewauk, N.B., Can....D4 74
Nava, lake, Sp....A3 20
Nava del Rey, Sp....B3 20
Navahermosa, Sp....C3 20
Navajo, Apache, Ariz....B6 80
Navajo, co., Ariz....B5 80
Navajo, creek, Utah....G4 119
*Navajo, Indian, res., Ariz.,
N. Mex*....A4 80
Navajo, mtn., Utah....F5 119
Navajo, nat. mon., Ariz....A5 80
Navajo, res., Colo., N. Mex...A2 107
Navajo, riv., Colo....D4 83
Navajo Mountain Trading Post,
San Juan, Utah....F5 119
Naval Base, Charleston,
S.C....F3 115
Navalcarnero, Sp....B3 20
Navalmoral de la Mata, Sp..C3 20
Navan, Ont., Can....B9, h13 72
Navarin, cape, Sov. Un....C20 28
Navarino, Shawano, Wis....D5 124
Navarino, isl., Chile....k12 54
Navarra (Navarre), prov.,
Sp....*A5 20
Navarre, Stark, Ohio....B4 111
Navarre, (Navarra), prov.,
Sp....*A5 20
Navarre, reg., Sp....A5 20
Navarro, Arg....A5, g7 54
Navarro, co., Tex....C4 118
Navas, de Tolosa, Sp....C4 20
Navasota, Grimes, Tex....D4 118
Navassa, Brunswick, N.C....C4 109
Navassa, isl., W.I.....E6 64
Navatu, reef, Fiji.... 52
Nave, isl., Scot....E2 13
Nävekvarn, Swe....u34 25
Naver, lake, Scot....B4 13
Naver, riv., Scot....B4 13
Navesink, Monmouth, N.J....C4 106
Navet, res., Trin....O23 65
Navia, Arg....A3 54
Navia, riv., Sp....A2 20
Navidad, Chile....A2 54
Naviti, isl., Fiji.... 52
Navojoa, Mex....B3 63
Navolato, Mex....C3 63
Navpaktos, Grc....C3 23
Navplion, Grc....D4 23
Navrongo, Ghana....D4 45
Navsāri, India....G4 40
Navy Yard City, Kitsap,
Wash....*B3 122
Nawā, Syr....B8 32
Nawābshāh, Pak....D2 40
Nawada, India....E10 40
Nāwah, Afg....E13 41
Naxos, Grc....D5 23
Naxos, isl., Grc....D5 23
Nay, Fr....F3 14
Nayarit, state, Mex....C4, m11 63
Nayau, isl., Fiji.... 52
Nāy Band, Iran....E8 41
Nāy Band, cape, Iran....F7 41
Nāy Band, mtn., Iran....E8 41
Naylor, Lowndes, Ga....F3 87
Naylor, Ripley, Mo....E7 101
Nayoro, Jap....D11 37
Naytahwaush, Mahnomen,
Minn....C3 99
Nazaka, Okinawa.... 52
Nazaré, Braz....D3 57
Nazaré, Port....C1 20
Nazaré da Mata, Braz....h6 57
Nazareth, Nelson, Ky....C4 94
Nazareth, Northampton, Pa.E11 114
Nazareth, Castro, Tex....B1 118
Nazareth, see Nazerat, Isr.
Nazas, Mex....B4 63
Nazas, riv., Mex....B4 63
Naze, cape, Nor....H2 25
Naze, The, headland, Eng....C9 12
Nazerat (Nazareth), Isr....B7 32
Nazeret, Eth....D4 47
Nāzik, Iran....B2 41
Nazilli, Tur....D7 23, D7 31
Nazimovo, Sov. Un....D27 9
Naziya, Sov. Un....s32 25
Nazko, riv., B.C., Can....C6 68
Nazlini, Apache, Ariz....B6 80
Nazyvayevsk, Sov. Un....B9 28
Ncheu, Malawi....D5 48
Ndala, Tan....B5 48
Ndéle, Cen. Afr. Rep....D4 46
Ndendé, Gabon....F2 46
Ndjamena (Fort Lamy),
Chad....C3 46
Ndjolé, Gabon....F2 46
Ndola, Zambia....D4 48
Ndravuni, isl., Fiji.... 52
Neagh, lake, N. Ire....C5 11
Neah Bay, Clallam, Wash...A1 122
Neal, Greenwood, Kans....E7 93
Néa Palátia, Grc....g11 23
Neapolis, Grc....D4 23
Neapolis, Grc....E5 23
Nea Psara (Eretria), Grc....g11 23
Near, is., Alsk....E2 79
Neath, Wales....C4 12
Neavitt, Talbot, Md....C5 85
Neba, Jap....n16 37
Nebel, riv., G.D.R....E6 24
Nebine, creek, Austl....D6 51
Nebit-Dag, Sov. Un....B7 41
Nebo, Pike, Ill....D3 90
Nebo, Hopkins, Ky....C2 94
Nebo, LaSalle, La....C3 95
Nebo, McDowell, N.C....*f10 109
Nebo, mtn., Utah....D4 119
Nebraska, Jennings, Ind....F7 96
Nebraska, state, U.S....B8 76, 103
Nebraska City, Otoe,
Nebr....D10, h13 103
Nebuzely, Czech....n18 26
Necedah, Juneau, Wis....D3 124
Nechako, range, B.C., Can....C5 68
Nechako, riv., B.C., Can....C5 68
Neche, Pembina, N. Dak....A8 110
Neches, riv., Tex....D5 118
Nechí, Col....B3 60
Nechi, riv., Col....B3 60
Nechranice, res., Czech....C8 17
Neckar, riv., F.R.G....D3 17
Neck City, Jasper, Mo....D3 101
Necker, isl., Haw....m15 88
Necochea, Arg....B5 54
Nederburgh, cape, Indon....F6 35
Nederland, Boulder, Colo....B5 83
Nederland, Jefferson, Tex....E6 118
Neder Rijn, riv., Neth....C5 15
Nedrow, Onondaga, N.Y....C4 108
Nee, res., Colo....C8 83
Needham, Norfolk, Mass....g11 97
Needle, mtn., Wyo....B3 125
Needle, mtn., Colo....D3 83
Needles, San Bernardino,
Calif....E6 82
Needmore, Lawrence, Ind...G4 91
Needmore, Fulton, Pa....G5 114
Needville, Fort Bend,
Tex....E5, r14 118
Neel, gap, Ga....B3 87
Neeley, Power, Idaho....G6 89
Neelin, Man., Can....E2 71
Neely, Greene, Miss....D5 100
Neelyville, Butler, Mo....E7 101
Ñeembucu, dept., Par....E4 55
Neenah, Winnebago,
Wis....D5, h9 124
Neepawa, Man., Can....D2 71
Neerpelt, Bel....C5 15
Neeses, Orangeburg, S.C....D5 115
Neffs, Belmont, Ohio....B5 111
Neffsville, Lancaster, Pa....F9 114
Neftegorsk, Sov. Un....G16 9
Nefyn, Wales....B3 12
Negaunee, Marquette, Mich.B3 98
Negele, Eth....D4 47
Negeri Sembilan, state,
Mala....K4 38
Negley, Columbiana, Ohio...B5 111
Negotin, Yugo....C6 22
Negra, range, Peru....C2 58
Negreira, Sp....A1 20
Negrine, Alg....G10 30
Negro, mtn., Md....k12 85
Negro, riv., Arg....B3 54
Negro, riv., Bol....B3 55
Negro, riv., Braz....B1 56
Negro, riv., Braz....D2 56
Negro, riv., S.A....D4 53
Negro, riv., Ur....E1 56
Negros, isl., Phil....D6 35
Negros Occidental, prov.,
Phil....*C6 35
Negros Oriental, prov.,
Phil....*D6 35
Negru Voda, Rom....D9 22
Neguac, N.B., Can....B4 74
Nehalem, Tillamook, Oreg...B3 113
Nehalem, riv., Oreg....B4 113
Nehawka, Cass, Nebr....D9, h13 103
Nehbandān, Iran....F10 41
Neheim-Hüsten, F.R.G....B2 17
Neiba, Dom. Rep....E8 64
Neichiang, China....F6 34
Neiden, Nor....C13 25
Neidpath, Sask., Can....G2 70
Neihart, Cascade, Mont....D6 102
Neihsiang, China....H5 36
Neihuang, China....G6 36
Neilburg, Sask., Can....E1 70
Neill, pt., Wash....f11 122
Neillsville, Clark, Wis....D3 124
Neisse, riv., F.R.G....B9 17
Neiva, Col....C2 60
Nejdek, Czech....C7 17
Nekemte, Eth....D4 47
Nekoma, Rush, Kans....D4 93
Nekoma, Cavalier, N. Dak....A7 110
Nekoosa, Wood, Wis....D4 124
Neksø, Den....A3 26
Nelagoney, Osage, Okla....A5 112
Nelidovo, Sov. Un....C9 27
Neligh, Antelope, Nebr....B7 103
Nell, isl., Kwajalein.... 52
Nellore, India....F6 39
Nellysford, Nelson, Va....C4 121
Nelma, Sov. Un....C9 37
Nelson, Yavapai, Ariz....B2 80
Nelson, B.C., Can....E9 68
Nelson, Eng....*G6 13
Nelson, Pickens and Cherokee,
Ga....B2 87
Nelson, Lee, Ill....B4 90
Nelson, Muhlenberg, Ky....*C2 94
Nelson, Saline, Mo....B4 101
Nelson, Nuckolls, Nebr....D7 103
Nelson, Clark, Nev....H7 104
Nelson, Cheshire, N.H....E2 105
Nelson, N.Z....N14 51
Nelson, Tioga, Pa....C7 114
Nelson, Buffalo, Wis....D1 124
Nelson, co., Ky....C4 94
Nelson, co., N. Dak....B7 110
Nelson, co., Va....C4 121
Nelson, lake, Man., Can....B1 71
Nelson, riv., Man., Can....A4 71
Nelson Forks, B.C., Can....m18 68
Nelson House, Man., Can...B2 71
Nelsonville, Athens, Ohio....C3 111
Nelspruit, S. Afr....C5 49
Néma, Maur....C3 45
Nemacolin, Greene, Pa....G2 114
*Nemadji, riv., Minn.,
Wis*....D6 99, B1 124
Nemaha, Sac, Iowa....B2 92
Nemaha, Nemaha, Nebr...D10 103
Nemaha, co., Kans....C7 93
Nemaha, co., Nebr....D10 103
Nemaksciai, Sov. Un....A7 26
Neman, Sov. Un....A7 26
Neman, riv., Sov. Un....E5 27
Nembe, Nig....F6 45
Nemeiben, lake, Sask., Can....B3 70
Nemi, lake, It....h9 21
Nemiscau, Que., Can....h11 73
Nemo, Lawrence, S. Dak....C2 116
Nemours, Fr....C5 14
Nemunas, riv., Sov. Un....A6 26
Nemuro, Jap....E12 37
Nemuro, strait, Jap....E12 37
Nen, riv., China....B2 37
Nenagh, Ire....E3 11
Nenana, Alsk....C10 79
Nenchiang, China....B10 34
Nene, riv., Eng....B7 12
Nenzel, Cherry, Nebr....B4 103
Neodesha, Wilson, Kans....E8 93
Neoga, Cumberland, Ill....D5 90
Neola, Pottawattamie, Iowa..C2 92
Neola, Duchesne, Utah....C5 119
Neon, Letcher, Ky....C7 94
Neopit, Shawano, Wis....D5 124
Neosho, Newton, Mo....E3 101
Neosho, Dodge, Wis....E5 124
Neosho, co., Kans....E8 93
*Neosho, riv., Kans.,
Okla*....E8 93, B6 112
Neosho Falls, Woodson,
Kans....D8 93
Neosho Rapids, Lyons, Kans.D8 93
Neotsu, Lincoln, Oreg....B3 113
Nepal, country,
Asia....G11 33, D10 40
Nepālganj, Nep....C8 40
Nepaug, res., Conn....B5 84
Nepewassi, lake, Ont., Can....A4 72
Nephi, Juab, Utah....D4 119
Nephton, Ont., Can....C7 72
Nepisiguit, bay, N.B., Can....B4 74
Nepisiguit, riv., N.B., Can....B3 74
Nepomuk, Czech....D8 17
Neponset, Bureau, Ill....B4 90
Neponset, riv., Mass....h11 97
Nepton, Fleming, Ky....B6 94
Neptune, Sask., Can....H3 70
Neptune, Monmouth, N.J....C4 106
Neptune Beach, Duval,
Fla....B5, m9 86
Neptune City, Monmouth,
N.J....C4 106
Nera, riv., It....C4 21
Nérac, Fr....E4 14
Nerchinsk, Sov. Un....D14 28
Nerekhta, Sov. Un....C13 27
Neretva, riv., Yugo....D3 22
Neris, riv., Sov. Un....A8 26
Nerja, Sp....D4 20
Nerpichye, Sov. Un....B12 37
Nerstrand, Rice, Minn....F5 99
Nerva, Sp....D2 20
Nes, Neth....A5 15
Nesbit, DeSoto, Miss....A3 100
Nesbitt, Man., Can....E2 71
Nesco, Atlantic, N.J....D3 106
Nesconset, Suffolk, N.Y....F4 84
Nescopeck, Luzerne, Pa....D9 114
Nesebur, Bul....D8 22
Neshaminy, creek, Pa....C2 106
Neshanic, riv., N.J.....C3 106
Neshanic Station, Somerset,
N.J....B3 106
Nesher, Isr....B7 32
Neshkoro, Marquette, Wis...E4 124
Neshoba, Neshoba, Miss....C4 100
Neshoba, co., Miss....C4 100
Nesika Beach, Curry, Oreg...E2 113
Neskaupstadur, Ice....n26 25
Neskowin, Tillamook, Oreg..B3 113
Nesle, Fr....E2 15
Nesmith, Williamsburg,
S.C....D8 115
Nesodden, Nor....p28 25
Nespelem, Okanogan, Wash.A7 122
Nesquehoning, Carbon, Pa..E10 114
Ness, co., Kans....D3 93
Ness, lake, Scot....C4 13
Ness City, Ness, Kans....D4 93
*Nesselrode, mtn., Alsk., B.C.,
Can*....E6 66
Nesselwang, F.R.G....E6 18
Nesslau, Switz....B7 19
Nessmersiel, F.R.G....A7 15
Nesterov, Sov. Un....A7 26
Nesterov, Sov. Un....C7 26
Nestorion, Grc....B3 23
Nestorville, Barbour, W. Va..B5 123
Nestos, riv., Grc....B5 23
Nesvizh, Sov. Un....E6 27
Nes Ziyyona, Isr....C6, h10 32
Netanya, Isr....B6, f10 32
Netarts, Tillamook, Oreg....B3 113
Netawaka, Jackson, Kans....C8 93
Netcong, Morris, N.J....B3 106
Netherhill, Sask., Can....F1 70
Netherlands, country,
Eur....E10 8, B5 15
Netherlands Antilles (Netherlands West Indies), dep.,
N.A....*B4 53, *A5 60
Netherlands Guiana, see Surinam,
Neth. dep., S.A.
Netherlands Indies, see
Indonesia, country, Asia
Netherlands West Indies, see
Netherlands Antilles, dep.,
N.A.
Nethy Bridge, Scot....C5 13
Netolice, Czech....D9 17
Netrakona, Bngl....E13 40
Nett, lake, Minn....B5 99
Nettie, Nicholas, W. Va....C4 123
*Nettilling, lake, N.W. Ter.,
Can*....C18 67
Nett Lake, St. Louis, Minn..B5 99
Nettleton, Lee and Monroe,
Miss....A5 100
Nettleton, Caldwell, Mo....B4 101
Nettuno, It....k9 21
Netvorice, Czech....o18 26
Neubeckum, F.R.G....B3 17
Neubrandenburg, G.D.R....B6 16
Neuburg, F.R.G....E6 17
Neuchâtel, Switz....B2 19
Neuchâtel, canton, Switz....C2 19
Neuchâtel, lake, Switz....C2 19
Neudorf, Sask., Can....G4 70
Neuenegg, Switz....C3 19
Neuenkirchen, F.R.G....E3 24
Neuenrade, F.R.G....B2 17
Neuerburg, F.R.G....D6 15
Neufchâteau, Bel....E5 15
Neufchâteau, Fr....C6 14
Neufchâtel-en-Bray, Fr....C4 14
Neufchâtel-sur-Aisne, Fr....E4 15
Neufelden, Aus....D6 17
Neugersdorf, G.D.R....C9 17
Neuharlingersiel, F.R.G....A7 15
Neuhaus, F.R.G....E4 24
Neuhaus, G.D.R....C6 17
Neuilly [-sur-Marne], Fr....g11 14
Neuilly-sur-Seine, Fr....g10 14
Neu-Isenburg, F.R.G....C3 17
Neukirchen am Grossvenediger,
Aus....B8 18
Neumarkt, F.R.G....A8 15
Neumarkt [in der Oberpfalz],
F.R.G....D6 17
Neumarkt-Sankt Veit,
F.R.G....A8 18
Neumarkt, see Sroda Slaska, Pol
Neumünster, F.R.G.A4 16, D3 24
Neunburg vorm Wald,
F.R.G....D7 17
Neunkirch, Switz....A6 19
Neunkirchen, Aus....E8 16
Neunkirchen, F.R.G....D6 15
Neuquén, Arg....B3 54
Neuquén, prov., Arg....B3 54
Neuquén, riv., Arg....B3 54
Neurara, Chile....D2 55
Neuruppin, G.D.R....B6 16
Neuse, riv., N.C....B4 109
Neusiedler, lake, Aus....E8 16
Neuss, F.R.G....B1 17
Neustadt, Ont., Can....C4 72
Neustadt am Rübenberge,
F.R.G....F3 24
Neustadt [an der Aisch],
F.R.G....D5 17
Neustadt [an der Dosse],
G.D.R....B6 16
Neustadt [an der Orla],
G.D.R....C6 17
Neustadt an der Waldnaab,
F.R.G....D7 17
Neustadt [an der Weinstrasse],
F.R.G....D3 17
Neustadt [bei Coburg],
F.R.G....C6 17
Neustadt-Glewe, G.D.R....E5 24
Neustadt [im Schwarzwald],
F.R.G....B4 18
Neustadt [in Holstein],
F.R.G....D4 24
Neustadt [in Sachsen],
G.D.R....B9 17
Neustadt [Kreis Marburg],
F.R.G....C4 17
Neustrelitz, G.D.R....B6 16
Neu-Ulm, F.R.G....D5 16
Neuville, Que., Can....C6, o16 73
Neuville-les-Dieppe, Fr....E9 12
Neuwerk, isl., F.R.G....E2 24
Neuwied, F.R.G....C2 17
Neva, Johnson, Tenn....C12 117
Neva, riv., Sov. Un....s31 25
Nevada, Story, Iowa....B4 92
Nevada, Vernon, Mo....D3 101
Nevada, Wyandot, Ohio....B2 111
Nevada, co., Ark....D2 81
Nevada, co., Calif....C3 82
Nevada, state, U.S....C4 76, 104
Nevada, mts., Sp....D4 20
Nevada City, Nevada, Calif..C3 82
Nevada Mills, Steuben, Ind..A7 91
Nevado, mtn., Arg....B3 54
Nevado del Huilo, mtn., Col...C2 60
Nevel, Sov. Un....C7 27
Nevelsk (Honto), Sov. Un....C10 37
Nevers, Fr....D5 14
Neversink, res., N.Y.....D6 108
Neversink, riv., N.Y.....D6 108
Neves, Braz....*C4 56
Nevesinje, Yugo....D4 22
Neville, Sask., Can....H2 70
Néville, Fr....E8 12
Neville Island, Allegheny,
Pa....*F2 114
Nevils, Bulloch, Ga....D5 87
Nevinnomyssk, Sov. Un....G17 9
Nevinville, Adams, Iowa....C3 92
Nevis, Hubbard, Minn....D4 99
Nevis, inlet, Scot....C3 13
*Nevis, isl., St. Kitts-Nevis-
Anguilla*....H13 64
Nevis, mtn., Scot....D3 13
Nevşehir, Tur....C10 25
New, chan., Sask., Can....D4 70
New, inlet, Fla....C2 86
New, inlet, N.C....D5 109
New, lake, N.C....B6 109
New, riv., Ariz....k8 80
New, riv., N.Z....P12 51
New, riv., N.C....C5 109
*New, riv.,
W. Va*....C3 123, C2 121
Newala, Tan....D6 48
New Albany, Floyd, Ind....H6 91
New Albany, Wilson, Kans..E8 93
New Albany, Union, Miss...A4 100
New Albany, Franklin,
Ohio....k11 111
New Albany, Bradford, Pa...C9 114
New Albin, Allamakee,
Iowa....A6 92
Newald, Forest, Wis....C5 124
New Alexandria, Fairfax,
Va....*B5 121
New Almelo, Norton, Kans..C3 93
New Alsace, Dearborn, Ind..F7 91
New Amsterdam, Guy....A3 59
Newark, Independence, Ark..B4 81
Newark, Alameda, Calif....h8 82
Newark, New Castle, Del....A6 85
Newark, Eng....A7 12
Newark, Kendall, Ill....B5 90
Newark, Greene, Ind....F4 91
Newark, Worcester, Md....D7 85
Newark, Knox, Mo....B6 101
Newark, Essex, N.J....B4, k8 106
Newark, Wayne, N.Y....B3 108
Newark, Licking, Ohio....B3 111
Newark, Wise, Tex....m9 118
Newark, bay, N.J....k8 106
Newark Valley, Tioga, N.Y..C4 108
New Ashford, Berkshire,
Mass....*A1 97
New Athens, St. Clair, Ill....E4 90
New Athens, Harrison, Ohio.B4 111
New Auburn, Sibley, Minn..F4 99
New Auburn, Chippewa,
Wis....C2 124
New Augusta, Marion, Ind..k10 91
New Augusta, Perry, Miss...D4 100
Newaygo, Newaygo, Mich..E5 98
Newaygo, co., Mich....E5 98
New Baden, Clinton and St.
Clair, Ill....E4 90
New Baltimore, Macomb and
St. Clair, Mich....F8 98
New Baltimore, Greene, N.Y.C7 108
New Baltimore, Hamilton,
Ohio....n12 111
New Baltimore, Somerset,
Pa....G4 114
New Beaver, Lawrence, Pa.*E1 114
New Bedford, Bureau, Ill....B4 90
New Bedford, Bristol, Mass..C6 97
Newberg, Yamhill, Oreg.B4, h12 113
New Berlin, Sangamon, Ill...D4 90
New Berlin, Chenango, N.Y.C5 108
New Berlin, Union, Pa....E8 114
New Berlin, Guadalupe, Tex.k7 118
New Berlin, Waukesha, Wis.n11 124
New Berlinville, Berks, Pa.*F10 114
Newbern, Hale, Ala....C2 78
Newbern, Jersey, Ill....D3 90
Newbern, Bartholomew, Ind.F6 91
New Bern, Craven, N.C....B5 109
Newbern, Dyer, Tenn....A2 117
Newberry, Alachua, Fla....C4 86
Newberry, Greene, Ind....G3 91
Newberry, Luce, Mich....B5 98
Newberry, Newberry, S.C....C4 115
Newberry, co., S.C....C4 115
Newberry Springs, San
Bernardino, Calif....E5 82
New Bethlehem, Clarion, Pa.D3 114
New Blaine, Logan, Ark....B2 81
New Bloomfield, Callaway,
Mo....C5 101
New Bloomfield (Bloomfield),
Perry, Pa....F7 114
New Bloomington, Marion,
Ohio....B2 111
Newborn, Newton, Ga....C3 87
Newboro, Ont., Can....C8 72
New Boston, Mercer, Ill....B3 90
New Boston, Lee, Iowa....D6 92
New Boston, Berkshire, Mass.B1 97
New Boston, Wayne, Mich..p15 98
New Boston, Hillsboro, N.H.E3 105
New Boston, Scioto, Ohio....D3 111
New Boston, Bowie, Tex....C5 118
New Braintree, Worcester,
Mass....B3 97
New Braunfels, Comal,
Tex....E3, h7 118
New Bremen, Lewis, N.Y....B5 108
New Bremen, Auglaize, Ohio.B1 111
Newbridge, Ire....D3 11
New Bridge, Baker, Oreg....C9 113
New Brigden, Alta., Can....D5 69
New Brighton, Ramsey,
Minn....m12 99
New Brighton, Beaver, Pa....E1 114
New Britain, Hartford, Conn.C5 84
New Britain, Bucks, Pa....*F11 114
*New Britain, isl.,
Pap. N. Gui*....G9 7, k13 50
New Brockton, Coffee, Ala..D4 78
Newbrook, Alta., Can....B4 69
New Brunswick, Middlesex,
N.J....C4 106
New Brunswick, prov.,
Can....G19 67, 74
New Brunswick Heights,
Middlesex, N.J....*C4 106
New Buffalo, Berrien, Mich..G4 98
Newburg, Warrick, Ind....I13 85
Newburg, Jasper, Iowa....C5 92
Newburg, Charles, Md....D4 85
Newburg, Phelps, Mo....D6 101
Newburg, Bottineau, N. Dak.A5 110
Newburg, Cumberland, Pa...F7 114
Newburg, Preston, W. Va....B5 123
Newburg, Washington and
Ozaukee, Wis....E5 124
Newburgh, Ont., Can....C8 72
Newburgh, Penobscot,
Maine....D3 96
Newburgh, Orange, N.Y....D6 108
Newburgh, Scot....C7 13
Newburgh Heights, Cuyahoga,
Ohio....h9 111
New Burnside, Johnson, Ill..F5 90
Newbury, Ont., Can....E3 72
Newbury, Eng....C6 12
Newbury, Essex, Mass....A6 97
Newbury, Merrimack, N.H..D2 105
Newbury, Orange, Vt....C4 120
Newburyport, Essex, Mass..A6 97
New Caledonia, Fr. dep.,
Oceania....H9 7
New Cambria, Saline, Kans.D6 93
New Cambria, Macon, Mo..B5 101
New Canaan, Fairfield,
Conn....E3 84
New Canton, Pike, Ill....D2 90
New Canton, Buckingham,
Va....C4 121
New Carlisle, Que., Can....A4 74
New Carlisle, St., Joseph,
Ind....A4 91

Nishinotoro, see Dalnyaya, Sov. Un.
Nishio, Jap...*I9 37
Nisiros, isl., Grc...D6 23
Niskayuna, Schenectady, N.Y...C7 108
Nisko, Pol...C7 26
Nisland, Butte, S. Dak...C2 116
Nisqually, riv., Wash...C3 122
Nissan, riv., Swe...B7 24
Nissum Bredning, fjord, Den...B2 24
Nisswa, Crow Wing, Minn...D4 99
Nistowiak, lake, Sask., Can...B3 70
Nisula, Houghton, Mich...C2 98
Niterói, Braz...C4, h6 56
Nith, riv., Scot...E5 13
Nitra, Czech...D5 26
Nitra, riv., Czech...D5 26
Nitro, Kanawha and Putnam, W. Va...C3 123
Nitta Yuma, Sharkey, Miss...B3 100
Nittenau, F.R.G...D7 17
Niue, N.Z. dep., Oceania...*H11 7
Nivelles, Bel...D4 15
Nivernais, former prov., Fr...D5 14
Nivernais, hills, Fr...D5 14
Niverville, Man., Can...E3 71
Nivskiy, Sov. Un...D15 25
Niwka, Pol...g10 26
Niwot, Boulder, Colo...A5 83
Nixa, Christian, Mo...D4 101
Nixburg, Coosa, Ala...C3 78
Nixon, Washoe, Nev...D2 104
Nixon, Hardin, Tenn...B3 117
Nixon, Gonzales, Tex...E4, k8 118
Nizāmābād, India...H7 40
Nizamsagar, lake, India...H6 40
Nizgān, riv., Afg...E11 41
Nizhmozero, Sov. Un...E17 25
Nizhne-Chirskaya, Sov. Un...G14 27
Nizhne-Kolymsk, Sov. Un...C19 28
Nizhneudinsk, Sov. Un...D12 28
Nizhneye, Sov. Un...q21 27
Nizhniye Narykary, Sov. Un...C21 9
Nizhniy-Lomov, Sov. Un...E14 27
Nizhniy Tagil, Sov. Un...B5 29
Nizhnyaya Tunguska, riv., Sov. Un...C12 28
Nizhnyaya Tura, Sov. Un...D21 9
Nizmennyy, cape, Sov. Un...E7 37
Nizza Monferrato, It...E4 18
Njombe, Tan...C5 48
Njurunda, Swe...F7 25
Nkai, Zimb...A4 49
Nkawkaw, Ghana...*E4 45
Nkhata Bay, Malawi...D5 48
Nkhota Kota, Malawi...D5 48
Nkongsamba, Cam...E1 46
Nnewi, Nig...E6 45
Noakhali, Bngl...F13 40
Noank, New London, Conn...D9 84
Noasca, It...D3 17
Noatak, Alsk...B7 79
Noatak, riv., Alsk...B7 79
Nobel, Ont., Can...B4 72
Nobeoka, Jap...J5 37
Noble, Walker, Ga...B1 87
Noble, Richland, Ill...E5 90
Noble, Sabine, La...C2 95
Noble, Cleveland, Okla...B4 112
Noble, co., Ind...B7 91
Noble, co., Ohio...C4 111
Noble, co., Okla...A4 112
Nobleboro, Lincoln, Maine...D3 96
Nobleford, Alta., Can...E4 69
Noble Lake, Jefferson, Ark...C4 81
Nobles, co., Minn...G3 99
Noblesville, Hamilton, Ind...D5 91
Nobleton, Hernando, Fla...D4 86
Noboribetsu, Jap...E10 37
Nobscot, hill, Mass...B5 97
Nocatee, De Soto, Fla...E5 86
Nocera Inferiore, It...*D5 21
Nochixtlán, Mex...o15 63
Nocona, Montague, Tex...C4 118
Noda, Jap...*I9 37
Noda, see Chekhov, Sov. Un.
Nodaway, Adams, Iowa...D3 92
Nodaway, co., Mo...A3 101
Nodaway, riv., Iowa, Mo...D2 92, A2 101
Node, Niobrara, Wyo...D8 125
Noel, McDonald, Mo...E3 101
Noel Paul's, brook, Newf., Can...D3 75
Noelville, Ont., Can...A4 72
Noemfoor, isl., Indon...F8 35
Nogal, Lincoln, N. Mex...D4 107
Nogal, riv., Som...D6 47
Nogales, Santa Cruz, Ariz...F5 80
Nogales, Mex...A2 63
Nogales, Mex...n15 63
Nogara, It...D7 18
Nōgata, Jap...J5 37
Nogent-en-Bassigny, Fr...C6 14
Nogent-le-Rotrou, Fr...C4 14
Nogent [-sur-Marne], Fr...g10 14
Nogent-sur-Seine, Fr...C5 14
Noginsk, Sov. Un...B1 29
Nogoa, riv., Austl...B6 51
Nogoyá, Arg...A5 54
Nógrád, co., Hung...*A4 22
Nogueira, Sp...A2 20
Nohar, India...C5 40
Noheji, Jap...F10 37
Noho, China...B2 37
Noire, riv., Que., Can...A7 72
Noire, riv., Upper Volta...D4 45
Noirmoutier, isl., Fr...D2 14
Noisy-le-Sec, Fr...g10 14
Nojima, cape, Jap...I9 37
Nokkeushi, see Kitami, Jap.
Nok Kundi, Pak...G11 41
Nokomis, Sask., Can...F3 70
Nokomis, Sarasota, Fla...E4 86
Nokomis, Montgomery, Ill...D4 90
Nokomis, lake, Wis...C4 124
Nokrek, peak, India...E13 40
Nola, Scott, Ark...C2 81
Nola, Cen. Afr. Rep...E3 46
Nola, It...D5 21
Nola, Lawrence, Miss...D3 100
Nolan, Nolan, Tex...C2 118
Nolan, Mingo, W. Va...D2 123
Nolan, co., Tex...C2 118
Nolensville, Williamson, Tenn...B5 117
Nolin, flood control res., Ky...C3 94
Nolin, riv., Ky...C3 94
Nolinsk, Sov. Un...B3 29
Noma, Holmes, Fla...u16 86
Noma, cape, Jap...K5 37
Nomans Land, isl., Mass...D6 97
Nombre de Dios, Pan...h12 62
Nome, Alsk...C6 79
Nome, Barnes, N. Dak...C8 110
Nomény, Fr...F6 15
Nominingue, Que., Can...C2 73
Nomme, Sov. Un...*B5 27
Nonacho, lake, N.W. Ter., Can...D11 66
Nonconnah, creek, Tenn...e9 117
Nondalton, Alsk...C8 79
Nonesuch, riv., Maine...g7 96
Nong Khai, Thai...D5 38
Nongoma, S. Afr...C5 49
Nonoava, Mex...B3 63
Nooksack, Whatcom, Wash...A3 122
Nooksack, riv., Wash...A3 122
Noonan, Divide, N. Dak...A2 110
Noord Pagai, isl., Indon...F2 35
Noordwijk-Binnen, Neth...B4 15
Noorvik, Alsk...B7 79
Nooseneck, Kent, R.I...C10 84
Nootka, isl., B.C., Can...E4 68
Nootka, sound, B.C., Can...E4 68
Nopal, De Witt, Tex...E4 118
No Point, pt., Md...D5 85
Noquebay, lake, Wis...C6 124
Nóqui, Ang...C1 48
Nora, Sask., Can...E4 70
Nora, Jo Daviess, Ill...A4 90
Nora, Swe...H6 25
Noranda, Que., Can...k11 73
Nora Springs, Floyd, Iowa...A5 92
Nor-Bayazet, Sov. Un...B15 29
Norbertville, Que., Can...C6 73
Norborne, Carroll, Mo...B4 101
Norcatur, Decatur, Kans...C3 93
Norco, Riverside, Calif...*F5 82
Norco, St. Charles, La...D5, h11 95
Norcross, Gwinnett, Ga...C2, h8 87
Norcross, Grant, Minn...E2 99
Nord, dept., Fr...D3 15
Nord, canal, Fr...D3 15
Nord, mts., Hai...E7 64
Nord, pt., Curaçao...H18 65
Nørdborg, Den...C3 24
Nordby, Den...C2 24
Nordby, Den...C4 24
Nordegg, Alta., Can...C2, g7 69
Nordegg, riv., Alta., Can...C3 69
Norden, F.R.G...B3 16
Nordenham, F.R.G...B4 16
Nordenskjöld, arch., Sov. Un...B4 4
Nordenskjöld, ice tongue, Ant...e39 5
Norderney, F.R.G...A7 15
Norderney, isl., F.R.G...A7 15
Nordfjord, fjord, Nor...G1 25
Nordhausen, G.D.R...B5 17
Nordheim, Winnebago, Wis...*D5 124
Nordhorn, F.R.G...B3 16
Nordjylland, co., Den...B3 24
Nordland, Jefferson, Wash...A3 122
Nordland, co., Nor...*D6 25
Nördlingen, F.R.G...E5 17
Nordmaling, Swe...F8 25
Nordman, Bonner, Idaho...A2 89
Nordreisa, Nor...C9 25
Nordrhein-Westfalen (North Rhine-Westphalia), state, F.R.G...B2 17
Nordstrand, isl., F.R.G...A4 16
Nord-Tröndelag, co., Nor...*E4 25
Nordvik, Sov. Un...B14 28
Nore, riv., Ire...E4 11
Norene, Wilson, Tenn...A5 117
Norfield, Lincoln, Miss...D3 100
Norfolk, Litchfield, Conn...B4 84
Norfolk, Norfolk, Mass...h10 97
Norfolk, Madison, Nebr...B8 103
Norfolk, St. Lawrence, N.Y...f9 108
Norfolk (Independent City), Va...D6, k15 121
Norfolk, co., Ont., Can...E4 72
Norfolk, co., Eng...B8 12
Norfolk, co., Mass...B5 97
Norfolk, is., Pac. O...H10 7
Norfolk Highlands, Norfolk, Va...*D6 121
Norfolk Island, Austl. dep., Oceania...H10 7
Norfork, Baxter, Ark...A3 81
Norfork, dam, Ark...A3 81
Norfork, lake, Ark...A3 81
Norge, Grady, Okla...C4 112
Norias, Kenedy, Tex...F4 118
Norilsk, Sov. Un...C11 28
Norland, Ont., Can...C6 72
Norland, Dade, Fla...s13 86
Norlina, Warren, N.C...A4 109
Norma, Salem, N.J...E2 106
Norma, Renville, N. Dak...A4 110
Norma, Scott, Tenn...C9 117
Normal, Madison, Ala...A3 78
Normal, McLean, Ill...C5 90
Norman, Montgomery, Ark...C2 81
Norman, Jackson, Ind...G5 91
Norman, Kearney, Nebr...D7 103
Norman, Richmond, N.C...B3 109
Norman, Cleveland, Okla...B4 112
Norman, co., Minn...C2 99
Norman, isl., Vir. Is. (Br)...B6 65
Norman, lake, N.C...B2 109
Norman, riv., Austl...C7 50
Normanby, riv., Austl...B7 50
Normandin, Que., Can...*D4 73
Normandy, Duval, Fla...*B5 86
Normandy, former prov., Fr...C4 14
Normandy, St. Louis, Mo...f13 101
Normandy, Bedford, Tenn...B5 117
Normandy, hills, Fr...C3 14
Normandy Beach, Ocean, N.J...C4 106
Normandy Park, King, Wash...*D2 122
Normangee, Madison and Leon, Tex...D4 118
Norman Park, Colquitt, Ga...E3 87
Norman's Cove, Newf., Can...*D5 75
Normanton, Austl...C7 50
Normantown, Toombs, Ga...D4 87
Norman Wells, N.W. Ter., Can...C7 66
Norphlet, Union, Ark...D3 81
Norquay, Sask., Can...F4 70
Ñorquincó, Arg...C2 54
Norrahammar, Swe...A8 24
Norrbotten, co., Swe...*E10 25
Nørre Åby, Den...C3 24
Nørre Alslev, Den...D5 24
Nørresundby, Den...A3 24
Norridge, Cook, Ill...k9 90
Norridgewock, Somerset, Maine...D3 96
Norrie, Marathon, Wis...D4 124
Norris, Fulton, Ill...C3 90
Norris, Madison, Mont...E5 102
Norris, Pickens, S.C...B2 115
Norris, Mellette, S. Dak...D4 116
Norris, Anderson, Tenn...C9 117
Norris, dam, Tenn...C9 117
Norris, lake, Tenn...C10 117
Norris Arm, Newf., Can...D4 75
Norris City, White, Ill...F5 90
Norris Point, Newf., Can...D3 75
Norristown, Montgomery, Pa...F11, o20 114
Norrisville, Harford, Md...A4 85
Norrköping, Swe...H7, u34 25
Norrtälje, Swe...H8, t36 25
Norseman, Austl...F3 50
Norsk, Sov. Un...A6 31
Norte, chan., Braz...B4 59
Norte, range, Braz...E3 59
Norte de Santander, dept., Col...B3 60
North, Orangeburg, S.C...D5 115
North, Mathews, Va...C6 121
North, div., Ice...*n23 25
North, bay, Utah...B3 119
North (Metedeconk, riv.) branch, N.J...C4 106
North (Lamoille, riv.) branch, Vt...B3 120
North (Winooski, riv.) branch, Vt...C3 120
North, cape, N.S., Can...B9 74
North, cape, N.Z...K14 51
North, cape, Nor...B11 25
North, cape, Svalbard...A12 4
North, chan., Ont., Can...A2 72
North, chan., N. Ire., Scot...C4 10
North, creek, Ga...h8 87
North (Flathead, riv.) fork, Mont...B2 102
North, fork, Wyo...B3 125
North, inlet, S.C...E9 115
North, isl., Ba...m17 64
North, isl., N.Z...M14 51
North, isl., S.C...E9 115
North, is., La...E7 95
North, mtn., Okla...C3 112
North, mtn., Pa...D9 114
North, park, Pa...A5 114
North, pass, La...E6 95
North, plains, N. Mex...C1 107
North, pt., Barb...K20 65
North, pt., P.E.I., Can...B6 74
North, pt., Md...B5 85
North, pt., Md...C5 85
North, pt., Mich...C7 98
North, pond, Maine...D3 96
North, pond, Mass...h9 97
North, riv., Ala...B2 78
North, riv., Newf., Can...B3 75
North, riv., Mass...h12 97
North, sea, Eur...D9 8
North, sound, Ire...D2 11
North, The, sound, Scot...A6 13
North Abington, Plymouth, Mass...B6, h12 97
North Acton, Middlesex, Mass...f10 97
North Adams, Berkshire, Mass...A1 97
North Adams, Hillsdale, Mich...G6 98
North Albany, Benton, Oreg...k11 113
Northallerton, Eng...C6 12
Northam, Austl...F2 50
Northam, Eng...*C3 12
North America, cont...C14 3, 61
North Amherst, Hampshire, Mass...B2 97
North Amity, Aroostook, Maine...C5 96
North Amityville, Suffolk, N.Y...*G3 84
Northampton, Austl...E1 50
Northampton, Eng...D6 10, B7 12
Northampton, Hampshire, Mass...B2 97
Northampton, Northampton, Pa...E11 114
Northampton, co., Eng...B6 12
Northampton, co., N.C...A5 109
Northampton, co., Pa...E11 114
Northampton, co., Va...C7 121
North Andaman, isl., India...F9 39
North Andover, Essex, Mass...A5 97
North Anna, riv., Va...B5 121
North Anson, Somerset, Maine...D3 96
North Apollo, Armstrong, Pa...E2 114
North Arlington, Bergen, N.J...h8 106
North Asheboro, Randolph, N.C...B3 109
North Atlanta, DeKalb, Ga...h8 87
North Atlantic, ocean...D18 3
North Attleboro, Bristol, Mass...C5 97
North Augusta, Ont., Can...C9 72
North Augusta, Aiken, S.C...D3 115
North Aulatsivik, isl., Newf., Can...f9 75
North Aurora, Kane, Ill...k8 90
North Babylon, Suffolk, N.Y...*G3 84
North Baltimore, Wood, Ohio...A2 111
North Bancroft, Aroostook, Maine...C5 96
North Bangor, Franklin, N.Y...f10 108
North Barrackpore, India...*F12 40
North Battleford, Sask., Can...E1, n7 70
North Bay, Ont., Can...A5, p20 72
North Bay, Dade, Fla...*G6 86
North Beach, Calvert, Md...C4 85
North Belle Vernon, Westmoreland, Pa...*F2 114
North Bellmore, Nassau, N.Y...*G2 84
North Bellport, Suffolk, N.Y...*G5 84
North Belmont, Gaston, N.C...B1 109
North Bend, B.C., Can...E7 68
North Bend, Dodge, Nebr...C9 103
North Bend, Hamilton, Ohio...o12 111
North Bend, Coos, Oreg...D2 113
North Bend, Clinton, Pa...D6 114
North Bend, King, Wash...B4 122
North Bend, Jackson, Wis...D2 124
North Bennington, Bennington, Vt...F2 120
North Bergen, Hudson, N.J...h8 106
North Berwick, York, Maine...E2 96
North Berwick, Scot...D6 13
North Billerica, Middlesex, Mass...A5, f10 97
North Bloomfield, Trumbull, Ohio...A5 111
North Bonneville, Skamania, Wash...D4 122
North Borneo, see Sabah, reg., Mala.
Northboro, Page, Iowa...D2 92
Northborough, Worcester, Mass...B4 97
North Brabant, prov., Neth...C5 15
North Bradford, Penobscot, Maine...C4 96
North Bradley, Midland, Mich...E6 98
North Branch, Allegany, Md...D2 85
North Branch, Lapeer, Mich...E7 98
North Branch, Chisago, Minn...E6 99
North Branch, Somerset, N.J...B3 106
North Branford, New Haven, Conn...D5 84
North Brewer, Penobscot, Maine (part of Brewer)...D4 96
Northbridge, Worcester, Mass...B4 97
North Bridgton, Cumberland, Maine...D2 96
Northbrook, Ont., Can...C7 72
Northbrook, Cook, Ill...h9 90
North Brookfield, Worcester, Mass...B3 97
North Brooksville, Hancock, Maine...D4 96
North Brother, mtn., Maine...C4 96
North Brunswick, Middlesex, N.J...C4 106
North Buena Vista, Clayton, Iowa...B7 92
North Calais, Washington, Vt...C4 120
North Caldwell, Essex, N.J...B4 106
North Canaan (Town of), Litchfield, Conn...A3 84
North Canadian, riv., Okla...B5 112
North Canton, Hartford, Conn...B5 84
North Canton, Cherokee, Ga...B2 87
North Canton, Stark, Ohio...B4 111
North Cape, Racine, Wis...n11 124
North Cape May, Cape May, N.J...F3 106
North Carolina, state, U.S...C12 77, 109
North Carrollton, Carroll, Miss...B4 100
North Carver, Plymouth, Mass...C6 97
North Cascades, nat. park, Wash...A3 76
North Catasauqua, Northampton, Pa...*E11 114
North Cedar, Black Hawk, Iowa...B5 92
North Charleroi, Washington, Pa...*F2 114
North Charleston, Charleston, S.C...F7, k12 115
North Charlestown, Sullivan, N.H...D2 105
North Chelmsford, Middlesex, Mass...A5 97
North Chicago, Lake, Ill...A6, h9 90
North Chili, Monroe, N.Y...*B3 108
North City, King, Wash...*B3 122
North Clarendon, Rutland, Vt...D3 120
North Cohasset, Norfolk, Mass...h12 97
North Cohocton, Steuben, N.Y...C3 108
North College Hill, Hamilton, Ohio...o12 111
North Collins, Erie, N.Y...C2 108
North Concord, Essex, Vt...C5 120
North Conway, Carroll, N.H...B4 105
North Corbin, Laurel, Ky...D5 94
North Cornville, Somerset, Maine...D3 96
Northcote, Austl...*H5 51
Northcraft, Fulton, Pa...G5 114
North Creek, Warren, N.Y...B7 108
Northcrest, Del Norte, Calif...*B1 82
North Dakota, state, U.S...A7 76, 110
North Danville, Caledonia, Vt...C4 120
North Dartmouth, Bristol, Mass...C6 97
North Decatur, De Kalb, Ga...*C2 87
North Derby, Orleans, Vt...B4 120
North Dighton, Bristol, Mass...C5 97
North Dixmont, Penobscot, Maine...D3 96
North Dorset, Bennington, Vt...E3 120
North Downs, hills, Eng...C8 12
North Druid Hills, De Kalb, Ga...*C2 87
North Eagle Butte, Dewey, S. Dak...B4 116
North East, Cecil, Md...A6 85
North East, Erie, Pa...B2 114
Northeast, cape, Alsk...C6 79
North East, isl., Nor...A12 4
North East, is., Truk...52
Northeast, pt., Newf., Can...B4 75
Northeast, pond, N.H...D5 105
Northeast, riv., Md...A6 85
North East Carry, Piscataquis, Maine...C3 96
Northeastern, reg., Ken...A6 48
Northeast Harbor, Hancock, Maine...D4 96
North Eastham, Barnstable, Mass...C8 97
North Easton, Bristol, Mass...B5 97
Northeast Providence, chan., Ba...B5 64
North Egremont, Berkshire, Mass...B1 97
Northeim, F.R.G...B5 17
North Emporia, Greensville, Va. (part of Emporia)...*D5 121
North End, Grafton, N.H...C3 105
North English, Iowa, Iowa...C5 92
North Enid, Garfield, Okla...A4 112
Northern, prov., Malawi...D5 48
Northern, prov., Zambia...D5 48
Northern, reg., Ghana...E4 45
Northern, reg., Nig...D6 45
Northern, reg., Tan...B6 48
Northern, reg., Ug...A5 48
Northern, head, N.B., Can...E3 74
Northern, range, Trin...N23 65
Northern Arm, Newf., Can...D4 75
Northern Cheyenne, Indian res., Mont...E10 102
Northern Dvina, riv., Sov. Un...C17 9
Northern Indian, lake, Man., Can...A3 71
Northern Ireland, reg., U.K...C3 10
Northern Light, lake, Ont., Can...A7 99
Northern Rhodesia, see Zambia, country, Afr.
Northern Sporades, is., Grc...C5 23
Northern Territory, ter., Austl...B5 50
North Esk, riv., Scot...D6 13
North Fabius, riv., Mo...A6 101
North Fairfield, Huron, Ohio...A3 111
North Falmouth, Barstable, Mass...C6 97
North Fayette, Kennebec, Maine...D2 96
North Ferrisburg, Addison, Vt...C2 120
Northfield, B.C., Can...f12 68
Northfield, Litchfield, Conn...C4 84
Northfield, Cook, Ill...*B6 90
Northfield, Washington, Maine...D5 96
Northfield, Franklin, Mass...A3 97
Northfield, Rice, Minn...F5 99
Northfield, Merrimack, N.H...D3 105
Northfield, Atlantic, N.J...E3 106
Northfield, Summit, Ohio...h9 111
Northfield (P.O.), Summit, Ohio...*A4 111
Northfield, Motley, Tex...B2 118
Northfield, Washington, Vt...C3 120
Northfield, Jackson, Wis...D2 124
Northfield, mts., Vt...C3 120
Northfield Center, Washington, Vt...C3 120
Northfield Falls, Washington, Vt...C3 120
North Fond du Lac, Fond du Lac, Wis...E5, k9 124
Northford, New Haven, Conn...D5 84
North Foreland, pt., Eng...C9 12
North Fork, Madera, Calif...D4 82
North Fork, Lemhi, Idaho...D5 89
North Fork Toutle, riv., Wash...C3 122
North Foster, Providence, R.I...B10 84
North Fox, isl., Mich...C5 98
North Franklin, New London, Conn...C8 84
North Freedom, Sauk, Wis...E4 124
North Frisian, is., F.R.G...A4 16
North Fryeburg, Oxford, Maine...D2 96
North Galiano, B.C., Can...f12 68
North Gamboa (Gamboa), C.Z...k11 62
Northgate, Sask., Can...H4 70
Northgate, Burke, N. Dak...A3 110
North Glen Ellyn, Du Page, Ill...*B5 90
Northglenn, Adams, Colo...B6 83
North Gower, Ont., Can...B9 72
North Grafton, Worcester, Mass...B4 97
North Granby, Hartford, Conn...B5 84
North Gray, Cumberland, Maine...E5 96
North Great River, Suffolk, N.Y...*G4 84
North Greenville, Washington, Miss...*B2 100
North Grosvenordale, Windham, Conn...B9 84
North Groton, Grafton, N.H...C3 105
North Guilford, New Haven, Conn...D6 84
North Guilford, Piscataquis, Maine...C3 96
North Gulfport, Harrison, Miss...E4, f7 100
North Halawa, riv., Haw...g10 88
North Haledon, Passaic, N.J...B4 106
North Hampton, Rockingham, N.H...E5 105
North Hanover, Plymouth, Mass...h12 97
North Hartland, Windsor, Vt...D4 120
North Hartland, res., Vt...D4 120
North Hartsville, Darlington, S.C...*C7 115
North Hatfield, Hampshire, Mass...B2 97
North Hatley, Que., Can...D6 73
North Haven, New Haven, Conn...D5 84
North Haven, Knox, Maine...D4 102
North Haven, pen., N.Y...E7 84
North Haverhill, Grafton, N.H...B2 105
North Havre, Hill, Mont...B7 102
North Head, N.B., Can...E3 74
North Henderson, Mercer, Ill...B3 90
North Henderson, Vance, N.C...*A4 109
North Hero, Grand Isle, Vt...B2 120
North Hero, isl., Vt...B2 120
North Highlands, Sacramento, Calif...*C3 82
North Holland (Noordholland), prov., Neth...B4 15
North Holston, Smyth, Va...f10 121
North Horn, lake, Tenn...e8 117
North Hornell, Steuben, N.Y...*C3 108
North Horr, Ken...A6 48
North Hudson, Essex, N.Y...B7 108
North Hudson, St. Croix, Wis...*D1 124
North Hyde Park, Lamoille, Vt...B3 120
North Industry, Stark, Ohio...B4 111
North Irwin, Westmoreland, Pa...*F2 114
North Jackson, Mahoning, Ohio...*A5 111
North Java, Wyoming, N.Y...C2 108
North Jay, Franklin, Maine...D2 96
North Judson, Starke, Ind...B4 91
North Kamloops, B.C., Can...D7 68
North Kansas City, Clay, Mo...h10 101
North Kennebunkport (Arundel), York, Maine...E2 96
North Kingstown (Wickford), Washington, R.I...C11 84
North Kingsville, Ashtabula, Ohio...A5 111
North La Junta, Otero, Colo...C7 83
Northlake, Cook, Ill...k9 90
North Lake, Marquette, Mich...B3 98
North Lake, Waukesha, Wis...m11 124
Northland, Marquette, Mich...B3 98
North Laramie, riv., Wyo...D7 125
North Las Vegas, Clark, Nev...G6 104
North Lawrence, St. Lawrence, N.Y...f10 108
North Lemmon, Adams, N. Dak...D3 110
North Lewisburg, Champaign, Ohio...B2 111
North Liberty, St. Joseph, Ind...A5 91
North Liberty, Johnson, Iowa...C6 92
North Lima, Mahoning, Ohio...B5 111
North Lindenhurst, Suffolk, N.Y...*G3 84
North Little Rock, Pulaski, Ark...C3, h10 81
North Logan, Cache, Utah...B4 119
North Loup, Valley, Nebr...C7 103
North Loup, riv., Nebr...B5 103
North Lubec, Washington, Maine...D5 96
North Madison, New Haven, Conn...D6 84
North Madison, Jefferson, Ind. (part of Madison)...G7 91
North Magnetic Pole, N.W. Ter., Can...A12 66
North Mam, peak, Colo...B3 83
North Manchester, Wabash, Ind...C6 91
North Manitou, isl., Mich...C4 98
North Mankato, Nicollet, Minn...F4 99
North Marshfield, Plymouth, Mass...h12 97
North Massapequa, Nassau, N.Y...*G3 84
North Merrick, Nassau, N.Y...*G2 84
North Merrydale, East Baton Rouge, La...*D4 95
North Miami, Dade, Fla...G6, s13 86
North Miami, Ottawa, Okla...A7 112
North Miami Beach, Dade, Fla...s13 86
North Middleboro, Plymouth, Mass...C6 97
North Middletown, Bourbon, Ky...B5 94
North Monmouth, Kennebec, Maine...D2 96
North Montpelier, Washington, Vt...C4 120
Northmoor, Platte, Mo...h10 101
North Muskegon, Muskegon, Mich...E4 98
North Myrtle Beach, Horry, S.C...D10 115
North Naples, Colliers, Fla...F5 86
North Negril, pt., Jam...E12 65
North Newcastle, Lincoln, Maine...D3 96
North New Hyde Park, Nassau, N.Y...*E7 108
North Newport, Sullivan, N.H...D2 105
North New Portland, Somerset, Maine...D2 96
North New River, canal, Fla...F6 86
North Newry, Oxford, Maine...D2 96
North Newton (Bethel College), Harvey, Kans...A5 93
North Norway, Oxford, Maine...D2 96
North Norwich, Chenango, N.Y...C5 108
North Oaks, Douglas, Nebr...*C10 103
North Ogden, Weber, Utah...B4 119
North Olmsted, Cuyahoga, Ohio...h9 111
North Omaha, Douglas, Nebr...g13 103
Northome, Koochiching, Minn...C4 99
North Orange, Franklin, Mass...A3 97
North Oxford, Worcester, Mass...B4 97
North Pacific, ocean...E9 2
North Palm Beach, Palm Beach, Fla...*F6 86
North Park, Winnebago, Ill...A4 90
North Park, basin, Colo...A4 83
North Parsonfield, York, Maine...E2 96
North Patchogue, Suffolk, N.Y...*G4 84
North Pekin, Tazewell, Ill...*C4 90
North Pembroke, Plymouth, Mass...B6 97
North Penobscot, Hancock, Maine...D4 96
North Pitcher, Chenango, N.Y...C5 108
North Plain, Middlesex, Conn...D7 84
North Plainfield, Somerset, N.J...B4 106
North Plains, Washington, Oreg...B4, g12 113
North Platte, Lincoln, Nebr...C5 103
North Platte, riv., U.S...B7 76
North Pleasanton, Atascosa, Tex...*E3 118
North Point, Hong Kong...*G7 34
North Pole, Arc. O...4
North Pole, mtn., Idaho...D3 89
North Pomfret, Windsor, Vt...D4 120
Northport, Tuscaloosa, Ala...B2 78
Northport, Leelanau, Mich...C5 98
Northport, Morrill, Nebr...C2 103
Northport, Stevens, Wash...A8 122
North Portal, Sask., Can...H4 70
North Powder, Union, Oreg...B9 113
North Pownal, Cumberland, Maine...g7 96
North Pownal, Bennington, Vt...F2 120
North Prairie, Waukesha, Wis...F5 124
North Providence, Providence, R.I...B11 84
North Quidnessett, Washington, R.I...*C11 84
North Raccoon, riv., Iowa...C3 92
North Range Corner, N.S., Can...E4 74
North Reading, Middlesex, Mass...f11 97
North Rhine-Westphalia, see Nordrhein-Westfalen, state, F.R.G.
North Richland Hills, Tarrant, Tex...*C4 118
Northridge, Clark, Ohio...C2 111

Northridge, Montgomery, Ohio ... *C1 111
North Ridgeville, Lorain, Ohio ... A3, h8 111
North Riding (York), co. part, Eng ... *A6 12
North Rim, Mohave, Ariz ... A3 80
North River Bridge, N.S., Can ... C9 74
North Riverside, Cook, Ill ... *B6 90
North Robinson, Crawford, Ohio ... B3 111
North Rockville Centre, Nassau, N.Y. ... *G2 84
North Ronaldsay, isl., Scot ... A5 10
North Rose, Wayne, N.Y ... B4 108
North Royalton, Cuyahoga, Ohio ... h9 111
North Rustico, P.E.I., Can ... C6 74
Norths, highland, Ant ... C25 5
North St. Paul, Ramsey, Minn ... m13 99
North Salem, Hendricks, Ind ... E4 91
North Salem, Rockingham, N.H ... E4 105
North Salt Lake, Davis, Utah ... C4 119
North Sandwich, Carroll, N.H ... C4 105
North Santee, riv., S.C. ... E9 115
North Santiam, riv., Oreg ... k12 113
North Saskatchewan, riv., Alta., Sask., Can ... C5 69
North Scarboro, Cumberland, Maine ... E5 96
North Scituate, Plymouth, Mass ... h12 97
North Scituate, Providence, R.I ... B10 84
North Searsmont, Waldo, Maine ... D3 90
North Shore, St. Tammany, La ... B8 95
North Shreveport, Caddo, La ... *B2 95
North Shrewsbury, Rutland, Vt ... D3 120
Northside, Granville, N.C ... A4 109
North Sioux City, Union, S. Dak ... E9 116
North Slidell, St. Tammany, La. (part of Slidell) ... B8 95
North Smithfield (Town of), Providence, R.I ... *B10 84
North Spicer, isl., N.W. Ter., Can ... C17 67
North Springfield, Erie, Pa ... C1 114
North Springfield, Windsor, Vt ... E3 120
North Springfield, Fairfax, Va ... *B5 121
North Springfield, res., Vt ... E4 120
North Star, Gratiot, Mich ... E6 98
North Star, Darke, Ohio ... B1 111
North Stonington, New London, Conn ... D9 84
North Stradbroke, isl., Austl ... C9 51
North Stratford, Coos, N.H ... A3, g6 105
North Street, St. Clair, Mich ... E8 98
North Sudbury, Middlesex, Mass ... g10 97
North Sumatra, see Sumatra, isl., Indon.
North Sunderland, Eng ... *E7 13
North Sutton, Merrimack, N.H ... D3 105
North Swansea, Bristol, Mass ... C5 97
North Sydney, Austl ... *F8 51
North Sydney, N.S., Can ... C9 74
North Syracuse, Onondaga, N.Y ... B4 108
North Tarrytown, Westchester, N.Y ... m15 108
North Tea, lake, Ont., Can ... B5 72
North Terre Haute, Vigo, Ind ... E3 91
North Tewksbury, Middlesex, Mass ... A5 97
North Thetford, Orange, Vt ... D4 120
North Thompson, riv., B.C., Can ... D8 68
North Tolsta, Scot ... B2 13
North Tonawanda, Niagara, N.Y ... B2 108
North Troy, Orleans, Vt ... B4 120
North Truro, Barnstable, Mass ... *B7 97
North Tunbridge, Orange, Vt ... D4 120
North Tunica, Tunica, Miss ... A3 100
North Turner, mtn., Maine ... C4 96
North Twin, lake, Newf., Can ... D3 75
North Twin, lake, Wis ... B4 124
North Tyne, riv., Eng ... E6 13
North Uist, isl., Scot ... C1 13
Northumberland, Coos, N.H ... A3 105
Northumberland, Northumberland, Pa ... E8 114
Northumberland, co., N.B., Can ... B3 74
Northumberland, co., Ont., Can ... C6 72
Northumberland, co., Eng ... E6 13
Northumberland, co., Pa ... D8 114
Northumberland, co., Va ... C6 121
Northumberland, is., Austl ... D9 50
Northumberland, strait, Can ... C5 74
North Umpqua, riv., Oreg ... D4 113
North Uvalde, Uvalde, Tex. (part of Uvalde) ... E3 118
North Uxbridge, Worcester, Mass ... B4 97
Northvale, Bergen, N.J ... g9 106
North Valley Stream, Nassau, N.Y ... *G2 84
North Vancouver, B.C., Can ... E6, f12 68
North Vandergrift, Armstrong, Pa ... *E2 114
North Vassalboro, Kennebec, Maine ... D3 96
North Vernon, Jennings, Ind ... F6 91
Northview, Webster, Mo ... D4 101
Northville, Litchfield, Conn ... C3 84
Northville, Wayne and Oakville, Mich ... p15 98
Northville, Fulton, N.Y ... B6 108
Northville, Spink, S. Dak ... B7 116
North Wabasca, lake, Alta., Can ... A3 69
North Waldoboro, Lincoln, Maine ... D3 96
North Wales, Montgomery, Pa ... F11 114
North Walpole, Cheshire, N.H ... D2 105
North Walsham, Eng ... B9 12
North Warren, Knox, Maine ... D3 96
North Warren, Warren, Pa ... C3 114
North Washington, Chickasaw, Iowa ... A5 92
North Waterford, Oxford, Maine ... D2 96
Northway, Alsk ... C11 79
North Weare, Hillsboro, N.H ... D3 105
North Webster, Kosciusko, Ind ... B6 91
North West, cape, Austl ... D1 50
North West, hbr., N.Y ... E7 84
North West, highlands, Scot ... C3 13
North Westchester, New London, Conn ... C7 84
North Western, prov., Zambia ... D4 48
North Westminster, Windham, Vt ... E4 120
North West Miramichi, riv., N.B., Can ... B3 74
Northwest Polder, reg., Neth ... B5 15
Northwest Providence, chan., Ba ... A4 64
North West River, Newf., Can ... B1, h9 75
Northwest Territories, ter., Can ... C9 66
North West Upsalquitch, riv., N.B., Can ... B2 74
Northwich, Eng ... A5 12
North Wildwood, Cape May, N.J ... E3 106
North Wilkesboro, Wilkes, N.C ... A1 109
North Wilmington, Middlesex, Mass ... f11 97
North Windham, Windham, Conn ... C8 84
North Windham, Cumberland, Maine ... E2, g7 96
North Winterport, Waldo, Maine ... D4 96
Northwood, Worth, Iowa ... A4 92
Northwood, Rockingham, N.H ... D4 105
Northwood, Grand Forks, N. Dak ... B8 110
Northwood Center, Rockingham, N.H ... D4 105
Northwood Narrows, Rockingham, N.H ... D4 105
Northwood Ridge, Rockingham, N.H ... D4 105
North Woodstock, Windham, Conn ... B8 84
North Woodstock, Grafton, N.H ... B3 105
North Yarmouth, Cumberland, Maine ... g7 96
North York, York, Pa ... G8 114
North York, moors, Eng ... C11 13
North Yorkshire, co., Eng ... F7 13
North Zurich, Madison, Tex ... D4 118
Norton, N.B., Can ... D4 74
Norton, Eng ... F8 13
Norton, Norton, Kans ... C4 93
Norton, Bristol, Mass ... C5 97
Norton, Jackson, N.C ... f9 109
Norton, Summit, Ohio ... A4 111
Norton, Zimb ... A5 49
Norton, Runnels, Tex ... D2 118
Norton, Essex, Vt ... A5 120
Norton (Independent City), Va ... f9 121
Norton, Randolph, W. Va ... C5 123
Norton, co., Kans ... C4 93
Norton, bay, Alsk ... C8 79
Norton, pond, Vt ... B5 120
Norton, res., Mass ... B12 84
Norton, sound, Alsk ... C6 79
Norton Acres, Minnehaha, S. Dak ... *D9 116
Norton Center, Summit, Ohio ... *A4 111
Nortons Corner, Maricopa, Ariz ... D4, m9 80
Norton Shores, Muskegon, Mich ... E4 98
Nortonville, Jefferson, Kans ... C8, k15 93
Nortonville, Hopkins, Ky ... C2 94
Nortonville, La Moure, N. Dak ... C7 110
Nortorf, F.R.G ... D3 24
Norvegia, cape, Ant ... B11 5
Norvell, Crittenden, Ark ... B5 81
Norvelt, Westmoreland, Pa ... *F3 114
Norwalk, Los Angeles, Calif ... n12 82
Norwalk, Fairfield, Conn ... E3 84
Norwalk, Warren, Iowa ... C4, f8 92
Norwalk, Huron, Ohio ... A3 111
Norwalk, Monroe, Wis ... E3 124
Norwalk, is., Conn ... E3 84
Norwalk, riv., Conn ... E3 84
Norway, Benton, Iowa ... C6 92
Norway, Republic, Kans ... C6 93
Norway, Oxford, Maine ... D2 96
Norway, Dickinson, Mich ... C3 98
Norway, Coos, Oreg ... D2 113
Norway, Orangeburg, S.C ... E5 115
Norway, country, Eur ... C11 8, E5 25
Norway, isl., Viet ... B7 38
Norway, lake, Minn ... E3 99
Norway House, Man., Can ... C3 71
Norwegian, bay, N.W. Ter., Can ... m33 67
Norwegian, sea, Eur ... C14 4
Norwell, Plymouth, Mass ... h12 97
Norwich, Ont., Can ... E4 72
Norwich, New London, Conn ... C8 84
Norwich, Eng ... B9 12
Norwich, Kingman, Kans ... E6, h11 93
Norwich, Chenango, N.Y ... C5 108
Norwich, McHenry, N. Dak ... A5 110
Norwich, Windsor, Vt ... D4 120
Norwichtown, New London, Conn. (part of Norwich) ... C8 84
Norwood, Ont., Can ... C7 72
Norwood, San Miguel, Colo ... C2 83
Norwood, Warren, Ga ... C4 87
Norwood, Polk, Iowa ... A7 92
Norwood, East Feliciana, La ... D4 95
Norwood, Norfolk, Mass ... B5, h11 97
Norwood, Carver, Minn ... F5 99
Norwood, Wright, Mo ... D5 101
Norwood, Bergen, N.J ... h9 106
Norwood, St. Lawrence, N.Y ... f10 108
Norwood, Stanly, N.C ... B2 109
Norwood, Hamilton, Ohio ... o13 111
Norwood, Delaware, Pa ... p20 114
Norwood, Knox, Tenn ... *D10 117
Norwottock, mtn., Mass ... B2 97
Nosbonsing, lake, Ont., Can ... A5 72
Noshiro, Jap ... F10 37
Nösjön, lake, Swe ... A6 24
Noss, head, Scot ... B5 13
Nossa Senhora das Dores, Braz ... D3 57
Nossen, G.D.R ... B8 17
Nossi-Bé, isl., Mad ... f9 49
Notasulga, Macon, Ala ... C4 78
Notch, mtn., Mass ... A3 97
Notch, peak, Utah ... D2 119
Notch Hill, B.C., Can ... D8 68
Notchland, Carroll, N.H ... B4 105
Notec, riv., Pol ... B3 26
Notikewin, Alta., Can ... A2 69
Notikewin, riv., Alta., Can ... A1 69
Noto, It ... F5 21
Noto, gulf, It ... F5 21
Noto, isl., Jap ... H8 37
Notodden, Nor ... H3 25
Notre-Dame, N.B., Can ... C5 74
Notre Dame, St. Joseph, Ind ... *A5 91
Notre Dame, bay, Newf., Can ... D4 75
Notre Dame, mts., Que., Can ... D6 73
Notre-Dame [-de-la-Salette], Que., Can ... D2 73
Notre-Dame-de-Lourdes, Man., Can ... E2 71
Notre-Dame-de-Rimouski, Que., Can ... A9 73
Notre-Dame-des-Bois, Que., Can ... D6 73
Notre-Dame-du-Lac, Que., Can ... B9 73
Notre-Dame-du-Laus, Que., Can ... C2 73
Nott, St. Tammany, La ... B7 95
Nottawa, Ont., Can ... C4 72
Nottawasaga, bay, Ont., Can ... C4 72
Nottaway, riv., Que., Can ... F17 67
Nottely, res., Ga ... B2 87
Nottingham, Eng ... B6 12
Nottingham Rockingham, N.H ... D4 105
Nottingham, Bucks, Pa ... *A12 114
Nottingham, co., Eng ... A7 12
Nottingham, isl., N.W. Ter., Can ... D17 67
Nottoway, Nottoway, Va ... C4 121
Nottoway, co., Va ... C4 121
Nottoway, riv., Va ... D5 121
Notukeu, creek, Sask., Can ... H2 70
Notus, Canyon, Idaho ... F2 89
Nouadhibou, Maur ... B1 45
Nouakchott, Maur ... C1 45
Nouamrhar, Maur ... C1 45
Nouméa, N. Cal ... H10 7
Nouna, Upper Volta ... D4 45
Nounan, Bear Lake, Idaho ... G7 89
Noupoort, S. Afr ... D3 49
Noutonice, Czech ... n17 26
Nouvelle-Anvers, Zaire ... A2 48
Nouvelle-France, cape, Que., Can ... D18 67
Nouzonville, Fr ... C6 14
Nova, Ashland, Ohio ... A3 111
Nova Caipemba, Ang ... C1 48
Nova Chaves, Ang ... D3 48
Nova Cruz, Braz ... C3, h6 57
Nova Freixo, Moz ... D6 48
Nova Friburgo, Braz ... C4, h6 56
Nova Gaia, Ang ... D2 48
Nova Granada, Braz ... C3 56
Nova Iguaçu, Braz ... h6 56
Nova Lima, Braz ... F2 57
Nova Lusitânia, Moz ... A5 49
Nova Mambone, Moz ... B6 49
Novar, Ont., Can ... B5 72
Novara, It ... D4 18, B2 21
Nova Russas, Braz ... B2 57
Nova Scotia, prov., Can ... H19 67, 74
Nova Sofala, Moz ... B5 49
Nova Soure, Braz ... D3 57
Novato, Marin, Calif ... C2 82
Nova Varos, Yugo ... D4 22
Nova Venécia, Braz ... E2 57
Novaya Astrakhan, Sov. Un ... p21 27
Novaya Kazanka, Sov. Un ... F18 9
Novaya Ladoga, Sov. Un ... A9 27
Novaya Lyalya, Sov. Un ... B6 29
Novaya Odessa, Sov. Un ... H8 27
Novaya Sibir, isl., Sov. Un ... B17 28
Novaya Zemlya, is., Sov. Un ... B8 28
Nova Zagora, Bul ... D8 22
Novelda, Sp ... C5 20
Novelty, Knox, Mo ... A5 101
Nové Mesto [nad Vahom], Czech ... D5 26
Nové Strašecí, Czech ... C8 17
Nové Zámky, Czech ... E5 26
Novgorod, Sov. Un ... B8 27
Novgorod-Severskiy, Sov. Un ... E9 27
Novi, Oakland, Mich ... p15 98
Novice, Coleman, Tex ... D3 118
Novigrad, Yugo ... C2 22
Novi Ligure, It ... B2 21
Novinger, Adair, Mo ... A5 101
Novi Pazar, Bul ... D8 22
Novi Pazar, Yugo ... D5 22
Novi Sad, Yugo ... C4 22
Noviye Senzhary, Sov. Un ... G10 27
Novo-Annenskiy, Sov. Un ... C2 29
Novoaydar, Sov. Un ... G12, q21 27
Novocherkassk, Sov. Un ... H12 27
Novoekonomicheskoye, Sov. Un ... q20 27
Novograd-Volynskiy, Sov. Un ... F6 27
Novogrudok, Sov. Un ... E5 27
Novo-Kazalinsk, Sov. Un ... D6 29
Novokurovka, Sov. Un ... B7 37
Novokuybyshevsk, Sov. Un ... *C3 29
Novokuznetsk, Sov. Un ... E26 9, D11 28
Novo Mesto, Yugo ... C2 22
Novomirgorod, Sov. Un ... G8 27
Novomoskovsk, Sov. Un ... C1 29
Novomoskovsk, Sov. Un ... G10 27
Novonazyvayevka, Sov. Un ... D23 9
Novopokrovskaya, Sov. Un ... F17 9
Novo Redondo, Ang ... D1 48
Novorossiysk, Sov. Un ... I11 27
Novo-Selo, Bul ... C6 22
Novoshakhtinsk, Sov. Un ... H12 27
Novosibirsk, Sov. Un ... B10 29
Novosibirskiye (New Siberian), is., Sov. Un ... B17 28
Novosil, Sov. Un ... E11 27
Novo-Troitsk, Sov. Un ... *C5 29
Novoukrainka, Sov. Un ... G8 27
Novouzensk, Sov. Un ... C3 29
Novoyeniseyskaya, Sov. Un ... B11 37
Novozybkov, Sov. Un ... E8 27
Nový Bohumín, Czech ... D5 26
Nový Bydzov, Czech ... C3 26
Nový Jicín, Czech ... D5 26
Novyy Oskol, Sov. Un ... F11 27
Novyy Port, Sov. Un ... C10 28
Novyy Vasyugan, Sov. Un ... B9 29
Nowagród, Pol ... B10 17
Nowa Sól, Pol ... C3 26
Nowata, Nowata, Okla ... A6 112
Nowata, co., Okla ... A6 112
Nowe Warpno, Pol ... B3 26
Nowogard, Pol ... B3 26
Nowood, riv., Wyo ... B5 125
Nowra-Bomaderry, Austl ... G8 51
Nowshera, Pak ... B5 39
Nowy Dwor, Pol ... k13 26
Nowy Sacz, Pol ... D6 26
Nowy Targ, Pol ... D6 26
Nowy Tomysl, Pol ... B4 26
Noxapater, Winston, Miss ... C4 100
Noxen, Wyoming, Pa ... D9, m16 114
Noxon, Sanders, Mont ... C1 102
Noxon, res., Mont ... C1 102
Noxontown, lake, Del ... B6 85
Noxubee, co., Miss ... B5 100
Noxubee, riv., Miss ... B5 100
Noxville, Kimble, Tex ... D3 118
Noya, Sp ... A1 20
Noyack, bay, N.Y ... E7 84
Noyes, Kittson, Minn ... B1 99
Noyon, Fr ... C5 14
Nsanje, Malawi ... E6 48
Nsawam, Ghana ... E4 45
Nsukka, Nig ... E6 45
Ntem, riv., Cam ... E6 45
Nuanetsi, Zimb ... B5 49
Nubansit, lake, N.H ... E2 105
Nuberg, Hart, Ga ... B4 87
Nubian, des., Sud ... A3 47
Ñuble, prov., Chile ... B2 54
Nuckolls, co., Nebr ... D7 103
Nucla, Montrose, Colo ... C2 83
Nudos Ojos del Salado, mtn., Arg ... E2 55
Nueces, co., Tex ... F4 118
Nueces, riv., Tex ... E3 118
Nueltin, lake, Man., N.W. Ter., Can ... D13 66
Nueva Casas Grandes, Mex ... A3 63
Nueva Ecija, prov., Phil ... *B6 35
Nueva Esparta, state, Ven ... A5 60
Nueva Esparta, is., Ven ... A5 60
Nueva Gerona, Cuba ... D2 64
Nueva Imperial, Chile ... B2 54
Nueva Lubecka, Arg ... C2 54
Nueva Palmira, Ur ... E1 56
Nueva Providencia, Pan ... k11 62
Nueva Rosita, Mex ... B4 63
Nueva San Salvador, Sal ... D3 62
Nueva Vizcaya, prov., Phil ... *B6 35
Nueve de Julio, Arg ... B4 54
Nuevitas, Cuba ... D5 64
Nuevo, gulf, Arg ... C4 54
Nuevo Emperador, Pan ... k11 62
Nuevo Laredo, Mex ... B5 63
Nuevo León, state, Mex ... B4 63
Nuevo Mundo, mtn., Bol ... D2 55
Nuevo San Juan, Pan ... k11 62
Nugget, Lincoln, Wyo ... E2 125
Nuits [-St Georges], Fr ... D6 14
Nukhaylah, oasis, Sud ... B2 47
Nukualofa, Tonga ... H11 7
Nukus, Sov. Un ... E5 29
Nulato, Alsk ... C8 79
Nules, Sp ... C5 20
Nulhegan, riv., Vt ... B5 120
Nullarbor, Austl ... F5 50
Nullarbor, plain, Austl ... F4 50
Numa, Appanoose, Iowa ... D5 92
Numan, Nig ... E7 45
Numazu, Jap ... I9, n17 37
Nu Mine, Armstrong, Pa ... E3 114
Nunda, Livingston, N.Y ... C3 108
Nunda, Lake, S. Dak ... C8 116
Nuneaton, Eng ... B6 12
Nunez, Emanuel, Ga ... D4 87
Nungan, China ... C10 34
Nunica, Ottawa, Mich ... E4 98
Nunivak, isl., Alsk ... C6 79
Nunn, Weld, Colo ... A6 83
Nunnelly, Hickman, Tenn ... B4 117
Nunukan Timur, isl., Indon ... E5 35
Nuoro, It ... D2 21
Nuquí, Col ... B2 60
Nuremberg, see Nürnberg, F.R.G.
Nuremberg, Luzerne and Schuylkill, Pa ... E9 114
Nuri, Mex ... B3 63
Nurmes, Fin ... F13 25
Nürnberg, F.R.G ... D6 17
Nurrari, lakes, Austl ... E5 50
Nursery, Victoria, Tex ... E4 118
Nürtingen, F.R.G ... E4 17
Nusaybin, Tur ... D13 31
Nushki, Pak ... C4 39
Nusle, Czech., (part of Prague) ... n17 26
Nut, lake, Sask., Can ... E4 70
Nuthe, riv., G.D.R ... A8 17
Nutley, Essex, N.J ... B4, h8 106
Nut Mountain, Sask., Can ... E4 70
Nutrioso, Apache, Ariz ... D6 80
Nutter Fort, Harrison, W. Va ... k10 123
Nutting Lake, Middlesex, Mass ... f10 97
Nuuanu Pali, pass, Haw ... g10 88
Nuutele, isl., W. Sam ... 52
Nuutoi, cape, W. Sam ... 52
Nuwara Eliya, Sri Lanka ... G7 39
Nuwaybi'al Muzayyinah, Eg ... H10 31
Nuweiba, Eg ... H10 31
Nūzvid, India ... I8 40
Nyac, Alsk ... C8 79
Nyack, Rockland, N.Y ... D7, m15 108
Nyala, Sud ... C1 47
Nyamandhlovu, Zimb ... A4 49
Nyamtumbo, Tan ... D6 48
Nyanda, Zimb ... B5 49
Nyandoma, Sov. Un ... A12 27
Nyanza, Rwanda ... B4 48
Nyanza, reg., Ken ... B5 48
Nyasa, lake, Afr ... H9 42
Nyasaland, see Malawi, country, Afr.
Nyborg, Den ... C4 24
Nybro, Swe ... I6 25
Nyda, Sov. Un ... B23 9
Nye, Stillwater, Mont ... E7 102
Nye, co., Nev ... E5 104
Nyeri, Ken ... B6 48
Nygami, lake, Bech ... B3 49
Nyimba, Zambia ... D5 48
Nyiregyhaza, Hung ... B5 26
Nykøbing [på] Falster, Den ... D5 24
Nykøbing [på Mors], Den ... B2 24
Nykøbing [på Sjaelland], Den ... C5 24
Nykoping, Swe ... H7, u34 25
Nyland Acres, Ventura, Calif ... *E4 82
Nylstroom, S. Afr ... B4 49
Nymagee, Austl ... F6 51
Nymburk, Czech ... C3, n19 26
Nymindegab, Den ... C2 24
Nynäshamn, Swe ... H7, u35 25
Nyngan, Austl ... E6 51
Nyon, Switz ... D1 19
Nyong, riv., Cam ... E2 46
Nyota, Blount, Ala ... B3 78
Nyrany, Czech ... D2 26
Nyrsko, Czech ... D8 17
Nysa, Pol ... C4 26
Nysa, riv., Pol ... C4 26
Nyssa, Malheur, Oreg ... D10 113
Nysted, Den ... D5 24
Nyunzu, Zaire ... C4 48
Nzega, Tan ... E5 48
Nzérékoré, Guinea ... E3 45

O

Oa, The, pen., Scot ... E2 13
Oacoma, Lyman, S. Dak ... D6 116
Oahe, Lake, res., S. Dak ... C5 116
Oahu, isl., Haw ... B4 88
Oak, Nuckolls, Nebr ... D8 103
Oak, hill, Mass ... f9 97
Oak, isl., Wis ... B3 124
Oak, lake, Man., Can ... E1 71
Oak, mtn., Ga ... D2 87
Oakalla, Burnet, Tex ... D4 118
Oak Bay, B.C., Can ... h12 68
Oak Bay, N.B., Can ... D2 74
Oak Bluffs, Dukes, Mass ... D6 97
Oakboro, Stanly, N.C ... B2 109
Oakburn, Man., Can ... D1 71
Oak City, Martin, N.C ... B5 109
Oak City, Millard, Utah ... D3 119
Oak Creek, Routt, Colo ... A4 83
Oak Creek, Milwaukee, Wis ... n12 124
Oakdale, Stanislaus, Calif ... D3 82
Oakdale, New London, Conn ... D8 84
Oakdale, Washington, Ill ... E4 90
Oakdale, Allen, La ... D3 95
Oakdale, Worcester, Mass ... B4 97
Oakdale, Antelope, Nebr ... B8 103
Oakdale, Suffolk, N.Y ... G4 84
Oakdale, Allegheny, Pa ... k13 114
Oakdale, Morgan, Tenn ... D9 117
Oakengates, Eng ... B5 12
Oakes, Dickey, N. Dak ... C7 110
Oakesdale, Whitman, Wash ... B8 122
Oakey, Austl ... C8 51
Oakfield, Worth, Ga ... E3 87
Oakfield, Aroostook, Maine ... B4 96
Oakfield, Genesee, N.Y ... B2 108
Oakfield, Madison, Tenn ... B3 117
Oakfield, Fond du Lac, Wis ... E5 124
Oakford, Menard, Ill ... C4 90
Oakford, Howard, Ind ... D5 91
Oak Forest, Cook, Ill ... k9 90
Oakgrove, Carroll, Ark ... h10 81
Oak Grove, De Kalb, Ga ... *C2 87
Oak Grove, Christian, Ky ... D2 94
Oak Grove, West Carroll, La ... B4 95
Oak Grove, Livingston, Mich ... F7 98
Oak Grove, Jackson, Mo ... *B3 101
Oak Grove, Clackamas, Oreg ... B4, h12 113
Oak Grove, Dillon, S.C ... C8 115
Oak Grove, Westmoreland, Va ... B6 121
Oakham, Eng ... B7 12
Oakham, Worcester, Mass ... B3 97
Oakharbor, Ottawa, Ohio ... A2 111
Oak Harbor, Island, Wash ... A3 122
Oak Hill, Volusia, Fla ... D6 86
Oak Hill, Manistee, Mich ... D4 98
Oak Hill, Crawford, Mo ... C6 101
Oak Hill, Jackson, Ohio ... D3 111
Oak Hill, Davidson, Tenn ... *A5 117
Oak Hill, Fayette, W. Va ... D3, n13 123
Oakhurst, Monmouth, N.J ... C4 106
Oakhurst, Tulsa and Creek, Okla ... *A5 112
Oak Lake, Man., Can ... E1 71
Oakland, Lauderdale, Ala ... A2 78
Oakland, Marion, Ark ... A3 81
Oakland, Alameda, Calif ... D2, h8 82
Oakland, Ont., Can ... D4 72
Oakland, Coles, Ill ... D5 90
Oakland, Pottawattamie, Iowa ... C2 92
Oakland, Warren, Ky ... C3 94
Oakland, Kennebec, Maine ... D3 96
Oakland, Garrett, Md ... m12 85
Oakland, Yalobusha, Miss ... A4 100
Oakland, St. Louis, Mo ... *C7 101
Oakland, Burt, Nebr ... C9 103
Oakland, Bergen, N.J ... A4 106
Oakland, Transylvania, N.C ... f10 109
Oakland, Marshall, Okla ... C5 112
Oakland, Douglas, Oreg ... D3 113
Oakland, Lawrence, Pa ... *D1 114
Oakland, Susquehanna, Pa ... C10 114
Oakland, Providence, R.I ... B10 84
Oakland, Fayette, Tenn ... B2 117
Oakland, co., Mich ... F7 98
Oakland City, Gibson, Ind ... H3 91
Oakland Gardens, Hartford, Conn ... *C5 84
Oaklandon, Marion, Ind ... k11 91
Oakland Park, Broward, Fla ... F6, r13 86
Oak Lawn, Cook, Ill ... B6, k9 90
Oaklawn, Sedgwick, Kans ... g12 93
Oaklawn, St. Tammany, La ... h12 95
Oakleigh, Austl ... *H5 51
Oakley, Cassia, Idaho ... G5 89
Oakley, Logan, Kans ... C3 93
Oakley, Saginaw, Mich ... E6 98
Oakley, Hinds, Miss ... C3 100
Oakley, Berkeley, S.C ... E7 115
Oakley, Summit, Utah ... C4 119
Oaklyn, Camden, N.J ... *D2 106
Oakman, Walker, Ala ... B2 78
Oakman, Gordon, Ga ... B2 87
Oakmont, Allegheny, Pa ... F2, h14 114
Oakner, Man., Can ... D1 71
Oak Orchard, Sussex, Del ... C7 85
Oak Park, Emanuel, Ga ... D4 87
Oak Park, Cook, Ill ... B6, k9 90
Oak Park, Oakland, Mich ... p15 98
Oak Point, Man., Can ... D2 71
Oak Ridge, Morehouse, La ... B4 95
Oak Ridge, Cape Girardeau, Mo ... D8 101
Oak Ridge, Guilford, N.C ... A3 109
Oakridge, Lane, Oreg ... D4 113
Oak Ridge, Armstrong, Pa ... E3 114
Oak Ridge, Anderson and Roane, Tenn ... C9 117
Oak Ridge, res., N.J ... A3 106
Oak Ridges, Ont., Can ... k15 72
Oak River, Man., Can ... D1 71
Oaks, Delaware, Okla ... A7 112
Oaks, Montgomery, Pa ... o20 114
Oakton, Hickman, Ky ... f8 94
Oakton, Fairfax, Va ... g12 121
Oaktown, Knox, Ind ... G3 91
Oak Vale, Lawrence and Jefferson Davis, Miss ... D4 100
Oakvale, Mercer, W. Va ... *D4 123
Oak Valley, Elk, Kans ... E8 93
Oak Valley, Gloucester, N.J ... D2 106
Oak View, Ventura, Calif ... *E4 82
Oak View, Montgomery, Md ... *C3 85
Oakville, Man., Can ... E2 71
Oakville, Ont., Can ... D5 72
Oakville, Litchfield, Conn ... C4 84
Oakville, Louisa, Iowa ... C6 92
Oakville, Delaware, Ind ... D7 91
Oakville, St. Louis, Mo ... g13 101
Oakville, Grays Harbor, Wash ... C2 122
Oakway, Oconee, S.C ... B1 115
Oakwood, Hall, Ga ... B3 87
Oakwood, Vermilion, Ill ... C6 90
Oakwood, Walsh, N. Dak ... A8 110
Oakwood, Marion, Mo. (part of Hannibal) ... B6 101
Oakwood (Far Hills), Montgomery, Ohio ... C1 111
Oakwood, Paulding, Ohio ... A1 111
Oakwood, Dewey, Okla ... B3 112
Oakwood, Lawrence, Pa ... *D1 114
Oakwood, Leon, Tex ... D5 118
Oakwood, Buchanan, Va ... e10 121
Oakwood, Milwaukee, Wis. (part of Oak Creek) ... F2 124
Oakwood Beach, Salem, N.J ... D1 106
Oakwood Villa, Duval, Fla ... *B5 86
Oamaru, N.Z ... P13 51
Oami, Jap ... n19 37
Oasis, Elko, Nev ... B7 104
Oasis, Millard, Utah ... D3 119
Oatman, Mohave, Ariz ... C1 80
Oats, Darlington, S.C ... C7 115
Oaxaca, Mex ... D5 63
Oaxaca, state, Mex ... D5 63
Ob, bay, Sov. Un ... C10 28
Ob, riv., Sov. Un ... D25 9
Oba, Ont., Can ... G16 67
Obama, Jap ... n14 37
Oban, Sask., Can ... E1 70
Oban, see Half-moon Bay, N.Z.
Oban, Scot ... D3 13
O'Bannon, Jefferson, Ky ... g12 94
Obbia, Som ... D6 47
Obed, Alta., Can ... C2 69
Obed, riv., Tenn ... C9 117
Oberá, Arg ... E4 55
Oberammergau, F.R.G ... B7 18
Oberdrauburg, Aus ... C8 18
Oberhausen, F.R.G ... B1 17
Oberkirch, F.R.G ... E3 17
Oberlin, Decatur, Kans ... C3 93
Oberlin, Allen, La ... D3 95
Oberlin, Gladwin, Mich ... D6 98
Oberlin, Lorain, Ohio ... A3 111
Oberlin, Bryan, Okla ... D6 112
Oberlin, Dauphin, Pa ... *F8 114
Obernai, Fr ... C7 14
Obernburg, F.R.G ... D4 17
Oberon, Benson, N. Dak ... B6 110
Oberösterreich (Upper Austria), state, Aus ... E9 17
Oberstaufen, F.R.G ... B6 18
Oberstdorf, F.R.G ... E5 15
Obert, Cedar, Nebr ... B8 103
Oberursel, F.R.G ... C3 17
Oberwald, Switz ... C5 19
Obetz, Franklin, Ohio ... C3, m11 111
Obiam, cape, Saipan ... 52
Obiam, inlet, Saipan ... 52
Óbidos, Braz ... C3 59
Obihiro, Jap ... E11 37
Obion, Obion, Tenn ... A2 117
Obion, co., Tenn ... A2 117
Obion, creek, Ky ... f9 94
Obion, riv., Tenn ... A7 117
Oblong, Crawford, Ill ... D6 90
Obluchye, Sov. Un ... E16 28
Obo, Cen. Afr. Rep ... D5 46
Obock, Dji ... C5 47
Oborniki, Pol ... B4 26
Obor Sumun, Mong ... B6 34
Oboyan, Sov. Un ... F11 27
O'Brien, Suwannee, Fla ... B4 86
O'Brien, Josephine, Oreg ... E3 113
O'Brien, co., Iowa ... A2 92
Observation, peak, Calif ... B3 82
Observation, peak, Oreg ... E4 113
Obsidian, Custer, Idaho ... F4 89
Obuasi, Ghana ... E4 45
Obwalden, sub canton, Switz ... C5 19
Ocala, Marion, Fla ... C4 86
Ocampo, Arg ... E4 55
Ocampo, Mex ... B3 63
Ocaña, Col ... B3 60
Ocaña, Sp ... C4 20
Ocate, Mora, N. Mex ... A5 107
Occidental Mindoro, prov., Phil ... *C6 35
Occoquan, Prince William, Va ... B5 121
Occum, New London, Conn. (part of Norwich) ... C8 84
Ocean, co., N.J ... D4 106
Oceana, Wyoming, W. Va ... D3 123
Oceana, co., Mich ... E4 98
Ocean Beach, Suffolk, N.Y ... G4 84
Ocean Bluff, Plymouth, Mass ... B6, h13 97
Ocean City, Okaloosa, Fla ... u15 86
Ocean City, Worcester, Md ... D7 85
Ocean City, Cape May, N.J ... E3 106
Ocean Falls, B.C., Can ... C4 68
Ocean Gate, Ocean, N.J ... D4 106
Ocean Grove, Bristol, Mass ... C5 97
Ocean Grove, Monmouth, N.J ... C4 106
Ocean Heights, Dukes, Mass ... D6 97
Oceanlake, Lincoln, Oreg ... C3 113

Pacolet, riv., S.C A4 115
Pacolet Mills, Spartanburg, S.C B4 115
Pacora, Pan k12 62
Pacora, riv., Pan k12 62
Pacov, Czech D9 17
Pacquet, Newf., Can C4 75
Pactola, res., S. Dak C2 116
Pactolus, Pitt, N.C B5 109
Paczkow, Pol C4 26
Padang, Indon F2 35
Padang Endau, Mala K5 38
Padangpanjang, Indon F2 35
Padangsidempuan, Indon m11, E1 35
Padauiri, riv., Braz C5 60
Paddle Prairie, Alta., Can f7 69
Paddling, lake, Sask., Can E2 70
Paddock Lake, Kenosha, Wis n11 124
Paddockwood, Sask., Can D3 70
Paddy Knob, mtn., W. Va C5 123
Paden, Tishomingo, Miss A5 100
Paden, Okfuskee, Okla B5 112
Paden City, Tyler and Wetzel, W. Va B4 123
Paderborn, F.R.G B3 17
Pad Idan, Pak D2 40
Padilla, Bol C3 55
Padova (Padua), It D7 18, B3 21
Padre, isl., Tex F4 118
Padroni, Logan, Colo A7 83
Padstow, Eng D3 12
Padua (Padova), It D7 18, B3 21
Paducah, McCracken, Ky e9 94
Paducah, Cottle, Tex B2 118
Paepaealeia, cape, W. Sam 52
Paeroa, N.Z L15 51
Paestum, ruins, It D5 21
Pafúri, Moz B5 49
Pag, isl., Yugo C2 22
Pagadian, Phil *D6 35
Pagai Selatan, isl., Indon F2 35
Pagai Utara, isl., Indon F2 35
Pagalu, isl., Equat. Gui F1 46
Pagan, isl., Mariana Is E8 7, F10 34
Pagat, pt., Guam 52
Pagatan, Indon F4 35
Pagato, riv., Sask., Can A4 70
Page, Coconino, Ariz A4 80
Page, Holt, Nebr B7 103
Page, Cass, N. Dak B8 110
Page, Le Flore, Okla C7 112
Page, Fayette, W. Va C3, m13 123
Page, co., Iowa D2 92
Page, co., Va B4 121
Pagedale, St. Louis, Mo *C7 101
Pageland, Chesterfield, S.C B7 115
Page Manor, Montgomery, Ohio *C1 111
Pageton, McDowell, W. Va *D3 123
Paglia, mtn., Switz D7 19
Pagny [-sur-Moselle], Fr F6 15
Pago, bay, Guam 52
Pago, pt., Guam 52
Pagoda, peak, Colo A3 83
Pagoda, pt., Burma E9 39
Pago Pago, Am. Sam 52
Pago Pago, hbr., Am. Sam 52
Pagosa Springs, Archuleta, Colo D3 83
Paguate, Valencia, N. Mex B2 107
Pahala, Hawaii, Haw D6 88
Pahang, state, Mala J5 38
Pahang, riv., Mala K5 38
Paharpur, Pak A3 40
Pahlavī, Iran C4 41
Pahoa, Hawaii, Haw D7 88
Pahokee, Palm Beach, Fla F6 86
Pahranagat, range, Nev F6 104
Pahrump, Nye, Nev G5 104
Pahute, mesa, Nev F5 104
Paia, Maui, Haw C5 88
Paicheng, China B9 34
Paichüan, China C3 37
Paignton, Eng D4 12
Paiho, China H4 36
Päijänne, lake, Fin G11 25
Pailingmiao, China D4 36
Pailo, Bledsoe, Tenn D8 117
Paincourt, Ont., Can E2 72
Paincourtville, Assumption, La k9 95
Paine Oeste, mtn., Chile E2 54
Painesville, Lake, Ohio A4 111
Paint, Somerset, Pa *F4 114
Paint, creek, Ohio C2 111
Paint, creek, W. Va m13 123
Paint, lake, Man., Can B3 71
Paint, mtn., W. Va n13 123
Paint, riv., Mich B2 98
Paint Bank, Craig, Va C2 121
Painted Desert, Ariz A4 80
Painted Post, Steuben, N.Y C3 108
Painter, Accomack, Va C7 121
Paint Lick, Garrard, Ky C5 94
Paint Rock, Jackson, Ala A3 78
Paint Rock, Concho, Tex D3 118
Paintsville, Johnson, Ky C7 94
Paise, China G6 34
Paisley, Ont., Can C3 72
Paisley, Lake, Fla D5 86
Paisley, Lake, Oreg E6 113
Paisley, Scot E4 13
Paita, Peru C1 58
Paiva Couceiro, Ang D1 48
Pajala, Swe D10 25
Pajardos, pt., Vir. Is. (Br.) A7 65
Pajarito, Bernalillo, N. Mex *B3 107
Pajaro, Monterey, Calif *D3 82
Pajaros, isl, Mariana Is E8 7
Pajon, pt., Guam 52
Pakanbaru, Indon E2 35
Pakaraima, mts., S.A B2 59
Pakenham, Ont., Can B8 72
Pakistan, country, Asia G9 33, C4 39
Pakli, see Peili, China
Pakokku, Bur D10 39
Pakowki, lake, Alta., Can E5 69
Pakra, riv., Yugo C3 22
Paks, Hung B4 22
Pakse, Laos E6 38
Pakwa, lake, Man., Can B2 71
Pala, Chad D2 46
Palacios, Matagorda, Tex E4 118
Palafrugell, Sp B7 20
Palagruza, is., Yugo D3 22
Palaiokhora, Grc E4 23
Palaion Faliron, Grc h11 23
Palaiseau, Fr h9 14
Palamas, Grc C4 23
Palamós, Sp B7 20
Palana, Sov. Un D18 28
Palanga, Sov. Un D3 27
Palangkaraya, Indon F4 35
Pālanpur, India E4 40
Palapag, Phil C7 35
Palapye, Bots B4 49
Palas de Rey, Sp A2 20
Palatine, Cook, Ill A5, h8 90
Palatka, Putnam, Fla C5 86
Palau, is., Pac. O 52
Palauig, Phil o12 35
Palauli, W. Sam 52
Palauli, bay, W. Sam 52
Palawan, prov., Phil *C5 35
Palawan, isl., Phil C5 35
Palayamcottai, India *G6 39
Palazzolo Acreide, It F5 21
Palco, Rooks, Kans C4 93
Palembang, Indon F2 35
Palena, riv., Chile C2 54
Palencia, Sp A3 20
Palencia, prov., Sp *A3 20
Palenque, ruins, Mex B1 62
Palenville, Greene, N.Y C6 108
Palermo, It E4 21
Palermo, Cape May, N.J E3 106
Palermo, Mountrail, N. Dak A3 110
Palestine, St. Francis, Ark C5 81
Palestine, Crawford, Ill D6 90
Palestine, Darke, Ohio B1 111
Palestine, Anderson, Tex D5 118
Palestine, Wirt, W. Va B3 123
Palestine, see Gaza Strip, Isr. occ., Asia
Palestine, reg., Asia C7 32
Palestrina, It h9 21
Paletwa, Bur D9 39
Palezgir Chauki, Pak B2 40
Pālghāt, India F6 39
Palgrave, Ont., Can D5 72
Palhoça, Braz D3 56
Pāli, India E4 40
Palidoro (Baebiana), It h8 21
Palikea, mtn., Haw g9 88
Palikir, pass, Ponape 52
Palikir, pt., Ponape 52
Palikun (Barkol), China C3 34
Palimé, Togo E5 45
Palisade, Mesa, Colo B2 83
Palisade, Aitkin, Minn D5 99
Palisade, Hitchcock, Nebr D4 103
Palisades, Bonneville, Idaho F7 89
Palisades, Douglas, Wash B6 122
Palisades, The, cliffs, N.J h9 106
Palisades Park, Bergen, N.J h8 106
Palisadoes, sandpit, Jam F15 65
Paliseul, Bel E5 15
Pālitāna, India G3 40
Palk, strait, India, Sri Lanka G6 39
Pallaskenry, Ire E3 11
Pallasovka, Sov. Un C3 29
Palling, B.C., Can B5 68
Palliser, cape, N.Z N15 51
Pal Mall, Fentriss, Tenn C9 117
Palma, Moz D7 48
Palma, isl., Sp. (Can. Is.) m13 20
Palma, riv., Braz D1 57
Palma del Río, Sp D3 20
Palma [de Mallorca], Sp C7 20
Palmares, Braz C3, k6 57
Palmar Sur, C.R F6 62
Palmas, Braz D2 56
Palmas, cape, I.C F3 45
Palmas de Monte Alto, Braz D2 57
Palma Soriano, Cuba D5 64
Palm Bay, Brevard, Fla D6 86
Palm Beach, Palm Beach, Fla F6 86
Palm Beach, co., Fla F6 86
Palm Beach Shores, Palm Beach, Fla *F6 86
Palmdale, Los Angeles, Calif E4 82
Palmdale, Glades, Fla F5 86
Palm Desert, Riverside, Calif *F5 82
Palmeira, Braz D3 56
Palmeira dos Indios, Braz C3, k5 57
Palmeir in Has, pt., Ang C1 48
Palmer, Alsk C10, g17 79
Palmer, Sask., Can H2 70
Palmer, Christian, Ill D4 90
Palmer, Pocahontas, Iowa B3 92
Palmer, Washington, Kans C6 93
Palmer, Hampden, Mass B3 97
Palmer, Marquette, Mich B3 98
Palmer, Merrick, Nebr C7 103
Palmer, Grundy, Tenn D8 117
Palmer, Ellis, Tex n10 118
Palmer, King, Wash f12 122
Palmer Heights, Northampton, Pa *E11 114
Palmer Lake, El Paso, Colo B6 83
Palmer Land, reg., Ant B6 5
Palmer Park, Prince Georges, Md *C4 85
Palmerston, Ont., Can D4 72
Palmerston, N.Z P13 51
Palmerston North, N.Z N15 51
Palmersville, Weakley, Tenn A3 117
Palmerton, Carbon, Pa E10 114
Palmerville, Austl C7 50
Palmetto, Manatee, Fla E4, q10 86
Palmetto, Fulton and Coweta, Ga C2 87
Palmetto, St. Laundry, La D4 95
Palm Harbor, Pinellas, Fla o10 86
Palmi, It E5 21
Palmira, Col C2 60
Palmira, Cuba C3 64
Palmira, Ec B2 58
Palms, Sanilac, Mich E8 98
Palms, is., S.C F8 115
Palm Springs, Riverside, Calif F5 82
Palm Springs, Palm Beach, Fla F6 86
Palm Valley, St. Johns, Fla m9 86
Palmyra, Macoupin, Ill D4 90
Palmyra, Harrison, Ind H5 91
Palmyra, Warren, Iowa f9 92
Palmyra, Marion, Mo B6 101
Palmyra, Otoe, Nebr D9, h12 103
Palmyra, Burlington, N.J C2 106
Palmyra, Wayne, N.Y B3 108
Palmyra, Halifax, N.C A5 109
Palmyra, Lebanon, Pa F8 114
Palmyra, Syr E12 31
Palmyra, Montgomery, Tenn A4 117
Palmyra, Fluvanna, Va C4 121
Palmyra, Jefferson, Wis F5 124
Palmyra, isl., Pac. O F12 7
Palmyras, pt., India G11 40
Palni, India *F6 39
Palo, Linn, Iowa B6 92
Palo, Ionia, Mich E4 98
Palo (Alsium), It h8 21
Palo Alto, Santa Clara, Calif D2, k8 82
Palo Alto, Schuylkill, Pa *E9 114
Palo Alto, co., Iowa A3 92
Palo Duro, canyon, Tex B2 118
Paloich, Sud C3 47
Palomar, mtn., Calif F5 82
Palomas, mtn., Ariz D2 80
Palombara Sabina, It g9 21
Palo Pinto, Palo Pinto, Tex C3 118
Palo Pinto, co., Tex C3 118
Palopo, Indon F6 35
Palos, cape, Sp D5 20
Palos Heights, Cook, Ill *B6 90
Palos Hills, Cook, Ill *B6 90
Palos Park, Cook, Ill k9 90
Palos Verdes Estates, Los Angeles, Calif n12 82
Palourde, lake, La k9 95
Palouse, Whitman, Wash C8 122
Palouse, riv., Wash C7 122
Palo Verde, Maricopa, Ariz D3, m7 80
Palo Verde, Imperial, Calif F6 82
Palpa, Peru D3 58
Pålsboda, Swe t33 25
Paluan, Phil *C6 35
Pama, Upper Volta D5 45
Pambrun, Sask., Can H2 70
Pamekasan, Indon G4 35
Pamiers, Fr F4 14
Pamir, mts., China, Sov. Un H23 9
Pamlico, co., N.C B6 109
Pamlico, riv., N.C B6 109
Pamlico, sound, N.C B6 109
Pampa, Gray, Tex B2 118
Pampa Grande, Bol C3 55
Pampanga, prov., Phil *B6 35
Pampanga, riv., Phil o13 35
Pampa Peñon, Chile D2 55
Pampas, Peru D3 58
Pampas, reg., Arg G4 55
Pampilhosa do Botão, Port B1 20
Pamplico, Florence, S.C D8 115
Pamplin, Appomattox and Prince Edward, Va C4 121
Pamplona, Col B3 60
Pamplona, Sp A5 20
Pamunkey, riv., Va C5 121
Pana, Ont., Can h13 72
Pana, Christian, Ill D4 90
Panaca, Lincoln, Nev F7 104
Panacea, Wakulla, Fla B2 86
Panache, lake, Ont., Can A3 72
Panagyurishte, Bul D7 22
Panaitan, isl., Indon G3 35
Panama, Montgomery, Ill D4 90
Panama, Shelby, Iowa C2 92
Panama, Lancaster, Nebr D9 103
Panama, Chautauqua, N.Y C1 108
Panama, LeFlore, Okla B7 112
Panamá, Pan F8, m11 62
Panama, country, N.A I12 61, F7 62
Panama, bay, Pan F8 62
Panama, canal, Pan F8, k11 62
Panama, gulf, Pan F8 62
Panama City, Bay, Fla u16 86
Panama City Beach, Bay, Fla u16 86
Panamint, range, Calif D5 82
Panao, Peru C2 58
Panarea, isl., It E5 21
Panaro, riv., It B3 21
Panay, isl., Phil C6 35
Pancake, range, Nev E5 104
Pancevo, Yugo C5 22
Pancoastburg, Fayette, Ohio C2 111
Panda, Moz B5 49
Pandan, Phil *C6 35
Pandharpur, India I5 40
Pāndhurna, India G7 40
Pando, Ur E1 56
Pando, dept., Bol B2 55
Pando, state, Braz E1 59
Pandora, Putnam, Ohio B2 111
Pandora, Wilson, Tex E4, k8 118
Pandu, Zaire A2 48
Panelas, Braz k6 57
Panet, Que., Can C7 73
Panevėžys, Sov. Un D5 27
Panfilov, Sov. Un E9 28
Pangala, Con F2 46
Pangani, Tan C6 48
Pangasinan, prov., Phil *B6 35
Pangburn, White, Ark B4 81
Pangfou (Pangpu), China H7 36
Pangi, Zaire B4 48
Pañginay, Phil o13 35
Pangkalanbuun, Indon F4 35
Pangkalangresik, Indon F2 35
Pangkalpinang, Indon F3 35
Pangkong, lake, China B6 39
Pangman, Sask., Can H3 70
Pangnirtung, N.W. Ter., Can C19 67
Pangong, lake, India B6 39
Pangpu, see Pangfou, China
Pangsau, pass, Bur C10 39
Panguitch, Garfield, Utah F3 119
Panhandle, Carson, Tex B2 118
Panihati, India *F12 40
Pānīpat, India C6 40
Paniqui, Phil o13 35
Panjāb, Afg D13 41
Panjang, isl., Viet H5 38
Panjgūr, Pak C3 39
Panjim, India E5 39
Panjpāi, Pak G13 41
Pankshin, Nig E6 45
Panmunjom, Kor H3 37
Panna, India E8 40
Panola, Sumter, Ala C1 78
Panola, co., Miss A3 100
Panola, co., Tex C5 118
Panora, Guthrie, Iowa C3 92
Panshan, China D9 36
Panshih, China E2 37
Pantar, isl., Indon G6 35
Pantego, Beaufort, N.C B6 109
Pantelleria, It F3 21
Pantelleria, isl., It F3 21
Pantin, Fr g10 14
Panton, Addison, Vt C2 120
Pantsyan, China C5 36
Pánuco, Mex C5, k14 63
Pánuco, riv., Mex k14 63
Panulcillo, Chile F1 55
Panzi, Zaire C2 48
Panzós, Guat C3 62
Paochang, China D6 36
Paocheng, China H2 36
Paochi, China G2 36
Paoching, China C6 37
Pão de Açúcar, Braz C3 57
Paokang, China I4 36
Paokuotu, China C9 36
Paola, It E6 21
Paola, Miami, Kans D9 93
Paoli, Phillips, Colo A8 83
Paoli, Orange, Ind G5 91
Paoli, Garvin, Okla C4 112
Paoli, Chester, Pa o20 114
Paonia, Delta, Colo C3 83
Paoshan, China F4 34
Paote, China E4 36
Paoti, China E7 36
Paoting (Tsingyuan), China E6 36
Paoting, China C8 38
Paotou, China D4 36
Paoua, Cen. Afr. Rep D3 46
Paoying, China H8 36
Papa, Hung B3 22
Papaaloa, Hawaii, Haw D6 88
Papagayo, gulf, C.R E5 62
Papago, Indian res., Ariz E3 80
Papaikou, Hawaii, Haw D6 88
Papalaulelei, cape, W. Sam 52
Papantla, Mex C5, m15 63
Papatele, mtn., Am. Sam 52
Papaya, Phil o13 35
Papeete, Fr. Polynesia, Oceania H13 7
Papenburg, F.R.G B3 16
Paper Mill Village, Bennington, Vt F2 120
Paphos, Cyp E9 31
Papillion, Sarpy, Nebr C9, g12 103
Papineau, co., Que., Can D2 73
Papineau, lake, Ont., Can B7 72
Papineauville, Que., Can D2 73
Paposo, Chile E1 55
Papua, gulf, Pap. N. Gui k11 50
Papua New Guinea, country, Oceania G8 7, h11 50
Papudo, Chile A2 54
Papun, Bur E10 39
Papy, pt., Fla E2 86
Paquette, Que., Can D6 73
Paquetville, N.B., Can B4 74
Para, dist., Sur A3 59
Pará, state, Braz B1 57
Pará, riv., Braz B1 57
Parabel, Sov. Un B10 29
Paracale, Phil o14 35
Paracatu, Braz E1 57
Paracatu, riv., Braz E1 57
Paracel, is., China B4 35
Pārachinār, Pak E15 41
Paraćin, Yugo D5 22
Paracurú, Braz B3 57
Paradis, St. Charles, La k11 95
Paradise, Butte, Calif C3 82
Paradise, Russell, Kans C5 93
Paradise, Sanders, Mont C2 102
Paradise, Clark, Nev G6 104
Paradise, Wallowa, Oreg B9 113
Paradise, Lancaster, Pa F9 114
Paradise, Cache, Utah B4 119
Paradise, riv., Newf., Can B3 75
Paradise Hill, Sask., Can D1 70
Paradise Hills, Bernalillo, N. Mex B3, k7 107
Paradise River, Newf., Can B3 75
Paradise Valley, Maricopa, Ariz m9 80
Paradise Valley, Alta., Can C5 69
Paradise Valley, Humboldt, Nev B4 104
Paradise Valley, Natrona, Wyo D6 125
Paradox, Montrose, Colo C2 83
Paradox, valley, Colo C2 83
Paragon, Morgan, Ind F4 91
Paragonah, Iron, Utah F3 119
Paragould, Greene, Ark A5 81
Paragua, riv., Ven B5 60
Paraguaçu, riv., Braz D3 57
Paraguaçu Paulista, Braz C2 56
Paraguai, riv., Braz B1 56
Paraguaná, pen., Ven A4 60
Paraguarí, Par E4 55
Paraguarí, dept., Par E4 55
Paraguay, country, S.A F5 53, D4 55
Paraguay, riv., Par D4 55
Paraíba, state, Braz C3, h6 57
Paraíba, riv., Braz C4 56
Paraíba do Sul, Braz h6 56
Paraiso, Pan k11 62
Paraíso, Mex D6 63
Paraisópolis, Braz C3 56
Parakhino-Poddubye, Sov. Un B9 27
Parakou, Benin E5 45
Paraloma, Sevier, Ark D1 81
Param, isl., Ponape 52
Paramaribo, Sur A3 59
Paramé, Fr C2 14
Paramirim, Braz D2 57
Paramithia, Grc C3 23
Paramonga, Peru D2 58
Paramount, Washington, Md A2 85
Paramus, Bergen, N.J h8 106
Paraná, Arg A4 54
Paranã, Braz D1 57
Paraná, state, Braz C2 56
Paraná, riv., Arg., Braz E4 55, C2 56
Paraná, riv., Braz D1 57
Paranaguá, Braz D3 56
Paranaíba, Braz B2 56
Paranaíba, riv., Braz B2 56
Paranam, Sur A3 59
Paranapanema, riv., Braz C2 56
Parañaque, Phil *C6 35
Paranatinga, riv., Braz E3 59
Parangaba, Braz *B3 57
Paraopeba, Braz E1 57
Parapeti, riv., Bol C3 55
Paratinga, Braz D2 57
Paray-le-Monial, Fr D6 14
Parbati, riv., India E6 40
Parbhani, India H6 40
Parchim, G.D.R B5 16
Parchment, Kalamazoo, Mich F5 98
Parcperdue, Iberia, La D4 95
Parczew, Pol C7 26
Pardeeville, Columbia, Wis E4 124
Pardes Hanna, Isr B6 32
Pardo, riv., Braz G2 56
Pardo, riv., Braz G3 56
Pardoe, Mercer, Pa D1 114
Pardoo, Austl D2 50
Pardubice, Czech C3 26
Pardum, Blaine, Nebr B5 103
Parecís, mts., Braz E2 59
Paredes, de Nava, Sp A3 20
Parent, Que., Can k12 73
Parepare, Indon F5 35
Parga, Grc C3 23
Pargolovo, Sov. Un r31 25
Parhams, Catahoula, La C4 95
Paria, gulf, Trin., Ven A5 60
Paria, pen., Ven A5 60
Paria, riv., Utah F4 119
Pariaguán, Ven B5 60
Paricutin, vol., Mex n12 63
Parigi, Indon F6 35
Parika, Guy A3 59
Parima, mts., Braz C5 60
Pariñas, pt., Peru B1 58
Parintins, Braz C3 59
Pario, riv., Ariz A4 80
Paris, Logan, Ark B2 81
Paris, Ont., Can D4 72
Paris, Fr C5, g10 14
Paris, Bear Lake, Idaho G7 89
Paris, Edgar, Ill D6 90
Paris, Bourbon, Ky B5 94
Paris, Oxford, Maine D2 96
Paris, Mecosta, Mich E5 98
Paris, Lafayette, Miss A4 100
Paris, Monroe, Mo B5 101
Paris, Greenville, S.C *B3 115
Paris, Henry, Tenn A3 117
Paris, Lamar, Tex C5 118
Paris, Fauquier, Va B5 121
Paris, Kenosha, Wis F1 124
Paris Crossing, Jennings, Ind G6 91
Parish, Oswego, N.Y B4 108
Parishville, St. Lawrence, N.Y f10 108
Parisville, Que., Can C5 73
Park, Grove, Kans C3 93
Park, co., Colo B5 83
Park, co., Mont E6 102
Park, co., Wyo B3 125
Park, plat., Colo D6 83
Park, range, Colo., Wyo A4 83
Park, riv., N. Dak A8 110
Parkbeg, Sask., Can G2 70
Park City, Lake, Ill *A6 90
Park City, Sedgwick, Kans g12 93
Park City, Barren, Ky C4 94
Park City, Stillwater, Mont E8 102
Park City, Summit, Utah C4 119
Parkdale, Ashley, Ark D4 81
Parkdale, P.E.I., Can C6 74
Parkdale, Manistee, Mich D4 98
Parkdale, Hood River, Oreg B5 113
Parkdale, Douglas, Wis B2 124
Parke, co., Ind E3 91
Parker, Yuma, Ariz C1 80
Parker, Douglas, Colo B6 83
Parker, Bay, Fla G3 86
Parker, Fremont, Idaho F7 89
Parker, Linn, Kans D8 93
Parker, Polk, Oreg C1 113
Parker, Armstrong, Pa D2 114
Parker, Turner, S. Dak D8 116
Parker, Spotsylvania, Va B5 121
Parker, Yakima, Wash C5 122
Parker, co., Tex C4 118
Parker, dam, Ariz C1 80
Parker, peak, S. Dak D2 116
Parker City, Randolph, Ind D7 91
Parker Dam, San Bernardino, Calif E6 82
Parker Head, Sagadahoc, Maine g8 96
Parkersburg, Richland, Ill E5 90
Parkersburg, Butler, Iowa B5 92
Parkersburg, Sampson, N.C C4 109
Parkersburg, Wood, W. Va B3 123
Parkers Prairie, Otter Tail, Minn D3 99
Parkertown, Ocean, N.J D4 106
Parkerview, Sask., Can F4 70
Parkerville, Morris, Kans D7 93
Parkes, Austl F7 51
Parkesburg, Chester, Pa G10 114
Park Falls, Price, Wis C3 124
Parkfield, Monterey, Calif E3 82
Park Forest, Cook and Will, Ill B6, m9 90
Park Hall, St. Marys, Md D5 85
Park Head, Ont., Can C3 72
Parkhill, Ont., Can D3 72
Park Hill, Cherokee, Okla B7 112
Park Hills, Kenton, Ky h13 94
Parkhurst, Aroostook, Maine (part of Presque Isle) B5 96
Parkin, Cross, Ark B5 81
Parkland, Alta., Can D4 69
Parkland, Bucks, Pa *F12 114
Parkland, Pierce, Wash f11 122
Park Lane, Litchfield, Conn *C3 84
Parklawn, Fairfax, Va *C5 121
Park Layne, Clark, Ohio C1 111
Parkman, Sask., Can H5 70
Parkman, Piscataquis, Maine C3 96
Parkman, Geauga, Ohio A4 111
Parkman, Sheridan, Wyo B5 125
Park Place, Clackamas, Oreg h12 113
Park Place, Greenville, S.C *B3 115
Park Rapids, Hubbard, Minn D3 99
Park Ridge, Cook, Ill A6, h9 90
Park Ridge, Bergen, N.J g8 106
Park Ridge Manor, Cook, Ill *B6 90
Park River, Walsh, N. Dak A8 110
Parkrose, Multnomah, Oreg B4 113
Parks, St. Martin, La D4 95
Parks, Dundy, Nebr D4 103
Parks, Stephens, Tex C3 118
Parkside, Sask., Can D2 70
Parkside, Delaware, Pa *G11 114
Parksley, Accomack, Va C7 121
Parkston, Hutchinson, S. Dak D8 116
Parksville, B.C., Can E5 68
Parksville, Sullivan, N.Y D6 108
Parksville, McCormick, S.C D3 115
Park Terrace, Salt Lake, Utah *C4 119
Parkton, Baltimore, Md A4 85
Parkton, Robeson, N.C C3 109
Park Valley, Box Elder, Utah B2 119
Park View, Rio Arriba, N. Mex A3 107
Parkview, Cuyahoga, Ohio *A4 111
Parkview, Allegheny, Pa *E2 114
Parkville, Baltimore, Md B4, g11 85
Parkville, Platte, Md B3, h10 101
Parkville, York, Pa *G8 114
Parkwater, Spokane, Wash g14 122
Parkwood, Montgomery, Md *B3 85
Parkwood, Durham, N.C B4 109
Parla, Sp p17 20
Parlākimidi, India H10 40
Parlier, Fresno, Calif D4 82
Parlin, Gunnison, Colo C4 83
Parma, Canyon, Idaho F2 89
Parma, It E6 18, B3 21
Parma, Jackson, Mich F6 98
Parma, New Madrid, Mo E8 101
Parma, Cuyahoga, Ohio A4, h9 111
Parma, riv., It E6 18
Parmachenee, lake, Maine C2 96
Parma Heights, Cuyahoga, Ohio h9 111
Parmele, Martin, N.C B5 109
Parmelee, Todd, S. Dak D4 116
Parmer, co., Tex B1 118
Parnaguá, Braz D2 57
Parnaíba, Braz B2 57
Parnaíba, riv., Braz B2 57
Parnassos, mtn., Grc C4 23
Parnell, Iowa, Iowa C6 92
Parnell, Nodaway, Mo A3 101
Parnis, mtn., Grc g11 23
Pärnu, Sov. Un B5 27
Paro, Bhu C8 39
Parole, Anne Arundel, Md. (part of Annapolis) C4 85
Paron, Saline, Ark C3 81
Paros, Grc D5 23
Paros, isl., Grc D5 23
Parow, S. Afr *D2 49
Parowan, Iron, Utah F3 119
Parr, Jasper, Ind B3 91
Parral, Chile B2 54
Parramatta, Austl *F8 51
Parramore, isl., Va C7 121
Parran, Calvert, Md C4 85
Parras de la Fuente, Mex B4 63
Parrett, riv., Eng C5 12
Parrish, Walker, Ala B2 78
Parrish, Manatee, Fla E4, p11 86
Parrish, Langlade, Wis C4 124
Parrott, Terrell, Ga E2 87
Parrott, Pulaski, Va C2 121
Parrottsville, Cocke, Tenn C10 117
Parrs, ridge, Md A3 85
Parrsboro, N.S., Can D5 74
Parry, Sask., Can H3 70
Parry, cape, N.W. Ter., Can B8 66
Parry, isl., Ont., Can B4 72
Parry, isl., Eniwetok 52
Parry, is., N.W. Ter., Can m29 67
Parry, mtn., B.C., Can C3 68
Parry Sound, Ont., Can B4, p20 72
Parry Sound, dist., Ont., Can B4 72
Parsberg, F.R.G D6 17
Parshall, Grand, Colo B4 83
Parshall, Mountrail, N. Dak B3 110
Parsippany, Morris, N.J B4 106
Parsippany-Troy Hills, Morris, N.J *B4 106
Parsnip, peak, Nev E7 104
Parsnip, riv., B.C., Can B6 68
Parsons, Labette, Kans E8 93
Parsons, Decatur, Tenn B3 117
Parsons, Tucker, W. Va B5 123
Parsonsburg, Wicomico, Md D7 85
Parson's Pond, Newf., Can C3, h10 75
Partābgarh, India E5 40
Parthenay, Fr D3 14
Parthenen, Aus C6 18
Parthenon, Newton, Ark B2 81
Partinico, It E4 21
Partizansk, Sov. Un E6 37
Partlow, Spotsylvania, Va B5 121
Partridge, Reno, Kans E5, g10 93
Partridge, pt., Newf., Can C3 75
Partry, Ire D2 11
Parys, S. Afr C4 49
Pasadena, Los Angeles, Calif E4, m12 82
Pasadena, Newf., Can D3 75
Pasadena, Anne Arundel, Md B2 85
Pasadena, Harris, Tex r14 118
Pasadena Hills, St. Louis, Mo *C7 101
Pasadena Park, Spokane, Wash *B8 122
Pasaje, Ec B2 58
Pasay (Rizal), Phil C6, o13 35
Pasayton, riv., B.C., Can., Wash A5 122
Pascagoula, Jackson, Miss E5, f8 100
Pascagoula, bay, Miss f8 100
Pascagoula, riv., Miss E5 100
Paşcani [-Gară], Rom B8 22
Paschall, Warren, N.C A4 109
Pasco, Franklin, Wash C6 122
Pasco, co., Fla D4 86
Pasco, dept., Peru D2 58
Pascoag, Providence, R.I B10 84
Pascoag, res., R.I B10 84
Pascola, Pemiscot, Mo E8 101
Pascualitos, Mex F6 82
Pas-de-Calais, dept., Fr D2 15
Paseley, cape, Austl F3 50
Pasewalk, G.D.R B7 16
Pashkovo, Sov. Un B5 37
Pasig, Phil o13 35
Pasión, riv., Guat B2 62
Paslek, Pol A5 26
Pasni, Pak C3 39
Paso del Limay, Arg C2 54
Paso de los Indios, Arg C3 54
Paso de los Libres, Arg E4 55
Paso de los Toros, Ur E1 56
Paso Río Mayo, Arg D2 54
Paso Robles, San Luis Obispo, Calif E3 82
Pasqua, Sask., Can G3 70
Pasque, isl., Mass D6 97
Pasquia, hills, Sask., Can D4 70
Pasquia, riv., Sask., Man., Can D5 70
Pasquo, Davidson, Tenn g10 117
Pasquotank, co., N.C A6 109
Pasrūr, Pak A5 40
Passaconaway, mtn., N.H C4 105
Passadumkeag, Penobscot, Maine C4 96
Passadumkeag, mtn., Maine C4 96
Passage East, Ire E5 11
Passage West, Ire F3 11
Passaic, Passaic, N.J B4, h8 106
Passaic, co., N.J A4 106
Passaic, riv., N.J h8 106
Passau, F.R.G E8 17
Pass Christian, Harrison, Miss E4, g7 100
Passekeag, N.B., Can D4 74
Passero, cape, It F5 21
Passo Fundo, Braz D2 56
Passos, Braz F1 57
Passugg-Araschgen, Switz C8 19
Passumpsic, Caledonia, Vt C4 120
Passumpsic, riv., Vt C4 120
Passwang, mtn., Switz B4 19
Passy, Fr E2 19
Pastaza, prov., Ec B2 58
Pastaza, riv., Ec., Peru B2 58
Pasto, Col C2 60
Pastora, peak, Ariz A6 80
Pastoria, Jefferson, Ark C3 81
Pastura, Guadalupe, N. Mex C5 107
Pasuruan, Indon G4 35

Paswegin, Sask., Can........F4 70
Patagonia, Santa Cruz, Ariz..F5 80
Patan, India..........F4 40
Patan, see Lalitpur, Nep.
Patang (Paan), China.......E4 34
Patapedia, riv., N.B., Que., Can..........B2 74
Patapsco, Carroll, Md.......A4 85
Patapsco, riv., Md.........B4 85
Pataskala, Licking, Ohio.....B3 111
Pataz, Peru.........C2 58
Patchewollock, Austl........G4 51
Patchogue, Suffolk, N.Y.....n15 108
Patea, N.Z.........M15 51
Pateley Bridge, Eng.........F7 13
Pateras, mtn., Grc.........g10 23
Paternò, It.........F5 21
Pateros, Okanogan, Wash....A6 122
Paterson, Passaic, N.J....B4, h8 106
Paterson, Benton, Wash......D6 122
Patesville, Hancock, Ky......C3 94
Pathānkot, India.........A5 40
Pathfinder, res., Wyo.......D6 125
Pathfork, Harlan, Ky.......D6 94
Pathlow, Sask., Can.........E3 70
Pati, pt., Guam............52
Patiāla, India.......B6 39, B6 40
Patiali, India..........D7 40
Patillas, mun., P.R.........*B3 65
Patmos, Hempstead, Ark......D2 81
Patmos, isl., Grc..........D6 23
Patna, India......C8 39, E10 40
Patnanongan, isl., Phil......o14 35
Patoka, Marion, Ill..........E4 90
Patoka, Gibson, Ind..........H2 91
Patoka, riv., Ind...........H2 91
Paton, Greene, Iowa.........B3 92
Patos, Braz..........C3 57
Patos de Minas, Braz.......E1 57
Patrai, Grc..........C3 23
Patrai, gulf, Grc..........C3 23
Patricia, Alta., Can........D5 69
Patricia, Dawson, Tex.......C1 118
Patrick, Chesterfield, S.C....B7 115
Patrick, co., Va..........D2 121
Patrick, mtn., Maine.......D3 96
Patricksburg, Owen, Ind.....F4 91
Patrick Springs, Patrick, Va..D2 121
Patriot, Switzerland, Ind.....G8 91
Patrocínio, Braz.........E1 57
Patroon, Shelby, Tex.......D6 118
Patsaliga, creek, Ala.......D3 78
Patsville, Elko, Nev.........B6 104
Pattagumpus, Penobscot, Maine..........C4 96
Pattani, Thai..........I4 38
Pattaquatic, hill, Mass......B3 97
Patten, Penobscot, Maine.....C4 96
Pattenburg, Hunterdon, N.J..B2 106
Patterson, Woodruff, Ark.....B4 81
Patterson, Pierce, Ga.......E4 87
Patterson, Lemhi, Idaho......E5 89
Patterson, Greene, Ill........D3 90
Patterson, Madison, Iowa.....C4 92
Patterson, St. Mary, La......E4 95
Patterson, Wayne, Mo.......D7 101
Patterson, Putnam, N.Y.....D7 108
Patterson, Buchanan, Va.....e10 121
Patterson, creek, W. Va.....B5 123
Patterson Knob, mtn., Tenn.....g10 117
Patterson Gardens, Monroe, Mich..........*G7 98
Pattison, Claiborne, Miss....D3 100
Patton, Bollinger, Mo.......D7 101
Patton, Cambria, Pa........E4 114
Pattonsburg, Daviess, Mo....A3 101
Pattullo, mtn., B.C., Can.....A3 68
Patu, Braz..........C3 57
Patuakhali, Bngl.........F13 40
Patuca, pt., Hond..........C5 62
Patuca, riv., Hond.........C5 62
Patung, China..........I4 36
Patuxent, Anne Arundel, Md..........B4 85
Patuxent, riv., Md.........B3 85
Patzau, Douglas, Wis........B1 124
Pátzcuaro, Mex.......D4, n13 63
Pátzcuaro, lake, Mex.......n13 63
Patzicía, Guat..........C2 62
Patzún, Guat..........C2 62
Pau, Fr..........F3 24
Paucarbamba, Peru........D3 58
Paucartambo, riv., Peru......D3 58
Paudalho, Braz.......C3, h6 57
Pau dos Ferros, Braz.......C3 57
Paugh Lake, Ont., Can.......B7 72
Pauillac, Fr..........E3 14
Pauk, Bur..........D9 39
Paul, Minidoka, Idaho.......G5 89
Paul, Midland, Tex.........C2 118
Paul, isl., Newf., Can.......g9 75
Paul, stream, Vt..........B5 120
Paulaya, riv., Hond........C5 62
Paulden, Yavapai, Ariz......C3 80
Paulding, Ontonagon, Mich..........n12 98
Paulding, Jasper, Miss......C4 100
Paulding, Paulding, Ohio.....A1 111
Paulding, co., Ga.........C2 87
Paulding, co., Ohio.........A1 111
Paulding, bay, Ant..........C25 5
Paulette, Noxubee, Miss.....B5 100
Paulina (Remy), St. James, La..........h10 95
Paulina, Warren, N.J.......B3 106
Paulina, Crook, Oreg........C7 113
Paulina, mts., Oreg.........D5 113
Paulina, peak, Oreg.........D5 113
Pauline, Adams, Nebr.......D7 103
Pauline, Spartanburg, S.C....B4 115
Pauline, mtn., B.C., Alta., Can..........C1 69
Paulins, kill, N.J.........A3 106
Paulis, see Isiro, Zaire
Paulistana, Braz.........C2 57
Paull, lake, Sask., Can......A3 70
Paull, riv., Sask., Can.......B3 70
Paullina, O'Brien, Iowa......B9 92
Paulo Afonso, falls, Braz.....C3 57
Paulsboro, Gloucester, N.J...D2 106
Paul Smiths, Franklin, N.Y..f10 108
Paul Spur, Cochise, Ariz......F6 80
Paulstown, Ire..........E4 11
Pauls Valley, Garvin, Okla..C4 112
Paungde, Bur..........E10 39
Paupack, Pike, Pa.........D11 114
Pauwela, Maui, Haw........C5 88
Pavant, range, Utah........E3 119
Pavia, It.........D5 18, B2 21
Pavilion, Genesee, N.Y......C2 108
Pavilion, key, Fla..........G5 86
Pavillion, Fremont, Wyo.....C4 125
Pavlodar, Sov. Un.........C9 29
Pavlof, vol., Alsk..........D7 79
Pavlograd, Sov. Un.........G10 27
Pavlovo, Sov. Un.........D14 27
Pavlovsk, Sov. Un..........s31 25
Pavlovsk, Sov. Un........F13 27
Pavlovskaya, Sov. Un.......H13 27
Pavlovskiy Posad, Sov. Un..n18 27
Pavo, Thomas and Brooks, Ga..........F3 87
Pavonia, Richland, Ohio.....B3 111
Pawcatuck, New London, Conn..........D9 84
Paw Creek, Mecklenburg, N.C..........B2 109
Pawhuska, Osage, Okla......A5 112
Pawlet, Rutland, Vt.........E2 120
Pawleys Island, Georgetown, S.C..........E9 115
Pawling, Dutchess, N.Y......D7 108
Pawnee, Sangamon, Ill.......D4 90
Pawnee, Pawnee, Okla........A5 112
Pawnee, Bee, Tex..........E4 118
Pawnee, co., Kans...........D4 93
Pawnee, co., Nebr..........D9 103
Pawnee, co., Okla...........A5 112
Pawnee, creek, Colo.........A7 83
Pawnee, riv., Kans.........D4 93
Pawnee City, Pawnee, Nebr..D9 103
Pawnee Rock, Barton, Kans.D5 93
Pawpaw, Lee, Ill..........B5 90
Paw Paw, Van Buren, Mich..F5 98
Paw Paw, Morgan, W. Va...B6 123
Pawpaw, creek, W. Va.......h10 123
Paw Paw, riv., Mich........F4 98
Paw Paw Lake, Berrien, Mich..........*F4 98
Pawtackaway, pond, N.H......D4 105
Pawtowicze, Pol.........h9 26
Pawtucket, Providence, R.I.B11 84
Pax, Fayette, W. Va........D6 123
Paxico, Wabaunsee, Kans....C7 93
Paxoí, isl., Grc...........C3 23
Paxtang, Dauphin, Pa.......*F8 114
Paxton, Walton, Fla........u15 86
Paxton, Ford, Ill..........C5 90
Paxton, Sullivan, Ind.......F3 91
Paxton, Worcester, Mass.....B4 97
Paxton, Keith, Nebr........C4 103
Paxtonville, Snyder, Pa......E7 114
Paxville, Clarendon, S.C.....D7 115
Payen, China..........C3 37
Payenhala, China.........A10 36
Payenhaote, see Alashantsochi, China
Payerne, Switz..........C2 19
Payette, Payette, Idaho......E2 89
Payette, co., Idaho.........E2 89
Payette, lake, Idaho........E2 89
Payette, riv., Idaho........E2 89
Payne, Bibb, Ga..........F2 87
Payne, Paulding, Ohio........A1 111
Payne, co., Okla..........A5 112
Payne, lake, Que., Can......g12 73
Paynes, Tallahatchie, Miss...B3 100
Paynes Creek, Tehama, Calif..........B3 82
Paynesville, Ontonagon, Mich..........n12 98
Paynesville, Stearns, Minn...E4 99
Paynesville, Pike, Mo........B7 101
Payneville, Meade, Ky.......C3 94
Paynton, Sask., Can.........D1 70
Paysandú, Ur..........E1 55
Paysandú, dept., Ur........*E1 56
Payson, Gila, Ariz..........C4 80
Payson, Adams, Ill..........D2 90
Payson, Lincoln, Okla.......B5 112
Payson, Utah, Utah..........C4 119
Paz, bay, Mex............C2 63
Pazardzhik, Bul..........D7 22
Pazin, Yugo..........C1 22
Pea, riv., Ala..........D3 78
Peabody, Marion, Kans.......D6 93
Peabody, Essex, Mass....A6, f12 97
Peabody, riv., N.H.........B4 105
Peace, riv., Alta., B.C., Can....E8 66
Peace, riv., Fla..........E5 86
Peace Dale, Washington, R.I..........D11 84
Peace River, Alta., Can..A2, f7 69
Peach, co., Ga..........D3 87
Peach, pt., Mass..........f12 97
Peacham, Caledonia, Vt......C4 120
Peach Creek, Logan, W. Va..D5 123
Peachland, B.C., Can.......E8 68
Peachland, Anson, N.C......C2 109
Peach Orchard, Clay, Ark....A5 81
Peach Orchard Knob, peak, Ky...C3 94
Peach Springs, Mohave, Ariz.B2 80
Peacock, Lake, Mich........D5 98
Peacock, hills, N.W. Ter., Can.C10 66
Peacock, pt., Wake Isl..........52
Peacock, sound, Ant..........B2 5
Peak, Newberry, S.C........C5 115
Peaked, mtn., Maine........B4 96
Peale, isl., Wake Isl..........52
Peale, mtn., Utah..........E6 119
Pea Patch, isl., Del.......D1 106
Pearce, Alta., Can.........E4 69
Pearcy, Garland, Ark.....C2, g7 81
Pea Ridge, Benton, Ark......A1 81
Pearisburg, Giles, Va.......C2 121
Pearl, Pike, Ill..........D3 90
Pearl, Rankin, Miss.........*C3 100
Pearl hbr., Haw..........B4 88
Pearl, riv., Miss..........C3 100
Pearland, Brazoria, Tex.....r14 118
Pearl and Hermes, reef, Haw...k12 88
Pearl Beach, St. Clair, Mich.*F8 98
Pearl City, Honolulu, Haw..........B4, g10 88
Pearl City, Stephenson, Ill...A4 90
Pearlington, Hancock, Miss..E4 100
Pearl River, St. Tammany, La..........D6 95
Pearl River, Rockland, N.Y.g12 109
Pearl River, co., Miss.......E4 100
Pear Ridge, Jefferson, Tex....E2 95
Pearsall, Frio, Tex.........E3 118
Pearsoll, peak, Oreg........E3 113
Pearson, Cleburne, Ark......B3 81
Pearson, Atkinson, Ga.......E4 87
Pearson, Langlade, Wis......C4 124
Pearsonia, Osage, Okla......A5 112
Peary, chan., N.W. Ter., Can.m30 67
Peary Land, reg., Grnld.......A18 4
Pease, Mille Lacs, Minn......E5 99
Pebane, Moz..........D7 49
Pebworth, Owsley, Ky.......C6 94
Peć, Yugo..........D5 22
Peçanha, Braz..........E2 57
Pecan Island, Vermilion, La.E3 95
Pecatonica, Winnebago, Ill..A4 90
Pecatonica, riv., Wis.......F3 124
Pechenga, Sov. Un.........C14 25
Pechora, Sov. Un..........C9 4
Pechora, riv., Sov. Un.......C20 9
Pechorskaya, bay, Sov. Un....B19 9
Peck, Nez Perce, Idaho......C2 89
Peck, Sedgwick and Sumner, Kans..........E6 93
Peck, Sanilac, Mich.........E8 98
Peckerwood Lake, res., Ark....C4 81
Peckham, Kay, Okla.........A4 112
Peckville (Blakely), Lackawanna, Pa..........A9 114
Peconic, Suffolk, N.Y.......E7 84
Peconic, riv., N.Y.........F7 84
Pecos, San Miguel, N. Mex..B4 107
Pecos, Reeves, Tex.....D1, o13 118
Pecos, co., Tex..........o13 118
Pecos, riv., N. Mex., Tex.....o13 76
Pécs, Hung..........B4 22
Peculiar, Cass, Mo..........C3 101
Pedasí, Pan..........G7 62
Peddocks, isl., Mass........g12 97
Pedley, Riverside, Calif.....*F5 82
Pedra Azul, Braz.........E2 57
Pedraza, see Ciudad Bolivia, Ven.
Pedregal, Pan..........F6 62
Pedregal, Pan..........k12 62
Pedregal, Ven..........A3 60
Pedreiras, Braz.........B2 57
Pedricktown, Salem, N.J....D2 106
Pedro Afonso, Braz........C1 57
Pedro Avelino, Braz........C3 57
Pedro de Valdivia, Chile....D2 55
Pedro Juan Caballero, Par..D4 55
Pedro Luro, Arg..........B4 54
Pedro Miguel, Pan.........k11 62
Pedro Velho, Braz..........h6 57
Peebinga, Austl..........G3 51
Peebles, Sask., Can.........G4 70
Peebles, Adams, Ohio........D2 111
Peebles, Scot..........E5 13
Peekaboo, mtn., Maine......C5 96
Peekskill, Westchester, N.Y..........D7, m15 108
Peel, N.B., Can..........C2 74
Peel, I. of Man..........F4 13
Peel, co., Ont., Can........D5 72
Peel, riv., Yukon, Can......C5 66
Peel, sound, N.W. Ter., Can..B13 69
Peel Fell, mtn., Scot......E6 13
Pe Ell, Lewis, Wash........C2 122
Peene, riv., G.D.R........B6 16
Peer, Bel..........C5 15
Peerless, Daniels, Mont....B11 102
Peerless, lake, Alta., Can....A3 69
Peers, Alta., Can..........C3 69
Peesane, Sask., Can.........E4 70
Peetz, Logan, Colo.........A7 83
Peever, Roberts, S. Dak......B9 116
Pefferlaw, Ont., Can........C5 72
Pegan, hill, Mass..........g10 97
Pegasus, bay, N.Z.........O14 51
Pegau, G.D.R..........B7 17
Peggs, Cherokee, Okla.......A6 112
Peggy, Atascosa, Tex.........E3 118
Pegnitz, F.R.G..........D6 17
Pegnitz, riv., F.R.G........D6 17
Pego, Sp..........C5 20
Pegram, Cheatham, Tenn....A4 117
Pegu, Bur..........E10 39
Pegu Yoma, mts., Bur.......C1 38
Pehčevo, Yugo..........E6 22
Pehuajo, Arg..........B4 54
Pei, China..........G7 36
Pei, China..........G7 36
Peian, China..........B10 34
Peichieh, China.........A8 40
Peihai, China..........G6 34
Peili (Pakli), China........C8 38
Peine, F.R.G..........A5 17
Peiping, see Peking, China
Peipus, lake, Sov. Un......B6 27
Peixe, Braz..........D1 57
Pejepscot, Sagadahoc, Maine..........E2, g7 96
Pekalongan, Indon.........G3 35
Pekan, Mala..........K5 38
Pekin, Tazewell, Ill.........C4 90
Pekin, Washington, Ind......G5 91
Pekin, Nelson, N. Dak.......B7 110
Peking (Peiping), China.........D8 34, E7 36
Pelagie, is., It..........G13 20
Pelagos, isl., Grc..........C5 23
Pelahatchie, Rankin, Miss...C4 100
Pelaihari, Indon..........F4 35
Pelat, mtn., Fr..........E7 14
Pelee, isl., Ont., Can.......F2 72
Pelée, mtn., Mart.........S10 65
Peleliu, isl., Palau Is..........52
Pelham, Shelby, Ala........B3 78
Pelham, Ont., Can..........D5 72
Pelham, Mitchell, Ga........E2 87
Pelham, Hampshire, Mass.....B3 97
Pelham, Hillsboro, N.H......E4 105
Pelham, Westchester, N.Y...*D7 108
Pelham, Caswell, N.C.......A3 109
Pelham, Greenville, S.C.....B3 115
Pelham, Grundy, Tenn.......D8 117
Pelham Manor, Westchester, N.Y..........h13 108
Pelhrimov, Czech..........D3 26
Pelican, Alsk..........k21 79
Pelican, De Soto, La........B2 95
Pelican, bay, Man., Can......C1 71
Pelican, butte, Oreg.......E4 113
Pelican, lake, Alta., Can....B4 69
Pelican, lake, Man., Can....C1 71
Pelican, lake, Sask., Can....B4 70
Pelican, lake, Minn........B6 99
Pelican, lake, Minn........D4 99
Pelican, lake, Minn........E5 99
Pelican, lake, Wis.........C4 124
Pelican, mtn., Alta., Can....B4 69
Pelican Lake, Palm Beach, Fla..........F6 86
Pelican Lake, Oneida, Wis...C4 124
Pelican Narrows, Sask., Can.B4 70
Pelican Rapids, Man., Can...C1 71
Pelican Rapids, Otter Tail, Minn..........D2 99
Peligre, res., Hai..........E8 64
Pelion, Lexington, S.C......D5 115
Pella, Marion, Iowa........C5 92
Pella, prov., Grc..........*B4 23
Pell City, Saint Clair, Ala...B3 78
Pellice, riv., It..........E3 18
Pell Lake, Walworth, Wis.....n11 124
Pellston, Emmet, Mich.......C6 98
Pellville, Hancock, Ky.......C3 94
Pellworm, isl., F.R.G........A4 16
Pelly, Sask., Can..........F5 70
Pelly, lake, N.W. Ter., Can...C12 66
Pelly, mts., Yukon, Can......D6 66
Pelly, riv., Yukon, Can......C5 66
Pelly Crossing, Yukon, Can..D5 66
Peloncillo, mts., Ariz., N. Mex..E6 80
Peloponnesos (Peloponnesus), reg., Grc..........D4 23
Pelotas, Braz..........E2 56
Pelotas, riv., Braz.........D2 56
Pelto, lake, La..........E5 95
Pelusium, see Tinah, bay, Eg.
Pelusium, ruins, Eg........C4 32
Pelzer, Anderson, S.C.......B3 115
Pelzer North, Anderson, S.C..........*B3 115
Pemadumcook, lake, Maine....C3 96
Pemanggil, isl., Mala........K6 38
Pemaquid, Lincoln, Maine...E3 96
Pematangsiantar, Indon.....K3 38
Pemba, see Porto Amélia, Moz.
Pemba, Zambia.........E4 48
Pemba, isl., Tan..........B6 48
Pemberton, B.C., Can.......D6 68
Pemberton, Burlington, N.J..D3 106
Pemberton, Shelby, Ohio....B1 111
Pemberville, Wood, Ohio.A2, f7 111
Pembina, Pembina, N. Dak..A8 110
Pembina, co., N. Dak.......A8 110
Pembina, mts., N. Dak.......A7 110
Pembina, riv., Alta., Can....C3 69
Pembina, riv., Man., Can.....E2 71
Pembina, riv., N. Dak.......A7 110
Pembine, Marinette, Wis.....C6 124
Pembroke, Ont., Can...B7, p20 72
Pembroke, Bryan, Ga........D5 87
Pembroke, Christian, Ky.....D2 94
Pembroke, Washington, Maine..........D5 96
Pembroke, Plymouth, Mass..B6 97
Pembroke, Genesee, N.Y.....C2 108
Pembroke, Robeson, N.C.....C3 109
Pembroke, Giles, Va.........C2 121
Pembroke, Wales..........C3 12
Pembroke, co., Wales.......C3 12
Pembroke Pines, Broward, Fla..........r13 86
Pembuang, Indon.........F4 35
Pemigewasset, riv., N.H.....C3 105
Pemiscot, co., Mo..........E8 101
Pemmican Portage, Sask., Can..........D4 70
Pemuco, Chile..........B2 54
Penablanca, Sandoval, N. Mex..........B3, h8 107
Penafiel, Port..........B1 20
Peñafiel, Sp..........B3 20
Peñalara, mtn., Sp..........B4 20
Penalosa, Kingman, Kans.....E5 93
Penamacor, Port..........B2 20
Peña Negra, mts., Sp........A2 20
Penang (Penang and Province Wellesley), state, Mala.....J4 38
Penang, isl., Mala..........J4 38
Penápolis, Braz..........C2 56
Peñaranda de Bracamonte, Sp..........B3 20
Pen Argyl, Northampton, Pa..........E11 114
Peña Roya, mtn., Sp.........B5 20
Peñarroya-Pueblonuevo, Sp..C3 20
Peñas, cape, Sp..........A3 20
Penas, gulf, Chile..........D2 54
Penasco, Taos, N. Mex.......A4 107
Penawawa, Whitman, Wash.C8 122
Penbrook, Dauphin, Pa.......F8 114
Pence, Warren, Ind.........D2 91
Penchi, China..........C9 34
Penck, trough, Ant........B12 5
Pendelikon (Pentelicus), mtn., Grc..........g11 23
Pendleton, Anderson, S.C....B2 115
Pendembu, S.L..........E2 45
Pender, Thurston, Nebr.....B9 103
Pender, co., N.C..........C4 109
Pender, isl., B.C., Can......g12 68
Pendergrass, Jackson, Ga....B3 87
Pender Island, B.C., Can...g12 68
Pendleton, Madison, Ind.....E6 91
Pendleton, Umatilla, Oreg..B8 113
Pendleton, co., Ky.........B5 94
Pendleton, co., W. Va.......C5 123
Pend Oreille, co., Wash.....A8 122
Pend Oreille, lake, Idaho....A2 89
Pend Oreille, riv., Wash......A8 122
Pendroy, Teton, Mont.......B4 102
Penedo, Braz..........D3 57
Penetanguishene, Ont., Can..C5 72
Penfield, Greene, Ga........C3 87
Penfield, Champaign, Ill.....C6 90
Penfield, Monroe, N.Y......*B3 108
Penfield, Clearfield, Pa......D4 114
Penfield Junction, Lorain, Ohio..........*A3 111
Pengan, China..........I2 36
Penganga, riv., India........H6 40
Penge, Zaire..........C3 48
Pengibu, isl., Indon.........L7 38
Penglai, China..........F9 36
Pengshui, China..........J3 36
Penguin, is., Newf., Can.....E3 75
Penhold, Alta., Can.........C4 69
Penhook, Franklin, Va.......D3 121
Peniche, Port..........C1 20
Penicuik, Scot..........E5 13
Peninsula, Washington, Minn..........E7 99
Peninsula, Summit, Ohio....A4 111
Penitas, Hidalgo, Tex.......F3 118
Penitente, mts., Braz.......C1 57
Penitentiary, mtn., Ala......A2 78
Penn, Sask., Can..........D2 70
Penn, Ramsey, N. Dak.......A6 110
Pennant, pt., N.S., Can......E6 74
Pennant Station, Sask., Can.G1 70
Pennask, mtn., B.C., Can.....E7 68
Penndel, Bucks, Pa.........*F12 114
Penne, It..........C4 21
Pennell, mtn., Utah.........F5 119
Pennellville, Oswego, N.Y...B4 108
Penneshaw, Austl..........G1 51
Penney Farms, Clay, Fla.....C5 86
Penn Grove, Sonoma, Calif.*C2 82
Penn Hills, Allegheny, Pa..........F2, k14 114
Penniac, N.B., Can.........C3 74
Pennine Alps, mts., It., Switz...D4 19
Pennines, mts., Eng........C5 10
Pennington, Choctaw, Ala....C1 78
Pennington, Mercer, N.J....C3 106
Pennington, co., Minn.......B2 99
Pennington, co., S. Dak.....D2 116
Pennington, mtn., Maine.....B4 96
Pennington Gap, Lee, Va......f8 121
Pennock, Kandiyohi, Minn...E3 99
Pennsauken, Camden, N.J...D2 106
Pennsboro, Ritchie, W. Va..B4 123
Pennsburg, Montgomery, Pa..........F11 114
Penns Grove, Salem, N.J....D2 106
Pennside, Berks, Pa........*F10 114
Pennsuco, Dade, Fla........s13 86
Pennsville, Salem, N.J......D1 106
Pennsville, Morgan, Ohio....C4 111
Pennsylvania, state, U.S..........B12 77, 114
Penn Valley, Montgomery, Pa..........*F11 114
Pennville, Jay, Ind..........D7 91
Pennville, York, Pa.........G8 114
Penn Wynne, Montgomery, Pa..........*G11 114
Penny, B.C., Can..........C7 68
Penn Yan, Yates, N.Y.......C3 108
Pennycutaway, riv., Man., Can..A5 71
Penny Hill, New Castle, Del..........*A6 85
Penobscot, Hancock, Maine..D4 96
Penobscot, co., Maine.......C4 96
Penobscot, bay, Maine.......D4 96
Penobscot, lake, Maine.......C2 96
Penobscot, riv., Maine.......C4 96
Penobsquis, N.B., Can......D4 74
Penokee, Graham, Kans......C4 93
Penong, Austl..........F5 50
Penonomé, Pan..........F7 62
Penrith, Eng..........F6 13
Pensacola, Escambia, Fla....u14 86
Pensacola, Mayes, Okla......A6 112
Pensacola, dam, Okla........A6 112
Pensacola, mts., Ant........A7 5
Pensaukee, Oconto, Wis.....D6 124
Pense, Sask., Can..........G3 70
Pentagon, mtn., Mont........C3 102
Pentecost, Sunflower, Miss...B3 100
Pentecoste, Braz..........B3 57
Penticton, B.C., Can.........E8 68
Pentland, firth, Scot........B5 13
Pentland, hills, Scot........E5 13
Penton, DeSota, Miss.......A3 100
Penton, Salem, N.J.........D2 106
Pentwater, Oceana, Mich......E4 98
Peñuelas, mun., P.R.........*B2 65
Penwell, Ector, Tex.........D1 118
Penza, Sov. Un..........C2 29
Penzance, Sask., Can........F3 70
Penzance, Eng..........D2 12
Penzberg, F.R.G..........E5 16
Penzhina, riv., Sov. Un......C19 28
Penzhino, Sov. Un.........C19 28
Penzlin, G.D.R..........E7 24
Peoa, Summit, Utah........C4 119
Peonan, pt., Man., Can......D2 71
Peone, Spokane, Wash.......D8 122
Peoples, Jackson, Ky........C5 94
Peoria, Maricopa, Ariz..D3, k8 80
Peoria, Peoria, Ill..........C4 90
Peoria, Amite, Miss.........D3 100
Peoria, Union, Ohio.........B2 111
Peoria, co., Ill..........C4 90
Peoria Heights, Peoria, Ill...C4 90
Peotone, Will, Ill..........B6 90
Pep, Roosevelt, N. Mex......D6 107
Pepacton, res., N.Y.........C6 108
Pepeekeo, Hawaii, Haw.......D6 88
Pepin, Pepin, Wis.........D1 124
Pepin, co., Wis..........D2 124
Pepin, lake, Wis..........D1 124
Pepperell, Middlesex, Mass..A4 97
Pepper Pike, Cuyahoga, Ohio..........*A4 111
Pepperton, Butts, Ga........C3 87
Peqin, Alb..........B2 23
Pequabuck, Litchfield, Conn.C5 84
Pequaming, Baraga, Mich....B2 98
Pequannock, Morris, N.J....B4 106
Pequeni, riv., Pan..........k12 62
Pequest, riv., N.J..........B3 106
Pequiri, riv., Braz..........B1 56
Pequiri, riv., Braz..........C2 56
Pequop, Elko, Nev.........B7 104
Pequot Lakes, Crow Wing, Minn..........D4 99
Perak, isl., Indon..........J2 38
Perak, riv., Mala..........J4 38
Perak, state, Mala.........J4 38
Perakhóra, Grc..........g9 23
Perales, riv., Sp..........p16 20
Perales de Tajuña, Sp.......p18 20
Peralta, Valencia, N. Mex....C3 107
Percival, Fremont, Iowa......D2 92
Percy, Fr..........C3 14
Percy, Randolph, Ill.........E4 90
Percy, Marion, Iowa.........C4 92
Percy, Washington, Miss.....B3 100
Percy, Coos, N.H..........A4 105
Perdido, Baldwin, Ala........D2 78
Perdido, bay, Fla..........u14 86
Perdido, mtn., Sp..........A6 20
Perdido, riv., Fla..........u14 86
Perdue, Sask., Can..........E2 70
Perea, McKinley, N. Mex.....B1 107
Pereira, Col..........C2 60
Pereira Barreto, Braz.......C2 56
Pereira de Eça, Ang........E2 48
Perekop, Sov. Un.........H9 27
Pere Marquette, riv., Mich.....E4 98
Peremennyy, cape, Ant........C23 5
Perené, riv., Peru..........D3 58
Pereslavl-Zalesskiy, Sov. Un..........C12 27
Pereyaslav-Khmelnitskiy, Sov. Un..........F8 27
Perez, Phil..........o13 35
Pergamino, Arg..........A4 54
Pergine, Valsugana, It.......A3 21
Perham, Aroostook, Maine..B4 96
Perham, Otter Tail, Minn....D3 99
Péribonca, Que., Can........A5 73
Périgueux, Fr..........E4 14
Perijá, mts., Ven..........B3 60
Perim, isl., P.D.R. of Yemen...C5 47
Peristérion, Grc..........*C4 23
Perkasie, Bucks, Pa.........F11 114
Perkins, Que., Can.........D2 73
Perkins, Jenkins, Ga.......D5 87
Perkins, Delta, Mich........C3 98
Perkins, Payne, Okla........B4 112
Perkins, co., Nebr..........D4 103
Perkins, co., S. Dak........B3 116
Perkinston, Stone, Miss.....E4 100
Perkinstown, Taylor, Wis....C3 124
Perkinsville, Windsor, Vt....E3 120
Perkiomen, creek, Pa........C2 106
Perla, Hot Spring, Ark....C3, g8 81
Perlas, is., Pan..........F8 62
Perlas, lagoon, Nic.........D6 62
Perleberg, G.D.R..........B5 16
Perley, Norman, Minn.......C2 99
Perlis, state, Mala..........I4 38
Perl-Mack, Adams, Colo.....*B6 83
Perm, Sov. Un.........D20 9
Perma, Sanders, Mont.......C2 102
Përmet, Alb..........B3 23
Pernambuco, state, Braz..C3, k6 57
Pernell, Garvin, Okla........C4 112
Pernik, Bul..........D6 22
Péronne, Fr..........C5 14
Perot, bayou, La..........k11 95
Perote, Bullock, Ala........D4 78
Perpignan, Fr..........F5 14
Perquimans, co., N.C.......A6 109
Perrégaux, Alg..........*B5 44
Perrin, Jack, Tex..........C3 118
Perrine, Dade, Fla......G6, s13 86
Perrineville, Monmouth, N.J.C4 106
Perris, Riverside, Calif.......F5 82
Perros-Guirec, Fr..........C2 14
Perrot, isl., Que., Can........q19 73
Perry, Perry, Ark..........B3 81
Perry, Taylor, Fla..........B3 86
Perry, Houston, Ga..........D3 87
Perry, Pike, Ill..........D3 90
Perry, Dallas, Iowa.........C3 92
Perry, Jefferson, Kans..C8, k15 93
Perry, Vermilion, La........E3 95
Perry, Washington, Maine...D5 96
Perry, Shiawassee, Mich.....F6 98
Perry, Ralls, Mo..........B6 101
Perry, Wyoming, N.Y.........C2 108
Perry, Lake, Ohio..........A4 111
Perry, Noble, Okla..........A4 112
Perry, Aiken, S.C..........D5 115
Perry, Box Elder, Utah......B3 119
Perry, co., Ala..........C2 78
Perry, co., Ark..........C3 81
Perry, co., Ill..........E4 90
Perry, co., Ind..........H4 91
Perry, co., Ky..........C6 94
Perry, co., Miss..........D4 100
Perry, co., Mo..........D8 101
Perry, co., Ohio..........C3 111
Perry, co., Pa..........F7 114
Perry, co., Tenn..........B4 117
Perry, peak, Mass..........B1 97
Perry, stream, N.H..........f7 105
Perrydale, Polk, Oreg...B3, h11 113
Perry Lake, res., Kans.......C8 93
Perryman, Harford, Md......B5 85
Perryopolis, Fayette, Pa.....*F2 114
Perry Point, Cecil, Md.......A5 85
Perrysburg, Cattaraugus, N.Y..........C1 108
Perrysburg, Wood, Ohio.A2, e6 111
Perry's Victory and International Peace Memorial, nat. mon., Ohio..........A2 111
Perrysville, Vermillion, Ind..D3 91
Perrysville, Ashland, Ohio...B3 111
Perrysville, Allegheny, Pa....h13 114
Perryton, Ochiltree, Tex.....A2 118
Perryvale, Alta., Can........B4 69
Perryville, Alsk..........D8 79
Perryville, Perry, Ark.......B3 81
Perryville, Boyle, Ky........C5 94
Perryville, Ouachita, La......B4 95
Perryville, Cecil, Md.........A5 85
Perryville, Perry, Mo........D8 101
Perryville, Washington, R.I..........D10 84
Perryville, Decatur, Tenn....B3 117
Persan, Fr..........E2 15
Persepolis, ruins, Iran.......G6 41
Pershing (East Germantown), Wayne, Ind..........E7 91
Pershing, Marion, Iowa......C5 92
Pershing, Gasconade, Mo....C6 101
Pershing, co., Nev..........C3 104
Persia, Harrison, Iowa......C2 92
Persia, see Iran, country, Asia
Persia, Hawkins, Tenn......C10 117
Persian, gulf, Asia..........J19 9
Persimmon Grove, Campbell, Ky..........k14 94
Person, co., N.C..........A3 109
Perstorp, Swe..........B7 24
Pertek, Tur..........C12 31
Perth, Austl..........F2 50
Perth, Ont., Can..........C8 72
Perth, Sumner, Kans........E6 93
Perth, Towner, N. Dak......A6 110
Perth, Scot..........D5 13
Perth, co., Ont., Can........D3 72
Perth Amboy, Middlesex, N.J..........B4, k7 106
Perth-Andover, N.B., Can....C2 74
Perthshire, Bolivar, Miss.....B3 100
Pertuis, Fr..........F6 14
Pertuis Breton, bay, Fr......D3 14
Peru, La Salle, Ill..........B4 90
Peru, Miami, Ind..........C5 91
Peru, Madison, Iowa........C4 92
Peru, Chautauqua, Kans.....E7 93
Peru, Berkshire, Mass.......B1 97
Peru, Nemaha, Nebr........D10 103
Peru, Clinton, N.Y.........f11 108
Peru, Bennington, Vt.......E3 120
Peru, country, S.A...E3 53, D3 58
Perugia, It..........C4 21
Peruque, St. Charles, Mo....f12 101
Peruvian Park, Salt Lake, Utah..........*C4 119
Péruwelz, Bel..........D3 15
Pervomaysk, Sov. Un........G8 27
Pervomaysk, Sov. Un........q21 27
Pervouralsk, Sov. Un........B5 29
Pesaro, It..........C4 21
Pescadero, San Mateo, Calif.D2 82
Pescara, It..........C5 21
Pescara, riv., It..........C4 21
Peschanyy, cape, Sov. Un....G19 9
Peschanyy, cape, Sov. Un....B10 37
Pesé, Pan..........G7 62
Peshastin, Chelan, Wash.....B5 122
Peshāwar, Pak..........B5 39
Peshkopi, Alb..........B3 23
Peshtera, Bul..........D7 22
Peshtigo, Martinette, Wis....C6 124
Peshtigo, riv., Wis.........C5 124
Peski, Sov. Un..........C7 29
Peski, Sov. Un..........F14 27
Peski, Sov. Un..........n18 27
Peski Muyun-Kum, des., Sov. Un..........C23 9
Peso da Régua, Port........B2 20
Pesotum, Champaign, Ill.....D5 90
Pesqueira, Braz.........C3, k5 57
Pest, co., Hung..........*B4 22
Petaca, Rio Arriba, N. Mex..........A3 107
Petah Tiqwa, Isr.......B6, g10 32
Petal, Forrest, Miss.........D4 100
Petaluma, Sonoma, Calif.....C2 82
Pétange, Lux..........E5 15
Petare, Ven..........*A4 60
Petatlán, Mex..........D4 63
Petauke, Zambia.........D5 48
Petawawa, Ont., Can........B7 72
Petawawa, riv., Ont., Can.....B6 72
Petenwell Lake, res., Wis......D4 124
Peter, isl., Vir. Is. (Br.)......B6 65
Peterborough, Austl........F2 51
Peterborough, Ont., Can.....C6 72
Peterborough, Eng..........B7 12
Peterborough (Peterboro), Hillsboro, N.H..........E3 105
Peterborough, co., Ont., Can..........C6 72
Peter I, isl., Ant..........C3 5
Petergof, see Petrodvorets, Sov. Un.
Peterhead, Scot..........C7 13
Peterman, Monroe, Ala......D2 78
Peter Pond, lake, Sask., Can....m7 70
Peters, creek, W. Va........m14 123
Peters, mtn., Va., W. Va.....D4 123
Peter's Arm, Newf., Can...*D3 75
Petersburg, Alsk.......D13, m23 79
Petersburg, Menard, Ill......C4 90
Petersburg, Pike, Ind........H3 91
Petersburg, Boone, Ky........h13 94
Petersburg, Monroe, Mich....G7 98
Petersburg, Boone, Nebr.....C7 103

Petersburg, Cape May, N.J. E3 106
Petersburg, Rensselaer, N.Y. C7 108
Petersburg, Nelson, N. Dak. A8 110
Petersburg, Mahoning, Ohio B5 111
Petersburg, Huntingdon, Pa. E5 114
Petersburg, Lincoln and Marshall, Tenn. B5 117
Petersburg, Hale, Tex. C2 118
Petersburg (Independent City), Va. C5, n18 121
Petersburg, Grant, W. Va. B5 123
Petersdorf, F.R.G. D5 24
Petersfield, Man., Can. D3 71
Petersfield, Eng. C7 12
Petersham, Worcester, Mass. B3 97
Peters Landing, Perry, Tenn. B4 117
Peterson, Clay, Iowa B2 92
Peterson, Fillmore, Minn. G7 99
Peterson, Morgan, Utah B4 119
Peterstown, Monroe, W. Va. D4 123
Petersville, Lewis, Ky. B6 94
Peter The Great, bay, Sov. Un. E5 37
Pétionville, Hai E7 64
Petit, lake, La k12 95
Petit Bois, isl., Miss g9 100
Petitcodiac, N.B., Can. D4 74
Petitcodiac, riv., N.B., Can. C5 74
Petit-de-Grat, N.S., Can. D9 74
Petite Amite, riv., La. h10 95
Petite-Rivière Bridge, N.S., Can. E5 74
Petite-Rivière-de-l'Artibonite, Hai E7 64
Petite-Rivière-de-l' Île, N.B., Can. B5 74
Petit-Étang, N.S., Can. C9 74
Petite-Vallée, Que., Can. *k14 73
Petit-Goâve, Hai E7 64
Petit Jean, creek, Ark B2 81
Petit Jean, mtn., Ark C2 81
Petit Jean, mtn., Ark B3 81
Petit Mécatina, isl., Que., Can. C2 75
Petit-Rocher, N.B., Can. B4 74
Petitsikapau, lake, Newf., Can. g8 75
Peto, Mex C7 63
Petorca, Chile A2 54
Petoskey, Emmet, Mich. C6 98
Petras, mtn., Ant B36 5
Petrey, Crenshaw, Ala. D3 78
Petrich, Bul E6 22
Petrified, forest, Miss C3 100
Petrified, forest, S. Dak D2 116
Petrified Forest, nat. park, Ariz. C6 80
Petrified Wood, park, S. Dak. B3 116
Petrikov, Sov. Un. E7 27
Petrinja, Yugo C3 22
Petrodvorets, Sov. Un. s30 25
Petrohué, Chile C2 54
Petrokrepost, Sov. Un. B8 27, s32 25
Petrolândia, Braz C3 57
Petroleum, Wells, Ind. C7 91
Petroleum, co., Mont. C8 102
Petrolia, Ont., Can. E2 72
Petrolia, Allen, Kans. E8 93
Petrolia, Butler, Pa. D2 114
Petrolia, Clay, Tex. B3 118
Petrolina, Braz C2 57
Petropavlovsk, Sov. Un. C7 29
Petropavlovskiy, Sov. Un. D3 29
Petropavlovsk [-Kamchatskiy], Sov. Un. D18 28
Petrópolis, Braz C4, h6 56
Petros, Morgan, Tenn. C9 117
Petroseni, Rom C6 22
Petrovgrad, see Zrenjanin, Yugo.
Petrovsk, Sov. Un. E15 27
Petrovskoye, Sov. Un. D2 29
Petrovsk-Zabaykalskiy, Sov. Un. D13 28
Petrozavodsk, Sov. Un. A10 27
Pettibone, Kidder, N. Dak. B6 110
Pettigoe, Ire C4 11
Pettigrew, Madison, Ark. B2 81
Pettis, co., Mo C4 101
Pettisville, Fulton, Ohio A1 111
Pettit, Washington, Miss. B2 100
Pettus, Lonoke, Ark. C4, k11 81
Pettus, Bee, Tex. E4 118
Petty Harbour, Newf., Can. E5 75
Petukhovo, Sov. Un. B7 29
Pevek, Sov. Un. C33 4
Pevely, Jefferson, Mo. g13 101
Pewamo, Ionia, Mich. E6 98
Pewaukee, Waukesha, Wis. E5, m11 124
Pewaukee, lake, Wis. m11 124
Pewee Valley, Oldham, Ky. B4, g12 94
Peyton, El Paso, Colo. B6 83
Pézenas, Fr F5 14
Pfaffenhofen, F.R.G. E6 17
Pfäffikon, Switz. B6 19
Pfarrkirchen, F.R.G. E7 17
Pfeifer, Ellis, Kans. D4 93
Pforzheim, F.R.G. E3 17
Pfunds, Aus C6 18
Pfungstadt, F.R.G. D3 17
Phair, Aroostook, Maine (part of Presque Isle) B5 96
Phalodi, India D4 40
Phaltan, India I5 40
Phangan, isl., Thai H4 38
Phan Rang, Viet. G8 38
Phan Thiet, Viet. G8 38
Pharoah, Okfuskee, Okla. B5 112
Pharr, Hidalgo, Tex. F3 118
Phatthalung, Thai I4 38
Pheba, Clay, Miss. B5 100
Phelps, Pike, Ky. C7 94
Phelps, Ontario, N.Y. C3 108
Phelps, Vilas, Wis. B4 124
Phelps, co., Mo. D6 101
Phelps, co., Nebr. D6 102
Phelps, lake, N.C. B6 109
Phelps City, Atchison, Mo. A2 101
Phenix, Charlotte, Va. C4 121
Phenix City, Russell, Ala. C4 78
Phet Buri, Thai F3 38
Phetchabun, Thai D4 38
Phichit, Thai D4 38
Philadelphia, Neshoba, Miss. C4 100
Philadelphia, Marion, Mo. B6 101
Philadelphia, Jefferson, N.Y. A5 108
Philadelphia, Philadelphia, Pa. G11, p21 114
Philadelphia, Loudon, Tenn. D9 117
Philadelphia, co., Pa. G11 114
Phil Campbell, Franklin, Ala. A2 78
Philip, Haakon, S. Dak. C4 116
Philipp, Tallahatchie, Miss. B3 100
Philippeville, see Skikda, Alg.
Philippeville, Bel D4 15
Philippi, Barbour, W. Va. B4 123
Philippi, glacier, Ant C21 5
Philippine, is., Phil B6 35
Philippine, sea, Phil A6 35
Philippine, trench, Phil C7 35
Philippines, country, Asia H15 33, B6 35
Philippolis, S. Afr D4 49
Philipsburg, Granite, Mont. D3 102
Philipsburg, Centre, Pa. E5 114
Philipsville, Ont., Can. C8 72
Philleo, lake, Wash h14 122
Phillip, isl., Austl I5 51
Phillippy, Lake, Tenn. A2 117
Phillips, Franklin, Maine D2 96
Phillips, Hamilton, Nebr. D7 103
Phillips, Coal, Okla C5 112
Phillips, Hutchinson, Tex. B2 118
Phillips, Price, Wis C3 124
Phillips, co., Ark C5 81
Phillips, co., Colo A8 83
Phillips, co., Kans C4 93
Phillips, co., Mont B8 102
Phillips, brook, N.H. A4 105
Phillips, isl., S.C G6 115
Phillipsburg, Que., Can. D4 73
Phillipsburg, Tift, Ga *E3 87
Phillipsburg, Phillips, Kans. C4 93
Phillipsburg, Laclede, Mo. D5 101
Phillipsburg, Warren, N.J. B2 106
Phillipsdale, Providence, R.I. (part of East Providence) B11 84
Phillipston, Worcester, Mass A3 97
Philmont, Columbia, N.Y. C7 108
Philo, Champaign, Ill D5 90
Philo, Muskingum, Ohio C4 111
Philomath, Benton, Oreg. C3 113
Philpott Lake, res., Va D2 121
Philrich, Hutchinson, Tex. *B2 118
Phippen, Sask., Can. E1 70
Phippsburg, Routt, Colo. A4 83
Phippsburg, Sagadahoc, Maine g8 96
Phitsanulok, Thai D4 38
Phlox, Langlade, Wis C4 124
Phnom Penh, Kam C2 39
Phocis (Fokis), prov., Grc. *C4 23
Phoenicia, Ulster, N.Y C6 108
Phoenix, Maricopa, Ariz. D3, m8 80
Phoenix, Cook, Ill k9 90
Phoenix, Baltimore, Md A4 85
Phoenix, Keweenaw, Mich. A2 98
Phoenix, Oswego, N.Y B4 108
Phoenix, Jackson, Oreg E4 113
Phoenix, is., Kir G11 7
Phoenixville, Windham, Conn B8 84
Phoenixville, Chester, Pa. F10, o20 114
Phong Saly, Laos B5 38
Phrae, Thai C4 38
Phthiotis (Fthiotis), prov., Grc *C4 23
Phuket, Thai I3 38
Phuket, isl., Thai I3 40
Phu Lai Leng, mtn., Laos C6 38
Phu Quoc, isl., Viet G6 38
Phutthaisong, Thai E5 38
Piaanu, pass, Truk 52
Piacenza, It B2 21, D5 18
Pialba, Austl B9 51
Pianosa, isl., It C3 21
Pianosa, isl., It C5 21
Piapot, Sask., Can. H1 70
Piaseczno, Pol m14 26
Piatra-Neamt, Rom B8 22
Piatt, co., Ill D5 90
Piauí, state, Braz C2 57
Piauí, mts., Braz C2 57
Piauí, riv., Braz C2 57
Piave, riv., It D8 18
Piazza Armerina, It F5 21
Pibor, riv., Sud D3 47
Pibor Post, Sud D3 47
Pibroch, Alta., Can B4 69
Picabo, Blaine, Idaho F4 89
Picacho, Pinal, Ariz E4 80
Picacho, Lincoln, N. Mex D4 107
Picard, Que., Can B8 73
Picardy (Picardie), former prov., Fr C5 14
Picayune, Pearl River, Miss. E4 100
Piccadilly, Newf., Can D2 75
Pic de Tibé, mtn., Guinea E3 45
Pic du Midi d'Ossau, mtn., Fr F3 14
Piceance, creek, Colo B2 83
Pichan, see Shanshan, China
Pichanal, Arg D3 55
Picher, Ottawa, Okla A7 112
Pichieh, China F6 36
Pichilemu, Chile A2 54
Pichincha, prov., Ec B2 58
Pickardville, Alta., Can B4 69
Pickaway, co., Ohio C2 111
Pick City, Mercer, N. Dak. B4 110
Pickens, Desha, Ark D4 81
Pickens, Holmes, Miss C4 100
Pickens, Pickens, S.C B2 115
Pickens, Randolph, W. Va C4 123
Pickens, co., Ala B1 78
Pickens, co., Ga B2 87
Pickens, co., S.C B2 115
Pickensville, Pickens, Ala B1 78
Pickerel, Ont., Can B4 72
Pickerel, Forest and Langlade, Wis C5 124
Pickerel, lake, Wis C4 124
Pickerel, riv., Ont., Can B4 72
Pickering, Ont., Can D5 72
Pickering, Eng F8 13
Pickering, Nodaway, Mo A3 101
Pickerington, Fairfield, Ohio C5, m11 111
Pickett, co., Tenn C8 117
Pickford, Chippewa and Mackinac, Mich B6 98
Pickle Crow, Ont., Can *E8 72
Pickleville, Rich, Utah B4 119
Pickrell, Gage, Nebr D9 103
Pickstown, Charles Mix, S. Dak E7 116
Pickwick, Winona, Minn G7 99
Pickwick Dam, Hardin, Tenn B3 117
Pickwick, lake, U.S A1 78
Pickworth, pt., Mass f12 97
Pico, isl., Port. (Azores) g8 44
Pico Rivera, Los Angeles, Calif n12 82
Picos, Braz C2 57
Pictograph Rocks, Ariz D1 80
Picton, Ont., Can D7 72
Picton, N.Z N15 51
Pictou, N.S., Can D7 74
Pictou, co., N.S., Can D7 74
Pictou, isl., N.S., Can D7 74
Pictou Landing, N.S., Can D7 74
Pic Touside, mtn., Chad A3 46
Picture, gorge, Oreg C7 113
Picture Butte, Alta., Can E4 69
Pictured Rocks, Ariz E4 80
Picture Rocks, Lycoming, Pa D8 114
Picuí, Braz h5 57
Picún-Leufú, Arg B3 54
Pidurutalagala, peak, Sri Lanka G7 39
Piedade, Braz m8 56
Piedmont, Calhoun, Ala B4 78
Piedmont, Alameda, Calif h8 82
Piedmont, Que., Can D3 73
Piedmont, Greenwood, Kans E7 93
Piedmont, Wayne, Mo D7 101
Piedmont, Canadian, Okla B4 112
Piedmont, Anderson and Greenville, S.C B3 115
Piedmont, Meade, S. Dak C2 116
Piedmont, Mineral, W. Va B5 123
Piedmont, reg., It B1 21
Piedmont, plat., U.S B1 109
Piedmont Lake, res., Ohio B4 111
Piedrabuena, Sp C3 20
Piedra Negra, pt., Mex D5 63
Piedras, pt., Arg B5 54
Piedras, riv., Pan k12 62
Piedras, riv., Peru D3 58
Piedras Blancas, pt., Calif E3 82
Piedras Negras, Guat B2 62
Piedras Negras, Mex B4 63
Piedra Sola, Ur E1 56
Piekietko, Pol k13 26
Pieksämäki, Fin F12 25
Piélagos, Sp A4 20
Pielinen, lake, Fin F13 25
Piemonte, pol. dist., It *B1 21
Piendamó, Col C2 60
Pienkaun, China E4 36
Pierce, Weld, Colo A6 83
Pierce, Polk, Fla E5 86
Pierce, Clearwater, Idaho C3 89
Pierce, Pierce, Nebr B8 103
Pierce, Obion, Tenn A3 117
Pierce, co., Ga E4 87
Pierce, co., Nebr B8 103
Pierce, co., N. Dak A5 110
Pierce, co., Wash C3 122
Pierce, co., Wis D1 124
Pierce, lake, Man., Can B5 71
Pierce, lake, Fla E5 86
Pierce, pond, Maine C2 96
Pierce Bridge, Grafton, N.H B3 105
Pierce City, Lawrence, Mo E3 101
Piercefield, St. Lawrence, N.Y A6, f10 108
Pierceland, Sask., Can *n7 70
Pierceton, Kosciusko, Ind B6 91
Pierceville, Finney, Kans E3 93
Piercy, Mendocino, Calif C2 82
Pieria, prov., Grc *B4 23
Piermont, Grafton, N.H C2 105
Piermont, mtn., N.H C2 105
Pierowall, Scot A6 13
Pierpont, Ashtabula, Ohio A5 111
Pierpont, Day, S. Dak B8 116
Pierre, Hughes, S. Dak C5 116
Pierre, bayou, Miss D3 100
Pierrefitte-sur-Aire, Fr F5 15
Pierrefitte [-sur-Seine], Fr g10 14
Pierrefonds, Que., Can q19 73
Pierreville, Que., Can C5 73
Pierron, Bond and Madison, Ill E4 100
Pierson, Man., Can E1 71
Pierson, Volusia, Fla C5 86
Pierson, Woodbury, Iowa B2 92
Pierz, Morrison, Minn E4 99
Piešťany, Czech D4 26
Pietermaritzburg, S. Afr C5 49
Pietersburg, S. Afr B4 49
Pie Town, Catron, N. Mex C1 107
Pietrasanta, It C3 21
Piet Retief, S. Afr C5 49
Pieve di Cadore, It A4 21
Pigeon, Huron, Mich E7 98
Pigeon, bay, Man., Can C3 71
Pigeon, creek, Ala D3 78
Pigeon, creek, Ind H3 91
Pigeon, lake, Alta., Can C3 69
Pigeon, mtn., Ga B1 87
Pigeon, mtn., N.Y B6 108
Pigeon, pt., U.S., Can h10 99
Pigeon, riv., Man., Can C3 71
Pigeon, riv., Ind A6 91
Pigeon, riv., Wis k10 124
Pigeon Cove, Essex, Mass A6 97
Pigeon Falls, Trempealeau, Wis D2 124
Pigeon Forge, Sevier, Tenn D10 117
Pigeon River, Cook, Minn k10 99
Pigg, riv., Va D3 121
Piggott, Clay, Ark A5 81
Pigüé, Arg B4 54
Piirai, isl., Eniwetok 52
Pijijiapan, Mex D6 63
Pike, Pike, Ark C2 81
Pike, Grafton, N.H B2 105
Pike, Wyoming, N.Y C2 108
Pike, Yamhill, Oreg B1 113
Pike, co., Ala D4 78
Pike, co., Ark C2 81
Pike, co., Ga C2 87
Pike, co., Ill D3 90
Pike, co., Ind H3 91
Pike, co., Ky C7 94
Pike, co., Miss D3 100
Pike, co., Mo B6 101
Pike, co., Ohio C2 111
Pike, co., Pa D11 114
Pike, riv., Wis C5 124
Pike Lake, St. Louis, Minn D6 99
Pike Road, Beaufort, N.C B6 109
Pikes, beach, N.Y G6 84
Pikes, peak, Colo C5 83
Pikes Rocks, mts., Pa C3 114
Pikesville, Baltimore, Md B4, g10 85
Piketberg, S. Afr D2 49
Piketon, Pike, Ohio C2 111
Pikeview, El Paso, Colo C6 83
Pikeville, Pike, Ky C7 94
Pikeville, Wayne, N.C B5 109
Pikeville, Bledsoe, Tenn D8 117
Pikwitonei, Man., Can B3 71
Piła, Pol B4 26
Pilar, Braz C3, k6 57
Pilar, Taos, N. Mex A4 107
Pilar, Par E4 55
Pilar de Goiás, Braz A3 56
Pilar [do Sul], Braz m8 56
Pilatus, peak, Switz C5 19
Pilcomayo, riv., Par D3 55
Pilger, Sask., Can E3 70
Pilger, Stanton, Nebr B8 103
Pilgrim Gardens, Delaware, Pa *B11 114
Pilgrims Knob, Buchanan, Va e10 121
Pilibhit, India C7 40
Pilica, riv., Pol C5 26
Pillager, Cass, Minn D4 99
Pillar, pt., Calif k7 82
Pillaro, Ec B2 58
Pillau, see Baltiysk, Sov. Un.
Pilley's Island, Newf., Can D4 75
Pillow (Uniontown), Dauphin, Pa E8 114
Pillsbury, Barnes, N. Dak B8 110
Pilos, Grc D3 23
Pilot, peak, Nev B7 104
Pilot, range, N.H A4 105
Pilot Butte, Sask., Can G3 70
Pilot Grove, Cooper, Mo C5 101
Pilot Knob, Iron, Mo D7 101
Pilot Knob, mtn., Ark B2 81
Pilot Knob, mtn., Ark C1 81
Pilot Knob, mtn., Idaho D3 89
Pilot Knob, mtn., Mo E4 101
Pilot Knob, ridge, Kans B8 93
Pilot Mound, Man., Can E2 71
Pilot Mound, Boone, Iowa B3 92
Pilot Mountain, Surry, N.C A2 109
Pilot Point, Alsk D8 79
Pilot Point, Denton, Tex C4 118
Pilot Rock, Umatilla, Oreg B8 113
Pilot Station, Alsk C7 79
Pilottown, Plaquemines, La E6 95
Pilsen, Kewaunee, Wis h10 124
Pilvo, Sov. Un A11 37
Pima, Graham, Ariz E6 80
Pima, co., Ariz E3 80
Pimba, Austl F6 50
Pimmit Hills, Fairfax, Va g12 121
Pimple, hill, Pa A2 106
Piña, Pan k10 62
Pinal, co., Ariz E4 80
Pinal, mts., Ariz D5 80
Pinang, see George Town, Mala.
Pinarbasi, Tur C11 31
Pinar del Río, Cuba C2 64
Pinar del Río, prov., Cuba C2 64
Pinardville, Hillsboro, N.H *E4 105
Pinas, Arg A3 54
Pincher Creek, Alta., Can E4 69
Pincher Station, Alta., Can E4 69
Pinckard, Dale, Ala D4 78
Pinckney, Crittenden, Ark f8 117
Pinckney, Livingston, Mich F7 98
Pinckney, isl., S.C G6 115
Pinckneyville, Perry, Ill E4 90
Pinckneyville, Wilkinson, Miss D2 100
Pinconning, Bay, Mich E7 98
Pinczow, Pol C6 26
Pindall, Searcy, Ark A3 81
Pindamonhangaba, Braz C3 56
Pindaré, riv., Braz B1 57
Pindus, mts., Grc C3 23
Pine, Gila, Ariz C4 80
Pine, Jefferson, Colo B5 83
Pine, Washington, La D5 95
Pine, co., Minn D6 99
Pine, creek, Alta., Can B4 69
Pine, creek, Nev C5 104
Pine, creek, Pa D7 114
Pine, creek, Wash B8 122
Pine, hill, Conn C4 84
Pine, key, Fla p10 86
Pine, lake, Ind A4 91
Pine, lake, Minn D3 99
Pine, lake, Wis C4 124
Pine, mtn., Conn B5 84
Pine, mtn., Ga D2 87
Pine, mtn., Ky., Tenn C9 117
Pine, mtn., Okla C6 112
Pine, mtn., Oreg D6 113
Pine, pt., Fla C3 86
Pine, ridge, Nebr B2 103
Pine, riv., B.C., Can B6 68
Pine, riv., Man., Can D1 71
Pine, riv., Mich D7 98
Pine, riv., N.H C4 105
Pine, riv., Wis C4 124
Pine Apple, Wilcox, Ala D3 78
Pine Bank, Greene, Pa G1 114
Pine Beach, Ocean, N.J *D4 106
Pine Bluff, Jefferson, Ark C3 81
Pinebluff, Moore, N.C B3 109
Pinebluff, lake, Sask., Can C4 70
Pine Bluffs, Laramie, Wyo E8 125
Pine Bluff Southeast, Jefferson, Ark *C4 81
Pinebur, Marion, Miss D4 100
Pine Bush, Orange, N.Y D6 108
Pine Castle, Orange, Fla D5 86
Pine City, Monroe, Ark C4 81
Pine City, Pine, Minn E6 99
Pine City, Whitman, Wash B8 122
Pine Creek, Austl B5 50
Pine Creek, gorge, Pa C7 114
Pinecrest, Tuolume, Calif C4 82
Pinecroft, Spokane, Wash D8 122
Pinedale, Navajo, Ariz C5 80
Pinedale, Sublette, Wyo D3 125
Pine Falls, Man., Can D3 71
Pine Forest, mts., Nev B3 104
Pinega, Sov. Un C17 9
Pine Grove, Appling, Ga E4 87
Pine Grove, St. Helena, La D5 95
Pine Grove, Burlington, N.J D3 106
Pine Grove, Schuylkill, Pa E9 114
Pine Grove, Wetzel, W. Va B4, h9 123
Pine Grove, Brown, Wis A6 124
Pine Grove Mills, Centre, Pa E6 114
Pine Hall, Stokes, N.C A2 109
Pine Hill, Wilcox, Ala D2 78
Pine Hill, Austl A6 51
Pine Hill, Rockcastle, Ky C5 94
Pine Hill, Camden, N.J D3 106
Pine Hills, Orange, Fla D5 86
Pinehouse, lake, Sask., Can B2 70
Pinehouse Lake, Sask., Can B2 70
Pinehurst, Dooly, Ga D3 87
Pinehurst, Shoshone, Idaho B2 89
Pinehurst, Middlesex, Mass f11 97
Pinehurst, Atlantic, N.J E3 106
Pinehurst, Moore, N.C B3 109
Pinehurst, Orange, Tex *D6 118
Pinehurst, Snohomish, Wash B3 122
Pinehurst, lake, Alta., Can B5 69
Pine Island, Goodhue, Minn F6 99
Pine Island, Orange, N.Y D6 108
Pine Island, bay, Ant B2 5
Pine Island, sound, Fla F4 86
Pine Knot, McCreary, Ky D5 94
Pine Lake, De Kalb, Ga h8 88
Pinelake, La Porte, Ind *A4 91
Pine Lake, Middlesex, Mass g10 97
Pineland, Jasper, S.C F5 115
Pineland, Sabine, Tex D6 118
Pine Lawn, St. Louis, Mo f13 101
Pine Level, Montgomery, Ala C3 78
Pine Level, Johnston, N.C B4 109
Pinellas, co., Fla E4 86
Pinellas, pt., Fla p10 86
Pinellas Park, Pinellas, Fla E4, p10 86
Pine Meadow, Litchfield, Conn B5 84
Pine Mountain, Harris, Ga D2 87
Pineora, Effingham, Ga D5 87
Pine Orchard, New Haven, Conn D5 84
Pine Park, Grady, Ga F2 87
Pine Plains, Dutchess, N.Y F7 108
Pine Point, N.W. Ter., Can D10 66
Pine Point, Cumberland, Maine E2, g7 96
Pine Prairie, Evangeline, La D3 95
Piner, bay, Ant C27 5
Pine Rest, Middlesex, Mass g10 97
Pine Ridge, Montgomery, Ark C2 81
Pine Ridge, Adams, Miss D2 100
Pine Ridge, Shannon, S. Dak D3 116
Pine Ridge, Indian res., S. Dak D3 116
Pine River, Man., Can D1 71
Pine River, Cass, Minn D4 99
Pinerolo, It B1 21
Pines, see Juventud, isl., Cuba
Pinesdale, Ravalli, Mont D2 102
Pinetop, Navajo, Ariz C6 80
Pinetops, Edgecombe, N.C B5 109
Pinetown, Beaufort, N.C B6 109
Pinetta, Madison, Fla B6 86
Pine Valley, San Diego, Calif F5 82
Pine Valley, Hillsboro, N.H E3 105
Pine Valley, LeFlore, Okla C7 112
Pine Valley, Washington, Utah F2 119
Pine Valley, mts., Utah F2 119
Pineview, Wilcox, Ga D3 87
Pine Village, Warren, Ind D3 91
Pineville, Bell, Ky D6 94
Pineville, Rapides, La C3 95
Pineville, Smith, Miss C4 100
Pineville, McDonald, Mo E3 101
Pineville, Mecklenburg, N.C B2 109
Pineville, Berkeley, S.C E2 115
Pineville, Wyoming, W. Va D3 123
Pinewald, Ocean, N.J D4 106
Pinewater, range, Nev G6 104
Pinewood, Beltrami, Minn C3 99
Pinewood, Sumter, S.C D7 115
Piney, Man., Can E4 71
Piney, creek, W. Va n13 123
Piney, fork, W. Va h9 123
Piney, pt. Fla C3 86
Piney Flats, Sullivan, Tenn C11 117
Piney Fork, Jefferson, Ohio B5 111
Piney Point, Manatee, Fla F2 86
Piney Point, Harris, Tex *E5 118
Piney Swamp Knob, mtn., W. Va B5 123
Piney View, Raleigh, W. Va n13 123
Piney Woods, Rankin, Miss C3 100
Pingchiang, China J5 36
Pingchuan, China D8 36
Pinghsiang, China K5 36
Pingliang, China G2 36
Pinglo, China G7 38
Pinglo, China E2 36
Pingnan, China G7 34
Pingree, Bingham, Idaho F6 89
Pingree, Stutsman, N. Dak B7 110
Pingting, China F5 36
Pingtingshan, China H5 36
Pingtu, China F8 36
Pingtung, Taiwan *G9 35
Pingwu, China E5 34
Pinhai, China E8 34
Pinhal, Braz C3, m8 56
Pinhal Novo, Port f10 20
Pinhead, buttes, Oreg C5 113
Pinheiro, Braz B1 57
Pinhel, Port B2 20
Pinhsien, China E1 35
Pinios, riv., Grc C4 23
Pink, cliffs, Utah F3 119
Pinkham, Sask., Can F1 70
Pink Hill, Lenoir, N.C B5 109
Pinkney (South Gastonia), Gaston, N.C *B1 109
Pinkstaff, Lawrence, Ill E6 90
Pinnacle, Pulaski, Ark C3, h10 81
Pinnacle, Stokes, N.C A2 109
Pinnacle, buttes, Wyo C3 125
Pinnacle, The, mtn., Conn B5 84
Pinnacle, mtn., Mo B7 101
Pinnacle, mtn., N.Y B6 108
Pinnacle, peaks, B.C., Can D1 69
Pinnacles, nat. mon., Calif D3 82
Pinnaroo, Austl G7 51
Pinneberg, F.R.G E3 24
Pinnebog, Huron, Mich E7 98
Pinó Hachado, pass, Arg B2 54
Pinola, Simpson, Miss D4 100
Pinole, Contra Costa, Calif h8 82
Pinon, Navajo, Ariz A5 80
Pinon, Fr E3 15
Pinon, Otero, N. Mex E4 107
Pinopolis, Berkeley, S.C E7 115
Pinopolis, dam, S.C E8 115
Pinos, Mex C4 63
Pinos, mtn., Calif E4 82
Pinos, pt., Calif D3 82
Pinos Altos, Grant, N. Mex E1 107
Pinoso, Sp C5 20
Pinos-Puente, Sp D4 20
Pinotpandian, Phil o13 35
Pinsk, Sov. Un E6 27
Pinsk, marshes, Sov. Un E6 27
Pinson, Jefferson, Ala f7 78
Pinson, Madison, Tenn B3 117
Pinta, isl., Ec f5 58
Pintados, Chile D2 55
Pintendre, Que., Can n17 73
Pinto, Allegany, Md D2 85
Pinto, Sp p17 20
Pinto, butte, Sask., Can H2 70
Pinto, creek, Sask., Can H2 70
Pintura, Washington, Utah F2 119
Pinware, riv., Newf., Can C3 75
Pinyon, peak, Idaho E4 89
Pinzolo, It C6 18
Pinzón, isl., Ec g5 58
Pioche, Lincoln, Nev F7 104
Piombino, It C3 21
Pioneer, Humboldt, Iowa B3 92
Pioneer, West Carroll, La B4 95
Pioneer, Williams, Ohio A1 111
Pioneer, mts., Idaho F5 89
Pioneer, mts., Mont E3 102
Pioneer Mine, B.C., Can D6 68
Pioneer, isl., Sov. Un B11 29
Piopolis, Que., Can D7 73
Piotrków [Trybunalski], Pol C5 26
Piove di Sacco, It D8 18
Pipe, Fond du Lac, Wis k9 124
Pipe, creek, Ind D6 91
Pipe, creek, Ohio g8 123
Piper, Bibb, Ala B2 78
Piper, Wyandotte, Kans k16 93
Piper City, Ford, Ill C5 90
Piperi, isl., Grc C5 23
Piperville, Ont., Can h12 72
Pipe Spring, nat. mon., Ariz A3 80
Pipestem, Summers, W. Va D4 123
Pipestem, creek, N. Dak B6 110
Pipestone, Man., Can E1 71
Pipestone, Pipestone, Minn G2 99
Pipestone, co., Minn F2 99
Pipestone, creek, Man., Can E1 71
Pipestone, creek, Sask., Can G5 70
Pipestone, nat. mon., Minn G2 99
Pipestone, pass, Mont E4 102
Pipmuacan, res., Que., Can k12 73
Piqua, Woodson, Kans E8 93
Piqua, Miami, Ohio B1 111
Piracanjuba, Braz E1 57
Piracicaba, Braz C3, m8 56
Piracicaba, riv., Braz m8 56
Piraçununga, Braz C3, k8 56
Piracuruca, Braz B2 57
Piraievs (Piraeus), Grc D4, h11 23
Pirajú, Braz C3 56
Pirajuí, Braz C3 56
Piramida, mtn., Sov. Un D12 28
Piran, Yugo B4 21
Pirané, Arg E4 55
Piranga, Braz F2 57
Piranhas, Braz C3 57
Pirapóra, Braz E2 57
Pireway, Columbus, N.C C4 109
Pirgos, Grc D3 23
Piriápolis, Ur E1 56
Pirin, mts., Bul E6 22
Piripiri, Braz B2 57
Pirmasens, F.R.G D2 17
Pirna, G.D.R C8 17
Pirot, Yugo D6 22
Pirovskoye, Sov. Un D27 9
Pirtleville, Cochise, Ariz F6 80
Piru, Indon F7 35
Piryatin, Sov. Un F9 27
Pis, isl., Truk 52
Pisa, It C3 21
Pisagua, Chile C1 55
Piscataqua, riv., N.H., Maine D5 105
Piscataquis, co., Maine C3 96
Piscataquis, riv., Maine C4 96
Piscataquog, riv., N.H D3 105
Piscataway, Middlesex, N.J B4 106
Piscataway, creek, Md C4 85
Pisciotta, It D5 21
Pisco, Peru D2 58
Piseco, lake, N.Y B6 108
Písek, Czech D3 26
Pisek, Walsh, N. Dak A8 110
Pisgah, Jackson, Ala A4 78
Pisgah, Harrison, Iowa C2 92
Pisgah, Charles, Md C3 85
Pisgah, mtn., Vt F3 120
Pisgah, mtn., Wyo C8 125
Pisgah Forest, Transylvania, N.C f10 109
Pishin, Pak F13 41
Pishin Lora, riv., Pak C4 39
Pishukan, cape, Pak I11 41
Pisia, riv., Pol m12 26
Pisinimo, Pima, Ariz E3 80
Pismo Beach, San Luis Obispo, Calif E3 82
Pisogne, It D6 18
Pissis, mtn., Arg E2 55
Pistal River, Curry, Oreg E2 113
Pisticci, It D6 21
Pistoia, It C3 21
Pistolet, bay, Newf., Can C4 75
Pisuerga, riv., Sp A3 20
Pisz, Pol B6 26
Pita, Guinea D2 45
Pitalito, Col C2 60
Pitangui, Braz E2 57
Pitcairn, Allegheny, Pa k14 114
Pitcairn, Br. dep., Oceania H14 7
Piteå, Swe E9 25
Piteälven, riv., Swe E9 25
Pitești, Rom C7 22
Pithiviers, Fr C5 14
Piti, Guam 52
Pitkin, Gunnison, Colo C4 83
Pitkin, Vernon, La D3 95
Pitkin, co., Colo B4 83
Pitlochry, Scot D5 13
Pitman, Gloucester, N.J D2 106
Pitons du Carbet, peaks, Mart S10 65
Pitrufquén, Chile B2 54
Pitsburg, Darke, Ohio C1 111
Pitt, Lake of the Woods, Minn B4 99
Pitt, co., N.C B5 109
Pitt, isl., B.C., Can C3 68
Pittenweem, Scot *D6 13
Pittman Center, Sevier, Tenn D10 117
Pitts, Wilcox, Ga E3 87
Pittsboro, Hendricks, Ind E5 91
Pittsboro, Calhoun, Miss B4 100
Pittsboro, Chatham, N.C B3 109
Pittsburg, Contra Costa, Calif g9 82
Pittsburg, Williamson, Ill F5 90
Pittsburg, Carroll, Ind C4 91
Pittsburg, Crawford, Kans E9 93
Pittsburg, Laurel, Ky C5 94
Pittsburg, Coos, N.H f7 105
Pittsburg, Pittsburg, Okla C6 112
Pittsburg, Camp, Tex C5 118
Pittsburg, co., Okla C6 112
Pittsburgh, Allegheny, Pa F1, k13 114
Pittsfield, Pike, Ill D3 90
Pittsfield, Somerset, Maine D3 96
Pittsfield, Berkshire, Mass B1 97
Pittsfield, Washtenaw, Mich *F7 98
Pittsfield, Merrimack, N.H D4 105
Pittsfield, Warren, Pa C3 114
Pittsfield, Rutland, Vt D3 120
Pittsford, Hillsdale, Mich G6 98
Pittsford, Rutland, Vt D2 120
Pittsford Mills, Rutland, Vt D2 120
Pittston, Luzerne, Pa D10, n17 114
Pittstown, Hunterdon, N.J B3 106
Pittsview, Russell, Ala C4 78
Pittsville, Wicomico, Md D7 85
Pittsville, Johnson, Mo C4 101
Pittsville, Wood, Wis D3 124
Pittsylvania, co., Va D3 121
Pitzuwo, China E10 36
Piuka, Jap D19 37
Piura, Peru C1 58
Piura, dept., Peru C1 58
Piute, co., Utah E3 119
Piute, res., Utah E3 119
Piuthān, Nep C9 40
Piva, riv., Yugo D4 21
Pixley, Tulare, Calif E4 82
Piyang, China H5 36
Pizzo, It E6 21

Port-Cartier-Ouest, Que., Can k13 73
Port Chalmers, N.Z P13 51
Port Charlotte, Charlotte, Fla F4 86
Port Chester, Westchester, N.Y E7, n15 108
Port Clements, B.C., Can C1 68
Port Clinton, Ottawa, Ohio A3 111
Port Clyde, N.S., Can F4 74
Port Clyde, Knox, Maine E3 96
Port Colborne, Ont., Can E5 72
Port Colden, Warren, N.J B3 106
Port Coquitlam, B.C., Can E6, f13 68
Port Credit, Ont., Can D5, m14 72
Port-Daniel, Que., Can A5 74
Port-de-Bouc, Fr F6 14
Port de Kindu, Zaire B4 48
Port-de-Paix, Hai E7 64
Port Deposit, Cecil, Md A5 85
Port Dickinson, Broome, N.Y C5 108
Port Dickson, Mala K4 38
Port Discovery, Jefferson, Wash A3 122
Port Douglas, Austl C8 50
Port Dover, Ont., Can E4 72
Port Eads, Plaquemines, La E6 95
Port Edward, B.C., Can B2 68
Port Edwards, Wood, Wis D4 124
Portel, Braz C4 59
Port Elgin, N.B., Can C5 74
Port Elgin, Ont., Can C3 72
Port Elizabeth, Cumberland, N.J E3 106
Port Elizabeth, S. Afr D4 49
Port Ellen, Scot E2 13
Porteña, Arg A4 54
Porter, Jefferson, Ala B3, f6 78
Porter, Porter, Ind A3 91
Porter, Yellow Medicine, Minn F2 98
Porter, Wagoner, Okla B6 112
Porter, Montgomery, Tex D5 118
Porter, Grays Harbor, Wash C2 122
Porter, co., Ind B3 91
Porter, lake, Sask., Can A2 70
Porter Corners, Saratoga, N.Y B7 108
Porterdale, Newton, Ga C3 87
Port Erin, I. of Man F4 13
Portersville, Butler, Pa E1 114
Porterville, Tulare, Calif D4 82
Porterville, Kemper, Miss C5 100
Porterville West (Burton), Tulare, Calif *D4 82
Port Essington, B.C., Can B3 68
Port Ewen, Ulster, N.Y D7 108
Port Fairy, Austl I4 51
Port Fouad (Port Fuad) (Būr Fu'ād), Eg C4 32
Port-Francqui, see Ilebo, Zaire
Port Fuad (Port Fouad) (Būr Fu'ād), Eg C4 32
Port Gamble, Kitsap, Wash B3 122
Port Gamble, Indian res., Wash B3 122
Port-Gentil, Gabon F1 46
Port George, N.S., Can D4 74
Port Gibson, Claiborne, Miss D3 100
Port Glasgow, Scot E4 13
Portglenone, N. Ire C5 11
Port Graham, Alsk D9, h16 79
Port Greville, N.S., Can D5 74
Port Hammond, B.C., Can f13 68
Port Harcourt, Nig F6 45
Port Hardy, B.C., Can D4 68
Port Hastings, N.S., Can D8 74
Port Hawkesbury, N.S., Can D8 74
Porthcawl, Wales C4 12
Port Hedland, Austl D2 50
Port Heiden, Alsk D8 79
Port Henry, Essex, N.Y A7 108
Port Hill, P.E.I., Can C6 74
Port Homer, Jefferson, Ohio e8 123
Port Hood, N.S., Can C8 74
Port Hope, Ont., Can D6 72
Port Hope, Huron, Mich E8 98
Port Hope Simpson, Newf., Can B3 75
Port Hueneme, Ventura, Calif E4 82
Port Huron, St. Clair, Mich F8 98
Portia, Lawrence, Ark A4 81
Portici, It *D5 21
Portimão, Port D1 20
Portis, Osborne, Kans C5 93
Port Isabel, Cameron, Tex F4 118
Port Jackson, bay, Austl F8 51
Port Jefferson, Suffolk, N.Y n15 108
Port Jefferson, Shelby, Ohio B1 111
Port Jefferson Station, Suffolk, N.Y *n15 108
Port Jervis, Orange, N.Y D6 108
Port Kent, Essex, N.Y f11 108
Portland, Ashley, Ark D4 81
Portland, Austl I3 51
Portland, Ont., Can C8 72
Portland, Fremont, Colo C5 83
Portland, Middlesex, Conn C6 84
Portland, Eng *D5 12
Portland, Walton, Fla u15 86
Portland, Jay, Ind D8 91
Portland, Cumberland, Maine E2, g7 96
Portland, Ionia, Mich F6 98
Portland, Callaway, Mo C6 101
Portland, Chautauqua, N.Y C1 108
Portland, Traill, N. Dak B8 110
Portland, Meigs, Ohio C4 111
Portland, Multnomah, Oreg B4, g12 113
Portland, Northampton, Pa E11 114
Portland, Sumner, Tenn A5 117
Portland, San Patricio, Tex F4 118
Portland, bight, Jam F14 65
Portland, canal, Alsk n24 79
Portland, canal, B.C., Can B2 68
Portland, inlet, B.C., Can B2 68
Portland, pt., Jam F14 65
Portland Creek, pond, Newf., Can C3 75
Portland Mills, Elk, Pa D4 114
Portlandville, Otsego, N.Y C6 108
Portlaoighise, Ire D4 11
Port Lavaca, Calhoun, Tex E4 118
Portlaw, Ire E4 11
Port Leyden, Lewis, N.Y B5 108
Port Lincoln, Austl F6 50
Port Lions, Alsk D9 79
Port Loko, S.L E2 45
Port Loring, Ont., Can B4 72
Port-Louis, Fr D2 14
Port-Louis, Guad Q8 65
Port Louis, Mauritius H24 3
Port Ludlow, Jefferson, Wash B3 122
Port McNicoll, Ont., Can C5 72
Port Macquarie, Austl E9 51
Portmadoc, Wales B3 12
Portmagee, Ire F1 11
Portmahomack, Scot C5 13
Port Mahon, Kent, Del B7 85
Port Maitland, N.S., Can F3 74
Port Maitland, Ont., Can E5 72
Port Maria, Jam E15 65
Port Matilda, Centre, Pa E5 114
Port Mayaca, Martin, Fla F6 86
Port Medway, N.S., Can E5 74
Port Mellon, B.C., Can E6 68
Port-Menier, Que., Can k8 75
Port Moller, Alsk D7 79
Port Monmouth, Monmouth, N.J C4 106
Port Morant, Jam F16 65
Port Moresby, Pap. N. Gui k12 50
Port Morien, N.S., Can C10 74
Port Morris, Morris, N.J B3 106
Port Mouton, N.S., Can F5 74
Port Murray, Warren, N.J B3 106
Port Musgrave, bay, Austl B7 50
Portnahaven, Scot E2 13
Port Neches, Jefferson, Tex E6 118
Port Nelson, Man., Can A5, f9 71
Portneuf, Que., Can C6 73
Portneuf, co., Que., Can C5 73
Portneuf, prov. park, Que., Can B5 73
Portneuf-sur-Mer, Que., Can A8 73
Port Nolloth, S. Afr C2 49
Portnoo, Ire C3 11
Port Norris, Cumberland, N.J E2 106
Port-Noveau-Québec, Que., Can f8 75
Pôrto (Oporto), Port B1 20
Pôrto Alegre, Braz E2 56
Pôrto Alexandre, Ang E1 48
Pôrto Amboim, Ang D1 48
Pôrto Amélia, Moz D7 48
Portobelo, Pan F8, h11 62
Pôrto Calvo, Braz C3, k6 57
Port O'Connor, Calhoun, Tex E4 118
Pôrto de Mós, Port C1 20
Pôrto de Moz, Braz C4 59
Pôrto Esperanca, Braz B1 56
Pôrto Feliz, Braz C3, m8 56
Portoferraio, It C3 21
Portofino, It B2 21
Port of Ness, Scot B2 13
Port of Spain, Trin N22 65
Porto Garibaldi, It E8 18
Portogruaro, It B4 21
Pôrto Guaíra, Braz C2 56
Portola, Plumas, Calif C3 82
Portomaggiore, It B3 21
Pôrto Mendes, Braz C2 56
Pôrto Murtinho, Braz D4 55
Pôrto Nacional, Braz D1 57
Porto-Novo, Benin E5 45
Port Orange, Volusia, Fla C6 86
Port Orchard, Kitsap, Wash B3, e10 122
Port Orford, Curry, Oreg E2 113
Porto Santo, isl., Port. (Madeira Is.) C1 44
Portoscuso, It E2 21
Pôrto Seguro, Braz E3 56
Porto Torres, It D2 21
Pôrto União, Braz D2 56
Porto-Vecchio, Fr D2 21
Pôrto Velho, Braz D2 59
Portoviejo, Ec B1 58
Portpatrick, Scot F3 13
Port Penn, New Castle, Del A6 85
Port Perry, Ont., Can C5 72
Port Phillip, bay, Austl G7 50
Port Pirie, Austl F1 51
Port Radium, N.W., Ter., Can C9 66
Port Reading, Middlesex, N.J k8 106
Portree, Scot C2 13
Portreeve, Sask., Can G1 70
Port Renfrew, B.C., Can E5 68
Port Republic, Atlantic, N.J D4 106
Port Republic, Rockingham, Va B4 121
Port Rexton, Newf., Can D5 75
Port Richey, Pasco, Fla D4 86
Port Rowan, Ont., Can E4 72
Port Royal, Henry, Ky B4 94
Port Royal, Juniata, Pa E7 114
Port Royal, Beaufort, S.C G6 115
Port Royal, Montgomery, Tenn A4 117
Port Royal, Caroline, Va B5 121
Port Royal, isl., S.C G6 115
Port Royal, sound, S.C G7 115
Portrush, N. Ire B5 11
Port Said (Būr Sa'īd), Eg C4 32
Port St. Joe, Gulf, Fla C1, v16 86
Port St. Johns, S. Afr D4 49
Port-St. Louis [-du-Rhône], Fr F6 14
Port Salerno, Martin, Fla E6 86
Portsalon, Ire B4 11
Port Sanilac, Sanilac, Mich E8 98
Port Saunders, Newf., Can C3, h10 75
Port Sewall, Martin, Fla E6 86
Port Shepstone, S. Afr D5 49
Port Simpson, B.C., Can B2 68
Portsmouth, Dominica I14 64
Portsmouth, Eng D6 12
Portsmouth, Shelby, Iowa C2 92
Portsmouth, Rockingham, N.H D5 105
Portsmouth, Scioto, Ohio D2 111
Portsmouth, Newport, R.I C12 84
Portsmouth (Independent City), Va D6, k15 121
Portsoy, Scot C6 13
Port Stanley, Ont., Can E3 72
Port Stanley (Stanley), Falk Is I5 53
Port Stephens, bay, Austl F9 52
Port Sudan (Būr Sūdān), Sud B4 47
Port Sulphur, Plaquemines, La E6 95
Port-sur-Saône, Fr B2 18
Port Sydney, Ont., Can B2 72
Port Talbot, Wales C4 12
Porttipahdan, res., Fin C11 25
Port Tobacco, Charles, Md C3 85
Port Townsend, Jefferson, Wash A3 122
Portugal, country, Eur H7 8, C1 20
Portugal Cove, Newf., Can *E5 75
Portugal Cove South, Newf., Can E5 75
Portugalete, Sp A4 20
Portugália, Ang C3 48
Portuguesa, riv., Ven B4 60
Portuguesa, state, Ven B4 60
Portuguese Guinea, see Guinea-Bissau, country, Afr.
Portuguese India, see Goa, Damān and Diu, ter., India
Portumna, Ire D3 11
Port Union, Newf., Can D5 75
Port Union, Butler, Ohio n13 111
Port-Vendres, Fr F5 14
Portville, Cattaraugus, N.Y C2 108
Port Vincent, Livingston, La D5, h10 95
Port Vue, Allegheny, Pa *F2 114
Port Wakefield, Austl G2 52
Port Washington, Nassau, N.Y h13 108
Port Washington, Tuscarawas, Ohio B4 111
Port Washington, Ozaukee, Wis E6 124
Port Wentworth, Chatham, Ga D5 87
Port William, Clinton, Ohio C2 111
Port William, Scot F4 13
Port Wing, Bayfield, Wis B2 124
Porum, Muskogee, Okla B6 112
Porvenir, Chile h11 54
Porvenir, Presidio, Tex F2 118
Porz, F.R.G C2 17
Posadas, Arg E4 55
Posadas, Sp D3 20
Poschiavo, Switz D9 19
Posen, Cook, Ill k9 90
Posen, Presque Isle, Mich C7 98
Posen, see Poznań, Pol.
Posey, co., Ind H2 91
Poseyville, Posey, Ind H2 91
Poshan, China F8 36
Poshekhonye-Volodarsk, Sov. Un B12 27
Poso, Indon F6 35
Poso, lake, Indon F6 35
Posse, Braz D1 57
Pössneck, G.D.R C6 17
Possuteng, lake, China C2 24
Post, Crook, Oreg C6 113
Post, Garza, Tex C2 118
Poste-de-la-Baleine, Que., Can g11 73
Poste-Mistassini, Que., Can h12 73
Post Falls, Kootenai, Idaho B2 89
Postmasburg, S. Afr C3 49
Post Maurice Cortier, Alg E5 44
Post Mills, Orange, Vt D4 120
Postojna, Yugo C2 22
Poston, Florence, S.C D9 115
Postville, Allamakee, Iowa A6 92
Potaro Landing, Guy A3 60
Potato Creek, Jackson, S. Dak D4 116
Potawatomi Indian res., Kans C8 93
Potchefstroom, S. Afr C4 49
Poteau, LeFlore, Okla B7 112
Poteau, mtn., Ark., Okla C1 81
Poteau, riv., Okla B7 112
Poteet, Atascosa, Tex E3 118
Potenza, It D5 21
Potenza, riv., It C4 21
Potgietersrus, S. Afr B4 49
Poth, Wilson, Tex E3 118
Potholes, res., Wash B6 122
Poti, Sov. Un G17 9
Poti, riv., Braz C2 57
Potiskum, Nig D7 45
Potlatch, Latah, Idaho C2 89
Poto, Peru D4 58
Potocho, China A11 40
Potomac, Vermillion, Ill C6 90
Potomac, Montgomery, Md B3 85
Potomac, Missoula, Mont D3 102
Potomac, riv., U.S D4 85
Potomac Park, Allegany, Md k13 85
Potosí, Bol C2 55
Potosi, Washington, Mo D7 101
Potosi, Grant, Wis F3 124
Potosí, dept., Bol C2 55
Potosi, Phil *C6 35
Potrerillos, Chile E2 55
Potrerillos, Hond C3 62
Potro, mtn., Arg E2 55
Potsdam, G.D.R A8 17
Potsdam, St. Lawrence, N.Y f10 108
Potsdam, Miami, Ohio C1 111
Pottawatomie, co., Kans C7 93
Pottawatomie, co., Okla B5 112
Pottawatomie, creek, Kans D8 93
Pottawattamie, co., Iowa C2 92
Pottawattamie Park, La Porte, Ind *A4 91
Potter, Polk, Ark C1 81
Potter, Atchison, Kans C8, k15 93
Potter, Cheyenne, Nebr C2 103
Potter, Calumet, Wis h9 124
Potter, co., Pa C6 114
Potter, co., S. Dak B6 116
Potter, co., Tex B2 118
Potter Hill, Washington, R.I D9 84
Potter Place, Merrimack, N.H D3 105
Potters Mills, Centre, Pa E6 114
Pottersville, Howell, Mo E5 101
Pottersville, Hunterdon and Somerset, N.J B3 106
Pottersville, Warren, N.Y B7 108
Potter Valley, Mendocino, Calif C2 82
Potterville, Taylor, Ga D2 87
Potterville, Eaton, Mich *F6 98
Potts, creek, Va., W. Va C2 121
Potts Camp, Marshall, Miss A4 100
Pottstown, Montgomery, Pa F10 114
Pottsville, Pope, Ark B2 81
Pottsville, Schuylkill, Pa E9 114
Pottsville, Hamilton, Tex D3 118
Potwin, Butler, Kans E6, g12 93
Pouce-Coupe, B.C., Can B7 68
Pouch Cove, Newf., Can E5 75
Poughkeepsie, Sharp, Ark A4 81
Poughkeepsie, Dutchess, N.Y D7 108
Poulan, Worth, Ga E3 87
Poulo Condore, is., Viet H7 38
Poulsbo, Kitsap, Wash B3 122
Poultney, Rutland, Vt D2 120
Poultney, riv., Vt D2 120
Pound, Wise, Va e9 121
Pound, Marinette, Wis C5 124
Pound Gap, pass, Va e9 121
Pouso Alegre, Braz C3, m9 56
Pouxeux, Fr A2 18
Povenets, Sov. Un F16 25
Poverty, bay, N.Z M17 51
Póvoa de Varzim, Port B1 20
Povorino, Sov. Un C2 29
Povorotnyy, cape, Sov. Un E6 37
Povungnituk, Que., Can f11 73
Powassan, Ont., Can A5 72
Poway, San Diego, Calif F5 82
Powder, riv., Mont., Wyo D11 102
Powder, riv., Oreg C9 113
Powderhorn, Gunnison, Colo C3 83
Powder River, Natrona, Wyo C6 125
Powder River, co., Mont E11 102
Powder River, pass, Wyo B5 125
Powder Springs, Cobb, Ga h7 87
Powderville, Powder River, Mont E11 102
Powe, Stoddard, Mo E7 101
Powell, McDonald, Mo E3 101
Powell, Delaware, Ohio B2 111
Powell, Bradford, Pa C8 114
Powell, Knox, Tenn m13 117
Powell, Navarro, Tex C4 118
Powell, Park, Wyo B4 125
Powell, co., Ky C6 94
Powell, co., Mont D4 102
Powell, lake, Utah F5 119
Powell, mtn., Colo B4 83
Powell, mtn., N. Mex B1 107
Powell, mtn., Tenn f8 171
Powell, riv., Tenn., Va C10 117
Powell Butte, Crook, Oreg C5 113
Powell Creek, Austl C5 50
Powellhurst, Multnomah, Oreg *B4 113
Powell Park, basin, Colo A2 83
Powell River, B.C., Can E5 68
Powellsville, Bertie, N.C A6 109
Powellton, Fayette, W. Va C3, m13 123
Powellville, Wicomico, Md D7 85
Powelton, Hancock, Ga C4 87
Powelton, Centre, Pa. (part of Sandy Ridge) E5 114
Power, Teton, Mont C5 102
Power, co., Idaho G6 89
Power, head, Ire F3 11
Powers, Jay, Ind D7 91
Powers, Menominee, Mich C3 98
Powers, Coos, Oreg E2 113
Powers Lake, Burke, N. Dak A3 110
Powersville, Putnam, Mo A4 101
Powerview, Man., Can *D3 71
Poweshiek, co., Iowa C5 92
Powhatan, Jefferson, Ala B2, f6 78
Powhatan, Lawrence, Ark A4 81
Powhatan, Natchitoches, La C2 95
Powhatan, Powhatan, Va C5 121
Powhatan, co., Va C5 121
Powhatan Point, Belmont, Ohio C5 111
Powhattan, Brown, Kans C8 93
Pownal, Cumberland, Maine g7 96
Pownal, Bennington, Vt F2 120
Pownal Center, Bennington, Vt F2 120
Poyang, China J7 36
Poyang, lake, China J7 36
Poyarkovo, Sov. Un B4 37
Poyen, Grant, Ark C3 81
Poygan, lake, Wis D5 124
Poynette, Columbia, Wis E8 124
Poynor, Ripley, Mo E7 101
Poyntzpass, N. Ire C5 11
Poy Sippi, Waushara, Wis D4 124
Požarevac, Yugo C5 22
Poznań, Pol B4 26
Poznan, prov., Pol A9 17
Pozo Almonte, Chile D2 55
Pozoblanco, Sp C3 20
Pozo Redondo, mts., Ariz E3 80
Pozuelo de Alarcón, Sp p17 20
Pozuzo, Peru D2 58
Pozzallo, It F5 21
Pozzuoli, It D5 21
Prachatice, Czech E9 17
Prachin Buri, Thai E4 38
Prachuap Khiri Khan, Thai G3 38
Praco, Jefferson, Ala f6 78
Prácticos, pt., Cuba C3 64
Prada, Switz C8 19
Prades, Fr F5 14
Praestø, co., Den C6 14
Praga, Pol. (part of Warsaw) k14 26
Prague, Czech C3, n17 26
Prague, Saunders, Nebr C9 103
Prague, Lincoln, Okla B5 112
Praha, see Prague, Czech.
Prahran, Austl *H5 51
Praia, C.V. Is *E3 42
Prainha, Braz C4 59
Prairie, Wilcox, Ala C2 78
Prairie, Monroe, Miss B5 100
Prairie, co., Ark C4 81
Prairie, co., Mont D11 102
Prairie, bayou, Ark g7 81
Prairie, riv., Minn C5 99
Prairie, riv., Wis C4 124
Prairie City, McDonough, Ill C3 90
Prairie City, Jasper, Iowa C4 92
Prairie City, Grant, Oreg C8 113
Prairie City, Perkins, S. Dak B3 116
Prairie Creek, Vigo, Ind F2 91
Prairie Dog, creek, Kans., Nebr D6 103
Prairie du Chien, Crawford, Wis E2 124
Prairie du Rocher, Randolph, Ill E3 90
Prairie du Sac, Sauk, Wis E4 124
Prairie Farm, Barron, Wis C2 124
Prairie Grove, Washington, Ark B1 81
Prairie Hill, Chariton, Mo B5 101
Prairie Home, Cooper, Mo C5 101
Prairie Home, Lancaster, Nebr h11 103
Prairie Point, Noxubee, Miss B5 100
Prairie River, Sask., Can E4 70
Prairieton, Vigo, Ind F3 91
Prairie View, Logan, Ark B2 81
Prairie View, Phillips, Kans C4 93
Prairie View, Waller, Tex D5 118
Prairie Village, Johnson, Kans m16 93
Prairieville, Ascension, La h10 95
Pralognan-la-Vanoise, Fr D2 18
Pran Buri, Thai F3 38
Praszka, Pol C5 26
Prata, Braz E1 57
Prather, Clark, Ind A4 94
Prato, It C3 21
Prats-de-Mollo, Fr F5 14
Pratt, Pratt, Kans E5 93
Pratt, Kanawha, W. Va *C3 123
Pratt, co., Kans E5 93
Pratteln, Switz A4 19
Prattsburg, Steuben, N.Y C3 108
Prattsville, Grant, Ark C3 81
Prattsville, Greene, N.Y C6 108
Prattville, Autauga, Ala C3 78
Prattville, Hillsdale, Mich G6 98
Prattville, Tulsa, Okla *A5 112
Pratum, Marion, Oreg k12 113
Pravdinsk (Friedland), Sov. Un A6 26
Pravia, Sp A2 20
Pray, Park, Mont E6 102
Preble, Adams, Ind C7 91
Preble, Brown, Wis A6 124
Preble, co., Ohio C1 111
Predazzo, It C7 18
Predivinsk, Sov. Un D27 9
Preeceville, Sask., Can F4 70
Preetz, F.R.G D4 24
Pregel, riv., Sov. Un A6 26
Pregnall, Dorchester, S.C E7 115
Prelate, Sask., Can G1 70
Premont, Jim Wells, Tex F3 118
Prémontré, Fr E5 15
Prenter, Boone, W. Va C3, m12 123
Prentice, Price, Wis C3 124
Prentiss, Penobscot, Maine C4 96
Prentiss, Jefferson Davis, Miss D4 100
Prentiss, Macon, N.C f9 109
Prentiss, co., Miss A5 100
Prenzlau, G.D.R B6 16
Prerov, Czech D4 26
Prescott, Yavapai, Ariz C3 80
Prescott, Nevada, Ark D2 81
Prescott, Ont., Can C9 72
Prescott, Adams, Iowa C3 92
Prescott, Linn, Kans D9 93
Prescott, Ogemaw, Mich D7 98
Prescott, Columbia, Oreg A4 113
Prescott, Walla Walla, Wash C7 122
Prescott, Pierce, Wis D1 124
Prescott, co., Ont., Can B10 72
Presho, Lyman, S. Dak D5 116
Presidencia Roque Sáenz Peña, Arg E3 55
Presidente Epitácio, Braz C2 56
Presidente Hayes, dept., Par D4 55
Presidente Prudente, Braz C2 56
Presidential, range, N.H B4 105
Presidents, isl., Tenn e8 117
Presidio, Presidio, Tex p12 118
Presidio, co., Tex F2 118
Preslav, Bul D8 22
Presov, Czech D6 26
Presque Isle, Aroostook, Maine B4 96
Presque Isle, Presque Isle, Mich C7 98
Presque Isle, Vilas, Wis B4 124
Presque Isle, co., Mich C6 98
Pressath, F.R.G D6 17
Prestatyn, Wales A4 12
Presteigne, Wales B4 12
Prestice, Czech D8 17
Preston, Austl *H5 51
Preston, New London, Conn C9 84
Preston, Eng A5 12
Preston, Webster, Ga D2 87
Preston, Franklin, Idaho G7 89
Preston, Jackson, Iowa B7 92
Preston, Pratt, Kans E5 93
Preston, Bath, Ky B6 94
Preston, Caroline, Md C6 85
Preston, Fillmore, Minn G6 99
Preston, Kemper, Miss C5 100
Preston, Hickory, Mo D4 101
Preston, Okmulgee, Okla B6 112
Preston, King, Wash e12 122
Preston, co., W. Va B5 123
Preston, peak, Calif B2 82
Prestonpans, Scot *E6 13
Prestonburg, Floyd, Ky C7 94
Prestonville, Carroll, Ky B4 94
Prestrud, inlet, Ant B32 5
Prestwick, Washington, Ala D2 78
Prestwick, Scot E4 13
Presumpscot, riv., Maine g7 96
Preti, mtn., It C8 18
Preto, riv., Braz h6 56
Prêto, riv., Braz D6 57
Prêto, riv., Braz C2 59
Pretoria, S. Afr C4 49
Prettyboy, res., Md A4 85
Pretty Prairie, Reno, Kans E5, g10 93
Preveza, Grc C3 22
Preveza, prov., Grc *C3 22
Prewitt, McKinley, N. Mex B1 107
Prewitt, res., Colo A7 83
Prey Veng, Kam G6 38
Pribilof, is., Alsk D5 79
Priboj, Yugo D4 22
Pribram, Czech D3 26
Price, Que., Can *k13 73
Price, Queen Annes, Md B6 85
Price, Rusk, Tex C5 118
Price, Carbon, Utah D5 119
Price, co., Wis C3 124
Price, isl., B.C., Can C3 68
Price, riv., Utah D5 119
Pricedale, Pike, Miss D3 100
Pricedale, Westmoreland, Pa *F2 114
Priceville, Ont., Can C4 72
Prichard, Mobile, Ala E1 78
Prichard, Wayne, W. Va C2 123
Priddy, Mills, Tex D3 118
Priego, Sp D3 20
Prienai, Sov. Un A7 26
Prieska, S. Afr C3 49
Priest, lake, Idaho A2 89
Priestley, mtn., B.C., Can B3 68
Priestly, mtn., Maine B3 96
Priest Rapids, dam, Wash C6 122
Priest Rapids Lake, res., Wash C6 122
Priest River, Bonner, Idaho A2 89
Prijedor, Yugo C3 22
Prijepolje, Yugo D4 22
Prikumsk, Sov. Un E7 29
Prilep, Yugo E5 22
Priluki, Sov. Un F9 27
Prim, pt., P.E.I., Can C6 74
Primate, Sask., Can E1 70
Primera, Cameron, Tex *F4 118
Primero, riv., Arg A4 54
Primghar, O'Brien, Iowa A2 92
Primolano, It D7 18
Primorsk, Sov. Un G13 25
Primorsk (Fischhausen), Sov. Un A6 26
Primorsko-Akhtarsk, Sov. Un H12 27
Primos, Delaware, Pa *G11 114
Primrose, Boone, Nebr C7 103
Primrose, Schuylkill, Pa *E9 114
Primrose, Providence, R.I B10 84
Primrose, lake, Sask., Can n7 70
Prince, Sask., Can E1 70
Prince, Lincoln, Nev F7 104
Prince, co., P.E.I., Can C5 74
Prince, inlet, S.C F4 115
Prince, lake, Va k14 121
Prince Albert, Sask., Can D3, n7 70
Prince Albert, mts., Ant B29 5
Prince Albert, nat. park, Sask., Can C2 70
Prince Albert, sound, N.W. Ter., Can B9 66
Prince Alfred, cape, N.W. Ter., Can B8 66
Prince Charles, isl., N.W. Ter., Can C17 67
Prince Charles, mts., Ant B19 5
Prince Charles Foreland, isl., Nor B14 4
Prince Edward, co., Ont., Can C7 72
Prince Edward, co., Va C4 121
Prince Edward, isl., P.E.I., Can C6 74
Prince Edward, is., Indian O J23 3
Prince Edward Island, prov., Can G20 67, C6 74
Prince Edward Island, nat. park, P.E.I., Can C6 74
Prince Frederick, Calvert, Md C4 85
Prince George, B.C., Can C6, n18 68
Prince George, Prince George, Va C5, n18 121
Prince George, co., Va C5 121
Prince Georges, co., Md C4 85
Prince of Wales, cape, Alsk B6 79
Prince of Wales, isl., Alsk n23 79
Prince of Wales, isl., Austl B7 50
Prince of Wales, isl., N.W. Ter., Can B13 66
Prince of Wales, strait, N.W. Ter., Can B9 66
Prince Olav, coast, Ant C17 5
Prince Patrick, isl., N.W. Ter., Can m27 67
Prince Regent, inlet, N.W. Ter., Can B14 66
Prince Rupert, B.C., Can B2, n16 68
Princesa Isabel, Braz C3 57
Prince's Lakes, Johnson, Ind F5 91
Princes Risborough, Eng C7 12
Princess Anne, Somerset, Md D6 85
Princess Charlotte, bay, Austl B7 50
Princess Martha, coast, Ant B11 5
Princess Ragnhild, coast, Ant B16 5
Princess Royal, isl., B.C., Can C3 68
Princes Town, Trin O23 65
Princeton, Jackson, Ala A3 78
Princeton, Dallas, Ark D3 81
Princeton, B.C., Can E7 68
Princeton, Newf., Can D5 75
Princeton, Ont., Can D4 72
Princeton, Colusa, Calif C2 82
Princeton, Dade, Fla G6, s13 86
Princeton, Latah, Idaho C2 89
Princeton, Gibson, Ind H2 91
Princeton, Scott, Iowa C7 92
Princeton, Franklin, Kans D8 93
Princeton, Caldwell, Ky C2 94
Princeton, Washington, Maine C5 96
Princeton, Worcester, Mass B4 97
Princeton, Marquette, Mich B3 98
Princeton, Mille Lacs, Minn E5 99
Princeton, Mercer, Mo A4 101
Princeton, Mercer, N.J C3 106
Princeton, Johnston, N.C B4 109
Princeton, Butler, Ohio *C1 111
Princeton, Harney, Oreg D8 113
Princeton, Greenville and Laurens, S.C B3 115
Princeton, Mercer, W. Va D3 123
Princeton, Green Lake, Wis E4 124
Princeton, mtn., Colo C4 83
Princeton Junction, Mercer, N.J C3 106
Princeton Township, Mercer, N.J *C3 106
Princeville, Que., Can C6 73
Princeville, Peoria, Ill C4 90
Princeville, Edgecombe, N.C B5 109
Prince William, N.B., Can D2 74
Prince William, co., Va B5 121
Prince William, sound, Alsk g18 79
Principe, chan., B.C., Can C2 68
Principe, isl., Sao Tome & Principe E1 46
Prineville, Crook, Oreg C6 113
Prineville, res., Oreg C6 113
Prineville Southeast, Crook, Oreg *C6 113
Pringle, Luzerne, Pa *D10 114
Pringle, Custer, S. Dak D2 116
Prinsburg, Kandiyohi, Minn F3 99
Prinzapolca, Nic D6 62
Prinzapolca, riv., Nic D5 62
Prior Lake, Scott, Minn F3 99
Priozersk, Sov. Un G14 25
Pripyat (Pripet), riv., Sov. Un E7 27
Prishib, Sov. Un B4 41
Pristina, Yugo D5 22
Pritchard, isl., S.C G7 115
Pritchardville, Beaufort, S.C G6 115
Pritchett, Baca, Colo D8 83
Pritchett, Upshur, Tex C5 118
Pritzerbe, G.D.R F6 24
Pritzwalk, G.D.R B6 16
Privas, Fr E6 14
Privert, lake, Que., Can g8 75
Privolnoye, Sov. Un H9 27
Prizren, Yugo D5 22
Prizzi, It F4 21
Probolinggo, Indon G4 35
Procious, Clay, W. Va m13 123
Procter, B.C., Can E9 68
Proctor, Logan, Colo A8 83
Proctor, St. Louis, Minn D6 99
Proctor, Lake, Mont C2 102
Proctor, Adair, Okla B7 112
Proctor, Comanche, Tex D3 118
Proctor, Rutland, Vt D2 120
Proctor, Wetzel, W. Va g8 123
Proctorsville, Windsor, Vt E3 120
Proctorville, Robeson, N.C C3 109
Proctorville, Lawrence, Ohio D3 111
Proddatur, India *F6 39
Proença-a-Nova, Port C2 20
Progreso, Mex C7 63
Prof. Dr. Ir. W. J. Van Blommestein Meer, res., Sur B4 59
Progreso, Hidalgo, Tex *F4 118
Progress, Dauphin, Pa *F8 114
Prokhladnyy, Sov. Un E2 29
Prokopyevsk, Sov. Un D11 28
Prokuplje, Yugo D5 22
Prole, Warren, Iowa f8 92
Proletarsk, Sov. Un q21 27
Proletarskaya, Sov. Un H13 27

Rainbow Bridge, nat. mon., Utah F5 119
Rainbow Flowage, res., Wis C4 124
Rainbow City, Etowah, Ala .*A3 78
Rainbow City, Pan k11 62
Rainelle, Greenbrier, W. Va .D4 123
Raines, Crisp, Ga E3 87
Rainier, Columbia, Oreg A4 113
Rainier, Thurston, Wash C3 122
Rainier, mtn., Wash C4 122
Rains, co., Tex C5 118
Rainsboro, Highland, Ohio . C2 111
Rainsville, DeKalb, Ala A4 78
Rainy, lake, Ont., Can., Minn . B5 99
Rainy, mtn., Okla C3 112
Rainy, riv., Ont., Can., Minn . B4 99
Rainy River, Ont., Can G14 66
Rainy River, dist., Ont., Can o16 72
Raipur, India G8 40
Ra'is, Sau. Ar E7 43
Raisin, Victoria, Tex E4 118
Raismes, Fr D3 15
Raivavae, isl., Fr. Polynesia . *H13 7
Raja, cape, Indon K2 38
Rājahmundry, India I8 40
Rājapālaiyam, India *G6 40
Rājasthān, state, India C5 39
Rājkot, India F3 40
Rājmahāl, India E11 40
Rāj-Nāndgaon, India G8 40
Rājpipla, India G4 40
Rājshāhi, Bngl E12 40
Rakaia, riv., N.Z. O13 51
Rake, Winnebago, Iowa A4 92
Rakhov, Sov. Un A7 22
Rakkestad, Nor p29 25
Rakovnik, Czech C2 26
Rakvere, Sov. Un B6 27
Raleigh, Newf., Can C4 75
Raleigh, Levy, Fla C4 86
Raleigh, Saline, Ill F5 90
Raleigh, Rush, Ind E7 91
Raleigh, Smith, Miss C4 100
Raleigh, Wake, N.C B4 109
Raleigh, Grant, N. Dak C4 110
Raleigh, Raleigh, W. Va ... n13 123
Raleigh, co., W. Va D3 123
Raleigh, bay, N.C C6 109
Raleigh Hills, Washington, Oreg *B4 113
Ralls, Crosby, Tex C2 117
Ralls, co., Mo B6 101
Ralph, Tuscaloosa, Ala B2 78
Ralph, Dickinson, Mich B3 98
Ralph, Harding, S. Dak B2 116
Ralston, Carroll and Greene, Iowa B3 92
Ralston, Douglas, Nebr g12 103
Ralston, Pawnee, Okla A5 112
Ralston, Lycoming, Pa D8 114
Ralston, Weakley, Tenn A3 117
Ralston, Park, Wyo B4 125
Ralston, val., Nev E4 104
Ram, riv., Alta., Can C3 69
Rama, Sask., Can F4 70
Rama, Isr B7 32
Rama, Nic D5 62
Ramah, El Paso, Colo B6 83
Ramah, McKinley, N. Mex .. B1 107
Rām Allāh, Jordan C7, h11 32
Ramapo, mts., N.J. A4 106
Ramapo, riv., N.J. A4 106
Ramat Gan, Isr B6, g10 32
Ramat HaKovesh, Isr g10 32
Ramat HaSharon, Isr g10 32
Rāmban, India B6 39
Rambervillers, Fr C7 14
Rambi, isl., Fiji 52
Ramblewood, Burlington, N.J D3 106
Rambouillet, Fr C4 14
Ramea, Newf., Can E3 75
Ramea, is., Newf., Can E3 75
Ramenskoye, Sov. Un . D12, n18 27
Ramer, Montgomery, Ala .. C3 78
Ramer, McNairy, Tenn B3 117
Rameshk, Iran H9 41
Rāmganga, riv., India D7 40
Rāmhormoz, Iran F4 41
Ramirez, Duval, Tex F3 118
Ramiriquí, Col B3 60
Ramirito, Jim Hogg, Tex ... F3 118
Ramla, Isr C6, h10 32
Ramm, mtn., Jordan E7 32
Ramnäs, Swe t34 25
Ramona, San Diego, Calif .. F5 82
Ramona, Marion, Kans D6 93
Ramona, Washington, Okla A6 112
Ramona, Lake, S. Dak C8 116
Ramor, lake, Ire D4 11
Rampart, Alsk B9 79
Rampart, range, Colo B5 83
Rāmpur, India C7 40
Ramsay, Gogebic, Mich A5 98
Ramsay, Silver Bow, Mont .D4 102
Ramsayville, Ont., Can h12 72
Ramseur, Randolph, N.C B3 109
Ramsey, Eng B7 12
Ramsey, Fayette, Ill D4 90
Ramsey, I. of Man F4 13
Ramsey, Bergen, N.J A4 106
Ramsey, co., Minn E5 99
Ramsey, co., N. Dak A7 110
Ramsgate, Eng C9 12
Rāmshīr, Iran F4 41
Ramshorn, peak, Mont E5 102
Ramu, riv., Pap. N. Gui k11 50
Ranaghat, India F12 40
Ranburne, Cleburne, Ala ... B4 78
Rancagua, Chile G3 53
Rancheria, rock, Oreg C6 113
Ranches of Taos, Taos, N. Mex A4 107
Ranchester, Sheridan, Wyo . B5 125
Rānchi, India F10 40
Ranchito, Taos, N. Mex A4 107
Rancho Cordova, Sacramento, Calif *C3 82
Ranco, Chile C2 54
Ranco, lake, Chile C2 54
Rancocas, Burlington, N.J .. C3 106
Rancocas, creek, N.J. C3 106
Rancocas Woods, Burlington, N.J D3 106
Rand, Jackson, Colo A4 83
Rand, Kanawha, W. Va ... m12 123
Randado, Jim Hogg, Tex ... F3 118
Randalia, Fayette, Iowa B6 92
Randall, Hamilton, Iowa B4 92
Randall, Jewell, Kans C5 93
Randall, Morrison, Minn D4 99
Randall, Burnett, Wis C1 124
Randall, co., Tex B2 118
Randallstown, Baltimore, Md B4 85
Randers, Den B4 24
Randfontein, S. Afr *C4 49
Randle, Lewis, Wash C4 122
Randleman, Randolph, N.C B3 109
Randlett, Cotton, Okla C3 112
Randlett, Uintah, Utah C6 119
Randolph, Pinal, Ariz E4 80
Randolph, Fremont, Iowa ... D2 92
Randolph, Kennebec, Maine D3 96
Randolph, Norfolk, Mass B5, h11 97
Randolph, Pontotoc, Miss .. A4 100
Randolph, Cedar, Nebr B8 103
Randolph, Coos, N.H B4 105
Randolph, Cattaraugus, N.Y C2 108
Randolph, Portage, Ohio A4 111
Randolph, Rich, Utah B4 119
Randolph, Orange, Vt D3 120
Randolph, Columbia and Dodge, Wis E4 124
Randolph, co., Ala B4 78
Randolph, co., Ark A4 81
Randolph, co., Ga E2 87
Randolph, co., Ill E4 90
Randolph, co., Ind D7 91
Randolph, co., Mo B5 101
Randolph, co., N.C B3 109
Randolph, co., W. Va C5 123
Randolph Center, Orange, Vt D3 120
Randolph Hills, Montgomery, Md B3 85
Random, isl., Newf., Can D5 75
Random Lake, Sheboygan, Wis E6 124
Randow, riv., G.D.R B7 16
Randsburg, Kern, Calif E5 82
Randwick, Austl *F8 51
Ranfurly, Alta., Can C5 69
Rangaunu, bay, N.Z. K14 51
Range, Grant, Oreg C8 113
Rangely, Rio Blanco, Colo A2 83
Rangeley, Franklin, Maine . D2 96
Rangeley, lake, Maine D2 96
Ranger, Gordon, Ga B2 87
Ranger, Eastland, Tex C3 118
Ranger, Lincoln, W. Va C2 123
Ranger, lake, N. Mex D6 107
Rangiora, N.Z O14 51
Rangitata, riv., N.Z. O13 51
Rangoon, Bur D2 38
Rangpur, Bngl E12 40
Rangsum, see Tungpu, China
Ranier, Koochiching, Minn . B5 99
Rānīganj, India D8 39
Rankin, Vermilion, Ill C6 90
Rankin, Allegheny, Pa k14 114
Rankin, Upton, Tex D2 118
Rankin, co., Miss C4 100
Ranlo, Gaston, N.C *B1 109
Rannes, Austl B8 51
Rannoch, lake, Scot D4 13
Rann of Kutch, swamp, India .. D4 39
Ranshaw, Northumberland, Pa *E9 114
Ransom, La Salle, Ill B5 90
Ransom, Ness, Kans D4 93
Ransom, Lackawanna, Pa .. m17 114
Ransom, co., N. Dak C8 110
Ransomville, Niagara, N.Y B2 108
Ranson, Jefferson, W. Va ... B7 123
Rantauparapat, Indon K3 38
Rantoul, Champaign, Ill C5 90
Rantoul, Franklin, Kans D8 93
Rantowles, Charleston, S.C . k11 115
Ranum, Den B3 24
Raon [-l'Etape], Fr A2 18
Raoui, sand dunes, Alg D4 44
Raoul, Habersham, Ga B3 87
Rapallo, It B2 21
Rapa, isl., Fr. Polynesia ... *H13 7
Rapa Nui (Easter), isl., Pac. O H15 7
Rapelje, Stillwater, Mont .. E7 102
Raphine, Rockbridge, Va ... C3 121
Raphoe, Ire C4 11
Rapid, riv., Minn B4 99
Rapidan, Culpepper, Va B4 121
Rapid City, Man., Can D1 71
Rapid City, Kalkaska, Mich D5 98
Rapid City, Pennington, S. Dak C2 116
Rapides, Rapides, La C3 95
Rapides, par., La C3 95
Rapid River, Delta, Mich ... C3 98
Rappahannock, co., Va B4 121
Rappahannock, riv., Va B5 121
Rappahannock Academy, Caroline, Va B5 121
Rapperswil, Switz B6 19
Raquette, lake, N.Y. B6 108
Raquette, riv., N.Y. f10 108
Raquette Lake, Hamilton, N.Y B6 108
Rarden, Scioto, Ohio D2 111
Rardin, Coles, Ill D5 90
Raritan, Henderson, Ill C3 90
Raritan, Somerset, N.J B3 106
Raritan, bay, N.J. C4 106
Raritan, riv., N.J. C4 106
Rasa, pt., Arg C4 54
Ra's al 'Ayn, Syr D13 31
Ra's al Khaymah, U.A.E I7 41
Ra's al Madrakah, cape, Om . E2 39
Ra's al 'Ushsh, Eg C4 32
Ra's an Naqb, Jordan E7 32
Ra's at Tin, cape, Libya F4 31
Rasbokil, Swe t35 25
Ras Dashan, mtn., Eth C4 47
Raseiniai, Sov. Un A7 26
Ra's al Hadd, cape, Om D2 39
Ra's al Milh, cape, Libya F5 31
Rashād, Sud C3 47
Rashid, see Rosetta, Eg.
Rashkov, Sov. Un B9 22
Rasht, Iran C4 41
Raška, Yugo D5 24
Raska, riv., Yugo D5 22
Raso, cape, Arg C3 54
Raso, cape, Braz B5 59
Raspberry, peak, Ark C1 81
Rasskazovo, Sov. Un E13 27
Rastatt, F.R.G E3 17
Rastede, F.R.G A8 15
Raszyn, Pol m13 26
Rat, is., Alsk E3 79
Rat, lake, Man., Can A2 71
Rat, lake, Man., Can B4 71
Rat, riv., Man., Can E3 71
Rat, riv., Man., Can A2 71
Ratangarh, India E5 40
Rat Buri, Thai F3 38
Ratcliff, Logan, Ark B2 81
Ratekau, F.R.G F4 24
Rathbun, Appanoose, Iowa . D5 92
Rathbun Lake, res., Iowa ... D5 92
Rathdrum, Kootenai, Idaho . B2 89
Rathdrum, Ire E5 11
Rathdrum, prairie, Idaho D8 122
Rathenow, G.D.R B6 16
Rathfriland, N. Ire C5 11
Rathkeale, Ire E3 11
Rathlin, isl., N. Ire B5 11
Rathlin, sound, N. Ire B5 11
Ráth Luirc, Ire E3 11
Rathmelton, Ire B4 11
Rathmore, Ire E2 11
Rathmullen, Ire B4 11
Rathnew, Ire D5 11
Rathowen, Ire D4 11
Rathwell, Man., Can E2 71
Ratibor, see Raciborz, Pol.
Ratingen, F.R.G B1 17
Ratlām, India F5 40
Ratnāgiri, India I4 40
Ratner, Sask., Can D3 70
Raton, Colfax, N. Mex A5 107
Raton, mesa, Colo D6 83
Raton, pass, Colo D6 83
Ratónes, is., P.R D5 61
Rattan, Pushmataha, Okla C6 112
Rattenberg, Aus E5 16
Rattlesnake, creek, Kans E4 93
Rattlesnake, creek, Ohio C2 111
Rattlesnake, creek, Wash C6 122
Rattlesnake, flat, Wash C7 122
Rattlesnake, hills, Wash C6 122
Rattlesnake, mtn., Conn C5 84
Rattlesnake, hills, Wyo C5 125
Rattling Brook, Newf., Can . D3 75
Rattray, head, Scot C7 13
Rättvik, Swe G6 25
Ratz, mtn., Alsk., B.C., Can .. E6 66
Ratzeburg, F.R.G E4 24
Ratzeburger, lake, F.R.G E4 24
Raub, Benton, Ind C3 91
Raub, McLean, N. Dak B3 110
Rauch, Arg B5 54
Rauch, Koochiching, Minn . C5 99
Rauer, isl., Nor p28 25
Raufarhofn, Ice m24 25
Rauland, Nor H3 25
Rauma, Fin G9 25
Rausu, Dake, peak, Jap D12 37
Rautalampi, Fin F12 25
Ravalli, Lake, Mont C2 102
Ravalli, co., Mont D2 102
Ravanna, Mercer, Mo A4 101
Rāvar, Iran F8 41
Rava-Russkaya, Sov. Un F4 27
Raven, Tazewell, Va e10 121
Raven, The, headland, Ire E5 11
Ravena, Albany, N.Y C7 108
Ravenden, Lawrence, Ark ... A4 81
Ravenden Springs, Randolph, Ark A4 81
Ravenel, Charleston, S.C .. k11 115
Ravenglass, Eng F5 13
Ravenna, It B4 21
Ravenna, Estill, Ky C6 94
Ravenna, Muskegon, Mich . E5 98
Ravenna, Buffalo, Nebr C7 103
Ravenna, Portage, Ohio A4 111
Raven Park, basin, Colo A2 83
Raven Rock, Hunterdon, N.J C2 106
Ravensburg, F.R.G E4 16
Ravenscrag, Sask., Can H1 70
Ravenscroft, White, Tenn .. D8 117
Ravensdale, King, Wash ... f12 122
Ravensthorpe, Austl F3 50
Ravenswood, Marion, Ind . k10 91
Ravenswood, Jackson, W. Va C3 123
Ravensworth, Ont., Can B5 72
Ravenwood, Nodaway, Mo . A3 101
Ravi, riv., Pak B4 40
Ravia, Johnston, Okla C5 112
Ravinia, Charles Mix., S. Dak D7 116
Rāwalpindi, Pak B5 39
Rawalpindi Cantonment, Pak *B5 39
Rawa Mazowiecka, Pol C6 26
Rawāndūz, Iraq C2 41
Rawdon, Que., Can C4 73
Rawhide, creek, Wyo D8 125
Rawhide, lake, Ont., Can B8 98
Rawicz, Pol C4 26
Rawlings, Allegany, Md k13 85
Rawlings, Brunswick, Va ... D5 121
Rawlinna, Austl F4 51
Rawlins, Carbon, Wyo E5 125
Rawlins, co., Kans C2 93
Rawson, Arg C3 54
Rawson, Arg g6 54
Rawson, McKenzie, N. Dak B2 110
Rawson, Hancock, Ohio B2 111
Rawsonville, Windham, Vt . E3 120
Ray, Steuben, Ind A8 91
Ray, Koochiching, Minn B5 99
Ray Williams, N. Dak A2 110
Ray, co., Mo B3 101
Ray, cape, Newf., Can E2 75
Raya, isl., Indon J1 38
Rayagada, India H9 40
Ray-Aleksandrovka, Sov. Un q20 27
Raybon, Brantley, Ga E5 87
Raychikhinsk, Sov. Un B4 37
Ray City, Berrien, Ga E3 87
Raygorodka, Sov. Un q22 27
Rayland, Jefferson, Ohio f8 123
Rayle, Wilkes, Ga C4 87
Raymond, Madera, Calif D4 82
Raymond, Alta., Can E4 69
Raymond, Coweta, Ga C2 87
Raymond, Montgomery, Ill . D4 90
Raymond, Rice, Kans D5 93
Raymond, Cumberland, Maine E2, g7 96
Raymond, Kandiyohi, Minn . E3 99
Raymond, Hinds, Miss C3 100
Raymond, Sheridan, Mont . B12 102
Raymond, Lancaster, Nebr . D9 103
Raymond, Rockingham, N.H D4 105
Raymond, Clark, S. Dak C8 116
Raymond, Pacific, Wash C2 122
Raymond Terrace, Austl F8 51
Raymondville, Texas, Mo .. D6 101
Raymondville, St. Lawrence, N.Y f10 108
Raymondville, Willacy, Tex . F4 118
Raymore, Sask., Can F3 70
Raymore, Cass, Mo C3 101
Rayne, Acadia, La D3 95
Rayner, glacier, Ant C17 5
Raynesford, Judith Basin, Mont C6 102
Raynham, Bristol, Mass C5 97
Raynham Center, Bristol, Mass C5 97
Rayón, Mex B2 63
Rayong, Thai F4 38
Raystown, branch, Pa F5 114
Raytown, Jackson, Mo h11 101
Rayville, Richland, La B4 95
Rayville, Ray, Mo B3 101
Razan, Iran D4 41
Razgrad, Bul D8 22
Razlog, Bul E6 22
Razmak, Pak B4 39
Razorback, mtn., B.C., Can ... D5 68
Ré, isl., Fr D3 14
Rea, Andrew, Mo A3 101
Rea, lake, Ire D3 11
Reader, Ouachita, Ark D2 81
Reader, Wetzel, W. Va . B4, h9 123
Reader, lake, Man., Can C1 71
Readfield, Kennebec, Maine D3 96
Reading, Eng C7 12
Reading, Lyon, Kans D8 93
Reading, Middlesex, Mass A5, f11 97
Reading, Hillsdale, Mich G6 98
Reading, Nobles, Minn G3 99
Reading, Hamilton, Ohio C1, o13 111
Reading, Berks, Pa F10 114
Reading, Windsor, Vt E3 120
Reading Center, Schuyler, N.Y C4 108
Readington, Hunterdon, N.J B3 106
Readland, Chicot, Ark D4 81
Readlyn, Sask., Can H3 70
Readlyn, Bremer, Iowa B5 92
Readsboro, Bennington, Vt . F3 120
Readstown, Vernon, Wis E3 124
Readyville, Cannon, Tenn .. B5 117
Reagan, Henderson, Tenn .. B3 117
Reagan, co., Tex D2 118
Real, co., Tex E3 118
Real, range, Bol C2 55
Realicó, Arg B4 54
Realitos, Duval, Tex F3 118
Ream, Camb G5 38
Ream, McDowell, W. Va .. *D3 123
Reamstown, Lancaster, Pa .. F9 114
Reardan, Lincoln, Wash B8 122
Reasnor, Jasper, Iowa C4 92
Reata, Mex B4 63
Reaville, Hunterdon, N.J ... C3 106
Rebecca, Turner, Ga E3 87
Rebersburg, Centre, Pa E7 114
Rebiana (Oasis), Libya E4 43
Rebiano, sand sea, Libya E3 43
Reboly, Sov. Un F14 25
Rebun, isl., Jap D10 37
Recalde, Arg B4 54
Recanati, It C4 21
Recherche, arch., Austl F3 50
Rechitsa, Sov. Un E8 27
Recife, Braz C4, k6 57
Recinto, Chile B2 54
Recklinghausen, F.R.G B2 17
Recluse, Campbell, Wyo B7 125
Recogne, Bel E5 15
Reconquista, Arg E4 55
Recovery, Decatur, Ga F2 87
Recreo, Arg E2 55
Rector, Clay, Ark A5 81
Red, bay, N. Ire B5 11
Red, creek, Miss E4 100
Red, isl., Newf., Can E4 75
Red, mtn., Ala g7 78
Red, mtn., Calif B2 82
Red, mtn., Mont C4 102
Red, peak, Colo B4 83
Red, peak, Idaho E3 89
Red, riv., Man., Can E3 71
Red, riv., Can., U.S G13 66
Red, riv., Ky C6 94
Red, riv., Tenn A4 117
Red, riv., U.S. D9 77
Red, riv., Viet B6 38
Red, riv., Wis D5 124
Red, sea, Afr., Asia D9 42
Redang, isl., Mala J5 38
Redange, Lux E5 15
Red Bank, Monmouth, N.J . C4 106
Red Bank, Lexington, S.C .. D5 115
Red Bank, Hamilton, Tenn . D8 117
Red Banks, Marshall, Miss .. A4 100
Red Bay, Franklin, Ala A1 78
Red Bay, Newf., Can ... C3, h10 75
Redbay, Walton, Fla u16 86
Redberry, lake, Sask., Can E2 70
Redbird, Holt, Nebr B7 103
Redbird, Lake, Ohio A4 111
Redbird, Wagoner, Okla B6 112
Red Bird, creek, Ky C6 94
Red Bluff, Tehama, Calif ... B2 82
Red Bluff, res., N. Mex., Tex . E6 107
Red Boiling Springs, Macon, Tenn C8 117
Red Bud, Randolph, Ill E4 90
Red Butte, mtn., Utah B2 119
Red Buttes Village, Natrona, Wyo D6 125
Redby, Beltrami, Minn C4 99
Redcar, Eng F7 13
Red Cedar, lake, Wis C2 124
Red Cedar, riv., Wis C2 124
Redcliff, Alta., Can D5 69
Redcliff, Eagle, Colo B4 83
Red Cliff, Bayfield, Wis B3 124
Red Cliff, Indian res., Wis B3 124
Red Cloud, Webster, Nebr . D7 103
Red Cloud, peak, Colo D3 83
Red Creek, Wayne, N.Y B4 108
Red Cross, lake, Man., Can .. B5 71
Red Deer, Alta., Can C4, g8 69
Red Deer, lake, Man., Can .. C1 71
Red Deer, riv., Alta., Sask., Can F10 66
Red Deer, riv., Man., Sask., Can E4 70
Reddell, Evangeline, La D3 95
Reddick, Marion, Fla C4 86
Reddick, Kankakee and Livingston, Ill B5 90
Redding, Jefferson, Ala E4 78
Redding, Shasta, Calif B2 82
Redding, Fairfield, Conn ... D3 84
Redding, Ringgold, Iowa ... D3 92
Redding Ridge, Fairfield, Conn D3 84
Redditch, Eng B6 12
Redditt, Ont., Can E4 71
Rede, riv., Eng E6 13
Redearth, lake, Sask., Can D4 70
Redenção, Braz D3 57
Redeye, riv., Minn D3 99
Redeyef, Tun G11 30
Red Feather Lakes, Larimer, Colo A5 83
Redfield, Jefferson, Ark C3 81
Redfield, Dallas, Iowa C3 92
Redfield, Bourbon, Kans E9 93
Redfield, Oswego, N.Y B5 108
Redfield, Spink, S. Dak C7 116
Redford, Clinton, N.Y f11 108
Redford, Presidio, Tex p12 118
Redford Township, Wayne, Mich p15 98
Redgranite, Waushara, Wis . D4 124
Redgut, bay, Ont., Can B6 99
Red Hill, Montgomery, Pa . *F11 114
Red Hook, Dutchess, N.Y ... C7 108
Redhouse, Madison, Ky C5 94
Red House, Charlotte, Va ... C4 121
Red House, Putnam, W. Va .C3 123
Redig, Harding, S. Dak B2 116
Red Indian, lake, Newf., Can .. D3 75
Redington Beach, Pinellas, Fla *E4 86
Redington Shores, Pinellas, Fla *E4 86
Red Jacket, Mingo, W. Va .. D2 123
Redkey, Jay, Ind D7 91
Red Lake, Ont., Can o16 72
Redlake, Beltrami, Minn C3 99
Red Lake, co., Minn C2 99
Red Lake, Indian res., Minn ... B3 99
Red Lake, riv., Minn C2 99
Red Lake Falls, Red Lake, Minn C2 99
Redlands, San Bernardino, Calif E5 82
Red Level, Covington, Ala .. D3 78
Red Lick, Jefferson, Miss ... D3 100
Red Lion, Logan, Colo A8 83
Red Lion, York, Pa G8 114
Red Lodge, Carbon, Mont .. E7 102
Redmon, Edgar, Ill D6 90
Redmond, Deschutes, Oreg .. C5 113
Redmond, Sevier, Utah E4 119
Redmond, King, Wash e11 122
Red Mountain, San Bernardino, Calif E5 82
Red Mountain, pass, Colo D3 83
Red Oak, Fulton, Ga h7 87
Red Oak, Montgomery, Iowa D2 92
Red Oak, Nash., N.C A5 109
Red Oak, Latimer, Okla C6 112
Red Oak, Ellis, Tex n10 118
Red Oak, Charlotte, Va D4 121
Red Oaks, East Baton Rouge, La h9 95
Redon, Fr D3 14
Redonda, isl., B.C., Can D5 68
Redondela, Sp A1 20
Redondo, Port C2 20
Redondo, King, Wash f11 122
Redondo Beach, Los Angeles, Calif n12 82
Redoubt, mtn., Alsk g15 79
Redowl, Meade, S. Dak C3 116
Red Pass, B.C., Can C8 68
Red Pheasant, Sask., Can .. E1 70
Red Rapids, N.B., Can C2 74
Red River, co., Tex C5 118
Red River, par., La B2 95
Red River, Hot Springs, Idaho D3 89
Red River, Taos, N. Mex ... A4 107
Red Rock, Pinal, Ariz E4 80
Red Rock, B.C., Can C6 68
Red Rock, Beaverhead, Mont F4 102
Redrock, Grant, N. Mex E1 107
Redrock, Noble, Okla A4 112
Red Rock, Bastrop, Tex E4 118
Red Rock, pass, Idaho, Mont .. E7 89
Red Rock, riv., Mont F4 102
Red Rock, Lake, res., Iowa C4 92
Redruth, Eng E2 12
Red Springs, Robeson, N.C . C3 109
Redstone, B.C., Can C6 68
Redstone, Pitkin, Colo B3 171
Redstone, Sheridan, Mont . B12 102
Redstone, Carroll, N.H B4 105
Redstone Park, Madison, Ala *A3 78
Red Sucker, lake, Man., Can .. B5 71
Red Sucker, riv., Man., Can .. B5 71
Red Table, mtn., Colo B4 83
Redvale, Montrose, Colo C2 83
Redvers, Sask., Can H5 70
Redwater, Alta., Can C4 69
Redwater, riv., Mont C11 102
Red Wing, Huerfano, Colo .. D5 83
Red Willow, Alta., Can C4 69
Red Willow, co., Nebr D5 103
Red Willow, creek, Nebr D5 103
Redwillow, riv., Alta., B.C., Can B7 68
Redwine, Morgan, Ky C6 94
Red Wing, Goodhue, Minn . F6 99
Redwood, Warren, Miss C3 100
Redwood, Jefferson, N.Y A5, f9 108
Redwood, Salt Lake, Utah *C4 119
Redwood, co., Minn F3 99
Redwood, riv., Minn F3 99
Redwood City, San Mateo, Calif D2, k8 82
Redwood Estates, Santa Clara, Calif *D3 82
Redwood Falls, Redwood, Minn F3 99
Redwood Valley, Mendocino, Calif C2 82
Ree, lake, Ire D4 11
Reed, Greer, Okla C2 112
Reed, Lane, Oreg C3 113
Reed, lake, Man., Can B1 71
Reed, lake, Sask., Can G1 70
Reed City, Osceola, Mich ... E5 98
Reeder, Adams, N. Dak C3 110
Reedley, Fresno, Calif D4 82
Reedpoint, Stillwater, Mont E7 102
Reeds, peak, N. Mex D2 107
Reeds Beach, Cape May, N.J E3 106
Reedsburg, Sauk, Wis E3 124
Reeds Ferry, Hillsboro, N.H E4 105
Reeds Lake, Kent, Mich F5 98
Reedsport, Douglas, Oreg .. D3 113
Reeds Spring, Stone, Mo E4 101
Reedsville, Meigs, Ohio C4 111
Reedsville, Mifflin, Pa E6 114
Reedsville, Preston, W. Va . B5 123
Reedsville, Manitowoc, Wis D6, h10 124
Reedville, Northumberland, Va C6 121
Reedy, Roane W. Va C3 123
Reedy, lake, Fla E5 86
Reedy, riv., S.C. C3 115
Reef, pt., N.Z. K14 51
Reefton, N.Z O13 51
Ree Heights, Hand, S. Dak . C6 116
Reelfoot, lake, Tenn A2 117
Reelsville, Putnam, Ind E4 91
Reeman, Newaygo, Mich E4 98
Reere, isl., Bikini 52
Reese, Greenwood, Kans E7 93
Reese, Tuscola, Mich E7 98
Reese, riv., Nev D4 104
Reese Station, Franklin, Ohio m11 111
Reese Village, Lubbock, Tex *C2 118
Reeseville, Dodge, Wis E5 124
Reesville, Clinton, Ohio C2 111
Reeth, Eng F7 13
Reeves, co., Tex o13 118
Reeves, mtn., Austl F7 51
Reevesville, Johnson, Ill F5 90
Reevesville, Dorchester, S.C . E6 115
Reform, Pickens, Ala B1 78
Reform, Choctaw, Miss B4 100
Refresco, Chile E2 55
Reftele, Swe A7 24
Refuge Cove, B.C., Can D5 68
Refugio, Refugio, Tex E4 118
Refugio, co., Tex E4 118
Rega, riv., Pol B3 26
Regan, Burleigh, N. Dak B5 110
Regat, riv., F.R.G D5 17
Regen, F.R.G E8 17
Regen, riv., F.R.G D6 16
Regency, Douglas, Nebr ... *C10 103
Regensburg, F.R.G D7 17
Regent, Man., Can E1 71
Regent, Hettinger, N. Dak .. C3 110
Register, Sullivan, Mo A4 101
Reggane, Alg D5 44
Reggio di Calabria, It E5 21
Reggio nell'Emilia, It B3 21
Reghin, Rom B7 22
Regina, Sask., Can G3, n8 70
Regina, Phillips, Mont C9 102
Regina, Sandoval, N. Mex .. A2 107
Regina Beach, Sask., Can .. G3 70
Register, Bulloch, Ga D5 87
Regla, Cuba C2 64
Regna, Swe u33 25
Rego, Orange, Ind H5 91
Reguengos de Monsaraz, Port C2 20
Rehau, F.R.G C7 17
Rehna, G.D.R E5 24
Rehoboth, Bristol, Mass C5 97
Rehoboth, McKinley, N. Mex B1 107
Rehoboth, Namibia B3 49
Rehoboth, bay, Del C7 85
Rehoboth Beach, Sussex, Del C7 85
Rehovot, Isr C6, h10 32
Reichenbach, F.R.G A4 18
Reichenbach, G.D.R C7 17
Reid, lake, Sask., Can G1 70
Reids Grove, Dorchester, Md C6 85
Reidsville, Tattnall, Ga D4 87
Reidsville, Rockingham, N.C A3 109
Reidville, Spartanburg, S.C . B3 115
Reigate, Eng C7 12
Reiley, East Feliciana, La .. D5 95
Reims, Fr C6 14, E4 15
Reina Adelaida, arch., Chile ... E2 54
Reinach, Switz B5 19
Reinbeck, Grundy, Iowa B5 92
Reindeer, isl., Man., Can C3 71
Reindeer, lake, Man., Sask., Can E12 66
Reindeer, riv., Sask., Can B4 70
Reinfeld, F.R.G E4 24
Reinosa, Sp A3 20
Reipetown, White Pine, Nev D6 104
Reisterstown, Baltimore, Md B4 85
Reit im Winkl, F.R.G B8 18
Reitz, S. Afr C4 49
Rekarne, Swe t34 25
Reliance, Lyman, S. Dak ... D6 116
Reliance, Polk, Tenn D9 117
Reliance, Sweetwater, Wyo . E3 125
Remada, Tun C7 44
Remagen, F.R.G C2 17
Remanso, Braz C2 57
Rembert, Sumter, S.C C6 115
Rembertow, Pol B6, k14 26
Rembrandt, Buena Vista, Iowa B2 92
Remecó, Arg B4 54
Remedios, Cuba C4 64
Remedios, Pan F7 62
Remer, Cass, Minn C5 99
Remerton, Lowndes, Ga F3 87
Remington, Jasper, Ind C3 91
Remington, Fauquier, Va ... B5 121
Remiremont, Fr C7 14
Remlap, Blount, Ala B3 78
Remmel, dam, Ark g8 81
Rems, riv., F.R.G E4 17
Remscheid, F.R.G B2 17
Remsen, Plymouth, Iowa ... B2 92
Remsen, Oneida, N.Y B5 108
Remus, Mecosta, Mich E5 98
Renaix, see Ronse, Bel.
Rena Lara, Coahoma, Miss . A3 100
Renault, Alg F7 30
Renault, Monroe, Ill E4 90
Rencona, San Miguel, N. Mex B4 107
Rencontre, East, Newf., Can E4 75
Rend, lake, Ill E5 90
Rendsburg, F.R.G A4 16
Rendville, Perry, Ohio C3 111
Renens, Switz C2 19
Renews, Newf., Can E5 75
Renforth, N.B., Can D4 74
Renfrew, Ont., Can B8 72
Renfrew, Scot *E4 13
Renfrew, Greenville, S.C ... B2 115
Renfrew, co., Ont., Can B7 72
Renfrow, Grant, Okla A4 112
Rengo, Chile A2 54
Reni, Sov. Un C9 22
Renick, Randolph, Mo B5 101
Renick (Falling Springs), Greenbrier, W. Va D4 123
Renish, pt., Scot C2 13
Renmark, Austl G3 51
Renner, Minnehaha, S. Dak D9 116
Renner, Collin, Tex m10 118
Rennerod, F.R.G C3 17
Rennert, Robeson, N.C C3 109
Rennes, Fr C3 14
Rennick, bay, Ant C29 5
Rennie, Man., Can E4 71
Reno, Bond, Ill E4 90
Reno, Leavenworth, Kans . k15 93
Reno, Washoe, Nev D2 104
Reno, Washington, Ohio C4 111
Reno, co., Kans E5 93
Reno, lake, Minn E3 99
Reno, riv., It B3 21
Renous, N.B., Can C3 74
Renous, riv., N.B., Can C3 74
Renovo, Clinton, Pa D6 114
Renown, Sask., Can F3 70
Rensselaer, Jasper, Ind C3 91
Rensselaer, Rensselaer, N.Y . C7 108
Rensselaer, co., N.Y C7 108
Rensselaer Falls, St. Lawrence, N.Y f9 108
Rensselaerville, Albany, N.Y C6 108
Rentiesville, McIntosh, Okla B6 112
Renton, King, Wash B3, f11 122
Rentz, Laurens, Ga D4 87

Roaring Branch, Lycoming, Pa C8 114
Roaring Creek, Columbia, Pa E9 114
Roaring Spring, Blair, Pa F5 114
Roaring Springs, Motley, Tex C2 118
Roaringwater, bay, Ire F2 11
Roark, Leslie, Ky C6 94
Roatán, Hond B4 62
Roba, Macon, Ala C4 78
Robards, Henderson, Ky C2 94
Robb, Alta., Can C2 69
Robbin, Kittson, Minn B1 99
Robbins, Cook, Ill k9 90
Robbins, Moore, N.C B3 109
Robbins, Scott, Tenn C9 117
Robbins, pt., Md B5 85
Robbinsdale, Hennepin, Minn m12 99
Robbinston, Washington, Maine C5 96
Robbinsville, Mercer, N.J C3 106
Robbinsville, Graham, N.C f9 109
Robbs, Pope, Ill F5 90
Robe, riv., Ire D2 11
Robeline, Natchitoches, La C2 95
Robersonville, Martin, N.C B5 109
Robert, Tangipahoa, La D5, g11 95
Robert, cape, Ont., Can A2 72
Roberta, Crawford, Ga D2 87
Robert Brown, cape, N.W. Ter., Can C16 67
Robert English, coast, Ant B5 5
Robert Lee, Coke, Tex D2 118
Roberts, Jefferson, Idaho F6 89
Roberts, Ford, Ill C5 90
Roberts, Newton, Miss C4 100
Roberts, Carbon, Mont E7 102
Roberts, St. Croix, Wis D1 124
Roberts, co., S. Dak B8 116
Roberts, co., Tex B2 118
Roberts, pt., Wash A2 122
Robert's Arm, Newf., Can D4 75
Robert Scott, glacier, Ant A32 5
Roberts Creek, mtn., Nev D5 104
Robertsdale, Baldwin, Ala E2 78
Robertsdale, Huntingdon, Pa F3 114
Robert S. Kerr Lake, res., Okla B6 112
Robertson, S. Afr D3 49
Robertson, Uinta, Wyo E2 125
Robertson, co., Ky B5 94
Robertson, co., Tenn A5 117
Robertson, co., Tex D4 118
Robertson, bay, Ant B29 5
Robertson, lake, Que., Can C2 75
Robertsonville, Que., Can C6 73
Robertsport, Lib E2 45
Robertstown, White, Ga B3 87
Robertville, Litchfield, Conn B4 84
Robertville, N.B., Can B4 74
Robert Williams, Ang D2 48
Roberval, Que., Can A5 73
Robeson, co., N.C C3 109
Robesonia, Berks, Pa *F9 114
Robinette, Baker, Oreg C9 113
Robin Hood's Bay, Eng F8 13
Robins, Linn, Iowa B6 92
Robins, Guernsey, Ohio C4 111
Robins, isl., N.Y F7 84
Robinson, Crawford, Ill D6 90
Robinson, Brown, Kans C8 93
Robinson, Aroostook, Maine B5 96
Robinson, Kidder, N. Dak B6 110
Robinson, Indiana, Pa F3 114
Robinson, McLennan, Tex *D4 118
Robinson, fork, W. Va k9 123
Robinson, fork, W. Va m14 123
Robinson, mtn., Wash A5 122
Robinsons, Newf., Can D2 75
Robinsonville, Tunica, Miss A3 100
Robinvale, Austl G4 51
Robinwood, Jefferson, Ala *B3 78
Roblin, Man., Can D1 71
Roblin, riv., Man., Can A5 71
Robsart, Sask., Can H1 70
Robson, B.C., Can E9 68
Robson, mtn., Alta., B.C., Can F9 66
Robstown, Nueces, Tex F4 118
Roby, Tex., Mo D5 101
Roby, Fisher, Tex C2 118
Roca, Lancaster, Nebr h11 103
Roca, cape, Port f9 20
Rocafuerte, Ec B1 58
Rocafuerte, Peru B2 58
Rocanville, Sask., Can G5 70
Rocas, is., Braz B4 57
Rocca Massima, It h9 21
Roccastrada, It C3 21
Rocha, Ur E2 56
Rocha, dept., Ur *E2 56
Rochdale, Eng A5 12
Rochdale, Worcester, Mass B4 97
Rochechouart, Fr E4 14
Rochefort, Bel D5 15
Rochefort, Fr E3 14
Roche Harbor, San Juan, Wash A2 122
Rochelle, Wilcox, Ga E3 87
Rochelle, Ogle, Ill B4 90
Rochelle, McCulloch, Tex D3 118
Rochelle Park, Bergen, N.J h8 106
Roche-Percée, Sask., Can H4 70
Rocheport, Boone, Mo C5 101
Rochester, Alta., Can B4 69
Rochester, Eng C8 12
Rochester, Sangamon, Ill D4 90
Rochester, Fulton, Ind B5 91
Rochester, Cedar, Iowa C6 92
Rochester, Butler, Ky C3 94
Rochester, Plymouth, Mass C6 97
Rochester, Oakland, Mich F7 98
Rochester, Olmsted, Minn F6 99
Rochester, Strafford, N.H D5 105
Rochester, Monroe, N.Y B3 108
Rochester, Lorain, Ohio A3 111
Rochester, Beaver, Pa E1 114
Rochester, Haskell, Tex C3 118
Rochester, Windsor, Vt D3 120
Rochester, Thurston, Wash C2 122
Rochester, Racine, Wis n11 124
Rochester, mtn., Vt D3 120
Rochfort Bridge, Alta., Can C3 69
Rochfort Bridge, Ire D4 11
Rochikarai, isl., Bikini 52
Rochlitz, G.D.R B7 17
Rociada, San Miguel, N. Mex B4 107
Rock, Cowley, Kans E7 93
Rock, Plymouth, Mass *C6 97
Rock, Delta, Mich B3 98
Rock, co., Minn G2 99
Rock, co., Nebr B6 103
Rock, co., Wis F4 124
Rock, creek, Sask., Can H2 70
Rock, creek, Ill B4 90
Rock, creek, Kans g10 93
Rock, creek, Md B3 85
Rock, creek, Nebr g11 103
Rock, creek, Nev C5 104
Rock, creek, Wash B8 122
Rock, creek, Wash E8 122
Rock, creek, Wash h14 122
Rock, creek, Wyo E6 125
Rock, isl., Fla C3 86
Rock, isl., Wis C7 124
Rock, lake, Man., Can E2 71
Rock, lake, Wash B8 122
Rock, mtn., Ala g6 78
Rock, riv., Ill., Wis B4 90, E5 124
Rock, riv., Iowa, Minn A1 92, G2 99
Rockall, isl., Scot D16 4
Rockawalkin, Wicomico, Md D6 85
Rockaway, Morris, N.J B3 106
Rockaway, Tillamook, Oreg B3 113
Rockaway, beach, N.Y k9 106
Rockaway, inlet, N.Y k9 106
Rockaway Beach, Taney, Mo E4 101
Rock Bay, B.C., Can D5 68
Rock Bluff, Liberty, Fla B2 86
Rockbridge, Greene, Ill D3 90
Rockbridge, Hocking, Ohio C3 111
Rockbridge, co., Va C3 121
Rockcastle, co., Ky C5 94
Rockcastle, riv., Ky C5 94
Rockcliffe Park, Ont., Can *B9 72
Rock Creek, B.C., Can E8 68
Rock Creek, Jefferson, Kans k14 93
Rock Creek, Ashtabula, Ohio A5 111
Rock Creek, Gilliam, Oreg B6 113
Rock Creek, butte, Oreg C8 113
Rock Creek Hills, Montgomery, Md *B3 85
Rockdale, Austl *G8 51
Rockdale, Will, Ill B5, m8 90
Rockdale, Dubuque, Iowa B7 92
Rockdale, Baltimore, Md B4 85
Rockdale, Maury, Tenn B4 117
Rockdale, Milam, Tex D4 118
Rockdale, co., Ga C3 87
Rock Eagle, mound, Ga C3 87
Rockefeller, plat., Ant A35 5
Rock Elm, Pierce, Wis D1 124
Rocker, Silver Bow, Mont D4 102
Rockerville, Pennington, S. Dak D2 116
Rockfall, Middlesex, Conn C6 84
Rock Falls, Whiteside, Ill B4 90
Rock Falls, Cerro Gordo, Iowa A4 92
Rockfield, Carroll, Ind C4 91
Rockfield, Warren, Ky D3 94
Rockfield, Washington, Wis m11 124
Rockford, Coosa, Ala C3 78
Rockford, Winnebago, Ill A4 90
Rockford, Floyd, Iowa A5 92
Rockford, Kent, Mich E5 98
Rockford, Wright and Hennepin, Minn m11 99
Rockford, Mercer, Ohio B1 111
Rockford, Blount, Tenn D10, n14 117
Rockford, Spokane, Wash B8 122
Rockford Bay, Kootenai, Idaho g15 122
Rockglen, Sask., Can H3 70
Rock Hall, Kent, Md B5 85
Rockham, Faulk, S. Dak C10 116
Rockhampton, Austl A8 51
Rockhaven, Sask., Can E1 70
Rock Hill, St. Louis, Mo *C7 101
Rock Hill, York, S.C B5 115
Rockhill Furnace, Huntingdon, Pa F6 114
Rockholds, Whitley, Ky D5 94
Rockingham, Bacon, Ga E4 87
Rockingham, Ray, Mo B4 101
Rockingham, Richmond, N.C C3 109
Rockingham, Windham, Vt E4 120
Rockingham, co., N.H D4 105
Rockingham, co., N.C A3 109
Rockingham, co., Va B4 121
Rock Island, Que., Can D5 73
Rock Island, Rock Island, Ill B3 90
Rock Island, Douglas, Wash B5 122
Rock Island, co., Ill B3 90
Rocklake, Towner, N. Dak A6 110
Rockland, Ont., Can B9 72
Rockland, Power, Idaho G6 89
Rockland, Knox, Maine D3 96
Rockland, Plymouth, Mass B6, h12 97
Rockland, Ontonagon, Mich m12 98
Rockland, Sullivan, N.Y D6 108
Rockland, co., N.Y D6 108
Rockledge, Brevard, Fla D6 86
Rockledge, Laurens, Ga D4 87
Rockledge, Montgomery, Pa o21 114
Rockleigh, Bergen, N.J g9 106
Rocklin, Placer, Calif C3 82
Rockmart, Polk, Ga C1 87
Rock Point, Apache, Ariz A6 80
Rock Point, Charles, Md D4 85
Rockport, Hot Springs, Ark g8 81
Rockport, Pike, Ill D2 90
Rockport, Spencer, Ind I3 91
Rockport, Ohio, Ky C3 94
Rockport, Knox, Maine D3 96
Rockport, Essex, Mass A6 97
Rockport, Copiah, Miss D3 100
Rock Port, Atchison, Mo A2 101
Rockport, Warren, N.J B3 106
Rockport, Aransas, Tex E4 118
Rockport, Skagit, Wash A4 122
Rock Rapids, Lyon, Iowa A1 92
Rock River, Albany, Wyo E7 125
Rock Run, Cherokee, Ala A4 78
Rock Springs, Rosebud, Mont D10 102
Rocksprings, Edwards, Tex D2 118
Rock Springs, Sauk., Wis E4 124
Rock Springs, Sweetwater, Wyo E3 125
Rockstone, Guy A3 59
Rockton, Winnebago, Ill A4 90
Rockton, Clearfield, Pa D4 114
Rockvale, Fremont, Colo C5 83
Rockvale, Rutherford, Tenn B5 117
Rock Valley, Sioux, Iowa A1 92
Rockville, Clarke, Ala D2 78
Rockville, Tolland, Conn B7 84
Rockville, Parke, Ind E3 91
Rockville, Montgomery, Md B3 85
Rockville, Norfolk, Mass h10 97
Rockville, Stearns, Minn E4 99
Rockville, Bates, Mo C3 101
Rockville, Sherman, Nebr C7 103
Rockville, Malheur, Oreg D9 113
Rockville, Washington, R.I D9 84
Rockville, Washington, Utah F2 119
Rockville Centre, Nassau, N.Y n15 108
Rockwall, Rockwall, Tex C4, n10 118
Rockwall, co., Tex C4 118
Rockwell, Cerro Gordo, Iowa B4 92
Rockwell, Rowan, N.C B2 109
Rockwell City, Calhoun, Iowa B3 92
Rockwell Park, Mecklenburg, N.C B2 109
Rockwood, Franklin, Ala A2 78
Rockwood, Ont., Can D4 72
Rockwood, Randolph, Ill F4 90
Rockwood, Somerset, Maine C3 96
Rockwood, Wayne, Mich F7 98
Rockwood, Multnomah, Oreg *B4 113
Rockwood, Somerset, Pa G3 114
Rockwood, Roane, Tenn D9 117
Rockwood, Coleman, Tex D3 118
Rocky, Washita, Okla B2 112
Rocky, bay, Newf., Can B4 75
Rocky, lake, Man., Can B1 71
Rocky, lake, Maine D5 96
Rocky, mtn., Mont C4 102
Rocky, mts., N.A D8 61
Rocky, pt., N.Y E7 84
Rocky, pt., N.Y F2 84
Rocky, riv., Alta., Can C2 69
Rocky, riv., N.C B2 109
Rocky, riv., Ohio h9 111
Rocky, riv., S.C C2 115
Rocky Bar, Elmore, Idaho F3 89
Rocky Boy, Hill, Mont B7 102
Rocky Boys, Indian res., Mont B7 102
Rocky Comfort, McDonald, Mo E3 101
Rocky Coulee, creek, Wash B6 122
Rockyford, Alta., Can D4 69
Rocky Ford, Otera, Colo C7 83
Rocky Ford, Screven, Ga D8 87
Rocky Fork, lake, Ohio C2 111
Rocky Gap, Bland, Va C1 121
Rocky Harbour, Newf., Can D3 75
Rocky Hill, Hartford, Conn C6 84
Rocky Hill, Edmonson, Ky C3 94
Rocky Hill, Somerset, N.J C3 106
Rocky Mount, Edgecombe and Nash, N.C B5 109
Rocky Mount, Franklin, Va C3 121
Rocky Mountain, nat. park, Colo A5 83
Rocky Mountain House, Alta., Can C3 69
Rocky Nook, Plymouth, Mass *C6 97
Rocky Point, Suffolk, N.Y F5 84
Rocky Point, Pender, N.C C5 109
Rocky Point, Kitsap, Wash *B3 122
Rockypoint, Campbell, Wyo B7 125
Rocky Ripple, Marion, Ind k10 91
Rocky River, Cuyahoga, Ohio A4, h9 111
Rocky Top, mtn., Oreg C4 113
Rocroi, Fr E4 15
Roda, Wise, Va f9 121
Rodach, F.R.G C5 17
Rodanthe, Dare, N.C B7 109
Rodarte, Taos, N. Mex *A4 107
Rødby, Den D5 24
Rødbyhavn, Den D5 24
Roddickton, Newf., Can C3, h10 75
Rødding, Den C3 24
Roddy, Rhea, Tenn D9 117
Rødekro, Den C3 24
Rodeo, Contra Costa, Calif *D2 82
Rodeo, Hidalgo, N. Mex F1 107
Roder, riv., G.D.R B8 17
Roderfield, McDowell, W. Va D3 123
Roderick, isl., B.C., Can C3 68
Rodessa, Caddo, La B1 95
Rodewisch, G.D.R C7 17
Rodey, Dona Ana, N. Mex E3 107
Rodez, Fr E5 14
Rodgers Forge, Baltimore, Md *C4 85
Rodhopi (Rhodope), prov., Grc *B5 23
Ródhos, Grc D7 23
Ródhos (Rhodes), isl., Grc D6 23
Roding, F.R.G D7 17
Rodinga, Austl D5 50
Rodman, Palo Alto, Iowa A3 92
Rodman, Chester, S.C B5 115
Rodnei, mts., Rom B7 22
Rodney, Ont., Can E3 72
Rodney, Jefferson, Miss D2 100
Rodney, pond, Newf., Can D4 75
Rodney Village, Kent, Del D6 85
Rödovre, Den *C6 24
Roduco, Gates, N.C A6 109
Roe, Monroe, Ark C4 81
Roebling, Burlington, N.J C3 106
Roebourne, Austl D2 50
Roebuck, Spartanburg, S.C B4 115
Roebuck, bay, Austl C3 50
Roebuck Plaza, Jefferson, Ala *B3 78
Roeland Park, Johnson, Kans k16 93
Roermond, Neth C5 15
Roeselare, Bel D3 15
Roessleville, Albany, N.Y *C7 108
Roes Welcome, sound, N.W. Ter., Can D15 66
Roetgen, F.R.G D6 15
Roff, Pontotoc, Okla C5 112
Rogachev, Sov. Un E8 27
Rogaland, co., Nor *H1 25
Roganville, Jasper, Tex D6 118
Rogatica, Yugo D4 22
Roger Mills, co., Okla B2 112
Rogers, Benton, Ark A1 81
Rogers, Windham, Conn B9 84
Rogers, Hennepin, Minn E5, m11 99
Rogers, Colfax, Nebr C9 103
Rogers, Roosevelt, N. Mex D6 107
Rogers, Barnes, N. Dak B7 110
Rogers, Columbiana, Ohio B5 111
Rogers, Bell, Tex D4 118
Rogers, co., Okla A6 112
Rogers, lake, Conn D7 84
Rogers, mtn., Va f10 121
Rogers, pass, Mont C4 102
Rogers City, Presque Isle, Mich C7 98
Rogers Heights, Prince Georges, Md *C4 85
Rogerson, Twin Falls, Idaho G4 89
Rogersville, Lauderdale, Ala A2 78
Rogersville, N.B., Can C4 74
Rogersville, Webster, Mo D4 101
Rogersville, Greene, Pa G1 114
Rogersville, Hawkins, Tenn C10 117
Roggen, Weld, Colo A6 83
Rogozno, Pol B4 26
Rogue, riv., Oreg E2 113
Rogue River, Jackson, Oreg E3 113
Rogue River, range, Oreg E3 113
Rohnerville, Humboldt, Calif *B1 82
Rohrersville, Washington, Md B2 85
Rohri, canal, Pak D2 40
Rohtak, India *C6 40
Rohwer, Desha, Ark D4 81
Roi Et, Thai D5 38
Roi isl., Kwajalein 52
Roissy-en-France, Fr g11 14
Roj, isl., Ponape 52
Rojas, Arg A4 54
Rojo, cape, P.R C1 65
Rokan, riv., Indon L4 38
Rokeby, Sask., Can F4 70
Rokel, riv., S.L E2 45
Rokitno, Sov. Un F6 27
Rokycany, Czech D2 26
Roland, Pulaski, Ark C3, h9 81
Roland, Man., Can E3 71
Roland, Story, Iowa B4 92
Roland, Sequoyah, Okla B7 112
Roland, lake, Md g10 85
Roland Terrace, Anne Arundel, Md *B4 85
Rolesville, Wake, N.C B4 109
Rolette, Rolette, N. Dak A6 110
Rolette, co., N. Dak A6 110
Rolfe, Pocahontas, Iowa B3 92
Roll, Yuma, Ariz D2 80
Roll, Blackford, Ind C7 91
Roll, Roger Mills, Okla B2 112
Rolla, B.C., Can B7 68
Rolla, Morton, Kans E2 93
Rolla, Phelps, Mo D6 101
Rolla, Rolette, N. Dak A6 110
Rolleville, Ba C6 64
Rolling, fork, Ark C1 81
Rollingbay, Kitsap, Wash e10 122
Rolling Fork, Sharkey, Miss C3 100
Rolling Fork, riv., Ky C4 94
Rolling Hills, Los Angeles, Calif *E4 82
Rolling Hills Estates, Los Angeles, Calif *E2 82
Rolling Meadows, Cook, Ill h8 90
Rollingstone, Winona, Minn F7 99
Rollingwood, Contra Costa, Calif *D2 82
Rollins, Lake, Mont C2 102
Rollinsford, Strafford, N.H D5 105
Rollo, Switz D1 19
Rolvsöya, isl., Nor B10 25
Roma, Austl C7 51
Roma, Alta., Can A2 69
Roma, see Rome, It.
Roma, Starr, Tex F3 118
Romain, cape, S.C F9 115
Romaine, riv., Que., Can h9 75
Roman, Rom B8 22
Romania, country, Eur F13 8, B7 22
Roman Nose, mtn., Md m12 85
Roman Nose, mtn., Oreg D3 113
Romano, cape, Fla G5 86
Romano, isl., Cuba C5 64
Romanshorn, Switz A7 19
Romans [-sur-Isère], Fr E6 14
Romanzof, cape, Alsk C6 79
Romanzof, mts., Alsk B11 79
Romayor, Liberty, Tex D5 118
Rombauer, Butler, Mo E7 101
Romblon, Phil *C6 35
Romblon, prov., Phil *C6 35
Rome, Floyd, Ga B1 87
Rome, Jefferson, Ill E5 90
Rome, Peoria, Ill C4 90
Rome, Perry, Ind I4 91
Rome, Henry, Iowa D6 92
Rome (Roma), It D4, h8 21
Rome, Sunflower, Miss B3 100
Rome, Oneida, N.Y B5 108
Rome, Franklin, Ohio *C3 111
Rome, Lawrence, Ohio D3 111
Rome, Bradford, Pa C9 114
Rome City, Noble, Ind B7 91
Romema, Isr m14 32
Romeo, Conejos, Colo D4 83
Romeo, Will, Ill *B5 90
Romeo, Macomb, Mich F7 98
Romeoville, Will, Ill B5, k8 90
Romeville, St. James, La h10 95
Romford, Eng. (part of London) k13 10
Romilly [-sur-Seine], Fr C5 14
Rominger, Watauga, N.C A1 109
Romita, Mex m13 63
Romney, Tippecanoe, Ind D4 91
Romney, Hampshire, W. Va B6 123
Romny, Sov. Un F9 27
Rømø, isl., Den C2 24
Romona, Owen, Ind F4 91
Romont, Switz C2 19
Romorantin, Fr D4 14
Rompin, riv., Mala K5 38
Romsey, Eng D6 12
Romulus, Wayne, Mich p15 98
Romulus, Seneca, N.Y C4 108
Romurikku, isl., Bikini 52
Ron, Viet D7 38
Rona, isl., Scot A3 13
Rona, isl., Scot C2 13
Ronald, Kittitas, Wash B4 122
Ronan, Lake, Mont C2 102
Roncador, mts., Braz E4 59
Roncador Bank, shoals, Caribbean Sea D7 62
Ronceverte, Greenbrier, W. Va D4 123
Ronciglione, It C4 21
Ronda, Wilkes, N.C A2 109
Ronda, Sp D3 20
Rønde, Den B4 24
Ronde, isl., Grenada W25 65
Rondo, Lee, Ark C5 81
Rondônia, prov., Braz E2 59
Rondout, Lake, Ill E2 90
Roneys Point, Ohio, W. Va f8 123
Rong, isl., Kam G5 38
Rongerik, atoll, Marshall Is F10 7
Ronkiti, Ponape 52
Ronkiti, hbr., Ponape 52
Ronkonkoma, Suffolk, N.Y F4 84
Ronkonkoma, lake, N.Y F4 84
Rønne, Den C8 24
Ronne, entrance, Ant B5 5
Rönne, riv., Swe B6 24
Rönneburg, G.D.R C7 17
Ronse, Bel D3 15
Ronuro, riv., Braz E7 59
Roodepoort-Maraisburg, S. Afr *C4 49
Roodeschool, Neth A6 15
Roodhouse, Greene, Ill D3 90
Roof, butte, Ariz A6 80
Rooks, co., Kans C4 93
Roopville, Carroll, Ga C1 87
Roorkee, India *C6 40
Roosendaal, Neth C4 15
Roosevelt, Gila, Ariz D4 80
Roosevelt, Roseau, Minn B3 99
Roosevelt, Monmouth, N.J C4 106
Roosevelt, Nassau, N.Y G2 84
Roosevelt, Kiowa, Okla C2 112
Roosevelt, Kimble, Tex D3 118
Roosevelt, Duchesne, Utah C5 119
Roosevelt, Klickitat, Wash D5 122
Roosevelt, co., Mont B11 102
Roosevelt, co., N. Mex C6 107
Roosevelt, isl., Ant B32 5
Roosevelt, riv., Braz D2 59
Roosevelt Campobello, international park, N.B., Can E3 74
Roosevelt Park, Muskegon, Mich E4 98
Root, riv., Minn G7 99
Root, riv., Wis n12 124
Rootstown, Portage, Ohio A4 111
Ropczyce, Pol C6 26
Roper, Washington, N.C B6 109
Roper, riv., Austl B5 50
Ropesville, Hockley, Tex C1 118
Roque Bluffs, Washington, Maine D5 96
Roquefort, Fr E3 14
Roques, is., Ven A4 60
Roquetas, Sp B6 20
Rora, head, Scot B5 13
Roraima, mtn., Ven B5 60
Rorke, lake, Man., Ont., Can B5 71
Rorketon, Man., Can D2 71
Röros, Nor F4 25
Rorschach, Switz B7 19
Rosa, St. Landry, La D3 95
Rosa, mtn., It., Switz D3 19
Rosa, pt., Mex B3 63
Rosales, Phil o13 35
Rosalia, Butler, Kans E7 93
Rosalia, Whitman, Wash B8 122
Rosalie, Thurston, Nebr B9 103
Rosalind, Alta., Can C4 69
Rosamond, Kern, Calif E4 82
Rosamond, Christian, Ill D4 90
Rosa Morada, Mex k11 63
Rosario, Arg A4 54
Rosário, Braz B2 57
Rosario, Mex C3 63
Rosario, Par D4 55
Rosario, Phil p13 35
Rosario, Ur E1 56
Rosario de la Frontera, Arg E3 55
Rosário do Sul, Braz E2 56
Rosário Oeste, Braz A1 56
Rosario Tala, Arg A5 54
Rosarti, Phelps, Mo C6 101
Rosboro, Pike, Ark C2 81
Rosburg, Wahkiakum, Wash C2 122
Roscoe, Winnebago, Ill A4 90
Roscoe, Stearns, Minn E4 99
Roscoe, St. Clair, Mo D4 101
Roscoe, Carbon, Mont E7 102
Roscoe, Keith, Nebr C4 103
Roscoe, Sullivan, N.Y D6 108
Roscoe, Washington, Pa F2 114
Roscoe, Edmunds, S. Dak B6 116
Roscoe, Nolan, Tex C2 118
Roscoe, glacier, Ant C22 5
Roscommon, Ire D3 11
Roscommon, Roscommon, Mich D6 98
Roscommon, co., Ire D3 11
Roscommon, co., Mich D6 98
Roscrea, Ire E4 11
Rose, Rock, Nebr B6 103
Rose, Wayne, N.C *B4 109
Rose, Mayes, Okla A6 112
Rose, peak, Ariz D6 80
Rose, pt., B.C., Can B2 68
Roseau, Dominica I14 64
Roseau, Roseau, Minn B3 99
Roseau, co., Minn B3 99
Roseau, riv., Man., Can E3 71
Roseau, riv., Minn B2 99
Rosebery, B.C., Can D9 68
Rose-Blanche, Newf., Can E2 75
Roseboro, Sampson, N.C C4 109
Rose Bud, White, Ark B3 81
Rosebud, Alta., Can D4 69
Rosebud, Gasconade, Mo C6 101
Rosebud, Rosebud, Mont D10 102
Rosebud, Todd, S. Dak D5 116
Rosebud, Falls, Tex D4 118
Rosebud, co., Mont D10 102
Rosebud, creek, Mont E10 102
Rosebud, Indian res., S. Dak D5 116
Rosebud, riv., Alta., Can D4 69
Roseburg, Douglas, Oreg D3 113
Rosebush, Isabella, Mich E6 98
Rose City, Ogemaw, Mich D6 98
Rose Creek, Mower, Minn G6 99
Rosedale, Alta., Can D4 69
Rosedale, B.C., Can f14 68
Rosedale, Manatee, Fla *E4 86
Rosedale, Parke, Ind E3 91
Rosedale, Bolivar, Miss B2 100
Rosedale, Anderson, Tenn C9 117
Rosedale, Pierce, Wash f10 122
Rosedale, Braxton, W. Va C4 123
Roseglen, McLean, N. Dak B4 110
Rosehearty, Scot C6 11
Rose Hill, Jasper, Ill D5 90
Rose Hill, Mahaska, Iowa C5 92
Rose Hill, Butler, Kans E6, g12 93
Rose Hill, Jasper, Miss C4 100
Rosehill, Duplin, N.C C4 109
Rose Hill, Fairfax, Va g12 121
Rose Hill, Lee, Va f8 121
Roseisle, Man., Can E2 71
Roseland, Sonoma, Calif *C2 82
Roseland, Indian River, Fla E6 86
Roseland, St. Joseph, Ind A5 91
Roseland, Tangipahoa, La D5 95
Roseland, Adams, Nebr D7 103
Roseland, Essex, N.J *B4 106
Roseland, Richland, Ohio B3 111
Roselawn, Newton, Ind B3 91
Roselle, DuPage, Ill k8 90
Roselle, Union, N.J k7 106
Roselle Park, Union, N.J k7 106
Rose Lynn, Alta., Can D5 69
Rosemark, Shelby, Tenn B2 117
Rosemary, Alta., Can D4 69
Rosemead, Los Angeles, Calif *F4 82
Rosemère, Que., Can p19 73
Rosemont, Cook, Ill *A6 90
Rosemont, St. Clair, Ill *E3 90
Rosemont, Hunterdon, N.J C3 106
Rosemont, Delaware and Montgomery, Pa *F11 114
Rosemont, Taylor, W. Va B7, k10 123
Rosemount, Dakota, Minn F5 99
Rosenberg, Fort Bend, Tex r14 118
Rosendael, Fr B5 14
Rosendale, Andrew, Mo A3 101
Rosendale, Ulster, N.Y *D6 108
Rosendale, Fond du Lac, Wis E5 124
Roseneath, Ont., Can C6 72
Rosenfeld, Man., Can E3 71
Rosenhayn, Cumberland, N.J E2 106
Rosenheim, F.R.G E6 16
Rosepine, Vernon, La D2 95
Rose Prairie, B.C., Can A7 68
Roseray, Sask., Can G1 70
Rosetown, Sask., Can F2, n7 70
Rosetta (Rashîd), Eg C6 43
Rosetta, Wilkinson, Miss D2 100
Rosetta, riv. mouth, Eg C2 32
Rose Valley, Sask., Can E4 70
Rosevear, Alta., Can C2 69
Roseville, Placer, Calif C3 82
Roseville, Warren, Ill C3 90
Roseville, Macomb, Mich o16 98
Roseville, Ramsey, Minn m12 99
Roseville, Muskingum and Perry, Ohio C3 111
Rosewood, Humboldt, Calif *B1 82
Rosewood, Champaign, Ohio B2 111
Rosewood Heights, Madison, Ill E3 90
Rosharon, Brazoria, Tex r14 118
Rosheim, Fr F7 15
Rosh Ha'Ayin, Isr B7, g10 32
Rosholt, Roberts, S. Dak B9 116
Rosholt, Portage, Wis D4 124
Rosh Pinna, Isr B7 32
Rosiclare, Hardin, Ill F5 90
Rosie, Independence, Ark B4 81
Rosier, Burke, Ga D4 87
Rosières-en-Santerre, Fr E2 15
Rosignol, Guy A3 59
Rosillo, peak, Tex E1 118
Rosine, Ohio, Ky C3 94
Roșiorii-de-Vede, Rom C7 22
Rosita, Custer, Colo C5 83
Roskilde, Den C6 24
Roskilde, co., Den C6 24
Roslavl, Sov. Un E9 27
Roslyn, Nassau, N.Y *F2 84
Roslyn, Montgomery, Pa o21 114
Roslyn, Day, S. Dak B8 116
Roslyn, Kittitas, Wash B4 122
Roslyn Estates, Nassau, N.Y *F2 84
Roslyn Harbor, Nassau, N.Y *F2 84
Roslyn Heights, Nassau, N.Y F2 84
Rosman, Transylvania, N.C f10 109
Rosny-sous-Bois, Fr g10 14
Ross, Marin, Calif *C2 82
Ross, Winston, Miss B4 100
Ross, N.Z O13 51
Ross, Mountrail, N. Dak A3 110
Ross, Butler, Ohio C1, n12 111
Ross, co., Ohio C2 111
Ross, dam, Wash A4 122
Ross, ice shelf, Ant B32 5
Ross, isl., Ant B29 5
Ross, isl., Bur F3 38
Ross, isl., Man., Can B3 71
Ross, lake, Wash A4 122
Ross, mtn., N.Z N15 51
Ross, sea, Ant B31 5
Rossa, Switz D7 19
Rossano, It E6 21
Rossburg, Darke, Ohio B1 111
Rossburn, Man., Can D1 71
Rosscarbery, Ire F2 11
Rosseau, Ont., Can B5 72
Rossendale, Man., Can E2 71
Rosser, Kaufman, Tex n10 118
Rosses, bay, Ire B3 11
Rosses Point, Ire C3 11
Rossford, Wood, Ohio A2, e6 111
Rossie, St. Lawrence, N.Y f9 108
Rossignol, lake, N.S., Can E4 74
Rossinière, Switz D3 19
Rossiter, Indiana, Pa E4 114
Rossland, B.C., Can E9 68
Rosslare, Ire E5 11
Rosslau, G.D.R B7 17
Rosslea, N. Ire C4 11
Rossmoor, Orange, Calif *F5 82
Rossmoyne, Hamilton, Ohio *C1 111
Rosso, Maur C1 45
Ross-on-Wye, Eng C5 12
Rossosh, Sov. Un F12 27
Ross River, Yukon, Can D6 66
Rosston, Nevada, Ark D2 81
Rosston, Harper, Okla A2 112
Rossville, Walker, Ga B1 87
Rossville, Vermilion, Ill C6 90
Rossville, Clinton, Ind D4 85
Rossville, Allamakee, Iowa A6 92
Rossville, Shawnee, Kans C8 93
Rossville, Fayette, Tenn B2 117
Rossville, Atascosa, Tex E3 118
Rossway, N.S., Can E4 74
Rosthern, Sask., Can E2 70
Rostock, G.D.R A6 16, D6 24
Rostov, Sov. Un C12 27
Rostov [-na-Donu], Sov. Un H12 27
Rosul, pass, Rom C6 22
Roswell, El Paso, Colo. (part of Colorado Springs) C6 83
Roswell, Fulton, Ga B2, g8 87
Roswell, Canyon, Idaho F2 89
Roswell, Chaves, N. Mex D5 107
Roswell, Miner, S. Dak C8 116
Rota, Sp D2 20
Rotan, Fisher, Tex C2 118
Rotenburg, F.R.G B4 16
Rotenburg [an der Fulda], F.R.G B4 17
Roth, Bottineau, N. Dak A5 110
Roth, F.R.G D6 17
Rothaargebirge, mts., F.R.G B3 17
Rothbury, Eng E7 13
Rothbury, Oceana, Mich E4 98
Röthenbach, F.R.G D6 17
Röthenbach im Emmental, Switz C4 19
Rothenburg [in der Lausitz], G.D.R B9 17
Rothenburg ob der Tauber, F.R.G D5 17
Rothenthurm, Switz B6 19

S

St. Barnabé-Nord, Que., Can...C5 73
St. Barnabé-Sud, Que., Can...D5 73
St. Barthélémy, Que., Can...C4 73
St. Barthélemy, isl., Guad...H13 64
St. Basile, N.B., Can...B1 74
St. Basile [-de-Portneuf], Que., Can...C6 73
St. Basile-le-Grand, Que., Can...*D4 73
Ste. Béatrix, Que., Can...C4 73
St. Bees, head, Eng...C5 10
St. Benedict, Sask., Can...E3 70
St. Benedict, Kossuth, Iowa...A3 92
St. Benedict, Nemaha, Kans...C7 93
St. Benedict, Marion, Oreg...h12 113
St. Benoît, Que., Can...p18 73
St. Benoît-Labre, Que., Can...C7 73
St. Bernard, Cullman, Ala...A3 78
St. Bernard, St. Bernard, La...E6, k12 95
St. Bernard, Platte, Nebr...C8 103
St. Bernard, Hamilton, Ohio...o12 111
St. Bernard, par., La...E6 95
St. Bernard, see Grand St. Bernard, pass, Switz., It.
St. Bernard [-de-Dorchester], Que., Can...C6 73
St. Bernice, Perry, Ind...E2 91
St. Bethlehem, Montgomery, Tenn...A4 117
Ste. Blandine, Que., Can...A9 73
St. Bonaventure, Que., Can...D5 73
St. Bonaventure, Cattaraugus, N.Y...*C2 108
St. Boswells, Sask., Can...G2 70
St. Brendan's, Newf., Can...D5 75
St. Bride, mtn., Alta., Can...D3 69
St. Bride's, Newf., Can...E4 75
St. Brides, bay, Wales...C2 12
St. Brieuc, Fr...C2 14
St. Brieux, Sask., Can...E3 70
Ste. Brigide, Que., Can...D4 73
Ste. Brigitte, Que., Can...C5 73
St. Bruno-de-Montarville, Que., Can...*D4 73
St. Bruno-Lac-St. Jean, Que., Can...A6 73
St. Calais, Fr...D4 14
St. Calixte, Que., Can...D4 73
St. Camille, Que., Can...D6 73
St. Camille [-de-Bellechasse], Que., Can...C7 73
St. Casimir, Que., Can...C5 73
St. Catharine, Washington, Ky...C4 94
St. Catharines, Ont., Can...D5 72
Ste. Catherine, Que., Can...C6, n16 73
St. Catherine, lake, Vt...E2 120
St. Catherine, mtn., Grenada...W25 65
St. Catherines, isl., Ga...E5 87
St. Catherine's, pt., Eng...D6 12
St. Catherines, sound, Ga...E5 87
Ste. Cécile, Que., Can...D7 73
St. Célestin, Que., Can...C5 73
St. Césaire, Que., Can...D4 73
St. Chamond, Fr...E6 14
St. Charles, Arkansas, Ark...C4 81
St. Charles, Bear Lake, Idaho...G4 89
St. Charles, Kane, Ill...B5, k8 90
St. Charles, Madison, Iowa...C4 92
St. Charles, Hopkins, Ky...C2 94
St. Charles, Saginaw, Mich...E6 98
St. Charles, Winona, Minn...G6 99
St. Charles, St. Charles, Mo...C3, f12 101
St. Charles, Gregory, S. Dak...D6 116
St. Charles, Lee, Va...f8 121
St. Charles, co., Mo...C7 101
St. Charles, par., La...E5 95
St. Charles, cape, Newf., Can...B4 75
St. Charles [-de-Bellechasse], Que., Can...C7 73
St. Chély-d'Apcher, Fr...E5 14
St. Chrysostome, Que., Can...D4 73
St. Clair, St. Clair, Mich...F8 98
St. Clair, Blue Earth, Minn...F5 99
St. Clair, Franklin, Mo...C6 101
St. Clair, Schuylkill, Pa...E9 114
St. Clair, co., Ala...B3 78
St. Clair, co., Ill...E4 90
St. Clair, co., Mich...F8 98
St. Clair, co., Mo...C4 101
St. Clair, lake, Ont., Can., Mich...E2 72
St. Clair, riv., Ont., Can., Mich...E2 72
St. Claire, Que., Can...C7 73
St. Clair Hills, St. Clair, Ill...B8 101
St. Clair Shores, Macomb, Mich...o16 98
St. Clairsville, Belmont, Ohio...B5 111
St. Claude, Man., Can...E2 71
St. Claude, Que., Can...D6 73
St. Claude [-sur-Bienne], Fr...D6 14
St. Clément, Que., Can...B8 73
St. Cléophas, Que., Can...*k13 73
Ste. Clothilde, Que., Can...D5 73
St. Cloud, Osceola, Fla...D5 86
St. Cloud, Fr...g9 14
St. Cloud, Stearns, Benton and Sherburne, Minn...E4 99
St. Cloud, Fond du Lac, Wis...E5, k9 124
St. Côme, Que., Can...C4 73
St. Constant, Que., Can...q19 73
St. Croix, N.B., Can...D2 74
Ste. Croix, Que., Can...C6, o16 73
Ste. Croix, Perry, Ind...H4 91
Ste. Croix, Switz...C2 19
St. Croix, co., Wis...C1 124
St. Croix, isl., Vir. Is. (U.S.)...C6 65
St. Croix, lake, Wis...D1 124
St. Croix, riv., N.B., Can...D2 74
St. Croix, riv., Maine...C5 96
St. Croix, riv., Minn., Wis...E6 99
St. Croix, stream, Maine...B4 96
St. Croix Falls, Polk, Wis...C1 124
St. Cuthbert, Que., Can...C4 73
St. Cyrille [-de-L'Islet], Que., Can...B7 73
St. Cyrille [-de-Wendover], Que., Can...D5 73
St. Damase, Que., Can...D4 73
St. Damase-de-Matane, Que., Can...*k13 73
St. Damase-des-Aulnaies, Que., Can...B7 73
St. Damien-de-Brandon, Que., Can...C4 73
St. Damien [-de-Buckland], Que., Can...C7 73
St. David, Cochise, Ariz...F5 80
St. David, Fulton, Ill...C3 90
St. David, Aroostook, Maine...A4 96
St. David [-de-l'Auberivière], Que., Can...n17 73
St. David [-d'Yamaska], Que., Can...D5 73
St. David's, Newf., Can...D2 75
St. Davids, Delaware, Pa...*G11 114
St. David's, Wales...C2 12
St. David's, head, Wales...C2 12
St. David's, isl., Bermuda...o21 64
St. Denis [-de-la-Bouteillerie], Que., Can...B8 73
St. Denis [River Richelieu], Que., Can...D4 73
St. Denis, Fr...C5, g10 14
St. Denis, Reunion...H24 3
St. Didace, Que., Can...C4 73
St. Dié, Fr...C7 14
St. Dizier, Fr...C6 14
St. Dominique, Que., Can...q18 73
St. Dominique-de-Bagot, Que., Can...D5 73
St. Donat-de-Montcalm, Que., Can...C3 73
St. Donatus, Jackson, Iowa...B7 92
Ste. Dorothée, Que., Can...*D4 73
St. Édouard, Que., Can...D4, q19 73
St. Edward, Boone, Nebr...C8 103
Ste. Edwidge, Que., Can...D6 73
St. Eleanor's, P.E.I., Can...C6 74
St. Éleuthère, Que., Can...B8 73
St. Elias, cape, Alsk...D11 79
St. Elias, mtn., Alsk., Yukon, Can...C11 79
St. Elias, mts., Alsk., B.C., Yukon, Can...C11 79
St.-Elie, Fr. Gu...B4 59
Ste. Élizabeth, Que., Can...C4 73
St. Elizabeth, Miller, Mo...C5 101
St. Elmo, Mobile, Ala...E1 78
St. Elmo, Fayette, Ill...D5 90
St. Éloi, Que., Can...A8 73
Ste. Émélie-de-l'Énergie, Que., Can...C4 73
St. Émile [-de-Suffolk], Que., Can...D3 73
St. Éphrem, Que., Can...C7 73
Saintes, Fr...E3 14
Saintes, is., Guad...R8 65
St. Esprit, Que., Can...D4 73
St. Étienne, Fr...E6 14
St. Étienne [-de-Beuharnois], Que., Can...q19 73
St.-Eugéne, Alg...*B5 44
Ste. Eulalie, Que., Can...C5 73
Ste. Euphémie, Que., Can...C7 73
St. Eusèbe, Que., Can...B9 73
St. Eustache, Que., Can...D4, p19 73
St. Eustatius, isl., Neth. Antilles...H13 64
St. Fabien, Que., Can...A9 73
Ste. Famille, Que., Can...C7 73
St. Famille d'Aumond, Que., Can...C2 73
St. Faustin, Que., Can...C3 73
St. Felicien, Que., Can...A5 73
Ste. Félicité, Que., Can...*k13 73
St. Félix-de-Valois, Que., Can...C4 73
St. Ferdinand, Que., Can...C6 73
St. Féréol, Que., Can...B7 73
St. Fidèle, Que., Can...B7 73
Saintfield, N. Ire...C6 11
St. Fintan's, Newf., Can...D2 75
St. Flavien, Que., Can...C6 73
St. Florent [-sur-Cher], Fr...D5 14
St. Florian, Lauderdale, Ala...A2 78
St. Flour, Fr...E5 14
St. Fortunat, Que., Can...D6 73
Ste. Foy, Que., Can...n17 73
Ste. Foy-la-Grande, Fr...E4 14
St. Francis, Clay, Ark...A5 81
St. Francis, Cheyenne, Kans...C2 93
St. Francis, Aroostook, Maine...A4 96
St. Francis, Anoka, Minn...E5 99
St. Francis, Todd, S. Dak...D4 116
St. Francis, Milwaukee, Wis...n12 124
St. Francis, co., Ark...B5 81
St. Francis, cape, Newf., Can...E5 75
St. Francis, lake, Que., Can...D6 73
St. Francis, riv., Ark...C5 81
St. Francis, riv., N.B., Que., Can., Maine...B8 73
St. Francis, riv., Que., Can...D5 73
St. Francis, riv., Mo...E7 101
St. Francisville, Lawrence, Ill...E6 90
St. Francisville, West Feliciana, La...D4 95
St. Francois, Que., Can...*p19 73
St. François, Guad...Q9 65
St. Francois, co., Mo...D7 101
St. François [-du-Lac], Que., Can...C5 73
Ste. Françoise, Que., Can...A8 73
St. François-Xavier, Que., Can...D5 73
St. Frédéric, Que., Can...C7 73
St. Froid, lake, Maine...B4 96
St. Fulgence, Que., Can...A7 73
St. Gabriel, Iberville, La...h9 95
St. Gabriel [-de-Brandon], Que., Can...C4 73
St. Gallen, see S[ank]t Gallen, Switz.
St. Gallen, see Sankt Gallen, canton, Switz.
St. Gaudens, Fr...F4 14
St. Gédéon, Que., Can...D7 73
Ste. Genevieve, Ste., Genevieve, Mo...D7 101
Ste. Genevieve, co., Mo...D7 101
Ste. Geneviève-de-Batiscan, Que., Can...C5 73
Ste. Geneviève-de-Pierrefonds, Que., Can...*D8 73
St. George, Austl...D7 51
St. George, Bermuda...o20 64
St. George, N.B., Can...D3 74
St. George, Ont., Can...D4 72
St. George, Charlton, Ga...F4 87
St. George, Pottawatomie, Kans...C7 93
St. George, St. Louis, Mo...*C7 101
St. George, Dorchester, S.C...E6 115
St. George, Washington, Utah...F2 119
St. George (Town of), Chittenden, Vt...*C2 120
St. George, cape, Newf., Can...D2 75
St. George, cape, Fla...C1 86
St. George, isl., Alsk...D6 79
St. George, isl., Fla...C2 86
St. George Island, St. Marys, Md...D4 85
St. Georges, Bel...D5 15
St. George's, Newf., Can...D2 75
St. Georges, Que., Can...C5 73
St. Georges, New Castle, Del...A6 85
St. Georges, Fr. Gu...B4 59
St. George's, Grenada...W25 65
St. George's, bay, Newf., Can...D2 75
St. Georges, bay, N.S., Can...D8 74
St. George's, chan., Ire., Wales...E3 10
St. George's, isl., Bermuda...o20 64
St. Georges-de-Malbaie, Que., Can...*k14 73
St. Georges [-de-Windsor], Que., Can...D6 73
St. Georges-Ouest, Que., Can...C7 73
St. Gérard, Que., Can...D6 73
St. Germain, forest, Fr...g9 14
St. Germain [-de-Grantham], Que., Can...D5 73
St. Germain-de-Kamouraska, Que., Can...B8 73
St. Germain-en-Laye, Fr...g9 14
Ste. Germaine-Station, Que., Can...C7 73
Ste. Gertrude, Que., Can...C5 73
St. Gertrude, St. Tammany, La...D5 95
St. Gervais, Que., Can...C7 73
St. Gervais-les-Bains, Fr...D2 18
St. Gilles, Bel...*D4 15
St. Gilles, Que., Can...C6 73
St. Gilles-du-Gard, Fr...F6 14
St. Gilles-sur-Vie, Fr...D3 14
St.-Gingolph, Switz...D2 19
St. Girons, Fr...F4 14
St. Goarshausen, see Sankt Goarshausen, F.R.G.
St. Gobain, Fr...C5 14
St. Gotthard, tunnel, Switz...C6 19
St. Goven's, head, Wales...C2 12
St. Grégoire, Que., Can...C5 73
St. Gregor, Sask., Can...E3 70
St. Gregory, mtn., Newf., Can...D2 75
St. Guillaume-d'Upton, Que., Can...D5 73
St. Helen, lake, Mich...D6 98
St. Helena, Napa, Calif...C2 82
St. Helena, Cedar, Nebr...B8 103
St. Helena, Br. dep., Afr...H5 42
St. Helena, par., La...D5 95
St. Helena, isl., Atl. O...H9 6
St. Helena, isl., S.C...G6 115
St. Helena, sound, S.C...G7 115
St. Helenabaai, bay, S. Afr...D2 49
St. Helène [-de-Kamouraska], Que., Can...B8 73
St. Helens, Eng...A5 12
St. Helens, Columbia, Oreg...B4 113
St. Helens, mtn., Wash...C3 122
St. Helier, Jersey...F5 10
Ste. Hénédine, Que., Can...C7 73
St. Henri, Que., Can...C6, o17 73
St. Henry, Mercer, Ohio...B1 111
St. Hermas, Que., Can...p18 73
St. Herménégilde, Que., Can...D6 73
St. Hilaire, Pennington, Minn...B2 99
St. Hilaire-de-Dorset, Que., Can...D7 73
St. Hilaire Est, Que., Can...*D4 73
St. Hilarion, Que., Can...B7 73
St. Honoré, Que., Can...D7 73
St. Honoré-de-Témiscouata, Que., Can...B8 73
St. Hubert, Que., Can...*D4 73
St. Hubert, Bel...D5 15
St. Hubert-de-Témiscouata, Que., Can...B8 73
St. Hugues, Que., Can...D5 73
St. Hyacinthe, Que., Can...D5 73
St. Hyacinthe, co., Que., Can...D4 73
St. Ignace, Mackinac, Mich...C6 98
St. Ignace, N.S., Can...C4 74
St. Ignatius, Lake, Mont...C2 102
St. Ignatius Mission, Guy...B3 59
St. Imier, Switz...B3 19
St. Inigoes, St. Marys, Md...D5 85
St. Irénée, Que., Can...B7 73
St. Isidore, N.B., Can...B4 74
St. Isidore-d'Auckland, Que., Can...D6 73
St. Isidore [-de-Laprairie], Que., Can...q19 73
St. Isidore-de-Prescott, Ont., Can...B10 72
St. Ives, Eng...B7 12
St. Ives, Eng...D2 12
St. Jacob, Madison, Ill...E4 90
St. Jacobs, Ont., Can...D4 72
St. Jacques, N.B., Can...B1 74
St. Jacques, Que., Can...D4 73
St. Jacques, cape, Viet...H7 38
St. Jacques-le-Mineur, Que., Can...q20 73
St. James, Stone, Ark...B4 81
St. James, St. James, La...k10 95
St. James, Charlevoix, Mich...C5 98
St. James, Watonwan, Minn...G4 99
St. James, Phelps, Mo...D6 101
St. James, Suffolk, N.Y...F4 84
St. James, par., La...D5 95
St. James, cape, B.C., Can...D2 68
St. James City, Lee, Fla...F4 86
St. Jean, Que., Can...D4 73
St. Jean, co., Que., Can...D4 73
St. Jean, lake, Que., Can...A5 73
St. Jean, riv., Que., Can...A7 73
St. Jean-Baptiste, Man., Can...E3 71
St. Jean-Chrysostome-de-Lévis, Que., Can...o17 73
St. Jean-d'Angély, Fr...E3 14
St. Jean-de-Dieu, Que., Can...A8 73
St. Jean-de-Luz, Fr...F3 14
St. Jean-de-Matha, Que., Can...C4 73
St. Jean [-de-Maurienne], Fr...D2 18
St. Jean-Eudes, Que., Can...*A7 73
St. Jean-Port-Joli, Que., Can...B7 73
St. Jérôme, Que., Can...D3 73
St. Jo, Montague, Tex...C4 118
St. Joachim [-de-Courval], Que., Can...D5 73
St. Joachim-de-Montmorency, Que., Can...B7 73
St. Joe, Searcy, Ark...A3 81
St. Joe, Benewah, Idaho...B2 89
St. Joe, DeKalb, Ind...B8 91
St. Joe, St. Tammany, La...h12 95
St. Joe, riv., Idaho...B3 89
Saint John, N.B., Can...D3 74
St. John, Lake, Ind...B3 91
St. John, Stafford, Kans...E5 93
St. John, Aroostook, Maine...A4 96
St. John, St. Louis, Mo...*C7 95
St. John, Rolette, N. Dak...A6 110
St. John, Tooele, Utah (part of Vernon)...C3 119
St. John, Whitman, Wash...B8 122
St. John, co., N.B., Can...D3 74
St. John, bay, Newf., Can...C3 75
St. John, cape, Newf., Can...D4 75
St. John, isl., Newf., Can...C3 75
St. John, isl., Vir. Is. (U.S.)...B6 65
St. John, lake, Newf., Can...D4 75
St. John, riv., Can., Maine...B5 96
St. John's, Antigua...H14 64
St. Johns, Apache, Ariz...C6 80
St. John's, Newf., Can...E5 75
St. Johns, Perry, Ill...E4 90
St. Johns, Clinton, Mich...E6 98
St. Johns, Auglaize, Ohio...B1 111
St. Johns, co., Fla...C5 86
St. John's, pt., Ire...C3 11
St. John's, pt., Ire...C6 11
St. Johns, riv., Fla...B5 86
St. Johnsbury, Caledonia, Vt...C4 120
St. Johnsbury Center, Caledonia, Vt...C4 120
St. Johns River, entrance, Fla...B6 86
St. Johnsville, Montgomery, N.Y...B6 108
St. John the Baptist, par., La...D5 95
St. Jones, riv., Del...B6 85
St. Joseph, N.B., Can...D5 74
St. Joseph, Dominica...J14 64
St. Joseph, Champaign, Ill...C5 90
St. Joseph, Tensas, La...C4 95
St. Joseph, Berrien, Mich...F4 98
St. Joseph, Stearns, Minn...E4 99
St. Joseph, Buchanan, Mo...B3 101
St. Joseph, Lawrence, Tenn...B4 117
St. Joseph, co., Ind...A5 91
St. Joseph, co., Mich...G5 98
St. Joseph, bay, Fla...C1 86
St. Joseph, isl., Ont., Can...B7 98
St. Joseph, isl., Mich...B6 98
St. Joseph, lake, Ont., Can...o17 72
St. Joseph, lake, Que., Can...n16 73
St. Joseph, pt., Fla...v16 86
St. Joseph, riv., U.S...A1 111
St. Joseph, sound, Fla...o10 86
St. Joseph-de-Beauce, Que., Can...C7 73
St. Joseph-de-la-Rive, Que., Can...B7 73
St. Joseph-de-St. Hyacinthe, Que., Can...*D4 73
St. Joseph-de-Sorel, Que., Can...*C4 73
St. Joseph-du-Lac, Que., Can...p18 73
St. Joseph's, Newf., Can...E5 75
St. Jovite, Que., Can...C3 73
St. Jovite-Station, Que., Can...C3 73
St. Jude, Que., Can...D5 73
St. Julien, Fr...D1 19
Ste. Julienne, Que., Can...D4 73
Ste. Julie-Station, Que., Can...C6 73
St. Junien, Fr...E4 14
St. Just, Eng...D2 12
St. Just-en-Chaussée, Fr...E2 15
Ste. Justine, Que., Can...D3 73
St. Keverne, Eng...*D2 12
St. Kilda, Austl...*H5 51
St. Kitts (St. Christopher), isl., St. Kitts-Nevis...H13 64
St. Kitts-Nevis, country, N.A....*H13 64
St. Lambert, Que., Can...p19 73
St. Lambert [-de-Lévis], Que., Can...C6 73
St. Landry, Evangeline, La...D3 95
St. Landry, par., La...D3 95
St. Laurent, Man., Can...D3 71
St. Laurent, Que., Can...p19 73
St. Laurent, Fr. Gu...A4 59
St. Laurent-Blangy, Fr...D2 15
St. Laurent-de-la-Salanque, Fr...F5 14
St. Laurent-du-Jura, Fr...C1 18
St. Lawrence, Austl...D8 50
St. Lawrence, Newf., Can...E4 75
St. Lawrence, Berks, Pa...*F10 114
St. Lawrence, Hand, S. Dak...C7 116
St. Lawrence, co., N.Y...A5 108
St. Lawrence, cape, N.S., Can...B9 74
St. Lawrence, gulf, Can...G20 67
St. Lawrence, isl., Alsk...C5 79
St. Lawrence, riv., Can., N.Y...G19 67
St. Lawrence Islands, nat. park, Ont., Can...C9 72
St. Lazare, Man., Can...D1 71
St. Lazare, Que., Can...q18 73
St. Leo, Pasco, Fla...D4 86
St. Leo, Yellow Medicine, Minn...F2 99
St. Léon, Que., Can...C5 73
St. Leon, Dearborn, Ind...F8 91
St. Léonard, N.B., Can...B2 74
St. Leonard, Calvert, Md...D4 85
St. Léonard [-d'Aston], Que., Can...C5 73
St. Léonard [-de-Noblat], Fr...E4 14
St. Léonard-de-Portneuf, Que., Can...C6 73
St. Léon-de-Standon, Que., Can...*C7 73
St. Lewis, riv., Newf., Can...B3 75
St. Lewis, sound, Newf., Can...B4 75
St. Libbory, St. Clair, Ill...E4 90
St. Liboire, Que., Can...D5 73
St. Libory, Howard, Nebr...C7 103
St. Lô, Fr...C3 14
St. Louis, P.E.I., Can...C5 74
St. Louis, Sask., Can...E3 70
St. Louis, Guad...R9 65
St. Louis, Gratiot, Mich...E6 98
St. Louis (Independent City), Mo...C7, f13 101
St. Louis, Pottawatomie, Okla...B5 102
St.-Louis, Sen...C1 45
St. Louis, co., Minn...C6 99
St. Louis, co., Mo...C7 101
St. Louis, bay, Miss...f7 100
St. Louis, lake, Que., Can...q19 73
St. Louis, riv., Minn...D6 99
St. Louis-de-Gonzague, Que., Can...D3, q19 73
St. Louis-de-Kent, N.B., Can...C5 74
St. Louis [-de-Richelieu], Que., Can...D5 73
St. Louis-du-Ha-Ha, Que., Can...B8 73
Ste. Louise, Que., Can...B7 73
St. Louis Park, Hennepin, Minn...n12 99
St. Louisville, Licking, Ohio...B3 111
St. Loup-sur-Semouse, Fr...B2 18
St.-Luc, Switz...D4 19
Saint Lucia, country, N.A....J14 64
St. Lucia, cape, S. Afr...C5 49
St. Lucia, chan., N.A...I14 64
St. Lucie, St. Lucie, Fla...E6 86
St. Lucie, co., Fla...E6 86
St. Lucie, canal, Fla...E6 86
St. Lucie, inlet, Fla...E6 86
Ste. Lucie-de-Beauregard, Que., Can...C7 73
St. Ludger, Que., Can...D7 73
Ste. Madeleine, Que., Can...D4 73
St. Magloire, Que., Can...C7 73
St. Magnus, bay, Scot...g10 10
St. Maixent-l'École, Fr...D3 14
St. Malachie, Que., Can...C7 73
St. Malo, Man., Can...E3 71
St. Malo, Fr...C2 14
St. Malo, gulf, Fr...C3 14
St. Mandé, Fr...g10 14
St. Marc, Que., Can...D4 73
St. Marc, Hai...E7 64
St. Marc [-des-Carrières], Que., Can...C5 73
St. Marcel-de-L'Islet, Que., Can...C7 73
St. Marcellin, Fr...E6 14
St. Margaret, bay, Newf., Can...C3 75
St. Margarets, Anne Arundel, Md...B5 85
St. Margaret's Hope, Scot...B6 13
Ste. Marguerite, riv., Que., Can...A7 73
Ste. Marguerite-de-Dorchester, Que., Can...C7 73
Ste. Marguerite Nord-Est, riv., Que., Can...A7 73
Ste. Marie, Que., Can...C5 73
Ste. Marie, Jasper, Ill...E5 90
Ste. Marie, Mart...S11 65
Ste. Marie, cape, Mad...K8 49
Ste.-Marie, isl., Que., Can...C2 75
Ste. Marie, isl., Mad...g9 49
Ste. Marie-aux-Mines, Fr...A3 18
Ste. Marie-Beauce, Que., Can...C6 73
St. Maries, Benewah, Idaho...B2 89
Ste. Marie-Sur-Mer, N.B., Can...B5 74
St. Mark, Sedgwick, Kans...g11 93
St. Marks, Wakulla, Fla...B2 86
Ste. Marthe, Que., Can...D3 73
St. Martin, par., La...D4 95
St. Martin, isl., Fr., Neth. Antilles...H13 64
St. Martin, isl., Mich...C4 98
St. Martin, lake, Man., Can...D2 71
St. Martin, riv., Md...D7 85
St. Martin-Boulogne, Fr...D9 12
St. Martin [-de-Ré], Fr...D3 14
Ste. Martine, Que., Can...D4, q19 73
St. Martins, N.B., Can...D4 74
St. Martin Station, Man., Can...D2, g8 71
St. Martinville, St. Martin, La...D4 95
St. Martory, Fr...F4 14
St. Mary, Marion, Ky...C4 94
St. Mary, par., La...E4 95
St. Mary, cape, N.S., Can...E3 74
St. Mary, res., Alta., Can...E4 69
St. Mary, riv., Alta., Can...E4 69
St. Mary, riv., B.C., Can...E2 69
St. Mary-of-the-Woods, Vigo, Ind...E3 91
St. Marys, Alsk...C7 79
St. Mary's, Newf., Can...E5 75
St. Mary's, Ont., Can...D3 72
St. Marys, Camden, Ga...F5 87
St. Marys, St. Joseph, Ind...A5 91
St. Marys, Pottawatomie, Kans...C7 93
St. Marys, Ste. Genevieve, Mo...D8 101
St. Marys, Auglaize, Ohio...B1 111
St. Marys, Elk, Pa...D4 114
St. Marys, Pleasants, W. Va...B3 123
St. Marys, co., Md...D4 85
St. Mary's, bay, Newf., Can...E5 75
St. Mary's, bay, N.S., Can...E3 74
St. Mary's, cape, Newf., Can...E4 75
St. Marys, entrance, Fla...B5 86
St. Mary's, riv., N.S., Can...D8 74
St. Marys, riv., Fla., Ga...B5 80, F5 87
St. Marys, riv., Ind., Ohio...C8 85, B1 111
St. Marys, riv., Md...D5 85
St. Marys, riv., Mich...B6 98
St. Marys City, St. Marys, Md...D5 85
St. Mathieu, Que., Can...A9 73
St. Mathieu [-de-Laprairie], Que., Can...q19 73
St. Matthew, isl., Alsk...C5 79
St. Matthew, isl., Bur...H3 38
St. Matthews, Jefferson, Ky...B4, g11 94
St. Matthews, Calhoun, S.C...D6 115
St. Maur-des-Fossés, Fr...g10 14, F2 15
St. Maurice, Que., Can...C5 73
St. Maurice, Switz...D3 19
St. Maurice, co., Que., Can...C4 73
St. Maurice, prov. park, Que., Can...B4 73
St. Maurice, riv., Que., Can...C5 73
St. Maxime, Que., Can...C6 73
St. Meinrad, Spencer, Ind...H4 91
Ste. Mélanie, Que., Can...C4 73
St Memmie, Fr...F4 15
Ste. Menehould, Fr...C6 14
St. Méthode, Que., Can...C6 73
St. Michael, Alsk...C7 79
St. Michael, Alta., Can...C4 69
St. Michael, Cambria, Pa...*F4 114
St. Michaels, Apache, Ariz...B6 80
St. Michaels, Talbot, Md...C5 85
St. Michael, Wright, Minn...E5 99
St. Michael, Benson, N. Dak...B7 110
St. Michaels, bay, Newf., Can...B4 75
St. Michel, Fr...E4 15
St. Michel [-de-Bellechasse], Que., Can...C7 73
St. Michel [-de-Maurienne], Fr...D2 18
St. Michel-de-Napierville, Que., Can...q19 73
St. Michel-des-Saints, Que., Can...C4 73
St. Mihiel, Fr...C6 14
St. Modeste, Que., Can...B8 73
St. Monance, Scot...*D6 13
Ste. Monique [-de-Nicolet], Que., Can...C5 73
St. Moritz, see Sankt Moritz, Switz.
St. Nazaire, Que., Can...D5 73
St. Nazaire, Fr...D2 14
St. Nazaire [-de-Buckland], Que., Can...C7 73
St. Nazaire-de-Chicoutimi, Que., Can...A6 73
St. Nazianz, Manitowoc, Wis...D6, h10 124
St. Neots, Eng...B7 12
St. Nérée, Que., Can...C7 73
St. Nicholas, Que., Can...o17 73
St. Nicolas, see Sint Niklaas, Bel.
St. Nicolas-de-Port, Fr...F6 15
St. Noël, Que., Can...*B3 73
St. Norbert, Man., Can...E3 71
Ste. Odile-sur-Rimouski, Que., Can...A9 73
St. Odilon, Que., Can...C7 73
St. Olaf, Clayton, Iowa...B6 92
St. Olof, Swe...C8 24
St. Omer, Que., Can...k13 73
St. Omer, Fr...B5 14
St. Onge, Lawrence, S. Dak...C2 116
Saintonge, former prov., Fr...E3 14
St. Ouen, Fr...g10 14
St. Ours, Que., Can...D4 73
St. Pacôme, Que., Can...B8 73
St. Pamphile, Que., Can...C8 73
St. Paris, Champaign, Ohio...B2 111
St. Pascal, Que., Can...B8 73
St. Patrick, lake, Que., Can...A7 72
St. Paul, Madison, Ark...B2 81
St. Paul, Alta., Can...B5 69
St. Paul, Decatur and Shelby, Ind...F6 91
St. Paul, Neosho, Kans...E8 93
St. Paul, Ramsey, Minn...F5, n12 99
St. Paul, St. Charles, Mo...f12 101
St. Paul, Howard, Nebr...C7 103
St. Paul, Marion, Oreg...h12 113
St. Paul, Clarendon, S.C...D7 115
St. Paul, Wise, Va...f9 121
St. Paul, isl., Alsk...D5 79
St. Paul, isl., N.S., Can...B9 74
St. Paul, isl., Indian O...I2 2
St. Paul, riv., Newf., Que., Can...C3 75
St. Paul, riv., Lib...E3 45
St. Paul, rocks, Atl. O...F8 6
St. Paul-de-Chester, Que., Can...D6 73
St. Paul-de-la-Croix, Que., Can...B8 73
St. Paul [-de-Montminy], Que., Can...C7 73
St. Paul-du-Nord, Que., Can...A8 73
St. Paulin, Que., Can...C4 73
St. Paul Island, Alsk...D5 79
St. Paul Park, Washington, Minn...n13 99
St. Pauls, Robeson, N.C...C4 109
Ste. Perpétue, Que., Can...C5 73
Ste. Perpétue-de-L'Islet, Que., Can...B8 73
St. Peter, Fayette, Ill...E5 90
St. Peter, Graham, Kans...C3 93
St. Peter, Nicollett, Minn...F5 99
St. Peter, lake, Que., Can...C5 73
St. Peter Port, Guernsey...F5 10
St. Peters, N.S., Can...D9 74
St. Peters, Franklin, Ind...F7 91
St. Peters, St. Charles, Mo...C3, f12 101
St. Peters Bay, P.E.I., Can...C7 74
St. Petersburg, Pinellas, Fla...E4, p10 86
St. Petersburg, Clarion, Pa...D2 114
St. Petersburg Beach, Pinellas, Fla...p10 86
Ste. Pétronille, Que., Can...n17 73
St. Philémon, Que., Can...C7 73
St. Philip, Posey, Ind...I2 91
St. Philippe [-de-Laprairie], Que., Can...D4, q20 73
St. Philippe-de-Neri, Que., Can...B8 73
St. Pie, Que., Can...D5 73
St. Pierre, Que., Can...*C3 73
St. Pierre, Que., Can...*D4 73
St. Pierre, Mart...S10 65
St. Pierre, St. Pierre & Miquelon...E3 75
St. Pierre, isl., St. Pierre & Miquelon...E3 75
St. Pierre & Miquelon, Fr. dep., N.A...E3 75
St. Pierre d'Albigny, Fr...D2 18
St. Pierre-en-Port, Fr...E8 12
St. Pierre-Jolys, Man., Can...E3 71
St. Pierre [-les-Becquets], Que., Can...C5 73
St. Pierre-Montmagny, Que., Can...C7 73
St. Pius, Stark, N. Dak...*C3 110
St. Placide, Que., Can...p18 73
St. Pol-de-Léon, Fr...C2 14
St. Pol-sur-Mer, Fr...C2 15
St. Pol [-sur-Ternoise], Fr...B5 14
St. Pourçain [-sur-Sioule], Fr...D5 14
St. Prime, Que., Can...A5 73
St. Prosper, Que., Can...C5 73
St. Prosper-de-Dorchester, Que., Can...C7 73
St. Quentin, N.B., Can...B2 74
St. Quentin, Fr...C5 14, E3 15
St. Raphaël, Que., Can...C7 73
St. Raphaël, Fr...F7 14
St. Raphaël-sur-Mer, N.B., Can...B5 74
St. Raymond, Que., Can...C6 73
St. Rédempteur, Que., Can...o17 73
St. Regis, Mineral, Mont...C1 102
St. Regis, Indian res., N.Y...f10 108
St. Regis, riv., N.Y...f10 108
St. Regis Falls, Franklin, N.Y...f10 108
St. Regis Park, Jefferson, Ky...*B4 94
St. Rémi, Que., Can...D4, q19 73
St. Remi-d'Amherst, Que., Can...C3 73
St. Rémi [-de-Tingwick], Que., Can...D6 73
St. Roch [-de-Richelieu], Que., Can...D4 73
St. Roch-des-Aulnaies, Que., Can...B7 73
St. Romuald, Que., Can...C6, n17 73
Ste. Rosalie, Que., Can...*D5 73
Ste. Rose, Que., Can...D4, p19 73
Ste. Rose, Guad...Q8 65
St. Rose, St. Charles, La...k11 95
Ste. Rose-du-Lac, Man., Can...D2 71
Ste. Sabine-de-Bellechasse, Que., Can...C7 73
St. Samuel, Que., Can...D7 73
St. Sauveur, N.B., Can...B4 74

SANI-SATA 139X

Sanibel, Lee, Fla....F4 86
Sanibel, isl., Fla....F4 86
San Ignacio, Bol....B2 55
San Ignacio, Bol....C3 55
San Ignacio, Mex....B2 63
San Ignacio, Par....E4 55
Sanilac, co., Mich....E8 98
San Ildefonso, Sp....B3 20
San Ildefonso, cape, Phil....n14 35
San Ildefonso, pen., Phil...B6, n14 35
San Isabel, Custer, Colo....D5 83
Sanish, Mountrail, N. Dak...B3 110
San Isidro, Arg....g7 54
San Isidro [del General], C.R.F6 62
San Isidro, Phil....*C6 35
San Isidro, Starr, Tex....F3 118
Sanitz, G.D.R....D6 24
Sanīyah, lake, Iraq....E3 41
San Jacinto, Riverside, Calif. F5 82
San Jacinto, Phil....*C6 35
San Jacinto, co., Tex....D5 118
San Jacinto, riv., Tex....r14 118
San Jaime, Arg....A5 54
San Javier, Arg....A5 54
San Javier, Bol....C3 55
San Javier, Chile....B2 54
San Javier, riv., Arg....A4 54
San Jerónimo [Aculco Lídice], Mex....h9 63
San Jerónimo, mts., Col....B2 60
Sanjo, Jap....H9 37
San Joao das Lampas, Port....f9 20
San Joaquín, Par....D4 55
San Joaquin, co., Calif....C3 82
San Joaquin, riv., Calif....D3 82
San Joaquin, val., Calif....D3 82
San Jon Quay, N. Mex....B6 107
San Jose, Graham, Ariz....E6 80
San Jose, Belize....B3 62
San Jose, Bol....C3 55
San Jose, Santa Clara, Calif....D3, k9 82
San José, C.R....F5 62
San José, Guat....D2 62
San Jose, Mason and Logan, Ill....C4 90
San Jose, Bernalillo, N. Mex.B3 107
San Jose, Rio Arriba, N. Mex....*A3 107
San Jose, Phil....o13 35
San Jose, Phil....o13 35
San Jose, Phil....C6 35
San Jose, Phil....*C6 35
San José, Ur....E1 56
San José, dept., Ur....*E1 56
San José, prov., C.R....*F5 62
San José, isl., Mex....B2 63
San Jose, isl., Tex....E4 118
San Jose, riv., B.C., Can....D7 68
San José, riv., Ur....g8 54
San José Boquerón, Arg....E3 55
San José de Feliciano, Arg...A5 54
San José de Guanipa, Ven...B5 60
San José de Cabo, Mex....C3 63
San José del Guaviare, Col...C3 60
San Jose [del Monte], Phil..o13 35
San José de los Molinos, Peru.D2 58
San Juan, Arg....A3 54
San Juan, Las Animas, Colo....D6 83
San Juan [de la Maguana], Dom. Rep....E8 64
San Juan, Grant, N. Mex....E2 107
San Juan, Phil....p13 35
San Juan, Phil....n13 35
San Juan, Phil....*D7 35
San Juan, P.R....B3 65
San Juan, Hidalgo, Tex....F3 118
San Juan, Ven....A4 60
San Juan, co., Colo....D3 83
San Juan, co., N. Mex....A1 107
San Juan, co., Utah....F5 119
San Juan, co., Wash....A3 122
San Juan, mun., P.R....*B3 65
San Juan, prov., Arg....A3 54
San Juan, isl., Wash....A2 122
San Juan, mts., Colo....D3 83
San Juan, pt., P.R....B4 65
San Juan, riv., Arg....A3 54
San Juan, riv., B.C., Can....g11 68
San Juan, riv., Colo....D3 83
San Juan, riv., C.R., Nic....E5 62
San Juan, riv., U.S....C5 76
San Juan Bautista, San Benito, Calif....C6 82
San Juan Bautista, Par....E4 55
San Juan Capistrano, Orange, Calif....F5 82
San Juan de Aragón, Mex...h9 63
San Juan de Colón, Ven....B3 60
San Juan del Monte, Phil...*C6 35
San Juan del Norte, Nic....E6 62
San Juan del Norte, bay, Nic...E6 62
San Juan de los Lagos, Mex....m12 63
San Juan de los Morros, Ven.B4 60
San Juan del Río, Mex....m13 63
San Juan del Sur, Nic....E5 62
San Juan Ixtayoapan, Mex.h10 63
San Juan Nepomuceno, Col..B2 63
San Juan Pueblo, Rio Arriba, N. Mex....*A3 107
San Juan y Martínez, Cuba..C2 64
San Julián, Arg....D3 54
San Justo, Arg....A4 54
San Justo, Arg....*A5 54
Sankarani, riv., Guinea, Mali...D3 45
Sankt Anton [am Arlberg], Aus....B6 18
Sankt Blasien, F.R.G....B4 18
S[ank]t Gallen, Switz....B7 19
Sankt Gallen, canton, Switz..B7 19
Sankt Georgen [im Attergau], Aus....B9 18
Sankt Goarshausen, F.R.G...C2 17
Sankt Johann [in Tirol], Aus.B8 18
S[ankt] Margrethen, Switz...B8 19
Sankt Michaelisdonn, F.R.G.E3 24
Sankt Moritz, Switz....C8 19
Sankt Pölten, Aus....D7 16
Sankt Veit [an der Glan], Aus....E7 16
Sankt Wendel, F.R.G....D2 17
Sankuru, riv., Zaire....B3 48
San Leandro, Alameda, Calif.h8 82
San Lorenzo, Arg....A4 54
San Lorenzo, Alameda, Calif....*D2 82
San Lorenzo, Ec....A2 58
San Lorenzo, Hond....D4 62
San Lorenzo, Grant, N. Mex.E2 107
San Lorenzo, P.R....B4 65
San Lorenzo, Ven....B3 60
San Lorenzo, mun., P.R....*B4 65
San Lorenzo del Escorial, Sp....B3, o16 20
San Lorenzo Tezonco, Mex..h9 63
Sanlúcar, Sp....D2 20
San Lucas, Bol....D2 55
San Lucas, Mex....C3 63
San Luis, Arg....A3 54
San Luis, Pima, Ariz....E3 80
San Luis, Yuma, Ariz....E1 80
San Luis, Costilla, Colo....D5 83
San Luis, Cuba....D6 64
San Luis, Guat....B3 62
San Luis, Mex....A2 63
San Luis, prov., Arg....A3 54
San Luis, creek, Colo....C5 83
San Luis, pass, Tex....r14 118
San Luis, peak, Colo....D4 83
San Luis, pt., Calif....E3 82
San Luis, riv., Mex....h9 63
San Luis, val., Colo....D4 83
San Luis de la Paz, Mex...m13 63
San Luis Jilotepeque, Guat..C3 62
San Luis Obispo, San Luis Obispo, Calif....E3 82
San Luis Obispo, co., Calif..E3 82
San Luis Potosí, Mex...C4, k13 63
San Lusi Potosí, state, Mex....C4, k13 63
San Manuel, Pinal, Ariz....E5 80
San Marco [in Lamis], It....D5 21
San Marcos, Col....B2 60
San Marcos, Guat....C2 62
San Marcos, Hays, Tex..E5, h8 118
San Marcos, riv., Tex....h8 118
San Marcos de Colón, Hond.D4 62
San Marino, Los Angeles, Calif....m12 82
San Marino, San Marino....C4 21
San Marino, country, Eur...C4 21
San Martín, Arg....A3 54
San Martín (General San Martín), Arg....g7 54
San Martín, Col....C3 60
San Martín, dept., Peru....C2 58
San Martín de la Vega, Sp...p17 20
San Martín de Los Andes, Arg....C2 54
San Martino dei Calvi, It...D5 18
San Martino do Castrozza, It.C7 18
San Mateo, San Mateo, Calif.h8 82
San Mateo, Putnam, Fla....C5 86
San Mateo, Valencia, N. Mex....B2 107
San Mateo, Sp....B6 20
San Mateo, Ven....B5 60
San Mateo, co., Calif....D2 82
San Mateo, cape, Ec....B1 58
San Mateo, mts., N. Mex....B2 107
San Mateo, mts., N. Mex....D2 107
San Mateo Xalpa, Mex....h9 63
San Matias, Bol....C4 55
San Matías, gulf, Arg....C4 54
Sanmenhsia, China....E7 34
San Miguel, Pima, Ariz....F4 80
San Miguel, San Luis Obispo, Calif....E3 82
San Miguel, Dona Ana, N. Mex....E3 107
San Miguel, San Miguel, N. Mex....B4 107
San Miguel, Pan....F8 62
San Miguel, Sal....D3 62
San Miguel, co., Colo....D2 83
San Miguel, co., N. Mex....B5 107
San Miguel, gulf, Pan....F8 62
San Miguel, isl., Calif....E3 82
San Miguel, mts., Colo....D2 83
San Miguel, riv., Colo....C2 83
San Miguel de Allende, Mex....m13 63
Sannār, Sud....C3 47
San Narciso, Phil....p14 35
San Narciso, Phil....o13 35
San Nicholas, Phil....o13 35
San Nicolás, Arg....A4 54
San Nicolas, Phil....n13 35
San Nicolas, isl., Calif....F4 82
San Nicolás [Totolapan], Mex....h9 63
Sannois, Fr....g10 14
Sano, Jap....*H9 37
Sanok, Pol....D7 26
San Onofre, Col....B2 60
San Pablo, Contra Costa, Calif....*D2 82
San Pablo, Costilla, Colo....D5 83
San Pablo, Phil....o13 35
San Pablo, bay, Calif....g8 82
San Patricio, Lincoln, N. Mex....D4 107
San Patricio, co., Tex....F4 118
San Patricio, bayou, La....C2 95
San Pedro, Arg....A5, f7 54
San Pedro, Arg....D3 55
San Pedro, Bol....B3 55
San Pedro, Bol....C2 55
San Pedro, Chile....D2 55
San Pedro, C.R....*F5 62
San Pedro, Rio Arriba, N. Mex....*B3 107
San Pedro, Par....D4 55
San Pedro, Nueces, Tex....*E4 118
San Pedro, dept., Par....D4 55
San Pedro, peaks, N. Mex....A3 107
San Pedro, riv., Ariz....E5 80
San Pedro, riv., Guat....B2 62
San Pedro, riv., Mex....C4 63
San Pedro, Mex....G2 107
San Pedro de Atacama, Chile....D2 55
San Pedro de las Colonias, Mex....B4 63
San Pedro de Lloc, Peru....C2 58
San Pedro de Macorís, Dom. Rep....E9 64
San Pedro Martir, mts., Mex...A1 63
San Pedro Sula, Hond....C3 62
Sanpete, co., Utah....D4 119
San Pierre, Starke, Ind....B4 91
San Pietro, isl., It....E2 21
San Pitch, mts., Utah....D4 119
Sanpoil, riv., Wash....A7 122
Sanquhar, Scot....E5 13
San Quintin, Phil....o13 35
San Rafael, Arg....A3 54
San Rafael, Marin, Calif.D2, h7 82
San Rafael, Valencia, N. Mex....B2 107
San Rafael, Ven....A3 61
San Rafael, des., Utah....E5 119
San Rafael, mts., Calif....E4 82
San Rafael, riv., Utah....D5 119
San Rafael, swell, Utah....E5 119
San Rafael del Norte, Nic...D4 62
San Rafael Knob, mtn., Utah...E5 119
San Ramón, Peru....D2 58
San Ramon, Ur....G9 54
San Remo, It....C1 21
San Roque, Sp....D3 20
San Rosendo, Chile....B2 54
San Saba, San Saba, Tex...D3 118
San Saba, co., Tex....D3 118
San Salvador, Arg....A5 54
San Salvador, Sal....D3 62
San Salvador (Watling), isl., Ba.B6 64
San Salvador (Santiago), isl., Ec....g5 58
Sansanné-Mango, Togo....D5 45
San Sebastián, C.R....F5 62
San Sebastián, Sp....A4 20
San Sebastián, mun., P.R...*B2 65
San Sebastián, cape, Arg....h12 54
San Sebastián de los Reyes, Sp....o17 20
San Sepolcro, It....C4 21
San Severo, It....D5 21
Sanshui, China....G7 34
San Simeon, San Luis Obispo, Calif....E3 82
San Simon, Cochise, Ariz....E6 80
San Simon, riv., Ariz....E6 80
Sansom Park Village, Tarrant, Tex....*B5 118
Sans Souci, Greenville, S.C.*B3 115
Santa, Benewah, Idaho....B2 89
Santa, Peru....C2 58
Santa, mtn., P.R....E13 65
Santa, riv., Peru....C2 58
Santa Amaro, isl., Braz....m8 58
Santa Ana, Bol....B2 55
Santa Ana, Bol....C2 55
Santa Ana, Orange, Calif....F3, n13 82
Santa Ana, Ec....B1 58
Santa Ana, Mex....A2 63
Santa Ana, Peru....D3 58
Santa Ana, Sal....D3 62
Santa Ana, Ven....B3 60
Santa Ana., Indian res., N. Mex.h7 107
Santa Ana, mts., Calif....n13 82
Santa Ana, riv., Calif....n13 82
Santa Ana Pueblo, Sandoval, N. Mex....B3, k7 107
Santa Anita, Mex....h9 63
Santa Anna, Coleman, Tex..D3 118
Santa Barbara, Braz....m8 56
Santa Bárbara, Braz....E2 57
Santa Barbara, Santa Barbara, Calif....E4 82
Santa Bárbara, Chile....B2 54
Santa Bárbara, Hond....C3 62
Santa Bárbara, Mex....B3 63
Santa Barbara, co., Calif....E3 82
Santa Barbara, chan., Calif....E3 82
Santa Barbara, is., Calif....F4 82
Santa Catalina, Arg....D2 55
Santa Catalina, Chile....E2 55
Santa Catalina, gulf, Calif....F5 82
Santa Catalina, isl., Calif....F4 82
Santa Catalina, mts., Ariz....E5 80
Santa Catarina, state, Braz..D2 56
Santa Catarina, isl., Braz....D3 56
Santa Clara, Santa Clara, Calif....D2, k9 82
Santa Clara, Cuba....C4 64
Santa Clara, Franklin, N.Y..f10 108
Santa Clara, Lane, Oreg...*C3 113
Santa Clara, Ur....E2 56
Santa Clara, Washington, Utah....F2 119
Santa Clara, co., Calif....D3 82
Santa Clara, riv., Calif....E4 82
Santa Clara Pueblo, Rio Arriba, N. Mex....*B3 107
Santa Claus, Spencer, Ind...H4 91
Santa Coloma de Farnés, Sp.B7 20
Santa Croce, cape, It....F5 21
Santa Cruz., Arg....E3 54
Santa Cruz, Pinal, Ariz....m8 80
Santa Cruz, Bol....C3 55
Santa Cruz, Braz....C3, h6 57
Santa Cruz, Santa Cruz, Calif....D2 82
Santa Cruz, Chile....A2 54
Santa Cruz, C.R....E5 62
Santa Cruz, Santa Fe, N. Mex....B3 107
Santa Cruz, Phil....p13 35
Santa Cruz, Phil....o12 35
Santa Cruz, Phil....o13 35
Santa Cruz, co., Ariz....F5 80
Santa Cruz, co., Calif....D2 82
Santa Cruz, dept., Bol....C3 55
Santa Cruz, prov., Arg....D3 54
Santa Cruz, isl., Calif....F4 82
Santa Cruz, is., Pac. O....G10 7
Santa Cruz, mtn., Jam....B3 65
Santa Cruz, riv., Ariz....E4 80
Santa Cruz de la Palma, Sp. (Can. Is.)...D1 44, m13 20
Santa Cruz de la Zarza, Sp..C4 20
Santa Cruz del Quiché, Guat....C2 62
Santa Cruz del Sur, Cuba...D5 64
Santa Cruz de Tenerife, Sp. (Can. Is.)....D1 44
Santa Cruz de Tenerife, prov., Sp....*m13 20
Santa Cruz do Rio Pardo, Braz....C3 56
Santa Cruz do Sul, Braz....D2 56
Santa Cruz (Indefatigable), isl., Ec....g5 58
Santa Elena, Ec....B1 58
Santa Elena, Starr, Tex....F3 118
Santa Elena, Ven....C5 60
Santa Elena, cape, C.R....E5 62
Santa Eugenia [de Ribeira], Sp....A1 20
Santa Eulalia del Río, Sp....C6 20
Santa Fe, Arg....A4 54
Santa Fé, Cuba....D2 64
Santa Fe, Mex....h9 63
Santa Fe, Santa Fe, N. Mex....B4, h9 107
Santa Fe, Auglaize and Logan, Ohio....B1 111
Santa Fe, Pan....F7 62
Santa Fe, Phil....*C6 35
Santafé, Sp....D4 20
Santa Fe, Maury, Tenn....B4 117
Santa Fe, co., N. Mex....B3 107
Santa Fe, prov., Arg....A4 54
Santa Fé, isl., Ec....g5 58
Santa Fe, lake, Fla....C4 86
Santa Fe, riv., N. Mex....h8 107
Santa Fe Baldy, mtn., N. Mex..B4 107
Santa Fe Springs, Los Angeles, Calif....E4 82
Santa Filomena, Braz....C1 57
Santai, China....E6 34
Santa Inés, isl., Chile....h11 54
Santa Inés Ahuatempan, Mex....n14 63
Santa Isabel, Arg....B3 54
Santa Isabel, Chile....D2 55
Santa Isabel, P.R....C3 65
Santa Isabel, see Paso de los Toros, Ur.
Santa Isabel, mun., P.R....*C3 65
Santa Isabel de Siguas, Peru.E3 58
Santa Lucía, Cuba....D6 64
Santa Lucia, Ur....E1 56
Santa Lucia, range, Calif....D3 82
Santa Margarita, San Luis Obispo, Calif....E3 82
Santa Margarita, isl., Mex....C2 63
Santa María, Arg....E2 55
Santa Maria, Braz....D2 56
Santa Maria, Santa Barbara, Calif....E3 82
Santa Maria, Phil....o13 35
Santa Maria, isl., Az. Is....h9 44
Santa María, isl., Ec....g5 58
Santa Maria, mts., Ariz....C3 80
Santa Maria, riv., Ariz....C2 80
Santa María, riv., Mex....m14 63
Santa María, riv., Mex....G2 107
Santa María, riv., Pan....F7 62
Santa Maria [Capua Vetere], It....D5 21
Santa María del Oro, Mex...B3 63
Santa Maria di Leuca, cape, It..E7 21
Santa Maria Madalena, Braz....C4 56
Santa Marta, Col....A3 60
Santa Marta, Sp....C2 20
Santa Marta, mts., Col....A3 60
Santa Monica, Los Angeles, Calif....m12 82
Santan, Pinal, Ariz....m9 80
Santan, mtn., Ariz....m9 80
Santana, Braz....D2 57
Santana, Port. (Madeira Is.).h12 20
Santana do Ipanema, Braz..C3 57
Santander, Col....C2 60
Santander, Sp....A4 20
Santander, prov., Sp....*A4 20
Santander, dept., Col....B3 60
Santander, mts., Col....B3 60
Santander Jiménez, Mex....C5 63
Sant'Angelo Romano, It....g9 21
Santanoni, peak, N.Y....A6 108
Santanópole, Braz....C3 57
Santañy, Sp....C7 20
Santa Paula, Ventura, Calif..E4 82
Santaquin, Utah, Utah....D4 119
Santa Quitéria, Braz....B2 57
Santarém, Braz....C4 59
Santarém, Port....C1 20
Santaren, chan., W.I....B4 64
Santa Rita, Braz....k8 56
Santa Rita, Braz....C4, h6 57
Santa Rita, Guam.... 52
Santa Rita, Glacier, Mont...B4 102
Santa Rita, Ven....A3 60
Santa Rita Park, Merced, Calif....D3 82
Santa Rosa, Arg....A3 54
Santa Rosa, Arg....A4 54
Santa Rosa, Arg....B4 54
Santa Rosa, Bol....B2 55
Santa Rosa, Braz....k8 56
Santa Rosa, Braz....D2 56
Santa Rosa, Sonoma, Calif...C2 82
Santa Rosa, Col....B2 60
Santa Rosa, Ec....B2 58
Santa Rosa, Walton, Fla....u15 86
Santa Rosa, DeKalb, Mo....B3 101
Santa Rosa, Guadalupe, N. Mex....C5 107
Santa Rosa, Phil....o13 35
Santa Rosa, Cameron, Tex.*F4 118
Santa Rosa, co., Fla....u14 86
Santa Rosa, isl., Calif....F3 82
Santa Rosa, mtn., Guam.... 52
Santa Rosa, range, Nev....B4 104
Santa Rosa Beach, Walton, Fla....u15 86
Santa Rosa de Aguán, Hond.C5 62
Santa Rosa de Copán, Hond.C3 62
Santa Rosalía, Mex....B2 63
Santa Rosalia, pt., Mex....B2 63
Santa Susana, Ventura, Calif....*E4 82
Santa Teresa, Gallura, It....D2 21
Santa Ursula, Mex....h9 63
Santa Venetia, Marin, Calif....*D2 82
Santa Vitória do Palmar, Braz....E2 56
Santa Ynez, Santa Barbara, Calif....E3 82
Santee, San Diego, Calif....o16 82
Santee, Knox, Nebr....B8 103
Santee, dam, S.C....E7 115
Santee, Indian res., Nebr....B8 103
Santee, riv., S.C....E8 115
Sant'Eufemia, gulf, It....E5 21
Santiago, Bol....C2 55
Santiago, Braz....D2 56
Santiago, Chile....A2 54
Santiago [de los Caballeros], Dom. Rep....E8 64
Santiago, Mex....C3 63
Santiago, Pan....F7 62
Santiago, Par....E4 55
Santiago, Phil....n13 35
Santiago, Sp....A1 20
Santiago, prov., Chile....A2 54
Santiago, cape, Phil....p13 35
Santiago, see San Salvador, isl., Ec.
Santiago, isl., Phil....n12 35
Santiago, peak, Calif....n14 82
Santiago, riv., Peru....B2 58
Santiago de Cao, Peru....C2 58
Santiago de Cuba, Cuba....E6 64
Santiago del Estero, Arg....E3 55
Santiago del Estero, prov., Arg....E3 55
Santiago, Ixcuintla, Mex....C3, m11 63
Santiago Morona, prov., Ec..B2 58
Santiago Papasquiaro, Mex..B3 63
Santiago Tepalcatlálpan, Mex....h9 63
Santipur, India....F12 40
Santis, mtn., Switz....B7 19
Santisteban del Puerto, Sp...C4 20
Santo, Palo Pinto, Tex....C3 118
Santo Amaro, Braz....D3 57
Santo André, Braz....*C3 56
Santo Angelo, Braz....D2 56
Santo Antão, isl., C.V. Is....*E2 42
Santo Antônio, Braz....C3, h6 57
Santo Antônio de Jesus, Braz.D3 57
Santo Antônio do Zaire, Ang....C1 48
Santo Domingo, Dom. Rep..E9 64
Santo Domingo, Nic....D5 62
Santo Domingo de la Calzada, Sp....A4 20
Santo Domingo de los Colorados, Ec....B2 58
Santo Domingo, Indian res., N. Mex....h8 107
Santo Domingo Pueblo, Sandoval, N. Mex....B3, k8 107
San Tomas, Santa Clara, Calif....*D3 82
Santoña, Sp....A4 20
Santos, Braz....C3, m8 56
Santos Dumont, Braz....C4, g6 56
Santo Tomás, Nic....D5 62
Santo Tomás, Peru....D3 58
Santo Tomas, Ven....B5 60
Santo Tomé, Arg....E4 55
Santuao, China....K8 36
Santuc, Union, S.C....B4 115
Santuit, Barnstable, Mass...*C7 97
San Valentín, mtn., Chile....D2 54
San Vicente, Col....C3 60
San Vicente, Sal....D3 62
San Vicente de Alcántara, Sp.C2 20
San Vicente de la Barquera, Sp....A3 20
San Vito al Tagliamento, It..B4 21
San Xavier, Indian res., Ariz...E4 80
San Ygnacio, Zapata, Tex...F3 118
San Ysidro, Sandoval, N. Mex....B3, h7 107
Sanza Pomba, Ang....C2 48
São Bento do Sul, Braz....D3 56
São Bento do Una, Braz....k5 57
São Bernardo [do Campo], Braz....C3, m8 56
São Borja, Braz....D1 56
São Caetano do Sul, Braz..*C3 56
São Carlos, Braz....C3, m8 56
São Cristovão, Braz....D3 57
São Domingos, Braz....D1 57
São Fidélis, Braz....C4 56
São Francisco, Braz....E2 57
São Francisco, Braz....C5 60
São Francisco, riv., Braz....C3 57
São Francisco do Sul, Braz..D3 56
São Gabriel, Braz....E2 56
São Gonçalo, Braz....*C4 56
São Gotardo, Braz....E1 57
São Jerônimo, Braz....D2 56
São Jeronimo, mts., Braz....B2 56
São João, isl., Braz....B2 57
São João da Barra, Braz....C4 56
São João da Boa Vista, Braz....C3, k8 56
São João das Lampas, Port...f9 20
São João del Rei, Braz...C4, g5 56
São João de Meriti. Braz...*C4 56
São João do Carirí, Braz.C3, h5 57
São João do Piauí, Braz....C2 57
São João Nepomuceno, Braz....C4, g6 56
São Joaquim, Braz....D3 56
São Jorge, isl., Port. (Azores)...g8 44
São José de Mipibú, Braz....h6 57
São José do Rio Pardo, Braz.k8 56
São José do Rio Prêto, Braz..C3 56
São José dos Campos, Braz....C3, m9 56
São José dos Pinhais, Braz...D3 56
São Leopoldo, Braz....D2 56
São Lourenço, Braz....C3 56
São Lourenço, riv., Braz....B1 56
São Lourenço do Sul, Braz...E2 56
São Luís, Braz....B2 57
São Luís do Quitunde, Braz..k6 57
São Luís Gonzaga, Braz....D2 56
São Manuel, Braz....C3, m7 56
São Mateus, Braz....E3 57
São Miguel, isl., Port. (Azores).h9 44
São Miguel Arcanjo, Braz...m8 56
São Miguel dos Campos, Braz....k5 57
Saona, isl., Dom. Rep....E9 64
Saône, riv., Fr....D6 14
Saône-et-Loire, dept., Fr...*D6 14
São Nicolau, isl., C.V. Is....*E3 42
São Paulo, Braz....C3, m8 56
São Paulo, state, Braz...C3, m8 56
São Paulo de Olivença, Braz....D4 60
São Pedro, Braz....m8 56
São Pedro do Piauí, Braz....C2 57
São Raimundo Nonato, Braz.C2 57
São Roque, Braz....m8 56
São Roque, cape, Braz....C3 57
Saorre, mtn., N.W. Ter., Can...D6 67
São Salvador do Congo, Ang.C1 48
São Sebastião, isl., Braz....C3 56
São Sebastião, pt., Mo....B6 49
São Sebastião do Paraíso, Braz....C3 56
São Simão, Braz....C3, k8 56
Saõ Tiago, isl., C.V. Is....*E3 42
São Tomé, Sao Tome & Principe....E1 46
São Tomé, isl., Sao Tome & Principe....E1 46
Sao Tome & Principe, country, Afr....F6 42, E1 46
Saoura, riv., Alg....D4 44
São Vicente, Braz....C3 56
São Vicente, Port. (Madeira Is.)....h11 20
São Vicente, isl., C.V. Is....*E3 42
Sapai, Grc....B5 23
Sapatu, isl., Viet....H8 38
Sapele, Nig....E6 45
Sapello, San Miguel, N. Mex.B4 107
Sapelo, isl., Ga....E5 87
Sapelo, sound, Ga....E5 87
Sapinero, Gunnison, Colo...C3 83
Sapitwa, peak, Malawi....E6 48
Saposoa, Peru....C2 58
Sapozhok, Sov. Un....E13 27
Sappa, creek, Nebr., Kans....C3 93
Sappemeer, Neth....A6 15
Sapphire, mts., Mont....D3 102
Sappho, Clallam, Wash....A1 122
Sappington, St. Louis, Mo...f12 101
Sapporo, Jap....E10 37
Sapri, It....D5 21
Sapulpa, Creek, Okla....B5 112
Saqqare, Eg....E3 32
Saqqez, Iran....C3 41
Sãquarema, Braz....C4, h6 56
Sarābiyūm, Eg....D4 32
Sara Buri, Thai....E4 38
Saragosa, Reeves, Tex..D1, o13 118
Saragossa, Walker, Ala....B2 78
Saragossa, see Zaragoza, prov. and city, Sp.
Saraguro, Ec....B2 58
Sarah, Tate, Miss....A3 100
Sarajevo, Yugo....D4 22
Sara Kaeo, Thai....F5 38
Saraktash, Sov. Un....E20 9
Sarala, Sov. Un....E26 9
Saraland, Mobile, Ala....E1 78
Saran, Sov. Un....*D8 29
Saranac, Ionia, Mich....F5 98
Saranac, Clinton, N.Y....f11 108
Saranac, lakes, N.Y....A6 108
Saranac, riv., N.Y....f11 108
Saranac Inn, Franklin, N.Y.f10 108
Saranac Lakes, Essex and Franklin, N.Y....f10 108
Saranap, Contra Costa, Calif....*D2 82
Sarandë, Alb....C2 23
Sarandí del Yí, Ur....E1 56
Sarandí Grande, Ur....E1 56
Sarangani, is., Phil....D6 35
Sarangpur, India....F6 40
Saransk, Sov. Un....C3 29
Sarapul, Sov. Un....B4 29
Sarasota, Sarasota, Fla..E4, q10 86
Sarasota, co., Fla....E4 86
Sarasota, bay, Fla....E4 86
Sarata, Sov. Un....B9 22
Saratoga, Howard, Ark....D2 81
Saratoga, Santa Clara, Calif....k8 82
Saratoga, Randolph, Ind....D8 91
Saratoga, Howard, Iowa....A5 92
Saratoga, Wilson, N.C....B5 109
Saratoga, Hardin, Tex....D5 118
Saratoga, Carbon, Wyo....E6 125
Saratoga, co., N.Y....B7 108
Saratoga, lake, N.Y....C7 108
Saratoga Place, Nansemond, Va....*D6 121
Saratoga Springs, Saratoga, N.Y....B7 108
Saratov, Sov. Un....C3 29
Saravane, Laos....E7 38
Sarawak, reg, Mala....I14 33, E4 35
Saray, Tur....B6 23
Saraykoy, Tur....D7 23
Sarbāz, Iran....H10 41
Sárbogárd, Hung....B4 22
Sarca, riv., It....D6 18
Sarcelles, Fr....g10 14
Sarcoxie, Jasper, Mo....D3 101
Sarda, riv., India....C8 40
Sardalas, Libya....D2 43
Sardegna, pol. dist., It....*E2 21
Sardinia, Decatur, Ind....F6 91
Sardinia, Brown, Ohio....C2 111
Sardinia, isl., It....D2 21
Sardis, Dallas, Ala....C3 78
Sardis, B.C., Can....f14 68
Sardis, Burke, Ga....D5 87
Sardis, Mason, Ky....B6 94
Sardis, Panola, Miss....A4 100
Sardis, Monroe, Ohio....C5 111
Sardis, Henderson, Tenn....B3 117
Sardis, dam, Miss....A4 100
Sardis, res., Miss....A4 100
Sarektjåkkå, mtn., Swe....D7 25
Sar-e Pol, Afg....C12 41
Sarepta, Webster, La....B2 95
Sarepta, Calhoun, Miss....A4 100
Sar-e Yazd, Iran....F7 41
Sargans, Switz....B7 19
Sargeant, Mower, Minn....G6 99
Sargent, Coweta, Ga....C2 87
Sargent, Custer, Nebr....C6 103
Sargent, co., N. Dak....C8 110
Sargents, Saguache, Colo....C4 83
Sargodha, Pak....A4 40
Sarh (Fort-Archambault), Chad....D3 46
Sarḫadd, Afg....k17 41
Sārī, Iran....C6 41
Saria, isl., Grc....E6 23
Sarikamis, Tur....B14 31
Sarina, Austl....D8 50
Sarine, riv., Switz....C3 19
Sariñena, Sp....B5 20
Sarita, Kenedy, Tex....F4 118
Sariwon, Kor....G2 37
Sark, isl., Guernsey....F5 10
Sarkand, Sov. Un....F24 9
Sarkisla, Tur....C11 31
Sarkoy, Tur....B6 23
Sarlat, Fr....E4 14
Sarles, Cavalier and Towner, N. Dak....A6 110
Särna, Swe....G5 25
Sarnen, Switz....C5 19
Sarnen, lake, Switz....C5 19
Sarnia, Ont., Can....E2 72
Sarny, Sov. Un....F6 27
Särö, Swe....A5 24
Sarona, Washburn, Wis....C2 124
Saronic, gulf, Grc....D4 23
Saronno, It....B2 21
Saronville, Clay, Nebr....D8 103
Saros, gulf, Tur....B6 23
Sarospatak, Hung....A5 22
Sarova, Sov. Un....D14 27
Sar Planina, mts., Yugo....D5 22
Sarpsborg, Nor....p29 25
Sarpy, co., Nebr....C9 103
Sarrebourg, Fr....F7 15
Sarreguemines, Fr....C7 14
Sarre-Union, Fr....F7 15
Sarria, Sp....A2 20
Sarsfield, Ont., Can....h13 72
Sarstedt, F.R.G....A4 17
Sarstún, riv., Belize, Guat....C3 62
Sartell, Stearns, Minn....E4 99
Sartène, Fr....D2 21
Sarthe, dept., Fr....*D4 14
Sarthe, riv., Fr....D3 14
Sartrouville, Fr....g9 14
Sarufutsu, Jap....D11 37
Sarus, see Seyhan, riv., Tur.
Sarvar, Hung....B3 22
Sarvestān, Iran....G6 41
Sarybyevo, Sov. Un....o18 27
Sary-Ishikotrau, des., Sov. Un..D9 29
Sary-Ozek, Sov. Un....E9 29
Sarysu, riv., Sov. Un....D7 29
Sarzana, It....B2 21
Sasabe, Pima, Ariz....F4 80
Sasaginnigak, lake, Man., Can....D4 71
Sasakwa, Seminole, Okla....C5 112
Sāsarām, India....E10 40
Sasebo, Jap....J4 37
Saskatchewan, prov., Can....F11 66, 70
Saskatchewan, riv., Man., Sask., Can....F12 66
Saskatoon, Sask., Can....E2, n7 70
Sasovo, Sov. Un....C2 29
Saspamco, Wilson, Tex....k7 118
Sassafras, mtn., S.C....A2 115
Sassafras, riv., Md....B5 85
Sassafras Knob, mtn., Tenn....D9 117
Sassandra, I.C....E3 45
Sassandra, riv., I.C....E3 45
Sassari, It....D2 21
Sassenberg, F.R.G....B3 17
Sasser, Terrell, Ga....E2 87
Sassnitz, G.D.R....A6 16
Sasso Marconi, It....E7 18
Sassuolo, It....E6 18
Sastre, Arg....A4 54
Sasuri, Kor....F3 37
Sasykkol, lake, Sov. Un....D10 29
Satah, mtn.; B.C., Can....C5 68
Satalo, W. Sam.... 52

Satanta, Haskell, Kans.....E3 93
Satapuala, W. Sam..... 52
Sātāra, India.....I4 40
Satartia, Yazoo, Miss.....C3 100
Sataua, bay, W. Sam..... 52
Säter, Swe.....G6 25
Saticoy, Ventura, Calif.....E4 82
Satilla, riv., Ga.....E4 87
Satipo, Peru.....D3 58
Satka, Sov. Un.....B5 29
Sātmāla, range, India.....H7 40
Satna, India.....E8 40
Satoraljaujhely, Hung.....A5 22
Sātpura, range, India.....G5 40
Sätrabrunn, Swe.....t34 25
Satrup, F.R.G.....D3 24
Satsop, Grays Harbor, Wash.B2 122
Satsuma, Mobile, Ala.....E1 78
Satsuma, Putnam, Fla.....C5 86
Sattahip, Thai.....F4 38
Sattler, Comal, Tex.....h7 118
Satu-Mare, Rom.....B6 22
Satun, Thai.....I4 38
Satupaitea, W. Sam..... 52
Saturna, isl., B.C., Can.....E6 68
Satus, creek, Wash.....C5 122
Sauce, Arg.....A5 54
Sauceda, mts., Ariz.....E3 80
Saucier, Harrison, Miss.....E4 100
Saucillo, Mex.....B3 63
Sauda, Nor.....H2 25
Saudi Arabia, country, Asia..G7 33
Saugatuck, Fairfield, Conn. (part of Westport).....E3 84
Saugatuck, Allegan, Mich.....F4 98
Saugatuck, riv., Conn.....D3 84
Saugerties, Ulster, N.Y.....C7 108
Saugus, Los Angeles, Calif..*E4 82
Saugus, Essex, Mass....B5, g11 98
Saugus, riv., Mass.....g11 97
Sauk, co., Wis.....E4 124
Sauk, riv., Minn.....E4 99
Sauk, riv., Wash.....A4 122
Sauk Centre, Stearns, Minn..E4 99
Sauk City, Sauk, Wis.....E4 124
Sauk Rapids, Benton, Minn..E4 99
Sauk Village, Cook, Ill.....*B6 90
Saukville, Ozaukee, Wis.....E6 124
Saulgrub, F.R.G.....B7 18
Saulnierville, N.S., Can.....E3 74
Saulsbury, Hardeman, Tenn .B2 117
Saulston, Wayne, N.C.....B5 109
Sault-au-Mouton, Que., Can.....A8 73
Sault Ste. Marie, Ont., Can .p18 72
Sault Ste. Marie, Chippewa, Mich.....B6 98
Saumlakki, Indon.....G8 35
Saumur, Fr.....D4 14
Saunders, Alta., Can.....C10 68
Saunders, co., Nebr.....C9 84
Saunderstown, Washington, R.I.....C11 84
Saundersville, Sumner, Tenn.....g10 117
Saunemin, Livingston, Ill.....C5 90
Saurashtra, pen., India.....D4 39
Saurimo, Ang.....C3 48
Sausalito, Marin, Calif...D2, h8 82
Sauveterre, Fr.....E5 14
Savá, Hond.....C4 62
Sava, riv., Yugo.....C4 22
Savage, Howard, Md.....B4 85
Savage, Scott, Minn.....n12 99
Savage, Tate, Miss.....A3 100
Savage, Richland, Mont.....C12 102
Savage, riv., Md.....k12 85
Savaii, isl., W. Sam..... 52
Savalou, Benin.....E5 45
Savana-la-Mar, Jam.....E12 65
Savanna, Carroll, Ill.....A3 90
Savanna, Pittsburg, Okla.....C6 112
Savannah, Chatham, Ga.....D5 87
Savannah, Andrew, Mo.....B3 101
Savannah, Wayne, N.Y.....B4 108
Savannah, Ashland, Ohio.....B3 111
Savannah, Hardin, Tenn.....B3 117
Savannah, lake, Md.....D6 85
Savannah, riv., Ga., S.C......F5 115
Savannah Beach, Chatham, Ga.....D6 87
Savannakhet, Laos.....D6 38
Savanna-la-Mar, Jam.....E4 64
Savé, Dah.....E5 45
Save, riv., Moz.....B5 49
Sāveh, Iran.....D5 41
Saveni, Rom.....B8 22
Saverne, Fr.....C7 14
Saverton, Ralls, Mo.....B6 101
Savery, Carbon, Wyo.....E5 125
Savigliano, It.....B1 21
Savigny [-sur-Orgel] Fr.....F2 15
Savo, riv., It.....h9 21
Savoie, dept., Fr.....D2 18
Savona, B.C., Can.....D7 68
Savona, It.....B2 21
Savona, Steuben, N.Y.....C3 108
Savonburg Allen, Kans.....E8 93
Savonlinna, Fin.....G13 25
Savoonga, Alsk.....C5 79
Savoy, Berkshire, Mass.....A1 97
Savoy, Blaine, Mont.....B8 102
Savoy (Savoie), former prov., Fr.....E7 14
Savran, Sov. Un.....G8 27
Sävsjö, Swe.....A8 24
Savu, is., Indon.....B3 50
Savu, sea, Indon.....G6 35
Savur, Tur.....D13 31
Savusavu, bay, Fiji..... 52
Saw, Bur.....D9 39
Sawākin, Sud.....B4 47
Sawankhalok, Thai.....D3 38
Sawara, Jap.....*I10 37
Sawatch, range, Colo.....B4 83
Sawdā, mtn., Libya.....D3 43
Sawdirī, Sud.....C2 47
Sawe, Indon.....L2 38
Sawhāj, Eg.....D6 43
Sawknah, Libya.....D3 43
Sawmill, Apache, Ariz.....B6 80
Saw Mill, riv., N.Y......D6 106
Sawn, lake, Alta., Can.....A3 69
Sawtooth, mts., Idaho.....E3 89
Sawtooth, ridge, Wash.....A5 122
Sawyer, Pratt, Kans.....E5 93
Sawyer, Berrien, Mich.....G4 98
Sawyer, Carlton, Minn.....D6 99
Sawyer, Ward, N. Dak.....A4 110
Sawyer, Choctaw, Okla.....C6 112
Sawyer, co., Wis.....C2 124
Sawyer, lake, Wash.....f11 122
Sawyers, hill, Newf., Can.....E5 75
Sawyerville, Que., Can.....D6 73
Sawyerwood, Summit, Ohio.....*A4 111
Saxe, Charlotte, Va.....D4 121
Saxis, Accomack, Va.....C7 121
Saxman, Alsk.....n24 79
Saxmundham, Eng.....B9 12
Saxon, Spartanburg, S.C.....B4 115
Saxon, Raleigh, W. Va.....n13 123
Saxon, Iron, Wis.....B3 124
Saxonburg, Butler, Pa.....E2 114
Saxony, reg., G.D.R.C6 16, B8 17
Saxony-Anhalt, reg., G.D.R..B6 17
Saxton, Whitley, Ky.....D5 94
Saxton, Bedford, Pa.....F5 114
Saxtons, riv., Vt.....E3 120
Saxtons River, Windham, Vt.....E3 120
Say, Niger.....D5 45
Sayaboury, Laos.....C4 38
Sayán, Peru.....D2 58
Sayan, mts., Sov. Un.....D12 28
Saybrook, McLean, Ill.....C5 90
Saybrook Point, Middlesex, Conn.....D7 84
Saybrook Manor, Middlesex, Conn.....*D7 84
Saydel, Polk, Iowa.....e8 92
Sayḩūt, P.D.R. of Yemen.....B7 47
Saylorsburg, Monroe, Pa...E11 114
Saylorville, Polk, Iowa.....e8 92
Saylorville Lake, res., Iowa..C4, e8 92
Sayner, Vilas, Wis.....B4 124
Sayre, Jefferson, Ala.....B3 78
Sayre, Beckham, Okla.....B2 112
Sayre, Bradford, Pa.....C8 114
Sayreton, Jefferson, Ala..C3, f7 78
Sayreville, Middlesex, N.J...C4 106
Sayr Usa, Mong.....C6 34
Sayula, Mex.....D4, n12 63
Sayula, lake, Mex.....n12 63
Say'ūn, P.D.R. of Yemen.....B6 47
Sayville, Suffolk, N.Y.....G4 84
Sazan, isl., Alb.....B2 23
Sazava, Czech.....o18 26
Sazava, riv., Czech.....o18 26
Sazliyka, riv., Bul.....D7 22
Sbeitla, prov., Tun.....*C6 44
Scafell Pike, mtn., Eng.....F5 13
Scalby, Eng.....*F8 13
Scales Mound, Jo Daviess, Ill.....A3 90
Scalp Level, Cambria, Pa.....F4 114
Scaly, Macon, N.C.....f9 109
Scamander, see Menderes, riv., Tur.
Scammon, Cherokee, Kans..E9 93
Scammon Bay, Alsk.....C6 79
Scandia, Alta., Can.....D4 69
Scandia, Republic, Kans.....C6 93
Scandia, Washington, Minn..E8 99
Scandinavia, Waupaca, Wis.D4 124
Scanlon, Carlton, Minn.....D6 99
Scansano, It.....C3 21
Scanterbury, Man., Can.....D3 71
Scantic, Hartford, Conn.....B6 84
Scanzano, It.....D6 21
Scapa, Alta., Can.....D5 69
Scapa Flow, bay, Scot.....B5 13
Scapegoat, mtn., Mont.....C4 102
Scappoose, Columbia, Oreg..B4 113
Scarba, isl., Scot.....D3 13
Scarboro, Jenkins, Ga.....D5 87
Scarborough, Cumberland, Maine.....E2, g7 96
Scarborough, Ont., Can.....m15 72
Scarborough, Eng.....C6 10
Scarborough, Trin.....M24 65
Scarbro, Fayette, W. Va.....n13 123
Scariff, isl., Ire.....F1 11
Scarriff, Ire.....E3 11
Scarsdale, Westchester, N.Y.h13 108
Scartaglen, Ire.....E2 11
Scarth, Man., Can.....E1 71
Scarville, Winnebago, Iowa..A4 92
Scauri, It.....F3 21
Sceaux, Fr.....g10 14
Scenic, Pennington, S. Dak..D3 116
Sceptre, Sask., Can.....G1 70
Schaal, lake, F.R.G.....E4 24
Schaefferstown, Lebanon, Pa.....F9 114
Schaerbeek, Bel.....*D4 15
Schaffer, Delta, Mich.....C3 98
Schaffhausen, Switz.....A6 19
Schaffhausen, canton, Switz..A5 19
Schagen, Neth.....B4 15
Schaghticoke, Rensselaer, N.Y.....C7 108
Schaller, Sac, Iowa.....B2 92
Schangnau Switz.....C4 19
Schārding, Aus.....E8 17
Scharhörn, isl., F.R.G.....E2 24
Schaumburg, Cook, Ill.....h8 90
Schefferville, Que., Can.....h13 73
Schell City, Vernon, Mo.....C3 101
Schell Creek, range, Nev.....E7 104
Schellsburg, Bedford, Pa.....F4 114
Schenectady, Schenectady, N.Y.....C7 108
Schenectady, co., N.Y.....C6 108
Schenefeld, F.R.G.....D3 24
Schenevus, Otsego, N.Y.....C6 108
Schererville, Lake, Ind.....B3 91
Scherfede, F.R.G.....B4 17
Schertz, Guadalupe, Tex.....h7 118
Scheveningen, Neth. (part of The Hague).....B4 15
Schiedam, Neth.....C4 15
Schiermonnikoog, isl., Neth.....A6 15
Schifferstadt, F.R.G.....D3 17
Schiltigheim, Fr.....C7 14
Schilpario, It.....C6 18
Schiller Park, Cook, Ill.....k9 90
Schio, It.....B3 21
Schivelbein, see Swidwin, Pol.
Schkeuditz, G.D.R.....B7 17
Schladming, Aus.....E6 16
Schlater, Leflore, Miss.....B3 100
Schlei, inlet, F.R.G.....D3 24
Schleicher, co., Tex.....D2 118
Schleiz, G.D.R.....C6 17
Schleswig, F.R.G.....A4 16
Schleswig, Crawford, Iowa...B2 92
Schleswig Holstein, reg., F.R.G.....A4 16
Schleswig-Holstein, state, F.R.G.....D3 24
Schley, Gloucester, Va.....C6 121
Schley, co., Ga.....D2 87
Schlieren, Switz.....B5 19
Schlitz, F.R.G.....C4 17
Schloss Neuhaus, F.R.G.....B3 17
Schlüchtern, F.R.G.....C4 17
Schmalkalden, G.D.R.....C5 17
Schmölln, G.D.R.....C7 17
Schnackenburg, F.R.G.....E3 24
Schneeberg, G.D.R.....C7 17
Schneeberg, mtn., F.R.G.....C6 17
Schneidemühl, see Piła, Pol.
Schneider, Lake, Ind.....B3 91
Schoenchen, Ellis, Kans.....D4 93
Schofield, Marathon, Wis...D4 124
Schofield Barracks, Honolulu, Haw.....B3, g9 88
Schoharie, Schoharie, N.Y...C6 108
Schoharie, co., N.Y.....C6 108
Schoharie, creek, N.Y......C6 108
Scholls, Washington, Oreg..h12 113
Schönbach, Aus.....D7 16
Schönebeck, G.D.R.....A6 17
Schöneck, G.D.R.....C7 17
Schongau, F.R.G.....E5 16
Schöningen, F.R.G.....A5 17
Schoodic, lake, Maine.....C4 96
Schoolcraft, Kalamazoo, Mich.....F5 98
Schoolcraft, co., Mich.....B4 98
Schooleys, mtn., N.J......B3 106
Schoonhoven, Neth.....C4 15
Schopfheim, F.R.G.....B3 18
Schorndorf, F.R.G.....E4 17
Schoten, Bel.....C4 15
Schötmar, F.R.G.....A3 17
Schouten, is., Indon.....F9 35
Schramberg, F.R.G.....D4 16
Schram City, Montgomery, Ill.....D4 90
Schriever, Terrebonne, La.....E5, k10 95
Schrobenhausen, F.R.G.....E6 17
Schroeder, Cook, Minn..C8, k9 99
Schroon, lake, N.Y......B7 108
Schroon Lake, Essex, N.Y...B7 108
Schuchk, Pima, Ariz.....E4 80
Schuchuli, Pima, Ariz.....E3 80
Schulenburg, Fayette, Tex...E4 118
Schuler, Alta., Can.....D5 69
Schull, Ire.....F2 11
Schulte, Sedgwick, Kans.....g12 93
Schulter, Okmulgee, Okla...B6 112
Schüpftheim, Switz.....B5 19
Schurz, Mineral, Nev.....E3 104
Schüttorf, F.R.G.....A2 17
Schuyler, Colfax, Nebr.....C8 103
Schuyler, Nelson, Va.....C4 121
Schuyler, co., Ill.....C3 90
Schuyler, co., Mo.....A5 101
Schuyler, co., N.Y.....C4 108
Schuyler Lake, Otsego, N.Y..C5 108
Schuylerville, Saratoga, N.Y.B7 108
Schuylkill, co., Pa.....E9 114
Schuylkill, riv., Pa.....A11 114
Schuylkill Haven, Schuylkill, Pa.....E9 114
Schwabach, F.R.G.....D6 17
Schwäbische Alb, plat., F.R.G..E4 17
Schwäbisch Gmünd, F.R.G..E4 17
Schwäbisch Hall, F.R.G.....D4 17
Schwabmünchen, F.R.G.....A6 18
Schwandorf, F.R.G.....D7 17
Schwaner, mts., Indon.....F4 35
Schwarmstedt, F.R.G.....F3 24
Schwarze Elster, riv., G.D.R...B8 17
Schwarzenbach [an der sächsischen Saale], F.R.G.....C6 17
Schwarzenbek, F.R.G.....E4 24
Schwarzenberg, G.D.R.....C7 17
Schwarzenfeld, F.R.G.....D7 17
Schwarzheide, G.D.R.....B8 17
Schwaz, Aus.....E5 16
Schwarzwald, mts., F.R.G.....E3 17
Schwedt, G.D.R.....B7 16
Schweibus, see Swiebodzin, Pol.
Schweinfurt, F.R.G.....C5 17
Schwenningen, F.R.G.....D4 16
Schwerin, G.D.R.....B5 16
Schweriner See, lake, G.D.R......E5 24
Schwetzingen, F.R.G.....D3 17
Schwyz, Switz.....B6 19
Schwyz, canton, Switz.....B6 19
Sciacca, It.....F4 21
Science Hill, Pulaski, Ky.....C5 94
Scilly, is., Eng.....F3 10
Scio, Allegany, N.Y.....C3 108
Scio, Harrison, Ohio.....B4 111
Scio, Linn, Oreg.....C4, k12 113
Sciota, McDonough, Ill.....C3 90
Scioto, co., Ohio.....D2 111
Scioto, riv., Ohio.....D2 111
Sciotodale, Scioto, Ohio.....*D3 111
Scioto Furnace, Scioto, Ohio.D3 111
Scipio, Jennings, Ind.....F6 91
Scipio, Millard, Utah.....D3 119
Scitico, Hartford, Conn.....B6 84
Scituate, Plymouth, Mass.....B6, h13 97
Scituate (Town of), Providence, R.I.....*B10 84
Scituate, res., R.I.....B10 84
Sciuēref, Libya.....D2 43
Scobey, Daniels, Mont.....B11 102
Scofield, Carbon, Utah.....D4 119
Scofield, res., Utah.....D4 119
Scollard, Alta., Can.....D4 69
Scone, Austl.....F8 51
Scooba, Kemper, Miss.....C5 100
Scopus, mtn., Jordan.....m14 32
Scoresbysund, Grnld.....B17 4
Scotch Plains, Union, N.J...B4 106
Scotch Village, N.S., Can..*D6 74
Scotia, Humboldt, Calif.....B1 82
Scotia, Ont., Can.....B5 72
Scotia, Greeley, Nebr.....C7 103
Scotia, Schenectady, N.Y.....C7 108
Scotia, Hampton, S.C.....F5 115
Scotland, Van Buren, Ark...B3 81
Scotland, Ont., Can.....D4 72
Scotland, Windham, Conn...C8 84
Scotland, Telfair, Ga.....D4 87
Scotland, Greene, Ind.....G4 91
Scotland, St. Marys, Md.....D5 85
Scotland, Cheshire, N.H.....E2 105
Scotland, Franklin, Pa.....G6 114
Scotland, Bon Homme, S. Dak.....D8 116
Scotland, reg., U.K..... 13
Scotland, co., Mo.....A5 101
Scotland, co., N.C.....C3 109
Scotland Neck, Halifax N.C.A5 109
Scotlandville, East Baton Rouge, La.....g9, D4 95
Scotrun, Monroe, Pa.....D11 114
Scotsburn, N.S., Can.....D7 74
Scotsguard, Sask., Can.....H1 70
Scotstown, Que., Can.....D6 73
Scott, N.Z. scientific station, Ant......B29 5
Scott, Lonoke and Pulaski, Ark.....C3, k10 81
Scott, Sask., Can.....E1 70
Scott, Johnson, Ga.....D4 87
Scott, Lafayette, La.....D3 95
Scott, Bolivar, Miss.....B2 100
Scott, Paulding and Van Wert, Ohio.....B1 111
Scott, co., Ark.....C1 81
Scott, co., Ill.....D3 90
Scott, co., Ind.....G6 91
Scott, co., Iowa.....C7 92
Scott, co., Kans.....D3 93
Scott, co., Ky.....B5 94
Scott, co., Minn.....F5 99
Scott, co., Miss.....C4 100
Scott, co., Mo.....D8 101
Scott, co., Tenn.....C9 117
Scott, co., Va.....f9 121
Scott, cape, B.C., Can.....D3 68
Scott, glacier, Ant.....C23 5
Scott, is., Ant.....C30 5
Scott, is., B.C., Can.....D3 68
Scott, mtn., Okla.....C3 112
Scott, res., N.C......A1 109
Scott City, Scott, Kans.....D3 93
Scott City, Scott, Mo.....D8 101
Scottdale, De Kalb, Ga.....h8 87
Scottdale, Westmoreland, Pa.....F2 114
Scottland, Edgar, Ill.....D6 90
Scotts, Kalamazoo, Mich.....F5 98
Scotts, mtn., N.J.....B2 106
Scottsbluff, Scotts Bluff, Nebr.....C2 103
Scotts Bluff, co., Nebr.....C2 103
Scotts Bluff, nat. mon., Nebr.....C2 103
Scottsboro, Jackson, Ala.....A3 78
Scottsburg, Scott, Ind.....G6 91
Scottsburg, Douglas, Oreg...D3 113
Scottsburg, Halifax, Va.....D4 121
Scottsdale, Maricopa, Ariz.....D4, m9 80
Scotts Hill, Pender, N.C.....C5 109
Scotts Hill, Henderson and Decatur, Tenn.....B3 117
Scotts Mills, Marion, Oreg.....B4, h12 113
Scottsville, Pope, Ark.....B3 81
Scottsville, Mitchell, Kans...C6 93
Scottsville, Allen, Ky.....D3 94
Scottsville, Monroe, N.Y.....B3 108
Scottsville, Albemarle and Fluvanna, Va.....C4 121
Scottville, Macoupin, Ill.....D3 90
Scottville, Mason, Mich.....E4 98
Scourie, Scot.....B3 13
Scout Lake, Sask., Can.....H3 70
Scow Bay, Alsk.....m23 79
Scraggly, lake, Maine.....B4 96
Scranton, Logan, Ark.....B2 81
Scranton, Greene, Iowa.....B3 92
Scranton, Osage, Kans.....D8 93
Scranton, Menifee, Ky.....C6 94
Scranton, Hyde, N.C.....B6 109
Scranton, Bowman, N. Dak..C2 110
Scranton, Lackawanna, Pa.....D10, m18 114
Scranton, Florence, S.C.....D8 115
Screven, Wayne, Ga.....E4 87
Screven, co., Ga.....D5 87
Scribner, Dodge, Nebr.....C9 103
Scridain inlet, Scot.....D2 13
Scrivia, riv., It.....E4 18
Scrolls Caves, Jordan.....C7 32
Scugog, lake, Ont., Can.....C6 72
Scullville, Atlantic, N.J.....E3 106
Scunthorpe, Eng.....A7 12
Scuol (Schuls), Switz.....C9 19
Scurry, co., Tex.....C2 118
Scutari (Shkodër), Alb.....A2 23
Scutari (Shkoder), pref., Alb.....*A2 23
Scutari, lake, Alb.....A2 23
Scyrene, Clarke, Ala.....D2 78
Seaboard, Northampton, N.C.....A5 109
Seábra, Braz.....C3 58
Sea Bright, Monmouth, N.J..C5 106
Seabrook, Prince Georges, Md.....*C4 85
Seabrook, Rockingham, N.H.E5 105
Seabrook, Cumberland, N.J..E2 106
Seabrook, Harris, Tex.....r14 118
Seabrook, isl., S.C......F7 115
Sea Cliff, Nassau, N.Y.....F2 84
Seadrift, Calhoun, Tex.....E4 118
Seaford, Sussex, Del.....C6 85
Seaford, Nassau, N.Y.....G3 84
Seaford, York, Va.....h15 121
Seaforth, Ont., Can.....D3 72
Sea Girt, Monmouth, N.J...C4 106
Seagoville, Dallas, Tex.....n10 118
Seagram, lake, Sask., Can.....E1 70
Seagrave, Ont., Can.....C6 72
Seagraves, Gaines, Tex.....C1 118
Seagrove, Randolph, N.C.....B3 109
Seaham, Eng.....F7 13
Sea Island, Glynn, Ga.....E5 87
Sea Isle City, Cape May, N.J.....E3 106
Seal, bay, Ant.....B11 5
Seal, lake, Newf., Can.....g9 75
Seal, pt., P.E.I., Can.....C5 74
Seal, riv., Man., Can.....f8 71
Seal Beach, Orange, Calif...*F5 82
Seal Cove, N.B., Can.....E3 74
Seal Cove, Newf., Can.....D3 75
Seal Cove, Hancock, Maine..D4 96
Seale, Russell, Ala.....C4 78
Sealevel, Carteret, N.C.....C6 109
Seal Harbor, Hancock, Maine.....D4 96
Seal Rock, Lincoln, Oreg.....C2 113
Sealston, King George, Va...B5 121
Sealy, Austin, Tex.....E4 118
Seama, Valencia, N. Mex.....B2 107
Seaman, Adams, Ohio.....D2 111
Seanor, Somerset, Pa.....F4 114
Searchlight, Clark, Nev.....H7 104
Searcy, White, Ark.....B4 81
Searcy, co., Ark.....B3 81
Searight, Crenshaw, Ala.....D3 78
Searles, Tuscaloosa, Ala.....B2 78
Searles, Brown, Minn.....F4 99
Searles, lake, Calif.....E5 82
Sears, Osceola, Mich.....E5 98
Sears, falls, Nebr.....B5 103
Searsboro, Poweshiek, Iowa..C5 92
Searsburg, Bennington, Vt...F3 120
Searsport, Waldo, Maine.....D4 96
Searston, Newf., Can.....E2 75
Seaside, Monterey, Calif...*D3 82
Seaside, Clatsop, Oreg.....B3 113
Seaside Heights, Ocean, N.J.D4 106
Seaside Park, Ocean, N.J.....D4 106
Seaton, Eng.....D4 12
Seaton, Mercer, Ill.....B3 90
Seat Pleasant, Prince Georges, Md.....C4, f9 85
Seattle, King, Wash.....B3, e11 122
Sea View, Plymouth, Mass..h13 97
Seaview, Pacific, Wash.....C1 122
Seaville, Cape May, N.J.....E3 106
Seba Beach, Alta., Can.....C3 69
Sébaco, Nic.....D4 62
Sebago, lake, Maine.....E2 96
Sebago Lake, Cumberland, Maine.....E2 96
Sebastian, Indian River, Fla .E6 86
Sebastian, co., Ark.....B1 81
Sebastian, cape, Oreg.....E2 113
Sebastian, inlet, Fla.....E6 86
Sebastián Vizcaíno, bay, Mex...B2 63
Sebasticook, lake, Maine.....D3 96
Sebastopol, Sonoma, Calif...C2 82
Sebastopol, Scott, Miss.....C4 100
Sebatik, isl., Indon.....E5 35
Sebderat, Eth.....B4 47
Sebec, Piscataquis, Maine...C3 96
Sebec, lake, Maine.....C3 96
Sebeka, Wadena, Minn.....D3 99
Sebeş, Rom.....C6 22
Sebewaing, Huron, Mich.....E7 98
Sebinkarahisar, Tur.....B12 31
Sebkha Mekerrhane, lake, Alg...D5 44
Sebnitz, G.D.R.....C9 17
Seboeis, Penobscot, Maine...C4 96
Seboeis, riv., Maine.....B4 96
Seboois, lake, Maine.....C4 96
Seboomook, Somerset, Maine.....C3 96
Seboomook, lake, Maine.....C3 96
Sebou, riv., Mor.....G4 30
Seboyeta, Valencia, N. Mex..B2 107
Sebree, Webster, Ky.....C2 94
Sebrell, Southampton, Va...D5 121
Sebring, Highlands, Fla.....E5 86
Sebring, Mahoning, Ohio.....B4 111
Sebringville, Ont., Can.....D3 72
Secane, Delaware, Pa.....*G11 114
Secaucus, Hudson, N.J.....h8 106
Secchia, riv., It.....B3 21
Sechelt, B.C., Can.....E6 68
Sechura, Peru.....C1 58
Sechura, bay, Peru.....C1 58
Seclin, Fr.....D3 15
Seco, Letcher, Ky.....C7 94
Second, lake, Maine.....B4 96
Second, lake, N.H.....f7 105
Second Mesa, Navajo, Ariz..B5 80
Secor, Woodford, Ill.....C4 90
Secor Gardens, Lucas, Ohio.*A2 111
Secretan, Sask., Can.....G2 70
Secretary, Dorchester, Md...C6 85
Secretary, isl., N.Z.....P11 51
Section, Jackson, Ala.....A4 78
Secunderabad Cantonment, India.....*I7 40
Security, El Paso, Colo.....C6 83
Sedalia, Alta., Can.....D5 69
Sedalia, Douglas, Colo.....B6 83
Sedalia, Clinton, Ind.....D4 91
Sedalia, Graves, Ky.....f9 94
Sedalia, Pettis, Mo.....C4 101
Sedalia (Midway), Madison, Ohio.....C2 111
Sedan, Fr.....C6 14
Sedan, Chautauqua, Kans...E7 93
Sedan, Pope, Minn.....E3 99
Sedan, Union, N. Mex.....A6 107
Sedbergh, Eng.....F6 13
Sederot, Isr.....C6 32
Sedgefield, Guilford, N.C...*A3 109
Sedgewick, Alta., Can.....C5 69
Sedgewick, Hancock, Maine.D4 96
Sedgewickville, Bollinger, Mo.....D8 101
Sedgwick, Lawrence, Ark.....B5 81
Sedgwick, Sedgwick, Colo...A8 83
Sedgwick, Harvey, Kans.E6, g12 93
Sedgwick, co., Colo.....A8 83
Sedgwick, co., Kans.....E6 93
Sedgwick, mtn., N. Mex.....B1 107
Sédhiou, Sen.....D1 45
Sedillo, Bernalillo, N. Mex...k8 107
Sedlčany, Czech.....D9 17
Sedley, Sask., Can.....G3 70
Sedley, Southampton, Va.....E6 121
Sedom, Isr.....C7 32
Sedona, Coconino, Ariz.....C4 80
Sedot Yam, Isr.....B6 32
Sedro Woolley, Skagit, Wash.....A3 122
Sedrun, Switz.....C6 19
Seebe, Alta., Can.....D3 69
Seeber, riv., Man., Ont., Can...C5 71
Seebert, Pocahontas, W. Va..C4 123
Seehausen, G.D.R.....F5 24
Seeheim, Namibia.....C2 49
Seeis, Namibia.....B2 49
Seekonk, Bristol, Mass.....C5 97
Seeley, Imperial, Calif.....F6 82
Seeley Lake, Missoula, Mont.C3 102
Seeleys Bay, Ont., Can.....C8 72
Seelow, G.D.R.....F8 24
Seelyville, Vigo, Ind.....F3 91
Seelyville, Wayne, Pa.....C11 114
Sées, Fr.....C4 14
Seesen, F.R.G.....B5 17
Sefadu, S.L.....E2 45
Seferihisar, Tur.....C6 23
Seffner, Hillsborough, Fla...D4 86
Sefid, riv., Iran.....C4 41
Segamat, Mala.....K5 38
Segbwema, S.L.....E2 45
Segesta, It.....F4 21
Segezha, Sov. Un.....F16 25
Segorbe, Sp.....C5 20
Ségou, Mali.....D3 45
Segovia, Sp.....B3 20
Segovia, prov., Sp.....*B3 20
Segozero, lake, Sov. Un.....F15 25
Segré, Fr.....D3 14
Segre, riv., Sp.....B6 20
Segreganset, Bristol, Mass...C5 97
Séguédine, Niger.....B7 45
Séguéla, I.C.....E3 45
Seguin, Guadalupe, Tex .E4, h8 118
Seguine, pt., N.Y......k8 106
Seguin Falls, Ont., Can.....B5 72
Segundo, Las Animas, Colo..D6 83
Segura, riv., Sp.....C5 20
Seh Konj, mtn., Iran.....F8 41
Sehore, India.....F6 40
Sehwān, Pak.....D1 40
Seibert, Kit Carson, Colo.....B8 83
Seiling, Dewey, Okla.....A3 112
Seille, riv., Fr.....F6 15
Seinäjoki, Fin.....F10 25
Seine, dept., Fr.....*C5 14
Seine, bay, Fr.....C3 14
Seine, riv., Fr.....C4 14
Seine-et-Marne, dept., Fr.....F2 15
Seine-et-Oise, dept., Fr.....F2 15
Seine-Maritime, dept., Fr.....E9 12
Seis de Septiembre, Arg.....g7 54
Seishin, see Chongjin, Kor.
Seixal, Port.....f9 20
Sejerby, Den.....C5 24
Sejerø, Den.....C5 24
Sejerø, isl., Den.....C5 24
Sekenke, Tan.....B5 48
Seki, Jap.....o15 37
Sekiu, Clallam, Wash.....A1 122
Sekondi-Takoradi, Ghana.....F4 45
Sekota, Eth.....C4 47
Selah, Yakima, Wash.....C5 122
Selangor, state, Mala.....K4 38
Selanovtsi, Bul.....D7 22
Selaru, isl., Indon.....G8 35
Selatan, cape, Indon.....F4 35
Selatpanjang, Indon.....L5 38
Selawik, Alsk.....B7 79
Selawik, lake, Alsk.....B7 79
Selb, F.R.G.....C7 17
Selborne, cape, Ant.....g40 5
Selbu, Nor.....F4 25
Selby, Eng.....A6 12
Selby, Walworth, S. Dak.....B5 116
Selbysport, Garrett, Md.....D1 85
Selbyville, Sussex, Del.....D7 85
Selbyville, Upshur, W. Va...C4 123
Selde, Den.....B3 24
Selden, Sheridan, Kans.....C3 93
Selden, Aroostook, Maine...C5 96
Seldovia, Alsk.....D9, h16 79
Selenge, riv., Mong.....B5 34
Selenicë, Alb.....B2 23
Selenter, lake, F.R.G.....D4 24
Sélestat, Fr.....C7 14
Seletytengiz, lake, Sov. Un.....C8 29
Selfridge, Sioux, N. Dak.....C5 110
Sélibaby, Maur.....C2 45
Selidovka, Sov. Un.....q20 27
Seligenstadt, F.R.G.....C3 17
Seliger, lake, Sov. Un.....C9 27
Seligman, Yavapai, Ariz.....B3 80
Seligman, Barry, Mo.....E4 101
Selinsgrove, Snyder, Pa.....E8 114
Selinunte, ruins, It.....F4 21
Selizharovo, Sov. Un.....C9 27
Selkirk, Man., Can.....D3 71
Selkirk, Ont., Can.....E5 72
Selkirk, Wichita, Kans.....D2 93
Selkirk, Scot.....E6 13
Selkirk, mtn., Idaho.....A2 89
Selkirk, mts., B.C., Can.....D9 68
Selleck, King, Wash.....B4, f12 122
Seller, lake, Man., Can.....B4 71
Sellers, Montgomery, Ala.....C3 78
Sellers, Dillon and Marion, S.C.....C9 115
Sellersburg, Clark, Ind.....H6 91
Sellersville, Bucks, Pa.....F11 114
Sells, Pima, Ariz.....F4 80
Selm, F.R.G.....B2 17
Selma, Dallas, Ala.....C2 78
Selma, Drew, Ark.....D4 81
Selma, Fresno, Calif.....D4 82
Selma, Delaware, Ind.....D7 91
Selma, Grant, La.....C3 95
Selma, Johnston, N.C.....B4 109
Selma, Josephine, Oreg.....E3 113
Selmah, N.S., Can.....D6 74
Selman, Harper, Okla.....A2 112
Selmer, McNairy, Tenn.....B3 117
Selsey, Eng.....D7 12
Selsey Bill, pt., Eng.....D7 12
Selukwe, Rh.....A5 49
Selva, Arg.....E3 55
Selvas, forests, Braz.....D4 53
Selvin, Warrick, Ind.....H3 91
Selway, riv., Idaho.....C3 89
Selwyn, Austl.....D7 50
Selwyn, lake, N.W. Ter., Sask. Can......k8 70
Selwyn, mtn., B.C., Can.....A6 68
Selwyn, mts., N.W. Ter., Yukon, Can......D6 66
Selz, Pierce, N. Dak.....B6 110
Seman, Elmore, Ala.....C3 78
Seman, riv., Alb.....B2 23
Semans, Sask., Can.....F3 70
Semara, W. Sahara.....D2 44
Semarang, Indon.....G4 35
Semenov, Sov. Un.....D17 9
Semenovka, Sov. Un.....E9 27
Seminary, Covington, Miss..D4 100
Seminoe, mts., Wyo.....D6 125
Seminoe, res., Wyo.....E6 125
Seminoe Dam, Carbon, Wyo.D6 125
Seminole, Baldwin, Ala.....E2 78
Seminole, Pinellas, Fla.....*E4 86
Seminole, Seminole, Okla.....B5 112
Seminole, Gaines, Tex.....C1 118
Seminole, co., Fla.....D5 86
Seminole, co., Ga.....F2 87
Seminole, co., Okla.....B5 112
Seminole, Indian res., Fla.....F6 86
Seminole (Big Cypress), Indian res., Fla.....F5 86
Seminole (Brighton), Indian res., Fla.....E5 86
Semipalatinsk, Sov. Un.....C10 29
Semitau, Indon.....E4 35
Semiyarskoye, Sov. Un.....C9 29
Semliki, riv., Zaire.....A4 48
Semmens, lake, Man., Can.....B4 71
Semmering, pass, Aus.....E7 16
Semnān, Iran.....D6 41
Semois, riv., Bel.....E5 15
Semora, Caswell, N.C.....A3 109
Sempach, Switz.....B5 19
Sempacher, lake, Switz.....B5 19
Semur-en-Auxois, Fr.....D6 14
Sen, riv., Kam.....F6 38
Sena, San Miguel, N. Mex...B4 107
Senaca, La Salle, Ill.....B5 90
Senachwine, lake, Ill.....B4 90
Senador Pompeu, Braz.....C3 57
Sena Madureira, Braz.....C4 58
Senanga, Zambia.....E3 48
Senate, Sask., Can.....H1 70
Senath, Dunklin, Mo.....E7 101
Senatobia, Tate, Miss.....A4 100
Sendai, Jap.....G10 37
Sendai (Kagoshima pref.), Jap.....K5 37
Sendai, bay, Jap.....G10 37
Seneca, Nemaha, Kans.....C7 93
Seneca, Newton, Mo.....E3 101
Seneca, Thomas, Nebr.....B5 103
Seneca, Union, N. Mex.....A6 107
Seneca, Grant, Oreg.....C8 113
Seneca, Venango, Pa.....D2 114
Seneca, Oconee, S.C.....B2 115
Seneca, Faulk, S. Dak.....B6 116
Seneca, Crawford, Wis.....E3 124
Seneca, co., N.Y.....C4 108
Seneca, co., Ohio.....A2 111
Seneca, caverns, W. Va.....C5 123
Seneca, lake, N.Y......C4 108
Seneca, rocks, W. Va.....C5 123
Seneca Falls, Seneca, N.Y...C4 108
Seneca Gardens, Jefferson, Ky.....*B4 94
Senecaville, Guernsey, Ohio..C4 111
Senecaville Lake, res., Ohio.....C4 111
Seneffe, Bel.....D4 15
Senegal, country, Afr.....E4 42, D1 45
Sénégal, riv., Maur., Sen.....C2 45
Seney, Schoolcraft, Mich.....B5 98
Senftenberg, G.D.R.....B9 17
Senga Hill, Zambia.....C5 48
Senguerr, riv., Arg.....D3 54
Senhor do Bonfim, Braz.....D2 57
Senhoshi, Jap.....D10 37

Senigallia, It....C4 21
Senj, Yugo....C2 22
Senja, isl., Nor....C7 25
Senlac, Sask., Can....E1 70
Senlis, Fr....C5 14
Senneterre, Que., Can....k11 73
Senneville, Que., Can....*p19 73
Senoia, Coweta, Ga....C2 87
Sens, Fr....C5 14
Sense, riv., Switz....C3 19
Senta, Yugo....C5 22
Sentery, Zaire....C4 48
Sentinel, Maricopa, Ariz....E2 80
Sentinel, Washita, Okla....B2 112
Sentinel, peak, B.C., Can....B6 68
Sentinel, butte, N. Dak....C2 110
Sentinel, range, Ant....B4 5
Sentinel Butte, Golden Valley, N. Dak....C2 110
Senzu, Jap....n17 37
Seo de Urgel, Sp....A6 20
Seoni, India....F7 40
Seoul (Sŏul), Kor....H3 37
Separ, Grant, N. Mex....E1 107
Sepik, riv., N. Gui....h11 50
Sepolno, Pol....B4 26
Sept Îles (Seven Islands), Que., Can....h13 73
Sepulga, riv., Ala....D3 78
Sequatchie, Marion, Tenn....D8 117
Sequatchie, co., Tenn....D8 117
Sequatchie, riv., Tenn....D7 117
Sequim, Clallam, Wash....A2 122
Sequoia, nat. park, Calif....D4 82
Sequoia, Tulare, Calif....D4 82
Sequoyah, co., Okla....B7 112
Serafimovich, Sov. Un....D2 29
Serafina, San Miguel, N. Mex....B4 107
Seraing, Bel....D5 15
Serakhs, Sov. Un....C10 41
Serampore, India....*F12 40
Serang, Indon....G3 35
Serasan, is., Indon....K8 38
Serbia, reg., Yugo....D5 22
Serbia, rep., Yugo....*D5 22
Serdo, Eth....C5 47
Serdobsk, Sov. Un....E15 27
Sered, Czech....D4 26
Sereflikochisar, Tur....C9 31
Seremban, Mala....K4 38
Serengeti, plain, Tan....B5 48
Serenje, Zambia....D5 48
Serenli, Som....E5 47
Sergeant, McKean, Pa....C4 114
Sergeant Bluff, Woodbury, Iowa....B1 92
Sergeantsville, Hunterdon, N.J....C3 106
Sergipe, state, Braz....D3 57
Seria, Brunei....E4 35
Serifos, Grc....D5 23
Serifos, isl., Grc....D5 23
Seringapatam, India....F6 39
Serles, Hardeman, Tenn....B2 117
Sermaize, Fr....F4 15
Sernyy Zavod, Sov. Un....B9 41
Seroei, Indon....F9 35
Serón, Sp....D4 20
Serov, Sov. Un....B6 29
Serowe, Bots....B4 49
Serpa, Port....D2 20
Serpentine, lakes, Austl....E4 50
Serpukhov, Sov. Un....C1 29
Serra dos Aimorés, disputed reg., Braz....*E2 57
Serrai, Grc....B4 23
Serrai, prov., Grc....*B4 23
Serrana Bank, shoals, Caribbean Sea....C7 62
Serra Negra, Braz....m8 56
Serranilla Bank, shoals, Caribbean Sea....C8 62
Serra Talhada, Braz....C3 57
Serres, Fr....E1 18
Serrezuela, Arg....A3 54
Serrinha, Braz....D3 57
Sêrro, Braz....E2 57
Sertã, Port....C1 20
Sertânia, Braz....C3 57
Serua, isl., Indon....G8 35
Serule, Bots....B4 49
Servia, Grc....B4 23
Servia, Wabash, Ind....C6 91
Service, Choctaw, Ala....D1 78
Service, buttes, Oreg....B7 113
Service Creek, Wheeler, Oreg....C7 113
Sese, isl., Ug....B5 48
Sesoko, isl., Okinawa....52
Sesheke, Zambia....E3 48
Sésia, riv., It....D4 18
Sesser, Franklin, Ill....E4 90
Sessums, Oktibbeha, Miss....B5 100
Sesto [Fiorentino], It....C3 21
Sesto, Sov. Un....A7 26
Sesto San Giovanni, It....D5 18
Sestriere, It....E2 18
Sestri Levante, It....B2 21
Sestroretsk, Sov. Un....A8 27
Setana, Jap....E9 37
Setauket, Suffolk, N.Y....F4 84
Sète (Cette), Fr....F5 14
Sete Lagoas, Braz....E2 57
Sete Quedas, falls, Braz....C5 55
Seth, Boone, W. Va....C3, m12 123
Seth Ward, Hale, Tex....*B2 118
Sétif, Alg....B6 44
Seto, Jap....I8, n16 37
Seton Portage, B.C., Can....D6 68
Settat, Mor....C3 44
Sette Cama, Gabon....F1 46
Settee, lake, Sask., Can....B3 70
Setting, lake, Man., Can....B2 71
Settle, Eng....F6 13
Setúbal, Port....C1 20
Setubal, bay, Port....C1 20
Seul, lake, Ont., Can....o16 72
Seul Choix, pt., Mich....C5 98
Sevan, lake, Sov. Un....G18 9
Sevastopol, Sov. Un....I9 27
Seven, heads, Ire....F3 11
Seven Devils, mts., Idaho....D2 89
Seven Harbors, Oakland, Mich....F7 98
Seven Hills, Cuyahoga, Ohio....h9 111
Seven Islands, see Sept Îles, Que., Can.
Seven Islands, bay, Newf., Can....f9 75
Seven Mile, Butler, Ohio....C1 111
Seven Mile, beach, N.J....E3 106
Sevenoaks, Eng....C8 12
Seven Persons, Alta., Can....E5 69
Seven Rivers, Eddy, N. Mex....E5 107
Seven Sisters, Duval, Tex....E3 118
Seven Sisters, peaks, B.C., Can....B3 68
Seven Springs, Wayne, N.C....B5 109
70 Mile House, B.C., Can....D7 68
Severance, Weld, Colo....A6 83
Severance, Doniphan, Kans....C8 93
Severka, riv., Sov. Un....n18 27
Severn, Anne Arundel, Md....B4 85
Severn, Northampton, N.C....A5 109
Severn, Gloucester, Va....C6 121
Severn, riv., Ont., Can....n17 72
Severn, riv., Eng., Wales....B4 12
Severn, riv., Md....B4 85
Severn, riv. mouth, Eng., Wales....C4 12
Severna Park, Anne Arundel, Md....B4 85
Severnaya Zemlya, is., Sov. Un....B13 28
Severodvinsk, Sov. Un....E18 25
Severomorsk, Sov. Un....C15 25
Severouralsk, Sov. Un....C20 9
Severy, Greenwood, Kans....E7 93
Sevier, Sevier, Utah....E3 119
Sevier, co., Ark....D1 81
Sevier, co., Tenn....D10 117
Sevier, co., Utah....E4 119
Sevier, des., Utah....D3 119
Sevier, lake, Utah....E2 119
Sevier, riv., Utah....D3 119
Sevier Bridge, res., Utah....D4 119
Sevierville, Sevier, Tenn....D10 117
Sevilla, Col....C2 60
Sevilla (Seville), Sp....D3 20
Sevilla (Seville), prov., Sp....*D3 20
Seville, Volusia, Fla....C5 86
Seville, Wilcox, Ga....E3 87
Seville, Medina, Ohio....A4 111
Sevlievo, Bul....D7 22
Sevogle, riv., N.B., Can....B3 74
Sevran, Fr....g11 14
Sèvre, riv., Fr....D3 14
Sèvre Niortaise, riv., Fr....D3 14
Sèvres, Fr....g9 14
Sewal, Wayne, Iowa....D4 92
Sewanee, Franklin, Tenn....B6 117
Seward, Alsk....C10, g17 79
Seward, Stafford, Kans....D5 93
Seward, Seward, Nebr....D8 103
Seward, Schoharie, N.Y....C6 108
Seward, Logan, Okla....B4 112
Seward, Westmoreland, Pa....F3 114
Seward, co., Kans....E3 93
Seward, co., Nebr....D8 103
Seward, pen., Alsk....B7 79
Seward Roads, chan., Midway Is....52
Sewaren, Middlesex, N.J....k7 106
Sewell, Chile....A2 54
Sewell, Gloucester, N.J....D2 106
Sewickley, Allegheny, Pa....E1, h13 114
Sewickley Heights, Allegheny, Pa....*E1 114
Sexsmith, Alta., Can....B1 69
Sextonville, Richland, Wis....E3 124
Seychelles, country, Afr....G24 3
Seychelles, is., Indian O....G24 3
Seydisehir, Tur....D8 31
Seydisfjördur, Ice....n25 25
Seyhan (Sarus), riv., Tur....C10 31
Seym, riv., Sov. Un....F9 27
Seymchan, Sov. Un....C18 28
Seymour, Austl....H5 51
Seymour, New Haven, Conn....D4 84
Seymour, Jackson, Ind....G6 91
Seymour, Wayne, Iowa....D4 92
Seymour, Webster, Mo....D5 101
Seymour, Sevier, Tenn....D10, n14 117
Seymour, Baylor, Tex....C3 118
Seymour, Outagamie, Wis....D5, g9 124
Seymour, inlet, B.C., Can....D4 68
Seymour, lake, Vt....B4 120
Seymourville, Iberville, La....h9 95
Sézanne, Fr....C5 14
Sezimbra, Port....C1 20
Sezze, It....D4 21
Sfax, Tun....C7 44
Sfax, prov., Tun....*C7 44
Sfîntul-Gheorghe, Rom....C7 22
's Gravenhage, see The Hague, Neth.
Sgùrr Alasdair, mtn., Scot....C2 13
Sgùrr Dhomhnuill, mtn., Scot....D3 13
Sgùrr Mor, mtn., Scot....C3 13
Sgùrr na Ciche, mtn., Scot....D3 13
Shabbona, DeKalb, Ill....B5 90
Shabogamo, lake, Newf., Can....h8 75
Shabrakhit, Eg....C2 32
Shabunda, Zaire....B4 48
Shabwah, P.D.R. of Yemen....B6 47
Shackelford, co., Tex....C3 118
Shackleton, Sask., Can....G1 70
Shackleton, glacier, Ant....A31 5
Shackleton, ice shelf, Ant....C22 5
Shackleton, range, Ant....A10 5
Shadehill, Perkins, S. Dak....B3 116
Shadehill, dam, S. Dak....B3 116
Shadehill, res., S. Dak....B3 116
Shades, creek, Ala....g7 78
Shades, mtn., Ala....g7 78
Shadeville, Franklin, Ohio....m10 111
Shadrinsk, Sov. Un....B6 29
Shady Cove, Jackson, Oreg....E4 113
Shady Dale, Jasper, Ga....C3 87
Shady Grove, Pike, Ala....D3 78
Shady Grove, Taylor, Fla....B3 86
Shady Grove, Crittenden, Ky....e10 94
Shady Grove, Franklin, Pa....G6 114
Shady Point, LeFlore, Okla....B7 112
Shady Rill, Washington, Vt....C3 120
Shady Side, Anne Arundel, Md....C4 85
Shadyside, Belmont, Ohio....C5 111
Shady Spring, Raleigh, W. Va....D3 123
Shady Valley, Johnson, Tenn....C12 117
Shafer, lake, Ind....C4 91
Shaft (William Penn), Schuylkill, Pa....*E9 114
Shafter, Kern, Calif....E4 82
Shafter, Elko, Nev....C7 104
Shafter, Presidio, Tex....p12 118
Shaftesbury, Eng....C5 12
Shaftsbury, Bennington, Vt....E2 120
Shaftsbury Center, Bennington, Vt....F2 120
Shag, rocks, Atl. O....J7 6
Shagamu, Nig....*E5 45
Shageluk, Alsk....C8 79
Shag Harbour, N.S., Can....F4 74
Shagwong, pt., N.Y....E9 84
Shah, riv., Iran....C5 41
Shahbanou Farah, dam, Iran....C4 41
Shāhdād (Khabīs), Iran....F8 41
Shāhdādkot, Pak....D1 40
Shahdol, India....F8 40
Shāhgarh, India....C4 39
Shaḥḥāt, Libya....C4 43
Shahi, isl., Iran....C2 41
Shāhjahānpur, India....D7 40
Shāh Jūy, Afg....E13 41
Shāhpur, India....I6 40
Shāhpur, Pak....C4 39
Shāhpura, India....E5 40
Shahrak, Afg....D12 41
Shahr-e Bābak, Iran....F7 41
Shahreẓā, Iran....E5 41
Shahsien, China....K7 36
Shaib al Qur, wadi, Sau. Ar....G13 31
Shaib Hub, riv., Iraq....G14 31
Shakawe, Bots....A3 49
Shaker Heights, Cuyahoga, Ohio....A4, n9 111
Shakhrisyabz, Sov. Un....B13 41
Shakhtersk, Sov. Un....*G12 27
Shakhty, Sov. Un....H13 27
Shakhunya, Sov. Un....B3 29
Shaki, Nig....E5 45
Shakopee, Scott, Minn....F5, n11 99
Shakotan, cape, Jap....E10 37
Shaktoolik, Alsk....C7 79
Shala, lake, Eth....D4 47
Shalalth, B.C., Can....D6 68
Shaler, mts., N.W. Ter., Can....B10 66
Shallmar, Garrett, Md....m12 85
Shallotte, Brunswick, N.C....D4 109
Shallotte, inlet, N.C....D4 109
Shallow Lake, Ont., Can....C3 72
Shallow Water, Scott, Kans....D3 93
Shallowater, Lubbock, Tex....C2 118
Shamattawa, Man., Can....B5 71
Shambat, Sud....B3 47
Shambaugh, Page, Iowa....D2 92
Shambe, Sud....D3 47
Shamīl, Iran....H8 41
Shamokin, Northumberland, Pa....E8 114
Shamokin Dam, Snyder, Pa....E8 114
Shamrock, Sask., Can....G2 70
Shamrock, Dixie, Fla....C3 86
Shamrock, Natchitoches, La....C2 95
Shamrock, Creek, Okla....B5 112
Shamrock, Wheeler, Tex....B2 118
Shamva, Zimb....A5 49
Shandaken, Ulster, N.Y....C6 108
Shandī, Sud....B3 47
Shandon, San Luis Obispo, Calif....E3 82
Shandon, Butler, Ohio....n12 111
Shanee, Park, Colo....B5 83
Shang, China....H4 36
Shangchiu, China....G6 36
Shanghai, China....I9 36
Shangjao, China....J8 36
Shangnan, China....H4 36
Shangshui, China....G6 36
Shangssu, China....A7 38
Shangtu, China....D5 36
Shanhaikuan, China....D8 36
Shaniko, Wasco, Oreg....B6 113
Shannock, Washington, R.I....D10 84
Shannon, Que., Can....n16 73
Shannon, Floyd, Ga....B1 87
Shannon, Carroll, Ill....A4 90
Shannon, Lee, Miss....A5 100
Shannon, Clay, Tex....C3 118
Shannon, co., Mo....D6 101
Shannon, co., S. Dak....D3 116
Shannon, airport, Ire....E3 11
Shannon, isl., Grnld....B16 4
Shannon, lake, Wash....A4 122
Shannon, riv., Ire....E2 11
Shannon, riv. mouth, Ire....E2 11
Shannon City, Union and Ringgold, Iowa....D3 92
Shannontown, Sumter, S.C....D7 115
Shanshan (Pichan), China....C3 34
Shansi, prov., China....D7 34
Shantar, is., Sov. Un....D16 28
Shantung, prov., China....D8 36
Shantung, pen., China....D9 34, F9 36
Shanwa, Tan....B5 48
Shaohsing, China....E9 34, I9 36
Shaokuan, China....G7 34
Shaopo, China....H8 36
Shaowu, China....K7 36
Shaoyang, China....F7 34, K4 36
Shap, Eng....F6 13
Shapinsay, isl., Scot....A6 13
Shapio, lake, Newf., Can....g9 75
Shapki, Sov. Un....s32 25
Sharafkhāneh, Iran....B2 41
Sharangad, Mong....B5 36
Sharasume, see Alotai, China
Sharbot Lake, Ont., Can....C8 72
Shari, Jap....E12 37
Sharita, cape, Om....H8 41
Shark, bay, Austl....E1 50
Shark, pt., Fla....G5 86
Sharkey, co., Miss....C3 100
Sharktooth, mtn., B.C., Can....E7 68
Sharon, Litchfield, Conn....B3 84
Sharon, Taliaferro, Ga....C4 87
Sharon, Barber, Kans....E5 93
Sharon, Norfolk, Mass....B5, h11 97
Sharon, Madison, Miss....C4 100
Sharon, Hillsboro, N.H....E3 105
Sharon, Steele, N. Dak....B8 110
Sharon, Woodward, Okla....A2 112
Sharon, Mercer, Pa....D1 114
Sharon, York, S.C....B5 115
Sharon, Weakley, Tenn....A3 117
Sharon, Windsor, Vt....D4 120
Sharon, Spokane, Wash....D7 122
Sharon, Kanawha, W. Va....m12 123
Sharon, Walworth, Wis....F5 124
Sharon Grove, Todd, Ky....D2 94
Sharon Hill, Delaware, Pa....p20 114
Sharon Park, Butler, Ohio....n12 111
Sharon Springs, Wallace, Kans....D2 93
Sharon Springs, Schoharie, N.Y....C6 108
Sharon Valley, Litchfield, Conn....B3 84
Sharonville, Hamilton, Ohio....n13 111
Sharp, co., Ark....A4 81
Sharpe, lake, Man., Can....B5 71
Sharpes, Brevard, Fla....D6 86
Sharples, Logan, W. Va....D3, n12 123
Sharpsburg, Taylor, Iowa....D3 92
Sharpsburg, Bath, Ky....B6 94
Sharpsburg, Washington, Md....B2 85
Sharpsburg, Nash, Edgecombe, and Wilson, N.C....B5 109
Sharpsburg, Allegheny, Pa....h14 114
Sharps Chapel, Union, Tenn....C10 117
Sharpsville, Tipton, Ind....D5 91
Sharpsville, Mercer, Pa....D1 114
Sharp Top, mtn., Ark....C2 81
Sharptown, Wicomico, Md....C6 85
Sharptown, Salem, N.J....D2 106
Sharya, Sov. Un....B3 29
Shashemene, Eth....D4 47
Shashi, riv., Bots., Zimb....B4 49
Shashke, Sov. Un....C7 29
Shashih, China....E7 34
Shasta, co., Calif....B3 82
Shasta, lake, Calif....B2 82
Shasta, mtn., Calif....B2 82
Shatsk, Sov. Un....D13 27
Shatney, mtn., N.H....f7 105
Shattuck, Ellis, Okla....A2 112
Shattuckville, Franklin, Mass....A2 97
Shatura, Sov. Un....D12 27
Shauck, Morrow, Ohio....B3 111
Shaunavon, Sask., Can....H1 70
Shavano, mtn., Colo....C4 83
Shavers, fork, W. Va....C5 123
Shavertown, Luzerne, Pa....*B8 114
Shaw, Lincoln, Colo....B7 83
Shaw, Bolivar, Miss....B3 100
Shaw, Marion, Oreg....k12 113
Shawanaga, Ont., Can....B4 72
Shawangunk, mts., N.Y....D6 108
Shawano, Shawano, Wis....D5 124
Shawano, co., Wis....D5 124
Shawano, lake, Wis....D5 124
Shawatun, China....D9 36
Shawboro, Currituck, N.C....A6 109
Shawbridge, Que., Can....D3 73
Shawhan, Bourbon, Ky....B5 94
Shawinigan, Que., Can....C5 73
Shawinigan Lake, B.C., Can....g12 68
Shawinigan-Sud, Que., Can....C5 73
Shawmut, Chambers, Ala....C4 78
Shawmut, Somerset, Maine....D3 96
Shawmut, Wheatland, Mont....D7 102
Shawnee, Johnson, Kansas....k16 93
Shawnee, Perry, Ohio....C3 111
Shawnee, Pottawatomie, Okla....B5 112
Shawnee, Converse, Wyo....D7 125
Shawnee, co., Kans....D8 93
Shawneetown, Gallatin, Ill....F5 90
Shawsheen, riv., Mass....f11 97
Shawsville, Hartford, Md....A4 85
Shawsville, Montgomery, Va....C2 121
Shawville, Que., Can....B8 73
Shayang, China....I5 36
Shchekino, Sov. Un....D11 27
Shchelkovo, Sov. Un....n18 27
Shchetovo, Sov. Un....q22 27
Shchigry, Sov. Un....F11 27
Shchors, Sov. Un....F8 27
Shchuchinsk, Sov. Un....C8 29
Shchurovo, Sov. Un....n18 27
Shearstown, Newf., Can....*E5 75
Sheaville, Malheur, Oreg....D9 113
Shebele, riv., Eth....D5 47
Shebelle, riv., Som....E5 47
Sheberghān, Afg....C12 41
Sheboygan, Sheboygan, Wis....B6, E6 124
Sheboygan, co., Wis....E6, k10 124
Sheboygan, riv., Wis....k10 124
Sheboygan Falls, Sheboygan, Wis....E6, k10 124
Shechichen, China....H5 36
Shedd, Linn, Oreg....C3 113
Shedden, Ont., Can....E3 72
Shediac, N.B., Can....C5 74
Sheelin, lake, Ire....D4 11
Sheenjek, riv., Alsk....B11 79
Sheep, creek, Alta., Can....C1 69
Sheep, mtn., Ariz....E1 80
Sheep, mtn., Wyo....C2 125
Sheep, mtn., Wyo....B5 125
Sheep, peak, Nev....G6 104
Sheep, range, Nev....G6 104
Sheep Haven, bay, Ire....B4 11
Sheep Heaven, mtn., Mass....A1 97
Sheerness, Alta., Can....D5 69
Sheerness, Eng....C8 12
Sheet Harbour, N.S., Can....E7 74
Shefar'am, Isr....B7 32
Shefayim, Isr....g10 32
Sheffield, Colbert, Ala....A2 78
Sheffield, Eng....A6 12
Sheffield, Bureau, Ill....B4 90
Sheffield, Franklin, Iowa....B4 92
Sheffield, Berkshire, Mass....B1 97
Sheffield, N.Z....O14 51
Sheffield, Lorain, Ohio....A3 111
Sheffield, Warren, Pa....C3 114
Sheffield, Pecos, Tex....D2 118
Sheffield, Caledonia, Vt....B4 120
Sheffield, lake, Newf., Can....D3 75
Sheffield Lake, Lorain, Ohio....*A3 111
Shefford, co., Que., Can....D5 73
Sheguiandah, Ont., Can....B3 72
Sheho, Sask., Can....F4 70
Shehsien, China....J8 36
Shehy, mts., Ire....F2 11
Sheikh, Som....D6 47
Sheikhūpura, Pak....B5 40
Sheila, N.B., Can....B5 74
Shelagski, cape, Sov. Un....B33 4
Shelagyote, peak, B.C., Can....B4 68
Shelbiana, Pike, Ky....C7 94
Shelbina, Shelby, Mo....B5 101
Shelburn, Sullivan, Ind....F3 91
Shelburn, Linn, Oreg....C4, k12 113
Shelburne, N.S., Can....F4 74
Shelburne, Ont., Can....C4 72
Shelburne, Franklin, Mass....A2 97
Shelburne, Coos, N.H....B4 105
Shelburne, Chittenden, Vt....C2 120
Shelburne, co., N.S., Can....F4 74
Shelburne, pond, Vt....C2 120
Shelburne Falls, Franklin, Mass....A2 97
Shelburne Falls, Chittenden, Vt....C2 120
Shelby, Shelby, Ala....B3 78
Shelby, Lake, Ind....B3 91
Shelby, Shelby, Iowa....C2 92
Shelby, Oceana, Mich....E4 98
Shelby, Bolivar, Miss....B3 100
Shelby, Toole, Mont....B5 102
Shelby, Polk, Nebr....C8 103
Shelby, Cleveland, N.C....B1 109
Shelby, Richland, Ohio....B3 111
Shelby, co., Ala....B3 78
Shelby, co., Ill....D5 90
Shelby, co., Ind....E6 91
Shelby, co., Iowa....C2 92
Shelby, co., Ky....B4 94
Shelby, co., Mo....B5 101
Shelby, co., Ohio....B1 111
Shelby, co., Tenn....B2 117
Shelby, co., Tex....D5 118
Shelby City, Boyle, Ky....C5 94
Shelby Village, Macomb, Mich....*F7 98
Shelbyville, Shelby, Ill....D5 90
Shelbyville, Shelby, Ind....E6 91
Shelbyville, Shelby, Ky....B4 94
Shelbyville, Shelby, Mo....B5 101
Shelbyville, Bedford, Tenn....B5 117
Shelbyville Lake, res., Ill....D5 90
Sheldahl, Boone, Polk, and Story, Iowa....e8 92
Sheldon, Iroquois, Ill....C6 90
Sheldon, O'Brien, Iowa....A2 92
Sheldon, Vernon, Mo....D3 101
Sheldon, Ransom, N. Dak....C8 110
Sheldon, Beaufort, S.C....F6 115
Sheldon, Harris, Tex....r14 118
Sheldon, Franklin, Vt....B3 120
Sheldon, Rusk, Wis....C3 124
Sheldon Springs, Franklin, Vt....B3 120
Sheldonville, Norfolk, Mass....B5 97
Shelekhov, gulf, Sov. Un....C18 28
Shelikof, strait, Alsk....D9 79
Shell, creek, Wyo....A5 125
Shell, inlet, Scot....C2 13
Shell, lake, Minn....D3 99
Shell, lake, Wis....C1 124
Shell, riv., Man., Can....D1 71
Shell Beach, San Luis Obispo, Calif....*E3 82
Shell Beach, St. Bernard, La....E6 95
Shellbrook, Sask., Can....D2 70
Shell Camp, Gregg, Tex....*C5 118
Shell Creek, Carter, Tenn....C11 117
Shelley, B.C., Can....C6 68
Shelley, Bingham, Idaho....F6 89
Shell Lake, Sask., Can....D2 70
Shell Lake, Washburn, Wis....C2 124
Shellman, Randolph, Ga....E2 87
Shellman Bluff, McIntosh, Ga....E5 87
Shellmouth, Man., Can....D1 71
Shell Rock, Butler, Iowa....B5 92
Shell Rock, riv., Iowa....A5 92
Shellsburg, Benton, Iowa....B6 92
Shelly, Norman, Minn....C2 99
Shelter, isl., N.Y....E7 84
Shelter Island, Suffolk, N.Y....E7 84
Shelter Island Heights, Suffolk, N.Y....E7 84
Shelton, Fairfield, Conn....D4 84
Shelton, Buffalo, Nebr....D7 103
Shelton, Mason, Wash....B2 122
Shemogue, N.B., Can....C5 74
Shenandoah, Page, Iowa....D2 92
Shenandoah, Schuylkill, Pa....E9 114
Shenandoah, Page, Va....B4 121
Shenandoah, co., Va....B4 121
Shenandoah, mtn., Va....B3 121
Shenandoah, nat. park, Va....B4 121
Shenandoah, riv., Va....A4 121
Shenandoah, val., Va....B3 121
Shenandoah Heights, Schuylkill, Pa....*E9 114
Shenango River Lake, res., Ohio....A5 111
Shencha, China....B12 40
Shenchiu, China....H6 36
Shenipsit, lake, Conn....B7 84
Shenmu, China....D7 34
Shenorock, Westchester, N.Y....*D7 108
Shensi, prov., China....E6 34
Shenyang (Mukden), China....C9 34
Sheopur, India....E6 40
Shepard, Alta., Can....D4 69
Shepard, isl., Ant....B35 5
Shepardsville, Vigo, Ind....E3 91
Shepaug, riv., Conn....C3 84
Shepetovka, Sov. Un....F6 27
Shepherd, Isabella, Mich....E6 98
Shepherd, Yellowstone, Mont....E8 102
Shepherd, San Jacinto, Tex....D5 118
Shepherd Brook, mtn., Maine....B3 96
Shepherdstown, Jefferson, W. Va....B7 123
Shepherdsville, Bullitt, Ky....C4, g11 94
Shepparton, Austl....H5 51
Sheppey, isl., Eng....C8 12
Sheppton, Schuylkill, Pa....E9 114
Shepton Mallet, Eng....C5 12
Sherard, Coahoma, Miss....A3 100
Sherborn, Middlesex, Mass....h10 97
Sherborne, Eng....D5 12
Sherbro, isl., S.L....E2 45
Sherbrooke, N.S., Can....D8 74
Sherbrooke, Que., Can....C2, k12 73
Sherbrooke, co., Que., Can....D5 73
Sherbrooke, lake, N.S., Can....E5 74
Sherburn, Martin, Minn....G4 99
Sherburne, Chenango, N.Y....C5 108
Sherburne (Town of), Rutland, Vt....*D3 120
Sherburne, co., Minn....E5 99
Shercock, Ire....D5 11
Shereshevo, Sov. Un....B8 26
Shergarh, India....D4 40
Sheridan, Grant, Ark....C3 81
Sheridan, Arapahoe, Colo....B6 82
Sheridan, La Salle, Ill....B5 90
Sheridan, Hamilton, Ind....D5 91
Sheridan, Crittenden, Ky....e9 94
Sheridan, Aroostook, Maine....B4 96
Sheridan, Montcalm, Mich....E5 98
Sheridan, Worth, Mo....A3 101
Sheridan, Madison, Mont....E4 102
Sheridan, Yamhill, Oreg....B3 113
Sheridan, Sheridan, Wyo....B6 125
Sheridan, co., Kans....C3 93
Sheridan, co., Mont....B12 102
Sheridan, co., Nebr....B3 103
Sheridan, co., N. Dak....B5 110
Sheridan, co., Wyo....B5 125
Sheridan, mtn., Wyo....B2 125
Sheridan Beach, King, Wash....*B3 122
Sheridan Gardens, Sheridan, Wyo....*B6 125
Sheridan Lake, Kiowa, Colo....C8 83
Sheringham, Eng....B9 12
Sherkaly, Sov. Un....C22 9
Sherman, Fairfield, Conn....C3 84
Sherman, Aroostook, Maine....C4 96
Sherman, Pontotoc and Union, Miss....A5 100
Sherman, St. Louis, Mo....f12 101
Sherman, Grant, N. Mex....E2 107
Sherman, Chautauqua, N.Y....C1 108
Sherman, Summit, Ohio....*B4 111
Sherman, Major, Okla....A3 112
Sherman, Minnehaha, S. Dak....D9 116
Sherman, Grayson, Tex....C4 118
Sherman, co., Kans....C2 93
Sherman, co., Nebr....C6 103
Sherman, co., Oreg....B6 113
Sherman, co., Tex....A2 118
Sherman, mtn., Ark....A2 81
Sherman, res., Nebr....C7 103
Sherman Mills, Aroostook, Maine....C4 96
Sherman Station, Penobscot, Maine....C4 96
Sherpur, Bngl....E12 40
Sherrard, Mercer, Ill....B3 90
Sherridon, Man., Can....B1 71
Sherrill, Jefferson, Ark....C4 81
Sherrill, Oneida, N.Y....B5 108
Sherrodsville, Carroll, Ohio....B4 111
's Hertogenbosch, Neth....C5 15
Sherwood, Pulaski, Ark....C3, h10 81
Sherwood, P.E.I., Can....C6 74
Sherwood, Choctaw, Miss....B5 100
Sherwood, Renville, N. Dak....A4 110
Sherwood, Defiance, Ohio....A1 111
Sherwood, Washington, Oreg....h12 113
Sherwood, Franklin, Tenn....B6 117
Sherwood, Calumet, Wis....h9 124
Sherwood Manor, Hartford, Conn....*B6 84
Sherwood Park, Alta., Can....C4 69
Sherwood Park, Salt Lake, Utah....*C4 119
Shetek, lake, Minn....F3 99
Shetland (Zetland), co., Scot....*g10 10
Shetland, is., Scot....g10 10
Shetucket, riv., Conn....C8 84
Shevchenko, Sov. Un....E4 29
Shevlin, Clearwater, Minn....C3 99
Shevlin, Klamath, Oreg....D5 113
Shewa, prov., Eth....D4 47
Shewa Gimira, Eth....D4 47
Sheyenne, Eddy, N. Dak....B6 110
Sheyenne, riv., N. Dak....C8 110
Shiant, isl., Scot....C2 13
Shiawassee, co., Mich....F6 98
Shibām, P.D.R. of Yemen....B6 47
Shibata, Jap....*H9 37
Shibetsu, Jap....D11 37
Shibīn al Kawm, Eg....D3 32
Shibīn al Qanāṭir, Eg....D3 32
Shichito, isl., Pac. O....D8 7
Shickley, Fillmore, Nebr....D8 103
Shickshinny, Luzerne, Pa....D9 114
Shideler, Delaware, Ind....D7 91
Shiderty, riv., Sov. Un....C8 29
Shidler, Osage, Okla....A5 112
Shiel, lake, Scot....D3 13
Shieldaig, Scot....C3 13
Shields, Lane, Kans....D3 93
Shields, Grant, N. Dak....C4 110
Shiga, pref., Jap....*I8 37
Shigawake, Que., Can....*B4 73
Shihchiachuang, China....D7 34
Shihchiachuang, China....E6 36
Shihchü, China....E4 34
Shihchüan, China....H3 36
Shihchüanho, China....A8 40
Shihmen, China....J4 36
Shihshou, China....J5 36
Shihtaokuo, China....F10 36
Shihtsuishan, China....D6 34
Shikārpur, Pak....D2 40
Shikoku, isl., Jap....J6 37
Shikuka, see Poronaysk, Sov. Un.
Shilka, Sov. Un....D14 28
Shillington, Berks, Pa....F10 114
Shillong, India....C9 39
Shiloh, Marengo, Ala....C2 78
Shiloh, Harris, Ga....D2 87
Shiloh, St. Clair, Ill....f14 101
Shiloh, Cumberland, N.J....E2 106
Shiloh, Camden, N.C. (part of Asheville)....A6 109
Shiloh, Montgomery, Ohio....C1 111
Shiloh, Richland, Ohio....B3 111
Shiloh, York, Pa....*G8 114
Shiloh, Hardin, Tenn....B3 117
Shiloh, Montgomery, Tenn....A4 117
Shiloh, nat. military park, Tenn....B3 117
Shimabara, Jap....J5 37
Shimada, Jap....o17 37
Shimane, pref., Jap....*I6 37
Shimanovsk, Sov. Un....D15 28
Shimizu, Jap....I9, n17 37
Shimo, isl., Jap....J5 37
Shimoda, Jap....o17 37
Shimodate, Jap....m18 37
Shimoga, India....F6 39
Shimonoseki, Jap....I5 37
Shimotsuma, Jap....m18 37
Shin, lake, Scot....B4 13
Shinall, mtn., Ark....h9 81
Shīndand, Afg....E11 41
Shiner, Lavaca, Tex....E4 118
Shingbwiyang, Bur....C10 39
Shinglehouse, Potter, Pa....C5 114
Shingleton, Alger, Mich....B4 98
Shingu, Jap....J7 37
Shinjo, Jap....G10 37
Shinkolobwe, Zaire....D4 48
Shinnecock, bay, N.Y....F6 84
Shinnston, Harrison, W. Va....B4, k10 123
Shin Pond, Penobscot, Maine....B4 96
Shinshiro, Jap....o16 37
Shinyanga, Tan....B5 48
Shio, cape, Jap....J7 37
Shiocton, Outagamie, Wis....D5, h8 124
Shiogama, Jap....G10 37
Shiojiri, Jap....m16 37
Shioya, cape, Jap....H10 37
Ship, isl., Miss....g7 100
Ship Bottom, Ocean, N.J....D4 106
Ship Cove, Newf., Can....E4 75
Ship Harbour, N.S., Can....E7 74
Shipiskan, lake, Newf., Can....g9 75
Ship Island, pass, Miss....g8 100
Shipka, pass, Bul....D7 22
Shipki, pass, India....B7 40
Shipman, Sask., Can....D3 70
Shipman, Macoupin, Ill....D3 90
Shipman, Nelson, Va....C4 121
Shippegan, N.B., Can....B5 74
Shippegan, isl., N.B., Can....B5 74
Shippegan Gully, N.B., Can....*B5 74
Shippensburg, Cumberland and Franklin, Pa....F6 114
Shippenville, Clarion, Pa....D3 114
Shiprock, San Juan, N. Mex....A1 107
Shipshaw, Que., Can....A6 73
Shipshewana, Lagrange, Ind....A6 91
Shipyard, Belize....B3 62
Shīr, mtn., Iran....F7 41
Shirabad, Sov. Un....C13 41
Shirase, glacier, Ant....B17 5
Shiratori, Jap....n15 37
Shīrāz, Iran....G6 41
Shirbīn, Eg....C8 31
Shire, riv., Malawi, Moz....E5 48
Shiremanstown, Cumberland, Pa....*F8 114
Shiretoko, cape, Jap....D12 37
Shiriya, cape, Jap....C4 39
Shirley, Van Buren, Ark....B3 81
Shirley, McLean, Ill....C4 90

Sligo, Clarion, Pa....D3 114
Sligo, co., Ire....C3 11
Sligo, bay, Ire....C2 10
Slinger, Washington, Wis....E5, m11 124
Slingerlands, Albany, N.Y..*C7 108
Slippery Rock, Butler, Pa...D1 114
Sliven, Bul....D8 22
Slivenec, Czech....n17 26
Sloan, Woodbury, Iowa....B1 92
Sloan, Clark, Nev....H6 104
Sloan, Erie, N.Y....C2 108
Sloans Valley, Pulaski, Ky...D5 94
Sloat, Plumas, Calif....C3 82
Sloatsburg, Rockland, N.Y..A4 106
Slobodskoy, Sov. Un....B4 29
Slobozia, Rom....C8 22
Slocan, B.C., Can....E9 68
Slocan, lake, B.C., Can....E9 68
Slocomb, Geneva, Ala....D4 78
Slocum, Washington, R.I...C10 84
Slöinge, Swe....B6 24
Slonim, Sov. Un....E5 27
Slope, co., N. Dak....C2 110
Slough, Eng....C7 12
Slovac, Prairie, Ark....C4 81
Slovakia (Slovensko), reg., Czech....D5 26
Slovaktown, Prairie, Ark....C4 81
Slovan, Washington, Pa....F1 114
Slovenia, reg., Yugo....C2 22
Slovenia, rep., Yugo....*C2 22
Slubice, Pol....A9 17
Sluch, riv., Sov. Un....F6 27
Slunj, Yugo....C2 22
Slupa, riv., Pol....A4 26
Slupca, Pol....B4 26
Słupsk, Pol....A4 26
Slutsk, Sov. Un....s31 25
Slutsk, Sov. Un....E6 27
Slyne, head, Ire....D1 11
Slyudyanka, Sov. Un....D13 28
Smackover, Union, Ark....D3 81
Smackover, creek, Ark....D2 81
Smaalandsfarvandet, bay, Den...C5 24
Small, pt., Maine....g8 96
Small Point Beach, Sagadahoc, Maine....E6 96
Smarr, Monroe, Ga....D3 87
Smarts, mtn., N.H....C2 105
Smartt, Warren, Tenn....D8 117
Smeaton, Sask., Can....D3 70
Smecno, Czech....n17 26
Smederevo, Yugo....C5 22
Smela, Sov. Un....G8 27
Smeltertown, El Paso, Tex. (part of El Paso)....E1 118
Smelterville, Shoshone, Idaho....B2 89
Smethport, McKean, Pa....C5 114
Smethwick (Warley), Eng...B6 12
Smicksburg, Indiana, Pa....E3 114
Smidovich, Sov. Un....B6 37
Smiley, Sask., Can....F1 70
Smiley, Gonzales, Tex...E4, k8 118
Smith, Alta., Can....B3, f8 69
Smith, Lyon, Nev....E2 104
Smith, co., Kans....C5 93
Smith, co., Miss....C4 100
Smith, co., Tenn....C8 117
Smith, co., Tex....C5 118
Smith, bay, Alsk....A9 79
Smith, cape, Ont., Can....B3 72
Smith, isl., Ant....C6 5
Smith, isl., Md., Va..D5 85, C6 121
Smith, isl., Va....C7 121
Smith, peak, Idaho....A2 89
Smith, pen., Ant....B6 5
Smith, pt., N.S., Can....D6 74
Smith, pt., Mass....D7 97
Smith, pt., Va....C6 121
Smith, res., Ala....A2 78
Smith, riv., Mont....D5 102
Smith, riv., Va....D3 121
Smith, sound, B.C., Can....D4 68
Smithboro, Bond, Ill....E4 90
Smithburg, Doddridge, W. Va....B4, k9 123
Smith Center, Smith, Kans..C5 93
Smith Creek, Wakulla, Fla...B2 86
Smithdale, Amite, Miss....D3 100
Smithers, B.C., Can....B4 68
Smithers, Fayette, W. Va....C3, m13 123
Smithfield (Town of), Providence, R.I....*B10 84
Smithfield, Fulton, Ill....C3 90
Smithfield, Somerset, Maine.D3 96
Smithfield, Jasper, Mo....D3 101
Smithfield, Gosper, Nebr....D6 103
Smithfield, Johnston, N.C....B4 109
Smithfield, Jefferson, Ohio...B5 111
Smithfield, Fayette, Pa....G2 114
Smithfield, Tarrant, Tex....n9 118
Smithfield, Cache, Utah....B4 119
Smithfield, Isle of Wight, Va....D6, k14 121
Smithfield, Wetzel, W. Va...h9 123
Smithland, Woodbury, Iowa.B2 92
Smithland, Livingston, Ky...e9 94
Smithland, Marion, Tex....C5 118
Smithmill, Clearfield, Pa....E5 114
Smith Mills, Henderson, Ky.C2 94
Smithonia, Oglethorpe, Ga..B3 87
Smith River, Del Norte, Calif....B1 82
Smiths, Lee, Ala....C4 78
Smithsburg, Washington, Md....A2 85
Smiths Cove, N.S., Can....E4 74
Smiths Falls, Ont., Can....C8 72
Smiths Ferry, Valley, Idaho..E2 89
Smiths Grove, Warren, Ky..C3 94
Smithshire, Warren, Ill....C3 90
Smiths Lake, McKinley, N. Mex....B1 107
Smithsons Valley, Comal, Tex....A4 118
Smithton, Clark, Ark....D2 81
Smithton, Austl....o15 50
Smithton, St. Clair, Ill....E4 90
Smithton, Pettis, Mo....g13 101
Smith Town, McCreary, Ky.D5 94
Smithtown, Rockingham, N.H....E5 105
Smithtown, Suffolk, N.Y....n15 108
Smithtown, bay, N.Y....F4 84
Smithville, Lawrence, Ark...A4 81
Smithville, Ont., Can....D5 72
Smithville, Lee, Ga....E2 87
Smithville, Monroe, Ind....F4 91
Smithville, Monroe, Miss....A5 100
Smithville, Clay, Mo...B3, h10 101
Smithville, Atlantic, N.J....E4 106
Smithville, Burlington, N.J..D3 106
Smithville, Wayne, Ohio....B4 111
Smithville, McCurtain, Okla.C7 112
Smithville, DeKalb, Tenn...D8 117
Smithville, Bastrop, Tex....D4 118
Smithville, Ritchie, W. Va...B3 123
Smithville Flats, Chenango, N.Y....C5 108
Smithwick, Fall River, S. Dak....D2 116
Smittle, cave, Mo....D5 101
Smoaks, Colleton, S.C....E6 115
Smock, Fayette, Pa....*G2 114
Smoke Creek, des., Nev....C2 104
Smokerun, Clearfield, Pa....E5 114
Smoky, cape, Austl....E9 51
Smoky, cape, N.S., Can....C9 74
Smoky, mts., Idaho....F4 89
Smoky, riv., Alta., Can....B1 69
Smoky Hill, riv., Kans....D5 93
Smoky Junction, Scott, Tenn.C9 117
Smoky Lake, Alta., Can....B4 69
Smöla, isl., Nor....F2 25
Smolan, Saline, Kans....D6 93
Smolensk, Sov. Un....D8 27
Smolyan, Bul....E7 22
Smoot, Lincoln, Wyo....D2 125
Smooth Rock Falls, Ont., Can....o19 72
Smoothstone, lake, Sask., Can....C2 70
Smoothstone, riv., Sask., Can....B2 70
Smoots, creek, Kans....g11 93
Smyadovo, Bul....D8 22
Smygehamn, Swe....C7 24
Smyley, cape, Ant....B4 5
Smyre, Gaston, N.C....*B2 109
Smyrna, Kent, Del....B6 85
Smyrna, Cobb, Ga....C2, h7 87
Smyrna, Chenango, N.Y....C5 108
Smyrna, York, S.C....A5 115
Smyrna, Rutherford, Tenn...h7 117
Smyrna, see Izmir, Tur.
Smyrna, riv., Del....B6 85
Smyrna Mills, Aroostook, Maine....B4 96
Smyth, co., Va....f10 121
Smythe, mtn., B.C., Can....E8 66
Snaefell, mtn., I of Man....F4 13
Snag, Yukon, Can....C29 4
Snake, creek, Nebr....B2 103
Snake, falls, Nebr....B5 103
Snake, mtn., Vt....C2 120
Snake, range, Nev....E7 104
Snake, riv., Idaho....D2 89
Snake, riv., Minn....B1 99
Snake, riv., Minn....D5 99
Snake, riv., Oreg....C9 113
Snake, riv., U.S....B4 76
Snake, riv., Wash....C7 122
Snake Indian, riv., Alta., Can...C1 69
Snake River, plain, Idaho....F2 89
Snake River, range, Idaho, Wyo....F7 89
Snares, is., N.Z....R11 51
Sneads, Jackson, Fla....B1 86
Sneads Ferry, Onslow, N.C..C5 109
Snedsted, Den....B2 24
Sneedville, Hancock, Tenn.C10 117
Sneek, Neth....A5 15
Sneem, Ire....F2 11
Snelling, Barnwell, S.C....E5 115
Snellville, Gwinnett, Ga....A6 87
Snezhnoye, Sov. Un....q21 27
Snezhnvy, peak, Sov. Un....D14 28
Sniardwy, lake, Pol....B7 26
Snipe, keys, Fla....H5 86
Snipe, lake, Alta., Can....B2 69
Snizort, bay, Scot....C2 13
Snöhetta, mtn., Nor....F3 25
Snohomish, Snohomish, Wash....B3 122
Snohomish, co., Wash....A4 122
Snomac, Seminole, Okla....B5 112
Snoqualmie, King, Wash....B4 122
Snötinden, mtn., Nor....D5 25
Snov, riv., Sov. Un....F8 27
Snover, Sanilac, Mich....E8 98
Snow, Pushmataha, Okla....C6 112
Snow, mtn., Maine....C2 96
Snow, peak, Wash....A7 122
Snowball, Searcy, Ark....B3 81
Snowbank, lake, Minn....B7 99
Snow Camp, Alamance, N.C....B3 109
Snowden, Sask., Can....D3 70
Snowdon, mtn., Wales....A3 12
Snowdonia, mts., Wales....A3 12
Snowdoun, Montgomery, Ala....C3 78
Snowfield, peak, Wash....A4 122
Snowflake, Navajo, Ariz....C5 80
Snowflake, Man., Can....E2 71
Snow Hill, Wilcox, Ala....D2 78
Snow Hill, Ouachita, Ark...D3 81
Snow Hill, Worcester, Md...D7 85
Snow Hill, Greene, N.C....B5 109
Snowking, mtn., Wash....A4 122
Snow Lake, Desha, Ark....C4 81
Snow Lake, Man., Can....B1 71
Snowmass, Petkin, Colo....B4 83
Snowmass, mtn., Colo....B3 83
Snow Road Station, Ont., Can....C8 72
Snow Shoe, Centre, Pa....D6 114
Snowshoe, lake, Maine....B4 96
Snowshoe, peak, Mont....B1 102
Snowville, Box Elder, Utah..B3 119
Snowville, Pulaski, Va....*C2 121
Snow Water, lake, Nev....C7 104
Snowy, mtn., N.Y....B6 108
Snowyside, mtn., Idaho....F4 89
Snyatyn, Sov. Un....A7 22
Snyder, Ashley, Ark....D4 81
Snyder, Morgan, Colo....A7 83
Snyder, Dodge, Nebr....C9 103
Snyder, Kiowa, Okla....C3 112
Snyder, Scurry, Tex....C2 118
Snyder, co., Pa....E7 114
Snyder Knob, mtn., W. Va....C5 123
Soai Rieng, Camb....G6 38
Soalala, Mad....g9 49
Soap Lake, Grant, Wash....B6 122
Soar, riv., Eng....B6 12
Soatá, Col....B3 60
Soay, isl., Scot....C2 13
Sobat, riv., Sud....D3 47
Sobeslav, Czech....D9 17
Sobieski, Oconto, Wis....D5 124
Sobinka, Sov. Un....D13 27
Sobota Rimavska, Czech....D6 26
Sobral, Braz....B2 57
Sobti, well, Mali....B4 45
Søby, Den....D4 24
Sochaczew, Pol....B6 26
Sochaux, Fr....A2 19
Soche (Yarkand), China...H24 9
Sochi, Sov. Un....G16 9
Social Circle, Walton, Ga....C3 87
Social Hill, Hot Spring, Ark..g8 81
Society, is., Fr. Polynesia....H12 7
Society Hill, Darlington, S.C.B8 115
Socmbawa, isl., Indon....G5 35
Socorro, Braz....m8 56
Socorro, Col....B3 60
Socorro, Socorro, N. Mex...C3 107
Socorro, El Paso, Tex....*F1 118
Socorro, co., N. Mex....D2 107
Socotra (Suqutra), isl., P.D.R. of Yemen....H8 33
Soc Trang, Viet....H6 38
Socuéllamos, Sp....C4 20
Soda Creek, B.C., Can....C6 68
Sodankylä, Fin....D12 25
Soda Springs, Caribou, Idaho....G7 89
Sodaville, Linn, Oreg....C4 113
Soddy-Daisy, Hamilton, Tenn....D8, h11 117
Söderala, Swe....G7 25
Söderhamn, Swe....G7 25
Söderköping, Swe....H7 25
Södermanland, co., Swe....H7 25
Södertälje, Swe....t35 25
Sodo, Eth....D4 47
Sodus, Berrien, Mich....F4 98
Sodus, Wayne, N.Y....B3 108
Sodus Point, Wayne, N.Y....B4 108
Soela, isl., Indon....F6 35
Soenda (Sunda), strait, Indon....G3 35
Soest, F.R.G....B3 17
Sofadhes, Grc....C4 23
Sofia (Sofiya), Bul....D6 22
Sofia, riv., Mad....g9 49
Sofiya, see Sofia, Bul.
Sofiya, co., Bul....*D6 22
Sofiyevka, Sov. Un....G9 27
Sofu-Gan, isl., Pac. O....E8 7
Sogamoso, Col....B3 60
Sögel, F.R.G....B7 15
Sognafjorden, fjord, Nor....G1 25
Sogn og Fjordane, co., Nor.*G1 25
Sogod, Phil....*C7 35
Sogut, Tur....C8 23
Soham, San Miguel, N. Mex.B4 107
Soignies, Bel....D4 15
Sointula, B.C., Can....D4 68
Soissons, Fr....C5 14
Sokal, Sov. Un....F5 27
Sokcho, Kor....*G4 37
Soke, Tur....D6 23
Sokhondo, mtn., Sov. Un....E14 28
Sokodé, Togo....E5 45
Sokol, Sov. Un....B13 27
Sokolka, Pol....B7 26
Sokolo, Mali....D3 45
Sokolov, Czech....C7 17
Sokolow, Pol....B7 26
Sokoto, Nig....D6 45
Solana, Charlotte, Fla....*F4 86
Solana Beach, San Diego, Calif....*F5 76
Solander, isl., N.Z....Q11 51
Solano, Harding, N. Mex....B5 107
Solano, Phil....n13 35
Solano, co., Calif....C2 82
Solbad Hall [in Tirol], Aus..E5 16
Soldatovo, Sov. Un....F26 9
Soldier, Monona, Iowa....C2 92
Soldier, Jackson, Kans....C8 93
Soldier, Carter, Ky....B6 94
Soldier, key, Fla....s13 86
Soldier, riv., Iowa....C2 92
Soldier Creek, Todd, S. Dak....*D5 116
Soldier Pond, Aroostook, Maine....A4 96
Soldiers Grove, Crawford, Wis....E3 124
Soldier Summit, Wasatch, Utah....D4 119
Soledad, Monterey, Calif....D3 82
Soledad, Col....A3 60
Soledad, Ven....B5 60
Soleduck, riv., Wash....B1 122
Solen, Sioux, N. Dak....C5 110
Solent, The, chan., Eng....D6 12
Solesmes, Fr....D3 15
Solihull, Eng....B6 12
Solikamsk, Sov. Un....B5 29
Sol-Iletsk, Sov. Un....C5 29
Soliman, Tun....F12 30
Solimões (Amazon), riv., Braz., Peru....B4 58
Solingen, F.R.G....B2 17
Solitar, mtn., Tex....B3 118
Sollas, Scot....C1 13
Sollefteå, Swe....F7 25
Sóller, Sp....C7 20
Sölleröd, Den....*C6 24
Sollihögda, Nor....p28 25
Sollyu-Bong, mts., Kor....G2 37
Solna, Swe....H7 25
Solok, Indon....F2 35
Solomea, W. Sam.... 52
Solomon, Graham, Ariz....E6 80
Solomon, Dickinson, Kans...D6 93
Solomon Is., country, Oceania....G9 7
Solomon, riv., Kans....C6 93
Solomons, Calvert, Md....D5 85
Solon, Johnson, Iowa....C6 92
Solon, Somerset, Maine....D3 96
Solon, Cuyahoga, Ohio....A4 111
Solonika, see Thessaloniki, Grc.
Solon Mills, McHenry, Ill...h8 90
Solon Springs, Douglas, Wis....B2 124
Solothurn, Switz....B4 19
Solothurn, Switz....B4 19
Solothurn, canton, Switz....B4 19
Solovyevsk, Sov. Un....D15 28
Solsberry, Greene, Ind....F4 91
Solsgirth, Man., Can....D1 71
Solta, isl., Yugo....D3 22
Soltau, F.R.G....B4 16
Solvang, Santa Barbara, Calif....*E3 82
Solvay, Onondaga, N.Y....B4 108
Sölvesborg, Swe....B8 24
Solway, Beltrami, Minn....C3 99
Solway, firth, Eng., Scot....F5 13
Solwezi, Zambia....D4 48
Soma, Tur....C6 23
Somalia, country, Afr....E10 42, E5 47
Sombor, Yugo....C4 22
Sombra, Ont., Can....E2 72
Sombrerete, Mex....C4 63
Sombrero, chan., India....G9 39
Somerdale, Camden, N.J....D2 106
Somers Tolland, Conn....B7 84
Somers, Calhoun, Iowa....B3 92
Somers, Flathead, Mont....B2 102
Somers, Kenosha, Wis..F6, n12 124
Somerset, Man., Can....E2 71
Somerset, Gunnison, Colo...C3 83
Somerset, Wabash, Ind....C6 91
Somerset, Pulaski, Ky....C5 94
Somerset, Montgomery, Md....*C3 85
Somerset, Bristol, Mass....C5 97
Somerset, Somerset, N.J....B3 106
Somerset, Perry, Ohio....C3 111
Somerset, Somerset, Pa....F3 114
Somerset, Bexar, Tex....k7 118
Somerset, St. Croix, Wis....C1 124
Somerset, co., Eng....C4 12
Somerset, co., Maine....C2 96
Somerset, co., Md....D6 85
Somerset, co., N.J....C3 106
Somerset, co., Pa....G3 114
Somerset, isl., Bermuda....p19 64
Somerset, isl., N.W. Ter., Can....B14 66
Somerset, res., Vt....E3 120
Somerset East, S. Afr....D4 49
Somerset Village, Bermuda..p19 64
Somers Point, Atlantic, N.J..E3 106
Somersville, Tolland, Conn..B7 84
Somersworth, Strafford, N.H....D5 105
Somerton, Yuma, Ariz....E1 80
Somervell, co., Tex....C4 118
Somerville, Morgan, Ala....A3 78
Somerville, Gibson, Ind....H3 91
Somerville, Middlesex, Mass....B5, g11 97
Somerville, Somerset, N.J....B3 106
Somerville, Butler, Ohio....C1 111
Somerville, Fayette, Tenn....B2 117
Somerville, Burleson, Tex...D4 118
Somesul, riv., Rom....B6 22
Somme, dept., Fr....E2 15
Somme, riv., Fr....B4 14
Sommepy, Fr....E4 15
Sömmerda, G.D.R....B6 17
Sommesous, Fr....F4 15
Somogy, co., Hung....*B3 22
Somonauk, DeKalb, Ill....B5 90
Somosomo, Fiji.... 52
Somosomo, strait, Fiji.... 52
Somoto, Nic....D4 62
Sompeta, India....H10 40
Somuncura, plat., Arg....C3 54
Somvix, Switz....C6 19
Son, riv., India....E9 40
Soná, Pan....F7 62
Sonchon, Kor....G2 40
Soncino, It....D5 15
Sønder, riv., Den....D3 24
Sønderborg, Den....D3 24
Sønderho, Den....C2 24
Sønderjylland, co., Den....C2 24
Sønder Omme, Den....C2 24
Sondershausen, G.D.R....B5 17
Søndervig, Den....B2 24
Sondheimer, East Carroll, La....B4 95
Sondrio, It....A2 21
Sonepur, India....G9 40
Sonestown, Sullivan, Pa....D8 114
Song, Nig....E7 45
Songadh, India....G4 40
Song Cau, Viet....F8 38
Songchon, Kor....G3 37
Songea, Tan....D6 48
Songjin, see Kimchaek, Kor.
Songkhla, Thai....I4 38
Songololo, Zaire....C1 48
Sonhāt, India....F9 40
Son La, Viet....B5 38
Sonmiāni, Pak....C4 39
Sonmiāni, bay, Pak....I12 41
Sonneberg, G.D.R....C6 17
Sonnette, Powder River, Mont....E11 102
Sonningdale, Sask, Can....E2 70
Sono, riv., Braz....C1 57
Sonobe, Jap....n14 37
Sonoita, Santa Cruz, Ariz....F5 80
Sonoita, Mex....A2 63
Sonoma, Sonoma, Calif....C2 82
Sonoma, co., Calif....C2 82
Sonoma, peak, Nev....C4 104
Sonoma, range, Nev....C4 104
Sonora, Tuolumne, Calif....D3 82
Sonora, Hardin, Ky....C4 94
Sonora, Muskingum, Ohio...C4 111
Sonora, Sutton, Tex....D2 118
Sonora, state, Mex....B2 63
Sonora, riv., Mex....G5 80
Sonqor, Iran....D3 41
Sonsón, Col....B2 60
Sonsonate, Sal....D3 62
Sontag, Lawrence, Miss....D3 100
Son Tay, Viet....B6 38
Sonyea, Livingston, N.Y....C3 108
Soo, locks, Mich....B6 98
Soo Junction, Luce, Mich...B5 98
Sooke, B.C., Can....E6, h12 68
Sopchoppy, Wakulla, Fla....B2 86
Soper, Choctaw, Okla....C6 112
Soperton, Treutlen, Ga....D4 87
Soperton, Forest, Wis. (part of Wabeno)....C5 124
Sophia, Randolph, N.C....B3 109
Sophia, Raleigh, W. Va....D3 123
Sopot, Pol....A5 26
Sopron, Hung....B3 22
Sôr, riv., Port....C1 20
Sora, It....D4 21
Sorak-San, peak, Kor....G4 37
Sorata, Bol....C2 55
Sorau, see Zary, Pol.
Sorbas, Sp....D4 20
Sorel, Que., Can....C4 73
Sorell, cape, Austl....o15 50
Sorento, Bond, Ill....E4 90
Soresina, It....B2 21
Soria, Sp....B4 20
Soria, prov., Sp....*B4 20
Soriano, Ur....f7 54
Soriano, dept., Ur....*E1 56
Sorø, Den....C5 24
Sorocaba, Braz....C3, m8 56
Sorochinsk, Sov. Un....C4 29
Soroki, Sov. Un....G7 27
Sorong, Indon....F8 35
Soroti, Ug....A5 48
Söröya, isl., Nor....B10 25
Sorraia, riv., Port....C1 20
Sorrento, Lake, Fla....D5 86
Sorrento, It....D5 21
Sorrento, Ascension, La.D5, h10 95
Sorris Sorris, Namibia....B1 49
Sør-Rondane, mts., Ant....B15 5
Sorsogon, Phil....C6 35
Sorsogon, prov., Phil....*C6 35
Sortavala, Sov. Un....G14 25
Sör-Tröndelag, co., Nor....*F4 25
Sorum, Perkins, S. Dak....B3 116
Sörumsand, Nor....p29 25
Sosan, Kor....H3 37
Sosnogorsk, Sov. Un....C19 9
Sosnovka, Sov. Un....E13 27
Sosnowiec, Pol....C5, g10 26
Soso, Jones, Miss....D4 100
Sosvinskaya, Sov. Un....C21 9
Sota, riv., Pol....h10 26
Sottern, lake, Swe....t33 25
Sotteville-lès-Rouen, Fr....C4 14
Souanké, Con....E2 46
Soubré, I.C....E3 45
Soucook, riv., N.H....D4 105
Soudan, St. Louis, Minn....C6 99
Souderton, Montgomery, Pa....F11 114
Souflion, Grc....B6 23
Soufriere, St. Lucia....J14 64
Soufrière, mtn., Guad....Q8 65
Soufrière, mtn., St. Vincent....U26 65
Souhegan, riv., Mass., N.H....E3 105
Souk Ahras, Alg....F10 30
Souk-el Arba, Tun....F11 30
Souk el Arba, prov., Tun...*C6 44
Sŏul, see Seoul, Kor.
Soulac [-sur-Mer], Fr....E3 14
Soulanges, co., Que., Can...D3 73
Sound Beach, Suffolk, N.Y..*F5 84
Sounding, creek, Alta., Can....D5 69
Sounding, lake, Alta., Can....C5 69
Sound View, New London, Conn....D7 84
Sources, mtn., Leso., S. Afr....C4 49
Sourdnahunk, lake, Maine....B3 96
Soure, Braz....C5 59
Soure, Port....B1 20
Souris, Man., Can....E1 71
Souris, P.E.I., Can....C7 74
Souris, Bottineau, N. Dak...A5 110
Souris, riv., Man., Sask., Can., N. Dak....G12 66
Sourlake, Hardin, Tex....D5 118
Sourland, mtn., N.J....C3 106
Sous, riv., Mor....C3 44
Sousa, Braz....C3 57
Sousse, Tun....B7 44
Sousse, prov., Tun....*B7 44
Soustons, Fr....F3 14
South, div., Ice....*n21 25
South, bay, Ont., Can....B3 72
South, bay, Utah....B3 119
South (Rancocas, creek) branch, N.J....D3 106
South (Raritan, riv.) branch, N.J....B3 106
South, cape, N.Z....Q11 51
South, cape, Nor....B13 4
South, chan., Eniwetok.... 52
South (Flathead, riv.) fork, Mont....C3 102
South, isl., N.Z....O12 51
South, isl., S.C....E9 115
South, isl., Truk.... 52
South, mtn., Idaho....G2 89
South, mtn., Md....A2 85
South, mtn., N. Mex....k8 107
South, mtn., Pa....C1 106
South, mts., N.C....B1 109
South, pass, Kwajalein.... 52
South, pass, La....F6 95
South, pass, Wyo....D4 125
South, pt., Barb....K21 65
South, pt., Newf., Can....C4 75
South, pt., Md....D7 85
South, pt., Mich....D7 98
South, riv., Ont., Can....A5 72
South, riv., Ga....h8 87
South, riv., Iowa....C4 92
South, riv., Md....C4 85
South, riv., N.C....C4 109
South Acton, Middlesex, Mass....g10 97
South Acworth, Sullivan, N.H....D2 105
South Addison, Washington, Maine....D5 96
South Africa, country, Afr....I8 42, C3 49
South Amboy, Middlesex, N.J....C4, m7 106
South America, cont....H17 3, 53
South Amherst, Hampshire, Mass....B2 97
South Amherst, Lorain, Ohio....A3 111
Southampton, N.S., Can....D5 74
Southampton, Ont., Can....C3 72
Southampton, Eng....D6 12
Southampton, Hampshire, Mass....B2 97
Southampton, Suffolk, N.Y.n16 108
Southampton, Bucks, Pa...*F11 114
Southampton, co., Va....D5 121
Southampton, beach, N.Y....F7 84
Southampton, cape, N.W. Ter., Can....D16 67
Southampton, isl., N.W. Ter., Can....D15 67
South Andaman, isl., India....F9 39
South Anna, riv., Va....C5 121
South Apopka, Orange, Fla.*D5 86
Southard, Blaine, Okla....A3 112
South Ashburnham, Worcester, Mass....A4 97
South Ashfield, Franklin, Mass....A2 97
South Atlantic, ocean....H20 3
South Aulatsivik, isl., Newf., Can....g9 75
South Australia, state, Austl..F6 50
South Baker, Baker, Oreg. (part of Baker)....C9 113
South Bald, mtn., Colo....A5 83
South Baldy, mtn., N. Mex....D2 107
South Bancroft, Aroostook, Maine....C5 96
Southbank, B.C., Can....C5 68
South Barnstead, Belknap, N.H....D4 105
South Barre, Worcester, Mass....B3 97
South Barre, Washington, Vt....C3 120
South Barrule, mtn., I. of Man..F4 13
South Bathurst, N.B., Can..*B4 74
South Bay, Palm Beach, Fla..F6 86
Southbeach, Lincoln, Oreg..C2 113
South Belmar, Monmouth, N.J....C4 106
South Belmont, Gaston, N.C.*B1 109
South Beloit, Winnebago, Ill.A4 90
South Bend, Lincoln, Ark..*C4 81
South Bend, St. Joseph, Ind.A5 91
South Bend, Cass, Nebr....h12 103
South Bend, Young, Tex....C3 118
South Bend, Pacific, Wash...C2 122
South Bennettsville, Marlboro, S.C....*B8 115
South Bentinck Arm, chan., B.C., Can....C4 68
South Berwick, York, Maine.E2 96
South Bethlehem, Albany, N.Y....C7 108
South Bloomfield, Pickaway, Ohio....C2 111
South Boardman, Kalkaska, Mich....D5 98
South Bocagrande, Lee, Fla..F4 86
South Boise, Ada, Idaho....*F2 89
South Bolton, Que., Can....D5 73
Southborough, Worcester, Mass....B4, g9 97
South Boston (Independent City), Va....D4 121
South Bound, Brook, Somerset, N.J....B3 106
South Branch, Newf., Can...E2 75
South Branch, Ogemaw, Mich....D7 98
South Branch, lake, Maine....C4 96
South Branch, mtn., W. Va....B6 123
Southbridge, Worcester, Mass....B3 97
South Bridgeview, Cook, Ill.*B6 90
South Bristol, Lincoln, Maine....E3 96
South Britain, New Haven, Conn....D3 84
South Broadway, Yakima, Wash....C5 122
South Brook, Newf., Can...*D3 75
South Brookfield, N.S., Can..E5 74
South Brooksville, Hancock, Maine....D4 96
South Burlington, Chittenden, Vt....C2 120
Southbury, New Haven, Conn....D4 84
South Byfield, Essex, Mass...A6 97
South Byron, Genesee, N.Y..B2 108
South Canaan, Wayne, Pa..C11 114
South Carolina, state, U.S....D11 77, 115
South Carver, Plymouth, Mass....C6 97
South Chaplin, Windham, Conn....*C8 84
South Charleston, Clark, Ohio....C2 111
South Charleston, Kanawha, W. Va....m12 123
South Charlestown, Sullivan, N.H....D2 105
South Chatham, Barnstable, Mass....C7 97
South Chatham, Carroll, N.H....B4 105
South Chelmsford, Middlesex, Mass....f10 97
South Cheney, Spokane, Wash....D7 122
South Chicago Heights, Cook, Ill....m9 90
South China, Kennebec, Maine....D3 96
South China, sea, Asia....H14 33
South Cle Elum, Kittitas, Wash....B5 122
South Clement, creek, Md....D4 85
South Cleveland, Bradley, Tenn....*D9 117
South Clinton, Anderson, Tenn....*C9 117
South Coatesville, Chester, Pa....*G10 114
South Coffeyville, Nowata, Okla....A6 112
South Colby, Kitsap, Wash..e10 122
South Colton, St. Lawrence, N.Y....f10 108
South Connellsville, Fayette, Pa....G2 114
South Corning, Steuben, N.Y....C3 108
South Dakota, state, U.S....B7 76, 116
South Danville, Rockingham, N.H....E4 105
South Dartmouth, Bristol, Mass....C6 97
South Dayton, Cattaraugus, N.Y....C1 108
South Daytona, Volusia, Fla.C5 86
South Decatur, De Kalb, Ga....*C2 87
South Deerfield, Franklin, Mass....B2 97
South Deerfield, Rockingham, N.H....D4 105
South Deer Isle, Hancock, Maine....D4 96
South Dennis, Barnstable, Mass....C7 97
South Dennis, Cape May, N.J....E3 106
South Dorset, Bennington, Vt....E2 120
South Dos Palos, Merced, Calif....D3 82
South Downs, hills, Eng....D7 12
South Dum-Dum, India...*F12 40
South Durham, Que., Can..D5 73
South Duxbury, Plymouth, Mass....B6 97
Southeast, pass, La....E6 95
South Easton, Bristol, Mass..B5 97
South Effingham, Carroll, N.H....C5 105
South Egremont, Berkshire, Mass....B1 97
South Elgin, Kane, Ill...B5, k8 90
South El Monte, Los Angeles, Calif....*E5 82
South Elwood, Madison, Ind.D6 91
Southend-on-Sea, Eng....C8 12
South English, Keokuk, Iowa....C5 92
Southern, prov., Malawi....E5 48
Southern, prov., Zambia....E4 48
Southern, reg., Tan....D6 48
Southern, uplands, Scot....E4 13
Southern Alps, mts., N.Z....O13 51
Southern Bug, riv., Sov. Un....H8 27
Southern Cross, Austl....F2 50
Southern Highlands, reg., Tan....C5 48
Southern Indian, lake, Man., Can....A2 71
Southern Pines, Moore, N.C.B3 109
Southern Rhodesia, see Rhodesia, Br. dep., Afr.
Southern Shops (Lone Oak), Spartanburg, S.C....*B4 115
Southern Ute, Indian res., Colo...D3 83
Southern View, Sangamon, Ill....*D4 90
Southern Yemen, see Yemen, P.D.R. of, Asia
South Esk., riv., Scot....D6 13
South Euclid, Cuyahoga, Ohio....g9 111
Southey, Sask., Can....G3 70
South Fabius, riv., Mo....A6 101
South Fallsburg, Sullivan, N.Y....D6 108
South Farmingdale, Nassau, N.Y....*G1 84

Stab, Pulaski, Ky....C5 94
Stacks, mts., Ire....E2 11
Stack Skerry, isl., Scot....A4 13
Stacy, Carteret, N.C....C6 109
Stacyville, Mitchell, Iowa....A5 92
Stacyville, Penobscot, Maine.C4 96
Stade, F.R.G....B4 16
Stadskanaal, Neth....A6 15
Stadthagen, F.R.G....A4 17
Stadtkyll, F.R.G....D6 15
Stadtlohn, F.R.G....B1 17
Stadtroda, G.D.R....C6 17
Stäfa, Switz....B6 19
Staffa, isl., Scot....B2 13
Stafford, Tolland, Conn....B7 84
Stafford, Eng....B5 12
Stafford, Stafford, Kans....E5 93
Stafford, Holt, Nebr....B7 103
Stafford, Genesee, N.Y....C2 108
Stafford, Monroe, Ohio....C4 111
Stafford, Custer, Okla....B2 112
Stafford, Fort Bend, Tex....*F5 118
Stafford, Stafford, Va....B5 121
Stafford, co., Eng....B5 12
Stafford, co., Kans....D5 93
Stafford, co., Va....B5 121
Stafford Springs, Tolland, Conn....B7 84
Stafford Springs, Jasper, Miss....D4 100
Staffordsville, Johnson, Ky..C7 94
Staffordville, Tolland, Conn..B7 84
Staffordville, Ocean, N.J....D4 106
Staines, Eng....m11 10
Stains, Fr....g10 14
Stalactite, cavern, Mo....E6 101
Stålboga, Swe....t34 25
Stalden, Switz....D4 19
Staley, Randolph, N.C....B3 109
Stalin, see Varna, Bul.
Stalinogród, see Katowice, Pol.
Stallcup, cave, Mo....D5 101
Stallo, Neshoba, Miss....C4 100
Stallworthy, cape, N.W. Ter., Can....k33 67
Stalwart, Sask., Can....F3 70
Stalwart, Chippewa, Mich....B6 98
Stambaugh, Iron, Mich....B2 98
Stamford, Fairfield, Conn....E2 84
Stamford, Eng....B7 12
Stamford, Harlan, Nebr....D6 103
Stamford, Delaware, N.Y....C6 108
Stamford, Jones, Tex....C3 118
Stamford, Bennington, Vt....F2 120
Stamping Ground, Scott, Ky.B5 94
Stampriet, Namibia....B2 49
Stamps, Lafayette, Ark....D2 81
Stanaford, Raleigh, W. Va....D3, n13 123
Stanardsville, Greene, Va....B4 121
Stanberry, Gentry, Mo....A3 101
Stanchfield, Isanti, Minn....E5 99
Standale, Kent, Mich....*F5 98
Standard, Alta., Can....D4 69
Standard, La Salle, La....C3 95
Standerton, S. Afr....C4 49
Standing Rock, Chambers, Ala....B4 78
Standing Rock, McKinley, N. Mex....B1 107
Standing Rock, Indian res., N.Dak., S.Dak....B4 116
Standish, Cumberland, Maine....E2 96
Standish, Arenac, Mich....E7 98
Standish, Clinton, N.Y....f11 108
Standon, Que., Can....C7 73
Stanfield, Pinal, Ariz....E3 80
Stanfield, Umatilla, Oreg....B7 113
Stanford, McLean, Ill....C4 90
Stanford, Monroe, Ind....F4 91
Stanford, Lincoln, Ky....C5 94
Stanford, Judith Basin, Mont.C6 102
Stangelville, Kewaunee, Wis....D5, h10 124
Stanger, S. Afr....C5 49
Stanhope, Que., Can....D6 73
Stanhope, Eng....F6 13
Stanhope, Hamilton, Iowa....B4 92
Stanhope, Sussex, N.J....B3 106
Staniard Creek, Ba....B5 64
Stanislaus, co., Calif....D3 82
Stanislawow, Pol....k15 26
Stanke Dimitrov, Bul....D6 22
Stanley, N.B., Can....C3 74
Stanley, Eng....*F7 13
Stanley (Port Stanley), Falk Is....53
Stanley, Custer, Idaho....E4 89
Stanley, Johnson, Kans....D9 93
Stanley, Daviess, Ky....C2 94
Stanley, Santa Fe, N. Mex....B4, k9 107
Stanley, Gaston, N.C....B1 109
Stanley, Mountrail, N. Dak..A3 110
Stanley, Pushmataha, Okla..C6 112
Stanley, Page, Va....B4 121
Stanley, Chippewa, Wis....D3 124
Stanley, co., S. Dak....C5 116
Stanley, see Boyoma, falls, Zaire
Stanleytown, Henry, Va....D3 121
Stanleyville, Forsyth, N.C....A2 109
Stanleyville, see Kisangani, Zaire
Stanly, co., N.C....B2 109
Stanmore, Alta., Can....D5 69
Stann Creek, Belize....B3 62
Stanovoi, mts., Sov. Un....D15 33
Stans, Switz....C5 19
Stansbury, mtn., Utah....C3 119
Stansbury Estates, Baltimore, Md....*B5 85
Stansbury Park, Tooele, Utah....*C3 119
Stanstead, Que., Can....D5 73
Stanstead, co., Que., Can....D5 73
Stanthorpe, Austl....D8 51
Stanton, Chilton, Ala....C3 78
Stanton, Orange, Calif....*F5 82
Stanton, New Castle, Del....*A6 85
Stanton, Montgomery, Iowa.D2 92
Stanton, Powell, Ky....C6 94
Stanton, Montcalm, Mich....E5 98
Stanton, Adams, Miss....D2 100
Stanton, Franklin, Mo....C6 101
Stanton, Stanton, Nebr....C8 103
Stanton, Hunterdon, N.J....B3 106
Stanton, Mercer, N. Dak....B4 110
Stanton, Haywood, Tenn....B2 117
Stanton, Martin, Tex....C2 118
Stanton, co., Kans....E2 93
Stanton, co., Nebr....C8 103
Stantonsburg, Wilson, N.C....B5 109
Stantonville, McNairy, Tenn.B3 117
Stanwood, Cedar, Iowa....C6 92
Stanwood, Mecosta, Mich....E5 98
Stanwood, Snohomish, Wash.A3 122
Staplehurst, Seward, Nebr....D8 103
Staples, Todd, Minn....D4 99
Staples, Guadalupe, Tex....h8 118
Stapleton, Baldwin, Ala....E2 78
Stapleton, Jefferson, Ga....C4 87
Stapleton, Logan, Nebr....C5 103
Stapp, Le Flore, Okla....C7 112
Star, Ada, Idaho....F2 89
Star, Rankin, Miss....C3 100
Star, Montgomery, N.C....B3 109
Star, Mills, Tex....D3 118
Star, lake, Minn....D3 99
Star, peak, Nev....C3 104
Stara Boleslav, Czech....n18 26
Starachowice, Pol....C6 26
Staraya Russa, Sov. Un....C8 27
Stara Zagora, Bul....D7 22
Stara-Zagora, co., Bul....*D7 22
Starbuck, Man., Can....E3 71
Starbuck, Pope, Minn....E3 99
Starbuck, Columbia, Wash....C7 122
Starbuck, isl., Kir....G12 7
Star City, Lincoln, Ark....D4 81
Star City, Sask., Can....E3 70
Star City, Pulaski, Ind....C4 91
Star City, Monongalia, W. Va....B5 123
Starford, Indiana, Pa....E4 114
Stargard, Pol....B3 26
Stargo, Greenlee, Ariz....D6 80
Staritsa, Sov. Un....C10 27
Starjunction, Fayette, Pa....*F2 114
Stark, Neosho, Kans....E3 93
Stark, Coos, N.H....A4 105
Stark, co., Ill....B4 90
Stark, co., N. Dak....C3 110
Stark, co., Ohio....B4 111
Starke, Bradford, Fla....C4 86
Starke, co., Ind....B4 91
Starkey, Union, Oreg....B8 113
Starks, Calcasieu, La....D2 95
Starks, Somerset, Maine....D3 96
Starksboro, Addison, Vt....C2 120
Starkville, Las Animas, Colo....D6 83
Starkville, Oktibbeha, Miss..B5 100
Starkville, Herkimer, N.Y....C6 108
Starkweather, Ramsey, N. Dak....A7 110
Starlight, Wayne, Pa....C11 114
Starnberg, F.R.G....B7 18
Starnberg, lake, F.R.G....E5 16
Starobelsk, Sov. Un....G12 27
Starodub, Sov. Un....E9 27
Starogard, Pol....B5 26
Starokonstantinov, Sov. Un..G6 27
Starominskaya, Sov. Un....F16 9, H12 27
Star Prairie, St. Croix, Wis..C1 124
Starr, Anderson, S.C....C2 115
Starr, co., Tex....F3 118
Starr, mtn., Tenn....D9 117
Starrking, Coos, N.H....A4 105
Starrucca, Wayne, Pa....C11 114
Start, bay, Eng....D4 12
Start, pt., Eng....D4 12
Startex, Spartanburg, S.C....B3 115
Startup, Snohomish, Wash....B4 122
Starý Plzenec, Czech....D8 17
Stary Sacz, Pol....D6 26
Staryy Oskol, Sov. Un....F11 27
Stassfurt, G.D.R....B6 17
Staszow, Pol....C6 26
State Center, Marshall, Iowa.B4 92
State College, Oktibbeha, Miss....B5 100
State College, Centre, Pa....E6 114
State Line, Warren, Ind....D2 91
State Line, Berkshire, Mass.B1 97
State Line, Greene, Miss....B5 100
Stateline, Douglas, Nev....E2 104
State Line, Cheshire, N.H....E2 105
State Line, Franklin, Pa....G6 114
Staten, isl., N.Y....k12 108
Staten Island, see Richmond, borough and co., N.Y.
Statenville, Echols, Ga....F4 87
State Road, Aroostook, Maine....B4 96
State Road, Surry, N.C....A3 109
Statesboro, Bulloch, Ga....D5 87
Statesville, Iredell, N.C....B2 109
Statham, Barrow, Ga....C3 87
Stathelle, Nor....p27 25
Statue of Liberty, nat. mon., N.Y....k12 108
Staufen, F.R.G....E3 18
Stauffer, Lake, Oreg....D6 113
Staunton, Macoupin, Ill....D4 90
Staunton, Clay, Ind....F3 91
Staunton (Independent City), Va....B3 121
Stavanger, Nor....H1 25
Stave, lake, B.C., Can....f13 68
Staveley, Eng....A6 12
Stavelot, Bel....D5 15
Stavely, Alta., Can....D4 69
Stavenisse, Neth....C4 15
Staveren, Neth....B5 15
Stavropol, Sov. Un....F17 9, D2 29
Stavropol, see Tolyatti, Sov. Un.
Stawell, Austl....H4 51
Stayner, Ont., Can....C4 72
Stayton, Marion, Oreg....C4, k12 113
Stead, Union, N. Mex....A6 107
Steady Brook, Newf., Can..*D3 75
Steamboat, Washoe, Nev....D2 104
Steamboat, mtn., Mont....C4 102
Steamboat Canyon, Apache, Ariz....B6 80
Steamboat Rock, Hardin, Iowa....B4 92
Steamboat Springs, Routt, Colo....A4 83
Stearns, McCreary, Ky....D5 94
Stearns, co., Minn....E4 99
Stearns, lake, Fla....E5 86
Stebbins, Alsk....C7 79
Stebbins, Aroostook, Maine.B5 96
Steblev, Sov. Un....G8 27
Stechovice, Czech....o17 26
Stecker, Caddo, Okla....C3 112
Stecoah, Graham, N.C....f9 109
Stedman, Cumberland, N.C..B4 109
Steel, mtn., Idaho....F3 89
Steele, St. Clair, Ala....B3 78
Steele, Pemiscot, Mo....E8 101
Steele, Kidder, N. Dak....C6 110
Steele, co., Minn....F5 99
Steele, co., N. Dak....B8 110
Steele, mtn., Wyo....E6 125
Steele City, Jefferson, Nebr.D8 103
Steeleville, Randolph, Ill....E4 90
Steelton, Dauphin, Pa....F8 114
Steelville, Crawford, Mo....D6 101
Steen, Rock, Minn....G2 99
Steenbergen, Neth....C4 15
Steenburg, Ont., Can....C7 72
Steens, Lowndes, Miss....B5 100
Steens, mtn., Oreg....E8 113
Steenwijk, Neth....B6 15
Steep Falls, Cumberland, Maine....E2 96
Steephill, lake, Sask., Can....B4 70
Steep Rock, Man., Can....D2 71
Steep Rock Lake, Ont., Can.o17 72
Stefanesti, Rom....B8 22
Stefanie, lake, Eth....E4 47
Stefansson, isl., N.W. Ter., Can....B11 66
Steffisburg, Switz....C4 19
Stege, Den....D6 24
Steger, Cook and Will, Ill....B6, m9 90
Stegi, Swaz....C5 49
Steiermark (Styria), state, Aus....*E7 16
Steilacoom, Pierce, Wash....f10 122
Stein, F.R.G....D6 17
Steinach, Aus....B7 18
Stein am Rhein, Switz....A6 19
Steinauer, Pawnee, Nebr....D9 103
Steinbach, Man., Can....E3 71
Steinbach-Hallenberg, G.D.R....C5 17
Steinfort, Lux....E5 15
Steinhatchee, Taylor, Fla....C3 86
Steinhatchee, riv., Fla....C3 86
Steinhausen, Namibia....B2 49
Steinhuder, lake, F.R.G....F3 24
Steinkjer, Nor....E4 25
Stella, Ont., Can....C8 72
Stella, Calloway, Ky....f9 94
Stella, Newton, Mo....E3 101
Stella, Richardson, Nebr....D10 103
Stella, mtn., It....C5 18
Stellarton, N.S., Can....D7 74
Stellenbosch, S. Afr....*D2 49
Stelvio, pass., Switz....C9 19
Stem, Granville, NC....A4 109
Stemmers Run, Baltimore, Md. (part of Essex)....B7 85
Stenay, Fr....E5 15
Stendal, G.D.R....B5 16
Stendal, Pike, Ind....H3 91
Stenen, Sask., Can....F4 70
Stenness, lake, Scot....A5 13
Stepanakert, Sov. Un....F3 29
Stepenitz, riv., G.D.R....E5 24
Stephan, Hyde, S. Dak....C6 116
Stephen, Marshall, Minn....B2 99
Stephens, Ouachita, Ark....D2 81
Stephens, Oglethorpe, Ga....C3 87
Stephens, co., Ga....B3 87
Stephens, co., Okla....C4 112
Stephens, co., Tex....C3 118
Stephens, passage, Alsk....m23 79
Stephensburg, Morris, N.J....B3 106
Stephens City, Frederick, Va.A4 121
Stephenson, Menominee, Mich....C3 98
Stephenson, co., Ill....A4 90
Stephensport, Breckinridge, Ky....D3 94
Stephenson, mtn., Ant....C6 5
Stephenston, Warrick, Ind....H3 91
Stephenville, Newf., Can....D2 75
Stephenville, Erath, Tex....C3 118
Stephenville Crossing, Newf., Can....D2 75
Stepnica, Pol....E8 24
Stepnoy, Sov. Un....D3 29
Stepnyak, Sov. Un....C8 29
Steps, pt., Am. Sam....52
Steptoe, White Pine, Nev....D7 104
Steptoe, Whitman, Wash....B8 122
Sterkstroom, S. Afr....D4 49
Sterley, Floyd, Tex....B2 118
Sterling, Logan, Colo....A7 83
Sterling, Windham, Conn....C9 84
Sterling, Bingham, Idaho....F6 89
Sterling, Whiteside, Ill....B4 90
Sterling, Fountain, Ind....D3 91
Sterling, Rice, Kans....D5 93
Sterling, Worcester, Mass....B4 97
Sterling, Arenac, Mich....D6 98
Sterling, Johnson, Nebr....D9 103
Sterling, Burleigh, N. Dak..C5 110
Sterling, Comanche, Okla....C3 112
Sterling, Sanpete, Utah....D4 119
Sterling, Loudoun, Va....A5, g12 121
Sterling, co., Tex....D2 118
Sterling, res., Colo....A7 83
Sterling City, Sterling, Tex..D2 118
Sterling Heights, Macomb, Mich....o15 98
Sterling Junction, Worcester, Mass....*B4 97
Sterling Run, Cameron, Pa..D5 114
Sterlington, Ouachita, La....B3 95
Sterlitamak, Sov. Un....D8 29
Sternberg, G.D.R....E5 24
Sternberk, Czech....D4 26
Sterrett, Shelby, Ala....B3 78
Steti, Czech....C9 17
Stetson, Penobscot, Maine..D3 96
Stetson, mtn., Maine....C5 96
Stetsonville, Taylor, Wis....C3 124
Stettin, see Szczecin, Pol.
Stettin, lagoon, G.D.R., Pol....E8 24
Stettler, Alta., Can....C4 69
Steuben, Washington, Maine....D5 96
Steuben, Schoolcraft, Mich..B4 98
Steuben, Crawford, Wis....E3 124
Steuben, co., Ind....A7 91
Steuben, co., N.Y....C3 108
Steubenville, Jefferson, Ohio.B5 111
Steve, Yell, Ark....C2 81
Stevenage, Eng....C7 12
Stevens, Burlington, N.J....C3 106
Stevens, co., Kans....E2 93
Stevens, co., Minn....E3 99
Stevens, co., Wash....A8 122
Stevens, peak, Idaho, Mont..C1 102
Stevenson, Jackson, Ala....A4 78
Stevenson, Fairfield, Conn..D4 84
Stevenson, Skamania, Wash.D4 122
Stevenson, lake, Man., Can....C4 71
Stevenson, mtn., Oreg....C6 113
Stevenson, riv., Man., Can....B4 71
Stevens Point, Portage, Wis.D4 124
Stevens Pottery, Baldwin, Ga....D3 87
Stevenston, Scot....*E4 13
Stevens Village, Alsk....B10 79
Stevensville, Queen Annes, Md....C5 85
Stevensville, Berrien, Mich....F4 98
Stevensville, Ravalli, Mont..D2 102
Stevensville, Bradford, Pa....C9 114
Steward, Lee, Ill....B4 90
Stewardson, Shelby, Ill....D5 90
Stewart, Hale, Ala....C2 78
Stewart, B.C., Can....B3, m17 68
Stewart, McLeod, Minn....F4 99
Stewart, Montgomery, Miss..B4 100
Stewart, Athens, Ohio....C4 111
Stewart, Houston, Tenn....A4 117
Stewart, co., Ga....D2 87
Stewart, co., Tenn....A4 117
Stewart, isl., N.Z....Q11 51
Stewart, riv., Yukon, Can....D5 66
Stewart Manor, Nassau, N.Y....*G2 84
Stewarton, Scot....E4 13
Stewartstown, Coos, N.H....f7 105
Stewartstown, N. Ire....C5 11
Stewartstown, York, Pa....G8 114
Stewartsville, Coosa, Ala....B3 78
Stewartsville, Posey, Ind....H2 91
Stewartsville, DeKalb, Mo..B3 101
Stewartsville, Warren, N.J..B2 106
Stewartsville, Bedford, Va..*D3 121
Stewart Valley, Sask., Can..G2 70
Stewartville, Olmsted, Minn.G6 99
Stewiacke, N.S., Can....D6 74
Steynsburg, S. Afr....D4 49
Steyr, Aus....D7 16
Stickney, Cook, Ill....*B6 90
Stickney, Aurora, S. Dak....D7 116
Stigler, Haskell, Okla....B6 112
Stikine, riv., Alsk., B.C., Can..E6 66
Stilesville, Hendricks, Ind....E4 91
Stilis, Grc....C4 23
Stillaguamish, riv., Wash....A4 122
Stillman Valley, Ogle, Ill....A4 90
Still Meadow, Douglas, Nebr....*C10 103
Stillmore, Emanuel, Ga....D4 87
Still Pond, Kent, Md....B5 85
Still River, Worcester, Mass..B4 97
Stillwater, B.C., Can....E5 68
Stillwater, Penobscot, Maine (part of Old Town)....D4 96
Stillwater, Washington, Minn....E6 99
Stillwater, Churchill, Nev....D3 104
Stillwater, Sussex, N.J....A3 106
Stillwater, Saratoga, N.Y....C7 108
Stillwater, Payne, Okla....A4 112
Stillwater, Columbia, Pa....D9 114
Stillwater, Providence, R.I..B10 84
Stillwater, co., Mont....E7 102
Stillwater, range, Nev....D3 104
Stillwater, res., N.Y....B5 108
Stillwell, Effingham, Ga....D5 87
Stillwell, LaPorte, Ind....A4 91
Stilson, Bullock, Ga....D5 87
Stilwell, Johnson, Kans....D9 93
Stilwell, Adair, Okla....B7 112
Stimson, mtn., Mont....B3 102
Stine, mtn., Mont....E4 102
Stinear Nunataks, peaks, Ant....C19 5
Stinesville, Monroe, Ind....F4 91
Stinking, lake, N. Mex....A3 107
Stinnett, Hutchinson, Tex....B2 118
Stinson Lake, Grafton, N.H..C3 105
Stip, Yugo....E6 22
Stirling, Alta., Can....E4 69
Stirling, Ont., Can....C7 72
Stirling, Morris, N.J....B4 106
Stirling, Scot....D5 13
Stirling City, Butte, Calif....C3 82
Stirrat, Logan, W. Va....D3 123
Stirum, Sargent, N. Dak....C8 110
Stissing, mtn., N.Y....B2 84
Stites, Idaho, Idaho....C2 89
Stittsville, Ont., Can....B9 72
Stjördalshalsen, Nor....F4 25
Stoa Pikt, Pima, Ariz....E3 80
Stockbridge, Henry, Ga....C2 87
Stockbridge, Berkshire, Mass.B1 97
Stockbridge, Ingham, Mich....F6 98
Stockbridge, Windsor, Vt....D3 120
Stockbridge, Calumet, Wis....B5, h9 124
Stockbridge-Munsee, Indian res., Wis....D5 124
Stockdale, Pike, Ohio....D3 111
Stockdale, Wilson, Tex....E4, k8 118
Stockerau, Aus....D8 16
Stockertown, Northampton, Pa....E11 114
Stockett, Cascade, Mont....C5 102
Stockham, Hamilton, Nebr....D8 103
Stockholm, Sask., Can....G4 70
Stockholm, Aroostook, Maine....A4 96
Stockholm, Sussex, N.J....A3 106
Stockholm, Grant, S. Dak....B9 116
Stockholm, Swe....H8, t36 25
Stockholm, Pepin, Wis....D1 124
Stockhorn, mtn., Switz....C4 19
Stockland, Iroquois, Ill....C6 90
Stockport, Eng....A5 12
Stockport, Van Buren, Iowa..D6 92
Stockport, Morgan, Ohio....C4 111
Stockton, Baldwin, Ala....E2 78
Stockton, San Joaquin, Calif....D3, h10 82
Stockton, Man., Can....E2 71
Stockton, Lanier, Ga....F4 87
Stockton, Jo Daviess, Ill....A3 90
Stockton, Rooks, Kans....C4 93
Stockton, Worcester, Md....D7 85
Stockton, Cedar, Mo....D4 101
Stockton, Hunterdon, N.J....C3 106
Stockton, Chautauqua, N.Y..C1 108
Stockton, Tooele, Utah....C3 119
Stockton, isl., Wis....B3 124
Stockton Lake, res., Mo....D4 101
Stockton Springs, Waldo, Maine....D4 96
Stockville, Frontier, Nebr....D5 103
Stockwell, Tippecanoe, Ind..D4 91
Stod, Czech....D8 17
Stoddard, Cheshire, N.H....D2 105
Stoddard, Vernon, Wis....E2 124
Stoddard, co., Mo....E8 101
Stoeckl, mtn., B.C., Can....A2 68
Stoer, pt., Scot....B3 13
Stoke Centre, Que., Can....D6 73
Stoke-on-Trent, Eng....D5 10
Stokes, Pitt, N.C....B5 109
Stokes, co., N.C....A2 109
Stokesdale, Guilford, N.C....A3 109
Stokesley, Eng....F7 13
Stokke, Nor....p28 25
Stolac, Yugo....D3 22
Stolberg, F.R.G....C3 16
Stolbovaya, Sov. Un....n17 27
Stolbovoy, isl., Sov. Un....B1 4
Stollberg, G.D.R....C7 17
Stollings, Logan, W. Va....n12 123
Stolzenau, F.R.G....F3 24
Stone, Eng....B5 12
Stone, Oneida, Idaho....G6 89
Stone, Pike, Ky....C7 94
Stone, co., Ark....B3 81
Stone, co., Miss....E4 100
Stone, co., Mo....E4 101
Stone, lake, Wis....C5 124
Stone, mtn., Ga....h8 89
Stone, mtn., Vt....B5 120
Stone, mts., Tenn....C12 117
Stonebluff, Fountain, Ind....D3 91
Stoneboro, Mercer, Pa....D1 114
Stone City, Jones, Iowa....B6 92
Stone Corral, lake, Oreg....E7 113
Stonefort, Saline and Williamson, Ill....F5 90
Stonega, Wise, Va....f9 121
Stoneham, Weld, Colo....A7 83
Stoneham, Middlesex, Mass.g11 97
Stone Harbor, Cape May, N.J....E3 106
Stonehaven, N.B., Can....B4 74
Stonehaven, Scot....D6 13
Stonehenge, Austl....B4 51
Stone Lake, Sawyer, Wis....C2 124
Stoneleigh, Baltimore, Md..*B4 85
Stone Mountain, De Kalb, Ga....C2, h8 87
Stone Park, Cook, Ill....*B6 90
Stoner, B.C., Can....C6 68
Stoner, Montezuma, Colo....D2 83
Stones, riv., Tenn....A5 117
Stones River, nat. battlefield, Tenn....B5 117
Stones River Homes, Rutherford, Tenn....*B5 117
Stoneville, Washington, Miss.B3 100
Stoneville, Rockingham, N.C.A3 109
Stoneville, Meade, S. Dak....C3 116
Stonewall, Man., Can....D3 71
Stonewall, Fulton, Ga....h7 87
Stonewall, De Soto, La....B2 95
Stonewall, Clarke, Miss....C5 100
Stonewall, Pontotoc, Okla....C5 112
Stonewall, Gillespie, Tex....D3 118
Stonewall, co., Tex....C2 118
Stonewood, Harrison, W. Va....k10 123
Stoney, creek, Va....C5 121
Stoney Creek, Ont., Can....D5 72
Stonington, Baca, Colo....D8 83
Stonington, New London, Conn....D8 84
Stonington, Christian, Ill....D4 90
Stonington, Hancock, Maine.D4 96
Stono, inlet, S.C....k12 115
Stono, riv., S.C....F2 115
Stony, brook, N.J....C3 106
Stony, isl., Newf., Can....B4 75
Stony, isl., N.Y....B4 108
Stony, lake, Ont., Can....C6 72
Stony Beach, Sask., Can....G3 70
Stony Brook, Suffolk, N.Y....n15 108
Stony Brook, hbr., N.Y....F6 84
Stony Creek, New Haven, Conn....D5 84
Stony Creek, Warren, N.Y....B7 108
Stony Creek, Sussex, Va....D5 121
Stony Creek Mills, Berks, Pa....*F10 114
Stonyford, Colusa, Calif....C2 82
Stony Mountain, Man., Can.D3 71
Stony Plain, Alta., Can....C3 69
Stony Point, Rockland, N.Y.A5 106
Stony Point, Alexander, N.C.B1 109
Stony Rapids, Sask., Can....m7 70
Stony Ridge, Wood, Ohio....e6 111
Stor, riv., F.R.G....B2 16
Storaa, riv., Den....B2 24
Stora Lulevatten, lake, Swe....D8 25
Stora Sundby, Swe....t34 25
Storavan, lake, Swe....E8 25
Storden, Cottonwood, Minn..F3 99
Store Baelt, strait, Den....C4 24
Store-Heddinge, Den....C6 24
Storey, co., Nev....D2 104
Storkow, G.D.R....A8 17
Storla, Aurora, S. Dak....D7 116
Storm, lake, Iowa....B2 92
Storm Lake, Buena Vista, Iowa....B2 92
Stormont, co., Ont., Can....B9 72
Stornoway, Sask., Can....F4 70
Stornoway, Scot....B2 13
Storozhinets, Sov. Un....G5 27
Storr, mtn., Scot....C2 13
Storrs, Tolland, Conn....B7 84
Storsjön, lake, Swe....F6 25
Storsjö, Swe....F5 25
Storstrøms, co., Den....D5 24
Storthoaks, Sask., Can....H5 70
Storuman, Swe....E7 25
Storuman, lake, Swe....E7 25
Story, Sheridan, Wyo....B6 125
Story, co., Iowa....B4 92
Story City, Story, Iowa....B4 92
Story Prairie, Sandusky, Ohio....*A2 111
Stotesbury, Vernon, Mo....D3 101
Stotts City, Lawrence, Mo....D4 101
Stottville, Columbia, N.Y....C7 108
Stoughton, Sask., Can....H4 70
Stoughton, Norfolk, Mass....B5, h11 97
Stoughton, Dane, Wis....F4 124
Stour, riv., Eng....C8 12
Stour, riv., Eng....F5 12
Stourbridge, Eng....B5 12
Stourport-on-Severn, Eng....B5 12
Stout (Rome), Adams, Ohio.D2 111
Stoutland, Camden, Mo....D5 101
Stoutsville, Monroe, Mo....B6 101
Stoutsville, Fairfield, Ohio....C3 111
Stovall, Meriwether, Ga....D2 87
Stovall, Coahoma, Miss....A3 100
Stovall, Granville, N.C....A4 109
Stove Creek, Sask., Can....E4 70
Stover, Morgan, Mo....C4 101
Støvring, Den....B3 24
Stow, Oxford, Maine....D2 96
Stow, Middlesex, Mass....B4, g9 97
Stow, Summit, Ohio....A4 111
Stow, creek, N.J....E2 106
Stowe Township, Allegheny, Pa....*E2 114
Stowe, Montgomery, Pa....F10 114
Stowe, Lamoille, Vt....C3 120
Stowmarket, Eng....B8 12
Stoy, Crawford, Ill....D6 90
Stoyoma, mtn., B.C., Can....E7 68
Stoystown, Somerset, Pa....F4 114
Strabane, N. Ire....C4 11
Strabane, Washington, Pa....F1 114
Strachur, Scot....D3 13
Stradbally, Ire....D4 11
Strader, Tangipahoa, La....h11 95
Stradone, Ire....D4 11
Strafford, Greene, Mo....D4 101
Strafford, Strafford, N.H....D4 105
Strafford, Chester, Pa....*G10 114
Strafford, Orange, Vt....D4 120
Strafford, co., N.H....D4 105
Straffordville, Ont., Can....E4 72
Strakonice, Czech....D2 26
Straldzha, Bul....D8 22
Stralsund, G.D.R....A6 16
Strand, S. Afr....D2 49
Strandburg, Grant, S. Dak....B9 116
Strandby, Den....A4 24
Strandhill, Ire....C3 11
Strandquist, Marshall, Minn.B2 99
Strang, Fillmore, Nebr....D8 103
Strang, Mayes, Okla....A6 112
Stranger, creek, Kans....k15 93
Strangford, N. Ire....C6 11
Strangford, lake, N. Ire....C6 11
Strängnäs, Swe....t35 25
Strångsjö, Swe....u34 25
Stranraer, Sask., Can....F1 70
Stranraer, Scot....F3 13
Strasbourg, Sask., Can....F3 70
Strasbourg, Fr....C7 14, F7 15
Strasburg, Adams and Arapahoe, Colo....B6 83
Strasburg, G.D.R....E7 24
Strasburg, Shelby, Ill....D5 90
Strasburg, Cass, Mo....C3 101
Strasburg, Emmons, N. Dak.C5 110
Strasburg, Tuscarawas, Ohio.B4 111
Strasburg, Lancaster, Pa....G9 114
Strasburg, Shenandoah, Va..B4 121
Strass, Aus....B7 18
Strasswalchen, Aus....B9 18
Stratford, Kings, Calif....D4 82
Stratford, Ont., Can....D3 72
Stratford, Fairfield, Conn....E4 84
Stratford, Hamilton and Webster, Iowa....B4 92
Stratford, Coos, N.H....A3 105
Stratford, Camden, N.J....D2 106
Stratford, Fulton, N.Y....B6 108
Stratford, N.Z....M15 51
Stratford, Garvin, Okla....C5 112
Stratford, Brown, S. Dak....B7 116
Stratford, Sherman, Tex....A1 118
Stratford, Marathon, Wis....D3 124
Stratford, pt., Conn....E4 84
Stratford Centre, Que., Can.D6 73
Stratford Hills, Chesterfield, Va....*C5 121
Stratford Landing, Fairfax, Va....*B5 121
Stratford-on-Avon, Eng....B6 12
Stratham, Rockingham, N.H....D5 105
Strathaven, Scot....E4 13
Strathclair, Man., Can....D1 71
Strathclyde, reg., Scot....D4 13
Strathcona, Ont., Can....C8 72
Strathcona, Roseau, Minn....B2 99
Strathcona, prov. park, B.C., Can....E5 68
Strathlorne, N.S., Can....C8 74
Strathmere, Cape May, N.J..E3 106
Strathmore, Tulare, Calif....D4 82
Strathmore, Alta., Can....D4 69
Strathroy, Ont., Can....E3 72
Strathy, pt., Scot....B4 13
Strattanville, Clarion, Pa....D3 114
Stratton, Ont., Can....*D5 72
Stratton, Kit Carson, Colo..B8 83
Stratton, Franklin, Maine....C2 96
Stratton, Hitchcock, Nebr....D4 103
Stratton, Jefferson, Ohio....B5 111
Stratton (Town of), Windham, Vt....*E3 120
Stratton, mtn., Vt....E3 120
Stratton Meadows, El Paso, Colo....C6 83
Straubing, F.R.G....E7 17
Straubille, Sargent, N. Dak..C8 110
Straughn, Henry, Ind....E7 91
Strausberg, G.D.R....F7 24
Strausstown, Berks, Pa....F9 114
Strawberry, Lawrence, Ark..B4 81
Strawberry, mtn., Oreg....C8 113
Strawberry, pt., Mass....B6 97
Strawberry, range, Oreg....C8 113
Strawberry, res., Utah....C4 119
Strawberry, riv., Ark....A4 81
Strawberry, riv., Utah....C5 119
Strawberry Plains, Jefferson, Tenn....C10 117
Strawberry Point, Marin, Calif....*C2 82
Strawberry Point, Clayton, Iowa....B6 92
Strawn, Livingston, Ill....B5 90
Strawn, Coffey, Kans....D8 93
Strawn, Palo Pinto, Tex....C3 118
Straznice, Czech....D4 26
Streamstown, Alta., Can....C5 69
Streamwood, Cook, Ill....*A5 90
Streator, La Salle and Livingston, Ill....B5 90
Streator East, La Salle, Ill..*B5 90
Streeter, Stutsman, N. Dak..C6 110
Streeter, Mason, Tex....D3 118
Streetman, Freestone and Navarro, Tex....D4 118
Streetsboro, Portage, Ohio..*A4 111
Streetsville, Ont., Can....m14 72
Strehaia, Rom....C6 22
Strehlen, see Strzelin, Pol.
Strelka, Sov. Un....C13 28
Strelka, Sov. Un....D27 9
Stresa, It....D4 18
Stretford, Eng....*A5 12
Stribro, Czech....D8 17
Strichen, Scot....C6 13
Strimon, gulf, Grc....B4 23
Strimon, riv., Grc....B4 23
Stringer, Jasper, Miss....D4 100
Stringtown, Lake, Colo....B4 83
Stringtown, Anderson, Ky....B5 94
Stringtown, Bolivar, Miss....B3 100
Stringtown, Atoka, Okla....C5 112
Strofadhes, isl., Grc....D3 23
Stroh, Lagrange, Ind....A7 91
Strokestown, Ire....D3 11
Stromboli, isl., It....E5 21
Strome, Alta., Can....C4 69
Strome Ferry, Scot....C3 13
Stromness, Scot....B5 13
Stromsburg, Polk, Nebr....C8 103
Stronach, Manistee, Mich....D4 98
Strong, Union, Ark....D3 81
Strong, Franklin, Maine....D2 96
Strong, Monroe, Miss....B5 100
Strong, riv., Miss....C4 100
Strong City, Chase, Kans....D7 93
Strong City, Roger Mills, Okla....B2 112
Strongfield, Sask., Can....F2 70
Stronghurst, Henderson, Ill..C2 90
Strongs, Chippewa, Mich....B6 98
Strongsville, Cuyahoga, Ohio....A4, h9 111
Stronsay, firth, Scot....A6 13
Stronsay, isl., Scot....A6 13
Strontian, Scot....D3 13
Stroud, Eng....C5 12
Stroud, Lincoln, Okla....B5 112
Stroudsburg, Monroe, Pa....E11 114
Stroudsburg West, Monroe, Pa....*E11 114
Struble, Plymouth, Iowa....B1 92
Struer, Den....B2 24
Struga, Yugo....E5 22

Sydney Mines, N.S., Can C9 74
Sykeston, Wells, N. Dak B6 110
Sykesville, Carroll, Md B4 85
Sykesville, Burlington N.J C3 106
Sykesville, Jefferson, Pa D4 114
Syktyvkar, Sov. Un C19 9
Sylacauga, Talladega, Ala B3 78
Sylamore, Izard, Ark B3 81
Sylhet, Pak D9 39
Sylling, Nor p28 25
Sylt, isl., F.R.G D2 24
Sylva, Jackson, N.C f9 109
Sylvan, Multnomah, Oreg g12 113
Sylvan, Franklin, Pa G5 114
Sylvan, lake, Alta., Can C10 68
Sylvan, lake, Ind B7 91
Sylvan Beach, Oneida, N.Y B5 108
Sylvan Grove, Lincoln, Kans C5 93
Sylvan Hills, Pulaski, Ark h10 81
Sylvania DeKalb, Ala A4 78
Sylvania, Sask., Can E3 70
Sylvania, Screven, Ga D5 87
Sylvania, Lucas, Ohio A2, e6 111
Sylvania, Bradford, Pa C8 114
Sylvan Lake, Alta., Can C3 69
Sylvan Lake, Oakland, Mich o15 98
Sylvan Shores, Lake, Fla *D5 86
Sylvarena, Smith, Miss C4 100
Sylvester, Worth, Ga E3 87
Sylvester, Fisher, Tex C2 118
Sylvester, mtn., Newf., Can D4 75
Sylvia, Reno, Kans E5 93
Sylvia, Dickson, Tenn A4 117
Sym, riv., Sov. Un C26 9
Symmes, creek, Ohio D3 111
Symsonia, Graves, Ky f9 94
Syosset, Nassau, N.Y F3 84
Syracuse, Kosciusko, Ind B6 91
Syracuse, Hamilton, Kans E2 93
Syracuse, Morgan, Mo C5 101
Syracuse, Otoe, Nebr D9, h12 103
Syracuse, Onondaga, N.Y B4 108
Syracuse, Meigs, Ohio D4 111
Syracuse, Davis, Utah B3 119
Syr Darya, riv., Sov. Un G22 9
Syria, country, Asia E12 31, F6 33
Syriam, Bur D2 38
Sysladobsis, lake, Maine C4 96
Sysola, riv., Sov. Un C19 9
Syzran, Sov. Un C3 29
Szabadszallas, Hung B4 22
Szabolcs-Szatmar, co., Hung *B5 22
Szamos, riv., Hung A6 22
Szamotuly, Pol B4 26
Szarvas, Hung B5 22
Szczakowa, Pol g10 26
Szczebrzeszyn, Pol C7 26
Szczecin (Stettin), Pol E8 24, B3 26
Szczecinek, Pol B4 26
Szczuczyn, Pol B7 26
Szczytno, Pol B6 26
Szechwan, prov., China E5 34
Szeged, Hung B5 22
Székesfehérvár, Hung B4 22
Szekszard, Hung B4 22
Szentendre, Hung B4 22
Szentes, Hung B5 22
Szigetvar, Hung B3 22
Szolnok, Hung B5 22
Szolnok, co., Hung *B5 22
Szombathely, Hung B3 22
Szprotawa, Pol C3 26
Sztum, Pol B5 26
Szubin, Pol B4 26
Szydlowiec, Pol C6 26
Szymanow, Pol m12 26

T

Taal, Phil p13 35
Taal, lake, Phil p13 35
Taasinge, isl., Den C4 24
Tab, Warren, Ind D3 91
Tabaco, Phil *C6 35
Ţābah, Sau. Ar I14 31
Tabas, Iran E8 41
Ţabas, Iran, E8 41
Ţabas, Iran E10 41
Tabasará, mts., Pan F7 62
Tabasco, state, Mex D6 63
Tabatinga, mts., Braz D2 57
Tabayoc, mtn., Phil n13 35
Tabbys, peak, Utah C3 119
Tabelbala, Alg D4 44
Taber, Alta., Can E4 69
Tabernacle, Burlington, N.J D3 106
Tabernas, Sp D4 20
Tabernash, Grand, Colo B5 83
Taberville, St. Clair, Mo C4 101
Tabik, isl., Kwajalein 52
Tabiona, Duchesne, Utah C5 119
Tabla, mtn., P.R B3 65
Tablas, cape, Chile A2 54
Tablas, isl., Phil C6 35
Table, bay, Newf., Can B3 75
Table, bay, S. Afr D2 49
Table, head, Newf., Can B4 75
Table, mtn., Ariz E5 80
Table, mtn., Newf., Can E2 75
Table, rock, Oreg C4 113
Table Grove, Fulton, Ill C3 90
Table Rock, Pawnee, Nebr D9 103
Table Rock, Jackson, Oreg E4 113
Table Top, mtn., Ariz E3 80
Taboada, Sp A2 20
Tabor, Czech D3 26
Tabor, Fremont and Mills, Iowa D2 92
Tabor, Polk, Minn B2 99
Tabor (Mount Tabor), Morris, N.J *B4 106
Tabor, Bon Homme, S. Dak E8 116
Tabor, see Tavor, mtn., Isr.
Tabora, Tan C5 48
Tabor City, Columbus, N.C C4 109
Tabou, I.C F3 45
Tabrīz, Iran B3 41
Tabūk, Sau. Ar D7 43
Tabusintac, riv., N.B., Can B4 74
Tacámbaro de Codallos, Mex n13 63
Tachaitan, China D4 34
Tacheng, China E7 36
Tacheng (Chuguchak), China B1 34
Tachie, riv., B.C., Can B5 68
Tachiiwa, pt., Iwo 52
Tachikawa, Jap n18 37
Táchira, state, Ven B3 60
Tachov, Czech D7 17
Tacloban, Phil C6 35
Tacna, Yuma, Ariz E1 80
Tacna, Peru E3 58
Tacna, dept., Peru E3 58
Tacoma, La Plata, Colo D3 83
Tacoma, Pierce, Wash B3, f11 122
Taconic, Litchfield, Conn A3 84
Taconic, range, Mass A1 97
Tacoronte, Sp. (Can. Is.) m13 20
Tacuarembó, Ur E1 56
Tacuarembó, dept., Ur *E1 56
Tacuatí, Par D4 55
Tacubaya, Mex. (part of Mexico City) h9 63
Tad, Kanawha, W. Va m13 123
Tadanac, B.C., Can *E9 68
Tademaït, plat., Alg D5 44
Tadjoura, Dji C5 47
Tadoule, lake, Man., Can f8 71
Tadoussac, Que., Can A8 73
Tadzhik, S.S.R., rep., Sov. Un F9 28
Taegu, Kor I4 37
Taejŏn, Kor H3 37
Taeyudong, Kor F2 37
Tafalla, Sp A5 20
Tafí Viejo, Arg E2 55
Tafresh, mtn., Iran D5 41
Taft, Kern, Calif E4 82
Taft, St. Charles, La k11 75
Taft, Muskogee, Okla B6 112
Taft, Lincoln, Oreg C3 113
Taft, Lincoln, Tenn B5 117
Taft, San Patricio, Tex F4 118
Taft Heights, Kern, Calif *E4 82
Taft Southwest, San Patricio, Texas *F4 118
Taftsville, Windsor, Vt D4 120
Taftville, New London, Conn. (part of Norwich) C8 84
Tagachan, pt., Guam 52
Taganrog, Sov. Un H12 27
Taganrog, gulf, Sov. Un H12 27
Tagawa, Jap *J5 37
Tagbileran, Phil D6 35
Taghrīfat, Libya D3 43
Taghmaconnell, Ire D3 11
Taghmon, Ire E5 11
Tagliamento, riv., It C8 18
Tagolo, pt., Phil D6 35
Taguan, pt., Guam 52
Taguatinga, Braz D1 57
Taguchi, Jap n16 37
Tagus, Mountrail, N. Dak A4 110
Tagus see Tejo, riv., Port.
Tagus, see Tajo, riv., Sp.
Tahan, mtn., Mala J5 38
Tahat, mtn., Alg E5 44
Tahiti, isl., Society Is H13 7
Tahlequah, Cherokee, Okla B7 112
Tahoe, lake, Calif., Nev C3 82
Tahoe City, Placer, Calif C3 82
Tahoka, Lynn, Tex C2 118
Taholah, Grays Harbor, Wash B1 122
Tahoma, Placer, Calif C3 82
Tahoua, Niger D6 45
Tahquamenon, falls, Mich B5 98
Tahsien, China I2 36
Tahsis, B.C., Can E4 68
Ţahţā, Eg D6 43
Tahtsa, lake, B.C., Can C4 68
Tahtsa, peak, B.C., Can C4 68
Tahuya, Mason, Wash B2 122
Tai, China E5 36
Taï, I.C E3 45
Tai, lake, China I9 36
Taian, China D10 36
Taian, China F7 36
Taiban, De Baca, N. Mex C5 107
Taichao (Giamda), China E3 34
Taichintala, China B9 36
Taichou, China H8 36
T'aichung, Taiwan G9 34
Taihape, N.Z M15 51
Taikang, China C2 37
Taiku, China F5 36
Tailagoin, mts., Mong C6 34
Tailai, China C1 37
Tailem Bend, Austl G2 51
Tailevu, pt., Fiji 52
Tain, Scot C4 13
T'ainan, Taiwan G9 34
Taining, China K7 36
Taipei (Taihoku), Taiwan G9 34
Taiping, Mala J4 38
Taipu, Braz g6 57
Taira, Jap H10 37
Taishun, China K8 36
Taitao, pen., Chile D1 54
T'aitung, Taiwan G9 34
Taivalkoski, Fin E13 25
Taiwan (Formosa), country (Nationalist China), Asia G15 33, G9 34
Taiwan, isl., Asia G9 34
Taiyüan (Yangkü), China D7 34, F5 36
Tajarḥī, Libya E2 43
Tajimi, Jap I8, n16 37
Tajique, Torrance, N. Mex C3 107
Tajo (Tagus), riv., Sp C3 20
Tajumulco, mtn., Guat C2 62
Tajuna, riv., Sp B4 20
Tājūrā', Libya C2 43
Tak, Thai D3 38
Takada, Jap H9 37
Takahe, mtn., Ant B1 5
Takaka, N.Z N14 51
Takamatsu, Jap I7 37
Takaoka, Jap H8 37
Takarazuka, Jap *I7 37
Takasago, Jap *I7 37
Takasaki, Jap H9, m18 37
Takata, Jap H9 37
Takato, Jap n17 37
Takatsuki, Jap o14 37
Takaw, Bur B3 38
Takawa, Jap *J5 37
Takayama, Jap H8, m16 37
Take, isl., Jap H5 37
Takefu, Jap n15 37
Takeo, Camb G6 38
Tākestān, Iran C4 41
Takhta-Bazar, Sov. Un D11 41
Takhta-Kupyr, Sov. Un E6 29
Takihara, Jap o15 37
Takijuq, lake, N.W. Ter., Can C10 66
Takilma, Josephine, Oreg E3 113
Takingeun, Indon J2 38
Takla, lake, B.C., Can B5 68
Taklakhar, see Pulan, China
Takla Makan, des., China F11 33
Takoma Park, Montgomery and Prince Georges, Md f9 85
Takotna, Alsk C8 79
Takouchen, China D7 36
Taku, China E7 36
Takua Pa, Thai H3 38
Takut, Bur A3 38
Talā, Eg D2 32
Tala, Mex m12 63
Tala, Ur E1 56
Talaga, Phil p13 35
Talagante, Chile A2 54
Talai, China D2 37
Talakan, Sov. Un B6 37
Talakmau, mtn., Indon E2 35
Talala, Rogers, Okla A6 112
Talamanca, mts., C.R F6 62
Talanga, Hond C4 62
Talara, Peru B1 58
Talas, Sov. Un E8 29
Talata Mafara, Nig D6 45
Talaud, is., Indon E7 35
Talavera de la Reina, Sp B2 20
Talawdī, Sud C3 47
Talayan, Phil *D6 35
Talbert, Breathitt, Ky C6 94
Talbiya, see Qomemiyyut, Isr.
Talbot, Benton, Ind D3 89
Talbot, Marion, Oreg k11 113
Talbot, co., Ga D2 87
Talbot, co., Md C5 85
Talbot, isl., Fla m9 86
Talbot, lake, Alta., Can C1 69
Talbot, lake, Man., Can B2 71
Talbottom, Talbot, Ga D2 87
Talca, Chile B2 54
Talca, prov., Chile B2 54
Talcahuano, Chile B2 54
Tālcher, India G10 40
Talco, Titus, Tex C5 118
Talcott, Summers, W. Va D4 123
Talcottville, Tolland, Conn B7 84
Talcottville, Lewis, N.Y B5 108
Taldy-Kurgan, Sov. Un D9 29, F24 9
Talent, Jackson, Oreg E4 113
Tali, China G4 36
Taliabu, isl., Indon F6 35
Taliaferro, co., Ga C4 87
Talihina, LeFlore, Okla C6 112
Talim, isl., Phil o13 35
Tali Post, Sud D3 47
Talisay, Phil o14 35
Talisayan, Phil *D6 35
Talish, mts., Iran, Sov. Un B4 41
Talitsa, Sov. Un B6 29
Talkeetna, Alsk C9, f16 79
Talkeetna, mts., Alsk f17 79
Talkhā, Eg C3 32
Talking Rock, Pickens, Ga B2 67
Tall, Jordan g11 32
Talladega, Talladega, Ala B3 78
Talladega, co., Ala B3 78
Talladega, mtn., Ala B4 78
Talladega Springs, Talladega, Ala B3 78
Tallahala, creek, Miss D4 100
Tallahassee, Leon, Fla B2 86
Tallahatchie, co., Miss B3 100
Tallahatchie, riv., Miss B3 100
Tallangatta, Austl H6 51
Tallant, Osage, Okla A5 112
Tallapoosa, Haralson, Ga C1 87
Tallapoosa, New Madrid, Mo E8 101
Tallapoosa, co., Ala C4 78
Tallapoosa, riv., Ala C3 78
Tallard, Fr E2 18
Tallassee, Elmore and Tallapoosa, Ala C4 78
Talleyville, New Castle, Del *A6 85
Tallieu, Assumption, La C5 95
Tallinn, Sov. Un B5 27
Tallmadge, Summit, Ohio A4 111
Tallow, Ire E3 11
Tallula, Menard, Ill D4 90
Tallula, Issaquena, Miss C2 100
Tallulah, Madison, La B4 95
Tallulah, mts., Ga B3 87
Tallūzā, Jordan f12 32
Talmage, Sask., Can H4 70
Talmage, Dickinson, Kans C6 93
Talmage, Otoe, Nebr D9 103
Talmage, Duchesne, Utah C5 119
Talnoye, Sov. Un G8 27
Talo, mtn., Eth C4 47
Talofofo, Guam 52
Talofofo, bay, Guam 52
Taloga, Dewey, Okla A3 112
Talon, lake, Ont., Can A5 72
Talowah, Lamar, Miss D4 100
Talpa, Coleman, Tex D3 118
Talpa de Allende, Mex m11 63
Talquin, lake, Fla B2 86
Talsi, Sov. Un C4 27
Taltal, Chile E1 55
Tama, Tama, Iowa C5 92
Tama, co., Iowa B5 92
Tamaha, Haskell, Okla B7 112
Tamalameque, Col B3 60
Tamale, Ghana E4 45
Tamalpais, mtn., Calif h7 82
Tamalpais Valley, Marin, Calif *C2 82
Taman, Sov. Un I11 27
Tamana, mtn., Trin O23 65
Tamanar, Mor C3 44
Tamano, Jap I6 37
Tamanrasset, Alg E6 44
Tamanrasset, wadi, Alg E5 44
Tamaqua, Shuylkill, Pa E10 114
Tamar, riv., Eng D3 12
Tamarack, Adams, Idaho E2 89
Tamarack, Aitkin, Minn D5 99
Tamarite, Sp B6 20
Tamaroa, Perry, Ill E4 90
Tamashima, Jap *I6 37
Tamassee, Oconee, S.C B1 115
Tamatave, prov., Mad g9 49
Tamaulipas, state, Mex C5 63
Tamazula de Gordiano, Mex n12 63
Tamazunchale, Mex C5, m14 63
Tambach, Ken A6 48
Tambacounda, Sen D2 45
També, Braz C3, h6 57
Tambelan, is., Indon E3 35
Tambo, Austl B6 51
Tambo, riv., Peru D3 58
Tambo, riv., Peru E3 58
Tambo Grande, Peru B1 58
Tambov, Sov. Un C2 29
Tambre, riv., Sp A1 20
Tamdy-Bulak, Sov. Un E6 29
Tambura, Sud D2 47
Tamchaket, Maur C2 45
Tame, Col B3 60
Tamega, riv., Port B2 20
Tamel Aike, Arg D2 54
Tamgue, mtn., Guinea D2 45
Tamiahua, Mex C5, m15 63
Tamiahua, lagoon, Mex C5 63
Tamiami, canal, Fla G6 86
Tamiao, China C4 36
Tamina, Montgomery, Tex D5 118
Tamina, riv., Switz C7 19
Taming, China F6 36
Tamins, Switz C7 19
Tamis, riv., Yugo C5 22
Tam Ky, Viet E8 38
Tamms, Alexander, Ill F4 90
Ţammūn, Jordan B7, f12 32
Tamney, Ire B4 11
Tamo, Jefferson, Ark C4 81
Tamora, Seward, Nebr D8 103
Tamora, Ponape 52
Tamoroi, Ponape 52
Tampa, Hillsborough, Fla E4, p11 86
Tampa, Marion, Kans D6 93
Tampa, bay, Fla E4 86
Tampasak, Mala D5 35
Tampere, Fin G10 25
Tampico, Whiteside, Ill B4 90
Tampico, Jackson, Ind G6 91
Tampico, Mex C5, k15 63
Tampico, Valley, Mont B10 102
Tams, Raleigh, W. Va D3 123
Tamuning, Guam 52
Tamworth, Austl E8 51
Tamworth, Ont., Can C8 72
Tamworth, Eng B6 12
Tamworth, Carroll, N.H C4 105
Tana, Chile C2 55
Tana, lake, Eth C4 47
Tana, riv., Fin., Nor C11 25
Tana, riv., Ken B7 48
Tanabe, Jap J7 37
Tanacross, Alsk C11 79
Tanafjorden, fjord, Nor B13 25
Tanaga, isl., Alsk E4 79
Tanahbala, isl., Indon F1 35
Tanahgrogot, Indon F5 35
Tanahmasa, isl., Indon F1 35
Tanakpur, India C8 40
Tanami, Austl D4 50
Tanana, Alsk B9 79
Tanana, riv., Alsk C11 79
Tananarive, prov., Mad g9 49
Tanapag, Saipan 52
Tanapag, hbr., Saipan 52
Tanaro, riv., It B2 21
Tanauan, Phil o13 35
Tanaunella, It D2 21
Tanavuso, pt., Fiji 52
Tancheng, China G8 36
Tanchon, Kor F4 37
Tancook Island, N.S., Can E5 74
Tānda, India D9 40
Tandag, Phil *D7 35
Tandaltī, Sud C2 47
Tăndărei, Rom C8 22
Tandil, Arg B5 54
Tando Ādam, Pak E2 40
Tandou, lake, Austl F4 51
Tanega, isl., Jap K5 37
Tanega, strait, Jap K5 37
Taney, co., Mo E9 101
Taneycomo, lake, Mo E5 101
Taneytown, Carroll, Md A3 85
Taneyville, Taney, Mo E4 101
Tanezrouft, des., Alg., Mali E4 44
Tanga, Tan C6 48
Tangancícuaro [de Aristа], Mex n12 63
Tanganyika, see Tanzania, country, Afr.
Tanganyika, lake, Afr C4 48
Tangent, Linn, Oreg C3, k11 113
Tanger (Tangier), Mor B3 44
Tangerhütte, G.D.R A6 17
Tangermünde, G.D.R B3 16
Tangho, China H5 36
Tangier, N.S., Can E7 74
Tangier, Parke, Ind E3 91
Tangier, see Tanger, Mor.
Tangier, Woodward, Okla A2 112
Tangier, Accomack, Va C7 121
Tangier, isl., Va C6 121
Tangier, sound, Md D6 85
Tangipahoa, Tangipahoa, La D5 95
Tangipahoa, par., La D5 95
Tangipahoa, riv., La g11 95
Tangkula, mts., China E2 34
Tangkulayuma, lake, China B8 39
Tangnaihai, China D4 34
Tangshan, China E8 36
Tangshan, China G7 36
Tangtan, China F5 34
Tangtu, China I8 36
Tanguiéta, Benin D5 45
Tanguisson, pt., Guam 52
Tangwang, riv., China B10 34
Tangyang, China I4 36
Tangyüan, China C4 37
Tanhsien (Nodoa), China C8 38
Tanimbar, is., Indon G8 35
Taninges, Fr C2 18
Tanjay, Phil *D6 35
Tanjore, see Thanjavure, India
Tanjung, Indon F5 35
Tanjungbalai, Indon E1, m11 35
Tanjungkarang-Telukbetung, Indon G3 35
Tanjungpandan, Indon F3 35
Tanjungselor, Indon E5 35
Tānk, Pak A3 40
Tank, cape, Iran I9 41
Tankābon, Iran C5 41
Tännäs, Swe F5 25
Tanner, Limestone, Ala A3 78
Tanner, Gilmer, W. Va C4 123
Tanner, mtn., B.C., Can E8 68
Tannersville, Greene, N.Y C6 108
Tannis, bay, Den A4 24
Tannu-Ola, mts., Sov. Un., Mong A3 34
Tânout, Niger C6 45
Tanque Verde, Pima, Ariz *E5 80
Tanshui, Taiwan *F9 34
Tantā, Eg G8 31, C6 43
Tantallon, Sask., Can G5 70
Tantoyuca, Mex m14 63
Tantung (Antung), China C9 34, F2 37
Tanum, Swe H4 25
Tanza, Phil o13 35
Tanzania, country, Afr G9 42, C5 48
Tao, riv., China B9 34
Taoan, China B10 36
Taoershan, China B9 36
Taohsien, China F7 34
Taokou, China G6 36
Taolakopa (Thog Daurakpa), China A10 40
Taopi, Mower, Minn G6 99
Taormina, It F5 21
Taos, Cole, Mo C6 101
Taos, Taos, N. Mex A4 107
Taos, co., N. Mex A4 107
Taos Pueblo, Taos, N. Mex A4 107
Taoudenni, Mali B4 45
Taoyuan, China J4 36
Taoyüan, Taiwan *G9 34
Tapacarí, Bol C2 55
Tapachula, Mex E6 63
Tapaga, cape, W. Sam 52
Tapajós, riv., Braz D3 59
Tapak, Ponape 52
Tapak, isl., Ponape 52
Tapaktuan, Indon m11 35
Tapalqué, Arg B4 54
Tapanahoni, riv., N. Gui B3 59
Tapanshang, China C8 36
Tapanui N.Z P12 51
Tapa Shan, mtn., China I4 36
Tapauá, riv., Braz C4 58
Taperoá, Braz h5 57
Tāpi, riv., India D5 39
Tapirapé, riv., Braz E4 59
Tapis, mtn., Mala K5 38
Tapotchau, mtn., Saipan 52
Tappahannock, Essex, Va C6 121
Tappan, Rockland, N.Y g13 108
Tappan, lake, N.J g8 106
Tappan Lake, res., Ohio B4 111
Tappen, Kidder, N. Dak C6 110
Tappita, Lib E3 45
Tapuaenuku, mtn., N.Z O14 51
Tapurucuara, Braz D4 60
Taputapu, cape, Am. Sam 52
Taqatu' Hayya, Sud B4 47
Taquara, Braz D2 56
Taquara, mts., Braz B2 56
Taquarí, riv., Braz B1 56
Taquarí, riv., Braz D2 56
Taquaritinga, Braz k7 56
Taquaritinga do Norte, Braz h5 57
Tar, riv., N.C B4 109
Tara, Ont., Can C3 72
Tara, St. Louis, Mo *C7 101
Tara, Sov. Un B8 29
Tara, hill, Ire D5 11
Tara, riv., Sov. Un B9 29
Tara, riv., Yugo D4 22
Tarabuco, Bol C3 55
Ţarābulus, see Tripoli, Leb.
Ţarābulus, see Tripoli, Libya
Ţarābulus, see Tripolitania, prov., Libya
Tarakan, Indon E5 35
Tarakliya, Sov. Un C9 22
Tarancón, Sp B4 20
Taransay, isl., Scot C1 13
Taranto, It D6 21
Taranto, gulf, It D6 21
Tarapaca, Col D4 60
Tarapacá, prov., Chile D1 55
Tarapoto, Peru C2 58
Tarare, Fr E6 14
Tarascon-sur-Ariège, Fr F4 14
Tarascon-sur-Rhône, Fr F6 14
Tarasp, Switz C9 19
Tarata, Bol C2 55
Tarata, Peru E3 58
Tarauacá, riv., Braz C3 58
Tarawa, isl., Kir 52
Tarawera, N.Z M16 51
Tarazona, Sp B5 20
Tarazona, Sp C5 20
Tarbagatay, range, Sov. Un D10 29
Tarbat Ness, pt., Scot C5 13
Tarbelville, Rutland, Vt E3 120
Tarbert, Ire E2 11
Tarbert, Scot C2 13
Tarbert, Scot E3 13
Tarbes, Fr F4 14
Tarbet, Scot D4 13
Tarboro, Camden, Ga F5 87
Tarboro, Edgecombe, N.C B5 109
Tarbū, Libya D3 43
Tarcento, It C9 18
Tarcoola, Austl F5 50
Taree, Austl E9 51
Tarentum, Pike, Ala D4 78
Tarentum, Allegheny, Pa E2, h14 114
Tarfaya, Mor D2 44
Tarfside, Scot D6 13
Targhee, pass, Idaho, Mont F5 102
Tarhūnah, Libya C2 43
Tarifa, Sp D3 20
Tariffville, Hartford, Conn B5 84
Tarigtig, pt., Phil n14 35
Tarija, Bol D3 55
Tarija, dept., Bol D3 55
Tarik, isl., Truk 52
Tarim Darya, riv., China E11 33
Taritai, isl., Tarawa 52
Tarkiln, hill, Maine g7 96
Tarkiln, Providence, R.I B10 84
Tarkio, Atchison, Mo A2 101
Tarkio, Mineral, Mont C2 102
Tarko-Sale, Sov. Un C24 9
Tarkwa, Ghana E4 45
Tarlac, Phil o13, B6 35
Tarlac, prov., Phil *B6 35
Tarland, Scot C6 13
Tarlton, Pickaway, Ohio C3 111
Tarm, Den C2 24
Tarma, Peru D2 58
Tarn, dept., Fr *F5 14
Tarn, riv., Fr F4 14
Tarna, riv., Hung B5 22
Tårnby, Den *C6 24
Tarn-et-Garonne, dept., Fr *E4 14
Tarnobrzeg, Pol C6 26
Tarnopol, Sask., Can E3 70
Tarnov, Platte, Nebr C8 103
Tarnów, Pol C6 26
Tarnowskie Gory, Pol C5, g9 26
Taro, riv., It B2 21
Taroom, Austl B7 51
Taroudant, Mor C3 44
Tarp, F.R.G D3 24
Tarpey, Fresno, Calif D4 82
Tarpley, Bandera, Tex E3 118
Tarpon Springs, Pinellas, Fla D4 86
Tarquí, Peru B2 58
Tarquinia, It C3 21
Tarragona, Sp B6 20
Tarragona, prov., Sp *B6 20
Tarrant, Jefferson, Ala C3, f7 78
Tarrant, co., Tex C4 118
Tarrasa, Sp B7 20
Tarratine, Somerset, Maine C3 96
Tárrega, Sp B6 20
Tarryall, Park, Colo B5 83
Tarryall, creek, Colo B5 83
Tarryall, mts., Colo B5 83
Tarrytown, Montgomery, Ga D4 87
Tarrytown, Westchester, N.Y D7, m15 108
Tårs, Den A4 24
Tarso Ahon, mtn., Chad A3 46
Tarsus, Tur D10 31
Tartagal, Arg D3 55
Tartu, Sov. Un B6 27
Tartuguan, pt., Guam 52
Tartūs, Syr E10 31
Tārūt, isl., Sau. Ar H5 41
Tarutung, Indon K3 38
Tarutao, isl., Thai I3 38
Tarver, Echols, Ga F4 87
Tarves, Scot C6 13
Tarya, riv., Bol D3 55
Tasāwah, Libya D2 43
Taseko, lakes, B.C., Can D6 68
Taseko, mtn., B.C., Can D6 68
Taseko, riv., B.C., Can D6 68
Tashauz, Sov. Un E5 29
Tashigong, see Chahsikang, China
Tashkent, Sov. Un G22 9, E7 29
Tashkumyr, Sov. Un E8 29
Taskan, Sov. Un C18 28
Taskopru, Tur B10 31
Tasman, bay, N.Z N14 51
Tasman, pen., Austl o15 50
Tasman, sea, Austl H8 51
Tasmania, state, Austl o15 50
Tassili du Ahaggar, plat., Alg E6 44
Tassili n'Ajjer, plat., Alg D6 44
Tasso, Bradley, Tenn D9 117
Taswell, Crawford, Ind H4 91
Tata, Hung B4 22
Tatabánya, Hung B4 22
Tatamagouche, N.S., Can D6 74
Tatar, strait, Sov. Un C10 37
Tatarbunary, Sov. Un C9 22
Tatarsk, Sov. Un B9 29
Tate, Sask., Can F3 70
Tate, Pickens, Ga B2 87
Tate, co., Miss A4 100
Tatebayashi, Jap *H9 37
Tate Cove, Evangeline, La D3 95
Tateville, Pulaski, Ky D5 94
Tateyama, Jap I9, o18 37
Tathlina, lake, N.W. Ter., Can D9 66
Tatien, China L7 36
Tatitlek, Alsk C10, g18 79
Tatla, lake, B.C., Can C5 68
Tatlayoko Lake, B.C., Can D5 68
Tatnam, cape, Man., Can f9 71
Tatra, mts., Pol., Czech D5 26
Tatta, Pak E1 40
Tattershall, Eng A7 12
Tattnall, co., Ga D4 87
Tatuí, Braz C3, m8 56
Tatuk, lake, B.C., Can C5 68
Tatum, Lea, N. Mex D6 107
Tatum, Marlboro, S.C B8 115
Tatumville, Dyer, Tenn A2 117
Tatung, China C7 34, D5 36
Tatvan, Tur C14 31
Tau, isl., Thai G3 38
Tauá, Braz C2 57
Taubaté, Braz C3 56
Tauber, riv., F.R.G D4 17
Tauberbischofsheim, F.R.G D4 17
Taucha, G.D.R B7 17
Tauern, tunnel, Aus C9 18
Taumatawhakatangihangakoauauotamateapokaiwhenuakitanatahu, hill, N.Z *N16 51
Taum Sauk, mtn., Mo D7 101
Taung, S. Afr C3 49
Taungdwingyi, Bur D10 39
Taunggyi, Bur D10 39
Taunton, Eng C4 12
Taunton, Bristol, Mass C5 97
Taunton, Lyon, Minn F2 99
Taunton Lakes, Burlington, N.J D3 106
Tauntor, riv., Mass C5 97
Taunus, mts., F.R.G D2 17
Taupo, lake, N.Z M15 51
Taurage, Sov. Un D4 27
Tauranga, N.Z L16 51
Taurianova, It E6 21
Taurus, mts., Tur D9 31
Tauste, Sp B5 20
Tavannes, Switz B3 19
Tavares, Lake, Fla D5 86
Tavas, Tur D7 23
Tavda, Sov. Un B7 29
Tavda, riv., Sov. Un D21 9
Tavernier, Monroe, Fla G6 86
Taveuni, isl., Fiji 52
Taviche, Mex D5 63
Tavira, Port D2 20
Tavistock, Ont., Can D4 72
Tavistock, Eng D3 12
Tavolzhan, Sov. Un C9 29
Tavor (Mt. Tabor), mtn., Isr B7 32
Tavoy, Bur F10 39
Tavoy, isl., Bur F3 38
Tavoy, pt., Bur F3 38
Tavsanli, Tur C7 23
Taw, riv., Eng D4 12
Tawas, lake, Mich D7 98
Tawas City, Iosco, Mich D7 98
Tawatinaw, Alta., Can B4 69
Tawe, riv, Wales C4 12
Tawi Tawi, isl., Phil D6 35
Tawi Tawi Group, is., Phil D6 35
Tawkar, Sud B4 47
Tāwurghā', Libya C3 43
Taxco de Alarcón, Mex n14 63
Tay, firth, Scot D5 13
Tay, lake, Scot D4 13
Tay, riv., Scot D5 13
Tayabamba, Peru C2 58
Tayabas, bay, Phil p13 35
Tayāsīr, Jordan f12 32
Taycheedah, Fond du Lac, Wis k9 124
Tayga, Sov. Un B11 29
Taylor, Columbia, Ark D2 81
Taylor, Navajo, Ariz C5 80
Taylor, B.C., Can A7 68
Taylor, Wayne, Mich p15 98
Taylor, Lafayette, Miss A4 100
Taylor, Loup, Nebr C6 103
Taylor, Stark, N. Dak C3 110
Taylor, Lackawanna, Pa D10, m18 114
Taylor, Williamson, Tex D4 118
Taylor, Jackson, Wis D2 124
Taylor, co., Fla B3 86
Taylor, co., Ga D2 87
Taylor, co., Iowa D3 92
Taylor, co., Ky C4 94
Taylor, co., Tex C3 118
Taylor, co., W. Va B4 123
Taylor, co., Wis C3 124
Taylor, dam, Nev C3 104
Taylor, mtn., Idaho E4 89
Taylor, mtn., N. Mex B2 107

Tieton, dam, Wash C4 122
Tieton, peak, Wash C4 122
Tieton, riv., Wash C4 122
Tiffany, mtn., Wash A6 122
Tiff City, McDonald, Mo E3 101
Tiffin, Johnson, Iowa C6 92
Tiffin, Seneca, Ohio A2 111
Tiffin, riv., Ohio A1 111
Tiflis, see Tbilisi, Sov. Un.
Tift, co., Ga E3 87
Tifton, Tift, Ga E3 87
Tiftona, Hamilton, Tenn *D8 117
Tigard, Washington, Oreg h12 113
Tiger, Rabun, Ga B3 87
Tiger, Pend Oreille, Wash A8 122
Tigerton, Shawano, Wis D4 124
Tigerville, Greenville, S.C A3 115
Tigh, ridge, Oreg B5 113
Tighnabruaich, Scot E3 13
Tigil, Sov. Un D18 28
Tignall, Wilkes, Ga C4 87
Tignere, Cam D2 46
Tignish, P.E.I., Can C5 74
Tigre, prov., Eth C4 47
Tigre, isl., Viet D7 38
Tigre, pt., La E5 95
Tigre, riv., Peru B2 58
Tigrett, Dyer, Tenn B2 117
Tigris, riv., Asia I18 9, E2 41
Tiguabos, Cuba D6 64
Tîh, mts., Eg E5 32
Tihuatlán, Mex m15 63
Tijeras, Bernalillo, N. Mex B3, k8 107
Tiji, Libya C2 43
Tijuana, Mex A1 63
Tijucas, Braz D3 56
Tikal, ruins, Guat B3 62
Tikamgarh, India E7 40
Tikhoretsk, Sov. Un I13 27
Tikhvin, Sov. Un B9 27
Tikrit, Iraq E14 31
Tiksi, Sov. Un B15 28
Tilamuta, Indon E6 35
Tilarán, C.R E5 62
Tilburg, Neth C5 15
Tilbury, Ont., Can E2 72
Tilbury, Eng C8 12
Tilcara, Arg D2 55
Tilden, Randolph, Ill E4 90
Tilden, Itawamba, Miss A5 100
Tilden, Madison and Antelope, Nebr B8 103
Tilden, McMullen, Tex E3 118
Tilemsès, Niger C5 45
Tilemsi, val., Mali C5 45
Tilford, Meade, S. Dak C2 116
Tilghman, Talbot, Md C5 85
Tilghman, isl., Md C5 85
Tiline, Livingston, Ky e9 94
Till, riv., Eng E6 13
Tillabéry, Niger D5 54
Tillamook, Tillamook, Oreg B3 113
Tillamook, co., Oreg B3 113
Tillar, Drew, Ark D4 81
Tillatoba, Yalobusha, Miss B4 100
Tillberga, Swe t34 25
Tiller, Douglas, Oreg D4 113
Tillery, lake, N.C B2 109
Tilley, Alta., Can D5 69
Tillicoultry, Scot *D5 13
Tillicum, Pierce, Wash *E1 122
Tillman, Jasper, S.C G5 115
Tillman, co., Okla C3 112
Tillson, Ulster, N.Y D6 108
Tillsonburg, Ont., Can E4 72
Tillyfourie, Scot C6 13
Tilmans Corner, Mobile, Ala E1 78
Tilos, isl., Grc D6 23
Tilpa, Austl E5 51
Tilrhemt, Alg C5 44
Tilsit, see Sovetsk, Sov. Un.
Tilston, Man., Can E1 71
Tilting, Newf., Can D4 75
Tilton, Whitefield, Ga B2 87
Tilton, Vermilion, Ill C6 90
Tilton, Belknap, N.H D3 105
Tiltonsville, Jefferson, Ohio B5 111
Tim, Sov. Un F11 27
Timaná, Col C2 60
Timaru, N.Z P13 51
Timashevskaya, Sov. Un I12 27
Timbalier, bay, La E5 95
Timbalier, isl., La E5 95
Timbaúba, Braz h6 57
Timbered Knob, mtn., Mo E5 101
Timberlake, Person, N.C A4 109
Timber Lake, Dewey, S. Dak B4 116
Timberlake, Campbell, Va C3 121
Timberville, Rockingham, Va B4 121
Timblin, Jefferson, Pa E3 114
Timbo, Stone, Ark B3 81
Timbuktu, see Tombouctou, Mali
Timerzit, Mor C4 44
Times Beach, St. Louis, Mo *C7 101
Timewell (Mound Station), Brown, Ill C3 90
Timimoun, Alg D5 44
Timiskaming, dist., Ont., Can o19 72
Timişoara, Rom C5 22
Timken, Rush, Kans D4 93
Timmendorfer Strand [an die Ostsee], F.R.G E4 24
Timmins, Ont., Can o19 72
Timmonsville, Florence, S.C C8 115
Timnath, Larimer, Colo A5 83
Timon, Natchitoches, La C2 95
Timor, isl., Indon G6 35
Timor, sea, Indon G7 35
Timpanogos Cave, nat. mon., Utah C4 119
Timpas, Otero, Colo D7 83
Timpson, Shelby, Tex D5 118
Timra, Swe F7 25
Timsâh, lake, Eg D4 32
Tims Ford, lake, Tenn B5 117
Tin, cape, Libya C4 43
Tina, Carroll, Mo B4 101
Tînah (Pelusium), bay, Eg C4 32
Tinahely, Ire E5 11
Tin Amzi, wadi, Alg E5 44
Tinaquillo, Ven B4 60
Tin City, Duplin, N.C C5 109
Tindouf, Alg D3 44
Tineo, Sp A2 20
Tinghai, China E9 34
Tinghert, plat., Alg., Libya D6 44
Tinghsien, China E6 36
Tinghsing, China E6 36
Tingjegaon, Nep C9 40
Tingjih (Tingri Dzong), China C11 40
Tinglev, Den D3 24
Tingley, Ringgold, Iowa D3 92
Tingmerkpuk, mtn., Alsk B7 79
Tingo Maria, Peru C2 58
Tingpien, China F2 36
Tingri Dzong, see Tingjih, China
Tingsryd, Swe B8 24
Tingwick, Que., Can D6 73
Tinian, Tinian 52
Tinian, hbr., Tinian 52
Tinian, isl., Mariana Is 52
Tinizong, Switz C8 19
Tinkisso, riv., Guinea D2 45
Tinley Park, Cook, Ill k9 90
Tinnie, Lincoln, N. Mex D4 107
Tinniswood, mtn., B.C., Can D6 68
Tinogasta, Arg E2 55
Tinos, Grc D5 23
Tinos, isl., Grc D5 23
Tinqueux, Fr E5 15
Tinquipaya, Bol C2 55
Tinrhert, plat., Alg D5 44
Tinsley, Yazoo, Miss C3 100
Tinsman, Calhoun, Ark D3 81
Tinsukia, India C10 39
Tintah, Traverse, Minn D2 99
Tintigny, Bel E5 15
Tintina, Arg E3 55
Tintinara, Austl G3 51
Tin Zaouatén, Alg E5 45
Tioga, Hancock, Ill C2 90
Tioga, Rapides, La C3 95
Tioga, Williams, N. Dak A3 110
Tioga, Tioga, Pa C7 114
Tioga, Nicholas, W. Va C4 123
Tioga, co., N.Y C4 108
Tioga, co., Pa C7 114
Tioga, riv., Pa C7 114
Tiogue, lake, R.I C10 84
Tioman, isl., Mala K6 38
Tiona, Warren, Pa C3 114
Tione di Trento, It C6 18
Tionesta, Forest, Pa C3 114
Tionesta, creek, Pa C3 114
Tionesta Lake, res., Pa C2 114
Tioughnioga, riv., N.Y C4 108
Tipler, Florence, Wis C5 124
Tiplersville, Tippah, Miss A5 100
Tippah, co., Miss A5 100
Tipp City, Miami, Ohio C1 111
Tippecanoe, Marshall, Ind B5 91
Tippecanoe, co., Ind D4 91
Tippecanoe, riv., Ind C4 91
Tipperary, Ire E3 11
Tipperary, co., Ire E3 11
Tippo, Tallahatchie, Miss B3 100
Tipton, Tulare, Calif D4 82
Tipton, Tipton, Ind D5 91
Tipton, Cedar, Iowa C6 92
Tipton, Mitchell, Kans C5 93
Tipton, Moniteau, Mo C5 101
Tipton, Tillman, Okla C2 112
Tipton, Tipton, Tenn B2 117
Tipton, co., Ind D5 91
Tipton, co., Tenn B2 117
Tipton, mtn., Ariz B1 80
Tiptonville, Lake, Tenn A2 117
Tiptop, Tazewell, Va C1, e10 121
Tip Top, mtn., Ont., Can o18 72
Tiquisate, Guat C2 62
Tirān, isl., Sau. Ar I10 31
Tiranë (Tirana), Alb B2 23
Tiranë (Tirana), pref., Alb *B2 23
Tirano, It A3 21
Tiraque Chico, Bol C2 55
Tiraspol, Sov. Un H7 27
Tirat Karmel, Isr B6 32
Tirat Ẕevi, Isr B7 32
Tire, Tur C6 23
Tirebolu, Tur B12 31
Tiree, isl., Scot D2 13
Tire Hill, Somerset, Pa F4 114
Tîrgovişte, Rom C7 22
Tîrgu-Frumos, Rom B8 22
Tîrgu-Jiu, Rom C6 22
Tîrgu-Mureş, Rom B7 22
Tîrgu-Neamţ, Rom B8 22
Tîrgu-Ocna, Rom B8 22
Tîrgu-Secuesc, Rom B8 22
Tiriro, Guinea D3 45
Tirlyanskiy, Sov. Un E20 9
Tîrnava Mică, riv., Rom B7 22
Tîrnăveni, Rom B7 22
Tirnavos, Grc C4 23
Tiro, Crawford, Ohio B3 111
Tirol, state, Aus B7 18
Tirol, reg., Aus E5 16
Tirschenreuth, F.R.G D7 17
Tirso, riv., It D2 21
Tirstrup, Den B4 24
Tiruchchirāppalli, India F6 39
Tirunelveli, India G6 39
Tiruppur, India *F6 39
Tisa, riv., Yugo C5 22
Tisaren, lake, Swe t33 25
Tisch Mills, Manitowoc, Wis h10 124
Tisdale, Sask., Can E3 70
Tishomingo, Tishomingo, Miss A5 100
Tishomingo, Johnston, Okla C5 112
Tishomingo, co., Miss A5 100
Tiskilwa Bureau, Ill B4 90
Tisnaren, lake, Swe u33 25
Tisonia, Duval, Fla B5 86
Tista, riv., India D12 40
Tisvildeleje, Den B6 24
Tisza, riv., Hung B5 22
Tiszafured, Hung B5 22
Tiszakecske, Hung B5 22
Titāgarh, India *F12 40
Titicaca, lake, Bol., Peru C2 55
Titicus, Fairfield, Conn D3 84
Titicus, res., N.Y D2 84
Titograd, Yugo D4 22
Titonka, Kossuth, Iowa A3 92
Titovo Užice, Yugo D4 22
Titov Veles, Yugo E5 22
Titule, Zaire A4 48
Titus, co., Tex C5 118
Titus, mtn., Conn B3 84
Titusville, Brevard, Fla D6 86
Titusville, Mercer, N.J C3 106
Titusville, Crawford, Pa C2 114
Tiuggi, is., Mala K6 38
Tivaouane, Sen D1 45
Tiverton, N.S., Can E3 74
Tiverton, Ont., Can C3 72
Tiverton, Eng D4 12
Tiverton, Newport, R.I C12 84
Tiverton Four Corners, Newport, R.I C12 84
Tivoli, It D4, h9 21
Tivoli, Dutchess, N.Y C7 108
Tivoli, Refugio, Tex E4 118
Tixtla, Mex o14 63
Tiyo, Eth C5 47
Tizapán, Mex h9 63
Tizimín, Mex C7 63
Tizi-Ouzou, Alg B5 44
Tiznit, Mor D3 44
Tjeukemeer, lake, Neth B5 15
Tjina, cape, Indon F2 35
Tlacolula, Mex D5 63
Tlacotalpan, Mex D5 63
Tlacotepec, Mex o14 63
Tláhuac, Mex h9 63
Tlahualilo de Zaragoza, Mex B4 63
Tlalnepantla, Mex g9 63
Tlalnepantla, riv., Mex g9 63
Tlalpan, Mex h9 63
Tlalpujahua, Mex n13 63
Tlaltenco, Mex h9 63
Tlapa, Mex o14 63
Tlapacoyan, Mex n15 63
Tlapaneco, riv., Mex o14 63
Tlaquepaque (San Pedro Tlaquepaque), Mex m12 63
Tlaxcala, Mex D5, n14 63
Tlaxcala, state, Mex D5 63
Tlaxco, Mex n14 63
Tlaxiaco, Mex D5 63
Tlemcen, Alg G6 30, C4 44
Tluszcz, Pol k14 26
Tmassah, Libya D3 43
To, isl., Jap I9 37
Toa Alta, mun., P.R *B3 65
Toa Baja, mun., P.R *B3 65
Toadlena, San Juan, N. Mex A1 107
Toamasina, Mad g9 49
Toano, James City, Va C6 121
Toast, Surry, N.C A2 109
Toay, Arg B4 54
Toba, Jap o15 37
Toba, inlet, B.C., Can D5 68
Toba, lake, Indon m11 35
Toba, riv., B.C., Can D5 68
Tobacco Root, mts., Mont E5 102
Tobago, isl., Trin M24 65
Tobago, is., St. Vincent V26 65
Tobarra, Sp C5 20
Tobaru, Okinawa 52
Tobercurry, Ire C3 11
Tobermory, Ont., Can B3 72
Tobermory, Scot D2 13
Tobi, isl., Jap G9 37
Tobias, Saline, Nebr D8 103
Tobin, lake, Sask., Can D4 70
Tobin, mtn., Nev C4 104
Tobinsport, Perry, Ind I4 91
Tobique, riv., N.B., Can B2 74
Tobol, Sov. Un C6 29
Tobol, riv., Sov. Un E21 9
Tobolsk, Sov. Un B7 29
Tobruk, see Ţubruq, Libya
Tobushi, pt., Iwo 52
Toby, mtn., Mass B2 84
Tobyhanna, Monroe, Pa D11 114
Tocantinópolis, Braz C1 57
Tocantins, riv., Braz C1 57
Toccoa, Stephens, Ga B3 87
Toccoa Falls, Stephens, Ga B3 87
Toccopola, Pontotoc, Miss A4 100
Toce, riv., It C4 18
Tochcha, lake, B.C., Can B5 68
Tochigi, Jap H9, m18 37
Tochigi, pref., Jap *H9 37
Tocito, San Juan, N. Mex A1 107
Toco, Trin N24 65
Tocoa, Hond C4 62
Tocopilla, Chile D1 55
Tocorpuri, hill, Bol D2 55
Tocsin, Wells, Ind C7 91
Tocúmen, Pan F8, k12 62
Tocumwal, Austl G5 51
Tocuyo, riv., Ven A4 60
Todd, Ashe and Watauga, N.C A1 109
Todd, co., Ky D2 94
Todd, co., Minn D4 99
Todd, co., S. Dak D5 116
Todd, fork, Ohio C1 111
Todd, riv., Austl D6 50
Toddville, Dorchester, Md D5 85
Toddy, pond, Maine D4 96
Todi, It C4 21
Tödi, mtn, Switz C6 19
Todoga, cape, Jap G11 37
Todos os Santos, bay, Braz D3 57
Todos Santos, Bol C2 55
Todos Santos, Mex C2 63
Todtnau, F.R.G B3 18
Toe, head, Ire F2 11
Toe, head, Scot C1 13
Toecane, Mitchell, N.C e10 109
Tofield, Alta., Can C4 69
Tofino, B.C., Can E5 68
Tofte, Cook, Minn C8, k9 99
Toftlund, Den C3 24
Togiak, Alsk D7 79
Togian, is., Indon F6 35
Togo, Sask., Can F5 70
Togo, country, Afr F6 42, E5 45
Toguchi, Okinawa 52
Tohakum, peak, Nev C2 104
Tohatchi, McKinley, N. Mex B1 107
Tohickon, creek, Pa C2 106
Tohopekaliga, lake, Fla D5 86
Toi, cape, Jap K5 37
Toivola, Houghton, Mich B2 98
Toivola, St. Louis, Minn C6 99
Toiyabe, range, Nev E4 104
Tok, Alsk C11 79
Tokaj, Hung A5 22
Tokara, is., Jap L4 37
Tokara, strait, Jap K5 37
Tokat, Tur B11 31
Tokeland, Pacific, Wash C2 122
Tokelau Islands, N.Z., dep., Oceania G11 7
Tokenon, Kor G3 37
Toki, Jap *I8 37
Toki, pt., Wake Isl 52
Tokio, Hempstead, Ark C2 81
Tokio, Benson, N. Dak B7 110
Tokio, Terry, Tex C1 118
Tokmak, Sov. Un E9 29
Tokoname, Jap *I8 37
Tokorosawa, Jap *I9 37
Tokoto, China C7 36
Tokuno, isl., Ryukyu Is F10 34
Tokushima, Jap I7 37
Tokushima, pref., Jap *I7 37
Tokuyama, Jap I5 37
Tōkyō, Jap I9, n18 37
Tōkyō, pref., Jap *I9 37
Tōkyō, bay, Jap n18 37
Tokzār, Afg D13 41
Tol, isl., Truk 52
Tolar, Roosevelt, N. Mex C6 107
Tolbukhin (Dobrich), Bul D8 22
Toleak, pt., Wash B1 122
Toledo, Ont., Can C8 72
Toledo, Cumberland, Ill D5 90
Toledo, Tama, Iowa C5 92
Toledo, Lucas, Ohio A2, e6 111
Toledo, Lincoln, Oreg C3 113
Toledo, Sp C3 20
Toledo, Lewis, Wash C3 122
Toledo, prov., Sp *C3 20
Toledo, mts., Sp C3 20
Toler, Pike, Ky C7 94
Tolga, Alg C6 44
Toliara, Mad h8 49
Tolima, dept. Col C2 60
Tolima, vol., Col C2 60
Tolimán, Mex m14 63
Tolken, lake, Swe A6 24
Tolland, Tolland, Conn B7 84
Tolland, co., Conn B7 84
Tollense, lake, G.D.R E7 24
Tollense, riv., G.D.R E7 24
Tollesboro, Lewis, Ky B6 94
Tolleson, Maricopa, Ariz m8 80
Tollette, Howard, Ark D2 81
Tolley, Renville, N. Dak A4 110
Tollhouse, Fresno, Calif D4 82
Tolloche, Arg E3 55
Tollville, Prairie, Ark C4 81
Tolmezzo, It A4 21
Tolmin, Yugo B1 22
Tolna, Hung B4 22
Tolna, Nelson, N. Dak B7 110
Tolna, co., Hung *B4 22
Tolo, Jackson, Oreg E4 113
Tolo, gulf, Indon F6 35
Tolocolme, peak, Ponape 52
Tolona, Champaign, Ill D5 90
Tolosa, Sp A4 20
Tolovana Park, Clatsop, Oreg B3 113
Tolsta, head, Scot B2 13
Tolstoi, Man., Can E3 71
Tolstoy, Potter, S. Dak B6 116
Tolten, Chile B2 54
Tolt-Seattle Water Supply, res., Wash B4 122
Tolu, Crittenden, Ky e9 94
Tolú, Col B2 60
Toluca, Marshall, Ill B4 90
Toluca, Mex D5, n14 63
Tolun, China C8 34
Tolyatti, Sov. Un C3 29
Tom, mtn., Conn C3 84
Tom, riv., Sov. Un E26 9
Tomah, Monroe, Wis E3 124
Tomahawk, Lincoln, Wis C4 124
Tomahawk, lake, Wis C4 124
Tomakomai, Jap E10 37
Tomakovka, Sov. Un H10 27
Tomar, Port C1 20
Tomari, Sov. Un C11 37
Tomaszow Lubelski, Pol C7 26
Tomaszow Mazowiecki, Pol C6 26
Tomatlán, Mex D3, n11 63
Tomato, Mississippi, Ark B6 81
Tomave, Bol D2 55
Tombador, mts., Braz C1 57
Tomball, Harris, Tex D5 118
Tombigbee, riv., Ala., Miss B5 100
Tombouctou (Timbuktu), Mali C4 45
Tombstone, Cochise, Ariz F5 80
Tombstone, mtn., Yukon, Can D5 66
Tomé, Chile B2 54
Tome, Valencia, N. Mex C3 107
Tomelilla, Swe C7 24
Tomelloso, Sp C4 20
Tom Green, co., Tex D2 118
Tomichi, creek, Colo C4 83
Tomini, gulf, Indon E6 35
Tomintoul, Scot C5 13
Tomkins Cove, Rockland, N.Y D6, m14 108
Tommot, Sov. Un D15 28
Tom Nevers, head, Mass D7 97
Tomnolen, Webster, Miss B4 100
Tomo, riv., Col B3 60
Tompkins, Newf., Can E2 75
Tompkins Sask., Can G1 70
Tompkins, co., N.Y C4 108
Tompkinsville, Monroe, Ky D4 94
Tompkinsville, Charles, Md D4 85
Tom Price, Austl D2 50
Tom Price, mtn., Austl D2 50
Toms, riv., N.J C4 106
Toms Creek, Wise, Va f9 121
Tomsk, Sov. Un B11 29
Toms River, Ocean, N.J D4 106
Tomy Town, Adair, Okla B7 112
Tonalá, Mex D6 63
Tonalea, Coconino, Ariz A5 80
Tonasket, Okanogan, Wash A6 122
Tonawanda, Erie, N.Y B2 108
Tonawanda, Indian res., N.Y B2 108
Tonbridge, Eng C8 12
Tondano, Indon E6 35
Tønder, Den D3 24
Tondī, salt lake, Afg E10 41
Toney, Madison, Ala A3 78
Tonga, country, Oceania H11 7
Tonganoxie, Leavenworth, Kans C8, k15 93
Tongareva, isl., Pac. O G12 7
Tongeren, Bel D5 15
Tongjoson, bay, Kor G3 37
Tongoi, Chile F1 55
Tongue, Scot B4 13
Tongue, riv., Mont., Wyo E10 102
Tonica, La Salle, Ill B4 90
Tónichi, Mex B3 63
Tonj, Sud D2 47
Tonk, India C6 39, D5 40
Tonka Bay, Hennepin, Minn *F5 99
Tonkawa, Kay, Okla A4 112
Tonkin, reg., Viet B6 38
Tonkin, gulf, Asia C7 38
Tonle Sap, lake, Kam F5 38
Tonneins, Fr E4 14
Tonnerre, Fr D5 14
Tönning, F.R.G D3 24
Tonoloway, ridge, Md A1 85
Tonopah, Nye, Nev E4 104
Tonosí, Pan G7 62
Tonpah, Maricopa, Ariz D3 80
Tonquin, Washington, Oreg B2 113
Tönsberg, Nor H4, p28 25
Tontitown, Washington, Ark A1 81
Tonto, natural bridge, Ariz C4 80
Tonto, nat. mon., Ariz D4 80
Tonto Basin, Gila, Ariz D4 80
Tontogany, Wood, Ohio f6 111
Tonton, Phil n13 35
Tony, Rusk, Wis C3 124
Tooele, Tooele, Utah C3 119
Tooele, co., Utah C3 119
Toole, co., Mont B5 102
Toombs, co., Ga D4 87
Toomevara, Ire E3 11
Toomsboro, Wilkinson, Ga D3 87
Toomsuba, Lauderdale, Miss C5 100
Toone, Hardeman, Tenn B3 117
Toormakeady, Ire D2 11
Toowoomba, Austl E8 51
Top, Grant, Oreg C7 113
Top, pond, Newf., Can E3 75
Topawa, Pima, Ariz F4 80
Topaz, Mono, Calif C4 82
Topaz Ranch Estates, Douglas, Nev *E2 104
Topeka, Lagrange, Ind A6 91
Topeka, Shawnee, Kans C8, k14 93
Topinabee, Cheboygan, Mich C6 98
Topki, Sov. Un B11 29
Topley, B.C., Can B4 68
Toplica, riv., Yugo D5 22
Topock, Mohave, Ariz C1 80
Topol'čany, Czech D5 26
Topolia, Grc g10 23
Topolnitsa, riv., Bul D7 22
Topolobampo, Mex B3 63
Topolovgrad, Bul D8 22
Toponas, Routt, Colo A4 83
Topozero, lake, Sov. Un E14 25
Toppenish, Yakima, Wash C5 122
Toppenish, ridge, Wash C5 122
Topsail, Newf., Can *E5 75
Topsfield, Washington, Maine C5 96
Topsfield, Essex, Mass A6 97
Topsham, Sagadahoc, Maine E3, g8 96
Topsham, Orange, Vt C4 120
Topton, Lauderdale, Miss C5 100
Topton, Berks, Pa C5 114
Toquerville, Washington, Utah F2 119
Toquima, range, Nev E4 104
Tor, Eg H9 31
Tor, bay, Eng D4 12
Torbali, Tur C6 23
Torbat-e Ḩeydarīyeh, Iran D9 41
Torbat-e Jām, Iran D10 41
Torbay, Newf., Can E5 75
Torbert, mtn., Alsk g15 79
Torbreck, mtn., Austl H5 51
Torbrook, N.S., Can E5 74
Torcello, It D8 18
Torch, lake, Mich D5 98
Torch, riv., Sask., Can C4 70
Torekov, Swe B6 24
Torez, Sov. Un q21 27
Torgau, G.D.R B7 17
Torhout, Bel C3 15
Tori, isl., Jap J4 37
Toride, Jap n19 37
Torino, see Turin, It.
Torit, Sud E3 47
Tórmes, riv., Sp B2 20
Tornado, mtn., Alta., B.C., Can E3 69
Torneälven, riv., Swe D10 25
Torneträsk, lake, Swe C9 25
Torngat, mts., Newf., Can f8 75
Tornillo, El Paso, Tex o11 118
Tornio, Fin E11 25
Tornquist, Arg B4 54
Toro, Sabine, La C2 95
Toro, Sp B3 20
Torö, Swe u35 25
Toro, lake, Que., Can C4 73
Toro, peak, Calif F5 82
Toroi, Mong C4 36
Törökszentmiklós, Hung B5 22
Toronto, Ont., Can D5, m15 72
Toronto, Woodson, Kans E8 93
Toronto, Jefferson, Ohio B5 111
Toronto, Deuel, S. Dak C9 116
Toronto Lake, res., Kans E7 93
Toropets, Sov. Un C8 27
Tororo, Ug A5 48
Torote, riv., Sp o18 20
Torpsbruk, Swe A8 24
Torquay, Sask., Can H4 70
Torquay (Torbay), Eng D4 12
Torr, head, N. Ire B5 11
Torrance, Los Angeles, Calif n12 82
Torrance, Ont., Can C5 72
Torrance, co., N. Mex C3 107
Torre Annunziata, It D5 21
Torrecilla, mtn., P.R B3 65
Torre de Cerredo, mtn., Sp A3 20
Torre del Greco, It D5 21
Torredonjimeno, Sp D4 20
Torrejoncillo, Sp C2 20
Torrejón de Ardoz, Sp p18 20
Torrelavega, Sp A3 20
Torremaggiore, It D5 21
Torrens, lake, Austl F6 50
Torrente, Sp C5 20
Torreon, Mex B4 63
Torreon, Torrance, N. Mex C3 107
Torre Pacheco, Sp D5 20
Tôrres, Braz D3 56
Torres, strait, Pap A7 50
Torres Novas, Port C1 20
Torres Vedras, Port C1 20
Torrevieja, Sp D5 20
Torrey, Wayne, Utah E4 119
Torridge, riv., Eng D3 12
Torridon, inlet, Scot C3 13
Torriglia, It E5 18
Tørring, Den C3 24
Torrington, Alta., Can D4 69
Torrington, Litchfield, Conn B4 84
Torrington, Eng D3 12
Torrington, Goshen, Wyo D8 125
Torrinha, Braz m7 56
Torrowangee, Austl E3 51
Torrox, Sp D4 20
Tors Cove, Newf., Can E5 75
Torshälla, Swe t34 25
Tortilla Flat, Maricopa, Ariz D4 80
Tortola, isl., Vir. Is. (Br.) B6 65
Tortona, It B2 21
Tortosa, Sp B6 20
Tortosa, cape, Sp B6 20
Tortue, isl., Hai D7 64
Tortuga, isl., Ven A4 60
Torun, Pol B5 26
Torup, Swe B7 24
Tory, isl., Ire B3 11
Tory, sound, Ire B3 11
Tory Hill, Ont., Can C6 72
Torysa, riv., Czech D6 26
Torzhok, Sov. Un C10 27
Torzym, Pol A10 17
Toscana, pol. dist., It *C3 21
Tosno, Sov. Un B8 27
Tostado, Arg E3 55
Toston, Broadwater, Mont D5 102
Tosya, Tur B10 31
Toszek, Pol g9 26
Totagatic, riv., Wis B2 124
Totana, Sp D5 20
Toteng, Bots B3 49
Totkomlos, Hung B5 22
Totnes, Eng D4 12
Totness, Sur A3 59
Totó, Guam 52
Totomi, sea, Jap o16 37
Totonicapan, Guat C2 62
Totorapalca, Bol C2 55
Totowa, Passaic, N.J B4 106
Totoya, isl., Fiji 52
Totten, glacier, Ant C24 5
Tottenham, Austl F6 51
Tottenham, Ont., Can C5 72
Tottenham, Eng., (part of London) k12 10
Tottori, Jap I7 37
Tottori, pref., Jap *I7 37
Totz, Harlan, Ky D6 94
Touba, I.C E3 45
Touba, Sen D1 45
Toubkal, mtn., Mor C3 44
Touchet, Walla Walla, Wash C7 122
Touchet, riv., Wash C8 122
Touchwood, lake, Man., Can B4 71
Tougaloo, Hinds, Miss C3 100
Tougan, Upper Volta D4 45
Touggourt, Alg C6 44
Touggourt, reg., Alg C6 44
Tougué, Guinea D2 45
Tougy, Saunders, Nebr C9 103
Touisset, Bristol, Mass C5 97
Toul, Fr C6 14
Toulépleu, I.C E3 45
Toulon, Fr F6 14
Toulon, Stark, Ill B4 90
Toulouse, Fr F4 14
Toungo, Nig E7 45
Toungoo, Bur E10 39
Tounin, Alg F7 30
Touraine, former prov., Fr D4 14
Tourane, see Da Nang, Viet.
Tourcoing, Fr B5 14, D3 15
Tourlaville, Fr C3 14
Tournai, Bel D3 15
Tournon [-sur-Rhône], Fr E6 14
Tournus, Fr D6 14
Touros, Braz C3 57
Tours, Fr D4 14
Tourville, Que., Can B8 73
Toussaint, creek, Ohio f7 111
Tovar, Ven B3 60
Tovey (Humphrey), Christian, Ill D4 90
Tow, Llano, Tex D3 118
Towaco, Morris, N.J B4 106
Towada, lake, Jap F10 37
Towanda, McLean, Ill C5 90
Towanda, Butler, Kans E7, g13 93
Towanda, Bradford, Pa C9 114
Towanda, creek, Pa C8 114
Towaoc, Montezuma, Colo D2 83
Tower, Cheboygan, Mich C6 98
Tower, St. Louis, Minn C6 99
Tower City, Cass, N. Dak C8 110
Tower City, Schuylkill, Pa E8 114
Tower Hill, Shelby, Ill D5 90
Town, creek, Md k13 85
Town, fork, Ohio f8 123
Town, hill, Bermuda p20 64
Town, hill, Md k13 85
Town and Country, St. Louis, Mo *C7 101
Town Creek, Lawrence, Ala A2 78
Towner, Kiowa, Colo C8 83
Towner, McHenry, N. Dak A5 110
Towner, co., N. Dak A6 110
Townley, Walker, Ala B2 78
Town of Tonawanda, Erie, N.Y *C2 108
Town Point, Cecil, Md B6 85
Towns, Telfair, Ga D4 87
Towns, co., Ga B3 87
Townsend, New Castle, Del B6 85
Townsend, McIntosh, Ga E5 87
Townsend, Middlesex, Mass A4 97
Townsend, Broadwater, Mont D5 102
Townsend, Blount, Tenn D10 117
Townsend, Northampton, Va C7 121
Townshend, Windham, Vt E3 120
Townshend, res., Vt E3 120
Townsville, Austl C8 50
Townsville, Vance, N.C A4 109
Townville, Crawford, Pa C2 114
Townville, Anderson, S.C B2 115
Towrzī, Afg F12 41
Towson, Baltimore, Md B4, g11 85
Towuti, lake, Indon F6 35
Toxey, Choctaw, Ala D1 78
Toyah, Reeves, Tex o13 118
Toyahvale, Reeves, Tex o13 118
Toyama, Jap H8 37
Toyama, pref., Jap *H8 37
Toyama, bay, Jap H8 37
Toyohashi, Jap I8, o16 37
Toyohira, Jap *E10 37
Toyokawa, Jap *o16 37
Toyonaka, Jap I7, o14 37
Tozeur, Tun C6 44
Tozghi, mtn., Pak G11 41
Trabancos, riv., Sp B3 20
Traben-Trarbach, F.R.G D2 17
Trabzon (Trebizond), Tur B12 31
Tracadie, N.B., Can B5 74
Tracadie, N.S., Can D8 74
Tracadie, riv., N.B., Can B4 74
Tracadie Cross, P.E.I., Can *C7 74
Tracy, San Joaquin, Calif D3, h10 82
Tracy, N.B., Can D3 74
Tracy, Que., Can C4 73
Tracy, New Haven, Conn. (part of Wallingford) C5 84
Tracy, Marion, Iowa C5 92
Tracy, Lyon, Minn F3 99
Tracy, Platte, Mo h10 101
Tracy City, Grundy, Tenn D8 117
Tracys, creek, Md C4 85
Tracyton, Kitsap, Wash e10 122
Trade, Johnson, Tenn C12 117
Trade, lake, Sask., Can B4 70
Tradewater, riv., Ky C2 94
Trading Post, Linn., Kans D9 93
Traer, Tama, Iowa B5 92
Traer, Decatur, Kans C3 93
Trafalgar, Johnson, Ind F5 91
Trafford, Westmoreland and Allegheny, Pa k14 114
Trafford, lake, Fla F5 86
Traiguén, Chile B2 54
Trail, B.C., Can E9, o19 68
Trail, Polk, Minn C3 99
Trail, Jackson, Oreg E4 113
Trail, ridge, Ga F4 87
Trail City, Dewey, S. Dak B5 116
Trail Creek, LaPorte, Ind A5 91
Traill, co., N. Dak B8 110
Traill, isl., Grnld B17 4
Traipu, Braz C3 57
Trairi, riv., Braz h6 57
Tralee, Ire E2 11
Tramelan Dessus, Switz B3 19

Victoria, Chile B2 54
Victoria, Grenada W25 65
Victoria, Hong Kong G7 34
Victoria, Knox, Ill B3 90
Victoria, Ellis, Kans D4 93
Victoria, Marshall, Miss A4 100
Victoria, Jefferson, Mo C7 101
Victoria, Phil o13 35
Victoria, Seychelles *G24 3
Victoria, Marion, Tenn D8 117
Victoria, Victoria, Tex E4 118
Victoria, Lunenburg, Va C4 121
Victoria, co., N.B., Can B2 74
Victoria, co., N.S., Can C9 74
Victoria, co., Ont., Can C6 72
Victoria, co., Tex E4 118
Victoria, state, Austl G7 51
Victoria, falls, Zambia, Zimb A4 49
Victoria, isl., N.W. Ter., Can B10 66
Victoria, lake, Afr B5 48
Victoria, lake, Austl F3 51
Victoria, lake, Newf., Can D3 75
Victoria, mtn., Pap. N. Gui k12 50
Victoria, peak, Belize B3 62
Victoria, riv., Austl C5 50
Victoria, riv., Newf., Can D3 75
Victoria, strait, N.W. Ter., Can C12 66
Victoria Beach, Man., Can D3 71
Victoria de las Tunas, Cuba D5 64
Victoria Falls, Zimb A4 49
Victoria Harbour, Ont., Can C5 72
Victoria Land, reg., Ant B29 5
Victoria Mine, Ont., Can A3 72
Victoria Park, Los Angeles, Calif *F2 82
Victoria Road, Ont., Can C6 72
Victoriaville, Que., Can C6 73
Victoria West, S. Afr D3 49
Victorica, Arg B3 54
Victorino de la Plaza, Arg B4 54
Victor Mills, Spartanburg, S.C *B3 115
Victorville, San Bernardino, Calif E5 82
Victory (Town of), Essex, Vt *C5 120
Victory, Vernon, Wis E2 124
Victory Gardens, Morris, N.J *B3 106
Victory Heights, Chemung, N.Y *C4 108
Vicuña, Chile F1 55
Vida, McCone, Mont C11 102
Vidalia, Toombs, Ga D4 87
Vidalia, Concordia, La C4 95
Vidette, Burke, Ga C4 87
Vidin, Bul D6 22
Vidisha, India F6 40
Vidor, Orange, Tex D5 118
Vidora, Sask., Can H1 70
Viechtach, F.R.G D7 17
Viedma, Arg C4 54
Vieja, peak, Tex F2 118
Vielsalm, Bel D5 15
Vienenburg, F.R.G B5 17
Vienna (Wien), Aus D8 16
Vienna, Ont., Can E4 72
Vienna, Dooly, Ga D3 87
Vienna, Johnson, Ill F5 90
Vienna, Dorchester, Md D6 85
Vienna, Maries, Mo C6 101
Vienna, Warren, N.J B3 106
Vienna, Clark, S. Dak C8 116
Vienna, Fairfax, Va B5, g12 121
Vienna, Wood, W. Va B3 123
Vienne, Fr E6 14
Vienne, dept., Fr *D4 14
Vienne, riv., Fr D4 14
Vientiane, Laos D5 38
Vieques, P.R B5 65
Vieques, mun., P.R *B5 65
Vieques, isl., P.R B5 65
Vieques, passage, P.R B4 65
Vieques, sound, P.R B4 65
Viernheim, F.R.G D3 17
Viersen, F.R.G C6 15
Vierzon, Fr D5 14
Viesca, Mex B4 63
Vieste, It D6 21
Vietnam, country, Asia E8 38, H13 33
Vieux Fort, St. Lucia J14 64
Vieux-Fort, pt., Guad R8 65
View Park, Los Angeles, Calif *E4 82
Vigan, Phil B6 35
Vigevano, It B2 21
Vignola, It E7 18
Vigo, Sp A1 20
Vigo, co., Ind F3 91
Vigsø, bay, Den A2 24
Vihowa, Pak B5 39, B3 40
Vijayapuri, India *E6 39
Vijayawāda, India E7 39
Vik, Ice o23 25
Viken, Swe B6 24
Vikesund, Nor p27 25
Viking, Alta., Can C5 69
Viking, Marshall, Minn B2 99
Vikramasingapuram, India *G6 39
Vila, New Hebr *H10 7
Vila Cabral, Moz D6 48
Vila da Feira, Port B1 20
Vila de Manica, Moz A5 49
Vila de Rei, Port C1 20
Vila do Conde, Port B1 20
Vila Fontes, Moz A6 49
Vila Franca de Xira, Port C1 20
Vila Junqueiro, Moz A6 49
Vilaine, riv., Fr D2 14
Vilanculos, Moz B6 49
Vila Nova de Foz Coa, Port B2 20
Vila Nova de Gaia, Port B1 20
Vila Nova de Milfontes, Port D1 20
Vila Nova de Seles, Ang D1 48
Vila Pery, Moz A5 49
Vila Real, Port B2 20
Vila Real de Santo António, Port D2 20
Vilas, Baca, Colo D8 83
Vilas, Liberty, Fla B2 86
Vilas, Miner, S. Dak C8 116
Vilas, co., Wis B4 124
Vila Vasco da Gama, Moz D5 48
Vila Viçosa, Port C2 20
Vila Vila, Bol C2 55
Vildbjerg, Den B2 24
Vildo, Hardeman, Tenn B2 117
Vileyka, Sov. Un D6 27
Vilhelmina, Swe E7 25
Viljandi, Sov. Un B5 27
Vilkaviskis, Sov. Un A7 26
Vilkitsky, isl., Sov. Un B7 4
Vilkovo, Sov. Un I7 27
Villa Acuña, Mex B4 63
Villa Ahumada, Mex A3 63
Villa Alhucemas, Mor G5 30
Villa Angela, Arg E3 55
Villa Aroma, Bol C2 55
Villa Bella, Bol B2 55
Villablino, Sp A2 20
Villacañas, Sp C4 20
Villacarrillo, Sp C4 20
Villach, Aus E6 16
Villacidro, It E2 21
Villa Cisneros, W. Sahara E1 44
Villa Constitución, Arg A4 54
Villa Crespo, Arg A4 54
Villa Cuauhtémoc, Mex k15 63
Villa de Cura, Ven A4 60
Villa del Rosario, Arg A4 54
Villa Dolores, Arg A3 54
Villafamés, Sp C5 20
Villa Federal, Arg A5 54
Villafranca, It B3 21
Villafranca del Bierzo, Sp A2 20
Villafranca de los Barros, Sp C2 20
Villafranca del Panadés, Sp B6 20
Villafranca di Verona, It D6 18
Villa García, Mex k13 63
Villagarcía de Arosa, Sp A1 20
Village, Columbia, Ark D2 81
Village, Richmond, Va C6 121
Village, creek, Ala E4 78
Village-Richelieu, Que., Can *D4 73
Village Springs, Blount, Ala B3 78
Villa Grove, Saguache, Colo C5 83
Villa Grove, Douglas, Ill D5 90
Villaguay, Arg A5 54
Villa Hayes, Par E4 55
Villa Heights, Prince Georges, Md *C4 85
Villahermosa, Mex D6 63
Villa Huidobro, Arg A4 54
Villa Iris, Arg B4 54
Villajoyosa, Sp C5 20
Villalba, Sp A2 20
Villalba, mun., P.R C5 65
Villaldama, Mex B4 63
Villalonga, Arg B4 54
Villalpando, Sp B3 20
Villa María, Arg A4 54
Villamartín, Sp D3 20
Villamil, Ec g5 58
Villa Montes, Bol D3 55
Villanova, Delaware, Pa *A10 114
Villanueva, Col A3 60
Villanueva, San Miguel, N. Mex B4 107
Villanueva de Córdoba, Sp C3 20
Villanueva del Arzobispo, Sp C4 20
Villanueva de la Serena, Sp C3 20
Villanueva [del Río y Minas], Sp D3 20
Villanueva y Geltrú, Sp B6 20
Villa Obregón, Mex h9 63
Villa Oliva, Par E4 55
Villa Park, DuPage, Ill k9 90
Villa Pedro Montoya, Mex m14 63
Villaputzu, It E2 21
Villard, Pope, Minn E3 99
Villard-Bonnot, Fr E6 14
Villa Rica, Carroll and Douglas, Ga C1 87
Villa Ridge, Pulaski, Ill F4 90
Villa Ridge, Franklin, Mo C7 101
Villarreal, Sp C5 20
Villarrica, Chile B2 54
Villarrica, Par E4 55
Villarrobledo, Sp C4 20
Villarrubia, Sp C4 20
Villars-le-Terroir, Switz D3 19
Villas, Cape May, N.J E3 106
Villa Unión, Arg E2 55
Villa Unión, Mex C3 63
Villa Valeria, Arg A4 54
Villavicencio, Col C3 60
Villaviciosa, Sp A3 20
Villazon, Bol D2 55
Villazón, Bol D3 55
Villé, Fr C7 14
Villefranche [-de-Rouergue], Fr E5 14
Villefranche-sur-Saône, Fr E6 14
Villegreen, Las Animas, Colo D7 83
Villejuif, Fr g10 14
Ville Marie, Que., Can p20 73
Villemomble, Fr g10 14
Villena, Sp C5 20
Villeneuve-la-Garenne, Fr F3 15
Villeneuve, Que., Can *C6 73
Villeneuve-le-Roi, Fr h10 14
Villeneuve-St. Georges, Fr h10 14
Villeneuve-sur-Lot, Fr E4 14
Villeneuve-sur-Yonne, Fr C5 14
Villepinte, Fr g11 14
Ville Platte, Evangeline, La D3 95
Villeroy, Que., Can C6 73
Villers-Bretonneux, Fr C5 14
Villers-Cotterêts, Fr C5 14
Villers-Outréaux, Fr D3 15
Villers-Semeuse, Fr C6 14
Villerupt, Fr C6 14
Ville St. Georges, Que., Can C7 73
Villeta, Par E4 55
Villeurbanne, Fr E6 14
Villia, Grc g10 23
Villingen, F.R.G D4 16
Villisca, Montgomery, Iowa D3 92
Vilna, Alta., Can B5 69
Vilnius, Sov. Un D5 27
Vilonia, Faulkner, Ark B3 81
Vilppula, Fin F11 25
Vils, riv., F.R.G E7 17
Vils, riv., F.R.G D6 17
Vilsbiburg, F.R.G E7 17
Vilseck, F.R.G D6 17
Vilshofen, F.R.G E8 17
Vilvoorde, Bel D4 15
Vilyuy, riv., Sov. Un C15 28
Vilyuysk, Sov. Un C14 28
Vimianzo, Sp A1 20
Vimmerby, Swe I6 25
Vimperk, Czech D2 26
Vina, Franklin, Ala A1 78
Vina, Tehama, Calif C2 82
Viña del Mar, Chile A2 54
Vinalhaven, Knox, Maine D4 96
Vinalhaven, isl., Maine D4 96
Vinaroz, Sp B6 20
Vincennes, Fr g10 14
Vincennes, Knox, Ind G2 91
Vincennes, bay, Ant C24 5
Vincent, Shelby, Ala B3 78
Vincent, Crittenden, Ark e9 117
Vincent, Webster, Iowa B3 92
Vincent, Lorain, Ohio *A3 111
Vincent, Washington, Ohio C4 111
Vincent, Howard, Tex C2 118
Vincentown, Burlington, N.J D3 106
Vinces, Ec B2 58
Vinchina, Arg E2 55
Vinco, Payne, Okla B4 112
Vindelälven, riv., Swe E8 25
Vindeln, Swe E8 25
Vinderup, Den B2 24
Vindex, Garrett, Md m12 85
Vindhya, range, India F6 40
Vine, brook, Mass g11 97
Vine Grove, Hardin, Ky C4 94
Vine Hill (Martinez East) Contra Costa, Calif *C2 82
Vineland, Orange, Fla D5 86
Vineland, Cumberland, N.J E2 106
Vinemont, Cullman, Ala A3 78
Vineyard, sound, Mass D6 97
Vineyard Haven (Tisbury), Dukes, Mass D6 97
Vingåker, Swe t33 25
Vinh, Viet C6 38
Vinhais, Port B2 20
Vinh Long, Viet G6 38
Vinh Yen, Viet B6 38
Vining, Clay, Kans C6 93
Vining, Otter Tail, Minn D3 99
Vinita, Craig, Okla A6 112
Vinita Park, St. Louis, Mo *C7 101
Vinkovci, Yugo C4 22
Vinnitsa, Sov. Un G7 27
Vinson, Harmon, Okla C2 112
Vinson Massif, mtn., Ant B4 5
Vinton, Benton, Iowa B5 92
Vinton, Calcasieu, La D2 95
Vinton, Gallia, Ohio D3 111
Vinton, Roanoke, Va C3 121
Vinton, co., Ohio C3 111
Vintondale, Cambria, Pa F4 114
Viola, Fulton, Ark A4 81
Viola, Kent, Del B6 85
Viola, Latah, Idaho C1 89
Viola, Mercer, Ill B3 90
Viola, Sedgwick, Kans E6, h11 93
Viola, Warren, Tenn D8 117
Viola, Richland and Vernon, Wis E3 124
Violet, St. Bernard, La k12 95
Vipiteno, It C7 18
Virac, Phil *C6 35
Virden, Man., Can E1 71
Virden, Macoupin, Ill D4 90
Virden, Hidalgo, N. Mex E1 107
Vire, Fr C3 14
Vire, riv., Fr C3 14
Virgenes, cape, Arg E3 54
Virgil, Greenwood, Kans E7 93
Virgil, Beadle, S. Dak C7 116
Virgil, Cortland, N.Y C4 108
Virgilina, Halifax, Va D4 121
Virgin, Washington, Utah F2 119
Virgin, mts., Nev G7 104
Virgin, passage, N.A B5 65
Virgin, riv., Utah G2 119
Virgin Gorda, isl., Vir. Is. (Br) B7 65
Virginia, Bannock, Idaho G6 89
Virginia, Cass, Ill D3 90
Virginia, Ire D4 11
Virginia, St. Louis, Minn C6 99
Virginia, Gage, Nebr D9 103
Virginia, S. Afr C4 49
Virginia, state, U.S C12 77, 121
Virginia, peak, Nev D2 104
Virginia Beach (Independent City), Va D7, k16 121
Virginia City, Madison, Mont E5 102
Virginia City, Storey, Nev D2 104
Virginia Gardens, Dade, Fla *G6 86
Virgin Islands, nat. park, Vir. Is. (U.S.) *B6 65
Virgin Islands, Br. dep., N.A B6 65
Virgin Islands of the U.S., dep., N.A B6 65
Viroflay, Fr g9 14
Viroqua, Vernon, Wis E3 124
Virovitica, Yugo C3 22
Vir-Pazar, Yugo D4 22
Virrat, Fin F10 25
Virserum, Swe I6 25
Virton, Bel E5 15
Virú, Peru C2 58
Virudhunagar, India *G6 39
Vis, Yugo D3 22
Vis, isl., Yugo D3 22
Visalia, Tulare, Calif D4 82
Visalia, Kenton, Ky k14 94
Visalia North (Crowley), Tulare, Calif *D4 82
Visayan, sea, Phil C6 35
Visby, Swe I8 25
Visconde do Rio Branco, Braz C4 56
Viscount, Sask., Can F3 70
Viscount Melville, sound, N.W. Ter., Can B10 66
Visé, Bel D5 15
Višegrad, Yugo D4 22
Viseu, Braz B1 57
Viseu, Port B2 20
Vishākhapatnam, India E7 39, I9 40
Vishera, riv., Sov. Un A5 29
Vislanda, Swe B8 24
Viso, mtn., It B1 21, E3 18
Visoko, Yugo D4 22
Visp, Switz D4 19
Vista, San Diego, Calif F5 82
Vista, Man., Can D1 71
Vista, St. Clair, Mo D4 101
Vista, Washoe, Nev *D2 104
Vista Park, Kern, Calif *E4 82
Vistillas, Lake, Ore E6 113
Vita, Man., Can E3 71
Vitanovak, Yugo D5 22
Vitebsk, Sov. Un D8 27
Viterbo, It C4 21
Viti Levu, bay, Fiji 52
Viti Levu, isl., Fiji 52
Vitim, Sov. Un D14 28
Vitim, riv., Sov. Un D14 28
Vitor, Peru E3 58
Vitória, Braz F2 57
Vitória, Braz k5 57
Vitória, Braz C4 56
Vitória, Spain A4 20
Vitória da Conquista, Braz D2 57
Vitória [de Santo Antão], Braz C3, k6 57
Vitória do Mearim, Braz B2 57
Vitré, Fr C3 14
Vitry-le-François, Fr C6 14
Vitry [-sur-Seine], Fr g10 14
Vittel, Fr C6 14
Vittoria, Ont., Can E4 72
Vittoria, It F5 21
Vittorio Veneto, It B4 21
Vivero, Sp A2 20
Vivian, Caddo, La B2 95
Vivian, Lyman, S. Dak D5 116
Vivian Park, Utah, Utah C4 119
Vivoratá, Arg B5 54
Viwa, isl., Fiji 52
Vizcaíno, des., Mex B2 63
Vizcaíno, mts., Mex B2 63
Vizcaya, prov., Sp *A4 20
Vize, Tur B6 23
Vizianagaram, India E7 39, H9 40
Vizille, Fr E6 14
Viziru, Rom C8 22
Vizzini, It F5 21
Vlaardingen, Neth C4 15
Vladimir, Sov. Un B2 29
Vladimiro-Aleksandrovskoye, Sov. Un E6 37
Vladimirovo, Sov. Un D3 29
Vladimir-Volynskiy, Sov. Un F5 27
Vladivostok, Sov. Un E5 37, E16 28
Vlasenica, Yugo C4 22
Vlasim, Czech D9 17
Vlasotince, Yugo D6 22
Vlčany, Czech D4 26
Vlieland, isl., Neth A4 15
Vlissingen, Neth C3 15
Vlkava, Czech n18 26
Vlkava, riv., Czech n18 26
Vlonë (Valona), Alb B2 23
Vlonë, pref., Alb *B2 23
Vlotho, F.R.G A3 17
Vltava, riv., Czech n17 26
Voca, McCulloch, Tex D3 118
Vodlozero, lake, Sov. Un F17 25
Vodnany, Czech D9 17
Voeune Sai, Camb F7 38
Voegelkop, pen., Indon F8 35
Voghera, It B2 21
Vohenstrauss, F.R.G D7 17
Vohipeno, Mad h9 49
Voi, Ken B6 48
Void, Fr F5 15
Voiotia (Boeotia), prov., Grc *C4 23
Voiron, Fr E6 14
Voisin, lake, Sask., Can C2 70
Voitsberg, Aus E7 16
Voïvis, lake, Grc C4 23
Vojens, Den C3 24
Vokhma, Sov. Un B3 29
Volary, Czech E8 17
Volborg, Custer, Mont E11 102
Volcano, Hawaii, Haw D6 88
Volcano, isl., Phil o13 35
Volchansk, Sov. Un F11 27
Volga, Clayton, Iowa B6 92
Volga, Brookings, S. Dak C9 116
Volga, Barbour, W. Va B4 123
Volga, plat., Sov. Un C3 29
Volga, riv., Sov. Un F18 9
Volga, riv. mouths, Sov. Un F18 9
Volgograd, res., Sov. Un D3 29
Volgograd, Sov. Un F17 9
Volin, Yankton, S. Dak E8 116
Volkach, F.R.G D5 17
Volkhov, Sov. Un B9 27
Volkhov, riv., Sov. Un B9 27
Völklingen, F.R.G D1 17
Volkovysk, Sov. Un E5 27
Vollenhove, Neth B5 15
Volney, Grayson, Va D1 121
Volnovakha, Sov. Un H11 27
Volo, Lake, Ill h8 90
Volochayevka Vtoraya, Sov. Un B7 37
Volochisk, Sov. Un G6 27
Volodarskiy, Sov. Un s31 25
Volodarskoye, Sov. Un C7 29
Vologda, Sov. Un B1 29
Volokolamsk, Sov. Un C10 27
Volos, Grc C4 23
Volos, gulf, Grc C4 23
Volsk, Sov. Un C3 29
Volta, reg., Ghana E5 45
Volta, lake, Ghana E4 45
Volta, riv., Ghana E4 45
Voltaire, McHenry, N. Dak A5 110
Volta Redonda, Braz C4, h5 56
Volterra, It C3 21
Volturno, riv., It D5 21
Voluntown, New London, Conn C9 84
Volusia, co., Fla C5 86
Volzhskiy, Sov. Un F17 9
Vona, Kit Carson, Colo B8 83
Vonda, Sask., Can E2 70
Von Frank, mtn., Alsk C8 79
Vonitsa, Grc C3 23
Vonore, Monroe, Tenn D9 117
Von Ormy, Bexar, Tex k7 118
Voorburg, Neth *B4 15
Voorheesville, Albany, N.Y *C7 108
Vopnafjorður, Ice n25 25
Vorarlberg, state, Aus E5 16
Vorderthal, Switz B6 19
Vordingborg, Den C5 24
Vorkuta, Sov. Un B21 9
Vorona, riv., Sov. Un E14 27
Voronezh, Sov. Un C1 29
Voronezh, riv., Sov. Un E12 27
Voronya, riv., Sov. Un C16 25
Voroshilov, see Ussuriysk, Sov. Un.
Voroshilovgrad (Lugansk), Sov. Un G12, q22 27
Vorskla, riv., Sov. Un G10 27
Vørterkaka, mtn., Ant B15 5
Vosburg, S. Afr D3 49
Vosges, dept., Fr A2 18
Vosges, mts., Fr C7 14
Voskresensk, Sov. Un n18 27
Voss, Nor G2 25
Voss, Walsh, N. Dak A8 110
Vossburg, Jasper, Miss D5 100
Vostochnyy, Sov. Un B11 37
Vostok, U.S.S.R. scientific station, Ant B23 5
Vostok, isl., Kir G12 7
Votaw, Hardin, Tex D5 118
Votice, Czech D3 26
Votkinsk, Sov. Un D8 29
Vouga, riv., Port B1 20
Vouliagmeni, Grc h11 23
Vouvray, Fr D4 14
Vouziers, Fr C6 14
Voyeykov, ice shelf, Ant C25 5
Vozhega, Sov. Un A13 27
Voznesensk, Sov. Un H8 27
Voznesenskoye, Sov. Un A8 37
Voznesenye, Sov. Un A10 27
Vrå, Den A3 24
Vranany, Czech n17 26
Vranje, Yugo D5 22
Vratsa, Bul D6 22
Vratsa, co., Bul D6 22
Vrbas, Yugo C4 22
Vrbas, riv., Yugo C3 22
Vrchlabi, Czech C3 26
Vrede, S. Afr C4 49
Vreden, F.R.G A1 17
Vredenburgh, Monroe, Ala D2 78
Vrena, Swe u34 25
Vriezenveen, Neth B6 15
Vrigstad, Swe A8 24
Vrin, Switz C7 19
Vršac, Yugo C5 22
Vršovice, Czech n17 26
Vryburg, S. Afr C3 49
Vryheid, S. Afr C5 49
Vsetaty, Czech n18 26
Vsetín, Czech D5 26
Vsevidof, mtn., Alsk E6 79
Vsevolozhsk, Sov. Un r31 25
Vuanggava, isl., Fiji 52
Vucha, riv., Bul E7 22
Vukovar, Yugo C4 22
Vulcan, Alta., Can D4 69
Vulcan, Dickinson, Mich C3 98
Vulcan, Iron, Mo D7 101
Vulcano, isl., It E5 21
Vulchedrum, Bul D6 22
Vunindawa, Fiji 52
Vuoloyarvi, Sov. Un r31 25
Vuya, pt., Fiji 52
Vyartsilya, Sov. Un F14 25
Vyatka, riv., Sov. Un D18 9
Vyatskiye Polyany, Sov. Un B4 29
Vyazemskiy, Sov. Un C7 37
Vyazma, Sov. Un D10 27
Vyazma, riv., Sov. Un n18 27
Vyazniki, Sov. Un C14 27
Vyborg, Sov. Un G13 25, A7 27
Vychegda, riv., Sov. Un C18 9
Vygozero, lake, Sov. Un F16 25
Vyksa, Sov. Un D14 27
Vym, riv., Sov. Un C19 9
Vyritsa, Sov. Un s31 25
Vyrovka, riv., Czech n19 26
Vyshniy Volochek, Sov. Un C10 27
Vyskov, Czech D4 26
Vysoka u Melnika, Czech n18 26
Vysoke Myto, Czech D4 26
Vysoké Tatry, Czech D6 26
Vyssi Brod., Czech E9 17
Vytegra, Sov. Un A11 27

W

Wa, Ghana D4 45
Waal, riv., Neth C5 15
Waalwijk, Neth C5 15
Wabamun, Alta., Can C3 69
Wabamun, lake, Alta., Can C3 69
Wabana (Bell Island) Newf., Can E5 75
Wabasca, Alta., Can B4 69
Wabasca, riv., Alta., Can A3 69
Wabash, Phillips, Ark C5 81
Wabash, Wabash, Ind C6 91
Wabash, Cass, Nebr h12 103
Wabash, co., Ill E6 90
Wabash, co., Ind C6 91
Wabash, riv., U.S C10 77
Wabasha, Wabasha, Minn F6 99
Wabasha, co., Minn F6 99
Wabasso, Indian River, Fla E6 86
Wabasso, Redwood, Minn F3 99
Wabaunsee, Wabaunsee, Kans C7 93
Wabaunsee, co., Kans D7 93
Wabbaseka, Jefferson, Ark C4 81
Wabeno, Forest, Wis C5 124
Wabigoon, Ont., Can E5 71
Wabigoon, lake, Ont., Can E5 71
Wabigoon, riv., Ont., Can E5 71
Wabowden, Man., Can B2, g8 71
Wąbrzeźno, Pol B5 26
Wabush, Newf., Can h8 75
Wabuska, Lyon, Nev D2 104
Waccamaw, riv., N.C., S.C C4 109
Waccasassa, bay, Fla C4 86
Wachapreague, Accomack, Va C7 121
Wachusett, mtn., Mass B4 97
Wachusett, res., Mass B4 97
Wacissa, Jefferson, Fla B3 86
Waco, Haralson, Ga C1 87
Waco, York, Nebr D8 103
Waco, Cleveland, N.C B1 109
Waco, McLennan, Tex D4 118
Waconia, Carver, Minn F5 99
Waddān, Libya D3 43
Waddān, mtn., Libya D3 43
Waddell, Maricopa, Ariz D3, k8 80
Wadden, sea, Neth A5 15
Wädenswil, Switz B6 19
Waddington, St. Lawrence, N.Y f9 108
Waddington, mtn., B.C., Can D5 68
Waddy, Shelby, Ky B4 94
Waddy, lake, Sask., Can A7 70
Wade, Cumberland, N.C B4 109
Wade, Bryan, Okla D5 112
Wade, mtn., Ant A31 5
Wadena, Sask., Can F4 70
Wadena, Fayette, Iowa B6 92
Wadena, Wadena, Minn D3 99
Wadena, co., Minn D4 99
Wadesboro, Tangipahoa, La h10 95
Wadesboro, Anson, N.C C2 109
Wadesville, Posey, Ind H2 91
Wadham, is., Newf., Can D5 75
Wadhams, Essex, N.Y A7, f11 108
Wadhwan, see Surendranagar, India
Wādī al Józ, Jordan m14 32
Wading, riv., N.J D3 106
Wading River, Burlington, N.J D4 106
Wading River, Suffolk, N.Y n16 108
Wadi Sirhān, val., Sau. Ar D8 43
Wadley, Randolph, Ala B4 78
Wadley, Jefferson, Ga D4 87
Wadmalaw, isl., S.C k11 115
Wad Medanī, Sud C3 47
Wadowice, Pol D5, h10 26
Wadsworth, Autauga, Ala C3 78
Wadsworth, Lake, Ill E2 90
Wadsworth, Washoe, Nev D2 104
Wadsworth, Medina, Ohio A4 111
Waelder, Gonzales, Tex E4 118
Wagener, Aiken, S.C D5 115
Wager, bay, N.W. Ter., Can C15 66
Wagga, Sud B4 47
Wagga Wagga, Austl G6 51
Waggoner, Montgomery, Ill D4 90
Waging [am See], F.R.G B8 18
Waginger See, lake, F.R.G E6 16
Wagner, Phillips, Mont B8 102
Wagner, Charles Mix, S. Dak D7 116
Wagoner, Yavapai, Ariz C3 80
Wagoner, Wagoner, Okla B6 112
Wagoner, co., Okla B6 112
Wagners Lake, Platte, Nebr *C8 103
Wagon Mound, Mora, N. Mex A5 107
Wagontire, mtn., Oreg D6 113
Wagon Wheel Gap, Mineral, Colo D4 83
Wagon Wheel Gap, res., Colo D4 83
Wagram, Scotland, N.C C3 109
Wągrowiec, Pol B4 26
Wahai, Indon F7 35
Wah Cantonment, Pak *B5 39
Wahiawa, Honolulu, Haw B3, f9 88
Wahkiakum, co., Wash C2 122
Wahkon, Mille Lacs, Minn D5 99
Wahlern, Switz C3 19
Wahneta, Polk, Fla *E5 86
Wahoo, Saunders, Nebr C9, g11 103
Wahoo creek, Nebr g11 103
Wahpeton, Richland, N. Dak C9 110
Wahsatch, Summit, Utah B4 119
Wah Wah mts., Utah E2 119
Waiakoa Maui Haw C5 88
Waialee Honolulu, Haw B3, f9 88
Waialua (Waialua Mill), Honolulu, Haw B3, f9 88
Waianae, Honolulu, Haw B3, g9 88
Waianae, range, Haw f9 88
Waiawa, riv., Haw g10 88
Waiblingen, F.R.G E4 17
Waidhofen, Aus D7 16
Waidhofen [an der Ybbs], Aus E7 16
Waigeo, isl., Indon E8 35
Waihee, Maui, Haw C5 88
Waikabubak, Indon G5 35
Waikalo, Indon G5 35
Waikapu, Maui, Haw C5 88
Waikari, N.Z O14 51
Waikato, riv., N.Z L15 51
Waikawa, N.Z Q12 51
Waikerie, Austl G2 51
Wailangilala, isl., Fiji 52
Wailea, Hawaii, Haw D6 88
Wailua, Kauai, Haw A2 88
Wailuku, Maui, Haw C5 88
Wailuku, riv., Haw D6 88
Waimanalo, Honolulu, Haw B4, g11 88
Waimanalo, bay, Haw g11 88
Waimanalo Beach, Honolulu, Haw g11 88
Waimate, N.Z P13 51
Waimea, Honolulu, Haw f9 88
Waimea, Kauai, Haw B2 88
Wainganga, riv., India G7 40
Waingapu, Indon G6 35
Waini, pt., Guy A3 59
Wainola, Ontonagon, Mich A6 98
Wainunu, bay, Fiji 52
Wainwright, Alsk A7 79
Wainwright, Alta., Can C5 69
Wainwright, East Carroll, La B4 95
Wainwright, Tuscarawas, Ohio B4 111
Wainwright, Muskogee, Okla B6 112
Waiohinu, Hawaii, Haw D6 88
Waipahu, Honolulu, Haw B3, g9 88
Waipara, N.Z O14 51
Waipawa, N.Z M16 51
Waipio Acres, Honolulu, Haw g9 88
Waipukurau, N.Z N16 51
Wairoa, N.Z M16 51
Waitaki, riv., N.Z P13 51
Waitara, N.Z M15 51
Waite, Washington, Maine C5 96
Waite Park, Stearns, Minn E4 99
Waiteville, Monroe, W. Va D4 123
Waits, riv., Vt C4 120
Waitsburg, Walla Walla, Wash C7 122
Waitsfield, Washington, Vt C3 120
Waits River, Orange, Vt C4 120
Waitville, Sask., Can E3 70
Waiwo, Indon F8 35
Wajima, Jap H8 37
Wajir, Ken A7 48
Waka, Ochiltree, Tex A2 118
Waka, Zaire A3 48
Wakamatsu, Jap H9 37
Wakarusa, Elkhart, Ind A5 91
Wakarusa, Shawnee, Kans D8, m14 93
Wakarusa, riv., Kans D8 93
Wakasa, bay, Jap I7 37
Wakatipu, lake, N.Z P12 51
Wakatomika, creek, Ohio B3 111
Wakaw, Sask., Can E3 70
Wakaya, isl., Fiji 52
Wakayama, Jap I7, o14 37
Wakayama, pref., Jap *I7 37
Wake, co., N.C B4 109
Wake, isl., Oceania 52
Wake, lagoon, Wake I 52
WaKeeney, Trego, Kans C4 93
Wakefield, Que., Can D2 73
Wakefield, Eng A6 12
Wakefield, Clay, Kans C6 93
Wakefield, Middlesex, Mass B5, f11 97
Wakefield, Gogebic, Mich n12 98
Wakefield, Dixon and Wayne, Nebr B9 103
Wakefield, Carroll, N.H C4 105
Wakefield, Pike, Ohio D2 111
Wakefield, Washington, R.I D11 84
Wakefield, Sussex, Va D6 121
Wake Forest, Wake, N.C B4 109
Wake Island, U.S. dep., Oceania 52
Wakeman, Huron, Ohio A3 111
Wakenda, Carroll, Mo B4 101
Wake Village, Bowie, Texas *C5 118
Wakita, Grant, Okla A4 112
Wakkanai, Jap D10 37
Wakkerstroom, S. Afr C5 49
Wakomata, lake, Ont., Can B7 98
Wakonda, Clay, S. Dak E8 116
Wakopa, Man., Can E2 71

Waukau, Winnebago, Wis...E5 124
Waukee, Dallas, Iowa.......C4 92
Waukeenah, Jefferson, Fla...B3 86
Waukegan, Lake, Ill.....A6, h9 90
Waukesha, Waukesha, Wis..........E5, m11 124
Waukesha, co., Wis.........E5 124
Waukomis, Garfield, Okla...A4 112
Waukon, Allamakee, Iowa...A6 92
Wauna, Clatsop, Oreg.......A3 113
Wauna, Pierce, Wash.......f11 122
Waunakee, Dane, Wis.......E4 124
Wauneta, Chase, Nebr......D4 103
Waupaca, Waupaca, Wis....D4 124
Waupaca, co., Wis.........D5 124
Waupun, Dodge and Fond du Lac, Wis..........E5 124
Wauregan, Windham, Conn .B9 84
Waurika, Jefferson, Okla...C4 112
Wausa, Knox, Nebr.........B8 103
Wausau, Washington, Fla...u16 86
Wausau, Marathon, Wis....D4 124
Wausaukee, Marinette, Wis..C6 124
Wauseon, Fulton, Ohio.....A1 111
Waushara, co., Wis.........D4 124
Wautoma, Waushara, Wis...D4 124
Wauwatosa, Milwaukee, Wis..........m12 124
Wauzeka, Crawford, Wis....E3 124
Wave, Dallas, Ark..........C3 81
Waveland, Montgomery, Ind.................E3 91
Waveland, Hancock, Miss..........E4, g7 100
Waveney, riv., Eng..........B9 12
Waverley, Austl...........*F8 51
Waverley, Austl...........*H5 51
Waverley, N.S., Can........E6 74
Waverly, Chambers and Lee, Ala...........C4 78
Waverly, Polk, Fla........*E5 86
Waverly, Camden, Ga.......E5 87
Waverly, Morgan, Ill........D4 90
Waverly, Morgan, Ind.......E5 91
Waverly, Bremer, Iowa......B5 92
Waverly, Coffey, Kans......D8 93
Waverly, Union, Ky.........C2 94
Waverly, Madison, La.......B4 95
Waverly, Wright, Minn......E5 99
Waverly, Lafayette, Mo.....B4 101
Waverly, Lancaster, Nebr..............D9, h11 103
Waverly, Tioga, N.Y........C4 108
Waverly, Pike, Ohio.........C2 111
Waverly, Humphreys, Tenn .A4 117
Waverly, Sussex, Va........C5 121
Waverly, Wood, W. Va......B3 123
Waverly Hall, Harris, Ga ...D2 87
Wavre, Bel..................D4 15
Wāw, Sud....................D2 47
Wawa, Ont., Can...........o18 72
Wawa, Nig..................D5 45
Wawaka, Noble, Ind........B7 91
Wāw al Kabīr, Libya........D3 43
Wawanesa, Man., Can......E2 71
Wawasee, lake, Ind..........B6 91
Wawayanda, lake, N.J.......A4 106
Wawayanda, mtn., N.J.......A4 106
Wawina, N.B., Can.........D2 74
Wawota, Sask., Can.........H4 70
Waxahachie, Ellis, Tex .C4, n10 118
Waxhaw, Union, N.C........C2 109
Waxia, St. Landry, La.......D4 95
Waxweiler, F.R.G...........D6 15
Way, Madison, Miss.........C3 100
Way, is., Viet................H5 38
Waya, isl., Fiji.................52
Wayagamack, lake, Que., Can...B5 73
Wayan, Caribou, Idaho......G7 89
Waycross, Ware, Ga.........E4 87
Wayland, Henry, Iowa.......C6 92
Wayland, Floyd, Ky..........C7 94
Wayland, Middlesex, Mass..g10 97
Wayland, Allegan, Mich.....F5 98
Wayland, Clark, Mo.........A6 101
Wayland, Steuben, N.Y......C3 108
Wayland Springs, Lawrence, Tenn.................B4 117
Waylyn, Charleston, S.C.....k12 115
Waymart, Wayne, Pa........C11 114
Wayne, Alta., Can..........D4 69
Wayne, Wayne, Mich........p15 98
Wayne, Wayne, Nebr........B8 103
Wayne, Passaic, N.J.........B4 106
Wayne, Schuyler, N.Y.......C3 108
Wayne, Wood, Ohio.........A2 111
Wayne, McClain, Okla.......C4 112
Wayne, Delaware, Pa. .F11, o20 114
Wayne, Wayne, W. Va.......C2 123
Wayne, co., Ga.............E5 87
Wayne, co., Ill..............E5 90
Wayne, co., Ind.............E7 91
Wayne, co., Iowa...........D4 92
Wayne, co., Ky.............D5 94
Wayne, co., Mich...........F7 98
Wayne, co., Miss...........D5 100
Wayne, co., Mo.............D7 101
Wayne, co., Nebr...........B8 103
Wayne, co., N.Y............B3 108
Wayne, co., N.C............B4 109
Wayne, co., Ohio...........B4 111
Wayne, co., Pa............C11 114
Wayne, co., Tenn...........B4 117
Wayne, co., Utah...........E4 119
Wayne, co., W. Va.........C2 123
Wayne City, Wayne, Ill......E5 90
Waynesboro, Burke, Ga.....C4 87
Waynesboro, Wayne, Miss...D5 100
Waynesboro, Franklin, Pa...G6 114
Waynesboro, Wayne, Tenn..B4 117
Waynesboro (Independent City), Va..............B4 121
Waynesburg, Lincoln, Ky...C5 94
Waynesburg, Stark, Ohio....B4 111
Waynesburg, Greene, Pa....G1 114
Waynesville, Brantley, Ga...E5 87
Waynesville, DeWitt, Ill.....C4 90
Waynesville, Pulaski, Mo....D5 101
Waynesville, Haywood, N.C.f10 109
Waynesville, Warren, Ohio..C1 111
Waynetown, Montgomery, Ind.................D3 91
Waynewood, Fairfax, Va.....g12 121
Waynoka, Woods, Okla......A3 112
Wayside, Montgomery, Kans.................E8 93
Wayside, Washington, Miss..B2 100
Wayside, Dawes, Nebr.......B2 103
Wayside, Armstrong, Tex....B2 118
Wayside, Brown, Wis.......h10 124
Wayzata, Hennepin, Minn..n11 99
We, isl., Indon...............J1 38
Weakley, co., Tenn.........A3 117
Weare, Hillsboro, N.H.......D3 105
Weatherby, De Kalb, Mo....B3 101
Weatherford, Custer, Okla...B3 112
Weatherford, Parker, Tex....C4 118
Weatherly, Carbon, Pa.....E10 114
Wethersfield (Town of), Windsor, Vt...........*E4 120
Weatogue, Hartford, Conn...B5 84
Weaubleau, Hickory, Mo....D4 101
Weaver, Calhoun, Ala.......B4 78
Weaver, lake, Man., Can......C3 71
Weaver, mts., Ariz...........C3 80
Weaversford, Ashe, N.C......A1 109
Weaverville, Trinity, Calif...B2 82
Weaverville, Buncombe, N.C...............f10 109
Webatuck, creek, N.Y.........B2 84
Webb, Houston, Ala.........D4 78
Webb, Sask., Can...........G1 70
Webb, Clay, Iowa...........B2 92
Webb, Tallahatchie, Miss....B3 100
Webb, co., Tex.............F3 118
Webb, hill, Mass.............B3 97
Webb, lake, Maine...........D2 96
Webb City, Franklin, Ark...B2 81
Webb City, Jasper, Mo......D3 101
Webb City, Osage, Okla.....A5 112
Webber, Jewell, Kans........C5 93
Webber, lake, Man., Can......B5 71
Webbers Falls, Muskogee, Okla.................B6 112
Webberville, Ingham, Mich..F6 98
Webb Lake, Burnett, Wis....B1 124
Webbville, Lawrence, Ky....B7 94
Webbwood, Ont., Can.......A3 72
Weber, co., Utah...........B4 119
Weber, mtn., B.C., Can.......B3 68
Weber City, Scott, Va.......f9 121
Webhannet, York, Maine....E2 96
Webster, Alta., Can.........B1 69
Webster, Sumter, Fla........D4 86
Webster, Keokuk, Iowa......C5 92
Webster, Androscoggin, Maine..................D5 96
Webster, Worcester, Mass....B4 97
Webster, Rice, Minn.........F5 99
Webster, Fallon, Mont.....D12 102
Webster, Merrimack, N.H....D3 105
Webster, Monroe, N.Y.......B3 108
Webster, Ramsey, N. Dak....A7 110
Webster, Darke, Ohio........B1 111
Webster, Westmoreland, Pa..F2 114
Webster, Say, S. Dak........B8 116
Webster, Harris, Tex.......r14 118
Webster, Burnett, Wis.......C1 124
Webster, co., Ga............D2 87
Webster, co., Iowa..........B3 92
Webster, co., Ky............C2 94
Webster, co., Miss..........B4 100
Webster, co., Mo............D5 101
Webster, co., Nebr..........D7 103
Webster, co., W. Va........C4 123
Webster, par., La...........B2 95
Webster, res., Kans.........C4 93
Webster City, Hamilton, Iowa..................B4 92
Webster Grove, Minnehaha, S. Dak.................*D9 116
Webster Groves, St. Louis, Mo...............f13 101
Webster Mills, Fulton, Pa....G5 114
Webster Springs (Addison), Webster, W. Va.........C4 123
Websterville, Washington, Vt....................C4 120
Wecota, Faulk, S. Dak.......B6 116
Weda, Indon................E7 35
Weddell, sea, Ant............C9 5
Wedgefield, Sumter, S.C....D7 115
Wedgeport, N.S., Can.......F4 74
Wedowee, Randolph, Ala....B4 78
Wedron, La Salle, Ill.........B5 90
Weed, Siskiyou, Calif........B2 82
Weed, Otero, N. Mex.......E4 107
Weed Heights, Lyon, Nev....E2 104
Weedon, Que., Can..........D6 73
Weedpatch, hill, Ind..........F5 91
Weedsport, Cayuga, N.Y.....B4 108
Weedville, Elk, Pa...........D5 114
Weehawken, Hudson, N.J.....h8 106
Weekapaug, Washington, R.I....................D10 84
Weekes, Sask., Can..........E4 70
Weeks, Iberia, La............E4 95
Weeksbury, Floyd, Ky.......C7 94
Weekstown, Atlantic, N.J....D3 106
Weeksville, Pasquotank, N.C.A6 109
Weems, Lancaster, Va.......C6 121
Weener, F.R.G..............A7 15
Weeping Water, Cass, Nebr.............D9, h12 103
Weert, Neth.................C5 15
Weesen, Switz..............B7 19
Weesp, Neth................B5 15
Weferlingen, G.D.R.........A6 17
Wegdahl, Chippewa, Minn ..F3 99
Weggis, Switz...............B5 19
Wegobork, see Wegorzewo, Pol.
Wegorzewo, Pol.............A6 26
Wegrow, Pol................B7 26
Weichang, China............C8 34
Wei-Chou, isl., China........B8 38
Weida, G.D.R...............C7 17
Weiden, F.R.G..............D7 17
Weidman, Isabella, Mich.....E5 98
Weifang, China.............D8 34
Weihai, China......D9 34, F10 36
Weihsi, China..............F4 34
Weilburg, F.R.G............C3 17
Weilheim, F.R.G............E5 16
Weimar, G.D.R.............C6 17
Weimar, Colorado, Tex.....E4 118
Wein, Marathon, Wis........D3 124
Weinan, China..............E6 34
Weinböhla, G.D.R..........B8 17
Weiner, Poinsett, Ark.......B5 81
Weinfelden, Switz...........A7 19
Weingarten, F.R.G..........E4 16
Weinheim, F.R.G...........D3 17
Weining, China.............F5 34
Weinsberg, F.R.G..........D4 17
Weipa, Austl...............B7 50
Weippe, Clearwater, Idaho..C3 89
Weir, Que., Can............D3 73
Weir, Cherokee, Kans.......E9 93
Weir, Muhlenberg, Ky.......C2 94
Weir, Choctaw, Miss........B4 100
Weir, lake, Fla...............C5 86
Weir, riv., Man., Can.........A4 71
Weirdale, Sask., Can........D3 70
Weir River, Man., Can.......A4 71
Weirsdale, Marion, Fla......D5 86
Weirton, Brooke and Hancock, W. Va...........A4, f10 123
Weiser, Washington, Idaho ..E2 89
Weiser, riv., Idaho...........E2 89
Weishan, lake, China.........G7 36
Weisner, mtn., Ala...........A4 78
Weiss, St. Helena, La.......D5 95
Weisse Elster, riv., G.D.R.....B7 17
Weissen, lake, Aus...........C9 18
Weissenburg, Switz.........C3 19
Weissenburg [in Bayern], F.R.G....................D5 17
Weissenfels, G.D.R.........B6 17
Weissenhorn, F.R.G........E5 16
Weissert, Custer, Nebr......C6 103
Weisshorn, mtn., Switz........D4 19
Weiss Lake, res., Ala.........A4 78
Weisswasser, G.D.R.........B9 17
Weitra, Aus.................E9 17
Wejherowo, Pol.............A5 26
Wekusko, lake, Man., Can.....B2 71
Welaka, Putnam, Fla........C5 86
Welch, Craig, Okla..........A6 112
Welch, Dawson, Tex.........C1 118
Welch, McDowell, W. Va....D3 123
Welches, Clackamas, Oreg...B5 113
Welcome, St. James, La.....h10 95
Welcome, Martin, Minn.....G4 99
Welcome, Greenville, S.C....B3 115
Weld, Franklin, Maine.......D2 96
Weld, co., Colo.............A6 83
Welda, Anderson, Kans......D8 93
Welden, F.R.G..............E5 17
Weldon, Sask., Can.........D3 70
Weldon, De Witt, Ill.........C5 90
Weldon, Decatur, Iowa......D4 92
Weldon, Halifax, N.C.......A5 109
Weldon, Houston, Tex.......D5 118
Weldona, Morgan, Colo......A7 83
Weldon Spring, St. Charles, Mo..................f12 101
Weleetka, Okfuskee, Okla....B5 112
Welega, prov., Eth..........D4 47
Welkom, S. Afr.............C4 49
Welland, Ont., Can..........E5 72
Welland, riv., Eng.....D6 10, B7 12
Wellandport, Ont., Can.....D5 72
Wellborn, Suwannee, Fla....B4 86
Wellborn, Brazos, Tex.......D4 118
Wellersburg, Somerset, Pa...G4 114
Welles, hbr., Midway Is..........52
Wellesley, Ont., Can........D4 72
Wellesley, Norfolk, Mass..............B5, g10 97
Wellesley, is., Austl..........C6 50
Wellfleet, Barnstable, Mass..C7 97
Wellfleet, Lincoln, Nebr.....D5 103
Wellford, Spartanburg, S.C..B3 115
Wellin, Bel.................D5 15
Welling, Cherokee, Okla.....B7 112
Wellingborough, Eng........D7 12
Wellington, Calhoun, Ala....B4 78
Wellington, Austl...........F7 51
Wellington, B.C., Can.......f11 68
Wellington, Ont., Can.......D7 72
Wellington, Larimer, Colo...A5 83
Wellington, Eng............B5 12
Wellington, Eng............E5 12
Wellington, Iroquois, Ill.....C6 90
Wellington, Sumner, Kans...E6 93
Wellington, Piscataquis, Maine..................C3 96
Wellington, Lafayette, Mo...B4 101
Wellington, Lyon, Nev......E2 104
Wellington, N.Z...........N15 51
Wellington, Lorain, Ohio....A3 111
Wellington, S. Afr..........D2 49
Wellington, Collingsworth, Tex....................B2 118
Wellington, Carbon, Utah...B5 119
Wellington, Fairfax, Va.....*B5 121
Wellington, co., Ont., Can ..D4 72
Wellington, chan., N.W., Ter., Can.................A14 66
Wellington, isl., Chile........D2 54
Wellington Station, N.S., Can...................E6 74
Wellington Station, P.E.I., Can...................C6 74
Wellman, Washington, Iowa.C6 92
Wellman, Terry, Tex........C1 118
Wellpinit, Stevens, Wash....B8 122
Wells, B.C., Can............C7 68
Wells, Eng.................C5 12
Wells [-next-the-sea], Eng...B8 12
Wells, Ottawa, Kans........C6 93
Wells, York, Maine..........E2 96
Wells, Delta, Mich..........C3 98
Wells, Fairbault, Minn......G5 99
Wells, Elko, Nev............B7 104
Wells, Hamilton, N.Y........B6 108
Wells, Cherokee, Tex.......D2 118
Wells, Rutland, Vt..........E2 120
Wells, co., Ind.............C7 91
Wells, co., N. Dak.........B6 110
Wells, lake, Austl............E3 50
Wells, lake, Man., Can.......A1 71
Wells, riv., Vt...............C4 120
Wells Beach, York, Maine...E2 96
Wellsboro, La Porte, Ind....B4 91
Wellsboro, Tioga, Pa........C7 114
Wellsburg, Grundy, Iowa....B5 92
Wellsburg, Chemung, N.Y...C4 108
Wellsburg, Brooke, W. Va.A4, f8 123
Wellsdale, Benton, Oreg.....C1 113
Wellsford, Kiowa, Kans......E4 93
Wells Gray, prov. park, B.C., Can...................C8 68
Wellshire, Arapahoe, Colo...*B6 83
Wells River, Orange, Vt....C4 120
Wells Tannery, Fulton, Pa...F5 114
Wellston, Manistee, Mich....D5 98
Wellston, Jackson, Ohio.....C3 111
Wellston, Lincoln, Okla......B4 112
Wellsville, Franklin, Kans...D8 93
Wellsville, Montgomery, Mo .B6 101
Wellsville, Allegany, N.Y....C3 108
Wellsville, Columbiana, Ohio...................B5 111
Wellsville, York, Pa.........F8 114
Wellsville, Cache, Utah.....B4 119
Wellton, Yuma, Ariz.........E1 80
Wellwood, Man., Can........D2 71
Welo, prov., Eth............C4 47
Wels, Aus..................D7 16
Welsford, N.B., Can.........D3 74
Welsh, Jefferson Davis, La...D3 95
Welshpool, N.B., Can.......*E3 74
Welshpool, Wales...........B4 12
Welton, Clinton, Iowa.......C7 92
Welty, Okfuskee, Okla......B5 112
Welview, Concho, Tex.......D3 118
Welwitschia, Namibia........B1 49
Welwyn, Sask., Can.........G5 70
Welwyn Garden City, Eng....C7 12
Welzow, G.D.R.............B9 17
Wem, Eng..................B5 12
Wema, Zaire...............B3 48
Wembere, riv., Tan...........B5 48
Wembley, Alta., Can.........B1 69
Wemding, F.R.G............E5 17
Wemme, Clackamas, Oreg...B5 113
Wenasoga, Alcorn, Miss.....A5 100
Wenatchee, Chelan, Wash...B5 122
Wenatchee, lake, Wash.......B5 122
Wenatchee, mts., Wash.......B5 122
Wenatchee, riv., Wash........B5 122
Wenceslau, Braz., Braz.....C3 56
Wenchang (Mencheong), China....................C9 38
Wenchi, Ghana.............E4 45
Wenchou, China...F9 34, K9 36
Wenchüan, see Aerhshan, China
Wendel, Lassen, Calif.......B3 82
Wendel, Taylor, W. Va......k10 123
Wendell, Gooding, Idaho....G4 89
Wendell, Franklin, Mass.....A3 97
Wendell, Grant, Minn.......D2 99
Wendell, Sullivan, N.H......D2 105
Wendell, Wake, N.C.........B4 109
Wenden, Yuma, Ariz........D2 80
Wendling, Lane, Oreg.......C4 113
Wendo, Eth.................D4 47
Wendover, Elko, Nev........C7 104
Wendover, Tooele, Utah.....C1 119
Wendover, Platte, Wyo......D8 125
Wenham, Essex, Mass...A6, f12 97
Wenham, lake, Mass..........f12 97
Wenham, swamp, Mass........f12 97
Wenlock, riv., Austl..........B7 50
Wennington, Eng...........*F6 13
Wenona, Marshall, Ill........B4 90
Wenona, Somerset, Md......D6 85
Wenonah, Gloucester, N.J...D2 106
Wenshan, China............G5 34
Wentworth, Austl...........G3 51
Wentworth, N.S., Can.......D6 74
Wentworth, Newton, Mo.....E3 101
Wentworth, Grafton, N.H....C3 105
Wentworth, Rockingham, N.C....................A3 109
Wentworth, Lake, S. Dak....C8 116
Wentworth, Douglas, Wis....B2 124
Wentworth, co., Ont., Can ..D4 72
Wentworth, lake, N.H.........C4 105
Wentzville, St. Charles, Mo..C7 101
Weohyakapka, lake, Fla.......E5 86
Weona, Poinsett, Ark.......B5 81
Weott, Humboldt, Calif......B2 82
Wepener, S. Afr............C4 49
Wequetequock, New London, Conn..................*D9 84
Werbomont, Bel............D5 15
Werdau, G.D.R............C7 17
Werder, G.D.R.............A7 17
Werdohl, F.R.G............B2 17
Werfen, Aus...............E6 16
Werl, F.R.G...............B2 17
Wernberg, F.R.G..........D7 17
Werne [an der Lippe], F.R.G....................B2 17
Wernersville, Berks, Pa.....*F9 114
Werneuchen, G.D.R........B6 16
Wernigerode, G.D.R........B5 17
Werra, riv., G.D.R...........C5 17
Wertach, riv., F.R.G..........D5 16
Wertheim, F.R.G...........D4 17
Wertingen, F.R.G..........E5 17
Wervik, Bel................D3 15
Wesco, Crawford, Mo.......D6 101
Wesel, F.R.G..............B1 17
Weser, riv., F.R.G...........A4 17
Weskan, Wallace, Kans.....D2 93
Weslaco, Hidalgo, Tex......F4 118
Weslaco North, Hidalgo, Tex....................*F3 118
Weslemkoon, lake, Ont., Can...C7 72
Wesley, Madison, Ark.......A2 81
Wesley, Emanuel, Ga.......D4 87
Wesley, Kassuth, Iowa......A4 92
Wesley, Washington, Maine. D5 96
Wesleyville, Newf., Can.....D5 75
Wesleyville, Erie, Pa........B2 114
Wessel, is., Austl............B6 50
Wesselburen, F.R.G........D2 24
Wessington, Beadle and Hand, S. Dak..................C7 116
Wessington Springs, Jerauld, S. Dak.................C7 116
Wesson, Union, Ark........D3 81
Wesson, Copiah, Miss.......D3 100
West, Holmes, Miss.........B4 100
West, McLennan, Tex.......D4 118
West, bay, Tex..............r14 118
West (Wading, riv.), branch, N.J.....................D3 106
West (Delaware, riv.), branch, N.Y.....................C5 108
West (St. Regis, riv.), branch N.Y.....................f10 108
West (Ompompanoosuc, riv.), branch, Vt..............D4 120
West, butte, Mont...........B5 102
West (Poplar, riv.), fork, Mont..................B10 102
West, fork, W. Va..........n12 123
West, ice shelf, Ant.........C21 5
West, isl., Mass.............C6 97
West, lake, Maine...........C4 96
West, mtn., N.Y.............B6 108
West, mtn., Vt..............B5 120
West, riv., N.S., Can........D7 74
West, riv., Mass.............h9 97
West, riv., Vt...............E3 120
West, spit, Eniwetok.............52
West Abington, Plymouth, Mass...................h12 97
West Acton, Middlesex, Mass...................g10 97
West Alexander, Washington, Pa......................F1 114
West Alexandria, Preble, Ohio....................C1 111
West Allis, Milwaukee, Wis .m11 124
West Alton, St. Charles, Mo .A8 101
West Alton, Belknap, N.H...C4 105
West Amityville, Nassau, N.Y....................*G3 84
West Andover, Essex, Mass...A5 97
West Andover, Merrimack, N.H....................D3 105
West Arichat, N.S., Can D8 74
West Athens, Somerset, Maine..................C3 96
West Auburn, Androscoggin, Maine..................D2 96
West Augusta, Augusta, Va..B3 121
West Ausdale, Richland, Ohio..................*B3 111
West Babylon, Suffolk, N.Y.*G4 84
West Baden Springs, Orange, Ind....................G4 91
West Bainbridge, Decatur, Ga.....................*F2 87
West Baldwin, Cumberland, Maine..................E2 96
Westbank, B.C., Can........E8 68
West Barnet, Caledonia, Vt..C4 120
West Barnstable, Barnstable, Mass...................C7 97
West Barrington, Bristol, R.I....................B11 84
West Bath, Sagadahoc, Maine..................E6 96
West Bathurst, N.B., Can....B4 74
West Baton Rouge, par., La..D4 95
West Battle, lake, Minn.......D3 99
West Bay, N.S., Can........D8 74
Westbay, Bay, Fla..........u16 86
West Belmar, Monmouth, N.J....................*C4 106
West Bend, Sask., Can.......F4 70
West Bend, Palo Alto, Iowa..B3 92
West Bend, Washington, Wis.E5 124
West Bengal, state, India....F11 40
West Berkshire, Franklin, Vt.B3 120
West Berlin, see Berlin, West, F.R.G.
West Berlin, Camden, N.J...D3 106
West Berlin, state, F.R.G...*B6 16
West Bethel, Oxford, Maine .D2 96
West Billerica, Middlesex, Mass..................f10 97
West Blocton, Bibb, Ala.....B2 78
West Bloomfield, Ontario, N.Y....................C3 108
West Bolton, Chittenden, Vt.C3 120
Westboro, Atchison, Mo.....A2 101
Westboro, Taylor, Wis......C3 124
Westborough, Worcester, Mass...............B4, g9 97
West Bountiful, Davis, Utah .C4 119
Westbourne, Man., Can......D2 71
West Bowdoin, Sagadahoc, Maine..................f7 96
West Boylston, Worcester, Mass...................B4 97
West Branch, Cedar, Iowa...C6 92
West Branch, Ogemaw, Mich....................D6 98
West Branch, res., Conn.......A4 84
West Branch, res., N.Y........D2 84
West Branch Farmington, riv., Conn...................B5 84
West Brentwood, Rockingham, N.H....................E4 105
West Bridgewater, Plymouth, Mass...................B5 97
West Bridgewater, Beaver, Pa.....................*E1 114
West Bridgewater, Rutland and Windsor, Vt.............D3 120
West Bromwich, Eng........B6 12
Westbrook, Middlesex, Conn.D7 84
Westbrook, Cumberland, Maine..............E2, g7 96
Westbrook, Cottonwood, Minn...................F3 99
Westbrook, Mitchell, Tex....C2 118
West Brookfield, Worcester, Mass...................B3 97
West Brooklyn, Lee, Ill......B4 90
Westbrook Park, Delaware, Pa.....................*G11 114
Westbrookville, Sullivan, N.Y....................D6 108
West Brownsville, Washington, Pa.....................*F2 114
West Burke, Caledonia, Vt...B5 120
West Burlington, Des Moines, Iowa...................D6 92
West Buxton, York, Maine...E2 96
Westby, Sheridan, Mont....B12 102
Westby, Vernon, Wis........E3 124
West Cache, creek, Okla.......C3 112
West Caldwell, Essex, N.J...B4 106
West Camp, Ulster, N.Y.....C7 108
West Campton, Grafton, N.H....................C3 105
West Canaan, Grafton, N.H .C2 105
West Cape May, Cape May, N.J....................F3 106
West Carroll, par., La.......B4 95
West Carrollton, Montgomery, Ohio....................C1 111
West Carry, pond, Maine......C2 96
West Carthage, Jefferson, N.Y....................B5 108
West Castleton, Rutland, Vt.D2 120
West Catasauqua, Lehigh, Pa.....................*E11 114
West Charleston, Orleans, Vt.....................B4 120
West Chatham, Barnstable, Mass...................C8 97
West Chazy, Clinton, N.Y....f11 108
West Chelmsford, Middlesex, Mass..................f10 97
West Cheshire, New Haven, Conn...................C5 84
Westchester, Cook, Ill.......k9 90
West Chester, Washington, Iowa...................C6 92
West Chester, Butler, Ohio..n13 111
West Chester, Chester, Pa..G10 114
Westchester, co., N.Y......D7 108
West Chesterfield, Cheshire, N.H....................E1 105
Westchester Station, N.S., Can...................D6 74
West Chicago, Du Page, Ill. .k8 90
West Chop, pt., Mass.........D6 97
West City, Franklin, Ill......E5 90
West Clarkston, Asotin, Wash..................*C8 122
Westcliffe, Custer, Colo.....C5 83
West College Corner, Union, Ind....................E8 91
West Collingswood Heights, Camden, N.J.............*D2 106
West Columbia, Lexington, S.C....................D5 115
West Columbia, Brazoria, Tex...................E5, r14 118
West Concord, Middlesex, Mass..............B5, g10 97
West Concord, Dodge, Minn .F6 99
West Concord, Cabarrus, N.C....................B3 109
Westconnaug, res., R.I.......C10 84
West Corners, Broome, N.Y.*C4 108
West Cornwall, Litchfield, Conn...................B3 84
West Cornwall, Addison, Vt .D2 120
West Cote Blanche, bay, La....E4 95
West Covina, Los Angeles, Calif...................m13 82
West Creek, Ocean, N.J.....D4 106
West Crossett, Ashley, Ark...D4 81
West Cumberland, Cumberland, Maine............E2, g7 96
West Cummington, Hampshire, Mass..........B2 97
Westdale, Cook, Ill.........*B5 90
West Danby, Tompkins, N.Y.C4 108
West Danville, Caledonia, Vt.....................C4 120
West Decatur, Clearfield, Pa.E5 114
West Dennis, Barnstable, Mass...................C7 97
West Derry, Westmoreland, Pa.....................*F3 114
West Des Moines, Polk, Iowa..............C4, e8 92
West Dover, Windham, Vt...F3 120
West Dudley, Worcester, Mass...................B4 97
West Dummerston, Windham, Vt......................F3 120
West Easton, Northampton, Pa....................*E11 114
West Eden, Hanock, Maine.D4 96
West Elizabeth, Allegheny, Pa.....................*F2 114
West Elk, mts., Colo..........C3 83
West Ellicott, Chautauqua, N.Y....................*C1 108
West Elmira, Chemung, N.Y....................*C4 108
West Elwood, Tipton, Ind...D6 91
West Eminence, Shannon, Mo...................D6 101
West Emma, creek, Kans.......D6 93
West End, Jefferson, Ark...*C3 81
West End, Ba...............A4 64
Westend, San Bernardino, Calif...................E5 82
West End, Marion, Fla.....*C4 86
West End, Winnebago, Ill...A4 90
West End, Moore, N.C......B3 109
West End, Otsego, N.Y....*C5 108
West End Anniston, Calhoun, Ala.....................*B4 78
West Endicott, Broome, N.Y....................*C4 108
West Enfield, Penobscot, Maine..................C4 96
West Enosburg, Franklin, Vt.....................B3 120
West Epping, Rockingham, N.H....................D4 105
Westerkappeln, F.R.G.......A2 17
Westerland, F.R.G..........A4 16
Westerly, Washington, R.I...D9 84
Western, Saline, Nebr.......D8 103
Western, reg., Ghana.......E4 45
Western, reg., Ken.........B6 48
Western, reg., Nig..........E5 45
Western, reg., Tan..........C5 48
Western, reg., Ug..........A5 48
Western, des., Eg...........D5 43
Western, head, Newf., Can....D2 75
Western, head, N.S., Can.....F5 74
Western, isl., Newf., Can......C4 75
Western Australia, state, Austl....................D3 50
Western Azerbaijan, see Azerbaijan, reg., Iran
Western Ghāts, range, India....E5 39
Western Grove, Newton, Ark.....................A3 81
Western Hills, Adams, Colo.*B6 83
Western Isles, reg., Scot.....B2 13
Western Peninsula, div., Ice......................*m21 25
Westernport, Allegany, Md .m12 85
Western Sahara, dep., Afr...................D4 42, E2 44
Western Samoa, country, Oceania......................52
Western Shore, N.S., Can...E5 74
Western Shoshone, Indian res., Idaho, Nev.................B5 104
Western Springs, Cook, Ill...k9 90
Westerschelde, chan., Neth....C3 15
Westerstede, F.R.G.........A7 15
Westervelt, Shelby, Ill.......D5 90
Westerville, Custer, Nebr...C6 103
Westerville, Franklin, Ohio .B3 111
Westerwald, mts., F.R.G......C2 17
West Fairlee, Orange, Vt....D4 120
West Fairview, Cumberland, Pa.....................F8 114
Westfall, Lincoln, Kans......D5 93
Westfall, Malheur, Oreg.....D9 113
West Falmouth, Barnstable, Mass...................C6 97
West Fargo, Cass, N. Dak ..C9 110
West Farmington, Franklin, Maine..................D2 96
West Farmington, Trumbull, Ohio....................A5 111
West Feliciana, par., La.....D4 95
Westfield, Jefferson, Ala.....E4 78
Westfield, N.B., Can........D3 74
Westfield, Clark, Ill.........D6 90
Westfield, Hamilton, Ind.....D5 91
Westfield, Plymouth, Iowa...B1 92
Westfield, Aroostook, Maine.B5 96
Westfield, Hampden, Mass..B2 97
Westfield, Union, N.J.......B4 106
Westfield, Chautauqua, N.Y .C1 108
Westfield, Surry, N.C.......A2 109
Westfield, Emmons, N. Dak .C5 110
Westfield, Tioga, Pa.........C6 114
Westfield, Orleans, Vt......B4 120
Westfield, Marquette, Wis...E4 124
Westfield, riv., Mass.........B2 97
Westfield Center, Medina, Ohio....................A4 111
Westfir, Lane, Oreg.........D4 113
West Flanders, prov., Bel......C3 15
Westford, Windham, Conn..B8 84
Westford, Middlesex, Mass..f10 97
Westford, Chittenden, Vt....B2 120
West Fork, Washington, Ark.B1 81
West Fork, riv., W. Va........B4 123
West Forks, Somerset, Maine..................C3 96
West Frankfort, Franklin, Ill......................F5 90
West Freehold, Monmouth, N.J....................C4 106
West Friendship, Howard, Md.....................B4 85
West Frisian, is., Neth........A5 15
West Gardiner, Kennebec, Maine..................D3 96
Westgate, Palm Beach, Fla...F6 86
Westgate, Fayette, Iowa.....B6 92
West Glacier, Flathead, Mont...................B3 102
West Glens Falls, Warren, N.Y....................*B7 108
West Glocester, Providence, R.I......................B9 84
West Glover, Orleans, Vt....B4 120
West Gorham, Cumberland, Maine..................g7 96
West Goshen, Litchfield, Conn...................B3 84
West Gouldsboro, Hancock, Maine..................D4 96
West Granby, Hartford, Conn...................B5 84
West Granville, Hampden, Mass...................B2 97
West Gravenhurst, Ont., Can...................C5 72
West Green, Coffee, Ga......E4 87
West Greene, Greene, Ala...C1 78
West Greenwich (Town of), Kent, R.I...........*C10 84

Whiting, Monona, Iowa B1 92
Whiting, Jackson, Kans C8 93
Whiting, Washington, Maine D5 96
Whiting, Ocean, N.J D4 106
Whiting, Addison, Vt D2 120
Whiting, Portage, Wis D4 124
Whiting Bay, Scot E3 13
Whitingham, Windham, Vt F3 120
Whitinsville, Worcester, Mass B4 97
Whitkow, Sask., Can E2 70
Whitla, Alta., Can E5 69
Whitlash, Liberty, Mont B5 102
Whitley, co., Ind B6 91
Whitley, co., Ky D5 94
Whitley City, McCreary, Ky D5 94
Whitlock, Henry, Tenn A3 117
Whitman, Plymouth, Mass B6, h12 97
Whitman, Grant, Nebr B4 103
Whitman, Nelson, N. Dak A7 110
Whitman, Logan, W. Va D2 123
Whitman, co., Wash B8 122
Whitman, nat. mon., Wash C7 122
Whitmans, pond, Mass h12 97
Whitman Square, Gloucester, N.J D2 106
Whitmell, Pittsylvania, Va D3 121
Whitmer, Randolph, W. Va C5 123
Whitmire, Newberry, S.C B4 115
Whitmore, mts., Ant A2 5
Whitmore City, Honolulu, Haw f9 88
Whitmore Lake, Washtenaw, Mich A6 98
Whitney, Ont., Can B6 72
Whitney, Franklin, Idaho G7 89
Whitney, Menominee, Mich C3 98
Whitney, Dawes, Nebr B2 103
Whitney, Baker, Oreg C8 113
Whitney, Westmoreland, Pa F3 114
Whitney, Spartanburg, S.C B4 115
Whitney, Hill, Tex D4 118
Whitney, mtn., Calif D4 82
Whitneyville, Washington, Maine D5 96
Whitsett, Guilford, N.C A3 109
Whitstable, Eng C9 12
Whitt, Parker, Tex C4 118
Whittemore, Kossuth, Iowa A3 92
Whittemore, Iosco, Mich D7 98
Whitten, Hardin, Iowa B4 92
Whittier, Alsk C10, g17 79
Whittier, Los Angeles, Calif F4, n12 82
Whittier, Jackson, N.C f9 109
Whittier Downs, Los Angeles, Calif *F4 82
Whittlesey, Eng B7 12
Whitwell, Marion, Tenn D8 117
Wholdaia, lake, N.W. Ter., Can D12 66
Whonock, B.C., Can f13 68
Whyalla, Austl F6 50
Whycocomagh, N.S., Can D8 74
Wiarton, Ont., Can C3 72
Wiau, lake, Alta., Can B5 69
Wiay, isl., Scot C1 13
Wibaux, Wibaux, Mont D12 102
Wibaux, co., Mont D12 102
Wiborg, McCreary, Ky D5 94
Wichita, Sedgwick, Kans E6, g12 93
Wichita, Clackamas, Oreg *B4 113
Wichita, co., Kans D2 93
Wichita, co., Tex B3 118
Wichita, mts., Okla C3 112
Wichita Falls, Wichita, Tex C3 118
Wick, Scot B5 13
Wickatunk, Monmouth, N.J C4 106
Wickenburg, Maricopa, Ariz D3 80
Wickes, Polk, Ark C1 81
Wickes, Jefferson, Mont D4 102
Wickett, Ward, Tex D1 118
Wickham, Que., Can D5 73
Wickiup, res., Oreg D5 113
Wickliffe, Ballard, Ky f8 94
Wickliffe, Lake, Ohio A4, g9 111
Wickliffe, Mahoning, Ohio *A5 111
Wicklow, Ire E5 11
Wicklow, co., Ire E5 11
Wicklow, head, Ire E6 11
Wicklow, mts., Ire E5 11
Wicomico, Charles, Md D4 85
Wicomico, co., Md D6 85
Wicomico, riv., Md D4 85
Wicomico, riv., Md D6 85
Wiconisco, Dauphin, Pa E8 114
Widefield, El Paso, Colo C6 83
Widen, Clay, W. Va m14 123
Widener, St. Francis, Ark B5 81
Widerøe, mtn., Ant B15 5
Wide Ruin, Apache, Ariz B6 80
Widnes, Eng A5 12
Widuchowa, Pol E8 24
Wiebelskirchen, F.R.G D2 17
Wiedenbrück, F.R.G B3 17
Wieliczka, Pol C6 26
Wielka Wies, Pol A5 26
Wielun, Pol C5 26
Wien (Vienna), state, Aus D8 16
Wiener Neustadt, Aus E8 16
Wieprz, riv., Pol C7 26
Wieprzowka, riv., Pol h10 26
Wiergate, Newton, Tex D6 118
Wiesau, F.R.G D7 17
Wiesbaden, F.R.G C3 17
Wiesenburg, G.D.R A7 17
Wiesental, F.R.G D3 17
Wiesloch, F.R.G D3 17
Wigan, Eng A5 12
Wiggins, Morgan, Colo A6 83
Wiggins, Stone, Miss E4 100
Wiggins, peak, Wyo C3 125
Wight, isl., Eng D6 12
Wigton, Eng F5 13
Wigtown, Scot F4 13
Wigtown, bay, Scot F4 13
Wijhe, Neth B6 15
Wikieup, Mohave, Ariz C2 80
Wikwemikong, Ont., Can B3 72
Wil, Switz B7 19
Wilbarger, co., Tex B3 118
Wilber, Saline, Nebr D9 103
Wilberforce, Ont., Can C6 72
Wilberforce, Greene, Ohio C2 111
Wilbraham, Hampden, Mass B3 97
Wilbur, Douglas, Oreg D3 113
Wilbur, Lincoln, Wash B7 122
Wilburn, Cleburne, Ark B4 81
Wilburton, Latimer, Okla C6 112
Wilcannia, Austl E4 51
Wilcox, Sask., Can G3 70
Wilcox, Gilchrist, Fla C4 86
Wilcox, Kearney, Nebr D6 103
Wilcox, Elk, Pa C4 114
Wilcox, co., Ala D2 78
Wilcox, co., Ga E3 87
Wilcox, mtn., Mass B1 97
Wilczek, isl., Sov. Un A8 4
Wild, branch, Vt B4 120
Wild Ammonoosuc, riv., N.H B4 105
Wildbad, F.R.G E3 17
Wildcat, creek, Ind D4 91
Wildcat, hill, Sask., Can D4 70
Wildcat Top, mtn., Tenn D10 117
Wild Cherry, Fulton, Ark A3 81
Wilden, Northampton, Pa *E11 114
Wilder, Canyon, Idaho F2 89
Wilder, Windsor, Vt D4 120
Wilder, dam, N.H C2 105
Wilderness, prov. park, Alta., Can C1 69
Wildersville, Henderson, Tenn B3 117
Wildervank, Neth A6 15
Wilderville, Josephine, Oreg E3 113
Wildeshausen, F.R.G F2 24
Wildhaus, Switz B7 19
Wildhay, riv., Alta., Can C2 69
Wildhorn, mtn., Switz D3 19
Wild Horse, Cheyenne, Colo C8 83
Wild Horse, creek, Wyo B7 125
Wild Horse, res., Nev B6 104
Wildnest, lake, Sask., Can C4 70
Wildomar, Riverside, Calif *F5 82
Wildorado, Oldham, Tex B1 118
Wild Rice, riv., Minn C2 99
Wild Rice, riv., N. Dak C8 110
Wildrose, Williams, N. Dak A2 110
Wild Rose, Waushara, Wis D4 124
Wildspitze, mtn., Aus C6 18
Wildsville, Concordia, La C4 95
Wildwood, Alta., Can C3 69
Wildwood, Sumter, Fla D4 86
Wildwood, Cape May, N.J F3 106
Wildwood, Allegheny, Pa *E2 114
Wildwood Crest, Cape May, N.J F3 106
Wiley, Prowers, Colo C8 83
Wilhelm, mtn., Pap. N. Gui k12 50
Wilhelmina, mts., Indon F9 35
Wilhelmina, mts., Sur B3 59
Wilhelm-Pieck-Stadt Guben, G.D.R B9 17
Wilhelmshaven, F.R.G B4 14, E2 24
Wilhoit, Yavapai, Ariz C3 80
Wilkau, G.D.R C7 17
Wilkes, co., Ga C4 87
Wilkes, co., N.C A1 109
Wilkes, isl., Wake Isl 52
Wilkes, lake, Ont., Can A6 72
Wilkes-Barre, Luzerne, Pa D10, n17 114
Wilkesboro, Wilkes, N.C A1 109
Wilkes Land, reg., Ant B27 5
Wilkeson, Pierce, Wash B3 122
Wilkesville, Vinton, Ohio C3 111
Wilkie, Sask., Can E1 70
Wilkin, co., Minn D2 99
Wilkins, sound, Ant B5 5
Wilkinsburg, Allegheny, Pa F2, k14 114
Wilkinson, Hancock, Ind E6 91
Wilkinson, Wilkinson, Miss D2 100
Wilkinson, Logan, W. Va D3 123
Wilkinson, co., Ga D3 87
Wilkinson, co., Miss D2 100
Wilkinsonville, Worcester, Mass *B4 97
Will, co., Ill B6 90
Willacoochee, Atkinson, Ga E3 87
Willacy, co., Tex F4 118
Willamette, riv., Oreg C3 113
Willamina, Yamhill, Oreg B3 113
Willapa, Pacific, Wash C2 122
Willapa, bay, Wash C1 122
Willard, Logan, Colo A7 83
Willard, Shawnee, Kans C8 93
Willard, Carter, Ky B7 94
Willard, Greene, Mo D4 101
Willard, Fallon, Mont D12 102
Willard, Torrance, N. Mex C3 107
Willard, Seneca, N.Y C4 108
Willard, Pender, N.C C4 109
Willard, Huron, Ohio A3 111
Willard, Box Elder, Utah B3 119
Willard, Clark, Wis D3 124
Willard, bay, Utah B3 119
Willard, stream, Vt B5 120
Willards, Wicomico, Md D7 85
Willcox, Cochise, Ariz E6 80
Willemstad, Neth Antilles H19 65
Willemstad, Neth C4 15
Willernie, Washington, Minn E7 99
Willet, Cortland, N.Y C5 108
Willette, Macon, Tenn C8 117
Willetts, Concordia, La C4 95
William, lake, Man., Can C2 71
William Creek, Austl E6 50
Williams, Coconino, Ariz B3 80
Williams, Colusa, Calif C2 82
Williams, Lawrence, Ind C4 91
Williams, Hamilton, Iowa B4 92
Williams, Lake of the Woods, Minn B4 99
Williams, Le Flore, Okla B7 112
Williams, Colleton, S.C E6 115
Williams, co., N. Dak A2 110
Williams, co., Ohio A1 111
Williams, cape, Ant C29 5
Williams, mtn., Okla C7 112
Williams, riv., Vt E3 120
Williams, riv., W. Va C4 123
Williams Bay, Walworth, Wis F5 124
Williamsburg, Ont., Can C9 72
Williamsburg, Wayne, Ind E8 91
Williamsburg, Iowa, Iowa C5 92
Williamsburg, Franklin, Kans D8 93
Williamsburg, Whitley, Ky D5 94
Williamsburg, Dorchester, Md C6 85
Williamsburg, Hampshire, Mass B2 97
Williamsburg, Grand Traverse, Mich D5 98
Williamsburg, Sierra, N. Mex D2 107
Williamsburg, Clermont, Ohio C1 111
Williamsburg, Blair, Pa F5 114
Williamsburg (Independent City), Va C6 121
Williamsburg, Greenbrier, W. Va D4 123
Williamsburg, co., S.C D8 115
Williamsfield, Knox, Ill C3 90
Williams Lake, B.C., Can C6, n18 68
Williamson, Pike, Ga C2 87
Williamson, Madison, Ill f14 101
Williamson, Lucas, Iowa C4 92
Williamson, Wayne, N.Y B3 108
Williamson, Mingo, W. Va D2 123
Williamson, co., Ill F5 90
Williamson, co., Tenn A5 117
Williamson, co., Tex D4 118
Williamson, head, Ant C28 5
Williams Park, Lake, Ill *A6 90
Williamsport, Newf., Can C3 75
Williamsport, Warren, Ind D3 91
Williamsport, Washington, Md A2 85
Williamsport, Pickaway, Ohio C2 111
Williamsport, Lycoming, Pa D7 114
Williamsport, Maury, Tenn B4 117
Williamston, Ingham, Mich F6 98
Williamston, Martin, N.C B5 109
Williamston, Anderson, S.C B3 115
Williamstown, Ont., Can B10 72
Williamstown, Jefferson, Kans k15 93
Williamstown, Grant, Ky B5 94
Williamstown, Berkshire, Mass A1 97
Williamstown, Lewis, Mo A6 101
Williamstown, Gloucester, N.J D3 106
Williamstown, Oswego, N.Y B5 108
Williamstown, Hancock, Ohio B2 111
Williamstown, Dauphin, Pa E8 114
Williamstown, Orange, Vt C3 120
Williamstown, Wood, W. Va B3 123
Williamsville, Sangamon, Ill D4 90
Williamsville, Attala, Miss B4 100
Williamsville, Wayne, Mo E7 101
Williamsville, Erie, N.Y C2 108
Williamsville, Windham, Vt F3 120
Williford, Sharp, Ark A4 81
Willimantic, Windham, Conn C8 84
Willimantic, riv., Conn B7 84
Willingboro, Burlington, N.J C3 106
Willingdon, Alta., Can C4 69
Willington (Town of), Tolland, Conn *B7 84
Willis, Brown, Kans C8 93
Willis, Washtenaw, Mich p14 98
Willis, Montgomery, Tex D5 118
Willis, Floyd, Va E2 121
Willis, isl., Newf., Can D5 75
Willisburg, Washington, Ky C4 94
Williston, Levy, Fla C4 86
Williston, Carteret, N.C C6 109
Williston, Williams, N. Dak A2 110
Williston, Ottawa, Ohio e7 111
Williston, Barnwell, S.C E5 115
Williston, Fayette, Tenn B2 117
Williston, Chittenden, Vt C2 120
Williston, S. Afr D3 49
Williston, basin, Mont., N. Dak B11 102
Williston, lake, B.C., Can B6 68
Williston Park, Nassau, N.Y G2 84
Willisville, Nevada, Ark D2 81
Willisville, Perry, Ill F4 90
Willis Wharf, Northampton, Va C7 121
Willits, Mendocino, Calif C2 82
Willmar, Sask., Can H4 70
Willmar, Kandiyohi, Minn E3 99
Willoughby, Austl *F8 51
Willoughby, Lake, Ohio A4 111
Willoughby, lake, Vt B4 120
Willoughby Hills, Lake, Ohio *A4 111
Willow, Alsk g16 79
Willow, Dallas, Ark C3 81
Willow, Greer, Okla B2 112
Willow, creek, Alta., Can D4 69
Willow, creek, Utah D6 119
Willow, creek, Wyo C6 125
Willow, res., Wis C3 124
Willow, riv., B.C., Can C6 68
Willow Beach, Clark, Nev *H7 104
Willow Branch, Hancock, Ind E6 91
Willow Brook, Los Angeles, Calif *n12 82
Willowbrook, Sask., Can F4 70
Willow Bunch, Sask., Can H3 70
Willow Bunch, lake, Sask., Can H3 70
Willow City, Bottineau, N. Dak A5 110
Willow City, Gillespie, Tex D3 118
Willow Creek, Gallatin, Mont E5 102
Willowdale, Ont., Can D5, k15 72
Willow Grove, Montgomery, Pa F11, o21 114
Willow Hill, Jasper, Ill E5 90
Willow Hill, Franklin, Pa F6 114
Willowick, Lake, Ohio g9 111
Willow Island, Dawson, Nebr D5 103
Willow Lake, Clark, S. Dak C8 116
Willow Lawn, Henrico, Va *C5 121
Willowmore, S. Afr D3 49
Willow Ranch, Modoc, Calif B3 82
Willow River, B.C., Can B6 68
Willow River, Pine, Minn D6 99
Willow Run, Washtenaw, Mich p14 98
Willows, Glenn, Calif C2 82
Willows, Sask., Can H3 70
Willows, Gilliam, Oreg B6 113
Willow Springs, Cook, Ill k9 90
Willow Springs, Howell, Mo E6 101
Wills, creek, W. Va m13 123
Wills, hill, Mass f11 97
Wills, mtn., Md k13 85
Wills, riv., Ala A3 78
Wills, val., Ala A4 78
Willsboro, Essex, N.Y f11 108
Willshire, Van Wert, Ohio B1 111
Wills Point, Van Zandt, Tex *C5 118
Willston, Fairfax, Va *B5 121
Wilmar, Drew, Ark D4 81
Wilmer, Mobile, Ala E1 78
Wilmer, Dallas, Tex n10 118
Wilmerding, Allegheny, Pa k14 114
Wilmersdorf, G.D.R E7 24
Wilmette, Cook, Ill A6, h9 90
Wilmington, New Castle, Del A6 85
Wilmington, Will, Ill B5 90
Wilmington, Middlesex, Mass A5, f11 97
Wilmington, Essex, N.Y f11 108
Wilmington, New Hanover, N.C C5 109
Wilmington, Clinton, Ohio C2 111
Wilmington, Windham, Vt F3 120
Wilmington, lake, Fla E6 86
Wilmont, Nobles, Minn G3 99
Wilmore, Comanche, Kans E4 93
Wilmore, Jessamine, Ky C5 94
Wilmot, Ashley, Ark D4 81
Wilmot, Cowley, Kans E7 93
Wilmot, Merrimack, N.H D3 105
Wilmot, Stark, Ohio B4 111
Wilmot, Roberts, S. Dak B9 116
Wilmot Flat, Merrimack, N.H D3 105
Wilmot Station, N.S., Can E4 74
Wilmslow, Eng A5 12
Wilno, Ont., Can B7 72
Wilno, see Vilnius, Sov. Un.
Wilsall, Park, Mont E6 102
Wilsey, Morris, Kans D7 93
Wilson, Mississippi, Ark B5 81
Wilson, Hartford, Conn B6 84
Wilson, Ellsworth, Kans D5 93
Wilson, East Feliciana, La D4 95
Wilson, Menominee, Mich C3 98
Wilson, Niagara, N.Y B2 108
Wilson, Wilson, N.C B5 109
Wilson, Carter, Okla C4 112
Wilson, Northampton, Pa E11 114
Wilson, Lynn, Tex C2 118
Wilson, Weber, Utah B3 119
Wilson, Teton, Wyo C2 125
Wilson, co., Kans E8 93
Wilson, co., N.C B5 109
Wilson, co., Tenn A5 117
Wilson, co., Tex E3 118
Wilson, creek, Wash B6 122
Wilson, creek, Wash B6 122
Wilson, dam, Ala A2 78
Wilson, mtn., Calif m12 82
Wilson, mtn., Nev E7 104
Wilson, mtn., Oreg B5 113
Wilson, peak, Colo D3 83
Wilson, pond, Maine C3 96
Wilson, riv., Austl C4 51
Wilson Creek, Grant, Wash B6 122
Wilson Mills, Johnston, N.C B4 109
Wilson Piedmont, glacier, Ant e39 5
Wilsons, Dinwiddie, Va C5 121
Wilson's, promontory, Austl I6 51
Wilsons Beach, N.B., Can E3 74
Wilsons Mills, Oxford, Maine D1 96
Wilsonville, Shelby, Ala B3 78
Wilsonville, Windham, Conn A9 84
Wilsonville, Macoupin, Ill D4 90
Wilsonville, Furnas, Nebr D5 103
Wilsonville, Clackamas, Oreg h12 113
Wilstedt, F.R.G E3 18
Wilster, F.R.G E3 18
Wilton, Shelby, Ala B3 78
Wilton, Little River, Ark D1 81
Wilton, Fairfield, Conn E3 84
Wilton, Muscatine, Iowa C6 92
Wilton, Franklin, Maine D2 96
Wilton, Beltrami, Minn C3 99
Wilton, Hillsboro, N.H E3 105
Wilton, Saratoga, N.Y B7 108
Wilton, Burleigh and McLean, N. Dak B5 110
Wilton, Monroe, Wis E3 124
Wiltshire, co., Eng C6 12
Wiltz, Lux E5 15
Wiluna, Austl E3 50
Wimapedi, riv., Man., Can B2 71
Wimauma, Hillsborough, Fla E4 86
Wimbledon, Eng. (part of London) m12 10
Wimbledon, Barnes, N. Dak B7 110
Wimborne, Alta., Can D4 69
Wimborne, Eng D6 12
Wimer, Jackson, Oreg E3 113
Wimico, lake, Fla C1 86
Winagami, lake, Alta., Can B2 69
Winamac, Pulaski, Ind B4 90
Winburg, S. Afr C4 49
Winburne, Clearfield, Pa E5 114
Wincheck, pond, R.I C9 84
Winchell, mtn., Mass B2 97
Winchendon, Worcester, Mass A3 97
Winchendon Springs, Worcester, Mass A3 97
Winchester, Drew, Ark D4 81
Winchester, Ont., Can B9 72
Winchester, Eng C6 12
Winchester, Lewis, Idaho C2 89
Winchester, Scott, Ill D3 90
Winchester, Randolph, Ind D8 91
Winchester, Jefferson, Kans k15 93
Winchester, Clark, Ky C5 94
Winchester, Middlesex, Mass g11 97
Winchester, Wayne, Miss D5 100
Winchester, Clark, Mo A6 101
Winchester, St. Louis, Mo *B7 101
Winchester, Clark, Nev G6 104
Winchester, Cheshire, N.H E2 105
Winchester, Adams, Ohio D2 111
Winchester, Franklin, Tenn B5 117
Winchester (Independent City), Va A4 121
Winchester Bay, Douglas, Oreg D2 113
Winchester Center, Litchfield, Conn B4 84
Wind, creek, Wyo C7 125
Wind, lake, Wis n11 124
Wind, riv., Wash D4 122
Wind, riv., Wyo C3 125
Windber, Somerset, Pa F4 114
Wind Cave, nat. park, S. Dak D2 116
Windemere, Ingham, Mich *F6 98
Winder, Barrow, Ga C3 87
Windermere, B.C., Can D10 68
Windermere, Ont., Can B5 72
Windermere, Eng C5 10
Windermere, lake, Eng F6 13
Windfall, Alta., Can B2 69
Windfall, Tipton, Ind D6 91
Windgap, Northampton, Pa E11 114
Windham, Windham, Conn C8 84
Windham, Judith Basin, Mont C6 102
Windham, Rockingham, N.H E4 105
Windham, Greene, N.Y C6 108
Windham, Portage, Ohio A4 111
Windham, co., Conn B8 84
Windham, co., Vt F3 120
Windhoek, Namibia B2 49
Windigo Lake, Ont., Can n17 72
Windigo, riv., Que., Can A4 73
Winding Stair, mtn., Okla C7 112
Wind Lake, Racine, Wis F5, n11 124
Windmill, pt., Va C6 121
Windom, McPherson, Kans D6 93
Windom, Cottonwood, Minn G3 99
Windom, peak, Colo D3 83
Window Rock, Apache, Ariz B6 80
Wind Point, Racine, Wis n12 124
Wind Ridge, Greene, Pa G1 114
Wind River, Indian res., Wyo C3 125
Wind River, range, Wyo C3 125
Windsbach, F.R.G D5 17
Windsor, Newf., Can D4 75
Windsor, N.S., Can E5 74
Windsor, Ont., Can E1 72
Windsor, Que., Can D5 73
Windsor, Weld, Colo A6 83
Windsor, Hartford, Conn B6 84
Windsor, Eng C7 12
Windsor, Shelby, Ill D5 90
Windsor, Berkshire, Mass A1 97
Windsor, Henry, Mo C4 101
Windsor, Mercer, N.J C3 106
Windsor, Broome, N.Y *C5 108
Windsor, Bertie, N.C A6 109
Windsor, Stutsman, N. Dak C6 110
Windsor, York, Pa G8 114
Windsor, Aiken, S.C E4 115
Windsor, Windsor, Vt E4 120
Windsor, Isle of Wight, Va D6, k14 121
Windsor, co., Vt D3 120
Windsor Heights, Polk, Iowa e8 92
Windsor Locks, Hartford, Conn B6 84
Windsorville, Hartford, Conn B6 84
Windthorst, Sask., Can G4 70
Windthorst, Archer, Tex C3 118
Windward, passage, N.A E6 64
Windward Islands, see Dominica, Grenada, St. Lucia, and St. Vincent, Br. dep., N.A.
Windy, lake, Sask., Can C4 70
Windy, peak, Wash A6 122
Windy, pt., Newf., Can C4 75
Windygates, Man., Can E2 71
Windy Hill, Florence, S.C C8 115
Winefred, lake, Alta., Can B5 69
Winefred, riv., Alta., Can B5 69
Winesap, Chelan, Wash B5 122
Winfall, Perquimans, N.C A6 109
Winfield, Marion, Ala B2 78
Winfield, Alta., Can C3 69
Winfield, Du Page, Ill *F2 90
Winfield, Henry, Iowa C6 92
Winfield, Cowley, Kans E7 93
Winfield, Carroll, Md B3 85
Winfield, Lincoln, Mo C7, f12 101
Winfield, Union, N.J k7 106
Winfield, Union, Pa E8 114
Winfield, Scott, Tenn C9 117
Winfield, Putnam, W. Va C3 123
Winfred, Lake, S. Dak C8 116
Wing, Covington, Ala D3 78
Wing, Yell, Ark C2 81
Wing, Burleigh, N. Dak B5 110
Wing, riv., Minn D3 99
Wingate, Eng *F7 13
Wingate, Montgomery, Ind D3 91
Wingate, Dorchester, Md D5 85
Wingate, Union, N.C C2 109
Winger, Polk, Minn C3 99
Wingham, Ont., Can D3 72
Wing Lake, Oakland, Mich *F7 98
Wingo, Graves, Ky f9 94
Winhall (Town of), Bennington, Vt *E3 120
Winifred, Fergus, Mont C7 102
Winifreda, Arg B4 54
Winifrede, Kanawha, W. Va m12 123
Winigan, Sullivan, Mo A5 101
Winisk, Ont., Can n18 72
Winisk, lake, Ont., Can n18 72
Winisk, riv., Ont., Can n18 72
Wink, Winkler, Tex D1 118
Winkelman, Gila, Ariz E5 80
Winkler, Man., Can E3 71
Winkler, co., Tex D1 118
Winlaw, B.C., Can E9 68
Winlock, Wheeler, Oreg C7 113
Winlock, Lewis, Wash C3 122
Winn, Penobscot, Maine C4 96
Winn, Isabella, Mich E6 98
Winn, par., La C3 95
Winnabow, Brunswick, N.C C4 109
Winneba, Ghana E4 45
Winnebago, Winnebago, Ill A4 90
Winnebago, Faribault, Minn G4 99
Winnebago, Thurston, Nebr B9 103
Winnebago, Winnebago, Wis h8 124
Winnebago, co., Ill A4 90
Winnebago, co., Iowa A4 92
Winnebago, co., Wis D5 124
Winnebago, Indian res., Nebr B9 103
Winnebago, lake, Wis D5 124
Winnebago, riv., Iowa A4 92
Winneconne, Winnebago, Wis D5 124
Winnemucca, Humboldt, Nev C4 104
Winnemucca, lake, Nev C2 104
Winner, Tripp, S. Dak D6 116
Winneshiek, co., Iowa A6 92
Winnetka, Cook, Ill A6, h9 90
Winnetoon, Knox, Nebr B8 103
Winnett, Petroleum, Mont D8 102
Winnfield, Winn, La C3 95
Winnibigoshish, lake, Minn C4 99
Winnifred, Alta., Can E5 69
Winning Pool, Austl D1 50
Winnipeg, Man., Can E3, h8 71
Winnipeg, lake, Man., Can C3 71
Winnipeg, riv., Man., Can D4 71
Winnipeg Beach, Man., Can D3 71
Winnipegosis, Man., Can D2 71
Winnipegosis, lake, Man., Can C2 71
Winnipesaukee, lake, N.H C4 105
Winnisquam, Belknap, N.H C3 105
Winnisquam, lake, N.H C3 105
Winnsboro, Franklin, La B4 95
Winnsboro, Fairfield, S.C C5 115
Winnsboro, Franklin and Wood, Tex C5 118
Winnsboro Mills, Fairfield, S.C C5 115
Winokur, Charlton, Ga E4 87
Winona, Ont., Can *D5 72
Winona, Starke, Ind B4 91
Winona, Logan, Kans C2 93
Winona, Houghton, Mich B2 98
Winona, Winona, Minn F7 99
Winona, Montgomery, Miss B4 100
Winona, Shannon, Mo D6 101
Winona, Whitman, Wash C8 122
Winona, Fayette, W. Va C4, m14 123
Winona, co., Minn F7 99
Winona, lake, Vt C2 120
Winona Lake, Kosciusko, Ind B6 91
Winooski, Chittenden, Vt C2 120
Winooski, riv., Vt C3 120
Winschoten, Neth A7 15
Winsen, F.R.G E4 24
Winsford, Eng A5 12
Winside, Wayne, Nebr B8 103
Winslow, Navajo, Ariz C5 80
Winslow, Washington, Ark B1 81
Winslow, Stephenson, Ill A4 90
Winslow, Pike, Ind H3 91
Winslow, Kennebec, Maine D3 96
Winslow, Dodge, Nebr C9 103
Winslow, Camden, N.J D3 106
Winslow, Kitsap, Wash e10 122
Winsted, Litchfield, Conn B4 84
Winsted, McLeod, Minn F4 99
Winston, Polk, Fla D4 86
Winston, Daviess, Mo B3 101
Winston, Broadwater, Mont D5 102
Winston, Sierra, N. Mex D2 107
Winston, Douglas, Oreg D3 113
Winston, co., Ala A2 78
Winston, co., Miss B4 100
Winston-Salem, Forsyth, N.C A2 109
Winstonville, Bolivar, Miss B3 100
Winsum, Neth A6 15
Winter, Sask., Can E1 70
Winter, Sawyer, Wis C2 124
Winter, ridge, Oreg E6 113
Winter Beach, Indian River, Fla E6 86
Winterberg, F.R.G B3 17
Winter Garden, Orange, Fla D5 86
Winter Harbor, Hancock, Maine D4 96
Winter Harbour, B.C., Can D3 68
Winter Haven, Polk, Fla D5 86
Wintering, lake, Man., Can B3 71
Winter Park, Grand, Colo B5 83
Winter Park, Orange, Fla D5 86
Winter Park, New Hanover, N.C C5 109
Winterpock, Chesterfield, Va C5 121
Winterport, Waldo, Maine D4 96
Winters, Yolo, Calif C2 82
Winters, Runnels, Tex D3 118
Winterset, Madison, Iowa C3 92
Wintersville, Jefferson, Ohio B5 111
Winterswijk, Neth C6 15
Winterthur, Switz A6 19
Winterton, Newf., Can E5 75
Winterville, Clarke, Ga C3 87
Winterville, Aroostook, Maine B4 96
Winterville, Washington, Miss B2 100
Winterville, Pitt, N.C B5 109
Winthrop, Little River, Ark D1 81
Winthrop, Middlesex, Conn *D7 84
Winthrop, Buchanan, Iowa B6 92
Winthrop, Kennebec, Maine D3 96
Winthrop, Suffolk, Mass B6, g12 97
Winthrop, Sibley, Minn F4 99
Winthrop, Buchanan, Mo B2 101
Winthrop, St. Lawrence, N.Y f10 108
Winthrop, Okanogan, Wash A5 122
Winthrop, lake, Mass h10 97
Winthrop Harbor, Lake, Ill A6, h9 90
Winton, Austl D7 50
Winton, Ba m18 64
Winton, St. Louis, Minn C7 99
Winton, Hertford, N.C A6 109
Wintzenheim, Fr A3 18
Winyah, bay, S.C E9 115
Wiota, Cass, Iowa C3 92
Wirral, N.B., Can D3 74
Wirt, Itasca, Minn C5 99
Wirt, Carter, Okla C4 112
Wirt, co., W. Va B3 123
Wirtz, Franklin, Va C3 121
Wisbech, Eng B8 12
Wiscasset, Lincoln, Maine D3 96
Wisconsin, state, U.S B10 77, 124
Wisconsin, riv., Wis E3 124
Wisconsin Dells, Columbia, Wis E4 124
Wisconsin Rapids, Wood, Wis D4 124
Wisdom, Beaverhead, Mont E3 102
Wise, Warren, N.C A4 109
Wise, Wise, Va f9 121
Wise, co., Tex C4 118
Wise, co., Va e9 121
Wiseman, Alsk B9 79
Wise River, Beaverhead, Mont E4 102
Wiseton, Sask., Can F2 70
Wishart, Sask., Can F3 70
Wishart, Polk, Mo D4 101
Wishaw, Scot E5 13
Wishek, McIntosh, N. Dak C6 110
Wishram, Klickitat, Wash D4 122
Wisła, riv., Pol B5 26
Wisłok, riv., Pol C6 26
Wisłoka, riv., Pol D6 26
Wismar, G.D.R B5 16
Wismar, bay, G.D.R D5 24
Wisner, Franklin, La C4 95
Wisner, Cuming, Nebr C9 103
Wissant, Fr D9 12
Wissembourg, Fr C7 14
Wissota, lake, Wis D2 124
Wister, LeFlore, Okla C7 112
Wister Lake, res., Okla C7 112
Witbank, S. Afr C4 49
Witchekan, lake, Sask., Can D2 70
Witch Lake, Marquette, Mich B2 98
Witham, Eng C8 12
Witham, riv., Eng A7 12
Withamsville, Clermont, Ohio h14 94
Withee, Clark, Wis D3 124
Witherbee, Essex, N.Y A7 108
Witherbee, Berkeley, S.C E8 115
Withernsea, Eng A8 12
Witherspoon, mtn., Alsk g18 79
Withlacoochee, riv., Fla., Ga B3 86
Withrow, Douglas, Wash B6 122
Witless Bay, Newf., Can E5 75
Witney, Eng C6 12
Witry-lès-Reims, Fr E4 15
Witt, Montgomery, Ill D4 90
Witt, Hamblen, Tenn C10 117
Witten, F.R.G B2 17
Witten, Tripp, S. Dak D6 116
Witten, lake, F.R.G D3 24

Wittenberg, G.D.R.....B7 17
Wittenberg, Shawano, Wis...D4 124
Wittenberge, G.D.R.....B5 16
Wittenheim, Fr.....B3 18
Wittingen, F.R.G.....B5 16
Wittlich, F.R.G.....D1 17
Wittman, Talbot, Md.....C5 85
Wittmann, Maricopa, Ariz.....D3, k7 80
Wittmund, F.R.G.....A7 15
Wittstock, G.D.R.....B6 16
Witvlei, Namibia.....B2 49
Witzenhausen, F.R.G.....B4 17
Wiveliscombe, Eng.....C4 12
Wiville, Woodruff, Ark.....B4 81
Wiwon, Kor.....F3 37
Wixom, Oakland, Mich.....o14 98
Wixom, lake, Mich......E6 98
Wkra, riv., Pol......B6 26
Włocławek, Pol.....B5 26
Wlodawa, Pol.....C7 26
Wloszczowa, Pol.....C5 26
Woburn, Que., Can.....D7 73
Woburn, Middlesex, Mass.....B5, g11 97
Woden, Hancock, Iowa.....A4 92
Woerden, Neth.....B4 15
Wohlen, Switz.....B7 19
Wohlthat, mts., Ant......B14 5
Woito, Ont., Can.....B7 72
Wokam, isl., Indon......G8 35
Woking, Alta., Can.....B1 69
Woking, Eng.....C7 12
Wokingham, Eng.....C7 12
Wolbach, Greeley, Nebr.....C7 103
Wolco, Osage, Okla.....A5 112
Wolcott, Eagle, Colo.....B4 83
Wolcott, New Haven, Conn.....C5 84
Wolcott, White, Ind.....C3 91
Wolcott, Wayne, N.Y.....B4 108
Wolcott, Lamoille, Vt.....B4 120
Wolcottville, Lagrange and Noble, Ind.....A7 91
Woldegk, G.D.R.....E7 24
Wolf, Sheridan, Wyo.....B5 125
Wolf, creek, Iowa.....B5 92
Wolf, creek, Mich......D7 98
Wolf, creek, Mont......C7 102
Wolf, creek, Okla......A2 112
Wolf, creek, W. Va.....m13 123
Wolf, isl., Ec......f5 58
Wolf, lake, Alta., Can......B5 69
Wolf, lake, Ill......k9 90
Wolf, riv., Miss., Tenn......A4 100
Wolf, riv., Miss......f7 100
Wolf, riv., Wis......D5 124
Wolf, swamp, N.C......C5 109
Wolf Creek, Lewis and Clark, Mont.....C4 102
Wolf Creek, Josephine, Oreg.....E3 113
Wolf Creek, pass, Colo.....D4 83
Wolf Creek Colony, Hutchinson, S. Dak.....*D8 116
Wolfe, Sask., Can.....E1 70
Wolfe, co., Que., Can.....D6 73
Wolfe, co., Ky.....C6 94
Wolfeboro, Carroll, N.H.....C4 105
Wolfeboro Center, Carroll, N.H.....C4 105
Wolfeboro Falls, Carroll, N.H.....C4 105
Wolfe City, Hunt, Tex.....C4 118
Wolfen, G.D.R.....B7 17
Wolfenbüttel, F.R.G.....A5 17
Wolfenschiessen, Switz.....C5 19
Wolfhagen, F.R.G.....B4 17
Wolf Island, Mississippi, Mo.....E8 101
Wolf Lake, Union, Ill.....F4 90
Wolflake, Noble, Ind.....B7 91
Wolf Lake, Muskegon, Mich.....E4 98
Wolf Lake, Becker, Minn.....D3 99
Wolford, Pierce, N. Dak.....A6 110
Wolf Point, Roosevelt, Mont.....B11 102
Wolfratshausen, F.R.G.....B7 18
Wolf Run, Jefferson, Ohio.....f8 123
Wolfsberg, Aus.....E7 16
Wolfsburg, F.R.G.....B5 16
Wolfsville, Frederick, Md.....A2 85
Wolfville, N.S., Can.....D5 74
Wolgast, G.D.R.....A6 16
Wolhusen, Switz.....B5 19
Wolin, Pol.....E8 24
Wolin, isl., Pol......E8 24
Wollaston, cape, N.W. Ter., Can......B9 66
Wollaston, isl., Chile.....k12 54
Wollaston, lake, Sask., Can......m8 70
Wollongong, Austl.....G8 51
Wolmaransstad, S. Afr.....C4 49
Wolmirstedt, G.D.R.....A6 17
Wolomin, Pol.....k14 26
Wolow, Pol.....C4 26
Wolseley, Sask., Can.....G4 70
Wolsey, Beadle, S. Dak.....C7 116
Wolsztyn, Pol.....B4 26
Wolverhampton, Eng.....B5 12
Wolverine, Cheboygan, Mich.....C6 98
Wolverton, Eng.....B7 12
Wolverton, Wilkin, Minn.....D2 99
Womack Hill, Choctaw, Ala.....D1 78
Womelsdorf, Berks, Pa.....F9 114
Women, lake, Minn......D4 99
Wompi, cave, Iowa.....A6 92
Wonalancet, Carroll, N.H.....C4 105
Wonder, cave, Iowa.....A6 92
Wonder Lake, McHenry, Ill.....A5, h8 90
Wonderland, Plumas, Calif.....B3 82
Wonewoc, Juneau, Wis.....E3 124
Wŏnju, Kor.....*H3 37
Wonowon, B.C., Can.....A7 68
Wonsan, Kor.....G3 37
Wonthaggi, Austl.....I5 51
Wood, Franklin, N.C.....A4 109
Wood, Huntingdon, Pa.....F5 114
Wood, Mellette, S. Dak.....D5 116
Wood, co., Ohio.....A2 111
Wood, co., Tex.....C5 118
Wood, co., W. Va.....B3 123
Wood, co., Wis.....D3 124
Wood, lake, Sask., Can......B4 70
Wood, mtn., Sask., Can......H2 70
Wood, mtn., Mont......E7 102
Wood, pond, Maine.....C2 96
Wood, riv., B.C., Can......C8 68
Wood, riv., Sask., Can......H2 70
Wood, riv., Wyo.....C3 125
Woodall, mtn., Miss......A5 100
Woodard, Bertie, N.C.....B6 109
Woodberry, Calhoun, Ark.....D3 81
Woodbine, Camden, Ga.....F5 87
Woodbine, Jo Daviess, Ill.....A3 90
Woodbine, Harrison, Iowa.....C2 92
Woodbine, Dickinson, Kans.....D7 93
Woodbine, Whitley, Ky.....D5 94
Woodbine, Carroll, Md.....B3 85
Woodbine, Cape May, N.J.....E3 106
Woodboro, Oneida, Wis.....C4 124
Woodbourne, Sullivan, N.Y.....D6 108
Woodbridge, New Haven, Conn.....D4 84
Woodbridge, Eng.....B9 12
Woodbridge, Middlesex, N.J.....B4, k7 106
Woodbridge, Prince William, Va.....B5 121
Wood Buffalo, nat. park, Alta., N.W. Ter., Can......D10 66
Woodburn, Allen, Ind.....B8 91
Woodburn, Clarke, Iowa.....C4 92
Woodburn, Warren, Ky.....D3 94
Woodburn, Marion, Oreg.....B4, h12 113
Woodbury, Litchfield, Conn.....C4 84
Woodbury, Meriwether, Ga.....D2 87
Woodbury, Butler, Ky.....C3 94
Woodbury, Washington, Minn.....F6 99
Woodbury, Gloucester, N.J.....D2 106
Woodbury, Nassau, N.Y.....*F3 84
Woodbury, Bedford, Pa.....F5 114
Woodbury, Cannon, Tenn.....B5 117
Woodbury, Washington, Vt.....C4 120
Woodbury, co., Iowa.....B1 92
Woodbury, mtn., Vt......C4 120
Woodcliff, Screven, Ga.....D5 87
Woodcliff, lake, N.J......g8 106
Woodcliff Lake, Bergen, N.J.....g8 106
Woodcroft, Marion, Ind.....*E5 91
Wood Dale, Du Page, Ill.....k9 90
Wood End, pt., Mass......B7 97
Woodfibre, B.C., Can.....E6 68
Woodfield, Richland, S.C.....C6 115
Woodford, Ire.....D3 11
Woodford, Orangeburg, S.C.....D5 115
Woodford, co., Ill.....C4 90
Woodford, co., Ky.....B5 94
Woodfords, Alpine, Calif.....C4 82
Woodhull, Henry, Ill.....B3 90
Woodhull, Steuben, N.Y.....C3 108
Woodlake, Tulare, Calif.....D4 82
Wood Lake, Yellow Medicine, Minn.....F3 99
Wood Lake, Cherry, Nebr.....B5 103
Woodlake, Trinity, Tex.....D5 118
Woodland, Randolph, Ala.....B4 78
Woodland, Yolo, Calif.....C3 82
Woodland, Talbot, Ga.....D2 87
Woodland, Iroquois, Ill.....C6 90
Woodland, Aroostook, Maine.....B4 96
Woodland, Washington, Maine.....C5 96
Woodland, Barry, Mich.....F5 98
Woodland, Chickasaw, Miss.....B4 100
Woodland, Northampton, N.C.....A5 109
Woodland, Clearfield, Pa.....E5 114
Woodland, Summit, Utah.....C4 119
Woodland, Cowlitz., Wash.....D3 122
Woodland Acres, Pueblo, Colo.....D6 83
Woodland Beach, Monroe, Mich.....G7 98
Woodland Mills, Obion, Tenn.....A2 117
Woodland Park, Teller, Colo.....C5 83
Woodlawn, Ont., Can.....h11 72
Woodlawn, Jefferson, Ill.....E4 90
Woodlawn, McCracken, Ky.....e9 94
Woodlawn, Baltimore, Md.....g10 85
Woodlawn, Prince Georges, Md.....*C4 85
Woodlawn, Hamilton, Ohio.....n13 111
Woodlawn, Montgomery, Tenn.....A4 117
Woodlawn, Carroll, Va.....D2 121
Woodlawn Park, Anne Arundel, Md.....*C4 85
Woodleaf, Rowan, N.C.....B2 109
Wood-Lynne, Camden, N.J.....*D2 106
Woodman, Carroll, N.H.....C5 105
Woodmere, Nassau, N.Y.....*G2 84
Woodmoor, Baltimore, Md.....B4 85
Wood Mountain, Sask., Can.....H2 70
Woodport, Morris, N.J.....B3 106
Woodridge, Man., Can.....E3 71
Woodridge, Du Page, Ill.....k8 90
Wood-Ridge, Bergen, N.J.....h8 106
Wood River, Madison, Ill.....E3 90
Wood River, Hall, Nebr.....D7 103
Wood River Junction, Washington, R.I.....D10 84
Woodroffe, mtn., Austl......E5 50
Woodrow, Cleburne, Ark.....B3 81
Woodrow, Sask., Can.....H2 70
Woodruff, Navajo, Ariz.....C5 80
Woodruff, Phillips, Kans.....C4 93
Woodruff, Spartanburg, S.C.....B3 115
Woodruff, Rich, Utah.....B4 119
Woodruff, Oneida, Wis.....C4 124
Woodruff, co., Ark.....B4 81
Woods, co., Okla.....A3 112
Woods, lake, Austl......C5 50
Woods, lake, Tenn.....B6 117
Woods, mtn., Ark......B2 81
Woodsboro, Frederick, Md.....A3 85
Woodsboro, Refugio, Tex.....E4 118
Woodsburgh, Nassau, N.Y.....*G2 84
Woods Cross, Davis, Utah.....C4 119
Woodsdale, Person, N.C.....A4 109
Woodsfield, Monroe, Ohio.....C4 111
Woods Hole, Barnstable, Mass.....C6 97
Woodside, Austl.....I6 51
Woodside, San Mateo, Calif.....*D2 82
Woodside, Kent, Del.....B6 85
Woodside, Emery, Utah.....D5 119
Wood's Island, Newf., Can.....D2 75
Woodson, Pulaski, Ark.....C3 81
Woodson, Morgan, Ill.....D3 90
Woodson, Throckmorton, Tex.....C3 118
Woodson, co., Kans.....E8 93
Woodstock, Bibb, Ala.....B2 78
Woodstock, N.B., Can.....C2 74
Woodstock, Ont., Can.....D4 72
Woodstock, Windham, Conn.....B9 84
Woodstock, Cherokee, Ga.....B2 87
Woodstock, McHenry, Ill.....A5 90
Woodstock, Howard and Baltimore, Md.....B4 85
Woodstock, Pipestone, Minn.....F2 99
Woodstock, Grafton, N.H.....C3 105
Woodstock, Ulster, N.Y.....C6 108
Woodstock, Champaign, Ohio.....B2 111
Woodstock, Shelby, Tenn.....e9 117
Woodstock, Windsor, Vt.....D3 120
Woodstock, Shenandoah, Va.....B4 121
Woodstock Valley, Windham, Conn.....B8 84
Woodston, Rooks, Kans.....C4 93
Woodstown, Salem, N.J.....D2 106
Woodsville, Grafton, N.H.....B2 105
Woodville, Austl.....*G2 51
Woodville, Ont., Can.....C5 72
Woodville, Leon, Fla.....B2 86
Woodville, Greene, Ga.....C3 87
Woodville, Bingham, Idaho.....F6 89
Woodville, McCracken, Ky.....e9 94
Woodville, Middlesex, Mass.....h9 97
Woodville, Jackson, Mich.....*F6 98
Woodville, Wilkinson, Miss.....D2 100
Woodville, N.Z.....N15 51
Woodville, Bertie, N.C.....A5 109
Woodville, Sandusky, Ohio.....A2, f7 111
Woodville, Marshall, Okla.....D5 112
Woodville, Washington, R.I.....D10 84
Woodville, Tyler, Tex.....D5 118
Woodville, St. Croix, Wis.....D1 124
Woodward, Jefferson, Ala.....B3, g7 78
Woodward, Dallas, Iowa.....C4 92
Woodward, Woodward, Okla.....A2 112
Woodward, co., Okla.....A2 112
Woodwards Cove, N.B., Can.....E3 74
Woodway, McLennan, Tex.....*D4 118
Woodway, Lee, Va.....f9 121
Woodworth, Rapides, La.....C3 95
Woodworth, Stutsman, N. Dak.....B6 110
Woody, riv., Man., Sask., Can......C1 71
Woolber, creek, Ky......h13 94
Wooldridge, Cooper, Mo.....C5 101
Wooler, Eng.....E6 13
Woolford, Dorchester, Md.....C5 85
Wool Market, Harrison, Miss.....E5, f7 100
Woolrich, Clinton, Pa.....D7 114
Woolsey, Washington, Ark.....B1 81
Woolsey, peak, Ariz......D3 80
Woolstock, Wright, Iowa.....B4 92
Woolwich, Eng., (part of London).....C8 12, m13 10
Woolwich, Sagadahoc, Maine.....g8 96
Woomera, Austl.....F6 50
Woonsocket, Providence, R.I.....A10 84
Woonsocket, Sanborn, S. Dak.....C7 116
Woonsocket, hill, R.I......B10 84
Wooramel, Austl.....E1 50
Wooster, Faulkner, Ark.....B3 81
Wooster, Wayne, Ohio.....B4 111
Woosung, Ogle, Ill.....B4 90
Worb, Switz.....C4 19
Worbis, G.D.R.....B5 17
Worcester, Eng.....B5 12
Worcester, Worcester, Mass.....B4 97
Worcester, Otsego, N.Y.....C6 108
Worcester, S. Afr.....D2 49
Worcester, Washington, Vt.....C3 120
Worcester, co., Eng.....B5 12
Worcester, co., Md.....D7 85
Worcester, co., Mass.....A3 97
Worcester, mts., Vt......C3 120
Worden, Madison, Ill.....E4 90
Worden, Yellowstone, Mont.....E8 102
Worden, Klamath, Oreg.....E5 113
Worden, pond, R.I......D10 84
Wordsworth, Sask., Can.....H4 70
Workington, Eng.....C5 10
Worksop, Eng.....A6 12
Workum, Neth.....B5 15
Worland, Bates, Mo.....C3 101
Worland, Washakie, Wyo.....B5 125
World..... 2
Worley, Kootenai, Idaho.....B2 89
Wormerveer, Neth.....B4 15
Worms, F.R.G.....D3 17
Worms, Merrick, Nebr.....C7 103
Worms, head, Wales.....C3 12
Woronoco, Hampden, Mass.....B2 97
Worsley, Eng.....*A5 12
Worth, Cook, Ill.....k9 90
Worth, Worth, Mo.....A3 101
Worth, co., Ga.....E3 87
Worth, co., Iowa.....A4 92
Worth, co., Mo.....A3 101
Wortham, Freestone, Tex.....D4 118
Worthing, Eng.....D7 12
Worthing, Lincoln, S. Dak.....D9 116
Worthington, Ont., Can.....A3 72
Worthington, Greene, Ind.....F4 91
Worthington, Dubuque, Iowa.....B6 92
Worthington, Greenup, Ky.....B7 94
Worthington, Hampshire, Mass.....B2 97
Worthington, Nobles, Minn.....G3 99
Worthington, Putnam, Mo.....A5 101
Worthington, Franklin, Ohio.....B2, k11 111
Worthington, Armstrong, Pa.....E2 114
Worthington, Marion, W. Va.....k10 123
Worthington, mtn., Nev.....F6 104
Worthington Knob, mtn., Tenn......D8 117
Worthington Springs, Union, Fla.....C4 86
Worthville, Carroll, Ky.....B4 94
Worthville, Randolph, N.C.....B3 109
Wortis, Sharp, Ark.....A4 81
Worton, Kent, Md.....B5 85
Wostok, Alta., Can.....C4 69
Wotton, Que., Can.....D6 73
Wounded Knee, Shannon, S. Dak.....D3 116
Wowoni, isl., Indon......F6 35
Wozniki, Pol.....f10 26
Wrangel, isl., Sov. Un......B21 28
Wrangell, Alsk.....D13, m23 79
Wrangell, isl., Alsk......m24 79
Wrangell, mtn., Alsk......f19 79
Wrangell, mts., Alsk......C11 79
Wrath, cape, Scot......B3 13
Wray, Yuma, Colo.....A8 83
Wray, Irwin, Ga.....E3 87
Wren, Van Wert, Ohio.....B1 111
Wrens, Jefferson, Ga.....C4 87
Wrenshall, Carlton, Minn.....D6 99
Wrentham, Alta., Can.....E4 69
Wrentham, Norfolk, Mass.....B5 97
Wrexham, Wales.....A5 12
Wriezen, G.D.R.....B7 16
Wright, Lauderdale, Ala.....A2 78
Wright, Mahaska, Iowa.....C5 92
Wright, Ford, Kans.....E4 93
Wright, Carlton, Minn.....D5 99
Wright, Campbell, Wyo.....*B7 125
Wright, co., Iowa.....B4 92
Wright, co., Minn.....E4 99
Wright, co., Mo.....D5 101
Wright, mtn., Mont......C4 102
Wright Brothers, nat. memorial, N.C......A7 109
Wright City, Warren, Mo.....C6 101
Wright City, McCurtain, Okla.....C6 112
Wright Patman, lake, Tex......C5 118
Wrightstown, Burlington, N.J.....C3 106
Wrightstown, Brown, Wis.....D5, h9 124
Wrightsville, Pulaski, Ark.....C3, k10 81
Wrightsville, Johnson, Ga.....D4 87
Wrightsville, York, Pa.....F8 114
Wrightsville, res., Vt......C3 120
Wrightsville Beach, New Hanover, N.C.....C5 109
Wrightwood, San Bernardino, Calif.....E5 82
Wrigley, N.W. Ter., Can.....D8 66
Wrigley, Hickman, Tenn.....B4 117
Wrigley, gulf, Ant......B36 5
Wrocław (Breslau), Pol.....C4 26
Wrong, lake, Man., Can......C3 71
Wroxeter, Ont., Can.....D3 72
Wroxham, Eng.....B9 12
Wroxton, Sask., Can.....F5 70
Wrzesnia, Pol.....B4 26
Wschowa, Pol.....C4 26
Wu, riv., China.....J3 36
Wuchan, China.....A2 37
Wuchang (part of Wuhan), China
Wuchang, China.....D3 37
Wuch'i, Taiwan.....G9 34
Wu Chin Shan, mtn., China.....C8 38
Wuchou, China.....G7 34
Wuchuan, China.....D4 36
Wuchuan, China.....J3 36
Wufeng, China.....I4 36
Wuhan, China.....E7 34, I6 36
Wuho, China.....H7 36
Wuhsi, China.....E9 34
Wuhsing, China.....I9 36
Wuhu, China.....I8 36
Wui, China.....F6 36
Wukang, China.....K4 36
Wukari, Nig.....E6 45
Wulumuchi, see Urumchi, China
Wulunku, riv., China.....B2 34
Wum, Cam.....D2 46
Wümme, riv., F.R.G......E3 24
Wunsiedel, F.R.G.....C7 17
Wunstorf, F.R.G.....A4 17
Wuntho, Bur.....D10 39
Wupatki, nat. mon., Ariz......B4 80
Wuppertal, F.R.G.....B2 17
Württemberg, reg., F.R.G.....D4 16
Wurtsboro, Sullivan, N.Y.....D6 108
Wurzach, F.R.G.....B5 18
Würzburg, F.R.G.....D4 17
Wurzen, G.D.R.....B7 17
Wushan, China.....I3 36
Wuskwatim, lake, Man., Can......B2 71
Wusu, China.....C1 34
Wusung, China.....I9 36
Wuta, China.....D6 34
Wutu, China.....E5 34
Wutungchiao, China.....F5 34
Wuwei, China.....D5 34
Wuwei, China.....I7 36
Wuyüan, China.....D3 36
Wuyun, China.....B10 34
Wyaconda, Clark, Mo.....A6 101
Wyaconda, riv., Mo......A6 101
Wyalusing, Bradford, Pa.....C9 114
Wyandanch, Suffolk, N.Y.....*G3 84
Wyandot, co., Ohio.....B2 111
Wyandotte, Wayne, Mich.....F7, p15 98
Wyandotte, Ottawa, Okla.....A7 112
Wyandotte, co., Kans.....C9 93
Wyandotte, cove, Ind......H5 91
Wyandra, Austl.....C5 51
Wyanet, Bureau, Ill.....B4 90
Wyarno, Sheridan, Wyo.....B6 125
Wyatt, St. Joseph, Ind.....A5 91
Wyatt, Mississippi, Mo.....E8 101
Wybark, Muskogee, Okla.....B6 112
Wyckoff, Bergen, N.J.....*A4 106
Wyco, Wyoming, W. Va.....D3 123
Wye, riv., Eng......C5 12
Wyebridge, Ont., Can.....C5 72
Wye Mills, Talbot, Md.....C5 85
Wyesocking, bay, N.C......B6 109
Wyevale, Ont., Can.....C5 72
Wyeville, Monroe, Wis.....D3 124
Wygietrzow, Pol.....g10 26
Wykoff, Fillmore, Minn.....G6 99
Wylie, Collin, Tex.....*C4 118
Wylie, lake, N.C., S.C......A5 115
Wylliesburg, Charlotte, Va.....D4 121
Wyman, Louisa, Iowa.....C6 92
Wyman, lake, Maine.....C3 96
Wymark, Sask., Can.....G2 70
Wymondham, Eng.....B9 12
Wymore, Gage, Nebr.....D9 103
Wynantskill, Rensselaer, N.Y.....*C7 108
Wyncote, Montgomery, Pa.....*F11 114
Wyndham, Austl.....C4 50
Wyndmere, Richland, N. Dak.....C8 110
Wynnburg, Lake, Tenn.....A2 117
Wynndel, B.C., Can.....E9 68
Wynne, Cross, Ark.....B5 81
Wynne Wood, Garvin, Okla.....C4 112
Wynona, Osage, Okla.....A5 112
Wynoochee, riv., Wash......B2 122
Wynot, Cedar, Nebr.....B8 103
Wynyard, Austl.....o15 50
Wynyard, Sask., Can.....F3, n8 70
Wyocena, Columbia, Wis.....E4 124
Wyodak, Campbell, Wyo.....B7 125
Wyola, Big Horn, Mont.....E9 102
Wyoming, Ont., Can.....E2 72
Wyoming, Kent, Del.....B6 85
Wyoming, Stark, Ill.....B4 90
Wyoming, Jones, Iowa.....B6 92
Wyoming, Kent, Mich.....F5 98
Wyoming, Chisago, Minn.....E6 99
Wyoming, Wyoming, N.Y.....C2 108
Wyoming, Hamilton, Ohio.....o13 111
Wyoming, Luzerne, Pa.....n17 114
Wyoming, Washington, R.I.....C10 84
Wyoming, co., N.Y.....C2 108
Wyoming, co., Pa.....D9 114
Wyoming, co., W. Va.....D3 123
Wyoming, state, U.S.....B6 76, 125
Wyoming, peak, Wyo.....D2 125
Wyoming, range, Wyo.....C2 125
Wyomissing, Berks, Pa.....F10 114
Wyrzsk, Pol.....B4 26
Wysokie, Mazowieckie, Pol.....B7 26
Wyszkow, Pol.....B6 26
Wythe, co., Va.....D1 121
Wytheville, Wythe, Va.....D1 121
Wytopitlock, Aroostook, Maine.....C4 96
Wyvis, mtn., Scot......C4 13

X-Y-Z

Xanthi, Grc.....B5 23
Xanthi, prov., Grc.....*B5 23
Xanthus, see Koca, riv., Tur.
Xapecó, riv., Braz......D2 56
Xapurí, Braz.....D4 58
Xau, lake, Bots.....B3 49
Xavantes, mts., Braz......E5 59
Xavier, Leavenworth, Kans.....k16 93
Xbonil, Mex.....D6 63
Xcalak, Mex.....D7 63
Xenia, Clay, Ill.....E5 90
Xenia, Greene, Ohio.....C2 111
Xieng Khouang, Laos.....C5 38
Xilitla, Mex.....m14 63
Xingú, riv., Braz......C4 59
Xique-Xique, Braz.....D2 57
Xochimilco, Mex.....h9 63

Yaan, China.....F5 34
Ya'bad, Jordan.....B7 32
Yabassi, Cam.....E1 46
Yabbenohr, isl., Kwajalein..... 52
Yablis, Nic.....C6 62
Yablonovy, mts., Sov. Un......D14 28
Yabu, Okinawa..... 52
Yabucoa, P.R.....B4 65
Yabucoa, mun., P.R.....*B4 65
Yachats, Lincoln, Oreg.....C2 113
Yaco, riv., Braz......C4 60
Yacolt, Clark, Wash.....D3 122
Yacuiba, Bol.....D3 55
Yad Eli'ezer, Isr.....h10 32
Yadkin, co., N.C.....A2 109
Yadkin, riv., N.C......B2 109
Yadkin Valley, Caldwell, N.C.....A1 109
Yadkinville, Yadkin, N.C.....A2 109
Yagi, Jap.....o14 37
Yagoua, Cam.....C3 46
Yaguachi, Ec.....B2 58
Yaguajay, Cuba.....C4 64
Yaguas, riv., Peru.....B3 58
Yahk, B.C., Can.....E9 68
Yahuma, Zaire.....A3 48
Yaicheng, China.....C8 38
Yaihsien (Sama), China.....C8 38
Yainax, butte, Oreg......E5 113
Yaizu, Jap.....o17 37
Yakima, Yakima, Wash.....C5 122
Yakima, co., Wash.....C5 122
Yakima, ridge, Wash......C5 122
Yakima, riv., Wash.....C5 122
Yakima, val., Wash......C5 122
Yako, Upper Volta.....D4 45
Yakoma, Zaire.....A3 48
Yaku, isl., Jap.....K5 37
Yakutat, Alsk.....D12 79
Yakutat, bay, Alsk......D12 79
Yakutsk, Sov. Un.....C15 28
Yalaha, Lake, Fla.....D5 86
Yale, B.C., Can.....E7 68
Yale, Jasper, Ill.....D5 90
Yale, Guthrie, Iowa.....C3 92
Yale, St. Clair, Mich.....E8 98
Yale, Payne, Okla.....A5 112
Yale, Beadle, S. Dak.....C8 116
Yale, Sussex, Va.....D5 121
Yale, lake, Wash.....D3 122
Yale, mtn., Colo.....C4 83
Yalesville, New Haven, Conn. (part of Wallingford).....D5 84
Yalinga, Cen. Afr. Rep.....D4 46
Yallahs, hill, Jam.....F15 65
Yalobusha, co., Miss.....A4 100
Yalobusha, riv., Miss......B4 100
Yalova, Tur.....B7 23
Yalta, Sov. Un.....I10 27
Yalu, see Putehachi, China
Yalu, riv., China, Kor......D11 36
Yalung, riv., China.....E5 34
Yalutrovsk, Sov. Un.....B7 29
Yalutsangpu, see Brahmaputra, riv., Asia
Yalvac, Tur.....C8 31
Yama, Sov. Un.....q21 27
Yamachiche, Que., Can.....C5 73
Yamagata, Jap.....G10 37
Yamagata, pref., Jap.....*G10 37
Yamaguchi, Jap.....I5 37
Yamaguchi, pref., Jap.....*I5 37
Yamanashi, pref., Jap.....*I9 37
Yamantau, mtn., Sov. Un......C5 29
Yamaska, Que., Can.....C5 73
Yamaska, co., Que., Can.....C5 73
Yambio, Sud.....E2 47
Yambol, Bul.....D8 22
Yamdena, isl., Indon.....G8 35
Yamethin, Bur.....D10 39
Yamhill, Yamhill, Oreg.....h11 113
Yamhill, co., Oreg.....B3 113
Yamkino, Sov. Un.....n18 27
Yamma Yamma, lake, Austl......C3 51
Yamoussoukro, I.C.....E3 45
Yampa, Routt, Colo.....A4 83
Yampa, mtn., Colo......A3 83
Yampa, plat., Colo., Utah.....C6 119
Yampa, riv., Colo......A2 83
Yamparaez, Bol.....C2 55
Yamsey, mtn., Oreg......E5 113
Yamsk, Sov. Un.....D18 28
Yana, riv., Sov. Un......C16 28
Yanam, India.....E7 39, I9 40
Yanao, Austl.....H3 51
Yanaoca, Peru.....D3 58
Yanaul, Sov. Un.....D20 9
Yanbu', Sau. Ar.....E7 43
Yancey, co., N.C.....f10 109
Yanceyville, Caswell, N.C.....A3 109
Yandua, isl., Fiji..... 52
Yanfolila, Mali.....D3 45
Yang, China.....H2 36
Yangambi, Zaire.....A3 48
Yangasa Cluster, is., Fiji..... 52
Yangchiang, China.....G7 34
Yangchou, China.....E8 34
Yangchoyung, lake, China.....C12 40
Yangchüan, China.....D7 34
Yangchun, China.....G7 34
Yangeshiri, isl., Jap.....D10 37
Yanggeta, isl., Fiji..... 52
Yangi-Yul, Sov. Un.....G22 9
Yangku, see Taiyuan, China
Yangtze (Chang), riv., China.....E6 34
Yangyang, Kor.....G4 37
Yankeetown, Citrus and Levy, Fla.....C4 86
Yankeetown, Warrick, Ind.....I3 91
Yankton, Yankton, S. Dak.....E8 116
Yankton, co., S. Dak.....D8 116
Yanonge, Zaire.....A3 48
Yantic, New London, Conn. (part of Norwich).....C8 84
Yantley, Choctaw, Ala.....C1 78
Yantra, riv., Bul......D7 22
Yanush, Latimer, Okla.....C6 112
Yao, Chad.....C3 46
Yao, Jap.....*I7 37
Yaosca, Nic.....D5 62
Yaoundé, Cam.....E2 46
Yap, isl., Pac. O......F8 7
Yapen, isl., Indon.....F9 35
Yaphank, Suffolk, N.Y.....F5 84
Yaque del Norte, riv., Dom. Rep......E8 64
Yaqui, riv., Mex......B3 63
Yar, Sov. Un.....B4 29
Yaracuy, state, Ven.....A4 60
Yaraka, Austl.....B5 52
Yarbo, Washington, Ala.....D1 78
Yardley, Bucks, Pa.....F12 114
Yardville, Mercer, N.J.....C3 106
Yarensk, Sov. Un.....C18 9
Yarí, riv., Col......C3 60
Yariga-Take, peak, Jap......H8 37
Yaritagua, Ven.....A4 60
Yarkand, see Soche, China
Yarker, Ont., Can.....C8 72
Yarkovo, Sov. Un.....B7 29
Yarmouth, N.S., Can.....F3 74
Yarmouth, Des Moines, Iowa.....C6 92
Yarmouth, Cumberland, Maine.....E2, g7 96
Yarmouth, Barnstable, Mass.....C7 97
Yarmouth, co., N.S., Can.....F4 74
Yarmouth Port, Barnstable, Mass.....*C7 97
Yarmuk, riv., Jordan and Syr......B7 32
Yarnell, Yavapai, Ariz.....C3 80
Yarnema, Sov. Un.....F18 25
Yaroslavl, Sov. Un.....B1 29
Yarovskoye, marsh, Sov. Un......B8 29
Yarqon, riv., Isr.....B6, g10 32
Yarraden, Austl.....B7 50
Yarram, Austl.....I6 51
Yarrow, B.C., Can.....f13 68
Yarrowsburg, Washington, Md.....B2 85
Yartsevo, Sov. Un.....D9 27
Yarumal, Col.....B2 60
Yasana, Zaire.....A4 48
Yasawa, isl., Fiji..... 52
Yasawa Group, is., Fiji..... 52
Yashan (Jiachan), China.....B8 40
Yashi, Nig.....D6 45
Yasinovataya, Sov. Un.....q20 27
Yasinya, Sov. Un.....A7 22
Yasothon, Thai.....E6 38
Yass, Austl.....G7 51
Yata, Bol.....B2 55
Yates, co., N.Y.....C3 108
Yatesboro, Armstrong, Pa.....E3 114
Yates Center, Woodson, Kans.....E8 93
Yates City, Knox, Ill.....C3 90
Yatesville, Upson, Ga.....D2 87
Yathata, isl., Fiji..... 52
Yathkyed, lake, N.W. Ter., Can......D13 66
Yatsuga Take, peak, Jap......I9 37
Yatsushiro, Jap.....J5 37
Yatsushiro, sea, Jap......J5 37
Yaṭṭah, Jordan.....C7 32
Yatung, China.....D12 40
Yauca, Peru.....E3 58
Yauco, P.R.....B2 65
Yauco, mun., P.R.....*B2 65
Yauco, res., P.R......B2 65
Yauli, Peru.....D2 58
Yaupi, Ec.....B2 58
Yauri, Peru.....D3 58
Yautepec, Mex.....n14 63
Yauyos, Peru.....D2 58
Yavapai, co., Ariz.....C3 80
Yavarí, riv., Braz., Peru.....B3 58
Yavatmāl (Yeotmal), India.....G7 40
Yaviza, Pan.....F9 62
Yavne, Isr.....C6, h9 32
Yavorov, Sov. Un.....G4 27
Yawata, isl., Truk..... 52
Yawatahama, Jap.....J6 37
Yawhee, plat., Oreg......E5 113
Yawngseng, Bur.....A3 38
Yazd (Yezd), Iran.....F7 41
Yazoo, co., Miss.....C3 100
Yazoo, riv., Miss......C3 100
Yazoo City, Yazoo, Miss.....C3 100
Ybbs, riv., Aus......D7 16
Yding Skovhøj, hill, Den......B3 24
Ye, Bur.....E10 39
Yeadon, Delaware, Pa.....p20 114
Yeager, Hughes, Okla.....B5 112
Yeagertown, Mifflin, Pa.....E6 114
Yebbi Bou, Chad.....A3 46
Yecla, Sp.....C5 20
Yeddo, Fountain, Ind.....D3 91
Yefremov, Sov. Un.....E12 27
Yegendybulak, Sov. Un.....D9 29
Yegoryevsk, Sov. Un.....B1 29
Yegus, pt., P.R......B4 65
Yehpaishou, see Chienping, China
Yehud, Isr.....g10 32
Yei, Sud.....E3 47
Yekaterinoslavka, Sov. Un.....A4 39
Yelabuga, Sov. Un.....D19 9
Yelan, Sov. Un.....F14 27
Yelanskoye, Sov. Un.....C15 28
Yelets, Sov. Un.....C1 29
Yélimané, Mali.....C2 45
Yelizarovo, Sov. Un.....C22 9
Yell, co., Ark.....B2 81
Yell, isl., Scot......g10 10
Yellandu, India.....I8 40
Yellow, creek, Tenn......A4 117
Yellow, lake, Wis......C1 124
Yellow, see Huang Ho, riv., China
Yellow, riv., Fla......u15 86
Yellow, riv., Ga......h8 87
Yellow, riv., Ind......B4 91
Yellow, riv., Wis......D3 124
Yellow, sea, China.....D9 34
Yellow Bluff, Wilcox, Ala.....D2 78
Yellow Creek, Sask., Can.....E3 70
Yellow Grass, Sask., Can.....H3 70
Yellowhead, pass, Alta., B.C., Can......C1 69
Yellow Jacket, Montezuma, Colo.....D2 83
Yellow Jacket, mts., Idaho.....D4 89

CHINESE PLACE-NAMES / Pinyin Conversion Chart

The language of geography defines geographic features in universally recognized terms. In creating this language, toponymy experts and cartographers have confronted complex problems in finding terms that are universally or regionally acceptable.

Sometimes the place-names most commonly recognized by English-speaking readers differ from the local, official name. The maps in this atlas generally show both conventional English and local names for these major features. For example, Yellow River (English) = Huang Ho (Chinese). Most places do not have English conventional names, so only one name is shown on the maps.

The problems encountered establishing local name-form policies are particularly complex for countries such as China, where the Roman alphabet is not used. The Chinese language uses ideographic characters instead of an alphabet, and these ideographic characters are transformed into the Roman alphabet through phonetic transcription.

The method used in this atlas for transforming Chinese names is the Wade-Giles system, named for its English authors. Another system, called "Pinyin", has been adopted by the Chinese government and incorporated into its official maps. In many instances, the English, Wade-Giles, and Pinyin names for a place are significantly different. For example, Peking (English) = Peiping (Wade-Giles) = Beijing (Pinyin). For some places, such as Shanghai, there is only one recognized name.

The Pinyin system is now used by the United States Board on Geographic Names and in official United Nations documents. However, despite rapidly growing popularity, Pinyin names are often accompanied by the more traditional Wade-Giles forms.

The table below equates the Pinyin names for some major features with the conventional English or Wade-Giles names shown on the China maps in this atlas. The table excludes places such as Shanghai, for which the Wade-Giles and Pinyin spellings are the same.

Pinyin	English or Wade-Giles	Map Reference	
Altay Shan	Altai Mountains	B–2	34
Altun Shan	Aerhchin Mountains	D–2	34
Anda	Anta	A–11	36
Anhui (province)	Anhwei	H–7	36
Anqing	Anching	I–7	36
Baicheng	Paicheng	B–10	36
Baoding	Paoting (Tsingyuan)	E–6	36
Baoji	Paochi	G–2	36
Baotou	Paotou	D–4	36
Baoying	Paoying	H–8	36
Bei'an	Peian	B–3	37
Beihai	Peihai	G–6	34
Beijing	Peking (Peiping)	E–7	36
Bengbu	Pangfou (Pangpu)	H–7	36
Benxi	Penchi	D–10	36
Bo Hai	Gulf of Chihli (Pohai)	E–8	36
Boshan	Poshan	F–7	36
Bo Xian	Pohsien	H–6	36
Butha Qi (Zalantun)	Putehachi (Yalu)	B–9	34
Cangzhou	Tsangchou	E–7	36
Chang (river)	Yangtze (Chang)	E–6	34
Changde	Changte	J–4	36
Changzhi	Changchih	F–5	36
Changzhou	Changchou	I–9	36
Chengde	Chengte (Jehol)	D–7	36
Chendu	Chengtu	E–5	34
Chen Xian	Chenhsien (Chenchou)	L–5	36
Chifeng (Ulanhad)	Chinfeng (Wulanhata)	C–8	36
Chongqing	Chungking	J–2	36
Da Hinggan Ling	Greater Khingan Range	B–8	34
Dandong	Tantung (Antung)	F–2	37
Datong	Tatung	D–5	36
Da Yunhe	Grand Canal	G–7	36
Dezhou	Techou	F–7	36
Ding Xian	Tinghsien	E–6	36
Dongtai	Tungtai	H–9	36
Dongting Hu (lake)	Tungting	J–5	36
Dunhua	Tunhua	E–4	37
Duyun	Tuyün	K–2	36
Ergun (river)	Argun	A–8	34
Fujian (province)	Fukien	F–8	34
Fuling	Fouling	J–2	36
Fu Xian	Fuhsien	E–9	36
Fuxin	Fouhsin	C–9	36
Fuyang	Fouyang	H–6	36
Fuzhou	Fuchou (Foochow)	K–8	36
Fuzhou	Linchuan (Fuchou)	J–7	36
Gangdisê Shan	Kailas Range	B–9	40
Gansu (province)	Kansu	C–4	34
Ganzhou	Kanchou (Kanhsien)	L–6	36
Gejiu	Kochiu	G–5	34
Guangdong (province)	Kwangtung	G–7	34
Guangxi Zhuangzu (auton. region)	Kwangsi Chuang	G–6	34
Guangzhou	Canton	G–7	34
Guilin	Kueilin	F–7	34
Guiyang	Kueiyang	K–2	36
Guizhou (province)	Kweichow	F–6	34
Hailar	Hailaerh (Hulun)	B–8	34
Handan	Hantan	F–6	36
Hangzhou	Hangchou	I–9	36
Hangzhou Wan	Hangchow Bay	I–9	36
Hanzhong	Hanchung	H–2	36
Harbin	Haerhpin (Harbin)	B–12	34
Hebei (province)	Hopeh	E–6	36
Hechuan	Hochuan	I–2	36
Hefei	Hofei	I–7	36
Hegang	Hokang	C–5	37
Heilong (river)	Amur (Heilungkiang)	B–10	34
Heilongjiang (province)	Heilungkiang	B–10	34
Helan Shan (mts.)	Holan Shan	D–6	34
Henan (province)	Honan	H–5	36
Hepu	Hopu	G–6	34
Hohhot	Huhohaote (Huhehot)	D–4	36
Horqin Youyi Qianqi (Ulanhot)	Koerhchinyuichienchi (Ulanhot)	A–10	36
Huadian	Huatien	E–3	37
Huaide (Gongzhuling)	Huaite (Kungchuling)	C–11	36
Huang Hai	Yellow Sea	D–9	34
Huang He (river)	Huang Ho (Yellow)	C–6	34
Huangshi	Huangshih	I–6	36
Huizhou	Huichou (Huiyang)	G–7	34
Hunjiang	Hunchiang	F–3	37
Jiamusi	Chiamussu	C–5	37
Ji'an	Chian	K–6	36
Jiangmen	Chiangmen	G–7	34
Jiangsu (province)	Kiangsu	H–8	36
Jiangxi (province)	Kiangsi	F–7	34
Jiao Xian	Chiaohsien	F–8	36
Jiaozhou Wan	Haichow Bay	G–8	36
Jiaozuo	Chiaotso	G–5	36
Jiaxing	Chiahsing	I–9	36
Jieyang	Chiehyang	G–8	34
Jilin (province)	Kirin	C–9	34
Jinan	Chinan (Tsinan)	F–7	36
Jingdezhen	Chingtechen	J–7	36
Jinhua	Chinhua	J–8	36
Jining	Chining	G–7	36
Jinsha (river)	Chinsha	F–5	34
Jinshi	Chingshih	J–4	36
Jinxi	Chinhsi	D–9	36
Jin Xian	Chinhsien	E–9	36
Jinzhou	Chinchou	D–9	36
Jiujiang	Chiuchiang	J–6	36
Jixi	Chihsi	D–5	37
Karamay	Kolamai (Karamai)	B–1	34
Kashi	Kashih (Kashgar)	F–10	33
Laizhou Wan	Laichow Bay	F–8	36
Lanzhou	Lanchou	D–5	34
Leshan	Loshan	F–5	34
Lianyungang (Xinpu)	Lienyünchiangshih (Sinhai)	G–8	36
Liaodong Bandao	Liaotung Peninsula	D–10	36
Liaodong Wan	Liaotung Bay	E–9	36
Linqing	Linching	F–6	36
Linxia	Linhsia	D–5	34
Linyi	Lini	G–8	36
Liuzhou	Liuchou	G–6	34
Lop Nur (lake)	Lop Nor	D–3	34
Lu'an	Liuan	I–7	36
Lüda (Dalian)	Lüta (Dairen)	E–9	36
Luohe	Loho	H–6	36
Luoyang	Loyang	G–5	36
Luzhou	Luchou (Luhsien)	I–2	36
Manzhouli	Manchouli (Lupin)	B–8	34
Mei Xian	Meihsien	G–8	34
Mianyang	Mienyang	E–5	34
Mudanjiang	Mutanchiang	D–4	37
Mu Us Shamo	Ordos Desert	D–6	36
Nanchong	Nanchung	I–2	36
Nanjing	Nanking	H–8	36
Nantong	Nantung	H–9	36
Neijiang	Neichiang	F–6	34
Nei Monggol (auton. region)	Inner Mongolia	C–7	34
Ningbo	Ningpo	J–9	36
Ningxia Huizu (auton. region)	Ningsia Hui	D–6	34
Nyainqêntanglha Shan (mts.)	Nienchi'ngt'angkula Shan	B–11	40
Pingdingshan	Pingtingshan	H–5	36
Pingxiang	Pinghsiang	K–5	36
Qaidam Pendi	Tsaidam Basin	D–3	34
Qilian Shan (mts.)	Nan Shan	D–4	34
Qingdao	Tsingtao (Chingtao)	F–9	36
Qinghai (province)	Tsinghai	D–3	34
Qinghai Hu (lake)	Koko Nor	D–4	34
Qingjiang	Chingchiang (Huaiyin)	H–8	36
Qing Zang Gaoyuan	Plateau of Tibet	B–7	39
Qinhuangdao	Chinhuangtao	E–8	36
Qin Ling (mts.)	Tsinling Shan	H–2	36
Qiqihar	Chichihaerh (Tsitsihar)	A–10	
Qomolangma Feng	Mount Everest	C–11	40
Quanzhou	Chüanchou	G–8	34
Qu Xian	Chühsien	J–8	36
Rugao	Jukao	H–9	36
Sanmenxia	Sanmenhsia	G–4	36
Shaanxi (province)	Shensi	G–2	36
Shandong (province)	Shantung	G–7	36
Shandong Bandao	Shantung Peninsula	F–9	36
Shangqiu (Zhuji)	Shangchiu	G–6	36
Shangrao	Shangjao	J–7	36
Shantou	Swatow (Shantou)	G–8	34
Shanxi (province)	Shansi	F–4	36
Shaoguan	Shaokuan	G–7	34
Shaoxing	Shaohsing	I–9	36
Shashi	Shashih	I–5	36
Shenyang	Mukden (Shenyang)	D–10	36
Shijiazhuang	Shihchiachuang	F–6	36
Sichuan (province)	Szechwan	E–5	34
Siping	Ssuping	C–11	36
Songhua (river)	Sungari	C–5	37
Songjiang	Sungchiang	I–9	36
Suoche (Yarkand)	Soche (Yarkand)	F–10	33
Su Xian	Suhsien	I–7	36
Suzhou	Suchou (Soochow)	I–9	36
Taiwan Haixia	Formosa Strait	G–8	34
Taizhou	Taichou	H–8	36
Taklimakan Shamo (desert)	Takla Makan	F–11	28
Tanggula Shan	Tangkula Mountains	E–2	34
Tarim He (river)	Tarim Darya	E–11	28
Tianjin	Tientsin (Tienching)	E–7	36
Tian Shan (mts.)	Tien Shan	E–10	33
Tianshui	Tienshui	E–6	34
Tieling	Tiehling	C–10	36
Tongchuan	Tungchuan	G–3	36
Tonghua	Tunghua	D–11	36
Tongliao	Tungliao	C–10	36
Tongling	Tungling	I–7	36
Tunxi	Tunchi	J–8	36
Turpan Pendi	Turfan Depression	C–3	34
Ürümqi	Urumchi (Wulumuchi)	C–2	34
Wanli Changchen	Great Wall	D–8	36
Wanxian	Wanhsien	I–3	36
Wenzhou	Wenchou	K–9	36
Wusuli (river)	Ussuri	C–7	37
Wutangqiao	Wutungchiao	F–5	34
Wuxi	Wuhsi	I–9	36
Wuxing (Huzhou)	Wuhsing	I–9	36
Wuzhou	Wuchou	G–7	34
Xiamen	Amoy	G–8	34
Xi (river)	Hsi (Si)	G–6	34
Xi'an	Hsian (Sian)	G–3	36
Xiangfan	Hsiangfan	H–5	36
Xiangtan (Shi)	Hsiangtan	K–5	36
Xianyang	Hsienyang	G–3	36
Xiao Hinggan Ling	Lesser Khingan Range	A–10	34
Xinghua	Hsinghua	H–8	36
Xinjiang Uygur (auton. region)	Sinkiang Uighur	C–2	34
Xingkai Hu	Lake Khanka	D–6	37
Xingtai	Hsingtai	F–6	36
Xining	Hsining (Sining)	D–5	34
Xinxiang	Hsinhsiang	G–5	36
Xinyang	Hsinyang	H–6	36
Xizang (auton. region)	Tibet	B–8	39
Xuanhua	Hsüanhua	D–6	36
Xuchang	Hsüchang	G–5	36
Xuzhou	Hsüchou (Süchow)	G–7	36
Yancheng	Yencheng	H–9	36
Yangjiang	Yangchiang	G–7	34
Yangquan	Yangchüan	E–5	36
Yangzhou	Yangchou	H–8	36
Yanji	Yenchi	E–4	37
Yantai	Yentai (Chefoo)	F–9	36
Yarlung Zangbo (river)	Brahmaputra (Yalutsangpu)	C–8	39
Yibin	Ipin	F–5	34
Yichang	Ichang	I–4	36
Yichun	Ichun	C–4	37
Yidu	Itu	F–8	36
Yining (Gulja)	Ining (Kuldja)	E–11	33
Yiyang	Iyang	J–5	36
Yuci	Yützu	F–5	36
Yueyang	Yüehyang	J–5	36
Yumen (Laojunmiao)	Yümenshih	D–4	34
Yungui Gaoyuan	Yunnan Plateau	F–5	34
Zhangjiakou	Changchiakou (Kalgan)	D–6	36
Zhangzhou	Changchou	G–8	36
Zhanjiang	Chanchiang (Tsamkong)	G–7	34
Zhaodong	Chaotung	C–2	37
Zhaoqing	Chaoching	G–7	34
Zhejiang (province)	Chekiang	J–8	36
Zhengzhou	Chengchou	G–5	36
Zhenjiang	Chenchiag	H–8	36
Zhoucun	Choutsun	F–7	36
Zhoukouzhen	Shangshui	H–6	36
Zhoushan Qundao	Choushan Islands	I–10	36
Zhuzhou	Chuchou	K–5	36
Zibo	Tzupo	D–8	34
Zigong	Tzukung	F–5	34
Zunyi	Tsuni	K–2	36